OECD
DEPARTMENT
OF ECONOMICS AND STATISTICS
DÉPARTEMENT DES
AFFAIRES ÉCONOMIQUES ET STATISTIQUES
OCDE

MAIN ECONOMIC INDICATORS

HISTORICAL STATISTICS

PRINCIPAUX INDICATEURS ÉCONOMIQUES

STATISTIQUES RÉTROSPECTIVES

1964-1983

ORGANISATION FOR ECONOMIC CO-OPERATION AND DEVELOPMENT
ORGANISATION DE COOPÉRATION ET DE DÉVELOPPEMENT ÉCONOMIQUES

Pursuant to article 1 of the Convention signed in Paris on 14th December, 1960, and which came into force on 30th September, 1961, the Organisation for Economic Co-operation and Development (OECD) shall promote policies designed:

- to achieve the highest sustainable economic growth and employment and a rising standard of living in Member countries, while maintaining financial stability, and thus to contribute to the development of the world economy;
- to contribute to sound economic expansion in Member as well as non-member countries in the process of economic development; and
- to contribute to the expansion of world trade on a multilateral, non-discriminatory basis in accordance with international obligations.

The Signatories of the Convention on the OECD are Austria, Belgium, Canada, Denmark, France, the Federal Republic of Germany, Greece, Iceland, Ireland, Italy, Luxembourg, the Netherlands, Norway, Portugal, Spain, Sweden, Switzerland, Turkey, the United Kingdom and the United States. The following countries acceded subsequently to this Convention (the dates are those on which the instruments of accession were deposited): Japan (28th April, 1964), Finland (28th January, 1969), Australia (7th June, 1971) and New Zealand (29th May, 1973).

The Socialist Federal Republic of Yugoslavia takes part in certain work of the OECD (agreement of 28th October, 1961).

En vertu de l'article 1er de la Convention signée le 14 décembre 1960, à Paris, et entrée en vigueur le 30 septembre 1961, l'Organisation de Coopération et de Développement Économiques (OCDE) a pour objectif de promouvoir des politiques visant :

- à réaliser la plus forte expansion de l'économie et de l'emploi et une progression du niveau de vie dans les pays Membres, tout en maintenant la stabilité financière, et à contribuer ainsi au développement de l'économie mondiale ;
- à contribuer à une saine expansion économique dans les pays Membres, ainsi que non membres, en voie de développement économique ;
- à contribuer à l'expansion du commerce mondial sur une base multilatérale et non discriminatoire conformément aux obligations internationales.

Les signataires de la Convention relative à l'OCDE sont : la République Fédérale d'Allemagne, l'Autriche, la Belgique, le Canada, le Danemark, l'Espagne, les Etats-Unis, la France, la Grèce, l'Irlande, l'Islande, l'Italie, le Luxembourg, la Norvège, les Pays-Bas, le Portugal, le Royaume-Uni, la Suède, la Suisse et la Turquie. Les pays suivants ont adhéré ultérieurement à cette Convention (les dates sont celles du dépôt des instruments d'adhésion) : le Japon (28 avril 1964), la Finlande (28 janvier 1969), l'Australie (7 juin 1971) et la Nouvelle-Zélande (29 mai 1973).

La République socialiste fédérative de Yougoslavie prend part à certains travaux de l'OCDE (accord du 28 octobre 1961).

INTRODUCTION

This volume of *Historical Statistics* is intended to supplement the monthly bulletin, *Main Economic Indicators,* by providing the user with a considerably longer run of homogeneous data for most of the series it includes.

This edition replaces those published previously. It includes therefore historical data for indicators which have been incorporated in the monthly publication since the previous edition. For other series, the data presented here take into account revisions effected by the compiling agency, as well as the most recent seasonal adjustments made either by these agencies or by the Statistics Division of the OECD. The base year for all indices is 1980.

The volume is arranged in chapters by country. The tables cover the period 1964 to 1983; they are followed by short notes describing some major characteristics of the series, and, where applicable, indicating breaks in continuity. Published sources are cited at the end of each chapter. They are selected on the grounds of the variety of subjects they cover, although they may not always be the primary source.

The Statistics Division of the OECD would like to express its gratitude to the statistical institutes and central banks of Member countries whose long-standing cooperation made it possible to compile the series presented in this volume.

Paris, July 1984

Le présent recueil de *Statistiques rétrospectives* complète le bulletin mensuel *Principaux indicateurs économiques* en fournissant, pour la plupart de ses rubriques, des séries homogènes beaucoup plus longues.

Ce volume remplace les éditions précédentes. Il comprend donc les données rétrospectives concernant les indicateurs qui ont été introduits, depuis la précédente édition, dans le bulletin mensuel. En ce qui concerne les autres séries, les données présentées tiennent compte des révisions effectuées par les organismes statistiques nationaux, ainsi que que des corrections des variations saisonnières les plus récentes effectuées, soit par ces organismes, soit par la Division statistique de l'OCDE. Toutes les séries d'indices sont présentées sur une année de base uniforme : 1980.

Cet ouvrage se compose de chapitres par pays. Les tableaux couvrent la période 1964-1983; ils sont suivis de notes brèves indiquant les caractéristiques principales des séries et, s'il y a lieu, les ruptures de continuité. Les sources publiées sont citées à la fin de chaque chapitre. Elles ont été sélectionnées pour la variété des sujets dont elles traitent et de ce fait ne sont pas toujours les sources primaires.

La Division statistique de l'OCDE tient à exprimer sa gratitude envers les instituts statistiques et les banques centrales des pays Membres, dont la coopération constante lui a permis d'établir les séries présentées dans ce recueil.

Paris, juillet 1984.

GUIDE TO USERS

1. The series presented in this volume are those shown in the tables *Indicators by Country,* and selected series shown in the tables *Indicators by subject* of *Main Economic Indicators.* The series shown are those published in the January 1984 issue. Future long-term revisions will be announced in *Main Economic Indicators* and historical data published in quarterly supplements.

2. Where there is no note to the contrary, quarterly and annual figures are averages or totals of monthly data. In some cases they are in fact calculated independently but deviations from the corresponding monthly data are not sufficiently important to warrant footnoting. The description *end of period* means that quarterly and annual figures refer to the last month of the period, but the monthly figure itself may not necessarily relate to the end of the month.

3. The sign for break (I or —) means that caution should be used when comparing figures on different sides of the bar. This sign is not always shown for seasonally adjusted series; nevertheless care should be taken when looking at periods separated by a break in the corresponding seasonally unadjusted series.

4. All series adjusted by the OECD. Secretariat are calculated using the X-11 variant of U.S. Bureau of the Census Method II. For a brief technical description of this method, see *Sources and Methods* No. 15, December 1972.

5. Notes on standard definitions and sources for a number of series are given below. References to other OECD publications, where detailed descriptions of some of theses series may be found, are also indicated.

Industrial production: Total production covers mining and quarrying, manufacturing, and electricity, gas and water, but not construction (major divisions 2 and 3, and groups 4101 and 4102 of the *International Standard Industrial Classification).* Unadjusted series are adjusted for unequal number of working days in the month except where otherwise indicated.

Production of Crude steel. Source: Industrial Iron and Steel Institute.

Ships completed. Source: Lloyd's Register.

Labour: Time lost through labour disputes excludes time lost due to shortages, or to strikes in related industries.

AVERTISSEMENT

1. Le présent volume reprend les séries des tableaux *Indicateurs par pays* et certaines séries des tableaux *Indicateurs par sujet* des *Principaux indicateurs économiques.* Les séries présentées sont celles publiées dans le numéro de janvier 1984. Les révisions sur le long terme qui, dans le futur, affecteront les séries présentées ici, seront annoncées dans les *Principaux indicateurs économiques,* et les rétrospectives rendant compte de ces révisions feront l'objet de suppléments trimestriels.

2. Sauf indication contraire, les chiffres trimestriels et annuels sont des moyennes ou des sommes de données mensuelles. Dans certains cas, ils sont en fait obtenus indépendemment, sans que les disparités par rapport aux données mensuelles correspondantes ne justifient une annotation. L'indication *fin de période* signifie que les chiffres trimestriels et annuels se réfèrent au dernier mois de la période; en revanche, les chiffres mensuels eux-mêmes ne concernent pas nécessairement la situation en fin de mois.

3. Le signe de rupture (I ou —) indique qu'il ne faut comparer qu'avec réserve les chiffres séparés par le trait. Bien que ce signe ne figure pas toujours dans les séries désaisonnalisées, il convient d'être prudent si l'on s'intéresse à des périodes situées de part et d'autre d'une rupture dans la série brute.

4. Toutes les séries désaisonnalisées par le Secrétariat de l'OCDE le sont par la variante X-11 de la méthode II du Bureau of the Census des États-Unis. Une brève description technique de cette méthode figure dans les *Sources et Méthodes,* n° 17, juin 1973.

5. Pour certains groupes de séries, on trouvera ci-dessous les définitions types, une indication des sources utilisées, ainsi que les titres des autres publications de l'OCDE qui en donnent une description détaillée.

Production industrielle : La production totale couvre les industries extractives et manufacturières, ainsi que l'électricité, le gaz et l'eau (branches 2 et 3, et groupes 4101 et 4102 de la *Classification internationale type par industrie)*; elle ne couvre pas la construction. Les séries brutes sont corrigées de l'inégalité du nombre de jours ouvrables dans le mois sauf indication contraire.

Production d'acier brut. Source : Industrial Iron and Steel Institute.

Navires achevés. Source : Lloyd's Register.

Conflits du travail : Non compris les arrêts de travail dûs à des conflits en cours dans d'autres secteurs de l'industrie (chômage technique) ou à la pénurie de produits de base.

Foreign trade: Special trade, as defined by the Economic and Social Council and the Statistical Commission of the United Nations.

Exchange rates and Official reserves: Source: *International Financial Statistics,* International Monetary Fund.

Index numbers: In the notes the term *original base* means the base year on which the index was originally calculated; in most cases it can be assumed that the same period was used both as reference base and as weight base. The period used to link indices calculated on different bases is indicated in the tables by = =.

6. **Sources and Methods.** Detailed descriptions of a number of series can be found in the *Sources and Methods* booklets published from time to time with issues of *Main Economic Indicators.* These booklets are arranged either by country, with each booklet covering all those series for a particular country that are published in the accompanying *Main Economic Indicators,* or by subject. This latter approach has the advantage of enabling comparisons to be made of the various definitions and calculation methods used in different countries for a particular type of statistic. Those studies published to date are listed below together with their dates of publication. It should however, be noted that following certain changes either to the selection of series shown in *Main Economic Indicators* or to the conceptual base of certain national statistics the information given in the earlier booklets may be partly outdated.

Commerce extérieur : Commerce spécial, tel que défini par le Conseil Économique et Social et la Commission Statistique des Nations Unies.

Taux de change et réserves officielles: Source: *International Financial Statistics,* Fonds Monétaire International.

Indices : Dans les notes, le terme *base originale* indique l'année de base sur laquelle l'indice a été calculé à l'origine; dans la plupart des cas cette période sert à la fois de base de référence et de base pour la pondération. La période utilisée pour les calculs de raccordements d'indices de bases différentes est indiquée dans les tableaux par les signes : = = .

6. **Sources et Méthodes.** La description détaillée des séries est exposée dans les brochures *Sources et Méthodes* diffusées à un rythme variable, avec certaines livraisons des *Principaux indicateurs économiques.* Ces brochures sont organisées soit par pays, chacune d'entre elles ayant trait à l'ensemble des statistiques présentées pour un pays donné dans le bulletin qu'elle accompagne, soit par sujet. Cette dernière présentation offre l'avantage de permettre des comparaisons de pays à pays quant aux définitions et méthodes de calcul utilisées pour établir un même type de statistique. Les études publiées jusqu'ici sont répertoriées ci-après avec indication de leur date de parution. Il convient d'observer que par suite de modifications apportées, soit à la sélection de séries retenue dans les *Principaux indicateurs économiques,* soit aux concepts selon lesquels les statistiques nationales sont élaborées, les brochures les plus anciennes peuvent être partiellement périmées.

CONVENTIONAL SIGNS

. .	Not available
—	Nil or negligible
I or —	Break in homogeneity of series
= =	Link
Adjusted	Adjusted for seasonal variations
Ton	Metric ton
$	U.S. dollar
£	Pound sterling
.	Decimal point
Billion	10^9
S	Strike

SIGNES CONVENTIONNELS

. .	Non disponible.
—	Nul ou négligeable.
I ou —	Rupture dans l'homogénéité de la série.
= =	Raccord.
Corrigé	Corrigé des variations saisonnières.
Tonne	Tonne métrique.
$	Dollar des États-Unis.
£	Livre sterling.
.	Séparation des décimales.
S	Grève.

SOURCES AND METHODS

SOURCES ET MÉTHODES

	Nº	Date		Nº	Date		Nº	Date
Canada			**Denmark** **Danemark**			**Netherlands** **Pays-Bas**	**35** **36**	June 82 Octobre 82
United States **États-Unis**	**10** **12**	January 71 Septembre 71	**Finland** **Finlande**	**16** **18**	February 73 Septembre 73	**Norway** **Norvège**		
Japan **Japon**	**10** **11**	January 71 Mars 71	**France**	**14** **13**	January 72 Novembre 71	**Portugal**		
Australia **Australie**	**30** **32**	June 79 Novembre 79	**Germany** **Allemagne**	**33** **34**	June 81 Juin 81	**Spain** **Espagne**		
New Zealand **Nlle-Zélande**			**Greece** **Grèce**	**27** **28**	February 78 Mars 78	**Sweden** **Suède**		
Austria **Autriche**			**Iceland** **Islande**			**Switzerland** **Suisse**	**25** **24**	May 76 Avril 76
Belgium **Belgique**			**Ireland** **Irlande**	**21** **23**	March 75 Novembre 75	**Turkey** **Turquie**		
Luxembourg			**Italy** **Italie**	**20** **19**	May 74 Janvier 74	**United Kingdom** **Royaume-Uni**	**15** **17**	December 72 Juin 73

Industrial production and price indices; foreign finance: No. 22, July 1975
Indices de production industrielle et de prix; finances extérieures : nº 22, juillet 1975

Money and credit: No. 26, January 1977
Monnaie et crédit : nº 26, janvier 1977

Employment, hours and wages: No. 29, July 1978
Emploi, durée du travail et salaires : nº 29, juillet 1978

Deliveries, orders and stocks in manufacturing: No. 31, September 1979
Livraisons, commandes et stocks: industries manufacturières : nº 31, décembre 1979

Business Surveys: No. 37, April 1983
Enquêtes de conjoncture : nº 37, décembre 1983

Consumer price indices: Special issue, March 1984
Indices des prix à la consommation : Numéro hors série, mars 1984.

TABLE OF CONTENTS

TABLE DES MATIÈRES

Canada

CANADA

Gross national product

at current market prices

million Canadian dollars, annual rates

Adjusted - Corrigé

Produit national brut

aux prix courants du marché

millions de dollars canadiens, taux annuels

	Year	Q.1	Q.2	Q.3	Q.4	JAN	FEB	MAR	APR	MAY	JUN	JUL	AUG	SEP	OCT	NOV	DEC
1964	50.28	49.02	49.60	50.81	51.69												
1965	55.36	53.40	54.42	56.06	57.57												
1966	61.83	60.19	61.49	62.31	63.32												
1967	66.41	64.78	66.43	65.54	67.89												
1968	72.59	69.60	71.65	73.52	75.57												
1969	79.82	77.73	78.68	80.46	82.39												
1970	85.69	83.94	84.38	86.68	87.24												
1971	94.45	89.87	93.16	95.02	98.75												
1972	105.23	100.58	104.04	105.05	110.24												
1973	123.56	116.65	120.39	124.57	132.62												
1974	147.53	139.87	145.51	150.71	154.02												
1975	165.34	157.28	161.33	168.34	174.43												
1976	191.86	183.59	191.93	193.46	198.45												
1977	210.19	202.67	207.54	212.49	218.06												
1978	232.21	222.95	228.30	236.04	241.55												
1979	264.28	249.74	260.12	269.71	277.55												
1980	296.56	285.75	290.74	298.62	311.11												
1981	339.06	326.47	336.55	342.54	350.66												
1982	356.60	351.74	353.38	359.11	362.17												
1983	388.69	373.21	384.17	396.80	400.57												

Domestic product: total (1)

1980 = 100

Produit intérieur : total (1)

1980 = 100

	Year	Q.1	Q.2	Q.3	Q.4	JAN	FEB	MAR	APR	MAY	JUN	JUL	AUG	SEP	OCT	NOV	DEC
1964	48.8	45.2	48.3	52.0	49.7	44.1	45.0	46.4	47.6	48.6	48.5	47.3	47.5	61.3	49.4	50.1	49.5
1965	52.3	48.2	51.3	55.8	54.0	47.4	47.8	49.4	50.9	51.4	51.5	50.5	50.3	66.2	53.7	54.4	53.8
1966	56.1	52.1	55.3	60.3	56.6	50.7	51.7	53.7	54.8	55.6	55.5	53.9	53.9	73.1	56.8	57.2	55.9
1967	58.0	54.0	57.8	61.1	59.2	53.4	53.4	55.2	57.1	58.3	58.0	56.0	56.5	70.7	58.8	59.8	58.9
1968	61.4	56.6	61.2	64.7	62.9	55.3	56.9	57.7	60.5	61.6	61.5	58.9	59.0	76.2	62.5	64.4	61.8
1969	65.0	61.2	64.7	63.4	65.7	59.1	61.5	62.9	64.8	64.6	64.7	61.6	62.0	81.6	65.4	66.7	65.1
1970	66.6	63.5	66.8	68.9	67.3	61.8	64.1	64.6	66.7	67.1	66.6	63.2	63.5	79.8	66.9	68.5	66.5
1971	70.5	64.6	70.7	74.3	72.2	62.2	65.4	66.1	69.5	70.8	71.7	67.4	70.1	86.8	73.2	73.2	70.2
1972	74.7	68.3	75.3	77.7	76.9	66.6	69.5	70.4	74.4	75.1	76.3	71.5	73.3	88.5	77.7	78.2	74.9
1973	80.5	75.0	81.2	83.3	82.7	71.5	76.1	77.5	80.8	81.2	81.4	77.3	77.7	94.3	83.1	84.0	80.9
1974	84.2	80.3	85.7	86.4	84.3	77.0	81.6	82.4	84.8	86.2	86.2	81.0	82.5	95.7	85.5	85.3	82.0
1975	85.0	79.7	85.7	88.3	86.1	77.0	81.3	80.8	85.3	85.9	86.1	81.8	83.3	99.8	86.0	87.3	85.1
1976	89.5	83.4	91.1	93.2	89.6	79.9	84.5	85.9	90.5	91.6	91.1	85.5	88.0	106.1	90.1	91.5	87.2
1977	92.0	87.0	93.0	95.4	91.9	83.7	88.3	88.8	92.2	93.1	93.6	87.7	90.1	108.3	92.9	93.4	89.3
1978	95.0	88.9	95.6	98.9	95.8	84.9	90.8	90.9	95.3	95.1	96.5	90.1	92.7	113.9	96.3	97.4	93.7
1979	98.8	93.5	99.6	102.6	98.5	89.3	94.9	96.2	98.3	99.7	100.9	95.0	97.1	115.6	100.2	99.9	95.4
1980	100.0	95.7	100.0	103.0	100.3	91.8	96.7	98.6	99.9	100.0	100.2	95.3	97.4	116.3	101.7	101.8	97.6
1981	103.0	98.5	105.0	106.4	101.0	93.9	100.0	101.4	104.1	105.0	105.9	98.5	100.1	120.6	102.9	102.4	97.6
1982	98.2	96.1	99.3	101.3	94.9	92.8	97.6	97.8	99.2	99.8	98.9	91.8	95.4	116.5	95.8	96.4	92.6
1983	100.5	93.8	100.9	105.7	101.5	90.4	94.6	96.4	99.0	100.9	102.9	96.2	99.7	121.3	102.5	103.1	98.8

Domestic product: agriculture (1)(2)

1980 = 100

Produit intérieur : agriculture (1)(2)

1980 = 100

	Year	Q.1	Q.2	Q.3	Q.4	JAN	FEB	MAR	APR	MAY	JUN	JUL	AUG	SEP	OCT	NOV	DEC
1964	64.9	36.9	47.7	130.4	44.4	31.3	35.6	43.8	60.2	53.7	29.3	48.2	34.1	308.9	41.2	48.8	43.1
1965	66.6	38.5	43.3	139.4	45.3	39.1	39.5	36.8	62.8	41.3	25.9	41.5	33.4	343.4	44.9	51.5	39.3
1966	75.3	35.8	50.1	170.1	45.2	33.5	37.0	36.9	64.7	55.1	30.6	52.3	34.5	423.4	43.9	53.3	38.5
1967	64.0	37.9	47.6	129.0	41.5	37.0	36.2	40.6	64.0	53.7	25.2	46.2	33.6	307.1	40.0	48.6	35.8
1968	67.4	34.1	55.0	140.3	40.2	29.3	35.0	38.0	69.4	63.7	31.8	46.4	29.9	344.7	31.6	55.8	33.4
1969	70.9	34.9	55.3	153.5	39.8	27.7	36.1	40.9	75.6	58.5	31.8	37.8	28.1	394.7	35.3	49.9	34.2
1970	69.9	39.9	64.4	130.0	45.2	31.0	41.0	47.8	82.3	73.6	37.5	40.1	28.9	321.0	40.8	57.1	37.8
1971	79.0	34.1	69.4	175.8	36.9	34.4	35.9	31.9	87.5	87.1	33.6	55.1	66.8	405.4	39.0	40.0	31.7
1972	72.8	30.9	69.5	153.4	37.4	30.1	34.1	28.3	90.6	84.9	33.1	52.8	63.9	343.5	39.5	41.3	31.4
1973	79.2	34.5	71.3	159.5	41.4	32.0	37.4	34.3	98.4	91.1	24.2	52.6	71.1	384.9	40.8	42.1	41.1
1974	74.1	36.7	75.2	146.9	37.5	35.8	39.4	35.0	104.3	95.0	26.3	52.6	67.0	321.1	34.7	39.4	38.3
1975	80.1	32.3	79.6	173.9	34.6	31.2	35.0	30.8	112.5	102.9	23.4	56.5	68.0	397.0	33.3	37.5	33.1
1976	85.9	31.7	80.4	192.4	39.2	28.7	35.0	31.5	115.6	105.1	20.6	55.6	66.1	455.6	39.6	46.0	31.9
1977	89.4	34.1	85.2	199.1	39.3	30.8	36.7	34.8	119.2	110.2	26.2	60.2	76.2	461.0	39.9	40.6	37.4
1978	89.3	35.3	79.2	205.1	37.7	33.8	39.8	32.2	109.5	102.0	26.1	55.4	74.0	486.0	35.9	35.7	41.5
1979	82.8	35.3	79.1	181.5	35.0	35.3	38.5	33.5	106.6	100.7	29.9	50.9	66.4	427.3	31.9	32.5	40.5
1980	100.0	42.2	83.0	190.7	84.2	38.5	45.7	42.4	114.8	105.3	28.7	60.6	72.7	438.8	34.2	33.3	185.1
1981	104.7	43.4	78.1	210.5	87.0	40.6	46.7	42.8	107.9	98.9	27.3	53.4	74.3	503.6	39.0	39.1	182.9
1982	103.3	37.9	72.5	221.3	81.5	35.6	41.1	37.1	101.9	91.8	23.8	45.4	71.2	547.4	31.8	31.5	181.4
1983	95.7	42.4	76.4	224.2	39.9	41.2	44.2	41.9	104.7	94.3	30.1	58.9	79.0	534.6	40.0	44.6	35.1

Gross national product implicit price level / Produit national brut niveau implicite des prix

1980 = 100

Adjusted - Corrigé

	Year	Q.1	Q.2	Q.3	Q.4	JAN	FEB	MAR	APR	MAY	JUN	JUL	AUG	SEP	OCT	NOV	DEC
1964	34.0	33.7	33.9	34.2	34.4												
1965	35.1	34.7	34.9	35.4	35.5												
1966	36.7	36.1	36.5	37.0	37.1												
1967	38.1	37.7	38.1	38.2	38.5												
1968	39.4	39.0	39.2	39.5	39.8												
1969	41.1	40.4	41.0	41.3	41.6												
1970	43.0	42.4	42.8	43.3	43.7												
1971	44.4	43.7	44.3	44.4	45.2												
1972	46.6	45.8	46.1	46.8	47.7												
1973	50.9	48.8	50.1	51.4	53.3												
1974	58.7	55.4	57.9	60.0	61.3												
1975	65.0	62.6	63.8	65.9	67.5												
1976	71.2	68.9	70.8	71.8	73.4												
1977	76.5	74.5	76.0	77.1	78.4												
1978	81.6	79.5	80.7	82.4	83.9												
1979	90.0	85.6	88.9	91.5	94.0												
1980	100.0	96.1	98.9	101.2	103.8												
1981	110.6	106.8	108.9	111.6	115.2												
1982	121.7	118.1	120.4	123.3	125.3												
1983	128.8	127.0	128.2	129.9	130.0												

Domestic product: total (1) / Produit intérieur : total (1)

1980 = 100

Adjusted - Corrigé

	Year	Q.1	Q.2	Q.3	Q.4	JAN	FEB	MAR	APR	MAY	JUN	JUL	AUG	SEP	OCT	NOV	DEC
1964		47.9	48.3	49.0	49.8	47.5	48.1	48.1	48.1	48.3	48.4	48.6	48.9	49.5	49.4	49.7	50.3
1965		51.1	51.4	52.5	54.1	50.9	50.9	51.3	51.5	51.1	51.5	52.5	52.3	52.8	53.6	54.0	54.7
1966		55.3	55.9	56.1	56.9	54.8	55.3	55.9	55.8	55.8	56.0	56.0	55.8	56.4	57.0	56.9	56.9
1967		56.7	57.9	58.5	59.0	57.1	56.4	56.6	57.7	57.9	58.0	58.1	58.6	58.7	58.7	59.0	59.2
1968		59.6	60.9	61.8	62.9	59.5	59.5	59.8	60.3	61.0	61.3	61.4	62.0	62.1	62.5	63.0	63.1
1969		64.4	64.7	65.1	65.9	63.6	64.5	65.2	64.9	64.3	64.7	65.0	64.9	65.4	65.3	65.7	66.5
1970		66.4	66.2	66.5	67.1	66.2	66.7	66.3	66.1	66.4	66.3	66.4	66.5	66.7	66.6	67.3	67.5
1971		68.4	69.3	71.5	72.4	67.9	68.4	68.7	69.0	69.8	70.5	70.6	71.8	72.2	72.4	72.2	72.5
1972		72.5	74.0	75.2	76.9	72.5	72.3	72.8	73.6	73.8	74.6	74.7	75.1	75.9	76.5	77.0	77.2
1973		78.9	79.9	80.6	82.7	77.9	79.0	79.9	79.9	79.9	79.9	81.0	79.7	81.0	82.0	82.8	83.2
1974		84.1	84.1	84.4	84.2	83.7	84.2	84.5	83.5	84.5	84.3	84.3	84.6	84.2	84.4	84.0	84.2
1975		83.6	84.2	85.5	86.4	83.7	84.0	83.2	84.1	84.0	84.6	85.4	85.4	85.7	85.4	86.2	87.8
1976		87.7	89.6	89.8	90.1	87.1	87.5	88.5	89.5	89.9	89.4	89.7	89.9	89.9	89.5	90.4	90.5
1977		91.2	91.5	91.9	92.5	91.1	91.1	91.3	91.1	91.5	91.9	91.8	92.1	91.9	92.3	92.6	92.6
1978		93.0	94.4	95.0	96.6	92.6	93.5	93.1	94.5	94.0	94.6	94.2	94.7	96.2	95.8	96.6	97.2
1979		97.4	98.1	99.4	99.3	97.1	97.1	97.9	97.4	98.1	98.7	99.2	99.5	99.6	99.5	99.2	99.3
1980		99.6	98.8	99.7	101.2	99.8	99.1	99.9	99.3	98.6	98.5	99.4	99.4	100.3	101.0	101.2	101.4
1981		102.7	103.7	102.5	101.7	102.3	102.6	103.1	103.6	103.6	104.1	103.0	102.2	102.4	102.0	101.9	101.2
1982		100.1	98.3	97.0	96.1	100.5	100.1	99.5	98.8	98.6	97.7	96.4	97.6	97.0	96.1	96.2	95.1
1983		97.8	99.7	101.8	102.5	98.1	97.1	98.0	98.6	99.5	101.2	101.4	101.7	102.2	102.3	102.5	102.7

Domestic product: agriculture (1)(2) / Produit intérieur : agriculture (1)(2)

1980 = 100

Adjusted - Corrigé

	Year	Q.1	Q.2	Q.3	Q.4	JAN	FEB	MAR	APR	MAY	JUN	JUL	AUG	SEP	OCT	NOV	DEC
1964		65.5	62.4	66.5	63.8	63.0	65.3	68.2	60.5	65.2	61.4	66.8	65.5	67.2	63.2	61.1	67.1
1965		70.0	62.5	66.2	66.8	71.6	70.8	67.5	68.6	56.9	62.0	64.4	67.2	67.1	67.8	66.3	66.4
1966		73.8	77.4	76.2	74.1	72.7	74.0	74.9	78.5	78.3	75.2	79.2	75.0	74.4	75.2	74.6	72.5
1967		64.7	66.9	63.5	62.0	68.4	62.5	63.2	68.6	69.3	62.7	64.7	64.3	61.5	64.4	62.3	59.4
1968		65.6	66.4	67.5	67.3	65.3	65.7	65.9	64.0	67.5	67.9	67.7	67.7	67.5	66.9	65.6	70.8
1969		70.4	71.4	69.8	71.6	66.9	71.8	72.4	76.4	65.7	72.2	67.1	68.5	73.7	71.4	72.2	71.1
1970		69.4	72.3	66.5	70.1	66.0	70.3	72.0	71.3	73.1	72.5	66.5	64.7	68.5	69.2	71.7	69.2
1971		79.1	78.7	79.3	78.5	79.8	78.5	78.9	76.4	78.8	80.7	80.3	80.6	78.6	79.8	77.9	77.6
1972		70.6	71.8	74.3	75.0	71.3	71.2	69.4	72.0	68.9	74.5	73.4	75.2	74.4	74.6	75.7	74.6
1973		77.8	76.6	78.6	82.3	76.5	77.4	79.5	77.6	77.5	74.7	78.0	77.7	80.1	81.4	80.9	84.8
1974		75.9	73.3	72.2	74.3	77.0	76.1	74.6	73.9	73.2	72.8	69.6	72.6	74.3	72.7	74.5	77.2
1975		79.3	80.6	82.0	78.4	79.7	79.2	78.9	80.4	78.7	82.8	84.2	80.9	80.8	77.5	77.3	80.5
1976		84.2	84.7	86.8	88.0	82.7	85.0	84.9	86.7	85.2	82.3	86.5	87.3	86.6	87.5	88.0	88.6
1977		86.1	89.1	91.5	88.9	83.8	86.1	88.4	87.7	89.1	90.3	91.0	92.0	91.5	88.5	89.1	89.2
1978		90.4	89.3	89.1	90.2	91.5	91.6	87.9	88.8	91.7	87.4	86.8	88.3	92.2	91.0	91.1	88.4
1979		82.4	82.9	82.2	84.5	83.8	80.8	82.6	82.6	82.6	83.6	80.7	83.2	82.5	83.3	84.0	86.3
1980		88.2	89.1	88.3	88.1	86.7	88.5	89.3	91.4	90.0	85.8	90.5	86.7	87.7	87.2	88.5	88.7
1981		95.8	91.6	89.9	92.3	97.0	95.8	94.5	92.3	92.1	90.3	88.8	89.2	91.6	91.6	95.1	90.2
1982		92.0	89.5	90.5	92.4	93.1	91.4	91.6	89.4	89.2	89.9	89.8	89.3	92.3	92.2	92.2	92.6
1983		94.6	94.1	96.4	93.9	97.7	94.1	92.2	93.0	93.7	95.6	97.1	95.0	97.3	95.2	94.1	92.5

CANADA

Domestic product: industry (1)

index of industrial production

1980 = 100

Produit intérieur : industrie (1)

indice de production industrielle

1980 = 100

	Year	Q.1	Q.2	Q.3	Q.4	JAN	FEB	MAR	APR	MAY	JUN	JUL	AUG	SEP	OCT	NOV	DEC
1964	50.4	48.6	51.2	50.0	51.9	47.3	49.6	49.0	50.1	51.1	52.4	47.8	50.0	52.2	52.1	53.4	50.3
1965	54.6	52.7	54.8	53.9	57.2	51.3	52.7	54.0	53.5	54.8	56.0	52.1	53.6	55.9	57.4	58.3	56.0
1966	58.2	57.4	59.0	56.6	59.6	55.9	58.2	58.2	58.2	58.8	60.0	54.4	56.3	59.1	60.2	60.7	57.9
1967	60.2	58.8	61.0	58.7	62.0	57.9	59.4	59.2	60.6	60.6	61.9	55.9	58.8	61.5	61.5	63.3	61.3
1968	64.3	61.5	65.4	62.6	67.8	60.3	61.9	62.2	64.2	65.2	66.7	59.7	61.5	66.5	67.8	69.4	66.1
1969	68.5	68.1	69.7	66.0	70.2	65.9	68.5	70.0	69.4	69.3	70.5	63.1	65.3	69.6	69.9	71.7	69.0
1970	69.6	70.4	70.3	66.8	70.3	68.5	71.7	71.0	70.5	70.5	71.4	63.9	66.6	69.9	70.3	71.9	68.8
1971	73.6	71.0	74.5	71.8	77.1	66.5	73.3	73.3	73.2	73.5	76.8	64.9	71.5	79.0	78.5	79.8	72.9
1972	79.2	76.3	80.5	75.9	84.3	72.1	78.0	78.6	80.3	78.5	82.6	69.8	74.3	83.7	85.2	87.8	79.8
1973	87.6	86.3	89.4	83.5	91.2	79.1	89.6	90.2	88.5	87.7	91.9	79.3	80.7	90.8	92.3	95.1	86.3
1974	90.4	92.4	93.5	85.6	90.0	86.6	95.3	95.3	92.5	92.6	95.3	80.7	84.1	92.0	92.8	93.0	84.3
1975	85.0	85.7	86.6	80.6	87.2	80.5	89.3	87.3	86.9	84.1	83.7	75.7	78.9	87.1	87.0	90.8	83.8
1976	90.2	89.4	93.5	85.9	92.2	83.1	92.1	93.1	92.6	92.4	95.4	78.6	85.7	93.4	91.9	96.4	88.1
1977	92.5	94.1	94.9	86.9	94.0	89.0	96.7	96.6	93.3	92.9	98.5	81.3	85.5	94.0	95.2	97.7	89.[illegible]
1978	95.6	95.2	97.3	89.9	100.0	88.7	98.8	98.2	97.2	94.1	100.6	82.3	87.3	100.0	100.5	103.9	95.6
1979	101.5	103.4	103.4	96.5	102.6	96.1	107.2	106.9	101.9	102.2	106.2	89.8	94.4	105.7	105.8	107.1	95.0
1980	100.0	104.2	100.2	93.6	102.0	97.5	106.4	108.9	101.7	97.2	101.6	86.5	90.8	103.3	104.4	106.1	95.6
1981	100.9	104.0	106.1	95.1	98.5	95.4	107.5	109.1	105.4	103.6	109.2	90.0	92.6	102.8	102.5	101.9	91.1
1982	90.2	96.5	93.5	84.0	86.7	90.8	100.0	98.9	93.6	92.5	94.2	75.9	84.9	91.1	88.3	90.7	81.0
1983	95.5	92.6	96.2	91.9	101.0	85.6	95.8	96.4	94.0	94.2	100.5	82.6	91.0	102.2	102.3	105.1	95.6

Domestic product: manufacturing (1)

index of industrial production

1980 = 100

Produit intérieur : industries manufacturières (1)

indice de production industrielle

1980 = 100

	Year	Q.1	Q.2	Q.3	Q.4	JAN	FEB	MAR	APR	MAY	JUN	JUL	AUG	SEP	OCT	NOV	DEC
1964	51.4	49.0	52.4	51.4	52.9	47.2	50.1	49.8	51.0	52.4	53.9	48.8	51.6	53.9	53.4	54.6	50.6
1965	56.1	53.1	56.8	55.8	58.8	51.3	53.1	55.0	54.8	56.9	58.7	54.0	55.5	57.8	59.5	59.9	56.9
1966	60.1	58.6	61.2	59.1	61.4	56.7	59.4	59.7	60.1	60.9	62.5	57.1	58.6	61.6	62.7	62.6	58.9
1967	61.6	59.7	63.1	60.5	63.2	58.4	60.2	60.4	62.5	62.4	64.3	57.7	60.4	63.8	63.1	64.8	61.9
1968	65.8	61.7	67.5	64.4	69.5	60.4	61.9	62.8	65.8	67.3	69.5	61.0	63.1	69.2	70.1	71.5	66.7
1969	70.6	68.6	72.7	69.2	71.8	65.7	68.9	71.1	71.1	72.4	74.5	65.8	68.7	73.2	72.7	73.8	68.9
1970	69.6	69.7	72.0	67.3	69.3	67.3	71.1	70.8	71.4	71.7	73.0	64.0	67.3	70.5	70.4	71.2	66.3
1971	73.7	69.4	75.6	72.5	77.3	63.6	72.2	72.4	73.6	74.4	78.9	64.0	72.2	81.2	80.2	80.7	71.1
1972	79.4	74.7	81.8	77.1	84.0	69.7	76.6	77.8	80.9	79.5	85.1	69.5	75.7	86.2	85.9	88.2	77.9
1973	87.8	85.1	90.5	84.2	91.3	76.7	88.8	89.8	88.9	88.6	94.0	78.9	80.9	92.8	93.8	95.8	84.3
1974	91.0	91.6	95.2	86.8	90.3	84.7	95.0	95.1	93.1	94.2	98.3	80.7	85.0	94.6	94.4	94.3	82.1
1975	85.6	84.4	88.6	81.9	87.7	77.8	88.2	87.1	87.8	86.0	91.8	76.0	79.0	89.9	89.0	92.1	82.1
1976	91.0	88.8	96.2	87.7	91.5	80.5	91.9	94.0	94.9	94.6	98.9	79.3	87.5	96.2	92.4	96.9	85.2
1977	92.8	92.8	97.0	88.0	93.4	85.7	95.7	97.0	95.0	94.5	101.5	81.5	85.7	96.8	96.7	98.1	85.3
1978	97.3	93.7	100.8	93.1	101.5	85.4	97.3	98.5	100.0	97.7	104.8	84.6	89.5	105.4	104.0	106.7	93.9
1979	102.9	103.5	107.1	98.3	102.8	94.3	107.3	109.1	104.4	105.9	110.9	90.1	95.2	109.5	108.3	108.3	91.9
1980	100.0	102.3	101.7	94.3	101.2	94.4	105.1	108.8	102.9	98.3	104.0	85.8	90.7	106.4	106.3	105.5	91.8
1981	101.6	102.5	109.5	97.0	97.3	91.3	106.3	109.8	107.3	106.8	114.5	91.7	93.3	106.1	104.0	101.4	85.4
1982	89.3	92.4	94.6	85.5	84.6	84.3	95.9	97.1	92.8	93.5	97.4	76.1	86.5	93.9	88.3	89.0	75.1
1983	94.9	90.1	97.6	92.7	99.2	81.3	93.3	95.6	94.5	95.6	102.8	82.6	91.5	104.1	103.1	104.1	90.3

Domestic product: durable manufactures (1)

index of industrial production

1980 = 100

Produit intérieur : biens durables (1)

indice de production industrielle

1980 = 100

	Year	Q.1	Q.2	Q.3	Q.4	JAN	FEB	MAR	APR	MAY	JUN	JUL	AUG	SEP	OCT	NOV	DEC
1964	47.9	46.3	49.3	46.8	49.1	44.6	47.2	47.1	47.8	49.4	50.6	44.7	46.3	49.3	48.9	51.0	47.4
1965	54.2	51.4	55.6	52.2	57.3	49.7	50.5	54.0	53.9	55.6	57.5	51.9	50.6	54.3	57.2	58.6	56.1
1966	58.6	57.9	60.1	56.0	60.1	56.3	58.4	59.1	59.4	59.9	61.1	54.9	53.8	59.4	61.0	61.4	58.0
1967	60.3	59.1	62.4	57.4	62.3	57.9	59.1	60.2	61.8	62.0	63.3	54.4	56.1	61.6	60.7	63.8	62.2
1968	65.2	60.2	67.8	62.7	70.0	60.7	59.6	60.3	65.5	63.5	69.4	59.1	59.7	69.2	70.9	72.6	66.6
1969	70.3	69.3	73.7	66.9	71.4	66.8	69.0	72.0	72.0	73.7	75.5	63.5	65.1	72.1	71.9	73.9	68.3
1970	67.8	69.3	71.7	64.2	65.7	67.6	71.0	70.7	71.9	70.7	72.6	60.9	63.3	68.3	66.9	67.2	62.8
1971	72.7	68.9	75.5	69.5	76.8	62.2	72.6	71.9	73.0	74.0	79.5	60.5	68.6	79.4	79.5	80.0	70.8
1972	78.0	74.2	81.1	73.4	83.5	69.3	76.2	77.1	80.5	78.9	83.9	65.3	70.4	84.4	83.7	88.5	78.3
1973	88.8	87.4	92.4	82.9	92.6	77.9	90.6	93.7	90.6	90.5	96.1	77.1	77.5	94.1	95.6	97.6	84.7
1974	93.3	94.8	98.2	86.7	93.6	87.4	98.2	98.7	95.5	98.0	101.1	79.9	83.1	97.1	97.2	98.6	85.2
1975	87.6	86.1	91.1	81.9	91.4	78.3	89.6	90.5	90.3	88.5	94.5	75.7	78.3	91.7	92.3	96.4	85.6
1976	92.4	92.0	98.9	85.9	92.9	83.8	95.5	96.6	97.7	97.8	101.2	75.9	85.0	96.6	91.6	99.3	87.8
1977	94.8	95.9	100.6	87.1	95.7	88.7	97.7	101.4	98.3	97.6	105.9	81.2	81.7	98.4	99.0	101.1	86.9
1978	99.1	95.3	104.7	92.0	104.6	86.0	98.4	101.4	103.8	101.2	109.1	84.3	85.5	106.2	105.9	110.5	97.3
1979	105.8	108.8	111.4	97.3	105.0	98.8	112.5	115.0	108.1	111.7	114.6	90.8	91.9	110.7	110.6	111.2	93.3
1980	100.0	104.9	101.6	91.3	102.2	95.8	107.1	111.8	104.0	97.8	103.1	83.5	85.1	105.4	107.3	107.1	92.1
1981	101.5	103.7	112.9	94.1	95.4	90.8	107.8	112.5	110.7	109.7	118.2	91.8	87.3	103.2	102.5	99.1	84.7
1982	85.8	90.7	94.0	80.1	78.2	81.5	94.5	96.1	93.7	93.2	95.2	70.8	81.1	88.4	82.5	81.9	70.3
1983	92.0	86.0	96.1	87.9	98.1	77.0	88.6	92.4	92.4	94.6	101.2	77.9	85.1	100.6	102.0	103.4	88.8

Domestic product: industry (1)

Produit intérieur : industrie (1)

index of industrial production / indice de production industrielle

1980 = 100

Adjusted - Corrigé

	Year	Q.1	Q.2	Q.3	Q.4	JAN	FEB	MAR	APR	MAY	JUN	JUL	AUG	SEP	OCT	NOV	DEC
1964		49.1	50.2	50.6	51.8	48.8	49.6	49.0	50.1	50.1	50.3	50.0	50.3	51.4	51.2	52.1	52.0
1965		53.0	53.6	54.8	56.9	52.9	52.5	53.7	53.3	53.7	53.9	55.2	53.9	55.3	56.4	56.7	57.5
1966		57.7	58.0	57.6	59.1	57.5	57.9	57.8	58.0	57.9	58.0	57.7	56.7	58.4	59.1	59.0	59.2
1967		59.1	59.9	60.5	61.1	59.4	59.0	58.8	60.2	59.6	59.9	60.1	60.8	60.7	60.2	61.3	61.9
1968		61.6	63.9	65.0	66.8	61.7	61.4	61.7	63.3	63.9	64.5	64.4	64.9	65.7	66.3	67.1	66.9
1969		68.2	68.3	68.5	69.1	67.4	68.0	69.2	68.4	68.3	68.3	69.1	68.1	68.3	68.1	68.9	70.2
1970		70.3	69.2	69.5	69.5	70.1	70.8	69.9	69.2	69.4	69.0	69.4	70.1	68.8	68.8	69.6	70.0
1971		71.1	72.5	74.8	75.9	70.6	71.2	71.5	71.6	72.6	73.2	73.4	75.4	75.7	76.0	75.4	76.3
1972		76.2	78.3	79.4	82.9	76.6	75.6	76.5	78.5	77.8	78.8	78.8	78.8	80.7	82.1	83.0	83.5
1973		86.0	87.0	88.0	89.7	84.1	86.5	87.4	86.6	86.9	87.4	89.3	86.9	87.7	88.9	90.2	90.0
1974		91.8	91.1	90.2	88.6	91.6	91.8	92.2	90.5	91.9	90.8	90.5	90.5	89.4	89.5	88.2	88.0
1975		84.9	84.2	85.2	85.9	85.0	85.4	84.2	85.0	83.3	84.4	85.5	84.9	85.1	84.1	86.0	87.6
1976		88.2	90.9	91.1	90.9	87.3	88.0	89.3	90.5	91.7	90.5	90.4	91.3	91.4	89.5	91.5	91.6
1977		92.5	92.3	92.5	92.9	93.4	91.9	92.2	91.3	92.4	93.2	92.7	92.6	92.1	92.8	92.9	93.0
1978		93.1	94.7	95.4	99.0	92.9	93.4	93.1	95.0	93.7	95.5	94.2	94.9	97.2	97.5	98.7	100.6
1979		100.9	101.2	102.5	101.5	100.8	101.1	100.7	100.1	102.2	101.3	102.4	102.6	102.7	102.5	101.8	100.7
1980		101.7	98.3	99.0	101.1	102.3	100.5	102.2	99.9	97.5	97.5	98.5	98.1	100.5	101.0	100.9	101.4
1981		101.6	103.6	100.8	97.6	100.4	101.6	102.7	103.2	103.3	104.3	102.8	99.9	99.9	99.3	97.0	96.6
1982		94.2	91.2	88.9	85.1	95.2	94.2	93.2	91.5	92.0	90.0	87.2	91.0	88.5	86.0	86.4	85.9
1983		90.5	93.4	97.4	100.5	90.4	90.3	90.9	91.9	93.0	95.2	95.6	97.4	99.2	99.6	100.5	101.4

Domestic product: manufacturing (1)

Produit intérieur : industries manufacturières (1)

index of industrial production / indice de production industrielle

1980 = 100

Adjusted - Corrigé

	Year	Q.1	Q.2	Q.3	Q.4	JAN	FEB	MAR	APR	MAY	JUN	JUL	AUG	SEP	OCT	NOV	DEC
1964		50.1	51.0	51.5	52.9	49.6	50.8	50.0	50.9	51.1	51.0	50.7	51.4	52.7	52.2	53.2	53.2
1965		54.2	55.2	56.3	58.6	53.9	53.6	55.0	54.6	55.5	55.7	57.2	55.0	56.6	58.2	58.2	59.4
1966		59.6	59.7	59.6	61.0	59.4	59.8	59.6	59.8	59.6	59.6	60.3	58.3	60.2	61.1	60.7	61.1
1967		60.8	61.3	62.0	62.4	61.2	60.8	60.5	62.1	60.8	61.1	61.8	62.1	62.1	61.2	62.6	63.4
1968		62.8	65.4	66.4	68.5	63.1	62.4	62.8	64.8	65.5	66.0	65.6	66.3	67.3	67.9	68.8	68.7
1969		69.8	70.5	71.1	70.8	68.7	69.6	71.0	70.0	70.7	70.7	72.0	70.8	70.5	70.1	70.8	71.5
1970		70.9	69.6	69.3	68.7	70.7	71.5	70.6	69.9	69.8	69.1	69.5	70.2	68.1	68.0	68.9	69.1
1971		71.0	72.6	74.9	76.3	70.2	71.3	71.4	71.7	72.8	73.4	73.1	75.6	76.1	76.7	75.8	76.4
1972		76.2	78.6	80.0	82.9	76.7	75.5	76.6	78.7	77.9	79.1	79.1	79.8	81.2	81.7	82.9	83.9
1973		86.3	86.9	88.0	90.1	84.4	86.9	87.7	86.5	86.8	87.3	89.5	86.9	87.6	89.3	90.4	90.5
1974		92.7	91.5	90.6	89.3	92.6	92.7	92.7	90.7	92.4	91.4	91.0	91.1	89.7	90.2	88.9	88.7
1975		85.2	85.0	85.7	86.9	85.2	85.7	84.6	85.4	84.4	85.1	86.1	85.4	85.5	85.1	86.8	88.9
1976		89.2	92.1	91.9	91.0	87.9	89.2	90.6	92.1	92.8	91.5	91.5	92.6	91.6	89.0	91.7	92.2
1977		93.0	92.7	92.5	93.0	93.6	92.4	92.9	92.0	92.6	93.6	93.2	92.4	92.1	93.2	92.9	92.9
1978		93.7	96.5	97.9	101.3	93.4	93.8	93.8	96.9	95.8	96.8	96.9	97.1	99.8	99.7	101.2	103.0
1979		103.1	102.8	103.4	102.6	103.1	103.1	103.1	101.4	104.1	102.8	103.0	103.7	103.5	103.5	102.8	101.6
1980		102.4	98.0	98.5	101.0	103.4	101.3	102.5	100.1	96.9	97.0	97.8	97.4	100.4	101.3	100.3	101.6
1981		102.3	105.0	101.5	97.2	100.8	102.5	103.6	104.3	104.7	106.1	104.7	100.0	99.9	99.3	96.6	95.8
1982		92.7	90.4	89.0	85.0	93.4	92.7	91.9	90.2	91.0	89.9	87.4	91.5	88.2	85.3	85.0	84.7
1983		90.5	92.6	96.5	99.3	90.4	90.4	90.6	91.6	92.4	93.8	94.9	96.9	98.1	98.5	100.0	101.1

Domestic product: durable manufactures (1)

Produit intérieur : biens durables (1)

index of industrial production / indice de production industrielle

1980 = 100

Adjusted - Corrigé

	Year	Q.1	Q.2	Q.3	Q.4	JAN	FEB	MAR	APR	MAY	JUN	JUL	AUG	SEP	OCT	NOV	DEC
1964		46.6	47.2	48.0	49.3	46.0	47.2	46.4	47.0	47.4	47.4	46.8	47.6	49.6	48.5	49.9	49.4
1965		51.6	53.4	53.9	57.2	51.3	50.5	53.0	52.8	53.3	54.0	56.0	51.4	54.3	56.6	56.9	58.1
1966		58.2	58.0	57.6	59.6	57.9	58.5	58.2	58.3	58.0	57.8	59.0	54.7	59.1	59.9	59.4	59.6
1967		59.5	59.8	60.4	61.1	59.6	59.4	59.6	60.5	59.4	59.4	60.0	60.7	60.6	59.2	61.3	62.8
1968		60.6	64.7	66.7	68.7	62.0	60.0	59.8	63.6	65.5	65.0	65.4	67.0	67.9	68.5	69.2	68.3
1969		69.7	70.5	70.5	70.2	68.5	69.4	71.2	69.8	71.1	70.6	72.0	70.1	69.5	69.0	70.3	71.4
1970		70.1	68.4	68.0	65.1	69.7	71.0	69.7	69.3	68.1	67.7	68.4	69.3	65.8	64.5	64.7	66.0
1971		69.6	71.6	74.0	75.5	68.2	70.6	69.9	70.1	71.5	73.1	72.3	74.7	74.9	76.3	74.3	75.8
1972		74.7	76.8	78.4	82.2	75.6	74.0	74.6	77.2	76.2	77.0	77.4	77.9	79.9	80.2	82.3	84.1
1973		87.5	87.5	89.5	91.0	85.0	87.6	89.7	87.1	87.2	83.3	90.9	88.4	89.5	91.2	91.3	90.5
1974		94.8	93.4	93.2	92.1	94.8	95.1	94.5	92.1	94.6	93.4	93.4	93.8	92.4	92.6	92.0	91.7
1975		85.9	86.5	88.4	90.0	85.2	86.4	86.1	86.9	85.8	86.8	88.9	88.1	88.2	88.0	90.0	92.1
1976		91.7	93.3	92.7	92.0	91.0	92.4	91.6	93.4	94.2	92.4	91.6	93.7	92.8	88.4	93.0	94.5
1977		95.3	94.6	94.7	94.9	96.6	94.1	95.1	93.7	94.0	96.1	95.8	93.7	94.5	95.6	94.9	94.4
1978		94.3	98.7	100.0	103.9	93.7	94.3	94.8	99.0	97.7	99.3	99.3	98.9	101.7	101.4	103.8	106.3
1979		107.2	105.5	106.1	104.5	107.8	107.5	106.3	103.5	108.1	105.0	106.1	106.6	105.7	105.3	104.9	103.3
1980		103.5	96.7	98.0	101.8	104.9	102.4	103.2	99.5	95.3	95.3	96.9	96.7	100.6	102.1	101.2	101.9
1981		102.8	106.6	101.3	95.2	100.8	103.3	104.3	105.5	105.9	108.3	106.5	99.0	98.4	98.0	94.1	93.7
1982		90.3	88.1	85.9	78.6	91.0	90.6	89.3	88.9	88.9	86.6	83.5	90.0	84.2	79.6	78.0	78.0
1983		86.2	88.8	93.9	99.3	87.0	85.5	86.1	87.0	88.9	90.5	91.5	94.3	95.9	97.7	99.6	100.7

Domestic product: non-durable manufactures (1)
index of industrial production
1980 = 100

Produit intérieur : biens non durables (1)
indice de production industrielle
1980 = 100

	Year	Q.1	Q.2	Q.3	Q.4	JAN	FEB	MAR	APR	MAY	JUN	JUL	AUG	SEP	OCT	NOV	DEC
1964	55.2	51.9	55.8	56.4	56.8	49.9	53.2	52.6	54.2	55.7	57.5	53.1	57.2	58.7	58.1	58.4	54.0
1965	58.2	54.9	58.0	59.5	60.3	53.0	55.8	56.0	55.8	58.4	60.0	56.3	60.6	61.6	62.0	61.2	57.7
1966	61.6	59.2	62.2	62.4	62.7	57.0	60.3	60.3	60.7	62.0	63.9	59.5	63.8	64.0	64.5	63.8	59.9
1967	63.1	60.3	63.8	64.0	64.2	58.8	61.5	60.6	63.1	62.8	65.5	61.1	64.7	66.1	65.5	65.7	61.5
1968	66.4	63.3	67.2	66.3	68.9	60.1	64.2	65.4	66.0	66.0	69.5	63.0	66.7	69.2	69.4	70.4	66.9
1969	70.8	67.9	71.5	71.5	72.2	64.5	68.9	70.3	70.2	70.9	73.5	68.2	72.5	74.2	73.6	73.6	69.6
1970	71.4	69.7	72.3	70.6	73.1	67.0	71.1	71.0	70.9	72.7	73.5	67.4	71.6	72.9	74.1	75.4	69.9
1971	74.8	70.0	75.8	75.7	78.0	65.1	71.9	73.0	74.3	74.8	78.2	67.6	76.2	83.1	81.0	81.5	71.5
1972	80.9	75.3	82.6	81.2	84.5	70.2	77.1	78.6	81.3	80.1	86.5	73.9	81.4	88.1	83.1	88.0	77.4
1973	86.7	82.7	88.4	85.5	89.9	75.5	86.9	85.7	87.1	86.5	91.7	80.8	84.3	91.4	92.0	94.0	83.8
1974	88.5	88.2	92.1	86.8	86.7	81.8	91.7	91.3	90.6	90.2	95.4	81.6	86.9	91.9	91.6	89.7	78.9
1975	83.5	82.5	85.9	81.9	83.8	77.4	86.6	83.6	85.2	83.4	89.0	76.2	81.6	87.9	85.5	87.5	78.4
1976	89.6	85.5	93.3	89.6	90.1	77.0	88.1	91.2	92.1	91.4	96.5	82.8	90.1	95.8	93.4	94.5	82.5
1977	90.6	89.5	93.2	88.9	90.9	82.5	93.6	92.3	91.4	91.2	97.0	81.8	89.9	95.1	94.2	94.9	83.6
1978	95.4	92.1	96.7	94.3	98.3	84.9	96.2	95.3	96.0	93.9	100.3	84.9	93.7	104.5	101.9	102.7	90.4
1979	99.9	98.0	102.4	98.8	100.5	89.4	101.7	102.8	100.4	99.8	107.0	89.4	98.9	108.3	105.8	105.2	90.5
1980	100.0	100.5	101.9	97.4	100.2	92.9	103.0	105.7	101.8	98.9	104.9	88.2	96.5	107.6	105.3	103.8	91.4
1981	101.6	101.1	106.0	100.1	99.2	91.8	104.7	106.9	103.7	103.8	110.4	91.6	99.7	109.2	105.5	103.9	88.2
1982	93.0	94.3	95.3	91.2	91.5	87.3	97.3	98.1	92.0	94.0	99.8	81.9	92.0	99.7	95.6	96.5	82.4
1983	98.0	94.4	96.8	97.9	100.1	85.8	98.4	99.0	96.8	96.7	96.9	87.5	98.3	107.7	103.4	104.8	92.0

Domestic product: construction (1)
1980 = 100

Produit intérieur : construction (1)
1980 = 100

	Year	Q.1	Q.2	Q.3	Q.4	JAN	FEB	MAR	APR	MAY	JUN	JUL	AUG	SEP	OCT	NOV	DEC
1964	58.8	50.5	56.1	65.4	63.3	48.6	52.0	50.8	52.4	54.5	61.3	64.0	66.2	66.0	66.8	64.1	58.9
1965	66.0	57.2	62.7	73.3	70.4	56.5	57.4	57.6	59.2	61.2	67.8	72.0	74.5	74.8	74.8	71.6	64.9
1966	71.1	64.0	70.4	78.1	71.8	62.1	64.1	65.9	67.2	69.0	74.8	77.9	77.8	78.5	77.2	73.5	64.8
1967	70.8	61.9	67.1	80.4	73.8	62.3	62.6	60.8	62.1	65.0	74.1	78.5	80.8	82.0	79.5	75.4	66.5
1968	73.9	63.0	72.4	84.2	75.9	60.1	64.1	64.7	67.2	71.6	78.5	82.8	84.5	85.4	83.9	79.4	64.3
1969	76.3	66.3	73.8	86.2	78.9	62.5	68.1	68.2	71.4	72.9	77.0	82.8	87.7	88.0	86.2	81.3	69.1
1970	75.5	65.6	71.7	84.4	80.3	63.0	67.8	66.0	67.4	71.1	76.7	80.9	84.1	88.2	86.2	83.8	70.9
1971	83.2	64.0	81.4	100.3	87.2	61.3	65.2	65.7	73.2	78.5	92.3	96.7	102.0	102.3	99.3	89.2	73.1
1972	85.5	69.0	85.1	101.8	86.2	67.3	69.8	69.7	78.9	82.0	94.3	98.5	103.9	103.0	97.2	88.7	72.7
1973	88.2	70.3	85.5	103.8	93.2	68.8	70.7	71.4	77.3	83.9	95.2	100.5	103.8	107.3	105.0	94.9	79.6
1974	91.5	77.6	88.6	105.9	93.8	75.6	78.4	78.8	83.2	85.7	96.8	102.4	106.2	109.3	106.4	96.1	79.0
1975	96.3	75.5	91.5	113.9	104.3	74.6	77.6	74.3	82.0	90.5	102.0	108.0	115.1	118.7	116.2	107.0	89.5
1976	100.9	84.8	104.0	114.7	100.2	82.0	85.7	86.9	94.2	101.9	116.1	114.0	116.1	114.1	110.7	103.7	86.1
1977	100.0	81.3	99.4	116.1	103.1	79.2	82.6	82.2	89.5	97.8	110.8	112.9	117.7	117.8	116.7	105.9	86.7
1978	97.9	81.3	98.7	113.1	98.7	77.9	83.2	82.9	89.9	96.6	109.4	109.6	114.5	115.2	110.7	101.9	83.4
1979	101.0	80.9	99.2	119.0	104.8	79.2	82.0	81.5	87.3	97.6	112.8	117.0	119.6	120.6	117.5	106.4	90.4
1980	100.0	84.4	97.9	114.6	103.2	83.9	85.2	84.2	89.2	98.1	106.3	111.8	114.7	117.2	115.2	104.8	89.5
1981	106.1	88.6	107.2	123.4	105.5	87.4	90.3	88.0	94.2	107.2	120.1	122.6	123.7	123.7	117.9	108.9	89.6
1982	94.3	85.7	95.2	103.7	92.4	84.3	87.7	85.3	92.0	91.8	101.8	103.7	103.5	104.0	102.5	92.6	82.0
1983	90.5	77.3	95.2	106.7	88.6	77.8	77.6	76.5	81.5	93.7	110.6	110.3	106.6	103.0	99.8	89.1	77.0

Domestic product: services (1)
1980 = 100

Produit intérieur : services (1)
1980 = 100

	Year	Q.1	Q.2	Q.3	Q.4	JAN	FEB	MAR	APR	MAY	JUN	JUL	AUG	SEP	OCT	NOV	DEC
1964	45.7	43.4	46.0	45.9	47.7	42.9	42.5	44.8	44.9	46.4	46.8	45.6	45.7	46.5	47.2	47.2	48.7
1965	48.8	45.7	49.0	48.9	51.5	45.1	44.9	47.2	47.8	49.4	49.6	48.6	48.7	49.4	50.6	51.1	52.7
1966	52.2	49.3	52.4	52.3	54.5	48.2	48.2	51.5	51.1	52.7	53.4	51.7	52.1	53.1	54.2	54.1	55.4
1967	55.3	51.8	56.0	55.5	57.7	51.4	50.6	53.5	54.2	56.8	57.0	54.9	55.1	56.5	57.1	57.4	58.7
1968	58.2	55.2	58.4	58.4	60.9	54.1	55.3	56.1	57.0	58.7	59.5	57.5	57.8	59.7	60.2	61.1	61.4
1969	61.6	58.8	61.9	61.5	64.2	57.4	58.9	60.2	60.8	61.8	63.0	60.8	60.7	63.3	63.5	64.0	65.0
1970	63.9	61.2	64.3	63.9	66.3	60.4	61.2	62.1	63.2	64.4	65.3	63.3	62.8	65.7	65.5	66.2	67.1
1971	67.2	63.3	67.8	67.4	70.4	61.8	63.4	64.7	66.2	67.7	69.5	66.2	66.4	69.6	70.1	70.4	70.8
1972	71.5	67.5	72.1	71.4	74.9	66.0	67.4	69.0	70.1	72.2	74.0	70.5	70.2	73.6	74.5	74.8	75.3
1973	76.4	72.6	77.4	75.7	79.9	70.4	72.7	74.7	76.5	77.2	78.5	75.4	74.0	77.8	79.1	80.1	80.7
1974	81.0	77.5	82.3	81.0	83.2	75.2	77.9	79.5	80.0	82.6	84.4	80.5	80.1	82.3	83.0	83.2	83.5
1975	83.9	79.9	84.9	83.9	85.8	78.1	80.5	81.1	83.0	85.0	86.8	83.3	82.9	85.7	85.6	86.5	88.2
1976	87.7	83.3	89.1	88.2	90.1	80.9	83.6	85.5	87.4	89.1	90.8	87.3	87.3	89.8	90.0	90.5	90.0
1977	90.5	87.1	91.6	90.6	92.7	84.6	87.9	88.9	90.0	91.4	93.5	89.5	90.0	92.4	92.5	93.1	92.5
1978	94.1	89.6	95.3	94.9	95.7	86.7	90.6	91.5	93.9	94.7	97.3	93.5	93.9	97.3	96.3	97.3	96.5
1979	97.6	93.3	98.8	98.5	99.6	90.2	93.6	96.1	96.9	98.4	101.2	97.6	97.8	100.5	99.9	99.7	99.1
1980	100.0	95.8	100.9	100.6	102.8	92.8	96.1	98.3	99.0	100.6	103.0	99.4	99.9	102.5	102.8	103.3	102.3
1981	103.4	99.9	105.6	103.3	104.8	96.7	100.5	102.5	103.9	105.4	107.3	102.3	102.4	105.1	104.5	105.3	104.5
1982	101.8	100.0	103.6	101.3	102.2	97.6	100.6	101.8	101.9	103.9	104.9	100.2	100.5	103.0	102.1	102.8	101.9
1983	103.5	98.6	104.7	104.4	106.2	96.3	98.4	101.2	102.3	104.7	107.2	103.0	103.9	106.4	106.2	106.6	105.9

Domestic product: non-durable manufactures (1)

index of industrial production

1980 = 100

Produit intérieur : biens non durables (1)

indice de production industrielle

1980 = 100

Adjusted - Corrigé

Year	Q.1	Q.2	Q.3	Q.4	JAN	FEB	MAR	APR	MAY	JUN	JUL	AUG	SEP	OCT	NOV	DEC
1964	53.8	55.0	55.4	56.7	53.4	54.4	53.7	55.1	55.0	54.9	54.8	55.5	55.9	56.1	56.8	57.1
1965	56.9	57.2	58.8	60.0	56.7	56.8	57.0	56.5	57.6	57.5	58.4	58.9	59.0	59.8	59.5	60.6
1966	61.1	61.4	61.7	62.4	60.9	61.2	61.2	61.5	61.3	61.4	61.7	62.0	61.4	62.4	62.2	62.7
1967	62.1	62.9	63.6	63.8	62.7	62.2	61.5	63.6	62.2	62.9	63.8	63.5	63.5	63.3	63.9	64.1
1968	65.1	66.2	66.0	68.2	64.3	65.1	65.9	66.0	65.5	67.1	65.9	65.5	66.6	67.3	68.4	69.0
1969	69.9	70.4	71.7	71.4	68.9	69.9	70.8	70.1	70.2	70.9	72.0	71.6	71.6	71.2	71.4	71.6
1970	71.3	70.9	70.5	72.4	71.7	72.1	71.6	70.5	71.7	70.5	70.7	70.6	70.4	71.7	73.3	72.3
1971	72.5	73.7	75.9	77.1	72.3	72.1	73.1	73.3	74.1	73.8	74.0	76.4	77.3	77.0	77.3	77.1
1972	77.9	80.4	81.7	83.6	77.9	77.0	78.7	80.1	79.8	81.3	81.0	81.8	82.4	83.4	83.6	83.7
1973	85.3	86.1	86.4	89.1	83.9	86.2	85.7	85.9	86.3	86.2	88.1	85.5	85.6	87.4	89.5	90.5
1974	90.4	89.5	87.9	86.2	90.4	90.2	90.7	89.3	90.2	89.2	88.5	88.2	86.9	87.6	85.6	85.5
1975	84.3	83.4	82.8	83.7	85.2	84.8	83.0	83.9	83.0	83.3	83.1	82.7	82.7	81.9	83.5	85.5
1976	86.7	90.9	91.1	89.9	84.6	85.8	89.6	90.7	91.4	90.5	91.4	91.5	90.5	89.8	90.2	89.8
1977	90.6	90.7	90.4	90.9	90.5	90.8	90.5	90.2	91.0	90.9	90.4	91.1	89.6	90.8	90.7	91.3
1978	93.0	94.2	95.7	98.6	93.0	93.2	92.9	94.7	93.8	94.1	94.2	95.2	97.8	97.8	98.5	99.4
1979	98.7	99.9	100.5	100.5	98.2	98.4	99.5	99.2	99.8	100.6	99.7	100.7	101.0	101.5	100.6	99.7
1980	101.2	99.4	99.1	100.3	101.8	100.1	101.3	100.8	98.7	98.7	98.8	98.2	100.2	100.4	99.2	101.2
1981	101.9	103.4	101.8	99.3	100.9	101.8	103.0	103.0	103.3	103.7	102.7	101.2	101.4	100.7	99.4	97.9
1982	95.2	92.8	92.4	91.3	96.0	95.0	94.7	91.7	93.3	93.5	91.5	93.1	92.6	91.2	92.3	91.7
1983	95.1	96.6	99.5	100.3	94.4	95.6	95.4	96.6	96.0	97.2	98.5	99.6	100.3	99.3	100.3	101.4

Domestic product: construction (1)

1980 = 100

Produit intérieur : construction (1)

1980 = 100

Adjusted - Corrigé

Year	Q.1	Q.2	Q.3	Q.4	JAN	FEB	MAR	APR	MAY	JUN	JUL	AUG	SEP	OCT	NOV	DEC
1964	57.6	57.5	57.9	61.9	56.6	58.9	57.2	57.5	57.2	57.8	57.4	58.1	58.3	60.1	61.7	63.8
1965	64.3	64.2	66.0	68.9	65.0	63.6	64.4	64.0	64.1	64.6	65.3	66.2	66.6	67.6	68.4	70.6
1966	71.8	72.0	70.1	71.7	71.5	70.5	73.5	72.6	72.0	71.3	70.9	69.6	69.6	70.0	72.4	72.6
1967	69.6	68.5	[illegible]	72.4	71.6	69.0	68.1	67.3	67.7	70.5	70.8	71.4	72.2	72.2	72.4	72.6
1968	71.4	74.9	74.9	73.4	70.3	70.8	73.1	74.3	75.4	74.8	75.5	74.8	74.4	74.9	74.7	70.5
1969	76.4	76.3	76.3	76.5	74.6	76.2	78.5	78.2	77.0	73.8	75.9	76.3	76.3	76.4	76.5	76.5
1970	75.2	73.6	74.5	77.6	74.5	76.2	74.8	73.5	74.3	73.1	73.7	73.9	76.1	76.2	78.7	78.0
1971	79.2	82.9	85.3	84.8	78.5	79.4	79.6	82.7	82.5	83.7	84.9	85.9	85.1	85.2	84.9	84.4
1972	84.3	87.0	86.4	84.1	84.5	84.1	84.1	88.9	86.4	85.7	86.5	86.9	85.6	83.9	84.5	83.9
1973	86.0	87.7	86.4	90.3	86.2	85.5	86.3	87.4	88.3	87.4	88.3	87.9	89.0	90.3	90.8	91.4
1974	94.0	91.1	90.8	91.3	93.7	93.8	94.3	93.2	90.8	89.2	90.8	90.7	90.9	91.8	91.1	90.9
1975	91.5	93.0	97.5	101.9	92.6	92.9	88.9	92.5	93.7	92.8	95.4	98.0	99.1	101.1	101.3	103.3
1976	102.8	105.7	99.1	97.5	101.7	102.5	104.1	105.8	105.2	106.0	101.7	99.7	95.7	96.3	97.6	98.6
1977	99.1	100.4	100.5	100.2	97.8	99.2	100.1	100.3	100.3	100.6	100.7	101.1	99.7	101.7	100.2	98.8
1978	97.6	99.1	97.3	96.6	95.2	98.6	99.1	100.3	98.4	98.7	96.8	97.5	97.6	96.4	97.1	96.2
1979	98.6	99.5	102.5	103.2	98.7	98.6	98.6	97.2	99.1	102.2	102.7	102.4	102.5	102.6	102.3	104.5
1980	101.7	98.9	99.1	101.7	103.0	101.7	100.4	100.3	99.5	96.8	98.3	98.9	100.1	101.0	101.5	102.8
1981	105.6	108.0	107.2	104.0	105.5	106.0	105.2	105.6	108.9	109.6	108.0	107.2	106.3	104.6	105.9	101.5
1982	100.8	96.1	90.6	91.2	101.0	[illegible]	100.4	101.9	92.6	93.7	92.4	89.7	89.8	90.3	89.8	93.5
1983	91.9	95.7	92.4	87.3	94.2	90.6	91.0	91.0	95.6	100.5	96.8	91.8	88.7	87.9	86.8	87.2

Domestic product: services (1)

1980 = 100

Produit intérieur : services (1)

1980 = 100

Adjusted - Corrigé

Year	Q.1	Q.2	Q.3	Q.4	JAN	FEB	MAR	APR	MAY	JUN	JUL	AUG	SEP	OCT	NOV	DEC
1964	45.0	45.3	46.1	46.6	44.8	45.0	45.2	45.2	45.2	45.5	45.8	46.0	46.4	46.4	46.5	46.9
1965	47.4	48.2	49.1	50.3	47.0	47.4	47.6	48.1	48.2	48.3	48.9	49.2	49.2	49.7	50.3	50.8
1966	51.1	51.6	52.6	53.3	50.4	51.1	51.8	51.5	51.4	52.0	52.1	52.7	52.8	53.3	53.2	53.3
1967	53.7	55.1	55.8	56.4	53.7	53.5	53.9	54.6	55.3	55.5	55.4	55.9	56.2	56.2	56.4	56.5
1968	57.0	57.6	58.5	59.4	56.8	57.1	57.2	57.2	57.7	57.9	58.1	58.8	58.6	59.0	59.6	59.7
1969	60.9	61.1	61.9	62.7	60.3	61.0	61.4	61.0	60.9	61.4	61.6	61.8	62.2	62.4	62.5	63.2
1970	63.3	63.5	64.2	64.7	63.4	63.3	63.2	63.4	63.5	63.6	64.1	64.0	64.5	64.4	64.7	65.2
1971	65.2	66.5	68.0	69.0	64.8	65.3	65.6	65.9	66.6	67.2	67.2	68.2	68.6	68.8	69.0	69.2
1972	69.6	70.7	72.1	73.4	69.3	69.5	70.0	69.7	70.9	71.5	71.6	71.9	72.7	73.2	73.3	73.7
1973	74.9	75.9	76.4	78.5	74.2	74.8	75.7	76.0	75.8	75.8	76.5	75.6	76.9	77.9	78.5	78.9
1974	80.0	80.7	81.5	81.8	79.3	80.1	80.5	79.7	81.0	81.3	81.5	81.8	81.4	81.9	81.8	81.9
1975	82.3	83.3	84.4	85.4	82.2	82.6	82.1	82.8	83.4	83.7	84.2	84.4	84.7	84.6	85.1	86.5
1976	86.0	87.4	88.3	88.9	85.7	85.7	86.5	87.3	87.5	87.5	88.1	88.3	88.5	88.7	89.0	89.1
1977	89.8	90.1	90.5	91.5	89.6	90.0	89.9	90.0	90.1	90.2	90.2	90.8	90.8	91.2	91.6	91.8
1978	92.4	93.7	94.7	95.6	91.9	92.8	92.4	93.8	93.5	94.0	94.2	94.5	95.4	94.9	95.7	96.0
1979	96.3	97.1	98.4	98.4	95.8	95.9	97.1	96.8	96.9	97.8	98.2	98.4	98.6	98.5	98.3	98.6
1980	98.3	99.2	100.4	101.7	98.8	98.5	99.0	99.0	99.1	99.5	100.1	100.5	100.7	101.4	101.9	101.7
1981	103.0	103.8	103.3	103.5	102.7	102.9	103.2	103.9	103.7	103.9	103.2	103.1	103.5	103.3	103.7	103.6
1982	102.8	102.0	102.4	101.0	103.0	102.9	102.5	102.0	102.3	101.7	101.1	101.5	101.5	101.0	101.2	100.8
1983	101.4	103.0	104.5	105.0	101.7	100.6	101.9	102.3	102.9	104.0	104.3	104.7	104.8	104.9	105.1	105.1

CANADA

Production: crude petroleum
million tons, monthly averages

Production : pétrole brut
millions de tonnes, moyennes mensuelles

	Year	Q.1	Q.2	Q.3	Q.4	JAN	FEB	MAR	APR	MAY	JUN	JUL	AUG	SEP	OCT	NOV	DEC
1964	3.36	3.46	3.22	3.29	3.48	3.54	3.37	3.46	2.99	3.35	3.32	3.33	3.28	3.24	3.37	3.42	3.66
1965	3.58	3.69	3.33	3.75	3.55	3.90	3.44	3.72	3.39	3.29	3.31	3.51	3.94	3.83	3.66	3.66	3.32
1966	3.91	3.80	3.77	3.97	4.11	3.83	3.63	3.93	3.72	3.81	3.78	4.06	4.03	3.81	3.86	4.14	4.34
1967	4.27	4.04	4.14	4.55	4.34	4.32	3.78	4.03	3.90	4.22	4.30	4.63	4.71	4.34	4.32	4.21	4.50
1968	4.61	4.55	4.32	4.79	4.80	4.46	4.42	4.76	4.32	4.30	4.34	4.76	4.93	4.68	4.65	4.64	5.10
1969	5.03	4.97	4.62	5.16	5.36	4.92	4.60	5.38	4.64	4.45	4.77	5.16	5.26	5.06	5.12	5.26	5.71
1970	5.65	5.90	4.92	5.63	6.16	6.21	5.65	5.84	4.60	4.95	5.22	5.61	5.54	5.74	5.69	6.02	6.78
1971	6.04	6.08	5.45	5.27	6.35	6.28	5.69	6.27	5.39	5.46	5.50	6.52	6.09	6.20	6.02	6.08	6.94
1972	6.96	6.88	6.28	7.05	7.64	7.18	6.52	6.94	6.17	6.32	6.36	7.11	7.21	6.84	7.66	7.26	8.00
1973	8.03	8.10	7.72	8.05	8.23	8.32	7.54	8.43	7.88	7.77	7.52	8.19	8.26	7.72	8.28	8.05	8.36
1974	7.54	8.08	7.58	7.34	7.17	8.31	7.38	8.54	7.76	7.61	7.37	7.57	7.38	7.07	7.31	6.67	7.52
1975	6.44	6.59	5.79	5.83	6.58	7.25	6.14	6.37	5.55	5.39	6.41	6.78	6.84	6.86	6.68	6.35	6.71
1976	5.89	5.67	5.84	5.62	6.43	6.06	5.38	5.58	5.10	6.04	6.37	5.78	5.61	5.49	6.21	5.98	7.10
1977	5.93	5.93	5.79	5.58	6.44	5.94	5.66	6.20	5.36	5.79	6.20	5.24	6.14	5.34	5.71	6.43	7.18
1978	5.85	5.68	5.62	5.58	6.50	5.71	5.36	5.97	4.89	5.30	6.66	5.31	5.93	5.51	6.17	6.51	6.83
1979	6.59	6.50	6.53	5.52	6.82	6.31	6.32	6.86	6.65	6.44	6.51	6.72	6.45	6.38	6.90	6.60	6.95
1980	6.30	6.53	6.24	5.27	6.19	6.70	6.22	6.66	5.88	6.43	6.41	6.54	6.44	5.81	5.91	6.37	6.30
1981	5.66	5.90	5.57	5.62	5.56	6.28	5.66	5.77	5.77	5.60	5.34	5.70	5.70	5.46	5.01	5.52	6.15
1982	5.59	5.38	5.02	5.87	6.08	5.58	5.19	5.37	4.15	5.14	5.76	5.71	6.26	5.65	5.94	6.11	6.19
1983		5.61	5.39	5.32		5.72	5.37	5.75	4.98	5.27	5.92	6.31	6.40	6.24	6.38	6.25	

Production: crude steel
thousand tons, monthly averages

Production : acier brut
milliers de tonnes, moyennes mensuelles

	Year	Q.1	Q.2	Q.3	Q.4	JAN	FEB	MAR	APR	MAY	JUN	JUL	AUG	SEP	OCT	NOV	DEC
1964																	
1965																	
1966																	
1967																	
1968																	
1969	767	881	909	523	757	895	816	932	919	923	884	855	349	365	481	860	929
1970	933	936	940	880	977	946	883	979	932	965	923	895	879	867	943	903	1085
1971	920	880	970	899	931	917	801	921	934	993	984	899	905	892	956	923	914
1972	988	987	1024	975	968	1005	940	1016	1003	1056	1014	978	981	965	888	981	1034
1973	1124	1100	1136	1118	1141	1107	1016	1178	1110	1140	1157	1073	1177	1103	1179	1104	1141
1974	1134	1127	1111	1115	1182	1143	1095	1142	1106	1079	1148	1102	1112	1134	1189	1194	1162
1975	1086	1134	1174	985	1049	1176	1050	1177	1178	1184	1159	1008	975	973	983	1072	1091
1976	1098	1077	1110	1109	1095	1071	1041	1120	1123	1152	1065	1122	1084	1120	1082	1104	1100
1977	1126	1136	1122	1107	1138	1117	1062	1228	1085	1151	1129	1023	1143	1155	1198	1113	1104
1978	1240	1212	1257	1203	1289	1202	1148	1287	1245	1290	1236	1233	1059	1316	1307	1231	1330
1979	1342	1325	1349	1297	1397	1372	1258	1346	1329	1409	1309	1266	1327	1297	1417	1395	1379
1980	1323	1353	1378	1238	1325	1413	1324	1322	1353	1435	1345	1194	1233	1287	1336	1325	1314
1981	1234	1409	1484	1027	1016	1396	1334	1497	1459	1511	1481	1390	703	989	1005	955	1087
1982	989	1232	1081	909	733	1219	1212	1265	1273	1090	980	833	930	965	814	761	623
1983	1070	883	1114	1104	1175	739	845	1081	1132	1079	1132	1019	1105	1187	1239	1198	1088

Production: natural gas
billion cubic metres, monthly averages

Production : gaz naturel
milliards de mètres cubes, moyennes mensuelles

	Year	Q.1	Q.2	Q.3	Q.4	JAN	FEB	MAR	APR	MAY	JUN	JUL	AUG	SEP	OCT	NOV	DEC
1964	3.11	3.32	2.86	2.75	3.49	3.49	3.23	3.25	3.11	2.88	2.59	2.70	2.80	2.80	3.07	3.34	4.06
1965	3.41	3.71	3.20	3.01	3.73	3.90	3.48	3.76	3.32	3.26	3.03	2.82	3.08	3.12	3.39	3.69	4.10
1966	3.67	3.99	3.43	3.16	4.09	4.33	3.69	3.94	3.60	3.50	3.20	3.18	3.21	3.10	3.77	4.15	4.35
1967	4.01	4.26	3.78	3.58	4.41	4.52	3.96	4.31	3.98	3.91	3.44	3.46	3.69	3.61	4.05	4.29	4.89
1968	4.52	4.30	4.15	4.00	5.15	4.99	4.64	4.78	4.38	4.12	3.96	3.31	4.12	4.06	4.71	5.09	5.65
1969	5.20	5.52	4.74	4.72	5.82	5.72	5.22	5.63	5.25	4.73	4.23	4.45	4.76	4.94	5.41	5.86	6.20
1970	5.99	6.25	5.60	5.42	6.67	6.45	5.84	6.47	6.07	5.75	4.99	5.14	5.39	5.72	6.12	6.62	7.27
1971	6.47	6.38	6.03	5.97	7.01	7.20	6.36	7.07	6.42	6.17	5.51	5.88	5.92	6.10	6.52	6.80	7.70
1972	7.63	7.80	7.11	7.13	8.48	7.88	7.68	7.86	7.36	7.13	6.85	6.96	7.07	7.36	8.17	8.31	8.97
1973	8.24	8.65	7.76	7.68	8.88	9.02	8.18	8.76	8.20	7.73	7.34	7.50	7.73	7.76	8.60	8.87	9.16
1974	8.09	8.66	7.32	7.43	8.41	9.04	8.06	8.87	8.25	7.88	7.33	7.47	7.76	7.22	8.12	8.27	8.84
1975	8.13	8.54	7.82	7.60	8.57	8.82	7.92	8.88	8.18	7.78	7.49	7.88	7.54	7.37	8.20	8.48	9.04
1976	8.17	8.80	7.92	7.26	8.71	9.04	8.43	8.93	8.24	7.98	7.53	7.44	7.28	7.07	8.33	8.60	9.21
1977	8.54	9.09	8.23	7.70	9.13	9.43	8.44	9.39	8.60	8.47	7.63	7.49	7.72	7.88	8.48	9.01	9.92
1978	8.30	9.12	7.61	7.37	9.12	9.88	8.55	8.92	8.21	7.63	6.99	7.38	7.52	7.21	8.13	9.14	10.08
1979	8.80	9.68	8.47	7.62	9.42	10.39	9.28	9.37	9.07	8.48	7.87	7.95	7.71	7.20	8.83	9.28	10.15
1980	8.23	9.54	7.40	5.95	9.02	10.47	8.88	9.28	7.74	7.63	6.82	6.96	7.09	6.82	8.06	8.94	10.06
1981	8.15	9.15	7.46	7.07	8.94	9.72	8.83	8.89	8.03	7.31	7.03	7.19	6.94	7.09	8.29	8.64	9.88
1982	8.23	9.60	7.49	6.86	8.97	10.57	9.10	9.13	8.19	7.34	6.94	6.87	6.85	6.87	7.93	9.05	9.93
1983		8.96	7.01	6.75		9.39	8.54	8.44	7.60	6.95	6.47	6.56	6.60	7.10	7.84	8.79	

Production: commercial vehicles — thousands, monthly averages

Production : véhicules utilitaires — milliers, moyennes mensuelles

	Year	Q.1	Q.2	Q.3	Q.4	JAN	FEB	MAR	APR	MAY	JUN	JUL	AUG	SEP	OCT	NOV	DEC
1964	9.2	10.5	11.6	6.7	8.2	10.7	10.2	10.6	11.8	11.5	11.6	5.8	4.4	9.8	7.0	10.2	7.3
1965	12.1	11.9	14.7	6.5	15.0	10.1	10.7	15.0	14.3	14.2	15.5	9.1	2.3	8.4	12.6	16.1	15.4
1966	16.7	16.0	18.8	12.3	19.9	16.6	14.5	16.9	16.7	17.5	22.1	19.9	4.1	12.7	16.1	22.7	20.8
1967	18.9	20.2	24.0	12.2	19.0	19.7	18.4	22.6	21.3	25.3	25.5	12.3	7.9	16.5	12.7	21.3	23.1
1968	23.3	21.2	26.0	18.7	27.2	26.2	19.4	18.1	23.0	29.4	25.5	23.3	8.7	24.0	30.2	28.5	22.8
1969	26.5	27.8	30.0	20.7	27.2	28.5	25.3	29.6	28.9	30.4	30.7	15.7	20.6	25.9	29.1	28.0	24.7
1970	20.9	24.5	27.9	16.2	14.9	24.5	23.4	25.5	28.2	26.6	29.0	9.5	18.4	20.6	16.3	14.4	14.0
1971	22.9	24.3	26.1	19.0	22.4	20.5	25.0	27.4	25.3	25.1	27.9	16.8	16.9	23.2	22.8	25.2	19.1
1972	26.4	27.8	32.5	18.3	27.1	26.8	27.7	29.0	28.3	34.6	34.6	16.9	18.3	19.7	27.0	30.6	23.8
1973	29.2	32.8	33.4	21.9	28.6	32.7	30.8	35.0	31.6	35.4	33.3	20.5	18.0	27.2	33.8	30.9	21.1
1974	31.4	33.7	33.9	24.8	33.2	36.5	31.1	33.4	33.2	37.0	31.5	30.7	16.8	26.8	35.5	38.2	25.9
1975	32.3	30.4	35.5	26.7	36.5	28.8	31.1	31.4	37.3	34.5	34.8	29.9	17.3	32.9	40.7	36.5	32.4
1976	41.7	42.4	47.7	35.6	41.1	38.6	40.5	48.3	47.4	45.3	50.5	30.3	31.9	44.7	33.3	48.7	41.2
1977	51.0	51.3	54.8	38.4	59.6	46.0	46.9	61.1	53.1	54.1	57.3	40.2	19.9	55.2	60.7	69.1	48.9
1978	56.3	58.4	63.7	41.2	61.6	51.4	57.2	66.7	62.1	64.8	64.3	41.3	28.0	54.5	62.5	70.0	52.4
1979	53.7	70.0	63.3	36.3	45.2	66.7	65.6	77.7	55.6	72.8	61.5	30.2	32.2	46.3	50.7	46.3	38.5
1980	44.0	48.6	45.7	33.0	48.6	44.5	44.9	56.4	49.6	44.1	43.3	23.1	26.4	49.4	56.0	45.9	44.0
1981	43.3	48.4	49.7	34.8	40.3	46.5	45.4	53.3	48.1	50.1	50.8	35.8	31.9	36.8	43.0	42.9	35.2
1982	39.0	39.6	52.8	33.4	30.4	29.6	34.8	54.4	52.5	50.5	55.5	26.2	39.0	35.0	36.0	29.6	25.5
1983		40.3	51.0	39.3		34.4	38.4	48.0	47.6	51.1	54.2	25.5	40.7	51.7	51.7		

Production: passenger cars — thousands, monthly averages

Production : voitures de tourisme — milliers, moyennes mensuelles

	Year	Q.1	Q.2	Q.3	Q.4	JAN	FEB	MAR	APR	MAY	JUN	JUL	AUG	SEP	OCT	NOV	DEC
1964	46.7	58.7	62.8	23.4	42.0	62.4	54.8	58.9	63.8	59.7	65.0	21.7	8.1	40.3	34.5	50.3	41.1
1965	59.2	62.0	72.0	32.5	70.4	56.2	53.9	75.9	71.3	70.7	74.1	53.5	6.0	38.2	60.2	77.1	73.8
1966	58.5	73.5	70.6	27.5	62.3	69.8	71.2	79.5	71.9	70.6	69.4	29.3	8.3	44.8	56.3	69.3	61.3
1967	60.1	59.9	71.6	38.5	70.2	60.8	55.7	63.1	63.2	74.6	77.0	32.0	25.2	58.7	58.0	76.0	76.5
1968	75.1	58.7	94.1	50.2	97.4	76.8	48.0	51.3	85.6	106.2	90.4	42.7	26.5	81.3	103.7	104.7	83.8
1969	86.3	85.5	98.1	63.9	97.8	96.0	73.6	86.8	89.7	102.6	101.9	42.2	44.4	105.1	109.7	98.6	85.0
1970	78.1	84.7	109.8	51.5	66.4	80.1	82.4	91.8	107.7	108.3	113.2	51.1	32.9	70.5	69.7	68.9	60.8
1971	91.2	96.1	103.5	71.5	93.6	78.5	98.4	111.3	98.6	102.4	109.6	38.1	74.2	102.6	99.9	101.8	79.3
1972	95.6	98.3	111.1	58.1	104.5	95.4	97.3	103.7	106.5	114.6	112.1	49.4	60.1	94.7	111.7	117.4	84.4
1973	102.9	112.9	123.0	59.9	105.8	112.1	105.7	120.9	114.5	128.4	126.1	75.5	39.8	94.3	131.2	117.8	68.4
1974	98.7	113.7	110.5	71.3	99.0	120.2	109.1	111.9	112.0	119.7	99.7	64.7	59.3	90.7	114.4	110.3	72.2
1975	87.8	81.3	99.1	73.3	97.1	66.4	79.1	98.4	104.3	97.5	95.4	63.2	66.4	91.9	109.7	99.6	82.1
1976	95.5	102.5	114.1	73.5	92.0	99.0	95.1	113.4	113.9	108.5	119.9	40.9	79.7	99.9	78.1	108.3	89.7
1977	96.9	108.9	120.1	54.3	93.7	98.2	96.4	132.1	113.7	116.8	129.9	65.9	47.8	80.8	92.2	106.7	82.0
1978	95.3	95.2	113.5	75.1	97.4	85.2	88.3	112.1	106.3	112.2	121.8	57.2	67.5	100.6	102.9	103.9	85.4
1979	82.3	101.9	94.8	57.5	75.9	102.1	94.8	108.9	83.9	104.6	96.0	55.9	36.9	79.9	82.2	83.8	58.9
1980	70.6	76.0	76.0	54.5	75.8	65.8	73.3	88.9	76.0	74.6	77.3	53.2	36.1	74.5	88.3	80.3	58.8
1981	66.9	61.7	93.4	54.1	58.6	47.2	52.5	85.3	94.1	85.1	101.2	60.7	45.9	55.6	59.2	65.7	50.8
1982	67.3	64.3	88.8	62.1	54.0	48.3	59.5	85.3	87.0	85.6	93.9	46.4	68.5	71.4	54.3	57.1	50.5
1983		79.4	99.0	60.3		73.3	77.9	87.0	89.6	105.4	101.9	52.8	56.1	72.0	81.9		

Rate of capacity utilization — manufacturing — per cent

Taux d'utilisation de capacité — industries manufacturières — pourcentage

Adjusted - Corrigé

	Year	Q.1	Q.2	Q.3	Q.4	JAN	FEB	MAR	APR	MAY	JUN	JUL	AUG	SEP	OCT	NOV	DEC
1964	85.0	84.6	84.6	84.8	86.0												
1965	87.7	86.8	87.1	87.5	89.5												
1966	88.1	89.9	88.7	87.0	85.9												
1967	84.6	85.5	84.5	84.5	83.8												
1968	85.0	83.1	84.8	85.1	86.9												
1969	86.9	87.6	87.6	86.9	85.6												
1970	82.0	85.0	82.2	80.9	79.7												
1971	82.6	80.8	81.8	83.5	84.2												
1972	85.6	83.4	85.1	85.9	88.0												
1973	90.5	90.6	90.0	90.2	91.3												
1974	89.5	92.8	90.6	88.5	86.1												
1975	80.6	81.4	80.3	80.1	80.5												
1976	82.6	81.9	83.9	83.0	81.4												
1977	81.4	82.4	81.6	80.9	80.7												
1978	83.1	80.7	82.5	83.3	85.7												
1979	85.7	86.6	85.9	85.7	84.6												
1980	80.8	83.9	79.7	79.2	80.2												
1981	78.6	80.4	81.5	78.2	74.2												
1982	67.0	70.1	67.8	66.4	63.5												
1983		66.7	68.1	70.5													

CANADA

Production: future tendency — Perspectives de production

manufacturing — industries manufacturières

per cent balance — solde en pourcentage

	Year	Q.1	Q.2	Q.3	Q.4	JAN	FEB	MAR	APR	MAY	JUN	JUL	AUG	SEP	OCT	NOV	DEC
1964																	
1965																	
1966																	
1967																	
1968																	
1969																	
1970																	
1971																	
1972																	
1973																	
1974																	
1975																	
1976		18	19	1	-11	18			19			1			-11		
1977		-4	17	-12	2	-4			17			-12			2		
1978		8	24	11	22	8			24			11			22		
1979		5	19	5	6	5			19			6			6		
1980		-10	-	-28	14	-10			-			-28			14		
1981		11	28	-10	-6	11			28			-10			-6		
1982		-33	-25	-41	-34	-33			-25			-41			-34		
1983		-3	26	1	6	-3			26			1			6		

Orders inflow: tendency — Commandes : tendance

manufacturing — industries manufacturières

per cent balance — solde en pourcentage

	Year	Q.1	Q.2	Q.3	Q.4	JAN	FEB	MAR	APR	MAY	JUN	JUL	AUG	SEP	OCT	NOV	DEC
1964																	
1965																	
1966																	
1967																	
1968																	
1969																	
1970																	
1971																	
1972																	
1973																	
1974																	
1975																	
1976		3	10	2	-10	3			10			2			-10		
1977		-7	-2	-7	-4	-7			-2			-7			-4		
1978		2	14	30	33	2			14			30			33		
1979		18	31	22	3	18			31			22			3		
1980		-16	-21	-34	-6	-16			-21			-34			-6		
1981		-8	10	-7	-35	-8			10			-7			-35		
1982		-48	-49	-59	-51	-48			-49			-59			-51		
1983		-18	15	15	19	-18			15			15			19		

Manufacturing deliveries: total — Livraisons des industries manufacturières : total

million Canadian dollars, monthly averages — millions de dollars canadiens, moyennes mensuelles

	Year	Q.1	Q.2	Q.3	Q.4	JAN	FEB	MAR	APR	MAY	JUN	JUL	AUG	SEP	OCT	NOV	DEC
1964	2571	2442	2637	2543	2664	2369	2359	2599	2592	2586	2733	2454	2430	2746	2711	2657	2622
1965	2824	2563	2889	2810	3035	2375	2409	2904	2786	2860	3022	2710	2724	2996	2994	3088	3022
1966	3109	2949	3201	3045	3240	2725	2822	3301	3067	3217	3318	2854	3042	3239	3254	3316	3149
1967	3246	3051	3345	3212	3377	2913	2928	3313	3179	3409	3449	2987	3239	3410	3420	3444	3267
1968	3505	3213	3583	3465	3759	3121	3136	3383	3460	3699	3589	3334	3357	3709	3985	3782	3510
1969	3828	3629	3954	3765	3966	3472	3489	3925	3826	4016	4020	3680	3573	4040	4176	3897	3825
1970	3865	3691	4045	3819	3906	3506	3659	3908	4003	3957	4174	3675	3683	4100	4061	3886	3770
1971	4190	3843	4308	4190	4417	3483	3772	4276	4164	4238	4522	3794	4142	4634	4491	4534	4225
1972	4687	4367	4847	4540	4995	4030	4336	4734	4595	4919	5028	4080	4542	4996	5129	5223	4633
1973	5563	5132	5626	5394	6101	4828	4949	5619	5354	5756	5767	5162	5244	5777	6344	6297	5662
1974	6871	6374	7044	6808	7259	6146	6224	6752	6761	7282	7091	6552	6627	7244	7695	7381	6701
1975	7372	6824	7552	7316	7794	6573	6735	7164	7423	7563	7671	7108	7044	7796	8074	7756	7552
1976	8190	7763	8590	8001	8409	7162	7533	8593	8393	8515	8862	7441	7990	8571	8309	8657	8260
1977	9083	8609	9382	8889	9454	7845	8289	9692	8924	9322	9398	8270	8784	9612	9666	9698	8997
1978	10775	9719	11085	10551	11744	8962	9405	10789	10342	11223	11689	9676	10326	11653	12038	12134	11059
1979	12707	12004	12942	12581	13302	11428	11459	13126	12133	13343	13349	11717	12752	13273	14219	13557	12131
1980	14030	13630	13830	13592	15069	12889	13454	14548	13670	13859	13962	12901	12842	15034	15790	14816	14600
1981	15926	14963	16915	15809	16017	13749	14516	16624	16486	16488	17772	15627	14894	16907	17023	15977	15052
1982	15234	15150	15628	15178	14978	13729	14739	16982	15210	15815	15861	14082	15245	16207	15282	15306	14344
1983	16666	15148	17058	16672	17776	13891	14624	16929	15841	17142	18221	15300	16599	18118	18191	18408	16729

Order books: level
manufacturing
per cent balance

Carnet de commandes : niveau
industries manufacturières
solde en pourcentage

Year	Q.1	Q.2	Q.3	Q.4	JAN	FEB	MAR	APR	MAY	JUN	JUL	AUG	SEP	OCT	NOV	DEC
1964																
1965																
1966																
1967																
1968																
1969																
1970																
1971																
1972																
1973																
1974																
1975																
1976	-22	-14	-21	-21	-22			-14			-21			-21		
1977	-31	-27	-25	-19	-31			-27			-25			-19		
1978	-12	-5	2	15	-12			-5			2			15		
1979	-7	17	21	10	-7			17			21			10		
1980	-6	-30	-40	-17	-6			-30			-40			-17		
1981	-19	-6	-20	-32	-19			-6			-20			-32		
1982	-55	-63	-69	-64	-55			-63			-69			-64		
1983	-60	-32	-14	-10	-60			-32			-14			-10		

Finished goods stocks: level
manufacturing
per cent balance

Stocks de produits finis : niveau
industries manufacturières
solde en pourcentage

Year	Q.1	Q.2	Q.3	Q.4	JAN	FEB	MAR	APR	MAY	JUN	JUL	AUG	SEP	OCT	NOV	DEC
1964																
1965																
1966																
1967																
1968																
1969																
1970																
1971																
1972																
1973																
1974																
1975																
1976	12	14	14	15	12			14			14			15		
1977	18	20	19	13	18			20			19			13		
1978	14	12	9	-	14			12			9			-		
1979	31	-1	5	6	31			-1			5			6		
1980	13	27	29	23	13			27			29			23		
1981	18	20	21	28	18			20			21			28		
1982	37	47	48	37	37			47			48			37		
1983	35	17	13	13	35			17			13			13		

Manufacturing deliveries: total
million Canadian dollars, monthly averages

Adjusted - Corrigé

Livraisons des industries manufacturières : total
millions de dollars canadiens, moyennes mensuelles

Year	Q.1	Q.2	Q.3	Q.4	JAN	FEB	MAR	APR	MAY	JUN	JUL	AUG	SEP	OCT	NOV	DEC
1964	2534	2535	2564	2618	2542	2523	2536	2550	2507	2547	2514	2562	2615	2592	2628	2632
1965	2675	2776	2854	2978	2641	2637	2746	2752	2780	2797	2866	2856	2840	2920	2974	3040
1966	3073	3082	3107	3177	3031	3085	3103	3063	3096	3088	3093	3128	3100	3162	3157	3212
1967	3178	3225	3305	3314	3206	3193	3136	3229	3200	3245	3259	3357	3300	3265	3281	3398
1968	3317	3447	3543	3670	3343	3273	3334	3408	3466	3467	3514	3499	3617	3688	3685	3637
1969	3790	3801	3851	3874	3722	3792	3857	3737	3827	3838	3869	3837	3847	3873	3873	3875
1970	3863	3879	3895	3838	3842	3943	3805	3874	3877	3887	3901	3933	3852	3829	3824	3859
1971	3998	4126	4282	4350	3902	4047	4045	4065	4142	4171	4084	4417	4343	4335	4356	4359
1972	4465	4642	4654	4959	4485	4448	4462	4622	4615	4690	4487	4664	4813	4890	4953	5035
1973	5247	5399	5575	6027	5108	5230	5403	5350	5372	5475	5623	5424	5677	5891	6036	6154
1974	6563	6761	7005	7154	6453	6595	6641	6620	6805	6859	6917	6991	7111	7151	7172	7141
1975	7030	7236	7540	7705	6940	7135	7016	7202	7190	7315	7484	7630	7506	7563	7713	7838
1976	7877	8201	8240	8358	7722	7852	8057	8195	8270	8138	7993	8543	8184	8095	8387	8590
1977	8791	8946	9179	9420	8617	8781	8974	8831	8928	9081	9168	9105	9266	9403	9340	9517
1978	9865	10619	10952	11698	9674	9918	10003	10450	10531	10875	10767	10734	11354	11474	11694	11925
1979	12128	12439	13111	13154	12020	12090	12274	12151	12521	12645	12887	13269	13178	13200	13199	13064
1980	13729	13358	13935	14901	13632	13740	13814	13387	13379	13307	13690	13744	14371	14645	14912	15147
1981	15271	16344	16225	15821	14861	15343	15610	16157	16286	16589	16707	15930	16037	16064	15897	15500
1982	15429	15440	15582	14822	15177	15589	15522	15101	15582	15636	15258	16171	15316	14733	14907	14827
1983	15443	16506	17149	17680	15347	15526	15457	15978	16694	16845	17020	17085	17343	17479	17790	17771

CANADA

Manufacturing deliveries: durable goods / Livraisons des industries manufacturières : biens durables

million Canadian dollars, monthly averages / millions de dollars canadiens, moyennes mensuelles

	Year	Q.1	Q.2	Q.3	Q.4	JAN	FEB	MAR	APR	MAY	JUN	JUL	AUG	SEP	OCT	NOV	DEC
1964	1121	1081	1178	1057	1167	1029	1040	1176	1144	1143	1246	1029	959	1184	1139	1170	1191
1965	1281	1148	1349	1221	1408	1045	1054	1345	1281	1329	1437	1218	1123	1320	1335	1427	1461
1966	1421	1358	1506	1328	1494	1240	1287	1547	1439	1510	1568	1266	1279	1439	1458	1531	1493
1967	1478	1391	1554	1407	1560	1323	1323	1528	1466	1591	1604	1301	1382	1537	1533	1596	1551
1968	1634	1456	1707	1574	1797	1436	1406	1527	1604	1789	1729	1526	1448	1748	1895	1811	1685
1969	1811	1746	1912	1705	1879	1660	1659	1920	1835	1952	1949	1692	1551	1875	1951	1848	1836
1970	1785	1734	1931	1717	1760	1627	1724	1850	1923	1857	2012	1660	1601	1891	1835	1749	1697
1971	1977	1800	2075	1937	2095	1585	1769	2047	1982	2026	2219	1711	1865	2233	2148	2157	1981
1972	2222	2088	2353	2065	2384	1921	2071	2273	2203	2394	2461	1824	1985	2384	2453	2518	2182
1973	2638	2504	2750	2449	2851	2355	2394	2761	2631	2819	2799	2355	2270	2722	3046	2953	2555
1974	3136	2966	3290	2993	3293	2880	2873	3145	3144	3417	3308	2889	2809	3295	3507	3371	3000
1975	3346	3073	3471	3250	3592	2921	2994	3305	3454	3441	3518	3157	3052	3541	3734	3590	3451
1976	3749	3623	4038	3534	3800	3290	3515	4065	3959	3964	4190	3173	3540	3890	3714	3977	3709
1977	4170	3996	4419	3940	4323	3625	3717	4646	4171	4331	4755	3633	3773	4414	4482	4479	4010
1978	5012	4531	5312	4735	5470	4109	4313	5170	4959	5304	5672	4345	4419	5441	5637	5702	5069
1979	5869	5659	6117	5668	6032	5305	5342	6329	5660	6419	6270	5212	5713	6078	6553	6171	5373
1980	6242	6265	6207	5818	6678	5856	6139	6789	6269	6172	6179	5468	5254	6731	7126	6605	6302
1981	6858	6560	7689	6571	6611	5718	6360	7602	7487	7461	8118	6624	5951	7139	7117	6606	6109
1982	6273	6437	6846	5034	5775	5600	6206	7506	6606	6670	7261	5414	6006	6681	5931	5947	5448
1983	7004	6213	7339	6815	7650	5563	5909	7168	6717	7376	7924	6142	6570	7733	7387	8048	7013

Manufacturing stocks: total (3) / Stocks des industries manufacturières : total (3)

million Canadian dollars, end of period / millions de dollars canadiens, fin de période

	Year	Q.1	Q.2	Q.3	Q.4	JAN	FEB	MAR	APR	MAY	JUN	JUL	AUG	SEP	OCT	NOV	DEC
1964	5345	5007	5082	5217	5345	4974	5036	5007	5041	5067	5082	5094	5175	5217	5222	5304	5345
1965	6005	5547	5607	5744	6005	5396	5503	5547	5564	5596	5607	5596	5686	5744	5793	5855	6005
1966	6707	6188	6310	6510	6707	6051	6138	6188	6238	6277	6310	6327	6444	6510	6586	6649	6707
1967	6919	6920	6890	6908	6919	6893	6898	6920	6876	6907	6890	6892	6953	6908	6892	6907	6919
1968	7230	6997	6888	7050	7230	6960	7012	6997	6955	6925	6888	6859	6969	7050	7067	7087	7230
1969	7950	7458	7514	7671	7950	7279	7391	7458	7458	7513	7514	7543	7633	7671	7764	7840	7950
1970	8169	8181	8039	8161	8169	8063	8170	8181	8155	8136	8039	8022	8175	8161	8138	8284	8169
1971	8421	8260	8170	8150	8421	8223	8271	8260	8206	8180	8170	8090	8159	8150	8221	8264	8421
1972	9090	8656	8721	8893	9090	8504	8599	8656	8713	8679	8721	8699	8873	8893	8947	8970	9090
1973	11022	9557	9890	10339	11022	9228	9408	9557	9605	9634	9890	9908	10217	10339	10493	10695	11022
1974	15057	12156	12957	13806	15057	11429	11802	12156	12454	12639	12957	13159	13568	13806	14192	14505	15057
1975	15940	15638	15579	15464	15940	15335	15391	15638	15632	15598	15579	15390	15422	15464	15446	15630	15940
1976	17117	16421	16474	16628	17117	15914	16163	16421	16501	16351	16474	16418	16504	16628	16693	16868	17117
1977	18783	17844	17969	18103	18783	17272	17602	17844	17873	17841	17969	17899	18114	18108	18301	18588	18783
1978	20801	19733	19729	19882	20801	19203	19660	19733	19835	19635	19729	19480	19810	19882	19938	20326	20801
1979	26064	22590	23586	24496	26064	21409	22010	22590	22802	23250	23586	23592	24120	24496	24881	25282	26064
1980	29597	27760	28529	28735	29597	26785	27261	27760	28393	28533	28529	28494	28861	28735	28934	29107	29597
1981	34213	31679	32669	33228	34213	30750	31152	31679	32132	32280	32669	32468	33197	33228	33503	33733	34213
1982	30885	35656	34696	33274	30885	34912	35457	35656	35406	34997	34696	34085	33712	33274	32703	32340	30885
1983	30767	30953	29714	30242	30767	30844	30940	30953	30862	30207	29714	29532	29991	30242	30386	30523	30767

Manufacturing stocks: finished goods / Stocks des industries manufacturières : produits finis

million Canadian dollars, end of period / millions de dollars canadiens, fin de période

Adjusted - Corrigé

	Year	Q.1	Q.2	Q.3	Q.4	JAN	FEB	MAR	APR	MAY	JUN	JUL	AUG	SEP	OCT	NOV	DEC
1964	1949	1853	1916	1931	1949	1864	1873	1853	1883	1898	1916	1919	1913	1931	1927	1953	1949
1965	2127	2005	2025	2092	2127	1968	2010	2005	2005	2014	2025	2069	2069	2092	2115	2116	2127
1966	2403	2168	2239	2315	2403	2124	2152	2168	2189	2221	2239	2268	2297	2315	2344	2373	2403
1967	2516	2509	2556	2561	2516	2497	2511	2509	2529	2544	2556	2577	2566	2561	2543	2532	2516
1968	2581	2497	2499	2537	2581	2508	2510	2497	2513	2496	2499	2528	2506	2537	2539	2541	2581
1969	2814	2629	2676	2728	2814	2581	2588	2629	2637	2671	2676	2692	2691	2728	2778	2806	2814
1970	3037	2963	2969	3053	3037	2915	2955	2963	2982	2996	2969	3015	3072	3053	3034	3111	3037
1971	3096	3009	3011	2972	3096	3022	3010	3009	2985	3016	3011	2979	2967	2972	3006	3032	3096
1972	3211	3113	3148	3221	3211	3096	3082	3113	3140	3113	3148	3170	3182	3221	3206	3184	3211
1973	3601	3213	3339	3514	3601	3183	3190	3213	3248	3229	3339	3380	3442	3514	3559	3544	3601
1974	4834	3829	4100	4296	4834	3632	3726	3829	3932	3972	4100	4145	4208	4296	4479	4659	4834
1975	5272	5069	5161	5093	5272	4927	4992	5069	5134	5143	5161	5114	5101	5093	5167	5216	5272
1976	6084	5479	5640	5964	6084	5284	5386	5479	5499	5564	5640	5781	5826	5964	5987	6030	6084
1977	6669	6228	6467	6558	6669	6085	6217	6228	6275	6345	6467	6519	6615	6558	6588	6716	6669
1978	6965	6795	6779	6856	6965	6810	6885	6795	6879	6830	6779	6744	6787	6856	6882	6918	6965
1979	8564	7368	7656	8052	8564	7019	7182	7368	7407	7539	7656	7752	7836	8052	8210	8391	8564
1980	10008	9044	9482	9846	10008	8676	8842	9044	9134	9316	9482	9667	9799	9846	9852	9964	10008
1981	11915	10524	10863	11289	11915	10211	10321	10524	10562	10751	10863	10973	11102	11289	11534	11714	11915
1982	11529	12066	12159	12066	11529	11993	11935	12066	12148	12118	12159	12156	12099	12066	11996	11887	11529
1983	11466	11259	10772	11274	11466	11327	11390	11259	11078	10926	10772	10861	10980	11274	11470	11470	11466

Manufacturing deliveries: durable goods

million Canadian dollars, monthly averages

Livraisons des industries manufacturières : biens durables

millions de dollars canadiens, moyennes mensuelles

Adjusted - Corrigé

Year	Q.1	Q.2	Q.3	Q.4	JAN	FEB	MAR	APR	MAY	JUN	JUL	AUG	SEP	OCT	NOV	DEC
1964	1116	1098	1109	1142	1110	1116	1123	1109	1075	1111	1070	1109	1149	1113	1156	1156
1965	1188	1259	1297	1373	1173	1159	1231	1249	1257	1270	1332	1291	1267	1331	1364	1425
1966	1405	1412	1417	1455	1386	1415	1413	1415	1418	1402	1417	1430	1405	1444	1433	1487
1967	1439	1459	1520	1519	1451	1451	1404	1467	1443	1466	1475	1576	1510	1486	1499	1571
1968	1496	1600	1672	1745	1529	1483	1477	1556	1624	1620	1656	1631	1730	1768	1745	1723
1969	1813	1791	1817	1824	1774	1818	1848	1751	1818	1805	1838	1814	1800	1821	1826	1825
1970	1808	1816	1803	1736	1789	1864	1770	1820	1818	1810	1813	1845	1765	1738	1722	1746
1971	1854	1936	2044	2072	1782	1898	1881	1902	1942	1964	1894	2155	2082	2081	2066	2069
1972	2119	2198	2182	2379	2143	2126	2088	2182	2183	2230	2064	2186	2297	2338	2375	2423
1973	2534	2573	2625	2820	2472	2533	2598	2585	2559	2574	2661	2524	2688	2800	2833	2827
1974	3029	3091	3186	3244	3005	3049	3032	3018	3131	3125	3126	3191	3241	3219	3256	3257
1975	3134	3255	3475	3543	3060	3182	3161	3261	3232	3272	3446	3565	3417	3452	3555	3623
1976	3640	3764	3771	3791	3553	3691	3678	3796	3784	3711	3553	4058	3702	3611	3830	3933
1977	4034	4108	4206	4326	3988	3969	4145	4035	4084	4206	4216	4132	4271	4342	4279	4356
1978	4549	4970	5086	5468	4461	4574	4610	4897	4859	5154	5043	4892	5323	5346	5451	5607
1979	5650	5736	6109	5995	5588	5659	5702	5525	5878	5805	5979	6259	6090	6026	6019	5940
1980	6256	5848	6138	6641	6264	6289	6215	5956	5855	5733	6022	5946	6446	6569	6692	6663
1981	6637	7231	6950	6597	6322	6715	6875	7091	7223	7379	7381	6752	6716	6728	6609	6456
1982	6473	6428	6432	5783	6356	6547	6516	6380	6412	6491	6225	6811	6259	5726	5832	5791
1983	6273	6878	7247	7691	6312	6272	6234	6574	6996	7065	7230	7105	7406	7564	7761	7748

Manufacturing stocks: total (3)

million Canadian dollars, end of period

Stocks des industries manufacturières : total (3)

millions de dollars canadiens, fin de période

Adjusted - Corrigé

Year	Q.1	Q.2	Q.3	Q.4	JAN	FEB	MAR	APR	MAY	JUN	JUL	AUG	SEP	OCT	NOV	DEC
1964	4965	5114	5258	5326	4953	4988	4965	5030	5069	5114	5172	5204	5258	5264	5319	5326
1965	5485	5629	5782	5981	5365	5471	5485	5539	5592	5629	5682	5704	5782	5841	5890	5981
1966	6135	6342	6549	6701	6020	6105	6135	6225	6271	6342	6419	6465	6549	6615	6662	6701
1967	6854	6938	6953	6892	6846	6860	6854	6856	6905	6938	7013	6985	6953	6912	6918	6892
1968	6916	6935	7081	7213	6915	6925	6916	6923	6927	6935	6968	6994	7081	7100	7105	7213
1969	7377	7566	7714	7938	7228	7297	7377	7421	7512	7566	7661	7655	7714	7806	7863	7938
1970	8081	8062	8255	8189	8018	8061	8081	8083	8111	8062	8146	8213	8256	8208	8353	8189
1971	8155	8202	8219	8433	8164	8153	8155	8135	8168	8202	8208	8179	8219	8275	8321	8433
1972	8536	8731	8966	9122	8453	8489	8536	8627	8652	8731	8801	8885	8966	9022	9038	9122
1973	9433	9906	10383	11029	9157	9303	9433	9534	9629	9906	10031	10230	10383	10557	10749	11029
1974	11995	12984	13847	15052	11357	11687	11995	12364	12640	12984	13300	13607	13847	14284	14588	15052
1975	15410	15599	15566	15925	15239	15251	15410	15505	15590	15599	15553	15520	15566	15627	15716	15925
1976	16145	16479	16795	17119	15804	15970	16145	16297	16318	16479	16589	16630	16795	16922	16999	17119
1977	17549	17946	18317	18830	17134	17351	17549	17623	17764	17946	18064	18266	18317	18582	18764	18830
1978	19365	19671	20164	20883	19054	19369	19365	19490	19483	19671	19683	19943	20164	20275	20582	20883
1979	22219	23470	24843	26254	21237	21700	22219	22385	23002	23470	23814	24249	24843	25334	25677	26254
1980	27251	28396	29156	29855	26563	26868	27251	27867	28214	28396	28757	29052	29156	29468	29591	29855
1981	31141	32531	33669	34508	30503	30752	31141	31573	31932	32531	32751	33369	33669	34115	34305	34508
1982	35033	34535	33784	31258	34630	35018	35033	34769	34592	34535	34402	33932	33784	33357	32953	31258
1983	30478	29557	30747	31165	30580	30640	30478	30405	29938	29557	29808	30232	30747	31014	31125	31165

CANADA

Manufacturing stocks: work in progress / Stocks des industries manufacturières : produits en cours de fabrication

million Canadian dollars, end of period — millions de dollars canadiens, fin de période

Adjusted - Corrigé

	Year	Q.1	Q.2	Q.3	Q.4	JAN	FEB	MAR	APR	MAY	JUN	JUL	AUG	SEP	OCT	NOV	DEC
1964	1402	1300	1311	1361	1402	1288	1294	1300	1321	1330	1311	1337	1361	1361	1364	1391	1402
1965	1607	1434	1473	1502	1607	1401	1429	1434	1448	1463	1473	1461	1476	1502	1537	1554	1607
1966	1958	1677	1751	1879	1958	1624	1666	1677	1713	1736	1751	1772	1805	1879	1925	1929	1958
1967	1947	1992	2009	1991	1947	1956	1994	1992	2001	2014	2009	2057	2034	1991	1985	1982	1947
1968	2086	1984	1984	2025	2086	1959	1967	1984	1967	1969	1984	1998	2041	2025	2015	2037	2086
1969	2265	2174	2246	2227	2265	2107	2145	2274	2206	2218	2246	2269	2232	2227	2244	2250	2265
1970	2409	2360	2388	2497	2409	2375	2375	2360	2353	2394	2388	2417	2431	2497	2472	2457	2409
1971	2386	2312	2327	2347	2386	2420	2346	2312	2331	2308	2327	2348	2309	2347	2373	2383	2386
1972	2531	2417	2464	2508	2531	2390	2399	2417	2445	2462	2464	2460	2476	2508	2522	2540	2531
1973	3070	2653	2792	2955	3070	2553	2596	2653	2671	2704	2792	2842	2945	2955	2989	3074	3070
1974	3969	3267	3488	3692	3969	3166	3215	3267	3340	3401	3488	3574	3643	3692	3764	3817	3969
1975	4300	3959	4085	4163	4300	3958	3942	3959	4010	4116	4085	4092	4123	4163	4177	4169	4300
1976	4639	4342	4428	4536	4639	4320	4348	4342	4387	4409	4428	4497	4474	4536	4594	4659	4639
1977	5238	4796	4812	5007	5238	4651	4746	4796	4763	4804	4812	4869	4965	5007	5050	5133	5238
1978	5897	5301	5488	5733	5897	5282	5306	5301	5426	5420	5488	5545	5644	5733	5769	5786	5897
1979	7297	6222	6573	6898	7297	6010	6136	6222	6253	6414	6573	6672	6829	6898	6970	7144	7297
1980	8632	7685	8009	8151	8632	7418	7535	7685	7763	7938	8009	8055	8169	8151	8322	8416	8632
1981	9688	9068	9453	9763	9688	8853	8971	9068	9183	9213	9453	9504	9646	9763	9884	9866	9688
1982	8739	10013	9965	10056	8739	9737	9910	10013	9985	10030	9965	10171	10047	10056	10050	9780	8739
1983	8269	8176	7878	8440	8269	8045	8140	8176	8142	8046	7878	8004	8287	8440	8234	8270	8269

Manufacturing new orders, net / Commandes nouvelles nettes : industries manufacturières

million Canadian dollars, monthly averages — millions de dollars canadiens, moyennes mensuelles

	Year	Q.1	Q.2	Q.3	Q.4	JAN	FEB	MAR	APR	MAY	JUN	JUL	AUG	SEP	OCT	NOV	DEC
1964	2601	2505	2669	2539	2691	2529	2350	2637	2621	2595	2791	2506	2413	2698	2737	2689	2646
1965	2867	2657	2917	2844	3050	2435	2500	3035	2827	2877	3047	2722	2783	3028	3005	3139	3005
1966	3181	3075	3274	3076	3297	2870	2904	3452	3160	3310	3352	2838	3191	3198	3250	3317	3325
1967	3241	3116	3291	3190	3369	3074	2894	3381	3114	3365	3394	3042	3216	3311	3428	3405	3272
1968	3508	3247	3560	3467	3760	3205	3089	3446	3418	3723	3538	3322	3391	3688	3983	3826	3469
1969	3885	3724	3978	3823	4017	3642	3577	3951	3833	4047	4054	3740	3626	4103	4126	3977	3948
1970	3849	3714	4008	3827	3847	3637	3615	3888	3960	3929	4136	3733	3742	4007	4000	3813	3729
1971	4215	3955	4314	4209	4383	3623	3837	4407	4252	4137	4553	3751	4171	4704	4393	4549	4208
1972	4736	4386	4908	4572	5080	3998	4360	4799	4662	4974	5087	4145	4531	5040	5214	5261	4765
1973	5793	5332	5720	5701	6421	5052	5127	5816	5498	5922	5740	5572	5506	6025	6625	6498	6139
1974	7125	6683	7339	7094	7382	6499	6538	7013	6995	7654	7368	6942	7059	7282	7844	7394	6909
1975	7297	6863	7314	7273	7736	6907	6627	7055	7105	7547	7290	7055	7082	7684	8059	7694	7455
1976	8117	7750	8518	7953	8245	7177	7575	8499	8432	8390	8732	7407	8141	8310	8135	8554	8047
1977	9212	8970	9533	8851	9492	8243	8682	9985	9201	9334	10063	8149	8955	9451	9839	9718	8920
1978	11035	10085	11278	10802	11977	9388	9616	11249	10592	11431	11811	9780	10356	12270	12306	12290	11334
1979	12965	12646	13099	12602	13513	12527	11673	13738	12468	13601	13229	11769	13059	12978	14413	14030	12095
1980	14091	14302	13378	13670	15013	14435	13770	14702	13397	13365	13373	13051	12840	15120	15727	14918	14394
1981	15931	15358	16932	15786	15650	14397	14933	16744	16621	16683	17492	15676	14683	16993	16645	15639	14664
1982	15117	15109	15769	14803	14786	13727	14779	16820	15330	15395	16582	13787	14830	15791	14886	15621	13850
1983	17046	15406	17045	18053	17679	14329	14968	16921	15999	17155	17982	15411	17135	21614	18138	18374	16527

Construction permits issued: total (4) / Permis de construire délivrés : total (4)

million Canadian dollars, monthly averages — millions de dollars canadiens, moyennes mensuelles

	Year	Q.1	Q.2	Q.3	Q.4	JAN	FEB	MAR	APR	MAY	JUN	JUL	AUG	SEP	OCT	NOV	DEC
1964	272	164	284	324	318	138	147	206	288	276	289	304	293	375	353	393	207
1965	318	194	385	351	340	152	162	268	328	386	441	395	312	346	388	343	289
1966	310	218	369	359	292	185	175	295	368	374	366	333	376	370	334	313	228
1967	339	209	422	371	354	162	210	254	358	468	440	349	379	384	412	336	315
1968	398	284	448	430	430	219	273	360	427	486	430	506	412	374	483	446	361
1969	408	289	475	477	392	213	252	403	480	480	464	588	388	454	417	363	395
1970	392	257	431	427	452	207	266	298	370	442	480	382	379	521	538	454	363
1971	478	339	551	535	485	249	311	458	471	524	659	528	569	509	555	454	445
1972	539	385	626	609	535	289	375	491	551	652	674	552	643	632	602	562	442
1973	713	494	777	816	766	368	457	656	677	884	770	775	920	754	860	792	647
1974	773	605	961	871	657	450	539	826	893	1187	803	824	918	870	848	607	515
1975	883	542	1005	1030	956	507	490	628	933	1048	1033	988	1051	1051	1138	892	839
1976	1017	752	1268	1081	965	542	696	1018	1155	1206	1444	1106	1099	1038	1066	1042	787
1977	1035	739	1265	1148	989	481	646	1090	1148	1295	1352	963	1275	1206	1032	1083	852
1978	1095	707	1313	1220	1139	538	624	959	1176	1409	1355	1116	1300	1244	1309	1089	1017
1979	1179	756	1396	1386	1176	534	625	1210	1173	1576	1439	1296	1518	1343	1329	1236	965
1980	1288	901	1306	1429	1517	789	852	1062	1202	1276	1439	1373	1361	1554	1661	1419	1471
1981	1563	1082	1898	1580	1685	751	995	1501	1877	1864	1954	1800	1585	1354	1358	1703	1995
1982	1066	952	1091	1092	1128	761	828	1266	1128	1058	1083	1187	1000	1089	1130	1206	1049
1983	1237	978	1419	1233	1317	652	853	1420	1653	1342	1263	1150	1311	1237	1334	1309	1309

nufacturing stocks:
ermediate goods
lion Canadian dollars, end of period

Stocks des industries manufacturières :
biens intermédiaires
millions de dollars canadiens, fin de période

Adjusted - Corrigé

	Year	Q.1	Q.2	Q.3	Q.4	JAN	FEB	MAR	APR	MAY	JUN	JUL	AUG	SEP	OCT	NOV	DEC
1964	2296	2121	2189	2241	2296	2091	2111	2121	2147	2161	2189	2209	2216	2241	2258	2275	2296
1965	2553	2346	2411	2479	2553	2305	2333	2346	2372	2412	2411	2426	2447	2479	2479	2511	2553
1966	2797	2611	2696	2762	2797	2590	2614	2611	2656	2663	2696	2721	2735	2762	2771	2793	2797
1967	2877	2852	2888	2903	2877	2860	2861	2852	2832	2868	2888	2906	2912	2903	2887	2898	2877
1968	3003	2895	2894	2955	3003	2891	2892	2895	2881	2897	2894	2888	2906	2955	2979	2970	3003
1969	3310	3054	3146	3229	3310	3005	3041	3054	3073	3117	3146	3192	3200	3229	3255	3272	3310
1970	3227	3220	3178	3210	3227	3184	3197	3220	3205	3186	3178	3193	3199	3210	3215	3295	3227
1971	3360	3251	3272	3315	3360	3218	3228	3251	3238	3265	3272	3288	3305	3315	3335	3333	3360
1972	3764	3425	3549	3655	3764	3387	3421	3425	3480	3511	3549	3588	3642	3655	3707	3726	3764
1973	4754	3950	4196	4358	4754	3811	3885	3950	4006	4098	4196	4243	4297	4358	4471	4628	4754
1974	6912	5372	5895	6452	6912	4986	5199	5372	5553	5747	5895	6112	6310	6452	6636	6755	6912
1975	7219	7124	7186	7205	7219	7026	7016	7124	7144	7125	7186	7152	7142	7205	7208	7201	7219
1976	7310	7192	7308	7260	7310	7070	7128	7192	7309	7262	7308	7235	7231	7260	7297	7287	7310
1977	7868	7427	7604	7754	7868	7318	7278	7427	7459	7512	7604	7613	7669	7754	7830	7861	7868
1978	9086	8241	8456	8668	9086	7937	8139	8241	8226	8286	8456	8465	8573	8668	8731	8964	9086
1979	11506	9637	10274	10957	11506	9219	9422	9637	9760	10044	10274	10483	10688	10957	11209	11246	11506
1980	12684	11765	12199	12417	12684	11634	11687	11765	12201	12225	12199	12298	12368	12417	12607	12584	12684
1981	14507	13233	13853	14318	14507	13016	13007	13233	13496	13563	13853	13945	14317	14318	14416	14447	14507
1982	12555	14571	14002	13232	12555	14399	14706	14571	14261	14013	14002	13718	13361	13232	12904	12805	12555
1983	12719	12493	12376	12553	12719	12717	12604	12493	12623	12438	12376	12416	12463	12553	12707	12732	12719

Manufacturing new orders, net
million Canadian dollars, monthly averages

Commandes nouvelles nettes :
industries manufacturières
millions de dollars canadiens, moyennes mensuelles

Adjusted - Corrigé

	Year	Q.1	Q.2	Q.3	Q.4	JAN	FEB	MAR	APR	MAY	JUN	JUL	AUG	SEP	OCT	NOV	DEC
1964		2572	2572	2577	2654	2673	2506	2537	2587	2512	2617	2572	2540	2618	2644	2676	2642
1965		2727	2813	2911	3010	2626	2736	2818	2810	2788	2840	2906	2894	2933	2955	3047	3027
1966		3148	3172	3162	3249	3073	3187	3182	3181	3179	3156	3098	3252	3135	3164	3174	3410
1967		3189	3197	3294	3316	3245	3183	3140	3176	3169	3245	3308	3304	3271	3281	3261	3406
1968		3300	3455	3550	3680	3321	3208	3371	3399	3515	3451	3498	3506	3646	3704	3757	3579
1969		3837	3855	3919	3937	3796	3854	3862	3777	3886	3902	3923	3866	3967	3852	3982	3979
1970		3798	3861	3914	3800	3762	3879	3752	3811	3903	3869	3947	3999	3796	3794	3789	3818
1971		4063	4146	4302	4331	3956	4085	4147	4153	4071	4214	4001	4460	4444	4245	4416	4331
1972		4438	4725	4702	5048	4368	4449	4497	4698	4684	4792	4541	4665	4900	4979	5028	5136
1973		5418	5520	5885	6355	5276	5393	5586	5529	5529	5503	5999	5679	5976	6149	6307	6610
1974		6830	7109	7281	7256	6677	6899	6914	6911	7160	7255	7249	7359	7236	7260	7237	7271
1975		6996	7054	7497	7667	7053	6988	6947	6955	7157	7051	7364	7616	7510	7583	7660	7757
1976		7761	8162	8204	8259	7501	7840	7942	8270	8153	8064	7935	8653	8025	7987	8348	8440
1977		9029	9133	9165	9517	8817	9087	9184	9118	8948	9333	9056	9225	9216	9563	9447	9542
1978		10054	10864	11245	12053	9743	10090	10330	10688	10761	11144	10909	10720	12105	11842	11958	12359
1979		12464	12739	13210	13480	12541	12132	12720	12423	12987	12807	13083	13584	12961	13577	13765	13098
1980		14032	13070	14067	14989	14454	13824	13818	13029	13222	12959	13961	13756	14483	14757	15097	15112
1981		15334	16495	16249	15602	14849	15526	15627	16178	16766	16542	16860	15735	16151	15880	15644	15283
1982		15078	15367	15238	14752	14538	15411	15284	15114	15421	15566	15012	15762	14939	14493	15326	14438
1983		15448	16589	18569	17693	15243	15695	15407	16039	16936	16791	17158	17651	20898	17580	17903	17595

Construction permits issued: total (4)
million Canadian dollars, monthly averages

Permis de construire délivrés : total (4)
millions de dollars canadiens, moyennes mensuelles

Adjusted - Corrigé

	Year	Q.1	Q.2	Q.3	Q.4	JAN	FEB	MAR	APR	MAY	JUN	JUL	AUG	SEP	OCT	NOV	DEC
1964		247	236	285	319	259	250	232	253	220	235	250	268	337	312	381	264
1965		281	321	312	348	284	271	287	289	321	352	342	276	318	353	326	365
1966		321	309	320	292	350	290	323	332	294	302	292	328	341	301	292	284
1967		306	347	340	355	285	347	286	332	352	356	313	349	359	352	330	382
1968		408	359	389	435	366	433	424	367	384	356	412	406	350	401	448	456
1969		415	404	428	389	373	396	476	420	418	374	493	385	405	340	386	442
1970		366	366	384	452	367	406	326	343	394	362	330	369	454	460	463	432
1971		472	467	481	487	453	471	491	444	458	499	473	518	452	493	451	516
1972		527	530	544	557	527	521	533	528	519	544	522	537	573	525	575	572
1973		671	661	721	813	625	673	713	650	690	644	717	757	688	724	859	857
1974		834	806	761	668	781	802	918	789	925	704	705	767	811	719	644	642
1975		754	841	909	1010	852	721	690	810	830	883	882	921	923	994	998	1039
1976		1060	1047	975	999	1046	1095	1038	1044	974	1122	1042	947	936	972	1043	983
1977		1043	1046	1011	1041	980	1018	1131	1030	1020	1089	913	1044	1075	937	1079	1106
1978		1024	1109	1081	1164	1057	993	1012	1133	1088	1106	1076	1078	1090	1145	1082	1265
1979		1098	1185	1255	1176	1081	1016	1197	1099	1273	1184	1225	1308	1232	1213	1255	1061
1980		1242	1096	1254	1558	1403	1223	1101	1067	1023	1199	1179	1233	1351	1463	1499	1712
1981		1482	1670	1473	1620	1439	1496	1512	1725	1634	1651	1647	1512	1258	1284	1621	1957
1982		1231	950	951	1131	1370	1138	1185	1039	926	885	1064	855	935	1070	1124	1197
1983		1302	1199	1134	1273	1303	1288	1315	1420	1105	1071	1129	1133	1136	1329	1256	1235

CANADA

Construction permits issued: residential (4)

million Canadian dollars, monthly averages

Permis de construire délivrés : bâtiments résidentiels (4)

millions de dollars canadiens, moyennes mensuelles

	Year	Q.1	Q.2	Q.3	Q.4	JAN	FEB	MAR	APR	MAY	JUN	JUL	AUG	SEP	OCT	NOV	DEC
1964	135	77	150	150	161	66	68	98	156	145	150	142	149	158	205	188	90
1965	146	84	183	155	163	65	68	120	160	184	205	161	143	163	203	172	114
1966	133	84	165	154	127	80	61	111	158	174	163	135	152	177	160	138	84
1967	160	86	229	183	143	64	80	116	212	260	216	196	174	180	182	147	99
1968	201	134	225	211	232	84	127	191	235	257	183	223	199	211	269	234	193
1969	202	146	274	215	175	95	142	201	276	274	271	244	201	201	230	166	128
1970	193	105	210	217	239	81	100	134	200	218	211	170	208	274	298	247	172
1971	267	169	328	299	272	104	169	233	289	332	362	287	304	306	357	275	186
1972	303	212	391	338	272	144	217	274	362	398	414	309	367	337	326	291	200
1973	397	266	463	441	419	174	233	391	394	528	466	416	512	393	476	464	316
1974	381	330	520	392	284	214	293	482	534	595	432	394	420	362	379	275	196
1975	511	249	629	635	530	164	224	360	571	665	652	619	636	649	664	517	408
1976	623	451	795	698	548	318	388	647	758	769	858	695	705	694	657	606	382
1977	634	445	806	683	603	262	354	719	774	836	808	627	734	689	631	673	506
1978	631	401	809	700	613	279	351	573	713	894	820	663	751	685	754	592	492
1979	647	393	821	763	612	268	307	604	727	941	795	720	852	716	750	632	455
1980	622	392	686	735	677	293	354	529	659	636	763	667	746	791	836	671	523
1981	818	588	1134	766	785	374	487	903	1153	1154	1093	901	759	637	623	676	1055
1982	511	366	540	500	638	345	287	467	572	545	503	465	501	535	624	714	575
1983	738	605	988	710	650	367	486	963	1330	889	746	716	692	723	755	688	506

Construction: housing starts

thousands, monthly averages

Construction : logements mis en chantier

milliers, moyennes mensuelles

	Year	Q.1	Q.2	Q.3	Q.4	JAN	FEB	MAR	APR	MAY	JUN	JUL	AUG	SEP	OCT	NOV	DEC
1964	13.8	7.8	13.3	15.7	18.5												
1965	13.9	7.5	15.4	16.5	16.2												
1966	11.2	7.7	11.6	12.4	13.2												
1967	13.7	5.7	17.2	17.5	14.3												
1968	16.4	8.9	19.0	17.5	20.2												
1969	17.5	13.0	21.2	19.5	16.4												
1970	15.9	8.1	13.4	18.2	23.8												
1971	19.5	9.9	21.6	23.4	23.0												
1972	20.8	12.7	23.9	24.6	22.1												
1973	22.4	12.9	26.2	26.5	23.9												
1974	18.5	14.4	24.0	20.3	15.4												
1975	19.3	8.0	19.6	24.1	25.4												
1976	22.8	14.5	26.8	25.6	24.1												
1977	20.5	11.9	23.5	24.1	22.5												
1978	19.0	15.7	19.0	21.2	19.9												
1979	16.4	10.7	18.3	18.2	18.5												
1980	13.2	9.0	13.3	15.3	15.3												
1981	14.8	9.5	20.1	16.9	12.8												
1982	10.5	10.1	10.7	8.9	12.3												
1983	13.6	9.0	21.2	12.3	11.7												

Wholesale sales

million Canadian dollars, monthly averages

Ventes du commerce de gros

millions de dollars canadiens, moyennes mensuelles

	Year	Q.1	Q.2	Q.3	Q.4	JAN	FEB	MAR	APR	MAY	JUN	JUL	AUG	SEP	OCT	NOV	DEC
1964	1260	1157	1311	1300	1273	999	1075	1397	1244	1273	1416	1214	1340	1348	1246	1232	1342
1965	1417	1247	1509	1467	1446	1052	1163	1525	1397	1484	1647	1355	1534	1512	1392	1436	1508
1966	1577	1462	1650	1603	1592	1213	1336	1837	1545	1633	1771	1421	1730	1660	1600	1599	1578
1967	1627	1471	1839	1595	1603	1323	1365	1725	1701	1986	1830	1584	1610	1591	1652	1585	1571
1968	1717	1499	1767	1796	1804	1399	1483	1614	1680	1885	1736	1749	1783	1851	1974	1786	1652
1969	1873	1640	1952	1961	1939	1533	1572	1815	1892	2014	1950	1943	1864	2074	2126	1856	1835
1970	1921	1696	1985	2032	1971	1614	1635	1838	1949	1973	2033	2002	1959	2134	2101	1972	1840
1971	2075	1736	2163	2174	2226	1565	1633	2011	2046	2167	2275	2094	2149	2279	2309	2248	2121
1972	2347	2006	2443	2429	2510	1797	1915	2306	2259	2584	2486	2313	2508	2466	2683	2542	2305
1973	2840	2434	2954	2899	3073	2209	2289	2804	2775	3135	2952	2844	2999	2855	3209	3140	2871
1974	3601	3138	3894	3769	3602	2869	3014	3532	3393	4351	3939	3818	3640	3849	3857	3705	3246
1975	3781	3292	3965	3977	3892	3059	3173	3644	3651	4271	3973	4076	3571	4285	4000	3858	3818
1976	4166	3799	4412	4328	4124	3465	3596	4338	4190	4495	4550	4208	4083	4692	4112	4383	3878
1977	4465	3981	4600	4648	4631	3582	3812	4550	4337	4599	4365	4383	4696	4864	4865	4716	4314
1978	5164	4374	5378	5389	5514	4018	4205	4899	5017	5503	5613	5064	5514	5590	5820	5712	5010
1979	6048	5231	6221	6383	6358	4879	4934	5878	5792	6431	6438	6134	6614	6400	6987	6400	5687
1980	6657	6004	6759	6858	7008	5632	5954	6428	6609	6895	6774	6657	6643	7274	7697	6713	6613
1981	7330	6639	7782	7638	7263	6162	6362	7393	7530	7677	8140	7649	7314	7951	7857	7283	6647
1982	6766	6527	7110	6761	6667	5974	6285	7321	6836	7169	7324	6447	6678	7158	6931	6856	6213
1983	7167	6503	7460	7446	7258	5945	6173	7390	7098	7471	7811	6950	7668	7719	7714	7543	6518

Construction permits issued: residential (4)
million Canadian dollars, monthly averages

Permis de construire délivrés : bâtiments résidentiels (4)
millions de dollars canadiens, moyennes mensuelles

	Year	Q.1	Q.2	Q.3	Q.4	JAN	FEB	MAR	APR	MAY	JUN	JUL	AUG	SEP	OCT	NOV	DEC
1964		125	117	135	160	134	125	117	123	112	115	123	143	138	167	184	129
1965		131	142	143	165	134	124	136	128	140	156	146	135	147	169	164	164
1966		136	128	140	130	165	110	132	126	131	127	123	135	164	131	131	127
1967		134	177	169	148	131	139	133	180	180	172	178	164	165	148	144	153
1968		203	174	192	246	162	215	231	184	183	154	183	195	198	216	232	291
1969		221	217	198	174	194	231	240	218	210	222	215	195	183	177	170	176
1970		162	167	197	244	172	157	158	164	173	164	151	197	243	239	248	246
1971		243	261	273	281	220	257	253	251	261	272	269	275	275	300	271	271
1972		306	314	304	290	301	312	306	322	290	331	293	310	309	273	286	311
1973		379	361	395	468	347	352	437	337	379	367	396	420	368	396	510	497
1974		473	403	345	317	432	452	534	432	428	350	347	349	339	331	302	318
1975		358	487	557	607	334	350	390	453	483	523	549	551	572	593	599	629
1976		661	614	625	602	682	651	650	626	578	637	638	613	624	603	617	585
1977		648	621	600	668	595	605	743	634	611	619	587	595	619	573	681	751
1978		614	633	617	659	627	609	606	625	641	633	627	618	606	651	595	731
1979		603	639	698	650	609	568	631	617	684	616	679	745	670	687	682	580
1980		571	521	650	747	586	578	549	509	447	608	579	673	692	722	766	753
1981		845	926	732	769	790	826	917	948	928	900	857	735	604	567	662	1077
1982		512	414	435	683	636	455	444	450	414	379	422	427	457	562	705	781
1983		826	773	665	719	793	786	898	1061	661	597	717	616	662	732	713	712

Cost of construction: (5)
residential
1980 = 100

Coût de la construction : (5)
bâtiments résidentiels
1980 = 100

	Year	Q.1	Q.2	Q.3	Q.4	JAN	FEB	MAR	APR	MAY	JUN	JUL	AUG	SEP	OCT	NOV	DEC
1964																	
1965																	
1966	31.4	30.6	31.2	31.7	32.2	30.5	30.6	30.8	30.9	31.3	31.4	31.4	31.3	31.8	32.2	32.2	32.3
1967	33.5	32.5	33.4	33.7	34.4	32.4	32.5	32.7	33.2	33.4	33.5	33.6	33.7	33.8	34.3	34.4	34.5
1968	35.8	34.9	35.8	36.2	36.5	34.9	34.9	35.0	35.5	35.9	36.0	36.1	36.2	36.3	36.4	36.5	36.6
1969	36.0	37.5	38.4	38.3	38.6	37.0	37.5	38.0	38.2	38.5	38.4	38.4	38.3	38.2	38.2	38.4	39.1
1970	40.9	39.4	40.6	41.2	42.3	39.2	39.3	39.8	40.1	40.8	41.0	41.0	41.2	41.3	41.9	42.5	42.5
1971	44.9	43.3	44.4	45.7	46.3	42.9	43.3	43.6	43.9	44.3	45.0	45.5	45.8	45.8	46.0	46.3	46.4
1972	49.4	47.3	48.7	50.2	51.6	47.0	47.4	47.6	48.1	48.8	49.2	49.8	50.1	50.6	51.1	51.8	51.8
1973	55.3	52.9	55.1	55.5	57.0	52.4	52.9	53.5	54.6	55.3	55.6	55.1	55.5	56.0	56.4	57.0	57.7
1974	60.5	58.3	60.8	61.6	61.1	57.8	58.2	59.0	60.1	61.2	61.3	61.9	61.5	61.4	61.5	61.8	60.1
1975	64.7	61.0	63.6	66.3	67.8	60.5	61.0	61.3	62.2	63.9	64.6	65.9	66.4	66.5	67.4	67.8	68.3
1976	72.1	69.4	71.6	73.0	74.4	68.9	69.2	70.0	70.5	72.0	72.1	72.4	73.1	73.5	73.7	74.5	74.9
1977	78.8	75.7	78.1	80.6	80.8	75.4	75.6	76.0	76.7	78.7	79.0	80.0	80.8	81.1	80.9	80.7	80.9
1978	86.2	82.7	85.3	87.3	89.5	81.9	82.9	83.4	84.2	85.7	86.0	86.7	87.4	87.9	88.8	90.0	89.9
1979	94.9	92.3	94.8	96.7	96.0	91.5	92.3	93.0	93.6	95.3	95.3	96.0	96.7	97.5	97.1	95.6	95.4
1980	100.0	97.5	98.6	101.6	102.5	96.5	98.1	97.8	97.1	98.4	100.1	101.6	101.7	101.5	102.0	102.5	103.0
1981	109.7	105.1	110.6	111.9	111.2	104.3	105.2	105.9	107.9	111.8	112.1	112.6	112.2	111.0	110.7	111.2	111.5
1982	115.9	112.1	114.2	117.5	119.5	112.2	111.9	112.2	112.6	113.8	116.2	117.5	117.4	117.7	118.0	120.2	120.8
1983	127.9	123.0	128.7	130.8	129.1	122.5	122.8	123.8	123.8	130.0	132.1	132.9	130.7	128.8	128.8	129.1	129.3

Wholesale sales
million Canadian dollars, monthly averages

Adjusted - Corrigé

Ventes du commerce de gros
millions de dollars canadiens, moyennes mensuelles

	Year	Q.1	Q.2	Q.3	Q.4	JAN	FEB	MAR	APR	MAY	JUN	JUL	AUG	SEP	OCT	NOV	DEC
1964		1241	1218	1264	1298	1206	1224	1293	1213	1214	1227	1244	1271	1276	1256	1294	1345
1965		1354	1405	1426	1471	1330	1348	1385	1373	1403	1440	1412	1440	1426	1433	1462	1519
1966		1578	1543	1567	1613	1511	1548	1674	1561	1509	1558	1519	1600	1582	1605	1611	1522
1967		1599	1699	1567	1613	1602	1582	1613	1746	1697	1656	1660	1491	1551	1591	1569	1681
1968		1637	1668	1747	1785	1643	1643	1624	1645	1696	1664	1726	1727	1787	1801	1823	1732
1969		1824	1850	1897	1913	1798	1837	1837	1846	1851	1851	1882	1873	1937	1933	1912	1895
1970		1895	1880	1963	1944	1937	1917	1833	1885	1872	1882	1948	1959	1983	1942	1988	1903
1971		1937	2041	2097	2219	1945	1913	1953	1997	2030	2096	2076	2111	2105	2217	2202	2240
1972		2199	2292	2373	2529	2222	2145	2230	2307	2283	2287	2348	2396	2376	2531	2469	2588
1973		2671	2759	2845	3099	2600	2661	2752	2781	2713	2781	2821	2925	2792	2996	3085	3217
1974		3456	3616	3675	3653	3334	3484	3550	3323	3765	3759	3685	3671	3668	3635	3749	3575
1975		3602	3683	3873	3980	3564	3639	3604	3593	3753	3704	3903	3765	3951	3863	3961	4116
1976		4057	4108	4211	4238	4080	4030	4061	4174	4044	4107	4167	4198	4268	4227	4295	4192
1977		4331	4388	4519	4636	4266	4354	4372	4354	4379	4432	4512	4486	4560	4587	4601	4719
1978		4735	5135	5271	5527	4727	4797	4680	5168	5070	5167	5188	5298	5328	5421	5551	5608
1979		5647	5940	6260	6313	5550	5616	5774	5836	5955	6028	6210	6322	6248	6303	6281	6356
1980		6445	6458	6688	6974	6430	6496	6409	6502	6529	6342	6560	6695	6808	6974	6856	7093
1981		7209	7429	7425	7261	7169	7187	7270	7374	7426	7487	7533	7331	7410	7319	7265	7198
1982		7040	6788	6595	6683	7074	7080	6966	6762	6894	6709	6526	6614	6648	6609	6710	6730
1983		6993	7118	7271	7304	6976	6942	7060	7136	7094	7125	7200	7365	7247	7319	7339	7253

Retail sales: value (6)
million Canadian dollars, monthly averages

Ventes au détail : valeur (6)
millions de dollars canadiens, moyennes mensuelles

	Year	Q.1	Q.2	Q.3	Q.4	JAN	FEB	MAR	APR	MAY	JUN	JUL	AUG	SEP	OCT	NOV	DEC
1964	1613	1441	1644	1562	1804	1445	1379	1500	1581	1720	1630	1622	1526	1537	1740	1653	2018
1965	1746	1490	1790	1690	2015	1473	1383	1614	1774	1822	1774	1781	1629	1659	1840	1892	2314
1966	1891	1692	1881	1832	2158	1614	1556	1905	1874	1853	1916	1836	1804	1855	1953	2038	2483
1967	2013	1750	2069	1961	2272	1714	1601	1936	1947	2119	2140	1931	1920	2032	2030	2193	2592
1968	2143	1878	2152	2084	2457	1848	1770	2015	2035	2257	2163	2114	2141	1998	2229	2443	2699
1969	2283	2018	2317	2205	2594	2020	1886	2148	2205	2464	2281	2221	2177	2216	2433	2429	2921
1970	2336	2064	2369	2271	2640	2151	1895	2146	2259	2457	2390	2371	2157	2287	2482	2416	3023
1971	2554	2129	2608	2497	2981	2098	1991	2299	2548	2636	2641	2606	2332	2552	2708	2837	3399
1972	2841	2314	2968	2825	3256	2166	2176	2599	2797	3039	3068	2771	2773	2930	2994	3106	3669
1973	3193	2632	3293	3144	3702	2459	2418	3009	3157	3332	3389	3128	3170	3136	3396	3632	4078
1974	3728	3051	3849	3785	4229	2916	2883	3352	3589	4064	3893	3769	3929	3657	3965	4100	4622
1975	4280	3455	4325	4295	5045	3395	3276	3695	4014	4605	4356	4385	4324	4176	4652	4708	5775
1976	4761	3922	4933	4737	5450	3865	3663	4239	4853	4890	5056	4931	4593	4687	5036	5011	6303
1977	5135	4287	5220	5143	5891	4105	4039	4717	5104	5203	5353	5114	5135	5181	5299	5598	6775
1978	5731	4704	5891	5820	6509	4365	4462	5283	5479	5991	6203	5620	5797	6043	5898	6215	7414
1979	6419	5388	6594	5455	7237	5008	4983	6173	6033	6771	6978	6374	6693	6296	6706	7001	8005
1980	7002	5847	6967	7089	8107	5651	5761	6128	6585	7362	6952	7070	7148	7048	7614	7625	9081
1981	7858	6680	8103	7840	8807	6684	6258	7098	7796	8256	8257	8110	7663	7748	8250	8199	9973
1982	8137	6880	8358	8164	9145	6666	6526	7449	8065	8528	8480	8428	7956	8107	8256	8538	10640
1983	8760	7281	8897	8893	9965	6882	6772	8189	8312	8860	9519	8985	8827	8881	8954	9340	11601

Retail sales: motor dealers (6)(7)
million Canadian dollars, monthly averages

Ventes au détail : commerce automobile (6)(7)
millions de dollars canadiens, moyennes mensuelles

	Year	Q.1	Q.2	Q.3	Q.4	JAN	FEB	MAR	APR	MAY	JUN	JUL	AUG	SEP	OCT	NOV	DEC
1964	282	279	347	248	253	254	269	313	347	350	344	287	227	229	273	258	228
1965	321	294	390	276	322	248	271	362	393	389	390	325	269	235	306	337	322
1966	362	372	396	322	356	299	334	482	393	387	408	345	331	290	354	370	344
1967	369	340	452	327	358	307	309	404	427	485	444	350	311	320	365	371	339
1968	393	363	445	363	401	327	351	411	420	478	436	417	349	324	433	420	349
1969	400	384	462	363	390	337	383	433	457	479	449	386	325	378	435	393	342
1970	350	329	422	329	319	304	310	373	408	429	428	370	291	328	382	308	267
1971	410	335	487	385	435	255	315	434	479	481	502	412	341	402	475	460	369
1972	520	425	630	484	542	360	396	519	588	674	627	504	459	488	611	544	471
1973	619	550	738	575	611	475	495	681	753	755	707	608	559	558	705	626	503
1974	692	582	827	698	661	511	564	670	787	903	791	752	713	628	744	656	584
1975	849	684	964	817	930	605	688	758	920	993	979	910	787	754	981	899	910
1976	922	774	1110	879	923	646	727	950	1115	1081	1136	959	872	806	976	904	888
1977	979	884	1139	943	951	773	839	1040	1107	1150	1158	958	976	896	1045	986	821
1978	1115	929	1301	1143	1087	775	897	1114	1159	1373	1372	1135	1144	1151	1265	1097	898
1979	1285	1120	1505	1277	1239	942	1045	1373	1404	1576	1535	1347	1323	1160	1443	1259	1014
1980	1308	1204	1417	1317	1295	1067	1247	1297	1414	1417	1422	1365	1286	1302	1479	1290	1115
1981	1379	1300	1625	1314	1277	1115	1254	1529	1673	1594	1609	1473	1196	1274	1301	1453	1076
1982	1201	1114	1387	1179	1124	876	1079	1388	1373	1391	1398	1180	1159	1198	1138	1204	1030
1983	1423	1186	1641	1414	1452	969	1081	1510	1498	1711	1712	1459	1409	1373	1509	1563	1283

Retail sales: volume
1980 = 100

Adjusted - Corrigé

Ventes au détail : volume
1980 = 100

	Year	Q.1	Q.2	Q.3	Q.4	JAN	FEB	MAR	APR	MAY	JUN	JUL	AUG	SEP	OCT	NOV	DEC
1964	60	61	60	61	61	61	63	59	59	61	59	61	60	61	65	59	61
1965	64	62	64	65	67	62	62	63	66	63	64	66	63	65	67	66	67
1966	67	67	64	66	67	65	66	69	64	63	65	65	67	67	67	67	66
1967	69	68	69	69	69	69	67	67	68	69	69	67	68	71	69	70	68
1968	71	68	69	71	72	71	66	68	68	69	70	72	71	72	71	73	73
1969	74	73	72	72	74	73	74	73	72	72	72	72	72	73	74	73	74
1970	74	72	72	74	75	73	71	71	71	72	73	74	73	75	74	74	77
1971	79	76	79	79	81	75	77	77	79	79	79	79	78	81	81	82	81
1972	84	80	85	84	87	80	78	82	85	85	85	83	82	86	87	87	87
1973	87	87	87	86	88	86	85	89	91	85	86	87	84	86	88	89	89
1974	90	90	91	91	89	90	91	90	91	91	90	91	92	92	89	88	88
1975	94	91	92	93	97	91	92	91	91	93	93	93	93	92	94	96	100
1976	99	95	99	99	101	95	94	97	101	98	99	99	99	99	100	100	103
1977	100	101	98	99	99	102	100	100	99	98	98	97	100	99	99	100	99
1978	101	100	101	101	101	99	101	100	101	101	101	99	100	105	101	101	101
1979	102	102	102	103	101	101	101	104	102	102	103	103	104	102	102	101	101
1980	100	100	98	100	100	100	100	100	98	97	99	99	101	101	100	102	99
1981	99	102	100	98	97	102	101	101	101	101	99	98	98	97	96	100	96
1982	94	95	94	93	93	96	96	93	94	96	92	93	93	93	93	92	94
1983	96	94	95	96	97	95	94	95	92	95	97	97	95	96	98	97	97

Retail sales: value (6)
million Canadian dollars, monthly averages

Adjusted - Corrigé

Ventes au détail : valeur (6)
millions de dollars canadiens, moyennes mensuelles

Year	Q.1	Q.2	Q.3	Q.4	JAN	FEB	MAR	APR	MAY	JUN	JUL	AUG	SEP	OCT	NOV	DEC
1964	1617	1598	1633	1650	1620	1662	1569	1581	1621	1593	1650	1611	1640	1737	1583	1629
1965	1677	1747	1769	1841	1655	1673	1703	1774	1721	1747	1808	1731	1767	1833	1824	1864
1966	1855	1809	1891	1907	1806	1845	1914	1805	1773	1848	1856	1912	1905	1913	1917	1890
1967	1928	1980	2013	2018	1961	1899	1922	1956	1983	1999	1969	2002	2066	2006	2036	2011
1968	2026	2070	2161	2197	2095	1946	2037	2048	2061	2101	2174	2137	2172	2159	2217	2214
1969	2235	2234	2263	2310	2213	2260	2231	2222	2237	2245	2242	2262	2284	2314	2284	2332
1970	2264	2286	2350	2361	2290	2258	2243	2263	2279	2314	2370	2325	2356	2343	2339	2400
1971	2403	2541	2582	2650	2350	2423	2436	2529	2536	2557	2564	2556	2625	2631	2667	2653
1972	2655	2841	2844	2969	2650	2594	2722	2827	2852	2844	2819	2787	2925	2973	2955	2978
1973	3034	3156	3195	3369	2983	2993	3125	3259	3080	3130	3194	3141	3251	3317	3390	3399
1974	3531	3689	3836	3830	3466	3564	3562	3629	3712	3725	3779	3855	3874	3816	3816	3859
1975	4023	4150	4329	4567	3981	4041	4045	4028	4177	4245	4330	4331	4325	4421	4550	4728
1976	4505	4744	4768	4895	4490	4445	4582	4784	4682	4765	4761	4742	4802	4857	4828	4999
1977	5003	5026	5150	5310	5021	4970	5019	5028	5017	5033	5057	5197	5197	5260	5347	5324
1978	5461	5675	5838	5924	5359	5489	5536	5607	5697	5722	5722	5760	6033	5879	5927	5967
1979	6191	6358	6524	6590	6044	6122	6408	6308	6347	6419	6520	6552	6501	6573	6552	6645
1980	6682	6745	7108	7369	6633	6698	6715	6644	6709	6882	6940	7164	7221	7265	7499	7342
1981	7709	7853	7862	7987	7645	7677	7804	7833	7840	7886	7858	7855	7874	7845	8190	7925
1982	7947	8107	8158	8252	7918	8014	7910	7977	8292	8052	8114	8185	8175	8208	8211	8337
1983	8409	8579	8855	9033	8365	8315	8548	8299	8579	8859	8938	8805	8824	9067	8980	9052

Retail sales: motor dealers (6)(7)
million Canadian dollars, monthly averages

Adjusted - Corrigé

Ventes au détail : commerce automobile (6)(7)
millions de dollars canadiens, moyennes mensuelles

Year	Q.1	Q.2	Q.3	Q.4	JAN	FEB	MAR	APR	MAY	JUN	JUL	AUG	SEP	OCT	NOV	DEC
1964	285	282	295	264	289	287	278	282	284	280	284	290	314	282	272	238
1965	303	319	325	335	295	298	315	316	317	323	321	333	320	328	334	342
1966	392	341	353	361	365	377	436	349	324	348	357	371	330	350	358	374
1967	364	389	357	371	377	350	366	403	383	379	361	356	353	359	367	387
1968	387	380	394	405	382	392	387	369	386	385	405	401	376	402	406	406
1969	420	393	393	395	410	441	410	397	387	397	381	391	407	398	405	382
1970	365	356	357	325	380	362	353	351	361	354	363	351	357	346	312	316
1971	364	408	421	443	337	371	385	406	402	415	406	413	443	442	445	442
1972	471	520	512	576	468	459	485	506	530	524	508	482	545	570	567	590
1973	612	611	609	642	595	597	645	641	591	601	599	586	643	648	644	634
1974	654	686	732	696	633	676	654	657	713	687	725	751	718	679	686	723
1975	772	803	850	992	748	816	751	775	799	835	866	841	843	897	966	1112
1976	851	929	911	980	806	840	908	935	908	942	919	911	902	925	934	1081
1977	989	957	974	1013	1001	979	985	957	954	961	944	992	986	996	1024	1018
1978	1025	1129	1184	1156	986	1041	1047	1126	1128	1133	1129	1144	1278	1177	1140	1151
1979	1230	1278	1312	1313	1186	1206	1299	1247	1286	1303	1315	1313	1306	1321	1302	1317
1980	1310	1223	1337	1374	1308	1366	1257	1219	1186	1265	1281	1355	1374	1359	1407	1357
1981	1420	1407	1325	1364	1397	1439	1424	1445	1398	1379	1386	1274	1315	1254	1541	1297
1982	1200	1204	1194	1202	1142	1236	1222	1187	1236	1190	1148	1203	1231	1161	1211	1235
1983	1275	1396	1422	1548	1277	1238	1309	1318	1434	1436	1444	1415	1407	1546	1546	1552

CANADA

Employment: manufacturing *(all employees)* (8) — Emploi : industries manufacturières *(salariés)* (8)

1980 = 100

	Year	Q.1	Q.2	Q.3	Q.4	JAN	FEB	MAR	APR	MAY	JUN	JUL	AUG	SEP	OCT	NOV	DEC
1964	86.1	83.1	85.8	88.4	87.1	82.7	83.1	83.6	83.9	85.8	87.8	86.7	89.3	89.2	87.4	87.9	86.1
1965	90.9	87.1	90.3	93.1	93.0	86.6	86.7	88.0	88.1	90.2	92.4	91.9	93.5	93.9	93.5	93.5	91.9
1966	95.7	92.9	95.9	97.7	96.3	92.3	93.0	93.5	93.8	95.8	98.1	96.1	98.7	98.3	97.7	97.0	94.3
1967	95.4	94.6	95.4	97.3	94.7	94.7	94.6	94.6	94.3	95.3	96.7	96.4	98.2	97.3	95.6	95.5	92.9
1968	94.7	92.2	94.4	96.4	95.6	92.8	91.2	92.6	93.2	94.5	95.6	94.4	97.1	97.5	96.6	96.1	94.1
1969	97.1	95.0	97.9	98.2	97.3	94.4	95.0	95.5	95.8	97.8	99.9	97.1	99.2	98.5	98.2	98.0	95.6
1970	95.2	95.0	95.7	96.2	93.8	95.0	95.0	95.0	94.7	95.2	97.3	94.7	98.0	95.9	95.0	93.6	92.8
1971	94.3	92.1	94.8	95.9	94.4	92.3	91.9	92.2	92.6	95.0	96.6	93.6	97.1	96.9	95.7	94.9	92.6
1972	95.9	93.2	96.1	97.5	95.9	92.6	93.0	94.0	94.7	96.6	97.0	95.8	98.2	98.7	97.8	97.5	95.3
1973	100.7	96.8	100.8	102.5	102.5	95.8	96.7	97.8	99.0	100.5	103.0	101.9	102.9	103.0	103.5	102.6	101.3
1974	103.8	102.0	105.1	105.4	102.3	101.7	101.6	102.6	103.3	105.1	107.0	105.2	105.7	105.4	104.6	102.7	99.5
1975	97.9	97.0	99.2	98.3	97.2	97.1	96.7	97.3	97.4	99.3	101.0	97.9	99.0	98.1	98.5	97.5	95.6
1976	99.3	97.5	100.5	100.7	98.3	96.2	97.8	98.5	99.2	100.9	101.3	100.3	101.6	100.2	99.5	98.8	96.6
1977	97.9	95.8	98.9	99.6	97.3	95.7	95.4	96.4	96.7	99.5	100.7	99.2	100.3	99.3	98.7	97.8	95.4
1978	98.9	95.8	99.2	100.8	99.9	95.3	95.5	96.7	97.3	99.5	100.8	100.0	101.5	101.0	100.8	100.2	98.7
1979	101.9	99.2	102.5	104.1	101.8	98.7	99.2	99.5	100.5	102.7	104.4	103.9	104.4	104.0	103.0	102.2	100.3
1980	100.0	99.5	100.6	100.5	99.4	99.1	99.4	100.2	100.0	99.9	101.9	99.8	100.8	100.9	100.4	99.5	98.3
1981	100.7	99.0	103.6	102.1	97.7	97.4	99.5	100.2	101.6	103.6	105.7	101.8	102.4	102.1	99.9	97.8	95.4
1982	91.2	93.9	93.8	91.6	85.7	94.2	93.8	93.6	93.1	94.0	94.3	92.3	92.1	90.5	87.5	85.7	83.7
1983	88.5	84.8	88.8	91.5	88.9	84.1	85.1	85.3	87.2	89.5	89.6	90.6	91.9	91.9	90.7	89.2	86.9

Unemployment (9) — Chômage (9)

thousands — milliers

	Year	Q.1	Q.2	Q.3	Q.4	JAN	FEB	MAR	APR	MAY	JUN	JUL	AUG	SEP	OCT	NOV	DEC
1964	324	463	326	243	266	466	467	456	403	293	282	265	246	217	257	257	284
1965	280	397	298	210	214	407	397	387	371	265	257	244	211	176	171	220	252
1966	251	303	237	236	230	315	302	293	255	230	225	254	239	214	204	240	246
1967	296	340	294	260	290	338	340	343	317	281	283	297	256	227	258	287	325
1968	358	411	365	332	324	407	408	417	374	340	382	390	332	274	295	334	343
1969	362	405	358	329	346	420	407	388	374	361	370	366	334	287	327	355	356
1970	476	455	490	479	479	438	456	472	471	480	518	549	472	416	437	489	512
1971	535	601	545	494	502	623	602	577	586	512	536	549	473	454	482	518	505
1972	553	591	540	536	545	623	567	582	532	528	561	580	535	493	518	549	567
1973	515	599	501	476	483	651	596	551	517	482	505	501	469	457	472	487	489
1974	514	564	494	488	512	592	562	539	509	500	472	510	489	464	460	507	568
1975	690	738	685	670	666	752	730	731	694	680	681	702	685	623	636	678	684
1976	726	776	717	709	703	790	789	749	759	699	692	766	700	661	670	697	741
1977	849	909	838	825	824	877	919	931	901	812	802	867	825	785	774	828	869
1978	909	999	930	878	827	975	992	1029	983	918	889	913	880	842	786	838	857
1979	836	966	856	759	762	974	951	973	940	833	796	790	770	718	741	769	777
1980	865	953	907	816	784	945	948	967	936	901	885	850	832	765	758	786	809
1981	898	951	854	840	937	944	927	983	885	852	856	835	792	892	889	931	991
1982	1314	1152	1266	1384	1455	1103	1121	1232	1242	1245	1310	1397	1398	1356	1402	1453	1510
1983	1448	1630	1515	1353	1295	1611	1604	1674	1582	1502	1462	1415	1375	1269	1253	1297	1336

Unemployment (9) — Chômage (9)

as per cent of civilian labour force — en pourcentage de la main-d'œuvre civile

	Year	Q.1	Q.2	Q.3	Q.4	JAN	FEB	MAR	APR	MAY	JUN	JUL	AUG	SEP	OCT	NOV	DEC
1964	4.7	6.9	4.7	3.4	3.8	6.9	7.0	6.8	5.9	4.2	4.0	3.7	3.4	3.1	3.7	3.7	4.1
1965	3.9	5.8	4.2	2.9	3.0	5.9	5.8	5.6	5.3	3.7	3.5	3.3	2.8	2.5	2.4	3.1	3.5
1966	3.6	4.2	3.2	3.0	3.1	4.4	4.2	4.1	3.5	3.1	3.0	3.2	3.0	2.8	2.7	3.2	3.3
1967	4.1	4.6	3.8	3.2	3.7	4.6	4.6	4.6	4.2	3.6	3.6	3.6	3.1	2.9	3.3	3.7	4.2
1968	4.8	5.4	4.6	4.0	4.0	5.4	5.4	5.5	4.9	4.3	4.7	4.7	4.0	3.4	3.6	4.1	4.3
1969	4.7	5.1	4.5	3.9	4.2	5.3	5.1	4.9	4.6	4.4	4.4	4.3	3.9	3.5	4.0	4.3	4.4
1970	5.7	5.7	5.8	5.5	5.7	5.5	5.7	5.9	5.8	5.7	6.0	6.2	5.4	4.9	5.1	5.8	6.1
1971	6.2	7.2	6.3	5.5	5.7	7.5	7.2	7.0	7.0	6.0	6.0	6.0	5.3	5.2	5.5	5.9	5.8
1972	6.2	6.9	6.1	5.8	6.1	7.3	6.7	6.8	6.2	6.0	6.1	6.2	5.8	5.5	5.8	6.1	6.3
1973	5.7	6.8	5.4	5.0	5.1	7.4	6.7	6.2	5.7	5.2	5.2	5.2	4.9	4.9	5.0	5.2	5.2
1974	5.5	6.1	5.1	4.9	5.2	6.4	6.1	5.8	5.4	5.2	4.8	5.0	4.8	4.8	4.7	5.2	5.8
1975	6.9	7.7	6.9	6.5	6.6	7.9	7.6	7.6	7.2	6.8	6.6	6.7	6.6	6.2	6.3	6.7	6.8
1976	7.1	7.9	7.0	6.7	6.9	8.0	8.0	7.6	7.6	6.9	6.6	7.1	6.6	6.4	6.5	6.8	7.3
1977	8.1	9.0	8.0	7.5	7.8	8.7	9.1	9.1	8.8	7.7	7.5	7.9	7.5	7.4	7.3	7.8	8.3
1978	8.4	9.5	8.6	7.3	7.6	9.4	9.5	9.7	9.3	8.4	8.0	8.0	7.7	7.7	7.2	7.7	7.9
1979	7.5	8.9	7.7	6.5	6.7	9.0	8.8	8.9	8.6	7.4	7.0	6.8	6.6	6.4	6.5	6.8	6.9
1980	7.5	8.5	7.8	6.9	6.8	8.5	8.4	8.5	8.3	7.8	7.4	7.1	6.9	6.6	6.5	6.8	7.0
1981	7.6	8.2	7.2	6.9	7.9	8.2	8.0	8.4	7.6	7.1	7.0	6.8	6.4	7.4	7.4	7.8	8.5
1982	11.0	9.9	10.6	11.3	12.2	9.5	9.7	10.5	10.6	10.4	10.7	11.2	11.3	11.3	11.7	12.2	12.8
1983	11.9	13.8	12.4	10.8	10.7	13.7	13.6	14.0	13.2	12.2	11.7	11.2	10.9	10.4	10.3	10.7	11.1

Employment: manufacturing *(all employees)* (8) — Emploi : industries manufacturières *(salariés)* (8)

1980 = 100 — Adjusted - Corrigé

Year	Q.1	Q.2	Q.3	Q.4	JAN	FEB	MAR	APR	MAY	JUN	JUL	AUG	SEP	OCT	NOV	DEC
1964	84.8	85.5	86.3	87.3	84.6	84.9	85.0	85.3	85.5	85.7	86.4	86.8	87.1	86.4	87.6	88.1
1965	88.8	90.0	91.5	93.2	88.4	88.5	89.5	89.5	90.0	90.3	91.6	91.0	91.8	92.5	93.1	93.9
1966	94.6	95.6	96.1	96.5	94.2	94.7	95.0	95.2	95.7	96.0	96.0	96.1	96.2	96.7	96.5	96.3
1967	96.3	95.1	95.8	94.8	96.5	96.4	96.1	95.7	95.1	94.5	96.3	95.8	95.3	94.6	95.0	94.7
1968	93.9	94.1	94.9	95.8	94.6	93.0	94.0	94.5	94.3	93.4	94.4	94.8	95.6	95.7	95.7	96.0
1969	96.7	97.4	96.9	97.4	96.3	96.7	97.0	97.1	97.4	97.6	97.2	96.8	96.5	97.2	97.5	97.5
1970	96.8	95.2	94.8	93.9	96.9	96.9	96.5	95.9	94.7	95.0	94.7	95.7	94.0	94.0	93.2	94.7
1971	93.9	94.1	94.5	94.6	94.3	93.7	93.6	93.6	94.3	94.3	93.5	95.0	95.1	94.7	94.6	94.6
1972	95.0	95.4	96.3	97.1	94.6	95.0	95.4	95.6	95.8	94.7	95.6	96.2	97.0	96.7	97.3	97.3
1973	98.7	100.0	101.2	102.8	98.0	98.9	99.3	99.9	99.6	100.5	101.6	100.9	101.2	102.3	102.5	103.5
1974	104.1	104.2	104.0	102.5	104.1	104.0	104.0	104.1	104.0	104.3	104.6	103.6	103.8	103.3	102.6	101.6
1975	99.0	98.3	97.0	97.5	99.5	99.0	98.7	98.2	98.2	98.5	97.1	97.1	96.7	97.4	97.4	97.6
1976	99.5	99.5	99.3	98.7	98.6	100.1	99.9	100.1	99.7	98.8	99.4	99.5	98.9	98.7	98.8	98.6
1977	97.9	98.0	98.1	97.7	98.1	97.7	97.8	97.5	98.2	98.3	98.2	98.2	98.0	97.8	97.8	97.4
1978	97.9	98.2	99.4	100.4	97.8	97.7	98.1	98.1	98.3	98.3	99.1	99.4	99.6	100.0	100.4	100.7
1979	101.2	101.5	102.6	102.4	101.2	101.3	101.0	101.2	101.4	101.9	102.9	102.4	102.4	102.3	102.5	102.4
1980	101.6	99.5	99.1	100.0	101.7	101.4	101.6	100.6	98.6	99.3	98.9	99.0	99.3	99.8	99.7	100.4
1981	101.2	102.4	100.7	98.4	100.7	101.4	101.6	102.0	102.3	102.9	100.9	100.6	100.5	99.3	98.5	97.4
1982	95.8	92.7	90.3	86.3	96.7	95.6	95.0	93.5	92.8	91.7	91.5	90.5	89.0	87.0	86.3	85.5
1983	86.6				86.4	86.8	86.4									

Unemployment (9) — Chômage (9)

thousands — milliers — Adjusted - Corrigé

Year	Q.1	Q.2	Q.3	Q.4	JAN	FEB	MAR	APR	MAY	JUN	JUL	AUG	SEP	OCT	NOV	DEC
1964	337	328	317	307	339	337	334	335	320	330	317	320	314	339	298	284
1965	293	296	269	245	299	291	288	312	286	290	282	269	255	225	256	255
1966	251	231	260	258	252	252	248	239	236	217	243	264	272	247	265	263
1967	285	288	287	325	275	287	294	298	288	278	290	284	287	315	316	344
1968	347	357	361	359	334	346	360	351	345	376	373	367	343	352	363	361
1969	351	360	357	380	352	354	347	354	364	363	348	367	357	387	379	373
1970	399	483	520	519	367	403	428	449	488	511	537	515	508	510	518	529
1971	533	537	529	539	529	542	529	564	520	528	530	515	541	551	545	521
1972	527	537	571	583	531	509	542	514	538	560	566	573	575	591	577	582
1973	535	499	501	520	557	536	512	506	490	502	486	494	523	533	518	508
1974	501	495	509	553	506	500	496	495	513	478	492	510	524	526	543	589
1975	658	679	701	724	674	652	649	643	692	703	693	714	695	726	732	715
1976	697	709	733	765	713	708	670	704	710	712	760	725	729	767	754	775
1977	818	826	868	890	794	831	830	833	818	828	869	863	873	876	890	904
1978	899	915	925	893	883	899	914	911	922	913	925	921	933	887	897	894
1979	873	842	797	820	884	869	865	878	837	811	803	798	789	825	820	814
1980	865	891	855	840	860	874	860	879	902	892	870	860	839	839	837	845
1981	869	849	879	995	862	865	879	837	851	860	855	810	973	974	984	1028
1982	1057	1246	1461	1534	1012	1051	1108	1176	1240	1322	1437	1457	1490	1537	1525	1540
1983	1503	1492	1421	1363	1486	1507	1515	1502	1497	1478	1454	1426	1383	1361	1362	1365

Unemployment (9) — Chômage (9)

as per cent of civilian labour force — en pourcentage de la main-d'œuvre civile — Adjusted - Corrigé

Year	Q.1	Q.2	Q.3	Q.4	JAN	FEB	MAR	APR	MAY	JUN	JUL	AUG	SEP	OCT	NOV	DEC
1964	4.9	4.8	4.6	4.4	4.9	4.9	4.8	4.9	4.6	4.8	4.6	4.6	4.5	4.9	4.3	4.1
1965	4.1	4.2	3.8	3.4	4.2	4.1	4.1	4.4	4.0	4.1	3.9	3.8	3.6	3.1	3.6	3.5
1966	3.4	3.1	3.4	3.4	3.4	3.4	3.3	3.2	3.2	2.9	3.2	3.5	3.6	3.3	3.5	3.4
1967	3.7	3.7	3.7	4.2	3.6	3.7	3.8	3.9	3.7	3.6	3.7	3.6	3.7	4.1	4.0	4.4
1968	4.4	4.5	4.5	4.5	4.3	4.4	4.6	4.5	4.4	4.7	4.7	4.6	4.3	4.4	4.5	4.5
1969	4.3	4.4	4.4	4.6	4.3	4.3	4.2	4.3	4.4	4.4	4.3	4.5	4.4	4.7	4.6	4.5
1970	4.9	5.8	6.2	6.1	4.5	4.9	5.2	5.4	5.8	6.1	6.4	6.1	6.0	6.0	6.1	6.2
1971	6.2	6.3	6.1	6.1	6.2	6.3	6.2	6.6	6.1	6.1	6.1	6.0	6.2	6.3	6.2	5.9
1972	6.0	6.1	6.4	6.5	6.0	5.8	6.1	5.8	6.1	6.3	6.3	6.4	6.4	6.6	6.4	6.4
1973	5.9	5.4	5.4	5.5	6.1	5.9	5.6	5.5	5.3	5.4	5.3	5.3	5.6	5.7	5.5	5.4
1974	5.2	5.2	5.3	5.7	5.3	5.2	5.2	5.2	5.4	5.0	5.1	5.3	5.4	5.4	5.6	6.0
1975	6.7	6.8	7.0	7.1	6.9	6.6	6.6	6.5	7.0	7.0	6.9	7.2	6.9	7.2	7.2	7.0
1976	6.9	7.0	7.2	7.4	7.0	7.0	6.6	6.9	7.0	7.0	7.4	7.1	7.1	7.5	7.3	7.5
1977	7.9	7.9	8.2	8.4	7.7	8.0	8.0	8.0	7.8	7.9	8.3	8.2	8.2	8.3	8.4	8.5
1978	8.4	8.4	8.4	8.1	8.3	8.4	8.5	8.4	8.5	8.4	8.4	8.4	8.5	8.1	8.1	8.1
1979	7.9	7.6	7.1	7.2	8.0	7.8	7.8	7.9	7.5	7.3	7.2	7.1	7.0	7.3	7.2	7.1
1980	7.5	7.7	7.4	7.2	7.5	7.6	7.5	7.6	7.8	7.7	7.5	7.5	7.2	7.2	7.2	7.2
1981	7.3	7.1	7.4	8.3	7.3	7.3	7.4	7.0	7.2	7.2	7.2	6.8	8.1	8.1	8.2	8.6
1982	8.9	10.5	12.2	12.8	8.5	8.8	9.3	9.9	10.4	11.1	11.9	12.2	12.4	12.8	12.7	12.8
1983	12.5	12.3	11.5	11.1	12.4	12.5	12.5	12.4	12.3	12.1	11.9	11.6	11.3	11.2	11.1	11.1

CANADA

Help wanted advertising (10) / Offres d'emploi par annonces (10)

1980 = 100 — Adjusted - Corrigé

	Year	Q.1	Q.2	Q.3	Q.4	JAN	FEB	MAR	APR	MAY	JUN	JUL	AUG	SEP	OCT	NOV	DEC
1964	50	47	51	48	55	46	49	46	52	52	49	44	50	52	58	51	56
1965	61	58	58	62	66	54	58	61	53	62	59	62	60	63	62	69	66
1966	65	66	67	63	64	64	66	69	69	64	68	66	63	60	65	61	65
1967	56	60	59	56	50	56	61	63	60	57	59	56	57	56	51	49	49
1968	50	48	51	49	51	49	48	48	53	56	44	46	51	51	51	55	48
1969	59	59	61	62	56	57	58	61	62	61	58	59	63	62	54	58	56
1970	50	56	48	47	47	57	58	54	49	48	47	46	46	51	47	44	50
1971	52	46	51	51	58	48	46	46	50	51	51	51	50	52	58	56	60
1972	66	60	64	69	72	60	59	61	63	64	65	69	71	66	73	73	72
1973	84	74	77	88	95	75	73	74	75	76	80	90	86	88	98	106	82
1974	113	105	118	121	106	98	107	111	107	123	124	120	118	125	117	108	93
1975	95	91	96	103	89	96	91	87	99	91	98	110	100	100	89	86	91
1976	87	91	84	83	84	99	88	87	68	96	89	88	88	87	79	87	87
1977	85	87	87	83	82	85	87	89	88	87	84	84	84	82	80	83	84
1978	89	85	84	88	98	83	87	85	84	79	88	86	90	86	88	102	104
1979	97	93	96	97	101	95	92	91	93	97	98	87	96	107	119	98	86
1980	100	104	95	99	103	107	105	101	103	90	91	102	97	98	105	105	100
1981	104	109	99	109	96	103	112	113	79	106	111	108	113	106	104	99	85
1982	51	74	52	39	37	79	76	68	57	56	42	41	42	35	36	35	39
1983	47	38	45	50	55	39	35	38	43	45	49	51	47	52	54	53	58

Weekly hours of work: manufacturing (8) / Durée hebdomadaire du travail : (8) industries manufacturières

hours / heures

	Year	Q.1	Q.2	Q.3	Q.4	JAN	FEB	MAR	APR	MAY	JUN	JUL	AUG	SEP	OCT	NOV	DEC
1964	41.0	41.0	41.3	41.3	40.5	41.2	41.2	40.7	41.2	41.5	41.2	40.9	41.3	41.7	41.6	41.2	38.7
1965	41.0	41.0	41.1	41.1	40.9	41.0	40.6	41.3	41.1	41.1	41.2	40.8	41.1	41.4	41.6	41.5	39.7
1966	40.8	41.1	40.9	40.9	40.2	40.9	41.2	41.2	41.0	40.9	40.7	40.6	41.0	41.2	41.2	41.0	38.5
1967	40.3	40.1	40.5	40.5	40.1	40.1	40.2	40.1	40.5	40.3	40.6	40.2	40.5	40.8	40.8	40.7	38.7
1968	40.3	40.2	40.6	40.5	39.9	40.0	40.4	40.1	40.7	40.6	40.4	40.0	40.4	41.0	40.9	40.9	38.0
1969	40.0	40.3	40.3	40.2	39.3	40.1	40.3	40.5	40.3	40.4	40.2	39.9	40.1	40.7	40.4	40.4	37.2
1970	39.7	39.8	40.0	39.8	39.3	39.8	40.0	39.5	39.8	40.0	40.1	39.3	39.9	40.1	40.1	39.9	38.0
1971	39.7	39.3	39.7	39.8	39.8	38.9	39.0	39.9	39.8	39.5	39.9	39.4	39.8	40.3	40.3	40.3	38.8
1972	40.0	39.8	40.1	40.1	39.9	39.8	39.7	39.9	40.3	39.8	40.2	39.5	40.0	40.7	40.7	40.5	38.5
1973	39.6	40.1	39.8	39.3	39.3	40.0	40.2	40.2	39.6	39.8	39.9	38.7	39.2	40.0	40.0	40.0	38.0
1974	38.9	39.5	39.1	38.7	38.3	39.5	39.4	39.5	39.2	39.0	39.0	38.4	38.7	39.1	39.2	39.0	36.8
1975	38.6	38.6	38.6	38.5	38.6	38.7	38.7	38.3	38.8	38.6	38.5	38.1	38.4	39.0	39.1	39.0	37.7
1976	38.7	38.9	38.7	38.5	38.7	38.7	38.9	39.0	38.9	38.5	38.7	38.2	38.5	38.9	38.9	39.1	38.2
1977	38.7	38.8	38.6	38.6	38.7	38.5	38.9	38.9	38.7	38.3	38.8	38.2	38.7	39.0	39.1	39.0	37.9
1978	38.8	38.5	38.8	38.8	39.0	37.8	39.0	38.6	38.9	38.7	38.9	38.5	38.8	39.2	39.2	39.4	38.3
1979	38.8	39.0	38.9	38.7	38.5	39.0	39.0	39.1	39.0	38.9	38.9	38.5	38.6	39.1	39.0	39.1	37.4
1980	38.5	38.9	38.4	38.2	38.6	38.9	38.8	38.9	38.5	38.4	38.3	37.6	38.1	38.9	39.1	39.0	37.8
1981	38.5	38.8	38.9	38.4	38.0	38.9	38.8	38.8	38.9	38.9	38.9	38.4	38.2	38.5	38.9	38.4	36.8
1982	37.7	38.2	37.8	37.4	37.3	38.2	38.3	38.1	38.0	37.6	37.8	37.3	37.3	37.5	37.8	37.6	36.5
1983	38.2	38.2	38.0	38.1	38.3	37.9	38.3	38.4	38.0	38.0	38.1	38.1	38.1	38.1	38.1	38.9	37.8

Hourly earnings: manufacturing (8) / Gains horaires : industries manufacturières (8)

1980 = 100

	Year	Q.1	Q.2	Q.3	Q.4	JAN	FEB	MAR	APR	MAY	JUN	JUL	AUG	SEP	OCT	NOV	DEC
1964	25	24	25	25	25	24	24	25	25	25	25	25	25	25	25	25	25
1965	26	26	26	25	26	25	25	26	26	26	26	26	26	26	26	26	27
1966	28	27	27	28	28	27	27	27	27	27	27	27	27	28	28	28	28
1967	29	29	29	30	30	29	29	29	29	29	29	29	29	30	30	30	31
1968	32	31	31	32	33	30	30	31	31	31	31	31	32	32	32	33	33
1969	34	33	34	34	35	33	33	34	34	34	34	34	34	35	35	35	36
1970	37	36	37	37	38	36	36	36	37	37	37	37	37	37	37	38	39
1971	40	39	40	40	41	39	39	39	40	40	40	40	40	41	41	41	42
1972	43	42	43	44	45	42	42	42	43	43	43	43	44	44	44	45	45
1973	47	46	47	47	49	45	46	46	46	47	47	47	47	48	49	49	49
1974	54	50	52	55	57	50	50	51	52	52	53	54	54	56	57	57	58
1975	62	59	61	62	65	58	59	60	61	61	62	62	62	63	64	65	65
1976	70	67	70	71	73	66	67	68	69	70	71	71	71	72	72	72	74
1977	78	75	78	79	80	75	75	76	77	78	78	78	78	80	80	80	81
1978	84	82	83	84	86	81	81	82	82	83	83	83	84	85	86	86	86
1979	91	88	90	92	94	87	88	89	90	90	91	91	91	93	94	94	94
1980	100	97	99	101	104	96	97	98	98	98	99	100	100	103	104	104	105
1981	112	107	111	112	117	106	108	109	110	111	112	111	112	112	117	117	118
1982	125	121	124	125	129	121	121	123	124	124	125	126	126	127	128	129	130
1983	130	130	128	129	132	131	131	127	128	128	129	129	129	130	131	132	133

Labour disputes: time lost (11) / Conflits du travail : journées perdues (11)

thousand man-days / milliers de journées-homme

	Year	Q.1	Q.2	Q.3	Q.4	JAN	FEB	MAR	APR	MAY	JUN	JUL	AUG	SEP	OCT	NOV	DEC
1964	1581	199	349	370	664	22	82	95	91	63	195	152	113	104	101	105	457
1965	2350	643	549	796	363	234	294	116	118	156	275	324	246	225	167	108	88
1966	5178	735	1207	2684	553	139	236	361	465	357	385	935	1057	692	165	232	155
1967	3975	805	1395	1104	671	236	477	91	149	501	746	314	368	422	314	210	147
1968	4947	1445	1246	1674	582	190	584	672	321	394	531	842	600	232	255	219	108
1969	7752	407	2334	3426	1585	119	128	160	277	1125	932	1048	1229	1148	1079	381	125
1970	6540	388	2178	2087	1887	96	122	170	431	958	789	846	621	620	759	704	424
1971	2862	609	568	983	702	208	172	230	160	118	290	327	370	287	317	233	153
1972	7754	745	3983	2196	829	135	239	372	1832	937	1213	1120	620	457	390	308	131
1973	5776	565	1477	2574	1160	178	169	218	231	542	704	624	1248	701	497	359	305
1974	9222	1123	4055	2589	1455	263	423	438	636	1395	2024	1017	857	714	683	471	301
1975	10909	1250	2056	3805	3797	410	361	480	559	692	805	1238	1294	1274	1277	1421	1099
1976	11685	1831	2670	4401	2783	819	564	449	710	661	1300	1270	1187	1944	2036	499	249
1977	3308	602	937	997	772	219	176	207	329	300	308	406	346	245	178	241	353
1978	7393	1055	1657	2788	1893	376	277	403	483	504	670	975	1039	774	842	580	471
1979	7834	1679	2305	2099	1751	529	472	679	680	756	869	783	899	417	623	674	454
1980	8976	2400	2120	2877	1578	690	1122	588	616	687	817	1061	998	817	780	466	333
1981	8879	1829	1513	4140	1396	352	698	779	563	457	494	1770	1685	685	655	546	195
1982	5795	643	1633	2297	1223	150	192	301	172	627	834	600	1258	440	332	627	264
1983		2253	823			451	1600	202	287	249	287	279					

Weekly hours of work: manufacturing (8) / Durée hebdomadaire du travail : (8) industries manufacturières

Adjusted - Corrigé

hours / heures

	Year	Q.1	Q.2	Q.3	Q.4	JAN	FEB	MAR	APR	MAY	JUN	JUL	AUG	SEP	OCT	NOV	DEC
1964		41.0	41.1	41.1	40.9	41.3	41.2	40.6	41.1	41.3	41.0	41.0	41.1	41.2	41.1	40.8	40.7
1965		41.0	41.0	40.9	41.3	41.1	40.6	41.2	41.0	40.9	41.1	41.0	40.9	40.9	41.0	41.1	41.7
1966		41.1	40.7	40.8	40.5	41.0	41.2	41.1	40.8	40.7	40.6	40.8	40.9	40.7	40.7	40.6	40.3
1967		40.2	40.3	40.3	40.4	40.3	40.2	40.0	40.3	40.1	40.5	40.4	40.3	40.2	40.3	40.3	40.5
1968		40.2	40.4	40.3	40.2	40.2	40.4	40.0	40.5	40.5	40.2	40.2	40.2	40.4	40.4	40.4	39.7
1969		40.3	40.1	40.1	39.6	40.3	40.3	40.4	40.1	40.3	40.0	40.2	40.0	40.1	39.9	40.0	38.8
1970		39.8	39.8	39.6	39.6	40.0	40.0	39.4	39.6	39.9	39.9	39.6	39.8	39.5	39.6	39.5	39.6
1971		39.3	39.6	39.8	40.0	39.1	39.0	39.8	39.6	39.5	39.7	39.8	39.8	39.8	39.8	39.9	40.4
1972		39.8	40.0	40.1	40.1	39.9	39.7	39.7	40.1	39.8	40.0	40.0	40.1	40.2	40.2	40.1	40.0
1973		40.0	39.6	39.3	39.5	40.0	40.1	40.0	39.3	39.8	39.7	39.2	39.3	39.5	39.5	39.6	39.4
1974		39.4	38.7	38.8	38.4	39.5	39.3	39.3	39.0	38.1	38.9	38.9	38.9	38.7	38.7	38.6	38.0
1975		38.4	38.6	38.5	38.7	38.7	38.5	38.1	38.6	38.7	38.4	38.6	38.5	38.6	38.7	38.6	38.8
1976		38.7	38.6	38.5	38.8	38.7	38.7	38.8	38.7	38.6	38.6	38.7	38.6	38.6	38.5	38.7	39.2
1977		38.6	38.5	38.7	38.7	38.5	38.7	38.7	38.5	38.4	38.7	38.6	38.8	38.7	38.7	38.6	38.9
1978		38.4	38.8	38.9	39.0	37.8	38.9	38.4	38.8	38.8	38.8	38.9	39.0	38.9	38.8	39.0	39.3
1979		38.9	38.9	38.8	38.6	39.0	38.9	38.9	38.9	38.9	38.8	38.9	38.8	38.8	38.6	38.7	38.4
1980		38.7	38.3	38.3	38.7	38.8	38.7	38.7	38.4	38.4	38.2	37.9	38.3	38.6	38.7	38.7	38.8
1981		38.7	38.8	38.5	38.1	38.8	38.7	38.6	38.8	38.9	38.8	38.7	38.5	38.2	38.5	38.1	37.8
1982		38.1	37.7	37.5	37.4	38.1	38.2	37.9	37.9	37.6	37.7	37.6	37.6	37.2	37.4	37.3	37.5
1983		38.0				37.8	38.1	38.2									

Hourly earnings: manufacturing (8) / Gains horaires : industries manufacturières (8)

Adjusted - Corrigé

1980 = 100

	Year	Q.1	Q.2	Q.3	Q.4	JAN	FEB	MAR	APR	MAY	JUN	JUL	AUG	SEP	OCT	NOV	DEC
1964		24	25	25	25	24	24	24	24	25	25	25	25	25	25	25	25
1965		26	26	25	26	25	25	26	26	26	26	26	26	26	26	26	26
1966		27	27	25	28	27	27	27	27	27	27	28	28	28	28	28	28
1967		29	29	30	30	28	29	29	29	29	29	30	30	30	30	30	30
1968		30	31	32	33	30	30	31	31	31	31	32	32	32	32	33	33
1969		33	34	34	35	33	33	33	34	34	34	34	34	35	35	35	35
1970		36	37	37	38	36	36	36	36	36	37	37	37	37	38	38	39
1971		39	40	41	41	39	39	39	39	40	40	40	41	41	41	41	41
1972		42	43	44	45	42	42	42	43	43	43	43	44	44	44	45	45
1973		46	47	48	49	45	46	46	46	47	47	47	47	48	49	49	49
1974		50	52	55	57	50	50	51	51	52	52	54	55	56	57	57	58
1975		59	61	63	65	58	59	60	61	61	62	62	63	63	64	65	65
1976		67	70	71	73	66	67	68	69	70	71	71	72	72	72	73	74
1977		75	77	79	80	75	75	76	77	77	78	79	79	80	80	80	81
1978		81	83	84	86	81	81	82	82	83	83	84	85	85	86	86	86
1979		88	90	92	94	87	88	88	89	90	91	91	92	92	93	94	95
1980		96	98	101	104	96	97	97	98	98	99	100	101	102	103	104	105
1981		107	111	113	117	106	107	108	109	111	112	112	113	115	116	117	119
1982		121	124	127	129	121	121	122	123	124	125	127	128	127	128	129	130
1983		131				131	131	132									

CANADA

Unit labour cost: (12) manufacturing

1980 = 100

Adjusted - Corrigé

Coût unitaire de la main-d'œuvre : (12) industries manufacturières

1980 = 100

	Year	Q.1	Q.2	Q.3	Q.4	JAN	FEB	MAR	APR	MAY	JUN	JUL	AUG	SEP	OCT	NOV	DEC
1964	41.1	41.0	40.9	41.5	41.0	41.2	40.5	41.3	40.6	40.9	41.2	41.4	42.0	41.1	41.2	40.8	41.0
1965	41.6	41.3	41.7	41.7	41.9	41.3	41.4	41.3	41.8	41.5	41.8	40.6	42.6	41.8	41.6	42.2	41.8
1966	43.3	42.1	43.1	44.2	43.7	41.7	42.0	42.5	42.7	43.2	43.5	43.7	45.1	43.9	43.6	44.0	43.4
1967	45.1	45.1	45.0	45.2	45.3	44.6	45.1	45.5	44.5	45.3	45.1	45.4	45.2	45.0	45.8	45.3	44.9
1968	45.1	45.3	44.9	45.0	45.1	45.2	45.5	45.2	45.7	44.8	44.4	44.9	45.1	45.1	45.0	45.0	45.2
1969	45.9	45.2	45.7	45.6	46.9	45.5	45.3	44.9	45.7	45.7	45.9	45.3	45.5	46.1	46.5	46.9	47.4
1970	48.6	47.5	48.5	48.9	49.3	47.6	47.0	47.8	48.3	48.2	49.1	48.9	48.5	49.4	49.4	49.1	49.5
1971	48.6	49.3	48.9	48.3	48.2	49.6	49.4	48.9	49.1	48.7	48.8	49.0	48.0	48.0	47.5	48.4	48.7
1972	49.9	49.5	49.7	50.0	50.2	48.8	49.9	49.9	49.7	50.1	49.4	49.7	50.3	50.1	50.2	50.2	50.2
1973	51.6	50.1	51.3	51.6	53.2	50.4	49.9	50.0	51.0	51.1	51.7	50.5	51.9	52.5	52.7	53.0	53.3
1974	58.1	53.9	56.7	59.6	62.3	53.5	53.7	54.6	56.6	56.1	57.3	58.5	59.1	61.2	61.2	62.7	63.1
1975	67.9	65.9	67.8	68.0	69.6	65.7	65.3	66.8	66.5	68.4	68.5	67.6	68.0	68.5	69.7	69.7	69.5
1976	73.4	72.2	72.6	73.2	75.6	71.5	72.5	72.6	72.4	71.9	73.5	73.7	72.5	73.3	75.6	75.1	76.1
1977	77.9	75.4	77.1	79.1	80.3	74.3	76.0	76.0	77.1	77.0	77.3	78.8	78.9	79.7	79.8	80.4	80.6
1978	81.5	80.9	81.1	82.0	81.9	79.9	81.1	81.7	79.4	81.4	82.5	82.0	82.7	81.4	82.3	82.3	81.2
1979	87.9	83.6	86.4	89.0	92.7	83.0	83.7	84.1	86.1	85.5	87.6	88.5	89.0	89.5	90.1	91.7	96.3
1980	100.0	94.8	99.7	102.0	103.7	93.4	95.4	95.5	97.0	100.3	101.8	102.8	101.6	101.5	102.3	103.4	105.4
1981	111.6	106.3	108.1	111.9	120.3	106.8	106.3	105.7	106.7	108.6	109.1	109.3	111.6	114.7	117.3	120.4	123.1
1982	127.9	123.2	126.9	127.8	131.8	123.5	120.2	125.9	127.2	125.0	128.5	133.8	132.2	127.5	130.1	130.7	134.7
1983	128.3	126.8	130.8	125.8	125.7	126.8	125.7	127.9	129.0	131.4	132.0	133.0	128.8	127.4	126.9	125.2	125.1

Producer prices: food and beverages (13)

1980 = 100

Prix à la production : produits alimentaires et boissons (13)

1980 = 100

	Year	Q.1	Q.2	Q.3	Q.4	JAN	FEB	MAR	APR	MAY	JUN	JUL	AUG	SEP	OCT	NOV	DEC
1964	32.6	32.8	32.7	32.6	32.3	32.8	32.8	32.7	32.7	32.7	32.6	32.6	32.6	32.5	32.4	32.3	32.2
1965	32.9	32.3	32.6	33.2	33.6	32.1	32.3	32.3	32.3	32.4	33.1	33.2	33.3	33.2	33.3	33.5	33.9
1966	34.7	34.5	34.4	35.0	34.8	34.3	34.7	34.6	34.3	34.3	34.6	34.7	35.1	35.1	34.9	34.6	34.8
1967	34.9	34.8	34.9	35.1	34.9	34.8	34.8	34.7	34.7	35.0	35.2	35.1	35.1	35.1	35.0	34.9	35.0
1968	35.4	34.9	35.1	35.7	36.0	35.0	34.9	34.7	34.8	35.0	35.4	35.5	35.8	35.9	35.9	35.9	36.1
1969	37.2	36.3	37.3	37.7	37.4	36.2	36.3	36.5	36.8	37.3	37.9	37.9	37.7	37.6	37.4	37.3	37.6
1970	38.1	38.2	38.2	38.1	38.0	38.1	38.4	38.3	38.2	38.2	38.1	38.2	38.0	38.0	38.0	37.9	38.0
1971	39.0	38.2	38.6	39.2	39.8	37.9	38.4	38.4	38.5	38.5	38.8	39.0	39.3	39.4	39.6	39.7	40.0
1972	42.4	41.0	42.0	42.7	43.7	40.5	41.1	41.5	41.7	42.1	42.2	42.4	42.6	43.0	43.2	43.5	44.2
1973	51.2	46.4	49.3	54.3	54.3	45.4	46.3	47.4	47.7	49.5	50.7	52.0	57.4	55.0	54.5	53.9	54.5
1974	60.4	56.8	57.8	61.5	65.4	56.2	57.2	57.1	57.8	57.9	57.8	59.3	62.4	63.1	64.3	66.3	65.6
1975	66.6	64.6	65.6	68.0	68.1	65.3	64.8	63.8	64.9	66.1	66.0	67.2	68.4	68.6	68.8	67.8	67.7
1976	67.7	67.4	67.8	68.1	67.4	67.5	67.4	67.2	67.1	68.0	68.5	68.4	67.7	68.2	67.2	67.1	68.0
1977	72.5	69.8	73.0	73.2	73.7	68.9	69.7	70.9	72.3	73.4	73.3	73.2	73.2	73.3	73.1	73.7	74.4
1978	80.1	76.0	79.7	81.3	83.5	75.1	76.1	76.9	78.2	80.1	80.9	80.9	81.2	81.7	83.1	83.5	83.9
1979	90.3	88.0	89.7	91.0	92.6	86.4	88.3	89.4	89.2	89.7	90.1	90.8	90.1	91.9	92.2	92.4	93.2
1980	100.0	95.2	96.6	101.5	106.7	94.5	96.0	94.9	95.4	97.2	97.2	98.4	102.0	104.3	106.0	107.2	106.9
1981	108.9	107.4	108.1	109.9	110.1	107.6	107.6	106.9	107.6	107.7	109.1	109.8	110.2	109.8	110.3	110.0	110.0
1982	114.7	111.5	115.5	116.4	115.6	110.5	111.8	112.1	114.3	115.7	116.4	116.6	116.5	116.3	115.7	115.3	115.8
1983	118.8	117.0	118.4	119.3	120.6	116.3	117.3	117.2	118.1	118.5	118.6	118.3	119.6	120.0	120.1	120.4	121.2

Producer prices: paper and allied industries (13)

1980 = 100

Prix à la production : papier et industries connexes (13)

1980 = 100

	Year	Q.1	Q.2	Q.3	Q.4	JAN	FEB	MAR	APR	MAY	JUN	JUL	AUG	SEP	OCT	NOV	DEC
1964	31.7	31.7	31.8	31.7	31.7	31.7	31.7	31.8	31.8	31.8	31.7	31.7	31.7	31.6	31.7	31.7	31.7
1965	31.9	31.8	31.9	32.0	31.9	31.7	31.8	31.8	31.8	31.9	32.0	32.0	31.9	31.9	31.9	31.9	32.0
1966	32.6	32.1	32.3	32.7	33.2	32.1	32.1	32.1	32.1	32.2	32.7	32.7	32.7	32.8	33.1	33.2	33.2
1967	33.5	33.3	33.4	33.6	33.6	33.3	33.3	33.4	33.4	33.4	33.4	33.7	33.6	33.6	33.5	33.5	33.7
1968	33.7	33.7	33.6	33.5	33.7	33.7	33.7	33.7	33.6	33.6	33.7	33.6	33.6	33.7	33.7	33.7	33.7
1969	34.7	34.4	34.6	35.0	35.0	34.3	34.3	34.4	34.6	34.6	34.8	35.0	35.0	35.0	35.0	35.0	34.9
1970	35.7	36.0	36.0	35.5	35.5	36.0	36.0	36.1	36.1	36.2	35.6	35.7	35.5	35.3	35.5	35.6	35.4
1971	36.1	35.7	36.2	36.3	36.1	35.8	35.7	35.7	36.1	36.2	36.4	36.4	36.2	36.2	36.1	36.1	36.1
1972	36.4	36.3	36.2	36.4	36.7	36.3	36.3	36.2	36.2	36.3	36.2	36.4	36.4	36.4	36.5	36.6	36.9
1973	40.4	37.5	39.0	41.2	44.0	37.3	37.5	37.8	38.8	39.1	39.1	40.5	41.2	41.9	43.0	44.4	44.8
1974	54.7	49.0	52.5	57.9	59.5	48.6	48.7	49.6	52.1	52.4	52.9	57.2	58.0	58.6	59.1	59.6	59.8
1975	64.4	63.8	64.4	64.6	64.7	63.6	63.9	63.8	64.1	64.7	64.6	64.5	64.8	64.6	64.8	64.6	64.5
1976	65.9	64.9	65.8	66.2	66.7	64.8	64.7	65.3	65.6	65.9	65.9	66.0	66.5	66.2	66.2	66.2	67.9
1977	69.8	68.6	69.6	70.4	70.6	68.2	68.4	69.3	69.6	69.6	69.8	70.5	70.4	70.3	70.9	71.0	70.0
1978	73.7	70.3	72.6	73.8	78.1	69.9	70.4	70.6	72.9	72.2	72.6	72.8	73.6	75.0	77.9	78.0	78.4
1979	86.4	82.0	84.9	87.0	91.8	80.8	82.4	82.7	84.1	85.0	85.8	86.5	87.3	87.4	90.6	92.5	92.4
1980	100.0	94.8	100.3	101.3	103.6	94.2	94.2	96.1	99.5	101.2	100.2	100.9	101.2	101.7	102.0	103.8	105.2
1981	110.4	107.1	108.6	112.0	114.0	106.7	107.5	107.3	108.0	108.6	109.2	110.4	113.1	112.6	114.0	113.7	114.2
1982	114.5	115.3	116.3	115.2	111.1	114.5	115.6	116.0	115.3	116.0	117.5	115.7	115.2	114.7	113.0	110.0	110.2
1983	110.9	109.2	109.9	111.5	112.8	109.1	109.2	109.2	109.8	109.9	110.2	111.4	111.5	111.5	112.2	112.9	113.4

Producer prices: chemicals (13) / Prix à la production : produits chimiques (13)

1980 = 100

	Year	Q.1	Q.2	Q.3	Q.4	JAN	FEB	MAR	APR	MAY	JUN	JUL	AUG	SEP	OCT	NOV	DEC
1964	38.3	38.3	38.3	38.3	38.5	38.4	38.2	38.2	38.3	38.3	38.3	38.3	38.2	38.3	38.4	38.5	38.5
1965	38.3	38.3	38.3	38.2	38.2	38.4	38.2	38.3	38.3	38.3	38.3	38.3	38.2	38.1	38.1	38.1	38.2
1966	38.1	38.1	38.1	38.1	38.3	38.0	38.1	38.2	38.2	38.0	38.2	38.0	38.1	38.2	38.3	38.2	38.5
1967	38.8	38.6	38.9	38.9	39.0	38.5	38.5	38.6	39.0	38.8	38.8	38.9	38.8	39.0	39.0	39.0	39.0
1968	39.2	39.2	39.3	39.2	39.2	39.0	39.1	39.3	39.4	39.3	39.3	39.1	39.2	39.2	39.2	39.2	39.2
1969	39.3	39.4	39.5	39.1	39.2	39.2	39.3	39.5	39.5	39.4	39.5	39.1	39.0	39.1	39.2	39.1	39.3
1970	39.4	39.3	39.3	39.3	39.8	39.3	39.3	39.2	39.3	39.3	39.4	39.3	39.2	39.5	39.7	39.8	39.8
1971	39.8	39.7	39.7	39.8	40.0	39.7	39.6	39.9	39.7	39.7	39.8	39.9	39.8	39.7	40.0	40.0	40.1
1972	40.4	40.1	40.5	40.4	40.5	40.1	40.1	40.3	40.6	40.4	40.5	40.5	40.4	40.3	40.5	40.5	40.7
1973	42.8	41.2	41.7	42.6	44.2	41.2	41.1	41.3	41.6	41.8	41.8	42.4	42.6	42.8	43.5	44.1	45.0
1974	54.5	48.9	52.7	56.6	60.0	47.8	48.9	50.0	51.6	52.8	53.8	55.6	56.2	58.0	59.0	60.1	61.0
1975	63.9	62.6	63.5	64.3	64.9	62.1	62.8	62.9	63.1	63.9	63.5	64.3	64.4	64.3	64.9	64.8	64.9
1976	66.6	65.6	66.5	66.3	67.5	65.5	65.5	65.8	66.2	66.6	66.6	66.7	66.9	66.8	67.2	67.5	67.7
1977	70.0	68.6	69.4	70.4	71.6	68.2	68.5	69.0	69.3	69.4	69.7	70.3	70.4	70.6	71.1	72.0	71.7
1978	75.3	73.3	74.7	76.0	77.4	73.1	73.4	73.5	74.4	74.8	74.8	75.6	76.0	76.4	77.2	77.4	77.8
1979	85.5	80.5	84.1	87.5	90.2	79.7	80.4	81.5	83.0	84.3	85.0	86.4	87.6	88.3	89.3	90.1	91.0
1980	100.0	95.9	100.5	101.3	103.0	95.1	95.4	97.2	100.1	100.8	100.6	101.0	101.2	101.6	102.5	102.6	103.9
1981	114.1	109.2	112.8	115.3	118.4	108.0	109.1	110.4	111.9	112.9	113.5	115.3	116.1	116.0	118.3	118.3	118.6
1982	122.2	120.5	122.0	123.1	123.1	120.5	120.6	120.3	121.6	122.1	122.4	123.0	123.2	123.2	123.0	123.2	123.0
1983	126.0	124.8	125.2	126.2	127.8	124.9	124.9	124.7	125.1	125.0	125.5	125.8	126.4	126.4	127.7	127.9	127.9

Producer prices: basic metals (13) / Prix à la production : métaux de base (13)

1980 = 100

	Year	Q.1	Q.2	Q.3	Q.4	JAN	FEB	MAR	APR	MAY	JUN	JUL	AUG	SEP	OCT	NOV	DEC
1964	26.0	25.6	25.8	26.0	26.4	25.5	25.5	25.7	25.8	25.9	25.9	25.9	26.0	26.2	26.3	26.4	26.5
1965	27.2	26.7	27.1	27.4	27.6	26.5	26.7	26.8	26.8	27.3	27.3	27.4	27.4	27.4	27.4	27.7	27.7
1966	28.3	28.2	28.2	28.2	28.4	28.2	28.2	28.2	28.2	28.2	28.3	28.2	28.2	28.2	28.2	28.5	28.5
1967	29.1	28.9	29.0	29.1	29.6	28.6	29.0	29.0	29.0	29.0	29.0	29.0	29.0	29.4	29.4	29.4	29.9
1968	29.5	30.2	29.7	29.1	29.2	29.9	30.3	30.5	29.8	29.5	29.7	29.1	29.0	29.1	29.0	29.1	29.3
1969	31.6	30.4	31.1	31.9	33.0	30.2	30.4	30.6	30.9	31.0	31.4	31.4	32.0	32.2	32.3	32.7	34.1
1970	33.5	34.4	34.3	33.0	32.5	34.2	34.3	34.7	34.8	34.4	33.8	33.3	32.9	32.7	32.6	32.5	32.3
1971	32.4	32.1	32.5	32.6	32.5	32.2	32.0	32.2	32.5	32.5	32.5	32.7	32.6	32.5	32.5	32.5	32.4
1972	33.1	32.8	33.0	33.1	33.7	32.6	32.8	33.0	33.1	33.1	32.9	33.0	32.9	33.3	33.6	33.6	33.9
1973	38.1	35.2	37.5	39.1	40.6	34.4	35.1	36.1	36.7	37.8	37.9	38.9	39.2	39.4	40.1	40.7	41.0
1974	47.8	44.6	48.4	48.3	49.8	42.7	44.5	46.5	48.0	48.8	48.6	48.4	48.9	49.0	49.5	49.9	49.9
1975	52.1	51.2	51.7	52.2	53.4	50.8	51.4	51.4	51.6	51.8	51.5	51.6	52.0	53.0	53.5	53.5	53.3
1976	54.9	53.2	54.5	55.6	57.1	53.1	53.1	53.3	54.1	54.4	54.9	55.5	55.7	55.7	56.1	56.6	58.5
1977	61.8	60.2	61.6	62.2	63.1	59.1	60.1	61.3	61.7	61.8	61.2	62.2	62.2	62.2	62.9	63.2	63.1
1978	67.3	64.1	66.0	67.8	71.5	63.8	64.1	64.5	66.0	65.6	66.3	66.7	68.0	68.8	71.2	71.5	71.7
1979	83.9	76.3	82.1	84.8	92.4	73.9	77.1	78.0	80.9	82.0	83.3	83.4	84.3	86.6	91.6	91.5	94.1
1980	100.0	101.0	97.6	99.6	101.6	102.0	103.4	97.7	97.9	97.0	97.8	98.6	99.2	101.0	102.9	101.5	100.3
1981	101.3	99.9	101.5	101.9	102.0	100.5	98.8	100.3	101.2	101.7	101.7	100.5	102.3	102.9	102.8	101.3	101.9
1982	100.7	101.6	100.8	100.3	100.3	101.6	102.4	100.7	101.9	100.6	99.8	99.9	99.4	101.5	100.6	99.7	100.5
1983	103.9	102.2	103.4	104.6	105.4	102.1	102.9	101.6	103.7	104.3	102.2	104.2	105.1	104.7	105.0	105.2	106.0

Producer prices: metal products / Prix à la production : ouvrages en métaux

1980 = 100

	Year	Q.1	Q.2	Q.3	Q.4	JAN	FEB	MAR	APR	MAY	JUN	JUL	AUG	SEP	OCT	NOV	DEC
1964																	
1965																	
1966																	
1967																	
1968																	
1969																	
1970																	
1971	43.1	42.4	42.9	43.3	43.7	42.2	42.4	42.5	42.8	42.8	42.9	43.0	43.4	43.5	43.7	43.7	43.7
1972	45.1	44.5	45.0	45.1	45.6	44.4	44.6	44.6	44.9	45.0	45.0	45.1	45.2	45.2	45.4	45.6	45.7
1973	48.6	46.6	47.6	49.4	50.8	46.5	46.6	46.7	47.3	47.6	47.8	49.1	49.3	49.7	50.5	50.6	51.2
1974	58.2	54.3	57.5	59.6	61.2	53.7	54.2	55.0	57.0	57.3	58.2	59.2	59.5	60.0	60.8	61.3	61.6
1975	65.6	63.6	64.9	65.3	68.0	62.8	63.8	64.1	64.7	64.8	65.1	65.2	65.4	66.7	67.6	68.1	68.3
1976	69.9	68.8	69.7	70.3	70.8	68.5	68.8	69.0	69.3	69.8	69.9	70.0	70.2	70.6	70.8	70.8	70.9
1977	74.1	71.8	73.7	74.9	76.0	71.3	71.9	72.2	72.9	74.1	74.2	74.6	74.7	75.3	75.7	76.0	76.2
1978	81.0	77.4	79.8	82.4	84.5	77.1	77.4	77.8	79.3	79.9	80.2	82.1	82.4	82.8	84.0	84.6	84.9
1979	91.0	87.6	90.0	91.9	94.6	86.7	87.9	88.3	89.5	89.8	90.8	91.2	91.9	92.6	93.9	94.7	95.2
1980	100.0	97.0	99.6	101.0	103.1	96.1	97.1	97.6	99.0	99.7	100.1	100.4	101.0	101.5	102.4	103.1	103.8
1981	110.0	106.5	109.3	110.7	114.4	105.8	106.4	107.2	108.7	109.4	109.8	110.6	110.5	110.9	113.8	114.5	115.0
1982	119.6	117.5	119.8	120.4	120.7	117.0	117.7	117.7	119.3	119.7	120.2	120.4	120.5	120.4	120.8	120.9	120.5
1983	122.2	120.7	121.9	122.9	123.4	120.8	120.5	120.7	121.4	121.6	122.6	122.5	123.0	123.0	123.1	123.5	123.6

CANADA

Producer prices: electrical machinery / Prix à la production : machines électriques

1980 = 100

	Year	Q.1	Q.2	Q.3	Q.4	JAN	FEB	MAR	APR	MAY	JUN	JUL	AUG	SEP	OCT	NOV	DEC
1964																	
1965																	
1966																	
1967																	
1968																	
1969																	
1970																	
1971	52.8	52.5	52.6	52.9	53.2	52.5	52.6	52.5	52.6	52.7	52.6	52.7	53.0	53.0	53.2	53.2	53.3
1972	53.3	53.4	53.5	53.2	53.1	53.3	53.4	53.5	53.6	53.6	53.4	53.3	53.3	53.0	53.1	53.1	53.0
1973	54.9	53.4	54.2	55.2	56.8	53.3	53.4	53.7	54.0	54.3	54.4	54.7	55.2	55.6	56.0	57.2	57.4
1974	64.3	59.4	62.5	65.9	69.3	58.6	59.4	60.3	61.4	62.6	63.5	64.9	65.6	67.2	69.0	69.4	69.6
1975	72.0	71.0	71.7	72.0	73.1	70.7	71.2	71.1	71.5	71.6	71.8	71.8	71.9	72.4	73.1	73.2	72.9
1976	74.1	73.4	73.9	74.2	74.7	73.4	73.3	73.4	73.8	73.9	74.1	74.1	74.2	74.3	74.3	74.5	75.3
1977	77.8	75.8	77.7	78.5	79.4	75.7	75.7	76.0	77.6	77.8	77.8	78.6	78.5	78.5	79.2	78.9	80.0
1978	82.9	81.3	82.5	83.2	84.8	80.9	81.2	81.8	82.4	82.5	82.7	82.9	83.0	83.5	84.3	84.9	85.2
1979	91.1	87.5	90.2	92.2	94.5	86.5	87.4	88.5	89.7	90.2	90.7	91.7	92.1	92.7	94.1	94.2	95.0
1980	100.0	97.4	99.6	101.0	102.5	96.8	97.3	98.2	98.6	99.8	100.4	100.4	101.0	101.5	102.5	102.3	102.8
1981	107.6	104.3	106.7	108.3	110.6	103.5	104.1	105.1	106.5	106.9	106.7	108.1	108.6	109.7	110.0	110.6	111.3
1982	114.7	112.3	114.5	115.7	116.1	112.0	112.5	112.5	114.2	114.5	114.8	115.6	115.6	115.9	116.1	116.1	116.2
1983	118.4	117.2	117.8	119.0	120.0	117.1	117.3	117.2	117.2	117.6	118.4	118.7	119.0	119.3	119.9	119.9	120.3

Producer prices: petroleum (13) / Prix à la production : pétrole (13)

1980 = 100

	Year	Q.1	Q.2	Q.3	Q.4	JAN	FEB	MAR	APR	MAY	JUN	JUL	AUG	SEP	OCT	NOV	DEC
1964	20.7	20.8	20.8	20.7	20.4	20.8	20.8	20.8	20.8	20.8	20.8	20.8	20.6	20.6	20.6	20.4	20.2
1965	20.3	19.9	20.4	20.4	20.5	19.1	20.3	20.4	20.4	20.4	20.4	20.4	20.5	20.5	20.5	20.5	20.5
1966	20.4	20.3	20.3	20.4	20.4	20.3	20.3	20.3	20.3	20.3	20.3	20.4	20.4	20.4	20.4	20.4	20.4
1967	20.5	20.5	20.6	20.5	20.5	20.4	20.5	20.6	20.6	20.6	20.6	20.6	20.6	20.5	20.5	20.5	20.5
1968	21.0	20.7	20.9	21.1	21.1	20.5	20.8	20.8	20.9	20.9	21.1	21.1	21.1	21.1	21.1	21.1	21.1
1969	21.4	21.1	21.2	21.5	21.7	21.1	21.1	21.1	21.1	21.2	21.2	21.2	21.6	21.6	21.6	21.7	21.8
1970	22.0	21.9	21.9	21.9	22.3	21.9	21.9	21.9	21.9	21.9	21.9	21.9	21.9	21.9	22.3	22.3	22.3
1971	24.4	23.5	24.6	24.7	24.7	23.5	23.5	23.5	24.5	24.6	24.6	24.6	24.6	24.8	24.8	24.8	24.6
1972	25.0	24.9	25.1	25.0	25.1	24.7	25.1	25.0	25.0	25.0	25.1	25.0	25.0	25.0	25.0	25.1	25.1
1973	28.6	26.6	27.3	29.1	31.4	26.5	26.6	26.6	26.6	27.6	27.8	28.2	29.4	29.9	30.1	31.2	33.0
1974	39.0	34.2	38.3	41.7	41.7	34.1	34.3	34.3	34.3	38.9	41.6	41.8	41.6	41.7	41.7	41.7	41.7
1975	44.9	42.3	43.6	45.4	48.6	41.7	41.8	43.3	43.6	43.6	43.5	43.5	45.9	46.7	47.5	48.9	49.2
1976	51.5	49.2	49.8	51.7	55.4	49.2	49.2	49.2	49.4	50.0	50.0	50.1	50.2	54.7	55.4	55.4	55.5
1977	60.1	56.5	59.4	60.8	63.7	55.6	55.6	58.2	59.4	59.3	59.6	59.6	59.6	63.1	63.8	63.7	63.6
1978	67.9	64.1	66.9	68.5	72.1	63.0	63.0	66.2	67.2	66.9	66.5	66.4	67.3	71.8	72.0	72.1	72.0
1979	79.4	73.4	75.2	81.2	87.7	72.8	73.6	73.8	74.3	75.2	76.1	78.1	80.8	84.8	86.0	87.4	89.5
1980	100.0	93.5	97.2	99.8	109.5	90.8	92.8	97.0	98.5	95.9	97.0	98.1	100.0	101.4	106.9	110.0	111.5
1981	136.3	124.2	133.0	142.3	145.9	121.6	122.6	128.4	129.4	131.8	137.9	140.5	141.5	144.9	145.8	145.3	146.4
1982	156.8	148.3	155.4	158.6	164.8	146.1	145.5	153.2	155.5	156.1	154.8	154.6	156.3	164.8	164.3	165.3	164.8
1983	166.9	158.4	167.7	171.1	169.9	155.7	153.1	166.3	167.4	166.3	169.4	170.0	171.0	172.3	170.5	170.2	168.9

Money supply (M1) (14) / Disponibilités monétaires (M1) (14)

billion Canadian dollars, end of period / milliards de dollars canadiens, fin de période

	Year	Q.1	Q.2	Q.3	Q.4	JAN	FEB	MAR	APR	MAY	JUN	JUL	AUG	SEP	OCT	NOV	DEC
1964	6.69	6.12	6.92	6.40	6.69	6.25	5.99	6.12	6.26	6.25	6.92	6.35	6.36	6.40	6.51	6.51	6.69
1965	7.13	6.40	6.73	6.87	7.13	6.53	6.32	6.40	6.60	6.60	6.73	6.82	6.90	6.87	6.93	7.03	7.13
1966	7.74	6.89	7.14	7.36	7.74	6.99	6.81	6.89	7.05	7.02	7.14	7.23	7.29	7.36	7.48	7.52	7.74
1967	8.37	7.61	7.85	8.17	8.37	7.56	7.50	7.61	7.80	7.78	7.85	7.97	7.99	8.17	8.26	8.13	8.37
1968	8.89	7.72	8.00	8.53	8.89	8.15	7.79	7.72	7.90	7.91	8.00	8.31	8.56	8.53	8.62	8.61	8.89
1969	9.22	8.49	8.84	8.92	9.22	8.81	8.37	8.49	8.78	8.79	8.84	8.99	8.87	8.92	9.07	8.87	9.22
1970	9.74	8.67	8.92	9.24	9.74	8.85	8.59	8.67	8.89	8.78	8.92	9.22	9.20	9.24	9.27	9.23	9.74
1971	11.46	9.51	10.26	10.78	11.46	9.44	9.26	9.51	9.70	9.86	10.26	10.34	10.48	10.78	10.75	10.81	11.46
1972	13.04	10.92	11.50	12.20	13.04	10.99	10.76	10.92	11.15	11.20	11.50	11.82	11.96	12.20	12.28	12.47	13.04
1973	14.49	12.47	13.31	13.93	14.49	12.73	12.44	12.47	12.90	13.09	13.31	13.71	13.79	13.93	13.99	13.84	14.49
1974	15.33	13.93	14.76	14.84	15.33	14.15	13.82	13.93	14.63	14.92	14.76	14.94	14.81	14.84	14.81	14.70	15.33
1975	18.87	15.61	16.40	17.27	18.87	15.24	15.24	15.61	15.86	15.92	16.40	16.95	17.19	17.27	17.49	18.17	18.87
1976	19.24	17.14	18.07	18.56	19.24	17.67	17.31	17.14	17.35	17.43	18.07	18.35	18.40	18.56	18.42	18.25	19.24
1977	21.48	18.46	19.76	20.18	21.48	18.55	18.29	18.46	18.70	18.80	19.76	19.95	20.09	20.18	20.15	20.12	21.48
1978	23.30	20.11	21.41	22.32	23.30	20.52	20.29	20.11	20.33	20.68	21.41	21.92	22.16	22.32	22.54	22.58	23.30
1979	24.14	21.35	23.31	23.99	24.14	22.12	21.80	21.35	21.73	22.46	23.31	23.70	24.06	23.99	23.96	23.43	24.14
1980	26.73	23.17	23.53	25.32	26.73	23.72	23.22	23.17	23.21	23.15	23.53	24.73	25.05	25.32	25.94	25.81	26.73
1981	27.14	24.79	25.26	25.26	27.14	25.22	24.64	24.79	25.43	25.31	25.26	27.06	26.00	25.26	24.77	23.90	27.14
1982	27.98	24.56	25.75	25.70	27.98	25.64	24.56	24.56	24.84	25.46	25.75	25.98	25.33	25.70	25.63	25.30	27.98
1983	30.18	26.74	28.43	29.14	30.18	26.59	26.58	26.74	27.19	27.21	28.43	29.21	29.17	29.14	28.77	28.65	30.18

Consumer prices: all items (15) — Prix à la consommation : total (15)

1980 = 100

	Year	Q.1	Q.2	Q.3	Q.4	JAN	FEB	MAR	APR	MAY	JUN	JUL	AUG	SEP	OCT	NOV	DEC
1964	37.3	37.0	37.2	37.4	37.5	37.0	37.0	37.1	37.2	37.2	37.2	37.5	37.5	37.3	37.3	37.5	37.7
1965	38.2	37.8	38.1	38.4	38.6	37.8	37.8	37.8	37.9	38.0	38.4	38.5	38.4	38.4	38.4	38.6	38.8
1966	39.6	39.1	39.5	39.9	40.1	38.9	39.1	39.3	39.5	39.5	39.6	39.7	39.9	39.9	40.0	40.0	40.2
1967	41.1	40.3	40.9	41.5	41.7	40.3	40.3	40.4	40.7	40.8	41.1	41.4	41.6	41.5	41.5	41.6	41.8
1968	42.7	42.1	42.5	43.0	43.4	42.1	42.1	42.2	42.4	42.4	42.6	42.9	43.0	43.1	43.2	43.4	43.5
1969	44.7	43.7	44.5	45.1	45.3	43.6	43.6	43.9	44.3	44.4	44.8	45.0	45.1	45.1	45.1	45.3	45.6
1970	46.2	45.8	46.2	46.4	46.3	45.7	45.8	45.9	46.1	46.1	46.2	46.5	46.5	46.3	46.3	46.3	46.2
1971	47.5	46.5	47.2	47.9	48.2	46.3	46.6	46.7	47.0	47.2	47.4	47.7	48.0	47.9	48.0	48.1	48.5
1972	49.7	48.8	49.2	50.2	50.7	48.7	48.8	48.9	49.2	49.3	49.3	49.9	50.3	50.5	50.5	50.6	51.0
1973	53.5	51.7	52.8	54.3	55.3	51.4	51.7	51.9	52.4	52.8	53.3	53.8	54.4	54.8	54.9	55.3	55.7
1974	59.4	56.7	58.5	60.3	61.9	56.1	56.7	57.3	57.6	58.6	59.4	59.7	60.4	60.7	61.3	62.0	62.5
1975	65.8	63.3	64.7	66.9	68.2	62.9	63.3	63.7	64.0	64.6	65.5	66.4	67.0	67.2	67.8	68.4	68.5
1976	70.7	69.1	70.2	71.2	72.3	68.8	69.2	69.4	69.7	70.3	70.6	70.9	71.2	71.5	72.0	72.2	72.6
1977	76.4	73.8	75.6	77.2	78.9	73.1	73.8	74.6	75.0	75.6	76.2	76.8	77.2	77.6	78.3	78.9	79.4
1978	83.2	80.3	82.3	84.4	85.7	79.6	80.2	81.1	81.3	82.4	83.1	84.4	84.5	84.2	85.1	85.8	86.0
1979	90.8	87.6	89.9	91.7	93.8	86.7	87.5	88.6	89.2	90.1	90.5	91.2	91.6	92.3	93.0	93.9	94.5
1980	100.0	95.9	98.5	101.3	104.2	95.0	95.8	96.8	97.4	98.5	99.7	100.4	101.3	102.2	103.1	104.5	105.1
1981	112.5	107.6	111.0	114.2	117.1	106.4	107.5	108.9	109.8	110.7	112.5	113.4	114.3	115.1	116.2	117.2	117.8
1982	124.6	120.0	123.7	126.4	128.4	118.6	120.0	121.5	122.2	123.8	125.1	125.8	126.3	127.0	127.8	128.7	128.7
1983	131.9	129.2	131.0	133.1	134.2	128.3	128.9	130.3	130.3	130.6	132.1	132.6	133.3	133.3	134.1	134.1	134.5

Money supply (M1) (14) — Disponibilités monétaires (M1) (14)

billion Canadian dollars, end of period — milliards de dollars canadiens, fin de période

Adjusted - Corrigé

	Year	Q.1	Q.2	Q.3	Q.4	JAN	FEB	MAR	APR	MAY	JUN	JUL	AUG	SEP	OCT	NOV	DEC
1964		6.30	6.36	6.36	6.50	6.22	6.20	6.30	6.31	6.32	6.36	6.34	6.36	6.36	6.39	6.39	6.50
1965		6.58	6.77	6.82	6.93	6.49	6.53	6.58	6.64	6.68	6.77	6.80	6.91	6.82	6.81	6.89	6.93
1966		7.10	7.16	7.25	7.47	6.97	7.05	7.10	7.12	7.18	7.16	7.19	7.22	7.25	7.36	7.46	7.47
1967		7.81	7.87	8.02	8.04	7.54	7.70	7.81	7.89	7.92	7.87	7.90	7.87	8.02	8.17	8.03	8.04
1968		7.98	8.04	8.45	8.61	8.10	8.07	7.98	8.04	8.02	8.04	8.23	8.47	8.45	8.48	8.58	8.61
1969		8.77	8.92	8.83	8.87	8.72	8.68	8.77	8.86	8.96	8.92	8.87	8.77	8.83	8.91	8.85	8.87
1970		9.00	8.98	9.08	9.34	8.84	8.95	9.00	8.96	8.94	8.98	9.06	9.12	9.08	9.17	9.26	9.34
1971		9.81	10.23	10.58	10.96	9.44	9.61	9.81	9.83	10.05	10.23	10.20	10.44	10.58	10.64	10.86	10.96
1972		11.20	11.49	12.03	12.55	11.01	11.11	11.20	11.32	11.38	11.49	11.66	11.81	12.03	12.25	12.41	12.55
1973		12.87	13.28	13.75	13.97	12.74	12.83	12.87	13.15	13.27	13.28	13.57	13.56	13.75	13.88	13.88	13.97
1974		14.39	14.73	14.71	14.84	14.12	14.23	14.39	14.92	15.10	14.73	14.68	14.63	14.71	14.66	14.76	14.84
1975		16.15	16.43	17.09	18.13	15.17	15.70	16.15	16.09	16.23	16.43	16.60	16.95	17.09	17.27	18.28	18.13
1976		17.71	17.93	18.16	18.35	17.68	17.89	17.71	17.73	17.82	17.93	18.04	18.20	18.16	18.27	18.42	18.35
1977		19.03	19.57	19.84	20.57	18.60	18.79	19.03	19.18	19.35	19.57	19.60	19.73	19.84	19.97	20.16	20.57
1978		20.67	21.37	21.95	22.28	20.59	20.71	20.67	20.92	21.16	21.37	21.56	21.67	21.95	22.40	22.61	22.28
1979		22.05	23.30	23.65	23.08	22.18	22.39	22.05	22.45	22.92	23.30	23.40	23.47	23.65	23.67	23.64	23.08
1980		23.92	23.66	25.12	25.49	23.74	23.84	23.92	23.72	23.66	23.66	24.19	24.58	25.12	25.57	26.16	25.49
1981		25.65	25.38	24.94	25.78	25.31	25.40	25.65	25.83	25.83	25.38	26.39	25.55	24.94	24.63	24.32	25.78
1982		25.23	25.66	25.33	26.53	25.75	25.27	25.23	25.32	25.96	25.66	25.48	25.00	25.38	25.56	25.75	26.53
1983		27.38	28.27	23.99	28.77	26.82	27.22	27.38	27.66	27.83	28.27	28.64	28.62	28.99	28.79	28.99	28.77

CANADA

M1 plus quasi-money (14) / M1 plus quasi-monnaie (14)

billion Canadian dollars, end of period / milliards de dollars canadiens, fin de période

	Year	Q.1	Q.2	Q.3	Q.4	JAN	FEB	MAR	APR	MAY	JUN	JUL	AUG	SEP	OCT	NOV	DEC
1964																	
1965																	
1966																	
1967																	
1968																	
1969																	
1970	34.41	31.26	32.14	33.50	34.41	31.04	30.99	31.26	31.74	31.89	32.14	32.82	33.11	33.50	33.91	33.97	34.41
1971	37.52	34.67	35.86	37.30	37.52	34.05	34.02	34.67	34.91	35.22	35.86	36.18	36.66	37.30	37.71	37.28	37.52
1972	43.11	39.13	41.51	42.32	43.11	37.86	38.12	39.13	39.96	40.68	41.51	41.73	42.07	42.32	43.10	43.05	43.11
1973	52.43	44.40	46.80	49.33	52.43	43.13	43.70	44.40	45.31	45.98	46.80	47.75	48.58	49.33	50.45	51.27	52.43
1974	63.83	55.35	59.68	63.57	63.83	52.83	53.74	55.35	56.91	58.84	59.68	61.47	62.78	63.57	64.41	64.05	63.83
1975	73.42	66.27	68.52	71.71	73.42	64.56	65.06	66.27	66.95	67.21	68.52	69.77	70.64	71.71	73.05	72.60	73.42
1976	88.35	76.89	82.45	85.91	88.35	73.57	74.74	76.89	79.76	81.09	82.45	83.76	84.80	85.91	86.73	87.04	88.35
1977	100.84	90.81	95.83	99.81	100.84	88.01	88.72	90.81	92.76	94.63	95.83	96.86	98.14	99.81	100.36	100.46	100.84
1978	118.68	102.97	108.69	114.12	118.68	100.26	100.86	102.97	105.91	106.97	108.69	110.20	111.91	114.12	114.87	118.43	118.68
1979	141.70	122.65	131.27	137.14	141.70	120.41	121.72	122.65	125.15	128.89	131.27	133.81	135.86	137.14	138.75	141.56	141.70
1980	161.93	146.41	154.29	157.65	161.93	143.17	144.76	146.41	149.39	152.07	154.29	158.02	157.25	157.65	159.80	161.30	161.93
1981	180.90	166.53	172.30	181.91	180.90	165.02	167.95	166.53	168.66	168.42	172.30	177.18	180.59	181.91	181.39	176.94	180.90
1982	186.61	178.59	182.29	187.34	186.61	177.99	175.81	178.59	179.49	180.36	182.29	184.44	185.57	187.34	187.32	185.85	186.61
1983	184.33	186.27	184.16	185.43	184.33	185.96	185.59	186.27	184.36	183.30	184.16	184.86	185.80	186.43	186.13	184.00	184.33

Savings deposits: commercial banks (14)(16) / Dépôts d'épargne : banques commerciales (16)(14)

billion Canadian dollars, end of period / milliards de dollars canadiens, fin de période

	Year	Q.1	Q.2	Q.3	Q.4	JAN	FEB	MAR	APR	MAY	JUN	JUL	AUG	SEP	OCT	NOV	DEC
1964	8.85	8.64	8.72	8.97	8.85	8.42	8.52	8.64	8.74	8.73	8.72	8.79	8.89	8.97	9.04	8.94	8.85
1965	9.64	9.21	9.33	9.65	9.64	8.92	9.06	9.21	9.32	9.33	9.33	9.39	9.55	9.65	9.74	9.74	9.64
1966	10.14	9.95	10.04	10.30	10.14	9.70	9.82	9.95	10.04	10.08	10.04	10.11	10.25	10.30	10.37	10.30	10.14
1967	11.63	10.56	10.97	11.47	11.63	10.24	10.42	10.56	10.72	10.91	10.97	11.13	11.32	11.47	11.62	11.71	11.63
1968	13.46	12.09	12.80	13.32	13.46	11.79	11.94	12.09	12.34	12.62	12.80	13.06	13.21	13.32	13.53	13.54	13.46
1969	14.89	14.01	14.44	14.93	14.89	13.66	13.85	14.01	14.23	14.35	14.44	14.60	14.73	14.93	15.09	15.05	14.89
1970	16.47	15.32	15.85	15.41	16.47	14.99	15.17	15.32	15.57	15.78	15.85	16.02	16.19	16.41	16.57	16.57	16.47
1971	17.53	17.07	17.48	18.08	17.53	16.66	16.89	17.07	17.28	17.39	17.48	17.65	17.85	18.08	18.28	17.81	17.53
1972	19.73	18.48	19.08	19.86	19.73	17.86	18.16	18.48	18.79	19.00	19.08	19.32	19.54	19.86	20.09	19.90	19.73
1973	24.28	20.69	21.66	22.85	24.28	20.13	20.48	20.69	21.00	21.31	21.66	22.13	22.54	22.86	23.35	23.95	24.28
1974	29.45	25.99	28.03	30.09	29.45	24.85	25.49	25.99	26.60	27.44	28.03	28.79	29.53	30.09	30.68	30.04	29.45
1975	32.98	30.95	32.13	33.46	32.98	30.16	30.69	30.95	31.56	31.89	32.13	32.64	33.05	33.46	33.89	33.00	32.98
1976	40.02	34.94	37.07	38.89	40.02	33.51	34.28	34.94	35.70	36.36	37.07	37.65	38.23	38.89	39.44	39.91	40.02
1977	44.58	41.84	43.42	44.82	44.58	40.75	41.31	41.84	42.59	43.03	43.42	43.94	44.46	44.82	45.18	45.02	44.58
1978	50.89	45.91	47.49	49.48	50.89	45.10	45.56	45.91	46.64	47.16	47.49	48.17	48.81	49.48	50.06	51.19	50.89
1979	63.43	53.78	56.66	60.08	63.43	52.27	53.14	53.78	54.81	55.88	56.66	57.78	58.98	60.08	61.33	63.17	63.43
1980	74.46	67.14	70.17	72.69	74.46	64.72	66.14	67.14	68.81	69.50	70.17	71.13	71.84	72.69	73.47	74.48	74.46
1981	91.34	77.47	81.54	86.77	91.34	75.15	76.40	77.47	79.19	80.24	81.54	82.88	84.74	86.77	88.11	91.91	91.34
1982	99.29	94.88	98.65	99.88	99.29	92.69	93.95	94.88	95.99	98.13	98.65	99.13	99.44	99.88	100.29	99.88	99.29
1983	100.66	100.74	101.17	102.61	100.66	100.01	100.65	100.74	100.92	101.34	101.17	101.85	102.39	102.61	102.65	101.39	100.66

Credit to economy: commercial banks (14)(16)(17) / Crédits à l'économie : banques commerciales (17)(16)(14)

billion Canadian dollars, end of period / milliards de dollars canadiens, fin de période

	Year	Q.1	Q.2	Q.3	Q.4	JAN	FEB	MAR	APR	MAY	JUN	JUL	AUG	SEP	OCT	NOV	DEC
1964	9.00	8.07	8.55	8.83	9.00	7.37	7.85	8.07	8.29	8.40	8.55	8.78	8.84	8.83	8.85	8.94	9.00
1965	11.02	9.29	10.00	10.55	11.02	8.96	9.06	9.29	9.59	9.74	10.00	10.39	10.60	10.55	10.67	10.68	11.02
1966	11.81	11.05	11.45	11.69	11.81	10.89	10.85	11.05	11.34	11.38	11.45	11.62	11.69	11.69	11.77	11.86	11.81
1967	13.53	12.15	12.36	13.02	13.53	11.82	12.04	12.15	12.30	12.38	12.36	12.63	12.81	13.02	13.35	13.59	13.53
1968	15.18	14.26	14.48	14.67	15.18	13.76	13.93	14.26	14.41	14.38	14.48	14.75	14.62	14.67	14.89	15.01	15.18
1969	17.36	15.98	16.80	15.99	17.36	15.38	15.60	15.98	16.46	16.60	16.80	16.96	16.99	16.99	17.21	17.22	17.36
1970	17.59	17.23	16.88	17.42	17.59	17.20	17.28	17.23	17.08	16.89	16.88	17.43	17.58	17.42	17.41	17.52	17.59
1971	20.41	18.01	18.74	19.55	20.41	17.59	17.75	18.01	18.17	18.37	18.74	19.11	19.27	19.55	19.74	20.10	20.41
1972	24.94	21.86	23.75	24.05	24.94	20.74	21.17	21.86	22.60	23.44	23.75	23.79	24.02	24.05	24.38	24.71	24.94
1973	31.58	26.61	28.41	29.69	31.58	25.29	25.92	26.61	27.40	28.09	28.41	28.92	29.29	29.69	30.25	30.66	31.58
1974	37.42	32.71	34.96	36.47	37.42	31.73	32.03	32.71	33.89	34.77	34.96	35.79	36.24	36.47	36.52	36.89	37.42
1975	43.38	39.12	40.44	41.99	43.38	37.95	38.50	39.12	39.78	40.03	40.44	41.23	41.61	41.99	42.41	43.17	43.38
1976	51.88	46.84	48.23	50.25	51.88	44.00	45.19	46.84	47.26	47.56	48.23	49.31	49.85	50.25	50.66	51.17	51.88
1977	57.88	54.96	56.25	57.32	57.88	52.44	53.52	54.96	55.25	55.70	56.25	56.97	57.11	57.32	57.77	58.03	57.88
1978	64.89	60.13	61.89	64.19	64.89	58.10	59.01	60.13	60.62	61.38	61.89	63.44	63.89	64.19	65.18	64.89	64.89
1979	80.83	69.18	74.33	78.13	80.83	66.25	67.44	69.18	70.43	72.42	74.33	76.44	77.51	78.13	79.60	79.64	80.83
1980	94.74	84.93	91.09	90.40	94.74	82.27	83.20	84.93	86.47	89.23	91.09	91.81	90.67	90.40	91.61	91.97	94.74
1981	124.24	103.02	110.08	118.55	124.24	100.04	102.38	103.02	106.02	105.97	110.08	113.28	117.60	118.56	119.44	121.07	124.24
1982	122.63	124.99	126.00	125.95	122.63	121.86	121.78	124.99	124.02	124.21	126.00	125.39	126.23	125.95	125.60	124.12	122.63
1983	112.72	119.79	116.13	113.03	112.72	120.03	119.90	119.79	118.19	117.20	116.13	115.02	114.19	113.03	112.95	112.75	112.72

M1 plus quasi-money (14) / M1 plus quasi-monnaie (14)

billion Canadian dollars, end of period — Adjusted - Corrigé — milliards de dollars canadiens, fin de période

Year	Q.1	Q.2	Q.3	Q.4	JAN	FEB	MAR	APR	MAY	JUN	JUL	AUG	SEP	OCT	NOV	DEC
1964																
1965																
1966																
1967																
1968																
1969																
1970	31.52	31.93	33.18	34.63	31.44	31.55	31.52	31.80	31.90	31.93	32.56	32.83	33.18	33.47	33.95	34.63
1971	34.95	35.64	36.94	37.76	34.47	34.61	34.95	34.98	35.21	35.64	35.88	36.34	36.94	37.24	37.27	37.76
1972	39.45	41.28	41.88	43.35	38.35	38.78	39.45	40.07	40.66	41.28	41.36	41.66	41.88	42.55	43.02	43.35
1973	44.79	46.55	48.81	52.73	43.76	44.50	44.79	45.46	45.92	46.55	47.30	48.07	48.81	49.85	51.29	52.73
1974	55.83	59.38	62.87	64.16	53.63	54.72	55.83	57.09	58.71	59.38	60.87	62.10	62.87	63.71	64.08	64.16
1975	66.88	68.16	70.89	73.75	65.58	66.28	66.88	67.15	66.99	68.16	69.10	69.88	70.89	72.34	72.61	73.75
1976	77.65	81.99	84.93	88.70	74.72	76.12	77.65	79.99	80.77	81.99	82.99	83.95	84.93	86.00	86.95	88.70
1977	91.79	95.26	98.75	101.21	89.28	90.30	91.79	93.06	94.24	95.26	96.04	97.24	98.75	99.63	100.21	101.21
1978	104.17	108.11	112.95	119.10	101.47	102.45	104.17	106.33	106.64	108.11	109.35	110.94	112.95	114.12	117.97	119.10
1979	124.12	130.76	135.72	142.18	121.56	123.40	124.12	125.79	128.77	130.76	132.85	134.68	135.72	137.82	140.94	142.18
1980	148.11	154.03	155.86	162.49	144.16	146.44	148.11	150.41	152.39	154.03	156.97	155.80	155.86	158.62	160.69	162.49
1981	168.27	172.31	179.52	181.25	165.84	169.60	168.27	170.00	169.24	172.31	176.04	178.77	179.52	179.69	176.32	181.25
1982	180.38	182.58	184.60	186.85	178.90	177.56	180.38	181.15	181.70	182.58	183.35	183.60	184.60	185.30	185.38	186.85
1983	188.04	184.61	183.56	184.74	186.89	187.46	188.04	186.09	184.88	184.61	183.83	183.81	183.56	184.03	183.73	184.74

Savings deposits: commercial banks (14)(16) / Dépôts d'épargne : banques commerciales (14)(16)

billion Canadian dollars, end of period — Adjusted - Corrigé — milliards de dollars canadiens, fin de période

Year	Q.1	Q.2	Q.3	Q.4	JAN	FEB	MAR	APR	MAY	JUN	JUL	AUG	SEP	OCT	NOV	DEC
1964	8.64	8.72	8.88	9.01	8.56	8.58	8.64	8.69	8.67	8.72	8.77	8.82	8.88	8.92	8.95	9.01
1965	9.21	9.34	9.55	9.81	9.06	9.13	9.21	9.28	9.28	9.34	9.38	9.47	9.55	9.62	9.73	9.81
1966	10.01	10.03	10.19	10.31	9.85	9.92	10.01	10.05	10.03	10.03	10.06	10.14	10.19	10.25	10.27	10.31
1967	10.63	10.95	11.35	11.82	10.38	10.52	10.63	10.73	10.86	10.95	11.08	11.21	11.35	11.49	11.67	11.82
1968	12.17	12.77	13.17	13.66	11.95	12.05	12.17	12.35	12.56	12.77	13.00	13.08	13.17	13.37	13.49	13.66
1969	14.12	14.40	14.77	15.12	13.85	13.99	14.12	14.26	14.28	14.40	14.53	14.66	14.77	14.92	15.01	15.12
1970	15.43	15.80	16.23	16.71	15.19	15.32	15.43	15.60	15.70	15.80	15.93	16.06	16.23	16.39	16.52	16.71
1971	17.20	17.43	17.88	17.80	16.88	17.04	17.20	17.32	17.30	17.43	17.55	17.71	17.88	18.08	17.76	17.80
1972	18.63	19.02	19.64	20.03	18.09	18.32	18.63	18.85	18.91	19.02	19.19	19.37	19.64	19.88	19.85	20.03
1973	20.88	21.58	22.62	24.65	20.39	20.66	20.88	21.08	21.19	21.58	21.97	22.33	22.62	23.11	23.88	24.65
1974	26.24	27.92	29.80	29.88	25.16	25.71	26.24	26.71	27.28	27.92	28.57	29.26	29.80	30.40	29.93	29.88
1975	31.26	31.99	33.19	33.43	30.52	30.96	31.26	31.70	31.69	31.99	32.40	32.77	33.19	33.61	32.86	33.43
1976	35.17	37.01	38.52	40.65	34.01	34.52	35.17	35.66	36.25	37.01	37.41	37.88	38.52	39.14	39.90	40.65
1977	42.07	43.36	44.47	45.23	41.19	41.55	42.07	42.50	42.89	43.36	43.71	44.14	44.47	44.91	44.96	45.23
1978	46.11	47.45	49.22	51.58	45.50	45.76	46.11	46.50	47.00	47.45	47.99	48.56	49.22	49.85	51.08	51.58
1979	53.95	56.62	59.85	64.14	52.62	53.28	53.95	54.60	55.70	56.62	57.64	58.76	59.85	61.11	62.90	64.14
1980	67.42	70.16	72.19	75.47	65.17	66.38	67.42	68.69	69.44	70.16	70.94	71.44	72.19	72.48	74.80	75.47
1981	77.75	81.53	85.99	92.26	75.71	76.68	77.75	79.03	80.23	81.53	82.62	84.17	85.99	86.79	91.86	92.26
1982	95.69	98.22	99.25	100.34	93.40	94.51	95.69	96.52	97.40	98.22	98.65	98.87	99.25	99.29	99.93	100.34
1983	101.60	100.71	101.90	101.81	100.84	101.30	101.60	101.47	100.61	100.71	101.35	101.77	101.90	101.64	101.55	101.81

Credit to economy: commercial banks (14)(16)(17) / Crédits à l'économie : banques commerciales (14)(16)(17)

billion Canadian dollars, end of period — Adjusted - Corrigé — milliards de dollars canadiens, fin de période

Year	Q.1	Q.2	Q.3	Q.4	JAN	FEB	MAR	APR	MAY	JUN	JUL	AUG	SEP	OCT	NOV	DEC
1964	8.21	8.50	8.74	9.07	8.03	8.05	8.21	8.32	8.39	8.50	8.59	8.66	8.74	8.79	8.93	9.07
1965	9.42	9.97	10.48	11.10	9.14	9.27	9.42	9.59	9.72	9.97	10.19	10.44	10.48	10.62	10.67	11.10
1966	11.06	11.45	11.72	11.86	11.02	10.94	11.06	11.21	11.32	11.45	11.54	11.68	11.72	11.73	11.86	11.86
1967	12.16	12.35	13.05	13.60	11.96	12.13	12.16	12.17	12.31	12.35	12.54	12.79	13.05	13.32	13.59	13.60
1968	14.05	14.48	14.70	15.23	13.66	13.81	14.05	14.27	14.36	14.48	14.63	14.60	14.70	14.86	15.01	15.23
1969	15.99	16.75	17.02	17.43	15.56	15.73	15.99	16.35	16.53	16.75	16.80	16.95	17.02	17.20	17.25	17.43
1970	17.25	16.79	17.44	17.68	17.40	17.41	17.25	16.98	16.81	16.79	17.25	17.53	17.44	17.43	17.57	17.68
1971	18.03	18.61	19.56	20.54	17.78	17.90	18.03	18.07	18.27	18.61	18.90	19.18	19.56	19.80	20.19	20.54
1972	21.89	23.56	24.05	25.13	20.97	21.36	21.89	22.46	23.29	23.56	23.53	23.88	24.05	24.48	24.85	25.13
1973	26.65	28.20	29.69	31.86	25.57	26.15	26.65	27.20	27.90	28.20	28.60	29.10	29.69	30.39	30.85	31.86
1974	32.74	34.73	36.46	37.78	32.08	32.29	32.74	33.61	34.55	34.73	35.39	35.99	36.46	36.68	37.15	37.78
1975	39.13	40.21	41.95	43.81	38.37	38.78	39.13	39.46	39.79	40.21	40.76	41.31	41.95	42.56	43.48	43.81
1976	46.82	47.97	50.17	52.43	44.52	45.48	46.82	46.95	47.33	47.97	48.70	49.47	50.17	50.76	51.57	52.43
1977	54.95	55.90	57.24	58.52	53.08	53.89	54.95	55.00	55.42	55.90	56.19	56.62	57.24	57.81	58.52	58.52
1978	60.16	61.38	64.18	65.64	58.30	59.45	60.16	60.45	61.02	61.38	62.48	63.37	64.18	65.15	65.50	65.64
1979	69.30	73.58	78.23	81.80	66.98	68.02	69.30	70.31	72.00	73.58	75.21	76.91	78.23	79.58	80.45	81.80
1980	84.99	90.42	90.53	95.53	82.87	83.78	84.99	86.53	88.92	90.42	90.77	90.08	90.53	91.42	92.54	95.53
1981	103.07	109.32	118.66	129.28	100.51	103.04	103.07	106.23	105.76	109.32	112.24	116.88	118.66	119.10	125.89	129.28
1982	130.08	130.42	131.22	128.28	126.83	127.46	130.08	129.36	129.26	130.42	129.64	130.67	131.22	130.33	129.46	128.28
1983	125.14	120.75	118.17	118.19	127.32	126.04	125.14	123.81	122.54	120.75	119.45	118.59	118.17	117.71	117.85	118.19

CANADA

Consumer credit outstanding (18)

billion Canadian dollars, end of period

Crédits à la consommation en cours (18)

milliards de dollars canadiens, fin de période

	Year	Q.1	Q.2	Q.3	Q.4	JAN	FEB	MAR	APR	MAY	JUN	JUL	AUG	SEP	OCT	NOV	DEC
1964	5.19	4.49	4.83	5.00	5.19	4.44	4.45	4.49	4.58	4.70	4.83	4.89	4.95	5.00	5.06	5.12	5.19
1965	6.05	5.23	5.63	5.80	6.05	5.17	5.17	5.23	5.36	5.47	5.63	5.68	5.75	5.80	5.92	5.94	6.05
1966	6.48	6.03	6.25	6.36	6.48	6.00	5.97	6.03	6.11	5.79	6.25	6.28	6.32	6.36	6.40	6.42	6.48
1967	7.12	6.41	6.77	6.90	7.12	6.42	6.38	6.41	6.51	6.61	6.77	6.79	6.82	6.90	7.01	7.03	7.12
1968	8.19	7.16	7.50	7.77	8.19	7.14	7.10	7.16	7.29	7.42	7.50	7.60	7.67	7.77	7.87	8.01	8.19
1969	9.23	8.39	8.91	9.03	9.23	8.20	8.25	8.39	8.55	8.74	8.91	8.89	8.97	9.03	9.07	9.11	9.23
1970	9.63	8.95	9.23	9.38	9.63	9.01	8.94	8.95	9.06	9.13	9.23	9.30	9.32	9.38	9.41	9.49	9.63
1971	10.44	9.20	9.66	9.98	10.44	9.14	9.15	9.20	9.30	9.46	9.66	9.81	9.87	9.98	10.12	10.28	10.44
1972	12.33	10.50	11.21	11.70	12.33	10.47	10.44	10.50	10.65	10.91	11.21	11.41	11.54	11.70	11.89	12.05	12.33
1973	14.66	12.66	13.71	14.17	14.66	12.47	12.52	12.66	13.00	13.42	13.71	13.87	14.01	14.17	14.39	14.53	14.66
1974	17.05	15.12	16.12	16.56	17.05	14.81	14.92	15.12	15.51	15.86	16.12	16.37	16.48	16.56	16.75	16.98	17.05
1975	19.74	17.41	18.25	18.97	19.74	17.25	17.32	17.41	17.59	17.93	18.25	18.53	18.81	18.97	19.17	19.52	19.74
1976	22.85	19.97	21.16	22.09	22.85	19.74	19.79	19.97	20.29	20.71	21.16	21.57	21.86	22.09	22.39	22.65	22.85
1977	25.53	23.32	24.23	24.90	25.53	23.00	23.12	23.32	23.61	23.93	24.23	24.51	24.72	24.90	25.09	25.27	25.53
1978	29.17	26.04	27.36	28.37	29.17	25.70	25.78	26.04	26.45	26.89	27.36	27.80	28.07	28.37	28.78	28.99	29.17
1979	33.26	29.58	31.48	32.72	33.26	29.33	29.33	29.58	30.09	30.78	31.48	31.99	32.37	32.72	33.00	33.14	33.26
1980	37.58	33.95	35.08	35.94	37.58	33.42	33.62	33.95	34.41	34.80	35.08	35.32	35.56	35.94	36.47	37.06	37.58
1981	40.79	38.60	40.61	41.81	40.79	37.91	38.13	38.60	39.30	40.12	40.61	41.09	41.65	41.81	41.88	40.62	40.79
1982	39.71	40.28	40.40	39.98	39.71	40.70	40.39	40.28	40.39	40.45	40.40	40.25	40.12	39.98	40.00	39.69	39.71
1983	42.04	39.06	40.00	40.99	42.04	39.80	39.28	39.06	39.32	39.55	40.00	40.51	40.75	40.99	41.43	41.54	42.04

Net new capital issues: corporations

billion Canadian dollars

Nouvelles émissions de titres, nettes : sociétés privées

milliards de dollars canadiens

	Year	Q.1	Q.2	Q.3	Q.4	JAN	FEB	MAR	APR	MAY	JUN	JUL	AUG	SEP	OCT	NOV	DEC
1964	1.10	0.05	0.42	0.13	0.50												
1965	1.78	0.34	0.59	0.44	0.41												
1966	1.55	0.56	0.41	0.26	0.32												
1967	1.28	0.25	0.36	0.24	0.43												
1968	1.28	0.12	0.48	0.35	0.34												
1969	1.81	0.46	0.66	0.41	0.28												
1970	1.86	0.49	0.37	0.30	0.70												
1971	2.21	0.63	0.77	0.34	0.46												
1972	2.20	0.53	0.54	0.44	0.70												
1973	2.14	0.40	0.64	0.48	0.63												
1974	2.59	0.46	0.71	0.52	0.92												
1975	4.08	1.05	1.41	0.68	0.94												
1976	5.26	1.42	1.25	1.59	1.00												
1977	8.21	1.12	2.86	1.77	2.46												
1978	11.62	2.59	1.99	1.62	5.42												
1979	7.30	1.75	2.18	2.45	0.91												
1980	9.10	1.86	2.69	2.16	2.39												
1981	12.99	3.23	4.25	2.23	3.28												
1982	9.17	2.78	1.43	2.38	2.58												
1983	10.31	2.06	3.07	2.75	2.41												

Official discount rate (19)

per cent per annum, end of period

Taux d'escompte officiel (19)

pourcentage par an, fin de période

	Year	Q.1	Q.2	Q.3	Q.4	JAN	FEB	MAR	APR	MAY	JUN	JUL	AUG	SEP	OCT	NOV	DEC
1964	4.25	4.00	4.00	4.00	4.25	4.00	4.00	4.00	4.00	4.00	4.00	4.00	4.00	4.00	4.00	4.25	4.25
1965	4.75	4.25	4.25	4.25	4.75	4.25	4.25	4.25	4.25	4.25	4.25	4.25	4.25	4.25	4.25	4.25	4.75
1966	5.25	5.25	5.25	5.25	5.25	4.75	4.75	5.25	5.25	5.25	5.25	5.25	5.25	5.25	5.25	5.25	5.25
1967	6.00	5.00	4.50	5.00	6.00	5.00	5.00	5.00	4.50	4.50	4.50	4.50	4.50	5.00	5.00	6.00	6.00
1968	6.50	7.50	7.50	6.00	6.50	7.00	7.00	7.50	7.50	7.50	7.50	6.50	6.50	6.00	6.00	6.00	6.50
1969	8.00	7.00	7.50	8.00	8.00	6.50	6.50	7.00	7.00	7.00	7.50	8.00	8.00	8.00	8.00	8.00	8.00
1970	6.00	8.00	7.00	6.50	6.00	8.00	8.00	8.00	8.00	7.50	7.00	7.00	6.50	6.50	6.50	6.00	6.00
1971	4.75	5.25	5.25	5.25	4.75	6.00	5.25	5.25	5.25	5.25	5.25	5.25	5.25	5.25	4.75	4.75	4.75
1972	4.75	4.75	4.75	4.75	4.75	4.75	4.75	4.75	4.75	4.75	4.75	4.75	4.75	4.75	4.75	4.75	4.75
1973	7.25	4.75	6.25	7.25	7.25	4.75	4.75	4.75	5.25	5.75	6.25	6.25	6.75	7.25	7.25	7.25	7.25
1974	8.75	7.25	8.75	9.25	8.75	7.25	7.25	7.25	8.25	8.75	8.75	9.25	9.25	9.25	9.25	8.75	8.75
1975	9.00	8.25	8.25	9.00	9.00	8.25	8.25	8.25	8.25	8.25	8.25	8.25	8.25	9.00	9.00	9.00	9.00
1976	8.50	9.50	9.50	9.50	8.50	9.00	9.00	9.50	9.50	9.50	9.50	9.50	9.50	9.50	9.50	9.00	8.50
1977	7.50	8.00	7.50	7.50	7.50	8.50	8.00	8.00	8.00	7.50	7.50	7.50	7.50	7.50	7.50	7.50	7.50
1978	10.75	8.00	8.50	9.50	10.75	7.50	7.50	8.00	8.50	8.50	8.50	9.00	9.00	9.50	10.25	10.75	10.75
1979	14.00	11.25	11.25	12.25	14.00	11.25	11.25	11.25	11.25	11.25	11.25	11.75	11.75	12.25	14.00	14.00	14.00
1980	17.26	15.49	10.63	11.20	17.26	14.00	14.00	15.49	15.67	11.83	10.63	10.18	10.74	11.20	12.16	13.95	17.26
1981	14.66	16.69	19.08	19.63	14.66	17.11	17.08	16.69	17.60	18.68	19.08	20.54	21.07	19.63	18.21	15.32	14.66
1982	10.05	15.11	16.58	12.98	10.05	14.59	14.83	15.11	15.23	15.43	16.58	15.50	13.95	12.98	11.46	10.97	10.05
1983	9.96	9.42	9.42	9.49	9.96	9.33	9.48	9.42	9.37	9.50	9.42	9.49	9.57	9.49	9.49	9.63	9.96

Consumer credit outstanding (18)

billion Canadian dollars, end of period

Adjusted - Corrigé

Crédits à la consommation en cours (18)

milliards de dollars canadiens, fin de période

	Year	Q.1	Q.2	Q.3	Q.4	JAN	FEB	MAR	APR	MAY	JUN	JUL	AUG	SEP	OCT	NOV	DEC
1964		4.58	4.78	4.97	5.14	4.47	4.53	4.58	4.63	4.71	4.78	4.83	4.90	4.97	5.04	5.09	5.14
1965		5.33	5.57	5.77	5.98	5.20	5.26	5.33	5.42	5.49	5.57	5.63	5.70	5.77	5.89	5.91	5.98
1966		6.15	6.19	6.32	6.40	6.04	6.07	6.15	6.18	5.81	6.19	6.23	6.28	6.32	6.36	6.38	6.40
1967		6.53	6.71	6.85	7.04	6.45	6.48	6.53	6.58	6.64	6.71	6.74	6.79	6.86	6.97	6.99	7.04
1968		7.28	7.43	7.73	8.10	7.17	7.22	7.28	7.37	7.44	7.43	7.55	7.64	7.73	7.83	7.97	8.10
1969		8.54	8.82	8.97	9.13	8.23	8.38	8.54	8.63	8.76	8.82	8.83	8.93	8.97	9.03	9.06	9.13
1970		9.08	9.13	9.34	9.54	9.05	9.07	9.08	9.13	9.14	9.13	9.24	9.30	9.34	9.39	9.46	9.54
1971		9.31	9.59	9.95	10.40	9.12	9.22	9.31	9.40	9.48	9.59	9.73	9.83	9.96	10.10	10.27	10.40
1972		10.64	11.13	11.67	12.29	10.45	10.53	10.64	10.76	10.93	11.13	11.31	11.48	11.67	11.84	12.02	12.29
1973		12.84	13.61	14.12	14.61	12.47	12.63	12.84	13.14	13.45	13.61	13.74	13.91	14.12	14.32	14.48	14.61
1974		15.31	16.05	16.52	16.97	14.83	15.03	15.31	15.68	15.91	16.05	16.26	16.40	16.52	16.68	16.82	16.97
1975		17.62	18.18	18.91	19.65	17.22	17.45	17.62	17.77	17.98	18.18	18.41	18.71	18.91	19.07	19.44	19.65
1976		20.21	21.10	22.01	22.76	19.73	19.95	20.21	20.49	20.78	21.10	21.43	21.73	22.01	22.27	22.56	22.76
1977		23.60	24.17	24.79	25.43	23.00	23.31	23.60	23.83	24.00	24.17	24.37	24.58	24.79	24.96	25.16	25.43
1978		26.34	27.30	28.24	29.07	25.71	26.01	26.34	26.67	26.96	27.30	27.65	27.92	28.24	28.62	28.87	29.07
1979		29.91	31.41	32.56	33.17	29.35	29.59	29.91	30.32	30.83	31.41	31.85	32.21	32.56	32.83	33.02	33.17
1980		34.30	34.99	35.74	37.46	33.46	33.92	34.30	34.63	34.82	34.99	35.18	35.38	35.74	36.26	36.91	37.46
1981		39.02	40.50	41.59	40.65	38.01	38.51	39.02	39.55	40.13	40.50	40.95	41.46	41.59	41.65	40.46	40.65
1982		40.70	40.29	39.78	39.59	40.81	40.78	40.70	40.63	40.45	40.29	40.14	39.94	39.78	39.79	39.62	39.59
1983		39.54	39.94	40.72	41.66	39.90	39.69	39.54	39.59	39.62	39.94	40.28	40.49	40.72	40.91	41.20	41.66

Call money rate (20)

per cent per annum, end of period

Taux de l'argent au jour le jour (20)

pourcentage par an, fin de période

	Year	Q.1	Q.2	Q.3	Q.4	JAN	FEB	MAR	APR	MAY	JUN	JUL	AUG	SEP	OCT	NOV	DEC
1964	3.81	3.75	3.55	3.63	3.81	3.48	3.75	3.75	3.33	3.15	3.55	3.55	3.80	3.63	3.73	3.68	3.81
1965	3.63	3.48	3.48	3.95	3.63	3.88	3.53	3.48	3.80	3.75	3.48	3.98	3.83	3.95	4.05	3.80	3.63
1966	4.42	5.10	4.73	4.68	4.42	3.85	3.90	5.10	5.05	5.13	4.73	4.98	4.05	4.68	5.03	4.93	4.42
1967	5.83	4.16	4.13	4.43	5.83	4.65	4.20	4.16	3.80	4.25	4.13	4.00	4.18	4.43	4.83	4.63	5.83
1968	5.47	6.95	5.50	5.33	5.47	5.20	6.70	6.95	6.70	6.95	5.50	6.00	4.15	5.33	4.55	5.20	5.47
1969	7.92	6.05	7.20	7.98	7.92	5.55	6.30	6.05	6.95	6.75	7.20	7.18	7.73	7.98	7.75	7.85	7.92
1970	5.19	6.70	5.95	5.30	5.19	7.88	7.85	6.70	6.85	6.40	5.95	5.90	5.50	5.30	5.05	4.38	5.19
1971	3.69	3.40	4.08	4.28	3.69	5.25	4.35	3.40	2.35	2.19	4.08	3.60	3.71	4.28	3.95	3.70	3.69
1972	3.50	3.75	3.75	3.50	3.50	3.65	3.70	3.75	3.65	3.70	3.75	3.45	3.58	3.50	3.70	3.75	3.50
1973	6.58	4.38	5.43	6.48	6.58	4.00	4.00	4.38	4.69	4.60	5.43	5.40	6.25	6.48	6.75	6.60	6.58
1974	7.25	6.50	8.50	8.85	7.25	6.50	6.50	6.50	7.45	8.50	8.50	9.00	9.05	8.85	8.50	7.35	7.25
1975	8.75	6.60	6.75	7.85	8.75	6.45	6.75	6.60	7.15	6.75	6.75	7.20	7.75	7.85	8.20	8.55	8.75
1976	8.41	9.00	8.95	9.25	8.41	8.75	8.75	9.00	8.75	8.75	8.95	9.03	9.15	9.25	9.15	8.95	8.41
1977	6.50	7.55	7.15	6.85	6.50	8.20	7.75	7.55	7.70	6.50	7.15	7.15	7.03	6.85	6.95	7.45	6.50
1978	8.50	7.38	7.65	9.05	8.50	6.90	7.13	7.38	7.25	8.00	7.65	8.18	8.05	9.05	9.55	9.30	8.50
1979	13.58	11.48	10.90	9.85	13.58	11.50	11.18	11.48	10.43	10.60	10.90	11.30	11.03	9.85	13.38	13.00	13.58
1980	17.17	12.90	10.73	9.15	17.17	13.73	11.15	12.90	16.25	11.70	10.73	9.68	10.03	9.15	11.75	12.40	17.17
1981	13.75	16.50	18.85	18.70	13.75	17.00	16.00	16.50	17.00	17.10	18.85	19.78	20.40	18.70	18.28	15.38	13.75
1982	9.83	14.78	14.20	13.13	9.83	14.48	13.50	14.78	15.00	15.25	14.20	15.50	14.65	13.13	11.50	10.60	9.83
1983	8.92	8.98	9.25	9.50	8.92	9.75	9.38	8.98	9.20	9.03	9.25	9.35	8.40	9.50	9.35	9.50	8.92

Treasury bill rate (3 months) (21)

per cent per annum, end of period

Bons du Trésor (3 mois) (21)

pourcentage par an, fin de période

	Year	Q.1	Q.2	Q.3	Q.4	JAN	FEB	MAR	APR	MAY	JUN	JUL	AUG	SEP	OCT	NOV	DEC
1964	3.82	3.88	3.59	3.73	3.82	3.77	3.88	3.88	3.70	3.58	3.59	3.67	3.80	3.73	3.70	3.87	3.82
1965	4.54	3.62	3.93	4.13	4.54	3.74	3.74	3.62	3.77	3.90	3.93	4.05	4.03	4.13	4.15	4.16	4.54
1966	4.96	5.06	5.00	5.01	4.96	4.63	4.69	5.06	5.08	5.11	5.00	5.02	5.04	5.01	5.19	5.15	4.96
1967	5.95	4.13	4.28	4.76	5.95	4.68	4.58	4.13	4.00	4.24	4.28	4.32	4.34	4.76	4.95	5.46	5.95
1968	6.24	6.98	6.56	5.66	6.24	6.29	6.80	6.98	6.99	6.95	6.56	6.03	5.48	5.66	5.57	5.66	6.24
1969	7.81	6.58	7.13	7.77	7.81	6.38	6.43	6.58	6.80	6.74	7.13	7.62	7.69	7.77	7.60	7.76	7.81
1970	4.44	7.00	5.94	5.39	4.44	7.78	7.60	7.00	6.78	6.34	5.94	5.70	5.51	5.39	5.01	4.40	4.44
1971	3.21	3.16	3.37	4.06	3.21	4.68	4.06	3.16	3.00	3.03	3.37	3.68	3.79	4.06	3.47	3.24	3.21
1972	3.65	3.57	3.50	3.62	3.65	3.36	3.45	3.57	3.64	3.73	3.50	3.46	3.50	3.62	3.57	3.68	3.65
1973	6.35	4.46	5.48	6.50	6.35	3.90	3.99	4.46	4.90	5.18	5.48	5.74	6.18	6.50	6.53	6.43	6.35
1974	7.12	6.51	8.75	8.94	7.12	6.22	6.07	6.51	7.64	8.63	8.75	9.10	9.11	8.94	8.31	7.49	7.12
1975	8.64	6.33	6.99	8.41	8.64	6.40	6.26	6.33	6.85	6.87	6.99	7.44	7.87	8.41	8.16	8.52	8.64
1976	8.14	9.07	8.98	9.11	8.14	8.59	8.79	9.07	8.99	8.94	8.98	9.07	9.13	9.11	9.01	8.59	8.14
1977	7.17	7.54	7.07	7.10	7.17	8.04	7.65	7.54	7.58	7.05	7.07	7.14	7.14	7.10	7.24	7.26	7.17
1978	10.46	7.73	8.26	9.17	10.46	7.13	7.30	7.73	8.19	8.20	8.26	8.66	8.80	9.17	9.85	10.36	10.46
1979	13.66	10.92	10.78	11.64	13.66	10.35	10.82	10.92	10.82	10.84	10.78	11.24	11.45	11.64	13.61	13.62	13.66
1980	17.01	15.24	10.38	10.95	17.01	13.50	13.55	15.24	15.15	11.58	10.38	10.06	10.20	10.95	11.91	13.70	17.01
1981	14.41	16.44	18.83	19.38	14.41	16.86	16.83	16.44	17.35	18.43	18.83	20.29	20.82	19.38	17.96	15.07	14.41
1982	9.80	14.86	16.33	12.73	9.80	14.34	14.58	14.86	14.98	15.18	16.33	15.25	13.70	12.73	11.21	10.72	9.80
1983	9.71	9.17	9.17	9.24	9.71	9.58	9.23	9.17	9.12	9.25	9.17	9.24	9.32	9.24	9.24	9.38	9.71

CANADA

Yield of long-term Government bonds (22)

per cent per annum, end of period

Rendement des bons d'État à long terme (22)

pourcentage par an, fin de période

	Year	Q.1	Q.2	Q.3	Q.4	JAN	FEB	MAR	APR	MAY	JUN	JUL	AUG	SEP	OCT	NOV	DEC
1964	5.03	5.25	5.20	5.21	5.03	5.17	5.17	5.25	5.24	5.21	5.20	5.22	5.23	5.21	5.16	5.11	5.03
1965	5.40	5.06	5.16	5.32	5.40	4.96	5.03	5.06	5.05	5.12	5.16	5.28	5.35	5.32	5.37	5.40	5.40
1966	5.76	5.58	5.66	5.75	5.76	5.41	5.61	5.58	5.60	5.61	5.66	5.74	5.94	5.75	5.71	5.91	5.76
1967	6.54	5.48	5.87	6.19	6.54	5.60	5.64	5.48	5.56	5.72	5.87	5.88	5.99	6.19	6.36	6.41	6.54
1968	7.27	6.91	6.62	6.60	7.27	6.54	6.72	6.91	6.62	6.97	6.62	6.49	6.43	6.60	6.83	6.95	7.27
1969	8.33	7.22	7.50	7.81	8.33	7.16	7.20	7.22	7.29	7.48	7.50	7.52	7.53	7.81	7.82	8.15	8.33
1970	6.99	7.93	8.09	7.88	6.99	8.31	8.13	7.93	8.04	8.23	8.09	7.91	8.00	7.83	7.94	7.50	6.99
1971	6.56	6.76	7.30	6.97	6.56	6.67	6.85	6.76	6.97	7.38	7.30	7.49	7.15	6.97	6.71	6.56	6.56
1972	7.12	7.24	7.45	7.46	7.12	6.73	6.90	7.24	7.27	7.34	7.45	7.49	7.44	7.46	7.26	7.08	7.12
1973	7.70	7.30	7.74	7.72	7.70	7.16	7.21	7.30	7.39	7.72	7.74	7.73	7.82	7.72	7.60	7.64	7.70
1974	8.77	8.19	9.46	9.67	8.77	7.75	7.74	8.19	8.81	8.91	9.46	9.63	9.84	9.67	9.20	8.87	8.77
1975	9.49	8.47	8.88	9.72	9.49	8.30	8.17	8.47	9.04	8.71	8.88	9.34	9.39	9.72	9.33	9.58	9.49
1976	8.47	9.39	9.35	9.16	8.47	9.29	9.27	9.39	9.34	9.32	9.35	9.37	9.24	9.16	9.09	8.32	8.47
1977	8.77	8.83	8.72	8.61	8.77	8.52	8.62	8.83	8.85	8.77	8.72	8.70	8.57	8.61	8.70	8.74	8.77
1978	9.68	9.17	9.23	9.15	9.68	9.06	9.15	9.17	9.22	9.23	9.23	9.17	9.16	9.15	9.48	9.54	9.68
1979	11.32	9.91	9.73	10.33	11.32	9.82	9.97	9.91	9.66	9.68	9.73	9.84	10.15	10.38	11.16	10.94	11.32
1980	12.67	13.45	11.29	12.98	12.67	12.13	12.91	13.45	12.01	11.42	11.29	12.32	12.40	12.98	13.22	13.01	12.67
1981	15.27	13.48	15.03	17.66	15.27	12.96	13.38	13.48	15.07	14.96	15.03	17.07	16.77	17.66	16.66	14.32	15.27
1982	11.69	15.06	16.03	13.48	11.69	15.94	15.01	15.06	14.75	14.72	16.03	15.62	13.96	13.48	12.63	12.18	11.69
1983	12.02	11.70	11.56	11.75	12.02	12.28	11.80	11.70	11.18	11.30	11.56	12.03	12.34	11.76	11.73	11.80	12.02

Prime corporate paper (90 days) (23)(24)

per cent per annum, end of period

Papier de premier choix des sociétés (90 jours) (24)(23)

pourcentage par an, fin de période

	Year	Q.1	Q.2	Q.3	Q.4	JAN	FEB	MAR	APR	MAY	JUN	JUL	AUG	SEP	OCT	NOV	DEC
1964	4.59	4.17	3.96	4.34	4.59	4.04	4.12	4.17	4.04	4.04	3.96	4.08	4.29	4.34	4.38	4.34	4.59
1965	6.09	4.43	4.81	5.22	6.09	4.47	4.38	4.43	4.59	4.73	4.81	4.99	5.25	5.22	5.50	5.76	6.09
1966	6.63	6.07	6.28	6.40	6.63	6.04	6.02	6.07	6.04	6.12	6.28	6.35	6.35	6.40	6.43	6.49	6.63
1967	6.57	5.39	5.54	5.95	6.57	6.37	5.94	5.39	4.89	5.27	5.54	5.59	5.65	5.95	6.50	6.50	6.57
1968	6.65	7.39	7.20	6.19	6.65	6.61	6.92	7.39	7.25	7.39	7.20	6.88	6.53	6.19	6.42	6.44	6.65
1969	9.17	7.04	7.82	8.43	9.17	6.89	6.85	7.04	7.08	7.13	7.82	8.17	8.37	8.43	8.56	8.67	9.17
1970	5.58	7.89	7.31	6.68	5.58	8.84	8.59	7.89	7.70	7.88	7.31	7.76	7.58	6.68	6.76	5.53	5.58
1971	4.32	3.53	3.98	4.99	4.32	5.61	5.08	3.53	3.83	4.09	3.98	4.51	4.61	4.99	4.98	4.60	4.32
1972	5.15	5.51	5.16	5.01	5.15	4.00	4.86	5.51	5.88	6.10	5.16	4.68	4.85	5.01	5.04	4.98	5.15
1973	10.25	5.24	7.40	8.95	10.25	5.08	4.92	5.24	6.00	6.48	7.40	7.77	8.65	8.95	9.50	9.20	10.25
1974	10.25	9.20	11.70	11.04	10.25	8.94	8.94	9.20	11.04	11.57	11.70	11.57	11.84	11.04	10.25	9.73	10.25
1975	9.34	6.86	7.25	8.94	9.34	7.12	6.61	6.86	7.64	7.12	7.25	7.64	8.55	8.94	8.81	9.34	9.34
1976	8.16	9.99	9.20	9.47	8.16	8.94	8.94	9.99	9.73	9.20	9.20	9.34	9.34	9.47	9.07	8.68	8.16
1977	7.23	7.77	6.99	7.25	7.23	8.16	7.77	7.77	7.64	7.12	6.99	7.25	7.51	7.25	7.51	7.51	7.23
1978	10.78	7.85	8.32	9.41	10.78	7.23	7.28	7.85	8.32	8.37	8.32	8.63	9.10	9.41	10.04	10.67	10.78
1979	14.20	11.31	11.15	12.00	14.20	11.10	10.99	11.31	11.20	11.15	11.15	11.55	11.85	12.00	14.65	13.70	14.20
1980	17.75	15.25	11.50	10.90	17.75	13.95	13.95	15.25	15.45	12.00	11.50	10.60	10.65	10.90	12.35	13.50	17.75
1981	15.65	17.00	19.20	19.60	15.65	17.25	17.15	17.00	17.50	19.00	19.20	21.25	22.20	19.60	18.80	15.40	15.65
1982	10.25	16.15	17.05	13.10	10.25	14.90	15.00	16.15	15.50	15.60	17.05	15.65	14.20	13.10	11.45	10.95	10.25
1983	9.85	9.30	9.30	9.30	9.85	10.05	9.50	9.30	9.30	9.35	9.30	9.35	9.35	9.30	9.30	9.50	9.85

Prime lending rate: commercial banks (23)

per cent per annum, end of period

Taux préférentiel des banques commerciales (23)

pourcentage par an, fin de période

	Year	Q.1	Q.2	Q.3	Q.4	JAN	FEB	MAR	APR	MAY	JUN	JUL	AUG	SEP	OCT	NOV	DEC
1964	5.75	5.75	5.75	5.75	5.75	5.75	5.75	5.75	5.75	5.75	5.75	5.75	5.75	5.75	5.75	5.75	5.75
1965	6.00	5.75	5.75	5.75	6.00	5.75	5.75	5.75	5.75	5.75	5.75	5.75	5.75	5.75	5.75	5.75	6.00
1966	6.00	6.00	6.00	6.00	6.00	6.00	6.00	6.00	6.00	6.00	6.00	6.00	6.00	6.00	6.00	6.00	6.00
1967	6.50	6.00	5.75	5.75	6.50	6.00	6.00	6.00	5.75	5.75	5.75	5.75	5.75	5.75	6.00	6.00	6.50
1968	6.75	7.00	7.25	6.75	6.75	6.50	7.00	7.00	7.00	7.25	7.25	7.00	7.00	6.75	6.75	6.75	6.75
1969	8.50	7.50	8.00	8.50	8.50	7.00	7.00	7.50	7.50	7.50	8.00	8.50	8.50	8.50	8.50	8.50	8.50
1970	7.50	8.50	8.50	8.00	7.50	8.50	8.50	8.50	8.50	8.50	8.50	8.00	8.00	8.00	8.00	7.50	7.50
1971	6.00	6.50	6.50	6.50	6.00	7.00	7.00	6.50	6.50	6.50	6.50	6.50	6.50	6.50	6.25	6.00	6.00
1972	6.00	6.00	6.00	6.00	6.00	6.00	6.00	6.00	6.00	6.00	6.00	6.00	6.00	6.00	6.00	6.00	6.00
1973	9.50	6.00	7.75	9.00	9.50	6.00	6.00	6.00	6.50	7.00	7.75	7.75	8.25	9.00	9.00	9.00	9.50
1974	11.00	9.50	11.00	11.50	11.00	9.50	9.50	9.50	10.50	11.00	11.00	11.50	11.50	11.50	11.50	11.00	11.00
1975	9.75	9.00	9.00	9.75	9.75	10.50	9.50	9.00	9.00	9.00	9.00	9.00	9.00	9.75	9.75	9.75	9.75
1976	9.75	10.25	10.25	10.25	9.75	9.75	9.75	10.25	10.25	10.25	10.25	10.25	10.25	10.25	10.25	9.75	9.75
1977	8.25	8.75	8.25	8.25	8.25	9.25	8.75	8.75	8.75	8.75	8.25	8.25	8.25	8.25	8.25	8.25	8.25
1978	11.50	8.75	9.25	10.25	11.50	8.25	8.25	8.75	9.25	9.25	9.25	9.25	9.75	10.25	11.00	11.50	11.50
1979	15.00	12.00	12.00	13.00	15.00	12.00	12.00	12.00	12.00	12.00	12.00	12.50	12.50	13.00	15.00	15.00	15.00
1980	18.25	15.75	13.25	12.25	18.25	15.00	15.00	15.75	16.75	13.75	13.25	12.25	12.25	12.25	12.75	13.75	18.25
1981	17.25	17.75	20.00	21.25	17.25	18.25	18.25	17.75	18.25	19.50	20.00	21.00	22.75	21.25	20.00	17.25	17.25
1982	12.50	17.00	18.25	15.00	12.50	16.50	16.50	17.00	17.00	17.00	18.25	17.25	16.00	15.00	13.75	13.00	12.50
1983	11.00	11.50	11.00	11.00	11.00	12.00	11.50	11.50	11.00	11.00	11.00	11.00	11.00	11.00	11.00	11.00	11.00

Share prices: Toronto Stock Exchange (25)

1980 = 100

Cours des actions : Bourse de Toronto (25)

1980 = 100

	Year	Q.1	Q.2	Q.3	Q.4	JAN	FEB	MAR	APR	MAY	JUN	JUL	AUG	SEP	OCT	NOV	DEC
1964	38	34	37	39	40	34	34	35	36	38	37	38	38	40	40	40	40
1965	41	42	42	40	41	42	42	42	43	43	40	39	40	41	42	41	41
1966	39	42	41	37	37	43	42	42	42	41	40	40	37	36	37	36	37
1967	42	40	42	43	42	40	40	41	42	41	42	43	43	43	41	42	42
1968	44	40	42	45	49	41	39	38	42	41	44	43	44	47	47	49	50
1969	49	50	51	45	48	51	49	50	52	53	48	45	47	47	47	49	48
1970	43	47	42	41	43	46	47	47	43	44	38	40	41	43	42	43	45
1971	46	46	47	46	43	46	46	47	48	46	46	46	46	45	41	42	47
1972	54	52	52	55	56	51	52	51	52	53	52	53	55	55	54	56	58
1973	57	59	55	58	58	59	59	58	56	54	54	58	56	59	62	56	56
1974	48	57	49	44	41	56	58	57	52	49	48	50	43	40	42	40	39
1975	47	47	49	43	45	46	47	47	48	49	50	50	49	46	44	46	45
1976	49	50	50	49	46	49	51	50	51	51	50	49	49	48	47	43	48
1977	48	48	47	43	48	47	48	48	47	46	49	49	47	47	46	48	50
1978	55	48	52	58	60	47	47	50	51	53	53	56	58	60	57	60	62
1979	74	66	73	79	80	64	65	69	70	72	76	73	80	82	74	80	85
1980	100	94	93	105	108	95	103	85	88	93	97	103	104	106	105	113	107
1981	102	106	110	99	91	105	103	110	109	112	111	106	102	89	87	95	92
1982	77	79	70	73	87	84	79	75	73	72	64	66	76	75	83	87	92
1983	111	105	113	117	117	116	98	101	110	114	115	117	117	118	111	120	120

Imports f.o.b. (26)(27) / Importations f.o.b. (26)(27)

million Canadian dollars, monthly averages / millions de dollars canadiens, moyennes mensuelles

	Year	Q.1	Q.2	Q.3	Q.4	JAN	FEB	MAR	APR	MAY	JUN	JUL	AUG	SEP	OCT	NOV	DEC
1964	624	552	682	607	655	566	513	576	704	658	686	638	566	616	637	673	656
1965	719	614	743	705	815	550	551	730	698	737	795	732	661	725	764	895	787
1966	839	735	887	812	923	707	668	830	822	938	901	793	818	826	936	961	872
1967	906	831	992	875	926	874	766	852	945	1054	978	916	842	868	925	974	880
1968	1030	937	1067	961	1155	943	965	902	1089	1127	985	976	876	1032	1212	1162	1090
1969	1178	1081	1263	1112	1255	1115	1032	1095	1234	1293	1261	1149	958	1231	1300	1223	1242
1970	1163	1112	1299	1115	1124	1068	1062	1207	1304	1283	1308	1174	988	1187	1129	1196	1046
1971	1301	1143	1368	1255	1440	1025	1044	1361	1278	1388	1438	1256	1203	1306	1456	1534	1330
1972	1556	1408	1671	1451	1694	1375	1335	1514	1527	1808	1678	1420	1443	1490	1773	1792	1516
1973	1944	1752	2018	1803	2202	1737	1645	1873	1819	2243	1991	1893	1739	1779	2334	2298	1976
1974	2644	2278	2698	2625	2974	2182	2165	2486	2432	2950	2711	2721	2524	2631	3114	3042	2764
1975	2893	2772	3104	2712	2984	2842	2608	2866	2897	3129	3286	2724	2576	2838	3112	2999	2342
1976	3125	3045	3343	2918	3193	2901	2992	3241	3153	3290	3586	2926	2881	2946	2976	3515	3087
1977	3530	3331	3832	3321	3637	3026	3223	3745	3567	3982	3948	3263	3386	3312	3738	3655	3518
1978	4176	3575	4542	3891	4695	3212	3933	3581	4731	4423	4473	3876	3771	4025	4821	4948	4316
1979	5239	4952	5261	5133	5611	4805	4503	5550	4950	5690	5142	4966	5621	4810	6174	5858	4801
1980	5773	5678	5980	5252	6182	5501	5467	6065	6480	5706	5753	5533	4835	5389	6809	5995	5742
1981	6624	6310	7280	5405	6498	6003	6033	6894	7169	7084	7587	6732	5800	6687	6868	6558	6068
1982	5661	5872	6081	5501	5189	4990	5878	6746	6185	5952	6105	5582	5408	5514	5154	5552	4860
1983	6299	5637	6361	5189	7009	5296	5446	6169	6184	6466	6433	5717	6249	6600	7323	7363	6340

Exports f.o.b. (26)(27) / Exportations f.o.b. (26)(27)

million Canadian dollars, monthly averages / millions de dollars canadiens, moyennes mensuelles

	Year	Q.1	Q.2	Q.3	Q.4	JAN	FEB	MAR	APR	MAY	JUN	JUL	AUG	SEP	OCT	NOV	DEC
1964	692	595	717	741	715	634	550	600	670	685	796	788	693	742	689	724	732
1965	731	617	723	733	845	587	557	706	665	766	737	790	704	719	791	925	819
1966	837	746	859	903	840	742	692	803	774	933	872	854	945	909	901	978	642
1967	952	878	1004	910	1015	952	829	854	903	1070	1038	965	906	859	976	1048	1020
1968	1135	1007	1172	1124	1238	994	999	1029	1178	1205	1134	1161	1076	1136	1255	1203	1255
1969	1239	1148	1284	1177	1348	1137	1106	1201	1199	1351	1301	1209	1031	1292	1353	1275	1417
1970	1402	1311	1492	1350	1454	1343	1252	1337	1464	1496	1516	1475	1209	1368	1450	1530	1381
1971	1485	1360	1544	1451	1585	1298	1255	1526	1429	1561	1642	1441	1431	1480	1547	1634	1575
1972	1679	1479	1789	1511	1938	1373	1504	1561	1532	1941	1892	1466	1531	1535	1984	2059	1771
1973	2118	1875	2218	1954	2426	1882	1791	1953	2056	2365	2233	2121	1837	1905	2472	2611	2196
1974	2704	2352	2807	2694	2962	2336	2233	2488	2558	3138	2726	2783	2586	2712	3118	3020	2747
1975	2777	2582	2937	2599	2992	2716	2530	2501	2646	3038	3127	2716	2302	2778	3042	2964	2969
1976	3205	2945	3381	3144	3348	2866	2971	2999	3110	3376	3657	3094	3084	3254	3222	3422	3401
1977	3713	3449	3874	3553	3976	3151	3281	3906	3525	3993	4103	3574	3540	3545	4116	3696	4115
1978	4432	3915	4681	4208	4924	3529	4119	4095	4694	4738	4611	3958	3977	4689	4847	5315	4612
1979	5470	5033	5375	5435	6037	5061	4598	5442	4935	5843	5347	5111	5503	5691	6326	6064	5722
1980	6347	6219	6325	5949	6892	5927	6185	6547	6308	6032	6587	6033	5564	6251	7259	6888	6531
1981	6984	6694	7472	6515	7256	6670	6370	7043	7030	7321	8064	6733	5990	6823	7246	7662	6860
1982	7045	6810	7550	6963	6855	6013	6779	7639	7186	7512	7951	6837	6486	7567	6674	6992	6898
1983	7580	6891	7888	7121	8421	6404	6822	7448	7383	7991	8291	6719	6995	7649	8263	8772	8227

Trade balance (f.o.b. — f.o.b.) (26)(27) / Balance commerciale (f.o.b. — f.o.b.) (26)(27)

million Canadian dollars, monthly averages / millions de dollars canadiens, moyennes mensuelles

	Year	Q.1	Q.2	Q.3	Q.4	JAN	FEB	MAR	APR	MAY	JUN	JUL	AUG	SEP	OCT	NOV	DEC
1964	68	43	35	134	60	68	37	24	-33	28	110	150	126	126	52	51	76
1965	11	3	-21	32	30	27	6	-24	-34	29	-58	58	44	-6	27	29	33
1966	-2	11	-28	91	-83	35	25	-28	-49	-6	-29	61	127	84	-36	17	-230
1967	46	48	12	35	88	78	63	2	-42	16	60	50	64	-9	51	74	140
1968	106	71	105	163	83	51	34	126	89	77	150	185	200	104	43	41	166
1969	62	67	21	65	94	21	74	107	-34	57	41	60	73	61	54	52	175
1970	239	198	194	234	330	275	190	130	160	212	209	301	221	180	321	334	335
1971	183	216	176	195	145	273	211	165	151	174	204	186	228	174	91	101	245
1972	123	71	118	60	245	-1	169	47	6	133	214	46	89	45	212	267	255
1973	175	123	200	151	224	144	146	80	237	122	242	228	98	126	139	313	220
1974	60	75	109	68	-12	154	68	2	125	188	15	63	62	80	3	-22	-18
1975	-116	-189	-167	-114	8	-125	-78	-364	-250	-91	-160	-8	-273	-60	-70	-35	127
1976	80	-99	38	226	156	-35	-21	-241	-43	86	71	168	203	308	247	-93	314
1977	183	118	41	232	339	134	58	161	-42	11	155	311	153	233	379	41	597
1978	256	340	139	317	230	318	186	515	-37	315	138	82	206	664	26	366	296
1979	231	81	114	302	426	256	95	-108	-15	152	205	145	-119	881	152	206	920
1980	574	542	345	697	711	426	718	482	-173	375	834	499	729	862	450	894	789
1981	361	385	192	109	758	668	337	150	-139	237	478	1	190	137	378	1104	792
1982	1384	939	1469	1463	1566	1023	900	893	1002	1560	1846	1255	1079	2054	1520	1439	2038
1983	1282	1254	1527	932	1412	1108	1376	1279	1199	1525	1858	1002	746	1049	940	1409	1887

Imports f.o.b. (26) / Importations f.o.b. (26)

million Canadian dollars, monthly averages — Adjusted - Corrigé — millions de dollars canadiens, moyennes mensuelles

Year	Q.1	Q.2	Q.3	Q.4	JAN	FEB	MAR	APR	MAY	JUN	JUL	AUG	SEP	OCT	NOV	DEC
1964	597	637	629	633	600	600	592	672	619	619	620	631	635	609	635	656
1965	670	691	730	786	636	652	722	665	677	733	730	720	740	769	803	787
1966	793	820	852	893	772	786	822	797	827	835	841	874	841	913	881	884
1967	885	913	927	900	912	893	851	945	897	896	958	912	911	867	891	941
1968	997	988	1012	1122	961	1060	972	999	988	977	961	1013	1063	1123	1125	1117
1969	1152	1162	1175	1222	1144	1169	1143	1141	1153	1191	1153	1143	1224	1198	1218	1248
1970	1176	1194	1189	1092	1125	1194	1210	1213	1195	1173	1199	1158	1209	1066	1138	1073
1971	1202	1256	1339	1410	1135	1170	1300	1201	1258	1308	1315	1356	1345	1435	1394	1401
1972	1455	1537	1561	1671	1492	1397	1477	1549	1518	1543	1515	1561	1607	1654	1656	1703
1973	1812	1867	1947	2148	1758	1815	1864	1803	1899	1901	1934	1938	1969	2125	2145	2175
1974	2366	2501	2803	2904	2222	2355	2521	2363	2561	2579	2734	2863	2813	2853	2926	2933
1975	2857	2867	2895	2952	2932	2795	2846	2802	2824	2976	2786	2948	2951	2908	2977	2973
1976	3077	3112	3154	3156	3110	3144	2977	3096	3049	3190	3143	3148	3169	2926	3249	3293
1977	3396	3566	3551	3609	3260	3415	3512	3572	3567	3557	3527	3588	3536	3618	3553	3656
1978	3659	4185	4232	4628	3653	3808	3516	4567	3878	4110	4207	4082	4406	4419	4642	4822
1979	4988	4979	5413	5573	4861	4805	5296	4875	5189	4873	5234	5549	5472	5575	5635	5508
1980	5668	5679	5640	6104	5576	5567	5862	6065	5439	5533	5637	5626	5656	6160	6046	6106
1981	6363	6726	6807	6431	6333	6404	6352	6756	6340	7082	6806	6769	6847	6414	6408	6472
1982	5859	5761	5806	5179	5315	6231	6031	5837	5798	5648	5890	5876	5653	4900	5353	5284
1983	5663	5990	6460	7083	5623	5726	5640	5952	6013	6005	6082	6563	6734	6968	7086	7196

Exports f.o.b. (26) / Exportations f.o.b. (26)

million Canadian dollars, monthly averages — Adjusted - Corrigé — millions de dollars canadiens, moyennes mensuelles

Year	Q.1	Q.2	Q.3	Q.4	JAN	FEB	MAR	APR	MAY	JUN	JUL	AUG	SEP	OCT	NOV	DEC
1964	656	701	729	682	658	664	637	714	651	738	734	722	731	671	671	704
1965	684	700	735	804	659	667	727	689	712	698	757	721	726	800	821	790
1966	817	823	902	900	812	808	831	803	838	827	850	941	915	891	904	906
1967	939	952	923	993	1006	941	869	963	927	966	947	937	885	963	989	1028
1968	1075	1127	1146	1193	1027	1094	1104	1146	1097	1138	1098	1151	1191	1200	1166	1214
1969	1226	1211	1221	1300	1194	1231	1253	1174	1242	1217	1195	1179	1288	1282	1274	1343
1970	1398	1403	1407	1399	1452	1389	1354	1457	1400	1353	1454	1355	1411	1412	1429	1354
1971	1441	1443	1534	1522	1436	1389	1498	1402	1433	1494	1483	1570	1549	1548	1463	1555
1972	1552	1669	1619	1877	1506	1581	1567	1616	1672	1718	1547	1651	1661	1863	1897	1872
1973	1990	2087	2093	2305	1963	1967	2039	2069	2067	2124	2145	2000	2133	2284	2353	2278
1974	2516	2614	2848	2836	2404	2445	2700	2568	2712	2563	2799	2935	2810	2860	2891	2756
1975	2719	2734	2733	2923	2772	2728	2657	2703	2740	2760	2726	2622	2850	2796	2967	3007
1976	3053	3188	3309	3275	3050	3152	2955	3099	3150	3314	3217	3407	3305	3231	3208	3387
1977	3543	3655	3722	3932	3415	3495	3718	3705	3604	3657	3850	3863	3452	4083	3753	3960
1978	4039	4369	4511	4809	3903	4138	4075	4619	4256	4231	4282	4334	4917	4558	4996	4873
1979	5092	5175	5705	5908	5168	4875	5234	5029	5295	5200	5481	5564	6072	5912	5756	6057
1980	6206	6064	6370	6746	5963	6356	6299	6320	5674	6199	6275	6543	6291	6718	6891	6631
1981	6777	7142	6924	7094	6913	6702	6717	6910	7080	7436	7058	6883	6825	6855	7506	6922
1982	6865	7196	7362	6783	6424	7107	7064	7188	7124	7277	7247	7323	7515	6571	6747	7031
1983	6977	7407	7603	8326	6822	7135	6974	7444	7450	7326	7383	7611	7813	8010	8433	8536

Trade balance (f.o.b. — f.o.b.) (26) / Balance commerciale (f.o.b. — f.o.b.) (26)

million Canadian dollars, monthly averages — Adjusted - Corrigé — millions de dollars canadiens, moyennes mensuelles

Year	Q.1	Q.2	Q.3	Q.4	JAN	FEB	MAR	APR	MAY	JUN	JUL	AUG	SEP	OCT	NOV	DEC
1964	59	64	100	49	58	64	45	42	31	119	114	91	96	62	36	48
1965	14	8	5	17	24	14	5	24	35	-34	28	1	-14	31	18	3
1966	24	3	50	8	40	22	9	6	11	-8	9	67	74	-22	23	22
1967	54	39	-4	94	94	48	19	18	30	70	-11	25	-26	95	98	88
1968	78	139	134	72	66	34	133	147	109	161	138	136	129	77	41	97
1969	74	50	45	78	50	62	110	33	90	26	43	30	64	83	56	95
1970	222	209	218	306	328	196	144	244	204	180	255	197	202	346	291	281
1971	240	187	195	112	302	219	198	201	175	186	168	213	204	113	69	154
1972	96	132	59	206	14	184	91	67	154	175	32	90	54	209	241	169
1973	177	219	145	156	205	152	175	266	169	223	211	62	164	159	208	102
1974	151	113	45	-68	182	90	179	205	151	-16	65	72	-3	7	-35	-177
1975	-139	-133	-162	-29	-160	-67	-189	-100	-84	-216	-60	-326	-100	-112	-10	34
1976	-24	76	155	119	-59	9	-22	3	100	124	74	259	136	304	-40	94
1977	147	90	171	323	155	80	206	133	37	100	322	275	-85	465	200	304
1978	380	184	280	182	250	330	559	52	379	122	75	252	512	139	354	52
1979	105	196	288	336	306	70	-62	154	106	327	248	15	601	337	121	549
1980	538	385	730	642	387	789	437	255	235	665	638	917	635	557	845	524
1981	414	416	117	663	580	298	365	154	740	354	252	119	-22	441	1097	450
1982	1006	1435	1555	1604	1109	876	1033	1351	1325	1629	1357	1447	1862	1671	1394	1747
1983	1314	1417	1143	1243	1199	1409	1334	1492	1438	1322	1301	1049	1079	1043	1347	1340

CANADA

U.S. dollar exchange rate: spot

cents per Canadian dollar, end of period

Taux de change du dollar É.-U. : au comptant

cents par dollar canadien, fin de période

	Year	Q.1	Q.2	Q.3	Q.4	JAN	FEB	MAR	APR	MAY	JUN	JUL	AUG	SEP	OCT	NOV	DEC
1964	93.13	92.54	92.49	93.02	93.13	92.57	92.57	92.54	92.38	92.52	92.49	92.57	92.81	93.02	93.05	93.21	93.13
1965	93.02	92.64	92.30	92.92	93.02	93.05	92.70	92.64	92.67	92.59	92.30	92.49	92.95	92.92	93.05	93.00	93.02
1966	92.27	92.83	92.97	92.78	92.27	93.05	92.89	92.83	92.92	92.81	92.97	93.10	92.95	92.78	92.54	92.24	92.27
1967	92.54	92.38	92.62	93.10	92.54	92.67	92.40	92.38	92.38	92.49	92.62	92.95	92.95	93.10	93.19	92.59	92.54
1968	93.21	92.38	92.95	93.21	93.21	92.01	91.98	92.38	92.73	92.76	92.95	93.21	93.21	93.21	93.24	93.19	93.21
1969	93.21	92.92	92.52	92.67	93.21	93.21	92.92	92.92	92.97	92.78	92.52	92.76	92.83	92.67	92.89	93.08	93.21
1970	98.89	93.21	96.67	93.19	98.89	93.24	93.24	93.21	93.21	93.08	96.67	97.50	98.22	98.19	98.04	98.13	98.89
1971	99.78	99.20	97.71	99.10	99.78	99.26	99.32	99.20	99.10	98.89	97.71	98.19	98.64	99.10	99.66	99.66	99.78
1972	100.44	100.31	101.49	101.69	100.44	99.44	99.91	100.31	100.79	101.95	101.49	101.69	101.72	101.69	101.72	100.56	100.44
1973	100.42	100.10	100.16	99.42	100.42	99.94	100.59	100.10	99.68	100.50	100.16	99.84	99.45	99.42	100.10	100.00	100.42
1974	100.89	102.84	102.86	101.44	100.89	101.19	103.22	102.84	104.12	103.95	102.86	102.12	101.26	101.44	101.56	101.28	100.89
1975	98.39	99.68	97.03	97.54	98.39	100.06	100.20	99.68	98.12	97.77	97.03	96.92	96.88	97.54	98.31	98.95	98.39
1976	99.09	101.61	103.24	102.75	99.09	99.90	101.56	101.61	102.19	102.17	103.24	102.54	101.90	102.75	102.86	96.62	99.09
1977	91.37	94.63	94.35	93.16	91.37	97.95	95.56	94.63	95.48	95.15	94.35	93.57	93.05	93.16	90.24	90.30	91.37
1978	84.32	88.32	88.93	84.52	84.32	90.28	89.71	88.32	88.42	89.05	88.93	88.41	86.87	84.52	85.70	85.36	84.32
1979	85.61	86.16	85.63	86.16	85.61	83.30	83.78	86.16	87.54	86.16	85.63	85.50	85.75	86.16	84.42	85.44	85.61
1980	83.70	83.94	86.88	85.43	83.70	86.33	87.35	83.94	84.19	86.29	86.88	86.09	86.41	85.43	85.06	84.07	83.70
1981	84.32	84.26	83.30	82.85	84.32	83.75	83.24	84.26	83.61	83.08	83.30	80.98	83.18	82.86	83.12	84.98	84.32
1982	81.34	81.28	77.34	80.89	81.34	83.56	81.33	81.28	82.02	80.37	77.34	79.65	80.68	80.89	81.57	80.83	81.34
1983	80.36	81.04	81.48	81.15	80.36	80.85	81.37	81.04	81.57	81.30	81.48	81.03	81.06	81.15	81.14	80.70	80.36

U.S. dollar exchange rate: forward (90 days)

cents per Canadian dollar, end of period

Taux de change du dollar É.-U. : à terme (90 jours)

cents par dollar canadien, fin de période

	Year	Q.1	Q.2	Q.3	Q.4	JAN	FEB	MAR	APR	MAY	JUN	JUL	AUG	SEP	OCT	NOV	DEC
1964	93.07	92.55	92.56	92.97	93.07	92.55	92.56	92.55	92.40	92.56	92.56	92.58	92.76	92.97	93.01	93.15	93.07
1965	92.87	92.72	92.37	92.78	92.87	93.00	92.70	92.72	92.75	92.64	92.37	92.44	92.88	92.78	92.89	92.83	92.87
1966	92.30	92.83	92.95	92.85	92.30	92.90	92.77	92.83	92.89	92.76	92.95	93.10	92.96	92.86	92.60	92.32	92.30
1967	92.39	92.42	92.57	92.83	92.39	92.57	92.38	92.42	92.35	92.44	92.57	92.79	92.71	92.83	92.91	92.59	92.39
1968	93.13	92.02	92.73	93.03	93.13	91.76	91.63	92.02	92.33	92.43	92.73	92.85	92.98	93.03	93.08	93.11	93.13
1969	93.18	93.08	92.85	92.81	93.18	93.20	93.04	93.08	93.17	93.11	92.85	92.92	92.95	92.81	92.89	93.08	93.18
1970	98.94	93.22	96.98	98.35	98.94	93.13	93.18	93.22	93.27	93.21	96.98	97.55	98.29	98.35	98.07	98.27	98.94
1971	99.94	99.24	98.02	99.29	99.94	98.96	99.05	99.24	99.32	99.19	98.02	98.52	98.95	99.29	99.70	99.78	99.94
1972	100.55	100.12	101.46	101.74	100.55	99.45	99.59	100.12	100.47	101.49	101.46	101.71	101.72	101.74	101.74	100.62	100.55
1973	100.50	100.73	100.56	99.78	100.50	100.29	101.06	100.73	100.09	100.77	100.56	100.47	100.10	99.78	100.08	100.09	100.50
1974	100.95	103.03	103.27	101.59	100.95	101.16	103.13	103.03	104.04	104.00	103.27	102.56	101.68	101.59	101.45	101.23	100.95
1975	97.54	99.75	96.88	97.20	97.54	100.19	100.30	99.75	98.02	97.51	96.88	96.73	96.55	97.20	97.78	98.19	97.54
1976	98.35	100.45	102.23	101.92	98.35	99.05	100.56	100.45	101.11	101.39	102.23	101.63	100.48	101.92	101.82	95.53	98.35
1977	91.42	94.24	94.08	92.99	91.42	97.49	94.98	94.24	94.99	94.81	94.08	93.19	92.75	92.99	90.32	90.12	91.42
1978	84.52	88.04	89.00	84.42	84.52	90.33	89.65	88.04	88.43	89.12	89.00	88.01	86.85	84.42	86.27	85.65	84.52
1979	85.84	86.15	85.45	85.41	85.84	83.26	83.79	86.15	87.33	86.04	85.45	85.32	85.85	86.41	84.63	85.65	85.84
1980	83.92	84.40	86.49	85.93	83.92	86.47	87.95	84.40	83.93	86.02	86.49	86.10	86.69	85.93	85.51	84.31	83.92
1981	84.03	83.98	82.96	82.43	84.03	83.72	83.17	83.98	83.46	82.91	82.96	80.42	82.48	82.43	82.75	84.21	84.03
1982	81.21	81.30	77.23	80.55	81.21	83.45	81.01	81.30	81.67	80.08	77.23	79.28	80.15	80.55	81.24	81.24	81.21
1983	80.41	80.82	81.52	81.22	80.41	80.76	81.24	80.82	81.63	81.26	81.52	81.26	81.26	81.22	81.20	80.74	80.41

Official reserves excluding gold

million SDR's, end of period

Réserves officielles, or exclu

millions de DTS, fin de période

	Year	Q.1	Q.2	Q.3	Q.4	JAN	FEB	MAR	APR	MAY	JUN	JUL	AUG	SEP	OCT	NOV	DEC
1964	1864	1644	1646	1733	1864	1764	1712	1644	1627	1638	1646	1627	1655	1733	1839	1892	1864
1965	1886	1781	1737	1921	1886	1847	1838	1781	1787	1763	1737	1754	1863	1921	1925	1925	1886
1966	1656	1827	1774	1709	1656	1885	1873	1827	1786	1818	1774	1789	1749	1709	1678	1678	1656
1967	1702	1605	1573	1590	1702	1668	1610	1605	1628	1607	1573	1575	1579	1590	1666	1614	1702
1968	2183	1285	1785	1874	2183	1593	1474	1285	1481	1823	1785	1723	1799	1874	1865	2022	2183
1969	2234	2148	2095	2084	2234	2227	2182	2148	2168	2149	2095	2069	2101	2084	2178	2203	2234
1970	3388	2718	3454	3673	3388	2441	2545	2718	2943	3204	3454	3564	3736	3673	3727	3764	3888
1971	4457	4054	4060	4200	4457	4008	4059	4054	4063	4087	4060	4132	4200	4200	4280	4482	4457
1972	4804	4631	4959	4962	4804	4545	4556	4631	4679	4800	4959	4934	4942	4962	4969	4801	4804
1973	4013	4332	4243	3973	4013	4725	4403	4332	4282	4317	4243	4186	4018	3973	4017	3986	4013
1974	3990	4289	4307	4125	3990	4084	4369	4289	4400	4396	4307	4231	4173	4125	4093	4035	3990
1975	3745	3841	3501	3661	3745	3867	3864	3841	3737	3527	3501	3566	3566	3661	3657	3823	3745
1976	4238	4237	4423	4252	4238	3978	4223	4237	4241	4297	4423	4239	4058	4252	4249	3632	4238
1977	3007	3599	3577	3320	3007	4122	3769	3599	3661	3715	3577	3471	3384	3320	2757	2769	3007
1978	2720	2429	3041	2077	2720	2839	2234	2429	2953	3106	3041	2859	2517	2077	2999	2747	2720
1979	2168	3429	2452	2644	2168	2637	2407	3429	3257	2433	2452	2477	2507	2644	2273	2261	2168
1980	2384	2162	2487	2239	2384	2316	2656	2162	2299	2453	2487	2295	2473	2239	2078	1937	2384
1981	3000	2238	1907	1865	3000	1983	1948	2238	1835	1969	1907	1297	2156	1865	1680	3098	3000
1982	2719	1919	1963	2815	2719	2987	2352	1919	2298	1834	1963	2275	2846	2815	2668	2675	2719
1983	3310	3225	3388	3632	3310	3065	3522	3225	3348	3211	3388	3427	3615	3632	3776	3603	3310

Balance of payments: net trade (28)
million Canadian dollars

Balance des paiements : balance commerciale (28)
millions de dollars canadiens

	Year	Q.1	Q.2	Q.3	Q.4	JAN	FEB	MAR	APR	MAY	JUN	JUL	AUG	SEP	OCT	NOV	DEC
1964	701	35	151	355	160												
1965	118	-40	-27	262	23												
1966	224	10	-49	223	40												
1967	566	115	28	100	323												
1968	1471	278	415	481	297												
1969	964	219	156	245	344												
1970	3052	646	636	747	1023												
1971	2563	733	610	664	556												
1972	1857	306	485	304	762												
1973	2735	531	735	594	875												
1974	1689	550	525	341	273												
1975	-451	-523	-213	-47	332												
1976	1559	-314	316	791	766												
1977	2975	404	422	782	1367												
1978	4315	1244	779	1184	1108												
1979	4425	580	596	1499	1750												
1980	8793	1821	1135	2593	3244												
1981	7368	2037	1242	986	3103												
1982	18338	3377	4645	4965	5350												
1983	18002	4099	5189	3621	5093												

Balance of payments: current balance (28)
million Canadian dollars

Balance des paiements : opérations courantes, nettes (28)
millions de dollars canadiens

	Year	Q.1	Q.2	Q.3	Q.4	JAN	FEB	MAR	APR	MAY	JUN	JUL	AUG	SEP	OCT	NOV	DEC
1964	-424	-336	-150	208	-146												
1965	-1130	-421	-364	34	-379												
1966	-1162	-387	-380	33	-428												
1967	-499	-313	-269	200	-117												
1968	-97	-210	12	299	-198												
1969	-917	-330	-387	-23	-172												
1970	1106	-8	119	417	578												
1971	431	135	124	304	-132												
1972	-386	-398	-50	5	55												
1973	108	-342	148	236	66												
1974	-1460	-528	-143	22	-811												
1975	-4757	-1854	-1126	-679	-1098												
1976	-4109	-1954	-1065	-165	-925												
1977	-4334	-1725	-1223	-575	-811												
1978	-4917	-1453	-1177	-298	-1989												
1979	-4840	-2237	-1478	45	-1170												
1980	-1069	-1434	-1024	1020	369												
1981	-5766	-1838	-1865	-1603	-460												
1982	3017	-1234	987	2059	1205												
1983	1578	-647	1120	255	849												

Balance of payments: net capital movements (28)
million Canadian dollars

Balance des paiements : mouvements de capitaux, nets (28)
millions de dollars canadiens

	Year	Q.1	Q.2	Q.3	Q.4	JAN	FEB	MAR	APR	MAY	JUN	JUL	AUG	SEP	OCT	NOV	DEC
1964	675	356	161	-28	186												
1965	1527	531	439	254	303												
1966	985	298	167	36	484												
1967	1020	647	116	-93	350												
1968	1230	50	659	284	237												
1969	1201	580	113	101	407												
1970	811	578	382	19	-168												
1971	1694	374	-10	545	785												
1972	2060	974	615	-37	508												
1973	75	377	-308	-324	330												
1974	2351	1057	57	307	930												
1975	5555	1578	870	867	2240												
1976	8398	2739	1915	436	3308												
1977	5174	595	2455	405	1718												
1978	4743	475	3482	-658	1444												
1979	9138	4615	1809	592	2122												
1980	982	370	1315	-180	-523												
1981	16030	5820	3369	1415	5426												
1982	332	2915	-3663	3422	-2342												
1983	5533	710	2699	1873	251												

NOTES

1. From 1971, index (original base 1971) linked on 1971 to previous index (original base 1961) covering period 1964 to 1970. Both indices are based on the 1970 version of the *Canadian Standard Industrial Classification*.
2. Including forestry, fishing and trapping.
3. Excluding payment received for work in progress.
4. The coverage of the series has been progressively broadened through the years. In 1983, the population of the municipalities covered accounted for about 89 per cent of the total population.
5. Index relating to the use of materials, labour and equipment in single detached houses in 1969.
6. Data up to 1965 based on 1948 *Canadian Standard Industrial Classification;* on the 1960 CSIC thereafter. Data from 1972 are based on a new survey method introduced in 1975.
7. New and used cars, including sales of car parts.
8. Establishment data referring to last pay period of month. To March 1983, firms employing 20 persons or more, and data based on the 1960 *Canadian Standard Industrial Classification*. From April 1983, firms of all sizes and the 1970 CSIC.
9. Labour force sample survey of population aged 15 or over, taken in the mid-month week. From 1970, new survey.
10. Data based on the space occupied by help wanted advertising in a monthly sample of 18 metropolitan newspapers.
11. Including all strikes, legal or illegal, lasting at least half a day and amounting to 10 or more man-days of time lost.
12. Wages and salaries per unit of output. From 1971, index (original base 1971) linked on 1971 to previous index.
13. From 1971, index based on 1970 *Canadian Standard Industrial Classification*. Previous index based on 1960 CSIC. The indices are linked on 1971.
14. Monthly data are averages of Wednesdays.
15. Weighting pattern based on 1957 to April 1973, on April 1973 from May 1973 to September 1978, on 1974 from October 1978 to March 1982, and on 1978 from April 1982.

NOTES

1. A partir de 1971, indice (base originale 1971) raccordé sur 1971 à l'indice précédent (base originale 1961), qui couvrait la période de 1964 à 1970. Les deux indices se réfèrent à la *Classification Canadienne Type de l'Industrie* de 1970.
2. Y compris la sylviculture, la pêche et le piégeage.
3. Non compris les acomptes versés sur les produits en cours de fabrication.
4. La couverture des séries a été progressivement étendue au cours des années. En 1983, la population des municipalités visées se montait à environ 89 % de la population totale.
5. Indice se rapportant aux matériaux, à la main-d'œuvre et au matériel employés dans la construction de maisons individuelles en 1969.
6. Les données jusqu'en 1965 se réfèrent à la *Classification Canadienne Type de l'Industrie* de 1948; à la CCTI de 1960 pour les années suivantes. A partir de 1972, les données sont établies selon une nouvelle méthode d'enquête introduite en 1975.
7. Voitures neuves et d'occasion, y compris les ventes de pièces détachées.
8. Statistiques d'établissement relatives à la dernière paie du mois. Jusqu'en mars 1983, entreprises employant au moins 20 personnes, les données se réfèrent à la *Classification Canadienne Type de l'Industrie* de 1960. A partir d'avril 1983, entreprises de toutes tailles, et la CCTI de 1970.
9. Enquête par sondage auprès de la population de 15 ans ou plus, effectuée au cours de la semaine médiane du mois. A partir de 1970, nouvelle enquête.
10. Données basées sur la place consacrée aux offres d'emploi dans un échantillon mensuel de 18 journaux d'agglomérations urbaines.
11. Y compris toute grève, légale ou non, qui dure au moins une demi-journée et qui représente un minimum de 10 journées-homme en temps de travail perdu.
12. Salaires par unité produite. A partir de 1971, indice (base originale 1971) raccordé sur 1971 à l'indice précédent.
13. A partir de 1971, indice se référant à la *Classification Canadienne Type de l'Industrie* de 1970. L'ancien indice se référait à la CCTI de 1960. Les deux indices ont été raccordés sur 1971.
14. Les données mensuelles représentent les moyennes des mercredis.
15. La pondération se réfère à 1957 jusqu'en avril 1973; de mai 1973 à septembre 1978, pondération d'avril 1973; d'octobre 1978 à mars 1982, pondération de 1974, et à partir d'avril 1982, pondération de 1978.

NOTES

16. From November 1981, new statistical reporting system.

17. Excluding short-term credit. Discontinuities in the series as from December 1965, November 1967 and January 1970 result from changes in the classification of certain assets. The revisions were of 2.2 per cent, 0.3 per cent and 0.7 per cent, respectively.

18. Excluding credit unions and "caisses populaires". From 1970, excluding loans for the financing of passenger cars used for commercial purposes. From 1971, excluding unearned interest and finance charges. From 1974, new estimation techniques. Monthly data are averages of Wednesdays, or, for certain components, averages of beginning- and end-of-month figures; prior to 1971, the data refer to end of period.

19. From 13th March 1980, the official discount rate is set at 0.25 per cent above the weekly average tender rate of 91-day Treasury bills.

20. Average of daily closing rates in the last week of the month.

21. Average yield of last weekly issue in month.

22. Based on average of buying and selling closing prices on last Wednesday of month.

23. Last Wednesday of month.

24. From April 1973, operative market trading levels. Previously, weighted averages of posted rates.

25. Closing prices on the last trading day of the month.

26. General trade.

27. Data for August 1979 affected by change in recording procedure.

28. Prior to 2nd quarter 1968, transactions in non-monetary gold were included in the capital account.

NOTES

16. A partir de novembre 1981, nouveau système de relevés des statistiques bancaires.

17. Crédits à court terme exclus. Les ruptures dans les séries à partir de décembre 1965, novembre 1967 et janvier 1970 résultent de changements dans la classification de certains avoirs. Les révisions étaient respectivement de 2,2 %, 0,3 % et 0,7 %.

18. Non compris les "credit unions" et les caisses populaires. A partir de 1970, non compris les prêts pour l'achat de voitures particulières destinées à des fins commerciales. A partir de 1971, non compris les intérêts non courus et les commissions de financement. A partir de 1974, nouvelles techniques d'estimation. Les données mensuelles sont des moyennes des mercredis ou, pour certaines composantes, des moyennes des données de début et de fin de mois; avant 1971, situation en fin de mois.

19. A partir du 13 mars 1980, le taux d'escompte officiel est fixé à 0,25 % au-dessus du dernier taux moyen hebdomadaire de soumission pour les bons du Trésor à 91 jours.

20. Moyenne des taux de clôture journaliers de la dernière semaine du mois.

21. Rendement moyen de la dernière émission hebdomadaire du mois.

22. Données établies à partir de la moyenne des cours acheteurs et vendeurs à la clôture, le dernier mercredi du mois.

23. Dernier mercredi du mois.

24. Avant avril 1973, moyennes pondérées des taux affichés; à partir d'avril 1973, taux effectivement pratiqués sur le marché.

25. Cours à la clôture du dernier jour ouvrable dans le mois.

26. Commerce général.

27. La donnée du mois d'août 1979 est affectée par un changement dans la procédure d'enregistrement.

28. Avant le 2e trimestre 1968, les transactions d'or non monétaire étaient comprises dans les mouvements des capitaux.

MAIN SOURCES

PRINCIPALES SOURCES

Series	Séries	Sources
National product	Produit national	Statistics Canada *Canadian Statistical Review*
Domestic product	Produit intérieur	
Production	Production	
Manufacturing deliveries, stocks, and orders	Livraisons, stocks et commandes, industries manufacturières	
Construction	Construction	
Internal trade	Commerce intérieur	
Labour and wages	Main-d'œuvre et salaires	
Prices	Prix	
Foreign trade	Commerce extérieur	
Balance of payments	Balance des paiements	
Rate of capacity utilization	Taux d'utilisation de capacité	*Statistics Canada daily*
Business surveys	Enquêtes de conjoncture	
Home finance	Finances internes	Bank of Canada *Bank of Canada Review*
Interest rates	Taux d'intérêts	
Share prices	Cours des actions	

United States — États-Unis

UNITED STATES

Gross national product — **Produit national brut**

at current market prices — *aux prix courants du marché*

billion dollars, annual rates — milliards de dollars, taux annuels

Adjusted - Corrigé

	Year	Q.1	Q.2	Q.3	Q.4	JAN	FEB	MAR	APR	MAY	JUN	JUL	AUG	SEP	OCT	NOV	DEC
1964	637.7	625.3	634.0	642.8	648.8												
1965	691.0	668.8	681.7	696.4	717.2												
1966	756.0	738.5	750.0	750.6	774.9												
1967	799.6	780.7	788.6	805.7	823.3												
1968	873.4	841.2	867.2	884.9	900.3												
1969	944.0	921.2	937.4	955.3	962.0												
1970	992.7	972.0	986.3	1003.5	1009.0												
1971	1077.7	1049.3	1068.9	1086.6	1105.8												
1972	1185.9	1142.4	1171.7	1196.1	1233.5												
1973	1326.4	1283.5	1307.6	1337.7	1376.7												
1974	1434.2	1387.7	1423.8	1451.5	1473.8												
1975	1549.2	1479.8	1516.7	1578.5	1621.8												
1976	1718.0	1672.0	1698.6	1729.0	1772.5												
1977	1918.3	1834.8	1895.1	1954.4	1988.9												
1978	2163.8	2031.7	2139.5	2202.5	2281.6												
1979	2417.8	2335.5	2377.9	2454.3	2502.9												
1980	2631.7	2572.9	2578.8	2639.1	2736.0												
1981	2954.1	2866.6	2912.5	3004.9	3032.2												
1982	3073.0	3021.4	3070.2	3090.7	3109.6												
1983	3310.5	3171.5	3272.0	3362.2	3436.2												

Gross national product — **Produit national brut**

implicit price level — niveau implicite des prix

1980 = 100

Adjusted - Corrigé

	Year	Q.1	Q.2	Q.3	Q.4	JAN	FEB	MAR	APR	MAY	JUN	JUL	AUG	SEP	OCT	NOV	DEC
1964	40.8	40.6	40.7	40.9	41.0												
1965	41.7	41.3	41.5	41.8	42.0												
1966	43.0	42.4	42.9	43.2	43.6												
1967	44.3	43.9	44.0	44.4	44.9												
1968	46.3	45.5	46.0	46.4	47.1												
1969	48.6	47.6	48.3	49.0	49.7												
1970	51.3	50.4	51.0	51.5	52.1												
1971	53.8	52.9	53.6	54.1	54.6												
1972	56.1	55.3	55.7	56.2	56.9												
1973	59.3	57.7	58.7	59.7	60.9												
1974	64.5	62.1	63.6	65.3	67.1												
1975	70.5	68.9	69.7	71.0	72.3												
1976	74.2	72.9	73.6	74.5	75.7												
1977	78.5	76.7	77.9	79.0	80.3												
1978	84.3	81.3	83.5	85.2	87.1												
1979	91.6	88.9	90.7	92.5	94.2												
1980	100.0	96.4	98.9	101.0	103.8												
1981	109.4	106.4	107.9	110.4	112.8												
1982	116.0	114.0	115.5	116.5	117.7												
1983	120.9	119.3	120.2	121.3	122.5												

Personal income: total
billion dollars, annual rates

Adjusted - Corrigé

Revenus individuels : total
milliards de dollars, taux annuels

	Year	Q.1	Q.2	Q.3	Q.4	JAN	FEB	MAR	APR	MAY	JUN	JUL	AUG	SEP	OCT	NOV	DEC
1964	499.2	485.8	494.9	504.0	512.1	483.4	485.7	488.3	491.8	495.1	497.7	500.5	504.4	507.2	507.8	511.4	517.3
1965	540.6	522.8	533.4	546.9	559.4	521.6	522.0	524.9	528.7	533.7	537.8	540.6	542.7	557.5	554.6	559.4	564.2
1966	588.2	571.4	581.4	594.1	605.7	566.5	572.0	575.8	578.2	580.6	585.4	589.0	594.1	599.2	602.5	606.6	608.2
1967	630.0	615.4	623.0	635.2	646.4	613.5	614.4	618.5	619.8	622.4	626.8	631.5	635.9	638.1	639.8	646.1	653.2
1968	690.6	663.7	682.7	700.4	715.6	656.3	663.7	671.2	676.1	683.1	688.8	695.1	700.6	705.6	710.6	715.8	720.4
1969	754.7	730.0	747.1	754.5	777.0	723.8	729.9	736.3	742.1	747.0	752.3	759.0	765.1	769.5	773.3	776.0	781.8
1970	811.1	788.2	810.4	819.3	826.4	783.3	788.1	793.3	812.8	808.7	809.7	814.3	819.2	824.4	823.0	825.0	831.2
1971	868.5	844.7	864.1	874.7	890.3	840.4	843.8	850.1	854.2	859.2	879.0	869.4	875.9	878.7	882.1	888.6	900.0
1972	951.4	919.7	934.4	957.1	994.2	910.1	921.7	927.4	933.2	938.9	931.0	948.3	958.7	964.2	982.5	996.1	1004.1
1973	1065.2	1024.2	1050.3	1077.9	1108.3	1011.7	1025.9	1034.9	1042.4	1049.9	1058.5	1068.0	1077.4	1088.3	1098.9	1110.3	1115.9
1974	1168.6	1124.9	1155.9	1187.4	1206.2	1118.4	1124.6	1131.6	1142.1	1157.1	1168.6	1181.9	1186.6	1193.7	1204.5	1204.2	1209.9
1975	1265.0	1214.2	1247.5	1283.5	1314.6	1208.7	1214.3	1219.7	1228.0	1242.1	1272.3	1269.5	1285.6	1295.5	1307.0	1315.2	1321.7
1976	1391.2	1348.5	1373.7	1404.2	1438.4	1338.6	1350.8	1356.2	1365.8	1375.0	1380.2	1394.3	1404.8	1413.5	1422.6	1440.5	1452.1
1977	1540.4	1476.9	1514.5	1551.1	1609.2	1460.4	1477.1	1493.1	1502.6	1514.1	1526.9	1548.2	1559.7	1575.3	1593.5	1608.9	1625.0
1978	1732.7	1644.9	1702.7	1751.8	1821.3	1628.5	1642.9	1663.4	1686.9	1700.9	1720.1	1745.9	1761.6	1777.8	1801.2	1819.5	1843.3
1979	1951.2	1871.8	1916.6	1981.9	2034.4	1853.4	1870.2	1891.8	1902.2	1915.8	1931.9	1965.3	1983.1	1997.4	2016.8	2034.2	2052.2
1980	2165.3	2092.1	2118.2	2186.0	2265.0	2079.2	2089.7	2107.5	2108.5	2116.2	2129.8	2165.4	2184.0	2208.5	2239.4	2264.5	2291.2
1981	2435.0	2338.3	2394.2	2490.9	2516.6	2316.9	2336.5	2361.4	2375.1	2390.6	2416.9	2463.7	2494.6	2514.3	2513.4	2518.7	2517.6
1982	2578.7	2528.1	2563.2	2591.3	2632.0	2518.1	2530.2	2535.8	2549.0	2568.0	2572.5	2589.8	2586.7	2597.4	2617.8	2633.1	2645.0
1983	2742.1	2657.7	2713.6	2761.9	2835.2	2652.6	2650.5	2670.1	2689.0	2719.3	2732.6	2747.6	2756.4	2781.6	2812.5	2833.5	2859.6

Personal income: non-agricultural
billion dollars, annual rates

Adjusted - Corrigé

Revenus individuels : secteur non agricole
milliards de dollars, taux annuels

	Year	Q.1	Q.2	Q.3	Q.4	JAN	FEB	MAR	APR	MAY	JUN	JUL	AUG	SEP	OCT	NOV	DEC
1964	483.7	470.6	479.4	488.5	496.2	468.0	470.6	473.3	476.5	479.5	482.2	484.9	489.0	491.8	491.8	495.5	501.2
1965	522.6	506.1	514.9	528.4	541.0	504.8	505.1	508.3	511.3	515.3	518.2	521.7	524.3	539.1	536.3	541.0	545.6
1966	568.9	550.6	562.0	575.1	587.7	546.2	550.8	554.9	558.6	561.3	566.2	570.0	575.1	580.2	584.4	588.5	590.1
1967	611.9	597.9	605.2	616.8	627.9	595.7	597.1	601.0	602.0	604.5	609.0	613.2	617.4	619.7	621.4	627.5	634.7
1968	672.1	645.6	664.9	681.7	696.2	637.9	645.7	653.3	658.5	665.4	670.8	676.6	681.8	686.8	691.4	696.5	700.8
1969	733.9	709.7	726.7	743.9	755.5	703.7	709.4	716.0	721.5	726.5	732.1	738.3	744.5	748.8	752.0	754.3	760.2
1970	790.0	766.5	789.1	798.7	805.8	761.8	766.2	771.5	791.2	787.4	788.6	793.7	798.7	803.7	802.6	804.3	810.6
1971	846.5	822.0	842.8	854.2	867.0	818.2	821.1	826.6	831.8	838.0	858.6	849.0	855.4	858.3	859.8	865.5	875.7
1972	925.3	894.7	908.3	931.3	966.1	885.5	896.7	902.0	907.7	912.7	904.5	922.4	933.4	939.7	956.2	968.0	974.2
1973	1023.7	989.1	1010.5	1034.3	1060.9	979.3	990.8	997.2	1003.4	1010.1	1017.9	1026.0	1033.8	1043.1	1051.9	1061.9	1068.9
1974	1131.8	1083.1	1119.1	1152.7	1172.4	1074.1	1082.8	1092.3	1103.9	1120.4	1133.0	1146.8	1151.9	1159.5	1170.3	1170.1	1176.7
1975	1229.1	1183.1	1212.3	1244.2	1276.6	1177.5	1183.5	1188.4	1194.7	1206.8	1235.3	1231.1	1246.0	1255.5	1267.5	1276.8	1285.6
1976	1359.3	1314.3	1340.6	1374.0	1408.4	1304.0	1316.6	1322.4	1332.4	1341.8	1347.5	1363.7	1374.7	1383.6	1392.5	1410.4	1422.3
1977	1506.5	1443.3	1483.4	1528.4	1570.9	1428.1	1443.4	1458.5	1470.4	1483.6	1496.3	1516.5	1526.7	1542.0	1557.9	1571.6	1583.3
1978	1689.7	1606.4	1660.6	1718.3	1773.5	1590.1	1604.6	1624.6	1646.6	1658.7	1676.4	1701.7	1718.3	1735.0	1756.6	1773.1	1791.0
1979	1899.3	1820.4	1861.9	1931.0	1983.9	1804.0	1819.0	1838.1	1847.8	1860.9	1876.9	1911.6	1932.1	1949.3	1966.7	1982.9	2002.2
1980	2119.5	2047.0	2076.6	2138.3	2215.6	2032.1	2045.0	2064.0	2066.4	2076.0	2087.3	2119.9	2136.4	2160.1	2190.7	2215.2	2240.9
1981	2377.0	2285.8	2337.9	2427.9	2456.6	2265.6	2284.1	2307.7	2320.4	2334.8	2358.6	2402.0	2430.1	2451.5	2452.4	2458.7	2458.7
1982	2527.6	2471.3	2516.8	2546.0	2576.5	2459.5	2472.4	2482.0	2499.9	2523.0	2527.4	2545.2	2543.1	2549.7	2564.5	2575.5	2589.4
1983	2674.9	2539.4	2663.3	2716.5	2780.2	2600.2	2599.7	2418.4	2637.5	2668.5	2683.8	2701.4	2711.8	2736.7	2761.8	2779.7	2799.2

Corporate profits after tax
billion dollars, annual rates

Adjusted - Corrigé

Bénéfices des sociétés après paiement des impôts
milliards de dollars, taux annuels

	Year	Q.1	Q.2	Q.3	Q.4	JAN	FEB	MAR	APR	MAY	JUN	JUL	AUG	SEP	OCT	NOV	DEC
1964	38.5	38.2	38.1	39.1	38.7												
1965	46.4	44.2	45.9	46.4	48.9												
1966	49.4	49.8	49.8	49.4	48.5												
1967	47.2	46.1	46.1	47.2	49.4												
1968	49.4	48.1	49.3	49.5	50.7												
1969	47.2	49.6	48.0	46.2	45.0												
1970	41.3	41.8	41.6	42.1	39.6												
1971	49.0	45.7	47.3	50.8	52.3												
1972	58.9	56.2	56.6	59.0	63.9												
1973	76.6	73.8	76.8	76.6	79.0												
1974	85.1	82.4	85.0	90.9	82.2												
1975	81.5	69.4	73.2	88.3	95.2												
1976	102.5	100.7	102.3	103.5	103.4												
1977	122.0	114.9	121.3	126.6	125.3												
1978	145.9	129.6	144.1	149.9	159.9												
1979	165.1	161.2	164.5	159.6	165.0												
1980	149.8	166.2	139.4	146.9	146.7												
1981	144.1	152.2	138.6	144.0	141.7												
1982	115.1	112.9	117.4	116.5	113.5												
1983	130.0	108.2	127.2	144.1	140.8												

UNITED STATES

Industrial production: total (1)
1980 = 100

Production industrielle : total (1)
1980 = 100

	Year	Q.1	Q.2	Q.3	Q.4	JAN	FEB	MAR	APR	MAY	JUN	JUL	AUG	SEP	OCT	NOV	DEC
1964	55.6	53.9	55.9	55.4	57.1	52.7	54.3	54.6	55.4	55.7	56.6	53.3	55.3	57.6	57.1	57.5	56.7
1965	61.1	59.1	61.2	60.9	63.2	57.7	59.2	60.4	60.4	60.9	62.4	59.0	60.8	62.9	64.3	63.3	62.2
1966	66.5	64.7	66.9	66.4	68.1	63.1	64.8	66.2	66.1	66.5	68.0	63.8	66.1	69.2	69.9	68.0	66.3
1967	68.0	67.2	67.9	67.3	69.8	66.7	67.4	67.4	67.8	67.1	68.6	64.2	67.8	69.9	70.3	70.1	69.0
1968	72.3	70.7	72.7	72.0	73.9	69.3	71.1	71.8	71.4	72.5	74.4	69.7	71.8	74.6	74.9	74.6	72.2
1969	75.6	74.7	76.0	75.7	76.1	73.0	75.1	75.9	75.2	75.2	77.6	73.0	75.9	78.3	78.3	76.2	73.7
1970	73.3	73.7	74.4	73.2	71.9	72.5	74.2	74.4	74.0	73.9	75.4	71.1	73.5	75.1	73.5	71.5	70.8
1971	74.6	73.3	75.0	74.3	75.7	71.8	74.4	73.9	74.0	74.5	76.5	71.7	74.0	77.2	77.5	75.9	73.8
1972	81.5	78.0	81.4	81.7	84.8	75.9	78.6	79.5	80.8	80.5	82.9	77.7	82.0	85.4	86.3	85.2	82.9
1973	88.3	86.1	88.7	88.8	89.6	83.5	87.1	87.6	87.5	88.2	90.5	86.0	88.6	91.7	92.0	90.4	86.2
1974	88.0	87.7	90.0	89.4	84.7	85.9	88.3	89.0	88.4	89.6	92.0	86.6	89.4	92.2	90.5	85.4	78.2
1975	80.1	76.3	78.5	82.0	83.7	76.1	76.9	76.1	76.9	77.4	81.1	77.9	82.6	85.7	85.3	84.2	81.5
1976	88.8	86.2	89.3	89.5	90.0	83.3	87.6	87.8	87.8	88.8	91.2	86.5	90.1	91.9	91.7	90.5	87.8
1977	94.0	91.0	94.8	94.9	95.3	88.4	91.6	92.9	93.3	94.1	97.0	92.0	95.0	97.6	97.9	95.5	92.4
1978	99.4	94.9	99.8	100.7	102.3	92.3	95.6	96.9	98.8	98.6	101.9	97.2	100.8	104.1	104.4	102.4	100.1
1979	103.8	103.0	104.5	104.0	103.5	99.9	103.9	105.1	102.9	104.0	106.7	101.4	103.9	106.9	106.3	103.7	100.5
1980	100.0	102.9	98.8	97.5	100.9	100.8	103.9	104.2	100.5	97.4	98.5	93.3	97.3	101.3	102.0	101.6	99.2
1981	102.7	102.2	104.4	104.8	99.3	99.6	103.2	103.9	103.1	103.8	106.5	102.7	105.7	106.0	103.7	99.6	94.6
1982	94.3	95.5	95.2	94.8	91.7	92.9	97.1	96.6	94.8	94.2	96.5	92.7	95.6	96.1	94.2	91.7	89.3
1983	100.4	93.5	98.8	104.0	105.3	90.8	94.0	95.6	96.5	97.9	101.8	100.0	104.3	107.8	107.8	105.2	103.0

Industrial production: manufacturing (1)
1980 = 100

Production industrielle : industries manufacturières (1)
1980 = 100

	Year	Q.1	Q.2	Q.3	Q.4	JAN	FEB	MAR	APR	MAY	JUN	JUL	AUG	SEP	OCT	NOV	DEC
1964	55.2	53.5	55.7	54.8	56.9	52.2	54.0	54.3	55.2	55.4	56.3	52.6	54.6	57.2	56.9	57.3	56.4
1965	61.2	59.1	61.4	60.7	63.4	57.3	59.2	60.6	60.6	61.2	62.5	58.8	60.5	62.9	64.6	63.5	62.2
1966	66.7	64.9	67.4	66.3	68.4	63.1	65.1	66.5	66.6	66.9	68.5	63.5	65.9	69.5	70.6	68.4	66.3
1967	68.2	67.3	68.2	67.1	70.1	66.6	67.6	67.6	68.0	67.5	69.0	63.7	67.6	70.1	70.8	70.6	68.9
1968	72.5	70.8	73.1	72.0	74.2	69.1	71.3	72.1	71.7	72.8	74.8	69.5	71.5	74.9	75.6	75.0	72.0
1969	75.6	74.8	76.3	75.6	75.9	72.7	75.3	76.3	75.7	75.5	77.7	72.6	75.6	78.5	78.7	76.1	73.0
1970	72.5	73.1	74.0	72.2	70.6	71.6	73.8	74.0	73.6	73.4	75.0	70.1	72.2	74.2	71.9	70.3	69.5
1971	73.8	72.0	74.4	73.3	75.4	70.4	72.7	73.1	73.3	74.0	75.9	70.6	72.8	76.6	77.6	75.7	72.8
1972	81.1	77.3	81.2	81.1	84.7	74.8	78.0	79.0	80.5	80.4	82.8	76.8	81.3	85.1	86.5	85.3	82.3
1973	88.5	86.1	89.3	88.7	90.0	83.0	87.2	88.1	88.1	88.8	91.1	85.6	88.3	92.0	92.7	91.1	86.1
1974	88.2	88.0	90.6	89.6	84.6	85.8	88.6	89.5	89.1	90.1	92.6	86.6	89.4	92.6	91.2	85.7	77.0
1975	79.3	74.9	77.7	81.2	83.3	74.5	75.5	74.7	75.9	76.8	80.4	76.6	81.6	85.5	85.4	84.0	80.6
1976	88.8	85.8	89.8	89.5	90.1	82.2	87.3	88.0	88.3	89.3	91.7	86.3	90.0	92.2	92.2	90.7	87.3
1977	94.3	90.8	95.6	95.1	95.9	87.5	91.5	93.4	94.0	94.9	97.8	91.8	95.2	98.3	98.9	96.3	92.6
1978	100.0	95.1	100.7	101.1	103.2	92.0	95.8	97.6	99.9	99.5	102.7	97.2	101.1	105.0	105.7	103.5	100.4
1979	104.7	103.6	106.1	104.3	104.4	99.9	104.5	106.4	104.2	105.6	108.4	102.0	104.4	108.1	107.8	104.7	100.6
1980	100.0	103.1	99.1	96.8	101.1	100.6	104.1	104.6	101.2	97.8	98.4	92.2	96.3	101.3	102.7	101.9	98.8
1981	102.5	101.8	105.1	104.4	98.8	98.7	102.7	104.0	103.9	104.6	106.8	101.9	105.2	106.0	103.9	99.3	93.4
1982	93.8	94.2	95.0	94.4	91.6	90.7	95.9	95.9	94.3	94.1	96.5	92.1	95.0	96.3	94.6	91.7	89.3
1983	101.1	93.5	99.9	104.6	106.3	89.8	94.1	96.5	97.5	99.1	103.1	100.1	104.6	109.1	109.5	106.4	103.0

Industrial production: durable goods (1)
1980 = 100

Production industrielle : biens durables (1)
1980 = 100

	Year	Q.1	Q.2	Q.3	Q.4	JAN	FEB	MAR	APR	MAY	JUN	JUL	AUG	SEP	OCT	NOV	DEC
1964	57.3	55.9	57.9	55.8	59.4	54.3	56.4	57.1	57.6	57.6	58.4	54.1	54.7	58.8	57.6	60.1	60.4
1965	65.1	62.8	65.7	63.7	68.1	60.6	63.0	64.9	64.8	65.4	66.8	62.7	62.5	66.0	68.4	68.0	67.9
1966	72.3	70.7	73.4	70.7	74.5	68.5	71.0	72.7	72.9	73.0	74.4	68.2	69.2	74.6	76.3	74.3	73.0
1967	73.2	73.2	73.6	70.7	75.2	72.6	73.5	73.5	73.5	73.2	74.1	67.9	70.5	73.7	74.5	75.8	75.3
1968	77.9	77.1	79.1	75.8	79.7	75.4	77.6	78.4	77.6	79.1	80.7	74.5	74.1	78.7	80.1	80.5	78.6
1969	80.9	81.1	82.0	79.5	80.9	79.1	81.4	82.8	81.8	81.1	83.3	76.7	78.7	83.0	83.5	80.9	78.2
1970	74.8	77.1	77.2	73.3	71.6	75.6	77.5	78.3	77.1	76.7	77.7	71.8	73.0	75.1	72.4	70.7	71.8
1971	74.9	74.5	76.4	72.7	76.1	72.6	75.2	75.6	75.4	76.3	77.4	70.6	71.3	76.3	77.8	76.3	74.0
1972	83.2	79.4	83.5	81.3	87.9	76.7	80.3	81.3	83.0	82.9	84.7	77.6	81.2	86.6	88.9	88.6	86.3
1973	93.0	90.9	94.1	92.0	94.9	87.6	92.2	93.0	92.9	93.5	95.9	89.8	90.3	95.9	97.0	96.2	91.5
1974	92.0	92.3	94.7	92.3	88.7	90.3	93.0	93.6	93.1	94.4	96.6	90.0	90.9	95.9	95.0	89.8	81.1
1975	80.0	77.7	79.0	80.3	82.9	77.7	78.1	77.5	78.1	78.3	80.5	76.2	80.0	84.6	84.5	83.3	81.0
1976	89.5	86.6	91.0	89.4	90.8	82.7	88.2	89.0	89.2	90.9	92.9	87.1	89.6	91.6	91.8	91.6	89.1
1977	95.1	91.7	96.7	94.3	97.3	88.5	92.3	94.4	95.3	96.1	98.8	92.4	93.7	98.3	99.6	97.4	94.8
1978	102.2	97.0	103.0	102.3	106.4	93.6	97.6	99.9	102.2	101.9	104.8	99.3	101.2	106.5	108.2	106.5	104.5
1979	107.1	107.5	109.1	105.5	106.3	103.9	108.4	110.2	107.0	109.1	111.3	104.0	103.7	108.9	109.1	106.4	103.3
1980	100.0	105.1	99.3	94.5	101.2	102.4	106.2	106.7	102.2	98.1	97.7	91.0	93.7	98.7	101.4	102.1	100.2
1981	102.8	102.9	106.1	103.5	98.5	99.8	103.4	105.4	104.9	105.9	107.5	102.1	103.9	104.7	102.9	98.7	93.9
1982	91.3	93.3	93.3	90.7	87.7	90.3	94.9	94.9	93.0	92.6	94.3	89.8	90.5	91.7	89.6	87.7	85.7
1983	98.4	90.7	97.1	100.7	105.1	87.2	91.1	93.7	94.9	96.4	99.9	96.9	100.0	105.3	106.7	105.2	103.4

Industrial production: total (1) — Adjusted - Corrigé — **Production industrielle : total (1)**

1980 = 100

	Year	Q.1	Q.2	Q.3	Q.4	JAN	FEB	MAR	APR	MAY	JUN	JUL	AUG	SEP	OCT	NOV	DEC
1964		54.0	55.2	56.1	56.9	53.7	54.1	54.1	55.0	55.3	55.4	55.8	56.2	56.4	55.6	57.3	58.0
1965		59.1	60.5	61.8	63.0	58.6	59.0	59.7	60.0	60.5	61.0	61.5	61.8	62.0	62.6	62.9	63.6
1966		64.8	66.2	67.2	67.8	64.2	64.6	65.5	65.7	66.3	66.6	66.9	67.0	67.6	68.1	67.6	67.8
1967		67.4	67.2	67.8	69.7	67.9	67.4	67.0	67.5	67.1	66.9	67.1	68.0	68.2	68.8	69.8	70.4
1968		70.9	72.0	72.7	73.6	70.5	71.0	71.2	71.4	72.2	72.5	72.5	72.9	72.9	73.1	73.9	73.9
1969		74.9	75.3	76.3	76.0	74.5	75.0	75.4	75.2	75.0	75.7	76.1	76.4	76.4	76.5	75.8	75.7
1970		74.1	73.7	73.5	72.0	74.2	74.0	74.0	73.9	73.7	73.5	73.7	73.7	73.2	71.7	71.3	72.9
1971		73.5	74.2	74.5	75.9	73.5	73.5	73.5	73.8	74.2	74.6	74.7	74.1	75.0	75.4	75.7	76.4
1972		78.6	80.4	82.0	84.7	78.0	78.4	79.3	80.1	80.3	80.8	81.2	82.1	82.9	84.0	84.6	85.6
1973		86.8	88.0	88.9	89.4	85.9	86.9	87.4	87.4	88.2	88.4	88.7	88.7	89.2	89.4	89.5	89.3
1974		88.3	89.1	89.6	84.7	88.4	88.2	88.4	88.4	89.3	89.7	89.7	89.6	89.7	88.1	85.0	81.2
1975		77.0	77.7	82.0	83.9	78.4	76.7	76.0	76.6	77.4	79.2	80.5	82.3	83.1	83.1	84.0	84.6
1976		86.8	88.4	89.5	90.1	85.8	87.1	87.6	87.8	88.5	88.9	89.3	89.8	89.3	89.3	90.2	90.9
1977		91.7	93.9	94.8	95.4	91.0	91.5	92.7	93.3	93.9	94.5	94.6	94.8	95.0	95.3	95.4	95.6
1978		95.8	98.7	100.6	102.5	95.2	95.4	96.7	98.2	98.5	99.4	100.1	100.7	101.1	101.8	102.5	103.3
1979		103.9	103.6	103.8	103.7	103.4	103.7	104.4	102.8	103.9	104.1	104.1	103.5	103.9	103.9	103.6	103.7
1980		103.8	98.3	96.3	101.2	104.1	104.0	103.5	100.8	97.8	96.2	95.4	96.7	98.2	99.7	101.5	102.3
1981		103.2	103.7	104.1	99.5	103.0	103.3	103.5	103.3	103.9	104.0	104.7	104.5	103.1	101.4	99.5	97.6
1982		96.4	94.8	94.0	92.0	95.7	97.2	96.4	95.4	94.7	94.4	94.4	94.2	93.4	92.3	91.8	92.0
1983		94.2	98.3	103.2	105.8	93.5	94.0	95.2	97.0	98.2	99.6	101.8	103.3	104.6	105.4	105.7	106.3

Industrial production: manufacturing (1) — Adjusted - Corrigé — **Production industrielle : industries manufacturières (1)**

1980 = 100

	Year	Q.1	Q.2	Q.3	Q.4	JAN	FEB	MAR	APR	MAY	JUN	JUL	AUG	SEP	OCT	NOV	DEC
1964		53.6	54.8	55.8	56.7	53.4	53.7	53.7	54.7	54.9	54.9	55.4	55.8	56.0	55.2	56.9	57.9
1965		59.1	60.5	61.9	63.0	58.6	59.0	59.7	60.1	60.5	60.9	61.8	61.8	62.0	62.5	62.8	63.7
1966		64.9	66.4	67.4	68.1	64.4	64.8	65.6	66.1	66.5	66.8	67.1	67.3	67.8	68.4	67.8	68.0
1967		67.5	67.4	67.9	69.8	68.0	67.4	67.0	67.6	67.1	67.3	67.1	68.2	68.3	68.9	70.0	70.6
1968		71.0	72.2	72.8	73.8	70.7	71.2	71.2	71.4	72.5	72.8	72.6	72.8	72.9	73.2	74.2	74.0
1969		75.1	75.4	76.4	75.8	74.6	75.1	75.5	75.4	75.1	75.7	76.3	76.4	76.4	76.4	75.7	75.4
1970		73.6	73.1	72.6	70.8	73.7	73.6	73.5	73.3	73.1	72.9	73.1	72.7	72.2	70.5	70.1	71.9
1971		72.5	73.4	73.7	75.4	72.5	72.5	72.4	72.8	73.5	73.8	73.9	73.0	74.2	75.1	75.3	75.9
1972		77.9	80.0	81.6	84.6	77.2	77.9	78.5	79.7	79.9	80.4	80.6	81.7	82.6	83.6	84.5	85.8
1973		86.7	88.4	89.1	89.9	85.7	87.0	87.5	87.5	88.3	88.5	89.0	88.9	89.4	89.7	90.0	89.9
1974		88.7	89.5	90.1	84.6	88.7	88.5	88.9	88.8	89.6	90.1	90.1	90.1	90.1	88.3	84.9	80.5
1975		75.8	76.6	81.4	83.6	77.3	75.5	74.5	75.6	76.2	78.1	79.8	81.6	82.8	82.6	83.6	84.4
1976		86.6	88.4	89.7	90.3	85.4	87.0	87.5	87.8	88.6	89.0	89.6	89.8	89.6	89.5	90.4	91.1
1977		91.8	94.1	95.3	96.2	91.1	91.4	92.9	93.4	94.1	94.8	95.1	95.2	95.5	96.0	96.1	96.5
1978		96.3	99.2	101.3	103.4	95.7	95.9	97.3	98.8	99.0	99.8	100.7	101.3	102.0	102.7	103.3	104.2
1979		104.9	104.6	104.3	104.6	104.3	104.7	105.6	103.5	105.0	105.1	105.3	104.2	104.9	104.8	104.5	104.4
1980		104.2	98.1	96.4	101.3	104.6	104.4	103.6	100.9	97.8	95.6	95.0	96.3	98.1	99.9	101.5	102.5
1981		103.1	103.9	104.0	98.8	103.0	103.1	103.3	103.6	104.2	103.9	104.4	104.4	103.0	100.9	98.8	96.8
1982		95.3	94.1	93.9	91.7	94.4	96.1	95.5	94.6	94.0	93.9	94.1	94.1	93.5	92.0	91.3	91.7
1983		94.4	99.0	104.2	105.7	93.2	94.2	95.7	97.6	98.9	100.5	102.7	104.2	105.7	106.5	106.6	107.0

Industrial production: durable goods (1) — Adjusted - Corrigé — **Production industrielle : biens durables (1)**

1980 = 100

	Year	Q.1	Q.2	Q.3	Q.4	JAN	FEB	MAR	APR	MAY	JUN	JUL	AUG	SEP	OCT	NOV	DEC
1964		55.5	56.7	58.0	59.0	55.2	55.5	55.7	56.5	56.7	56.8	57.5	57.9	58.5	56.7	59.5	60.9
1965		62.2	64.4	66.2	67.5	61.5	62.0	63.1	63.7	64.4	65.0	66.2	66.2	66.3	66.8	67.1	68.5
1966		70.1	72.1	73.1	74.0	69.4	69.9	71.0	71.8	72.1	72.4	72.7	72.9	73.7	74.7	73.4	73.8
1967		72.7	72.4	72.5	74.8	73.5	72.6	72.1	72.5	72.4	72.2	72.1	73.1	72.7	73.2	75.2	75.9
1968		76.6	77.8	78.0	79.1	76.4	76.8	76.6	76.9	78.1	78.4	78.2	77.9	77.8	78.3	79.4	79.6
1969		80.7	80.7	81.5	80.7	80.3	80.5	81.1	80.9	80.2	81.0	81.4	81.6	81.9	81.9	80.5	79.7
1970		76.8	75.8	75.0	71.7	77.0	76.7	76.7	76.2	75.8	75.4	75.5	75.4	74.2	71.0	70.6	73.4
1971		74.2	74.8	74.4	76.1	74.2	74.3	74.0	74.2	75.1	75.1	74.8	73.4	75.0	75.9	75.9	76.5
1972		79.2	81.7	83.9	87.8	78.3	79.2	80.0	81.4	81.7	82.2	82.6	83.8	85.2	86.6	87.8	89.1
1973		90.6	92.3	93.9	94.8	89.6	90.9	91.3	91.7	92.4	93.0	93.9	93.3	94.5	94.6	95.0	94.9
1974		92.2	93.2	94.2	88.5	92.4	91.9	92.2	92.2	93.3	94.0	94.0	94.1	94.4	92.6	89.0	83.9
1975		77.9	77.5	81.7	83.0	79.7	77.3	76.6	77.1	77.2	78.3	80.0	82.2	83.0	82.4	83.0	83.7
1976		86.6	89.3	90.9	91.1	85.2	86.9	87.7	88.2	89.6	90.0	90.9	91.5	90.1	89.7	91.2	92.4
1977		92.0	94.8	96.3	97.5	91.2	91.4	93.3	93.9	94.8	95.6	96.1	96.2	96.6	97.2	97.3	98.0
1978		97.4	101.1	103.8	105.5	96.6	96.8	98.8	100.7	100.9	101.7	103.2	103.7	104.5	105.8	106.4	107.4
1979		108.0	107.2	106.7	106.3	107.5	107.7	108.7	105.7	108.0	108.0	107.7	105.6	106.7	106.8	106.2	105.9
1980		105.5	98.0	95.3	101.2	105.9	105.6	105.0	101.3	97.5	95.0	94.2	95.0	96.6	99.3	101.8	102.6
1981		103.4	104.7	104.3	98.4	103.2	103.0	104.0	104.2	105.0	104.8	105.1	104.9	103.1	100.8	98.3	96.1
1982		93.8	92.3	91.3	87.7	93.0	94.6	93.8	92.7	92.3	91.8	92.1	91.4	90.3	88.0	87.3	87.7
1983		90.9	94.0	101.7	105.2	89.6	90.6	92.4	88.6	95.8	97.4	100.1	101.5	103.5	104.5	105.1	105.9

UNITED STATES

Industrial production: non-durable goods (1)
1980 = 100

Production industrielle : biens non durables (1)
1980 = 100

	Year	Q.1	Q.2	Q.3	Q.4	JAN	FEB	MAR	APR	MAY	JUN	JUL	AUG	SEP	OCT	NOV	DEC
1964	52.8	50.6	53.1	53.7	54.0	49.6	51.2	50.9	52.5	52.9	54.0	50.9	54.7	55.3	56.1	54.2	51.6
1965	56.4	54.5	56.3	57.1	57.7	53.4	54.7	55.4	55.5	55.9	57.4	54.0	58.1	59.2	60.0	58.0	55.2
1966	60.0	57.8	60.0	61.0	61.0	56.4	58.0	59.1	59.1	59.6	61.4	57.8	61.9	63.2	63.6	61.4	58.1
1967	62.0	60.0	61.5	62.8	63.8	59.2	60.3	60.4	61.4	60.4	62.7	58.6	64.0	65.8	66.3	64.1	61.1
1968	65.9	63.1	65.7	67.2	67.4	61.5	63.6	64.3	64.5	65.1	67.5	63.3	68.2	70.1	70.1	68.2	64.0
1969	69.2	66.9	69.2	70.7	69.9	65.0	67.7	68.2	68.2	68.6	71.0	67.6	71.7	73.0	72.8	70.2	66.6
1970	69.7	68.2	70.1	70.7	69.7	66.8	69.0	68.8	69.2	69.3	71.7	67.9	71.2	73.1	72.8	69.8	66.6
1971	72.3	69.0	71.9	74.0	74.5	67.5	69.5	69.9	70.7	71.0	74.0	70.4	74.6	76.9	77.4	74.9	71.2
1972	78.5	74.6	78.4	80.1	80.7	72.4	75.2	76.2	77.4	77.4	80.3	75.7	81.3	83.3	83.6	81.2	77.4
1973	83.0	80.2	83.4	84.5	83.9	77.2	81.1	82.2	82.1	83.0	85.1	80.4	85.9	87.2	87.5	84.7	79.4
1974	83.5	82.6	85.6	86.2	79.7	80.3	83.1	84.4	84.1	84.9	87.8	82.5	87.5	88.7	86.5	80.6	72.0
1975	78.4	71.4	76.1	82.3	83.9	70.6	72.2	71.3	73.3	74.8	80.2	77.2	83.4	86.4	86.5	84.7	80.3
1976	88.0	85.0	88.2	89.5	89.1	81.6	86.4	86.9	87.2	87.3	90.1	85.2	90.4	93.0	92.8	89.6	85.0
1977	93.4	89.6	94.1	95.4	94.3	86.3	90.5	92.2	92.5	93.4	96.5	91.1	97.0	98.3	98.0	95.0	89.8
1978	97.4	92.7	97.9	99.5	99.3	89.8	93.6	94.7	96.9	96.5	100.2	94.6	101.0	103.2	102.6	99.8	95.4
1979	101.8	98.8	102.3	104.0	102.0	95.0	99.6	101.7	100.8	101.4	104.7	99.6	105.2	107.1	106.1	102.6	97.3
1980	100.0	100.6	98.8	99.6	101.0	98.2	101.5	102.2	99.8	97.3	99.3	93.7	100.6	104.4	104.3	101.7	97.1
1981	102.2	100.5	103.8	105.4	99.2	97.3	101.9	102.2	102.5	103.0	105.8	101.7	106.8	107.6	105.0	99.9	92.7
1982	96.9	95.2	97.0	99.0	96.3	91.3	97.2	97.2	96.0	95.8	99.2	94.9	100.4	101.8	100.7	96.6	91.5
1983	104.3	96.8	103.4	109.3	107.7	93.0	97.7	99.8	100.7	102.4	107.1	104.0	110.2	113.7	113.0	107.9	102.4

Industrial production: investment goods (1)
(including defence)
1980 = 100

Production industrielle : biens d'équipement (1)
(y compris ceux pour la défense nationale)
1980 = 100

	Year	Q.1	Q.2	Q.3	Q.4	JAN	FEB	MAR	APR	MAY	JUN	JUL	AUG	SEP	OCT	NOV	DEC
1964	49.2	48.4	49.2	48.3	50.8	47.9	48.4	48.9	49.2	49.0	49.6	47.6	47.6	49.7	49.8	50.9	51.7
1965	55.6	52.8	55.1	55.4	59.2	51.4	53.0	53.9	54.0	54.8	56.3	54.6	54.5	57.2	58.4	59.0	60.1
1966	64.8	61.9	64.4	65.0	67.8	60.7	61.9	63.2	63.2	64.1	65.8	64.1	63.9	66.9	67.8	67.4	68.1
1967	68.9	68.4	68.7	67.8	70.6	67.6	68.7	68.9	68.5	68.4	69.3	66.2	67.4	69.7	69.8	71.0	71.1
1968	73.4	72.5	73.3	73.2	74.5	71.2	72.9	73.3	72.0	73.1	74.7	71.8	72.5	75.2	74.9	74.7	73.9
1969	75.3	75.0	75.9	75.3	75.0	74.2	74.9	75.9	75.6	75.1	76.9	74.7	74.2	77.1	76.9	74.7	73.4
1970	69.0	71.8	70.2	67.9	66.0	71.4	72.3	71.8	70.5	69.6	70.5	67.7	67.4	68.5	66.7	65.8	65.4
1971	65.2	64.7	64.7	64.9	66.5	64.2	65.2	64.7	64.1	64.1	65.8	63.3	64.2	67.2	67.3	66.6	65.6
1972	71.5	68.4	70.9	71.7	75.0	66.7	69.0	69.6	70.0	70.2	72.7	69.4	71.1	74.6	75.1	75.6	74.3
1973	78.9	76.5	78.4	79.3	81.3	74.8	77.6	77.0	77.1	77.8	80.2	77.8	78.4	81.8	82.1	82.0	79.8
1974	82.7	80.8	83.0	83.8	83.2	79.2	81.5	81.6	81.3	82.8	84.9	82.4	82.1	86.8	85.5	84.2	79.8
1975	75.9	75.8	75.3	76.3	76.3	76.4	76.2	74.9	74.3	74.7	77.0	74.5	75.6	78.7	76.9	76.4	75.6
1976	78.9	77.3	78.2	79.5	80.8	75.5	78.4	78.1	77.0	77.6	80.0	78.4	78.9	81.1	80.2	81.4	80.7
1977	84.7	81.7	84.7	86.1	86.3	80.2	82.6	82.4	83.3	83.9	86.9	84.4	85.2	88.8	87.1	86.3	85.6
1978	91.4	87.0	90.6	93.2	95.1	84.8	87.2	88.9	89.3	89.4	93.0	91.1	92.4	96.0	95.8	95.2	94.2
1979	98.0	96.3	97.3	98.5	99.7	94.0	97.0	97.9	95.3	97.0	99.5	96.6	97.0	101.7	100.6	99.9	98.7
1980	100.0	100.3	99.3	99.2	101.3	98.1	101.7	101.1	99.1	98.5	100.3	97.5	98.5	101.5	101.3	101.5	101.2
1981	104.6	102.1	104.7	106.5	104.9	100.1	102.9	103.2	102.7	104.0	107.4	105.6	106.1	108.1	106.3	104.8	103.7
1982	96.3	100.3	96.7	95.0	93.1	99.0	101.7	100.3	97.0	95.8	97.1	94.6	95.0	95.5	93.3	93.0	93.0
1983	97.0	91.4	94.1	99.4	103.0	91.0	91.3	91.9	92.2	93.1	96.9	96.9	98.6	102.8	102.8	103.0	103.2

Industrial production: consumer goods (1)
1980 = 100

Production industrielle : biens de consommation (1)
1980 = 100

	Year	Q.1	Q.2	Q.3	Q.4	JAN	FEB	MAR	APR	MAY	JUN	JUL	AUG	SEP	OCT	NOV	DEC
1964	59.1	57.4	59.3	59.3	60.2	56.6	58.3	57.3	58.8	58.7	60.5	57.0	58.8	62.0	61.0	60.6	59.1
1965	63.7	62.5	63.5	63.1	65.6	61.2	62.8	63.6	62.6	62.7	65.1	60.9	62.4	66.0	68.2	65.9	62.8
1966	67.0	65.9	66.9	66.5	68.5	64.5	66.4	66.9	66.3	65.8	68.6	63.3	65.5	70.6	71.8	68.6	65.0
1967	68.8	67.0	68.6	68.5	71.0	66.4	67.1	67.4	68.4	67.0	70.4	64.3	68.2	73.1	73.0	71.1	68.9
1968	72.9	70.8	72.7	72.9	75.1	69.1	71.3	72.1	70.9	71.7	75.5	69.4	71.5	77.9	78.1	75.9	71.2
1969	75.5	74.7	75.2	76.5	75.6	72.9	75.3	75.9	74.1	73.7	77.9	72.3	76.5	80.8	79.9	75.5	71.6
1970	75.0	73.8	76.2	76.0	73.9	71.9	74.6	74.7	74.6	75.2	78.8	73.2	75.7	79.3	76.9	72.8	71.9
1971	78.9	76.2	78.5	80.1	80.6	74.8	76.9	77.0	77.0	77.4	81.1	75.9	79.9	84.7	84.7	81.1	76.1
1972	85.6	81.8	85.7	86.6	88.2	79.7	82.7	82.9	85.1	83.9	88.0	80.4	87.1	92.4	92.3	88.5	83.7
1973	90.5	88.7	91.1	91.8	90.2	85.8	89.8	90.5	89.6	90.1	93.7	87.6	90.7	97.0	96.2	91.6	82.8
1974	88.6	87.0	90.3	91.6	85.7	85.0	87.4	88.6	88.1	89.1	93.7	87.2	91.9	95.6	93.6	86.6	77.0
1975	85.3	78.7	84.1	89.5	88.9	77.2	79.5	79.4	81.6	82.2	88.6	84.2	90.0	94.4	92.8	89.7	84.3
1976	94.3	91.3	94.8	95.8	95.3	88.1	93.3	92.6	92.7	94.0	97.7	91.0	96.6	99.7	99.3	95.7	90.9
1977	100.0	96.9	100.6	102.0	100.3	94.1	97.8	98.9	98.6	99.0	104.3	97.7	101.9	106.4	106.3	100.3	94.4
1978	102.5	98.7	103.3	104.8	103.4	95.1	99.9	101.0	103.2	101.0	105.8	99.1	104.9	110.4	108.9	103.4	97.9
1979	103.7	103.5	104.6	105.0	101.9	99.9	104.6	105.9	102.1	103.7	108.1	100.7	104.3	109.9	107.6	102.0	96.0
1980	100.0	100.5	98.2	100.9	100.4	97.6	101.5	102.3	98.5	95.9	100.3	95.1	101.4	106.0	104.9	101.4	95.0
1981	101.7	99.9	103.2	105.1	98.5	96.8	101.1	101.9	101.2	102.1	106.2	101.6	106.4	107.4	104.9	98.6	92.4
1982	98.1	95.4	98.4	101.7	96.9	92.2	96.9	97.0	96.4	97.0	101.9	98.6	102.8	103.9	101.6	96.6	92.4
1983	104.4	97.3	103.1	110.0	107.1	94.8	97.9	99.1	100.1	101.7	107.6	104.8	110.5	114.5	112.5	106.6	102.3

Industrial production: non-durable goods (1) / Production industrielle : biens non durables (1)

1980 = 100

Adjusted - Corrigé

Year	Q.1	Q.2	Q.3	Q.4	JAN	FEB	MAR	APR	MAY	JUN	JUL	AUG	SEP	OCT	NOV	DEC
1964	51.4	52.7	53.3	54.0	51.3	51.6	51.4	52.5	52.9	52.7	53.2	53.4	53.4	53.7	53.9	54.4
1965	55.4	55.9	56.6	57.7	55.2	55.3	55.7	55.6	55.9	56.1	56.4	56.6	56.9	57.3	57.6	58.0
1966	58.8	59.6	60.5	60.9	58.4	58.6	59.4	59.1	59.8	59.9	60.4	60.5	60.6	60.7	60.9	61.0
1967	61.0	61.2	62.0	63.7	61.3	61.0	60.7	61.7	60.7	61.2	60.9	62.2	62.9	63.4	63.7	64.1
1968	64.3	65.4	66.4	67.2	63.8	64.3	64.7	64.8	65.5	65.9	65.7	66.5	66.9	67.1	67.6	67.0
1969	68.2	68.9	69.8	69.8	67.6	68.4	68.7	68.6	68.9	69.2	70.0	69.9	69.7	69.7	69.7	70.0
1970	69.6	69.7	69.7	69.7	69.6	69.9	69.4	69.6	69.7	69.7	70.2	69.3	69.7	69.7	69.4	70.0
1971	70.4	71.5	72.9	74.6	70.5	70.4	70.4	71.1	71.4	72.0	72.7	72.6	73.3	74.1	74.5	75.0
1972	76.2	77.8	78.9	80.8	75.7	76.1	76.7	77.6	77.6	78.1	78.2	79.1	79.4	80.0	80.6	81.7
1973	81.9	82.9	83.2	83.8	80.8	82.1	82.7	82.4	83.4	82.8	83.0	83.4	83.1	83.8	83.8	83.9
1974	84.4	85.1	85.0	79.7	84.1	84.2	84.9	84.7	85.3	85.4	85.2	85.1	84.6	82.9	80.0	76.4
1975	73.3	75.5	81.0	84.1	74.3	73.5	72.0	73.7	74.9	77.9	79.5	81.0	82.4	82.9	84.5	84.9
1976	86.6	87.4	88.2	89.4	85.6	87.0	87.2	87.4	87.1	87.6	87.8	87.7	89.0	89.3	89.3	89.6
1977	91.6	93.3	94.0	94.5	90.9	91.4	92.5	92.7	93.4	93.7	93.9	94.0	94.1	94.5	94.5	94.5
1978	94.9	96.8	98.2	99.6	94.5	94.9	95.4	96.5	96.7	97.4	97.5	98.3	98.8	99.0	99.5	100.3
1979	101.0	101.3	102.4	102.4	100.3	101.1	101.7	100.9	101.5	101.6	102.2	102.5	102.6	102.2	102.4	102.5
1980	102.6	98.2	97.9	101.3	103.0	102.9	101.9	100.3	98.1	96.2	95.9	97.8	99.9	100.6	101.1	102.4
1981	102.8	103.0	103.5	99.4	102.7	103.1	102.5	102.9	103.2	102.9	103.7	103.8	102.9	101.0	99.4	97.6
1982	97.2	96.4	97.0	96.6	96.2	97.9	97.6	96.8	96.2	96.3	96.6	97.3	97.2	96.9	96.3	96.5
1983	98.6	102.7	107.1	108.4	97.6	98.6	99.6	101.3	102.6	104.1	105.8	107.3	108.3	108.9	108.1	108.2

Industrial production: investment goods (1) / Production industrielle : biens d'équipement (1)

(including defence) / (y compris ceux pour la défense nationale)

1980 = 100

Adjusted - Corrigé

Year	Q.1	Q.2	Q.3	Q.4	JAN	FEB	MAR	APR	MAY	JUN	JUL	AUG	SEP	OCT	NOV	DEC
1964	48.0	48.8	49.3	50.6	48.1	47.8	48.1	48.8	48.8	48.8	49.1	49.2	49.6	49.5	50.8	51.5
1965	52.3	54.6	56.6	58.8	51.6	52.3	53.1	53.7	54.6	55.3	56.2	56.5	57.2	57.9	58.8	59.8
1966	61.5	63.8	66.3	67.4	61.0	61.3	62.3	63.0	63.9	64.7	65.6	66.2	66.9	67.2	67.1	67.9
1967	68.3	68.5	68.3	70.3	68.2	68.3	68.3	68.7	68.7	68.3	67.6	68.6	68.9	68.9	70.7	71.4
1968	72.4	73.1	73.8	74.1	71.9	72.5	72.7	72.2	73.4	73.7	73.1	74.0	74.2	74.0	74.2	74.2
1969	75.0	75.7	75.9	74.5	75.0	74.6	75.4	75.8	75.6	75.7	76.1	75.7	75.9	75.8	74.1	73.8
1970	71.9	70.0	68.2	65.7	72.4	72.0	71.4	70.8	70.0	69.3	69.0	68.3	67.3	65.6	65.4	66.0
1971	64.9	64.4	65.3	66.2	65.1	64.9	64.5	64.4	64.5	64.4	64.9	65.1	65.8	66.1	66.1	66.5
1972	68.6	70.7	71.9	74.6	67.6	68.6	69.7	70.2	70.6	71.3	70.9	72.0	72.7	73.7	74.8	75.4
1973	76.8	78.3	79.5	80.7	76.2	77.3	77.1	77.7	78.2	78.9	79.2	79.4	80.0	80.4	80.5	81.0
1974	81.0	82.8	84.0	82.7	80.5	81.1	81.5	81.8	83.3	83.2	83.9	83.7	84.6	83.9	83.1	81.1
1975	76.1	75.2	76.4	76.1	77.6	75.8	74.8	74.9	75.2	75.6	75.8	76.7	76.7	75.8	75.8	76.8
1976	77.7	78.1	79.3	80.4	77.2	78.0	78.0	77.8	78.1	78.4	79.3	79.6	79.0	79.0	80.8	81.5
1977	82.4	84.6	85.9	86.0	82.1	82.4	82.6	84.1	84.5	85.1	85.4	85.8	86.4	85.5	85.7	86.7
1978	87.7	90.5	93.0	94.7	86.9	87.1	89.1	90.0	90.2	91.1	92.3	93.2	93.6	94.1	94.4	95.5
1979	97.0	97.3	98.2	99.4	96.4	96.8	97.7	96.5	97.7	97.6	97.9	97.7	99.0	98.9	99.3	100.0
1980	101.0	99.3	98.7	101.0	100.6	101.3	101.1	100.4	99.2	98.4	98.4	99.0	98.9	99.7	100.9	102.5
1981	102.8	104.8	105.3	104.6	102.7	102.4	103.3	104.3	104.8	105.4	106.1	106.1	105.3	104.8	104.3	104.8
1982	101.1	96.9	94.2	92.8	101.4	101.5	100.5	98.8	96.7	95.3	95.0	94.6	93.1	92.3	92.4	93.7
1983	92.2	94.3	98.5	102.7	93.2	91.4	92.2	93.8	94.0	95.2	97.1	98.6	99.8	101.2	102.7	104.2

Industrial production: consumer goods (1) / Production industrielle : biens de consommation (1)

1980 = 100

Adjusted - Corrigé

Year	Q.1	Q.2	Q.3	Q.4	JAN	FEB	MAR	APR	MAY	JUN	JUL	AUG	SEP	OCT	NOV	DEC
1964	57.6	59.1	59.7	59.9	57.8	57.6	57.4	58.8	59.3	59.2	60.0	59.9	59.2	58.1	60.3	61.5
1965	62.7	63.2	63.8	65.1	62.4	62.5	63.1	62.9	63.3	63.5	63.5	63.4	64.4	64.7	65.1	65.4
1966	66.1	66.7	66.8	68.0	65.8	66.0	66.4	66.6	66.6	66.9	66.9	66.6	66.9	68.2	67.9	67.7
1967	67.9	68.1	68.4	70.8	68.1	67.7	68.0	68.3	68.1	68.0	67.8	68.6	68.8	69.8	70.9	71.5
1968	71.5	72.3	73.2	74.5	71.1	71.6	71.7	71.9	72.4	72.7	72.6	73.5	73.7	74.1	74.9	74.5
1969	75.4	74.9	76.3	75.5	74.9	75.5	75.7	75.0	74.4	75.2	76.3	76.6	76.0	76.1	75.2	75.3
1970	74.7	75.7	75.2	74.2	74.3	74.8	75.0	75.4	75.7	75.9	76.0	75.1	74.6	73.5	73.1	76.0
1971	77.2	78.0	79.4	81.1	77.2	77.1	77.2	77.7	77.9	78.3	79.4	79.2	79.6	80.5	81.1	81.7
1972	83.0	84.5	86.1	88.6	82.4	82.9	83.6	84.3	84.6	84.7	85.3	86.3	86.8	87.7	88.3	89.7
1973	89.7	90.4	90.4	90.8	89.1	89.8	90.4	90.2	90.9	90.2	90.4	89.6	91.4	91.5	91.1	89.8
1974	88.2	89.7	90.4	86.4	88.2	87.9	88.4	89.1	89.6	90.2	90.2	90.9	90.2	89.2	86.8	83.2
1975	80.3	83.4	87.8	89.9	80.5	79.9	80.5	81.8	82.8	85.5	87.1	87.7	88.7	88.5	90.2	91.0
1976	92.5	94.2	94.5	95.9	91.5	92.9	93.2	93.7	94.3	94.6	94.6	94.8	94.1	94.6	95.9	97.3
1977	98.1	100.0	100.3	100.9	97.3	97.7	99.4	99.5	99.9	100.6	101.0	100.8	100.7	101.2	100.8	100.6
1978	99.9	102.7	103.4	104.1	98.5	99.9	101.4	102.8	102.5	102.7	103.0	103.6	103.7	104.0	104.1	104.2
1979	104.7	104.0	103.1	102.6	104.1	104.4	105.5	102.7	104.7	104.6	104.0	102.3	103.2	103.2	102.5	102.2
1980	101.8	98.4	98.5	101.2	101.7	101.9	101.8	99.9	97.7	97.5	97.7	98.3	99.4	100.6	101.9	101.2
1981	101.6	103.1	102.7	99.2	101.0	101.7	102.0	102.4	103.7	103.4	103.7	102.9	101.7	100.8	99.0	97.7
1982	97.0	98.7	99.3	97.6	96.0	97.5	97.3	97.7	98.8	99.6	100.3	99.1	98.6	97.8	97.2	97.7
1983	98.9	103.3	107.4	107.8	98.8	98.6	99.2	101.6	103.4	104.8	106.5	107.5	108.2	107.9	107.4	108.2

UNITED STATES

Industrial production: intermediate goods (1)(2)

1980 = 100

Production industrielle : biens intermédiaires (1)(2)

1980 = 100

	Year	Q.1	Q.2	Q.3	Q.4	JAN	FEB	MAR	APR	MAY	JUN	JUL	AUG	SEP	OCT	NOV	DEC
1964	56.0	53.0	57.1	57.2	56.6	51.0	53.3	54.7	56.2	57.0	58.2	56.0	56.8	58.8	58.3	57.0	54.5
1965	59.7	56.3	59.9	61.4	61.2	54.1	56.4	58.3	58.7	59.7	61.3	59.4	62.0	62.7	62.8	61.2	59.6
1966	63.3	60.5	64.3	65.1	63.4	58.5	60.4	62.5	63.2	64.1	65.7	63.5	65.3	66.6	65.8	63.6	60.9
1967	65.9	62.6	65.9	67.5	67.5	61.1	62.6	64.2	65.3	65.4	66.9	64.3	68.5	70.1	70.2	67.7	64.4
1968	70.0	66.2	70.3	71.8	71.7	63.9	66.6	68.1	69.3	70.1	71.7	69.1	72.8	73.5	73.3	72.4	69.4
1969	74.3	71.2	75.0	75.8	75.3	68.7	71.7	73.2	73.9	74.5	76.6	73.3	76.4	77.9	78.0	75.5	72.3
1970	74.3	71.3	75.3	76.3	74.3	69.3	71.5	73.1	74.8	74.7	76.4	74.2	76.7	78.0	77.2	74.5	71.2
1971	76.9	72.6	77.1	79.2	78.6	69.9	73.6	74.3	76.1	76.6	78.7	77.4	78.7	81.4	81.4	78.9	75.4
1972	83.3	78.0	83.1	85.4	86.7	74.9	78.5	80.5	82.1	82.4	84.8	82.0	85.9	88.4	89.3	87.6	83.2
1973	90.3	85.7	91.4	92.7	91.6	81.4	86.6	88.9	89.8	91.1	93.2	90.3	93.1	94.7	94.3	92.8	87.8
1974	89.1	87.7	92.4	92.1	84.0	85.1	88.4	89.7	91.8	91.4	94.0	89.7	93.1	93.5	90.3	85.0	76.8
1975	81.0	74.8	79.1	85.1	85.0	73.3	75.6	75.4	77.2	78.3	81.9	81.4	86.1	87.8	87.4	85.9	81.7
1976	90.3	85.7	90.6	93.2	91.7	82.4	87.0	87.8	89.3	89.9	92.6	90.6	93.5	95.5	94.5	92.2	88.4
1977	95.5	90.0	95.5	98.8	97.7	87.6	90.3	92.2	93.4	95.1	98.2	95.5	99.9	101.1	100.7	98.1	94.3
1978	101.5	95.9	101.7	104.5	103.8	93.1	96.5	98.0	99.9	100.7	104.5	101.6	105.3	106.7	106.3	104.1	101.1
1979	105.7	102.9	106.7	108.1	105.2	99.4	103.9	105.3	105.2	105.8	109.0	105.0	109.4	109.7	109.0	105.6	100.9
1980	100.0	101.7	97.0	100.1	101.1	99.6	102.4	103.1	98.2	95.5	97.4	95.3	101.3	103.8	103.6	101.1	98.6
1981	101.6	100.4	103.3	105.4	97.4	97.5	101.5	102.1	102.2	102.6	105.1	103.3	106.7	106.3	102.6	97.8	91.7
1982	94.3	92.8	94.5	97.3	92.8	89.7	94.3	94.3	93.6	93.6	96.3	94.5	98.5	98.8	95.7	93.2	89.6
1983	103.1	93.4	100.9	109.5	108.6	90.0	93.8	96.3	98.1	99.8	104.8	104.6	110.7	113.4	112.2	108.8	104.8

Industrial production: raw materials (1)

1980 = 100

Production industrielle : matières premières (1)

1980 = 100

	Year	Q.1	Q.2	Q.3	Q.4	JAN	FEB	MAR	APR	MAY	JUN	JUL	AUG	SEP	OCT	NOV	DEC
1964	56.1	54.5	56.4	55.5	58.2	53.1	54.9	55.4	56.0	56.5	56.8	52.5	55.9	58.0	57.6	58.7	58.4
1965	62.6	60.9	63.3	61.9	64.3	59.6	60.8	62.3	62.9	63.1	63.8	59.8	62.5	63.5	65.0	64.2	63.8
1966	68.2	66.8	69.0	67.4	69.6	64.9	66.9	68.5	68.3	69.2	69.7	64.0	68.0	70.2	71.1	69.4	68.2
1967	67.7	68.2	67.5	65.9	69.4	68.4	68.6	67.6	67.8	67.2	67.6	62.9	67.3	67.4	69.0	69.9	69.4
1968	72.2	71.3	73.2	70.8	73.4	70.1	71.6	72.0	72.1	73.4	74.2	69.1	71.2	72.2	73.1	74.2	73.0
1969	76.2	75.6	76.9	75.3	77.1	73.9	76.2	76.8	76.4	76.4	77.9	72.5	76.1	77.2	78.1	77.5	75.7
1970	74.0	75.4	75.0	72.8	72.7	74.4	75.9	76.0	75.0	74.8	75.1	70.3	73.8	74.5	73.1	72.3	72.6
1971	75.4	75.3	77.1	73.3	76.0	74.1	75.7	76.2	76.1	77.1	78.0	71.0	73.2	75.5	76.3	75.9	75.7
1972	82.9	80.0	83.0	81.9	86.6	77.9	80.6	81.6	82.6	82.7	83.6	78.5	82.5	84.8	86.7	86.8	86.3
1973	90.7	89.2	91.2	90.1	92.4	86.7	90.3	90.5	90.5	90.9	92.3	87.5	90.7	92.0	93.2	92.9	91.1
1974	89.6	91.7	92.0	89.8	84.9	90.1	92.3	92.6	91.0	92.6	92.4	87.3	90.0	91.9	91.0	85.3	78.5
1975	78.3	75.4	75.8	78.6	83.2	76.0	75.8	74.5	74.7	75.1	77.6	74.0	79.6	82.3	83.7	83.7	82.2
1976	89.2	87.2	90.5	89.0	90.3	84.0	88.4	89.3	89.2	90.4	91.8	86.1	90.1	90.7	91.1	90.7	89.0
1977	93.9	91.7	95.5	93.0	95.3	88.8	92.2	94.2	94.4	95.4	96.5	90.8	93.4	94.8	96.4	95.9	93.6
1978	100.5	95.9	101.1	100.3	104.5	93.8	96.4	97.5	100.1	100.6	102.6	97.4	100.7	102.8	104.9	104.7	104.0
1979	106.0	105.9	107.3	104.3	105.9	103.1	106.7	107.9	106.4	107.0	108.6	102.9	105.1	106.3	107.3	106.1	104.3
1980	100.0	106.3	99.5	93.3	101.0	104.5	107.1	107.3	103.3	98.4	96.8	89.2	93.6	97.0	99.8	101.8	101.4
1981	102.7	104.5	105.4	103.4	97.5	101.9	105.3	106.2	104.7	105.1	106.5	101.8	104.5	103.8	101.7	98.1	92.6
1982	90.6	94.1	92.3	88.8	87.0	91.5	95.9	95.1	93.0	91.7	92.3	86.9	89.8	89.8	89.0	87.1	85.0
1983	98.4	91.8	97.3	100.2	104.3	88.2	92.6	94.7	95.5	97.0	99.3	96.5	100.6	103.6	105.4	104.3	103.1

Industrial production: construction (1)

1980 = 100

Adjusted - Corrigé

Production industrielle : construction (1)

1980 = 100

	Year	Q.1	Q.2	Q.3	Q.4	JAN	FEB	MAR	APR	MAY	JUN	JUL	AUG	SEP	OCT	NOV	DEC
1964	62.7	61.7	62.6	63.0	63.4	60.6	62.1	62.4	62.6	62.9	62.4	63.6	63.0	62.5	62.7	64.2	63.4
1965	66.6	65.1	65.6	67.0	68.5	63.8	65.5	66.0	65.1	65.8	65.8	67.7	67.0	66.4	67.4	68.4	69.9
1966	69.4	69.8	70.3	69.1	68.4	69.7	69.1	70.4	70.4	70.8	69.8	70.4	68.4	68.4	68.5	68.5	68.4
1967	70.9	69.1	70.3	71.7	72.4	69.5	68.6	69.2	69.7	70.5	70.6	70.8	71.8	72.6	71.9	72.6	72.6
1968	75.5	73.8	75.1	76.1	77.1	73.2	73.8	74.5	74.5	75.3	75.5	76.3	76.5	75.4	75.5	77.3	78.4
1969	79.6	79.8	79.2	78.9	80.3	79.2	80.0	80.3	79.2	79.2	79.4	78.5	78.9	79.4	80.1	80.4	80.3
1970	78.7	77.1	78.6	79.8	79.1	77.3	76.5	77.4	78.9	78.5	78.5	79.6	80.1	79.7	79.1	78.4	79.8
1971	82.8	80.2	82.1	83.8	84.9	79.7	80.4	80.4	81.2	82.1	83.1	84.4	82.8	84.2	84.8	84.2	85.8
1972	90.9	87.5	89.5	91.9	94.9	86.9	87.2	88.3	89.3	89.2	89.9	91.1	91.6	92.9	94.7	95.6	94.3
1973	99.1	97.4	98.9	99.5	100.4	95.2	97.9	99.0	98.2	99.2	99.4	99.1	99.5	100.1	100.0	100.1	101.1
1974	95.3	99.1	98.7	96.6	86.9	99.8	98.8	98.6	99.1	98.9	98.0	96.9	98.0	95.0	91.8	87.1	81.7
1975	82.5	78.4	78.9	85.1	87.4	79.0	78.8	77.5	78.1	78.9	79.8	82.8	86.0	86.7	85.9	87.2	87.9
1976	93.9	91.4	93.4	95.2	95.6	90.1	92.3	91.9	92.5	93.6	94.2	94.9	95.6	95.0	95.4	95.8	95.6
1977	99.6	95.8	98.1	101.1	103.5	95.5	95.4	96.6	97.1	98.3	98.8	99.9	101.5	102.0	102.8	103.3	104.5
1978	107.6	104.5	106.4	108.6	110.8	105.1	104.4	104.1	105.5	106.2	107.4	108.0	109.0	108.8	109.5	110.6	112.2
1979	112.0	113.0	111.7	112.1	111.3	113.1	113.0	113.0	111.3	111.7	112.0	111.9	112.5	111.8	111.9	111.5	110.3
1980	100.0	109.6	94.5	94.7	101.2	111.0	109.4	108.3	98.8	93.5	91.2	91.0	95.0	98.1	99.6	101.1	102.9
1981	100.6	105.4	103.4	101.1	92.7	105.2	105.5	105.6	104.8	103.8	101.6	102.3	102.0	99.0	95.8	92.2	90.0
1982	88.1	89.1	87.1	89.0	87.1	88.0	90.4	89.0	87.6	86.6	87.2	87.9	90.1	88.9	86.8	87.4	87.2
1983	100.9	92.1	98.5	105.4	107.5	90.0	91.9	94.3	96.7	98.1	100.7	103.3	105.6	107.3	107.9	107.4	107.3

Industrial production: intermediate goods (1)(2) / Production industrielle : biens intermédiaires (1)(2)

Adjusted - Corrigé

1980 = 100

	Year	Q.1	Q.2	Q.3	Q.4	JAN	FEB	MAR	APR	MAY	JUN	JUL	AUG	SEP	OCT	NOV	DEC
1964		55.0	56.2	56.4	56.8	54.4	55.2	55.4	56.0	56.3	56.2	56.8	56.3	56.2	56.3	57.1	57.1
1965		58.3	59.0	60.0	61.4	57.5	58.3	58.9	58.5	59.1	59.3	60.0	60.1	59.8	60.6	61.2	62.3
1966		62.7	63.4	63.7	63.6	62.3	62.4	63.3	63.0	63.6	63.6	64.3	63.3	63.5	63.5	63.7	63.6
1967		64.7	65.4	66.4	67.2	64.9	64.4	64.8	65.2	65.0	65.0	65.3	66.5	67.2	67.0	67.3	67.4
1968		68.4	69.5	70.4	71.7	67.9	68.4	68.8	69.1	69.6	69.8	70.1	70.7	70.4	70.6	71.9	72.6
1969		73.5	74.1	74.4	75.2	73.0	73.5	73.9	73.7	74.1	74.5	74.1	74.4	74.6	75.1	75.0	75.6
1970		73.8	74.4	74.3	74.3	74.0	73.4	73.9	74.5	74.3	74.3	75.0	74.8	74.7	74.3	74.0	74.5
1971		75.0	76.1	77.7	78.6	74.6	75.4	75.0	75.8	76.2	76.4	78.2	76.8	78.0	78.5	78.3	79.0
1972		80.6	82.0	83.8	86.5	80.1	80.5	81.2	81.7	82.0	82.3	82.9	83.7	84.7	86.0	86.8	86.6
1973		88.6	90.0	91.0	91.6	87.2	88.8	89.8	89.3	90.3	90.4	91.2	90.9	90.8	91.1	91.6	92.2
1974		90.8	91.0	90.4	83.9	91.2	90.7	90.6	91.3	90.5	91.2	90.7	91.1	89.3	87.1	84.2	80.4
1975		77.5	78.1	83.5	85.0	78.7	77.6	76.3	77.0	77.8	79.5	82.3	84.2	84.0	84.3	85.1	85.5
1976		88.5	89.6	91.1	91.8	87.6	88.9	88.8	89.3	89.5	89.9	90.7	91.1	91.6	91.5	91.8	92.2
1977		93.0	94.5	96.5	98.0	93.2	92.7	93.2	93.6	94.6	95.3	95.7	96.8	97.0	97.4	97.9	98.6
1978		99.0	100.6	102.2	104.0	99.1	98.9	99.0	100.1	100.3	101.4	101.8	102.4	102.4	103.0	103.9	105.3
1979		106.1	105.5	105.8	105.4	106.0	106.2	106.3	105.4	105.4	105.8	105.5	106.2	105.7	105.7	105.5	105.1
1980		105.0	96.5	97.5	101.2	105.9	104.8	104.3	99.0	95.8	94.6	95.2	98.0	99.5	100.3	101.0	102.3
1981		103.6	102.6	102.5	97.9	103.7	103.8	103.4	102.9	102.8	102.0	102.8	103.2	101.8	99.7	97.9	96.1
1982		95.4	94.0	94.5	93.2	94.4	96.3	95.6	94.6	93.9	93.4	94.0	95.3	94.6	93.2	93.4	93.2
1983		95.9	100.4	106.6	109.1	94.6	95.7	97.3	99.3	100.2	101.7	104.1	106.8	108.9	109.6	109.0	108.8

Industrial production: raw materials (1) / Production industrielle : matières premières (1)

Adjusted - Corrigé

1980 = 100

	Year	Q.1	Q.2	Q.3	Q.4	JAN	FEB	MAR	APR	MAY	JUN	JUL	AUG	SEP	OCT	NOV	DEC
1964		54.1	55.4	57.0	58.3	53.5	54.3	54.3	55.0	55.4	55.8	55.9	57.1	57.9	56.8	58.6	59.4
1965		60.5	62.2	63.6	64.2	60.0	60.2	61.1	61.8	62.0	62.7	63.4	64.0	63.4	64.1	63.8	64.6
1966		66.3	67.9	69.2	69.4	65.5	66.2	67.3	67.2	68.0	68.4	68.6	69.1	69.8	70.1	69.1	69.1
1967		67.5	66.7	67.5	69.4	68.5	67.4	66.5	67.1	66.5	66.4	66.8	67.8	67.8	68.6	69.4	70.2
1968		70.6	72.2	72.5	73.4	70.3	70.5	70.9	71.4	72.5	72.8	72.8	72.4	72.5	72.6	73.7	73.9
1969		75.0	75.7	77.1	77.1	74.3	75.1	75.5	75.5	75.3	76.4	76.5	77.2	77.4	77.4	77.1	76.8
1970		74.8	73.9	74.5	72.8	75.1	74.8	74.7	74.1	73.9	73.6	74.1	74.3	74.6	72.6	72.1	73.6
1971		74.7	75.9	74.3	76.0	74.8	74.5	74.8	75.1	76.1	76.4	74.9	74.0	75.5	75.5	75.8	76.8
1972		79.5	81.8	83.6	86.5	78.9	79.3	80.2	81.4	81.7	82.2	82.7	83.6	84.6	85.8	86.5	87.3
1973		89.0	90.4	91.8	92.0	88.0	89.2	89.6	89.7	90.5	91.0	91.5	92.0	91.7	91.6	92.1	92.1
1974		91.2	91.2	91.5	84.8	91.4	91.1	91.1	90.0	91.6	91.9	91.7	91.3	91.7	89.7	84.8	80.0
1975		75.0	74.8	80.1	83.2	77.0	74.6	73.4	73.7	74.4	76.3	77.6	80.6	82.0	82.7	83.4	83.5
1976		86.8	89.1	90.5	90.4	85.4	87.1	88.0	88.1	89.2	89.9	90.1	90.9	90.3	90.1	90.5	90.7
1977		91.5	94.0	94.4	95.4	90.2	91.3	93.0	93.4	94.1	94.6	94.3	94.2	94.5	95.3	95.7	95.4
1978		95.8	99.4	101.8	104.8	95.7	95.3	96.3	98.5	99.3	100.5	101.2	101.8	102.4	103.8	104.7	105.8
1979		105.9	105.7	106.3	106.0	105.5	105.8	106.3	105.0	105.8	106.2	106.6	106.1	106.1	106.1	105.8	106.1
1980		106.2	98.2	94.3	101.2	106.8	106.3	105.5	102.2	97.7	94.7	92.4	94.0	96.5	98.9	101.7	103.1
1981		104.5	104.0	104.6	97.6	104.2	104.5	104.6	103.6	103.9	104.3	105.2	105.2	103.3	100.6	98.0	94.2
1982		94.0	91.2	89.8	87.2	93.0	95.1	93.8	92.3	91.0	90.5	90.1	90.0	89.4	88.1	87.0	86.6
1983		91.4	96.0	101.5	104.6	89.4	91.4	93.2	94.7	96.0	97.4	100.1	101.4	103.1	104.3	104.7	104.7

Production: crude steel (3) / Production : acier brut (3)

thousand tons, monthly averages / milliers de tonnes, moyennes mensuelles

	Year	Q.1	Q.2	Q.3	Q.4	JAN	FEB	MAR	APR	MAY	JUN	JUL	AUG	SEP	OCT	NOV	DEC
1964																	
1965																	
1966																	
1967																	
1968																	
1969	10665	10402	10980	10375	10902	10055	9902	11250	11016	11209	10714	10310	10361	10454	11179	10810	10716
1970	9942	10162	10367	9759	9481	10200	9524	10763	10329	10500	10272	9780	9766	9731	9706	9108	9628
1971	9075	10521	11182	7074	7521	10228	9865	11471	11399	11721	10425	9019	5238	6965	7321	7306	7936
1972	10062	9546	10434	9705	10564	9073	9054	10512	10512	10829	9961	9381	9836	9900	10575	10340	10776
1973	11372	11215	11627	11098	11547	11225	10547	11873	11602	11951	11329	11149	11050	11094	11681	11419	11542
1974	10999	11214	11303	10838	10642	11545	10522	11574	11287	11569	11054	11027	10739	10749	11446	10537	9943
1975	8829	10410	8853	7957	8095	10509	9854	10868	9677	8949	7932	7593	7845	8432	8359	7901	8025
1976	9694	9385	10638	9975	8775	8922	8988	10246	10377	11010	10528	10342	10095	9492	9340	8613	8372
1977	9429	8769	10509	9302	9135	8246	8037	10023	10131	11069	10327	9361	9427	9117	9473	8843	9088
1978	10312	9322	10782	10379	10764	9312	8653	10002	10428	11171	10747	10329	10457	10350	11005	10573	10713
1979	10277	10355	11254	10182	9315	10074	9582	11409	11064	11602	11095	10724	10260	9563	9807	9070	9068
1980	8397	9806	8281	6526	8975	9708	9373	10337	9669	8370	6805	6165	6367	7046	8566	9124	9235
1981	9073	9787	10014	9041	7450	9607	9097	10657	10199	10363	9481	9217	9181	8725	8167	7223	6959
1982	5533	6962	5838	5001	4332	7002	6551	7332	6365	6065	5084	5167	5028	4808	4769	4162	4064
1983	6291	5559	6561	5373	6669	5061	5149	6466	6615	6724	6344	6279	6369	6472	6978	6589	6440

UNITED STATES

Production: crude petroleum / Production : pétrole brut

million tons, monthly averages / millions de tonnes, moyennes mensuelles

	Year	Q.1	Q.2	Q.3	Q.4	JAN	FEB	MAR	APR	MAY	JUN	JUL	AUG	SEP	OCT	NOV	DEC
1964	31.4	31.5	31.3	31.0	31.8	31.9	30.1	32.3	31.4	31.7	30.7	31.3	31.2	30.5	31.9	31.0	32.6
1965	32.1	31.7	31.9	31.5	33.2	32.6	29.5	33.0	32.0	32.2	31.4	32.1	32.5	30.1	33.0	32.4	34.3
1966	34.1	33.2	34.1	34.2	34.9	33.7	31.2	34.8	33.5	35.0	33.8	34.5	34.6	33.5	34.9	34.2	35.7
1967	36.2	34.8	34.7	38.3	37.1	35.9	32.6	35.8	34.4	35.1	34.6	38.4	39.5	36.9	37.7	36.4	37.3
1968	37.5	37.8	37.5	37.5	37.0	37.8	36.5	39.0	37.0	38.6	37.1	38.4	38.3	36.2	37.4	36.4	37.3
1969	38.0	36.3	38.6	38.2	38.8	37.2	33.8	37.9	37.5	39.2	39.0	39.0	38.0	37.7	38.6	37.9	39.9
1970	39.6	38.6	38.9	39.5	41.5	39.7	36.2	39.8	38.9	39.9	38.0	38.5	40.1	40.0	42.0	40.7	41.7
1971	38.9	39.4	39.7	38.7	37.9	40.5	36.8	40.9	39.6	40.4	38.9	39.6	39.4	37.0	38.4	37.1	38.1
1972	38.9	38.1	39.2	39.4	39.0	38.2	36.6	39.6	38.6	40.3	38.6	39.8	39.7	38.5	39.7	38.2	39.1
1973	37.9	37.6	38.0	37.9	37.9	38.5	35.6	38.8	37.7	38.8	37.4	38.6	38.4	36.8	38.6	37.1	38.0
1974	36.1	36.5	36.4	35.8	35.5	37.4	34.6	37.6	36.3	37.3	35.6	36.8	36.5	34.2	36.1	34.8	35.7
1975	34.4	34.5	34.5	34.4	34.3	35.4	32.5	35.6	34.3	35.1	34.1	34.9	34.6	33.6	34.9	33.6	34.6
1976	33.5	33.7	33.2	33.7	33.4	34.5	32.1	34.5	32.8	34.0	32.8	34.0	34.0	33.0	33.8	32.8	33.8
1977	33.9	32.5	33.2	34.4	35.4	32.9	30.8	33.9	33.0	33.8	32.9	34.0	34.8	34.4	35.9	34.8	35.6
1978	35.8	34.4	36.2	36.4	36.2	35.0	31.7	36.5	35.8	37.0	35.8	36.7	36.7	35.7	37.0	35.4	36.3
1979	35.1	34.5	34.9	35.3	35.7	35.4	32.2	36.0	34.6	36.0	34.1	35.0	36.5	34.3	35.9	35.1	36.0
1980	35.4	35.6	35.4	35.4	35.4	36.2	34.1	36.5	35.2	36.2	34.7	35.8	35.3	35.0	35.8	34.5	36.1
1981	35.2	34.8	35.1	35.4	35.6	35.8	32.5	36.0	34.6	35.6	34.9	35.3	35.9	34.8	35.8	34.8	36.1
1982	35.7	35.1	35.5	36.0	36.0	36.3	32.9	36.0	35.1	36.3	35.2	36.2	36.5	35.4	36.4	35.2	36.3
1983		35.1	35.6	35.9	35.8	36.2	32.8	36.4	35.2	36.4	35.2	36.2	36.3	35.1	36.3	35.0	36.1

Production: passenger cars (4) / Production : voitures de tourisme (4)

thousands, monthly averages / milliers, moyennes mensuelles

	Year	Q.1	Q.2	Q.3	Q.4	JAN	FEB	MAR	APR	MAY	JUN	JUL	AUG	SEP	OCT	NOV	DEC
1964																	
1965				513	883							754	333	453	856	908	884
1966	716	828	806	418	811	798	766	920	811	788	819	488	144	622	835	823	775
1967	620	620	725	420	714	651	526	684	660	750	765	426	232	601	645	683	814
1968	735	764	838	491	848	787	703	801	783	917	814	625	193	656	935	877	732
1969	684	762	737	521	717	815	707	763	714	720	777	465	346	752	857	682	612
1970	546	584	730	416	452	571	555	626	661	724	805	482	272	494	393	364	599
1971	715	778	776	577	730	711	758	865	750	767	810	490	484	758	793	773	623
1972	735	751	808	557	825	698	748	807	779	842	804	412	399	859	896	873	706
1973	805	899	902	624	795	900	855	941	844	941	921	714	440	717	956	888	540
1974	611	589	696	549	609	600	552	616	681	737	670	542	444	662	832	548	448
1975	559	431	610	552	644	391	410	493	586	613	632	504	485	668	746	606	579
1976	708	721	805	576	730	647	682	835	789	776	850	559	518	652	691	766	733
1977	766	771	878	641	776	683	676	953	816	868	951	679	505	739	874	767	686
1978	764	747	891	618	799	657	675	909	869	919	886	589	528	738	894	842	660
1979	702	776	834	555	641	737	709	883	761	922	820	587	449	630	787	641	494
1980	533	594	545	420	575	513	619	649	572	518	544	432	299	529	675	560	490
1981	521	511	676	460	438	439	475	620	645	670	712	513	345	522	520	425	370
1982	421	354	520	408	401	273	320	469	488	510	561	439	356	429	431	407	366
1983	562	502	587	527	632	457	474	575	529	587	644	461	492	627	678	636	581

Manufacturing deliveries: total / Livraisons des industries manufacturières : total

billion dollars, monthly averages / milliards de dollars, moyennes mensuelles

	Year	Q.1	Q.2	Q.3	Q.4	JAN	FEB	MAR	APR	MAY	JUN	JUL	AUG	SEP	OCT	NOV	DEC
1964	37.33	36.30	38.17	36.76	38.09	34.44	37.08	37.39	38.24	37.61	38.67	35.05	36.18	39.04	38.54	37.86	37.88
1965	41.00	39.64	41.77	40.15	42.41	36.93	40.00	42.01	42.03	40.79	42.51	38.49	40.11	41.86	43.00	42.50	41.73
1966	44.87	43.74	45.99	44.00	45.75	40.71	44.34	46.16	45.74	45.17	47.07	41.13	43.82	47.04	47.27	45.54	44.46
1967	46.49	45.42	47.20	45.51	47.81	42.64	46.06	47.57	46.66	46.52	48.43	42.52	45.80	48.22	47.76	47.78	47.89
1968	50.23	48.82	51.25	49.09	51.75	46.06	49.51	50.90	50.18	50.63	52.96	47.29	47.48	52.49	53.71	51.87	49.67
1969	53.50	52.19	54.40	52.94	54.48	48.86	53.09	54.62	53.67	53.28	56.25	49.81	52.40	56.61	57.08	54.28	52.06
1970	52.81	52.87	54.49	52.23	51.63	49.98	53.92	54.70	53.19	53.72	56.55	49.64	51.88	55.19	53.47	50.61	50.82
1971	55.91	54.13	57.55	54.97	56.98	50.12	55.15	57.11	56.15	56.48	60.00	51.82	54.67	58.43	58.26	57.30	55.39
1972	63.02	59.36	63.53	62.50	66.71	55.29	60.24	62.54	62.33	62.45	65.82	57.19	62.46	67.86	68.23	67.36	64.53
1973	72.94	69.63	74.11	72.19	75.81	64.42	70.93	73.56	72.46	72.98	76.89	68.35	71.98	76.25	78.04	77.17	72.22
1974	84.79	78.81	86.04	85.66	87.67	73.06	79.94	83.43	83.30	85.21	89.60	80.81	86.83	92.34	93.67	89.13	80.21
1975	86.60	82.74	87.03	87.03	89.54	78.44	84.58	85.18	86.38	84.81	89.88	80.68	87.22	93.34	93.49	89.47	85.66
1976	98.80	93.66	100.80	98.67	102.08	86.26	94.91	99.80	98.82	99.03	104.56	91.95	98.70	105.34	103.43	102.48	100.34
1977	113.20	107.89	115.56	112.29	117.06	97.98	108.78	116.92	113.68	113.38	119.61	104.22	112.27	120.38	121.21	116.48	113.57
1978	126.91	118.41	129.49	125.02	133.70	106.97	121.00	127.28	128.37	126.56	133.53	115.46	127.36	135.25	137.98	133.60	129.51
1979	143.94	138.75	145.65	143.01	148.33	126.35	138.87	151.04	139.73	147.06	150.15	133.88	142.77	152.38	154.14	146.99	143.87
1980	154.39	154.00	150.96	150.15	162.45	143.16	157.44	161.41	151.16	147.85	153.88	137.81	148.72	163.94	167.08	161.77	158.48
1981	168.13	166.25	174.83	167.44	164.00	153.30	168.37	176.57	171.93	171.15	181.40	157.95	168.32	176.07	171.93	162.87	157.20
1982	159.18	159.18	165.15	157.93	154.39	146.65	162.62	168.26	160.45	163.86	171.15	149.36	157.05	167.55	159.49	153.63	150.07
1983	171.08	158.70	171.94	172.37	181.28	146.61	159.49	170.01	164.35	168.94	182.54	158.50	172.16	186.46	183.31	180.27	180.26

Ships completed / Navires achevés

thousand gross register tons, quarterly averages / milliers de tonneaux de jauge brute, moyennes trimestrielles

	Year	Q.1	Q.2	Q.3	Q.4	JAN	FEB	MAR	APR	MAY	JUN	JUL	AUG	SEP	OCT	NOV	DEC
1964	62	42	33	35	140												
1965	55	23	115	50	31												
1966	48	31	65	41	54												
1967	52	31	41	57	80												
1968	92	38	115	109	106												
1969	116	135	145	35	160												
1970	94	39	119	89	124												
1971	123	111	76	215	83												
1972	120	57	164	124	130												
1973	241	167	161	263	225												
1974	183	55	199	114	268												
1975	119	134	46	115	190												
1976	204	141	275	236	157												
1977	253	64	357	178	337												
1978	258	241	349	193	283												
1979	338	376	305	197	509												
1980	139	29	150	299	72												
1981	90	22	102	124	110												
1982	54	13	60	22	127												
1983	205	214	57	81	35												

Rate of capacity utilization / Taux d'utilisation de capacité

manufacturing / industries manufacturières

per cent / pourcentage

Adjusted - Corrigé

	Year	Q.1	Q.2	Q.3	Q.4	JAN	FEB	MAR	APR	MAY	JUN	JUL	AUG	SEP	OCT	NOV	DEC
1964	85.7	84.5	85.5	86.1	86.5												
1965	89.6	88.9	89.4	89.9	90.0												
1966	91.1	91.1	91.6	91.2	90.6												
1967	86.9	88.2	86.6	85.9	86.9	89.5	88.1	87.2	87.5	86.4	86.1	85.3	86.3	85.9	86.2	87.1	87.5
1968	87.1	87.1	87.4	86.9	86.9	87.1	87.3	87.0	86.8	87.7	87.7	87.1	86.9	86.7	86.7	87.4	86.8
1969	86.4	87.3	86.6	86.5	85.0	87.1	87.4	87.5	87.0	86.3	86.6	86.9	86.6	86.3	85.9	84.8	84.2
1970	79.5	81.7	80.4	79.3	76.7	82.0	81.7	81.3	80.9	80.4	80.0	80.0	79.3	78.6	76.5	75.9	77.6
1971	78.4	77.9	78.3	78.1	79.4	78.2	78.0	77.6	77.9	78.4	78.6	78.5	77.4	78.5	79.2	79.3	79.7
1972	83.5	81.3	82.8	83.7	85.0	80.8	81.3	81.8	82.7	82.7	82.9	82.9	83.8	84.4	85.2	85.9	86.8
1973	87.5	87.2	87.6	87.7	87.5	86.4	87.5	87.6	87.3	87.9	87.7	87.9	87.5	87.7	87.7	87.6	87.3
1974	83.8	85.5	85.4	85.1	79.1	85.8	85.3	85.4	85.0	85.5	85.7	85.4	85.1	84.8	82.8	79.5	75.1
1975	72.9	70.3	70.7	74.5	76.1	71.9	70.1	69.0	69.9	70.3	71.9	73.3	74.8	75.7	75.5	76.2	76.7
1976	79.6	78.5	79.5	80.1	80.2	77.5	78.8	79.1	79.2	79.6	79.8	80.2	80.2	79.9	79.6	80.2	80.7
1977	82.2	80.9	82.3	82.7	82.9	80.4	80.5	81.7	81.9	82.3	82.7	82.7	82.7	82.7	82.9	82.8	82.9
1978	84.7	82.4	84.2	85.5	86.6	82.1	82.1	83.0	84.1	84.1	84.6	85.1	85.4	85.8	86.2	86.6	87.1
1979	86.0	87.2	86.2	85.7	84.8	86.9	87.1	87.5	85.6	86.6	86.4	86.3	85.2	85.5	85.2	84.7	84.5
1980	79.6	83.8	78.3	76.4	79.7	84.4	84.0	83.2	80.7	78.1	76.1	75.5	76.3	77.6	78.8	79.9	80.5
1981	79.4	80.6	80.8	80.3	75.9	80.7	80.6	80.6	80.7	81.0	80.6	80.9	80.7	79.4	77.7	75.9	74.2
1982	71.1	72.9	71.6	71.0	69.0	72.3	73.4	72.9	72.0	71.5	71.3	71.4	71.2	70.6	69.4	68.8	68.9
1983	75.2	70.7	73.8	77.4	78.9	70.0	70.6	71.6	72.9	73.8	74.9	76.4	77.3	78.4	78.9	78.8	78.9

Manufacturing deliveries: total / Livraisons des industries manufacturières : total

billion dollars, monthly averages / milliards de dollars, moyennes mensuelles

Adjusted - Corrigé

	Year	Q.1	Q.2	Q.3	Q.4	JAN	FEB	MAR	APR	MAY	JUN	JUL	AUG	SEP	OCT	NOV	DEC
1964		36.48	37.12	37.68	38.15	36.75	36.54	36.17	37.17	37.21	36.97	37.80	37.37	37.87	37.29	37.91	39.26
1965		39.75	40.59	41.30	42.34	39.34	39.43	40.48	40.89	40.29	40.60	41.48	41.25	41.17	41.50	42.43	43.08
1966		43.85	44.73	45.10	45.70	43.36	43.75	44.45	44.64	44.65	44.89	44.65	45.27	45.37	45.69	45.53	45.88
1967		45.58	45.93	46.59	47.83	45.43	45.50	45.82	45.68	46.01	46.09	46.08	47.17	46.54	46.19	47.83	49.47
1968		49.17	49.87	50.23	51.62	49.32	49.04	49.16	49.33	50.07	50.23	51.02	49.34	50.49	51.69	51.76	51.40
1969		52.54	52.93	54.13	54.49	52.26	52.59	52.77	52.88	52.68	53.24	54.14	53.93	54.33	55.03	54.26	54.20
1970		53.29	53.00	53.12	51.85	53.48	53.43	52.94	52.46	53.07	53.46	53.37	52.85	53.14	51.62	50.68	53.25
1971		54.54	55.93	55.95	57.20	53.73	54.65	55.22	55.37	55.76	56.65	56.32	55.64	55.90	56.01	57.14	58.46
1972		59.90	61.72	63.32	67.07	59.39	59.79	60.52	61.39	61.60	62.17	62.12	63.50	64.35	65.50	67.19	68.52
1973		70.31	71.97	73.27	76.10	69.37	70.43	71.14	71.35	71.90	72.67	73.41	73.30	73.09	74.90	76.91	76.50
1974		79.60	83.59	87.79	88.04	78.82	79.44	80.55	81.90	84.03	84.83	87.07	87.89	88.42	90.24	89.21	84.68
1975		83.56	84.63	88.25	90.06	84.76	84.02	81.91	84.87	83.71	85.30	87.20	88.16	89.37	89.99	89.74	90.44
1976		94.44	97.94	100.25	102.65	93.46	94.35	95.52	96.93	97.69	99.20	100.05	100.21	100.48	99.57	102.81	105.57
1977		108.48	112.26	114.45	117.50	106.22	107.95	111.27	111.43	111.95	113.40	113.56	114.36	115.46	116.30	116.84	119.37
1978		118.96	125.81	128.60	134.02	116.18	119.97	120.72	125.74	125.11	126.57	126.03	130.00	129.77	132.39	134.12	135.56
1979		139.19	141.77	146.05	148.60	137.02	137.46	143.10	137.34	145.50	142.48	146.17	145.52	146.50	148.50	147.89	149.42
1980		154.49	147.57	152.80	152.65	154.41	155.63	153.42	149.26	146.96	146.48	149.83	151.24	157.33	161.31	162.76	163.89
1981		166.51	170.94	170.85	163.98	165.27	166.36	167.91	170.04	170.09	172.68	171.89	171.74	168.95	166.28	163.84	161.83
1982		159.47	161.75	160.95	154.35	157.50	160.74	160.16	159.12	163.01	163.12	162.42	160.02	160.46	154.19	154.32	154.54
1983		159.37	168.32	175.73	181.52	158.24	158.08	161.80	163.07	167.97	173.92	172.60	175.99	178.59	176.79	181.08	186.68

UNITED STATES

Manufacturing deliveries: durable goods
billion dollars, monthly averages

Livraisons des industries manufacturières : biens durables
milliards de dollars, moyennes mensuelles

	Year	Q.1	Q.2	Q.3	Q.4	JAN	FEB	MAR	APR	MAY	JUN	JUL	AUG	SEP	OCT	NOV	DEC
1964	19.64	19.10	20.52	18.87	20.06	17.95	19.56	19.79	20.53	20.11	20.92	18.31	18.08	20.23	19.69	19.91	20.58
1965	22.22	21.41	22.95	21.22	23.30	19.68	21.59	22.97	23.08	22.26	23.51	20.66	20.96	22.05	23.23	23.31	23.35
1966	24.65	24.02	25.71	23.53	25.35	22.10	24.35	25.60	25.45	25.20	26.46	22.07	22.97	25.53	26.02	25.21	24.83
1967	25.27	24.70	26.00	24.23	26.13	23.08	24.99	26.04	25.36	25.58	27.05	22.53	24.18	25.99	25.43	25.92	27.05
1968	27.66	27.11	28.68	25.19	28.65	25.40	27.38	28.55	27.96	28.40	29.69	25.67	24.49	28.41	29.65	28.74	27.57
1969	29.44	29.13	30.27	28.43	29.92	26.99	29.73	30.66	29.87	29.47	31.47	26.45	27.76	31.09	31.32	29.72	28.73
1970	28.19	28.44	29.78	27.50	27.03	26.62	29.14	29.58	28.72	29.47	31.16	26.08	26.93	29.49	27.64	26.21	27.23
1971	29.95	29.08	31.48	28.82	30.45	26.49	29.59	31.16	30.34	30.91	33.19	27.07	28.24	31.14	30.97	30.63	29.74
1972	34.02	32.09	34.85	33.13	36.03	29.43	32.66	34.16	34.09	34.41	36.05	30.04	32.64	36.73	37.05	36.37	34.66
1973	39.69	37.85	41.14	38.81	40.95	34.74	38.58	40.24	39.84	40.64	42.93	37.05	37.83	41.55	42.80	42.03	38.02
1974	44.23	41.16	45.86	44.49	45.41	37.87	41.70	43.90	43.90	45.27	48.40	41.21	43.98	48.27	48.92	46.15	41.16
1975	43.66	42.21	44.80	43.08	44.53	39.83	43.18	43.62	44.51	43.67	46.22	39.59	42.67	46.98	47.03	44.16	42.41
1976	50.69	47.34	52.56	50.17	52.69	42.64	47.90	51.49	50.95	51.88	54.83	46.36	50.17	53.99	53.20	52.90	51.97
1977	59.27	56.05	61.23	58.06	51.73	50.03	56.13	62.00	59.65	60.04	64.01	53.73	57.18	63.27	64.74	61.05	59.39
1978	67.85	62.52	70.03	65.47	72.38	55.39	63.73	68.44	69.27	68.23	72.58	60.04	66.60	72.78	74.97	72.12	70.04
1979	76.06	75.10	78.82	73.84	76.43	67.10	75.30	82.92	75.33	80.00	81.12	68.89	73.08	79.55	81.30	75.18	72.97
1980	77.55	78.81	75.89	73.70	81.79	72.04	81.15	83.25	76.93	73.66	77.09	66.72	71.58	82.81	85.38	81.16	78.83
1981	83.87	82.57	89.52	82.43	80.98	74.20	83.44	90.06	87.73	87.37	93.45	77.19	82.22	87.87	85.60	80.09	77.25
1982	76.84	77.60	81.71	74.82	73.24	69.16	79.35	84.29	79.59	80.87	84.66	70.64	73.67	80.16	75.89	72.46	71.37
1983	85.22	77.83	86.17	84.49	92.39	69.98	78.27	85.25	82.05	83.95	92.51	76.66	83.45	93.35	92.88	91.76	92.54

Manufacturing stocks: total
billion dollars, end of period

Stocks des industries manufacturières : total
milliards de dollars, fin de période

	Year	Q.1	Q.2	Q.3	Q.4	JAN	FEB	MAR	APR	MAY	JUN	JUL	AUG	SEP	OCT	NOV	DEC
1964	63.29	61.04	61.16	61.29	63.29	60.37	60.82	61.04	61.20	61.38	61.16	60.70	61.02	61.29	62.12	62.76	63.29
1965	68.03	64.69	65.49	65.35	68.03	63.92	64.39	64.69	64.92	65.29	65.49	65.58	65.97	66.35	66.68	67.22	68.03
1966	77.75	70.52	72.74	74.80	77.75	69.06	69.88	70.52	71.23	72.08	72.74	73.00	74.15	74.80	75.71	76.78	77.75
1967	84.39	81.01	82.09	82.38	84.39	79.40	80.46	81.01	81.77	82.36	82.09	81.94	82.57	82.38	82.83	83.57	84.39
1968	90.24	86.19	87.66	88.41	90.24	85.03	85.92	86.19	87.01	87.75	87.66	87.25	88.21	88.41	88.93	89.40	90.24
1969	97.75	93.12	94.79	95.73	97.75	91.36	92.34	93.12	94.00	95.10	94.79	95.00	95.59	95.73	96.44	97.04	97.75
1970	101.25	99.62	100.32	100.18	101.25	98.30	99.19	99.62	100.78	100.84	100.32	100.21	100.49	100.18	100.82	101.46	101.25
1971	102.27	102.51	102.41	101.39	102.27	102.19	102.49	102.51	102.90	103.29	102.41	101.56	101.66	101.39	102.05	102.11	102.27
1972	107.91	104.12	105.04	105.88	107.91	103.31	103.94	104.12	104.56	105.17	105.04	104.69	106.02	105.88	106.68	107.30	107.91
1973	124.33	112.46	115.31	117.93	124.33	109.69	111.15	112.46	113.34	114.58	115.31	115.79	117.05	117.93	119.74	121.52	124.33
1974	157.59	132.30	139.40	147.77	157.59	127.49	130.18	132.30	135.02	137.57	139.40	142.07	145.27	147.77	150.49	153.41	157.59
1975	159.84	161.28	158.26	156.65	159.84	160.77	161.85	161.28	160.76	160.02	158.26	157.03	156.93	156.65	157.89	158.87	159.84
1976	174.87	163.78	166.24	169.15	174.87	161.85	162.78	163.78	164.23	165.29	166.24	166.60	167.92	169.16	171.76	173.28	174.87
1977	188.44	179.60	182.28	184.48	188.44	177.29	178.96	179.60	180.94	182.69	182.28	182.38	183.81	184.48	185.96	187.30	188.44
1978	209.12	194.50	198.69	202.09	209.12	191.39	193.36	194.50	196.17	198.01	198.69	199.31	201.64	202.09	204.03	206.88	209.12
1979	239.10	219.19	225.78	231.17	239.10	214.04	217.32	219.19	222.42	224.18	225.78	226.81	230.13	231.17	234.31	236.92	239.10
1980	261.70	253.29	259.02	257.80	261.70	245.92	249.57	253.29	258.08	259.97	259.02	258.82	259.02	257.80	258.18	259.80	261.70
1981	279.45	272.95	275.52	279.23	279.45	267.73	271.08	272.95	274.90	276.86	275.52	276.34	277.85	279.23	281.26	282.59	279.45
1982	261.99	281.52	275.46	269.21	261.99	281.28	282.95	281.52	281.49	278.88	275.46	273.88	272.64	269.21	268.92	266.31	261.99
1983	257.75	259.43	257.93	257.44	257.75	262.43	262.70	259.43	260.17	260.48	257.93	257.42	258.56	257.44	259.03	259.38	257.75

Manufacturing stocks: durable goods
billion dollars, end of period

Stocks des industries manufacturières : biens durables
milliards de dollars, fin de période

	Year	Q.1	Q.2	Q.3	Q.4	JAN	FEB	MAR	APR	MAY	JUN	JUL	AUG	SEP	OCT	NOV	DEC
1964	38.24	36.57	37.04	37.14	38.24	35.97	36.31	36.57	36.79	36.99	37.04	36.66	36.93	37.14	37.54	37.92	38.24
1965	41.98	39.56	40.56	41.30	41.98	38.65	39.15	39.56	39.88	40.27	40.56	40.62	40.92	41.30	41.40	41.58	41.98
1966	49.62	43.85	45.63	47.55	49.62	42.63	43.28	43.85	44.46	45.13	45.63	45.78	46.90	47.55	48.21	48.97	49.62
1967	54.65	52.07	53.09	53.40	54.65	50.71	51.62	52.07	52.66	53.20	53.09	53.00	53.64	53.40	53.72	54.21	54.65
1968	58.44	56.01	57.15	57.59	58.44	54.87	55.74	56.01	56.67	57.17	57.15	56.55	57.33	57.59	57.74	57.93	58.44
1969	64.22	60.82	62.29	62.95	64.22	59.35	60.08	60.82	61.43	62.29	62.29	62.53	62.91	62.95	63.43	63.74	64.22
1970	66.28	65.58	65.98	66.21	66.28	64.55	65.09	65.58	66.36	66.36	65.98	66.10	66.47	66.21	66.34	66.61	66.28
1971	65.76	67.17	66.87	66.08	65.76	66.69	67.00	67.17	67.51	67.66	66.87	66.29	66.34	66.08	65.98	65.79	65.76
1972	69.69	67.29	67.91	68.67	69.69	66.50	67.04	67.29	67.62	68.04	67.91	67.69	68.75	68.67	69.06	69.42	69.69
1973	80.74	73.00	74.91	77.15	80.74	70.92	71.99	73.00	73.73	74.43	74.91	75.18	76.38	77.15	77.94	78.87	80.74
1974	100.91	85.98	90.39	95.53	100.91	82.69	84.51	85.98	87.60	89.24	90.39	92.06	93.83	95.53	97.08	98.34	100.91
1975	102.10	105.17	104.43	102.16	102.10	103.37	105.11	105.17	105.60	105.58	104.43	103.55	102.87	102.16	102.00	102.06	102.10
1976	111.55	105.12	106.60	107.93	111.55	103.32	104.14	105.12	105.47	106.06	106.60	106.61	107.21	107.93	109.35	110.37	111.55
1977	120.35	115.56	117.13	118.30	120.35	113.57	115.13	115.56	116.15	117.29	117.13	117.06	118.03	118.30	118.44	119.48	120.35
1978	136.28	126.08	129.57	131.89	136.28	122.59	124.70	126.08	127.23	128.94	129.57	129.92	131.55	131.89	132.98	134.97	136.28
1979	158.47	145.42	150.55	153.12	158.47	140.55	143.78	145.42	147.80	149.41	150.55	151.13	153.17	153.12	155.40	157.39	158.47
1980	172.19	168.10	171.43	169.91	172.19	162.90	165.61	168.10	171.22	172.41	171.43	171.11	171.56	169.91	169.49	170.54	172.19
1981	183.62	179.93	181.47	184.37	183.62	176.54	179.05	179.93	181.06	181.70	181.47	182.27	183.46	184.37	185.49	186.22	183.62
1982	172.62	186.11	183.58	178.83	172.62	185.09	186.77	186.11	186.22	185.37	183.58	181.97	181.15	178.83	177.98	175.40	172.62
1983	168.73	171.12	170.62	168.84	168.73	172.24	173.01	171.12	171.82	172.59	170.62	169.59	170.22	168.84	169.08	169.29	168.73

Manufacturing deliveries: durable goods

billion dollars, monthly averages

Adjusted - Corrigé

Livraisons des industries manufacturières : biens durables

milliards de dollars, moyennes mensuelles

Year	Q.1	Q.2	Q.3	Q.4	JAN	FEB	MAR	APR	MAY	JUN	JUL	AUG	SEP	OCT	NOV	DEC
1964	19.21	19.50	19.88	20.07	19.34	19.32	18.97	19.61	19.45	19.42	20.03	19.60	20.00	19.24	19.95	21.02
1965	21.43	21.84	22.45	23.15	21.12	21.26	21.91	22.10	21.56	21.85	22.59	22.46	22.32	22.54	23.22	23.70
1966	24.02	24.55	24.72	25.22	23.70	23.97	24.41	24.53	24.50	24.62	24.50	24.78	24.86	25.26	25.16	25.23
1967	24.72	24.88	25.42	26.06	24.76	24.60	24.81	24.56	24.90	25.16	25.03	25.91	25.32	24.73	25.93	27.53
1968	27.25	27.49	27.48	28.42	27.42	27.04	27.30	27.25	27.66	27.55	28.29	26.70	27.46	28.54	28.58	28.13
1969	29.25	29.03	29.73	29.85	29.08	29.33	29.33	29.20	28.73	29.16	29.64	29.64	29.89	30.24	29.69	29.61
1970	28.61	28.55	28.49	27.15	28.74	28.76	28.33	28.13	28.69	28.84	28.68	28.29	28.51	26.75	26.31	28.39
1971	29.23	30.12	29.89	30.53	28.58	29.22	29.81	29.67	30.02	30.67	30.37	29.61	29.71	29.68	30.53	31.39
1972	32.37	33.33	34.09	36.28	31.96	32.39	32.78	33.30	33.38	33.29	33.58	34.18	34.52	35.46	36.37	37.01
1973	38.24	39.29	39.93	41.11	37.82	38.32	38.58	38.86	39.34	39.66	40.46	39.66	39.82	40.85	41.92	40.57
1974	41.67	43.81	45.67	45.64	41.44	41.57	42.00	42.74	43.91	44.78	45.38	45.56	46.07	46.80	46.31	43.81
1975	42.78	42.83	44.25	44.84	43.70	43.10	41.55	43.32	42.43	42.75	43.85	44.12	44.83	44.86	44.47	45.19
1976	47.86	50.21	51.71	53.05	46.98	47.87	48.72	49.48	50.42	50.74	51.74	52.21	51.17	50.75	53.27	55.13
1977	56.46	58.50	60.11	61.98	55.19	55.98	58.21	57.74	58.43	59.32	59.86	59.80	60.68	61.42	61.51	63.00
1978	62.88	67.00	68.87	72.59	61.25	63.44	63.95	67.04	66.56	67.39	66.95	69.82	69.83	71.15	72.68	73.92
1979	75.40	75.59	75.50	76.53	74.19	74.74	77.25	73.03	78.25	75.50	76.90	76.30	76.30	77.40	75.98	76.21
1980	79.24	73.12	76.02	81.78	79.64	80.43	77.67	74.92	72.48	71.97	74.28	74.55	79.22	81.43	81.99	81.91
1981	82.91	86.25	85.44	80.74	82.04	82.62	84.07	85.47	85.94	87.35	86.10	86.16	84.05	81.81	80.87	79.54
1982	77.91	78.90	77.51	72.99	76.46	78.53	78.73	77.81	79.68	79.20	78.86	77.25	76.42	72.48	73.01	73.50
1983	78.37	83.16	87.85	92.21	77.74	77.77	79.60	80.24	82.67	86.58	85.65	87.92	89.97	88.23	92.25	96.15

Manufacturing stocks: total

billion dollars, end of period

Adjusted - Corrigé

Stocks des industries manufacturières : total

milliards de dollars, fin de période

Year	Q.1	Q.2	Q.3	Q.4	JAN	FEB	MAR	APR	MAY	JUN	JUL	AUG	SEP	OCT	NOV	DEC
1964	60.64	61.03	61.72	63.44	60.15	60.37	60.64	60.83	61.01	61.03	61.12	61.38	61.72	62.52	63.04	63.44
1965	64.24	65.35	66.83	68.22	63.66	63.91	64.24	64.47	64.84	65.35	66.05	66.31	66.83	67.16	67.61	68.22
1966	70.05	72.59	75.40	78.00	68.82	69.39	70.05	70.69	71.53	72.59	73.43	74.46	75.40	76.28	77.26	78.00
1967	80.52	81.93	83.09	84.66	79.18	79.96	80.52	81.10	81.67	81.93	82.35	82.88	83.09	83.43	84.04	84.66
1968	85.74	87.57	89.09	90.62	84.81	85.48	85.74	86.35	86.95	87.57	87.66	88.47	89.09	89.50	89.89	90.62
1969	92.65	94.62	95.53	98.20	91.14	91.88	92.65	93.25	94.19	94.62	95.43	95.90	96.53	97.06	97.57	98.20
1970	99.11	100.11	101.05	101.65	98.06	98.69	99.11	99.97	99.92	100.11	100.66	100.83	101.06	101.48	102.00	101.65
1971	101.94	102.21	102.32	102.66	101.83	101.87	101.94	102.10	102.45	102.21	102.08	102.03	102.32	102.72	102.69	102.66
1972	103.49	104.91	105.92	108.24	102.83	103.18	103.49	103.76	104.37	104.91	105.34	106.52	106.92	107.38	107.91	108.24
1973	111.65	115.25	119.16	124.63	109.04	110.19	111.65	112.46	113.78	115.25	116.54	117.71	119.16	120.54	122.14	124.63
1974	131.31	139.47	149.30	157.79	126.64	129.00	131.31	134.07	136.73	139.47	143.01	146.16	149.30	151.53	154.20	157.79
1975	160.00	158.50	158.38	159.94	159.57	160.28	160.00	159.64	159.14	158.50	158.12	158.00	158.38	158.98	159.59	159.94
1976	162.51	166.45	171.00	175.19	160.57	161.13	162.51	163.21	164.38	166.45	167.76	168.80	171.00	172.94	174.02	175.19
1977	178.22	182.38	185.30	189.20	176.07	177.30	178.22	179.74	181.56	182.38	183.52	184.69	186.30	187.31	188.37	189.20
1978	192.94	198.54	204.05	210.42	190.25	191.72	192.94	194.62	196.47	198.54	200.30	202.46	204.06	205.67	208.27	210.42
1979	217.43	225.45	233.33	241.11	213.02	215.55	217.43	220.44	222.27	225.45	227.84	231.02	233.33	236.19	238.53	241.11
1980	251.27	258.52	260.15	264.11	244.97	247.62	251.27	255.51	257.64	258.52	259.61	259.93	260.15	259.95	261.19	264.11
1981	270.87	275.04	281.71	282.33	267.15	269.18	270.87	272.13	274.55	275.04	277.12	279.02	281.71	283.23	284.32	282.33
1982	279.34	274.91	271.68	264.90	280.79	280.94	279.34	278.47	276.36	274.91	274.63	273.81	271.68	270.79	267.92	264.90
1983	257.30	257.39	260.02	260.83	262.12	260.86	257.30	257.40	258.15	257.39	258.18	259.83	260.02	260.82	261.02	260.83

Manufacturing stocks: durable goods

billion dollars, end of period

Adjusted - Corrigé

Stocks des industries manufacturières : biens durables

milliards de dollars, fin de période

Year	Q.1	Q.2	Q.3	Q.4	JAN	FEB	MAR	APR	MAY	JUN	JUL	AUG	SEP	OCT	NOV	DEC
1964	36.28	36.78	37.33	38.53	36.03	36.12	36.28	36.46	36.59	36.78	36.85	37.05	37.33	37.82	38.27	38.53
1965	39.27	40.31	41.49	42.28	38.69	38.94	39.27	39.51	39.84	40.31	40.87	41.01	41.49	41.71	41.95	42.28
1966	43.56	45.38	47.81	49.95	42.69	43.07	43.56	44.05	44.66	45.38	46.00	46.96	47.81	48.57	49.38	49.95
1967	51.78	52.84	53.73	55.01	50.80	51.40	51.78	52.16	52.62	52.84	53.22	53.69	53.73	54.10	54.60	55.01
1968	55.75	56.98	57.83	58.88	54.99	55.60	55.75	56.21	56.53	56.98	56.74	57.32	57.83	58.10	58.33	58.88
1969	60.51	62.07	63.31	64.74	59.48	59.91	60.51	60.88	61.59	62.07	62.71	62.95	63.31	63.82	64.18	64.74
1970	65.21	65.74	66.63	66.78	64.66	64.89	65.21	65.74	65.66	65.74	66.28	66.55	66.63	66.79	67.08	66.78
1971	66.76	66.64	66.51	66.29	66.70	66.72	66.76	66.89	67.02	66.64	66.50	66.43	66.51	66.47	66.32	66.29
1972	66.83	67.71	69.15	70.25	66.43	66.68	66.83	66.97	67.41	67.71	67.96	68.90	69.15	69.58	70.02	70.25
1973	72.41	74.68	77.73	81.40	70.78	71.49	72.41	72.99	73.71	74.68	75.47	76.65	77.73	78.61	79.60	81.40
1974	85.20	90.08	96.37	101.74	82.47	83.86	85.20	86.70	88.35	90.08	92.38	94.25	96.37	98.08	99.40	101.74
1975	104.10	104.13	103.15	102.87	103.04	104.16	104.10	104.51	104.56	104.13	103.91	103.41	103.15	103.09	103.09	102.87
1976	104.06	106.22	109.03	112.58	102.95	103.14	104.06	104.49	105.03	106.22	106.95	107.52	109.03	110.58	111.46	112.58
1977	114.34	116.64	119.50	121.58	113.32	114.11	114.34	115.05	116.09	116.64	117.42	118.40	119.50	119.82	120.71	121.58
1978	124.65	128.97	133.21	137.83	122.27	123.61	124.65	125.90	127.50	128.97	130.26	131.85	133.21	134.56	136.36	137.83
1979	143.84	149.92	154.59	160.55	140.28	142.52	143.84	146.25	147.77	149.92	151.58	153.43	154.59	157.18	159.00	160.55
1980	166.28	170.70	171.46	174.55	162.70	164.13	166.28	169.25	170.49	170.70	171.30	171.83	171.46	171.24	172.14	174.55
1981	178.13	180.70	185.07	186.22	176.52	177.55	178.13	178.98	179.77	180.70	182.47	183.82	186.07	187.26	187.96	186.22
1982	184.32	182.81	180.52	175.20	185.24	185.20	184.32	184.05	183.38	182.81	182.10	181.54	180.52	179.68	177.06	175.20
1983	169.38	169.84	170.39	171.47	172.51	171.57	169.38	169.81	170.74	169.84	169.69	170.58	170.39	170.63	170.96	171.47

UNITED STATES

Manufacturing stocks: finished goods
billion dollars, end of period

Stocks des industries manufacturières : produits finis
milliards de dollars, fin de période

Adjusted - Corrigé

	Year	Q.1	Q.2	Q.3	Q.4	JAN	FEB	MAR	APR	MAY	JUN	JUL	AUG	SEP	OCT	NOV	DEC
1964	21.62	20.96	21.10	21.13	21.62	20.76	20.87	20.96	21.07	21.14	21.10	21.19	21.19	21.18	21.43	21.50	21.62
1965	22.54	21.83	21.87	22.15	22.54	21.74	21.78	21.83	21.63	21.74	21.87	22.04	22.01	22.15	22.25	22.40	22.54
1966	25.19	23.03	23.59	24.31	25.19	22.75	22.87	23.03	23.08	23.32	23.59	23.83	24.00	24.31	24.52	24.88	25.19
1967	27.07	25.88	26.43	26.81	27.07	25.51	25.74	25.88	26.20	26.41	26.43	26.51	26.71	26.81	26.84	26.91	27.07
1968	28.77	27.31	27.57	28.18	28.77	27.22	27.25	27.31	27.32	27.46	27.57	27.65	27.89	28.18	28.33	28.51	28.77
1969	30.26	29.30	30.14	30.70	31.26	28.78	29.05	29.30	29.59	29.95	30.14	30.30	30.51	30.70	30.74	31.08	31.26
1970	34.20	32.05	32.98	33.65	34.20	31.53	31.85	32.05	32.69	32.71	32.98	33.24	33.45	33.65	33.99	34.24	34.20
1971	34.90	34.82	34.65	34.74	34.90	34.49	34.60	34.82	34.65	34.66	34.65	34.38	34.53	34.74	35.11	35.01	34.90
1972	35.93	35.15	35.82	36.19	35.93	34.86	34.94	35.15	35.34	35.53	35.82	35.83	36.36	36.19	35.96	35.95	35.93
1973	38.21	36.16	36.95	37.17	38.21	35.72	35.82	36.16	36.21	36.60	36.95	37.04	36.93	37.17	37.39	37.64	38.21
1974	48.16	40.00	41.71	44.62	48.16	38.87	39.37	40.00	40.59	40.99	41.71	42.71	43.65	44.62	45.65	46.96	48.16
1975	50.27	49.68	49.30	49.63	50.27	49.08	49.37	49.68	49.54	49.43	49.30	48.98	49.28	49.63	49.81	49.98	50.27
1976	55.54	51.09	52.62	54.45	55.54	50.21	50.67	51.09	51.44	51.76	52.62	53.16	53.79	54.45	55.45	55.13	55.54
1977	59.94	56.12	57.59	58.50	59.94	55.76	55.94	56.12	56.33	57.24	57.59	58.06	58.10	58.50	59.35	59.86	59.94
1978	65.31	61.00	62.21	63.59	65.31	60.69	60.67	61.00	61.40	61.79	62.21	62.62	63.43	63.59	63.74	64.58	65.31
1979	72.89	67.32	69.38	71.32	72.89	66.26	67.10	67.32	68.26	68.62	69.38	70.05	70.52	71.32	71.48	71.71	72.89
1980	80.08	76.14	79.34	79.88	80.08	74.13	75.05	76.14	77.89	79.00	79.34	79.91	80.23	79.88	79.57	80.04	80.08
1981	89.55	82.63	85.30	88.30	89.55	79.89	81.01	82.63	82.96	84.65	85.30	85.50	87.08	88.30	89.34	90.00	89.55
1982	85.07	89.90	87.56	87.79	85.07	89.14	89.78	89.90	89.19	88.32	87.56	88.22	88.30	87.79	87.61	86.40	85.07
1983	80.79	82.41	81.93	82.09	80.79	83.79	83.29	82.41	82.04	82.12	81.93	82.49	82.62	82.09	82.12	82.06	80.79

Manufacturing stocks: work in progress
billion dollars, end of period

Stocks des industries manufacturières : produits en cours de fabrication
milliards de dollars, fin de période

Adjusted - Corrigé

	Year	Q.1	Q.2	Q.3	Q.4	JAN	FEB	MAR	APR	MAY	JUN	JUL	AUG	SEP	OCT	NOV	DEC
1964	19.71	18.68	18.96	19.29	19.71	18.37	18.50	18.68	18.82	18.91	18.96	18.99	19.15	19.29	19.46	19.61	19.71
1965	21.89	19.89	20.45	21.24	21.89	19.74	19.84	19.89	19.96	20.07	20.45	20.81	21.06	21.24	21.42	21.61	21.89
1966	26.15	22.77	23.81	25.09	26.15	22.16	22.41	22.77	23.13	23.42	23.81	24.16	24.59	25.09	25.54	25.92	26.15
1967	29.43	27.27	28.11	28.55	29.43	26.61	27.01	27.27	27.56	27.93	28.11	28.27	28.43	28.55	28.77	29.08	29.43
1968	32.18	30.01	30.79	31.24	32.18	29.36	29.83	30.01	30.26	30.42	30.79	30.56	30.98	31.24	31.38	31.71	32.18
1969	35.53	33.26	34.05	35.01	35.53	32.66	33.05	33.26	33.41	33.77	34.05	34.57	34.81	35.01	35.25	35.31	35.53
1970	35.12	35.35	35.57	35.62	35.12	35.25	35.26	35.35	35.65	35.68	35.67	35.92	35.76	35.62	35.54	35.54	35.12
1971	34.32	34.75	34.24	34.34	34.32	35.04	34.88	34.75	34.63	34.62	34.24	34.13	34.08	34.34	34.36	34.38	34.32
1972	36.77	34.83	35.33	35.90	36.77	34.50	34.61	34.83	34.81	34.99	35.33	35.21	35.47	35.90	36.38	36.56	36.77
1973	42.25	38.27	39.23	40.59	42.25	37.27	37.65	38.27	38.51	38.78	39.23	39.55	40.16	40.59	41.01	41.64	42.25
1974	50.78	44.35	46.76	49.12	50.78	42.89	43.78	44.35	45.20	45.97	46.76	47.60	48.46	49.12	49.66	50.20	50.78
1975	52.21	50.97	51.74	51.83	52.21	50.73	51.03	50.97	51.46	51.73	51.74	52.04	51.81	51.83	52.01	52.19	52.21
1976	56.28	52.60	53.57	54.69	56.28	52.12	52.07	52.60	52.71	52.97	53.57	53.69	54.00	54.69	55.28	55.66	56.28
1977	61.60	57.36	57.63	59.86	61.60	56.72	57.27	57.36	57.89	57.80	57.63	58.43	59.09	59.86	60.00	60.87	61.60
1978	70.59	63.70	65.87	67.55	70.59	62.13	63.10	63.70	64.57	65.22	65.87	66.91	67.39	67.55	68.92	69.68	70.59
1979	83.06	72.79	76.71	79.72	83.06	71.12	72.39	72.79	74.18	75.18	76.71	77.55	78.18	79.72	81.00	82.03	83.06
1980	92.70	86.62	89.10	90.42	92.70	84.10	84.91	86.62	87.88	88.66	89.10	89.71	90.31	90.42	90.39	90.99	92.70
1981	97.10	95.02	95.63	97.17	97.10	94.19	94.59	95.02	95.42	96.33	95.63	96.40	96.56	97.17	97.72	98.21	97.10
1982	92.15	95.62	95.10	93.73	92.15	96.32	95.97	95.62	95.45	95.16	95.10	94.41	94.20	93.73	93.75	92.92	92.15
1983	91.77	90.06	90.13	90.75	91.77	91.52	90.90	90.06	90.37	90.86	90.13	90.52	90.56	90.75	91.57	91.45	91.77

Manufacturing new orders, net: total
billion dollars, monthly averages

Commandes nouvelles nettes (industries manufacturières) : total
milliards de dollars, moyennes mensuelles

	Year	Q.1	Q.2	Q.3	Q.4	JAN	FEB	MAR	APR	MAY	JUN	JUL	AUG	SEP	OCT	NOV	DEC
1964	38.34	37.46	39.10	37.93	38.87	36.19	37.89	38.30	38.99	38.50	39.80	37.02	36.73	40.04	39.79	38.24	38.59
1965	42.11	41.19	42.47	41.29	43.49	39.04	41.51	43.02	42.83	41.24	43.35	39.74	40.86	43.27	44.37	43.24	42.86
1966	46.40	46.30	47.54	45.87	45.89	43.63	46.52	48.76	47.53	46.10	49.00	43.48	44.79	49.33	48.17	45.12	44.39
1967	47.06	45.70	47.80	45.32	48.41	43.60	46.41	47.08	46.78	46.85	49.77	43.92	46.26	48.78	48.83	47.46	48.93
1968	50.69	45.88	50.59	49.73	52.55	46.87	50.27	52.49	50.16	49.21	52.40	47.43	48.18	53.58	55.20	51.76	50.70
1969	53.95	53.15	54.96	53.42	54.27	49.88	54.28	55.29	55.75	53.30	55.83	52.02	52.10	57.15	56.91	53.81	52.08
1970	52.04	52.30	52.95	51.67	51.23	49.95	53.22	53.74	51.74	51.84	55.27	49.97	50.56	54.47	52.15	49.99	51.55
1971	55.98	55.21	55.98	55.40	57.35	51.98	56.41	57.24	55.40	54.19	58.37	52.35	54.71	59.13	58.53	57.57	55.94
1972	64.17	60.30	63.85	64.30	68.23	56.45	61.38	63.05	62.37	62.58	66.59	59.41	63.44	70.05	69.26	68.59	66.83
1973	76.26	73.62	77.16	75.29	78.98	67.39	74.72	78.23	76.12	75.68	79.69	72.04	75.31	78.50	81.11	80.61	75.22
1974	87.27	83.12	89.53	91.23	85.19	77.96	84.61	86.81	86.46	89.03	93.10	87.10	93.09	93.49	91.58	86.94	77.06
1975	85.15	80.28	84.49	87.42	88.40	76.32	82.46	82.07	83.63	81.92	87.93	83.23	87.35	91.69	92.15	88.69	84.37
1976	99.54	94.17	101.23	99.38	103.40	85.90	95.54	101.06	99.82	98.49	105.38	95.02	98.25	104.86	105.00	102.85	102.36
1977	115.06	109.51	116.92	113.49	120.33	100.72	109.85	117.96	115.72	113.84	121.20	105.37	113.37	121.72	124.37	118.58	118.04
1978	131.62	123.15	133.62	129.83	139.87	112.01	124.86	132.58	132.93	131.03	136.90	118.96	131.28	139.24	145.70	139.60	134.31
1979	147.47	147.14	148.64	143.65	150.44	134.73	147.89	158.80	145.42	147.72	152.77	134.52	142.53	153.91	155.92	148.47	146.92
1980	156.14	159.19	148.18	151.87	165.33	151.51	161.81	164.25	150.94	142.43	151.19	140.81	149.09	165.71	170.78	161.69	163.52
1981	167.92	169.22	174.69	165.34	161.44	158.81	170.70	178.16	173.86	171.02	179.20	158.38	166.17	174.47	169.38	159.39	155.56
1982	157.37	160.85	160.55	153.14	154.95	150.66	162.28	169.61	158.84	157.65	165.16	144.95	150.99	163.48	159.05	150.60	155.18
1983	173.86	162.52	173.02	173.73	186.16	154.56	160.30	172.69	166.87	168.38	183.82	160.11	172.88	188.19	189.77	183.71	184.98

Manufacturing stocks: intermediate goods / Stocks des industries manufacturières : biens intermédiaires

billion dollars, end of period — milliards de dollars, fin de période

Adjusted - Corrigé

	Year	Q.1	Q.2	Q.3	Q.4	JAN	FEB	MAR	APR	MAY	JUN	JUL	AUG	SEP	OCT	NOV	DEC
1964	22.12	21.01	20.96	21.25	22.12	21.02	21.00	21.01	20.94	20.96	20.96	20.94	21.04	21.25	21.63	21.92	22.12
1965	23.79	22.52	23.03	23.44	23.79	22.19	22.29	22.52	22.88	23.02	23.03	23.19	23.23	23.44	23.49	23.60	23.79
1966	26.66	24.25	25.20	25.01	26.66	23.90	24.11	24.25	24.48	24.79	25.20	25.44	25.86	26.01	26.22	26.45	26.66
1967	28.17	27.37	27.39	27.73	28.17	27.06	27.21	27.37	27.33	27.33	27.39	27.57	27.75	27.73	27.82	28.05	28.17
1968	29.67	28.42	29.21	29.67	29.67	28.22	28.41	28.42	28.77	29.07	29.21	29.46	29.61	29.67	29.79	29.67	29.67
1969	31.42	30.09	30.43	30.82	31.42	29.70	29.78	30.09	30.25	30.47	30.43	30.56	30.58	30.82	31.07	31.18	31.42
1970	32.33	31.71	31.47	31.79	32.33	31.28	31.57	31.71	31.63	31.53	31.47	31.51	31.63	31.79	31.96	32.22	32.33
1971	33.44	32.38	33.32	33.24	33.44	32.31	32.39	32.38	32.83	33.17	33.32	33.56	33.42	33.24	33.26	33.29	33.44
1972	35.54	33.51	33.77	34.84	35.54	33.48	33.64	33.51	33.61	33.86	33.77	34.31	34.70	34.84	35.04	35.40	35.54
1973	44.16	37.22	39.07	41.40	44.16	36.05	36.71	37.22	37.73	38.39	39.07	39.95	40.62	41.40	42.14	42.87	44.16
1974	58.85	46.96	51.00	55.56	58.85	44.88	45.85	46.96	48.27	49.77	51.00	52.70	54.05	55.56	56.22	57.05	58.85
1975	57.46	59.36	57.47	56.93	57.46	59.75	59.88	59.36	58.64	57.97	57.47	57.10	56.92	56.93	57.16	57.42	57.46
1976	63.38	58.83	60.26	61.86	63.38	58.24	58.40	58.83	59.06	59.64	60.26	60.91	61.01	61.86	62.21	63.23	63.38
1977	67.66	64.73	67.16	67.93	67.66	63.60	64.10	64.73	65.52	66.51	67.16	67.04	67.50	67.93	67.97	67.64	67.66
1978	74.52	68.24	70.45	72.92	74.52	67.43	67.95	68.24	58.65	69.46	70.45	70.77	71.65	72.92	73.01	74.01	74.52
1979	85.16	77.33	79.36	82.29	85.16	75.64	76.06	77.33	78.00	78.48	79.36	80.24	82.32	82.29	83.72	84.79	85.16
1980	91.33	88.51	90.08	89.85	91.33	86.75	87.65	88.51	39.74	89.98	90.08	89.99	89.44	89.86	90.00	90.16	91.33
1981	95.68	93.22	94.11	95.25	95.68	93.08	93.58	93.22	93.76	93.57	94.11	95.23	95.37	96.25	96.17	96.11	95.68
1982	87.68	93.82	92.25	90.16	87.68	95.34	95.19	93.82	93.83	92.88	92.25	92.00	91.32	90.16	89.43	88.61	87.68
1983	88.27	84.83	85.32	87.18	88.27	86.31	86.67	84.83	84.99	85.17	85.32	85.17	86.66	87.18	87.13	87.51	88.27

Manufacturing new orders, net: total / Commandes nouvelles nettes (industries manufacturières) : total

billion dollars, monthly averages — milliards de dollars, moyennes mensuelles

Adjusted - Corrigé

	Year	Q.1	Q.2	Q.3	Q.4	JAN	FEB	MAR	APR	MAY	JUN	JUL	AUG	SEP	OCT	NOV	DEC
1964		37.29	38.18	38.83	39.24	37.75	37.17	36.95	37.98	38.37	38.20	39.39	38.03	39.07	38.53	38.83	40.36
1965		40.79	41.54	42.33	43.76	40.34	40.67	41.35	41.83	41.18	41.61	42.30	42.06	42.64	42.84	43.82	44.62
1966		45.98	46.54	46.80	46.15	45.27	45.72	46.95	46.46	46.18	46.98	46.42	46.32	47.66	46.43	45.92	46.11
1967		45.48	46.82	47.10	48.72	45.39	45.71	45.33	45.82	47.03	47.62	46.76	47.65	46.90	47.22	48.34	50.60
1968		49.77	49.85	50.54	52.59	49.33	49.28	50.69	49.64	49.73	50.17	49.86	50.02	51.73	53.18	52.19	52.39
1969		53.11	54.11	54.29	54.42	52.46	53.32	53.55	55.25	53.77	53.30	54.04	53.69	55.13	54.87	54.26	54.13
1970		52.32	52.02	52.18	51.66	52.57	52.35	52.03	51.20	52.24	52.62	52.41	51.50	52.62	50.43	50.55	53.98
1971		55.25	54.87	55.98	57.84	54.96	55.54	55.25	54.80	54.49	55.31	55.58	55.57	56.79	56.48	57.96	59.09
1972		60.49	62.51	64.68	68.96	59.35	60.70	60.93	61.63	62.70	63.21	62.83	64.30	66.90	66.88	69.00	71.01
1973		73.88	75.50	75.91	79.76	72.22	73.77	75.65	75.12	75.65	75.73	75.35	76.21	76.16	78.48	81.19	79.61
1974		83.40	87.57	91.86	86.14	83.06	83.41	83.73	85.07	89.03	88.61	91.26	93.44	90.89	88.80	87.97	81.65
1975		80.56	82.61	83.04	89.51	81.31	81.21	78.66	82.34	82.09	83.41	87.53	87.73	88.87	88.98	90.05	89.50
1976		94.33	98.79	100.84	104.21	92.14	94.28	96.57	98.02	98.45	99.89	101.50	99.56	101.47	101.28	103.80	107.56
1977		109.44	113.98	116.02	121.00	107.93	108.46	111.93	112.90	113.17	115.88	114.53	115.98	117.53	119.70	119.54	123.74
1978		122.46	130.59	133.09	140.25	118.85	123.07	125.45	129.79	130.68	131.30	129.57	134.92	134.78	140.09	140.89	139.76
1979		145.66	146.03	147.58	150.62	142.09	145.09	149.79	142.72	148.09	147.30	146.97	146.51	149.26	149.75	150.72	151.39
1980		157.31	146.49	155.45	165.08	158.54	158.63	154.76	149.28	143.96	146.24	152.95	153.14	160.24	163.85	164.18	167.20
1981		167.11	172.79	170.69	160.84	166.36	167.44	167.54	172.10	172.67	173.60	172.66	171.33	168.09	162.60	161.82	158.10
1982		158.80	159.10	157.05	154.12	157.69	159.12	159.58	157.85	159.47	159.99	158.91	155.70	156.57	152.36	152.60	157.38
1983		161.07	171.46	173.24	185.26	162.87	157.76	162.59	166.03	169.87	178.49	175.46	178.30	180.96	181.80	185.47	188.51

UNITED STATES

Manufacturing new orders, net: durable goods
billion dollars, monthly averages

Commandes nouvelles nettes (industries manufacturières) : biens durables
milliards de dollars, moyennes mensuelles

	Year	Q.1	Q.2	Q.3	Q.4	JAN	FEB	MAR	APR	MAY	JUN	JUL	AUG	SEP	OCT	NOV	DEC
1964	20.63	20.29	21.42	20.03	20.79	19.76	20.43	20.69	21.31	20.91	22.02	20.28	18.63	21.20	20.86	20.21	21.29
1965	23.29	22.92	23.58	22.34	24.31	21.79	23.02	23.96	23.81	22.68	24.26	21.87	21.71	23.43	24.55	23.95	24.44
1966	26.18	26.48	27.23	25.47	25.53	24.95	26.37	28.13	27.16	26.09	28.45	24.42	24.05	27.93	26.88	24.83	24.87
1967	25.83	25.01	26.62	24.99	26.68	24.04	25.38	25.61	25.47	25.94	28.46	23.87	24.58	26.53	26.45	25.51	28.07
1968	28.12	28.18	27.99	26.85	29.45	26.22	28.12	30.18	27.92	26.97	29.08	25.77	25.32	29.47	31.11	28.60	28.64
1969	29.87	30.04	30.78	28.95	29.72	28.01	30.81	31.29	31.87	29.47	30.99	27.70	27.51	31.64	31.16	29.22	26.77
1970	27.39	27.90	28.24	25.89	26.52	26.68	28.42	28.60	27.23	27.54	29.94	26.38	25.63	28.67	26.16	25.49	27.92
1971	30.00	30.10	29.91	29.30	30.68	28.29	30.81	31.19	29.55	28.63	31.55	27.59	28.37	31.94	31.05	30.75	30.24
1972	35.06	32.87	35.17	34.89	37.32	30.45	33.52	34.64	34.19	34.50	36.82	32.21	33.65	38.83	37.87	37.28	36.82
1973	42.93	41.54	44.12	42.03	44.03	37.98	42.06	44.59	43.29	43.23	45.83	40.89	41.26	43.94	45.80	45.38	40.91
1974	46.85	45.31	49.40	49.33	43.37	42.51	46.22	47.20	46.86	49.20	52.14	47.66	50.45	49.38	47.22	44.40	38.50
1975	42.02	39.78	42.04	43.13	43.13	37.86	41.09	40.39	41.50	40.59	44.02	41.83	42.56	45.01	45.14	43.04	41.20
1976	51.40	47.65	52.91	51.11	53.92	41.96	48.40	52.58	51.65	51.26	55.83	49.66	50.09	53.59	54.62	53.37	53.78
1977	61.11	57.44	62.65	59.32	65.03	52.43	57.24	62.67	61.71	60.63	65.60	54.85	58.53	64.58	67.97	63.13	64.01
1978	72.41	66.99	73.96	70.20	78.49	59.94	67.59	73.44	73.58	72.40	75.89	63.38	70.40	76.81	82.62	78.16	74.71
1979	79.51	83.37	81.75	74.33	78.56	75.40	84.13	90.59	80.71	80.76	83.78	69.65	72.59	80.89	83.10	76.26	76.31
1980	79.34	83.73	73.47	75.45	84.72	79.96	85.46	85.76	76.83	68.77	74.82	69.93	71.89	84.53	89.03	81.33	83.79
1981	83.73	85.39	89.30	81.46	78.76	78.99	85.56	91.63	89.38	87.07	91.45	77.68	80.17	86.52	83.38	77.08	75.82
1982	75.10	79.32	77.32	70.01	73.75	72.96	79.42	85.59	78.08	74.91	78.96	66.44	67.63	75.96	75.56	69.48	76.25
1983	87.87	81.38	87.15	85.55	97.40	77.67	79.06	87.41	84.38	83.30	93.79	77.99	83.88	94.81	99.45	95.41	97.32

Construction: value of contracts, total including civil engineering (F.W. Dodge Corporation)
1980 = 100

Adjusted - Corrigé

Construction : valeur des contrats, total y compris les travaux publics (F.W. Dodge Corporation)
1980 = 100

	Year	Q.1	Q.2	Q.3	Q.4	JAN	FEB	MAR	APR	MAY	JUN	JUL	AUG	SEP	OCT	NOV	DEC
1964	33	34	33	31	34	35	34	33	33	33	33	33	29	31	32	34	36
1965	34	33	34	34	35	32	33	33	36	34	33	35	33	35	35	33	36
1966	35	37	37	34	32	36	37	37	38	37	35	35	33	35	33	31	31
1967	37	33	36	38	40	30	34	35	33	36	39	35	39	40	40	40	39
1968	41	38	39	44	44	39	36	40	39	41	38	44	45	43	47	43	42
1969	46	47	46	45	47	48	48	43	43	50	44	43	51	41	46	42	52
1970	46	50	44	45	48	49	51	49	48	41	44	43	49	43	43	48	52
1971	54	49	55	57	57	46	47	53	59	52	55	56	57	57	53	58	60
1972	62	59	61	65	63	59	58	59	64	62	57	58	67	69	64	65	61
1973	67	71	66	68	65	69	71	73	67	64	68	65	73	67	70	71	55
1974	64	64	64	65	63	57	68	67	62	69	60	65	62	69	69	56	64
1975	63	55	73	65	56	61	51	54	69	77	74	61	77	58	61	56	51
1976	75	70	76	75	78	70	68	72	77	77	74	80	71	76	90	78	67
1977	95	78	110	95	99	77	80	78	95	120	115	80	99	106	91	96	111
1978	107	100	108	110	113	106	100	94	104	125	94	107	109	112	119	107	114
1979	115	129	115	109	105	120	143	124	125	110	109	112	101	114	106	96	113
1980	100	106	84	104	116	117	106	96	80	80	93	91	119	101	103	127	119
1981	103	116	107	95	93	129	107	112	118	98	104	95	95	96	97	88	110
1982	103	102	94	105	114	113	93	101	84	90	106	98	105	112	101	117	126
1983	132	120	137	135	133	122	114	126	124	142	145	131	140	137	133	139	128

Construction: value of contracts, total (F.W. Dodge Corporation)
billion dollars

Construction : valeur des contrats, total (F.W. Dodge Corporation)
milliards de dollars

	Year	Q.1	Q.2	Q.3	Q.4	JAN	FEB	MAR	APR	MAY	JUN	JUL	AUG	SEP	OCT	NOV	DEC
1964	36.06	8.28	10.23	9.45	8.48	2.53	2.51	3.24	3.43	3.41	3.40	3.55	2.95	2.95	3.13	2.75	2.60
1965	38.47	8.06	11.15	10.34	9.38	2.43	2.36	3.26	3.67	3.85	3.63	3.64	3.48	3.22	3.48	3.02	2.88
1966	37.22	9.05	11.47	9.50	7.78	2.55	2.78	3.73	3.96	3.80	3.71	3.30	3.24	2.96	3.02	2.50	2.26
1967	41.29	7.90	11.34	10.85	10.02	2.11	2.49	3.30	3.46	3.81	4.07	3.58	3.76	3.53	3.76	3.30	2.95
1968	47.35	9.61	12.88	13.05	12.41	2.81	2.75	4.06	3.83	4.77	4.27	4.70	4.42	3.94	4.78	4.04	3.59
1969	50.90	11.33	14.89	13.52	11.95	3.89	3.71	3.73	4.68	5.30	4.91	4.70	4.85	3.97	4.79	3.24	3.91
1970	49.29	11.64	12.90	13.62	11.55	3.73	3.75	4.17	4.88	3.87	4.14	4.82	4.68	4.12	4.17	3.65	3.74
1971	60.30	11.74	17.11	16.80	15.32	3.34	3.47	4.93	5.25	5.57	6.29	5.98	5.38	5.44	5.24	5.13	4.96
1972	72.00	14.60	20.19	19.62	17.67	4.37	4.45	5.77	6.16	7.30	6.73	6.21	7.04	6.37	6.64	5.73	5.30
1973	77.23	18.31	22.12	21.05	16.94	5.62	5.51	7.19	7.15	7.38	7.59	7.22	7.47	6.36	6.43	5.95	4.55
1974	67.46	15.60	20.28	19.13	13.88	4.54	4.94	6.13	6.77	6.98	6.54	7.05	6.31	5.82	5.17	4.55	4.17
1975	62.91	11.96	20.02	15.94	14.09	3.87	3.65	4.45	5.78	6.84	7.40	6.14	5.39	5.41	5.74	4.31	4.04
1976	74.20	14.88	20.17	20.43	18.41	4.29	4.49	6.10	6.55	6.67	6.94	7.14	6.70	6.59	6.75	6.43	5.24
1977	97.10	18.69	26.08	27.67	24.52	5.12	5.34	8.24	8.40	8.69	8.98	8.59	9.88	9.19	8.64	8.32	7.55
1978	120.00	23.15	34.42	33.74	28.70	6.70	6.75	9.70	10.31	12.32	11.80	11.28	11.22	11.24	11.36	9.60	7.74
1979	124.76	27.45	35.91	33.59	27.59	8.49	7.82	11.14	11.48	12.53	11.91	11.45	11.48	10.66	11.55	8.44	7.60
1980	115.54	24.67	26.90	31.85	32.36	8.33	7.85	8.49	8.22	8.62	10.06	10.96	10.35	10.55	11.68	10.67	10.01
1981	120.04	27.49	34.14	31.05	26.62	8.23	8.10	11.17	11.92	10.90	11.33	11.37	9.79	9.91	10.53	8.06	8.04
1982	115.00	23.48	30.55	31.57	29.96	6.86	6.75	9.87	9.65	9.19	11.72	10.16	10.65	10.75	10.66	10.15	9.16
1983	155.26	31.62	42.19	43.13	38.33	9.43	8.99	13.20	12.22	13.48	16.49	13.78	15.26	14.08	14.02	13.09	11.22

Manufacturing new orders, net: durable goods
billion dollars, monthly averages

Commandes nouvelles nettes (industries manufacturières) : biens durables
milliards de dollars, moyennes mensuelles

Adjusted - Corrigé

	Year	Q.1	Q.2	Q.3	Q.4	JAN	FEB	MAR	APR	MAY	JUN	JUL	AUG	SEP	OCT	NOV	DEC
1964		20.06	20.56	20.99	21.10	20.41	20.03	19.75	20.46	20.59	20.63	21.62	20.21	21.15	20.43	20.84	22.04
1965		22.44	22.73	23.44	24.52	22.12	22.44	22.76	22.99	22.45	22.77	23.37	23.21	23.74	23.85	24.54	25.15
1966		26.05	26.35	26.45	25.72	25.51	25.81	26.83	26.29	26.00	26.77	26.28	25.87	27.25	25.99	25.64	25.54
1967		24.65	25.81	25.85	26.91	24.71	24.87	24.38	24.72	25.96	26.74	25.65	26.27	25.63	25.74	26.39	28.61
1968		27.87	27.43	27.73	29.40	27.41	27.30	28.90	27.57	27.31	27.41	27.11	27.44	28.64	30.04	29.03	29.14
1969		29.78	30.15	29.89	29.80	29.26	29.99	30.08	31.52	29.80	29.14	29.60	29.39	30.67	30.13	29.71	29.55
1970		27.68	27.56	27.47	26.87	27.92	27.69	27.43	26.86	27.80	28.02	27.68	26.90	27.83	25.43	26.12	29.04
1971		29.91	29.05	29.94	31.05	29.85	30.10	29.79	29.12	28.75	29.29	29.61	29.56	30.66	30.00	31.25	31.92
1972		32.86	34.12	35.35	37.95	32.32	33.06	33.21	33.66	34.42	34.29	34.21	34.92	36.91	36.67	37.87	39.30
1973		41.59	42.75	42.65	44.67	40.52	41.42	42.85	42.53	42.99	42.72	42.50	42.53	42.95	44.41	46.10	43.51
1974		45.41	47.85	49.94	44.15	45.56	45.48	45.18	45.86	49.02	48.66	49.71	51.17	48.93	45.78	45.47	41.21
1975		39.89	40.60	43.71	43.98	41.06	40.37	38.24	40.64	40.64	40.52	43.88	43.32	43.94	43.33	44.35	44.27
1976		47.66	50.98	52.47	54.48	45.55	47.73	49.72	50.43	51.08	51.44	53.46	51.77	52.17	52.34	54.27	56.82
1977		57.32	60.26	61.68	65.45	56.82	56.55	58.59	59.36	59.74	61.68	60.82	61.53	62.69	64.89	64.09	67.37
1978		66.24	71.56	73.23	78.69	63.68	66.56	68.47	70.94	71.80	71.94	70.34	74.50	74.85	78.79	79.36	77.93
1979		81.89	79.76	77.87	78.46	79.47	82.23	83.96	78.21	80.87	80.20	77.82	76.98	78.80	78.69	78.22	78.46
1980		81.95	72.34	78.67	84.18	83.52	83.44	78.80	75.16	69.93	71.94	77.63	76.35	82.03	83.96	83.41	85.18
1981		83.50	87.97	85.39	77.87	83.17	83.55	83.77	87.38	88.31	88.21	86.94	85.84	83.38	78.47	79.03	76.11
1982		77.41	76.42	73.63	72.66	76.70	77.36	78.18	76.74	76.35	76.16	75.56	72.97	72.35	70.74	71.07	76.18
1983		79.92	86.15	89.74	96.11	82.36	77.45	79.95	83.10	84.46	90.91	88.23	89.93	91.00	93.37	96.51	98.44

Construction: housing starts
thousands, monthly averages

Construction : logements mis en chantier
milliers, moyennes mensuelles

	Year	Q.1	Q.2	Q.3	Q.4	JAN	FEB	MAR	APR	MAY	JUN	JUL	AUG	SEP	OCT	NOV	DEC
1964	130.1	111.3	156.4	135.8	116.8	99.3	102.2	132.3	150.9	155.9	162.4	143.0	141.3	123.2	142.9	113.1	94.5
1965	125.8	97.6	155.9	133.1	116.6	85.8	83.0	124.1	151.3	157.7	158.6	141.5	131.6	126.2	135.2	112.7	101.9
1966	99.7	94.4	133.5	98.5	72.2	81.9	79.0	122.4	143.0	133.9	123.5	100.0	103.7	91.9	79.1	75.1	62.3
1967	110.2	72.6	127.2	127.4	113.4	61.7	63.2	92.9	115.9	134.2	131.6	126.1	130.2	125.8	137.0	120.2	83.1
1968	128.8	99.5	150.8	140.9	124.0	82.7	87.2	128.6	164.9	144.5	142.9	142.3	141.0	139.5	143.3	129.5	99.3
1969	125.0	112.0	156.0	129.0	102.8	105.8	94.6	135.6	159.9	157.7	150.5	126.5	127.5	132.9	125.8	97.4	85.3
1970	122.4	88.1	133.3	136.3	132.1	69.2	77.2	117.8	130.6	127.3	141.9	143.5	131.5	133.8	143.8	128.3	124.1
1971	173.7	129.6	201.3	192.8	171.1	114.8	104.6	169.3	203.6	203.5	196.8	197.0	205.9	175.6	181.7	176.4	155.3
1972	198.2	170.1	222.4	214.3	186.0	150.9	153.6	205.8	213.2	227.9	226.2	207.5	231.0	204.4	218.2	187.1	152.7
1973	171.5	162.6	214.3	184.0	124.9	147.3	139.5	201.1	205.4	234.2	203.4	203.2	199.9	148.9	149.5	134.6	90.6
1974	112.7	107.7	153.4	113.5	76.1	86.2	109.6	127.2	160.9	149.9	149.5	127.2	114.0	99.6	97.2	75.6	55.4
1975	97.1	64.7	106.7	117.2	99.8	56.9	56.2	81.1	99.2	110.1	110.9	120.1	118.7	112.8	125.0	97.2	77.1
1976	129.0	94.4	146.9	145.8	128.7	72.9	91.6	118.8	137.4	148.3	155.1	137.5	146.8	153.1	149.8	128.2	108.1
1977	166.8	123.2	195.0	188.7	160.2	81.5	113.4	174.7	183.4	203.2	198.5	190.9	195.3	180.0	194.2	155.9	130.5
1978	169.7	121.6	209.6	190.2	157.2	89.5	101.9	173.4	199.0	212.9	217.0	193.5	192.0	185.2	192.1	159.5	120.1
1979	146.7	109.2	181.4	159.1	126.9	88.9	85.0	153.6	161.9	189.5	192.9	165.8	172.0	169.6	169.5	119.3	92.0
1980	109.4	80.5	102.5	133.4	121.2	73.8	80.8	86.8	96.8	93.0	117.7	121.6	131.7	147.0	153.7	113.5	96.3
1981	91.7	88.8	113.9	93.1	70.9	85.2	72.4	108.9	124.0	110.6	107.0	101.1	87.3	90.9	88.1	64.9	59.7
1982	89.3	59.4	92.1	104.3	101.6	47.6	52.0	78.7	85.1	99.2	91.9	107.2	97.2	108.4	111.5	109.9	83.4
1983	143.0	108.5	162.6	156.1	134.9	92.9	96.7	135.8	136.4	175.5	175.8	163.6	177.8	156.8	159.9	136.4	108.5

Construction: value of contracts residential (F.W. Dodge Corporation)
billion dollars

Construction : valeur des contrats bâtiments résidentiels (F.W. Dodge Corporation)
milliards de dollars

	Year	Q.1	Q.2	Q.3	Q.4	JAN	FEB	MAR	APR	MAY	JUN	JUL	AUG	SEP	OCT	NOV	DEC
1964	20.56	4.79	6.05	5.40	4.49	1.37	1.43	1.99	2.01	2.05	2.00	2.00	1.68	1.72	1.70	1.48	1.31
1965	21.25	4.45	6.29	5.68	5.04	1.28	1.30	1.88	2.14	2.07	2.08	1.95	1.97	1.76	1.90	1.70	1.45
1966	17.83	4.75	5.83	4.23	3.20	1.34	1.41	2.00	2.08	1.97	1.83	1.48	1.52	1.28	1.23	1.08	0.90
1967	21.16	3.58	5.63	5.48	5.01	0.94	1.06	1.58	1.63	2.00	2.00	1.83	1.91	1.74	1.89	1.72	1.40
1968	24.84	5.18	7.10	5.71	6.19	1.46	1.50	2.22	2.31	2.54	2.24	2.29	2.30	2.13	2.41	2.04	1.74
1969	25.26	5.52	7.71	5.64	5.71	1.75	1.82	1.96	2.55	2.62	2.55	2.30	2.39	1.95	2.29	1.68	1.74
1970	24.84	4.93	6.81	6.87	6.29	1.48	1.48	1.97	2.47	2.12	2.22	2.35	2.35	2.18	2.30	1.95	2.05
1971	34.71	6.18	9.96	9.81	9.17	1.63	1.82	2.73	3.17	3.31	3.49	3.36	3.26	3.20	3.17	3.00	3.00
1972	44.98	8.92	12.71	12.45	10.95	2.65	2.66	3.61	3.96	4.42	4.33	3.81	4.61	4.03	4.25	3.58	3.12
1973	45.70	11.03	13.88	12.10	9.31	3.20	3.28	4.56	4.51	4.75	4.61	4.22	4.23	3.64	3.67	3.30	2.34
1974	34.40	8.28	11.33	8.91	6.10	2.23	2.68	3.37	3.92	3.86	3.55	3.35	3.06	2.50	2.46	1.93	1.72
1975	31.26	5.34	9.18	8.87	7.90	1.54	1.53	2.27	2.99	3.07	3.12	3.08	2.83	2.95	3.17	2.48	2.26
1976	44.17	8.36	12.12	12.22	11.14	2.17	2.56	3.64	4.02	3.93	4.18	4.19	4.20	3.82	4.12	3.76	3.26
1977	62.02	11.81	17.35	17.54	15.23	2.97	3.52	5.33	5.50	5.80	6.04	5.70	6.20	5.64	5.53	5.36	4.34
1978	74.95	14.12	22.57	20.44	17.77	3.93	3.86	6.33	6.85	7.80	7.92	6.82	7.12	6.50	7.08	5.97	4.72
1979	74.56	16.10	22.58	20.14	15.69	4.53	4.59	6.98	7.19	8.08	7.31	6.88	7.08	6.18	6.81	4.70	4.17
1980	63.08	12.86	13.80	18.49	18.19	4.06	4.37	4.44	4.32	4.41	5.07	6.14	6.09	6.26	6.80	5.85	5.54
1981	60.64	14.35	18.28	15.24	12.04	4.23	4.17	5.96	6.62	5.86	5.81	5.81	4.73	4.70	4.72	3.65	3.68
1982	58.50	10.73	15.31	16.08	16.44	2.99	3.14	4.60	4.65	5.06	5.60	5.14	5.41	5.53	5.63	5.63	5.18
1983	92.22	17.51	26.06	25.37	22.28	4.97	4.78	7.76	7.67	8.24	10.16	8.47	9.26	8.64	8.22	7.58	6.48

UNITED STATES

Construction, work put in place: total — billion dollars

Construction, travaux effectués : total — milliards de dollars

	Year	Q.1	Q.2	Q.3	Q.4	JAN	FEB	MAR	APR	MAY	JUN	JUL	AUG	SEP	OCT	NOV	DEC
1964	48.14	9.83	12.28	13.50	12.54	3.31	3.10	3.43	3.87	4.03	4.38	4.54	4.55	4.42	4.34	4.19	4.01
1965	52.34	10.30	13.12	14.72	14.20	3.47	3.23	3.60	4.01	4.38	4.73	4.82	4.96	4.93	4.89	4.74	4.58
1966	52.91	11.53	13.62	14.76	13.01	3.90	3.62	4.01	4.31	4.49	4.82	4.89	4.97	4.39	4.59	4.36	4.06
1967	53.14	10.55	13.26	14.75	14.57	3.50	3.33	3.63	4.08	4.48	4.70	4.84	4.91	5.01	5.01	4.93	4.63
1968	59.17	12.12	15.03	15.18	15.83	4.07	3.82	4.23	4.76	5.10	5.17	5.22	5.45	5.51	5.50	5.35	4.98
1969	65.58	13.91	17.10	18.14	16.44	4.60	4.46	4.85	5.34	5.76	6.00	6.08	6.01	6.05	5.74	5.56	5.14
1970	63.93	13.76	16.05	17.10	17.03	4.51	4.41	4.74	5.11	5.33	5.60	5.55	5.78	5.77	5.71	5.77	5.54
1971	77.14	15.08	19.41	21.55	21.10	5.02	4.82	5.24	6.02	6.52	6.87	7.06	7.30	7.18	7.21	7.16	6.74
1972	89.85	18.67	22.50	24.66	24.03	6.21	5.99	6.47	7.04	7.56	7.90	8.04	8.26	8.36	8.22	8.02	7.78
1973	100.19	21.99	25.43	27.45	25.32	7.33	7.00	7.65	8.08	8.48	8.86	9.11	9.26	9.09	8.99	8.62	7.72
1974	95.01	20.74	24.79	26.01	23.46	6.83	6.73	7.18	7.88	8.43	8.48	8.70	8.82	8.50	8.38	7.88	7.20
1975	88.35	18.32	21.74	24.65	23.64	6.30	5.88	6.14	6.78	7.33	7.62	8.05	8.25	8.36	8.34	8.02	7.29
1976	100.37	20.37	25.41	27.29	27.30	6.56	6.45	7.36	7.94	8.53	8.95	8.89	9.10	9.30	9.56	9.34	8.40
1977	122.45	22.69	31.31	35.63	32.83	7.15	7.14	8.40	9.53	10.49	11.28	11.65	11.99	11.99	11.72	11.25	9.86
1978	148.29	29.71	37.12	42.25	39.20	11.67	8.25	9.79	11.17	12.51	13.45	13.92	14.27	14.07	13.92	13.40	11.89
1979	161.89	31.62	40.72	45.93	43.57	10.44	9.75	11.42	12.44	13.64	14.63	15.16	15.40	15.42	15.54	14.81	13.22
1980	158.21	35.56	38.62	41.38	42.65	12.10	11.35	12.12	12.52	12.90	13.20	13.25	13.84	14.30	14.61	14.49	13.55
1981	165.18	36.76	43.07	44.43	40.88	12.25	11.55	12.96	13.94	14.36	14.77	14.92	14.85	14.71	14.45	13.81	12.62
1982	156.94	32.79	40.11	41.63	42.41	10.31	10.37	11.62	12.59	13.32	14.19	13.80	13.92	13.91	14.33	14.56	13.52
1983	191.18	37.58	46.60	55.47	51.53	12.40	11.90	13.28	14.29	15.44	16.87	17.68	18.83	18.96	17.93	17.60	16.00

Construction, work put in place: residential, private sector — billion dollars

Construction, travaux effectués : bâtiments résidentiels, secteur privé — milliards de dollars

	Year	Q.1	Q.2	Q.3	Q.4	JAN	FEB	MAR	APR	MAY	JUN	JUL	AUG	SEP	OCT	NOV	DEC
1964	28.01	5.79	7.08	7.99	7.15	2.00	1.80	2.00	2.21	2.33	2.54	2.69	2.71	2.59	2.47	2.41	2.27
1965	27.93	5.62	7.01	8.09	7.22	1.96	1.75	1.90	2.12	2.32	2.57	2.72	2.74	2.63	2.52	2.42	2.29
1966	25.72	5.65	6.77	7.40	5.90	1.98	1.76	1.91	2.10	2.25	2.42	2.52	2.52	2.36	2.14	1.96	1.79
1967	25.57	4.49	6.34	7.34	7.40	1.53	1.39	1.57	1.87	2.14	2.33	2.40	2.46	2.48	2.52	2.51	2.36
1968	30.57	5.84	7.80	8.72	8.20	2.00	1.81	2.04	2.38	2.64	2.78	2.86	2.95	2.92	2.84	2.75	2.62
1969	33.20	6.90	8.85	9.38	8.07	2.34	2.18	2.39	2.71	2.98	3.16	3.20	3.16	3.01	2.84	2.70	2.53
1970	31.86	6.52	7.91	8.64	8.80	2.25	2.05	2.21	2.48	2.65	2.78	2.84	2.88	2.92	2.97	2.96	2.86
1971	43.27	7.76	10.86	12.47	12.18	2.59	2.44	2.73	3.24	3.66	3.95	4.09	4.18	4.20	4.18	4.09	3.92
1972	54.29	10.75	13.69	15.14	14.70	3.57	3.40	3.78	4.24	4.58	4.88	4.99	5.07	5.09	5.04	4.94	4.72
1973	59.73	13.03	15.32	16.84	14.53	4.35	4.13	4.55	4.81	5.11	5.40	5.61	5.70	5.53	5.28	4.97	4.28
1974	50.38	10.93	13.24	14.40	11.80	3.72	3.43	3.78	4.14	4.48	4.63	4.86	4.88	4.66	4.40	4.01	3.39
1975	46.47	8.63	11.45	13.61	12.78	2.98	2.67	2.97	3.43	3.85	4.17	4.42	4.58	4.61	4.56	4.38	3.84
1976	60.52	11.02	15.43	16.71	17.36	3.51	3.41	4.10	4.71	5.22	5.50	5.47	5.52	5.73	6.08	6.02	5.26
1977	80.96	14.06	21.11	24.12	21.66	4.35	4.35	5.35	6.26	7.16	7.69	7.97	8.14	8.02	7.81	7.43	6.42
1978	93.42	16.68	24.54	27.53	24.63	5.24	5.16	6.27	7.29	8.30	8.95	9.17	9.32	9.10	8.85	8.48	7.30
1979	99.03	19.32	25.49	28.48	25.74	6.49	5.92	6.91	7.73	8.55	9.21	9.43	9.59	9.46	9.38	8.85	7.52
1980	87.26	19.74	20.87	22.63	24.02	6.82	6.22	6.71	6.88	7.00	6.99	7.12	7.54	7.97	8.28	8.31	7.43
1981	86.57	19.82	23.74	23.12	19.88	6.66	6.14	7.02	7.64	7.99	8.11	7.95	7.70	7.47	7.20	6.75	5.93
1982	74.81	14.62	19.32	17.80	21.07	4.96	4.45	5.21	5.89	6.56	6.87	6.64	6.61	6.56	7.00	7.27	6.80
1983	112.82	19.48	27.61	34.45	31.32	6.23	6.08	7.16	8.22	9.22	10.17	10.99	11.60	11.87	11.19	10.73	9.41

Wholesale sales (5) — billion dollars, monthly averages

Ventes du commerce de gros (5) — milliards de dollars, moyennes mensuelles

	Year	Q.1	Q.2	Q.3	Q.4	JAN	FEB	MAR	APR	MAY	JUN	JUL	AUG	SEP	OCT	NOV	DEC
1964	14.53	13.37	14.39	14.80	15.56	13.30	12.83	13.98	14.24	14.25	14.67	14.80	14.45	15.14	15.79	15.14	15.74
1965	15.60	14.24	15.60	15.83	16.71	13.42	13.26	16.05	15.53	15.21	16.05	15.45	15.82	16.22	16.41	16.82	16.90
1966	16.98	15.99	17.19	17.28	17.47	15.02	15.06	17.90	16.69	16.96	17.90	16.35	18.04	17.44	17.56	17.61	17.22
1967	19.45	18.55	19.49	19.46	20.29	18.01	17.46	20.18	18.63	19.90	19.94	18.61	20.30	19.48	20.48	20.65	19.74
1968	20.85	19.58	20.69	21.20	21.92	19.18	19.23	20.32	20.59	21.09	20.39	21.04	21.43	21.15	22.70	21.51	21.54
1969	22.61	20.37	22.93	23.11	24.03	19.96	19.19	21.95	22.82	23.12	22.85	22.86	22.80	23.65	25.33	22.82	23.95
1970	23.94	22.43	23.95	24.37	25.02	21.77	21.52	24.00	23.67	23.52	24.67	24.28	23.90	24.91	25.55	24.29	25.22
1971	26.26	24.01	26.59	26.94	27.50	22.65	22.75	26.62	25.90	26.04	27.83	26.27	27.00	27.54	26.93	27.61	27.95
1972	29.58	27.27	29.20	29.85	32.02	25.84	26.25	29.72	27.38	30.10	30.11	27.86	31.40	30.29	32.15	32.49	31.43
1973	38.01	33.92	37.33	38.14	42.67	32.69	31.88	37.18	35.75	38.93	37.33	37.16	40.08	37.18	43.02	43.08	41.90
1974	47.75	44.70	48.18	49.03	49.08	43.09	42.25	48.75	48.27	49.31	46.96	48.81	50.09	48.20	50.56	48.06	48.62
1975	46.62	45.64	46.04	46.94	47.87	46.46	43.94	46.52	46.37	46.07	45.70	46.55	46.44	47.82	50.11	45.44	48.05
1976	50.69	48.13	50.88	51.41	52.36	45.76	45.83	52.80	51.08	49.09	52.46	50.17	51.56	52.51	51.14	51.92	54.01
1977	55.57	52.73	57.26	55.12	56.17	48.73	50.20	59.27	56.12	57.30	58.36	53.67	58.00	56.69	56.46	53.50	58.56
1978	66.12	58.63	67.47	67.55	70.82	54.58	55.33	65.97	63.55	69.65	69.20	63.86	71.35	67.44	72.90	71.44	68.14
1979	78.68	70.37	78.38	80.29	85.69	67.32	65.31	78.47	74.80	81.40	78.94	78.28	83.87	78.71	88.32	86.06	82.69
1980	92.66	86.29	88.23	93.57	102.53	85.30	84.10	89.48	88.51	89.01	87.18	91.61	91.97	97.15	105.98	97.40	104.22
1981	100.67	100.26	102.48	99.43	100.51	99.46	94.62	106.71	103.89	101.03	102.54	99.88	97.43	100.94	103.13	97.80	100.60
1982	95.36	94.95	98.93	93.73	93.84	89.34	89.23	106.28	98.69	97.71	100.39	93.27	94.29	93.63	93.07	94.18	94.28
1983	98.78	91.12	97.58	100.09	106.33	87.42	84.97	100.95	91.15	98.52	103.06	94.64	102.79	102.83	105.69	105.93	107.36

Cost of construction / Coût de la construction

(Engineering News-Record) / (Engineering News-Record)

1980 = 100 / 1980 = 100

	Year	Q.1	Q.2	Q.3	Q.4	JAN	FEB	MAR	APR	MAY	JUN	JUL	AUG	SEP	OCT	NOV	DEC
1964	32	31	32	32	32	31	31	31	32	32	32	32	32	32	32	32	32
1965	32	32	32	33	33	32	32	32	32	32	32	33	33	33	33	33	33
1966	34	33	34	34	34	33	33	33	34	34	34	34	34	34	34	34	34
1967	35	34	34	35	36	34	34	34	34	35	35	35	35	35	35	36	36
1968	37	36	37	38	39	36	36	36	36	37	37	37	38	38	39	39	39
1969	41	40	41	41	41	40	40	40	41	41	41	41	41	41	41	41	42
1970	43	42	43	44	45	42	42	42	42	43	43	44	44	44	45	45	45
1971	49	46	48	50	51	45	45	47	47	48	49	49	50	51	51	51	51
1972	54	52	53	55	56	52	52	53	53	53	54	54	54	55	55	56	56
1973	59	57	59	59	60	57	57	58	58	59	59	59	59	59	60	59	60
1974	62	59	61	64	64	59	59	59	61	61	62	63	64	64	64	64	64
1975	67	65	66	68	70	64	65	65	65	66	67	68	68	69	70	69	70
1976	73	71	72	75	76	70	71	71	72	72	73	73	75	76	76	76	76
1977	79	77	78	80	83	77	77	77	78	78	78	79	80	82	83	82	83
1978	86	83	85	88	89	83	83	83	83	85	86	87	88	89	89	89	89
1979	94	90	91	96	98	90	90	90	90	90	93	94	95	98	98	98	98
1980	100	98	98	101	103	98	98	99	98	97	99	101	102	102	102	103	104
1981	108	104	107	109	112	104	104	104	106	107	107	109	109	110	111	112	112
1982	116	113	114	115	117	112	113	113	113	113	115	116	116	116	116	117	118
1983	123	120	122	125	124	119	121	121	121	121	123	124	125	125	124	125	124

Construction, work put in place: / Construction, travaux effectués :

residential, private sector / bâtiments résidentiels, secteur privé

billion dollars, annual rates / milliards de dollars, taux annuels

Adjusted - Corrigé

	Year	Q.1	Q.2	Q.3	Q.4	JAN	FEB	MAR	APR	MAY	JUN	JUL	AUG	SEP	OCT	NOV	DEC
1964		29.3	28.2	27.7	27.3	29.0	29.2	29.7	29.0	27.9	27.7	27.9	27.8	27.4	27.0	27.2	27.6
1965		28.5	27.8	28.0	27.6	28.5	28.5	28.3	27.8	27.8	27.9	28.2	28.0	27.8	27.6	27.5	27.8
1966		28.7	26.9	25.8	23.0	28.8	28.8	28.5	27.5	26.9	26.3	26.4	25.9	25.2	23.8	22.8	22.4
1967		22.5	24.6	25.6	28.9	22.2	22.3	22.9	23.8	24.8	25.2	25.1	25.3	26.4	28.0	29.2	29.4
1968		29.1	30.4	30.6	31.8	28.9	28.9	29.6	30.3	30.7	30.3	30.2	30.5	31.1	31.5	31.8	32.3
1969		33.8	34.2	33.5	31.4	33.3	34.1	34.1	34.0	34.2	34.4	34.2	33.7	32.8	31.8	31.2	31.2
1970		31.8	30.4	31.1	34.5	32.0	31.9	31.5	30.7	30.2	30.2	30.5	30.9	31.9	33.4	34.5	35.6
1971		37.3	41.9	45.0	47.6	36.3	37.1	38.4	40.4	42.2	43.3	44.1	45.1	45.9	45.8	47.5	48.4
1972		51.7	53.2	54.5	57.3	50.2	51.7	53.1	53.0	53.1	53.5	53.7	54.3	55.3	56.2	57.2	58.5
1973		62.7	60.1	60.0	57.0	62.1	63.2	62.8	60.7	59.9	59.8	60.4	60.2	59.4	58.3	57.2	55.6
1974		53.5	51.6	50.4	46.4	53.8	53.5	53.3	52.3	51.6	51.0	51.1	50.4	49.6	47.5	46.2	45.5
1975		43.3	43.7	46.9	50.8	44.3	43.1	42.3	42.8	43.6	44.7	45.8	46.8	48.2	49.4	51.1	52.0
1976		56.3	58.8	57.6	69.2	54.2	56.7	58.1	58.7	59.2	58.4	56.6	56.3	59.9	66.1	70.0	71.6
1977		72.1	80.7	83.2	85.2	68.3	72.4	75.5	78.7	81.5	81.9	82.5	83.3	83.8	84.5	84.7	86.5
1978		84.7	94.6	96.1	96.1	80.8	85.1	88.1	92.6	95.1	96.1	96.6	96.3	95.4	95.1	96.3	96.8
1979		96.6	98.7	101.5	99.0	98.8	95.6	95.4	97.1	98.2	100.7	101.7	101.8	101.2	100.9	98.9	97.4
1980		95.9	80.2	82.0	93.0	99.3	96.7	91.7	84.7	79.5	76.5	77.7	81.8	86.4	90.1	93.9	95.2
1981		95.6	92.1	84.5	76.8	96.3	95.6	94.8	94.7	92.2	89.5	87.8	84.6	81.5	78.8	76.2	75.3
1982		69.7	74.2	72.7	81.2	71.2	68.3	69.6	71.9	75.2	75.5	73.8	72.7	71.7	76.4	81.3	86.0
1983		93.1	107.7	122.8	120.0	89.7	93.6	96.1	102.0	107.5	113.5	112.3	127.1	129.1	121.7	119.1	119.3

Wholesale sales (5) / Ventes du commerce de gros (5)

billion dollars, monthly averages / milliards de dollars, moyennes mensuelles

Adjusted - Corrigé

	Year	Q.1	Q.2	Q.3	Q.4	JAN	FEB	MAR	APR	MAY	JUN	JUL	AUG	SEP	OCT	NOV	DEC
1964		14.08	14.31	14.58	14.92	14.13	14.07	14.05	14.08	14.44	14.43	14.56	14.58	14.59	14.80	14.94	15.02
1965		15.14	15.50	15.64	16.03	15.05	14.79	15.59	15.44	15.51	15.54	15.66	15.58	15.68	15.78	16.16	16.15
1966		17.03	17.10	17.06	16.91	16.98	16.78	17.33	16.97	16.88	17.44	16.99	17.22	16.98	17.03	16.70	17.00
1967		19.35	19.24	19.38	19.99	19.55	19.26	19.25	19.32	19.19	19.21	19.28	19.43	19.42	19.63	20.08	20.25
1968		20.33	20.39	20.93	21.43	20.29	20.31	20.40	20.30	20.24	20.63	20.74	20.96	21.25	21.08	21.52	21.68
1969		21.46	22.56	22.85	23.54	21.11	21.22	22.04	22.48	22.58	22.61	22.47	23.01	23.08	23.65	23.48	23.50
1970		23.53	23.54	24.17	24.53	23.37	23.74	23.49	23.31	23.63	23.68	24.00	24.17	24.34	24.40	24.53	24.66
1971		25.09	26.10	25.68	27.09	24.97	25.01	25.27	25.51	26.14	26.65	26.51	26.65	26.89	26.54	27.14	27.58
1972		28.08	28.63	29.82	31.85	28.50	27.65	28.09	28.33	28.74	28.83	29.07	30.01	30.37	31.07	31.85	32.64
1973		34.85	36.61	38.49	42.21	34.30	34.86	35.39	36.27	36.72	36.83	38.00	38.83	38.63	40.89	42.08	43.66
1974		45.88	47.34	49.24	48.32	44.37	45.73	47.55	47.16	47.10	47.77	49.21	49.14	49.37	47.62	48.44	48.89
1975		47.17	45.18	45.75	47.54	48.30	47.52	45.69	45.18	44.66	45.71	46.15	46.89	47.23	47.64	47.12	47.84
1976		48.99	49.81	51.23	51.86	48.52	48.99	49.48	49.45	49.41	50.57	50.83	50.74	52.13	50.74	51.27	53.56
1977		54.46	55.91	55.95	57.68	53.82	54.79	54.78	55.77	55.64	56.34	55.99	55.98	55.86	56.23	57.86	58.96
1978		60.23	66.22	67.93	70.34	58.32	60.39	61.48	65.02	66.90	66.73	67.07	68.16	68.56	70.64	70.23	70.14
1979		72.14	77.11	81.15	84.31	70.78	71.31	74.33	75.54	77.30	78.48	80.41	81.16	81.89	83.54	84.42	84.98
1980		88.08	86.89	93.97	100.67	88.11	88.82	87.30	87.07	87.15	86.44	91.13	94.13	96.66	99.74	100.23	102.03
1981		103.40	101.18	100.04	98.00	105.06	103.55	101.59	102.38	102.26	98.90	100.44	99.49	100.19	98.47	98.49	97.03
1982		97.39	96.91	93.51	91.57	96.77	97.05	98.36	97.22	97.73	95.78	94.81	93.66	92.05	91.21	92.05	91.45
1983		93.10	96.04	101.00	104.97	94.34	92.35	92.61	92.89	96.65	98.58	99.94	100.89	102.17	104.21	103.79	106.89

UNITED STATES

Retail sales: total (6)
billion dollars, monthly averages

Ventes au détail : total (6)
milliards de dollars, moyennes mensuelles

	Year	Q.1	Q.2	Q.3	Q.4	JAN	FEB	MAR	APR	MAY	JUN	JUL	AUG	SEP	OCT	NOV	DEC
1964	21.82	19.49	22.00	21.77	24.03	19.17	18.78	20.52	21.21	22.53	22.27	22.17	21.80	21.33	22.62	21.74	27.74
1965	23.68	20.72	23.75	23.31	26.93	20.60	19.63	21.94	23.55	23.85	23.85	24.15	23.01	22.75	25.09	25.18	30.53
1966	25.33	22.71	25.42	25.20	27.99	22.10	21.28	24.74	25.50	24.79	25.98	25.35	25.37	24.89	25.95	26.18	31.83
1967	24.41	21.60	24.38	24.45	27.23	21.06	20.11	23.63	23.03	24.51	25.59	24.15	24.60	24.59	24.55	25.85	31.28
1968	27.03	23.67	27.03	27.16	30.27	22.73	22.81	25.47	25.94	27.66	27.48	27.26	28.30	25.91	28.21	29.20	33.39
1969	28.89	25.68	29.05	28.73	32.06	25.56	24.22	27.26	27.99	30.07	29.10	28.74	29.22	28.36	30.37	29.74	36.07
1970	30.70	27.14	30.90	30.94	33.82	27.11	25.55	28.78	29.61	31.40	31.68	31.53	30.92	30.36	32.23	30.79	38.45
1971	33.85	29.37	33.95	34.06	38.04	28.64	27.71	31.74	33.36	33.79	34.70	34.46	33.80	33.92	35.40	35.89	42.83
1972	37.42	32.62	37.35	37.69	42.04	30.74	31.05	36.08	35.27	38.02	38.75	37.17	38.25	37.65	38.93	39.94	47.24
1973	42.46	37.96	42.98	42.45	46.46	36.43	35.58	41.86	41.24	43.58	44.11	42.19	43.79	41.37	44.01	44.94	50.44
1974	45.08	39.30	45.80	45.50	48.73	38.23	36.85	42.82	44.28	47.12	46.01	46.40	48.95	44.14	46.58	46.67	52.93
1975	49.01	42.33	48.86	50.03	54.84	41.66	40.15	45.17	45.88	51.19	49.50	50.39	51.20	48.48	51.97	50.97	61.59
1976	54.78	48.42	55.04	55.03	60.64	47.46	45.77	52.02	54.49	54.71	55.92	56.52	55.01	53.55	56.16	56.62	69.13
1977	60.44	52.72	60.80	60.95	67.26	49.89	49.88	58.40	60.19	60.57	61.63	61.12	62.07	59.68	62.26	63.48	76.06
1978	67.29	57.46	67.58	68.19	75.90	53.35	53.85	65.19	64.36	68.59	69.80	67.37	70.04	67.17	69.65	72.38	85.68
1979	75.05	66.06	74.69	75.65	83.80	62.93	61.73	73.51	71.78	76.09	76.19	73.51	79.38	74.05	77.92	80.43	93.04
1980	80.06	72.71	77.69	80.15	89.71	70.90	70.92	76.30	75.55	79.71	77.80	80.29	82.21	77.95	84.20	84.03	100.91
1981	86.96	78.48	86.88	87.96	94.52	77.12	74.06	84.27	85.62	87.38	87.64	88.60	89.42	85.87	89.18	87.75	106.63
1982	89.55	79.92	89.15	89.54	99.58	77.18	76.10	86.47	87.87	90.71	88.87	91.05	89.50	88.07	91.33	94.18	113.24
1983	97.83	84.63	97.43	99.17	110.09	81.29	78.86	93.74	93.86	97.83	100.61	99.44	100.13	97.93	100.66	103.87	125.76

Retail sales: total
billion 1972 dollars, monthly averages

Adjusted - Corrigé

Ventes au détail : total
milliards de dollars de 1972, moyennes mensuelles

	Year	Q.1	Q.2	Q.3	Q.4	JAN	FEB	MAR	APR	MAY	JUN	JUL	AUG	SEP	OCT	NOV	DEC
1964	27.60	26.89	27.53	28.10	27.88	26.74	26.87	27.06	27.25	27.65	27.67	27.78	28.17	28.36	27.37	27.55	28.73
1965	29.59	28.88	29.12	29.65	30.70	28.86	29.05	28.72	28.96	29.34	29.05	29.53	29.66	29.77	30.50	30.80	30.79
1966	30.97	31.09	30.68	31.17	30.92	30.99	30.93	31.36	30.82	30.29	30.95	31.04	31.24	31.23	31.02	30.99	30.77
1967	29.24	28.83	29.03	29.28	29.83	29.08	28.62	28.80	28.90	28.83	29.36	29.13	29.13	29.57	29.35	29.69	30.46
1968	31.02	30.23	30.76	31.31	31.80	29.86	30.15	30.69	30.60	30.61	31.06	31.38	31.62	30.93	31.61	31.99	31.80
1969	31.92	31.77	31.73	31.92	32.25	31.82	31.93	31.56	31.71	31.84	31.64	31.63	31.90	32.21	32.28	32.14	32.33
1970	32.59	32.25	32.56	32.91	32.65	32.18	32.28	32.29	32.23	32.64	32.82	32.92	32.89	32.92	32.76	32.20	32.98
1971	34.67	33.73	34.25	34.81	35.87	33.60	33.78	33.81	34.22	34.05	34.49	34.39	34.80	35.25	35.53	36.21	35.87
1972	37.32	35.93	36.88	37.49	38.97	35.60	35.74	36.44	36.53	37.02	37.09	37.25	37.52	37.70	38.58	38.78	39.56
1973	39.91	40.55	39.86	39.71	39.51	40.47	40.72	40.47	40.09	39.83	39.68	39.98	39.29	39.87	39.83	40.00	38.69
1974	38.19	38.41	38.57	38.74	37.03	38.61	38.29	38.35	38.68	38.54	38.50	38.74	39.32	38.16	37.46	37.01	36.61
1975	38.46	37.44	38.15	38.89	39.35	37.45	37.96	36.92	37.22	38.63	38.60	38.68	38.91	39.10	38.94	39.37	39.73
1976	40.88	40.34	40.69	40.96	41.55	40.34	40.35	40.34	40.81	40.25	41.01	40.97	41.03	40.81	40.99	41.40	42.26
1977	43.02	42.30	42.79	43.21	43.79	41.85	42.46	42.58	42.86	42.93	42.58	43.14	43.20	43.29	43.82	43.98	43.57
1978	44.98	43.55	45.18	45.16	46.05	42.75	43.62	44.26	45.05	45.18	45.30	45.01	45.22	45.25	45.79	46.00	46.36
1979	45.92	45.90	45.68	45.03	46.05	45.87	45.72	46.12	45.74	45.73	45.57	45.30	46.38	46.41	46.03	46.14	45.99
1980	44.58	45.55	43.65	44.35	44.79	46.50	45.74	44.41	43.68	43.45	43.81	44.44	44.38	44.22	44.69	44.86	44.80
1981	45.09	45.72	45.10	45.28	44.26	45.55	45.91	45.70	45.29	44.70	45.31	44.98	45.71	45.17	44.36	44.25	44.16
1982	44.62	44.27	44.50	44.38	45.32	43.54	44.89	44.39	44.54	45.12	43.83	44.29	44.27	44.59	44.65	45.85	45.45
1983	47.62	45.85	47.46	47.97	49.19	45.67	45.63	46.25	46.65	47.55	48.19	48.09	47.66	48.16	48.76	49.32	49.49

Retail sales: durable goods (6)
billion dollars, monthly averages

Ventes au détail : biens durables (6)
milliards de dollars, moyennes mensuelles

	Year	Q.1	Q.2	Q.3	Q.4	JAN	FEB	MAR	APR	MAY	JUN	JUL	AUG	SEP	OCT	NOV	DEC
1964	7.05	6.27	7.55	7.05	7.32	6.00	6.10	6.71	7.33	7.66	7.68	7.36	6.97	6.85	7.08	6.76	8.12
1965	7.85	6.99	8.20	7.57	8.64	6.64	6.64	7.68	8.02	8.19	8.40	8.11	7.49	7.12	8.46	8.43	9.02
1966	8.19	7.57	8.45	8.06	8.69	7.02	7.03	8.65	8.41	8.11	8.82	8.20	8.28	7.70	8.67	8.45	8.96
1967	7.39	6.49	7.84	7.42	7.83	6.26	5.99	7.21	7.23	7.96	8.33	7.56	7.42	7.29	7.64	7.66	8.17
1968	8.48	7.35	8.83	8.53	9.20	6.84	7.13	8.07	8.31	9.14	9.04	8.92	8.67	7.99	9.31	9.01	9.28
1969	9.05	8.18	9.62	8.93	9.48	7.93	7.83	8.76	9.25	9.81	9.79	9.18	8.61	9.02	9.74	8.93	9.77
1970	9.10	8.09	9.83	9.35	9.12	7.72	7.78	8.77	9.39	9.75	10.34	9.89	9.18	9.00	9.45	8.33	9.60
1971	10.73	9.06	11.19	10.93	11.75	8.22	8.57	10.40	10.85	10.95	11.78	11.06	10.68	11.04	11.75	11.61	11.90
1972	12.37	10.58	12.96	12.53	13.41	9.59	10.08	12.06	11.96	13.25	13.67	12.56	12.71	12.31	13.35	13.14	13.75
1973	14.41	13.34	15.46	14.45	14.38	12.42	12.51	15.09	14.82	15.84	15.70	14.78	14.84	13.74	15.20	14.28	13.68
1974	14.12	12.23	15.26	15.14	13.84	11.59	11.39	13.71	14.63	15.76	15.39	15.71	15.83	13.87	14.48	13.27	13.78
1975	15.25	12.64	15.83	15.91	16.61	12.11	12.41	13.41	14.76	16.32	16.42	16.62	15.74	15.37	16.91	15.49	17.42
1976	18.15	15.83	19.34	18.51	18.94	14.46	15.03	18.01	18.99	19.01	20.01	19.35	18.51	17.64	18.30	18.16	20.34
1977	20.72	17.95	21.98	21.29	21.67	15.97	16.89	21.01	21.39	21.85	22.71	21.34	22.09	20.43	21.75	20.97	22.30
1978	23.21	19.32	24.77	23.85	24.89	17.04	18.02	22.90	23.30	25.21	25.81	24.05	24.89	22.61	24.66	24.43	25.60
1979	25.20	22.78	26.42	25.81	25.78	21.12	21.13	26.08	25.60	27.14	26.52	25.31	27.52	24.60	26.19	24.86	26.30
1980	24.37	22.84	23.81	24.77	26.05	22.25	22.50	23.76	23.25	23.87	24.32	25.54	24.77	24.00	26.04	24.53	27.57
1981	26.31	24.17	27.07	27.57	26.41	22.42	22.95	27.14	26.60	26.63	27.98	27.83	28.22	26.66	26.22	24.89	28.13
1982	27.04	23.67	28.00	27.33	29.17	21.03	22.71	27.26	27.24	28.80	27.94	27.55	27.28	27.16	27.20	28.81	31.50
1983	32.10	26.67	33.20	33.25	35.26	24.18	24.54	31.31	30.83	33.20	35.57	33.39	33.59	32.77	33.59	34.00	38.19

Retail sales: total (6) — Ventes au détail : total (6)

billion dollars, monthly averages — Adjusted - Corrigé — milliards de dollars, moyennes mensuelles

Year	Q.1	Q.2	Q.3	Q.4	JAN	FEB	MAR	APR	MAY	JUN	JUL	AUG	SEP	OCT	NOV	DEC
1964	21.16	21.67	22.16	22.01	21.05	21.14	21.30	21.47	21.76	21.78	21.89	22.20	22.40	21.54	21.74	22.75
1965	22.94	23.22	23.69	24.60	22.92	23.06	22.83	23.03	23.38	23.24	23.62	23.70	23.76	24.37	24.67	24.76
1966	25.11	24.99	25.54	25.50	24.92	24.99	25.43	25.08	24.65	25.22	25.33	25.62	25.67	25.56	25.57	25.38
1967	23.76	24.05	24.54	25.21	23.98	23.57	23.73	23.91	23.84	24.39	24.37	24.37	24.89	24.74	25.13	25.77
1968	25.84	26.56	27.26	28.03	25.44	25.73	26.34	26.30	26.42	26.97	27.23	27.49	27.06	27.78	28.22	28.09
1969	28.31	28.60	28.92	29.62	28.22	28.45	28.28	28.55	28.64	28.61	28.61	28.93	29.23	29.45	29.59	29.83
1970	29.92	30.47	31.00	31.15	29.81	29.99	29.95	30.09	30.59	30.74	30.93	30.98	31.10	31.14	30.69	31.64
1971	32.47	33.30	34.07	35.22	32.26	32.52	32.62	33.15	33.10	33.66	33.63	34.10	34.48	34.84	35.50	35.34
1972	35.53	36.67	37.61	39.44	35.10	35.38	36.11	36.24	36.84	36.94	37.21	37.63	38.00	38.92	39.24	40.15
1973	41.73	42.00	42.58	43.32	41.32	41.86	42.02	41.97	41.98	42.06	42.46	42.32	42.98	43.26	43.88	42.83
1974	43.47	44.90	45.33	45.53	43.17	43.34	43.91	44.59	44.90	45.20	45.79	46.98	46.21	45.78	45.53	45.29
1975	46.58	48.03	49.95	51.16	46.36	47.18	46.18	46.67	48.56	48.86	49.47	50.03	50.36	50.42	51.14	51.92
1976	52.92	53.81	54.84	56.44	52.88	52.90	52.97	53.71	53.30	54.42	54.61	54.93	54.97	55.55	56.22	57.55
1977	58.24	59.56	60.80	62.30	57.33	58.51	58.89	59.44	59.71	59.52	60.52	60.82	61.04	62.01	62.63	62.25
1978	62.94	66.81	68.11	70.66	61.64	62.82	64.35	65.85	66.94	67.65	67.63	67.90	68.81	69.86	70.57	71.55
1979	72.01	73.98	75.07	77.71	71.49	71.62	72.94	73.49	74.01	74.45	74.49	76.46	77.27	77.10	77.77	78.26
1980	78.86	77.37	80.25	82.85	79.69	79.08	77.80	77.01	76.99	78.11	79.54	80.33	80.88	82.10	82.99	83.47
1981	86.22	86.41	88.00	87.03	85.37	86.50	86.78	86.36	85.73	87.14	86.99	88.71	88.30	86.95	87.04	87.12
1982	87.73	88.70	89.51	91.71	86.47	88.85	87.88	88.27	89.79	88.05	89.25	89.25	90.02	90.51	92.75	91.86
1983	92.85	97.00	98.83	101.75	92.53	92.21	93.80	95.13	97.24	98.63	98.83	98.28	99.54	100.92	101.90	102.44

Retail sales: durable goods (6) — Ventes au détail : biens durables (6)

billion dollars, monthly averages — Adjusted - Corrigé — milliards de dollars, moyennes mensuelles

Year	Q.1	Q.2	Q.3	Q.4	JAN	FEB	MAR	APR	MAY	JUN	JUL	AUG	SEP	OCT	NOV	DEC
1964	6.88	7.06	7.27	6.95	6.83	6.92	6.89	6.99	7.17	7.03	7.04	7.25	7.52	6.53	6.73	7.58
1965	7.68	7.68	7.78	8.20	7.71	7.74	7.60	7.66	7.69	7.68	7.77	7.81	7.76	7.99	8.24	8.39
1966	8.32	7.95	8.25	8.25	8.20	8.18	8.59	8.09	7.70	8.04	8.06	8.37	8.34	8.24	8.26	8.26
1967	7.14	7.33	7.46	7.66	7.37	6.98	7.06	7.30	7.29	7.40	7.49	7.44	7.46	7.52	7.56	7.90
1968	8.01	8.26	8.50	8.99	7.82	7.94	8.27	8.10	8.27	8.41	8.54	8.72	8.25	8.87	9.09	9.01
1969	9.04	8.99	8.94	9.24	9.03	9.12	8.95	9.02	9.03	8.93	8.79	8.87	9.16	9.16	9.29	9.28
1970	8.99	9.19	9.29	8.85	8.97	9.06	8.94	9.02	9.26	9.29	9.36	9.35	9.16	9.01	8.50	9.05
1971	10.04	10.42	10.82	11.62	9.93	9.99	10.20	10.41	10.27	10.57	10.56	10.86	11.05	11.54	11.88	11.43
1972	11.58	12.05	12.38	13.47	11.52	11.51	11.70	11.91	12.07	12.18	12.16	12.44	12.54	13.06	13.31	14.05
1973	14.67	14.36	14.31	14.23	14.53	14.71	14.77	14.48	14.45	14.14	14.27	14.22	14.45	14.45	14.67	13.57
1974	13.68	14.22	14.77	13.75	13.64	13.49	13.92	14.11	14.22	14.33	14.61	15.28	14.43	13.89	13.73	13.62
1975	14.12	14.71	15.65	16.48	14.15	14.71	13.50	14.15	14.88	15.09	15.48	15.58	15.88	16.10	16.55	16.79
1976	17.43	17.91	18.11	18.90	17.20	17.63	17.47	17.94	17.70	18.10	18.09	18.21	18.02	18.27	18.84	19.58
1977	19.88	20.45	20.93	21.47	19.42	19.93	20.28	20.47	20.55	20.33	20.73	20.97	21.10	21.44	21.58	21.39
1978	21.12	23.37	23.46	24.64	20.51	20.98	21.88	22.97	23.46	23.67	23.47	23.34	23.58	24.33	24.60	24.99
1979	24.72	25.22	25.41	25.22	24.69	24.37	25.11	25.36	25.25	25.03	24.70	25.74	25.80	25.30	25.08	25.29
1980	25.06	22.77	24.28	25.27	26.02	25.48	23.69	22.82	22.45	23.05	24.26	24.12	24.47	25.04	25.50	25.27
1981	26.77	25.89	25.95	25.63	26.37	27.04	26.89	25.89	25.59	26.19	26.30	27.53	27.06	25.65	25.66	25.58
1982	26.07	26.82	26.72	28.49	25.20	26.70	26.30	26.70	27.65	26.10	26.38	26.54	27.24	27.32	29.51	28.64
1983	29.26	31.72	32.43	34.69	28.96	28.84	29.99	30.67	31.71	32.79	32.60	31.95	32.91	33.88	34.64	35.53

UNITED STATES

Employment in manufacturing (7)
(employees on payrolls)
millions

Emploi dans les industries manufacturières (7)
(salariés sur bordereaux)
millions

	Year	Q.1	Q.2	Q.3	Q.4	JAN	FEB	MAR	APR	MAY	JUN	JUL	AUG	SEP	OCT	NOV	DEC
1964	17.27	16.91	17.15	17.50	17.54	16.86	16.90	16.97	17.02	17.10	17.31	17.27	17.47	17.77	17.41	17.62	17.58
1965	18.06	17.52	17.87	18.31	18.55	17.43	17.52	17.62	17.71	17.81	18.10	18.10	18.30	18.53	18.52	18.56	18.55
1966	19.21	18.60	19.11	19.49	19.66	18.42	18.62	18.76	18.89	19.03	19.39	19.26	19.54	19.69	19.70	19.68	19.60
1967	19.45	19.38	19.33	19.45	19.61	19.41	19.38	19.36	19.28	19.24	19.49	19.26	19.55	19.57	19.51	19.69	19.64
1968	19.78	19.46	19.70	19.92	20.05	19.42	19.46	19.49	19.54	19.61	19.94	19.77	19.93	20.07	20.04	20.06	20.04
1969	20.17	19.93	20.14	20.38	20.23	19.84	19.93	20.02	20.00	20.03	20.39	20.16	20.49	20.48	20.39	20.19	20.10
1970	19.35	19.78	19.53	19.37	18.70	19.81	19.76	19.78	19.61	19.40	19.59	19.29	19.39	19.44	18.78	18.56	18.76
1971	18.57	18.46	18.53	18.63	18.67	18.51	18.45	18.41	18.41	18.50	18.69	18.42	18.64	18.83	18.71	18.70	18.61
1972	19.15	18.63	19.01	19.29	19.68	18.53	18.62	18.73	18.81	18.94	19.28	18.92	19.38	19.56	19.62	19.70	19.72
1973	20.15	19.72	20.07	20.31	20.52	19.59	19.73	19.84	19.90	19.99	20.32	20.05	20.37	20.50	20.54	20.57	20.45
1974	20.08	20.07	20.21	20.29	19.74	20.14	20.04	20.03	20.07	20.14	20.42	20.13	20.33	20.41	20.20	19.81	19.21
1975	18.32	18.23	18.08	18.36	18.62	18.55	18.14	18.00	17.96	18.04	18.24	17.98	18.42	18.67	18.67	18.62	18.58
1976	19.00	18.58	18.97	19.20	19.25	18.49	18.55	18.69	18.84	18.91	19.15	18.91	19.23	19.46	19.24	19.30	19.20
1977	19.68	19.13	19.62	19.91	20.07	19.07	19.08	19.25	19.40	19.57	19.88	19.69	19.92	20.12	20.06	20.06	20.08
1978	20.51	20.02	20.42	20.65	20.94	19.95	19.98	20.12	20.24	20.36	20.65	20.42	20.66	20.87	20.88	20.96	20.97
1979	21.04	20.89	21.12	21.12	21.03	20.83	20.85	20.97	20.99	21.07	21.31	21.03	21.07	21.26	21.15	21.01	20.93
1980	20.29	20.70	20.28	19.95	20.21	20.72	20.67	20.72	20.48	20.21	20.13	19.67	19.99	20.19	20.20	20.25	20.19
1981	20.17	20.03	20.29	20.37	19.99	20.01	19.99	20.09	20.18	20.26	20.45	20.24	20.37	20.50	20.26	20.02	19.70
1982	18.85	19.28	19.06	18.76	18.32	19.34	19.29	19.21	19.08	19.05	19.04	18.70	18.75	18.81	18.50	18.30	18.16
1983	18.68	18.10	18.49	18.89	19.24	18.05	18.08	18.17	18.30	18.47	18.71	18.65	18.89	19.14	19.22	19.25	19.24

Unemployment (8)
thousands

Chômage (8)
milliers

	Year	Q.1	Q.2	Q.3	Q.4	JAN	FEB	MAR	APR	MAY	JUN	JUL	AUG	SEP	OCT	NOV	DEC
1964	3786	4401	3937	3495	3308	4518	4461	4225	3831	3528	4453	3675	3551	3262	3198	3318	3409
1965	3366	3938	3588	3145	2794	3942	4172	3699	3492	3214	4057	3429	3165	2842	2709	2888	2786
1966	2878	3114	3038	2791	2566	3244	3109	2990	2730	2793	3592	3050	2821	2503	2465	2579	2655
1967	2976	3099	2917	3029	2858	3159	3184	2954	2664	2458	3628	3249	2942	2895	2952	2903	2720
1968	2817	3097	2803	2865	2501	3074	3287	2929	2491	2304	3615	3217	2772	2607	2510	2576	2418
1969	2831	2848	2747	3003	2726	2875	2923	2747	2542	2300	3399	3182	2870	2958	2840	2711	2627
1970	4093	3644	3869	4347	4512	3406	3794	3732	3552	3385	4671	4514	4226	4300	4269	4618	4650
1971	5016	5359	4879	5102	4724	5429	5458	5190	4712	4415	5511	5354	5086	4867	4599	4846	4728
1972	4882	5392	4860	4941	4335	5481	5446	5250	4732	4382	5467	5216	4901	4705	4518	4317	4169
1973	4365	4731	4330	4372	4029	4730	4898	4564	4227	3855	4907	4613	4273	4230	3830	4127	4130
1974	5156	5040	4683	5193	5702	5081	5212	4826	4372	4219	5459	5341	4967	5287	5131	5775	6199
1975	7928	8372	8097	7911	7333	8272	8399	8446	7908	7715	8667	8311	7799	7624	7350	7341	7307
1976	7406	8020	7061	7429	7112	8286	8143	7631	6996	6415	7772	7697	7443	7148	6958	7224	7154
1977	6992	7966	6854	6852	6297	7980	8237	7680	6692	6280	7589	7081	6897	6579	6365	6495	6031
1978	6202	6852	5971	6215	5772	7048	6886	6621	5826	5605	6481	6597	6090	5958	5624	5797	5896
1979	6138	6525	5849	6192	5985	6602	6649	6325	5720	5419	6409	6282	6315	5978	5964	5964	6027
1980	7637	7131	7668	8153	7595	7234	7177	6983	7023	7501	8481	8603	8202	7655	7674	7682	7430
1981	8273	8544	7926	7987	8635	8746	8614	8271	7561	7731	8485	8130	7947	7884	8216	8676	9013
1982	10678	10284	10267	10814	11349	10183	10378	10290	9957	9957	10886	11036	10710	10695	10942	11476	11628
1983	10717	12259	11123	10316	9168	12517	12382	11879	11035	10765	11570	10707	10411	9830	9383	9129	8992

Unemployment (8)
as per cent of civilian labour force

Chômage (8)
en pourcentage de la main-d'œuvre civile

	Year	Q.1	Q.2	Q.3	Q.4	JAN	FEB	MAR	APR	MAY	JUN	JUL	AUG	SEP	OCT	NOV	DEC
1964	5.2	6.2	5.3	4.7	4.5	6.4	6.2	5.9	5.3	4.8	5.9	4.9	4.8	4.5	4.4	4.5	4.7
1965	4.5	5.4	4.8	4.2	3.7	5.5	5.7	5.1	4.7	4.3	5.3	4.5	4.2	3.8	3.6	3.9	3.7
1966	3.8	4.2	4.0	3.6	3.4	4.4	4.2	4.0	3.6	3.7	4.6	3.9	3.6	3.3	3.2	3.4	3.5
1967	3.8	4.1	3.8	3.8	3.7	4.2	4.2	3.9	3.5	3.2	4.6	4.1	3.7	3.7	3.8	3.7	3.5
1968	3.6	4.0	3.5	3.6	3.2	4.0	4.2	3.8	3.2	2.9	4.5	4.0	3.5	3.3	3.2	3.3	3.1
1969	3.5	3.6	3.4	3.7	3.3	3.7	3.7	3.5	3.2	2.9	4.1	3.8	3.5	3.7	3.5	3.3	3.2
1970	4.9	4.5	4.7	5.2	5.4	4.2	4.7	4.6	4.3	4.1	5.6	5.3	5.0	5.2	5.1	5.5	5.6
1971	5.9	6.5	5.8	6.0	5.5	6.6	6.6	6.3	5.7	5.3	6.5	6.2	5.9	5.8	5.4	5.7	5.5
1972	5.6	6.3	5.6	5.5	4.9	6.5	6.4	6.1	5.5	5.1	6.2	5.9	5.5	5.4	5.1	4.9	4.8
1973	4.9	5.4	4.9	4.8	4.5	5.5	5.6	5.2	4.8	4.4	5.4	5.0	4.7	4.7	4.2	4.6	4.6
1974	5.6	5.6	5.1	5.5	6.1	5.7	5.8	5.3	4.8	4.6	5.8	5.7	5.3	5.7	5.5	6.2	6.7
1975	8.5	9.1	8.7	8.3	7.8	9.0	9.1	9.1	8.6	8.3	9.1	8.7	8.2	8.1	7.8	7.8	7.8
1976	7.7	8.5	7.4	7.5	7.3	8.8	8.7	8.1	7.4	6.8	8.0	7.8	7.6	7.4	7.2	7.4	7.4
1977	7.1	8.2	6.9	6.8	6.3	8.3	8.5	7.9	6.9	6.4	7.5	7.0	6.8	6.6	6.4	6.5	6.0
1978	6.0	6.9	5.8	6.0	5.6	7.1	6.9	6.6	5.8	5.5	6.2	6.3	5.9	5.8	5.4	5.6	5.7
1979	5.8	6.3	5.6	5.8	5.6	6.4	6.4	6.1	5.5	5.2	6.0	5.9	5.9	5.7	5.6	5.6	5.7
1980	7.1	6.8	7.2	7.6	7.0	6.9	6.8	6.6	6.7	7.1	7.8	7.9	7.6	7.2	7.1	7.1	6.9
1981	7.6	8.0	7.3	7.3	7.9	8.2	8.0	7.7	7.0	7.1	7.7	7.3	7.2	7.3	7.5	7.9	8.3
1982	9.7	9.5	9.4	9.7	10.3	9.4	9.6	9.5	9.2	9.1	9.8	9.8	9.6	9.7	9.9	10.4	10.5
1983	9.6	11.2	10.0	9.1	8.2	11.4	11.3	10.8	10.0	9.8	10.2	9.4	9.2	8.8	8.4	8.1	8.0

Employment in manufacturing (7) / Emploi dans les industries manufacturières (7)

(employees on payrolls) / (salariés sur bordereaux)

millions / millions

Adjusted - Corrigé

Year	Q.1	Q.2	Q.3	Q.4	JAN	FEB	MAR	APR	MAY	JUN	JUL	AUG	SEP	OCT	NOV	DEC
1964	17.11	17.20	17.37	17.43	17.07	17.11	17.14	17.18	17.20	17.22	17.28	17.34	17.48	17.20	17.50	17.59
1965	17.72	17.92	18.18	18.43	17.65	17.71	17.78	17.86	17.91	17.98	18.11	18.16	18.27	18.31	18.44	18.54
1966	18.79	19.16	19.37	19.53	18.63	18.81	18.92	19.05	19.15	19.27	19.31	19.42	19.39	19.48	19.55	19.57
1967	19.54	19.39	19.36	19.51	19.59	19.54	19.48	19.43	19.37	19.36	19.35	19.37	19.36	19.35	19.57	19.60
1968	19.62	19.75	19.81	19.94	19.60	19.62	19.62	19.70	19.75	19.80	19.81	19.82	19.82	19.88	19.94	20.01
1969	20.09	20.19	20.27	20.12	20.02	20.10	20.16	20.16	20.17	20.24	20.28	20.29	20.25	20.22	20.06	20.07
1970	19.96	19.60	19.29	18.64	20.00	19.94	19.94	19.79	19.56	19.46	19.40	19.27	19.20	18.65	18.49	18.77
1971	18.67	18.63	18.55	18.63	18.74	18.68	18.60	18.62	18.67	18.60	18.56	18.51	18.62	18.59	18.64	18.65
1972	18.82	19.07	19.16	19.56	18.73	18.82	18.91	18.99	19.07	19.14	19.09	19.16	19.24	19.42	19.56	19.70
1973	19.93	20.12	20.13	20.39	19.81	19.96	20.03	20.08	20.10	20.17	20.15	20.20	20.18	20.32	20.41	20.43
1974	20.30	20.25	20.17	19.61	20.36	20.29	20.24	20.26	20.24	20.26	20.25	20.16	20.09	19.98	19.66	19.18
1975	18.46	18.12	18.21	18.50	18.77	18.40	18.22	18.13	18.14	18.09	18.06	18.20	18.35	18.45	18.47	18.57
1976	18.80	18.99	19.07	19.13	18.70	18.80	18.89	19.00	18.98	18.99	19.02	19.03	19.15	19.05	19.16	19.18
1977	19.34	19.64	19.81	19.95	19.28	19.32	19.44	19.55	19.64	19.72	19.80	19.79	19.85	19.88	19.93	20.06
1978	20.21	20.43	20.57	20.83	20.14	20.20	20.28	20.36	20.42	20.49	20.53	20.57	20.62	20.71	20.84	20.94
1979	21.05	21.13	21.06	20.92	21.01	21.05	21.10	21.10	21.13	21.17	21.16	21.01	21.02	20.98	20.89	20.90
1980	20.86	20.29	19.90	20.11	20.89	20.84	20.84	20.58	20.28	20.01	19.80	19.93	19.96	20.03	20.13	20.16
1981	20.17	20.31	20.30	19.92	20.17	20.15	20.20	20.28	20.33	20.33	20.36	20.30	20.24	20.11	19.93	19.72
1982	19.43	19.05	18.67	18.26	19.53	19.45	19.31	19.16	19.08	18.92	18.80	18.67	18.56	18.36	18.22	18.19
1983	18.25	18.48	18.80	19.17	18.24	18.25	18.27	18.38	18.49	18.58	18.73	18.79	18.87	19.06	19.17	19.28

Unemployment (8) / Chômage (8)

thousands / milliers

Adjusted - Corrigé

Year	Q.1	Q.2	Q.3	Q.4	JAN	FEB	MAR	APR	MAY	JUN	JUL	AUG	SEP	OCT	NOV	DEC
1964	3970	3832	3653	3643	4029	3932	3950	3918	3764	3814	3608	3655	3712	3726	3551	3651
1965	3604	3471	3257	3082	3572	3730	3510	3595	3432	3387	3301	3254	3216	3143	3073	3031
1966	2898	2883	2858	2827	2988	2820	2887	2828	2950	2872	2876	2900	2798	2798	2770	2912
1967	2924	2939	2949	3076	2968	2915	2889	2895	2929	2992	2944	2945	2958	3143	3066	3018
1968	2919	2796	2779	2696	2878	3001	2877	2709	2740	2938	2883	2768	2686	2689	2715	2685
1969	2707	2762	2921	2930	2718	2692	2712	2758	2713	2816	2868	2856	3040	3049	2856	2884
1970	3430	3929	4296	4855	3201	3453	3635	3797	3919	4071	4175	4256	4456	4591	4898	5076
1971	4959	4958	5070	5090	4986	4903	4987	4959	4996	4949	5035	5134	5042	4954	5161	5154
1972	4995	4935	4900	4673	5019	4928	5038	4959	4922	4923	4913	4939	4849	4875	4602	4543
1973	4391	4384	4320	4343	4326	4452	4394	4459	4329	4363	4305	4305	4350	4144	4396	4489
1974	4670	4750	5174	6100	4644	4731	4634	4618	4705	4927	5063	5022	5437	5523	6140	6636
1975	7666	8288	7993	7812	7501	7520	7978	8210	8433	8220	8127	7928	7923	7897	7794	7744
1976	7363	7235	7463	7532	7534	7326	7230	7330	7053	7322	7490	7518	7380	7430	7620	7545
1977	7343	7035	6835	6655	7280	7443	7307	7059	6911	7134	6829	6925	6751	6763	6815	6386
1978	6381	6112	6171	6084	6489	6318	6337	6180	6127	6028	6309	6080	6125	5947	6077	6228
1979	6130	5958	6161	6302	6112	6173	6104	6062	5861	5950	5986	6313	6183	6298	6248	6361
1980	6699	7734	8234	7953	6684	6684	6729	7369	7938	8075	8375	8287	8039	8101	8021	7737
1981	8037	8019	8057	8988	8074	8050	7988	7891	8111	8055	7884	8043	8244	8653	9014	9297
1982	9665	10382	11024	11775	9393	9693	9910	10303	10363	10480	10896	10910	11267	11544	11887	11894
1983	11486	11240	10529	9507	11523	11516	11419	11369	11188	11162	10600	10633	10353	9896	9429	9195

Unemployment (8) / Chômage (8)

as per cent of civilian labour force / en pourcentage de la main-d'œuvre civile

Adjusted - Corrigé

Year	Q.1	Q.2	Q.3	Q.4	JAN	FEB	MAR	APR	MAY	JUN	JUL	AUG	SEP	OCT	NOV	DEC
1964	5.5	5.2	5.0	5.0	5.6	5.4	5.4	5.3	5.1	5.2	4.9	5.0	5.1	5.1	4.8	5.0
1965	4.9	4.7	4.4	4.1	4.9	5.1	4.7	4.8	4.6	4.6	4.4	4.4	4.3	4.2	4.1	4.0
1966	3.9	3.8	3.8	3.7	4.0	3.8	3.8	3.8	3.9	3.8	3.8	3.8	3.7	3.7	3.6	3.8
1967	3.8	3.8	3.8	3.9	3.9	3.8	3.8	3.8	3.8	3.9	3.8	3.8	3.8	4.0	3.9	3.8
1968	3.7	3.6	3.5	3.4	3.7	3.8	3.7	3.5	3.5	3.7	3.7	3.5	3.4	3.4	3.4	3.4
1969	3.4	3.4	3.5	3.6	3.4	3.4	3.4	3.4	3.4	3.5	3.5	3.5	3.7	3.7	3.5	3.5
1970	4.2	4.8	5.2	5.8	3.9	4.2	4.4	4.6	4.8	4.9	5.0	5.1	5.4	5.5	5.9	6.1
1971	5.9	5.9	6.0	5.9	5.9	5.9	6.0	5.9	5.9	5.9	6.0	6.1	6.0	5.8	6.0	6.0
1972	5.8	5.7	5.6	5.4	5.8	5.7	5.8	5.7	5.7	5.7	5.6	5.6	5.5	5.6	5.3	5.2
1973	4.9	4.9	4.8	4.8	4.9	5.0	4.9	5.0	4.9	4.9	4.8	4.8	4.8	4.6	4.8	4.9
1974	5.1	5.2	5.6	6.6	5.1	5.2	5.1	5.1	5.1	5.4	5.5	5.5	5.9	6.0	6.6	7.2
1975	8.3	8.9	8.5	8.3	8.1	8.1	8.6	8.8	9.0	8.8	8.6	8.4	8.4	8.4	8.3	8.2
1976	7.7	7.6	7.7	7.8	7.9	7.7	7.6	7.7	7.4	7.6	7.8	7.8	7.6	7.7	7.8	7.8
1977	7.5	7.1	6.9	6.7	7.5	7.6	7.4	7.2	7.0	7.2	6.9	7.0	6.8	6.8	6.8	6.4
1978	6.3	6.0	6.0	5.9	6.4	6.3	6.3	6.1	6.0	5.9	6.2	5.9	6.0	5.8	5.9	6.0
1979	5.9	5.7	5.9	6.0	5.9	5.9	5.8	5.8	5.6	5.7	5.7	6.0	5.9	6.0	5.9	6.0
1980	6.3	7.3	7.7	7.4	6.3	6.3	6.3	6.9	7.4	7.6	7.8	7.7	7.5	7.5	7.5	7.2
1981	7.4	7.3	7.4	8.2	7.5	7.4	7.4	7.2	7.4	7.4	7.3	7.4	7.6	7.9	8.3	8.5
1982	8.8	9.4	10.0	10.6	8.6	8.9	9.0	9.4	9.4	9.5	9.9	9.9	10.2	10.4	10.7	10.7
1983	10.4	10.1	9.4	8.5	10.4	10.4	10.3	10.2	10.1	10.0	9.5	9.5	9.2	8.8	8.4	8.2

UNITED STATES

Help-wanted advertising (9)

(The Conference Board)

1980 = 100

Offres d'emploi par annonces (9)

(The Conference Board)

1980 = 100

Adjusted - Corrigé

	Year	Q.1	Q.2	Q.3	Q.4	JAN	FEB	MAR	APR	MAY	JUN	JUL	AUG	SEP	OCT	NOV	DEC
1964	52	48	51	53	55	48	47	48	50	50	52	54	53	54	54	56	56
1965	65	59	62	66	74	57	59	61	61	63	64	64	66	68	71	75	77
1966	81	80	81	81	80	78	79	84	81	81	82	82	81	80	80	80	79
1967	78	79	77	77	78	80	79	77	78	77	77	75	78	78	78	78	78
1968	85	80	82	86	92	80	80	81	82	83	82	85	86	88	92	92	91
1969	94	95	96	93	92	95	95	95	97	97	93	92	91	96	95	92	89
1970	72	83	74	63	63	85	85	80	78	73	72	69	68	67	63	63	63
1971	64	62	63	65	67	61	62	62	62	63	65	64	65	64	65	67	68
1972	80	72	76	81	90	71	72	74	75	76	77	79	81	82	86	88	95
1973	98	98	98	98	97	98	98	98	97	98	98	100	98	97	98	98	95
1974	85	90	93	88	71	91	90	91	93	92	92	92	88	83	77	71	66
1975	62	59	59	65	67	60	59	57	57	57	63	65	64	64	64	67	68
1976	74	71	73	75	78	67	72	73	71	73	74	76	75	73	74	77	81
1977	92	82	87	94	104	81	82	84	85	87	88	94	95	93	99	103	109
1978	116	108	113	117	126	107	108	109	113	112	114	116	115	118	125	125	128
1979	122	123	119	121	125	125	123	121	120	119	119	120	120	123	130	123	123
1980	100	116	90	92	101	119	117	112	95	87	89	92	91	95	98	104	101
1981	92	99	92	92	85	99	100	97	92	92	94	95	92	87	85	86	85
1982	67	79	67	61	61	82	80	74	68	67	66	64	61	57	59	61	64
1983	74	64	67	76	89	64	64	64	63	67	71	78	75	76	86	88	94

Weekly hours of work: manufacturing (7)

gross hours per production worker

Durée hebdomadaire du travail : (7)

industries manufacturières

heures brutes par ouvrier

	Year	Q.1	Q.2	Q.3	Q.4	JAN	FEB	MAR	APR	MAY	JUN	JUL	AUG	SEP	OCT	NOV	DEC
1964	40.7	40.2	40.7	40.8	41.1	39.8	40.3	40.4	40.5	40.7	41.0	40.7	40.9	40.7	40.8	40.9	41.5
1965	41.2	41.0	41.1	41.1	41.5	40.9	41.0	41.2	40.7	41.2	41.3	41.0	41.1	41.1	41.3	41.4	41.7
1966	41.4	41.3	41.4	41.3	41.3	41.2	41.4	41.4	41.2	41.5	41.6	41.1	41.4	41.5	41.4	41.3	41.3
1967	40.6	40.4	40.4	40.7	40.9	40.8	40.1	40.3	40.2	40.4	40.6	40.3	40.7	41.0	40.8	40.8	41.1
1968	40.7	40.4	40.6	40.9	41.0	40.0	40.6	40.6	39.8	40.9	41.1	40.7	40.7	41.2	41.1	40.9	41.1
1969	40.6	40.4	40.7	40.7	40.8	40.4	40.0	40.7	40.5	40.7	40.9	40.4	40.6	41.0	40.7	40.6	41.0
1970	39.8	39.9	39.9	39.8	39.8	40.0	39.8	40.0	39.7	39.8	40.1	39.9	39.8	39.6	39.6	39.7	40.0
1971	39.9	39.6	39.9	39.8	40.3	39.6	39.4	39.7	39.5	40.0	40.2	39.8	39.8	39.8	40.0	40.2	40.7
1972	40.6	40.0	40.6	40.6	41.0	39.8	40.0	40.3	40.5	40.5	40.8	40.4	40.6	40.9	40.8	41.0	41.1
1973	40.7	40.4	40.8	40.7	40.9	39.9	40.5	40.7	40.7	40.7	40.9	40.6	40.5	41.0	40.7	40.9	41.2
1974	40.0	40.1	39.9	40.1	39.9	40.0	40.1	40.2	39.1	40.3	40.4	40.0	40.1	40.3	40.1	39.7	39.9
1975	39.5	38.6	39.1	39.7	40.3	38.7	38.5	38.7	38.9	39.0	39.5	39.2	39.7	40.2	40.0	40.1	40.9
1976	40.1	40.0	40.0	40.1	40.4	40.0	40.0	40.1	39.2	40.3	40.5	40.1	40.1	40.1	40.1	40.3	40.7
1977	40.3	39.7	40.4	40.4	40.8	39.1	39.9	40.2	40.1	40.4	40.8	40.1	40.3	40.7	40.6	40.7	41.1
1978	40.4	39.7	40.5	40.5	41.0	39.2	39.6	40.4	40.4	40.4	40.8	40.3	40.4	40.7	40.6	40.9	41.4
1979	40.2	40.3	39.8	40.1	40.5	40.1	40.2	40.6	38.9	40.1	40.4	39.9	40.0	40.3	40.3	40.4	40.9
1980	39.7	39.8	39.4	39.3	40.3	39.8	39.8	39.8	39.4	39.3	39.4	38.8	39.4	39.8	39.8	40.2	40.8
1981	39.8	39.8	40.0	39.7	39.8	39.9	39.5	39.9	39.7	40.1	40.2	39.6	39.9	39.5	39.7	39.7	39.9
1982	38.9	38.5	39.0	38.9	39.3	37.1	39.2	39.1	38.7	39.0	39.3	38.9	39.0	38.9	39.0	39.3	39.7
1983	40.1	39.2	40.0	40.3	40.9	39.2	38.8	39.6	39.8	39.9	40.3	40.0	40.2	40.8	40.7	40.8	41.2

Hourly earnings: manufacturing (7)

gross earnings per production worker

1980 = 100

Gains horaires : industries manufacturières (7)

gains bruts par ouvrier

1980 = 100

	Year	Q.1	Q.2	Q.3	Q.4	JAN	FEB	MAR	APR	MAY	JUN	JUL	AUG	SEP	OCT	NOV	DEC
1964	35	35	35	35	35	35	34	35	35	35	35	35	35	35	35	35	36
1965	36	36	36	36	37	36	36	36	36	36	36	36	36	36	36	37	37
1966	37	37	37	37	38	37	37	37	37	37	37	37	37	38	38	38	38
1967	39	38	39	39	40	38	38	38	39	39	39	39	39	39	39	40	40
1968	41	41	41	42	42	40	40	41	41	41	41	41	42	42	42	42	43
1969	44	43	44	44	45	43	43	43	43	44	44	44	44	45	45	45	45
1970	46	45	46	47	47	45	45	46	46	46	46	46	46	47	46	47	48
1971	49	48	49	49	50	48	48	48	49	49	49	49	49	50	49	49	51
1972	53	51	52	53	54	51	51	52	52	52	52	52	53	53	53	54	55
1973	56	55	56	57	58	55	55	55	55	56	56	56	55	57	57	58	58
1974	61	58	60	62	64	58	58	59	59	60	61	61	62	63	63	63	64
1975	66	65	66	67	68	64	65	65	65	66	66	66	67	68	68	68	69
1976	72	70	71	73	74	69	70	70	70	71	71	72	72	74	73	74	75
1977	78	76	77	79	81	76	75	76	77	77	78	78	78	80	80	81	82
1978	85	82	84	86	88	82	82	83	83	84	84	85	85	87	87	88	89
1979	92	90	91	93	95	89	90	90	90	91	92	92	92	94	94	95	96
1980	100	97	98	101	105	96	96	97	98	98	99	100	101	102	103	105	106
1981	110	107	109	111	113	106	107	107	108	109	110	110	111	112	112	113	114
1982	117	115	116	118	119	116	115	115	116	116	117	118	117	118	118	118	119
1983	122	120	121	122	124	120	120	120	121	121	121	122	121	122	123	124	125

Labour disputes: time lost (10) / Conflits du travail : journées perdues (10)

thousand man-days / milliers de journées-homme

	Year	Q.1	Q.2	Q.3	Q.4	JAN	FEB	MAR	APR	MAY	JUN	JUL	AUG	SEP	OCT	NOV	DEC
1964	22934	2754	5470	5330	9380	898	1040	816	1170	2400	1900	1740	1200	2390	6590	1730	1060
1965	23297	4950	6280	8010	4057	1740	1440	1770	1840	1850	2590	3670	2230	2110	1770	1380	907
1966	25378	3428	7690	8250	6010	1090	928	1410	2600	2870	2220	3100	3370	1780	2190	2150	1670
1967	42140	4040	11880	13350	12870	1250	1280	1510	2540	4410	4930	4330	2860	6160	7110	3210	2550
1968	49019	10455	18706	11742	8116	2669	4104	3682	5677	7452	5577	4612	4049	3081	3992	2431	1693
1969	42870	8151	13223	10138	11358	3173	2566	2412	3755	4745	4723	4311	3634	2193	3168	4308	3882
1970	66416	8293	17928	17634	22561	3711	2111	2471	5431	6651	5846	5112	3852	8670	11574	7798	3189
1971	47590	7291	10483	16162	13654	2868	1934	2489	2389	4000	4094	7895	5037	3230	5511	5034	3109
1972	27068	6209	8468	8680	3711	2530	1849	1830	2258	2604	3606	3437	2840	2403	1342	1351	1018
1973	27950	4339	7444	8521	7646	1660	1335	1344	1832	2709	2903	2996	2571	2954	2485	3026	2135
1974	47992	4852	15936	17864	9340	1363	1370	2119	2945	6050	6941	8954	5882	3028	2854	3807	2679
1975	31237	4936	8858	11525	5918	1605	1557	1774	2177	3319	3362	4465	3377	3684	2327	1737	1854
1976	37996	3909	11342	13609	9136	1191	1030	1688	3148	3706	4488	5219	3824	4566	4138	3228	1770
1977	35823	5182	8815	10292	11534	1297	1475	2410	2519	3323	2973	3212	3995	3085	3347	3158	5029
1978	26202	11834	2542	9174	2652	4443	3811	3580	729	912	901	1897	2662	4615	1203	742	707
1979	20410	2673	7196	4546	5995	1167	795	711	3649	2074	1473	1424	1739	1383	2048	2273	1674
1980	20846	7167	4190	7167	2322	2432	2580	2155	1498	1096	1596	2697	2151	2319	1273	604	445
1981	16910	1239	11157	3493	1021	258	119	862	4085	4454	2618	1576	1018	899	734	141	146
1982	9060	801	2098	3688	2474	203	241	357	533	658	907	845	754	2089	905	805	764
1983	17461	2771	1967	10510	2213	795	844	1132	790	489	689	1270	8673	567	1143	605	464

Weekly hours of work: manufacturing (7) / Durée hebdomadaire du travail : (7) industries manufacturières

Adjusted - Corrigé

gross hours per production worker / heures brutes par ouvrier

	Year	Q.1	Q.2	Q.3	Q.4	JAN	FEB	MAR	APR	MAY	JUN	JUL	AUG	SEP	OCT	NOV	DEC
1964		40.4	40.7	40.7	40.8	40.1	40.6	40.6	40.8	40.7	40.7	40.8	40.9	40.5	40.6	40.8	41.1
1965		41.3	41.1	41.0	41.3	41.2	41.2	41.4	41.0	41.2	41.1	41.1	41.0	40.8	41.2	41.3	41.4
1966		41.5	41.4	41.3	41.1	41.4	41.6	41.5	41.5	41.4	41.4	41.2	41.4	41.3	41.3	41.2	40.9
1967		40.6	40.4	40.6	40.6	41.0	40.4	40.4	40.5	40.4	40.4	40.5	40.6	40.7	40.6	40.6	40.7
1968		40.6	40.6	40.8	40.8	40.3	40.9	40.7	40.0	40.9	40.9	40.8	40.7	40.9	40.9	40.8	40.7
1969		40.6	40.7	40.6	40.5	40.7	40.4	40.8	40.7	40.7	40.7	40.6	40.6	40.7	40.6	40.4	40.5
1970		40.2	39.9	39.7	39.5	40.4	40.2	40.1	39.9	39.8	39.9	40.0	39.8	39.3	39.5	39.5	39.5
1971		39.8	39.9	39.7	40.0	39.9	39.7	39.8	39.7	39.9	40.0	39.9	39.8	39.4	39.9	40.0	40.2
1972		40.3	40.6	40.5	40.7	40.2	40.4	40.4	40.7	40.5	40.6	40.5	40.6	40.6	40.7	40.8	40.6
1973		40.7	40.7	40.6	40.6	40.4	40.9	40.8	40.9	40.7	40.6	40.7	40.5	40.7	40.6	40.7	40.6
1974		40.4	39.9	40.1	39.6	40.5	40.4	40.4	39.3	40.3	40.2	40.2	40.2	40.0	40.0	39.5	39.3
1975		39.0	39.1	39.7	40.0	39.2	38.9	38.8	39.2	39.0	39.2	39.4	39.7	39.9	39.8	39.8	40.3
1976		40.3	40.0	40.1	40.0	40.5	40.3	40.2	39.6	40.3	40.2	40.3	40.1	39.8	40.0	40.1	40.0
1977		40.1	40.4	40.4	40.4	39.7	40.3	40.2	40.4	40.4	40.5	40.3	40.4	40.4	40.5	40.4	40.4
1978		40.0	40.6	40.5	40.6	39.7	39.9	40.4	40.8	40.4	40.5	40.6	40.5	40.5	40.5	40.6	40.6
1979		40.6	39.9	40.2	40.1	40.7	40.5	40.5	39.2	40.2	40.2	40.3	40.1	40.2	40.1	40.0	40.1
1980		40.0	39.5	39.4	39.8	40.3	40.0	39.8	39.8	39.4	39.2	39.2	39.4	39.6	39.6	39.8	40.0
1981		40.0	40.1	39.8	39.4	40.3	39.8	39.9	40.0	40.2	40.0	39.9	39.9	39.5	39.6	39.4	39.2
1982		38.7	39.1	39.0	39.0	37.5	39.5	39.0	39.0	39.1	39.1	39.1	39.0	38.8	38.9	39.0	39.0
1983		39.5	40.1	40.4	40.6	39.7	39.2	39.5	40.1	40.0	40.1	40.2	40.3	40.8	40.6	40.6	40.5

Unit labour cost: manufacturing / Coût unitaire de la main-d'œuvre : industries manufacturières

Adjusted - Corrigé

1980 = 100

	Year	Q.1	Q.2	Q.3	Q.4	JAN	FEB	MAR	APR	MAY	JUN	JUL	AUG	SEP	OCT	NOV	DEC
1964	50	50	50	50	50	50	50	50	50	50	50	50	50	50	50	49	49
1965	49	49	49	48	49	49	49	49	49	48	49	48	48	48	49	49	49
1966	50	49	50	50	50	49	49	49	49	49	50	50	50	50	50	51	50
1967	51	51	51	51	51	51	51	51	51	51	51	51	51	51	51	51	51
1968	52	52	52	53	53	51	52	52	52	52	52	52	52	53	53	53	53
1969	55	53	54	55	55	53	53	54	54	54	54	54	55	55	55	55	56
1970	57	57	57	58	58	57	57	57	57	57	57	57	58	58	58	57	57
1971	58	58	58	58	57	58	58	58	58	58	58	57	58	57	57	57	58
1972	58	58	58	58	58	57	58	58	58	58	58	58	58	58	58	58	58
1973	60	59	59	60	61	59	59	59	60	59	60	60	60	60	61	61	62
1974	65	63	64	65	69	62	63	63	63	64	64	65	65	65	67	69	72
1975	73	74	74	72	73	73	74	75	74	74	73	72	72	72	73	72	73
1976	74	73	73	74	75	73	73	73	73	74	73	74	74	75	75	75	76
1977	79	77	78	79	81	76	77	77	77	78	78	79	79	80	80	81	81
1978	84	83	83	84	85	82	83	83	83	83	83	84	84	84	85	85	86
1979	90	87	89	91	92	87	87	87	89	88	89	90	91	91	91	92	93
1980	100	95	100	103	102	94	95	96	98	100	103	103	103	103	102	102	102
1981	106	103	105	107	111	103	103	104	105	105	106	106	106	108	110	111	112
1982	116	115	116	115	117	116	114	114	116	117	117	116	115	116	117	117	118
1983	115	118	116	113	114	118	118	117	116	116	115	114	113	113	113	114	114

UNITED STATES

Producer prices: total (11)
1980 = 100

Prix à la production : total (11)
1980 = 100

	Year	Q.1	Q.2	Q.3	Q.4	JAN	FEB	MAR	APR	MAY	JUN	JUL	AUG	SEP	OCT	NOV	DEC
1964	35.3	35.3	35.1	35.2	35.3	35.4	35.3	35.2	35.2	35.1	35.1	35.2	35.2	35.3	35.4	35.3	35.3
1965	36.0	35.5	35.9	36.1	36.3	35.4	35.5	35.6	35.7	35.8	36.1	36.1	36.1	36.2	36.2	36.3	36.5
1966	37.2	36.9	37.0	37.4	37.2	36.7	37.0	37.0	37.0	37.0	37.1	37.3	37.5	37.5	37.3	37.2	37.2
1967	37.2	37.2	37.1	37.3	37.4	37.3	37.2	37.1	36.9	37.1	37.3	37.3	37.2	37.3	37.3	37.3	37.5
1968	38.2	37.9	38.1	38.3	38.5	37.6	37.9	38.0	38.0	38.1	38.2	38.3	38.2	38.3	38.3	38.5	38.6
1969	39.7	39.0	39.5	39.3	40.2	38.8	39.0	39.2	39.3	39.6	39.7	39.8	39.8	39.9	40.0	40.3	40.4
1970	41.1	40.8	41.0	41.3	41.3	40.7	40.8	40.9	40.9	41.0	41.1	41.3	41.1	41.3	41.3	41.3	41.3
1971	42.4	41.9	42.4	42.7	42.7	41.6	42.0	42.1	42.2	42.4	42.6	42.7	42.8	42.6	42.6	42.6	43.0
1972	44.3	43.6	44.0	44.7	45.1	43.3	43.7	43.7	43.8	44.0	44.2	44.6	44.6	44.8	44.7	44.9	45.8
1973	50.2	47.3	49.6	51.6	52.1	46.4	47.2	48.3	48.6	49.6	50.6	50.0	52.9	52.0	51.6	51.8	52.8
1974	59.6	55.5	57.5	61.6	63.7	54.6	55.7	56.4	56.9	57.7	58.0	60.2	62.3	62.3	63.4	64.0	63.9
1975	65.1	63.7	64.4	55.3	66.5	64.0	63.8	63.4	64.1	64.5	64.7	65.4	65.8	66.2	66.6	66.3	66.5
1976	68.1	66.8	67.8	68.6	69.3	66.8	66.8	66.9	67.5	67.7	68.2	68.7	68.4	68.8	69.0	69.1	69.7
1977	72.3	70.8	72.5	72.6	73.4	70.0	70.8	71.5	72.3	72.7	72.4	72.5	72.5	72.7	73.1	73.4	73.8
1978	77.9	75.2	77.5	78.5	80.4	74.5	75.2	75.8	76.9	77.4	78.0	78.4	78.4	79.1	80.0	80.3	81.0
1979	87.5	83.4	86.3	89.0	92.1	82.2	83.4	84.4	85.6	86.4	86.9	88.2	88.7	90.1	91.4	92.0	93.0
1980	100.0	96.4	98.4	101.6	104.0	94.9	96.9	97.5	97.8	98.4	98.9	100.7	101.9	102.1	103.4	103.9	104.5
1981	109.2	107.0	109.5	110.2	110.1	106.0	107.1	108.1	109.2	109.5	109.8	110.3	110.4	110.1	110.2	110.0	110.1
1982	111.4	111.1	111.2	111.7	111.8	111.1	111.2	111.0	111.0	111.2	111.4	111.8	111.8	111.4	111.6	111.8	112.0
1983	112.8	111.9	112.3	113.3	113.9	111.7	112.0	111.9	111.9	112.3	112.6	112.9	113.4	113.7	113.9	113.8	113.9

Producer prices: food (11)(12)
1980 = 100

Prix à la production : alimentation (11)(12)
1980 = 100

	Year	Q.1	Q.2	Q.3	Q.4	JAN	FEB	MAR	APR	MAY	JUN	JUL	AUG	SEP	OCT	NOV	DEC
1964	38.1	38.4	37.8	38.3	38.0	38.8	38.2	38.2	38.0	37.6	37.8	38.2	38.0	38.6	38.2	38.0	37.8
1965	39.7	38.3	39.5	40.3	40.7	38.2	38.4	38.5	38.9	39.3	40.3	40.3	40.2	40.3	40.3	40.5	41.4
1966	42.3	42.4	42.0	43.1	41.8	41.9	42.7	42.5	42.3	42.0	41.9	42.7	43.3	43.4	42.3	41.6	41.5
1967	40.9	41.1	40.9	41.2	40.5	41.6	41.1	40.6	40.2	40.9	41.5	41.7	40.9	40.9	40.5	40.2	40.7
1968	41.9	41.3	41.9	42.2	42.0	40.9	41.5	41.6	41.5	42.0	42.0	42.5	41.9	42.2	41.8	42.1	42.2
1969	44.1	42.8	44.1	44.5	44.9	42.7	42.8	43.0	43.1	44.4	44.9	44.9	44.5	44.5	44.5	45.0	45.2
1970	45.6	46.1	45.6	46.0	44.9	46.0	46.1	46.2	45.7	45.5	45.7	46.4	45.5	46.1	45.1	45.0	44.7
1971	46.5	46.0	46.8	46.7	46.7	45.3	46.5	46.4	46.3	46.8	47.2	47.0	46.9	46.2	46.2	46.5	47.4
1972	50.1	48.6	49.0	50.3	52.0	48.0	48.9	48.7	48.4	49.1	49.6	50.7	50.6	50.9	50.4	51.3	54.2
1973	65.1	58.4	63.6	70.2	68.1	56.0	58.2	60.9	60.5	63.4	66.9	64.2	75.5	71.0	68.2	67.2	68.7
1974	72.5	72.9	68.0	73.0	76.0	72.7	73.9	72.1	69.4	68.5	66.1	70.6	75.0	73.3	75.7	76.1	76.3
1975	75.3	73.4	73.9	77.4	76.7	75.2	73.4	71.5	73.1	74.1	74.6	77.0	77.3	77.9	77.9	76.1	76.1
1976	74.9	74.5	75.8	75.4	73.9	75.5	74.4	73.6	75.1	75.6	76.7	76.9	74.3	74.8	73.4	72.9	75.2
1977	77.3	76.9	79.7	75.9	76.4	75.6	77.1	78.1	80.1	80.5	78.3	77.2	75.4	75.3	75.3	76.5	77.5
1978	84.5	80.3	85.0	85.2	87.5	78.6	80.5	81.8	84.1	84.9	86.1	86.0	84.0	85.6	87.2	86.8	88.4
1979	93.9	92.3	94.2	94.3	95.1	90.4	92.9	93.7	94.6	94.4	93.7	95.0	93.1	94.8	94.3	95.0	96.0
1980	100.0	96.0	95.0	103.4	105.9	94.9	96.9	96.1	93.5	95.6	95.8	100.9	104.3	104.9	106.1	106.5	105.1
1981	102.9	104.5	103.8	103.8	99.5	105.5	104.3	103.7	103.8	103.4	104.0	105.0	104.0	102.4	100.6	99.2	98.6
1982	101.8	101.2	104.0	102.2	99.9	100.6	101.6	101.2	102.9	104.6	104.4	103.2	102.1	101.2	99.7	99.8	100.1
1983	103.8	101.8	103.9	104.4	105.2	100.5	102.4	102.5	104.2	104.2	103.3	102.9	104.5	106.0	105.3	104.7	105.4

Producer prices: textiles and clothing (11)
1980 = 100

Prix à la production : textiles et habillement (11)
1980 = 100

	Year	Q.1	Q.2	Q.3	Q.4	JAN	FEB	MAR	APR	MAY	JUN	JUL	AUG	SEP	OCT	NOV	DEC
1964	54.1	54.1	54.0	54.1	54.2	54.1	54.1	54.1	54.0	54.1	54.0	54.0	54.1	54.1	54.2	54.2	54.3
1965	54.4	54.3	54.3	54.5	54.5	54.3	54.3	54.3	54.3	54.3	54.5	54.5	54.5	54.6	54.5	54.5	54.5
1966	54.6	54.5	54.6	54.7	54.5	54.5	54.5	54.6	54.6	54.6	54.6	54.7	54.7	54.6	54.6	54.6	54.4
1967	54.5	54.5	54.3	54.3	55.0	54.6	54.5	54.4	54.3	54.2	54.3	54.2	54.3	54.5	54.6	55.0	55.5
1968	56.5	55.9	56.1	56.8	57.3	55.8	55.9	55.9	56.0	56.1	56.3	56.6	56.8	57.0	57.2	57.4	57.4
1969	57.7	57.3	57.2	58.0	58.4	57.4	57.3	57.3	57.3	57.1	57.3	57.6	58.1	58.3	58.3	58.4	58.4
1970	58.5	58.5	58.5	58.5	58.4	58.6	58.5	58.6	58.5	58.5	58.5	58.4	58.6	58.6	58.5	58.4	58.2
1971	59.2	58.3	58.9	59.7	60.0	58.3	58.2	58.3	58.6	58.8	59.2	59.5	59.3	59.8	59.8	59.9	60.3
1972	61.9	61.0	61.7	52.2	62.8	60.7	61.1	61.1	61.4	61.8	61.9	62.2	62.2	62.3	62.6	62.8	63.0
1973	67.5	64.2	66.7	58.4	70.9	63.6	64.0	64.9	65.9	66.7	67.5	67.7	68.3	69.1	70.1	70.9	71.7
1974	75.9	73.6	76.0	77.5	76.1	73.0	73.7	74.2	75.0	75.9	77.3	77.5	77.6	77.5	76.6	76.2	75.5
1975	75.2	74.2	73.7	75.0	77.9	75.0	74.4	73.2	73.3	73.7	74.1	74.6	75.0	75.5	77.0	78.1	78.5
1976	80.8	79.7	80.5	81.3	81.7	79.4	79.8	80.0	80.3	80.3	80.9	81.2	81.5	81.2	81.4	81.8	81.7
1977	83.9	82.7	84.0	84.4	84.8	82.2	82.7	83.1	83.8	84.0	84.3	84.2	84.3	84.6	84.6	84.7	85.0
1978	87.1	85.6	86.5	87.5	88.9	85.3	85.6	85.8	86.1	86.5	86.8	87.2	87.5	88.0	88.5	89.0	89.2
1979	91.9	89.7	91.2	92.9	94.1	89.5	89.5	90.1	90.7	91.2	91.8	92.3	93.0	93.4	93.8	94.2	94.4
1980	100.0	96.5	99.3	101.2	103.3	95.5	96.2	97.8	98.8	99.2	99.8	100.7	101.2	101.7	102.6	103.4	103.8
1981	108.7	105.8	108.5	110.3	111.1	105.3	105.7	106.4	107.7	108.6	109.1	109.8	110.4	110.6	111.2	111.0	110.9
1982	111.5	111.9	111.9	111.3	111.0	111.8	112.1	111.8	112.0	112.0	111.8	111.3	111.3	111.4	111.3	111.2	110.5
1983	111.7	110.6	111.3	112.2	112.9	110.5	110.5	110.9	111.0	111.4	111.6	111.9	112.3	112.4	112.9	112.9	113.0

Producer prices: chemicals (11)
Prix à la production : produits chimiques (11)

1980 = 100

	Year	Q.1	Q.2	Q.3	Q.4	JAN	FEB	MAR	APR	MAY	JUN	JUL	AUG	SEP	OCT	NOV	DEC
1964	37.8	37.7	37.7	37.7	37.9	37.6	37.7	37.7	37.7	37.8	37.7	37.7	37.7	37.7	37.9	37.9	38.0
1965	38.1	38.1	38.1	38.0	38.1	38.0	38.1	38.1	38.1	38.1	38.1	38.1	37.9	38.0	38.1	38.1	38.1
1966	38.2	38.1	38.1	38.3	38.3	38.1	38.1	38.1	38.1	38.2	38.1	38.2	38.2	38.3	38.2	38.3	38.4
1967	38.4	38.5	38.6	38.3	38.4	38.4	38.5	38.5	38.6	38.6	38.5	38.4	38.3	38.2	38.4	38.4	38.4
1968	38.4	38.4	38.5	38.3	38.2	38.3	38.3	38.5	38.6	38.6	38.5	38.4	38.3	38.2	38.2	38.2	38.2
1969	38.4	38.2	38.3	38.5	38.6	38.1	38.2	38.3	38.2	38.3	38.4	38.4	38.6	38.6	38.5	38.6	38.6
1970	39.3	38.9	39.2	39.4	39.7	38.7	38.9	39.1	39.2	39.3	39.2	39.4	39.5	39.4	39.6	39.7	39.7
1971	40.1	40.0	40.1	40.1	39.9	39.9	40.1	40.2	40.2	40.1	40.1	40.1	40.1	40.1	40.1	39.9	39.7
1972	40.1	39.8	40.1	40.1	40.2	39.7	39.8	39.7	40.0	40.1	40.1	40.1	40.1	40.1	40.1	40.2	40.3
1973	42.3	40.7	41.9	42.7	43.8	40.4	40.6	41.0	41.4	42.0	42.4	42.6	42.7	42.9	43.3	43.6	44.4
1974	56.4	46.9	52.8	60.0	66.0	45.4	46.2	48.9	50.9	52.7	54.9	57.0	60.9	62.1	64.8	66.5	66.9
1975	69.7	68.7	69.9	69.9	70.3	67.6	68.5	69.9	70.1	70.0	69.6	69.7	70.0	70.0	70.1	70.3	70.5
1976	71.9	71.2	71.9	72.2	72.4	70.9	71.1	71.4	71.9	71.9	72.0	71.9	72.3	72.5	72.5	72.5	72.3
1977	74.1	73.1	74.4	74.4	74.5	72.6	73.1	73.5	74.1	74.6	74.5	74.4	74.4	74.3	74.4	74.5	74.6
1978	76.4	75.0	76.2	76.8	77.7	74.6	75.0	75.4	75.7	76.3	76.4	76.8	76.7	77.0	77.5	77.8	77.8
1979	85.1	79.7	83.6	87.7	90.8	78.8	79.7	80.7	82.7	83.8	84.2	86.5	87.8	88.7	90.0	90.7	91.5
1980	100.0	95.8	100.6	101.4	102.4	94.5	95.6	97.2	99.9	100.9	101.0	101.2	101.6	101.2	101.8	102.5	103.0
1981	110.6	106.6	110.8	112.5	112.3	105.4	106.7	107.8	109.9	110.9	111.6	112.0	112.7	112.7	112.4	112.2	112.1
1982	112.3	112.9	113.1	112.0	111.5	112.6	112.8	113.2	113.1	113.4	112.7	112.1	112.1	111.7	111.4	111.6	111.3
1983	112.6	111.4	111.9	113.3	113.8	111.2	111.6	111.4	112.0	111.9	111.8	112.9	113.1	113.7	113.6	113.9	114.0

Producer prices: metal and metal products (11)
Prix à la production : métaux et ouvrages en métaux (11)

1980 = 100

	Year	Q.1	Q.2	Q.3	Q.4	JAN	FEB	MAR	APR	MAY	JUN	JUL	AUG	SEP	OCT	NOV	DEC
1964	32.8	32.5	32.6	32.8	33.3	32.5	32.5	32.6	32.6	32.6	32.6	32.7	32.9	32.9	33.1	33.3	33.4
1965	33.7	33.4	33.7	33.8	34.0	33.3	33.4	33.4	33.6	33.7	33.8	33.7	33.9	33.9	33.9	34.1	34.0
1966	34.6	34.3	34.6	34.5	34.7	34.1	34.3	34.4	34.5	34.6	34.7	34.7	34.6	34.6	34.7	34.8	34.8
1967	38.3	35.0	34.8	34.9	35.3	34.9	35.0	34.9	34.8	34.8	34.8	34.8	34.8	35.0	35.1	35.4	35.5
1968	35.9	36.1	35.8	35.5	35.9	35.8	36.2	36.3	36.1	35.6	35.6	35.5	35.5	35.8	35.9	35.8	36.0
1969	37.9	36.7	37.4	38.4	39.3	36.5	36.8	37.0	37.2	37.5	37.6	37.9	38.4	38.8	39.1	39.2	39.5
1970	40.8	40.2	41.0	41.1	40.9	39.9	40.2	40.5	40.8	41.1	41.2	41.2	41.1	41.1	41.2	40.8	40.6
1971	41.6	40.7	41.4	42.1	42.3	40.7	40.7	40.7	41.2	41.4	41.4	41.8	42.3	42.3	42.3	42.3	42.2
1972	43.2	42.8	43.2	43.3	43.4	42.5	42.9	43.2	43.2	43.2	43.2	43.2	43.3	43.4	43.4	43.4	43.5
1973	46.4	44.5	46.0	46.7	48.5	43.9	44.4	45.2	45.6	46.1	46.3	46.4	46.8	47.0	47.5	48.4	49.6
1974	60.1	52.2	58.7	64.5	65.1	50.7	51.8	54.1	56.4	59.0	60.8	63.0	64.9	65.4	65.4	65.3	64.6
1975	64.9	65.0	64.7	64.5	65.4	64.9	65.1	65.1	64.9	64.7	64.5	64.1	64.4	64.9	65.5	65.4	65.4
1976	68.5	66.2	68.0	69.8	70.1	65.7	66.2	66.7	67.5	67.9	68.7	69.6	69.8	70.0	69.9	70.0	70.2
1977	73.1	71.3	72.8	74.0	74.3	70.7	71.1	72.2	72.8	72.9	72.6	73.6	74.0	74.3	74.1	74.1	74.6
1978	79.4	76.4	78.6	80.4	82.3	75.2	76.6	77.3	78.3	78.5	79.0	79.5	80.8	80.9	81.9	82.3	82.7
1979	90.8	86.4	89.8	91.5	94.9	84.6	86.5	88.0	89.5	89.6	90.3	91.2	91.5	92.2	94.3	94.8	95.7
1980	100.0	100.3	98.9	99.5	101.8	99.5	101.0	100.3	99.4	98.5	98.6	98.8	99.7	100.5	102.1	101.8	101.6
1981	105.0	103.1	104.5	106.2	106.4	102.8	102.8	103.6	104.5	104.6	104.3	105.6	106.3	106.6	106.8	106.4	106.1
1982	105.5	106.3	105.5	105.0	105.1	106.5	106.4	105.9	106.0	105.9	104.7	104.7	104.6	105.5	105.5	105.1	104.9
1983	107.4	106.0	106.9	108.0	108.7	105.0	106.5	106.4	106.5	107.0	107.1	107.5	107.8	108.6	108.7	108.5	108.9

Producer prices: machinery and equipment (11)
Prix à la production : équipement et outillage (11)

1980 = 100

	Year	Q.1	Q.2	Q.3	Q.4	JAN	FEB	MAR	APR	MAY	JUN	JUL	AUG	SEP	OCT	NOV	DEC
1964	38.7	38.7	38.8	38.7	38.8	38.7	38.7	38.7	38.9	38.9	38.7	38.7	38.7	38.7	38.8	38.9	38.8
1965	39.2	39.0	39.2	39.2	39.4	39.0	39.0	39.0	39.1	39.2	39.2	39.2	39.2	39.2	39.3	39.4	39.4
1966	40.4	39.8	40.2	40.5	41.1	39.6	39.8	39.9	40.0	40.2	40.4	40.4	40.5	40.7	40.9	41.2	41.3
1967	41.7	41.5	41.7	41.7	42.1	41.5	41.6	41.6	41.6	41.7	41.7	41.7	41.7	41.7	41.9	42.1	42.3
1968	43.1	42.6	43.0	43.2	43.5	42.5	42.7	42.7	42.9	43.0	43.0	43.1	43.2	43.3	43.5	43.5	43.6
1969	44.4	43.8	44.2	44.5	45.2	43.7	43.8	44.0	44.0	44.2	44.3	44.4	44.5	44.7	45.0	45.2	45.5
1970	46.5	45.8	46.2	46.5	47.3	45.7	45.8	46.0	46.1	46.2	46.3	46.5	46.6	46.8	47.0	47.2	47.5
1971	48.2	47.8	48.1	48.4	48.4	47.7	47.8	48.0	48.0	48.1	48.2	48.3	48.5	48.4	48.4	48.4	48.5
1972	49.2	48.8	49.2	49.4	49.5	48.6	48.9	49.0	49.1	49.2	49.3	49.4	49.4	49.4	49.4	49.5	49.5
1973	50.8	49.9	50.7	51.0	51.7	49.6	49.8	50.1	50.4	50.7	50.9	50.9	51.0	51.2	51.4	51.7	52.0
1974	58.2	53.1	55.9	60.0	63.5	52.6	53.0	53.8	54.6	56.0	57.3	58.6	60.2	61.3	62.6	63.7	64.3
1975	67.4	65.8	66.9	67.8	68.9	65.4	65.8	66.3	66.7	66.9	67.2	67.5	67.7	68.1	68.5	69.0	69.2
1976	71.4	70.0	70.8	71.7	72.9	69.7	70.0	70.3	70.6	70.8	71.1	71.5	71.6	72.1	72.6	72.8	73.2
1977	75.8	74.1	75.1	76.3	77.9	73.8	74.1	74.4	74.7	75.1	75.4	75.9	76.3	76.7	77.5	78.0	78.3
1978	81.8	79.5	81.0	82.5	84.5	79.0	79.4	80.0	80.4	80.9	81.5	82.0	82.4	83.0	83.7	84.6	85.1
1979	89.1	86.2	88.2	90.2	92.5	85.6	86.2	86.8	87.6	88.2	88.7	89.7	90.2	90.9	91.8	92.4	93.2
1980	100.0	96.0	99.2	101.4	103.6	95.0	96.1	97.0	98.7	99.2	99.8	100.8	101.3	102.1	103.0	103.6	104.3
1981	109.8	106.6	108.9	111.2	112.9	105.7	106.6	107.5	108.4	108.8	109.4	110.5	111.1	111.9	112.4	112.9	113.5
1982	116.3	114.9	116.1	116.3	117.6	114.4	114.9	115.3	115.9	116.1	116.3	116.7	116.8	116.9	117.3	117.6	117.9
1983	119.5	118.6	119.3	120.0	120.3	118.2	118.7	118.8	119.1	119.4	119.5	120.0	120.0	120.2	120.0	120.2	120.5

UNITED STATES

Producer prices: industrial goods (11)
1980 = 100

Prix à la production : produits industriels (11)
1980 = 100

	Year	Q.1	Q.2	Q.3	Q.4	JAN	FEB	MAR	APR	MAY	JUN	JUL	AUG	SEP	OCT	NOV	DEC
1964	34.7	34.7	34.6	34.6	34.8	34.7	34.7	34.6	34.6	34.6	34.6	34.6	34.6	34.6	34.8	34.8	34.9
1965	35.1	34.9	35.0	35.1	35.3	34.9	34.9	35.0	35.0	35.0	35.1	35.1	35.2	35.2	35.2	35.4	35.4
1966	35.9	35.5	35.8	36.0	36.1	35.5	35.5	35.6	35.7	35.9	35.9	36.0	36.0	36.0	36.1	36.1	36.1
1967	36.4	36.3	36.3	36.4	36.7	36.2	36.3	36.3	36.3	36.3	36.3	36.3	36.4	36.5	36.6	36.7	36.8
1968	37.3	37.1	37.3	37.3	37.7	37.0	37.1	37.2	37.3	37.2	37.3	37.3	37.3	37.4	37.6	37.6	37.8
1969	38.6	38.2	38.4	38.6	39.1	38.0	38.2	38.4	38.4	38.4	38.4	38.5	38.6	38.8	39.0	39.1	39.2
1970	40.0	39.6	39.9	40.1	40.6	39.4	39.6	39.6	39.8	39.9	40.0	40.0	40.1	40.2	40.5	40.5	40.7
1971	41.5	41.0	41.4	41.8	41.9	40.8	41.0	41.1	41.2	41.4	41.5	41.7	41.9	41.9	41.9	41.8	42.0
1972	42.9	42.4	42.8	43.1	43.4	42.2	42.4	42.5	42.7	42.8	42.9	43.0	43.1	43.2	43.3	43.4	43.5
1973	45.8	44.2	45.6	46.1	47.4	43.7	44.2	44.7	45.2	45.6	45.9	45.9	46.1	46.4	46.8	47.4	48.1
1974	56.0	50.5	54.7	58.5	60.3	49.3	50.3	51.8	53.4	54.8	55.9	57.4	58.8	59.3	60.0	60.4	60.5
1975	62.4	61.3	62.0	62.7	63.9	61.0	61.3	61.5	61.8	62.0	62.1	62.3	62.7	63.0	63.6	63.9	64.1
1976	66.4	64.9	65.8	66.9	68.1	64.6	64.8	65.2	65.6	65.7	66.1	66.5	66.9	67.3	67.8	68.1	68.2
1977	71.0	69.2	70.7	71.7	72.6	68.6	69.2	69.8	70.4	70.7	70.9	71.3	71.7	72.0	72.5	72.6	72.8
1978	76.3	73.9	75.5	77.0	78.6	73.4	73.9	74.3	75.0	75.5	76.0	76.7	77.0	77.4	78.2	78.6	79.1
1979	85.9	81.1	84.3	87.7	91.3	80.1	81.0	82.1	83.4	84.3	85.2	86.5	87.6	88.9	90.6	91.2	92.1
1980	100.0	96.5	99.1	101.1	103.4	94.9	96.8	97.8	98.8	99.0	99.6	100.6	101.3	101.5	102.7	103.2	104.3
1981	110.7	107.6	110.8	111.7	112.6	106.1	107.6	109.1	110.5	110.9	111.1	111.5	111.8	111.9	112.5	112.6	112.9
1982	113.7	113.4	112.9	113.9	114.6	113.5	113.4	113.2	112.8	112.7	113.1	113.9	114.0	113.8	114.4	114.7	114.7
1983	114.9	114.2	114.2	115.4	115.9	114.3	114.3	114.1	113.7	114.2	114.8	115.2	115.5	115.4	115.9	115.9	115.9

Producer prices: refined petroleum products (11)
1980 = 100

Prix à la production : produits de raffineries de pétrole (11)
1980 = 100

	Year	Q.1	Q.2	Q.3	Q.4	JAN	FEB	MAR	APR	MAY	JUN	JUL	AUG	SEP	OCT	NOV	DEC
1964	13.5	13.8	13.3	13.2	13.5	14.0	13.8	13.5	13.2	13.4	13.4	13.4	13.3	13.0	13.3	13.5	13.6
1965	13.9	13.7	13.8	14.0	14.2	13.8	13.6	13.6	13.7	13.8	13.9	13.9	14.0	14.0	14.0	14.2	14.3
1966	14.4	14.2	14.3	14.5	14.6	14.3	14.2	14.1	14.2	14.3	14.5	14.5	14.6	14.7	14.7	14.7	14.5
1967	14.8	14.7	14.9	15.1	14.6	14.6	14.8	14.9	14.8	15.1	15.0	15.0	15.2	15.1	14.7	14.6	14.5
1968	14.6	14.4	14.7	14.7	14.4	14.3	14.4	14.4	14.6	14.6	15.0	15.0	14.7	14.6	14.4	14.4	14.4
1969	14.8	14.5	14.9	14.9	14.8	14.4	14.4	14.8	14.9	14.9	15.0	15.0	14.9	14.8	14.7	14.7	14.8
1970	15.0	14.7	14.9	15.0	15.4	14.7	14.7	14.6	14.7	15.1	14.8	14.9	15.0	15.1	15.1	15.3	15.9
1971	15.8	15.9	15.8	15.9	15.8	16.0	15.9	15.7	15.6	15.9	15.9	15.9	15.9	15.9	15.8	15.8	15.7
1972	16.2	15.7	15.9	16.4	16.6	15.7	15.6	15.8	15.8	15.9	16.1	16.2	16.4	16.5	16.5	16.5	16.6
1973	19.1	17.4	18.5	19.4	21.1	16.7	17.6	17.9	18.2	18.5	18.9	19.3	19.3	19.5	19.9	20.8	22.5
1974	33.1	27.7	33.2	35.9	35.6	24.7	27.9	30.6	32.0	33.3	34.4	35.5	36.2	36.0	36.2	35.3	35.4
1975	38.2	35.9	36.7	39.5	40.7	35.9	35.7	35.9	36.1	36.5	37.4	38.4	39.8	40.4	40.7	40.8	40.7
1976	41.0	40.3	39.8	41.6	42.4	40.5	40.4	40.0	39.6	39.6	40.1	41.0	41.6	42.1	42.3	42.4	42.7
1977	45.7	43.9	45.9	46.5	46.6	42.9	43.8	44.8	45.5	46.0	46.3	46.5	46.4	46.4	46.6	46.5	46.6
1978	47.6	46.4	46.7	48.0	49.4	46.6	46.4	46.1	46.2	46.6	47.2	47.6	47.9	48.3	48.8	49.2	50.2
1979	65.6	52.1	59.4	71.5	80.8	51.0	51.9	53.4	56.1	59.3	62.8	66.7	71.6	76.2	79.1	80.9	82.3
1980	100.0	92.1	100.9	103.2	104.0	86.5	92.0	97.7	100.5	101.0	101.1	102.9	103.4	103.3	102.4	103.4	106.3
1981	119.5	115.3	123.8	120.4	118.6	109.3	114.1	122.4	124.7	123.9	122.8	121.0	120.6	119.5	119.0	118.4	118.4
1982	112.9	116.8	108.1	115.2	112.0	118.9	117.1	114.3	108.8	105.8	109.6	115.1	115.9	114.5	111.9	112.4	111.8
1983	101.9	102.8	98.3	103.1	102.6	106.9	102.7	98.8	95.8	97.8	101.5	103.0	103.0	103.1	103.3	103.0	101.5

Money supply (M1) (13)
billion dollars, end of period

Disponibilités monétaires (M1) (13)
milliards de dollars, fin de période

	Year	Q.1	Q.2	Q.3	Q.4	JAN	FEB	MAR	APR	MAY	JUN	JUL	AUG	SEP	OCT	NOV	DEC
1964	166.4	154.6	155.5	159.4	166.4	159.4	155.4	154.6	156.8	154.2	155.5	157.1	157.0	159.4	161.3	163.2	166.4
1965	174.3	161.5	162.2	165.6	174.3	166.9	161.9	161.5	164.2	160.3	162.2	163.5	162.8	165.6	168.2	169.9	174.3
1966	178.6	170.4	171.7	172.7	178.6	175.6	170.3	170.4	174.1	169.6	171.7	171.0	170.0	172.7	173.4	174.6	178.6
1967	190.3	174.6	177.4	181.7	190.3	178.4	173.4	174.6	176.6	174.1	177.4	179.1	179.0	181.7	183.9	185.7	190.3
1968	204.8	185.4	190.2	193.9	204.8	191.0	184.9	185.4	189.3	186.6	190.2	191.8	191.4	193.9	196.3	199.6	204.8
1969	211.4	199.8	202.3	203.3	211.4	205.9	199.3	199.8	203.5	199.3	202.3	203.3	201.4	203.3	205.0	207.0	211.4
1970	222.2	205.5	208.9	212.8	222.2	213.0	204.0	205.5	210.1	206.2	208.9	210.1	210.0	212.8	214.4	216.7	222.2
1971	236.9	218.6	225.2	227.7	236.9	222.7	216.6	218.6	223.8	221.1	225.2	227.5	225.9	227.7	229.1	231.2	236.9
1972	258.9	234.2	238.8	244.6	258.9	237.6	231.4	234.2	239.6	234.8	238.8	241.9	241.4	244.6	247.1	250.5	258.9
1973	273.2	251.7	259.3	259.5	273.2	259.3	251.2	251.7	257.0	253.6	259.3	261.1	258.7	259.5	261.4	265.6	273.2
1974	285.1	266.5	271.4	272.6	285.1	271.7	264.1	266.5	271.5	266.3	271.4	273.3	271.1	272.6	274.7	278.8	285.1
1975	298.9	276.3	285.8	287.7	298.9	281.9	273.3	276.3	281.3	278.0	285.8	288.0	286.2	287.7	288.4	293.5	298.9
1976	318.7	291.4	299.5	302.6	318.7	296.9	289.0	291.4	300.0	295.2	299.5	302.4	301.1	302.6	307.1	309.8	318.7
1977	344.3	312.3	321.7	327.9	344.3	317.7	309.0	312.3	322.7	315.7	321.7	326.3	324.3	327.9	332.2	335.7	344.3
1978	372.5	335.0	349.6	357.1	372.5	343.7	332.2	335.0	347.6	342.5	349.6	354.1	351.9	357.1	359.6	363.1	372.5
1979	398.8	360.9	376.8	385.7	398.8	367.9	356.4	360.9	376.2	367.1	376.8	383.4	381.8	385.7	388.0	389.7	398.8
1980	424.7	387.8	393.0	411.0	424.7	395.9	386.2	387.8	392.6	383.4	393.0	400.5	404.1	411.0	417.1	420.7	424.7
1981	452.1	416.9	427.8	432.0	452.1	422.1	410.4	416.9	436.2	423.5	427.8	432.5	430.8	432.0	435.2	440.4	452.1
1982	491.0	440.9	450.8	451.0	491.0	454.3	438.1	440.9	456.3	445.8	450.8	454.3	454.3	461.0	470.6	479.1	491.0
1983	525.3	496.4	510.9	518.9	525.3	485.1	491.1	496.4	497.9	506.9	510.9	514.9	517.4	518.9	521.6	523.0	525.3

Consumer prices: all items (14) — Prix à la consommation : total (14)

1980 = 100

	Year	Q.1	Q.2	Q.3	Q.4	JAN	FEB	MAR	APR	MAY	JUN	JUL	AUG	SEP	OCT	NOV	DEC
1964	37.7	37.5	37.6	37.7	37.9	37.5	37.5	37.5	37.6	37.6	37.6	37.7	37.7	37.8	37.8	37.9	37.9
1965	38.3	38.0	38.2	38.4	38.6	37.9	37.9	38.0	38.1	38.2	38.4	38.4	38.3	38.4	38.5	38.5	38.7
1966	39.4	38.9	39.3	39.6	39.9	38.7	38.9	39.0	39.2	39.2	39.3	39.5	39.7	39.8	39.9	39.9	40.0
1967	40.5	40.0	40.3	40.7	41.1	40.0	40.0	40.1	40.2	40.3	40.4	40.6	40.7	40.8	40.9	41.1	41.2
1968	42.2	41.5	41.9	42.5	43.0	41.3	41.5	41.7	41.8	41.9	42.1	42.3	42.5	42.6	42.8	43.0	43.1
1969	44.5	43.5	44.2	44.9	45.5	43.2	43.4	43.8	44.0	44.2	44.5	44.7	44.9	45.1	45.2	45.5	45.8
1970	47.1	46.2	46.9	47.4	48.0	45.9	46.2	46.4	46.7	46.9	47.1	47.3	47.4	47.6	47.9	48.0	48.3
1971	49.2	48.4	49.0	49.5	49.7	48.3	48.4	48.5	48.7	49.0	49.2	49.4	49.5	49.5	49.6	49.7	49.9
1972	50.8	50.1	50.5	51.0	51.4	49.9	50.2	50.2	50.4	50.5	50.7	50.9	50.9	51.1	51.3	51.4	51.6
1973	53.9	52.2	53.3	54.5	55.7	51.7	52.1	52.6	53.0	53.3	53.7	53.8	54.7	54.9	55.4	55.8	56.1
1974	59.9	57.3	58.9	60.7	62.5	56.6	57.3	58.0	58.3	59.0	59.5	60.0	60.7	61.5	62.0	62.5	63.0
1975	65.3	63.6	64.6	66.0	67.1	63.3	63.7	63.9	64.3	64.6	65.1	65.8	66.0	66.3	66.7	67.1	67.4
1976	69.1	67.7	68.5	69.6	70.4	67.5	67.7	67.9	68.2	68.6	68.9	69.3	69.7	69.9	70.2	70.4	70.6
1977	73.5	71.7	73.2	74.3	75.1	71.0	71.8	72.2	72.8	73.2	73.7	74.0	74.3	74.6	74.8	75.1	75.4
1978	79.1	76.3	78.3	80.1	81.7	75.8	76.3	76.8	77.5	78.3	79.1	79.6	80.0	80.6	81.3	81.7	82.2
1979	88.1	83.8	86.8	89.7	92.2	82.9	83.9	84.7	85.8	86.8	87.8	88.8	89.7	90.6	91.3	92.2	93.1
1980	100.0	95.8	99.3	101.2	103.8	94.5	95.8	97.1	98.2	99.2	100.3	100.4	101.1	102.0	102.9	103.8	104.7
1981	110.2	106.5	109.0	112.0	113.5	105.6	106.7	107.4	108.0	109.0	109.9	111.2	111.9	113.0	113.2	113.5	113.8
1982	116.8	114.4	116.1	118.4	118.6	114.2	114.5	114.4	114.9	116.0	117.5	118.1	118.4	118.5	118.9	118.7	118.2
1983	120.4	118.4	119.9	121.3	122.0	118.3	118.3	118.6	119.4	120.0	120.3	120.7	121.3	121.8	122.0	122.0	122.1

New capital issues: corporations — Nouvelles émissions de titres : sociétés privées

billion dollars — milliards de dollars

	Year	Q.1	Q.2	Q.3	Q.4	JAN	FEB	MAR	APR	MAY	JUN	JUL	AUG	SEP	OCT	NOV	DEC
1964	13.38	2.50	4.85	2.73	3.31	0.99	0.71	0.80	2.24	1.15	1.46	0.87	0.73	1.13	1.03	0.70	1.58
1965	15.99	3.01	5.04	3.91	4.03	0.86	0.79	1.36	1.23	1.77	2.04	1.44	0.93	1.54	0.99	1.40	1.65
1966	18.17	5.19	5.12	4.20	3.67	1.41	1.30	2.48	1.58	1.10	2.43	1.09	1.71	1.40	0.89	1.12	1.66
1967	24.80	5.46	6.21	6.83	6.29	1.68	1.42	2.36	2.02	1.52	2.67	2.59	2.48	1.77	2.41	1.50	2.39
1968	21.96	5.18	5.71	5.13	5.95	1.77	1.61	1.80	1.43	1.87	2.41	2.14	1.43	1.55	2.13	1.77	2.06
1969	26.70	6.22	7.30	6.33	6.84	2.08	2.05	2.10	2.75	2.07	2.48	2.48	1.43	2.43	1.93	2.38	2.53
1970	37.45	7.60	10.22	8.28	11.36	2.40	1.74	3.46	3.14	3.81	3.28	2.61	2.15	3.52	3.61	4.09	3.66
1971	43.23	11.58	11.13	10.16	10.36	2.99	2.85	5.74	3.76	3.16	4.20	3.87	2.61	3.68	3.20	3.64	3.52
1972	40.23	9.33	11.00	8.99	10.91	2.98	3.28	3.07	3.22	3.45	4.33	3.47	2.73	2.75	3.68	3.63	3.61
1973	32.03	8.03	8.18	6.17	9.66	2.32	1.90	3.81	2.41	2.39	3.38	2.56	1.77	1.84	3.22	3.36	3.07
1974	38.31	9.39	9.29	7.61	12.02	3.40	2.72	3.27	3.07	3.20	3.02	3.26	2.70	1.66	4.68	3.85	3.50
1975	53.62	15.27	15.69	9.57	13.09	5.37	4.53	5.38	4.29	5.80	5.60	4.33	2.41	2.84	4.71	4.08	4.31
1976	53.49	13.88	14.13	11.39	14.09	3.38	3.86	6.63	3.51	4.19	6.44	3.22	3.36	4.82	4.51	3.07	6.50
1977	53.79	12.73	13.29	11.89	15.88	4.36	2.79	5.58	3.93	3.73	5.63	4.25	3.45	4.18	4.03	5.34	6.52
1978	47.23	10.67	13.16	12.03	11.37	3.33	2.77	4.57	3.40	4.23	5.54	4.41	3.38	4.24	3.80	3.21	4.37
1979	51.53	11.29	15.09	12.91	12.25	3.77	3.17	4.35	4.69	4.16	6.24	4.10	4.21	4.59	4.60	3.87	3.78
1980	73.69	15.13	24.38	18.49	15.69	6.17	4.51	4.45	5.66	9.07	9.65	8.03	5.44	5.03	5.82	3.94	5.93
1981	70.44	16.88	22.13	11.83	19.60	5.74	4.41	6.74	6.87	5.66	9.60	3.84	3.11	4.88	4.63	8.79	6.18
1982	84.20	14.21	17.39	23.89	28.71	3.10	3.85	7.26	4.93	7.53	4.93	6.22	9.42	8.25	9.99	8.89	9.83
1983	98.54	27.93	30.12	18.98	21.51	7.71	8.49	11.73	10.47	11.49	8.17	6.47	5.94	6.57	6.59	8.10	6.81

Money supply (M1) (13) — Disponibilités monétaires (M1) (13)

Adjusted - Corrigé

billion dollars, end of period — milliards de dollars, fin de période

	Year	Q.1	Q.2	Q.3	Q.4	JAN	FEB	MAR	APR	MAY	JUN	JUL	AUG	SEP	OCT	NOV	DEC
1964		156.0	157.2	160.3	161.8	155.3	155.8	156.0	156.3	156.9	157.2	158.4	159.4	160.3	160.9	161.5	161.8
1965		163.1	163.9	166.5	169.5	162.3	162.5	163.1	163.7	163.3	163.9	164.7	165.3	166.5	167.7	168.4	169.5
1966		172.2	173.3	173.7	173.7	170.8	171.3	172.2	173.5	173.0	173.3	172.1	172.5	173.7	172.9	173.1	173.7
1967		176.6	178.9	182.5	185.1	173.6	174.8	176.6	176.0	177.5	178.9	180.0	181.6	182.5	183.6	184.2	185.1
1968		187.4	191.4	194.8	199.4	186.0	186.6	187.4	188.6	190.0	191.4	192.5	193.8	194.8	196.1	198.0	199.4
1969		202.1	203.4	204.2	205.8	200.7	201.4	202.1	202.7	202.8	203.4	203.8	203.7	204.2	205.0	205.6	205.8
1970		207.9	209.9	213.9	216.5	208.0	206.4	207.9	209.3	209.6	209.9	210.3	212.3	213.9	214.6	215.4	216.5
1971		221.2	226.2	228.9	230.7	217.8	219.3	221.2	222.8	224.7	226.2	227.3	228.2	228.9	229.4	229.9	230.7
1972		236.8	239.4	245.7	251.9	232.8	234.6	236.8	238.2	238.6	239.4	241.3	243.6	245.7	247.6	248.9	251.9
1973		254.6	259.9	260.9	265.8	254.4	254.8	254.6	255.4	257.8	259.9	260.5	260.8	260.9	261.9	263.9	265.8
1974		269.8	271.9	274.1	277.5	267.1	268.3	269.8	269.9	270.7	271.9	272.4	273.2	274.1	275.2	276.8	277.5
1975		280.1	286.4	289.1	291.1	277.4	278.1	280.1	279.4	282.5	286.4	286.9	288.1	289.1	288.4	291.3	291.1
1976		295.8	300.0	303.5	310.4	292.7	294.6	295.8	297.6	299.9	300.0	300.8	302.9	303.5	306.4	307.5	310.4
1977		317.7	322.1	328.5	335.5	313.1	315.5	317.7	319.9	320.7	322.1	324.5	326.2	328.5	331.2	333.2	335.5
1978		341.1	350.3	357.4	363.2	339.3	339.8	341.1	344.3	348.0	350.3	352.2	353.9	357.4	358.3	360.4	363.2
1979		367.9	377.8	386.0	389.0	363.6	365.1	367.9	371.7	373.1	377.8	381.8	384.0	386.0	386.5	386.6	389.0
1980		395.0	394.3	411.7	414.1	391.4	395.6	395.0	387.1	389.1	394.3	399.2	406.3	411.7	415.2	416.6	414.1
1981		424.5	429.9	433.5	440.6	416.7	419.9	424.5	429.7	429.7	429.9	432.0	433.9	433.5	433.3	435.9	440.6
1982		448.6	453.4	463.2	480.5	447.8	448.0	448.6	449.3	452.4	453.4	451.3	458.3	463.2	470.2	476.4	480.5
1983		496.4	510.9	518.9	525.3	485.1	491.1	496.4	497.9	506.6	510.9	514.9	517.4	518.9	521.6	523.0	525.3

M1 plus quasi-money (13)
billion dollars, end of period

M1 plus quasi-monnaie (13)
milliards de dollars, fin de période

	Year	Q.1	Q.2	Q.3	Q.4	JAN	FEB	MAR	APR	MAY	JUN	JUL	AUG	SEP	OCT	NOV	DEC
1964	443.0	410.9	418.7	429.5	443.0	410.7	409.4	410.9	414.8	414.4	418.7	422.7	424.8	429.5	434.0	437.3	443.0
1965	483.7	449.1	456.6	468.0	483.7	448.2	446.6	449.1	453.6	451.7	456.6	460.7	462.7	468.0	473.7	476.9	483.7
1966	506.5	488.0	493.9	499.3	506.5	488.4	485.3	488.0	493.6	490.5	493.9	495.4	495.6	499.3	500.0	500.4	506.5
1967	558.8	516.4	529.8	544.2	558.8	511.5	510.9	516.4	521.6	522.4	529.8	535.2	538.8	544.2	548.8	552.1	558.8
1968	607.3	563.1	572.5	587.0	607.3	562.3	559.1	563.1	568.0	566.6	572.5	577.5	581.3	587.0	593.2	598.8	607.3
1969	615.6	606.1	609.2	605.3	615.6	609.4	603.5	606.1	610.3	605.9	609.2	607.9	603.8	605.3	606.5	610.4	615.6
1970	676.1	612.5	626.3	650.0	676.1	615.7	607.3	612.5	621.3	620.9	626.3	634.3	641.0	650.0	657.9	664.0	676.1
1971	773.9	703.9	729.7	747.6	773.9	686.5	690.5	703.9	716.4	720.3	729.7	737.3	740.7	747.6	755.8	762.2	773.9
1972	882.7	797.5	823.8	851.1	882.7	783.4	786.3	797.5	810.1	812.4	823.8	834.5	842.5	851.1	860.0	868.4	882.7
1973	980.0	910.0	938.2	959.5	980.0	894.0	897.1	910.0	922.8	926.3	938.2	947.9	954.0	959.5	964.7	968.3	980.0
1974	1062.9	1003.5	1032.6	1045.4	1062.9	989.3	991.4	1003.5	1018.4	1021.1	1032.6	1039.5	1042.1	1045.4	1050.2	1053.0	1062.9
1975	1164.1	1080.5	1113.0	1135.5	1164.1	1069.0	1068.4	1080.5	1092.8	1096.8	1113.0	1123.9	1127.0	1135.5	1142.9	1152.6	1164.1
1976	1299.6	1190.8	1225.0	1253.4	1299.6	1172.6	1175.8	1190.8	1209.9	1213.9	1225.0	1236.9	1245.3	1253.4	1267.0	1277.9	1299.6
1977	1457.2	1330.9	1371.6	1409.7	1457.2	1310.8	1313.7	1330.9	1351.2	1355.4	1371.6	1388.2	1396.9	1409.7	1425.2	1437.7	1457.2
1978	1621.1	1486.6	1528.5	1570.5	1621.1	1468.6	1467.4	1486.6	1509.5	1514.6	1528.5	1544.9	1554.3	1570.5	1584.3	1599.8	1621.1
1979	1766.7	1643.2	1684.1	1734.9	1766.7	1627.6	1625.8	1643.2	1666.2	1665.2	1684.1	1703.2	1714.4	1734.9	1749.1	1750.3	1766.7
1980	1944.9	1795.5	1827.7	1885.7	1944.9	1775.7	1781.4	1795.5	1802.9	1805.2	1827.7	1851.8	1869.5	1885.7	1906.9	1926.0	1944.9
1981	2175.9	1994.7	2044.9	2105.4	2175.9	1966.0	1971.6	1994.7	2022.3	2023.5	2044.9	2067.4	2088.0	2105.4	2126.7	2149.5	2175.9
1982	2385.3	2211.0	2257.2	2324.4	2385.3	2193.5	2189.2	2211.0	2235.3	2237.3	2257.2	2280.8	2308.8	2324.4	2350.4	2369.2	2385.3
1983	2713.1	2532.3	2593.0	2631.0	2713.1	2489.9	2517.1	2532.3	2550.6	2571.0	2593.0	2604.0	2617.2	2631.0	2655.1	2690.0	2713.1

Loans and investments including U.S. Government securities: (15)
commercial banks
billion dollars

Prêts et placements y compris les fonds d'État : (15)
banques commerciales
milliards de dollars

	Year	Q.1	Q.2	Q.3	Q.4	JAN	FEB	MAR	APR	MAY	JUN	JUL	AUG	SEP	OCT	NOV	DEC
1964	279.2	254.0	261.9	256.9	279.2	250.3	251.3	254.0	254.8	255.7	261.9	258.8	260.7	266.9	267.1	271.0	279.2
1965	307.6	279.2	289.3	292.1	307.6	274.4	276.0	279.2	281.3	282.5	289.3	286.5	288.5	292.1	295.5	297.7	307.6
1966	324.0	303.8	315.9	314.5	324.0	302.4	301.6	303.8	307.1	307.8	315.9	312.6	313.1	314.6	313.8	314.8	324.0
1967	360.8	325.9	335.3	344.7	360.8	319.8	320.4	325.9	328.3	329.4	335.3	337.7	340.1	344.7	347.6	350.0	360.8
1968	400.4	357.4	367.7	380.6	400.4	356.3	356.6	357.4	360.5	361.3	367.7	371.9	373.8	380.6	385.4	387.6	400.4
1969	412.1	392.3	403.2	398.0	412.1	391.4	390.4	392.3	398.3	397.1	403.2	399.4	396.2	398.0	398.7	402.0	412.1
1970	446.8	400.5	411.7	424.7	446.8	399.1	397.2	400.5	404.8	405.3	411.7	414.1	416.8	424.7	425.6	429.3	446.8
1971	497.9	447.7	464.8	472.0	497.9	439.5	442.4	447.7	450.9	453.6	464.8	463.0	466.1	472.0	476.5	479.9	497.9
1972	577.1	501.5	521.6	535.0	577.1	490.1	492.4	501.5	506.6	513.7	521.6	521.4	525.8	535.0	540.3	549.9	577.1
1973	653.2	590.8	613.3	633.2	653.2	575.2	580.1	590.8	597.8	604.1	613.3	620.5	627.8	633.2	637.0	642.3	653.2
1974	719.8	666.2	694.2	708.5	719.8	654.7	655.4	666.2	679.7	685.6	694.2	699.9	704.8	708.5	708.8	711.2	719.8
1975	751.3	713.2	723.6	733.0	751.3	714.3	707.4	713.2	716.7	717.8	723.6	724.2	726.1	733.0	736.3	740.0	751.3
1976	811.5	750.9	769.5	781.1	811.5	744.8	743.0	750.9	757.8	761.0	769.5	769.7	775.1	781.1	789.4	797.8	811.5
1977	899.0	821.6	848.0	869.7	899.0	809.9	810.7	821.6	831.3	838.3	848.0	852.6	861.2	869.7	877.6	887.2	899.0
1978	1022.5	915.7	953.4	982.3	1022.5	900.8	902.8	915.7	930.1	938.6	953.4	962.1	968.2	982.3	994.5	1007.4	1022.5
1979	1145.0	1044.0	1083.6	1126.4	1145.0	1029.5	1031.5	1044.0	1060.0	1066.4	1083.6	1094.5	1103.9	1126.4	1133.1	1131.5	1145.0
1980	1249.5	1162.0	1159.7	1195.3	1249.5	1147.1	1153.2	1162.0	1163.5	1156.0	1159.7	1164.9	1180.4	1195.3	1208.7	1226.8	1249.5
1981	1326.1	1256.7	1293.1	1320.5	1326.1	1254.8	1251.4	1256.7	1267.0	1278.5	1293.1	1297.3	1306.2	1320.5	1329.9	1333.4	1326.1
1982	1422.5	1337.3	1366.3	1391.0	1422.5	1322.6	1328.2	1337.3	1351.4	1356.0	1366.3	1370.4	1377.7	1391.0	1402.8	1405.4	1422.5
1983	1578.1	1445.0	1485.6	1521.6	1578.1	1430.5	1432.2	1445.0	1460.0	1468.1	1485.6	1493.6	1507.0	1521.6	1538.2	1555.8	1578.1

Loans: commercial banks (15)
billion dollars

Prêts : banques commerciales (15)
milliards de dollars

	Year	Q.1	Q.2	Q.3	Q.4	JAN	FEB	MAR	APR	MAY	JUN	JUL	AUG	SEP	OCT	NOV	DEC
1964	177.4	157.0	166.2	168.4	177.4	153.6	154.7	157.0	158.9	160.9	166.2	164.0	164.3	168.4	167.7	170.2	177.4
1965	203.2	179.9	190.2	192.3	203.2	173.8	175.8	179.9	181.6	184.2	190.2	187.7	189.6	192.3	192.9	195.1	203.2
1966	219.0	203.0	213.6	212.2	219.0	198.4	199.2	203.0	205.2	207.1	213.6	211.2	211.0	212.2	211.6	212.5	219.0
1967	236.8	216.1	224.4	226.3	236.8	214.4	213.1	216.1	218.2	218.9	224.4	223.9	223.2	226.3	226.2	227.4	236.8
1968	264.4	233.0	244.8	250.5	264.4	232.3	231.3	233.0	236.8	237.5	244.8	246.8	246.3	250.5	251.8	255.3	264.4
1969	286.1	262.3	276.8	273.6	286.1	257.7	260.1	262.3	268.0	269.9	276.8	273.5	271.0	273.6	273.9	276.1	286.1
1970	299.0	276.3	284.5	289.5	299.0	275.6	275.0	276.3	278.2	278.4	284.5	284.9	284.7	289.5	287.5	288.4	299.0
1971	328.3	294.6	307.1	313.4	328.3	290.9	292.1	294.6	296.7	300.0	307.1	305.6	309.3	313.4	315.1	317.3	328.3
1972	393.6	330.5	349.8	360.7	393.6	322.7	324.3	330.5	335.1	341.6	349.8	350.3	353.7	360.7	365.2	371.8	393.6
1973	464.5	411.2	434.0	452.1	464.5	392.3	400.0	411.2	418.0	425.4	434.0	441.6	448.4	452.1	454.2	456.5	464.5
1974	524.8	473.4	502.4	518.4	524.8	464.4	465.1	473.4	486.6	494.0	502.4	510.1	514.4	518.4	519.1	519.6	524.8
1975	521.9	512.8	512.1	512.5	521.9	519.2	512.3	512.8	511.3	510.4	512.1	511.1	509.7	512.5	514.3	514.7	521.9
1976	560.1	517.5	530.9	540.4	560.1	515.0	512.4	517.5	519.9	523.5	530.9	532.3	535.8	540.4	547.0	551.6	560.1
1977	638.2	566.4	590.0	612.4	638.2	558.8	558.5	566.4	573.5	581.0	590.0	596.2	604.9	612.4	621.2	629.0	638.2
1978	754.2	653.4	688.8	716.3	754.2	641.8	642.8	653.4	664.6	675.0	688.8	699.3	705.1	716.3	728.8	740.8	754.2
1979	857.4	769.4	806.3	845.1	857.4	758.5	760.1	769.4	782.6	790.3	806.3	817.9	826.4	845.1	850.6	847.4	857.4
1980	923.3	869.7	859.0	882.1	923.3	859.6	863.2	869.7	869.5	859.4	859.0	861.1	870.7	882.1	892.4	905.6	923.3
1981	981.8	923.3	954.7	982.1	981.8	925.2	920.2	923.3	931.4	942.3	954.7	960.6	968.7	982.1	989.4	992.0	981.8
1982	1050.4	988.6	1014.6	1035.5	1050.4	977.3	981.1	988.6	998.7	1005.1	1014.6	1020.1	1024.9	1035.5	1044.0	1043.5	1050.4
1983	1140.7	1049.5	1068.0	1098.2	1140.7	1047.7	1044.4	1049.5	1056.0	1057.6	1068.0	1077.2	1087.5	1098.2	1110.4	1123.4	1140.7

M1 plus quasi-money (13) / M1 plus quasi-monnaie (13)

billion dollars, end of period / milliards de dollars, fin de période

Adjusted - Corrigé

Year	Q.1	Q.2	Q.3	Q.4	JAN	FEB	MAR	APR	MAY	JUN	JUL	AUG	SEP	OCT	NOV	DEC
1964	411.6	420.0	430.8	439.9	406.5	409.3	411.6	413.7	416.8	420.0	423.4	427.0	430.8	433.7	437.0	439.9
1965	449.9	458.0	469.3	480.3	443.5	446.8	449.9	452.5	454.6	458.0	461.4	465.0	469.3	473.2	476.5	480.3
1966	489.1	495.3	500.4	503.2	483.5	486.1	489.1	492.3	493.7	495.3	496.0	497.7	500.4	499.5	499.9	503.2
1967	517.8	530.9	544.9	555.7	506.8	512.3	517.8	520.4	525.6	530.9	535.7	540.5	544.9	548.2	551.8	555.7
1968	564.7	573.1	587.4	604.3	557.9	561.4	564.7	566.6	569.7	573.1	577.4	582.5	587.4	592.6	598.7	604.3
1969	607.9	609.4	605.9	613.2	605.1	606.3	607.9	608.6	608.7	609.4	607.3	604.9	605.9	606.1	610.9	613.2
1970	614.2	625.7	650.7	674.5	612.0	610.5	614.2	619.0	623.1	625.7	632.9	641.6	650.7	657.9	665.4	674.5
1971	706.0	728.6	748.6	773.0	683.3	694.3	706.0	713.6	721.8	728.6	735.4	740.8	748.6	756.1	764.7	773.0
1972	799.4	822.0	852.4	882.0	780.8	790.6	799.4	806.2	813.4	822.0	831.5	842.2	852.4	860.7	871.7	882.0
1973	912.2	936.2	960.9	979.2	891.5	901.8	912.2	918.3	927.0	936.2	944.7	953.2	960.9	965.2	972.2	979.2
1974	1006.0	1031.1	1047.2	1061.4	986.5	996.5	1006.0	1013.8	1021.8	1031.1	1036.6	1041.3	1047.2	1050.5	1056.6	1061.4
1975	1082.8	1111.1	1137.9	1161.7	1066.1	1073.9	1082.8	1087.7	1098.0	1111.1	1120.7	1127.2	1137.9	1143.6	1156.1	1161.7
1976	1192.7	1223.1	1255.6	1296.3	1169.9	1181.8	1192.7	1203.9	1215.8	1223.1	1233.1	1246.3	1255.6	1266.7	1280.7	1296.3
1977	1333.7	1370.3	1411.5	1451.8	1307.9	1320.7	1333.7	1344.7	1358.3	1370.3	1384.4	1398.9	1411.5	1424.2	1439.6	1451.8
1978	1489.9	1529.4	1573.1	1613.5	1464.4	1475.4	1489.9	1502.8	1519.2	1529.4	1541.8	1557.7	1573.1	1582.9	1600.7	1613.5
1979	1646.6	1686.3	1739.3	1758.4	1621.3	1633.1	1646.6	1658.1	1669.9	1686.3	1701.8	1719.6	1739.3	1748.8	1750.8	1758.4
1980	1797.5	1830.1	1892.1	1936.7	1767.6	1787.2	1797.5	1793.7	1808.9	1830.1	1851.7	1875.9	1892.1	1907.1	1926.2	1936.7
1981	1995.6	2047.9	2114.0	2167.9	1955.9	1975.3	1995.6	2011.4	2026.7	2047.9	2069.2	2096.6	2114.0	2128.3	2150.0	2167.9
1982	2210.9	2260.2	2409.5	2460.3	2181.8	2191.6	2210.9	2224.1	2240.7	2260.2	2364.2	2389.6	2409.5	2452.9	2448.6	2460.3
1983	2532.3	2593.0	2636.4	2706.8	2489.9	2517.1	2532.3	2550.6	2571.0	2593.0	2604.0	2617.2	2636.4	2657.1	2688.9	2706.8

Loans and investments including U.S. Government securities: (15) commercial banks / Prêts et placements y compris les fonds d'État : (15) banques commerciales

billion dollars / milliards de dollars

Adjusted - Corrigé

Year	Q.1	Q.2	Q.3	Q.4	JAN	FEB	MAR	APR	MAY	JUN	JUL	AUG	SEP	OCT	NOV	DEC
1964	254.1	259.5	266.6	272.3	250.9	252.6	254.1	255.8	257.5	259.5	260.6	263.4	266.6	267.1	270.3	272.3
1965	279.2	286.7	292.0	300.1	275.1	277.8	279.2	282.5	284.5	286.7	289.0	290.6	292.0	295.6	297.3	300.1
1966	304.8	313.0	315.0	316.1	302.9	303.9	304.8	308.3	309.9	313.0	313.6	314.3	315.0	314.1	314.1	316.1
1967	327.2	333.4	345.3	352.0	319.9	323.2	327.2	329.3	330.9	333.4	337.9	342.2	345.3	347.8	350.0	352.0
1968	359.4	365.6	381.3	390.2	355.5	359.3	359.4	361.2	363.6	365.6	371.4	376.4	381.3	386.0	387.8	390.2
1969	394.6	400.8	398.5	401.7	392.2	393.6	394.6	398.7	399.2	400.8	399.8	399.0	398.5	400.1	402.3	401.7
1970	403.0	409.2	423.7	435.5	400.0	400.5	403.0	406.1	407.5	409.2	415.2	419.6	423.7	426.7	429.3	435.5
1971	449.4	462.0	471.9	485.7	440.2	446.1	449.4	452.6	456.1	462.0	464.5	468.7	471.9	477.7	480.1	485.7
1972	502.8	518.5	535.1	572.5	491.2	496.5	502.8	508.2	514.5	518.5	523.1	528.8	535.1	541.7	549.4	572.5
1973	593.7	611.4	631.7	647.8	575.7	585.1	593.7	598.2	604.9	611.4	619.7	627.4	631.7	636.8	640.6	647.8
1974	668.7	692.1	706.7	713.6	655.8	662.5	668.7	680.6	686.8	692.1	699.0	704.4	706.7	708.1	709.2	713.6
1975	716.1	721.4	731.5	745.2	715.2	714.7	716.1	717.6	719.0	721.4	723.7	725.8	731.5	735.5	738.6	745.2
1976	753.6	767.5	780.3	804.6	745.5	749.8	753.6	757.8	762.5	767.5	770.2	775.8	780.3	788.8	796.0	804.6
1977	824.2	846.5	869.0	891.5	809.9	816.7	824.2	830.9	840.2	846.5	853.8	862.3	869.0	876.1	884.5	891.5
1978	918.8	952.8	981.3	1013.5	900.1	908.2	918.8	930.2	941.6	952.8	964.3	971.0	981.3	992.1	1004.1	1013.5
1979	1047.5	1084.0	1124.3	1135.9	1027.2	1036.2	1047.5	1060.4	1070.7	1084.0	1097.6	1107.5	1124.3	1128.5	1126.2	1135.9
1980	1166.4	1161.3	1192.8	1239.6	1144.5	1157.9	1166.4	1164.7	1161.4	1161.3	1169.2	1185.2	1192.8	1203.4	1221.1	1239.6
1981	1261.0	1295.4	1317.8	1316.3	1251.4	1255.7	1261.0	1267.9	1285.1	1295.4	1302.8	1312.2	1317.8	1324.0	1327.5	1316.3
1982	1342.5	1368.8	1389.4	1412.1	1320.0	1332.4	1342.5	1352.6	1362.0	1368.8	1376.1	1383.1	1389.4	1397.5	1398.5	1412.1
1983	1450.1	1488.0	1520.3		1428.2	1436.3	1450.1	1460.6	1474.4	1488.0	1499.9	1513.2	1520.3	1533.1	1548.6	

Loans: commercial banks (15) / Prêts : banques commerciales (15)

billion dollars / milliards de dollars

Adjusted - Corrigé

Year	Q.1	Q.2	Q.3	Q.4	JAN	FEB	MAR	APR	MAY	JUN	JUL	AUG	SEP	OCT	NOV	DEC
1964	158.1	162.9	167.7	172.9	155.3	156.6	158.1	159.5	161.2	162.9	164.3	166.0	167.7	168.6	170.6	172.9
1965	180.3	186.5	191.7	198.2	175.7	178.0	180.3	182.5	184.5	186.5	188.5	190.1	191.7	194.1	195.8	198.2
1966	203.8	209.4	211.9	213.9	200.2	202.2	203.8	206.1	207.9	209.4	210.3	211.1	211.9	212.8	213.1	213.9
1967	217.7	220.3	226.1	231.3	215.9	216.4	217.7	218.8	219.3	220.3	222.4	223.9	226.1	227.3	228.8	231.3
1968	235.2	240.7	250.2	258.2	233.2	234.4	235.2	237.2	238.6	240.7	244.5	247.3	250.2	253.0	256.5	258.2
1969	264.8	272.1	273.2	279.4	260.6	263.2	264.8	268.5	270.8	272.1	272.1	272.2	273.2	275.5	277.5	279.4
1970	279.0	280.3	287.6	292.0	278.6	278.4	279.0	279.7	279.3	280.3	283.7	285.5	287.6	288.9	289.7	292.0
1971	296.3	302.9	312.4	320.9	293.7	295.7	296.3	298.8	301.0	302.9	305.2	309.1	312.4	315.8	318.3	320.9
1972	333.0	345.4	359.8	390.3	325.6	328.4	333.0	337.1	341.8	345.4	349.2	353.5	359.8	365.9	372.8	390.3
1973	414.8	432.7	449.4	460.5	393.2	405.0	414.8	420.5	426.9	432.7	439.5	447.2	449.4	452.2	454.9	460.5
1974	476.6	500.9	515.7	520.1	465.8	471.8	476.6	489.3	495.5	500.9	508.0	513.2	515.7	516.9	517.7	520.1
1975	516.2	510.5	510.0	517.4	520.3	519.1	516.2	514.1	512.1	510.5	509.3	508.5	510.0	511.6	513.0	517.4
1976	521.2	529.7	538.6	555.0	515.7	518.7	521.2	522.7	525.4	529.7	531.2	535.2	538.6	544.3	549.2	555.0
1977	570.2	589.3	610.9	632.5	558.7	564.1	570.2	576.2	583.4	589.3	595.9	605.0	610.9	618.0	625.7	632.5
1978	657.6	688.8	714.8	747.0	641.0	647.9	657.6	667.3	678.2	688.8	700.0	706.2	714.8	724.9	737.0	747.0
1979	773.9	807.1	842.7	849.9	756.2	764.6	773.9	785.3	794.6	807.1	819.5	828.5	842.7	845.3	842.1	849.9
1980	875.1	860.6	879.4	915.1	856.8	867.7	875.1	872.6	864.6	860.6	863.6	873.7	879.4	886.6	899.9	915.1
1981	928.8	957.2	979.0	973.9	921.6	924.4	928.8	934.5	948.5	957.2	964.0	972.7	979.0	982.8	986.1	973.9
1982	995.0	1017.1	1033.5	1042.0	974.5	985.2	995.0	1002.0	1010.8	1017.1	1023.7	1028.3	1033.5	1038.1	1036.4	1042.0
1983	1056.3	1070.6	1096.3		1045.0	1048.7	1056.3	1059.5	1063.3	1070.6	1080.9	1091.0	1096.3	1104.2	1115.6	

UNITED STATES

Consumer credit outstanding:
financial institutions
billion dollars, end of period

Crédits à la consommation en cours :
établissements financiers
milliards de dollars, fin de période

	Year	Q.1	Q.2	Q.3	Q.4	JAN	FEB	MAR	APR	MAY	JUN	JUL	AUG	SEP	OCT	NOV	DEC
1964	56.78	51.03	53.62	55.45	56.78	50.29	50.63	51.03	51.78	52.67	53.62	54.34	55.00	55.45	55.84	56.04	56.78
1965	64.09	57.70	60.80	62.77	64.09	56.87	57.15	57.70	58.79	59.74	60.80	61.59	62.43	62.77	63.05	63.43	64.09
1966	68.52	64.35	66.35	67.62	68.52	63.91	63.93	64.35	64.93	65.52	66.35	66.94	67.58	67.62	67.75	68.01	68.52
1967	71.66	67.88	69.35	70.57	71.66	68.09	67.81	67.88	68.17	68.63	69.35	69.78	70.45	70.57	70.78	71.10	71.66
1968	79.66	71.55	74.71	77.36	79.66	70.81	71.07	71.55	72.42	73.51	74.71	75.74	76.92	77.36	78.17	78.74	79.66
1969	88.05	80.41	84.22	85.59	88.05	79.51	79.85	80.41	81.63	82.84	84.22	85.09	86.01	86.59	87.17	87.56	88.05
1970	91.63	86.98	89.16	91.23	91.63	87.24	87.07	86.98	87.53	88.12	89.16	90.01	90.77	91.23	91.35	91.16	91.63
1971	104.10	93.72	97.24	100.95	104.10	93.44	93.36	93.72	94.85	95.92	97.24	98.43	99.86	100.95	101.69	102.74	104.10
1972	118.19	104.40	110.33	114.66	118.19	103.32	103.48	104.40	106.03	107.91	110.33	111.53	113.58	114.66	115.52	116.62	118.19
1973	138.52	122.48	129.40	135.14	138.52	120.34	121.12	122.48	124.31	126.77	129.40	131.48	133.99	135.14	136.41	137.62	138.52
1974	146.48	137.73	142.89	147.34	146.48	138.07	137.81	137.73	139.04	140.85	142.89	144.61	146.73	147.34	147.19	146.72	146.48
1975	153.80	143.57	145.71	150.85	153.80	145.29	144.71	143.57	143.83	144.36	145.71	147.94	149.67	150.85	151.65	152.19	153.80
1976	174.27	154.62	162.09	169.51	174.27	153.67	153.68	154.62	156.92	159.04	162.09	164.72	167.35	169.51	170.61	171.71	174.27
1977	207.07	177.58	188.18	198.73	207.07	174.33	174.96	177.58	180.68	183.77	188.18	191.25	195.68	198.73	200.71	203.39	207.07
1978	247.66	211.53	226.76	238.84	247.66	207.30	208.29	211.53	215.36	220.58	226.76	230.68	235.62	238.84	240.57	243.60	247.66
1979	283.91	253.57	266.00	277.49	283.91	248.94	250.57	253.57	257.42	261.72	266.00	269.18	273.64	277.49	279.43	281.53	283.91
1980	285.02	283.51	279.42	282.60	285.02	283.70	283.78	283.51	282.56	280.63	279.42	279.44	281.45	282.60	282.49	282.52	285.02
1981	302.15	284.97	292.40	301.58	302.15	283.32	282.88	284.97	287.41	289.39	292.40	293.71	297.67	301.58	301.17	300.45	302.15
1982	314.60	299.74	305.66	310.64	314.60	300.58	299.29	299.74	301.40	302.82	305.66	306.58	308.22	310.64	309.43	310.73	314.60
1983	354.74	315.10	325.21	339.29	354.74	314.29	312.61	315.10	317.29	319.65	325.21	330.12	335.60	339.29	342.85	346.72	354.74

Consumer credit outstanding:
retail outlets
billion dollars, end of period

Crédits à la consommation en cours :
commerces de détail
milliards de dollars, fin de période

	Year	Q.1	Q.2	Q.3	Q.4	JAN	FEB	MAR	APR	MAY	JUN	JUL	AUG	SEP	OCT	NOV	DEC
1964	8.79	7.35	7.56	7.77	8.79	7.56	7.29	7.35	7.38	7.47	7.56	7.60	7.68	7.77	7.92	8.08	8.79
1965	9.79	8.24	8.45	8.65	9.79	8.62	8.37	8.24	8.32	8.38	8.45	8.48	8.54	8.65	8.80	9.03	9.79
1966	10.82	9.34	9.46	9.71	10.82	9.63	9.40	9.34	9.36	9.39	9.46	9.52	9.61	9.71	9.79	10.01	10.82
1967	11.48	10.15	10.19	10.27	11.48	10.55	10.21	10.15	10.04	10.00	10.19	10.04	10.15	10.27	10.20	10.51	11.48
1968	12.02	10.73	10.83	10.58	12.02	11.10	10.85	10.73	10.80	10.76	10.83	10.69	10.54	10.58	10.67	11.03	12.02
1969	13.12	11.28	11.54	11.69	13.12	11.65	11.49	11.28	11.30	11.42	11.54	11.52	11.60	11.69	11.76	12.08	13.12
1970	13.90	12.25	12.31	12.48	13.90	12.74	12.40	12.25	12.22	12.21	12.31	12.29	12.37	12.48	12.53	12.67	13.90
1971	14.15	12.72	12.65	12.80	14.15	13.25	12.92	12.72	12.68	12.62	12.65	12.56	12.61	12.80	12.80	13.16	14.15
1972	14.98	13.04	13.04	13.36	14.98	13.58	13.17	13.04	13.03	13.06	13.04	12.97	13.13	13.36	13.39	13.91	14.98
1973	16.59	14.22	14.50	14.71	16.59	14.64	14.37	14.22	14.25	14.35	14.50	14.52	14.63	14.71	15.00	15.41	16.59
1974	18.11	15.49	15.79	16.30	18.11	15.98	15.75	15.49	15.55	15.75	15.79	15.83	16.12	16.30	16.37	16.80	18.11
1975	18.20	16.48	16.29	16.43	18.20	17.34	16.81	16.48	16.41	16.44	16.29	16.17	16.33	16.43	16.37	16.66	18.20
1976	19.26	16.62	16.60	16.85	19.26	17.32	16.97	16.62	16.62	16.50	16.60	16.44	16.61	16.85	16.97	17.55	19.26
1977	23.49	19.59	20.37	20.57	23.49	19.97	19.58	19.59	19.93	20.37	20.37	20.35	20.46	20.57	20.87	21.53	23.49
1978	25.99	21.64	21.81	22.29	25.99	22.53	21.87	21.64	21.57	21.74	21.81	21.83	22.02	22.29	22.71	23.48	25.99
1979	28.12	23.75	23.93	24.48	28.12	24.92	24.20	23.75	23.77	24.00	23.93	23.97	24.37	24.48	24.94	25.81	28.12
1980	28.45	25.50	24.79	24.95	28.45	27.22	26.25	25.50	25.07	24.97	24.79	24.62	24.92	24.95	25.06	25.78	28.45
1981	29.55	26.10	26.39	26.59	29.55	27.44	26.51	26.10	26.26	26.29	26.39	26.94	26.43	26.59	26.92	27.51	29.55
1982	30.20	26.53	26.65	26.83	30.20	28.18	27.01	26.53	26.54	26.54	26.65	26.71	26.75	26.83	27.05	27.64	30.20
1983	33.18	27.47	27.80	28.32	33.18	28.86	27.73	27.47	27.46	27.54	27.80	27.90	28.07	28.32	28.71	29.67	33.18

Official discount rate
(Federal Reserve Bank of New York)
per cent per annum, end of period

Taux d'escompte officiel
(Federal Reserve Bank of New York)
pourcentage par an, fin de période

	Year	Q.1	Q.2	Q.3	Q.4	JAN	FEB	MAR	APR	MAY	JUN	JUL	AUG	SEP	OCT	NOV	DEC
1964	4.00	3.50	3.50	3.50	4.00	3.50	3.50	3.50	3.50	3.50	3.50	3.50	3.50	3.50	3.50	4.00	4.00
1965	4.50	4.00	4.00	4.00	4.50	4.00	4.00	4.00	4.00	4.00	4.00	4.00	4.00	4.00	4.00	4.00	4.50
1966	4.50	4.50	4.50	4.50	4.50	4.50	4.50	4.50	4.50	4.50	4.50	4.50	4.50	4.50	4.50	4.50	4.50
1967	4.50	4.50	4.00	4.00	4.50	4.50	4.50	4.50	4.00	4.00	4.00	4.00	4.00	4.00	4.00	4.50	4.50
1968	5.50	5.00	5.50	5.25	5.50	4.50	4.50	5.00	5.50	5.50	5.50	5.50	5.25	5.25	5.25	5.25	5.50
1969	6.00	5.50	6.00	6.00	6.00	5.50	5.50	5.50	6.00	6.00	6.00	6.00	6.00	6.00	6.00	6.00	6.00
1970	5.50	6.00	6.00	6.00	5.50	6.00	6.00	6.00	6.00	6.00	6.00	6.00	6.00	6.00	6.00	5.75	5.50
1971	4.50	4.75	4.75	5.00	4.50	5.00	4.75	4.75	4.75	4.75	4.75	5.00	5.00	5.00	5.00	4.75	4.50
1972	4.50	4.50	4.50	4.50	4.50	4.50	4.50	4.50	4.50	4.50	4.50	4.50	4.50	4.50	4.50	4.50	4.50
1973	7.50	5.50	6.50	7.50	7.50	5.00	5.50	5.50	5.50	6.00	6.50	7.00	7.50	7.50	7.50	7.50	7.50
1974	7.75	7.50	8.00	8.00	7.75	7.50	7.50	7.50	8.00	8.00	8.00	8.00	8.00	8.00	8.00	8.00	7.75
1975	6.00	6.25	6.00	6.00	6.00	7.25	6.75	6.25	6.25	6.00	6.00	6.00	6.00	6.00	6.00	6.00	6.00
1976	5.25	5.50	5.50	5.50	5.25	5.50	5.50	5.50	5.50	5.50	5.50	5.50	5.50	5.50	5.50	5.25	5.25
1977	6.00	5.25	5.25	5.75	6.00	5.25	5.25	5.25	5.25	5.25	5.25	5.25	5.75	5.75	6.00	6.00	6.00
1978	9.50	6.50	7.00	8.00	9.50	6.50	6.50	6.50	6.50	7.00	7.00	7.25	7.75	8.00	8.25	9.50	9.50
1979	12.00	9.50	9.50	11.00	12.00	9.50	9.50	9.50	9.50	9.50	9.50	10.00	10.50	11.00	12.00	12.00	12.00
1980	13.00	13.00	11.00	11.00	13.00	12.00	13.00	13.00	13.00	12.00	11.00	10.00	10.00	11.00	11.00	12.00	13.00
1981	12.00	13.00	14.00	14.00	12.00	13.00	13.00	13.00	13.00	14.00	14.00	14.00	14.00	14.00	14.00	13.00	12.00
1982	8.50	12.00	12.00	10.00	8.50	12.00	12.00	12.00	12.00	12.00	12.00	11.50	10.00	10.00	9.50	9.00	8.50
1983	8.50	8.50	8.50	8.50	8.50	8.50	8.50	8.50	8.50	8.50	8.50	8.50	8.50	8.50	8.50	8.50	8.50

Treasury bill rate (3 months) (16) — Bons du Trésor (3 mois) (16)

per cent per annum, end of period — pourcentage par an, fin de période

	Year	Q.1	Q.2	Q.3	Q.4	JAN	FEB	MAR	APR	MAY	JUN	JUL	AUG	SEP	OCT	NOV	DEC
1964	3.86	3.53	3.48	3.56	3.86	3.50	3.55	3.53	3.45	3.48	3.48	3.48	3.51	3.56	3.57	3.87	3.86
1965	4.46	3.92	3.78	3.93	4.46	3.85	3.99	3.92	3.92	3.89	3.78	3.80	3.89	3.98	4.04	4.10	4.46
1966	4.75	4.56	4.44	5.50	4.75	4.60	4.66	4.56	4.63	4.64	4.44	4.82	5.09	5.50	5.41	5.20	4.75
1967	4.99	4.15	3.46	4.63	4.99	4.49	4.54	4.15	3.72	3.48	3.46	4.18	4.49	4.63	4.54	4.96	4.99
1968	6.20	5.19	5.24	5.18	6.20	4.85	5.06	5.19	5.50	5.70	5.24	5.19	5.17	5.18	5.47	5.45	6.20
1969	8.10	6.07	6.46	7.11	8.10	6.17	6.08	6.07	6.05	6.12	6.46	7.17	7.01	7.11	7.03	7.48	8.10
1970	4.83	6.26	6.35	6.03	4.83	7.89	6.81	6.26	6.88	6.82	6.35	6.41	6.34	6.03	5.65	5.08	4.83
1971	3.73	3.52	5.08	4.68	3.73	4.20	3.50	3.52	3.87	4.34	5.08	5.55	4.55	4.68	4.44	4.32	3.73
1972	5.11	3.85	4.14	4.64	5.11	3.37	3.45	3.85	3.60	3.86	4.14	3.79	4.33	4.64	4.77	4.89	5.11
1973	7.41	6.25	7.23	7.33	7.41	5.69	5.81	6.25	6.28	6.69	7.23	8.32	8.67	7.33	7.20	7.70	7.41
1974	7.11	8.30	7.84	6.39	7.11	7.78	7.19	8.30	8.91	7.98	7.84	8.51	9.91	6.39	7.89	7.33	7.11
1975	5.21	5.56	6.01	6.55	5.21	5.61	5.46	5.56	5.72	5.21	6.01	6.32	6.59	6.55	5.69	5.52	5.21
1976	4.30	4.93	5.37	5.07	4.30	4.76	4.87	4.93	4.91	5.58	5.37	5.19	5.09	5.07	4.93	4.47	4.30
1977	6.14	4.61	4.97	5.98	6.14	4.72	4.71	4.61	4.52	4.99	4.97	5.16	5.57	5.98	6.28	6.06	6.14
1978	9.34	6.31	6.97	8.11	9.34	6.44	6.43	6.31	6.29	6.66	6.97	6.90	7.32	8.11	8.45	9.17	9.34
1979	12.11	9.50	8.80	9.99	12.11	9.32	9.45	9.50	9.50	9.53	8.80	9.15	9.68	9.99	12.26	11.93	12.11
1980	13.60	15.04	8.15	11.52	13.60	12.04	15.14	15.04	10.79	7.68	8.15	8.22	10.03	11.52	12.33	14.38	13.60
1981	12.97	12.50	13.91	14.67	12.97	15.20	14.10	12.50	14.19	16.75	13.91	15.07	15.58	14.67	12.97	10.40	12.97
1982	7.98	13.40	13.27	7.85	7.98	13.36	12.43	13.40	12.47	11.52	13.27	10.56	7.75	7.85	8.03	8.28	7.98
1983	8.94	8.68	9.09	8.73	8.94	8.12	7.94	8.68	8.15	8.65	9.09	9.13	9.28	8.73	8.41	8.90	8.94

Yield of long-term Government bonds (17) — Rendement des bons d'État à long terme (17)

per cent per annum, end of period — pourcentage par an, fin de période

	Year	Q.1	Q.2	Q.3	Q.4	JAN	FEB	MAR	APR	MAY	JUN	JUL	AUG	SEP	OCT	NOV	DEC
1964	4.14	4.18	4.13	4.16	4.14	4.15	4.14	4.18	4.20	4.16	4.13	4.13	4.14	4.16	4.16	4.12	4.14
1965	4.43	4.15	4.14	4.25	4.43	4.14	4.16	4.15	4.15	4.14	4.14	4.15	4.19	4.25	4.27	4.34	4.43
1966	4.65	4.63	4.63	4.79	4.65	4.43	4.61	4.63	4.55	4.57	4.63	4.74	4.80	4.79	4.70	4.74	4.65
1967	5.36	4.45	4.86	4.99	5.36	4.40	4.47	4.45	4.51	4.76	4.86	4.86	4.95	4.99	5.18	5.44	5.36
1968	5.66	5.39	5.23	5.09	5.66	5.18	5.16	5.39	5.28	5.40	5.23	5.09	5.04	5.09	5.24	5.36	5.66
1969	6.81	6.05	6.05	6.32	6.81	5.74	5.86	6.05	5.84	5.85	6.05	6.07	6.02	6.32	6.27	6.52	6.81
1970	5.97	6.39	6.99	6.63	5.97	6.86	6.44	6.39	6.53	6.94	6.99	6.57	6.75	6.63	6.59	6.24	5.97
1971	5.62	5.71	5.94	5.56	5.62	5.92	5.84	5.71	5.75	5.96	5.94	5.91	5.78	5.56	5.46	5.48	5.62
1972	5.63	5.66	5.59	5.70	5.63	5.62	5.67	5.66	5.74	5.64	5.59	5.59	5.59	5.70	5.69	5.51	5.63
1973	6.35	6.20	6.32	6.41	6.35	5.96	6.14	6.20	6.11	6.25	6.32	6.53	6.85	6.41	6.25	6.30	6.35
1974	6.77	6.81	7.02	7.30	6.77	6.56	6.54	6.81	7.04	7.09	7.02	7.18	7.33	7.30	7.22	6.93	6.77
1975	7.17	6.77	6.86	7.28	7.17	6.68	6.66	6.77	7.05	7.01	6.86	6.89	7.11	7.28	7.29	7.21	7.17
1976	6.38	6.88	6.92	6.70	6.38	6.93	6.92	6.88	6.73	7.01	6.92	6.85	6.82	6.70	6.65	6.62	6.38
1977	7.24	7.20	6.99	6.94	7.24	6.68	7.16	7.20	7.13	7.17	6.99	6.98	7.01	6.94	7.08	7.16	7.24
1978	8.36	7.63	7.94	7.82	8.36	7.51	7.60	7.63	7.74	7.87	7.94	8.10	7.88	7.82	8.07	8.16	8.36
1979	9.58	8.45	8.32	8.68	9.58	8.43	8.43	8.45	8.44	8.55	8.32	8.35	8.42	8.68	9.44	9.80	9.58
1980	11.89	11.87	9.40	10.94	11.89	10.03	11.55	11.87	10.83	9.82	9.40	9.83	10.53	10.94	11.20	11.83	11.89
1981	12.88	12.15	12.39	14.14	12.88	11.65	12.23	12.15	12.62	12.96	12.39	13.05	13.61	14.14	14.13	12.68	12.88
1982	10.33	12.98	13.32	11.48	10.33	13.73	13.63	12.98	12.84	12.67	13.32	12.97	12.15	11.48	10.51	10.18	10.33
1983	11.44	10.34	10.64	11.26	11.44	10.37	10.60	10.34	10.19	10.21	10.64	11.10	11.42	11.26	11.21	11.32	11.44

Share prices: industrials (Standard and Poor) (18) — Cours des actions : industrielles (Standard and Poor) (18)

1980 = 100

	Year	Q.1	Q.2	Q.3	Q.4	JAN	FEB	MAR	APR	MAY	JUN	JUL	AUG	SEP	OCT	NOV	DEC
1964	64	61	63	65	67	60	61	62	63	64	63	66	64	66	67	67	66
1965	70	68	69	69	73	68	68	68	69	70	67	67	68	71	72	73	73
1966	68	73	70	65	63	74	74	71	73	69	69	68	64	62	61	64	64
1967	74	69	73	75	77	67	69	71	73	74	73	75	75	77	77	75	77
1968	80	74	80	81	85	77	73	72	78	80	82	81	79	82	84	85	86
1969	80	82	83	77	77	83	82	80	82	85	81	77	77	77	78	79	75
1970	68	72	64	64	70	74	71	72	70	62	62	62	64	67	69	69	73
1971	81	79	83	81	79	76	79	81	85	84	82	81	80	82	80	76	82
1972	91	87	90	91	95	85	87	89	90	89	90	89	92	91	91	95	97
1973	90	96	89	88	85	99	96	94	92	89	87	88	87	88	92	85	79
1974	69	79	76	63	58	80	77	81	77	75	76	70	64	57	58	60	56
1975	71	65	74	73	73	60	66	70	71	75	77	77	72	71	74	75	71
1976	85	83	85	87	85	81	84	85	85	85	85	87	86	83	85	84	86
1977	81	84	81	80	77	86	83	83	82	81	81	82	80	79	77	77	77
1978	79	73	79	84	80	74	73	73	76	80	80	80	85	86	83	78	79
1979	85	82	84	88	88	83	81	83	85	83	84	84	88	90	87	86	90
1980	100	93	90	104	113	93	97	88	86	90	96	101	104	107	110	116	113
1981	107	111	112	105	101	112	108	112	113	111	111	108	108	99	100	102	103
1982	99	95	95	95	114	97	95	91	96	96	91	91	91	102	110	114	115
1983	134	123	136	139	139	120	123	127	131	137	139	140	136	140	140	138	138

UNITED STATES

Official reserves excluding gold

million SDR's, end of period

Réserves officielles, or exclu

millions de DTS, fin de période

	Year	Q.1	Q.2	Q.3	Q.4	JAN	FEB	MAR	APR	MAY	JUN	JUL	AUG	SEP	OCT	NOV	DEC
1964	1201	1344	968	878	1201	1341	1253	1344	1172	1163	968	999	1033	878	780	1449	1201
1965	1385	1191	1454	1537	1385	1135	1002	1191	1112	1058	1454	1338	1675	1537	1443	1410	1385
1966	1647	1288	1429	1520	1647	1155	1151	1288	1248	1323	1429	1735	1696	1520	1569	1453	1647
1967	2765	671	1105	1572	2765	994	837	671	672	729	1105	1088	1530	1572	1888	2473	2765
1968	4818	3224	3382	3879	4818	2617	2890	3224	3293	3880	3382	3690	3746	3879	3640	4763	4818
1969	5105	4922	4904	5579	5105	4626	4698	4922	5012	4917	4904	4792	5041	5579	5126	4829	5105
1970	3415	5448	4439	4034	3415	5515	5764	5448	5017	4265	4439	4131	3979	4034	3625	3412	3415
1971	1942	3379	2997	1923	1942	3659	3495	3379	3382	3243	2997	2830	1919	1923	1939	1924	1942
1972	2453	2591	2624	2514	2453	2651	2646	2591	2589	2629	2624	2394	2427	2514	2602	2597	2453
1973	2260	2250	2235	2247	2260	2364	2245	2250	2226	2236	2235	2239	2244	2247	2251	2255	2260
1974	3456	2434	2731	3573	3456	2415	2480	2434	2479	2667	2731	2710	3215	3573	3546	3469	3456
1975	3952	3716	3738	4031	3952	3481	3579	3716	3675	3737	3738	3750	3806	4031	4190	4264	3952
1976	6153	4620	6002	6350	6153	4298	4332	4620	5074	5565	6002	5796	6073	6350	6422	6800	6153
1977	6250	6438	6431	6300	6250	6447	6457	6438	6203	6488	6431	6205	6367	6300	6262	6335	6250
1978	5357	6043	5775	5605	5357	6367	6240	6043	5811	5941	5775	5667	5590	5606	5397	4971	5357
1979	5909	7910	7703	5562	5909	6906	6785	7910	7846	8625	7703	6731	6757	5562	5306	6248	5909
1980	12228	8247	8133	9011	12228	7462	7451	8247	8089	8194	8133	8135	8758	9011	9925	11366	12228
1981	16258	15674	16016	16218	16258	13790	15144	15674	15467	15589	16016	15714	15989	16218	16588	16811	16258
1982	20677	16884	17874	18506	20677	16506	16781	16884	18064	17583	17874	18385	18544	18506	19356	21174	20677
1983	21612	21436	21290	20759	21612	20978	21188	21436	21302	21162	21290	21069	20578	20759	20908	21447	21612

Balance of payments: net trade (19)(20)

billion dollars

Adjusted - Corrigé

Balance des paiements : balance commerciale (19) (20)

milliards de dollars

	Year	Q.1	Q.2	Q.3	Q.4	JAN	FEB	MAR	APR	MAY	JUN	JUL	AUG	SEP	OCT	NOV	DEC
1964	6.8	1.8	1.6	1.7	1.7												
1965	5.0	1.0	1.5	1.3	1.2												
1966	3.8	1.2	1.0	0.8	0.9												
1967	3.8	1.0	1.2	1.1	0.5												
1968	0.6	0.1	0.3	0.3	-0.1												
1969	0.6	0.0	0.0	0.0	0.6												
1970	2.6	0.7	1.0	0.6	0.3												
1971	-2.3	0.3	-0.7	-0.6	-1.2												
1972	-6.4	-1.7	-1.6	-1.7	-1.4												
1973	0.9	-0.8	-0.1	0.6	1.2												
1974	-5.5	0.7	-1.8	-2.7	-1.5												
1975	8.9	-8.4	3.1	1.7	1.8												
1976	-9.5	-0.6	-1.9	-3.1	-3.8												
1977	-31.1	-6.9	-7.2	-7.3	-9.7												
1978	-34.0	-11.2	-8.4	-7.6	-6.9												
1979	-27.6	-4.8	-7.3	-7.0	-8.4												
1980	-25.5	-9.7	-6.6	-4.0	-5.2												
1981	-28.1	-4.5	-7.3	-8.4	-7.8												
1982	-36.4	-6.1	-5.9	-13.1	-11.4												
1983	-60.6	-8.9	-14.7	-18.2	-18.8												

Balance of payments: net capital movements, assets

billion dollars

Adjusted - Corrigé

Balance des paiements : mouvements nets de capitaux, avoirs

milliards de dollars

	Year	Q.1	Q.2	Q.3	Q.4	JAN	FEB	MAR	APR	MAY	JUN	JUL	AUG	SEP	OCT	NOV	DEC
1964	-9.7	-2.0	-2.3	-2.3	-3.1												
1965	-6.9	-2.4	-1.4	-1.5	-1.7												
1966	-7.9	-1.9	-2.0	-1.3	-2.2												
1967	-9.8	-2.2	-1.9	-2.8	-3.0												
1968	-10.1	-2.2	-2.4	-2.9	-2.6												
1969	-10.4	-2.6	-3.1	-2.7	-2.0												
1970	-11.8	-3.1	-2.7	-3.0	-3.0												
1971	-14.8	-3.6	-3.4	-4.9	-2.9												
1972	-14.5	-4.2	-2.1	-4.1	-4.2												
1973	-23.0	-8.1	-4.2	-3.2	-7.6												
1974	-33.3	-5.7	-10.0	-6.7	-11.0												
1975	-38.9	-10.3	-9.6	-4.8	-14.3												
1976	-48.7	-11.6	-10.1	-10.2	-16.8												
1977	-34.4	-0.8	-12.2	-6.4	-15.1												
1978	-61.9	-15.4	-5.9	-9.8	-30.8												
1979	-63.2	-4.6	-16.1	-28.9	-13.6												
1980	-77.9	-9.7	-25.4	-18.4	-24.5												
1981	-105.4	-18.8	-21.3	-17.3	-48.1												
1982	-113.1	-30.4	-39.8	-25.3	-17.6												
1983	-49.1	-20.9	-1.7	-9.5	-17.0												

Liabilities to foreigners (21)

billion dollars, end of period

Dette envers l'étranger (21)

milliards de dollars, fin de période

	Year	Q.1	Q.2	Q.3	Q.4	JAN	FEB	MAR	APR	MAY	JUN	JUL	AUG	SEP	OCT	NOV	DEC
1964	24.01	21.15	21.40	22.35	23.94	21.38	21.28	21.15	21.56	21.55	21.40	22.00	22.37	22.35	23.01	24.00	23.94
1965	24.22	23.36	23.06	23.85	24.22	23.93	24.10	23.36	22.88	22.67	23.06	22.79	23.54	23.85	24.18	24.18	24.22
1966	26.62	23.82	24.62	25.64	26.72	24.01	23.76	23.82	24.11	24.46	24.62	25.60	25.82	25.64	26.62	26.96	26.72
1967	30.87	26.15	27.35	28.79	31.00	25.81	25.93	26.15	26.60	26.85	27.35	27.75	28.57	28.79	30.02	31.35	31.00
1968	31.99	30.38	30.63	31.57	31.99	30.96	31.28	30.38	30.88	31.21	30.63	30.76	31.43	31.57	31.99	33.52	31.99
1969	37.96	33.40	37.27	40.55	39.80	32.13	32.76	33.40	34.38	35.94	37.27	38.28	39.67	40.56	40.90	40.82	39.80
1970	41.09	40.96	41.30	42.17	41.04	40.81	40.96	40.96	41.39	41.28	41.30	41.24	41.52	42.17	42.21	42.41	41.04
1971	53.70	42.55	45.04	51.17	53.68	41.19	41.55	42.55	44.49	48.60	45.04	44.57	50.44	51.17	52.33	52.27	53.68
1972	59.21	56.18	56.08	57.41	59.21	54.51	55.84	56.18	54.94	54.51	56.08	56.00	57.53	57.41	58.75	59.03	59.21
1973	67.22	64.45	65.09	65.45	67.22	57.63	62.84	64.45	63.71	65.12	65.09	66.51	65.96	65.45	66.50	66.48	67.22
1974	91.30	71.61	79.23	85.57	91.39	65.28	67.51	71.61	74.06	77.35	79.23	82.27	84.77	85.57	86.37	89.22	91.39
1975	89.89	89.68	89.16	83.72	89.89	89.08	90.09	89.68	90.78	90.23	89.16	88.80	90.13	88.72	88.40	91.97	89.89
1976	104.94	91.45	94.69	97.35	104.94	91.19	94.57	91.45	97.64	99.76	94.69	97.84	97.02	97.35	98.77	98.35	104.94
1977	122.89	102.66	109.00	112.63	122.89	101.39	101.96	102.66	105.97	108.44	109.00	114.25	107.37	112.63	114.02	115.90	122.89
1978	164.24	135.71	134.53	143.49	164.24	122.75	127.00	135.71	140.30	135.38	134.53	135.69	135.15	143.49	143.32	156.99	164.24
1979	185.16	164.25	164.74	182.61	185.16	162.08	161.89	164.25	157.95	156.36	164.74	165.22	187.57	182.61	178.05	181.44	185.16
1980	202.95	184.54	183.38	189.60	202.95	184.13	192.45	184.54	178.79	181.14	183.38	185.56	199.09	189.60	193.30	202.32	202.95
1981	241.17	204.06	207.84	214.72	241.17	200.44	199.51	204.06	211.91	212.31	207.84	212.56	206.83	214.72	197.33	206.85	241.17
1982	302.10	260.26	285.49	296.01	302.10	249.11	253.16	260.26	265.41	274.18	285.49	283.75	290.10	296.01	295.08	296.85	302.10
1983	366.27	313.36	316.14	332.60	366.27	299.27	300.34	313.36	303.04	310.86	316.14	321.62	329.38	332.60	333.15	345.18	366.27

Balance of payments: current balance (20)

billion dollars

Adjusted - Corrigé

Balance des paiements : opérations courantes, nettes (20)

milliards de dollars

	Year	Q.1	Q.2	Q.3	Q.4	JAN	FEB	MAR	APR	MAY	JUN	JUL	AUG	SEP	OCT	NOV	DEC
1964	6.8	1.9	1.5	1.7	1.7												
1965	5.4	1.2	1.6	1.5	1.1												
1966	3.0	0.9	0.8	0.6	0.7												
1967	2.6	0.8	0.6	0.7	0.5												
1968	0.6	0.1	0.4	0.3	-0.2												
1969	0.4	0.2	-0.1	0.1	0.3												
1970	2.3	0.6	1.0	0.5	0.2												
1971	-1.4	0.7	-0.4	-0.5	-1.2												
1972	-5.8	-1.7	-1.7	-1.3	-1.1												
1973	7.1	0.2	0.9	2.7	3.4												
1974	2.1	1.6	0.2	-0.3	0.6												
1975	18.3	4.3	5.1	4.1	4.8												
1976	4.4	2.6	1.7	-0.1	0.2												
1977	-14.5	-2.7	-3.1	-2.8	-5.9												
1978	-15.5	-6.2	-4.5	-3.4	-1.4												
1979	-1.0	0.8	-1.3	0.6	-1.0												
1980	0.4	-2.1	-1.5	3.3	0.7												
1981	4.6	3.3	0.7	-0.1	0.6												
1982	-12.2	0.6	0.4	-6.5	-6.6												
1983	-40.8	-3.7	-9.8	-12.1	-15.3												

Balance of payments:

net capital movements, liabilities

billion dollars

Adjusted - Corrigé

Balance des paiements :

mouvements nets de capitaux, dettes

milliards de dollars

	Year	Q.1	Q.2	Q.3	Q.4	JAN	FEB	MAR	APR	MAY	JUN	JUL	AUG	SEP	OCT	NOV	DEC
1964	3.6	0.5	0.6	0.8	1.8												
1965	0.8	0.3	-0.3	0.4	0.3												
1966	3.7	0.5	1.0	0.8	1.3												
1967	7.4	0.5	2.0	2.4	2.6												
1968	9.9	1.4	2.3	2.7	3.6												
1969	12.7	3.7	3.9	3.3	1.3												
1970	6.4	2.2	0.9	1.9	1.4												
1971	23.0	3.1	5.2	8.7	6.0												
1972	21.5	4.4	4.3	6.4	6.4												
1973	18.4	10.7	3.1	2.2	2.4												
1974	29.2	1.3	9.7	9.1	9.2												
1975	15.7	2.6	4.0	2.7	6.4												
1976	36.5	7.5	8.0	8.3	12.3												
1977	51.3	2.9	14.2	14.3	20.0												
1978	64.0	18.2	0.9	16.9	28.1												
1979	38.8	2.3	6.9	24.5	5.1												
1980	54.9	8.0	8.8	12.7	25.4												
1981	80.7	8.4	14.0	16.7	41.6												
1982	87.9	27.1	31.6	17.6	11.5												
1983	83.0	16.5	11.0	19.5	36.2												

UNITED STATES

Imports f.o.b. (19)(22)
million dollars, monthly averages

Importations f.o.b. (19)(22)
millions de dollars, moyennes mensuelles

	Year	Q.1	Q.2	Q.3	Q.4	JAN	FEB	MAR	APR	MAY	JUN	JUL	AUG	SEP	OCT	NOV	DEC
1964	1557	1457	1536	1555	1680	1445	1337	1590	1559	1456	1594	1612	1491	1562	1613	1672	1755
1965	1781	1536	1829	1790	1967	1113	1463	2033	1857	1724	1906	1710	1804	1856	1877	2017	2007
1966	2129	1965	2111	2182	2257	1829	1823	2242	2071	2074	2189	2072	2180	2293	2277	2252	2240
1967	2234	2205	2193	2135	2404	2261	2004	2351	2091	2219	2270	2127	2166	2112	2339	2442	2431
1968	2769	2588	2752	2819	2917	2739	2456	2570	2754	2841	2661	2827	2751	2880	2936	2804	3010
1969	3004	2470	3260	3064	3221	2022	2399	2988	3330	3237	3214	3152	2909	3130	3429	2987	3246
1970	3329	3152	3356	3291	3518	3125	2947	3382	3390	3175	3504	3311	3116	3447	3597	3405	3553
1971	3797	3506	4001	3925	3755	3421	3187	3910	3837	3845	4271	3693	3838	4246	3463	3522	4279
1972	4632	4434	4581	4511	5002	4279	4179	4844	4252	4726	4766	4314	4727	4491	5009	5201	4796
1973	5790	5323	5767	5661	6408	5406	4959	5604	5353	6037	5911	5659	6017	5307	6403	6845	5974
1974	8354	7013	8557	8803	9040	6614	6645	7781	8334	8835	8502	8965	9097	8361	9094	8885	9139
1975	8048	8210	7632	7889	8459	10033	7187	7409	8218	7382	7296	7938	7531	8198	8533	7933	8911
1976	10084	9126	9841	10495	10873	9027	8131	10221	9918	8986	10618	10588	10476	10425	10050	11085	11484
1977	12307	11793	12413	12309	12713	10643	11594	13142	11935	11258	14046	12431	12045	12452	12498	12270	13372
1978	14332	13506	14400	14381	15040	12718	13252	14548	14486	14199	14514	14702	14022	14418	15118	15049	14952
1979	17188	15130	16704	17707	19211	15847	13779	15765	16172	16510	17429	17113	17931	18078	19233	18656	19744
1980	20406	20998	20576	19398	20652	20705	21057	21231	20089	20770	20869	19529	19125	19539	20645	19796	21514
1981	21749	21672	22232	21211	21880	22559	21110	21348	22747	21434	22514	20328	22589	20715	23510	22507	19622
1982	20329	20565	20166	20940	19647	22606	18265	20823	17882	20805	21311	19763	22868	20138	21219	19002	18720
1983	21504	19351	21168	22125	23371	20149	17593	20311	19808	21933	21763	21584	23059	21736	25130	23305	21678

Exports f.o.b. (19)(22)
million dollars, monthly averages

Exportations f.o.b. (19)(22)
millions de dollars, moyennes mensuelles

	Year	Q.1	Q.2	Q.3	Q.4	JAN	FEB	MAR	APR	MAY	JUN	JUL	AUG	SEP	OCT	NOV	DEC
1964	2141	2062	2138	2012	2352	2036	2008	2141	2140	2224	2049	2048	1902	2086	2290	2190	2576
1965	2225	1864	2377	2160	2499	1188	1514	2891	2530	2381	2219	2217	2125	2139	2463	2438	2594
1966	2448	2359	2478	2342	2614	2130	2208	2741	2463	2505	2467	2326	2275	2424	2624	2572	2646
1967	2578	2560	2656	2425	2671	2471	2416	2794	2665	2683	2619	2377	2397	2500	2442	2760	2812
1968	2839	2674	2902	2809	2970	2636	2690	2647	2961	2961	2783	2675	2804	2947	2732	3134	3046
1969	3111	2529	3384	3086	3446	2058	2160	3368	3505	3548	3098	2995	3151	3110	3563	3413	3362
1970	3555	3398	3740	3384	3698	3230	3387	3577	3598	3906	3715	3554	3264	3335	3916	3494	3684
1971	3629	3705	3802	3641	3368	3480	3528	4108	3813	3907	3687	3338	3366	4220	2826	3221	4056
1972	4100	3963	4013	3857	4567	3807	3778	4305	3888	4137	4015	3677	3929	3963	4436	4578	4686
1973	5902	5174	5816	5694	6924	4732	4866	5925	5563	6025	5860	5331	5785	5965	6751	7100	6921
1974	8159	7538	8376	7731	8990	6825	7292	8498	8372	8428	8328	7655	7929	7611	8926	9343	8703
1975	8966	9079	8892	8364	9529	9245	8546	9445	9085	8921	8669	8226	8501	8364	9736	9526	9326
1976	9596	9214	9887	9154	10228	8764	8750	9829	9835	9970	9858	9346	8908	9207	10155	9695	10834
1977	10096	9880	10593	9697	10214	9120	9470	11051	10528	10970	10279	9740	8984	10368	9555	9690	11396
1978	11966	10316	12342	11760	13446	9364	9511	12074	12065	12481	12480	10936	11632	12714	13156	13652	13531
1979	15138	13691	14806	14875	17178	12558	12929	15585	14257	14813	15345	14728	14979	14922	17277	17302	16954
1980	18386	17666	18863	17642	19370	16355	16964	19680	19142	18766	18682	17181	17939	17807	19953	18614	19543
1981	19473	19906	20250	18382	19355	17962	18338	22918	20509	19986	20255	18565	17764	18816	19894	19040	19130
1982	17683	18432	19004	15738	16558	17508	17636	20152	18605	18992	19413	17252	16250	16713	17267	15689	16716
1983	16707	16687	16830	15126	17186	16201	15532	18328	16708	16229	17555	15894	15640	16844	17244	16812	17501

Trade balance (f.o.b. — f.o.b.) (19)(22)
million dollars, monthly averages

Balance commerciale (f.o.b. — f.o.b.) (19)(22)
millions de dollars, moyennes mensuelles

	Year	Q.1	Q.2	Q.3	Q.4	JAN	FEB	MAR	APR	MAY	JUN	JUL	AUG	SEP	OCT	NOV	DEC
1964	584	604	601	457	672	591	671	551	581	768	455	436	411	525	677	519	822
1965	445	328	548	370	532	75	51	858	673	658	313	507	321	283	587	421	588
1966	320	395	367	160	357	301	385	499	392	430	278	254	94	131	347	320	406
1967	344	355	462	290	268	209	412	443	575	464	349	250	231	389	103	318	381
1968	70	86	150	-11	54	-53	234	77	206	120	122	-152	53	67	-204	330	35
1969	107	59	123	22	226	36	-239	380	175	312	-116	-157	243	-20	134	426	117
1970	226	246	383	93	180	105	440	195	208	731	211	243	149	-112	319	89	132
1971	-168	199	-199	-285	-387	59	341	198	-75	62	-584	-355	-472	-26	-638	-301	-223
1972	-532	-471	-568	-654	-435	-472	-401	-538	-363	-589	-751	-637	-799	-528	-572	-623	-110
1973	112	-149	49	33	516	-674	-93	321	210	-12	-51	-328	-231	657	348	254	947
1974	-195	525	-181	-1076	-49	211	648	716	39	-406	-174	-1311	-1168	-750	-168	457	-437
1975	918	869	1260	475	1070	-789	1359	2037	867	1540	1372	288	970	166	1203	1593	415
1976	-488	-12	47	-1343	-645	-263	619	-392	-84	984	-760	-1243	-1567	-1218	105	-1390	-651
1977	-2211	-1913	-1820	-2612	-2500	-1523	-2124	-2092	-1406	-288	-3767	-2691	-3061	-2085	-2943	-2580	-1976
1978	-2365	-3190	-2058	-2620	-1593	-3354	-3741	-2474	-2421	-1719	-2034	-3766	-2390	-1704	-1962	-1397	-1421
1979	-2050	-1440	-1898	-2831	-2034	-3289	-850	-180	-1914	-1696	-2083	-2385	-2952	-3156	-1956	-1354	-2790
1980	-2020	-3331	-1713	-1755	-1282	-4351	-4093	-1551	-947	-2004	-2187	-2348	-1186	-1732	-693	-1182	-1971
1981	-2275	-1766	-1982	-2829	-2525	-4597	-2272	1570	-2238	-1448	-2259	-1763	-4825	-1899	-3617	-3467	-492
1982	-2647	-2133	-1162	-4201	-3090	-5098	-629	-672	723	-1812	-2398	-2511	-6613	-3475	-3952	-3313	-2004
1983	-4797	-2664	-4338	-5000	-6185	-3948	-2061	-1984	-3100	-5704	-4208	-5690	-7419	-4892	-7886	-6493	-4177

Imports f.o.b. (19)(22) — million dollars, monthly averages

Adjusted - Corrigé

Importations f.o.b. (22) (19) — millions de dollars, moyennes mensuelles

Year	Q.1	Q.2	Q.3	Q.4	JAN	FEB	MAR	APR	MAY	JUN	JUL	AUG	SEP	OCT	NOV	DEC
1964	1467	1528	1573	1631	1421	1462	1518	1525	1535	1524	1576	1585	1559	1551	1688	1655
1965	1555	1819	1808	1912	1199	1606	1861	1811	1797	1848	1742	1825	1858	1885	1941	1911
1966	2010	2084	2214	2231	1956	2013	2050	2091	2061	2102	2216	2137	2288	2303	2195	2196
1967	2233	2167	2196	2381	2317	2216	2166	2198	2118	2184	2245	2145	2198	2254	2396	2493
1968	2622	2717	2849	2842	2687	2592	2588	2604	2755	2792	2725	2872	2951	2736	2883	2908
1969	2552	3197	3105	3150	2002	2672	2982	3183	3257	3152	3074	3163	3078	3192	3180	3078
1970	3240	3288	3341	3443	3222	3279	3219	3262	3337	3265	3254	3346	3423	3498	3428	3402
1971	3598	3906	3975	3698	3599	3564	3629	3774	3908	4037	3832	3913	4179	3469	3456	4169
1972	4475	4457	4634	4963	4436	4473	4515	4417	4486	4468	4565	4726	4612	4738	5148	5002
1973	5380	5613	5828	6324	5244	5483	5414	5360	5703	5775	5829	6011	5644	5996	6684	6291
1974	7186	8289	8962	9001	6498	7318	7742	8025	8265	8577	8922	9267	8696	8773	8973	9257
1975	8422	7462	7994	8322	9848	7947	7471	7986	7280	7120	7850	7890	8241	8191	8227	8547
1976	9187	9694	10645	10761	9019	9054	9487	9666	9226	10190	10742	10500	10692	10584	10645	11053
1977	11827	12101	12509	12823	10444	12613	12424	11798	11170	13334	12483	12101	12942	12587	12407	13474
1978	13776	14158	14498	14899	13103	14221	14005	14491	14013	13970	14543	14131	14821	14852	14818	15028
1979	15498	16369	17830	19062	16528	14607	15358	15841	16437	16829	16804	18277	18409	19027	18546	19612
1980	21289	20235	19597	20548	21142	21779	20947	19766	20587	20353	19139	19713	19941	20347	19860	21436
1981	21854	21828	21544	21777	22616	21916	21029	22249	21232	22005	20114	23242	21274	23077	22508	19746
1982	20720	19793	21120	19684	22573	19570	20019	17714	20477	21187	19849	22930	20581	21006	18892	19154
1983	19486	20759	22331	23474	20127	18804	19528	19914	21446	20916	21828	22714	22451	24333	23115	22976

Exports f.o.b. (19)(22) — million dollars, monthly averages

Adjusted - Corrigé

Exportations f.o.b. (22) (19) — millions de dollars, moyennes mensuelles

Year	Q.1	Q.2	Q.3	Q.4	JAN	FEB	MAR	APR	MAY	JUN	JUL	AUG	SEP	OCT	NOV	DEC
1964	2065	2079	2150	2242	2052	2076	2067	2081	2077	2080	2118	2095	2237	2150	2183	2394
1965	1863	2313	2307	2363	1228	1623	2739	2406	2299	2235	2300	2329	2291	2349	2378	2362
1966	2394	2406	2477	2508	2298	2353	2530	2317	2416	2485	2469	2460	2503	2616	2491	2417
1967	2582	2580	2588	2588	2639	2582	2525	2608	2549	2582	2601	2566	2597	2415	2671	2677
1968	2676	2822	3006	2860	2815	2775	2439	2855	2740	2870	2858	2950	3211	2631	2972	2977
1969	2538	3255	3295	3340	2161	2266	3188	3318	3268	3179	3182	3366	3341	3342	3398	3280
1970	3442	3599	3615	3586	3406	3547	3375	3410	3661	3727	3704	3591	3553	3688	3499	3569
1971	3695	3683	3909	3249	3601	3695	3790	3631	3746	3672	3573	3667	4487	2669	3196	3881
1972	3922	3891	4147	4444	4074	3824	3869	3820	3882	3971	4074	4191	4176	4312	4468	4553
1973	5112	5594	6109	6804	4955	5070	5311	5494	5561	5728	5865	6042	6420	6585	6879	6949
1974	7442	8026	8362	8836	7150	7549	7625	8108	7652	8317	8307	8379	8399	8673	8973	8862
1975	9005	8559	9013	9311	9497	8804	8715	8713	8241	8755	8885	9038	9116	9241	9421	9272
1976	9022	9560	9885	9940	9108	8932	9026	9377	9570	9734	9989	9826	9839	9770	9602	10448
1977	9909	10186	10365	9945	9667	9898	10164	9940	10529	10091	10372	9683	11039	9357	9478	10999
1978	10315	11889	12405	13210	9363	9939	11143	11628	11776	12264	11656	12286	13275	12901	13448	13282
1979	13726	14294	15745	16784	13265	13616	14298	13979	14084	14819	15692	15717	15825	16682	16929	16742
1980	17556	18218	18727	19060	17419	16984	18265	18567	17647	18440	18267	19087	18828	19214	18715	19251
1981	19989	19478	19290	19057	18902	19788	21278	19786	18899	19750	19289	19031	19551	19163	19153	18885
1982	18553	18318	17614	16290	18584	18614	18462	18005	18124	18823	18060	17463	17320	16671	15852	16347
1983	16745	16236	16775	17131	17232	16312	16690	16095	15655	16959	16486	16582	17257	17033	17063	17298

Trade balance (f.o.b. — f.o.b.) (19)(22) — million dollars, monthly averages

Adjusted - Corrigé

Balance commerciale (f.o.b. — f.o.b.) (22) (19) — millions de dollars, moyennes mensuelles

Year	Q.1	Q.2	Q.3	Q.4	JAN	FEB	MAR	APR	MAY	JUN	JUL	AUG	SEP	OCT	NOV	DEC
1964	598	551	577	611	631	614	549	556	542	556	542	510	678	600	495	739
1965	308	495	498	451	29	17	878	595	503	387	558	504	433	465	438	451
1966	384	321	263	277	332	339	480	226	355	383	253	323	214	313	296	221
1967	349	413	392	207	322	366	359	410	432	398	357	421	399	161	275	184
1968	54	105	157	18	128	184	-150	251	-15	78	133	78	261	-105	89	70
1969	-13	58	192	190	159	-406	206	136	11	27	108	204	263	150	218	202
1970	202	311	275	143	183	267	156	148	324	462	450	245	130	190	71	168
1971	98	-223	-65	-450	2	130	160	-143	-161	-365	-259	-247	308	-800	-260	-288
1972	-552	-566	-487	-518	-351	-649	-647	-596	-604	-497	-491	-535	-436	-426	-680	-449
1973	-268	-19	281	480	-289	-413	-103	133	-142	-47	37	32	776	589	195	658
1974	256	-263	-600	-165	652	231	-117	83	-612	-260	-615	-888	-297	-100	-0	-395
1975	584	1107	1019	990	-351	857	1244	727	961	1634	1035	1143	875	1051	1194	725
1976	-165	-133	-760	-821	89	-122	-461	-289	345	-456	-753	-674	-853	-814	-1043	-605
1977	-1918	-1914	-2144	-2878	-777	-2715	-2260	-1858	-641	-3244	-2111	-2418	-1903	-3230	-2929	-2475
1978	-3462	-2269	-2093	-1689	-3240	-4282	-2863	-2863	-2236	-1707	-2887	-1844	-1546	-1950	-1371	-1745
1979	-1772	-2075	-2085	-2278	-3263	-992	-1060	-1862	-2353	-2011	-1112	-2560	-2585	-2345	-1618	-2871
1980	-3733	-2017	-870	-1488	-3723	-4794	-2682	-1198	-2941	-1912	-872	-626	-1112	-1134	-1145	-2185
1981	-1864	-2350	-2253	-2710	-3714	-2127	249	-2463	-2333	-2255	-825	-4212	-1724	-3914	-3356	-861
1982	-2168	-1475	-3506	-3394	-3989	-956	-1557	291	-2353	-2364	-1790	-5467	-3261	-4335	-3041	-2808
1983	-2742	-4522	-5555	-6343	-2895	-2493	-2837	-3819	-5791	-3957	-5341	-6132	-5195	-7300	-6052	-5678

NOTES

1. Index (original base 1967) consistent with the *Standard Industrial Classification* (SIC) 1957, which was revised in 1967. The year 1963 has been used as the weight base for the period to 1966, and 1967 for the period from 1967.
2. Construction materials and other products leaving the industrial sector.
3. Excluding about 200 thousand tons per month of steel for casting produced by independent foundries.
4. Factory sales.
5. From 1967, new sample design.
6. From 1967, the series excludes turnover tax and is based on a new sample design.
7. Establishment data referring to pay period including the 12th of month. 1972 *Standard Industrial Classification* (SIC) from 1972; 1967 SIC previously.
8. Labour force sample survey of population aged 16 and over, referring to the week including the 12th of the month.
9. Index of advertisements in newspapers representing 52 metropolitan areas.
10. From 1978, strikes involving 1,000 or more workers; previously, strikes involving 6 or more workers.
11. Weighting pattern based on 1958 to 1966, on 1963 from 1967 to 1975, and on 1967 from 1976.
12. Farm products and processed foods and feeds.
13. Monthly data are daily averages except for part of quasi-money, which is an average of beginning- and end-of-month figures.
14. Wage and salary earners only. Weighting pattern based on 1960-61 to 1977 and on 1973-74 from 1978.
15. To December 1972, monthly data refer to last Wednesday of month except for 30th June and 31st December. From January 1973, monthly data are averages of Wednesday figures.
16. Rate on last issue of month.
17. Ten years and over; monthly data are averages of daily rates.
18. Monthly data are daily averages.
19. Excluding military.

NOTES

1. Indice (base originale 1967) établi selon la *Classification Industrielle Standard* (CIS) de 1957 qui a été révisée en 1967. Les années de base de pondération sont 1963 jusqu'en 1966 et 1967 à partir de 1967.
2. Matériaux de construction et autres produits quittant le secteur industriel.
3. Non compris environ 200000 tonnes d'acier par mois destinées à la fabrication des pièces moulées par des fonderies indépendantes.
4. Ventes effectuées par les producteurs.
5. A partir de 1967, nouvelle méthode de sondage.
6. A partir de 1967, la série ne comprend pas la taxe sur le chiffre d'affaires, et elle est basée sur une nouvelle méthode de sondage.
7. Statistiques d'établissement se référant à la période de paie comprenant le 12 du mois. *Classification Industrielle Standard* (CIS) de 1972 à partir de 1972; avant cette date, CIS de 1967.
8. Enquête par sondage auprès de la population âgée de 16 ans ou plus, se référant à la semaine comprenant le 12 du mois.
9. Indices des annonces parues dans les journaux de 52 agglomérations urbaines.
10. Depuis 1978, grèves impliquant 1000 personnes ou plus; auparavant, grèves impliquant au moins 6 personnes.
11. La pondération se réfère à 1958 jusqu'en 1966, à 1963 de 1967 à 1975, et à 1967 à partir de 1976.
12. Produits agricoles et produits alimentaires manufacturés.
13. Les données mensuelles sont des moyennes journalières, sauf pour certains éléments de la quasi-monnaie, pour lesquels les moyennes mensuelles sont les moyennes des données de début et de fin de mois.
14. Salariés seulement. La pondération se réfère à 1960-61 jusqu'en 1977, et à 1973-74 à partir de 1978.
15. Jusqu'en décembre 1972, les données mensuelles se réfèrent au dernier mercredi du mois, sauf pour le 30 juin et le 31 décembre. A partir de janvier 1973, les données mensuelles sont la moyenne des mercredis.
16. Rendement de la dernière émission du mois.
17. Dix ans et plus; les données mensuelles sont des moyennes journalières.
18. Les données mensuelles sont la moyenne de chiffres journaliers.
19. Secteur militaire exclu.

NOTES

20. From 1970, the data incorporate the results of the US-Canadian trade reconciliation. The result of the revision was about +1.2 per cent for Exports and +0.3 per cent for Imports in 1970.

21. Excluding international agencies. Annual figures may differ from data for December and 4th quarter because of changes in reporting coverage and classification of liabilities.

22. General trade. Prior to 1970, excluding silver ore and bullion. From 1977, including non-monetary gold.

NOTES

20. A partir de 1970, les données tiennent compte des résultats de l'harmonisation des statistiques de commerce entre le Canada et les États-Unis. La révision effectuée était de +1,2 % pour les exportations et +0,3 % pour les importations en 1970.

21. Non compris les organismes internationaux. Les chiffres annuels peuvent être différents des données de décembre et du 4e trimestre en raison de modifications dans la couverture et la classification de la dette.

22. Commerce général. Avant 1970, non compris minerai et lingots d'argent. A partir de 1977, y compris l'or non monétaire.

MAIN SOURCES

PRINCIPALES SOURCES

Series	Séries	Sources
National income and product	Revenu et produit national	U.S. Department of Commerce *Survey of Current Business*
Manufacturing deliveries, stocks and orders	Livraisons, stocks et commandes, industries manufacturières	
Construction	Construction	
Internal trade	Commerce intérieur	
Producer prices	Prix à la production	
Balance of payments	Balance des paiements	
Foreign trade	Commerce extérieur	
Industrial production	Production industrielle	Board of Governors of the Federal Reserve System *Federal Reserve Bulletin*
Rate of capacity utilization	Taux d'utilisation de capacité	
Home finance	Finances internes	
Interest rates	Taux d'intérêts	
Share prices	Cours des actions	
Liabilities to foreigners	Dette envers l'étranger	
Production	Production	Council of Economic Advisers *Economic Indicators*
Labour and wages	Main-d'œuvre et salaires	U.S. Department of Labor *Monthly Labor Review*
Consumer prices	Prix à la consommation	
Unit labour cost	Coût unitaire de la main-d'œuvre	U.S. Department of Commerce *Business Conditions Digest*

Japan — Japon

JAPAN

Gross national product
at current market prices
billion yen, annual rates

Adjusted - Corrigé

Produit national brut
aux prix courants du marché
milliards de yens, taux annuels

	Year	Q.1	Q.2	Q.3	Q.4	JAN	FEB	MAR	APR	MAY	JUN	JUL	AUG	SEP	OCT	NOV	DEC
1964	28917	27360	28404	29358	30057												
1965	32657	31767	32221	33273	33367												
1966	37932	35305	37498	38926	39777												
1967	44463	41787	43062	45310	47255												
1968	52703	49005	51049	53023	57180												
1969	62018	57429	60428	62914	66505												
1970	73128	69361	71503	74587	76265												
1971	80522	77680	79349	81612	82788												
1972	92313	87000	89667	93824	97598												
1973	112441	104573	109273	113568	120045												
1974	133922	123327	131574	137562	140876												
1975	147874	141548	146199	149264	153394												
1976	165695	158519	163862	168623	170964												
1977	184368	178020	182205	185936	190717												
1978	202708	196278	200251	204857	208919												
1979	218894	212969	217467	220415	223248												
1980	235834	226931	233003	239066	243029												
1981	252000	246627	249741	253754	255899												
1982	264775	259287	264491	267525	267743												
1983	274639	270144	273190	275421	278537												

Industrial production: total (1)(2)
1980 = 100

Production industrielle : total (1)(2)
1980 = 100

	Year	Q.1	Q.2	Q.3	Q.4	JAN	FEB	MAR	APR	MAY	JUN	JUL	AUG	SEP	OCT	NOV	DEC
1964	31.4	30.5	30.9	31.5	32.8	28.2	30.6	32.5	30.4	30.6	31.7	31.5	30.5	32.6	32.6	32.0	33.8
1965	32.7	32.8	32.1	32.2	33.5	30.8	32.4	35.2	32.2	31.4	32.8	32.5	31.4	32.8	32.9	33.2	34.4
1966	36.9	34.5	35.8	37.2	40.1	32.0	34.0	37.6	35.4	35.4	36.8	37.0	36.3	38.3	38.9	39.5	41.9
1967	44.0	41.4	42.6	44.4	47.7	38.7	40.5	44.9	41.7	42.1	43.9	44.0	43.2	46.1	46.4	47.2	49.3
1968	50.7	47.7	49.5	51.1	54.5	44.4	47.7	51.1	48.8	49.2	50.4	51.3	49.7	52.2	53.5	54.4	55.7
1969	58.8	54.5	57.4	59.4	63.7	50.8	54.4	58.2	56.9	56.6	58.7	59.9	57.0	61.4	63.1	62.4	65.6
1970	66.8	64.0	66.4	67.7	69.1	59.7	63.6	68.7	65.8	64.7	68.7	69.2	64.9	69.0	68.9	67.6	71.0
1971	68.6	67.8	67.5	69.1	70.2	63.8	67.0	72.5	68.3	64.7	69.4	70.1	66.4	70.7	69.6	69.7	71.3
1972	73.6	69.8	71.7	74.1	78.9	64.8	69.2	75.4	71.1	70.2	73.9	74.0	71.7	76.5	77.0	77.7	82.0
1973	84.6	80.0	83.7	85.5	89.0	74.2	78.8	87.0	82.5	82.5	86.0	86.2	82.9	87.8	88.9	88.6	89.5
1974	81.3	84.1	82.8	80.5	77.8	79.5	83.8	89.1	83.2	82.2	82.9	83.2	76.8	81.6	79.5	77.2	76.9
1975	72.8	69.0	72.0	74.4	75.8	65.3	68.3	73.4	71.8	70.5	73.8	75.8	70.6	76.7	76.4	74.1	76.8
1976	80.8	75.3	80.2	82.8	84.8	68.9	74.5	82.7	80.1	78.1	82.5	84.6	79.0	84.8	84.2	84.3	86.0
1977	84.1	81.4	83.8	84.5	86.6	76.4	79.5	88.5	84.3	81.5	85.7	85.1	81.5	87.3	85.5	86.2	88.1
1978	89.3	84.8	88.8	90.6	92.8	79.0	82.8	92.6	89.2	86.9	90.3	91.7	87.4	92.8	91.6	91.9	94.9
1979	95.6	90.4	95.4	96.3	99.9	84.2	88.7	98.3	94.8	94.0	97.5	98.7	93.8	98.0	98.8	99.4	101.4
1980	100.0	98.9	102.0	98.7	100.4	90.9	99.9	106.0	103.8	100.2	102.1	102.9	92.4	100.7	100.5	98.4	102.2
1981	101.0	97.6	100.3	101.8	104.5	91.2	96.4	105.1	101.5	97.0	102.4	104.8	95.9	104.6	104.4	103.5	105.6
1982	101.4	100.3	101.6	101.7	102.1	93.6	98.6	108.7	103.0	98.0	103.7	104.4	96.0	104.6	100.5	102.2	103.5
1983	105.0	99.5	103.2	106.5	110.7	92.3	97.4	108.8	104.0	100.1	105.6	107.2	101.1	111.4	108.5	110.2	113.4

Industrial production: (1)(2)
finished investment goods
1980 = 100

Production industrielle : (1)(2)
produits finis, biens d'équipement
1980 = 100

	Year	Q.1	Q.2	Q.3	Q.4	JAN	FEB	MAR	APR	MAY	JUN	JUL	AUG	SEP	OCT	NOV	DEC
1964	23.6	22.4	23.2	24.5	24.2	19.4	22.6	25.1	22.8	22.8	24.1	24.0	23.0	26.5	24.2	23.4	24.9
1965	24.7	25.1	24.4	24.9	24.5	22.6	24.7	27.8	24.9	23.5	24.9	24.5	23.8	26.3	24.6	24.3	24.6
1966	27.6	25.3	27.1	28.2	29.8	22.3	24.8	28.8	26.5	26.7	28.1	27.9	26.9	29.8	29.4	29.3	30.7
1967	35.6	32.0	34.1	37.0	39.3	28.7	31.2	36.0	33.0	33.8	35.4	35.9	34.8	40.5	37.7	39.1	41.1
1968	44.0	39.4	42.9	45.5	48.0	35.2	39.0	43.9	41.1	42.4	45.3	45.1	43.7	47.8	47.8	47.9	48.4
1969	51.3	47.4	50.3	52.9	54.7	41.7	48.4	52.2	50.8	48.9	51.4	52.9	49.2	56.6	56.2	53.2	54.7
1970	61.0	58.0	60.5	63.0	62.3	52.4	57.5	64.2	58.9	58.3	64.2	64.0	58.3	66.3	62.0	60.4	64.6
1971	61.6	62.6	61.2	62.5	59.8	55.5	62.4	70.1	62.6	57.5	63.5	62.5	58.2	67.2	60.1	59.8	59.5
1972	64.2	60.4	61.7	66.1	68.6	53.7	58.7	68.9	60.3	59.9	64.9	64.0	62.1	72.3	68.2	66.8	70.8
1973	80.4	76.3	77.2	84.5	83.6	66.6	74.0	88.3	76.4	75.0	80.2	81.8	80.6	91.1	84.7	82.6	83.5
1974	80.0	82.7	80.8	81.3	75.0	73.8	80.8	93.4	79.1	79.5	83.8	82.2	75.1	86.8	77.2	73.9	74.0
1975	67.0	70.6	66.3	66.7	64.2	62.7	69.9	79.2	67.1	64.3	67.6	67.1	62.2	70.9	66.3	62.1	64.1
1976	70.6	68.1	69.0	72.7	72.7	59.0	66.6	78.8	69.2	66.2	71.5	71.6	67.9	78.7	73.2	70.7	74.1
1977	75.0	75.2	72.3	76.7	76.0	66.2	71.2	88.2	73.5	68.6	74.8	73.3	72.7	84.0	77.2	74.6	76.1
1978	81.5	80.8	79.9	83.2	82.2	71.0	75.7	95.7	83.1	76.3	80.3	79.6	77.5	92.4	82.0	80.3	84.4
1979	89.0	86.1	86.3	91.3	91.9	74.7	83.2	100.3	87.5	83.3	88.1	89.8	87.4	98.1	91.7	92.4	91.5
1980	100.0	97.7	99.1	102.8	100.4	83.7	96.5	112.9	100.5	95.7	101.1	103.3	92.3	112.9	102.0	98.3	100.8
1981	106.0	104.9	102.1	109.8	107.1	93.2	101.6	119.8	102.4	98.8	105.1	110.4	100.2	118.9	107.2	106.1	108.0
1982	106.4	111.1	103.0	108.5	102.7	96.6	107.0	129.8	106.4	96.5	106.2	106.5	99.5	119.7	100.7	103.1	104.3
1983	106.7	105.6	101.0	109.2	111.0	91.2	100.7	124.8	102.0	97.1	103.9	105.0	99.9	122.6	108.6	110.7	113.8

Gross national product
implicit price level
1980 = 100

Adjusted - Corrigé

Produit national brut
niveau implicite des prix
1980 = 100

	Year	Q.1	Q.2	Q.3	Q.4	JAN	FEB	MAR	APR	MAY	JUN	JUL	AUG	SEP	OCT	NOV	DEC
1964																	
1965	38.1	38.1	38.0	38.3	38.4												
1966	40.0	39.0	39.8	40.3	40.7												
1967	42.3	41.6	41.8	42.3	43.2												
1968	44.5	43.6	44.1	44.6	45.3												
1969	46.6	45.2	46.0	47.2	47.7												
1970	50.1	48.8	49.5	50.3	51.2												
1971	52.6	51.9	52.2	52.9	53.2												
1972	55.4	53.8	54.6	55.9	56.7												
1973	62.0	58.1	60.1	62.5	66.1												
1974	74.8	70.1	73.5	76.0	78.2												
1975	80.6	79.1	80.0	80.8	81.9												
1976	85.8	83.3	85.1	86.7	87.6												
1977	90.6	88.7	89.9	91.2	92.3												
1978	94.8	93.2	94.3	95.4	95.9												
1979	97.3	96.6	97.2	97.4	97.5												
1980	100.0	97.6	99.7	100.9	101.4												
1981	102.7	102.0	102.1	102.8	103.7												
1982	104.5	104.0	104.6	104.9	104.6												
1983	105.2	105.3	105.4	105.0	105.0												

Industrial production: total (1)(2)
1980 = 100

Adjusted - Corrigé

Production industrielle : total (1)(2)
1980 = 100

	Year	Q.1	Q.2	Q.3	Q.4	JAN	FEB	MAR	APR	MAY	JUN	JUL	AUG	SEP	OCT	NOV	DEC
1964		30.2	31.0	32.0	32.6	29.8	30.5	30.4	30.6	31.0	31.5	31.7	31.7	32.5	32.5	32.2	33.0
1965		32.6	32.3	32.5	33.2	32.6	32.3	32.8	32.3	32.0	32.5	32.5	32.5	32.8	32.8	33.3	33.3
1966		34.2	36.0	37.7	39.8	33.8	33.9	34.9	35.4	36.0	36.5	37.1	37.8	38.3	38.9	39.8	40.6
1967		41.1	42.8	45.0	47.3	40.9	40.5	41.8	41.9	42.8	43.6	44.0	44.8	46.1	46.4	47.5	47.9
1968		48.3	49.8	51.1	53.5	47.7	48.5	48.7	49.0	50.5	49.8	50.3	51.7	51.4	52.7	54.1	53.9
1969		55.1	57.8	59.4	62.5	54.5	55.4	55.5	57.1	58.3	57.9	58.7	59.2	60.4	62.1	62.2	63.4
1970		64.7	66.8	67.7	68.0	64.1	64.7	65.4	65.9	66.7	67.8	67.8	67.5	67.8	67.9	67.3	68.7
1971		68.5	67.9	69.0	69.1	68.6	68.2	68.9	68.5	66.8	68.3	68.5	68.9	69.5	68.7	69.5	69.2
1972		70.5	72.1	74.1	77.6	69.6	70.4	71.6	71.2	72.3	72.6	72.6	74.5	75.3	76.1	77.5	79.3
1973		82.3	84.0	85.1	86.9	81.4	82.1	83.5	83.1	84.1	84.8	84.0	86.2	85.0	86.5	87.2	87.0
1974		86.6	83.0	79.9	76.0	87.3	87.3	85.3	83.7	83.8	81.7	80.9	79.3	79.0	77.2	76.0	74.7
1975		71.2	72.2	73.7	74.0	71.9	71.3	70.3	72.0	71.9	72.7	73.5	73.4	74.2	74.3	73.1	74.7
1976		77.6	80.3	82.0	82.9	76.0	77.9	79.0	80.1	79.7	81.2	81.9	82.1	82.0	81.9	83.2	83.7
1977		83.9	83.8	83.8	84.9	84.3	83.1	84.3	83.8	83.6	84.1	82.8	84.4	84.2	83.7	85.2	85.8
1978		86.8	88.1	90.3	91.7	86.6	86.2	87.6	87.9	88.0	88.5	89.5	90.4	90.9	91.1	91.5	92.4
1979		92.4	94.7	96.5	98.6	92.2	92.0	93.1	93.3	95.2	95.7	96.1	97.7	96.1	98.0	99.1	98.8
1980		101.1	101.3	98.5	99.1	99.6	103.3	100.4	102.1	101.5	100.2	99.9	96.9	98.7	99.5	98.1	99.6
1981		99.6	99.5	101.8	103.2	99.9	99.4	99.6	99.8	98.3	100.5	101.6	101.1	102.6	103.3	103.3	103.0
1982		102.3	101.2	101.6	100.4	102.4	101.8	102.7	101.4	100.4	101.8	101.2	101.7	102.0	99.3	101.5	100.5
1983		101.4	102.9	106.6	108.9	101.0	100.3	102.8	102.6	102.6	103.6	103.9	107.1	108.7	107.2	109.4	110.1

Industrial production: (1)(2)
finished investment goods
1980 = 100

Adjusted - Corrigé

Production industrielle : (1)(2)
produits finis, biens d'équipement
1980 = 100

	Year	Q.1	Q.2	Q.3	Q.4	JAN	FEB	MAR	APR	MAY	JUN	JUL	AUG	SEP	OCT	NOV	DEC
1964		22.2	23.2	24.3	24.6	21.6	22.4	22.5	22.6	23.0	23.8	24.0	23.7	25.1	24.4	24.2	25.1
1965		24.9	24.4	24.7	24.9	25.2	24.6	24.9	24.8	23.9	24.6	24.4	24.7	24.9	24.7	25.2	24.8
1966		25.1	26.9	28.0	30.3	24.8	24.8	25.8	26.3	27.0	27.5	27.9	28.0	28.2	29.5	30.3	31.0
1967		31.8	34.0	36.7	40.0	31.9	31.2	32.2	32.8	34.3	34.9	35.8	36.0	38.2	38.0	40.5	41.5
1968		40.0	42.9	44.7	48.2	39.7	39.8	40.4	41.3	43.7	43.7	43.9	45.8	44.5	47.6	48.8	48.2
1969		48.0	50.4	52.0	55.0	47.0	49.2	47.9	50.9	50.6	49.6	51.5	51.7	52.8	56.1	54.2	54.7
1970		58.7	60.6	61.9	62.8	59.0	58.3	58.7	59.1	60.5	62.1	62.2	61.2	62.2	62.0	61.5	64.8
1971		63.1	61.3	61.4	60.3	62.2	63.1	64.0	62.9	59.7	61.3	60.8	61.1	62.3	60.2	60.8	59.9
1972		61.0	62.0	64.8	68.9	60.4	59.6	63.0	60.7	62.4	62.8	62.4	65.0	67.0	67.6	68.1	71.0
1973		76.0	78.6	82.8	84.1	74.9	75.6	77.5	78.2	78.6	79.0	80.6	84.7	83.2	84.0	84.8	83.6
1974		82.4	82.2	79.8	75.6	83.0	82.4	81.8	80.7	83.3	82.4	81.0	79.0	79.4	76.6	76.0	74.1
1975		70.3	67.4	65.5	64.7	70.6	71.3	69.0	68.2	67.4	66.6	66.2	65.4	64.9	65.8	64.1	64.3
1976		67.6	70.0	71.3	73.4	66.5	67.8	68.6	70.1	69.5	70.4	70.6	71.5	72.0	72.6	73.1	74.3
1977		74.7	73.7	74.9	75.7	74.4	72.8	76.8	74.3	72.9	74.0	72.6	75.7	76.3	76.3	77.2	76.8
1978		79.7	81.0	81.5	83.8	80.2	77.6	81.2	82.0	80.6	80.4	80.3	80.9	83.4	82.2	83.3	86.0
1979		85.0	87.5	90.0	93.6	84.3	85.0	85.7	86.5	87.9	88.2	89.5	91.9	88.6	92.1	95.6	93.1
1980		96.6	100.6	100.6	102.1	94.5	98.3	97.1	99.7	100.8	101.2	102.0	97.6	102.1	102.5	101.3	102.4
1981		103.9	103.7	107.4	108.9	105.2	103.0	103.5	101.9	104.1	105.1	108.3	106.3	107.7	107.6	109.2	109.8
1982		109.3	105.2	106.2	104.2	108.9	108.2	110.9	106.7	102.6	106.4	104.7	106.5	107.5	101.7	105.9	105.1
1983		103.8	103.2	106.8	112.7	102.8	101.8	106.7	102.3	103.2	104.1	103.2	107.0	110.2	109.7	113.7	114.7

JAPAN

Industrial production: (1)(2)
finished consumer durable goods
1980 = 100

Production industrielle : (1)(2)
produits finis, biens de consommation durables
1980 = 100

	Year	Q.1	Q.2	Q.3	Q.4	JAN	FEB	MAR	APR	MAY	JUN	JUL	AUG	SEP	OCT	NOV	DEC
1964	15.7	14.8	16.4	15.4	16.4	13.0	15.3	16.0	16.2	16.1	17.0	15.8	14.6	15.8	16.6	16.0	16.6
1965	15.1	14.9	15.4	14.8	15.3	13.5	15.1	16.2	15.5	15.1	15.7	15.2	13.9	15.3	15.1	15.1	15.7
1966	18.3	15.8	17.6	18.5	21.1	14.1	16.0	17.4	17.3	17.0	18.6	18.6	17.5	19.3	19.8	20.9	22.5
1967	23.9	21.3	23.2	23.9	27.1	19.3	21.4	23.1	22.7	22.1	24.7	23.8	22.4	25.4	26.1	27.0	28.2
1968	30.1	26.1	30.1	30.6	33.7	23.0	27.4	27.8	29.0	29.2	32.0	31.1	28.5	32.3	32.5	34.5	34.1
1969	37.7	32.2	37.2	38.2	43.3	28.9	33.7	34.0	36.3	36.0	39.3	38.8	35.6	40.3	41.7	43.0	45.2
1970	42.1	38.6	42.7	42.8	44.3	34.2	39.9	41.6	41.2	41.2	45.7	44.8	39.8	43.6	44.1	43.9	44.8
1971	44.8	40.6	43.8	45.4	49.4	36.5	41.8	43.6	44.5	40.2	46.7	46.6	41.9	47.8	48.7	49.0	50.5
1972	50.5	46.5	50.6	50.4	54.5	42.0	47.4	50.0	50.0	48.7	53.0	52.1	46.3	52.8	53.4	53.8	56.3
1973	55.1	50.8	55.4	55.0	59.4	45.8	52.1	54.6	54.1	52.7	59.3	57.3	50.8	56.9	58.9	59.4	59.7
1974	54.2	53.9	54.7	53.5	54.9	49.3	55.9	56.4	52.7	54.1	57.2	57.9	47.7	55.0	55.6	55.3	53.7
1975	50.5	44.3	50.0	52.0	55.8	42.7	44.8	45.4	47.9	48.4	53.8	54.1	46.6	55.3	56.8	55.5	55.0
1976	64.0	55.9	64.7	66.1	69.5	49.4	55.9	62.4	64.2	61.7	68.3	70.4	59.5	68.3	69.7	70.1	68.7
1977	71.9	65.3	72.9	71.7	77.8	59.4	64.6	71.9	72.1	69.7	76.8	74.4	65.0	75.6	75.9	79.1	78.3
1978	81.0	73.9	82.8	81.5	86.0	66.7	73.5	81.4	81.6	79.2	87.5	85.8	73.4	85.3	86.6	86.4	85.0
1979	88.8	78.6	90.4	89.8	96.2	70.7	79.3	85.7	87.0	87.5	96.8	96.5	81.1	91.8	95.6	96.6	96.4
1980	100.0	92.8	103.9	99.2	104.1	81.6	97.1	99.7	104.0	99.8	107.9	106.5	86.2	105.0	105.0	102.0	105.2
1981	107.8	100.3	110.4	106.0	114.6	90.3	101.3	109.3	111.2	103.7	116.4	114.2	91.7	112.1	116.7	115.4	111.6
1982	110.1	104.8	112.1	110.2	113.4	94.6	105.0	114.9	112.2	106.7	117.3	120.3	95.9	114.4	113.1	116.5	110.5
1983	117.5	107.6	119.0	117.3	125.6	96.7	106.9	119.2	119.2	112.3	125.5	125.4	103.4	124.7	121.6	127.3	127.8

Industrial production: (1)(2)
finished consumer non-durable goods
1980 = 100

Production industrielle : (1)(2)
produits finis, biens de consommation non durables
1980 = 100

	Year	Q.1	Q.2	Q.3	Q.4	JAN	FEB	MAR	APR	MAY	JUN	JUL	AUG	SEP	OCT	NOV	DEC
1964	47.9	50.0	45.6	46.0	49.9	46.1	50.5	53.5	45.3	44.9	46.6	46.1	44.6	47.3	48.3	47.3	54.2
1965	50.6	53.7	47.9	47.8	52.9	49.3	53.1	58.7	48.5	46.5	48.6	47.9	46.7	48.8	50.3	51.8	56.6
1966	55.7	57.5	53.5	53.4	58.3	52.7	57.0	62.8	53.6	52.7	54.2	54.0	52.6	53.8	55.6	56.7	62.5
1967	59.6	61.3	56.3	57.1	63.5	56.3	60.1	67.6	55.8	55.2	57.8	56.6	56.5	58.3	60.9	62.3	67.4
1968	63.2	65.9	60.6	60.3	65.9	60.2	65.7	71.7	61.7	60.2	60.0	61.3	60.0	59.8	62.5	64.7	70.6
1969	67.9	69.3	65.8	65.9	70.5	63.9	68.3	75.6	65.2	65.1	67.2	67.6	64.1	66.1	67.7	67.7	76.2
1970	73.3	75.3	71.1	71.8	75.0	68.9	74.9	82.1	71.5	68.1	73.6	74.6	69.8	70.9	72.9	71.2	81.1
1971	74.8	79.4	72.8	71.4	75.7	75.2	77.4	85.5	74.4	69.5	74.5	74.4	69.1	70.7	71.5	74.1	81.4
1972	77.7	79.5	75.5	74.8	81.1	73.1	78.7	86.5	76.3	72.0	78.2	76.6	73.5	74.4	75.6	78.8	88.9
1973	83.4	76.5	83.6	82.9	90.8	70.1	75.9	83.4	82.5	84.0	84.2	83.6	81.1	84.0	86.9	89.5	96.1
1974	83.0	80.2	84.8	82.0	84.9	74.9	80.3	85.6	88.6	84.2	81.5	84.6	79.8	81.7	83.7	84.0	87.1
1975	81.2	72.2	81.8	84.2	86.7	65.4	70.7	80.5	83.1	80.4	81.9	86.7	80.4	85.6	84.5	82.7	92.9
1976	87.1	78.9	88.7	88.1	92.6	70.0	78.1	88.7	89.2	86.7	90.2	91.5	83.6	89.2	88.2	91.6	98.0
1977	90.6	83.2	92.5	92.1	95.4	75.3	82.3	92.0	92.5	89.9	95.1	92.5	88.1	92.9	90.1	94.9	101.2
1978	95.3	87.2	97.9	96.1	99.9	76.9	86.8	98.0	99.5	95.4	98.8	98.0	93.9	96.5	96.2	97.7	105.9
1979	98.6	90.4	101.6	98.7	103.5	81.3	89.1	100.9	102.6	100.0	102.1	101.4	95.5	99.1	100.4	101.4	108.8
1980	100.0	95.2	102.1	98.1	104.6	85.5	98.8	101.2	106.2	98.8	101.3	102.6	92.8	98.9	101.5	101.2	111.2
1981	103.3	96.3	104.1	103.1	109.8	87.0	95.9	106.0	107.3	99.4	105.5	106.0	97.7	105.6	106.9	106.8	115.8
1982	106.5	97.7	109.7	107.7	110.9	88.5	96.4	108.3	110.0	105.7	113.3	110.7	102.8	109.6	107.4	109.8	115.6
1983	109.7	101.3	112.7	110.9	113.7	91.1	99.9	113.0	115.6	109.5	113.1	110.6	106.1	115.9	111.2	111.2	118.8

Industrial production: intermediate goods (1)(2)
1980 = 100

Production industrielle : biens intermédiaires (1)(2)
1980 = 100

	Year	Q.1	Q.2	Q.3	Q.4	JAN	FEB	MAR	APR	MAY	JUN	JUL	AUG	SEP	OCT	NOV	DEC
1964	34.2	32.4	33.8	34.6	36.0	30.9	32.2	34.0	33.1	33.9	34.4	34.6	33.8	35.4	36.0	35.7	36.4
1965	35.6	34.8	35.3	35.5	36.7	33.6	34.3	36.4	34.9	34.9	36.0	35.9	34.8	35.7	36.3	36.6	37.1
1966	40.5	36.8	39.4	41.5	44.4	34.9	36.0	39.4	38.8	39.0	40.4	41.0	40.8	42.6	43.5	44.1	45.5
1967	48.1	44.7	47.2	48.9	51.4	42.7	43.7	47.7	46.2	47.2	48.1	48.6	48.2	50.1	51.0	51.0	52.2
1968	55.3	52.0	54.1	55.9	59.3	49.5	51.6	54.9	53.8	54.1	54.5	56.1	54.6	56.9	58.7	59.3	59.9
1969	64.4	59.0	62.9	65.3	70.3	56.4	58.3	62.2	62.3	62.6	63.9	65.7	63.3	67.0	69.7	69.5	71.8
1970	73.2	69.5	73.2	74.2	76.0	66.2	68.8	73.6	73.3	71.9	74.4	75.4	72.2	75.0	76.4	75.1	76.7
1971	75.1	73.0	73.9	76.1	77.5	70.7	71.7	76.6	74.6	72.1	75.1	77.0	74.3	77.0	77.3	77.2	77.9
1972	81.3	76.2	79.4	82.0	87.3	72.2	75.7	80.7	78.9	78.5	80.7	81.7	80.7	83.5	85.9	87.1	90.4
1973	93.1	88.9	93.1	93.1	97.4	84.7	87.6	94.4	91.7	92.3	95.2	94.4	90.7	94.2	98.2	97.4	96.7
1974	86.9	92.4	89.2	84.7	81.2	89.7	92.2	95.1	90.3	89.0	88.2	87.9	81.7	84.4	84.0	80.7	79.0
1975	76.6	71.4	75.7	78.2	81.1	69.8	70.7	73.8	75.1	74.5	77.6	79.7	75.0	80.0	82.0	80.2	81.2
1976	86.0	80.4	85.3	88.0	90.2	75.6	79.7	85.9	85.0	83.7	87.2	90.0	85.1	88.9	90.2	90.4	90.1
1977	87.5	85.7	87.7	87.2	89.4	83.0	84.2	89.8	88.3	86.3	88.5	88.4	85.1	88.0	88.8	89.2	90.2
1978	91.2	86.7	90.5	92.0	95.7	83.2	85.1	91.8	90.1	89.8	91.7	93.3	89.4	93.2	94.8	95.5	96.7
1979	98.1	93.4	98.1	98.5	102.5	89.4	92.0	98.9	97.1	97.6	99.6	100.8	96.2	98.8	101.8	102.2	103.4
1980	100.0	101.0	103.4	97.0	98.6	95.3	101.6	106.0	105.3	102.9	102.2	102.0	92.6	96.5	99.3	97.4	99.1
1981	97.3	94.3	97.3	97.1	100.4	90.3	93.6	98.9	98.5	94.9	98.6	99.5	93.1	98.5	101.2	99.9	100.2
1982	96.4	95.8	97.2	95.4	97.2	92.4	94.6	100.3	98.7	94.8	97.9	98.7	91.1	96.4	96.3	97.5	97.8
1983	100.5	94.4	98.9	101.5	107.3	90.6	93.1	99.6	99.3	96.5	100.9	103.0	97.4	103.9	105.9	107.2	108.6

Industrial production: (1)(2) finished consumer durable goods

Production industrielle : (1)(2) produits finis, biens de consommation durables

Adjusted - Corrigé

1980 = 100

	Year	Q.1	Q.2	Q.3	Q.4	JAN	FEB	MAR	APR	MAY	JUN	JUL	AUG	SEP	OCT	NOV	DEC
1964		15.4	15.9	15.7	15.9	15.1	15.7	15.5	15.8	15.9	16.1	15.6	15.7	15.8	16.1	15.8	16.0
1965		15.5	15.0	15.1	14.9	15.6	15.3	15.6	15.1	15.0	14.9	15.0	15.0	15.3	14.8	14.9	15.1
1966		16.4	17.1	18.9	20.6	16.3	16.3	16.7	16.8	16.8	17.6	18.3	18.3	19.4	19.5	20.7	21.5
1967		22.1	22.5	24.3	26.5	22.3	21.8	22.2	22.1	21.9	23.4	23.4	24.0	25.5	25.7	26.7	27.0
1968		27.8	29.6	30.7	32.1	27.0	28.1	28.3	28.8	30.0	30.1	30.1	30.8	31.3	31.3	32.9	32.1
1969		34.3	36.7	38.3	41.2	33.9	34.5	34.5	36.1	37.0	37.0	37.4	38.4	39.0	40.1	41.1	42.5
1970		41.1	42.2	42.8	42.2	40.1	41.0	42.1	41.0	42.5	43.0	43.2	42.9	42.2	42.3	42.0	42.2
1971		43.2	43.3	45.4	47.1	42.7	42.9	44.0	44.3	41.6	44.0	44.8	45.1	46.2	46.6	46.9	47.6
1972		49.4	50.0	50.5	51.9	49.2	48.7	50.3	49.6	50.3	49.9	50.2	50.0	51.1	51.4	51.4	53.0
1973		53.9	54.6	55.1	56.7	52.8	54.4	54.5	54.7	53.8	55.4	53.9	56.3	55.1	56.0	56.8	57.4
1974		57.1	54.0	53.5	52.6	56.8	58.5	56.1	53.0	55.4	53.6	54.3	52.9	53.3	52.9	52.9	51.9
1975		47.1	49.2	51.9	53.5	49.2	47.3	44.9	47.8	49.5	50.4	50.7	51.7	53.4	53.9	53.1	53.5
1976		59.3	63.6	65.9	66.9	57.0	59.4	61.6	63.7	63.0	64.0	65.8	66.0	65.9	66.3	67.2	67.3
1977		69.4	71.1	71.7	75.2	68.6	68.9	70.7	70.7	71.2	71.4	70.3	72.0	72.9	72.6	75.8	77.1
1978		78.2	79.8	82.4	83.6	78.2	77.0	79.3	79.1	79.6	80.6	81.3	82.8	83.1	83.9	83.4	83.4
1979		83.1	87.0	91.0	93.5	82.9	82.7	83.6	84.1	87.9	89.1	91.2	92.3	89.6	92.4	93.5	94.7
1980		98.0	99.9	100.6	101.3	95.7	100.8	97.4	100.2	100.3	99.3	100.4	98.9	102.4	101.3	99.1	103.5
1981		105.8	106.0	107.5	111.6	105.9	104.8	106.8	106.9	104.2	107.0	107.4	105.8	109.5	112.5	112.3	110.0
1982		110.7	108.8	111.3	109.7	110.9	109.1	112.0	108.7	108.9	108.7	112.4	111.0	110.5	108.6	111.4	109.2
1983		113.6	115.5	119.1	121.6	113.4	111.1	116.2	115.5	114.6	116.3	117.2	119.7	120.5	116.8	121.7	126.3

Industrial production: (1)(2) finished consumer non-durable goods

Production industrielle : (1)(2) produits finis, biens de consommation non durables

Adjusted - Corrigé

1980 = 100

	Year	Q.1	Q.2	Q.3	Q.4	JAN	FEB	MAR	APR	MAY	JUN	JUL	AUG	SEP	OCT	NOV	DEC
1964		45.7	47.3	49.0	49.8	45.8	46.1	45.3	46.5	47.0	48.6	48.1	48.6	50.2	49.9	49.0	50.5
1965		49.5	49.6	50.7	52.6	49.2	49.0	50.1	49.6	48.9	50.3	49.9	50.8	51.4	51.7	53.3	52.7
1966		53.0	55.4	56.5	58.0	52.7	52.7	53.5	54.9	55.4	55.9	56.2	57.0	56.5	57.1	58.3	58.4
1967		56.5	58.3	60.5	63.2	56.3	55.5	57.6	57.2	58.0	59.6	59.0	61.3	61.3	62.5	64.0	63.1
1968		62.5	62.2	62.8	65.1	61.6	63.1	63.0	62.6	63.3	60.6	61.7	63.9	63.0	64.2	66.1	65.2
1969		65.7	67.5	68.6	69.8	65.3	65.5	66.4	66.1	68.6	67.8	68.0	68.3	69.6	69.6	69.3	70.4
1970		71.5	72.8	74.5	74.3	70.4	72.0	72.2	72.6	72.0	73.9	74.8	74.4	74.6	75.1	72.8	75.0
1971		75.5	74.5	74.2	75.0	76.9	74.4	75.2	75.3	73.6	74.5	74.4	73.9	74.3	73.8	75.6	75.5
1972		75.3	77.3	78.1	80.3	74.3	75.6	75.9	77.0	76.4	78.5	77.1	78.6	78.5	78.6	80.4	81.9
1973		82.3	82.6	82.8	85.0	82.3	82.3	82.2	79.9	83.7	84.1	81.2	83.5	83.5	85.0	86.1	87.0
1974		86.5	83.7	81.7	80.6	88.2	87.1	84.2	85.7	84.0	81.2	81.9	82.2	81.0	82.0	80.9	78.8
1975		77.8	80.8	83.8	82.3	77.4	76.8	79.1	80.4	80.4	81.5	83.7	83.0	84.7	83.0	79.9	84.2
1976		85.0	87.6	87.4	88.0	83.2	84.9	86.8	86.4	86.9	89.6	88.0	86.3	87.9	86.6	88.6	88.7
1977		89.9	90.9	90.1	91.3	90.2	89.9	89.8	89.7	90.2	92.7	89.0	90.5	90.8	89.8	92.1	92.0
1978		92.7	94.9	96.8	96.5	91.1	92.8	94.2	94.5	94.5	95.6	96.0	97.7	96.7	96.3	96.5	96.7
1979		96.1	98.6	99.5	99.9	96.1	95.0	97.1	97.3	99.6	99.0	99.2	100.0	99.3	100.0	100.3	99.3
1980		101.1	99.3	99.0	100.7	100.8	105.0	97.4	100.7	98.6	98.4	100.2	97.7	99.1	100.6	100.1	101.3
1981		102.1	101.3	104.2	105.6	102.4	101.7	102.1	101.7	99.6	102.6	103.5	103.4	105.8	105.6	105.7	105.5
1982		104.1	107.3	108.2	106.3	104.2	103.2	105.0	104.8	107.2	109.9	107.6	108.6	108.5	105.9	107.8	105.2
1983		108.0	110.3	111.4	109.0	107.3	107.0	109.6	110.1	111.1	109.7	107.5	112.0	114.8	109.7	109.1	108.1

Industrial production: intermediate goods (1)(2)

Production industrielle : biens intermédiaires (1)(2)

Adjusted - Corrigé

1980 = 100

	Year	Q.1	Q.2	Q.3	Q.4	JAN	FEB	MAR	APR	MAY	JUN	JUL	AUG	SEP	OCT	NOV	DEC
1964		33.0	33.8	34.5	35.3	32.7	33.3	33.1	33.3	34.0	34.2	34.4	34.5	35.0	35.1	35.1	35.6
1965		35.5	35.3	35.5	35.9	35.5	35.5	35.4	35.1	35.1	35.7	35.6	35.5	35.3	35.5	36.1	36.3
1966		37.4	39.4	41.5	43.5	36.8	37.2	38.3	39.0	39.3	40.0	40.7	41.5	42.2	42.6	43.4	44.4
1967		45.6	47.2	49.0	50.4	45.1	45.3	46.3	46.5	47.4	47.7	48.2	49.0	49.6	49.9	50.4	51.0
1968		53.1	54.3	55.8	58.0	52.4	53.2	53.7	53.7	54.9	54.3	55.0	56.0	56.3	57.1	58.3	58.4
1969		60.2	63.2	65.2	68.8	59.7	60.2	60.7	62.2	63.7	63.7	64.3	64.9	66.3	67.8	68.5	70.0
1970		71.0	73.4	73.9	74.4	70.1	71.0	71.9	73.2	73.1	74.1	73.7	73.9	74.1	74.4	74.1	74.8
1971		74.6	74.2	75.8	75.8	74.9	74.1	74.9	74.5	73.4	74.7	75.2	76.0	76.1	75.3	76.3	76.0
1972		77.7	79.5	81.9	86.1	76.4	78.0	78.6	78.6	79.7	80.2	80.4	82.5	82.8	84.2	86.1	88.0
1973		91.3	93.1	93.0	95.0	90.3	91.0	92.6	92.3	93.1	93.9	92.4	93.9	92.7	94.6	95.3	95.1
1974		95.0	89.2	84.5	79.2	95.8	95.8	93.3	90.8	89.9	87.0	85.9	84.6	83.1	80.9	79.0	77.7
1975		73.6	75.7	78.0	79.1	74.8	73.6	72.4	75.3	75.3	76.6	77.7	77.6	78.7	79.0	78.4	79.9
1976		82.9	85.2	87.5	88.0	81.0	83.2	84.5	85.0	84.6	86.1	87.4	88.1	87.4	87.0	88.4	88.5
1977		88.3	87.5	86.8	87.4	88.9	88.0	88.1	87.9	87.4	87.2	86.0	87.6	86.6	86.3	87.4	88.6
1978		88.5	89.8	92.4	94.0	88.5	88.0	89.1	89.1	89.9	90.3	91.4	92.4	93.4	93.3	94.3	94.5
1979		95.4	97.2	99.2	100.7	95.2	94.9	96.0	95.8	97.7	98.2	98.8	99.8	99.1	99.9	101.0	101.1
1980		103.0	102.4	97.8	96.9	101.6	104.6	102.9	103.8	102.9	100.6	99.8	96.7	96.9	97.3	96.3	97.0
1981		96.2	96.2	97.9	98.7	96.2	96.1	96.1	96.8	94.9	96.9	97.4	97.4	99.0	99.0	98.9	98.1
1982		97.6	96.2	96.3	95.4	98.4	97.3	97.2	96.6	95.7	96.4	96.5	95.9	96.4	94.3	96.2	95.8
1983		96.2	98.0	102.4	105.3	96.4	95.7	96.6	97.3	97.4	99.4	100.6	102.6	103.9	103.8	105.8	106.4

JAPAN

Industrial production: manufacturing (1)(2) / Production industrielle : industries manufacturières (1)(2)

1980 = 100

	Year	Q.1	Q.2	Q.3	Q.4	JAN	FEB	MAR	APR	MAY	JUN	JUL	AUG	SEP	OCT	NOV	DEC
1964	30.8	29.8	30.4	30.9	32.2	27.5	30.0	32.0	29.9	30.1	31.1	30.9	29.9	32.0	32.0	31.4	33.2
1965	32.0	32.2	31.6	31.5	32.8	30.1	31.8	34.6	31.6	30.9	32.2	31.8	30.7	32.2	32.2	32.5	33.6
1966	36.1	33.8	34.5	36.5	39.5	31.2	33.3	36.9	32.6	34.8	36.2	36.4	35.6	37.7	38.5	39.0	41.1
1967	43.5	40.8	42.1	44.0	47.2	38.0	40.0	44.4	41.2	41.7	43.4	43.4	42.6	45.8	46.0	46.8	48.8
1968	50.3	47.2	49.2	50.7	54.2	43.8	47.1	50.7	48.5	48.8	50.2	50.9	49.2	52.0	53.2	54.1	55.3
1969	58.5	54.1	57.3	59.2	63.5	50.2	54.1	57.9	57.0	56.4	58.5	59.6	56.7	61.2	62.9	62.3	65.2
1970	66.6	63.7	66.3	67.5	68.9	59.2	63.4	68.5	65.7	64.5	68.7	69.0	64.7	68.9	68.7	67.4	70.7
1971	68.4	67.5	67.3	68.3	70.0	63.4	66.7	72.3	68.3	64.5	69.2	69.8	66.0	70.7	69.4	69.6	71.1
1972	73.4	69.5	71.6	73.8	78.8	64.4	69.0	75.2	71.0	70.0	73.9	73.7	71.3	76.5	76.9	77.6	81.8
1973	84.6	79.9	83.8	85.5	89.1	73.9	78.8	87.0	82.6	82.6	86.2	85.9	82.5	88.0	89.1	88.7	89.6
1974	81.2	84.1	82.9	80.2	77.6	79.3	83.9	89.2	83.4	82.3	83.0	82.9	76.3	81.5	79.4	77.0	76.4
1975	72.3	68.4	71.7	73.7	75.3	64.5	67.7	73.0	71.5	70.3	73.4	75.1	69.8	76.2	76.0	73.7	76.2
1976	80.4	74.7	80.0	82.3	84.4	68.0	73.9	82.3	79.9	77.8	82.2	84.1	78.2	84.6	84.0	83.9	85.4
1977	83.7	80.9	83.6	84.0	86.3	75.5	78.9	88.2	84.1	81.2	85.4	84.3	80.7	86.9	85.2	85.9	87.6
1978	88.9	84.2	88.8	89.8	92.7	78.0	82.2	92.4	89.3	86.9	90.1	90.6	86.1	92.7	91.6	91.8	94.6
1979	95.5	90.0	95.5	96.4	99.9	83.3	88.5	98.1	95.1	94.1	97.4	98.3	92.9	98.0	99.0	99.5	101.2
1980	100.0	98.6	102.4	98.5	100.4	90.1	99.6	106.0	104.4	100.5	102.4	102.8	92.0	101.0	100.7	98.6	102.0
1981	101.0	97.2	100.6	101.5	104.7	90.3	96.2	105.2	102.0	97.2	102.7	104.2	95.2	105.1	104.8	103.8	105.4
1982	101.4	100.0	101.8	101.4	102.1	92.8	98.4	108.9	103.4	98.1	104.0	104.3	95.1	104.9	100.6	102.5	103.2
1983	104.9	99.0	103.6	106.2	110.8	91.3	97.1	108.7	104.5	100.3	105.9	106.9	100.0	111.6	108.9	110.4	113.2

Industrial production: construction (1)(2) / Production industrielle : construction (1)(2)

Adjusted - Corrigé

1980 = 100

	Year	Q.1	Q.2	Q.3	Q.4	JAN	FEB	MAR	APR	MAY	JUN	JUL	AUG	SEP	OCT	NOV	DEC
1964	40.9	39.3	40.9	41.5	41.8	39.7	39.3	38.9	39.4	41.7	41.6	41.5	41.5	41.5	41.2	41.9	42.2
1965	41.8	42.4	41.7	41.1	42.1	42.4	43.0	41.8	41.9	41.8	41.5	42.0	41.4	41.0	42.0	42.2	42.3
1966	47.4	43.7	46.2	48.3	50.7	42.4	43.3	45.4	45.6	45.4	47.4	47.9	48.6	50.0	49.6	50.6	51.9
1967	55.8	53.0	55.6	56.8	58.0	51.7	53.0	54.3	54.2	56.3	56.3	56.2	57.1	57.2	57.5	58.1	58.4
1968	65.4	62.8	64.3	66.2	68.1	61.6	62.5	64.5	63.5	65.0	64.5	64.5	66.7	67.4	67.4	68.6	68.2
1969	75.2	70.4	73.8	76.4	80.1	69.9	70.6	70.6	72.4	74.2	74.7	75.7	76.3	77.3	79.4	79.8	81.1
1970	84.1	81.9	85.4	84.4	84.7	80.7	82.0	83.1	87.1	84.0	85.1	84.2	84.4	84.7	84.9	84.2	84.9
1971	84.8	84.4	83.4	85.3	86.3	85.3	84.5	83.5	83.2	83.4	83.5	85.1	85.4	85.2	84.9	86.6	87.4
1972	94.0	88.9	91.0	95.4	100.8	87.4	88.9	90.5	89.5	90.8	92.6	92.9	97.1	96.4	99.1	100.3	103.0
1973	108.3	106.6	107.7	108.2	110.8	106.0	106.3	107.5	106.8	107.7	108.6	107.6	108.7	108.2	110.4	111.1	110.9
1974	96.1	108.5	98.6	92.5	84.9	111.1	109.0	105.2	100.7	99.1	96.0	94.9	92.6	90.0	86.6	84.7	83.5
1975	83.0	80.1	83.5	84.1	84.5	80.2	80.1	79.9	83.1	83.6	83.7	83.7	83.5	85.1	84.9	83.9	84.7
1976	90.9	88.4	89.7	92.3	93.4	85.9	88.8	90.5	89.4	88.6	91.0	92.0	92.4	92.5	93.3	93.6	93.3
1977	91.4	92.7	91.1	89.7	91.9	93.7	91.8	92.5	92.0	90.9	90.5	89.3	89.9	90.0	90.8	91.8	93.0
1978	96.1	92.9	94.5	97.8	99.2	92.6	92.3	93.7	93.4	94.9	95.3	96.3	97.5	99.6	97.5	99.7	100.3
1979	102.9	100.9	101.8	104.1	104.9	101.1	100.2	101.5	100.1	102.1	103.3	104.1	104.7	103.5	104.5	105.9	104.2
1980	100.0	105.9	103.7	96.7	93.9	103.4	107.9	106.3	106.6	104.3	100.1	99.0	96.1	95.0	94.8	93.6	93.3
1981	92.0	91.2	90.9	93.1	92.8	92.0	91.3	90.2	90.9	89.5	92.2	92.6	92.6	94.2	93.4	92.3	92.6
1982	90.5	90.8	89.5	90.9	90.8	92.1	90.2	90.0	88.5	89.4	90.6	91.6	89.9	91.1	90.1	91.2	91.2
1983	89.6	89.2	88.9	90.5	89.6	89.3	89.3	89.1	87.9	88.4	90.5	89.7	91.4	90.3	89.9	89.8	89.2

Production : passenger cars (3) / Production : voitures de tourismes (3)

thousands, monthly averages / milliers, moyennes mensuelles

	Year	Q.1	Q.2	Q.3	Q.4	JAN	FEB	MAR	APR	MAY	JUN	JUL	AUG	SEP	OCT	NOV	DEC
1964	48.3	42.6	47.2	44.5	58.9	37.5	43.2	47.1	48.0	45.9	47.7	42.2	42.0	49.3	57.4	57.4	62.0
1965	58.0	55.8	61.4	54.3	60.5	49.8	55.7	62.0	61.1	61.5	61.5	56.3	48.6	58.1	59.6	60.7	61.3
1966	73.1	64.3	70.7	70.4	87.2	55.6	66.8	70.4	69.2	70.6	72.2	73.3	64.0	74.0	78.5	87.0	96.1
1967	114.7	98.4	108.5	109.1	142.5	84.8	98.4	112.1	108.5	101.7	115.4	108.2	91.9	127.1	135.1	141.1	151.4
1968	171.3	149.2	173.5	158.9	193.7	127.8	152.5	167.4	167.2	173.2	180.1	174.7	156.8	175.1	196.1	193.9	191.1
1969	217.6	192.4	206.8	217.8	256.4	174.2	193.6	209.3	217.0	201.7	201.8	216.3	191.2	246.0	259.0	252.8	257.3
1970	264.9	236.3	265.4	261.2	296.7	207.9	238.6	262.3	245.2	262.6	288.3	282.4	226.3	275.0	291.5	291.9	306.8
1971	309.8	294.8	296.9	293.3	353.4	252.6	299.3	332.4	303.9	277.9	309.0	306.0	240.0	333.8	349.8	358.6	351.9
1972	335.2	318.0	332.9	314.5	375.3	281.4	324.3	348.2	326.5	334.7	337.5	318.8	270.1	354.9	391.4	369.4	365.2
1973	372.6	361.2	383.3	362.1	383.4	320.6	365.4	397.6	345.9	392.2	411.9	376.1	324.2	386.1	402.5	393.9	353.9
1974	327.7	315.9	296.2	316.0	382.5	315.6	326.7	305.5	277.1	310.9	300.6	336.7	252.8	358.5	390.2	386.8	370.4
1975	380.6	344.3	380.8	391.2	406.3	330.9	340.3	361.8	378.9	374.8	383.7	401.4	341.8	430.5	454.6	411.2	353.0
1976	419.0	382.3	433.6	419.0	441.0	343.0	373.6	430.3	434.8	410.0	456.1	464.4	346.8	445.7	453.2	450.2	419.7
1977	452.4	414.3	458.5	448.4	488.5	374.8	401.7	466.3	448.3	442.2	484.9	474.4	378.1	492.7	475.4	512.7	477.5
1978	498.0	476.0	511.2	483.0	521.8	436.9	449.8	541.2	490.4	503.6	539.5	508.8	417.2	523.1	533.4	539.5	492.4
1979	514.7	468.8	523.0	495.3	571.0	430.7	468.1	507.5	490.6	538.3	540.1	538.1	432.8	516.5	587.0	585.8	540.3
1980	566.5	551.6	606.7	588.2	599.5	490.8	578.4	585.6	615.7	580.5	624.0	665.7	450.1	648.7	641.9	566.3	590.4
1981	581.4	572.9	612.1	545.9	594.7	538.2	558.2	622.3	629.5	569.7	637.2	631.5	408.6	597.7	609.5	595.0	579.5
1982	573.9	567.2	594.6	556.0	577.9	501.6	560.3	639.8	603.7	549.9	630.1	627.8	429.4	610.7	581.2	600.1	552.4
1983	596.1	589.5	600.0	586.9	608.2	521.1	577.6	669.7	587.6	575.5	636.8	643.3	469.8	647.5	583.9	645.2	595.6

Industrial production: manufacturing (1)(2) / Production industrielle : industries manufacturières (1)(2)

Adjusted - Corrigé

1980 = 100

	Year	Q.1	Q.2	Q.3	Q.4	JAN	FEB	MAR	APR	MAY	JUN	JUL	AUG	SEP	OCT	NOV	DEC
1964		29.6	30.5	31.3	31.9	29.3	29.9	29.6	30.1	30.4	30.9	30.9	31.0	32.0	31.9	31.6	32.3
1965		31.9	31.7	32.0	32.5	32.0	31.7	32.0	31.7	31.4	31.9	31.8	32.0	32.2	32.1	32.7	32.7
1966		33.6	35.3	37.1	39.2	33.2	33.3	34.2	34.8	35.3	35.9	36.6	37.1	37.7	38.3	39.3	40.1
1967		40.5	42.2	44.5	46.9	40.3	40.0	41.1	41.3	42.3	43.1	43.6	44.3	45.6	46.0	47.1	47.5
1968		47.9	49.4	50.7	53.2	47.3	48.0	48.4	48.6	50.1	49.4	49.9	51.2	51.1	52.3	53.7	53.5
1969		54.8	57.5	59.2	62.3	54.2	55.1	55.2	56.8	58.0	57.6	58.4	58.9	60.1	61.9	61.9	63.1
1970		64.5	66.6	67.4	67.8	63.9	64.5	65.1	65.8	66.5	67.6	67.5	67.1	67.6	67.7	67.1	68.5
1971		68.3	67.6	68.7	68.9	68.4	67.9	68.7	68.3	66.6	68.0	68.3	68.5	69.3	68.5	69.3	69.0
1972		70.4	71.9	73.9	77.5	69.5	70.1	71.5	70.9	72.1	72.6	72.4	74.2	75.0	76.0	77.3	79.3
1973		82.3	84.0	85.0	86.9	81.4	82.0	83.3	83.1	84.0	84.8	83.8	86.2	85.1	86.4	87.2	87.2
1974		86.8	83.0	79.7	75.7	87.5	87.5	85.4	83.6	83.8	81.6	80.7	79.7	78.7	77.1	75.8	74.4
1975		70.7	71.7	73.1	73.5	71.5	70.8	69.8	71.5	71.5	72.2	73.0	72.9	73.5	73.8	72.6	74.2
1976		77.1	79.9	81.7	82.5	75.5	77.4	78.6	79.7	79.3	80.8	81.5	81.7	81.7	81.5	82.8	83.3
1977		83.5	83.4	83.2	84.5	83.8	82.6	84.0	83.4	83.1	83.7	82.1	83.9	83.7	83.2	84.9	85.4
1978		86.4	87.3	89.7	91.5	86.2	85.6	87.3	87.5	87.7	88.2	88.8	89.8	90.6	90.8	91.3	92.3
1979		92.2	94.5	96.5	98.5	92.0	91.9	92.7	93.1	95.0	95.4	96.1	97.6	95.8	97.9	99.0	98.7
1980		101.0	101.3	98.7	99.0	99.6	103.1	100.3	102.1	101.4	100.3	100.2	97.3	98.7	99.4	98.1	99.6
1981		99.6	99.4	101.8	103.3	99.8	99.3	99.6	99.6	98.1	100.5	101.4	101.1	102.8	103.4	103.4	103.0
1982		102.3	101.4	101.5	100.4	102.4	101.8	102.8	101.3	100.3	101.8	101.3	101.5	101.9	99.1	101.6	100.5
1983		101.3	102.9	106.3	109.0	100.8	100.4	102.6	102.4	102.6	103.6	103.8	106.7	108.5	107.3	109.6	110.2

Production: crude steel / Production : acier brut

thousand tons, monthly averages / milliers de tonnes, moyennes mensuelles

	Year	Q.1	Q.2	Q.3	Q.4	JAN	FEB	MAR	APR	MAY	JUN	JUL	AUG	SEP	OCT	NOV	DEC
1964																	
1965																	
1966																	
1967																	
1968																	
1969	6847	6093	6667	6990	7539	6053	5773	6453	6505	6779	6717	6843	6970	7156	7630	7444	7844
1970	7777	7713	7820	7901	7673	7832	7241	8066	7682	7927	7852	7959	7802	7943	8074	7400	7544
1971	7380	7408	7156	7431	7524	7491	7103	7630	7094	7330	7044	7273	7445	7576	7637	7426	7509
1972	8075	7369	7709	8163	9059	7401	7156	7550	7535	7880	7712	8251	8166	8072	8821	8789	9567
1973	9944	9393	9878	10082	10423	9548	8823	9808	9656	10100	9877	10116	9958	10171	10659	10305	10305
1974	9761	9625	9916	9952	9550	10022	8914	9939	9783	10095	9871	10141	10010	9705	9950	9302	9399
1975	8526	8593	8709	8781	8020	8867	8079	8333	8412	8865	8849	8936	8789	8618	8498	7715	7848
1976	8948	8354	8562	9333	9539	8022	7846	9193	8641	8542	8504	9430	9446	9137	9757	9450	9409
1977	8534	8668	8621	8523	8322	8871	8171	8962	8590	8732	8542	8657	8487	8426	8499	8218	8250
1978	8508	8082	8386	8688	8877	8328	7646	8272	8367	8466	8326	8799	8705	8561	9053	8770	8807
1979	9313	9067	9337	9363	9485	9234	8711	9256	9329	9524	9158	9553	9312	9225	9707	9445	9303
1980	9283	9488	9759	9109	8776	9648	9237	9579	9801	9969	9506	9481	8905	8940	9192	8609	8528
1981	8473	8151	8457	8554	8730	8314	7785	8354	8438	8516	8416	8748	8516	8398	9006	8668	8516
1982	8296	8602	8669	7994	7917	8787	8206	8813	8788	8766	8453	8191	7925	7867	8060	7889	7803
1983	8097	7519	8059	8250	8561	7677	7121	7759	7964	8207	8005	8408	8139	8202	8913	8458	8311

Production : commercial vehicles / Production : véhicules utilitaires

thousands, monthly averages / milliers, moyennes mensuelles

	Year	Q.1	Q.2	Q.3	Q.4	JAN	FEB	MAR	APR	MAY	JUN	JUL	AUG	SEP	OCT	NOV	DEC
1964	93.7	88.5	97.7	89.5	98.7	80.0	89.6	95.8	98.6	95.1	99.4	87.2	85.0	96.3	105.3	93.4	97.4
1965	98.3	91.9	98.2	98.4	104.3	81.4	90.4	103.8	98.0	94.1	102.5	98.7	91.6	105.0	107.7	103.1	102.0
1966	117.4	104.6	117.8	118.7	128.5	90.0	102.9	120.8	119.7	112.5	121.3	120.5	112.1	123.4	130.2	128.8	126.5
1967	147.6	130.4	146.9	149.9	163.0	116.1	128.7	146.5	139.2	143.8	157.8	148.4	135.6	165.8	161.8	162.6	164.6
1968	169.2	166.3	171.4	170.2	168.8	147.4	173.6	177.8	173.3	166.5	174.5	171.2	163.9	175.4	173.5	172.2	160.8
1969	172.0	160.7	177.2	173.7	176.2	145.0	161.0	176.0	179.2	175.9	176.5	182.1	160.0	179.2	185.5	169.1	174.0
1970	175.9	175.2	180.8	169.3	178.2	150.2	179.3	196.1	178.9	177.1	186.4	181.6	150.5	175.8	182.0	172.1	180.5
1971	174.4	171.8	176.9	172.0	177.0	149.3	171.8	194.1	178.1	165.4	187.4	186.9	143.1	185.9	179.9	174.6	176.6
1972	189.4	172.9	189.9	190.1	204.6	143.8	170.2	204.6	177.2	184.3	208.1	194.6	179.7	195.9	207.6	197.7	208.5
1973	217.7	209.3	221.6	212.2	227.7	182.6	211.5	233.7	214.5	217.9	232.4	220.0	193.4	223.1	241.9	232.3	209.0
1974	218.3	225.2	222.5	212.9	212.7	199.2	226.6	249.7	225.7	222.2	219.5	229.8	180.6	228.5	232.4	207.7	198.1
1975	197.8	180.9	192.7	206.8	210.7	172.3	175.4	195.0	195.7	182.9	199.4	216.0	180.7	223.7	224.0	208.1	200.1
1976	234.5	206.4	239.9	239.0	252.7	189.9	200.3	229.1	248.3	218.1	253.4	254.7	206.2	256.1	257.7	255.7	244.6
1977	257.2	244.2	255.3	255.4	273.9	220.0	228.5	284.2	254.4	241.1	270.4	254.1	220.6	291.5	280.3	279.9	261.7
1978	274.4	269.8	281.9	270.9	275.1	242.8	259.0	307.6	266.9	278.0	300.9	281.8	243.6	287.2	283.5	280.9	261.0
1979	288.2	259.0	292.0	234.8	317.1	228.2	256.8	292.1	275.9	288.8	311.1	304.1	255.9	294.3	324.6	320.7	306.2
1980	333.7	319.5	343.6	329.8	341.8	289.0	333.0	336.4	350.1	326.0	354.6	374.0	260.7	354.8	363.9	328.5	333.0
1981	350.4	342.5	353.8	358.2	347.1	313.4	338.9	375.2	361.7	325.2	374.5	404.4	281.0	389.2	361.1	346.3	334.0
1982	320.8	326.4	326.5	318.3	311.6	292.4	319.9	366.8	341.7	300.7	337.2	345.5	253.5	357.4	309.4	321.3	304.2
1983	329.9	323.7	346.9	322.3	326.8	278.9	312.4	379.6	351.0	326.9	362.8	354.0	253.5	359.4	340.4	329.5	310.5

JAPAN

Ships completed
thousand gross register tons, quarterly averages

Navires achevés
milliers de tonneaux de jauge brute, moyennes trimestrielles

	Year	Q.1	Q.2	Q.3	Q.4	JAN	FEB	MAR	APR	MAY	JUN	JUL	AUG	SEP	OCT	NOV	DEC
1964	941	559	911	864	1430												
1965	1221	846	1062	1538	1441												
1966	1624	1458	1291	1713	2033												
1967	1804	1567	1626	2121	1904												
1968	2087	1968	2146	1917	2319												
1969	2292	2396	1968	2444	2285												
1970	2525	2657	2032	2787	2535												
1971	2783	2502	2856	3265	2496												
1972	3214	3511	2713	3729	2907												
1973	3688	3518	3221	4261	3663												
1974	4224	3322	4760	3425	5458												
1975	4248	3921	4566	3983	4364												
1976	3967	4842	4001	3697	3303												
1977	2927	3579	3011	2572	2539												
1978	1577	2142	1622	1222	1295												
1979	1174	1275	1017	1193	1187												
1980	1524	1308	1730	1605	1451												
1981	2100	2068	1721	2702	1928												
1982	2041	2760	1597	2296	1584												
1983	1675	1957	1441	2011	1200												

Business situation: current
manufacturing

per cent balance

État actuel des affaires
industries manufacturières

solde en pourcentage

	Year	Q.1	Q.2	Q.3	Q.4	JAN	FEB	MAR	APR	MAY	JUN	JUL	AUG	SEP	OCT	NOV	DEC
1964																	
1965																	
1966		-7	3	13	29		-7			3			13			29	
1967		34	46	50	52		34			44			50			51	
1968		43	38	32	36		43			38			32			36	
1969		33	38	38	39		33			38			38			39	
1970		42	41	35	21		42			41			35			21	
1971		-3	-19	-23	-34		-3			-19			-23			-34	
1972		-34	-27	-18	-		-34			-27			-28			-	
1973		25	44	51	52		25			44			51			52	
1974		27	6	-23	-37		27			6			-23			-37	
1975		-65	-66	-67	-63		-65			-66			-67			-63	
1976		-57	-37	-17	-18		-57			-37			-17			-18	
1977		-28	-27	-32	-36		-28			-27			-32			-36	
1978		-29	-22	-9	-3		-29			-22			-9			-3	
1979		6	21	30	30		6			21			30			30	
1980		22	23	8	-5		22			23			8			-5	
1981		-16	-18	-19	-15		-16			-18			-19			-15	
1982		-12	-17	-26	-35		-12			-17			-26			-35	
1983		-34	-33	-29	-17		-34			-33			-29			-17	

Business situation: prospects
manufacturing

per cent balance

État des affaires : perspectives
industries manufacturières

solde en pourcentage

	Year	Q.1	Q.2	Q.3	Q.4	JAN	FEB	MAR	APR	MAY	JUN	JUL	AUG	SEP	OCT	NOV	DEC
1964																	
1965																	
1966																	
1967			49	50	47					49			50			47	
1968		34	28	34	39		34			28			34			39	
1969		35	36	40	41		35			36			40			41	
1970		45	44	35	16		45			44			35			16	
1971		-5	-12	-11	-39		-5			-12			-11			-39	
1972		-33	-26	-7	10		-33			-26			-7			10	
1973		31	40	48	41		31			40			48			41	
1974		-5	-23	-28	-47		-5			-23			-28			-47	
1975		-65	-56	-55	-51		-65			-56			-55			-51	
1976		-42	-21	-4	-15		-42			-21			-4			-15	
1977		-23	-23	-25	-29		-23			-23			-25			-29	
1978		-26	-18	-8	-5		-26			-18			-8			-5	
1979		7	18	12	9		7			18			12			9	
1980		-1	6	-3	-8		-1			6			-3			-8	
1981		-13	-13	-3	-4		-13			-13			-3			-4	
1982		-10	-13	-20	-28		-10			-13			-20			-28	
1983		-29	-23	-12	3		-29			-23			-12			3	

Finished goods stocks: level / Stocks de produits finis : niveau

manufacturing — industries manufacturières

per cent balance — solde en pourcentage

	Year	Q.1	Q.2	Q.3	Q.4	JAN	FEB	MAR	APR	MAY	JUN	JUL	AUG	SEP	OCT	NOV	DEC
1964		7	13	11	19		7			13			11			19	
1965		18	50	46	40		18			50			46			40	
1966		33	25	11	2		33			25			11			2	
1967		-	5	1	3		-			5			1			3	
1968		13	12	3	7		13			12			3			7	
1969		11	10	-2	-4		11			10			-2			3	
1970		1	10	4	16		1			10			13			16	
1971		32	39	39	43		32			39			39			43	
1972		40	34	23	13		40			34			23			13	
1973		-4	-17	-34	-33		-4			-17			-34			-33	
1974		-28	14	51	63		-28			14			51			63	
1975		72	66	62	51		72			66			62			51	
1976		48	36	30	31		48			36			30			31	
1977		34	32	35	32		34			32			35			32	
1978		37	28	23	21		37			28			23			21	
1979		16	8	3	5		16			8			3			5	
1980		11	5	25	43		11			6			25			43	
1981		42	37	38	31		42			37			38			31	
1982		26	30	30	31		26			30			30			31	
1983		32	26	26	18		32			26			26			18	

Judgment on capacity utilization / Appréciation sur l'utilisation des capacités

manufacturing — industries manufacturières

per cent balance — solde en pourcentage

	Year	Q.1	Q.2	Q.3	Q.4	JAN	FEB	MAR	APR	MAY	JUN	JUL	AUG	SEP	OCT	NOV	DEC
1964																	
1965																	
1966		-24	-12	-	9		-24			-12			-			9	
1967		12	16	16	14		12			16			16			14	
1968		9	12	15	20		9			11			16			20	
1969		16	21	22	28		16			21			22			28	
1970		31	29	26	21		31			29			26			21	
1971		5	-2	-7	-20		5			-2			-7			-20	
1972		-19	-24	-19	-10		-19			-24			-19			-10	
1973		5	18	29	34		5			18			29			34	
1974		22	11	-2	-25		22			11			-2			-25	
1975		-43	-52	-49	-51		-43			-52			-49			-51	
1976		-55	-50	-44	-41		-55			-50			-44			-41	
1977		-42	-41	-44	-42		-42			-41			-44			-42	
1978		-44	-43	-42	-38		-44			-43			-42			-38	
1979		-32	-25	-13	-14		-32			-25			-18			-14	
1980		-12	-9	-11	-16		-12			-9			-21			-16	
1981		-21	-24	-23	-22		-21			-24			-23			-22	
1982		-23	-29	-32	-35		-23			-29			-32			-35	
1983		-36	-34	-33	-30		-36			-34			-33			-30	

JAPAN

Mining and manufacturing deliveries: (1)
total (volume)
1980 = 100

Livraisons des industries extractives (1)
et manufacturières : total (volume)
1980 = 100

	Year	Q.1	Q.2	Q.3	Q.4	JAN	FEB	MAR	APR	MAY	JUN	JUL	AUG	SEP	OCT	NOV	DEC
1964	31.6	29.4	31.3	32.2	33.4	26.6	29.1	32.6	31.0	31.0	32.0	31.8	31.1	33.7	32.8	32.4	34.9
1965	32.9	31.6	32.4	33.1	34.4	29.0	31.2	34.6	32.4	31.8	32.8	32.8	32.5	34.0	34.1	33.7	35.5
1966	37.3	33.5	36.4	38.3	41.3	30.4	32.9	37.2	36.2	35.7	37.3	37.7	37.6	39.5	39.7	40.7	43.4
1967	43.9	39.9	42.7	45.4	47.6	36.7	39.1	44.0	41.7	42.3	44.2	44.7	44.2	47.2	46.1	47.1	49.6
1968	50.9	46.5	50.4	52.0	55.0	42.4	46.0	50.9	50.0	50.2	50.8	51.5	50.6	53.7	53.4	55.0	56.7
1969	59.3	53.2	58.4	61.1	64.7	48.3	52.1	59.2	57.8	57.6	59.7	61.0	58.4	63.8	64.0	62.8	67.3
1970	67.1	63.2	66.5	68.9	69.6	57.7	61.7	70.4	66.1	64.5	68.9	69.9	65.7	71.2	69.0	67.0	72.8
1971	69.2	65.9	68.8	70.5	71.4	60.2	63.7	73.8	69.7	66.3	70.3	71.4	66.5	73.6	69.3	70.5	74.4
1972	75.1	69.6	73.6	76.5	80.9	62.9	68.0	78.0	72.5	72.6	75.6	76.0	73.2	80.3	77.4	79.0	86.3
1973	85.8	80.9	85.2	86.5	90.4	73.5	79.5	89.7	83.9	84.9	87.0	87.7	82.6	89.4	89.9	89.5	91.8
1974	81.2	82.6	82.1	80.8	79.2	80.0	81.2	86.7	82.5	82.2	81.6	82.5	77.4	82.5	80.7	77.6	79.3
1975	75.1	70.4	74.6	76.4	78.9	64.5	69.0	77.7	76.0	72.6	75.3	78.0	72.0	79.2	79.3	75.8	81.7
1976	82.8	77.4	82.6	84.9	86.5	68.2	75.9	88.0	82.2	81.0	84.6	86.4	80.7	87.4	85.0	85.5	89.0
1977	86.1	83.3	85.5	86.5	89.0	76.8	80.7	92.5	86.6	83.1	86.7	86.7	83.0	89.8	86.7	87.7	92.6
1978	91.1	87.5	90.3	92.0	94.6	79.0	84.7	98.7	90.5	88.6	91.7	92.7	88.3	95.1	91.9	93.5	98.3
1979	97.2	92.8	97.1	97.6	101.5	84.1	90.5	103.7	98.2	96.4	98.7	99.5	94.2	99.0	99.2	99.9	105.3
1980	100.0	100.0	101.8	97.7	100.5	90.3	100.6	109.1	104.5	99.6	101.3	101.7	90.9	100.5	99.6	97.7	104.1
1981	100.6	97.8	99.7	101.5	103.4	89.3	96.0	108.0	102.0	95.8	101.2	104.2	95.2	105.2	102.0	101.8	106.4
1982	99.9	99.0	99.5	100.2	100.9	90.1	96.6	110.2	100.6	96.1	101.8	102.2	93.6	104.7	99.1	100.1	103.4
1983	103.4	98.7	101.3	105.0	108.5	89.5	96.1	110.5	102.4	98.1	103.3	104.4	100.7	109.9	106.4	107.3	111.7

Mining and manufacturing deliveries: (1)
investment goods (volume)
1980 = 100

Livraisons des industries extractives et manufacturières : (1)
biens d'équipement (volume)
1980 = 100

	Year	Q.1	Q.2	Q.3	Q.4	JAN	FEB	MAR	APR	MAY	JUN	JUL	AUG	SEP	OCT	NOV	DEC
1964	22.0	20.4	21.4	23.1	23.4	17.4	20.1	23.7	22.0	19.9	22.2	22.6	21.6	25.1	23.5	22.4	24.3
1965	23.5	23.2	22.5	24.0	24.1	20.6	23.0	25.8	23.9	21.6	21.9	22.9	22.9	26.1	24.8	23.7	23.9
1966	26.6	24.7	25.0	27.5	29.3	21.3	24.4	28.3	25.0	23.5	26.4	26.2	26.2	29.9	28.2	29.5	30.7
1967	33.2	29.2	31.2	36.1	36.0	25.7	28.6	33.2	31.7	29.6	32.3	34.0	33.6	40.8	35.1	36.2	36.7
1968	42.3	38.4	41.5	43.7	45.5	33.8	37.4	44.0	40.6	40.9	42.9	42.5	40.8	47.8	44.3	46.6	45.7
1969	49.7	46.1	49.1	51.4	51.9	38.7	43.9	55.8	49.6	46.3	51.4	51.6	46.5	56.1	54.9	49.5	51.3
1970	58.8	57.4	57.0	61.1	59.9	49.7	53.6	68.8	56.2	52.8	62.0	61.8	55.9	65.7	61.4	56.3	62.1
1971	59.8	59.9	59.9	61.4	58.1	50.7	56.6	72.2	63.3	55.7	60.7	59.9	53.4	71.0	58.4	57.8	58.2
1972	63.4	61.3	60.3	66.3	65.8	52.4	56.2	75.3	59.0	58.6	63.4	63.3	58.3	77.3	62.8	63.2	71.3
1973	77.7	73.7	75.0	82.8	79.3	59.2	71.0	90.9	74.4	74.3	76.3	82.1	73.1	93.1	81.1	79.5	77.3
1974	76.1	76.6	78.2	77.2	72.6	71.6	72.0	86.1	79.2	77.2	78.2	78.2	70.1	83.4	77.7	69.2	71.0
1975	67.4	68.8	66.9	67.5	66.2	57.1	66.3	83.1	70.6	60.9	69.2	68.5	61.3	73.0	71.4	61.1	66.0
1976	73.1	71.8	70.8	75.9	73.8	55.6	70.1	89.8	70.5	69.4	72.6	74.1	70.8	83.0	72.8	72.0	75.5
1977	78.4	78.8	77.3	79.0	78.3	68.3	73.1	95.0	81.3	72.0	78.7	76.2	74.5	86.2	77.0	76.8	81.3
1978	84.9	87.6	83.2	86.3	82.7	70.8	79.4	112.6	86.2	79.3	84.2	83.4	79.1	96.3	80.8	83.6	83.6
1979	91.4	91.1	88.7	93.1	92.8	74.2	86.0	113.0	88.9	86.0	91.2	92.9	86.6	99.8	92.3	91.7	94.5
1980	100.0	98.5	99.4	103.8	98.3	80.6	96.9	118.1	99.3	96.9	101.9	106.2	91.7	113.6	100.2	94.1	100.7
1981	106.5	106.2	103.4	112.7	103.8	88.5	102.8	127.2	104.7	98.2	107.2	111.1	100.9	126.0	102.1	103.1	106.1
1982	105.4	112.4	101.4	108.7	99.0	94.1	106.6	136.5	104.5	94.9	104.9	104.6	97.6	123.9	99.0	96.9	101.2
1983	106.3	109.1	101.0	109.2	106.0	92.9	101.4	133.1	100.9	95.8	106.3	103.5	102.4	121.6	105.4	106.4	106.3

Mining and manufacturing deliveries: (1)
consumer goods (volume)
1980 = 100

Livraisons des industries extractives et manufacturières : (1)
biens de consommation (volume)
1980 = 100

	Year	Q.1	Q.2	Q.3	Q.4	JAN	FEB	MAR	APR	MAY	JUN	JUL	AUG	SEP	OCT	NOV	DEC
1964	31.4	28.5	31.9	31.9	33.5	24.7	28.0	32.7	31.2	31.9	32.7	31.5	30.9	33.2	32.0	32.3	36.5
1965	32.0	29.7	32.0	32.1	34.4	26.5	29.2	33.4	31.5	31.5	32.9	32.2	31.7	32.2	32.9	33.2	37.1
1966	36.2	31.2	36.3	36.9	40.6	27.8	30.3	35.6	36.1	35.7	37.0	37.0	36.6	37.1	38.1	39.3	44.3
1967	41.2	36.6	40.6	42.1	45.5	32.7	35.6	41.4	38.9	40.1	42.9	42.4	41.4	42.3	43.1	44.1	49.3
1968	46.6	39.9	47.5	47.7	51.1	34.6	39.9	45.3	48.0	47.3	47.3	47.5	47.5	48.0	47.7	50.1	55.5
1969	53.8	45.2	53.7	55.8	60.2	40.0	44.7	51.0	52.4	53.7	55.0	56.0	54.0	57.6	56.7	57.6	66.2
1970	59.0	52.0	59.4	61.9	62.5	45.4	51.3	59.2	58.1	58.0	62.2	63.2	59.3	63.0	59.4	59.5	68.7
1971	62.2	54.9	62.9	64.1	66.7	48.8	52.8	63.2	62.9	60.5	65.4	67.1	60.5	64.7	61.9	64.7	73.5
1972	66.8	58.7	67.9	67.8	73.0	51.2	58.5	66.4	66.6	66.0	71.1	69.4	64.9	69.1	67.6	70.9	80.3
1973	72.4	65.4	72.7	72.4	79.1	58.4	65.2	72.5	71.3	72.4	73.9	73.9	69.4	74.0	75.3	76.6	85.3
1974	70.7	66.5	70.5	71.5	74.1	63.6	65.2	70.6	69.9	70.8	70.8	73.0	68.7	73.2	71.6	72.9	77.8
1975	71.3	62.9	72.1	72.6	77.6	56.1	62.2	70.2	74.7	70.6	71.1	74.3	68.4	75.1	74.5	73.9	84.3
1976	78.0	68.6	79.2	79.7	84.4	59.3	67.4	79.1	79.0	77.8	81.0	82.7	75.1	81.3	79.7	82.8	90.6
1977	83.6	76.1	83.8	84.9	89.7	67.6	74.8	86.0	83.4	82.0	86.0	86.0	80.1	88.7	84.4	87.4	97.2
1978	89.1	82.4	90.0	90.7	93.5	70.8	81.2	95.1	90.4	87.4	92.2	93.4	86.1	92.6	88.3	90.7	101.5
1979	94.2	85.8	96.4	94.5	100.2	74.2	85.1	98.2	95.3	95.0	98.9	97.4	89.9	96.2	95.7	97.1	107.8
1980	100.0	94.7	102.2	98.2	104.9	82.4	96.9	104.8	107.3	96.6	102.7	102.6	90.6	101.5	101.1	100.1	113.4
1981	104.8	99.1	105.1	104.8	110.4	87.7	97.8	111.8	109.9	99.1	106.3	109.2	97.6	107.6	105.8	107.6	117.7
1982	106.5	99.7	108.2	107.1	110.9	86.8	98.0	114.4	108.9	104.8	110.8	111.2	98.5	111.5	106.5	109.6	116.6
1983	111.1	103.7	111.7	112.3	116.6	89.5	102.4	119.3	115.8	106.9	112.5	113.8	107.4	115.6	112.3	113.2	124.2

Mining and manufacturing deliveries: (1) total (volume)

Livraisons des industries extractives (1) et manufacturières : total (volume)

1980 = 100

Adjusted - Corrigé

Year	Q.1	Q.2	Q.3	Q.4	JAN	FEB	MAR	APR	MAY	JUN	JUL	AUG	SEP	OCT	NOV	DEC
1964	30.3	31.4	32.1	32.4	29.9	30.4	30.7	30.9	31.3	31.8	31.8	31.6	32.8	32.2	32.2	32.9
1965	32.6	32.4	33.0	33.5	32.7	32.7	32.6	32.3	32.2	32.6	32.7	33.1	33.1	33.5	33.5	33.4
1966	34.6	36.4	38.1	40.1	34.3	34.6	35.1	36.1	36.1	37.1	37.6	38.2	38.5	39.1	40.4	40.9
1967	41.2	42.8	45.2	46.3	41.3	40.9	41.5	41.5	42.8	44.0	44.6	44.9	46.0	45.5	46.6	46.6
1968	48.5	50.2	51.3	53.8	48.2	49.0	48.2	49.6	50.9	50.0	50.2	52.3	51.3	52.7	54.8	53.8
1969	55.5	58.2	60.2	63.2	54.8	55.5	56.0	57.4	58.5	58.7	59.3	60.3	60.9	63.2	62.6	63.9
1970	65.8	66.3	67.9	68.1	65.4	65.6	66.3	65.6	65.6	67.5	67.8	68.0	68.0	68.3	67.0	69.0
1971	68.4	68.5	69.5	70.0	68.3	67.7	69.3	69.3	67.5	68.9	69.3	69.0	70.2	68.6	70.5	70.7
1972	72.2	73.4	75.5	79.2	71.3	72.3	72.9	72.1	73.9	74.1	73.9	75.8	76.8	76.8	79.2	81.6
1973	83.9	85.4	85.8	87.7	82.2	84.2	85.2	84.3	85.7	86.2	85.5	86.1	85.9	87.0	88.6	87.5
1974	86.0	82.3	80.1	76.9	90.1	86.0	82.1	82.8	83.2	80.8	80.3	80.6	79.3	78.2	76.9	75.6
1975	73.1	74.8	75.5	76.7	72.9	73.2	73.2	76.0	73.7	74.7	75.7	75.0	76.2	76.9	75.3	78.0
1976	80.2	82.8	83.9	84.2	77.3	80.7	82.6	81.9	82.5	83.9	83.7	84.0	84.0	82.5	85.0	84.9
1977	86.3	85.5	85.5	87.0	87.3	85.6	86.1	85.8	85.2	85.6	84.4	86.0	86.2	85.3	87.5	88.1
1978	89.2	89.3	92.0	93.1	88.6	88.2	90.8	89.2	89.9	90.4	91.2	92.1	92.8	92.4	93.4	93.6
1979	94.5	96.6	97.6	100.0	94.2	94.0	95.4	94.6	97.9	97.4	97.5	98.8	96.6	99.5	100.0	100.4
1980	101.9	101.3	97.3	99.0	101.1	104.2	100.5	102.6	101.1	100.1	99.5	96.0	98.0	99.7	97.9	99.3
1981	99.5	99.1	101.8	101.9	99.9	99.2	99.5	99.8	97.4	100.0	101.9	101.0	102.6	102.0	102.1	101.5
1982	100.6	99.6	100.2	99.1	100.8	100.0	101.1	99.0	99.2	100.5	99.6	99.9	101.1	99.0	99.8	98.5
1983	100.3	101.3	105.1	106.6	100.1	99.5	101.4	100.8	101.2	102.0	101.8	107.5	106.1	106.3	107.0	106.4

Mining and manufacturing deliveries: (1) investment goods (volume)

Livraisons des industries extractives et manufacturières : (1) biens d'équipement (volume)

1980 = 100

Adjusted - Corrigé

Year	Q.1	Q.2	Q.3	Q.4	JAN	FEB	MAR	APR	MAY	JUN	JUL	AUG	SEP	OCT	NOV	DEC
1964	20.4	21.9	22.7	23.0	19.8	20.4	21.1	22.0	21.3	22.5	22.8	22.2	23.0	22.8	22.7	23.5
1965	23.3	23.1	23.5	23.7	23.5	23.5	23.0	23.7	23.4	22.1	23.1	23.6	23.9	24.1	24.0	23.1
1966	24.8	25.7	27.0	28.8	24.3	24.8	25.2	24.9	25.4	26.7	26.6	27.1	27.4	27.4	29.7	29.4
1967	29.3	32.1	35.5	35.4	29.2	29.0	29.6	31.5	32.0	32.8	34.4	34.7	37.4	34.2	36.4	35.8
1968	39.0	41.3	42.9	46.2	39.6	39.9	37.5	40.1	42.7	41.1	41.4	43.9	43.3	43.8	48.6	46.3
1969	46.5	49.0	50.3	52.7	45.4	46.8	47.3	48.8	48.7	49.4	50.3	50.0	50.7	54.2	51.8	52.0
1970	57.6	57.0	59.9	60.9	58.0	56.9	57.8	55.4	55.8	59.8	60.4	60.4	59.0	60.7	59.0	63.0
1971	59.7	60.1	60.0	59.2	59.0	60.0	60.2	62.4	59.2	53.8	58.8	57.3	63.3	57.9	60.7	59.1
1972	61.2	60.6	64.5	67.0	60.9	59.9	62.9	58.4	62.1	61.5	61.9	63.1	68.4	62.7	66.5	72.0
1973	73.4	75.1	81.2	80.7	70.4	74.2	75.5	73.0	76.9	75.4	80.0	79.8	83.8	78.8	83.8	79.4
1974	77.3	78.4	75.9	73.9	85.7	75.1	71.0	77.8	80.2	77.3	76.3	76.3	75.1	75.9	73.2	72.8
1975	68.6	67.0	66.4	67.4	68.2	69.3	68.2	69.3	63.4	68.4	66.9	66.5	65.8	69.9	64.8	67.5
1976	71.0	71.1	74.5	75.4	66.3	73.5	73.3	68.9	72.7	71.6	72.4	76.6	74.9	71.3	76.6	78.3
1977	78.5	77.9	77.0	80.3	81.7	76.6	77.1	79.3	76.9	77.4	74.9	78.4	77.8	77.6	81.2	82.1
1978	84.9	84.4	84.9	84.9	83.6	81.0	90.2	85.1	84.2	83.9	83.0	84.6	87.2	83.5	86.4	84.7
1979	88.7	90.1	91.3	95.5	87.6	87.4	91.0	88.3	91.3	90.8	91.6	92.7	89.7	95.4	95.3	95.9
1980	96.2	101.2	101.2	101.5	95.0	98.1	95.4	99.3	102.6	101.6	103.8	98.3	101.6	103.6	98.4	102.4
1981	103.8	105.2	109.7	107.2	104.2	103.6	103.5	105.0	104.0	106.7	108.0	108.3	112.7	105.4	108.3	107.8
1982	109.0	103.6	104.6	103.9	110.1	107.2	109.7	104.9	101.7	104.3	102.2	104.3	107.4	104.1	103.7	104.0
1983	105.9	103.2	105.3	111.3	108.7	102.0	107.0	101.3	102.7	105.7	101.2	109.4	105.4	110.8	113.9	109.2

Mining and manufacturing deliveries: (1) consumer goods (volume)

Livraisons des industries extractives et manufacturières : (1) biens de consommation (volume)

1980 = 100

Adjusted - Corrigé

Year	Q.1	Q.2	Q.3	Q.4	JAN	FEB	MAR	APR	MAY	JUN	JUL	AUG	SEP	OCT	NOV	DEC
1964	30.5	31.1	31.9	32.1	29.7	30.7	31.1	30.6	31.2	31.7	31.1	31.4	33.1	32.1	31.9	32.4
1965	31.8	31.4	32.1	32.8	31.9	31.9	31.7	31.2	31.0	31.9	31.8	32.2	32.2	32.9	32.7	32.9
1966	33.6	35.5	36.9	38.7	33.6	33.2	33.9	35.6	35.3	35.7	36.5	37.2	37.0	38.0	38.7	39.4
1967	39.3	39.7	42.0	43.4	39.4	39.0	39.5	38.2	39.4	41.5	41.8	42.0	42.3	43.0	43.4	43.8
1968	44.3	46.6	46.5	48.4	43.4	44.9	44.6	47.1	47.1	45.4	45.3	48.1	46.3	47.6	49.2	48.5
1969	50.3	52.6	54.5	57.0	50.1	50.5	50.3	51.5	53.6	52.8	53.1	54.7	55.6	56.7	56.6	57.7
1970	57.7	58.2	60.2	59.4	56.9	58.0	58.4	57.2	58.1	59.3	59.6	60.2	60.8	59.5	58.7	60.0
1971	61.1	61.6	62.3	63.4	61.2	59.7	62.2	62.0	60.6	62.1	62.9	61.5	62.4	62.2	63.9	64.2
1972	64.9	66.2	66.4	69.2	63.9	65.8	65.1	65.2	66.1	67.5	66.1	66.4	66.9	67.9	69.8	70.0
1973	71.6	72.0	71.6	74.1	70.3	72.4	72.1	71.6	71.9	72.5	71.2	72.1	71.5	73.5	74.1	74.8
1974	73.1	69.8	70.8	69.6	77.0	72.5	69.9	69.4	70.5	69.4	70.2	71.4	70.7	69.9	70.5	68.4
1975	68.3	71.3	71.7	72.9	68.1	69.1	69.1	73.9	70.4	69.6	71.4	71.2	72.6	72.9	71.5	74.4
1976	74.9	78.3	78.7	79.5	72.4	74.8	77.4	77.8	77.7	79.3	79.3	78.3	78.4	78.0	80.3	80.1
1977	83.2	82.5	83.9	84.8	83.0	83.0	83.5	81.8	82.2	83.7	82.8	83.8	85.1	83.4	85.1	85.8
1978	87.1	88.1	90.7	90.4	86.0	86.5	88.9	87.7	87.8	88.7	90.2	91.1	90.8	89.7	90.5	91.0
1979	90.6	94.4	94.7	96.9	89.8	90.3	91.7	91.7	96.1	95.3	94.0	95.7	94.4	96.9	96.8	97.0
1980	100.0	100.0	98.5	101.4	99.4	102.6	97.9	102.6	98.3	99.1	98.9	97.0	99.8	101.9	99.8	102.4
1981	104.4	102.8	105.4	106.7	105.4	103.3	104.5	104.6	101.1	102.6	105.3	105.1	105.9	106.3	107.3	106.5
1982	105.2	106.3	107.4	106.8	104.7	104.5	106.4	104.1	107.7	107.2	106.9	106.7	108.7	106.5	108.4	105.5
1983	109.4	109.8	112.8	112.2	108.0	109.2	111.0	110.7	109.9	108.8	109.4	116.4	112.7	112.3	112.0	112.4

JAPAN

Mining and manufacturing deliveries: (1)
semi-manufactured goods (volume)
1980 = 100

Livraisons des industries extractives et manufacturières : (1)
demi-produits (volume)
1980 = 100

	Year	Q.1	Q.2	Q.3	Q.4	JAN	FEB	MAR	APR	MAY	JUN	JUL	AUG	SEP	OCT	NOV	DEC
1964	35.0	33.4	34.5	35.5	36.7	31.6	33.2	35.3	34.0	34.7	34.9	35.4	34.7	36.7	36.4	36.2	37.4
1965	36.7	35.7	36.1	36.9	38.0	33.7	35.3	38.0	35.9	35.8	36.6	36.7	36.5	37.5	37.9	37.7	38.5
1966	41.9	38.1	40.6	42.9	45.8	35.7	37.7	40.9	40.3	40.2	41.3	42.2	42.1	44.2	44.8	45.5	47.2
1967	49.2	46.0	48.1	50.0	52.6	43.6	45.1	49.2	46.9	48.4	49.0	49.4	49.4	51.2	51.7	52.5	53.6
1968	56.0	52.6	54.6	56.6	60.0	49.8	52.3	55.8	54.0	54.7	55.0	56.3	55.4	58.1	59.3	60.1	60.7
1969	65.3	59.5	63.6	66.8	71.3	56.2	58.6	63.8	63.0	63.4	64.3	66.5	64.3	69.1	70.5	70.0	73.3
1970	73.6	70.6	73.0	74.5	76.1	66.9	69.6	75.3	73.4	71.9	73.8	75.3	72.0	76.3	76.1	74.2	77.9
1971	75.5	73.2	74.2	76.4	78.1	69.6	71.5	78.5	74.5	72.7	75.4	77.1	74.2	77.8	76.5	77.6	80.2
1972	83.2	77.7	80.8	84.0	90.1	72.7	77.1	83.3	80.2	80.6	81.7	83.4	82.8	85.7	87.6	88.7	94.2
1973	94.8	90.6	94.7	94.4	99.5	85.7	89.1	97.1	92.9	94.5	96.8	96.1	92.1	94.9	99.7	99.1	99.7
1974	87.6	92.3	88.7	86.0	83.5	90.7	92.0	94.2	89.4	89.1	87.6	88.3	83.8	86.0	85.6	82.4	82.6
1975	79.3	74.2	78.2	81.0	83.8	70.9	72.9	78.8	78.1	77.5	79.2	82.7	77.3	83.1	84.1	81.7	85.7
1976	88.3	83.2	88.1	90.2	91.7	76.8	81.8	91.0	87.6	86.3	90.3	92.3	86.7	91.5	91.7	91.3	92.3
1977	89.5	87.9	88.7	89.4	92.1	84.0	85.7	94.0	89.5	87.2	89.5	90.3	87.0	91.1	90.9	91.4	93.9
1978	93.7	89.7	92.3	94.2	98.4	85.0	87.8	96.3	91.7	91.7	93.6	94.9	91.9	95.9	96.7	97.6	101.1
1979	100.2	96.3	99.8	100.2	104.5	91.3	94.1	103.6	98.8	99.9	100.7	102.2	98.3	100.1	102.8	103.4	107.3
1980	100.0	102.8	102.4	95.7	99.1	96.6	103.3	108.5	104.8	101.6	100.6	100.0	90.9	96.3	98.8	97.5	100.8
1981	97.0	94.9	96.2	96.9	100.2	90.3	93.4	100.9	97.8	93.6	97.2	100.0	92.5	98.3	100.3	98.8	101.4
1982	95.4	94.8	95.1	94.7	96.9	90.4	93.2	100.9	95.9	92.4	96.9	97.4	90.3	96.4	95.7	96.8	98.2
1983	98.9	93.5	96.7	99.8	105.5	88.6	91.8	100.2	96.8	94.9	98.4	100.6	97.1	101.7	104.1	104.8	107.7

Stocks, manufacturing output: total (1)
(volume)
1980 = 100

Stocks, produits manufacturés : total (1)
(volume)
1980 = 100

	Year	Q.1	Q.2	Q.3	Q.4	JAN	FEB	MAR	APR	MAY	JUN	JUL	AUG	SEP	OCT	NOV	DEC
1964	26.5	25.6	26.3	27.0	27.2	24.6	26.2	25.9	26.0	26.2	26.7	27.3	27.2	26.4	27.1	27.3	27.2
1965	30.1	29.9	30.3	30.7	29.6	29.0	30.3	30.3	30.0	30.1	30.7	31.1	30.5	30.4	29.6	30.0	29.1
1966	31.5	32.0	31.8	31.7	30.6	31.1	32.2	32.7	31.9	31.7	31.9	32.1	31.6	31.3	31.0	31.0	29.7
1967	34.1	32.9	34.0	34.1	35.2	31.8	33.3	33.8	34.1	33.9	34.0	34.2	33.8	34.4	34.9	35.7	35.0
1968	41.4	39.8	40.9	42.2	42.9	38.3	40.3	41.0	40.3	41.0	41.4	42.6	42.0	41.9	42.7	43.3	42.6
1969	49.0	47.8	49.1	49.5	49.8	46.2	48.5	48.7	48.7	49.0	49.8	50.4	49.7	48.3	49.1	50.5	49.8
1970	57.4	54.2	56.0	58.0	61.3	53.1	54.8	54.7	55.1	55.6	57.3	58.1	58.5	57.5	60.4	62.4	60.9
1971	67.9	67.9	68.2	67.4	67.9	66.0	69.2	68.4	68.4	68.0	68.3	67.8	68.0	66.6	68.4	68.8	66.5
1972	68.1	70.5	68.9	67.2	65.6	69.6	71.3	70.5	69.9	68.4	68.3	68.0	67.4	66.2	66.8	66.7	63.3
1973	65.9	65.6	65.2	65.7	66.8	65.6	66.0	65.2	65.2	65.0	65.4	65.2	66.1	65.8	67.1	67.9	65.3
1974	84.7	71.9	82.9	89.8	94.1	68.3	72.1	75.3	79.9	82.7	86.2	89.1	89.9	90.3	93.6	95.3	93.6
1975	90.5	95.0	89.2	89.4	88.4	95.9	95.8	93.2	89.5	89.0	89.1	89.4	89.6	89.2	90.1	89.9	85.2
1976	89.1	88.6	87.5	88.7	91.7	88.7	89.8	87.2	87.6	87.3	87.5	88.6	88.7	89.0	90.9	92.8	91.5
1977	94.8	93.8	94.3	95.7	95.5	94.5	94.8	92.1	93.2	94.1	95.6	96.0	96.5	94.7	95.5	96.9	94.2
1978	93.2	95.9	92.3	91.3	93.3	98.8	97.0	91.9	92.5	92.6	91.7	91.3	91.7	91.0	93.2	94.6	92.2
1979	92.5	93.3	89.6	91.0	96.2	95.4	94.7	89.8	90.4	89.6	83.7	89.9	90.7	92.5	95.6	97.7	95.2
1980	100.0	96.7	96.9	102.0	104.4	98.0	97.8	94.4	95.0	97.4	98.3	100.9	102.3	102.7	104.4	105.6	103.1
1981	102.0	104.0	102.3	100.8	101.0	105.3	105.1	101.7	101.6	102.1	103.1	101.8	100.4	100.2	101.5	102.2	99.4
1982	101.4	102.6	101.6	101.3	99.8	103.4	104.2	100.2	101.3	101.9	101.5	102.5	102.2	100.6	100.9	100.5	97.9
1983	96.2	99.0	96.2	95.5	94.2	101.4	100.4	95.2	95.3	96.4	96.9	97.5	94.9	94.1	94.4	95.2	92.9

Stocks, manufacturing output: investment goods (1)
(volume)
1980 = 100

Stocks, produits manufacturés : biens d'équipements (1)
(volume)
1980 = 100

	Year	Q.1	Q.2	Q.3	Q.4	JAN	FEB	MAR	APR	MAY	JUN	JUL	AUG	SEP	OCT	NOV	DEC
1964	20.3	19.2	20.0	20.8	21.2	18.3	19.6	19.7	19.3	19.8	20.8	21.1	20.9	20.3	20.3	21.1	22.1
1965	23.4	23.4	22.6	24.2	23.3	23.0	24.0	23.1	22.1	22.0	23.7	24.6	24.0	24.0	22.9	23.5	23.4
1966	22.8	23.5	21.7	23.2	22.8	24.1	23.5	22.8	21.4	21.6	22.1	23.0	23.0	23.5	23.0	22.4	23.1
1967	24.1	23.7	22.7	24.2	25.6	23.6	24.2	23.4	22.4	22.6	23.2	23.6	24.1	24.8	24.7	25.3	27.0
1968	34.0	31.4	29.7	34.6	40.3	30.3	31.8	32.0	29.7	29.3	29.9	32.7	34.7	36.4	38.0	40.2	42.8
1969	42.4	43.6	39.5	41.3	45.2	43.1	45.4	42.3	40.2	38.8	39.6	41.1	41.9	41.1	41.8	45.1	48.6
1970	50.5	50.3	45.8	50.0	56.1	51.9	51.5	47.4	44.8	44.8	47.7	49.8	50.4	49.9	52.8	56.1	59.4
1971	64.5	66.0	63.4	53.1	65.4	65.3	68.6	64.2	62.6	62.8	64.7	63.6	63.9	61.7	63.6	65.2	67.3
1972	57.5	66.4	56.2	53.5	53.9	69.2	68.5	61.6	58.0	55.3	55.1	53.4	54.2	53.0	53.6	53.9	54.3
1973	52.1	54.1	48.9	48.0	56.8	54.3	56.2	51.7	50.4	47.9	48.4	47.9	49.7	49.0	52.6	56.8	61.0
1974	84.7	69.4	79.6	89.4	100.3	65.1	71.3	71.9	76.5	78.8	83.6	89.0	88.9	90.2	96.5	101.6	102.8
1975	92.7	102.5	90.1	88.0	90.1	105.6	105.5	96.3	91.3	90.2	88.8	89.7	88.2	86.0	87.7	91.4	91.1
1976	89.2	92.0	83.5	85.0	96.5	96.6	94.7	84.6	84.5	82.4	83.5	85.2	83.5	86.2	92.6	97.0	100.1
1977	97.3	100.5	93.6	93.5	101.5	101.4	103.8	96.4	93.8	92.6	94.6	95.1	92.6	93.1	97.4	102.9	104.1
1978	90.8	103.7	89.1	82.3	88.3	110.5	106.8	93.8	92.4	87.6	87.2	84.5	81.6	80.7	84.4	89.0	91.6
1979	86.9	91.5	83.0	81.3	91.9	95.4	94.5	84.5	84.0	82.5	82.6	82.2	80.5	81.2	87.0	93.5	95.1
1980	100.0	99.0	94.7	96.3	110.0	101.4	103.5	92.2	94.6	94.0	95.6	97.0	93.9	97.9	107.0	111.0	112.0
1981	108.7	113.9	103.9	105.5	111.6	117.8	117.1	106.7	104.3	101.6	105.7	108.6	103.0	105.2	108.1	110.9	115.7
1982	111.9	118.7	110.7	108.7	109.3	120.4	121.1	114.7	112.4	108.8	110.9	112.7	108.9	104.5	108.1	109.9	109.8
1983	105.5	109.6	103.3	104.1	104.9	114.1	111.5	103.3	102.6	102.7	104.6	107.4	102.2	102.7	103.0	106.3	105.3

Mining and manufacturing deliveries: (1) semi-manufactured goods (volume)
1980 = 100

Livraisons des industries extractives et manufacturières : (1) demi-produits (volume)
1980 = 100

Adjusted - Corrigé

	Year	Q.1	Q.2	Q.3	Q.4	JAN	FEB	MAR	APR	MAY	JUN	JUL	AUG	SEP	OCT	NOV	DEC
1964		33.9	34.8	35.5	35.8	33.9	34.0	33.9	34.3	35.0	35.2	35.4	35.1	35.9	35.6	35.7	36.2
1965		36.3	36.3	36.8	37.2	36.2	36.2	36.6	36.1	36.2	36.8	36.7	37.0	36.8	37.1	37.3	37.3
1966		38.8	40.9	42.7	44.9	38.2	38.7	39.4	40.5	40.6	41.5	42.2	42.7	43.4	44.0	45.1	45.7
1967		46.7	48.4	49.9	51.5	46.7	46.2	47.2	47.2	48.8	49.2	49.4	50.0	50.2	50.6	52.0	52.0
1968		53.8	54.9	56.3	58.7	53.4	54.3	53.8	54.1	55.5	55.0	55.4	56.8	56.8	58.1	59.5	58.6
1969		60.9	63.9	66.4	69.7	60.3	60.8	61.5	63.0	64.4	64.4	65.3	66.4	67.5	69.1	69.3	70.9
1970		72.1	73.4	74.1	74.5	71.7	72.1	72.6	73.5	73.0	73.8	74.0	73.7	74.6	74.6	73.7	75.2
1971		74.8	74.6	75.9	76.6	74.6	74.1	75.5	74.6	73.8	75.3	75.7	75.9	76.0	75.2	77.1	77.5
1972		79.1	81.1	83.3	88.3	78.0	79.4	80.0	80.1	81.6	81.7	82.3	84.7	84.3	86.1	88.4	90.5
1973		93.2	95.0	94.1	96.8	91.7	93.2	94.7	93.9	94.9	96.2	94.0	95.1	93.3	96.3	97.4	96.7
1974		95.1	88.9	85.6	81.4	97.6	96.1	91.6	90.2	89.7	86.9	86.2	86.4	84.4	82.7	81.2	80.2
1975		76.5	78.4	80.5	81.7	76.6	76.4	76.4	78.6	78.0	78.6	80.5	79.7	81.4	81.4	80.7	83.2
1976		85.8	88.2	89.5	89.6	83.3	85.9	88.1	87.9	87.0	89.7	89.6	89.4	89.5	88.8	90.3	89.8
1977		90.4	88.9	88.3	90.1	91.1	89.9	90.4	89.3	88.6	88.7	87.9	89.6	89.0	88.7	90.3	91.1
1978		91.1	92.5	94.7	96.4	90.9	90.8	91.5	91.7	92.5	93.2	93.7	94.7	95.7	95.6	96.5	97.0
1979		97.7	99.8	100.9	102.2	97.5	97.2	98.5	98.5	100.7	100.2	100.8	102.0	100.0	101.3	102.4	102.9
1980		104.3	102.3	96.5	96.8	103.3	106.6	103.2	104.1	102.5	100.2	98.4	95.0	96.5	97.2	96.5	96.7
1981		96.2	96.1	98.0	97.9	96.4	96.0	96.0	96.9	94.4	96.9	98.4	97.1	98.5	98.5	97.9	97.4
1982		96.2	95.1	95.7	94.5	96.7	96.0	95.9	95.0	94.2	96.2	95.6	95.5	95.9	94.1	95.3	94.1
1983		94.9	96.8	100.9	102.9	94.7	94.6	95.3	95.9	96.8	97.7	98.6	102.7	101.2	102.3	103.2	103.3

Stocks, manufacturing output: total (1) (volume)
1980 = 100

Stocks, produits manufacturés : total (1) (volume)
1980 = 100

Adjusted - Corrigé

	Year	Q.1	Q.2	Q.3	Q.4	JAN	FEB	MAR	APR	MAY	JUN	JUL	AUG	SEP	OCT	NOV	DEC
1964		25.0	26.0	26.9	28.3	24.7	25.2	25.2	25.6	26.1	26.2	26.7	27.1	26.9	27.7	28.1	29.0
1965		29.2	30.0	30.5	30.7	29.0	29.2	29.4	29.7	30.0	30.2	30.4	30.3	30.9	30.2	30.9	31.0
1966		31.3	31.4	31.5	31.8	31.1	31.1	31.7	31.4	31.4	31.4	31.4	31.5	31.8	31.9	31.9	31.7
1967		32.2	33.6	34.1	36.7	31.8	32.0	32.7	33.7	33.7	33.5	33.5	33.8	34.9	35.8	36.7	37.4
1968		38.7	40.5	42.7	44.1	37.8	38.6	39.6	39.6	40.7	41.0	42.4	42.4	43.5	43.7	43.9	44.6
1969		46.4	48.7	50.1	51.1	45.7	46.4	47.1	48.0	48.7	49.3	50.0	50.1	50.2	50.2	51.1	52.0
1970		52.7	55.4	58.9	62.9	52.5	52.5	53.1	54.2	55.3	56.8	57.8	59.1	59.7	61.7	63.2	63.7
1971		66.0	67.6	68.4	69.6	65.2	66.4	66.5	67.3	67.7	67.9	67.5	68.5	69.1	69.7	69.5	69.5
1972		68.6	68.3	68.1	67.1	68.7	68.3	68.7	68.9	68.2	67.8	67.9	68.0	68.4	68.0	67.1	66.1
1973		65.3	65.5	65.8	66.7	65.2	65.2	65.3	65.4	65.5	65.5	65.3	66.1	66.1	66.3	66.7	67.1
1974		71.5	83.4	90.0	94.0	67.9	71.1	75.5	80.3	83.4	86.6	89.3	89.9	90.9	92.7	93.7	95.7
1975		94.2	89.8	89.7	88.2	95.0	94.2	93.5	90.0	89.9	89.6	89.6	89.7	89.8	89.3	88.3	87.0
1976		87.7	88.3	89.0	91.6	87.5	88.0	87.7	88.3	88.3	88.1	88.7	88.8	89.6	90.1	91.3	93.3
1977		93.1	95.2	95.8	95.3	93.4	93.1	92.8	94.4	95.2	96.0	95.9	96.1	95.4	94.9	95.4	95.6
1978		95.0	93.6	92.0	92.2	95.8	94.9	94.2	94.1	93.8	93.0	92.3	92.2	91.6	92.0	92.3	92.3
1979		92.5	90.9	91.7	95.0	92.7	92.8	91.9	92.1	90.8	89.9	90.7	91.2	93.1	94.3	95.3	95.3
1980		95.9	98.4	102.5	103.1	95.4	95.9	96.5	96.7	98.7	99.7	101.7	103.0	103.1	102.9	103.0	103.3
1981		103.2	103.8	101.4	99.8	102.7	103.0	103.9	103.6	103.4	104.5	102.5	101.1	100.5	100.0	99.7	99.6
1982		101.8	102.6	102.0	99.3	101.3	102.1	102.0	102.7	102.7	102.4	102.5	102.5	101.1	100.1	98.9	98.9
1983		98.2	97.2	95.8	93.7	99.3	98.3	96.9	96.7	97.2	97.8	97.5	95.2	94.6	93.7	93.7	93.8

Stocks, manufacturing output: investment goods (1) (volume)
1980 = 100

Stocks, produits manufacturés : biens d'équipements (1) (volume)
1980 = 100

Adjusted - Corrigé

	Year	Q.1	Q.2	Q.3	Q.4	JAN	FEB	MAR	APR	MAY	JUN	JUL	AUG	SEP	OCT	NOV	DEC
1964		18.4	20.5	20.8	21.6	17.4	18.3	19.5	19.9	20.7	20.9	20.9	20.9	20.7	21.2	21.5	22.0
1965		22.5	23.3	24.0	23.7	22.1	22.5	22.8	23.0	22.9	24.0	24.1	23.7	24.2	23.8	24.0	23.4
1966		22.6	22.4	23.0	23.1	23.1	22.2	22.5	22.2	22.6	22.4	22.5	22.8	23.7	23.7	22.7	22.9
1967		22.9	23.5	24.0	26.0	22.7	22.8	23.1	23.4	23.6	23.4	23.3	23.8	24.9	25.6	25.7	26.8
1968		29.0	31.5	36.1	39.8	27.4	28.5	31.0	31.0	31.6	31.9	34.1	35.8	38.4	39.1	39.7	40.5
1969		40.3	41.8	43.2	44.6	39.1	40.7	41.1	41.8	41.7	41.9	42.7	43.3	43.5	43.1	44.6	46.1
1970		46.5	48.2	52.2	55.5	47.1	46.2	46.1	46.4	47.9	50.1	51.7	52.1	52.9	54.6	55.5	56.4
1971		61.2	66.3	66.0	64.8	59.2	61.5	62.7	64.7	66.8	67.5	66.0	66.1	65.9	65.7	64.8	64.0
1972		61.6	59.1	55.3	53.2	62.9	61.6	60.3	60.3	59.1	57.9	55.5	55.9	56.0	54.9	53.3	51.5
1973		51.3	50.4	50.9	55.7	50.8	51.7	51.3	51.1	49.7	50.3	49.3	51.6	51.9	53.4	55.2	58.4
1974		66.0	82.5	93.3	98.2	60.8	65.6	71.5	77.9	82.5	87.0	91.7	92.7	95.4	97.8	98.5	98.4
1975		97.2	93.4	91.8	88.1	98.4	97.1	96.1	93.2	94.5	92.4	92.3	92.2	90.8	88.8	88.5	87.1
1976		87.2	86.6	88.6	94.3	89.9	87.1	84.6	86.7	86.2	86.9	87.7	87.4	90.8	93.5	93.9	95.6
1977		95.3	97.3	97.8	99.0	94.2	95.3	96.3	96.5	97.0	98.2	97.9	97.5	98.1	98.6	99.2	99.1
1978		96.8	92.4	87.7	85.9	99.0	96.5	94.8	94.5	91.9	90.8	88.9	87.7	86.5	85.9	85.4	86.5
1979		85.5	86.2	86.5	89.2	85.7	85.4	85.5	85.9	86.6	86.0	86.3	86.7	86.9	88.2	89.8	89.7
1980		92.8	98.3	102.6	106.8	91.3	93.7	93.4	96.7	98.6	99.6	101.7	101.3	104.7	108.3	106.5	105.7
1981		106.8	107.9	112.3	108.3	106.3	106.0	108.0	106.9	106.6	110.2	113.6	111.1	112.3	109.2	106.5	109.2
1982		111.7	114.5	114.4	107.3	109.7	110.2	115.3	114.3	114.4	114.8	115.2	116.5	111.4	109.5	107.2	105.2
1983		103.1	106.9	109.4	103.0	103.9	101.5	103.8	104.4	108.0	108.3	109.8	109.3	109.2	104.4	103.7	100.9

Stocks, manufacturing output: consumer goods (1) (volume)

Stocks, produits manufacturés : (1) biens de consommation (volume)

1980 = 100

	Year	Q.1	Q.2	Q.3	Q.4	JAN	FEB	MAR	APR	MAY	JUN	JUL	AUG	SEP	OCT	NOV	DEC
1964	26.7	26.7	27.2	27.1	26.0	25.0	27.7	27.3	27.2	27.1	27.2	27.9	27.5	26.0	26.6	26.0	25.2
1965	29.5	30.2	30.6	29.6	27.6	28.0	30.8	31.7	31.0	30.6	30.3	30.3	29.0	29.5	28.0	28.5	26.3
1966	32.0	32.8	33.0	32.2	30.2	30.1	33.2	35.0	33.4	32.8	32.8	32.9	32.0	31.6	31.2	31.0	28.4
1967	35.1	34.7	36.0	34.5	35.0	32.2	35.2	36.9	36.7	35.9	35.2	35.1	34.0	34.6	34.9	36.1	34.0
1968	42.9	41.6	43.5	43.7	42.7	37.8	42.4	44.6	42.9	43.9	43.8	44.9	43.3	42.9	43.8	43.9	40.5
1969	50.9	49.5	52.4	51.9	49.6	46.3	50.0	52.1	52.1	52.1	53.1	53.5	52.1	50.0	50.8	51.2	46.9
1970	57.9	55.7	58.9	58.1	58.9	52.2	56.2	58.6	58.7	58.4	59.5	59.2	58.5	56.8	60.1	61.0	55.6
1971	61.9	65.3	65.0	60.4	56.9	61.4	67.0	67.6	66.3	64.8	64.0	61.9	61.3	58.0	59.2	58.4	53.1
1972	62.0	62.2	63.2	62.6	59.8	58.6	62.9	65.2	64.6	62.8	62.3	63.0	63.0	61.8	62.4	61.3	55.6
1973	63.7	61.5	62.7	64.8	66.0	60.4	62.1	62.0	62.2	62.3	63.6	64.3	65.6	64.5	66.9	68.7	62.3
1974	78.5	69.3	79.2	82.3	82.8	65.1	70.3	72.6	77.9	79.2	80.7	83.7	82.3	80.8	84.2	84.8	79.4
1975	74.8	80.6	71.5	75.1	72.0	81.6	80.4	79.9	71.9	70.7	71.9	74.3	74.9	76.1	77.5	74.6	63.9
1976	76.8	71.5	75.7	80.2	79.7	68.6	72.1	73.7	74.9	74.9	77.3	80.7	80.2	79.8	81.6	82.0	75.5
1977	81.9	78.5	81.4	84.7	82.9	78.8	78.9	77.9	80.0	80.6	83.7	85.0	86.1	82.9	84.1	85.9	78.9
1978	86.0	83.9	82.9	85.9	91.4	86.8	85.2	79.8	81.6	83.2	83.8	84.7	86.1	86.9	91.4	94.6	88.3
1979	91.4	89.7	85.4	90.6	99.8	92.3	91.1	85.7	86.3	85.3	84.6	88.3	90.2	93.2	98.9	103.0	97.6
1980	100.0	98.8	95.2	101.3	104.7	99.8	100.8	95.8	92.9	96.1	96.6	100.5	100.7	102.8	105.5	108.4	100.1
1981	99.2	99.5	97.6	98.6	101.0	101.3	100.8	96.4	95.6	97.4	99.8	100.1	97.1	98.6	102.6	103.8	96.5
1982	100.5	99.6	97.4	102.4	102.6	101.3	102.0	95.6	96.6	96.7	98.8	102.3	102.3	102.6	104.7	105.0	98.0
1983	95.4	97.6	93.7	97.0	93.2	101.9	99.4	91.4	90.4	93.4	97.2	99.3	95.8	95.8	95.8	95.6	88.2

Stocks, manufacturing output: semi-manufactured goods (1) (volume)

Stocks, produits manufacturés : (1) demi-produits (volume)

1980 = 100

	Year	Q.1	Q.2	Q.3	Q.4	JAN	FEB	MAR	APR	MAY	JUN	JUL	AUG	SEP	OCT	NOV	DEC
1964	27.6	25.8	26.8	28.1	29.6	25.6	26.0	25.8	26.1	26.8	27.5	28.0	28.1	28.0	29.0	29.8	30.0
1965	32.0	30.8	31.6	32.9	32.5	30.9	31.2	30.4	31.0	31.4	32.4	33.1	33.1	32.5	32.3	32.7	32.6
1966	33.0	33.2	33.1	33.1	32.5	33.6	33.2	32.6	32.8	33.0	33.5	33.5	33.1	32.7	32.7	32.8	32.2
1967	35.4	33.2	34.8	36.0	37.5	33.2	33.3	33.2	34.3	34.7	35.3	35.8	36.0	36.3	37.3	37.5	37.6
1968	41.7	40.1	41.3	42.4	43.0	40.2	40.2	40.0	40.6	41.2	42.0	42.8	42.3	42.0	42.6	42.9	43.5
1969	48.7	46.9	48.6	49.0	50.4	46.4	47.4	47.0	47.9	48.5	49.4	49.7	49.2	48.2	49.1	50.7	51.5
1970	58.0	53.7	55.7	59.2	63.5	54.3	53.7	53.1	54.3	55.6	57.3	58.5	59.9	59.2	61.8	64.4	64.4
1971	72.2	69.2	70.9	72.8	75.8	68.5	70.1	69.1	70.5	70.8	71.5	72.2	73.0	73.2	75.6	76.4	75.2
1972	74.3	76.6	75.3	73.3	72.0	76.8	77.2	75.8	75.8	75.0	75.1	74.5	73.3	72.0	72.6	73.0	70.3
1973	69.5	70.1	69.8	69.4	68.7	70.8	69.9	69.5	69.8	69.9	69.7	69.1	69.4	69.7	69.6	69.2	67.4
1974	87.5	73.2	85.0	93.5	98.5	70.1	72.6	76.8	80.9	84.8	89.2	91.5	93.8	95.1	97.5	99.1	99.0
1975	98.6	100.9	98.8	97.5	97.1	101.3	101.8	99.5	98.8	98.8	98.8	97.7	97.8	97.0	97.4	97.9	95.9
1976	95.6	97.3	94.6	93.7	96.9	98.2	98.4	95.1	95.1	95.1	93.6	93.1	94.1	94.1	95.2	97.2	98.2
1977	101.1	100.6	101.2	101.9	100.7	101.5	101.5	98.8	100.0	101.6	102.0	101.8	102.6	101.2	100.8	101.2	100.2
1978	97.0	100.3	97.2	95.3	95.0	102.6	101.1	97.3	97.6	97.9	96.1	95.5	95.9	94.6	95.4	95.5	94.2
1979	93.9	95.3	92.6	92.8	95.1	96.9	96.4	92.6	93.3	92.7	91.6	91.8	92.6	93.9	95.4	95.8	94.2
1980	100.0	95.4	98.0	103.2	103.4	96.6	95.6	94.1	96.0	98.4	99.7	101.7	104.4	103.5	103.4	103.5	103.2
1981	102.3	104.6	104.3	101.1	99.4	105.2	105.3	103.4	104.1	104.4	104.3	101.5	101.6	100.1	99.9	100.1	98.1
1982	100.2	101.4	102.2	100.4	97.0	101.7	102.5	100.0	101.8	103.4	101.4	101.0	101.1	99.0	97.9	96.9	96.0
1983	95.1	98.0	96.3	93.5	92.6	99.2	99.1	95.7	96.5	96.7	95.6	95.1	93.3	92.1	91.5	93.2	93.1

Stocks, manufacturing input: (1) total (volume)

Stocks, produits de base pour les industries manufacturières : (1) total (volume)

1980 = 100

	Year	Q.1	Q.2	Q.3	Q.4	JAN	FEB	MAR	APR	MAY	JUN	JUL	AUG	SEP	OCT	NOV	DEC
1964	37.8	37.1	37.2	38.5	38.5	37.6	37.0	36.7	36.3	36.8	38.4	37.9	38.7	38.8	38.8	38.7	38.1
1965	36.3	36.0	35.0	37.0	37.4	36.9	36.0	35.0	34.6	34.9	35.6	36.5	37.5	37.0	37.8	37.4	36.9
1966	37.8	35.7	36.4	39.0	40.2	36.2	35.5	35.4	35.4	36.0	37.8	38.7	39.3	38.9	40.3	40.3	40.1
1967	44.6	40.2	43.4	46.7	48.0	40.0	40.1	40.5	41.7	42.9	45.5	45.7	46.9	47.6	47.8	48.0	48.1
1968	47.8	47.0	46.4	48.3	49.6	48.4	46.7	45.9	45.7	46.0	47.6	47.8	48.7	48.2	49.2	49.6	50.0
1969	51.0	49.3	49.1	51.7	53.8	50.0	49.2	48.6	48.7	48.4	50.1	50.4	52.3	52.6	53.6	53.8	54.1
1970	57.9	53.9	55.3	59.9	62.5	54.1	53.9	53.8	54.4	55.1	56.4	58.7	60.1	61.0	62.3	62.8	62.3
1971	67.0	64.0	65.9	68.7	69.5	63.8	63.7	64.4	64.9	65.4	67.5	69.3	68.5	68.4	69.7	69.6	69.2
1972	68.7	68.0	68.3	68.7	69.6	68.0	67.9	68.0	67.7	69.3	68.0	67.6	68.6	69.8	70.7	69.7	68.5
1973	73.6	67.4	71.0	76.4	79.3	67.3	67.6	67.2	69.2	70.5	73.2	74.4	76.7	78.1	79.9	78.7	79.5
1974	86.6	80.7	84.5	90.0	90.5	79.9	80.2	81.9	83.2	84.1	86.4	89.6	90.2	90.2	90.9	90.5	89.9
1975	90.1	87.5	87.8	91.5	93.6	89.1	87.1	86.2	86.2	88.1	89.0	90.0	92.0	92.4	95.3	91.5	94.0
1976	94.5	90.9	93.3	96.7	97.1	91.6	90.5	90.7	91.3	93.2	95.5	96.2	96.9	96.9	97.1	97.3	96.9
1977	99.4	97.3	98.9	100.5	100.8	99.4	95.2	97.4	96.9	99.4	100.5	100.9	99.6	101.1	101.1	100.5	100.7
1978	98.2	99.5	99.6	97.3	96.6	100.3	98.3	99.8	97.9	101.8	99.0	97.7	97.0	97.1	96.9	96.1	96.8
1979	96.8	94.2	96.2	97.0	99.8	94.7	94.1	93.9	94.3	97.3	97.1	97.1	97.2	96.8	99.0	99.7	100.6
1980	100.0	97.3	99.4	102.0	101.3	98.5	96.5	97.0	97.9	99.1	101.2	102.6	101.7	101.8	101.3	101.3	101.2
1981	98.5	97.9	99.1	99.1	97.8	99.6	97.9	96.3	98.1	99.3	100.0	99.7	99.6	97.9	98.1	97.8	97.4
1982	94.9	95.7	95.2	94.7	94.1	96.0	95.7	95.4	96.0	94.8	94.7	95.3	94.3	94.5	94.7	93.6	94.1
1983	87.1	89.6	86.1	86.1	86.5	91.2	88.9	88.7	86.7	84.9	86.6	85.7	86.6	85.9	86.2	86.1	87.2

Stocks, manufacturing output: consumer goods (1)
(volume)
1980 = 100

Adjusted - Corrigé

Stocks, produits manufacturés : (1)
biens de consommation (volume)
1980 = 100

	Year	Q.1	Q.2	Q.3	Q.4	JAN	FEB	MAR	APR	MAY	JUN	JUL	AUG	SEP	OCT	NOV	DEC
1964		25.5	26.7	27.2	27.7	25.2	25.7	25.5	26.4	26.7	26.9	27.4	27.6	26.6	27.3	27.3	28.4
1965		28.9	29.7	29.6	29.8	28.5	28.7	29.5	29.5	29.8	29.8	29.5	29.2	30.1	29.2	30.2	30.1
1966		31.3	32.0	32.2	32.7	30.6	30.9	32.4	31.9	31.9	32.1	32.1	32.3	32.3	32.6	32.8	32.5
1967		33.2	34.9	34.7	37.9	32.6	32.8	34.1	35.1	35.0	34.6	34.3	34.3	35.5	36.4	38.2	39.0
1968		40.3	41.9	44.1	45.6	38.9	40.6	41.4	40.8	42.3	42.5	44.0	43.4	44.9	45.2	45.4	46.1
1969		48.0	50.4	52.5	52.9	47.6	47.9	48.5	49.5	50.2	51.5	52.5	52.3	52.6	52.2	52.9	53.5
1970		54.0	56.6	58.9	62.6	53.7	53.8	54.5	55.7	56.3	57.7	58.1	58.7	59.8	61.8	63.0	63.2
1971		63.4	62.5	61.2	60.5	63.2	64.0	62.9	62.9	62.5	62.1	60.9	61.5	61.1	60.8	60.4	60.3
1972		60.5	61.1	63.2	63.3	60.3	60.2	60.9	61.4	61.0	60.7	62.0	63.1	64.4	63.8	63.1	63.1
1973		62.3	62.8	63.6	66.1	62.1	62.4	62.4	62.4	62.9	63.3	62.7	64.0	64.2	65.0	66.6	66.8
1974		70.3	79.5	80.7	83.0	67.2	70.7	73.0	78.0	80.2	80.4	81.4	80.3	80.5	81.7	82.3	85.0
1975		81.8	71.8	73.6	71.9	84.1	80.8	80.3	72.1	71.8	71.6	72.1	73.1	75.5	75.2	72.4	68.2
1976		72.4	76.3	78.5	79.9	70.5	72.5	74.1	75.3	76.2	77.3	78.3	78.2	79.1	79.2	79.7	80.7
1977		79.9	82.0	82.4	83.3	81.4	79.8	78.5	81.1	82.0	82.9	82.0	83.2	81.9	82.0	83.5	84.4
1978		83.9	85.6	86.3	88.2	84.4	83.8	83.4	84.5	86.2	86.1	85.8	86.5	86.7	87.5	88.3	88.7
1979		89.7	88.3	91.0	96.3	90.0	89.7	89.4	89.7	88.4	86.9	89.2	90.8	92.9	94.6	96.2	98.0
1980		98.8	98.6	101.7	100.8	97.5	99.2	99.7	97.0	99.5	99.4	101.3	101.6	102.3	100.8	101.2	100.5
1981		99.5	101.1	98.9	97.3	99.2	99.1	100.1	99.9	100.8	102.6	100.6	98.1	98.0	98.0	97.0	96.9
1982		99.4	100.8	102.4	99.4	99.2	99.6	99.4	101.0	100.1	101.4	102.1	103.1	101.9	100.4	98.7	99.2
1983		97.3	97.0	96.9	90.3	99.8	97.1	95.0	94.6	96.7	99.8	99.1	96.6	95.1	91.9	89.8	89.3

Stocks, manufacturing output: semi-manufactured goods (1)
(volume)
1980 = 100

Adjusted - Corrigé

Stocks, produits manufacturés : (1)
demi-produits (volume)
1980 = 100

	Year	Q.1	Q.2	Q.3	Q.4	JAN	FEB	MAR	APR	MAY	JUN	JUL	AUG	SEP	OCT	NOV	DEC
1964		25.8	26.8	27.7	29.8	25.4	25.9	26.2	26.5	26.8	27.1	27.3	27.7	28.2	29.1	30.0	30.5
1965		30.8	31.7	32.6	32.8	30.5	30.9	31.0	31.4	31.6	32.0	32.3	32.7	32.7	32.5	32.8	33.2
1966		33.1	33.1	32.8	32.8	33.1	33.1	33.3	33.2	33.1	33.0	32.7	32.7	32.9	32.9	32.9	32.7
1967		33.3	34.8	35.7	37.9	32.7	33.2	33.8	34.7	34.8	34.8	35.1	35.5	36.6	37.6	37.7	38.2
1968		39.5	41.2	42.7	43.5	39.2	39.3	40.0	40.4	41.2	41.8	42.4	42.6	43.2	43.3	43.2	44.1
1969		46.2	48.5	49.5	50.9	45.3	46.3	47.0	47.6	48.6	49.2	49.3	49.5	49.6	49.9	50.8	52.1
1970		52.6	55.6	59.8	64.0	52.2	52.4	53.1	54.1	55.7	57.2	58.3	60.3	60.8	62.6	64.3	65.1
1971		68.2	70.9	73.6	76.1	66.9	68.5	69.0	70.4	71.0	71.4	71.9	73.6	75.3	76.4	76.2	75.8
1972		75.5	75.2	74.0	72.4	75.3	75.4	75.9	75.6	75.1	74.9	74.3	73.8	74.0	73.1	72.8	71.2
1973		70.0	69.5	69.6	68.8	70.4	69.7	69.8	69.7	69.6	69.3	69.3	69.3	70.1	69.6	68.7	68.2
1974		73.0	84.7	93.8	98.7	69.7	72.1	77.1	80.8	84.5	88.8	91.9	93.8	95.8	97.5	98.5	100.0
1975		100.4	98.6	98.0	97.3	100.3	100.3	100.0	98.9	98.4	98.5	98.2	98.0	97.8	97.6	97.4	96.7
1976		96.5	94.6	94.4	97.1	96.9	96.8	95.6	95.4	94.9	93.6	93.7	94.3	95.0	95.6	96.7	98.9
1977		99.8	101.4	102.4	100.9	100.0	99.6	99.6	100.6	101.4	102.1	102.4	102.7	102.1	101.4	100.8	100.5
1978		99.7	97.5	95.6	95.1	100.5	99.7	99.0	98.3	97.6	96.5	96.0	95.7	95.1	95.4	95.0	95.0
1979		94.7	92.8	92.9	95.2	94.9	95.3	94.0	93.9	92.5	92.0	92.2	92.4	94.2	95.4	95.3	95.0
1980		94.9	98.3	103.4	103.5	94.8	94.6	95.4	96.5	98.2	100.1	102.3	104.2	103.7	103.4	103.0	104.2
1981		104.2	104.4	101.2	99.5	103.5	104.2	104.9	104.5	104.2	104.6	102.1	101.4	100.2	99.9	99.6	99.0
1982		101.0	101.8	100.2	97.9	100.5	101.4	101.2	101.8	102.5	101.1	101.0	100.2	99.4	98.6	97.5	97.7
1983		97.6	95.9	93.4	93.8	97.9	98.0	96.9	96.5	95.9	95.3	95.1	92.5	92.5	93.0	93.7	94.7

Stocks, manufacturing input: (1)
total (volume)
1980 = 100

Adjusted - Corrigé

Stocks, produits de base pour les industries manufacturières : (1)
total (volume)
1980 = 100

	Year	Q.1	Q.2	Q.3	Q.4	JAN	FEB	MAR	APR	MAY	JUN	JUL	AUG	SEP	OCT	NOV	DEC
1964		37.8	38.2	37.8	37.3	37.8	37.6	38.0	38.0	38.2	38.5	37.8	37.7	37.9	37.2	37.4	37.4
1965		36.6	36.1	36.3	36.2	37.1	36.6	36.2	36.4	36.2	35.8	36.3	36.4	36.2	36.2	36.2	36.2
1966		36.5	37.5	38.2	39.0	36.4	36.2	36.8	37.1	37.4	37.8	38.5	38.2	38.0	38.7	39.0	39.5
1967		41.0	44.7	45.9	46.6	40.1	40.9	42.1	43.8	44.7	45.5	45.4	45.7	46.5	46.0	46.5	47.3
1968		47.4	47.2	47.7	48.9	48.0	47.2	46.9	46.9	47.0	47.8	47.6	47.8	47.6	48.2	48.9	49.6
1969		49.6	49.9	51.1	53.1	49.6	49.7	49.6	49.9	49.6	50.3	50.0	51.4	52.1	52.5	53.0	53.9
1970		54.5	56.2	59.2	61.7	54.0	54.6	54.9	55.7	56.3	56.5	58.2	59.0	60.4	61.1	61.8	62.1
1971		64.7	66.8	67.9	68.7	63.7	64.5	65.8	66.4	66.6	67.5	68.5	67.4	67.8	68.3	68.7	69.1
1972		68.6	69.5	68.0	68.6	67.9	68.7	69.3	69.3	70.5	68.7	67.3	67.8	68.8	69.0	68.6	68.2
1973		68.7	71.8	75.1	78.2	67.9	69.1	69.2	70.8	71.6	73.1	73.6	75.1	76.6	77.4	78.1	79.1
1974		82.3	85.6	88.4	89.2	80.5	82.1	84.2	85.2	85.2	86.2	88.5	88.2	88.5	88.3	89.8	89.5
1975		89.3	88.9	89.9	92.3	89.7	89.4	88.7	88.6	89.3	88.7	88.8	90.0	90.7	92.6	90.8	93.5
1976		92.3	94.5	95.0	95.8	92.2	92.9	93.2	93.8	94.4	95.2	95.0	94.8	95.1	94.5	96.5	96.5
1977		99.2	99.7	98.9	99.8	99.9	97.8	99.9	99.5	99.9	99.7	99.6	97.7	99.5	99.0	99.8	100.5
1978		100.9	99.5	96.8	95.8	101.0	100.6	101.1	99.5	100.8	93.1	97.0	96.8	96.5	96.1	95.5	95.8
1979		95.7	96.1	96.4	98.9	95.3	96.2	95.5	95.8	96.5	96.1	96.2	96.8	96.2	98.1	99.0	99.6
1980		99.0	99.4	101.3	100.4	99.1	98.7	99.1	99.5	98.5	100.2	101.5	101.1	101.3	100.4	100.5	100.3
1981		99.6	99.1	98.2	96.9	100.2	100.0	98.6	99.6	98.9	98.9	98.5	98.8	97.4	97.2	96.9	96.5
1982		96.9	95.4	94.1	93.4	96.5	97.3	97.0	97.0	95.1	94.0	94.3	93.8	94.1	93.9	93.1	93.1
1983		90.7	86.3	85.5	85.8	91.7	90.3	90.2	87.6	85.2	86.0	84.8	86.2	85.6	85.5	85.7	86.3

JAPAN

Net new orders: machinery (4)
(value, 178 corporations)
billion yen, monthly averages

Commandes nouvelles nettes : construction mécanique (4)
(valeur, 178 sociétés)
milliards de yens, moyennes mensuelles

	Year	Q.1	Q.2	Q.3	Q.4	JAN	FEB	MAR	APR	MAY	JUN	JUL	AUG	SEP	OCT	NOV	DEC
1964	135	129	122	149	140	100	124	163	118	125	124	138	128	180	130	122	167
1965	142	138	126	150	156	107	130	177	135	114	129	135	140	175	142	115	211
1966	172	150	151	209	180	119	131	200	145	150	158	177	157	292	152	157	231
1967	230	210	211	244	257	163	190	277	226	190	217	211	235	288	258	251	261
1968	267	242	236	302	288	227	188	310	259	223	227	268	297	342	277	282	306
1969	387	307	380	426	436	265	274	384	373	386	380	375	415	488	426	416	467
1970	539	529	519	547	562	394	490	702	592	507	460	541	432	667	595	455	635
1971	544	587	501	569	519	486	492	784	525	473	504	500	523	684	441	495	621
1972	526	542	425	527	609	449	378	799	440	398	436	424	423	733	562	571	693
1973	864	804	694	965	994	671	672	1068	648	636	797	871	787	1238	1087	995	901
1974	703	724	659	825	604	651	570	950	684	630	663	795	663	1017	601	549	662
1975	703	781	562	757	714	511	607	1226	546	562	577	504	632	1135	603	546	992
1976	779	836	642	940	697	474	603	1431	656	575	697	722	638	1461	589	681	821
1977	833	884	781	902	762	704	589	1360	705	684	954	727	785	1195	648	668	971
1978	876	980	722	1013	790	657	794	1490	699	635	830	869	819	1350	646	730	993
1979	1047	1111	853	1231	995	724	703	1905	856	879	825	861	950	1881	964	919	1102
1980	1180	1228	1122	1191	1178	849	856	1979	1084	1220	1062	1153	936	1483	1188	949	1396
1981	1213	1390	1090	1282	1090	985	999	2186	1116	962	1194	974	984	1888	1179	902	1188
1982	1179	1380	1075	1276	986	906	1102	2133	930	968	1325	1072	1016	1739	891	811	1257
1983	1168	1324	1047	1268	1034	730	907	2335	958	980	1204	920	964	1899	1025	975	1103

Net new orders: machinery excl. ships, (4)
(value, 178 corporations)
billion yen, monthly averages

Commandes nouvelles nettes : construction mécanique (4)
non compris les navires (valeur, 178 sociétés)
milliards de yens, moyennes mensuelles

	Year	Q.1	Q.2	Q.3	Q.4	JAN	FEB	MAR	APR	MAY	JUN	JUL	AUG	SEP	OCT	NOV	DEC
1964	112	110	107	121	111	88	103	138	111	105	103	114	103	148	102	99	132
1965	110	111	96	122	110	90	90	152	94	99	96	108	103	155	109	93	127
1966	134	122	122	143	149	101	103	161	125	119	121	122	126	179	129	131	185
1967	194	173	193	202	209	146	163	210	202	173	206	188	186	231	204	201	222
1968	228	202	212	250	248	182	173	250	235	201	199	223	238	289	251	236	258
1969	333	261	331	364	377	230	227	328	338	322	334	322	355	416	366	364	399
1970	428	433	433	455	390	316	393	590	490	437	373	414	375	575	406	312	452
1971	408	461	350	471	349	376	354	651	335	325	390	438	408	567	298	335	415
1972	438	466	371	467	450	341	349	708	376	363	372	358	384	659	399	422	528
1973	626	602	551	645	704	485	484	839	559	508	586	578	543	815	753	749	610
1974	625	580	594	761	566	434	462	842	625	565	593	702	622	958	574	508	614
1975	629	695	499	732	590	431	543	1110	475	502	520	479	587	1128	510	493	768
1976	734	796	625	878	638	422	556	1410	644	570	661	678	575	1382	567	615	732
1977	776	848	711	823	724	661	567	1316	672	558	903	619	707	1142	617	613	941
1978	828	914	687	963	747	646	708	1387	669	605	788	803	787	1298	615	681	944
1979	992	1085	838	1164	881	711	682	1863	880	830	803	820	881	1790	888	856	899
1980	1059	1090	971	1093	1084	773	768	1730	930	1015	967	1026	843	1409	1127	838	1287
1981	1099	1254	981	1165	998	911	860	1991	1006	864	1074	876	942	1676	1074	810	1111
1982	1124	1299	1034	1202	960	882	1031	1985	881	939	1281	1027	954	1625	848	768	1264
1983	1073	1234	937	1150	973	699	836	2168	857	873	1080	816	893	1742	1004	908	1006

Net new domestic orders: (4)(5)
machinery (value, 178 corporations)
billion yen, monthly averages

Commandes nouvelles nettes (marché intérieur) : (4)(5)
construction mécanique (valeur, 178 sociétés)
milliards de yens, moyennes mensuelles

	Year	Q.1	Q.2	Q.3	Q.4	JAN	FEB	MAR	APR	MAY	JUN	JUL	AUG	SEP	OCT	NOV	DEC
1964	103	100	96	112	105	84	93	123	98	98	93	98	110	123	106	84	125
1965	100	96	97	108	98	79	82	129	99	94	99	106	90	127	104	74	117
1966	116	110	102	123	128	93	90	146	105	101	100	110	107	152	104	125	157
1967	171	153	162	180	189	126	141	192	173	146	168	162	172	206	192	175	199
1968	198	172	187	218	214	159	147	209	209	172	180	195	209	249	214	210	218
1969	294	235	293	318	328	199	195	311	294	295	290	275	299	381	337	311	337
1970	377	391	359	410	350	280	367	525	397	371	310	364	350	516	387	297	365
1971	380	412	328	435	347	341	274	620	334	295	354	364	411	529	290	250	500
1972	361	395	305	384	361	321	246	618	325	298	292	270	340	543	323	331	430
1973	534	496	445	576	620	371	414	703	452	395	487	536	445	746	684	607	568
1974	498	465	473	615	440	351	362	682	486	452	481	591	486	768	443	415	460
1975	437	524	378	458	387	342	410	821	377	369	389	352	400	624	378	342	442
1976	463	490	387	530	444	269	378	823	389	361	410	416	377	798	421	429	480
1977	505	562	446	558	452	382	412	892	458	404	476	426	489	760	457	377	521
1978	607	654	491	732	550	390	467	1105	492	431	551	639	593	965	497	529	625
1979	679	802	577	735	602	410	493	1503	647	520	564	559	533	1114	612	606	588
1980	761	751	685	793	817	503	538	1212	692	728	633	696	599	1085	895	593	962
1981	762	925	667	765	689	509	617	1648	734	608	659	570	602	1124	737	557	773
1982	720	843	625	754	657	515	733	1283	607	658	611	582	600	1079	609	543	818
1983	745	902	658	753	665	481	553	1672	606	598	770	563	605	1092	662	663	669

Net new orders: machinery (4)
(value, 178 corporations)
billion yen, monthly averages

Commandes nouvelles nettes : construction mécanique (4)
(valeur, 178 sociétés)
milliards de yens, moyennes mensuelles

Adjusted - Corrigé

Year	Q.1	Q.2	Q.3	Q.4	JAN	FEB	MAR	APR	MAY	JUN	JUL	AUG	SEP	OCT	NOV	DEC
1964	133	131	136	141	132	140	126	126	141	126	135	134	139	140	145	140
1965	141	135	138	154	138	147	137	142	130	134	134	145	134	152	133	178
1966	151	163	188	180	149	148	157	152	169	167	179	162	222	161	178	200
1967	210	225	228	259	197	214	219	229	212	233	217	243	225	267	277	234
1968	241	250	287	290	264	214	244	256	246	247	278	308	274	283	305	283
1969	304	410	425	442	304	312	297	377	427	425	409	466	400	445	462	420
1970	493	564	539	561	448	552	479	608	569	514	590	488	538	614	496	572
1971	551	552	555	517	551	560	541	550	544	562	536	594	535	454	534	563
1972	498	478	491	611	512	437	546	479	470	486	452	475	546	585	617	632
1973	764	795	893	1031	789	798	706	728	772	887	928	886	864	1162	1096	835
1974	693	766	758	635	787	689	603	796	777	726	859	740	675	667	619	620
1975	713	654	659	762	644	743	753	643	700	620	543	704	729	706	642	937
1976	731	745	806	774	610	740	843	778	717	741	793	704	919	721	829	772
1977	810	900	810	851	925	731	773	829	852	1019	803	880	748	811	831	912
1978	894	829	920	876	854	996	832	814	786	887	975	932	854	784	913	932
1979	963	982	1088	1114	940	880	1069	990	1083	873	954	1097	1212	1139	1166	1039
1980	1091	1288	1217	1300	1109	1065	1098	1254	1491	1120	1297	1093	962	1355	1224	1321
1981	1249	1239	1166	1210	1319	1227	1200	1295	1173	1249	1100	1168	1228	1323	1182	1124
1982	1248	1209	1195	1081	1232	1353	1158	1076	1177	1375	1218	1224	1141	986	1072	1185
1983	1123	1180	1165	1153	998	1100	1270	1106	1189	1244	1049	1193	1252	1126	1295	1038

Net new orders: machinery excl. ships, (4)
(value, 178 corporations)
billion yen, monthly averages

Commandes nouvelles nettes : construction mécanique (4)
non compris les navires (valeur, 178 sociétés)
milliards de yens, moyennes mensuelles

Adjusted - Corrigé

Year	Q.1	Q.2	Q.3	Q.4	JAN	FEB	MAR	APR	MAY	JUN	JUL	AUG	SEP	OCT	NOV	DEC
1964	110	110	114	114	108	117	107	114	113	103	117	111	114	111	114	118
1965	109	100	115	113	108	102	117	96	106	98	112	111	121	117	106	114
1966	121	125	135	151	118	117	126	125	127	125	128	134	143	137	148	169
1967	174	198	193	214	170	184	167	194	185	215	195	197	188	211	224	207
1968	201	217	238	257	210	196	197	223	215	212	230	250	235	261	262	249
1969	257	357	345	414	264	257	251	350	356	365	338	380	319	418	437	387
1970	399	467	425	424	372	445	379	509	486	406	436	403	436	463	372	438
1971	424	378	440	382	446	404	422	348	363	424	459	441	419	341	402	402
1972	421	409	418	496	408	403	452	408	415	403	375	414	467	466	510	512
1973	564	612	584	801	604	569	519	605	590	640	612	592	547	895	917	591
1974	537	670	687	636	556	553	503	690	673	649	761	684	617	693	627	590
1975	625	570	629	658	569	659	647	529	610	572	527	653	707	627	617	732
1976	679	724	749	727	557	683	798	730	709	732	760	638	848	711	776	693
1977	769	823	732	814	873	706	728	766	696	1006	696	798	701	772	777	894
1978	830	795	875	833	831	897	761	760	749	875	916	898	812	739	863	898
1979	936	959	1031	995	903	866	1041	1000	1009	869	922	1015	1158	1032	1097	857
1980	972	1102	1022	1197	986	971	960	1064	1217	1025	1164	976	924	1270	1090	1230
1981	1122	1099	1072	1107	1190	1076	1099	1165	1022	1111	992	1109	1114	1193	1071	1057
1982	1130	1145	1134	1030	1171	1286	1084	1021	1101	1313	1168	1138	1095	928	1025	1137
1983	1050	1038	1062	1085	930	1033	1187	992	1020	1102	931	1071	1183	1089	1219	946

Net new domestic orders: (4)(5)
machinery (value, 178 corporations)
billion yen, monthly averages

Commandes nouvelles nettes (marché intérieur) : (4)(5)
construction mécanique (valeur, 178 sociétés)
milliards de yens, moyennes mensuelles

Adjusted - Corrigé

Year	Q.1	Q.2	Q.3	Q.4	JAN	FEB	MAR	APR	MAY	JUN	JUL	AUG	SEP	OCT	NOV	DEC
1964	101	100	106	107	103	104	96	99	107	95	100	117	101	110	101	110
1965	96	101	102	99	94	93	100	99	102	102	109	95	102	107	87	104
1966	109	106	117	130	108	103	115	104	109	105	114	112	124	107	140	142
1967	153	157	172	192	147	161	153	166	157	178	169	178	170	197	193	185
1968	172	193	207	220	184	170	162	200	185	195	206	213	203	220	234	206
1969	230	320	297	364	227	228	234	305	328	326	302	305	283	363	387	342
1970	365	392	380	382	324	444	328	413	415	347	400	360	380	416	363	366
1971	375	360	400	371	399	333	392	349	336	396	394	426	380	314	301	497
1972	358	339	341	391	383	303	389	346	348	324	287	355	381	355	394	424
1973	470	498	516	680	463	513	434	489	469	537	568	474	507	763	717	560
1974	438	534	558	479	457	445	411	535	544	525	632	526	514	495	488	455
1975	483	430	409	426	470	497	483	420	448	424	376	439	411	426	407	444
1976	434	444	461	497	382	456	464	437	447	447	450	415	519	481	520	490
1977	512	513	502	509	551	502	482	511	500	527	466	549	491	527	464	535
1978	573	564	675	616	565	576	578	540	532	619	718	682	625	560	657	632
1979	666	658	662	674	595	621	782	704	628	641	631	627	729	681	761	580
1980	683	780	747	884	736	692	621	748	863	729	808	719	713	976	750	926
1981	798	754	718	744	750	803	841	794	701	766	674	736	744	796	712	724
1982	792	706	721	701	763	964	649	657	746	714	701	744	719	649	703	752
1983	763	744	723	724	713	728	847	656	673	904	684	754	731	701	863	609

JAPAN

Net new export orders: (4)(5)
machinery (value, 178 corporations)
billion yen, monthly averages

Commandes nouvelles nettes en provenance de l'étranger : (4)(5)
construction mécanique (valeur, 178 sociétés)
milliards de yens, moyennes mensuelles

	Year	Q.1	Q.2	Q.3	Q.4	JAN	FEB	MAR	APR	MAY	JUN	JUL	AUG	SEP	OCT	NOV	DEC
1964	24	22	19	28	27	10	25	33	13	20	23	31	11	42	16	30	34
1965	34	32	22	33	49	21	41	36	28	14	24	20	42	38	30	32	85
1966	46	31	39	75	42	17	31	44	30	38	48	56	39	128	40	21	64
1967	45	44	34	49	53	27	36	70	40	29	34	34	47	66	53	59	46
1968	51	54	31	65	54	53	26	83	32	32	28	53	70	72	44	51	67
1969	68	51	60	80	80	47	58	49	53	64	62	73	90	76	62	76	101
1970	129	106	126	104	180	89	92	138	162	102	116	146	51	114	173	127	241
1971	132	141	142	101	144	118	187	117	161	148	117	101	82	120	124	217	91
1972	127	115	82	105	208	102	104	139	82	60	102	111	51	151	203	198	222
1973	267	253	186	326	303	262	192	306	141	182	235	277	288	413	337	322	251
1974	154	199	132	155	129	230	156	209	152	121	125	152	135	179	121	98	168
1975	224	219	143	253	282	141	157	360	133	154	142	110	200	448	184	148	513
1976	272	303	211	364	209	172	169	567	225	171	238	258	223	610	126	205	295
1977	280	276	286	292	267	277	136	414	199	229	430	247	250	380	147	246	406
1978	213	273	173	222	184	226	280	312	159	146	215	169	178	320	94	145	315
1979	307	252	211	437	328	266	153	336	145	298	191	240	362	710	284	251	450
1980	353	404	368	338	303	280	250	680	317	427	359	390	291	335	237	303	368
1981	387	398	363	453	336	424	326	445	324	296	468	338	329	691	365	287	355
1982	398	472	386	460	276	339	313	766	265	246	647	428	363	587	228	214	384
1983	360	361	326	447	306	201	295	586	297	318	364	290	317	735	296	251	370

Construction, new orders: total
(83 contractors)
billion yen, monthly averages

Construction, commandes nouvelles : total
(83 entreprises)
milliards de yens, moyennes mensuelles

	Year	Q.1	Q.2	Q.3	Q.4	JAN	FEB	MAR	APR	MAY	JUN	JUL	AUG	SEP	OCT	NOV	DEC
1964	89	85	93	92	87	72	77	107	92	99	88	86	88	101	87	85	89
1965	80	83	71	87	78	76	73	100	71	67	77	74	82	104	71	78	86
1966	88	76	75	99	102	52	67	109	62	72	91	86	93	119	91	96	118
1967	114	99	102	123	131	81	81	136	99	96	111	117	115	138	123	138	131
1968	138	122	129	143	158	100	107	159	124	129	133	133	128	168	151	144	178
1969	176	147	174	182	202	116	127	198	173	172	177	175	169	203	208	194	204
1970	229	196	219	236	239	170	184	233	224	216	216	223	208	278	229	231	256
1971	260	222	224	276	263	166	162	339	188	234	250	221	238	368	216	279	292
1972	309	279	255	313	323	204	223	410	225	277	263	274	278	386	259	348	362
1973	384	343	373	431	405	253	299	478	344	387	388	422	407	464	400	439	376
1974	381	327	368	415	357	211	244	526	379	346	380	361	380	504	365	338	368
1975	336	386	282	380	326	255	287	615	271	252	322	294	342	503	293	348	336
1976	360	355	271	405	375	202	265	599	247	266	300	321	346	547	346	375	402
1977	367	391	307	424	385	238	333	603	274	345	301	343	378	552	365	390	400
1978	431	418	406	476	424	273	332	648	326	461	432	403	442	583	403	437	433
1979	480	427	468	522	503	298	374	609	441	459	503	482	465	619	474	510	526
1980	545	558	516	574	533	415	504	754	530	488	531	541	514	668	516	542	541
1981	593	608	607	608	563	392	459	973	528	670	624	513	501	811	532	558	600
1982	580	607	509	666	537	347	497	976	425	552	550	523	530	945	466	583	561
1983	591	595	510	653	601	341	429	1014	359	591	578	512	523	924	517	668	619

Construction, buildings started: total (6)
billion yen, monthly averages

Construction, bâtiments mis en chantier : total (6)
milliards de yens, moyennes mensuelles

	Year	Q.1	Q.2	Q.3	Q.4	JAN	FEB	MAR	APR	MAY	JUN	JUL	AUG	SEP	OCT	NOV	DEC
1964	188	186	199	177	191	207	166	185	195	197	206	168	177	186	197	188	189
1965	188	189	181	179	204	200	202	164	187	168	189	186	162	188	211	218	182
1966	205	163	194	228	236	147	169	174	190	183	210	242	227	217	239	249	220
1967	277	215	270	299	326	207	215	222	280	251	280	278	314	305	320	340	317
1968	357	294	356	370	410	287	295	300	354	353	360	353	368	389	381	413	436
1969	445	346	462	492	480	332	355	350	448	460	479	482	488	505	467	493	481
1970	556	472	556	600	596	457	442	517	564	513	590	603	592	605	584	604	599
1971	608	540	550	658	684	722	398	500	539	513	596	669	640	664	671	708	673
1972	809	659	784	862	932	567	560	851	757	708	888	836	848	904	921	926	948
1973	1221	966	1166	1352	1400	867	884	1145	1208	1107	1183	1315	1297	1444	1397	1366	1438
1974	1136	991	1027	1371	1154	1062	950	960	970	977	1134	1385	1373	1356	1235	1084	1143
1975	1223	1034	1156	1374	1328	865	1081	1157	1193	1111	1165	1462	1376	1284	1360	1168	1455
1976	1367	1164	1336	1558	1412	1131	1131	1230	1324	1253	1430	1706	1549	1419	1402	1337	1498
1977	1481	1292	1468	1649	1513	1265	1178	1434	1535	1393	1476	1680	1773	1495	1538	1488	1512
1978	1652	1409	1718	1750	1731	1250	1375	1602	1743	1482	1929	1961	1680	1610	1699	1732	1761
1979	1862	1436	1932	2168	1911	1209	1356	1744	2103	1723	1969	2267	2144	2093	2005	1841	1886
1980	1903	1633	2060	2066	1854	1436	1493	1969	2270	1837	2072	2230	2027	1940	1915	1737	1911
1981	1874	1562	2281	1888	1763	1258	1623	1805	2211	2566	2066	1836	1896	1932	1767	1668	1854
1982	1848	1517	1960	2049	1866	1303	1478	1771	1997	1805	2077	2119	2055	1973	1943	1891	1765
1983	1805	1529	1829	1961	1902	1374	1559	1654	1900	1623	1963	2052	1903	1929	1951	1922	1834

Net new export orders: (4)(5) machinery (value, 178 corporations)

Commandes nouvelles nettes en provenance de l'étranger : (4)(5) construction mécanique (valeur, 178 sociétés)

Adjusted - Corrigé

billion yen, monthly averages — milliards de yens, moyennes mensuelles

	Year	Q.1	Q.2	Q.3	Q.4	JAN	FEB	MAR	APR	MAY	JUN	JUL	AUG	SEP	OCT	NOV	DEC
1964		24	22	23	25	20	27	24	18	27	22	28	12	30	20	33	23
1965		36	27	29	44	37	44	26	37	19	26	19	41	25	35	36	59
1966		31	49	59	39	26	34	33	39	51	56	54	38	85	45	24	46
1967		43	43	42	51	37	41	52	48	38	42	33	48	45	57	61	36
1968		53	37	60	50	66	29	64	36	40	36	53	73	53	45	49	56
1969		52	63	91	73	54	63	40	49	71	70	78	115	80	59	79	83
1970		97	135	111	163	90	86	114	157	117	130	154	64	116	159	129	200
1971		131	158	108	135	117	180	97	163	180	132	105	103	115	112	217	77
1972		104	95	103	193	100	103	111	90	76	118	120	62	127	185	201	194
1973		228	229	316	297	260	203	222	168	242	277	306	341	300	325	344	222
1974		183	169	147	130	232	180	138	197	164	145	174	152	114	132	111	147
1975		190	182	205	280	148	198	224	176	213	158	126	221	267	237	181	423
1976		250	263	298	228	182	223	346	305	225	259	307	242	345	186	266	232
1977		245	338	260	292	302	183	251	271	284	458	291	274	216	239	324	312
1978		271	204	193	194	236	380	197	218	170	222	197	195	187	149	188	246
1979		234	242	366	377	276	205	220	199	341	185	264	395	439	432	329	368
1980		354	420	315	355	290	323	449	438	486	334	421	314	210	334	411	321
1981		388	401	384	409	469	413	282	447	343	415	354	360	440	498	399	329
1982		417	399	409	324	391	390	471	358	283	556	441	404	383	305	297	369
1983		317	358	379	367	237	358	357	398	366	309	297	355	485	391	347	362

Construction, new orders: residential (83 contractors)

Construction, commandes nouvelles : bâtiments résidentiels (83 entreprises)

billion yen, monthly averages — milliards de yens, moyennes mensuelles

	Year	Q.1	Q.2	Q.3	Q.4	JAN	FEB	MAR	APR	MAY	JUN	JUL	AUG	SEP	OCT	NOV	DEC
1964	11	9	9	14	11	8	7	12	8	8	10	10	13	17	12	10	11
1965	10	8	9	11	11	7	8	10	9	8	10	9	12	11	10	11	13
1966	12	12	9	14	12	7	11	17	7	7	14	10	10	21	12	13	12
1967	16	12	14	20	17	11	8	17	12	14	15	18	20	22	16	18	16
1968	21	19	16	22	26	14	18	25	14	18	15	17	21	27	28	23	26
1969	28	25	23	32	33	16	20	39	21	23	23	25	33	39	30	33	35
1970	38	34	32	44	43	28	30	46	36	24	34	36	44	51	42	43	44
1971	41	43	33	44	46	26	23	80	38	30	33	31	36	65	32	53	53
1972	54	57	42	55	63	32	41	97	43	46	38	44	47	73	41	70	78
1973	89	73	85	110	90	46	65	108	75	84	97	115	87	128	89	104	78
1974	79	71	75	78	69	42	43	130	101	58	67	66	81	85	51	75	81
1975	70	93	57	72	65	53	49	178	71	43	56	58	60	100	55	57	82
1976	71	87	47	86	68	37	46	178	53	42	45	47	82	129	63	63	78
1977	74	84	54	82	80	58	51	142	50	65	48	57	75	114	83	80	76
1978	88	89	76	94	92	65	66	135	64	82	81	63	99	120	97	82	97
1979	94	88	86	95	106	59	64	143	68	90	100	80	84	121	112	98	109
1980	120	148	119	104	109	86	99	258	131	111	114	85	95	133	110	93	123
1981	118	146	114	107	106	68	87	284	125	130	97	100	79	141	113	110	94
1982	121	140	91	144	108	58	108	254	94	99	80	78	84	269	95	123	104
1983	106	125	88	108	105	74	71	229	69	88	107	84	84	155	95	106	113

Construction, buildings started: total

Construction, bâtiments mis en chantier : total

Adjusted - Corrigé

billion yen, monthly averages — milliards de yens, moyennes mensuelles

	Year	Q.1	Q.2	Q.3	Q.4	JAN	FEB	MAR	APR	MAY	JUN	JUL	AUG	SEP	OCT	NOV	DEC
1964		198	199	176	182	212	176	207	192	207	197	165	180	182	184	178	185
1965		202	181	177	193	207	214	184	184	176	181	181	164	184	196	202	180
1966		178	193	223	223	159	182	194	185	191	203	234	225	212	224	229	218
1967		238	267	289	310	229	236	248	271	260	270	269	305	294	304	312	313
1968		328	351	355	393	319	334	330	343	362	347	338	354	371	368	383	428
1969		387	455	467	463	364	418	380	436	473	457	458	465	477	455	465	470
1970		525	551	568	572	487	536	551	553	538	563	570	567	567	561	566	588
1971		608	553	610	656	825	473	526	532	555	573	617	605	608	639	671	658
1972		737	797	790	894	652	675	886	754	772	866	755	791	823	867	893	923
1973		1090	1198	1222	1352	1003	1075	1192	1214	1214	1165	1161	1191	1313	1308	1351	1396
1974		1131	1057	1227	1122	1236	1159	998	975	1068	1126	1199	1239	1244	1160	1098	1109
1975		1177	1186	1221	1305	1013	1316	1203	1191	1211	1156	1241	1223	1199	1291	1210	1415
1976		1329	1355	1383	1403	1337	1376	1275	1295	1357	1412	1429	1368	1351	1343	1402	1463
1977		1480	1464	1473	1516	1525	1438	1477	1458	1499	1434	1402	1573	1445	1489	1572	1488
1978		1621	1675	1580	1744	1539	1689	1634	1598	1578	1848	1649	1509	1582	1654	1833	1746
1979		1653	1854	1963	1933	1523	1673	1765	1877	1826	1858	1917	1954	2020	1969	1956	1874
1980		1893	1956	1852	1380	1842	1850	1987	1990	1939	1938	1827	1871	1858	1887	1853	1900
1981		1822	2183	1723	1792	1630	2016	1820	1920	2706	1924	1559	1763	1847	1753	1772	1852
1982		1784	1825	1876	1830	1751	1323	1778	1733	1853	1890	1836	1915	1878	1906	1947	1783
1983		1798	1715	1805	1915	1844	1866	1685	1697	1680	1770	1785	1792	1838	1915	1971	1860

Construction: housing starts / Construction : logements mis en chantier

thousands, monthly averages / milliers, moyennes mensuelles

	Year	Q.1	Q.2	Q.3	Q.4	JAN	FEB	MAR	APR	MAY	JUN	JUL	AUG	SEP	OCT	NOV	DEC
1964	62.6	55.0	63.1	65.6	66.9	50.2	58.4	56.3	61.3	62.3	65.7	66.6	64.6	65.7	73.1	67.1	60.4
1965	70.2	59.4	70.2	72.3	79.1	54.8	62.1	61.2	72.9	64.4	73.2	74.5	69.6	72.8	84.2	83.5	69.5
1966	71.4	60.2	72.3	77.6	75.5	54.3	62.4	63.9	69.3	67.6	79.8	84.6	74.5	73.6	77.4	82.2	66.8
1967	82.6	68.5	82.0	89.3	90.6	65.2	64.6	75.7	89.1	76.7	80.3	85.9	94.2	87.7	38.4	95.5	87.8
1968	100.1	85.4	101.7	104.3	109.2	82.1	85.2	88.9	104.1	99.8	101.1	97.3	102.3	113.2	107.7	114.3	105.7
1969	112.2	89.3	115.8	128.3	115.4	86.0	89.3	92.7	111.1	106.9	129.4	128.7	127.5	128.7	112.6	117.6	116.0
1970	123.7	109.7	128.6	133.1	123.4	100.2	108.1	120.8	129.1	117.7	139.1	139.4	136.0	123.9	119.6	125.2	125.4
1971	122.0	111.8	115.9	132.8	127.4	128.2	90.8	116.5	114.9	111.8	121.0	138.0	131.2	129.2	131.6	125.5	125.0
1972	150.6	134.3	144.7	157.6	165.5	102.4	106.6	195.3	139.6	139.1	155.5	159.4	153.4	160.0	162.6	166.8	167.0
1973	158.8	153.2	159.5	165.7	156.6	142.4	141.5	175.6	170.2	151.9	156.5	165.0	159.0	173.1	160.7	154.2	155.0
1974	109.7	105.9	101.7	131.4	99.7	107.3	103.2	107.1	99.0	99.9	106.2	138.7	134.2	121.4	107.0	95.5	96.5
1975	113.0	87.6	111.5	128.0	124.9	70.5	82.6	109.7	114.7	105.2	114.7	141.4	128.9	113.8	120.6	109.5	144.7
1976	127.0	111.4	130.0	139.5	127.1	107.0	107.5	119.8	131.0	122.0	137.0	158.0	138.6	121.8	124.1	117.7	139.4
1977	125.7	113.6	126.4	135.3	127.4	116.5	106.0	118.4	143.7	116.6	118.8	139.6	145.7	120.7	121.5	128.0	132.7
1978	129.1	121.5	136.8	125.7	132.4	109.5	117.9	137.2	139.7	115.1	155.6	151.7	116.2	109.3	124.0	140.0	133.1
1979	124.4	104.5	138.5	138.2	116.5	85.6	97.3	130.7	156.2	117.1	142.2	158.4	133.9	122.2	118.0	114.3	117.1
1980	105.7	102.4	120.9	105.6	93.9	89.5	94.5	123.3	139.9	106.1	116.6	116.6	102.9	97.4	94.1	88.4	99.3
1981	96.0	84.2	115.9	94.1	89.7	67.7	87.6	97.2	119.6	119.3	108.9	97.2	93.1	92.0	88.0	86.6	94.5
1982	95.5	81.2	102.0	100.2	98.6	66.2	79.4	97.9	106.1	93.0	106.9	104.7	97.7	98.3	101.0	98.4	96.5
1983	94.7	84.8	97.1	97.3	99.7	79.9	83.5	91.1	102.0	82.6	106.7	101.2	96.0	94.7	99.0	96.9	103.1

Retail sales: value (7) / Ventes au détail : valeur (7)

1980 = 100

	Year	Q.1	Q.2	Q.3	Q.4	JAN	FEB	MAR	APR	MAY	JUN	JUL	AUG	SEP	OCT	NOV	DEC
1964	14	13	14	14	16	12	12	14	14	14	13	15	14	14	14	14	20
1965	16	14	15	15	18	13	13	15	15	15	15	16	15	15	16	16	23
1966	18	15	17	17	21	14	14	17	17	17	17	18	17	17	18	18	26
1967	20	17	19	20	24	16	16	20	19	19	19	21	20	20	21	21	30
1968	23	20	22	23	27	19	19	23	23	22	22	24	23	23	23	24	34
1969	26	22	25	26	31	21	20	25	25	25	25	27	25	25	27	27	39
1970	29	25	28	29	34	24	23	28	28	27	28	31	29	28	30	30	43
1971	34	30	33	34	39	28	28	33	33	33	33	36	33	33	35	35	48
1972	37	31	34	37	44	30	29	34	34	34	35	39	36	36	38	39	55
1973	47	39	44	47	56	36	36	45	44	43	44	49	45	46	49	51	69
1974	55	46	51	56	68	45	42	50	49	51	53	58	54	57	58	60	85
1975	66	57	64	66	76	53	52	65	65	64	64	70	65	62	68	67	93
1976	70	62	67	69	82	59	59	68	67	67	68	73	69	66	72	73	100
1977	78	69	76	78	89	66	64	77	77	75	75	83	78	74	79	79	109
1978	85	74	83	85	97	70	69	84	85	82	83	92	82	81	86	86	117
1979	93	82	90	92	106	80	76	90	90	90	90	97	91	89	93	96	128
1980	100	92	100	97	111	88	88	101	103	99	97	102	95	94	99	101	133
1981	102	95	100	100	112	92	88	105	104	99	97	107	97	95	100	101	135
1982	100	94	99	97	111	92	86	103	100	99	97	102	96	94	100	100	133
1983	100	92	98	99	111	91	85	101	101	98	95	104	99	94	101	100	132

Wholesale sales (7) / Ventes du commerce de gros (7)

1980 = 100

	Year	Q.1	Q.2	Q.3	Q.4	JAN	FEB	MAR	APR	MAY	JUN	JUL	AUG	SEP	OCT	NOV	DEC
1964	10	9	10	11	11	8	9	10	9	10	10	10	10	11	11	11	12
1965	11	11	11	12	13	10	10	12	11	11	11	11	11	12	12	12	14
1966	13	12	13	14	14	11	12	14	13	13	13	13	13	14	14	14	15
1967	15	14	14	15	16	12	13	15	14	14	15	15	15	16	15	16	18
1968	17	15	17	18	20	14	15	18	16	17	17	17	17	19	18	20	22
1969	23	20	22	24	26	18	19	23	21	22	23	23	23	26	24	25	28
1970	28	26	27	29	29	23	24	29	26	27	28	28	27	30	27	28	32
1971	29	27	28	30	32	25	25	32	27	28	29	30	28	33	29	31	34
1972	34	31	33	36	38	28	30	37	31	33	34	34	34	39	35	37	42
1973	45	40	41	47	54	34	38	47	39	41	43	45	44	53	49	52	60
1974	57	54	54	60	61	49	51	61	51	55	56	58	56	67	57	61	66
1975	61	57	58	64	66	51	54	67	56	58	60	61	59	72	63	64	72
1976	70	67	67	73	75	57	61	81	65	66	70	71	68	80	70	74	80
1977	74	72	71	75	77	63	66	86	70	70	72	72	71	83	71	76	83
1978	78	75	75	80	82	65	69	91	72	75	77	77	76	86	77	81	87
1979	87	79	83	89	96	70	74	94	79	84	85	87	84	98	88	95	105
1980	100	100	99	101	101	87	95	116	99	100	98	98	92	113	96	97	109
1981	102	99	97	106	108	87	90	120	95	96	100	102	96	120	101	107	115
1982	106	106	101	109	109	91	97	131	100	100	103	104	98	124	101	108	118
1983	105	105	100	108	108	91	96	129	97	100	102	101	100	125	101	107	118

Retail sales: volume

1980 = 100

Adjusted - Corrigé

Ventes au détail : volume

1980 = 100

	Year	Q.1	Q.2	Q.3	Q.4	JAN	FEB	MAR	APR	MAY	JUN	JUL	AUG	SEP	OCT	NOV	DEC
1964	34	33	34	35	35	32	35	33	33	34	34	35	36	36	34	35	34
1965	36	36	36	37	36	36	36	36	36	37	36	36	38	37	37	36	36
1966	40	38	39	40	41	38	38	38	39	39	39	40	40	41	41	41	41
1967	45	42	44	46	47	42	43	43	44	44	44	45	46	47	47	47	46
1968	50	49	49	51	51	48	49	50	49	48	51	50	52	53	52	51	52
1969	57	53	56	59	60	53	53	54	55	56	57	58	60	60	59	62	60
1970	65	62	64	68	67	62	62	63	63	66	65	67	68	68	66	69	65
1971	72	69	70	74	74	71	69	66	69	70	70	73	73	77	75	74	72
1972	80	77	78	82	84	78	78	74	78	78	80	81	81	83	85	84	83
1973	91	89	90	92	92	87	90	91	92	90	89	92	92	93	94	93	91
1974	89	88	88	91	88	89	87	88	87	88	90	89	91	92	87	88	89
1975	91	90	91	92	92	90	89	92	90	90	93	91	94	91	92	93	93
1976	92	93	92	92	91	91	97	93	93	93	91	91	94	90	92	91	91
1977	93	92	92	94	94	93	93	92	92	92	91	93	96	92	93	93	94
1978	97	95	96	98	100	94	96	96	96	95	96	97	98	98	100	99	100
1979	101	101	101	101	100	99	102	102	102	100	100	100	102	101	99	100	101
1980	100	104	98	99	99	103	105	103	99	98	98	97	101	98	99	99	99
1981	102	101	101	103	101	100	102	102	102	102	100	102	104	102	101	102	101
1982	103	104	103	103	101	104	104	103	103	102	102	103	105	101	102	101	101
1983	104	103	103	105	104	103	103	102	104	103	101	106	107	103	106	103	103

Retail sales: value (7)

1980 = 100

Adjusted - Corrigé

Ventes au détail : valeur (7)

1980 = 100

	Year	Q.1	Q.2	Q.3	Q.4	JAN	FEB	MAR	APR	MAY	JUN	JUL	AUG	SEP	OCT	NOV	DEC
1964		14	14	15	15	13	14	14	14	14	14	14	15	15	14	15	15
1965		15	15	16	16	15	15	15	15	15	16	16	16	16	16	16	16
1966		16	17	18	19	16	16	17	17	17	17	18	18	18	18	19	19
1967		19	20	21	21	18	19	19	19	20	20	21	21	21	21	21	22
1968		22	23	24	24	22	22	22	23	23	23	23	23	24	24	24	24
1969		24	25	26	27	24	24	24	25	25	26	26	26	26	27	27	28
1970		27	28	30	30	27	27	28	28	28	29	29	30	30	30	31	31
1971		32	34	35	35	32	33	32	33	34	34	34	34	35	36	35	35
1972		35	35	37	39	34	35	35	35	35	36	37	37	37	38	39	39
1973		43	45	48	50	41	43	44	45	45	46	47	47	48	49	50	50
1974		50	52	57	60	51	50	50	50	53	54	56	57	60	58	60	61
1975		63	66	66	67	61	62	65	66	66	66	66	67	66	67	67	67
1976		68	68	71	74	68	70	67	67	69	69	69	71	71	73	75	75
1977		75	77	79	80	75	75	76	76	77	77	78	80	79	80	80	81
1978		81	84	86	87	79	81	83	83	83	85	86	85	87	87	87	88
1979		89	91	94	96	89	88	89	89	91	92	92	95	95	94	97	97
1980		100	101	99	101	98	102	99	101	101	100	97	99	100	101	102	100
1981		102	101	102	102	102	101	103	102	101	101	102	102	101	102	101	102
1982		101	100	100	100	101	100	100	99	101	100	99	100	100	101	100	100
1983		99	99	102	100	100	99	98	101	100	98	101	103	100	102	100	99

Wholesale sales (7)

1980 = 100

Adjusted - Corrigé

Ventes du commerce de gros (7)

1980 = 100

	Year	Q.1	Q.2	Q.3	Q.4	JAN	FEB	MAR	APR	MAY	JUN	JUL	AUG	SEP	OCT	NOV	DEC
1964		9	10	10	11	9	9	9	10	10	10	10	10	11	11	11	11
1965		11	11	12	12	11	11	11	11	11	11	11	12	12	12	12	12
1966		13	13	14	14	13	13	13	13	13	14	14	14	14	14	14	14
1967		14	15	15	16	14	14	14	14	15	15	15	15	15	15	16	16
1968		16	17	18	19	15	16	17	16	17	17	17	17	18	18	19	20
1969		20	22	24	25	20	21	21	21	22	23	23	24	24	24	24	25
1970		27	27	28	28	26	27	27	27	27	28	28	28	28	27	28	28
1971		28	28	30	30	28	28	29	28	28	29	29	29	30	30	31	31
1972		32	33	35	37	31	32	33	32	33	34	34	35	36	36	37	38
1973		40	43	46	51	39	40	41	42	43	44	45	47	48	50	51	53
1974		55	57	59	59	56	55	54	55	58	57	58	59	60	59	60	59
1975		58	61	63	64	58	58	58	60	61	61	62	62	64	64	63	65
1976		68	69	71	73	67	67	70	69	69	70	71	71	72	73	74	73
1977		73	73	74	75	73	73	73	73	72	73	73	74	75	74	75	75
1978		76	77	78	80	75	76	78	76	77	78	78	78	78	80	80	79
1979		80	85	88	94	80	81	80	82	86	86	88	89	88	91	94	95
1980		101	102	100	98	100	104	99	104	103	99	99	99	100	99	96	99
1981		99	100	104	105	99	98	101	100	99	102	103	104	106	105	106	105
1982		106	106	106	106	105	106	108	106	105	106	106	106	107	106	107	107
1983		106	104	106	106	105	105	106	102	105	104	103	108	108	106	105	107

Employment: manufacturing (8)
(regular workers)
1980 = 100

Emploi : industries manufacturières (8)
(travailleurs réguliers)
1980 = 100

	Year	Q.1	Q.2	Q.3	Q.4	JAN	FEB	MAR	APR	MAY	JUN	JUL	AUG	SEP	OCT	NOV	DEC
1964	94.3	91.0	96.0	95.3	94.9	90.7	90.6	91.8	96.1	96.0	95.9	95.9	95.2	94.8	94.6	95.1	95.1
1965	96.4	94.4	98.4	96.8	96.0	94.5	93.8	94.8	98.9	98.4	98.0	97.5	96.8	96.2	95.9	96.0	96.0
1966	96.9	95.2	98.4	97.3	96.9	95.2	94.6	95.7	98.9	98.2	98.2	97.8	97.3	96.3	96.6	96.9	97.1
1967	100.1	97.1	101.3	100.7	101.1	96.6	96.6	98.2	101.6	101.1	101.1	101.1	100.7	100.4	100.5	101.3	101.6
1968	104.2	101.3	105.5	104.8	105.3	101.0	100.8	102.0	105.9	105.3	105.2	105.2	104.5	104.6	104.5	105.5	105.8
1969	108.0	105.3	109.5	108.6	108.6	105.2	104.8	105.9	109.3	109.4	109.3	109.2	108.3	108.2	108.1	108.8	109.0
1970	112.1	109.2	113.6	112.8	112.9	108.7	108.8	110.0	113.8	113.5	113.5	113.5	112.6	112.4	112.3	113.1	113.2
1971	112.9	111.9	114.5	113.1	112.0	112.2	111.6	111.9	115.1	114.4	114.1	113.7	113.1	112.4	112.0	112.1	111.8
1972	110.7	110.2	111.8	110.6	110.2	110.6	110.0	109.9	112.2	111.7	111.5	111.3	110.4	110.0	110.0	110.3	110.4
1973	111.0	109.9	111.9	111.1	111.3	109.9	109.7	110.0	112.1	111.8	111.8	111.7	110.9	110.7	110.8	111.6	111.5
1974	110.5	110.4	112.4	110.6	108.9	110.5	110.2	110.4	113.0	112.3	111.9	111.4	110.3	110.0	109.5	108.9	108.2
1975	104.8	105.6	105.5	104.4	103.7	106.6	105.5	104.6	105.9	105.3	105.2	104.7	104.3	104.1	103.7	103.8	103.6
1976	102.7	102.4	103.2	102.6	102.5	102.8	102.2	102.1	103.5	103.1	103.0	102.9	102.5	102.4	102.3	102.6	102.5
1977	101.7	101.6	102.9	101.7	100.7	101.9	101.6	101.4	103.2	102.9	102.7	102.3	101.7	101.1	100.9	100.7	100.4
1978	99.4	99.4	100.4	99.3	98.7	99.7	99.2	99.2	100.7	100.3	100.1	99.7	99.3	99.0	98.7	98.8	98.7
1979	99.0	98.1	99.8	99.2	98.9	98.2	98.0	98.2	99.8	99.8	99.7	99.6	99.0	98.9	98.9	99.0	98.8
1980	100.0	98.4	100.9	100.5	100.2	98.3	98.2	98.7	101.0	100.9	100.9	100.7	100.5	100.3	100.2	100.3	100.1
1981	101.1	99.4	102.2	101.6	101.2	99.4	99.2	99.5	102.3	102.1	102.3	102.0	101.5	101.4	101.2	101.3	101.0
1982	101.8	100.3	103.1	102.2	101.6	100.4	100.2	100.3	103.2	103.1	102.9	102.7	102.1	101.9	101.7	101.7	101.3
1983	101.7	100.5	102.7	102.0	101.6	100.7	100.4	100.4	103.0	102.7	102.5	102.2	101.9	101.8	101.7	101.7	101.5

Unemployment (9)
millions

Chômage (9)
millions

	Year	Q.1	Q.2	Q.3	Q.4	JAN	FEB	MAR	APR	MAY	JUN	JUL	AUG	SEP	OCT	NOV	DEC
1964	0.55	0.71	0.51	0.51	0.46	0.63	0.68	0.82	0.56	0.48	0.49	0.52	0.53	0.47	0.43	0.46	0.49
1965	0.58	0.66	0.57	0.56	0.54	0.59	0.63	0.75	0.60	0.52	0.58	0.57	0.56	0.56	0.51	0.53	0.58
1966	0.64	0.82	0.61	0.58	0.54	0.76	0.71	1.00	0.62	0.63	0.57	0.54	0.60	0.61	0.54	0.55	0.54
1967	0.63	0.83	0.59	0.55	0.55	0.69	0.64	1.15	0.64	0.54	0.59	0.56	0.57	0.51	0.51	0.57	0.56
1968	0.59	0.77	0.57	0.57	0.47	0.72	0.75	0.83	0.64	0.54	0.52	0.60	0.59	0.53	0.47	0.45	0.48
1969	0.58	0.69	0.59	0.55	0.47	0.64	0.69	0.75	0.60	0.58	0.59	0.58	0.54	0.53	0.48	0.45	0.48
1970	0.59	0.65	0.56	0.59	0.57	0.63	0.66	0.67	0.64	0.53	0.50	0.57	0.59	0.62	0.61	0.56	0.54
1971	0.64	0.73	0.62	0.60	0.61	0.66	0.72	0.80	0.68	0.60	0.57	0.60	0.64	0.57	0.59	0.60	0.64
1972	0.73	0.87	0.70	0.71	0.64	0.85	0.84	0.93	0.78	0.69	0.64	0.67	0.70	0.77	0.64	0.63	0.66
1973	0.67	0.80	0.71	0.63	0.55	0.80	0.78	0.82	0.75	0.69	0.68	0.63	0.61	0.64	0.54	0.56	0.55
1974	0.74	0.83	0.66	0.69	0.77	0.74	0.84	0.91	0.70	0.64	0.63	0.61	0.75	0.70	0.76	0.71	0.84
1975	1.00	1.07	0.95	0.94	1.03	1.00	1.09	1.13	0.99	0.92	0.93	0.88	0.95	1.00	1.04	0.99	1.06
1976	1.08	1.26	1.08	1.01	0.96	1.25	1.26	1.26	1.14	1.07	1.04	0.99	1.03	1.01	1.00	0.97	0.92
1977	1.10	1.21	1.09	1.05	1.05	1.14	1.22	1.27	1.06	1.09	1.11	1.05	1.06	1.05	1.00	1.03	1.11
1978	1.24	1.34	1.24	1.20	1.16	1.26	1.36	1.41	1.23	1.23	1.26	1.15	1.21	1.25	1.17	1.16	1.16
1979	1.17	1.28	1.15	1.14	1.10	1.27	1.21	1.35	1.24	1.11	1.11	1.16	1.18	1.08	1.11	1.11	1.07
1980	1.14	1.16	1.11	1.12	1.17	1.13	1.11	1.24	1.18	1.09	1.05	1.12	1.15	1.09	1.13	1.21	1.18
1981	1.26	1.33	1.32	1.19	1.20	1.23	1.35	1.42	1.37	1.32	1.26	1.21	1.15	1.20	1.22	1.19	1.19
1982	1.36	1.38	1.38	1.32	1.36	1.31	1.35	1.47	1.43	1.34	1.37	1.32	1.30	1.34	1.39	1.34	1.35
1983	1.56	1.66	1.59	1.53	1.46	1.62	1.65	1.72	1.70	1.58	1.48	1.44	1.58	1.57	1.49	1.47	1.43

Unemployment (9)
as per cent of total labour force

Chômage (9)
en pourcentage de la population active

	Year	Q.1	Q.2	Q.3	Q.4	JAN	FEB	MAR	APR	MAY	JUN	JUL	AUG	SEP	OCT	NOV	DEC
1964	1.2	1.6	1.1	1.1	1.0	1.4	1.5	1.8	1.2	1.0	1.0	1.1	1.1	1.0	0.9	1.0	1.1
1965	1.2	1.4	1.2	1.2	1.1	1.3	1.4	1.6	1.3	1.1	1.2	1.2	1.2	1.1	1.0	1.1	1.2
1966	1.3	1.8	1.2	1.2	1.1	1.7	1.5	2.1	1.3	1.3	1.1	1.1	1.2	1.2	1.1	1.1	1.1
1967	1.3	1.7	1.2	1.1	1.1	1.5	1.4	2.3	1.3	1.1	1.1	1.1	1.1	1.0	1.0	1.1	1.1
1968	1.2	1.6	1.1	1.1	0.9	1.5	1.6	1.7	1.3	1.0	1.0	1.2	1.1	1.0	0.9	0.9	1.0
1969	1.1	1.4	1.1	1.1	0.9	1.3	1.4	1.5	1.2	1.1	1.1	1.1	1.0	1.0	0.9	0.9	1.0
1970	1.1	1.3	1.1	1.1	1.1	1.3	1.3	1.3	1.2	1.0	1.0	1.1	1.1	1.2	1.2	1.1	1.1
1971	1.2	1.4	1.2	1.2	1.2	1.3	1.5	1.6	1.3	1.1	1.1	1.1	1.2	1.1	1.1	1.2	1.3
1972	1.4	1.7	1.3	1.4	1.2	1.7	1.7	1.8	1.5	1.3	1.2	1.3	1.3	1.5	1.2	1.2	1.3
1973	1.3	1.5	1.3	1.2	1.0	1.6	1.5	1.6	1.4	1.3	1.3	1.2	1.1	1.2	1.0	1.0	1.1
1974	1.4	1.6	1.2	1.3	1.4	1.4	1.6	1.7	1.3	1.2	1.1	1.1	1.4	1.3	1.4	1.3	1.6
1975	1.9	2.1	1.8	1.8	1.9	2.0	2.1	2.2	1.9	1.7	1.7	1.6	1.8	1.9	1.9	1.9	2.0
1976	2.0	2.4	2.0	1.9	1.8	2.4	2.4	2.4	2.1	2.0	1.9	1.8	1.9	1.9	1.8	1.8	1.7
1977	2.0	2.3	2.0	1.9	1.9	2.2	2.3	2.4	1.9	2.0	2.0	1.9	1.9	1.9	1.8	1.9	2.1
1978	2.2	2.5	2.2	2.2	2.1	2.4	2.5	2.6	2.2	2.2	2.2	2.1	2.2	2.2	2.1	2.1	2.1
1979	2.1	2.3	2.0	2.0	2.0	2.3	2.2	2.5	2.2	2.0	1.9	2.0	2.1	1.9	2.0	2.0	1.9
1980	2.0	2.1	1.9	1.9	2.1	2.1	2.0	2.2	2.1	1.9	1.8	1.9	2.0	1.9	2.0	2.1	2.1
1981	2.2	2.4	2.3	2.1	2.1	2.2	2.4	2.5	2.4	2.3	2.2	2.1	2.0	2.1	2.1	2.1	2.1
1982	2.4	2.4	2.4	2.3	2.3	2.3	2.4	2.6	2.5	2.3	2.3	2.3	2.2	2.3	2.4	2.3	2.3
1983	2.7	2.9	2.7	2.6	2.5	2.8	2.9	3.0	2.9	2.6	2.5	2.4	2.7	2.6	2.5	2.5	2.5

Employment: manufacturing (8) / Emploi : industries manufacturières (8)

(regular workers) / (travailleurs réguliers)

1980 = 100

Adjusted - Corrigé

Year	Q.1	Q.2	Q.3	Q.4	JAN	FEB	MAR	APR	MAY	JUN	JUL	AUG	SEP	OCT	NOV	DEC
1964	92.7	94.0	95.0	95.7	92.4	92.8	92.9	93.6	94.0	94.3	94.9	94.9	95.1	95.4	95.7	95.9
1965	96.0	96.5	96.5	96.7	96.1	95.9	95.9	96.4	96.5	96.5	96.5	96.5	96.6	96.7	96.6	96.7
1966	96.7	96.5	97.0	97.5	96.7	96.6	96.8	96.4	96.4	96.8	96.8	97.1	97.2	97.4	97.4	97.7
1967	98.6	99.4	100.6	101.7	98.0	98.5	99.2	99.2	99.3	99.7	100.2	100.6	100.9	101.3	101.8	102.1
1968	102.7	103.7	104.6	105.8	102.4	102.6	103.0	103.5	103.6	103.9	104.3	104.5	105.1	105.3	105.9	106.2
1969	106.7	107.7	108.5	109.1	106.5	106.6	106.9	107.4	107.8	108.0	108.3	108.4	108.7	108.9	109.1	109.3
1970	110.5	111.9	112.7	113.3	109.9	110.5	111.1	111.5	112.0	112.3	112.6	112.7	112.9	113.0	113.4	113.4
1971	113.2	113.0	113.0	112.3	113.3	113.2	113.0	113.0	113.0	113.0	112.9	113.2	112.8	112.6	112.3	111.9
1972	111.3	110.5	110.5	110.4	111.6	111.4	111.0	110.4	110.6	110.5	110.6	110.5	110.4	110.5	110.4	110.4
1973	111.0	110.8	111.0	111.4	110.8	111.0	111.1	110.5	110.9	111.0	111.0	111.0	111.0	111.2	111.6	111.5
1974	111.4	111.4	110.4	109.0	111.3	111.4	111.5	111.5	111.5	111.2	110.8	110.3	110.2	109.8	108.9	108.2
1975	106.5	104.6	104.2	103.8	107.3	106.6	105.7	104.7	104.6	104.6	104.2	104.3	104.2	103.9	103.8	103.6
1976	103.3	102.4	102.4	102.6	103.5	103.2	103.1	102.4	102.4	102.4	102.4	102.4	102.5	102.5	102.6	102.6
1977	102.5	102.1	101.5	100.8	102.6	102.6	102.4	102.1	102.2	102.0	101.8	101.6	101.1	101.1	100.7	100.5
1978	100.3	99.5	99.1	98.9	100.4	100.2	100.2	99.7	99.5	99.4	99.1	99.1	99.0	98.8	98.9	98.9
1979	99.1	98.9	98.9	99.1	99.0	99.1	99.2	98.8	98.9	98.9	99.0	98.8	98.9	99.1	99.1	99.2
1980	99.4	99.9	100.2	100.4	99.2	99.3	99.7	99.9	99.9	100.0	100.0	100.3	100.3	100.3	100.4	100.4
1981	100.5	101.2	101.3	101.4	100.4	100.5	100.6	101.2	101.1	101.4	101.3	101.3	101.3	101.3	101.4	101.4
1982	101.5	102.0	101.9	101.8	101.5	101.6	101.4	102.1	102.1	101.9	102.0	101.9	101.9	101.9	101.8	101.7
1983	101.7	101.7	101.6	101.9	101.8	101.8	101.5	101.9	101.7	101.5	101.4	101.7	101.8	101.9	101.8	102.0

Unemployment (9) / Chômage (9)

millions

Adjusted - Corrigé

Year	Q.1	Q.2	Q.3	Q.4	JAN	FEB	MAR	APR	MAY	JUN	JUL	AUG	SEP	OCT	NOV	DEC
1964	0.57	0.54	0.55	0.53	0.56	0.59	0.55	0.55	0.53	0.54	0.56	0.57	0.52	0.53	0.53	0.54
1965	0.52	0.60	0.61	0.62	0.53	0.55	0.49	0.59	0.57	0.63	0.62	0.59	0.62	0.62	0.61	0.64
1966	0.65	0.64	0.63	0.63	0.67	0.62	0.66	0.61	0.69	0.62	0.58	0.63	0.67	0.65	0.64	0.61
1967	0.65	0.62	0.59	0.64	0.61	0.56	0.78	0.62	0.59	0.64	0.60	0.60	0.56	0.60	0.67	0.64
1968	0.62	0.58	0.61	0.54	0.64	0.65	0.58	0.61	0.58	0.56	0.63	0.62	0.58	0.55	0.53	0.55
1969	0.57	0.61	0.58	0.54	0.57	0.59	0.55	0.57	0.62	0.65	0.61	0.56	0.57	0.55	0.53	0.55
1970	0.54	0.57	0.62	0.65	0.56	0.56	0.51	0.60	0.56	0.55	0.60	0.61	0.66	0.69	0.65	0.61
1971	0.61	0.63	0.64	0.69	0.58	0.61	0.63	0.63	0.63	0.63	0.64	0.67	0.60	0.66	0.70	0.72
1972	0.73	0.71	0.76	0.73	0.75	0.71	0.74	0.72	0.72	0.70	0.73	0.73	0.81	0.72	0.73	0.73
1973	0.67	0.72	0.67	0.61	0.71	0.66	0.65	0.70	0.72	0.74	0.70	0.64	0.67	0.60	0.64	0.60
1974	0.70	0.67	0.73	0.85	0.66	0.71	0.73	0.67	0.67	0.67	0.68	0.79	0.73	0.83	0.80	0.91
1975	0.92	0.96	1.01	1.12	0.89	0.93	0.93	0.96	0.95	0.98	0.98	1.00	1.05	1.12	1.10	1.14
1976	1.09	1.10	1.07	1.04	1.13	1.09	1.05	1.11	1.10	1.08	1.09	1.07	1.06	1.07	1.06	0.98
1977	1.07	1.10	1.11	1.11	1.04	1.08	1.08	1.04	1.12	1.15	1.13	1.09	1.10	1.06	1.10	1.17
1978	1.21	1.25	1.26	1.23	1.17	1.24	1.22	1.20	1.26	1.30	1.22	1.24	1.31	1.24	1.22	1.22
1979	1.16	1.17	1.18	1.15	1.19	1.12	1.17	1.21	1.14	1.15	1.21	1.20	1.13	1.18	1.16	1.12
1980	1.06	1.12	1.16	1.23	1.07	1.04	1.08	1.15	1.12	1.08	1.16	1.17	1.14	1.20	1.26	1.23
1981	1.23	1.33	1.23	1.24	1.17	1.27	1.24	1.33	1.36	1.30	1.24	1.18	1.26	1.27	1.22	1.24
1982	1.30	1.36	1.38	1.44	1.29	1.30	1.30	1.33	1.34	1.40	1.38	1.35	1.40	1.45	1.42	1.45
1983	1.56	1.54	1.61	1.50	1.58	1.56	1.53	1.56	1.55	1.51	1.51	1.65	1.66	1.54	1.52	1.43

Unemployment (9) / Chômage (9)

as per cent of total labour force / en pourcentage de la population active

Adjusted - Corrigé

Year	Q.1	Q.2	Q.3	Q.4	JAN	FEB	MAR	APR	MAY	JUN	JUL	AUG	SEP	OCT	NOV	DEC
1964	1.2	1.2	1.2	1.1	1.2	1.3	1.2	1.2	1.1	1.2	1.2	1.2	1.1	1.1	1.1	1.1
1965	1.1	1.3	1.3	1.3	1.1	1.2	1.1	1.2	1.2	1.3	1.3	1.2	1.3	1.3	1.3	1.3
1966	1.3	1.3	1.3	1.3	1.4	1.3	1.4	1.3	1.4	1.3	1.2	1.3	1.4	1.3	1.3	1.2
1967	1.3	1.2	1.2	1.3	1.2	1.1	1.6	1.3	1.2	1.3	1.2	1.2	1.1	1.2	1.3	1.3
1968	1.2	1.2	1.2	1.1	1.3	1.3	1.2	1.2	1.2	1.1	1.3	1.2	1.1	1.1	1.0	1.1
1969	1.1	1.2	1.1	1.1	1.1	1.2	1.1	1.1	1.2	1.3	1.2	1.1	1.1	1.1	1.0	1.1
1970	1.1	1.1	1.2	1.3	1.1	1.1	1.0	1.2	1.1	1.1	1.2	1.2	1.3	1.3	1.3	1.2
1971	1.2	1.2	1.2	1.3	1.1	1.2	1.2	1.2	1.2	1.2	1.2	1.3	1.2	1.3	1.3	1.4
1972	1.4	1.4	1.5	1.4	1.5	1.4	1.4	1.4	1.4	1.4	1.4	1.4	1.5	1.4	1.4	1.4
1973	1.3	1.4	1.3	1.2	1.3	1.2	1.2	1.3	1.4	1.4	1.3	1.2	1.3	1.1	1.2	1.1
1974	1.3	1.3	1.4	1.6	1.2	1.3	1.4	1.3	1.3	1.3	1.3	1.5	1.4	1.6	1.5	1.7
1975	1.7	1.8	1.9	2.1	1.7	1.8	1.8	1.3	1.8	1.8	1.8	1.9	2.0	2.1	2.1	2.1
1976	2.0	2.1	2.0	1.9	2.1	2.0	2.0	2.1	2.1	2.0	2.0	2.0	2.0	2.0	2.0	1.8
1977	2.0	2.0	2.0	2.0	1.9	2.0	2.0	1.9	2.1	2.1	2.1	2.0	2.0	1.9	2.0	2.1
1978	2.2	2.3	2.3	2.2	2.1	2.2	2.2	2.2	2.3	2.3	2.2	2.3	2.4	2.2	2.2	2.2
1979	2.1	2.1	2.1	2.1	2.1	2.0	2.1	2.2	2.0	2.1	2.2	2.1	2.0	2.1	2.1	2.0
1980	1.9	2.0	2.0	2.2	1.9	1.9	1.9	2.0	2.0	1.9	2.1	2.1	2.0	2.1	2.2	2.2
1981	2.2	2.3	2.2	2.2	2.1	2.3	2.2	2.3	2.4	2.3	2.2	2.1	2.2	2.2	2.1	2.2
1982	2.3	2.4	2.4	2.4	2.3	2.3	2.3	2.3	2.3	2.4	2.4	2.4	2.5	2.5	2.4	2.4
1983	2.6	2.6	2.7	2.6	2.7	2.7	2.6	2.7	2.6	2.6	2.6	2.8	2.8	2.6	2.6	2.6

JAPAN

Unemployment insurance beneficiaries (10) — Bénéficiaires de l'assurance chômage (10)

thousands — milliers

	Year	Q.1	Q.2	Q.3	Q.4	JAN	FEB	MAR	APR	MAY	JUN	JUL	AUG	SEP	OCT	NOV	DEC
1964	625	847	656	545	452	798	849	894	806	585	578	579	546	510	472	434	451
1965	592	798	613	509	446	721	809	864	788	535	516	526	514	487	457	436	446
1966	583	793	614	503	422	714	806	860	774	550	519	519	512	479	435	413	418
1967	556	777	587	471	389	702	787	841	746	526	488	486	483	443	410	376	380
1968	531	727	558	464	375	664	741	776	721	494	460	488	472	433	407	360	359
1969	512	699	537	449	364	650	702	746	693	471	448	472	450	425	393	346	352
1970	491	666	515	431	353	622	671	706	664	446	436	450	430	412	375	336	349
1971	547	695	566	497	429	634	696	755	716	481	501	512	498	482	447	418	422
1972	584	783	612	529	414	729	785	834	747	546	544	543	541	502	451	405	386
1973	527	723	558	466	362	678	717	773	705	494	474	484	477	438	402	351	333
1974	574	699	571	517	510	644	698	754	724	504	484	523	526	502	[illegible]	489	535
1975	870	993	910	863	714	905	988	1087	1049	838	842	886	871	833	[illegible]	683	689
1976	754	991	793	643	588	961	982	1031	974	711	694	676	639	[illegible]	593	580	591
1977	632	572	633	668	655	559	553	603	608	621	670	675	671	658	642	655	669
1978	709	668	738	744	685	649	647	707	696	744	774	760	756	716	690	686	678
1979	658	639	680	682	630	643	617	657	640	690	711	702	695	648	641	629	619
1980	649	587	650	692	664	589	578	595	609	661	681	713	694	669	675	652	666
1981	731	645	747	790	743	640	625	670	705	736	800	820	785	766	750	734	746
1982	811	724	827	873	819	718	698	757	774	815	892	894	878	846	815	824	819
1983	865	791	886	925	857	793	774	807	833	884	940	938	941	896	869	861	841

Jobs vacant, new vacancies (11) — Offres d'emploi nouvelles (11)

thousands — milliers

	Year	Q.1	Q.2	Q.3	Q.4	JAN	FEB	MAR	APR	MAY	JUN	JUL	AUG	SEP	OCT	NOV	DEC
1964	393	451	421	412	290	441	452	461	469	407	387	361	413	461	384	261	224
1965	309	400	321	291	222	380	382	437	378	314	270	253	310	311	299	210	158
1966	361	380	347	404	314	333	372	434	392	337	311	308	441	462	404	310	228
1967	437	488	431	486	341	499	458	508	471	439	382	382	531	546	427	347	248
1968	444	513	431	473	357	541	501	496	482	429	383	402	507	511	451	360	260
1969	493	528	471	536	436	554	507	522	527	468	419	450	547	612	564	416	327
1970	521	615	514	543	413	637	592	617	560	510	472	449	542	638	545	381	314
1971	452	553	444	471	341	556	520	582	502	428	402	398	494	521	423	337	263
1972	517	534	470	570	496	515	520	566	489	472	449	444	625	640	608	471	409
1973	687	784	673	747	542	800	774	778	691	691	638	636	807	799	753	530	343
1974	477	636	483	463	324	628	639	641	560	489	401	415	485	488	447	298	227
1975	338	425	329	346	254	385	405	484	390	318	279	300	347	392	338	231	192
1976	348	409	355	365	264	364	388	476	408	336	320	319	384	393	333	263	195
1977	315	399	303	319	237	367	388	442	357	285	266	260	341	357	308	232	171
1978	331	375	322	356	271	323	351	451	368	306	293	299	380	390	344	268	201
1979	386	429	374	417	322	389	401	498	414	376	333	349	446	455	414	315	237
1980	390	455	392	409	302	430	438	497	454	384	339	364	430	432	380	285	241
1981	372	423	363	405	297	404	396	469	409	347	332	358	442	415	369	279	242
1982	351	410	340	374	278	371	388	472	384	323	312	326	411	384	335	275	225
1983	361	399	337	396	310	358	365	475	356	331	324	333	446	408	368	313	250

Monthly hours of work: manufacturing (8)(12) (regular workers) — Durée mensuelle du travail : industries manufacturières (8)(12) (travailleurs réguliers)

1980 = 100

	Year	Q.1	Q.2	Q.3	Q.4	JAN	FEB	MAR	APR	MAY	JUN	JUL	AUG	SEP	OCT	NOV	DEC
1964	109.7	106.9	111.4	109.8	110.7	97.7	114.4	108.7	113.2	106.4	114.7	110.6	107.1	111.7	109.9	111.8	110.4
1965	107.6	104.9	108.3	108.1	109.0	98.5	111.6	104.7	111.5	102.6	110.8	109.6	105.1	109.7	107.9	110.4	108.7
1966	108.3	104.1	109.6	109.1	110.2	97.4	109.7	105.1	112.2	104.4	112.2	110.4	106.2	110.7	108.6	110.4	111.7
1967	108.7	105.5	109.9	109.1	110.1	99.9	110.3	106.2	112.6	104.5	112.5	110.8	104.4	112.2	109.0	110.4	111.0
1968	108.0	104.8	109.6	108.3	109.4	97.0	110.4	107.1	113.0	103.6	112.2	109.9	103.7	111.3	106.2	112.7	109.4
1969	106.4	102.0	107.9	107.1	108.5	94.0	108.7	103.4	109.6	102.5	111.5	108.5	103.4	109.4	105.6	109.7	110.1
1970	105.1	101.9	107.1	105.1	106.2	93.4	108.5	103.7	109.5	101.4	110.4	107.7	101.4	106.3	105.3	107.5	105.9
1971	103.3	100.9	103.9	103.9	104.6	94.2	106.2	102.2	107.8	97.1	106.8	106.8	99.6	105.2	104.0	105.8	104.1
1972	102.7	99.5	103.8	103.3	104.4	92.7	103.8	102.1	107.1	97.0	107.2	105.9	97.7	106.2	102.3	105.2	105.7
1973	102.1	99.7	103.7	101.7	103.1	92.3	105.8	101.0	106.0	96.8	108.4	104.9	96.2	104.1	101.8	104.4	103.1
1974	97.2	95.0	98.9	97.0	97.8	86.4	102.0	96.7	100.8	92.8	103.0	100.6	91.3	99.2	95.5	100.4	97.6
1975	94.3	89.2	94.6	95.4	97.9	82.0	95.3	90.4	95.4	89.2	99.3	97.8	90.5	97.9	96.2	99.5	98.0
1976	97.6	93.6	98.6	98.3	99.3	84.7	98.8	97.4	101.6	92.5	101.7	102.0	93.6	99.2	98.5	101.5	99.5
1977	97.9	94.4	99.2	98.2	99.9	88.5	98.0	96.7	102.4	93.1	102.2	101.3	93.5	99.7	98.2	100.5	101.0
1978	98.6	94.8	99.8	98.9	101.0	86.5	98.7	97.3	102.3	93.6	103.4	101.8	93.3	101.6	99.3	101.8	101.9
1979	99.7	95.7	101.1	99.8	102.3	88.6	100.5	98.1	103.3	94.6	105.4	103.2	94.1	102.2	100.3	104.3	102.3
1980	100.0	96.9	102.2	99.7	101.3	87.7	103.2	99.7	104.3	97.1	105.2	102.8	94.6	101.6	99.7	102.6	101.6
1981	99.7	96.1	101.2	99.2	102.1	88.8	101.4	98.1	104.0	95.4	104.2	103.2	94.0	100.5	102.2	103.0	101.0
1982	99.3	96.3	100.6	99.1	101.0	90.0	100.1	98.9	103.6	95.0	103.1	103.5	94.0	99.9	100.0	102.5	100.6
1983	99.8	95.8	101.1	100.0	102.3	89.9	98.7	98.7	104.7	94.6	104.1	103.5	94.7	101.7	100.7	102.9	103.3

Jobs vacant, new vacancies (11) / Offres d'emploi nouvelles (11)

thousands / milliers

Adjusted - Corrigé

	Year	Q.1	Q.2	Q.3	Q.4	JAN	FEB	MAR	APR	MAY	JUN	JUL	AUG	SEP	OCT	NOV	DEC
1964		388	404	403	379	407	395	361	399	397	415	393	393	423	388	351	400
1965		338	312	285	289	345	333	334	323	315	297	293	285	277	299	281	286
1966		319	346	384	407	294	327	338	342	340	357	365	390	399	402	407	412
1967		414	438	457	436	423	402	417	422	449	443	445	461	465	423	444	440
1968		442	440	444	446	445	449	432	438	437	445	453	448	432	436	456	446
1969		458	482	504	535	458	455	460	484	483	480	505	493	513	536	531	538
1970		535	529	509	508	539	539	528	518	533	536	506	492	530	519	493	510
1971		477	458	444	428	479	468	484	476	448	449	457	436	437	422	440	422
1972		460	489	532	617	452	463	465	471	493	503	503	546	548	575	613	664
1973		680	699	705	651	717	678	644	664	707	725	716	706	692	694	697	562
1974		556	495	436	393	585	563	521	518	502	464	455	437	416	413	395	384
1975		368	334	327	321	365	360	379	347	331	323	329	318	333	324	307	332
1976		349	361	348	340	341	350	356	357	358	367	357	352	334	328	348	343
1977		326	308	303	304	339	318	321	314	307	302	296	308	307	306	303	303
1978		314	330	338	346	296	320	327	327	328	336	339	338	338	339	348	350
1979		364	384	393	403	360	365	368	372	398	383	385	397	398	407	407	393
1980		393	401	384	376	398	403	378	410	405	388	392	376	383	376	371	381
1981		368	373	377	369	375	368	360	373	369	377	380	380	370	373	363	372
1982		356	351	347	347	344	363	362	353	350	350	346	348	346	343	353	345
1983		346	350	365	387	331	342	364	328	361	361	353	373	369	379	399	383

Monthly hours of work: manufacturing (8)(12) / Durée mensuelle du travail : industries manufacturières (8)(12)

(regular workers) / (travailleurs réguliers)

1980 = 100

Adjusted - Corrigé

	Year	Q.1	Q.2	Q.3	Q.4	JAN	FEB	MAR	APR	MAY	JUN	JUL	AUG	SEP	OCT	NOV	DEC
1964		110.6	110.1	109.2	109.0	107.9	111.6	112.2	109.3	110.5	110.6	109.0	109.6	108.9	109.5	109.5	108.1
1965		108.5	107.0	107.5	107.3	108.9	108.9	107.7	107.6	106.7	106.8	107.8	107.8	106.9	107.5	108.0	106.5
1966		107.7	108.3	108.4	108.5	107.9	107.3	107.8	108.2	108.6	108.2	108.4	109.1	107.8	108.3	107.9	109.4
1967		109.2	108.5	108.5	108.4	110.8	108.0	108.7	108.6	108.7	108.3	108.7	107.5	109.2	108.8	107.8	108.7
1968		108.5	108.3	107.7	107.7	107.8	108.2	109.5	109.0	108.0	107.9	107.6	107.1	108.3	106.0	109.9	107.2
1969		105.5	106.6	106.6	106.7	104.5	106.6	105.5	105.6	107.1	107.1	106.1	107.1	106.5	105.4	106.8	107.9
1970		105.3	105.9	104.6	104.5	103.8	106.4	105.6	105.6	106.4	105.8	105.0	105.3	103.6	105.1	104.5	103.9
1971		104.2	102.8	103.4	102.8	104.7	104.0	104.0	104.0	102.2	102.1	103.9	103.8	102.5	103.7	102.8	101.9
1972		102.9	102.8	102.8	102.5	103.1	101.6	103.9	103.6	102.4	102.3	102.8	102.2	103.4	102.0	102.1	103.4
1973		103.1	102.7	101.3	101.1	102.8	103.6	102.8	102.6	102.3	103.2	101.6	101.0	101.3	101.4	101.2	100.7
1974		98.3	97.9	96.6	95.9	96.4	99.9	98.5	97.7	98.0	98.0	97.2	95.9	96.6	95.1	97.2	95.3
1975		92.4	93.7	95.0	96.0	91.5	93.6	92.1	92.4	94.1	94.5	94.4	95.1	95.5	95.9	96.3	95.7
1976		97.0	97.5	97.9	97.9	94.5	97.2	99.2	98.2	97.5	96.8	98.5	98.4	96.9	98.1	98.3	97.2
1977		97.9	98.0	97.9	98.1	98.7	96.7	98.2	98.7	98.0	97.4	97.8	98.4	97.5	97.9	97.5	98.8
1978		98.3	98.4	98.7	99.2	98.7	97.5	98.6	98.4	98.3	98.6	98.4	98.3	99.5	99.0	98.8	99.7
1979		99.1	99.6	99.8	100.5	98.8	99.3	99.2	99.2	99.2	100.5	99.8	99.4	100.3	100.0	101.2	100.2
1980		100.1	100.7	99.7	99.4	97.8	101.9	100.7	100.1	101.6	100.3	99.4	100.0	99.8	99.3	99.4	99.5
1981		99.4	99.7	99.3	100.2	99.1	100.2	99.0	99.8	99.7	99.5	99.7	99.4	98.9	101.7	99.7	99.1
1982		99.7	99.0	99.3	99.2	100.5	98.8	99.8	99.4	99.2	98.5	99.9	99.4	98.5	99.5	99.2	98.8
1983		99.1	99.6	100.1	100.4	100.4	97.4	99.6	100.5	98.8	99.5	99.9	100.1	100.4	100.2	99.6	101.5

JAPAN

Monthly earnings: manufacturing (8) — Gains mensuels : industries manufacturières (8)
(regular workers) — (travailleurs réguliers)
1980 = 100

	Year	Q.1	Q.2	Q.3	Q.4	JAN	FEB	MAR	APR	MAY	JUN	JUL	AUG	SEP	OCT	NOV	DEC
1964	13.6	10.5	12.4	14.5	17.1	10.6	10.5	10.5	10.8	11.0	15.3	19.7	12.4	11.4	11.6	11.8	27.8
1965	14.8	11.7	13.4	15.7	18.3	12.1	11.6	11.5	11.8	11.8	16.5	21.3	13.6	12.3	12.3	12.6	29.9
1966	16.5	12.7	15.0	17.5	20.3	13.0	12.5	12.5	13.0	13.2	18.8	23.9	14.9	13.7	13.8	14.2	34.4
1967	18.7	14.1	17.1	19.7	23.3	14.2	14.0	14.0	14.6	14.9	21.7	27.3	16.5	15.4	15.4	16.0	39.9
1968	21.4	15.9	19.6	22.4	27.8	16.1	15.7	16.0	16.4	16.9	25.5	31.2	18.6	17.4	17.5	18.2	47.7
1969	24.9	17.8	22.7	26.5	32.8	18.0	17.6	17.8	18.4	19.4	30.3	37.7	21.5	20.2	20.0	20.8	57.6
1970	29.4	20.5	26.7	31.6	38.8	20.5	20.5	20.6	21.5	22.9	35.7	44.7	26.5	23.5	23.7	24.8	67.8
1971	33.5	24.1	30.5	36.2	43.0	24.6	23.9	23.9	24.5	25.3	41.7	51.4	30.2	26.9	26.7	27.9	74.5
1972	38.7	27.6	35.2	41.0	51.0	28.1	27.1	27.5	28.2	29.7	47.7	58.3	33.6	31.0	31.0	32.7	89.2
1973	47.8	32.2	42.8	50.1	65.9	32.6	31.8	32.3	33.1	36.5	58.8	72.4	40.5	37.5	37.7	40.0	120.0
1974	60.2	38.2	55.6	66.6	80.6	38.1	37.9	38.5	41.1	48.7	77.0	99.4	53.2	47.2	47.0	49.9	144.9
1975	67.2	48.0	58.8	75.0	87.0	49.2	47.0	47.9	48.3	50.6	77.4	113.1	58.8	53.1	53.1	54.5	153.3
1976	75.4	54.6	66.7	82.7	97.6	55.2	54.0	54.7	55.8	58.0	86.4	123.4	65.7	59.1	59.6	61.4	171.7
1977	81.9	60.2	73.7	89.5	104.3	61.1	59.3	60.2	61.3	63.8	96.0	133.2	71.2	64.1	64.1	66.1	182.7
1978	86.7	65.1	78.1	93.7	110.1	66.1	64.1	65.0	65.8	67.1	101.4	139.3	73.9	67.9	67.7	70.6	192.0
1979	93.0	68.7	83.6	101.4	118.5	69.1	68.0	69.1	69.7	72.0	109.0	147.3	84.6	72.2	72.1	74.9	208.5
1980	100.0	73.8	90.3	109.2	126.7	74.6	72.9	73.9	75.0	77.9	118.0	160.1	90.6	76.9	76.8	80.5	222.7
1981	105.6	77.9	94.7	115.4	134.4	79.5	76.8	77.4	79.0	81.8	123.3	172.6	92.8	80.8	81.3	85.2	236.6
1982	110.7	82.1	100.2	120.2	140.2	83.6	81.0	81.8	83.0	86.1	131.4	174.3	101.4	85.0	85.1	88.5	246.9
1983	115.0	86.1	104.7	123.6	145.5	87.2	84.8	86.4	87.3	87.9	139.0	182.7	99.3	88.7	88.3	93.8	253.8

Unit labour cost (13) — Coût unitaire de la main-d'œuvre (13)
1980 = 100

	Year	Q.1	Q.2	Q.3	Q.4	JAN	FEB	MAR	APR	MAY	JUN	JUL	AUG	SEP	OCT	NOV	DEC
1964	47	44	48	48	47	46	44	42	48	48	48	48	49	47	47	49	46
1965	50	47	51	52	50	49	48	43	51	52	51	52	53	51	50	51	49
1966	49	49	51	50	47	52	50	45	51	51	51	50	51	49	48	48	46
1967	48	46	49	48	47	48	47	43	50	49	49	49	49	47	47	47	46
1968	48	46	49	49	47	48	46	44	49	49	49	48	49	48	47	47	47
1969	48	47	50	50	48	49	47	44	49	50	50	49	51	49	47	49	47
1970	51	48	52	53	53	50	49	45	51	53	52	52	55	52	53	54	52
1971	58	54	58	60	59	56	55	50	56	60	59	59	62	58	59	59	58
1972	61	59	62	63	60	62	59	54	61	63	63	63	64	61	61	61	58
1973	63	60	64	65	64	63	61	55	61	64	66	66	67	64	64	65	64
1974	82	67	82	88	91	70	68	64	75	84	87	86	92	87	89	92	91
1975	100	99	100	101	100	104	100	92	97	101	102	100	106	99	99	103	99
1976	100	101	100	100	99	109	102	92	98	102	100	98	104	98	99	100	97
1977	104	102	105	105	103	108	105	94	102	107	105	106	108	102	104	103	101
1978	102	104	103	102	99	111	106	94	101	104	102	102	106	98	99	100	97
1979	99	101	100	99	96	108	103	93	100	101	100	99	102	98	97	97	95
1980	100	97	100	103	100	105	97	90	97	102	101	100	110	100	100	102	99
1981	104	102	106	105	102	108	104	95	103	109	105	103	112	101	101	102	101
1982	112	108	113	113	113	114	110	99	109	116	112	111	119	110	114	113	111
1983		115	115	113		122	117	105	114	118	114	112	118	108	111	109	

Producer prices (manufactured goods): (14) total — Prix à la production (produits manufacturés) : (14) total
1980 = 100

	Year	Q.1	Q.2	Q.3	Q.4	JAN	FEB	MAR	APR	MAY	JUN	JUL	AUG	SEP	OCT	NOV	DEC
1964																	
1965																	
1966																	
1967	49.4	49.6	49.3	49.4	49.5	49.6	49.6	49.5	49.3	49.2	49.3	49.3	49.4	49.4	49.4	49.6	49.6
1968	49.5	49.6	49.4	49.5	49.6	49.5	49.6	49.6	49.3	49.4	49.5	49.4	49.5	49.6	49.6	49.6	49.7
1969	50.3	49.7	50.0	50.4	51.0	49.7	49.7	49.7	49.8	50.0	50.1	50.1	50.3	50.6	50.8	51.0	51.2
1970	52.1	51.9	52.3	52.2	51.9	51.6	51.8	52.1	52.4	52.4	52.2	52.2	52.2	52.1	52.1	51.9	51.7
1971	51.4	51.5	51.6	51.5	51.1	51.6	51.5	51.4	51.6	51.6	51.5	51.5	51.5	51.4	51.2	51.1	51.1
1972	51.9	51.2	51.4	51.8	53.3	51.2	51.2	51.2	51.3	51.4	51.5	51.6	51.8	52.1	52.5	53.4	54.0
1973	59.8	55.8	57.8	60.2	65.1	54.8	55.7	57.0	57.4	57.8	58.3	59.2	60.1	61.2	62.4	64.0	69.0
1974	75.6	73.7	75.3	76.3	77.1	72.6	73.9	74.5	75.2	75.2	75.5	76.1	76.5	76.4	76.8	77.2	77.3
1975	77.3	77.2	77.0	77.3	77.9	77.4	77.1	77.0	77.0	77.1	77.0	77.0	77.3	77.5	77.8	77.8	78.0
1976	81.4	79.4	80.8	82.4	83.1	78.9	79.4	80.0	80.5	80.7	81.1	81.8	82.6	82.8	83.0	83.1	83.2
1977	83.7	83.5	83.8	83.7	83.7	83.3	83.5	83.6	83.8	83.8	83.8	83.7	83.8	83.8	83.9	83.7	83.5
1978	83.0	83.4	83.4	82.8	82.3	83.4	83.4	83.4	83.4	83.5	83.4	83.1	82.8	82.4	82.3	82.2	82.3
1979	87.2	83.2	85.3	88.9	91.3	82.7	83.1	83.7	84.5	85.3	86.2	87.8	88.9	90.0	90.6	91.0	92.3
1980	100.0	96.2	100.5	101.8	101.5	94.5	96.2	97.8	99.6	100.7	101.3	101.4	101.9	102.0	101.7	101.6	101.3
1981	101.1	100.7	100.8	101.2	101.6	101.1	100.6	100.3	100.5	101.0	100.9	100.8	101.3	101.5	101.5	101.6	101.7
1982	101.6	101.6	101.3	101.5	101.8	101.6	101.6	101.5	101.5	101.4	101.1	101.2	101.6	101.7	101.8	101.9	101.8
1983	100.8	101.4	100.6	100.4	100.6	101.5	101.5	101.3	100.3	100.8	100.8	100.8	100.2	100.3	100.5	100.6	100.7

Monthly earnings: manufacturing (8) / Gains mensuels : industries manufacturières (8)

(regular workers) / (travailleurs réguliers)

1980 = 100

Adjusted - Corrigé

	Year	Q.1	Q.2	Q.3	Q.4	JAN	FEB	MAR	APR	MAY	JUN	JUL	AUG	SEP	OCT	NOV	DEC
1964		13.1	13.3	13.9	14.0	12.9	13.1	13.2	13.2	13.5	13.3	13.8	14.0	13.9	14.1	14.1	13.7
1965		14.7	14.4	15.1	14.9	14.8	14.6	14.6	14.5	14.5	14.3	14.8	15.4	15.1	15.1	15.1	14.6
1966		15.9	16.1	16.8	17.0	16.0	15.8	15.9	16.1	16.2	16.1	16.5	17.0	16.9	17.1	17.2	16.6
1967		17.8	18.4	18.9	19.3	17.6	17.9	18.0	18.3	18.4	18.4	18.7	18.9	19.1	19.2	19.5	19.1
1968		20.4	21.0	21.4	22.3	20.1	20.3	20.8	20.8	20.9	21.2	21.1	21.4	21.7	22.0	22.3	22.6
1969		23.0	24.1	25.2	26.0	22.7	23.0	23.3	23.6	24.0	24.8	25.3	24.9	25.4	25.3	25.6	27.1
1970		26.8	28.4	30.0	30.9	26.0	27.1	27.3	27.9	28.4	28.9	29.6	30.7	29.7	30.3	30.6	31.7
1971		31.7	32.3	34.3	34.5	31.4	31.9	31.9	32.1	31.5	33.4	33.7	35.0	34.3	34.3	34.6	34.6
1972		36.5	37.5	38.8	40.7	36.1	36.5	36.9	37.3	37.1	38.0	37.7	39.0	39.7	40.1	40.7	41.3
1973		42.8	45.5	47.2	51.5	42.0	43.0	43.4	43.9	45.7	46.9	46.2	47.0	48.3	49.0	50.1	55.4
1974		50.8	59.3	61.8	63.6	49.2	51.4	51.7	54.6	51.3	61.9	62.7	61.7	61.0	61.2	62.8	66.7
1975		63.8	63.7	69.2	69.5	63.6	63.7	64.2	64.1	64.0	62.9	70.5	68.3	68.9	69.3	68.8	70.5
1976		72.4	72.9	76.5	78.2	71.4	72.9	73.0	73.8	73.7	71.1	76.4	76.3	76.8	77.8	77.7	79.0
1977		79.5	80.7	82.8	83.8	79.0	79.6	80.0	80.7	81.3	80.0	82.3	82.6	83.4	83.6	83.7	84.0
1978		85.7	85.7	86.7	88.6	85.3	85.6	86.1	86.3	85.5	85.2	86.1	85.6	88.4	88.4	89.2	88.2
1979		90.4	91.7	94.4	94.8	89.1	90.7	91.4	91.3	91.7	92.0	91.1	97.8	94.2	94.3	94.5	95.7
1980		97.0	99.0	101.4	101.3	96.2	97.1	97.7	98.2	99.1	99.7	99.1	104.5	100.5	100.6	101.5	101.9
1981		102.6	104.0	106.5	107.3	102.7	102.5	102.5	103.6	104.1	104.2	106.9	106.9	105.8	106.6	107.4	108.0
1982		108.2	109.9	112.1	112.0	108.0	108.2	108.5	108.9	109.6	111.1	108.0	116.7	111.5	111.7	111.7	112.6
1983		113.5	114.7	114.6	116.9	112.7	113.3	114.6	114.6	111.9	117.5	113.2	114.2	116.4	116.6	118.4	115.7

Unit labour cost (13) / Coût unitaire de la main-d'œuvre (13)

1980 = 100

Adjusted - Corrigé

	Year	Q.1	Q.2	Q.3	Q.4	JAN	FEB	MAR	APR	MAY	JUN	JUL	AUG	SEP	OCT	NOV	DEC
1964		46	46	47	48	46	46	47	46	46	46	47	47	46	47	48	47
1965		49	50	50	51	48	49	49	50	50	50	50	51	50	51	50	51
1966		51	49	49	48	51	51	50	50	49	49	49	49	49	48	47	47
1967		48	48	47	47	48	49	48	48	48	47	48	47	47	47	46	47
1968		47	48	48	48	47	47	48	48	47	48	48	47	48	48	47	48
1969		48	48	49	48	48	48	48	48	48	49	49	49	49	48	49	48
1970		49	51	52	54	48	49	49	50	51	51	52	52	52	53	54	54
1971		55	57	59	60	55	56	56	56	57	57	58	59	59	60	59	60
1972		60	61	61	61	61	61	60	61	60	61	62	61	61	61	61	61
1973		61	62	64	66	60	61	60	61	63	64	64	63	65	65	66	67
1974		68	80	87	93	66	68	70	75	81	85	85	87	89	91	93	94
1975		99	98	100	103	99	99	100	97	98	99	99	100	101	101	104	102
1976		101	98	99	101	102	101	100	98	99	98	98	99	100	101	101	101
1977		102	103	105	105	101	103	102	103	104	103	106	104	105	106	104	105
1978		104	101	101	101	104	104	103	102	101	101	102	101	101	101	101	101
1979		100	99	99	98	101	100	101	100	99	99	98	98	100	98	98	98
1980		97	99	102	102	98	95	98	97	99	100	100	105	102	101	103	102
1981		102	105	104	103	102	103	103	104	106	104	103	105	103	103	103	104
1982		108	111	112	115	108	109	108	111	112	110	112	112	112	116	113	115
1983		115	114	112		115	116	114	115	113	112	113	111	111			

Producer prices (manufactured goods): (14) / Prix à la production (produits manufacturés) : (14)

food / alimentation

1980 = 100

	Year	Q.1	Q.2	Q.3	Q.4	JAN	FEB	MAR	APR	MAY	JUN	JUL	AUG	SEP	OCT	NOV	DEC
1964																	
1965																	
1966																	
1967	45.0	44.9	45.0	44.9	45.3	44.7	45.0	45.1	45.1	44.9	44.9	44.9	44.9	45.1	45.2	45.4	45.3
1968	47.0	45.3	46.3	47.7	48.0	45.3	45.3	45.3	45.2	47.4	47.7	47.6	47.7	47.9	47.9	48.0	48.1
1969	48.5	48.2	48.4	48.5	49.0	48.1	48.2	48.3	48.4	48.3	48.4	48.4	48.5	48.7	48.7	49.1	49.2
1970	50.3	49.3	49.9	50.5	51.4	49.2	49.4	49.4	49.7	50.1	50.0	50.2	50.3	50.9	51.2	51.4	51.5
1971	52.3	51.7	52.2	52.6	52.9	51.6	51.7	51.8	51.9	52.4	52.3	52.4	52.6	52.7	52.9	52.8	52.9
1972	53.0	53.0	52.9	53.1	53.3	53.0	53.0	52.9	52.7	53.0	52.9	53.0	53.0	53.2	53.2	53.3	53.4
1973	57.1	54.4	55.8	57.6	60.3	53.8	54.4	55.1	55.1	56.0	56.4	57.1	57.6	58.1	59.2	60.5	62.6
1974	72.6	68.4	70.8	73.8	77.2	67.2	68.5	69.4	69.9	71.0	71.4	72.7	73.8	74.9	75.9	77.4	78.3
1975	79.0	78.3	78.9	78.9	79.9	78.4	78.0	78.3	78.8	79.0	79.0	78.6	78.6	79.5	79.8	79.2	80.7
1976	86.3	84.7	86.1	86.8	87.6	83.9	84.7	85.6	85.9	86.1	86.3	86.5	86.9	87.0	87.1	87.4	88.2
1977	90.0	88.8	90.0	90.5	90.6	88.6	88.6	89.2	89.7	90.1	90.3	90.4	90.4	90.8	90.6	90.7	90.6
1978	91.1	90.6	91.4	91.3	90.9	90.4	90.6	90.6	90.7	91.9	91.8	91.6	91.2	91.1	91.0	90.8	90.8
1979	91.6	91.0	91.4	91.8	92.3	90.9	91.1	91.1	91.2	91.4	91.6	91.7	91.8	91.9	92.1	92.3	92.5
1980	100.0	95.1	100.2	101.9	102.9	93.7	95.1	96.4	98.0	101.1	101.4	101.5	101.8	102.4	102.8	102.9	103.0
1981	104.7	103.0	104.6	105.7	105.7	103.1	102.9	103.0	103.4	105.1	105.2	105.6	105.7	105.7	105.7	105.8	105.7
1982	105.6	105.9	105.6	105.5	105.5	105.8	105.9	106.0	105.8	105.6	105.3	105.4	105.5	105.5	105.5	105.6	105.5
1983	108.3	105.4	107.8	109.3	110.5	105.3	105.4	105.5	106.1	108.5	108.9	108.9	109.3	109.7	110.3	110.5	110.8

Producer prices (manufactured goods): (14)
textiles
1980 = 100

Prix à la production (produits manufacturés) : (14)
textiles
1980 = 100

	Year	Q.1	Q.2	Q.3	Q.4	JAN	FEB	MAR	APR	MAY	JUN	JUL	AUG	SEP	OCT	NOV	DEC
1964																	
1965																	
1966																	
1967	59.3	57.9	58.8	60.1	60.4	57.9	57.9	58.0	58.1	59.0	59.5	59.6	60.1	60.6	60.7	60.5	60.0
1968	60.0	60.7	59.7	59.8	59.5	60.3	61.1	60.7	59.9	59.3	60.0	59.5	59.9	60.0	59.6	59.5	59.3
1969	59.3	59.0	59.0	59.4	60.0	59.4	59.0	58.6	58.8	58.9	59.3	59.3	59.5	59.4	59.5	59.8	60.7
1970	62.4	62.4	62.6	62.8	62.0	62.3	62.2	62.6	62.9	62.6	62.4	62.7	63.0	62.6	62.4	62.1	61.4
1971	59.7	60.5	60.1	59.5	58.8	60.6	60.6	60.3	60.1	60.0	60.1	60.0	59.5	59.0	58.8	58.7	58.8
1972	61.3	59.3	60.1	61.1	64.6	59.1	59.3	59.5	59.8	60.1	60.4	60.3	61.1	62.1	63.9	64.1	65.9
1973	83.5	76.5	83.2	86.6	87.8	70.1	75.5	83.9	81.9	83.4	84.3	86.1	87.6	86.1	85.3	86.7	91.4
1974	82.5	89.9	84.7	78.9	76.5	92.1	90.1	87.5	86.2	84.9	83.0	81.1	78.9	76.6	75.6	76.7	77.3
1975	81.3	77.6	80.3	83.1	84.1	77.2	77.5	78.1	79.3	80.4	81.3	82.6	83.5	83.3	83.9	84.2	84.2
1976	90.4	86.3	90.1	92.5	92.7	84.9	86.4	87.6	89.4	90.2	90.7	91.5	92.6	93.3	93.3	92.8	92.2
1977	89.1	90.1	89.7	88.3	88.5	90.7	89.8	89.8	89.8	89.9	89.3	88.3	88.4	88.3	88.9	88.3	88.2
1978	91.8	90.2	92.1	92.3	92.6	89.0	90.2	91.4	91.9	92.1	92.2	92.1	92.4	92.3	92.2	92.6	93.1
1979	95.2	94.1	94.9	95.4	96.3	93.5	94.2	94.6	94.8	94.9	94.9	94.6	95.5	96.0	96.4	96.3	96.3
1980	100.0	98.0	100.6	101.0	100.4	96.8	98.3	98.9	100.5	100.9	100.5	100.3	101.1	101.6	100.8	100.4	99.9
1981	101.1	100.2	100.5	101.2	102.6	99.9	100.2	100.5	100.5	100.6	100.4	100.6	101.3	101.6	102.3	102.5	103.0
1982	102.9	103.2	103.0	102.9	102.4	103.4	103.3	103.0	102.9	103.1	103.1	103.0	102.9	102.9	102.7	102.5	102.0
1983	101.1	100.7	100.7	101.2	101.8	101.2	100.8	100.1	100.2	100.7	101.1	101.0	101.1	101.5	101.3	101.7	102.4

Producer prices (manufactured goods): (14)
chemicals
1980 = 100

Prix à la production (produits manufacturés) : (14)
produits chimiques
1980 = 100

	Year	Q.1	Q.2	Q.3	Q.4	JAN	FEB	MAR	APR	MAY	JUN	JUL	AUG	SEP	OCT	NOV	DEC
1964																	
1965																	
1966																	
1967	46.1	46.5	46.3	45.9	45.6	46.4	46.5	46.4	46.3	46.4	46.3	46.0	45.9	45.9	45.6	45.6	45.5
1968	45.0	45.4	45.1	44.8	44.8	45.4	45.4	45.3	45.1	45.1	45.0	44.8	44.9	44.9	44.9	44.8	44.7
1969	44.6	44.7	44.8	44.5	44.5	44.7	44.6	44.7	44.8	44.7	44.7	44.6	44.5	44.6	44.6	44.4	44.5
1970	44.8	44.9	45.0	44.8	44.6	44.9	44.9	44.9	44.9	45.1	45.0	45.0	44.8	44.7	44.7	44.6	44.5
1971	44.2	44.3	44.1	44.2	44.0	44.4	44.2	44.2	44.1	44.1	44.2	44.2	44.2	44.2	44.2	44.1	43.9
1972	43.9	43.8	43.7	43.9	44.4	43.8	43.8	43.8	43.6	43.7	43.8	43.8	43.9	44.0	44.2	44.4	44.5
1973	49.3	44.8	46.5	48.6	57.3	44.6	44.7	45.1	46.0	46.6	46.8	47.4	48.4	49.9	51.6	55.0	65.3
1974	70.5	68.5	68.2	71.1	74.1	68.9	68.5	68.2	67.9	67.7	69.1	70.1	71.3	72.0	73.7	74.3	74.5
1975	74.7	74.5	74.5	74.4	75.3	74.6	74.4	74.5	74.5	74.5	74.5	74.6	74.3	74.2	74.8	75.3	75.8
1976	78.3	76.6	78.1	79.0	79.5	76.4	76.5	76.9	77.7	78.0	78.5	78.9	78.9	79.2	79.4	79.4	79.7
1977	79.4	79.7	79.7	79.3	78.8	79.7	79.7	79.6	79.8	79.7	79.7	79.4	79.3	79.3	79.2	78.9	78.4
1978	75.7	77.2	76.1	75.1	74.3	78.0	77.0	76.5	76.4	76.0	76.0	75.4	75.1	74.8	74.5	74.2	74.3
1979	82.8	74.8	79.8	85.9	90.3	74.2	74.5	75.8	78.6	80.0	81.0	83.6	86.1	88.1	89.5	90.3	91.0
1980	100.0	95.3	101.2	102.4	101.1	93.5	95.2	97.3	100.0	101.4	102.1	102.5	102.3	102.3	101.6	100.9	100.7
1981	98.1	99.0	97.8	97.3	98.2	99.8	98.8	98.4	98.3	98.3	96.8	97.1	97.3	97.4	97.9	98.3	98.3
1982	96.9	98.3	97.2	96.0	96.2	98.4	98.3	98.2	97.7	97.2	96.7	96.1	95.9	95.9	96.0	96.2	96.5
1983	95.0	95.8	95.0	94.3	94.7	95.8	95.9	95.7	95.4	95.0	94.6	94.3	94.2	94.4	94.5	94.7	95.0

Producer prices (manufactured goods): (14)
iron and steel
1980 = 100

Prix à la production (produits manufacturés) : (14)
sidérurgie
1980 = 100

	Year	Q.1	Q.2	Q.3	Q.4	JAN	FEB	MAR	APR	MAY	JUN	JUL	AUG	SEP	OCT	NOV	DEC
1964																	
1965																	
1966																	
1967	50.1	52.9	49.9	49.3	48.1	53.8	53.2	51.7	50.6	49.7	49.3	49.8	49.4	48.7	48.3	48.2	47.8
1968	46.5	46.9	45.9	46.3	46.9	47.4	47.1	46.3	45.7	45.9	46.1	46.0	46.2	46.6	46.9	47.0	46.8
1969	48.6	46.4	47.6	49.2	51.1	46.5	46.4	46.5	46.8	47.6	48.2	48.4	49.0	50.2	51.0	51.1	51.3
1970	52.0	52.8	52.7	51.9	50.8	52.1	53.0	53.2	53.3	52.9	51.9	51.9	52.0	51.7	51.3	50.7	50.4
1971	48.8	50.0	48.9	48.9	47.4	50.6	50.1	49.3	49.1	49.0	48.7	48.9	49.0	48.7	47.7	47.2	47.4
1972	49.8	48.7	49.6	50.2	50.6	48.3	48.7	49.0	49.5	49.6	49.8	50.0	50.3	50.4	50.5	50.6	50.8
1973	55.6	52.3	52.8	56.1	61.3	51.9	52.4	52.5	52.5	52.6	53.2	54.0	55.7	58.5	60.2	60.7	62.9
1974	70.8	65.5	67.6	76.2	74.1	65.4	65.3	65.7	66.0	66.5	70.3	75.4	76.4	76.8	74.9	74.2	73.3
1975	73.5	72.3	72.5	74.1	75.2	72.2	72.2	72.6	72.9	72.6	71.8	72.3	74.7	75.4	75.4	74.9	75.4
1976	82.2	78.1	80.2	84.4	86.0	76.5	78.4	79.3	79.8	80.3	80.5	82.4	85.4	85.5	85.9	86.3	85.8
1977	87.0	86.0	85.7	87.7	88.5	85.9	86.3	85.8	85.4	85.8	86.0	86.0	88.3	88.7	88.9	88.4	88.3
1978	90.6	89.4	90.9	91.0	91.0	88.5	89.5	90.3	90.7	90.8	91.0	91.1	91.1	90.9	91.0	90.9	91.1
1979	92.4	91.4	91.8	92.8	93.3	91.4	91.4	92.4	91.7	91.8	92.0	92.5	92.8	93.0	93.1	93.2	93.5
1980	100.0	95.1	102.2	101.8	100.8	94.2	95.1	95.9	102.0	102.6	102.0	101.6	102.0	101.9	101.3	100.7	100.4
1981	99.2	99.4	99.4	99.4	98.6	100.2	99.3	98.8	99.3	99.3	99.7	99.7	99.4	99.0	98.6	98.6	98.6
1982	99.4	98.5	98.8	99.7	100.6	98.2	98.5	98.7	98.9	98.8	98.6	98.6	100.0	100.4	100.7	100.8	100.4
1983	99.5	99.5	99.3	99.4	99.7	100.0	99.4	99.1	99.2	99.3	99.3	99.4	99.3	99.5	99.7	99.7	99.6

Producer prices (manufactured goods): (14)
machinery and equipment
1980 = 100

Prix à la production (produits manufacturés) : (14)
équipement et outillage
1980 = 100

	Year	Q.1	Q.2	Q.3	Q.4	JAN	FEB	MAR	APR	MAY	JUN	JUL	AUG	SEP	OCT	NOV	DEC
1964																	
1965																	
1966																	
1967	70.7	70.6	70.8	70.8	70.8	70.6	70.6	70.7	70.7	70.7	70.8	70.8	70.8	70.8	70.8	70.7	70.7
1968	70.8	70.7	70.9	70.9	70.7	70.7	70.7	70.7	70.8	70.9	71.0	70.9	70.9	70.9	70.7	70.7	70.7
1969	70.7	70.7	70.6	70.7	71.0	70.7	70.7	70.7	70.7	70.6	70.6	70.6	70.7	70.8	70.9	71.0	71.1
1970	72.0	71.6	72.0	72.2	72.2	71.5	71.7	71.8	72.0	72.0	72.1	72.2	72.2	72.2	72.2	72.2	72.1
1971	71.8	71.9	71.9	71.8	71.6	72.0	71.9	71.8	71.8	71.9	72.0	72.0	71.8	71.7	71.6	71.6	71.6
1972	71.6	71.4	71.5	71.6	71.8	71.5	71.5	71.3	71.5	71.5	71.5	71.6	71.6	71.7	71.7	71.7	71.8
1973	76.0	72.5	74.8	76.3	80.2	72.0	72.4	73.0	74.3	74.8	75.4	75.8	76.2	77.0	78.3	79.6	82.8
1974	92.9	89.8	92.7	94.1	95.1	86.7	90.9	91.9	92.1	92.6	93.4	93.9	94.1	94.4	94.5	95.1	95.8
1975	95.6	96.2	95.8	95.4	95.0	96.6	96.2	95.7	95.8	95.9	95.6	95.6	95.4	95.3	95.2	95.1	94.8
1976	95.3	95.0	95.2	95.5	95.8	94.9	94.9	95.0	95.0	95.2	95.2	95.3	95.5	95.6	95.8	95.8	95.9
1977	96.6	96.2	96.6	96.9	96.8	96.0	96.2	96.3	96.5	96.7	96.7	96.8	96.9	96.9	96.9	96.8	96.7
1978	96.9	96.8	96.9	96.9	96.8	96.8	96.8	96.9	96.9	96.9	96.9	96.8	96.9	96.9	96.9	96.8	96.6
1979	97.1	96.7	96.9	97.2	97.5	96.7	96.7	96.8	96.9	96.9	96.9	97.1	97.2	97.3	97.4	97.4	97.6
1980	100.0	98.4	99.4	100.9	101.3	98.3	98.4	98.6	99.0	99.5	99.8	100.6	100.9	101.1	101.3	101.3	101.3
1981	101.2	101.4	101.3	101.2	101.0	101.5	101.4	101.4	101.2	101.3	101.3	101.3	101.2	101.2	101.0	101.0	101.0
1982	100.7	101.0	100.8	100.6	100.4	101.0	101.1	101.0	100.9	100.8	100.7	100.7	100.6	100.5	100.5	100.5	100.3
1983	99.9	100.2	99.9	99.7	99.7	100.3	100.2	100.2	100.1	99.9	99.8	99.8	99.8	99.7	99.8	99.6	99.6

Producer prices (manufactured goods): (14)
petroleum and coal products
1980 = 100

Prix à la production (produits manufacturés) : (14)
dérivés du pétrole et du charbon
1980 = 100

	Year	Q.1	Q.2	Q.3	Q.4	JAN	FEB	MAR	APR	MAY	JUN	JUL	AUG	SEP	OCT	NOV	DEC
1964																	
1965																	
1966																	
1967	19.0	18.9	18.7	19.0	19.4	18.9	18.9	18.9	18.9	18.7	18.6	18.7	19.1	19.2	19.3	19.4	19.4
1968	19.1	19.3	19.1	18.9	18.8	19.3	19.3	19.4	19.2	19.1	19.0	18.9	18.9	18.9	18.8	18.8	18.8
1969	18.5	18.6	18.4	18.5	18.6	18.7	18.6	18.5	18.4	18.4	18.4	18.4	18.5	18.5	18.5	18.6	18.6
1970	19.1	18.7	18.8	19.0	19.7	18.7	18.7	18.7	18.8	18.8	18.8	18.9	19.0	19.1	19.5	19.7	19.8
1971	21.0	20.2	21.3	21.3	21.1	20.1	20.2	20.4	21.3	21.3	21.3	21.3	21.3	21.3	21.2	21.2	21.1
1972	21.1	20.9	21.0	21.1	21.4	20.9	20.9	20.9	20.9	21.0	21.0	21.1	21.1	21.1	21.3	21.4	21.4
1973	22.9	21.6	22.2	22.5	25.2	21.5	21.6	21.8	22.0	22.3	22.3	22.4	22.5	22.6	22.9	24.5	28.3
1974	40.7	30.4	41.2	43.3	48.0	28.7	29.0	33.5	40.6	40.8	42.2	43.2	43.3	43.4	47.7	48.0	48.4
1975	50.5	49.1	49.3	51.1	52.2	48.7	48.9	49.6	49.7	49.7	49.9	50.8	51.1	51.5	51.9	51.9	52.7
1976	55.7	54.0	55.2	56.6	56.9	53.5	53.8	54.6	55.1	55.1	55.3	56.5	56.6	56.6	56.8	56.9	57.2
1977	57.4	57.2	57.7	57.7	57.0	57.2	57.2	57.2	57.7	57.7	57.7	57.9	57.6	57.5	57.3	57.1	56.8
1978	52.7	55.7	53.9	51.9	49.3	56.4	55.9	54.7	54.2	53.9	53.5	52.9	52.0	50.9	50.1	49.0	48.8
1979	60.6	49.2	54.0	66.0	73.4	48.8	48.9	49.8	51.0	53.9	57.1	62.4	66.1	69.4	70.5	71.1	78.7
1980	100.0	87.4	100.4	105.7	106.6	82.7	86.6	92.9	97.0	100.5	103.6	102.0	107.5	107.5	106.7	106.9	106.3
1981	111.1	105.3	108.4	114.0	116.6	106.2	105.2	104.5	105.4	108.8	110.9	110.9	114.8	116.4	116.5	116.6	116.6
1982	119.7	116.4	118.0	120.9	123.4	116.6	116.4	116.3	117.7	118.1	118.1	118.5	121.6	122.6	123.4	123.4	123.4
1983	114.2	123.5	115.5	110.0	108.0	123.4	123.5	123.6	115.5	115.5	115.4	114.7	107.7	107.7	108.0	108.0	107.9

Wholesale prices: total (15)
1980 = 100

Prix de gros : total (15)
1980 = 100

	Year	Q.1	Q.2	Q.3	Q.4	JAN	FEB	MAR	APR	MAY	JUN	JUL	AUG	SEP	OCT	NOV	DEC
1964	43.1	43.3	43.0	43.1	43.2	43.4	43.3	43.2	43.1	43.0	42.9	42.9	43.0	43.2	43.1	43.3	43.3
1965	43.5	43.5	43.4	43.4	43.6	43.6	43.6	43.5	43.5	43.5	43.3	43.3	43.3	43.5	43.5	43.6	43.7
1966	44.5	44.2	44.4	44.7	44.9	44.0	44.3	44.3	44.3	44.3	44.5	44.6	44.7	44.7	44.8	44.8	44.9
1967	45.3	45.3	45.0	45.2	45.7	45.4	45.4	45.2	45.1	45.0	45.1	45.1	45.2	45.4	45.6	45.8	45.8
1968	45.7	45.9	45.6	45.6	45.9	45.8	45.9	45.9	45.5	45.5	45.6	45.5	45.5	45.8	45.8	45.9	45.9
1969	46.7	46.0	46.4	46.9	47.5	45.9	46.0	46.1	46.2	46.4	46.5	46.6	46.8	47.2	47.3	47.5	47.7
1970	48.4	48.3	48.6	48.4	48.3	48.1	48.3	48.5	48.6	48.6	48.4	48.4	48.4	48.4	48.3	48.3	48.2
1971	48.0	48.0	48.2	48.2	47.8	48.1	48.0	48.0	48.2	48.2	48.1	48.2	48.3	48.0	47.8	47.7	47.7
1972	48.4	47.7	47.9	48.3	49.7	47.7	47.7	47.7	47.9	47.9	48.0	48.0	48.3	48.6	48.9	49.7	50.5
1973	56.1	52.1	53.9	56.7	61.6	51.2	52.1	53.0	53.3	53.8	54.5	55.5	56.7	57.7	58.9	60.8	65.1
1974	73.7	70.6	72.9	75.1	76.0	68.7	71.3	71.8	72.3	72.8	73.8	74.6	75.3	75.4	75.8	76.0	76.2
1975	75.9	75.7	75.4	75.8	76.6	76.2	75.6	75.3	75.5	75.5	75.3	75.4	75.8	76.0	76.4	76.4	76.9
1976	79.7	78.0	79.1	80.5	81.2	77.5	78.0	78.4	78.8	79.1	79.4	80.1	80.5	80.8	81.0	81.3	81.4
1977	81.2	81.5	81.6	81.2	80.6	81.3	81.6	81.6	81.6	81.7	81.4	81.0	81.2	81.3	81.0	80.5	80.2
1978	79.1	80.2	79.9	78.5	78.0	80.1	80.2	80.1	79.8	80.1	79.7	79.0	78.3	78.2	77.8	77.9	78.4
1979	84.9	79.5	82.8	86.8	90.5	78.8	79.5	80.2	81.6	82.9	83.9	85.5	86.9	88.1	89.1	90.4	92.1
1980	100.0	97.1	100.9	101.4	100.6	95.1	97.3	98.8	101.4	100.8	100.4	101.0	101.8	101.4	100.6	100.8	100.5
1981	101.4	100.0	101.1	102.4	102.1	100.0	99.9	100.0	100.5	101.3	101.5	102.1	102.6	102.5	102.4	102.1	101.8
1982	103.2	102.5	102.8	103.8	103.7	101.9	102.6	102.9	103.1	102.4	102.9	103.5	103.8	104.2	104.4	104.1	102.7
1983	100.9	101.7	100.7	100.9	100.3	101.8	101.9	101.5	100.8	100.5	100.8	101.0	100.8	100.9	100.2	100.3	100.4

Consumer prices: all items (16) / Prix à la consommation : total (16)

including imputed rent / loyers imputés inclus

1980 = 100

	Year	Q.1	Q.2	Q.3	Q.4	JAN	FEB	MAR	APR	MAY	JUN	JUL	AUG	SEP	OCT	NOV	DEC
1964																	
1965																	
1966																	
1967																	
1968																	
1969																	
1970	42.3	41.6	42.1	42.2	43.4	41.3	41.5	41.9	42.3	42.1	42.1	42.0	42.0	42.6	43.3	43.4	43.7
1971	45.0	44.0	44.8	45.3	45.9	44.0	44.0	44.1	44.7	44.8	45.0	45.0	44.9	46.1	46.2	45.7	45.8
1972	47.2	46.1	47.1	47.5	48.2	45.8	46.0	46.4	47.0	47.1	47.2	47.2	47.6	47.8	48.2	48.1	48.4
1973	52.7	49.5	52.0	53.5	55.8	48.9	49.2	50.4	51.4	52.2	52.3	52.8	53.2	54.7	54.9	55.4	57.2
1974	65.0	61.0	63.7	66.1	68.9	59.6	61.5	61.9	63.5	63.7	64.0	65.3	66.0	67.0	68.5	69.0	69.3
1975	=72.6	=70.3	72.2	72.9	74.9	70.0	70.1	70.8	72.0	72.4	72.3	72.5	72.4	73.9	75.1	74.8	74.8
1976	79.4	76.6	79.0	80.0	82.0	76.1	76.6	76.9	78.7	79.0	79.3	79.7	79.2	81.1	81.6	81.6	82.6
1977	85.9	83.8	86.0	86.4	87.2	83.3	83.7	84.3	85.6	86.4	86.1	85.9	86.0	87.4	87.9	86.9	86.7
1978	89.5	87.6	89.5	90.2	90.5	87.1	87.5	88.3	89.3	89.8	89.4	89.8	89.9	90.9	91.2	90.2	90.1
1979	92.8	90.3	92.5	93.4	95.0	90.2	90.0	90.7	91.9	92.7	92.8	93.6	92.7	93.8	95.0	94.7	95.2
1980	=100.0	=96.9	99.9	101.0	102.2	96.2	96.9	97.5	99.2	100.1	100.5	100.6	100.3	102.0	102.2	102.4	102.1
1981	104.9	103.2	104.9	105.2	106.4	103.1	103.0	103.4	104.2	105.1	105.3	105.0	104.5	106.1	106.5	106.3	106.5
1982	107.8	106.4	107.6	108.1	109.0	106.5	106.3	106.5	107.3	107.7	107.7	107.0	107.8	109.5	109.8	108.7	108.6
1983	109.8	108.7	110.0	109.7	110.9	108.7	108.4	109.0	109.5	110.6	109.9	109.5	109.2	110.5	111.4	110.8	110.5

Money supply (M1) (17) / Disponibilités monétaires (M1) (17)

billion yen, end of period / milliards de yens, fin de période

	Year	Q.1	Q.2	Q.3	Q.4	JAN	FEB	MAR	APR	MAY	JUN	JUL	AUG	SEP	OCT	NOV	DEC
1964	8704	7316	7385	7576	8704	7058	6900	7316	7298	7445	7385	7349	7271	7576	7542	7756	8704
1965	10287	8423	8617	8919	10287	8187	8141	8423	8402	8454	8617	8527	8510	8919	9032	9140	10287
1966	11716	10065	10073	10376	11716	9441	9359	10065	9885	9910	10073	10196	9918	10376	10210	10529	11716
1967	13369	11378	11485	11648	13369	10625	10659	11378	11445	11241	11485	11347	11220	11648	11647	11981	13369
1968	15155	12946	13443	13256	15155	12182	12124	12946	12989	12955	13443	13123	12941	13256	13315	13753	15155
1969	18283	14817	15633	15865	18283	14068	14057	14817	15128	15168	15633	15525	15707	15865	15992	17098	18283
1970	21360	17798	18578	18576	21360	16883	16873	17798	18191	18579	18578	18423	18233	18576	18754	19406	21360
1971	27693	21187	23254	24098	27693	20282	20548	21187	22000	22500	23254	23315	23685	24098	24427	25204	27693
1972	34526	27063	27878	28813	34526	25627	25682	27063	27633	27419	27878	26967	27349	28813	29644	31010	34526
1973	40312	34475	36205	36588	40312	31896	32482	34475	36221	35777	36205	35716	35082	36588	36378	37267	40312
1974	43780	39779	41900	40295	43780	37728	37603	39779	40047	40994	41900	40356	39421	40295	38893	40327	43780
1975	48677	42250	44254	43939	48677	42608	41430	42250	43564	43482	44254	44385	43947	43939	43551	43889	48677
1976	55023	47998	50847	49882	55023	47629	46640	47998	49010	49284	50847	50481	49774	49882	49758	50617	55023
1977	58907	52492	53428	53030	58907	52985	51108	52492	52730	51152	53428	53590	52817	53030	52452	53771	58907
1978	65256	56764	59457	59244	65256	56588	54723	56764	56833	56965	59457	59655	59004	59244	58472	59923	65256
1979	70381	63105	66066	64502	70381	62807	60745	63105	65654	65998	66066	65789	65188	64502	63371	64609	70381
1980	69312	68192	68017	64462	69312	66916	64979	68192	70266	68715	68017	66136	64411	64462	62886	64043	69312
1981	76343	67177	70243	69161	76343	65723	64249	67177	67397	68495	70243	69842	68707	69161	68115	69299	76343
1982	80107	71933	73719	72792	80107	70310	68266	71933	72946	72957	73719	73734	72113	72792	71336	72341	80107
1983	81810	75956	76525	75093	81810	75018	72353	75956	76201	75604	76525	75997	73949	75093	72892	72952	81810

M1 plus quasi-money (17)(18) / M1 plus quasi-monnaie (17)(18)

billion yen, end of period / milliards de yens, fin de période

	Year	Q.1	Q.2	Q.3	Q.4	JAN	FEB	MAR	APR	MAY	JUN	JUL	AUG	SEP	OCT	NOV	DEC
1964	21523	18734	19237	19965	21523	18161	18163	18734	18834	19101	19237	19354	19420	19965	19992	20309	21523
1965	25394	21678	22398	23376	25394	21136	21233	21678	21792	21967	22398	22496	22663	23376	23604	23872	25394
1966	29523	25687	26355	27502	29523	24684	24754	25687	25699	25866	26355	26724	26724	27502	27426	27900	29523
1967	34098	29731	30529	31661	34098	28586	28794	29731	29923	29873	30529	30699	30880	31661	31804	32307	34098
1968	39154	34169	35482	36302	39154	33054	33155	34169	34420	34598	35482	35463	35586	36302	36534	37236	39154
1969	46400	39435	41347	42818	46400	38242	38410	39435	40067	40376	41347	41631	42173	42818	43150	44568	46400
1970	54237	46613	48810	50285	54237	45200	45428	46613	47404	48184	48810	49153	49391	50285	50720	51615	54237
1971	67398	55002	58845	61908	67398	53381	54008	55002	56276	57200	58845	59604	60680	61908	62702	63829	67398
1972	84041	68225	72261	75534	84041	65897	66404	68225	69750	70357	72261	73012	73680	75534	77068	79060	84041
1973	98189	85346	90134	92832	98189	81968	83115	85346	87973	88399	90134	90649	90793	92832	92929	94212	98189
1974	107500	98236	102159	102908	107500	96103	96187	98236	99417	99854	102159	101565	101333	102908	101760	103618	107500
1975	123068	107993	112508	115710	123068	107388	106705	107993	109996	110639	112508	114006	114710	115710	116267	118010	123068
1976	140072	124917	130755	133117	140072	123463	123020	124917	126695	127793	130755	131710	132109	133117	133545	134890	140072
1977	155015	140154	145103	148144	155015	139601	138311	140154	141249	142075	145103	146452	146553	148144	147731	149458	155015
1978	173918	155674	162526	165947	173918	154343	153106	155674	158124	158406	162526	164096	164650	165947	165635	167811	173918
1979	193133	174732	181753	184885	193133	173282	171947	174732	177472	178725	181753	183563	184180	184885	184597	186412	193133
1980	208275	193258	199192	199765	208275	191589	190478	193258	195905	197196	199192	199692	199375	199765	198682	201051	208275
1981	230137	208085	215796	219980	230137	205830	204395	208085	211326	211907	215796	217659	218581	219980	220066	222058	230137
1982	248254	229899	234802	239449	248254	227872	226605	229899	231023	231816	234802	237793	238272	239449	238382	239866	248254
1983	266997	247319	252842	256743	266997	245391	243435	247319	248538	249301	252842	254603	254739	256743	255522	256250	266997

Money supply (M1) (17)

billion yen, end of period

Adjusted - Corrigé

Disponibilités monétaires (M1) (17)

milliards de yens, fin de période

	Year	Q.1	Q.2	Q.3	Q.4	JAN	FEB	MAR	APR	MAY	JUN	JUL	AUG	SEP	OCT	NOV	DEC
1964		7201	7354	7642	7922	7045	7069	7201	7239	7464	7354	7469	7556	7642	7755	7839	7922
1965		8269	8576	8993	9389	8204	8356	8269	8331	8477	8576	8658	8838	8993	9274	9229	9389
1966		9869	10029	10477	10725	9498	9614	9869	9785	9936	10029	10340	10285	10477	10473	10620	10725
1967		11162	11392	11788	12287	10728	10961	11162	11306	11257	11392	11486	11612	11788	11943	12069	12287
1968		12721	13305	13454	13981	12329	12472	12721	12806	12953	13305	13263	13363	13454	13648	13842	13981
1969		14584	15447	16142	16930	14259	14465	14584	14889	15129	15447	15678	16200	16142	16382	17195	16930
1970		17549	18332	18923	19841	17121	17352	17549	17880	18477	18332	18610	18808	18923	19199	19512	19841
1971		20904	22919	24550	25794	20575	21116	20904	21610	22297	22919	23564	24478	24550	25012	25341	25794
1972		26698	27745	29357	32233	26008	26362	26698	27130	27090	27745	27266	28323	29357	30385	31166	32233
1973		33984	35588	37302	37720	32382	33302	33984	35559	35274	35588	36111	36412	37302	37334	37406	37720
1974		39175	41113	41139	41448	38308	38491	39175	39344	40414	41113	40765	40922	41139	40273	41007	41448
1975		42418	43483	44935	46152	41843	42299	42418	43138	43375	43483	44030	44562	44935	45087	44604	46152
1976		48258	50026	50816	51935	46846	47487	48258	48532	49234	50026	50048	50464	50816	51454	51774	51935
1977		52583	52483	53976	55677	52142	52335	52583	52166	51202	52483	52994	53529	53976	54379	54987	55677
1978		56581	58350	60304	61584	55924	56253	56581	55899	57003	58350	59119	59712	60304	60766	61302	61584
1979		62846	64850	65495	66583	62468	62629	62846	64314	65573	64850	65297	65890	65495	66127	66302	66583
1980		67673	66597	65786	65803	66745	67036	67673	68816	67829	66597	65737	65178	65786	65466	65753	65803
1981		66655	69077	70405	72320	65622	66309	66655	65807	67232	69077	69260	69799	70405	71031	71332	72320
1982		71490	72331	73953	75320	70078	70449	71490	71174	71667	72331	73192	73427	73953	74193	74515	75320
1983		75271	75062	76028	76123	75176	74954	75271	74729	74715	75062	75089	75488	76028	75794	75065	76123

M1 plus quasi-money (17)(18)

billion yen, end of period

Adjusted - Corrigé

M1 plus quasi-monnaie (17) (18)

milliards de yens, fin de période

	Year	Q.1	Q.2	Q.3	Q.4	JAN	FEB	MAR	APR	MAY	JUN	JUL	AUG	SEP	OCT	NOV	DEC
1964		18607	19225	19948	20635	18124	18340	18607	18810	19201	19225	19492	19728	19948	20203	20423	20635
1965		21528	22378	23350	24377	21120	21450	21528	21772	22095	22378	22637	23000	23350	23835	23995	24377
1966		25517	26314	27482	28379	24700	25020	25517	25672	26028	26314	26867	27087	27482	27670	28026	28379
1967		29565	30456	31661	32836	28641	29120	29565	29881	30055	30456	30829	31255	31661	32067	32429	32836
1968		34029	35364	36331	37767	33148	33545	34029	34361	34790	35364	35578	35971	36331	36810	37357	37767
1969		39339	41170	42892	44829	38375	38880	39339	39983	40565	41170	41725	42588	42892	43454	44700	44829
1970		46576	48560	50402	52470	45368	45986	46576	47296	48356	48560	49235	49853	50402	51062	51771	52470
1971		55022	58495	62074	65280	53587	54668	55022	56125	57343	58495	59666	61250	62074	63146	64040	65280
1972		68283	71786	75751	81474	66156	67185	68283	69530	70475	71786	73057	74388	75751	77672	79343	81474
1973		85422	89478	93134	95284	82296	84061	85422	87647	88499	89478	90662	91687	93134	93751	94546	95284
1974		98317	101348	103266	105375	96495	97241	98317	99001	99942	101348	101524	102319	103266	102799	104277	105375
1975		108570	111723	116107	120649	106444	107643	108570	110118	110996	111723	113424	114894	116107	117500	118916	120649
1976		125547	129791	133499	137344	122417	124084	125547	126855	128282	129791	130944	132229	133499	134968	136014	137344
1977		140841	144032	148434	152076	138532	139627	140841	141369	142647	144032	145469	146569	148434	149353	150743	152076
1978		156425	161299	166219	170710	153376	154744	156425	158104	158944	161299	162907	164535	166219	167540	169294	170710
1979		175555	180363	185231	189634	172436	173919	175555	177261	179145	180363	182197	183939	185231	186780	188152	189634
1980		194110	197594	200214	204521	190859	192708	194110	195512	197514	197594	198234	199098	200214	201051	203015	204521
1981		208949	214029	220521	225988	205134	207285	208949	210831	212187	214029	216090	218300	220521	222665	224283	225988
1982		230822	232869	240074	243339	227145	229241	230822	230447	232094	232869	236094	237987	240074	241179	242038	243339
1983		248238	251109	257077	261635	244901	245869	248238	248389	250026	251109	252959	254485	257077	258182	258457	261635

JAPAN

Loans and discounts: commercial banks
billion yen, end of period

Prêts et escomptes : banques commerciales
milliards de yens, fin de période

	Year	Q.1	Q.2	Q.3	Q.4	JAN	FEB	MAR	APR	MAY	JUN	JUL	AUG	SEP	OCT	NOV	DEC
1964	18626	16586	17059	17792	18626	16125	16290	16586	16617	16816	17059	17294	17504	17792	17906	18180	18626
1965	21411	19195	19635	20458	21411	18681	18846	19195	19176	19370	19635	19877	20060	20458	20529	20760	21411
1966	24525	21942	22308	23403	24525	21301	21455	21942	21730	21929	22308	22668	22862	23403	23390	23692	24525
1967	28323	25328	25936	27193	28323	24415	24683	25328	25217	25438	25936	26319	26663	27193	27283	27635	28323
1968	32641	29057	29650	30676	32641	28312	28536	29057	29008	29261	29650	30005	30276	30676	30891	31313	32641
1969	38097	33636	34722	36289	38097	32709	33001	33636	33676	34124	34722	35270	35738	36289	36551	37127	38097
1970	44634	39233	40512	42283	44634	38225	38567	39233	39375	39874	40512	41165	41639	42283	42650	43300	44634
1971	55398	46563	48864	51746	55398	45043	45577	46563	46904	47778	48864	49984	50742	51746	52421	53304	55398
1972	69575	57806	60245	64461	69575	55681	56431	57806	58199	58958	60245	61823	62702	64461	65496	66839	69575
1973	81254	72432	74787	78023	81254	69859	70818	72432	72966	73612	74787	76001	76838	78023	78374	79198	81254
1974	90282	83259	85039	87371	90282	81566	82097	83259	83238	83841	85039	85811	86427	87371	87720	88363	90282
1975	100782	92307	93995	97083	100782	90525	91076	92307	92306	92937	93995	95199	96184	97083	97728	98605	100782
1976	112148	103300	105107	108286	112148	101116	102044	103300	103242	103684	105107	106228	107038	108286	109261	109844	112148
1977	122571	114541	115806	118670	122571	112276	112961	114541	114097	114397	115806	117251	117488	118670	118928	119937	122571
1978	134634	124914	125984	129284	134634	122263	123019	124914	125020	124150	125984	126970	127581	129284	129265	130830	134634
1979	143547	136152	137496	140941	143547	133648	134484	136152	136466	135778	137496	138393	139039	140941	140255	141163	143547
1980	153999	145980	147312	149723	153999	143729	144473	145980	145621	145985	147312	148399	149761	149723	150339	152212	153999
1981	169845	157202	158659	163668	169845	154709	155753	157202	157330	157947	158659	160238	161399	163668	163926	165324	169845
1982	187152	173705	174892	181213	187152	170914	172048	173705	172707	172607	174892	176895	177906	181213	181697	182813	187152
1983	206483	191102	192653	199055	206483	186869	188035	191102	190207	190088	192653	195428	195437	199055	198222	200375	206483

New loans for equipment:
commercial banks
billion yen, monthly averages

Nouveaux prêts pour l'équipement :
banques commerciales
milliards de yens, moyennes mensuelles

	Year	Q.1	Q.2	Q.3	Q.4	JAN	FEB	MAR	APR	MAY	JUN	JUL	AUG	SEP	OCT	NOV	DEC
1964	137	132	133	145	139	105	117	173	127	129	144	129	132	173	126	127	164
1965	161	150	154	172	166	116	126	209	141	153	170	155	153	209	150	156	192
1966	173	161	161	178	194	120	130	232	143	170	170	152	158	224	158	176	247
1967	235	208	216	265	250	153	178	293	177	230	240	224	241	331	230	234	286
1968	278	243	262	296	311	200	217	312	236	257	294	274	265	348	286	287	359
1969	360	319	349	380	391	252	283	423	324	345	377	344	344	453	358	351	465
1970	425	385	409	440	466	316	343	497	398	389	439	411	391	518	427	421	549
1971	628	523	592	693	702	395	451	724	553	588	636	652	627	800	622	631	853
1972	795	680	702	873	925	513	603	923	639	712	754	778	819	1022	851	823	1102
1973	875	906	859	861	874	696	807	1215	821	835	922	838	781	965	854	756	1013
1974	781	737	765	808	814	645	633	932	752	716	828	745	741	937	803	717	921
1975	901	868	885	918	932	692	745	1166	859	850	946	899	829	1026	888	809	1100
1976	937	963	939	957	887	802	848	1238	926	899	993	921	890	1061	825	813	1022
1977	944	897	872	982	1023	694	772	1225	817	869	930	935	949	1061	933	954	1182
1978	1031	998	972	1077	1079	701	904	1388	890	1052	973	1020	1005	1207	971	1031	1234
1979	1166	1200	1250	1130	1083	824	962	1816	1381	1224	1146	1199	1105	1086	1041	992	1217
1980	1130	1175	1138	1050	1158	817	1038	1670	1185	1095	1133	1028	948	1175	1040	991	1444
1981	1266	1201	1272	1328	1263	995	1024	1583	1174	1239	1401	1280	1191	1514	1266	1132	1391
1982	1285	1280	1250	1393	1219	931	1149	1760	1182	1244	1325	1338	1458	1382	1012	1204	1440
1983	1333	1417	1246	1386	1284	926	1206	2120	1186	1198	1354	1125	1169	1863	1043	1197	1612

Net new bond issues: (19)
corporations
billion yen

Nouvelles émissions d'obligations, nettes : (19)
sociétés privées
milliards de yens

	Year	Q.1	Q.2	Q.3	Q.4	JAN	FEB	MAR	APR	MAY	JUN	JUL	AUG	SEP	OCT	NOV	DEC
1964	564	124	130	143	168	40	43	41	43	42	44	46	48	49	44	56	68
1965	786	164	174	224	224	57	52	56	55	55	64	70	70	84	74	73	78
1966	795	203	190	192	211	69	55	79	58	67	65	58	54	80	57	71	83
1967	909	201	237	219	252	69	70	63	67	72	98	68	63	88	70	86	95
1968	730	74	155	214	287	44	19	11	53	48	54	69	66	79	87	96	104
1969	971	230	240	255	246	81	75	74	80	81	79	85	81	89	64	90	92
1970	1185	193	240	298	454	60	61	72	57	86	96	98	106	94	137	140	178
1971	1887	273	370	573	672	84	110	78	122	114	134	191	228	154	219	216	237
1972	2294	551	265	555	924	200	190	161	124	95	46	147	161	247	292	320	312
1973	2660	607	659	668	727	248	192	167	207	226	225	208	253	207	288	209	230
1974	2452	443	513	409	1087	195	157	91	146	97	271	251	109	49	359	221	508
1975	3918	654	1002	902	1361	248	217	190	271	322	409	369	160	373	487	389	485
1976	3018	563	717	628	1110	288	153	122	237	212	267	251	139	238	291	372	447
1977	3101	754	639	618	1089	285	246	224	363	81	196	180	160	278	242	372	476
1978	3086	728	614	715	1029	225	343	160	295	115	204	220	245	250	331	277	422
1979	2919	584	710	681	944	278	294	13	198	287	225	33	-182	829	316	270	359
1980	2515	123	1049	265	1078	219	31	-128	441	256	352	112	264	-111	284	444	350
1981	2599	295	749	253	1302	136	31	129	387	123	239	144	58	51	25	532	745
1982	10737	1012	1730	3186	4810	313	223	475	229	340	1161	950	681	1554	1331	1242	2236
1983	16635	3455	4265	3766	5149	1369	888	1198	1545	1273	1447	1328	883	1556	1777	1215	2157

Loans and discounts: commercial banks
billion yen, end of period

Adjusted - Corrigé

Prêts et escomptes : banques commerciales
milliards de yens, fin de période

	Year	Q.1	Q.2	Q.3	Q.4	JAN	FEB	MAR	APR	MAY	JUN	JUL	AUG	SEP	OCT	NOV	DEC
1964		16487	17131	17749	18323	16054	16276	16487	16725	16950	17131	17336	17565	17749	17981	18204	18323
1965		19075	19717	20402	21065	18607	18837	19075	19299	19526	19717	19918	20127	20402	20614	20798	21065
1966		21801	22396	23337	24139	21223	21453	21801	21866	22105	22396	22707	22933	23337	23489	23748	24139
1967		25165	26028	27127	27898	24327	24685	25165	25370	25634	26028	26351	26735	27127	27406	27712	27898
1968		28876	29746	30616	32182	28205	28539	28876	29177	29476	29746	30027	30344	30616	31032	31411	32182
1969		33435	34831	36240	37590	32578	33002	33435	33859	34362	34831	35281	35805	36240	36720	37253	37590
1970		39006	40643	42237	44066	38062	38562	39006	39574	40142	40643	41169	41708	42237	42839	43456	44066
1971		46295	49033	51696	54717	44846	45560	46295	47124	48098	49033	49982	50826	51696	52639	53508	54717
1972		57470	60466	64396	68756	55434	56400	57470	58451	59357	60466	61823	62810	64396	65746	67100	68756
1973		71998	75069	77953	80340	69560	70757	71998	73251	74116	75069	76015	76981	77953	78656	79498	80340
1974		82734	85354	87306	89307	81233	82000	82734	83537	84421	85354	85838	86604	87306	88031	88684	89307
1975		91692	94321	97024	99722	90185	90940	91692	92604	93588	94321	95239	96407	97024	98094	98941	99722
1976		102573	105439	108208	110988	100771	101872	102573	103538	104426	105439	106280	107322	108208	109713	110208	110988
1977		113700	116140	118575	121366	111926	112749	113700	114374	115228	116140	117335	117859	118575	119513	120370	121366
1978		123929	126321	129071	133192	121845	122732	123929	125254	125046	126321	127069	127995	129071	129889	131209	133192
1979		135140	137862	140660	142020	133316	134262	135140	136747	136782	137862	138528	139518	140660	140980	141574	142020
1980		144882	147695	149428	152446	143375	144241	144882	145896	147055	147695	148576	150316	149428	151195	152725	152446
1981		156008	159071	163245	167988	154328	155510	156008	157620	159099	159071	160452	161947	163245	164925	166092	167988
1982		172544	175457	180744	185155	169448	171684	172544	172736	173769	175457	177242	178517	180744	182833	183344	185155
1983		190691	193282	198549	204557	186401	187630	190691	190241	191381	193282	195824	196282	198549	199291	201356	204557

New loans for equipment: commercial banks
billion yen, monthly averages

Adjusted - Corrigé

Nouveaux prêts pour l'équipement : banques commerciales
milliards de yens, moyennes mensuelles

	Year	Q.1	Q.2	Q.3	Q.4	JAN	FEB	MAR	APR	MAY	JUN	JUL	AUG	SEP	OCT	NOV	DEC
1964		134	137	138	137	132	134	136	138	134	139	137	139	140	136	135	139
1965		154	158	164	165	151	151	160	155	157	163	164	161	167	165	165	164
1966		163	165	169	191	155	156	179	157	175	162	163	164	179	173	187	212
1967		213	220	251	250	199	212	227	197	232	230	237	253	265	250	250	250
1968		251	267	282	308	253	249	249	255	261	285	281	279	285	304	308	312
1969		331	355	364	385	322	335	336	349	354	363	353	369	370	378	385	393
1970		401	418	421	459	404	404	395	427	409	416	420	414	430	448	462	467
1971		535	607	668	689	515	531	558	596	619	605	666	668	670	658	684	726
1972		686	720	843	915	661	685	713	697	739	724	800	863	866	887	901	959
1973		919	882	842	861	875	950	933	885	882	379	864	823	838	866	841	877
1974		759	785	784	808	816	741	721	794	758	803	749	784	819	825	797	803
1975		876	906	896	927	878	867	883	906	899	915	910	889	889	923	915	944
1976		965	962	936	892	1032	962	901	982	944	959	929	943	935	889	893	894
1977		893	892	962	1035	916	881	881	858	903	916	954	980	953	1012	1051	1043
1978		982	994	1055	1102	948	1023	976	947	1052	983	1025	1049	1092	1063	1135	1107
1979		1150	1281	1125	1099	1107	1084	1261	1453	1225	1164	1209	1161	1005	1117	1102	1078
1980		1134	1164	1035	1167	1119	1127	1157	1223	1097	1171	1020	1021	1063	1130	1117	1254
1981		1207	1299	1307	1290	1377	1148	1094	1213	1260	1425	1272	1272	1376	1382	1269	1221
1982		1271	1240	1411	1204	1313	1321	1179	1191	1239	1291	1363	1610	1260	1116	1212	1283
1983		1371	1236	1363	1293	1305	1387	1420	1195	1193	1319	1154	1208	1725	1115	1333	1431

Official discount rate
per cent per annum, end of period

Taux d'escompte officiel
pourcentage par an, fin de période

	Year	Q.1	Q.2	Q.3	Q.4	JAN	FEB	MAR	APR	MAY	JUN	JUL	AUG	SEP	OCT	NOV	DEC
1964	6.57	6.57	6.57	6.57	6.57	5.84	5.84	6.57	6.57	6.57	6.57	6.57	6.57	6.57	6.57	6.57	6.57
1965	5.48	6.21	5.48	5.48	5.48	6.21	6.21	6.21	5.84	5.84	5.48	5.48	5.48	5.48	5.48	5.48	5.48
1966	5.48	5.48	5.48	5.48	5.48	5.48	5.48	5.48	5.48	5.48	5.48	5.48	5.48	5.48	5.48	5.48	5.48
1967	5.84	5.48	5.48	5.84	5.84	5.48	5.48	5.48	5.48	5.48	5.48	5.48	5.48	5.84	5.84	5.84	5.84
1968	5.84	6.21	6.21	5.84	5.84	6.21	6.21	6.21	6.21	6.21	6.21	6.21	5.84	5.84	5.84	5.84	5.84
1969	6.25	5.84	5.84	6.25	6.25	5.84	5.84	5.84	5.84	5.84	5.84	5.84	5.84	6.25	6.25	6.25	6.25
1970	6.00	6.25	6.25	6.25	6.00	6.25	6.25	6.25	6.25	6.25	6.25	6.25	6.25	6.25	6.00	6.00	6.00
1971	4.75	5.75	5.50	5.25	4.75	5.75	5.75	5.75	5.75	5.50	5.50	5.25	5.25	5.25	5.25	5.25	4.75
1972	4.25	4.75	4.25	4.25	4.25	4.75	4.75	4.75	4.75	4.75	4.25	4.25	4.25	4.25	4.25	4.25	4.25
1973	9.00	4.25	5.50	7.00	9.00	4.25	4.25	4.25	5.00	5.50	5.50	6.00	7.00	7.00	7.00	7.00	9.00
1974	9.00	9.00	9.00	9.00	9.00	9.00	9.00	9.00	9.00	9.00	9.00	9.00	9.00	9.00	9.00	9.00	9.00
1975	6.50	9.00	8.00	7.50	6.50	9.00	9.00	9.00	8.50	8.50	8.00	8.00	7.50	7.50	6.50	6.50	6.50
1976	6.50	6.50	6.50	6.50	6.50	6.50	6.50	6.50	6.50	6.50	6.50	6.50	6.50	6.50	6.50	6.50	6.50
1977	4.25	6.00	5.00	4.25	4.25	6.50	6.50	6.00	5.00	5.00	5.00	5.00	5.00	4.25	4.25	4.25	4.25
1978	3.50	3.50	3.50	3.50	3.50	4.25	4.25	3.50	3.50	3.50	3.50	3.50	3.50	3.50	3.50	3.50	3.50
1979	6.25	3.50	4.25	5.25	6.25	3.50	3.50	3.50	4.25	4.25	4.25	5.25	5.25	5.25	5.25	6.25	6.25
1980	7.25	9.00	9.00	8.25	7.25	6.25	7.25	9.00	9.00	9.00	9.00	9.00	8.25	8.25	8.25	7.25	7.25
1981	5.50	6.25	6.25	6.25	5.50	7.25	7.25	6.25	6.25	6.25	6.25	6.25	6.25	6.25	6.25	6.25	5.50
1982	5.50	5.50	5.50	5.50	5.50	5.50	5.50	5.50	5.50	5.50	5.50	5.50	5.50	5.50	5.50	5.50	5.50
1983	5.00	5.50	5.50	5.50	5.00	5.50	5.50	5.50	5.50	5.50	5.50	5.50	5.50	5.50	5.00	5.00	5.00

JAPAN

Call money rate (20) — Taux de l'argent au jour le jour (20)

per cent per annum, end of period — pourcentage par an, fin de période

	Year	Q.1	Q.2	Q.3	Q.4	JAN	FEB	MAR	APR	MAY	JUN	JUL	AUG	SEP	OCT	NOV	DEC
1964	10.95	8.76	10.59	11.32	10.95	7.67	8.21	8.76	9.13	9.49	10.59	10.95	11.32	11.32	10.95	10.95	10.95
1965	5.84	8.40	6.94	6.21	5.84	8.40	8.40	8.40	7.30	7.30	6.94	6.57	6.57	6.21	5.84	5.84	5.84
1966	5.84	5.84	5.84	5.84	5.84	5.84	5.84	5.84	5.84	5.84	5.84	5.84	5.84	5.84	5.84	5.84	5.84
1967	7.30	6.21	6.21	6.94	7.30	5.84	5.84	6.21	5.84	5.84	6.21	6.21	6.57	6.94	6.94	6.94	7.30
1968	7.67	8.03	8.03	8.03	7.67	7.67	7.67	8.03	8.03	8.03	8.03	8.40	8.03	8.03	7.67	7.30	7.67
1969	8.50	7.67	6.94	8.25	8.50	7.30	7.30	7.67	7.30	6.94	6.94	7.67	8.03	8.25	8.25	8.25	8.50
1970	8.00	8.50	8.25	8.50	8.00	8.25	8.50	8.50	8.25	8.25	8.25	8.50	8.50	8.50	8.25	7.75	8.00
1971	5.50	7.25	6.50	6.00	5.50	7.50	7.25	7.25	6.75	6.50	6.50	6.50	6.25	6.00	5.50	5.50	5.50
1972	4.71	5.25	4.64	4.50	4.71	5.00	5.10	5.25	5.00	4.81	4.64	4.39	4.50	4.50	4.43	4.32	4.71
1973	10.47	5.43	6.55	8.72	10.47	4.96	5.17	5.43	5.89	5.96	6.55	7.32	7.61	8.72	8.82	9.04	10.47
1974	13.46	12.48	12.48	13.00	13.46	11.65	12.10	12.48	12.04	12.00	12.48	12.63	13.48	13.00	12.50	12.65	13.46
1975	7.96	12.92	10.72	9.67	7.96	12.67	13.00	12.92	12.02	11.06	10.72	11.00	10.69	9.67	8.73	7.61	7.96
1976	7.11	7.00	6.90	7.05	7.11	7.28	7.00	7.00	6.75	6.75	6.90	7.08	7.25	7.05	6.77	6.77	7.11
1977	5.01	6.69	5.48	4.98	5.01	7.00	7.00	6.69	5.87	5.18	5.48	5.66	5.75	4.98	4.92	4.62	5.01
1978	4.57	4.62	4.11	4.25	4.57	4.79	4.80	4.62	4.14	4.06	4.11	4.44	4.39	4.25	4.18	3.93	4.57
1979	8.05	4.64	5.34	6.81	8.05	4.29	4.35	4.64	4.39	5.12	5.34	5.80	6.69	6.81	6.74	7.58	8.05
1980	9.49	10.73	12.64	11.40	9.49	8.06	8.74	10.73	12.21	12.56	12.64	12.70	12.09	11.40	11.04	9.50	9.49
1981	6.70	8.04	7.12	7.26	6.70	8.91	8.60	8.04	7.19	7.05	7.12	7.26	7.24	7.26	7.05	6.80	6.70
1982	6.92	6.68	7.19	6.99	6.92	6.58	6.58	6.68	7.16	7.17	7.19	7.19	7.18	6.99	6.92	6.68	6.92
1983	6.44	6.69	6.20	6.53	6.44	6.64	6.57	6.69	6.30	6.08	6.20	6.39	6.46	6.53	6.43	5.99	6.44

"Gensaki" rate (3 months) (21) — Taux «Gensaki» (3 mois) (21)

per cent per annum, end of period — pourcentage par an, fin de période

	Year	Q.1	Q.2	Q.3	Q.4	JAN	FEB	MAR	APR	MAY	JUN	JUL	AUG	SEP	OCT	NOV	DEC
1964																	
1965																	
1966																	
1967																	
1968																	
1969																	
1970																	
1971																	
1972																	
1973																	
1974																	
1975																	
1976																	
1977	6.06	7.52	6.44	6.25	6.06	..	7.11	7.52	6.23	6.35	6.44	6.21	6.34	6.25	5.37	5.17	6.06
1978	4.86	6.07	5.03	4.93	4.86	5.62	6.09	6.07	5.10	4.93	5.03	4.86	4.94	4.93	4.46	4.57	4.86
1979	8.13	4.97	5.32	6.46	8.13	4.69	4.73	4.97	4.91	5.07	5.32	5.58	6.32	6.46	6.69	7.37	8.13
1980	9.90	11.51	11.55	11.27	9.90	7.96	8.77	11.51	12.67	12.30	11.55	11.21	11.30	11.27	10.20	9.58	9.90
1981	6.75	7.87	7.41	7.26	6.75	8.47	8.39	7.87	6.82	7.24	7.41	7.16	7.22	7.26	7.13	7.15	6.75
1982	6.96	6.43	7.14	7.19	6.96	6.41	6.38	6.43	6.57	6.82	7.14	7.15	7.14	7.19	6.97	6.98	6.96
1983	6.45	6.72	6.46	5.68	6.45	6.48	6.64	6.72	6.35	6.26	6.46	6.47	6.57	6.68	5.52	6.36	6.45

Yield of Central Government bonds — Rendement des obligations du gouvernement central

per cent per annum, end of period — pourcentage par an, fin de période

	Year	Q.1	Q.2	Q.3	Q.4	JAN	FEB	MAR	APR	MAY	JUN	JUL	AUG	SEP	OCT	NOV	DEC
1964																	
1965																	
1966	6.86				6.86										6.85	6.86	6.86
1967	6.98	6.87	6.88	6.97	6.98	6.85	6.86	6.87	6.87	6.88	6.88	6.89	6.96	6.97	6.97	6.97	6.98
1968	7.05	7.02	7.03	7.05	7.05	7.01	7.01	7.02	7.02	7.03	7.03	7.04	7.04	7.05	7.05	7.05	7.05
1969	7.13	7.07	7.09	7.12	7.13	7.05	7.06	7.07	7.07	7.08	7.09	7.08	7.09	7.12	7.12	7.13	7.13
1970	7.24	7.16	7.19	7.21	7.24	7.14	7.15	7.16	7.16	7.17	7.19	7.19	7.20	7.21	7.22	7.23	7.24
1971	7.24	7.28	7.32	7.27	7.24	7.25	7.26	7.28	7.28	7.30	7.32	7.29	7.25	7.27	7.28	7.30	7.24
1972	6.40	7.10	6.58	6.43	6.40	7.18	7.12	7.10	6.90	6.84	6.68	6.45	6.44	6.43	6.41	6.39	6.40
1973	8.78	6.64	7.09	7.52	8.78	6.43	6.58	6.64	7.04	7.08	7.09	7.24	7.43	7.52	7.61	7.71	8.78
1974	9.60	9.20	9.18	9.53	9.60	9.00	8.94	9.20	9.16	9.12	9.18	9.07	9.33	9.53	9.41	9.59	9.60
1975	9.02	9.35	9.17	9.12	9.02	9.70	9.15	9.35	9.29	9.08	9.17	9.10	9.17	9.12	9.09	9.16	9.02
1976	8.73	8.70	8.77	8.76	8.73	8.60	8.61	8.70	8.67	8.77	8.77	8.75	8.71	8.76	8.76	8.79	8.73
1977	6.27	8.41	7.31	6.86	6.27	8.58	8.50	8.41	7.73	7.42	7.31	6.74	6.81	6.86	6.72	6.58	6.27
1978	6.10	6.03	6.36	6.19	6.10	6.14	6.20	6.03	5.97	6.00	6.06	6.06	6.21	6.19	6.05	6.10	6.10
1979	8.64	6.95	8.07	7.86	8.64	6.11	6.37	6.95	7.66	7.75	8.07	7.75	7.92	7.86	8.41	8.76	8.64
1980	9.41	10.00	8.61	9.21	9.41	8.50	9.32	10.00	10.30	8.75	8.61	8.88	9.09	9.21	8.99	9.52	9.41
1981	7.93	8.29	8.78	9.02	7.93	8.81	8.79	8.29	8.41	8.81	8.78	8.93	9.15	9.02	8.79	8.21	7.93
1982	7.50	7.58	8.53	8.41	7.50	7.86	7.85	7.58	7.60	8.04	8.53	8.34	8.39	8.41	8.45	8.13	7.50
1983	6.94	7.56	7.49	7.28	6.94	7.77	7.52	7.56	7.46	7.61	7.49	7.59	7.54	7.28	7.22	7.09	6.94

Share prices: (22) / Cours des actions : (22)

Tokyo Stock Exchange / Bourse de Tokyo

1980 = 100

	Year	Q.1	Q.2	Q.3	Q.4	JAN	FEB	MAR	APR	MAY	JUN	JUL	AUG	SEP	OCT	NOV	DEC
1964	21	21	21	21	20	21	21	21	20	21	22	22	21	21	20	20	20
1965	20	20	19	19	22	21	20	20	19	19	18	17	19	21	20	22	23
1966	25	25	26	24	24	24	25	26	26	26	25	25	25	24	24	24	23
1967	23	24	24	23	22	24	24	24	24	24	25	25	23	22	23	22	21
1968	25	22	24	27	28	22	22	22	23	24	24	25	27	29	29	27	28
1969	32	29	32	32	35	29	29	30	31	32	32	32	31	33	34	35	36
1970	35	38	35	33	32	37	37	38	38	33	33	34	34	33	33	33	31
1971	38	34	39	40	38	33	34	36	38	39	41	43	40	38	37	38	40
1972	60	46	54	64	74	44	46	48	52	54	58	61	65	67	69	73	79
1973	77	83	76	78	69	87	82	81	77	76	76	80	79	75	73	70	64
1974	65	68	70	64	58	66	69	68	68	71	71	69	63	61	56	57	60
1975	66	63	69	66	66	58	63	66	68	70	69	68	65	63	65	67	67
1976	71	71	72	75	75	71	71	72	71	72	74	74	75	75	74	73	77
1977	80	80	79	80	79	80	80	80	79	80	79	79	80	82	83	78	77
1978	88	81	87	89	93	79	81	84	87	86	87	89	89	90	92	93	94
1979	95	95	94	95	95	96	96	95	94	96	94	93	95	96	95	94	96
1980	100	98	98	100	104	98	99	96	97	99	99	99	100	102	104	104	103
1981	116	107	117	123	117	107	107	109	115	117	120	125	126	119	115	118	119
1982	116	118	115	112	119	121	120	113	113	117	114	112	110	112	114	119	123
1983	137	125	133	142	146	124	124	127	130	134	136	140	141	144	145	145	149

U.S. dollar exchange rate: spot / Taux de change du dollar É.-U. : au comptant

cents per yen, end of period / cents par yen, fin de période

	Year	Q.1	Q.2	Q.3	Q.4	JAN	FEB	MAR	APR	MAY	JUN	JUL	AUG	SEP	OCT	NOV	DEC
1964	0.2791	0.2763	0.2758	0.2772	0.2791	0.2759	0.2758	0.2763	0.2758	0.2758	0.2758	0.2758	0.2759	0.2772	0.2761	0.2772	0.2791
1965	0.2771	0.2770	0.2762	0.2760	0.2771	0.2786	0.2776	0.2770	0.2758	0.2762	0.2762	0.2761	0.2760	0.2760	0.2762	0.2769	0.2771
1966	0.2759	0.2762	0.2759	0.2759	0.2759	0.2768	0.2765	0.2762	0.2759	0.2760	0.2759	0.2758	0.2758	0.2759	0.2758	0.2758	0.2759
1967	0.2763	0.2764	0.2763	0.2765	0.2763	0.2758	0.2760	0.2764	0.2763	0.2763	0.2763	0.2761	0.2761	0.2765	0.2763	0.2762	0.2763
1968	0.2796	0.2762	0.2766	0.2787	0.2796	0.2762	0.2763	0.2762	0.2760	0.2762	0.2766	0.2778	0.2782	0.2787	0.2793	0.2795	0.2796
1969	0.2795	0.2794	0.2786	0.2796	0.2795	0.2794	0.2795	0.2794	0.2792	0.2789	0.2786	0.2780	0.2784	0.2796	0.2795	0.2795	0.2795
1970	0.2796	0.2797	0.2738	0.2794	0.2796	0.2796	0.2797	0.2797	0.2790	0.2786	0.2788	0.2788	0.2792	0.2794	0.2796	0.2796	0.2796
1971	0.3177	0.2798	0.2798	0.2992	0.3177	0.2797	0.2798	0.2798	0.2798	0.2798	0.2798	0.2798	0.2950	0.2992	0.3037	0.3052	0.3177
1972	0.3311	0.3287	0.3321	0.3321	0.3311	0.3221	0.3287	0.3287	0.3281	0.3284	0.3321	0.3321	0.3321	0.3321	0.3321	0.3321	0.3311
1973	0.3571	0.3762	0.3769	0.3764	0.3571	0.3321	0.3704	0.3762	0.3766	0.3774	0.3769	0.3796	0.3769	0.3764	0.3748	0.3571	0.3571
1974	0.3323	0.3623	0.3520	0.3350	0.3323	0.3344	0.3477	0.3623	0.3575	0.3547	0.3520	0.3358	0.3304	0.3350	0.3335	0.3332	0.3323
1975	0.3277	0.3404	0.3374	0.3304	0.3277	0.3357	0.3489	0.3404	0.3409	0.3432	0.3374	0.3363	0.3357	0.3304	0.3313	0.3300	0.3277
1976	0.3415	0.3337	0.3362	0.3479	0.3415	0.3293	0.3309	0.3337	0.3340	0.3334	0.3362	0.3408	0.3463	0.3479	0.3405	0.3381	0.3415
1977	0.4167	0.3604	0.3736	0.3767	0.4167	0.3457	0.3537	0.3604	0.3601	0.3606	0.3736	0.3759	0.3741	0.3767	0.3990	0.4070	0.4167
1978	0.5139	0.4496	0.4885	0.5287	0.5139	0.4143	0.4189	0.4496	0.4486	0.4476	0.4885	0.5244	0.5258	0.5287	0.5682	0.5063	0.5139
1979	0.4172	0.4778	0.4608	0.4478	0.4172	0.4968	0.4946	0.4778	0.4577	0.4550	0.4608	0.4604	0.4545	0.4478	0.4207	0.4019	0.4172
1980	0.4926	0.4005	0.4596	0.4713	0.4926	0.4188	0.4003	0.4005	0.4184	0.4458	0.4596	0.4405	0.4566	0.4713	0.4728	0.4615	0.4926
1981	0.4548	0.4739	0.4429	0.4297	0.4548	0.4885	0.4789	0.4739	0.4651	0.4462	0.4429	0.4176	0.4386	0.4297	0.4277	0.4666	0.4548
1982	0.4255	0.4057	0.3937	0.3711	0.4255	0.4338	0.4219	0.4057	0.4254	0.4125	0.3937	0.3883	0.3821	0.3711	0.3606	0.3951	0.4255
1983	0.4307	0.4177	0.4172	0.4235	0.4307	0.4203	0.4247	0.4177	0.4219	0.4196	0.4172	0.4137	0.4055	0.4235	0.4280	0.4274	0.4307

Official reserves excluding gold / Réserves officielles, or exclu

million SDR's, end of period / millions de DTS, fin de période

	Year	Q.1	Q.2	Q.3	Q.4	JAN	FEB	MAR	APR	MAY	JUN	JUL	AUG	SEP	OCT	NOV	DEC
1964	1715	1707	1647	1649	1715	1746	1692	1707	1685	1640	1647	1625	1637	1649	1616	1634	1715
1965	1824	1770	1698	1687	1824	1743	1766	1770	1735	1731	1698	1668	1682	1687	1716	1803	1824
1966	1790	1827	1821	1760	1790	1799	1826	1827	1815	1813	1821	1770	1779	1760	1735	1760	1790
1967	1692	1792	1769	1712	1692	1768	1766	1792	1807	1805	1769	1730	1675	1712	1682	1652	1692
1968	2550	1647	1646	2025	2550	1658	1686	1647	1578	1603	1646	1742	1888	2025	2219	2437	2550
1969	3241	2861	2766	2928	3241	2594	2735	2861	2749	2742	2766	2711	2803	2928	2936	3178	3241
1970	4308	3590	3612	3467	4308	3320	3351	3590	3645	3619	3612	3475	3494	3467	3688	3895	4308
1971	13468	5360	7160	12705	13468	4440	4774	5360	5456	6477	7160	7458	11835	12705	13421	14157	13468
1972	16177	14613	13855	14449	16177	14018	14466	14613	14495	14029	13855	13891	14341	14449	15652	16220	16177
1973	9412	14287	11861	11526	9412	15708	15123	14287	13218	12416	11861	11826	11800	11526	10907	10200	9412
1974	10303	9561	10393	10354	10303	8849	9125	9561	9800	10175	10393	10233	10154	10354	10517	10644	10303
1975	10208	10606	11073	10658	10208	10165	10344	10606	10810	10936	11073	11550	11132	10658	10386	10327	10208
1976	13553	11526	12696	13511	13553	10515	11199	11526	12244	12576	12696	13159	13417	13511	13618	13807	13553
1977	18392	14113	14443	14948	18392	13752	14003	14113	14353	14379	14443	14586	14883	14948	16182	18308	18392
1978	24875	23128	21558	22318	24875	18819	19299	23128	21964	22225	21558	22803	22473	22318	21139	24893	24875
1979	14819	21921	18711	18624	14819	25287	24885	21921	19888	18420	18711	18676	18752	18624	17498	14814	14819
1980	19316	14228	16568	17581	19316	15360	15340	14228	14093	15748	16568	16845	16995	17581	18647	19040	19316
1981	24235	21573	23869	24143	24235	20834	21393	21573	22465	23315	23869	24084	24095	24143	24409	24207	24235
1982	21153	24362	23283	22389	21153	24440	24788	24362	23764	23646	23283	23454	22542	22389	21518	21302	21153
1983	23498	22425	23468	23617	23498	21780	21955	22425	22701	23100	23468	23896	23621	23617	23587	23617	23498

JAPAN

Imports c.i.f. (23)
billion yen, monthly averages

Importations c.a.f. (23)
milliards de yens, moyennes mensuelles

	Year	Q.1	Q.2	Q.3	Q.4	JAN	FEB	MAR	APR	MAY	JUN	JUL	AUG	SEP	OCT	NOV	DEC
1964	238	239	247	223	243	235	236	247	243	259	241	234	214	221	245	228	256
1965	245	237	260	238	245	226	238	248	251	266	264	240	238	237	240	240	254
1966	286	267	289	280	307	240	269	292	287	301	280	276	286	278	303	308	308
1967	350	327	358	340	376	310	323	347	337	382	355	323	352	344	365	370	392
1968	390	374	391	380	413	362	374	386	380	423	368	395	372	374	406	409	426
1969	451	411	432	466	494	404	400	428	403	455	439	458	462	479	501	473	509
1970	566	528	562	580	596	506	509	570	531	564	591	593	560	587	617	559	613
1971	576	585	600	553	565	569	565	620	596	594	610	601	534	525	566	566	563
1972	602	556	567	603	685	511	536	619	574	601	525	545	629	633	665	663	727
1973	867	699	829	881	1059	675	682	741	743	858	887	867	913	862	1003	1006	1168
1974	1505	1354	1561	1522	1585	1131	1408	1523	1481	1652	1549	1604	1535	1427	1601	1540	1612
1975	1431	1421	1390	1399	1513	1473	1340	1449	1370	1484	1317	1467	1329	1402	1555	1355	1631
1976	1602	1496	1585	1631	1698	1461	1439	1589	1532	1590	1633	1676	1603	1615	1635	1698	1760
1977	1594	1657	1640	1567	1513	1654	1514	1804	1585	1724	1611	1556	1617	1529	1522	1470	1547
1978	1394	1450	1431	1299	1396	1444	1397	1508	1394	1619	1282	1292	1303	1301	1315	1348	1526
1979	2020	1559	1860	2121	2541	1476	1474	1728	1754	1972	1854	1986	2158	2220	2322	2576	2725
1980	2666	2682	2885	2529	2569	2481	2640	2923	3043	2947	2665	2709	2518	2361	2566	2399	2743
1981	2622	2509	2636	2616	2728	2437	2403	2687	2630	2747	2529	2740	2610	2497	2608	2731	2845
1982	2721	2769	2669	2674	2774	2692	2623	2993	2911	2643	2454	2734	2689	2598	2715	2857	2749
1983	2501	2471	2404	2436	2694	2544	2283	2586	2428	2316	2470	2345	2417	2545	2552	2628	2902

Exports f.o.b. (23)
billion yen, monthly averages

Exportations f.o.b. (23)
milliards de yens, moyennes mensuelles

	Year	Q.1	Q.2	Q.3	Q.4	JAN	FEB	MAR	APR	MAY	JUN	JUL	AUG	SEP	OCT	NOV	DEC
1964	200	157	189	208	247	113	165	194	185	185	196	215	202	205	240	219	283
1965	254	219	253	268	275	160	232	264	247	252	259	273	276	254	268	250	308
1966	293	252	281	303	338	201	254	300	279	275	287	311	293	304	317	306	393
1967	313	273	306	327	347	209	289	322	310	297	310	322	330	331	341	306	394
1968	389	313	380	407	457	238	325	376	362	400	379	385	412	422	425	431	515
1969	480	397	465	509	549	302	395	493	455	458	481	510	497	520	512	498	636
1970	580	494	559	605	660	393	489	600	550	537	589	616	574	625	639	562	781
1971	699	606	701	750	741	452	594	772	682	683	736	778	744	729	706	680	838
1972	734	632	674	772	858	481	629	785	693	651	678	754	747	814	770	778	1026
1973	836	720	763	850	1011	562	800	798	747	749	791	878	791	882	887	964	1181
1974	1352	1003	1279	1474	1651	763	1019	1227	1185	1286	1365	1484	1499	1439	1630	1532	1792
1975	1379	1293	1328	1359	1536	1108	1319	1450	1402	1281	1301	1418	1302	1356	1472	1337	1798
1976	1661	1453	1637	1701	1855	1113	1451	1795	1596	1597	1718	1760	1581	1761	1757	1652	2155
1977	1804	1698	1809	1829	1880	1386	1688	2019	1889	1702	1837	1942	1733	1812	1838	1724	2077
1978	1713	1745	1759	1651	1687	1364	1793	2078	1750	1751	1806	1714	1540	1699	1595	1552	1914
1979	1878	1556	1792	1929	2235	1195	1549	1925	1674	1795	1906	1935	1797	2055	2006	2049	2650
1980	2449	2205	2488	2461	2640	1656	2304	2655	2535	2494	2435	2495	2336	2553	2501	2349	3071
1981	2789	2430	2777	2965	2984	1925	2464	2903	2725	2748	2857	3083	2784	3028	3094	2692	3166
1982	2869	2728	2882	2918	2950	2284	2704	3196	3032	2750	2862	3060	2685	3010	2974	2741	3135
1983	2909	2607	2862	2994	3174	2134	2616	3069	2912	2738	2935	3030	2824	3130	3032	2908	3581

Trade balance (f.o.b. — c.i.f.) (23)
billion yen, monthly averages

Balance commerciale (f.o.b. — c.a.f.) (23)
milliards de yens, moyennes mensuelles

	Year	Q.1	Q.2	Q.3	Q.4	JAN	FEB	MAR	APR	MAY	JUN	JUL	AUG	SEP	OCT	NOV	DEC
1964	-38	-82	-59	-16	4	-122	-72	-52	-58	-74	-45	-19	-12	-16	-4	-9	26
1965	9	-18	-8	30	30	-66	-5	17	-4	-13	-5	34	38	17	28	10	54
1966	8	-15	-9	23	32	-39	-15	8	-7	-27	8	36	7	26	13	-2	84
1967	-37	-53	-53	-12	-29	-101	-34	-25	-27	-85	-45	-1	-22	-13	-24	-65	2
1968	-1	-61	-10	26	43	-125	-49	-9	-18	-23	11	-10	40	48	19	22	89
1969	29	-14	33	43	54	-101	-5	65	52	3	42	52	35	41	11	24	127
1970	13	-34	-3	25	64	-113	-20	30	19	-26	-2	24	14	38	22	3	168
1971	124	21	100	197	176	-117	29	152	86	89	126	177	210	204	140	114	274
1972	131	76	108	169	173	-30	93	166	119	50	154	209	117	181	106	115	299
1973	-31	21	-67	-30	-48	-113	119	57	4	-109	-96	11	-122	20	-116	-42	13
1974	-154	-351	-282	-48	67	-369	-388	-295	-296	-366	-184	-120	-36	13	29	-8	179
1975	-52	-128	-62	-40	22	-365	-20	1	32	-203	-16	-49	-27	-45	-82	-18	167
1976	59	-43	52	69	157	-347	12	206	64	7	85	84	-22	146	123	-47	395
1977	210	40	170	262	367	-268	173	215	304	-22	227	387	116	283	317	254	530
1978	319	295	338	352	291	-80	396	570	356	133	525	422	236	398	279	205	388
1979	-142	-3	-68	-192	-306	-282	75	198	-80	-176	53	-51	-361	-165	-316	-527	-75
1980	-218	-477	-397	-68	71	-825	-336	-269	-508	-454	-230	-214	-182	191	-66	-50	328
1981	167	-78	141	350	256	-512	61	216	94	1	328	343	174	532	486	-39	321
1982	148	-41	212	245	176	-408	82	203	121	107	409	326	-5	412	259	-116	386
1983	408	136	458	559	480	-410	334	483	484	423	466	684	407	585	480	280	679

Imports c.i.f. (23) — Importations c.a.f. (23)

billion yen, monthly averages — milliards de yens, moyennes mensuelles

Adjusted - Corrigé

Year	Q.1	Q.2	Q.3	Q.4	JAN	FEB	MAR	APR	MAY	JUN	JUL	AUG	SEP	OCT	NOV	DEC
1964	239	237	232	245	245	238	233	235	237	238	237	222	238	245	240	250
1965	237	249	249	246	237	239	235	243	244	261	246	247	253	241	249	248
1966	266	278	292	307	251	270	278	280	276	278	284	297	295	303	315	302
1967	327	347	352	374	322	325	333	335	352	353	332	365	360	363	376	383
1968	376	382	391	410	376	381	371	383	395	367	400	385	388	400	414	415
1969	413	426	475	490	418	410	410	409	430	438	459	474	492	491	482	496
1970	531	556	589	590	523	526	544	539	539	588	591	573	603	602	571	595
1971	539	593	563	559	595	584	589	602	569	608	598	546	544	554	578	544
1972	559	558	616	677	538	554	586	577	572	525	546	641	661	650	681	699
1973	706	815	900	1045	710	702	705	748	811	885	863	929	910	983	1034	1117
1974	1364	1538	1556	1562	1188	1452	1451	1498	1560	1556	1593	1567	1510	1571	1583	1533
1975	1437	1374	1423	1488	1530	1398	1384	1393	1404	1327	1446	1355	1466	1523	1397	1543
1976	1513	1576	1652	1670	1505	1515	1518	1567	1518	1643	1648	1630	1678	1611	1737	1663
1977	1673	1633	1584	1488	1693	1616	1710	1627	1653	1618	1540	1640	1572	1505	1498	1462
1978	1468	1409	1317	1378	1479	1493	1433	1429	1486	1312	1303	1320	1329	1325	1375	1434
1979	1640	1832	2152	2510	1510	1580	1829	1796	1794	1907	2012	2184	2261	2346	2627	2556
1980	2670	2840	2586	2567	2508	2761	2740	3033	2741	2748	2762	2565	2431	2619	2493	2588
1981	2509	2569	2694	2685	2489	2508	2530	2530	2558	2620	2769	2677	2637	2675	2692	2687
1982	2788	2618	2755	2751	2756	2744	2863	2812	2486	2556	2713	2764	2789	2786	2840	2626
1983	2472	2365	2516	2667	2606	2388	2421	2343	2181	2573	2323	2487	2740	2617	2610	2775

Exports f.o.b. (23) — Exportations f.o.b. (23)

billion yen, monthly averages — milliards de yens, moyennes mensuelles

Adjusted - Corrigé

Year	Q.1	Q.2	Q.3	Q.4	JAN	FEB	MAR	APR	MAY	JUN	JUL	AUG	SEP	OCT	NOV	DEC
1964	175	191	202	226	165	176	184	188	189	197	206	197	202	228	225	226
1965	243	255	260	254	233	248	249	249	257	259	261	268	251	254	257	250
1966	281	282	294	313	289	272	282	281	279	287	298	286	299	302	315	322
1967	304	307	318	322	299	311	301	311	301	309	308	322	323	326	315	325
1968	347	382	394	426	338	353	350	364	405	377	369	404	410	411	444	425
1969	439	468	492	511	429	433	453	458	467	478	487	489	501	499	513	521
1970	547	565	586	613	537	535	549	557	552	586	586	569	602	624	578	637
1971	663	713	727	689	638	647	704	695	707	735	737	739	704	690	695	681
1972	691	688	750	791	674	677	722	706	678	680	712	749	789	752	791	830
1973	790	779	829	933	779	849	741	763	782	793	826	800	861	863	978	958
1974	1086	1303	1445	1530	1037	1080	1141	1201	1340	1367	1399	1522	1415	1574	1553	1462
1975	1411	1349	1338	1420	1489	1399	1347	1407	1336	1304	1339	1335	1341	1422	1364	1474
1976	1556	1656	1682	1725	1480	1540	1648	1591	1665	1713	1664	1637	1745	1698	1698	1779
1977	1819	1822	1816	1763	1825	1801	1832	1862	1778	1826	1837	1807	1805	1778	1785	1726
1978	1836	1765	1647	1612	1799	1870	1839	1738	1802	1755	1640	1624	1678	1575	1637	1624
1979	1568	1785	1930	2139	1575	1608	1520	1664	1845	1846	1858	1904	2029	1992	2168	2257
1980	2318	2458	2476	2528	2230	2399	2327	2576	2459	2338	2428	2500	2498	2540	2478	2565
1981	2573	2689	2963	2880	2598	2556	2565	2565	2711	2790	2980	2965	2943	3143	2858	2640
1982	2938	2836	2889	2847	3101	2839	2875	2954	2719	2837	2916	2844	2907	2958	2923	2662
1983	2805	2817	2965	3053	2900	2747	2768	2829	2707	2916	2883	2989	3024	3011	3105	3044

Trade balance (f.o.b. — c.i.f.) (23) — Balance commerciale (f.o.b. — c.a.f.) (23)

billion yen, monthly averages — milliards de yens, moyennes mensuelles

Adjusted - Corrigé

Year	Q.1	Q.2	Q.3	Q.4	JAN	FEB	MAR	APR	MAY	JUN	JUL	AUG	SEP	OCT	NOV	DEC
1964	-63	-45	-31	-19	-80	-61	-49	-47	-48	-41	-31	-26	-35	-18	-16	-23
1965	7	6	11	8	-4	9	14	6	13	-2	16	21	-3	14	8	2
1966	15	4	2	6	39	2	3	0	3	9	14	-11	4	-2	0	20
1967	-23	-40	-35	-52	-23	-14	-32	-24	-51	-44	-24	-43	-37	-37	-61	-57
1968	-29	0	3	17	-38	-28	-21	-19	10	10	-31	19	21	11	30	10
1969	26	42	17	22	11	23	43	50	37	40	28	15	9	8	31	26
1970	16	10	-3	23	33	9	4	18	14	-3	-5	-4	-1	21	6	42
1971	74	119	164	130	43	63	115	93	138	127	139	193	160	137	118	137
1972	132	130	134	115	136	124	136	130	106	155	167	108	129	102	111	131
1973	84	-36	-71	-112	69	147	37	15	-29	-93	-37	-129	-48	-121	-57	-160
1974	-277	-235	-111	-32	-150	-372	-310	-297	-220	-189	-194	-45	-94	4	-29	-71
1975	-26	-26	-84	-68	-41	1	-38	14	-68	-23	-108	-20	-125	-102	-32	-70
1976	44	80	30	55	-25	24	131	24	147	70	16	7	67	87	-39	117
1977	146	189	232	275	132	185	122	234	126	208	297	166	233	273	286	265
1978	367	356	330	234	320	376	406	310	316	443	337	304	349	250	262	190
1979	-72	-47	-222	-371	65	28	-310	-132	51	-60	-154	-281	-232	-354	-459	-299
1980	-351	-383	-110	-39	-279	-362	-413	-457	-282	-410	-333	-65	68	-79	-15	-23
1981	64	119	268	196	109	49	35	35	152	170	211	288	306	468	165	-47
1982	151	218	134	97	345	95	12	142	233	281	204	79	119	172	83	36
1983	333	452	449	386	293	359	346	487	526	343	560	502	284	394	495	269

JAPAN

Balance of payments: net trade (24)
million dollars

Balance des paiements : balance commerciale (24)
millions de dollars

	Year	Q.1	Q.2	Q.3	Q.4	JAN	FEB	MAR	APR	MAY	JUN	JUL	AUG	SEP	OCT	NOV	DEC
1964	377	-309	-57	246	497	-215	-74	-20	-18	-58	19	77	89	80	139	116	242
1965	••	••	401	652	661	••	••	••	118	118	165	226	235	191	215	169	277
1966	2275	370	449	691	765	26	146	198	149	106	194	263	192	236	217	171	377
1967	1160	152	171	450	387	-105	121	136	119	-21	73	173	121	156	145	33	209
1968	2529	118	546	845	1020	-147	80	185	144	166	236	194	309	342	283	285	452
1969	3699	560	913	1067	1159	-63	220	403	349	230	334	367	325	375	286	291	582
1970	3963	579	845	1105	1434	-44	223	400	307	197	341	369	331	405	392	298	744
1971	7787	1055	1748	2489	2495	-3	363	695	542	558	648	787	851	851	714	614	1167
1972	8971	1688	1984	2637	2662	177	626	885	718	509	757	986	727	924	662	701	1299
1973	3688	1050	593	1005	1040	20	738	292	428	59	106	484	-8	529	125	345	570
1974	1436	-1849	-848	1517	2616	-819	-690	-340	-344	-529	25	332	559	626	796	602	1218
1975	5028	655	1082	1402	1889	-620	595	680	654	-71	499	494	495	413	329	444	1116
1976	9887	1470	2383	2715	3319	-572	635	1407	759	683	941	998	557	1160	1129	518	1672
1977	17311	2731	3852	4717	6011	-68	1233	1566	1766	603	1483	1996	1074	1647	1800	1565	2646
1978	24596	5755	6532	7351	4958	348	2312	3095	2270	1327	2935	2721	1950	2680	1029	1356	2573
1979	1845	1690	1523	-355	-1013	-885	1088	1487	471	-4	1056	148	-680	177	-407	-1268	662
1980	2125	-2593	-1300	2259	3759	-2329	-228	-36	-759	-665	124	154	305	1800	828	615	2316
1981	19967	2048	4846	7388	5685	-1412	1382	2078	1433	809	2604	2375	1738	3275	2952	559	2174
1982	18079	2439	5312	5760	4568	-859	1276	2022	1431	1363	2518	2370	950	2440	1939	117	2512
1983	31649	4501	8379	9697	9072	-634	2194	2941	2816	2748	2815	3832	2480	3385	3094	2115	3863

Balance of payments: current balance
million dollars

Balance des paiements : opérations courantes, nettes
millions de dollars

	Year	Q.1	Q.2	Q.3	Q.4	JAN	FEB	MAR	APR	MAY	JUN	JUL	AUG	SEP	OCT	NOV	DEC
1964																	
1965	••	••	141	433	391	••	••	••	21	28	92	152	168	113	135	88	168
1966	1254	84	192	478	500	-62	68	78	55	22	115	193	121	164	132	88	280
1967	-190	-174	-173	137	20	-200	34	-8	8	-134	-47	71	26	40	36	-85	69
1968	1048	-295	191	504	648	-275	-47	27	26	34	131	73	206	225	171	165	312
1969	2119	130	551	672	766	-195	101	224	236	104	211	245	201	226	165	173	428
1970	1970	55	373	599	943	-201	87	169	154	43	176	191	185	223	254	128	561
1971	5797	434	1262	2100	2001	-190	178	446	372	396	494	610	817	673	568	450	983
1972	6624	958	1212	2084	2370	-21	393	586	506	177	529	752	625	707	545	655	1170
1973	-136	494	-416	101	-315	-189	690	-7	158	-316	-258	194	-330	237	-256	-78	19
1974	-4693	-3288	-2404	-134	1133	-1260	-1213	-815	-778	-1040	-586	-205	29	42	290	126	717
1975	-682	-925	-300	-23	566	-1164	109	130	185	-574	89	-4	22	-41	-156	37	685
1976	3680	-109	941	983	1865	-1081	147	825	292	226	423	410	13	560	637	40	1188
1977	10918	893	2183	3261	4581	-650	683	860	1226	85	872	1494	669	1098	1316	1111	2154
1978	16534	3971	4579	5146	2838	-266	1835	2402	1680	634	2265	1989	1246	1921	393	592	1853
1979	-8754	-711	-1126	-3229	-3688	-1462	262	489	-345	-889	108	-939	-1510	-780	-1086	-2294	-308
1980	-10746	-5810	-4533	-1011	608	-3372	-1250	-1188	-1734	-1861	-888	-951	-913	853	-17	-506	1131
1981	4770	-2076	1455	3531	1860	-2724	-129	777	449	-382	1388	940	477	2114	1788	-1061	1133
1982	6850	-912	2582	2924	2256	-1892	3	977	562	147	1873	1496	-40	1468	1433	-1021	1844
1983	21024	1373	6272	5915	6464	-1532	896	2009	2270	1667	2335	2902	1352	2661	2281	868	3315

Balance of payments: net capital movements
million dollars

Balance des paiements : mouvements de capitaux, nets
millions de dollars

	Year	Q.1	Q.2	Q.3	Q.4	JAN	FEB	MAR	APR	MAY	JUN	JUL	AUG	SEP	OCT	NOV	DEC
1964																	
1965	••	••	-73	-216	-162	••	••	••	-62	10	-21	-62	-103	-51	-59	-46	-57
1966	-873	-143	-143	-229	-358	-35	-13	-95	-18	-33	-92	-71	-45	-113	-151	-89	-118
1967	-306	-51	4	-146	-113	-28	-24	1	-33	26	11	-83	-22	-41	-117	-17	21
1968	-30	4	-38	38	-34	-15	87	-68	-31	-41	34	72	45	-79	38	17	-89
1969	23	42	63	-45	-37	33	43	-34	-50	76	37	-90	-5	50	-10	103	-130
1970	-867	-253	-314	-71	-229	-147	-18	-88	-39	-136	-139	-76	-8	13	-37	-49	-143
1971	1353	-63	837	1687	-1108	-179	116	-	-21	769	89	-160	2137	-290	-374	-325	-409
1972	-2521	68	-942	-724	-923	190	371	-493	-329	-273	-340	-365	-106	-253	147	-128	-942
1973	-7343	-1235	-1650	-1633	-2825	-517	-378	-340	-613	-545	-492	-805	-344	-484	-428	-1274	-1123
1974	-2103	-719	-879	-84	-421	-819	-1	101	-92	32	-819	-114	-285	315	152	-242	-331
1975	-1410	202	-738	-117	-757	-50	189	63	-416	68	-390	92	-109	-100	-524	-227	-6
1976	-873	-24	127	-27	-949	-246	374	-152	70	141	-84	368	-107	-288	-694	159	-414
1977	-3832	-355	-901	-1529	-1047	-257	-154	56	-926	53	-28	-553	-276	-700	-980	204	-271
1978	-10851	579	-3672	-3355	-4403	-112	44	647	-1105	-917	-1650	-1276	-1029	-1050	-1631	-1162	-1610
1979	-10241	-3306	-3713	-609	-2613	37	-1108	-2235	-2415	-663	-835	42	1188	-1839	-2139	58	-532
1980	5469	1500	-57	3089	947	1296	1330	-1126	-2956	1424	1465	1164	1387	538	-482	1616	-187
1981	-7407	3496	-5646	-2742	-2515	1834	832	830	-2909	-542	-2195	-1954	-243	-545	-3076	2229	-1668
1982	-14088	-4940	-7420	-4726	2998	-2102	-1470	-1368	-4226	-76	-3118	-1587	-1185	-1954	1230	2734	-966
1983	-13758	-3424	-655	-5847	-3832	-959	-339	-2126	1172	-31	-1796	-1719	-1831	-2297	-1997	180	-2015

NOTES

1. The original base of the index is 1965 to 1967, 1970 from 1968 to 1972, 1975 from 1973 to 1977, and 1980 from 1978. The indices were linked on January 1968, on 1973 and on 1978 respectively.
2. Series not adjusted for unequal number of working days in the month.
3. Four-wheeled vehicles only.
4. The number of enterprises covered was increased from 127 to 178 from April 1969.
5. Excluding purchasing agencies.
6. Figures refer to construction scheduled to start in period.
7. The original base of the index is 1965 to 1969, 1970 from 1970 to 1971, 1975 from 1972 to 1976, and 1980 from 1977. The indices are linked on 1970, 1972 and 1977 respectively.
8. Establishments employing 30 persons or more; survey conducted during the last pay period of month. Prior to July 1972, excluding Okinawa.
9. Labour force sample survey of population aged 15 or over, taken during the last seven days of the month. Prior to 1973, excluding Okinawa.
10. Unemployed who received benefits during the month. Prior to June 1972, excluding Okinawa. From April 1975, excluding seasonal workers.
11. Prior to April 1972, excluding Okinawa.
12. Excluding paid leave.
13. Regular wages and salaries per unit of output.
14. Excluding imports and exports. Weighting pattern based on 1965 to 1969, 1970 from 1970 to 1979, and 1980 from 1980.
15. Weighting pattern based on 1960 to 1964, 1965 from 1965 to 1969, 1970 from 1970 to 1974, 1975 from 1975 to 1979, and 1980 from 1980.
16. Weighting pattern based on 1970 to 1974, 1975 from 1975 to 1979, and 1980 from 1980.
17. Monthly data are daily averages from 1974, and end-of-month figures previously.
18. From May 1979, including certificates of deposit.
19. From August 1979, excluding convertible bonds.
20. Monthly figures refer to arithmetic averages of daily rates in Tokyo from May 1972, and to mode of daily rates previously.

NOTES

1. La base originale de l'indice est 1965 jusqu'en 1967, 1970 de 1968 à 1972, 1975 de 1973 à 1977, et 1980 à partir de 1978. Les indices ont été raccordés sur janvier 1968, l'année 1973 et l'année 1978 respectivement.
2. La série n'est pas corrigée de l'inégalité du nombre de jours ouvrables dans le mois.
3. Véhicules à quatre roues seulement.
4. Le nombre d'entreprises a été porté de 127 à 178 à partir d'avril 1969.
5. Non compris les sociétés d'achat.
6. Données concernant les mises en chantier prévues pour la période de référence.
7. La base originale de l'indice est 1965 jusqu'en 1969, 1970 de 1970 à 1971, 1975 de 1972 à 1976, et 1980 à partir de 1977. Les indices ont été raccordés sur 1970, 1972 et 1977 respectivement.
8. Établissements employant 30 personnes ou plus; enquête effectuée pendant la dernière période de paie du mois. Avant juillet 1972, non compris la préfecture d'Okinawa.
9. Enquête par sondage auprès de la population de 15 ans ou plus, effectuée au cours des sept derniers jours du mois. Avant 1973, non compris la préfecture d'Okinawa.
10. Chômeurs secourus durant le mois. Avant juin 1972, non compris la préfecture d'Okinawa. A partir d'avril 1975, non compris les travailleurs saisonniers.
11. Avant avril 1972, non compris la préfecture d'Okinawa.
12. Non compris les congés payés.
13. Salaires (à l'exclusion des primes) par unité produite.
14. Non compris les importations et les exportations. La pondération se réfère à 1965 jusqu'en 1969; de 1970 à 1979, pondération de 1970, et à partir de 1980, pondération de 1980.
15. La pondération se réfère à 1960 en 1964; de 1965 à 1969, pondération de 1965, de 1970 à 1974, pondération de 1970, de 1975 à 1979, pondération de 1975, et à partir de 1980, pondération de 1980.
16. La pondération se réfère à 1970 jusqu'en 1974; de 1975 à 1979, pondération de 1975, et à partir de 1980, pondération de 1980.
17. Les données mensuelles sont des moyennes journalières à partir de 1974; avant cette date, situation en fin de mois.
18. A partir de mai 1979, y compris les certificats de dépôts.
19. A partir d'août 1979, non compris les obligations convertibles.
20. A partir de mai 1972, les données mensuelles sont la moyenne arithmétique des taux quotidiens à Tokyo et, avant cette date, le mode de ces taux.

NOTES

21. The "Gensaki" market is a short-term money market where the instrument is a repurchase agreement in securities.
22. From 1968, index (original base 4th January 1968) linked on 1968 to previous index (original base 5th January 1959). Monthly data are averages of daily indices.
23. General trade.
24. Excluding military. Prior to July 1979, including processing fees and merchanting.

NOTES

21. Le "Marché Gensaki" est un marché monétaire à court terme qui assure la prise en pension des titres.
22. A partir de 1968, indice (base originale 4 janvier 1968) raccordé sur l'année 1968 à l'indice précédent (base originale 5 janvier 1959). Les données mensuelles sont la moyenne d'indices journaliers.
23. Commerce général.
24. Secteur militaire exclu. Avant juillet 1979, y compris les frais de transformation et le courtage international.

MAIN SOURCES

PRINCIPALES SOURCES

Series	Séries	Sources
National product	Produit national	
Monthly hours of work	Durée mensuelle du travail	
Producer prices	Prix à la production	
Wholesale prices	Prix de gros	Bank of Japan
Home finance	Finances internes	*Economic Statistics Monthly*
Interest rates	Taux d'intérêts	
Share prices	Cours des actions	
Balance of payments	Balance des paiements	
Industrial production	Production industrielle	Ministry of international Trade and Industry
Deliveries and stocks	Livraisons et stocks	
Internal trade	Commerce intérieur	*Industrial Statistics Monthly*
Business surveys	Enquêtes de conjoncture	Bank of Japan *Short-term Economic Survey of Principal Enterprises in Japan*
Orders	Commandes	Economic Planning Agency
Unit labour cost	Coût unitaire de la main-d'œuvre	*Japanese Economic Indicators*
Construction	Construction	Ministry of Construction *Monthly of Construction Statistics*
Labour (except hours), and wages	Mains d'œuvre (sauf heures) et salaires	Office of the Prime Minister Bureau of statistics
Consumer prices	Prix à la consommation	*Monthly Statistics of Japan*
Foreign trade	Commerce extérieur	Ministry of international Trade and Industry *Monthly Foreign Trade Statistics*

Australia — Australie

AUSTRALIA

Gross domestic product / Produit intérieur brut

at current market prices / *aux prix courants du marché*

million Australian dollars, annual rates / millions de dollars australiens, taux annuels

Adjusted - Corrigé

	Year	Q.1	Q.2	Q.3	Q.4	JAN	FEB	MAR	APR	MAY	JUN	JUL	AUG	SEP	OCT	NOV	DEC
1964	18790	17972	18460	19136	19592												
1965	20340	19884	20400	20532	20544												
1966	21633	20808	21256	21952	22516												
1967	23635	23200	23648	23620	24072												
1968	25973	24752	25388	26268	27484												
1969	29061	28020	28676	29348	30200												
1970	31981	30844	31808	32236	33036												
1971	35783	34440	35104	36604	36984												
1972	39814	37756	39160	40236	42104												
1973	47354	44172	45680	48792	50772												
1974	56251	52372	53192	58264	61176												
1975	66780	62348	65608	67968	71196												
1976	78646	73900	77932	80424	82328												
1977	86616	83672	86612	87712	88468												
1978	95989	91040	94204	97952	100760												
1979	108246	104480	106392	109320	112792												
1980	122946	116548	120876	124336	130024												
1981	139526	132288	137300	142560	145956												
1982	155553	148376	154756	157472	161608												
1983		160936	163848	171340													

Industrial production: total (1)(2) / Production industrielle : total (1)(2)

1980 = 100

	Year	Q.1	Q.2	Q.3	Q.4	JAN	FEB	MAR	APR	MAY	JUN	JUL	AUG	SEP	OCT	NOV	DEC
1964	60	55	59	63	63	43	61	60	60	60	59	62	63	65	63	66	60
1965	63	59	64	66	64	47	64	65	63	64	63	65	65	67	67	67	58
1966	64	59	64	66	67	46	65	67	63	65	64	65	65	67	68	70	61
1967	68	63	68	70	69	50	71	70	68	69	67	68	69	72	72	73	63
1968	71	65	71	74	75	51	72	73	71	72	71	73	73	76	78	80	67
1969	76	71	76	79	79	56	79	79	75	75	76	78	79	81	83	81	72
1970	80	75	80	80	82	59	84	82	81	80	80	80	79	83	84	87	76
1971	83	78	83	85	85	63	85	84	83	81	85	84	85	88	88	89	77
1972	84	75	84	87	89	60	77	87	84	85	84	83	86	91	92	93	83
1973	92	84	91	99	95	67	91	94	89	94	89	97	98	103	98	98	39
1974	95	92	97	98	92	73	102	99	94	100	98	98	96	100	99	97	81
1975	88	83	87	90	92	68	91	89	86	87	87	88	90	93	96	97	83
1976	93	87	94	96	95	66	98	96	93	95	93	92	95	100	101	98	86
1977	93	87	96	96	93	69	98	95	99	94	94	96	93	98	91	102	87
1978	94	89	95	96	98	70	100	98	97	93	94	97	93	99	101	103	90
1979	100	91	100	105	103	72	102	101	102	99	99	101	103	110	107	107	93
1980	100	94	100	104	102	76	103	104	102	99	99	103	105	103	103	109	92
1981	102	97	105	105	103	76	107	107	105	106	103	102	109	105	105	108	95
1982	97	96	101	97	93	76	108	104	101	100	102	100	96	96	99	97	83
1983	92	85	92	95	96	64	96	94	93	90	93	95	94	96	98	101	90

Industrial production: manufacturing (1) / Production industrielle : industries manufacturières (1)

1980 = 100

	Year	Q.1	Q.2	Q.3	Q.4	JAN	FEB	MAR	APR	MAY	JUN	JUL	AUG	SEP	OCT	NOV	DEC
1964	64	58	63	67	67	45	65	64	64	63	62	66	66	70	67	70	64
1965	67	62	67	69	68	49	68	70	67	68	67	68	69	71	71	71	62
1966	68	63	68	69	71	49	69	72	67	69	68	68	69	70	72	74	65
1967	71	67	72	73	74	52	75	74	72	73	70	71	73	76	77	78	66
1968	75	69	75	78	79	54	76	78	75	76	74	76	77	81	83	85	71
1969	80	75	79	83	83	59	83	83	80	79	80	82	83	85	87	86	76
1970	83	79	84	84	86	62	89	86	85	84	83	83	82	87	88	92	79
1971	86	81	87	88	89	66	90	88	87	85	88	86	88	91	92	94	80
1972	86	77	87	89	93	62	80	90	87	88	86	85	88	94	95	97	86
1973	95	87	93	103	99	68	95	98	92	97	91	99	101	107	102	102	92
1974	98	95	100	100	95	75	107	103	97	103	101	100	98	103	102	100	84
1975	90	85	88	91	94	69	94	91	88	89	88	88	91	95	98	100	85
1976	94	88	95	97	97	66	100	98	95	96	94	93	95	102	103	100	87
1977	94	89	97	96	95	69	99	97	101	95	94	95	94	99	93	104	88
1978	95	90	95	96	99	69	101	99	98	94	94	96	93	100	102	104	91
1979	100	92	100	105	104	71	103	102	103	98	98	100	104	112	109	109	94
1980	100	95	100	103	102	74	105	106	103	99	97	102	105	103	104	111	92
1981	102	97	105	104	103	74	109	108	106	106	102	99	109	105	105	109	95
1982	96	96	99	95	92	74	109	105	100	98	99	96	95	95	98	95	82
1983	90	83	90	92	94	61	95	93	93	87	90	92	91	94	95	99	88

Gross domestic product / Produit intérieur brut

implicit price level / niveau implicite des prix

1980 = 100

Adjusted - Corrigé

	Year	Q.1	Q.2	Q.3	Q.4	JAN	FEB	MAR	APR	MAY	JUN	JUL	AUG	SEP	OCT	NOV	DEC
1964																	
1965																	
1966																	
1967																	
1968																	
1969				34.1	34.7												
1970	35.5	35.1	35.1	35.6	36.0												
1971	37.6	37.0	37.2	37.9	38.2												
1972	40.4	39.2	39.7	40.9	41.7												
1973	45.3	42.6	44.4	46.4	47.6												
1974	53.1	49.3	51.0	55.1	57.0												
1975	61.6	58.2	59.9	62.6	65.8												
1976	70.1	66.7	69.7	71.4	72.6												
1977	76.5	74.3	76.1	77.3	78.5												
1978	82.0	79.6	81.4	82.6	84.3												
1979	89.7	86.0	88.8	91.6	92.5												
1980	100.0	96.4	98.8	101.1	103.6												
1981	109.1	104.7	107.7	110.5	113.4												
1982	121.8	115.6	120.7	123.2	127.7												
1983		127.7	131.8	132.1													

Industrial production: total (1)(2) / Production industrielle : total (1)(2)

1980 = 100

Adjusted - Corrigé

	Year	Q.1	Q.2	Q.3	Q.4	JAN	FEB	MAR	APR	MAY	JUN	JUL	AUG	SEP	OCT	NOV	DEC
1964		57	59	61	62	57	57	58	59	59	60	60	61	61	61	62	63
1965		63	63	63	63	63	63	62	63	63	63	63	63	63	63	63	63
1966		63	64	64	65	63	63	63	63	64	64	64	64	64	64	65	65
1967		67	67	68	68	67	67	67	67	67	67	68	68	68	68	68	68
1968		69	70	72	73	68	69	69	70	71	71	71	72	72	73	73	73
1969		75	75	77	77	74	75	75	75	75	76	77	77	77	77	77	77
1970		80	79	79	81	79	79	80	79	80	79	79	79	79	80	80	82
1971		82	82	83	83	83	83	82	81	83	83	84	83	83	83	83	82
1972		80	83	84	87	79	80	81	84	84	83	83	84	85	86	88	88
1973		89	91	95	94	89	89	90	91	90	92	93	96	95	94	93	95
1974		97	97	94	91	97	97	97	96	97	97	96	94	93	93	91	89
1975		88	86	87	90	89	88	87	87	86	86	87	87	88	89	91	91
1976		91	93	93	94	90	92	92	90	95	93	90	93	95	96	92	92
1977		93	95	93	91	93	92	92	96	94	94	94	91	93	87	93	94
1978		94	94	93	96	94	95	94	94	93	94	94	91	94	95	96	97
1979		97	99	101	101	96	97	97	99	99	99	98	101	105	103	101	101
1980		100	99	101	100	101	99	101	100	99	99	101	103	99	99	103	100
1981		103	104	102	101	102	103	103	103	106	103	99	105	102	101	101	103
1982		101	100	94	92	102	103	100	99	100	102	98	93	92	95	90	90
1983		90	91	92	95	86	91	92	91	90	93	92	90	93	94	94	97

Industrial production: manufacturing (1) / Production industrielle : industries manufacturières (1)

1980 = 100

Adjusted - Corrigé

	Year	Q.1	Q.2	Q.3	Q.4	JAN	FEB	MAR	APR	MAY	JUN	JUL	AUG	SEP	OCT	NOV	DEC
1964		55	56	58	59	54	55	55	56	55	57	57	58	58	57	59	62
1965		59	60	60	60	59	58	59	60	60	60	61	60	60	59	60	60
1966		59	60	60	62	59	59	60	59	60	61	60	61	60	61	61	64
1967		63	63	64	64	63	64	63	63	64	63	63	64	64	65	64	64
1968		65	66	68	69	65	65	66	67	67	66	68	68	68	69	70	69
1969		71	70	73	72	70	71	71	69	71	71	73	72	73	73	70	74
1970		75	74	73	75	74	76	74	74	74	75	73	72	73	74	76	76
1971		77	77	77	77	77	76	76	77	75	78	78	78	76	77	79	76
1972		73	77	77	81	74	68	77	77	78	77	76	77	79	80	80	82
1973		83	83	89	86	82	81	85	82	85	81	89	89	89	85	86	89
1974		90	89	87	83	90	91	87	88	89	89	89	87	86	84	83	81
1975		81	78	79	82	83	80	79	78	78	79	78	79	80	81	82	82
1976		93	94	95	95	91	95	95	92	96	95	92	95	96	97	94	94
1977		94	96	94	93	95	94	94	97	95	95	95	94	94	88	96	95
1978		95	94	94	97	95	95	95	95	94	95	95	92	95	95	96	98
1979		98	99	102	102	97	97	98	99	99	99	99	102	106	103	101	101
1980		101	99	101	100	101	99	101	99	99	98	101	104	99	99	102	99
1981		102	104	102	101	101	102	103	102	106	103	97	107	101	100	100	102
1982		101	99	93	90	101	102	99	97	98	100	95	93	90	94	89	88
1983		87	89	90	93	83	89	88	90	87	91	90	90	91	92	93	95

AUSTRALIA

Industrial production: durable manufactures (1)
1980 = 100

Production industrielle : biens durables (1)
1980 = 100

	Year	Q.1	Q.2	Q.3	Q.4	JAN	FEB	MAR	APR	MAY	JUN	JUL	AUG	SEP	OCT	NOV	DEC
1964	72	64	73	78	74	49	72	70	72	73	73	76	77	81	75	80	66
1965	75	68	77	80	75	53	74	77	76	78	76	79	79	81	79	79	68
1966	75	68	77	78	78	51	75	77	76	79	77	79	77	78	79	82	72
1967	79	71	79	82	82	55	80	79	77	81	79	80	82	85	86	87	74
1968	85	75	85	90	89	57	83	86	83	87	85	87	90	93	94	94	79
1969	89	81	89	94	92	64	90	90	88	90	89	92	94	96	98	94	84
1970	91	85	93	93	94	66	96	92	94	94	92	93	92	96	96	100	87
1971	93	85	94	99	96	67	94	94	95	93	95	97	98	102	101	101	84
1972	91	78	92	96	98	62	80	92	91	94	92	92	97	100	100	102	91
1973	101	91	99	110	105	68	102	104	98	104	94	107	110	114	109	109	97
1974	103	99	107	109	99	77	112	108	103	111	107	108	107	110	109	104	86
1975	94	86	95	99	98	68	96	94	92	97	94	95	100	102	103	103	88
1976	98	89	100	102	100	64	102	101	98	101	99	99	100	107	108	104	89
1977	95	88	99	99	93	65	99	98	103	97	96	100	97	100	89	104	88
1978	95	88	96	97	99	65	99	98	97	95	96	98	92	100	101	104	92
1979	102	90	103	108	106	65	101	102	102	102	104	103	108	114	111	111	96
1980	100	93	99	105	103	71	104	103	98	99	99	106	107	102	104	112	94
1981	103	95	106	108	104	69	109	106	105	109	103	104	113	108	108	109	95
1982	93	94	100	93	85	69	108	105	100	99	99	96	94	90	91	88	76
1983	84	73	85	89	89	49	87	85	85	84	87	90	89	89	90	94	84

Industrial production: non-durable manufactures (1)
1980 = 100

Production industrielle : biens non-durables (1)
1980 = 100

	Year	Q.1	Q.2	Q.3	Q.4	JAN	FEB	MAR	APR	MAY	JUN	JUL	AUG	SEP	OCT	NOV	DEC
1964	57	55	55	58	59	42	61	62	58	55	53	56	57	61	61	63	54
1965	60	59	60	61	63	47	64	66	61	60	59	59	59	64	65	67	56
1966	62	60	60	62	65	47	66	68	61	60	60	59	62	64	67	69	60
1967	66	66	65	65	67	51	72	74	69	65	62	64	65	68	69	72	60
1968	67	66	65	66	70	52	72	75	68	65	63	65	65	69	72	76	64
1969	73	71	71	73	75	55	79	80	75	68	70	72	72	75	78	79	69
1970	76	75	75	74	80	59	83	83	79	74	73	73	73	77	81	86	73
1971	81	80	80	80	83	65	88	86	82	77	82	77	79	83	85	87	76
1972	83	79	83	83	89	63	82	91	86	82	81	80	81	89	91	93	83
1973	91	85	89	96	95	70	90	95	88	91	88	92	94	102	97	97	90
1974	93	94	95	93	92	75	105	101	93	94	97	92	91	97	95	97	83
1975	85	84	80	85	91	70	92	89	82	79	80	82	85	89	93	97	82
1976	91	87	91	91	93	68	99	95	93	91	88	86	91	96	99	95	86
1977	94	90	94	93	97	73	101	97	99	92	91	91	91	98	98	104	89
1978	95	92	94	95	98	73	102	100	99	91	91	93	93	100	102	103	90
1979	99	95	97	102	102	76	106	102	104	94	92	97	99	109	105	108	91
1980	100	97	101	102	101	78	106	108	108	99	95	98	103	104	103	109	90
1981	101	99	102	103	102	79	108	110	105	102	100	95	103	102	102	108	94
1982	98	97	98	97	100	79	110	103	100	97	99	96	94	100	107	105	88
1983	96	92	94	96	100	73	103	101	100	91	92	94	94	100	103	105	92

Industrial production: fuel and power (1)(3)
1980 = 100

Production industrielle : combustibles et énergie (1)(3)
1980 = 100

	Year	Q.1	Q.2	Q.3	Q.4	JAN	FEB	MAR	APR	MAY	JUN	JUL	AUG	SEP	OCT	NOV	DEC
1964	30	27	31	33	30	26	28	28	29	32	33	34	33	31	31	31	29
1965	33	30	34	36	33	28	31	31	31	34	36	38	36	35	34	34	32
1966	36	32	36	40	36	31	33	33	33	36	38	41	41	38	36	37	35
1967	39	36	40	42	38	34	37	36	38	41	40	42	42	40	39	40	35
1968	42	37	42	46	42	34	39	39	38	44	44	48	46	44	44	43	39
1969	45	40	46	50	46	37	42	42	41	46	50	52	47	50	49	45	44
1970	51	46	53	56	51	41	49	48	49	52	58	55	54	58	53	52	47
1971	55	49	56	58	55	46	50	52	51	57	61	59	58	56	56	57	53
1972	60	54	62	64	63	47	55	58	56	64	66	62	65	64	66	65	58
1973	66	59	67	73	65	55	61	62	61	70	71	75	73	70	67	68	61
1974	71	63	72	77	71	58	66	64	64	75	77	80	72	77	76	73	66
1975	73	69	76	74	73	62	74	70	72	77	78	77	72	73	77	74	67
1976	80	71	81	88	77	67	73	74	75	81	88	90	90	86	81	77	75
1977	84	76	87	93	79	71	79	78	79	86	95	97	93	90	78	81	79
1978	89	81	91	98	85	76	84	83	84	91	99	102	99	92	88	87	81
1979	94	86	96	105	91	82	89	87	88	98	102	108	108	99	94	92	87
1980	100	91	102	110	98	87	94	93	94	100	111	116	109	104	99	99	95
1981	108	99	111	118	103	94	101	102	102	111	122	126	122	108	106	103	100
1982	103	103	113	100	98	99	107	104	102	109	126	107	99	94	108	93	92
1983	113	102	117	123	110	94	103	108	108	115	127	130	122	118	113	112	105

Industrial production: durable manufactures (1) — Production industrielle : biens durables (1)

1980 = 100

Adjusted - Corrigé

	Year	Q.1	Q.2	Q.3	Q.4	JAN	FEB	MAR	APR	MAY	JUN	JUL	AUG	SEP	OCT	NOV	DEC
1964		69	71	73	74	68	69	70	70	70	71	72	73	73	74	73	74
1965		74	75	75	74	74	75	75	75	75	75	75	76	75	75	75	74
1966		74	75	75	75	74	74	75	75	75	76	75	75	75	75	75	77
1967		78	78	79	80	77	78	77	78	78	78	79	79	79	80	80	80
1968		81	83	86	87	81	81	82	83	83	84	85	86	87	88	87	88
1969		88	88	90	90	88	88	88	88	88	88	89	90	90	90	90	90
1970		92	92	90	91	92	92	92	92	92	92	91	90	90	90	92	92
1971		93	93	94	93	93	93	94	92	93	94	94	94	94	94	94	92
1972		87	90	92	95	88	87	88	88	91	91	91	92	92	94	95	96
1973		98	100	102	105	97	99	99	101	99	99	101	102	104	104	104	108
1974		107	106	104	99	107	107	107	107	106	106	105	104	103	101	98	97
1975		94	93	94	96	95	94	94	93	93	93	94	94	94	96	96	96
1976		97	98	98	98	95	98	98	96	99	97	96	97	100	101	96	95
1977		95	98	95	91	96	95	94	102	96	95	97	94	93	83	96	93
1978		96	95	92	97	96	96	95	96	94	95	95	89	93	95	96	99
1979		98	102	103	103	96	97	99	101	101	103	99	103	106	105	102	103
1980		102	98	100	101	104	100	100	97	98	98	102	102	96	99	103	101
1981		103	105	103	102	101	104	103	104	108	102	98	107	103	102	102	102
1982		102	100	90	82	102	103	101	101	99	98	94	91	84	86	81	81
1983		79	84	84	88	71	83	83	84	83	86	85	83	86	85	90	91

Industrial production: non-durable manufactures (1) — Production industrielle : biens non-durables (1)

1980 = 100

Adjusted - Corrigé

	Year	Q.1	Q.2	Q.3	Q.4	JAN	FEB	MAR	APR	MAY	JUN	JUL	AUG	SEP	OCT	NOV	DEC
1964		55	56	58	58	55	55	56	56	56	56	57	58	58	58	58	59
1965		59	60	61	61	59	59	59	60	60	60	61	61	61	61	62	61
1966		61	61	62	64	61	61	60	61	61	61	62	62	62	63	63	65
1967		66	66	66	66	65	66	66	66	66	66	66	66	66	66	66	66
1968		66	66	67	69	66	66	66	66	66	66	66	67	67	68	69	69
1969		71	72	73	74	70	70	72	72	72	73	73	74	74	74	74	74
1970		75	76	76	78	74	75	75	76	76	76	75	75	76	76	78	79
1971		80	80	81	81	80	80	80	79	81	81	81	82	81	81	81	81
1972		80	83	84	86	79	80	81	81	84	83	83	83	85	85	87	87
1973		87	90	94	93	86	87	87	87	90	92	93	95	95	94	93	93
1974		95	96	94	90	94	95	95	95	96	96	95	95	92	91	90	88
1975		86	83	84	87	87	86	85	83	82	82	83	85	86	87	87	88
1976		90	91	91	91	88	91	91	88	93	91	87	93	91	93	89	92
1977		93	94	93	95	94	92	91	93	94	94	93	91	93	92	97	95
1978		94	94	95	96	93	94	94	93	93	94	95	94	96	97	96	96
1979		97	97	101	100	97	98	97	99	96	97	99	100	104	101	100	99
1980		99	100	101	99	99	98	102	102	100	100	100	103	101	99	101	97
1981		101	102	100	100	101	101	102	100	104	103	96	104	99	98	100	102
1982		99	98	96	98	100	102	97	93	98	102	98	93	96	102	97	95
1983		95	94	96	99	94	96	93	94	91	96	96	95	96	100	97	101

Industrial production: fuel and power (1)(3) — Production industrielle : combustibles et énergie (1)(3)

1980 = 100

Adjusted - Corrigé

	Year	Q.1	Q.2	Q.3	Q.4	JAN	FEB	MAR	APR	MAY	JUN	JUL	AUG	SEP	OCT	NOV	DEC
1964		30	30	31	31	29	29	30	30	31	31	31	31	31	31	32	32
1965		32	33	34	34	32	32	33	33	33	33	34	34	34	34	34	35
1966		35	35	37	37	34	34	35	35	35	36	37	37	37	37	37	38
1967		39	39	39	39	39	38	39	39	39	38	38	39	39	39	39	39
1968		40	41	43	43	39	40	40	41	41	42	42	43	43	43	43	43
1969		44	45	46	47	43	44	44	44	44	46	46	46	47	47	47	47
1970		50	51	52	53	49	50	51	50	51	51	51	52	53	53	52	53
1971		53	54	55	56	53	54	53	54	55	55	55	54	55	55	57	57
1972		58	60	60	64	57	58	59	60	60	59	59	60	62	63	64	65
1973		64	66	68	67	64	65	65	65	65	66	67	68	67	67	67	68
1974		68	70	72	73	68	68	68	69	70	71	71	72	72	73	72	73
1975		75	73	70	74	74	75	75	74	73	71	70	70	71	73	74	75
1976		77	79	81	82	76	76	78	79	79	78	78	81	83	82	81	82
1977		82	84	85	84	81	83	83	83	84	85	85	84	86	81	85	87
1978		87	89	89	90	86	87	88	89	89	89	89	90	90	90	91	90
1979		93	93	96	97	94	92	92	93	95	91	94	97	96	97	97	96
1980		98	99	100	103	98	98	98	99	99	99	101	99	101	102	103	105
1981		106	108	108	109	105	105	107	108	108	109	108	111	106	109	108	110
1982		111	110	109	110	111	111	110	108	108	113	113	110	105	113	114	103
1983		111	114	113	117	110	110	114	113	113	114	113	113	115	117	117	116

AUSTRALIA

Production: crude petroleum / **Production : pétrole brut**

thousand tons, monthly averages / milliers de tonnes, moyennes mensuelles

	Year	Q.1	Q.2	Q.3	Q.4	JAN	FEB	MAR	APR	MAY	JUN	JUL	AUG	SEP	OCT	NOV	DEC
1964	17	6	17	22	21												
1965	29	25	29	31	33												
1966	38	38	40	39	35												
1967	85	35	73	98	135	33	29	44	62	80	79	92	82	119	130	129	144
1968	156	148	156	162	157	150	140	154	151	172	146	168	163	154	162	152	155
1969	177	153	160	176	220	156	141	161	154	162	163	175	168	184	223	224	212
1970	706	246	700	862	1017	182	182	375	691	706	701	636	939	1009	1031	945	1074
1971	1201	986	1115	1333	1369	1029	966	963	1043	1043	1259	1358	1345	1295	1320	1369	1419
1972	1298	1330	1170	1140	1551	1429	1282	1279	1409	1359	741	447	1472	1503	1557	1518	1579
1973	1564	1364	1563	1673	1656	1537	1337	1218	1517	1599	1572	1705	1713	1602	1595	1633	1739
1974	1613	1644	1559	1467	1784	1773	1494	1665	1578	1581	1517	1358	1257	1785	1807	1731	1813
1975	1680	1717	1680	1602	1721	1788	1635	1728	1662	1620	1758	1744	1803	1260	1827	1665	1670
1976	1710	1676	1722	1842	1598	1801	1502	1724	1678	1789	1700	1676	1838	1812	1624	1493	1678
1977	1762	1737	1747	1796	1766	1774	1605	1833	1552	1873	1816	1832	1858	1697	1867	1680	1752
1978	1776	1814	1765	1761	1763	1876	1679	1887	1704	1778	1812	1804	1833	1647	1693	1770	1825
1979	1789	1683	1802	1840	1829	1800	1585	1664	1799	1796	1811	1951	1884	1686	1894	1741	1851
1980	1568	1578	1428	1687	1580	1863	1366	1503	1693	1339	1250	1817	1679	1566	1797	1072	1870
1981	1609	1695	1533	1452	1756	1902	1459	1724	1729	1682	1188	1667	1445	1245	1877	1690	1700
1982	1527	1558	1545	1335	1672	1599	1676	1398	1414	1679	1543	1424	1446	1135	1679	1639	1698
1983		1516	1689	1711		1736	1318	1495	1672	1737	1658	1732	1678	1723	1860	1935	

Production: crude steel / **Production : acier brut**

thousand tons, monthly averages / milliers de tonnes, moyennes mensuelles

	Year	Q.1	Q.2	Q.3	Q.4	JAN	FEB	MAR	APR	MAY	JUN	JUL	AUG	SEP	OCT	NOV	DEC
1964																	
1965																	
1966																	
1967																	
1968																	
1969	586	578	571	587	607	590	525	620	582	559	572	599	603	560	603	602	617
1970	570	535	569	587	589	579	497	528	523	607	576	612	582	567	592	573	603
1971	563	543	552	594	562	569	469	590	581	504	570	618	588	577	601	570	516
1972	563	507	509	596	638	494	497	530	492	543	491	556	627	606	646	656	613
1973	642	596	583	688	699	601	551	637	618	645	487	691	694	679	706	671	719
1974	651	671	534	655	745	692	643	677	531	541	530	686	653	626	751	730	753
1975	656	679	628	677	639	681	662	694	642	666	576	595	737	698	591	664	663
1976	650	655	681	655	606	674	585	707	633	735	676	697	636	632	637	556	626
1977	611	604	632	609	599	680	567	566	639	653	605	589	621	618	640	560	596
1978	632	651	659	593	626	670	605	677	574	708	696	630	553	595	662	600	617
1979	678	635	659	699	719	665	598	641	667	674	637	686	706	705	734	674	749
1980	633	683	531	678	639	763	658	628	529	488	575	736	685	614	630	635	653
1981	636	684	650	664	547	728	634	691	678	675	596	712	736	544	576	501	564
1982	531	596	616	512	400	631	497	661	601	655	592	606	561	368	372	414	413
1983	467	399	451	513	505	368	399	430	396	472	486	518	519	503	518	485	511

Business situation: prospects (4) / **État des affaires : perspectives (4)**

manufacturing / industries manufacturières

per cent balance / solde en pourcentage

	Year	Q.1	Q.2	Q.3	Q.4	JAN	FEB	MAR	APR	MAY	JUN	JUL	AUG	SEP	OCT	NOV	DEC
1964		68		52	27			68				52				27	
1965		21		-25	-4			21				-25				-4	
1966		9	16	6	53			9			16			6			53
1967		44	38	43	17			44			38			43			17
1968		8	44	45	28			8			44			45			28
1969		37	34	32	24			37			34			32			24
1970		27	-36	13	16			27			-36			13			16
1971		-37	-19	-26	-41			-37			-19			-26			-41
1972		19	44	58	58			19			44			58			58
1973		46	32	6	-44			46			32			6			-44
1974		-27	-70	-74	-60			-27			-70			-74			-60
1975		14	-2	-17	-7			14			-2			-17			-7
1976		39	44	36	-			39			44			36			-
1977		7	23	11	24			7			23			11			24
1978		36	25	15	30			36			25			15			30
1979		52	15	26	18			52			15			26			18
1980		22	11	24	30			22			11			24			30
1981		43	30	4	-15			43			30			4			-15
1982		-50	-42	-56	-74			-50			-42			-56			-74
1983		-36	-4	31	55			-36			-4			31			55

Production: future tendency (4) manufacturing per cent balance

Perspectives de production (4) industries manufacturières solde en pourcentage

	Year	Q.1	Q.2	Q.3	Q.4	JAN	FEB	MAR	APR	MAY	JUN	JUL	AUG	SEP	OCT	NOV	DEC
1964		39		44	27			39				44				27	
1965		31		19	7			31				19				7	
1966		21	21	21	24			21			21			21			24
1967		34	28	34	4			34			28			34			4
1968		17	28	40	17			17			28			40			17
1969		34	38	39	20			34			38			39			20
1970		35	8	40	16			35			8			40			16
1971		7	13	17	-22			7			13			17			-22
1972		7	21	38	27			7			21			38			27
1973		31	38	38	4			31			38			38			4
1974		18	-3	-27	-39			18			-3			-27			-39
1975		4	3	3	-18			4			3			3			-18
1976		22	18	28	-5			22			18			28			-5
1977		8	18	20	5			8			18			20			5
1978		29	17	23	11			29			17			23			11
1979		36	22	26	9			36			22			26			9
1980		22	14	35	13			22			14			35			13
1981		38	32	23	-4			38			32			23			
1982		-6	-17	-32	-52			-6			-17			-32			-52
1983		-23	6	21	13			-23			6			21			13

Orders inflow: tendency (4) manufacturing per cent balance

Commandes : tendance (4) industries manufacturières solde en pourcentage

	Year	Q.1	Q.2	Q.3	Q.4	JAN	FEB	MAR	APR	MAY	JUN	JUL	AUG	SEP	OCT	NOV	DEC
1964		44		42	45			44				42				45	
1965		34		5	4			34				5				4	
1966		-10	-8	-7	22			-10			-8			-7			22
1967		8	10	17	22			8			10			17			22
1968		7	10	18	24			7			10			18			24
1969		16	16	29	38			16			16			29			38
1970		29	9	1	16			29			9			1			16
1971		10	-11	-18	-14			10			-11			-18			-14
1972		-38	-19	1	32			-38			-19			1			32
1973		26	49	57	52			26			49			57			52
1974		33	6	-45	-50			33			6			-45			-50
1975		-47	-24	-20	-15			-47			-24			-20			-15
1976		-9	-4	-5	1			-9			-4			-5			1
1977		-2	-11	-12	-3			-2			-11			-12			-3
1978		1	5	10	19			1			5			10			19
1979		12	16	11	21			12			16			11			21
1980		13	3	6	15			13			3			6			15
1981		13	17	12	4			13			17						
1982		-18	-41	-51	-53			-18			-41			-51			-53
1983		-55	-25	-4	21			-55			-25			-4			21

Finished goods stocks: tendency (4) manufacturing per cent balance

Stocks de produits finis : tendance (4) industries manufacturières solde en pourcentage

	Year	Q.1	Q.2	Q.3	Q.4	JAN	FEB	MAR	APR	MAY	JUN	JUL	AUG	SEP	OCT	NOV	DEC
1964		-4		6	6			-4				6				6	
1965		6		19	19			6				19				19	
1966		7	2	6	4			7			2			6			4
1967		-3	1	5	13			-3			1			5			13
1968		-2	5	10	6			-2			5			10			6
1969		-7	2	5	2			-7			2			5			2
1970		-4	5	17	3			-4			5			17			3
1971		-4	7	15	7			-4			7			15			7
1972		-2	-	1	-1			-2			-			1			-1
1973		-13	-22	-19	-33			-13			-22			-19			-33
1974		-30	-16	18	21			-30			-16			18			21
1975		7	-9	-9	-17			7			-9			-9			-17
1976		-5	-1	2	6			-5			-1			2			6
1977		-6	11	14	-4			-6			11			14			-4
1978		-4	1	-2	2			-4			1			-2			2
1979		-3	4	9	14			-3			4			9			14
1980		2	7	6	2			2			7			6			2
1981		-	3	7	5			-			3						
1982		-4	6	-	-5			-4			6			-			-5
1983		-16	-21	-18	-4			-16			-21			-18			-4

Firms operating at full capacity (4)

manufacturing

per cent

Entreprises travaillant à pleine capacité (4)

industries manufacturières

pourcentage

	Year	Q.1	Q.2	Q.3	Q.4	JAN	FEB	MAR	APR	MAY	JUN	JUL	AUG	SEP	OCT	NOV	DEC
1964		59		64	74			59				64				74	
1965		65		60	56			65				60				56	
1966		49	44	41	47			49			44			41			47
1967		48	45	51	51			48			45			51			51
1968		49	50	47	54			49			50			47			54
1969		54	52	56	57			54			52			56			57
1970		57	55	52	54			57			55			52			54
1971		53	45	38	39			53			45			38			39
1972		32	30	33	47			32			30			33			47
1973		49	56	63	58			49			56			63			58
1974		52	48	39	29			52			48			39			29
1975		24	23	25	28			24			23			25			28
1976		24	23	24	30			24			23			24			30
1977		29	28	26	33			29			28			26			33
1978		30	27	32	36			30			27			32			36
1979		39	40	40	43			39			40			40			43
1980		46	40	41	43			46			40			41			43
1981		45	42	45	47			45			42			45			47
1982		38	27	22	19			38			27			22			19
1983		15	18	21	33			15			18			21			33

Manufacturing stocks: (5)

finished goods

million Australian dollars, end of period

Stocks des industries manufacturières : (5)

produits finis

millions de dollars australiens, fin de période

	Year	Q.1	Q.2	Q.3	Q.4	JAN	FEB	MAR	APR	MAY	JUN	JUL	AUG	SEP	OCT	NOV	DEC
1964																	
1965																	
1966																	
1967																	
1968																	
1969																	
1970																	
1971																	
1972																	
1973	1855				1855												
1974	2588	1875	1993	2327	2588												
1975	2838	2678	2758	2817	2838												
1976	3515	3031	3331	3448	3515												
1977	4018	3672	3893	4013	4018												
1978	4255	4104	4174	4274	4255												
1979	4984	4449	4534	4803	4984												
1980	5648	5187	5466	5659	5648												
1981	6156	5752	5922	6090	6156												
1982	6816	6262	5813	6933	6816												
1983	6631	6585	6503	6653	6631												

Construction permits issued: total (6)

million Australian dollars, monthly averages

Permis de construire délivrés : total (6)

millions de dollars australiens, moyennes mensuelles

	Year	Q.1	Q.2	Q.3	Q.4	JAN	FEB	MAR	APR	MAY	JUN	JUL	AUG	SEP	OCT	NOV	DEC
1964	141.9	117.6	153.1	148.0	149.0	111.7	107.6	133.5	165.4	126.9	167.1	139.8	147.9	156.3	144.3	140.7	162.0
1965	151.4	144.5	155.6	159.6	145.8	133.8	136.3	163.3	139.4	154.5	173.0	151.6	160.5	166.8	156.7	150.2	130.4
1966	142.5	122.3	150.6	151.4	145.8	90.2	118.5	158.1	115.3	154.4	182.1	157.2	152.6	144.5	162.9	155.0	119.6
1967	167.0	146.6	175.2	172.4	173.7	149.8	147.7	142.4	153.6	195.5	176.6	158.3	168.1	190.7	180.4	181.6	159.0
1968	188.0	170.9	200.3	196.4	184.4	165.1	165.2	182.4	175.0	223.4	202.6	198.7	203.3	187.2	193.8	179.0	180.4
1969	226.0	187.7	234.7	234.5	247.1	162.3	193.1	207.6	225.5	233.1	245.6	249.8	215.0	238.8	251.2	226.1	264.0
1970	247.5	232.6	264.2	239.3	254.0	224.3	214.3	259.1	273.7	239.1	279.8	256.1	208.7	253.1	276.0	253.0	233.1
1971	260.0	237.5	254.0	282.5	266.1	223.4	228.3	260.7	246.2	260.3	255.6	254.0	303.6	290.0	266.9	284.7	246.8
1972	297.1	236.6	302.1	321.1	328.4	189.9	238.9	280.9	232.5	332.0	341.9	361.1	302.5	299.8	373.9	322.1	289.2
1973	400.1	360.7	398.7	422.8	418.0	287.4	344.6	450.1	340.3	399.3	456.5	447.8	434.1	386.5	462.0	445.3	346.7
1974	355.8	365.6	398.0	335.9	323.8	339.0	376.9	380.8	354.4	421.9	417.7	426.3	304.9	276.6	344.2	325.1	302.1
1975	393.1	281.5	436.6	450.1	404.3	263.2	257.1	324.2	398.6	426.6	484.6	461.1	359.6	529.5	402.1	405.5	405.2
1976	484.2	405.6	521.4	492.3	517.6	343.2	396.2	477.4	487.3	551.5	525.5	494.4	439.2	543.3	495.9	535.0	521.9
1977	505.2	455.5	523.0	512.7	529.7	405.7	450.8	510.0	472.5	563.5	533.0	502.1	526.1	509.8	542.3	554.2	492.6
1978	516.4	447.4	555.6	521.5	540.9	407.2	434.9	500.2	518.9	562.3	585.5	468.6	573.1	522.8	582.5	580.2	460.1
1979	605.8	523.8	608.8	614.7	675.9	439.1	550.0	582.4	507.2	667.5	651.7	606.8	611.5	625.9	620.0	848.3	559.3
1980	727.8	642.1	720.2	763.5	785.4	568.5	656.8	701.0	659.0	730.4	771.1	760.9	762.4	767.3	821.7	770.8	763.7
1981	894.7	738.3	910.7	1033.5	896.3	625.2	714.1	875.6	828.2	933.8	970.0	959.4	873.7	1267.3	915.1	795.9	977.8
1982	801.2	810.5	862.5	792.9	738.8	717.3	744.2	970.1	766.2	877.5	943.7	861.0	792.2	725.5	722.3	753.9	740.2
1983	867.7	736.5	841.0	941.0	952.2	570.8	829.1	809.6	714.9	930.4	877.7	830.4	1014.5	978.1	975.5	992.7	888.3

Manufacturing stocks: (5) work in progress / Stocks des industries manufacturières : (5) produits en cours de fabrication

million Australian dollars, end of period / millions de dollars australiens, fin de période

	Year	Q.1	Q.2	Q.3	Q.4	JAN	FEB	MAR	APR	MAY	JUN	JUL	AUG	SEP	OCT	NOV	DEC
1964																	
1965																	
1966																	
1967																	
1968																	
1969																	
1970																	
1971																	
1972																	
1973	943				943												
1974	1179	1039	1111	1182	1179												
1975	1223	1252	1266	1250	1223												
1976	1437	1312	1376	1438	1437												
1977	1615	1547	1587	1650	1615												
1978	1769	1672	1759	1783	1769												
1979	2075	1867	1914	2019	2075												
1980	2425	2309	2316	2422	2425												
1981	2709	2615	2608	2743	2709												
1982	2658	2745	2775	2805	2658												
1983	2658	2723	2727	2736	2658												

Manufacturing stocks: (5) intermediate goods / Stocks des industries manufacturières : (5) biens intermédiaires

million Australian dollars, end of period / millions de dollars australiens, fin de période

	Year	Q.1	Q.2	Q.3	Q.4	JAN	FEB	MAR	APR	MAY	JUN	JUL	AUG	SEP	OCT	NOV	DEC
1964																	
1965																	
1966																	
1967																	
1968																	
1969																	
1970																	
1971																	
1972																	
1973	1928				1928												
1974	2876	2167	2491	2695	2876												
1975	2921	2973	2967	2903	2921												
1976	3300	3008	3183	3241	3300												
1977	3520	3448	3519	3589	3520												
1978	3712	3538	3558	3640	3712												
1979	4575	3820	4107	4181	4575												
1980	5204	4798	5008	5097	5204												
1981	5477	5249	5432	5386	5477												
1982	5649	5661	6542	5694	5649												
1983	5668	5558	5571	5665	5668												

Construction permits issued: total (6) / Permis de construire délivrés : total (6)

Adjusted - Corrigé

million Australian dollars, monthly averages / millions de dollars australiens, moyennes mensuelles

	Year	Q.1	Q.2	Q.3	Q.4	JAN	FEB	MAR	APR	MAY	JUN	JUL	AUG	SEP	OCT	NOV	DEC
1964		130.8	140.3	140.5	154.2	126.5	123.0	143.0	151.4	124.7	144.8	134.4	147.1	140.1	138.4	144.3	179.8
1965		157.0	148.1	151.4	149.8	165.2	155.5	150.2	143.1	149.8	151.3	150.6	153.2	150.5	157.5	147.6	144.4
1966		130.0	142.0	145.6	150.4	109.9	134.8	145.4	124.7	142.6	158.6	162.9	142.2	131.8	161.7	153.5	136.0
1967		163.6	160.9	158.4	178.7	174.3	167.9	148.5	155.0	174.2	153.4	161.2	158.6	185.3	169.6	179.1	187.5
1968		182.3	190.7	190.0	186.5	186.6	176.7	183.7	181.2	199.6	191.2	185.2	203.8	181.1	175.0	185.6	198.8
1969		202.4	224.2	227.9	249.8	187.2	215.8	204.2	238.2	215.8	218.5	230.1	229.5	224.0	227.9	241.6	279.8
1970		261.9	242.7	233.4	253.5	271.5	237.1	277.2	259.2	231.3	237.6	236.7	222.5	241.0	260.5	254.7	245.3
1971		259.5	242.2	277.0	265.9	286.4	252.4	239.7	260.0	248.5	218.2	243.3	311.4	276.3	264.6	273.0	260.2
1972		257.0	278.3	320.5	329.3	243.2	251.2	276.6	251.3	291.9	291.6	357.3	301.7	302.4	348.4	309.5	330.0
1973		386.5	376.2	422.3	410.1	342.0	383.2	434.2	367.7	350.5	410.3	422.6	439.0	405.2	414.4	424.7	391.3
1974		403.6	376.2	328.7	319.1	405.4	419.8	385.6	366.4	372.6	389.5	390.2	320.5	275.4	308.3	323.2	325.8
1975		323.8	397.8	441.0	404.2	319.9	286.8	364.7	373.7	390.8	429.0	423.3	394.4	505.4	364.4	413.6	434.5
1976		442.3	503.6	490.6	515.9	435.7	433.9	452.3	510.4	524.8	475.7	482.3	458.5	531.0	498.8	500.2	548.6
1977		502.4	495.3	506.9	527.5	534.0	503.3	470.0	518.4	508.8	458.8	509.5	521.8	489.3	534.8	511.7	536.0
1978		508.2	507.8	521.3	551.9	510.7	488.5	525.4	524.4	489.8	509.1	472.7	564.9	526.3	549.5	583.2	522.9
1979		576.6	573.9	614.3	656.4	532.5	633.5	563.9	540.9	578.5	602.4	587.8	604.3	650.9	566.1	775.1	627.9
1980		701.9	678.1	752.9	776.8	690.7	712.3	702.8	677.8	664.0	692.5	711.1	830.6	717.0	766.0	767.0	797.4
1981		810.4	866.9	1003.0	880.1	792.9	806.7	831.5	852.8	893.0	855.0	904.0	897.3	1207.6	894.4	742.9	1003.0
1982		894.3	829.2	768.6	726.9	942.4	851.5	889.1	811.1	837.2	839.3	844.1	772.6	689.0	741.3	672.3	767.1
1983		807.6	803.6	913.3	951.6	740.5	939.0	743.3	797.0	832.2	781.5	834.8	953.0	952.2	993.6	917.4	943.7

Construction permits issued: dwellings (7)
thousands, monthly averages

Permis de construire délivrés : logements (7)
milliers, moyennes mensuelles

	Year	Q.1	Q.2	Q.3	Q.4	JAN	FEB	MAR	APR	MAY	JUN	JUL	AUG	SEP	OCT	NOV	DEC
1964	10.4	8.7	11.3	11.4	10.1	7.5	8.8	9.8	11.0	9.8	13.2	10.7	12.2	11.4	10.4	10.8	9.3
1965	9.6	9.0	10.4	10.1	8.9	7.4	9.0	10.7	9.6	10.4	11.1	9.6	10.0	10.6	9.5	8.9	8.2
1966	9.7	8.2	9.7	10.8	10.2	5.9	8.2	10.4	8.6	10.3	10.1	10.3	11.6	10.4	11.3	10.4	8.9
1967	10.3	8.7	10.6	10.8	11.0	7.4	9.8	9.0	9.8	11.8	10.3	10.2	11.7	10.4	11.8	11.7	9.4
1968	11.8	10.7	11.7	12.9	12.2	9.4	10.9	11.7	10.6	12.9	11.6	12.7	13.0	12.9	12.7	12.6	11.3
1969	13.1	11.3	13.2	14.2	13.9	9.6	11.2	12.9	11.8	14.7	13.1	15.0	13.8	13.7	14.4	13.7	13.7
1970	12.1	11.6	12.3	12.0	12.4	10.0	12.2	12.6	13.6	11.3	12.0	11.3	11.7	13.1	13.0	11.9	12.2
1971	12.0	10.8	12.1	12.8	12.4	9.6	10.2	12.7	11.7	11.3	13.3	12.5	13.3	12.8	12.4	13.1	11.7
1972	13.8	11.8	13.4	14.9	15.0	9.3	12.4	13.7	10.9	14.6	14.6	13.7	15.6	15.4	15.7	16.1	13.2
1973	16.8	15.5	17.4	18.3	15.9	13.2	14.6	18.7	14.7	19.8	17.8	18.9	18.8	17.1	18.4	16.4	12.8
1974	11.4	12.5	13.3	10.6	9.3	11.7	12.2	13.6	12.8	14.6	12.5	13.2	9.5	9.1	9.4	8.9	9.6
1975	11.1	8.6	12.0	11.7	12.1	7.5	8.3	9.9	11.1	11.9	12.9	12.5	10.4	12.4	12.1	12.4	11.8
1976	12.6	11.4	13.4	12.9	12.6	8.8	11.7	13.6	12.2	13.3	14.7	12.6	12.2	14.0	12.9	13.5	11.6
1977	10.8	10.4	11.1	10.9	10.8	9.8	10.8	10.7	9.9	11.6	11.9	10.7	11.4	10.7	11.0	11.4	9.9
1978	10.1	8.9	10.7	9.9	10.3	7.8	8.7	10.1	10.0	11.1	11.1	9.4	10.4	9.9	11.1	11.4	9.8
1979	11.4	9.9	11.9	12.0	11.9	8.1	9.8	11.9	10.2	13.6	12.0	12.4	11.9	11.6	12.9	13.0	9.8
1980	12.7	11.6	13.0	13.0	13.3	10.1	11.3	13.3	12.7	13.3	13.1	13.2	12.8	13.0	14.1	13.1	12.5
1981	12.9	12.1	13.8	13.2	12.4	10.4	11.6	14.3	13.3	13.2	14.9	13.2	12.9	13.5	13.4	12.5	11.2
1982	9.8	10.3	10.3	9.7	8.9	9.4	9.4	12.2	10.3	10.3	10.2	10.2	9.6	9.3	8.7	9.6	8.4
1983	11.1	9.3	10.9	11.8	12.5	7.1	9.6	11.4	9.7	11.7	11.2	10.4	12.4	12.5	12.5	12.9	12.0

Construction: housing starts (8)
thousands, monthly averages

Construction : logements mis en chantier (8)
milliers, moyennes mensuelles

	Year	Q.1	Q.2	Q.3	Q.4	JAN	FEB	MAR	APR	MAY	JUN	JUL	AUG	SEP	OCT	NOV	DEC
1964	9.6	8.9	9.6	10.4	9.3												
1965	9.3	9.7	9.4	9.6	8.3												
1966	9.2	8.5	9.4	9.5	9.6												
1967	9.8	9.4	9.9	10.5	9.5												
1968	11.0	10.2	10.9	11.4	11.5												
1969	12.2	11.3	12.3	12.9	12.2												
1970	12.3	12.0	12.3	12.9	12.2												
1971	11.9	11.5	11.7	12.4	11.8												
1972	13.1	11.9	13.3	13.8	13.3												
1973	14.7	14.1	15.6	15.6	13.3												
1974	11.2	13.4	12.5	9.8	9.1												
1975	10.7	9.5	11.0	11.7	10.5												
1976	12.0	11.4	12.1	12.8	11.7												
1977	10.8	11.5	11.3	11.0	9.2												
1978	9.5	9.2	10.2	9.7	8.9												
1979	10.7	10.3	10.8	10.9	10.7												
1980	12.2	11.4	11.6	13.0	12.8												
1981	12.2	11.6	12.3	13.0	11.9												
1982	9.1	9.7	9.4	8.9	8.3												
1983		8.0	9.8														

Construction, work in progress (8)
(new buildings): dwellings
thousands, end of period

Construction, travaux en cours (8)
(nouveaux bâtiments) : logements
milliers, fin de période

	Year	Q.1	Q.2	Q.3	Q.4	JAN	FEB	MAR	APR	MAY	JUN	JUL	AUG	SEP	OCT	NOV	DEC
1964	58.2	52.5	55.5	60.3	58.2												
1965	54.1	61.0	59.5	59.4	54.1												
1966	52.9	54.0	54.0	55.1	52.9												
1967	54.8	56.5	57.2	58.8	54.8												
1968	61.6	58.4	60.1	62.0	61.6												
1969	68.7	65.9	68.2	71.6	68.7												
1970	63.3	72.5	69.4	67.7	63.3												
1971	61.5	65.1	65.0	65.9	61.5												
1972	70.3	65.4	68.1	71.0	70.3												
1973	92.5	77.6	86.6	93.6	92.5												
1974	77.1	98.8	98.1	90.5	77.1												
1975	71.5	72.8	71.6	75.2	71.5												
1976	71.1	75.6	74.9	75.5	71.1												
1977	60.6	73.2	70.1	68.7	60.6												
1978	53.0	59.6	58.6	58.5	53.0												
1979	56.3	56.8	59.0	59.5	56.3												
1980	71.2	60.7	62.2	71.3	71.2												
1981	70.4	73.2	75.2	74.8	70.4												
1982	47.4	68.9	64.2	56.1	47.4												
1983		48.5	52.7														

Construction permits issued: dwellings (7)

thousands, monthly averages

Adjusted - Corrigé

Permis de construire délivrés : logements (7)

milliers, moyennes mensuelles

	Year	Q.1	Q.2	Q.3	Q.4	JAN	FEB	MAR	APR	MAY	JUN	JUL	AUG	SEP	OCT	NOV	DEC
1964		9.9	10.6	10.7	10.2	10.1	9.5	10.1	10.2	9.5	12.2	10.1	11.7	10.2	9.9	10.7	9.8
1965		10.1	10.0	9.4	9.0	10.1	10.4	9.8	10.1	9.9	10.1	9.4	9.2	9.6	9.4	8.4	9.0
1966		8.9	9.4	10.2	10.3	8.3	8.9	9.3	9.5	9.3	9.4	10.4	10.3	9.8	11.1	9.7	10.0
1967		9.9	10.1	10.2	11.0	9.8	10.7	9.1	10.1	10.4	9.8	10.2	10.3	10.2	11.0	11.0	10.9
1968		11.6	11.4	12.2	12.1	12.0	11.3	11.6	11.1	11.6	11.6	11.8	12.3	12.5	11.3	12.7	12.2
1969		12.5	12.9	13.3	13.9	12.5	12.3	12.6	12.3	13.7	12.8	13.7	13.5	12.7	13.3	13.9	14.4
1970		13.2	11.7	11.4	12.3	13.3	13.5	12.7	13.2	10.8	11.1	10.6	11.4	12.1	12.5	11.7	12.6
1971		11.9	11.8	12.2	12.4	12.5	11.8	11.4	12.7	10.6	12.1	12.2	12.5	11.9	12.3	12.3	12.6
1972		12.9	12.8	14.4	14.9	12.5	13.0	13.1	11.9	12.8	13.6	13.6	14.2	15.4	14.7	15.1	15.0
1973		16.8	16.8	17.7	15.6	16.5	16.3	17.6	16.1	17.1	17.2	18.0	18.0	17.1	16.8	15.8	14.3
1974		13.7	12.8	10.2	9.2	14.4	13.6	13.2	13.4	13.1	12.0	12.3	9.5	8.9	8.5	8.9	10.2
1975		9.7	11.2	11.3	12.0	9.6	9.3	10.4	10.5	11.1	12.1	11.5	10.8	11.7	11.4	12.3	12.4
1976		12.2	12.8	12.6	12.5	11.7	12.8	12.1	13.0	12.6	13.0	12.4	12.1	13.3	12.9	12.5	12.2
1977		11.6	10.6	10.8	10.7	13.2	12.1	9.3	10.9	10.5	10.5	11.0	11.0	10.4	10.9	10.4	10.8
1978		9.9	10.0	9.8	10.6	10.0	9.8	10.0	10.1	9.8	10.0	9.5	9.9	10.1	10.4	10.5	10.9
1979		10.8	11.4	11.9	11.6	10.2	11.0	11.2	10.9	11.9	11.4	12.0	11.9	11.8	11.7	12.3	10.8
1980		12.6	12.5	12.7	12.9	12.8	12.4	12.7	12.8	12.4	12.2	12.1	13.6	12.4	13.2	13.0	12.7
1981		13.3	13.2	13.0	12.1	13.7	13.0	13.0	13.4	12.9	13.4	12.8	13.3	12.8	12.7	12.1	11.5
1982		11.3	9.9	9.5	8.8	11.8	11.3	10.8	10.6	10.0	9.1	10.3	9.3	9.0	8.5	8.9	8.9
1983		10.0	10.4	11.7	12.5	9.3	10.7	9.9	10.3	10.6	10.2	10.9	11.7	12.3	12.3	11.9	13.3

Construction, work in progress (8)(9) (new buildings): total

million Australian dollars, end of period

Construction, travaux en cours (8)(9) (nouveaux bâtiments) : total

millions de dollars australiens, fin de période

	Year	Q.1	Q.2	Q.3	Q.4	JAN	FEB	MAR	APR	MAY	JUN	JUL	AUG	SEP	OCT	NOV	DEC
1964	1156	1001	1082	1170	1156												
1965	1303	1223	1256	1336	1303												
1966	1264	1307	1302	1327	1264												
1967	1370	1322	1383	1432	1370												
1968	1508	1464	1542	1571	1508												
1969	1807	1625	1695	1804	1807												
1970	2133	1992	2049	2048	2133												
1971	2360	2256	2335	2398	2360												
1972	2685	2454	2514	2673	2685												
1973	3714	2957	3270	3590	3714												
1974	4173	4051	4331	4412	4173												
1975	4590	4287	4534	4794	4590												
1976	5022	4714	4893	5103	5022												
1977	4907	5120	5096	5129	4907												
1978	5105	4962	5063	5234	5105												
1979	5152	5359	5503	5482	5152												
1980	7024	5706	5894	6929	7024												
1981	8281	7607	8276	8150	8281												
1982	7564	8620	8479	8469	7564												
1983		7276	7697														

Construction, work in progress (8) (new buildings): dwellings

thousands, end of period

Adjusted - Corrigé

Construction, travaux en cours (8) (nouveaux bâtiments) : logements

milliers, fin de période

	Year	Q.1	Q.2	Q.3	Q.4	JAN	FEB	MAR	APR	MAY	JUN	JUL	AUG	SEP	OCT	NOV	DEC
1964		52.5	55.7	58.5	60.0												
1965		60.9	59.6	57.7	55.9												
1966		53.9	53.8	53.6	54.7												
1967		56.3	56.9	57.3	56.9												
1968		58.1	59.7	60.6	63.9												
1969		65.6	67.6	70.0	71.3												
1970		72.2	68.7	66.2	65.5												
1971		64.8	64.2	64.4	64.0												
1972		65.2	67.2	69.4	73.2												
1973		77.5	85.5	91.4	96.3												
1974		98.7	96.9	88.3	80.2												
1975		72.7	70.8	73.2	74.3												
1976		75.5	74.3	73.4	74.0												
1977		73.1	69.5	66.5	63.1												
1978		59.5	58.1	56.7	55.3												
1979		56.8	58.5	57.6	58.8												
1980		60.8	60.8	68.7	74.6												
1981		73.4	74.4	72.3	73.9												
1982		68.8	63.0	56.0	49.1												
1983		48.1	51.5														

AUSTRALIA

Retail sales: value (10)

million Australian dollars, monthly averages

Ventes au détail : valeur (10)

millions de dollars australiens, moyennes mensuelles

	Year	Q.1	Q.2	Q.3	Q.4	JAN	FEB	MAR	APR	MAY	JUN	JUL	AUG	SEP	OCT	NOV	DEC
1964	509	461	490	497	586	477	449	457	484	510	477	503	491	499	529	532	698
1965	539	490	522	526	618	497	466	508	527	530	508	531	519	529	546	567	741
1966	569	516	549	555	655	511	498	538	542	566	538	543	557	565	570	604	790
1967	609	554	586	597	699	549	535	579	563	614	582	579	602	609	614	656	825
1968	646	595	621	624	742	595	584	605	605	667	593	623	645	603	663	695	867
1969	712	633	667	707	842	653	597	648	646	711	645	705	710	706	764	755	1008
1970	793	721	765	767	919	743	693	726	753	799	744	773	758	770	839	829	1089
1971	867	782	839	846	999	787	740	820	831	862	823	852	834	853	892	926	1180
1972	933	843	894	909	1085	811	830	889	845	947	891	876	921	930	949	1016	1291
1973	1083	939	1028	1065	1300	938	885	994	969	1082	1033	1021	1111	1064	1164	1239	1496
1974	1303	1141	1255	1296	1522	1157	1087	1178	1215	1341	1209	1279	1335	1273	1380	1429	1757
1975	1524	1324	1465	1497	1810	1355	1264	1354	1442	1548	1404	1484	1494	1512	1644	1637	2149
1976	1717	1570	1632	1668	1998	1576	1487	1646	1613	1674	1608	1670	1649	1686	1731	1833	2430
1977	1877	1658	1820	1837	2195	1628	1589	1757	1765	1889	1806	1785	1850	1876	1911	2022	2651
1978	2078	1826	2024	2037	2424	1780	1759	1941	1929	2139	2003	1959	2072	2081	2110	2244	2918
1979	2288	2063	2199	2229	2662	2049	1955	2185	2098	2348	2151	2182	2322	2182	2334	2501	3151
1980	2613	2321	2488	2565	3078	2324	2268	2370	2399	2666	2399	2552	2552	2591	2735	2747	3751
1981	2944	2613	2805	2890	3468	2644	2492	2705	2728	2936	2753	2880	2852	2937	3080	3077	4248
1982	3249	2916	3145	3144	3789	2922	2741	3084	3137	3215	3084	3190	3080	3163	3283	3494	4589
1983	3538	3227	3370	3444	4112	3129	3078	3473	3376	3418	3317	3373	3472	3487	3523	3781	5034

Retail sales: volume (11)

million 1979-80 Australian dollars, quarterly averages

Ventes au détail : volume (11)

millions de dollars australiens de 1979-80, moyennes trimestrielles

	Year	Q.1	Q.2	Q.3	Q.4	JAN	FEB	MAR	APR	MAY	JUN	JUL	AUG	SEP	OCT	NOV	DEC
1964																	
1965																	
1966																	
1967																	
1968																	
1969																	
1970																	
1971																	
1972																	
1973																	
1974																	
1975																	
1976				6872	7971												
1977	7091	6517	6950	6878	8019												
1978	7234	6635	7171	7092	8037												
1979	7193	6746	6991	6931	8103												
1980	7464	6864	7200	7262	8531												
1981	7755	7117	7522	7570	8812												
1982	7900	7344	7771	7584	8901												
1983		7464															

New passenger car registrations

thousands, monthly averages

Immatriculations de voitures de tourisme neuves

milliers, moyennes mensuelles

	Year	Q.1	Q.2	Q.3	Q.4	JAN	FEB	MAR	APR	MAY	JUN	JUL	AUG	SEP	OCT	NOV	DEC
1964	27.8	24.5	28.1	29.7	28.8	21.3	24.6	27.6	29.9	27.4	27.0	31.1	29.7	28.2	29.4	26.2	30.8
1965	27.7	27.3	30.1	28.6	24.6	23.7	25.7	32.4	29.7	30.7	29.9	30.6	31.4	24.0	22.7	24.7	26.3
1966	25.6	23.4	26.1	25.7	27.1	20.5	22.6	26.9	25.7	28.2	24.5	24.9	26.4	25.7	25.6	28.3	27.4
1967	28.0	24.4	27.6	28.7	31.2	22.2	23.4	27.7	26.0	29.1	27.5	27.3	30.2	28.6	31.4	32.5	29.6
1968	30.7	29.0	33.4	29.1	31.5	25.7	29.7	31.6	31.7	36.8	31.6	31.8	28.2	27.2	32.8	30.9	30.8
1969	33.4	30.8	33.3	34.9	34.6	27.5	30.3	34.5	31.2	37.0	31.8	36.1	32.9	35.6	36.0	33.6	34.3
1970	34.4	32.4	34.5	35.0	35.8	29.7	34.3	33.1	37.8	32.4	33.4	37.0	34.2	33.7	35.3	34.4	37.8
1971	34.8	32.6	34.1	37.6	34.7	32.3	29.9	35.7	32.2	34.6	35.6	38.7	40.0	34.1	34.0	35.6	34.4
1972	33.8	30.7	34.5	34.1	36.0	28.6	30.5	32.9	30.9	38.3	34.4	34.0	35.0	33.2	34.8	38.8	34.4
1973	38.3	34.5	38.7	40.2	40.0	32.5	32.4	38.6	33.4	44.8	37.8	39.1	43.8	37.7	46.1	42.2	31.7
1974	39.6	34.5	40.3	43.2	40.5	35.4	33.1	35.1	36.3	49.4	35.3	44.4	43.4	41.9	46.3	40.7	34.5
1975	39.4	39.8	44.1	38.9	34.7	30.4	44.4	44.4	51.6	42.7	38.2	43.3	39.4	34.0	39.6	31.7	32.9
1976	39.1	36.1	41.8	37.2	41.1	30.1	33.4	44.8	40.4	42.4	42.6	38.2	35.6	37.8	37.0	40.3	46.2
1977	35.9	34.9	35.8	37.6	35.2	31.6	34.5	38.5	29.3	37.7	40.5	38.1	40.1	34.5	34.0	36.5	35.2
1978	37.6	32.9	38.5	41.4	37.7	30.1	33.6	34.9	37.1	40.3	38.1	38.2	44.5	41.6	38.8	39.1	35.2
1979	38.4	34.9	40.5	41.6	36.8	30.0	34.2	40.4	36.2	45.4	40.0	44.6	43.7	36.3	39.8	38.4	32.2
1980	37.8	35.5	36.8	40.0	38.8	33.2	36.3	37.0	36.3	37.7	36.5	43.2	39.4	37.5	40.2	36.4	39.9
1981	38.6	35.5	39.9	40.9	38.0	31.8	35.9	38.7	37.2	39.6	42.8	45.1	39.8	37.9	35.4	37.5	41.0
1982	40.0	37.1	41.1	41.7	40.2	33.6	33.4	44.1	38.0	41.2	44.2	41.9	43.8	39.3	36.5	36.3	47.7
1983	36.1	33.1	36.2	38.0	37.1	26.2	29.7	43.5	31.4	38.0	39.3	35.1	42.6	36.5	34.2	38.9	38.2

Retail sales: value (10) — Ventes au détail : valeur (10)

million Australian dollars, monthly averages — millions de dollars australiens, moyennes mensuelles

Adjusted - Corrigé

Year	Q.1	Q.2	Q.3	Q.4	JAN	FEB	MAR	APR	MAY	JUN	JUL	AUG	SEP	OCT	NOV	DEC
1964	488	502	513	521	487	484	491	498	503	505	510	513	515	517	523	523
1965	527	536	542	547	524	526	530	541	530	536	539	543	545	547	547	549
1966	555	563	571	582	551	556	557	560	564	566	566	571	576	578	580	587
1967	595	600	616	626	591	597	596	598	599	605	612	613	624	623	628	626
1968	629	633	646	661	627	627	633	635	639	640	647	650	640	655	662	667
1969	676	685	732	749	673	668	688	677	680	698	728	734	734	741	747	759
1970	773	782	792	819	769	773	777	776	785	783	785	792	799	817	819	821
1971	835	859	871	878	830	834	840	852	860	864	868	871	875	877	879	879
1972	896	913	941	972	876	907	907	902	917	921	933	939	951	963	970	982
1973	1002	1050	1108	1165	990	1001	1014	1033	1047	1071	1085	1109	1130	1146	1167	1182
1974	1227	1277	1335	1366	1220	1227	1232	1258	1272	1300	1319	1337	1348	1359	1352	1388
1975	1428	1485	1544	1619	1409	1428	1446	1478	1474	1504	1529	1539	1564	1594	1615	1647
1976	1671	1658	1723	1762	1652	1665	1697	1636	1658	1678	1704	1729	1736	1743	1768	1775
1977	1801	1854	1890	1947	1789	1802	1812	1806	1876	1880	1873	1885	1910	1952	1948	1941
1978	1978	2056	2107	2170	1962	1992	1979	2044	2063	2061	2083	2109	2128	2165	2151	2195
1979	2209	2240	2323	2367	2197	2214	2216	2237	2260	2224	2322	2324	2324	2330	2372	2399
1980	2476	2536	2654	2729	2489	2438	2501	2498	2534	2576	2634	2640	2688	2681	2729	2778
1981	2824	2862	2985	3074	2796	2820	2856	2824	2871	2890	2922	2990	3041	3034	3049	3139
1982	3148	3219	3248	3349	3146	3134	3163	3221	3198	3237	3249	3242	3254	3344	3389	3314
1983	3478	3456	3544	3650	3429	3479	3525	3489	3416	3462	3534	3552	3546	3637	3661	3651

Retail sales: volume (11) — Ventes au détail : volume (11)

million 1979-80 Australian dollars, quarterly averages — millions de dollars australiens de 1979-80, moyennes trimestrielles

Adjusted - Corrigé

Year	Q.1	Q.2	Q.3	Q.4	JAN	FEB	MAR	APR	MAY	JUN	JUL	AUG	SEP	OCT	NOV	DEC
1964																
1965																
1966																
1967																
1968																
1969																
1970																
1971																
1972																
1973																
1974																
1975																
1976			7082	7070												
1977	7058	7093	7064	7137												
1978	7134	7338	7326	7209												
1979	7208	7149	7220	7208												
1980	7303	7375	7499	7576												
1981	7664	7713	7800	7826												
1982	7906	7972	7814	7883												
1983	8067															

New passenger car registrations — Immatriculations de voitures de tourisme neuves

thousands, monthly averages — milliers, moyennes mensuelles

Adjusted - Corrigé

Year	Q.1	Q.2	Q.3	Q.4	JAN	FEB	MAR	APR	MAY	JUN	JUL	AUG	SEP	OCT	NOV	DEC
1964	26.7	27.8	28.4	27.6	24.8	26.6	28.7	28.3	27.3	27.7	28.7	29.8	26.7	27.5	25.9	29.4
1965	29.2	30.4	27.6	23.7	29.8	28.4	29.5	31.0	30.4	30.0	29.2	30.7	23.0	22.4	23.5	25.3
1966	25.0	26.3	24.9	26.3	25.6	25.1	24.3	27.3	27.0	24.5	24.8	24.5	25.4	25.4	26.3	27.1
1967	26.8	26.8	28.0	30.6	26.8	26.1	27.4	26.4	26.1	28.0	27.1	27.8	29.2	30.6	30.5	30.6
1968	30.8	33.0	28.4	30.5	29.2	31.8	31.4	32.6	32.8	33.8	29.2	27.4	28.6	30.0	30.4	31.0
1969	33.2	32.8	34.0	33.5	31.2	34.0	34.5	31.3	33.8	33.4	32.9	33.4	35.7	33.4	34.2	32.9
1970	36.0	33.2	34.0	34.9	34.8	38.5	34.8	35.3	30.7	33.4	34.2	34.6	33.1	33.7	34.6	36.3
1971	35.3	33.5	36.7	34.0	39.4	33.5	32.9	33.1	32.7	34.7	37.1	39.3	33.7	33.9	34.3	33.8
1972	33.0	33.4	33.5	35.8	34.8	32.5	31.5	32.3	33.5	34.3	33.8	32.1	34.4	33.9	36.8	36.7
1973	36.6	37.7	39.6	39.2	36.4	36.2	37.2	35.7	38.9	38.4	37.7	40.4	40.5	42.6	41.1	33.9
1974	37.1	39.2	42.0	39.8	39.2	36.9	35.3	36.9	43.6	37.0	40.3	41.3	44.4	42.6	40.8	36.1
1975	44.1	41.9	37.4	34.2	34.2	49.5	48.5	47.4	39.1	39.2	38.9	38.9	34.5	37.0	33.0	32.7
1976	38.0	40.8	35.8	41.1	35.2	37.1	41.6	41.1	40.7	40.6	35.9	34.0	37.6	37.5	39.7	46.1
1977	37.4	34.8	36.1	35.4	38.8	38.1	35.4	30.6	35.4	38.5	37.2	36.0	35.1	34.6	35.3	36.3
1978	36.1	36.8	39.9	38.2	36.1	36.9	35.1	37.3	36.1	36.8	37.1	39.3	43.4	38.8	38.1	37.9
1979	36.8	39.5	40.1	36.9	34.2	37.5	38.9	39.0	40.4	39.2	42.1	39.0	39.3	38.1	38.2	34.4
1980	37.7	36.1	38.0	38.8	37.5	38.2	37.3	36.8	35.3	36.2	38.1	37.7	38.2	38.9	38.3	39.1
1981	38.3	39.2	38.6	38.2	37.7	38.9	38.1	38.3	38.8	40.4	40.1	37.9	37.6	35.8	39.0	39.7
1982	39.7	40.4	39.4	40.4	41.7	36.3	41.1	40.2	40.4	40.7	38.6	40.5	39.1	38.6	36.0	46.8
1983	34.9	35.6	36.0	37.6	32.6	32.2	40.1	34.2	36.3	36.2	33.7	37.2	37.2	36.2	37.7	38.8

Employment: manufacturing (12) — Emploi : industries manufacturières (12)

thousands — milliers

	Year	Q.1	Q.2	Q.3	Q.4	JAN	FEB	MAR	APR	MAY	JUN	JUL	AUG	SEP	OCT	NOV	DEC
1964																	
1965																	
1966				1233										1233			
1967				1261										1261			
1968				1264										1264			
1969				1302										1302			
1970				1320										1320			
1971				1365										1365			
1972				1330										1330			
1973				1382										1382			
1974				1374										1374			
1975				1263										1263			
1976				1282	1279									1282			1279
1977	1277	1301	1281	1277	1248			1301			1281			1277			1248
1978	1209	1227	1235	1185	1189			1227			1235			1185			1189
1979	1213	1195	1217	1221	1221			1195			1217			1221			1221
1980	1240	1239	1257	1234	1229			1239			1257			1234			1229
1981	1248	1238	1262	1231	1259			1238			1262			1231			1259
1982	1211	1243	1245	1193	1162			1243			1245			1193			1162
1983		1147	1151	1134				1147			1151			1134			

Unemployment (13) — Chômage (13)

thousands — milliers

	Year	Q.1	Q.2	Q.3	Q.4	JAN	FEB	MAR	APR	MAY	JUN	JUL	AUG	SEP	OCT	NOV	DEC
1964	63.3	83.0	64.6	52.4	53.2		83.0			64.6			52.4			53.2	
1965	60.7	67.3	55.5	54.2	65.8		67.3			55.5			54.2			65.8	
1966	76.5	86.2	65.4	78.6	75.7		86.2			65.4			78.6			75.7	
1967	94.5	108.7	100.3	86.8	82.3		108.7			100.3			86.8			82.3	
1968	93.8	112.1	100.3	81.1	81.8		112.1			100.3			81.1			81.8	
1969	96.1	112.2	95.9	78.9	97.5		112.2			95.9			78.9			97.5	
1970	90.6	105.5	92.9	78.2	85.7		105.5			92.9			78.2			85.7	
1971	107.3	116.8	107.7	92.7	111.9		116.8			107.7			92.7			111.9	
1972	150.1	167.4	134.2	144.0	154.9		167.4			134.2			144.0			154.9	
1973	136.3	182.9	132.5	105.8	123.8		182.9			132.5			105.8			123.8	
1974	161.6	155.6	124.0	140.9	226.0		155.6			124.0			140.9			226.0	
1975	302.5	333.1	288.2	278.4	310.1		333.1			288.2			278.4			310.1	
1976	298.1	342.1	275.9	292.7	281.5		342.1			275.9			292.7			281.5	
1977	358.1	372.3	353.8	359.3	346.8		372.3			353.8			359.3			346.8	
1978	413.3	477.0	397.2	386.1	392.8		477.0	420.3	401.1	395.3	392.3	378.0	395.7	384.5	367.5	369.7	441.2
1979	404.7	441.7	400.9	384.2	391.8	446.2	453.9	425.0	416.8	396.6	389.3	382.4	373.8	396.5	387.8	360.6	426.9
1980	405.6	431.6	408.0	394.4	388.2	437.8	444.5	412.4	404.5	413.6	406.0	385.4	392.3	405.5	375.7	357.0	432.0
1981	390.4	421.5	367.2	382.0	391.9	430.4	424.1	409.9	376.0	375.5	350.2	374.8	377.1	391.1	370.4	371.9	433.3
1982	491.3	461.2	444.6	471.6	587.6	439.6	484.4	459.7	436.2	449.9	447.8	450.3	458.5	505.9	536.8	552.0	674.0
1983	697.0	726.2	707.7	698.3	655.9	694.6	750.1	733.9	709.3	720.5	693.2	687.2	686.8	720.9	653.1	624.7	690.0

Unemployment (13) — Chômage (13)

as per cent of civilian labour force — en pourcentage de la main-d'œuvre civile

	Year	Q.1	Q.2	Q.3	Q.4	JAN	FEB	MAR	APR	MAY	JUN	JUL	AUG	SEP	OCT	NOV	DEC
1964																	
1965																	
1966				1.6	1.5								1.6			1.5	
1967	1.9	2.2	2.0	1.7	1.6		2.2			2.0			1.7			1.6	
1968	1.9	2.2	2.0	1.6	1.6		2.2			2.0			1.6			1.6	
1969	1.8	2.1	1.8	1.5	1.8		2.1			1.8			1.5			1.8	
1970	1.6	1.9	1.7	1.4	1.5		1.9			1.7			1.4			1.5	
1971	1.9	2.1	1.9	1.7	2.0		2.1			1.9			1.7			2.0	
1972	2.6	2.9	2.4	2.5	2.7		2.9			2.4			2.5			2.7	
1973	2.3	3.1	2.3	1.8	2.1		3.1			2.3			1.8			2.1	
1974	2.7	2.6	2.1	2.4	3.7		2.6			2.1			2.4			3.7	
1975	4.9	5.4	4.7	4.6	5.0		5.4			4.7			4.6			5.0	
1976	4.8	5.4	4.4	4.7	4.5		5.4			4.4			4.7			4.5	
1977	5.7	5.9	5.5	5.7	5.5		5.9			5.5			5.7			5.5	
1978	6.4	7.4	6.2	6.0	6.1		7.4	6.6	6.3	6.2	6.1	5.9	6.2	6.0	5.8	5.8	6.7
1979	6.2	6.9	6.2	5.9	6.0	7.0	7.0	6.6	6.4	6.2	6.0	5.9	5.8	6.1	6.0	5.5	6.4
1980	6.1	6.5	6.1	5.9	5.8	6.7	6.7	6.2	6.1	6.2	6.1	5.8	5.9	6.0	5.6	5.4	6.3
1981	5.8	6.3	5.5	5.6	5.8	6.5	6.3	6.0	5.6	5.6	5.2	5.5	5.6	5.7	5.5	5.5	6.3
1982	7.1	6.7	6.5	6.9	8.4	6.5	7.0	6.6	6.4	6.6	6.6	6.6	6.7	7.3	7.7	8.0	9.5
1983	10.0	10.4	10.2	10.0	9.3	10.1	10.7	10.4	10.2	10.3	10.0	9.8	9.9	10.2	9.3	8.9	9.7

Jobs vacant, unfilled vacancies (14) — Offres d'emploi non satisfaites (14)

thousands — milliers

	Year	Q.1	Q.2	Q.3	Q.4	JAN	FEB	MAR	APR	MAY	JUN	JUL	AUG	SEP	OCT	NOV	DEC
1964																	
1965																	
1966																	
1967																	
1968																	
1969																	
1970																	
1971																	
1972																	
1973																	
1974	165.2																
1975	55.2																
1976	50.8																
1977	41.6	49.6	39.3	41.0	36.4					39.3			41.0			36.4	
1978	34.1	35.6	32.2	..	..		49.6			32.2			..			..	
1979	33.9	..	34.3	33.0	34.3		35.6			34.3			33.0			34.3	
1980	32.8	36.9	29.8	30.1	34.3		36.9			29.8			30.1			34.3	
1981	35.2	33.5	35.7	34.7	36.7		33.0			35.7			34.7			36.7	
1982	24.2	33.7	25.3	21.5	16.4		33.7			25.3			21.5			16.4	
1983	17.6	16.9	17.5	16.7	19.1		16.9			17.5			16.7			19.1	

Unemployment (13) — Chômage (13)

Adjusted - Corrigé

thousands — milliers

	Year	Q.1	Q.2	Q.3	Q.4	JAN	FEB	MAR	APR	MAY	JUN	JUL	AUG	SEP	OCT	NOV	DEC
1964		69.5	70.6	61.1	58.3		69.5			70.6			61.1			58.3	
1965		56.5	58.4	61.5	71.0		56.5			58.4			61.5			71.0	
1966		72.7	69.0	90.3	85.7		72.7			69.0			90.3			85.7	
1967		91.0	98.4	97.7	92.9		91.0			98.4			97.7			92.9	
1968		94.3	97.6	95.5	88.1		94.3			97.6			95.5			88.1	
1969		94.9	92.5	91.8	104.1		94.9			92.5			91.8			104.1	
1970		88.3	91.6	91.9	90.8		88.3			91.6			91.9			90.8	
1971		97.3	106.1	107.7	121.8		97.3			106.1			107.7			121.8	
1972		139.0	135.0	168.6	160.9		139.0			135.0			168.6			160.9	
1973		151.8	135.3	125.3	126.9		151.8			135.3			125.3			126.9	
1974		128.9	129.4	165.1	247.1		128.9			129.4			165.1			247.1	
1975		296.5	294.2	287.6	334.8		296.5			294.2			287.6			334.8	
1976		303.6	281.4	302.0	304.6		303.6			281.4			302.0			304.6	
1977		329.7	359.7	372.2	375.9		329.7			359.7			372.2			375.9	
1978		423.4	402.9	402.7	402.8		423.4	406.1	404.2	398.2	406.4	398.2	416.8	393.2	392.7	405.8	409.8
1979		406.5	409.0	402.1	402.3	406.6	402.4	410.6	421.8	400.2	404.9	404.6	394.8	406.8	414.2	395.7	397.0
1980		397.2	416.2	412.3	397.9	401.3	394.3	396.0	408.5	417.0	423.2	407.2	413.7	416.0	401.1	391.1	401.4
1981		388.3	373.6	397.0	401.1	395.7	377.5	391.7	378.8	377.2	364.9	395.7	396.2	399.2	394.0	407.0	402.2
1982		426.0	453.1	490.3	602.9	407.6	431.5	439.0	440.0	451.5	467.9	474.8	481.3	514.9	570.0	600.9	637.7
1983		668.9	718.1	724.5	680.0	640.4	671.0	695.3	711.6	718.8	723.9	724.3	718.9	730.2	697.0	679.4	663.7

Unemployment (13) — Chômage (13)

Adjusted - Corrigé

as per cent of civilian labour force — en pourcentage de la main-d'œuvre civile

	Year	Q.1	Q.2	Q.3	Q.4	JAN	FEB	MAR	APR	MAY	JUN	JUL	AUG	SEP	OCT	NOV	DEC
1964																	
1965																	
1966				1.8	1.7								1.8			1.7	
1967		1.8	2.0	1.9	1.8		1.8			2.0			1.9			1.8	
1968		1.9	1.9	1.8	1.7		1.9			1.9			1.8			1.7	
1969		1.8	1.8	1.7	1.9		1.8			1.8			1.7			1.9	
1970		1.6	1.7	1.7	1.6		1.6			1.7			1.7			1.6	
1971		1.7	1.9	1.9	2.2		1.7			1.9			1.9			2.2	
1972		2.4	2.4	2.9	2.8		2.4			2.4			2.9			2.8	
1973		2.6	2.3	2.1	2.1		2.6			2.3			2.1			2.1	
1974		2.1	2.1	2.7	4.0		2.1			2.1			2.7			4.0	
1975		4.8	4.8	4.7	5.4		4.8			4.8			4.7			5.4	
1976		4.9	4.5	4.8	4.9		4.9			4.5			4.8			4.9	
1977		5.2	5.6	5.8	5.9		5.2			5.6			5.8			5.9	
1978		6.6	6.3	6.3	6.3		6.6	6.4	6.3	6.2	6.3	6.2	6.5	6.2	6.1	6.3	6.4
1979		6.3	6.3	6.2	6.1	6.3	6.3	6.4	6.5	6.2	6.3	6.3	6.1	6.3	6.3	6.0	6.1
1980		6.0	6.3	6.2	5.9	6.1	6.0	6.0	6.2	6.3	6.4	6.1	6.2	6.2	6.0	5.8	6.0
1981		5.8	5.5	5.8	5.9	5.9	5.6	5.8	5.6	5.6	5.4	5.8	5.8	5.8	5.8	6.0	5.9
1982		6.2	6.6	7.1	8.7	6.0	6.3	6.4	6.4	6.6	6.8	6.9	7.0	7.5	8.2	8.7	9.2
1983		9.6	10.3	10.3	9.7	9.2	9.6	10.0	10.2	10.3	10.3	10.3	10.3	10.4	9.9	9.7	9.4

Weekly hours of work: manufacturing (15)

hours

Durée hebdomadaire du travail : industries manufacturières (15)

heures

	Year	Q.1	Q.2	Q.3	Q.4	JAN	FEB	MAR	APR	MAY	JUN	JUL	AUG	SEP	OCT	NOV	DEC
1964																	
1965																	
1966																	
1967																	
1968																	
1969			38.4	39.2	39.5					38.4			39.2			39.5	
1970	39.5	39.7	39.3	39.1	39.9		39.7			39.3			39.1			39.9	
1971	39.5	39.4	39.1	39.6	39.8		39.4			39.1			39.6			39.8	
1972	38.7	37.4	38.9	39.0	39.4		37.4			38.9			39.0			39.4	
1973	38.8	38.3	38.7	39.4	38.9		38.3			38.7			39.4			38.9	
1974	38.8	39.3	38.7	38.4	38.9		39.3			38.7			38.4			38.9	
1975	38.0	38.2	37.3	38.0	38.4		38.2			37.3			38.0			38.4	
1976	37.7	38.1	37.2	37.8	37.8		38.1			37.2			37.8			37.8	
1977	37.4	36.7	37.1	37.8	38.0		36.7			37.1			37.8			38.0	
1978	36.9	34.9	37.5	38.1	37.2		34.9			37.5			38.1			37.2	
1979	37.8	38.0	37.8	38.1	37.3		38.0			37.8			38.1			37.3	
1980	37.5	38.0	36.7	38.1	37.2		38.0			36.7			38.1			37.2	
1981	37.6	38.4	37.3	37.9	36.7		38.4			37.3			37.9			36.7	
1982	36.2	35.4	36.8	37.1	35.5		35.4			36.8			37.1			35.5	
1983	35.6	33.8	35.4	37.1	36.2		33.8			35.4			37.1			36.2	

Labour disputes: time lost (16)

thousand man-days

Conflits du travail : journées perdues (16)

milliers de journées-homme

	Year	Q.1	Q.2	Q.3	Q.4	JAN	FEB	MAR	APR	MAY	JUN	JUL	AUG	SEP	OCT	NOV	DEC
1964	911	154	196	180	382	16	58	81	60	102	35	55	45	80	248	68	66
1965	816	260	143	289	124	59	91	110	79	25	40	127	103	59	44	66	14
1966	732	221	160	177	174	22	127	72	34	71	55	45	58	74	51	53	70
1967	705	97	166	334	108	18	45	35	73	30	63	115	159	60	38	56	14
1968	1080	379	222	237	241	95	206	78	44	78	101	57	112	69	148	73	20
1969	1958	333	969	285	372	106	125	102	84	849	36	88	78	119	130	188	54
1970	2394	389	759	667	579	69	110	210	158	425	176	191	333	144	220	248	111
1971	3069	403	926	1284	456	85	139	179	156	648	121	517	358	409	154	110	192
1972	2010	303	557	789	361	54	132	117	122	267	168	245	356	189	137	171	53
1973	2635	562	860	660	553	82	248	232	192	304	364	225	219	216	245	258	50
1974	6292	2483	1731	1598	481	54	418	2011	936	560	235	526	816	255	239	162	81
1975	3510	323	1556	1115	516	37	117	169	416	505	635	558	293	265	206	270	40
1976	3799	507	867	2021	405	71	193	243	166	129	573	1673	204	143	183	160	62
1977	1655	307	411	659	278	28	110	169	99	154	158	161	224	274	166	89	23
1978	2131	184	792	663	492	31	70	84	228	414	151	160	250	253	207	171	115
1979	3964	507	1968	1065	425	51	233	223	152	233	1582	613	241	211	171	195	59
1980	3311	1071	761	849	631	116	419	535	132	409	219	318	317	214	254	250	127
1981	4192	657	760	1090	1685	90	319	248	176	216	367	511	237	342	518	945	223
1982	2158	750	307	779	322	462	132	156	107	118	82	199	413	167	151	102	70
1983	1642	388	511	398	345	106	102	180	236	175	101	148	147	103	124	137	83

Hourly rates: all activities (17)

(wage earners)

1980 = 100

Taux horaires : ensemble des activités (17)

(ouvriers)

1980 = 100

	Year	Q.1	Q.2	Q.3	Q.4	JAN	FEB	MAR	APR	MAY	JUN	JUL	AUG	SEP	OCT	NOV	DEC
1964																	
1965																	
1966																	
1967																	
1968																	
1969																	
1970																	
1971																	
1972																	
1973																	
1974																	
1975																	
1976				72.3	73.9						71.3	71.3	72.8	72.8	72.8	74.4	74.4
1977	78.6	75.6	78.6	80.2	81.2	74.4	74.6	77.6	77.7	79.1	79.1	79.1	80.8	80.8	80.8	80.8	82.0
1978	83.9	82.9	83.7	84.6	86.2	82.0	83.3	83.3	83.3	83.3	84.5	84.5	84.5	85.0	85.0	85.0	88.5
1979	90.1	88.6	89.7	91.9	92.7	88.5	88.6	88.6	88.7	88.7	91.7	91.8	91.9	92.0	92.0	92.9	93.1
1980	100.0	97.6	98.2	103.1	103.8	97.4	97.7	97.8	98.1	98.2	98.3	102.9	103.1	103.4	103.7	103.8	103.9
1981	111.3	107.9	110.6	112.9	116.5	107.8	107.9	107.9	107.9	111.8	112.1	112.3	112.9	113.5	114.2	115.7	119.5
1982	127.5	122.9	127.0	132.6	134.2	120.9	123.0	124.7	125.5	126.2	129.4	131.5	132.9	133.4	133.7	134.1	134.7
1983	136.7	134.9	135.3	135.8	141.6	134.9	134.9	135.1	135.1	135.2	135.5	135.7	135.8	135.8	141.6	141.6	141.6

Producer prices: food, beverages and tobacco (manufacturing output)

Prix à la production : alimentation, boissons et tabac (produits manufacturés)

1980 = 100

	Year	Q.1	Q.2	Q.3	Q.4	JAN	FEB	MAR	APR	MAY	JUN	JUL	AUG	SEP	OCT	NOV	DEC
1964																	
1965																	
1966																	
1967																	
1968				36.0	35.4							36.2	35.8	35.9	35.5	35.4	35.3
1969	36.5	35.6	36.1	37.2	37.2	35.6	35.5	35.7	35.9	36.1	36.3	37.0	37.3	37.2	37.5	37.2	36.8
1970	38.6	37.7	38.3	38.8	39.4	37.3	37.7	38.0	38.2	38.3	38.6	38.5	38.8	39.1	39.3	39.3	39.5
1971	41.0	40.2	40.9	41.2	41.5	39.7	40.3	40.6	40.8	41.1	40.9	41.0	41.2	41.3	41.4	41.6	41.6
1972	43.3	42.4	42.8	43.6	44.3	42.2	42.4	42.6	42.6	42.8	43.1	43.3	43.6	43.8	44.0	44.2	44.6
1973	48.8	46.5	48.3	49.8	50.4	45.4	46.5	47.6	48.1	48.3	48.4	49.2	49.8	50.4	50.2	50.4	50.6
1974	53.2	52.0	52.1	53.9	54.6	51.9	52.1	52.1	52.1	52.2	51.9	53.2	54.2	54.3	54.7	52.9	56.1
1975	56.2	55.2	55.2	56.4	57.9	55.2	54.7	55.7	55.3	55.0	55.4	55.9	56.6	56.7	57.4	58.0	58.3
1976	61.1	59.5	60.2	61.7	63.1	58.9	59.7	59.8	60.3	60.1	60.1	61.1	61.9	62.3	62.6	62.7	63.9
1977	67.3	65.6	67.1	67.8	68.6	64.6	65.7	66.6	67.1	67.1	67.2	67.7	67.7	68.1	68.6	68.4	68.7
1978	74.0	70.4	73.1	74.9	77.5	69.4	70.5	71.2	72.1	73.1	74.0	74.7	74.5	75.5	76.8	77.4	78.4
1979	89.5	82.1	89.4	91.9	94.3	80.2	82.2	84.0	87.1	89.2	91.8	92.2	91.7	91.9	93.5	94.2	95.1
1980	100.0	97.0	98.0	101.2	104.0	96.1	97.1	97.8	97.5	97.9	98.7	99.7	101.0	102.9	102.9	103.6	105.3
1981	106.1	105.3	105.7	106.3	107.1	105.3	105.4	105.3	105.7	105.3	106.0	105.5	106.6	106.9	106.9	106.9	107.4
1982	111.5	108.1	110.4	112.4	115.0	107.0	108.3	108.9	109.8	110.4	111.2	111.5	112.0	113.6	114.5	115.1	115.3
1983		117.4	124.8	126.0		115.5	117.5	119.2	123.1	125.1	126.1	126.7	125.8	125.3	126.2	126.2	

Producer prices: machinery and equipment (manufacturing output)

Prix à la production : équipement et outillage (produits manufacturés)

1980 = 100

	Year	Q.1	Q.2	Q.3	Q.4	JAN	FEB	MAR	APR	MAY	JUN	JUL	AUG	SEP	OCT	NOV	DEC
1964																	
1965																	
1966																	
1967																	
1968				36.6	36.7							36.6	36.6	36.6	36.6	36.7	36.8
1969	37.3	37.0	37.2	37.4	37.6	36.9	37.0	37.0	37.2	37.2	37.1	37.3	37.4	37.5	37.6	37.7	37.7
1970	38.5	38.1	38.4	38.6	38.7	38.0	38.2	38.3	38.4	38.4	38.5	38.5	38.6	38.6	38.6	38.8	38.8
1971	40.3	39.4	39.8	40.6	41.3	39.1	39.4	39.6	39.7	39.8	40.0	40.3	40.6	41.0	41.1	41.3	41.6
1972	42.6	42.0	42.4	42.8	43.2	41.9	41.9	42.2	42.2	42.4	42.5	42.8	42.8	42.9	43.0	43.1	43.5
1973	45.1	43.8	44.3	45.7	46.4	43.7	43.8	44.0	44.2	44.2	44.5	45.5	45.7	46.0	46.1	46.5	46.8
1974	52.2	47.5	50.6	54.1	56.6	47.2	47.4	48.0	49.2	50.1	52.4	53.4	53.9	54.9	55.8	56.7	57.3
1975	61.4	58.4	60.1	62.6	64.6	57.9	58.2	59.0	59.5	59.8	61.1	61.9	62.7	63.1	64.1	64.4	65.2
1976	69.2	66.2	68.6	70.4	71.5	65.7	66.1	66.8	67.7	68.6	69.4	69.9	70.4	70.9	71.1	71.3	72.1
1977	75.9	73.8	75.4	76.6	77.8	73.0	73.7	74.6	75.1	75.3	75.8	76.3	76.6	77.0	77.4	77.7	78.4
1978	81.8	79.4	81.0	82.6	84.3	79.0	79.5	79.8	80.6	80.9	81.5	82.1	82.7	83.0	83.6	84.3	84.9
1979	89.4	86.3	87.8	90.3	93.2	85.7	86.4	86.9	87.2	87.9	88.3	89.4	90.5	91.1	92.1	93.2	94.2
1980	100.0	96.8	99.0	101.1	103.1	95.3	97.0	98.0	98.3	99.1	99.5	100.4	101.4	101.7	102.5	103.2	103.8
1981	109.4	105.4	108.2	111.0	112.9	104.4	105.5	106.3	107.2	107.8	109.5	110.4	111.0	111.5	112.3	113.1	113.5
1982	121.9	117.0	120.5	123.8	126.4	115.5	117.1	118.4	119.5	120.2	121.7	122.9	124.0	124.5	125.9	126.3	127.0
1983		128.4	130.5	132.2		127.9	128.3	129.0	129.9	130.5	131.0	131.6	132.2	132.9	133.7	134.1	

Producer prices: total (manufacturing input)

Prix à la production : total (produits de base pour les industries manufacturières)

1980 = 100

	Year	Q.1	Q.2	Q.3	Q.4	JAN	FEB	MAR	APR	MAY	JUN	JUL	AUG	SEP	OCT	NOV	DEC
1964																	
1965																	
1966																	
1967																	
1968				29.3	28.4							29.8	29.2	28.8	28.6	28.2	28.4
1969	29.5	29.0	29.5	29.9	29.5	28.6	29.1	29.2	29.6	29.4	29.5	29.9	29.9	29.8	29.4	29.4	29.6
1970	29.4	29.7	30.0	29.3	28.7	29.6	29.7	29.9	30.2	30.1	29.8	29.7	29.1	29.0	28.8	28.4	28.7
1971	29.5	29.0	29.4	30.1	29.4	28.7	29.0	29.1	29.2	29.3	29.6	30.2	30.3	30.0	29.7	29.3	29.3
1972	30.6	29.7	29.8	31.4	31.6	29.4	29.8	29.8	29.6	29.9	30.0	30.9	31.6	31.8	31.6	31.6	31.7
1973	36.1	33.9	35.4	37.3	37.9	31.7	34.2	35.7	35.1	35.3	35.7	36.5	37.7	37.8	37.4	37.8	38.4
1974	41.2	40.0	41.1	41.9	41.7	39.2	40.5	40.5	41.3	41.5	40.7	42.3	42.4	40.9	41.5	41.5	42.0
1975	43.6	42.0	42.9	44.0	45.7	41.9	41.9	42.3	43.2	43.0	42.6	43.2	43.9	44.8	45.6	45.6	45.8
1976	48.9	46.8	47.7	50.3	50.8	46.6	46.8	46.9	47.0	47.5	48.6	49.6	50.5	50.7	50.7	49.7	52.0
1977	55.9	54.3	56.1	56.4	56.1	53.2	54.4	55.4	56.0	56.1	56.3	56.1	56.4	56.6	56.2	55.5	56.4
1978	62.5	58.0	60.0	64.5	67.5	57.4	58.4	58.2	59.1	59.4	61.6	62.9	64.4	66.2	66.8	67.4	68.4
1979	83.5	73.8	82.9	86.5	90.9	71.5	73.4	76.6	79.5	83.7	85.6	86.5	85.1	87.8	89.8	90.1	92.7
1980	100.0	99.3	96.9	101.9	102.0	98.7	100.3	98.8	95.2	97.2	98.2	101.3	102.5	102.0	101.4	102.1	102.4
1981	103.1	103.6	103.4	103.9	101.6	104.2	103.5	103.1	102.9	102.6	104.6	103.6	104.4	103.7	102.0	101.7	101.3
1982	106.7	103.6	106.8	108.1	109.2	102.7	103.5	104.6	106.9	106.9	106.7	107.4	108.1	108.9	109.8	109.1	108.8
1983		113.2	119.7	117.5		111.9	112.4	115.3	118.2	120.4	120.6	118.5	117.0	117.0	115.4	114.7	

Producer prices: domestic goods (manufacturing input)
1980 = 100

Prix à la production : produits d'origine nationale (produits de base pour les industries manufacturières)
1980 = 100

	Year	Q.1	Q.2	Q.3	Q.4	JAN	FEB	MAR	APR	MAY	JUN	JUL	AUG	SEP	OCT	NOV	DEC
1964																	
1965																	
1966																	
1967																	
1968				31.2	30.0							31.9	31.1	30.5	30.3	29.7	29.9
1969	31.4	30.7	31.5	32.0	31.4	30.2	30.8	31.1	31.6	31.3	31.5	32.1	32.1	32.0	31.3	31.3	31.6
1970	31.3	31.8	32.2	31.1	30.1	31.6	31.8	32.1	32.4	32.3	31.9	31.8	30.9	30.7	30.4	29.9	30.1
1971	31.0	30.4	30.8	31.9	31.0	30.1	30.5	30.5	30.5	30.8	31.2	31.9	32.2	31.7	31.4	30.8	30.7
1972	32.6	31.4	31.5	33.7	33.9	31.0	31.5	31.5	31.2	31.6	31.7	33.0	34.0	34.3	34.0	33.9	33.9
1973	40.2	37.4	39.5	41.9	42.2	34.2	37.9	40.1	39.2	39.4	39.8	40.9	42.4	42.5	41.9	42.1	42.6
1974	41.9	43.0	42.6	42.2	39.9	42.9	43.4	42.6	43.2	43.0	41.4	43.1	42.9	40.5	40.3	39.6	39.9
1975	41.4	39.6	40.6	41.8	43.6	39.6	39.3	39.9	41.0	40.6	40.1	40.7	41.7	42.9	43.8	43.4	43.6
1976	46.8	44.4	45.4	48.8	48.7	44.4	44.4	44.5	44.5	45.2	46.4	47.9	49.1	49.4	49.3	47.7	49.0
1977	52.5	50.9	52.8	52.9	52.4	50.1	50.8	51.9	52.8	52.7	52.9	52.7	52.8	53.1	52.6	51.7	53.0
1978	61.1	55.0	57.7	63.9	67.9	54.2	55.6	55.2	56.4	56.7	60.0	61.7	63.7	66.2	67.1	67.7	69.0
1979	85.7	76.1	86.1	88.0	92.3	73.1	75.4	79.7	82.7	87.1	88.5	89.0	85.8	89.2	91.7	91.7	93.5
1980	100.0	100.7	95.2	102.1	102.0	100.5	102.3	99.2	93.4	95.4	96.8	101.5	103.0	101.9	101.3	102.3	102.4
1981	101.7	103.2	102.1	102.5	99.0	104.6	103.0	101.9	101.5	101.0	103.7	101.9	103.4	102.1	100.0	98.9	98.0
1982	103.6	100.8	104.1	104.9	105.5	99.8	100.9	101.7	104.6	104.0	103.8	104.3	105.0	105.5	106.5	105.2	104.9
1983		112.1	120.4	116.8		110.3	111.0	115.0	118.6	121.3	121.4	118.5	116.0	116.0	113.9	113.1	

Producer prices: fuel and electricity (manufacturing input)
1980 = 100

Prix à la production : combustibles et électricité (produits de base pour les industries manufacturières)
1980 = 100

	Year	Q.1	Q.2	Q.3	Q.4	JAN	FEB	MAR	APR	MAY	JUN	JUL	AUG	SEP	OCT	NOV	DEC
1964																	
1965																	
1966																	
1967																	
1968				15.6	15.3							15.7	15.6	15.5	15.4	15.3	15.1
1969	15.6	15.5	15.9	15.8	15.4	15.4	15.6	15.5	15.9	15.9	15.9	15.9	15.7	15.7	15.5	15.5	15.3
1970	15.0	15.0	15.0	15.2	14.9	14.9	14.9	15.1	15.0	15.1	15.0	15.3	15.3	15.1	15.0	14.8	14.8
1971	15.3	15.1	15.4	15.5	15.3	15.0	15.2	15.1	15.3	15.5	15.5	15.6	15.5	15.5	15.4	15.3	15.3
1972	15.4	15.5	15.4	15.5	15.3	15.4	15.6	15.4	15.4	15.5	15.3	15.5	15.5	15.3	15.2	15.3	15.3
1973	16.0	15.4	15.5	16.0	17.0	15.5	15.5	15.3	15.3	15.6	15.6	16.0	16.0	15.9	16.3	17.1	17.5
1974	24.5	21.2	24.4	25.3	27.4	19.0	21.6	22.9	24.0	24.4	24.8	25.1	25.3	25.4	26.8	27.5	28.0
1975	31.8	28.6	30.4	32.3	36.0	28.5	28.7	28.6	30.4	30.4	30.5	30.7	31.7	34.4	35.3	36.2	36.5
1976	37.5	37.0	37.3	37.5	38.1	36.9	37.1	37.0	37.2	37.3	37.5	38.0	37.3	37.3	37.5	37.5	39.3
1977	43.1	41.2	41.9	43.7	45.5	40.2	41.9	41.7	41.8	42.0	41.8	41.8	43.8	45.5	45.7	45.6	45.3
1978	49.6	45.8	46.1	51.1	55.3	45.9	45.8	45.7	46.1	46.3	45.8	47.3	51.2	54.9	55.2	55.4	55.4
1979	67.9	57.5	61.6	74.5	78.1	57.2	57.6	57.6	59.0	62.0	63.7	72.5	75.4	75.6	76.5	76.8	80.9
1980	100.0	94.2	98.4	103.3	104.1	92.7	94.2	95.6	96.7	99.3	99.4	102.5	103.1	104.3	103.8	103.8	104.9
1981	114.7	111.8	113.6	116.0	117.4	110.5	111.7	113.0	112.9	113.5	114.4	115.5	116.0	116.5	116.7	117.7	117.9
1982	129.7	122.4	124.5	134.2	137.5	122.0	122.1	123.0	123.8	124.6	125.2	131.4	134.9	136.4	137.8	137.8	137.0
1983		140.0	136.3	136.4		140.5	140.2	139.3	136.1	136.5	136.3	136.3	136.3	136.5	136.6	136.3	

Money supply (M1) (18)
million Australian dollars, end of period

Disponibilités monétaires (M1) (18)
millions de dollars australiens, fin de période

	Year	Q.1	Q.2	Q.3	Q.4	JAN	FEB	MAR	APR	MAY	JUN	JUL	AUG	SEP	OCT	NOV	DEC
1964	3991	3943	3731	3760	3991	3838	3872	3943	3893	3743	3731	3723	3659	3760	3799	3870	3991
1965	3907	4034	3791	3689	3907	3957	4032	4034	3920	3810	3791	3671	3670	3689	3733	3788	3907
1966	4203	3933	3816	3882	4203	3894	3996	3933	3927	3830	3816	3759	3815	3882	3967	4061	4203
1967	4495	4291	4074	4113	4495	4182	4246	4291	4169	4106	4074	4035	4073	4113	4189	4300	4495
1968	4752	4507	4414	4421	4752	4530	4495	4507	4488	4379	4414	4374	4359	4421	4526	4581	4752
1969	5205	4885	4750	4756	5205	4820	4858	4885	4864	4752	4750	4747	4740	4756	4865	4989	5205
1970	5446	5337	4985	5036	5446	5160	5235	5337	5204	5041	4985	4984	4961	5036	5112	5213	5446
1971	5749	5415	5312	5397	5749	5368	5419	5415	5366	5273	5312	5228	5298	5397	5416	5498	5749
1972	6899	5774	5795	6054	6899	5703	5738	5774	5848	5735	5795	5821	5920	6054	6269	6468	6899
1973	8050	7038	7317	7587	8050	6927	6977	7038	7223	7190	7317	7357	7433	7587	7719	7717	8050
1974	7990	7899	7451	7294	7990	7956	8017	7899	7902	7649	7451	7324	7209	7294	7465	7548	7990
1975	9807	8362	8389	8743	9807	8116	8133	8362	8625	8267	8389	8559	8630	8743	9059	9279	9807
1976	10681	10041	9572	9785	10681	9890	9823	10041	10025	9573	9572	9531	9601	9785	9839	10029	10681
1977	11378	10863	10377	10512	11378	10674	10805	10863	10707	10343	10377	10348	10423	10512	10647	10896	11378
1978	12709	11509	11216	11539	12709	11311	11334	11509	11480	11203	11216	11327	11411	11539	11725	12010	12709
1979	14661	13195	13146	13540	14661	12900	13012	13195	13434	13003	13146	13304	13491	13540	13759	13925	14661
1980	17220	15170	14843	15284	17220	15149	15107	15170	15170	14618	14843	15079	15141	15284	15792	16311	17220
1981	18063	16871	16627	16797	18063	16920	16777	16871	16911	16376	16627	16818	16726	16797	16924	17082	18063
1982	18031	17734	16895	16684	18031	17917	17802	17784	17320	16772	16895	16724	16618	16684	16800	16896	18031
1983	20801	18102	17881	18242	20801	18081	17981	18102	17932	17565	17881	17880	17976	18242	18521	18903	20801

Consumer prices: all items (19)

Prix à la consommation : total (19)

1980 = 100

	Year	Q.1	Q.2	Q.3	Q.4	JAN	FEB	MAR	APR	MAY	JUN	JUL	AUG	SEP	OCT	NOV	DEC
1964	30.6	30.2	30.4	30.8	31.2		30.2			30.4			30.8			31.2	
1965	31.9	31.4	31.7	32.0	32.4		31.4			31.7			32.0			32.4	
1966	32.8	32.5	32.7	32.9	33.1		32.5			32.7			32.9			33.1	
1967	33.8	33.3	33.7	34.1	34.2		33.3			33.7			34.1			34.2	
1968	34.7	34.4	34.6	34.8	35.1		34.4			34.6			34.8			35.1	
1969	35.7	35.4	35.6	35.8	36.1		35.4			35.6			35.8			36.1	
1970	37.1	36.5	37.0	37.2	37.9		36.5			37.0			37.2			37.9	
1971	39.4	38.3	39.0	39.7	40.6		38.3			39.0			39.6			40.6	
1972	41.7	41.0	41.4	42.0	42.5		41.0			41.4			42.0			42.5	
1973	45.6	43.4	44.8	46.4	48.1		43.4			44.8			46.4			48.1	
1974	52.6	49.2	51.2	53.9	55.9		49.2			51.2			54.0			55.9	
1975	60.5	57.9	59.9	60.4	63.7		57.9			59.9			60.4			63.7	
1976	68.7	65.6	67.3	68.8	72.9		65.6			67.3			68.8			72.9	
1977	77.1	74.6	76.3	77.8	79.7		74.6			76.3			77.8			79.7	
1978	83.2	80.7	82.4	83.9	85.8		80.7			82.4			83.9			85.8	
1979	90.8	87.3	89.6	91.7	94.5		87.3			89.6			91.7			94.5	
1980	100.0	96.5	99.2	101.1	103.2		96.5			99.2			101.1			103.2	
1981	109.7	105.6	108.0	110.2	114.8		105.6			108.0			110.2			114.8	
1982	121.9	116.8	119.6	123.8	127.4		116.8			119.6			123.8			127.4	
1983	134.3	130.2	133.0	135.3	138.4		130.2			133.0			135.3			138.4	

Money supply (M1) (18)

Disponibilités monétaires (M1) (18)

million Australian dollars, end of period

millions de dollars australiens, fin de période

Adjusted - Corrigé

	Year	Q.1	Q.2	Q.3	Q.4	JAN	FEB	MAR	APR	MAY	JUN	JUL	AUG	SEP	OCT	NOV	DEC
1964		3815	3832	3840	3851	3708	3733	3815	3803	3801	3832	3837	3858	3840	3859	3880	3851
1965		3875	3848	3767	3767	3854	3888	3875	3858	3871	3848	3825	3829	3767	3794	3799	3767
1966		3776	3871	4007	4095	3802	3853	3776	3866	3895	3871	3916	3934	4007	4036	4029	4095
1967		4110	4178	4241	4374	4081	4103	4110	4121	4130	4178	4199	4193	4241	4263	4265	4374
1968		4386	4524	4559	4620	4373	4350	4386	4423	4403	4524	4498	4530	4559	4558	4595	4620
1969		4763	4864	4902	5000	4558	4710	4763	4741	4834	4864	4875	4918	4902	4898	5004	5000
1970		5199	5098	5130	5230	5042	5084	5199	5090	5128	5098	5109	5140	5130	5200	5232	5230
1971		5253	5368	5492	5518	5248	5276	5253	5281	5263	5368	5407	5490	5492	5507	5527	5518
1972		5600	5915	6225	6691	5576	5594	5600	5759	5771	5915	6016	6076	6225	6383	6447	6691
1973		6904	7471	7807	7796	6694	6804	6904	7077	7239	7471	7604	7638	7807	7788	7791	7796
1974		7739	7613	7498	7726	7886	7825	7739	7728	7705	7613	7481	7474	7498	7546	7625	7726
1975		8152	8583	9000	9376	7842	7952	8152	8378	8418	8583	8739	8949	9000	9172	9386	9376
1976		9713	9712	9974	10211	9627	9589	9713	9789	9759	9712	9823	9948	9974	10070	10152	10211
1977		10505	10533	10820	10989	10388	10540	10505	10463	10563	10533	10651	10682	10820	10896	10928	10989
1978		11084	11543	11877	12278	10996	11052	11084	11307	11351	11543	11641	11683	11877	11996	12050	12278
1979		12899	13458	13954	14164	12398	12666	12899	13207	13193	13458	13666	13803	13954	13933	14113	14164
1980		14834	15187	15770	16465	14532	14687	14834	14814	14986	15187	15325	15620	15770	15980	16528	16465
1981		16504	17009	17179	17273	16370	16308	16504	16562	16800	17009	17084	17224	17179	17277	17305	17273
1982		17248	17113	17065	17245	17332	17318	17248	17167	17189	17113	17136	17077	17065	17126	17106	17245
1983		17520	18110	18841	20095	17499	17515	17520	17865	17994	18110	18313	18288	18841	18867	18956	20095

M1 plus quasi-money (18)(20) — M1 plus quasi-monnaie (18)(20)

million Australian dollars, end of period — millions de dollars australiens, fin de période

	Year	Q.1	Q.2	Q.3	Q.4	JAN	FEB	MAR	APR	MAY	JUN	JUL	AUG	SEP	OCT	NOV	DEC
1964	10313	9542	9555	9878	10313	9338	9429	9542	9543	9477	9555	9656	9734	9878	9991	10142	10313
1965	10845	10488	10337	10459	10845	10300	10439	10488	10403	10287	10337	10319	10378	10459	10560	10690	10845
1966	11686	11000	10937	11218	11686	10875	11052	11000	10963	10876	10937	10980	11104	11218	11356	11516	11686
1967	12739	11895	11824	12154	12739	11706	11829	11895	11770	11748	11824	11903	12020	12154	12312	12506	12739
1968	13635	12824	12805	13096	13635	12802	12800	12824	12772	12684	12805	12878	12955	13096	13271	13422	13635
1969	15185	13947	14112	14452	15185	13756	13869	13947	14010	13998	14112	14196	14325	14452	14677	14942	15185
1970	15766	15371	14982	15148	15766	15150	15244	15371	15221	15050	14982	14977	14999	15148	15316	15503	15766
1971	17097	15984	15907	16370	17097	15717	15881	15984	15943	15847	15907	15891	16080	16370	16543	16747	17097
1972	20794	17589	17621	18958	20794	17266	17499	17589	17663	17489	17621	17989	18463	18958	19581	20133	20794
1973	25579	21827	22449	23903	25579	21209	21648	21827	22067	22109	22449	22830	23388	23903	24325	24680	25579
1974	28251	27248	27260	26658	28251	26123	26825	27248	27415	27482	27260	26799	26531	26658	27454	27959	28251
1975	32333	28228	28504	30380	32333	27153	27715	28228	28502	28184	28504	29247	29810	30380	31149	31689	32333
1976	36395	32911	32672	34449	36395	32604	32525	32911	32924	32467	32672	33202	33747	34449	35059	35559	36395
1977	38659	37384	36264	37028	38659	36694	37187	37384	36868	36166	36264	36344	36669	37028	37588	38087	38659
1978	42743	39726	39151	40988	42743	38784	39156	39726	39481	38937	39151	39592	40393	40988	41507	41960	42743
1979	47668	44243	43778	45174	47668	43179	43711	44243	44190	43560	43778	44061	44687	45174	45920	46622	47668
1980	53856	49311	49159	51068	53856	48628	49057	49311	49009	48509	49159	49860	50449	51068	51969	52657	53856
1981	59558	55080	55387	56963	59558	54144	54452	55080	55012	54724	55387	55780	56129	56963	57778	58334	59558
1982	65967	60738	61653	63413	65967	59827	60167	60738	61048	61433	61653	62115	62428	63413	63666	64351	65967
1983	74725	68277	69373	71443	74725	65918	66547	68277	68167	68283	69373	70169	70544	71443	71984	72830	74725

Bank credit to private sector — Crédits bancaires au secteur privé

million Australian dollars, end of period — millions de dollars australiens, fin de période

	Year	Q.1	Q.2	Q.3	Q.4	JAN	FEB	MAR	APR	MAY	JUN	JUL	AUG	SEP	OCT	NOV	DEC
1964	4088	3844	3955	3988	4088	3646	3749	3844	3918	3930	3955	4000	3978	3988	4037	4075	4088
1965	4695	4419	4675	4669	4695	4149	4278	4419	4550	4632	4675	4708	4689	4669	4696	4697	4695
1966	5244	4917	5078	5105	5244	4765	4837	4917	5001	5020	5078	5126	5085	5105	5162	5190	5244
1967	6026	5623	5892	5921	6026	5318	5468	5623	5764	5827	5892	5948	5939	5921	5987	5972	6026
1968	6677	6237	6493	6560	6677	6100	6169	6237	6386	6434	6493	6562	6567	6560	6636	6644	6677
1969	7650	7035	7385	7424	7650	6802	6920	7035	7218	7283	7385	7462	7419	7424	7517	7566	7650
1970	8022	7942	7855	7893	8022	7767	7851	7942	7947	7814	7855	7893	7859	7893	8024	8007	8022
1971	8717	8355	8511	8546	8717	8171	8258	8355	8421	8453	8511	8557	8535	8546	8645	8659	8717
1972	9990	8961	9325	9506	9990	8834	8841	8961	9089	9214	9325	9461	9449	9506	9659	9806	9990
1973	13015	10746	11729	12438	13015	10159	10473	10746	11143	11444	11729	11922	12134	12438	12725	12763	13015
1974	15525	13948	14819	14628	15525	13299	13637	13948	14426	14600	14819	14758	14649	14628	15107	15292	15525
1975	18147	16253	17070	17554	18147	15916	16168	16253	16584	16996	17070	17322	17409	17554	17851	17864	18147
1976	21478	18952	19899	20658	21478	18456	18621	18952	19608	19796	19899	20162	20431	20658	21251	21350	21478
1977	24529	22031	23032	23677	24529	21472	21528	22031	22531	22844	23032	23323	23408	23677	24266	24393	24529
1978	27546	25428	25830	26753	27546	24731	24945	25428	25555	25952	25830	26003	26405	26753	27225	27243	27546
1979	31496	28865	29212	30186	31496	28021	26554	28865	29364	29336	29212	29569	29787	30186	30808	31149	31496
1980	35192	32654	32963	33677	35192	32187	32402	32654	33006	33108	32963	33493	33632	33677	34431	34629	35192
1981	40057	35819	37226	38548	40057	35379	35460	35819	36638	37216	37226	37894	37864	38548	39238	39465	40057
1982	44395	41154	41951	43611	44395	40245	40359	41154	42189	42353	41951	42629	42930	43611	44174	44010	44395
1983	50730	46544	47516	48540	50730	45066	45353	46544	46870	47024	47516	47589	48074	48540	45471	49792	50730

Consumer credit outstanding (21) — Crédits à la consommation en cours (21)

million Australian dollars, end of period — millions de dollars australiens, fin de période

	Year	Q.1	Q.2	Q.3	Q.4	JAN	FEB	MAR	APR	MAY	JUN	JUL	AUG	SEP	OCT	NOV	DEC
1964	1445	1345	1356	1385	1445			1345			1356			1385			1445
1965	1485	1437	1451	1463	1485			1437			1451			1463			1485
1966	1469	1445	1434	1426	1469			1445			1434			1426			1469
1967	1528	1433	1443	1462	1528			1433			1443			1462			1528
1968	1689	1535	1576	1603	1689			1535			1576			1603			1689
1969	1852	1688	1733	1768	1852			1688			1733			1768			1852
1970	2017	1869	1908	1940	2017			1869			1908			1940			2017
1971	2163	2035	2077	2106	2163			2035			2077			2106			2163
1972	2189	2139	2135	2136	2189			2139			2135			2136			2189
1973	1888	2185	2225	1824	1888			2185			2225	1801	1811	1824	1842	1871	1888
1974	2078	1887	1936	2018	2078	1890	1884	1887	1893	1920	1936	1974	1998	2018	2052	2069	2078
1975	2245	2077	2097	2156	2245	2068	2066	2077	2082	2092	2097	2120	2140	2156	2181	2208	2245
1976	2646	2312	2427	2535	2646	2266	2280	2312	2358	2383	2427	2472	2503	2535	2575	2585	2646
1977	2914	2695	2766	2835	2914	2672	2686	2695	2713	2735	2766	2789	2810	2835	2857	2885	2914
1978	3032	2911	2934	2967	3032	2922	2912	2911	2907	2924	2934	2943	2956	2967	2983	3005	3032
1979	3046	3024	3041	3019	3046	3032	3028	3024	3022	3036	3041	3043	3026	3019	3024	3038	3046
1980	3049	3032	3035	3003	3049	3043	3039	3032	3020	3018	3035	3007	3001	3003	3020	3029	3049
1981	3457	3105	3170	3314	3457	3073	3089	3105	3118	3141	3170	3212	3234	3314	3361	3411	3457
1982	3901	3542	3706	3823	3901	3496	3513	3542	3585	3638	3706	3761	3791	3823	3839	3868	3901
1983	3888	3818	3841	3830	3888	3909	3817	3818	3811	3830	3841	3833	3824	3830	3839	3859	3888

M1 plus quasi-money (18)(20)

million Australian dollars, end of period

Adjusted - Corrigé

M1 plus quasi-monnaie (20) (18)

millions de dollars australiens, fin de période

	Year	Q.1	Q.2	Q.3	Q.4	JAN	FEB	MAR	APR	MAY	JUN	JUL	AUG	SEP	OCT	NOV	DEC
1964		9422	9704	9935	10136	9191	9270	9422	9500	9607	9704	9774	9882	9935	10019	10100	10136
1965		10334	10451	10511	10664	10185	10272	10334	10394	10431	10451	10482	10525	10511	10589	10642	10664
1966		10845	11051	11319	11537	10761	10880	10845	10960	11026	11051	11147	11212	11319	11387	11420	11537
1967		11720	11987	12256	12570	11581	11657	11720	11782	11659	11987	12081	12134	12256	12342	12401	12570
1968		12709	12975	13206	13450	12619	12625	12709	12770	12798	12975	13026	13125	13206	13257	13358	13450
1969		13818	14156	14391	14673	13587	13687	13818	13866	14052	14156	14215	14337	14391	14455	14634	14673
1970		14975	15021	15111	15418	14732	14786	14975	14924	15040	15021	15019	15077	15111	15252	15361	15418
1971		15669	16087	16463	16763	15493	15633	15669	15825	15983	16087	16200	16341	16463	16558	16657	16763
1972		17162	17835	18918	20127	16948	17025	17162	17457	17547	17835	18208	18526	18918	19326	19644	20127
1973		21064	22424	23740	24406	20402	20744	21064	21448	21700	22424	22863	23284	23740	23892	24069	24406
1974		25090	25210	24870	26135	24563	24859	25090	25305	25541	25210	24911	24770	24870	25337	25898	26135
1975		27751	29162	30749	31727	26536	27196	27751	28250	28624	29162	29780	30355	30749	31125	31552	31727
1976		32274	33258	34705	35724	32087	31954	32274	32705	33006	33258	33881	34327	34705	35124	35414	35724
1977		36628	36907	37383	38102	36144	36543	36628	36646	36789	36907	37050	37130	37383	37658	37861	38102
1978		38929	39883	41331	42157	38244	38545	38929	39347	39494	39883	40299	40858	41331	41573	41754	42157
1979		43578	44511	45546	47032	42479	43051	43578	44032	44135	44511	44805	45172	45546	45892	46579	47032
1980		48606	49917	51487	52951	47646	48272	48606	48725	49221	49917	50497	51120	51487	51966	52649	52951
1981		54346	56166	57229	58605	53467	53805	54346	54728	55434	56166	56395	56848	57229	57937	58306	58605
1982		59824	62272	63622	65024	59195	59605	59824	60974	62085	62272	62901	63157	63622	63764	64278	65024
1983		67369	69971	71841	73844	65379	66137	67369	68181	68873	69971	70832	71128	71841	72150	72607	73844

Commercial bills (90 days) (22)

per cent per annum, end of period

Effets commerciaux (90 jours) (22)

pourcentage par an, fin de période

	Year	Q.1	Q.2	Q.3	Q.4	JAN	FEB	MAR	APR	MAY	JUN	JUL	AUG	SEP	OCT	NOV	DEC
1964																	
1965																	
1966																	
1967																	
1968	4.90	5.15	5.50	5.05	4.90	5.10	5.15	5.15	5.15	5.30	5.50	5.10	5.10	5.05	5.00	4.90	4.90
1969	5.65	5.15	5.90	5.80	5.65	5.10	5.10	5.15	5.40	5.50	5.90	5.80	6.10	5.80	5.60	5.70	5.65
1970	6.50	7.15	8.70	6.35	6.50	5.80	6.30	7.15	8.60	9.10	8.70	7.40	6.80	6.35	6.40	6.20	6.50
1971	5.90	8.00	8.15	6.45	5.90	6.60	7.60	8.00	7.80	7.80	8.15	6.80	6.70	6.45	6.30	6.00	5.90
1972	4.45	5.50	5.75	4.50	4.45	5.60	5.50	5.50	5.50	5.60	5.75	4.60	4.60	4.50	4.30	5.10	4.45
1973	9.25	5.45	6.40	9.25	9.25	4.70	4.80	5.45	5.80	6.40	6.40	6.50	6.40	9.25	9.65	9.20	9.25
1974	9.75	10.10	18.80	12.60	9.75	9.25	9.50	10.10	16.25	21.75	18.80	15.00	14.20	12.60	10.40	10.30	9.75
1975	7.70	8.75	8.80	8.10	7.70	8.95	9.00	8.75	9.80	8.90	8.80	8.15	8.15	8.10	7.95	8.05	7.70
1976	9.15	8.40	10.45	9.35	9.15	7.65	8.35	8.40	10.30	9.80	10.45	9.55	9.40	9.35	9.00	9.75	9.15
1977	9.95	9.85	11.10	10.60	9.95	8.90	9.60	9.85	11.10	10.75	11.10	10.80	10.90	10.60	9.95	9.95	9.95
1978	8.75	10.70	10.80	9.80	8.75	9.50	9.65	10.70	10.90	10.60	10.80	9.65	9.90	9.80	9.80	8.95	8.75
1979	10.25	9.30	10.35	10.00	10.25	8.50	8.75	9.30	10.80	10.15	10.35	9.85	9.85	10.00	10.15	10.25	10.25
1980	12.60	12.70	13.85	11.50	12.60	10.20	10.10	12.70	13.30	14.05	13.85	12.80	12.20	11.50	11.25	11.40	12.60
1981	15.75	14.80	16.00	15.20	15.75	12.65	13.90	14.80	16.65	15.50	16.00	15.75	15.60	15.20	14.75	14.70	15.75
1982	9.85	19.95	18.75	14.10	9.85	16.60	17.15	19.95	21.65	17.95	18.75	16.55	17.60	14.10	15.20	14.35	9.85
1983	9.05	15.95	13.60	10.70	9.05	10.85	14.85	15.95	12.85	12.95	13.60	11.95	12.10	10.70	11.10	10.35	9.05

Yield of long-term Government bonds (23)

per cent per annum, end of period

Rendement des bons d'État à long terme (23)

pourcentage par an, fin de période

	Year	Q.1	Q.2	Q.3	Q.4	JAN	FEB	MAR	APR	MAY	JUN	JUL	AUG	SEP	OCT	NOV	DEC
1964																	
1965																	
1966																	
1967																	
1968	5.35				5.35											5.40	5.35
1969	6.00	5.41	5.87	5.99	6.00	5.41	5.41	5.41	5.43	5.41	5.87	5.99	5.97	5.99	5.98	5.99	6.00
1970	6.99	6.04	6.99	6.99	6.99	6.00	6.00	6.04	7.00	7.00	6.99	7.00	6.99	6.99	6.99	7.00	6.99
1971	6.50	6.99	6.99	6.98	6.50	6.99	7.00	6.99	6.99	7.00	6.99	7.00	7.00	6.98	6.90	6.70	6.50
1972	6.01	6.02	5.99	6.01	6.01	6.23	6.02	6.02	6.02	5.99	5.99	5.99	6.02	6.01	6.02	6.02	6.01
1973	8.50	6.02	6.99	8.50	8.50	6.00	6.02	6.02	6.40	6.50	6.99	7.00	7.00	8.50	8.50	8.50	8.50
1974	9.50	8.50	9.49	9.50	9.50	8.50	8.50	8.50	8.50	8.80	9.49	9.50	9.50	9.50	9.50	9.50	9.50
1975	10.00	9.50	9.50	10.00	10.00	9.50	9.50	9.50	9.50	9.50	9.50	10.00	10.00	10.00	10.00	10.00	10.00
1976	10.50	10.20	10.20	10.20	10.50	10.02	10.20	10.20	10.20	10.20	10.20	10.20	10.20	10.20	10.20	10.20	10.50
1977	9.50	10.50	10.49	10.20	9.50	10.50	10.50	10.50	10.50	10.48	10.49	10.49	10.49	10.20	10.05	9.80	9.50
1978	8.80	9.20	9.10	9.00	8.80	9.36	9.20	9.20	9.16	9.10	9.10	9.10	9.00	9.00	8.89	8.80	8.80
1979	10.08	9.35	10.10	10.07	10.08	8.85	9.00	9.35	9.65	9.70	10.10	10.07	10.07	10.07	10.08	10.08	10.08
1980	12.60	11.20	11.79	11.78	12.60	10.45	10.50	11.20	11.60	11.80	11.79	11.78	11.80	11.78	11.88	12.42	12.60
1981	15.00	13.10	13.15	15.00	15.00	13.10	13.10	13.10	13.10	13.10	13.15	14.20	15.00	15.00	15.00	15.00	15.00
1982	13.00	16.30	16.40	14.00	13.00	15.15	16.00	16.30	16.30	16.40	16.40	16.40	16.10	14.00	13.70	14.40	13.00
1983	13.70	15.10	15.00	14.30	13.70	13.30	14.75	15.10	13.80	14.80	15.00	14.75	14.95	14.30	13.95	13.60	13.70

AUSTRALIA

Share prices: industrials (24)
Australian Stock Exchange
1980 = 100

Cours des actions industrielles (24)
Bourse d'Australie
1980 = 100

	Year	Q.1	Q.2	Q.3	Q.4	JAN	FEB	MAR	APR	MAY	JUN	JUL	AUG	SEP	OCT	NOV	DEC
1964																	
1965																	
1966																	
1967																	
1968																	
1969																	
1970	62	67	59	62	58	68	67	66	63	57	59	62	63	62	60	57	56
1971	56	56	57	56	55	57	57	55	56	58	57	58	56	55	55	55	57
1972	78	68	78	80	84	64	68	73	76	77	82	79	81	79	81	85	88
1973	78	85	80	77	69	88	83	83	79	79	81	81	80	71	70	71	65
1974	56	72	65	45	41	70	72	74	72	66	57	51	44	40	39	42	40
1975	52	48	49	50	59	44	49	51	49	49	51	50	49	52	57	58	62
1976	64	66	64	67	59	67	66	66	63	64	64	67	69	66	61	58	57
1977	62	58	60	62	65	58	57	57	58	61	62	62	61	62	63	65	67
1978	71	68	69	73	74	69	69	66	68	70	70	70	73	77	76	73	73
1979	79	77	75	80	85	76	77	76	74	76	75	76	79	84	84	85	86
1980	100	94	93	104	109	90	97	93	91	93	96	101	104	106	106	110	112
1981	124	118	130	123	123	115	117	122	130	130	130	126	123	120	119	123	129
1982	111	115	112	108	110	123	115	108	110	115	111	107	106	110	113	111	106
1983	136	114	128	143	160	115	113	113	122	131	129	134	143	152	153	159	169

U.S. dollar exchange rate: spot
cents per Australian dollar, end of period

Taux de change du dollar É.-U. : au comptant
cents par dollar australien, fin de période

	Year	Q.1	Q.2	Q.3	Q.4	JAN	FEB	MAR	APR	MAY	JUN	JUL	AUG	SEP	OCT	NOV	DEC
1964	111.4	111.7	111.4	111.1	111.4	111.7	111.7	111.7	111.8	111.7	111.4	111.3	111.1	111.1	111.2	111.4	111.4
1965	111.9	111.5	111.4	111.8	111.9	111.5	111.6	111.5	111.8	111.5	111.4	111.5	111.4	111.8	111.9	111.9	111.9
1966	111.4	111.5	111.4	111.4	111.4	111.9	111.8	111.5	111.5	111.4	111.4	111.4	111.3	111.4	111.4	111.3	111.4
1967	112.1	111.6	111.4	111.1	112.1	111.5	111.5	111.6	111.7	111.5	111.4	111.2	111.2	111.1	111.1	112.7	112.1
1968	111.0	111.7	111.0	111.3	111.0	112.3	112.0	111.7	111.6	111.0	111.0	111.5	111.0	111.3	111.3	111.1	111.0
1969	111.8	111.4	111.3	110.9	111.8	111.3	111.4	111.4	111.2	111.3	111.3	111.4	110.9	110.9	111.6	111.6	111.8
1970	111.5	112.1	111.6	111.2	111.5	111.8	112.1	112.1	112.1	111.9	111.6	111.3	111.0	111.2	111.3	111.3	111.5
1971	119.1	112.6	112.7	115.7	119.1	112.6	112.6	112.6	112.6	112.6	112.7	113.0	114.9	115.7	116.2	116.2	119.1
1972	127.5	119.1	119.1	119.1	127.5	119.1	119.1	119.1	119.1	119.1	119.1	119.1	119.1	119.1	119.1	119.1	127.5
1973	148.8	141.7	141.7	149.0	148.8	127.5	141.7	141.7	141.7	141.7	141.7	141.7	141.7	149.0	148.8	149.0	148.8
1974	132.7	148.8	148.8	131.0	132.7	148.8	148.8	148.8	148.8	148.8	148.8	148.8	148.8	131.0	131.0	131.6	132.7
1975	125.7	135.4	132.6	125.6	125.7	133.8	136.7	135.4	134.1	134.3	132.6	129.8	127.9	125.6	127.1	125.9	125.7
1976	108.6	124.9	123.6	123.7	108.6	125.9	126.1	124.9	123.9	122.7	123.6	124.1	124.6	123.7	122.6	101.2	108.6
1977	114.1	110.3	111.6	110.8	114.1	108.7	109.7	110.3	110.5	110.4	111.6	112.3	110.5	110.8	112.4	112.7	114.1
1978	115.1	114.3	114.8	115.7	115.1	113.8	113.7	114.3	113.6	113.0	114.8	115.5	115.2	115.7	118.9	113.6	115.1
1979	110.6	111.8	112.1	113.0	110.6	113.3	112.8	111.8	110.2	110.5	112.1	113.0	112.8	113.0	109.7	109.4	110.6
1980	118.1	108.3	115.8	116.9	118.1	110.7	109.9	108.3	111.5	114.3	115.8	115.3	116.6	116.9	117.3	116.4	118.1
1981	112.8	116.8	114.8	114.1	112.8	117.1	115.7	116.8	115.1	113.9	114.8	113.6	115.1	114.1	113.5	115.1	112.8
1982	98.1	105.0	102.2	94.9	98.1	109.9	107.4	105.0	106.1	105.1	102.2	99.6	96.4	94.9	93.7	95.5	98.1
1983	89.3	86.3	87.5	89.7	89.3	97.2	96.1	86.3	86.8	88.2	87.5	88.1	87.9	89.7	91.7	91.3	89.3

Official reserves excluding gold
million SDR's, end of period

Réserves officielles, or exclu
millions de DTS, fin de période

	Year	Q.1	Q.2	Q.3	Q.4	JAN	FEB	MAR	APR	MAY	JUN	JUL	AUG	SEP	OCT	NOV	DEC
1964	1680	1692	1755	1709	1680	1661	1706	1692	1714	1781	1755	1738	1706	1709	1729	1731	1680
1965	1317	1510	1412	1287	1317	1627	1607	1510	1470	1432	1412	1346	1307	1287	1290	1340	1317
1966	1344	1341	1488	1386	1344	1313	1339	1341	1402	1476	1488	1491	1466	1386	1388	1375	1344
1967	1133	1198	1243	1187	1133	1271	1266	1198	1202	1229	1243	1180	1192	1187	1217	1175	1133
1968	1185	1160	1173	1172	1185	1167	1171	1160	1152	1198	1173	1159	1159	1172	1201	1241	1185
1969	998	1336	1332	1123	998	1262	1358	1336	1378	1383	1332	1245	1173	1123	1115	1111	998
1970	1454	1111	1453	1402	1454	1107	1133	1111	1236	1354	1453	1440	1462	1402	1437	1491	1454
1971	2794	1838	2300	2582	2794	1574	1694	1838	2000	2190	2300	2379	2495	2582	2682	2804	2794
1972	5397	3315	3955	4668	5397	2953	3129	3315	3533	3758	3955	4156	4349	4668	4850	5047	5397
1973	4465	4468	4639	4507	4465	5436	4601	4468	4457	4576	4639	4910	4671	4507	4556	4537	4465
1974	3229	4275	4049	3432	3229	4277	4259	4275	4212	4185	4049	3854	3672	3432	3398	3380	3229
1975	2524	3236	3490	3323	2524	3127	3104	3236	3327	3398	3490	3604	3445	3323	3145	3198	2524
1976	2470	2518	2519	2556	2470	2564	2615	2518	2432	2456	2519	2701	2552	2556	2251	2106	2470
1977	1694	2591	2263	1720	1694	2732	2750	2591	2622	2465	2263	2006	1633	1720	1847	1771	1694
1978	1583	1879	1852	1690	1583	1590	1621	1879	1892	1837	1852	1874	1763	1690	1645	1643	1583
1979	1081	1663	1689	1208	1081	1600	1774	1663	1715	1743	1689	1592	1380	1208	1132	1136	1081
1980	1325	1360	1367	1021	1325	1300	1425	1360	1307	1462	1367	1315	1120	1021	1472	1580	1325
1981	1436	1681	2519	1406	1436	1700	1648	1681	2213	2447	2519	2153	1901	1406	1449	1277	1436
1982	5775	1482	3821	4198	5775	1093	1123	1482	2373	3465	3821	3711	3307	4198	4684	5261	5775
1983	8472	5206	5734	5963	8472	6191	5221	5206	5935	5839	5734	5877	6233	5963	7102	6933	8472

Balance of payments: net trade (25)
million Australian dollars

Balance des paiements : balance commerciale (25)
millions de dollars australiens

	Year	Q.1	Q.2	Q.3	Q.4	JAN	FEB	MAR	APR	MAY	JUN	JUL	AUG	SEP	OCT	NOV	DEC
1964	150	139	81	-64	-6												
1965	-326	-38	-57	-164	-67												
1966	66	-21	57	-8	38												
1967	23	6	54	-55	18												
1968	-260	-141	-40	-101	22												
1969	236	53	41	69	73												
1970	445	158	116	76	95												
1971	519	85	171	138	125							58	29	58	14	66	53
1972	1640	240	429	426	545	67	66	111	113	184	137	90	151	194	180	194	183
1973	1968	643	569	375	381	249	190	210	183	189	205	102	177	103	186	123	88
1974	53	174	24	-166	21	97	96	-12	-10	21	28	-54	-81	-16	-75	41	70
1975	1626	313	623	381	309	49	137	148	181	190	270	143	179	74	123	100	101
1976	1656	318	516	502	320	89	113	116	255	55	206	172	103	222	224	93	63
1977	918	43	230	176	469	116	-85	13	101	77	61	29	47	77	72	158	239
1978	80	-11	222	-96	-35	-54	82	-38	103	9	130	53	-107	-40	-133	23	76
1979	2256	285	532	546	893	69	119	46	134	210	133	184	75	274	280	247	367
1980	1237	534	787	-102	18	63	223	261	328	107	368	136	-25	-195	-137	115	96
1981	-2024	-329	-38	-800	-857	151	-93	-341	9	51	-136	-458	-98	-297	-468	-306	-115
1982	-2513	-946	-695	-603	-269	-229	-288	-423	-261	-196	-231	-75	-308	-230	-258	50	-59
1983	263	-54	11	-119	425	235	-120	-169	-35	165	-119	88	-162	-45	63	91	271

Balance of payments: current balance (25)
million Australian dollars

Balance des paiements : opérations courantes, nettes (25)
millions de dollars australiens

	Year	Q.1	Q.2	Q.3	Q.4	JAN	FEB	MAR	APR	MAY	JUN	JUL	AUG	SEP	OCT	NOV	DEC
1964	-418	16	-88	-197	-149												
1965	-1021	-202	-241	-339	-239												
1966	-634	-176	-142	-176	-140												
1967	-844	-178	-169	-265	-232												
1968	-1228	-357	-292	-343	-236												
1969	-827	-183	-250	-171	-223												
1970	-745	-119	-204	-196	-226							-75	-79	-63	-57	-59	-91
1971	-772	-225	-154	-160	-233	-59	-56	-87	-45	-46	-53	-61	-63	-33	-80	-43	-107
1972	339	-46	83	127	175	-32	-25	12	-11	71	23	-19	42	105	71	66	38
1973	290	239	150	-33	-66	114	66	60	36	59	54	-37	29	-23	44	-6	-103
1974	-1962	-281	-537	-659	-485	-80	-11	-182	-192	-209	-165	-227	-257	-173	-251	-97	-151
1975	-783	-127	52	-289	-419	-108	8	-22	13	-37	42	-68	-97	-120	-96	-113	-224
1976	-1600	-418	-278	-403	-501	-159	-88	-150	12	-232	-91	-116	-218	-56	-128	-139	-246
1977	-2803	-794	-733	-920	-356	-213	-301	-245	-231	-253	-281	-336	-300	-292	-188	-69	-103
1978	-3969	-872	-905	-1145	-1047	-369	-152	-334	-283	-375	-236	-328	-453	-366	-483	-267	-302
1979	-2371	-822	-675	-594	-280	-336	-199	-331	-275	-205	-258	-235	-355	-85	-150	-118	-36
1980	-3607	-581	-548	-1293	-1185	-380	-139	-91	-165	-347	-82	-323	-490	-598	-620	-228	-285
1981	-7205	-1505	-1472	-2073	-2155	-264	-413	-742	-487	-424	-593	-916	-533	-771	-969	-734	-544
1982	-8415	-2259	-2386	-2088	-1682	-719	-673	-904	-826	-760	-788	-564	-755	-725	-776	-336	-450
1983	-5790	-1326	-1565	-1789	-1110	-282	-495	-549	-547	-329	-689	-482	-715	-592	-523	-358	-229

Balance of payments: net capital movements
million Australian dollars

Balance des paiements : mouvements de capitaux, nets
millions de dollars australiens

	Year	Q.1	Q.2	Q.3	Q.4	JAN	FEB	MAR	APR	MAY	JUN	JUL	AUG	SEP	OCT	NOV	DEC
1964	465	92	141	163	69												
1965	621	74	180	168	199												
1966	496	147	195	48	106												
1967	821	114	117	224	366												
1968	1122	225	389	246	262												
1969	635	304	190	8	133												
1970	907	246	279	160	222												
1971	1636	449	552	318	317												
1972	1452	353	300	483	316												
1973	-400	-361	-105	10	56												
1974	546	61	241	70	174												
1975	531	114	465	127	-175												
1976	1519	257	384	174	704												
1977	1775	551	334	428	462												
1978	3251	854	637	927	833												
1979	1867	698	667	154	348												
1980	3542	519	761	950	1312												
1981	6113	1297	1882	693	2241												
1982	11589	2014	4360	2115	3100												
1983		1643	1655	1735													

AUSTRALIA

Imports f.o.b. (26) | **Importations f.o.b.** (26)

million Australian dollars, monthly averages | millions de dollars australiens, moyennes mensuelles

	Year	Q.1	Q.2	Q.3	Q.4	JAN	FEB	MAR	APR	MAY	JUN	JUL	AUG	SEP	OCT	NOV	DEC
1964	217	193	212	227	236	209	189	181	220	202	215	227	233	220	241	229	237
1965	246	232	253	260	239	247	203	247	232	263	264	237	267	275	224	252	242
1966	236	239	222	255	229	242	210	264	222	217	226	201	282	281	223	244	221
1967	255	249	261	270	242	273	228	245	260	258	264	231	308	270	260	264	203
1968	285	277	276	296	289	271	281	280	246	315	267	292	292	304	320	289	258
1969	296	265	281	319	318	294	265	237	273	283	287	344	296	316	345	304	304
1970	331	308	322	355	339	322	317	285	337	308	321	371	333	360	353	334	329
1971	338	319	341	355	335	326	283	349	356	340	328	338	382	344	359	325	322
1972	316	319	298	306	340	318	319	321	303	307	285	299	337	283	369	354	299
1973	395	343	354	413	469	348	348	333	295	379	390	420	415	403	493	456	458
1974	634	505	599	719	712	487	493	533	544	687	567	700	741	716	780	705	650
1975	623	604	601	639	646	696	580	536	641	629	534	675	621	622	672	622	642
1976	754	692	712	805	806	686	667	723	639	731	765	810	855	750	761	879	778
1977	920	926	934	943	876	884	917	976	886	976	939	940	1011	877	921	951	758
1978	1027	935	969	1061	1145	986	854	965	897	1020	988	1068	1135	981	1194	1206	1034
1979	1233	1136	1242	1218	1338	1213	1051	1144	1120	1318	1288	1227	1325	1102	1476	1371	1167
1980	1487	1465	1390	1557	1535	1621	1445	1331	1277	1489	1403	1592	1463	1617	1735	1325	1545
1981	1725	1538	1691	1854	1815	1406	1613	1594	1705	1623	1746	1922	1794	1846	2007	1815	1624
1982	1982	1947	2053	2003	1923	1751	1932	2158	1904	2225	2030	2085	2048	1876	2079	1992	1698
1983	1791	1617	1712	1959	1875	1383	1627	1840	1565	1712	1858	2013	2014	1850	1924	1916	1787

Exports f.o.b. (26) | **Exportations f.o.b.** (26)

million Australian dollars, monthly averages | millions de dollars australiens, moyennes mensuelles

	Year	Q.1	Q.2	Q.3	Q.4	JAN	FEB	MAR	APR	MAY	JUN	JUL	AUG	SEP	OCT	NOV	DEC
1964	227	236	237	205	231	245	236	228	237	242	231	234	182	199	235	230	228
1965	224	220	228	220	227	221	207	232	221	228	235	225	203	230	217	243	220
1966	236	219	241	239	244	212	214	232	209	255	260	226	245	247	244	259	228
1967	259	252	273	248	263	256	260	239	270	285	264	249	248	246	266	284	239
1968	262	237	268	257	288	216	259	234	240	293	272	264	268	239	298	263	302
1969	314	282	298	338	338	283	288	275	283	307	304	350	333	332	370	324	320
1970	355	350	353	362	355	356	344	349	297	395	368	407	342	337	372	358	335
1971	383	343	398	408	383	362	309	360	400	401	395	418	409	397	373	391	386
1972	452	397	443	453	514	380	381	429	413	487	430	392	495	471	520	543	477
1973	560	555	550	550	585	594	523	547	478	601	571	532	590	528	637	583	535
1974	640	563	608	669	723	581	587	521	513	713	598	652	648	705	715	737	717
1975	760	720	780	780	762	747	735	676	769	801	770	788	862	689	817	698	771
1976	898	777	894	994	926	763	768	800	897	805	981	1000	986	997	916	1000	862
1977	1004	952	1011	1026	1028	984	913	958	1024	1029	979	980	1087	1012	966	1119	1000
1978	1049	975	1060	1017	1144	1018	957	951	1013	1042	1126	1077	1038	937	1137	1209	1088
1979	1393	1203	1383	1360	1625	1303	1130	1176	1248	1495	1406	1400	1301	1379	1635	1679	1562
1980	1614	1669	1652	1523	1613	1742	1655	1609	1620	1538	1799	1679	1487	1402	1667	1594	1579
1981	1577	1573	1681	1560	1493	1671	1570	1476	1659	1725	1659	1494	1690	1497	1551	1505	1422
1982	1807	1653	1819	1850	1906	1558	1682	1719	1812	1814	1830	2012	1818	1719	1870	2031	1817
1983	1911	1785	1861	1950	2046	1925	1656	1774	1619	2079	1884	2051	1956	1843	1998	2098	2043

Trade balance (f.o.b. — f.o.b.) (26) | **Balance commerciale** (f.o.b. — f.o.b.) (26)

million Australian dollars, monthly averages | millions de dollars australiens, moyennes mensuelles

	Year	Q.1	Q.2	Q.3	Q.4	JAN	FEB	MAR	APR	MAY	JUN	JUL	AUG	SEP	OCT	NOV	DEC
1964	10	44	25	-22	-5	36	47	47	18	40	16	7	-51	-21	-6	1	-9
1965	-22	-12	-25	-40	-12	-27	4	-14	-10	-35	-29	-12	-63	-45	-7	-9	-21
1966	-0	-19	20	-16	15	-30	4	-32	-14	38	34	25	-37	-34	22	15	7
1967	4	3	13	-22	21	-17	32	-6	11	26	1	18	-60	-24	6	20	36
1968	-22	-41	-8	-39	-1	-55	-22	-46	-7	-22	5	-28	-24	-65	-22	-26	45
1969	18	17	17	20	20	-11	23	38	10	24	17	6	37	16	24	20	16
1970	24	42	32	7	17	34	28	64	-40	87	47	35	9	-23	20	24	5
1971	46	24	57	53	48	36	25	11	43	61	67	81	27	53	14	66	64
1972	136	77	145	146	173	62	62	107	110	181	145	93	158	188	152	189	179
1973	165	212	196	137	116	246	175	214	183	222	182	112	175	125	144	127	77
1974	7	58	8	-50	11	94	93	-13	-32	26	31	-47	-93	-11	-65	32	67
1975	138	116	179	140	117	51	155	141	128	173	236	113	241	67	145	76	129
1976	144	85	183	189	120	77	102	77	259	73	217	191	131	246	155	122	84
1977	85	26	77	84	152	99	-4	-18	138	53	40	41	76	135	45	168	243
1978	22	40	92	-44	-0	32	103	-14	116	22	138	9	-97	-44	-57	3	54
1979	160	67	141	142	288	90	80	32	128	177	118	173	-24	277	160	309	395
1980	127	203	262	-35	78	121	211	278	343	48	396	87	23	-214	-68	269	34
1981	-148	35	-10	-294	-323	265	-43	-118	-45	102	-86	-428	-104	-349	-456	-310	-202
1982	-175	-294	-234	-153	-17	-193	-250	-439	-92	-411	-200	-74	-229	-157	-208	39	119
1983	120	169	149	-9	171	542	30	-67	54	367	26	38	-57	-7	74	182	257

Imports f.o.b. (26)
million Australian dollars, monthly averages

Adjusted - Corrigé *

Importations f.o.b. (26)
millions de dollars australiens, moyennes mensuelles

Year	Q.1	Q.2	Q.3	Q.4	JAN	FEB	MAR	APR	MAY	JUN	JUL	AUG	SEP	OCT	NOV	DEC
1964	194	210	220	239	188	207	187	211	208	212	223	224	212	245	230	243
1965	238	251	249	245	242	225	247	228	268	259	244	247	257	236	247	252
1966	243	221	245	236	236	233	259	229	216	218	218	254	264	230	238	239
1967	252	261	261	247	264	248	244	271	250	263	245	274	264	257	254	230
1968	281	277	286	291	255	283	304	244	304	284	287	275	294	295	297	282
1969	271	284	308	318	280	279	254	267	283	302	326	296	301	316	316	321
1970	316	327	343	334	319	329	300	327	323	331	351	332	346	325	339	337
1971	329	349	343	331	340	293	353	356	352	340	327	372	329	342	318	332
1972	323	308	299	335	328	317	323	324	298	301	298	309	290	337	338	328
1973	349	368	404	459	340	365	342	313	357	432	407	383	422	440	441	497
1974	518	613	697	699	465	519	569	570	652	633	653	701	738	694	710	692
1975	615	620	619	639	671	614	560	673	610	577	614	611	631	617	632	669
1976	694	729	778	807	674	699	710	672	728	786	770	810	755	759	846	815
1977	932	951	929	878	887	971	939	970	947	935	938	933	917	901	908	826
1978	934	981	1057	1150	960	896	945	988	963	993	1055	1039	1078	1123	1137	1188
1979	1131	1256	1218	1324	1149	1091	1153	1204	1218	1346	1183	1245	1226	1324	1321	1329
1980	1456	1401	1550	1519	1528	1456	1383	1322	1434	1447	1463	1493	1695	1531	1355	1671
1981	1557	1705	1842	1786	1408	1661	1602	1747	1622	1747	1798	1812	1915	1815	1811	1731
1982	1977	2064	1978	1916	1859	1984	2089	1994	2184	2016	2011	2015	1909	1965	1934	1848
1983	1623	1720	1957	1882	1459	1668	1741	1710	1635	1815	2033	1920	1917	1793	1846	2007

Exports f.o.b. (26)
million Australian dollars, monthly averages

Adjusted - Corrigé *

Exportations f.o.b. (26)
millions de dollars australiens, moyennes mensuelles

Year	Q.1	Q.2	Q.3	Q.4	JAN	FEB	MAR	APR	MAY	JUN	JUL	AUG	SEP	OCT	NOV	DEC
1964	234	233	215	223	232	240	229	238	236	224	229	212	203	233	214	221
1965	222	224	228	221	226	214	227	228	221	223	227	225	232	222	224	218
1966	221	237	246	241	218	220	226	224	242	244	236	252	251	246	241	237
1967	254	269	254	263	259	267	236	299	257	252	258	245	259	259	267	263
1968	237	264	258	289	209	253	250	252	263	276	253	269	253	274	263	329
1969	288	293	338	338	273	297	294	290	284	305	329	342	342	343	336	336
1970	358	347	357	357	353	357	364	299	381	362	382	348	342	357	366	347
1971	352	391	404	387	373	323	360	403	385	385	409	407	398	373	386	401
1972	401	433	454	520	391	382	430	438	438	423	401	468	492	510	523	526
1973	566	534	555	583	577	549	572	493	534	575	537	562	566	601	570	580
1974	582	588	670	722	560	615	572	509	642	612	633	638	739	671	741	753
1975	750	755	779	756	728	771	751	746	753	767	751	884	702	777	717	775
1976	802	863	992	922	763	802	840	874	791	924	982	989	1004	940	969	857
1977	992	977	1032	1028	1014	967	995	1023	996	912	992	1053	1051	994	1061	1029
1978	1005	1026	1035	1147	1011	1018	986	1043	968	1067	1086	1002	1016	1142	1135	1166
1979	1226	1338	1402	1617	1232	1196	1251	1264	1372	1380	1369	1275	1560	1569	1599	1683
1980	1687	1606	1549	1601	1617	1681	1762	1574	1453	1790	1553	1575	1519	1587	1612	1604
1981	1605	1633	1595	1486	1610	1642	1564	1606	1683	1610	1382	1790	1611	1525	1493	1441
1982	1682	1767	1880	1910	1555	1758	1735	1787	1756	1758	1921	1879	1841	1918	1951	1860
1983	1805	1803	1993	2066	1920	1725	1770	1642	1967	1801	2036	1935	2008	2047	1985	2167

Trade balance (f.o.b. — f.o.b.) (26)
million Australian dollars, monthly averages

Adjusted - Corrigé *

Balance commerciale (f.o.b. — f.o.b.) (26)
millions de dollars australiens, moyennes mensuelles

Year	Q.1	Q.2	Q.3	Q.4	JAN	FEB	MAR	APR	MAY	JUN	JUL	AUG	SEP	OCT	NOV	DEC
1964	40	23	-5	-16	44	32	42	27	29	12	6	-13	-9	-12	-16	-22
1965	-16	-28	-21	-24	-16	-12	-21	0	-47	-36	-16	-23	-25	-14	-23	-34
1966	-21	16	1	6	-18	-13	-33	-5	26	26	18	-2	-13	16	3	-2
1967	2	8	-7	-6	-5	19	-8	29	7	-11	13	-29	-5	2	13	32
1968	-44	-14	-27	-3	-46	-31	-54	8	-42	-7	-34	-6	-41	-21	-34	47
1969	17	9	30	21	-7	18	40	23	1	3	3	46	41	27	20	15
1970	42	20	14	23	35	28	65	-28	58	31	30	16	-5	32	27	11
1971	23	41	62	56	33	30	7	47	32	44	82	35	69	31	67	70
1972	78	125	154	185	63	65	107	114	139	122	103	158	202	173	185	198
1973	217	167	151	124	237	184	230	180	176	144	129	179	144	161	129	83
1974	65	-31	-27	23	95	96	3	-61	-11	-21	-20	-63	1	-23	31	62
1975	135	135	160	117	57	157	191	73	143	190	136	273	71	159	85	106
1976	107	134	214	116	89	104	130	202	63	138	213	179	249	182	123	42
1977	60	26	103	150	127	-5	56	52	49	-23	55	120	134	93	153	203
1978	71	45	-23	-2	51	122	41	55	6	74	31	-37	-62	18	-2	-23
1979	95	82	184	293	83	105	98	60	153	34	186	30	335	246	279	354
1980	231	205	-1	82	89	224	379	252	20	344	90	82	-175	56	257	-67
1981	48	-72	-247	-300	202	-19	-39	-140	61	-138	-415	-22	-304	-290	-318	-291
1982	-295	-297	-98	-6	-304	-226	-354	-207	-428	-258	-39	-137	-68	-47	17	12
1983	182	83	37	184	461	57	29	-68	332	-14	4	16	91	254	139	160

* Adjusted by the O.E.C.D.

* Corrigé par l'O.C.D.E.

NOTES

1. From 1976, index (original base 1976-77) linked on 1976 to previous index (original base 1963-64).
2. Manufacturing, electricity and gas.
3. Prior to 1976, fuel and power.
4. Quarterly series from 1966; previously three surveys per year.
5. From 2nd quarter 1980, new sample.
6. Including alterations and additions valued at 10,000 Australian dollars or more. Prior to July 1975, new buildings are included if the value is at least 2,000 Australian dollars. From July 1975, all new dwellings are included, and other new buildings if the value is at least 10,000 Australian dollars.
7. Prior to July 1973, alterations and additions valued at 10,000 Australian dollars or more are included. Prior to July 1975 new dwellings valued at under 2,000 Australian dollars are excluded.
8. From 3rd quarter 1980, sample survey. From 3rd quarter 1981, slight changes in definition.
9. From 3rd quarter 1966, including alterations valued at 10,000 Australian dollars or more. From 3rd quarter 1973, excluding alterations and additions.
10. Up to June 1969, data are based on the 1961-62 census of retail establishments; from July 1969 to March 1976, they are based on the 1968-69 census; from April 1976 to March 1982, data are based on the 1973-74 census, and from April 1982, the 1979-80 census.
11. From 2nd quarter 1982, new census.
12. Labour force sample survey of population aged 15 and over.
13. Sample survey referring to the first half of the month from February 1978, and to the midmonth of the quarter previously. From 1975, new definition. From August 1976, new survey. From 2nd quarter 1978, quarterly data are averages of monthly data.
14. Sample survey of establishments. From May 1979, new survey.
15. Excluding hours paid for, but not worked.
16. Stoppages of 10 man-days or more.
17. Monthly data refer to end of period.

NOTES

1. A partir de 1976, indice (base originale 1976-77) raccordé sur 1976 à l'indice précédent (base originale 1963-64).
2. Industries manufacturières, électricité et gaz.
3. Avant 1976, combustibles et énergie.
4. Série trimestrielle à partir de 1966; auparavant enquêtes quadrimestrielles.
5. A partir du 2e trimestre 1980, nouvel échantillon.
6. Y compris les transformations et les agrandissements d'une valeur de 10000 dollars australiens ou plus. Avant juillet 1975, les nouveaux bâtiments sont inclus si la valeur est d'au moins 2000 dollars australiens. A partir de juillet 1975, tous les nouveaux logements sont compris, les autres bâtiments n'étant inclus que si la valeur est d'au moins 10000 dollars australiens.
7. Avant juillet 1973, y compris les transformations et les agrandissements d'une valeur de 10000 dollars australiens ou plus. Avant juillet 1975, non compris les logements nouveaux d'une valeur inférieure à 2000 dollars australiens.
8. A partir du 3e trimestre 1980, enquête par sondage. A partir du 3e trimestre 1981 changements minimes dans la définition.
9. A partir du 3e trimestre 1966, y compris les transformations d'une valeur supérieure à 10000 dollars australiens. A partir du 3e trimestre 1973, non compris les transformations et les agrandissements.
10. Jusqu'en juin 1969, les données sont basées sur le recensement des établissements de ventes au détail de 1961-62; de juillet 1969 à mars 1976, les données sont basées sur le recensement de 1968-69; d'avril 1976 à mars 1982 elles se réfèrent au recensement de 1973-74, et à partir d'avril 1982, à celui de 1979-80.
11. A partir du 2e trimestre 1982, nouveau recensement.
12. Enquête par sondage auprès de la population de 15 ans ou plus.
13. Enquête par sondage se référant à la première quinzaine du mois à partir de février 1978, et au mois du milieu du trimestre auparavant. A partir de 1975, nouvelle définition. A partir d'août 1976, nouvelle enquête. A partir du 2e trimestre 1978, les données trimestrielles sont des moyennes des données mensuelles.
14. Enquête par sondage des établissements. A partir de mai 1979, nouvelle enquête.
15. Non compris les heures payées mais non ouvrées.
16. Arrêts d'au moins 10 journées-homme.
17. Situation en fin de mois.

NOTES

18. Prior to July 1973, including Papua New Guinea. The amount attributable to this area in June 1973 is 86 million Australian dollars for M1 and 145 million Australian dollars for M1 plus quasi-money.

19. Weightling pattern based on 1961-62 to 1968, on 1966-67 from 1969 to 1973, on 1971-72 from 1974 to 3rd quarter 1976, on 1974-75 from 4th quarter 1976 to 1981, and on 1st quarter 1982 from 1982.

20. From July 1974, excluding certificates of deposit held by state governments and other banks. These amounted to 297 million Australian dollars in June 1974.

21. Prior to July 1973, including balances outstanding on agreements financing sales of plant, machinery and commercial vehicles. From April 1978, only finance companies with outstanding balance of 5 million Australian dollars or more.

22. Average of daily yields for week ended last Wednesday of the month.

23. From June 1981, 15-year Treasury bonds; previously, 20-year Government bonds.

24. Monthly data are averages of daily indices.

25. Monthly data are provisional.

26. General trade.

NOTES

18. Avant juillet 1973, y compris Papuasie, Nouvelle-Guinée. Le montant attribuable à cette région en juin 1973 est de 86 millions de dollars australiens pour la M1, et de 145 millions de dollars australiens pour M1 plus quasi-monnaie.

19. La pondération se réfère à 1961-62 jusqu'en 1968; de 1969 à 1973, pondération de 1966-67, de 1974 au 3e trimestre 1976, pondération de 1971-72, du 4e trimestre 1976 à 1981, pondération de 1974-75, et à partir de 1982, pondération du 1er trimestre 1982.

20. A partir de juillet 1974, non compris les certificats de dépôts détenus par les administrations des états et par les autres banques. Leur montant s'élevait à 297 millions de dollars australiens en juin 1974.

21. Avant juillet 1973, y compris les balances en cours des accords de financement des ventes d'usine, d'outillage et de véhicules commerciaux. A partir d'avril 1978, seulement les établissements financiers dont le montant des crédits est égal ou supérieur à 5 millions de dollars australiens.

22. Moyenne journalière des rendements de la semaine se terminant le dernier mercredi du mois.

23. A partir de juin 1981, bons du Trésor à 15 ans; auparavant, bons d'État à 20 ans.

24. Les données mensuelles sont des moyennes d'indices journaliers.

25. Les données mensuelles sont provisoires.

26. Commerce général.

MAIN SOURCES
PRINCIPALES SOURCES

Series	Séries	Sources
National product	Produit national	Australian Bureau of Statistics *Quarterly Estimates of National Income and Expenditure*
Industrial production	Production industrielle	Australia and New Zealand Banking Group Limited *Quarterly Survey*
Production	Production	
Construction permits issued	Permis de construire délivrés	
Construction, housing starts	Construction, logements mis en chantier	
Internal trade, value............	Commerce intérieur, valeur	Australian Bureau of Statistics *Monthly Summary of Statistics*
Labour, except hours	Main-d'œuvre sauf heures	
Prices	Prix	
Consumer credit	Crédits à la consommation	
Foreign trade	Commerce extérieur	
Business surveys	Enquêtes de conjoncture	Confederation of Australian Industry, Bank of New South Wales *Survey of Industrial Trends in Australia*
Manufacturing stocks	Stocks des industries manufacturières	
Construction, work in progress ..	Construction, travaux en cours	Australian Bureau of Statistics
Internal trade, volume..........	Commerce intérieur, volume.......	
Weekly hours of work	Durée hebdomadaire du travail	Australian Bureau of Statistics *The Labour Force*
Wages	Salaires	Australian Bureau of Statistics *Award Rates of Pay Indexes*
Money supply	Disponibilités monétaires..........	
Bank credit	Crédits bancaires	
Interest rates	Taux d'intérêts	Reserve Bank of Australia *Statistical Bulletin*
Share prices...................	Cours des actions..................	
Balance of payments	Balance des paiements.............	Australian Bureau of Statistics *Balance of Payments*

New Zealand — Nouvelle-Zélande

NEW ZEALAND

Production: passenger cars assembled
thousands, monthly averages

Production : voitures de tourisme montées
milliers, moyennes mensuelles

	Year	Q.1	Q.2	Q.3	Q.4	JAN	FEB	MAR	APR	MAY	JUN	JUL	AUG	SEP	OCT	NOV	DEC
1964	4.77	3.96	4.86	5.32	4.94	2.63	4.50	4.76	4.61	4.94	5.03	5.19	5.32	5.44	5.20	5.31	4.30
1965	4.78	4.15	5.08	5.25	4.64	2.56	4.66	5.22	4.65	4.86	5.73	5.32	5.25	5.18	4.78	5.14	3.98
1966	4.55	4.38	4.51	4.93	4.37	2.70	5.05	5.39	4.38	4.77	4.38	4.83	4.94	5.03	4.56	4.69	3.85
1967	4.17	3.85	4.49	4.65	3.67	2.55	4.66	4.36	4.66	4.70	4.12	4.58	4.76	4.61	4.07	3.94	3.02
1968	3.60	3.30	3.37	4.06	3.67	2.25	3.89	3.76	2.92	3.84	3.34	4.14	3.82	4.23	3.80	3.83	3.38
1969	4.28	3.65	4.15	4.88	4.45	2.82	3.94	4.17	3.60	4.36	4.48	4.68	4.64	5.31	4.75	4.45	4.15
1970	4.64	3.69	4.88	5.14	4.86	2.31	4.56	4.19	4.63	4.68	5.34	4.85	5.05	5.51	5.51	5.56	3.50
1971	4.95	4.37	4.80	5.47	5.16	3.49	3.95	5.67	4.12	5.14	5.13	5.59	4.99	5.84	5.40	5.82	4.28
1972	5.71	4.96	5.97	6.01	5.92	3.15	5.55	6.18	4.75	6.81	6.34	5.63	6.67	5.72	6.13	6.86	4.77
1973	6.03	5.33	5.35	7.24	6.19	3.78	5.61	6.60	4.28	5.87	5.30	7.09	7.82	6.82	7.04	6.62	4.93
1974	5.64	5.22	5.61	5.79	5.95	3.64	5.55	6.47	4.88	6.85	5.09	6.42	6.23	4.71	6.29	6.61	4.94
1975	5.62	4.23	5.82	6.57	5.87	3.04	4.71	4.94	5.36	6.14	5.97	6.40	6.49	6.81	6.28	6.47	4.85
1976	5.80	5.23	6.43	6.01	5.51	2.62	5.84	7.23	6.36	6.80	6.12	6.13	6.04	5.85	5.24	6.10	5.20
1977	5.24	4.43	5.44	6.35	4.73	1.68	5.65	5.97	4.23	6.42	5.68	6.01	6.94	6.09	4.87	5.62	3.71
1978	4.32	2.95	4.13	5.19	5.01	1.13	3.29	4.44	3.72	4.14	4.53	4.73	5.43	5.39	5.01	5.84	4.18
1979	5.87	4.55	5.66	6.76	6.54	2.17	4.91	6.55	4.70	6.20	6.06	6.22	7.77	6.28	7.65	7.33	4.63
1980	6.11	4.93	6.02	7.24	6.27	2.38	5.86	6.54	5.55	6.59	5.92	7.37	6.61	7.73	7.08	6.65	5.09
1981	7.96	5.66	8.65	9.39	8.13	2.86	5.94	8.17	7.88	9.03	9.03	9.75	8.90	9.51	8.84	9.02	6.53
1982	7.25	6.61	8.03	9.11	5.26	3.14	7.65	9.03	7.67	8.78	7.64	9.06	9.47	8.81	6.02	6.33	3.43
1983	5.27	3.91	4.90	6.10	6.17	1.81	4.58	5.35	4.24	5.70	4.75	5.29	6.56	6.44	6.08	7.40	5.03

Production: cement
thousand tons, monthly averages

Production : ciment
milliers de tonnes, moyennes mensuelles

	Year	Q.1	Q.2	Q.3	Q.4	JAN	FEB	MAR	APR	MAY	JUN	JUL	AUG	SEP	OCT	NOV	DEC
1964	65.7	60.2	72.7	66.2	63.6	51.1	65.3	64.1	77.0	70.9	70.0	69.1	63.5	65.9	66.0	68.2	56.6
1965	70.2	63.6	75.9	70.0	71.2	47.4	64.3	79.1	76.0	78.1	73.5	70.7	65.8	73.6	72.7	77.1	63.7
1966	73.2	68.5	78.5	76.4	69.4	49.9	70.7	84.7	75.4	82.4	77.6	76.3	76.7	76.2	74.1	74.9	59.3
1967	67.8	63.9	76.2	67.6	63.5	48.7	69.5	73.7	74.3	81.9	72.6	67.5	67.6	67.9	70.6	68.2	51.7
1968	63.6	62.6	62.7	65.7	63.3	50.5	70.1	67.2	57.6	69.9	60.5	66.3	64.4	66.5	56.6	68.3	55.1
1969	66.9	66.1	67.4	67.4	66.6	55.9	67.1	75.3	65.1	72.3	64.8	71.3	63.2	67.8	72.3	67.2	60.2
1970	69.1	62.6	73.7	69.4	70.7	50.3	68.7	68.7	77.7	70.9	72.6	70.7	67.1	70.3	74.1	76.8	61.2
1971	68.6	65.0	70.0	70.4	68.9	49.9	66.5	78.7	68.7	71.6	69.8	74.1	66.6	70.6	66.1	74.5	65.9
1972	75.0	67.8	74.9	77.1	80.0	49.0	77.0	77.5	66.9	83.1	74.6	71.3	79.1	80.9	80.0	92.2	68.0
1973	88.2	80.2	85.5	92.4	94.5	57.7	85.4	97.4	78.4	88.8	89.3	94.7	92.7	89.8	103.6	102.3	77.6
1974	92.6	87.2	93.8	95.6	93.7	70.2	90.4	100.9	89.2	107.5	84.6	94.2	99.2	93.3	99.2	102.5	79.4
1975	89.5	80.6	93.8	92.0	91.5	65.5	87.4	89.0	95.7	101.6	84.2	96.1	88.2	91.7	100.4	90.0	84.2
1976	83.3	82.4	84.3	79.2	87.2	53.9	87.8	105.4	82.5	87.4	83.1	76.7	75.8	85.0	84.5	95.3	81.8
1977	75.9	78.6	77.1	74.8	73.0	53.9	84.9	97.1	73.8	84.1	73.3	72.6	78.1	73.6	72.9	80.2	65.9
1978	66.5	62.8	69.0	65.8	68.4	42.0	68.0	78.5	64.5	77.8	64.8	62.3	68.5	66.7	73.3	76.0	56.0
1979	62.7	58.2	67.1	60.9	64.5	45.0	61.4	68.3	66.0	71.3	64.1	65.0	60.4	57.4	69.0	70.6	53.8
1980	60.0	56.4	60.7	60.0	62.8	38.5	63.2	67.4	60.7	66.5	54.8	67.2	51.9	61.0	56.2	62.3	60.0
1981	63.3	55.9	62.8	65.6	68.8	45.2	53.5	69.1	63.7	63.3	61.4	69.5	59.4	67.9	73.1	71.0	62.4
1982	65.1	62.6	66.9	65.1	65.8	43.4	64.7	79.8	70.3	66.1	64.4	64.8	66.2	64.3	61.9	74.8	60.7
1983	63.3	61.6	59.8	67.8	64.0	47.4	61.6	75.9	53.6	69.2	56.6	64.3	69.8	69.3	62.4	73.6	55.9

Production: wood pulp
thousand tons, quarterly averages

Production : pâte à papier
millions de tonnes, moyennes trimestrielles

	Year	Q.1	Q.2	Q.3	Q.4	JAN	FEB	MAR	APR	MAY	JUN	JUL	AUG	SEP	OCT	NOV	DEC
1964	100.4	88.6	103.1	106.7	103.1												
1965	101.7	90.5	100.4	107.4	108.5												
1966	105.3	101.2	117.8	113.5	88.5												
1967	121.9	116.4	117.9	125.8	127.3												
1968	119.2	110.2	119.8	124.8	122.1												
1969	136.7	127.1	135.3	143.5	141.0												
1970	144.4	142.1	145.2	148.5	141.7												
1971	144.6	140.6	146.6	151.9	139.1												
1972	147.7	141.8	144.5	149.8	154.8												
1973	153.4	138.3	181.2	126.8	167.1												
1974	210.1	203.0	199.1	238.1	200.1												
1975	227.1	226.8	226.1	235.9	219.4												
1976	252.4	232.0	259.2	260.3	258.0												
1977	273.7	277.5	282.0	286.3	248.9												
1978	257.7	279.7	216.8	263.0	271.1												
1979	300.7	291.9	294.5	312.2	304.2												
1980	285.5	213.3	304.8	316.4	307.4												
1981	290.1	284.7	298.7	282.8	294.0												
1982	251.3	223.2	233.2	293.7	255.0												
1983	268.4	269.2	248.2	293.7	262.4												

Business situation: prospects
manufacturing and construction
per cent balance

État des affaires : perspectives
industries manufacturières et construction
solde en pourcentage

Year	Q.1	Q.2	Q.3	Q.4	JAN	FEB	MAR	APR	MAY	JUN	JUL	AUG	SEP	OCT	NOV	DEC
1964	28	33	42	17	28			33			42			17		
1965	21	6	-9	-34	21			6			-9			-34		
1966	-20	-35	-24	-57	-20			-35			-24			-57		
1967	-72	-65	-40	-55	-72			-65			-40			-55		
1968	-19	20	64	58	-19			20			64			58		
1969	45	43	43	32	45			43			43			32		
1970	5	-8	-10	-44	5			-8			-10			-44		
1971	-42	-5	7	16	-42			-5			7			16		
1972	8	64	67	72	8			64			67			72		
1973	50	42	10	-51	50			42			10			-51		
1974	-21	-59	-58	-76	-21			-59			-58			-76		
1975	-38	-31	-39	-44	-38			-31			-39			-44		
1976	-28	-34	-7	-49	-28			-34			-7			-49		
1977	-44	-53	-62	-56	-44			-53			-62			-56		
1978	-15	28	29	-23	-15			28			29			-23		
1979	-35	-38	-19	-48	-35			-38			-19			-48		
1980	-30	-36	-27	-13	-30			-36			-27			-13		
1981	26	38	36	-9	26			38			36			-9		
1982	-26	-41	-47	-62	-26			-41			-47			-62		
1983	-23	11	48	43	-23			11			48			43		

Production: future tendency
manufacturing and construction
per cent balance

Perspectives de production
industries manufacturières et construction
solde en pourcentage

Year	Q.1	Q.2	Q.3	Q.4	JAN	FEB	MAR	APR	MAY	JUN	JUL	AUG	SEP	OCT	NOV	DEC
1964	38	34	49	32	38			34			49			32		
1965	43	44	31	9	43			44			31			9		
1966	26	18	30	5	26			18			30			5		
1967	-15	-23	-8	-31	-15			-23			-8			-31		
1968	-2	20	50	31	-2			20			50			31		
1969	43	39	49	30	43			39			49			30		
1970	33	28	34	6	33			28			34			6		
1971	7	16	20	7	7			16			20			7		
1972	16	49	58	49	16			49			58			49		
1973	52	59	46	16	52			59			46			16		
1974	30	22	20	-29	30			22			20			-29		
1975	-13	-2	-1	-8	-13			-2			-1			-8		
1976	13	1	18	-5	13			1			18			-5		
1977	1	-11	-22	-28	1			-11			-22			-28		
1978	-9	12	30	3	-9			12			30			3		
1979	10	6	7	-8	10			6			7			-8		
1980	3	-9	-4	-9	3			-9			-4			-9		
1981	16	34	38	14	16			34			-38			14		
1982	14	-8	-14	-43	14			-8			-14			-43		
1983	-24	-1	35	46	-24			-1			35			46		

Orders inflow: tendency
manufacturing and construction
per cent balance

Commandes : tendance
industries manufacturières et construction
solde en pourcentage

Year	Q.1	Q.2	Q.3	Q.4	JAN	FEB	MAR	APR	MAY	JUN	JUL	AUG	SEP	OCT	NOV	DEC
1964	31	27	37	47	31			27			37			47		
1965	32	36	33	40	32			36			33			40		
1966	16	19	18	23	16			19			18			23		
1967	-13	-22	-45	-35	-13			-22			-45			-35		
1968	-21	-6	30	53	-21			-6			30			53		
1969	39	35	47	49	39			35			47			49		
1970	40	35	34	35	40			35			34			35		
1971	11	-9	-7	-4	11			-9			-7			-4		
1972	-13	2	30	47	-13			2			30			47		
1973	61	67	57	61	61			67			57			61		
1974	45	37	12	-27	45			37			12			-27		
1975	-56	-30	-34	-13	-56			-30			-34			-13		
1976	-3	-6	-6	16	-3			-6			-6			16		
1977	4	-18	-40	-44	4			-18			-40			-44		
1978	-47	-33	-3	18	-47			-33			-3			18		
1979	23	18	-1	4	23			-18			-1			4		
1980	-17	-32	-26	-16	-17			-32			-26			-16		
1981	-3	20	33	41	-3			20			33			-41		
1982	25	13	-18	-44	25			13			-18			-44		
1983	-48	-24	4	40	-48			-24			4			40		

NEW ZEALAND

Finished goods stocks: tendency / Stocks de produits finis : tendance

manufacturing and construction / industries manufacturières et construction

per cent balance / solde en pourcentage

	Year	Q.1	Q.2	Q.3	Q.4	JAN	FEB	MAR	APR	MAY	JUN	JUL	AUG	SEP	OCT	NOV	DEC
1964		-	5	12	-23	-			5			12			-23		
1965		-4	3	9	6	4			3			9			6		
1966		-2	-	10	-9	-2			-			10			-9		
1967		1	7	8	9	1			7			8			9		
1968		-5	2	6	-2	-5			2			6			-2		
1969		3	-3	18	-1	3			-3			18			-1		
1970		4	1	7	10	4			1			7			10		
1971		14	22	17	10	14			22			17			10		
1972		-3	-7	-2	-7	-3			-7			-2			-7		
1973		-14	-17	-17	-19	-14			-17			-17			-19		
1974		-26	-16	11	25	-26			-16			11			25		
1975		24	10	13	-	24			10			13			-		
1976		-	-	4	-1	-			-			4			-1		
1977		-3	18	34	19	-3			18			34			19		
1978		8	7	3	-8	8			7			3			-8		
1979		-3	-17	11	9	-3			-17			11			9		
1980		16	23	20	9	16			23			20			9		
1981		2	-11	-2	16	2			-11			-2			16		
1982		12	15	10	22	12			15			10			22		
1983		4	-13	-8	-22	4			-13			-8			-22		

Firms operating at full capacity (1) / Entreprises travaillant à pleine capacité (1)

manufacturing and construction / industries manufacturières et construction

per cent / pourcentage

	Year	Q.1	Q.2	Q.3	Q.4	JAN	FEB	MAR	APR	MAY	JUN	JUL	AUG	SEP	OCT	NOV	DEC
1964		11	10	14	11	11			10			14			11		
1965		12	14	11	14	12			14			11			14		
1966		12	10	9	11	12			10			9			11		
1967		8	7	8	7	8			7			8			7		
1968		7	7	6	7	7			7			6			7		
1969		8	8	8	8	8			8			8			8		
1970		10	11	12	12	10			11			12			12		
1971		11	7	8	10	11			7			8			10		
1972		8	10	9	12	8			10			9			12		
1973		12	19	19	17	12			19			19			17		
1974		21	21	14	11	21			21			14			11		
1975		9	10	8	8	9			10			8			8		
1976		8	7	4	8	8			7			4			8		
1977		8	6	6	3	8			6			6			3		
1978		5	6	4	5	5			6			4			5		
1979		7	7	8	8	7			7			8			8		
1980		6	6	5	4	6			6			5			4		
1981		2	3	5	7	2			3			5			7		
1982		6	8	8	4	6			8			8			4		
1983		4	4	6	7	4			4			6			7		

Manufacturing stocks: total (2) / Stocks des industries manufacturières : total (2)

million NZ dollars, end of period / millions de dollars néo-zélandais, fin de période

	Year	Q.1	Q.2	Q.3	Q.4	JAN	FEB	MAR	APR	MAY	JUN	JUL	AUG	SEP	OCT	NOV	DEC
1964																	
1965																	
1966																	
1967	393	386	392	412	393												
1968	420	407	410	425	420												
1969	475	448	463	485	475												
1970	536	501	522	544	536												
1971	713	714	713	722	713												
1972	770	796	798	750	770												
1973	872	856	872	853	872												
1974	1282	1057	1125	1176	1282												
1975	1493	1460	1466	1460	1493												
1976	1681	1666	1743	1699	1681												
1977	2005	1978	1989	1993	2005												
1978	2011	2114	2103	1993	2011												
1979	2383	2236	2359	2333	2383												
1980	2732	2597	2699	2709	2732												
1981	3122	2893	3010	3104	3122												
1982	3628	3312	3486	3658	3628												
1983	3399	3560	3437	3389	3399												

Construction permits issued: total (3) / Permis de construire délivrés : total (3)

million NZ dollars, monthly averages / millions de dollars néo-zélandais, moyennes mensuelles

	Year	Q.1	Q.2	Q.3	Q.4	JAN	FEB	MAR	APR	MAY	JUN	JUL	AUG	SEP	OCT	NOV	DEC
1964																	
1965			30.9	32.6	33.3				28.9	33.7	30.0	34.0	29.6	34.3	28.7	36.9	34.3
1966	32.3	28.8	30.4	37.9	32.3	19.1	34.2	33.0	28.7	28.9	33.5	28.8	37.5	47.5	28.7	32.6	35.6
1967	27.7	29.9	27.1	28.6	25.4	28.9	27.7	33.0	25.1	30.3	25.9	29.8	26.2	29.7	29.4	27.3	19.5
1968	30.8	29.0	24.7	35.7	33.7	24.0	25.9	37.2	20.3	27.6	26.2	32.1	35.5	39.6	32.4	30.6	38.1
1969	37.9	37.7	32.8	38.1	43.1	42.0	33.0	38.1	30.9	32.2	35.4	37.5	37.5	39.2	55.4	41.4	32.4
1970	40.4	35.4	41.0	44.2	41.2	29.8	36.6	39.7	46.3	35.9	40.7	41.5	46.8	44.2	39.3	46.5	37.9
1971	44.7	44.7	38.9	45.9	49.3	35.6	37.1	61.5	34.1	41.3	41.4	47.2	42.3	48.2	53.5	52.4	41.9
1972	56.1	45.6	53.0	60.2	65.7	33.2	55.1	48.4	42.6	54.0	62.4	62.6	58.8	59.1	74.8	68.0	54.3
1973	81.1	69.8	75.8	90.1	88.9	58.3	60.9	90.1	64.0	83.3	80.0	86.3	98.6	85.3	99.8	95.3	71.6
1974	91.1	77.7	98.5	101.9	86.2	58.5	73.4	101.3	79.7	117.9	97.9	91.8	108.4	105.5	92.2	93.1	73.4
1975	92.1	73.7	85.6	103.5	105.4	52.9	84.5	83.8	79.5	86.4	90.8	132.7	86.6	91.3	122.2	96.8	97.2
1976	99.4	91.7	97.6	100.2	107.9	65.2	85.3	124.6	90.3	103.6	99.0	97.3	98.0	105.4	106.9	110.9	105.9
1977	101.8	104.9	103.9	104.0	94.5	66.3	114.7	133.7	93.4	102.8	115.5	100.3	98.0	113.7	88.8	106.8	88.0
1978	95.1	83.4	91.1	101.2	104.9	53.6	72.0	124.5	83.3	108.3	81.7	93.8	105.2	104.5	105.6	107.1	101.9
1979	91.7	86.0	83.0	93.9	104.1	67.5	85.3	105.3	71.5	95.3	82.1	84.5	97.4	99.7	111.0	113.8	87.5
1980	109.6	106.0	104.7	114.8	112.8	93.8	95.7	128.4	86.3	126.6	101.1	115.5	108.4	120.6	110.3	110.3	117.7
1981	155.0	119.7	142.7	164.9	192.4	94.3	125.6	139.3	123.0	145.2	160.0	167.5	142.0	185.2	164.9	236.6	175.8
1982	175.8	167.7	168.2	162.2	205.0	124.6	162.6	215.8	157.9	170.5	176.3	165.8	166.2	154.6	271.6	180.3	163.2
1983	172.7	131.2	160.9	185.2	213.3	92.8	127.0	173.9	131.7	191.1	159.9	188.2	186.6	180.8	199.2	223.4	217.4

Construction permits issued: (3) residential / Permis de construire délivrés : (3) bâtiments résidentiels

million NZ dollars, monthly averages / millions de dollars néo-zélandais, moyennes mensuelles

	Year	Q.1	Q.2	Q.3	Q.4	JAN	FEB	MAR	APR	MAY	JUN	JUL	AUG	SEP	OCT	NOV	DEC
1964																	
1965			17.2	18.1	16.4				17.0	17.2	17.3	17.5	17.0	19.7	16.6	17.4	15.3
1966	16.9	15.7	16.9	17.8	17.1	11.0	16.4	19.6	15.8	18.2	16.8	16.5	17.6	19.2	17.2	17.8	16.2
1967	15.8	15.9	15.4	16.4	15.5	12.3	16.4	18.9	15.1	15.9	15.2	15.3	17.1	16.9	18.0	16.6	11.9
1968	16.3	15.2	14.7	18.3	16.9	12.0	16.2	17.3	13.2	16.8	14.1	17.7	18.4	18.7	19.1	17.6	14.1
1969	18.4	17.4	18.1	19.5	18.4	14.3	17.6	20.4	17.1	19.6	17.7	19.5	18.7	20.4	19.8	18.9	16.4
1970	20.3	17.7	20.5	21.8	21.3	14.5	17.5	21.1	21.1	20.2	20.1	21.6	20.7	23.1	22.4	22.6	18.9
1971	22.9	20.2	21.5	24.5	25.4	15.7	19.9	25.1	20.1	22.4	21.9	23.7	24.2	25.6	24.8	28.4	23.1
1972	31.0	24.1	30.2	34.8	35.0	15.6	27.4	29.3	24.0	35.2	31.5	31.0	37.7	35.7	37.3	38.0	29.8
1973	48.4	38.3	45.5	53.5	56.4	26.6	37.5	50.8	38.7	51.6	46.1	52.9	55.5	52.0	62.8	61.4	44.9
1974	53.0	48.8	57.1	56.5	49.4	37.2	48.3	61.0	47.1	69.1	55.1	55.7	58.9	55.0	55.9	51.3	41.0
1975	53.6	44.5	52.0	59.4	58.4	34.7	39.2	59.5	51.1	55.0	49.9	61.2	56.9	60.2	62.1	55.6	57.4
1976	52.6	58.6	58.6	63.2	69.9	39.8	55.8	80.1	53.9	61.8	60.2	61.7	61.4	66.5	66.4	75.1	68.3
1977	55.6	58.1	55.7	54.5	54.0	40.7	61.3	72.3	49.7	62.8	54.6	50.1	59.1	54.3	52.0	59.3	50.7
1978	51.8	42.6	48.9	56.6	59.0	30.4	41.5	55.8	41.0	55.2	50.6	50.8	60.1	58.9	60.8	66.2	49.9
1979	50.5	48.1	47.6	51.8	54.7	36.9	48.3	59.0	43.2	52.1	47.4	50.5	52.6	52.3	59.8	60.4	44.0
1980	57.6	51.2	54.7	60.9	63.8	40.6	52.6	60.3	49.5	62.9	51.6	60.2	57.8	64.7	64.4	62.0	65.1
1981	84.6	60.8	78.1	90.0	109.4	45.6	59.5	77.4	70.0	83.6	80.8	85.5	84.5	100.1	106.7	111.8	109.6
1982	94.3	96.0	98.6	90.4	92.2	71.2	92.7	124.2	99.3	100.5	95.9	90.7	91.9	88.7	86.6	98.4	91.6
1983	104.7	81.9	97.6	109.0	130.2	56.7	81.3	107.6	87.8	108.2	96.7	93.0	108.2	125.7	127.7	137.2	125.7

Construction: housing starts / Construction : logements mis en chantier

thousands, monthly averages / milliers, moyennes mensuelles

	Year	Q.1	Q.2	Q.3	Q.4	JAN	FEB	MAR	APR	MAY	JUN	JUL	AUG	SEP	OCT	NOV	DEC
1964																	
1965																	
1966																	
1967																	
1968																	
1969																	
1970																	
1971																	
1972																	
1973																	
1974																	
1975																	
1976			2.5	2.5	2.5				2.4	2.6	2.5	2.6	2.4	2.6	2.4	2.8	2.3
1977	2.0	2.3	2.0	1.8	1.7	1.6	2.5	2.9	1.8	2.2	1.9	1.7	1.8	1.8	1.8	1.9	1.5
1978	1.5	1.3	1.5	1.6	1.6	1.1	1.3	1.6	1.3	1.7	1.5	1.4	1.7	1.7	1.7	1.8	1.2
1979	1.2	1.2	1.2	1.3	1.3	1.0	1.4	1.3	1.1	1.3	1.1	1.3	1.4	1.2	1.4	1.4	1.0
1980	1.2	1.1	1.2	1.3	1.1	0.8	1.1	1.4	1.1	1.3	1.1	1.3	1.3	1.3	1.2	1.1	1.0
1981	1.4	1.2	1.4	1.5	1.7	0.8	1.6	1.3	1.2	1.4	1.4	1.4	1.4	1.7	1.8	1.8	1.6
1982	1.4	1.6	1.5	1.3	1.2	1.2	1.6	1.9	1.7	1.5	1.4	1.3	1.3	1.3	1.3	1.3	1.1
1983	1.4	1.2	1.4	1.6	1.7	0.8	1.2	1.5	1.2	1.5	1.3	1.5	1.6	1.6	1.8	1.8	1.4

NEW ZEALAND

Construction, work put in place: total (3)

million NZ dollars, quarterly averages

Construction, travaux effectués : total (3)

millions de dollars néo-zélandais, moyennes trimestrielles

	Year	Q.1	Q.2	Q.3	Q.4	JAN	FEB	MAR	APR	MAY	JUN	JUL	AUG	SEP	OCT	NOV	DEC
1964																	
1965			96.4	103.2	98.9												
1966	95.3	87.5	95.0	100.8	98.0												
1967	92.7	89.2	94.9	95.2	91.6												
1968	88.0	80.5	82.8	90.1	98.7												
1969	102.4	88.6	99.0	110.7	111.4												
1970	119.2	99.6	121.2	126.4	129.7												
1971	134.2	130.0	122.7	140.4	143.9												
1972	154.6	128.3	154.9	156.0	179.1												
1973	197.5	170.9	178.7	216.0	224.6												
1974	253.5	219.9	251.7	273.5	268.8												
1975	281.7	252.2	295.3	300.4	279.0												
1976	312.8	285.9	299.0	322.9	343.5												
1977	331.8	331.5	347.6	345.8	302.4												
1978	293.4	269.8	288.5	308.5	306.7												
1979	317.5	303.2	306.3	333.7	327.0												
1980	350.9	315.5	343.4	371.7	373.0												
1981	430.4	345.8	413.8	454.9	497.0												
1982	541.3	505.5	560.3	553.2	546.2												
1983		447.7	588.8	589.7													

Construction, work put in place: (3) residential

million NZ dollars, quarterly averages

Construction, travaux effectués : (3) bâtiments résidentiels

millions de dollars néo-zélandais, moyennes trimestrielles

	Year	Q.1	Q.2	Q.3	Q.4	JAN	FEB	MAR	APR	MAY	JUN	JUL	AUG	SEP	OCT	NOV	DEC
1964																	
1965			52.3	56.6	54.7												
1966	51.0	46.7	50.8	53.3	53.2												
1967	49.2	48.4	48.9	48.1	51.4												
1968	47.7	42.0	45.2	47.9	55.6												
1969	54.3	47.1	55.0	59.1	55.8												
1970	59.6	50.3	61.0	61.3	65.9												
1971	67.5	61.1	59.4	72.5	76.9												
1972	85.9	68.6	85.9	83.9	105.1												
1973	115.9	96.6	105.7	127.7	133.5												
1974	152.0	136.1	153.4	159.5	159.1												
1975	167.7	146.5	177.7	176.2	170.2												
1976	185.7	168.8	173.7	195.7	204.7												
1977	189.9	201.8	202.7	191.9	163.1												
1978	158.6	153.0	148.3	165.6	167.6												
1979	163.4	161.3	157.6	163.2	171.7												
1980	177.2	153.8	177.8	185.4	191.3												
1981	217.1	173.5	208.1	231.0	255.8												
1982	289.9	282.0	311.3	291.3	275.0												
1983		235.2	280.9	328.8													

Retail sales: value (4)

million NZ dollars, monthly averages

Ventes au détail : valeur (4)

millions de dollars néo-zélandais, moyennes mensuelles

	Year	Q.1	Q.2	Q.3	Q.4	JAN	FEB	MAR	APR	MAY	JUN	JUL	AUG	SEP	OCT	NOV	DEC
1964	115.7	105.6	111.7	112.0	133.5												
1965	126.8	116.5	122.4	122.5	145.6												
1966	136.0	126.1	133.4	132.9	151.4												
1967	137.5	130.8	135.8	131.5	151.9												
1968	144.5	135.3	140.0	138.3	164.5												
1969	156.2	142.9	151.6	151.6	178.8												
1970	174.9	155.8	171.8	170.5	201.5	151.6	151.7	164.0	173.8	177.2	164.3	172.7	164.7	174.3	181.8	180.6	242.2
1971	189.3	169.9	184.1	186.1	217.1	157.1	164.7	187.8	189.4	184.4	173.3	186.5	183.6	188.3	187.2	205.0	259.0
1972	213.0	188.8	204.9	210.1	248.4	168.0	186.3	212.3	188.6	218.8	207.1	200.2	216.5	213.5	219.5	238.9	286.7
1973	253.6	222.1	238.8	249.4	303.9	212.0	212.2	242.2	223.9	258.2	234.4	239.4	264.3	244.5	275.2	296.9	339.6
1974	295.6	263.6	283.5	293.4	341.8	255.3	252.5	283.1	272.7	314.1	263.8	295.3	296.6	288.4	317.6	319.2	388.7
1975	330.3	280.9	313.2	327.5	399.5	277.5	275.6	289.6	311.9	330.4	297.4	322.5	318.6	341.5	370.2	351.1	477.3
1976	554.4	336.4	571.5	593.3	716.5	310.8	323.9	374.6	568.7	578.5	567.3	586.0	584.8	609.2	616.5	668.0	865.0
1977	654.9	610.9	639.6	659.9	709.1	579.7	578.6	674.3	616.2	671.5	631.0	633.7	670.1	676.0	636.1	682.5	808.8
1978	724.2	633.9	701.1	725.3	836.4	601.0	605.6	695.1	655.6	742.3	705.3	691.5	746.2	738.1	755.7	816.5	936.9
1979	824.5	747.5	798.0	800.6	951.8	729.3	712.0	801.3	736.1	859.9	797.9	777.1	848.9	775.9	832.8	943.3	1029.4
1980	994.4	895.6	945.5	997.4	1139.1	878.8	876.8	931.1	900.1	1021.1	915.2	1005.4	981.8	1004.9	1075.0	1044.3	1298.1
1981	1210.6	1058.6	1158.6	1244.4	1380.9	1007.1	1019.6	1149.1	1134.5	1178.1	1163.2	1268.9	1207.7	1256.6	1299.9	1259.6	1583.1
1982	1345.7	1270.5	1330.0	1343.5	1438.7	1201.4	1193.2	1417.0	1339.9	1337.6	1312.6	1375.4	1343.3	1311.7	1294.2	1370.8	1651.2
1983	1424.4	1304.9	1358.0	1434.6	1600.2	1185.1	1213.4	1516.2	1316.1	1413.4	1344.6	1377.1	1440.1	1486.6	1441.6	1535.5	1823.4

Construction, work put in place: total (3) — Adjusted - Corrigé — **Construction, travaux effectués : total** (3)

million NZ dollars, quarterly averages — millions de dollars néo-zélandais, moyennes trimestrielles

	Year	Q.1	Q.2	Q.3	Q.4	JAN	FEB	MAR	APR	MAY	JUN	JUL	AUG	SEP	OCT	NOV	DEC
1964																	
1965			97.1	98.6	95.8												
1966		94.2	95.8	96.3	94.7												
1967		96.2	95.7	91.0	88.3												
1968		87.0	83.5	86.2	94.8												
1969		96.0	100.0	106.1	106.7												
1970		107.8	123.0	120.8	124.0												
1971		139.7	124.7	134.8	137.6												
1972		138.3	156.2	150.1	171.0												
1973		185.0	180.5	205.6	213.5												
1974		233.9	256.5	250.1	258.6												
1975		269.3	296.5	288.4	273.4												
1976		304.7	297.9	305.5	341.4												
1977		351.1	344.3	334.4	304.5												
1978		285.8	284.5	294.9	306.3												
1979		319.3	305.1	317.9	325.3												
1980		330.9	344.5	353.6	370.0												
1981		365.8	413.5	439.7	489.3												
1982		537.3	564.1	535.6	541.3												
1983		471.0	584.3	567.7													

Wholesale sales: value — **Ventes du commerce de gros : valeur**

million NZ dollars, quarterly averages — millions de dollars néo-zélandais, moyennes trimestrielles

	Year	Q.1	Q.2	Q.3	Q.4	JAN	FEB	MAR	APR	MAY	JUN	JUL	AUG	SEP	OCT	NOV	DEC
1964	329.8	288.5	321.6	343.6	365.5												
1965	369.7	330.2	358.6	389.6	400.4												
1966	400.7	364.2	391.7	415.8	430.8												
1967	405.4	387.4	405.9	407.9	420.5												
1968	440.6	411.5	406.1	452.5	492.1												
1969	506.7	456.3	484.8	525.4	560.1												
1970	584.9	518.9	572.8	604.0	643.8												
1971	637.7	580.7	622.6	642.0	705.5												
1972	707.4	634.0	680.9	719.7	794.9												
1973	863.7	764.9	816.8	898.8	974.3												
1974	996.9	881.5	950.5	1072.2	1083.4												
1975	1080.1	947.4	1032.2	1137.1	1204.0												
1976	1272.4	1130.5	1232.2	1321.6	1405.2												
1977	1363.6	1315.0	1375.1	1376.3	1388.2												
1978	1464.0	1279.3	1454.1	1493.3	1629.4												
1979	1725.4	1518.2	1706.5	1742.8	1934.2												
1980	1962.1	1816.4	1919.4	1985.2	2127.2												
1981	2319.9	2016.9	2228.5	2429.5	2604.6												
1982	2580.5	2412.0	2673.7	2645.1	2591.0												
1983	2650.2	2408.0	2628.1	2700.2	2864.3												

Retail sales: value (4) — Adjusted - Corrigé — **Ventes au détail : valeur** (4)

million NZ dollars, monthly averages — millions de dollars néo-zélandais, moyennes mensuelles

	Year	Q.1	Q.2	Q.3	Q.4	JAN	FEB	MAR	APR	MAY	JUN	JUL	AUG	SEP	OCT	NOV	DEC
1964		111.1	113.9	116.4	120.6												
1965		122.6	124.7	127.5	131.6												
1966		132.7	135.7	138.5	136.8												
1967		137.7	138.0	137.1	137.3												
1968		142.3	142.2	144.3	148.9												
1969		150.2	153.9	158.2	161.8												
1970		169.5	173.4	174.9	179.9	168.3	169.3	170.8	170.5	176.3	173.3	172.0	175.5	177.3	178.7	177.3	183.6
1971		182.9	188.0	190.6	192.9	180.8	183.6	184.2	189.4	187.1	187.5	190.5	190.9	190.4	190.7	194.5	193.5
1972		199.8	209.5	217.2	224.2	196.9	199.3	203.1	205.9	209.4	213.1	216.4	216.0	219.2	221.1	223.7	227.9
1973		236.4	244.9	258.6	272.2	234.7	236.8	237.7	240.5	245.0	249.1	251.7	260.1	264.0	257.4	273.6	275.4
1974		272.2	291.1	301.3	305.2	246.7	281.8	288.0	284.6	294.1	294.7	300.7	299.5	303.6	305.0	303.7	306.8
1975		305.3	319.0	335.9	355.2	299.3	307.9	308.8	315.0	317.3	324.7	326.0	334.0	347.8	349.6	351.1	364.9
1976		356.9	582.8	600.2	653.0	344.2	359.9	366.5	583.5	578.5	586.5	591.8	598.7	610.2	624.2	638.1	696.8
1977		651.1	651.9	666.4	653.4	652.5	642.0	658.7	650.0	656.4	649.3	662.9	667.3	668.9	655.7	651.6	653.0
1978		666.6	715.2	740.3	775.1	660.1	670.3	669.5	724.0	706.8	714.7	732.9	736.4	751.6	762.8	775.1	787.5
1979		784.5	814.5	819.1	878.2	780.5	789.0	784.1	795.6	814.7	833.2	803.3	827.4	826.7	866.3	883.9	884.5
1980		935.4	965.6	1010.4	1049.7	933.1	920.1	953.0	941.5	978.1	977.2	1001.5	1008.7	1020.9	1033.5	1050.6	1065.0
1981		1115.2	1184.7	1259.8	1271.3	1074.0	1128.7	1142.9	1178.1	1169.5	1206.4	1246.2	1260.1	1273.2	1274.8	1242.9	1296.1
1982		1337.6	1361.1	1359.1	1317.2	1323.7	1321.3	1367.8	1370.3	1353.0	1359.9	1378.9	1373.0	1325.1	1312.7	1312.2	1326.6
1983		1374.0	1390.2	1442.3	1501.0	1323.9	1343.7	1454.5	1384.2	1397.5	1388.8	1416.8	1428.3	1481.7	1492.8	1488.7	1521.4

Retail sales: volume (5)

million 4th quarter 1980 NZ dollars, quarterly averages

Ventes au détail : volume (5)

millions de dollars néo-zélandais du 4e trimestre 1980, moyennes trimestrielles

	Year	Q.1	Q.2	Q.3	Q.4	JAN	FEB	MAR	APR	MAY	JUN	JUL	AUG	SEP	OCT	NOV	DEC
1964	2327.2	2164.2	2263.4	2244.1	2637.0												
1965	2468.4	2303.1	2412.1	2402.1	2836.2												
1966	2617.8	2446.3	2580.7	2552.8	2891.0												
1967	2515.9	2440.8	2478.6	2382.5	2761.5												
1968	2538.3	2429.2	2475.3	2414.3	2834.3												
1969	2611.0	2430.0	2547.5	2511.8	2954.6												
1970	2788.5	2578.0	2791.5	2706.2	3078.1												
1971	2756.4	2573.5	2692.0	2690.8	3069.2												
1972	2925.8	2627.8	2832.5	2874.6	3368.3												
1973	3228.3	2934.7	3086.3	3124.6	3767.5												
1974	3454.3	3210.1	3381.7	3399.2	3826.3												
1975	3334.9	3034.5	3245.8	3253.8	3805.6												
1976	3251.9	3067.8	3199.8	3092.9	3647.0												
1977	3082.3	2966.7	3091.2	2977.9	3293.2												
1978	3036.6	2764.6	2930.5	2952.9	3498.4												
1979	3069.3	2901.7	3054.2	2896.9	3424.5												
1980	3101.4	2966.7	3045.0	2976.4	3417.4												
1981	3327.4	3078.1	3243.5	3367.7	3620.1												
1982	3277.8	3236.6	3271.5	3212.3	3390.9												
1983	3280.0	3055.1	3153.3	3285.1	3626.6												

Employment: total (employees on payrolls) (6)

thousands

Emploi : total (salariés sur bordereaux) (6)

milliers

	Year	Q.1	Q.2	Q.3	Q.4	JAN	FEB	MAR	APR	MAY	JUN	JUL	AUG	SEP	OCT	NOV	DEC
1964	663	659	660	661	673	655	661	661	659	662	660	659	661	662	662	672	686
1965	691	686	688	688	700	682	688	688	686	689	688	686	688	690	690	697	714
1966	715	711	713	712	722	707	712	714	713	714	713	710	712	713	713	719	735
1967	723	733	728	714	717	727	735	736	734	729	722	716	714	712	710	717	725
1968	718	721	716	712	723	719	723	722	719	716	713	711	711	713	713	721	736
1969	739	737	736	734	747	733	740	740	738	737	735	734	734	736	735	745	761
1970	764	761	764	759	773	755	763	764	763	766	762	758	759	759	758	771	789
1971	779	785	780	771	780	781	786	787	784	781	776	771	772	770	771	777	794
1972	788	790	787	781	794	785	793	793	791	787	783	781	781	781	781	792	810
1973	811	810	815	808	813	803	812	815	815			808			813		
1974	840	837	846	836	840	837			846			836			840		
1975	852	853	860	847	847	853			860			847			847		
1976	861	862	870	857	855	862			870			857			855		
1977	865	869	878	861	852	869			878			861			852		
1978	860	861	866	857	855	861			866			857			855		
1979	••	876	879	••	866	876			879			••			866		
1980	873	888	885	857	863		888			885			857			863	
1981	870	874	873	860	873		874			873			860			873	
1982	874	878	882	867	868		878			882			867			868	
1983	857	863	861	847	859		863			861			847			859	

Unemployment (registered unemployed) (7)

thousands

Chômage (chômeurs inscrits) (7)

milliers

	Year	Q.1	Q.2	Q.3	Q.4	JAN	FEB	MAR	APR	MAY	JUN	JUL	AUG	SEP	OCT	NOV	DEC
1964	0.65	0.54	0.73	0.82	0.46	0.60	0.51	0.51	0.63	0.78	0.94	0.96	0.76	0.73	0.51	0.43	0.45
1965	0.51	0.52	0.66	0.53	0.34	0.52	0.52	0.52	0.61	0.59	0.76	0.58	0.55	0.47	0.37	0.33	0.34
1966	0.46	0.38	0.46	0.54	0.47	0.39	0.36	0.40	0.39	0.47	0.53	0.57	0.54	0.51	0.41	0.46	0.53
1967	3.85	0.60	2.83	6.15	5.83	0.60	0.61	0.59	0.97	2.30	5.23	6.29	6.51	5.64	4.86	5.74	6.89
1968	6.88	6.92	8.31	7.56	4.74	7.66	6.53	6.56	8.53	8.26	8.13	8.56	7.65	6.47	5.15	4.51	4.55
1969	2.93	3.67	3.35	2.94	1.75	4.64	3.49	2.89	2.97	3.50	3.58	3.26	3.04	2.51	1.84	1.60	1.80
1970	1.60	1.53	1.61	1.78	1.48	1.82	1.45	1.33	1.45	1.57	1.80	1.72	1.88	1.76	1.66	1.26	1.51
1971	3.12	1.29	2.58	4.03	4.57	1.52	1.22	1.12	1.67	2.54	3.53	4.14	4.07	3.88	3.56	4.66	5.48
1972	5.68	5.07	5.86	6.79	5.02	5.75	4.73	4.74	4.93	5.69	6.95	7.26	6.79	6.33	5.15	4.69	5.22
1973	2.32	3.24	2.78	2.25	1.02	4.57	2.81	2.34	2.27	2.75	3.32	2.72	2.18	1.84	1.25	0.88	0.92
1974	0.96	0.72	0.94	1.14	1.03	0.80	0.65	0.70	0.69	0.94	1.20	1.30	1.06	1.05	0.93	0.87	1.29
1975	4.17	3.09	4.11	5.16	4.30	3.14	3.09	3.06	3.28	3.88	5.16	5.13	5.27	5.09	3.30	3.95	5.67
1976	5.36	5.74	5.32	5.85	4.52	6.42	5.78	5.02	4.52	5.13	6.31	6.33	5.84	5.39	4.08	4.45	5.02
1977	7.39	4.68	5.06	7.29	12.50	5.28	4.67	4.11	4.39	4.96	5.84	6.59	7.21	8.08	9.03	13.05	15.42
1978	22.33	19.11	22.82	25.40	21.99	18.82	18.65	19.84	21.50	22.94	24.04	26.31	25.49	24.41	21.76	21.06	23.14
1979	25.24	24.26	24.92	26.10	25.68	24.90	24.14	23.73	24.90	24.51	25.36	26.13	25.92	26.24	24.44	25.71	26.39
1980	36.50	28.59	30.81	40.00	46.61	28.17	28.59	29.00	28.80	29.90	33.73	37.12	40.35	42.53	41.48	48.49	49.85
1981	48.31	48.25	46.54	47.62	50.84	47.85	45.43	47.46	46.68	46.02	46.93	48.46	47.60	46.32	45.97	56.31	50.24
1982	52.10	49.31	46.07	50.25	62.76	50.77	50.17	46.98	46.08	45.14	47.00	48.49	50.47	51.80	55.42	63.21	69.66
1983	75.82	74.40	75.22	78.21	75.44	74.05	76.37	72.77	73.87	74.93	76.87	79.34	78.34	76.96	75.50	74.66	76.16

Retail sales: volume (5)

Ventes au détail : volume (5)

million 4th quarter 1980 NZ dollars, quarterly averages

millions de dollars néo-zélandais du 4e trimestre 1980, moyennes trimestrielles

Adjusted - Corrigé

	Year	Q.1	Q.2	Q.3	Q.4	JAN	FEB	MAR	APR	MAY	JUN	JUL	AUG	SEP	OCT	NOV	DEC
1964		2330.3	2360.0	2386.2	2436.7												
1965		2479.9	2512.5	2556.9	2620.8												
1966		2634.6	2685.5	2720.1	2671.4												
1967		2628.3	2576.7	2541.3	2554.1												
1968		2612.9	2570.6	2575.2	2623.7												
1969		2613.8	2645.6	2681.9	2735.0												
1970		2869.6	2882.3	2840.4	2310.9												
1971		2833.9	2813.1	2819.1	2790.6												
1972		2844.2	2963.2	3041.5	3111.1												
1973		3196.0	3237.3	3315.2	3452.2												
1974		3527.4	3553.1	3571.0	3495.2												
1975		3374.7	3382.5	3414.4	3461.7												
1976		3329.5	3372.7	3237.9	3281.2												
1977		3292.9	3244.2	3107.7	3004.1												
1978		3061.9	3041.2	3137.6	3218.3												
1979		3180.4	3193.5	3077.7	3143.7												
1980		3261.3	3169.3	3135.3	3149.1												
1981		3243.8	3316.7	3410.5	3330.6												
1982		3410.7	3348.0	3249.8	3102.1												
1983		3220.4	3227.7	3303.3	3398.5												

Jobs vacant, unfilled vacancies (7)(8)

Offres d'emploi non satisfaites (7)(8)

thousands

milliers

	Year	Q.1	Q.2	Q.3	Q.4	JAN	FEB	MAR	APR	MAY	JUN	JUL	AUG	SEP	OCT	NOV	DEC
1964	6.61	6.42	6.16	6.30	7.58	6.30	6.48	6.47	6.41	6.04	6.03	6.05	6.21	6.64	7.30	7.69	7.76
1965	7.94	7.87	7.70	7.53	8.64	7.82	8.09	7.70	7.90	7.46	7.73	7.45	7.43	7.72	8.32	8.63	8.98
1966	7.75	8.47	7.61	7.05	7.88	8.89	8.23	8.29	7.94	7.62	7.27	7.02	7.04	7.11	7.34	8.25	8.06
1967	4.13	7.05	3.84	2.70	2.92	7.72	7.12	6.30	5.43	3.41	2.70	2.81	2.59	2.71	2.64	3.22	2.88
1968	2.68	2.47	2.11	2.14	4.00	2.91	2.48	2.01	2.03	2.22	2.10	2.04	2.14	2.25	3.64	4.57	3.79
1969	4.17	3.58	3.61	3.73	5.74	3.55	3.62	3.58	3.52	3.67	3.64	3.63	3.74	3.83	5.24	6.28	5.70
1970	5.25	5.44	5.03	4.87	5.65	5.60	5.73	4.99	5.04	4.91	5.13	5.05	4.81	4.75	5.18	6.15	5.63
1971	3.16	4.70	2.50	2.25	3.18	5.42	4.70	3.99	2.82	2.28	2.39	2.22	2.25	2.29	2.60	3.72	3.23
1972	2.65	2.69	2.14	2.42	3.34	2.88	2.71	2.48	2.35	1.90	2.16	2.37	2.31	2.59	3.64	3.57	2.81
1973	3.54	2.85	3.19	3.88	4.24	2.61	2.89	3.03	3.43	2.94	3.18	3.50	3.74	4.39	4.78	4.53	3.43
1974	4.56	4.20	4.64	4.93	4.45	3.94	4.40	4.27	4.61	4.67	4.66	4.47	4.84	5.48	5.80	4.45	3.09
1975	2.05	2.49	2.07	2.00	1.65	2.46	2.54	2.46	2.18	1.92	2.11	2.06	2.02	1.91	2.05	1.53	1.36
1976	1.67	1.80	1.57	1.64	1.56	1.52	1.87	2.01	1.75	1.59	1.65	1.62	1.62	1.69	1.83	1.57	1.28
1977	1.52	1.70	1.60	1.45	1.34	1.59	1.69	1.82	1.84	1.61	1.37	1.38	1.47	1.51	1.45	1.39	1.18
1978	1.74	1.41	1.41	1.81	2.33	1.38	1.50	1.34	1.41	1.35	1.47	1.54	1.69	2.20	1.98	2.85	2.15
1979	1.69	1.90	1.85	1.53	1.46	1.89	2.17	1.64	1.80	2.01	1.76	1.44	1.65	1.50	1.74	1.41	1.25
1980	1.48	1.38	1.18	1.66	1.68	1.62	1.38	1.14	1.09	1.12	1.33	1.49	1.66	1.82	1.81	1.75	1.48
1981	3.44	2.29	3.53	3.81	4.13	1.76	1.97	3.15	3.25	3.55	3.78	3.77	3.63	4.02	4.35	4.13	3.90
1982	3.68	4.12	4.01	3.30	3.29	3.95	4.32	4.08	4.20	3.98	3.86	3.52	3.44	2.95	2.88	3.32	3.68
1983	2.78	2.12	1.66	2.31	5.02	2.36	2.01	1.99	1.12	1.97	1.88	1.98	2.27	2.69	3.49	5.11	6.46

Unemployment (registered unemployed) (7)

Chômage (chômeurs inscrits) (7)

thousands

milliers

Adjusted - Corrigé *

	Year	Q.1	Q.2	Q.3	Q.4	JAN	FEB	MAR	APR	MAY	JUN	JUL	AUG	SEP	OCT	NOV	DEC
1964		0.67	0.67	0.65	0.60	0.70	0.66	0.65	0.67	0.69	0.67	0.67	0.61	0.66	0.61	0.59	0.58
1965		0.65	0.58	0.43	0.43	0.60	0.67	0.68	0.65	0.53	0.55	0.41	0.44	0.43	0.45	0.43	0.42
1966		0.47	0.41	0.44	0.57	0.44	0.47	0.52	0.42	0.43	0.39	0.41	0.44	0.47	0.49	0.59	0.63
1967		0.73	2.39	5.00	6.87	0.66	0.77	0.77	1.06	2.11	3.98	4.62	5.19	5.20	5.74	7.09	7.79
1968		8.36	7.90	6.14	5.47	8.08	8.27	8.72	9.64	7.70	6.37	6.37	6.08	5.96	6.02	5.49	4.91
1969		4.34	3.20	2.40	1.97	4.77	4.42	3.82	3.42	3.31	2.87	2.46	2.44	2.30	2.12	1.94	1.87
1970		1.80	1.55	1.48	1.66	1.84	1.83	1.74	1.70	1.50	1.44	1.32	1.53	1.60	1.89	1.54	1.54
1971		1.49	2.41	3.38	5.12	1.52	1.51	1.43	1.99	2.44	2.81	3.20	3.39	3.55	4.08	5.78	5.51
1972		5.79	5.60	5.78	5.73	5.72	5.75	5.90	5.91	5.46	5.43	5.67	5.77	5.88	6.01	5.95	5.23
1973		3.52	2.65	1.93	1.18	4.49	3.28	2.80	2.71	2.65	2.58	2.15	1.90	1.75	1.50	1.12	0.92
1974		0.76	0.88	1.01	1.18	0.77	0.72	0.81	0.81	0.90	0.94	1.06	0.95	1.02	1.13	1.12	1.30
1975		3.19	3.89	4.73	4.90	2.94	3.24	3.40	3.73	3.77	4.16	4.32	4.85	5.01	4.07	4.98	5.65
1976		5.70	5.10	5.48	5.13	5.88	5.82	5.41	4.97	5.03	5.31	5.53	5.51	5.39	5.00	5.44	4.97
1977		4.56	4.98	6.97	13.51	4.77	4.59	4.33	4.70	4.99	5.26	5.98	6.92	8.02	10.65	14.80	15.07
1978		18.60	22.92	24.62	23.22	17.06	18.13	20.60	22.55	23.43	22.77	24.68	24.87	24.30	24.76	22.50	22.40
1979		23.51	25.37	25.64	26.39	22.83	23.41	24.30	25.82	25.34	24.94	25.13	25.56	26.23	26.86	26.39	25.91
1980		27.73	31.62	39.80	46.85	26.13	27.60	29.45	29.66	31.18	34.02	36.53	40.11	42.76	44.35	48.39	47.80
1981		46.68	48.16	47.78	50.52	44.72	47.40	47.94	48.15	48.37	47.95	48.39	47.56	47.39	48.43	55.15	47.96
1982		47.60	47.92	50.68	61.84	47.55	47.77	47.48	47.70	47.64	48.41	48.94	50.57	52.53	58.06	61.24	66.21
1983		71.85	78.51	79.05	74.35	69.35	72.57	73.63	76.73	79.30	79.50	80.43	78.59	78.12	78.86	71.95	72.24

* Adjusted by the O.E.C.D.

* Corrigé par l'O.C.D.E.

Labour disputes: time lost / Conflits du travail : journées perdues

thousand man-days / milliers de journées-homme

	Year	Q.1	Q.2	Q.3	Q.4	JAN	FEB	MAR	APR	MAY	JUN	JUL	AUG	SEP	OCT	NOV	DEC
1964	66.8	15.1	25.4	6.4	19.9												
1965	21.8	6.3	5.1	8.4	2.0												
1966	99.1	15.8	19.0	8.8	55.6												
1967	139.5	55.7	71.0	0.6	12.2												
1968	130.3	46.9	20.3	44.8	18.3												
1969	138.7	67.6	38.8	9.8	22.5												
1970	277.4	86.8	40.2	74.4	75.9												
1971	162.6	39.0	46.0	53.2	24.4												
1972	140.7	41.7	27.1	18.7	53.2												
1973	271.7	125.5	65.9	39.7	40.7												
1974	183.7	88.5	54.1	23.6	17.6												
1975	214.6	46.3	81.8	31.5	55.1												
1976	488.4	94.8	55.3	121.9	216.5												
1977	436.8	72.5	115.3	86.4	162.6												
1978	380.6	88.2	208.8	29.0	54.6												
1979	381.9	91.2	86.0	106.1	98.5												
1980	360.1	159.5	37.6	21.5	141.5												
1981	245.4	117.7	56.3	44.7	26.7												
1982	328.2	188.6	80.4	21.9	37.3												
1983		87.9	114.4	72.8													

Weekly wage rates: (9) / Taux de salaires hebdomadaires : (9)

all activities / ensemble des activités

1980 = 100

	Year	Q.1	Q.2	Q.3	Q.4	JAN	FEB	MAR	APR	MAY	JUN	JUL	AUG	SEP	OCT	NOV	DEC
1964	18.7	18.0	18.1	19.2	19.4			18.0			18.1			19.2			19.4
1965	19.6	19.4	19.5	19.7	19.8			19.4			19.5			19.7			19.8
1966	20.1	19.8	19.9	20.4	20.9			19.8			19.9			20.4			20.9
1967	21.1	20.9	21.1	21.2	21.3			20.9			21.1			21.2			21.3
1968	22.0	21.4	21.5	22.6	22.8			21.4			21.5			22.6			22.8
1969	23.2	22.9	23.3	23.4	23.8			22.9			23.3			23.4			23.8
1970	26.2	24.5	25.5	27.2	30.7			24.5			25.5			27.2			30.7
1971	32.1	31.0	31.3	33.0	34.1			31.0			31.3			33.0			34.1
1972	35.1	34.6	34.6	34.8	37.4			34.6			34.6			34.8			37.4
1973	39.2	37.6	38.4	41.0	41.1			37.6			38.4			41.0			41.1
1974	44.6	42.2	42.2	47.4	47.8			42.2			42.2			47.4			47.8
1975	50.6	49.4	49.4	52.1	52.6			49.4			49.4			52.1			52.6
1976	56.6	54.6	58.1	58.1	60.2			54.6			58.1			58.1			60.2
1977	64.0	64.0	64.3	64.6	67.7			64.0			64.3			64.6		67.8	67.7
1978	73.0	69.7	70.6	75.2	76.5		69.7			70.6			75.2			76.5	
1979	84.5	81.0	82.5	82.9	91.5		81.0			82.5			82.9			91.5	
1980	100.0	94.9	96.1	100.3	108.5		94.9			96.1			100.3			108.5	
1981	119.3	113.3	115.0	121.2	127.9		113.3			115.0			121.2			127.9	
1982	133.4	132.3	133.6	133.8	133.8		132.3			133.6			133.8			133.8	
1983	133.8	133.8	133.8	133.8	133.8		133.8			133.8			133.8			133.8	

Producer prices: manufactured goods (10) / Prix à la production : produits manufacturés (10)

1980 = 100

	Year	Q.1	Q.2	Q.3	Q.4	JAN	FEB	MAR	APR	MAY	JUN	JUL	AUG	SEP	OCT	NOV	DEC
1964																	
1965																	
1966																	
1967																	
1968																	
1969																	
1970																	
1971																	
1972																	
1973																	
1974																	
1975																	
1976																	
1977					66.7											66.7	
1978	71.6	68.3	70.0	73.1	74.9		68.3			70.0			73.1			74.9	
1979	83.6	77.9	81.3	85.6	89.7		77.9			81.3			85.6			89.7	
1980	100.0	93.5	98.3	102.4	105.7		93.5			98.3			102.4			105.7	
1981	116.0	109.9	113.3	118.5	122.1		109.9			113.3			118.5			122.1	
1982	130.4	125.9	129.9	132.7	133.3		125.9			129.9			132.7			133.3	
1983	135.7	134.1	134.5	136.5	137.5		134.1			134.5			136.5			137.5	

Producer prices: agricultural goods (10) — Prix à la production produits agricoles (10)

1980 = 100

	Year	Q.1	Q.2	Q.3	Q.4	JAN	FEB	MAR	APR	MAY	JUN	JUL	AUG	SEP	OCT	NOV	DEC
1964																	
1965																	
1966																	
1967																	
1968																	
1969																	
1970																	
1971																	
1972																	
1973																	
1974																	
1975																	
1976																	
1977					63.8											63.8	
1978	70.9	65.4	67.3	73.0	78.3		65.4			67.3			73.0			78.3	
1979	92.4	83.1	96.0	92.4	98.4		83.1			96.0			92.4			98.4	
1980	100.0	102.8	95.7	98.0	103.4		102.8			95.7			98.0			103.4	
1981	107.5	102.2	101.9	108.5	117.2		102.2			101.9			108.5			117.2	
1982	122.4	120.0	119.1	123.9	126.4		120.0			119.1			123.9			126.4	
1983	134.3	126.9	132.6	138.6	138.7		126.9			132.6			138.6			138.7	

Producer prices: input to manufacturing (10) — Prix à la production : produits de base (10) pour les industries manufacturières

1980 = 100

	Year	Q.1	Q.2	Q.3	Q.4	JAN	FEB	MAR	APR	MAY	JUN	JUL	AUG	SEP	OCT	NOV	DEC
1964																	
1965																	
1966																	
1967																	
1968																	
1969																	
1970																	
1971																	
1972																	
1973																	
1974																	
1975																	
1976																	
1977					64.3											64.3	
1978	68.7	65.8	67.5	69.6	71.9		65.8			67.5			69.6			71.9	
1979	82.1	74.8	80.2	84.3	89.2		74.8			80.2			84.3			89.2	
1980	100.0	94.5	98.1	101.8	105.7		94.5			98.1			101.8			105.7	
1981	115.2	108.4	111.9	117.9	122.6					111.9			117.9			122.6	
1982	131.5	126.0	130.5	134.1	135.3		126.0			130.5			134.1			135.3	
1983	139.0	136.0	138.6	140.2	141.3		136.0			138.6			140.2			141.3	

Consumer prices: all items (11) — Prix à la consommation : total (11)

1980 = 100

	Year	Q.1	Q.2	Q.3	Q.4	JAN	FEB	MAR	APR	MAY	JUN	JUL	AUG	SEP	OCT	NOV	DEC
1964	23.6	23.1	23.2	23.6	24.0		23.1			23.2			23.6			24.0	
1965	24.3	24.0	24.1	24.4	24.6		24.0			24.1			24.4			24.6	
1966	24.9	24.7	24.9	25.0	25.1		24.7			24.9			25.0			25.1	
1967	26.4	25.8	26.5	26.8	26.8		25.8			26.5			26.8			26.8	
1968	27.6	27.1	27.4	27.7	28.1		27.1			27.4			27.7			28.1	
1969	28.9	28.5	28.8	29.1	29.3		28.5			28.8			29.1			29.3	
1970	30.8	29.9	30.4	30.9	32.2		29.9			30.4			30.9			32.2	
1971	34.0	33.0	33.7	34.4	35.1		33.0			33.7			34.4			35.1	
1972	36.4	35.8	36.2	36.6	37.0		35.8			36.2			36.6			37.0	
1973	39.4	37.9	38.9	39.8	40.8		37.9			38.9			39.8			40.8	
1974	43.7	41.8	42.8	44.4	45.9		41.8			42.8			44.4			45.9	
1975	50.2	47.3	49.2	51.0	53.1		47.3			49.2			51.0			53.1	
1976	58.7	55.5	57.9	59.8	61.4		55.5			57.9			59.8			61.4	
1977	67.1	63.0	66.1	68.4	70.8		63.0			66.1			68.4			70.8	
1978	75.1	72.2	74.2	76.0	78.0		72.2			74.2			76.0			78.0	
1979	85.4	79.8	83.4	87.5	90.9		79.8			83.4			87.5			90.9	
1980	100.0	94.4	98.3	101.8	105.5		94.4			98.3			101.8			105.5	
1981	115.4	108.8	113.1	117.6	122.1		108.8			113.1			117.6			122.1	
1982	134.0	126.0	132.3	137.1	140.8		126.0			132.3			137.1			140.8	
1983	143.9	141.9	143.3	144.5	145.8		141.9			143.3			144.5			145.8	

NEW ZEALAND

Money supply (M1) (7)(12)(13) — Disponibilités monétaires (M1) (7)(12)(13)

million NZ dollars, end of period — millions de dollars néo-zélandais, fin de période

	Year	Q.1	Q.2	Q.3	Q.4	JAN	FEB	MAR	APR	MAY	JUN	JUL	AUG	SEP	OCT	NOV	DEC
1964																	
1965	766				766												766
1966	776	703	732	704	776			703			732			704			776
1967	762	706	695	668	762			706			695			668			762
1968	756	685	702	690	756			685			702			690			756
1969	777	713	731	723	777			713			731			723			777
1970	838	764	788	765	838			764			788			765			838
1971	920	802	833	821	920			802			833			821			920
1972	1165	908	959	978	1165			908			959			978			1165
1973	1422	1135	1244	1270	1422			1135			1244			1270			1422
1974	1436	1298	1351	1285	1436			1298			1351			1285			1436
1975	1580	1332	1424	1407	1580			1332			1424			1407			1580
1976	1792	1596	1655	1548	1792			1596			1655			1548			1792
1977	1820	1690	1692	1586	1820			1690	1708	1706	1692	1650	1711	1586	1620	1690	1820
1978	2189	1720	1843	1834	2189	1716	1851	1720	1791	1844	1843	1836	1908	1834	1960	1995	2189
1979	2371	2035	2072	2005	2371	2074	2223	2035	2113	2090	2072	2061	2075	2005	2030	2090	2371
1980	2482	2147	2294	2184	2482	2160	2310	2147	2232	2286	2294	2260	2320	2184	2202	2360	2482
1981	2863	2452	2650	2570	2863	2420	2710	2452	2530	2600	2650	2610	2650	2570	2550	2690	2863
1982	3030	2881	2906	2643	3030	2760	2941	2881	2785	2845	2906	2834	2840	2643	2675	2756	3030
1983	3498	3002	2940	2955	3498	2865	3036	3002	2980	3011	2940	2919	3057	2955	3036	3206	3498

M1 plus quasi-money (7)(12)(13) — M1 plus quasi-monnaie (7)(12)(13)

million NZ dollars, end of period — millions de dollars néo-zélandais, fin de période

	Year	Q.1	Q.2	Q.3	Q.4	JAN	FEB	MAR	APR	MAY	JUN	JUL	AUG	SEP	OCT	NOV	DEC
1964																	
1965	2298				2298												2298
1966	2435	2243	2297	2315	2435			2243			2297			2315			2435
1967	2510	2355	2378	2369	2510			2355			2378			2369			2510
1968	2666	2445	2515	2540	2666			2445			2515			2540			2666
1969	2905	2622	2708	2758	2905			2622			2708			2758			2905
1970	3135	2861	2956	2997	3135			2861			2956			2997			3135
1971	3380	3077	3156	3197	3380			3077			3156			3197			3380
1972	4100	3395	3571	3712	4100			3395			3571			3712			4100
1973	4976	4183	4513	4693	4976			4183			4513			4693			4976
1974	5110	4838	4920	4878	5110			4838			4920			4878			5110
1975	5734	4971	5206	5350	5734			4971			5206			5350			5734
1976	6767	5818	6223	6284	6767			5818			6223			6284			6767
1977	7613	6726	7041	7123	7613			6726	6920	6980	7041	7100	7220	7123	7190	7340	7613
1978	9238	7621	8159	8509	9238	7550	7779	7621	7799	7994	8159	8323	8492	8509	8778	8934	9238
1979	10999	9296	9743	10142	10999	9216	9487	9296	9296	9608	9743	9973	10135	10142	10340	10520	10999
1980	12402	10800	11388	11667	12402	10970	11180	10800	11010	11230	11388	11556	11720	11667	11730	11980	12402
1981	14448	12336	13310	13750	14448	12340	12770	12336	12646	13010	13310	13600	13810	13750	13869	14070	14448
1982	16004	14401	15001	14984	16004	14456	14763	14401	14699	14947	15001	15055	15144	14984	15086	15389	16004
1983	17954	16107	16254	16814	17954	16151	16615	16107	16134	16028	16254	16635	16844	16814	16917	17344	17954

Credit to private sector: (7)(13)(14) — Crédits au secteur privé : (7)(13)(14)

commercial banks — banques commerciales

million NZ dollars, end of period — millions de dollars néo-zélandais, fin de période

	Year	Q.1	Q.2	Q.3	Q.4	JAN	FEB	MAR	APR	MAY	JUN	JUL	AUG	SEP	OCT	NOV	DEC
1964	401	465	425	412	401			465			425			412			401
1965	421	505	471	451	421			505			471			451			421
1966	434	528	499	472	434			528			499			472			434
1967	418	527	506	469	418			527			506			469			418
1968	494	510	506	482	494			510			506			482			494
1969	542	578	575	544	542			578			575			544			542
1970	635	669	654	658	635			669			654			658			635
1971	665	766	740	701	665			766			740			701			665
1972	750	803	770	758	750			803			770			758			750
1973	1151	952	993	1049	1151			952			993			1049			1151
1974	1475	1401	1471	1535	1475			1401			1471			1535			1475
1975	1582	1604	1553	1562	1582			1604			1553			1562			1582
1976	1933	1740	1741	1868	1933			1740			1741			1868			1933
1977	2278	2289	2260	2342	2278			2289			2260			2342			2278
1978	2792	2487	2459	2670	2792	2282	2314	2487	2513	2540	2459	2549	2536	2670	2698	2762	2792
1979	3439	3081	3226	3378	3439	2863	2867	3081	3165	3188	3226	3277	3232	3378	3510	3440	3439
1980	3966	3670	3628	3761	3966	3480	3460	3670	3770	3630	3628	3620	3680	3761	3910	3915	3966
1981	5018	4325	4480	5225	5018	4035	4125	4325	4410	4430	4480	4610	4635	5225	5100	4995	5018
1982	5553	5822	5720	5828	5553	5141	5230	5822	5595	5592	5720	5690	5720	5828	5904	5730	5553
1983	6223	5798	5757	5820	6223	5614	5483	5798	5852	5698	5757	5749	5618	5820	5940	6148	6223

Money supply (M1) (7)(12)(13)

million NZ dollars, end of period

Adjusted - Corrigé *

Disponibilités monétaires (M1) (7)(12)(13)

millions de dollars néo-zélandais, fin de période

	Year	Q.1	Q.2	Q.3	Q.4	JAN	FEB	MAR	APR	MAY	JUN	JUL	AUG	SEP	OCT	NOV	DEC
1964																	
1965					720												720
1966		718	736	731	732			718			736			731			732
1967		720	698	693	721			720			698			693			721
1968		698	704	715	717			698			704			715			717
1969		725	733	749	739			725			733			749			739
1970		777	790	792	796			777			790			792			796
1971		816	833	852	873			816			833			852			873
1972		925	958	1015	1102			925			958			1015			1102
1973		1159	1240	1324	1341			1159			1240			1324			1341
1974		1327	1344	1346	1351			1327			1344			1346			1351
1975		1362	1416	1481	1482			1362			1416			1481			1482
1976		1629	1647	1636	1678			1629			1647			1636			1678
1977		1719	1693	1683	1702			1719	1698	1689	1693	1682	1718	1683	1695	1702	1702
1978		1756	1843	1947	2048	1714	1736	1756	1780	1826	1843	1872	1915	1947	2052	2007	2048
1979		2077	2068	2126	2218	2072	2083	2077	2105	2067	2068	2103	2085	2126	2126	2103	2218
1980		2193	2287	2314	2322	2160	2165	2193	2221	2261	2287	2301	2334	2314	2308	2377	2322
1981		2505	2642	2723	2678	2420	2540	2505	2517	2572	2642	2658	2669	2723	2673	2709	2678
1982		2943	2897	2800	2834	2760	2759	2943	2771	2814	2897	2886	2860	2800	2804	2775	2834
1983		3066	2931	3130	3272	2865	2848	3066	2965	2978	2931	2973	3119	3130	3182	3229	3272

M1 plus quasi-money (7)(12)(13)

million NZ dollars, end of period

Adjusted - Corrigé *

M1 plus quasi-monnaie (7)(12)(13)

millions de dollars néo-zélandais, fin de période

	Year	Q.1	Q.2	Q.3	Q.4	JAN	FEB	MAR	APR	MAY	JUN	JUL	AUG	SEP	OCT	NOV	DEC
1964																	
1965					2244												2244
1966		2270	2304	2336	2378			2270			2304			2336			2378
1967		2383	2386	2391	2451			2383			2386			2391			2451
1968		2475	2523	2563	2606			2475			2523			2563			2606
1969		2653	2716	2780	2840			2653			2716			2780			2840
1970		2896	2962	3022	3065			2896			2962			3022			3065
1971		3118	3162	3223	3304			3118			3162			3223			3304
1972		3440	3575	3746	4008			3440			3575			3746			4008
1973		4242	4513	4735	4859			4242			4513			4735			4859
1974		4912	4920	4927	4990			4912			4920			4927			4990
1975		5047	5200	5404	5600			5047			5200			5404			5600
1976		5906	6216	6347	6602			5906			6216			6347			6602
1977		6828	7063	7195	7427			6828	7025	7015	7063	7093	7177	7195	7248	7318	7427
1978		7785	8184	8595	9013	7505	7627	7785	7910	8034	8184	8306	8442	8595	8849	8907	9013
1979		9505	9772	10244	10731	9161	9292	9505	9438	9666	9772	9953	10075	10244	10423	10489	10731
1980		11043	11411	11773	12100	10905	10950	11043	11178	11298	11411	11521	11650	11773	11825	11944	12100
1981		12626	13350	13889	14109	12266	12507	12626	12839	13089	13350	13573	13741	13889	13981	14042	14109
1982		14740	15046	15135	15629	14370	14459	14740	14923	15037	15046	15025	15069	15135	15208	15358	15629
1983		16486	16303	16984	17533	16055	16273	16486	16380	16125	16303	16602	16760	16984	17053	17309	17533

Credit to private sector: (7)(13)(14)

other credit institutions

million NZ dollars, end of period

Crédits au secteur privé : (7)(13)(14)

autres institutions de crédit

millions de dollars néo-zélandais, fin de période

	Year	Q.1	Q.2	Q.3	Q.4	JAN	FEB	MAR	APR	MAY	JUN	JUL	AUG	SEP	OCT	NOV	DEC
1964	268	242	242	262	268			242			242			262			268
1965	328	280	286	314	328			280			286			314			328
1966	362	328	319	345	362			328			319			345			362
1967	370	349	342	359	370			349			342			359			370
1968	389	357	354	379	389			357			354			379			389
1969	436	396	393	422	436			396			393			422			436
1970	524	458	454	494	524			458			454			494			524
1971	605	540	532	578	605			540			532			578			605
1972	713	613	627	669	713			613			627			669			713
1973	917	746	777	868	917			746			777			868			917
1974	1024	962	980	1023	1024			962			980			1023			1024
1975	1192	1039	1050	1130	1192			1039			1050			1130			1192
1976	1474	1225	1247	1358	1474			1225			1247			1358			1474
1977	1776	1527	1567	1666	1776			1527			1567			1666			1776
1978	2267	1867	1950	2089	2267	1810	1820	1867	1894	1925	1950	1986	2027	2089	2140	2207	2267
1979	2796	2361	2461	2603	2796	2290	2337	2361	2389	2427	2461	2500	2549	2603	2670	2720	2796
1980	3418	2938	3008	3216	3418	2840	2880	2938	2990	3020	3008	3080	3105	3216	3285	3345	3418
1981	4397	3633	3790	4110	4397	3470	3520	3633	3670	3725	3790	3875	3985	4110	4120	4280	4397
1982	4854	4602	4608	4814	4854	4436	4473	4602	4556	4560	4608	4666	4727	4814	4846	4843	4854
1983	5642	4967	4914	5282	5642	4876	4930	4967	4944	4926	4914	4966	5109	5282	5393	5512	5642

* Adjusted by the O.E.C.D.

* Corrigé par l'O.C.D.E.

NEW ZEALAND

Instalment credit outstanding (15)
million NZ dollars, end of period

Crédits remboursables par tranches : en cours (15)
millions de dollars néo-zélandais, fin de période

	Year	Q.1	Q.2	Q.3	Q.4	JAN	FEB	MAR	APR	MAY	JUN	JUL	AUG	SEP	OCT	NOV	DEC
1964	52.4	48.2	47.8	49.0	52.4			48.2			47.8			49.0			52.4
1965	61.8	54.6	55.4	56.8	61.8			54.6			55.4			56.8			61.8
1966	66.0	61.7	62.7	64.3	66.0			61.7			62.7			64.3			66.0
1967	59.0	62.4	62.4	58.1	59.0			62.4			62.4			58.1			59.0
1968	59.0	57.1	56.7	58.4	59.0			57.1			56.7			58.4			59.0
1969	84.9	66.7	74.6	73.7	84.9			66.7			74.6			73.7			84.9
1970	108.5	88.4	94.6	97.3	108.5			88.4			94.6			97.3			108.5
1971	131.0	112.8	115.4	122.9	131.0			112.8			115.4			122.9			131.0
1972	153.4	129.9	143.8	140.3	153.4			129.9			143.8			140.3			153.4
1973	192.9	158.7	157.7	177.9	192.9			158.7			157.7			177.9			192.9
1974	190.8	192.6	195.8	195.5	190.8			192.6			195.8			195.5			190.8
1975	220.1	192.5	185.5	200.2	220.1			192.5			185.5			200.2			220.1
1976	297.5	224.0	226.6	234.3	297.5			224.0			226.6			234.3			297.5
1977	434.8	284.2	349.8	366.5	434.8			284.2			349.8			366.5			434.8
1978	505.8	450.2	432.9	506.7	505.8			450.2			432.9			506.7			505.8
1979	621.8	542.6	558.7	580.7	621.8			542.6			558.7			580.7			621.8
1980	724.0	649.4	684.3	680.1	724.0			649.4			684.3			680.1			724.0
1981	890.3	763.8	790.3	848.9	890.3			763.8			790.3			848.9			890.3
1982	1089.8	945.9	1010.0	1060.5	1089.8			945.9			1010.0			1060.5			1089.8
1983	1273.2	1109.9	1104.6	1125.2	1273.2			1109.9			1104.6			1125.2			1273.2

Yield of long-term Government bonds (16)
per cent per annum, end of period

Rendement des bons d'État à long terme (16)
pourcentage par an, fin de période

	Year	Q.1	Q.2	Q.3	Q.4	JAN	FEB	MAR	APR	MAY	JUN	JUL	AUG	SEP	OCT	NOV	DEC
1964	5.03	5.12	5.07	5.02	5.03	5.11	5.10	5.12	5.14	5.11	5.07	5.03	5.01	5.02	5.01	5.02	5.03
1965	5.12	5.08	5.13	5.11	5.12	5.03	5.04	5.08	5.10	5.11	5.13	5.12	5.12	5.11	5.12	5.12	5.12
1966	5.36	5.16	5.28	5.38	5.36	5.13	5.14	5.16	5.19	5.25	5.28	5.38	5.38	5.38	5.37	5.35	5.36
1967	5.54	5.49	5.52	5.53	5.54	5.36	5.43	5.49	5.50	5.51	5.52	5.53	5.53	5.53	5.55	5.54	5.54
1968	5.53	5.54	5.53	5.50	5.53	5.53	5.53	5.54	5.55	5.54	5.53	5.52	5.50	5.50	5.53	5.54	5.53
1969	5.53	5.56	5.55	5.54	5.53	5.54	5.55	5.56	5.55	5.55	5.55	5.55	5.55	5.54	5.54	5.53	5.53
1970	5.49	5.54	5.50	5.49	5.49	5.54	5.53	5.54	5.55	5.53	5.50	5.47	5.47	5.49	5.49	5.49	5.49
1971	5.53	5.51	5.51	5.52	5.53	5.51	5.51	5.51	5.51	5.51	5.51	5.52	5.53	5.52	5.52	5.52	5.53
1972	5.54	5.53	5.52	5.54	5.54	5.52	5.53	5.53	5.53	5.52	5.52	5.45	5.54	5.54	5.52	5.53	5.54
1973	6.08	5.55	5.66	6.03	6.08	5.54	5.53	5.55	5.55	5.55	5.66	5.99	6.01	6.03	6.02	6.05	6.08
1974	6.11	6.04	6.14	6.08	6.11	6.06	6.04	6.04	6.05	6.05	6.14	6.12	6.09	6.08	6.10	6.11	6.11
1975	6.66	6.10	6.11	6.63	6.66	6.11	6.11	6.10	6.10	6.10	6.11	6.10	6.63	6.63	6.63	6.64	6.66
1976	8.70	8.60	8.60	8.58	8.70	6.92	6.92	8.60	8.60	8.60	8.60	8.58	8.58	8.58	8.72	8.70	8.70
1977	10.00	8.71	8.53	..	10.00	8.70	8.70	8.71	8.71	8.71	8.53	8.53	10.04	..	10.33	9.92	10.00
1978	10.02	10.00	9.99	9.97	10.02	10.00	9.98	10.00	9.99	9.99	9.99	9.79	9.99	9.97	10.02	10.02	10.02
1979	12.98	10.02	12.64	..	12.98	10.10	10.05	10.02	12.64	12.95	12.64	12.08	12.35	..	13.00	12.96	12.98
1980	12.99	13.57	13.49	12.98	12.99	13.44	13.45	13.57	13.47	13.44	13.49	13.40	13.25	12.98	12.96	12.96	12.99
1981	12.55	12.88	12.90	12.77	12.55	12.81	12.97	12.88	12.85	12.85	12.90	12.90	13.02	12.77	12.57	12.92	12.55
1982	12.84	12.98	12.99	12.94	12.84	12.78	12.78	12.98	12.92	12.97	12.99	12.97	12.73	12.94	12.82	13.00	12.84
1983	10.50	12.69	13.59	10.13	10.50	12.77	12.95	12.69	13.95	14.00	13.59	14.02	10.41	10.13	10.57	10.61	10.50

Share prices: all shares (RBNZ) (17)
1980 = 100

Cours des actions : ensemble des actions (RBNZ) (17)
1980 = 100

	Year	Q.1	Q.2	Q.3	Q.4	JAN	FEB	MAR	APR	MAY	JUN	JUL	AUG	SEP	OCT	NOV	DEC
1964																	
1965																	
1966																	
1967	55	56	55	55	53	58	55	55	54	56	56	57	55	54	53	53	54
1968	65	56	64	69	73	53	55	58	61	64	66	66	69	72	72	73	74
1969	81	77	81	82	85	77	78	76	81	82	81	82	81	83	85	85	85
1970	85	89	86	85	80	89	89	88	88	84	86	86	85	85	82	80	79
1971	75	77	76	74	73	78	78	75	76	76	77	76	73	72	73	72	73
1972	79	75	77	79	83	77	75	74	74	77	79	79	80	80	81	82	86
1973	94	91	96	99	89	90	90	93	93	95	98	102	100	96	93	90	85
1974	78	89	89	73	63	87	87	92	92	91	84	75	74	70	63	62	64
1975	72	71	78	69	72	66	72	74	77	80	78	70	68	69	70	72	74
1976	79	78	77	82	78	76	79	79	76	76	78	81	83	83	80	79	75
1977	70	75	73	66	64	75	74	75	75	74	71	67	66	66	65	65	63
1978	71	67	71	73	72	65	67	68	70	71	73	74	73	72	72	71	72
1979	77	73	75	79	83	73	72	74	76	74	75	76	79	81	83	84	81
1980	100	85	94	102	119	83	84	87	91	95	96	100	103	104	109	123	125
1981	142	131	149	146	143	128	131	133	143	150	154	147	146	146	139	142	147
1982	139	152	140	136	129	153	155	148	139	140	140	136	138	135	135	128	124
1983	184	140	169	198	230	130	139	150	160	170	176	188	201	205	213	233	244

U.S. dollar exchange rate: spot / Taux de change du dollar É.-U. : au comptant

cents per NZ dollar, end of period / cents par dollar néo-zélandais, fin de période

	Year	Q.1	Q.2	Q.3	Q.4	JAN	FEB	MAR	APR	MAY	JUN	JUL	AUG	SEP	OCT	NOV	DEC
1964	138.5	138.9	138.6	138.1	138.5	138.9	138.9	138.9	139.0	138.9	138.6	138.4	138.2	138.1	138.2	138.5	138.5
1965	139.1	138.6	138.5	139.0	139.1	138.6	138.7	138.6	138.9	138.6	138.5	138.6	138.5	139.0	139.2	139.1	139.1
1966	138.5	138.7	138.5	138.5	138.5	139.2	139.0	138.7	138.7	138.6	138.5	138.5	138.4	138.5	138.5	138.5	138.5
1967	112.3	138.8	138.5	138.2	112.3	138.7	138.6	138.8	138.9	138.7	138.5	138.3	138.3	138.2	138.1	112.9	112.3
1968	111.2	111.9	111.1	111.4	111.2	112.5	112.2	111.9	111.8	111.2	111.1	111.7	111.2	111.4	111.5	111.3	111.2
1969	112.0	111.6	111.5	112.1	112.0	111.5	111.6	111.6	111.3	111.4	111.5	111.5	111.1	111.1	111.8	111.8	112.0
1970	111.6	112.2	111.8	111.4	111.6	112.0	112.3	112.2	112.2	112.0	111.8	111.5	111.2	111.4	111.5	111.5	111.6
1971	119.5	112.7	112.8	115.9	119.5	112.7	112.8	112.7	112.8	112.8	112.8	113.4	115.8	115.9	116.4	116.4	119.5
1972	119.5	119.5	119.5	119.5	119.5	119.5	119.5	119.5	119.5	119.5	119.5	119.5	119.5	119.5	119.5	119.5	119.5
1973	142.8	132.7	132.7	147.8	142.8	119.5	132.7	132.7	132.7	132.7	132.7	135.2	133.8	147.8	148.0	144.4	142.8
1974	131.6	146.7	145.4	130.2	131.6	139.5	142.2	146.7	146.8	145.6	145.4	144.7	142.4	130.2	130.4	130.7	131.6
1975	104.4	134.3	129.6	104.6	104.4	132.9	135.4	134.3	132.7	132.2	129.6	126.9	106.7	104.6	105.8	104.5	104.4
1976	95.0	102.3	99.2	97.6	95.0	104.7	104.7	102.3	100.5	98.5	99.2	99.9	100.2	97.6	94.6	90.6	95.0
1977	102.0	96.1	96.3	97.1	102.0	95.1	95.6	96.1	96.3	96.2	96.8	97.5	97.0	97.1	98.8	99.5	102.0
1978	106.7	102.3	103.1	106.2	106.7	102.3	102.3	102.3	101.5	101.1	103.1	104.9	105.2	106.2	110.1	104.9	106.7
1979	98.6	105.5	101.1	101.1	98.6	105.6	105.6	105.5	104.3	104.2	101.1	102.2	101.3	101.1	96.7	97.5	98.6
1980	96.2	94.3	98.9	97.9	96.2	98.4	97.3	94.3	96.7	98.4	98.9	97.6	98.2	97.9	97.8	96.0	96.2
1981	82.4	92.0	85.3	81.9	82.4	95.3	92.3	92.0	89.9	87.4	85.3	82.9	83.1	81.9	82.1	84.2	82.4
1982	73.3	76.7	74.3	71.8	73.3	80.4	78.7	76.7	77.2	76.1	74.3	73.7	72.6	71.8	70.9	71.8	73.3
1983	65.5	65.1	65.5	65.7	65.5	72.0	71.9	65.1	66.0	66.4	65.5	65.4	65.0	65.7	66.3	65.7	65.5

Official reserves excluding gold / Réserves officielles, or exclu

million SDR's, end of period / millions de DTS, fin de période

	Year	Q.1	Q.2	Q.3	Q.4	JAN	FEB	MAR	APR	MAY	JUN	JUL	AUG	SEP	OCT	NOV	DEC
1964																	
1965																	
1966																	
1967	218	-	-	196	218	-	-	-	-	-	-	-	-	196	183	196	218
1968	161	246	254	228	161	235	242	246	270	262	254	263	274	228	229	213	161
1969	209	201	251	223	209	156	179	201	237	254	251	240	226	223	240	250	209
1970	257	252	267	287	257	231	220	252	260	269	267	285	271	287	291	282	257
1971	453	298	409	487	453	276	283	298	358	393	409	448	452	487	484	481	453
1972	766	610	756	769	766	481	530	610	668	711	756	763	779	769	807	753	766
1973	866	882	1117	1051	866	846	862	882	967	1093	1117	1083	1066	1051	982	933	866
1974	522	867	613	586	522	866	842	867	858	745	613	604	523	586	540	550	522
1975	365	546	493	392	365	545	529	546	478	473	493	495	489	392	428	495	365
1976	422	502	378	381	422	358	474	502	459	426	378	485	409	381	387	334	422
1977	364	481	444	467	364	417	440	481	477	567	444	419	401	467	447	438	364
1978	346	673	647	487	346	373	500	673	640	664	647	609	521	487	479	380	346
1979	342	470	542	478	342	490	452	470	462	630	542	505	482	478	525	461	342
1980	276	378	246	269	276	356	393	378	373	301	246	402	315	269	440	291	276
1981	579	338	303	302	579	354	334	338	[illegible]	329	303	299	326	302	432	277	579
1982	576	367	367	467	576	396	375	367	535	334	367	438	447	467	660	522	576
1983	743	996	818	603	743	723	815	996	1079	790	818	778	711	603	641	701	743

Net foreign position: commercial banks / Position extérieure nette : banques commerciales

million NZ dollars, end of period / millions de dollars néo-zélandais, fin de période

	Year	Q.1	Q.2	Q.3	Q.4	JAN	FEB	MAR	APR	MAY	JUN	JUL	AUG	SEP	OCT	NOV	DEC
1964	50	81	67	45	50	58	75	81	81	76	67	67	55	45	51	49	50
1965	44	61	44	43	44	58	63	61	40	53	44	43	46	43	38	38	44
1966	32	47	51	35	32	39	41	47	49	53	51	38	35	35	31	32	32
1967	37	52	38	37	37	32	38	52	50	36	38	42	39	37	34	34	37
1968	56	67	76	55	56	46	67	67	68	65	76	72	59	56	55	58	56
1969	56	39	87	70	56	66	81	89	90	85	87	..	77	70	67	55	56
1970	63	91	89	78	63	67	88	91	88	85	89	77	74	78	66	62	63
1971	57	88	76	54	57	76	80	88	87	91	76	95	81	54	71	64	57
1972	59	67	64	73	59	63	84	67	69	63	64	76	73	73	77	73	59
1973	58	99	94	60	58	70	81	99	109	97	94	76	71	60	67	48	58
1974	62	48	48	43	62	50	54	48	52	49	48	57	42	43	50	51	62
1975	89	62	66	72	89	64	67	62	60	62	66	67	78	72	79	76	89
1976	111	98	125	110	111	89	94	98	93	88	125	111	112	110	104	119	111
1977	142	130	146	115	142	114	115	130	135	130	146	138	126	115	122	144	142
1978	193	154	162	163	193	146	145	154	161	174	162	158	163	163	175	172	193
1979	224	219	230	209	224	184	231	219	217	225	230	198	176	209	199	183	224
1980	295	252	311	296	295	209	261	252	252	274	311	280	255	296	237	311	295
1981	338	322	334	287	338	283	249	322	332	334	334	348	363	287	296	299	338
1982	301	273	411	267	301	255	360	273	320	384	411	326	312	267	335	275	301
1983		243	245	257		350	220	243	240	380	245	320	271	257			

NEW ZEALAND

Imports c.i.f. (18) / Importations c.a.f. (18)

million NZ dollars, monthly averages / millions de dollars néo-zélandais, moyennes mensuelles

	Year	Q.1	Q.2	Q.3	Q.4	JAN	FEB	MAR	APR	MAY	JUN	JUL	AUG	SEP	OCT	NOV	DEC
1964	58	56	54	61	59	55	57	55	54	52	57	68	59	57	58	62	58
1965	63	55	60	72	65	56	51	59	60	57	65	72	67	76	63	75	57
1966	66	65	65	68	65	61	69	65	55	66	74	58	77	69	65	67	61
1967	58	65	64	57	46	65	64	65	58	60	74	53	63	57	47	47	44
1968	67	61	58	73	74	62	65	56	51	62	63	78	68	74	79	73	69
1969	75	67	69	86	76	79	60	62	61	77	69	91	74	93	84	69	76
1970	93	75	99	98	100	78	65	81	100	99	96	99	96	99	101	103	95
1971	99	94	95	109	98	84	89	108	95	91	98	116	103	107	93	107	95
1972	106	101	104	102	118	94	98	112	97	113	100	101	113	92	114	128	111
1973	133	117	119	148	147	119	108	123	93	127	132	163	141	141	152	152	137
1974	218	164	212	235	260	172	159	162	176	232	228	228	235	244	252	266	261
1975	218	215	203	201	252	216	238	190	206	188	215	199	189	216	256	251	250
1976	273	268	255	275	293	229	198	376	260	247	257	277	242	306	255	353	272
1977	289	286	299	306	264	247	293	320	268	303	324	281	331	304	272	260	260
1978	280	249	272	276	323	227	250	269	233	259	324	233	332	264	391	317	262
1979	372	304	372	382	431	313	304	296	315	385	415	318	449	379	477	429	385
1980	468	455	444	489	485	411	503	452	405	441	484	510	428	529	472	469	513
1981	553	441	577	580	614	417	382	526	446	673	613	558	575	607	601	597	642
1982	650	596	699	697	609	495	604	690	589	677	729	688	756	647	600	624	602
1983	666	600	627	724	713	562	562	675	531	701	649	706	742	724	646	834	660

Exports f.o.b. (18) / Exportations f.o.b. (18)

million NZ dollars, monthly averages / millions de dollars néo-zélandais, moyennes mensuelles

	Year	Q.1	Q.2	Q.3	Q.4	JAN	FEB	MAR	APR	MAY	JUN	JUL	AUG	SEP	OCT	NOV	DEC
1964	64	76	77	47	58	76	86	64	91	79	60	42	56	45	50	52	72
1965	60	71	70	45	56	58	78	77	73	83	54	34	43	57	44	62	63
1966	65	77	76	55	51	79	75	76	72	73	84	57	52	55	46	48	58
1967	60	72	64	49	56	58	90	69	63	68	62	55	55	36	44	68	58
1968	75	79	83	64	75	65	86	87	84	75	89	60	79	53	72	70	82
1969	90	99	92	83	87	91	114	91	104	83	89	87	78	85	75	93	91
1970	91	103	90	83	89	89	105	114	80	85	105	91	85	72	77	76	115
1971	100	97	108	104	91	75	132	84	120	111	93	115	123	75	89	76	106
1972	125	128	136	115	121	123	146	114	143	130	136	112	107	127	102	111	149
1973	159	183	177	140	138	137	190	221	158	183	192	124	155	141	146	113	155
1974	145	161	157	131	129	144	164	175	182	141	149	125	152	115	127	118	143
1975	150	120	158	144	177	115	130	114	164	155	154	141	141	150	179	172	180
1976	235	194	276	221	248	157	199	225	221	226	379	176	260	229	219	249	275
1977	275	279	324	252	244	284	286	266	319	308	347	277	249	229	232	210	290
1978	300	287	321	268	326	252	300	309	334	244	384	264	279	261	319	354	304
1979	384	367	396	347	426	319	373	410	361	418	408	318	369	353	397	439	443
1980	464	464	480	436	476	386	479	528	463	524	455	481	382	445	415	493	520
1981	529	470	621	487	537	520	381	508	660	576	627	522	462	476	494	560	556
1982	611	578	642	575	647	498	608	630	553	738	637	665	490	571	570	659	712
1983	658	647	695	647	642	494	640	808	576	746	764	652	695	592	591	659	674

Trade balance (f.o.b. — c.i.f.) (18) / Balance commerciale (f.o.b. — c.a.f.) (18)

million NZ dollars, monthly averages / millions de dollars néo-zélandais, moyennes mensuelles

	Year	Q.1	Q.2	Q.3	Q.4	JAN	FEB	MAR	APR	MAY	JUN	JUL	AUG	SEP	OCT	NOV	DEC
1964	7	20	22	-14	-1	21	29	9	37	28	3	-27	-3	-12	-7	-10	14
1965	-3	16	9	-27	-9	2	27	18	13	26	-11	-39	-24	-19	-19	-13	7
1966	-1	12	11	-14	-14	19	6	11	16	7	10	-1	-25	-14	-20	-19	-3
1967	3	8	1	-9	10	-7	27	4	5	8	-12	2	-8	-20	-3	21	13
1968	9	18	24	-9	1	3	21	31	34	13	26	-18	11	-21	-8	-3	13
1969	15	32	23	-3	10	12	54	29	43	6	20	-4	4	-8	-9	25	15
1970	-2	28	-9	-15	-10	11	40	33	-21	-14	9	-8	-11	-27	-24	-27	20
1971	1	3	13	-5	-8	-9	43	-24	26	20	-5	-1	19	-32	-4	-31	11
1972	19	26	33	13	3	29	48	2	45	17	36	11	-5	34	-11	-18	38
1973	27	66	58	-8	-9	18	82	98	60	56	59	-39	14	-0	-6	-39	18
1974	-73	-3	-55	-105	-130	-28	5	13	6	-91	-80	-103	-82	-129	-125	-148	-118
1975	-68	-94	-45	-57	-75	-100	-107	-76	-42	-33	-61	-58	-48	-66	-77	-80	-70
1976	-38	-74	21	-54	-45	-72	1	-151	-38	-19	121	-102	18	-77	-35	-104	3
1977	-14	-8	26	-54	-20	37	-7	-54	50	4	22	-5	-82	-75	-40	-50	30
1978	20	39	49	-8	2	24	51	41	102	-15	60	32	-53	-4	-72	37	42
1979	12	63	24	-35	-4	6	69	114	46	32	-7	0	-79	-27	-81	10	58
1980	-4	9	37	-53	-9	-25	-24	76	58	82	-30	-29	-46	-33	-58	24	7
1981	-24	28	44	-93	-77	103	-1	-18	215	-97	14	-36	-113	-130	-107	-37	-86
1982	-39	-18	-56	-121	38	3	4	-61	-137	61	-92	-23	-266	-75	-31	35	110
1983	-8	48	68	-78	-72	-68	78	133	45	45	114	-54	-47	-131	-55	-175	14

Imports c.i.f. (18) — Importations c.a.f. (18)

million NZ dollars, monthly averages — Adjusted - Corrigé * — millions de dollars néo-zélandais, moyennes mensuelles

Year	Q.1	Q.2	Q.3	Q.4	JAN	FEB	MAR	APR	MAY	JUN	JUL	AUG	SEP	OCT	NOV	DEC
1964	57	56	57	60	57	58	58	57	55	55	59	59	53	58	60	60
1965	58	62	66	66	61	52	60	65	61	62	64	64	70	67	71	62
1966	66	67	63	67	64	71	64	64	68	70	54	71	64	69	65	68
1967	66	66	53	48	65	66	67	68	59	71	50	56	55	46	46	52
1968	62	60	68	75	59	65	62	55	60	65	68	65	70	74	76	76
1969	70	71	79	78	77	65	66	66	75	71	78	76	84	81	73	79
1970	77	101	92	99	79	72	81	107	102	95	88	97	91	99	104	96
1971	98	96	103	98	92	98	105	101	92	96	108	100	99	97	100	97
1972	104	105	99	117	102	101	109	112	107	97	101	104	92	111	117	122
1973	120	120	147	142	121	116	123	108	119	133	159	137	144	144	138	145
1974	171	215	232	251	173	166	173	186	228	231	220	235	242	232	257	263
1975	224	205	198	245	226	245	202	217	191	208	191	200	203	242	249	244
1976	273	257	269	286	250	200	369	275	264	232	286	235	287	259	327	272
1977	295	299	302	262	284	298	304	299	310	287	312	306	289	271	245	269
1978	256	270	271	321	252	256	260	267	255	287	254	294	266	371	302	290
1979	315	369	374	426	339	316	291	356	366	386	329	405	390	443	418	418
1980	472	441	471	483	436	515	464	442	435	447	493	418	503	444	492	513
1981	463	575	558	606	472	404	512	488	692	544	544	552	579	585	609	624
1982	629	702	660	610	598	641	649	772	674	660	676	696	609	627	604	600
1983	629	627	695	716	673	597	618	631	661	588	731	664	691	667	809	672

Exports f.o.b. (18) — Exportations f.o.b. (18)

million NZ dollars, monthly averages — Adjusted - Corrigé * — millions de dollars néo-zélandais, moyennes mensuelles

Year	Q.1	Q.2	Q.3	Q.4	JAN	FEB	MAR	APR	MAY	JUN	JUL	AUG	SEP	OCT	NOV	DEC
1964	64	66	59	65	72	62	58	68	72	57	52	67	57	62	67	67
1965	62	60	54	66	58	63	65	60	68	52	40	55	67	60	75	62
1966	65	67	68	56	72	61	63	61	66	73	72	62	69	58	56	56
1967	64	57	56	63	59	74	59	53	61	58	62	61	46	59	70	61
1968	69	75	73	84	63	64	81	73	71	80	66	85	67	87	79	86
1969	88	83	97	96	91	92	80	90	77	82	91	91	108	92	106	88
1970	95	82	93	96	87	83	114	63	87	97	97	90	92	88	91	107
1971	89	97	115	102	83	105	80	102	103	87	118	141	85	111	95	101
1972	117	123	127	134	125	118	108	119	124	126	116	112	152	122	129	151
1973	167	160	157	148	148	159	195	135	169	177	145	163	162	161	140	142
1974	155	141	142	140	153	144	168	157	134	133	141	150	134	133	140	146
1975	115	142	161	186	127	120	99	145	142	140	157	153	175	194	189	174
1976	187	249	240	263	166	192	203	195	206	345	192	282	248	250	268	272
1977	270	291	287	247	300	273	236	287	303	284	331	261	269	241	223	276
1978	287	288	294	342	291	285	285	303	222	338	283	294	304	369	335	323
1979	353	357	394	434	347	349	361	345	365	359	366	415	400	437	443	423
1980	447	438	491	482	409	468	464	464	445	405	494	467	511	457	478	512
1981	465	573	537	535	550	359	486	621	536	562	534	520	555	522	555	528
1982	578	592	616	672	587	579	568	578	613	586	636	610	601	674	650	692
1983	618	641	726	642	528	613	711	609	676	637	682	821	674	636	663	626

Trade balance (f.o.b. — c.i.f.) (18) — Balance commerciale (f.o.b. — c.a.f.) (18)

million NZ dollars, monthly averages — Adjusted - Corrigé * — millions de dollars néo-zélandais, moyennes mensuelles

Year	Q.1	Q.2	Q.3	Q.4	JAN	FEB	MAR	APR	MAY	JUN	JUL	AUG	SEP	OCT	NOV	DEC
1964	7	10	2	6	16	5	0	11	17	2	-7	8	4	4	6	7
1965	4	-3	-12	-1	-3	11	5	-5	7	-10	-24	-8	-4	-7	4	1
1966	-1	-0	5	-11	8	-10	-1	-3	-2	3	18	-9	6	-11	-9	-12
1967	-2	-9	3	15	-6	8	-8	-15	3	-13	12	5	-9	13	24	9
1968	7	15	5	9	4	-1	19	18	11	15	-2	20	-3	13	3	11
1969	18	12	17	18	14	27	13	24	1	12	13	15	24	11	33	9
1970	18	-19	1	-4	9	11	33	-44	-15	2	9	-7	1	-11	-12	11
1971	-9	1	12	5	-9	6	-25	1	11	-9	10	41	-14	14	-4	4
1972	13	18	27	17	23	17	-1	7	17	29	15	8	60	11	12	29
1973	47	40	10	5	27	43	72	27	50	44	-14	26	18	17	2	-3
1974	-16	-74	-90	-111	-20	-22	-5	-29	-94	-98	-79	-85	-107	-99	-117	-117
1975	-109	-63	-37	-60	-99	-124	-103	-72	-49	-68	-34	-47	-28	-49	-60	-70
1976	-86	-8	-29	-23	-83	-8	-166	-79	-58	113	-95	48	-39	-10	-60	0
1977	-25	-7	-15	-15	16	-25	-68	-12	-7	-3	20	-45	-21	-31	-22	7
1978	31	18	23	22	39	29	25	36	-33	51	29	0	39	-2	33	33
1979	37	-13	19	8	8	33	70	-11	-1	-26	37	10	10	-6	25	6
1980	-25	-3	19	-0	-27	-47	0	22	10	-42	0	50	8	14	-14	-1
1981	3	-2	-22	-71	78	-45	-26	133	-156	18	-10	-32	-24	-63	-54	-96
1982	-51	-110	-45	62	-11	-61	-81	-194	-61	-75	-40	-87	-8	47	46	92
1983	-12	14	31	-74	-144	16	93	-21	15	49	-48	156	-17	-31	-146	-46

* Adjusted by the O.E.C.D. — * Corrigé par l'O.C.D.E.

NEW ZEALAND

Balance of payments: net trade (19)

million NZ dollars

Balance des paiements : balance commerciale (19)

millions de dollars néo-zélandais

	Year	Q.1	Q.2	Q.3	Q.4	JAN	FEB	MAR	APR	MAY	JUN	JUL	AUG	SEP	OCT	NOV	DEC
1964	133	67	70	8	-11	18	26	23	33	26	10	6	2	-0	-4	-6	-2
1965	49	46	41	-14	-23	1	11	33	11	24	6	-7	-1	-6	-5	-19	-
1966	84	28	58	16	-19	-0	10	19	19	20	19	10	5	1	2	-7	-14
1967	74	18	34	10	12	-3	4	17	7	11	17	8	3	-1	5	4	3
1968	238	100	77	38	23	19	36	45	23	38	17	20	9	9	15	2	5
1969	282	71	97	73	41	9	24	39	44	24	30	39	24	10	26	3	12
1970	177	61	92	33	-8	12	21	28	32	32	28	12	-3	24	7	-8	-6
1971	221	39	104	57	20	14	6	19	29	38	37	31	19	6	13	8	-1
1972	405	97	140	106	63	16	28	53	47	54	39	40	38	28	43	-3	23
1973	359	162	194	37	-34	42	41	80	69	94	31	18	17	2	-6	-23	-5
1974	-530	-18	-86	-189	-237	-24	14	-9	5	-49	-42	-51	-78	-60	-64	-38	-85
1975	-600	-162	-128	-108	-202	-63	-70	-29	-54	-30	-45	-39	3	-72	-54	-74	-74
1976	-10	44	30	-48	-34	-30	31	43	3	26	1	-7	-15	-27	20	-24	-30
1977	221	96	170	23	-69	21	38	38	64	52	54	34	18	-29	-15	-36	-18
1978	607	202	265	63	77	33	66	103	59	88	118	32	32	-1	63	9	5
1979	711	256	312	64	79	59	77	119	85	142	85	67	48	-50	34	-29	73
1980	885	353	260	209	64	125	87	140	74	70	116	126	18	65	12	29	23
1981	812	236	368	220	-13	8	132	97	48	137	183	187	35	-2	-75	25	38
1982	263	93	94	32	44	-22	61	53	51	-48	91	-81	51	61	43	58	-57
1983	1277	319	673	332	-47	113	80	126	275	284	113	119	171	42	-20	-34	6

Balance of payments: current balance (19)

million NZ dollars

Balance des paiements : opérations courantes, nettes (19)

millions de dollars néo-zélandais

	Year	Q.1	Q.2	Q.3	Q.4	JAN	FEB	MAR	APR	MAY	JUN	JUL	AUG	SEP	OCT	NOV	DEC
1964	2	44	30	-25	-47	12	15	17	22	12	-3	-7	-7	-11	-16	-14	-18
1965	-96	17	0	-48	-66	-6	4	20	-1	10	-9	-21	-11	-17	-16	-32	-18
1966	-87	-4	10	-30	-63	-8	-3	7	6	2	1	-5	-10	-15	-9	-20	-34
1967	-107	-24	-16	-33	-34	-10	-15	0	-6	-7	-3	-4	-12	-17	-9	-8	-18
1968	73	66	39	-7	-24	10	28	28	12	20	7	4	-7	-5	4	-14	-15
1969	96	38	44	15	-0	-2	13	27	30	1	13	18	6	-9	21	-7	-13
1970	-26	20	27	-17	-55	1	9	11	17	9	1	-4	-21	7	-9	-20	-27
1971	42	7	51	9	-25	3	-3	7	15	25	12	11	2	-5	-0	-7	-18
1972	208	60	87	49	13	10	14	37	34	28	25	18	21	10	30	-19	1
1973	152	138	126	-31	-81	39	35	64	51	72	3	-5	-8	-18	-18	-32	-31
1974	-816	-45	-178	-281	-312	-30	14	-28	-19	-83	-76	-86	-116	-79	-85	-99	-128
1975	-985	-221	-252	-241	-271	-79	-79	-63	-94	-76	-82	-85	-45	-111	-68	-84	-119
1976	-623	-50	-142	-253	-178	-57	14	-7	-43	-34	-66	-81	-82	-89	-10	-54	-113
1977	-603	-18	-82	-214	-289	-6	8	-20	7	-43	-47	-41	-78	-95	-70	-105	-115
1978	-392	76	-62	-230	-177	12	24	40	-19	-20	-24	-57	-88	-85	1	-85	-93
1979	-537	42	-89	-275	-216	16	-12	38	6	-2	-93	-48	-74	-153	-51	-142	-22
1980	-549	97	-139	-221	-287	60	5	32	-22	-52	-65	-18	-115	-88	-88	-96	-103
1981	-954	-69	-148	-340	-397	-96	45	-19	-99	-39	-10	-12	-126	-202	-194	-114	-89
1982	-1845	-256	-494	-601	-494	-130	-40	-86	-113	-234	-148	-334	-143	-124	-130	-97	-268
1983	-961	-121	97	-326	-610	-34	-38	-50	90	112	-106	-159	37	-204	-201	-204	-205

Balance of payments: net capital movements (19)

million NZ dollars

Balance des paiements : mouvements de capitaux, nets (19)

millions de dollars néo-zélandais

	Year	Q.1	Q.2	Q.3	Q.4	JAN	FEB	MAR	APR	MAY	JUN	JUL	AUG	SEP	OCT	NOV	DEC
1964	5	4	-1	-0	1	1	1	2	0	-1	-0	0	-1	-0	-0	0	2
1965	71	12	-3	15	47	10	-0	2	-1	-3	0	13	-2	4	-1	45	2
1966	71	11	-3	36	27	5	5	1	-1	-0	-2	4	15	17	4	23	-0
1967	148	52	13	24	60	15	41	-5	-1	2	11	21	0	3	41	2	18
1968	-101	-11	-33	-28	-28	4	-16	1	1	-33	-1	4	3	-36	-2	-3	-24
1969	-34	26	-23	-23	-14	0	21	5	1	-3	-21	-0	-19	-3	-0	-7	-7
1970	75	29	-3	35	13	26	0	3	2	-2	-3	15	1	20	3	0	11
1971	103	43	32	47	-19	25	10	8	28	10	-6	23	5	20	4	-5	-18
1972	111	82	50	-11	-9	34	38	10	22	3	26	-9	9	-11	24	-35	2
1973	-21	20	8	-23	-25	5	15	-1	1	3	4	-21	4	-6	-35	5	4
1974	425	-30	17	228	210	-15	-21	6	2	5	11	63	57	108	55	42	113
1975	664	151	239	28	246	69	35	47	29	84	127	6	98	-77	100	132	15
1976	446	130	-55	197	175	2	125	2	-76	9	13	162	2	33	63	-46	157
1977	473	51	58	202	161	-7	4	54	0	102	-44	17	67	119	46	114	2
1978	459	317	25	2	115	3	143	172	-53	20	58	-20	12	10	-22	30	108
1979	660	110	185	237	127	149	-14	-25	-4	208	-19	6	55	176	112	51	-36
1980	520	-101	0	393	229	-174	117	-44	1	-34	33	307	-54	139	157	130	-59
1981	1710	151	175	381	1003	-10	111	50	30	141	5	50	258	74	288	-16	731
1982	1896	-79	308	790	878	-191	89	23	389	-152	71	365	296	130	500	96	281
1983	1229	515	-302	197	818	170	80	266	61	-305	-58	11	43	143	321	97	400

NOTES

1. Percentage of firms unable to increase production, given existing capacity, without raising unit costs.
2. Up to 1970, data are based on 1969-70 survey of manufacturers; from 1971, they are based on the 1974-75 survey.
3. Including alterations and additions.
4. From April 1976 new sample with greater coverage. The figures for April 1976 according to the old sample were 367.8 million NZ dollars for the unadjusted series, and 376.5 million NZ dollars for the seasonally adjusted series.
5. Up to 1969, data are based on the 1962-63 census; from 1970 to 1980, they are based on the 1972-73 census, and from 1981 on the 1977-78 census.
6. Excluding agriculture. Monthly data refer to the 15th of the month.
7. Monthly data refer to end of period.
8. From March 1981, due to administrative changes data are not comparable with those for previous periods.
9. Prior to November 1977, monthly data refer to end of period and only males are included. The present index refers to mid-month. Annual averages are calculated from daily rates.
10. Weighting pattern based on 1975-76 to 3rd quarter 1982 and on 1981-82 from 4th quarter 1982.
11. Weighting pattern based on 1952-53 to 1965, on 1962-63 from 1966 to 1974, on July 1973-June 1974 from 1975 to 1977, on April 1976-March 1977 from 1978 to 1980, and on 1979-80 from 1981.
12. Quarterly data refer to last day of quarter.
13. Monthly data, other than those for last month of quarter, are partly estimated.
14. Including credit to local authorities.
15. From June 1977, restricted survey of businesses which accounted for 92 per cent of instalment credit sales in 1977-78. The businesses surveyed previously accounted for 72 per cent of instalment credit sales in 1967-68. On this basis the figure for June 1977 was 302.6 million NZ dollars.
16. Bonds with term of over 5 years from June 1977, and over 10 years previously.

NOTES

1. Pourcentage d'entreprises qui, étant donné leurs capacités de production disponibles, ne peuvent augmenter leur production sans augmenter leurs coûts unitaires.
2. Jusqu'en 1970, les données sont basées sur l'enquête auprès des producteurs de 1969-70; à partir de 1971, elles sont basées sur l'enquête de 1974-75.
3. Y compris les transformations et les agrandissements.
4. A partir d'avril 1976, nouvel échantillon couvrant un plus grand nombre de points de vente. Les chiffres d'avril 1976 calculés à partir de l'ancien échantillon étaient de 367,8 millions de dollars néo-zélandais pour la série brute, et de 376,5 millions de dollars néo-zélandais pour la série corrigée des variations saisonnières.
5. Jusqu'en 1969, les données sont basées sur le recensement de 1962-63; de 1970 à 1980 elles sont basées sur celui de 1972-73, et à partir de 1981, sur celui de 1977-78.
6. Non compris l'agriculture. Les données mensuelles se réfèrent au 15 du mois.
7. Situation en fin de mois.
8. A partir de mars 1981, en raison de changements administratifs, les données ne sont pas comparables à celles des périodes précédentes.
9. Avant novembre 1977, situation en fin de mois et comprenant seulement les hommes. L'indice actuel se réfère à la situation en milieu de mois. Les moyennes annuelles sont calculées à partir de données journalières.
10. La pondération se réfère à 1975-76 jusqu'au 3e trimestre 1982, et à 1981-82 à partir du 4e trimestre 1982.
11. La pondération se réfère à 1952-53 jusqu'en 1965, à 1962-63 de 1966 à 1974, à juillet 1973-juin 1974 de 1975 à 1977, à avril 1976-mars 1977 de 1978 à 1980, et à 1979-80 à partir de 1981.
12. Les données trimestrielles se réfèrent au dernier jour du trimestre.
13. Les données mensuelles, autres que celles du dernier mois du trimestre, sont en partie estimées.
14. Y compris les crédits aux administrations locales.
15. A partir de juin 1977 enquête qui portait, en 1977-78, sur environ 92 % du total des ventes à tempérament. Avant juin 1977, enquête qui portait en 1967-68 sur environ 72 % du total des ventes à tempérament. Sur l'ancienne base le chiffre de juin 1977 était de 302,6 millions de dollars néo-zélandais.
16. Bons à plus de 5 ans à partir de juin 1977, à plus de 10 ans auparavant.

NOTES

17. Monthly data are daily averages from April 1977, and averages of Thursdays previously.
18. General trade.
19. Settlements basis.

NOTES

17. Les données mensuelles sont des moyennes journalières à partir d'avril 1977 et des moyennes des jeudis auparavant.
18. Commerce général.
19. Sur la base des règlements.

MAIN SOURCES

PRINCIPALES SOURCES

Series	Séries	Sources
Production	Production	Department of Statistics *Monthly Abstract of Statistics*
Manufacturing stocks	Stocks, industries manufacturières	
Construction	Construction	
Internal trade	Commerce intérieur	
Labour and wages	Main-d'œuvre et salaires	
Prices	Prix	
Instalment credit	Crédits remboursables par tranches	
Interest rates	Taux d'intérêts	
Foreign trade	Commerce extérieur	
Business surveys	Enquêtes de conjoncture	New Zealand Institute of Economic Research *Quarterly Survey of Business Opinion*
Money supply	Disponibilités monétaires	Reserve Bank of New Zealand *Bulletin*
Credit to private sector	Crédits au secteur privé	
Share prices	Cours des actions	
Net foreign position of commercial banks	Position extérieure nette des banques commerciales	
Balance of payments	Balance des paiements	

Austria — Autriche

AUSTRIA

Industrial production: total (1)(2) / Production industrielle : total (1)(2)

1980 = 100

	Year	Q.1	Q.2	Q.3	Q.4	JAN	FEB	MAR	APR	MAY	JUN	JUL	AUG	SEP	OCT	NOV	DEC
1964	47.7	45.1	48.7	45.9	51.2	43.6	45.6	46.0	46.7	51.1	48.5	44.1	45.1	48.5	51.1	53.0	49.5
1965	49.8	47.3	50.6	48.3	53.1	47.2	47.1	47.4	49.2	51.2	51.4	45.9	47.2	51.8	53.6	55.8	49.8
1966	52.1	49.3	53.3	49.4	56.4	47.7	49.5	50.8	52.4	53.8	53.8	47.9	47.4	53.0	56.3	57.4	55.4
1967	52.5	49.3	54.2	49.5	56.5	48.0	50.0	51.3	53.3	54.7	54.2	47.7	47.5	53.4	55.6	57.6	56.4
1968	56.4	51.9	58.1	55.0	60.8	49.5	51.7	54.4	56.0	57.8	60.5	51.6	53.8	59.5	60.9	64.9	56.6
1969	62.8	57.6	64.2	61.1	68.1	54.4	58.5	60.0	61.6	65.2	65.9	57.5	60.2	65.4	68.1	73.1	63.0
1970	68.2	63.5	70.2	65.8	73.3	59.0	65.2	66.4	67.9	73.7	69.0	62.4	65.0	70.1	73.3	76.9	69.9
1971	72.2	68.3	74.8	69.0	76.9	65.9	68.7	70.3	73.2	76.6	74.7	65.4	67.5	74.2	78.2	80.8	71.6
1972	78.1	72.0	78.4	73.8	88.2	69.4	71.8	74.8	77.6	78.1	79.6	70.0	71.7	79.6	85.1	88.3	91.3
1973	81.0	75.2	83.0	77.3	83.5	70.2	77.6	77.7	81.5	82.5	85.0	73.3	74.4	84.2	85.4	88.6	91.4
1974	85.4	82.5	89.3	81.2	88.6	76.4	84.8	86.2	87.0	87.6	93.2	78.1	79.1	86.5	86.6	91.0	88.3
1975	80.0	78.7	81.5	74.6	85.1	73.9	81.8	80.5	80.5	82.0	81.9	71.2	73.0	79.6	80.3	87.7	87.4
1976	85.3	79.1	87.3	81.5	93.2	75.0	80.7	81.8	83.6	88.7	89.5	77.7	78.2	88.6	91.5	94.3	94.0
1977	88.6	85.8	91.3	83.4	93.8	82.7	85.7	89.2	90.9	90.9	92.2	82.5	80.0	87.8	93.9	94.6	92.9
1978	90.4	85.4	92.7	85.9	97.5	81.5	86.7	88.1	93.5	92.4	92.2	82.7	82.2	92.9	95.7	97.4	99.5
1979	97.4	91.1	98.8	94.1	105.6	86.7	92.5	94.2	96.7	97.3	102.3	90.8	89.9	101.5	98.2	102.3	116.2
1980	100.0	98.1	102.6	92.7	106.6	92.1	98.9	103.2	101.5	102.3	104.1	89.6	91.3	97.2	100.6	107.5	111.7
1981	98.4	95.9	101.5	92.0	104.2	89.7	98.1	99.8	100.3	102.5	101.8	88.9	88.0	99.0	100.9	104.1	107.5
1982	97.6	97.3	101.5	90.9	100.6	94.7	99.0	98.3	99.1	103.4	102.0	89.4	86.2	97.0	98.9	101.5	101.5
1983	98.2	92.8	101.7	93.8	104.5	87.8	95.5	95.3	99.9	102.6	102.7	93.2	88.0	100.3	103.4	105.9	104.3

Industrial production: investment goods (1) / Production industrielle : biens d'équipement (1)

1980 = 100

	Year	Q.1	Q.2	Q.3	Q.4	JAN	FEB	MAR	APR	MAY	JUN	JUL	AUG	SEP	OCT	NOV	DEC
1964	36.6	33.4	37.7	34.2	41.1	30.5	33.9	35.9	35.4	40.8	36.9	33.4	32.9	36.3	38.3	39.8	45.2
1965	38.8	35.9	39.8	37.0	42.5	33.1	36.2	38.5	38.4	39.7	41.3	36.1	34.2	40.8	40.2	42.6	44.7
1966	39.6	36.8	40.9	36.4	44.3	34.3	37.0	39.2	40.6	41.1	41.0	36.0	34.1	39.1	40.7	42.0	50.3
1967	41.3	37.1	43.6	37.3	47.1	33.2	37.2	41.0	43.0	43.8	43.9	36.4	34.0	41.5	45.7	44.4	51.3
1968	42.3	37.7	43.9	40.8	46.7	35.9	36.8	40.4	42.6	44.4	44.7	39.7	38.6	44.0	44.6	47.6	47.9
1969	50.4	43.5	52.1	49.3	56.8	38.0	45.1	47.4	48.9	53.5	53.8	48.0	46.7	53.3	53.7	57.5	59.3
1970	56.1	51.3	59.5	52.9	60.8	44.4	52.7	56.9	56.7	63.1	58.9	52.6	48.9	57.3	58.9	60.7	62.8
1971	60.9	55.7	63.2	55.7	68.8	50.8	57.1	59.2	63.2	64.4	62.0	55.1	50.0	62.1	64.3	69.8	72.5
1972	66.3	59.5	66.2	59.7	79.9	56.1	59.1	63.5	65.4	66.5	66.7	57.4	56.2	65.4	71.6	70.8	97.2
1973	67.2	58.2	68.5	64.4	77.7	51.1	60.9	62.6	65.7	66.8	73.0	60.7	60.9	71.6	71.4	71.7	89.9
1974	74.0	68.9	76.3	68.5	82.3	63.4	68.8	74.5	75.1	73.6	80.3	68.0	64.8	72.8	72.6	80.5	93.9
1975	72.2	67.3	72.4	65.4	83.6	59.7	73.4	68.8	70.6	72.5	74.0	62.2	63.5	70.5	69.6	78.5	102.6
1976	75.3	68.1	75.2	69.3	88.7	64.3	68.9	71.1	71.2	78.1	76.4	67.3	64.8	75.8	80.2	84.7	101.1
1977	79.1	71.1	79.4	75.2	90.7	68.8	68.5	75.8	78.6	79.5	80.1	79.1	70.6	76.1	85.3	85.9	100.9
1978	79.7	72.3	80.3	73.0	93.2	66.3	75.4	75.3	82.7	77.7	80.5	72.1	67.2	79.7	83.0	86.4	110.4
1979	96.0	82.6	94.7	91.7	115.2	75.5	84.3	88.0	94.8	91.0	98.3	88.8	83.2	102.9	94.1	100.5	150.9
1980	100.0	93.9	98.2	87.1	120.8	85.9	94.9	100.9	99.4	94.2	100.9	85.9	84.4	91.2	107.0	108.5	146.9
1981	97.4	90.0	97.3	88.2	113.9	75.7	92.3	102.0	95.7	98.4	97.9	85.6	82.1	97.0	101.0	105.9	134.7
1982	101.0	91.1	102.9	93.6	116.3	85.1	91.7	96.3	102.7	103.9	102.1	91.0	87.8	102.1	105.0	111.4	132.6
1983	98.9	87.3	101.9	92.4	113.8	78.8	90.7	92.4	102.6	103.2	99.8	91.2	85.3	100.8	106.8	106.7	127.9

Industrial production: consumer goods (1)(2) / Production industrielle : biens de consommation (1)(2)

1980 = 100

	Year	Q.1	Q.2	Q.3	Q.4	JAN	FEB	MAR	APR	MAY	JUN	JUL	AUG	SEP	OCT	NOV	DEC
1964	48.4	46.8	48.9	44.7	53.4	46.0	47.5	46.9	47.5	50.6	48.5	41.4	43.7	49.1	53.3	56.7	50.2
1965	50.8	49.4	51.2	46.4	56.3	50.6	49.0	48.6	50.3	51.6	51.8	41.7	45.5	51.9	56.5	61.8	50.5
1966	53.8	51.2	54.0	48.4	61.7	50.1	51.2	52.1	53.5	54.0	54.6	44.8	45.9	54.5	61.7	64.5	58.9
1967	54.1	51.9	54.8	48.6	61.1	51.2	52.3	52.3	54.9	55.0	54.6	44.7	46.1	55.1	58.8	64.4	60.1
1968	59.1	54.9	60.0	55.2	66.4	52.7	55.2	56.9	57.9	59.2	63.0	49.4	53.4	62.8	66.7	73.6	58.9
1969	65.8	61.0	66.4	61.2	74.8	57.9	62.0	63.2	64.2	66.9	68.2	54.9	60.1	68.4	75.1	83.0	66.2
1970	70.7	66.5	71.3	65.5	79.4	61.6	69.1	68.9	70.6	74.7	68.5	58.6	65.3	72.7	78.9	86.9	72.4
1971	75.6	71.4	77.9	70.0	82.9	69.9	71.2	73.0	76.1	80.0	77.5	62.8	69.5	77.7	85.4	89.7	73.6
1972	82.5	76.7	83.2	75.2	95.1	74.1	77.5	78.4	82.6	82.6	84.3	67.9	73.6	84.2	92.3	98.0	94.9
1973	85.6	80.9	87.4	79.1	95.2	75.4	84.3	83.0	86.7	87.4	88.0	71.3	76.3	89.9	91.8	98.0	95.8
1974	88.7	87.9	93.0	81.2	92.8	81.6	91.6	90.6	89.9	91.5	97.7	74.9	78.0	90.5	92.4	98.2	88.0
1975	80.9	80.8	81.5	72.8	88.7	76.0	83.6	83.0	80.7	82.1	81.7	66.4	70.0	82.0	85.4	94.4	86.2
1976	87.6	82.6	89.1	81.2	97.4	78.6	84.8	84.4	86.6	89.3	91.5	74.6	77.5	91.6	96.4	101.5	94.5
1977	92.3	91.8	94.6	83.2	99.5	88.6	92.3	94.5	94.2	93.9	95.7	79.0	78.3	92.4	100.7	102.7	95.0
1978	93.9	90.9	96.3	86.3	102.1	87.7	91.8	93.3	98.2	95.7	94.9	78.9	82.9	97.2	102.1	104.7	99.5
1979	96.2	91.0	98.3	91.2	104.3	85.3	93.2	94.5	94.7	97.7	102.5	84.8	86.0	102.8	101.4	104.3	107.3
1980	100.0	98.1	102.8	92.3	106.9	91.1	99.0	104.2	100.7	101.6	106.0	85.0	89.3	102.5	103.4	111.3	106.0
1981	98.5	97.0	103.3	90.0	103.5	90.9	100.5	99.5	101.6	104.9	103.5	85.1	83.4	101.6	103.9	107.6	98.9
1982	98.4	100.1	101.6	89.3	102.6	95.5	102.8	102.0	99.2	103.0	102.6	83.8	82.0	102.1	103.3	106.4	98.0
1983	99.1	97.1	102.3	92.2	104.9	93.0	98.7	99.4	99.8	101.5	105.6	88.9	84.6	103.1	105.9	110.8	98.0

Industrial production: total (1)(2) — Adjusted - Corrigé * — Production industrielle : total (1)(2)

1980 = 100

	Year	Q.1	Q.2	Q.3	Q.4	JAN	FEB	MAR	APR	MAY	JUN	JUL	AUG	SEP	OCT	NOV	DEC
1964		47.0	47.1	47.9	48.5	46.9	47.0	47.0	46.3	47.4	47.5	48.3	47.7	47.8	48.6	48.2	48.7
1965		49.4	49.3	50.4	50.2	50.4	49.1	48.6	48.9	49.0	50.0	50.1	50.3	50.9	50.4	51.3	49.0
1966		51.6	51.9	51.7	53.3	51.1	51.5	52.1	51.7	51.9	52.0	52.0	50.7	52.3	53.0	52.4	54.6
1967		52.2	52.7	51.7	53.5	52.2	51.9	52.4	52.7	52.9	52.5	51.9	50.9	52.2	52.8	52.5	55.3
1968		54.1	55.8	57.5	57.8	54.1	53.3	54.9	55.6	55.5	56.2	56.9	57.3	58.2	58.1	58.9	56.4
1969		60.2	62.2	63.9	64.5	59.2	60.6	60.6	60.9	62.4	63.5	63.5	63.7	64.6	64.7	65.9	63.0
1970		66.5	67.1	68.8	69.7	64.2	67.5	67.7	66.9	67.2	67.1	68.7	68.9	68.9	69.5	69.6	70.1
1971		71.4	72.4	72.3	73.0	71.1	71.1	71.9	72.4	72.6	72.2	71.8	72.2	72.8	73.7	73.9	71.6
1972		75.1	76.4	78.0	82.6	76.7	72.9	75.7	76.5	76.4	76.3	77.4	78.1	78.4	82.4	80.8	84.7
1973		78.3	80.9	81.7	82.9	77.5	78.8	78.6	80.5	80.6	81.4	81.1	81.0	83.0	82.6	81.3	84.8
1974		85.8	86.9	85.9	83.1	84.1	86.3	87.0	86.0	85.6	89.3	86.2	86.3	85.3	83.6	83.6	82.1
1975		81.9	79.4	78.9	80.0	81.2	83.4	81.0	79.6	80.0	78.5	78.4	79.8	78.6	77.3	81.0	81.5
1976		82.1	85.0	86.1	87.9	81.8	82.3	82.2	82.7	86.5	85.8	85.0	85.7	87.6	88.0	87.6	87.9
1977		88.9	88.9	88.2	88.6	89.3	87.4	89.5	89.7	88.7	88.4	90.1	87.8	86.8	90.4	88.3	87.0
1978		88.3	90.2	90.9	92.2	88.3	88.4	88.2	92.1	90.0	88.4	90.1	90.5	92.0	92.3	91.5	93.0
1979		94.0	95.9	99.6	99.9	94.0	93.9	94.3	95.2	94.5	98.0	99.1	99.2	100.5	95.0	96.4	108.4
1980		101.1	99.5	98.4	101.0	100.0	100.0	103.2	99.8	99.0	99.7	97.8	101.1	96.4	97.6	101.5	104.0
1981		98.7	98.2	97.8	93.8	97.6	93.7	99.8	98.5	98.5	97.5	97.4	97.7	98.3	98.1	98.3	100.0
1982		100.3	98.0	96.8	95.5	103.1	99.4	98.3	97.3	99.0	97.7	98.1	95.9	96.6	96.3	95.9	94.3
1983		95.6	98.1	100.1	99.2	95.7	95.8	95.3	98.0	98.0	98.3	102.3	98.0	99.9	100.7	100.0	97.0

Industrial production: investment goods (1) — Adjusted - Corrigé * — Production industrielle : biens d'équipement (1)

1980 = 100

	Year	Q.1	Q.2	Q.3	Q.4	JAN	FEB	MAR	APR	MAY	JUN	JUL	AUG	SEP	OCT	NOV	DEC
1964		35.9	36.6	36.5	37.2	35.7	36.0	36.1	35.3	39.4	35.1	36.3	37.1	36.3	37.4	36.6	37.7
1965		38.8	38.5	39.5	38.5	38.9	38.7	38.8	38.0	38.2	39.2	39.3	38.6	40.7	39.0	39.3	37.2
1966		39.9	39.4	38.9	40.2	40.5	39.6	39.5	40.1	39.3	38.9	39.3	38.5	39.0	39.6	39.1	41.9
1967		40.1	41.8	39.8	43.0	39.4	39.6	41.3	42.2	41.7	41.6	39.6	38.5	41.3	44.7	41.6	42.7
1968		40.8	42.1	43.7	42.8	42.7	39.0	40.7	41.7	42.0	42.5	43.3	43.9	43.8	43.8	44.6	39.9
1969		46.8	49.9	53.0	51.9	45.2	47.6	47.6	47.8	50.4	51.3	52.4	53.2	53.2	52.8	53.8	49.3
1970		55.1	57.2	56.9	55.4	52.6	55.4	57.3	55.5	59.7	56.4	57.7	55.9	57.1	58.0	56.4	51.8
1971		59.8	60.9	60.0	62.4	59.7	60.3	59.6	62.0	61.4	59.3	60.8	57.3	61.9	63.4	64.5	59.2
1972		64.0	63.9	64.5	71.4	65.5	62.5	64.1	64.3	63.9	63.6	63.8	64.4	65.3	70.7	65.0	78.4
1973		62.5	66.4	69.7	69.2	59.3	64.7	63.5	65.0	64.7	69.5	67.8	69.8	71.6	70.7	65.5	71.5
1974		74.1	74.4	74.4	73.0	73.2	73.0	76.0	74.9	71.9	76.5	76.1	74.0	73.2	71.7	73.5	73.9
1975		72.3	70.9	71.1	73.4	68.9	77.7	70.4	70.6	71.3	70.8	69.5	72.7	71.1	68.3	71.8	79.9
1976		73.3	74.1	75.3	78.1	74.2	72.6	73.0	71.2	77.4	73.6	74.8	74.4	76.7	78.0	78.0	78.2
1977		76.4	73.5	82.1	79.7	79.4	71.8	77.9	78.2	79.6	77.9	87.8	81.6	77.0	82.2	79.4	77.4
1978		77.6	79.7	79.6	81.2	76.4	79.0	77.2	81.9	78.4	73.7	80.3	78.1	80.3	79.3	80.1	84.1
1979		88.7	94.1	100.0	98.9	87.4	88.5	90.1	93.7	92.1	96.6	99.2	97.5	103.3	89.7	93.1	113.8
1980		101.2	97.6	95.5	104.0	99.9	100.3	103.3	98.2	95.1	99.5	96.3	99.1	91.2	102.1	100.2	109.9
1981		97.0	96.7	96.7	98.0	88.3	98.3	104.4	94.6	98.8	96.7	96.5	96.7	96.8	96.4	97.4	100.2
1982		98.9	102.1	102.8	100.2	99.7	98.3	98.8	101.7	103.6	101.0	103.0	103.4	102.0	100.1	102.1	98.5
1983		95.0	101.0	101.5	98.1	92.6	97.5	95.0	101.8	102.5	98.8	103.5	100.4	100.7	101.8	97.6	94.9

Industrial production: consumer goods (1)(2) — Adjusted - Corrigé * — Production industrielle : biens de consommation (1)(2)

1980 = 100

	Year	Q.1	Q.2	Q.3	Q.4	JAN	FEB	MAR	APR	MAY	JUN	JUL	AUG	SEP	OCT	NOV	DEC
1964		48.0	48.4	48.9	48.6	47.9	48.4	47.5	47.4	49.8	47.8	49.4	48.5	48.6	49.0	48.3	48.6
1965		50.7	50.6	50.6	51.2	52.9	49.9	49.3	50.1	50.7	50.9	49.9	50.6	51.3	51.9	52.5	49.2
1966		52.6	53.2	52.9	56.3	52.5	52.2	53.0	53.1	52.9	53.6	53.8	51.2	53.7	56.7	54.5	57.7
1967		53.4	53.9	53.2	55.8	54.0	53.3	53.1	54.5	53.8	53.4	53.8	51.6	54.2	53.9	54.3	59.1
1968		56.6	58.9	60.3	60.5	55.9	56.3	57.8	57.5	57.6	61.5	59.6	59.6	61.8	61.2	62.0	58.2
1969		62.9	65.0	67.0	68.2	61.5	63.2	64.1	63.7	64.7	66.5	66.5	67.0	67.4	68.8	70.1	65.6
1970		68.6	69.6	71.8	72.5	65.6	70.4	69.9	69.9	72.1	66.7	71.0	72.7	71.6	72.2	73.7	71.7
1971		73.7	75.9	76.7	75.8	74.6	72.4	74.1	75.3	77.3	75.3	76.1	77.6	76.5	78.3	76.6	72.6
1972		79.0	81.1	82.4	87.4	79.2	78.4	79.4	81.6	79.8	81.9	82.0	82.4	82.7	85.1	84.2	93.0
1973		83.1	85.2	86.5	87.8	80.8	84.8	83.7	85.6	84.8	85.3	85.6	85.9	88.0	85.1	84.8	93.3
1974		90.0	90.8	88.8	85.6	87.7	91.7	90.7	88.8	89.1	94.6	89.5	88.6	88.4	86.2	85.5	85.2
1975		82.5	79.6	79.5	61.9	81.5	83.3	82.6	79.9	80.1	78.9	78.8	79.8	80.0	80.0	82.8	83.1
1976		84.2	87.1	88.6	90.4	84.4	84.5	83.8	85.9	87.1	88.3	88.0	88.6	89.2	90.6	89.7	90.8
1977		93.6	92.4	90.8	92.4	94.9	92.2	93.6	93.5	94.6	92.1	92.8	89.6	89.9	94.9	91.4	90.9
1978		92.9	93.8	93.9	95.2	94.2	91.8	92.5	97.2	93.2	90.8	92.2	95.2	94.4	96.6	93.9	95.2
1979		92.9	95.4	99.2	97.6	91.8	93.1	93.7	93.7	94.8	97.8	98.8	99.2	99.6	96.1	94.2	102.6
1980		100.0	99.6	100.5	100.3	98.1	98.6	103.2	99.6	98.3	101.0	98.9	103.5	98.9	98.4	100.9	101.6
1981		98.5	100.0	98.1	97.4	97.5	99.6	98.3	100.4	101.1	98.5	99.1	97.3	98.0	99.1	97.9	95.1
1982		101.5	98.1	97.4	96.7	102.2	101.6	100.7	97.9	98.9	97.5	97.6	96.0	98.6	98.8	96.9	94.4
1983		98.3	98.7	100.8	98.9	99.2	97.5	98.1	98.5	97.4	100.3	103.7	99.2	99.5	101.3	101.0	94.5

* Adjusted by the O.E.C.D. — * Corrigé par l'O.C.D.E.

AUSTRIA

Industrial production: intermediate goods (1) / Production industrielle : biens intermédiaires (1)

1980 = 100

	Year	Q.1	Q.2	Q.3	Q.4	JAN	FEB	MAR	APR	MAY	JUN	JUL	AUG	SEP	OCT	NOV	DEC
1964	53.5	48.8	56.0	54.8	54.5	46.3	49.2	50.8	52.8	59.9	55.2	54.1	54.6	55.7	56.4	56.4	50.7
1965	54.6	50.8	56.2	55.6	56.0	51.0	50.2	51.2	54.6	57.5	56.3	53.8	55.2	57.8	59.4	57.0	51.6
1966	56.8	53.8	59.4	56.7	57.3	50.9	54.0	56.5	58.6	60.7	59.0	57.0	54.6	58.6	58.8	58.7	54.2
1967	56.9	53.7	59.9	56.6	57.5	51.2	54.0	56.0	59.3	61.3	59.2	55.7	55.5	58.4	59.3	58.4	55.0
1968	61.7	55.9	64.7	62.7	63.4	52.1	55.3	60.4	62.2	64.4	67.4	60.2	62.1	65.8	64.8	66.8	58.5
1969	67.6	61.4	70.7	69.5	68.8	58.0	61.7	64.4	67.9	72.1	72.1	67.5	69.1	71.9	71.8	74.2	60.6
1970	72.9	66.4	77.0	73.4	74.9	62.8	66.9	69.5	73.1	81.9	75.9	71.9	72.4	75.9	78.1	76.9	69.8
1971	77.7	71.9	81.8	79.2	77.9	67.8	73.2	74.6	79.2	83.5	82.7	77.8	77.9	81.9	83.5	80.6	69.7
1972	84.4	75.9	85.2	85.0	91.5	72.1	74.4	8[illegible].0	84.3	85.0	86.2	83.3	82.5	89.3	92.6	93.1	83.3
1973	87.9	81.8	91.1	87.3	91.2	76.4	83.9	85.0	89.8	91.2	92.4	85.0	84.8	92.1	91.3	93.7	88.7
1974	91.7	87.1	97.8	91.2	90.6	77.6	90.4	93.2	95.5	97.5	100.3	88.0	90.8	94.7	92.3	93.8	85.7
1975	83.3	83.5	86.1	79.9	83.7	78.3	84.9	87.4	86.7	86.0	85.5	77.2	79.6	83.0	83.9	89.3	77.8
1976	90.6	80.5	96.3	91.8	93.9	74.1	81.8	85.6	91.7	98.1	99.2	90.1	89.2	96.1	97.5	95.6	88.6
1977	91.2	87.3	97.4	88.3	91.7	82.3	87.7	91.9	97.5	96.9	97.6	89.3	85.7	90.0	96.0	94.1	84.9
1978	94.3	86.6	99.1	93.8	97.5	81.9	86.1	91.8	99.3	101.3	96.7	91.3	90.0	100.1	100.1	99.8	92.7
1979	99.8	92.8	102.7	98.7	104.3	85.7	94.2	93.5	102.1	101.7	104.2	95.0	95.5	105.3	102.3	103.7	108.4
1980	100.0	98.6	106.9	96.2	98.3	91.5	99.1	105.3	104.2	110.2	106.4	94.8	94.8	99.0	97.9	103.0	93.8
1981	96.9	92.5	103.3	93.9	97.8	85.5	93.2	98.6	101.3	105.6	102.9	90.9	91.4	99.3	100.6	98.3	94.5
1982	91.3	90.3	99.0	86.7	89.2	87.5	89.7	93.7	98.1	103.1	96.0	85.9	83.4	90.8	93.5	91.4	82.8
1983	94.5	84.1	99.5	94.3	100.0	78.3	85.0	89.2	98.1	101.3	99.1	93.7	89.2	100.0	104.5	102.1	93.3

Industrial production: construction (3) / Production industrielle : construction (3)

1980 = 100

	Year	Q.1	Q.2	Q.3	Q.4	JAN	FEB	MAR	APR	MAY	JUN	JUL	AUG	SEP	OCT	NOV	DEC
1964																	
1965																	
1966																	
1967																	
1968																	
1969	68.4	46.8	79.3	79.9	67.5	39.4	43.5	57.5	71.5	85.4	80.8	80.1	78.0	81.8	79.4	77.0	46.0
1970	71.8	47.4	82.0	83.7	74.2	38.9	47.5	55.7	74.3	90.5	81.2	81.5	83.8	85.9	84.9	77.1	60.7
1971	83.8	60.1	95.3	96.9	83.0	47.7	64.5	68.1	87.9	102.5	95.4	95.4	95.9	99.4	99.8	84.3	65.0
1972	96.4	71.2	102.7	106.7	105.1	62.6	65.8	85.4	103.3	99.7	105.0	103.2	102.0	115.1	112.5	105.8	97.1
1973	95.1	76.9	105.2	104.8	93.4	66.2	78.5	86.1	103.0	106.1	106.4	101.6	103.0	109.9	101.9	97.6	80.7
1974	98.8	82.8	112.7	104.7	95.0	66.2	84.6	97.7	110.2	111.0	116.9	101.6	103.7	108.7	103.6	98.9	82.5
1975	90.2	77.4	99.8	96.2	87.4	65.5	75.8	91.0	98.3	102.4	98.8	89.6	98.0	100.9	94.6	93.8	73.8
1976	95.0	68.3	108.9	106.3	96.6	56.6	66.9	81.5	99.4	112.4	114.8	104.8	102.9	111.1	109.0	99.9	80.9
1977	95.1	74.6	108.3	103.9	93.6	61.5	72.3	89.9	104.6	111.7	108.8	105.1	100.2	106.4	109.2	97.9	73.7
1978	93.7	71.7	106.0	104.3	92.8	62.9	67.8	84.4	102.7	108.6	106.8	102.2	99.8	110.9	106.1	96.8	75.4
1979	96.0	72.1	102.9	105.3	103.8	56.4	73.1	86.7	97.8	102.6	108.4	101.6	101.9	112.4	108.1	101.9	101.3
1980	100.0	81.4	113.1	108.9	96.6	66.5	78.9	98.8	104.5	117.8	116.9	105.5	107.4	114.0	109.3	104.5	76.0
1981	99.4	78.1	119.0	108.9	91.8	61.5	77.4	95.4	113.8	124.2	113.8	109.4	105.7	111.6	106.0	98.2	71.2
1982	90.4	67.5	108.0	98.4	87.6	51.0	67.2	84.3	103.3	113.8	107.0	98.4	93.5	103.3	101.4	93.3	68.0
1983	91.2	64.9	106.5	101.8	91.6	53.5	61.7	79.5	103.1	109.4	107.1	101.8	97.8	105.9	105.7	97.6	71.4

Industrial production: manufacturing (1)(2) / Production industrielle : industries manufacturières (1)(2)

1980 = 100

	Year	Q.1	Q.2	Q.3	Q.4	JAN	FEB	MAR	APR	MAY	JUN	JUL	AUG	SEP	OCT	NOV	DEC
1964	47.1	44.3	48.2	45.2	50.3	42.6	44.8	45.5	46.1	50.7	47.7	43.2	44.3	48.0	50.7	52.7	48.9
1965	48.4	45.9	49.3	46.3	52.1	45.9	45.6	46.2	48.1	49.8	49.9	43.3	45.1	50.3	52.8	55.0	48.6
1966	50.6	47.8	51.7	47.3	55.6	45.9	48.0	49.6	51.2	52.1	51.9	45.6	45.0	51.3	55.7	56.6	54.5
1967	51.1	48.2	52.8	47.6	55.9	46.3	48.5	49.9	52.5	53.4	52.6	45.3	45.4	52.0	54.9	57.0	55.6
1968	55.2	50.5	56.8	53.3	60.1	47.9	50.2	53.3	54.8	56.5	59.2	49.6	51.8	58.5	60.1	64.6	55.5
1969	62.0	56.9	63.4	60.0	67.6	53.6	57.5	59.5	61.0	64.2	65.0	56.0	59.1	64.9	67.9	72.8	62.1
1970	67.3	62.5	69.9	64.1	72.8	57.8	64.1	65.6	68.0	72.5	69.1	60.0	62.9	69.3	72.9	77.0	68.4
1971	72.2	68.6	74.5	68.5	77.1	65.9	69.7	70.2	72.9	76.0	74.6	64.3	66.5	74.7	78.2	82.2	70.9
1972	78.5	71.6	79.2	73.3	89.9	68.0	71.8	75.0	78.5	79.1	79.9	68.5	71.0	80.3	85.3	88.0	96.6
1973	82.3	75.9	84.4	78.5	90.6	69.7	78.9	79.1	83.1	84.0	86.0	72.8	75.6	87.0	87.3	91.1	93.6
1974	86.6	83.6	91.0	81.2	90.6	76.3	86.3	88.3	88.6	89.6	94.9	77.0	78.6	88.1	88.1	93.5	90.1
1975	79.6	78.7	80.7	72.6	86.4	72.6	81.9	81.5	80.2	81.0	80.8	67.6	70.6	79.5	81.3	89.4	88.5
1976	85.5	78.0	88.0	81.3	94.8	73.1	79.6	81.2	84.4	89.5	90.2	77.3	77.6	89.0	93.2	96.1	94.9
1977	88.5	84.9	91.4	82.2	95.4	81.5	84.5	88.7	91.2	90.9	92.2	81.7	77.8	87.2	96.0	96.2	93.9
1978	90.4	84.7	93.1	84.8	99.0	79.8	85.9	88.3	94.9	92.9	91.4	80.1	80.5	93.8	97.1	99.0	100.8
1979	97.5	89.7	99.0	93.8	107.5	83.1	91.5	94.4	97.4	97.5	102.0	89.0	88.4	104.0	99.9	103.4	119.4
1980	100.0	97.2	102.9	92.0	107.8	89.4	98.4	103.8	102.0	102.5	104.4	87.8	89.9	98.4	102.0	108.2	113.2
1981	97.6	94.1	101.5	90.7	104.0	86.0	96.3	100.0	99.8	103.2	101.6	87.0	85.8	99.2	101.6	103.8	106.6
1982	96.4	94.9	100.7	89.1	101.0	91.0	95.9	97.8	99.4	103.0	99.7	86.0	83.7	97.6	100.0	101.9	101.0
1983	97.3	90.3	100.8	92.8	105.3	84.7	92.2	94.1	99.5	101.4	101.5	91.1	86.2	101.1	105.5	106.6	103.9

Industrial production: intermediate goods (1) — Production industrielle : biens intermédiaires (1)

Adjusted - Corrigé *

1980 = 100

Year	Q.1	Q.2	Q.3	Q.4	JAN	FEB	MAR	APR	MAY	JUN	JUL	AUG	SEP	OCT	NOV	DEC
1964	52.2	52.5	54.2	54.5	51.1	52.9	52.6	50.6	53.5	53.6	54.0	54.5	54.0	54.7	54.9	54.1
1965	53.8	53.4	55.3	56.2	56.7	52.8	52.0	52.7	53.6	53.9	54.4	55.6	55.8	57.0	55.5	56.0
1966	56.9	56.5	56.4	57.5	56.4	56.7	57.4	56.6	56.5	56.4	57.7	54.9	56.5	56.6	57.1	58.9
1967	56.8	57.0	56.2	57.7	56.9	56.7	56.8	57.3	57.1	56.5	56.4	55.9	56.3	57.0	56.5	59.6
1968	59.3	61.5	62.3	63.4	58.0	58.3	61.5	60.3	60.1	64.1	61.0	62.5	63.4	62.3	64.7	63.2
1969	65.1	67.3	69.1	68.6	64.7	64.9	65.6	65.8	67.4	68.6	68.4	69.7	69.3	69.0	71.5	65.3
1970	70.4	73.4	73.1	74.6	70.1	70.2	70.8	71.0	76.9	72.1	72.9	73.3	73.2	74.9	74.1	74.7
1971	76.1	78.1	79.2	77.2	75.9	76.5	75.8	77.1	78.9	78.5	79.2	79.2	79.1	80.1	77.5	74.1
1972	80.2	81.4	85.2	90.7	81.0	77.4	82.1	82.0	80.6	81.7	85.1	84.3	86.2	89.0	89.4	93.8
1973	86.2	87.1	87.7	90.4	86.1	86.9	85.8	87.2	86.6	87.4	87.2	86.9	89.0	87.9	90.0	93.2
1974	91.6	93.2	91.9	89.8	87.7	93.5	93.7	92.4	92.6	94.4	90.8	93.4	91.5	89.1	90.2	90.2
1975	88.1	81.7	80.8	83.0	88.5	88.1	87.7	83.6	81.4	80.2	79.8	82.3	80.2	81.1	86.1	81.9
1976	84.9	91.0	93.0	93.4	83.7	85.1	85.9	87.9	92.2	93.0	93.3	92.8	92.9	94.2	92.6	93.5
1977	92.1	91.7	89.7	91.2	92.8	91.7	91.9	93.1	90.5	91.6	92.5	89.6	87.0	92.7	91.4	89.5
1978	91.3	93.1	95.4	97.1	92.4	90.1	91.4	94.5	94.0	90.9	94.9	94.5	96.9	96.9	97.4	97.2
1979	97.7	96.3	100.9	104.5	96.7	93.5	97.9	96.9	93.8	98.1	99.2	100.7	102.7	99.3	101.4	112.8
1980	103.7	100.1	98.7	97.7	103.3	103.5	104.2	99.0	100.9	100.5	99.6	100.1	96.4	95.2	100.9	97.1
1981	97.1	96.6	96.7	97.1	96.7	97.2	97.5	96.3	96.0	97.4	96.0	96.8	97.2	97.9	96.3	97.2
1982	95.0	92.5	89.4	88.5	99.0	93.5	92.6	93.3	93.2	91.0	90.8	88.4	89.1	90.9	89.6	84.9
1983	88.5	92.9	97.3	99.1	88.6	88.7	88.2	93.3	91.4	94.0	99.1	94.5	98.2	101.6	100.1	95.6

Industrial production: construction (3) — Production industrielle : construction (3)

Adjusted - Corrigé *

1980 = 100

Year	Q.1	Q.2	Q.3	Q.4	JAN	FEB	MAR	APR	MAY	JUN	JUL	AUG	SEP	OCT	NOV	DEC
1964																
1965																
1966																
1967																
1968																
1969	63.9	68.8	70.5	67.9	65.6	58.7	67.5	66.6	68.9	70.9	71.3	70.0	70.3	69.6	77.0	57.2
1970	64.2	71.2	74.1	75.6	64.1	63.8	64.8	68.9	73.5	71.3	72.9	75.6	73.9	74.8	76.9	75.1
1971	80.4	83.1	86.4	84.0	77.1	86.0	78.2	81.0	84.6	83.7	86.3	87.1	85.9	88.9	83.6	79.6
1972	93.9	90.3	95.8	107.8	98.7	86.4	96.5	94.8	83.9	92.2	94.6	93.1	99.6	101.4	104.2	117.7
1973	99.9	92.7	94.9	94.9	101.9	102.2	95.6	94.2	90.9	93.1	94.4	94.9	95.5	92.6	95.2	96.9
1974	105.8	99.8	95.2	96.1	100.7	109.4	107.4	101.2	96.2	102.0	95.0	96.1	94.6	94.1	95.6	98.5
1975	99.2	88.3	87.6	88.1	99.5	98.7	99.4	90.3	88.9	85.7	83.8	91.3	87.9	85.7	90.1	88.5
1976	87.8	96.2	96.7	97.2	86.9	87.6	88.8	91.7	97.2	99.6	97.5	95.9	96.7	98.0	95.9	97.7
1977	96.4	95.5	94.6	93.8	96.0	95.8	97.4	96.5	95.9	94.2	97.5	93.7	92.5	97.6	94.1	89.5
1978	93.6	93.2	94.7	93.6	99.7	90.3	90.8	94.6	92.6	92.4	94.5	93.5	96.2	94.9	93.4	92.5
1979	93.7	89.9	95.8	106.6	90.6	97.7	93.0	89.4	86.9	93.5	94.0	95.8	97.6	97.0	98.5	124.4
1980	106.3	98.1	99.4	97.8	107.8	105.4	105.8	95.1	98.7	100.7	97.7	101.2	99.2	98.6	101.2	93.5
1981	102.0	102.6	99.7	93.0	100.3	103.3	102.3	102.8	102.8	102.1	101.8	100.0	97.4	96.1	95.2	87.6
1982	88.0	92.7	90.3	88.7	83.6	89.8	90.5	93.0	93.3	91.8	91.7	88.6	90.5	92.1	90.4	83.7
1983	85.3	91.2	93.5	92.3	87.8	82.4	85.7	92.5	89.4	91.8	95.0	92.7	93.0	96.1	94.6	87.8

Industrial production: manufacturing (1)(2) — Production industrielle : industries manufacturières (1)(2)

Adjusted - Corrigé *

1980 = 100

Year	Q.1	Q.2	Q.3	Q.4	JAN	FEB	MAR	APR	MAY	JUN	JUL	AUG	SEP	OCT	NOV	DEC
1964	46.3	46.5	47.5	47.7	46.1	46.4	46.3	45.7	47.0	46.8	48.0	47.3	47.3	47.8	47.2	48.0
1965	48.1	48.0	48.8	48.8	49.3	47.7	47.2	47.7	47.7	48.5	48.4	48.6	49.5	49.0	49.8	47.7
1966	50.2	50.3	49.8	52.2	49.7	50.0	50.9	50.3	50.2	50.4	50.4	48.6	50.5	51.8	51.0	53.9
1967	50.6	51.2	50.1	52.5	50.6	50.4	50.7	51.3	51.4	51.0	50.3	49.4	50.7	51.5	51.4	54.7
1968	52.7	54.4	56.3	56.8	52.6	51.9	53.5	54.2	54.2	54.9	55.7	56.1	56.9	56.9	57.8	55.6
1969	59.3	61.3	63.4	63.7	58.8	59.3	59.8	59.9	61.7	62.3	63.2	63.3	63.8	63.9	64.8	62.6
1970	65.3	66.6	67.5	69.0	63.6	65.9	66.5	66.8	66.1	67.0	67.1	67.7	67.8	68.9	68.7	69.5
1971	71.4	72.0	72.5	72.9	71.6	71.6	71.2	71.8	72.3	71.9	72.0	72.2	73.1	73.1	74.1	71.6
1972	74.9	76.9	78.2	83.5	77.0	72.5	75.3	77.0	76.9	76.8	77.9	78.3	78.3	82.1	79.9	88.5
1973	79.4	81.9	83.7	84.2	78.9	79.7	79.5	81.5	81.5	82.6	82.7	83.4	85.1	84.0	82.7	85.8
1974	87.3	88.3	86.9	84.1	86.0	87.4	88.5	87.1	86.8	91.1	87.4	87.0	86.2	84.7	84.9	82.7
1975	82.1	78.3	77.7	80.2	81.4	83.4	81.7	78.9	78.4	77.6	76.5	78.5	78.0	77.9	81.2	81.5
1976	81.4	85.4	87.0	88.1	81.5	81.4	81.3	83.0	86.5	86.6	87.2	86.5	87.3	89.1	87.6	87.5
1977	88.6	88.7	88.2	88.6	90.5	86.7	88.7	89.6	87.9	88.5	91.9	87.0	85.6	91.5	88.0	86.4
1978	88.3	90.2	90.7	92.0	88.7	88.3	88.0	93.0	89.9	87.7	89.9	90.2	92.0	92.5	91.0	92.6
1979	93.5	95.9	100.3	100.0	92.7	94.1	93.8	95.4	94.2	98.0	99.7	99.2	101.8	95.4	95.5	109.2
1980	101.4	99.6	98.6	100.3	100.3	100.8	103.0	99.9	98.7	100.3	98.4	101.1	96.3	97.6	100.3	103.1
1981	98.1	98.1	97.2	96.9	96.9	98.5	99.0	97.7	98.7	97.8	97.6	96.8	97.2	97.5	96.4	96.8
1982	99.2	97.1	95.6	94.1	102.7	98.0	96.9	97.4	98.0	95.9	96.6	94.5	95.7	96.1	94.7	91.6
1983	94.4	97.1	99.7	98.2	95.7	94.2	93.3	97.5	96.1	97.6	102.3	97.5	99.3	101.5	99.0	94.2

* Adjusted by the O.E.C.D. — * Corrigé par l'O.C.D.E.

AUSTRIA

Production: crude steel
thousand tons, monthly averages

Production : acier brut
milliers de tonnes, moyennes mensuelles

	Year	Q.1	Q.2	Q.3	Q.4	JAN	FEB	MAR	APR	MAY	JUN	JUL	AUG	SEP	OCT	NOV	DEC
1964																	
1965																	
1966																	
1967																	
1968																	
1969	327	326	318	340	324	320	317	342	307	322	326	349	323	348	355	337	280
1970	340	333	346	347	333	343	321	336	360	324	355	359	325	358	350	341	307
1971	330	339	330	345	305	323	328	366	330	318	343	348	347	340	324	310	281
1972	339	341	321	350	344	321	335	366	295	323	346	356	342	352	358	355	320
1973	353	356	347	361	348	352	341	376	334	369	339	357	357	369	374	367	303
1974	392	388	380	408	390	375	380	409	379	394	367	426	393	405	427	393	351
1975	339	373	341	316	327	385	371	364	369	296	357	334	286	327	366	337	277
1976	373	353	391	401	349	319	339	400	379	399	394	401	394	407	363	357	326
1977	341	362	357	324	320	355	349	383	358	355	359	331	307	335	349	330	282
1978	361	359	387	337	361	342	346	390	392	375	395	320	322	368	377	358	347
1979	410	397	411	415	416	399	363	428	419	423	391	415	416	414	441	417	391
1980	385	421	397	376	347	428	410	426	396	405	389	382	357	339	364	350	307
1981	388	365	364	403	400	333	357	405	367	386	399	408	397	405	410	404	385
1982	355	405	384	324	306	393	389	434	403	374	374	338	319	315	325	318	274
1983	368	344	368	373	385	305	341	387	368	369	366	373	350	396	403	390	363

Production: wood fellings
thousand cubic metres, quarterly averages

Production : abattage d'arbres
milliers de mètres cubes, moyennes trimestrielles

	Year	Q.1	Q.2	Q.3	Q.4	JAN	FEB	MAR	APR	MAY	JUN	JUL	AUG	SEP	OCT	NOV	DEC
1964	2484	2063	2138	2090	3645												
1965	2600	1629	2399	2426	3944												
1966	2506	2073	2168	2186	3597												
1967	2670	2149	2453	2301	3777												
1968	2409	1769	2152	2082	3632												
1969	2617	1799	2427	2307	3936												
1970	2781	1587	2710	2598	4228												
1971	2649	2146	2196	2169	4085												
1972	2538	2074	1987	1970	4122												
1973	2429	1831	2008	2137	3738												
1974	2506	2379	2123	1983	3540												
1975	2400	2068	1858	1916	3757												
1976	2895	2535	2374	2446	4224												
1977	2677	2342	2124	2064	4176												
1978	2637	2126	2033	2219	4169												
1979	3188	2280	2881	2487	5104												
1980	3183	2857	2635	2652	4588												
1981	3042	2609	2648	2522	4390												
1982	2773	2415	2370	2152	4154												
1983	2920	2225	2319	2538	4599												

Production: future tendency
mining and manufacturing
per cent balance

Perspectives de production
industries extractives et manufacturières
solde en pourcentage

	Year	Q.1	Q.2	Q.3	Q.4	JAN	FEB	MAR	APR	MAY	JUN	JUL	AUG	SEP	OCT	NOV	DEC
1964		21	20	21	12	21			20			21			12		
1965		22	21	14	9	22			21			14			9		
1966		15	20	18	2	15			20			18			2		
1967		-9	-1	-1	-10	-9			-1			-1			-10		
1968		15	17	15	21	15			17			15			21		
1969		26	22	24	19	26			22			24			19		
1970		32	16	20	13	32			16			20			13		
1971		17	13	10	3	17			13			10			3		
1972		6	12	14	13	6			12			14			13		
1973		16	12	4	-	16			12			4			-		
1974		8	4	6	-16	8			4			6			-16		
1975		-16	-21	-19	-13	-16			-21			-19			-13		
1976		5	14	14	-12	5			14			14			-12		
1977		4	5	-3	-14	4			5			-3			-14		
1978		1	-2	-1	-6	1			-2			-1			-6		
1979		4	13	8	3	4			13			8			3		
1980		12	6	-7	-16	12			6			-7			-16		
1981		-7	-5	-8	-8	-7			-5			-8			-8		
1982		3	-8	-2	-22	3			-8			-2			-22		
1983		-11	-7	-9	-14	-11			-7			-9			-14		

Order books: level
mining and manufacturing
per cent balance

Carnet de commandes : niveau
industries extractives et manufacturières
solde en pourcentage

Year	Q.1	Q.2	Q.3	Q.4	JAN	FEB	MAR	APR	MAY	JUN	JUL	AUG	SEP	OCT	NOV	DEC
1964	-2	8	5	-1	-2			8			5			-1		
1965	-3	-10	-1	-12	-3			-10			-1			-12		
1966	-19	-10	-13	-21	-19			-10			-13			-21		
1967	-27	-39	-37	-38	-27			-39			-37			-38		
1968	-38	-10	-7	-2	-38			-10			-7			-2		
1969	3	13	20	28	3			13			20			28		
1970	22	19	30	25	22			19			30			25		
1971	16	10	11	1	16			10			11			1		
1972	-5	1	3	18	-5			1			3			18		
1973	13	7	5	5	13			7			5			5		
1974	7	18	9	-10	7			18			9			-10		
1975	-36	-59	-59	-55	-36			-59			-59			-55		
1976	-45	-30	-25	-33	-45			-30			-25			-33		
1977	-39	-32	-40	-46	-39			-32			-40			-46		
1978	-37	-34	-28	-33	-37			-34			-28			-33		
1979	-14	6	13	11	-14			6			13			11		
1980	6	-	-11	-32	6			-			-11			-32		
1981	-28	-36	-25	-26	-30			-32								
1982	-30	-36	-34	-51	-30			-36			-34			-51		
1983	-45	-44	-37	-34	-45			-44			-37			-34		

Finished goods stocks: level
mining and manufacturing
per cent balance

Stocks de produits finis : niveau
industries extractives et manufacturières
solde en pourcentage

Year	Q.1	Q.2	Q.3	Q.4	JAN	FEB	MAR	APR	MAY	JUN	JUL	AUG	SEP	OCT	NOV	DEC
1964	-1	-	-	-	-1			-			-			-		
1965	10	9	9	6	10			9			9			6		
1966	18	16	18	18	18			16			18			18		
1967	25	29	28	25	25			29			28			25		
1968	25	10	17	13	25			10			17			13		
1969	6	4	1	-8	6			4			1			-8		
1970	-6	-5	-11	-13	-6			-5			-11			-13		
1971	2	7	7	15	2			7			7			15		
1972	13	8	4	-9	13			8			4			-9		
1973	-2	2	5	8	-2			2			5			8		
1974	-	-8	4	18	-			-8			4			18		
1975	37	53	54	47	37			53			54			47		
1976	39	35	24	23	39			35			24			23		
1977	16	24	29	35	16			24			29			35		
1978	32	31	34	29	32			31			34			29		
1979	20	19	9	1	20			19			9			1		
1980	8	9	13	28	8			9			13			28		
1981	26	32	35	29	26			25								
1982	27	34	39	34	27			34			39			34		
1983	27	27	26	20	27			27			26			20		

Firms operating at full capacity
mining and manufacturing
per cent

Entreprises travaillant à pleine capacité
industries extractives et manufacturières
solde en pourcentage

Year	Q.1	Q.2	Q.3	Q.4	JAN	FEB	MAR	APR	MAY	JUN	JUL	AUG	SEP	OCT	NOV	DEC
1964	55	54	61	58	55			54			61			58		
1965	54	58	59	57	54			58			59			57		
1966	48	46	52	51	48			46			52			51		
1967	35	32	36	35	35			32			36			35		
1968	39	46	44	48	39			46			44			48		
1969	49	59	66	71	49			59			66			71		
1970	68	70	71	71	68			70			71			71		
1971	67	72	71	59	67			72			71			59		
1972	59	64	63	72	59			64			63			72		
1973	62	67	65	60	62			67			65			60		
1974	65	69	60	52	65			69			60			52		
1975	37	25	18	17	37			25			18			17		
1976	24	31	37	35	24			31			37			35		
1977	35	34	31	25	35			34			31			25		
1978	28	28	37	34	28			28			37			34		
1979	38	41	48	51	38			41			48			51		
1980	49	57	44	35	49			57			44			35		
1981	23	22	21	20	32			32								
1982	17	17	15	12	17			17			15			12		
1983	12	13	19	20	12			13			19			20		

AUSTRIA

Manufacturing new orders, net: (4) — Commandes nouvelles nettes (industries manufacturières) : (4)
domestic — marché intérieur
million schilling, monthly averages — millions de schillings, moyennes mensuelles

	Year	Q.1	Q.2	Q.3	Q.4	JAN	FEB	MAR	APR	MAY	JUN	JUL	AUG	SEP	OCT	NOV	DEC
1964																	
1965																	
1966																	
1967																	
1968																	
1969																	
1970																	
1971																	
1972					10229										11282	10655	8750
1973	9346	8598	9497	8778	10512	7914	7958	9923	9265	10210	9015	8015	8745	9574	11772	11171	8592
1974	10497	10018	11108	10363	10497	9714	9382	10960	11783	11521	10019	10093	10445	10549	12235	10404	8853
1975	10051	9914	10080	9777	10431	10154	10001	9587	10375	9415	10450	9413	9226	10693	11158	10296	9838
1976	11277	10531	11664	11410	11503	9825	9488	12280	12185	11335	11473	10916	10850	12465	11481	12469	10559
1977	11839	12141	11843	11493	11879	11287	11224	13912	12050	11840	11640	10473	10984	13021	12667	11891	11078
1978	11625	11268	12011	10926	12294	11622	10187	11996	12589	11696	11749	10346	10936	11497	13077	13361	10443
1979	13365	12677	13702	13442	13640	12557	11319	13655	13743	13772	13592	12960	13342	14024	16202	13348	11365
1980	13762	13439	14209	13427	13923	13627	12615	14224	14188	14105	14334	12863	11581	15839	16295	13224	12249
1981	14673	14349	14381	14477	15485	13264	13587	16196	15684	13449	14010	14510	13185	15735	16974	15599	13883
1982	14385	14863	14029	14094	14555	13763	13374	17454	14820	13016	14251	13446	14074	14764	14330	16541	12794
1983	15169	14881	14958	15340	15498	13837	13733	17073	15132	14601	15140	14361	14188	17473	15200	15408	15886

Manufacturing new orders, net: (4) — Commandes nouvelles nettes (industries manufacturières) : (4)
export — étranger
million schilling, monthly averages — millions de schillings, moyennes mensuelles

	Year	Q.1	Q.2	Q.3	Q.4	JAN	FEB	MAR	APR	MAY	JUN	JUL	AUG	SEP	OCT	NOV	DEC
1964																	
1965																	
1966																	
1967																	
1968																	
1969																	
1970																	
1971																	
1972					6852										7112	6895	6548
1973	6858	6912	6942	6054	7524	6207	7181	7349	6515	7366	6946	6272	5502	6388	7836	7655	7080
1974	8981	8874	9799	8735	8517	8244	9144	9233	9227	10739	9429	9350	7201	9654	9212	8636	7704
1975	8999	10007	8394	8511	9085	8314	12703	9004	9705	8055	7422	7749	7049	10735	9648	8422	9186
1976	9720	10632	9102	8842	10303	9519	9149	13229	9423	8618	9264	10053	7806	8666	9968	9911	11030
1977	10376	11101	10480	9666	10256	10654	9805	12844	11213	10872	9355	10367	8466	10166	9907	10417	10443
1978	11165	10254	12155	9595	12655	10049	9651	11061	11385	12792	12289	9775	8728	10282	12962	13097	11906
1979	12868	12794	12218	12209	14251	13616	11659	13107	12391	12690	11573	12472	11525	12631	15333	13428	13991
1980	13954	14458	13860	12245	15253	14985	14001	14388	14606	12247	14727	13069	10104	13561	16206	12203	17348
1981	16548	15618	19036	15289	16250	15366	15062	16425	20609	14934	21566	16131	13439	16298	16209	15055	17484
1982	15860	18167	15640	13617	16016	15865	18146	20491	17776	14333	14812	15143	11242	14466	14451	16625	16974
1983	16399	16058	16406	15058	18075	16039	15203	16932	15773	15045	18398	14818	12979	17378	17459	15330	21436

Wholesale sales (5) — Ventes du commerce de gros (5)
1980 = 100 — 1980 = 100

	Year	Q.1	Q.2	Q.3	Q.4	JAN	FEB	MAR	APR	MAY	JUN	JUL	AUG	SEP	OCT	NOV	DEC
1964	25	21	24	27	27	20	20	23	24	22	26	26	28	27	28	27	27
1965	27	22	26	29	30	20	22	25	26	25	27	27	30	29	30	31	29
1966	29	25	28	31	31	23	24	29	27	28	29	29	33	30	30	32	32
1967	30	26	29	31	32	24	25	29	27	28	33	29	34	31	32	33	32
1968	32	28	30	35	34	27	27	30	30	31	30	35	37	33	36	33	33
1969	34	29	32	36	37	29	27	31	33	32	33	36	36	37	39	36	36
1970	38	32	37	41	42	30	31	35	38	35	38	41	42	42	43	41	42
1971	42	36	41	45	46	33	35	41	41	39	42	44	46	47	45	47	46
1972	47	41	44	50	54	38	40	45	42	44	46	47	51	51	55	56	53
1973	50	40	49	53	59	35	39	47	46	51	50	50	57	52	59	59	60
1974	61	54	60	66	66	52	52	58	60	61	58	64	67	65	71	64	64
1975	64	56	61	68	73	54	54	60	62	56	64	69	64	70	74	67	78
1976	74	61	70	80	84	54	58	72	68	68	73	76	82	82	79	83	90
1977	79	68	76	82	88	59	66	81	73	75	81	82	82	84	82	90	91
1978	79	67	77	84	88	61	63	78	73	76	83	78	89	85	87	90	87
1979	88	75	86	92	99	68	71	86	82	89	86	91	93	92	102	100	95
1980	100	87	98	104	111	80	86	96	98	95	102	104	100	108	113	106	113
1981	108	96	107	112	116	83	95	109	109	101	111	115	108	114	112	116	120
1982	111	98	109	115	120	84	95	117	109	104	114	115	115	116	115	121	125
1983	124	102	122	129	144	89	96	121	122	116	127	124	132	132	137	142	154

Construction: work put in place (6)(7) / Construction : travaux effectués (6)(7)

million schilling, monthly averages / millions de schillings, moyennes mensuelles

	Year	Q.1	Q.2	Q.3	Q.4	JAN	FEB	MAR	APR	MAY	JUN	JUL	AUG	SEP	OCT	NOV	DEC
1964																	
1965																	
1966																	
1967																	
1968	1768	1099	1933	2143	1895	849	1029	1420	1753	2012	2034	2128	2142	2160	2117	1970	1599
1969	1771	1006	1849	2197	2029	807	911	1302	1664	1825	2059	2202	2121	2268	2404	2190	1493
1970	2112	1090	2139	2669	2548	881	1061	1329	1870	2142	2407	2628	2599	2780	2655	2750	2238
1971	2618	1528	2723	3214	3003	1250	1510	1824	2399	2762	3024	3121	3202	3318	3170	3130	2707
1972	3410	2168	3315	3918	4238	1772	2018	2716	2996	3332	3616	3698	3937	4120	4210	4307	4198
1973	3634	2477	3695	4384	3980	2167	2283	2979	3369	3892	3825	4338	4383	4433	4450	4225	3265
1974	3972	2897	4075	4593	4321	2472	2810	3409	3830	4203	4193	4535	4399	4844	4613	4490	3860
1975	3996	3014	3907	4573	4491	2693	2999	3349	3619	3786	4317	4620	4415	4685	4865	4573	4033
1976	4202	2900	4206	4913	4791	2572	2313	3316	3748	4371	4498	4716	4952	5070	5015	5005	4355
1977	4779	3260	4784	5548	5523	2841	3023	3918	4343	4828	5181	5403	5471	5770	5779	5623	5169
1978	5060	3625	5175	5828	5614	3367	3363	4146	4825	5001	5700	5906	5690	5887	5936	5857	5047
1979	5419	3672	5431	6345	6229	3127	3483	4405	5084	5499	5710	6123	6432	6480	6762	6216	5710
1980	5621	3888	5667	6690	6240	3280	3705	4678	5210	5520	6270	6588	6456	7026	6915	6456	5348
1981	5941	4066	6245	7053	6401	3173	3873	5151	5841	6324	6570	6857	7004	7297	6975	6673	5554
1982	5773	3638	5987	6907	6561	2767	3459	4687	5540	5897	6524	6725	6868	7129	6754	6928	6001
1983	6036	3718	6164	7318	6942	3097	3277	4779	5511	6114	6869	7051	7257	7647	7397	7312	6119

Cost of construction: (5)(6) / Coût de la construction : (5)(6)

residential / bâtiments résidentiels

1980 = 100

	Year	Q.1	Q.2	Q.3	Q.4	JAN	FEB	MAR	APR	MAY	JUN	JUL	AUG	SEP	OCT	NOV	DEC
1964																	
1965																	
1966																	
1967																	
1968																	
1969																	
1970																	
1971				44.2	45.0												
1972	50.4	46.8	50.1	51.8	53.1												
1973	60.7	57.2	59.7	61.8	63.9												
1974	70.2	66.2	70.5	71.5	72.4												
1975	75.2	74.2	75.5	75.6	75.6												
1976	78.9	76.5	78.7	80.1	80.4												
1977	83.5	80.9	83.6	84.5	84.8												
1978	88.2	85.8	87.9	89.3	89.6												
1979	92.8	90.1	92.2	93.5	95.5												
1980	100.0	96.8	100.0	100.9	102.3												
1981	108.3	104.6	107.9	109.7	111.1												
1982	115.3	112.5	115.8	116.2	116.7												
1983	119.5	117.6	119.9	120.4	119.5												

Wholesale sales (5) / Ventes du commerce de gros (5)

Adjusted - Corrigé *

1980 = 100

	Year	Q.1	Q.2	Q.3	Q.4	JAN	FEB	MAR	APR	MAY	JUN	JUL	AUG	SEP	OCT	NOV	DEC
1964		24	24	25	25	24	24	24	24	24	25	24	25	25	26	25	25
1965		26	27	27	28	25	26	26	27	27	27	26	27	27	28	28	28
1966		28	29	29	30	28	28	29	29	30	29	29	28	29	29	29	31
1967		30	30	29	30	29	30	29	29	29	32	29	30	30	30	30	32
1968		31	31	32	32	31	31	31	31	31	31	32	33	32	32	32	33
1969		33	33	33	35	33	33	33	33	33	33	33	33	34	35	35	35
1970		38	36	38	41	37	39	37	37	37	35	36	38	39	41	41	41
1971		43	40	41	46	43	44	41	40	40	39	39	41	44	45	46	46
1972		49	42	45	55	51	49	46	43	41	41	42	43	50	54	55	55
1973		43	48	48	59	45	50	48	46	46	51	45	49	52	57	59	62
1974		65	56	60	65	66	66	62	58	56	56	55	60	65	69	65	62
1975		67	58	62	70	69	68	64	60	57	59	60	60	67	70	69	72
1976		70	69	75	79	70	70	70	68	69	69	70	77	77	78	80	81
1977		78	77	78	82	77	79	77	76	78	77	80	76	78	79	83	83
1978		76	78	81	82	77	75	76	77	78	78	78	82	82	81	82	81
1979		84	87	89	92	84	84	85	86	87	87	88	87	91	93	91	91
1980		98	99	100	103	97	98	98	98	99	101	97	100	102	103	103	102
1981		108	107	108	108	104	112	107	108	106	109	109	108	107	105	110	108
1982		110	109	111	112	108	111	111	109	111	108	111	113	109	111	111	113
1983		113	122	125	135	115	112	113	125	120	121	124	126	125	133	130	144

* Adjusted by the O.E.C.D. / * Corrigé par l'O.C.D.E.

AUSTRIA

Retail sales: value (7)(8)
1980 = 100

Ventes au détail : valeur (7)(8)
1980 = 100

	Year	Q.1	Q.2	Q.3	Q.4	JAN	FEB	MAR	APR	MAY	JUN	JUL	AUG	SEP	OCT	NOV	DEC
1964	31	27	28	30	38	26	27	28	27	28	29	31	31	30	33	32	49
1965	33	28	31	33	41	27	28	29	32	29	32	34	33	32	35	36	51
1966	35	30	33	34	42	29	29	32	34	33	34	35	34	34	34	38	54
1967	37	32	34	36	44	31	30	35	32	35	36	35	37	36	36	40	56
1968	38	33	36	38	46	33	32	35	36	37	35	38	40	35	39	43	56
1969	40	34	37	40	49	34	32	35	37	39	36	40	41	38	42	43	61
1970	43	37	40	43	53	36	35	40	39	40	41	44	44	42	46	47	66
1971	48	39	44	48	58	39	37	42	45	44	44	49	48	47	49	53	73
1972	53	44	48	53	65	42	42	50	46	50	49	53	54	53	54	59	82
1973	59	47	55	59	73	43	45	54	54	55	56	59	59	58	64	70	86
1974	66	56	63	68	79	55	52	60	63	64	61	68	69	67	73	74	91
1975	73	62	68	74	89	60	58	68	66	69	68	76	72	74	81	79	107
1976	80	66	74	80	97	63	63	73	75	73	74	81	78	82	82	90	119
1977	89	74	82	88	110	70	70	83	81	82	83	87	86	91	94	101	135
1978	86	73	82	87	103	69	67	82	77	82	86	84	86	89	91	96	121
1979	93	82	90	91	110	80	75	91	88	92	90	91	92	90	101	104	127
1980	100	89	96	98	118	88	84	94	95	98	94	101	94	99	109	106	139
1981	106	92	103	104	125	92	87	99	106	100	103	108	100	106	113	115	147
1982	112	100	109	110	130	95	93	111	113	105	109	114	106	108	116	121	153
1983	121	105	115	117	147	99	95	121	113	116	114	116	113	121	126	133	182

Retail sales: durable goods (7)(8)
1980 = 100

Ventes au détail : biens durables (7)(8)
1980 = 100

	Year	Q.1	Q.2	Q.3	Q.4	JAN	FEB	MAR	APR	MAY	JUN	JUL	AUG	SEP	OCT	NOV	DEC
1964	28	22	24	27	38	21	21	22	24	23	25	27	25	30	31	33	49
1965	30	23	26	30	40	22	22	24	26	26	27	30	28	31	32	36	52
1966	32	25	29	32	42	22	24	28	29	29	30	31	30	35	33	38	56
1967	33	27	30	32	45	26	25	29	28	30	31	30	31	35	34	40	59
1968	35	28	32	34	47	27	28	30	32	33	31	34	34	36	38	43	60
1969	38	29	34	37	49	28	28	31	33	35	34	37	35	39	41	44	64
1970	41	31	37	41	54	30	31	33	36	36	38	40	38	43	43	48	70
1971	46	35	41	46	61	32	35	38	40	41	43	45	43	49	47	55	81
1972	54	40	46	53	75	36	39	45	43	49	48	51	51	58	55	67	102
1973	58	44	56	58	76	33	44	54	54	57	56	60	55	58	66	71	92
1974	68	57	65	66	82	54	53	64	67	67	63	70	64	65	74	74	97
1975	77	64	72	73	99	60	61	70	71	70	75	79	67	74	85	85	126
1976	85	70	80	83	108	59	69	82	79	80	81	84	79	86	87	101	136
1977	104	82	90	97	148	69	80	97	89	93	89	103	89	98	118	134	193
1978	84	63	83	84	107	54	57	77	77	82	91	84	82	85	93	101	128
1979	94	84	91	90	111	77	77	99	90	94	90	94	87	88	102	105	127
1980	100	90	98	98	115	84	85	99	97	99	98	104	88	101	108	102	134
1981	101	88	100	98	118	82	83	101	103	98	100	104	89	100	106	110	133
1982	106	94	105	103	123	83	88	112	110	98	106	110	97	101	105	117	146
1983	123	106	119	113	157	94	92	131	117	116	120	125	106	117	122	139	209

New passenger car registrations
thousands, monthly averages

Immatriculations de voitures de tourisme neuves
milliers, moyennes mensuelles

	Year	Q.1	Q.2	Q.3	Q.4	JAN	FEB	MAR	APR	MAY	JUN	JUL	AUG	SEP	OCT	NOV	DEC
1964	8.0	7.2	10.0	7.3	7.5	4.1	6.5	11.1	10.4	10.3	9.2	8.2	7.2	6.4	8.5	7.4	6.6
1965	9.2	7.5	12.0	8.7	8.7	4.7	6.6	11.1	13.8	12.2	10.1	10.3	7.6	8.3	9.5	8.8	7.9
1966	10.1	9.1	12.9	9.5	9.0	5.2	8.8	13.3	14.5	13.5	10.8	11.1	7.7	9.3	11.0	8.6	7.3
1967	10.2	10.0	12.7	8.4	9.6	6.3	8.8	15.0	13.0	13.0	12.2	9.8	6.3	9.3	9.5	9.0	10.3
1968	10.9	10.2	14.2	16.8	2.4	8.2	10.5	11.8	12.0	14.7	15.8	15.4	33.5	1.6	1.7	2.8	2.7
1969	8.4	5.0	10.8	8.9	8.9	2.9	4.0	8.1	10.4	11.9	10.1	9.8	8.2	8.6	11.3	9.1	6.4
1970	10.6	9.3	14.7	11.4	7.1	6.6	8.4	12.8	14.0	16.0	14.0	13.5	10.5	10.3	11.2	9.3	0.8
1971	16.3	18.0	19.4	14.6	13.1	23.0	12.8	18.1	21.3	18.7	18.1	18.0	13.1	12.8	16.7	13.1	9.6
1972	18.5	15.9	20.5	15.3	22.2	12.4	15.2	20.3	21.4	19.5	20.6	20.2	15.1	10.5	20.2	23.1	23.3
1973	15.6	15.0	18.0	15.1	14.2	11.7	13.1	20.1	19.0	17.8	17.4	16.9	13.2	15.3	16.9	15.6	10.0
1974	13.9	15.0	16.2	13.3	11.1	13.1	12.4	19.7	18.0	15.8	14.8	14.4	13.2	12.4	14.1	12.5	6.6
1975	15.4	16.4	17.0	14.6	13.8	13.7	15.1	20.4	16.2	16.0	16.7	16.2	13.5	14.1	16.5	14.4	10.4
1976	18.8	18.7	20.2	17.6	18.7	15.4	18.1	22.6	21.0	20.8	18.7	20.7	14.2	17.9	20.0	17.9	18.3
1977	24.7	20.6	22.1	21.9	34.1	16.0	18.8	26.9	24.6	22.4	19.2	26.6	17.6	21.6	29.5	30.2	42.6
1978	13.2	9.3	15.4	14.3	13.7	8.5	6.6	12.9	13.0	16.3	16.8	16.3	12.7	14.0	14.2	16.3	10.7
1979	17.9	17.8	21.3	16.4	15.9	15.6	14.7	23.1	23.4	20.2	20.3	17.9	15.4	16.1	16.7	18.9	12.0
1980	19.0	20.3	22.7	17.7	15.3	16.9	19.7	24.3	22.8	23.9	21.3	19.5	17.0	16.5	20.4	16.2	9.3
1981	16.6	17.7	21.6	14.8	12.1	15.7	16.1	21.5	24.3	22.6	17.8	18.2	12.9	13.3	16.0	12.5	7.3
1982	16.8	16.2	21.4	16.1	13.3	14.2	14.6	19.9	24.8	22.2	17.3	19.6	14.2	14.5	15.7	14.3	10.0
1983	21.4	19.6	26.7	20.6	18.7	16.9	16.5	25.3	34.0	23.6	22.5	24.1	17.0	20.6	19.9	21.0	15.3

Retail sales: value (7)(8) — Adjusted - Corrigé * — Ventes au détail : valeur (7)(8)

1980 = 100

	Year	Q.1	Q.2	Q.3	Q.4	JAN	FEB	MAR	APR	MAY	JUN	JUL	AUG	SEP	OCT	NOV	DEC
1964		30	30	31	32	30	31	30	30	30	31	31	31	31	32	31	32
1965		32	33	34	34	32	33	32	33	32	33	34	34	34	34	34	34
1966		35	35	35	35	34	35	35	35	36	35	35	34	34	35	36	35
1967		36	37	36	37	37	36	36	36	36	37	36	36	37	36	37	38
1968		38	38	38	38	38	37	38	38	38	38	38	38	38	38	39	38
1969		39	40	40	41	39	39	38	40	40	40	40	40	40	41	41	41
1970		42	43	44	45	41	42	42	42	42	43	43	44	44	44	45	45
1971		45	47	48	49	46	46	45	47	47	48	47	48	49	48	48	49
1972		50	51	53	55	50	49	51	51	52	51	53	53	53	54	54	57
1973		54	58	59	62	50	55	57	57	58	59	59	58	60	62	63	61
1974		64	66	68	67	65	64	64	66	66	66	67	68	69	69	67	65
1975		71	73	74	75	70	71	71	72	71	74	74	73	73	75	75	75
1976		76	78	81	82	73	77	78	77	79	78	79	81	82	78	83	84
1977		85	86	88	93	84	86	86	84	88	87	87	88	89	91	93	95
1978		82	86	87	88	83	82	81	86	85	88	86	88	88	87	89	89
1979		93	93	93	95	94	91	93	93	95	91	93	94	94	95	94	95
1980		99	99	100	102	102	97	98	98	99	100	100	98	101	102	101	103
1981		104	106	107	108	103	105	105	107	105	106	106	106	108	105	111	109
1982		111	112	112	112	110	112	112	112	112	113	112	113	111	111	113	113
1983		117	119	119	126	116	115	120	115	122	118	117	118	122	122	125	132

Retail sales: durable goods (7)(8) — Adjusted - Corrigé * — Ventes au détail : biens durables (7)(8)

1980 = 100

	Year	Q.1	Q.2	Q.3	Q.4	JAN	FEB	MAR	APR	MAY	JUN	JUL	AUG	SEP	OCT	NOV	DEC
1964		27	27	28	28	28	27	27	27	27	27	28	28	28	28	28	28
1965		29	29	30	30	30	29	29	30	29	30	30	30	30	30	30	30
1966		32	32	32	32	30	32	33	32	33	32	33	32	33	32	32	33
1967		34	33	33	34	34	33	33	32	33	32	32	32	33	33	34	36
1968		35	35	35	36	35	34	36	35	35	35	35	35	35	36	36	36
1969		36	37	38	33	36	36	37	37	37	37	38	38	37	38	39	38
1970		39	40	41	42	38	40	39	40	40	40	41	41	42	41	42	42
1971		43	45	46	47	44	44	42	44	45	45	45	46	47	46	47	49
1972		49	50	54	59	49	48	49	48	51	50	52	54	57	54	59	64
1973		53	59	60	61	44	56	58	59	59	59	61	59	59	62	63	59
1974		69	69	68	66	72	66	68	70	68	68	69	69	67	70	66	63
1975		76	76	76	80	80	75	74	75	74	78	77	75	75	79	79	81
1976		82	84	86	87	78	83	83	83	84	86	82	89	88	82	90	89
1977		96	95	100	120	93	97	97	94	99	92	104	98	99	112	120	130
1978		72	87	87	90	72	69	76	84	86	92	85	89	87	87	91	91
1979		96	94	94	94	97	94	97	96	95	93	94	94	93	94	94	94
1980		101	101	101	98	104	99	100	99	101	102	101	98	103	100	97	98
1981		100	102	101	102	100	100	100	103	102	102	100	100	102	99	104	102
1982		106	106	106	106	104	106	107	108	104	107	106	109	103	102	107	108
1983		118	120	117	135	117	111	125	115	124	121	115	117	118	119	129	156

Retail sales: volume (7)(8) — Adjusted - Corrigé * — Ventes au détail : volume (7)(8)

1980 = 100

	Year	Q.1	Q.2	Q.3	Q.4	JAN	FEB	MAR	APR	MAY	JUN	JUL	AUG	SEP	OCT	NOV	DEC
1964	67	66	66	68	68	66	67	65	66	66	67	67	68	68	69	67	69
1965	70	69	69	72	71	68	70	69	69	67	70	72	72	71	72	71	70
1966	72	72	73	71	71	71	72	72	73	74	73	73	71	70	70	72	70
1967	72	72	73	72	72	73	72	72	72	73	75	72	72	72	71	72	74
1968	73	73	73	73	73	74	71	73	73	74	72	73	74	72	73	74	73
1969	75	73	75	75	76	74	73	73	75	75	75	75	76	74	76	76	76
1970	79	77	78	79	80	76	78	77	77	77	79	78	80	79	79	80	80
1971	83	81	83	83	84	81	81	80	82	83	83	82	84	85	83	83	85
1972	87	85	85	87	88	85	83	86	85	87	84	88	87	87	87	87	91
1973	91	86	91	92	93	80	87	89	90	92	92	92	90	93	94	94	92
1974	94	94	94	95	91	96	94	92	95	94	93	95	96	96	95	90	88
1975	95	93	94	95	96	93	93	93	94	92	96	96	94	94	96	95	96
1976	97	94	95	98	97	91	95	95	94	95	95	95	98	99	94	99	99
1977	102	100	100	101	107	98	101	100	98	102	100	101	101	102	104	107	109
1978	96	92	97	98	98	94	92	92	96	95	98	96	98	98	97	98	98
1979	100	101	101	100	100	103	100	101	101	103	99	100	100	99	100	99	100
1980	100	101	100	99	100	105	99	100	100	100	100	99	97	100	100	99	100
1981	99	99	99	99	99	99	100	99	100	98	99	99	98	100	96	101	100
1982	99	100	100	98	98	99	101	100	99	99	101	98	99	98	97	98	98
1983	104	101	102	102	107	101	99	104	99	106	102	100	101	104	104	105	112

* Adjusted by the O.E.C.D. — * Corrigé par l'O.C.D.E.

AUSTRIA

Employment: mining and manufacturing (9)(10)
(all employees)
thousands

Emploi : industries extractives et manufacturières (9)(10)
(salariés)
milliers

	Year	Q.1	Q.2	Q.3	Q.4	JAN	FEB	MAR	APR	MAY	JUN	JUL	AUG	SEP	OCT	NOV	DEC
1964	629	626	627	629	635	625	626	627	628	627	626	627	629	631	635	637	633
1965	630	628	627	631	635	628	628	627	626	627	627	628	630	635	634	636	634
1966	626	629	626	625	625	629	629	628	627	625	625	625	625	525	627	628	619
1967	606	613	606	602	601	615	613	611	609	607	603	603	602	603	605	604	593
1968	596	589	591	598	605	590	589	589	590	591	591	594	596	602	507	608	599
1969	614	603	609	619	625	600	602	605	608	609	611	616	618	623	627	628	620
1970	634	624	630	637	643	621	625	626	630	630	631	634	637	640	645	646	639
1971	648	640	643	652	657	635	640	643	644	641	643	649	652	656	658	661	650
1972	663	654	657	667	673	653	654	657	657	658	657	662	669	670	674	678	665
1973	676	672	672	679	682	670	672	673	673	673	670	676	680	682	686	685	676
1974	673	673	671	676	672	674	672	672	672	671	670	676	674	673	680	676	662
1975	639	654	640	635	628	658	654	650	645	640	637	636	633	634	633	630	622
1976	629	621	624	634	639	619	620	623	623	624	625	629	634	639	641	641	635
1977	634	634	630	637	635	632	634	635	630	630	630	634	638	639	639	636	631
1978	623	626	619	624	624	628	626	625	619	619	618	621	624	627	627	626	619
1979	621	615	615	624	628	617	614	615	614	615	617	621	625	627	629	629	625
1980	627	625	624	630	630	624	624	626	624	623	625	629	629	633	633	631	627
1981	614	619	614	615	608	620	619	619	615	614	613	616	615	613	612	609	603
1982	589	596	591	590	580	597	595	595	592	590	590	591	591	589	585	580	574
1983	565	565	563	567	565	567	564	565	564	562	564	566	567	569	567	556	562

Unemployment (registered unemployed) (9)(11)
thousands

Chômage (chômeurs inscrits) (9)(11)
milliers

	Year	Q.1	Q.2	Q.3	Q.4	JAN	FEB	MAR	APR	MAY	JUN	JUL	AUG	SEP	OCT	NOV	DEC
1964	66	122	41	33	66	144	131	92	50	39	35	33	32	35	45	60	94
1965	66	117	43	34	68	132	129	91	52	42	36	33	32	36	46	63	95
1966	61	103	44	35	65	126	114	67	52	42	38	35	33	36	45	61	89
1967	65	101	46	37	74	118	112	72	54	44	39	37	36	39	51	68	105
1968	71	122	49	39	73	140	132	92	58	47	42	39	38	40	51	69	100
1969	67	120	48	36	65	136	131	94	58	45	40	37	33	37	45	59	90
1970	58	101	44	33	56	114	104	85	53	42	37	34	32	33	44	54	69
1971	52	77	42	34	56	90	79	62	47	41	38	34	32	35	45	56	67
1972	49	68	42	34	52	80	73	52	47	41	37	35	33	35	45	54	57
1973	41	56	32	28	50	62	59	46	37	32	27	27	27	29	40	49	61
1974	41	61	33	24	48	71	64	49	39	33	26	25	22	24	35	48	60
1975	56	69	46	38	69	75	73	61	56	45	37	37	36	40	54	68	84
1976	55	89	43	32	57	97	95	76	54	42	33	32	31	34	46	56	68
1977	51	75	38	31	62	87	80	56	47	37	28	29	29	34	49	61	75
1978	59	84	47	37	67	92	91	68	50	45	35	36	36	40	55	67	79
1979	57	87	46	34	60	99	93	68	56	47	34	34	33	36	50	62	69
1980	53	77	39	31	66	91	82	58	49	38	29	30	30	34	51	66	82
1981	69	91	43	43	95	105	99	71	56	49	38	41	41	48	71	94	120
1982	105	139	81	72	129	156	146	116	96	81	66	69	69	79	104	128	156
1983	127	171	111	90	137	182	181	152	133	110	91	89	88	93	114	136	160

Unemployment (registered unemployed) (9)(11)(12)
as per cent of total labour force

Chômage (chômeurs inscrits) (9)(11)(12)
en pourcentage de la population active

	Year	Q.1	Q.2	Q.3	Q.4	JAN	FEB	MAR	APR	MAY	JUN	JUL	AUG	SEP	OCT	NOV	DEC
1964	2.7	5.0	1.7	1.3	2.7	5.9	5.4	3.8	2.1	1.6	1.4	1.3	1.3	1.4	1.8	2.4	3.8
1965	2.7	4.8	1.8	1.4	2.7	5.4	5.3	3.8	2.1	1.7	1.5	1.4	1.3	1.5	1.8	2.5	3.9
1966	2.5	4.2	1.8	1.4	2.7	5.2	4.7	2.8	2.1	1.7	1.5	1.4	1.4	1.4	1.8	2.5	3.7
1967	2.7	4.2	1.9	1.5	3.1	4.9	4.6	3.0	2.3	1.8	1.6	1.5	1.5	1.6	2.1	2.8	4.3
1968	2.9	5.1	2.1	1.6	3.0	5.9	5.5	3.9	2.4	2.0	1.8	1.6	1.5	1.7	2.1	2.8	4.2
1969	2.8	5.0	2.0	1.5	2.7	5.7	5.5	3.9	2.4	1.9	1.7	1.5	1.4	1.5	1.9	2.4	3.7
1970	2.4	4.2	1.8	1.3	2.3	4.7	4.3	3.5	2.2	1.7	1.5	1.4	1.3	1.3	1.8	2.2	2.8
1971	2.1	3.1	1.7	1.4	2.2	3.7	3.2	2.5	1.9	1.7	1.5	1.4	1.3	1.4	1.8	2.2	2.7
1972	1.9	2.7	1.7	1.3	2.0	3.2	2.9	2.1	1.9	1.6	1.5	1.3	1.3	1.3	1.7	2.1	2.2
1973	1.6	2.2	1.2	1.0	1.9	2.4	2.3	1.8	1.4	1.2	1.0	1.0	1.0	1.1	1.5	1.8	2.3
1974	1.5	2.3	1.2	0.9	1.7	2.7	2.4	1.8	1.5	1.2	1.0	0.9	0.8	0.9	1.3	1.7	2.2
1975	2.1	2.6	1.7	1.4	2.5	2.8	2.7	2.2	2.1	1.7	1.4	1.3	1.3	1.5	2.0	2.5	3.1
1976	2.0	3.3	1.6	1.2	2.0	3.6	3.5	2.8	2.0	1.6	1.2	1.2	1.1	1.2	1.6	2.0	2.5
1977	1.8	2.7	1.3	1.1	2.2	3.2	2.9	2.0	1.7	1.3	1.0	1.0	1.0	1.2	1.7	2.2	2.7
1978	2.1	3.0	1.7	1.3	2.4	3.3	3.2	2.4	2.1	1.6	1.3	1.3	1.3	1.4	1.9	2.4	2.8
1979	2.0	3.1	1.6	1.2	2.1	3.5	3.3	2.4	2.0	1.7	1.2	1.2	1.2	1.2	1.7	2.2	2.4
1980	1.9	2.7	1.4	1.1	2.3	3.2	2.9	2.1	1.7	1.4	1.0	1.0	1.0	1.2	1.8	2.3	2.8
1981	2.4	3.2	1.7	1.5	3.2	3.7	3.5	2.5	2.0	1.7	1.3	1.4	1.4	1.7	2.4	3.2	4.1
1982	3.7	4.8	2.8	2.5	4.5	5.4	5.1	4.0	3.4	2.8	2.3	2.4	2.4	2.7	3.6	4.4	5.4
1983	4.5	6.0	3.9	3.1	4.8	6.3	6.3	5.3	4.7	3.9	3.2	3.1	3.0	3.3	4.0	4.7	5.6

Employment: foreign workers / Emploi : main-d'œuvre étrangère

thousands / milliers

	Year	Q.1	Q.2	Q.3	Q.4	JAN	FEB	MAR	APR	MAY	JUN	JUL	AUG	SEP	OCT	NOV	DEC
1964																	
1965																	
1966																	
1967																	
1968																	
1969																	
1970	112	83	101	127	136	81	81	86	93	99	113	121	128	132	135	138	134
1971	150	117	143	165	175	114	114	124	132	144	154	160	165	172	174	177	174
1972	187	143	180	208	217	140	140	151	167	180	192	202	209	213	214	219	218
1973	227	182	222	248	254	176	176	194	210	222	235	242	249	253	254	256	253
1974	222	211	224	229	225	209	209	216	224	223	226	227	230	229	227	228	221
1975	191	188	196	194	186	187	187	192	194	196	198	194	195	192	189	187	183
1976	172	151	168	181	187	147	150	156	160	169	175	177	182	184	188	188	186
1977	189	172	191	198	196	168	170	178	187	191	194	197	198	198	197	196	194
1978	177	169	179	182	178	164	170	171	176	179	181	182	183	182	180	177	176
1979	171	160	171	177	175	156	161	163	168	171	175	176	177	177	176	174	173
1980	175	161	175	183	180	157	161	164	171	175	179	181	183	184	182	181	178
1981	172	164	174	178	171	161	165	167	171	174	177	178	179	176	174	172	169
1982	156	151	159	161	153	148	152	154	157	159	162	162	161	158	156	153	151
1983	145	140	147	150	145	139	140	141	144	146	149	150	151	149	148	145	142

Unemployment (registered unemployed) (9)(11) / Chômage (chômeurs inscrits) (9)(11)

Adjusted - Corrigé *

thousands / milliers

	Year	Q.1	Q.2	Q.3	Q.4	JAN	FEB	MAR	APR	MAY	JUN	JUL	AUG	SEP	OCT	NOV	DEC
1964		68	64	64	63	70	68	67	64	64	64	63	64	64	65	63	63
1965		67	65	63	64	65	68	67	66	67	63	63	62	64	64	65	64
1966		58	66	63	61	63	61	51	65	66	65	64	63	61	61	62	61
1967		59	67	66	69	60	61	55	67	68	66	66	66	66	68	68	72
1968		73	70	67	68	73	74	72	71	71	69	68	68	66	66	68	70
1969		75	66	59	59	73	76	75	69	65	65	61	58	58	57	56	64
1970		65	60	54	51	63	63	69	61	59	59	56	54	51	52	50	50
1971		51	55	53	51	51	50	51	53	55	59	55	53	52	51	51	49
1972		46	54	53	47	47	48	44	52	53	58	54	54	52	51	49	42
1973		39	41	43	45	38	39	39	40	41	42	42	43	43	45	44	45
1974		42	41	37	42	43	42	42	42	41	40	39	37	36	39	43	44
1975		48	58	60	61	46	48	52	59	57	59	59	61	61	60	61	62
1976		62	54	52	50	59	61	65	56	54	53	52	52	52	51	50	50
1977		51	48	50	54	53	51	48	49	47	47	49	50	52	54	54	55
1978		57	60	61	59	55	57	58	61	59	60	60	61	62	60	60	58
1979		58	59	57	54	59	58	58	58	61	58	58	57	55	55	55	51
1980		52	50	51	58	53	52	50	50	50	49	50	51	52	56	59	60
1981		61	62	71	84	61	62	61	58	63	65	68	71	75	79	84	88
1982		94	105	119	115	91	92	99	99	104	112	115	119	122	117	115	115
1983		117	144	148	123	106	114	130	137	141	153	149	151	144	129	123	118

Monthly hours of work: industry (10)(13) (wage earners) / Durée mensuelle du travail : industrie (10) (ouvriers) (13)

hours / heures

	Year	Q.1	Q.2	Q.3	Q.4	JAN	FEB	MAR	APR	MAY	JUN	JUL	AUG	SEP	OCT	NOV	DEC
1964																	
1965	168	167	169	162	173	166	164	172	171	171	165	159	161	167	175	172	171
1966	168	171	169	161	171	169	165	178	169	170	167	160	155	168	172	171	169
1967	166	169	167	158	170	171	165	172	174	159	169	157	154	164	173	172	164
1968	168	170	167	161	172	167	168	175	169	169	163	157	156	169	177	174	166
1969	167	168	166	162	172	165	164	174	170	163	166	160	157	170	178	177	161
1970	162	161	164	158	165	155	160	169	170	156	165	157	155	163	166	171	159
1971	161	163	161	155	163	155	159	175	164	158	162	145	155	166	164	166	160
1972	157	163	157	150	160	158	159	172	157	154	159	143	148	160	166	165	148
1973	156	161	155	150	153	159	155	168	158	161	147	145	147	158	166	164	145
1974	156	162	155	150	157	162	157	166	159	159	147	148	140	161	169	159	144
1975	147	149	147	141	151	147	147	151	158	131	153	140	130	153	163	155	134
1976	149	150	149	145	152	140	149	162	153	150	145	137	141	156	151	157	147
1977	147	151	149	141	148	142	146	164	148	148	150	132	136	154	149	155	140
1978	145	148	146	138	146	148	142	154	150	136	153	132	135	147	152	154	133
1979	146	150	144	140	148	148	145	157	146	148	139	137	136	147	156	153	134
1980	146	151	145	140	149	148	149	155	152	138	144	140	129	152	159	154	133
1981	145	146	145	141	148	137	144	157	150	141	143	139	130	153	151	156	136
1982	145	148	146	140	146	138	144	163	150	140	147	134	133	152	144	154	140
1983	144	146	145	139	147	138	141	160	145	144	147	131	133	153	147	155	139

* Adjusted by the O.E.C.D.

* Corrigé par l'O.C.D.E.

AUSTRIA

Jobs vacant, unfilled vacancies (9)
thousands

Offres d'emploi non satisfaites (9)
milliers

	Year	Q.1	Q.2	Q.3	Q.4	JAN	FEB	MAR	APR	MAY	JUN	JUL	AUG	SEP	OCT	NOV	DEC
1964	40	34	47	44	34	26	33	42	47	45	48	46	44	43	39	35	29
1965	42	35	48	46	38	29	33	43	48	46	49	47	47	45	43	38	32
1966	46	41	53	50	40	33	41	48	52	52	54	52	50	49	46	41	34
1967	32	36	39	32	23	33	35	40	40	39	38	34	33	31	26	23	19
1968	28	25	31	30	25	21	26	29	31	30	32	32	29	29	27	25	22
1969	34	28	38	36	34	23	27	33	37	37	41	37	36	35	36	35	31
1970	45	38	49	49	45	33	39	43	47	48	53	50	49	48	47	46	41
1971	56	49	63	60	52	44	49	54	61	63	66	62	59	58	56	53	47
1972	62	55	68	65	61	50	56	58	66	68	70	66	64	65	62	63	57
1973	66	61	75	70	59	58	61	64	73	74	77	71	69	69	64	62	52
1974	58	55	69	61	46	51	55	57	67	69	69	64	63	57	50	46	41
1975	31	36	37	30	22	38	36	36	38	38	35	32	31	28	23	22	20
1976	29	23	34	32	29	21	22	26	33	35	34	33	32	31	30	31	25
1977	32	29	40	33	27	24	29	34	39	42	38	34	33	32	29	29	24
1978	29	27	36	29	26	24	26	31	35	38	35	30	29	28	26	28	24
1979	31	26	37	32	31	23	24	30	35	39	36	32	32	31	31	33	31
1980	37	35	45	36	30	31	34	39	44	47	44	38	37	34	31	31	27
1981	25	27	34	24	17	25	27	30	33	37	31	26	24	21	18	17	15
1982	17	19	23	15	13	17	18	21	24	25	20	15	15	14	13	14	12
1983	15	13	19	15	14	11	12	16	19	21	16	15	15	15	14	14	14

Monthly earnings: mining and manufacturing (10)
(wage earners)
1980 = 100

Gains mensuels : industries extractives et manufacturières (10)
(ouvriers)
1980 = 100

	Year	Q.1	Q.2	Q.3	Q.4	JAN	FEB	MAR	APR	MAY	JUN	JUL	AUG	SEP	OCT	NOV	DEC
1964	23.1	20.7	22.5	23.4	25.9	21.6	19.8	20.7	21.2	22.3	24.1	25.1	23.3	21.8	21.4	27.1	29.2
1965	25.1	21.6	24.0	26.6	28.3	22.1	20.8	21.8	22.6	23.8	25.6	28.2	26.8	24.9	24.9	28.9	31.2
1966	28.1	24.1	26.5	29.1	32.8	24.5	23.2	24.6	24.6	26.5	28.5	31.1	28.9	27.4	27.8	34.6	36.0
1967	30.3	26.9	29.6	30.8	34.0	28.2	25.5	27.0	27.7	29.5	31.6	33.7	30.1	28.5	29.2	36.1	36.6
1968	32.1	28.7	31.5	32.5	35.9	29.5	28.1	28.6	29.0	31.5	34.0	35.1	31.7	30.8	31.1	37.8	38.7
1969	34.1	30.0	33.2	34.8	38.4	31.6	28.6	29.8	30.2	32.6	36.9	37.1	35.0	32.2	33.7	41.5	40.0
1970	37.3	32.8	36.8	37.5	42.0	33.6	31.5	33.4	33.8	36.0	40.6	40.7	36.8	35.1	38.4	45.6	42.1
1971	42.4	36.1	43.2	41.6	48.5	36.2	34.5	37.5	38.1	44.2	47.3	45.4	41.0	38.5	44.1	55.3	46.3
1972	47.3	38.8	47.6	46.8	56.0	38.4	37.4	40.5	40.0	48.4	54.3	50.6	46.6	43.2	52.9	63.3	51.8
1973	53.3	43.7	53.2	51.5	64.9	44.7	42.0	44.5	45.6	55.1	58.9	54.8	50.5	49.3	63.1	73.7	58.0
1974	61.8	50.8	62.3	59.4	74.6	52.5	48.4	51.6	53.8	64.8	68.4	64.5	58.0	55.7	71.4	85.1	67.2
1975	70.0	60.1	71.8	67.9	80.4	63.0	57.1	60.2	62.4	75.2	77.6	74.3	67.5	61.8	82.6	86.3	72.2
1976	76.4	64.2	79.4	73.1	88.8	63.2	62.4	67.0	69.6	82.0	86.5	76.4	74.0	69.1	89.4	99.3	77.8
1977	82.9	69.0	87.7	80.0	94.9	68.5	65.2	73.5	74.9	91.5	96.7	82.8	81.9	75.3	96.9	106.4	81.3
1978	87.6	74.6	90.1	84.6	101.2	77.3	70.2	76.2	76.7	95.9	97.5	87.3	87.8	78.8	106.5	110.4	86.9
1979	92.7	79.6	95.4	88.7	107.2	84.3	75.2	79.1	82.3	102.5	101.4	92.3	91.0	82.7	114.1	114.4	93.1
1980	100.0	85.5	102.4	94.2	118.0	88.9	82.8	84.6	90.7	103.4	113.1	101.1	93.2	88.1	123.7	127.9	102.4
1981	106.2	89.7	111.0	100.3	123.8	91.0	86.1	92.1	95.8	117.7	119.4	104.8	100.7	95.4	132.5	131.3	107.7
1982	112.7	97.0	118.7	105.8	129.5	97.4	93.0	100.6	104.1	124.7	127.4	108.1	108.9	100.3	137.6	139.6	111.2
1983	117.8	100.5	124.6	111.2	134.9	101.1	96.5	103.7	106.5	132.1	135.2	111.4	116.1	106.2	147.9	142.4	114.3

Hourly rates: (14)
mining and manufacturing
1980 = 100

Taux horaires : (14)
industries extractives et manufacturières
1980 = 100

	Year	Q.1	Q.2	Q.3	Q.4	JAN	FEB	MAR	APR	MAY	JUN	JUL	AUG	SEP	OCT	NOV	DEC
1964	24.6	24.6	24.6	24.6	24.6	24.6	24.6	24.6	24.6	24.6	24.6	24.6	24.6	24.6	24.6	24.6	24.6
1965	26.9	25.5	26.7	27.6	27.6	25.4	25.4	25.7	25.9	26.6	27.6	27.6	27.6	27.6	27.5	27.6	27.6
1966	28.4	27.6	27.6	28.9	29.3	27.6	27.6	27.6	27.6	27.6	27.6	28.4	29.2	29.3	29.3	29.3	29.3
1967	30.3	30.2	30.3	30.3	30.4	30.1	30.1	30.3	30.3	30.3	30.3	30.3	30.3	30.3	30.4	30.4	30.5
1968	32.4	31.8	32.6	32.6	32.7	31.1	32.1	32.2	32.5	32.6	32.6	32.6	32.6	32.6	32.6	32.6	32.7
1969	34.3	32.7	33.7	35.2	35.5	32.7	32.7	32.7	33.0	33.2	34.8	35.1	35.1	35.4	35.4	35.5	35.6
1970	37.8	37.3	37.8	37.9	38.1	37.3	37.3	37.3	37.8	37.7	37.8	37.8	37.9	38.0	38.1	38.1	38.2
1971	42.0	41.3	42.0	42.2	42.3	41.1	41.2	41.5	41.8	42.0	42.2	42.2	42.2	42.2	42.2	42.3	42.3
1972	47.0	43.9	46.4	48.8	49.0	43.6	43.7	44.3	44.6	45.9	48.7	48.7	48.9	48.9	49.0	49.0	49.0
1973	52.3	49.2	50.1	53.1	56.7	49.1	49.1	49.4	49.5	50.0	51.0	51.3	51.5	56.5	56.7	56.7	56.8
1974	58.8	57.1	58.0	59.3	60.9	56.8	56.8	57.5	57.6	58.3	58.3	59.1	59.2	59.6	60.4	61.2	61.2
1975	70.5	69.1	70.1	71.0	71.8	68.9	69.1	69.4	69.9	69.9	70.6	70.7	70.9	71.3	71.5	71.5	72.3
1976	=77.4	= 75.1	77.5	78.1	78.9	72.5	76.4	76.4	77.3	77.3	77.9	77.9	78.2	78.2	78.7	79.1	79.1
1977	84.4	81.0	85.4	85.6	85.7	79.4	79.7	83.8	85.1	85.5	85.5	85.5	85.7	85.7	85.7	85.7	85.8
1978	89.4	86.1	88.0	91.7	91.8	85.9	86.2	86.2	87.5	88.2	88.4	91.6	91.7	91.8	91.8	91.8	91.8
1979	94.3	91.9	93.1	94.9	97.2	91.8	91.9	92.1	92.7	93.3	93.3	93.7	93.8	97.1	97.1	97.1	97.2
1980	100.0	97.4	98.3	99.9	104.0	97.2	97.2	97.7	98.2	99.1	99.2	99.6	99.8	100.2	104.0	104.0	104.0
1981	107.3	104.3	106.4	107.6	110.8	104.1	104.1	104.7	105.7	106.7	106.8	107.4	107.6	107.7	107.9	112.2	112.2
1982	115.3	112.5	114.6	115.6	118.2	112.3	112.3	112.9	113.8	114.9	115.0	115.3	115.7	115.9	115.9	119.3	119.4
1983	121.6	119.5	121.3	122.0	123.7	119.4	119.4	119.5	120.7	121.5	121.6	121.8	121.9	122.2	122.2	124.4	124.5

Jobs vacant, unfilled vacancies (9) / Offres d'emploi non satisfaites (9)

Adjusted - Corrigé *

thousands / milliers

	Year	Q.1	Q.2	Q.3	Q.4	JAN	FEB	MAR	APR	MAY	JUN	JUL	AUG	SEP	OCT	NOV	DEC
1964		39	40	41	39	37	39	40	40	39	41	41	41	40	39	39	39
1965		40	42	43	43	40	38	41	41	43	42	43	43	43	43	43	43
1966		45	46	47	45	43	46	46	46	46	46	47	47	47	47	46	44
1967		40	33	30	28	42	40	38	35	33	30	30	30	29	27	27	29
1968		29	25	27	30	29	30	27	26	25	25	27	27	28	28	29	31
1969		31	32	34	38	31	31	32	32	32	33	33	34	34	37	38	40
1970		42	43	47	49	41	43	42	42	43	45	46	47	47	48	50	50
1971		53	57	57	57	52	54	54	56	57	57	58	57	56	57	57	56
1972		59	61	63	65	58	61	60	61	61	61	62	62	64	64	66	66
1973		66	68	67	64	66	66	65	67	67	69	67	67	67	66	65	61
1974		60	62	59	50	59	60	59	62	62	62	60	60	56	53	50	49
1975		41	30	28	26	45	41	37	32	30	28	28	29	27	25	25	27
1976		27	28	30	33	27	27	27	28	27	28	30	30	30	32	34	32
1977		33	33	32	31	31	34	34	33	34	32	32	32	32	32	32	30
1978		30	30	28	30	30	30	30	30	29	30	28	28	29	29	30	30
1979		29	30	32	35	30	28	29	29	30	30	31	32	33	34	35	37
1980		38	38	37	34	37	38	38	38	38	38	37	37	36	35	33	33
1981		30	27	24	21	31	31	28	28	28	25	25	24	23	22	19	21
1982		21	16	15	17	23	21	20	18	16	15	14	14	15	17	16	17
1983		16	12	15	18	17	16	15	13	12	11	14	14	17	18	16	20

Monthly earnings: mining and manufacturing (10) / Gains mensuels : industries extractives et manufacturières (10)

(wage earners) / (ouvriers)

Adjusted - Corrigé *

1980 = 100

	Year	Q.1	Q.2	Q.3	Q.4	JAN	FEB	MAR	APR	MAY	JUN	JUL	AUG	SEP	OCT	NOV	DEC
1964		22.8	23.3	22.9	23.5	22.7	22.7	22.9	23.1	23.3	23.4	22.7	23.0	22.9	22.8	24.1	23.6
1965		23.8	24.8	26.1	25.8	23.4	23.9	24.1	24.7	24.8	24.8	25.5	26.6	26.2	26.4	25.3	25.6
1966		26.6	27.2	28.7	29.7	26.0	25.6	27.2	26.9	27.4	27.4	28.2	28.9	28.9	29.3	30.0	30.0
1967		29.7	30.2	30.3	30.9	30.0	29.2	29.9	30.3	30.3	30.1	30.6	30.2	30.2	30.5	30.9	31.1
1968		31.8	31.9	32.3	32.6	31.5	32.3	31.6	31.7	32.0	32.0	32.1	32.0	32.3	32.0	32.0	33.7
1969		33.3	33.4	34.8	34.8	33.8	33.1	32.9	33.2	32.7	34.2	34.1	35.7	34.6	34.1	34.6	35.6
1970		36.6	36.6	37.9	37.9	36.3	36.6	36.9	37.1	35.6	37.2	37.7	37.8	38.2	38.0	37.4	38.4
1971		40.4	42.6	42.4	43.5	39.3	40.4	41.6	42.0	43.0	42.9	42.5	42.5	42.3	42.5	44.5	43.3
1972		43.7	46.5	48.2	49.9	42.1	44.0	45.2	44.6	46.3	48.5	47.7	48.8	48.1	49.9	50.1	49.6
1973		49.6	51.8	53.5	57.5	49.0	49.8	50.0	50.8	52.1	52.5	52.0	53.2	55.2	58.3	57.7	56.5
1974		57.9	60.4	61.9	65.9	57.8	57.8	58.2	59.8	60.6	60.8	61.5	61.3	63.0	64.9	66.5	66.3
1975		68.8	69.2	71.2	71.2	68.9	69.2	68.2	69.1	70.2	68.2	72.8	71.0	69.8	72.8	68.2	72.6
1976		72.7	76.2	76.9	78.4	70.1	72.8	75.3	76.2	75.8	76.7	76.1	76.6	78.1	78.3	78.4	78.5
1977		79.0	84.1	84.1	83.9	75.1	78.8	83.0	82.7	83.5	86.1	82.6	84.7	85.1	83.9	84.4	83.3
1978		85.3	86.1	89.2	89.3	85.1	84.7	86.2	84.5	87.0	86.8	87.6	91.1	88.9	90.2	88.8	89.0
1979		91.2	91.1	93.7	94.5	93.1	90.6	89.7	90.6	92.6	90.2	93.1	94.5	93.4	95.7	92.5	95.3
1980		98.1	97.8	99.7	103.9	98.5	99.5	96.2	99.8	93.0	100.6	102.3	97.1	99.7	103.2	103.9	104.6
1981		103.0	105.7	106.4	108.9	101.1	103.3	104.8	105.3	105.7	106.2	106.3	105.1	108.0	110.1	106.8	109.9
1982		111.5	113.2	112.4	113.7	108.4	111.6	114.6	114.2	112.0	113.2	109.8	113.8	113.6	114.2	113.6	113.4
1983		115.5	118.6	118.4	118.4	112.6	115.8	118.2	116.9	118.7	120.2	113.3	121.4	120.5	122.6	116.2	116.5

Wholesale prices: agricultural goods (7) (15) / Prix de gros : produits agricoles (7)(15)

1980 = 100

	Year	Q.1	Q.2	Q.3	Q.4	JAN	FEB	MAR	APR	MAY	JUN	JUL	AUG	SEP	OCT	NOV	DEC
1964	53.5																
1965	60.0																
1966	57.2	62.4	63.1	51.8	51.4	63.3	61.9	61.9	62.8	65.5	61.1	52.2	50.3	52.9	54.3	50.6	49.3
1967	58.2	53.1	65.0	61.8	52.8	52.5	54.2	52.6	57.5	63.4	74.0	63.8	63.7	57.9	55.1	52.0	51.5
1968	56.1	54.6	60.5	56.4	53.1	52.1	53.6	57.9	58.6	60.3	62.5	57.7	56.0	55.4	53.1	53.4	52.8
1969	57.8	55.3	60.4	60.5	54.7	55.4	55.5	55.1	58.0	58.8	64.3	64.8	61.2	55.6	54.8	55.2	54.2
1970	60.0	56.9	62.6	60.7	59.9	57.2	56.2	57.2	60.5	64.0	63.2	61.5	59.4	61.1	61.2	60.1	58.3
1971	60.5	59.2	64.0	61.9	57.0	58.4	59.0	60.2	61.5	62.8	67.6	62.2	64.1	59.4	58.1	56.2	56.7
1972	65.5	56.8	63.2	73.1	69.1	57.2	55.7	57.3	61.3	59.9	68.3	77.1	70.9	71.1	71.2	69.3	66.9
1973	70.5	69.3	77.2	68.7	66.9	69.7	68.8	69.5	72.0	80.0	79.6	72.6	65.1	68.4	66.4	68.1	66.1
1974	65.8	63.4	65.2	68.3	66.1	64.5	61.8	64.0	60.9	64.4	70.4	68.3	67.0	69.6	68.5	67.2	62.7
1975	73.2	64.6	77.1	76.1	75.0	63.9	64.1	65.8	69.8	75.6	85.9	77.0	77.3	74.1	75.1	75.0	75.0
1976	= 86.7 =	90.4	89.1	82.8	84.4	86.5	91.8	92.8	90.6	89.3	87.3	83.6	85.5	79.2	81.0	84.7	87.4
1977	88.7	92.5	95.2	84.3	82.9	90.6	92.5	94.4	100.5	93.7	91.3	92.3	84.7	76.9	81.9	81.1	85.8
1978	88.7	90.2	94.7	84.4	85.5	86.0	91.4	93.1	92.7	98.1	93.2	89.2	86.1	78.1	81.2	85.4	89.9
1979	91.9	95.1	98.0	89.1	85.6	90.6	94.8	100.0	98.3	99.5	96.4	96.6	90.0	80.7	79.1	88.3	89.3
1980	100.0	95.9	108.6	99.3	96.2	95.3	95.2	97.2	103.0	106.6	116.4	106.7	104.3	86.7	88.7	98.4	101.4
1981	108.2	111.7	112.9	105.1	103.1	109.2	111.2	114.6	115.8	112.6	110.5	108.5	104.3	102.4	100.6	101.3	107.5
1982	108.7	114.1	123.8	101.1	95.7	110.5	112.9	118.9	125.8	126.9	118.7	114.5	99.8	89.1	91.6	98.4	97.1
1983	108.5	109.9	113.3	104.5	106.3	103.8	111.9	114.0	119.8	108.8	111.2	103.5	106.9	103.1	102.5	106.9	109.5

* Adjusted by the O.E.C.D. / * Corrigé par l'O.C.D.E.

Wholesale prices: food (7)(15) — Prix de gros : produits alimentaires (7)(15)

1980 = 100

	Year	Q.1	Q.2	Q.3	Q.4	JAN	FEB	MAR	APR	MAY	JUN	JUL	AUG	SEP	OCT	NOV	DEC
1964	56.6																
1965	57.9																
1966	58.2	57.6	57.7	58.4	59.2	58.6	56.7	57.6	57.7	57.6	57.7	58.0	58.5	58.6	59.0	59.5	59.0
1967	63.4	63.5	62.8	63.3	64.0	64.1	63.4	62.9	62.7	62.8	62.8	62.8	63.2	63.9	64.0	64.0	64.0
1968	64.2	63.6	63.5	64.5	65.4	64.1	63.6	62.9	62.9	63.5	64.1	64.3	64.6	64.7	64.9	65.3	66.2
1969	64.9	65.2	64.4	64.8	65.4	65.2	65.2	65.2	64.8	64.2	64.1	64.6	64.8	65.0	64.9	64.9	66.2
1970	65.8	65.8	65.6	65.7	66.0	66.2	65.7	65.5	65.8	65.7	65.5	65.4	65.8	65.8	65.9	65.9	66.2
1971	67.8	66.2	66.9	68.5	69.5	66.4	66.0	66.1	66.2	66.2	68.2	68.3	68.5	68.8	69.2	69.0	70.4
1972	69.8	69.1	68.7	69.5	71.9	69.2	69.1	69.0	68.9	68.8	68.4	69.1	69.8	69.7	70.8	71.2	73.8
1973	70.4	69.0	69.0	70.7	72.8	68.9	69.0	69.0	69.0	69.0	68.9	69.6	71.2	71.4	71.5	72.5	74.5
1974	77.0	73.7	76.4	77.8	80.1	74.4	73.1	73.5	76.8	76.0	76.4	76.6	77.9	78.9	79.2	80.0	81.1
1975	83.8	82.5	82.6	84.8	85.5	80.7	83.1	83.7	83.2	82.8	81.8	84.3	84.9	85.1	85.3	85.2	85.8
1976	=87.3	86.2	86.5	87.6	89.1	86.1	86.3	86.1	86.2	86.6	86.6	86.8	87.5	88.4	88.7	88.9	89.7
1977	94.1	91.1	93.9	96.1	95.3	90.4	91.1	91.7	92.6	93.6	95.6	96.4	96.5	95.5	95.1	95.5	95.2
1978	96.6	96.3	96.6	96.9	96.6	95.2	96.7	96.9	96.9	96.4	96.6	96.9	97.0	96.7	96.5	96.6	96.7
1979	97.6	97.3	97.0	97.6	98.1	97.3	97.6	97.0	97.0	97.0	97.0	97.3	97.7	97.7	97.7	98.1	98.6
1980	100.0	99.6	99.8	100.2	100.3	99.5	99.7	99.6	99.9	99.7	99.8	100.0	100.4	100.3	100.4	100.2	100.3
1981	103.0	100.7	102.5	103.9	104.7	100.2	100.6	101.2	102.0	102.5	103.0	103.4	104.0	104.3	104.6	104.4	105.0
1982	108.4	106.1	108.4	109.5	109.5	105.2	105.9	107.2	107.5	108.5	109.2	109.4	109.5	109.4	109.4	109.3	109.7
1983	111.2	110.3	110.4	111.0	112.9	109.6	110.7	110.6	110.6	110.4	110.2	110.4	111.2	111.4	112.1	113.1	113.5

Wholesale prices: transport equipment (7)(15) — Prix de gros : matériel de transport (7)(15)

1980 = 100

	Year	Q.1	Q.2	Q.3	Q.4	JAN	FEB	MAR	APR	MAY	JUN	JUL	AUG	SEP	OCT	NOV	DEC
1964	58.2																
1965	58.5																
1966	59.8	58.9	59.5	60.0	60.8	58.9	58.9	58.9	59.5	59.5	59.5	59.5	59.5	60.8	60.8	60.8	60.8
1967	61.1	61.0	61.2	61.2	61.2	60.9	60.9	61.2	61.2	61.2	61.2	61.2	61.2	61.2	61.2	61.2	61.2
1968	63.0	62.1	62.9	63.3	63.6	61.0	62.5	62.6	62.8	62.7	63.2	63.2	63.2	63.5	63.5	63.7	63.7
1969	65.9	64.4	65.7	66.1	67.1	63.7	63.9	65.8	65.8	65.6	65.6	65.8	66.2	66.2	66.2	67.6	67.6
1970	69.9	67.2	70.3	70.7	71.5	67.4	67.2	66.9	70.3	70.4	70.3	70.3	70.3	71.4	71.5	71.5	71.5
1971	73.4	72.1	72.9	73.8	74.9	71.5	72.4	72.4	72.4	73.2	73.2	73.2	73.2	74.8	74.8	74.8	74.9
1972	77.6	76.2	77.0	78.1	78.7	75.8	76.5	76.5	77.0	77.0	77.0	77.2	77.3	79.9	78.7	78.7	78.7
1973	71.4	70.4	71.4	71.5	72.3	69.9	69.9	71.3	71.4	71.4	71.4	71.4	71.4	71.8	72.0	72.5	72.5
1974	77.7	74.8	77.7	78.7	79.7	73.5	74.1	76.7	77.3	77.8	77.8	78.5	78.7	79.1	79.1	79.1	80.9
1975	83.9	81.4	82.9	85.2	86.2	80.9	81.6	81.7	82.0	83.3	83.3	83.3	86.2	86.2	86.2	86.2	86.2
1976	=86.2	84.0	86.3	87.1	87.4	83.4	83.9	84.7	85.6	86.6	86.7	86.7	87.2	87.3	87.3	87.4	87.6
1977	89.3	88.4	90.2	89.1	89.4	87.5	88.5	89.1	90.0	90.3	90.4	89.0	89.1	89.1	89.2	89.6	89.5
1978	91.0	89.5	90.2	91.6	92.6	89.3	89.6	89.6	89.5	90.0	91.0	91.2	91.6	92.1	92.4	92.7	92.8
1979	95.7	94.2	95.3	96.6	96.8	94.0	94.0	94.6	94.8	95.4	95.5	95.9	96.7	97.2	96.8	96.8	96.6
1980	100.0	97.6	99.8	100.9	101.8	97.1	97.2	98.6	99.4	99.9	100.2	100.4	100.9	101.3	101.6	101.9	101.9
1981	103.4	101.5	102.3	104.2	105.3	101.7	101.6	101.2	101.8	102.2	102.9	103.8	104.0	104.9	105.0	105.4	105.4
1982	109.2	107.5	108.8	109.6	111.0	106.4	107.9	108.2	108.5	108.8	109.0	109.3	109.3	110.3	110.7	110.8	111.4
1983	113.2	112.0	112.1	113.7	115.1	111.6	112.1	112.2	112.0	112.2	112.2	112.5	113.5	115.0	114.9	115.2	115.2

Money supply (M1) — Disponibilités monétaires (M1)

billion schilling, end of period — milliards de schillings, fin de période

	Year	Q.1	Q.2	Q.3	Q.4	JAN	FEB	MAR	APR	MAY	JUN	JUL	AUG	SEP	OCT	NOV	DEC
1964	47.67	44.96	46.36	48.30	47.67	43.43	43.54	44.96	45.43	45.88	46.36	47.19	48.54	48.30	47.05	47.74	47.67
1965	51.80	47.44	50.13	52.08	51.80	46.07	46.75	47.44	47.71	49.21	50.13	50.71	51.49	52.08	50.55	52.06	51.80
1966	54.17	51.85	54.49	55.43	54.17	50.57	51.11	51.85	52.80	53.14	54.49	55.51	55.17	55.43	54.49	56.11	54.17
1967	57.78	54.18	55.79	57.59	57.78	52.90	53.84	54.18	54.66	55.24	55.79	57.06	57.54	57.59	56.20	58.83	57.78
1968	61.73	56.83	61.18	62.94	61.73	56.39	57.72	56.83	58.37	60.25	61.18	62.04	63.80	62.94	61.16	62.69	61.73
1969	66.52	62.49	65.55	67.44	66.52	60.17	61.55	62.49	63.78	64.56	65.55	67.00	67.34	67.44	64.61	68.08	66.52
1970	70.98	67.24	70.28	73.97	70.98	65.79	66.69	67.24	67.81	69.70	70.28	71.07	73.69	73.97	71.13	74.48	70.98
1971	82.88	74.92	81.04	84.98	82.88	70.67	71.78	74.92	75.45	77.41	81.04	81.73	83.82	84.98	80.44	84.57	82.88
1972	102.06	85.66	92.48	103.49	102.06	82.29	84.50	85.66	85.83	88.23	92.48	96.22	98.95	103.49	98.57	105.43	102.06
1973	108.29	98.21	104.20	105.73	108.29	100.78	100.62	98.21	98.13	100.81	104.20	103.24	104.27	105.73	100.12	106.96	108.29
1974	114.05	102.26	109.22	113.05	114.05	101.50	103.59	102.26	103.21	106.21	109.22	109.70	111.97	113.05	107.60	113.13	114.05
1975	134.30	115.66	121.51	128.54	134.30	110.98	115.64	115.66	116.63	121.31	121.51	124.91	126.22	128.54	120.88	131.32	134.30
1976	146.98	139.97	144.54	145.12	146.98	132.95	139.83	139.97	138.51	138.10	144.54	145.56	145.32	146.12	140.48	151.52	146.98
1977	153.66	141.41	152.30	156.39	153.66	140.45	141.04	141.41	148.34	151.32	152.30	151.25	156.04	156.39	150.47	161.19	153.66
1978	165.63	145.75	162.49	166.10	165.63	149.05	150.00	145.75	152.90	157.23	162.49	157.38	160.87	166.10	160.61	169.03	165.63
1979	153.95	159.54	155.20	164.24	153.95	158.61	167.78	159.54	144.17	150.14	155.20	155.17	155.92	164.24	156.72	160.66	153.95
1980	170.28	152.10	163.62	170.37	170.28	148.26	146.86	152.10	155.36	154.96	163.62	165.14	163.32	170.37	163.78	173.92	170.28
1981	167.98	167.32	167.44	167.81	167.98	160.89	167.15	167.32	168.37	169.84	167.44	163.91	164.12	167.81	158.90	163.88	167.98
1982	181.97	161.92	175.53	180.31	181.97	159.85	162.55	161.92	167.29	169.55	175.53	171.12	172.67	180.31	170.93	177.88	181.97
1983	202.62	182.57	203.19	203.70	202.62	177.38	179.23	182.57	189.39	192.70	203.19	198.56	193.91	203.70	193.62	198.45	202.62

Wholesale prices: petroleum products (7)(15) / Prix de gros : dérivés du pétrole (7)(15)

1980 = 100

	Year	Q.1	Q.2	Q.3	Q.4	JAN	FEB	MAR	APR	MAY	JUN	JUL	AUG	SEP	OCT	NOV	DEC
1964	35.4																
1965	35.4																
1966	37.0	35.4	36.3	38.2	38.2	35.4	35.4	35.4	35.4	35.4	38.2	38.2	38.2	38.2	38.2	38.2	38.2
1967	37.7	37.9	37.7	37.7	37.7	38.2	37.7	37.7	37.7	37.7	37.7	37.7	37.7	37.7	37.7	37.7	37.7
1968	37.7	37.7	37.7	37.7	37.7	37.7	37.7	37.7	37.7	37.7	37.7	37.7	37.7	37.7	37.7	37.7	37.7
1969	37.7	37.7	37.7	37.7	37.7	37.7	37.7	37.7	37.7	37.7	37.7	37.7	37.7	37.7	37.7	37.7	37.7
1970	37.7	37.7	37.7	37.7	37.7	37.7	37.7	37.7	37.7	37.7	37.7	37.7	37.7	37.7	37.7	37.7	37.7
1971	43.7	43.7	43.7	43.7	43.7	43.7	43.7	43.7	43.7	43.7	43.7	43.7	43.7	43.7	43.7	43.7	43.7
1972	44.7	44.7	44.7	44.7	44.7	44.7	44.7	44.7	44.7	44.7	44.7	44.7	44.7	44.7	44.7	44.7	44.7
1973	43.2	38.6	40.2	43.6	50.7	38.6	38.6	38.6	38.6	38.6	43.6	43.6	43.6	43.6	43.6	54.3	54.3
1974	63.3	57.9	65.1	65.1	65.1	54.3	54.3	65.1	65.1	65.1	65.1	65.1	65.1	65.1	65.1	65.1	65.1
1975	65.1	65.1	65.1	65.1	65.1	65.1	65.1	65.1	65.1	65.1	65.1	65.1	65.1	65.1	65.1	65.1	65.1
1976	=71.3	= 66.5	72.6	73.0	73.2	66.6	66.5	66.5	72.4	72.8	72.8	72.8	73.1	73.1	73.1	73.2	73.2
1977	73.2	73.1	73.2	73.2	73.2	73.3	73.0	73.2	73.3	73.3	73.2	73.2	73.2	73.2	73.2	73.2	73.2
1978	73.2	73.2	73.2	73.2	73.2	73.2	73.2	73.2	73.2	73.2	73.2	73.2	73.2	73.3	73.2	73.2	73.2
1979	80.0	73.3	77.2	84.3	85.1	73.3	73.3	73.3	75.4	75.3	80.9	83.2	84.6	85.0	85.0	85.0	85.5
1980	100.0	91.7	99.6	102.5	106.3	85.6	94.7	94.7	94.8	101.9	102.1	102.6	102.5	102.5	102.4	102.7	113.8
1981	124.6	116.4	122.9	128.3	130.9	113.4	113.4	122.3	122.5	123.2	123.2	128.2	128.3	128.3	131.0	130.9	130.8
1982	126.9	128.8	127.6	125.5	125.6	130.9	128.0	127.5	127.4	127.6	127.8	126.4	125.0	125.0	125.2	125.3	126.3
1983	124.5	125.7	120.9	124.2	126.9	126.9	126.5	123.8	120.8	120.9	121.0	122.5	124.5	125.7	125.8	126.6	128.5

Consumer prices: all items (16) / Prix à la consommation : total (16)

1980 = 100

	Year	Q.1	Q.2	Q.3	Q.4	JAN	FEB	MAR	APR	MAY	JUN	JUL	AUG	SEP	OCT	NOV	DEC
1964	44.1	43.4	44.2	44.5	44.3	43.4	43.5	43.4	43.7	44.1	44.8	45.0	44.2	44.2	44.1	44.4	44.4
1965	46.3	44.6	46.8	47.0	46.7	44.6	44.5	44.8	45.2	46.4	48.7	47.6	46.9	46.7	46.2	46.7	47.1
1966	=47.3	= 46.7	47.5	47.3	47.7	46.8	46.5	46.6	47.1	47.1	48.2	47.6	47.2	47.3	47.3	47.8	48.0
1967	49.2	48.8	48.8	49.4	49.7	48.9	48.8	48.7	48.7	48.9	48.9	49.2	49.3	49.6	49.7	49.7	49.8
1968	50.6	50.0	50.2	50.7	51.3	49.8	50.0	50.2	50.2	50.0	50.4	50.5	50.7	50.8	51.2	51.3	51.3
1969	52.1	51.5	51.8	52.3	52.7	51.5	51.5	51.5	51.7	51.7	52.0	52.4	52.3	52.3	52.5	52.7	53.1
1970	54.4	53.5	54.0	54.8	55.3	53.5	53.4	53.5	53.6	53.9	54.4	54.8	54.7	54.8	55.0	55.2	55.5
1971	56.9	55.8	56.4	57.5	58.1	55.7	55.8	55.9	56.2	56.1	56.7	57.2	57.6	57.7	58.0	58.0	58.2
1972	60.5	59.0	59.8	61.1	62.3	58.7	59.0	59.3	59.3	59.5	60.4	60.7	61.1	61.4	62.0	62.3	62.7
1973	65.1	63.7	64.4	65.3	67.1	63.4	63.7	63.8	64.1	64.3	64.8	65.0	65.4	65.4	66.4	67.3	67.6
1974	71.3	69.1	70.7	71.8	73.6	68.6	69.0	69.6	70.3	70.5	71.4	71.5	71.9	72.1	73.0	73.6	74.1
1975	77.3	75.5	76.8	78.2	78.8	74.9	75.7	76.0	76.4	76.6	77.4	77.9	78.2	78.4	78.6	78.8	79.1
1976	=83.0	= 81.1	82.6	83.7	84.5	80.3	81.2	81.9	82.3	82.3	83.1	83.0	84.0	84.0	84.3	84.4	84.8
1977	87.6	86.3	87.3	88.2	88.4	85.9	86.4	86.6	86.8	87.1	87.9	88.2	88.3	88.1	88.6	88.1	88.4
1978	90.7	89.7	90.4	91.2	91.4	89.3	89.7	90.0	90.2	90.4	90.7	90.9	91.5	91.1	91.3	91.4	91.6
1979	94.0	92.8	93.3	94.5	95.5	92.5	93.0	93.1	93.2	93.2	93.6	94.4	94.4	94.5	95.0	95.4	95.9
1980	100.0	97.8	99.4	101.0	101.7	97.1	97.9	98.3	98.7	99.2	100.3	100.7	101.3	101.1	101.4	101.5	102.3
1981	106.8	104.6	106.1	107.7	108.7	103.9	104.5	105.3	106.0	105.9	106.6	107.2	107.8	108.1	108.7	108.6	108.9
1982	112.6	110.9	112.4	113.3	113.8	110.3	110.7	111.6	112.1	112.3	112.9	113.1	113.3	113.4	113.7	113.7	114.0
1983	116.4	115.2	115.4	116.8	118.0	114.8	115.3	115.5	115.4	115.1	115.7	116.3	116.9	117.1	117.8	117.9	118.3

Money supply (M1) / Disponibilités monétaires (M1)

billion schilling, end of period / milliards de schillings, fin de période

Adjusted - Corrigé *

	Year	Q.1	Q.2	Q.3	Q.4	JAN	FEB	MAR	APR	MAY	JUN	JUL	AUG	SEP	OCT	NOV	DEC
1964		46.02	46.08	47.12	47.34	44.59	44.57	46.02	46.31	46.16	46.08	46.31	47.22	47.12	47.10	47.08	47.34
1965		48.46	49.79	50.86	51.69	47.50	47.90	48.46	48.54	49.41	49.79	49.72	50.09	50.86	50.75	51.24	51.69
1966		52.91	54.00	54.13	54.22	52.30	52.36	52.91	53.60	53.30	54.00	54.37	53.62	54.13	54.87	55.12	54.22
1967		55.29	55.29	56.24	58.07	54.76	55.11	55.29	55.44	55.29	55.29	55.83	55.81	56.24	56.76	57.68	58.07
1968		57.93	60.57	61.35	62.10	58.43	59.08	57.93	59.20	60.31	60.57	60.70	61.83	61.35	61.97	61.34	62.10
1969		63.70	64.90	65.54	66.99	62.35	62.93	63.70	64.88	64.62	64.90	65.68	65.19	65.54	65.52	66.48	66.99
1970		68.54	69.51	71.61	71.41	68.10	68.19	68.54	69.20	69.91	69.51	69.74	71.33	71.61	72.36	72.59	71.41
1971		76.45	80.08	82.11	83.22	73.01	73.24	76.45	77.23	77.72	80.08	80.36	81.30	82.11	82.00	82.27	83.22
1972		87.50	91.29	99.99	102.17	84.84	86.05	87.50	88.03	88.67	91.29	94.71	96.26	99.99	100.79	102.45	102.17
1973		100.31	102.96	102.46	108.08	103.79	102.05	100.31	100.75	101.21	102.96	101.71	101.83	102.46	102.59	103.84	108.08
1974		104.45	107.93	109.97	113.49	104.43	104.74	104.45	105.85	106.43	107.93	108.19	109.67	109.97	110.47	109.62	113.49
1975		118.27	120.19	125.41	133.23	114.06	116.69	118.27	119.25	121.31	120.19	123.67	123.99	125.41	123.98	126.88	133.23
1976		142.97	143.11	142.56	145.67	136.78	141.24	142.97	141.20	138.24	143.11	144.69	143.03	142.56	143.64	145.98	145.67
1977		144.30	150.79	151.98	152.14	144.49	142.75	144.30	151.06	152.23	150.79	150.65	154.19	151.98	152.91	154.85	152.14
1978		148.72	161.04	160.64	163.99	153.50	152.13	148.72	155.70	158.98	161.04	157.22	159.43	160.64	162.23	161.91	163.99
1979		162.80	153.32	157.92	152.28	163.68	170.50	162.80	146.97	152.58	153.82	155.17	154.69	157.92	157.67	153.89	152.28
1980		155.21	162.48	163.03	168.43	153.32	149.40	155.21	158.53	157.96	162.48	165.14	162.18	163.03	164.43	166.59	168.43
1981		170.56	166.44	160.43	166.15	166.56	169.87	170.56	171.81	173.67	166.44	163.74	163.31	160.43	159.38	156.97	166.15
1982		164.89	174.48	172.22	179.99	165.48	165.19	164.89	170.88	173.54	174.48	170.95	171.82	172.22	171.45	170.38	179.99
1983		185.91	201.93	194.55	200.41	183.63	182.14	185.91	193.45	197.23	201.98	198.36	192.94	194.55	194.20	190.09	200.41

* Adjusted by the O.E.C.D. / * Corrigé par l'O.C.D.E.

AUSTRIA

Quasi-money

billion schilling, end of period

Quasi-monnaie

milliards de schillings, fin de période

	Year	Q.1	Q.2	Q.3	Q.4	JAN	FEB	MAR	APR	MAY	JUN	JUL	AUG	SEP	OCT	NOV	DEC
1964	73.75	65.71	67.22	70.51	73.75	63.77	65.03	65.71	66.02	66.43	67.22	68.61	69.47	70.51	71.72	71.80	73.75
1965	84.57	77.39	79.18	81.99	84.57	75.27	76.49	77.39	77.49	77.86	79.18	80.34	81.46	81.99	82.31	82.62	84.57
1966	96.12	88.30	89.95	91.93	96.12	86.38	87.45	88.30	88.67	89.04	89.95	90.77	91.54	91.93	93.70	93.49	96.12
1967	107.02	99.12	100.63	103.53	107.02	97.37	98.68	99.12	99.59	99.86	100.63	101.71	103.00	103.53	105.18	104.41	107.02
1968	119.18	110.14	111.49	113.96	119.18	108.01	109.71	110.14	110.67	110.68	111.49	112.60	113.47	113.96	115.94	115.83	119.18
1969	135.98	123.90	126.41	129.46	135.98	121.38	122.70	123.90	124.98	125.28	126.41	127.11	128.64	129.46	132.34	132.05	135.98
1970	157.27	142.20	145.02	148.74	157.27	138.63	140.48	142.20	143.26	144.17	145.02	146.44	147.82	148.74	152.22	151.58	157.27
1971	181.26	163.55	166.72	171.88	181.26	159.80	161.74	163.55	164.09	165.53	166.72	168.59	171.31	171.38	175.91	175.09	181.26
1972	206.06	187.43	191.54	197.70	206.06	183.93	185.14	187.43	189.37	189.94	191.54	193.81	196.47	197.70	201.79	199.72	206.06
1973	237.46	216.12	220.63	226.64	237.46	210.57	214.16	216.12	217.49	220.08	220.63	223.02	226.05	226.64	231.34	230.00	237.46
1974	273.79	247.41	251.16	258.71	273.79	241.63	245.58	247.41	247.82	249.15	251.16	254.73	257.83	258.71	263.36	261.76	273.79
1975	327.83	285.32	293.75	304.37	327.83	277.19	280.39	285.32	288.53	290.37	293.75	298.01	302.49	304.37	312.42	311.80	327.83
1976	392.79	340.99	347.18	360.04	392.79	333.41	337.06	340.99	343.60	345.18	347.18	352.30	357.14	360.04	369.38	369.20	392.79
1977	436.70	399.68	410.92	417.88	436.70	393.07	396.24	399.68	404.29	406.04	410.92	415.47	419.06	417.88	421.80	417.83	436.70
1978	506.97	451.88	462.72	476.80	506.97	439.73	444.94	451.88	456.22	460.50	462.72	468.25	473.82	476.80	483.70	483.42	506.97
1979	575.34	523.91	545.02	550.70	575.34	516.42	515.42	523.91	539.52	542.32	545.02	548.46	552.92	550.70	554.03	549.91	575.34
1980	642.71	599.55	606.52	604.92	642.71	574.48	592.37	599.55	606.20	610.01	606.52	598.75	606.89	604.92	614.97	614.27	642.71
1981	719.91	666.96	661.73	671.53	719.91	650.86	660.17	666.96	665.64	666.60	661.73	669.34	676.40	671.53	681.45	675.99	719.91
1982	804.96	743.45	744.22	761.80	804.96	729.80	738.99	743.45	746.69	745.10	744.22	749.89	765.33	761.80	767.77	763.64	804.96
1983	847.05	812.12	815.72	833.43	847.05	807.92	808.50	812.12	813.48	815.32	815.72	822.83	835.26	833.43	831.82	824.18	847.05

Domestic credit (17)

billion schilling, end of period

Crédits au secteur intérieur (17)

milliards de schillings, fin de période

	Year	Q.1	Q.2	Q.3	Q.4	JAN	FEB	MAR	APR	MAY	JUN	JUL	AUG	SEP	OCT	NOV	DEC
1964	77.8	68.6	71.5	74.1	77.8	67.1	67.6	68.6	69.4	70.3	71.5	73.0	73.4	74.1	74.9	76.6	77.8
1965	92.0	80.9	84.7	87.1	92.0	78.6	79.4	80.9	81.8	83.2	84.7	85.8	86.3	87.1	88.5	90.3	92.0
1966	106.7	95.8	99.9	102.9	106.7	93.8	94.7	95.8	97.0	98.2	99.9	101.2	101.4	102.9	104.3	105.6	106.7
1967	116.3	109.8	112.9	114.3	116.3	107.7	108.5	109.8	110.5	111.3	112.9	114.4	114.2	114.3	114.8	116.0	116.3
1968	129.1	117.7	121.2	123.7	129.1	116.4	117.3	117.7	118.2	119.3	121.2	121.5	122.4	123.7	124.7	127.1	129.1
1969	150.4	132.7	140.0	144.7	150.4	129.7	130.8	132.7	134.1	136.9	140.0	142.0	143.3	144.7	146.2	148.2	150.4
1970	175.7	155.6	163.0	167.0	175.7	150.9	153.2	155.6	157.7	159.8	163.0	164.9	166.5	167.0	169.1	172.2	175.7
1971	210.6	181.0	191.4	198.4	210.6	176.1	178.4	181.0	184.0	187.7	191.4	194.1	196.5	198.4	201.5	205.8	210.6
1972	254.9	216.6	228.2	237.5	254.9	211.3	213.2	216.6	220.1	222.9	228.2	231.9	233.8	237.5	241.4	248.1	254.9
1973	282.7	257.3	266.4	271.6	282.7	253.4	254.8	257.3	260.3	262.2	266.4	267.2	269.1	271.6	274.7	279.0	282.7
1974	323.5	290.2	298.9	308.6	323.5	283.1	286.8	290.2	292.4	294.8	298.9	303.2	305.4	308.6	311.6	315.8	323.5
1975	366.0	328.6	342.4	349.9	366.0	322.4	326.6	328.6	332.6	337.1	342.4	345.1	346.5	349.9	354.8	356.5	366.0
1976	445.3	374.3	392.4	410.6	445.3	364.1	368.6	374.3	378.4	381.9	392.4	399.1	404.2	410.6	419.1	430.7	445.3
1977	511.5	451.7	476.6	490.0	511.5	441.5	444.6	451.7	461.8	469.4	476.6	481.2	484.4	490.0	498.0	504.4	511.5
1978	588.5	520.1	540.7	561.6	588.5	511.1	516.2	520.1	527.1	534.0	540.7	546.9	552.6	561.6	567.3	574.9	588.5
1979	685.3	602.0	628.5	648.7	685.3	587.0	594.0	602.0	607.3	613.9	628.5	634.3	638.4	648.7	657.3	668.3	685.3
1980	773.5	699.4	726.8	752.4	773.5	683.7	689.6	699.4	706.8	713.9	726.8	737.1	743.5	752.4	758.7	764.9	773.5
1981	867.6	789.5	816.9	834.0	867.6	772.9	778.6	789.5	799.3	803.9	816.9	824.8	824.2	834.0	843.1	848.9	867.6
1982	934.7	879.3	898.1	916.7	934.7	868.0	873.5	879.3	881.5	881.9	898.1	899.5	910.6	916.7	919.0	922.4	934.7
1983	1000.9	936.7	960.8	974.1	1000.9	934.7	932.6	936.7	942.2	944.4	960.8	965.2	964.3	974.1	975.3	981.4	1000.9

Official discount rate

per cent per annum, end of period

Taux d'escompte officiel

pourcentage par an, fin de période

	Year	Q.1	Q.2	Q.3	Q.4	JAN	FEB	MAR	APR	MAY	JUN	JUL	AUG	SEP	OCT	NOV	DEC
1964	4.50	4.50	4.50	4.50	4.50	4.50	4.50	4.50	4.50	4.50	4.50	4.50	4.50	4.50	4.50	4.50	4.50
1965	4.50	4.50	4.50	4.50	4.50	4.50	4.50	4.50	4.50	4.50	4.50	4.50	4.50	4.50	4.50	4.50	4.50
1966	4.50	4.50	4.50	4.50	4.50	4.50	4.50	4.50	4.50	4.50	4.50	4.50	4.50	4.50	4.50	4.50	4.50
1967	3.75	4.50	4.25	4.25	3.75	4.50	4.50	4.50	4.25	4.25	4.25	4.25	4.25	4.25	3.75	3.75	3.75
1968	3.75	3.75	3.75	3.75	3.75	3.75	3.75	3.75	3.75	3.75	3.75	3.75	3.75	3.75	3.75	3.75	3.75
1969	4.75	3.75	3.75	4.75	4.75	3.75	3.75	3.75	3.75	3.75	3.75	3.75	3.75	4.75	4.75	4.75	4.75
1970	5.00	5.00	5.00	5.00	5.00	5.00	5.00	5.00	5.00	5.00	5.00	5.00	5.00	5.00	5.00	5.00	5.00
1971	5.00	5.00	5.00	5.00	5.00	5.00	5.00	5.00	5.00	5.00	5.00	5.00	5.00	5.00	5.00	5.00	5.00
1972	5.50	5.00	5.00	5.00	5.50	5.00	5.00	5.00	5.00	5.00	5.00	5.00	5.00	5.00	5.00	5.50	5.50
1973	5.50	5.50	5.50	5.50	5.50	5.50	5.50	5.50	5.50	5.50	5.50	5.50	5.50	5.50	5.50	5.50	5.50
1974	6.50	5.50	6.50	6.50	6.50	5.50	5.50	5.50	5.50	6.50	6.50	6.50	6.50	6.50	6.50	6.50	6.50
1975	6.00	6.50	6.00	6.00	6.00	6.50	6.50	6.50	6.00	6.00	6.00	6.00	6.00	6.00	6.00	6.00	6.00
1976	4.00	5.00	4.00	4.00	4.00	5.00	5.00	5.00	5.00	5.00	4.00	4.00	4.00	4.00	4.00	4.00	4.00
1977	5.50	4.00	5.50	5.50	5.50	4.00	4.00	4.00	4.00	4.00	5.50	5.50	5.50	5.50	5.50	5.50	5.50
1978	4.50	5.50	4.50	4.50	4.50	5.50	5.50	5.50	5.50	5.50	4.50	4.50	4.50	4.50	4.50	4.50	4.50
1979	3.75	3.75	3.75	3.75	3.75	3.75	3.75	3.75	3.75	3.75	3.75	3.75	3.75	3.75	3.75	3.75	3.75
1980	6.75	6.75	6.75	6.75	6.75	5.25	5.25	6.75	6.75	6.75	6.75	6.75	6.75	6.75	6.75	6.75	6.75
1981	6.75	6.75	6.75	6.75	6.75	6.75	6.75	6.75	6.75	6.75	6.75	6.75	6.75	6.75	6.75	6.75	6.75
1982	4.75	6.75	6.75	6.25	4.75	6.75	6.75	6.75	6.75	6.75	6.75	6.75	6.25	6.25	5.75	5.75	4.75
1983	3.75	3.75	3.75	3.75	3.75	4.75	4.75	3.75	3.75	3.75	3.75	3.75	3.75	3.75	3.75	3.75	3.75

M1 plus quasi-money — M1 plus quasi-monnaie

billion schilling, end of period — milliards de schillings, fin de période

Adjusted - Corrigé *

	Year	Q.1	Q.2	Q.3	Q.4	JAN	FEB	MAR	APR	MAY	JUN	JUL	AUG	SEP	OCT	NOV	DEC
1964		108.6	111.2	115.5	118.3	105.7	106.6	108.6	109.4	110.4	111.2	112.6	114.2	115.5	116.4	117.4	118.3
1965		122.3	126.2	130.1	133.3	119.4	120.9	122.3	122.8	124.6	126.2	127.2	128.3	130.1	130.6	132.2	133.3
1966		137.1	141.0	143.7	147.0	135.0	136.0	137.1	138.7	139.4	141.0	142.0	142.1	143.7	145.5	146.8	147.0
1967		150.2	153.0	157.3	161.3	148.3	149.4	150.2	151.4	152.1	153.0	154.7	155.7	157.3	158.6	160.3	161.3
1968		163.3	168.6	172.3	176.4	161.9	164.2	163.3	165.5	167.4	168.6	169.8	171.7	172.3	173.9	174.8	176.4
1969		181.9	186.7	190.8	196.9	178.1	180.0	181.9	184.4	185.2	186.7	188.3	189.1	190.3	192.7	195.0	196.9
1970		203.2	208.6	216.0	221.8	199.4	201.5	203.2	205.5	207.7	208.6	210.6	213.7	216.0	218.7	220.7	221.8
1971		232.1	241.0	249.4	256.6	224.9	227.3	232.1	234.1	236.9	241.0	243.3	246.5	249.4	251.5	253.6	256.6
1972		266.9	277.2	293.6	299.8	260.3	263.2	266.9	270.1	272.3	277.2	283.1	287.2	293.6	296.1	299.4	299.8
1973		307.2	317.2	324.6	335.2	304.7	306.6	307.2	310.1	314.0	317.2	318.1	321.0	324.6	327.6	330.9	335.2
1974		341.2	351.5	363.1	375.1	335.5	339.6	341.2	344.2	347.4	351.5	355.3	359.8	363.1	366.5	368.0	375.1
1975		392.1	406.3	424.6	448.3	379.9	385.4	392.1	397.7	403.0	406.3	414.3	419.4	424.6	430.6	437.8	448.3
1976		471.8	482.6	498.8	522.6	457.8	466.5	471.8	474.4	474.2	482.6	489.7	492.9	498.8	507.0	515.0	522.6
1977		531.2	552.8	564.5	571.7	523.2	525.5	531.2	544.3	547.8	552.8	556.8	564.3	564.5	567.7	571.6	571.7
1978		586.8	613.6	632.2	652.4	576.3	581.8	586.8	600.1	606.9	613.6	614.7	623.0	632.2	639.0	645.6	652.4
1979		673.6	687.5	701.4	705.9	662.2	669.8	673.6	676.5	683.9	687.5	692.6	695.9	701.4	704.0	702.8	705.9
1980		722.2	735.5	752.9	782.0	708.1	713.9	722.2	730.9	733.3	735.5	740.9	745.9	752.9	763.0	772.5	782.0
1981		810.5	815.8	825.8	863.3	789.0	803.3	810.5	815.2	817.4	815.8	821.7	826.4	825.8	834.2	833.4	863.3
1982		891.0	904.3	926.3	959.0	874.1	884.9	891.0	905.0	906.0	904.3	906.4	922.7	926.3	931.3	934.5	959.0
1983		980.3	1002.3	1020.1	1017.9	967.8	970.2	980.3	993.5	998.2	1002.3	1006.3	1012.3	1020.1	1018.2	1012.9	1017.9

Share prices: Vienna Stock Exchange — Cours des actions : Bourse de Vienne

1980 = 100

	Year	Q.1	Q.2	Q.3	Q.4	JAN	FEB	MAR	APR	MAY	JUN	JUL	AUG	SEP	OCT	NOV	DEC
1964																	
1965																	
1966																	
1967																	
1968	78	79	77	77	77	79	80	79	78	77	77	76	76	80	78	76	77
1969	78	78	76	77	82	77	78	78	78	76	75	75	76	78	78	83	85
1970	87	84	84	90	91	84	84	83	84	84	85	87	90	92	92	91	89
1971	88	89	90	88	86	89	90	89	90	90	90	89	89	87	87	86	85
1972	96	87	91	102	105	86	87	87	87	90	95	96	107	104	105	104	106
1973	114	112	118	117	109	109	112	115	119	117	117	121	125	115	110	111	106
1974	108	111	110	106	104	108	111	114	113	108	110	107	106	105	104	104	104
1975	107	107	108	107	107	104	106	109	109	108	107	107	107	106	106	107	107
1976	109	110	110	108	106	109	110	111	111	110	109	108	109	109	109	105	105
1977	102	106	105	102	96	105	106	105	105	105	104	103	103	101	97	96	95
1978	96	95	95	96	96	96	96	94	95	94	95	96	96	96	97	95	95
1979	96	94	97	95	99	95	94	94	96	97	96	94	95	96	97	99	101
1980	100	102	101	99	98	102	102	102	101	101	100	99	100	99	99	97	98
1981	90	95	92	87	84	96	95	94	93	93	91	89	88	85	84	84	85
1982	80	84	81	77	77	85	84	83	81	82	80	78	77	77	76	76	78
1983	86	80	88	88	87	79	78	82	85	91	89	88	87	88	87	87	87

U.S. dollar exchange rate: spot — Taux de change du dollar É.-U. : au comptant

cents per schilling, end of period — cents par schilling, fin de période

	Year	Q.1	Q.2	Q.3	Q.4	JAN	FEB	MAR	APR	MAY	JUN	JUL	AUG	SEP	OCT	NOV	DEC
1964	3.866	3.864	3.864	3.864	3.866	3.864	3.861	3.864	3.861	3.866	3.864	3.869	3.867	3.864	3.864	3.864	3.866
1965	3.863	3.864	3.867	3.866	3.863	3.863	3.864	3.864	3.864	3.864	3.867	3.869	3.869	3.866	3.864	3.863	3.863
1966	3.860	3.863	3.867	3.867	3.860	3.861	3.861	3.863	3.863	3.864	3.867	3.867	3.867	3.867	3.863	3.858	3.860
1967	3.864	3.863	3.867	3.867	3.864	3.858	3.863	3.863	3.863	3.864	3.867	3.869	3.867	3.867	3.858	3.861	3.864
1968	3.864	3.858	3.867	3.864	3.864	3.855	3.861	3.858	3.861	3.863	3.867	3.867	3.864	3.864	3.861	3.860	3.864
1969	3.864	3.855	3.858	3.858	3.864	3.855	3.855	3.855	3.858	3.858	3.858	3.867	3.861	3.858	3.858	3.857	3.864
1970	3.864	3.855	3.858	3.864	3.864	3.857	3.860	3.855	3.852	3.855	3.858	3.867	3.866	3.864	3.866	3.861	3.864
1971	4.218	3.863	4.016	4.139	4.218	3.857	3.855	3.863	3.867	3.994	4.016	4.003	4.070	4.139	4.119	4.146	4.218
1972	4.322	4.340	4.367	4.320	4.322	4.294	4.314	4.340	4.322	4.333	4.367	4.359	4.340	4.320	4.307	4.318	4.322
1973	5.038	4.840	5.447	5.580	5.038	4.373	4.859	4.840	4.822	5.018	5.447	5.764	5.495	5.580	5.507	5.187	5.038
1974	5.838	5.342	5.465	5.314	5.838	4.869	5.097	5.342	5.495	5.513	5.465	5.441	5.297	5.314	5.435	5.631	5.838
1975	5.403	6.004	6.011	5.306	5.403	5.995	6.154	6.004	5.933	6.011	6.011	5.507	5.483	5.306	5.526	5.377	5.403
1976	5.964	5.486	5.432	5.783	5.964	5.451	5.444	5.486	5.507	5.394	5.432	5.539	5.589	5.783	5.856	5.857	5.964
1977	6.607	5.901	6.030	6.058	6.607	5.811	5.875	5.901	5.965	5.958	6.030	6.149	6.055	6.058	6.226	6.281	6.607
1978	7.481	6.866	6.678	7.123	7.481	6.595	6.821	6.866	6.719	6.618	6.678	6.797	6.969	7.123	7.873	7.100	7.481
1979	8.044	7.301	7.362	7.972	8.044	7.338	7.372	7.301	7.158	7.107	7.362	7.423	7.486	7.972	7.689	8.016	8.044
1980	7.242	7.190	8.005	7.797	7.242	8.003	7.890	7.190	7.782	7.848	8.005	7.908	7.881	7.797	7.401	7.327	7.242
1981	6.295	6.723	5.931	6.136	6.295	6.678	6.637	6.723	6.387	6.082	5.931	5.776	5.862	6.136	6.323	6.459	6.295
1982	5.993	5.891	5.775	5.622	5.993	6.177	5.983	5.891	6.092	6.055	5.775	5.798	5.694	5.622	5.551	5.716	5.993
1983	5.170	5.864	5.579	5.390	5.170	5.822	5.880	5.864	5.782	5.635	5.579	5.380	5.257	5.390	5.412	5.259	5.170

* Adjusted by the O.E.C.D. — * Corrigé par l'O.C.D.E.

AUSTRIA

Official reserves excluding gold
million SDR's, end of period

Réserves officielles, or exclu
millions de DTS, fin de période

	Year	Q.1	Q.2	Q.3	Q.4	JAN	FEB	MAR	APR	MAY	JUN	JUL	AUG	SEP	OCT	NOV	DEC
1964	717	640	628	673	717	641	609	640	599	648	628	660	682	673	656	672	717
1965	611	636	621	639	611	653	637	636	631	626	621	649	666	639	657	653	611
1966	632	550	571	626	632	540	540	550	551	552	571	651	628	626	612	618	632
1967	783	649	685	738	783	566	606	649	626	649	685	719	719	738	725	725	783
1968	796	704	780	824	796	651	660	704	722	718	780	806	834	824	809	741	796
1969	822	751	699	731	822	710	746	751	719	712	699	789	743	731	829	798	822
1970	1044	786	826	958	1044	797	813	786	768	787	826	971	942	958	1045	960	1044
1971	1424	1069	1139	1509	1424	1016	1004	1069	1085	1078	1139	1262	1458	1509	1479	1456	1424
1972	1775	1454	1559	1977	1775	1416	1434	1454	1457	1501	1559	1744	1907	1977	1928	1806	1775
1973	1652	1706	1844	1988	1652	1745	1706	1706	1667	1711	1844	1989	1991	1988	1872	1655	1652
1974	2070	1556	1524	1872	2070	1523	1557	1556	1427	1506	1524	1708	1808	1872	1853	1858	2070
1975	3060	2261	2415	2814	3060	2182	2256	2261	2348	2342	2415	2704	2793	2814	2805	2764	3060
1976	3065	3064	3111	2908	3065	3037	3205	3064	3037	3020	3111	3315	3054	2908	2745	2818	3065
1977	2758	2657	2606	2496	2758	2533	2629	2657	2661	2472	2606	2689	2795	2496	2409	2659	2758
1978	3874	2674	3076	3366	3874	2313	2463	2674	2737	3038	3076	3256	3418	3366	3329	3466	3874
1979	3094	3441	2939	2946	3094	3399	3417	3441	3063	2713	2939	2972	3096	2946	2741	2778	3094
1980	4140	3014	2813	3611	4140	2856	3019	3014	3005	2756	2813	3183	3485	3611	3846	3779	4140
1981	4540	3630	3670	3802	4540	3970	3623	3630	3668	3735	3670	3990	4147	3802	4018	3887	4540
1982	4805	4378	4592	4332	4805	4383	4328	4378	4275	4134	4592	4156	4512	4332	4410	4418	4805
1983	4313	4680	4396	4463	4313	4529	4506	4680	4653	4593	4396	4614	4498	4463	4399	4267	4313

Net foreign position: commercial banks
million schilling, end of period

Position extérieure nette : banques commerciales
millions de schillings, fin de période

	Year	Q.1	Q.2	Q.3	Q.4	JAN	FEB	MAR	APR	MAY	JUN	JUL	AUG	SEP	OCT	NOV	DEC
1964	355	1227	1599	3691	355	796	1370	1227	2306	1230	1599	2397	3328	3691	3557	2574	355
1965	-663	1771	1510	2479	-663	1805	1912	1771	1581	1074	1510	1611	2260	2479	1290	45	-663
1966	-2603	-45	-938	-401	-2603	284	673	-45	-81	-928	-938	-1223	-219	-401	-120	-933	-2603
1967	-1547	-2333	-2123	749	-1547	-1313	-1661	-2333	-1306	-1920	-2123	-1634	335	749	1332	1297	-1547
1968	1880	1681	1401	4306	1880	1417	2491	1681	1511	2283	1401	2946	3494	4306	3675	3925	1880
1969	4384	5004	4873	5982	4384	4783	4648	5004	5144	3572	4873	3718	5456	5982	3861	4414	4384
1970	2115	5424	4453	6588	2115	5927	5356	5424	5892	5432	4458	4166	5983	6588	3853	4820	2115
1971	-3072	2375	1657	-1235	-3072	4065	4771	2375	1015	1196	1657	1724	-474	-1235	-974	-2574	-3072
1972	-4555	-3736	-3876	-3838	-4555	-3435	-3509	-3736	-3580	-3604	-3876	-3823	-3889	-3838	-4485	-4136	-4555
1973	-348	-4577	-3890	-1263	-348	-3601	-3917	-4577	-4110	-4319	-3890	-2022	-1430	-1263	-1148	-375	-348
1974	-3077	2170	2725	2458	-3077	-246	770	2170	3214	2000	2725	2584	3018	2458	1005	999	-3077
1975	-1082	-1284	-22	2584	-1082	-2340	-2619	-1284	-2180	-1959	-22	189	1222	2584	2328	2350	-1082
1976	-8023	1485	-1404	3390	-8023	90	-2559	1485	2286	1260	-1404	-2203	3026	3390	4509	-1346	-8023
1977	-13449	-3748	-4641	-1141	-13449	1237	-744	-3748	-3520	-3378	-4641	-2215	-2510	-1141	-4198	-7123	-13449
1978	-16093	-6799	-9336	-7076	-16093	-4315	-4491	-6799	-6935	-11413	-9386	-8948	-8508	-7076	-6772	-9413	-16093
1979	-14829	-6926	-4508	-295	-14829	-8346	-7149	-6926	-3338	-698	-4508	-845	-835	-295	-68	-4285	-14829
1980	-47895	-10928	-23337	-35609	-47895	-7030	-10414	-10928	-17771	-19876	-23337	-28323	-31325	-35609	-41510	-41340	-47895
1981	-53536	-35609	-43780	-35577	-53536	-46910	-36110	-35609	-41696	-46086	-43780	-46172	-38547	-35577	-39888	-42821	-53536
1982	-24723	-38759	-42710	-23082	-24723	-45434	-41817	-38759	-37384	-35642	-42710	-29875	-32305	-23082	-23041	-23490	-24723
1983	-16638	-13160	-15837	-3711	-16638	-16682	-19566	-13160	-15880	-16739	-15837	-14116	-10186	-3711	-4769	-11275	-16638

Balance of payments: net services (18)
million schilling

Balance des paiements : services, nets (18)
millions de schillings

	Year	Q.1	Q.2	Q.3	Q.4	JAN	FEB	MAR	APR	MAY	JUN	JUL	AUG	SEP	OCT	NOV	DEC
1964																	
1965																	
1966	10809																
1967	9660																
1968	10386																
1969	12257	2691	2214	5446	1906	865	948	878	508	514	1192	2410	2023	1013	605	513	788
1970	17636	3268	3551	8150	2220	1002	936	1330	823	1019	1709	3344	3101	1705	806	364	1050
1971	22648	3634	4968	10462	2763	1142	881	1611	1390	956	2622	4173	3932	2357	1023	599	1143
1972	27198	4798	5884	11937	2955	1324	1453	2021	1327	1691	2866	4905	4549	2483	1210	490	1255
1973	28198	4884	6491	11931	2096	1821	1202	1861	1728	1494	3269	5211	4617	2103	632	237	1227
1974	26445	3958	4420	11570	2477	1281	1094	1583	1278	1213	1929	4587	3984	2999	1277	-93	1293
1975	27620	4907	4804	11534	2931	1543	1112	2252	1325	1241	2238	5861	4033	1640	1222	-244	1953
1976	28053	6032	5456	11020	2685	1890	1708	2434	1552	1491	2413	5182	4354	1484	813	-239	2111
1977	24414	6243	4414	10838	705	1939	1876	2428	1030	593	2791	5544	4406	888	56	-610	1259
1978	30465	8563	5899	11460	2886	2623	2446	3494	1525	1819	2555	5234	4460	1766	1155	-136	1867
1979	34855	8554	6289	14797	2791	3396	2549	2609	1955	1468	2866	5350	6507	2940	939	87	1765
1980	42159	11456	6926	15288	5999	4131	3498	3827	2604	1555	2767	5924	5999	3365	2889	375	2735
1981	41393	12365	6170	16209	4087	4132	3968	4265	2653	1006	2511	7084	6185	2940	596	-271	3762
1982	46158	14013	7038	18229	5018	5786	3475	4752	2026	1447	3565	7082	6995	4152	1819	237	2962
1983	37466	12769	7490	14565	2643	4552	3792	4425	3124	1912	2454	4978	5682	3905	1041	708	894

Balance of payments: current balance (18)
million schilling

Balance des paiements : opérations courantes, nettes (18)
millions de schillings

	Year	Q.1	Q.2	Q.3	Q.4	JAN	FEB	MAR	APR	MAY	JUN	JUL	AUG	SEP	OCT	NOV	DEC
1964	1159																
1965	-1024																
1966	-4935																
1967	-2977																
1968	-2500																
1969	2322	243	-466	3237	-433	-462	328	377	-565	-381	480	1705	1161	371	-167	-89	-177
1970	-1727	-582	-1223	3338	-3217	-182	-310	-90	-1343	-273	393	2036	1744	-442	-697	-1501	-1019
1971	-1973	-1584	-948	5276	-4791	-270	-555	-759	-495	-1423	970	2701	2473	102	-1306	-1976	-1509
1972	-3423	-1640	12	5713	-7559	-747	-996	103	-879	-465	1356	3001	2486	226	-2190	-2974	-2395
1973	-5295	-2877	-587	3737	-5597	-176	-1840	-861	-839	-698	950	2739	1476	-478	-2134	-2115	-1348
1974	-2704	-4898	-1439	3024	-5451	-1502	-1709	-1687	-1689	-841	1041	2160	1308	-444	-2347	-2202	-902
1975	-3346	-1789	-3710	7490	-5418	-426	-1005	-358	-1883	-901	-926	5408	1845	237	-1401	-2361	-1656
1976	-13901	-1888	-5120	-408	-11487	-184	-415	-1289	-2225	-2015	-880	2272	128	-2808	-2958	-5092	-3437
1977	-35283	-5783	-6744	-2368	-16042	-1800	-2523	-1460	-3217	-3535	8	2218	198	-4784	-4095	-5692	-6255
1978	-9211	-1874	-1960	2712	-8230	-712	-887	-275	-499	-69	-1292	3427	1240	-1955	-2341	-4290	-1599
1979	-14098	-2353	-2597	1376	-15044	-43	-1464	-846	-1109	-2808	1320	1799	1723	-2146	-3520	-6365	-5159
1980	-21376	-4019	-9830	-4290	-6287	-270	-672	-3077	-3079	-5819	-932	18	-3002	-1306	-2071	-4131	-85
1981	-21408	-2405	-7591	-1511	-10819	-265	-1990	-150	-4330	-3716	455	563	2279	-4353	-3422	-5247	-2150
1982	12184	4833	-7072	8928	1240	3743	-54	1144	-2884	-2618	-1570	5690	3311	-73	-1214	-85	2539
1983	-1324	6018	-1599	4837	-10578	3815	-1007	3210	-889	452	-1162	3270	1919	-352	-881	-5441	-4256

Balance of payments: net capital movements (18)
million schilling

Balance des paiements : mouvements de capitaux, nets (18)
millions de schillings

	Year	Q.1	Q.2	Q.3	Q.4	JAN	FEB	MAR	APR	MAY	JUN	JUL	AUG	SEP	OCT	NOV	DEC
1964	1704																
1965	-109																
1966	1593																
1967	7429																
1968	4293																
1969	-1141	1520	-1912	-756	7	488	549	483	-334	-1786	208	-78	-268	-410	309	-157	-145
1970	-514	-142	-838	-659	1175	63	257	-462	-204	-239	-445	677	-912	-424	389	91	695
1971	10	-402	-274	885	-199	43	-97	-348	703	-55	-922	771	519	-405	539	-538	-200
1972	1824	3	809	798	214	41	104	-142	-458	1083	184	40	411	347	-60	-121	395
1973	-3055	915	1173	-2500	-2643	156	917	-158	-100	442	831	485	-1325	-1660	-2459	-703	519
1974	6930	1397	300	-546	5776	-467	2230	-366	-90	390	-	6	-947	395	1540	2979	1257
1975	13222	8592	4833	679	4118	4843	3362	387	3657	-660	1836	352	-39	366	-136	149	4105
1976	-1998	-275	703	-3546	1117	-61	-137	-77	973	-543	273	214	-2910	-850	-324	1877	-436
1977	15501	-912	3611	-19	7560	-669	1757	-2000	3343	-917	1185	1327	338	-1684	270	7575	-285
1978	20059	4195	8012	3347	4326	345	2971	879	2901	970	4141	598	691	2058	3533	-558	1341
1979	-11184	-1642	-3633	-1607	321	15	800	-2457	-741	-1951	-941	-1362	-1360	1115	1788	-167	-1300
1980	1375	-4262	998	3807	3507	-2255	-1226	-781	-57	583	472	2254	264	1239	2465	1112	-70
1981	17043	5028	-1337	3838	9879	767	2913	1348	-1772	1057	-622	-1640	4352	1126	4418	1006	4455
1982	-10490	1855	-6435	697	-8368	-1703	-1002	4560	-370	177	-6242	1623	-1229	303	-5800	-2799	231
1983	-21262	-6009	-5436	-1731	-8037	-4348	-192	-1469	-1417	989	-5058	-1008	-904	181	-3618	-1642	-2777

AUSTRIA

Imports c.i.f. (19)
billion schilling, monthly averages

Importations c.a.f. (19)
milliards de schillings, moyennes mensuelles

	Year	Q.1	Q.2	Q.3	Q.4	JAN	FEB	MAR	APR	MAY	JUN	JUL	AUG	SEP	OCT	NOV	DEC
1964	4.0	3.8	4.0	4.0	4.5	3.6	3.6	4.1	4.1	3.7	4.2	4.1	3.6	4.1	4.5	4.5	4.5
1965	4.6	4.1	4.4	4.6	5.1	3.8	3.9	4.6	4.7	4.4	4.1	4.6	4.4	4.7	4.9	5.1	5.4
1966	5.0	4.9	5.1	5.0	5.2	4.7	4.6	5.4	5.0	5.0	5.2	4.9	4.8	5.2	5.3	5.3	5.1
1967	5.0	4.9	5.0	4.7	5.4	4.8	4.7	5.3	4.9	4.8	5.3	4.8	4.6	4.8	5.2	5.4	5.5
1968	5.4	5.3	5.1	5.4	5.7	6.3	4.8	4.9	5.0	5.6	4.8	5.6	5.5	5.2	6.0	5.8	5.5
1969	6.1	5.6	6.0	6.2	6.7	5.5	5.3	5.9	6.1	6.0	5.9	6.3	5.7	6.5	7.2	6.5	6.4
1970	7.7	6.9	7.6	7.8	8.5	6.5	6.8	7.4	7.8	6.9	8.2	8.1	7.2	8.0	8.6	8.5	8.4
1971	8.7	8.3	8.7	8.7	9.2	7.3	8.0	9.4	8.8	8.4	9.0	8.6	8.1	9.2	8.8	9.4	9.5
1972	10.1	9.0	9.7	9.2	12.3	8.4	8.8	9.8	9.1	9.7	10.2	9.6	8.9	9.2	12.1	12.4	12.3
1973	11.5	10.7	11.4	11.4	12.5	10.2	10.0	11.8	11.2	11.9	11.2	12.1	10.6	11.5	13.0	13.1	11.4
1974	14.0	14.0	14.0	14.1	14.1	13.2	13.8	14.9	14.0	15.1	12.8	14.9	13.0	14.4	15.5	14.0	12.7
1975	13.6	13.4	13.5	13.0	14.6	13.0	13.4	13.9	14.1	12.4	13.9	13.2	11.7	13.9	15.2	13.9	14.7
1976	17.2	15.6	16.6	17.3	19.2	14.7	14.3	17.8	16.4	17.0	16.5	17.1	16.7	18.2	18.2	20.2	19.0
1977	19.6	18.4	18.5	19.8	21.5	17.1	17.7	20.5	18.2	18.5	19.1	20.2	18.9	20.3	20.6	23.0	20.8
1978	19.3	18.1	19.4	18.9	21.0	18.0	17.0	19.4	19.0	18.4	20.8	18.7	18.5	19.4	21.5	22.5	18.9
1979	22.5	20.1	21.8	22.8	25.3	19.0	18.7	22.5	20.9	23.4	21.1	24.0	22.6	21.9	26.2	27.4	22.2
1980	26.3	25.6	26.5	26.1	27.1	25.2	24.7	26.9	27.1	25.5	26.9	27.6	23.3	27.5	29.6	27.2	24.5
1981	27.9	26.5	27.8	28.9	28.3	24.6	26.2	28.8	28.0	27.1	28.3	30.3	26.7	29.7	29.3	29.0	26.7
1982	27.7	27.3	28.3	27.9	27.3	24.3	25.9	31.7	28.8	26.7	29.4	29.4	26.3	28.1	26.4	28.6	26.9
1983	29.1	26.9	27.9	29.1	32.5	24.9	24.9	31.0	25.9	27.6	30.4	27.9	28.4	30.9	30.5	33.2	33.9

Exports f.o.b. (19)
billion schilling, monthly averages

Exportations f.o.b. (19)
milliards de schillings, moyennes mensuelles

	Year	Q.1	Q.2	Q.3	Q.4	JAN	FEB	MAR	APR	MAY	JUN	JUL	AUG	SEP	OCT	NOV	DEC
1964	3.1	2.8	3.1	3.2	3.4	2.4	2.9	3.2	3.1	3.0	3.2	3.2	3.1	3.4	3.6	3.4	3.3
1965	3.5	3.1	3.4	3.6	3.8	2.8	3.1	3.5	3.4	3.4	3.3	3.8	3.3	3.7	3.8	3.6	3.8
1966	3.7	3.4	3.6	3.7	3.9	3.0	3.3	3.8	3.6	3.6	3.7	3.9	3.4	3.9	3.9	3.7	4.1
1967	3.9	3.6	3.9	4.0	4.2	3.3	3.5	3.9	4.0	3.7	4.1	4.1	3.7	4.3	4.3	4.1	4.1
1968	4.3	3.9	4.2	4.3	4.8	3.4	3.9	4.5	4.2	4.3	4.2	4.3	4.1	4.5	5.0	4.8	4.7
1969	5.2	4.6	5.0	5.4	5.9	4.1	4.5	5.1	4.9	5.0	5.2	5.6	4.8	5.9	6.3	5.9	5.5
1970	6.2	5.6	6.2	6.3	6.7	4.9	5.6	6.4	6.4	5.7	6.7	6.5	5.7	6.7	6.7	6.7	6.6
1971	6.6	6.2	6.5	6.6	7.0	5.2	6.0	7.3	6.7	6.2	6.7	6.6	6.2	7.1	6.8	7.1	7.1
1972	7.5	6.5	7.1	7.3	9.0	5.5	6.6	7.4	6.8	7.2	7.4	7.2	7.1	7.6	8.0	8.4	10.6
1973	8.5	7.2	8.5	8.6	9.7	6.3	7.1	8.2	8.4	8.9	8.2	9.0	8.0	8.9	9.9	10.1	9.1
1974	11.1	10.4	11.2	11.2	11.6	9.4	10.3	11.6	11.4	11.9	10.4	11.9	10.1	11.7	12.5	11.9	10.4
1975	10.9	10.4	10.7	10.6	11.9	9.3	10.9	11.0	11.3	10.0	10.9	11.0	8.8	11.9	12.2	11.3	12.3
1976	12.7	11.2	12.4	12.9	14.2	8.7	11.5	13.4	12.0	13.2	12.1	12.8	12.3	13.7	13.9	13.9	14.7
1977	13.5	12.8	13.4	13.5	14.3	10.6	12.2	15.4	13.3	13.3	13.7	13.4	12.0	15.0	13.9	14.4	14.7
1978	14.7	13.5	14.7	14.2	16.2	11.7	13.4	15.5	14.2	13.7	16.3	14.2	13.0	15.5	16.1	15.5	17.1
1979	17.2	15.2	16.9	17.4	19.2	13.8	14.4	17.6	15.6	17.9	17.1	18.4	16.3	17.7	19.2	20.1	18.3
1980	18.9	18.0	18.5	18.9	20.0	16.4	17.7	19.8	18.6	17.4	19.6	20.6	15.7	20.4	20.8	19.7	19.5
1981	21.0	19.4	20.7	20.9	22.9	16.2	19.9	22.1	21.3	19.2	21.5	22.1	18.1	22.4	23.8	21.9	23.1
1982	22.2	21.6	22.8	21.3	23.3	17.4	21.2	26.2	23.5	20.7	24.1	22.9	18.4	22.6	22.2	23.9	24.0
1983	23.1	21.6	22.9	23.0	24.9	19.2	20.4	25.1	22.6	22.5	23.7	23.3	19.1	26.5	24.2	24.7	25.9

Trade balance (f.o.b. — c.i.f.) (19)
billion schilling, monthly averages

Balance commerciale (f.o.b. — c.a.f.) (19)
milliards de schillings, moyennes mensuelles

	Year	Q.1	Q.2	Q.3	Q.4	JAN	FEB	MAR	APR	MAY	JUN	JUL	AUG	SEP	OCT	NOV	DEC
1964	-0.9	-0.9	-0.9	-0.7	-1.0	-1.2	-0.7	-0.9	-1.1	-0.7	-1.0	-0.9	-0.6	-0.8	-0.8	-1.1	-1.2
1965	-1.1	-1.0	-1.0	-1.0	-1.4	-1.0	-0.8	-1.1	-1.3	-1.0	-0.8	-0.9	-1.1	-1.0	-1.0	-1.5	-1.6
1966	-1.4	-1.5	-1.5	-1.2	-1.4	-1.7	-1.3	-1.6	-1.4	-1.5	-1.5	-1.1	-1.4	-1.2	-1.4	-1.6	-1.1
1967	-1.1	-1.4	-1.1	-0.7	-1.2	-1.5	-1.2	-1.4	-0.9	-1.2	-1.2	-0.8	-1.0	-0.4	-0.9	-1.3	-1.4
1968	-1.1	-1.4	-0.9	-1.1	-0.9	-2.9	-0.9	-0.5	-0.8	-1.4	-0.6	-1.3	-1.4	-0.7	-0.9	-1.0	-0.8
1969	-0.9	-1.0	-1.0	-0.8	-0.8	-1.4	-0.8	-0.7	-1.2	-1.0	-0.7	-0.7	-0.9	-0.7	-0.9	-0.7	-0.9
1970	-1.5	-1.3	-1.4	-1.5	-1.9	-1.6	-1.2	-1.1	-1.5	-1.2	-1.5	-1.7	-1.5	-1.3	-1.9	-1.9	-1.8
1971	-2.1	-2.1	-2.2	-2.0	-2.2	-2.2	-2.0	-2.1	-2.0	-2.2	-2.4	-2.1	-1.9	-2.2	-2.0	-2.2	-2.4
1972	-2.6	-2.5	-2.6	-1.9	-3.3	-2.9	-2.3	-2.4	-2.3	-2.5	-2.8	-2.4	-1.9	-1.6	-4.1	-4.0	-1.7
1973	-3.0	-3.5	-2.9	-2.8	-2.8	-3.9	-3.0	-3.6	-2.8	-3.0	-3.0	-3.1	-2.6	-2.6	-3.1	-3.0	-2.2
1974	-2.9	-3.5	-2.8	-2.9	-2.5	-3.8	-3.4	-3.3	-2.7	-3.2	-2.4	-3.1	-2.9	-2.7	-3.0	-2.1	-2.2
1975	-2.7	-3.0	-2.8	-2.4	-2.7	-3.6	-2.6	-2.9	-2.9	-2.4	-3.0	-2.2	-3.0	-2.1	-3.0	-2.6	-2.4
1976	-4.5	-4.4	-4.2	-4.4	-5.0	-6.0	-2.8	-4.4	-4.4	-3.8	-4.4	-4.4	-4.4	-4.5	-4.3	-6.3	-4.4
1977	-6.1	-5.7	-5.2	-6.3	-7.2	-6.4	-5.5	-5.1	-4.9	-5.2	-5.4	-6.8	-6.9	-5.3	-6.8	-8.6	-6.2
1978	-4.7	-4.6	-4.7	-4.6	-4.7	-6.2	-3.6	-4.0	-4.8	-4.7	-4.5	-4.5	-5.5	-3.9	-5.4	-7.0	-1.9
1979	-5.3	-4.8	-4.9	-5.4	-6.1	-5.2	-4.3	-4.9	-5.3	-5.5	-4.0	-5.6	-6.3	-4.3	-7.1	-7.3	-3.9
1980	-7.5	-7.6	-8.0	-7.2	-7.1	-8.8	-7.0	-7.0	-8.5	-8.1	-7.4	-7.0	-7.6	-7.1	-8.9	-7.4	-5.0
1981	-6.9	-7.1	-7.1	-8.0	-5.4	-8.3	-6.3	-6.8	-6.6	-7.8	-6.8	-8.2	-8.5	-7.2	-5.6	-7.0	-3.6
1982	-5.5	-5.7	-5.5	-6.7	-4.0	-6.9	-4.7	-5.6	-5.4	-5.9	-5.3	-6.4	-8.0	-5.6	-4.3	-4.7	-2.9
1983	-6.0	-5.4	-5.0	-6.1	-7.6	-5.7	-4.5	-5.9	-3.3	-5.1	-6.7	-4.7	-9.2	-4.4	-6.3	-8.5	-8.0

Imports c.i.f. (19)
billion schilling, monthly averages

Adjusted - Corrigé *

Importations c.a.f. (19)
milliards de schillings, moyennes mensuelles

Year	Q.1	Q.2	Q.3	Q.4	JAN	FEB	MAR	APR	MAY	JUN	JUL	AUG	SEP	OCT	NOV	DEC
1964	3.8	4.0	4.0	4.2	3.7	3.9	3.9	3.9	4.0	4.0	4.0	4.0	4.1	4.2	4.2	4.2
1965	4.2	4.4	4.7	4.9	4.2	4.2	4.3	4.6	4.4	4.3	4.6	4.7	4.7	4.8	4.8	5.1
1966	5.0	5.1	5.1	5.1	5.1	5.0	5.0	5.1	5.1	5.1	5.0	5.1	5.1	5.2	5.0	5.0
1967	5.0	5.0	4.9	5.2	5.0	5.0	5.0	5.0	4.9	5.1	4.9	4.9	4.9	4.9	5.1	5.5
1968	5.4	5.2	5.6	5.5	6.5	4.8	4.8	4.9	5.3	5.3	5.4	5.9	5.3	5.5	5.6	5.3
1969	5.7	6.0	6.3	6.5	5.7	5.7	5.7	6.0	6.1	5.9	6.1	6.4	6.5	6.6	6.6	6.2
1970	7.1	7.5	7.9	8.1	6.9	7.2	7.2	7.4	7.4	7.8	7.9	8.0	8.0	8.0	8.2	8.1
1971	8.5	8.7	8.8	8.8	8.1	8.5	8.7	8.5	8.8	8.8	8.6	8.9	9.1	8.4	8.8	9.2
1972	9.1	9.6	9.6	11.9	9.2	9.1	9.0	9.5	9.6	9.8	9.8	9.7	9.3	11.2	11.8	12.6
1973	10.8	11.4	11.8	11.9	10.7	10.8	11.0	11.2	11.3	11.7	12.0	11.4	11.9	11.9	12.3	11.6
1974	14.3	14.0	14.4	13.5	13.7	15.0	14.2	13.8	14.3	13.7	14.6	14.4	14.4	14.1	13.6	12.6
1975	13.9	13.4	13.2	14.0	13.4	14.6	13.6	13.7	13.0	13.5	12.9	13.2	13.6	13.8	13.7	14.4
1976	15.7	16.7	17.6	18.3	15.6	15.3	16.2	16.1	17.2	16.9	17.1	17.9	17.7	17.6	18.5	18.7
1977	18.9	18.7	20.1	20.7	18.7	19.4	18.7	18.6	18.8	18.7	20.7	19.8	19.7	19.8	21.0	21.3
1978	18.7	19.3	19.3	20.1	19.2	18.7	18.3	19.4	19.0	19.6	18.9	19.2	19.6	20.0	20.3	20.2
1979	20.7	21.8	23.1	24.2	20.1	20.6	21.3	21.0	22.5	22.0	23.3	23.3	22.7	24.0	24.7	23.9
1980	26.3	26.5	26.0	26.3	26.8	26.1	26.0	26.9	26.2	26.4	26.0	25.4	26.6	27.0	26.5	25.3
1981	27.6	27.7	28.8	27.6	26.9	29.0	26.9	27.5	27.5	28.0	28.3	29.0	29.0	27.6	27.5	27.7
1982	28.3	28.1	27.7	26.8	27.5	28.5	28.9	28.1	28.1	28.1	28.2	27.7	27.2	25.7	26.8	27.9
1983	27.9	27.7	28.8	32.4	28.0	27.4	28.1	26.2	28.2	28.6	27.6	29.3	29.6	29.6	31.5	36.1

Exports f.o.b. (19)
billion schilling, monthly averages

Adjusted - Corrigé *

Exportations f.o.b. (19)
milliards de schillings, moyennes mensuelles

Year	Q.1	Q.2	Q.3	Q.4	JAN	FEB	MAR	APR	MAY	JUN	JUL	AUG	SEP	OCT	NOV	DEC
1964	3.0	3.1	3.2	3.3	2.8	3.1	3.1	3.0	3.1	3.0	3.0	3.3	3.2	3.3	3.3	3.2
1965	3.3	3.4	3.5	3.6	3.4	3.4	3.3	3.4	3.4	3.4	3.6	3.5	3.5	3.6	3.5	3.7
1966	3.6	3.6	3.7	3.7	3.6	3.6	3.6	3.6	3.7	3.6	3.7	3.6	3.7	3.6	3.5	4.0
1967	3.8	3.9	4.0	4.0	3.9	3.8	3.7	4.0	3.9	3.9	4.0	3.9	4.1	4.0	4.0	4.1
1968	4.1	4.2	4.3	4.6	4.0	4.0	4.2	4.2	4.2	4.4	4.1	4.4	4.3	4.6	4.6	4.6
1969	4.8	5.0	5.4	5.6	4.9	4.8	4.8	4.9	5.1	5.1	5.4	5.2	5.5	5.8	5.7	5.3
1970	6.0	6.1	6.3	6.3	5.9	6.0	6.1	6.1	6.1	6.3	6.3	6.2	6.4	6.3	6.4	6.3
1971	6.5	6.5	6.7	6.6	6.4	6.5	6.6	6.5	6.5	6.5	6.4	6.8	6.8	6.5	6.7	6.7
1972	6.7	7.1	7.4	8.6	6.8	6.6	6.8	6.9	7.2	7.2	7.3	7.6	7.3	7.6	8.0	10.2
1973	7.5	8.5	8.8	9.2	7.6	7.5	7.5	8.4	8.5	8.6	8.8	8.7	8.8	9.2	9.5	8.8
1974	11.0	11.2	11.4	10.9	11.3	10.9	10.8	11.2	11.3	11.1	11.6	11.2	11.4	11.6	11.4	9.8
1975	12.1	10.6	10.7	11.3	11.2	11.4	10.6	10.9	10.4	10.7	10.8	10.0	11.2	11.2	11.1	11.4
1976	11.5	12.5	13.1	13.3	10.5	11.9	12.1	11.9	13.1	12.5	12.6	13.9	12.9	13.2	13.2	13.5
1977	13.3	13.5	13.6	13.6	13.0	13.0	13.8	13.5	13.6	13.5	13.4	13.5	13.9	13.3	13.7	13.7
1978	14.2	14.6	14.5	15.5	13.9	14.4	14.3	14.3	14.5	15.1	14.2	14.5	14.8	15.2	14.8	16.5
1979	15.8	16.9	17.8	18.2	16.1	15.5	15.8	15.9	17.7	17.1	17.8	18.4	17.3	17.9	18.9	17.9
1980	18.6	18.5	19.1	19.1	19.0	18.4	18.3	18.5	18.2	18.8	19.5	18.4	19.3	19.4	19.4	18.6
1981	20.1	20.6	21.3	21.9	18.9	21.6	19.9	21.1	19.9	20.8	20.9	21.5	21.6	22.3	21.2	22.1
1982	22.3	22.6	21.6	22.3	20.7	22.9	23.3	22.7	22.6	22.5	21.7	21.4	21.7	21.3	22.5	23.0
1983	22.4	22.8	23.3	24.0	23.0	22.1	22.3	22.1	24.2	22.2	22.5	22.2	25.1	23.4	23.5	24.9

Trade balance (f.o.b. — c.i.f.) (19)
billion schilling, monthly averages

Adjusted - Corrigé *

Balance commerciale (f.o.b. — c.a.f.) (19)
milliards de schillings, moyennes mensuelles

Year	Q.1	Q.2	Q.3	Q.4	JAN	FEB	MAR	APR	MAY	JUN	JUL	AUG	SEP	OCT	NOV	DEC
1964	-0.8	-0.9	-0.9	-1.0	-0.8	-0.8	-0.9	-1.0	-0.9	-1.0	-0.9	-0.7	-0.9	-0.9	-1.0	-1.0
1965	-0.8	-1.0	-1.1	-1.3	-0.8	-0.8	-1.0	-1.2	-1.0	-0.9	-1.0	-1.2	-1.2	-1.2	-1.3	-1.4
1966	-1.4	-1.5	-1.4	-1.3	-1.5	-1.4	-1.5	-1.4	-1.5	-1.5	-1.3	-1.5	-1.5	-1.5	-1.5	-1.0
1967	-1.2	-1.1	-0.9	-1.2	-1.1	-1.2	-1.3	-1.0	-1.1	-1.2	-0.9	-1.0	-0.8	-0.9	-1.1	-1.4
1968	-1.3	-0.9	-1.3	-0.9	-2.5	-0.9	-0.6	-0.7	-1.2	-0.9	-1.3	-1.5	-1.0	-0.9	-1.0	-0.7
1969	-0.9	-1.0	-1.0	-0.8	-0.8	-0.8	-0.9	-1.1	-1.0	-0.8	-0.8	-1.2	-0.9	-0.8	-0.8	-0.9
1970	-1.1	-1.4	-1.7	-1.8	-1.0	-1.2	-1.2	-1.3	-1.3	-1.5	-1.6	-1.8	-1.6	-1.8	-1.8	-1.8
1971	-2.0	-2.2	-2.2	-2.2	-1.7	-2.1	-2.1	-2.0	-2.3	-2.3	-2.2	-2.1	-2.3	-1.9	-2.2	-2.4
1972	-2.4	-2.5	-2.2	-3.3	-2.4	-2.4	-2.2	-2.6	-2.4	-2.6	-2.6	-2.1	-1.9	-3.7	-3.8	-2.4
1973	-3.3	-2.9	-3.0	-2.8	-3.1	-3.4	-3.5	-2.8	-2.8	-3.1	-3.2	-2.7	-3.1	-2.7	-2.9	-2.8
1974	-3.3	-2.8	-3.1	-2.5	-2.4	-4.1	-3.4	-2.7	-3.0	-2.6	-3.0	-3.2	-3.0	-2.6	-2.2	-2.8
1975	-2.8	-2.8	-2.6	-2.7	-2.2	-3.2	-3.0	-2.8	-2.7	-2.8	-2.1	-3.2	-2.4	-2.6	-2.6	-3.0
1976	-4.2	-4.2	-4.5	-5.0	-5.2	-3.5	-4.1	-4.2	-4.0	-4.5	-4.6	-4.0	-4.8	-4.4	-5.3	-5.2
1977	-5.7	-5.2	-6.5	-7.1	-5.7	-6.4	-4.9	-5.1	-5.2	-5.3	-7.3	-6.4	-5.7	-6.5	-7.3	-7.6
1978	-4.5	-4.7	-4.8	-4.7	-5.3	-4.3	-4.0	-5.1	-4.5	-4.5	-4.8	-4.6	-4.9	-4.8	-5.5	-3.7
1979	-4.9	-4.9	-5.3	-6.0	-4.0	-5.1	-5.5	-5.1	-4.8	-4.9	-5.5	-5.0	-5.4	-6.1	-5.9	-6.0
1980	-7.8	-8.0	-6.9	-7.2	-7.8	-7.8	-7.7	-8.4	-8.0	-7.6	-6.5	-7.0	-7.3	-7.7	-7.2	-6.7
1981	-7.5	-7.1	-7.5	-5.7	-8.0	-7.4	-7.0	-6.4	-7.6	-7.2	-7.5	-7.5	-7.4	-5.3	-6.4	-5.6
1982	-6.0	-5.5	-6.1	-4.5	-6.8	-5.6	-5.6	-5.4	-5.5	-5.6	-6.5	-6.3	-5.5	-4.4	-4.3	-4.9
1983	-5.4	-4.9	-5.6	-8.4	-5.1	-5.3	-5.9	-4.1	-4.1	-6.5	-5.1	-7.2	-4.5	-6.1	-8.0	-11.2

* Adjusted by the O.E.C.D.

* Corrigé par l'O.C.D.E.

NOTES

1. The original base of the index is 1956 to 1964, 1964 from 1965 to 1968, 1976 from 1969 to 1972, and 1981 from 1973.
2. Excluding sawmills and film industries.
3. The original base of the index is 1976 to 1972 and 1981 from 1973.
4. Excluding sawmills, film industries, petroleum refining, food, beverages and tobacco.
5. From 1973, including value added tax.
6. Including civil engineering.
7. From 1973, excluding indirect taxes.
8. From 1973, new index.
9. Monthly figures refer to end of period.
10. Excluding sawmills and electricity. Prior to 1965 sample survey covering 30 per cent of employment in the industries concerned. Prior to 1971, excluding establishments with less than 6 employees. From 1971, census-based postal survey with compulsory participation.
11. Administrative changes in January 1973 and April 1974 produced a slight decrease in the level of the series.
12. The self-employed are excluded from the total labour force.
13. Excluding hours paid for but not worked.
14. From 1977, new index linked on 1976 to previous index.
15. Weighting pattern based on 1958 from 1966 to 1975, and on 1975 from 1976.
16. Weighting pattern based on 1954-55 to 1966, on 1964 from 1967 to 1976, and on 1974 from 1977.
17. Including instalment credit.
18. Annual data are based on more complete information than quarterly and monthly data.
19. From 1978, including non-monetary gold.

NOTES

1. La base originale de l'indice est 1956 en 1964, 1964 de 1965 à 1968, 1976 de 1969 à 1972, et 1981 à partir de 1973.
2. Non compris les scieries et l'industrie du film.
3. La base originale de l'indice est 1976 jusqu'en 1972 et 1981 à partir de 1973.
4. Non compris les scieries, l'industrie du film, le raffinage du pétrole, l'alimentation, les boissons et le tabac.
5. A partir de 1973, y compris la taxe sur la valeur ajoutée.
6. Y compris les travaux publics.
7. A partir de 1973, non compris les impôts indirects.
8. A partir de 1973, nouvel indice.
9. Situation en fin de mois.
10. Non compris les scieries et l'électricité. Avant 1965, enquête par sondage couvrant 30% de l'emploi dans les industries concernées. Avant 1971, non compris les établissements de moins de 6 employés. A partir de 1971, enquête par courrier basée sur un recensement, avec participation obligatoire.
11. Des changements d'ordre administratif en janvier 1973 et avril 1974 ont entraîné une légère baisse dans le niveau de la série.
12. Les travailleurs indépendants ne sont pas compris dans la population active.
13. Non compris les heures payées mais non ouvrées.
14. A partir de 1977, nouvel indice raccordé sur 1976 à l'indice précédent.
15. La pondération se réfère à 1958 de 1966 à 1975, et à 1975 à partir de 1976.
16. La pondération se réfère à 1954-55 jusqu'en 1966, à 1964 de 1967 à 1976, et à 1974 à partir de 1977.
17. Y compris les crédits remboursables par tranches.
18. Les données annuelles sont établies à partir d'informations plus complètes que les données trimestrielles et mensuelles.
19. A partir de 1978, y compris l'or non monétaire.

MAIN SOURCES

PRINCIPALES SOURCES

Series	Séries	Sources
Industrial production	Production industrielle	Österreichisches Institut für Wirtschaftsforschung *Statistische Übersichten, Beilage zu den Monatsberichten*
Manufacturing new orders	Commandes nouvelles, industries manufacturières	
Internal trade	Commerce intérieur	
Construction....................	Construction	
Labour and wages	Main-d'œuvre et salaires	
Prices	Prix	
Share prices....................	Cours des actions..................	
Foreign trade	Commerce extérieur	
Business surveys	Enquêtes de conjoncture	Österreichisches Institut für Wirtschaftsforschung *Konjunkturtest*
Home finance	Finances internes	Österreichische Nationalbank *Mitteilungen*
Interest rates	Taux d'intérêts	
Net foreign position of commercial banks	Position extérieure nette des banques commerciales	
Balance of payments	Balance des paiements	

Belgium — Belgique

BELGIUM

Industrial production: total (1) — Production industrielle : total (1)

1980 = 100

	Year	Q.1	Q.2	Q.3	Q.4	JAN	FEB	MAR	APR	MAY	JUN	JUL	AUG	SEP	OCT	NOV	DEC
1964	63.4	62.2	64.2	59.6	66.6	59.8	63.3	63.6	64.6	64.2	63.7	54.1	59.8	64.7	67.9	68.3	63.7
1965	64.6	63.9	66.2	59.8	69.1	63.2	65.0	63.4	66.5	66.8	65.4	53.4	59.9	66.0	69.4	70.3	67.6
1966	65.9	65.4	67.7	61.8	69.2	63.0	66.8	66.4	68.9	66.9	67.4	54.5	61.8	69.1	69.5	71.3	66.8
1967	67.0	66.6	68.3	62.5	71.3	63.5	68.3	67.9	68.8	68.4	67.7	54.1	62.6	70.9	70.7	72.3	70.8
1968	70.7	68.7	72.4	66.3	76.1	65.7	69.0	71.5	71.5	71.4	74.2	53.8	67.7	77.5	74.4	79.2	74.7
1969	77.5	75.3	80.6	73.2	82.1	72.7	75.0	78.2	79.6	82.0	80.2	63.4	75.3	81.1	81.9	86.5	77.9
1970	80.2	79.0	82.5	75.0	84.0	74.2	80.0	83.0	81.1	86.0	80.4	65.0	76.3	83.6	84.7	85.5	82.0
1971	82.3	82.5	82.4	75.7	85.6	80.7	84.2	82.7	84.4	79.9	82.8	65.2	75.8	86.2	88.2	87.8	80.7
1972	87.3	85.4	90.5	80.1	94.8	83.3	85.3	87.6	92.1	90.5	88.8	66.8	80.5	92.9	93.8	95.3	95.4
1973	92.8	92.9	95.7	85.5	97.7	88.7	94.8	95.4	96.7	95.8	94.7	69.5	87.7	99.2	96.9	100.2	96.1
1974	96.2	99.8	102.5	88.1	96.3	96.0	101.7	101.8	101.8	100.4	105.1	72.1	90.6	101.4	97.6	102.9	90.0
1975	87.0	92.0	89.0	77.7	89.8	89.2	92.5	94.5	87.6	90.6	88.9	64.8	79.4	89.0	88.2	96.2	85.1
1976	94.6	93.6	99.0	85.8	98.4	89.7	96.9	94.3	100.6	98.3	98.2	71.6	86.2	99.5	102.0	102.4	90.8
1977	94.5	97.3	98.1	85.5	97.2	94.6	93.6	98.6	100.6	98.0	95.6	72.4	88.4	95.7	97.9	102.0	91.7
1978	96.8	96.0	98.9	88.4	104.0	91.6	97.2	99.3	101.8	100.0	94.9	72.7	89.5	103.0	103.7	105.5	102.7
1979	101.2	98.9	106.8	93.7	105.3	91.7	102.4	102.6	107.9	104.7	107.9	75.4	95.4	110.4	104.3	107.7	103.8
1980	100.0	107.1	105.6	89.3	98.4	104.2	107.4	109.6	107.0	106.5	103.3	72.7	95.0	100.2	99.5	105.0	90.6
1981	97.2	98.3	101.9	87.5	100.4	95.0	101.2	100.1	101.8	103.3	100.6	70.3	90.4	102.0	102.7	105.6	92.9
1982	97.0	99.4	102.9	87.4	98.8	101.4	101.3	95.5	104.1	105.1	99.6	72.6	87.7	101.8	105.0	103.1	88.3
1983	99.4	100.1	103.0	91.0	103.3	98.4	101.9	99.8	104.0	101.4	103.7	74.7	93.8	104.6	107.1	110.3	92.5

Industrial production: investment goods (1) — Production industrielle : biens d'équipement (1)

1980 = 100

	Year	Q.1	Q.2	Q.3	Q.4	JAN	FEB	MAR	APR	MAY	JUN	JUL	AUG	SEP	OCT	NOV	DEC
1964	52.0	52.3	51.8	49.7	54.1	51.7	52.0	53.2	53.7	49.2	52.6	44.6	49.7	54.9	55.9	52.7	53.9
1965	56.4	54.1	53.6	54.4	63.5	52.5	53.4	56.3	54.2	53.2	53.6	47.3	54.2	61.7	62.9	61.6	65.9
1966	59.3	59.6	60.1	55.7	62.0	58.6	57.0	63.3	60.9	58.4	60.9	47.9	56.1	63.0	62.7	60.5	62.8
1967	60.0	59.5	59.3	56.9	64.4	59.2	58.4	60.8	58.9	58.1	60.9	48.1	58.6	64.1	65.5	64.8	63.1
1968	60.7	60.4	58.6	57.7	66.0	59.5	59.1	62.7	59.4	58.1	58.2	49.6	59.1	64.4	66.5	63.4	68.1
1969	71.8	68.5	71.1	69.4	78.1	67.1	66.5	71.8	71.2	69.6	72.5	61.6	68.5	78.2	80.9	75.5	77.7
1970	77.8	75.7	76.1	74.7	84.8	73.9	74.6	78.5	76.7	73.8	77.7	63.2	75.3	85.6	87.9	81.8	84.6
1971	75.9	76.8	77.0	70.8	78.8	72.4	76.4	81.7	78.6	75.3	77.2	59.5	72.3	80.8	79.2	75.8	81.3
1972	80.9	80.7	78.4	75.7	89.0	78.1	79.8	84.1	77.7	76.6	80.8	59.5	79.7	87.9	90.8	88.1	87.9
1973	88.2	86.8	85.3	84.0	96.5	83.8	84.7	91.8	85.0	87.5	83.5	66.9	89.4	95.7	99.6	97.4	92.6
1974	95.3	96.1	94.2	90.2	100.9	95.6	94.3	98.2	96.5	95.3	90.8	74.5	93.3	102.9	107.2	98.8	96.6
1975	92.1	94.9	91.2	86.9	95.6	96.3	93.7	94.6	95.5	86.9	91.4	72.0	87.9	100.7	94.6	94.6	97.6
1976	97.2	98.7	95.6	90.8	103.8	95.6	97.7	102.8	98.8	93.2	94.9	71.9	95.3	105.1	104.8	101.8	104.8
1977	97.2	101.3	95.3	90.9	101.4	99.5	100.5	103.9	98.0	91.0	96.9	71.1	97.4	104.3	103.8	101.2	99.2
1978	100.4	100.6	102.3	95.2	103.4	97.7	93.4	105.8	102.7	99.6	104.7	73.9	103.0	108.8	108.1	103.4	98.7
1979	103.3	103.5	99.5	98.5	111.8	101.6	102.3	106.6	101.1	99.0	98.4	78.5	106.0	110.9	116.9	112.8	105.7
1980	100.0	110.5	99.6	91.6	98.3	111.6	111.2	108.7	104.6	94.6	99.6	72.8	95.7	106.2	107.5	95.1	92.3
1981	96.6	98.1	96.3	89.9	102.1	94.2	97.7	102.5	101.5	91.9	95.5	70.8	92.8	106.1	107.7	101.6	97.0
1982	98.6	102.1	97.9	92.4	102.0	99.7	101.3	105.4	102.5	92.2	98.8	72.2	97.0	107.9	108.3	99.1	98.4
1983	101.6	105.0	100.2	97.0	104.3	101.6	104.3	109.3	100.1	94.3	106.1	71.1	104.2	115.7	109.1	103.8	99.8

Industrial production: consumer durable goods (1) — Production industrielle : biens de consommation durables (1)

1980 = 100

	Year	Q.1	Q.2	Q.3	Q.4	JAN	FEB	MAR	APR	MAY	JUN	JUL	AUG	SEP	OCT	NOV	DEC
1964	61.7	62.8	62.8	58.0	63.0	60.0	62.9	65.4	66.7	59.0	62.9	50.5	57.1	66.4	68.2	59.8	61.1
1965	63.8	63.0	64.6	59.6	68.1	56.3	62.7	70.0	67.8	63.0	62.9	48.5	58.4	71.9	70.9	65.0	68.4
1966	66.8	66.9	66.7	63.6	70.0	62.0	64.0	74.7	67.0	64.0	69.2	49.0	64.9	76.8	73.3	67.8	69.0
1967	67.8	69.5	67.2	62.5	72.0	65.9	68.1	74.4	68.2	64.4	69.0	47.5	65.8	74.3	75.5	71.4	69.0
1968	71.4	71.7	70.4	66.4	77.3	68.1	71.7	75.2	73.5	70.7	67.0	53.8	66.5	78.8	83.5	73.5	74.9
1969	79.8	78.4	80.7	75.5	84.6	75.7	75.7	83.8	83.0	77.4	81.5	62.5	73.2	90.7	92.6	80.2	80.9
1970	82.6	82.6	82.7	76.9	88.3	76.3	81.6	89.8	88.6	76.3	83.4	62.3	75.1	93.3	94.3	84.6	85.9
1971	88.6	87.8	90.4	81.5	94.6	77.8	85.4	100.3	94.5	85.0	91.7	61.6	81.3	101.7	99.2	90.7	94.0
1972	95.4	98.8	95.9	85.7	101.1	87.9	96.8	111.8	93.6	93.8	100.3	61.4	89.8	105.9	107.8	99.9	95.7
1973	99.6	104.4	100.1	89.5	104.3	97.7	102.7	112.7	100.0	103.0	97.4	66.0	95.2	107.4	116.5	103.2	93.3
1974	101.5	106.9	104.8	92.6	101.7	102.6	104.6	113.4	109.7	104.4	100.3	71.8	93.4	112.7	115.4	96.5	93.1
1975	96.3	101.2	95.8	87.7	100.6	97.9	101.0	104.6	104.4	86.9	96.0	67.2	85.4	110.5	111.8	93.5	96.6
1976	103.1	108.9	106.5	93.1	104.2	98.0	106.8	121.8	112.8	100.1	106.5	63.9	95.5	119.7	112.7	100.1	99.7
1977	99.1	108.1	100.3	91.1	97.0	100.3	104.0	120.0	103.8	93.1	104.0	61.5	98.5	113.2	102.8	94.4	93.7
1978	97.7	101.7	99.6	88.7	100.6	96.9	98.7	109.5	101.2	92.5	105.2	60.0	96.5	109.6	108.6	99.3	93.9
1979	100.6	103.1	99.8	92.4	107.3	94.1	103.1	112.2	101.0	98.3	100.2	65.5	100.3	111.3	118.9	105.7	97.3
1980	100.0	112.5	99.8	91.0	96.8	112.6	110.7	114.4	108.4	91.7	99.3	68.5	92.5	112.1	109.9	90.0	90.4
1981	97.4	102.1	98.8	89.8	99.0	94.8	101.1	110.3	104.7	90.3	101.3	65.4	91.1	113.0	108.7	95.0	93.1
1982	100.2	105.4	101.7	92.3	101.5	96.4	103.8	116.1	107.1	92.5	105.5	66.1	93.7	117.1	109.5	97.9	96.9
1983	102.7	110.0	103.6	94.8	102.5	101.8	106.0	122.0	104.0	96.0	110.8	63.8	100.6	120.0	109.9	103.4	94.0

Industrial production: total (1) — Adjusted - Corrigé * — Production industrielle : total (1)

1980 = 100

Year	Q.1	Q.2	Q.3	Q.4	JAN	FEB	MAR	APR	MAY	JUN	JUL	AUG	SEP	OCT	NOV	DEC
1964	63.0	62.4	63.1	64.3	63.0	62.8	63.1	62.5	62.4	62.2	63.7	63.0	62.8	65.5	63.6	63.7
1965	64.4	64.3	63.7	66.6	66.3	64.2	62.7	64.1	64.9	63.9	63.7	63.4	63.9	66.7	65.5	67.6
1966	65.7	65.8	66.1	66.6	65.9	65.9	65.3	66.4	64.9	66.1	65.9	65.7	66.8	66.7	66.4	66.7
1967	66.7	66.3	66.9	68.8	66.1	67.4	66.5	66.4	66.2	66.4	66.0	66.5	68.3	68.0	67.6	70.7
1968	68.6	70.3	70.9	73.5	68.0	68.1	69.7	69.2	68.8	72.9	66.3	71.8	74.6	71.5	74.3	74.7
1969	75.0	78.2	78.9	79.3	74.9	74.1	75.9	77.1	78.6	78.9	78.7	80.0	78.1	78.6	81.4	78.0
1970	78.4	79.9	81.1	81.4	76.0	78.8	80.5	78.4	82.1	79.1	81.7	81.3	80.5	81.2	80.8	82.2
1971	81.6	79.7	82.3	83.0	82.2	82.6	80.0	81.4	76.2	81.4	83.0	81.1	82.7	84.6	83.1	81.2
1972	84.1	87.3	87.2	92.2	84.7	83.2	84.5	88.5	86.4	87.0	86.3	86.4	88.9	90.3	90.0	96.4
1973	91.2	92.2	93.4	95.2	90.0	91.8	91.7	92.4	91.8	92.5	91.1	94.5	94.7	93.6	94.1	97.8
1974	97.7	98.6	96.6	94.3	97.4	98.1	97.7	96.7	96.5	102.5	95.3	97.7	96.9	94.8	96.1	92.2
1975	89.9	85.5	85.6	87.7	90.4	88.9	90.3	82.7	87.2	86.7	86.0	85.7	85.0	85.7	89.5	87.7
1976	91.4	94.9	94.5	96.1	91.0	93.1	90.2	94.6	94.5	95.7	95.0	93.1	95.2	99.1	95.2	94.1
1977	94.9	93.8	94.5	95.1	95.7	94.9	94.2	94.3	94.1	93.1	96.3	95.6	91.6	94.9	94.8	95.5
1978	93.7	94.5	97.5	102.0	92.5	93.5	95.0	95.4	95.7	92.3	97.0	96.7	98.7	100.4	98.3	107.2
1979	96.2	101.9	103.5	103.4	92.2	98.5	98.0	101.3	99.6	104.9	101.4	103.3	105.9	100.8	100.6	108.9
1980	104.1	100.6	99.1	96.6	104.2	103.3	104.8	100.5	100.9	100.5	98.4	102.9	96.0	96.1	98.2	95.4
1981	95.8	97.0	97.1	98.8	94.4	97.3	95.6	95.7	97.3	97.9	95.4	98.2	97.8	99.2	98.9	98.2
1982	96.3	97.9	97.3	97.1	100.3	97.2	91.3	97.9	98.6	97.1	98.8	95.3	97.7	101.4	96.4	93.5
1983	96.8	98.1	101.4	101.6	97.2	97.7	95.5	97.9	95.0	101.2	101.8	102.1	100.4	103.5	103.2	98.0

Industrial production: investment goods (1) — Adjusted - Corrigé * — Production industrielle : biens d'équipement (1)

1980 = 100

Year	Q.1	Q.2	Q.3	Q.4	JAN	FEB	MAR	APR	MAY	JUN	JUL	AUG	SEP	OCT	NOV	DEC
1964	52.1	51.5	51.7	52.0	51.8	52.2	52.2	52.1	50.9	51.4	51.1	52.3	51.8	52.2	52.2	51.5
1965	54.2	53.8	56.8	60.6	53.8	54.9	53.8	53.3	54.5	53.5	55.9	56.5	58.0	59.4	59.7	62.8
1966	59.4	60.3	58.6	59.1	60.0	58.4	59.8	61.0	60.2	59.7	58.6	58.2	59.0	59.0	58.5	59.9
1967	59.3	59.4	60.4	61.3	59.8	59.7	58.3	59.2	59.3	59.7	59.9	60.5	61.0	60.7	62.3	61.1
1968	59.3	59.1	61.3	62.4	59.3	57.7	60.8	59.1	58.1	60.0	60.9	61.6	61.5	60.5	61.6	65.0
1969	68.0	71.8	73.9	73.8	66.8	67.6	69.5	71.0	71.4	72.9	75.9	72.6	73.2	73.8	74.3	73.4
1970	75.2	76.5	79.5	79.9	74.2	75.8	75.7	75.3	77.3	77.0	78.9	79.7	80.0	80.8	79.6	79.4
1971	75.9	78.0	75.4	74.4	73.8	77.4	76.7	78.0	79.1	77.0	75.6	75.5	75.1	74.0	72.5	76.7
1972	78.9	79.1	80.6	84.5	79.5	77.4	79.7	78.3	78.5	80.5	77.9	81.6	82.4	83.9	84.1	85.5
1973	84.9	86.6	89.9	91.4	83.0	85.2	86.5	85.8	87.7	86.4	87.3	91.5	90.9	90.8	92.7	90.6
1974	94.2	95.7	96.5	95.5	93.8	94.5	94.3	95.5	96.0	95.4	96.7	95.9	96.8	97.1	95.8	93.8
1975	93.4	92.2	92.7	91.2	94.4	93.4	92.4	93.0	90.2	93.3	93.5	91.4	93.1	85.9	93.2	94.4
1976	95.2	97.0	96.4	99.0	94.2	94.6	96.7	96.5	97.3	97.0	95.0	97.2	97.1	97.7	97.8	101.6
1977	98.8	96.6	96.6	97.4	100.2	99.2	96.9	97.0	96.1	96.8	96.4	97.6	95.9	97.0	97.5	97.7
1978	97.9	103.3	101.7	99.6	97.0	96.7	100.1	101.4	104.4	104.0	101.4	102.0	101.5	99.4	99.5	99.9
1979	100.0	100.8	105.7	107.5	99.7	100.3	100.0	100.1	101.4	101.0	107.3	105.3	104.6	106.0	108.2	108.3
1980	105.8	100.7	97.9	94.6	108.7	104.8	104.0	101.6	99.8	100.6	98.4	97.8	97.4	96.6	94.1	93.0
1981	94.9	97.2	96.2	93.2	92.4	95.7	96.6	98.1	97.2	96.4	96.4	95.2	97.1	97.2	99.7	97.8
1982	98.9	98.7	98.8	98.3	99.5	99.1	98.2	98.6	99.5	97.9	99.3	98.5	98.4	99.4	95.6	99.8
1983	101.6	101.0	103.2	100.9	101.6	102.0	101.2	97.7	99.6	105.5	99.7	104.7	105.3	100.2	100.3	102.2

Industrial production: (1) consumer durable goods — Adjusted - Corrigé * — Production industrielle : (1) biens de consommation durables

1980 = 100

Year	Q.1	Q.2	Q.3	Q.4	JAN	FEB	MAR	APR	MAY	JUN	JUL	AUG	SEP	OCT	NOV	DEC
1964	61.5	61.7	61.6	60.9	61.4	61.9	61.4	61.3	62.0	61.6	62.2	61.8	60.8	61.6	61.2	59.9
1965	62.0	64.0	63.1	65.8	60.8	62.4	62.9	63.7	65.2	63.2	62.8	62.1	64.5	65.8	65.3	66.3
1966	65.5	66.3	67.7	68.1	66.7	63.8	66.0	65.4	66.2	67.3	66.4	67.9	68.7	68.2	67.4	68.6
1967	67.8	66.5	67.5	69.6	68.9	68.1	66.5	66.9	66.3	66.3	65.6	68.1	68.7	68.6	69.5	70.8
1968	69.1	70.0	71.7	74.4	69.3	68.3	69.7	70.4	69.5	70.2	71.9	71.1	72.3	73.2	74.4	75.7
1969	76.4	80.0	82.1	81.3	75.5	76.1	77.5	78.9	79.7	81.6	83.5	81.1	81.8	80.6	82.8	80.4
1970	80.8	81.2	83.8	84.9	78.5	81.9	82.1	81.5	81.4	80.6	84.2	83.9	83.5	84.4	85.3	85.0
1971	85.0	89.1	88.6	91.6	82.4	85.1	87.5	88.9	89.5	88.8	87.4	89.0	89.4	91.2	90.5	93.3
1972	94.2	93.9	94.6	98.3	93.2	92.2	97.1	91.6	94.2	95.8	91.9	95.1	96.8	96.9	97.9	101.7
1973	99.3	98.6	99.3	101.5	98.7	100.6	98.7	96.9	100.5	98.4	97.9	100.3	99.7	102.3	101.8	100.2
1974	102.0	103.1	102.8	99.2	102.3	101.9	102.0	104.2	101.7	103.4	105.6	101.3	101.4	100.2	99.4	98.0
1975	97.0	93.5	97.0	98.3	97.0	98.1	95.8	96.2	90.7	93.6	98.5	95.0	97.5	96.8	98.7	99.5
1976	101.9	104.7	101.1	102.1	100.1	101.3	104.3	104.3	105.6	104.4	96.9	103.5	103.0	103.9	101.7	100.6
1977	102.7	98.8	99.2	96.1	105.8	100.8	101.5	99.8	98.1	98.5	96.5	103.6	97.6	95.4	95.4	97.4
1978	96.4	97.7	97.4	99.5	99.6	95.6	93.9	97.9	97.1	98.1	94.6	99.3	98.3	98.6	99.0	100.8
1979	97.2	98.7	101.6	105.7	94.2	99.8	97.6	97.3	99.2	99.7	100.8	102.1	102.0	105.6	105.8	105.7
1980	105.5	98.4	100.0	95.4	110.9	102.4	103.2	102.3	96.6	96.3	101.6	99.8	98.5	95.8	95.6	94.6
1981	96.7	97.4	97.9	97.8	95.7	97.3	97.1	97.4	96.6	98.3	96.5	98.7	98.6	97.7	98.6	96.9
1982	99.9	100.2	100.0	100.9	100.2	99.6	99.8	99.9	101.0	99.9	100.4	99.1	100.5	101.6	100.1	100.9
1983	103.7	102.1	102.4	102.9	106.2	101.7	103.4	100.8	101.8	103.6	99.8	104.0	103.3	102.5	105.0	101.1

* Adjusted by the O.E.C.D.

* Corrigé par l'O.C.D.E.

BELGIUM

Industrial production: (1) consumer non-durable goods
Production industrielle : (1) biens de consommation non durables

1980 = 100

	Year	Q.1	Q.2	Q.3	Q.4	JAN	FEB	MAR	APR	MAY	JUN	JUL	AUG	SEP	OCT	NOV	DEC
1964	67.0	61.8	65.6	65.0	75.6	64.2	59.0	62.2	66.5	60.7	69.6	63.6	64.3	67.1	79.9	75.0	72.0
1965	67.3	64.8	66.5	64.1	73.9	64.7	61.2	68.4	67.1	63.9	68.6	61.2	64.7	66.3	72.8	73.9	74.9
1966	68.6	65.7	68.1	67.1	73.4	63.3	62.2	71.4	66.0	64.4	73.9	59.3	68.8	73.2	74.3	76.0	70.0
1967	70.7	68.6	70.2	68.4	75.8	66.9	65.6	73.2	66.6	68.3	75.6	61.3	71.5	72.4	78.3	78.6	70.5
1968	73.5	70.0	73.5	72.6	78.0	70.1	67.7	72.1	72.2	76.0	72.4	69.1	73.6	75.2	83.2	76.7	74.2
1969	77.1	72.9	77.3	76.0	82.2	75.7	68.5	74.5	78.2	73.6	80.1	73.5	75.3	79.1	88.3	79.2	79.1
1970	= 79.8 =	74.4	81.1	80.3	83.4	71.0	72.4	79.7	82.8	74.0	86.5	77.0	79.5	84.4	88.1	79.6	82.6
1971	82.6	80.0	80.6	82.6	87.1	74.8	77.1	88.2	80.8	75.8	85.3	75.4	84.4	87.9	89.9	85.6	85.8
1972	86.5	83.6	87.3	83.2	92.1	79.4	80.4	91.1	82.8	86.1	92.9	71.4	86.7	91.4	95.7	93.2	87.5
1973	93.0	91.5	92.5	90.9	97.0	90.6	86.5	97.5	88.9	95.8	92.8	83.4	94.3	95.0	105.4	100.2	85.5
1974	95.4	95.5	98.4	93.4	94.3	97.9	92.5	96.0	98.6	100.2	96.4	86.7	93.7	99.8	104.2	92.9	85.8
1975	89.8	90.0	91.1	86.9	91.2	95.9	85.9	88.0	96.7	84.1	92.6	81.2	85.9	93.5	99.0	89.8	84.7
1976	94.6	91.5	96.1	92.2	98.5	87.5	89.0	97.9	96.6	90.3	101.4	84.7	91.5	100.4	100.2	98.3	97.1
1977	97.1	96.3	99.3	93.0	100.0	91.9	89.4	107.5	96.7	95.8	105.3	76.6	97.7	102.6	101.3	100.7	97.8
1978	96.7	94.7	97.1	90.5	104.6	92.7	88.7	102.6	95.8	96.8	98.8	77.2	94.6	99.8	108.0	109.7	96.2
1979	100.1	100.0	102.7	95.6	102.3	98.2	94.8	106.9	100.1	103.1	104.9	85.7	102.2	98.9	112.4	104.1	90.4
1980	100.0	103.0	102.2	94.0	100.9	103.1	101.0	105.0	104.3	97.8	104.6	85.4	90.9	105.6	113.7	98.2	90.8
1981	101.0	100.4	101.4	96.2	106.0	100.5	96.7	104.0	102.4	95.9	105.9	86.6	96.1	105.8	112.6	105.1	100.2
1982	104.4	103.4	106.7	99.7	107.9	102.0	96.7	111.6	107.4	100.1	112.5	88.3	101.0	109.8	114.0	107.8	101.8
1983	106.5	105.8	106.8	103.1	110.2	105.1	101.0	111.3	103.8	104.2	112.3	86.1	110.0	113.3	114.3	114.1	102.2

Industrial production: intermediate goods (1)
Production industrielle : biens intermédiaires (1)

1980 = 100

	Year	Q.1	Q.2	Q.3	Q.4	JAN	FEB	MAR	APR	MAY	JUN	JUL	AUG	SEP	OCT	NOV	DEC
1964	66.6	65.0	67.8	63.6	69.9	65.1	63.3	66.5	70.3	64.0	68.9	58.7	62.3	69.9	72.9	67.5	69.2
1965	66.9	66.8	68.0	63.2	69.7	65.3	64.0	71.2	69.0	67.0	68.0	55.8	64.0	69.9	71.2	67.5	70.3
1966	67.2	67.9	68.7	63.1	69.0	65.2	65.2	73.3	68.8	66.5	70.7	53.8	64.6	71.0	69.7	67.5	69.9
1967	67.9	67.9	69.1	63.1	71.4	67.9	65.0	70.8	67.9	68.0	71.3	52.9	64.7	71.7	73.3	71.2	69.7
1968	72.7	71.4	72.9	68.5	78.0	70.5	70.1	73.7	73.2	73.7	71.9	59.3	70.3	76.0	82.0	75.0	77.1
1969	79.1	76.9	80.4	75.0	84.1	78.4	71.5	80.7	80.7	78.9	81.5	66.2	74.0	84.7	88.8	80.4	83.1
1970	= 81.0 =	78.8	82.6	76.9	85.9	76.6	76.0	83.7	85.2	78.5	84.2	67.8	76.4	86.4	89.0	82.1	86.6
1971	82.7	83.1	84.0	77.6	86.2	80.4	80.2	88.8	84.1	81.0	86.8	65.6	78.6	88.7	88.5	83.8	86.2
1972	87.9	87.7	88.6	80.0	95.5	84.6	84.4	94.2	85.9	87.6	92.2	64.8	82.7	92.4	97.5	94.7	94.2
1973	93.0	94.4	93.1	84.9	99.5	93.8	89.6	99.8	92.7	96.0	90.7	71.2	90.5	93.0	103.8	99.8	94.9
1974	96.3	100.3	100.0	89.0	95.8	101.3	96.7	102.9	101.9	100.7	97.4	78.6	89.6	98.8	104.4	93.8	89.2
1975	83.7	88.0	84.7	73.5	88.7	91.2	84.8	87.9	87.1	81.2	85.8	63.6	69.6	87.4	92.3	85.9	88.0
1976	92.8	92.3	95.9	86.3	96.9	88.4	83.5	99.9	98.6	93.1	95.9	70.6	87.4	100.8	99.1	96.1	95.5
1977	93.0	96.4	95.3	84.4	96.0	92.9	91.4	104.9	94.6	93.4	98.0	68.5	88.3	96.3	95.8	96.2	96.1
1978	96.0	96.2	96.0	87.4	104.4	95.6	90.9	102.0	96.4	95.0	96.6	69.5	90.7	101.9	108.1	104.9	100.0
1979	101.4	99.6	104.7	94.2	107.0	94.8	96.0	107.9	104.0	105.4	104.9	78.9	98.2	105.4	112.3	107.5	101.2
1980	100.0	109.7	103.3	88.6	98.6	110.4	107.5	111.1	107.5	98.9	103.5	75.3	89.6	100.9	105.8	95.7	94.3
1981	96.1	97.8	97.6	87.7	101.1	94.8	95.1	103.7	100.0	93.8	99.1	72.0	87.1	104.1	105.4	99.9	97.8
1982	94.3	95.2	99.6	86.3	96.3	94.4	92.6	98.5	102.0	94.8	101.9	69.8	87.0	102.0	100.6	94.8	93.4
1983	95.5	96.5	97.7	87.6	100.3	94.5	91.1	103.9	96.5	94.7	101.9	69.2	92.1	101.6	104.0	102.4	94.5

Industrial production: manufacturing (1)
Production industrielle : industries manufacturières (1)

1980 = 100

	Year	Q.1	Q.2	Q.3	Q.4	JAN	FEB	MAR	APR	MAY	JUN	JUL	AUG	SEP	OCT	NOV	DEC
1964	60.0	58.2	60.4	57.6	63.6	57.5	57.0	59.9	62.4	56.9	62.0	53.4	56.6	62.9	67.4	61.4	62.1
1965	61.6	60.2	61.7	58.6	65.7	57.5	58.3	64.7	62.9	60.4	61.8	51.8	58.7	65.4	67.4	63.9	65.8
1966	63.5	63.0	64.2	60.7	66.2	59.8	60.4	68.7	64.0	61.7	67.0	51.2	61.9	69.1	67.9	65.3	65.5
1967	64.6	64.3	64.7	60.9	68.5	62.7	62.3	67.8	63.8	63.0	67.3	50.7	62.9	69.1	71.1	68.5	65.9
1968	68.7	67.1	68.2	65.5	74.3	65.2	66.1	69.8	69.0	68.9	66.6	56.5	66.6	73.3	78.8	71.3	72.7
1969	76.6	73.5	77.4	73.7	81.8	73.3	69.7	77.6	78.1	75.2	78.8	65.5	72.3	83.4	87.6	78.1	79.9
1970	= 79.7 =	77.2	80.6	76.5	84.5	74.5	75.3	81.8	83.1	75.9	82.9	67.1	75.8	86.7	88.7	80.7	84.2
1971	81.6	81.0	82.9	77.4	85.1	76.1	73.7	88.1	84.4	79.3	85.0	65.1	78.1	88.8	88.1	82.4	84.9
1972	86.7	86.0	87.2	80.2	93.6	81.2	83.3	93.6	84.3	85.8	91.5	63.9	83.6	93.0	96.7	93.2	90.8
1973	93.0	93.2	93.0	86.7	99.2	90.8	89.4	99.4	91.7	95.9	91.4	71.8	92.1	96.2	105.3	100.1	92.2
1974	97.1	100.3	100.5	90.7	96.7	100.4	97.4	103.1	102.6	101.2	97.7	78.5	91.7	102.0	106.1	94.3	89.9
1975	87.1	90.6	88.1	79.3	90.6	92.9	88.3	90.7	91.6	83.4	89.3	67.8	76.5	93.6	95.6	87.1	89.0
1976	94.8	94.4	97.4	88.6	98.9	89.1	91.7	102.4	100.5	93.3	98.5	71.3	90.2	104.2	102.6	97.4	96.8
1977	95.0	98.5	96.8	87.8	97.0	93.7	94.3	107.5	96.4	93.3	100.6	69.4	93.1	100.9	98.6	96.9	95.6
1978	96.9	97.0	97.7	89.5	103.3	94.8	92.8	103.5	97.8	95.6	99.7	69.7	94.5	104.4	108.6	104.0	97.3
1979	101.9	100.1	104.0	96.0	107.4	94.4	97.8	108.0	103.2	104.0	105.0	78.2	101.8	107.9	114.9	107.7	99.5
1980	100.0	108.6	103.0	90.8	97.3	108.2	107.4	110.1	107.2	98.0	103.8	75.1	91.9	105.3	108.5	93.6	91.3
1981	97.7	98.4	99.6	90.9	101.3	94.0	95.9	105.2	102.8	94.4	101.6	73.2	91.2	108.2	108.9	100.3	96.3
1982	97.8	99.2	101.9	91.0	99.3	96.0	96.8	104.7	104.7	95.8	105.1	72.8	92.3	108.0	105.6	97.3	95.2
1983	100.0	101.3	102.5	93.2	103.0	97.7	96.8	109.5	100.5	97.4	109.7	70.3	98.7	110.7	107.8	105.0	96.3

Industrial production: (1) consumer non-durable goods

Production industrielle : (1) biens de consommation non durables

1980 = 100

Adjusted - Corrigé *

	Year	Q.1	Q.2	Q.3	Q.4	JAN	FEB	MAR	APR	MAY	JUN	JUL	AUG	SEP	OCT	NOV	DEC
1964		64.7	65.9	65.9	70.2	64.7	64.9	64.5	65.6	65.6	66.5	65.6	67.4	64.8	71.6	69.3	69.7
1965		68.0	67.3	65.1	69.0	69.1	68.1	66.9	67.8	67.8	66.3	65.9	66.2	63.3	67.5	67.3	72.1
1966		68.6	68.6	68.2	69.4	68.2	69.1	68.7	68.8	67.4	69.5	66.3	68.5	69.8	69.6	69.2	69.6
1967		71.4	70.0	70.3	72.0	70.0	72.5	71.6	69.4	70.6	70.0	69.4	70.2	71.4	71.7	72.0	72.3
1968		71.6	74.0	74.1	74.1	71.5	71.0	72.3	73.7	75.3	73.0	73.9	73.9	74.6	73.5	73.7	75.2
1969		75.3	77.6	77.3	78.5	76.0	75.1	74.8	78.8	76.2	77.8	77.7	77.8	76.4	78.0	79.2	78.4
1970		77.2	80.5	81.6	80.2	73.5	78.6	79.4	80.6	79.5	81.3	81.1	83.0	80.5	80.4	78.6	81.6
1971		81.8	80.6	83.8	84.4	79.6	82.9	82.8	80.5	81.0	80.3	82.3	86.2	82.9	84.7	83.2	85.4
1972		84.4	86.3	85.3	90.6	84.9	82.2	86.2	85.2	86.5	87.1	81.7	85.5	88.6	88.8	89.4	93.6
1973		91.9	91.8	93.7	95.0	91.2	91.6	92.7	91.0	93.3	91.2	93.6	93.0	94.4	95.4	96.4	93.3
1974		96.3	97.2	96.0	92.5	97.0	97.9	94.1	97.8	96.8	97.2	95.6	95.5	96.9	93.5	92.4	91.7
1975		91.6	88.6	89.5	89.5	94.3	91.0	89.5	91.7	85.7	88.4	89.3	90.3	88.9	88.4	91.8	88.2
1976		91.0	94.0	95.2	96.8	88.8	93.0	91.4	93.0	93.1	95.7	96.9	94.5	94.3	94.9	95.9	99.5
1977		96.9	97.0	96.4	99.0	97.2	95.0	98.5	96.2	97.7	96.9	93.8	98.4	96.9	96.6	97.1	103.2
1978		94.9	94.3	95.5	103.0	95.2	93.9	95.6	95.6	97.4	89.9	94.1	94.2	98.1	99.7	104.7	104.5
1979		99.1	100.6	101.5	99.8	97.7	99.9	99.8	100.4	100.2	101.2	102.6	101.6	100.3	100.5	99.4	99.4
1980		101.4	100.3	99.1	93.1	100.8	101.0	102.3	101.5	99.3	100.2	98.7	96.0	102.5	99.8	99.7	94.7
1981		99.9	99.6	101.4	103.2	100.3	100.3	99.0	99.0	99.2	100.7	100.0	102.4	101.9	101.8	104.3	103.3
1982		102.7	104.9	105.0	105.1	104.5	99.8	103.7	104.2	106.2	104.3	105.3	104.6	105.0	106.1	104.5	104.6
1983		105.0	105.2	108.4	108.4	108.5	104.1	102.4	104.5	107.5	103.6	105.9	110.8	108.6	107.5	109.3	108.3

Industrial production: intermediate goods (1)

Production industrielle : biens intermédiaires (1)

1980 = 100

Adjusted - Corrigé *

	Year	Q.1	Q.2	Q.3	Q.4	JAN	FEB	MAR	APR	MAY	JUN	JUL	AUG	SEP	OCT	NOV	DEC
1964		64.9	66.0	66.9	67.6	64.6	64.9	65.2	66.4	65.3	66.4	67.4	66.2	67.1	67.7	68.1	66.9
1965		67.1	66.7	66.7	67.4	67.6	67.0	66.8	66.3	67.3	66.5	66.3	67.4	66.4	67.8	66.7	67.6
1966		67.7	67.3	67.0	67.0	67.0	67.9	68.2	67.6	67.1	67.2	66.6	66.7	67.5	66.1	66.6	68.2
1967		67.7	67.5	67.4	69.3	68.8	67.8	66.6	67.2	67.3	67.9	66.2	66.7	69.4	68.5	69.7	69.6
1968		70.2	71.6	73.2	75.1	69.7	69.8	71.1	71.1	71.3	72.5	72.4	73.6	73.7	74.6	75.0	75.8
1969		76.3	78.9	80.4	81.0	76.8	74.5	77.5	78.4	78.9	79.5	81.1	79.6	80.4	80.7	82.0	80.2
1970		78.5	80.8	82.6	82.6	76.1	79.2	80.3	81.1	80.7	80.4	83.6	82.1	82.0	82.0	82.2	83.5
1971		82.2	82.5	83.4	83.0	81.7	83.3	81.6	81.7	83.0	82.9	83.1	83.5	83.6	83.6	82.0	83.5
1972		85.7	86.6	86.6	92.7	85.6	84.0	87.4	85.6	86.7	87.5	84.9	85.7	89.2	90.8	91.6	95.6
1973		92.0	91.4	92.9	95.8	91.4	92.2	92.3	92.3	92.9	89.2	93.0	94.2	91.6	94.5	96.4	96.5
1974		98.3	98.1	97.3	92.3	98.3	99.1	97.6	99.3	97.2	97.7	101.2	95.0	95.7	94.8	92.2	89.8
1975		86.4	82.5	80.4	85.5	88.3	86.8	84.2	83.2	80.9	83.3	82.2	76.1	83.0	83.9	86.1	86.6
1976		88.9	93.7	94.1	93.5	86.9	89.0	90.8	95.0	93.4	92.7	93.1	94.1	95.0	94.3	92.7	93.5
1977		94.0	93.1	92.5	93.1	93.6	93.6	94.8	92.6	94.0	92.5	93.3	93.2	90.9	91.0	92.6	95.7
1978		93.9	93.2	96.1	101.3	95.2	93.0	93.3	94.5	93.8	91.4	94.8	95.3	98.2	101.3	100.1	102.6
1979		96.4	102.2	104.5	103.1	92.5	98.0	98.6	101.4	102.3	102.9	106.7	103.4	103.5	102.7	102.8	103.9
1980		105.7	100.6	97.8	95.0	107.7	105.4	104.0	102.5	99.3	100.0	99.6	98.6	95.1	95.9	95.4	93.6
1981		95.5	95.0	96.5	97.3	94.2	96.7	95.6	94.4	95.3	95.4	95.6	95.8	98.0	96.8	98.2	96.9
1982		93.2	96.9	94.6	92.9	96.5	94.1	88.8	96.5	97.9	96.4	94.2	94.5	95.2	94.7	91.3	92.7
1983		94.1	95.1	96.3	97.2	96.5	92.6	93.1	93.3	95.7	96.3	96.0	97.7	95.1	97.7	98.6	95.4

Industrial production: manufacturing (1)

Production industrielle : industries manufacturières (1)

1980 = 100

Adjusted - Corrigé *

	Year	Q.1	Q.2	Q.3	Q.4	JAN	FEB	MAR	APR	MAY	JUN	JUL	AUG	SEP	OCT	NOV	DEC
1964		58.6	59.5	59.8	61.1	58.1	58.8	59.0	59.4	59.5	59.6	59.9	59.8	59.6	61.9	60.9	60.4
1965		61.0	61.1	60.9	63.1	60.9	61.2	60.8	60.9	61.6	60.8	60.5	61.4	61.0	63.4	62.4	63.6
1966		63.4	63.6	63.5	63.9	63.1	63.3	63.8	63.6	63.0	64.2	62.2	63.7	64.5	63.8	63.5	64.4
1967		64.7	63.7	64.2	66.1	64.9	65.5	63.6	63.5	63.9	63.8	62.5	64.2	66.0	65.6	66.1	66.4
1968		66.5	67.5	69.0	71.3	66.0	66.2	67.3	67.5	67.2	67.9	67.8	69.5	69.8	70.6	71.1	72.3
1969		73.6	76.5	78.0	78.6	73.0	73.2	74.7	76.0	76.1	77.5	78.6	77.4	78.0	78.2	79.4	78.1
1970		77.7	79.1	81.1	81.2	75.7	78.8	78.7	78.7	79.6	79.0	81.2	81.3	80.9	81.0	80.5	82.1
1971		80.7	81.7	82.0	82.2	79.0	81.8	81.2	81.8	82.0	81.5	81.4	82.5	82.1	82.5	80.8	83.1
1972		84.5	85.4	85.8	91.0	83.9	82.8	86.8	84.0	85.4	86.9	82.9	85.9	88.6	89.4	89.8	93.9
1973		91.3	91.6	93.5	96.0	90.2	91.6	92.3	91.1	93.2	90.4	92.8	94.6	93.1	95.3	96.9	95.8
1974		98.7	99.0	97.9	93.7	98.8	99.3	97.9	100.1	98.3	98.4	100.6	96.3	96.8	95.3	93.7	92.0
1975		89.4	86.0	85.6	87.6	91.0	89.9	87.5	87.0	85.3	85.7	87.0	82.5	87.3	85.6	88.3	89.0
1976		91.2	95.7	95.1	95.8	89.1	91.3	93.3	96.4	95.3	95.3	94.2	95.5	95.7	96.5	95.4	95.7
1977		96.4	94.9	94.8	94.6	96.2	96.0	97.0	94.8	95.3	94.6	95.1	96.4	92.9	92.6	94.6	96.6
1978		95.0	95.3	97.2	100.6	95.8	94.5	94.8	96.1	97.0	92.8	96.1	96.8	98.6	100.1	100.6	101.3
1979		97.4	101.9	104.8	104.2	93.4	99.5	99.2	101.0	101.7	103.0	106.6	104.1	103.6	103.5	104.6	104.4
1980		105.0	100.7	98.5	94.9	106.3	105.0	103.7	102.6	99.4	100.1	99.7	98.6	97.3	96.6	95.0	93.0
1981		96.3	97.3	98.2	99.0	94.2	97.3	97.2	97.2	96.9	97.8	97.2	98.2	99.4	98.9	100.0	98.0
1982		97.1	99.5	98.2	96.9	98.8	98.1	94.4	99.3	100.0	99.0	98.9	97.7	98.1	98.4	95.5	96.9
1983		98.8	100.1	100.3	101.2	100.7	98.1	97.7	97.8	100.0	102.5	98.0	102.1	100.8	100.5	102.6	100.4

* Adjusted by the O.E.C.D.

* Corrigé par l'O.C.D.E.

BELGIUM

Industrial production: construction (1)(2)

1980 = 100

Production industrielle : construction (1)(2)

1980 = 100

	Year	Q.1	Q.2	Q.3	Q.4	JAN	FEB	MAR	APR	MAY	JUN	JUL	AUG	SEP	OCT	NOV	DEC
1964	114.8	105.4	122.9	113.5	117.5	95.0	110.1	111.3	126.4	114.3	128.0	100.5	112.8	127.2	128.0	118.2	106.3
1965	110.8	96.9	122.8	111.5	112.1	91.2	86.8	112.8	123.5	117.1	127.6	84.1	122.7	127.8	126.5	102.0	107.8
1966	114.4	103.4	122.4	113.8	118.1	74.4	106.8	128.8	119.5	117.3	130.5	77.8	129.3	134.4	123.5	120.4	110.5
1967	120.6	113.3	131.7	116.4	121.0	97.6	108.2	134.2	126.3	130.2	138.6	81.5	132.5	135.1	139.2	133.3	90.3
1968	113.5	102.5	115.0	116.0	120.7	90.1	99.9	117.4	115.7	108.8	120.5	90.6	124.6	132.8	141.0	122.0	99.1
1969	117.9	101.8	130.9	121.0	117.8	108.8	71.7	124.9	136.9	121.5	134.4	93.1	127.1	143.0	150.3	125.9	77.3
1970	=136.1	=113.4	146.2	134.2	150.6	100.4	109.5	130.2	151.2	132.5	155.0	94.2	147.5	161.0	169.5	147.2	135.0
1971	137.0	117.9	154.2	129.8	146.2	97.1	122.5	134.2	156.3	144.5	161.6	75.7	149.7	164.0	155.9	141.2	141.4
1972	134.5	126.5	148.7	119.6	143.3	99.2	121.0	159.5	145.4	142.7	157.8	53.2	156.1	149.5	157.8	147.4	124.8
1973	126.8	125.5	137.6	115.9	128.1	119.2	115.4	142.0	131.2	145.3	136.5	55.9	147.6	144.2	155.2	132.4	96.7
1974	134.1	132.7	146.4	119.6	137.7	132.0	126.7	139.3	149.8	149.0	140.4	64.2	144.8	149.3	160.7	131.7	120.8
1975	132.0	126.3	147.0	119.6	134.9	127.8	125.6	125.4	152.9	133.1	155.1	67.9	131.6	159.3	165.9	131.2	107.8
1976	129.1	112.6	146.9	120.8	136.1	104.9	88.8	144.1	151.8	137.7	151.0	56.1	145.2	161.1	154.2	140.8	113.3
1977	126.9	120.1	144.3	120.9	122.2	96.5	112.1	151.7	140.1	136.2	156.6	59.3	147.2	156.2	141.8	121.9	102.9
1978	118.1	103.2	138.9	111.0	119.4	100.8	71.7	137.1	137.1	129.5	149.9	43.1	140.3	149.5	152.0	131.3	74.8
1979	95.1	55.1	118.6	94.0	112.5	19.5	45.0	100.8	113.9	120.3	121.8	38.6	122.2	121.1	142.7	115.1	79.6
1980	100.0	93.6	118.4	96.4	91.7	64.0	100.8	116.1	123.0	108.0	124.2	44.8	113.7	130.6	129.0	84.9	61.2
1981	82.4	72.2	102.7	79.3	75.5	59.6	52.2	104.8	108.6	94.2	105.3	35.2	93.9	108.7	98.0	81.6	46.9
1982	79.2	68.7	95.5	75.1	77.6	41.9	70.9	93.2	97.8	84.5	104.1	33.3	91.3	100.5	88.7	77.6	66.5
1983	64.2	56.7	75.5	61.7	62.8	55.5	38.9	75.7	71.4	69.3	85.9	23.4	79.3	82.3	75.9	66.5	46.0

Production: crude steel

thousand tons, monthly averages

Production : acier brut

milliers de tonnes, moyennes mensuelles

	Year	Q.1	Q.2	Q.3	Q.4	JAN	FEB	MAR	APR	MAY	JUN	JUL	AUG	SEP	OCT	NOV	DEC
1964																	
1965																	
1966																	
1967																	
1968																	
1969	1069	1038	1079	1030	1131	1026	971	1117	1085	1076	1076	955	1014	1120	1173	1088	1132
1970	1051	1030	1148	1044	981	962	929	1199	1199	1142	1103	1012	1006	1113	1068	850	1024
1971	1037	1099	1109	1070	871	1143	1045	1108	1106	1119	1101	1046	1040	1123	1019	819	776
1972	1211	1188	1239	1107	1309	1141	1153	1271	1222	1224	1272	1044	1077	1201	1276	1302	1350
1973	1294	1318	1318	1178	1361	1385	1164	1405	1371	1361	1223	1239	1280	1014	1279	1411	1392
1974	1352	1426	1465	1250	1268	1475	1372	1430	1484	1488	1422	1290	1200	1261	1374	1297	1134
1975	965	1209	1058	671	923	1237	1146	1194	998	1070	1105	699	413	902	922	888	958
1976	1012	988	1074	1020	966	975	892	1097	1180	1033	1008	943	1016	1102	1041	979	879
1977	938	995	971	879	905	955	948	1083	904	1060	949	881	863	892	827	951	937
1978	1050	1052	1013	935	1202	1044	999	1114	1103	1101	834	829	907	1068	1241	1195	1169
1979	1120	1134	1221	1053	1071	1068	1097	1238	1237	1234	1193	1043	1044	1073	1023	1052	1139
1980	1027	1215	1208	851	832	1190	1184	1271	1215	1261	1149	866	926	761	862	820	815
1981	1024	972	1073	966	1083	914	930	1071	1005	1132	1082	888	896	1115	1040	1116	1094
1982	824	844	1021	723	709	1072	889	572	1023	1028	1012	698	644	827	692	657	779
1983	846	849	900	737	899	859	766	923	922	890	887	700	759	751	974	880	844

Prospects for total economy (3)

manufacturing

average July 1974-June 1981 = 100

Perspectives économiques (3)

industries manufacturières

moyenne juillet 1974-juin 1981 = 100

	Year	Q.1	Q.2	Q.3	Q.4	JAN	FEB	MAR	APR	MAY	JUN	JUL	AUG	SEP	OCT	NOV	DEC
1964																	
1965																	
1966																	
1967																	
1968																	
1969																	
1970																	
1971																	
1972																	
1973																	
1974												120.90	110.89	105.04	96.81	85.96	81.84
1975						79.05	75.47	74.02	79.43	83.94	83.02	82.92	83.26	89.07	98.48	103.28	110.23
1976						110.85	113.37	115.37	114.09	112.74	113.20	113.20	111.43	109.28	103.91	100.49	96.73
1977						96.27	97.88	97.81	95.58	95.67	96.23	94.65	95.22	91.67	92.48	95.55	97.69
1978						98.81	96.31	94.78	98.22	100.01	100.04	100.86	104.04	105.96	105.34	105.49	105.82
1979						103.50	105.30	109.84	110.79	115.13	115.68	116.34	118.04	118.88	120.45	118.51	114.69
1980						115.04	114.37	109.61	104.74	98.00	94.63	94.45	89.52	88.41	89.05	87.43	87.32
1981						84.89	86.77	88.52	90.72	92.72	95.86	98.49	100.10	100.27	99.23	98.00	100.86
1982						98.66	98.74	101.22	103.23	104.36	104.58	103.08	100.13	98.30	96.79	100.10	99.58
1983						97.16	96.30	100.87	98.52	100.72	101.43	104.29	105.48	106.34	104.21	106.40	105.95

Industrial production: construction (1)(2)
1980 = 100

Adjusted - Corrigé *

Production industrielle : construction (1)(2)
1980 = 100

	Year	Q.1	Q.2	Q.3	Q.4	JAN	FEB	MAR	APR	MAY	JUN	JUL	AUG	SEP	OCT	NOV	DEC
1964		119.9	112.0	114.1	113.8	115.4	132.3	111.9	111.5	108.6	116.0	117.7	112.8	111.7	112.9	115.0	113.5
1965		110.3	112.4	111.7	109.0	118.4	104.1	108.6	110.6	115.9	110.8	108.4	116.1	110.5	114.1	97.3	115.7
1966		114.5	112.6	113.9	116.9	98.8	127.2	117.6	113.2	112.0	112.7	107.8	117.9	115.9	114.4	109.9	126.4
1967		123.8	121.7	119.7	116.9	123.0	127.6	120.8	122.5	122.1	120.6	121.8	116.2	121.2	122.3	121.2	107.0
1968		111.2	106.6	121.7	116.6	109.4	110.7	113.6	108.2	99.3	112.2	131.1	115.1	119.0	115.3	117.8	116.7
1969		111.5	120.8	127.0	111.7	127.3	83.4	123.8	122.3	117.3	122.9	135.7	120.0	125.4	122.3	124.1	88.5
1970		124.2	134.3	141.0	146.0	122.8	127.2	122.6	133.9	130.6	138.4	144.4	143.2	135.4	144.5	143.8	149.8
1971		128.4	141.1	134.8	142.9	121.0	142.2	121.8	139.0	146.0	138.5	129.3	137.8	137.3	135.9	136.3	156.4
1972		133.0	135.6	122.9	140.5	125.9	133.4	139.6	138.3	132.9	135.7	102.1	134.5	132.0	135.2	136.4	149.8
1973		134.4	125.1	121.5	124.5	139.4	133.1	130.8	122.1	130.0	123.2	108.6	127.0	128.8	128.7	124.1	120.6
1974		141.9	132.8	129.4	134.6	148.5	145.9	131.4	136.3	133.1	128.8	126.9	131.0	130.1	128.0	130.3	145.4
1975		137.4	132.3	130.3	130.2	144.7	145.0	122.5	132.3	125.3	139.4	135.8	121.5	133.8	130.8	132.1	127.7
1976		119.6	131.5	127.6	132.9	127.3	100.4	131.0	131.6	137.1	125.8	123.7	131.6	127.5	129.2	136.9	132.7
1977		130.5	128.2	130.8	121.5	127.8	130.7	133.0	127.1	129.5	128.0	140.6	128.6	123.2	120.5	113.6	130.5
1978		111.9	122.7	116.3	114.9	132.8	83.9	119.1	126.8	119.3	122.2	109.2	117.3	122.6	121.9	122.8	99.9
1979		56.6	104.3	99.1	110.9	26.0	52.7	9[illegible].2	103.2	106.5	103.1	95.9	101.2	100.2	111.0	109.4	112.4
1980		102.9	102.9	103.4	88.6	86.2	112.6	109.9	103.9	100.3	104.6	105.3	101.0	103.9	97.6	87.0	81.2
1981		80.9	88.7	83.9	74.0	87.8	61.0	94.0	90.5	89.3	86.2	83.1	85.7	82.8	78.9	82.6	60.4
1982		76.0	82.0	79.2	78.9	65.0	82.6	80.5	81.9	82.7	81.5	82.3	79.3	76.1	73.8	77.4	85.4
1983		66.0	64.7	62.9	63.9	89.7	45.3	62.9	62.7	64.7	66.8	59.1	66.7	62.9	65.5	64.0	62.1

Domestic orders inflow: tendency
manufacturing
per cent balance

Commandes intérieures : tendance
industries manufacturières
solde en pourcentage

	Year	Q.1	Q.2	Q.3	Q.4	JAN	FEB	MAR	APR	MAY	JUN	JUL	AUG	SEP	OCT	NOV	DEC
1964																	
1965																	
1966						-15	1	-6	-17	-19	-11	-21	-11	-20	-31	-22	-29
1967						-20	-18	-23	-33	-26	-16	-22	-13	-21	-20	-17	-21
1968						-17	-11	-25	-16	-8	-8	-4	-	11	15	3	2
1969						25	3	15	14	12	20	7	14	17	13	1	5
1970						-4	-2	-11	-6	-27	-	-21	-2	-7	-18	-8	5
1971						-14	-2	-8	-22	-11	-8	-19	-5	-18	-23	-17	-11
1972						-11	-3	-11	-22	-1	1	-16	9	-9	5	4	6
1973						10	7	-	-3	19	1	-5	17	-7	13	-1	-8
1974						15	-4	-1	-4	1	-13	-6	-23	-24	-35	-44	-40
1975						-36	-40	-47	-34	-31	-25	-33	-33	-27	-10	-20	-9
1976						-2	-	4	-14	-13	-4	-13	-8	-14	-20	-24	-23
1977						-20	-15	-19	-22	-29	-19	-29	-18	-35	-25	-25	-19
1978						-6	-18	-11	-16	-12	-13	-18	-12	-17	-14	-13	-13
1979						-23	-6	1	-9	1	4	-3	4	2	12	1	-2
1980						6	5	-7	-19	-24	-17	-18	-27	-28	-26	-33	-28
1981						-22	-20	-25	-23	-21	-14	-11	-13	-13	-20	-15	-13
1982						-16	-14	-16	-14	-11	-9	-10	-9	-17	-11	-6	-4
1983						-16	-15	-4	-22	-14	-9	-12	-11	-12	-18	-6	-11

Order books or demand: level
manufacturing
per cent balance

Carnet de commandes ou demande globale : niveau
industries manufacturières
solde en pourcentage

	Year	Q.1	Q.2	Q.3	Q.4	JAN	FEB	MAR	APR	MAY	JUN	JUL	AUG	SEP	OCT	NOV	DEC
1964																	
1965																	
1966						-25	-25	-19	-22	-25	-26	-21	-23	-34	-35	-35	-44
1967						-40	-39	-40	-40	-42	-42	-46	-40	-38	-39	-43	-42
1968						-41	-35	-35	-31	-25	-21	-17	-13	-7	-4	-4	-2
1969						7	7	11	13	16	20	16	19	18	21	10	6
1970						5	-4	-5	-5	-16	-16	-14	-21	-18	-17	-16	-14
1971						-17	-14	-17	-15	-18	-14	-14	-16	-22	-29	-32	-22
1972						-30	-23	-20	-22	-17	-18	-19	-20	-17	-14	-14	-14
1973						-4	-	1	2	12	8	7	6	4	9	2	-4
1974						3	5	4	3	3	-4	-5	-17	-25	-38	-55	-56
1975						-59	-62	-63	-61	-60	-63	-65	-61	-60	-57	-51	-48
1976						-46	-42	-32	-34	-32	-28	-33	-34	-32	-42	-43	-49
1977						-47	-47	-47	-51	-50	-49	-53	-49	-54	-55	-51	-53
1978						-50	-50	-49	-44	-45	-43	-46	-40	-41	-41	-42	-43
1979						-36	-34	-32	-30	-30	-27	-24	-23	-22	-16	-18	-24
1980						-21	-18	-18	-25	-31	-37	-39	-44	-46	-46	-45	-47
1981						-47	-45	-45	-45	-44	-41	-43	-41	-36	-38	-43	-41
1982						-44	-39	-38	-36	-35	-36	-37	-42	-39	-43	-45	-41
1983						-43	-36	-35	-34	-33	-34	-32	-34	-29	-32	-27	-28

* Adjusted by the O.E.C.D.

* Corrigé par l'O.C.D.E.

BELGIUM

Finished goods stocks: level — Stocks de produits finis : niveau

manufacturing — industries manufacturières

per cent balance — solde en pourcentage

	Year	Q.1	Q.2	Q.3	Q.4	JAN	FEB	MAR	APR	MAY	JUN	JUL	AUG	SEP	OCT	NOV	DEC
1964																	
1965																	
1966						8	9	6	8	6	8	4	8	8	7	13	16
1967						21	21	18	11	19	15	12	13	16	18	14	15
1968						17	14	12	10	9	3	2	-2	-5	-3	-11	-6
1969						-6	-	-5	-6	-8	-10	-9	-11	-10	-13	-7	-5
1970						2	1	5	11	7	8	8	11	15	8	5	3
1971						10	12	13	14	16	12	11	15	10	13	16	10
1972						9	12	8	6	7	9	3	3	6	3	5	4
1973						-2	1	-3	-	-2	-12	-5	-5	-12	-8	-2	-1
1974						-2	-2	-1	-6	-7	-6	-3	2	7	21	25	23
1975						27	28	29	21	21	24	30	29	21	17	13	15
1976						4	-4	-1	1	5	-3	5	2	3	3	8	8
1977						2	9	9	7	25	22	24	26	21	16	17	15
1978						22	14	21	20	22	25	20	22	15	14	14	14
1979						21	20	18	18	14	10	10	4	1	3	2	6
1980						7	9	10	11	11	12	13	15	15	14	17	16
1981						15	12	15	16	13	8	2	7	6	8	5	9
1982						6	8	3	7	4	14	9	11	12	10	7	10
1983						7	6	9	11	12	14	6	6	9	9	6	12

Rate of capacity utilization — Taux d'utilisation de capacité

manufacturing — industries manufacturières

per cent — pourcentage

	Year	Q.1	Q.2	Q.3	Q.4	JAN	FEB	MAR	APR	MAY	JUN	JUL	AUG	SEP	OCT	NOV	DEC
1964		83.4	83.7		84.3	83.4				83.7					84.3		
1965		81.3	82.4		81.9	81.3				82.4					81.9		
1966		82.6	82.2		82.0	82.6				82.2					82.0		
1967		79.4	77.5		77.9	79.4				77.5					77.9		
1968		76.4	78.1		82.4	76.4				78.1					82.4		
1969		84.1	86.5		87.4	84.1				86.5					87.4		
1970		86.5	86.7		85.6	86.5				86.7					85.6		
1971		84.6	83.8		82.6	84.6				83.8					82.6		
1972		82.1	83.1		82.9	82.1				83.1					82.9		
1973		83.7	85.4		85.0	83.7				85.4					85.0		
1974		83.8	85.1		80.9	83.8				85.1					80.9		
1975		74.2	71.5		71.0	74.2				71.5					71.0		
1976		72.0	76.6		76.8	72.0				76.6					76.8		
1977		73.5	73.7		72.0	73.5				73.7					72.0		
1978		72.1	72.6	74.7	73.6	72.1			72.6			74.7			73.6		
1979		75.4	77.8	78.0	77.8	75.4			77.8			78.0			77.8		
1980		78.7	77.9	74.5	73.7	78.7			77.9			74.5			73.7		
1981		74.9	75.3	75.6	74.6	74.9			75.3			75.6			74.6		
1982		75.9	76.4	76.7	75.2	75.9			76.4			76.7			75.2		
1983		75.6	76.4	76.2	74.6	75.6			76.4			76.2			74.6		

Sales: metal products — Ventes : ouvrages en métaux

billion francs, monthly averages — milliards de francs, moyennes mensuelles

	Year	Q.1	Q.2	Q.3	Q.4	JAN	FEB	MAR	APR	MAY	JUN	JUL	AUG	SEP	OCT	NOV	DEC
1964	11.53	10.86	11.70	10.77	12.79	10.24	10.72	11.62	12.22	10.48	12.39	9.93	9.31	13.08	12.18	11.94	14.24
1965	12.76	12.02	13.31	11.41	14.32	11.19	11.60	13.26	12.72	13.53	13.67	10.23	9.96	14.05	13.88	12.91	16.16
1966	13.43	13.22	14.27	11.65	14.59	11.64	12.97	15.05	13.83	13.59	15.39	9.95	10.84	14.17	13.92	13.87	15.98
1967	13.69	13.42	14.20	12.18	14.95	12.83	12.70	14.73	13.98	13.31	15.30	10.03	12.08	14.41	14.43	14.51	15.92
1968	14.92	14.72	15.23	13.21	16.54	14.02	14.13	16.01	15.61	15.23	14.86	12.13	11.86	15.63	17.15	14.93	17.54
1969	18.12	16.43	18.92	15.34	20.78	15.96	15.88	17.44	18.67	17.58	20.50	14.85	14.07	20.09	21.66	18.32	22.37
1970	21.27	19.02	21.22	18.69	26.15	17.59	18.02	21.44	21.50	19.59	22.58	16.97	15.98	23.10	23.41	23.21	31.84
1971	23.30	22.13	24.48	21.23	25.36	18.97	21.83	25.59	24.15	22.47	26.84	18.23	19.31	26.17	25.30	23.94	26.83
1972	26.03	25.86	26.73	22.65	28.88	23.32	25.46	28.81	25.04	26.66	28.50	16.22	22.67	29.07	28.72	28.51	29.41
1973	30.21	29.71	31.02	26.65	33.45	26.83	28.92	33.37	30.04	32.93	30.11	21.34	26.18	32.43	35.01	33.08	32.26
1974	34.40	33.03	35.28	30.96	38.34	31.48	31.79	35.81	35.93	35.67	34.25	28.15	28.25	36.48	40.54	35.73	38.75
1975	37.17	35.93	38.50	32.59	41.64	34.06	36.35	37.38	39.39	35.16	40.94	26.83	27.85	43.10	43.03	37.45	44.44
1976	43.59	43.27	45.83	37.10	48.16	37.07	42.31	50.43	44.51	44.51	48.48	28.62	35.03	47.66	47.14	44.07	53.26
1977	44.27	45.64	47.16	37.74	46.53	42.14	43.41	51.37	44.64	44.20	52.63	26.45	37.59	49.19	45.11	40.59	53.90
1978	46.95	46.05	49.30	39.92	52.51	44.83	44.14	49.17	46.57	45.75	55.59	26.86	40.22	52.69	56.13	47.33	54.09
1979	50.01	48.21	52.05	42.22	57.54	40.09	48.05	56.50	48.10	53.04	55.00	30.05	45.45	51.16	61.05	56.33	55.25
1980	52.33	56.61	55.14	43.48	54.08	54.33	54.25	61.24	56.81	49.30	59.30	34.65	42.25	53.55	56.42	48.53	57.28
1981	54.39	50.77	58.20	47.21	61.39	45.10	48.93	58.27	59.20	52.85	62.56	34.56	46.06	61.01	62.27	59.61	62.28
1982	62.51	60.37	67.43	53.59	68.64	54.93	57.82	68.36	68.43	59.95	73.92	40.41	45.88	70.47	69.39	64.92	71.60
1983		67.88	70.13	61.15		60.59	67.78	75.26	66.65	66.61	77.14	44.54	63.72	75.18	69.30	70.10	

Net new orders: metal products / Commandes nouvelles nettes : ouvrages en métaux

billion francs, monthly averages / milliards de francs, moyennes mensuelles

	Year	Q.1	Q.2	Q.3	Q.4	JAN	FEB	MAR	APR	MAY	JUN	JUL	AUG	SEP	OCT	NOV	DEC
1964	11.22	11.34	11.26	10.46	11.82	10.56	12.06	11.39	11.08	10.86	11.86	9.57	9.84	11.97	11.78	11.48	12.21
1965	12.60	12.67	12.80	11.12	13.80	11.14	13.16	13.73	12.99	13.04	12.37	9.67	10.73	12.96	13.83	12.77	14.79
1966	13.49	13.63	13.71	12.11	14.51	12.63	13.84	14.43	13.55	13.09	14.48	10.33	13.10	12.92	13.85	14.07	15.62
1967	13.42	13.79	13.48	11.92	14.48	13.19	13.22	14.96	12.69	13.13	14.63	10.04	11.69	14.05	14.48	13.45	15.52
1968	15.95	15.28	15.19	14.93	18.39	15.14	15.21	15.48	14.95	16.80	13.82	13.28	14.50	17.01	19.01	16.08	20.07
1969	20.09	19.94	20.04	17.92	22.44	21.89	19.07	18.87	19.98	19.14	21.01	15.28	16.70	21.79	22.99	19.98	24.35
1970	22.35	21.77	22.01	19.68	25.93	22.03	20.15	23.12	22.84	20.42	22.77	17.66	18.71	22.67	26.57	25.11	26.10
1971	23.66	24.13	25.15	21.62	23.73	23.43	23.28	25.67	24.43	25.14	25.88	19.20	19.09	26.57	24.00	23.72	23.47
1972	25.69	25.32	26.59	22.90	27.93	24.29	24.25	27.44	25.58	27.64	26.54	16.35	24.22	28.13	27.94	25.97	29.87
1973	33.11	31.23	33.03	29.98	38.20	29.16	30.51	34.03	31.61	35.62	31.87	24.57	31.61	33.76	39.96	37.95	36.69
1974	36.68	37.54	37.86	32.17	39.13	35.57	36.20	40.85	37.14	40.14	36.29	28.14	31.32	37.06	40.96	37.06	39.37
1975	38.22	39.99	38.24	33.72	40.93	39.63	38.70	41.65	39.59	35.86	39.27	28.05	32.43	40.70	40.12	35.29	47.37
1976	45.05	45.74	44.77	39.67	50.03	42.50	45.83	48.90	45.12	43.19	45.98	30.48	43.31	45.22	47.05	43.98	59.06
1977	45.85	47.47	47.59	37.51	50.86	43.31	46.21	52.89	46.25	44.88	51.61	27.17	40.60	44.75	45.91	47.35	55.33
1978	47.42	48.29	47.14	41.86	52.39	48.15	47.77	48.94	44.66	46.02	50.76	28.81	46.56	50.21	46.33	47.36	63.47
1979	55.16	55.09	55.43	46.38	63.68	53.09	51.78	60.41	49.47	54.47	62.51	35.14	49.05	54.94	66.86	65.66	58.53
1980	53.07	63.00	54.82	42.02	52.43	60.10	60.19	68.70	58.19	49.51	56.74	33.75	42.09	50.23	50.38	52.87	54.04
1981	55.61	53.94	58.01	50.78	59.71	49.36	52.40	60.05	56.88	51.81	65.35	36.18	54.33	61.83	57.46	56.81	64.85
1982	61.16	63.02	64.22	52.65	64.76	59.54	57.55	71.99	63.33	59.08	70.25	40.15	52.50	65.29	61.56	60.56	72.16
1983		68.91	64.65	60.81		66.72	66.36	73.65	62.85	61.25	69.85	50.05	60.79	71.60	67.29	69.75	

Net new orders: metal products export / Commandes nouvelles nettes : ouvrages en métaux, en provenance de l'étranger

billion francs, monthly averages / milliards de francs, moyennes mensuelles

	Year	Q.1	Q.2	Q.3	Q.4	JAN	FEB	MAR	APR	MAY	JUN	JUL	AUG	SEP	OCT	NOV	DEC
1964	4.92	4.83	4.75	4.54	5.57	4.34	5.47	4.67	4.50	4.87	4.77	4.20	4.35	5.06	5.39	5.58	5.74
1965	6.02	6.24	5.93	5.35	6.54	5.31	6.68	6.73	5.86	6.13	5.79	4.61	4.90	6.54	6.72	6.28	6.63
1966	6.60	6.96	6.86	5.45	7.12	6.39	7.32	7.17	6.87	6.62	7.08	5.02	4.82	6.50	7.21	6.99	7.15
1967	6.70	6.90	6.74	5.77	7.39	6.72	6.76	7.23	6.32	6.98	6.92	4.51	5.63	7.17	7.42	6.85	7.90
1968	8.60	8.21	8.13	8.07	9.98	8.27	8.36	7.99	8.06	9.01	7.32	6.21	8.14	9.87	10.18	8.56	11.20
1969	11.52	11.32	11.37	9.94	13.45	12.15	11.05	10.75	11.55	10.95	11.61	8.16	8.85	12.80	14.03	11.57	14.74
1970	13.00	12.84	13.00	11.17	14.93	13.12	11.26	14.14	13.05	12.77	13.18	10.50	10.33	12.69	14.81	15.28	14.84
1971	14.24	15.00	15.00	12.83	14.12	14.70	14.79	15.51	14.54	13.93	16.54	12.43	10.94	15.11	14.62	14.38	13.36
1972	15.51	15.48	16.08	14.01	16.49	14.45	14.90	17.09	14.88	16.78	16.58	9.62	14.80	17.60	17.22	13.95	18.29
1973	20.46	19.29	20.63	18.60	23.30	18.18	18.39	21.30	19.51	22.13	20.24	15.20	19.46	21.15	23.03	25.19	21.68
1974	22.54	23.40	23.27	19.73	23.77	22.77	22.99	24.43	22.76	24.25	22.80	18.06	18.96	22.16	25.10	24.30	21.90
1975	24.27	24.51	25.00	21.16	26.41	23.08	22.32	28.13	24.14	24.96	25.89	16.37	19.44	27.68	26.67	23.51	29.05
1976	30.56	31.26	30.69	27.04	33.25	28.33	32.00	33.45	30.54	30.54	30.99	21.24	29.41	30.48	30.85	30.28	39.63
1977	30.02	31.79	31.17	24.59	32.51	29.24	31.71	34.42	29.78	30.68	33.07	18.58	25.25	29.94	30.18	33.36	33.98
1978	31.45	32.22	31.87	27.64	34.06	32.77	31.21	32.67	29.92	32.15	33.54	19.49	31.27	32.14	31.72	32.39	38.08
1979	37.24	38.42	36.38	31.31	42.83	36.69	37.20	41.37	34.27	37.90	36.96	24.14	32.40	37.38	44.61	46.15	37.74
1980	35.60	43.67	36.22	27.36	35.15	41.51	42.39	47.12	39.07	30.03	39.56	22.78	27.11	32.19	33.18	35.69	36.58
1981	37.88	36.79	40.56	32.14	42.05	33.90	35.67	40.79	40.01	34.39	47.28	23.38	30.47	42.57	41.20	41.17	43.79
1982	43.28	45.61	43.87	36.95	46.71	40.06	42.29	54.47	43.60	42.13	45.88	28.75	34.93	47.17	43.78	45.32	51.02
1983		49.08	47.20	42.13		47.21	47.93	52.08	46.22	44.43	50.96	30.88	43.02	52.49	50.71	52.45	

Construction permits issued: total / Permis de construire délivrés : total

thousand cubic metres, monthly averages / milliers de mètres cubes, moyennes mensuelles

	Year	Q.1	Q.2	Q.3	Q.4	JAN	FEB	MAR	APR	MAY	JUN	JUL	AUG	SEP	OCT	NOV	DEC
1964																	
1965																	
1966																	
1967																	
1968	4586	3912	4878	4729	4827	3234	3004	5498	4852	4529	5253	6601	4394	3192	5226	4675	4579
1969	5500	4932	6204	6246	4613	4319	4784	5693	6586	5707	6320	7274	5551	5912	5320	3806	4727
1970	5304	4704	6844	5364	4306	3952	5318	4843	7305	6706	6520	5574	5283	5235	4458	4082	4377
1971	4260	3812	4039	4659	4530	4384	3129	3922	3949	3154	5015	4175	5654	4149	4695	3491	5405
1972	6032	4690	6273	6464	6701	4165	4499	5405	6092	6716	6012	6624	7446	5323	7203	6756	6143
1973	6516	6271	6956	7129	5710	5881	5872	7060	6848	7560	6460	7429	7074	6893	6956	5116	5057
1974	7302	7752	8015	7360	6082	7357	6811	9089	8389	8540	7115	8480	6619	6982	6088	5542	6617
1975	5698	6195	5749	5239	5608	5106	5430	8050	6757	5442	5047	4908	5420	5388	5553	5156	6115
1976	6105	6324	7074	5512	5510	6039	5744	7190	6872	7198	7152	4545	6299	5691	5166	4932	6383
1977	5465	4809	7058	4976	5017	4213	4446	5768	8832	6095	6248	4522	5142	5264	4893	5441	4717
1978	5619	5614	5866	6146	4852	5510	5783	5549	5701	5701	6196	5512	5649	7276	4908	4639	5008
1979	5290	5736	5572	4879	4970	4911	4891	7407	5347	5257	6113	5303	4373	4962	6730	4165	4016
1980	4224	5068	4599	3748	3481	4544	5048	5613	4808	3822	5166	4103	3726	3414	3342	3246	3855
1981	3472	3495	3570	4001	2820	3098	3374	4014	3532	3420	3759	4735	4308	2960	2765	3653	2042
1982	3257	2843	3731	3520	2933	2466	2370	3193	3104	3450	4639	2652	4181	3726	3052	2881	2867
1983		2875	3183	2885		2850	2470	3304	3697	3136	2717	3129	3010	2516	2932	2330	

BELGIUM

Construction permits issued: residential

thousand cubic metres, monthly averages

Permis de construire délivrés : bâtiments résidentiels

milliers de mètres cubes, moyennes mensuelles

	Year	Q.1	Q.2	Q.3	Q.4	JAN	FEB	MAR	APR	MAY	JUN	JUL	AUG	SEP	OCT	NOV	DEC
1964																	
1965																	
1966																	
1967																	
1968	2598	2509	2889	2412	2583	1929	1686	3911	2365	3379	2922	2900	2562	1775	2304	2460	2484
1969	3074	2869	3537	3315	2574	2359	2238	3310	3796	3250	3565	3947	2994	3005	2901	2120	2702
1970	2506	2373	2945	2647	2058	2055	2501	2563	3444	2647	2743	2945	2436	2560	2310	1781	2084
1971	1992	1944	1893	2017	2115	2108	1597	2128	1922	1499	2267	1897	2477	1677	2070	1806	2470
1972	3231	2707	3355	2966	3898	2293	2786	3041	3535	3173	3356	2847	3022	3028	3925	3806	3964
1973	3483	3607	3822	3463	3039	3192	3610	4018	3488	4233	3746	3470	3182	3736	3420	3012	2685
1974	3844	3874	4691	4133	2676	3691	3795	4137	4857	5090	4127	4770	3536	4093	2972	2624	2433
1975	3336	3251	3508	3171	3413	3151	3519	3082	3898	3238	3387	3041	2890	3533	3220	3346	3673
1976	4021	4197	4469	3609	3809	3834	4286	4472	4448	4549	4410	3238	3859	3730	3720	3352	4355
1977	3362	3034	4040	3258	3116	2514	2924	3665	4483	3544	4093	3254	3329	3192	2916	3263	3169
1978	3357	3740	3647	3029	3011	3297	3926	3997	3462	3754	3726	2904	3367	2817	3153	2894	2937
1979	2920	3246	3003	2754	2677	2786	3364	3588	3016	3059	2934	3172	2433	2658	3637	2074	2320
1980	2358	2923	2672	2110	1724	2762	2803	3205	2841	2339	2836	2426	1934	1991	1589	1750	1834
1981	1672	1896	1761	1583	1449	1707	1311	2171	1936	1689	1657	1801	1679	1269	1437	1564	1345
1982	1341	1453	1589	1154	1170	1335	1467	1556	1493	1483	1791	1068	1204	1190	1165	1141	1203
1983		1191	1292	1080		1114	1148	1311	1369	1366	1142	1203	1086	951	1291	1024	

Construction: buildings started

thousand cubic metres, monthly averages

Construction : bâtiments mis en chantier

milliers de mètres cubes, moyennes mensuelles

	Year	Q.1	Q.2	Q.3	Q.4	JAN	FEB	MAR	APR	MAY	JUN	JUL	AUG	SEP	OCT	NOV	DEC
1964																	
1965																	
1966																	
1967																	
1968	3379	2166	3309	3768	4274	1578	2221	2700	3367	3010	3550	3705	4199	3400	4816	4297	3710
1969	4095	3161	4937	4833	3450	2739	2105	4638	5210	5343	4259	4043	5466	4990	5044	3364	1943
1970	3795	3173	4622	3800	3535	2518	2780	4222	4768	4337	4761	2942	3992	4465	3486	4341	2928
1971	4057	2814	4628	4648	4133	1584	2713	4145	4614	3505	5766	3351	5157	5437	4753	4474	3187
1972	4611	4353	4881	4365	4843	4163	4207	4689	5945	4980	3718	3255	4376	5465	6039	5577	2914
1973	4958	4379	6660	4571	4220	4379	3372	5387	7662	7187	5130	2916	4464	6334	5477	4481	2702
1974	5387	4537	7159	5255	4599	2716	4929	5965	8149	3462	4866	3925	6388	5453	3946	5384	4466
1975	5873	6368	7247	4894	4984	3448	6565	9090	8451	6948	6342	4174	5250	5257	5699	4876	4377
1976	5420	5270	7259	4753	4396	4815	5506	5488	7278	8658	5841	3769	4974	5516	5240	4659	3290
1977	4988	3982	4856	5971	5144	3736	3333	4377	4076	5246	5245	5617	6294	6001	5794	4704	4935
1978	4956	5512	5673	4680	3959	5133	5497	5907	4979	5221	6819	3461	4566	6014	4081	3633	4163
1979	5117	3537	5955	6133	4841	1132	4009	5470	5386	5099	7380	4454	6843	7102	7042	3891	3591
1980	3845	4819	3942	3491	3127	3404	3650	7402	4332	4301	3192	2504	3493	4477	3548	3563	2271
1981	3052	2575	3487	3085	3061	2289	1625	3811	4882	2990	2590	1458	2504	5292	4274	3192	1716
1982	2827	2580	3551	2986	2189	1417	2507	3816	4399	1918	4336	2345	2840	3773	1955	2803	1809
1983		2610	3974	2756		2581	2122	3127	3526	3709	4687	2301	3144	2822	5024	3261	

Retail sales: value (4)

1980 = 100

Ventes au détail : valeur (4)

1980 = 100

	Year	Q.1	Q.2	Q.3	Q.4	JAN	FEB	MAR	APR	MAY	JUN	JUL	AUG	SEP	OCT	NOV	DEC
1964																	
1965																	
1966																	
1967																	
1968	31																
1969	34	30	35	34	37	30	28	33	35	36	34	34	33	34	36	34	41
1970	37	33	37	36	42	33	31	35	37	37	37	36	35	37	37	38	49
1971	40	34	42	41	45	32	32	39	41	41	43	41	39	42	44	42	49
1972	46	41	46	45	50	37	39	46	44	47	48	43	44	48	47	47	58
1973	52	47	53	49	59	45	44	52	51	54	55	48	48	52	57	54	66
1974	61	53	62	60	68	52	50	58	61	64	63	59	58	62	67	61	77
1975	67	60	68	64	76	60	56	65	68	68	67	62	61	69	74	66	87
1976	74	70	78	74	85	68	65	76	78	77	80	72	70	80	80	76	98
1977	82	76	84	77	89	74	71	84	83	83	86	73	75	84	84	80	103
1978	86	81	89	81	92	76	76	90	86	88	91	76	78	88	88	84	105
1979	93	85	96	87	101	81	80	95	92	97	98	92	87	92	98	93	113
1980	100	96	103	94	108	93	92	102	102	104	102	91	91	99	106	95	123
1981	105	96	108	99	115	96	91	102	107	104	113	95	97	106	114	99	133
1982	113	105	116	107	125	100	99	116	119	112	117	103	105	113	119	110	148
1983	113	108	113	109	122	104	102	117	112	111	117	102	108	117	114	111	140

Construction: housing starts / Construction : logements mis en chantier

thousands, monthly averages / milliers, moyennes mensuelles

	Year	Q.1	Q.2	Q.3	Q.4	JAN	FEB	MAR	APR	MAY	JUN	JUL	AUG	SEP	OCT	NOV	DEC
1964																	
1965																	
1966																	
1967																	
1968	4.0	2.7	4.2	4.5	4.5	1.9	2.5	3.8	5.0	3.2	4.4	4.8	4.5	4.1	6.4	4.5	2.5
1969	4.7	3.8	5.5	5.5	3.9	3.4	2.6	5.4	5.9	5.5	5.2	4.2	6.4	5.8	5.6	3.8	2.2
1970	3.6	2.9	5.0	3.7	2.7	1.9	2.2	4.5	5.3	4.3	5.3	2.8	3.9	4.3	3.0	2.6	2.7
1971	3.5	2.5	4.2	3.9	3.3	1.4	2.2	3.9	4.0	4.3	4.4	3.0	4.4	4.3	3.4	3.7	2.9
1972	4.3	3.8	5.0	4.0	4.5	3.7	3.2	4.7	6.6	4.1	4.2	3.3	4.2	4.6	5.3	5.5	2.8
1973	5.1	4.8	6.4	4.9	4.4	4.9	3.5	6.1	6.8	7.1	5.4	2.9	5.5	6.3	4.9	5.2	3.2
1974	5.4	4.9	7.2	5.6	4.1	3.2	5.4	6.0	8.0	8.0	5.5	4.6	6.6	5.6	4.6	4.2	3.6
1975	6.5	7.0	8.0	5.7	5.3	5.0	6.8	9.3	9.5	7.7	6.7	4.8	5.3	6.9	5.9	5.1	4.9
1976	6.4	5.8	8.0	5.8	5.8	4.8	6.0	6.7	7.9	9.2	6.9	4.7	5.5	7.2	7.0	6.7	3.7
1977	6.0	5.3	6.1	6.7	6.0	4.1	6.3	5.6	6.0	6.0	6.3	4.3	7.7	8.1	6.6	5.5	6.1
1978	5.5	6.6	6.2	5.2	4.0	6.3	6.3	7.1	6.2	6.1	6.3	3.8	5.7	6.0	4.8	4.2	3.1
1979	5.7	4.0	6.8	6.4	5.7	1.4	4.2	6.5	6.8	5.6	7.9	4.8	7.1	7.2	3.7	4.7	3.6
1980	3.9	5.2	4.5	3.3	2.6	3.7	3.6	3.3	5.1	5.0	3.5	2.7	3.2	4.2	3.3	2.6	1.8
1981	2.7	2.6	3.4	2.4	2.5	2.0	1.7	4.1	5.0	2.8	2.5	1.5	1.8	3.8	3.8	2.6	1.3
1982	2.4	2.1	3.4	2.5	1.5	1.1	2.0	3.2	4.0	1.6	4.6	2.2	2.8	2.5	1.3	1.7	1.6
1983		2.0	2.8	2.1		2.1	1.9	2.1	3.0	2.3	3.0	2.2	1.8	2.3	3.0	2.5	

Retail sales: value (4) / Ventes au détail : valeur (4)

1980 = 100

Adjusted - Corrigé *

	Year	Q.1	Q.2	Q.3	Q.4	JAN	FEB	MAR	APR	MAY	JUN	JUL	AUG	SEP	OCT	NOV	DEC
1964																	
1965																	
1966																	
1967																	
1968																	
1969		33	34	34	34	33	33	34	34	34	34	34	35	34	34	35	34
1970		36	36	37	39	36	36	36	36	36	36	36	37	37	36	39	41
1971		37	40	42	42	35	38	39	40	40	41	42	42	42	43	43	40
1972		43	45	47	47	42	43	45	44	45	45	46	47	48	46	47	49
1973		50	51	52	55	50	50	51	50	51	52	51	51	53	55	55	56
1974		57	60	63	64	57	58	57	59	60	61	63	62	63	63	63	65
1975		64	65	67	71	64	64	65	66	64	66	66	68	69	70	70	72
1976		73	75	78	79	73	73	74	74	76	76	77	78	79	78	79	79
1977		80	81	82	83	81	80	80	80	81	81	81	82	82	83	84	84
1978		85	85	86	87	84	86	85	85	85	85	85	85	88	86	87	87
1979		89	92	93	95	87	89	89	91	93	93	92	94	94	95	96	95
1980		99	99	100	101	99	99	100	98	99	99	100	100	100	101	102	101
1981		101	104	106	107	102	102	99	103	103	108	104	107	107	108	106	108
1982		110	112	114	117	109	110	111	112	111	112	112	116	113	115	115	120
1983		113	109	116	114	115	113	111	108	110	111	115	117	116	112	117	113

* Adjusted by the O.E.C.D.

* Corrigé par l'O.C.D.E.

BELGIUM

Retail sales: department stores (5) — Ventes au détail : grands magasins (5)

1980 = 100

	Year	Q.1	Q.2	Q.3	Q.4	JAN	FEB	MAR	APR	MAY	JUN	JUL	AUG	SEP	OCT	NOV	DEC
1964	27	24	26	25	33	23	24	25	26	26	25	26	23	25	30	31	38
1965	29	25	28	28	35	25	23	26	29	28	27	30	25	28	31	33	41
1966	31	27	30	29	37	27	25	28	31	30	30	31	28	29	33	34	45
1967	32	29	31	30	37	28	26	31	31	30	32	31	28	32	31	35	45
1968	33	29	33	32	40	28	28	32	33	33	32	33	31	31	34	39	46
1969	36	32	36	34	43	32	29	34	35	38	35	35	34	34	38	41	51
1970	40	35	39	38	50	35	32	37	38	39	39	40	35	38	44	44	61
1971	43	36	42	42	52	37	34	38	43	41	43	45	40	41	46	49	62
1972	49	43	48	48	53	41	40	48	45	47	51	48	45	52	48	53	71
1973	55	48	54	52	66	45	45	53	51	53	58	52	49	54	57	60	82
1974	63	54	61	62	75	53	51	58	59	62	63	64	61	61	67	72	86
1975	68	59	66	66	82	59	55	62	63	70	66	67	63	69	74	74	98
1976	76	67	74	74	90	70	61	69	74	74	73	78	68	76	79	81	109
1977	83	72	81	81	96	73	69	75	80	80	83	83	78	82	83	87	118
1978	88	78	86	87	101	76	72	85	82	86	91	86	82	92	87	92	125
1979	94	83	93	91	111	77	79	91	89	92	97	90	92	92	97	104	130
1980	100	90	93	96	116	87	88	93	95	103	98	99	95	94	105	104	139
1981	108	97	109	102	123	101	92	100	109	108	110	103	101	102	122	107	141
1982	117	106	118	111	133	105	100	111	121	113	120	116	108	121	126	117	155
1983	130	120	130	126	142	116	113	131	131	124	134	127	121	130	135	124	166

Retail sales: volume (4) — Ventes au détail : volume (4)

1980 = 100

	Year	Q.1	Q.2	Q.3	Q.4	JAN	FEB	MAR	APR	MAY	JUN	JUL	AUG	SEP	OCT	NOV	DEC
1964																	
1965																	
1966	57																
1967	58																
1968	61																
1969	65	59	67	64	69	59	54	63	67	69	66	65	62	64	67	65	77
1970	69	61	68	66	78	61	58	65	68	68	69	67	64	68	73	70	91
1971	73	63	76	73	80	58	59	70	75	75	77	74	69	75	78	75	86
1972	79	72	81	77	85	67	68	80	77	81	84	75	76	82	79	78	96
1973	85	78	87	80	94	75	72	86	83	88	89	77	78	84	91	86	104
1974	88	82	92	84	94	81	78	88	91	94	91	85	82	87	93	84	106
1975	87	81	90	83	95	81	76	87	90	90	89	81	79	88	94	83	108
1976	92	86	95	89	100	84	80	93	94	93	96	87	84	94	95	89	115
1977	93	88	98	88	100	85	82	97	97	95	103	83	85	95	95	90	116
1978	95	91	99	90	102	86	85	100	97	99	102	85	87	98	97	93	115
1979	99	93	104	93	106	88	87	103	100	106	107	88	93	98	103	98	113
1980	100	98	104	94	105	96	94	104	104	105	104	92	91	99	104	93	119
1981	97	92	102	91	103	92	87	96	101	99	107	88	89	96	103	89	118
1982	96	92	99	89	103	88	87	101	103	96	99	86	88	93	97	90	121
1983	89	87	91	85	93	84	82	94	90	89	93	80	84	90	88	85	107

New passenger car registrations — Immatriculations de voitures de tourisme neuves

thousands, monthly averages — milliers, moyennes mensuelles

	Year	Q.1	Q.2	Q.3	Q.4	JAN	FEB	MAR	APR	MAY	JUN	JUL	AUG	SEP	OCT	NOV	DEC
1964	16.8	17.3	19.8	16.0	14.1	13.5	17.1	21.2	21.1	17.5	20.8	19.4	13.7	14.9	15.2	12.7	14.3
1965	19.5	19.5	22.8	17.4	18.4	14.0	18.6	26.0	24.7	21.0	22.6	19.6	16.5	16.2	18.3	17.8	19.3
1966	19.3	19.5	22.5	18.3	16.9	15.2	17.7	25.7	21.7	21.0	24.8	19.3	18.2	17.3	18.6	16.0	16.0
1967	19.9	21.8	23.4	17.7	16.5	16.9	22.1	26.5	23.2	23.1	24.0	19.6	16.7	16.8	19.4	16.0	14.1
1968	22.5	22.7	28.4	20.7	18.2	19.8	23.1	25.1	30.4	29.6	25.2	26.0	18.0	18.2	22.0	16.9	15.9
1969	25.9	25.7	32.9	24.6	20.5	21.7	24.7	30.7	33.2	29.7	35.8	28.9	20.6	24.3	26.8	18.5	16.2
1970	25.1	23.9	27.6	22.3	26.5	21.1	24.1	26.6	28.5	24.6	29.6	26.0	19.5	21.3	26.9	24.3	28.3
1971	22.1	21.3	25.7	20.6	21.0	18.8	17.4	27.8	25.0	23.1	29.1	23.1	17.2	21.3	20.4	20.2	22.3
1972	28.0	29.6	32.5	25.7	24.0	26.5	28.4	34.1	28.3	31.8	37.5	28.4	25.0	23.8	27.1	25.1	19.8
1973	28.4	33.2	32.9	25.7	21.8	33.4	29.3	37.0	32.1	33.4	33.2	29.4	25.2	22.6	29.5	22.4	13.6
1974	28.0	30.8	33.2	25.5	22.4	30.3	29.6	32.4	35.2	32.9	31.7	30.9	21.6	23.9	27.3	21.8	17.6
1975	30.4	31.3	33.9	29.3	27.1	32.9	29.5	31.4	37.2	31.2	33.4	30.3	28.6	29.0	32.9	25.6	22.8
1976	35.1	39.0	39.5	32.1	29.7	38.7	33.0	45.2	41.0	37.3	40.3	35.5	28.1	32.6	32.8	30.0	26.3
1977	35.7	41.7	42.7	30.0	28.5	39.3	38.7	47.1	40.5	44.5	43.2	31.6	28.2	30.3	34.5	28.3	22.6
1978	35.4	43.5	41.5	29.6	26.8	45.3	40.3	45.0	42.0	38.5	44.1	30.9	28.7	29.1	32.5	29.7	18.3
1979	35.8	38.3	47.1	30.8	26.8	34.2	32.7	48.1	54.2	44.3	42.9	34.1	28.9	29.5	36.3	27.9	16.0
1980	33.9	44.0	38.9	28.9	24.0	41.6	43.6	46.8	40.7	32.5	43.6	35.0	24.1	27.6	31.7	22.7	17.5
1981	30.0	34.1	37.1	26.0	22.9	34.9	30.5	37.0	38.3	31.8	41.2	30.1	21.0	26.8	29.0	23.6	16.2
1982	30.2	36.7	36.7	24.8	22.5	29.8	34.3	46.0	45.0	32.3	32.8	26.7	24.3	23.6	27.0	21.3	18.3
1983	29.7	34.9	35.6	23.6	24.8	33.6	27.9	43.3	35.6	34.4	36.8	25.6	22.9	22.1	32.1	24.6	17.6

Retail sales: department stores (5) — Ventes au détail : grands magasins (5)

1980 = 100

Adjusted - Corrigé *

	Year	Q.1	Q.2	Q.3	Q.4	JAN	FEB	MAR	APR	MAY	JUN	JUL	AUG	SEP	OCT	NOV	DEC
1964		26	26	26	28	25	27	26	26	26	26	26	26	27	28	28	28
1965		28	28	29	29	28	28	28	28	28	29	29	29	30	29	29	29
1966		30	31	31	32	30	30	30	30	31	31	31	31	30	32	31	31
1967		32	32	32	32	32	32	32	33	30	32	31	31	33	32	32	32
1968		32	33	34	34	32	32	33	33	33	33	34	33	34	34	34	34
1969		35	36	37	37	35	35	36	36	37	36	36	37	36	37	37	38
1970		39	39	40	42	38	39	39	40	39	39	40	39	41	41	42	44
1971		41	43	44	45	41	41	40	43	41	44	43	45	44	44	45	45
1972		47	48	51	50	46	46	49	47	48	49	49	50	53	48	50	51
1973		53	54	55	57	51	53	54	54	54	56	54	53	56	56	56	60
1974		60	62	65	65	59	60	60	62	62	62	66	64	65	66	66	65
1975		65	67	69	72	65	65	65	68	67	67	68	68	71	72	71	72
1976		73	74	77	78	74	71	75	74	75	74	76	76	78	77	78	79
1977		80	82	83	84	80	81	80	80	82	83	83	85	82	82	86	84
1978		85	87	89	91	85	84	86	87	87	88	88	88	92	89	90	93
1979		90	92	96	99	86	92	92	92	93	92	93	97	97	98	100	99
1980		96	98	100	105	96	96	96	97	99	99	101	100	99	102	105	108
1981		105	108	107	112	105	104	106	108	107	108	104	108	110	114	111	110
1982		114	117	117	120	113	113	115	117	114	119	113	119	119	122	119	119
1983		129	129	132	129	126	127	133	126	128	131	128	132	136	133	128	124

Retail sales: volume (4) — Ventes au détail : volume (4)

1980 = 100

Adjusted - Corrigé *

	Year	Q.1	Q.2	Q.3	Q.4	JAN	FEB	MAR	APR	MAY	JUN	JUL	AUG	SEP	OCT	NOV	DEC
1964																	
1965																	
1966																	
1967																	
1968																	
1969		64	65	65	65	64	64	65	65	65	65	66	66	64	64	66	65
1970		67	66	68	72	66	67	66	66	66	66	68	69	68	69	72	76
1971		68	73	75	74	65	69	70	72	73	74	75	74	75	75	76	71
1972		76	78	80	79	75	75	79	77	78	79	79	80	82	77	80	82
1973		83	84	84	87	82	83	84	83	83	85	82	83	86	87	87	88
1974		88	89	89	88	88	89	88	88	89	88	90	87	89	88	87	89
1975		87	86	87	89	87	87	87	88	85	86	85	87	88	89	88	89
1976		90	91	93	93	90	90	91	90	91	91	93	93	94	93	93	94
1977		93	94	93	94	94	93	93	93	93	97	92	93	94	94	94	94
1978		95	95	96	96	95	96	96	95	96	95	95	94	98	95	97	96
1979		97	100	100	100	96	98	98	99	101	100	98	100	100	100	101	100
1980		102	100	100	99	102	101	102	100	100	100	101	100	99	100	99	98
1981		96	98	97	96	98	97	93	97	97	100	97	98	97	98	95	96
1982		97	95	95	96	96	97	97	97	95	94	95	96	94	94	94	99
1983		91	87	90	88	93	92	89	87	88	87	91	90	90	87	89	87

Unemployment: insured unemployed (6) — Chômage : chômeurs assurés (6)

as per cent of insured labour force — en pourcentage de la main-d'œuvre assurée

	Year	Q.1	Q.2	Q.3	Q.4	JAN	FEB	MAR	APR	MAY	JUN	JUL	AUG	SEP	OCT	NOV	DEC
1964	2.2	2.6	2.1	2.0	2.4	2.8	2.6	2.3	2.2	2.1	1.9	2.0	1.9	2.0	2.1	2.3	2.7
1965	2.4	2.7	2.3	2.2	2.5	2.8	2.7	2.5	2.4	2.3	2.2	2.2	2.2	2.2	2.3	2.5	2.8
1966	2.7	2.9	2.5	2.4	2.9	3.0	3.0	2.8	2.7	2.5	2.3	2.4	2.4	2.4	2.5	2.8	3.3
1967	3.7	3.7	3.6	3.4	4.2	3.6	3.7	3.7	3.7	3.6	3.4	3.4	3.4	3.5	3.8	4.2	4.6
1968	4.5	4.9	4.4	4.1	4.5	5.0	4.9	4.8	4.6	4.4	4.2	4.2	4.1	4.1	4.3	4.4	4.7
1969	3.7	4.5	3.6	3.3	3.4	4.8	4.6	4.2	3.9	3.7	3.3	3.4	3.2	3.3	3.3	3.3	3.6
1970	3.0	3.4	2.9	2.8	3.0	3.5	3.4	3.3	3.2	3.0	2.5	2.9	2.8	2.8	2.8	2.9	3.2
1971	2.9	3.1	2.7	2.7	3.1	3.2	3.1	3.0	2.9	2.8	2.5	2.7	2.6	2.7	2.8	3.1	3.5
1972	3.4	3.6	3.3	3.3	3.7	3.6	3.6	3.5	3.4	3.3	3.2	3.3	3.2	3.3	3.6	3.7	3.9
1973	3.6	3.9	3.4	3.4	3.8	4.0	3.9	3.7	3.6	3.4	3.3	3.4	3.4	3.5	3.7	3.8	4.0
1974	4.0	4.0	3.6	3.9	4.9	4.1	4.0	3.8	3.7	3.6	3.5	3.8	3.8	4.1	4.5	4.8	5.4
1975	6.7	5.9	6.2	6.7	8.3	5.7	5.9	6.0	6.2	6.2	6.3	6.5	6.6	7.0	7.9	8.2	8.7
1976	8.6	8.6	8.2	8.4	9.3	8.7	8.6	8.4	8.3	8.2	8.1	8.4	8.4	8.4	8.7	9.4	9.8
1977	9.8	9.7	9.4	9.7	10.7	9.9	9.7	9.6	9.5	9.4	9.3	9.7	9.6	9.7	10.1	10.9	11.0
1978	10.5	10.8	10.2	10.0	10.8	11.1	10.8	10.6	10.4	10.3	9.9	10.1	10.0	9.9	10.4	11.0	11.1
1979	10.9	11.1	10.5	10.6	11.3	11.2	11.1	10.9	10.7	10.6	10.2	10.6	10.6	10.6	10.9	11.4	11.6
1980	11.8	11.3	11.0	11.7	13.2	11.6	11.3	11.1	11.2	11.0	10.9	11.6	11.7	11.9	12.7	13.3	13.7
1981	14.2	13.7	13.8	14.5	15.1	13.7	13.7	13.7	13.7	13.8	13.8	14.4	14.4	14.6	14.8	15.0	15.4
1982	16.6	16.3	16.1	16.7	17.3	16.0	16.4	16.4	16.2	16.1	16.1	16.8	16.6	16.7	17.0	17.3	17.6
1983	18.4	18.3	18.1	18.6	18.5	18.1	18.5	18.4	18.3	18.0	17.9	18.6	18.6	18.6	18.6	18.5	18.5

* Adjusted by the O.E.C.D. — * Corrigé par l'O.C.D.E.

BELGIUM

Unemployment: insured unemployed (6) / Chômage : chômeurs assurés (6)

thousands / milliers

	Year	Q.1	Q.2	Q.3	Q.4	JAN	FEB	MAR	APR	MAY	JUN	JUL	AUG	SEP	OCT	NOV	DEC
1964	50	57	47	44	53	62	58	52	50	47	44	44	44	45	47	52	60
1965	55	61	52	51	58	63	62	57	54	52	50	51	50	51	53	57	65
1966	62	67	57	56	66	70	68	63	61	58	53	56	55	56	58	65	75
1967	85	84	81	79	97	83	86	84	84	82	78	79	78	80	88	96	107
1968	103	113	101	95	102	115	114	110	106	102	95	97	94	94	97	101	109
1969	85	104	84	76	78	109	107	97	90	84	76	78	74	75	75	77	82
1970	71	78	69	66	71	80	79	76	73	70	65	68	65	66	67	70	76
1971	71	74	65	66	78	77	75	71	68	66	63	67	66	66	70	78	86
1972	87	89	82	83	94	90	89	87	85	82	79	83	81	84	90	94	100
1973	92	97	86	87	97	100	98	93	90	86	82	87	85	88	93	95	102
1974	105	100	92	99	127	104	101	96	94	92	90	97	97	105	116	125	140
1975	177	152	161	178	218	148	153	156	160	161	162	172	174	186	209	217	229
1976	229	226	217	224	248	229	226	221	220	217	215	225	223	223	231	251	261
1977	264	260	250	260	287	265	260	256	253	251	247	259	259	261	273	293	296
1978	282	292	274	271	293	300	291	284	280	277	265	273	271	269	280	297	301
1979	294	299	284	288	307	303	301	294	290	285	276	289	288	287	296	309	315
1980	322	307	297	319	364	314	306	302	300	297	295	313	317	327	350	365	377
1981	392	377	378	398	414	378	377	375	377	378	379	397	396	401	407	413	424
1982	457	448	445	460	474	439	452	451	447	445	443	462	457	460	466	474	484
1983	505	504	496	511	509	497	509	506	502	495	491	511	511	511	512	508	503

Jobs vacant, unfilled vacancies (6)(7) / Offres d'emploi non satisfaites (6)(7)

thousands / milliers

	Year	Q.1	Q.2	Q.3	Q.4	JAN	FEB	MAR	APR	MAY	JUN	JUL	AUG	SEP	OCT	NOV	DEC
1964	13.1	14.7	15.4	13.2	9.0	14.0	14.8	15.2	15.6	15.1	15.6	13.9	13.1	12.7	10.8	9.3	7.0
1965	8.4	7.8	9.6	9.0	7.2	6.6	7.4	9.5	9.7	9.3	9.9	9.1	9.0	9.0	8.6	6.9	6.2
1966	7.5	7.3	8.9	8.1	5.6	6.2	7.5	8.1	8.6	9.0	9.0	7.8	8.4	8.1	6.6	5.6	4.6
1967	4.4	4.4	4.9	4.8	3.4	4.5	4.3	4.4	4.8	5.0	4.9	4.7	5.1	4.5	3.7	3.3	3.2
1968	4.9	3.8	4.8	5.4	5.6	3.5	3.8	4.2	4.4	4.9	5.2	4.9	5.6	5.7	5.4	5.7	5.7
1969	11.6	7.3	12.0	13.9	13.2	6.6	6.9	8.3	9.8	11.8	14.5	12.3	13.6	15.8	14.9	12.5	12.2
1970	23.9	23.3	28.3	25.0	19.0	20.4	23.5	26.1	26.7	23.4	29.9	26.7	24.4	23.8	22.0	19.5	15.5
1971	13.4	15.7	15.6	13.4	8.8	15.6	15.6	15.9	16.0	15.7	15.0	13.9	13.9	12.5	10.5	8.6	7.4
1972	8.5	7.5	9.0	9.1	8.3	7.5	7.2	7.7	8.6	9.2	9.1	8.6	9.8	9.0	9.0	7.8	8.2
1973	14.2	10.8	14.0	16.5	15.3	9.5	10.4	12.6	12.4	14.2	15.5	15.1	16.8	17.5	17.4	15.4	13.2
1974	13.5	14.3	17.6	14.9	7.2	12.6	14.7	15.7	16.7	17.9	18.3	16.9	15.6	12.1	8.9	7.0	5.7
1975	4.1	5.0	4.2	3.7	3.3	5.3	4.8	4.9	4.3	4.2	4.2	3.4	4.0	3.8	3.5	3.2	3.2
1976	4.1	3.9	4.3	4.6	3.6	3.6	3.8	4.3	4.0	4.4	4.4	4.2	4.8	4.7	3.9	3.5	3.4
1977	3.4	3.6	3.9	3.4	2.8	3.6	3.9	3.4	3.6	4.0	4.0	3.5	3.5	3.1	2.8	2.8	2.7
1978	4.2	3.1	3.8	5.0	5.1	3.0	3.2	3.0	3.1	3.7	4.5	4.5	4.9	5.6	4.7	5.5	5.1
1979	5.7	5.4	5.9	5.8	5.6	5.4	5.3	5.6	5.3	6.3	6.2	5.6	5.9	6.0	5.5	5.7	5.5
1980	5.9	6.4	6.8	5.6	5.0	5.9	6.5	6.7	6.6	6.5	7.3	6.2	5.5	5.1	5.1	5.5	4.3
1981	4.4	5.2	5.0	4.3	3.1	4.8	5.3	5.4	4.9	5.3	4.8	4.0	4.3	4.7	3.4	3.1	2.8
1982	4.0	3.3	4.1	4.5	4.0	2.9	3.3	3.7	3.6	4.3	4.5	4.1	4.9	4.6	4.5	3.7	3.7
1983	6.2	5.1	6.2	6.6	6.7	4.4	5.1	5.9	6.0	5.8	6.8	6.3	6.7	6.8	6.4	6.8	6.9

Monthly hours worked: mining and manufacturing (8) (wage earners) / Heures effectuées par mois : industries extractives et manufacturières (ouvriers) (8)

1980 = 100

	Year	Q.1	Q.2	Q.3	Q.4	JAN	FEB	MAR	APR	MAY	JUN	JUL	AUG	SEP	OCT	NOV	DEC
1964	174	178	177	161	180	181	173	179	185	163	182	144	158	182	189	172	179
1965	169	175	172	152	177	172	168	185	177	167	172	127	151	176	179	169	181
1966	165	170	169	148	170	171	157	182	170	160	177	117	154	175	173	167	171
1967	157	165	161	140	162	166	158	172	159	155	168	112	146	162	168	163	156
1968	154	159	156	139	163	161	154	162	158	158	151	115	141	159	172	157	160
1969	159	160	161	145	168	166	151	163	164	155	165	123	142	169	181	159	165
1970	159	162	164	143	165	163	157	167	171	151	169	118	144	163	172	156	166
1971	155	161	158	142	158	156	155	172	163	149	164	108	150	167	164	153	156
1972	149	159	152	129	155	153	156	168	146	149	160	93	139	154	161	156	147
1973	143	150	146	126	148	148	142	160	142	153	142	95	139	144	160	151	134
1974	144	153	148	126	147	157	147	154	153	150	142	101	129	149	163	145	132
1975	123	134	127	104	125	142	127	132	136	119	126	84	98	132	140	117	118
1976	122	127	125	108	124	124	121	137	130	119	127	77	113	133	129	120	122
1977	114	124	118	101	113	121	117	133	119	110	125	70	109	123	116	112	110
1978	107	114	106	95	110	116	109	119	110	105	104	69	102	114	117	113	101
1979	106	110	109	97	109	108	106	116	105	109	109	76	104	110	121	111	95
1980	100	111	105	87	97	111	111	111	110	96	110	65	89	107	111	90	91
1981	92	98	95	81	93	95	94	104	98	89	99	59	83	102	102	91	87
1982	88	93	93	78	88	92	90	97	95	85	99	54	81	98	95	86	83
1983		91	88	75		89	85	99	87	82	96	49	81	93			

Unemployment: insured unemployed (6) — Adjusted - Corrigé * — **Chômage :** chômeurs assurés (6)

thousands / milliers

Year	Q.1	Q.2	Q.3	Q.4	JAN	FEB	MAR	APR	MAY	JUN	JUL	AUG	SEP	OCT	NOV	DEC
1964	50	50	50	52	51	50	49	51	50	50	49	49	50	51	52	53
1965	53	55	56	57	53	54	54	54	55	56	56	56	56	57	58	58
1966	59	60	62	65	59	59	59	61	60	60	61	62	62	62	66	68
1967	75	85	87	95	71	75	79	83	85	87	86	87	88	93	96	97
1968	101	105	104	101	99	100	104	105	105	106	105	104	103	102	101	99
1969	94	87	82	76	96	95	91	89	87	85	84	82	82	78	76	74
1970	71	73	72	69	71	71	72	73	73	72	73	72	71	70	69	69
1971	68	69	71	75	68	68	68	68	69	70	71	72	71	72	76	78
1972	82	86	89	91	81	82	84	85	86	87	88	88	89	91	91	91
1973	90	91	93	93	90	91	90	91	91	91	92	92	93	94	92	93
1974	94	97	105	122	94	94	94	95	96	99	102	104	111	117	121	128
1975	144	169	187	210	135	144	153	162	169	177	180	185	196	210	208	211
1976	215	227	234	238	211	215	218	222	226	233	234	235	234	232	239	243
1977	249	261	270	277	247	249	253	255	261	265	268	270	272	274	278	279
1978	281	284	280	283	281	280	282	284	287	283	280	281	279	281	284	285
1979	290	294	296	298	286	290	293	293	295	293	295	297	297	298	297	299
1980	298	307	326	357	299	295	300	304	306	311	318	325	336	352	357	362
1981	366	389	405	410	362	364	372	381	388	397	401	405	410	409	409	411
1982	435	455	466	472	422	436	448	450	455	461	464	465	468	469	475	472
1983	490	507	518	508	478	491	501	505	505	510	513	519	520	516	511	496

Jobs vacant, unfilled vacancies (6)(7) — Adjusted - Corrigé * — **Offres d'emploi non satisfaites** (6)(7)

thousands / milliers

Year	Q.1	Q.2	Q.3	Q.4	JAN	FEB	MAR	APR	MAY	JUN	JUL	AUG	SEP	OCT	NOV	DEC
1964	17.2	13.5	12.0	10.1	18.9	17.2	15.4	13.8	13.3	13.4	13.0	12.0	11.0	10.6	10.7	9.1
1965	8.9	8.5	8.2	8.2	8.7	8.5	9.7	8.8	8.2	8.5	8.5	8.1	8.0	8.6	7.9	8.0
1966	8.2	7.8	7.4	6.4	7.9	8.5	8.3	7.9	7.9	7.7	7.2	7.6	7.3	6.7	6.5	5.9
1967	5.0	4.4	4.4	3.9	5.5	4.9	4.5	4.5	4.4	4.2	4.4	4.6	4.1	3.8	3.8	4.1
1968	4.2	4.3	4.9	6.5	4.2	4.3	4.3	4.1	4.3	4.5	4.6	5.0	5.2	5.6	6.6	7.2
1969	7.9	10.7	12.8	15.1	7.7	7.7	8.4	9.2	10.3	12.5	11.5	12.1	14.6	15.5	14.5	15.3
1970	25.4	25.4	22.9	21.6	23.6	26.3	26.2	25.2	25.0	25.9	25.0	21.7	22.1	22.7	22.8	19.4
1971	17.1	14.0	12.3	10.0	18.0	17.4	15.9	15.2	13.9	13.0	13.0	12.2	11.7	10.7	10.1	9.3
1972	8.1	8.1	8.3	9.6	8.7	8.1	7.7	8.2	8.2	7.9	8.1	8.5	8.4	9.2	9.2	10.3
1973	11.7	12.7	15.0	17.5	11.0	11.6	12.5	12.0	12.7	13.4	14.2	14.5	16.3	17.9	18.2	16.4
1974	15.4	16.1	13.6	8.1	14.4	16.2	15.5	16.4	16.1	15.9	16.1	13.5	11.2	9.2	8.2	7.0
1975	5.3	3.9	3.4	3.7	6.0	5.2	4.8	4.3	3.8	3.7	3.3	3.5	3.5	3.7	3.7	3.8
1976	4.1	4.0	4.2	4.0	4.0	4.0	4.2	4.1	4.0	3.9	4.1	4.3	4.4	4.2	4.0	4.0
1977	3.8	3.6	3.2	3.1	3.9	4.0	3.4	3.7	3.7	3.5	3.4	3.2	2.9	3.0	3.1	3.1
1978	3.2	3.5	4.7	5.7	3.2	3.3	3.0	3.2	3.4	4.0	4.4	4.6	5.2	5.1	6.0	5.9
1979	5.5	5.6	5.6	6.2	5.8	5.3	5.5	5.4	5.8	5.5	5.5	5.6	5.6	5.9	6.2	6.5
1980	6.5	6.3	5.4	5.5	6.4	6.5	6.5	6.7	5.9	6.4	6.2	5.2	4.8	5.5	6.0	5.1
1981	5.3	4.6	4.2	3.5	5.3	5.3	5.2	4.9	4.8	4.2	4.0	4.0	4.5	3.6	3.4	3.4
1982	3.4	3.8	4.4	4.5	3.2	3.3	3.5	3.5	3.9	4.0	4.1	4.6	4.4	4.8	4.1	4.6
1983	5.2	5.7	6.3	7.7	5.0	5.1	5.5	5.8	5.2	6.0	6.3	6.2	6.5	6.8	7.5	8.6

Monthly hours worked: mining and manufacturing (8) (wage earners) — Adjusted - Corrigé * — **Heures effectuées par mois :** industries extractives et (8) manufacturières (ouvriers)

1980 = 100

Year	Q.1	Q.2	Q.3	Q.4	JAN	FEB	MAR	APR	MAY	JUN	JUL	AUG	SEP	OCT	NOV	DEC
1964	176	174	172	174	175	179	174	177	167	177	168	171	176	177	172	173
1965	173	170	162	170	173	171	174	171	170	167	156	163	168	171	167	173
1966	167	167	160	165	172	160	169	167	164	168	151	162	167	165	163	167
1967	161	157	153	156	163	160	161	158	156	159	149	154	157	157	157	155
1968	155	153	151	157	156	154	156	154	155	151	147	151	155	157	156	158
1969	156	159	157	162	159	153	157	159	157	160	154	155	162	165	161	160
1970	159	161	156	159	159	158	160	163	156	162	150	157	159	160	156	160
1971	157	156	154	151	156	156	160	158	154	156	145	160	157	154	150	150
1972	154	149	142	150	153	157	153	147	149	152	134	144	149	150	150	150
1973	145	143	139	143	143	143	149	141	148	141	133	143	141	145	145	139
1974	148	146	138	142	150	148	146	150	146	144	136	136	143	147	143	135
1975	130	124	116	120	134	128	128	128	121	124	116	107	124	124	119	118
1976	123	123	118	119	120	123	126	124	124	122	111	120	123	121	118	120
1977	120	116	111	110	121	117	121	116	114	118	107	113	112	109	108	111
1978	110	104	106	107	114	108	108	108	106	97	106	104	108	108	108	105
1979	105	106	107	106	104	104	107	103	107	107	109	105	107	109	106	101
1980	107	103	96	95	108	110	102	107	97	105	96	94	99	101	88	94
1981	93	93	90	91	92	92	95	95	91	94	90	88	94	92	90	91
1982	88	91	87	85	89	88	88	92	86	94	85	85	90	84	84	87
1983	87	86	84		86	83	90	84	84	91	80	85	85			

* Adjusted by the O.E.C.D. — * Corrigé par l'O.C.D.E.

BELGIUM

Hourly rates: manufacturing (6)(9) — Taux horaires : industries manufacturières (6)(9)

1980 = 100

	Year	Q.1	Q.2	Q.3	Q.4	JAN	FEB	MAR	APR	MAY	JUN	JUL	AUG	SEP	OCT	NOV	DEC
1964	20		20	20	21			19			20			20			21
1965	22	21	22	22	22			21			22			22			22
1966	24	23	24	24	24			23			24			24			24
1967	25	25	25	26	26			25			25			26			26
1968	27	26	26	27	27			26			26			27			27
1969	29	28	29	29	30			28			29			29			30
1970	32	31	31	32	32			31			31			32			32
1971	35	34	35	35	36			34			35			35			36
1972	40	38	39	40	42			38			39			40			42
1973	46	44	46	47	49			44			46			47			49
1974	56	51	55	58	61			51			55			58			61
1975	66	63	65	67	70			63			65			67			70
1976	75	72	74	76	77			72			74			76			77
1977	82	80	81	82	84			80			81			82			84
1978	87	85	86	87	88			85			86			87			88
1979	92	89	91	93	95			89			91			93			95
1980	100	97	99	101	103			97			99			101			103
1981	109	106	107	109	113			106			107			109			113
1982	117	115	116	118	120			115			116			118			120
1983	124	122	123	124	127			122			123			124			127

Hourly earnings: mining, manufacturing and transport (10) — Gains horaires : industries extractives et manufacturières, et transports (10)

1980 = 100

	Year	Q.1	Q.2	Q.3	Q.4	JAN	FEB	MAR	APR	MAY	JUN	JUL	AUG	SEP	OCT	NOV	DEC
1964	19	18	18	19	19			18			18			19			19
1965	20	20	20	21	21			20			20			21			21
1966	22	21	22	23	23			21			22			23			23
1967	24	24	24	24	25			24			24			24			25
1968	25	24	25	25	26			24			25			25			26
1969	27	26	27	27	28			26			27			27			28
1970	30	29	30	31	32			29			30			31			32
1971	34	32	34	34	36			32			34			34			36
1972	39	36	38	39	41			36			38			39			41
1973	45	42	45	45	48			42			45			45			48
1974	55	49	54	56	59			49			54			56			59
1975	65	62	64	65	70			62			64			65			70
1976	73	70	73	73	76			70			73			73			76
1977	79	76	79	80	83			76			79			80			83
1978	85	82	84	84	88			82			84			84			88
1979	92	88	92	91	95			88			92			91			95
1980	100	95	99	100	105			95			99			100			105
1981	110	105	109	109	116			105			109			109			116
1982	117	114	116	116	122			114			116			116			122
1983	122	118	120	122	126			118			120			122			126

Wholesale prices: total (11) — Prix de gros : total (11)

1980 = 100

	Year	Q.1	Q.2	Q.3	Q.4	JAN	FEB	MAR	APR	MAY	JUN	JUL	AUG	SEP	OCT	NOV	DEC
1964																	
1965																	
1966																	
1967																	
1968	54.7	54.3	54.2	54.6	55.7	54.3	54.2	54.3	54.3	54.3	54.1	54.2	54.6	55.0	55.4	55.7	55.9
1969	57.4	56.3	57.1	57.5	58.6	56.1	56.4	56.4	57.1	57.1	57.2	57.2	57.6	57.8	57.9	58.5	59.3
1970	60.1	59.9	60.3	60.1	60.3	59.7	59.9	60.1	60.4	60.3	60.1	60.2	60.0	60.0	60.0	60.4	60.3
1971	59.8	59.5	59.7	60.1	59.9	59.6	59.4	59.5	59.4	59.4	60.3	59.9	60.2	60.1	59.8	59.9	59.9
1972	62.3	60.7	61.6	62.4	64.3	60.3	60.8	61.0	61.4	61.7	61.8	61.8	62.4	62.9	63.6	64.3	65.0
1973	69.9	66.9	68.8	70.9	73.0	66.1	67.0	67.6	68.1	69.0	69.5	70.5	71.0	71.3	71.5	72.9	74.5
1974	81.5	79.2	82.0	82.4	82.6	78.4	79.4	79.9	81.8	82.1	82.0	82.0	82.1	83.0	82.9	82.7	82.2
1975	82.6	81.6	81.4	82.9	84.3	82.0	81.4	81.5	81.7	81.5	81.1	82.2	83.0	83.5	83.8	84.1	85.1
1976	88.5	86.6	88.1	89.2	89.9	85.8	86.2	87.7	87.4	87.7	89.1	88.9	89.1	89.6	90.0	90.0	89.8
1977	90.6	91.7	91.6	90.0	89.1	91.5	91.8	91.9	91.8	91.6	91.3	90.6	90.0	89.4	89.4	89.2	88.8
1978	88.8	88.1	88.6	89.0	90.1	88.3	87.7	88.2	88.5	88.6	88.6	88.7	88.7	89.6	89.4	90.2	90.6
1979	94.4	92.2	94.1	95.2	95.8	91.3	92.2	93.1	93.2	94.3	94.7	95.4	94.8	95.4	96.1	96.8	94.5
1980	100.0	99.8	99.3	99.2	101.6	98.8	100.1	100.6	99.9	99.0	99.0	99.2	98.5	99.9	100.7	102.0	102.3
1981	108.1	104.3	107.3	110.4	110.6	103.4	104.3	105.1	106.3	107.5	108.1	110.1	110.5	110.6	110.1	110.5	111.2
1982	116.5	113.5	116.9	118.1	117.5	112.6	113.4	114.6	116.1	117.0	117.7	118.2	118.5	117.5	117.6	117.6	117.2
1983	122.6	117.8	120.0	124.5	128.0	117.4	117.7	118.3	118.9	119.8	121.4	121.8	124.8	126.7	126.8	128.1	129.1

Wholesale prices: agricultural goods (11)
1980 = 100

Prix de gros : produits agricoles (11)
1980 = 100

	Year	Q.1	Q.2	Q.3	Q.4	JAN	FEB	MAR	APR	MAY	JUN	JUL	AUG	SEP	OCT	NOV	DEC
1964	53.6	53.3	54.1	52.9	54.2	54.9	52.3	52.8	53.9	54.1	54.2	52.8	53.0	53.0	53.7	54.3	54.6
1965	55.2	54.7	55.7	53.7	57.0	55.5	54.1	54.6	55.7	56.1	55.1	53.7	53.4	54.1	55.0	57.6	58.3
1966	57.7	57.2	58.3	57.2	58.0	57.4	56.5	57.6	58.4	59.4	57.1	57.0	56.9	57.7	57.5	58.4	58.0
1967	57.6	58.3	59.6	56.7	56.0	57.6	57.7	59.7	59.6	60.2	59.1	56.4	57.5	56.1	55.2	56.2	56.5
1968	57.0	55.5	55.4	57.1	60.1	56.0	55.0	55.4	55.8	55.9	54.5	55.2	57.1	58.9	59.1	60.3	61.0
1969	61.7	60.7	61.8	60.9	63.4	60.9	60.5	60.7	62.2	61.3	61.8	60.4	60.9	61.5	61.8	63.9	64.4
1970	=62.8=	64.1	63.8	61.9	61.4	64.3	63.6	64.4	64.4	64.1	62.8	62.5	61.8	61.5	61.1	61.8	61.4
1971	60.1	60.6	59.6	60.3	59.8	62.2	60.1	59.6	59.0	58.5	61.3	59.7	60.4	60.9	59.6	60.1	59.7
1972	63.5	60.5	62.5	63.7	67.2	60.6	60.5	60.4	61.4	63.1	63.1	62.3	64.2	64.6	65.6	67.2	68.7
1973	76.5	72.0	77.7	78.4	78.0	70.6	72.0	73.4	76.5	78.3	78.2	79.3	78.3	77.8	77.4	77.9	78.6
1974	80.2	81.5	79.8	78.2	81.2	81.2	81.2	82.2	80.2	79.8	79.3	78.0	76.0	80.7	81.9	81.6	80.0
1975	82.9	77.9	79.2	84.8	89.5	78.6	76.8	78.2	79.2	79.3	79.0	82.8	84.6	87.0	88.4	88.6	91.3
1976	94.2	92.9	92.7	93.0	98.4	92.5	92.3	94.0	91.6	92.6	94.0	91.8	93.2	93.9	98.6	98.6	97.9
1977	98.5	100.8	102.6	96.9	93.8	100.8	100.4	101.3	102.5	102.4	102.8	99.6	98.1	93.2	93.2	94.5	93.5
1978	91.7	91.5	91.7	90.5	92.9	92.0	90.8	91.8	92.0	92.0	91.0	90.7	88.9	92.0	90.5	93.3	94.9
1979	98.2	95.6	96.8	99.8	100.9	95.5	95.6	95.7	95.1	96.9	98.4	101.6	98.4	99.3	98.9	101.9	101.8
1980	100.0	102.8	98.8	96.5	102.0	102.6	102.6	103.1	100.1	98.5	97.7	97.1	93.3	99.1	99.5	102.6	104.0
1981	110.6	106.2	110.9	113.3	111.9	105.6	106.3	106.9	109.5	111.3	111.9	113.8	112.9	113.3	110.6	111.9	113.2
1982	118.5	115.6	120.8	120.2	117.2	114.5	115.1	117.2	118.6	120.5	123.2	121.4	121.5	117.6	116.2	117.7	117.8
1983	127.6	118.1	120.4	130.9	140.9	118.2	117.7	118.3	117.7	119.2	124.4	123.3	130.8	138.6	138.6	141.1	142.9

Wholesale prices: manufactured goods (11)
1980 = 100

Prix de gros : produits manufacturés (11)
1980 = 100

	Year	Q.1	Q.2	Q.3	Q.4	JAN	FEB	MAR	APR	MAY	JUN	JUL	AUG	SEP	OCT	NOV	DEC
1964	53.9	53.1	53.8	54.2	54.4	52.6	53.3	53.6	53.6	53.5	54.2	54.0	54.2	54.5	54.6	54.3	54.2
1965	54.6	54.5	54.5	54.6	54.9	54.4	54.5	54.5	54.6	54.5	54.5	54.4	54.6	54.7	54.9	54.9	55.0
1966	55.9	55.9	55.9	55.6	56.1	55.7	56.1	56.0	56.0	55.9	55.6	55.7	55.6	55.6	56.0	56.1	56.2
1967	56.5	56.6	56.4	56.4	56.5	56.5	56.7	56.6	56.4	56.2	56.5	56.5	56.3	56.4	56.4	56.6	56.6
1968	56.8	56.7	56.7	56.7	57.1	56.7	56.8	56.8	56.8	56.6	56.6	56.5	56.7	56.8	57.2	57.0	57.1
1969	58.5	57.6	58.0	58.5	59.8	57.3	57.8	57.7	58.2	57.9	58.0	58.0	58.5	58.9	59.4	59.5	60.6
1970	=62.1=	61.3	61.5	62.4	63.3	61.0	61.4	61.4	61.5	61.4	61.7	62.0	62.4	62.8	63.0	63.3	63.4
1971	62.8	62.1	62.3	63.0	63.7	62.0	62.2	62.2	62.1	62.2	62.5	62.7	63.0	63.3	63.5	63.7	63.9
1972	65.0	64.4	64.6	65.1	65.7	64.3	64.4	64.3	64.5	64.5	64.9	64.9	65.2	65.3	65.6	65.7	65.8
1973	67.2	66.1	66.3	67.5	68.7	65.9	66.2	66.3	66.1	66.1	66.7	67.1	67.6	67.8	68.0	68.7	69.4
1974	78.8	72.8	77.9	81.4	83.0	72.1	73.0	73.3	76.2	78.3	79.3	80.3	81.8	82.1	82.7	82.9	83.3
1975	84.2	83.6	84.0	84.1	85.2	83.3	83.6	83.9	84.0	84.0	83.9	83.7	84.0	84.7	84.9	85.2	85.5
1976	87.5	86.3	87.0	88.0	88.6	85.9	86.0	87.1	86.9	86.8	87.1	87.6	88.0	88.5	88.6	88.5	88.6
1977	90.3	90.0	90.1	90.4	90.4	89.9	90.1	90.0	90.1	90.0	90.1	90.2	90.4	90.6	90.6	90.4	90.3
1978	91.0	90.3	90.8	91.1	91.7	90.2	90.3	90.6	90.9	90.6	90.9	90.9	91.1	91.4	91.4	91.7	91.9
1979	95.0	93.2	94.5	95.6	96.7	92.5	93.2	93.9	94.1	94.5	94.8	95.4	95.5	95.9	96.5	96.7	97.0
1980	100.0	98.6	99.8	99.8	101.8	98.1	98.7	99.1	99.8	99.7	99.9	99.9	99.7	99.9	101.1	102.1	102.1
1981	106.7	104.1	105.6	107.8	109.2	103.6	104.0	104.7	105.1	105.7	106.0	107.0	108.0	108.3	108.8	109.2	109.6
1982	114.1	111.5	113.8	115.0	116.1	110.6	111.6	112.3	113.0	114.0	114.4	114.5	115.0	115.4	116.0	116.3	116.1
1983	117.9	116.5	117.2	118.3	119.4	116.7	115.5	116.3	117.1	117.0	117.5	117.6	118.5	118.9	119.1	119.5	119.6

Wholesale prices: semi-manufactured goods (11)
1980 = 100

Prix de gros : demi-produits (11)
1980 = 100

	Year	Q.1	Q.2	Q.3	Q.4	JAN	FEB	MAR	APR	MAY	JUN	JUL	AUG	SEP	OCT	NOV	DEC
1964	50.7	49.8	50.4	51.1	51.4	49.4	49.9	50.0	50.3	50.3	50.6	51.0	51.1	51.4	51.6	51.5	51.1
1965	50.9	50.8	50.6	50.8	51.2	50.8	50.8	50.6	50.7	50.7	50.5	50.7	50.9	50.9	51.1	51.1	51.3
1966	52.5	52.0	53.2	52.7	52.0	51.7	52.1	52.1	53.1	53.3	53.3	53.3	52.3	52.3	52.1	52.1	51.9
1967	51.7	52.0	51.5	51.4	51.8	51.7	52.2	52.0	51.7	51.5	51.3	51.4	51.3	51.4	51.6	51.9	52.0
1968	52.4	52.4	52.1	52.3	52.9	52.1	52.5	52.5	52.0	52.0	52.2	52.2	52.2	52.5	52.7	53.0	53.0
1969	56.1	54.2	55.8	57.0	57.4	53.9	54.3	54.4	55.2	55.9	56.2	56.7	57.1	57.1	56.9	57.4	58.0
1970	=58.0=	58.5	58.3	57.6	57.8	58.1	58.6	58.7	58.6	58.3	58.0	57.7	57.5	57.6	57.6	57.8	57.9
1971	57.1	56.7	57.2	57.4	57.1	56.6	56.7	56.9	57.3	57.1	57.3	57.3	57.5	57.3	57.1	57.0	57.1
1972	59.5	58.1	59.1	60.0	61.1	57.4	58.2	58.5	59.1	59.1	59.1	59.4	60.0	60.5	60.9	61.1	61.3
1973	68.2	64.4	66.0	69.1	73.6	63.3	64.3	65.4	65.1	66.1	66.8	67.7	69.2	70.2	70.8	73.7	76.1
1974	85.8	83.3	88.8	86.3	84.7	80.6	83.9	85.4	88.8	88.8	88.8	86.7	86.4	86.0	84.7	85.0	84.3
1975	81.8	83.0	81.3	81.5	81.5	83.9	83.0	82.3	81.8	81.2	80.9	81.5	81.7	81.3	81.0	81.3	82.2
1976	87.1	84.0	87.2	88.9	88.0	83.1	83.9	85.1	86.2	86.6	88.9	89.2	88.7	88.8	87.9	88.0	88.2
1977	88.1	89.5	88.5	87.3	87.2	89.2	89.7	89.6	89.0	88.8	87.9	87.5	87.1	87.4	87.6	87.0	86.9
1978	86.5	85.5	86.0	86.9	87.8	86.0	85.3	85.4	85.6	86.1	86.1	86.3	86.8	87.4	87.7	87.9	87.8
1979	91.7	89.7	91.7	91.5	93.9	88.5	89.7	90.7	90.9	92.3	91.9	91.2	91.4	91.9	93.6	93.6	94.5
1980	100.0	100.0	99.4	100.1	100.6	98.3	100.9	100.8	99.7	99.4	99.0	99.9	99.9	100.4	100.5	100.6	100.7
1981	108.3	102.4	105.3	110.8	114.5	101.2	102.8	103.2	104.5	105.2	106.3	108.6	109.5	114.3	114.5	114.2	114.9
1982	120.9	117.5	122.1	123.2	120.9	116.2	117.1	119.3	120.9	122.7	122.7	123.7	123.7	122.3	122.4	121.0	119.3
1983	130.5	121.8	127.1	134.0	139.0	119.6	121.6	124.2	125.4	127.6	128.4	130.5	135.5	135.9	136.4	139.0	141.5

Wholesale prices: raw materials (11)

1980 = 100

Prix de gros : matières premières (11)

1980 = 100

	Year	Q.1	Q.2	Q.3	Q.4	JAN	FEB	MAR	APR	MAY	JUN	JUL	AUG	SEP	OCT	NOV	DEC
1964	55.4	54.7	55.0	55.9	55.9	54.3	55.1	54.9	54.7	55.1	55.1	55.6	56.3	55.7	56.0	55.9	55.9
1965	55.1	55.6	54.9	54.7	55.0	55.7	55.6	55.4	55.1	55.0	54.7	54.9	54.6	54.6	55.1	54.8	55.3
1966	54.8	55.7	55.5	54.3	53.7	55.5	55.9	55.8	55.8	55.8	54.9	54.8	54.2	53.8	53.6	53.7	53.6
1967	52.2	53.2	52.1	51.8	51.6	53.4	53.2	52.9	52.2	52.1	51.9	52.0	51.7	51.6	51.5	51.6	51.7
1968	51.9	51.6	51.8	51.9	52.5	51.6	51.6	51.6	51.6	51.8	51.9	52.0	51.9	51.8	52.5	52.4	52.5
1969	53.5	52.8	53.4	53.7	53.9	52.5	52.9	52.8	53.4	53.5	53.3	53.8	53.9	53.5	53.4	53.9	54.5
1970	57.0	55.7	57.5	57.6	57.4	55.2	55.9	56.0	57.2	57.3	57.9	58.2	57.4	57.1	57.2	57.6	57.3
1971	57.9	57.5	58.6	58.3	57.4	57.0	57.6	57.9	58.1	58.5	59.2	59.0	58.5	57.4	57.4	57.5	57.3
1972	59.9	58.2	59.0	59.6	62.9	57.3	58.4	59.1	59.1	59.1	59.0	59.3	59.3	60.3	61.7	63.2	63.9
1973	70.6	66.5	68.6	72.2	75.1	65.6	66.6	67.3	67.4	68.8	69.6	71.6	72.1	72.7	72.7	74.7	77.9
1974	83.5	84.2	83.9	84.2	81.6	84.9	84.1	83.6	86.0	83.8	82.0	84.2	84.6	83.9	82.6	81.5	80.7
1975	81.0	80.8	79.9	81.2	81.9	81.3	80.9	80.2	80.4	80.2	79.1	80.4	81.8	81.4	81.5	81.8	82.3
1976	86.8	84.4	86.9	88.5	87.4	83.1	83.9	86.2	86.2	86.4	88.2	88.6	87.9	88.8	87.6	87.6	86.8
1977	87.3	89.3	88.2	86.4	85.1	88.8	89.6	89.6	88.9	88.3	87.6	87.2	85.9	86.2	85.8	85.2	84.4
1978	86.0	84.1	85.4	86.8	87.6	84.5	83.8	84.0	85.1	85.2	85.9	86.3	86.9	87.0	87.4	87.5	88.0
1979	93.6	90.5	93.6	94.6	95.6	88.8	90.4	92.3	92.6	93.8	94.5	94.3	94.5	95.0	95.7	95.9	95.1
1980	100.0	99.1	98.9	99.8	102.2	97.2	99.5	100.5	99.9	98.3	98.5	99.0	99.8	100.5	101.2	102.6	102.9
1981	108.4	104.7	109.1	111.8	107.9	103.4	104.5	106.3	107.4	109.6	110.4	113.6	113.6	108.2	107.8	107.7	103.4
1982	114.4	111.1	113.9	116.1	116.4	110.7	111.1	111.6	114.0	114.1	113.7	116.1	116.1	116.0	116.6	116.3	116.2
1983	118.8	115.8	117.7	120.1	121.3	115.6	115.8	116.1	116.9	117.8	118.5	119.2	120.3	120.8	120.6	121.4	121.9

Money supply (M1) (12)

billion francs, end of period

Disponibilités monétaires (M1) (12)

milliards de francs, fin de période

	Year	Q.1	Q.2	Q.3	Q.4	JAN	FEB	MAR	APR	MAY	JUN	JUL	AUG	SEP	OCT	NOV	DEC
1964																	
1965																	
1966																	
1967																	
1968																	
1969	361.0				361.0												
1970	389.6	358.8	380.0	370.6	389.3												
1971	428.3	386.9	425.2	414.2	428.3												
1972	498.5	439.6	492.8	479.0	498.5												
1973	536.2	509.6	545.7	522.5	536.2												
1974	576.2	547.8	576.7	563.4	576.2												
1975	673.5	591.3	653.6	642.6	673.5												
1976	719.5	668.2	728.7	699.6	719.5												
1977	791.8	730.8	778.6	768.3	791.8												
1978	836.4	795.1	849.5	822.7	836.4												
1979	868.7	837.8	896.4	840.3	868.7												
1980	868.7	833.0	895.7	860.9	868.7												
1981	900.8	865.8	949.0	878.1	900.8												
1982	941.0	853.9	964.7	943.3	941.0												
1983		926.2	1012.1	995.8													

M1 plus quasi-money (12)

billion francs, end of period

M1 plus quasi-monnaie (12)

milliards de francs, fin de période

	Year	Q.1	Q.2	Q.3	Q.4	JAN	FEB	MAR	APR	MAY	JUN	JUL	AUG	SEP	OCT	NOV	DEC
1964																	
1965																	
1966																	
1967																	
1968																	
1969	776.7				776.7												
1970	846.9	786.0	815.8	818.0	846.9												
1971	962.5	864.0	912.7	918.5	962.5												
1972	1130.5	991.1	1059.1	1069.3	1130.5												
1973	1297.4	1175.5	1231.8	1239.5	1297.4												
1974	1442.4	1349.6	1334.2	1386.6	1442.4												
1975	1689.3	1491.2	1570.3	1596.7	1689.3												
1976	1919.7	1745.6	1820.3	1835.9	1919.7												
1977	2104.2	1952.6	2002.9	2011.7	2104.2												
1978	2299.2	2157.9	2218.1	2228.7	2299.2												
1979	2447.0	2347.3	2416.8	2373.7	2447.0												
1980	2504.9	2457.5	2486.6	2440.5	2504.9												
1981	2642.6	2524.3	2626.9	2569.7	2642.6												
1982	2795.6	2662.9	2746.4	2759.1	2795.6												
1983		2797.9	2887.0	2917.2													

Consumer prices: all items (13) — Prix à la consommation : total (13)

1980 = 100

	Year	Q.1	Q.2	Q.3	Q.4	JAN	FEB	MAR	APR	MAY	JUN	JUL	AUG	SEP	OCT	NOV	DEC
1964	39.8	39.1	39.5	40.1	40.4	39.2	39.2	39.0	39.2	39.3	39.8	40.1	40.1	40.2	40.3	40.4	40.6
1965	41.4	40.8	41.2	41.6	42.0	40.7	40.8	40.8	40.9	41.4	41.5	41.6	41.6	41.7	41.8	42.0	42.2
1966	=43.1=	42.5	43.3	43.2	43.5	42.4	42.5	42.7	43.1	43.3	43.5	43.1	43.1	43.3	43.4	43.5	43.6
1967	44.4	43.8	44.2	44.6	45.0	43.7	43.8	43.9	44.1	44.2	44.3	44.4	44.5	44.8	44.9	45.0	45.0
1968	45.6	45.2	45.4	45.7	46.1	45.1	45.2	45.2	45.3	45.4	45.5	45.6	45.7	45.8	46.0	46.0	46.2
1969	47.3	46.6	47.1	47.5	48.0	46.4	46.6	46.8	47.0	47.1	47.2	47.4	47.5	47.6	47.8	48.0	48.2
1970	49.1	48.6	49.0	49.4	49.6	48.4	48.6	48.8	49.0	49.0	49.0	49.3	49.4	49.4	49.5	49.6	49.7
1971	=51.3=	50.3	50.9	51.6	52.3	50.0	50.4	50.6	50.8	51.0	51.1	51.4	51.6	51.9	52.1	52.2	52.5
1972	54.1	52.9	53.5	54.4	55.4	52.7	53.0	53.1	53.3	53.3	53.9	54.3	54.4	54.7	55.0	55.4	55.8
1973	57.8	56.6	57.3	58.1	59.3	56.3	56.6	56.8	57.1	57.3	57.6	57.9	58.1	58.4	58.8	59.2	59.9
1974	65.2	61.4	63.9	66.6	68.7	60.6	61.4	62.1	63.0	63.9	64.9	65.8	66.6	67.5	68.1	68.8	69.3
1975	73.5	70.7	72.6	74.2	76.4	70.0	70.8	71.3	72.1	72.7	73.0	73.7	74.2	74.9	75.7	76.5	76.9
1976	80.2	78.0	79.5	81.0	82.4	77.6	77.9	78.4	79.1	79.7	79.8	80.5	80.8	81.8	82.0	82.3	82.8
1977	85.9	84.0	85.4	86.7	87.7	83.6	84.2	84.2	84.6	85.5	86.0	86.3	86.5	87.1	87.3	87.6	88.0
1978	89.8	88.7	89.2	90.1	91.0	88.4	88.8	89.0	89.1	89.2	89.2	89.7	90.1	90.5	90.7	91.0	91.4
1979	93.8	92.2	92.8	94.4	95.7	91.9	92.2	92.3	92.5	92.8	93.2	94.0	94.5	94.7	95.3	95.7	96.1
1980	100.0	98.0	98.7	100.5	102.8	97.4	98.2	98.3	98.5	98.8	99.0	100.2	100.4	101.0	102.0	103.0	103.3
1981	107.6	105.1	105.9	108.7	110.9	104.2	105.1	105.8	105.8	105.7	106.3	108.0	108.5	109.5	109.9	111.0	111.8
1982	117.0	113.1	115.7	118.5	120.8	112.8	113.1	113.3	114.7	115.7	116.7	117.6	118.3	119.8	120.7	120.9	120.8
1983	126.0	122.9	124.5	127.5	129.1	122.3	123.0	123.4	123.8	124.4	125.2	126.4	127.6	128.5	128.6	129.2	129.4

Money supply (M1) (12) — Disponibilités monétaires (M1) (12)

billion francs, end of period — milliards de francs, fin de période

Adjusted - Corrigé *

	Year	Q.1	Q.2	Q.3	Q.4	JAN	FEB	MAR	APR	MAY	JUN	JUL	AUG	SEP	OCT	NOV	DEC
1964																	
1965																	
1966																	
1967																	
1968																	
1969					363.2												
1970		366.1	365.0	376.2	392.2												
1971		394.4	408.5	420.5	431.3												
1972		447.7	473.9	486.3	502.5												
1973		518.4	524.7	530.5	540.5												
1974		556.7	555.1	572.0	580.3												
1975		600.9	630.3	651.7	678.3												
1976		679.1	703.4	708.8	723.8												
1977		744.2	751.5	777.6	795.8												
1978		810.5	820.0	832.7	840.6												
1979		854.9	865.3	849.7	873.1												
1980		850.0	864.6	869.6	873.1												
1981		884.4	916.0	887.0	904.4												
1982		912.1	931.2	953.8	943.8												
1983		945.1	976.9	1006.9													

M1 plus quasi-money (12) — M1 plus quasi-monnaie (12)

billion francs, end of period — milliards de francs, fin de période

Adjusted - Corrigé *

	Year	Q.1	Q.2	Q.3	Q.4	JAN	FEB	MAR	APR	MAY	JUN	JUL	AUG	SEP	OCT	NOV	DEC
1964																	
1965																	
1966																	
1967																	
1968																	
1969					776.7												
1970		789.2	803.7	827.1	846.9												
1971		866.6	899.2	929.7	962.5												
1972		994.1	1044.5	1082.3	1130.5												
1973		1177.9	1216.0	1255.8	1296.1												
1974		1351.0	1367.8	1404.9	1439.5												
1975		1489.7	1553.2	1617.7	1685.9												
1976		1743.9	1802.3	1862.0	1914.0												
1977		1950.7	1983.1	2040.3	2097.9												
1978		2153.6	2196.1	2262.6	2292.3												
1979		2342.6	2392.9	2409.9	2439.7												
1980		2452.6	2459.6	2480.2	2497.4												
1981		2519.3	2598.3	2611.5	2634.7												
1982		2657.6	2713.8	2804.0	2787.2												
1983		2792.3	2852.8	2964.6													

* Adjusted by the O.E.C.D. — * Corrigé par l'O.C.D.E.

New capital issues (14)

billion francs

Nouvelles émissions sur le marché des capitaux (14)

milliards de francs

	Year	Q.1	Q.2	Q.3	Q.4	JAN	FEB	MAR	APR	MAY	JUN	JUL	AUG	SEP	OCT	NOV	DEC
1964	12.4	1.2	4.5	2.1	4.6	0.4	0.3	0.5	1.8	2.1	0.6	1.4	0.2	0.5	1.9	1.2	1.5
1965	13.5	3.9	3.1	2.0	4.5	1.5	0.3	2.1	1.7	1.0	0.4	1.0	0.3	0.7	1.8	1.2	1.5
1966	13.0	4.4	2.3	1.4	4.9	0.9	0.9	2.6	0.5	0.6	1.0	0.2	0.5	0.7	0.6	3.3	1.0
1967	12.4	2.4	1.6	1.9	6.5	0.4	0.4	1.6	0.7	0.4	0.5	0.6	0.1	1.2	1.0	3.8	1.7
1968	20.6	3.1	5.9	2.1	9.5	0.5	1.8	0.8	0.7	2.1	3.1	1.6	0.2	0.3	0.7	6.5	2.3
1969	20.1	2.7	6.1	2.6	8.7	1.2	0.6	0.9	2.1	1.5	2.5	1.3	0.7	0.6	1.7	0.8	6.2
1970	18.9	2.7	9.8	1.9	4.5	0.6	1.4	0.7	1.0	2.6	6.2	0.8	0.3	0.8	1.4	0.5	2.6
1971	26.9	6.9	10.9	3.6	5.5	1.1	3.2	2.6	0.8	3.0	7.1	1.2	0.3	2.1	0.4	1.7	3.4
1972	37.1	5.6	10.7	9.1	11.7	0.3	2.2	3.1	2.3	3.7	4.7	7.0	1.3	0.8	1.7	4.4	5.6
1973	29.0	7.5	6.2	5.0	10.3	1.0	1.3	5.2	1.2	2.9	2.1	3.2	1.0	0.8	2.6	2.0	5.7
1974	28.9	4.2	7.1	6.2	11.4	1.5	1.2	1.5	2.3	1.4	3.4	4.1	1.0	1.1	5.5	2.4	3.5
1975	39.3	3.9	15.0	6.4	14.0	1.2	1.4	1.3	3.0	3.2	8.8	2.9	1.6	1.9	4.7	1.3	8.0
1976	33.0	5.1	6.9	6.1	14.9	1.5	1.9	1.7	2.7	1.8	2.4	2.7	1.4	2.0	5.2	1.2	8.5
1977	58.9	7.7	11.8	15.9	23.5	1.7	1.8	4.2	1.0	7.3	3.5	5.5	6.7	3.7	4.5	1.7	17.3
1978	43.8	10.4	10.4	12.4	10.6	4.9	1.3	4.2	3.1	4.9	2.4	6.8	3.0	2.6	1.7	1.7	7.2
1979	64.0	7.8	35.8	7.4	13.0	0.9	2.9	4.0	2.8	3.0	30.0	3.5	2.6	1.3	3.9	1.8	7.3
1980	52.7	8.5	19.4	8.4	16.4	1.9	2.2	4.4	4.4	10.8	4.2	4.4	1.7	2.3	4.0	3.5	8.9
1981	94.2	6.9	56.4	9.4	21.5	1.2	3.3	2.4	3.8	2.2	50.4	5.0	1.4	3.0	2.2	9.7	9.6
1982	108.4	13.2	26.3	14.2	54.7	2.0	4.4	6.8	12.4	2.6	11.3	5.9	2.1	6.2	10.6	6.7	37.4
1983	..	38.0	34.2	..		7.9	18.1	12.0	7.8	11.2	15.2	..	..	13.5			

Credit to economy: monetary institutions

billion francs, end of period

Crédits à l'économie : organismes monétaires

milliards de francs, fin de période

	Year	Q.1	Q.2	Q.3	Q.4	JAN	FEB	MAR	APR	MAY	JUN	JUL	AUG	SEP	OCT	NOV	DEC
1964																	
1965																	
1966																	
1967																	
1968																	
1969	217.3				217.3												
1970	246.4	219.9	228.4	228.4	246.4												
1971	283.1	248.8	257.3	260.9	283.1												
1972	342.8	285.3	300.9	311.5	342.8												
1973	400.1	349.2	363.8	380.6	400.1												
1974	452.5	414.9	423.1	429.5	452.5												
1975	526.9	461.0	477.3	488.4	526.9												
1976	616.6	546.8	570.6	592.7	616.6												
1977	727.6	625.6	658.0	673.8	727.6												
1978	803.7	713.2	754.8	773.7	803.7												
1979	942.5	802.8	855.8	881.2	942.5												
1980	1022.0	941.9	976.0	979.9	1022.0												
1981	1088.0	1030.7	1040.4	1053.1	1088.0												
1982	1107.2	1102.7	1100.4	1092.3	1107.2												
1983	1160.0	1089.9	1088.3	1102.4	1160.0												

Credit to economy: non-monetary institutions (15)

billion francs, end of period

Crédits à l'économie : organismes non monétaires (15)

milliards de francs, fin de période

	Year	Q.1	Q.2	Q.3	Q.4	JAN	FEB	MAR	APR	MAY	JUN	JUL	AUG	SEP	OCT	NOV	DEC
1964	230.9	209.0	216.9	223.1	230.9												
1965	253.5	233.0	238.3	245.6	253.5												
1966	287.9	258.0	265.4	276.6	287.9												
1967	322.5	292.2	301.1	310.2	322.5												
1968	358.6	327.9	334.0	347.1	358.6												
1969	394.9	363.3	375.2	389.9	394.9												
1970	437.3	404.5	415.7	427.4	437.3												
1971	477.8	447.6	462.6	472.0	477.8												
1972	528.1	485.6	500.6	514.3	528.1												
1973	605.4	548.1	569.0	586.9	605.4												
1974	683.5	625.0	649.1	671.9	683.5												
1975	772.0	694.4	717.7	738.7	772.0												
1976	893.0	799.6	829.6	854.7	893.0												
1977	999.2	917.2	948.4	974.9	999.2												
1978	1130.1	1030.0	1069.3	1096.7	1130.1												
1979	1259.3	1156.8	1184.0	1218.0	1259.3												
1980	1360.3	1290.5	1321.9	1341.8	1360.3												
1981	1419.0	1380.1	1393.3	1406.8	1419.0												
1982	1465.3	1434.2	1452.9	1457.8	1465.3												
1983		1474.2	1488.5	1489.5													

Official discount rate / Taux d'escompte officiel

per cent per annum, end of period / pourcentage par an, fin de période

	Year	Q.1	Q.2	Q.3	Q.4	JAN	FEB	MAR	APR	MAY	JUN	JUL	AUG	SEP	OCT	NOV	DEC
1964	4.75	4.25	4.25	4.75	4.75	4.25	4.25	4.25	4.25	4.25	4.25	4.75	4.75	4.75	4.75	4.75	4.75
1965	4.75	4.75	4.75	4.75	4.75	4.75	4.75	4.75	4.75	4.75	4.75	4.75	4.75	4.75	4.75	4.75	4.75
1966	5.25	4.75	5.25	5.25	5.25	4.75	4.75	4.75	4.75	4.75	5.25	5.25	5.25	5.25	5.25	5.25	5.25
1967	4.00	4.75	4.50	4.25	4.00	5.25	5.00	4.75	4.75	4.50	4.50	4.50	4.50	4.25	4.00	4.00	4.00
1968	4.50	3.75	3.75	3.75	4.50	4.00	4.00	3.75	3.75	3.75	3.75	3.75	3.75	3.75	3.75	3.75	4.50
1969	7.50	5.00	6.00	7.50	7.50	4.50	4.50	5.00	5.50	6.00	6.00	7.00	7.00	7.50	7.50	7.50	7.50
1970	6.50	7.50	7.50	7.50	6.50	7.50	7.50	7.50	7.50	7.50	7.50	7.50	7.50	7.50	7.00	7.00	6.50
1971	5.50	6.00	6.00	5.50	5.50	6.50	6.50	6.00	6.00	6.00	6.00	6.00	6.00	5.50	5.50	5.50	5.50
1972	5.00	4.00	4.00	4.00	5.00	5.00	4.50	4.00	4.00	4.00	4.00	4.00	4.00	4.00	4.00	4.50	5.00
1973	7.75	5.00	5.50	6.50	7.75	5.00	5.00	5.00	5.00	5.50	5.50	6.00	6.50	6.50	7.00	7.75	7.75
1974	8.75	8.75	8.75	8.75	8.75	8.75	8.75	8.75	8.75	8.75	8.75	8.75	8.75	8.75	8.75	8.75	8.75
1975	6.00	7.50	6.50	6.00	6.00	8.25	8.25	7.50	7.00	6.50	6.50	6.50	6.00	6.00	6.00	6.00	6.00
1976	9.00	7.00	7.00	9.00	9.00	6.00	6.00	7.00	7.00	7.00	7.00	8.00	9.00	9.00	9.00	9.00	9.00
1977	9.00	7.00	6.00	6.00	9.00	8.00	7.00	7.00	7.00	6.50	6.00	6.00	6.00	6.00	6.00	6.00	9.00
1978	6.00	5.50	5.50	6.00	6.00	7.50	6.50	5.50	5.50	5.50	5.50	6.00	6.00	6.00	6.00	6.00	6.00
1979	10.50	6.00	9.00	9.00	10.50	6.00	6.00	6.00	6.00	8.00	9.00	9.00	9.00	9.00	10.00	10.00	10.50
1980	12.00	14.00	13.00	12.00	12.00	10.50	12.00	14.00	14.00	14.00	13.00	12.00	12.00	12.00	12.00	12.00	12.00
1981	15.00	16.00	13.00	13.00	15.00	12.00	12.00	16.00	14.00	13.00	13.00	13.00	13.00	13.00	13.00	13.00	15.00
1982	11.50	13.00	14.00	12.50	11.50	14.00	14.00	13.00	14.00	14.00	14.00	13.50	13.00	12.50	12.00	11.50	11.50
1983	10.00	11.00	9.00	9.00	10.00	11.50	11.50	11.00	10.00	9.50	9.00	9.00	9.00	9.00	9.00	10.00	10.00

Call money rate (16) / Taux de l'argent au jour le jour (16)

per cent per annum, end of period / pourcentage par an, fin de période

	Year	Q.1	Q.2	Q.3	Q.4	JAN	FEB	MAR	APR	MAY	JUN	JUL	AUG	SEP	OCT	NOV	DEC
1964	4.25	3.35	3.88	3.60	4.25	4.13	4.30	3.35	3.08	4.13	3.88	4.25	4.38	3.60	4.00	3.25	4.25
1965	4.15	3.25	3.60	2.30	4.15	4.25	2.45	3.25	4.15	3.50	3.60	3.50	3.00	2.30	5.25	2.85	4.15
1966	4.10	2.45	3.15	5.85	4.10	3.20	3.55	2.45	4.75	4.05	3.15	4.25	3.85	5.85	6.15	3.70	4.10
1967	3.25	5.00	4.15	3.00	3.25	3.75	3.35	5.00	5.75	3.25	4.15	3.05	3.00	3.00	2.85	2.55	3.25
1968	3.30	2.80	3.00	2.90	3.30	2.85	2.80	2.80	3.00	3.05	3.00	2.75	3.35	2.90	3.10	5.25	3.30
1969	5.55	3.85	7.50	7.00	5.55	5.60	3.40	3.85	3.40	4.00	7.50	4.05	8.50	7.00	7.05	6.40	5.55
1970	5.70	6.45	6.35	6.25	5.70	9.00	6.55	6.45	6.35	6.50	6.35	6.20	7.10	6.25	6.30	5.85	5.70
1971	3.80	4.65	4.40	2.35	3.80	5.05	6.00	4.65	5.95	5.25	4.40	4.20	4.75	2.35	5.65	4.10	3.80
1972	6.00	2.45	2.15	3.05	6.00	4.95	1.60	2.45	3.85	2.90	2.15	2.30	4.00	3.05	4.00	1.25	6.00
1973	8.50	3.00	6.55	4.05	8.50	1.80	3.70	3.00	2.15	2.85	6.55	6.00	7.80	4.05	5.95	8.50	8.50
1974	9.55	9.50	9.75	11.85	9.55	8.50	9.50	9.50	9.50	9.50	9.75	9.60	9.50	11.85	9.50	9.50	9.55
1975	4.00	4.55	5.50	4.20	4.00	9.00	4.00	4.55	4.30	4.95	5.50	4.10	5.55	4.20	4.30	4.00	4.00
1976	7.75	9.95	7.00	12.50	7.75	7.50	3.50	9.95	7.05	6.75	7.00	7.95	13.00	12.50	12.00	8.50	7.75
1977	7.65	4.90	6.25	4.50	7.65	5.50	5.50	4.90	7.05	5.25	6.25	5.00	5.40	4.50	4.10	3.90	7.65
1978	6.65	4.15	5.50	4.65	6.65	7.40	4.60	4.15	3.50	4.00	5.50	3.60	6.00	4.65	8.00	6.15	6.65
1979	12.45	5.95	9.00	11.20	12.45	5.30	6.70	5.95	5.65	5.75	9.00	11.25	8.15	11.20	9.05	8.45	12.45
1980	9.60	14.00	13.75	12.00	9.60	12.90	12.50	14.00	15.00	12.45	13.75	11.00	8.25	12.00	10.10	8.55	9.60
1981	17.00	9.65	9.10	8.85	17.00	9.65	7.50	9.65	15.50	12.85	9.10	12.20	10.55	8.85	9.90	8.85	17.00
1982	9.30	10.35	13.60	10.05	9.30	12.00	11.40	10.35	13.95	10.95	13.60	13.60	10.25	10.05	11.80	12.25	9.30
1983	6.55	12.00	9.50	5.85	6.55	12.00	10.30	12.00	9.60	6.45	9.50	8.20	5.90	5.85	7.60	9.30	6.55

Treasury bill rate (3 months) (16) / Bons du Trésor (3 mois) (16)

per cent per annum, end of period / pourcentage par an, fin de période

	Year	Q.1	Q.2	Q.3	Q.4	JAN	FEB	MAR	APR	MAY	JUN	JUL	AUG	SEP	OCT	NOV	DEC
1964	4.75	4.25	4.30	4.50	4.75	4.20	4.25	4.25	4.30	4.30	4.30	4.50	4.50	4.50	4.50	4.75	4.75
1965	4.75	4.50	4.60	4.60	4.75	4.70	4.65	4.50	4.50	4.50	4.60	4.80	4.60	4.60	4.60	4.60	4.75
1966	5.85	4.75	5.30	5.50	5.85	4.75	4.75	4.75	4.90	5.10	5.30	5.30	5.40	5.50	5.70	5.75	5.85
1967	4.40	5.50	5.45	5.00	4.40	5.75	5.70	5.50	5.30	5.20	5.45	5.50	5.25	5.00	4.50	4.45	4.40
1968	5.00	3.95	3.75	3.80	5.00	4.35	4.10	3.95	3.75	3.75	3.75	3.75	3.75	3.80	4.10	4.50	5.00
1969	8.50	6.00	6.55	8.50	8.50	5.40	5.70	6.00	6.10	6.25	6.55	7.50	7.75	8.50	8.50	8.50	8.50
1970	6.95	8.10	8.00	7.65	6.95	8.50	8.25	8.10	8.05	8.00	8.00	8.00	7.80	7.65	7.30	7.10	6.95
1971	4.80	4.85	4.80	4.60	4.80	6.80	5.80	4.85	4.80	4.80	4.80	4.90	4.70	4.60	4.60	4.60	4.80
1972	4.50	3.45	3.50	3.65	4.50	4.80	4.00	3.45	3.50	3.50	3.50	3.50	3.65	3.65	3.85	4.05	4.50
1973	7.65	5.20	5.70	7.35	7.65	5.20	5.20	5.20	5.20	5.25	5.70	6.55	6.85	7.35	7.65	7.65	7.65
1974	10.50	9.00	11.25	11.75	10.50	7.65	8.50	9.00	9.40	10.00	11.25	11.75	11.75	11.75	11.25	10.75	10.50
1975	6.05	7.30	6.00	6.05	6.05	9.50	8.50	7.30	7.15	6.60	6.00	6.25	6.05	6.05	6.05	6.05	6.05
1976	10.00	9.00	9.00	13.00	10.00	6.05	6.40	9.00	9.25	9.50	9.00	10.00	11.50	13.00	13.50	11.50	10.00
1977	9.25	7.25	6.75	6.25	9.25	8.25	7.50	7.25	7.25	7.00	6.75	6.65	6.25	6.25	6.25	6.00	9.25
1978	9.25	5.75	5.75	7.50	9.25	7.75	6.75	5.75	5.60	5.60	5.75	6.35	7.00	7.50	9.50	8.75	9.25
1979	14.40	7.90	11.25	13.00	14.40	8.75	8.15	7.90	7.90	8.50	11.25	12.00	12.00	13.00	14.00	14.30	14.40
1980	12.75	17.50	13.75	12.25	12.75	14.40	15.00	17.50	17.00	15.50	13.75	13.00	12.35	12.25	12.10	12.75	12.75
1981	16.00	15.00	14.75	15.75	16.00	12.10	13.25	15.00	17.00	16.75	14.75	16.25	15.75	15.75	15.65	15.00	16.00
1982	12.25	14.25	15.75	12.75	12.25	15.15	14.25	14.25	15.00	15.00	15.75	14.50	13.75	12.75	12.75	12.25	12.25
1983	10.85	12.00	9.25	9.25	10.85	12.25	12.25	12.00	10.45	10.00	9.25	9.25	9.25	9.25	9.50	10.50	10.85

Yield of long-term Government bonds (17) / Rendement des bons d'État à long terme (17)

per cent per annum, end of period / pourcentage par an, fin de période

	Year	Q.1	Q.2	Q.3	Q.4	JAN	FEB	MAR	APR	MAY	JUN	JUL	AUG	SEP	OCT	NOV	DEC
1964	6.43	6.42	6.42	6.45	6.43	6.38	6.47	6.42	6.45	6.45	6.42	6.54	6.44	6.45	6.48	6.49	6.43
1965	6.45	6.39	6.49	6.45	6.45	6.46	6.40	6.39	6.44	6.45	6.49	6.34	6.39	6.45	6.50	6.50	6.45
1966	6.76	6.54	6.68	6.76	6.76	6.50	6.53	6.54	6.59	6.64	6.68	6.69	6.73	6.76	6.67	6.73	6.76
1967	6.58	6.76	6.77	6.66	6.58	6.75	6.76	6.76	6.77	6.77	6.77	6.64	6.64	6.66	6.57	6.54	6.58
1968	6.65	6.51	6.52	6.58	6.65	6.60	6.51	6.51	6.47	6.44	6.52	6.45	6.59	6.58	6.59	6.63	6.65
1969	7.80	6.84	7.16	7.86	7.80	6.71	6.76	6.84	7.06	7.19	7.16	7.22	7.37	7.86	7.82	7.73	7.80
1970	7.79	7.64	7.83	8.05	7.79	7.82	7.65	7.64	7.78	7.77	7.83	7.76	8.01	8.05	7.83	7.72	7.79
1971	7.17	7.37	7.28	7.29	7.17	7.72	7.42	7.37	7.41	7.35	7.28	7.32	7.15	7.29	7.21	7.17	7.17
1972	7.21	6.84	7.07	6.95	7.21	7.18	7.01	6.84	7.07	7.07	7.07	6.96	6.93	6.95	7.06	7.18	7.21
1973	7.92	7.33	7.21	7.62	7.92	7.33	7.28	7.33	7.34	7.29	7.21	7.45	7.71	7.62	7.66	7.79	7.92
1974	9.03	8.36	8.86	9.12	9.03	8.14	8.22	8.36	8.71	8.78	8.86	8.82	9.26	9.12	8.92	9.00	9.03
1975	8.72	8.71	8.07	8.50	8.72	9.24	8.79	8.71	8.42	8.09	8.07	8.21	8.41	8.50	8.50	8.53	8.72
1976	9.22	9.00	8.94	9.11	9.22	8.80	8.96	9.00	9.19	9.35	8.94	8.81	9.21	9.11	9.17	9.30	9.22
1977	8.76	9.06	8.61	8.42	8.76	9.24	9.08	9.06	8.94	8.93	8.61	8.62	8.68	8.42	8.39	8.42	8.76
1978	8.80	8.30	8.22	8.40	8.80	8.71	8.54	8.30	8.25	8.22	8.22	8.25	8.45	8.40	8.62	8.69	8.80
1979	11.13	8.90	9.42	9.90	11.13	9.05	8.83	8.90	8.99	9.21	9.42	9.63	9.80	9.90	10.58	11.00	11.13
1980	13.04	12.45	11.84	12.43	13.04	11.42	11.93	12.45	12.02	12.26	11.84	11.77	12.08	12.43	12.56	12.61	13.04
1981	13.99	13.57	14.18	13.97	13.99	13.19	13.44	13.57	13.52	13.85	14.18	13.97	14.06	13.97	13.80	13.87	13.99
1982	12.66	13.93	13.59	13.20	12.66	14.25	13.83	13.93	13.66	13.56	13.59	13.44	13.13	13.20	13.23	12.87	12.66
1983	11.89	12.49	11.55	11.39	11.89	12.48	12.60	12.49	11.59	11.63	11.55	11.42	11.46	11.39	11.32	11.75	11.89

Share prices: industrials (18) / Cours des actions industrielles (18)

1980 = 100

	Year	Q.1	Q.2	Q.3	Q.4	JAN	FEB	MAR	APR	MAY	JUN	JUL	AUG	SEP	OCT	NOV	DEC
1964	113	117	112	110	111	118	117	115	114	113	109	109	111	110	111	111	111
1965	105	110	104	103	98	111	110	108	106	106	102	102	104	102	100	98	97
1966	87	98	90	81	77	99	98	96	94	87	88	83	83	78	77	78	75
1967	86	79	84	90	90	74	80	82	84	83	84	86	90	94	90	90	90
1968	92	90	91	94	95	89	88	92	92	91	91	92	95	96	94	95	95
1969	100	99	103	101	96	98	100	100	103	106	100	100	103	99	98	96	95
1970	94	95	92	95	95	96	95	96	96	89	91	94	96	96	96	94	97
1971	105	106	108	108	98	104	108	106	107	109	109	111	109	103	97	99	99
1972	118	109	115	123	125	105	109	114	116	113	115	122	124	124	125	123	126
1973	140	138	147	139	134	136	143	136	144	144	152	143	139	134	141	134	128
1974	112	130	120	104	95	134	129	126	127	119	113	112	105	93	97	98	90
1975	108	103	113	109	105	99	104	105	115	114	110	111	111	106	102	105	108
1976	99	111	101	95	89	113	111	109	106	100	98	99	93	93	85	91	93
1977	92	93	91	92	89	93	94	92	91	90	93	93	92	91	90	89	88
1978	93	88	95	96	94	88	89	89	97	94	93	94	95	97	94	94	93
1979	102	100	103	104	102	97	101	101	105	102	102	103	103	105	102	100	103
1980	100	105	102	98	93	109	109	98	104	102	100	98	99	97	95	92	92
1981	81	90	80	75	78	91	91	89	87	76	76	76	76	75	74	75	87
1982	96	95	93	96	100	90	97	97	100	90	91	91	94	103	100	99	100
1983	123	106	124	131	130	103	104	111	120	123	128	129	132	132	125	126	138

U.S. dollar exchange rate: spot (19) / Taux de change du dollar É.-U. : au comptant (19)

cents per franc, end of period / cents par franc, fin de période

	Year	Q.1	Q.2	Q.3	Q.4	JAN	FEB	MAR	APR	MAY	JUN	JUL	AUG	SEP	OCT	NOV	DEC
1964	2.0148	2.0071	2.0049	2.0135	2.0148	2.0080	2.0060	2.0071	2.0087	2.0085	2.0049	2.0109	2.0116	2.0135	2.0151	2.0151	2.0148
1965	2.0144	2.0151	2.0151	2.0134	2.0144	2.0151	2.0151	2.0151	2.0151	2.0149	2.0151	2.0150	2.0142	2.0134	2.0135	2.0144	2.0144
1966	1.9979	2.0076	2.0062	2.0008	1.9979	2.0110	2.0104	2.0076	2.0080	2.0089	2.0062	2.0151	2.0086	2.0008	1.9995	2.0032	1.9979
1967	2.0150	2.0118	2.0151	2.0151	2.0150	2.0074	2.0097	2.0118	2.0143	2.0150	2.0151	2.0151	2.0151	2.0151	2.0151	2.0147	2.0150
1968	1.9968	2.0132	2.0022	1.9875	1.9968	2.0145	2.0139	2.0132	2.0150	2.0070	2.0022	2.0030	1.9925	1.9875	1.9881	1.9968	1.9968
1969	2.0134	1.9863	1.9888	1.9904	2.0134	1.9944	1.9920	1.9863	1.9902	1.9917	1.9888	1.9908	1.9851	1.9904	2.0129	2.0122	2.0134
1970	2.0131	2.0136	2.0133	2.0147	2.0131	2.0137	2.0134	2.0136	2.0145	2.0141	2.0133	2.0148	2.0143	2.0147	2.0151	2.0149	2.0131
1971	2.2344	2.0151	2.0098	2.1265	2.2344	2.0151	2.0150	2.0151	2.0151	2.0144	2.0098	2.0151	2.0705	2.1265	2.1450	2.1645	2.2344
1972	2.2665	2.2749	2.2813	2.2637	2.2665	2.2738	2.2822	2.2749	2.2655	2.2808	2.2813	2.2826	2.2763	2.2637	2.2663	2.2703	2.2665
1973	2.4201	2.4950	2.7739	2.7100	2.4201	2.2813	2.5332	2.4950	2.4800	2.5934	2.7739	2.7882	2.6560	2.7100	2.7113	2.5289	2.4201
1974	2.7684	2.5674	2.6307	2.5491	2.7684	2.3557	2.4774	2.5674	2.6638	2.6226	2.6307	2.6147	2.5411	2.5491	2.6216	2.6874	2.7684
1975	2.5299	2.8850	2.8369	2.5003	2.5299	2.8555	2.9330	2.8850	2.8425	2.8523	2.8369	2.6015	2.5996	2.5003	2.5955	2.5278	2.5299
1976	2.7791	2.5608	2.5191	2.6589	2.7791	2.5484	2.5549	2.5608	2.5760	2.5096	2.5191	2.5445	2.5723	2.6589	2.7071	2.7124	2.7791
1977	3.0358	2.7319	2.7751	2.7978	3.0358	2.6896	2.7235	2.7319	2.7733	2.7728	2.7751	2.8273	2.7999	2.7978	2.8391	2.8436	3.0358
1978	3.4722	3.1766	3.0572	3.2733	3.4722	3.0574	3.1598	3.1766	3.0981	3.0416	3.0572	3.1075	3.1946	3.2733	3.6802	3.2941	3.4722
1979	3.5654	3.3852	3.3767	3.5480	3.5654	3.4130	3.4168	3.3852	3.3063	3.2581	3.3767	3.4060	3.4136	3.5480	3.4352	3.5492	3.5654
1980	3.1723	3.2082	3.5562	3.4459	3.1723	3.5392	3.4758	3.2082	3.4412	3.4941	3.5562	3.5032	3.4746	3.4459	3.2677	3.2300	3.1723
1981	2.6001	2.9030	2.5471	2.6352	2.6001	2.9483	2.8727	2.9030	2.7751	2.6354	2.5471	2.4769	2.5167	2.6352	2.6505	2.6989	2.6001
1982	2.1313	2.1949	2.1334	2.0375	2.1313	2.5437	2.2843	2.1949	2.2676	2.2550	2.1334	2.1334	2.0887	2.0375	2.0145	2.0511	2.1313
1983	1.7973	2.0718	1.9633	1.8692	1.7973	2.0839	2.0964	2.0718	2.0408	1.9871	1.9633	1.8896	1.8375	1.3692	1.8716	1.8260	1.7973

BELGIQUE

U.S. dollar exchange rate: forward (90 days) (19) / Taux de change du dollar É.-U : à terme (90 jours) (19)

cents per franc, end of period / cents par franc, fin de période

	Year	Q.1	Q.2	Q.3	Q.4	JAN	FEB	MAR	APR	MAY	JUN	JUL	AUG	SEP	OCT	NOV	DEC
1964	2.0113	2.0040	2.0020	2.0080	2.0113	2.0060	2.0036	2.0040	2.0064	2.0068	2.0020	2.0048	2.0060	2.0080	2.0105	2.0105	2.0113
1965	2.0141	2.0153	2.0129	2.0133	2.0141	2.0145	2.0133	2.0153	2.0141	2.0121	2.0129	2.0133	2.0141	2.0133	2.0129	2.0129	2.0141
1966	1.9988	2.0084	2.0060	2.0048	1.9988	2.0113	2.0097	2.0084	2.0092	2.0084	2.0060	2.0145	2.0129	2.0048	2.0024	2.0036	1.9988
1967	2.0235	2.0105	2.0117	2.0161	2.0235	2.0044	2.0080	2.0105	2.0113	2.0125	2.0117	2.0121	2.0133	2.0161	2.0178	2.0255	2.0235
1968	1.9944	2.0243	2.0129	1.9936	1.9944	2.0157	2.0165	2.0243	2.0235	2.0198	2.0129	2.0105	1.9996	1.9936	1.9920	2.0000	1.9944
1969	2.0153	1.9905	1.9833	2.0044	2.0153	1.9984	1.9980	1.9905	1.9893	1.9877	1.9833	1.9885	1.9964	2.0044	2.0129	2.0133	2.0153
1970	2.0113	2.0129	2.0165	2.0161	2.0113	2.0137	2.0133	2.0129	2.0133	2.0141	2.0165	2.0165	2.0153	2.0161	2.0165	2.0157	2.0113
1971	2.2371	2.0153	2.0210	2.1423	2.2371	2.0121	2.0125	2.0153	2.0182	2.0276	2.0210	2.0243	2.1008	2.1423	2.1468	2.1654	2.2371
1972	2.2712	2.2852	2.2925	2.2758	2.2712	2.2764	2.2784	2.2852	2.2702	2.2821	2.2925	2.3020	2.2883	2.2758	2.2671	2.2738	2.2712
1973	2.4361	2.5329	2.7910	2.7609	2.4361	2.2899	2.5813	2.5329	2.5000	2.6089	2.7910	2.8137	2.6810	2.7609	2.7233	2.5400	2.4361
1974	2.7571	2.5240	2.6192	2.5478	2.7571	2.3408	2.4390	2.5240	2.6413	2.5733	2.6192	2.6062	2.5400	2.5478	2.6103	2.6653	2.7571
1975	2.5278	2.8670	2.8353	2.5082	2.5278	2.8329	2.9095	2.8670	2.8329	2.8490	2.8353	2.6049	2.5913	2.5082	2.6015	2.5329	2.5278
1976	2.7450	2.5063	2.5019	2.5820	2.7450	2.5246	2.5368	2.5063	2.5407	2.4944	2.5019	2.5767	2.5031	2.5820	2.6469	2.6624	2.7450
1977	3.0057	2.7196	2.7686	2.8027	3.0057	2.6681	2.7078	2.7196	2.7594	2.7579	2.7686	2.8241	2.7988	2.8027	2.8441	2.8466	3.0057
1978	3.4928	3.1929	3.0798	3.2712	3.4928	3.0553	3.1626	3.1929	3.1114	3.0600	3.0798	3.1240	3.2051	3.2712	3.6778	3.3069	3.4928
1979	3.5663	3.4106	3.3750	3.5448	3.5663	3.4294	3.4400	3.4106	3.3322	3.2712	3.3750	3.4002	3.4165	3.5448	3.4471	3.5474	3.5663
1980	3.2134	3.2248	3.5224	3.4590	3.2134	3.5398	3.4941	3.2248	3.4294	3.4542	3.5224	3.4807	3.4734	3.4590	3.2960	3.2712	3.2134
1981	2.5615	2.8612	2.5549	2.5940	2.5615	2.9878	2.8952	2.8612	2.7693	2.6392	2.5549	2.4631	2.5031	2.5940	2.6261	2.6702	2.5615
1982	2.1035	2.1872	2.1317	2.0300	2.1035	2.5132	2.2836	2.1872	2.2568	2.2447	2.1317	2.1286	2.0764	2.0300	1.9988	2.0334	2.1035
1983	1.7921	2.0585	1.9670	1.8688	1.7921	2.0631	2.0695	2.0585	2.0346	1.9849	1.9670	1.8957	1.8409	1.8688	1.8727	1.8208	1.7921

Official reserves excluding gold (19) / Réserves officielles, or exclu (19)

million SDR's, end of period / millions de DTS, fin de période

	Year	Q.1	Q.2	Q.3	Q.4	JAN	FEB	MAR	APR	MAY	JUN	JUL	AUG	SEP	OCT	NOV	DEC
1964	771	609	588	631	771	591	589	609	590	611	588	593	612	631	657	710	771
1965	776	756	731	803	776	775	772	756	775	772	731	786	794	803	791	791	776
1966	825	753	769	797	825	755	733	753	769	768	769	828	826	797	835	828	825
1967	1110	824	935	1037	1110	843	813	824	847	859	935	973	1016	1037	1045	1112	1110
1968	663	1149	1020	892	663	1092	1078	1149	1086	1062	1020	990	975	892	902	800	663
1969	868	580	689	656	868	675	647	580	649	665	689	580	648	656	755	808	868
1970	1377	1010	1078	1260	1377	953	976	1010	1039	1054	1078	1196	1225	1260	1307	1359	1377
1971	1655	1607	1612	1852	1655	1639	1646	1607	1594	1706	1612	1689	1856	1852	1769	1767	1655
1972	2056	1840	1992	2203	2056	1746	1865	1840	1811	1725	1992	2142	2208	2203	2171	2107	2056
1973	2751	2557	2715	2844	2751	2270	2431	2557	2634	2734	2715	2688	2605	2844	2718	2675	2751
1974	2890	2485	2359	2870	2890	2475	2471	2485	2445	2327	2359	2581	2765	2870	2947	3009	2890
1975	3476	3248	3366	3472	3476	2986	3167	3248	3309	3397	3366	3407	3456	3472	3459	3454	3476
1976	3004	3139	3067	2598	3004	3268	3170	3139	3001	3086	3067	2922	2892	2598	2594	2750	3004
1977	3257	3235	3377	3458	3257	3100	3171	3235	3295	3362	3377	3425	3453	3458	3432	3383	3257
1978	3044	3322	3295	2957	3044	3289	3309	3322	3348	3354	3295	2881	2737	2957	2995	3088	3044
1979	4132	4658	4291	4469	4132	3184	3177	4658	4514	4274	4291	4490	4510	4469	4771	4771	4132
1980	6133	3307	5700	6361	6133	4215	3566	3307	4277	4949	5700	6558	6492	6361	6138	6385	6133
1981	4254	4957	5310	4510	4254	6386	6168	4957	5663	5898	5310	5117	4735	4510	4446	4503	4254
1982	3560	3581	3103	4159	3560	3862	3645	3581	2972	2970	3103	3392	3764	4159	4089	3890	3560
1983	4502	4474	5006	4571	4502	3938	3880	4474	4689	4675	5006	5130	4947	4571	4638	4584	4502

Net foreign position: commercial banks (20) / Position extérieure nette : banques commerciales (20)

billion francs, end of period / milliards de francs, fin de période

	Year	Q.1	Q.2	Q.3	Q.4	JAN	FEB	MAR	APR	MAY	JUN	JUL	AUG	SEP	OCT	NOV	DEC
1964	-27	-24	-24	-24	-27			-24			-24			-24			-27
1965	-28	-26	-28	-30	-28			-26			-28			-30			-28
1966	-35	-26	-30	-32	-35			-26			-30			-32			-35
1967	-40	-33	-36	-39	-40			-33			-36			-39			-40
1968	-37	-39	-37	-39	-37			-39			-37			-39			-37
1969	-35	-34	-33	-29	-35			-34			-33			-29			-35
1970	-38	-33	-34	-35	-38			-33			-34			-35			-38
1971	-32	-40	-33	-33	-32			-40			-33			-33			-32
1972	-46	-36	-35	-50	-46			-36			-35			-50			-46
1973	-67	-65	-70	-76	-67	-56	-69	-65	-65	-67	-70	-74	-72	-76	-74	-67	-67
1974	-96	-71	-78	-89	-96	-64	-70	-71	-67	-68	-78	-82	-90	-89	-96	-97	-96
1975	-93	-96	-90	-96	-93	-99	-100	-96	-98	-98	-90	-84	-96	-96	-101	-96	-93
1976	-86	-77	-99	-79	-86	-89	-79	-77	-81	-97	-99	-86	-85	-79	-86	-91	-86
1977	-108	-87	-102	-134	-108	-82	-92	-87	-96	-100	-102	-108	-121	-134	-123	-119	-108
1978	-146	-118	-136	-126	-146	-104	-122	-118	-123	-138	-136	-128	-125	-126	-129	-125	-146
1979	-266	-167	-200	-218	-266	-138	-157	-167	-172	-196	-200	-214	-225	-218	-237	-244	-266
1980	-384	-275	-327	-352	-384	-262	-279	-275	-296	-329	-327	-337	-347	-352	-379	-385	-384
1981	-506	-396	-424	-450	-506	-389	-396	-396	-427	-417	-424	-430	-436	-450	-471	-476	-506
1982	-592	-593	-570	-621	-592	-529	-570	-593	-550	-550	-570	-572	-601	-621	-626	-606	-592
1983	-774	-644	-721	-755	-774	-601	-616	-644	-652	-698	-721	-728	-757	-755	-761	-757	-774

BELGIUM

Imports c.i.f. (19) — Importations c.a.f. (19)

billion francs, monthly averages — milliards de francs, moyennes mensuelles

	Year	Q.1	Q.2	Q.3	Q.4	JAN	FEB	MAR	APR	MAY	JUN	JUL	AUG	SEP	OCT	NOV	DEC
1964	24.50	24.19	25.10	23.07	25.65	24.58	23.77	24.22	25.74	23.93	25.64	24.29	20.93	23.99	25.60	24.57	26.80
1965	26.38	24.64	26.48	25.19	29.23	22.76	23.83	27.33	27.83	25.72	25.88	25.25	22.68	27.64	28.04	28.92	30.73
1966	29.79	28.89	29.92	28.97	31.38	26.55	28.43	31.69	28.46	30.01	31.30	26.43	29.99	30.48	31.30	30.93	31.91
1967	29.81	29.38	30.58	25.25	33.04	29.50	27.27	31.38	28.70	30.33	32.70	23.11	29.91	25.73	31.91	34.61	32.60
1968	34.14	33.82	32.77	32.22	37.76	31.07	35.08	35.31	32.26	35.17	30.88	31.26	31.89	33.52	40.83	35.38	37.07
1969	41.53	38.42	42.31	40.07	45.33	37.14	36.81	41.30	40.56	41.62	44.76	40.44	36.40	43.36	48.55	41.44	46.01
1970	47.25	44.82	47.78	44.85	51.56	39.84	47.15	47.47	51.05	43.16	49.12	46.22	39.92	48.40	51.76	49.21	53.70
1971	49.89	49.07	51.37	46.44	52.67	42.48	49.19	55.54	52.03	47.50	54.57	45.61	45.11	48.59	54.62	50.27	53.12
1972	56.45	55.50	56.68	52.06	61.56	50.55	52.85	63.09	52.43	57.00	60.61	45.13	54.20	56.86	62.17	61.12	61.40
1973	71.34	66.40	70.16	68.13	80.69	65.06	64.17	69.98	66.36	73.54	70.58	63.19	70.05	71.16	85.76	79.10	77.19
1974	96.72	91.31	102.94	95.08	97.57	88.55	89.21	96.17	99.50	108.89	100.42	96.90	90.74	97.59	106.34	93.52	92.86
1975	94.25	90.39	94.78	87.60	104.22	90.19	88.71	92.26	98.77	88.49	97.08	85.57	77.46	99.75	111.21	97.44	104.11
1976	114.16	108.57	118.12	110.33	119.64	104.34	102.14	119.23	119.52	112.39	122.45	101.80	107.22	121.97	121.95	118.54	118.42
1977	120.67	124.43	125.33	110.20	122.70	116.55	118.29	138.46	124.35	119.95	131.69	94.03	114.25	122.31	124.89	121.09	122.14
1978	127.17	126.84	127.61	118.23	136.01	123.21	123.62	133.69	122.64	126.94	133.24	107.65	120.65	126.39	142.30	137.33	128.39
1979	148.70	138.70	149.74	138.94	167.41	126.46	136.88	152.76	141.07	160.37	147.78	127.48	145.11	144.22	176.25	165.60	160.39
1980	173.40	184.00	174.88	154.65	180.08	184.11	189.25	178.62	184.39	165.74	174.50	148.95	137.57	177.41	188.57	168.44	183.23
1981	192.48	190.72	188.88	189.31	201.02	175.80	188.93	207.42	195.80	176.34	194.49	184.90	183.48	199.55	202.04	197.26	203.75
1982	221.11	221.05	229.92	205.65	227.84	193.59	201.15	268.41	239.42	216.14	234.19	198.87	192.16	225.93	221.29	239.66	222.56
1983		239.73	226.65	207.02		218.08	229.02	272.10	229.18	212.36	238.42	189.91	195.89	235.27	248.16		

Exports f.o.b. (19) — Exportations f.o.b. (19)

billion francs, monthly averages — milliards de francs, moyennes mensuelles

	Year	Q.1	Q.2	Q.3	Q.4	JAN	FEB	MAR	APR	MAY	JUN	JUL	AUG	SEP	OCT	NOV	DEC
1964	23.28	22.80	23.33	21.77	25.22	22.54	22.44	23.42	24.49	21.31	24.19	22.65	18.83	23.84	26.02	24.55	25.10
1965	26.62	26.21	25.75	25.53	29.00	24.12	25.98	28.53	25.47	24.20	27.57	25.65	21.61	29.32	27.60	28.82	30.58
1966	28.44	27.43	29.11	27.01	30.21	24.65	26.38	31.26	27.98	27.90	31.45	26.17	23.81	31.05	30.01	29.48	31.15
1967	29.30	29.76	29.67	25.14	32.61	30.40	28.52	30.35	29.94	29.31	29.77	26.18	22.82	26.43	34.85	30.84	32.15
1968	33.96	33.23	33.20	31.85	37.55	31.17	33.51	35.01	35.02	33.14	31.43	34.33	27.48	33.74	35.63	35.08	37.94
1969	41.70	39.02	41.06	39.62	47.10	42.04	34.88	40.15	40.12	41.24	41.81	43.09	30.48	45.29	48.90	45.34	47.06
1970	47.97	45.48	49.48	44.34	52.58	43.83	43.75	48.86	53.24	45.06	50.15	49.60	34.49	48.93	53.46	48.76	55.51
1971	49.99	47.80	51.23	48.33	52.61	43.62	44.07	55.71	47.25	49.75	56.68	51.47	37.00	56.52	51.86	50.10	55.87
1972	58.82	55.45	58.76	52.85	68.00	52.22	52.08	62.05	54.88	59.41	62.60	51.66	46.81	60.09	68.20	63.85	71.93
1973	72.51	66.35	71.35	69.27	83.07	59.94	63.60	75.50	68.71	74.26	71.09	70.19	60.67	76.94	87.40	77.23	84.58
1974	91.65	84.42	97.26	88.80	96.13	82.60	75.67	94.98	97.27	101.41	93.09	97.69	75.93	92.79	105.32	91.78	91.29
1975	88.07	89.35	87.94	77.61	97.40	91.22	87.38	89.45	91.01	83.08	89.72	82.72	63.30	86.80	99.22	93.57	99.42
1976	105.54	99.50	107.55	98.77	116.33	90.23	95.68	112.58	104.94	102.39	115.32	92.48	85.72	118.11	123.40	103.42	122.18
1977	112.06	113.80	116.56	101.67	116.20	100.50	105.99	134.92	113.11	109.91	126.66	95.95	85.42	123.65	119.53	107.82	121.24
1978	117.27	115.76	117.75	108.72	126.85	113.15	108.50	125.63	116.27	112.32	124.66	106.16	95.27	124.74	134.58	124.70	121.26
1979	138.44	130.00	140.46	130.11	153.17	116.12	127.64	146.24	130.78	147.91	142.70	126.16	121.85	142.32	170.22	149.72	139.57
1980	157.53	169.46	161.57	137.33	161.76	159.10	173.25	176.03	177.86	152.99	153.87	143.33	113.30	155.35	165.96	151.68	163.64
1981	171.86	158.90	171.62	165.65	191.27	143.88	158.06	174.76	172.83	161.19	180.85	165.80	131.65	199.49	200.78	179.63	193.43
1982	199.51	185.48	202.24	190.49	219.83	156.37	181.11	218.96	203.36	188.74	214.63	192.36	144.35	234.77	237.26	203.45	218.78
1983		216.16	219.91	200.91		218.36	192.99	237.12	216.60	205.28	237.85	191.65	183.80	227.29	246.51		

Trade balance (f.o.b. — c.i.f.) (19) — Balance commerciale (f.o.b. — c.a.f.) (19)

billion francs, monthly averages — milliards de francs, moyennes mensuelles

	Year	Q.1	Q.2	Q.3	Q.4	JAN	FEB	MAR	APR	MAY	JUN	JUL	AUG	SEP	OCT	NOV	DEC
1964	-1.22	-1.39	-1.77	-1.30	-0.43	-2.04	-1.33	-0.80	-1.25	-2.62	-1.45	-1.64	-2.10	-0.15	0.42	-0.01	-1.71
1965	0.24	1.57	-0.73	0.34	-0.23	1.36	2.14	1.20	-2.36	-1.53	1.69	0.40	-1.07	1.67	-0.43	-0.10	-0.15
1966	-1.35	-1.46	-0.82	-1.96	-1.17	-1.90	-2.05	-0.43	-0.48	-2.12	0.14	-0.26	-6.18	0.57	-1.29	-1.45	-0.76
1967	-0.51	0.38	-0.91	-1.10	-0.42	0.90	1.25	-1.02	1.24	-1.02	-2.94	3.07	-7.09	0.70	2.95	-3.78	-0.44
1968	-0.19	-0.59	0.43	-0.37	-0.21	0.10	-1.56	-0.30	2.76	-2.02	0.55	3.07	-4.41	0.22	-1.20	-0.30	0.87
1969	0.17	0.61	-1.25	-0.45	1.77	4.90	-1.93	-1.15	-0.43	-0.37	-2.96	2.65	-5.93	1.93	0.35	3.90	1.05
1970	0.72	0.66	1.70	-0.51	1.02	3.99	-3.40	1.39	2.19	1.90	1.02	3.38	-5.43	0.53	1.70	-0.45	1.81
1971	0.11	-1.27	-0.14	1.89	-0.06	1.14	-5.11	0.17	-4.77	2.25	2.12	5.87	-8.11	7.92	-2.76	-0.17	2.75
1972	2.36	-0.05	2.28	0.79	6.43	1.67	-0.78	-1.04	2.45	2.41	1.99	6.53	-7.39	3.24	6.03	2.73	10.54
1973	1.17	-0.06	1.20	1.14	2.38	-5.12	-0.56	5.52	2.36	0.72	0.52	7.01	-9.38	5.79	1.64	-1.88	7.39
1974	-5.07	-6.89	-5.68	-6.28	-1.44	-5.95	-13.54	-1.19	-2.23	-7.48	-7.33	0.79	-14.81	-4.81	-1.01	-1.74	-1.57
1975	-6.17	-1.04	-6.84	-9.99	-6.82	1.03	-1.34	-2.81	-7.76	-5.41	-7.36	-2.85	-14.16	-12.96	-11.89	-3.87	-4.69
1976	-8.63	-9.07	-10.57	-11.56	-3.30	-14.11	-6.46	-6.65	-14.58	-10.00	-7.13	-9.32	-21.50	-3.86	1.45	-15.12	3.76
1977	-8.61	-10.63	-8.77	-8.52	-6.51	-16.05	-12.30	-3.54	-11.24	-10.04	-5.03	1.92	-28.83	1.34	-5.36	-13.27	-0.89
1978	-9.90	-11.08	-9.86	-9.51	-9.16	-10.06	-15.11	-8.06	-6.37	-14.62	-8.58	-1.49	-25.38	-1.65	-7.72	-12.63	-7.13
1979	-10.26	-8.70	-9.27	-8.83	-14.24	-10.34	-9.24	-6.52	-10.28	-12.46	-5.08	-1.32	-23.27	-1.89	-6.03	-15.87	-20.82
1980	-15.87	-14.54	-13.30	-17.32	-18.32	-25.01	-16.00	-2.60	-6.52	-12.76	-20.63	-5.62	-24.28	-22.06	-18.61	-16.77	-19.59
1981	-20.62	-31.82	-17.26	-23.66	-9.74	-31.92	-30.87	-32.66	-22.98	-15.15	-13.65	-19.10	-51.83	-0.06	-1.25	-17.63	-10.34
1982	-21.60	-35.57	-27.67	-15.16	-8.01	-37.22	-20.04	-49.45	-36.06	-27.40	-19.56	-6.52	-47.80	8.84	15.97	-36.21	-3.78
1983		-23.57	-6.75	-6.11		0.28	-36.02	-34.98	-12.59	-7.08	-0.57	1.75	-12.09	-7.99	-1.67		

Imports c.i.f. (19) — Adjusted - Corrigé * — **Importations c.a.f.** (19)

billion francs, monthly averages — milliards de francs, moyennes mensuelles

	Year	Q.1	Q.2	Q.3	Q.4	JAN	FEB	MAR	APR	MAY	JUN	JUL	AUG	SEP	OCT	NOV	DEC
1964		24.26	24.33	24.24	24.71	24.51	24.45	23.81	23.81	24.69	24.49	24.86	23.52	24.35	24.17	24.86	25.09
1965		24.66	26.09	26.50	28.09	24.55	24.57	24.85	27.05	25.67	25.55	27.06	24.68	27.75	27.51	28.32	28.43
1966		28.86	29.54	30.58	30.48	28.64	29.22	28.71	28.89	30.01	29.73	29.69	31.47	30.57	30.57	30.33	30.56
1967		29.35	29.88	28.12	32.08	31.02	27.86	29.19	29.32	29.30	31.03	26.02	31.58	26.77	30.07	33.64	32.53
1968		33.20	32.36	34.28	36.31	31.61	34.12	33.86	31.82	32.93	32.34	33.01	35.00	34.81	36.89	35.96	36.09
1969		38.09	41.63	42.78	43.65	37.55	37.53	39.18	39.84	41.82	43.38	42.75	41.89	43.71	43.46	44.00	43.48
1970		45.06	46.14	47.79	49.99	41.63	48.11	45.42	47.49	45.15	45.78	48.60	46.04	48.74	48.11	50.52	51.34
1971		48.40	50.04	49.59	51.41	45.78	50.19	49.24	50.12	49.38	50.62	49.95	50.45	48.35	53.03	50.32	50.89
1972		53.90	55.03	56.15	61.21	53.84	51.97	55.88	54.39	55.18	55.51	51.63	58.15	58.68	58.65	60.88	64.09
1973		64.78	67.94	73.69	79.38	64.23	65.68	64.44	65.96	68.86	68.99	70.84	74.28	75.94	78.10	79.02	81.00
1974		90.26	99.57	101.52	96.43	86.99	91.40	92.38	95.67	101.20	101.84	105.67	99.39	99.48	96.85	97.01	95.43
1975		90.15	90.28	93.58	102.77	87.56	90.80	92.07	91.03	87.96	91.85	94.03	88.33	98.38	100.55	104.67	103.08
1976		105.07	114.25	118.04	117.83	105.07	103.49	106.65	113.50	112.95	116.29	116.07	118.34	119.70	118.86	118.18	116.44
1977		121.53	121.61	118.21	122.07	121.79	119.72	123.08	122.51	121.29	121.04	112.34	121.67	120.62	121.49	120.60	124.12
1978		123.54	122.96	129.09	135.43	125.47	123.62	121.54	120.83	124.33	123.71	128.62	128.62	130.03	135.27	135.44	135.57
1979		132.12	146.60	152.22	164.97	124.47	135.12	136.76	138.57	153.17	148.07	147.72	154.38	154.57	162.74	162.99	169.19
1980		174.13	171.66	167.14	178.26	182.11	176.87	163.43	175.44	169.13	170.41	165.32	158.86	177.23	174.93	178.44	181.42
1981		181.84	185.45	205.12	199.65	179.76	183.97	181.79	183.51	182.17	190.68	203.41	212.61	199.35	196.15	199.66	203.14
1982		208.69	225.81	222.29	226.96	206.16	195.67	224.23	223.97	230.43	223.04	226.77	216.64	223.47	224.66	235.19	221.01
1983		226.82	223.65	223.71		231.51	222.56	226.37	222.72	220.52	227.71	225.28	212.92	232.95	251.96		

Exports f.o.b. (19) — Adjusted - Corrigé * — **Exportations f.o.b.** (19)

billion francs, monthly averages — milliards de francs, moyennes mensuelles

	Year	Q.1	Q.2	Q.3	Q.4	JAN	FEB	MAR	APR	MAY	JUN	JUL	AUG	SEP	OCT	NOV	DEC
1964		22.42	22.62	23.16	24.40	22.32	22.24	22.69	22.30	22.64	22.91	22.81	23.68	22.99	24.07	24.88	24.25
1965		25.85	25.34	27.16	28.09	25.58	26.40	25.56	24.63	24.94	26.43	26.55	27.01	27.92	26.72	28.28	29.27
1966		26.86	28.61	29.11	29.19	26.14	26.86	27.59	27.81	28.82	29.20	28.26	29.14	29.94	28.97	28.65	29.95
1967		29.78	28.75	27.39	31.52	31.83	29.28	28.24	29.13	29.04	28.08	28.00	28.00	26.17	33.00	29.71	31.84
1968		32.64	32.48	34.60	35.80	31.61	33.05	33.25	33.90	31.62	31.91	34.40	35.50	33.91	35.51	35.36	36.52
1969		39.04	40.03	42.64	44.86	42.55	36.79	37.77	38.40	40.92	40.79	42.08	41.58	44.27	44.05	46.99	43.53
1970		46.32	47.36	47.71	50.00	45.37	46.64	46.93	48.67	46.35	47.04	48.68	47.18	47.27	49.10	50.27	50.65
1971		47.89	49.66	51.75	50.49	47.16	47.29	49.22	45.79	50.82	52.39	51.52	49.60	54.13	49.63	50.25	51.59
1972		55.09	56.75	57.71	66.05	56.21	53.47	55.60	54.88	57.35	58.02	53.98	59.17	59.97	63.86	63.28	71.01
1973		65.43	69.23	76.06	80.01	61.04	67.59	67.65	69.33	69.14	69.22	72.82	76.60	78.75	78.45	78.24	83.33
1974		83.73	94.43	96.68	92.40	82.94	79.65	88.60	94.90	95.94	92.45	99.18	97.22	93.63	92.63	96.20	88.37
1975		90.11	84.22	84.24	93.60	92.70	91.21	86.42	83.88	82.83	85.94	83.90	84.40	84.43	87.57	100.40	92.83
1976		96.95	104.41	107.49	111.80	94.28	98.34	98.24	101.49	104.16	107.58	98.17	112.34	111.96	115.65	106.29	113.45
1977		111.28	113.20	111.50	111.86	109.60	108.82	115.41	112.33	112.96	114.31	107.56	108.27	118.67	111.19	109.13	115.25
1978		115.06	113.07	120.37	122.63	121.93	110.27	112.98	113.10	111.54	114.58	119.69	119.24	122.18	123.02	124.21	120.66
1979		126.28	137.14	145.37	146.39	121.08	128.92	128.84	130.52	141.54	139.36	139.87	154.63	141.61	149.84	150.02	139.29
1980		164.88	157.77	150.34	154.46	164.02	168.53	162.09	169.23	154.85	149.25	150.40	153.94	146.70	148.70	158.99	155.70
1981		156.77	167.79	179.71	182.16	153.23	158.22	158.87	162.28	165.35	174.73	175.45	178.62	185.06	178.95	185.76	181.78
1982		182.78	197.46	205.15	210.50	174.13	181.47	192.74	193.49	198.68	200.21	207.73	192.73	214.99	220.70	203.05	207.77
1983		214.05	215.24	221.12		242.36	193.96	205.83	211.52	212.94	221.25	216.07	236.24	211.04	228.47		

Trade balance (f.o.b. — c.i.f.) (19) — Adjusted - Corrigé * — **Balance commerciale** (f.o.b. — c.a.f.) (19)

billion francs, monthly averages — milliards de francs, moyennes mensuelles

	Year	Q.1	Q.2	Q.3	Q.4	JAN	FEB	MAR	APR	MAY	JUN	JUL	AUG	SEP	OCT	NOV	DEC
1964		-1.84	-1.71	-1.08	-0.31	-2.19	-2.22	-1.12	-1.51	-2.05	-1.58	-2.05	0.17	-1.37	-0.10	0.01	-0.85
1965		1.19	-0.75	0.67	0.00	1.03	1.83	0.72	-2.42	-0.73	0.89	-0.51	2.34	0.17	-0.79	-0.04	0.84
1966		-1.99	-0.94	-1.46	-1.30	-2.51	-2.36	-1.12	-1.08	-1.19	-0.53	-1.43	-2.33	-0.63	-1.60	-1.68	-0.61
1967		0.43	-1.13	-0.73	-0.56	0.81	1.43	-0.95	-0.19	-0.26	-2.95	1.98	-3.58	-0.60	2.93	-3.93	-0.70
1968		-0.56	0.12	0.33	-0.51	0.00	-1.07	-0.61	2.09	-1.30	-0.43	1.39	0.50	-0.90	-1.37	-0.59	0.42
1969		0.95	-1.65	-0.14	1.21	5.00	-0.73	-1.42	-1.44	-0.91	-2.59	-0.67	-0.31	0.57	0.59	2.99	0.05
1970		1.26	1.22	-0.09	0.02	3.74	-1.47	1.51	1.18	1.21	1.26	0.08	1.13	-1.47	0.99	-0.26	-0.69
1971		-0.51	-0.38	2.17	-0.92	1.38	-2.90	-0.02	-4.33	1.44	1.77	1.57	-0.86	5.78	-3.40	-0.07	0.70
1972		1.20	1.72	1.56	4.84	2.37	1.50	-0.28	0.49	2.17	2.51	2.35	1.02	1.30	5.21	2.40	6.92
1973		0.65	1.30	2.37	0.63	-3.19	1.91	3.21	3.38	0.29	0.24	1.98	2.32	2.81	0.35	-0.78	2.33
1974		-6.53	-5.14	-4.84	-4.03	-4.05	-11.75	-3.78	-0.77	-5.26	-9.40	-6.49	-2.17	-5.85	-4.21	-0.81	-7.06
1975		-0.03	-6.06	-9.34	-9.17	5.14	0.41	-5.65	-7.15	-5.13	-5.91	-10.14	-3.93	-13.95	-12.98	-4.27	-10.25
1976		-8.12	-9.84	-10.55	-6.03	-10.79	-5.15	-8.41	-12.01	-8.79	-8.71	-17.90	-6.00	-7.74	-3.21	-11.90	-2.99
1977		-10.25	-8.41	-6.71	-10.22	-12.19	-10.90	-7.66	-10.19	-8.33	-6.72	-4.78	-13.40	-1.95	-10.30	-11.47	-8.87
1978		-8.48	-9.83	-8.72	-12.80	-3.53	-13.35	-8.56	-7.73	-12.79	-9.14	-8.93	-9.39	-7.85	-12.25	-11.23	-14.92
1979		-5.83	-9.47	-6.85	-18.59	-3.39	-6.20	-7.91	-8.05	-11.63	-8.72	-7.85	0.25	-12.96	-12.90	-12.97	-29.90
1980		-9.25	-13.88	-16.79	-23.80	-18.09	-8.34	-1.34	-6.21	-14.28	-21.17	-14.92	-4.92	-30.54	-26.23	-19.44	-25.72
1981		-25.06	-17.67	-25.41	-17.49	-26.53	-25.74	-22.92	-21.23	-15.83	-15.95	-27.96	-33.98	-14.29	-17.20	-13.90	-21.36
1982		-25.91	-28.35	-17.14	-16.45	-32.03	-14.20	-31.49	-30.47	-31.75	-22.83	-19.04	-23.91	-8.48	-3.96	-32.15	-13.25
1983		-12.76	-8.41	-2.60		10.85	-28.60	-20.54	-11.21	-7.58	-6.46	-9.21	23.32	-21.91	-23.49		

* Adjusted by the O.E.C.D. — * Corrigé par l'O.C.D.E.

BELGIUM

Balance of payments: net trade (19)(21) — Balance des paiements : balance commerciale (21) (19)

billion francs — milliards de francs

	Year	Q.1	Q.2	Q.3	Q.4	JAN	FEB	MAR	APR	MAY	JUN	JUL	AUG	SEP	OCT	NOV	DEC
1964																	
1965																	
1966																	
1967																	
1968																	
1969																	
1970	39.7	12.3	7.0	7.6	12.8												
1971	34.3	7.0	8.3	10.8	8.2												
1972	56.0	12.8	10.4	15.6	17.2												
1973	51.7	17.5	18.6	7.4	8.2												
1974	24.2	16.5	-5.7	15.5	-2.1												
1975	2.6	7.0	5.5	-11.3	1.4												
1976	-25.7	-5.6	-10.8	-17.6	8.3												
1977	-48.9	-5.9	-17.8	-21.7	-3.5												
1978	-40.4	-8.8	-12.7	-18.2	-0.7												
1979	-73.7	-7.1	-14.5	-17.7	-34.4												
1980	-114.1	-21.6	-30.7	-28.0	-33.8												
1981	-109.3	-27.3	-26.4	-34.9	-20.7												
1982	-91.4	-68.3	-21.4	9.6	-11.3												
1983		-35.5	32.3	19.6													

Balance of payments: current balance (19) — Balance des paiements : opérations courantes, nettes (19)

billion francs — milliards de francs

	Year	Q.1	Q.2	Q.3	Q.4	JAN	FEB	MAR	APR	MAY	JUN	JUL	AUG	SEP	OCT	NOV	DEC
1964																	
1965																	
1966																	
1967																	
1968																	
1969																	
1970	34.1	11.5	6.1	5.7	10.8												
1971	32.5	5.8	6.1	7.5	13.1												
1972	57.6	12.8	10.0	14.1	20.7												
1973	51.8	17.3	13.8	6.0	14.7												
1974	29.5	23.0	-10.5	12.7	4.3												
1975	6.0	12.2	0.6	-15.7	8.9												
1976	15.0	-0.6	-1.5	-8.4	25.5												
1977	-19.9	8.8	-14.5	-18.2	4.0												
1978	-26.4	-0.9	-8.0	-23.3	5.8												
1979	-89.4	-5.7	-14.8	-33.2	-35.7												
1980	-144.4	-29.9	-44.1	-36.4	-34.0												
1981	-155.5	-32.7	-43.7	-44.8	-34.3												
1982	-120.3	-80.7	-29.2	0.3	-10.7												
1983		-53.9	27.4	27.0													

Balance of payments: net capital movements (19) — Balance des paiements : mouvements de capitaux, nets (19)

billion francs — milliards de francs

	Year	Q.1	Q.2	Q.3	Q.4	JAN	FEB	MAR	APR	MAY	JUN	JUL	AUG	SEP	OCT	NOV	DEC
1964																	
1965																	
1966																	
1967																	
1968																	
1969																	
1970	-15.6	-4.4	-2.4	-0.3	-8.5												
1971	-13.4	-2.8	-1.5	-1.1	-8.0												
1972	-40.5	-15.0	-6.9	-10.0	-8.6												
1973	-20.9	-15.6	-8.3	0.9	2.1												
1974	1.6	-5.4	8.3	-2.0	0.7												
1975	4.7	7.6	-9.2	8.8	-2.5												
1976	-5.6	-18.3	14.5	-6.2	4.4												
1977	16.1	11.8	3.7	8.1	-7.5												
1978	-11.2	8.9	-10.5	3.3	-12.9												
1979	-11.8	-11.3	0.6	-3.0	1.9												
1980	60.7	-2.1	41.0	15.3	6.5												
1981	93.4	10.9	49.9	2.4	30.2												
1982	119.2	54.7	34.5	14.1	15.9												
1983		35.0	-23.4	-60.0													

NOTES

1. Original chain index with reference base 1963 to 1969 and 1970 from 1970. 1962 has been used as the weight base to 1966, 1964 from 1967 to 1969, 1966 from 1970 to 1971, 1968 from 1972 to 1973, and 1970 from 1974. Seasonally unadjusted series other than *Total industrial production* are not adjusted for unequal number of working days in the month.
2. Not included in total index.
3. Synthesis of results of several series (excluding price series) covering manufacturing, construction and internal trade, from the survey of the Banque Nationale de Belgique. See *Bulletin de la Banque Nationale de Belgique*, September 1983.
4. From 1970, new index (original base 1970).
5. The original base of the index is 1953 to 1964, 1964 from 1965 to 1968, 1966 for 1969 and 1970 from 1970. From 1981 including chain stores.
6. Monthly data refer to end of period.
7. A change in legislation led to a rise in the level of the series from 1970.
8. Excluding hours paid for but not worked.
9. Data compiled according to the classification of the European Communities from 1971, and the *United Nations' International Standard Industrial Classification* previously. The weighting pattern is based on 1958 to 1966, 1961 from 1967 to 1975, and 1971 from 1976.
10. The weighting pattern is based on 1963 to 1971. From 1972, the weighting pattern is revised each year. Sample enlarged in 1974.
11. From 1971, excluding indirect taxes. From 1974, index (original base 1970) linked on 1970 to previous index.
12. From 1972, new reporting system.
13. Excluding rent before June 1976. Weighting pattern based on 1973-74 from June 1976, linked on March- April 1976 to previous indices (based on 1971, 1966 and 1953), whose weighting patterns were based on number of items.
14. Gross bond and net share issues of corporations operating mainly in Belgium.
15. From 4th quarter 1969, including financing of instalment credit.
16. Last Friday of month.
17. Monthly data refer to beginning of following month in source.

NOTES

1. Indice original en chaîne avec 1963 comme base de référence jusqu'en 1969 et 1970 à partir de 1970. Les années de base de pondération sont 1962 jusqu'en 1966, 1964 de 1967 à 1969, 1966 de 1970 à 1971, 1968 de 1972 à 1973 et 1970 à partir de 1974. Les indices bruts ne sont pas corrigés de l'inégalité du nombre de jours ouvrables à l'exception de l'indice de *Production industrielle totale*.
2. Non compris dans l'indice total.
3. Synthèse des résultats de plusieurs séries (à l'exclusion des séries de prix) couvrant les industries manufacturières, la construction et le commerce intérieur, de l'enquête de la Banque Nationale de Belgique. Voir *Bulletin de la Banque Nationale de Belgique,* septembre 1983.
4. A partir de 1970, nouvel indice (base originale 1970).
5. La base originale de l'indice est 1953 en 1964, 1964 de 1965 à 1968, 1966 en 1969 et 1970 à partir de 1970. A partir de 1981 y compris les magasins populaires.
6. Situation en fin de mois.
7. Une modification dans la législation a entraîné une hausse du niveau de la série à partir de 1970.
8. Non compris les heures payées mais non ouvrées.
9. Les données ont été recueillies d'après la classification des Communautés Européennes à partir de 1971; d'après la *Classification Internationale Type de l'Industrie des Nations Unies* auparavant. La pondération se réfère à 1958 jusqu'en 1966, à 1961 de 1967 à 1975, et à 1971 à partir de 1976.
10. La pondération se réfère à 1963 jusqu'en 1971. A partir de 1972, la pondération est révisée chaque année. Échantillon élargi en 1974.
11. A partir de 1971, non compris les impôts indirects. A partir de 1974, indice (base originale 1970) raccordé sur 1970 à l'indice précédent.
12. A partir de 1972, nouveau système de notification.
13. Avant juin 1976, non compris les loyers. La pondération se réfère à 1973-74 à partir de juin 1976, raccordé sur mars-avril 1976 aux indices précédents (années de base 1971, 1966 et 1953), dont les pondérations se référaient au nombre de produits.
14. Émissions brutes d'obligations et émissions nettes d'actions des sociétés ayant leur principale exploitation en Belgique.
15. A partir du 4e trimestre 1969, y compris le financement des ventes à tempérament.
16. Dernier vendredi du mois.
17. Les données mensuelles concernent, dans la source originale, le début du mois suivant.

NOTES

18. Brussels and Antwerp Stock Exchange. Monthly figures refer to the 25th of the month.
19. Data refer to the Belgo-Luxembourg Economic Union.
20. Including Belgian commercial banks' position vis-à-vis Luxembourg.
21. Calculated partly on a c.i.f. basis.

NOTES

18. Bourses de Bruxelles et d'Anvers. Les données mensuelles se réfèrent au 25 du mois.
19. Données relatives à l'Union Économique Belgo-Luxembourgeoise.
20. Y compris la situation des banques commerciales belges vis-à-vis du Luxembourg.
21. Commerce en partie évalué sur la base c.a.f.

MAIN SOURCES

PRINCIPALES SOURCES

Series	Séries	Sources
Industrial production	Production industrielle	
Labour	Main-d'œuvre	
Consumer prices	Prix à la consommation	Institut national de Statistique
Share prices	Cours des actions	*Bulletin de statistique*
Foreign trade	Commerce extérieur	
Business surveys	Enquêtes de conjoncture	Banque Nationale de Belgique *Enquête sur la conjoncture*
Sales and orders	Ventes et commandes	Institut national de Statistique
Internal trade	Commerce intérieur	*Communiqué hebdomadaire*
Construction	Construction	
Job vacancies	Offres d'emploi	
Hourly earnings	Gains horaires	
Wholesale prices	Prix de gros	Banque nationale de Belgique
Home finance	Finances internes	*Bulletin*
Interest rates	Taux d'intérêts	
Net foreign position of commercial banks	Position extérieure nette des banques commerciales	
Balance of payments	Balance des paiements	
Hourly rates	Taux horaires	Ministère de l'Emploi et du Travail *Revue du Travail*

Denmark — Danemark

DENMARK

Output: animal products (1)
1980 = 100

Production : produits d'origine animale (1)
1980 = 100

	Year	Q.1	Q.2	Q.3	Q.4	JAN	FEB	MAR	APR	MAY	JUN	JUL	AUG	SEP	OCT	NOV	DEC
1964	87	83	92	86	85	84	80	84	92	89	95	87	80	91	82	84	90
1965	90	87	94	90	87	84	84	92	90	90	103	90	90	90	82	90	90
1966	90	91	92	89	88	88	88	97	85	91	100	87	91	88	86	94	84
1967	90	89	96	87	89	85	90	91	91	99	96	84	90	87	90	94	83
1968	89	91	92	86	85	95	89	89	91	97	89	90	84	84	90	84	81
1969	86	83	90	85	84	84	82	84	90	89	91	90	79	86	87	81	84
1970	85	86	90	85	81	86	83	88	90	90	89	84	85	84	82	81	81
1971	86	86	91	85	83	85	85	89	88	92	92	84	85	84	86	82	82
1972	85	82	90	84	82	82	81	83	90	91	90	81	85	85	84	83	78
1973	87	85	93	83	86	83	86	85	89	96	95	81	83	86	86	89	82
1974	88	89	93	84	85	91	86	90	94	91	94	84	85	84	85	87	82
1975	87	85	94	86	84	89	84	82	96	95	92	84	85	87	86	85	82
1976	87	88	93	84	83	85	83	97	91	93	95	81	87	85	81	86	83
1977	89	89	95	86	87	86	82	99	90	97	99	82	91	85	87	90	84
1978	93	88	99	93	92	90	83	92	95	103	98	90	98	90	94	97	84
1979	98	97	102	96	96	99	90	102	97	108	102	96	102	91	102	99	86
1980	100	99	102	100	98	104	94	100	100	99	108	102	97	100	105	94	96
1981	100	100	102	101	97	102	95	104	76	111	118	104	98	101	98	98	96
1982	101	99	102	101	102	99	94	104	98	97	110	97	102	103	100	104	101
1983	105	103	108	105	105	103	98	109	103	109	112	98	110	107	106	109	100

Ships completed
thousand gross register tons, quarterly averages

Navires achevés
milliers de tonneaux de jauge brute, moyennes trimestrielles

	Year	Q.1	Q.2	Q.3	Q.4	JAN	FEB	MAR	APR	MAY	JUN	JUL	AUG	SEP	OCT	NOV	DEC
1964	70	100	55	24	99												
1965	52	59	60	41	49												
1966	118	124	112	85	151												
1967	106	67	150	108	101												
1968	130	154	79	157	128												
1969	148	125	139	153	182												
1970	130	9	148	154	207												
1971	182	143	136	202	197												
1972	238	324	185	227	216												
1973	251	200	334	186	233												
1974	269	179	354	263	249												
1975	242	195	224	256	287												
1976	259	215	282	274	263												
1977	177	132	249	217	110												
1978	86	82	108	83	72												
1979	66	118	49	42	54												
1980	52	75	50	16	67												
1981	88	72	139	52	92												
1982	113	145	79	52	162												
1983	108	138	166	68	61												

Production: crude steel
thousand tons, monthly averages

Production : acier brut
milliers de tonnes, moyennes mensuelles

	Year	Q.1	Q.2	Q.3	Q.4	JAN	FEB	MAR	APR	MAY	JUN	JUL	AUG	SEP	OCT	NOV	DEC
1964																	
1965																	
1966																	
1967																	
1968																	
1969	40	43	39	39	40	44	42	43	32	41	43	41	36	40	40	40	40
1970	39	41	37	40	40	49	42	32	41	33	36	40	40	40	40	40	40
1971	39	42	35	38	42	39	39	49	35	24	46	37	37	41	45	40	40
1972	42	44	41	41	42	46	46	41	40	38	44	39	41	44	46	43	37
1973	38	38	33	36	45	49	39	25	23	42	34	29	45	33	51	48	35
1974	45	46	42	44	47	48	46	44	43	49	33	29	53	49	45	54	43
1975	46	47	45	46	48	42	47	51	42	44	49	36	55	46	45	50	50
1976	60	63	56	51	71	60	62	66	47	64	58	18	64	71	70	73	69
1977	57	72	53	45	59	73	68	75	49	54	55	16	47	71	49	71	57
1978	72	69	76	67	76	76	68	62	79	75	75	35	85	81	88	81	58
1979	67	70	66	58	73	72	68	70	42	81	76	28	70	77	78	79	62
1980	61	83	70	40	51	83	76	91	66	72	73	23	47	50	54	48	51
1981	51	51	46	50	57	57	48	49	48	58	32	33	59	57	62	58	51
1982	47	58	53	32	43	56	56	63	49	57	52	9	59	29	47	45	38
1983	41	39	39	33	54	39	36	42	37	38	41	7	40	52	56	59	46

Production: future tendency — Perspectives de production

mining and manufacturing — industries extractives et manufacturières

per cent balance — solde en pourcentage

Year	Q.1	Q.2	Q.3	Q.4	JAN	FEB	MAR	APR	MAY	JUN	JUL	AUG	SEP	OCT	NOV	DEC
1964	35	25	33	24	35			25			33			24		
1965	31	18	14	1	31			18			14			1		
1966	20	7	21	-7	20			7			21			-7		
1967	4	1	5	3	4			1			5			3		
1968	19	6	31	18	19			6			31			18		
1969	36	20	38	20	36			20			38			20		
1970	33	19	21	-3	33			19			21			-3		
1971	14	6	8	1	14			6			8			1		
1972	19	7	40	29	19			7			40			29		
1973	33	23	37	2	33			23			37			2		
1974	14	-20	-13	-32	14			-20			-13			-32		
1975	3	-12	16	4	3			-12			16			4		
1976	23	7	23	-3	23			7			23			-3		
1977	10	-5	12	-6	10			-5			12			-6		
1978	19	3	20	15	19			3			20			15		
1979	25	-	25	-6	25						25			-6		
1980	14	-12	-4	-20	14			-12			-4			-20		
1981	4	-	7	-16	4						7			-16		
1982	18	-5	19	-11	18			-5			19			-11		
1983	16	-	24	15	16			-			24			15		

Orders inflow: tendency — Commandes : tendance

mining and manufacturing — industries extractives et manufacturières

per cent balance — solde en pourcentage

Year	Q.1	Q.2	Q.3	Q.4	JAN	FEB	MAR	APR	MAY	JUN	JUL	AUG	SEP	OCT	NOV	DEC
1964																
1965																
1966																
1967																
1968																
1969																
1970																
1971																
1972																
1973																
1974																
1975																
1976																
1977																
1978																
1979				23										23		
1980	1	-13	-36	-12	1			-13			-36			-12		
1981	-12	5	8	4	-12			5			8			4		
1982	-8	9	-2	16	-8			9			-2			16		
1983	-11	20	22	27	-11			20			22			27		

Order books or demand: level — Carnet de commandes ou demande globale : niveau

mining and manufacturing — industries extractives et manufacturières

per cent balance — solde en pourcentage

Year	Q.1	Q.2	Q.3	Q.4	JAN	FEB	MAR	APR	MAY	JUN	JUL	AUG	SEP	OCT	NOV	DEC
1964																
1965																
1966																
1967																
1968																
1969																
1970																
1971																
1972																
1973																
1974																
1975																
1976																
1977																
1978																
1979				9										9		
1980	9	-15	-30	-33	9			-15			-30			-33		
1981	-21	-16	-15	-13	-21			-16			-15			-13		
1982	-13	-13	-12	-12	-13			-18			-12			-12		
1983	-9	-	7	22	-9			-			7			22		

DENMARK

Finished goods stocks: level
mining and manufacturing
per cent balance

Stocks de produits finis : niveau
industries extractives et manufacturières
solde en pourcentage

	Year	Q.1	Q.2	Q.3	Q.4	JAN	FEB	MAR	APR	MAY	JUN	JUL	AUG	SEP	OCT	NOV	DEC
1964																	
1965																	
1966																	
1967																	
1968																	
1969																	
1970																	
1971																	
1972																	
1973																	
1974																	
1975																	
1976																	
1977																	
1978																	
1979					2										2		
1980		11	20	21	21	11			20			21			21		
1981		23	12	11	14	23			12			11			14		
1982		16	16	18	10	16			16			18			10		
1983		12	10	4	2	12			10			4			2		

Manufacturing sales: total (2)(3)
(volume)
1980 = 100

Ventes des industries manufacturières : total (2)(3)
(volume)
1980 = 100

	Year	Q.1	Q.2	Q.3	Q.4	JAN	FEB	MAR	APR	MAY	JUN	JUL	AUG	SEP	OCT	NOV	DEC
1964																	
1965																	
1966																	
1967																	
1968																	
1969																	
1970	81	74	83	81	84												
1971	82	79	82	82	87												
1972	89	84	91	86	94												
1973	92	90	90	90	100												
1974	89	94	92	83	86	90	91	101	91	92	91	62	92	94	94	88	76
1975	= 83 =	79	84	80	91	78	79	81	84	81	87	61	85	94	98	90	87
1976	93	89	95	90	97	80	88	100	92	93	102	64	99	107	98	99	93
1977	93	93	92	92	97	86	88	106	84	88	103	61	107	109	99	99	93
1978	96	90	100	93	102	88	86	95	96	97	107	63	108	107	107	105	94
1979	100	93	100	96	109	86	87	108	93	101	107	70	110	107	118	112	99
1980	100	102	101	94	101	98	98	110	99	97	108	73	100	108	108	98	98
1981	99	97	99	98	103	91	93	108	97	93	109	75	105	115	108	104	97
1982	102	100	106	96	106	90	96	113	102	96	119	70	105	113	104	111	103
1983	106	101	108	102	112	93	97	114	99	103	122	70	114	121	110	117	109

Manufacturing sales: investment goods (2)(3)
(volume)
1980 = 100

Ventes des industries manufacturières : biens d'équipement (2)(3)
(volume)
1980 = 100

	Year	Q.1	Q.2	Q.3	Q.4	JAN	FEB	MAR	APR	MAY	JUN	JUL	AUG	SEP	OCT	NOV	DEC
1964																	
1965																	
1966																	
1967																	
1968																	
1969																	
1970	68	61	71	66	74												
1971	71	68	71	67	81												
1972	80	75	83	73	87												
1973	83	80	79	76	98												
1974	84	87	86	76	86	80	84	98	81	84	93	55	82	91	87	86	86
1975	= 76 =	77	75	68	84	72	78	81	73	71	81	49	72	83	81	77	94
1976	86	79	86	80	100	68	76	93	80	79	99	53	85	104	91	94	115
1977	91	92	87	83	101	84	88	105	80	77	105	44	96	108	95	98	111
1978	94	86	91	86	113	82	82	92	86	86	100	50	101	108	105	109	124
1979	99	93	97	88	120	82	88	109	86	93	112	58	102	103	116	115	129
1980	100	104	104	85	108	95	103	115	103	94	114	59	90	105	107	95	121
1981	98	94	100	90	107	82	93	107	99	92	111	63	93	114	104	103	115
1982	101	99	105	89	109	82	99	116	105	90	121	58	99	109	99	109	119
1983	104	101	105	93	119	91	95	118	95	98	123	53	108	119	104	121	132

Judgment on capacity utilization
mining and manufacturing
per cent balance

Appréciation sur l'utilisation des capacités
industries extractives et manufacturières
solde en pourcentage

Year	Q.1	Q.2	Q.3	Q.4	JAN	FEB	MAR	APR	MAY	JUN	JUL	AUG	SEP	OCT	NOV	DEC
1964																
1965																
1966																
1967																
1968																
1969																
1970																
1971																
1972																
1973																
1974																
1975																
1976																
1977																
1978																
1979				-13										13		
1980	-16	-15	-26	-35	-16			-15			-26			-35		
1981	-30	-22	-26	-33	-30			-22			-26			-33		
1982	-30	-30	-33	-32	-30			-30			-33			-32		
1983	-28	-28	-33	-22	-28			-28			-33			-22		

Manufacturing sales: total (2)(3)
(volume)
1980 = 100

Ventes des industries manufacturières : total (2)(3)
(volume)
1980 = 100

Adjusted - Corrigé

Year	Q.1	Q.2	Q.3	Q.4	JAN	FEB	MAR	APR	MAY	JUN	JUL	AUG	SEP	OCT	NOV	DEC
1964																
1965																
1966																
1967																
1968																
1969																
1970	75	81	83	83												
1971	81	80	83	85												
1972	86	89	88	88												
1973	93	88	93	93												
1974	95	91	87	83	98	95	93	92	93	87	90	87	84	87	84	78
1975	80	83	84	83	84	83	74	84	82	82	89	79	84	89	85	89
1976	90	94	94	93	87	93	92	93	93	95	95	92	95	90	94	95
1977	95	90	96	93	93	94	97	85	89	96	91	98	98	91	94	95
1978	92	98	96	98	97	93	87	98	98	98	93	100	95	98	99	97
1979	95	99	99	105	93	93	98	95	103	98	101	103	95	107	106	102
1980	104	100	98	97	106	106	101	103	98	100	103	94	97	98	93	100
1981	99	98	103	99	98	101	99	100	94	101	105	99	103	98	99	100
1982	102	104	100	102	98	103	104	105	98	110	98	99	103	93	106	107
1983	102	105	106	104	102	102	103	101	108	111	101	110	107	100	103	109

Manufacturing sales: investment goods (2)(3)
(volume)
1980 = 100

Ventes des industries manufacturières : biens d'équipement (2)(3)
(volume)
1980 = 100

Adjusted - Corrigé

Year	Q.1	Q.2	Q.3	Q.4	JAN	FEB	MAR	APR	MAY	JUN	JUL	AUG	SEP	OCT	NOV	DEC
1964																
1965																
1966																
1967																
1968																
1969																
1970	63	70	72	69												
1971	70	70	73	74												
1972	76	82	79	80												
1973	80	78	82	90												
1974	88	88	85	78	88	87	89	87	91	85	90	84	80	83	82	70
1975	78	76	76	75	80	81	73	78	76	73	82	73	73	76	73	76
1976	80	88	88	89	76	79	84	86	86	91	89	85	91	86	89	92
1977	93	89	89	90	94	92	94	86	84	95	76	95	95	89	92	89
1978	88	92	94	100	92	87	83	91	95	91	84	102	95	98	102	100
1979	95	98	98	106	92	93	101	90	102	101	98	105	92	107	107	105
1980	108	104	95	95	109	110	104	108	102	103	99	93	93	98	88	99
1981	97	101	101	94	95	99	97	102	99	100	105	97	102	95	95	93
1982	102	105	99	96	95	105	105	108	97	109	98	102	98	89	101	97
1983	104	103	103	106	107	99	105	95	107	107	88	113	107	96	112	111

DENMARK

Manufacturing sales: consumer goods (2)(3)
(volume)
1980 = 100

Ventes des industries manufacturières : biens de consommation (2)(3)
(volume)
1980 = 100

	Year	Q.1	Q.2	Q.3	Q.4	JAN	FEB	MAR	APR	MAY	JUN	JUL	AUG	SEP	OCT	NOV	DEC
1964																	
1965																	
1966																	
1967																	
1968																	
1969																	
1970	83	78	84	84	86												
1971	84	81	83	85	88												
1972	89	85	89	88	94												
1973	92	91	91	92	96												
1974	89	92	90	86	88	90	90	97	91	91	87	68	95	95	97	90	76
1975	87	82	86	86	94	83	82	83	89	83	86	70	92	97	103	92	85
1976	93	91	95	93	93	84	90	100	92	92	99	74	104	103	98	97	84
1977	92	93	88	95	94	87	89	102	82	87	97	72	108	105	98	97	88
1978	94	89	95	94	97	88	86	94	91	95	99	74	104	104	103	100	87
1979	97	94	97	97	101	89	88	104	91	101	98	79	109	104	110	104	90
1980	100	101	98	100	100	98	97	109	95	96	104	85	104	110	110	98	92
1981	104	102	99	106	106	98	97	111	95	92	109	89	112	117	114	109	96
1982	108	106	109	105	111	101	100	117	103	102	123	84	112	119	112	116	106
1983	110	107	112	110	114	98	104	119	104	110	122	86	118	124	113	118	110

Manufacturing sales: intermediate goods (2)(3)
(volume)
1980 = 100

Ventes des industries manufacturières : biens intermédiaires (2)(3)
(volume)
1980 = 100

	Year	Q.1	Q.2	Q.3	Q.4	JAN	FEB	MAR	APR	MAY	JUN	JUL	AUG	SEP	OCT	NOV	DEC
1964																	
1965																	
1966																	
1967																	
1968																	
1969																	
1970	87	76	92	90	92												
1971	90	86	93	89	91												
1972	97	90	101	94	101												
1973	101	100	101	100	108												
1974	94	105	101	85	85	101	101	112	101	105	98	61	98	96	99	88	69
1975	86	77	88	81	95	76	77	79	86	85	93	57	87	100	103	96	85
1976	98	95	104	94	101	86	92	106	99	102	110	60	106	115	106	109	89
1977	99	97	102	96	100	89	90	114	92	97	116	58	113	116	106	107	88
1978	102	94	114	96	104	95	88	99	110	109	122	57	118	113	113	113	86
1979	105	93	110	102	114	86	86	107	103	110	117	68	122	116	131	122	90
1980	100	102	106	94	98	99	96	110	104	102	111	68	104	111	109	101	85
1981	97	94	102	95	96	88	89	105	100	96	111	67	105	115	105	99	84
1982	96	92	102	92	98	80	87	108	99	93	113	59	102	115	99	108	86
1983	101	94	106	98	105	89	89	105	96	100	121	62	115	119	111	113	92

Manufacturing new orders, net: total (2)(4)
1980 = 100

Commandes nouvelles nettes (industries (2)(4)
manufacturières) : total
1980 = 100

	Year	Q.1	Q.2	Q.3	Q.4	JAN	FEB	MAR	APR	MAY	JUN	JUL	AUG	SEP	OCT	NOV	DEC
1964																	
1965																	
1966																	
1967																	
1968																	
1969																	
1970																	
1971																	
1972																	
1973																	
1974	57	59	58	52	58	58	55	62	59	59	54	42	56	59	63	59	52
1975	58	54	57	55	66	55	54	52	59	56	58	45	57	63	72	64	62
1976	69	68	70	67	72	63	65	76	68	70	72	53	70	78	74	74	70
1977	74	72	73	73	77	68	67	82	70	72	78	53	81	84	78	81	72
1978	81	76	83	77	86	76	70	83	82	83	85	58	87	87	90	86	82
1979	91	84	91	89	100	79	78	96	86	94	94	71	99	96	110	103	88
1980	100	104	101	94	102	103	98	111	102	98	105	79	98	104	108	102	97
1981	114	110	112	113	121	105	103	122	107	109	121	94	118	125	126	121	114
1982	127	125	127	122	135	116	116	143	121	121	139	95	131	141	133	143	129
1983	141	132	143	138	153	126	124	147	135	141	153	102	151	160	153	157	151

Manufacturing sales: consumer goods (2)(3) / Ventes des industries manufacturières : biens de consommation (2)(3)

(volume)

1980 = 100

Adjusted - Corrigé

	Year	Q.1	Q.2	Q.3	Q.4	JAN	FEB	MAR	APR	MAY	JUN	JUL	AUG	SEP	OCT	NOV	DEC
1964																	
1965																	
1966																	
1967																	
1968																	
1969																	
1970		80	84	84	84												
1971		83	84	86	85												
1972		87	89	89	91												
1973		92	91	93	93												
1974		92	93	87	86	94	92	90	93	92	92	87	87	86	90	86	84
1975		83	86	87	92	87	84	77	90	85	83	90	84	88	95	89	93
1976		92	95	94	92	88	95	93	95	94	96	94	95	93	91	93	91
1977		93	89	95	93	92	93	94	84	89	93	91	98	96	91	93	96
1978		90	96	94	95	93	90	86	95	97	96	92	96	94	95	97	95
1979		95	98	97	100	93	93	97	96	104	95	97	100	94	102	100	98
1980		102	100	99	99	103	104	99	100	98	101	104	95	100	100	95	102
1981		102	100	106	105	103	103	102	100	95	105	107	104	107	104	105	106
1982		106	110	105	111	105	106	107	109	104	118	102	104	109	103	112	117
1983		106	113	110	113	102	109	109	110	114	117	108	111	112	104	114	119

Manufacturing sales: intermediate goods (2)(3) / Ventes des industries manufacturières : biens intermédiaires (2)(3)

(volume)

1980 = 100

Adjusted - Corrigé

	Year	Q.1	Q.2	Q.3	Q.4	JAN	FEB	MAR	APR	MAY	JUN	JUL	AUG	SEP	OCT	NOV	DEC
1964																	
1965																	
1966																	
1967																	
1968																	
1969																	
1970		80	88	92	91												
1971		89	89	92	90												
1972		92	97	97	100												
1973		102	97	103	106												
1974		108	96	90	83	111	108	104	100	102	87	97	90	85	88	83	78
1975		80	84	86	93	83	82	74	86	82	83	92	80	87	93	90	97
1976		97	98	98	99	93	100	99	97	99	97	96	96	102	95	101	102
1977		101	96	99	98	97	99	106	91	95	102	94	102	103	95	98	101
1978		99	107	99	101	105	98	92	109	106	107	91	106	99	102	103	99
1979		97	104	106	111	95	97	101	102	108	103	106	110	102	118	113	103
1980		107	100	98	96	109	108	103	103	100	98	103	94	97	97	93	97
1981		99	97	99	94	97	100	98	97	94	98	101	96	100	94	92	97
1982		96	96	94	96	89	98	101	97	92	101	89	92	101	88	100	100
1983		98	100	101	104	100	98	97	93	100	106	95	106	101	101	106	106

Manufacturing new orders, net: investment goods (2)(4) / Commandes nouvelles nettes (industries manufacturières) : biens d'équipement (2)(4)

1980 = 100

	Year	Q.1	Q.2	Q.3	Q.4	JAN	FEB	MAR	APR	MAY	JUN	JUL	AUG	SEP	OCT	NOV	DEC
1964																	
1965																	
1966																	
1967																	
1968																	
1969																	
1970																	
1971																	
1972																	
1973																	
1974	56	62	59	49	54	61	59	67	62	59	56	37	56	56	58	56	48
1975	54	55	50	48	63	59	60	47	57	43	49	35	50	57	64	61	62
1976	70	71	67	66	78	62	69	81	67	62	71	48	65	84	75	76	84
1977	74	75	70	70	82	73	68	83	67	66	77	41	82	87	77	86	82
1978	84	82	81	77	96	81	72	94	77	78	88	46	97	88	93	93	101
1979	96	89	93	91	110	84	82	101	87	92	101	63	111	98	116	107	107
1980	100	112	100	84	103	118	108	109	104	94	104	65	92	96	103	102	104
1981	112	110	112	102	122	104	109	118	101	115	121	78	113	116	123	121	122
1982	126	134	119	113	130	112	129	160	108	115	136	86	123	131	124	145	144
1983	145	140	140	133	168	126	143	151	136	130	154	75	158	166	148	174	182

DENMARK

Manufacturing new orders, net: (2)(4) — **Commandes nouvelles nettes** (industries manufacturières) : biens de consommation (2)(4)

consumer goods

1980 = 100

	Year	Q.1	Q.2	Q.3	Q.4	JAN	FEB	MAR	APR	MAY	JUN	JUL	AUG	SEP	OCT	NOV	DEC
1964																	
1965																	
1966																	
1967																	
1968																	
1969																	
1970																	
1971																	
1972																	
1973																	
1974	55	55	56	52	58	55	51	59	58	58	51	44	54	57	62	61	50
1975	60	54	60	58	67	54	54	54	61	61	59	51	60	64	75	66	60
1976	69	66	72	68	72	62	62	73	68	74	73	57	71	76	77	74	64
1977	75	71	76	76	78	67	65	81	72	77	79	63	81	84	81	82	71
1978	83	77	86	82	86	75	71	84	95	87	86	69	86	91	92	87	79
1979	89	83	91	88	94	78	77	95	87	96	90	75	95	94	106	98	80
1980	100	100	99	99	104	98	92	110	98	97	102	85	102	108	116	101	95
1981	116	110	110	121	123	104	100	125	105	105	119	104	126	134	134	122	114
1982	131	126	131	128	139	120	116	141	124	126	143	104	137	144	142	146	130
1983	143	131	144	144	154	122	122	150	135	145	153	117	150	164	158	156	147

Manufacturing new orders, net: (2)(4) — **Commandes nouvelles nettes** (industries manufacturières) : biens intermédiaires (2)(4)

intermediate goods

1980 = 100

	Year	Q.1	Q.2	Q.3	Q.4	JAN	FEB	MAR	APR	MAY	JUN	JUL	AUG	SEP	OCT	NOV	DEC
1964																	
1965																	
1966																	
1967																	
1968																	
1969																	
1970																	
1971																	
1972																	
1973																	
1974	57	59	57	52	59	60	56	63	58	59	55	42	55	60	66	55	55
1975	56	50	55	53	64	52	50	50	54	53	58	41	55	62	68	62	63
1976	66	67	67	62	68	63	63	75	66	67	68	45	67	75	67	71	67
1977	69	71	70	67	71	65	67	80	67	67	77	45	76	81	71	74	67
1978	74	71	79	69	79	72	67	74	79	77	81	46	82	77	82	81	73
1979	91	81	90	89	103	78	75	91	84	91	96	69	99	98	111	109	89
1980	100	105	105	90	98	103	101	112	106	101	109	76	93	101	97	103	96
1981	111	109	115	104	115	104	104	117	112	111	122	87	108	118	116	117	111
1982	121	116	124	117	126	111	104	133	123	114	134	87	124	141	126	136	118
1983	136	128	142	131	144	133	114	138	133	142	151	92	148	151	146	148	136

Construction permits issued: dwellings (5)(6) — **Permis de construire délivrés** : logements (5)(6)

thousands, monthly averages — milliers, moyennes mensuelles

	Year	Q.1	Q.2	Q.3	Q.4	JAN	FEB	MAR	APR	MAY	JUN	JUL	AUG	SEP	OCT	NOV	DEC
1964	1.69	1.46	1.23	1.97	2.10	1.69	1.15	1.55	1.33	1.16	1.19	2.00	1.26	2.64	1.64	2.17	2.48
1965	1.72	1.54	2.03	1.80	1.52	0.97	0.96	2.68	1.45	1.74	2.91	1.31	2.58	1.50	1.16	2.28	1.14
1966	2.09	1.91	2.63	2.13	1.71	1.73	1.50	2.50	1.92	2.42	3.54	1.36	2.27	2.76	1.39	2.58	1.05
1967	2.08	1.56	2.88	1.83	2.05	1.77	1.11	1.78	2.26	2.83	3.55	2.02	2.02	1.45	1.46	1.82	2.88
1968	2.10	1.80	2.21	2.12	2.29	2.12	0.90	2.37	1.86	1.96	2.81	2.59	1.38	2.38	2.04	0.78	4.05
1969	2.56	1.81	2.61	3.53	2.28	1.91	1.34	2.18	2.90	1.87	3.07	4.26	2.97	3.36	2.86	2.35	1.63
1970	2.59	3.20	2.60	3.07	1.48	4.84	2.34	2.42	1.68	1.93	4.20	3.00	3.26	2.97	2.06	1.17	1.21
1971	2.64	2.10	2.56	3.20	2.70	2.31	1.62	2.39	2.67	1.85	3.15	2.51	4.27	2.30	3.68	2.32	2.12
1972	2.93	2.59	4.00	2.51	2.64	1.68	3.85	2.24	3.00	3.63	5.37	1.53	2.64	3.35	2.47	2.58	2.86
1973	4.28	5.21	4.29	3.88	3.72	4.25	4.79	6.60	3.93	4.73	4.21	3.12	3.86	4.66	4.85	2.83	3.47
1974	2.02	2.70	2.58	1.43	1.38	3.10	2.41	2.59	3.29	1.69	2.76	1.11	1.22	1.94	1.69	1.07	1.38
1975	2.70	1.93	2.86	2.61	3.40	1.92	1.72	2.14	2.38	2.93	3.26	2.27	2.36	3.18	3.56	3.46	3.18
1976	2.92	4.36	2.22	2.43	2.65	3.12	3.22	6.73	1.61	1.91	3.16	2.10	2.25	2.93	2.06	2.91	2.98
1977	3.00	3.28	2.99	2.91	2.82	4.90	1.48	3.47	2.58	2.69	3.69	2.30	3.00	3.43	2.66	3.09	2.71
1978	2.71	2.23	3.45	2.67	2.47	2.72	1.53	2.43	3.68	3.17	3.50	2.18	2.76	3.09	2.51	2.40	2.56
1979	2.64	2.23	3.11	2.91	2.30	2.65	1.75	2.28	2.67	3.01	3.66	2.66	2.89	3.17	2.81	2.04	2.04
1980	1.96	2.14	2.39	1.67	1.64	1.54	2.09	2.78	1.99	2.88	2.30	1.87	1.51	1.63	1.92	1.58	1.42
1981	1.71	1.53	2.07	1.83	1.40	1.29	1.16	2.13	2.15	2.43	1.64	1.82	1.72	1.95	1.66	1.44	1.12
1982	1.53	1.16	1.83	1.35	1.83	0.82	1.10	1.57	1.95	1.86	1.69	1.13	1.42	1.51	1.84	1.91	1.73
1983	2.08	1.43	2.52	1.89	1.79	0.82	1.29	2.18	1.43	3.42	2.71	1.99	2.06	1.61	1.80	1.67	1.89

Construction, buildings started: total (6) / Construction, bâtiments mis en chantier : total (6)

million square metres, quarterly averages / millions de mètres carrés, moyennes trimestrielles

	Year	Q.1	Q.2	Q.3	Q.4	JAN	FEB	MAR	APR	MAY	JUN	JUL	AUG	SEP	OCT	NOV	DEC
1964	1.61	1.35	1.64	1.61	1.86												
1965	1.52	1.44	1.83	1.36	1.47												
1966	1.83	1.52	2.03	2.02	1.75												
1967	1.84	1.53	2.11	2.05	1.69												
1968	1.74	1.36	1.71	2.07	1.80												
1969	2.58	2.29	2.91	2.85	2.27												
1970	2.41	2.31	2.46	2.85	2.01												
1971	2.52	1.98	2.61	3.03	2.47												
1972	3.33	2.56	4.79	2.80	3.16												
1973	3.24	3.54	3.48	3.22	2.74												
1974	2.07	2.52	2.35	1.85	1.55												
1975	2.21	1.62	2.19	2.25	2.76												
1976	2.72	3.48	2.46	2.52	2.43												
1977	2.61	2.33	2.91	2.77	2.45												
1978	2.66	0.95	3.16	2.83	2.35												
1979	2.53	1.98	3.07	2.75	2.34												
1980	1.94	1.89	2.58	1.87	1.42												
1981	1.42	1.26	1.81	1.51	1.09												
1982	1.32	1.04	1.68	1.42	1.12												
1983		0.99	1.77	1.66													

Construction: housing starts (6) / Construction : logements mis en chantier (6)

thousands, monthly averages / milliers, moyennes mensuelles

	Year	Q.1	Q.2	Q.3	Q.4	JAN	FEB	MAR	APR	MAY	JUN	JUL	AUG	SEP	OCT	NOV	DEC
1964	3.7	3.2	3.9	3.8	4.0												
1965	3.5	3.5	4.5	2.7	3.2												
1966	4.1	3.8	4.3	4.6	4.0												
1967	3.8	3.0	4.4	4.7	3.1												
1968	3.7	2.9	3.8	4.6	3.5												
1969	4.5	4.2	4.8	5.2	3.8												
1970	3.7	3.5	3.9	4.8	2.7												
1971	3.9	3.0	4.3	4.6	3.8												
1972	5.3	4.1	7.7	4.4	5.0												
1973	4.2	5.3	4.3	3.8	3.5	4.7	3.9	7.2	3.9	4.7	4.3	2.7	3.5	5.1	4.9	3.0	2.5
1974	2.1	2.8	2.5	1.8	1.5	2.5	2.8	3.0	2.8	2.1	2.5	1.7	1.8	2.0	1.6	1.6	1.3
1975	2.8	2.0	2.9	2.8	3.5	1.4	2.6	2.1	2.3	2.4	3.9	2.5	2.5	3.4	3.5	2.8	4.3
1976	3.0	4.1	2.7	2.6	2.6	2.8	2.8	6.6	2.1	2.1	3.8	1.9	2.7	3.2	2.1	2.6	3.2
1977	2.9	2.5	3.4	3.0	2.7	2.0	1.7	3.6	3.1	2.9	4.0	1.8	3.8	3.4	2.9	2.9	2.5
1978	2.8	2.5	3.4	2.9	2.5	2.8	2.0	2.7	3.3	3.2	3.8	2.3	3.4	3.0	2.9	2.5	2.1
1979	2.6	2.0	3.2	2.8	2.4	1.4	1.4	3.4	3.0	3.3	3.3	2.3	2.9	3.0	2.6	2.2	2.3
1980	1.9	1.8	2.4	1.8	1.6	1.7	1.5	2.0	2.5	2.0	2.6	1.8	1.8	1.9	1.8	1.4	1.8
1981	1.6	1.3	2.0	1.8	1.3	1.4	1.2	1.4	2.3	1.9	1.7	1.5	1.9	1.9	1.6	1.4	0.9
1982	1.4	1.0	1.8	1.6	1.4	1.0	1.1	0.9	2.4	1.5	1.5	1.4	1.8	1.5	1.4	1.6	1.3
1983	2.0	1.4	2.1	2.3	1.9	1.4	0.9	1.8	1.4	2.7	2.3	1.5	3.2	2.1	2.1	1.6	1.9

Construction, work in progress: total (6) / Construction, travaux en cours : total (6)

million square metres, end of period / millions de mètres carrés, fin de période

	Year	Q.1	Q.2	Q.3	Q.4	JAN	FEB	MAR	APR	MAY	JUN	JUL	AUG	SEP	OCT	NOV	DEC
1964	7.95	7.29	7.68	7.68	7.95												
1965	8.20	8.17	8.87	8.48	8.20												
1966	9.75	8.50	9.16	9.65	9.75												
1967	10.33	9.83	10.35	10.55	10.33												
1968	10.71	10.16	10.30	10.78	10.71												
1969	11.99	10.98	11.87	12.47	11.99												
1970	11.57	11.93	11.99	12.52	11.57												
1971	11.43	10.92	11.08	11.64	11.43												
1972	14.13	11.62	13.98	14.13	14.13												
1973	15.24	14.85	15.65	15.74	15.24												
1974	11.27	14.64	13.91	12.76	11.27												
1975	10.63	10.36	10.40	10.32	10.63												
1976	10.98	11.67	11.66	11.51	10.98												
1977	10.51	10.49	10.88	11.13	10.51												
1978	10.85	10.37	11.14	11.31	10.85												
1979	11.38	10.65	11.66	11.84	11.38												
1980	9.44	11.28	11.15	10.58	9.44												
1981	7.67	8.50	8.52	8.30	7.67												
1982	6.50	6.98	7.08	7.05	6.50												
1983		5.96	6.41	6.77													

DENMARK

Construction, work in progress: dwellings (5)(6) — Construction, travaux en cours : logements (5)(6)

thousands, end of period — milliers, fin de période

	Year	Q.1	Q.2	Q.3	Q.4	JAN	FEB	MAR	APR	MAY	JUN	JUL	AUG	SEP	OCT	NOV	DEC
1964	24.28	22.49	23.25	23.24	24.28	22.42	21.98	22.49	23.15	23.60	23.25	23.16	23.53	23.24	23.92	24.33	24.28
1965	25.53	24.66	26.32	25.21	25.53	24.28	23.98	24.66	24.97	24.66	26.32	26.36	26.31	25.21	24.82	25.68	25.53
1966	31.43	26.48	27.04	30.07	31.43	25.89	25.93	26.48	25.50	26.33	27.04	27.62	29.47	30.07	30.88	32.44	31.43
1967	33.52	30.37	30.91	34.02	33.52	31.45	31.41	30.37	30.74	31.50	30.91	31.90	32.92	34.02	34.73	33.99	33.52
1968	31.61	32.09	32.09	33.39	31.61	33.38	33.35	32.09	32.64	32.41	32.09	32.40	33.12	33.39	33.63	32.39	31.61
1969	40.21	40.86	40.84	43.44	40.21	41.10	40.95	40.86	40.65	40.76	40.84	41.89	42.32	43.44	43.08	43.09	40.21
1970	36.35	37.61	39.66	42.12	36.35	39.19	38.89	37.61	41.51	40.84	39.66	39.52	40.26	42.12	41.25	39.51	36.35
1971	33.87	32.85	32.87	35.94	33.87	36.31	34.03	32.85	32.85	32.90	32.87	33.63	34.49	35.94	36.52	36.16	33.87
1972	38.77	33.19	39.22	38.56	38.77	33.48	33.12	33.19	33.46	34.83	39.22	39.03	38.54	38.56	40.50	40.08	38.77
1973	61.25	68.70	68.33	64.42	61.25	66.49	66.26	68.70	68.81	69.56	68.33	67.33	66.46	64.42	65.62	63.90	61.25
1974	38.36	56.98	51.74	45.51	38.36	60.14	59.05	56.98	55.37	54.01	51.74	49.51	47.73	45.51	43.35	41.16	38.36
1975	36.47	34.99	34.80	34.94	36.47	36.45	35.89	34.99	35.06	34.97	34.80	34.99	35.28	34.94	35.38	35.93	36.47
1976	33.18	38.67	37.60	35.55	33.18	36.95	36.27	38.67	38.50	37.52	37.60	36.92	36.65	35.55	35.18	34.42	33.18
1977	31.55	31.13	32.56	33.46	31.55	32.15	31.26	31.13	31.94	32.36	32.56	32.32	33.60	33.46	33.54	32.61	31.55
1978	31.09	30.60	32.48	33.01	31.09	31.58	31.11	30.60	31.62	32.38	32.48	32.76	33.23	33.01	32.87	32.59	31.09
1979	31.04	30.21	32.85	32.86	31.04	30.00	29.30	30.21	31.25	32.22	32.85	33.11	33.42	32.86	32.88	31.83	31.04
1980	23.71	28.45	27.42	25.70	23.71	30.11	29.33	28.45	28.29	27.94	27.42	27.44	26.43	25.70	25.23	24.31	23.71
1981	20.50	21.55	22.39	22.60	20.50	23.11	22.57	21.55	22.41	22.97	22.39	22.49	22.93	22.60	22.36	22.13	20.50
1982	17.31	18.74	18.72	18.87	17.31	20.11	19.85	18.74	19.31	19.22	18.72	18.79	19.09	18.87	18.69	18.06	17.31
1983	16.27	15.75	16.80	17.95	16.27	17.16	16.69	15.75	16.09	16.94	16.80	16.62	18.03	17.95	17.52	17.02	16.27

Retail sales: value (7) — Ventes au détail : valeur (7)

1980 = 100

	Year	Q.1	Q.2	Q.3	Q.4	JAN	FEB	MAR	APR	MAY	JUN	JUL	AUG	SEP	OCT	NOV	DEC
1964	21	19	20	21	24	19	18	19	19	21	20	21	21	21	22	20	29
1965	23	20	23	23	27	21	19	21	22	23	23	24	23	22	24	24	33
1966	25	23	25	26	29	24	21	23	24	25	25	26	26	25	25	25	36
1967	28	25	29	27	31	25	23	26	25	29	33	25	28	28	27	27	38
1968	30	28	29	30	35	28	26	29	28	31	28	30	31	29	31	31	42
1969	33	30	32	33	38	31	27	31	31	34	32	34	34	33	35	33	47
1970	37	33	37	37	42	35	31	34	35	38	37	39	36	36	39	36	51
1971	40	35	39	40	46	37	33	36	40	40	39	42	40	40	42	40	55
1972	44	39	43	45	50	38	37	42	41	44	44	44	45	46	44	44	61
1973	50	44	48	50	58	45	40	46	45	48	50	50	52	50	52	52	69
1974	55	49	54	55	62	51	46	51	53	57	52	56	57	52	56	57	72
1975	62	55	60	62	73	58	52	56	58	62	60	63	62	59	69	64	86
1976	71	65	68	71	81	67	67	61	68	66	70	75	70	70	73	72	99
1977	80	71	77	83	89	71	67	73	76	74	80	81	83	86	76	81	111
1978	86	78	83	86	97	81	71	83	80	85	85	84	85	89	85	89	117
1979	93	84	90	92	107	88	78	86	85	93	93	93	96	87	96	99	125
1980	100	91	97	99	114	94	87	92	93	101	96	103	102	93	105	101	135
1981	109	96	105	109	125	105	88	96	105	107	103	117	107	102	116	108	151
1982	121	107	118	119	138	111	99	110	118	118	118	126	117	115	124	124	167
1983	129	118	125	132	151	119	107	127	120	124	130	135	131	131	132	137	183

Retail sales: durable goods (7) — Ventes au détail : biens durables (7)

1980 = 100

	Year	Q.1	Q.2	Q.3	Q.4	JAN	FEB	MAR	APR	MAY	JUN	JUL	AUG	SEP	OCT	NOV	DEC
1964	25	21	23	25	31	22	20	21	22	24	23	25	26	25	26	24	42
1965	28	25	26	28	34	24	24	26	26	26	26	28	30	27	28	27	48
1966	30	27	27	31	37	27	25	28	27	27	28	29	33	30	28	30	52
1967	33	29	34	31	37	29	27	30	30	33	40	28	33	32	30	31	51
1968	34	32	30	34	42	31	30	34	28	32	28	33	37	33	34	34	57
1969	38	34	34	39	47	36	31	34	33	36	34	38	39	39	40	38	64
1970	43	38	41	42	49	43	37	36	39	42	43	44	43	40	43	40	66
1971	46	41	42	45	55	43	38	41	42	42	44	45	46	45	47	46	73
1972	52	44	46	53	62	44	43	46	44	48	47	49	58	54	52	53	82
1973	58	53	50	60	70	60	47	52	47	52	51	56	65	59	64	62	86
1974	61	58	58	61	70	64	54	56	56	66	52	61	64	59	61	61	87
1975	71	62	61	67	91	71	58	58	64	63	57	68	69	65	83	77	114
1976	80	80	67	78	93	83	95	61	66	68	68	80	79	75	78	82	118
1977	85	76	74	93	97	82	71	76	74	72	75	85	97	98	77	85	129
1978	85	78	76	92	96	93	70	73	74	75	78	87	93	97	80	88	120
1979	98	86	88	99	117	96	76	87	84	92	89	99	108	92	98	106	147
1980	100	95	90	98	116	105	89	90	87	88	94	99	101	93	99	99	151
1981	106	98	96	107	124	111	88	94	95	98	96	113	108	100	108	106	158
1982	120	109	111	120	141	115	102	109	112	108	112	121	123	115	120	125	177
1983	138	118	117	132	153	131	106	117	112	117	121	128	139	129	125	136	198

Cost of construction: multiple dwellings (8)
1980 = 100

Coût de la construction : immeubles résidentiels (8)
1980 = 100

	Year	Q.1	Q.2	Q.3	Q.4	JAN	FEB	MAR	APR	MAY	JUN	JUL	AUG	SEP	OCT	NOV	DEC
1964	25	24	25	25	26	24			25			25			26		
1965	28	26	28	28	29	26			28			28			29		
1966	30	29	30	30	30	29			30			30			30		
1967	32	30	31	32	33	30			31			32			33		
1968	34	33	34	34	34	=33=			34			34			34		
1969	36	34	35	35	37	34			35			35			37		
1970	38	37	38	38	39	37			38			38			39		
1971	40	39	39	40	41	39			39			40			41		
1972	43	41	42	43	43	41			42			43			43		
1973	48	44	46	48	51	44			46			48			51		
1974	58	54	56	58	61	54			56			58			61		
1975	65	62	64	65	66	62			64			65			66		
1976	69	66	68	69	71	66			68			69			71		
1977	75	72	74	75	77	72			74			75			77		
1978	81	77	80	81	82	77			80			81			82		
1979	87	83	85	88	92	83			85			88			92		
1980	100	94	97	100	103	94			97			100			103		
1981	112	104	109	110	117	104			109			110			117		
1982	123	118	121	124	128	118			121			124			128		
1983	134	130	134	135	137	130			134			135			137		

Retail sales: value (7)
1980 = 100

Adjusted - Corrigé

Ventes au détail : valeur (7)
1980 = 100

	Year	Q.1	Q.2	Q.3	Q.4	JAN	FEB	MAR	APR	MAY	JUN	JUL	AUG	SEP	OCT	NOV	DEC
1964		20	21	21	22	20	20	20	21	21	21	21	21	22	22	22	22
1965		22	23	23	24	22	22	22	23	23	23	23	23	24	24	24	24
1966		25	25	26	26	25	25	25	25	25	25	25	26	26	26	26	26
1967		27	28	28	28	27	27	27	27	28	28	28	28	28	28	29	29
1968		30	29	31	32	29	29	31	29	29	29	30	32	30	31	31	32
1969		32	33	34	35	32	32	33	33	32	33	34	34	34	34	35	35
1970		36	37	37	38	36	36	36	36	37	38	38	37	38	38	38	38
1971		38	40	41	42	38	39	38	40	40	40	40	41	42	42	42	41
1972		42	44	46	46	41	42	44	44	44	44	45	45	47	45	46	46
1973		47	48	51	53	47	47	48	48	48	49	50	51	53	52	52	54
1974		53	55	56	57	53	53	53	55	56	54	55	56	56	56	57	57
1975		60	61	62	67	59	60	60	61	61	62	63	62	62	68	66	67
1976		69	69	72	74	67	76	65	70	68	71	71	71	73	73	73	75
1977		76	77	83	81	75	76	77	76	76	80	80	83	88	78	83	83
1978		84	84	87	89	85	81	85	85	85	83	85	85	91	86	90	91
1979		90	92	94	96	91	89	89	90	94	92	94	94	94	96	97	96
1980		97	99	101	103	96	96	99	99	100	99	102	102	99	103	103	103
1981		104	108	111	112	104	104	104	110	107	106	113	109	110	111	111	113
1982		117	120	121	124	114	118	118	120	119	122	120	121	123	122	125	124
1983		128	127	135	135	124	126	135	121	127	132	132	133	139	132	138	135

Retail sales: durable goods (7)
1980 = 100

Adjusted - Corrigé

Ventes au détail : biens durables (7)
1980 = 100

	Year	Q.1	Q.2	Q.3	Q.4	JAN	FEB	MAR	APR	MAY	JUN	JUL	AUG	SEP	OCT	NOV	DEC
1964																	
1965																	
1966																	
1967																	
1968		33	33	35	36	33	33	33	33	33	31	34	35	35	35	35	37
1969		37	37	39	41	36	36	37	37	37	37	39	39	41	40	41	41
1970		41	44	43	43	42	43	40	43	44	46	44	43	42	43	43	43
1971		44	46	46	47	43	45	44	46	45	48	45	46	46	48	47	47
1972		47	51	53	54	45	47	49	50	50	51	52	53	53	53	54	55
1973		55	55	61	61	55	54	55	55	55	56	59	61	62	63	61	60
1974		62	64	61	61	61	62	61	63	70	60	62	61	61	60	60	61
1975		65	68	68	79	66	65	65	72	67	67	69	68	67	82	79	76
1976		83	76	78	79	76	108	66	75	77	77	79	78	77	78	81	78
1977		81	83	93	83	78	81	83	82	82	85	85	94	99	79	85	85
1978		83	86	92	83	87	81	81	86	85	87	89	89	97	81	86	81
1979		92	99	99	101	90	91	94	97	103	98	99	100	97	99	102	101
1980		101	101	97	100	99	101	101	99	97	107	97	96	97	99	100	101
1981		104	107	106	107	102	105	105	106	109	107	108	105	106	108	107	107
1982		116	121	120	122	111	120	118	121	120	123	117	121	122	123	124	120
1983		126	128	132	133	128	124	126	122	129	132	127	134	135	130	134	134

DENMARK

Retail sales: volume (7) / Ventes au détail : volume (7)

1980 = 100

Adjusted - Corrigé

	Year	Q.1	Q.2	Q.3	Q.4	JAN	FEB	MAR	APR	MAY	JUN	JUL	AUG	SEP	OCT	NOV	DEC
1964																	
1965																	
1966																	
1967																	
1968	75	74	73	75	73	74	74	75	73	73	72	74	75	75	77	77	79
1969	81	79	79	82	84	78	78	81	80	78	80	81	81	83	84	84	84
1970	85	85	86	85	86	85	84	84	84	87	87	86	84	84	86	85	87
1971	88	86	88	89	90	86	87	86	90	98	87	88	89	90	91	90	88
1972	92	90	91	94	92	87	90	93	92	91	91	92	93	96	91	92	93
1973	95	94	93	96	96	94	93	93	93	92	94	94	96	98	96	95	96
1974	93	94	94	92	91	95	95	93	96	96	91	93	93	91	91	90	90
1975	96	94	94	94	103	93	94	93	94	93	94	96	94	93	107	103	103
1976	=101=	105	100	102	99	104	116	93	100	97	103	103	102	100	99	99	100
1977	101	102	101	105	97	101	102	102	100	99	103	102	105	110	94	99	99
1978	100	99	99	101	100	101	96	100	99	99	98	99	98	105	98	101	102
1979	102	101	103	102	102	102	101	100	101	105	102	104	102	100	102	102	101
1980	=100=	101	101	99	100	100	100	102	101	101	100	101	100	97	100	100	100
1981	99	100	99	100	98	101	100	98	102	99	96	103	98	98	98	97	99
1982	101	101	102	101	101	99	102	101	103	101	103	101	100	101	100	102	101
1983	103	100	102	105	103	99	100	102	101	101	103	104	104	103	101	105	103

New passenger car registrations / Immatriculations de voitures de tourisme neuves

thousands, monthly averages / milliers, moyennes mensuelles

	Year	Q.1	Q.2	Q.3	Q.4	JAN	FEB	MAR	APR	MAY	JUN	JUL	AUG	SEP	OCT	NOV	DEC
1964	8.09	7.64	9.84	7.32	7.55	5.16	6.97	10.81	10.18	9.87	9.46	8.15	6.43	7.38	7.39	8.82	6.45
1965	6.92	10.84	6.73	4.86	5.22	6.02	7.87	18.65	7.26	6.34	6.59	4.32	4.56	5.71	5.72	5.04	4.91
1966	8.22	7.34	9.59	9.00	6.94	3.95	5.56	12.51	8.63	9.77	10.37	9.32	8.05	9.65	7.21	6.63	6.99
1967	7.90	8.67	10.89	5.16	5.37	5.55	7.18	13.28	10.68	12.03	9.95	6.08	5.70	6.69	6.67	6.28	4.66
1968	7.47	9.75	6.87	6.47	6.81	4.70	6.82	17.72	4.51	8.54	7.56	7.07	5.27	7.07	7.70	6.89	5.84
1969	9.74	9.95	12.76	8.80	7.43	7.06	8.01	14.79	13.14	13.03	12.10	10.18	7.53	8.71	9.88	6.90	5.50
1970	9.05	9.24	15.22	5.78	5.97	7.14	8.30	12.26	12.97	13.77	18.93	4.75	5.45	7.13	6.89	5.83	5.20
1971	8.65	8.84	10.26	7.77	7.73	6.14	9.01	11.36	10.60	10.14	10.03	8.13	7.13	8.06	10.46	8.11	4.63
1972	7.71	7.20	9.24	7.34	7.07	5.58	6.09	9.94	7.99	9.13	10.61	6.75	7.46	7.82	8.29	7.27	5.64
1973	10.11	10.54	12.46	9.97	7.47	8.21	10.45	12.96	10.12	14.23	13.03	10.36	9.21	10.34	10.94	7.84	3.62
1974	6.57	10.08	10.28	3.80	2.12	5.91	10.11	14.23	11.47	12.81	6.57	4.43	3.62	3.34	3.09	2.09	1.19
1975	9.64	9.01	9.68	9.87	10.03	8.90	7.82	10.30	9.26	9.74	10.02	9.52	9.42	10.66	11.26	9.80	9.03
1976	12.67	15.48	14.83	12.83	7.48	12.14	14.87	19.42	15.50	14.51	14.63	11.56	17.80	9.13	8.15	7.63	6.66
1977	11.78	12.88	14.62	15.34	4.30	9.14	12.80	16.69	15.17	14.16	14.53	13.59	18.76	13.66	3.11	4.83	4.97
1978	11.12	10.17	14.32	13.69	6.29	8.09	7.97	14.46	14.93	14.47	13.55	10.38	12.27	18.41	5.64	7.27	5.95
1979	10.59	13.61	13.34	8.87	6.56	8.56	22.43	9.86	13.25	13.83	12.92	8.87	9.44	8.29	3.36	6.58	4.73
1980	6.16	8.72	7.85	4.08	4.01	6.81	8.46	10.88	8.47	6.74	8.35	2.98	4.44	4.31	4.67	4.02	3.34
1981	5.98	7.01	7.32	5.26	4.34	5.42	7.01	8.61	8.12	7.18	6.64	5.57	5.12	5.09	5.50	4.08	3.43
1982	7.13	8.37	8.12	7.08	4.93	5.02	8.47	11.63	10.09	8.56	5.70	9.15	6.12	5.97	5.97	5.09	3.73
1983	9.70	9.98	10.96	9.06	8.78	7.38	8.55	14.02	10.27	11.18	11.44	9.25	8.75	9.18	9.66	9.26	7.42

Unemployment: registered unemployed (9) / Chômage : chômeurs inscrits (9)

thousands / milliers

	Year	Q.1	Q.2	Q.3	Q.4	JAN	FEB	MAR	APR	MAY	JUN	JUL	AUG	SEP	OCT	NOV	DEC
1964	19.3	44.9	10.8	5.7	15.6	48.4	46.7	39.7	20.5	7.2	4.7	6.2	4.9	6.1	7.5	9.6	29.8
1965	16.1	29.8	5.9	5.3	23.6	31.7	30.5	27.1	9.6	4.8	3.2	4.1	4.3	7.1	8.3	20.6	41.8
1966	19.2	43.4	10.3	5.2	17.6	51.0	52.0	27.1	21.2	7.1	4.0	4.5	5.6	5.6	7.3	13.7	31.7
1967	22.7	30.7	12.3	11.9	36.0	34.1	32.7	25.3	18.3	10.7	7.8	9.2	10.6	15.9	24.4	27.4	56.3
1968	40.2	62.1	30.8	22.7	45.1	68.5	62.0	55.7	42.2	27.6	22.7	22.4	22.9	22.7	30.4	32.4	72.6
1969	32.4	60.2	21.5	13.3	34.7	63.8	62.8	54.0	32.2	18.8	13.4	13.7	13.0	13.2	16.9	22.0	65.1
1970	24.9	48.4	14.6	9.6	26.8	48.8	50.5	46.0	25.4	10.9	7.4	8.9	8.1	11.9	17.5	21.9	40.9
1971	32.1	44.3	22.9	20.5	40.5	48.2	41.8	43.0	30.1	21.1	17.6	19.5	21.4	20.7	27.4	39.3	54.9
1972	33.0	57.9	28.8	18.2	27.2	61.0	63.9	48.8	36.5	30.9	19.0	20.1	17.9	16.5	18.0	21.9	41.6
1973	21.6	30.9	19.2	11.9	24.2	35.2	31.6	25.9	32.2	14.8	10.7	13.2	11.4	11.0	12.8	19.4	40.4
1974	50.5	34.7	27.9	44.3	95.1	42.0	34.7	27.4	27.2	27.4	29.1	33.6	43.4	55.8	76.7	91.9	116.7
1975	123.1	132.8	114.8	108.8	135.9	140.7	127.7	130.1	128.2	113.2	103.1	95.3	114.2	116.8	123.1	127.3	157.3
1976	126.0	143.0	108.3	110.7	142.1	155.3	143.8	129.8	119.0	106.1	99.9	111.7	108.4	111.9	128.9	130.4	167.1
1977	164.5	171.5	152.1	153.5	180.7	177.6	175.8	161.2	162.9	147.4	145.9	147.5	153.5	159.6	164.2	174.2	203.8
1978	190.4	215.9	182.3	173.2	190.1	218.6	215.0	214.2	199.8	178.9	168.2	167.7	175.3	176.7	180.8	190.7	198.9
1979	163.9	210.1	155.6	141.1	148.8	218.8	213.5	197.9	173.7	152.6	140.6	137.4	146.7	139.1	141.3	147.1	157.9
1980	184.0	185.6	160.3	170.6	219.5	187.9	188.4	180.6	171.7	156.0	153.2	156.0	173.9	181.9	200.1	220.5	237.8
1981	240.6	265.5	225.6	214.2	257.2	276.6	264.9	255.1	243.4	224.8	208.5	199.0	216.5	227.0	242.3	256.9	272.5
1982	257.9	290.4	245.2	230.1	265.6	303.3	289.2	278.8	265.1	246.2	224.3	208.0	235.7	246.7	254.7	265.1	277.1
1983	280.6	310.2	274.9	256.2	281.0	319.3	309.6	301.6	296.9	271.1	256.7	241.4	259.6	267.5	277.1	279.8	286.1

Employment: mining and manufacturing (wage earners) (10) (11) (12)

Emploi : industries extractives et manufacturières (ouvriers) (10) (11) (12)

thousands / milliers

	Year	Q.1	Q.2	Q.3	Q.4	JAN	FEB	MAR	APR	MAY	JUN	JUL	AUG	SEP	OCT	NOV	DEC
1964	304	298	304	306	308	297	298	299	301	303	306	305	306	308	308	310	305
1965	308	310	309	309	305	310	310	311	308	308	312	310	309	308	307	306	301
1966	288	290	291	288	283	289	289	290	289	290	292	288	288	287	285	284	279
1967	288	292	290	288	280	294	292	291	289	290	292	290	288	286	283	281	276
1968	285	281	284	288	288	281	281	281	280	283	288	288	288	289	289	289	286
1969	298	292	299	302	302	289	292	294	295	298	304	301	302	302	304	304	298
1970	317	315	317	318	316	313	316	317	316	315	321	318	318	318	319	318	311
1971	304	308	307	304	298	309	308	307	305	305	310	306	304	303	301	299	294
1972	308	302	307	311	314	300	302	303	302	306	314	310	311	312	313	316	313
1973	321	316	321	325	322	315	317	315	314	320	328	326	324	324	325	323	318
1974	307	319	317	306	285	319	319	319	316	316	319	314	306	300	293	285	276
1975	274	275	276	275	270	277	276	274	274	275	278	276	275	273	272	270	267
1976	278	274	279	281	273	272	274	276	276	279	283	281	281	281	280	279	275
1977	276	278	278	276	271	279	279	278	276	277	280	278	276	276	274	272	268
1978	274	269	275	277	274	270	270	269	271	274	280	277	277	277	277	275	271
1979	278	272	278	282	279	270	271	273	274	277	283	282	281	282	282	281	275
1980	268	273	274	271	256	272	273	273	272	273	277	274	270	268	262	256	250
1981	251	250	249	256	251	249	249	250	243	246	258	257	256	255	253	252	247
1982	249	246	252	251	245	243	246	247	249	251	256	252	252	250	248	246	242
1983	247	243	248	249	247	242	244	243	245	246	252	250	249	248	248	248	245

Unemployment: registered unemployed (9)

Chômage : chômeurs inscrits (9)

Adjusted - Corrigé

thousands / milliers

	Year	Q.1	Q.2	Q.3	Q.4	JAN	FEB	MAR	APR	MAY	JUN	JUL	AUG	SEP	OCT	NOV	DEC
1964		18.4	17.1	15.0	11.5	21.9	18.1	15.1	20.4	15.7	15.2	15.3	15.1	14.5	13.7	12.1	8.6
1965		10.3	12.4	15.1	15.3	9.7	9.4	11.8	9.8	13.0	14.4	14.8	15.0	15.4	15.4	15.9	15.3
1966		14.0	15.1	15.7	13.9	10.0	16.3	15.6	14.3	15.5	15.5	15.7	15.8	15.5	14.4	14.2	12.9
1967		12.3	18.0	22.0	30.2	8.9	14.8	13.3	16.3	18.7	19.0	20.1	21.7	24.2	26.9	29.4	34.4
1968		38.8	35.2	32.9	32.4	37.9	34.1	44.4	37.1	34.8	33.8	33.1	33.1	32.6	33.1	32.9	31.2
1969		31.7	26.2	24.0	23.1	35.1	29.9	30.1	28.0	25.6	25.1	24.4	24.0	23.5	23.0	23.1	23.2
1970		20.6	19.9	19.8	16.5	16.6	13.7	26.4	22.1	18.1	19.5	19.8	19.8	19.7	18.3	17.5	13.6
1971		24.8	28.1	30.3	32.3	22.0	27.4	25.1	26.5	28.2	29.7	30.1	30.1	30.6	32.6	33.9	32.0
1972		34.4	32.5	28.7	22.0	30.5	37.3	35.3	34.1	32.8	30.6	30.2	28.8	27.1	24.4	22.3	19.3
1973		15.1	20.9	22.8	18.5	14.1	16.1	15.1	18.0	21.4	23.2	23.8	23.0	21.7	18.4	17.5	19.7
1974		18.0	33.4	55.4	89.3	16.3	16.5	21.1	25.7	33.6	41.0	45.2	55.2	65.9	78.1	90.1	99.7
1975		111.5	119.8	123.0	122.6	105.5	111.4	117.6	121.8	120.4	117.3	118.5	124.0	126.6	124.3	122.9	120.6
1976		118.4	114.8	120.3	126.4	121.0	120.8	113.3	115.9	114.0	114.6	119.0	119.9	122.0	124.4	125.7	129.1
1977		147.0	156.2	163.0	172.0	142.3	147.0	151.8	152.5	156.3	159.7	161.3	163.0	164.8	168.1	171.8	176.0
1978		183.1	184.3	185.7	188.0	179.3	181.3	188.6	185.2	184.0	183.8	185.0	185.2	186.8	187.3	187.0	189.7
1979		170.7	156.8	148.5	140.3	171.7	168.8	171.5	164.6	154.1	151.7	150.3	148.6	146.6	143.6	140.3	137.1
1980		147.6	162.0	183.3	210.8	140.9	146.4	155.5	157.8	160.4	167.7	175.9	182.9	191.2	200.7	210.0	221.7
1981		229.9	230.6	233.2	251.1	226.4	231.5	231.7	233.1	231.5	227.3	225.6	233.2	240.8	246.2	251.1	256.0
1982		254.6	252.0	251.5	261.4	257.8	253.1	252.8	253.6	253.3	249.2	246.9	249.6	257.9	258.9	262.5	262.7
1983		272.8	281.8	279.5	278.1	268.5	273.9	275.9	283.7	280.9	280.9	275.9	280.9	281.8	281.3	277.5	275.5

DENMARK

Unemployment: registered unemployed (9)(13)
as per cent of insured labour force

Chômage: chômeurs inscrits (9)(13)
en pourcentage de la main-d'œuvre assurée

	Year	Q.1	Q.2	Q.3	Q.4	JAN	FEB	MAR	APR	MAY	JUN	JUL	AUG	SEP	OCT	NOV	DEC
1964																	
1965																	
1966																	
1967																	
1968																	
1969																	
1970	1.3	2.6	0.8	0.5	1.4	2.6	2.7	2.4	1.3	0.6	0.4	0.5	0.4	0.6	0.9	1.2	2.2
1971	1.7	2.3	1.2	1.1	2.1	2.5	2.2	2.3	1.6	1.1	0.9	1.0	1.1	1.1	1.4	2.0	2.8
1972	1.7	3.0	1.3	0.9	1.4	3.2	3.3	2.5	1.9	1.0	1.0	1.0	0.9	0.8	0.9	1.1	2.1
1973	1.1	1.6	0.9	0.6	1.2	1.8	1.6	1.3	1.6	0.7	0.5	0.7	0.6	0.6	0.6	1.0	2.0
1974	2.5	1.7	1.4	2.2	4.6	2.1	1.7	1.4	1.4	1.4	1.5	1.7	2.2	2.8	3.7	4.5	5.7
1975	6.0	6.5	5.6	5.3	6.6	6.9	6.2	6.3	6.3	5.5	5.0	4.6	5.6	5.7	6.0	6.2	7.7
1976	6.1	7.0	5.3	5.4	6.9	7.6	7.0	6.3	5.8	5.2	4.9	5.4	5.3	5.5	6.3	6.4	3.1
1977	7.7	8.2	7.2	7.3	8.4	8.4	8.4	7.7	7.7	7.0	6.9	7.0	7.3	7.6	7.6	8.1	9.5
1978	7.4	8.4	7.0	6.7	7.2	8.5	8.3	8.3	7.7	5.9	5.5	6.5	6.8	6.9	6.8	7.2	7.5
1979	6.1	8.0	5.9	5.3	5.7	8.3	8.1	7.5	6.6	5.8	5.3	5.2	5.5	5.3	5.4	5.6	6.0
1980	7.0	7.1	6.1	6.5	8.4	7.2	7.2	6.9	6.5	5.9	5.8	5.9	6.6	6.9	7.6	8.4	9.1
1981	9.2	10.1	8.6	8.1	9.8	10.5	10.1	9.7	9.3	8.6	7.9	7.6	8.2	8.6	9.2	9.8	10.4
1982	9.8	11.0	9.3	8.8	10.1	11.5	11.0	10.6	10.1	9.4	8.5	7.9	9.0	9.4	9.7	10.1	10.5
1983	10.7	11.8	10.5	9.8	10.7	12.2	11.8	11.5	11.3	10.3	9.8	9.2	9.9	10.2	10.5	10.7	10.9

Jobs vacant, unfilled vacancies (10)(14)
number

Offres d'emploi non satisfaites (10)(14)
nombre

	Year	Q.1	Q.2	Q.3	Q.4	JAN	FEB	MAR	APR	MAY	JUN	JUL	AUG	SEP	OCT	NOV	DEC
1964																	
1965																	
1966																	
1967																	
1968																	
1969			6414	6497	5109				5112	7468	6662	6243	6969	6230	5788	4965	4574
1970	8914	6628	12430	9958	6640	5994	6422	7467	11309	14042	11940	10311	10035	9527	8739	6357	4823
1971	4238	4390	4983	4532	3048	4517	4267	4387	4881	5384	4683	5281	4523	3791	3311	2953	2881
1972	5688	3291	5700	7438	6321	3159	3130	3583	4840	6394	5867	6997	7691	7627	6943	6284	5737
1973	8870	6742	10371	11139	7230	6702	8223	5300	9060	11845	10207	10057	11782	11579	9961	7303	4426
1974	2886	4685	3979	1914	966	4711	4745	4598	5070	3855	3011	2354	1989	1399	1212	961	726
1975	1044	735	1063	1176	1201	622	796	788	949	1088	1152	1216	1245	1067	1225	1341	2038
1976	1914	1697	2592	2040	1327	1270	1732	2088	2514	2816	2445	2158	2172	1789	1619	1251	1112
1977	1569	1340	2011	1597	1328	1110	1254	1656	2132	2069	1831	1593	1887	1312	1692	1272	1020
1978	1881	1390	2262	1985	1865	1439	1330	1402	1881	2410	2494	2216	1978	1761	2413	1700	1543
1979	2021	2069	2539	2021	1452	2123	1903	2181	2436	2928	2254	2035	2254	1775	1790	1527	1040
1980	864	1100	1128	802	425	1300	1054	947	1255	1136	993	894	880	633	489	435	302
1981	368	411	476	333	254	470	403	360	542	522	363	309	392	297	292	267	203
1982	208	204	235	240	154	241	187	184	226	249	230	209	301	210	199	151	111
1983	199	154	152	317	174	129	211	123	145	184	128	193	403	354	165	173	184

Monthly hours worked: (11)(12)
mining and manufacturing (wage earners)
1980 = 100

Durée mensuelle du travail : (11)(12)
industries extractives et manufacturières (ouvriers)
1980 = 100

	Year	Q.1	Q.2	Q.3	Q.4	JAN	FEB	MAR	APR	MAY	JUN	JUL	AUG	SEP	OCT	NOV	DEC
1964	152.0	153.3	157.8	139.4	157.8	147.9	156.0	156.0	157.3	157.3	158.7	102.2	154.7	161.4	161.4	162.8	149.2
1965	153.4	158.3	159.6	139.9	153.8	154.7	160.1	160.1	160.1	157.3	161.4	103.5	156.0	160.1	158.7	158.7	143.9
1966	145.3	153.4	150.5	131.2	145.2	152.4	153.9	153.9	149.5	151.0	151.0	95.8	146.7	151.0	151.0	149.5	135.1
1967	136.5	143.3	142.4	123.0	134.6	143.8	143.8	142.4	143.8	140.9	142.4	88.5	138.0	142.4	139.4	139.4	124.9
1968	130.7	135.1	135.6	119.8	132.5	132.0	136.0	137.3	136.0	136.0	134.7	87.6	133.3	138.5	137.3	138.5	121.5
1969	135.6	136.3	142.4	124.6	138.8	133.6	137.2	138.1	142.4	142.0	142.9	91.7	138.4	143.5	144.1	144.6	127.8
1970	132.5	135.8	140.2	121.5	132.6	130.2	136.1	141.0	142.1	139.2	139.3	92.6	134.8	138.2	137.8	137.3	122.7
1971	125.9	131.9	133.2	114.7	124.0	131.5	132.8	131.5	134.4	132.8	132.3	85.5	124.1	130.7	129.9	128.2	113.9
1972	124.7	126.2	130.9	111.7	130.2	120.6	127.2	130.8	132.1	129.1	131.4	78.7	124.6	131.8	131.8	132.8	126.1
1973	122.2	126.5	119.9	112.4	129.9	127.1	133.2	119.0	92.1	134.3	133.3	76.9	126.2	134.3	133.6	134.4	121.5
1974	115.7	125.0	125.6	102.8	109.3	120.1	128.6	126.3	128.3	121.8	126.1	71.0	117.0	120.5	116.5	113.9	97.6
1975	100.0	103.6	105.9	88.9	101.4	98.3	106.3	106.3	106.6	104.5	106.6	60.8	99.6	106.3	106.0	106.0	92.2
1976	103.9	105.5	112.1	92.9	105.2	101.7	107.4	107.6	111.9	112.2	112.2	61.7	105.1	111.8	112.1	111.6	91.9
1977	103.0	109.1	109.1	91.0	102.9	106.9	109.9	110.4	109.8	108.0	109.4	59.2	104.9	109.0	108.5	107.3	92.9
1978	102.0	104.2	107.3	91.3	104.9	103.1	104.0	105.5	108.1	104.8	109.1	59.2	105.7	109.0	109.1	108.8	96.7
1979	103.2	104.0	109.3	93.2	106.6	102.5	104.0	105.4	109.5	107.5	110.8	60.8	107.0	111.8	111.9	111.2	96.6
1980	100.0	106.8	107.0	89.7	96.7	105.2	107.1	108.1	109.0	105.2	106.7	61.3	102.1	105.6	103.1	100.8	86.1
1981	92.6	95.6	96.8	85.0	92.6	92.6	96.6	97.5	94.9	95.5	99.1	57.9	96.5	100.7	96.7	98.7	82.5
1982	93.0	96.7	100.3	84.2	90.7	95.0	96.9	98.0	100.3	99.1	101.6	57.6	95.0	99.9	94.5	98.2	79.4
1983	94.4	97.2	100.1	84.7	95.7	96.7	97.1	97.9	100.7	97.7	101.9	55.7	97.0	101.4	97.2	101.8	83.2

Unemployment: registered unemployed (9)(13)
as per cent of insured labour force

Adjusted - Corrigé

Chômage: chômeurs inscrits (9)(13)
en pourcentage de la main-d'œuvre assurée

	Year	Q.1	Q.2	Q.3	Q.4	JAN	FEB	MAR	APR	MAY	JUN	JUL	AUG	SEP	OCT	NOV	DEC
1964																	
1965																	
1966																	
1967																	
1968																	
1969																	
1970		1.1	1.0	1.0	0.9	0.9	1.0	1.4	1.2	0.9	1.0	1.0	1.0	1.0	1.0	0.9	0.7
1971		1.3	1.5	1.6	1.7	1.2	1.4	1.3	1.4	1.5	1.5	1.6	1.6	1.6	1.7	1.7	1.7
1972		1.8	1.7	1.5	1.1	1.6	1.9	1.8	1.8	1.7	1.6	1.5	1.5	1.4	1.2	1.1	1.0
1973		0.8	1.1	1.2	0.9	0.7	0.8	0.8	0.9	1.1	1.2	1.2	1.2	1.1	0.9	0.9	1.0
1974		0.9	1.7	2.8	4.4	0.8	0.8	1.1	1.3	1.7	2.1	2.3	2.8	3.3	3.9	4.4	4.9
1975		5.4	5.9	6.0	6.0	5.2	5.4	5.7	6.0	5.9	5.7	5.8	6.1	6.2	6.1	6.0	5.9
1976		5.8	5.6	5.9	6.0	5.9	5.9	5.5	5.7	5.5	5.6	5.8	5.9	5.9	5.9	6.0	6.1
1977		7.0	7.4	7.7	8.0	6.8	7.0	7.2	7.2	7.4	7.6	7.7	7.7	7.8	7.8	8.0	8.2
1978		7.1	7.1	7.2	7.1	7.0	7.0	7.3	7.2	7.1	7.1	7.2	7.2	7.2	7.1	7.1	7.2
1979		6.5	5.9	5.6	5.3	6.5	6.4	6.5	6.2	5.8	5.7	5.7	5.6	5.5	5.5	5.3	5.2
1980		5.6	6.2	7.0	8.0	5.4	5.6	5.9	6.0	6.1	6.4	6.7	6.9	7.3	7.6	8.0	8.4
1981		8.7	8.8	8.9	9.6	8.6	8.8	8.8	8.9	8.8	8.7	8.6	8.9	9.2	9.4	9.6	9.7
1982		9.7	9.6	9.6	10.0	9.8	9.6	9.6	9.7	9.6	9.5	9.4	9.6	9.8	9.9	10.0	10.0
1983		10.4	10.7	10.6	10.6	10.2	10.4	10.5	10.8	10.7	10.7	10.5	10.7	10.7	10.7	10.6	10.5

Hourly earnings: mining and manufacturing (11)(12)
(wage earners)
1980 = 100

Gains horaires : industries extractives et manufacturières (12)(11)
(ouvriers)
1980 = 100

	Year	Q.1	Q.2	Q.3	Q.4	JAN	FEB	MAR	APR	MAY	JUN	JUL	AUG	SEP	OCT	NOV	DEC
1964																	
1965																	
1966																	
1967																	
1968																	
1969																	
1970	26.6																
1971	30.4	28.4	30.4	31.2	32.1	28.0	28.1	29.0	30.3	30.4	30.4	31.3	30.7	31.5	31.7	31.9	32.7
1972	34.3	32.6	34.0	34.7	35.7	32.1	32.3	33.3	33.9	34.2	34.1	35.0	34.0	35.0	35.2	35.6	36.4
1973	40.7	36.3	40.0	42.4	44.6	35.9	36.2	36.8	38.5	40.4	41.1	42.3	40.8	44.2	44.2	44.4	45.4
1974	49.4	45.8	49.0	50.3	53.4	44.3	44.8	48.3	49.1	48.7	49.1	50.5	48.8	51.8	52.5	52.6	55.2
1975	58.9	55.6	58.7	59.7	62.0	54.4	54.8	57.7	58.7	58.8	58.7	60.8	57.8	60.3	61.3	61.6	63.0
1976	66.4	63.6	66.1	67.1	69.2	61.9	63.0	65.8	66.2	66.0	66.3	68.7	65.0	67.5	68.3	68.6	70.7
1977	73.2	69.5	72.8	74.1	76.3	69.1	69.1	70.3	72.1	73.3	73.0	75.2	72.4	74.7	75.3	75.9	77.8
1978	80.7	77.7	80.2	81.3	83.9	76.4	77.3	79.5	79.7	80.7	80.1	82.3	79.5	81.9	83.0	83.3	85.5
1979	89.9	85.3	88.5	90.4	95.4	84.3	85.0	86.6	88.2	88.8	88.8	90.9	87.5	92.8	94.1	94.8	97.2
1980	100.0	96.6	99.5	100.8	103.8	95.6	96.4	97.8	99.6	99.6	99.2	102.3	98.7	101.6	102.3	103.3	105.9
1981	109.5	105.5	108.2	110.3	114.6	103.8	104.8	107.8	107.6	108.0	109.1	111.8	107.2	111.8	113.3	113.3	117.1
1982	120.3	115.6	119.7	121.1	125.4	114.0	114.1	118.7	119.7	119.9	119.6	122.6	118.1	122.7	124.3	124.4	127.5
1983	128.5	125.4	128.6	129.5	130.5	123.9	124.6	127.6	128.4	129.1	128.5	132.7	127.0	128.9	129.6	129.8	132.0

Monthly hours worked: (12)
mining and manufacturing (wage earners)
1980 = 100

Adjusted - Corrigé *

Durée mensuelle du travail : (12)
industries extractives et manufacturières (ouvriers)
1980 = 100

	Year	Q.1	Q.2	Q.3	Q.4	JAN	FEB	MAR	APR	MAY	JUN	JUL	AUG	SEP	OCT	NOV	DEC
1964		149.7	152.4	151.6	154.8	147.5	150.9	150.8	152.3	152.5	152.3	150.1	151.6	153.2	154.1	155.2	155.1
1965		154.7	154.1	152.0	150.9	154.1	155.1	154.8	154.7	152.3	155.1	150.9	153.1	152.1	151.5	151.2	150.0
1966		149.8	144.9	143.1	142.5	151.7	149.1	148.7	143.8	146.0	144.9	142.3	143.8	143.2	144.0	142.1	141.4
1967		139.9	136.8	134.6	132.1	143.0	139.5	137.2	137.9	135.9	136.5	133.7	135.2	134.8	132.5	132.2	131.5
1968		131.9	129.9	131.2	130.1	131.1	132.2	132.4	129.8	130.9	128.9	131.6	130.8	131.1	130.4	131.4	128.5
1969		133.2	136.6	135.8	136.5	132.8	133.7	133.1	135.9	136.8	137.1	134.8	136.3	136.2	137.2	137.5	134.9
1970		132.8	134.3	132.7	130.2	129.4	132.7	136.4	135.4	134.0	133.4	134.2	133.1	130.9	130.8	130.1	129.6
1971		129.1	127.2	125.9	121.4	130.9	129.3	127.1	127.6	128.0	126.1	132.2	122.5	123.2	122.7	120.9	120.6
1972		123.5	125.0	122.9	127.5	120.2	123.4	126.9	125.3	124.8	124.9	121.6	123.0	124.0	124.5	125.5	132.6
1973		123.9	114.0	123.6	127.1	127.2	129.1	115.2	85.4	130.2	126.5	120.1	124.6	126.2	126.2	127.1	128.0
1974		122.5	119.7	113.9	106.7	120.4	124.3	122.7	122.3	117.6	119.1	114.1	115.3	112.4	109.1	106.7	104.3
1975		101.2	100.0	99.8	98.9	99.5	101.9	102.3	100.0	100.6	99.5	103.5	97.6	98.3	98.7	99.0	99.0
1976		103.1	106.2	103.6	103.0	102.7	103.2	103.4	105.3	108.2	105.1	103.7	102.8	104.1	104.9	104.9	99.1
1977		106.7	103.2	101.5	100.8	107.8	106.2	106.0	103.3	103.9	102.3	100.5	102.4	101.6	101.4	100.8	100.3
1978		101.7	101.5	101.4	103.1	103.5	100.5	101.2	101.7	100.7	102.2	99.6	103.0	101.7	102.1	102.6	104.4
1979		101.5	103.6	102.9	105.0	102.6	100.8	101.2	103.3	103.6	104.0	100.3	104.0	104.4	105.0	105.3	104.6
1980		104.4	101.5	99.1	95.3	105.1	104.0	103.9	102.9	101.4	100.1	100.1	98.9	98.1	96.3	95.1	94.4
1981		93.1	91.4	94.2	91.3	92.4	93.6	93.4	88.9	92.8	92.5	96.1	93.4	93.3	89.9	93.0	90.9
1982		94.2	94.9	93.3	89.4	94.9	93.9	93.9	94.3	95.4	95.1	95.5	92.0	92.4	87.8	92.6	87.8
1983		94.8	94.8	93.8	94.4	96.5	94.2	93.8	94.8	94.0	95.5	93.5	93.9	93.9	90.5	96.2	96.6

* Adjusted by the O.E.C.D.

* Corrigé par l'O.C.D.E.

DENMARK

Wholesale prices: agricultural raw materials (15) — Prix de gros : matières premières agricoles (15)

1980 = 100

	Year	Q.1	Q.2	Q.3	Q.4	JAN	FEB	MAR	APR	MAY	JUN	JUL	AUG	SEP	OCT	NOV	DEC
1964	39	39	40	39	39	40	39	39	40	39	40	40	40	38	38	39	39
1965	41	40	41	41	41	40	40	40	40	41	42	42	42	41	40	41	40
1966	42	42	43	43	42	43	42	42	42	43	43	43	43	42	42	42	42
1967	41	42	43	41	40	42	42	42	42	43	43	42	41	39	39	40	42
1968	41	42	42	40	39	42	42	42	42	42	43	41	41	38	39	39	39
1969	40	40	40	38	42	40	40	40	40	40	40	38	38	39	41	42	42
1970	=44=	43	44	44	45	43	44	44	44	44	44	42	44	45	45	45	45
1971	45	46	46	44	44	46	46	45	45	46	47	45	43	43	44	45	45
1972	49	45	47	49	55	45	45	45	47	47	48	47	48	51	52	54	59
1973	72	64	77	76	71	65	65	62	66	76	88	90	74	65	65	71	76
1974	69	73	65	70	71	79	70	69	66	65	63	69	70	69	73	71	70
1975	67	65	56	69	69	68	64	64	66	66	66	69	71	69	69	68	69
1976	77	72	77	78	80	71	73	74	74	77	80	76	78	80	79	80	82
1977	84	85	92	77	80	85	85	86	95	93	88	78	76	77	78	80	81
1978	80	81	83	78	79	80	81	82	84	84	81	79	78	78	78	79	80
1979	86	83	87	85	88	81	83	84	85	86	90	85	85	85	86	89	90
1980	100	95	97	99	109	=94=	95	97	97	98	96	96	98	102	106	111	111
1981	117	115	120	118	116	114	115	115	118	121	120	120	119	116	114	116	118
1982	125	123	128	124	127	122	122	125	128	129	127	124	124	124	125	128	129
1983	135	131	132	137	141	132	131	131	131	131	133	131	138	141	141	140	143

Wholesale prices: machinery and transport equipment (15) — Prix de gros : machines et matériel de transport (15)

1980 = 100

	Year	Q.1	Q.2	Q.3	Q.4	JAN	FEB	MAR	APR	MAY	JUN	JUL	AUG	SEP	OCT	NOV	DEC
1964	33	33	33	33	33	33	33	33	33	33	33	33	33	33	33	33	33
1965	34	34	34	34	34	33	33	34	34	34	34	34	34	34	34	34	34
1966	35	35	35	35	35	35	35	35	35	35	35	35	35	35	35	35	35
1967	37	36	36	37	37	36	36	36	36	36	36	37	37	37	37	37	37
1968	38	38	38	38	38	38	38	38	38	38	38	38	38	38	38	38	38
1969	39	39	39	39	40	39	39	39	39	39	39	39	39	39	39	40	40
1970	=44=	44	44	45	45	43	43	44	44	44	45	45	45	45	45	45	45
1971	45	44	44	45	46	44	44	44	44	44	45	45	45	45	46	46	46
1972	49	48	49	50	50	48	49	49	49	49	49	49	50	50	50	50	50
1973	52	51	51	52	54	51	51	51	51	51	51	52	52	53	54	54	54
1974	60	56	58	61	63	56	56	57	57	58	59	61	61	62	63	63	64
1975	68	66	67	68	69	66	66	66	67	67	68	68	68	69	69	69	69
1976	72	70	71	73	74	70	70	71	71	71	72	73	73	73	74	74	74
1977	79	75	77	80	82	75	75	76	77	77	78	79	79	80	82	82	82
1978	85	83	85	86	87	83	83	84	84	85	85	85	85	86	86	87	87
1979	91	89	90	91	94	88	89	89	89	90	90	91	91	92	93	94	94
1980	100	97	99	101	103	=96=	97	97	99	99	100	101	101	102	103	103	104
1981	113	107	111	114	117	106	107	108	110	112	112	114	114	115	116	118	118
1982	126	121	124	128	131	120	120	122	124	124	125	126	128	129	131	131	131
1983	137	133	136	139	141	133	133	133	135	136	137	138	139	139	140	141	141

Wholesale prices: consumer goods (15) — Prix de gros : biens de consommation (15)

1980 = 100

	Year	Q.1	Q.2	Q.3	Q.4	JAN	FEB	MAR	APR	MAY	JUN	JUL	AUG	SEP	OCT	NOV	DEC
1964	37	36	37	37	37	36	36	37	37	37	37	37	37	37	37	37	37
1965	39	38	39	39	39	37	38	38	39	39	40	39	39	39	39	39	39
1966	40	40	40	40	40	39	40	40	40	40	40	40	39	40	40	40	40
1967	41	40	41	41	41	40	40	40	40	40	42	41	41	41	41	41	41
1968	41	41	42	41	41	41	41	41	41	42	42	41	42	41	41	41	41
1969	43	42	43	43	44	42	42	43	42	42	44	43	44	43	43	44	44
1970	=45=	45	46	45	45	45	45	46	45	45	46	46	45	45	45	45	45
1971	48	46	47	48	49	46	46	46	47	47	48	48	48	48	48	49	48
1972	51	50	52	52	52	49	50	50	50	51	53	52	52	52	52	52	53
1973	57	55	58	58	59	53	54	56	56	58	60	58	58	59	60	59	59
1974	62	61	62	62	65	60	60	62	61	62	62	62	62	63	65	65	65
1975	69	67	69	70	72	67	67	67	68	68	71	69	69	70	71	72	73
1976	76	74	76	76	79	74	74	75	76	76	75	76	75	77	78	79	79
1977	84	80	83	85	86	79	79	81	82	83	85	86	84	86	86	86	87
1978	88	88	88	88	89	87	88	88	88	87	90	88	89	88	88	89	88
1979	92	90	91	92	94	89	90	90	89	91	93	91	91	92	94	95	94
1980	100	97	100	101	102	=96=	97	99	99	99	102	100	100	101	101	101	102
1981	111	105	109	113	117	103	105	107	109	109	110	112	113	115	117	117	117
1982	124	119	122	125	127	118	120	120	120	122	124	124	125	127	127	127	127
1983	130	127	129	131	134	127	127	128	127	129	130	129	131	133	134	134	134

Wholesale prices: industrial raw materials (15)(16) — Prix de gros : matières premières industrielles (16)(15)

1980 = 100

	Year	Q.1	Q.2	Q.3	Q.4	JAN	FEB	MAR	APR	MAY	JUN	JUL	AUG	SEP	OCT	NOV	DEC
1964	34	34	34	35	35	34	34	34	34	34	34	34	34	35	35	35	35
1965	36	35	36	35	36	35	35	35	36	36	36	35	35	35	36	36	36
1966	36	36	36	36	36	36	36	36	36	36	36	36	36	36	36	36	36
1967	36	36	36	36	37	36	36	36	35	36	36	36	36	36	36	37	37
1968	38	38	38	37	38	37	38	38	38	38	37	37	37	37	37	38	38
1969	39	38	39	40	41	38	38	38	38	39	39	39	40	40	40	41	41
1970	=42=	42	42	42	42	41	41	42	42	42	42	42	42	42	42	42	42
1971	43	43	43	44	44	43	43	43	43	43	43	44	44	44	44	44	43
1972	45	44	44	45	46	44	44	44	44	44	44	45	45	45	46	46	46
1973	52	48	51	54	56	47	48	49	49	51	52	53	53	54	55	56	58
1974	67	64	67	69	69	61	64	66	66	67	67	69	69	70	70	69	69
1975	68	69	68	67	67	70	69	68	68	67	67	67	68	67	67	67	67
1976	71	68	71	72	73	68	68	69	70	71	71	72	73	73	73	73	73
1977	76	75	76	76	77	74	74	75	76	76	76	76	76	76	76	77	77
1978	80	78	79	80	81	77	77	79	79	80	80	80	81	81	81	81	81
1979	88	83	86	89	92	82	83	84	85	86	87	88	89	90	91	92	93
1980	100	97	99	101	103	=96=	97	98	99	99	100	101	101	102	103	103	103
1981	111	105	110	114	116	103	105	107	109	110	111	113	114	115	115	115	116
1982	123	119	123	125	126	117	119	120	122	122	123	124	125	125	126	127	126
1983	131	127	129	133	135	127	127	127	129	129	129	131	133	134	135	135	136

Wholesale prices: liquid fuel (15) — Prix de gros : combustibles liquides (15)

1980 = 100

	Year	Q.1	Q.2	Q.3	Q.4	JAN	FEB	MAR	APR	MAY	JUN	JUL	AUG	SEP	OCT	NOV	DEC
1964	14	14	14	14	14	14	14	14	14	14	14	14	14	14	14	14	14
1965	14	14	14	14	14	14	14	14	14	14	14	14	14	14	14	14	14
1966	14	14	14	14	14	14	14	14	14	14	14	14	14	14	14	14	14
1967	14	14	14	15	15	14	14	14	14	14	14	15	15	15	15	15	15
1968	15	15	15	15	15	15	15	15	15	15	15	15	15	15	15	15	15
1969	15	15	15	15	16	15	15	15	15	15	15	15	15	15	15	16	16
1970	=18=	16	17	18	19	16	16	17	17	17	18	18	18	19	19	20	20
1971	18	18	18	18	17	17	18	18	18	18	18	18	18	18	18	17	17
1972	17	17	17	17	17	17	17	17	17	17	17	17	17	17	17	17	17
1973	20	18	19	19	24	18	18	18	18	19	19	19	19	20	21	25	28
1974	42	42	42	42	42	41	43	41	43	42	42	42	42	42	42	42	42
1975	42	41	41	42	45	42	41	41	41	41	41	41	42	43	44	45	45
1976	46	46	46	47	47	45	46	47	46	46	46	47	47	47	47	46	46
1977	49	47	48	50	50	47	47	48	48	48	49	49	50	50	50	50	50
1978	48	49	48	48	47	49	49	48	48	48	47	48	48	48	47	47	47
1979	63	50	57	68	75	47	49	52	54	57	61	65	68	72	72	73	80
1980	100	91	101	100	108	=84=	90	98	100	102	101	100	99	101	103	107	115
1981	136	125	139	144	137	117	124	133	134	138	144	145	145	140	136	137	139
1982	149	145	141	151	159	142	146	147	143	139	143	147	150	155	160	161	155
1983	148	147	141	149	153	151	149	141	140	140	142	146	149	153	152	153	155

Consumer prices: all items, (17) excluding indirect taxes — Prix à la consommation : total, (17) non compris les impôts indirects

1980 = 100

	Year	Q.1	Q.2	Q.3	Q.4	JAN	FEB	MAR	APR	MAY	JUN	JUL	AUG	SEP	OCT	NOV	DEC
1964	31.2	30.7	31.2	31.4	31.7	30.7			31.2			31.4			31.7		
1965	33.1	32.3	32.8	33.5	33.8	32.3			32.8			33.5			33.8		
1966	35.1	34.6	35.0	35.2	35.6	34.6			35.0			35.2			35.6		
1967	37.0	36.1	36.6	37.3	37.8	36.0	36.1	36.2	36.5	36.6	36.8	37.2	37.3	37.4	37.5	38.0	38.0
1968	38.6	38.2	38.6	38.8	39.0	38.1	38.2	38.3	38.3	38.7	38.8	38.8	38.7	38.8	38.9	39.0	39.0
1969	40.0	39.2	39.8	40.2	40.9	39.1	39.2	39.3	39.4	39.9	40.1	40.1	40.2	40.4	40.5	41.0	41.1
1970	42.4	41.5	42.2	42.6	43.3	41.2	41.5	41.8	41.9	42.4	42.4	42.5	42.5	42.9	43.0	43.4	43.4
1971	44.8	43.4	44.5	45.2	45.9	=43.4=	43.4	43.5	43.9	44.8	44.9	44.9	45.1	45.5	45.7	46.0	46.1
1972	47.9	46.4	47.6	48.3	49.2	46.2	46.4	46.8	47.1	47.7	48.0	48.1	48.3	48.6	48.8	49.2	49.4
1973	52.3	50.0	51.6	52.9	54.9	49.6	50.0	50.3	50.9	51.7	52.1	52.5	52.8	53.4	53.9	55.0	55.7
1974	60.2	57.0	59.4	60.9	63.2	56.6	56.9	57.5	58.6	59.6	59.9	60.4	60.7	61.6	62.5	63.5	63.8
1975	66.8	64.6	66.0	67.1	69.3	=64.1=	64.6	64.9	65.3	66.2	66.5	66.9	67.0	67.6	68.3	69.8	69.9
1976	72.6	70.7	72.0	72.7	74.9	70.1	70.7	71.2	71.4	72.5	72.2	72.1	72.6	73.5	74.1	75.3	75.4
1977	78.8	75.7	78.0	79.8	81.7	75.3	75.3	76.3	76.8	78.5	78.8	79.2	79.8	80.5	81.2	82.0	82.1
1978	84.7	82.6	84.3	85.3	86.6	82.2	82.6	83.1	83.4	84.6	84.8	84.9	85.3	85.8	86.1	86.9	86.8
1979	91.1	87.3	89.8	92.5	94.9	86.7	87.3	88.0	88.3	90.1	90.9	91.4	92.5	93.5	94.0	95.3	95.3
1980	100.0	96.9	99.3	101.1	102.7	=96.2=	96.8	97.6	98.2	99.7	100.0	100.5	101.1	101.6	102.0	103.0	103.1
1981	109.2	104.4	108.4	110.4	113.5	103.5	104.2	105.7	106.9	108.8	109.5	109.6	110.2	111.4	112.5	113.9	114.1
1982	120.0	115.4	119.1	121.4	123.9	114.6	115.3	116.3	117.2	119.9	120.2	120.6	121.2	122.3	123.1	124.4	124.3
1983	128.5	125.2	127.6	129.2	132.0	124.8	125.2	125.5	126.4	128.1	128.5	128.4	129.0	130.1	130.9	132.4	132.6

DENMARK

Money supply (M1) (18)(19)

billion kroner, end of period

Disponibilités monétaires (M1) (18)(19)

milliards de couronnes, fin de période

	Year	Q.1	Q.2	Q.3	Q.4	JAN	FEB	MAR	APR	MAY	JUN	JUL	AUG	SEP	OCT	NOV	DEC
1964																	
1965																	
1966																	
1967																	
1968	26.69																
1969	29.95																
1970	29.36	29.14	29.10	28.17	29.11		28.67	29.14	30.66	29.24	29.10	29.44	28.43	28.17	29.09	29.12	29.11
1971	31.85	28.24	31.81	32.86	31.57	28.34	30.08	28.24	29.60	29.78	31.81	32.23	31.63	32.86	30.68	32.29	31.57
1972	37.26	31.69	34.59	34.58	37.07	30.45	30.24	31.69	33.36	33.46	34.59	33.71	33.94	34.58	34.82	36.77	37.07
1973	41.05	35.71	39.46	39.41	41.01	35.50	34.69	35.71	37.18	37.71	39.46	38.00	38.37	39.41	39.67	40.67	41.01
1974	43.44	37.58	40.37	40.50	43.42	38.54	37.96	37.58	39.48	39.33	40.37	39.31	39.16	40.50	40.71	42.88	43.42
1975	54.77	41.10	47.76	47.43	54.75	39.49	39.55	41.10	42.29	43.09	47.76	46.86	45.56	47.43	50.86	52.40	54.75
1976	58.14	52.05	56.55	53.80	58.16	50.73	52.30	52.05	53.98	54.56	56.55	54.00	52.01	53.80	54.35	55.30	58.16
1977	63.39	55.31	60.43	57.57	63.41	54.27	53.10	55.31	56.61	57.35	60.43	56.23	54.46	57.57	59.26	59.73	63.41
1978	73.45	60.33	67.73	65.55	73.51	57.34	56.55	60.33	62.31	62.30	67.73	62.83	62.07	65.55	66.48	67.21	73.51
1979	80.31	71.13	75.83	72.91	80.31	66.44	65.40	71.13	71.48	71.36	75.83	71.28	69.24	72.91	75.41	75.57	80.31
1980	87.75	75.85	79.46	77.03	87.81	72.63	70.27	75.85	74.44	74.26	79.46	72.92	71.78	77.03	79.25	81.06	87.81
1981	97.32	82.94	90.77	87.00	97.36	78.03	77.60	82.94	84.74	83.57	90.77	82.72	88.26	87.00	88.06	90.94	97.36
1982	110.42	93.47	100.57	96.92	110.38	87.99	87.20	93.47	92.63	93.23	100.57	92.21	91.20	96.92	97.68	99.77	110.38
1983	136.93	109.93	122.99	123.47	136.93	99.77	98.76	109.93	109.73	110.23	122.99	114.98	113.63	123.47	121.64	121.29	136.93

M1 plus quasi-money (18)(19)

billion kroner, end of period

M1 plus quasi-monnaie (18)(19)

milliards de couronnes, fin de période

	Year	Q.1	Q.2	Q.3	Q.4	JAN	FEB	MAR	APR	MAY	JUN	JUL	AUG	SEP	OCT	NOV	DEC
1964																	
1965																	
1966																	
1967																	
1968	49.71																
1969	54.89																
1970	56.47	54.75	55.76	55.29	56.22		54.28	54.75	56.80	55.57	55.76	56.41	55.39	55.29	56.19	56.26	56.22
1971	61.45	55.59	59.76	61.22	61.16	55.60	57.36	55.59	57.24	57.53	59.76	60.28	59.77	61.22	59.20	61.47	61.16
1972	70.69	61.68	65.34	66.38	70.49	60.49	60.05	61.68	63.78	64.18	65.34	64.87	65.55	66.38	66.61	69.59	70.49
1973	79.67	69.97	74.92	76.30	79.63	69.35	68.91	69.97	71.96	73.11	74.92	74.06	74.82	76.30	76.97	78.87	79.63
1974	86.75	76.97	80.64	81.51	86.67	77.31	76.99	76.97	79.03	79.61	80.64	79.32	79.86	81.51	82.41	86.20	86.67
1975	108.55	86.49	94.99	97.65	108.46	83.88	84.47	86.49	88.84	90.74	94.99	94.78	95.43	97.65	102.69	106.32	108.46
1976	120.94	109.60	116.19	114.64	120.95	106.35	109.17	109.60	112.21	113.98	116.19	114.73	113.16	114.64	115.83	117.74	120.95
1977	132.77	119.43	126.33	126.16	132.74	117.20	116.74	119.43	122.48	124.30	126.83	123.56	122.81	126.16	128.73	129.61	132.74
1978	141.62	128.44	136.37	134.05	141.66	126.85	125.11	128.44	130.46	131.17	136.37	132.30	130.87	134.05	135.12	135.87	141.66
1979	155.66	141.35	149.11	146.78	155.65	135.38	135.43	141.35	143.63	145.14	149.11	144.99	143.24	146.78	149.96	150.52	155.65
1980	172.54	153.42	159.18	158.28	172.59	148.37	146.72	153.42	153.20	153.88	159.18	153.07	152.73	158.28	162.43	165.46	172.59
1981	190.50	170.71	179.70	176.25	190.55	163.88	164.16	170.71	173.30	173.27	179.70	172.71	177.94	176.25	179.09	183.47	190.55
1982	212.01	188.89	196.19	195.23	211.97	181.30	180.75	188.89	189.11	189.44	196.19	191.36	190.10	195.23	196.72	197.93	211.97
1983	270.33	216.28	237.00	241.76	270.33	202.78	202.43	216.28	219.23	223.57	237.00	228.66	229.43	241.76	242.38	246.09	270.33

Net new bond issues (20)

billion kroner

Nouvelles émissions d'obligations, nettes (20)

milliards de couronnes

	Year	Q.1	Q.2	Q.3	Q.4	JAN	FEB	MAR	APR	MAY	JUN	JUL	AUG	SEP	OCT	NOV	DEC
1964	4.39	1.00	0.89	1.24	1.26	0.32	0.34	0.34	0.32	0.36	0.22	0.44	0.42	0.39	0.44	0.41	0.43
1965	6.99	1.20	1.69	2.07	2.04	0.31	0.37	0.52	0.39	0.49	0.82	0.68	0.73	0.65	0.67	0.67	0.70
1966	5.95	1.28	1.34	1.35	1.99	0.36	0.44	0.48	0.46	0.45	0.44	0.24	0.54	0.57	0.55	0.61	0.82
1967	6.43	1.26	1.44	1.63	2.10	0.26	0.42	0.58	0.41	0.56	0.47	0.40	0.68	0.56	0.77	0.91	0.42
1968	9.27	1.56	1.74	2.42	3.55	0.36	0.61	0.60	0.50	0.69	0.55	0.62	0.89	0.91	1.25	1.20	1.11
1969	11.78	3.70	2.84	2.50	2.74	0.95	1.21	1.54	1.20	0.86	0.87	0.82	0.77	0.92	0.86	1.05	0.84
1970	10.76	2.29	2.93	2.83	2.71	0.49	0.89	0.92	0.88	0.76	1.29	0.98	0.92	0.93	0.96	1.01	0.74
1971	14.03	3.03	4.08	3.29	3.64	0.47	1.11	1.45	1.57	1.07	1.44	1.00	1.22	1.08	1.14	1.20	1.30
1972	16.85	3.69	4.27	4.22	4.67	0.68	1.32	1.69	1.30	1.57	1.40	0.80	1.53	1.89	1.27	2.11	1.29
1973	23.13	6.91	4.96	5.31	5.95	1.87	2.04	3.00	1.62	1.59	1.75	1.47	1.95	1.89	2.10	2.59	1.27
1974	26.37	6.60	6.57	6.51	6.60	1.76	2.23	2.62	1.95	2.04	2.67	1.61	2.07	2.83	3.72	1.37	1.51
1975	33.88	6.04	7.66	11.96	8.21	0.98	2.42	2.65	2.20	2.64	2.82	3.96	2.74	5.26	3.38	2.59	2.24
1976	37.55	8.61	7.97	3.49	12.47	1.65	3.54	3.43	2.36	2.68	2.93	1.70	3.56	3.23	3.39	4.69	4.39
1977	42.16	12.00	11.14	8.29	10.73	2.66	4.41	4.94	3.47	3.81	3.86	1.70	2.80	3.73	2.77	6.18	1.78
1978	52.50	9.42	13.86	15.06	14.17	1.90	4.61	2.90	4.53	5.49	3.84	5.89	4.50	4.67	4.60	5.41	4.16
1979	55.20	15.31	16.60	10.06	13.23	5.42	3.57	6.32	7.27	4.87	4.46	4.68	2.13	3.26	6.50	5.08	1.65
1980	62.34	9.96	18.14	17.44	16.80	5.58	2.50	1.89	5.86	6.78	5.49	8.09	4.08	5.27	8.36	5.42	3.02
1981	67.90	15.00	20.37	18.22	14.32	8.73	3.53	2.74	5.68	8.33	6.37	5.40	6.41	6.41	2.74	5.07	6.51
1982	94.15	19.63	22.82	23.36	28.35	2.90	8.49	8.24	3.29	5.58	9.05	8.16	8.78	6.42	8.59	9.24	10.52
1983	112.76	27.58	25.25	33.56	26.38	13.14	8.90	5.54	10.36	4.55	10.34	10.70	12.06	10.80	12.75	3.48	10.15

Money supply (M1) (18)

billion kroner, end of period

Adjusted - Corrigé *

Disponibilités monétaires (M1) (18)

milliards de couronnes, fin de période

	Year	Q.1	Q.2	Q.3	Q.4	JAN	FEB	MAR	APR	MAY	JUN	JUL	AUG	SEP	OCT	NOV	DEC
1964																	
1965																	
1966																	
1967																	
1968																	
1969																	
1970		30.10	28.09	28.09	28.56		30.27	30.10	30.48	29.21	28.09	29.12	28.43	28.09	28.79	28.33	28.56
1971		29.14	30.70	32.76	30.36	29.22	31.69	29.14	29.42	29.75	30.70	31.94	31.70	32.76	30.38	31.41	30.86
1972		32.74	33.32	34.41	35.99	31.39	31.83	32.74	33.23	33.39	33.32	33.58	34.15	34.41	34.48	35.70	35.99
1973		36.39	37.94	39.21	39.47	36.64	36.51	36.89	37.07	37.60	37.94	38.03	38.87	39.21	39.32	39.49	39.47
1974		38.74	38.67	40.34	41.44	39.81	39.91	38.74	39.40	39.13	38.67	39.55	40.05	40.34	40.31	41.67	41.44
1975		42.24	45.58	47.33	51.80	40.88	41.59	42.24	42.80	42.83	45.58	47.29	47.02	47.33	50.35	51.07	51.80
1976		53.22	53.75	53.85	54.61	52.57	55.05	53.22	53.82	54.29	53.75	54.66	54.12	53.85	53.77	54.11	54.61
1977		56.26	57.28	57.74	59.20	56.24	56.01	56.26	56.39	57.12	57.28	57.09	57.03	57.74	58.62	58.56	59.20
1978		61.00	64.08	65.88	68.26	59.36	59.78	61.00	61.94	62.17	64.08	64.05	65.33	65.88	65.70	65.96	68.26
1979		71.63	71.67	73.28	74.30	68.71	69.21	71.63	70.98	71.50	71.67	72.88	72.96	73.28	74.59	74.16	74.30
1980		76.15	75.10	77.42	81.08	75.11	74.44	76.15	73.92	74.64	75.10	74.71	75.72	77.42	78.31	79.55	81.08
1981		83.19	85.80	87.44	89.32	80.61	82.20	83.19	84.15	84.08	85.80	84.84	93.20	87.44	87.02	89.24	89.82
1982		93.75	95.14	97.50	101.82	90.90	92.47	93.75	91.99	93.89	95.14	94.57	96.31	97.50	96.53	97.91	101.82
1983		110.26	116.35	124.22	126.32	103.07	104.72	110.26	108.96	111.01	116.36	117.93	119.99	124.22	120.20	119.02	126.32

M1 plus quasi-money (18)

billion kroner, end of period

Adjusted - Corrigé *

M1 plus quasi-monnaie (18)

milliards de couronnes, fin de période

	Year	Q.1	Q.2	Q.3	Q.4	JAN	FEB	MAR	APR	MAY	JUN	JUL	AUG	SEP	OCT	NOV	DEC
1964																	
1965																	
1966																	
1967																	
1968																	
1969																	
1970		55.81	54.88	55.23	55.28		55.72	55.81	56.63	55.46	54.88	56.29	55.39	55.23	56.41	55.21	55.28
1971		56.61	58.81	61.16	60.08	56.28	58.83	56.61	57.07	57.42	58.81	60.22	59.83	61.16	59.38	60.33	60.08
1972		62.82	64.31	66.32	69.11	61.22	61.52	62.82	63.65	63.99	64.31	64.94	65.75	66.32	66.74	68.29	69.11
1973		71.26	73.74	76.30	77.84	70.12	70.60	71.26	71.89	72.89	73.74	74.29	75.35	76.30	77.05	77.40	77.84
1974		78.22	79.21	81.59	84.56	78.25	78.81	78.22	78.95	79.29	79.21	79.64	80.74	81.59	82.41	84.67	84.56
1975		87.81	93.22	97.85	105.51	84.90	86.45	87.81	88.75	90.29	93.22	95.16	96.78	97.85	102.58	104.65	105.51
1976		110.93	113.80	114.99	117.42	107.86	111.85	110.93	112.20	113.30	113.80	115.31	115.12	114.99	115.48	116.23	117.42
1977		120.51	123.86	126.67	128.63	118.99	119.85	120.51	122.24	123.56	123.86	124.18	125.31	126.67	128.22	128.20	128.63
1978		129.21	133.04	134.72	137.00	128.91	128.71	129.21	129.94	130.51	133.04	133.10	133.81	134.72	134.32	134.52	137.00
1979		141.92	145.19	147.52	150.38	137.72	139.47	141.92	142.92	144.56	145.19	146.01	146.61	147.52	145.22	149.17	150.38
1980		153.73	154.85	159.08	166.59	151.09	151.26	153.73	152.44	153.26	154.85	154.30	156.48	159.08	161.62	163.98	166.59
1981		170.88	174.81	177.31	183.75	167.06	169.24	170.88	172.44	172.75	174.81	174.28	182.50	177.31	178.02	181.83	183.75
1982		188.89	190.84	196.41	204.40	184.81	186.34	188.89	188.17	188.87	190.84	193.10	194.98	196.41	195.55	196.17	204.40
1983		216.28	230.55	243.22	260.69	206.71	208.69	216.28	218.14	222.90	230.55	230.74	235.32	243.22	240.94	243.90	260.69

Domestic credit (18)(19)(21)

billion kroner, end of period

Crédits au secteur intérieur (18)(19)(21)

milliards de couronnes, fin de période

	Year	Q.1	Q.2	Q.3	Q.4	JAN	FEB	MAR	APR	MAY	JUN	JUL	AUG	SEP	OCT	NOV	DEC
1964	25.08	22.42	23.72	24.18	25.02	21.73	21.75	22.42	22.75	22.89	23.72	23.58	23.44	24.18	24.20	24.56	25.02
1965	27.50	26.00	26.73	26.85	27.40	25.11	25.20	26.00	25.96	25.79	26.73	26.41	26.11	26.85	26.62	26.72	27.40
1966	31.63	28.25	29.49	30.33	31.46	27.24	27.17	28.25	28.14	28.03	29.49	29.31	29.29	30.33	30.14	30.53	31.46
1967	34.51	32.74	33.72	33.91	34.38	31.36	31.40	32.74	32.64	32.42	33.72	33.29	33.05	33.91	33.38	33.74	34.38
1968	37.48	35.30	36.25	36.61	37.38	34.02	34.26	35.30	34.81	35.15	36.25	35.46	35.91	36.61	36.17	37.01	37.38
1969	43.11	38.32	40.57	41.96	42.97	36.84	37.46	38.32	38.31	39.24	40.57	40.19	41.00	41.96	41.64	42.39	42.97
1970	46.02	43.56	44.70	44.80	45.86	42.14	42.73	43.56	43.22	43.88	44.70	43.88	43.97	44.80	44.62	45.15	45.86
1971	47.81	46.97	47.27	47.22	47.87	45.92	46.15	46.97	46.36	46.55	47.27	46.75	46.37	47.22	46.65	47.17	47.87
1972	53.70	48.96	50.52	52.07	53.83	47.71	47.92	48.96	48.60	49.18	50.52	50.18	50.69	52.07	51.77	53.02	53.83
1973	62.21	56.45	58.46	60.54	62.17	54.24	55.06	56.45	56.37	57.27	58.46	58.48	58.89	60.54	60.34	61.33	62.17
1974	66.57	65.26	66.90	66.34	66.56	62.45	63.54	65.26	64.61	65.33	66.90	65.31	65.12	66.34	64.98	66.10	66.56
1975	68.16	67.63	67.11	66.60	68.24	65.99	66.36	67.63	66.08	65.14	67.11	65.83	65.79	66.60	66.67	67.21	68.24
1976	79.80	72.27	75.81	78.88	79.75	68.69	69.39	72.27	72.78	73.39	75.81	74.72	76.02	78.88	78.05	78.17	79.75
1977	89.24	82.05	85.68	87.48	89.19	79.16	79.99	82.05	81.84	82.63	85.68	85.22	86.24	87.48	86.15	87.57	89.19
1978	98.66	92.14	94.83	96.28	98.70	88.94	89.60	92.14	91.98	92.50	94.83	93.26	94.52	96.28	95.08	101.28	98.70
1979	103.54	100.86	105.37	107.34	108.78	97.72	98.69	100.86	100.53	101.78	105.37	102.66	104.07	107.34	105.11	106.62	108.78
1980	117.80	111.65	115.72	115.32	118.67	107.76	108.87	111.65	111.73	112.53	115.72	112.73	113.34	115.32	112.39	115.30	118.67
1981	128.47	120.01	127.42	127.92	129.52	116.14	117.19	120.01	120.17	122.63	127.42	123.24	124.34	127.92	125.28	124.81	129.52
1982	137.18	131.72	138.86	140.53	141.27	125.25	125.63	131.72	131.11	134.17	138.86	134.96	135.78	140.53	137.96	137.39	141.27
1983	158.30	142.54	148.21	148.63	158.30	136.95	137.86	142.54	142.74	143.24	148.21	143.41	144.54	148.63	147.45	145.89	158.30

* Adjusted by the O.E.C.D.

* Corrigé par l'O.C.D.E.

DENMARK

Official discount rate — Taux d'escompte officiel

per cent per annum, end of period — pourcentage par an, fin de periode

	Year	Q.1	Q.2	Q.3	Q.4	JAN	FEB	MAR	APR	MAY	JUN	JUL	AUG	SEP	OCT	NOV	DEC
1964	6.50	5.50	6.50	5.50	6.50	5.50	5.50	5.50	5.50	5.50	6.50	6.50	6.50	6.50	6.50	6.50	6.50
1965	6.50	6.50	6.50	6.50	6.50	6.50	6.50	6.50	6.50	6.50	6.50	6.50	6.50	6.50	6.50	6.50	6.50
1966	6.50	6.50	6.50	6.50	6.50	6.50	6.50	6.50	6.50	6.50	6.50	6.50	6.50	6.50	6.50	6.50	6.50
1967	7.50	6.50	6.50	6.50	7.50	6.50	6.50	6.50	6.50	6.50	6.50	6.50	6.50	6.50	6.50	6.50	7.50
1968	6.00	7.00	6.50	6.00	6.00	7.50	7.50	7.00	7.00	7.00	6.50	6.50	6.00	6.00	6.00	6.00	6.00
1969	9.00	7.00	9.00	9.00	9.00	6.00	6.00	7.00	7.00	9.00	9.00	9.00	9.00	9.00	9.00	9.00	9.00
1970	9.00	9.00	9.00	9.00	9.00	9.00	9.00	9.00	9.00	9.00	9.00	9.00	9.00	9.00	9.00	9.00	9.00
1971	7.50	8.00	7.50	7.50	7.50	8.00	8.00	8.00	7.50	7.50	7.50	7.50	7.50	7.50	7.50	7.50	7.50
1972	7.00	7.00	8.00	8.00	7.00	7.00	7.00	7.00	7.00	7.00	8.00	8.00	8.00	8.00	7.00	7.00	7.00
1973	9.00	7.00	7.00	8.00	9.00	7.00	7.00	7.00	7.00	7.00	7.00	8.00	8.00	8.00	8.00	8.00	9.00
1974	10.00	10.00	10.00	10.00	10.00	10.00	10.00	10.00	10.00	10.00	10.00	10.00	10.00	10.00	10.00	10.00	10.00
1975	7.50	9.00	8.00	7.50	7.50	9.00	9.00	9.00	8.00	8.00	8.00	8.00	7.50	7.50	7.50	7.50	7.50
1976	10.00	8.50	8.50	8.50	10.00	7.50	7.50	8.50	8.50	8.50	8.50	8.50	8.50	8.50	11.00	11.00	10.00
1977	9.00	9.00	9.00	9.00	9.00	10.00	10.00	9.00	9.00	9.00	9.00	9.00	9.00	9.00	9.00	9.00	9.00
1978	8.00	9.00	9.00	8.00	8.00	9.00	9.00	9.00	9.00	9.00	9.00	8.00	8.00	8.00	8.00	8.00	8.00
1979	11.00	8.00	9.00	11.00	11.00	8.00	8.00	8.00	8.00	8.00	9.00	9.00	9.00	11.00	11.00	11.00	11.00
1980	11.00	13.00	13.00	12.00	11.00	11.00	13.00	13.00	13.00	13.00	13.00	13.00	13.00	12.00	11.00	11.00	11.00
1981	11.00	11.00	11.00	11.00	11.00	11.00	11.00	11.00	11.00	11.00	11.00	11.00	11.00	11.00	11.00	11.00	11.00
1982	10.00	11.00	11.00	11.00	10.00	11.00	11.00	11.00	11.00	11.00	11.00	11.00	11.00	11.00	11.00	10.00	10.00
1983	7.00	8.50	7.50	7.50	7.00	10.00	10.00	8.50	7.50	7.50	7.50	7.50	7.50	7.50	7.00	7.00	7.00

Yield of long-term bonds (22) — Rendement des obligations à long terme (22)

per cent per annum, end of period — pourcentage par an, fin de période

	Year	Q.1	Q.2	Q.3	Q.4	JAN	FEB	MAR	APR	MAY	JUN	JUL	AUG	SEP	OCT	NOV	DEC
1964	8.18	6.36	6.92	7.56	8.18	6.13	6.39	6.36	6.46	6.60	6.92	6.97	7.26	7.56	7.39	8.18	8.18
1965	8.66	8.22	8.65	8.89	8.66	8.22	8.34	8.22	8.48	8.97	8.65	8.78	8.82	8.89	8.82	8.62	8.66
1966	8.89	8.62	8.63	8.84	8.89	8.62	8.59	8.62	8.62	8.59	8.63	8.64	8.85	8.84	8.96	9.05	8.89
1967	9.37	8.85	8.99	9.17	9.37	8.90	8.90	8.85	8.85	8.90	8.99	9.04	9.13	9.17	9.26	9.40	9.37
1968	8.50	8.81	8.56	8.45	8.50	9.26	9.39	8.81	8.63	8.60	8.56	8.57	8.38	8.45	8.49	8.49	8.50
1969	10.06	8.72	9.82	10.61	10.06	8.50	8.58	8.72	8.72	9.86	9.82	10.10	10.25	10.61	10.62	10.21	10.06
1970	11.30	10.57	10.81	11.84	11.30	10.02	10.23	10.57	10.58	10.53	10.81	12.06	11.48	11.84	12.27	11.41	11.30
1971	10.91	11.05	11.49	10.56	10.91	10.78	10.90	11.05	11.17	11.42	11.49	10.96	11.02	10.56	10.51	10.68	10.91
1972	11.24	11.15	11.04	11.04	11.24	11.41	11.39	11.15	11.11	11.07	11.04	10.99	10.71	11.04	10.33	10.65	11.24
1973	13.78	11.99	12.01	13.41	13.78	11.50	11.73	11.99	11.76	11.88	12.01	12.30	13.33	13.41	13.56	13.51	13.78
1974	14.54	15.29	17.59	15.79	14.54	14.21	15.25	15.29	16.37	17.25	17.59	17.68	16.68	15.79	15.23	14.28	14.54
1975	12.66	12.57	12.67	12.05	12.66	13.08	13.35	12.57	13.09	13.03	12.67	12.86	12.45	12.05	12.43	12.39	12.66
1976	16.37	14.40	14.56	15.93	16.37	12.98	13.62	14.40	14.76	14.98	14.56	15.03	15.42	15.93	15.57	15.51	16.37
1977	17.54	16.06	16.07	16.21	17.54	16.23	15.86	16.06	15.28	15.69	16.07	16.67	16.60	16.21	16.57	16.63	17.54
1978	17.96	16.58	17.87	17.17	17.96	17.41	17.56	16.58	17.23	17.58	17.87	17.00	16.59	17.17	17.97	18.25	17.96
1979	17.98	16.50	17.41	18.04	17.98	17.48	17.15	16.50	15.89	17.29	17.41	17.55	17.65	18.04	17.89	18.05	17.98
1980	18.60	19.56	19.30	19.33	18.60	18.34	19.49	19.56	19.73	19.80	19.30	18.76	19.83	19.33	18.62	18.34	18.60
1981	19.45	18.48	19.54	20.44	19.45	18.02	18.26	18.48	18.92	19.36	19.54	20.29	20.22	20.44	19.33	19.14	19.45
1982	19.40	20.58	21.18	21.16	19.40	19.84	20.57	20.58	20.76	21.28	21.18	20.67	20.67	21.16	19.81	19.61	19.40
1983	12.77	14.67	14.22	13.56	12.77	18.12	15.67	14.67	13.66	13.83	14.22	14.39	14.31	13.56	13.71	13.92	12.77

Share prices: industrials (10)(23) — Cours des actions : industrielles (10)(23)

1980 = 100

	Year	Q.1	Q.2	Q.3	Q.4	JAN	FEB	MAR	APR	MAY	JUN	JUL	AUG	SEP	OCT	NOV	DEC
1964	59	56	60	61	58	55	56	58	59	60	60	61	61	60	59	58	58
1965	60	61	62	59	59	59	61	62	64	61	60	60	59	59	58	59	60
1966	63	63	65	65	58	62	63	64	65	65	66	67	66	63	61	57	56
1967	51	54	52	49	49	55	55	53	54	52	51	50	50	48	48	49	50
1968	53	49	51	54	55	50	49	49	50	52	52	54	54	54	55	55	55
1969	60	60	63	59	57	58	58	62	65	62	61	61	59	57	56	58	58
1970	54	57	56	52	50	57	57	57	57	56	55	53	53	51	50	50	50
1971	50	49	49	51	50	50	49	48	49	49	49	51	51	51	51	49	51
1972	71	55	64	70	94	53	55	57	61	64	67	68	70	72	85	98	101
1973	109	110	113	116	98	111	110	109	110	112	116	117	117	113	108	91	95
1974	81	91	87	76	71	94	94	85	88	88	86	80	72	75	73	66	73
1975	89	78	88	92	99	76	79	79	86	89	89	92	92	92	96	99	104
1976	116	109	118	125	113	109	108	111	114	119	120	127	127	121	116	111	111
1977	119	119	123	119	117	115	118	122	122	123	122	117	119	121	120	115	115
1978	113	116	114	116	107	114	116	118	112	115	115	117	117	113	105	109	107
1979	109	111	112	110	103	110	110	112	112	113	111	112	111	108	105	104	100
1980	100	89	90	101	121	93	87	87	89	90	92	97	99	106	121	119	122
1981	168	137	163	180	191	134	135	141	151	160	179	182	155	173	188	190	194
1982	213	203	207	217	227	202	207	201	212	206	203	207	220	225	230	217	233
1983	373	269	345	425	455	249	265	291	321	347	366	375	447	454	454	447	463

U.S. dollar exchange rate: spot — Taux de change du dollar É.-U. : au comptant

cents per krone, end of period — cents par couronne, fin de période

	Year	Q.1	Q.2	Q.3	Q.4	JAN	FEB	MAR	APR	MAY	JUN	JUL	AUG	SEP	OCT	NOV	DEC
1964	14.45	14.48	14.45	14.43	14.45	14.45	14.45	14.48	14.48	14.46	14.45	14.44	14.41	14.43	14.41	14.44	14.45
1965	14.51	14.43	14.41	14.49	14.51	14.44	14.45	14.43	14.46	14.42	14.41	14.40	14.38	14.49	14.48	14.50	14.51
1966	14.46	14.48	14.45	14.48	14.46	14.49	14.47	14.48	14.46	14.43	14.45	14.42	14.43	14.48	14.46	14.47	14.46
1967	13.40	14.45	14.41	14.41	13.40	14.45	14.43	14.45	14.45	14.42	14.41	14.39	14.40	14.41	14.39	13.39	13.40
1968	13.33	13.41	13.34	13.33	13.33	13.39	13.41	13.41	13.39	13.39	13.34	13.29	13.29	13.33	13.30	13.32	13.33
1969	13.35	13.31	13.28	13.28	13.35	13.29	13.30	13.31	13.27	13.28	13.28	13.28	13.28	13.28	13.31	13.34	13.35
1970	13.35	13.33	13.33	13.33	13.35	13.33	13.33	13.33	13.31	13.33	13.33	13.32	13.32	13.33	13.33	13.35	13.35
1971	14.16	13.37	13.34	13.73	14.16	13.35	13.36	13.37	13.33	13.34	13.34	13.33	13.61	13.73	13.78	13.84	14.16
1972	14.61	14.34	14.37	14.44	14.61	14.27	14.30	14.34	14.28	14.41	14.37	14.38	14.51	14.44	14.46	14.55	14.61
1973	15.90	16.11	17.58	17.45	15.90	14.63	16.19	16.11	16.01	16.55	17.58	18.12	17.26	17.45	17.51	16.31	15.90
1974	17.70	16.52	16.67	16.31	17.70	15.14	15.94	16.52	16.98	16.91	16.67	16.72	16.31	16.31	16.79	17.24	17.70
1975	16.19	18.38	18.27	16.07	16.19	17.91	18.43	18.38	18.26	18.31	18.27	16.77	16.73	16.07	16.74	16.30	16.19
1976	17.28	16.47	16.26	17.04	17.28	16.24	16.22	16.47	16.63	16.33	16.26	16.34	16.51	17.04	16.99	17.00	17.28
1977	17.31	17.09	16.59	16.24	17.31	16.86	16.99	17.09	16.77	16.63	16.59	16.70	16.13	16.24	16.45	16.27	17.31
1978	19.65	17.97	17.73	18.65	19.65	17.49	17.92	17.97	17.72	17.66	17.73	18.04	18.14	18.65	20.83	18.76	19.65
1979	18.64	19.26	18.83	19.64	18.64	19.41	19.31	19.26	18.84	18.22	18.83	18.91	18.95	19.64	18.80	18.69	18.64
1980	16.63	16.60	18.33	17.90	16.63	18.39	18.14	16.60	17.73	17.99	18.33	18.11	18.02	17.90	17.04	16.92	16.63
1981	13.65	15.10	13.34	13.69	13.65	15.38	15.01	15.10	14.33	13.67	13.34	12.92	13.14	13.69	13.78	14.08	13.65
1982	11.93	12.14	11.76	11.29	11.93	13.22	12.54	12.14	12.59	12.52	11.76	11.75	11.47	11.29	11.10	11.40	11.93
1983	10.13	11.62	10.95	10.50	10.13	11.63	11.61	11.62	11.42	11.09	10.95	10.52	10.27	10.50	10.55	10.25	10.13

Official reserves excluding gold — Réserves officielles, or exclu

million SDR's, end of period — millions de DTS, fin de période

	Year	Q.1	Q.2	Q.3	Q.4	JAN	FEB	MAR	APR	MAY	JUN	JUL	AUG	SEP	OCT	NOV	DEC
1964	553	378	423	481	553	350	334	378	395	390	423	450	439	481	490	496	553
1965	490	480	413	398	490	507	481	480	436	402	413	399	360	398	405	440	490
1966	489	520	480	451	439	490	477	520	489	469	480	434	408	451	433	440	489
1967	427	430	435	426	427	472	471	480	475	433	435	397	384	426	377	379	427
1968	335	403	355	371	335	396	416	403	374	338	355	315	294	371	296	320	335
1969	357	218	283	226	357	275	260	218	207	361	283	267	198	226	257	307	357
1970	419	360	253	304	419	311	320	360	290	274	253	235	282	304	363	399	419
1971	601	530	360	358	601	443	479	530	410	360	360	370	359	358	405	525	601
1972	724	726	661	595	724	653	718	726	686	682	661	640	668	596	585	667	724
1973	1034	827	902	714	1034	759	795	827	902	909	902	858	690	714	738	947	1034
1974	701	783	598	583	701	898	826	783	816	653	598	584	625	583	585	628	701
1975	686	681	636	672	686	677	620	681	614	616	636	603	626	672	693	691	686
1976	724	972	810	466	724	677	666	972	940	847	810	546	645	466	613	621	724
1977	1308	1131	1739	1682	1308	867	980	1131	1540	1655	1739	1554	1525	1682	1829	1797	1308
1978	2402	1745	2150	2270	2402	1862	1749	1745	1755	1915	2150	2290	2287	2270	2151	2282	2402
1979	2456	3267	3061	2560	2456	2727	2951	3267	3653	3637	3061	3015	2708	2560	2537	2388	2456
1980	2655	1470	1883	2413	2655	2103	1608	1470	1576	1712	1883	2287	2250	2413	2489	2564	2655
1981	2189	2484	2380	2144	2189	2643	2556	2484	2316	2222	2380	2529	2256	2144	2079	2268	2189
1982	2054	1889	1904	1706	2054	2009	2031	1389	1710	1787	1904	1806	1872	1706	1509	1947	2054
1983	3458	2317	2900	3287	3458	2692	2682	2317	3111	3105	2900	2990	2989	3287	3768	3953	3458

Net foreign position (24) — Position extérieure nette (24)

million kroner, end of period — millions de couronnes, fin de période

	Year	Q.1	Q.2	Q.3	Q.4	JAN	FEB	MAR	APR	MAY	JUN	JUL	AUG	SEP	OCT	NOV	DEC
1964	-680	-300	-482	-520	-859	-272	-59	-300	-378	-381	-482	-494	-379	-520	-569	-584	-859
1965	-260	-661	-602	-325	-304	-645	-536	-661	-588	-537	-602	-526	-221	-325	-181	-218	-304
1966	-113	-326	-276	-156	-178	-180	-69	-326	-218	-10	-276	-62	90	-156	-19	26	-178
1967	8	-233	-204	-77	-70	-103	-95	-233	-132	18	-204	-70	90	-77	254	120	-70
1968	602	18	190	463	507	322	220	18	159	359	190	617	804	463	960	631	507
1969	42	687	313	235	42	1066	900	687	565	559	313	400	417	235	148	103	42
1970	4	97	57	142	-118	432	232	97	173	194	57	273	234	142	154	110	-118
1971	-264	-110	174	150	-426	-46	2	-110	28	106	174	227	239	150	167	162	-426
1972	452	-169	43	-151	277	-224	-146	-169	-37	95	43	44	-50	-151	216	372	277
1973	190	-256	-134	1065	-313	716	-60	-256	-520	-294	-134	1472	1489	1065	1345	472	-313
1974	2350	1412	2011	1961	2012	694	1083	1412	1888	2961	2011	2169	1816	1961	2094	2548	2012
1975	839	2155	1463	1737	483	2071	2597	2155	2235	2025	1463	1505	1457	1737	1241	1639	483
1976	2018	2949	2112	3946	1717	1006	1561	2949	2791	2540	2112	2585	3415	3946	3216	2238	1717
1977	3202	807	437	-353	2862	1477	1492	807	-233	586	437	500	-28	-353	-770	897	2862
1978	791	1607	920	2042	352	2109	1846	1607	1005	1082	920	632	2297	2042	3366	1779	352
1979	2249	437	2241	4596	1864	297	-63	437	-111	311	2241	2278	2460	4596	3521	3372	1864
1980	255	3236	2623	1526	-238	2157	3683	3236	2823	2820	2623	1630	1086	1526	805	1526	-238
1981	419	-1300	-1693	1064	-42	-1913	2371	-1300	-56	-972	-1693	-621	64	1064	237	1477	-42
1982	820	-833	-2512	2262	181	-213	-2236	-833	-304	-2099	-2512	-1307	-716	2262	4234	589	181
1983	-4271	695	-1074	-3742	-4271	-2147	-2571	695	-2968	-3109	-1074	-1436	-1962	-3742	-3620	-4508	-4271

DENMARK

Imports c.i.f. (25) — Importations c.a.f. (25)

billion kroner, monthly averages — milliards de couronnes, moyennes mensuelles

	Year	Q.1	Q.2	Q.3	Q.4	JAN	FEB	MAR	APR	MAY	JUN	JUL	AUG	SEP	OCT	NOV	DEC
1964	1.50	1.39	1.38	1.41	1.64	1.50	1.31	1.36	1.72	1.40	1.61	1.35	1.46	1.41	1.58	1.63	1.70
1965	1.62	1.62	1.67	1.52	1.66	1.54	1.54	1.78	1.62	1.78	1.62	1.53	1.55	1.48	1.54	1.64	1.80
1966	1.72	1.70	1.70	1.61	1.88	1.62	1.61	1.86	1.74	1.65	1.71	1.58	1.63	1.62	1.94	1.71	2.00
1967	1.82	1.78	1.85	1.70	1.96	1.81	1.71	1.83	1.86	1.97	1.72	1.46	1.82	1.82	1.92	1.94	2.01
1968	2.02	1.93	1.98	1.91	2.24	1.86	1.92	2.02	2.13	2.11	1.70	1.97	1.79	1.98	2.19	1.98	2.54
1969	2.38	2.19	2.40	2.31	2.59	2.16	2.06	2.36	2.42	2.20	2.59	2.20	2.13	2.60	2.48	2.41	2.89
1970	2.74	2.54	2.89	2.52	3.02	2.44	2.52	2.66	3.03	2.69	2.94	2.46	2.46	2.64	2.79	3.16	3.12
1971	2.83	2.82	2.90	2.62	2.99	2.40	2.58	3.49	2.47	3.00	3.24	2.48	2.58	2.81	2.90	2.98	3.08
1972	2.93	2.85	2.77	2.82	3.28	2.60	2.86	3.08	2.61	2.91	2.79	2.72	2.78	2.96	3.34	3.40	3.10
1973	3.91	3.58	3.83	3.67	4.59	3.89	3.31	3.53	3.42	4.37	3.69	3.44	3.76	3.80	4.78	4.63	4.35
1974	5.04	5.34	5.16	4.73	4.93	5.40	5.15	5.47	5.56	5.25	4.66	4.80	4.77	4.61	5.27	4.85	4.68
1975	4.98	4.56	4.72	4.61	6.01	4.79	4.66	4.24	5.14	4.46	4.54	4.47	4.33	5.04	5.84	5.81	6.39
1976	6.25	6.07	6.12	5.99	6.83	5.38	5.92	6.90	6.26	5.87	6.24	5.16	6.20	6.61	6.45	7.10	6.94
1977	6.64	6.69	6.54	6.42	6.89	6.27	6.07	7.72	6.18	6.38	7.07	5.54	6.67	7.07	6.74	7.12	6.81
1978	6.68	6.52	6.58	6.35	7.29	6.46	6.23	6.85	6.36	6.61	6.76	5.34	6.86	6.86	7.25	7.51	7.10
1979	8.07	7.32	7.81	7.99	9.16	6.97	6.68	8.31	7.42	8.37	7.64	7.67	8.40	7.90	9.58	9.22	8.68
1980	9.12	10.08	9.01	8.23	9.15	10.00	9.94	10.31	9.60	6.97	10.46	8.09	7.47	9.12	9.18	8.60	9.67
1981	10.35	9.93	10.21	9.86	11.38	9.49	8.98	11.34	10.54	10.23	9.87	10.11	8.92	10.56	10.73	12.14	11.28
1982	11.57	11.69	11.38	10.87	12.35	10.47	11.57	13.04	11.81	10.10	12.24	9.41	10.99	12.20	11.63	12.46	12.96
1983	12.40	11.72	12.07	11.71	14.09	9.76	11.56	13.83	11.23	11.97	13.02	9.58	11.95	13.62	13.08	13.76	15.44

Exports f.o.b. (25) — Exportations f.o.b. (25)

billion kroner, monthly averages — milliards de couronnes, moyennes mensuelles

	Year	Q.1	Q.2	Q.3	Q.4	JAN	FEB	MAR	APR	MAY	JUN	JUL	AUG	SEP	OCT	NOV	DEC
1964	1.20	1.12	1.13	1.16	1.39	1.11	1.08	1.15	1.10	1.10	1.17	1.15	1.08	1.26	1.32	1.50	1.37
1965	1.31	1.24	1.29	1.24	1.46	1.13	1.23	1.36	1.28	1.27	1.34	1.17	1.27	1.28	1.44	1.48	1.47
1966	1.38	1.36	1.41	1.29	1.48	1.29	1.32	1.47	1.48	1.39	1.35	1.17	1.31	1.39	1.53	1.38	1.53
1967	1.44	1.36	1.44	1.37	1.59	1.34	1.43	1.31	1.47	1.43	1.43	1.15	1.46	1.50	1.54	1.61	1.61
1968	1.62	1.58	1.56	1.59	1.74	1.42	1.52	1.79	1.60	1.58	1.49	1.49	1.55	1.74	1.74	1.69	1.77
1969	1.85	1.76	1.86	1.75	2.03	1.67	1.75	1.87	1.91	1.65	2.02	1.60	1.61	2.03	2.01	1.93	2.15
1970	2.06	1.89	2.07	2.00	2.26	1.76	1.84	2.09	2.19	1.88	2.14	1.85	2.00	2.15	2.30	2.34	2.14
1971	2.23	2.04	2.29	2.16	2.43	1.82	1.97	2.33	2.10	2.36	2.40	1.88	2.30	2.30	2.49	2.36	2.43
1972	2.51	2.43	2.56	2.29	2.75	2.31	2.40	2.57	2.34	2.69	2.65	2.13	2.25	2.49	2.88	2.65	2.74
1973	3.13	2.85	2.95	3.12	3.59	2.59	2.94	3.02	2.63	3.19	3.04	2.88	2.74	3.74	3.70	3.39	3.69
1974	3.91	3.76	3.87	3.76	4.26	3.24	3.87	4.16	3.77	4.04	3.80	3.36	3.73	4.13	4.56	4.25	3.96
1975	4.17	3.93	4.25	3.80	4.70	3.68	4.11	4.01	4.32	4.01	4.41	3.56	3.63	4.20	5.45	4.23	4.43
1976	4.59	4.39	4.67	4.36	4.92	4.10	4.29	4.78	4.31	4.83	4.88	3.91	4.43	4.76	4.82	5.02	4.90
1977	5.04	4.99	4.89	4.72	5.54	4.46	4.83	5.68	4.92	4.58	5.19	3.99	4.83	5.33	5.39	5.64	5.60
1978	5.40	5.07	5.59	5.07	5.85	4.71	5.28	5.21	5.35	5.42	6.02	4.06	5.28	5.87	5.95	5.79	5.81
1979	6.45	5.93	6.36	6.22	7.27	5.36	5.33	7.10	6.37	6.23	6.48	5.31	6.44	6.93	7.85	7.57	6.41
1980	7.97	8.05	7.86	7.51	8.47	7.75	8.03	8.36	7.59	7.67	8.33	6.58	7.31	8.66	8.98	8.08	8.36
1981	9.48	9.07	9.54	9.17	10.15	8.61	8.58	10.03	9.35	9.04	10.24	8.21	9.21	10.10	10.25	10.76	9.43
1982	10.69	10.61	10.88	10.05	11.20	8.89	10.45	12.50	10.47	10.16	12.02	8.36	9.85	11.95	11.20	11.84	10.57
1983	12.16	11.83	11.84	11.44	13.46	10.44	12.33	12.89	10.99	11.47	13.05	9.39	11.53	13.41	13.15	14.69	12.53

Trade balance (f.o.b. — c.i.f.) (25) — Balance commerciale (f.o.b. — c.a.f.) (25)

billion kroner, monthly averages — milliards de couronnes, moyennes mensuelles

	Year	Q.1	Q.2	Q.3	Q.4	JAN	FEB	MAR	APR	MAY	JUN	JUL	AUG	SEP	OCT	NOV	DEC
1964	-0.30	-0.27	-0.45	-0.25	-0.24	-0.38	-0.23	-0.21	-0.62	-0.30	-0.44	-0.20	-0.38	-0.15	-0.26	-0.14	-0.33
1965	-0.31	-0.38	-0.38	-0.27	-0.20	-0.41	-0.31	-0.43	-0.34	-0.52	-0.28	-0.35	-0.27	-0.20	-0.11	-0.17	-0.34
1966	-0.34	-0.34	-0.30	-0.32	-0.40	-0.33	-0.29	-0.40	-0.27	-0.26	-0.36	-0.41	-0.32	-0.23	-0.41	-0.32	-0.46
1967	-0.38	-0.42	-0.41	-0.33	-0.37	-0.47	-0.28	-0.52	-0.40	-0.54	-0.30	-0.31	-0.36	-0.32	-0.38	-0.33	-0.40
1968	-0.40	-0.36	-0.42	-0.32	-0.50	-0.44	-0.40	-0.23	-0.53	-0.53	-0.21	-0.48	-0.24	-0.24	-0.45	-0.29	-0.77
1969	-0.53	-0.43	-0.55	-0.56	-0.56	-0.50	-0.30	-0.49	-0.51	-0.56	-0.57	-0.60	-0.52	-0.57	-0.47	-0.48	-0.74
1970	-0.69	-0.65	-0.82	-0.52	-0.76	-0.68	-0.68	-0.57	-0.83	-0.82	-0.80	-0.61	-0.46	-0.50	-0.49	-0.82	-0.98
1971	-0.61	-0.78	-0.62	-0.47	-0.56	-0.58	-0.61	-1.16	-0.37	-0.65	-0.84	-0.60	-0.28	-0.51	-0.41	-0.62	-0.65
1972	-0.42	-0.42	-0.21	-0.53	-0.53	-0.29	-0.46	-0.52	-0.27	-0.22	-0.14	-0.59	-0.53	-0.47	-0.46	-0.75	-0.37
1973	-0.79	-0.73	-0.88	-0.55	-0.99	-1.31	-0.37	-0.51	-0.80	-1.17	-0.65	-0.55	-1.03	-0.06	-1.08	-1.24	-0.66
1974	-1.13	-1.58	-1.29	-0.97	-0.68	-2.16	-1.29	-1.30	-1.79	-1.21	-0.86	-1.44	-1.04	-0.43	-0.71	-0.60	-0.72
1975	-0.81	-0.63	-0.47	-0.82	-1.31	-1.11	-0.55	-0.24	-0.82	-0.45	-0.13	-0.91	-0.70	-0.84	-0.39	-1.58	-1.96
1976	-1.67	-1.67	-1.45	-1.62	-1.91	-1.28	-1.63	-2.12	-1.95	-1.04	-1.36	-1.25	-1.76	-1.85	-1.63	-2.07	-2.04
1977	-1.60	-1.70	-1.65	-1.71	-1.35	-1.81	-1.24	-2.04	-1.25	-1.81	-1.89	-1.54	-1.84	-1.74	-1.35	-1.48	-1.21
1978	-1.29	-1.45	-0.98	-1.28	-1.44	-1.75	-0.95	-1.65	-1.01	-1.20	-0.74	-1.28	-1.58	-0.98	-1.30	-1.72	-1.29
1979	-1.62	-1.39	-1.45	-1.77	-1.89	-1.61	-1.35	-1.21	-1.04	-2.14	-1.15	-2.36	-1.97	-0.97	-1.74	-1.65	-2.27
1980	-1.14	-2.04	-1.15	-0.71	-0.67	-2.26	-1.90	-1.96	-2.01	0.70	-2.13	-1.51	-0.16	-0.47	-0.20	-0.51	-1.31
1981	-0.86	-0.86	-0.67	-0.69	-1.23	-0.88	-0.40	-1.31	-1.18	-1.19	0.37	-1.90	0.29	-0.47	-0.48	-1.37	-1.85
1982	-0.89	-1.08	-0.50	-0.81	-1.15	-1.58	-1.12	-0.54	-1.33	0.06	-0.23	-1.04	-1.14	-0.26	-0.43	-0.62	-2.39
1983	-0.24	0.17	-0.23	-0.27	-0.64	0.68	0.77	-0.95	-0.23	-0.50	0.03	-0.19	-0.41	-0.21	0.07	0.93	-2.92

Imports c.i.f. (25) — billion kroner, monthly averages

Adjusted - Corrigé *

Importations c.a.f. (25) — milliards de couronnes, moyennes mensuelles

	Year	Q.1	Q.2	Q.3	Q.4	JAN	FEB	MAR	APR	MAY	JUN	JUL	AUG	SEP	OCT	NOV	DEC
1964		1.41	1.51	1.48	1.58	1.44	1.39	1.41	1.50	1.47	1.56	1.34	1.61	1.49	1.59	1.61	1.54
1965		1.62	1.65	1.60	1.61	1.62	1.63	1.62	1.54	1.80	1.60	1.61	1.63	1.56	1.61	1.60	1.62
1966		1.69	1.67	1.71	1.85	1.67	1.70	1.69	1.75	1.59	1.67	1.75	1.67	1.70	1.98	1.70	1.85
1967		1.81	1.76	1.83	1.91	1.81	1.80	1.82	1.76	1.86	1.67	1.60	1.91	1.98	1.88	1.92	1.91
1968		1.92	1.93	2.02	2.14	1.84	1.93	1.97	2.00	2.01	1.77	2.05	1.98	2.04	2.10	2.07	2.26
1969		2.20	2.34	2.47	2.48	2.20	2.17	2.24	2.33	2.19	2.50	2.36	2.46	2.59	2.37	2.56	2.51
1970		2.64	2.73	2.71	2.39	2.61	2.65	2.66	2.67	2.77	2.75	2.67	2.78	2.67	2.76	3.11	2.80
1971		2.80	2.84	2.82	2.86	2.64	2.68	3.09	2.41	3.02	3.11	2.83	2.80	2.83	2.94	2.83	2.82
1972		2.73	2.74	3.09	3.17	2.73	2.82	2.78	2.76	2.74	2.71	3.14	2.96	3.17	3.14	3.23	3.12
1973		3.47	3.82	4.00	4.34	3.75	3.35	3.32	3.39	4.22	3.84	3.82	3.98	4.20	4.34	4.38	4.30
1974		5.25	5.19	5.06	4.70	5.22	5.20	5.34	5.37	5.16	5.03	5.21	5.24	4.73	4.85	4.79	4.45
1975		4.57	4.63	4.93	5.71	4.60	4.72	4.39	4.66	4.65	4.59	4.97	4.86	4.97	5.41	5.84	5.88
1976		5.82	6.22	6.34	6.49	5.45	6.01	6.00	6.23	6.20	6.23	6.05	6.44	6.53	6.50	6.49	6.49
1977		6.50	6.64	6.80	6.67	6.48	6.29	6.74	6.51	6.46	6.96	6.76	6.70	6.96	6.65	6.67	6.69
1978		6.49	6.46	6.82	7.09	6.44	6.50	6.52	6.31	6.46	6.61	6.32	7.05	7.08	6.93	7.03	7.30
1979		7.05	7.84	8.63	8.81	6.73	6.95	7.48	7.45	8.29	7.78	8.74	8.74	8.39	8.95	8.74	8.74
1980		9.66	8.94	8.83	8.91	9.76	9.87	9.34	9.47	7.22	10.13	9.09	8.54	8.38	8.76	8.84	9.13
1981		9.54	10.16	10.68	11.08	9.63	9.13	9.86	10.20	11.05	9.22	11.45	10.07	10.53	10.74	11.68	10.82
1982		11.23	11.21	11.77	12.07	10.97	11.71	10.99	11.45	10.64	11.55	11.21	12.02	12.08	12.10	11.67	12.45
1983		11.14	11.91	12.75	13.97	9.92	11.67	11.84	11.43	12.18	12.11	11.93	12.72	13.59	13.25	13.13	15.52

Exports f.o.b. (25) — billion kroner, monthly averages

Adjusted - Corrigé *

Exportations f.o.b. (25) — milliards de couronnes, moyennes mensuelles

	Year	Q.1	Q.2	Q.3	Q.4	JAN	FEB	MAR	APR	MAY	JUN	JUL	AUG	SEP	OCT	NOV	DEC
1964		1.15	1.12	1.22	1.29	1.16	1.13	1.16	1.05	1.16	1.16	1.23	1.17	1.26	1.24	1.41	1.23
1965		1.26	1.31	1.31	1.36	1.23	1.29	1.25	1.29	1.29	1.36	1.30	1.35	1.27	1.38	1.38	1.32
1966		1.38	1.42	1.35	1.40	1.37	1.36	1.40	1.50	1.40	1.35	1.34	1.35	1.36	1.43	1.33	1.43
1967		1.41	1.41	1.44	1.51	1.43	1.47	1.33	1.42	1.40	1.41	1.30	1.54	1.49	1.43	1.54	1.54
1968		1.59	1.55	1.65	1.65	1.49	1.52	1.75	1.55	1.56	1.54	1.65	1.64	1.67	1.63	1.66	1.66
1969		1.79	1.83	1.84	1.94	1.79	1.83	1.77	1.91	1.63	1.96	1.84	1.74	1.93	1.85	1.96	2.00
1970		1.98	1.98	2.11	2.17	1.93	1.91	2.09	2.05	1.87	2.02	2.11	2.12	2.11	2.16	2.28	2.06
1971		2.06	2.23	2.29	2.32	2.05	2.03	2.10	2.12	2.26	2.32	2.19	2.43	2.26	2.35	2.29	2.33
1972		2.44	2.48	2.46	2.66	2.53	2.38	2.42	2.42	2.49	2.52	2.48	2.41	2.50	2.61	2.62	2.75
1973		2.83	2.89	3.37	3.42	2.74	2.95	2.80	2.69	3.05	2.94	3.33	2.90	3.87	3.29	3.32	3.64
1974		3.77	3.80	3.99	4.09	3.54	3.84	3.93	3.80	3.83	3.78	3.82	4.05	4.10	4.20	4.20	3.87
1975		4.00	4.09	4.08	4.49	3.96	4.07	3.97	4.16	3.92	4.17	4.20	4.01	4.04	4.98	4.24	4.23
1976		4.33	4.60	4.68	4.69	4.52	4.21	4.26	4.36	4.76	4.67	4.68	4.72	4.64	4.63	4.70	4.75
1977		4.98	4.81	5.02	5.35	4.90	4.84	5.21	5.04	4.50	4.89	4.93	5.00	5.13	5.07	5.44	5.55
1978		5.16	5.37	5.42	5.67	5.12	5.31	5.06	5.20	5.25	5.65	4.92	5.62	5.72	5.57	5.54	5.92
1979		5.85	6.25	5.67	6.96	5.70	5.34	6.50	6.30	6.26	6.19	6.39	6.74	6.88	7.18	7.23	6.47
1980		7.92	7.71	8.00	8.25	8.49	7.70	7.55	7.61	7.80	7.72	8.00	7.98	8.03	8.35	8.08	8.34
1981		8.97	9.35	9.77	9.93	9.47	8.55	8.91	9.34	9.41	9.29	9.85	9.85	9.61	9.73	10.23	9.84
1982		10.38	10.64	10.66	10.98	9.94	10.40	10.79	10.43	10.32	11.16	10.25	10.45	11.28	10.85	11.10	10.97
1983		11.68	11.58	12.11	13.32	11.37	12.26	11.42	11.20	11.57	11.97	11.75	11.99	12.60	12.45	14.16	13.34

Trade balance (f.o.b. — c.i.f.) (25) — billion kroner, monthly averages

Adjusted - Corrigé *

Balance commerciale (f.o.b. — c.a.f.) (25) — milliards de couronnes, moyennes mensuelles

	Year	Q.1	Q.2	Q.3	Q.4	JAN	FEB	MAR	APR	MAY	JUN	JUL	AUG	SEP	OCT	NOV	DEC
1964		-0.27	-0.39	-0.26	-0.29	-0.28	-0.27	-0.25	-0.45	-0.31	-0.41	-0.11	-0.44	-0.23	-0.35	-0.21	-0.31
1965		-0.37	-0.34	-0.29	-0.25	-0.39	-0.34	-0.37	-0.25	-0.51	-0.25	-0.31	-0.28	-0.29	-0.24	-0.22	-0.30
1966		-0.31	-0.25	-0.36	-0.45	-0.29	-0.34	-0.29	-0.25	-0.20	-0.32	-0.41	-0.33	-0.34	-0.55	-0.37	-0.43
1967		-0.40	-0.35	-0.39	-0.40	-0.39	-0.32	-0.49	-0.34	-0.46	-0.26	-0.30	-0.37	-0.50	-0.45	-0.38	-0.37
1968		-0.33	-0.38	-0.37	-0.49	-0.35	-0.42	-0.22	-0.45	-0.45	-0.24	-0.40	-0.34	-0.36	-0.47	-0.42	-0.60
1969		-0.41	-0.51	-0.63	-0.54	-0.42	-0.35	-0.47	-0.42	-0.56	-0.54	-0.52	-0.72	-0.66	-0.51	-0.60	-0.51
1970		-0.67	-0.75	-0.59	-0.73	-0.68	-0.74	-0.57	-0.62	-0.90	-0.73	-0.56	-0.66	-0.56	-0.61	-0.83	-0.74
1971		-0.74	-0.61	-0.53	-0.54	-0.59	-0.64	-0.99	-0.29	-0.76	-0.79	-0.64	-0.37	-0.57	-0.59	-0.54	-0.49
1972		-0.33	-0.26	-0.63	-0.51	-0.20	-0.44	-0.35	-0.34	-0.25	-0.19	-0.66	-0.55	-0.68	-0.53	-0.61	-0.38
1973		-0.64	-0.92	-0.63	-0.92	-1.01	-0.40	-0.52	-0.70	-1.17	-0.90	-0.48	-1.09	-0.33	-1.05	-1.06	-0.66
1974		-1.48	-1.38	-1.07	-0.61	-1.68	-1.36	-1.40	-1.57	-1.33	-1.25	-1.39	-1.19	-0.63	-0.66	-0.59	-0.59
1975		-0.57	-0.55	-0.85	-1.22	-0.64	-0.64	-0.43	-0.50	-0.73	-0.42	-0.77	-0.85	-0.93	-0.42	-1.60	-1.65
1976		-1.49	-1.63	-1.66	-1.80	-0.93	-1.80	-1.74	-1.87	-1.44	-1.56	-1.37	-1.73	-1.89	-1.87	-1.79	-1.74
1977		-1.52	-1.83	-1.78	-1.32	-1.59	-1.44	-1.53	-1.47	-1.96	-2.07	-1.83	-1.69	-1.83	-1.58	-1.24	-1.14
1978		-1.33	-1.09	-1.40	-1.41	-1.33	-1.20	-1.46	-1.10	-1.21	-0.96	-1.41	-1.43	-1.36	-1.36	-1.49	-1.39
1979		-1.20	-1.59	-1.96	-1.85	-1.02	-1.60	-0.98	-1.14	-2.04	-1.59	-2.35	-2.01	-1.52	-1.76	-1.51	-2.27
1980		-1.74	-1.23	-0.83	-0.65	-1.27	-2.17	-1.79	-1.87	0.58	-2.41	-1.08	-0.57	-0.85	-0.41	-0.76	-0.79
1981		-0.57	-0.81	-0.91	-1.14	-0.16	-0.58	-0.95	-0.87	-1.64	0.07	-1.59	-0.22	-0.93	-1.00	-1.45	-0.98
1982		-0.85	-0.58	-1.11	-1.10	-1.03	-1.32	-0.20	-1.02	-0.31	-0.39	-0.96	-1.57	-0.80	-1.25	-0.56	-1.47
1983		0.54	-0.33	-0.63	-0.65	1.45	0.59	-0.42	-0.24	-0.61	-0.14	-0.18	-0.73	-0.99	-0.81	1.04	-2.18

* Adjusted by the O.E.C.D.

* Corrigé par l'O.C.D.E.

DENMARK

Balance of payments: net trade
million kroner

Balance des paiements : balance commerciale
millions de couronnes

	Year	Q.1	Q.2	Q.3	Q.4	JAN	FEB	MAR	APR	MAY	JUN	JUL	AUG	SEP	OCT	NOV	DEC
1964	-2583	-555	-1111	-477	-440												
1965	-2495	-862	-849	-524	-260												
1966	-2781	-701	-585	-677	-818												
1967	-3193	-928	-913	-643	-719												
1968	-3407	-727	-932	-628	-1120												
1969	-4720	-938	-1250	-1304	-1228												
1970	-5702	-1456	-1903	-1050	-1293												
1971	-5314	-1838	-1357	-919	-1200												
1972	-3007	-758	-157	-1119	-973												
1973	-7175	-1644	-2140	-1034	-2357												
1974	-11079	-4016	-3340	-2220	-1503												
1975	-7627	-1365	-943	-1954	-3365												
1976	-17368	-4378	-3747	-4179	-5064												
1977	-16285	-4405	-4200	-4315	-3365												
1978	-12945	-3765	-2330	-3150	-3700												
1979	-16120	-3385	-3560	-4465	-4710												
1980	-11790	-5335	-4010	-1075	-1370												
1981	-6835	-1835	-1110	-1160	-2730												
1982	-7385	-2310	-1660	-1210	-2205												
1983	2015	1520	435	870	-810												

Balance of payments: current balance
million kroner

Balance des paiements : opérations courantes, nettes
millions de couronnes

	Year	Q.1	Q.2	Q.3	Q.4	JAN	FEB	MAR	APR	MAY	JUN	JUL	AUG	SEP	OCT	NOV	DEC
1964																	
1965																	
1966	-1453	-396	-337	-271	-449												
1967	-2004	-672	-660	-266	-406												
1968	-1616	-194	-566	-166	-690												
1969	-3082	-542	-975	-802	-763												
1970	-4077	-1060	-1582	-416	-1019												
1971	-3169	-1380	-919	-170	-700												
1972	-402	-232	378	-226	-322												
1973	-2816	-961	-1109	527	-1273												
1974	-5787	-3310	-1896	-631	50												
1975	-3176	-539	242	-523	-2356												
1976	-13052	-3963	-2892	-2789	-3408												
1977	-12106	-3305	-2880	-2925	-2996												
1978	-8345	-3135	-750	-1615	-2845												
1979	-16065	-3720	-3020	-4430	-4395												
1980	-13400	-6570	-3795	-1070	-1965												
1981	-12500	-3715	-1935	-1895	-4955												
1982	-18725	-5460	-4420	-3360	-5485												
1983	-10860	-2495	-2615	-1145	-4605												

NOTES

1. The original base of the index is 1964 to 1975, 1975 from 1976 to 1979 and 1980 from 1980.
2. Excluding shipbuilding.
3. From 1976, new index linked on 1975 to previous index.
4. Including mining. From 1977, new index linked on 1977 to previous index.
5. The breaks in the series are due to increases in coverage. From 1973 the series cover all Denmark.
6. From 1980, new definition.
7. The original base of the index is 1968 to 1975, 1975 from 1976 to 1980, and 1980 from 1981. The break in the series between 1971 and 1972 is due to a change in sample. The other breaks are due to changes in the value added tax rate.
8. From 1968, new definition.
9. Monthly data are averages of weekly data from 1978, and averages of Wednesdays previously. The registered unemployed include unemployed insured for loss of part-time jobs from 1977, and partially unemployed from 1978.
10. Monthly data refer to end of period.
11. A sample revision, effective from 1970, increased the level of the series by about 4 per cent in 1970.
12. Data compiled according to the *United Nations International Standard Industrial Classification,* 1968 edition from 1972, 1958 edition previously.
13. The self-employed are excluded from the total labour force prior to 1978.
14. Full-time jobs only.
15. Weighting pattern based on 1954 to 1970, on 1966 from 1971 to 1980, and on 1975 from 1981.
16. Excluding liquid fuel.
17. From 1980, excluding heating, energy and motor vehicle fuels and lubricants.
18. The major savings banks included are those whose net capital plus deposits exceed 25 million kroner from January 1982, 10 million kroner from April 1975 to December 1981, and 5 million kroner prior to April 1975.
19. Because of adjustments made in connection with the drawing up of annual balance sheets, end-year data do not necessarily equal end-December data.

NOTES

1. La base originale de l'indice est 1964 jusqu'en 1975, 1975 de 1976 à 1979, et 1980 à partir de 1980.
2. Non compris la construction navale.
3. A partir de 1976, nouvel indice raccordé sur 1975 à l'indice précédent.
4. Y compris les industries extractives. A partir de 1977, nouvel indice raccordé sur 1977 à l'indice précédent.
5. Les discontinuités dans les séries sont dues à des élargissements successifs de la couverture géographique. A partir de 1973 les séries couvrent tout le Danemark.
6. A partir de 1980, nouvelle définition.
7. La base originale de l'indice est 1968 jusqu'en 1975, 1975 de 1976 à 1980, et 1980 à partir de 1981. La discontinuité entre 1971 et 1972 est due à un changement d'échantillon. Les autres discontinuités indiquent des changements dans le niveau de la taxe sur la valeur ajoutée.
8. A partir de 1968, nouvelle définition.
9. Les données mensuelles sont les moyennes des données hebdomadaires à partir de 1978 et les moyennes des données relatives aux mercredis auparavant. Les chômeurs assurés contre la perte d'un emploi à temps partiel sont compris à partir de 1977, et le chômage partiel à partir de 1978.
10. Situation en fin de mois.
11. Une révision de l'échantillon à partir de 1970 a augmenté le niveau de la série d'environ 4 % en 1970.
12. Les données ont été recueillies d'après la *Classification Internationale Type de l'Industrie des Nations Unies,* édition de 1968 à partir de 1972, édition de 1958 auparavant.
13. Les travailleurs indépendants ne sont pas compris dans la population active avant 1978.
14. Emplois à temps complet seulement.
15. La pondération se réfère à 1954 jusqu'en 1970, à 1966 de 1971 à 1980, et à 1975 à partir de 1981.
16. Non compris les combustibles liquides.
17. A partir de 1980, non compris le chauffage, l'énergie et les produits pétroliers destinés aux véhicules à moteur.
18. Les grandes banques d'épargne prises en considération sont celles dont la somme capital net + dépôts dépasse un certain seuil : jusqu'en mars 1975, 5 millions de couronnes, d'avril 1975 à décembre 1981, 10 millions de couronnes et à partir de janvier 1982, 25 millions de couronnes.
19. Les différences entre les données annuelles et celles de décembre sont dues à des ajustements effectués à l'occasion de l'établissement des bilans annuels.

NOTES

20. Nominal value.
21. Commercial and major savings banks. Prior to 1971, including credit to foreigners. From 1982, excluding fixed-interest private mortgage term loans.
22. Government and first mortgage bonds, last Wednesday of month. Prior to 1972, first mortgage bonds only, last day of month. The other break indicated is due to changes in the selection of mortgage bonds.
23. The original base of the index is 1960 to 1972, 1971 from 1973 to 1982, and 1983 from 1983.
24. Annual data are based on more complete information than quarterly and monthly data. Prior to August 1973, excluding savings banks.
25. Prior to 1978, general trade.

NOTES

20. Valeur nominale.
21. Banques commerciales et grandes banques d'épargne. Avant 1971, y compris les crédits consentis aux étrangers. A partir de 1982, non compris les prêts hypothécaires privés à taux d'intérêt fixe.
22. Bons d'état et obligations hypothécaires de premier rang, dernier mercredi du mois. Avant 1972, obligations hypothécaires de premier rang seulement, dernier jour du mois. L'autre rupture dans la série est due à un changement dans la sélection des obligations hypothécaires.
23. La base originale de l'indice est 1960 jusqu'en 1972, 1971 de 1973 à 1982, et 1983 à partir de 1983.
24. Les données annuelles sont établies à partir d'informations plus complètes que les données trimestrielles et mensuelles. Avant août 1973, non compris les banques d'épargne.
25. Avant 1978, commerce général.

MAIN SOURCES

PRINCIPALES SOURCES

Series	Séries	Sources
Output of animal products	Production : produits d'origine animale	Danmarks Statistik *Statistiske efterretninger*
Manufacturing sales and orders	Ventes et commandes, industries manufacturières	
Construction	Construction	
Labour and wages	Main-d'œuvre et salaires	
Consumer prices	Prix à la consommation	
Business surveys	Enquêtes de conjoncture	Danmarks Statistik *Konjunkturbarometer for industri*
Internal trade	Commerce intérieur	Danmarks Statistik *Statistisk Månedsoversigt*
Wholesale prices	Prix de gros	
Bond issues	Emissions d'obligations	
Yield of long-term bonds	Rendement des obligations à long terme	
Share prices	Cours des actions	
Balance of payments	Balance des paiements	
Home finance	Finances internes	Danmarks Nationalbank *Monetary review*
Official discount rate	Taux d'escompte officiel	
Net foreign position	Position extérieure nette	
Foreign trade	Commerce extérieur	Danmarks Statistik *Månedsstatistik over udenrigshandelen*

Finland — Finlande

Indicators of domestic product: total (1) — Indicateurs du produit intérieur : total (1)

at factor cost — *au coût des facteurs*

1980 = 100

Adjusted - Corrigé

	Year	Q.1	Q.2	Q.3	Q.4	JAN	FEB	MAR	APR	MAY	JUN	JUL	AUG	SEP	OCT	NOV	DEC
1964	53	53	53	54	53												
1965	56	55	56	57	55												
1966	57	55	56	58	59												
1967	59	58	59	59	58												
1968	60	59	60	61	61												
1969	66	64	64	66	67												
1970	71	68	70	71	73												
1971	72	68	73	74	75												
1972	77	76	76	78	79												
1973	82	82	79	83	84												
1974	85	85	85	85	86												
1975	85	86	86	85	85												
1976	85	84	85	86	87												
1977	86	86	85	86	85												
1978	88	87	88	87	90												
1979	94	93	94	94	96												
1980	100	99	98	103	101												
1981	102	100	101	102	103												
1982	104	102	104	104	106												
1983		106	107	107													

Indicators of domestic product: industry (2) — Indicateurs du produit intérieur : industrie (2)

index of industrial production — indice de production industrielle

1980 = 100

	Year	Q.1	Q.2	Q.3	Q.4	JAN	FEB	MAR	APR	MAY	JUN	JUL	AUG	SEP	OCT	NOV	DEC
1964	42	42	42	38	44	41	42	43	43	43	41	30	41	44	45	45	43
1965	45	45	46	41	46	44	46	45	47	47	45	33	43	47	46	47	45
1966	47	47	48	42	50	46	47	48	49	49	46	33	44	49	51	51	49
1967	49	50	49	43	51	50	51	51	52	51	45	34	46	49	52	52	50
1968	51	52	53	45	55	51	52	52	55	54	49	35	48	52	54	56	56
1969	58	58	60	52	63	58	58	59	62	62	56	42	56	60	61	64	64
1970	64	66	67	58	66	66	66	66	69	69	62	47	62	65	65	67	67
1971	67	70	70	60	70	70	69	70	71	71	67	48	64	69	70	69	69
1972	73	75	75	63	79	75	74	76	77	77	72	50	67	74	78	78	81
1973	78	81	78	69	85	79	82	83	81	79	75	52	74	81	83	85	87
1974	82	87	84	72	86	85	87	87	87	85	81	53	79	82	85	86	85
1975	79	85	81	66	82	84	86	86	87	82	74	45	76	73	80	86	81
1976	80	82	82	68	86	80	82	83	83	86	78	42	77	85	86	86	86
1977	80	83	81	69	87	85	87	78	79	84	81	42	78	87	88	89	84
1978	84	86	86	72	92	84	88	87	87	89	82	43	82	90	92	94	92
1979	93	95	96	81	100	93	95	97	98	98	93	55	91	97	99	103	98
1980	100	102	104	89	106	100	101	104	105	103	104	66	98	104	106	108	105
1981	103	104	107	92	108	102	105	105	109	112	101	66	102	107	110	109	107
1982	104	107	110	91	103	107	107	108	110	110	109	65	101	107	107	110	107
1983	107	106	114	95	113	104	106	107	113	115	115	67	105	112	112	116	110

Indicators of domestic product: (1) — Indicateurs du produit intérieur : (1)

transport and communication — transports et communications

1980 = 100

Adjusted - Corrigé

	Year	Q.1	Q.2	Q.3	Q.4	JAN	FEB	MAR	APR	MAY	JUN	JUL	AUG	SEP	OCT	NOV	DEC
1964	53	54	52	53	55												
1965	56	56	55	56	56												
1966	58	57	58	57	59												
1967	58	59	57	57	57												
1968	61	59	60	61	62												
1969	65	64	64	67	68												
1970	70	68	70	72	72												
1971	71	70	71	72	72												
1972	76	73	76	77	78												
1973	82	82	80	84	84												
1974	87	86	87	87	87												
1975	84	86	86	82	81												
1976	82	80	81	82	86												
1977	83	82	80	86	84												
1978	85	83	86	85	86												
1979	94	90	95	94	93												
1980	100	101	96	102	101												
1981	103	102	101	104	104												
1982	104	103	104	103	104												
1983		105	106	106													

Indicators of domestic product: (1) agriculture — Indicateurs du produit intérieur : (1) agriculture

1980 = 100

Adjusted - Corrigé

	Year	Q.1	Q.2	Q.3	Q.4	JAN	FEB	MAR	APR	MAY	JUN	JUL	AUG	SEP	OCT	NOV	DEC
1964	95	94	108	98	79												
1965	90	88	90	93	87												
1966	92	93	93	91	91												
1967	91	90	86	92	94												
1968	92	92	93	93	90												
1969	92	92	94	92	89												
1970	91	96	85	88	94												
1971	91	84	96	92	92												
1972	89	94	91	88	82												
1973	84	84	82	84	85												
1974	84	92	78	84	82												
1975	92	82	90	91	105												
1976	94	96	94	99	87												
1977	95	103	97	86	95												
1978	93	93	94	86	99												
1979	95	101	98	88	96												
1980	100	97	97	106	100												
1981	96	97	106	87	95												
1982	103	95	99	107	109												
1983		112	110	121													

Indicators of domestic product: industry (2) — Indicateurs du produit intérieur : industrie (2)

index of industrial production — indice de production industrielle

1980 = 100

Adjusted - Corrigé

	Year	Q.1	Q.2	Q.3	Q.4	JAN	FEB	MAR	APR	MAY	JUN	JUL	AUG	SEP	OCT	NOV	DEC
1964		40	40	42	42	39	39	40	40	41	41	42	42	42	42	42	42
1965		43	44	45	44	43	43	43	44	44	45	45	45	45	44	44	44
1966		44	46	46	48	44	45	45	45	46	46	46	46	47	48	48	48
1967		48	47	48	49	48	48	48	47	47	46	47	48	48	49	49	49
1968		49	50	50	53	49	49	49	50	50	50	49	50	51	52	53	54
1969		55	57	58	60	54	55	56	56	57	57	58	59	59	59	60	61
1970		62	65	66	65	63	63	62	64	65	64	67	66	65	64	65	65
1971		57	68	69	67	67	54	50	67	68	69	69	68	69	68	67	67
1972		71	73	73	76	71	70	72	71	73	73	73	72	74	76	75	78
1973		77	76	79	81	75	77	77	76	75	77	80	78	80	80	81	83
1974		81	82	84	81	81	81	81	81	81	83	87	84	81	82	82	81
1975		82	78	79	77	82	82	81	81	77	76	83	78	75	76	78	76
1976		78	79	79	81	78	78	78	78	80	79	77	79	81	81	79	82
1977		79	78	80	81	82	83	73	74	79	82	77	80	83	83	82	80
1978		83	83	82	87	82	84	83	83	83	82	76	84	86	87	87	88
1979		91	93	93	95	90	91	93	93	92	92	94	93	93	94	96	95
1980		98	100	104	102	98	97	99	100	97	102	110	101	100	101	101	103
1981		101	102	105	104	101	102	101	103	105	99	106	105	104	106	102	104
1982		105	104	104	104	106	104	105	103	103	105	104	104	104	103	104	105
1983		104	108	108	109	103	104	104	107	108	110	107	108	109	109	110	107

FINLAND

Industrial production: investment goods (2) (3) (4)
1980 = 100

Production industrielle : biens d'équipement (2)(3)(4)
1980 = 100

	Year	Q.1	Q.2	Q.3	Q.4	JAN	FEB	MAR	APR	MAY	JUN	JUL	AUG	SEP	OCT	NOV	DEC
1964	35	35	35	30	38	36	36	34	37	33	35	19	33	39	38	39	38
1965	37	39	33	33	40	37	39	42	37	37	38	23	33	41	42	40	39
1966	37	40	38	31	41	39	39	44	37	38	37	17	35	41	41	41	40
1967	38	41	39	31	42	40	40	42	41	39	37	19	36	39	44	43	39
1968	41	45	41	34	44	44	45	46	42	43	37	20	39	42	46	46	41
1969	45	49	44	38	50	48	46	53	45	46	43	24	40	50	52	50	48
1970	=54=	52	56	47	60	52	52	52	61	53	54	32	51	58	61	60	59
1971	67	71	69	57	71	67	68	80	69	67	69	37	63	72	72	72	69
1972	63	69	64	52	67	68	67	72	65	65	61	33	59	65	69	68	62
1973	65	70	65	53	73	69	67	73	61	70	64	30	63	67	78	77	63
1974	76	80	79	63	81	81	77	83	81	83	72	35	75	78	87	85	71
1975	=96=	102	101	76	104	102	101	104	107	100	97	40	91	97	101	110	100
1976	96	106	104	75	101	112	102	105	109	104	99	37	88	93	101	102	101
1977	89	95	94	72	97	102	100	84	87	93	100	38	81	98	99	99	92
1978	82	88	85	64	90	86	88	88	86	86	84	28	75	87	89	92	90
1979	90	92	94	74	98	90	92	93	93	95	93	41	86	95	98	101	96
1980	=100=	100	108	84	111	96	101	103	107	103	113	49	95	108	103	115	114
1981	115	112	124	96	127	108	114	113	117	132	122	53	112	124	123	126	131
1982	121	127	135	94	130	128	129	125	132	133	140	49	108	125	126	135	128
1983	125	127	144	99	132	127	129	126	143	141	148	51	111	135	128	136	132

Industrial production: consumer goods (2)(3)
1980 = 100

Production industrielle : biens de consommation (2)(3)
1980 = 100

	Year	Q.1	Q.2	Q.3	Q.4	JAN	FEB	MAR	APR	MAY	JUN	JUL	AUG	SEP	OCT	NOV	DEC
1964	36	35	37	35	37	35	36	35	39	36	36	27	39	39	39	38	35
1965	38	37	38	37	40	35	37	41	38	39	38	28	40	42	41	41	38
1966	40	40	41	38	42	37	38	43	41	41	41	28	43	44	44	44	39
1967	42	42	43	40	44	42	41	42	45	43	42	29	46	45	48	45	39
1968	44	44	44	41	45	44	43	46	45	47	41	32	45	45	50	46	42
1969	52	51	53	49	55	51	49	54	53	55	51	38	54	55	59	54	53
1970	=63=	63	66	57	66	65	61	63	73	62	62	43	62	65	68	66	65
1971	67	65	69	61	70	67	61	68	71	58	70	44	68	71	71	72	68
1972	70	71	71	63	75	68	69	75	70	73	69	43	74	71	77	78	70
1973	74	77	74	65	80	77	73	81	72	81	71	45	78	73	86	84	70
1974	85	87	84	76	91	91	83	88	86	90	77	55	88	87	99	93	80
1975	=82=	86	83	71	87	84	87	86	90	81	79	49	80	83	80	89	85
1976	82	82	85	71	89	81	83	82	83	88	84	45	81	88	89	89	90
1977	82	85	83	72	89	86	90	79	78	86	85	45	81	89	90	92	86
1978	88	91	89	75	97	88	93	92	90	90	87	47	87	93	96	98	98
1979	93	95	96	80	101	93	95	97	100	96	92	51	91	96	99	104	100
1980	=100=	102	102	88	109	102	100	104	105	103	99	62	99	104	110	108	108
1981	104	104	107	92	111	103	104	107	110	111	100	64	104	108	114	111	109
1982	104	108	108	90	109	109	107	108	111	108	104	63	100	106	108	110	107
1983	103	103	108	91	111	102	103	105	108	110	105	64	101	107	111	116	106

Industrial production: intermediate goods (2)(4)
1980 = 100

Production industrielle : biens intermédiaires (2)(4)
1980 = 100

	Year	Q.1	Q.2	Q.3	Q.4	JAN	FEB	MAR	APR	MAY	JUN	JUL	AUG	SEP	OCT	NOV	DEC
1964	47	46	45	45	50	46	45	45	48	45	44	38	46	50	52	51	48
1965	50	51	49	48	52	49	49	55	49	51	46	41	51	54	54	53	49
1966	53	53	51	50	58	51	51	58	51	54	49	41	52	56	60	59	54
1967	55	56	54	51	57	57	55	56	58	55	48	42	55	56	60	59	53
1968	58	60	56	53	62	59	58	61	58	60	49	45	56	59	65	64	58
1969	65	65	62	61	70	65	62	68	63	65	58	52	64	68	73	70	68
1970	=68=	68	68	64	70	70	66	68	72	67	63	55	67	71	72	70	69
1971	73	72	73	69	77	76	67	72	73	74	72	57	73	77	78	78	74
1972	77	79	75	70	83	78	77	83	75	78	74	57	76	78	86	84	80
1973	83	88	79	77	89	89	83	92	78	86	74	63	83	85	94	92	81
1974	85	91	84	77	88	91	88	95	85	92	74	61	82	87	94	89	79
1975	=74=	82	76	62	76	80	83	82	82	79	68	44	70	72	73	79	75
1976	75	76	76	65	82	73	77	79	77	82	71	41	73	81	82	82	82
1977	77	80	73	67	83	80	84	75	77	81	76	41	76	84	84	85	81
1978	83	84	84	71	91	82	85	85	86	88	80	44	81	89	90	92	85
1979	94	96	97	82	100	93	96	98	98	100	94	59	91	97	99	102	98
1980	=100=	102	104	91	104	100	101	103	105	103	105	72	98	103	104	106	103
1981	100	103	104	91	104	101	105	103	106	109	98	69	100	104	106	104	101
1982	101	103	106	91	103	102	103	104	105	107	105	69	100	104	102	105	104
1983	105	103	112	96	110	100	104	105	110	112	113	71	105	110	110	113	107

Industrial production: investment goods (2)(4)
1980 = 100

Adjusted - Corrigé

Production industrielle : biens d'équipement (2)(4)
1980 = 100

	Year	Q.1	Q.2	Q.3	Q.4	JAN	FEB	MAR	APR	MAY	JUN	JUL	AUG	SEP	OCT	NOV	DEC
1964		34	35	36	36	35	34	32	36	34	35	35	36	36	35	36	37
1965		37	37	39	38	35	37	39	36	38	39	43	36	39	39	38	38
1966		37	38	37	39	37	37	39	36	38	38	33	38	38	38	39	39
1967		37	38	37	39	37	38	37	39	38	38	36	39	37	40	40	39
1968		41	40	41	42	41	42	41	40	42	38	39	42	40	42	43	41
1969		45	44	46	48	45	43	47	42	45	44	46	44	48	48	47	48
1970		48	55	57	57	48	49	46	58	52	56	60	55	56	56	56	60
1971		36	66	73	68	62	27	21	64	65	70	82	68	70	66	68	71
1972		63	62	63	64	62	63	63	61	62	62	65	62	63	63	64	64
1973		64	62	64	69	63	64	65	57	65	64	62	67	65	70	71	66
1974		73	75	77	76	73	73	74	76	76	72	78	79	75	78	77	74
1975		95	95	97	95	92	95	98	97	94	94	101	98	94	94	98	93
1976		99	98	94	93	101	95	100	101	98	95	93	95	94	94	91	95
1977		89	88	91	89	94	93	80	82	88	96	93	87	93	92	89	86
1978		83	80	77	84	81	83	85	81	81	79	68	81	83	84	83	85
1979		88	88	93	92	86	87	90	88	89	86	96	93	91	93	93	91
1980		96	100	106	104	93	95	99	101	95	104	114	102	103	100	106	108
1981		108	113	121	120	105	108	109	108	120	110	123	122	118	120	117	124
1982		123	121	117	123	124	123	122	120	120	124	114	119	119	123	125	121
1983		123	128	124	125	123	123	123	129	126	128	122	123	128	125	125	125

Industrial production: consumer goods (2)
1980 = 100

Adjusted - Corrigé

Production industrielle : biens de consommation (2)
1980 = 100

	Year	Q.1	Q.2	Q.3	Q.4	JAN	FEB	MAR	APR	MAY	JUN	JUL	AUG	SEP	OCT	NOV	DEC
1964		36	36	37	37	37	37	34	38	35	36	37	37	37	37	37	37
1965		37	38	39	39	36	37	39	36	38	38	39	38	39	38	39	40
1966		39	40	41	42	38	39	41	39	40	41	39	41	42	41	42	42
1967		41	42	43	43	42	42	40	43	42	43	41	44	43	44	43	42
1968		43	43	44	46	43	44	43	42	45	41	45	44	43	46	45	45
1969		50	51	54	55	49	49	51	49	53	52	55	53	54	55	53	56
1970		61	63	63	65	61	62	60	68	59	63	64	61	63	63	64	68
1971		62	67	68	68	63	61	63	67	65	70	67	67	70	66	69	71
1972		68	69	70	72	64	69	70	66	69	70	67	72	70	70	74	73
1973		74	73	73	76	73	73	76	68	77	73	71	76	72	77	78	73
1974		84	83	86	86	86	83	82	83	85	79	88	86	84	89	86	83
1975		83	81	82	80	82	83	85	86	78	79	86	81	79	81	81	79
1976		79	83	82	83	80	79	79	80	84	84	80	82	84	82	81	84
1977		82	81	83	83	84	84	77	75	83	84	81	82	85	83	84	81
1978		87	86	87	91	85	88	88	87	86	86	83	88	89	89	91	93
1979		91	93	92	94	90	91	93	95	92	92	89	93	93	92	96	95
1980		99	99	103	102	99	97	100	100	99	100	106	101	101	103	101	103
1981		102	104	106	105	100	102	102	104	106	102	108	106	105	107	103	105
1982		106	104	103	102	107	106	105	105	103	105	104	103	104	102	102	103
1983		101	104	104	105	101	102	102	102	105	105	104	104	104	105	107	103

Industrial production: intermediate goods (2)(4)
1980 = 100

Adjusted - Corrigé

Production industrielle : biens intermédiaires (2)(4)
1980 = 100

	Year	Q.1	Q.2	Q.3	Q.4	JAN	FEB	MAR	APR	MAY	JUN	JUL	AUG	SEP	OCT	NOV	DEC
1964		45	46	47	49	45	46	43	48	44	47	48	46	48	48	49	49
1965		50	50	51	50	48	49	51	48	51	50	51	51	51	50	50	51
1966		51	52	53	55	49	51	54	50	53	54	52	53	54	55	55	56
1967		54	55	54	55	55	54	52	57	54	54	53	56	54	55	56	54
1968		57	56	57	60	56	58	57	56	59	54	57	57	58	60	60	59
1969		63	63	65	68	62	62	65	61	64	63	66	65	66	67	66	69
1970		65	69	69	67	66	66	64	71	66	69	70	68	69	66	67	69
1971		63	74	74	74	71	60	58	72	72	77	74	74	75	72	74	75
1972		76	76	76	80	73	77	77	74	75	80	76	77	76	79	79	81
1973		83	80	85	85	83	82	85	78	82	81	87	85	83	86	86	82
1974		86	85	86	83	85	86	88	84	88	82	90	83	84	86	83	81
1975		77	74	73	71	78	77	77	77	73	72	78	72	69	70	73	71
1976		73	74	75	77	71	72	74	73	75	74	73	75	78	78	76	78
1977		76	75	77	79	78	78	71	73	75	78	72	78	80	80	79	78
1978		80	81	81	86	79	80	81	82	82	81	75	83	85	86	86	87
1979		92	93	94	96	90	91	94	93	93	94	96	93	93	94	97	97
1980		98	100	104	101	98	97	99	100	97	104	111	100	100	100	101	102
1981		100	100	102	101	100	101	99	101	103	96	103	102	101	103	100	100
1982		101	101	101	101	102	101	101	100	100	102	102	101	101	100	100	103
1983		102	106	106	108	100	102	102	105	105	108	105	107	107	108	109	106

FINLAND

Industrial production: manufacturing (2) / Production industrielle : industries manufacturières (2)

1980 = 100

	Year	Q.1	Q.2	Q.3	Q.4	JAN	FEB	MAR	APR	MAY	JUN	JUL	AUG	SEP	OCT	NOV	DEC
1964	42	42	44	39	45	41	42	44	44	45	42	30	41	44	45	46	44
1965	45	46	48	41	47	45	46	46	48	48	47	32	43	47	48	48	46
1966	47	47	49	42	51	46	47	48	51	50	47	33	44	49	51	52	50
1967	49	51	50	43	52	50	51	52	53	52	46	33	47	50	52	53	51
1968	52	52	54	45	56	52	52	53	57	55	50	35	48	53	54	56	57
1969	59	59	61	52	64	58	58	60	63	64	57	41	56	60	62	64	65
1970	66	67	69	59	68	67	67	67	71	72	64	47	63	65	66	68	69
1971	67	62	73	61	71	73	58	54	75	74	70	48	65	70	71	70	71
1972	75	76	77	64	81	76	75	78	79	80	74	49	68	75	80	79	82
1973	80	82	80	69	86	80	83	84	83	81	77	49	76	83	85	85	88
1974	84	88	87	72	87	87	89	90	90	88	83	52	80	84	85	88	87
1975	80	86	83	67	83	84	87	88	89	84	77	44	77	80	81	86	81
1976	80	82	84	68	86	80	82	84	84	87	80	40	78	86	86	87	86
1977	79	82	82	68	86	83	86	77	79	84	82	39	78	87	87	88	82
1978	83	85	86	71	92	82	85	86	87	89	82	41	81	90	92	93	89
1979	92	93	97	81	99	90	93	96	98	99	93	53	92	98	99	102	97
1980	100	100	105	90	107	98	99	103	106	105	104	65	99	105	106	108	106
1981	103	104	109	91	109	101	105	105	110	114	103	63	103	108	111	109	106
1982	104	107	111	90	109	106	107	108	112	112	109	60	101	109	108	111	108
1983	107	106	116	94	114	104	106	107	115	118	116	64	105	115	114	117	109

Production: wood fellings (5) / Production : abattage d'arbres (5)

million cubic metres, monthly averages / millions de mètres cubes, moyennes mensuelles

	Year	Q.1	Q.2	Q.3	Q.4	JAN	FEB	MAR	APR	MAY	JUN	JUL	AUG	SEP	OCT	NOV	DEC
1964	3.21	4.80	3.69	1.30	3.06	3.94	5.03	5.43	5.03	3.74	2.30	1.08	1.21	1.59	2.33	2.90	3.94
1965	3.29	5.28	3.88	1.40	2.60	4.01	5.47	6.35	5.83	3.75	2.07	1.31	1.26	1.64	1.94	2.62	3.24
1966	2.71	4.00	3.22	1.13	2.47	3.55	4.24	4.21	3.44	4.04	2.17	0.83	1.06	1.51	2.07	2.32	3.01
1967	2.74	4.20	3.24	1.12	2.38	3.24	4.44	4.92	4.63	3.17	1.93	0.84	1.14	1.40	2.11	2.27	2.77
1968	2.90	4.07	3.15	1.05	3.33	3.01	4.38	4.83	4.63	3.12	1.70	0.83	1.04	1.30	2.29	3.07	4.64
1969	3.26	4.88	3.38	1.21	3.57	4.47	4.82	5.36	4.68	3.43	2.02	0.90	1.12	1.60	2.65	3.28	4.79
1970	3.71	5.26	3.93	1.64	4.03	4.44	5.66	5.68	5.22	3.79	2.77	1.27	1.51	2.14	3.01	3.74	5.33
1971	3.36	5.30	3.60	1.53	2.99	4.70	5.56	5.64	4.64	3.49	2.66	1.20	1.41	1.93	2.52	2.89	3.53
1972	3.12	4.61	3.35	1.42	3.09	3.59	4.68	5.56	4.48	3.37	2.19	0.90	1.41	1.95	2.49	2.91	3.96
1973	3.09	4.41	3.20	1.46	3.29	3.93	4.25	5.05	4.91	2.93	1.75	0.99	1.47	1.94	2.83	3.40	3.62
1974	2.85	3.78	3.24	1.61	2.75	3.48	3.89	3.98	3.94	3.50	2.29	1.29	1.53	2.00	2.46	2.75	3.05
1975	2.49	3.91	3.01	1.10	1.92	3.10	3.99	4.64	3.89	2.71	2.44	0.96	1.05	1.30	1.74	1.93	2.08
1976	2.40	2.56	2.74	1.42	2.89	1.78	2.46	3.45	3.40	2.89	1.92	1.11	1.22	1.94	2.42	2.94	3.30
1977	2.59	3.33	2.96	1.40	2.67	2.74	3.28	3.98	3.61	3.19	2.09	0.77	1.39	2.04	2.34	2.63	3.03
1978	2.69	3.46	2.69	1.31	3.30	2.92	3.42	4.05	3.83	2.71	1.53	0.68	1.20	2.03	2.85	3.39	3.66
1979	3.67	4.50	4.68	1.70	3.79	3.87	4.60	5.04	5.60	5.26	3.20	1.14	1.59	2.38	3.49	3.96	3.91
1980	3.92	4.90	4.02	2.50	4.28	4.48	5.63	4.59	3.13	5.09	3.84	2.02	2.31	3.16	4.00	4.18	4.64
1981	3.70	4.66	4.29	2.04	3.32	4.11	4.65	5.21	5.52	4.34	3.01	1.60	1.73	2.79	3.44	3.68	4.34
1982	3.48	4.44	3.80	1.65	4.04	3.28	4.26	5.78	5.24	3.56	2.58	1.17	1.38	2.40	3.16	4.17	4.79
1983	3.30	4.75	3.46	1.52	3.45	3.73	4.55	5.96	5.23	3.07	2.09	1.08	1.30	2.17	2.86	3.39	4.11

Production: paper (6) / Production : papier (6)

thousand tons, monthly averages / milliers de tonnes, moyennes mensuelles

	Year	Q.1	Q.2	Q.3	Q.4	JAN	FEB	MAR	APR	MAY	JUN	JUL	AUG	SEP	OCT	NOV	DEC
1964	249	241	232	259	269	239	234	250	245	237	215	255	254	267	283	275	248
1965	263	271	246	272	265	264	258	291	246	271	220	259	273	282	281	268	246
1966	281	266	265	299	296	250	252	297	260	278	258	300	299	298	313	298	278
1967	297	279	256	286	274	297	265	275	296	262	209	277	296	285	291	272	257
1968	301	289	276	310	315	285	278	303	284	300	243	307	315	307	333	331	281
1969	338	324	308	355	348	316	311	346	317	312	294	349	364	351	366	357	321
1970	356	243	228	254	239	256	233	239	236	227	221	259	259	244	255	244	216
1971	371	247	212	256	265	248	233	259	215	218	203	247	264	258	279	270	247
1972	423	275	238	282	302	275	263	286	223	250	240	275	280	292	314	306	286
1973	464	315	270	313	317	319	298	327	266	310	234	303	321	315	331	322	299
1974	443	481	406	481	404	495	446	502	373	465	379	486	481	475	490	324	399
1975	325	354	308	294	343	353	359	350	371	353	199	274	356	251	330	360	339
1976	377	397	318	372	419	363	392	435	260	414	281	246	433	438	455	424	378
1977	383	369	362	383	419	371	389	348	355	402	330	270	432	449	438	436	383
1978	423	410	412	410	461	429	405	398	443	418	374	330	416	483	477	476	430
1979	462	476	417	478	478	471	448	509	403	482	365	455	489	491	509	494	431
1980	477	480	428	505	494	479	457	505	420	438	424	507	519	489	503	500	430
1981	500	509	443	522	522	519	478	532	441	512	390	509	554	504	556	533	475
1982	480	489	447	512	471	509	425	533	403	490	450	510	539	437	473	467	472
1983	524	478	437	565	567	419	463	552	472	510	480	572	586	538	629	604	469

Industrial production: manufacturing (2) / Production industrielle : industries manufacturières (2)

1980 = 100

Adjusted - Corrigé

	Year	Q.1	Q.2	Q.3	Q.4	JAN	FEB	MAR	APR	MAY	JUN	JUL	AUG	SEP	OCT	NOV	DEC
1964		41	42	43	44	41	41	42	41	42	42	43	44	43	44	44	44
1965		45	46	47	46	45	45	44	45	45	47	47	46	46	46	46	46
1966		46	47	48	49	45	46	46	47	47	48	47	47	49	49	49	49
1967		49	48	49	50	49	49	50	48	48	47	48	50	49	50	50	50
1968		50	52	51	54	50	50	51	52	51	51	50	51	53	53	54	56
1969		56	58	60	62	55	56	57	58	59	58	60	60	60	60	62	63
1970		64	66	68	66	64	64	64	65	67	66	69	68	66	65	66	67
1971		59	70	72	69	69	56	52	69	69	71	73	70	71	70	69	68
1972		72	74	75	78	73	71	74	73	75	75	76	73	75	78	77	80
1973		78	77	81	83	77	79	79	77	76	78	81	80	82	82	82	84
1974		83	83	85	83	84	83	83	83	82	84	87	85	82	83	83	83
1975		81	80	80	78	82	83	79	80	81	79	85	79	76	77	79	77
1976		77	81	80	81	78	77	76	77	83	82	77	80	82	81	79	83
1977		78	78	79	81	81	81	71	73	80	82	75	80	82	82	81	79
1978		81	82	81	86	80	81	82	81	83	82	75	83	85	86	86	87
1979		90	92	94	94	89	89	91	92	92	92	95	94	93	93	95	94
1980		97	100	105	102	97	96	99	100	98	102	113	101	101	101	101	104
1981		102	103	105	104	101	103	101	103	105	100	107	106	103	105	102	104
1982		105	104	103	105	106	105	105	104	103	105	101	104	104	103	104	106
1983		104	109	108	109	103	104	105	107	108	110	108	108	110	109	110	107

Production: wood fellings (5) / Perspectives économiques (5)

million cubic metres, monthly averages / solde en pourcentage

Adjusted - Corrigé

	Year	Q.1	Q.2	Q.3	Q.4	JAN	FEB	MAR	APR	MAY	JUN	JUL	AUG	SEP	OCT	NOV	DEC
1964		3.15	3.18	3.11	3.20	3.18	3.18	3.09	3.14	3.14	3.27	3.22	3.08	3.02	3.15	3.14	3.32
1965		3.43	3.22	3.40	2.75	3.27	3.43	3.60	3.65	3.11	2.90	3.87	3.19	3.14	2.61	2.87	2.76
1966		2.63	2.86	2.70	2.62	2.89	2.63	2.37	2.14	3.35	3.09	2.51	2.69	2.91	2.77	2.55	2.54
1967		2.72	2.73	2.75	2.49	2.61	2.75	2.81	2.93	2.63	2.78	2.62	2.92	2.71	2.76	2.46	2.24
1968		2.64	2.72	2.59	3.28	2.39	2.73	2.80	2.99	2.70	2.46	2.63	2.66	2.48	2.92	3.26	3.65
1969		3.25	3.03	2.92	3.49	3.56	3.03	3.15	3.10	3.08	2.91	2.87	2.85	3.02	3.35	3.45	3.66
1970		3.53	3.66	3.53	3.86	3.49	3.63	3.48	3.68	3.64	3.65	3.64	3.46	3.49	3.67	3.82	4.10
1971		3.60	3.37	3.26	2.92	3.73	3.63	3.45	3.22	3.31	3.58	3.45	3.13	3.18	3.02	2.93	2.81
1972		3.15	3.08	2.88	3.00	2.89	3.14	3.41	3.09	3.17	2.96	2.54	3.03	3.06	2.93	2.84	3.24
1973		3.13	2.80	2.92	3.27	3.30	2.96	3.13	3.37	2.70	2.33	2.68	3.08	3.00	3.31	3.42	3.07
1974		2.79	2.95	3.21	2.74	3.06	2.82	2.48	2.70	3.17	2.98	3.45	3.16	3.02	2.84	2.74	2.65
1975		2.92	2.73	2.21	1.91	2.85	2.99	2.93	2.66	2.39	3.14	2.56	2.15	1.91	1.99	1.90	1.82
1976		1.92	2.42	2.80	2.83	1.67	1.89	2.21	2.33	2.49	2.44	3.10	2.52	2.79	2.72	2.85	2.92
1977		2.57	2.62	2.66	2.59	2.59	2.53	2.60	2.49	2.70	2.67	2.21	2.88	2.88	2.58	2.52	2.67
1978		2.71	2.31	2.45	3.16	2.72	2.67	2.73	2.67	2.28	1.98	2.01	2.51	2.84	3.07	3.20	3.20
1979		3.56	4.19	3.31	3.60	3.57	3.62	3.48	3.93	4.47	4.19	3.29	3.34	3.29	3.71	3.72	3.37
1980		3.93	3.88	5.01	4.02	4.16	4.46	3.18	2.18	4.43	5.02	5.66	5.00	4.39	4.24	3.90	3.93
1981		3.68	3.89	4.01	3.55	3.88	3.68	3.49	3.79	3.93	3.95	4.31	3.83	3.90	3.66	3.40	3.59
1982		3.42	3.42	3.20	3.68	3.17	3.38	3.71	3.51	3.33	3.43	3.11	3.13	3.36	3.40	3.82	3.82
1983		3.62	3.06	3.01	3.11	3.68	3.57	3.61	3.39	2.96	2.84	2.95	3.03	3.04	3.10	3.05	3.18

Production: crude steel / Production : acier brut

thousand tons, monthly averages / milliers de tonnes, moyennes mensuelles

	Year	Q.1	Q.2	Q.3	Q.4	JAN	FEB	MAR	APR	MAY	JUN	JUL	AUG	SEP	OCT	NOV	DEC
1964																	
1965																	
1966																	
1967																	
1968																	
1969	75	81	74	64	80	74	83	85	71	76	75	28	81	82	80	80	80
1970	97	103	98	84	105	105	99	105	98	104	92	43	103	105	112	106	97
1971	85	45	94	83	117	105	28	3	79	106	97	41	97	111	119	122	109
1972	121	119	121	104	140	119	120	119	122	128	113	90	95	126	138	145	136
1973	135	142	137	112	147	148	137	141	135	150	127	79	120	137	156	146	139
1974	138	150	142	115	145	152	145	153	153	152	121	80	142	124	149	147	138
1975	135	152	129	120	139	155	143	154	151	144	92	86	133	142	149	142	125
1976	137	142	136	111	162	141	132	152	136	151	120	92	102	138	164	158	163
1977	180	166	179	171	203	152	168	179	174	191	172	121	193	200	179	214	217
1978	192	205	202	155	206	209	181	226	201	217	189	85	172	209	214	204	201
1979	205	216	209	175	220	218	198	232	223	224	180	137	187	201	227	218	216
1980	207	214	207	195	213	214	211	218	217	212	193	186	188	211	216	209	213
1981	201	216	193	178	217	219	208	221	209	200	169	152	170	212	216	217	218
1982	202	219	200	183	204	234	195	228	217	222	161	151	190	208	205	199	209
1983	201	201	200	187	217	214	190	199	180	219	201	154	197	211	222	211	219

FINLAND

Business situation: prospects (7) — **État des affaires :** perspectives (7)
manufacturing — industries manufacturières
per cent balance — solde en pourcentage

	Year	Q.1	Q.2	Q.3	Q.4	JAN	FEB	MAR	APR	MAY	JUN	JUL	AUG	SEP	OCT	NOV	DEC
1964																	
1965																	
1966		15	3	-1	-10	15			3			-1			-10		
1967		1	2	-6	5	1			2			-6			5		
1968		1	15	28	37	1			15			28			37		
1969		56	42	35	18	56			42			35			18		
1970		5	10	-6	-5	5			10			-6			-5		
1971		-32	-29	-21	-22	-32			-29			-21			-22		
1972		-1	48	37	52	-1			48			37			52		
1973		51	38	12	-22	51			38			12			-22		
1974		-15	-10	-28	-41	-15			-10			-28			-41		
1975		-51	-30	-32|	-17	-51			-30			-32|			-17		
1976		9	19	16	-23	9			19			16			-23		
1977		-14	-13	-16	-27	-14			-13			-16			-27		
1978		-25	21	35	20	-25			21			35			20		
1979		33	19	11	-	33			19			11			-		
1980		-3	-29	-30	-35	-3			-29			-30			-35		
1981		-24	-37	-40	-45	-24			-37			-40			-46		
1982		-34	-28	-42	-25	-34			-28			-42			-25		
1983		8	6	11	15	8			6			11			15		

Production: future tendency (7) — **Perspectives de production** (7)
manufacturing — industries manufacturières
per cent balance — solde en pourcentage

	Year	Q.1	Q.2	Q.3	Q.4	JAN	FEB	MAR	APR	MAY	JUN	JUL	AUG	SEP	OCT	NOV	DEC
1964																	
1965																	
1966		40	21	25	1	40			21			25			1		
1967		19	-9	7	-9	19			-9			7			-9		
1968		43	8	19	34	43			8			19			34		
1969		35	7	50	42	35			7			50			42		
1970		45	23	36	30	45			23			36			30		
1971		42	-6	20	20	42			-6			20			20		
1972		11	-13	36	31	11			-13			36			31		
1973		55	32	48	15	55			32			48			15		
1974		14	30	33	23	14			30			33			23		
1975		-15	-	-13|	6	-15						-13|			6		
1976		28	27	-2	-14	28			27			-2			-14		
1977		-8	7	17	-17	-8			7			17			-17		
1978		-11	6	4	17	-11			6			4			17		
1979		4	21	29	22	4			21			29			22		
1980		14	7	-1	-2	14			7			-1			-2		
1981		4	-9	10	-21	4			-9			10			-21		
1982		-3	-12	-2	-9	-3			-12			-2			-9		
1983		19	-8	9	7	19			-8			9			7		

Orders inflow: tendency (7) — **Commandes :** tendance (7)
manufacturing — industries manufacturières
per cent balance — solde en pourcentage

	Year	Q.1	Q.2	Q.3	Q.4	JAN	FEB	MAR	APR	MAY	JUN	JUL	AUG	SEP	OCT	NOV	DEC
1964																	
1965																	
1966		43	15	18	-6	43			15			18			-6		
1967		-17	-14	-10	-31	-17			-14			-10			-31		
1968		3	2	6	7	3			2			6			7		
1969		42	22	57	29	42			22			57			29		
1970		30	31	-	-	30			31			-			-		
1971		-3	-17	-14	-29	-3			-17			-14			-29		
1972		12	24	-8	16	12			24			-8			16		
1973		47	39	29	36	47			39			29			36		
1974		19	-	-14	-20	19			-			-14			-20		
1975		-11	-37	-11|	5	-11			-37			-11|			5		
1976		-	26	-3	-30	-			26			-3			-30		
1977		-12	-10	-11	-23	-12			-10			-11			-23		
1978		-16	21	15	7	-16			21			15			7		
1979		44	37	14	17	44			37			14			17		
1980		23	15	3	-13	23			15			3			-13		
1981		-9	-7	-18	-38	-9			-7			-18			-38		
1982		-24	-27	-42	-41	-24			-27			-42			-41		
1983		16	-5	-10	17	16			-5			-10			17		

Order books: level / Carnet de commandes : niveau

manufacturing — industries manufacturières

per cent balance — solde en pourcentage

	Year	Q.1	Q.2	Q.3	Q.4	JAN	FEB	MAR	APR	MAY	JUN	JUL	AUG	SEP	OCT	NOV	DEC
1964																	
1965																	
1966		15	7	12	-11	15			7			12			-11		
1967		-13	-16	2	-3	-13			-16			2			-8		
1968		1	-14	-6	-17	1			-14			-6			-17		
1969		-2	20	41	35	-2			20			41			35		
1970		38	47	33	10	38			47			33			10		
1971		6	-3	1	-3	6			-3						-3		
1972		1	8	13	13	1			8			13			13		
1973		28	26	31	37	28			26			31			37		
1974		14	10	-	-4	14			10						-4		
1975		-34	-37	-59	-16	-34			-37			-59			-16		
1976		-61	-56	-62	-64	-61			-56			-62			-64		
1977		-68	-66	-78	-72	-68			-66			-78			-72		
1978		-67	-49	-44	-39	-57			-49			-44			-39		
1979		-23	-8	-7	-5	-23			-8			-7			-5		
1980		5	20	-7	-22	5			20			-7			-22		
1981		-14	-8	-21	-40	-14			-8			-21			-40		
1982		-38	-45	-51	-50	-38			-45			-51			-50		
1983		-30	-20	-32	-24	-30			-20			-32			-24		

Finished goods stocks: tendency / Stocks de produits finis : tendance

manufacturing — industries manufacturières

per cent balance — solde en pourcentage

	Year	Q.1	Q.2	Q.3	Q.4	JAN	FEB	MAR	APR	MAY	JUN	JUL	AUG	SEP	OCT	NOV	DEC
1964																	
1965																	
1966																	
1967																	
1968																	
1969																	
1970																	
1971																	
1972																	
1973																	
1974					43										43		
1975		51	4	32	-5	51			4			32			-5		
1976		-19	-7	-14	4	-19			-7			-14			4		
1977		15	19	-11	-9	-15			19			-11			-9		
1978		-5	5	-10	-26	-5			5			-10			-26		
1979		11	-15	-8	7	11			-15			-8			7		
1980		18	-1	9	29	18			-1			9			29		
1981		38	25	9	24	38			25			9			24		
1982		5	9	-1	2	5			9			-1			2		
1983		-2	-3	1	2	-2			-3			1			2		

Firms operating at full capacity (7) / Entreprises travaillant à pleine capacité (7)

per cent — pourcentage

	Year	Q.1	Q.2	Q.3	Q.4	JAN	FEB	MAR	APR	MAY	JUN	JUL	AUG	SEP	OCT	NOV	DEC
1964																	
1965																	
1966		38	46	40	43	38			46			40			43		
1967		40	41	42	33	40			41			42			33		
1968		28	26	36	30	28			26			36			30		
1969		36	37	40	43	36			37			40			43		
1970		55	52	55	49	55			52			55			49		
1971		41	43	35	41	41			43			35			41		
1972		48	40	45	50	48			40			45			50		
1973		46	64	66	71	46			64			66			71		
1974		69	67	70	46	69			67			70			46		
1975		35	38	43	19	35			38			43			19		
1976		16	18	14	15	16			18			14			15		
1977		12	17	10	8	12			17			10			8		
1978		12	13	16	18	12			13			16			18		
1979		21	30	42	48	21			30			42			48		
1980		48	50	46	36	48			50			46			36		
1981		41	41	36	31	41			41			36			31		
1982		23	20	18	20	23			20			18			20		
1983		20	25	27	28	20			25			27			28		

FINLAND

Construction permits issued: total (8) (9)

million cubic metres

Permis de construire délivrés : total (8) (9)

millions de mètres cubes

	Year	Q.1	Q.2	Q.3	Q.4	JAN	FEB	MAR	APR	MAY	JUN	JUL	AUG	SEP	OCT	NOV	DEC
1964	29.23	4.80	8.82	7.29	8.32	1.59	1.67	1.55	2.94	3.09	2.79	2.47	2.02	2.30	2.55	2.36	2.91
1965	31.71	5.50	10.41	9.33	6.47	1.49	1.84	2.17	3.38	3.36	3.17	2.84	3.93	2.57	2.47	1.62	2.38
1966	34.75	6.25	10.40	8.61	9.49	2.34	2.35	2.52	3.18	3.66	3.56	2.31	2.69	3.61	3.04	3.14	4.31
1967	28.82	4.34	9.03	7.30	8.15	1.16	1.14	2.04	2.74	3.60	2.70	1.85	2.77	2.67	4.03	2.02	2.10
1968	31.58	4.34	8.87	9.40	8.97	1.17	1.27	1.90	2.56	3.47	2.83	2.81	2.85	3.74	3.96	2.98	2.03
1969	38.95	5.43	11.98	11.78	9.76	1.48	1.72	2.23	3.57	4.08	4.33	4.44	3.65	3.69	3.25	3.86	2.65
1970	41.42	6.58	14.25	11.52	9.07	1.75	2.09	2.74	4.24	4.69	5.32	4.02	3.97	3.53	3.18	3.41	2.48
1971	42.63	6.52	13.59	12.90	9.62	1.47	2.34	2.71	3.35	4.63	5.61	3.69	4.94	4.26	3.36	3.41	2.85
1972	47.81	7.31	13.52	13.44	13.54	2.09	2.17	3.05	4.40	4.69	4.40	4.04	4.54	4.86	4.15	4.38	4.86
1973	54.96	10.62	16.97	16.24	11.13	2.78	3.24	4.51	6.04	5.26	5.68	4.93	6.27	5.02	4.56	3.79	2.78
1974	53.23	10.33	16.64	14.53	11.73	3.21	3.56	3.53	5.50	6.71	4.44	4.04	5.77	4.72	4.96	3.29	3.48
1975	51.36	10.51	16.46	13.68	10.71	4.90	3.03	4.67	5.48	5.88	4.55	3.52	3.81	4.88	3.92	3.55	3.24
1976	46.90	8.52	14.00	12.42	11.96	2.51	2.75	3.26	3.89	5.15	4.96	3.57	4.12	4.73	4.08	3.71	4.17
1977	41.88	6.73	13.22	11.41	10.52	1.87	2.50	2.36	3.80	4.97	4.45	3.42	4.24	3.75	3.40	3.46	3.67
1978	41.99	10.21	12.92	11.07	7.79	2.52	2.43	5.25	2.90	5.58	4.44	2.60	4.28	4.20	2.90	2.65	2.24
1979	48.64	7.75	19.16	11.74	9.99	1.89	2.80	3.06	4.56	7.55	7.02	3.57	3.52	4.65	4.25	2.75	2.99
1980	50.53	8.55	18.92	11.97	11.09	2.16	2.69	3.71	6.24	6.67	6.01	3.84	4.07	4.05	5.80	2.95	2.34
1981	44.92	7.25	16.95	10.77	9.95	1.28	2.58	3.39	5.49	6.47	5.00	3.15	3.82	3.80	3.73	2.99	3.23
1982	51.70	9.10	19.17	12.80	10.63	1.91	2.32	4.31	6.18	6.39	6.07	4.13	3.88	3.89	3.98	3.30	2.90
1983	51.17	9.77	18.94	14.14	8.32	1.81	4.50	4.51	5.93	6.80	4.86	3.26	4.00	4.75	3.65	3.04	1.70

Construction permits issued: residential (8) (9)

million cubic metres

Permis de construire délivrés : bâtiments résidentiels (8) (9)

millions de mètres cubes

	Year	Q.1	Q.2	Q.3	Q.4	JAN	FEB	MAR	APR	MAY	JUN	JUL	AUG	SEP	OCT	NOV	DEC
1964	11.73	1.42	3.59	2.63	4.09	0.41	0.46	0.55	1.14	1.38	1.07	0.83	0.74	1.06	1.31	1.03	1.75
1965	12.12	1.89	3.97	3.21	3.05	0.45	0.66	0.79	1.33	1.50	1.13	1.01	0.87	1.33	1.05	0.74	1.26
1966	14.03	2.00	4.17	3.21	4.65	0.37	0.96	1.12	1.22	1.45	1.50	0.92	0.82	1.47	1.43	1.70	2.53
1967	11.51	1.35	3.72	3.26	3.18	0.34	0.46	0.55	1.17	1.41	1.14	0.70	1.19	1.37	1.97	0.67	0.55
1968	14.00	1.72	3.80	4.31	4.17	0.33	0.56	0.83	1.11	1.53	1.15	1.15	1.43	1.73	2.01	1.24	0.92
1969	15.38	2.12	4.95	4.94	3.37	0.50	0.64	0.98	1.42	1.83	1.71	1.62	1.57	1.75	1.44	1.36	0.57
1970	17.96	2.57	6.04	5.12	4.23	0.62	0.84	1.11	1.82	1.87	2.36	1.64	1.87	1.61	1.73	1.53	0.96
1971	17.54	2.86	5.54	6.66	4.48	0.77	0.97	1.11	1.42	2.09	2.03	1.92	2.30	2.44	2.00	1.43	1.04
1972	20.56	2.73	6.22	6.11	5.50	0.73	0.73	1.28	1.87	2.25	2.09	1.68	2.29	2.14	1.88	2.19	1.43
1973	24.68	3.99	7.35	7.86	4.98	1.09	1.21	1.68	2.58	2.61	2.66	1.93	3.19	2.75	2.25	1.51	1.22
1974	22.34	3.65	7.96	6.15	4.58	1.13	1.24	1.28	2.52	3.18	2.27	2.03	1.86	2.26	1.99	1.46	1.13
1975	20.53	3.47	7.81	5.10	4.15	0.88	1.07	1.37	2.32	2.94	2.20	1.57	1.50	1.77	1.55	1.24	1.24
1976	20.71	3.16	7.80	5.61	4.14	0.86	1.03	1.14	1.88	2.76	2.75	1.47	1.82	2.14	1.65	1.30	1.15
1977	19.81	3.00	7.40	5.03	4.38	0.94	0.87	1.11	1.93	2.97	2.10	1.31	1.83	1.52	1.52	1.36	1.34
1978	19.00	3.90	6.92	4.44	3.74	0.92	1.12	1.68	1.45	2.92	2.14	1.16	1.52	1.44	1.48	1.10	0.97
1979	19.83	3.51	7.88	4.77	3.67	0.93	1.13	1.26	1.78	3.15	2.52	1.47	1.53	1.48	1.49	1.14	0.83
1980	20.71	3.57	8.60	4.95	3.59	0.80	1.24	1.54	2.78	3.52	2.29	1.67	1.56	1.72	1.74	1.00	0.85
1981	18.76	3.07	7.85	4.64	3.20	0.56	1.01	1.50	2.41	3.05	2.39	1.49	1.56	1.59	1.43	1.04	0.73
1982	19.20	3.36	7.96	4.59	3.29	0.63	0.82	1.72	2.63	2.81	2.29	1.42	1.30	1.51	1.29	1.06	0.83
1983	19.45	4.14	7.91	4.20	3.20	0.60	2.14	2.14	2.67	2.78	1.89	1.11	1.21	1.48	1.13	1.08	0.76

Construction, work in progress: total (8)

million cubic metres, end of period

Construction, travaux en cours : total (8)

millions de mètres cubes, fin de période

	Year	Q.1	Q.2	Q.3	Q.4	JAN	FEB	MAR	APR	MAY	JUN	JUL	AUG	SEP	OCT	NOV	DEC
1964	28.75	25.39	29.45	30.74	28.75												
1965	31.41	28.31	32.78	35.75	31.41												
1966	36.19	30.31	36.69	38.79	36.19												
1967	31.40	33.15	34.14	33.00	31.40												
1968	34.09	29.47	33.70	34.29	34.09												
1969	36.40	32.29	37.06	38.14	36.40												
1970	36.56	35.82	41.20	42.55	36.56												
1971	37.64	32.98	37.90	41.76	37.64												
1972	40.57	34.34	39.33	41.87	40.57												
1973	51.42	38.65	48.56	55.01	51.42												
1974	52.84	49.20	54.56	56.89	52.84												
1975	52.45	50.24	54.44	56.38	52.45												
1976	51.85	48.82	51.73	55.22	51.85												
1977	48.12	47.95	51.52	52.69	48.12												
1978	42.78	44.62	47.46	48.76	42.78												
1979	47.62	38.86	47.27	51.91	47.62												
1980	49.57	42.93	51.89	53.39	49.57												
1981	47.14	44.44	50.83	53.71	47.14												
1982	50.32	44.41	51.52	56.52	50.32												
1983	52.62	45.37	52.12	57.94	52.62												

Construction permits issued: total (8)

million cubic metres

Adjusted - Corrigé

Permis de construire délivrés : total (8)

millions de mètres cubes

	Year	Q.1	Q.2	Q.3	Q.4	JAN	FEB	MAR	APR	MAY	JUN	JUL	AUG	SEP	OCT	NOV	DEC
1964		6.90	7.07	7.08	7.82												
1965		8.12	8.34	8.93	5.99												
1966		11.02	8.28	8.01	9.39												
1967		6.73	7.18	6.65	7.76												
1968		6.89	7.01	8.36	8.75												
1969		8.64	9.44	10.34	9.75												
1970		10.38	11.22	9.94	9.51												
1971		9.38	10.73	11.20	10.40												
1972		10.61	10.74	11.80	14.97												
1973		14.73	13.65	14.54	12.24												
1974		14.14	13.51	13.22	12.85												
1975		15.16	13.43	12.41	11.45												
1976		12.19	11.19	11.44	13.[illegible]7												
1977		9.43	10.23	10.77	11.80												
1978		14.34	9.56	10.76	8.94												
1979		10.81	13.63	11.68	11.64												
1980		12.01	12.85	11.94	13.27												
1981		10.16	11.28	10.68	12.11												
1982		12.86	12.63	12.49	13.28												
1983		13.66	12.58	13.53	10.65												

Construction permits issued: residential (8)

million cubic metres

Adjusted - Corrigé

Permis de construire délivrés : bâtiments résidentiels (8)

millions de mètres cubes

	Year	Q.1	Q.2	Q.3	Q.4	JAN	FEB	MAR	APR	MAY	JUN	JUL	AUG	SEP	OCT	NOV	DEC
1964		2.40	3.02	2.69	3.25												
1965		3.36	3.30	3.19	2.45												
1966		5.45	3.41	3.02	4.88												
1967		2.46	3.00	2.95	2.90												
1968		3.12	3.06	3.70	4.04												
1969		3.77	3.97	4.13	3.39												
1970		4.48	4.82	4.16	4.50												
1971		4.79	4.36	5.46	4.89												
1972		4.48	4.81	5.06	6.14												
1973		6.44	5.90	6.71	5.63												
1974		5.83	5.79	5.42	5.29												
1975		5.46	5.27	5.00	5.05												
1976		4.89	5.25	5.59	5.09												
1977		4.52	4.94	5.08	5.49												
1978		5.79	4.52	4.54	4.83												
1979		5.12	5.03	4.93	4.91												
1980		5.06	5.33	5.12	4.94												
1981		4.26	4.78	4.85	4.53												
1982		4.57	4.79	4.86	4.74												
1983		5.49	4.75	4.51	4.65												

Construction, work in progress: total (8)

million cubic metres, end of period

Adjusted - Corrigé

Construction, travaux en cours : total (8)

millions de mètres cubes, fin de période

	Year	Q.1	Q.2	Q.3	Q.4	JAN	FEB	MAR	APR	MAY	JUN	JUL	AUG	SEP	OCT	NOV	DEC
1964		27.93	28.06	28.76	29.76												
1965		30.97	31.43	33.68	32.26												
1966		33.02	35.40	36.70	37.04												
1967		36.06	32.96	31.31	32.03												
1968		32.04	32.58	32.49	34.73												
1969		35.20	35.84	35.95	37.03												
1970		39.29	39.93	39.73	37.24												
1971		36.40	36.77	38.70	38.36												
1972		37.98	38.27	38.70	41.29												
1973		42.55	47.45	51.04	52.12												
1974		53.80	53.51	53.06	53.44												
1975		53.72	53.95	52.98	52.68												
1976		52.45	51.06	51.67	52.23												
1977		51.93	50.56	49.04	48.58												
1978		48.85	46.24	45.10	43.33												
1979		42.93	45.80	47.70	48.36												
1980		47.94	50.26	48.83	50.51												
1981		49.83	49.30	48.91	48.01												
1982		49.85	50.17	51.29	51.25												
1983		50.80	50.99	52.46	53.55												

FINLAND

Construction, work in progress: residential (8)

million cubic metres, end of period

Construction, travaux en cours : bâtiments résidentiels (8)

millions de mètres cubes, fin de période

	Year	Q.1	Q.2	Q.3	Q.4	JAN	FEB	MAR	APR	MAY	JUN	JUL	AUG	SEP	OCT	NOV	DEC
1964	11.84	9.87	12.42	13.05	11.84												
1965	12.31	11.59	14.12	14.73	12.31												
1966	14.81	11.83	14.39	15.42	14.81												
1967	13.30	13.14	14.68	14.79	13.30												
1968	14.00	11.84	14.28	14.54	14.00												
1969	15.48	12.98	15.60	16.53	15.48												
1970	14.95	14.25	16.69	17.04	14.95												
1971	17.09	13.04	15.87	17.76	17.09												
1972	18.10	15.53	17.74	19.10	18.10												
1973	21.29	16.58	20.82	23.18	21.29												
1974	20.66	19.85	22.24	23.51	20.66												
1975	19.76	19.37	21.50	22.24	19.76												
1976	20.34	17.81	20.85	23.05	20.34												
1977	19.90	14.84	21.61	23.28	19.90												
1978	17.91	17.71	20.34	21.05	17.91												
1979	18.99	16.22	20.37	22.19	18.99												
1980	19.36	16.71	21.35	22.49	19.36												
1981	19.43	16.35	20.07	21.96	19.43												
1982	19.43	17.28	20.94	22.07	19.43												
1983	20.00	16.90	20.97	22.59	20.00												

Cost of construction (10)

1980 = 100

Coût de la construction (10)

1980 = 100

	Year	Q.1	Q.2	Q.3	Q.4	JAN	FEB	MAR	APR	MAY	JUN	JUL	AUG	SEP	OCT	NOV	DEC
1964	23.6	22.7	23.5	23.8	24.1	22.3	22.7	23.0	23.3	23.6	23.6	23.6	23.9	23.9	24.1	24.1	24.2
1965	24.9	24.6	25.0	25.0	24.9	24.5	24.5	24.7	24.9	25.0	25.0	25.0	25.0	25.0	25.0	24.9	24.9
1966	25.5	24.8	25.5	25.8	25.8	24.8	24.8	24.8	24.9	25.7	25.8	25.8	25.8	25.8	25.8	25.8	25.8
1967	27.0	26.4	26.5	26.8	28.0	26.4	26.4	26.4	26.4	26.4	26.8	26.8	26.8	26.8	27.6	28.2	29.3
1968	29.7	29.3	29.6	29.9	30.0	29.2	29.3	29.4	29.5	29.4	29.9	29.9	29.9	29.9	29.9	30.0	30.0
1969	30.9	30.5	30.7	31.0	31.4	30.5	30.5	30.5	30.5	30.7	30.7	30.8	30.9	31.2	31.3	31.5	31.5
1970	32.6	32.4	32.6	32.6	32.7	32.3	32.5	32.6	32.6	32.6	32.6	32.6	32.6	32.6	32.6	32.7	32.9
1971	35.1	33.4	35.1	35.6	36.2	33.2	33.4	33.7	34.8	35.1	35.2	35.3	35.4	36.1	36.1	36.2	36.3
1972	38.0	36.4	37.9	38.7	39.0	36.4	36.3	36.4	37.2	38.2	38.3	38.6	38.6	38.8	38.8	39.0	39.1
1973	44.4	40.6	42.6	46.1	48.1	40.2	40.5	41.0	41.9	42.6	43.3	45.2	46.1	47.0	47.5	47.9	49.0
1974	55.6	51.8	55.9	56.8	57.9	50.3	51.8	53.3	55.3	56.1	56.3	56.4	56.5	57.4	57.7	57.8	58.3
1975	61.8	59.6	62.2	62.4	63.1	59.1	59.6	60.2	62.0	62.3	62.2	62.3	62.4	62.6	63.0	63.0	63.3
1976	67.2	64.3	65.8	68.4	70.5	64.0	64.4	64.5	64.8	66.2	66.4	67.3	68.2	69.7	70.1	70.5	70.8
1977	76.0	73.6	75.2	77.3	77.9	73.1	73.8	74.0	74.4	74.8	76.4	76.6	77.7	77.7	77.7	78.0	77.9
1978	80.2	78.7	79.6	80.4	82.1	78.6	78.6	78.9	79.1	79.8	79.9	79.8	79.9	81.5	81.9	82.1	82.2
1979	88.2	84.4	87.4	89.3	91.5	83.4	84.2	85.6	86.5	87.4	88.3	88.6	89.1	90.2	90.9	91.4	92.4
1980	100.0	95.3	99.1	101.3	104.4	94.5	95.3	96.1	97.2	99.6	100.4	100.5	101.1	102.2	104.0	104.4	104.9
1981	110.1	107.0	109.1	111.0	113.1	106.7	107.0	107.4	108.6	108.9	109.7	110.3	110.4	112.2	113.0	113.1	113.3
1982	117.7	114.6	117.1	118.0	121.1	113.9	114.1	115.7	116.8	117.0	117.5	117.4	118.1	118.6	120.7	121.1	121.5
1983	128.7	123.9	127.6	130.7	132.8	123.3	123.8	124.5	125.9	127.1	129.7	130.1	130.7	131.2	132.6	132.8	133.0

Wholesale sales: value (11)

1980 = 100

Ventes du commerce de gros : valeur (11)

1980 = 100

	Year	Q.1	Q.2	Q.3	Q.4	JAN	FEB	MAR	APR	MAY	JUN	JUL	AUG	SEP	OCT	NOV	DEC
1964	10	9	10	10	11	8	9	10	11	10	10	10	11	11	11	11	12
1965	11	10	12	11	12	8	10	11	11	12	11	11	11	12	12	12	13
1966	12	10	12	12	13	9	10	12	11	12	12	10	12	12	12	12	13
1967	13	11	13	12	14	9	11	12	13	13	12	11	13	13	14	14	14
1968	13	12	14	13	15	11	12	13	13	15	13	12	14	14	15	14	15
1969	16	14	16	17	19	13	14	15	16	16	16	15	17	18	19	17	20
1970	19	17	19	20	22	15	17	18	20	19	19	18	19	22	21	20	23
1971	21	19	22	22	23	17	19	21	22	23	21	19	22	24	23	23	25
1972	25	22	24	25	29	20	22	25	23	25	25	22	26	26	28	29	30
1973	32	28	30	32	38	25	27	32	29	33	29	27	34	34	38	37	39
1974	42	37	40	42	49	34	36	40	40	42	39	38	45	44	50	47	50
1975	52	49	51	51	57	46	47	54	56	51	46	46	51	57	59	53	59
1976	58	51	56	58	67	46	49	58	55	55	58	51	58	66	63	63	76
1977	62	54	62	62	68	46	53	63	61	65	60	52	65	69	66	66	73
1978	68	61	68	67	77	55	60	69	67	70	68	54	72	74	77	73	80
1979	82	71	82	83	93	68	66	78	73	86	80	72	90	87	96	97	98
1980	100	92	96	100	112	89	89	98	92	101	96	89	99	113	115	103	119
1981	114	104	113	114	127	96	102	114	111	116	112	101	114	126	126	118	136
1982	127	112	125	123	146	100	109	128	125	124	125	107	124	138	142	143	153
1983	138	122	141	134	153	108	118	142	137	166	120	107	143	151	148	150	163

Construction, work in progress: residential (8) — Construction, travaux en cours : bâtiments résidentiels (8)

million cubic metres, end of period — millions de mètres cubes, fin de période

Adjusted - Corrigé

	Year	Q.1	Q.2	Q.3	Q.4	JAN	FEB	MAR	APR	MAY	JUN	JUL	AUG	SEP	OCT	NOV	DEC
1964		11.25	11.74	11.92	12.35												
1965		13.13	13.39	13.55	12.74												
1966		13.34	13.70	14.23	15.24												
1967		14.80	14.01	13.73	13.58												
1968		13.33	13.70	13.50	14.21												
1969		14.63	15.01	15.33	15.63												
1970		16.11	16.10	15.71	15.07												
1971		14.73	15.35	16.31	17.22												
1972		17.53	17.23	17.47	18.24												
1973		18.66	20.28	21.15	21.49												
1974		22.33	21.67	21.38	20.94												
1975		22.49	21.12	19.81	19.71												
1976		20.90	20.20	20.45	20.54												
1977		17.48	20.73	20.58	20.23												
1978		20.96	19.31	18.56	18.36												
1979		19.08	19.28	19.59	19.49												
1980		19.64	20.30	20.04	19.92												
1981		19.70	19.17	19.66	19.95												
1982		20.23	20.05	19.80	19.39												
1983		19.78	20.10	20.31	20.43												

Wholesale sales: value (11) — Ventes du commerce de gros : valeur (11)

1980 = 100

Adjusted - Corrigé

	Year	Q.1	Q.2	Q.3	Q.4	JAN	FEB	MAR	APR	MAY	JUN	JUL	AUG	SEP	OCT	NOV	DEC
1964		9	10	10	11	9	10	9	10	9	10	10	10	10	10	11	11
1965		11	11	11	11	10	11	11	11	11	11	11	11	11	11	11	12
1966		11	11	12	12	11	11	11	11	11	12	11	12	12	11	12	12
1967		12	12	12	14	12	12	12	13	12	12	12	13	13	15	14	13
1968		13	13	13	14	13	13	13	13	14	13	13	14	13	14	14	14
1969		15	16	17	18	16	15	15	15	15	16	17	15	18	18	17	18
1970		18	19	20	20	18	18	18	19	18	20	20	19	20	20	20	21
1971		20	21	22	22	20	20	21	21	22	21	21	22	23	22	22	23
1972		23	24	25	27	23	24	24	23	24	26	25	26	25	26	28	27
1973		29	30	33	36	28	29	30	29	32	30	31	34	33	36	36	36
1974		38	40	43	46	38	39	38	39	41	41	43	44	42	46	46	45
1975		51	52	52	53	52	51	51	56	50	49	53	50	54	55	51	53
1976		54	56	59	62	54	54	55	54	53	61	58	57	62	58	61	68
1977		57	62	62	63	53	58	60	61	62	62	60	63	64	61	64	65
1978		65	68	67	71	63	66	66	67	66	70	62	70	69	71	70	72
1979		75	81	84	87	77	72	75	79	84	81	84	88	81	88	93	80
1980		97	95	102	104	100	97	94	92	96	97	104	97	105	106	99	108
1981		110	112	116	117	108	111	110	111	112	114	118	113	117	115	114	121
1982		119	124	126	134	116	120	122	124	120	127	125	124	128	131	136	134
1983		131	140	136	140	128	130	134	135	162	122	127	143	140	138	142	140

FINLAND

Wholesale sales: volume (11)
1980 = 100

Ventes du commerce de gros : volume (11)
1980 = 100

	Year	Q.1	Q.2	Q.3	Q.4	JAN	FEB	MAR	APR	MAY	JUN	JUL	AUG	SEP	OCT	NOV	DEC
1964	45	39	46	46	50	33	40	43	48	45	45	44	47	48	50	47	52
1965	47	41	48	47	51	34	41	47	47	50	47	45	47	50	50	49	53
1966	48	43	49	48	53	38	43	47	47	50	50	42	49	52	51	50	57
1967	50	45	53	51	52	39	46	51	52	55	51	46	52	54	54	52	51
1968	47	43	49	48	52	38	44	46	47	52	46	45	50	49	52	49	54
1969	56	49	55	57	62	46	47	54	55	57	54	52	57	62	64	57	65
1970	62	53	62	63	69	49	54	57	64	61	61	59	61	69	67	65	74
1971	65	58	67	65	70	51	58	65	66	71	63	58	66	71	67	68	74
1972	71	65	70	70	80	59	65	72	68	72	71	62	75	74	77	80	[illegible]
1973	80	74	78	78	88	67	71	84	75	84	73	68	84	82	91	86	88
1974	82	75	79	81	91	71	74	81	79	83	76	73	86	83	92	88	92
1975	91	88	90	88	96	84	84	96	99	91	81	81	87	97	100	89	99
1976	90	83	89	89	100	76	80	94	86	89	93	79	88	99	94	94	113
1977	85	78	87	85	92	67	77	90	86	91	84	72	90	93	89	88	98
1978	87	80	88	85	96	72	78	90	87	90	88	69	93	94	97	91	100
1979	96	85	97	96	104	83	80	93	93	105	93	84	104	99	108	107	98
1980	100	96	98	100	107	94	92	101	94	102	97	89	98	111	111	98	113
1981	104	98	103	102	112	92	96	105	101	106	102	91	102	112	111	105	120
1982	108	98	108	106	119	88	95	112	109	107	108	92	107	119	120	127	109
1983	110	100	114	106	119	89	96	116	112	135	95	85	113	119	116	117	125

Retail sales: value (12) (13)
1980 = 100

Ventes au détail : valeur (12) (13)
1980 = 100

	Year	Q.1	Q.2	Q.3	Q.4	JAN	FEB	MAR	APR	MAY	JUN	JUL	AUG	SEP	OCT	NOV	DEC
1964	14	11	14	13	16	10	12	12	14	15	14	12	13	13	14	15	20
1965	15	13	16	15	18	12	13	13	16	17	16	14	15	15	16	16	22
1966	17	14	17	16	19	14	14	14	17	18	18	15	16	17	17	17	24
1967	18	15	19	17	22	14	15	16	18	19	19	16	16	18	19	19	27
1968	20	17	20	19	23	16	17	18	20	21	21	18	19	20	20	21	28
1969	22	19	23	21	26	18	19	20	22	24	24	20	21	22	22	24	33
1970	24	20	25	23	28	20	20	21	24	25	26	23	22	24	25	25	34
1971	27	23	29	25	30	22	23	24	27	31	27	24	25	26	27	27	36
1972	31	26	31	30	37	27	26	27	30	30	33	29	29	31	32	33	48
1973	38	32	37	37	45	30	32	33	36	37	39	35	37	39	39	40	56
1974	46	37	45	45	57	35	38	39	43	46	46	44	45	47	47	51	72
1975	59	51	59	58	67	49	51	53	59	55	61	57	57	59	61	59	80
1976	67	57	69	66	76	55	57	59	66	71	70	66	64	67	69	68	92
1977	64	60	72	70	76	57	59	63	70	74	74	70	69	71	69	71	90
1978	76	66	78	73	85	62	65	69	80	76	79	73	73	75	75	78	103
1979	86	73	90	85	99	69	72	77	88	93	88	85	84	85	85	90	121
1980	100	85	103	98	115	83	83	89	99	104	105	97	97	99	100	102	143
1981	111	95	117	109	123	93	95	97	111	121	117	111	108	107	112	112	145
1982	125	107	127	122	144	107	106	109	125	131	125	123	122	122	131	133	168
1983	136	122	139	133	150	120	120	126	132	142	142	135	127	135	134	140	177

Retail sales: volume (12) (13)
1980 = 100

Ventes au détail : volume (12) (13)
1980 = 100

	Year	Q.1	Q.2	Q.3	Q.4	JAN	FEB	MAR	APR	MAY	JUN	JUL	AUG	SEP	OCT	NOV	DEC
1964	55	46	59	52	65	40	48	49	55	63	58	50	54	53	55	60	80
1965	60	51	64	56	69	48	52	51	62	66	62	54	56	58	61	63	84
1966	62	53	66	58	72	52	54	54	64	68	66	56	58	61	63	64	89
1967	64	54	67	59	75	52	56	55	65	69	66	56	58	62	68	64	93
1968	64	56	66	61	75	54	55	58	63	68	68	58	60	64	66	67	91
1969	69	59	73	65	81	55	58	63	68	75	75	63	64	67	69	74	100
1970	70	60	73	67	81	58	60	62	70	75	75	66	65	69	71	73	98
1971	73	65	79	67	81	62	64	67	76	86	75	67	67	69	73	72	97
1972	80	70	80	76	94	71	68	71	77	78	84	75	74	78	81	83	120
1973	89	79	88	86	101	75	79	82	86	87	91	83	85	89	89	90	125
1974	91	79	90	88	107	75	80	82	88	87	93	86	88	90	90	96	136
1975	98	91	100	95	107	89	92	93	102	94	104	95	94	96	98	94	129
1976	99	88	104	95	108	86	87	90	100	107	105	97	92	97	98	96	130
1977	90	80	95	89	98	75	81	84	98	92	95	90	88	89	86	89	118
1978	91	81	95	89	101	79	80	85	98	91	95	88	88	89	88	92	123
1979	97	85	101	94	107	81	84	89	100	105	99	95	94	94	93	98	132
1980	100	90	103	97	111	90	88	92	101	104	106	97	96	97	97	99	133
1981	101	90	107	98	109	89	90	90	102	112	107	101	98	96	100	99	123
1982	106	93	108	103	120	93	92	94	106	111	107	104	103	103	111	111	137
1983	107	99	112	101	114	98	97	101	105	127	103	101	98	104	103	107	133

Wholesale sales: volume (11)
1980 = 100

Adjusted - Corrigé

Ventes du commerce de gros : volume (11)
1980 = 100

Year	Q.1	Q.2	Q.3	Q.4	JAN	FEB	MAR	APR	MAY	JUN	JUL	AUG	SEP	OCT	NOV	DEC
1964	44	45	46	46	43	44	43	46	43	45	46	46	45	46	46	46
1965	46	46	47	47	45	45	47	45	47	46	47	46	47	47	47	47
1966	48	47	47	49	49	47	47	46	47	49	46	48	49	47	49	51
1967	50	51	50	52	48	50	51	51	52	51	50	51	50	57	51	46
1968	47	47	47	48	47	48	46	46	49	46	48	49	45	49	48	49
1969	54	54	57	58	56	52	54	53	53	54	56	56	58	60	56	59
1970	58	61	63	64	58	58	57	61	58	62	65	61	64	64	63	66
1971	62	66	65	65	60	62	64	65	67	64	64	66	67	64	65	66
1972	69	70	71	74	68	70	70	67	69	73	70	73	71	72	77	74
1973	78	78	79	82	76	77	81	76	81	76	77	82	79	84	82	80
1974	79	80	82	84	81	80	77	79	80	80	83	85	79	85	85	82
1975	93	91	90	88	96	92	91	99	88	86	92	85	92	92	85	88
1976	88	90	89	93	88	88	89	87	85	97	90	86	93	87	91	99
1977	83	87	86	85	78	85	86	86	87	87	83	87	86	83	85	86
1978	85	87	85	89	83	86	87	88	85	89	79	90	87	90	88	89
1979	91	96	97	97	94	88	90	94	100	94	97	101	92	100	103	89
1980	102	97	101	101	107	101	98	95	97	98	104	96	104	103	95	105
1981	104	103	104	105	105	106	102	102	102	103	106	101	103	102	100	113
1982	105	108	106	111	103	105	107	109	104	110	107	106	110	112	120	102
1983	108	113	107	111	106	107	110	110	132	97	100	112	109	108	109	117

Retail sales: value (12)
1980 = 100

Adjusted - Corrigé

Ventes au détail : valeur (12)
1980 = 100

Year	Q.1	Q.2	Q.3	Q.4	JAN	FEB	MAR	APR	MAY	JUN	JUL	AUG	SEP	OCT	NOV	DEC
1964	13	13	14	14	12	13	14	13	14	14	14	14	14	14	14	14
1965	15	15	16	16	15	15	15	15	16	15	16	16	15	16	16	15
1966	16	16	17	17	16	16	16	16	16	17	17	17	17	17	17	17
1967	17	17	18	19	17	17	17	18	17	18	18	18	18	19	18	20
1968	19	19	20	20	19	19	20	19	19	20	20	21	21	20	20	21
1969	21	22	22	23	21	21	22	22	22	23	22	22	23	23	24	24
1970	23	24	25	25	22	23	23	23	23	24	24	24	25	25	26	25
1971	26	27	27	27	25	25	26	27	29	26	26	27	27	28	27	27
1972	29	30	32	34	30	28	29	29	28	31	31	31	32	33	33	35
1973	35	36	39	41	34	35	36	35	35	37	38	39	40	40	41	41
1974	41	44	47	51	39	42	42	43	45	44	46	47	48	48	52	53
1975	57	57	60	61	56	57	57	59	53	59	59	60	60	62	60	60
1976	64	67	68	70	64	63	64	65	68	67	68	66	68	70	69	70
1977	67	69	72	70	66	67	67	68	70	71	71	72	72	70	71	69
1978	73	75	75	78	72	73	75	77	71	75	74	76	77	77	79	79
1979	81	85	87	90	79	82	83	84	87	84	86	87	88	87	91	93
1980	95	97	101	105	95	93	96	95	96	101	99	101	102	102	103	109
1981	105	110	112	113	104	106	104	108	110	113	113	112	111	114	113	112
1982	118	121	126	132	118	118	118	122	118	122	126	127	126	132	134	131
1983	134	132	137		132	133	136	130	126	140	138	133	139	134	141	

Retail sales: volume (12)
1980 = 100

Adjusted - Corrigé

Ventes au détail : volume (12)
1980 = 100

Year	Q.1	Q.2	Q.3	Q.4	JAN	FEB	MAR	APR	MAY	JUN	JUL	AUG	SEP	OCT	NOV	DEC
1964	52	55	56	57	48	54	55	54	55	55	55	57	56	55	58	57
1965	58	60	60	61	58	59	58	61	61	59	60	60	60	61	61	60
1966	61	62	62	63	62	61	60	62	62	62	62	62	63	63	62	63
1967	62	63	63	65	61	63	62	63	63	62	62	62	64	68	62	66
1968	64	63	65	65	64	63	64	62	62	64	64	65	66	66	66	65
1969	67	69	69	71	65	67	69	68	70	70	69	69	69	69	72	72
1970	67	69	72	73	66	67	68	68	68	72	72	72	73	73	74	73
1971	72	76	72	73	70	71	73	75	80	72	72	72	72	74	73	72
1972	77	78	81	84	80	76	77	77	75	81	81	80	81	82	83	88
1973	87	86	90	91	84	87	88	86	86	87	88	91	92	90	91	91
1974	87	83	92	95	85	88	88	87	86	89	90	93	92	91	96	99
1975	101	98	98	96	102	101	100	100	93	100	98	99	98	99	95	94
1976	98	101	98	98	99	97	97	97	105	100	100	96	98	100	97	96
1977	89	92	91	89	87	91	91	95	89	91	92	91	91	89	90	88
1978	91	91	91	92	91	90	92	94	88	91	90	92	91	91	93	92
1979	95	97	97	98	93	95	96	96	99	95	97	97	97	95	99	100
1980	100	99	100	102	101	99	100	97	98	102	99	100	101	100	100	105
1981	99	103	101	100	100	101	98	100	105	103	102	102	99	101	99	99
1982	102	104	106	110	103	102	102	105	104	103	104	108	106	112	110	107
1983	109	108	104	104	108	108	110	105	119	99	101	103	107	103	106	105

FINLAND

New passenger car registrations
thousands, monthly averages

Immatriculations de voitures de tourisme neuves
milliers, moyennes mensuelles

	Year	Q.1	Q.2	Q.3	Q.4	JAN	FEB	MAR	APR	MAY	JUN	JUL	AUG	SEP	OCT	NOV	DEC
1964	6.8	3.4	8.4	9.6	6.0	1.8	3.2	5.1	8.2	8.5	8.5	9.7	10.3	8.8	9.2	5.5	3.2
1965	8.3	4.7	10.1	10.0	8.6	3.5	4.3	6.2	6.5	10.2	13.6	11.4	9.3	9.3	11.8	8.7	5.4
1966	6.6	5.9	7.6	7.5	5.3	4.5	4.1	9.1	6.9	10.0	5.9	9.9	8.8	3.8	6.4	5.0	4.6
1967	5.5	4.3	7.6	6.0	4.1	3.0	3.6	6.4	7.4	8.3	7.0	7.4	6.0	4.6	6.6	2.7	2.8
1968	4.0	2.1	6.1	4.1	4.0	1.6	1.4	3.2	8.6	6.4	5.2	4.1	6.0	2.1	5.7	2.8	3.5
1969	7.1	5.0	10.2	7.6	5.5	3.0	4.4	7.6	9.4	10.1	11.1	8.7	7.8	6.2	6.7	5.6	4.1
1970	7.7	7.4	10.2	7.8	5.3	6.0	8.2	3.2	9.7	11.4	9.4	6.7	8.9	7.8	5.3	6.8	3.8
1971	6.3	7.7	13.3	2.3	1.9	7.7	6.3	8.5	10.4	23.9	5.6	2.1	2.0	2.9	2.7	2.3	0.7
1972	8.5	10.4	8.9	7.4	7.1	15.1	8.0	7.9	7.7	9.6	9.4	6.9	7.9	7.4	8.6	7.5	5.3
1973	9.9	12.8	10.1	10.2	6.4	13.4	11.8	13.3	10.5	9.6	10.3	8.2	9.4	12.9	9.6	6.6	3.1
1974	8.1	6.8	8.6	9.7	7.1	8.0	5.7	6.7	8.3	9.2	8.3	9.1	10.5	9.5	10.2	7.7	3.5
1975	9.8	13.0	11.4	9.6	5.2	14.0	11.5	13.4	13.7	10.8	9.8	9.8	9.2	9.9	10.1	3.2	2.3
1976	7.7	8.1	9.1	8.0	5.7	9.7	6.4	8.2	8.6	8.6	10.2	7.4	7.4	9.3	8.5	5.8	2.7
1977	7.6	8.8	8.5	7.8	5.0	10.9	6.7	8.7	10.4	7.9	7.3	6.7	8.3	8.6	6.5	5.9	2.8
1978	6.8	8.6	7.0	6.4	5.0	10.6	7.7	7.6	7.9	6.7	6.4	5.5	6.5	7.2	7.1	5.2	2.7
1979	8.3	9.1	9.9	8.1	6.3	10.9	7.3	9.2	9.7	11.1	8.9	7.8	8.3	8.2	8.7	7.1	3.1
1980	8.7	10.4	9.7	8.0	6.4	13.4	3.8	9.0	10.4	10.2	8.6	8.2	7.5	8.4	8.4	6.0	4.9
1981	8.8	10.1	10.4	8.0	6.7	10.6	9.8	9.9	11.0	10.2	10.1	8.5	7.2	8.2	9.4	6.8	4.0
1982	10.7	11.4	11.3	10.0	10.2	13.3	9.5	11.4	12.3	10.2	11.5	9.9	9.3	10.8	14.8	10.6	5.2
1983	10.0	12.6	11.5	8.6	7.4	15.6	9.9	12.3	11.2	16.7	6.5	7.2	8.0	10.6	9.7	8.3	4.2

Unemployment (14)
thousands

Chômage (14)
milliers

	Year	Q.1	Q.2	Q.3	Q.4	JAN	FEB	MAR	APR	MAY	JUN	JUL	AUG	SEP	OCT	NOV	DEC
1964	33	48	28	24	33	58	47	39	32	25	28	26	24	22	29	33	36
1965	30	39	27	23	29	45	36	37	36	23	23	27	26	17	23	27	37
1966	33	48	31	21	32	47	53	45	42	28	22	20	22	20	28	29	40
1967	64	64	51	56	86	67	68	56	55	48	50	52	56	60	71	87	99
1968	85	110	84	70	75	122	108	101	95	79	79	80	66	65	66	74	84
1969	62	91	65	44	47	96	92	86	81	62	52	49	46	37	38	43	61
1970	41	57	43	32	32	59	57	54	52	38	39	32	35	28	29	30	38
1971	49	57	49	42	47	50	58	62	57	50	39	45	42	40	41	47	53
1972	55	71	54	48	48	70	72	72	63	49	50	52	49	43	44	48	53
1973	52	68	53	42	43	72	69	63	60	49	50	46	42	38	41	40	48
1974	40	50	39	36	34	53	53	44	45	36	35	38	37	32	30	32	39
1975	51	48	44	48	62	49	48	47	48	40	45	48	48	49	52	61	72
1976	91	91	95	90	86	94	96	84	104	89	91	100	99	71	73	84	102
1977	137	131	136	137	143	129	133	132	137	134	138	148	141	122	126	145	159
1978	169	189	167	159	160	192	186	188	168	155	179	175	155	147	153	163	164
1979	139	176	140	124	118	185	181	162	149	135	135	141	120	110	116	106	131
1980	114	126	109	105	114	134	118	127	115	98	113	119	106	91	121	107	115
1981	125	129	120	125	127	132	126	128	114	118	127	134	124	118	122	126	132
1982	149	166	144	142	146	175	160	163	165	130	136	142	143	140	152	139	147
1983	156	170	159	141	153	180	165	164	167	145	166	153	128	143	151	152	157

Unemployment (14)
as per cent of civilian labour force

Chômage (14)
en pourcentage de la main-d'œuvre civile

	Year	Q.1	Q.2	Q.3	Q.4	JAN	FEB	MAR	APR	MAY	JUN	JUL	AUG	SEP	OCT	NOV	DEC
1964	1.5	2.2	1.3	1.1	1.5	2.7	2.2	1.8	1.5	1.2	1.2	1.1	1.1	1.0	1.3	1.5	1.7
1965	1.4	1.8	1.3	1.1	1.5	2.1	1.6	1.7	1.7	1.1	1.0	1.2	1.2	0.9	1.2	1.4	2.0
1966	1.6	2.3	1.4	1.0	1.6	2.2	2.5	2.2	2.0	1.3	1.0	1.0	1.1	1.0	1.4	1.5	2.0
1967	2.9	2.9	2.2	2.4	3.9	3.1	3.1	2.6	2.5	2.1	2.1	2.2	2.4	2.6	3.2	4.0	4.5
1968	4.1	5.3	3.9	3.3	3.6	5.8	5.2	5.0	4.7	3.5	3.6	3.6	3.2	3.2	3.2	3.6	4.0
1969	2.9	4.4	3.0	2.0	2.1	4.6	4.4	4.1	3.8	2.9	2.3	2.1	2.1	1.8	1.8	2.0	2.4
1970	1.9	2.7	2.0	1.4	1.5	2.8	2.7	2.6	2.5	1.8	1.7	1.4	1.5	1.3	1.4	1.4	1.8
1971	2.3	2.7	2.2	1.9	2.2	2.4	2.8	3.0	2.7	2.3	1.7	1.9	1.9	1.8	1.9	2.2	2.5
1972	2.6	3.4	2.5	2.2	2.3	3.3	3.4	3.4	3.0	2.3	2.2	2.3	2.2	2.0	2.1	2.2	2.6
1973	2.3	3.2	2.4	1.8	1.9	3.4	3.3	3.0	2.8	2.3	2.1	1.9	1.8	1.7	1.8	1.8	2.2
1974	1.7	2.3	1.7	1.5	1.5	2.4	2.4	2.0	2.0	1.6	1.4	1.6	1.6	1.4	1.3	1.4	1.7
1975	2.2	2.2	1.9	2.1	2.8	2.2	2.2	2.1	2.2	1.8	1.8	2.0	2.1	2.2	2.3	2.8	3.2
1976	3.9	4.0	4.0	3.6	3.8	4.1	4.3	3.7	4.6	3.9	3.6	3.9	4.0	3.0	3.2	3.7	4.5
1977	5.9	5.8	5.8	5.6	6.3	5.7	5.9	5.9	6.1	5.9	5.5	5.8	5.8	5.2	5.5	6.4	7.0
1978	7.3	8.3	7.2	6.7	7.1	8.4	8.3	8.3	7.5	6.8	7.2	7.1	6.5	6.4	6.8	7.2	7.3
1979	6.0	7.8	5.9	5.1	5.1	8.2	8.1	7.2	6.6	5.8	5.3	5.6	4.9	4.7	5.0	4.6	5.7
1980	4.7	5.5	4.5	4.3	4.5	5.8	5.1	5.5	5.0	4.1	4.4	4.7	4.3	3.8	4.3	4.5	4.8
1981	5.1	5.4	4.9	4.9	5.2	5.6	5.3	5.4	4.9	5.0	4.9	5.1	4.9	4.8	5.0	5.2	5.5
1982	5.9	6.7	5.7	5.5	5.8	7.0	6.5	6.6	6.7	5.2	5.1	5.4	5.5	5.5	5.6	5.7	6.2
1983	6.1	6.9	6.2	5.4	6.1	7.3	6.7	6.6	6.7	5.7	6.1	5.6	5.1	5.6	6.0	6.1	6.2

Employment: industry (14) / Emploi : industrie (14)

thousands / milliers

	Year	Q.1	Q.2	Q.3	Q.4	JAN	FEB	MAR	APR	MAY	JUN	JUL	AUG	SEP	OCT	NOV	DEC
1964	501	484	510	513	498	481	485	486	497	501	532	525	516	499	498	499	497
1965	505	488	512	521	498	485	487	491	498	503	536	532	521	510	500	497	496
1966	526	500	530	549	524	495	500	505	509	518	563	563	551	532	527	524	520
1967	527	515	535	542	517	513	515	517	519	525	561	558	544	523	521	517	513
1968	522	504	523	538	522	507	503	502	507	518	544	548	541	524	526	520	521
1969	540	514	549	560	538	512	510	519	527	541	578	578	562	539	536	542	537
1970	563	541	572	581	557	540	541	543	547	565	605	608	574	562	558	559	555
1971	560	528	564	582	565	525	528	531	537	555	601	594	583	568	570	564	562
1972	570	545	578	585	571	545	544	546	552	567	614	604	581	569	572	573	567
1973	584	555	589	603	537	555	553	558	561	580	625	625	602	583	587	588	587
1974	613	588	619	633	612	584	592	587	594	606	658	659	633	608	613	614	608
1975	609	600	628	619	588	600	597	602	604	621	660	655	611	591	590	590	585
1976	587	568	595	602	582	578	569	556	589	578	618	627	597	582	591	579	576
1977	578	567	586	590	569	573	564	564	566	574	618	608	588	574	570	574	563
1978	562	544	565	575	566	546	535	550	557	544	594	597	569	559	570	564	563
1979	581	560	589	597	576	562	559	559	565	585	618	614	601	576	574	575	580
1980	606	579	616	624	605	584	580	573	588	610	649	633	638	601	610	602	602
1981	620	605	629	642	605	598	609	607	597	622	667	646	648	633	621	588	607
1982	605	602	617	608	593	594	609	604	589	623	639	608	611	604	596	593	589
1983	606	601	612	622	588	578	618	607	588	616	633	638	623	604	586	578	599

Unemployment (14) / Chômage (14)

Adjusted - Corrigé *

thousands / milliers

	Year	Q.1	Q.2	Q.3	Q.4	JAN	FEB	MAR	APR	MAY	JUN	JUL	AUG	SEP	OCT	NOV	DEC
1964		34	34	33	33	37	33	30	29	34	38	34	32	33	35	34	31
1965		28	31	32	29	29	25	29	33	30	31	35	35	25	28	28	32
1966		35	33	28	33	31	38	37	37	34	28	25	29	29	34	31	36
1967		47	55	73	90	46	50	46	48	56	62	64	71	84	87	94	90
1968		84	88	89	80	88	80	83	82	89	94	96	82	89	82	80	78
1969		71	66	54	51	71	69	71	70	68	59	57	56	50	48	47	58
1970		45	43	38	36	45	44	45	44	42	43	36	42	37	37	33	37
1971		45	49	50	53	39	45	52	49	54	43	50	49	52	52	53	53
1972		57	54	56	54	55	56	61	54	53	54	57	56	55	55	55	53
1973		55	53	48	43	57	54	54	52	53	54	49	47	47	51	46	48
1974		41	39	40	38	42	42	39	40	39	37	39	41	39	37	37	39
1975		40	44	54	68	39	39	42	43	43	47	48	53	59	63	69	72
1976		77	95	97	94	77	80	75	95	95	94	99	108	85	87	94	102
1977		113	137	147	156	107	113	118	128	143	141	144	153	145	147	160	159
1978		164	169	170	172	162	161	169	160	166	181	169	167	173	174	178	165
1979		154	142	131	126	158	159	147	144	145	136	135	129	128	129	115	132
1980		112	111	111	122	115	105	115	113	105	114	114	114	105	133	116	117
1981		114	122	132	135	113	113	116	112	127	128	128	133	135	133	137	134
1982		147	146	150	155	150	144	149	162	140	137	135	153	160	165	151	149
1983		151	162	149	163	154	149	150	164	157	167	146	137	163	164	165	160

Unemployment (14) / Chômage (14)

Adjusted - Corrigé *

as per cent of civilian labour force / en pourcentage de la main-d'œuvre civile

	Year	Q.1	Q.2	Q.3	Q.4	JAN	FEB	MAR	APR	MAY	JUN	JUL	AUG	SEP	OCT	NOV	DEC
1964		1.6	1.5	1.5	1.5	1.9	1.5	1.3	1.3	1.6	1.7	1.5	1.5	1.6	1.6	1.6	1.3
1965		1.1	1.5	1.6	1.5	1.3	0.8	1.2	1.4	1.5	1.5	1.7	1.7	1.5	1.5	1.5	1.6
1966		1.6	1.6	1.6	1.7	1.4	1.7	1.7	1.7	1.7	1.5	1.5	1.6	1.6	1.8	1.6	1.7
1967		2.2	2.4	2.9	4.0	2.2	2.3	2.0	2.1	2.4	2.6	2.7	2.9	3.2	3.6	4.1	4.2
1968		4.6	4.1	3.9	3.7	4.9	4.4	4.4	4.3	3.8	4.1	4.1	3.7	3.9	3.7	3.8	3.7
1969		3.6	3.1	2.5	2.2	3.8	3.6	3.5	3.3	3.1	2.8	2.6	2.6	2.4	2.3	2.2	2.2
1970		2.0	2.1	1.9	1.7	2.0	1.9	2.0	2.0	2.0	2.2	1.9	1.9	1.9	1.9	1.6	1.6
1971		2.0	2.3	2.3	2.4	1.7	2.0	2.4	2.2	2.5	2.1	2.3	2.3	2.4	2.4	2.4	2.4
1972		2.7	2.5	2.6	2.6	2.6	2.6	2.9	2.5	2.5	2.6	2.6	2.6	2.5	2.6	2.5	2.6
1973		2.6	2.4	2.1	2.2	2.7	2.6	2.5	2.4	2.5	2.4	2.2	2.1	2.1	2.3	2.1	2.2
1974		1.7	1.7	1.8	1.7	1.7	1.7	1.6	1.6	1.7	1.7	1.8	1.9	1.8	1.8	1.7	1.7
1975		1.6	1.9	2.4	3.1	1.5	1.5	1.7	1.8	1.9	2.1	2.2	2.4	2.6	2.8	3.1	3.3
1976		3.3	4.0	4.1	4.1	3.2	3.5	3.1	4.2	4.0	3.9	4.1	4.5	3.8	3.8	4.1	4.5
1977		5.0	5.9	6.1	6.6	4.7	5.0	5.3	5.7	6.1	5.8	6.0	6.3	6.1	6.1	6.8	7.0
1978		7.4	7.3	7.2	7.4	7.3	7.4	7.6	7.1	7.0	7.6	7.3	7.1	7.3	7.4	7.5	7.2
1979		6.9	6.0	5.6	5.3	7.1	7.2	6.5	6.3	6.1	5.7	5.8	5.5	5.5	5.5	4.9	5.6
1980		4.6	4.7	4.8	4.8	4.7	4.2	4.8	4.7	4.5	4.8	4.9	4.8	4.6	4.7	4.8	4.7
1981		4.6	5.1	5.4	5.5	4.5	4.5	4.7	4.6	5.5	5.3	5.3	5.4	5.5	5.4	5.5	5.4
1982		5.9	5.9	5.9	6.0	5.9	5.7	5.9	6.4	5.7	5.5	5.6	5.9	6.2	6.0	6.0	6.1
1983		6.0	6.4	5.9	6.3	6.2	5.9	5.9	6.4	6.2	6.5	5.8	5.5	6.3	6.3	6.4	6.1

* Adjusted by the O.E.C.D. / * Corrigé par l'O.C.D.E.

FINLAND

Jobs vacant, unfilled vacancies (15)
thousands

Offres d'emploi non satisfaites (15)
milliers

	Year	Q.1	Q.2	Q.3	Q.4	JAN	FEB	MAR	APR	MAY	JUN	JUL	AUG	SEP	OCT	NOV	DEC
1964	5.1	3.7	6.7	5.7	4.2	3.5	3.6	3.8	5.6	8.1	6.3	5.0	5.8	6.4	4.8	3.8	4.0
1965	5.3	4.2	6.6	6.0	4.4	3.9	4.2	4.4	5.5	8.5	5.8	4.9	6.1	6.8	5.3	4.0	4.0
1966	6.0	4.4	6.8	7.2	5.6	4.1	4.3	4.7	5.4	8.2	6.9	5.9	7.7	8.2	6.7	5.5	4.7
1967	5.2	5.0	6.9	5.5	3.4	4.6	4.7	5.6	7.3	8.0	5.4	4.9	6.3	5.2	3.6	3.3	3.3
1968	5.0	3.9	5.7	5.6	4.9	3.6	3.8	4.3	5.3	6.5	5.4	4.7	6.1	5.9	5.1	4.5	5.0
1969	8.5	5.7	9.4	9.9	9.1	5.2	5.5	6.4	8.0	11.4	8.6	8.1	10.7	11.0	9.6	9.1	8.6
1970	13.3	9.4	14.6	15.9	13.1	8.8	9.2	10.3	12.2	16.8	14.8	12.5	17.1	18.1	15.2	12.8	11.4
1971	11.7	8.8	13.6	13.8	10.3	9.9	8.4	8.2	11.5	16.9	12.4	11.0	16.5	13.9	12.0	10.4	10.0
1972	15.8	10.8	17.1	20.4	14.7	10.1	10.5	11.8	14.3	20.5	16.6	18.1	23.6	19.7	15.5	14.2	14.5
1973	22.8	16.8	22.5	28.8	23.2	14.9	16.7	18.8	24.3	20.6	22.6	24.1	32.9	29.5	24.3	22.9	21.9
1974	29.8	23.6	33.6	35.8	26.4	22.0	24.0	24.7	31.6	37.3	31.9	33.2	38.8	35.4	30.3	26.3	22.4
1975	18.5	20.7	23.3	19.6	10.5	20.7	20.5	20.8	23.5	26.1	20.4	19.9	23.1	16.0	12.6	10.0	8.9
1976	11.2	10.1	13.7	13.8	7.4	9.3	10.1	11.0	12.1	15.7	13.1	13.4	15.7	12.2	9.2	7.2	5.9
1977	6.4	6.3	8.2	7.0	4.1	5.8	6.1	7.1	7.7	9.1	7.7	7.3	7.9	5.8	4.4	4.1	3.8
1978	5.5	4.3	7.0	6.0	4.6	4.0	4.2	4.8	6.2	7.9	6.8	6.3	6.6	5.2	4.7	4.7	4.5
1979	8.3	6.0	10.2	9.5	7.4	5.3	5.6	7.3	9.3	11.0	10.4	8.9	10.1	9.6	7.7	7.4	7.3
1980	12.2	9.4	15.3	14.4	9.8	8.5	9.6	10.2	13.5	16.7	15.7	13.2	16.5	13.5	10.7	9.0	9.8
1981	13.0	12.9	17.2	13.4	8.6	11.3	13.3	14.0	16.8	19.7	15.0	14.3	14.4	11.6	9.5	8.4	7.8
1982	11.3	9.7	14.7	12.9	8.0	8.8	9.2	11.0	15.0	16.5	12.6	13.1	14.5	11.0	8.6	7.5	7.9
1983	11.8	9.7	14.5	13.7	9.5	8.8	9.0	11.3	14.7	15.4	13.3	13.1	15.5	12.3	10.8	9.0	8.6

Labour disputes: time lost (16)
thousand man-days

Conflits du travail : journées perdues (16)
milliers de journées-homme

	Year	Q.1	Q.2	Q.3	Q.4	JAN	FEB	MAR	APR	MAY	JUN	JUL	AUG	SEP	OCT	NOV	DEC
1964	58.3	13.8	16.1	24.5	3.9	1.3	2.1	10.4	1.4	5.9	8.8	5.9	8.8	9.3	3.3	0.2	0.4
1965	16.1	3.0	2.1	7.8	3.2	-	2.8	0.2	1.1	0.7	0.3	1.3	6.3	0.2	0.2	1.4	1.6
1966	127.4	74.2	38.0	7.1	8.1	26.0	22.3	25.9	11.0	10.6	16.4	3.7	2.0	1.4	6.2	0.6	1.3
1967	320.8	167.2	34.4	98.7	20.5	1.9	1.0	164.3	0.8	14.0	19.6	42.8	47.2	8.7	19.5	0.5	0.5
1968	282.4	255.6	13.6	11.8	1.4	40.5	93.4	116.7	0.7	4.1	8.8	8.1	0.9	2.8	0.5	0.6	0.3
1969	161.1	38.2	41.4	10.2	71.3	31.8	6.0	0.4	10.4	14.3	16.7	7.7	2.1	0.4	9.2	30.9	31.2
1970	233.2	23.7	42.8	30.3	136.4	3.5	3.5	16.7	12.7	26.5	3.6	2.1	4.9	23.3	62.2	68.9	5.3
1971	2711.1	2481.0	185.9	28.4	15.8	86.6	1063.1	1331.3	168.0	12.2	7.7	2.6	2.1	23.7	6.1	8.0	1.7
1972	473.1	28.0	402.1	15.1	27.9	7.0	9.5	11.5	45.2	285.2	71.7	4.4	2.5	8.2	11.2	14.3	2.4
1973	2497.1	55.0	2393.9	17.0	31.2	7.9	14.0	33.1	273.0	743.5	1377.4	3.3	2.9	10.8	17.7	5.0	8.5
1974	411.1	63.0	182.4	76.8	88.9	8.5	29.6	24.9	125.6	45.2	11.6	4.6	8.0	64.2	46.2	32.6	10.1
1975	284.2	116.4	97.2	35.7	34.9	25.1	61.0	30.3	22.5	68.7	6.0	1.1	18.6	16.0	15.5	15.7	3.7
1976	1325.6	360.0	846.0	59.0	60.6	15.0	244.2	100.8	645.9	182.3	17.8	1.8	8.9	48.3	35.4	18.5	6.7
1977	2374.7	573.6	1742.1	20.9	38.1	8.6	41.2	523.8	394.8	1338.2	9.1	0.9	9.0	11.0	14.5	4.7	18.9
1978	132.4	37.0	49.5	11.1	34.8	9.0	9.3	18.7	31.1	9.9	8.5	4.3	3.4	3.4	9.7	17.8	7.3
1979	243.4	30.8	61.7	42.3	108.6	8.3	9.7	12.8	21.2	17.6	22.9	2.8	10.3	29.2	76.7	26.8	5.1
1980	1598.7	100.3	1291.0	48.9	158.5	12.8	13.6	73.9	433.4	845.5	12.1	3.5	9.2	36.2	63.2	20.3	75.0
1981	643.1	114.8	326.9	46.4	155.0	16.4	27.9	70.5	299.4	13.8	13.7	1.8	21.3	23.3	13.1	23.2	118.7
1982	198.9	30.4	107.4	20.1	41.0	8.6	9.3	12.5	6.2	19.0	82.2	0.6	13.9	5.6	10.6	16.2	14.2
1983	759.7	101.6	567.2	26.1	64.8	20.3	22.0	59.3	115.8	413.8	37.6	0.6	6.5	19.0	19.8	7.9	37.1

Hourly earnings: industry (17)
1980 = 100

Gains horaires : industrie (17)
1980 = 100

	Year	Q.1	Q.2	Q.3	Q.4	JAN	FEB	MAR	APR	MAY	JUN	JUL	AUG	SEP	OCT	NOV	DEC
1964	15	15	15	15	16												
1965	17	16	17	17	17												
1966	18	17	18	18	18												
1967	19	19	19	20	20												
1968	22	21	21	22	22												
1969	23	23	23	23	24												
1970	26	25	26	26	27												
1971	30	28	30	30	32												
1972	34	32	35	35	35												
1973	40	36	40	41	42												
1974	49	44	49	50	53												
1975	59	55	60	60	62												
1976	68	64	69	69	70												
1977	74	70	75	75	76												
1978	79	76	79	80	83												
1979	89	86	90	89	90												
1980	100	94	102	100	105												
1981	113	107	115	113	116												
1982	125	121	125	123	129												
1983		130	138	136													

Jobs vacant, unfilled vacancies (15) — Offres d'emploi non satisfaites (15)

thousands — milliers

Adjusted - Corrigé *

	Year	Q.1	Q.2	Q.3	Q.4	JAN	FEB	MAR	APR	MAY	JUN	JUL	AUG	SEP	OCT	NOV	DEC
1964		5.4	5.3	4.8	5.0	5.2	5.5	5.4	5.8	5.2	5.0	4.9	4.8	4.9	4.3	4.9	5.8
1965		5.7	5.3	5.2	5.3	5.6	5.9	5.7	5.5	5.6	4.8	5.0	5.1	5.4	5.1	5.2	5.5
1966		5.7	5.5	6.4	6.6	5.6	5.7	5.7	5.2	5.5	5.9	6.0	6.4	6.7	6.6	7.0	6.3
1967		6.2	5.7	4.9	4.0	6.1	6.0	6.5	7.0	5.5	4.7	5.1	5.3	4.3	3.6	4.1	4.2
1968		4.8	4.8	5.0	5.6	4.6	4.8	4.9	5.1	4.6	4.8	4.9	5.0	4.9	5.2	5.4	6.3
1969		6.9	8.0	8.7	10.4	6.6	6.9	7.3	7.8	8.3	7.8	8.5	8.5	9.2	9.6	10.8	10.7
1970		11.5	12.7	13.7	14.3	11.2	11.5	11.9	12.0	12.5	13.7	13.0	13.1	15.1	15.4	15.0	14.0
1971		10.9	11.9	11.7	12.2	12.6	10.5	9.6	11.5	12.7	11.6	11.2	12.3	11.6	12.1	12.1	12.3
1972		13.4	15.2	17.1	17.0	13.0	13.2	13.9	14.2	15.7	15.6	17.6	17.2	16.6	15.9	16.8	18.3
1973		20.8	20.3	23.8	27.4	19.4	20.9	22.0	23.9	15.9	21.2	22.5	23.5	25.4	25.9	27.9	28.4
1974		29.2	29.5	29.6	31.9	29.2	29.9	28.5	30.3	28.7	29.6	30.0	27.6	31.2	32.6	32.9	30.1
1975		25.7	20.0	16.2	13.1	27.8	25.5	23.7	22.0	19.8	18.3	17.5	16.7	14.4	13.9	12.9	12.3
1976		12.5	11.4	11.5	9.4	12.6	12.7	12.2	11.0	11.7	11.4	11.7	11.6	11.3	10.5	9.4	8.3
1977		7.7	6.6	5.9	5.4	7.8	7.6	7.8	6.9	6.6	6.4	6.4	6.0	5.5	5.3	5.5	5.5
1978		5.3	5.5	5.2	6.2	5.4	5.3	5.2	5.4	5.6	5.6	5.5	5.1	5.0	5.7	6.3	6.5
1979		7.2	8.0	8.4	10.0	6.9	7.0	7.7	8.0	7.8	8.4	7.9	8.0	9.4	9.5	10.0	10.5
1980		11.2	11.9	12.8	13.2	11.0	11.9	10.7	11.4	11.7	12.6	11.8	13.4	13.3	13.3	12.1	14.1
1981		15.1	13.3	12.0	11.5	14.4	16.3	14.7	14.1	13.8	12.1	12.6	11.8	11.4	11.9	11.4	11.2
1982		11.3	11.5	11.5	10.7	11.2	11.3	11.5	12.6	11.6	10.2	11.8	11.9	10.9	10.7	10.1	11.3
1983		11.3	11.3	12.2	12.7	11.1	11.0	11.8	12.3	10.8	10.8	11.8	12.7	12.2	13.5	12.2	12.3

Producer prices: investment goods (18) — Prix à la production : biens d'équipement (18)

1980 = 100

	Year	Q.1	Q.2	Q.3	Q.4	JAN	FEB	MAR	APR	MAY	JUN	JUL	AUG	SEP	OCT	NOV	DEC
1964																	
1965																	
1966																	
1967																	
1968																	
1969																	
1970																	
1971																	
1972																	
1973																	
1974																	
1975	66.9	64.5	66.6	67.8	68.9	64.3	64.5	64.7	65.7	66.9	67.3	67.3	67.8	68.1	68.6	68.9	69.1
1976	72.9	70.5	72.0	73.6	75.4	70.1	70.6	71.0	71.4	72.1	72.6	72.8	73.7	74.4	75.0	75.5	75.6
1977	79.0	76.8	78.1	79.9	81.2	76.6	76.8	76.8	77.5	77.8	78.9	79.2	80.0	80.6	81.1	81.1	81.3
1978	84.8	82.8	84.1	85.2	87.0	82.6	82.9	83.1	83.7	84.1	84.3	84.9	85.0	85.7	86.5	87.0	87.6
1979	91.4	89.2	90.8	91.9	93.7	88.4	89.2	89.8	90.3	90.8	91.2	91.4	91.9	92.4	93.0	93.8	94.2
1980	=100.0=	96.5	99.7	100.8	102.7	94.9	96.6	97.9	99.3	99.8	100.1	100.4	100.9	101.1	102.0	102.7	103.3
1981	108.8	105.3	108.0	110.1	111.9	104.1	105.5	106.2	107.0	107.7	109.2	109.5	110.1	110.7	111.3	112.1	112.3
1982	117.4	114.5	116.3	118.0	120.3	112.9	114.9	115.6	116.4	116.9	117.1	117.3	118.2	118.5	119.7	120.6	120.7
1983	125.0	122.4	124.5	126.0	127.0	121.7	122.4	123.2	123.9	124.3	125.3	125.7	126.0	126.4	126.6	127.0	127.4

Producer prices: consumer goods (18) — Prix à la production : biens de consommation (18)

1980 = 100

	Year	Q.1	Q.2	Q.3	Q.4	JAN	FEB	MAR	APR	MAY	JUN	JUL	AUG	SEP	OCT	NOV	DEC
1964																	
1965																	
1966																	
1967																	
1968																	
1969																	
1970																	
1971																	
1972																	
1973																	
1974																	
1975	60.9	58.8	60.1	61.6	63.2	58.4	58.6	59.4	60.0	60.2	60.2	60.7	61.6	62.6	62.8	63.4	63.4
1976	68.9	65.1	67.5	70.8	72.0	64.2	64.3	66.9	67.5	67.3	67.7	69.8	71.1	71.4	71.9	72.0	72.0
1977	79.5	75.1	79.3	81.3	82.0	73.7	74.9	76.8	77.3	80.3	80.4	80.9	81.5	81.4	81.9	82.2	82.0
1978	83.1	81.7	82.2	83.5	84.9	81.5	81.7	81.8	82.2	82.1	82.2	82.6	83.1	84.8	84.9	85.0	84.6
1979	89.2	86.6	87.9	90.0	92.4	86.0	86.7	87.1	87.5	88.1	88.2	89.3	90.1	90.6	91.8	92.6	92.8
1980	=100.0=	96.0	98.7	101.8	103.5	95.0	96.3	96.6	97.4	98.9	99.8	101.0	101.7	102.8	103.0	103.6	103.9
1981	112.4	107.4	110.4	114.6	117.3	106.5	107.1	108.5	109.5	110.5	111.1	114.0	114.3	115.5	116.9	117.3	117.6
1982	123.5	121.1	123.2	123.9	125.7	120.4	121.0	121.8	122.8	123.3	123.5	123.6	123.8	124.4	125.4	125.8	125.8
1983	131.9	129.5	131.4	132.7	133.9	129.0	129.5	130.0	131.0	131.9	131.4	132.4	132.5	133.1	133.5	134.0	134.3

* Adjusted by the O.E.C.D. — * Corrigé par l'O.C.D.E.

FINLAND

Producer prices: intermediate goods (18)
1980 = 100

Prix à la production : biens intermédiaires (18)
1980 = 100

	Year	Q.1	Q.2	Q.3	Q.4	JAN	FEB	MAR	APR	MAY	JUN	JUL	AUG	SEP	OCT	NOV	DEC
1964																	
1965																	
1966																	
1967																	
1968																	
1969																	
1970																	
1971																	
1972																	
1973																	
1974																	
1975	65.8	65.8	66.2	65.5	65.5	65.7	65.8	65.9	66.3	66.3	65.9	65.4	65.6	65.6	65.5	65.7	65.4
1976	68.2	66.2	67.6	69.2	69.9	65.6	66.3	66.7	67.2	67.7	68.0	68.8	69.7	69.8	69.9	69.9	70.0
1977	72.7	71.2	72.7	71.0	73.8	70.7	71.3	71.5	72.4	72.8	72.8	66.3	73.0	73.7	73.8	74.0	73.4
1978	75.4	73.7	74.8	75.9	77.2	73.4	73.6	74.1	74.6	74.8	75.0	75.1	76.0	76.6	76.9	77.3	77.4
1979	84.0	79.5	82.5	85.8	88.3	78.6	79.4	80.4	81.6	82.1	83.6	84.8	85.5	87.1	87.9	88.4	88.7
1980	100.0	95.1	99.7	101.8	103.5	91.8	94.7	98.7	99.0	99.9	100.1	100.9	102.0	102.4	102.8	103.5	104.3
1981	112.1	107.7	111.3	113.7	115.8	105.6	107.6	110.0	110.7	111.0	112.1	112.8	113.7	114.7	114.8	116.4	116.1
1982	118.5	117.5	118.1	118.0	120.3	116.7	117.5	118.4	118.2	117.9	118.2	118.1	118.2	117.7	119.0	120.1	121.8
1983	123.0	121.0	122.0	123.7	125.2	121.2	121.2	120.7	121.3	122.2	122.4	122.9	123.3	124.9	124.8	125.2	125.5

Producer prices: petroleum products (18)
1980 = 100

Prix à la production : dérivés du pétrole (18)
1980 = 100

	Year	Q.1	Q.2	Q.3	Q.4	JAN	FEB	MAR	APR	MAY	JUN	JUL	AUG	SEP	OCT	NOV	DEC
1964																	
1965																	
1966																	
1967																	
1968																	
1969																	
1970																	
1971																	
1972																	
1973																	
1974																	
1975	39.3	39.5	39.1	39.2	39.6	39.7	39.4	39.4	39.0	39.1	39.1	39.0	39.2	39.3	39.4	39.7	39.7
1976	43.4	41.5	43.7	44.3	44.2	39.6	42.4	42.5	42.6	44.3	44.3	44.3	44.3	44.3	44.3	44.2	44.2
1977	49.5	46.3	49.0	50.4	52.4	44.1	47.4	47.3	47.7	48.8	50.4	50.4	50.3	50.4	52.3	52.3	52.4
1978	52.6	52.3	52.6	52.6	52.9	52.2	52.2	52.4	52.5	52.6	52.6	52.6	52.6	52.6	52.6	52.8	53.4
1979	64.7	54.7	59.6	69.8	74.6	53.3	53.7	57.2	57.2	55.4	66.6	66.6	67.7	74.9	74.6	74.6	74.6
1980	100.0	91.0	102.4	101.4	105.1	80.5	83.9	108.6	100.2	103.9	103.1	103.6	100.4	100.3	102.5	104.4	108.5
1981	125.2	116.0	125.5	129.4	129.0	111.2	111.4	125.5	125.5	126.5	127.4	128.1	129.8	130.3	129.8	129.0	128.1
1982	129.0	130.1	122.9	124.9	138.2	131.0	130.3	129.0	122.1	123.6	122.9	125.2	124.4	125.1	133.7	134.4	146.5
1983	136.8	140.2	132.6	135.6	139.0	143.2	142.2	135.2	132.5	133.0	132.3	133.1	133.8	140.0	139.3	138.9	133.7

Consumer prices: all items (19)
1980 = 100

Prix à la consommation : total (19)
1980 = 100

	Year	Q.1	Q.2	Q.3	Q.4	JAN	FEB	MAR	APR	MAY	JUN	JUL	AUG	SEP	OCT	NOV	DEC
1964	26	26	26	26	27	25	26	26	26	26	26	26	26	27	27	27	27
1965	28	27	27	28	28	27	27	27	27	27	28	28	28	28	28	28	28
1966	29	28	29	29	29	28	28	28	28	29	29	29	29	29	29	29	29
1967	30	30	30	30	31	30	30	30	30	30	30	30	30	30	31	31	31
1968	33	32	33	33	33	32	32	33	33	33	33	33	33	33	33	33	33
1969	34	33	34	34	34	33	33	33	34	34	34	34	34	34	34	34	34
1970	35	34	34	35	35	34	34	34	34	34	35	35	35	35	35	35	35
1971	37	36	36	37	38	35	36	36	36	36	37	37	37	38	38	38	38
1972	39	38	39	40	40	38	38	38	39	39	39	40	40	40	40	41	41
1973	44	41	43	45	46	41	41	42	42	43	43	44	45	45	45	46	46
1974	51	48	50	52	54	47	48	48	50	50	50	51	52	53	54	54	54
1975	60	57	59	61	64	56	57	57	59	59	59	60	61	62	63	64	64
1976	69	66	67	70	72	65	66	67	67	68	68	69	70	70	71	72	72
1977	77	74	77	79	80	73	74	75	76	77	77	78	79	79	80	80	80
1978	83	81	83	84	85	80	81	82	82	83	83	84	84	85	85	86	85
1979	90	87	89	90	92	86	87	88	89	89	89	90	90	91	92	92	93
1980	100	95	99	101	105	94	95	96	98	99	100	100	101	103	104	105	106
1981	112	108	111	113	116	106	107	109	110	112	112	113	113	115	116	116	116
1982	122	119	122	124	125	118	118	120	121	123	123	124	124	124	124	125	126
1983	133	128	132	135	137	128	128	129	131	132	134	134	135	135	136	137	137

Official discount rate / Taux d'escompte officiel

per cent per annum, end of period / pourcentage par an, fin de période

	Year	Q.1	Q.2	Q.3	Q.4	JAN	FEB	MAR	APR	MAY	JUN	JUL	AUG	SEP	OCT	NOV	DEC
1964	7.00	7.00	7.00	7.00	7.00	7.00	7.00	7.00	7.00	7.00	7.00	7.00	7.00	7.00	7.00	7.00	7.00
1965	7.00	7.00	7.00	7.00	7.00	7.00	7.00	7.00	7.00	7.00	7.00	7.00	7.00	7.00	7.00	7.00	7.00
1966	7.00	7.00	7.00	7.00	7.00	7.00	7.00	7.00	7.00	7.00	7.00	7.00	7.00	7.00	7.00	7.00	7.00
1967	7.00	7.00	7.00	7.00	7.00	7.00	7.00	7.00	7.00	7.00	7.00	7.00	7.00	7.00	7.00	7.00	7.00
1968	7.00	7.00	7.00	7.00	7.00	7.00	7.00	7.00	7.00	7.00	7.00	7.00	7.00	7.00	7.00	7.00	7.00
1969	7.00	7.00	7.00	7.00	7.00	7.00	7.00	7.00	7.00	7.00	7.00	7.00	7.00	7.00	7.00	7.00	7.00
1970	7.00	7.00	7.00	7.00	7.00	7.00	7.00	7.00	7.00	7.00	7.00	7.00	7.00	7.00	7.00	7.00	7.00
1971	8.50	7.00	8.50	8.50	8.50	7.00	7.00	7.00	7.00	7.00	8.50	8.50	8.50	8.50	8.50	8.50	8.50
1972	7.75	7.75	7.75	7.75	7.75	7.75	7.75	7.75	7.75	7.75	7.75	7.75	7.75	7.75	7.75	7.75	7.75
1973	9.25	7.75	7.75	9.25	9.25	7.75	7.75	7.75	7.75	7.75	7.75	9.25	9.25	9.25	9.25	9.25	9.25
1974	9.25	9.25	9.25	9.25	9.25	9.25	9.25	9.25	9.25	9.25	9.25	9.25	9.25	9.25	9.25	9.25	9.25
1975	9.25	9.25	9.25	9.25	9.25	9.25	9.25	9.25	9.25	9.25	9.25	9.25	9.25	9.25	9.25	9.25	9.25
1976	9.25	9.25	9.25	9.25	9.25	9.25	9.25	9.25	9.25	9.25	9.25	9.25	9.25	9.25	9.25	9.25	9.25
1977	8.25	9.25	9.25	9.25	8.25	9.25	9.25	9.25	9.25	9.25	9.25	9.25	9.25	9.25	8.25	8.25	8.25
1978	7.25	8.25	7.25	7.25	7.25	8.25	8.25	8.25	8.25	7.25	7.25	7.25	7.25	7.25	7.25	7.25	7.25
1979	8.50	7.25	7.25	7.25	8.50	7.25	7.25	7.25	7.25	7.25	7.25	7.25	7.25	7.25	7.25	8.50	8.50
1980	9.25	9.25	9.25	9.25	9.25	8.50	9.25	9.25	9.25	9.25	9.25	9.25	9.25	9.25	9.25	9.25	9.25
1981	9.25	9.25	9.25	9.25	9.25	9.25	9.25	9.25	9.25	9.25	9.25	9.25	9.25	9.25	9.25	9.25	9.25
1982	8.50	9.25	8.50	8.50	8.50	9.25	9.25	9.25	9.25	9.25	8.50	8.50	8.50	8.50	8.50	8.50	8.50
1983	9.50	8.50	8.50	9.50	9.50	8.50	8.50	8.50	8.50	8.50	8.50	9.50	9.50	9.50	9.50	9.50	9.50

Yield of long-term Government bonds (20) / Rendement des bons d'État à long terme (20)

per cent per annum, end of period / pourcentage par an, fin de période

	Year	Q.1	Q.2	Q.3	Q.4	JAN	FEB	MAR	APR	MAY	JUN	JUL	AUG	SEP	OCT	NOV	DEC
1964	8.45																
1965	8.75																
1966	8.00	8.25	8.75	..	8.00												
1967	8.00	8.38	..	..	8.00												
1968	8.04	8.09	8.25	8.25	8.04												
1969	7.66	8.05	7.55	8.25	7.66												
1970	7.81	7.70	7.60	8.25	7.81												
1971	8.30	7.64	7.54	9.25	8.30												
1972	7.91	8.08	7.98	7.95	7.91	7.66	8.16	8.08	8.20	7.65	7.98	8.20	8.14	7.95	7.86	7.79	7.91
1973	8.25	8.25	8.25	8.25	8.25	8.06	8.19	8.25	8.25	8.25	8.25	8.40	8.39	8.25	8.32	8.25	8.25
1974	8.62	8.79	8.94	9.35	8.62	8.89	8.86	8.79	8.72	8.67	8.94	9.30	8.54	9.35	8.47	8.34	8.62
1975	..	9.55	9.57	9.75	..	9.52	9.51	9.55	9.55	9.50	9.67	9.60	9.72	9.75	9.75	9.73	..
1976	9.82	9.79	10.49	9.23	9.82	9.86	9.85	9.79	9.77	10.86	10.49	10.36	10.52	9.23	10.76	10.69	9.82
1977	10.41	10.99	10.81	10.96	10.41	10.99	10.97	10.99	10.92	10.98	10.81	10.80	10.71	10.96	10.25	10.25	10.41
1978	9.27	10.54	9.63	9.40	9.27	10.56	10.53	10.54	10.28	9.70	9.63	9.62	9.63	9.40	9.33	9.10	9.27
1979	9.58	9.48	9.52	9.51	9.53	9.29	9.66	9.48	9.64	9.46	9.52	9.54	9.42	9.51	9.36	9.53	9.58
1980	10.46	10.38	10.48	10.41	10.46	9.94	10.29	10.38	10.58	10.49	10.48	10.54	10.54	10.41	10.49	10.46	10.46
1981	11.15	11.01	10.95	10.96	11.15	10.92	10.95	11.01	11.06	10.92	10.95	11.01	11.00	10.96	10.92	10.96	11.15
1982	11.24	11.04	10.86	10.69	11.24	10.98	11.55	11.04	11.07	11.12	10.86	11.14	10.69	10.69	10.72	10.75	11.24
1983	11.00	10.59	10.66	10.44	11.00	10.58	10.70	10.59	10.63	10.71	10.66	10.99	10.59	10.44	11.10	11.13	11.00

Share prices: industrials (21) / Cours des actions industrielles (21)

Helsinki Stock Exchange / Bourse d'Helsinki

1980 = 100

	Year	Q.1	Q.2	Q.3	Q.4	JAN	FEB	MAR	APR	MAY	JUN	JUL	AUG	SEP	OCT	NOV	DEC
1964	34	34	34	34	33	33	34	35	35	33	34	34	35	34	34	33	34
1965	32	34	33	32	31	33	34	34	33	33	32	32	32	32	31	30	31
1966	30	32	32	29	28	32	32	32	33	32	31	30	29	28	27	29	29
1967	27	28	27	27	26	29	28	28	27	27	28	28	27	26	27	26	26
1968	34	27	36	38	37	26	26	28	35	35	37	37	38	39	38	37	38
1969	46	44	45	48	47	42	44	44	43	46	47	46	49	49	48	46	48
1970	53	50	53	54	56	50	50	51	52	53	53	54	54	54	54	57	58
1971	60	60	60	61	61	60	59	60	60	61	59	60	61	62	61	60	61
1972	80	69	74	86	92	66	69	73	71	74	76	84	87	87	88	93	95
1973	125	118	120	124	137	110	120	124	122	119	118	117	122	132	142	138	131
1974	121	128	124	122	109	131	126	126	127	123	122	124	122	119	114	110	104
1975	109	109	105	113	107	111	108	110	107	103	107	114	114	111	109	105	108
1976	98	106	99	96	89	109	105	103	101	100	97	99	95	95	94	88	86
1977	80	86	83	79	72	89	85	85	85	83	80	80	79	77	72	72	73
1978	77	76	78	76	78	74	75	79	80	78	76	76	77	76	76	78	79
1979	95	87	91	100	98	84	88	89	89	90	95	97	103	101	98	98	99
1980	100	101	105	101	95	100	101	103	105	105	103	102	102	99	96	94	95
1981	103	98	103	105	108	97	98	99	101	103	105	105	104	104	107	108	111
1982	139	124	140	145	145	114	123	135	135	142	144	147	148	140	141	145	149
1983	211	165	195	226	257	151	163	180	183	196	207	217	223	239	242	261	269

FINLAND

Money supply (M1) (22)

billion markkaa, end of period

Disponibilités monétaires (M1) (22)

milliards de markkas, fin de période

	Year	Q.1	Q.2	Q.3	Q.4	JAN	FEB	MAR	APR	MAY	JUN	JUL	AUG	SEP	OCT	NOV	DEC
1964	2.04	1.85	1.90	1.95	2.04	1.83	1.80	1.85	1.83	1.91	1.90	1.89	1.90	1.95	1.93	2.01	2.04
1965	2.07	1.99	2.01	1.99	2.07	1.93	2.00	1.99	1.94	2.03	2.01	1.94	1.98	1.99	1.90	2.03	2.07
1966	2.18	1.90	2.04	2.00	2.18	1.97	2.04	1.90	1.92	2.07	2.04	2.04	2.02	2.00	1.95	2.02	2.18
1967	2.15	2.00	2.07	1.98	2.15	2.02	2.08	2.00	2.05	2.04	2.07	2.00	2.00	1.98	2.04	2.02	2.15
1968	2.64	2.12	2.29	2.35	2.64	2.17	2.14	2.12	2.24	2.23	2.29	2.28	2.28	2.35	2.29	2.33	2.64
1969	3.13	2.54	2.72	2.72	3.13	2.47	2.58	2.54	2.60	2.66	2.72	2.62	2.66	2.72	2.75	2.78	3.13
1970	3.45	3.02	3.09	3.09	3.45	3.02	3.06	3.02	3.11	3.10	3.09	3.03	3.02	3.09	3.05	3.17	3.45
1971	4.03	3.22	3.42	3.42	4.03	3.29	3.31	3.22	3.17	3.47	3.42	3.30	3.38	3.42	3.50	3.61	4.03
1972	4.96	3.95	4.28	4.41	4.96	3.82	3.93	3.95	3.96	4.02	4.28	4.24	4.27	4.41	4.42	4.42	4.96
1973	6.12	4.64	5.17	5.00	6.12	4.63	4.76	4.64	5.58	5.23	5.17	4.88	4.79	5.00	4.75	4.91	6.12
1974	7.28	5.38	5.90	6.15	7.28	5.39	5.48	5.38	5.46	5.65	5.90	5.97	6.04	6.15	6.09	6.38	7.28
1975	9.77	7.67	8.10	7.68	9.77	7.39	7.53	7.67	7.54	7.60	8.10	7.70	7.81	7.68	7.65	7.91	9.77
1976	9.60	8.91	8.98	8.80	9.60	8.96	9.07	8.91	8.95	8.77	8.98	8.98	9.20	8.80	8.77	8.96	9.60
1977	9.87	9.50	10.00	9.67	9.87	9.38	9.40	9.50	9.62	9.79	10.00	9.68	9.82	9.67	9.73	9.93	9.87
1978	11.50	10.06	11.25	11.07	11.50	9.88	10.14	10.06	10.27	10.68	11.25	11.35	11.18	11.07	11.13	11.11	11.50
1979	14.09	11.44	13.27	13.01	14.09	11.54	11.10	11.44	11.56	12.44	13.27	13.16	13.27	13.01	13.00	13.13	14.09
1980	14.98	13.35	14.59	14.14	14.98	13.77	13.39	13.35	13.40	13.59	14.59	14.44	13.83	14.14	14.23	13.76	14.98
1981	17.19	15.09	15.76	16.05	17.19	14.31	13.65	15.09	14.35	14.63	15.76	15.47	15.86	16.05	15.88	16.13	17.19
1982	19.92	16.35	18.66	18.96	19.92	17.11	16.21	16.35	17.34	17.62	18.66	18.34	18.65	18.96	19.09	18.98	19.92
1983	21.43	19.40	21.36	21.40	21.43	20.33	19.86	19.40	19.37	21.33	21.36	20.63	21.01	21.40	21.77	21.11	21.43

M1 plus quasi-money (22)(23)

billion markkaa, end of period

M1 plus quasi-monnaie (22)(23)

milliards de markkas, fin de période

	Year	Q.1	Q.2	Q.3	Q.4	JAN	FEB	MAR	APR	MAY	JUN	JUL	AUG	SEP	OCT	NOV	DEC
1964	10.20	9.29	9.41	9.60	10.20	9.08	9.16	9.29	9.32	9.49	9.41	9.43	9.49	9.60	9.63	9.81	10.20
1965	11.27	10.55	10.58	10.70	11.27	10.21	10.44	10.55	10.53	10.66	10.58	10.56	10.63	10.70	10.64	10.89	11.27
1966	12.62	11.49	11.67	11.85	12.62	11.27	11.53	11.49	11.48	11.73	11.67	11.71	11.78	11.85	11.87	12.05	12.62
1967	13.69	12.79	12.90	12.98	13.69	12.58	12.76	12.79	12.90	12.97	12.90	12.95	12.93	12.98	13.08	13.11	13.69
1968	15.38	13.92	14.17	14.44	15.38	13.67	13.86	13.92	14.12	14.11	14.17	14.19	14.28	14.44	14.43	14.61	15.38
1969	17.36	15.56	15.91	16.18	17.36	15.29	15.52	15.56	15.72	15.91	15.91	15.85	16.00	16.18	16.33	16.49	17.36
1970	19.71	17.78	18.12	18.47	19.71	17.44	17.73	17.78	18.03	18.16	18.12	18.11	18.22	18.47	18.52	18.81	19.71
1971	22.44	19.91	20.15	20.55	22.44	19.73	19.99	19.91	19.92	20.22	20.15	20.12	20.31	20.55	20.63	21.21	22.44
1972	26.31	22.85	23.57	24.42	26.31	22.37	22.71	22.85	23.02	23.28	23.57	23.76	24.03	24.42	24.63	24.92	26.31
1973	30.41	26.54	27.38	27.84	30.41	26.30	26.64	26.54	27.23	27.31	27.38	27.16	27.37	27.84	27.84	28.20	30.41
1974	35.65	30.27	31.41	32.44	35.65	30.13	30.41	30.27	30.42	30.91	31.41	31.72	32.20	32.44	32.74	33.48	35.65
1975	43.17	37.29	38.60	39.43	43.17	36.11	36.88	37.29	37.38	37.85	38.60	38.82	39.39	39.43	39.42	39.91	43.17
1976	47.01	43.05	43.89	43.98	47.01	42.85	43.30	43.05	43.44	43.42	43.89	44.09	44.49	43.98	44.33	44.92	47.01
1977	52.58	47.69	49.38	50.26	52.58	47.44	47.26	47.69	48.16	48.85	49.38	49.51	50.10	50.26	50.61	51.44	52.58
1978	60.68	54.27	57.37	58.33	60.68	52.72	53.71	54.27	54.99	55.96	57.37	58.03	58.50	58.33	58.61	59.30	60.68
1979	71.16	62.46	65.83	67.12	71.16	61.06	61.62	62.46	63.20	64.35	65.83	66.29	67.14	67.12	67.92	69.01	71.16
1980	81.60	72.41	75.75	77.67	81.60	71.81	72.42	72.41	73.24	74.14	75.75	77.33	77.07	77.67	78.29	78.49	81.60
1981	94.58	82.99	87.30	89.79	94.58	81.62	81.71	82.99	84.11	85.19	87.30	88.41	89.51	89.79	90.23	90.51	94.58
1982	107.55	95.92	101.00	102.48	107.55	95.47	95.99	95.92	98.00	98.89	101.00	101.35	102.09	102.48	103.52	103.58	107.55
1983	121.91	110.10	115.24	115.47	121.91	108.49	109.71	110.10	110.89	113.73	115.24	115.28	115.63	116.47	116.99	117.01	121.91

Bank credit to economy

billion markkaa, end of period

Crédits bancaires à l'économie

milliards de markkas, fin de période

	Year	Q.1	Q.2	Q.3	Q.4	JAN	FEB	MAR	APR	MAY	JUN	JUL	AUG	SEP	OCT	NOV	DEC
1964	9.9	8.8	9.2	9.5	9.9	8.7	8.8	8.8	9.0	9.1	9.2	9.3	9.3	9.5	9.6	9.7	9.9
1965	11.0	10.2	10.5	10.7	11.0	9.9	10.0	10.2	10.3	10.4	10.5	10.6	10.6	10.7	10.7	10.9	11.0
1966	12.4	11.2	11.6	11.9	12.4	11.0	11.1	11.2	11.2	11.4	11.6	11.7	11.8	11.9	11.9	12.2	12.4
1967	13.6	12.4	12.7	13.0	13.6	12.2	12.3	12.4	12.6	12.6	12.7	12.8	12.9	13.0	13.3	13.4	13.6
1968	14.2	13.3	13.4	13.6	14.2	13.3	13.4	13.3	13.4	13.4	13.4	13.5	13.5	13.6	13.8	14.0	14.2
1969	16.3	14.5	15.0	15.6	16.3	14.2	14.3	14.5	14.6	14.8	15.0	15.1	15.3	15.6	15.8	16.1	16.3
1970	18.8	16.7	17.3	18.0	18.8	16.4	16.6	16.7	17.0	17.2	17.3	17.5	17.7	18.0	18.4	18.6	18.8
1971	21.8	19.4	20.1	20.9	21.8	19.0	19.2	19.4	19.7	20.0	20.1	20.3	20.5	20.9	21.2	21.5	21.8
1972	25.6	22.3	23.2	24.1	25.6	21.9	22.0	22.3	22.6	22.9	23.2	23.5	23.7	24.1	24.5	24.9	25.6
1973	31.6	27.0	28.5	29.9	31.6	26.0	26.4	27.0	27.8	28.0	28.5	28.8	29.3	29.9	30.5	31.1	31.6
1974	38.3	32.8	34.6	36.2	38.3	32.0	32.4	32.8	33.4	34.0	34.6	35.0	35.4	36.2	37.0	37.7	38.3
1975	45.0	40.2	41.8	43.5	45.0	39.0	39.7	40.2	40.9	41.4	41.8	42.1	42.5	43.5	44.1	44.6	45.0
1976	50.7	46.2	47.6	48.8	50.7	45.5	45.8	46.2	46.6	47.0	47.6	47.8	48.3	48.8	49.4	49.9	50.7
1977	56.4	51.1	52.4	53.9	56.4	50.9	51.0	51.1	51.4	51.9	52.4	52.8	53.3	53.9	54.7	55.3	56.4
1978	62.0	56.9	58.1	59.6	62.0	57.0	57.2	56.9	57.2	57.6	58.1	58.4	58.8	59.6	60.3	60.9	62.0
1979	72.1	63.3	65.3	68.2	72.1	62.3	63.2	63.3	64.0	64.7	65.3	66.3	67.1	68.2	69.6	70.8	72.1
1980	83.3	74.9	78.2	81.2	83.3	72.8	74.1	74.9	75.6	76.6	78.2	79.1	79.6	81.2	82.0	82.6	83.3
1981	96.7	85.7	89.0	92.6	96.7	83.8	84.9	85.7	86.6	87.5	89.0	90.1	91.2	92.6	94.4	96.2	96.7
1982	112.9	100.6	104.7	109.0	112.9	97.9	98.9	100.6	101.8	103.7	104.7	105.7	107.0	109.0	110.5	111.9	112.9
1983	127.7	117.2	120.8	125.3	127.7	115.0	116.4	117.2	118.3	119.5	120.8	121.5	123.0	125.3	125.3	127.1	127.7

Money supply (M1) (22) — Disponibilités monétaires (M1) (22)

billion markkaa, end of period — milliards de markkas, fin de période

Adjusted - Corrigé *

	Year	Q.1	Q.2	Q.3	Q.4	JAN	FEB	MAR	APR	MAY	JUN	JUL	AUG	SEP	OCT	NOV	DEC
1964		1.85	1.89	1.95	1.96	1.86	1.78	1.85	1.85	1.88	1.89	1.93	1.92	1.95	1.99	1.98	1.96
1965		2.00	1.99	2.01	1.98	1.96	1.98	2.00	1.96	1.99	1.99	1.97	2.00	2.01	1.96	2.02	1.98
1966		1.92	2.01	2.02	2.06	2.00	2.02	1.92	1.93	2.03	2.01	2.07	2.05	2.02	2.02	2.03	2.06
1967		2.02	2.04	2.01	2.02	2.04	2.05	2.02	2.05	2.01	2.04	2.03	2.04	2.01	2.12	2.05	2.02
1968		2.14	2.25	2.39	2.47	2.18	2.10	2.14	2.23	2.20	2.25	2.32	2.32	2.39	2.38	2.38	2.47
1969		2.56	2.68	2.77	2.92	2.47	2.54	2.56	2.58	2.63	2.68	2.67	2.73	2.77	2.85	2.84	2.92
1970		3.04	3.04	3.15	3.21	3.01	3.01	3.04	3.09	3.06	3.04	3.09	3.10	3.15	3.16	3.25	3.21
1971		3.23	3.36	3.48	3.76	3.26	3.25	3.23	3.15	3.42	3.36	3.37	3.49	3.43	3.64	3.71	3.76
1972		3.95	4.19	4.50	4.63	3.79	3.86	3.95	3.95	3.97	4.19	4.32	4.39	4.50	4.62	4.57	4.63
1973		4.63	5.04	5.12	5.73	4.57	4.67	4.63	5.57	5.17	5.04	4.96	4.91	5.12	4.98	5.09	5.73
1974		5.34	5.74	6.30	6.86	5.30	5.38	5.34	5.45	5.61	5.74	6.04	6.15	6.30	6.40	6.63	6.86
1975		7.63	7.39	7.88	9.27	7.26	7.39	7.63	7.54	7.58	7.89	7.76	7.89	7.88	8.00	8.19	9.27
1976		8.91	8.71	9.02	9.17	8.81	8.94	8.91	8.98	8.76	8.71	8.98	9.21	9.02	9.10	9.24	9.17
1977		9.57	9.68	9.87	9.48	9.26	9.34	9.57	9.72	9.81	9.68	9.60	9.77	9.87	9.99	10.20	9.48
1978		10.22	10.84	11.22	11.08	9.81	10.19	10.22	10.43	10.71	10.84	11.17	11.08	11.22	11.32	11.38	11.08
1979		11.72	12.71	13.13	13.61	11.53	11.26	11.72	11.78	12.50	12.71	12.84	13.10	13.13	13.16	13.47	13.61
1980		13.75	13.91	14.24	14.49	13.81	13.68	13.75	13.70	13.68	13.91	14.02	13.62	14.24	14.38	14.12	14.49
1981		15.58	15.00	16.14	16.62	14.36	13.99	15.58	15.22	14.74	15.00	14.99	15.62	16.14	16.02	16.56	16.62
1982		16.89	17.74	19.07	19.26	17.18	16.62	16.89	17.77	17.76	17.74	17.75	18.38	19.07	19.26	19.49	19.26
1983		20.04	20.31	21.53	20.72	20.42	20.37	20.04	19.85	21.50	20.31	19.98	20.70	21.53	21.97	21.67	20.72

M1 plus quasi-money (22)(23)(24) — M1 plus quasi-monnaie (22)(23)(24)

billion markkaa, end of period — milliards de markkas, fin de période

Adjusted - Corrigé

	Year	Q.1	Q.2	Q.3	Q.4	JAN	FEB	MAR	APR	MAY	JUN	JUL	AUG	SEP	OCT	NOV	DEC
1964		9.15	9.43	9.73	10.03	9.03	9.02	9.15	9.24	9.36	9.43	9.55	9.62	9.73	9.86	9.95	10.03
1965		10.40	10.59	10.86	11.07	10.16	10.27	10.40	10.44	10.52	10.59	10.68	10.77	10.86	10.89	11.06	11.07
1966		11.33	11.69	12.03	12.37	11.20	11.34	11.33	11.38	11.60	11.69	11.85	11.94	12.03	12.13	12.24	12.37
1967		12.63	12.92	13.16	13.42	12.49	12.55	12.63	12.77	12.84	12.92	12.99	13.11	13.16	13.36	13.33	13.42
1968		13.76	14.19	14.65	15.04	13.55	13.63	13.76	13.98	13.98	14.19	14.36	14.48	14.65	14.72	14.86	15.04
1969		15.40	15.93	16.41	16.93	15.14	15.26	15.40	15.57	15.78	15.93	16.04	16.24	16.41	16.65	16.76	16.93
1970		17.62	18.15	18.73	19.22	17.23	17.42	17.62	17.88	18.03	18.15	18.35	18.51	18.73	18.87	19.12	19.22
1971		19.73	20.19	20.84	21.87	19.45	19.62	19.73	19.80	20.11	20.19	20.38	20.62	20.84	21.22	21.55	21.87
1972		22.63	23.60	24.77	25.61	22.00	22.28	22.63	22.95	23.18	23.60	24.06	24.37	24.77	25.12	25.34	25.61
1973		26.30	27.38	28.23	29.60	25.83	26.12	26.30	27.20	27.24	27.38	27.45	27.68	28.23	28.41	28.69	29.60
1974		30.03	31.37	32.89	34.77	29.58	29.85	30.03	30.43	30.87	31.37	31.99	32.46	32.89	33.42	34.08	34.77
1975		37.26	38.37	39.95	42.70	35.83	36.55	37.26	37.34	37.81	38.37	38.82	39.35	39.95	40.02	40.35	42.70
1976		43.00	43.63	44.51	46.50	42.55	42.92	43.00	43.40	43.38	43.63	44.05	44.45	44.51	44.96	45.38	46.50
1977		47.69	49.04	50.77	52.01	47.16	46.93	47.69	48.16	48.80	49.04	49.41	50.00	50.77	51.23	51.90	52.01
1978		54.33	56.91	58.80	60.08	52.51	53.50	54.33	55.10	55.96	56.91	57.85	58.33	58.80	59.26	59.84	60.08
1979		62.59	65.25	67.66	70.52	60.82	61.49	62.59	63.33	64.35	65.25	65.90	66.87	67.66	68.61	69.64	70.52
1980		72.62	75.00	78.22	80.87	71.67	72.35	72.62	73.46	74.14	75.00	76.79	76.68	78.22	79.08	79.20	80.87
1981		83.33	86.44	90.42	93.83	81.45	81.63	83.33	84.36	85.27	86.44	87.79	89.06	90.42	91.15	91.34	93.83
1982		96.30	100.10	103.20	106.70	95.28	95.90	96.30	98.40	98.99	100.10	100.65	101.58	103.20	104.57	104.52	106.70
1983		110.54	114.21	117.29	120.94	108.27	109.60	110.54	111.34	113.84	114.21	114.48	115.05	117.29	118.17	118.07	120.94

Bank credit to economy — Crédits bancaires à l'économie

billion markkaa, end of period — milliards de markkas, fin de période

Adjusted - Corrigé

	Year	Q.1	Q.2	Q.3	Q.4	JAN	FEB	MAR	APR	MAY	JUN	JUL	AUG	SEP	OCT	NOV	DEC
1964		8.9	9.1	9.5	9.8	8.8	8.8	8.9	9.0	9.0	9.1	9.2	9.3	9.5	9.6	9.7	9.8
1965		10.2	10.5	10.7	10.9	9.9	10.0	10.2	10.3	10.4	10.5	10.6	10.7	10.7	10.7	10.8	10.9
1966		11.2	11.6	12.0	12.3	11.1	11.1	11.2	11.2	11.4	11.6	11.7	11.8	12.0	11.9	12.1	12.3
1967		12.5	12.7	13.0	13.4	12.3	12.4	12.5	12.6	12.7	12.7	12.8	12.9	13.0	13.3	13.3	13.4
1968		13.3	13.5	13.6	14.1	13.4	13.4	13.3	13.4	13.4	13.5	13.5	13.6	13.6	13.8	13.9	14.1
1969		14.5	15.0	15.6	16.1	14.2	14.3	14.5	14.6	14.9	15.0	15.2	15.4	15.6	15.8	16.0	16.1
1970		16.8	17.4	18.0	18.7	16.4	16.6	16.8	17.0	17.2	17.4	17.6	17.8	18.0	18.3	18.6	18.7
1971		19.5	20.2	21.0	21.6	19.0	19.2	19.5	19.6	20.0	20.2	20.4	20.6	21.0	21.2	21.4	21.6
1972		22.3	23.3	24.1	25.5	21.9	22.0	22.3	22.5	22.9	23.3	23.5	23.8	24.1	24.4	34.8	25.5
1973		27.0	28.5	29.9	31.4	25.9	26.4	27.0	27.8	28.0	28.5	28.9	29.5	29.9	30.5	31.0	31.4
1974		32.8	34.6	36.3	38.1	31.9	32.4	32.8	33.3	34.0	34.6	35.2	35.7	36.3	36.9	37.6	38.1
1975		40.3	41.8	43.6	44.7	38.8	39.6	40.3	40.8	41.4	41.8	42.3	42.8	43.6	44.1	44.5	44.7
1976		46.2	47.7	48.9	50.3	45.2	45.6	46.2	46.6	47.1	47.7	48.1	48.6	48.9	49.3	49.7	50.3
1977		51.2	52.6	54.0	56.0	50.6	50.8	51.2	51.6	52.1	52.6	53.0	53.6	54.0	54.6	55.2	56.0
1978		57.0	58.3	59.7	61.5	55.7	57.0	57.0	57.4	57.8	58.3	58.7	59.1	59.7	60.1	60.7	61.5
1979		63.4	65.5	68.2	71.7	62.0	62.9	63.4	64.3	65.0	65.5	66.5	67.4	68.2	69.4	70.5	71.7
1980		75.1	78.4	81.2	83.0	72.6	73.8	75.1	75.9	76.9	78.4	79.4	80.0	81.2	81.8	82.2	83.0
1981		85.8	89.1	92.4	96.5	83.6	84.7	85.8	86.3	87.6	89.1	90.4	91.6	92.4	94.2	95.9	96.5
1982		100.7	104.3	108.7	112.8	97.8	93.8	100.7	102.0	103.8	104.8	106.0	107.4	108.7	110.3	111.4	112.8
1983		117.2	120.8	124.9	127.6	114.8	116.3	117.2	118.6	119.5	120.8	122.0	123.4	124.9	125.1	126.6	127.6

* Adjusted by the O.E.C.D. — * Corrigé par l'O.C.D.E.

FINLAND

U.S. dollar exchange rate: spot
cents per markka, end of period

Taux de change du dollar É.-U. : au comptant
cents par markka, fin de période

	Year	Q.1	Q.2	Q.3	Q.4	JAN	FEB	MAR	APR	MAY	JUN	JUL	AUG	SEP	OCT	NOV	DEC
1964	31.056	31.056	31.056	31.056	31.056	31.056	31.056	31.056	31.056	31.056	31.056	31.056	31.056	31.056	31.056	31.056	31.056
1965	31.056	31.056	31.056	31.056	31.056	31.056	31.056	31.056	31.056	31.056	31.056	31.056	31.056	31.056	31.056	31.056	31.056
1966	31.056	31.056	31.056	31.056	31.056	31.056	31.056	31.056	31.056	31.056	31.056	31.056	31.056	31.056	31.056	31.056	31.056
1967	23.810	31.056	31.056	31.056	23.810	31.056	31.056	31.056	31.056	31.056	31.056	31.056	31.056	31.056	23.810	23.810	23.810
1968	23.810	23.810	23.810	23.810	23.810	23.810	23.810	23.810	23.810	23.810	23.810	23.810	23.810	23.810	23.810	23.810	23.810
1969	23.810	23.810	23.810	23.810	23.810	23.810	23.810	23.810	23.810	23.810	23.810	23.810	23.810	23.810	23.810	23.810	23.810
1970	23.923	23.810	23.923	23.923	23.923	23.810	23.810	23.810	23.810	23.810	23.923	23.923	23.923	23.923	23.923	23.923	23.923
1971	24.096	23.923	23.810	24.039	24.096	23.923	23.923	23.923	23.810	23.810	23.810	23.923	24.039	24.039	24.039	24.039	24.096
1972	23.923	24.155	24.155	24.155	23.923	24.096	24.096	24.155	24.155	24.155	24.155	24.213	24.155	24.155	24.039	23.981	23.923
1973	26.008	25.840	27.390	26.961	26.008	23.981	25.575	25.840	25.707	26.042	27.390	27.541	27.181	26.961	27.196	26.434	26.008
1974	28.161	26.803	27.617	26.158	28.161	25.214	25.833	26.803	27.315	26.983	27.617	27.020	26.344	26.158	26.448	27.144	28.161
1975	25.974	28.281	28.151	25.349	25.974	28.604	28.893	28.281	28.082	28.241	28.161	26.413	26.378	25.349	26.103	25.700	25.974
1976	26.546	26.069	25.727	25.873	26.546	26.035	26.137	26.069	26.008	25.628	25.727	25.780	25.720	25.873	26.001	26.158	26.546
1977	24.888	26.316	24.679	24.067	24.888	26.103	26.240	26.316	24.685	24.516	24.679	24.851	24.777	24.067	24.149	23.838	24.888
1978	25.471	24.004	23.568	24.832	25.471	25.031	23.964	24.004	23.691	23.250	23.568	24.015	24.396	24.832	26.575	24.649	25.473
1979	26.947	25.132	25.661	26.911	26.947	25.132	25.189	25.132	24.851	25.006	25.661	26.055	26.035	26.911	26.206	26.810	26.947
1980	26.042	25.733	27.548	27.263	26.042	26.969	26.610	25.733	26.918	27.248	27.548	27.337	27.322	27.263	26.631	26.295	26.042
1981	22.952	24.594	22.492	22.312	22.952	25.031	24.456	24.594	23.759	22.957	22.492	21.863	21.993	22.312	22.660	23.305	22.952
1982	18.900	21.636	21.160	20.619	18.900	22.635	21.988	21.636	22.090	21.949	21.160	21.178	20.934	20.619	18.132	18.308	18.900
1983	17.212	18.273	18.047	17.674	17.212	18.491	18.577	18.278	18.406	18.258	18.047	17.724	17.361	17.674	17.627	17.304	17.212

Official reserves excluding gold
million SDR's, end of period

Réserves officielles, or exclu
millions de DTS, fin de période

	Year	Q.1	Q.2	Q.3	Q.4	JAN	FEB	MAR	APR	MAY	JUN	JUL	AUG	SEP	OCT	NOV	DEC
1964	299	265	252	257	299	232	254	265	257	261	252	249	251	257	271	279	299
1965	206	262	204	190	206	288	288	262	256	227	204	205	204	190	217	210	206
1966	144	190	158	143	144	189	190	190	180	172	158	159	148	143	131	118	144
1967	139	114	142	157	139	146	142	114	145	137	142	143	136	157	151	141	139
1968	293	207	261	267	293	146	185	207	231	238	261	260	262	267	280	293	293
1969	282	298	223	199	282	301	298	298	290	229	223	217	220	199	241	245	282
1970	425	302	325	354	425	291	322	302	307	315	325	332	349	354	381	378	425
1971	574	481	469	501	574	445	453	481	459	437	469	526	510	501	512	546	574
1972	615	676	659	704	615	649	691	676	698	670	659	702	700	704	670	650	615
1973	476	473	401	395	476	576	528	473	448	462	401	389	419	395	373	455	476
1974	487	501	544	513	487	473	491	501	490	490	544	572	577	513	502	489	487
1975	370	357	406	435	370	393	358	357	326	273	406	366	458	435	432	394	370
1976	398	331	422	398	398	351	314	331	389	442	422	489	457	398	365	355	398
1977	437	383	306	327	437	328	356	383	376	346	306	282	248	327	336	285	437
1978	939	697	777	950	939	418	579	697	706	840	777	839	977	950	897	809	939
1979	1169	1140	1545	1469	1169	1062	1091	1140	1214	1288	1545	1564	1740	1469	1254	1100	1169
1980	1466	1337	1492	1479	1466	1325	1408	1337	1353	1389	1492	1555	1535	1479	1470	1495	1466
1981	1275	1448	1391	1319	1275	1306	1469	1448	1547	1341	1391	1368	1376	1319	1171	1177	1275
1982	1376	1382	1058	971	1376	1111	1187	1382	1313	1139	1058	1048	919	971	1055	1210	1376
1983	1182	1045	946	750	1182	1207	1031	1045	953	929	946	957	931	750	919	1003	1182

Net foreign position: commercial banks
million markkaa, end of period

Position extérieure nette : banques commerciales
millions de markkas, fin de période

	Year	Q.1	Q.2	Q.3	Q.4	JAN	FEB	MAR	APR	MAY	JUN	JUL	AUG	SEP	OCT	NOV	DEC
1964	-152	-192	-176	-177	-152	-156	-175	-192	-189	-206	-176	-158	-159	-177	-143	-166	-152
1965	-156	-157	-124	-159	-156	-136	-151	-157	-142	-150	-124	-184	-176	-159	-191	-178	-156
1966	-269	-207	-223	-228	-269	-153	-172	-207	-196	-213	-223	-228	-222	-228	-197	-213	-269
1967	-264	-220	-246	-258	-264	-184	-214	-220	-255	-251	-246	-228	-226	-253	-251	-241	-264
1968	-301	-313	-386	-283	-301	-297	-337	-313	-346	-335	-386	-318	-323	-283	-267	-298	-301
1969	-141	-293	-179	-93	-141	-288	-243	-293	-247	-235	-179	-124	-121	-93	-147	-117	-141
1970	-525	-322	-528	-758	-525	-191	-285	-322	-473	-555	-528	-632	-723	-758	-845	-716	-525
1971	-550	-513	-619	-523	-550	-471	-405	-513	-600	-610	-619	-604	-587	-523	-546	-415	-550
1972	-234	-612	-588	-597	-234	-633	-680	-612	-705	-739	-588	-513	-539	-597	-405	-432	-234
1973	-395	-395	-324	-421	-395	-156	-422	-395	-461	-560	-324	-235	-422	-421	-390	-461	-395
1974	-1124	-539	-711	-748	-1124	-266	-296	-539	-584	-582	-711	-543	-703	-748	-984	-942	-1124
1975	-2798	-1704	-2153	-2286	-2798	-1176	-1243	-1704	-1753	-1969	-2153	-1823	-2084	-2286	-2481	-2672	-2798
1976	-2711	-2335	-2447	-2316	-2711	-2577	-2540	-2335	-2695	-2724	-2447	-2532	-2438	-2316	-2264	-2599	-2711
1977	-2652	-3087	-3221	-3515	-2652	-2678	-2857	-3087	-3405	-3466	-3221	-3127	-2931	-3515	-3123	-2327	-2652
1978	-2353	-3348	-2966	-2642	-2353	-2329	-2889	-3348	-3153	-3007	-2966	-2677	-2757	-2642	-2168	-2196	-2353
1979	-3310	-3013	-4573	-3692	-3310	-2186	-2552	-3013	-3448	-4112	-4573	-4109	-4658	-3692	-3237	-2734	-3310
1980	-6108	-3848	-4793	-5478	-6108	-3794	-3786	-3848	-3544	-4350	-4793	-5306	-5540	-5478	-5971	-5804	-6108
1981	-6781	-6832	-6803	-6380	-6781	-5971	-6466	-6832	-7068	-6643	-6803	-6248	-6184	-6380	-6325	-6386	-6781
1982	-10039	-5587	-5839	-6004	-10039	-6264	-5583	-5587	-5552	-5525	-5839	-6107	-6463	-6004	-6898	-8105	-10039
1983	-12697	-9418	-10242	-9795	-12697	-10492	-9896	-9418	-9088	-10215	-10242	-10733	-10812	-9795	-11142	-12100	-12697

Balance of payments: net services
million markkaa

Balance des paiements : services, nets
millions de markkas

	Year	Q.1	Q.2	Q.3	Q.4	JAN	FEB	MAR	APR	MAY	JUN	JUL	AUG	SEP	OCT	NOV	DEC
1964	159	21	57	38	43												
1965	137	25	43	54	15												
1966	135	22	40	20	53												
1967	136	15	30	30	61												
1968	172	36	56	112	-32												
1969	247	40	33	60	114												
1970	512	101	106	186	119												
1971	564	94	108	241	121												
1972	627	93	136	274	124												
1973	708	164	120	363	61												
1974	676	169	224	270	13												
1975	156	-45	-79	190	90												
1976	27	22	-81	159	-73												
1977	-226	-65	-280	253	-134												
1978	349	5	-65	271	138												
1979	711	202	-251	448	312												
1980	704	326	7	522	-151												
1981	725	-55	-425	795	410												
1982	-1877	-227	-829	-47	-774												
1983	-2150	-452	-806	-189	-703												

Balance of payments: current balance
million markkaa

Balance des paiements : opérations courantes, nettes
millions de markkas

	Year	Q.1	Q.2	Q.3	Q.4	JAN	FEB	MAR	APR	MAY	JUN	JUL	AUG	SEP	OCT	NOV	DEC
1964	-563	-253	-174	-4	-132												
1965	-607	-302	-225	-23	-57												
1966	-633	-347	-114	-65	-107												
1967	-489	-245	-125	18	-137												
1968	269	-93	34	291	37												
1969	87	-128	20	207	-12												
1970	-1004	-150	-195	-43	-616												
1971	-1424	-288	-417	-144	-575												
1972	-461	-25	-326	60	-170												
1973	-1481	-454	-588	-99	-340												
1974	-4628	-997	-890	-1519	-1222												
1975	-7952	-2389	-2150	-2047	-1366												
1976	-4455	-1409	-541	-1347	-1158												
1977	-580	1	-1248	385	282												
1978	2606	233	434	607	1332												
1979	-761	537	312	-933	-677												
1980	-5155	-668	-1597	-2359	-531												
1981	-1211	661	-873	-951	-48												
1982	-4698	845	-795	-2291	-2457												
1983	-5300	-272	-1331	-1957	-1740												

Balance of payments: net long-term capital
million markkaa

Balance des paiements : capitaux à long terme, nets
millions de markkas

	Year	Q.1	Q.2	Q.3	Q.4	JAN	FEB	MAR	APR	MAY	JUN	JUL	AUG	SEP	OCT	NOV	DEC
1964	492	108	173	110	101												
1965	98	43	24	-37	68												
1966	154	16	31	55	52												
1967	484	143	259	150	-68												
1968	129	24	146	-29	-12												
1969	101	37	-13	-11	38												
1970	330	70	-44	66	238												
1971	1582	359	354	533	336												
1972	1304	597	278	235	194												
1973	412	-21	-13	448	-2												
1974	947	-91	295	84	659												
1975	5132	893	1388	1888	963												
1976	4202	1046	1600	635	921												
1977	3239	321	414	360	2144												
1978	2265	839	1115	1042	-731												
1979	509	522	-578	100	465												
1980	182	759	-46	31	-562												
1981	2325	-13	513	844	981												
1982	619	2552	151	602	-2686												
1983	2300	1632	-387	214	841												

FINLAND

Imports c.i.f. (25) — Importations c.a.f. (25)

billion markkaa, monthly averages — milliards de markkas, moyennes mensuelles

	Year	Q.1	Q.2	Q.3	Q.4	JAN	FEB	MAR	APR	MAY	JUN	JUL	AUG	SEP	OCT	NOV	DEC
1964	0.40	0.36	0.42	0.39	0.43	0.36	0.35	0.37	0.45	0.40	0.41	0.36	0.39	0.42	0.42	0.43	0.45
1965	0.44	0.42	0.47	0.43	0.45	0.38	0.41	0.46	0.44	0.53	0.43	0.43	0.39	0.46	0.43	0.45	0.47
1966	0.46	0.41	0.46	0.45	0.51	0.43	0.37	0.45	0.44	0.49	0.46	0.41	0.44	0.51	0.49	0.49	0.56
1967	0.48	0.45	0.46	0.42	0.60	0.47	0.44	0.43	0.49	0.48	0.42	0.40	0.43	0.42	0.54	0.62	0.65
1968	0.56	0.50	0.61	0.50	0.62	0.53	0.47	0.51	0.56	0.66	0.61	0.45	0.47	0.58	0.59	0.61	0.67
1969	0.71	0.65	0.67	0.67	0.85	0.63	0.67	0.64	0.62	0.74	0.65	0.65	0.59	0.78	0.87	0.75	0.92
1970	0.92	0.77	0.91	0.90	1.12	0.77	0.74	0.79	0.98	0.91	0.83	0.87	0.80	1.02	0.97	0.99	1.41
1971	0.98	0.84	0.93	0.95	1.19	0.88	0.74	0.91	0.96	1.02	0.81	0.87	0.88	1.11	1.08	1.02	1.46
1972	1.09	0.98	1.10	1.06	1.23	0.96	0.96	1.03	1.09	1.08	1.12	1.10	1.00	1.09	1.22	1.26	1.21
1973	1.38	1.29	1.29	1.36	1.59	1.39	1.11	1.39	1.29	1.46	1.11	1.20	1.41	1.43	1.69	1.62	1.46
1974	2.14	1.90	2.07	2.28	2.30	1.95	1.89	1.87	2.13	2.27	1.81	2.16	2.27	2.42	2.40	2.30	2.20
1975	2.33	2.46	2.24	2.22	2.42	2.75	2.54	2.10	2.30	2.36	2.05	2.27	2.16	2.24	2.46	2.25	2.55
1976	2.38	2.11	2.08	2.51	2.82	2.13	1.95	2.25	1.85	1.94	2.44	2.54	2.36	2.63	2.36	2.78	3.31
1977	2.56	2.26	2.57	2.56	2.84	2.39	1.99	2.40	2.17	2.42	3.12	2.44	2.40	2.85	2.58	2.89	3.05
1978	2.70	2.46	2.68	2.61	3.03	2.63	2.19	2.57	2.43	2.94	2.68	2.64	2.47	2.72	3.04	3.14	2.91
1979	3.69	3.04	3.38	3.84	4.48	3.57	2.39	3.16	3.16	3.65	3.33	3.79	3.86	3.87	4.30	4.40	4.75
1980	4.85	4.53	4.67	5.21	5.01	4.94	4.23	4.41	4.50	3.79	5.74	5.01	5.48	5.13	5.31	4.17	5.55
1981	5.11	4.51	5.23	5.21	5.48	4.50	4.40	4.62	4.92	5.91	4.86	4.41	5.94	5.28	5.22	5.50	5.71
1982	5.40	4.92	5.09	5.11	6.46	5.00	4.79	4.98	5.38	4.92	4.99	4.85	5.46	5.00	5.85	6.17	7.35
1983	5.96	5.45	5.76	5.95	6.68	5.55	5.07	5.73	5.71	6.25	5.34	5.80	5.51	6.54	6.57	6.38	7.08

Exports f.o.b. (25) — Exportations f.o.b. (25)

billion markkaa, monthly averages — milliards de markkas, moyennes mensuelles

	Year	Q.1	Q.2	Q.3	Q.4	JAN	FEB	MAR	APR	MAY	JUN	JUL	AUG	SEP	OCT	NOV	DEC
1964	0.34	0.27	0.35	0.38	0.38	0.28	0.30	0.23	0.34	0.34	0.37	0.37	0.35	0.41	0.40	0.37	0.38
1965	0.38	0.31	0.38	0.40	0.43	0.32	0.27	0.34	0.34	0.40	0.41	0.40	0.39	0.43	0.43	0.39	0.47
1966	0.40	0.29	0.42	0.43	0.47	0.31	0.23	0.34	0.37	0.45	0.42	0.41	0.42	0.45	0.46	0.44	0.52
1967	0.44	0.36	0.42	0.42	0.55	0.37	0.34	0.38	0.40	0.40	0.46	0.37	0.41	0.47	0.56	0.53	0.54
1968	0.57	0.47	0.61	0.56	0.65	0.47	0.40	0.54	0.56	0.66	0.60	0.52	0.58	0.60	0.67	0.68	0.61
1969	0.69	0.57	0.67	0.73	0.81	0.59	0.49	0.62	0.56	0.75	0.70	0.74	0.70	0.73	0.89	0.71	0.84
1970	0.81	0.70	0.81	0.83	0.89	0.76	0.60	0.73	0.81	0.82	0.81	0.78	0.83	0.88	0.91	0.85	0.91
1971	0.83	0.73	0.77	0.84	0.97	0.87	0.66	0.66	0.69	0.78	0.83	0.85	0.81	0.86	0.92	0.96	1.02
1972	1.01	0.96	0.96	1.00	1.11	0.87	0.96	1.05	0.86	0.89	1.12	0.99	0.83	1.17	1.02	1.14	1.18
1973	1.22	1.10	1.07	1.23	1.48	1.06	1.08	1.17	0.94	1.34	0.93	1.09	1.22	1.37	1.54	1.56	1.33
1974	1.72	1.54	1.73	1.71	1.92	1.54	1.47	1.60	1.78	1.85	1.56	1.80	1.55	1.78	2.24	1.81	1.72
1975	1.69	1.71	1.57	1.50	1.96	2.01	1.55	1.58	1.74	1.59	1.38	1.65	1.14	1.71	1.84	1.67	2.37
1976	2.04	1.67	1.97	2.04	2.49	1.56	1.48	1.97	1.45	2.21	2.23	2.26	1.76	2.12	2.39	2.46	2.61
1977	2.58	2.34	2.29	2.66	3.04	2.47	1.92	2.62	2.08	2.23	2.54	2.83	2.24	2.90	2.99	2.96	3.16
1978	2.93	2.60	2.89	2.76	3.48	2.51	2.52	2.75	2.89	2.94	2.82	2.68	2.40	3.24	3.44	3.64	3.36
1979	3.62	3.24	3.63	3.41	4.20	3.44	2.81	3.46	3.38	4.01	3.49	3.52	3.36	3.36	4.38	4.38	3.85
1980	4.40	4.26	4.15	4.28	4.91	4.25	3.80	4.74	3.79	4.17	4.50	4.35	3.92	4.58	4.64	4.49	5.59
1981	5.03	4.82	5.17	4.71	5.41	5.00	4.43	5.04	4.66	5.54	5.31	4.25	4.78	5.10	5.63	5.65	4.94
1982	5.25	5.37	5.20	4.44	6.00	5.33	5.47	5.29	5.08	5.12	5.42	4.28	4.26	4.79	5.63	6.34	6.03
1983	5.81	5.60	5.73	5.43	6.49	5.03	5.57	6.21	5.74	6.15	5.29	5.68	5.13	5.48	6.09	6.51	6.86

Trade balance (f.o.b. — c.i.f.) (25) — Balance commerciale (f.o.b. — c.a.f.) (25)

billion markkaa, monthly averages — milliards de markkas, moyennes mensuelles

	Year	Q.1	Q.2	Q.3	Q.4	JAN	FEB	MAR	APR	MAY	JUN	JUL	AUG	SEP	OCT	NOV	DEC
1964	-0.06	-0.09	-0.07	-0.02	-0.05	-0.08	-0.05	-0.14	-0.11	-0.06	-0.05	0.01	-0.04	-0.01	-0.02	-0.07	-0.07
1965	-0.06	-0.11	-0.09	-0.02	-0.02	-0.07	-0.14	-0.12	-0.09	-0.14	-0.03	-0.03	-	-0.04	0.00	-0.06	0.00
1966	-0.06	-0.12	-0.05	-0.03	-0.04	-0.12	-0.14	-0.11	-0.07	-0.04	-0.04	-0.01	-0.02	-0.05	-0.03	-0.05	-0.04
1967	-0.05	-0.09	-0.04	-0.00	-0.06	-0.10	-0.10	-0.06	-0.09	-0.08	0.04	-0.03	-0.02	0.05	0.02	-0.09	-0.11
1968	0.02	-0.04	-0.00	0.07	0.03	-0.07	-0.07	0.03	0.00	0.01	-0.01	0.07	0.11	0.02	0.08	0.07	-0.05
1969	-0.01	-0.08	0.00	0.05	-0.03	-0.04	-0.18	-0.02	-0.06	0.01	0.06	0.09	0.12	-0.05	0.02	-0.03	-0.09
1970	-0.12	-0.07	-0.09	-0.07	-0.23	-0.01	-0.15	-0.06	-0.17	-0.09	-0.02	-0.08	0.03	-0.14	-0.05	-0.14	-0.50
1971	-0.15	-0.12	-0.16	-0.12	-0.22	-0.01	-0.08	-0.26	-0.27	-0.24	0.02	-0.02	-0.07	-0.25	-0.15	-0.06	-0.44
1972	-0.09	-0.02	-0.14	-0.07	-0.12	-0.09	0.01	0.02	-0.24	-0.19	0.01	-0.11	-0.17	0.08	-0.20	-0.12	-0.03
1973	-0.17	-0.19	-0.22	-0.14	-0.11	-0.34	-0.03	-0.22	-0.35	-0.13	-0.18	-0.11	-0.19	-0.12	-0.15	-0.07	-0.13
1974	-0.42	-0.36	-0.35	-0.58	-0.38	-0.41	-0.41	-0.27	-0.35	-0.42	-0.26	-0.37	-0.72	-0.64	-0.16	-0.49	-0.48
1975	-0.65	-0.75	-0.66	-0.72	-0.46	-0.74	-0.99	-0.52	-0.56	-0.76	-0.67	-0.62	-1.03	-0.53	-0.62	-0.58	-0.17
1976	-0.34	-0.44	-0.11	-0.47	-0.33	-0.57	-0.47	-0.28	-0.40	0.28	-0.21	-0.29	-0.60	-0.51	0.03	-0.32	-0.70
1977	0.02	0.07	-0.28	0.10	0.19	0.08	-0.08	0.22	-0.09	-0.19	-0.58	0.39	-0.16	0.05	0.41	0.07	0.11
1978	0.24	0.13	0.21	0.17	0.45	-0.12	0.34	0.18	0.47	0.01	0.15	0.05	-0.07	0.52	0.40	0.50	0.46
1979	-0.07	0.20	0.24	-0.42	-0.28	-0.13	0.42	0.30	0.22	0.35	0.16	-0.27	-0.49	-0.51	0.08	-0.02	-0.90
1980	-0.46	-0.27	-0.52	-0.92	-0.10	-0.70	-0.44	0.33	-0.71	0.36	-1.24	-0.66	-1.56	-0.55	-0.67	0.32	0.04
1981	-0.08	0.32	-0.06	-0.51	-0.07	0.50	0.03	0.42	-0.26	-0.37	0.45	-0.17	-1.16	-0.19	0.41	0.14	-0.77
1982	-0.14	0.44	0.11	-0.66	-0.47	0.33	0.69	0.31	-0.30	0.20	0.43	-0.57	-1.20	-0.22	-0.23	0.16	-1.33
1983	-0.15	0.15	-0.04	-0.52	-0.13	-0.53	0.50	0.48	0.03	-0.09	-0.05	-0.12	-0.39	-1.06	-0.47	0.14	-0.22

Imports c.i.f. (25) — billion markkaa, monthly averages

Adjusted - Corrigé *

Importations c.a.f. (25) — milliards de markkas, moyennes mensuelles

Year	Q.1	Q.2	Q.3	Q.4	JAN	FEB	MAR	APR	MAY	JUN	JUL	AUG	SEP	OCT	NOV	DEC
1964	0.38	0.39	0.41	0.41	0.37	0.38	0.40	0.41	0.37	0.41	0.36	0.45	0.42	0.40	0.42	0.42
1965	0.44	0.45	0.45	0.43	0.42	0.45	0.44	0.42	0.48	0.44	0.46	0.44	0.44	0.43	0.43	0.41
1966	0.43	0.45	0.48	0.49	0.45	0.41	0.44	0.44	0.45	0.46	0.46	0.48	0.48	0.48	0.47	0.51
1967	0.47	0.44	0.45	0.57	0.48	0.49	0.45	0.47	0.42	0.44	0.45	0.49	0.41	0.53	0.57	0.60
1968	0.52	0.60	0.52	0.58	0.53	0.49	0.54	0.54	0.57	0.69	0.48	0.54	0.55	0.55	0.59	0.59
1969	0.67	0.66	0.72	0.77	0.62	0.74	0.66	0.60	0.69	0.70	0.70	0.70	0.74	0.78	0.76	0.78
1970	0.83	0.89	0.93	1.03	0.78	0.82	0.87	0.87	0.87	0.91	0.91	0.93	0.97	0.91	0.96	1.21
1971	0.88	0.93	0.99	1.09	0.92	0.82	0.89	0.92	0.97	0.91	0.95	1.00	1.03	1.05	1.00	1.22
1972	1.01	1.11	1.12	1.15	0.96	1.05	1.03	1.10	0.98	1.26	1.21	1.07	1.07	1.16	1.20	1.10
1973	1.32	1.31	1.41	1.47	1.30	1.23	1.41	1.29	1.37	1.29	1.29	1.43	1.51	1.55	1.56	1.30
1974	1.97	2.14	2.30	2.15	1.84	2.12	1.97	2.19	2.10	2.15	2.18	2.38	2.34	2.26	2.25	1.95
1975	2.58	2.28	2.26	2.22	2.53	2.89	2.32	2.28	2.31	2.25	2.29	2.33	2.15	2.27	2.23	2.16
1976	2.18	2.17	2.50	2.58	2.07	2.24	2.22	1.98	1.93	2.61	2.57	2.49	2.45	2.36	2.58	2.79
1977	2.39	2.67	2.54	2.65	2.38	2.35	2.43	2.42	2.40	3.17	2.51	2.41	2.70	2.53	2.67	2.73
1978	2.65	2.72	2.60	2.84	2.64	2.61	2.70	2.63	2.77	2.74	2.65	2.49	2.67	2.97	2.84	2.72
1979	3.18	3.48	3.83	4.15	3.43	2.82	3.29	3.41	3.52	3.52	3.82	3.68	3.97	4.00	4.08	4.37
1980	4.76	4.82	5.18	4.63	4.87	4.72	4.69	4.74	3.73	6.01	4.96	5.52	5.05	4.89	4.17	4.85
1981	4.84	5.37	5.11	5.10	4.54	5.05	4.92	4.96	6.04	5.11	4.30	5.74	5.29	5.05	5.23	5.03
1982	5.26	5.24	5.02	6.00	5.27	5.43	5.09	5.46	4.95	5.31	4.98	5.18	4.89	5.88	5.85	6.26
1983	5.83	5.93	5.88	6.28	5.78	5.71	5.99	5.97	6.27	5.54	6.19	4.95	6.50	6.48	6.06	6.31

Exports f.o.b. (25) — billion markkaa, monthly averages

Adjusted - Corrigé *

Exportations f.o.b. (25) — milliards de markkas, moyennes mensuelles

Year	Q.1	Q.2	Q.3	Q.4	JAN	FEB	MAR	APR	MAY	JUN	JUL	AUG	SEP	OCT	NOV	DEC
1964	0.34	0.33	0.35	0.36	0.33	0.39	0.31	0.34	0.33	0.33	0.33	0.34	0.36	0.34	0.37	0.35
1965	0.37	0.37	0.38	0.39	0.38	0.36	0.38	0.37	0.38	0.37	0.38	0.39	0.38	0.39	0.37	0.42
1966	0.35	0.41	0.41	0.43	0.37	0.30	0.37	0.40	0.43	0.39	0.41	0.41	0.41	0.42	0.42	0.46
1967	0.44	0.40	0.41	0.51	0.43	0.45	0.43	0.41	0.37	0.42	0.39	0.41	0.43	0.52	0.50	0.50
1968	0.52	0.60	0.56	0.60	0.51	0.50	0.56	0.61	0.59	0.59	0.52	0.57	0.60	0.59	0.63	0.58
1969	0.63	0.67	0.73	0.75	0.62	0.62	0.64	0.61	0.69	0.69	0.75	0.73	0.71	0.77	0.71	0.76
1970	0.78	0.80	0.83	0.83	0.79	0.73	0.82	0.82	0.80	0.78	0.77	0.88	0.85	0.82	0.83	0.84
1971	0.77	0.78	0.85	0.90	0.93	0.76	0.63	0.76	0.78	0.82	0.84	0.88	0.81	0.86	0.91	0.92
1972	0.98	0.99	1.01	1.05	0.93	1.04	0.98	1.00	0.86	1.10	1.04	0.90	1.09	0.96	1.07	1.13
1973	1.11	1.10	1.28	1.38	1.05	1.18	1.10	1.07	1.30	0.93	1.14	1.33	1.36	1.38	1.44	1.31
1974	1.56	1.79	1.76	1.79	1.51	1.61	1.56	1.95	1.74	1.69	1.76	1.78	1.75	2.00	1.68	1.69
1975	1.78	1.57	1.55	1.81	1.88	1.73	1.74	1.71	1.52	1.48	1.61	1.39	1.64	1.58	1.65	2.21
1976	1.67	2.03	2.13	2.27	1.47	1.70	1.85	1.54	2.22	2.32	2.15	2.20	2.05	2.16	2.29	2.38
1977	2.39	2.34	2.76	2.80	2.45	2.23	2.49	2.20	2.23	2.59	2.81	2.67	2.79	2.76	2.73	2.90
1978	2.76	2.84	2.91	3.26	2.50	2.95	2.83	2.95	2.79	2.80	2.74	2.83	3.17	3.22	3.32	3.22
1979	3.26	3.65	3.66	3.89	3.29	3.24	3.26	3.72	3.82	3.41	3.70	3.75	3.54	3.96	3.92	3.78
1980	4.29	4.15	4.57	4.58	4.13	4.02	4.73	4.02	3.88	4.56	4.52	4.52	4.66	4.14	4.29	5.30
1981	4.91	5.11	5.05	5.06	4.80	4.91	5.03	4.89	5.34	5.11	4.38	5.53	5.25	5.15	5.29	4.75
1982	5.44	5.15	4.78	5.58	5.33	5.97	5.02	5.27	5.01	5.16	4.54	4.90	4.92	5.39	5.75	5.61
1983	5.70	5.67	5.82	6.12	5.12	6.03	5.94	6.01	6.03	4.98	6.31	5.60	5.55	5.96	5.92	6.48

Trade balance (f.o.b. — c.i.f.) (25) — billion markkaa, monthly averages

Adjusted - Corrigé *

Balance commerciale (f.o.b. — c.a.f.) (25) — milliards de markkas, moyennes mensuelles

Year	Q.1	Q.2	Q.3	Q.4	JAN	FEB	MAR	APR	MAY	JUN	JUL	AUG	SEP	OCT	NOV	DEC
1964	-0.04	-0.06	-0.06	-0.06	-0.04	0.01	-0.08	-0.07	-0.04	-0.08	-0.03	-0.10	-0.06	-0.06	-0.06	-0.06
1965	-0.06	-0.07	-0.07	-0.03	-0.04	-0.09	-0.06	-0.06	-0.10	-0.07	-0.08	-0.05	-0.06	-0.04	-0.06	0.01
1966	-0.09	-0.04	-0.07	-0.05	-0.08	-0.10	-0.07	-0.04	-0.01	-0.07	-0.06	-0.07	-0.08	-0.06	-0.06	-0.04
1967	-0.04	-0.05	-0.04	-0.06	-0.06	-0.04	-0.02	-0.06	-0.05	-0.02	-0.06	-0.07	0.02	-0.01	-0.07	-0.09
1968	0.00	-0.00	0.04	0.02	-0.02	0.01	0.02	0.07	0.02	-0.10	0.04	0.03	0.05	0.04	0.04	-0.01
1969	-0.05	0.00	0.02	-0.03	0.00	-0.12	-0.02	0.01	0.01	-0.01	0.05	0.03	-0.03	-0.01	-0.05	-0.02
1970	-0.05	-0.09	-0.10	-0.20	0.01	-0.10	-0.04	-0.06	-0.07	-0.14	-0.14	-0.05	-0.12	-0.09	-0.13	-0.37
1971	-0.10	-0.15	-0.14	-0.19	0.01	-0.06	-0.26	-0.17	-0.19	-0.09	-0.10	-0.12	-0.21	-0.19	-0.09	-0.31
1972	-0.03	-0.12	-0.11	-0.10	-0.03	-0.01	-0.05	-0.10	-0.12	-0.15	-0.17	-0.17	0.02	-0.20	-0.13	0.03
1973	-0.21	-0.22	-0.14	-0.09	-0.25	-0.06	-0.31	-0.22	-0.07	-0.36	-0.16	-0.10	-0.16	-0.18	-0.12	0.01
1974	-0.42	-0.35	-0.54	-0.36	-0.33	-0.51	-0.41	-0.23	-0.35	-0.46	-0.43	-0.60	-0.60	-0.26	-0.56	-0.26
1975	-0.80	-0.71	-0.71	-0.41	-0.65	-1.16	-0.58	-0.57	-0.79	-0.77	-0.67	-0.95	-0.51	-0.69	-0.58	0.05
1976	-0.51	-0.15	-0.37	-0.30	-0.60	-0.54	-0.37	-0.44	0.29	-0.29	-0.42	-0.29	-0.40	-0.20	-0.29	-0.41
1977	0.01	-0.33	0.22	0.15	0.07	-0.12	0.07	-0.22	-0.17	-0.58	0.31	0.26	0.09	0.23	0.06	0.17
1978	0.12	0.13	0.31	0.41	-0.13	0.34	0.14	0.32	0.02	0.05	0.10	0.34	0.50	0.25	0.48	0.51
1979	0.08	0.17	-0.16	-0.27	-0.14	0.42	-0.03	0.32	0.30	-0.11	-0.12	0.07	-0.43	-0.04	-0.16	-0.59
1980	-0.47	-0.67	-0.61	-0.06	-0.75	-0.70	0.04	-0.73	0.15	-1.45	-0.45	-1.00	-0.39	-0.75	0.11	0.46
1981	0.08	-0.26	-0.06	-0.04	0.26	-0.14	0.11	-0.07	-0.70	-0.01	0.08	-0.21	-0.04	0.11	0.05	-0.28
1982	0.18	-0.09	-0.23	-0.41	0.06	0.55	-0.07	-0.19	0.06	-0.15	-0.45	-0.28	0.03	-0.49	-0.10	-0.65
1983	-0.13	-0.25	-0.06	-0.15	-0.66	0.32	-0.05	0.04	-0.24	-0.56	0.12	0.66	-0.95	-0.52	-0.14	0.17

* Adjusted by the O.E.C.D.

* Corrigé par l'O.C.D.E.

NOTES

1. The original base of the index is 1964 to 1975 and 1975 from 1976.
2. The original base of the index is 1959 to 1969, 1970 from 1970 to 1974, 1975 from 1975 to 1979, and 1980 from 1980.
3. Prior to 1975, the series is not adjusted for unequal number of working days in the month.
4. Machinery and transport equipment only.
5. Solid, with bark, excluding firewood.
6. Sample revision in 1968.
7. Prior to 4th quarter 1975, excluding forestry.
8. Including alterations and additions.
9. Annual and quarterly data are based on more complete information than monthly data.
10. The original base of the index is 1951 to 1965, 1964 from 1966 to 1972, 1973 from 1973 to 1979 and 1980 from 1980.
11. Sample revision in 1979.
12. Sample revision in 1969 and 1979.
13. Series adjusted for unequal number of working days in the month.
14. Monthly labour force sample survey of population aged 15 to 74. From 1982, new method of data collection; including part-time workers and the self-employed.
15. Monthly data refer to a date near mid-month.
16. Man-days lost are calculated by multiplying the length of the dispute by the number of participants on the day on which they were most numerous.
17. Survey of all enterprises affiliated with the "Finnish Employers Confederation" accounting for approximately three quarters of total employment in industry. Excluding hours paid for but not worked.
18. The original base of the index is 1975 to 1979, and 1980 from 1980.
19. Weighting pattern based on 1955-56 to 1966, on 1966 from 1967 to 1971, on 1971 from 1972 to 1976, on 1976 from 1977 to 1980, and on 1980 from 1981. Prior to 1967, the index refers to wage and salary earners only.
20. Weighted average of nominal rates on new issues. Prior to 1966, annual averages.

NOTES

1. La base originale de l'indice est 1964 jusqu'en 1975 et 1975 à partir de 1976.
2. La base originale de l'indice est 1959 jusqu'en 1969, 1970 de 1970 à 1974, 1975 de 1975 à 1979, et 1980 à partir de 1980.
3. Avant 1975, la série n'est pas corrigée de l'inégalité du nombre de jours ouvrables dans le mois.
4. La série ne couvre que les machines et le matériel de transport.
5. Volume net, non écorcé, non compris le bois de chauffage.
6. Révision de l'échantillon en 1968.
7. Avant le 4e trimestre 1975, non compris la sylviculture.
8. Y compris les transformations et les agrandissements.
9. Les données annuelles et trimestrielles sont établies à partir d'informations plus complètes que les données mensuelles.
10. La base originale de l'indice est 1951 jusqu'en 1965, 1964 de 1966 à 1972, 1973 de 1973 à 1979 et 1980 à partir de 1980.
11. Révision de l'échantillon en 1979.
12. Révision de l'échantillon en 1969 et 1979.
13. Série corrigée de l'inégalité du nombre de jours ouvrables dans le mois.
14. Enquête mensuelle par sondage auprès de la population âgée de 15 à 74 ans. A partir de 1982, nouvelle méthode de relevé des données; y compris les travailleurs à temps partiel et les travailleurs indépendants.
15. Les données mensuelles concernent une date proche du 15.
16. Le nombre de journées-homme perdues est le produit de la durée du conflit et le nombre de participants le jour de la plus forte participation.
17. Enquête de la "Confédération du patronat finlandais " auprès de ses membres, soit environ les trois quarts des effectifs dans l'industrie. Non compris les heures payées mais non ouvrées.
18. La base originale de l'indice est 1975 jusqu'en 1979, et 1980 à partir de 1980.
19. La pondération se réfère à 1955-56 jusqu'en 1966, à 1966 de 1967 à 1971, à 1971 de 1972 à 1976, à 1976 de 1977 à 1980, et à 1980 à partir de 1981. Avant 1967, l'indice se réfère aux salariés seulement.
20. Rendement nominal moyen pondéré des nouvelles émissions. Avant 1966, moyennes annuelles.

NOTES

21. The original base of the index is 1948 to 1969, 1970 from 1970 to 1974, and 1975 from 1975. Monthly data are daily averages from 1970 and averages of Fridays previously.
22. From 1975, including foreign currency deposits.
23. Prior to 1975, excluding time and savings deposits with the Central Bank.
24. Prior to 1975, seasonally adjusted by the national authorities.
25. General trade.

NOTES

21. La base originale de l'indice est 1948 jusqu'en 1969, 1970 de 1970 à 1974, et 1975 à partir de 1975. Les données mensuelles sont les moyennes journalières à partir de 1970 et les moyennes des vendredis auparavant.
22. A partir de 1975, y compris les dépôts en devises.
23. Avant 1975, non compris les dépôts à terme et d'épargne auprès de la Banque Centrale.
24. Avant 1975, série corrigée des variations saisonnières par les autorités nationales.
25. Commerce général.

MAIN SOURCES

PRINCIPALES SOURCES

Series	Séries	Sources
Indicators of domestic product	Indicateurs du produit intérieur	Central Statistical Office *Bulletin of Statistics*
Industrial production	Production industrielle	
Construction	Construction	
Labour and wages	Main-d'œuvre et salaires	
Prices	Prix	
Share prices	Cours des actions	
Credit	Crédits	
Foreign trade	Commerce extérieur	
Business surveys	Enquêtes de conjoncture	Confédération of Finnish Industries *Economic Barometer*
Internal trade	Commerce intérieur	Central Statistical Office
Official discount rate	Taux d'escompte officiel	Bank of Finland *Monthly Bulletin*
Money supply	Disponibilités monétaires	
Balance of payments	Balance des paiements	
Yield of long-term Government bonds	Rendement des bons d'État à long terme	Bank of Finland
Net foreign position of commercial banks	Position extérieure nette des banques commerciales	

France

FRANCE

Industrial production: total (1) — Production industrielle : total (1)

1980 = 100

	Year	Q.1	Q.2	Q.3	Q.4	JAN	FEB	MAR	APR	MAY	JUN	JUL	AUG	SEP	OCT	NOV	DEC
1964	56	57	59	48	59	58	59	58	59	59	59	51	32	58	59	60	58
1965	57	57	59	49	62	57	59	58	59	59	60	52	34	59	62	62	62
1966	60	60	63	52	64	60	63	63	62	62	64	57	36	63	64	65	65
1967	61	62	64	53	67	63	64	64	64	63	65	56	37	64	65	67	68
1968	63	66	58	57	73	66	68	69	69	46	58	62	41	67	72	74	75
1969	70	71	74	60	76	72	73	73	75	75	75	67	42	73	73	76	77
1970	74	75	78	64	81	77	79	79	80	77	78	69	44	77	80	80	82
1971	79	80	81	68	87	79	82	83	82	79	81	72	46	82	85	87	87
1972	84	84	86	72	91	86	86	88	87	87	87	75	53	87	91	93	94
1973	89	91	92	77	97	92	95	95	92	96	95	82	59	92	97	99	96
1974	91	96	97	80	93	98	101	98	99	99	98	86	61	93	96	95	92
1975	85	87	87	72	93	90	92	90	89	85	88	75	52	85	90	91	94
1976	92	95	95	80	100	94	96	97	96	95	97	83	58	98	97	103	100
1977	94	99	97	80	98	102	103	103	99	96	101	83	60	96	97	102	97
1978	96	98	99	81	104	99	101	103	104	99	99	84	60	98	101	106	105
1979	100	102	101	88	109	104	106	107	103	103	105	92	67	104	105	109	108
1980	100	108	102	86	105	108	110	110	108	101	103	91	64	98	101	103	106
1981	99	102	102	86	106	101	105	105	102	99	102	87	62	99	101	105	105
1982	97	102	101	83	104	101	104	105	102	99	102	85	59	96	99	103	102
1983		102	101	84		101	103	104	102	101	101	87	63	99	100	103	109

Industrial production: investment goods (1) — Production industrielle : biens d'équipement (1)

1980 = 100

	Year	Q.1	Q.2	Q.3	Q.4	JAN	FEB	MAR	APR	MAY	JUN	JUL	AUG	SEP	OCT	NOV	DEC
1964	50	50	52	43	55	46	47	48	50	50	51	47	22	48	50	51	59
1965	52	51	55	43	57	46	50	52	55	55	56	50	23	47	54	52	63
1966	54	54	57	46	59	49	53	57	56	56	61	52	25	55	56	57	65
1967	56	55	59	47	64	51	56	59	59	56	63	52	25	55	55	59	75
1968	58	57	61	51	70	53	56	61	65	37	53	58	32	60	64	71	83
1969	65	61	70	55	73	57	61	64	70	67	74	66	31	63	68	70	80
1970	70	65	74	61	80	61	66	72	75	70	76	58	47	65	73	69	96
1971	80	74	82	70	93	65	69	73	73	75	81	61	49	74	78	82	93
1972	82	78	88	71	92	72	75	82	84	83	90	69	55	81	90	84	104
1973	87	84	90	76	100	77	83	88	88	93	101	70	65	86	89	96	113
1974	94	92	100	83	103	89	91	97	97	97	104	80	69	89	100	101	115
1975	92	88	96	79	103	91	94	100	98	97	108	80	69	91	102	94	126
1976	96	98	101	82	105	96	93	102	103	103	108	84	71	96	102	108	120
1977	97	98	99	84	105	100	100	109	103	104	111	89	76	95	104	108	127
1978	98	95	103	84	111	96	98	100	105	105	111	80	70	98	102	109	133
1979	101	95	101	90	118	91	91	100	97	96	109	80	74	100	97	104	139
1980	100	99	105	87	117	84	94	99	105	91	115	82	75	92	101	105	159
1981	106	101	111	94	119	85	101	103	108	97	123	84	79	107	99	109	140
1982	103	101	106	89	117	86	102	101	108	100	114	79	72	104	97	113	145
1983		99	102	88		93	92	97	99	104	109	83	76	95	95	114	150

Industrial production: consumer goods (1) — Production industrielle : biens de consommation (1)

1980 = 100

	Year	Q.1	Q.2	Q.3	Q.4	JAN	FEB	MAR	APR	MAY	JUN	JUL	AUG	SEP	OCT	NOV	DEC
1964	54	55	58	48	56	49	51	51	52	50	50	43	21	48	49	49	47
1965	55	54	57	49	60	46	48	50	49	49	49	41	24	50	52	53	52
1966	59	59	63	53	63	51	55	55	55	55	56	50	24	55	55	58	56
1967	61	61	65	54	66	54	56	57	59	56	57	50	25	56	56	58	58
1968	63	64	59	58	72	57	60	61	60	40	49	55	29	60	65	67	63
1969	69	68	73	59	74	63	65	66	68	69	68	62	28	63	72	68	66
1970	72	71	75	63	77	68	72	71	71	70	71	63	30	70	73	73	71
1971	76	77	79	66	82	74	76	77	78	72	77	70	33	79	81	81	78
1972	80	82	84	69	86	81	82	82	83	83	82	70	39	83	86	87	86
1973	85	87	88	73	90	87	88	89	81	91	89	78	40	87	90	92	85
1974	86	90	90	74	89	91	93	89	91	92	92	79	42	87	89	88	85
1975	84	85	87	72	92	86	88	84	83	82	85	74	39	83	89	89	87
1976	91	92	94	79	99	91	93	93	95	95	96	83	42	97	100	102	96
1977	93	98	97	79	99	100	100	103	99	96	101	79	43	100	98	103	93
1978	96	99	99	82	104	97	99	103	104	101	99	87	50	101	106	109	101
1979	100	103	102	87	107	104	105	107	104	107	108	93	55	107	108	110	100
1980	100	107	102	87	104	108	110	111	109	103	106	91	54	102	105	105	97
1981	98	101	100	86	104	101	104	106	101	102	104	87	52	102	102	105	100
1982	100	102	103	87	108	103	102	109	104	105	105	88	54	106	111	112	101
1983		107	107	89		106	108	115	113	109	109	91	60	107	109	115	103

Industrial production: total (1) — Adjusted - Corrigé — **Production industrielle : total (1)**

1980 = 100

	Year	Q.1	Q.2	Q.3	Q.4	JAN	FEB	MAR	APR	MAY	JUN	JUL	AUG	SEP	OCT	NOV	DEC
1964		56	56	55	55	56	56	56	57	56	56	55	55	56	56	56	55
1965		55	56	57	58	55	56	56	56	56	57	57	57	57	59	59	59
1966		59	60	61	60	58	59	60	59	60	61	61	61	61	61	61	61
1967		61	61	62	63	61	61	61	60	61	62	62	62	63	62	63	64
1968		64	55	66	69	64	64	65	65	44	56	68	68	66	69	70	70
1969		68	71	71	72	70	69	69	71	73	72	72	72	71	74	72	72
1970		72	74	75	76	74	75	75	76	75	75	75	75	76	76	76	77
1971		77	78	80	82	76	78	78	78	77	78	79	79	81	81	82	81
1972		81	83	84	86	82	81	83	83	84	83	85	85	86	87	87	89
1973		88	88	90	91	88	89	90	88	93	91	93	93	91	92	93	90
1974		92	93	93	88	94	95	93	94	96	94	97	97	92	92	89	87
1975		84	84	84	87	86	86	84	85	82	84	83	83	84	86	85	90
1976		90	92	93	93	90	90	91	92	92	92	93	93	97	93	96	95
1977		95	94	93	93	97	96	96	94	93	97	94	94	95	93	95	93
1978		94	96	96	98	95	94	96	99	97	96	96	96	97	99	99	99
1979		97	99	103	102	98	99	100	93	101	102	105	105	102	102	102	102
1980		102	100	100	99	102	102	102	102	99	99	101	101	97	99	98	99
1981		98	99	99	99	96	99	97	96	97	99	97	97	99	93	98	99
1982		98	98	96	97	97	96	96	97	97	97	95	95	95	96	97	95
1983		98	98	98		97	96	96	96	99	97	99	99	97	96	99	99

Industrial production: investment goods (1) — Adjusted - Corrigé — **Production industrielle : biens d'équipement (1)**

1980 = 100

	Year	Q.1	Q.2	Q.3	Q.4	JAN	FEB	MAR	APR	MAY	JUN	JUL	AUG	SEP	OCT	NOV	DEC
1964		50	50	51	51	48	46	47	47	46	46	48	48	49	49	48	49
1965		51	53	51	52	48	49	50	51	51	51	50	50	48	54	49	52
1966		54	55	54	54	52	53	53	52	53	53	53	53	55	54	55	51
1967		56	56	56	58	54	57	55	55	54	55	53	53	56	54	55	62
1968		59	49	60	63	57	56	58	60	35	48	60	60	61	62	67	63
1969		62	67	65	66	62	63	62	64	65	66	65	65	64	65	67	64
1970		67	70	71	71	66	66	68	70	67	68	70	70	68	70	64	78
1971		76	77	81	83	70	70	70	69	73	72	74	74	78	75	77	76
1972		79	83	81	83	79	75	80	81	81	80	83	83	85	87	78	86
1973		85	85	88	89	81	85	85	84	90	91	88	88	89	85	90	92
1974		93	95	96	93	93	93	93	94	94	94	96	96	93	96	95	93
1975		89	93	92	95	94	97	96	95	94	98	96	96	96	98	88	101
1976		97	96	95	96	100	96	98	100	100	98	99	99	101	99	100	95
1977		97	95	98	96	104	104	106	100	102	100	106	106	100	101	101	99
1978		95	98	98	102	100	102	98	102	103	100	96	96	102	100	102	102
1979		97	96	104	106	96	95	99	94	97	97	99	99	105	96	97	105
1980		101	102	101	103	95	97	98	101	93	100	101	101	91	103	99	115
1981		104	108	108	105	98	104	103	103	100	106	105	105	104	102	103	101
1982		105	104	101	104	101	103	101	102	103	99	98	98	100	101	106	105
1983		101	100	100		109	93	97	93	106	94	103	103	92	97	106	106

Industrial production: consumer goods (1) — Adjusted - Corrigé — **Production industrielle : biens de consommation (1)**

1980 = 100

	Year	Q.1	Q.2	Q.3	Q.4	JAN	FEB	MAR	APR	MAY	JUN	JUL	AUG	SEP	OCT	NOV	DEC
1964		54	55	56	53	48	48	47	48	48	47	46	46	47	46	46	45
1965		53	54	57	57	45	45	46	46	46	46	47	47	48	49	49	50
1966		58	59	62	59	51	55	55	55	55	56	37	37	55	55	58	56
1967		60	61	63	62	54	56	57	59	56	57	38	38	56	56	58	58
1968		63	56	67	67	57	60	61	60	40	49	42	42	60	65	67	63
1969		67	69	69	69	63	65	66	68	69	68	45	45	63	72	68	66
1970		69	71	74	72	68	72	71	71	70	71	46	46	70	73	73	71
1971		75	75	78	77	74	76	77	78	72	77	51	51	79	81	81	78
1972		79	79	81	81	81	82	82	83	83	82	55	55	83	86	87	86
1973		84	84	85	84	82	82	83	76	85	84	85	85	84	84	86	82
1974		86	87	87	84	86	86	83	85	87	86	87	87	84	83	82	82
1975		81	84	84	87	81	81	79	78	78	80	81	81	80	83	82	85
1976		88	91	91	93	86	87	87	89	90	90	90	90	93	93	94	94
1977		93	94	92	93	94	94	96	93	91	96	90	90	96	92	95	92
1978		94	97	96	97	92	93	95	97	96	94	97	97	98	99	100	100
1979		98	99	102	100	99	99	99	97	102	102	103	103	103	101	101	100
1980		102	99	100	98	103	103	102	104	97	100	101	101	98	98	97	97
1981		97	98	98	99	96	97	97	96	97	98	97	97	97	96	97	99
1982		99	100	100	102	98	95	100	99	99	99	100	100	101	104	104	100
1983		103	103	102		101	101	106	107	103	102	107	107	103	101	106	102

FRANCE

Industrial production: intermediate goods (1) — **Production industrielle** : biens intermédiaires (1)

1980 = 100

	Year	Q.1	Q.2	Q.3	Q.4	JAN	FEB	MAR	APR	MAY	JUN	JUL	AUG	SEP	OCT	NOV	DEC
1964	60	62	65	51	63	63	66	65	68	68	68	58	36	65	67	67	62
1965	61	61	64	52	65	61	64	64	65	66	68	59	37	66	68	68	65
1966	64	65	68	55	68	63	68	69	69	70	72	63	39	70	71	70	68
1967	64	66	68	55	69	67	69	69	68	69	72	62	39	71	72	72	69
1968	67	70	62	60	77	69	73	74	75	52	66	67	43	75	80	80	78
1969	76	77	81	65	80	78	79	80	83	84	84	72	47	81	85	83	79
1970	79	81	84	66	84	82	86	85	88	87	86	73	48	84	86	86	80
1971	82	83	86	69	88	81	86	87	87	87	88	76	50	89	90	89	86
1972	86	88	91	73	94	87	90	92	93	93	94	80	54	94	95	97	95
1973	93	96	98	79	99	95	100	101	104	103	103	88	61	99	103	102	94
1974	95	102	103	82	93	104	108	106	108	110	108	93	64	102	101	96	87
1975	82	88	87	68	87	89	93	91	90	86	91	74	49	86	88	90	86
1976	92	94	97	80	97	90	95	98	98	99	103	85	57	101	99	101	92
1977	93	100	99	78	94	97	102	103	100	98	105	84	56	93	95	97	86
1978	95	100	101	79	99	95	99	102	104	102	105	87	57	101	102	103	95
1979	101	103	105	87	108	96	103	107	104	106	110	96	65	108	107	109	102
1980	100	112	105	83	99	107	112	111	111	106	107	94	61	101	101	100	90
1981	96	101	101	82	101	94	101	103	102	101	104	88	57	101	100	101	93
1982	94	99	101	79	96	95	100	101	102	102	103	85	53	95	97	96	86
1983		99	100	81		92	96	98	98	98	101	86	53	98	97	99	90

Industrial production: manufacturing — **Production industrielle** : industries manufacturières

1980 = 100

	Year	Q.1	Q.2	Q.3	Q.4	JAN	FEB	MAR	APR	MAY	JUN	JUL	AUG	SEP	OCT	NOV	DEC
1964	55	56	58	46	58	55	57	57	58	56	58	51	31	57	58	58	57
1965	56	57	58	48	61	55	58	57	58	58	59	52	33	57	61	61	60
1966	59	61	62	51	64	58	62	62	61	61	63	57	35	62	63	64	64
1967	60	62	63	52	65	61	63	63	63	61	64	56	36	63	64	65	66
1968	63	66	67	56	73	63	66	68	68	45	57	62	39	66	72	73	73
1969	71	72	75	60	76	71	72	72	75	75	75	67	41	72	77	75	75
1970	75	77	78	63	80	75	78	78	79	77	78	68	44	77	80	80	81
1971	78	80	81	67	86	78	82	82	82	79	82	71	47	82	85	86	86
1972	85	86	88	72	93	84	85	87	88	88	88	76	53	88	92	93	94
1973	91	94	96	79	98	91	94	95	92	98	97	83	59	94	98	99	95
1974	94	100	100	81	95	98	101	99	100	100	100	87	61	95	97	95	92
1975	85	89	88	71	91	89	90	88	88	85	90	75	51	86	90	90	93
1976	93	94	97	80	100	92	95	96	97	97	99	84	58	99	98	102	99
1977	95	102	99	80	98	100	102	104	99	96	103	84	60	97	97	101	96
1978	96	99	102	82	104	97	99	102	104	100	101	86	60	99	102	105	104
1979	101	103	105	89	106	100	103	106	102	104	108	93	68	105	105	108	106
1980	100	107	106	85	102	104	108	109	109	102	106	91	65	99	101	102	103
1981	96	100	101	83	101	96	101	102	101	99	104	86	62	101	100	102	102
1982	95	99	101	80	100	95	99	101	101	100	103	84	59	97	99	102	99
1983	95	97	100	82	100	95	97	100	99	100	102	86	61	93	97	103	103

Industrial production: energy (1) — **Production industrielle** : énergie (1)

1980 = 100

	Year	Q.1	Q.2	Q.3	Q.4	JAN	FEB	MAR	APR	MAY	JUN	JUL	AUG	SEP	OCT	NOV	DEC
1964	57	60	55	50	62	62	60	57	56	55	55	50	43	57	60	62	63
1965	60	62	58	54	65	65	64	59	59	58	58	53	48	61	63	67	67
1966	62	64	60	56	67	67	65	61	60	60	60	56	50	62	63	69	70
1967	65	68	62	59	71	71	68	64	63	61	62	57	53	67	67	72	74
1968	66	72	57	61	74	74	72	70	68	45	59	61	55	65	70	74	77
1969	72	75	69	64	78	78	77	71	71	69	66	65	56	72	75	78	83
1970	77	82	74	67	84	85	82	81	78	73	72	67	61	75	80	84	89
1971	80	87	76	68	88	88	88	86	81	75	72	65	62	76	82	90	93
1972	85	90	81	75	95	93	90	87	84	82	77	74	69	81	91	97	99
1973	91	97	88	81	100	101	99	93	92	89	84	80	76	87	96	102	102
1974	90	99	87	81	95	99	102	95	91	86	84	82	77	84	93	95	96
1975	84	91	80	72	94	94	92	88	86	77	76	74	64	79	87	93	103
1976	91	100	83	82	101	101	103	96	90	81	79	78	76	91	88	105	109
1977	92	105	87	80	101	113	108	99	93	84	87	82	73	84	91	105	107
1978	95	106	90	80	103	112	110	103	101	88	83	78	75	87	93	104	111
1979	101	116	94	88	106	123	119	110	101	94	90	87	84	92	97	102	112
1980	100	114	91	85	109	118	113	110	100	93	87	87	78	88	95	110	121
1981	99	114	90	83	109	120	119	105	97	91	85	83	75	89	98	108	117
1982	94	110	83	78	100	117	111	106	97	86	85	81	69	79	88	99	111
1983		107	88	81		110	113	100	94	91	84	81	74	85	91	102	120

Industrial production: intermediate goods (1) — Production industrielle : biens intermédiaires (1)

1980 = 100

Adjusted - Corrigé

	Year	Q.1	Q.2	Q.3	Q.4	JAN	FEB	MAR	APR	MAY	JUN	JUL	AUG	SEP	OCT	NOV	DEC
1964		60	61	60	60	62	63	63	64	64	63	62	62	62	63	63	61
1965		59	60	61	62	61	61	61	61	61	63	63	63	63	64	64	64
1966		63	64	65	65	63	65	65	65	65	66	67	67	67	67	66	67
1967		64	63	65	65	66	65	66	64	65	67	67	67	67	67	68	68
1968		68	53	70	73	69	69	70	70	49	61	73	73	71	75	76	77
1969		74	76	76	76	77	75	76	77	79	79	79	79	78	80	79	78
1970		78	78	78	80	81	81	80	82	81	80	80	80	81	81	82	80
1971		80	80	82	84	80	82	82	82	81	83	83	83	85	86	85	86
1972		84	86	87	89	86	85	87	88	87	88	89	89	90	90	92	94
1973		92	94	95	95	93	95	95	94	97	96	98	98	95	98	98	94
1974		98	99	98	87	103	102	100	101	103	100	104	104	98	96	92	88
1975		83	81	80	84	87	87	85	85	81	84	81	81	82	84	86	87
1976		88	91	92	94	89	89	92	92	93	95	94	94	97	94	96	94
1977		94	93	91	90	96	96	96	93	93	96	93	93	93	92	93	88
1978		94	97	94	97	93	93	95	98	97	96	95	95	96	97	98	97
1979		97	100	104	104	94	96	98	98	100	100	106	106	103	102	104	105
1980		104	99	98	96	106	105	103	103	100	98	101	101	97	97	95	94
1981		95	95	97	97	94	95	96	95	95	95	95	95	97	96	96	96
1982		95	96	91	93	94	94	94	95	95	95	91	91	91	92	92	90
1983		95	94	94		92	91	91	91	91	93	92	92	93	92	95	93

Industrial production: manufacturing — Production industrielle : industries manufacturières

1980 = 100

Adjusted - Corrigé

	Year	Q.1	Q.2	Q.3	Q.4	JAN	FEB	MAR	APR	MAY	JUN	JUL	AUG	SEP	OCT	NOV	DEC
1964		54	55	54	55	54	54	54	55	56	54	54	54	55	55	55	54
1965		54	55	56	57	55	54	54	55	55	55	56	56	56	58	57	57
1966		58	59	61	60	57	59	59	58	59	60	60	60	61	60	60	60
1967		60	60	61	61	60	59	60	59	59	60	60	60	62	60	61	62
1968		63	54	66	69	62	63	64	64	43	54	67	67	64	68	69	69
1969		69	71	71	72	69	68	68	70	73	71	72	72	70	73	71	71
1970		74	74	74	76	73	74	74	75	74	74	74	74	75	76	75	76
1971		77	77	79	81	76	77	77	77	76	78	78	78	81	80	81	81
1972		82	83	85	88	82	81	83	83	84	84	85	85	86	87	88	89
1973		90	91	93	92	89	89	91	87	94	92	94	94	92	93	94	90
1974		95	95	96	90	96	96	94	95	96	95	98	98	93	92	89	88
1975		85	83	84	86	86	86	84	84	81	84	83	83	84	86	84	89
1976		90	93	95	95	90	90	91	92	93	93	93	93	97	94	96	95
1977		97	94	94	93	97	97	97	94	93	97	94	94	94	93	95	92
1978		95	97	95	99	94	94	95	99	97	95	95	95	97	98	99	100
1979		99	100	104	101	99	98	99	97	101	101	104	104	103	102	101	101
1980		103	101	99	97	103	103	102	103	99	100	101	101	97	98	97	98
1981		96	96	96	96	95	96	96	96	95	97	95	95	97	96	97	96
1982		95	96	93	95	95	95	95	96	96	96	92	92	94	96	96	93
1983		94	95	95	96	95	93	95	94	96	95	95	95	95	94	97	96

Industrial production: energy (1) — Production industrielle : énergie (1)

1980 = 100

Adjusted - Corrigé

	Year	Q.1	Q.2	Q.3	Q.4	JAN	FEB	MAR	APR	MAY	JUN	JUL	AUG	SEP	OCT	NOV	DEC
1964		56	56	56	58	56	56	57	57	57	57	56	56	57	59	58	57
1965		58	60	60	61	58	59	58	59	59	61	60	60	61	61	62	61
1966		60	62	63	63	60	61	60	61	62	63	63	63	63	62	63	64
1967		63	64	66	66	64	62	63	64	63	66	66	66	67	66	66	67
1968		67	59	69	69	66	66	68	68	47	63	70	70	67	68	69	69
1969		70	71	73	73	69	71	69	71	73	71	72	72	74	73	71	75
1970		76	77	77	78	75	75	78	77	76	78	76	76	78	78	77	79
1971		80	79	78	81	78	80	82	80	78	79	76	76	80	79	83	83
1972		82	84	86	88	83	82	83	83	85	84	85	85	86	88	88	88
1973		89	92	93	92	90	89	89	91	94	92	93	93	92	93	93	91
1974		90	91	93	87	88	92	91	90	92	92	95	95	90	91	87	85
1975		84	84	83	86	84	81	83	85	83	84	83	83	85	87	85	91
1976		91	88	94	92	88	90	90	90	87	88	92	92	99	88	96	96
1977		97	93	91	93	97	95	92	92	91	97	94	94	92	92	96	94
1978		95	96	93	96	95	95	94	100	95	93	92	92	95	96	95	98
1979		102	101	103	99	103	102	102	100	102	102	103	103	102	100	100	99
1980		99	99	100	101	98	98	101	99	101	99	101	101	99	99	101	104
1981		99	98	98	99	100	103	96	96	98	99	98	98	100	101	98	99
1982		97	96	92	91	97	96	96	97	93	99	94	94	91	91	90	93
1983		93	96	96		92	97	90	93	98	97	96	96	98	94	93	101

FRANCE

Industrial production: construction

1980 = 100

Production industrielle : construction

1980 = 100

	Year	Q.1	Q.2	Q.3	Q.4	JAN	FEB	MAR	APR	MAY	JUN	JUL	AUG	SEP	OCT	NOV	DEC
1964	88	81	95	86	93	73	83	86	96	94	95	94	68	97	97	96	85
1965	94	84	103	91	98	81	80	91	100	103	105	98	73	102	102	98	94
1966	98	91	107	94	100	78	92	101	105	108	107	102	74	107	105	102	94
1967	101	95	110	97	104	87	93	105	109	112	109	103	78	109	109	107	95
1968	101	98	103	97	105	94	97	104	110	97	102	103	82	107	113	105	98
1969	106	98	115	103	107	99	88	108	115	117	112	112	81	116	117	113	91
1970	109	102	119	105	112	99	100	105	120	119	119	114	82	120	120	113	103
1971	106	97	114	102	112	89	100	101	114	110	117	111	80	117	116	110	109
1972	109	106	113	101	111	102	106	109	122	116	115	107	82	114	112	113	106
1973	108	107	118	102	106	98	114	109	120	117	117	107	83	116	110	114	93
1974	110	112	122	99	108	104	118	114	121	119	126	105	80	114	110	115	98
1975	104	108	115	93	101	100	116	109	112	116	116	103	70	106	108	105	90
1976	104	103	116	92	104	97	109	104	116	115	116	101	68	106	110	114	89
1977	103	106	112	92	102	100	113	106	111	113	111	102	69	106	107	110	87
1978	99	98	108	88	101	96	96	102	109	107	107	96	67	101	107	107	90
1979	98	94	109	88	102	77	105	98	111	106	109	99	58	107	105	107	94
1980	100	102	111	87	101	93	109	104	111	106	113	99	57	106	105	110	87
1981	100	102	113	85	101	94	108	106	112	114	112	98	53	105	102	113	88
1982	95	100	107	80	94	93	109	98	106	112	104	92	50	99	100	105	76
1983	91	93	100	78	91	93	92	94	99	102	100	90	47	95	99	102	73

Production: passenger cars (2)(3)

thousands, monthly averages

Production : voitures de tourisme (2)(3)

milliers, moyennes mensuelles

	Year	Q.1	Q.2	Q.3	Q.4	JAN	FEB	MAR	APR	MAY	JUN	JUL	AUG	SEP	OCT	NOV	DEC
1964	139.7	131.1	127.0	77.4	103.4	139.0	125.5	128.7	137.1	111.0	133.1	110.9	9.2	112.0	104.7	97.0	108.5
1965	114.5	110.1	119.5	90.1	138.2	104.6	106.1	119.7	115.0	115.6	128.0	87.4	45.4	137.5	130.4	130.8	153.4
1966	146.8	154.5	165.2	112.5	155.0	141.4	150.1	171.9	157.3	158.2	179.6	159.2	12.8	165.3	153.9	151.4	159.8
1967	146.0	160.7	159.3	102.5	161.5	163.7	150.6	167.8	158.5	150.5	168.8	139.1	12.5	155.8	164.3	162.6	157.6
1968	152.7	177.2	115.3	127.1	191.4	179.4	174.0	178.0	180.8	96.0	69.2	191.5	20.1	169.6	208.1	175.2	190.9
1969	180.5	186.2	198.8	136.4	201.4	195.2	180.4	183.0	207.5	190.1	198.7	211.7	8.7	188.8	226.7	174.1	203.5
1970	204.8	213.5	220.9	152.8	232.1	213.3	204.4	222.7	234.6	189.3	238.9	47.9	186.1	224.4	236.6	217.6	242.1
1971	224.5	239.8	226.1	176.4	255.7	225.5	230.9	263.1	248.4	167.6	262.2	249.6	19.2	260.5	255.2	245.5	266.3
1972	249.4	270.5	265.1	180.4	281.7	264.8	259.7	286.9	245.3	262.0	288.0	203.5	71.0	266.5	293.0	279.8	272.3
1973	266.9	294.0	268.1	208.2	297.2	297.6	275.3	309.1	197.9	308.2	298.0	284.1	56.5	284.1	332.9	305.0	253.6
1974	253.6	286.2	275.2	189.5	263.5	305.1	269.6	283.9	284.8	283.8	257.1	295.5	20.9	252.0	301.9	245.2	243.4
1975	245.9	246.7	258.2	190.9	287.9	272.0	243.8	224.4	243.7	248.4	282.5	284.5	22.7	265.3	316.6	254.2	293.0
1976	293.6	288.9	302.8	214.5	323.1	288.4	261.0	317.4	306.7	291.2	310.6	299.7	19.1	324.6	320.5	307.7	341.0
1977	296.7	330.4	317.6	221.6	316.7	323.3	310.3	357.5	307.1	299.7	345.9	221.0	109.3	334.3	318.3	318.0	313.8
1978	301.6	324.5	316.6	226.1	339.4	331.6	301.3	340.6	319.8	312.8	317.1	256.6	100.1	321.6	357.2	348.8	312.3
1979	310.8	332.7	328.1	250.2	332.4	335.0	306.3	356.8	302.8	351.1	330.3	..	427.6	323.1	369.6	349.9	277.6
1980	290.6	340.9	311.0	222.4	288.2	361.5	322.4	338.8	333.3	282.2	317.5	..	359.9	307.3	332.0	265.8	266.9
1981	246.1	266.8	254.2	192.4	271.0	272.5	250.2	277.7	233.6	239.9	289.2	235.5	65.3	276.0	275.2	257.7	280.2
1982	257.2	274.6	256.3	199.8	297.6	263.8	248.4	311.6	265.5	242.2	262.7	230.8	75.1	293.4	308.6	295.4	288.7
1983	269.0	257.3	296.2	206.8	275.7	263.2	280.3	343.5	293.4	283.5	311.7	225.3	109.1	286.1	278.7	296.7	251.6

Production: commercial vehicles (3)

thousands, monthly averages

Production : véhicules utilitaires (3)

milliers, moyennes mensuelles

	Year	Q.1	Q.2	Q.3	Q.4	JAN	FEB	MAR	APR	MAY	JUN	JUL	AUG	SEP	OCT	NOV	DEC
1964	22.1	24.3	23.1	15.9	25.2	26.0	23.4	23.6	25.3	20.3	23.8	21.1	2.4	24.2	25.5	26.3	23.8
1965	20.2	22.8	21.3	14.4	22.3	20.1	22.8	25.6	22.3	20.9	20.7	14.5	7.8	20.8	21.3	21.2	24.3
1966	21.9	23.9	23.7	16.6	23.5	23.6	23.3	24.7	22.9	22.6	25.5	23.3	2.7	23.7	22.5	23.9	24.2
1967	21.5	23.6	22.7	16.0	23.7	24.4	21.9	24.6	21.2	21.2	25.7	21.5	2.3	24.2	23.8	24.1	23.2
1968	20.2	22.5	15.1	17.5	25.9	22.6	21.8	23.2	23.1	13.3	9.0	24.0	4.6	23.7	28.6	23.5	25.5
1969	24.2	24.6	26.9	18.0	27.5	26.3	24.1	23.3	27.7	25.5	27.3	28.4	2.1	23.6	30.1	24.4	28.1
1970	24.4	27.7	24.6	18.2	27.1	28.9	26.4	27.9	27.4	21.3	25.0	9.1	19.5	25.9	27.6	24.8	29.0
1971	26.4	27.0	24.9	22.6	31.0	26.2	25.5	29.2	26.0	19.6	28.9	32.1	2.9	33.0	29.9	29.8	33.3
1972	28.0	31.4	29.3	20.3	30.8	30.2	30.8	33.2	27.4	28.4	32.0	19.6	11.7	29.3	30.3	31.9	30.4
1973	32.8	34.0	33.8	24.3	39.1	31.3	33.0	37.7	28.3	36.0	37.1	36.0	5.7	31.3	42.7	40.3	34.3
1974	34.8	39.3	39.0	24.4	36.6	41.9	37.4	38.5	42.5	38.6	35.9	37.0	3.0	33.3	42.1	35.3	32.4
1975	28.9	32.5	24.6	19.8	38.4	34.0	32.7	30.8	33.8	22.9	17.2	25.7	1.9	31.8	41.4	33.3	40.4
1976	38.7	41.2	41.9	26.2	42.2	41.4	37.9	44.2	44.6	39.8	41.5	37.4	3.1	38.2	41.0	40.5	45.2
1977	34.2	41.3	39.9	28.0	41.2	40.7	38.3	44.9	37.8	37.7	44.2	30.5	10.1	43.4	41.8	40.5	41.2
1978	37.4	41.9	42.3	24.8	40.5	39.5	40.4	45.6	42.0	40.6	44.4	21.8	12.5	40.0	42.3	41.0	38.2
1979	38.5	41.8	40.0	29.1	43.3	41.3	39.3	44.7	38.9	41.6	39.6	..	46.9	40.2	46.0	45.0	38.9
1980	41.8	45.8	44.8	29.8	46.6	45.7	46.3	45.5	49.2	40.7	44.6	..	42.7	46.6	49.5	43.4	47.0
1981	39.5	42.5	43.1	29.6	43.6	40.6	39.8	44.2	41.0	42.2	46.0	38.3	7.3	43.3	42.6	43.3	44.8
1982	38.8	41.6	43.4	28.3	41.9	40.4	36.7	47.8	42.5	41.0	46.6	38.3	5.8	40.9	43.3	41.0	41.5
1983	38.7	37.0	47.3	30.2	40.2	32.9	28.0	50.1	45.3	45.5	51.1	34.9	12.5	43.2	39.3	43.6	37.6

Industrial production: construction / Production industrielle : construction

1980 = 100

Adjusted - Corrigé

	Year	Q.1	Q.2	Q.3	Q.4	JAN	FEB	MAR	APR	MAY	JUN	JUL	AUG	SEP	OCT	NOV	DEC
1964		86	87	89	91	83	88	86	88	85	87	89	89	91	90	93	91
1965		89	94	95	97	91	65	91	92	94	97	94	94	96	95	95	101
1966		95	98	99	99	88	98	100	97	98	99	98	98	100	98	98	101
1967		100	101	101	102	98	99	103	100	102	101	101	101	102	101	104	101
1968		103	95	102	103	105	103	103	102	89	95	104	104	100	105	101	104
1969		103	106	108	105	109	93	107	106	108	105	108	108	103	108	109	98
1970		106	110	111	111	108	105	106	110	110	111	110	110	112	112	109	110
1971		101	105	108	111	97	103	102	104	103	108	108	108	110	110	106	117
1972		109	103	108	111	111	107	109	111	108	106	108	108	107	108	109	116
1973		108	108	110	106	106	111	109	109	108	108	110	110	110	106	109	102
1974		112	112	109	103	112	113	112	110	110	115	108	108	109	105	109	109
1975		108	105	103	101	107	109	107	101	107	106	104	104	103	104	99	101
1976		103	106	102	104	104	102	102	105	105	106	102	102	103	105	106	102
1977		105	102	104	101	106	106	104	101	104	101	104	104	102	102	102	99
1978		97	98	99	101	102	90	100	99	99	97	100	100	97	101	99	102
1979		92	99	99	102	82	98	96	100	98	99	97	97	102	99	100	107
1980		101	100	100	99	100	101	101	100	98	102	100	100	100	100	100	99
1981		101	101	100	99	101	99	103	101	102	101	100	100	100	96	101	100
1982		98	96	95	91	99	99	95	96	99	94	96	96	95	94	93	86
1983		92	90	93	88	100	84	92	90	90	91	94	94	91	92	90	82

Production: passenger cars (2) / Production : voitures de tourisme (2)

thousands, monthly averages / milliers, moyennes mensuelles

Adjusted - Corrigé *

	Year	Q.1	Q.2	Q.3	Q.4	JAN	FEB	MAR	APR	MAY	JUN	JUL	AUG	SEP	OCT	NOV	DEC
1964		120.5	114.8	103.2	98.5	126.4	121.7	113.5	126.5	101.8	116.1	102.4	103.3	104.0	99.2	96.2	100.1
1965		100.3	108.2	118.0	131.0	95.5	101.8	105.3	105.7	107.9	110.8	113.0	113.8	127.3	122.8	129.5	140.7
1966		141.3	149.4	150.5	146.2	129.5	143.2	151.1	144.0	149.3	155.0	148.2	149.3	154.1	142.8	149.6	146.3
1967		147.0	144.4	136.7	151.3	149.9	143.3	147.9	143.4	143.8	146.0	130.9	132.0	147.1	149.2	160.0	144.7
1968		162.6	104.8	176.1	177.7	164.0	166.0	157.8	161.8	92.5	60.2	182.5	184.2	161.7	185.7	171.8	175.7
1969		171.0	181.2	187.3	185.8	178.2	172.0	162.8	185.6	184.6	173.4	190.0	191.5	180.5	199.8	170.0	187.6
1970		196.0	201.6	206.2	213.9	195.1	195.5	197.3	211.2	183.7	210.0	201.3	203.0	214.3	207.0	210.8	223.8
1971		220.2	206.5	237.1	235.3	206.7	221.7	232.2	226.8	162.0	230.8	230.6	232.1	248.5	222.1	236.1	247.6
1972		248.4	244.6	241.6	258.3	242.1	250.9	252.1	228.0	251.7	254.1	234.3	235.5	255.0	253.2	267.2	254.6
1973		270.1	248.0	284.2	271.3	270.7	268.2	271.3	186.9	294.3	262.8	289.0	290.1	273.6	285.3	290.2	238.4
1974		263.1	256.4	259.8	239.6	275.8	264.5	249.0	271.3	270.5	227.3	267.2	268.1	244.1	257.4	232.4	229.1
1975		227.4	239.8	259.0	261.9	245.0	240.7	196.3	231.8	237.4	250.3	259.9	260.4	256.8	270.1	239.3	276.4
1976		264.3	283.2	284.4	294.2	259.6	257.7	275.5	292.3	280.7	276.6	270.1	270.8	312.2	274.9	287.0	320.7
1977		302.0	298.7	293.1	287.7	290.9	306.1	309.0	293.2	292.0	310.8	280.4	280.7	318.1	273.5	293.8	295.8
1978		295.6	301.6	301.2	307.4	297.9	295.6	293.5	307.6	309.0	288.1	301.1	300.8	301.8	307.2	320.3	294.7
1979		302.9	316.0	337.4	300.2	300.9	300.2	307.6	291.8	351.5	304.7	357.2	356.0	298.9	316.4	321.0	263.2
1980		310.9	301.8	291.1	260.4	325.6	316.4	290.6	323.3	286.1	296.0	296.8	295.9	280.8	283.0	244.8	253.3
1981		243.3	247.8	247.4	246.2	246.6	246.8	236.6	226.4	245.6	271.4	246.6	245.9	249.8	234.0	238.7	266.0
1982		249.9	251.3	254.0	270.4	240.2	246.1	263.4	257.8	249.3	246.8	249.5	248.7	263.8	262.3	275.2	273.8
1983		270.8	290.0	266.7	250.9	240.6	278.2	293.7	234.3	292.2	293.5	272.2	271.3	256.4	236.9	277.2	238.5

Production: crude steel / Production : acier brut

thousand tons, monthly averages / milliers de tonnes, moyennes mensuelles

	Year	Q.1	Q.2	Q.3	Q.4	JAN	FEB	MAR	APR	MAY	JUN	JUL	AUG	SEP	OCT	NOV	DEC
1964																	
1965																	
1966																	
1967																	
1968																	
1969	1876	1943	1950	1615	1996	2024	1835	1971	1901	1965	1985	1546	1321	1987	2007	1939	2041
1970	1981	2100	2072	1746	2006	2196	1994	2111	2127	2035	2005	1780	1386	2072	2127	1964	1927
1971	1905	2064	1855	1664	2038	2127	1957	2107	1979	1801	1784	1553	1434	2004	2109	1999	2005
1972	2005	2062	2066	1761	2129	2062	2023	2101	1970	2166	2062	1623	1591	2068	2210	2113	2065
1973	2105	2220	2153	1788	2260	2227	2103	2330	2078	2176	2205	1672	1663	2029	2259	2251	2269
1974	2252	2390	2206	2047	2364	2466	2296	2408	2253	2416	1948	1978	1755	2408	2420	2401	2272
1975	1795	2041	1813	1559	1763	2236	1905	1981	1994	1439	2005	1417	1339	1921	1779	1846	1678
1976	1936	1887	1992	1848	2015	1721	1728	2213	1866	2165	1945	1769	1498	2277	2161	2091	1792
1977	1842	1898	2009	1697	1764	1788	1778	2129	1846	2018	2164	1659	1385	2046	2014	1795	1492
1978	1904	1960	2139	1677	1838	1752	1897	2231	2231	2155	2030	1773	1366	1893	1890	1839	1785
1979	1947	2029	1707	1865	2187	1979	1941	2167	1329	1734	2057	1960	1551	2085	2308	2192	2060
1980	1930	2259	2103	1730	1630	2238	2187	2351	2190	2096	2022	1985	1428	1778	1706	1664	1520
1981	1763	1783	1894	1680	1697	1748	1712	1890	1843	1977	1861	1726	1449	1864	1738	1649	1704
1982	1535	1782	1743	1238	1372	1798	1531	1918	1768	1840	1637	1430	965	1319	1580	1391	1144
1983	1468	1419	1531	1288	1634	1357	1282	1618	1433	1560	1599	1447	817	1599	1674	1644	1584

* Adjusted by the O.E.C.D. / * Corrigé par l'O.C.D.E.

FRANCE

Ships completed / Navires achevés

thousand gross register tons, quarterly averages / milliers de tonneaux de jauge brute, moyennes trimestrielles

	Year	Q.1	Q.2	Q.3	Q.4	JAN	FEB	MAR	APR	MAY	JUN	JUL	AUG	SEP	OCT	NOV	DEC
1964	133	165	77	89	200												
1965	121	121	132	108	125												
1966	110	68	158	73	143												
1967	105	73	168	94	85												
1968	158	161	203	41	225												
1969	173	54	242	130	245												
1970	215	224	146	224	184												
1971	272	224	376	83	373												
1972	258	270	320	278	161												
1973	293	490	300	159	222												
1974	262	295	338	211	199												
1975	287	455	302	280	111												
1976	418	409	387	140	735												
1977	277	133	215	203	286												
1978	110	134	162	20	84												
1979	180	137	175	49	360												
1980	71	85	44	75	46												
1981	125	75	42	251	130												
1982	66	58	76	122	21												
1983	77	115	98	59	34												

Construction permits issued: residential / Permis de construire délivrés : bâtiments résidentiels

thousands / milliers

	Year	Q.1	Q.2	Q.3	Q.4	JAN	FEB	MAR	APR	MAY	JUN	JUL	AUG	SEP	OCT	NOV	DEC
1964	575	122	137	129	183	40	39	43	48	42	48	51	33	44	68	47	73
1965	598	129	139	136	194	39	45	46	44	45	51	42	44	50	53	58	83
1966	510	120	134	123	133	41	36	42	48	37	49	44	41	33	42	44	47
1967	466	109	120	114	124	32	36	41	38	42	40	41	36	37	37	40	47
1968	556	108	117	135	197	35	31	42	36	37	45	46	47	41	54	57	85
1969	585	123	137	159	166	42	37	44	41	44	52	56	45	58	54	43	69
1970	593	129	146	138	180	36	45	48	46	42	57	45	42	51	39	43	98
1971	667	151	161	152	204	38	46	67	46	48	67	52	48	52	53	60	91
1972	637	141	152	147	200	48	44	49	43	54	56	50	47	50	60	68	72
1973	670	161	150	171	188	..	..	..	..	..	..	..	..	..	..	..	..
1974	628	159	155	166	154	53	50	56	37	60	59	70	46	51	50	49	55
1975	542	123	131	137	150	34	49	40	39	47	46	40	51	47	49	46	56
1976	576	146	141	142	146	49	45	52	49	46	46	46	47	49	46	40	60
1977	503	133	118	123	129	41	40	52	34	41	43	35	44	45	42	39	49
1978	469	113	113	112	131	37	38	39	37	36	41	35	40	38	45	41	45
1979	464	109	112	117	125	33	38	39	32	40	40	42	37	38	39	44	42
1980	503	118	118	126	141	36	41	42	37	37	44	44	40	42	48	42	52
1981	489	125	120	122	122	42	39	45	38	40	42	42	42	38	44	38	40
1982	425	113	91	104	117	33	41	39	26	28	37	30	35	39	37	35	46
1983	93	96	95	89	92	32	29	35	29	30	36	29	30	30	29	30	33

Construction: housing starts / Construction : logements mis en chantier

thousands, monthly averages / milliers, moyennes mensuelles

	Year	Q.1	Q.2	Q.3	Q.4	JAN	FEB	MAR	APR	MAY	JUN	JUL	AUG	SEP	OCT	NOV	DEC
1964	35.8	32.6	34.5	36.2	39.8	32.6	32.6	32.6	34.5	34.5	34.5	36.2	36.2	36.2	39.8	39.8	39.3
1965	37.1	34.6	38.8	35.4	39.5	34.6	34.6	34.6	38.8	38.8	38.8	35.4	35.4	35.4	39.5	39.5	39.5
1966	35.4	31.2	36.3	33.1	41.1	31.2	31.2	31.2	36.3	36.3	36.3	33.1	33.1	33.1	41.1	41.1	41.1
1967	36.3	36.8	36.8	32.3	39.4	36.8	36.8	36.8	36.8	36.8	36.8	32.3	32.3	32.3	39.4	39.4	39.4
1968	36.2	34.1	32.6	33.4	44.6	34.1	34.1	34.1	32.6	32.6	32.6	33.4	33.4	33.4	44.6	44.6	44.6
1969	41.6	37.0	43.6	37.3	48.6	37.0	37.0	37.0	43.6	43.6	43.6	37.3	37.3	37.3	48.6	48.6	48.6
1970	40.1	31.7	43.6	38.1	47.1	31.7	31.7	31.7	43.6	43.6	43.6	38.1	38.1	38.1	47.1	47.1	47.1
1971	43.1	37.3	47.6	38.2	49.1	37.3	37.3	37.3	47.6	47.6	47.6	38.2	38.2	38.2	49.1	49.1	49.1
1972	46.3	42.8	47.7	38.2	56.4	42.8	42.8	42.8	47.7	47.7	47.7	38.2	38.2	38.2	56.4	56.4	56.4
1973	46.3	44.1	47.4	36.5	57.3	44.1	44.1	44.1	47.4	47.4	47.4	36.5	36.5	36.5	57.3	57.3	57.3
1974	46.0	45.4	49.7	43.5	45.2	39.4	35.4	61.5	31.0	45.0	73.1	34.5	32.6	63.3	25.9	36.1	73.6
1975	43.1	43.5	46.2	39.3	43.5	41.8	35.5	53.1	41.9	45.7	50.9	42.0	32.0	43.8	43.6	39.6	47.3
1976	41.1	40.1	44.4	36.9	42.9	37.1	35.8	47.5	40.0	41.6	51.6	36.7	31.5	42.5	38.6	36.8	52.9
1977	39.5	42.9	40.5	37.1	37.6	32.7	38.8	57.2	35.7	39.4	46.5	36.6	33.2	41.5	35.4	33.0	44.5
1978	36.7	34.4	37.9	34.9	39.6	30.5	32.5	40.1	33.4	37.5	42.7	31.4	33.9	39.3	39.4	36.6	42.9
1979	35.9	37.3	34.6	33.3	38.3	42.4	32.1	37.4	28.6	35.7	39.4	34.9	28.9	36.0	38.4	42.1	34.5
1980	33.5	34.7	32.1	31.1	36.1	29.3	37.2	37.6	29.3	30.4	36.5	30.3	26.4	36.5	36.4	33.9	38.1
1981	33.3	34.1	33.3	31.4	34.4	31.0	34.0	37.3	30.5	33.2	36.1	31.6	29.9	32.7	38.0	32.2	33.0
1982	28.6	28.3	26.9	25.5	33.8	26.1	29.3	29.7	27.8	32.3	20.6	26.0	26.0	24.4	33.9	33.0	34.5
1983	27.7	27.0	28.1	25.3	30.4	27.8	30.4	22.8	26.1	25.2	32.9	25.3	20.9	29.8	30.9	30.5	29.7

Cost of construction: multiple dwellings / Coût de la construction : immeubles résidentiels

1980 = 100

	Year	Q.1	Q.2	Q.3	Q.4	JAN	FEB	MAR	APR	MAY	JUN	JUL	AUG	SEP	OCT	NOV	DEC
1964	30.1	29.2	29.7	30.4	31.1												
1965	31.8	31.4	31.7	31.9	32.1												
1966	32.6	32.2	32.6	32.7	32.7												
1967	33.1	32.9	33.1	33.3	33.3												
1968	34.6	33.1	33.9	35.3	36.0												
1969	36.6	36.5	36.5	36.6	37.0												
1970	37.6	37.1	37.5	37.8	38.1												
1971	39.9	39.0	39.7	40.2	40.7												
1972	42.2	41.2	41.9	42.5	43.4												
1973	45.7	44.2	45.2	46.2	47.3												
1974	52.9	49.1	51.0	54.4	57.2												
1975	59.9	58.2	59.6	60.3	61.4												
1976	66.8	63.3	66.0	68.0	70.0												
1977	73.1	70.2	72.6	73.9	75.8												
1978	79.5	76.3	77.8	79.7	84.2												
1979	88.0	84.7	86.1	88.6	92.5												
1980	100.0	96.0	99.1	101.9	103.0												
1981	109.3	106.3	107.3	110.0	113.6												
1982	121.2	117.6	121.0	123.5	122.7												
1983		125.9	128.3	131.0													

Construction permits issued: residential / Permis de construire délivrés : bâtiments résidentiels

thousands / milliers

Adjusted - Corrigé *

	Year	Q.1	Q.2	Q.3	Q.4	JAN	FEB	MAR	APR	MAY	JUN	JUL	AUG	SEP	OCT	NOV	DEC
1964		135	139	130	163	46	45	44	49	45	46	46	38	45	65	45	53
1965		145	143	139	164	47	52	47	46	50	47	40	49	50	51	55	57
1966		136	139	125	114	51	43	43	53	40	46	43	43	39	41	41	33
1967		123	125	118	105	39	44	41	43	45	37	41	38	39	36	37	33
1968		122	122	138	167	41	36	44	41	39	43	44	51	43	51	56	59
1969		139	142	165	140	48	45	46	46	49	48	54	50	61	50	43	46
1970		147	151	142	153	44	53	50	52	47	52	43	48	52	38	43	66
1971		169	166	157	174	46	53	67	53	54	59	53	53	51	53	59	61
1972		153	158	153	175	57	49	48	51	56	51	53	49	51	59	64	54
1973		175	156	176	167	..	..	..	..	..	..	..	..	..	..	..	..
1974		166	158	170	145	54	56	56	42	57	59	77	42	50	43	52	45
1975		130	135	137	141	35	54	42	44	46	45	43	48	46	46	48	47
1976		151	147	140	135	51	47	53	53	48	46	49	45	47	45	42	48
1977		138	123	123	121	45	43	50	40	42	41	38	43	42	41	40	40
1978		116	119	114	121	39	40	37	43	38	38	38	38	38	43	41	38
1979		114	118	117	116	37	40	37	37	41	40	43	36	38	37	43	36
1980		121	124	126	130	38	41	42	43	39	42	43	40	42	43	43	45
1981		129	127	122	112	45	41	43	42	44	41	41	44	39	40	38	34
1982		113	96	102	108	36	45	38	29	32	35	30	35	38	35	36	37
1983		99	100	89	86	35	32	32	33	33	34	30	31	28	28	31	27

* Adjusted by the O.E.C.D.

* Corrigé par l'O.C.D.E.

FRANCE

Prospects for industrial sector (4)
manufacturing
per cent balance

Perspectives dans l'industrie (4)
industries manufacturières
solde en pourcentage

	Year	Q.1	Q.2	Q.3	Q.4	JAN	FEB	MAR	APR	MAY	JUN	JUL	AUG	SEP	OCT	NOV	DEC
1964						12	14	7	18	12	-3	-6		-10	-19	-17	-28
1965						-34	-42	-44	-15	-12	-24	-12		3	16	21	25
1966						35	42	37	35	32	23	29		38	37	22	23
1967						8	6	10	-1	-13	-20	-23		-3	8	-5	2
1968						-3	1	13	25	31	18	4		49	54	50	34
1969						38	42	40	44	38	40	36		19	19	23	20
1970						22	23	23	20	18	19	12		20	12	15	17
1971						16	25	29	31	33	29	26		24	12	1	4
1972						14	17	27	30	34	29	28		42	45	44	35
1973						40	41	44	43	52	50	43		43	32	20	-28
1974						-26	-8	3	4	3	9	-3		-14	-35	-66	-52
1975						-38	-21	-46	-37	-31	-37	-36		-25	-2	15	26
1976						35	39	40	48	56	47	28		14	-16	-28	-32
1977						-20	-1	-10	-5	-10	-14	-17		-11	-8	-12	-20
1978						-13	-7	-1	37	29	9	-		4	-7	3	6
1979						7	10	10	15	14	-3	-8		-6	-	1	6
1980						-4	6	-4	-	-12	-24	-45		-39	-47	-46	-47
1981						-51	-42	-42	-32	-25	-46	-43		-33	-34	-21	-11
1982						-5	-3	-12	-13	-18	-32	-46		-46	-47	-42	-33
1983						-42	-35	-36	-46	-52	-59	-63		-50	-54	-43	-47

Production: future tendency (4)(5)
manufacturing
per cent balance

Perspectives de production (4)(5)
industries manufacturières
solde en pourcentage

	Year	Q.1	Q.2	Q.3	Q.4	JAN	FEB	MAR	APR	MAY	JUN	JUL	AUG	SEP	OCT	NOV	DEC
1964						25	26	26	24	20	16	11		11	12	9	-2
1965						-1	-	6	10	10	10	8		18	19	19	13
1966						21	22	29	26	24	19	19		22	20	14	17
1967						8	11	14	9	7	-1	-2		6	9	7	7
1968						8	8	20	20	20	22	24		37	31	28	24
1969						24	25	29	30	31	27	29		29	28	23	23
1970						23	25	24	21	17	16	14		13	15	16	16
1971						19	26	31	31	23	22	19		25	21	13	10
1972						13	20	21	24	26	23	24		30	33	28	25
1973						26	28	34	32	33	27	22		30	23	22	8
1974						5	10	14	15	12	10	4		-4	-16	-32	-27
1975						-22	-11	-16	-13	-9	-14	-17		-8	4	15	18
1976						22	28	28	29	29	25	15		13	6	-5	-10
1977						-3	-2	5	2	-4	-5	-7		-2	-7	-8	-11
1978						-2	1	11	20	12	11	3		6	5	8	7
1979						6	9	15	15	12	10	8		10	11	9	8
1980						12	9	11	6	3	-6	-19		-22	-28	-23	-20
1981						-10	-15	-10	-13	-12	-16	-13		-10	-7	-3	-3
1982						-2	2	6	3	3	-7	-8		-19	-18	-16	-12
1983						-10	-7	4	-6	-10	-19	-29		-23	-14	-29	-19

Orders inflow or demand: tendency (6)
manufacturing
per cent balance

Commandes ou demande globale : tendance (6)
industries manufacturières
solde en pourcentage

	Year	Q.1	Q.2	Q.3	Q.4	JAN	FEB	MAR	APR	MAY	JUN	JUL	AUG	SEP	OCT	NOV	DEC
1964		24	18		-2			24			18					-2	
1965		-21	-3		14			-21			-8					14	
1966		16	17		13			16			17					13	
1967		4	-8		-6			4			-8					-6	
1968		5	20		40			5			20					40	
1969		35	41		34			35			41					34	
1970		17	9		3			17			9					3	
1971		3	13		6			3			13					6	
1972		10	22		20			10			22					20	
1973		26	32		28			26			32					28	
1974		32	28		-34			32			28					-34	
1975		-47	-46		-9			-47			-46					-9	
1976		17	26		8			17			26					8	
1977		6	-13		-18			6			-13					-18	
1978		-12	1		-2			-12			1					-2	
1979		9	10	20	9	9			10			20			9		
1980		9	14	-1	-24	9			14			-1			-24		
1981		-31	-33	-29	-23	-31			-33			-29			-23		
1982		-8	-14	-3	-20	-8			-14			-3			-20		
1983		-13	-20	-11	-19	-13			-20			-11			-19		

Order books: level (4)(5)
manufacturing
per cent balance

Carnet de commandes : niveau (4)(5)
industries manufacturières
solde en pourcentage

Year	Q.1	Q.2	Q.3	Q.4	JAN	FEB	MAR	APR	MAY	JUN	JUL	AUG	SEP	OCT	NOV	DEC
1964					5	-2	-1	-	-1	-4	-7		-13	-21	-31	-33
1965					-39	-43	-46	-42	-41	-38	-36		-33	-20	-15	-15
1966					-18	-15	-11	-4	-4	-5	-4		-9	-13	-19	-19
1967					-23	-24	-30	-28	-34	-35	-35		-36	-35	-33	-34
1968					-32	-33	-31	-24	-16	-13	-9		6	13	21	20
1969					21	23	27	31	34	37	43		40	35	31	27
1970					22	18	10	10	5	8	-3		1	-8	-11	-11
1971					-6	-10	-13	-10	-	-7	-3		-5	-5	-11	-11
1972					-8	-9	-9	-5	-3	-4	2		9	7	9	8
1973					6	10	14	20	19	22	28		23	24	24	20
1974					15	19	18	16	19	12	15		3	-6	-36	-40
1975					-43	-41	-47	-48	-46	-49	-49		-50	-47	-36	-32
1976					-23	-14	-14	-10	-3	-5	-6		-7	-16	-22	-21
1977					-23	-22	-20	-25	-32	-36	-36		-38	-41	-43	-40
1978					-42	-40	-39	-22	-18	-16	-21		-22	-17	-22	-19
1979					-21	-14	-13	-11	-7	-4	-4		-7	-10	-3	-5
1980					-8	-7	-	-8	-10	-15	-23		-38	-38	-42	-48
1981					-44	-48	-43	-42	-41	-41	-40		-36	-38	-25	-26
1982					-24	-23	-23	-13	-17	-23	-25		-35	-30	-25	-28
1983					-26	-25	-31	-33	-38	-39	-44		-51	-42	-41	-42

Finished goods stocks: level (4)(5)
manufacturing
per cent balance

Stocks de produits finis : niveau (4)(5)
industries manufacturières
solde en pourcentage

Year	Q.1	Q.2	Q.3	Q.4	JAN	FEB	MAR	APR	MAY	JUN	JUL	AUG	SEP	OCT	NOV	DEC
1964					-5	1	-1	2	3	7	7		9	14	23	23
1965					26	34	31	33	31	25	27		25	17	15	14
1966					13	14	15	11	10	10	8		7	6	7	11
1967					15	19	23	22	23	29	27		21	23	27	22
1968					21	20	21	22	15	7	-1		-13	-16	-18	-17
1969					-16	-15	-15	-18	-17	-21	-26		-18	-17	-18	-13
1970					-12	-5	4	3	1	9	13		14	16	8	18
1971					21	22	17	22	23	19	17		10	11	11	11
1972					13	14	9	10	11	6	6		-1	-1	-3	-
1973					-2	-3	-7	-8	-12	-9	-12		-16	-13	-11	-8
1974					-6	-5	-8	-7	-6	-5	1		9	21	41	43
1975					46	50	50	46	44	40	35		29	27	18	11
1976					9	9	13	4	-5	-2	-5		-5	-	2	9
1977					12	19	19	21	24	25	27		27	31	33	34
1978					32	32	27	24	28	26	19		17	14	13	16
1979					16	13	16	11	8	7	2		4	4	-1	4
1980					36	37	39	34	36	34	32		26	20	20	18
1981					36	37	39	34	36	34	32		26	20	20	18
1982					16	21	22	14	12	14	15		16	14	19	15
1983					17	12	16	15	26	22	26		25	18	15	18

Rate of capacity utilization (6)
manufacturing
per cent

Taux d'utilisation de capacité (6)
industries manufacturières
pourcentage

Year	Q.1	Q.2	Q.3	Q.4	JAN	FEB	MAR	APR	MAY	JUN	JUL	AUG	SEP	OCT	NOV	DEC
1964	82.7	82.7		78.4			82.7			82.7					78.4	
1965	79.1	79.1		79.9			79.1			79.1					79.9	
1966	79.9	81.1		80.4			79.9			81.1					80.4	
1967	79.4	79.3		79.8			79.4			79.3					79.8	
1968	78.7	79.8		81.9			78.7			79.8					81.9	
1969	83.5	83.6		84.4			83.5			83.6					84.4	
1970	84.1	83.3		83.0			84.1			83.3					83.0	
1971	83.3	83.5		83.5			83.3			83.5					83.5	
1972	83.3	83.9		84.9			83.3			83.9					84.9	
1973	85.5	86.1		85.8			85.5			86.1					85.8	
1974	85.8	85.3		79.6			85.8			85.3					79.6	
1975	74.6	69.4		73.5			74.6			69.4					73.5	
1976	76.2	79.2		79.9			76.2			79.2					79.9	
1977	79.3	79.0		79.4			79.3			79.0					79.4	
1978	79.6	80.3		79.3			79.6			80.3					79.8	
1979	81.3	81.5	81.3	81.1	81.3			81.5			81.3			81.1		
1980	82.5	82.3	81.6	79.7	82.5			82.3			81.6			79.7		
1981	78.2	78.0	77.3	76.3	78.2			78.0			77.3			76.8		
1982	77.1	77.5	78.4	77.4	77.1			77.5			78.4			77.4		
1983	77.5	77.3	77.0	77.1	77.5			77.3			77.0			77.1		

FRANCE

Retail sales: major outlets (7)(8) — Ventes au détail : grande distribution (7)(8)

(value) — (valeur)

1980 = 100

	Year	Q.1	Q.2	Q.3	Q.4	JAN	FEB	MAR	APR	MAY	JUN	JUL	AUG	SEP	OCT	NOV	DEC
1964																	
1965																	
1966																	
1967																	
1968																	
1969																	
1970																	
1971	36.8	32.4	35.2	34.9	44.8	32.3	29.5	35.4	36.0	34.1	35.6	34.5	31.5	38.7	39.2	39.3	55.8
1972	40.3	36.5	37.9	39.0	47.3	34.7	34.4	40.4	36.6	37.9	39.3	37.1	35.6	44.5	41.7	41.9	59.9
1973	44.3	39.2	42.2	40.8	55.1	37.6	35.7	43.3	40.5	42.9	43.3	39.4	38.0	44.9	48.5	49.2	67.6
1974	51.5	46.1	48.7	49.6	61.4	46.5	42.6	49.4	47.3	51.0	47.9	47.9	45.8	55.0	57.9	51.8	74.5
1975	58.8	52.0	55.5	56.2	71.3	51.5	48.8	55.8	55.7	57.9	52.9	53.6	51.7	63.4	65.8	61.3	86.6
1976	65.0	57.0	61.7	62.7	78.6	57.8	52.4	60.9	62.3	61.8	60.8	60.4	56.8	71.0	69.7	69.1	96.9
1977	71.6	63.6	68.1	69.3	85.6	62.1	59.0	69.7	67.8	65.6	70.9	65.9	65.3	76.6	76.0	74.3	106.1
1978	79.5	70.2	76.2	76.9	94.8	68.2	65.2	77.2	74.8	76.3	77.6	73.4	70.9	85.4	83.1	84.4	116.8
1979	89.3	80.2	84.6	84.5	107.9	78.4	74.1	88.0	80.4	86.6	86.7	78.2	81.9	93.4	98.5	97.6	127.5
1980	100.0	90.3	93.4	95.0	121.4	89.2	86.9	94.7	92.0	97.5	90.8	93.1	86.8	105.2	112.2	105.9	145.9
1981	114.1	100.3	106.7	108.7	140.7	102.5	93.8	104.5	106.1	107.2	106.7	107.3	98.5	120.3	130.8	122.8	168.5
1982	128.6	116.5	121.9	120.5	154.5	113.9	110.3	125.3	122.7	117.2	126.4	120.4	111.7	129.4	142.5	135.4	185.7
1983	136.4	126.8	128.6	129.0	161.3	121.0	118.5	140.9	127.8	129.3	128.8	123.4	120.3	143.3	140.1	144.3	199.5

Retail sales: major outlets (7) — Ventes au détail : grande distribution (7)

(volume) — (volume)

1980 = 100

	Year	Q.1	Q.2	Q.3	Q.4	JAN	FEB	MAR	APR	MAY	JUN	JUL	AUG	SEP	OCT	NOV	DEC
1964																	
1965																	
1966																	
1967																	
1968																	
1969																	
1970																	
1971																	
1972																	
1973																	
1974																	
1975	93.6	85.2	89.0	88.8	110.4	85.0	79.9	90.7	89.8	92.7	84.4	85.1	81.8	99.6	102.6	95.0	133.4
1976	96.1	86.9	92.4	92.3	112.6	88.6	80.0	92.2	93.8	92.5	90.7	89.7	83.6	103.5	100.6	99.1	138.3
1977	96.2	89.7	92.4	91.6	111.0	88.5	83.4	97.3	93.2	89.0	95.1	87.8	86.3	100.5	99.0	96.9	137.0
1978	98.0	89.7	95.0	94.4	113.5	87.8	83.4	97.9	93.7	95.1	96.3	90.7	87.1	105.3	100.4	101.0	139.2
1979	100.4	94.1	96.8	94.3	116.5	92.7	87.1	102.5	92.8	99.0	98.5	88.0	91.6	103.3	107.5	105.4	136.6
1980	100.0	94.3	94.9	94.1	116.3	94.1	90.7	98.0	94.2	99.0	91.5	93.0	86.1	103.3	109.1	102.1	139.3
1981	100.9	93.2	96.0	94.9	118.9	96.2	87.2	96.2	96.5	96.5	95.0	94.6	86.1	103.9	111.6	103.7	141.4
1982	102.5	96.4	97.8	95.5	120.5	95.0	91.3	102.7	98.9	93.9	100.7	95.7	88.7	102.3	108.3	102.8	149.8
1983	99.8	96.5	95.3	93.5	113.8	93.2	90.2	106.3	95.1	95.8	94.9	90.2	87.3	103.0	99.6	101.5	140.3

New motor vehicle registrations (9) — Immatriculations de voitures neuves (9)

thousands, monthly averages — milliers, moyennes mensuelles

	Year	Q.1	Q.2	Q.3	Q.4	JAN	FEB	MAR	APR	MAY	JUN	JUL	AUG	SEP	OCT	NOV	DEC
1964	87.7	98.9	109.0	61.3	81.8	84.6	94.4	117.7	117.4	100.0	109.5	83.8	31.3	68.2	93.4	80.7	71.4
1965	88.1	86.4	101.4	65.9	98.7	67.9	80.5	110.8	106.3	94.4	103.4	85.6	36.2	76.0	59.8	96.2	100.0
1966	100.8	107.4	118.6	72.8	104.6	83.4	101.7	137.2	116.6	116.0	123.1	89.9	46.3	82.3	107.4	108.5	97.8
1967	102.6	111.9	119.3	68.9	110.0	97.0	102.0	136.8	121.9	116.3	119.6	81.7	40.9	84.2	118.2	113.2	93.7
1968	103.3	105.8	97.9	78.4	131.1	90.8	101.1	125.4	135.9	90.4	67.4	109.5	47.1	78.6	129.4	120.3	143.5
1969	113.8	115.2	141.9	86.4	111.6	115.6	103.0	127.1	148.4	133.7	143.6	108.3	61.2	89.7	128.6	104.4	101.7
1970	108.0	108.8	121.2	79.8	122.3	96.8	95.6	134.0	128.2	108.1	127.2	86.5	46.8	106.0	123.5	117.1	126.4
1971	122.4	126.7	127.3	96.7	138.9	100.5	110.3	169.3	145.1	112.8	124.1	104.8	60.4	124.8	145.7	139.2	131.7
1972	136.5	145.9	146.5	100.8	152.6	114.7	142.9	180.2	136.3	142.7	160.6	109.5	70.7	122.2	163.2	158.5	136.2
1973	145.1	154.5	161.2	111.3	153.6	138.2	138.2	187.2	161.8	158.4	163.4	140.8	74.3	118.2	173.2	164.1	123.4
1974	127.6	142.3	147.4	94.1	124.3	149.8	127.9	149.3	153.7	157.9	130.7	110.8	64.2	107.4	138.9	110.1	123.8
1975	123.6	115.0	132.3	98.3	148.6	101.5	124.3	119.1	137.8	117.7	141.3	111.7	69.4	113.9	160.6	136.7	143.6
1976	155.0	150.1	174.0	121.5	174.6	151.6	129.9	168.7	180.3	164.9	176.8	142.9	83.0	138.6	176.2	176.5	171.0
1977	158.9	171.5	174.4	120.5	169.3	161.2	154.5	198.7	190.9	148.6	183.8	129.2	98.4	134.0	172.7	169.9	165.3
1978	162.1	156.7	189.6	126.9	175.1	136.5	147.7	186.0	185.9	199.0	183.9	136.7	103.0	141.0	173.3	186.4	165.5
1979	164.7	172.4	189.0	126.8	170.6	157.2	161.6	198.3	187.6	198.2	181.3	150.7	113.5	116.3	182.3	180.7	149.7
1980	156.1	168.5	171.0	126.0	159.0	155.5	163.1	186.8	213.7	147.5	151.8	149.2	103.6	125.1	175.5	149.2	152.3
1981	152.9	149.3	175.4	120.1	167.1	135.1	134.2	173.6	179.6	175.2	171.4	131.4	105.7	123.1	173.6	164.9	165.8
1982	171.4	175.2	176.9	138.3	194.9	144.5	152.7	228.4	184.8	162.0	184.0	151.0	126.5	137.5	182.3	201.2	201.2
1983	168.1	167.9	186.4	135.0	183.5	149.0	148.0	206.8	189.6	182.4	187.3	150.5	126.5	128.1	169.8	193.2	187.5

Retail sales: major outlets (7)(8)
(value)
1980 = 100

Ventes au détail : grande distribution (7)(8)
(valeur)
1980 = 100

Adjusted - Corrigé

	Year	Q.1	Q.2	Q.3	Q.4	JAN	FEB	MAR	APR	MAY	JUN	JUL	AUG	SEP	OCT	NOV	DEC
1964																	
1965																	
1966																	
1967																	
1968																	
1969																	
1970																	
1971		34.9	36.8	37.2	38.1	35.0	34.2	35.5	37.2	36.2	36.9	36.5	37.4	37.6	37.2	37.8	39.3
1972		38.9	39.3	41.3	41.4	38.4	39.1	39.3	38.1	39.3	40.4	40.7	41.4	41.8	40.7	42.6	41.0
1973		41.4	43.8	44.2	47.1	40.5	42.1	41.6	43.3	43.5	44.5	45.2	44.1	43.1	46.1	48.0	47.3
1974		49.0	50.7	52.7	52.9	49.8	48.7	48.5	49.9	51.4	50.9	51.6	52.2	54.3	54.4	50.4	53.7
1975		56.8	57.2	59.0	61.4	56.1	57.1	57.1	56.9	58.5	56.1	58.3	58.6	60.1	62.1	60.8	61.3
1976		61.5	64.1	65.3	67.3	61.9	61.2	61.3	64.4	64.0	64.0	64.8	64.5	66.6	65.8	66.8	69.5
1977		68.9	70.3	72.7	72.9	68.5	68.6	69.7	69.5	68.0	73.4	71.7	73.9	72.6	72.1	73.3	73.3
1978		75.7	78.7	80.6	81.7	73.9	75.3	78.0	77.3	79.0	80.0	80.3	80.1	81.3	79.7	83.2	82.3
1979		85.3	87.9	90.0	92.5	84.1	85.0	86.8	85.7	88.5	89.4	87.4	92.8	89.8	92.7	93.1	91.8
1980		96.0	96.9	100.4	104.6	95.1	97.4	95.4	96.7	98.2	96.0	100.3	99.0	102.0	104.4	104.2	105.4
1981		107.0	111.3	115.5	120.3	107.3	106.6	107.1	111.4	109.7	112.9	115.3	114.4	116.6	119.7	119.5	121.7
1982		124.3	127.9	127.2	133.8	120.9	125.4	126.7	128.0	123.5	132.1	127.6	128.4	125.6	132.5	131.6	137.2
1983		135.8	133.3	137.5	136.3	131.2	134.1	142.1	132.0	135.7	133.0	132.5	138.5	141.4	129.5	140.9	138.5

Retail sales: major outlets (7)
(volume)
1980 = 100

Ventes au détail : grande distribution (7)
(volume)
1980 = 100

Adjusted - Corrigé

	Year	Q.1	Q.2	Q.3	Q.4	JAN	FEB	MAR	APR	MAY	JUN	JUL	AUG	SEP	OCT	NOV	DEC
1964																	
1965																	
1966																	
1967																	
1968																	
1969																	
1970																	
1971																	
1972																	
1973																	
1974																	
1975																	
1976		93.7	96.0	96.1	96.5	95.0	93.3	93.0	96.9	95.8	95.4	96.2	95.0	97.1	95.0	95.6	99.1
1977		97.2	95.4	96.2	94.5	97.5	96.7	97.3	95.5	92.2	98.5	95.5	97.8	95.2	93.8	95.0	94.8
1978		96.7	98.2	98.9	97.9	95.0	96.4	98.9	96.8	98.4	99.3	99.2	98.5	99.2	96.3	99.5	98.0
1979		100.1	100.6	100.5	100.0	99.4	99.8	101.1	98.9	101.2	101.6	98.4	103.7	99.4	101.1	100.6	98.4
1980		100.3	98.4	99.5	100.8	100.4	101.7	98.8	99.0	99.6	96.7	100.2	98.1	100.2	101.4	100.3	100.7
1981		99.4	100.2	100.8	101.7	100.7	99.2	98.5	101.3	98.7	100.6	101.7	100.1	100.8	102.2	100.9	102.1
1982		102.9	102.6	100.9	103.6	100.9	103.7	103.9	103.7	99.0	105.2	101.5	102.0	99.3	103.5	102.4	105.0
1983		103.4	98.8	99.7	96.4	101.0	102.2	107.1	97.5	100.8	98.0	96.8	100.5	101.7	92.1	99.6	97.3

New motor vehicle registrations (9)
thousands, monthly averages

Emploi : industries manufacturières (salariés) (9)
1980 = 100

Adjusted - Corrigé

	Year	Q.1	Q.2	Q.3	Q.4	JAN	FEB	MAR	APR	MAY	JUN	JUL	AUG	SEP	OCT	NOV	DEC
1964		94.3	89.9	84.2	80.5	92.2	96.7	94.0	89.9	92.5	87.3	85.7	82.7	84.1	83.0	81.8	76.8
1965		82.1	85.0	91.1	95.9	81.7	83.3	81.4	86.2	80.5	88.3	92.2	88.1	93.1	93.6	93.1	101.0
1966		99.9	100.2	104.0	101.5	94.6	104.9	100.3	99.2	100.2	101.3	104.6	108.4	99.1	100.3	103.9	100.3
1967		104.4	101.7	97.6	105.2	104.2	105.0	104.1	103.6	101.9	99.6	95.1	93.4	104.3	105.0	102.4	108.3
1968		99.2	84.6	106.8	125.8	97.5	99.7	100.3	110.7	77.0	66.2	114.3	109.9	96.3	110.3	120.2	147.0
1969		110.2	125.8	122.7	136.4	123.0	106.3	101.2	120.8	127.6	129.0	119.6	145.4	103.1	109.2	103.3	196.8
1970		103.9	106.8	108.0	113.6	106.0	101.3	104.5	102.7	110.6	107.2	99.1	103.3	121.6	108.0	109.7	123.1
1971		118.1	113.3	130.8	129.2	115.8	116.9	121.5	123.5	111.5	105.0	125.9	125.4	141.1	133.6	130.6	123.3
1972		134.0	132.1	138.3	141.7	126.1	142.9	132.9	128.3	134.6	133.3	135.7	139.8	139.5	139.9	141.1	144.1
1973		146.5	146.4	148.1	140.5	146.9	144.2	148.3	148.1	143.8	149.4	158.3	144.4	141.5	145.3	146.5	129.7
1974		139.4	132.3	121.8	116.0	153.4	136.3	128.5	131.2	141.2	124.4	115.4	127.0	123.1	113.5	108.1	126.5
1975		115.4	116.3	129.5	137.0	102.7	132.6	110.8	112.1	115.5	121.3	120.8	142.4	125.3	131.8	134.5	144.7
1976		147.2	154.5	157.9	162.3	161.1	140.5	140.0	155.1	155.2	153.3	163.6	155.7	154.4	160.5	167.3	159.0
1977		167.8	153.0	157.3	158.9	172.4	165.9	165.1	165.9	137.0	156.1	155.4	158.7	157.9	161.5	159.0	156.2
1978		152.8	166.5	166.9	163.7	139.5	153.0	161.0	160.1	182.3	157.1	163.9	158.9	177.9	155.6	164.9	170.7
1979		167.0	170.8	162.0	160.3	162.8	170.3	168.0	167.5	174.1	170.7	163.1	166.9	155.9	158.7	161.4	160.9
1980		164.2	152.7	159.8	150.1	163.3	165.2	164.1	174.6	147.9	135.7	161.2	166.3	152.0	152.5	148.4	149.3
1981		145.5	159.1	152.0	156.0	147.2	142.4	147.0	149.2	172.0	156.1	147.5	154.5	153.9	159.2	152.6	156.3
1982		170.2	159.0	174.0	183.5	165.3	163.8	181.6	154.0	160.9	162.2	170.9	177.1	173.9	176.1	191.0	183.5
1983		159.1	166.5	173.5	175.3	159.7	157.3	160.2	165.9	169.9	163.7	186.0	174.3	160.1	169.9	180.4	177.0

FRANCE

Households' consumption of industrial products

(1970 prices)
1980 = 100

Adjusted - Corrigé

Consommation des ménages de produits industriels

(prix de 1970)
1980 = 100

	Year	Q.1	Q.2	Q.3	Q.4	JAN	FEB	MAR	APR	MAY	JUN	JUL	AUG	SEP	OCT	NOV	DEC
1964	46.7	46.8	46.3	46.0	47.7	45.7	43.3	46.4	45.9	46.6	44.6	46.7	44.9	46.4	50.1	46.2	46.8
1965	48.7	46.7	48.3	50.0	49.8	47.4	46.2	46.4	48.6	47.8	48.5	49.3	48.6	52.2	49.4	49.6	50.4
1966	52.4	51.8	52.5	52.4	52.9	50.7	53.0	51.7	52.1	51.8	53.8	51.9	53.2	52.2	53.9	52.5	52.2
1967	54.6	54.6	53.6	54.9	55.4	54.0	54.3	55.5	53.8	53.2	53.8	53.9	53.1	57.7	53.8	55.0	57.4
1968	58.0	55.5	54.0	59.9	62.6	54.3	55.9	56.4	57.4	48.9	55.6	60.2	60.5	58.9	59.7	65.7	62.4
1969	62.1	60.9	62.8	64.0	60.7	61.8	60.3	60.5	62.1	65.1	61.3	63.0	67.3	61.8	61.9	61.0	59.3
1970	63.4	61.2	62.6	63.2	66.5	61.8	60.9	60.9	60.8	63.6	63.1	61.2	63.1	65.4	68.1	63.6	67.3
1971	69.0	66.5	68.3	69.9	71.6	66.6	66.4	66.4	69.7	67.4	67.7	70.0	68.9	70.7	71.2	72.3	71.2
1972	75.1	73.8	73.4	76.6	76.7	72.0	74.5	74.8	72.4	73.2	74.5	75.2	76.9	77.7	75.1	76.5	78.4
1973	80.3	79.0	80.3	78.8	83.4	76.7	78.6	81.6	78.6	80.2	82.0	79.3	79.6	77.5	82.1	84.1	83.9
1974	84.6	86.2	85.2	84.9	82.3	89.1	85.1	84.3	85.7	86.4	83.6	84.1	86.3	84.2	84.8	80.3	81.8
1975	85.9	83.5	83.6	86.3	89.9	82.7	85.8	82.2	84.2	84.8	81.9	85.6	86.0	87.3	92.2	87.6	90.0
1976	92.1	90.3	91.5	92.9	93.5	93.0	88.9	89.0	91.4	90.9	92.3	93.3	89.5	95.8	92.6	93.6	94.4
1977	93.1	93.2	90.9	94.7	93.7	92.8	93.8	92.9	91.7	87.0	94.0	93.7	95.1	95.3	92.3	94.0	94.8
1978	97.3	94.5	97.8	98.5	98.4	92.3	94.3	96.8	97.1	98.4	97.9	96.8	98.0	100.6	96.4	98.9	99.9
1979	99.6	99.0	99.3	99.5	100.5	98.8	98.3	99.5	96.8	100.4	100.7	97.6	102.1	98.9	99.9	101.5	100.2
1980	100.0	101.6	98.4	100.0	100.0	103.0	103.1	98.9	100.8	98.8	95.8	103.4	98.9	97.6	101.4	99.2	99.4
1981	102.3	100.2	102.0	103.2	103.8	102.0	99.2	99.3	101.5	101.8	102.7	104.7	101.1	103.9	105.0	102.3	104.0
1982	108.0	106.7	107.7	108.1	109.7	105.5	106.7	107.9	105.9	104.0	113.1	107.8	109.0	107.5	111.0	108.8	109.2
1983	105.6	106.3	105.4	105.4	105.3	105.5	105.3	108.2	105.4	103.7	107.1	104.6	105.5	106.1	101.7	106.1	108.2

Unemployment (registered unemployed) (10)(11)

thousands

Chômage (chômeurs inscrits) (10)(11)

milliers

	Year	Q.1	Q.2	Q.3	Q.4	JAN	FEB	MAR	APR	MAY	JUN	JUL	AUG	SEP	OCT	NOV	DEC
1964	98	107	87	82	116	111	109	101	97	86	77	76	81	90	106	117	126
1965	132	144	122	117	146	144	147	142	131	123	113	110	113	127	139	147	151
1966	142	157	128	122	159	164	160	149	139	128	117	116	119	132	148	161	168
1967	192	188	174	175	231	189	190	184	184	175	164	164	171	190	214	235	245
1968	255	270	..	240	261	272	274	264	251	.. S	243	232	238	251	261	262	258
1969	223	261	210	195	226	272	264	246	227	210	193	190	193	204	218	226	232
1970	262	253	235	248	313	253	256	250	244	234	227	231	243	270	297	319	322
1971	337	343	301	312	390	352	346	331	325	300	289	291	305	341	377	395	398
1972	380	405	351	350	415	418	410	389	375	352	327	324	339	386	414	417	413
1973	394	398	346	376	456	417	400	378	365	343	330	346	364	419	452	455	461
1974	498	461	395	454	682	479	466	439	416	389	379	398	428	534	628	694	723
1975	840	764	744	836	1015	766	770	755	757	737	738	766	797	946	1016	1020	1010
1976	933	978	853	869	1035	1017	978	938	897	848	813	809	842	955	1025	1041	1037
1977	1073	1048	931	1081	1181	1068	1055	1021	1000	976	968	1004	1064	1175	1212	1183	1148
1978	1167	1108	1047	1179	1334	1126	1108	1088	1065	1037	1039	1094	1157	1285	1344	1330	1328
1979	1350	1337	1261	1328	1474	1356	1342	1313	1291	1259	1233	1257	1303	1424	1480	1473	1469
1980	1451	1443	1336	1408	1610	1485	1448	1412	1375	1337	1296	1330	1374	1519	1585	1613	1632
1981	1773	1668	1634	1778	2011	1680	1668	1657	1646	1631	1626	1681	1742	1912	2002	2016	2014
1982	2008	2001	1894	1981	2156	2034	2004	1965	1928	1885	1867	1899	1944	2099	2177	2161	2131
1983	2042	2076	1913	1972	2205	2130	2080	2017	1950	1913	1878	1893	1934	2087	2165	2223	2227

Jobs vacant, unfilled vacancies (10)(12)

thousands

Offres d'emploi non satisfaites (10)(12)

milliers

	Year	Q.1	Q.2	Q.3	Q.4	JAN	FEB	MAR	APR	MAY	JUN	JUL	AUG	SEP	OCT	NOV	DEC
1964	45	48	54	48	29	42	48	53	52	53	53	49	46	50	37	27	22
1965	30	26	33	32	28	22	25	30	31	32	35	32	32	33	30	27	25
1966	38	34	43	42	34	27	35	39	39	43	48	43	40	44	39	34	30
1967	32	32	35	33	27	30	31	34	36	34	36	35	32	33	30	27	24
1968	36	30	..	34	46	26	29	34	37	.. S	29	30	30	41	46	44	47
1969	78	59	85	86	84	50	58	67	77	85	93	88	78	93	85	87	80
1970	93	87	98	99	95	83	90	88	92	98	103	95	95	105	93	98	94
1971	123	105	134	135	117	95	104	116	123	136	143	137	134	136	126	118	107
1972	167	124	153	176	213	114	124	134	142	150	168	167	170	191	216	215	209
1973	252	227	264	270	245	214	228	240	246	267	279	263	264	281	279	249	208
1974	205	218	251	212	138	206	216	231	236	257	261	228	211	196	160	129	126
1975	109	120	110	109	98	138	114	109	106	111	114	107	105	115	105	96	92
1976	124	107	141	140	107	98	103	120	129	142	153	139	138	143	121	105	95
1977	104	100	105	113	98	96	98	105	103	105	107	104	113	123	109	98	87
1978	87	85	94	90	79	84	83	88	91	95	96	88	89	95	87	79	71
1979	88	74	91	97	91	70	72	80	85	91	96	92	96	104	93	92	83
1980	89	92	100	89	75	86	91	97	100	101	100	98	88	91	84	75	66
1981	69	71	76	71	60	67	70	76	79	75	74	68	69	74	66	59	56
1982	84	68	83	90	94	61	67	76	79	83	87	85	90	96	96	94	94
1983	80	105	88	69	57	105	107	103	95	89	81	70	70	67	65	59	49

Employment: manufacturing (all employees) (13) / Emploi : industries manufacturières (salariés) (13)

1980 = 100

	Year	Q.1	Q.2	Q.3	Q.4	JAN	FEB	MAR	APR	MAY	JUN	JUL	AUG	SEP	OCT	NOV	DEC
1964	108.1	107.7	108.0	108.3	108.6	107.7			108.0			108.3			108.6		
1965	106.5	107.3	106.4	106.1	106.6	107.3			106.4			106.1			106.6		
1966	106.6	106.0	106.2	106.9	107.1	106.0			106.2			106.9			107.1		
1967	105.3	106.4	105.9	105.5	104.9	106.4			105.9			105.5			104.9		
1968	102.9	103.5	103.1	102.5	102.8	103.5			103.1			102.5			102.8		
1969	104.9	103.1	103.9	105.1	106.1	103.1			103.9			105.1			106.1		
1970	106.7	106.3	106.3	107.0	107.1	106.3			106.3			107.0			107.1		
1971	107.2	106.7	106.7	107.4	107.9	106.7			106.7			107.4			107.9		
1972	107.8	107.3	107.1	107.8	108.4	107.3			107.1			107.8			108.4		
1973	109.8	108.7	109.3	110.0	110.3	108.7			109.3			110.0			110.3		
1974	110.6	110.6	110.5	111.1	110.8	110.6			110.5			111.1			110.8		
1975	107.7	109.7	108.3	107.8	106.8	109.7			108.4			107.8			106.8		
1976	106.6	106.2	106.2	107.0	106.9	106.2			106.2			107.0			106.9		
1977	105.7	106.6	106.2	106.1	105.3	106.6			106.2			106.1			105.3		
1978	103.4	104.2	103.3	103.6	103.2	104.2			103.3			103.6			103.2		
1979	101.9	102.5	102.0	102.1	101.6	102.5			102.0			102.1			101.6		
1980	100.0	101.0	100.6	100.7	99.6	101.0			100.6			100.7			99.6		
1981	96.0	98.0	96.6	96.1	95.1	98.0			96.6			96.1			95.1		
1982	93.8	94.1	93.9	94.7	93.6	94.1			93.9			94.7			93.6		
1983	91.4	92.7	91.8	91.8	90.6	92.7			91.8			91.8			90.6		

Unemployment (registered unemployed) (10)(11) / Chômage (chômeurs inscrits) (10)(11)

Adjusted - Corrigé

thousands / milliers

	Year	Q.1	Q.2	Q.3	Q.4	JAN	FEB	MAR	APR	MAY	JUN	JUL	AUG	SEP	OCT	NOV	DEC
1964		84	96	103	109	83	83	87	93	95	99	102	105	103	106	109	113
1965		121	131	138	139	115	121	127	128	132	135	135	138	140	139	139	138
1966		135	137	143	152	135	134	134	136	136	139	141	143	145	149	152	156
1967		165	183	196	225	160	164	170	181	183	186	190	195	203	214	226	235
1968		248	..	266	246	243	249	250	252	.. S	278	269	267	261	252	245	241
1969		236	225	216	212	239	237	234	228	227	221	220	216	211	210	211	216
1970		230	254	273	292	222	230	238	247	253	262	269	273	277	284	295	298
1971		313	327	344	361	309	312	317	319	327	336	340	345	347	355	362	365
1972		371	385	384	380	367	372	375	383	388	383	380	384	389	386	379	376
1973		367	375	407	421	371	365	365	373	375	376	396	405	420	422	417	424
1974		428	428	486	624	428	428	427	426	425	432	455	475	529	578	630	665
1975		722	810	889	924	694	723	748	783	805	843	870	881	916	923	922	927
1976		929	928	925	942	927	925	934	930	926	928	919	930	925	931	941	952
1977		1003	1052	1100	1114	984	1007	1019	1036	1051	1068	1083	1104	1114	1117	1116	1110
1978		1081	1121	1202	1257	1073	1077	1094	1103	1115	1146	1180	1203	1223	1244	1253	1274
1979		1304	1346	1359	1388	1288	1306	1318	1334	1348	1356	1354	1360	1363	1375	1387	1403
1980		1412	1425	1443	1515	1409	1410	1417	1421	1430	1424	1433	1437	1458	1476	1518	1552
1981		1622	1732	1833	1900	1591	1619	1655	1693	1733	1771	1807	1833	1859	1880	1903	1917
1982		1945	2003	2043	2038	1928	1946	1962	1982	2000	2027	2039	2046	2045	2046	2039	2028
1983		2018	2024	2034	2084	2019	2020	2014	2004	2029	2038	2033	2035	2033	2035	2097	2119

Jobs vacant, unfilled vacancies (10)(12) / Offres d'emploi non satisfaites (10)(12)

Adjusted - Corrigé

thousands / milliers

	Year	Q.1	Q.2	Q.3	Q.4	JAN	FEB	MAR	APR	MAY	JUN	JUL	AUG	SEP	OCT	NOV	DEC
1964		52	48	46	34	50	52	52	49	47	48	46	46	45	38	33	30
1965		29	27	30	33	30	29	29	28	27	25	28	32	29	31	33	34
1966		37	37	40	39	35	39	38	36	37	39	39	40	40	40	39	39
1967		35	29	31	32	38	35	33	33	29	27	31	33	29	31	32	33
1968		33	..	31	50	34	33	33	34	.. S	20	26	31	36	47	50	55
1969		62	79	82	89	58	62	66	74	79	83	83	78	85	84	91	94
1970		92	92	94	95	93	94	90	91	92	92	91	94	97	96	91	98
1971		111	126	130	123	106	110	118	122	126	128	131	133	125	123	122	124
1972		132	145	168	224	127	131	136	141	141	151	161	167	175	210	222	241
1973		242	246	254	261	240	242	244	245	248	246	249	255	260	272	269	243
1974		234	234	198	148	228	237	238	236	237	229	214	201	179	157	141	147
1975		132	103	100	105	158	126	112	106	103	100	101	98	102	103	104	108
1976		117	132	129	115	113	115	123	130	132	134	132	128	126	119	114	112
1977		110	98	105	105	111	110	108	104	98	94	99	105	113	106	106	102
1978		93	88	83	85	97	94	90	91	89	84	83	82	83	85	86	84
1979		82	85	89	93	81	82	83	85	85	85	87	89	91	95	98	99
1980		101	94	82	80	100	103	100	100	95	88	84	81	80	81	82	77
1981		76	69	66	66	77	76	75	74	68	66	67	66	65	64	65	68
1982		73	77	85	100	71	73	74	74	77	79	83	87	87	95	100	106
1983		110	82	65	63	115	112	102	91	83	73	69	67	59	64	65	61

FRANCE

Foreign workers: new immigration (14) / Travailleurs étrangers : nouveaux immigrants (14)

thousands / milliers

	Year	Q.1	Q.2	Q.3	Q.4	JAN	FEB	MAR	APR	MAY	JUN	JUL	AUG	SEP	OCT	NOV	DEC
1964	153.7	33.0	44.9	32.7	43.1	9.4	11.1	12.5	14.8	14.4	15.7	12.0	8.4	12.3	14.4	15.1	13.6
1965	152.1	42.1	43.3	29.7	37.0	12.8	14.3	15.1	15.6	14.8	12.9	11.9	8.2	9.6	11.2	11.6	14.2
1966	131.7	34.3	39.3	26.1	31.5	10.7	10.9	12.7	14.0	13.6	12.3	9.1	7.6	9.4	9.2	10.7	11.6
1967	107.8	28.8	32.3	20.8	26.0	9.2	7.8	11.8	12.8	9.1	10.4	7.7	5.7	7.3	8.9	8.6	8.5
1968	93.2	25.4	22.9	19.0	25.8	8.3	8.9	8.2	9.4	6.4	7.1	7.0	4.6	7.5	9.0	9.1	7.8
1969	167.8	30.4	40.6	41.8	55.1	7.8	9.9	12.7	14.4	13.5	12.6	12.4	10.8	18.5	22.2	17.5	15.3
1970	174.2	45.9	46.1	37.7	44.6	14.4	15.2	16.3	18.2	14.0	13.9	11.7	9.8	16.2	15.9	13.5	14.2
1971	136.0	39.6	36.5	29.0	30.9	13.1	11.1	15.3	13.3	10.6	12.7	9.6	7.6	11.8	11.0	10.3	9.6
1972	98.1	27.1	23.4	22.7	24.9	8.7	8.4	10.0	7.7	7.8	7.9	6.9	6.4	9.4	10.4	7.9	6.7
1973	132.1	24.9	25.4	37.7	44.1	8.4	8.0	8.6	8.0	8.7	8.7	11.6	11.9	14.1	17.5	14.5	12.1
1974	64.5	26.1	19.2	12.5	6.6	10.0	8.3	7.8	6.1	7.3	5.9	5.0	3.4	4.1	2.6	1.2	2.9
1975	25.6	6.0	6.5	6.0	7.2	2.1	1.9	2.0	2.0	2.4	2.1	2.0	1.7	2.3	2.4	2.5	2.3
1976	27.0	7.1	6.6	6.0	7.2	2.3	2.6	2.2	2.1	2.4	2.1	1.9	1.6	2.5	2.3	2.5	2.5
1977	22.8	7.4	5.7	4.7	5.0	2.5	2.6	2.4	1.8	1.8	2.1	1.5	1.5	1.7	2.0	1.5	1.6
1978	18.4	5.1	4.7	4.0	4.6	1.7	1.5	1.9	1.5	1.6	1.6	1.3	1.1	1.7	1.5	1.8	1.3
1979	17.0	4.3	4.3	3.8	4.7	1.4	1.4	1.5	1.3	1.5	1.5	1.3	1.1	1.4	1.5	1.7	1.5
1980	17.4	4.8	4.4	3.8	4.4	1.6	1.5	1.8	1.5	1.5	1.5	1.3	1.0	1.5	1.8	1.5	1.1
1981	33.4	4.1	2.8	2.3	24.3	1.6	1.2	1.3	1.0	1.0	0.9	0.8	0.6	0.9	4.4	9.3	10.6
1982	39.0	36.9	38.8	9.2	4.2	10.3	14.0	12.6	16.4	11.3	11.1	3.9	3.1	2.2	1.6	1.4	1.2
1983																	

Weekly hours of work: manufacturing (13) (wage earners) / Durée hebdomadaire du travail : industries manufacturières (13) (ouvriers)

hours / heures

	Year	Q.1	Q.2	Q.3	Q.4	JAN	FEB	MAR	APR	MAY	JUN	JUL	AUG	SEP	OCT	NOV	DEC
1964	46.3	46.4	46.0	46.3	46.3	46.4			46.0			46.3			46.3		
1965	45.5	45.5	44.9	45.7	45.9	45.5			44.9			45.7			45.9		
1966	45.9	46.0	45.5	46.2	46.0	46.0			45.5			46.2			46.0		
1967	45.5	45.8	45.4	45.4	45.4	45.8			45.4			45.4			45.4		
1968	45.3	45.0	45.2	45.3	45.6	45.0			45.2			45.3			45.6		
1969	45.5	45.5	45.4	45.6	45.3	45.5			45.4			45.6			45.3		
1970	44.9	45.1	44.8	44.8	44.7	45.1			44.8			44.8			44.7		
1971	44.5	44.6	44.5	44.5	44.5	44.6			44.5			44.5			44.5		
1972	44.0	44.3	44.0	44.0	44.0	44.3			44.0			44.0			44.0		
1973	43.6	43.8	43.7	43.7	43.5	43.8			43.7			43.7			43.5		
1974	42.9	43.1	43.1	43.0	42.8	43.1			43.1			43.0			42.8		
1975	41.7	42.0	41.7	41.8	41.5	42.0			41.7			41.8			41.5		
1976	41.6	41.5	41.7	41.8	41.6	41.5			41.7			41.8			41.6		
1977	41.3	41.4	41.3	41.4	41.2	41.4			41.3			41.4			41.2		
1978	41.0	40.9	41.0	41.1	40.9	40.9			41.0			41.1			40.9		
1979	40.8	40.8	40.8	40.8	40.8	40.8			40.8			40.8			40.8		
1980	40.6	40.7	40.6	40.7	40.6	40.7			40.6			40.7			40.6		
1981	40.3	40.4	40.3	40.3	40.3	40.4			40.3			40.3			40.3		
1982	39.2	40.1	39.3	39.3	39.2	40.1			39.3			39.3			39.2		
1983	38.9	39.0	38.9	39.0	38.8	39.0			38.9			39.0			38.8		

Labour disputes: time lost (15) / Conflits du travail : journées perdues (15)

thousand man-days / milliers de journées-homme

	Year	Q.1	Q.2	Q.3	Q.4	JAN	FEB	MAR	APR	MAY	JUN	JUL	AUG	SEP	OCT	NOV	DEC
1964	2497	759	705	136	897	53	126	580	354	199	153	40	12	84	195	57	645
1965	980	402	411	39	128	306	46	50	172	135	105	10	9	20	54	54	20
1966	2524	760	1487	51	225	21	104	635	517	713	257	18	6	27	69	102	54
1967	4204	1298	2304	77	525	82	712	504	1174	1089	41	42	15	20	86	157	282
1968	150426	257	150072	125	72	105	65	87	72		150000	13	3	9	19	23	30
1969	2224	851	204	354	815	23	76	752	76	49	79	35	14	304	327	423	65
1970	1742	475	643	153	472	57	227	191	275	118	250	43	11	100	222	119	130
1971	4388	840	2854	150	544	165	397	278	512	968	1374	56	26	68	185	116	244
1972	3755	531	1444	177	1604	77	165	289	161	196	1086	87	15	75	837	599	168
1973	3915	396	1428	440	1651	148	110	138	352	542	534	120	47	273	528	254	870
1974	3377	1349	835	209	984	80	211	1058	544	144	147	86	21	102	226	652	106
1975	3870	462	1687	635	1086	69	175	218	364	613	710	296	65	274	352	353	381
1976	5001	1539	1748	322	1393	225	459	856	733	677	288	136	43	143	870	175	348
1977	3666	881	1686	221	879	172	314	395	537	906	243	96	20	105	190	95	594
1978	2187	623	394	235	435	74	134	414	153	281	461	92	20	123	152	163	120
1979	3626	1060	1004	306	1256	180	442	439	294	297	413	101	22	133	668	419	170
1980	1671	474	772	192	233	139	145	190	223	224	324	112	16	63	114	56	63
1981	1442	441	279	195	527	94	114	233	116	60	103	34	8	104	206	195	126
1982	2251	893	716	159	473	125	451	322	225	260	231	78	13	68	140	210	129
1983	1325	374	393	227	332	151	122	101	93	128	172	84	34	109	78	74	179

Hourly rates: manufacturing (13) / Taux horaire : industries manufacturières (13)

1980 = 100

	Year	Q.1	Q.2	Q.3	Q.4	JAN	FEB	MAR	APR	MAY	JUN	JUL	AUG	SEP	OCT	NOV	DEC
1964	16.3	15.7	16.0	16.3	16.5	15.7			16.0			16.3			16.5		
1965	17.2	16.7	17.0	17.2	17.4	16.7			17.0			17.2			17.4		
1966	18.2	17.7	18.0	18.2	18.5	17.7			18.0			18.2			18.5		
1967	19.3	18.7	19.0	19.3	19.6	18.7			19.0			19.3			19.6		
1968	21.7	19.9	20.2	22.3	22.8	19.9			20.2			22.3			22.8		
1969	24.2	23.1	23.6	24.1	24.7	23.1			23.6			24.1			24.7		
1970	26.7	25.3	26.1	26.7	27.4	25.3			26.1			26.7			27.4		
1971	29.7	28.1	29.0	29.7	30.4	28.1			29.0			29.7			30.4		
1972	33.0	31.2	32.2	33.0	34.0	31.2			32.2			33.0			34.0		
1973	37.8	35.1	36.4	37.8	39.2	35.1			36.4			37.8			39.2		
1974	45.2	40.7	42.9	45.5	47.3	40.7			42.9			45.5			47.3		
1975	53.0	49.2	50.8	53.4	54.8	49.2			50.8			53.4			54.8		
1976	60.4	56.3	58.3	60.5	62.6	56.3			58.3			60.5			62.6		
1977	68.1	64.3	65.8	68.0	70.1	64.3			65.8			68.0			70.1		
1978	76.9	72.2	74.0	77.2	79.5	72.2			74.0			77.2			79.5		
1979	86.9	81.6	83.9	86.7	89.9	81.6			83.9			86.7			89.9		
1980	100.0	92.9	96.3	100.3	103.5	92.9			96.3			100.3			103.5		
1981	114.5	106.6	109.5	114.3	118.8	106.6			109.5			114.3			118.8		
1982	131.9	123.7	129.4	133.4	133.6	123.7			129.4			133.4			133.6		
1983	146.7	139.1	143.4	147.1	150.1	139.1			143.4			147.1			150.1		

Labour cost: (16) engineering industries / Coût de la main-d'œuvre : (16) industries mécaniques et électriques

1980 = 100

	Year	Q.1	Q.2	Q.3	Q.4	JAN	FEB	MAR	APR	MAY	JUN	JUL	AUG	SEP	OCT	NOV	DEC
1964	14.6	14.3	14.5	14.6	15.0	14.2	14.3	14.4	14.4	14.6	14.6	14.6	14.6	14.7	14.9	15.0	15.0
1965	15.5	15.2	15.5	15.5	15.7	15.2	15.2	15.2	15.4	15.5	15.5	15.5	15.5	15.5	15.6	15.7	15.7
1966	16.3	16.0	16.2	16.4	16.7	15.9	15.9	16.0	16.2	16.2	16.2	16.3	16.4	16.4	16.6	16.7	16.7
1967	17.4	17.0	17.3	17.5	17.9	16.9	17.0	17.0	17.2	17.3	17.4	17.5	17.5	17.5	17.7	18.0	18.1
1968	19.3	18.2	18.9	19.9	20.3	18.1	18.2	18.3	18.5	18.5	19.9	19.9	19.9	19.9	20.5	20.4	20.0
1969	21.0	20.3	20.8	21.0	21.9	20.2	20.3	20.4	20.6	20.9	20.9	20.9	20.9	21.2	21.6	22.0	22.0
1970	23.5	22.5	23.4	23.7	24.4	22.2	22.5	22.8	23.1	23.4	23.5	23.6	23.6	23.8	24.2	24.3	24.5
1971	26.4	25.3	26.1	26.6	27.3	25.0	25.4	25.6	26.0	26.2	26.3	26.5	26.5	26.8	27.2	27.4	27.5
1972	29.5	28.2	29.1	29.7	30.8	27.9	28.1	28.6	28.9	29.1	29.4	29.6	29.6	29.9	30.5	30.7	31.2
1973	34.3	32.7	33.7	34.7	36.2	32.5	32.7	33.0	33.5	33.7	34.0	34.5	34.5	35.0	35.9	36.2	36.5
1974	40.9	38.5	40.3	41.7	43.2	38.0	38.5	39.1	39.8	40.4	40.7	41.5	41.5	42.1	42.6	43.2	43.8
1975	49.2	46.6	48.2	50.4	51.7	46.1	46.5	47.2	47.8	48.1	48.6	50.2	50.2	50.8	51.3	51.7	52.0
1976	57.3	54.4	56.7	57.8	60.5	53.8	54.1	55.4	56.3	56.7	57.0	57.5	57.5	58.2	60.0	60.4	61.0
1977	65.5	62.7	64.4	66.4	68.5	62.5	62.6	63.1	64.1	64.3	64.8	66.2	66.2	66.8	68.1	68.3	69.1
1978	74.8	71.3	73.3	76.4	78.1	70.8	71.4	71.8	72.7	73.2	74.0	76.2	76.2	76.8	77.8	78.1	78.5
1979	86.2	81.9	85.1	87.3	90.6	81.2	81.5	83.0	84.6	85.2	85.5	87.0	87.0	87.9	89.8	90.5	91.4
1980	100.0	94.1	98.4	102.1	105.4	93.3	94.0	95.0	97.5	98.4	99.4	101.8	101.8	102.7	104.9	105.4	106.0
1981	114.4	109.1	112.1	115.8	120.6	108.6	109.1	109.6	111.6	112.0	112.6	115.2	115.2	116.9	119.3	120.7	121.8
1982	137.5	128.3	136.8	140.8	144.2	125.6	127.9	131.3	136.2	136.6	137.7	141.0	141.0	140.6	141.1	145.2	146.3
1983	155.1	148.6	153.5	157.6	160.6	148.2	148.6	148.9	152.9	153.3	154.5	157.3	157.3	158.1	160.0	160.6	161.2

Labour cost: textile industries (16) / Coût de la main-d'œuvre : industries textiles (16)

1980 = 100

	Year	Q.1	Q.2	Q.3	Q.4	JAN	FEB	MAR	APR	MAY	JUN	JUL	AUG	SEP	OCT	NOV	DEC
1964	15.3	14.9	15.3	15.5	15.6	14.7	14.7	15.2	15.2	15.3	15.4	15.5	15.5	15.5	15.6	15.6	15.6
1965	16.1	15.7	16.0	16.3	16.5	15.7	15.7	15.8	15.9	15.9	16.2	16.3	16.3	16.4	16.4	16.5	16.5
1966	17.3	16.9	17.2	17.4	17.8	16.7	17.0	17.1	17.2	17.2	17.3	17.3	17.4	17.4	17.6	17.9	18.0
1967	18.6	18.1	18.4	18.8	19.1	18.1	18.1	18.2	18.2	18.3	18.7	18.7	18.8	18.8	18.9	19.2	19.3
1968	20.8	19.4	20.2	21.7	22.0	19.3	19.4	19.4	19.4	19.4	21.6	21.6	21.7	21.7	22.2	22.2	21.6
1969	22.6	21.8	22.4	22.8	23.6	21.7	21.8	21.8	22.0	22.5	22.6	22.7	22.8	22.9	23.1	23.7	23.8
1970	25.2	24.2	25.1	25.4	26.3	24.1	24.2	24.3	24.9	25.1	25.2	25.3	25.4	25.5	26.1	26.3	26.4
1971	28.6	27.1	28.4	28.8	30.1	27.0	27.1	27.2	28.0	28.5	28.6	28.7	28.8	28.9	29.7	30.3	30.4
1972	32.2	30.6	32.0	32.4	33.8	30.5	30.6	30.6	31.8	32.0	32.1	32.3	32.4	32.4	33.6	33.9	34.0
1973	36.4	34.5	35.8	37.0	38.5	34.0	34.5	34.9	35.4	35.8	36.1	36.5	37.0	37.5	38.1	38.5	38.9
1974	44.1	40.7	43.2	45.2	47.4	39.9	40.7	41.5	42.6	43.2	43.8	44.3	45.2	46.0	47.0	47.4	47.7
1975	52.3	49.5	51.1	53.5	55.0	49.1	49.5	49.9	50.3	51.1	51.9	52.9	53.5	54.1	54.6	55.0	55.4
1976	60.3	56.8	59.2	61.3	63.7	56.1	56.8	57.6	58.5	59.2	59.9	60.6	61.3	62.0	63.1	63.7	64.3
1977	68.7	66.2	67.7	69.5	71.4	65.5	66.3	66.7	67.2	67.7	68.2	68.8	69.5	70.2	70.9	71.5	72.0
1978	77.5	73.5	75.9	79.2	81.6	73.0	73.5	74.0	74.5	76.0	77.2	78.4	79.2	80.0	81.1	81.6	82.2
1979	87.4	83.3	85.6	89.0	91.9	82.8	83.3	83.8	84.4	85.6	86.8	88.1	89.0	89.9	90.7	91.9	93.0
1980	100.0	95.2	98.4	101.7	104.7	94.2	95.2	96.2	97.2	98.4	99.6	100.9	101.7	102.5	103.4	104.7	106.0
1981	113.1	108.2	110.6	114.0	119.7	107.4	108.2	109.0	109.8	111.4	110.7	112.2	114.0	115.8	117.6	119.7	121.8
1982	133.9	126.3	133.1	136.9	139.2	123.9	126.3	128.7	131.1	133.1	135.1	136.8	136.9	137.0	137.1	139.2	141.4
1983	152.4	145.1	150.2	155.7	159.1	143.6	145.1	146.6	148.0	150.2	152.3	154.4	155.7	157.0	158.4	159.1	159.9

FRANCE

Producer prices: agricultural goods (17)
1980 = 100

Adjusted - Corrigé

Prix à la production : produits agricoles (17)
1980 = 100

	Year	Q.1	Q.2	Q.3	Q.4	JAN	FEB	MAR	APR	MAY	JUN	JUL	AUG	SEP	OCT	NOV	DEC
1964	38.9	38.9	39.0	39.2	38.6	39.7	38.7	38.4	37.9	38.9	40.2	38.8	39.2	39.5	38.1	38.5	39.2
1965	39.3	38.9	39.6	40.1	40.8	38.9	39.0	39.0	39.3	39.0	40.3	39.8	39.8	40.8	40.5	41.2	40.8
1966	41.2	40.7	41.0	41.4	41.7	40.7	40.8	40.6	41.4	40.8	40.8	41.1	41.5	41.6	41.2	42.1	41.6
1967	41.4	41.4	41.4	40.9	41.1	41.1	41.3	41.6	41.9	41.3	40.9	40.8	41.0	41.0	41.0	41.3	41.7
1968	41.8	40.4	41.2	42.1	42.9	40.5	40.3	40.5	40.7	41.3	41.5	41.7	42.2	42.5	42.7	43.0	43.1
1969	44.5	43.2	44.4	45.0	46.3	43.0	43.3	43.4	44.0	44.5	44.7	44.7	44.8	45.4	46.3	46.0	46.9
1970	=47.1=	47.0	47.7	47.5	47.1	46.6	47.0	47.4	47.9	47.6	47.5	47.6	47.6	47.3	47.2	47.0	47.2
1971	49.1	47.6	48.2	49.3	51.0	47.5	47.7	47.7	47.8	48.3	48.5	48.8	49.3	49.8	50.4	51.1	51.5
1972	55.5	52.1	54.0	56.5	58.7	51.5	52.2	52.5	53.1	54.3	54.6	55.5	56.6	57.2	58.1	58.7	59.3
1973	61.7	60.9	62.7	62.1	62.7	60.4	60.9	61.5	62.7	62.8	62.7	61.6	62.2	62.4	62.8	62.8	62.5
1974	63.9	62.9	61.3	62.2	66.2	62.7	63.1	62.8	61.4	62.1	62.0	60.8	62.2	63.6	65.7	66.7	66.1
1975	=68.7=	65.5	67.5	70.3	71.6	64.6	65.3	66.5	67.6	66.9	67.8	70.5	70.1	70.3	71.1	71.5	72.2
1976	78.7	74.2	74.9	80.7	84.1	73.3	74.4	74.9	75.1	74.9	74.8	77.7	80.5	83.8	84.1	84.2	84.1
1977	85.6	84.3	84.3	84.4	85.3	85.5	84.5	82.9	84.1	83.9	84.7	84.3	84.1	84.8	84.4	84.9	86.7
1978	88.7	88.0	88.2	88.4	89.2	87.4	88.5	88.0	87.8	87.8	89.0	89.3	88.7	87.3	88.2	89.2	90.2
1979	94.4	92.3	92.6	93.5	94.8	91.7	91.9	93.2	92.5	93.6	91.7	92.0	93.9	94.3	94.2	95.7	94.4
1980	100.0	94.9	95.5	99.3	103.5	95.7	94.7	94.2	94.0	95.7	96.9	99.7	98.6	99.7	101.4	104.4	104.7
1981	111.3	105.2	108.0	112.3	118.5	104.3	105.9	105.3	105.2	108.3	110.5	112.1	111.0	113.7	117.5	119.2	118.9
1982	124.5	121.5	124.9	125.0	128.5	119.1	120.6	124.9	125.7	125.2	123.8	124.5	125.0	125.5	127.5	129.5	128.5
1983	134.1	127.7	130.7	136.9	141.2	126.7	128.0	128.4	127.6	130.9	133.5	133.7	136.8	140.1	139.9	141.8	141.7

Wholesale prices (manufacturing): (18)(19)
textiles
1980 = 100

Prix de gros (industries manufacturières) : (18) (19)
textiles
1980 = 100

	Year	Q.1	Q.2	Q.3	Q.4	JAN	FEB	MAR	APR	MAY	JUN	JUL	AUG	SEP	OCT	NOV	DEC
1964	55.5	55.8	55.8	55.5	54.9	55.3	55.9	56.2	56.1	55.8	55.7	55.5	55.6	55.4	55.3	55.1	54.2
1965	53.1	53.4	53.0	52.8	53.3	53.7	53.5	53.0	52.8	53.0	53.0	52.9	52.8	52.8	53.0	53.3	53.5
1966	54.3	53.8	54.7	54.6	53.9	53.7	53.8	54.0	54.6	54.8	54.6	54.6	54.6	54.6	54.2	53.9	53.6
1967	53.5	53.8	53.6	53.5	53.1	53.8	54.1	53.5	53.5	53.5	53.8	53.4	53.6	53.5	53.3	53.5	52.5
1968	53.2	51.5	52.3	53.3	55.9	51.5	51.4	51.5	51.8	52.0	53.0	53.0	52.9	53.9	55.5	55.5	56.6
1969	58.7	56.8	58.1	58.9	60.9	56.7	56.8	56.8	57.4	58.3	58.5	58.6	58.6	59.7	61.0	61.0	60.8
1970	60.8	61.2	61.4	61.1	59.6	61.3	61.5	60.8	61.3	61.2	61.6	61.2	61.2	60.9	59.7	59.3	59.7
1971	62.2	60.0	61.6	62.7	64.6	60.1	59.9	60.0	61.3	61.2	62.1	62.1	62.7	63.4	64.0	64.5	65.3
1972	70.2	66.7	68.7	70.0	75.2	65.6	66.6	67.9	68.2	69.0	69.0	69.2	69.6	71.3	74.5	74.6	76.4
1973	85.4	82.8	83.8	85.8	89.2	80.4	83.4	84.8	85.1	82.8	83.3	84.0	85.6	87.0	88.0	86.7	92.8
1974	98.5	95.8	102.1	100.4	95.9	96.4	96.3	94.5	100.2	102.8	103.4	102.0	99.8	99.6	97.4	97.4	93.1
1975	84.7	88.7	83.1	83.3	83.5	92.7	86.8	86.6	83.8	83.1	82.5	83.0	83.7	83.3	82.4	83.7	84.4
1976	89.5	85.3	87.5	91.2	94.1	84.9	85.0	86.0	86.5	87.5	88.7	89.7	91.8	92.1	93.6	95.0	93.6
1977	90.2	91.1	91.7	90.4	87.6	90.5	90.9	91.9	91.9	92.6	90.6	90.8	90.6	89.8	87.9	87.5	87.4
1978	88.7	87.8	88.6	89.1	89.3	87.7	87.5	88.0	88.0	88.9	88.8	88.9	89.1	89.4	89.1	89.3	89.6
1979	94.6	90.9	94.9	95.9	96.8	89.4	89.5	93.8	94.2	94.9	95.5	95.9	95.7	96.0	97.1	96.6	96.6
1980	100.0	97.2	98.7	99.9	103.6	97.3	97.7	98.5	98.7	98.2	99.1	98.8	98.8	102.2	102.3	103.5	104.9
1981	109.8	105.9	109.6	113.1	110.4	105.4	105.8	106.6	107.8	108.7	112.4	113.2	113.5	112.7	112.3	108.5	110.5
1982	120.8	114.6	119.3	123.4	125.9	113.6	114.4	115.9	118.5	118.6	120.8	123.2	123.2	123.8	124.3	126.1	127.3
1983	139.4	129.2	136.3	143.8	148.2	126.9	128.7	132.0	132.2	136.6	140.0	141.9	143.9	145.6	144.9	143.5	151.0

Wholesale prices (manufacturing): (18)(19)
chemicals
1980 = 100

Prix de gros (industries manufacturières) : (18) (19)
produits chimiques
1980 = 100

	Year	Q.1	Q.2	Q.3	Q.4	JAN	FEB	MAR	APR	MAY	JUN	JUL	AUG	SEP	OCT	NOV	DEC
1964	37.0	37.2	37.0	36.8	37.0	37.1	37.2	37.2	37.2	36.9	36.9	36.7	36.9	36.9	36.9	37.0	37.1
1965	37.2	37.4	37.2	37.1	37.1	37.3	37.4	37.4	37.5	37.1	37.1	37.0	37.1	37.1	37.1	37.2	37.2
1966	37.3	37.4	37.4	37.1	37.3	37.3	37.4	37.4	37.6	37.2	37.3	37.0	37.2	37.1	37.2	37.3	37.4
1967	37.0	37.3	36.9	36.8	37.2	37.3	37.4	37.4	37.4	36.6	36.7	36.6	36.8	36.9	37.0	37.2	37.3
1968	36.3	36.2	36.0	36.3	36.8	36.2	36.3	36.3	36.2	35.9	35.9	36.3	36.4	36.3	36.4	36.4	37.5
1969	37.7	37.8	37.6	37.4	38.2	37.7	37.8	37.8	37.8	37.7	37.2	37.3	37.4	37.6	37.8	38.4	38.5
1970	39.1	39.1	39.0	38.8	39.5	38.7	39.2	39.3	39.4	39.2	38.6	38.7	38.7	39.0	39.3	39.6	39.8
1971	40.4	40.2	40.3	40.4	40.8	39.9	40.2	40.4	40.5	40.4	40.0	40.3	40.5	40.6	40.8	40.8	40.9
1972	41.8	41.3	41.4	41.9	42.7	41.1	41.5	41.5	41.5	41.5	41.3	41.8	41.9	42.1	42.3	42.6	43.2
1973	44.7	43.2	43.9	44.3	47.2	42.7	43.2	43.6	44.0	43.9	43.7	44.0	44.1	44.9	46.3	47.2	48.2
1974	58.8	53.5	58.4	60.3	62.9	51.1	53.3	56.1	57.3	58.4	59.4	59.7	60.6	60.5	62.8	62.9	62.9
1975	63.6	63.7	63.6	63.2	64.0	63.0	63.7	64.4	64.1	63.9	62.9	63.0	63.2	63.4	63.7	64.0	64.5
1976	66.6	65.1	66.2	67.0	67.9	64.6	65.3	65.5	66.2	66.9	65.5	66.6	66.9	67.6	67.6	68.1	68.1
1977	69.8	68.9	69.9	69.7	70.9	67.7	69.1	69.8	70.2	70.1	69.3	69.4	69.5	70.3	70.9	70.8	71.1
1978	72.8	71.6	72.2	72.9	74.4	71.1	71.6	72.2	72.3	72.1	72.0	72.1	72.9	73.6	73.9	74.2	75.2
1979	84.0	77.8	82.2	85.7	90.0	75.7	77.4	80.2	81.4	82.4	82.9	84.4	85.7	87.1	89.5	89.9	90.3
1980	100.0	95.9	99.7	100.1	104.4	92.9	96.8	98.0	99.7	99.9	99.6	99.6	99.9	100.9	104.2	104.2	104.6
1981	114.2	106.6	112.9	116.0	121.4	105.9	106.5	107.4	112.5	112.9	113.3	114.0	115.8	118.2	121.0	121.2	121.9
1982	128.6	123.4	128.0	130.3	132.9	122.4	123.0	124.7	127.2	127.4	129.5	129.8	131.0	130.1	131.6	133.2	133.8
1983	140.8	135.0	140.2	142.5	145.6	134.3	134.4	136.3	139.2	139.9	141.5	139.8	143.7	144.0	144.3	145.9	146.6

Wholesale prices (manufacturing): (18)(19) — Prix de gros (industries manufacturières) : (19)(18)

metal products — ouvrages en métaux

1980 = 100 — 1980 = 100

	Year	Q.1	Q.2	Q.3	Q.4	JAN	FEB	MAR	APR	MAY	JUN	JUL	AUG	SEP	OCT	NOV	DEC
1964	34.9	33.4	34.5	35.4	36.2	33.2	33.5	33.6	34.2	34.5	34.7	35.0	35.5	35.8	36.2	36.4	36.0
1965	36.3	35.7	36.2	36.1	37.2	35.5	35.8	35.8	36.2	36.4	36.1	36.1	36.1	36.3	37.4	37.1	37.1
1966	40.0	38.9	42.7	39.3	39.2	38.5	39.0	39.3	41.7	43.5	42.7	41.2	37.8	38.9	39.3	39.1	39.2
1967	37.9	38.3	36.5	37.1	39.6	39.1	38.5	37.3	36.3	36.9	36.4	36.9	37.0	37.6	39.0	40.0	39.7
1968	37.2	39.4	36.1	36.3	37.2	38.6	41.0	38.6	35.8	36.0	36.5	35.9	36.3	36.6	36.3	36.9	38.5
1969	44.4	39.7	42.0	46.1	49.7	39.6	39.5	40.0	41.5	41.8	42.7	43.6	47.3	47.3	48.4	49.8	50.8
1970	50.3	52.3	52.4	49.7	46.8	50.9	51.6	54.3	53.9	52.4	51.1	51.0	49.1	49.0	47.3	46.9	46.3
1971	47.3	47.0	47.8	47.5	46.8	46.0	46.1	48.9	48.7	47.2	47.6	47.9	47.6	47.1	47.2	46.7	46.4
1972	46.8	47.0	46.5	46.5	47.1	46.7	47.1	47.2	46.8	46.4	46.2	46.1	46.5	46.9	46.9	46.8	47.7
1973	55.0	49.2	52.7	56.1	61.9	47.6	48.6	51.6	52.5	52.0	53.6	55.0	56.5	56.9	58.4	65.1	62.2
1974	73.6	73.5	79.8	72.8	68.2	67.5	72.2	80.7	83.7	78.4	77.4	74.9	72.3	71.2	69.6	68.5	66.4
1975	63.8	66.2	63.0	63.7	62.1	65.9	66.7	66.2	64.3	62.5	62.1	63.4	63.8	63.8	62.1	62.2	62.1
1976	71.2	64.2	70.4	76.0	74.2	62.6	63.3	66.7	69.2	70.5	71.6	76.7	75.8	75.5	73.9	74.0	74.8
1977	75.2	76.6	75.5	74.0	74.8	75.5	76.9	77.3	76.8	75.2	74.3	73.8	73.4	74.9	74.6	74.6	75.1
1978	78.4	74.6	76.6	79.7	82.7	74.1	74.3	75.5	75.6	76.2	77.8	78.6	80.2	80.2	82.1	82.8	83.3
1979	93.4	89.1	93.0	95.1	96.6	86.0	89.1	92.0	92.5	92.7	93.7	93.0	94.7	97.6	95.7	96.3	97.7
1980	100.0	102.9	98.8	98.9	99.3	102.5	103.9	102.2	100.3	98.4	97.9	99.6	98.3	98.8	99.2	100.4	98.2
1981	106.3	99.5	103.9	109.8	111.8	99.4	99.4	99.7	101.3	103.9	106.6	109.1	110.2	110.1	110.6	110.5	114.5
1982	121.7	117.6	120.2	124.0	125.0	115.8	117.1	120.0	119.9	119.8	121.0	123.0	124.2	124.8	125.0	125.0	125.2
1983	138.1	129.2	135.8	142.1	146.0	127.0	128.9	131.8	134.2	135.4	137.8	140.3	142.5	143.4	143.0	146.6	148.2

Wholesale prices (manufacturing): (18) — Prix de gros (industries manufacturières) : (18)

semi-manufactured goods — demi-produits

1980 = 100 — 1980 = 100

	Year	Q.1	Q.2	Q.3	Q.4	JAN	FEB	MAR	APR	MAY	JUN	JUL	AUG	SEP	OCT	NOV	DEC
1964	38.0	37.7	38.0	38.1	38.2	37.6	37.8	37.8	38.0	37.9	38.0	38.0	38.1	38.2	38.2	38.2	38.1
1965	38.3	38.1	38.2	38.1	38.5	38.1	38.2	38.1	38.2	38.2	38.2	38.1	38.1	38.2	38.5	38.5	38.6
1966	39.2	39.0	39.6	39.1	39.1	38.8	39.1	39.2	39.5	39.8	39.6	39.3	38.9	39.0	39.0	39.0	39.1
1967	39.1	39.2	38.9	39.0	39.3	39.2	39.3	39.1	39.0	38.8	38.8	38.8	39.0	39.1	39.2	39.5	39.3
1968	38.6	38.3	37.8	38.5	39.6	38.2	38.5	38.2	37.8	37.7	38.1	38.3	38.4	38.8	39.1	39.3	40.3
1969	42.2	40.8	41.6	42.5	43.7	40.7	40.8	41.0	41.4	41.6	41.8	42.0	42.7	42.8	43.4	43.8	44.1
1970	45.0	44.8	45.2	44.9	45.0	44.3	44.7	45.4	45.5	45.1	45.0	44.9	44.7	45.0	44.9	45.0	45.2
1971	46.8	45.8	46.7	47.2	47.5	45.5	45.7	46.4	46.7	46.6	46.8	46.9	47.2	47.4	47.6	47.5	47.6
1972	49.3	48.1	48.8	49.5	51.0	47.7	48.0	48.4	48.7	48.8	48.8	49.1	49.3	50.0	50.6	50.9	51.5
1973	54.8	52.2	53.6	55.2	57.9	51.4	52.2	53.1	53.3	53.3	54.2	54.9	55.2	55.6	56.3	57.8	59.7
1974	69.9	64.6	71.1	72.0	71.8	61.9	64.5	67.5	70.1	71.2	72.0	72.2	72.0	71.9	72.3	72.2	70.8
1975	69.1	70.6	68.7	68.5	68.7	70.7	70.7	70.3	69.3	68.7	68.2	68.4	68.6	68.6	68.5	68.7	68.8
1976	73.0	69.9	72.2	74.6	75.2	69.1	69.8	70.7	71.6	72.5	72.7	74.3	74.5	75.0	75.0	75.2	75.5
1977	76.5	75.7	76.8	76.6	76.3	74.9	75.8	76.4	77.0	77.1	76.5	76.5	76.4	76.8	76.8	76.7	76.9
1978	80.5	77.9	79.6	81.1	83.4	77.3	78.0	78.5	79.2	79.4	80.1	80.5	80.8	82.0	82.7	83.3	84.0
1979	91.3	87.0	90.2	93.0	95.3	85.3	86.5	89.1	89.4	90.1	91.1	92.2	93.1	93.7	94.6	95.3	95.8
1980	100.0	97.7	99.1	99.9	103.3	96.7	97.8	98.6	99.0	99.1	99.2	99.4	99.8	100.5	103.4	103.3	103.3
1981	114.0	110.0	114.6	113.8	117.6	108.9	110.2	111.0	113.4	114.5	116.0	112.2	113.5	115.7	116.8	117.0	118.9
1982	125.2	121.4	124.8	126.5	128.2	120.1	121.0	123.1	124.4	124.4	125.7	126.2	126.6	126.8	127.2	128.3	129.1
1983	136.5	131.1	134.6	138.1	142.1	130.0	130.8	132.5	133.7	134.3	135.8	136.3	138.6	139.5	140.2	142.9	143.3

Wholesale prices (manufacturing): (18) — Prix de gros (industries manufacturières) : (18)

raw materials — matières premières

1980 = 100 — 1980 = 100

	Year	Q.1	Q.2	Q.3	Q.4	JAN	FEB	MAR	APR	MAY	JUN	JUL	AUG	SEP	OCT	NOV	DEC
1964	39.2	38.4	39.0	39.5	40.0	38.0	38.5	38.7	38.9	39.0	39.1	39.2	39.6	39.8	40.1	40.2	39.6
1965	39.6	39.5	39.7	39.4	39.7	39.2	39.6	39.7	39.8	39.8	39.5	39.5	39.4	39.5	39.7	39.7	39.8
1966	41.0	40.4	42.2	40.9	40.6	40.5	40.5	40.3	41.9	42.3	42.3	41.7	40.5	40.6	40.7	40.6	40.6
1967	40.0	40.5	39.6	39.5	40.2	40.8	40.5	40.1	39.5	39.8	39.4	39.4	39.5	39.7	40.1	40.5	40.0
1968	39.0	39.3	38.3	38.6	39.7	38.9	39.9	39.1	38.0	38.3	38.6	38.4	38.6	38.9	38.6	39.7	40.9
1969	44.7	41.6	43.1	45.7	48.3	41.4	41.5	41.9	42.7	43.2	43.4	43.8	46.0	47.2	47.6	48.5	48.8
1970	49.0	50.0	50.3	48.6	47.1	49.5	50.0	50.5	51.0	50.4	49.4	49.0	48.6	48.1	47.1	47.1	47.2
1971	47.5	47.7	47.7	47.3	47.2	47.6	47.3	48.2	48.3	47.4	47.5	47.6	47.4	46.9	47.3	47.2	47.2
1972	48.6	47.5	47.9	48.3	50.6	47.2	47.5	47.9	48.0	48.1	47.7	47.9	48.2	48.8	49.9	50.1	51.7
1973	61.2	55.1	57.5	62.5	69.7	53.5	55.4	56.4	57.3	56.8	58.4	60.9	63.0	63.6	66.1	70.8	72.0
1974	81.5	81.7	86.4	81.6	76.1	79.2	80.9	85.1	88.7	86.2	84.2	83.3	81.6	80.0	78.2	76.4	73.6
1975	67.0	70.1	65.7	66.7	65.7	72.4	69.0	68.9	67.5	65.2	64.4	66.2	67.0	66.7	64.4	66.0	66.7
1976	75.8	68.6	74.2	79.8	80.4	67.5	68.3	70.1	72.3	74.4	75.8	79.0	80.3	80.2	80.0	80.9	80.2
1977	81.9	82.9	83.1	81.0	80.3	81.7	82.9	84.1	84.2	83.6	81.4	80.9	80.8	81.3	79.8	80.5	80.6
1978	83.1	80.6	82.0	83.6	86.3	80.2	80.7	80.8	81.0	82.8	82.1	82.4	83.7	84.7	85.7	86.7	86.4
1979	93.9	90.3	93.8	95.7	95.9	87.9	90.7	92.3	93.2	93.8	94.3	94.7	95.8	96.6	95.7	96.2	95.7
1980	100.0	99.9	98.7	98.9	102.5	99.7	100.4	99.7	99.7	98.3	98.1	98.3	98.0	100.4	101.5	102.7	103.2
1981	111.6	106.9	112.7	114.6	112.0	106.1	106.8	108.0	109.6	112.5	115.9	114.7	115.9	113.2	113.3	111.2	111.5
1982	117.7	113.8	116.4	120.5	120.3	112.9	113.7	114.8	115.9	116.3	117.1	120.4	120.5	120.6	120.2	120.5	120.1
1983	138.5	124.3	134.4	143.9	152.2	120.1	125.0	127.9	131.5	135.0	136.8	140.0	144.0	147.8	148.5	151.3	156.9

FRANCE

Wholesale prices (manufacturing): (18)
imported raw materials
1980 = 100

Prix de gros (industries manufacturières) : (18)
matières premières importées
1980 = 100

	Year	Q.1	Q.2	Q.3	Q.4	JAN	FEB	MAR	APR	MAY	JUN	JUL	AUG	SEP	OCT	NOV	DEC
1964	43.7	42.5	43.5	44.2	44.6	41.8	42.6	43.0	43.2	43.5	43.7	43.7	44.3	44.5	44.8	45.0	44.0
1965	44.7	44.4	45.1	44.4	44.6	44.1	44.5	44.6	45.3	45.3	44.8	44.6	44.4	44.3	44.6	44.6	44.7
1966	47.8	45.5	50.4	48.1	47.4	45.7	45.6	45.3	49.2	51.1	50.9	49.7	46.7	47.8	47.6	47.4	47.3
1967	46.2	46.7	45.2	45.4	47.3	47.4	46.9	45.9	45.2	45.6	44.9	45.3	45.2	45.8	47.0	47.8	47.2
1968	45.4	46.7	44.6	44.3	45.9	45.8	48.0	46.3	44.2	44.9	44.8	43.9	44.4	44.7	44.1	46.2	47.5
1969	53.3	48.8	50.7	55.3	58.6	48.5	48.7	49.2	50.2	50.9	51.0	51.9	56.5	57.6	57.7	59.0	59.3
1970	56.4	60.0	58.2	55.1	52.3	59.5	60.1	60.4	59.6	58.5	56.6	56.2	55.1	54.1	52.6	51.9	52.4
1971	52.7	53.3	52.7	52.5	52.3	53.3	52.5	54.1	53.4	52.1	52.7	53.0	52.6	51.8	52.4	52.2	52.3
1972	53.9	52.6	52.8	52.9	57.2	52.2	52.5	53.1	52.7	53.1	52.6	52.5	52.8	53.5	56.0	56.3	59.4
1973	75.4	67.1	70.5	78.0	85.2	63.9	67.7	69.7	70.9	68.7	71.7	76.3	78.8	78.7	81.8	88.1	88.7
1974	96.2	102.7	103.0	93.5	85.6	101.6	101.6	105.0	109.5	102.2	97.4	96.5	93.1	91.0	88.0	86.1	82.7
1975	70.5	74.8	67.5	70.6	68.9	80.1	72.3	72.0	70.2	66.9	65.5	70.0	71.3	70.5	67.4	68.8	70.4
1976	84.3	74.2	81.5	89.6	91.8	72.1	73.3	76.8	79.4	80.9	84.1	88.4	90.3	90.0	91.0	93.1	91.2
1977	91.5	95.6	94.7	89.4	86.4	94.3	95.8	96.6	96.4	96.0	91.6	89.9	88.7	89.7	85.9	86.6	86.8
1978	87.9	86.0	87.3	88.1	90.1	85.8	86.4	85.7	85.9	88.4	87.7	86.7	87.9	89.5	89.6	91.0	89.8
1979	96.7	94.1	98.1	98.7	95.9	91.9	94.5	95.8	97.3	98.3	98.6	97.9	99.1	99.1	96.3	96.4	95.0
1980	100.0	101.8	97.4	97.6	103.2	102.4	102.9	100.2	99.2	97.1	95.9	96.6	96.4	99.6	101.3	103.8	104.4
1981	117.9	111.1	121.0	124.7	114.5	209.5	111.1	112.7	115.3	121.3	126.4	125.6	127.6	121.0	120.1	111.8	111.9
1982	119.8	113.9	117.4	124.8	123.0	113.2	113.5	115.0	116.9	116.3	118.9	124.3	125.1	125.1	124.6	123.5	121.0
1983	147.0	125.1	141.6	157.0	164.5	120.0	124.4	131.0	135.5	142.5	146.8	150.1	159.1	161.8	158.8	164.8	169.8

Money supply (M1) (20)
billion francs, end of period

Disponibilités monétaires (M1) (20)
milliards de francs, fin de période

	Year	Q.1	Q.2	Q.3	Q.4	JAN	FEB	MAR	APR	MAY	JUN	JUL	AUG	SEP	OCT	NOV	DEC
1964	160.6	147.1	150.6	153.8	160.6	146.0	145.2	147.1	147.1	147.5	150.6	154.9	152.3	153.8	154.1	153.0	160.6
1965	175.7	158.5	164.6	168.7	175.7	157.9	156.5	158.5	160.4	160.9	164.6	168.5	167.6	168.7	169.7	168.3	175.7
1966	189.3	174.0	180.3	183.2	189.3	173.0	171.9	174.0	175.6	175.9	180.3	184.6	182.3	183.2	183.1	180.9	189.3
1967	199.6	188.3	194.8	194.7	199.6	187.8	185.6	186.3	192.5	189.6	194.8	197.6	193.7	194.7	193.7	190.0	199.6
1968	216.2	190.9	207.6	209.2	216.2	192.5	189.3	190.9	192.2	.. S	207.6	209.3	205.9	209.2	209.0	206.8	216.2
1969	211.1	209.9	214.4	215.0	211.1	207.0	206.6	209.9	212.9	209.1	214.4	217.4	214.6	215.0	211.9	209.3	211.1
1970	235.1	204.3	211.2	215.0	235.1	203.6	201.1	204.3	207.5	205.8	211.2	216.0	213.5	215.0	220.5	220.7	235.1
1971	262.9	232.1	244.3	247.5	262.9	227.1	227.5	232.1	233.2	235.5	244.3	250.4	245.6	247.5	251.5	248.0	262.9
1972	302.4	260.5	276.9	285.5	302.4	252.6	250.1	260.5	261.3	262.2	276.9	285.0	277.3	285.5	286.6	288.2	302.4
1973	331.9	288.1	306.6	307.2	331.9	285.8	281.5	288.1	296.1	296.7	306.6	308.0	301.2	307.2	309.4	303.1	331.9
1974	370.5	321.3	333.3	333.1	370.5	312.0	308.4	321.3	322.5	318.7	333.3	337.4	327.0	333.1	339.4	346.6	370.5
1975	432.2	354.3	374.8	387.7	432.2	348.0	341.7	354.3	351.6	353.4	374.8	381.3	374.7	387.7	391.3	394.6	432.2
1976	465.7	415.3	437.4	437.0	465.7	407.5	404.9	415.3	422.1	420.5	437.4	443.8	430.3	437.0	443.3	437.8	465.7
1977	519.6	446.9	463.1	474.6	519.6	442.5	433.5	446.9	452.9	454.0	463.1	476.9	464.1	474.6	481.3	472.9	519.6
1978	577.1	495.8	517.5	534.6	577.1	488.1	490.5	495.8	508.2	494.2	517.5	529.4	515.3	534.6	538.2	534.2	577.1
1979	647.3	568.0	593.9	595.6	647.3	548.5	545.4	568.0	570.4	567.3	593.9	595.7	576.8	595.6	598.9	582.1	647.3
1980	692.7	616.6	637.2	645.7	692.7	600.6	593.1	616.6	618.4	616.6	637.2	635.8	628.5	645.7	648.7	646.5	692.7
1981	794.2	667.5	710.6	748.1	794.2	659.7	659.1	667.5	683.9	690.8	710.6	717.4	709.2	748.1	754.4	741.8	794.2
1982	878.4	773.1	812.0	830.9	878.4	765.8	759.0	773.1	733.1	794.8	812.0	828.9	810.3	830.9	858.8	830.9	878.4
1983	982.2	856.0	900.7	907.3	982.2	849.2	834.8	856.0	[illegible]	877.4	900.7	915.5	890.9	907.3	924.8	901.9	982.2

M1 plus quasi-money (20)
billion francs, end of period

M1 plus quasi-monnaie (20)
milliards de francs, fin de période

	Year	Q.1	Q.2	Q.3	Q.4	JAN	FEB	MAR	APR	MAY	JUN	JUL	AUG	SEP	OCT	NOV	DEC
1964	184.3	168.4	172.4	176.6	184.3	166.4	166.1	168.4	168.6	169.3	172.4	177.3	176.0	176.6	177.5	176.7	184.3
1965	204.4	184.0	190.8	196.5	204.4	182.5	181.6	184.0	186.4	187.1	190.8	195.8	195.2	196.5	197.9	196.8	204.4
1966	226.1	205.8	213.3	218.2	226.1	203.0	202.9	205.8	207.9	208.5	213.3	218.4	216.7	218.2	218.5	217.2	226.1
1967	256.9	228.2	236.5	246.2	256.9	226.1	225.1	228.2	233.1	230.9	236.5	242.5	242.1	246.2	247.8	245.8	256.9
1968	287.2	256.0	272.9	278.0	287.2	252.4	252.1	256.0	258.3	.. S	272.9	276.1	274.5	278.0	280.0	278.8	287.2
1969	307.2	286.6	293.0	299.1	307.2	280.3	282.2	286.6	290.9	287.7	293.0	298.2	298.0	299.1	297.8	296.3	307.2
1970	354.3	308.1	317.9	327.7	354.3	303.3	302.5	308.1	313.0	312.0	317.9	325.2	324.7	327.7	335.4	338.5	354.3
1971	417.2	361.5	378.7	390.4	417.2	350.5	352.5	361.5	365.0	369.1	378.7	388.3	386.4	390.4	398.1	398.4	417.2
1972	494.6	425.6	451.9	469.2	494.6	409.6	411.5	425.6	429.6	433.8	451.9	463.1	460.8	469.2	472.8	478.1	494.6
1973	569.0	488.4	514.1	529.9	569.0	479.7	473.1	488.4	501.7	504.5	514.1	524.3	523.9	529.9	535.3	535.4	569.0
1974	659.7	573.7	592.1	610.7	659.7	557.3	556.7	573.7	578.5	579.3	592.1	608.0	603.0	610.7	622.7	633.6	659.7
1975	779.7	662.1	688.4	718.1	779.7	648.5	648.5	662.1	665.1	666.6	688.4	703.6	703.0	718.1	733.1	742.1	779.7
1976	879.8	785.4	818.7	832.7	879.8	767.0	768.5	785.4	799.6	802.0	818.7	832.8	824.6	832.7	846.6	845.8	879.8
1977	1002.0	883.0	904.9	939.8	1002.0	869.3	867.3	883.0	892.7	893.6	904.9	927.1	926.2	939.8	953.3	953.8	1002.0
1978	1124.5	999.9	1033.7	1063.3	1124.5	980.7	985.3	999.9	1013.7	1008.2	1033.7	1052.7	1049.2	1063.3	1072.9	1082.2	1124.5
1979	1286.4	1139.4	1174.1	1201.5	1286.4	1107.5	1110.9	1139.4	1147.3	1154.1	1174.1	1187.2	1186.9	1201.5	1218.4	1220.6	1286.4
1980	1412.4	1284.2	1308.5	1333.8	1412.4	1253.8	1255.5	1284.2	1291.0	1293.4	1308.5	1321.0	1323.1	1333.8	1346.5	1353.2	1412.4
1981	1573.7	1421.6	1479.7	1509.6	1573.7	1397.4	1405.9	1421.6	1450.5	1461.4	1479.7	1509.4	1517.0	1509.6	1523.7	1516.1	1573.7
1982	1754.6	1602.6	1663.2	1676.3	1754.6	1568.0	1575.4	1602.6	1623.9	1639.3	1663.2	1692.3	1689.8	1696.3	1731.2	1709.4	1754.6
1983	1956.8	1769.0	1814.8	1829.4	1956.8	1757.6	1753.4	1769.0	1787.9	1806.0	1814.8	1839.9	1828.7	1829.4	1863.0	1873.3	1956.8

Consumer prices: all items (21)

1980 = 100

Prix à la consommation : total (21)

1980 = 100

	Year	Q.1	Q.2	Q.3	Q.4	JAN	FEB	MAR	APR	MAY	JUN	JUL	AUG	SEP	OCT	NOV	DEC
1964	31.4	31.2	31.3	31.5	31.7	31.1	31.2	31.2	31.2	31.2	31.3	31.4	31.4	31.6	31.7	31.7	31.7
1965	32.2	31.9	32.3	32.3	32.5	31.9	31.9	32.0	32.0	32.1	32.6	32.3	32.3	32.3	32.4	32.5	32.6
1966	33.1	32.8	33.0	33.2	33.4	32.7	32.8	32.8	32.9	33.0	33.0	33.1	33.2	33.2	33.3	33.4	33.5
1967	34.0	33.7	33.8	34.0	34.5	33.6	33.6	33.7	33.8	33.8	33.8	33.9	34.0	34.1	34.3	34.6	34.6
1968	35.5	35.0	35.2	35.6	36.3	35.0	35.0	35.0	35.1	35.2	35.3	35.4	35.6	35.9	36.2	36.3	36.4
1969	37.8	37.0	37.5	37.9	38.4	36.8	37.0	37.1	37.3	37.5	37.6	37.8	37.9	38.1	38.3	38.5	38.6
1970	39.8	39.1	39.6	40.0	40.4	39.0	39.1	39.2	39.4	39.6	39.7	39.8	40.0	40.1	40.3	40.4	40.6
1971	42.0	42.0	41.6	42.2	42.8	40.8	41.0	41.2	41.4	41.7	41.8	42.0	42.2	42.4	42.6	42.8	43.0
1972	44.6	43.3	43.9	44.8	45.7	43.1	43.3	43.5	43.7	43.9	44.2	44.5	44.8	45.1	45.4	45.7	46.0
1973	47.8	46.1	47.1	48.2	49.5	46.0	46.1	46.3	46.6	47.1	47.4	47.8	48.2	48.6	49.1	49.5	49.9
1974	54.4	51.4	53.4	55.2	56.9	50.7	51.4	52.0	52.8	53.4	54.0	54.7	55.2	55.8	56.4	56.9	57.4
1975	60.8	58.5	59.9	61.2	62.6	58.1	58.5	59.0	59.5	59.9	60.4	60.8	61.2	61.7	62.2	62.6	63.0
1976	66.7	64.1	65.6	67.1	68.8	63.6	64.1	64.6	65.2	65.6	65.9	66.5	67.0	67.7	68.4	68.9	69.2
1977	72.9	69.9	72.0	73.7	75.1	69.4	69.8	70.5	71.4	72.1	72.6	73.3	73.7	74.3	74.9	75.2	75.4
1978	79.5	76.3	78.5	80.6	82.3	75.7	76.3	77.0	77.8	78.6	79.2	80.1	80.6	81.1	81.9	82.3	82.7
1979	88.1	84.1	86.4	89.2	91.8	83.5	84.0	84.8	85.6	86.5	87.2	88.4	89.3	90.1	91.1	91.7	92.4
1980	100.0	95.3	98.3	101.4	104.2	94.2	95.2	96.3	97.5	98.3	99.0	100.4	101.4	102.3	103.4	104.1	105.1
1981	113.4	107.3	110.9	115.2	118.9	106.3	107.2	108.4	109.8	110.8	111.9	113.9	115.2	116.6	118.0	119.1	119.8
1982	126.8	122.3	126.1	127.8	130.2	121.0	122.2	123.7	125.1	126.1	127.0	127.4	127.8	128.3	129.0	130.2	131.3
1983	139.0	133.6	137.4	140.3	143.0	132.6	133.5	134.8	136.5	137.4	138.2	139.4	140.2	141.3	142.4	143.0	143.5

Money supply (M1) (20)

billion francs, end of period

Adjusted - Corrigé

Disponibilités monétaires (M1) (20)

milliards de francs, fin de période

	Year	Q.1	Q.2	Q.3	Q.4	JAN	FEB	MAR	APR	MAY	JUN	JUL	AUG	SEP	OCT	NOV	DEC
1964		1.5	1.5	1.5	1.6	1.5	1.5	1.5	1.5	1.5	1.5	1.5	1.5	1.5	1.5	1.6	1.6
1965		160.1	164.1	168.4	169.2	157.7	158.6	160.1	160.9	162.7	164.1	164.8	166.9	168.4	169.6	170.9	169.2
1966		174.3	175.8	178.7	182.1	172.0	173.5	174.3	173.9	175.7	175.8	177.2	178.7	178.7	180.1	180.7	182.1
1967		186.9	188.3	188.6	190.5	184.9	185.4	186.9	188.5	187.6	188.3	188.2	188.0	188.6	188.9	188.1	190.5
1968		189.3	200.7	202.9	205.4	189.8	189.9	189.3	188.6	..	200.7	199.4	200.5	202.9	203.6	204.6	205.4
1969		209.7	209.1	210.3	203.3	206.4	208.8	209.7	210.8	209.1	209.1	209.0	210.9	210.3	207.9	208.5	203.3
1970		206.2	208.3	214.9	225.9	205.8	206.9	206.2	209.5	209.1	208.3	210.6	214.7	214.9	219.3	222.5	225.9
1971		234.1	240.8	247.5	251.8	229.5	234.0	234.1	235.2	239.2	240.8	244.5	247.3	247.5	250.2	250.0	251.8
1972		262.5	272.6	285.2	288.6	255.4	257.6	262.5	263.6	266.6	272.6	278.5	279.8	285.2	285.3	290.3	288.6
1973		290.1	301.8	307.0	315.4	289.1	290.4	290.1	298.8	302.1	301.8	301.0	304.6	307.0	308.5	305.5	315.4
1974		323.3	328.0	333.0	351.1	315.3	328.0	323.3	325.4	324.9	328.0	330.1	331.4	333.0	338.7	349.7	351.1
1975		356.6	369.1	387.7	408.5	351.4	351.7	356.6	354.4	360.7	369.1	373.3	380.3	387.7	390.6	398.7	408.5
1976		418.1	431.0	436.6	440.3	411.2	415.7	418.1	425.3	429.3	431.0	434.9	437.2	436.6	442.3	443.2	440.3
1977		450.0	456.7	473.7	491.3	446.4	449.1	450.0	456.0	463.4	456.7	467.9	472.0	473.7	479.3	479.1	491.3
1978		499.2	510.8	532.7	547.4	492.5	501.6	499.2	511.2	503.6	510.8	520.7	524.3	532.7	535.8	541.6	547.4
1979		572.2	586.8	592.7	615.5	553.5	557.0	572.2	573.4	576.8	586.8	587.5	587.3	592.7	595.7	590.1	615.5
1980		621.7	630.0	643.2	658.0	605.9	606.5	621.7	621.9	625.5	630.0	627.0	640.1	643.2	643.8	655.5	658.0
1981		673.4	703.3	745.1	754.1	664.7	674.2	673.4	688.2	699.0	703.3	708.0	721.9	745.1	747.1	751.2	754.1
1982		781.4	804.4	828.3	833.7	771.7	777.7	781.4	789.0	802.8	804.4	818.5	824.3	828.3	849.0	841.9	833.7
1983		866.2	893.0	905.1	932.5	855.4	855.5	866.2	874.8	885.5	893.0	904.1	906.3	905.1	913.8	914.5	932.5

M1 plus quasi-money (20)

billion francs, end of period

Adjusted - Corrigé

M1 plus quasi-monnaie (20)

milliards de francs, fin de période

	Year	Q.1	Q.2	Q.3	Q.4	JAN	FEB	MAR	APR	MAY	JUN	JUL	AUG	SEP	OCT	NOV	DEC
1964		168.7	172.5	176.7	180.8	166.5	167.7	168.7	169.8	171.1	172.5	174.1	175.0	176.7	177.3	179.2	180.8
1965		185.4	190.6	196.4	203.0	182.3	183.5	185.4	186.6	188.6	190.6	192.1	194.6	196.4	197.8	199.4	203.0
1966		209.5	214.8	218.6	224.4	205.9	207.8	209.5	210.0	212.9	214.8	216.7	218.0	218.6	220.0	221.5	224.4
1967		230.5	236.4	245.3	253.6	227.4	228.6	230.5	233.3	234.0	236.4	239.1	241.7	245.3	247.8	248.8	253.6
1968		258.7	272.9	277.2	282.9	254.4	256.7	258.7	259.2	..	272.9	272.4	274.7	277.2	280.1	282.1	282.9
1969		291.2	294.9	300.4	299.7	285.0	289.4	291.2	293.8	293.6	294.9	296.2	300.2	300.4	299.6	301.3	299.7
1970		309.4	315.9	328.2	345.5	304.9	308.1	309.4	314.2	315.1	315.9	319.9	325.7	328.2	334.8	340.5	345.5
1971		362.6	376.4	391.2	406.4	352.2	358.9	362.6	366.1	372.6	376.4	382.4	387.8	391.2	397.6	400.6	406.4
1972		426.6	449.4	469.9	481.3	411.5	418.8	426.6	430.7	438.0	449.4	456.5	462.7	469.9	472.5	480.3	481.3
1973		489.4	511.4	531.2	553.0	481.8	486.6	489.4	503.0	509.8	511.4	517.3	526.6	531.2	535.5	538.1	553.0
1974		574.5	589.8	612.4	641.0	558.8	565.7	574.5	579.5	585.3	589.8	600.8	606.5	612.4	623.3	636.9	641.0
1975		662.8	686.4	720.5	757.1	649.3	657.5	662.8	665.6	673.3	686.4	696.1	707.7	720.5	733.7	746.5	757.1
1976		786.1	816.7	835.6	856.0	767.4	778.0	786.1	799.9	810.8	816.7	825.0	830.3	835.6	847.2	851.5	856.0
1977		883.3	903.3	943.3	976.0	869.4	876.2	883.3	892.6	902.5	903.3	919.5	932.0	943.3	954.1	960.9	976.0
1978		1000.0	1032.1	1067.0	1097.1	981.1	994.2	1000.0	1013.0	1016.4	1032.1	1043.9	1054.8	1067.0	1074.3	1091.6	1097.1
1979		1139.7	1172.0	1205.7	1257.7	1108.8	1119.8	1139.7	1146.0	1161.6	1172.0	1178.3	1191.8	1205.7	1220.3	1232.6	1257.7
1980		1284.6	1306.3	1339.7	1384.8	1255.3	1264.4	1284.6	1289.0	1299.1	1306.3	1310.7	1327.1	1339.7	1350.3	1368.6	1384.8
1981		1422.0	1477.2	1516.3	1542.1	1398.5	1414.8	1422.0	1447.7	1465.2	1477.2	1496.2	1519.5	1516.3	1527.0	1533.6	1542.1
1982		1605.4	1660.1	1705.2	1721.3	1570.5	1587.2	1605.4	1621.6	1642.4	1660.1	1676.2	1691.9	1705.2	1734.8	1730.2	1721.3
1983		1773.0	1811.2	1839.6	1921.1	1760.1	1765.9	1773.0	1785.2	1808.5	1811.2	1821.8	1831.0	1839.6	1867.5	1897.6	1921.1

FRANCE

Total liquidity (20)
billion francs, end of period

Total des liquidités (20)
milliards de francs, fin de période

	Year	Q.1	Q.2	Q.3	Q.4	JAN	FEB	MAR	APR	MAY	JUN	JUL	AUG	SEP	OCT	NOV	DEC
1964	265.7	243.8	249.0	255.1	265.7	240.8	241.4	243.8	244.9	246.0	249.0	254.7	254.2	255.1	256.8	256.4	265.7
1965	293.0	267.0	274.6	281.8	293.0	265.0	264.5	267.0	270.0	271.0	274.6	280.3	280.4	281.8	283.8	283.2	293.0
1966	322.5	296.7	305.1	311.6	322.5	292.9	293.4	296.7	299.5	300.3	305.1	311.0	309.9	311.6	312.6	311.4	322.5
1967	362.3	325.4	334.2	345.7	362.3	322.0	321.6	325.4	330.5	328.7	334.2	341.1	341.5	345.7	349.2	348.2	362.3
1968	401.1	365.4	380.3	387.8	401.1	359.0	360.4	365.4	368.4	.. S	380.3	384.6	384.4	387.8	390.8	390.0	401.1
1969	437.6	404.8	411.6	421.6	437.6	397.8	401.0	404.8	409.6	406.8	411.6	418.0	419.2	421.6	422.2	422.0	437.6
1970	501.0	442.0	452.6	466.1	501.0	436.7	436.7	442.0	447.7	447.4	452.6	461.7	462.6	466.1	475.8	479.8	501.0
1971	585.2	512.1	533.4	549.0	585.2	500.1	503.2	512.1	518.5	523.2	533.4	544.7	543.8	549.0	558.1	559.7	585.2
1972	684.2	597.4	626.3	647.6	684.2	580.5	582.9	597.4	602.4	606.9	626.3	639.1	638.2	647.6	653.0	660.3	684.2
1973	782.4	682.8	711.1	731.4	782.4	671.8	671.1	682.8	696.8	700.2	711.1	723.0	724.5	731.4	738.7	739.8	782.4
1974	902.2	792.3	813.5	838.6	902.2	773.7	774.5	792.3	798.1	799.0	813.5	832.1	829.4	838.6	851.9	863.2	902.2
1975	1076.5	913.6	947.7	988.4	1076.5	895.7	897.8	913.6	920.0	923.2	947.7	967.2	970.0	988.4	1008.3	1020.4	1076.5
1976	1234.4	1095.7	1137.1	1162.8	1234.4	1070.5	1075.4	1095.7	1113.5	1117.6	1137.1	1155.8	1151.9	1162.8	1180.4	1181.5	1234.4
1977	1414.0	1247.3	1275.5	1319.8	1414.0	1228.5	1228.6	1247.3	1260.4	1261.7	1275.5	1301.2	1303.8	1319.8	1336.6	1340.3	1414.0
1978	1605.2	1424.2	1465.5	1509.2	1605.2	1398.8	1406.2	1424.2	1441.6	1437.4	1465.5	1487.7	1490.0	1509.2	1523.9	1536.2	1605.2
1979	1837.4	1636.6	1678.9	1717.4	1837.4	1596.0	1603.3	1636.6	1648.1	1656.0	1678.9	1696.2	1700.6	1717.4	1737.6	1741.2	1837.4
1980	2029.0	1841.5	1869.3	1907.9	2029.0	1808.5	1811.4	1841.5	1350.9	1853.2	1869.8	1887.6	1894.5	1907.9	1923.4	1933.3	2029.0
1981	2267.1	2050.4	2111.8	2149.1	2267.1	2020.3	2031.2	2050.4	2082.5	2093.6	2111.8	2143.5	2154.5	2149.1	2171.1	2165.6	2267.1
1982	2532.2	2306.8	2371.5	2418.7	2532.2	2267.2	2276.4	2306.8	2331.2	2345.2	2371.5	2406.4	2409.9	2418.7	2456.3	2434.9	2532.2
1983	2811.4	2552.5	2604.3	2627.2	2811.4	2539.3	2535.4	2552.5	2577.7	2595.2	2604.3	2633.6	2626.4	2627.2	2663.0	2672.7	2811.4

Bank credit to economy: total (20)
billion francs, end of period

Crédits bancaires à l'économie : total (22) (20)
milliards de francs, fin de période

	Year	Q.1	Q.2	Q.3	Q.4	JAN	FEB	MAR	APR	MAY	JUN	JUL	AUG	SEP	OCT	NOV	DEC
1964	126.4	113.2	115.7	119.0	126.4	111.4	111.2	113.2	115.4	115.9	115.7	120.1	118.6	119.0	121.8	122.3	126.4
1965	143.1	125.3	130.6	133.4	143.1	123.6	124.3	125.8	127.8	128.9	130.6	133.8	132.2	133.4	137.5	138.8	143.1
1966	165.0	143.6	150.0	154.3	165.0	141.6	142.2	143.6	146.3	147.6	150.0	153.4	152.3	154.3	158.7	160.9	165.0
1967	195.3	167.6	176.2	182.5	195.3	164.5	165.3	167.6	171.8	173.1	176.2	181.3	180.5	182.5	187.0	188.5	195.3
1968	231.3	197.9	210.3	217.1	231.3	192.3	193.3	197.9	199.5	206.1	210.3	212.8	212.7	217.1	222.6	226.4	231.3
1969	284.1	236.5	244.6	252.0	284.1	228.7	231.3	236.5	239.3	242.1	244.6	247.2	247.7	252.0	255.3	255.4	284.1
1970	332.0	283.6	291.8	298.6	332.0	279.3	280.2	283.6	287.6	286.8	291.8	294.1	293.1	298.6	308.1	317.3	332.0
1971	398.9	342.7	359.1	367.1	398.9	332.1	333.5	342.7	345.8	353.3	359.1	365.2	360.6	367.1	374.5	378.7	398.9
1972	499.0	410.5	439.5	456.4	499.0	395.2	397.1	410.5	418.8	423.3	439.5	448.9	445.6	456.4	467.1	477.5	499.0
1973	597.0	496.3	527.8	550.5	597.0	492.6	490.3	496.3	512.2	522.1	527.8	538.1	537.2	550.5	563.5	569.0	597.0
1974	705.1	603.7	632.4	651.8	705.1	585.1	584.6	603.7	627.5	625.9	632.4	643.3	641.6	651.8	662.4	670.0	705.1
1975	790.4	697.3	708.5	728.3	790.4	687.5	688.6	697.3	700.8	695.6	708.5	721.1	717.0	728.3	742.4	750.9	790.4
1976	915.4	797.0	827.9	849.0	915.4	769.8	777.9	797.0	812.3	811.6	827.9	848.9	841.8	849.0	873.6	879.2	915.4
1977	1041.9	915.6	952.0	972.5	1041.9	915.5	913.7	915.6	929.9	951.2	952.0	966.4	960.9	972.5	993.7	994.9	1041.9
1978	1154.6	1030.0	1052.7	1069.2	1154.6	1026.8	1035.3	1030.0	1048.1	1038.1	1052.7	1067.7	1056.6	1069.2	1091.7	1093.0	1154.6
1979	1331.6	1153.9	1197.2	1226.6	1331.6	1127.4	1125.4	1153.9	1168.5	1178.5	1197.2	1210.8	1205.2	1226.6	1250.7	1257.2	1331.6
1980	1548.0	1323.6	1371.2	1410.1	1548.0	1308.4	1310.4	1323.6	1343.2	1354.2	1371.2	1384.5	1387.6	1410.1	1440.8	1452.4	1548.0
1981	1786.3	1573.5	1628.5	1660.6	1786.3	1539.2	1559.7	1573.5	1593.8	1621.7	1628.5	1657.4	1651.7	1660.6	1700.7	1710.5	1786.3
1982	2103.6	1814.5	1915.4	1957.5	2103.6	1783.1	1802.2	1814.5	1841.0	1870.6	1915.4	1959.7	1950.9	1967.5	2020.0	2015.7	2103.6
1983	2375.6	2136.9	2189.7	2220.6	2375.6	2093.9	2104.4	2136.9	2150.1	2155.7	2189.7	2216.8	2207.7	2220.6	2271.6	2286.2	2375.6

Net new capital issues (23)
billion francs, end of period

Nouvelles émissions sur le marché des capitaux, nettes (23)
milliards de francs, fin de période

	Year	Q.1	Q.2	Q.3	Q.4	JAN	FEB	MAR	APR	MAY	JUN	JUL	AUG	SEP	OCT	NOV	DEC
1964																	
1965																	
1966																	
1967																	
1968																	
1969																	
1970																	
1971																	
1972	23.17	7.60	3.00	4.00	8.57												
1973	29.34	3.91	10.00	4.88	10.56	3.41	2.02	0.48	4.01	3.46	2.53	1.86	0.66	2.37	2.77	5.57	2.23
1974	23.18	6.76	3.56	4.54	8.31	2.48	1.67	2.60	0.74	1.23	1.60	1.98	0.69	1.87	1.40	4.50	2.32
1975	33.77	8.39	9.42	5.87	9.59	1.95	2.81	4.14	5.06	0.72	3.65	1.73	0.60	3.54	2.06	2.85	4.64
1976	32.23	11.52	6.50	5.06	9.15	3.83	3.03	4.65	1.97	2.69	1.84	2.13	0.17	2.75	1.16	4.64	3.34
1977	34.56	11.01	5.55	6.85	11.16	3.55	2.75	4.71	0.82	0.80	3.94	2.50	0.62	3.72	2.98	4.11	4.06
1978	38.88	8.99	7.94	8.05	13.91	4.05	2.40	2.54	1.97	3.49	2.48	2.71	0.30	5.05	2.73	8.57	2.61
1979	42.81	9.01	8.39	4.79	20.62	4.35	1.93	2.73	3.21	4.05	1.13	2.65	0.78	1.36	12.11	4.31	4.20
1980	73.70	16.84	20.34	20.22	16.30	4.39	6.08	6.37	5.83	5.52	8.99	11.25	1.40	7.57	4.04	7.28	4.99
1981	110.29	30.76	11.28	28.46	39.79	14.49	7.79	8.48	5.63	4.09	1.57	3.39	3.30	21.78	16.82	9.09	13.88
1982	145.26	35.86	20.60	37.38	51.41	16.24	10.26	9.36	3.10	5.74	11.77	14.77	6.93	15.68	15.97	21.35	14.10
1983	196.74	53.41	30.85	54.95	57.54	18.71	19.86	14.63	7.21	17.39	6.25	13.01	9.95	32.00	21.51	12.20	23.93

Total liquidity (20)

billion francs, end of period

Adjusted - Corrigé

Total des liquidités (20)

milliards de francs, fin de période

	Year	Q.1	Q.2	Q.3	Q.4	JAN	FEB	MAR	APR	MAY	JUN	JUL	AUG	SEP	OCT	NOV	DEC
1964																	
1965					290.0												290.0
1966		298.1	305.7	312.2	319.1	293.6	295.9	298.1	299.5	303.0	305.7	309.1	310.8	312.2	314.0	316.0	319.1
1967		327.0	335.2	347.9	358.7	322.8	324.5	327.0	330.5	331.8	335.2	339.3	342.9	347.9	351.3	354.0	358.7
1968		368.0	382.0	389.6	397.1	360.6	364.3	368.0	369.3		382.0	383.2	386.4	389.6	393.2	396.1	397.1
1969		407.7	413.7	424.5	428.5	400.1	405.8	407.7	410.9	411.7	413.7	416.9	422.2	424.5	425.4	429.1	428.5
1970		442.0	451.3	468.7	490.2	435.7	440.2	442.0	448.1	450.5	451.3	457.3	464.7	468.7	477.3	484.1	490.2
1971		511.9	532.0	552.0	572.2	498.8	507.3	511.9	518.7	526.8	532.0	539.9	546.5	552.0	560.1	564.7	572.2
1972		596.7	624.7	650.9	668.6	578.8	587.5	596.7	602.5	611.1	624.7	633.6	641.4	650.9	655.2	665.7	668.6
1973		681.9	709.6	735.6	763.6	670.1	676.7	681.9	696.9	705.6	709.6	717.3	728.9	735.6	742.0	746.3	763.6
1974		790.6	812.4	843.8	380.1	770.6	780.0	790.6	797.5	805.2	812.4	826.4	834.9	843.8	856.1	871.3	880.1
1975		911.4	947.2	995.0	1049.4	891.2	902.6	911.4	918.5	930.5	947.2	961.6	977.2	995.0	1013.5	1030.7	1049.4
1976		1092.4	1137.0	1171.1	1204.5	1064.2	1079.8	1092.4	1111.1	1126.3	1137.0	1150.6	1160.9	1171.1	1186.9	1194.7	1204.5
1977		1242.8	1276.4	1329.5	1380.2	1220.5	1231.2	1242.8	1257.0	1270.5	1276.4	1297.0	1313.6	1329.5	1344.6	1356.2	1380.2
1978		1418.5	1466.9	1520.1	1568.0	1389.7	1407.6	1418.5	1436.9	1445.3	1466.9	1484.7	1500.7	1520.1	1533.9	1556.0	1568.0
1979		1629.9	1680.6	1730.3	1797.8	1586.0	1603.2	1629.9	1641.9	1663.0	1680.6	1693.9	1712.3	1730.3	1750.7	1765.5	1797.8
1980		1834.3	1871.5	1923.9	1986.4	1796.9	1810.4	1834.3	1843.4	1858.8	1871.5	1883.0	1905.3	1923.9	1939.0	1964.3	1986.4
1981		2042.1	2113.8	2166.9	2217.5	2006.2	2028.7	2042.1	2073.3	2097.2	2113.8	2136.8	2164.7	2166.9	2187.5	2200.4	2217.5
1982		2300.3	2373.6	2440.4	2478.2	2253.3	2275.6	2300.3	2321.9	2348.1	2373.6	2397.7	2420.8	2440.4	2474.9	2475.3	2478.2
1983		2546.2	2606.6	2652.0	2753.0	2523.2	2533.8	2546.2	2567.1	2597.4	2606.6	2623.8	2638.8	2652.0	2684.3	2719.2	2753.0

Bank credit to economy: total (20)(22)

billion francs, end of period

Adjusted - Corrigé

Crédits bancaires à l'économie : total (20)(22)

milliards de francs, fin de période

	Year	Q.1	Q.2	Q.3	Q.4	JAN	FEB	MAR	APR	MAY	JUN	JUL	AUG	SEP	OCT	NOV	DEC
1964																	
1965					146.1												146.1
1966		150.2	155.7	161.6	168.4	147.8	149.4	150.2	151.8	153.5	155.7	158.3	159.7	161.6	164.2	166.7	168.4
1967		175.2	182.8	191.1	199.1	171.5	173.5	175.2	178.3	180.1	182.8	187.2	189.5	191.1	193.7	195.5	199.1
1968		206.7	218.3	227.3	235.6	200.3	202.6	206.7	206.9	214.3	218.3	219.9	223.3	227.3	230.7	234.8	235.6
1969		246.9	254.0	264.2	276.3	238.0	242.3	246.9	248.2	251.9	254.0	255.8	260.5	264.2	265.1	265.1	276.3
1970		283.2	290.6	302.4	322.5	278.3	282.6	283.2	286.4	287.7	290.6	292.6	298.3	302.4	309.5	318.0	322.5
1971		342.2	357.9	371.5	387.1	330.8	336.3	342.2	344.3	354.3	357.9	363.5	366.8	371.5	376.1	379.6	387.1
1972		410.1	438.5	461.1	484.0	393.8	400.5	410.1	417.2	424.7	438.5	446.7	452.7	461.1	468.5	478.4	484.0
1973		496.2	527.3	556.1	578.0	491.8	494.8	496.2	510.5	524.3	527.3	535.4	545.3	556.1	565.0	570.5	578.0
1974		603.6	632.7	658.2	682.0	584.4	589.5	603.6	625.5	629.3	632.7	640.1	650.7	658.2	663.6	672.3	682.0
1975		697.9	709.5	736.0	764.6	687.0	653.1	697.9	698.0	700.0	709.5	717.7	726.7	736.0	743.3	754.2	764.6
1976		798.0	829.4	858.3	886.0	769.1	781.2	798.0	808.9	816.9	829.4	845.3	853.2	858.3	874.4	884.2	886.0
1977		917.0	953.4	983.7	1009.7	913.8	916.0	917.0	925.8	957.3	953.4	962.8	974.1	983.7	954.6	1001.7	1009.7
1978		1031.7	1053.7	1081.8	1120.9	1023.5	1036.3	1031.7	1043.9	1043.6	1053.7	1064.3	1071.2	1081.8	1092.9	1101.5	1120.9
1979		1155.9	1197.7	1241.8	1295.6	1122.3	1125.1	1155.9	1164.7	1193.0	1197.7	1207.4	1221.7	1241.8	1252.8	1268.4	1295.6
1980		1326.7	1370.5	1427.0	1510.6	1301.4	1309.1	1326.7	1341.0	1358.3	1370.5	1378.8	1404.3	1427.0	1443.2	1466.0	1510.6
1981		1575.9	1626.7	1680.7	1744.3	1529.7	1557.5	1575.9	1592.5	1615.8	1626.7	1649.2	1669.4	1680.7	1702.5	1725.5	1744.3
1982		1817.6	1912.9	1992.3	2056.6	1773.6	1800.8	1817.6	1341.5	1375.6	1912.9	1948.7	1969.8	1992.3	2022.2	2033.2	2056.6
1983		2140.5	2186.8	2250.1	2325.2	2082.7	2102.2	2140.5	2151.2	2161.6	2186.8	2203.4	2228.2	2250.1	2274.5	2307.1	2325.2

Bank credit to economy: short-term (20)(22)(24)

billion francs, end of period

Crédits bancaires à l'économie : court terme (20)(22)(24

milliards de francs, fin de période

	Year	Q.1	Q.2	Q.3	Q.4	JAN	FEB	MAR	APR	MAY	JUN	JUL	AUG	SEP	OCT	NOV	DEC
1964																	
1965	83.5				83.5												83.5
1966	96.5	83.8	88.1	89.8	96.5	81.8	82.0	83.8	86.0	86.6	88.1	90.8	88.8	89.8	93.1	93.9	96.5
1967	112.7	97.0	102.5	104.9	112.7	95.3	95.7	97.0	100.1	100.3	102.5	106.3	104.2	104.9	103.3	108.4	112.7
1968	129.6	112.5	121.0	123.1	129.6	109.1	109.4	112.5	113.8	118.9	121.0	122.3	120.4	123.1	126.7	128.9	129.6
1969	134.8	129.3	131.5	132.3	134.8	126.5	126.8	129.3	130.8	131.5	131.5	131.9	130.4	132.3	132.5	132.5	134.8
1970	164.1	133.6	134.1	136.8	164.1	134.5	134.2	133.6	134.8	134.8	134.1	136.4	136.4	136.8	144.9	154.3	164.1
1971	197.0	167.4	176.8	178.3	197.0	163.2	163.9	167.4	171.7	173.7	176.8	180.7	175.6	178.3	182.4	185.2	197.0
1972	229.1	197.5	209.4	217.0	229.1	193.0	192.7	197.5	201.0	200.6	209.4	215.3	217.0	217.0	217.4	219.2	229.1
1973	242.6	212.3	224.7	228.5	242.6	218.6	202.4	212.3	219.7	220.6	224.7	228.5	224.1	228.5	230.4	233.5	242.6
1974	256.9	..	258.5	268.1	286.9	238.6	232.7	..S	..S	..S	258.5	264.9	266.5	268.1	271.2	275.0	286.9
1975	318.0	289.9	297.4	295.8	318.0	283.4	283.4	289.9	292.3	293.6	297.4	299.6	295.4	295.8	301.9	306.3	318.0
1976	353.0	317.0	322.4	328.1	353.0	313.0	310.4	317.0	322.3	318.3	322.4	338.7	330.1	328.1	337.0	337.9	353.0
1977	382.8	353.1	358.2	363.8	382.8	353.4	352.7	353.1	353.4	361.7	358.2	364.7	362.6	363.8	368.1	372.0	382.8
1978	410.0	372.8	375.3	383.4	410.0	372.3	377.1	372.8	377.1	371.5	375.3	383.5	377.0	383.4	388.8	396.1	410.0
1979	438.4	405.0	417.2	417.6	438.4	396.6	356.5	405.0	411.2	409.5	417.2	422.0	416.4	417.6	422.4	426.5	438.4
1980	504.1	447.4	456.6	466.0	504.1	438.2	439.1	447.4	451.0	451.1	456.6	464.7	467.0	466.0	478.5	486.1	504.1
1981	577.5	514.4	523.7	531.9	577.5	506.3	513.6	514.4	525.2	526.4	523.7	533.5	533.8	531.9	544.3	555.6	577.5
1982	681.3	588.7	622.9	638.8	681.3	583.5	584.4	588.7	598.6	603.3	622.9	646.8	645.8	638.8	645.8	656.4	681.3
1983		685.0	693.6	696.7		675.9	672.9	685.0	696.8	685.4	693.6	709.3	703.8	696.7	710.0	714.3	

FRANCE

Bank credit to economy: medium term (22) (negotiable)

Crédits bancaires à l'économie : moyen terme (22) (mobilisables)

billion francs, end of period — milliards de francs, fin de période

	Year	Q.1	Q.2	Q.3	Q.4	JAN	FEB	MAR	APR	MAY	JUN	JUL	AUG	SEP	OCT	NOV	DEC
1964																	
1965																	
1966																	
1967																	
1968																	
1969	43.1				43.1												43.1
1970	47.1	43.6	44.8	45.5	47.1			43.6			44.8			45.5			47.1
1971	51.8	46.5	46.6	47.9	51.8			46.5			46.6			47.9			51.8
1972	56.8	51.4	53.0	53.3	56.8			51.4			53.0			53.3			56.8
1973	60.9	58.3	57.9	58.3	60.9			58.3			57.9			58.3			60.9
1974	64.1	61.1	61.7	62.5	64.1			61.1			61.7			62.5			64.1
1975	69.7	64.2	65.7	67.2	69.7			64.2			65.7			67.2			69.7
1976	85.4	73.7	76.6	80.6	85.4			73.7			76.6			80.6			85.4
1977	100.2	86.9	91.2	93.6	100.2			86.9			91.2			93.6			100.2
1978	112.7	101.6	107.1	107.4	112.7			101.6			107.1			107.4			112.7
1979	123.8	112.3	115.9	118.8	123.8			112.3			115.9			118.8			123.8
1980	136.1	125.0	130.2	132.0	136.1			125.0			130.2			132.0			136.1
1981	151.0	138.0	142.5	145.2	151.0			138.0			142.5			145.2			151.0
1982	170.7	155.8	161.6	164.6	170.7	151.5	153.5	155.8	157.7	159.4	161.6	162.1	162.6	164.6	166.0	167.0	170.7
1983		172.0	173.4	176.6		169.3	171.5	172.0	172.2	171.9	173.4	174.0	175.3	176.6	177.5	177.6	

Consumer credit outstanding: all credit institutions

Crédits à la consommation en cours : ensemble des institutions de crédit

billion francs, end of period — milliards de francs, fin de période

	Year	Q.1	Q.2	Q.3	Q.4	JAN	FEB	MAR	APR	MAY	JUN	JUL	AUG	SEP	OCT	NOV	DEC
1964	4.0	3.9	4.1	4.0	4.0			3.9			4.1			4.0			4.0
1965	4.3	4.0	4.2	4.1	4.3			4.0			4.2			4.1			4.3
1966	5.2	4.5	5.0	5.0	5.2			4.5			5.0			5.0			5.2
1967	6.1	5.4	5.9	5.8	6.1			5.4			5.9			5.8			6.1
1968	7.2	6.2	6.7	6.8	7.2			6.2			6.7			6.8			7.2
1969	6.9	7.4	7.9	7.6	6.9			7.4			7.9			7.6			6.9
1970	6.3	6.3	6.2	6.0	6.3			6.3			6.2			6.0			6.3
1971	8.1	6.7	7.5	7.6	8.1			6.7			7.5			7.6			8.1
1972	8.5	8.2	8.6	8.4	8.5			8.2			8.6			8.4			8.5
1973	9.5	8.7	9.1	9.1	9.5			8.7			9.1			9.1			9.5
1974	11.3	10.3	11.0	11.2	11.3			10.3			11.0			11.2			11.3
1975	14.7	11.6	12.5	12.9	14.7			11.6			12.5			12.9			14.7
1976	19.2	16.0	17.5	18.1	19.2			16.0			17.5			18.1			19.2
1977	20.2	19.5	20.3	19.7	20.2			19.5			20.3			19.7			20.2
1978	21.1	20.3	21.3	20.5	21.1			20.3			21.3			20.5			21.1
1979	28.1	21.9	24.0	25.5	28.1			21.9			24.0			25.5			28.1
1980	30.2	29.4	27.3	27.3	30.2			29.4			27.3			27.3			30.2
1981	33.3	31.3	32.6	32.0	33.3			31.3			32.6			32.0			33.3
1982	40.2	34.5	36.1	36.3	40.2			34.5			36.1			36.3			40.2
1983		41.3	42.7	44.0				41.3			42.7			44.0			

Official discount rate

Taux d'escompte officiel

per cent per annum, end of period — pourcentage par an, fin de période

	Year	Q.1	Q.2	Q.3	Q.4	JAN	FEB	MAR	APR	MAY	JUN	JUL	AUG	SEP	OCT	NOV	DEC
1964	4.00	4.00	4.00	4.00	4.00	4.00	4.00	4.00	4.00	4.00	4.00	4.00	4.00	4.00	4.00	4.00	4.00
1965	3.50	4.00	3.50	3.50	3.50	4.00	4.00	4.00	3.50	3.50	3.50	3.50	3.50	3.50	3.50	3.50	3.50
1966	3.50	3.50	3.50	3.50	3.50	3.50	3.50	3.50	3.50	3.50	3.50	3.50	3.50	3.50	3.50	3.50	3.50
1967	3.50	3.50	3.50	3.50	3.50	3.50	3.50	3.50	3.50	3.50	3.50	3.50	3.50	3.50	3.50	3.50	3.50
1968	6.00	3.50	3.50	5.00	6.00	3.50	3.50	3.50	3.50	3.50	3.50	5.00	5.00	5.00	5.00	6.00	6.00
1969	8.00	6.00	7.00	7.00	8.00	6.00	6.00	6.00	6.00	6.00	7.00	7.00	7.00	7.00	8.00	8.00	8.00
1970	7.00	8.00	8.00	7.50	7.00	8.00	8.00	8.00	8.00	8.00	8.00	8.00	7.50	7.50	7.00	7.00	7.00
1971	6.50	6.50	6.75	6.75	6.50	6.50	6.50	6.50	6.50	6.75	6.75	6.75	6.75	6.75	6.50	6.50	6.50
1972	7.50	6.00	5.75	5.75	7.50	6.00	6.00	6.00	5.75	5.75	5.75	5.75	5.75	5.75	5.75	6.50	7.50
1973	11.00	7.50	7.50	11.00	11.00	7.50	7.50	7.50	7.50	7.50	7.50	8.50	9.50	11.00	11.00	11.00	11.00
1974	13.00	11.00	13.00	13.00	13.00	11.00	11.00	11.00	11.00	11.00	13.00	13.00	13.00	13.00	13.00	13.00	13.00
1975	8.00	11.00	9.50	8.00	8.00	12.00	11.00	11.00	10.00	10.00	9.50	9.50	9.50	8.00	8.00	8.00	8.00
1976	10.50	8.00	8.00	10.50	10.50	8.00	8.00	8.00	8.00	8.00	8.00	9.50	9.50	10.50	10.50	10.50	10.50
1977	9.50	10.50	10.50	9.50	9.50	10.50	10.50	10.50	10.50	10.50	10.50	10.50	9.50	9.50	9.50	9.50	9.50
1978	9.50	9.50	9.50	9.50	9.50	9.50	9.50	9.50	9.50	9.50	9.50	9.50	9.50	9.50	9.50	9.50	9.50
1979	9.50	9.50	9.50	9.50	9.50	9.50	9.50	9.50	9.50	9.50	9.50	9.50	9.50	9.50	9.50	9.50	9.50
1980	9.50	9.50	9.50	9.50	9.50	9.50	9.50	9.50	9.50	9.50	9.50	9.50	9.50	9.50	9.50	9.50	9.50
1981	9.50	9.50	9.50	9.50	9.50	9.50	9.50	9.50	9.50	9.50	9.50	9.50	9.50	9.50	9.50	9.50	9.50
1982	9.50	9.50	9.50	9.50	9.50	9.50	9.50	9.50	9.50	9.50	9.50	9.50	9.50	9.50	9.50	9.50	9.50
1983	9.50	9.50	9.50	9.50	9.50	9.50	9.50	9.50	9.50	9.50	9.50	9.50	9.50	9.50	9.50	9.50	9.50

Call money rate (25)

per cent per annum, end of period

Taux de l'argent au jour le jour (25)

pourcèntage par an, fin de période

	Year	Q.1	Q.2	Q.3	Q.4	JAN	FEB	MAR	APR	MAY	JUN	JUL	AUG	SEP	OCT	NOV	DEC
1964	4.18	5.06	4.86	4.75	4.18	4.27	4.36	5.06	5.05	5.28	4.86	4.77	4.72	4.75	4.36	4.14	4.18
1965	4.48	4.42	4.40	3.81	4.48	3.87	4.21	4.42	3.98	4.31	4.40	4.35	4.00	3.81	3.96	4.66	4.48
1966	5.70	4.55	4.78	4.60	5.70	3.92	4.34	4.55	4.37	4.83	4.78	4.79	4.77	4.60	5.27	5.41	5.70
1967	4.76	5.00	4.50	4.31	4.76	5.57	5.04	5.00	5.06	4.93	4.50	4.79	4.48	4.31	4.48	4.65	4.76
1968	8.25	5.08	5.77	6.72	8.25	5.00	4.77	5.08	5.11	5.67	5.77	6.00	5.93	6.72	7.15	8.93	8.25
1969	10.42	8.18	9.47	9.40	10.42	8.07	7.87	8.18	8.33	8.98	9.47	9.20	8.87	9.40	9.37	9.57	10.42
1970	7.48	9.46	9.34	8.12	7.48	10.32	9.70	9.46	9.02	8.92	9.34	8.63	8.13	8.12	7.83	7.29	7.48
1971	5.29	5.77	6.45	5.98	5.29	6.52	6.00	5.77	5.52	5.88	6.45	5.61	5.70	5.98	5.95	5.51	5.29
1972	7.31	4.78	3.85	3.88	7.31	5.32	5.23	4.78	4.84	5.32	3.85	3.81	3.75	3.88	5.18	6.30	7.31
1973	11.52	7.51	7.66	10.13	11.52	7.22	7.73	7.51	7.46	7.72	7.66	8.52	9.16	10.13	11.20	11.12	11.52
1974	11.87	12.15	13.57	13.43	11.87	13.53	12.48	12.15	11.83	12.91	13.57	13.84	13.75	13.43	13.15	12.43	11.87
1975	6.45	9.17	7.32	6.92	6.45	11.42	9.96	9.17	8.28	7.60	7.32	7.28	7.18	6.92	6.68	6.74	6.45
1976	10.44	7.63	7.63	9.25	10.44	6.36	7.20	7.63	7.54	7.54	7.63	8.29	9.42	9.25	10.74	10.68	10.44
1977	9.30	9.73	8.92	8.30	9.30	9.94	9.83	9.73	9.22	9.07	8.92	8.67	8.52	8.30	8.36	8.97	9.30
1978	6.67	9.96	7.76	7.20	6.67	8.88	10.18	9.96	8.48	8.08	7.76	7.43	7.25	7.20	6.99	6.89	6.67
1979	12.17	6.77	8.01	11.00	12.17	6.64	6.68	6.77	6.82	7.20	8.01	9.34	10.44	11.00	11.47	11.95	12.17
1980	10.88	12.96	12.43	11.37	10.88	11.99	12.18	12.96	12.40	12.62	12.43	12.04	11.32	11.37	11.22	10.74	10.88
1981	15.46	11.72	19.93	17.78	15.46	10.74	10.91	11.72	12.23	16.03	19.93	18.49	17.50	17.78	17.09	15.72	15.46
1982	12.88	15.72	15.98	14.11	12.88	15.25	14.56	15.72	16.21	16.41	15.98	15.05	14.58	14.11	13.91	13.18	12.88
1983	12.27	12.84	12.61	12.56	12.27	12.71	12.77	12.84	12.55	12.46	12.61	12.41	12.54	12.56	12.36	12.37	12.27

Bond yields: private corporations

per cent per annum, end of period

Rendement des obligations : sociétés privées

pourcentage par an, fin de période

	Year	Q.1	Q.2	Q.3	Q.4	JAN	FEB	MAR	APR	MAY	JUN	JUL	AUG	SEP	OCT	NOV	DEC
1964	5.73	5.69	..	5.73	5.73	..	5.71	5.69	..	..	..	..	5.72	5.73	5.72	5.72	5.73
1965	6.56	6.55	6.56	..	6.56	..	..	6.55	..	..	6.56	6.56	6.56	..	6.50	6.56	6.56
1966	7.08	..	..	7.08	7.08	..	6.55	..	..	6.54	..	7.20	7.06	7.08	7.04	..	7.08
1967	7.05	7.07	..	..	7.05	..	7.08	7.07	7.08	7.08	..	7.08	7.08	..	7.02	7.05	7.05
1968	7.73	..	..	7.40	7.73	7.10	7.04	..	7.38	..	..	7.50	..	7.40	7.39	7.40	7.73
1969	8.88	8.42	..	8.49	8.83	8.20	8.21	8.42	8.49	..	..	8.52	..	8.49	8.66	8.80	8.88
1970	8.84	9.10	9.04	8.67	8.84	..	9.05	9.10	9.02	9.01	9.04	..	8.78	8.67	8.79	8.82	8.84
1971	8.78	8.75	8.75	8.77	8.78	8.82	8.69	8.75	8.74	8.79	8.75	8.79	8.79	8.77	8.80	8.80	8.78
1972	8.19	8.62	8.11	8.03	8.19	8.70	8.74	8.62	8.38	8.15	8.11	8.06	8.00	8.03	8.01	8.10	8.19
1973	9.66	8.71	8.95	9.52	9.66	..	8.52	8.71	8.76	8.79	8.95	8.94	9.43	9.52	9.62	9.63	9.66
1974	12.05	10.99	..	12.00	12.05	10.44	10.81	10.99	..	11.26	..	12.02	..	12.00	..	11.98	12.05
1975	10.85	11.56	11.23	10.79	10.85	12.00	11.92	11.56	11.34	..	11.23	11.04	10.83	10.79	10.76	10.82	10.85
1976	11.39	10.77	10.77	11.06	11.39	10.74	10.76	10.77	10.78	10.78	10.77	10.81	..	11.06	11.24	11.29	11.39
1977	11.64	11.12	11.64	11.45	11.64	10.34	11.10	11.12	11.45	11.61	11.64	11.59	11.44	11.45	11.47	11.65	11.64
1978	10.46	11.88	11.12	10.71	10.46	11.65	11.76	11.88	11.51	11.20	11.12	10.89	10.73	10.71	10.75	10.45	10.46
1979	12.42	9.90	10.99	11.93	12.42	..	9.86	9.90	9.88	9.83	10.99	11.01	11.80	11.93	11.85	11.96	12.42
1980	15.23	14.65	14.16	14.03	15.23	13.21	12.70	14.65	14.63	14.39	14.16	13.93	13.86	14.03	14.69	14.83	15.23
1981	17.33	15.39	..	17.64	17.33	14.62	15.13	15.39	15.39	15.35	..	18.20	17.80	17.64	17.60	17.51	17.33
1982	15.91	16.97	16.67	16.59	15.91	17.20	17.08	16.97	17.04	16.80	16.67	16.61	16.83	16.59	16.41	16.33	15.91
1983	14.06	15.00	14.86	14.36	14.06	15.64	15.12	15.00	14.87	14.85	14.86	14.73	14.54	14.36	14.32	14.29	14.06

Bond yields: issues guaranteed by the Government

per cent per annum, end of period

Rendement des obligations : émissions garanties par le gouvernement

pourcentage par an, fin de période

	Year	Q.1	Q.2	Q.3	Q.4	JAN	FEB	MAR	APR	MAY	JUN	JUL	AUG	SEP	OCT	NOV	DEC
1964	5.59	4.60	5.63	5.59	5.59	5.62	5.63	4.60	5.56	5.64	5.63	5.59	5.59	5.59	5.65	5.59	5.59
1965	6.25	..	..	6.21	6.25	6.17	6.25	..	6.23	..	..	..	..	6.21	6.08	6.28	6.25
1966	6.80	6.27	6.75	6.77	6.80	6.24	6.25	6.27	6.25	6.26	6.75	6.84	7.04	6.77	6.68	6.84	6.80
1967	6.81	6.82	6.85	6.81	6.81	6.81	6.83	6.82	6.74	6.63	6.85	6.82	6.82	6.81	6.81	6.82	6.81
1968	7.42	6.82	..	7.35	7.42	6.80	6.82	6.82	7.03	7.01	..	7.50	7.25	7.35	7.31	7.24	7.42
1969	8.64	8.07	8.17	8.41	8.64	7.93	7.93	8.07	8.09	8.20	8.17	8.33	..	8.41	8.46	8.52	8.64
1970	8.64	8.94	8.87	8.76	8.64	8.97	8.90	8.94	8.87	8.83	8.87	8.84	..	8.76	8.62	8.72	8.64
1971	8.45	8.49	8.56	..	8.45	8.82	8.48	8.49	8.52	8.54	8.56	..	..	..	8.53	8.57	8.45
1972	8.03	8.37	8.01	7.92	8.03	8.51	8.46	8.37	8.13	8.03	8.01	7.96	..	7.92	7.93	7.95	8.03
1973	9.51	8.62	8.80	9.34	9.51	7.18	8.37	8.62	8.62	8.69	8.80	8.93	9.32	9.34	9.46	9.49	9.51
1974	11.29	10.60	11.30	11.44	11.29	9.99	10.45	10.60	10.70	10.68	11.30	..	..	11.44	11.36	11.25	11.29
1975	10.16	10.65	10.44	10.17	10.16	11.32	11.19	10.65	10.46	..	10.44	10.44	..	10.17	10.15	10.13	10.16
1976	10.95	10.17	10.25	10.62	10.95	10.15	10.17	10.17	10.26	10.26	10.25	10.36	..	10.62	..	10.91	10.95
1977	11.12	10.85	11.14	11.01	11.12	10.86	10.73	10.85	10.97	..	11.14	11.10	..	11.01	11.02	11.04	11.12
1978	10.04	11.10	10.73	10.35	10.04	11.07	11.24	11.10	10.96	10.84	10.73	10.61	10.48	10.35	10.29	10.18	10.04
1979	12.14	9.65	..	11.65	12.14	9.83	9.66	9.65	9.66	9.64	..	10.65	..	11.65	11.65	11.77	12.14
1980	14.71	14.53	13.95	13.99	14.71	12.54	12.47	14.53	14.56	14.26	13.95	13.71	..	13.99	14.59	14.55	14.71
1981	17.06	15.25	17.56	17.49	17.06	..	14.72	15.25	15.15	15.19	17.56	17.48	17.58	17.49	17.42	17.31	17.06
1982	15.71	16.84	16.88	16.36	15.71	16.97	16.95	16.84	16.91	16.81	16.88	16.48	16.78	16.36	16.43	16.32	15.71
1983	13.99	14.92	14.91	14.27	13.99	15.25	15.06	14.92	14.84	14.79	14.91	14.61	14.37	14.27	14.24	14.19	13.99

FRANCE

Share prices: industrials (I.N.S.E.E.) (26)

1980 = 100

Cours des actions industrielles (I.N.S.E.E.) (26)

1980 = 100

	Year	Q.1	Q.2	Q.3	Q.4	JAN	FEB	MAR	APR	MAY	JUN	JUL	AUG	SEP	OCT	NOV	DEC
1964	62	66	59	62	62	70	65	62	63	59	56	63	64	60	61	62	62
1965	58	60	59	57	56	61	59	62	61	60	57	55	57	57	55	55	57
1966	54	60	55	52	51	62	60	57	56	54	54	53	53	50	49	53	51
1967	49	49	48	49	52	49	50	48	47	49	48	46	49	54	53	52	50
1968	53	53	55	51	52	52	51	55	57	54	52	50	52	51	51	52	53
1969	66	63	67	65	70	58	62	67	66	70	64	63	66	66	70	69	72
1970	69	74	67	68	67	76	73	72	69	67	65	67	68	67	68	66	67
1971	66	68	69	67	60	67	69	68	68	70	69	70	67	63	59	61	61
1972	74	66	74	79	77	63	64	69	73	77	73	77	80	81	81	76	74
1973	82	80	87	82	78	79	78	83	86	89	86	82	81	81	83	75	75
1974	61	74	..	55	52	78	75	69	..	65	61	61	56	49	51	51	53
1975	66	62	66	66	69	62	61	65	70	64	63	65	68	66	67	70	69
1976	65	73	68	64	55	71	75	72	69	68	67	64	65	63	56	54	57
1977	52	54	49	52	54	57	54	50	46	46	51	49	52	54	55	55	52
1978	68	52	66	77	78	49	50	59	65	66	67	74	74	82	78	77	78
1979	87	..	92	94	93	80	74	..	81	80	85	86	93	102	93	93	92
1980	100	98	97	99	105	101	102	92	93	99	100	98	99	100	108	106	102
1981	88	99	84	86	83	94	99	103	98	80	75	84	88	87	81	84	84
1982	86	86	89	82	86	92	95	72	92	91	83	80	84	83	85	86	86
1983	116	95	110	123	134	90	93	101	107	113	111	117	125	127	127	135	140

U.S. dollar exchange rate: spot

cents per franc, end of period

Taux de change du dollar É.-U. : au comptant

cents par franc, fin de période

	Year	Q.1	Q.2	Q.3	Q.4	JAN	FEB	MAR	APR	MAY	JUN	JUL	AUG	SEP	OCT	NOV	DEC
1964	20.408	20.408	20.408	20.408	20.408	20.408	20.400	20.408	20.408	20.408	20.408	20.408	20.408	20.408	20.408	20.408	20.408
1965	20.400	20.408	20.408	20.387	20.400	20.408	20.404	20.408	20.396	20.408	20.408	20.408	20.404	20.387	20.400	20.404	20.400
1966	20.194	20.408	20.408	20.272	20.194	20.396	20.404	20.408	20.408	20.400	20.408	20.408	20.375	20.272	20.235	20.218	20.194
1967	20.375	20.202	20.400	20.392	20.375	20.186	20.210	20.202	20.268	20.354	20.400	20.396	20.387	20.392	20.400	20.387	20.375
1968	20.210	20.325	20.105	20.109	20.210	20.338	20.309	20.325	20.263	.. S	20.105	20.105	20.105	20.109	20.105	20.182	20.210
1969	17.992	20.165	20.125	17.940	17.992	20.190	20.194	20.165	20.105	20.105	20.125	20.113	18.038	17.940	17.928	17.947	17.992
1970	18.116	18.047	18.119	18.113	18.116	18.041	18.034	18.047	18.109	18.116	18.119	18.119	18.129	18.113	18.113	18.123	18.116
1971	19.142	18.136	18.132	18.083	19.142	18.126	18.129	18.136	18.136	18.064	18.132	18.139	18.136	18.083	18.070	18.139	19.142
1972	19.512	19.889	19.992	19.952	19.512	19.497	19.739	19.889	19.873	19.992	19.992	19.992	19.976	19.952	19.837	19.830	19.512
1973	21.240	22.022	24.361	23.529	21.240	19.897	22.080	22.022	21.882	22.676	24.361	24.225	23.121	23.529	23.518	22.262	21.240
1974	22.500	20.991	20.734	21.093	22.500	19.608	20.764	20.991	20.513	20.363	20.734	21.304	20.730	21.093	21.299	21.537	22.500
1975	22.294	23.722	24.753	22.047	22.294	23.128	23.991	23.722	24.173	24.713	24.753	22.857	22.729	22.047	22.975	22.415	22.294
1976	20.122	21.418	21.096	20.297	20.122	22.337	22.279	21.418	21.455	21.136	21.096	20.328	20.326	20.297	20.008	20.028	20.122
1977	21.254	20.124	20.328	20.395	21.254	20.098	20.052	20.124	20.166	20.216	20.328	20.498	20.385	20.395	20.623	20.583	21.254
1978	23.923	21.832	22.215	23.089	23.923	21.131	20.984	21.832	21.683	21.706	22.215	22.868	22.973	23.089	25.078	22.668	23.923
1979	24.876	23.272	23.337	24.387	24.876	23.395	23.425	23.272	22.868	22.630	23.337	23.397	23.463	24.387	23.607	24.570	24.876
1980	22.144	22.329	24.468	23.812	22.144	24.564	24.078	22.329	23.790	24.039	24.468	24.166	24.010	23.812	22.983	22.366	22.144
1981	17.397	20.169	17.490	17.963	17.397	20.498	19.976	20.169	19.033	18.041	17.490	17.088	17.167	17.963	17.641	18.003	17.397
1982	14.870	16.021	14.643	14.010	14.870	17.021	16.449	16.021	16.422	16.365	14.643	14.637	14.248	14.010	13.751	14.244	14.870
1983	11.980	13.756	13.093	12.486	11.980	14.417	14.571	13.756	13.556	13.227	13.093	12.566	12.271	12.486	12.541	12.192	11.980

U.S. dollar exchange rate: forward (90 days)

cents per franc, end of period

Taux de change du dollar É.-U. : à terme (90 jours)

cents par franc, fin de période

	Year	Q.1	Q.2	Q.3	Q.4	JAN	FEB	MAR	APR	MAY	JUN	JUL	AUG	SEP	OCT	NOV	DEC
1964	20.404	20.358	20.346	20.363	20.404	20.383	20.375	20.358	20.354	20.300	20.346	20.354	20.358	20.363	20.396	20.408	20.404
1965	20.417	20.417	20.408	20.417	20.417	20.412	20.404	20.417	20.417	20.421	20.408	20.417	20.417	20.417	20.412	20.412	20.417
1966	20.222	20.421	20.417	20.367	20.222	20.417	20.417	20.421	20.425	20.417	20.417	20.458	20.450	20.367	20.276	20.227	20.222
1967	20.450	20.218	20.417	20.425	20.450	20.202	20.227	20.218	20.259	20.356	20.417	20.404	20.408	20.425	20.433	20.467	20.450
1968	20.153	20.392	20.068	20.024	20.153	20.354	20.338	20.392	20.321	.. S	20.068	20.101	20.092	20.024	20.083	20.141	20.153
1969	17.976	20.153	20.125	17.973	17.976	20.161	20.182	20.153	20.068	20.129	20.125	20.117	18.090	17.973	17.918	17.966	17.976
1970	18.090	18.012	18.103	18.109	18.090	18.018	18.021	18.012	18.093	18.126	18.103	18.113	18.123	18.109	18.083	18.116	18.090
1971	19.157	18.103	18.126	18.376	19.157	18.103	18.096	18.103	18.136	18.096	18.126	18.159	18.505	18.376	18.335	18.325	19.157
1972	19.418	19.912	20.024	19.992	19.418	19.482	19.720	19.912	19.881	19.980	20.024	20.048	20.024	19.992	19.810	19.755	19.418
1973	21.133	22.060	24.378	23.436	21.133	19.853	22.104	22.060	21.891	22.712	24.378	24.343	23.229	23.436	23.365	22.193	21.133
1974	22.427	20.816	20.568	20.956	22.427	19.365	20.513	20.816	20.526	20.243	20.568	21.213	20.683	20.955	21.128	21.515	22.427
1975	22.242	23.618	24.710	22.080	22.242	22.999	23.849	23.618	24.108	24.618	24.710	22.836	22.748	22.080	22.962	22.407	22.242
1976	19.861	21.299	20.991	20.097	19.861	22.262	22.153	21.299	21.327	21.044	20.991	20.141	20.145	20.097	19.724	19.755	19.861
1977	21.119	19.908	20.178	20.317	21.119	19.861	19.853	19.908	19.960	20.072	20.178	20.383	20.292	20.317	20.551	20.433	21.119
1978	24.242	21.911	22.232	23.036	24.242	20.773	20.807	21.911	21.636	21.617	22.232	22.920	23.057	23.036	25.297	22.946	24.242
1979	25.013	23.485	23.392	24.456	25.013	23.602	23.652	23.485	23.095	22.743	23.392	23.425	23.491	24.456	23.804	24.657	25.013
1980	22.472	22.655	24.313	23.918	22.472	24.704	24.096	22.655	23.883	23.889	24.313	24.073	24.044	23.918	23.047	22.743	22.472
1981	17.397	20.276	17.489	17.934	17.397	20.820	20.133	20.276	19.260	17.928	17.489	17.162	17.200	17.934	17.612	18.002	17.397
1982	14.741	15.990	14.676	13.922	14.741	16.992	16.491	15.990	16.356	16.300	14.676	14.573	14.156	13.922	13.684	14.128	14.741
1983	11.909	13.671	13.004	12.396	11.909	14.360	14.426	13.671	13.443	13.129	13.004	12.511	12.206	12.396	12.463	12.127	11.909

Official reserves excluding gold
million SDR's, end of period

Réserves officielles, or exclu
millions de DTS, fin de période

	Year	Q.1	Q.2	Q.3	Q.4	JAN	FEB	MAR	APR	MAY	JUN	JUL	AUG	SEP	OCT	NOV	DEC
1964	1995	1681	1833	1813	1995	1722	1706	1681	1669	1779	1833	1863	1830	1813	1823	1886	1995
1965	1637	1761	1719	1692	1637	1884	1920	1761	1762	1741	1719	1723	1713	1692	1649	1695	1637
1966	1495	1655	1723	1637	1495	1620	1614	1655	1705	1699	1723	1780	1734	1637	1605	1546	1495
1967	1760	1480	1453	1516	1760	1488	1495	1480	1491	1422	1453	1496	1503	1516	1537	1826	1760
1968	324	1671	778	208	324	1702	1682	1671	1681	1372	778	274	235	208	137	110	324
1969	286	160	59	461	286	339	249	160	49	86	59	44	231	461	366	442	286
1970	1428	582	904	1206	1428	504	578	582	653	766	904	1114	1176	1206	1247	1424	1428
1971	4078	1963	2132	3787	4078	1814	1873	1963	2035	2105	2132	2630	4105	3787	3749	3971	4078
1972	5700	4277	5132	5704	5700	4223	4283	4277	4276	4283	5132	5616	5650	5704	5701	5704	5700
1973	3538	5738	6071	5771	3538	5688	5289	5738	5970	6092	6071	6083	5783	5771	4870	3555	3538
1974	3697	3203	3233	3643	3697	3332	3188	3203	3202	3218	3238	3365	3569	3643	3921	3915	3697
1975	7224	3983	4974	5612	7224	3737	3788	3983	4195	4558	4974	5007	5317	5612	6391	6901	7224
1976	4837	6097	4846	4563	4837	6986	6209	6097	4875	4879	4846	4618	4562	4563	4768	4805	4837
1977	4834	4945	5215	5026	4834	4949	4966	4945	5033	5097	5215	4945	5017	5026	4983	4904	4834
1978	7122	4715	5787	6647	7122	4846	4587	4715	5088	5636	5787	6343	6516	6647	6373	6910	7122
1979	13345	11783	11911	12007	13345	7762	7961	11783	12010	12059	11911	12221	12254	12007	12820	12736	13345
1980	21436	16836	19437	21095	21436	14878	15433	16836	19617	19565	19437	20773	20966	21095	22126	22386	21436
1981	19126	24506	22117	19129	19126	23086	24226	24506	25069	25205	22117	22040	20781	19129	18870	18494	19126
1982	14985	17489	13897	12047	14985	17768	18243	17489	15326	14034	13897	14066	12803	12047	12277	12365	14985
1983	18961	14843	16587	19339	18961	17927	15700	14848	17069	17359	16587	19174	19747	19339	19365	19638	18961

Net foreign position: commercial banks (24)(27)
billion francs, end of period

Position extérieure nette : banques commerciales (24)(27)
milliards de francs, fin de période

	Year	Q.1	Q.2	Q.3	Q.4	JAN	FEB	MAR	APR	MAY	JUN	JUL	AUG	SEP	OCT	NOV	DEC
1964	-2.0	-1.9	-2.3	-1.8	-2.0	-1.8	-1.6	-1.9	-2.0	-2.4	-2.3	-2.3	-2.0	-1.8	-1.8	-2.1	-2.0
1965	-0.6	-2.1	-1.5	-1.6	-0.6	-2.3	-2.2	-2.1	-1.8	-1.5	-1.5	-1.9	-2.0	-1.6	-1.2	-1.1	-0.6
1966	-0.9	-0.2	-0.1	-1.2	-0.9	-0.3	-0.2	-0.2	0.1	-0.0	-0.1	-0.4	-0.6	-1.2	-1.0	-0.9	-0.9
1967	-5.2	-2.7	-2.2	-2.8	-5.2	..	..	-2.7	..	..	-2.2	..	..	-2.8	..	..	-5.2
1968	-2.1	-5.3	1.1	2.7	-2.1	-5.1	-5.5	-5.3	-6.0	-4.6	1.1	1.2	2.0	2.7	0.3	-0.2	-2.1
1969	-4.7	-6.1	-5.5	-5.1	-4.7	-3.9	-5.4	-6.1	-5.8	-6.4	-5.5	-6.2	-6.4	-5.1	-5.9	-5.7	-4.7
1970	-7.5	-5.5	-3.7	-5.2	-7.5	-5.6	-5.5	-5.5	-6.4	-5.2	-3.7	-4.3	-4.3	-5.2	-6.5	-7.6	-7.5
1971	-15.0	-8.7	-9.9	-16.6	-15.0	-8.6	-8.9	-8.7	-8.2	-10.6	-9.9	-12.2	-16.7	-16.6	-15.1	-14.4	-15.0
1972	-21.2	-17.4	-19.6	-20.8	-21.2	-16.5	-16.8	-17.4	-15.3	-15.8	-19.6	-21.1	-21.0	-20.8	-20.4	-20.2	-21.2
1973	-16.2	-23.1	-20.4	-15.4	-16.2	-21.4	-21.6	-23.1	-24.0	-23.4	-20.4	-21.5	-23.3	-15.4	-12.6	-14.2	-16.2
1974	-26.1	..	-21.1	-26.1	-26.1	-11.1	..	..	..	..	-21.1	-24.6	-24.5	-26.1	-26.1	-26.3	-26.1
1975	-24.5	-23.9	-19.8	-19.2	-24.5	-28.1	-28.1	-23.9	-22.1	-21.3	-19.8	-16.4	-18.8	-19.2	-21.0	-23.2	-24.5
1976	-35.2	-23.2	-25.7	-32.9	-35.2	-26.8	-26.4	-23.2	-24.2	-25.3	-25.7	-27.2	-28.9	-32.9	-35.2	-38.1	-35.2
1977	-29.1	-39.1	-37.0	-34.7	-29.1	-38.4	-40.1	-39.1	-39.5	-39.7	-37.0	-35.4	-33.9	-34.7	-31.0	-29.4	-29.1
1978	-43.1	-51.5	-43.6	-46.9	-43.1	-51.4	-50.2	-51.5	-52.9	-50.3	-43.6	-43.1	-46.4	-46.9	-49.1	-41.6	-43.1
1979	-51.1	-49.1	-46.6	-45.8	-51.1	-44.3	-45.6	-49.1	-48.1	-47.5	-46.6	-46.2	-45.9	-45.8	-44.6	-53.5	-51.1
1980	-116.5	-66.6	-78.3	-99.0	-116.5	-55.1	-61.3	-66.6	-74.0	-78.7	-78.3	-82.6	-92.0	-99.0	-107.2	-111.7	-116.5
1981	-207.6	-145.0	-147.6	-165.6	-207.6	-128.4	-135.8	-145.0	-150.8	-134.8	-147.6	-158.1	-162.1	-165.6	-182.9	-197.9	-207.6
1982	-259.3	-221.6	-250.9	-262.2	-259.3	-212.0	-215.4	-221.6	-225.7	-234.7	-250.9	-251.1	-264.0	-262.2	-274.9	-267.2	-259.3
1983	-316.4	-301.6	-325.3	-327.2	-316.4	-281.5	-268.3	-301.6	-321.2	-318.8	-325.8	-332.9	-330.9	-327.2	-316.8	-308.0	-316.4

FRANCE

Imports f.o.b. (28) — Importations f.o.b. (28)

billion francs, monthly averages — milliards de francs, moyennes mensuelles

	Year	Q.1	Q.2	Q.3	Q.4	JAN	FEB	MAR	APR	MAY	JUN	JUL	AUG	SEP	OCT	NOV	DEC
1964	4.14	4.26	4.39	3.67	4.25	4.25	4.18	4.36	4.59	4.15	4.42	4.02	3.11	3.97	4.15	4.08	4.53
1965	4.25	4.19	4.34	3.81	4.67	4.03	3.94	4.60	4.44	4.31	4.27	4.08	3.35	4.00	4.39	4.57	5.05
1966	4.89	4.82	5.03	4.45	5.25	4.43	4.61	5.42	4.91	4.95	5.24	4.58	3.85	4.90	5.09	5.21	5.45
1967	5.09	5.39	5.14	4.46	5.38	5.27	5.13	5.79	5.17	5.22	5.03	4.57	3.81	4.99	5.22	5.26	5.66
1968	5.74	5.62	5.06	5.51	6.77	5.37	5.45	6.02	5.75	3.96	5.47	6.13	4.61	5.79	6.50	6.67	7.15
1969	7.39	6.34	7.60	6.84	8.28	6.74	6.51	7.26	7.73	7.53	7.53	7.31	5.51	7.69	8.56	7.65	8.64
1970	8.30	7.91	8.64	7.65	8.99	7.60	7.80	8.34	9.33	7.41	9.17	8.20	6.45	8.30	8.66	8.72	9.60
1971	9.15	8.73	9.31	8.56	10.01	7.79	8.34	10.05	9.49	8.55	9.89	9.13	7.23	9.31	9.64	9.58	10.80
1972	10.58	10.45	10.73	9.39	11.69	9.14	10.59	11.63	10.73	11.13	10.87	9.43	8.16	10.60	11.20	11.35	12.53
1973	12.96	12.28	13.04	12.03	14.49	11.74	11.80	13.29	11.93	13.94	13.24	12.76	10.68	12.66	14.75	14.47	14.23
1974	19.93	18.79	21.43	19.31	20.19	17.41	18.26	20.68	21.80	22.24	20.26	22.04	16.41	19.49	20.98	18.94	20.65
1975	18.46	19.01	18.20	16.46	20.16	19.14	18.78	19.11	19.86	16.63	18.12	18.45	13.11	17.82	20.28	18.48	21.71
1976	24.48	22.33	24.19	23.35	28.03	20.34	21.74	24.92	24.45	23.97	24.14	23.75	20.14	26.16	27.22	27.58	29.30
1977	27.58	28.34	28.33	25.12	28.55	26.48	27.09	31.44	27.46	27.26	30.27	25.66	22.59	27.11	27.17	29.16	29.31
1978	29.59	30.15	30.19	26.32	31.69	28.59	28.64	33.23	29.99	29.99	30.60	26.98	23.34	28.63	31.42	31.96	31.69
1979	36.50	33.92	35.92	35.00	41.17	32.07	33.02	36.68	33.83	38.30	35.62	36.94	31.32	36.73	43.00	41.52	39.01
1980	45.91	46.67	46.32	42.03	48.64	42.75	46.32	50.93	46.49	46.12	46.36	46.38	33.74	45.46	49.94	45.97	50.00
1981	52.27	49.75	51.57	49.79	57.97	45.67	49.17	54.42	51.48	49.82	53.42	53.54	40.19	55.63	56.81	57.03	60.08
1982	60.53	58.48	61.19	57.38	65.03	54.24	57.38	63.82	61.63	54.77	67.18	59.93	48.62	63.59	63.04	66.12	66.08
1983	63.88	64.67	64.42	57.90	68.52	62.48	60.65	70.89	59.88	66.09	67.28	60.16	51.25	62.29	64.72	69.28	71.55

Exports f.o.b. (28) — Exportations f.o.b. (28)

billion francs, monthly averages — milliards de francs, moyennes mensuelles

	Year	Q.1	Q.2	Q.3	Q.4	JAN	FEB	MAR	APR	MAY	JUN	JUL	AUG	SEP	OCT	NOV	DEC
1964	3.70	3.70	3.74	3.30	4.05	3.61	3.71	3.80	3.81	3.48	3.94	3.73	2.73	3.44	4.12	3.98	4.07
1965	4.14	3.93	4.14	3.87	4.63	3.40	3.86	4.52	4.15	4.22	4.06	4.33	3.21	4.07	4.52	4.42	4.96
1966	4.48	4.40	4.65	4.15	4.75	3.82	4.31	5.05	4.67	4.52	4.74	4.69	3.60	4.16	4.69	4.54	5.00
1967	4.68	4.57	4.80	4.24	5.12	4.36	4.46	4.90	4.79	4.55	5.06	4.72	3.47	4.53	5.13	5.04	5.18
1968	5.22	5.29	4.40	5.28	5.91	4.86	5.26	5.75	5.37	3.93	3.91	6.39	4.53	4.94	6.19	5.60	5.94
1969	6.41	5.91	6.41	5.83	7.50	5.69	5.82	6.21	6.47	6.08	6.66	6.72	4.61	6.16	7.70	6.88	7.93
1970	8.35	7.95	8.71	7.61	9.15	7.28	7.89	8.67	8.99	7.49	9.66	8.50	6.24	8.08	9.09	8.94	9.42
1971	9.61	9.11	9.70	9.01	10.64	8.17	8.98	10.20	9.82	9.26	10.01	10.19	7.64	9.19	10.57	10.26	11.09
1972	11.12	10.42	11.60	9.90	12.58	9.37	10.27	11.61	11.47	12.19	12.15	10.69	8.25	10.75	12.83	12.25	12.66
1973	13.54	12.66	13.85	12.47	15.19	11.99	12.24	13.74	13.11	14.21	14.22	14.13	10.48	12.79	15.16	15.31	15.10
1974	18.59	17.33	19.56	17.56	19.93	16.60	16.63	18.75	19.28	19.78	19.61	20.36	14.32	18.01	20.06	19.00	20.73
1975	18.89	19.24	19.58	16.87	19.35	18.52	19.51	19.69	20.31	17.84	20.61	19.76	13.38	17.46	20.14	18.55	20.85
1976	22.77	21.12	23.59	20.97	25.41	18.97	21.00	23.39	23.22	23.14	24.41	23.43	17.41	22.07	24.66	24.43	27.13
1977	26.66	26.06	27.61	24.10	28.87	23.48	25.52	29.19	26.60	26.55	29.70	25.56	20.12	26.63	28.57	27.15	30.88
1978	29.80	29.35	31.29	26.68	31.88	25.90	28.82	33.32	30.92	29.84	33.11	29.64	21.25	29.16	32.58	31.96	32.09
1979	35.66	33.49	36.29	33.25	39.61	30.13	33.07	37.28	34.85	36.98	37.06	37.60	27.31	34.84	40.20	39.06	39.58
1980	40.88	40.57	42.35	36.77	43.83	35.67	41.55	44.48	44.24	33.37	44.44	41.49	28.85	39.98	44.98	40.07	46.43
1981	43.06	44.78	49.65	45.70	52.09	37.89	45.91	50.55	50.25	47.17	51.54	50.42	38.84	47.84	51.92	51.38	52.97
1982	52.76	51.65	53.55	47.93	57.90	45.35	51.52	58.08	53.38	51.85	55.40	53.87	39.64	50.28	57.18	57.35	59.17
1983	60.26	55.63	61.42	55.74	68.22	50.94	53.32	62.64	59.79	58.92	65.56	59.27	47.97	59.99	66.51	65.81	72.35

Trade balance (f.o.b. — f.o.b.) (28) — Balance commerciale (f.o.b. — f.o.b.) (28)

billion francs, monthly averages — milliards de francs, moyennes mensuelles

	Year	Q.1	Q.2	Q.3	Q.4	JAN	FEB	MAR	APR	MAY	JUN	JUL	AUG	SEP	OCT	NOV	DEC
1964	-0.44	-0.56	-0.65	-0.37	-0.20	-0.64	-0.47	-0.56	-0.78	-0.67	-0.49	-0.29	-0.38	-0.43	-0.03	-0.11	-0.46
1965	-0.11	-0.27	-0.20	0.06	-0.04	-0.63	-0.08	-0.08	-0.30	-0.09	-0.21	0.25	-0.14	0.07	0.13	-0.15	-0.09
1966	-0.40	-0.43	-0.39	-0.29	-0.50	-0.61	-0.30	-0.37	-0.24	-0.43	-0.49	0.11	-0.25	-0.75	-0.40	-0.66	-0.45
1967	-0.41	-0.32	-0.34	-0.22	-0.26	-0.91	-0.67	-0.89	-0.38	-0.67	0.03	0.15	-0.35	-0.46	-0.09	-0.22	-0.48
1968	-0.52	-0.32	-0.66	-0.23	-0.86	-0.51	-0.19	-0.27	-0.38	-0.03	-1.56	0.25	-0.08	-0.85	-0.32	-1.07	-1.20
1969	-0.98	-0.93	-1.19	-1.01	-0.78	-1.05	-0.69	-1.05	-1.26	-1.45	-0.87	-0.60	-0.90	-1.53	-0.86	-0.77	-0.71
1970	0.06	0.04	0.07	-0.04	0.16	-0.32	0.10	0.33	-0.35	0.08	0.49	0.30	-0.21	-0.22	0.43	0.22	-0.18
1971	0.46	0.39	0.39	0.45	0.63	0.37	0.64	0.15	0.34	0.71	0.12	1.06	0.40	-0.11	0.93	0.68	0.28
1972	0.54	-0.04	0.83	0.50	0.89	0.23	-0.33	-0.02	1.15	0.05	1.28	1.26	0.09	0.15	1.63	0.90	0.13
1973	0.58	0.38	0.81	0.44	0.71	0.25	0.44	0.45	1.18	0.27	0.98	1.37	-0.20	0.13	0.41	0.84	0.87
1974	-1.34	-1.46	-1.88	-1.75	-0.26	-0.81	-1.63	-1.94	-2.53	-2.46	-0.65	-1.68	-2.09	-1.48	-0.93	0.07	0.08
1975	0.43	0.24	1.38	0.41	-0.31	-0.62	0.74	0.59	0.45	1.21	2.49	1.31	0.28	-0.36	-0.13	0.07	-0.85
1976	-1.71	-1.22	-0.50	-2.38	-2.63	-1.37	-0.74	-1.53	-1.24	-0.84	0.27	-0.32	-2.73	-4.09	-2.56	-3.15	-2.17
1977	-0.92	-2.27	-0.72	-1.02	0.32	-3.00	-1.57	-2.25	-0.87	-0.71	-0.58	-0.11	-2.47	-0.48	1.39	-2.01	1.58
1978	0.21	-0.31	1.10	0.37	0.19	-2.69	0.17	0.10	0.93	-0.15	2.52	2.67	-2.09	0.52	1.16	-0.00	-0.60
1979	-0.84	-0.43	0.38	-1.75	-1.56	-1.94	0.05	0.60	1.02	-1.33	1.44	0.66	-4.00	-1.89	-2.80	-2.46	0.57
1980	-5.04	-6.10	-3.97	-5.26	-4.81	-7.08	-4.78	-6.45	-2.25	-7.75	-1.92	-5.39	-4.90	-5.49	-4.96	-5.90	-3.57
1981	-4.22	-4.97	-1.92	-4.09	-5.88	-7.78	-3.26	-3.88	-1.23	-2.65	-1.88	-3.13	-1.36	-7.79	-4.89	-5.65	-7.11
1982	-7.78	-6.83	-7.65	-9.45	-7.18	-8.88	-5.86	-5.74	-8.25	-2.92	-11.78	-6.06	-8.98	-13.31	-5.86	-8.77	-6.91
1983	-3.62	-9.04	-2.99	-2.16	-0.29	-11.54	-7.33	-8.25	-0.09	-7.17	-1.72	-0.89	-3.28	-2.30	1.79	-3.47	0.80

Imports f.o.b. (28)(29) — Importations f.o.b. (29)(28)

billion francs, monthly averages — milliards de francs, moyennes mensuelles

Adjusted - Corrigé

Year	Q.1	Q.2	Q.3	Q.4	JAN	FEB	MAR	APR	MAY	JUN	JUL	AUG	SEP	OCT	NOV	DEC
1964	4.06	4.22	4.12	4.11	4.05	4.14	4.00	4.26	4.12	4.27	4.07	4.16	4.13	4.05	4.18	4.09
1965	4.05	4.19	4.30	4.47	4.07	3.98	4.09	4.10	4.35	4.11	4.25	4.41	4.24	4.41	4.46	4.54
1966	4.67	4.87	4.98	5.06	4.55	4.67	4.81	4.64	4.89	5.07	4.96	4.92	5.07	5.16	5.04	4.99
1967	5.21	4.98	5.04	5.20	5.29	5.20	5.13	5.15	5.00	4.79	5.03	4.88	5.20	5.14	5.11	5.37
1968	5.42	4.90	6.16	6.47	5.26	5.33	5.68	5.37	3.78	5.55	6.31	6.02	6.14	6.15	6.58	6.67
1969	6.74	7.32	7.56	7.95	6.64	6.63	6.96	7.18	7.35	7.43	7.48	7.43	7.77	8.10	7.95	7.78
1970	7.92	8.13	8.47	8.76	7.95	7.90	7.90	8.33	7.56	8.50	8.29	8.64	8.49	8.42	9.10	8.77
1971	8.61	8.78	9.46	9.65	8.55	8.43	8.84	8.70	8.50	9.12	9.47	9.29	9.64	9.66	9.84	9.44
1972	10.01	10.39	10.51	11.55	9.77	10.18	10.09	10.25	10.93	10.00	10.25	10.39	10.89	11.06	11.49	12.11
1973	11.88	12.59	13.38	14.06	11.98	11.85	11.80	11.58	13.29	12.90	13.00	13.46	13.69	14.01	14.09	14.07
1974	18.36	20.75	20.96	19.94	17.85	18.34	18.89	20.40	20.92	20.93	21.32	20.95	20.60	20.00	19.81	20.01
1975	18.85	17.36	18.09	19.60	19.37	18.81	18.36	17.93	16.49	17.66	18.58	17.59	18.09	19.09	19.58	20.14
1976	21.37	23.33	25.45	27.13	20.84	21.65	21.63	23.02	23.50	23.46	24.33	25.37	26.66	27.02	27.50	26.85
1977	27.44	27.27	27.49	28.07	27.79	27.04	27.48	26.41	26.67	28.75	26.79	28.35	27.33	27.34	29.52	27.36
1978	29.06	29.14	29.32	31.30	28.76	28.59	29.83	29.38	29.26	28.78	29.10	29.61	29.25	30.77	31.24	31.88
1979	32.56	35.18	38.68	39.82	32.14	32.92	32.64	33.70	36.37	35.47	37.32	35.34	39.37	40.52	38.98	39.97
1980	44.73	45.29	45.93	47.25	43.18	43.70	47.29	44.36	45.89	45.63	46.83	45.35	45.60	46.94	47.29	47.53
1981	48.24	50.86	53.74	56.57	46.46	48.97	49.30	49.79	50.32	52.47	53.01	52.82	55.40	54.78	56.25	58.67
1982	56.98	59.57	62.09	62.80	58.09	57.14	55.70	59.10	56.26	63.34	60.85	61.60	63.83	62.58	64.16	61.64
1983	62.52	62.71	63.43	66.34	64.78	60.68	62.11	59.87	64.83	63.44	63.06	64.74	62.48	65.06	67.37	68.09

Exports f.o.b. (28)(29) — Exportations f.o.b. (29)(28)

billion francs, monthly averages — milliards de francs, moyennes mensuelles

Adjusted - Corrigé

Year	Q.1	Q.2	Q.3	Q.4	JAN	FEB	MAR	APR	MAY	JUN	JUL	AUG	SEP	OCT	NOV	DEC
1964	3.63	3.65	3.63	3.84	3.69	3.69	3.51	3.66	3.56	3.73	3.55	3.62	3.74	3.83	3.92	3.76
1965	3.89	4.05	4.26	4.38	3.66	3.92	4.09	3.90	4.31	3.93	4.17	4.25	4.35	4.35	4.27	4.51
1966	4.35	4.54	4.59	4.51	4.08	4.37	4.61	4.48	4.62	4.51	4.69	4.69	4.40	4.43	4.50	4.59
1967	4.51	4.58	4.72	4.89	4.61	4.51	4.42	4.72	4.56	4.75	4.67	4.57	4.92	4.80	4.91	4.95
1968	5.19	4.26	5.83	5.61	5.02	5.06	5.49	4.97	3.92	3.89	6.10	6.02	5.38	5.67	5.56	5.59
1969	5.86	6.20	6.48	7.12	5.85	5.86	5.87	6.09	6.13	6.37	6.49	6.41	6.54	6.96	7.09	7.32
1970	8.10	8.16	8.45	8.71	7.73	8.18	8.38	8.33	7.65	8.49	8.28	8.46	8.61	8.51	8.78	8.84
1971	9.16	9.16	9.94	10.16	9.08	9.28	9.11	9.39	9.12	8.97	9.99	9.99	9.85	10.23	10.23	10.01
1972	10.16	11.08	11.16	12.33	10.14	9.92	10.41	11.58	10.94	10.73	10.94	11.09	11.45	12.25	12.15	12.57
1973	12.51	13.14	13.95	14.51	12.75	12.32	12.47	12.75	13.29	13.39	13.75	13.86	14.25	14.08	14.70	14.76
1974	17.32	18.57	19.17	19.55	17.77	16.70	17.49	18.03	18.23	19.43	18.92	19.25	19.34	18.99	19.88	19.77
1975	19.44	18.41	18.85	19.24	19.54	19.55	19.21	18.87	17.61	18.75	19.63	18.90	18.02	18.90	19.47	19.36
1976	20.61	22.32	23.03	24.59	20.29	20.91	20.62	21.90	22.04	23.03	22.86	22.94	23.28	24.15	24.46	25.16
1977	25.70	25.99	26.78	28.11	25.50	25.45	26.15	25.40	25.73	26.85	25.66	27.08	27.59	27.87	27.82	28.65
1978	28.94	29.51	29.82	31.23	27.15	28.67	31.00	29.39	29.60	29.54	30.15	28.75	30.56	31.12	31.71	30.88
1979	32.84	34.73	37.00	37.95	32.26	32.84	33.41	33.70	35.12	35.36	36.30	36.37	38.33	37.22	37.41	39.23
1980	39.50	40.44	40.91	42.45	38.52	39.12	40.85	42.01	38.34	40.96	40.96	40.86	40.92	41.96	41.92	43.51
1981	43.93	47.77	50.57	50.36	40.82	45.50	45.46	48.04	46.99	48.30	48.57	53.20	49.93	49.03	50.47	51.57
1982	51.03	51.09	52.46	55.99	51.33	51.03	50.73	50.13	52.62	50.52	52.22	52.33	52.83	55.52	57.01	55.44
1983	54.59	58.44	61.96	66.42	55.19	52.85	55.74	57.63	57.91	59.78	59.82	63.92	62.16	64.51	66.19	68.56

Trade balance (f.o.b. — f.o.b.) (28)(29) — Balance commerciale (f.o.b. — f.o.b.) (29)(28)

billion francs, monthly averages — milliards de francs, moyennes mensuelles

Adjusted - Corrigé

Year	Q.1	Q.2	Q.3	Q.4	JAN	FEB	MAR	APR	MAY	JUN	JUL	AUG	SEP	OCT	NOV	DEC
1964	-0.43	-0.57	-0.49	-0.27	-0.36	-0.45	-0.48	-0.61	-0.56	-0.54	-0.52	-0.55	-0.40	-0.22	-0.26	-0.33
1965	-0.16	-0.14	-0.04	-0.09	-0.41	-0.06	0.00	-0.19	-0.05	-0.18	-0.08	-0.16	0.11	-0.07	-0.19	-0.02
1966	-0.32	-0.33	-0.39	-0.55	-0.47	-0.30	-0.19	-0.17	-0.27	-0.56	-0.27	-0.24	-0.67	-0.72	-0.55	-0.39
1967	-0.70	-0.30	-0.32	-0.32	-0.68	-0.70	-0.71	-0.43	-0.44	-0.04	-0.36	-0.31	-0.28	-0.34	-0.20	-0.41
1968	-0.24	-0.64	-0.33	-0.86	-0.25	-0.27	-0.19	-0.40	0.14	-1.66	-0.21	0.00	-0.77	-0.48	-1.02	-1.07
1969	-0.88	-1.12	-1.08	-0.82	-0.79	-0.77	-1.09	-1.09	-1.23	-1.06	-0.99	-1.02	-1.24	-1.14	-0.86	-0.47
1970	0.18	0.03	-0.02	-0.05	-0.22	0.28	0.48	-0.01	0.09	-0.01	-0.01	-0.17	0.12	0.09	-0.32	0.07
1971	0.55	0.39	0.48	0.51	0.53	0.85	0.27	0.69	0.62	-0.15	0.52	0.71	0.22	0.58	0.39	0.57
1972	0.15	0.69	0.65	0.78	0.37	-0.26	0.33	1.32	0.01	0.73	0.69	0.70	0.56	1.20	0.66	0.47
1973	0.63	0.55	0.57	0.46	0.77	0.47	0.66	1.17	-0.00	0.49	0.75	0.40	0.56	0.07	0.60	0.70
1974	-1.04	-2.18	-1.79	-0.40	-0.08	-1.64	-1.40	-2.36	-2.69	-1.50	-2.39	-1.71	-1.26	-1.01	0.07	-0.25
1975	0.59	1.05	0.76	-0.36	0.17	0.74	0.86	0.94	1.11	1.09	1.05	1.31	-0.07	-0.20	-0.11	-0.77
1976	-0.77	-1.01	-2.43	-2.54	-0.56	-0.74	-1.01	-1.12	-1.47	-0.43	-1.47	-2.43	-3.39	-2.87	-3.04	-1.69
1977	-1.74	-1.28	-0.71	0.04	-2.29	-1.59	-1.33	-1.00	-0.94	-1.90	-1.13	-1.27	0.26	0.53	-1.70	1.29
1978	-0.12	0.37	0.50	-0.07	-1.61	0.09	1.17	0.01	0.35	0.76	1.06	-0.87	1.32	0.35	0.46	-1.00
1979	0.27	-0.46	-1.68	-1.87	0.13	-0.09	0.77	0.01	-1.26	-0.12	-1.02	-2.97	-1.04	-3.30	-1.57	-0.74
1980	-5.23	-4.86	-5.02	-4.79	-4.66	-4.58	-6.44	-2.34	-7.56	-4.67	-5.88	-4.49	-4.68	-4.98	-5.38	-4.02
1981	-4.31	-3.09	-3.18	-6.21	-5.63	-3.47	-3.84	-1.75	-3.34	-4.18	-4.44	0.39	-5.47	-5.76	-5.77	-7.10
1982	-5.94	-8.48	-9.63	-6.81	-6.75	-6.11	-4.97	-8.96	-3.64	-12.82	-8.63	-9.27	-11.00	-7.07	-7.15	-6.20
1983	-7.93	-4.27	-1.46	-0.42	-9.60	-7.83	-6.36	-2.24	-6.92	-3.65	-3.25	-0.82	-0.33	-0.55	-1.18	0.47

FRANCE

Balance of payments: net trade
billion francs

Balance des paiements : balance commerciale
milliards de francs

	Year	Q.1	Q.2	Q.3	Q.4	JAN	FEB	MAR	APR	MAY	JUN	JUL	AUG	SEP	OCT	NOV	DEC
1964																	
1965																	
1966																	
1967																	
1968																	
1969																	
1970																	
1971																	
1972																	
1973	2.2	0.3	2.0	0.2	-0.3												
1974	-21.2	-6.4	-7.8	-5.4	-1.6												
1975	6.2	0.8	5.5	1.3	-1.3												
1976	-22.3	-3.5	-2.3	-8.1	-8.5												
1977	-13.9	-7.1	-2.2	-4.2	-0.4												
1978	3.4	-2.2	3.6	1.7	0.3												
1979	-8.9	-0.7	1.1	-4.4	-4.8												
1980	-55.1	-15.7	-8.9	-15.7	-14.8												
1981	-55.0	-16.9	-4.7	-14.2	-19.2												
1982	-102.1	-21.7	-26.4	-29.7	-24.3												
1983	-57.2	-29.7	-13.9	-10.8	-2.8												

Balance of payments: current balance
billion francs

Balance des paiements : opérations courantes, nettes
milliards de francs

	Year	Q.1	Q.2	Q.3	Q.4	JAN	FEB	MAR	APR	MAY	JUN	JUL	AUG	SEP	OCT	NOV	DEC
1964																	
1965																	
1966																	
1967																	
1968																	
1969																	
1970																	
1971																	
1972																	
1973	6.6	1.2	3.8	0.0	1.6												
1974	-18.8	-5.7	-6.7	-6.8	0.4												
1975	11.5	0.9	7.6	2.0	1.0												
1976	-16.4	-3.0	0.1	-8.4	-5.0												
1977	-2.1	-5.3	1.7	-2.5	3.9												
1978	31.6	2.4	12.5	6.7	10.0												
1979	22.1	4.7	10.5	3.6	3.3												
1980	-17.6	-9.9	3.3	-6.8	-4.2												
1981	-25.8	-11.7	6.0	-9.5	-10.6												
1982	-79.3	-15.7	-22.6	-25.5	-15.6												
1983	-29.1	-31.0	-1.7	-0.5	4.0												

Balance of payments: net capital movements
billion francs

Balance des paiements : mouvements de capitaux, nets
milliards de francs

	Year	Q.1	Q.2	Q.3	Q.4	JAN	FEB	MAR	APR	MAY	JUN	JUL	AUG	SEP	OCT	NOV	DEC
1964																	
1965																	
1966																	
1967																	
1968																	
1969																	
1970																	
1971																	
1972																	
1973	-5.5	-0.4	-5.0	1.0	-1.2												
1974	13.3	6.2	3.5	6.8	-3.3												
1975	-19.1	-3.0	-9.8	-5.0	-1.3												
1976	11.4	3.8	-2.5	7.6	2.5												
1977	-2.5	4.0	-3.8	2.1	-4.7												
1978	-31.4	-4.5	-10.9	-6.0	-10.1												
1979	-24.5	-5.1	-12.0	-2.6	-4.3												
1980	8.0	7.4	-6.3	5.9	0.9												
1981	37.9	14.7	-0.4	8.1	15.6												
1982	38.8	8.2	0.8	12.8	16.9												
1983	36.1	8.8	10.1	21.0	-3.3												

NOTES

1. Annual and quarterly data have more complete coverage than monthly data.
2. The series includes unassembled vehicles for export.
3. Data for August 1979 and 1980 include production in July.
4. No survey in August.
5. Excluding food. From February 1976, new weighting pattern.
6. From 1st quarter 1976, new weighting pattern.
7. Department stores, chain stores, mail order houses and hypermarkets.
8. The original base of the index is 1971 to 1974, and 1975 from 1975.
9. Passenger cars and commercial vehicles.
10. Monthly data refer to end of period.
11. Numerous administrative changes have had impacts on the level of the series, particularly since 1977.
12. Full-time jobs only. An official attempt to find employment for those repatriated from North Africa was made in 1962, and the resulting number of job vacancies was excluded from the data from October 1962 to March 1963.
13. Sample survey providing employment data for last day of preceding quarter, hours worked for first week of quarter (last week of preceding quarter before 1973) and wage rates applicable from first day of quarter. Annual data are centred averages from January of current year to January of following year. Weighting pattern based on 1954 to 1972, 1970 from 1973 to 1975, and 1975 from 1976.
14. Permanent workers. Excluding immigration from some former French possessions. Data for January to April 1975 have been estimated by distributing a cumulative total over the four months for one of the components. From 1982, excluding nationals of EEC countries.
15. Excluding civil servants and agricultural workers.
16. From 1973, index (original base 1st January 1973) linked to previous index (original base 1st January 1960) by means of a coefficient provided by national authorities.
17. The original base of the index is 1955 to 1969, 1970 from 1970 to 1974, and 1975 from 1975.

NOTES

1. Les données annuelles et trimestrielles ont une couverture plus étendue que les données mensuelles.
2. La série prend en compte les véhicules incomplets destinés à être montés à l'étranger.
3. Les chiffres d'août 1979 et 1980 couvrent également la production de juillet.
4. Pas d'enquête au mois d'août.
5. Non compris l'alimentation. A partir de février 1976 nouvelle pondération.
6. A partir du 1er trimestre 1976, nouvelle pondération.
7. Grands magasins, magasins populaires, ventes par correspondance et hypermarchés.
8. La base originale de l'indice est 1971 jusqu'en 1974 et 1975 à partir de 1975.
9. Voitures particulières et commerciales.
10. Situation en fin de mois.
11. Le niveau de la série a été affecté de façon ponctuelle par de nombreux changements administratifs, surtout à partir de 1977.
12. Emplois à temps complet seulement. Le nombre d'emplois vacants, obtenus à la suite de démarches officielles en vue de procurer un emploi en 1962 aux rapatriés de l'Afrique du Nord a été exclu de la série d'octobre 1962 à mars 1963.
13. Enquête par sondage fournissant des chiffres concernant l'emploi au dernier jour du trimestre précédent, la durée du travail au cours de la première semaine du trimestre (avant 1973, dernière semaine du trimestre précédent), et les taux de salaires en vigueur au premier jour du trimestre. Les données annuelles sont des moyennes centrées de janvier de l'année en cours à janvier de l'année suivante. La pondération se réfère à 1954 jusqu'en 1972, à 1970 de 1973 à 1975, et à 1975 à partir de 1976.
14. Travailleurs permanents. Non compris les ressortissants de certains pays anciennement sous administration française. Les chiffres de janvier à avril 1975 d'une des composantes de la série sont estimés en répartissant un total cumulé sur les quatre mois. A partir de 1982, non compris les ressortissants des pays de la CEE.
15. Non compris l'administration publique et l'agriculture.
16. A partir de 1973, indice (base originale 1er janvier 1973) raccordé à l'indice précédent (base originale 1er janvier 1960) à l'aide d'un coefficient fourni par les autorités nationales.
17. La base originale de l'indice est 1955 jusqu'en 1969, 1970 de 1970 à 1974, et 1975 à partir de 1975.

FRANCE

NOTES

18. Excluding food, fuel and power.

19. Raw materials and semi-manufactured goods.

20. From December 1969, new accounting system.

21. Weighting pattern revised each January from 1970. Previously weights based on 1962.

22. Including credit to non-residents.

23. Prior to 1982, excluding bonds issued by the Treasury, local authorities and insurance companies.

24. From 1978, new accounting system.

25. On collateral of private bills; monthly data are averages of daily opening quotations.

26. Monthly data refer to last Friday of month. The original base of the index is 29th December 1961 to 1972 and 29th December 1972 from 1973.

27. Net short-term position in foreign exchange and in francs. Prior to 1967, excluding franc area. From 1976, improved statistical methods.

28. From 1970, including non-monetary gold.

29. Prior to 1970, seasonally adjusted by the OECD Secretariat.

NOTES

18. Non compris les produits alimentaires, les combustibles et l'énergie.

19. Matières premières et demi-produits.

20. A partir de décembre 1969, nouveau système de comptabilité.

21. A partir de 1970, la pondération est révisée chaque mois de janvier. Auparavant, la pondération se référait à 1962.

22. Y compris les crédits consentis aux non-résidents.

23. Avant 1982, non compris les obligations émises par le Trésor, les collectivités locales et les compagnies d'assurance.

24. A partir de 1978, nouveau système de comptabilité.

25. Contre effets privés; les données mensuelles sont la moyenne des taux quotidiens d'ouverture.

26. Les données mensuelles se réfèrent au dernier vendredi du mois. La base originale de l'indice est le 29 décembre 1961 jusqu'en 1972 et le 29 décembre 1972 à partir de 1973.

27. Position nette à court terme en devises et en francs. Avant 1967, zone franc exclue. A partir de 1976, méthodes statistiques améliorées.

28. A partir de 1970, y compris l'or non monétaire.

29. Avant 1970, corrigée des variations saisonnières par le Secrétariat de l'OCDE.

MAIN SOURCES

PRINCIPALES SOURCES

Series	Séries	Sources
Industrial production New motor vehicle registrations Labour cost Prices New capital issues Share prices Foreign trade	Production industrielle Immatriculations de voitures neuves Coût de la main-d'œuvre Prix Nouvelles émissions de capitaux Cours des actions Commerce extérieur	Institut national de la Statistique et des Études économiques *Bulletin mensuel de statistique*
Construction	Construction	Ministère de l'Environnement et du Cadre de Vie *Statistiques de la Construction*
Business surveys	Enquêtes de conjoncture	Institut national de la Statistique et des Études économiques *Enquête mensuelle (trimestrielle) dans l'industrie*
Retail sales	Ventes au détail	Chambre de Commerce et d'Industrie de Paris *Lettre mensuelle de conjoncture*
Households' consumption	Consommation des ménages	Institut national de la Statistique et des Études économiques *Tendances de la conjoncture*
Labour Hourly rates	Main-d'œuvre Taux horaires	Ministère du Travail *Statistiques du Travail*
Home finance Interest rates Net foreign position of commercial banks Balance of payments	Finances internes Taux d'intérêts Position extérieure nette des banques commerciales Balance des paiements	Banque de France *Bulletin trimestriel*

Germany — Allemagne

GERMANY

Gross national product / Produit national brut

at current market prices / *aux prix courants du marché*

billion DM, annual rates / milliards de DM, taux annuels

Adjusted - Corrigé

	Year	Q.1	Q.2	Q.3	Q.4	JAN	FEB	MAR	APR	MAY	JUN	JUL	AUG	SEP	OCT	NOV	DEC
1964	419.6	404.8	416.4	423.2	434.0												
1965	458.3	446.0	454.8	461.6	470.8												
1966	487.4	485.6	486.8	492.8	484.4												
1967	493.7	486.8	490.8	492.8	504.4												
1968	533.6	509.6	523.2	542.4	559.2												
1969	597.9	565.2	584.4	610.0	632.0												
1970	675.6	633.6	676.3	686.0	706.0												
1971	751.8	727.2	746.0	761.2	772.8												
1972	825.0	799.6	813.2	830.0	857.2												
1973	918.8	900.0	905.2	923.2	946.8												
1974	985.5	961.6	975.6	1000.4	1004.4												
1975	1028.8	996.4	1022.0	1036.8	1060.0												
1976	1123.0	1089.6	1119.2	1129.2	1154.0												
1977	1196.3	1175.2	1183.2	1196.4	1230.4												
1978	1290.0	1252.0	1277.6	1302.4	1328.0												
1979	1395.3	1345.6	1386.0	1411.6	1438.0												
1980	1485.7	1472.0	1478.8	1496.0	1496.0												
1981	1543.7	1512.8	1529.2	1560.0	1572.8												
1982	1598.9	1575.6	1592.4	1607.2	1620.4												
1983	1671.3	1634.4	1658.0	1676.8	1716.0												

Industrial production: total (1) / Production industrielle : total (1)

1980 = 100

	Year	Q.1	Q.2	Q.3	Q.4	JAN	FEB	MAR	APR	MAY	JUN	JUL	AUG	SEP	OCT	NOV	DEC
1964	61.0	58.3	62.1	58.4	65.4	55.4	58.7	61.0	60.2	64.8	61.5	57.4	55.5	62.4	64.9	67.8	63.7
1965	64.9	62.3	66.2	61.0	68.2	61.8	63.0	62.1	66.3	66.4	65.9	59.6	57.5	65.9	68.9	70.1	65.6
1966	65.0	63.9	68.3	61.5	66.8	62.0	63.9	65.7	69.0	67.8	68.0	61.8	56.9	65.7	67.5	68.7	64.1
1967	63.4	60.2	63.4	60.2	70.2	58.3	60.5	61.9	63.9	63.7	62.5	60.1	54.9	65.4	67.2	70.7	72.6
1968	69.4	62.9	71.2	66.8	77.6	59.5	62.8	66.5	68.9	69.4	75.1	62.8	64.4	73.2	73.8	81.5	77.7
1969	78.5	73.5	81.2	74.3	85.4	69.8	74.0	76.8	79.6	81.7	82.2	71.5	71.5	79.3	82.4	90.4	83.5
1970	83.2	81.2	87.2	77.9	86.8	76.8	81.5	85.2	84.5	91.9	85.3	77.0	73.8	82.9	86.0	89.9	84.5
1971	83.9	83.1	88.1	78.4	86.4	82.0	83.8	83.5	88.3	88.5	87.5	78.6	72.1	84.4	88.3	90.3	80.6
1972	86.9	83.6	90.0	81.0	93.9	80.3	83.4	86.9	91.8	89.5	88.5	80.2	74.9	87.9	90.6	96.6	94.4
1973	92.4	90.1	96.6	85.9	98.2	84.9	93.0	92.4	97.6	95.0	97.1	80.9	80.9	96.1	94.6	100.9	99.0
1974	90.8	90.8	97.3	83.8	92.4	86.3	92.4	93.7	96.3	95.2	100.4	82.4	77.8	91.2	91.2	97.5	88.7
1975	85.2	84.9	87.6	77.6	91.7	79.6	84.9	90.1	85.7	89.7	87.3	73.0	74.3	85.3	88.2	96.8	90.2
1976	91.1	88.4	95.4	84.3	96.7	84.1	91.3	89.8	95.0	94.7	96.5	80.1	79.3	93.5	96.7	100.7	92.5
1977	93.4	92.5	97.4	85.5	98.8	89.0	93.8	94.8	99.0	95.6	97.5	81.6	80.1	94.9	97.5	101.9	96.9
1978	95.1	92.7	96.8	88.6	102.7	89.7	93.6	94.9	97.5	97.0	95.8	84.8	81.5	99.5	100.3	105.6	102.3
1979	100.0	95.7	104.5	93.4	107.9	90.1	96.7	100.4	104.8	101.8	106.9	90.7	85.0	104.4	103.6	111.0	109.1
1980	100.0	102.8	101.4	93.3	102.8	98.5	105.6	104.4	103.9	98.7	101.5	92.7	85.2	102.0	105.0	104.9	98.4
1981	98.5	99.1	98.6	93.0	103.5	90.5	104.2	102.5	100.7	96.5	98.6	91.2	83.7	104.0	104.5	106.7	99.3
1982	95.6	98.5	98.6	88.2	96.9	89.5	101.0	105.0	101.1	96.2	98.6	84.2	81.7	98.8	96.7	99.7	94.2
1983	96.3	95.0	97.5	90.1	102.8	87.2	96.9	101.0	96.9	94.9	100.6	84.7	82.9	102.6	100.9	106.4	101.1

Industrial production: investment goods (1) / Production industrielle : biens d'équipement (1)

1980 = 100

	Year	Q.1	Q.2	Q.3	Q.4	JAN	FEB	MAR	APR	MAY	JUN	JUL	AUG	SEP	OCT	NOV	DEC
1964	58.3	56.2	60.3	54.0	63.5	52.4	56.8	59.5	56.9	63.5	60.4	52.8	50.0	59.1	60.9	65.5	64.1
1965	62.3	60.4	65.3	57.0	66.6	59.2	61.7	60.3	64.6	65.4	65.9	55.8	51.7	63.6	65.4	67.3	67.0
1966	62.3	61.7	66.8	56.6	64.8	59.8	62.1	63.1	67.3	65.8	67.3	57.4	50.4	61.9	63.8	65.9	64.6
1967	58.6	55.2	58.7	53.4	67.8	53.7	55.2	56.6	58.5	59.3	58.4	53.5	45.9	60.8	61.3	65.8	76.2
1968	63.9	56.3	66.1	60.0	75.0	52.9	55.6	60.4	62.5	63.7	72.3	55.4	55.5	69.1	67.9	78.3	78.8
1969	75.5	69.8	79.6	69.2	84.2	64.6	71.0	73.8	76.8	80.1	82.0	66.5	63.9	77.2	78.8	88.9	84.9
1970	82.0	79.5	88.0	74.2	87.3	73.3	80.3	85.0	83.4	93.8	86.9	74.0	67.1	81.7	84.4	90.2	87.3
1971	81.4	81.6	88.1	73.8	82.8	81.1	82.1	81.7	86.7	89.0	88.5	76.1	63.4	82.0	85.1	86.6	76.5
1972	83.6	80.2	88.0	75.2	92.1	76.6	80.2	83.8	89.5	87.4	87.2	75.5	66.4	83.6	86.0	94.3	95.8
1973	89.6	86.5	95.1	80.5	98.4	80.3	89.8	89.2	95.2	93.0	97.0	74.8	72.0	94.8	91.1	99.4	104.6
1974	87.3	87.1	95.3	78.0	90.6	81.8	89.3	90.2	92.4	92.7	101.0	76.5	69.2	88.2	85.7	95.7	90.5
1975	83.2	80.8	87.9	74.2	91.3	73.1	80.6	88.7	84.0	90.8	88.8	68.5	69.6	84.5	85.2	95.8	92.9
1976	88.6	85.4	94.7	78.3	96.7	80.6	88.9	86.8	92.0	94.5	97.5	72.3	71.7	90.9	94.6	100.3	95.1
1977	92.9	91.1	98.7	82.3	100.5	85.8	92.9	94.6	99.1	97.0	100.0	77.5	74.2	95.2	97.1	102.8	101.8
1978	93.3	90.3	95.5	85.1	103.3	87.2	91.8	91.9	94.1	95.6	96.9	81.1	74.2	100.1	97.6	104.0	108.4
1979	97.8	92.1	103.5	88.3	109.9	85.7	92.7	98.1	102.5	99.7	103.2	86.1	75.4	103.5	100.8	111.4	117.4
1980	100.0	99.6	102.2	92.9	105.9	93.5	102.9	102.3	103.9	98.0	104.6	92.6	81.2	104.8	107.1	105.8	104.7
1981	100.4	97.7	101.7	93.1	109.1	85.6	104.3	103.1	103.0	99.3	102.9	91.1	80.0	108.1	106.8	110.5	109.9
1982	99.1	99.8	104.4	89.9	102.3	86.0	103.8	109.6	105.2	101.9	106.2	84.9	80.6	104.3	99.9	102.9	104.1
1983	98.7	95.3	101.6	90.2	107.5	84.6	98.0	103.4	100.0	98.9	106.0	83.7	79.6	107.3	102.4	108.7	111.3

Gross national product
implicit price level
1980 = 100

Adjusted - Corrigé

Produit national brut
niveau implicite des prix
1980 = 100

	Year	Q.1	Q.2	Q.3	Q.4	JAN	FEB	MAR	APR	MAY	JUN	JUL	AUG	SEP	OCT	NOV	DEC
1964	48.4	47.8	48.1	48.7	49.0												
1965	50.1	49.5	49.9	50.4	50.7												
1966	51.9	51.3	51.6	52.6	52.2												
1967	52.6	52.4	52.7	52.8	52.7												
1968	53.6	53.1	53.4	53.5	54.4												
1969	55.9	54.8	55.2	56.0	57.3												
1970	60.1	58.5	59.9	60.6	61.4												
1971	64.8	63.2	64.5	65.4	66.1												
1972	68.3	67.1	67.8	68.7	69.5												
1973	72.7	71.3	72.1	73.0	74.6												
1974	77.7	75.2	76.8	78.5	80.2												
1975	82.4	81.0	82.4	82.9	83.2												
1976	85.2	83.8	85.0	85.5	86.4												
1977	88.3	87.1	88.0	88.5	89.7												
1978	92.0	90.8	91.5	92.4	93.5												
1979	95.7	94.3	94.9	96.5	97.2												
1980	100.0	97.9	100.0	100.9	101.3												
1981	104.2	102.0	103.9	104.9	106.0												
1982	109.2	107.2	108.6	109.9	111.0												
1983	112.7	111.6	111.8	113.2	114.3												

Industrial production: total (1)
1980 = 100

Adjusted - Corrigé

Production industrielle : total (1)
1980 = 100

	Year	Q.1	Q.2	Q.3	Q.4	JAN	FEB	MAR	APR	MAY	JUN	JUL	AUG	SEP	OCT	NOV	DEC
1964		60	60	62	63	60	61	60	60	60	60	62	61	62	63	62	63
1965		64	64	65	65	65	64	64	64	64	63	64	65	65	65	64	66
1966		66	66	65	64	65	66	67	66	66	66	65	65	65	64	64	64
1967		62	62	64	67	62	62	61	62	61	62	64	63	64	65	66	70
1968		65	68	71	74	64	65	66	66	68	69	69	73	72	72	74	75
1969		75	77	79	81	75	75	76	77	78	78	78	80	80	81	82	81
1970		82	84	84	83	81	83	83	84	84	84	84	84	83	83	83	84
1971		85	85	84	83	85	85	84	85	84	85	85	83	84	84	83	81
1972		86	87	87	89	85	86	86	87	86	87	86	87	87	88	89	91
1973		92	93	92	93	91	92	92	92	93	93	89	94	93	93	93	93
1974		92	93	91	88	93	92	91	92	93	92	93	90	90	90	89	85
1975		85	84	84	87	85	84	85	84	84	84	84	85	85	87	87	87
1976		90	92	92	92	88	90	90	91	91	93	91	92	93	93	93	92
1977		94	93	93	94	93	93	94	93	92	94	92	94	94	94	94	95
1978		93	93	96	98	96	94	91	93	93	94	95	96	97	96	97	100
1979		97	100	101	102	98	97	97	99	100	101	102	101	100	100	102	104
1980		103	100	99	98	103	104	101	101	100	100	100	100	97	99	99	98
1981		99	98	99	99	97	100	99	98	98	97	99	98	99	100	99	97
1982		98	97	94	93	97	98	99	98	97	96	94	95	94	93	93	92
1983		94	96	96	99	94	94	95	95	95	98	95	96	97	97	99	99

Industrial production: investment goods (1)
1980 = 100

Adjusted - Corrigé

Production industrielle : biens d'équipement (1)
1980 = 100

	Year	Q.1	Q.2	Q.3	Q.4	JAN	FEB	MAR	APR	MAY	JUN	JUL	AUG	SEP	OCT	NOV	DEC
1964		57	58	59	60	57	57	57	57	57	58	59	58	58	60	60	60
1965		62	62	62	63	62	62	62	62	63	62	62	62	63	63	62	64
1966		63	63	62	61	64	63	64	63	63	63	63	62	61	61	60	61
1967		56	56	58	63	58	56	55	56	56	57	58	56	59	60	60	68
1968		58	62	66	69	58	57	59	60	62	63	63	67	67	67	70	71
1969		71	74	76	73	70	71	72	73	74	75	75	77	77	78	79	78
1970		80	83	82	82	78	81	82	83	83	83	83	82	81	82	82	82
1971		83	83	82	78	85	83	82	83	82	83	84	79	81	81	79	73
1972		82	83	83	85	82	82	83	83	82	83	84	84	81	84	86	86
1973		89	89	89	91	88	89	89	89	90	88	86	90	90	90	90	91
1974		89	88	87	83	90	90	87	88	89	87	92	85	85	85	85	81
1975		81	83	83	84	80	81	82	83	82	82	83	84	83	84	85	84
1976		87	89	88	90	86	88	87	88	89	90	87	88	89	90	91	89
1977		93	92	92	93	92	93	94	92	92	93	91	93	93	93	93	94
1978		92	91	95	95	97	92	87	90	90	92	93	94	97	93	94	98
1979		94	97	97	101	96	93	94	96	97	98	99	97	97	98	101	104
1980		101	99	101	99	102	102	99	101	99	99	102	101	98	100	99	98
1981		99	100	100	102	97	101	100	100	100	99	101	100	101	102	102	101
1982		101	101	98	95	99	102	103	102	102	100	97	99	97	96	95	94
1983		96	99	98	100	96	96	98	98	98	101	97	97	100	98	100	103

GERMANY

Industrial production: consumer goods (1)(2) — Production industrielle : biens de consommation (1)(2)

1980 = 100

	Year	Q.1	Q.2	Q.3	Q.4	JAN	FEB	MAR	APR	MAY	JUN	JUL	AUG	SEP	OCT	NOV	DEC
1964	69.4	67.9	70.2	64.8	75.6	63.6	68.4	71.7	69.8	74.8	66.0	61.2	60.5	72.9	77.4	79.5	69.7
1965	73.7	71.9	75.1	68.9	79.5	71.1	72.9	71.5	77.7	76.0	71.6	64.5	63.7	78.4	82.2	83.8	72.5
1966	74.3	74.6	77.6	69.3	76.1	72.5	74.4	77.0	81.2	77.4	74.3	68.5	61.7	77.7	79.8	79.4	69.2
1967	70.5	69.0	68.2	66.5	78.8	66.4	69.4	71.3	72.0	67.8	64.9	64.7	59.4	75.6	77.1	80.7	78.7
1968	77.2	70.5	79.3	72.8	87.6	64.9	70.7	75.8	78.0	77.4	82.4	64.4	70.8	83.1	84.6	93.7	84.4
1969	85.5	81.4	87.6	79.3	94.7	76.5	81.7	86.1	88.5	88.7	85.6	73.4	76.6	87.9	92.0	102.2	89.9
1970	88.0	87.2	90.6	81.0	94.2	81.6	87.1	92.9	90.0	97.1	84.6	76.7	76.3	90.0	94.9	99.3	88.4
1971	90.8	88.6	93.7	83.3	98.2	87.5	88.9	89.5	96.2	94.7	90.1	79.7	76.7	93.5	101.1	103.9	89.6
1972	96.2	93.3	98.3	88.5	105.4	90.3	92.3	97.3	103.2	97.6	94.1	84.8	80.7	99.9	103.0	108.8	104.3
1973	98.0	98.2	103.3	89.6	102.4	91.4	102.3	100.9	107.3	101.6	101.0	80.5	84.4	103.8	100.6	105.5	100.9
1974	93.3	94.7	100.8	83.7	95.8	87.7	96.2	100.3	102.4	98.2	101.8	80.4	75.6	95.1	95.3	102.5	89.6
1975	88.3	89.6	89.2	79.8	95.9	82.3	89.6	97.1	88.6	92.3	86.6	72.9	76.0	90.5	93.9	103.0	90.8
1976	93.9	92.4	97.1	85.9	100.9	87.0	95.9	94.3	100.6	96.1	94.7	79.0	78.5	100.1	104.2	106.9	91.6
1977	97.3	96.2	100.2	88.7	104.7	92.8	97.1	98.9	104.0	98.8	97.8	80.6	82.7	102.7	107.1	108.6	98.2
1978	97.7	96.4	99.0	89.4	106.7	92.3	96.6	100.2	103.3	98.3	95.5	81.9	82.4	103.9	106.7	110.9	102.5
1979	101.2	97.7	105.5	93.6	109.6	91.7	98.1	103.3	106.0	101.9	108.5	88.0	82.7	110.1	108.1	113.7	107.0
1980	100.0	104.9	100.3	94.1	101.4	99.7	108.0	106.9	104.4	97.8	98.6	91.3	84.9	106.2	106.2	104.8	93.1
1981	94.9	97.8	94.7	90.3	96.6	89.8	102.5	101.2	99.2	92.6	92.4	88.2	78.2	104.5	102.8	101.1	85.8
1982	90.3	93.8	91.2	85.0	91.1	85.5	95.2	100.7	95.6	88.8	89.3	78.3	77.9	98.9	94.4	95.4	83.6
1983	91.5	92.1	92.2	86.4	95.4	84.8	93.0	98.4	92.7	89.0	94.9	79.8	77.6	101.9	97.6	100.2	88.3

Industrial production: food, beverages and tobacco (1) — Production industrielle : alimentation, boissons et tabac (1)

1980 = 100

	Year	Q.1	Q.2	Q.3	Q.4	JAN	FEB	MAR	APR	MAY	JUN	JUL	AUG	SEP	OCT	NOV	DEC
1964	66.0	59.6	66.5	64.7	71.5	58.6	58.9	61.3	62.4	71.1	66.2	65.3	64.1	64.6	70.5	74.1	70.0
1965	68.7	62.6	69.1	66.7	75.3	63.1	62.4	62.2	68.5	68.1	70.8	66.1	65.9	68.1	74.3	79.3	72.2
1966	70.9	64.3	73.0	69.2	75.8	62.3	65.3	65.3	72.3	72.7	74.1	69.4	67.7	70.4	77.1	78.3	72.1
1967	72.8	65.6	73.0	71.8	79.2	61.9	66.2	68.9	71.2	77.0	70.8	73.2	69.2	72.9	78.8	80.8	78.1
1968	76.1	68.0	78.9	74.0	82.8	65.3	67.9	70.8	78.0	76.0	82.8	72.8	72.7	76.4	80.9	86.9	80.8
1969	80.2	74.3	82.6	77.9	85.3	72.8	74.8	75.2	80.4	85.0	82.5	75.9	78.5	79.2	83.5	90.2	82.3
1970	82.6	78.0	85.7	79.9	86.2	76.4	76.2	81.5	80.5	91.3	85.3	78.2	80.2	81.4	85.4	89.4	83.9
1971	86.4	81.1	88.4	83.7	91.5	81.7	81.4	80.2	87.8	89.6	87.7	83.6	82.7	84.9	92.1	95.4	87.0
1972	87.2	81.9	90.6	83.6	92.1	79.7	81.3	84.8	90.9	92.9	88.0	85.3	80.9	84.7	91.3	96.7	88.4
1973	90.0	83.1	93.7	88.0	94.7	80.6	84.9	83.8	93.4	92.0	95.8	86.0	86.0	91.8	91.8	99.5	92.7
1974	90.5	85.9	95.3	86.5	94.0	84.8	86.6	86.1	94.2	92.6	99.0	84.4	85.3	89.9	92.4	100.3	89.3
1975	90.4	87.9	91.8	86.2	95.3	85.7	87.0	91.1	87.0	96.9	91.4	82.0	87.6	88.8	92.8	100.2	92.8
1976	93.1	86.7	96.7	90.6	97.7	86.5	88.7	84.8	96.4	94.8	98.9	89.0	89.9	92.9	98.5	102.8	91.8
1977	93.1	87.4	96.5	89.4	98.3	85.6	88.0	88.6	96.8	94.6	98.0	88.6	87.5	92.2	98.0	103.3	93.7
1978	95.8	90.1	97.7	91.8	102.3	87.3	88.6	94.4	97.2	101.8	94.1	90.8	90.0	94.6	100.5	106.3	100.1
1979	98.0	91.3	101.8	94.0	104.4	89.0	92.7	92.2	101.7	99.8	103.9	92.9	90.4	98.5	102.0	108.4	103.0
1980	100.0	97.2	98.4	95.8	108.7	95.5	99.4	96.7	99.7	95.8	99.7	94.8	91.8	100.7	112.8	112.8	100.5
1981	101.7	99.9	99.4	99.2	108.2	94.7	103.6	101.5	99.8	96.3	102.2	98.0	92.6	107.0	112.7	113.5	98.5
1982	98.7	100.3	97.6	93.4	103.6	94.1	102.3	104.5	100.2	94.5	98.0	89.4	90.3	100.4	105.2	109.6	95.9
1983	99.3	94.4	97.6	99.1	106.1	89.3	94.4	99.4	94.1	93.1	105.6	97.4	97.6	102.4	109.1	113.6	95.6

Industrial production: intermediate goods (1) — Production industrielle : biens intermédiaires (1)

1980 = 100

	Year	Q.1	Q.2	Q.3	Q.4	JAN	FEB	MAR	APR	MAY	JUN	JUL	AUG	SEP	OCT	NOV	DEC
1964	58.6	54.1	60.4	59.3	61.1	51.1	54.4	56.7	59.0	61.5	60.7	59.1	57.3	61.4	62.2	63.3	57.7
1965	61.7	59.1	64.2	61.8	61.7	59.0	59.0	59.5	63.8	64.6	64.1	61.5	60.3	63.7	64.4	63.3	57.3
1966	63.4	60.9	66.9	63.3	62.6	57.8	60.6	64.4	66.4	67.0	67.4	64.1	60.9	65.0	65.0	64.5	58.4
1967	64.5	60.2	66.3	64.0	67.5	57.4	60.5	62.8	66.0	66.3	66.7	64.8	61.0	66.2	68.0	70.2	64.4
1968	72.8	65.8	75.3	73.7	77.0	61.5	66.4	69.6	73.1	74.5	78.4	71.6	72.8	76.6	76.6	81.3	73.3
1969	81.6	75.0	84.6	81.6	85.4	72.0	74.4	78.5	82.3	84.6	87.1	80.0	80.4	84.4	85.9	90.6	79.7
1970	85.4	82.1	90.1	85.0	84.5	78.5	83.0	84.8	87.6	93.3	89.3	85.3	83.8	86.1	86.8	86.9	79.6
1971	85.3	82.8	90.0	83.9	84.8	79.1	84.9	84.4	90.4	89.4	90.1	84.3	80.9	86.4	87.8	87.9	78.5
1972	89.4	83.8	92.7	88.4	93.2	78.5	84.0	88.8	93.2	91.4	93.4	87.5	85.0	92.6	93.6	95.9	90.1
1973	97.6	93.6	102.1	96.0	99.1	87.6	96.0	97.2	101.7	101.4	103.2	92.7	94.1	101.2	101.3	103.8	92.3
1974	96.5	96.0	104.2	94.8	91.6	91.2	97.7	99.3	104.0	102.5	106.0	95.0	91.5	97.8	96.9	95.8	82.2
1975	83.9	83.5	85.8	79.9	86.9	80.7	84.4	85.4	84.8	86.2	86.5	77.6	76.9	85.1	86.9	92.5	81.3
1976	92.2	87.6	97.7	91.2	92.5	81.5	89.8	91.6	97.1	97.1	98.8	89.6	87.8	96.3	96.1	96.5	85.0
1977	92.7	92.2	97.7	89.1	92.2	87.3	93.6	95.6	98.1	96.3	98.8	88.4	85.3	93.6	93.7	95.9	86.9
1978	95.9	91.7	100.0	94.2	93.1	87.7	92.0	95.4	100.6	99.2	100.3	92.2	89.9	100.6	101.8	103.8	88.8
1979	103.8	96.2	110.2	103.1	106.0	87.0	98.3	103.2	110.3	108.6	111.8	101.4	99.1	108.9	108.3	110.5	99.3
1980	100.0	105.4	104.2	95.4	94.9	100.3	108.6	107.4	106.0	102.8	103.8	95.5	90.8	100.0	99.8	98.4	86.6
1981	95.8	96.5	97.7	94.5	94.5	88.5	100.6	100.5	99.9	96.0	97.1	93.4	89.6	100.6	99.3	99.3	84.9
1982	91.1	94.2	96.7	87.1	86.4	86.8	95.9	99.9	99.1	94.0	97.0	85.1	82.7	93.4	88.9	90.5	79.7
1983	94.1	91.3	96.7	91.6	96.2	84.2	92.6	97.0	96.0	94.6	99.4	87.0	87.3	100.6	97.9	101.7	89.1

Industrial production: consumer goods (1)(2) — Production industrielle : biens de consommation (1)(2)

Adjusted - Corrigé

1980 = 100

	Year	Q.1	Q.2	Q.3	Q.4	JAN	FEB	MAR	APR	MAY	JUN	JUL	AUG	SEP	OCT	NOV	DEC
1964		69	69	70	72	68	70	69	70	68	70	71	69	70	72	71	71
1965		73	74	75	75	73	73	73	74	74	74	73	75	76	75	75	76
1966		77	76	75	72	76	76	78	76	75	77	77	74	75	73	71	71
1967		71	68	72	74	71	71	70	69	65	69	73	70	72	72	73	77
1968		73	77	79	82	71	73	74	75	77	79	75	82	80	81	83	82
1969		83	85	87	89	82	83	84	84	85	86	86	87	86	88	90	89
1970		88	88	89	89	86	88	88	89	88	88	90	88	89	89	89	89
1971		90	91	92	93	91	90	90	92	90	91	92	91	92	93	94	93
1972		95	96	97	99	96	95	96	96	95	97	97	97	97	97	98	102
1973		100	100	98	96	99	101	100	99	101	100	95	101	98	96	95	96
1974		96	97	93	90	95	96	96	97	98	95	97	90	91	91	91	88
1975		89	87	88	91	88	89	89	87	87	87	88	89	88	90	91	91
1976		93	95	95	96	91	94	94	95	94	95	94	94	97	97	97	95
1977		97	97	98	100	97	96	98	97	97	98	95	99	100	100	99	101
1978		97	97	99	101	100	97	95	97	95	98	98	101	98	99	100	103
1979		100	102	102	102	100	99	99	100	102	105	104	101	101	101	102	104
1980		103	100	99	97	104	105	102	101	101	100	100	100	97	97	98	97
1981		96	95	95	92	95	97	96	96	96	93	97	93	95	96	93	89
1982		92	91	90	88	92	91	93	92	91	90	88	91	90	89	88	87
1983		90	93	91	92	90	89	91	90	91	97	91	90	92	92	93	92

Industrial production: food, beverages and tobacco (1) — Production industrielle : alimentation, boissons et tabac (1)

Adjusted - Corrigé

1980 = 100

	Year	Q.1	Q.2	Q.3	Q.4	JAN	FEB	MAR	APR	MAY	JUN	JUL	AUG	SEP	OCT	NOV	DEC
1964		64	65	66	67	65	64	63	64	65	64	67	65	66	66	65	69
1965		67	67	68	70	68	66	68	67	66	67	67	68	69	68	71	71
1966		69	70	70	71	68	70	70	70	70	72	69	71	71	71	70	70
1967		70	71	73	74	68	71	72	70	73	70	73	72	73	74	73	74
1968		73	75	75	77	72	74	73	77	74	75	75	75	76	77	78	77
1969		79	79	79	79	80	79	78	79	79	78	78	80	80	79	79	80
1970		82	82	82	81	82	80	82	81	83	83	81	82	82	81	80	83
1971		85	84	86	87	86	85	85	85	83	84	86	86	86	86	86	88
1972		86	87	85	86	84	86	88	87	88	86	87	85	85	87	88	85
1973		87	89	90	89	86	87	88	89	89	91	89	90	90	88	90	89
1974		90	90	89	88	91	90	88	91	90	90	89	89	89	89	89	86
1975		90	88	89	89	92	90	90	87	90	87	87	90	90	89	87	91
1976		91	92	94	92	91	91	90	93	90	94	94	94	94	92	92	93
1977		91	92	93	93	90	91	92	92	91	95	93	93	93	92	92	94
1978		92	94	94	98	92	91	93	94	96	92	94	94	94	98	99	97
1979		96	98	98	100	95	97	95	97	98	98	99	97	97	101	101	98
1980		100	100	99	101	101	101	99	101	100	99	99	100	99	100	101	103
1981		103	101	103	100	102	103	103	101	100	103	102	101	105	102	99	100
1982		103	99	97	96	103	103	103	101	99	97	95	97	98	96	97	95
1983		96	99	103	99	96	95	98	96	96	105	106	104	100	100	100	96

Industrial production: intermediate goods (1) — Production industrielle : biens intermédiaires (1)

Adjusted - Corrigé

1980 = 100

	Year	Q.1	Q.2	Q.3	Q.4	JAN	FEB	MAR	APR	MAY	JUN	JUL	AUG	SEP	OCT	NOV	DEC
1964		57	58	60	62	57	58	57	58	57	59	60	59	61	61	61	62
1965		63	62	63	62	64	61	62	62	62	61	62	63	63	63	61	63
1966		64	64	64	63	63	63	66	64	64	65	64	64	65	64	63	64
1967		63	64	65	68	63	63	64	64	63	65	65	64	66	67	68	69
1968		70	72	75	78	68	71	71	71	72	73	73	76	75	76	79	78
1969		79	81	83	86	80	77	80	80	81	83	82	84	84	85	87	86
1970		86	87	87	86	87	86	85	86	88	86	88	87	85	86	84	86
1971		86	86	86	86	86	87	86	87	85	87	87	85	86	86	85	86
1972		88	89	90	94	86	88	90	89	88	90	90	90	92	92	93	97
1973		97	98	98	100	96	97	99	97	99	98	96	100	99	100	101	99
1974		99	100	98	92	100	99	99	100	100	99	99	98	96	96	93	88
1975		86	82	83	88	88	86	84	83	82	83	82	82	84	87	89	88
1976		91	94	95	94	89	91	92	93	94	94	94	95	95	95	93	93
1977		95	94	93	94	95	94	96	93	93	94	93	93	93	93	93	95
1978		95	95	98	100	96	94	93	95	95	95	97	98	98	99	100	102
1979		99	104	106	107	98	100	100	103	104	104	106	106	105	105	106	109
1980		106	101	97	96	107	108	105	101	102	100	98	98	96	96	97	96
1981		97	94	97	95	96	97	97	95	95	93	97	97	96	97	96	93
1982		94	93	89	87	95	93	95	94	93	92	90	89	89	88	88	87
1983		91	93	94	98	91	90	91	92	92	94	93	94	96	97	98	98

GERMANY

Industrial production: manufacturing (1)

Production industrielle : industries manufacturières (1)

1980 = 100

	Year	Q.1	Q.2	Q.3	Q.4	JAN	FEB	MAR	APR	MAY	JUN	JUL	AUG	SEP	OCT	NOV	DEC
1964	61.1	57.9	62.7	58.6	65.7	54.6	58.3	61.0	60.3	65.7	62.1	57.4	55.5	62.7	65.2	68.2	63.7
1965	64.7	62.2	67.0	61.5	68.2	61.6	62.9	62.1	67.0	67.3	66.8	60.0	57.8	66.6	68.9	70.2	65.6
1966	65.6	63.9	69.3	62.1	67.2	61.6	64.1	66.1	70.0	68.9	69.2	62.6	57.3	66.4	68.3	69.1	64.3
1967	63.8	60.1	64.1	60.7	70.8	57.8	60.4	62.2	64.4	64.7	63.3	60.9	55.2	66.2	67.9	71.2	73.3
1968	70.1	62.8	72.5	67.7	78.6	58.9	62.7	66.8	70.0	70.5	76.9	63.6	65.1	74.5	74.7	82.7	78.3
1969	79.5	73.9	82.8	75.5	86.6	69.8	74.3	77.4	80.8	83.5	84.2	72.6	72.6	81.3	83.7	91.9	84.1
1970	84.1	81.4	88.8	79.0	87.6	76.4	81.7	86.0	85.4	94.0	87.1	78.0	74.7	84.3	87.0	90.8	85.1
1971	84.6	83.1	89.6	79.3	86.9	81.7	84.0	83.6	89.5	90.2	89.2	79.8	72.6	85.5	89.4	90.9	80.4
1972	87.7	83.6	91.4	82.0	94.7	79.8	83.4	87.6	93.0	90.9	90.2	81.4	75.5	89.0	91.5	97.5	94.9
1973	93.3	90.1	98.2	87.1	98.9	84.3	93.1	92.8	98.8	96.6	99.3	81.9	81.7	97.7	95.5	101.7	99.4
1974	91.2	90.7	98.7	84.5	92.2	85.7	92.5	94.0	97.5	96.4	102.3	83.1	78.2	92.3	91.2	97.5	88.0
1975	85.1	83.8	88.0	78.0	91.4	78.1	83.9	89.5	85.4	90.5	88.2	73.2	74.6	86.2	88.0	96.6	89.4
1976	91.0	87.3	96.2	84.5	96.4	82.6	90.3	89.1	95.4	95.5	97.5	80.1	79.3	94.1	97.1	100.7	91.5
1977	93.6	91.8	98.5	86.1	98.8	87.4	93.3	94.8	99.4	96.8	99.2	82.3	80.3	95.7	98.0	102.0	96.3
1978	95.1	91.6	97.6	89.1	102.4	88.2	92.3	94.5	97.7	97.8	97.3	85.4	81.7	100.2	100.6	105.4	101.2
1979	100.0	94.0	105.4	93.8	108.2	87.4	95.1	99.6	105.0	102.5	108.7	91.3	84.8	105.4	104.2	111.2	109.1
1980	100.0	101.8	102.0	94.1	102.4	96.6	105.0	103.9	104.1	99.1	102.9	93.5	85.6	103.3	105.5	104.3	97.3
1981	98.3	97.6	99.2	93.7	102.9	88.0	102.9	101.9	101.2	97.0	99.5	92.0	83.7	105.3	104.7	106.1	97.8
1982	95.4	97.3	99.4	88.7	96.2	87.0	100.1	104.9	101.4	96.8	100.0	84.3	81.7	100.0	96.5	98.9	93.2
1983	96.3	93.8	98.3	90.9	102.2	85.6	95.3	100.4	97.1	95.5	102.3	85.4	83.3	104.0	101.0	105.9	99.8

Industrial production: construction (1)(3)

Production industrielle : construction (1)(3)

1980 = 100

	Year	Q.1	Q.2	Q.3	Q.4	JAN	FEB	MAR	APR	MAY	JUN	JUL	AUG	SEP	OCT	NOV	DEC
1964	77.5	59.4	86.3	83.9	80.5	49.9	59.2	69.2	78.7	92.5	87.6	83.7	82.5	85.4	87.0	86.2	68.3
1965	79.1	61.9	88.4	86.9	79.2	61.9	58.7	65.1	85.4	90.1	89.8	86.4	84.8	89.7	92.5	81.3	63.8
1966	80.2	64.4	91.3	87.1	78.0	52.4	61.9	78.8	89.3	92.1	92.5	90.2	82.6	88.5	90.2	81.5	62.3
1967	76.2	57.8	81.8	84.2	80.4	49.8	55.2	68.5	79.5	83.3	82.5	84.2	80.0	88.4	87.7	86.9	66.6
1968	79.8	57.2	89.9	88.0	85.2	46.6	56.9	68.1	82.6	88.6	98.6	84.5	87.8	91.5	89.8	95.4	70.4
1969	87.0	64.2	98.0	95.8	90.0	59.3	59.1	74.3	90.3	101.5	102.1	94.3	95.3	97.9	99.3	102.5	68.1
1970	91.8	64.0	102.9	102.4	97.7	56.1	60.9	75.0	90.4	112.1	106.3	100.2	101.6	105.3	105.0	104.6	83.5
1971	94.8	70.9	107.7	102.9	98.1	61.7	72.9	77.9	101.8	110.7	110.5	103.0	98.5	107.1	110.3	102.4	81.7
1972	101.5	78.0	113.2	107.7	107.3	65.3	72.9	95.8	112.8	113.1	113.7	106.8	102.4	114.0	113.6	112.8	95.5
1973	102.3	83.7	117.7	108.9	99.1	71.5	83.5	96.0	112.2	117.7	123.1	103.6	104.2	119.0	105.8	107.5	80.0
1974	95.2	81.9	110.7	96.8	92.6	69.8	82.4	93.6	106.6	107.8	117.6	93.3	91.9	105.3	99.8	100.6	77.2
1975	84.6	70.7	92.5	87.6	87.7	62.9	68.8	80.4	85.2	96.4	96.0	84.1	83.8	94.8	95.1	96.4	71.5
1976	87.6	69.1	98.6	90.4	92.7	61.7	65.9	79.6	95.0	100.4	100.4	87.9	85.0	98.3	104.4	99.5	74.3
1977	90.6	72.0	101.2	93.6	95.9	61.4	69.6	84.9	98.2	101.1	104.3	92.6	86.2	102.2	106.0	100.6	81.1
1978	96.3	71.6	106.2	102.0	105.1	67.3	63.1	84.4	104.5	106.2	107.9	100.4	92.4	113.1	113.8	114.5	86.9
1979	102.8	69.0	118.0	112.6	112.7	53.5	64.2	89.2	109.9	115.7	128.5	106.6	103.2	126.1	119.4	118.7	99.9
1980	100.0	85.4	115.3	105.9	94.9	61.1	89.2	105.8	118.6	112.4	114.8	103.8	93.9	119.9	121.1	100.7	62.8
1981	92.7	68.3	110.5	103.8	88.2	48.0	64.8	92.0	113.5	108.0	110.0	100.9	92.7	117.7	108.5	98.0	58.2
1982	88.4	63.2	103.1	97.2	90.1	38.3	61.0	90.3	101.5	100.2	107.5	89.2	91.8	110.5	102.0	98.1	70.2
1983	86.3	59.4	98.9	97.4	89.3	54.1	44.1	79.9	92.5	97.9	106.3	90.6	93.6	108.0	103.2	101.8	63.0

Production: commercial vehicles

thousands, monthly averages

Production : véhicules utilitaires

milliers, moyennes mensuelles

	Year	Q.1	Q.2	Q.3	Q.4	JAN	FEB	MAR	APR	MAY	JUN	JUL	AUG	SEP	OCT	NOV	DEC
1964	43.9	49.2	46.3	37.4	42.6	49.7	49.8	48.1	52.5	40.7	45.7	32.2	34.5	45.5	46.1	41.4	40.4
1965	43.6	47.7	45.6	34.8	46.3	44.4	46.3	52.5	45.8	46.2	44.7	26.6	31.2	46.6	44.2	47.7	46.9
1966	43.3	48.5	46.0	33.5	45.3	46.3	46.8	52.4	44.1	46.1	47.7	22.1	36.4	42.0	43.9	48.1	44.0
1967	35.4	31.9	36.6	29.8	43.2	38.9	30.1	26.8	32.1	37.2	40.4	19.9	25.7	43.8	47.6	44.9	37.0
1968	46.0	47.8	44.5	41.0	50.8	50.3	45.2	47.8	42.6	48.5	42.4	34.4	36.3	52.2	56.7	53.1	42.6
1969	52.9	54.4	53.0	49.8	57.8	55.9	50.3	57.1	53.7	51.3	54.0	43.3	42.3	63.6	66.5	55.7	51.2
1970	57.0	57.1	61.3	45.6	61.7	57.5	55.1	58.6	67.3	54.0	62.8	36.6	44.6	55.6	63.6	63.8	57.9
1971	55.6	62.4	61.7	50.1	48.1	56.6	60.3	70.2	62.0	57.8	65.2	59.6	28.2	62.6	60.7	58.3	25.2
1972	52.0	53.1	57.6	45.3	52.1	46.9	51.8	60.8	55.7	58.5	58.7	44.4	34.4	57.2	54.7	59.1	42.5
1973	46.6	55.9	52.3	35.7	42.0	55.9	52.2	59.6	50.7	56.3	51.5	29.5	36.0	41.5	49.9	41.1	35.1
1974	41.0	43.2	50.9	34.8	35.2	38.4	42.8	48.5	52.9	52.8	47.0	31.6	34.9	37.9	42.5	37.6	25.6
1975	38.5	36.3	41.5	35.4	40.8	33.6	36.2	39.1	43.5	38.2	42.7	26.4	36.3	43.6	45.9	40.3	36.1
1976	44.2	46.2	48.7	37.1	44.7	43.4	45.1	50.0	49.4	49.0	47.8	22.5	40.6	48.2	45.9	48.0	40.9
1977	41.6	46.1	43.9	32.5	44.1	46.5	43.2	48.5	42.3	47.4	42.1	19.8	35.9	41.7	42.3	48.4	41.4
1978	44.3	45.6	43.1	39.8	48.5	51.5	43.1	42.3	39.2	41.1	49.2	38.6	31.2	49.5	52.8	53.2	39.7
1979	46.3	51.9	48.3	36.6	48.3	53.6	47.2	54.9	47.2	49.5	48.2	34.1	32.5	43.2	52.0	53.0	39.9
1980	49.7	54.2	53.0	45.0	46.7	54.2	53.8	54.4	53.7	50.5	54.8	36.9	40.6	57.6	54.3	45.0	40.8
1981	47.1	48.6	47.0	44.1	48.9	45.1	46.7	54.0	47.7	47.9	45.2	34.0	42.6	55.5	51.4	51.3	43.9
1982	44.3	51.1	46.3	37.7	41.9	49.3	47.5	56.6	46.9	47.1	45.0	27.1	36.8	49.3	40.5	46.6	38.5
1983	47.8	49.4	49.7	40.9	51.2	43.2	47.0	58.0	49.9	50.1	49.1	23.3	46.3	53.0	50.7	55.4	47.5

Industrial production: manufacturing (1) — Production industrielle : industries manufacturières (1)

1980 = 100 — Adjusted - Corrigé

	Year	Q.1	Q.2	Q.3	Q.4	JAN	FEB	MAR	APR	MAY	JUN	JUL	AUG	SEP	OCT	NOV	DEC
1964		60	60	62	63	59	61	60	60	60	61	62	61	62	63	63	63
1965		65	65	65	65	65	65	65	65	65	64	64	65	66	65	65	66
1966		67	66	66	64	66	66	68	66	66	67	66	65	66	65	64	64
1967		62	62	64	67	63	62	62	62	62	63	65	63	65	65	66	70
1968		66	69	72	75	64	66	66	67	69	70	70	74	73	73	75	75
1969		76	79	80	82	76	76	77	78	79	79	80	81	81	82	83	82
1970		83	85	84	84	82	84	84	85	86	85	85	84	84	84	83	84
1971		86	85	85	83	86	86	85	86	85	85	87	83	85	85	84	81
1972		87	87	88	90	86	86	88	87	87	87	88	88	87	88	90	91
1973		93	93	93	94	92	93	93	93	95	93	91	95	94	94	94	94
1974		93	93	91	87	94	93	92	93	94	92	94	90	90	89	88	84
1975		84	84	85	87	85	84	84	84	84	84	84	85	85	86	87	87
1976		89	92	92	93	88	90	90	91	92	92	91	92	93	93	93	92
1977		94	94	93	94	93	93	95	93	93	94	92	94	94	94	94	95
1978		93	93	96	98	97	93	91	93	93	94	95	96	97	96	97	100
1979		97	100	101	103	97	96	97	99	100	101	102	101	99	101	102	105
1980		103	100	99	98	104	104	101	101	100	99	101	100	97	99	99	98
1981		98	97	99	98	97	100	98	98	98	96	99	98	99	100	99	97
1982		98	97	94	92	97	98	99	98	97	96	93	94	94	93	92	91
1983		94	96	96	98	93	93	95	95	95	99	96	96	97	97	99	99

Industrial production: construction (1)(3) — Production industrielle : construction (1)(3)

1980 = 100 — Adjusted - Corrigé

	Year	Q.1	Q.2	Q.3	Q.4	JAN	FEB	MAR	APR	MAY	JUN	JUL	AUG	SEP	OCT	NOV	DEC
1964		85	84	83	86	83	88	85	84	83	85	85	83	83	84	86	89
1965		89	86	86	84	94	87	86	88	87	84	86	86	87	88	80	85
1966		92	88	86	82	86	91	100	90	87	87	88	84	85	85	80	83
1967		85	79	82	84	85	85	86	82	77	79	82	81	83	83	85	85
1968		85	85	87	89	83	88	85	84	85	86	84	89	86	86	92	89
1969		91	94	97	96	96	88	90	92	95	95	98	97	96	98	100	88
1970		90	100	105	104	92	90	90	95	101	102	105	105	103	103	104	106
1971		99	104	106	105	97	103	97	104	104	105	108	104	105	107	102	106
1972		107	110	111	114	103	105	115	112	108	110	111	110	111	112	113	116
1973		114	114	112	105	111	114	116	121	115	115	110	113	114	109	107	99
1974		111	105	100	98	110	115	109	107	105	103	101	98	100	97	98	98
1975		98	87	90	93	102	101	90	86	87	88	91	89	90	91	93	94
1976		92	96	96	100	97	89	90	96	96	95	93	98	96	98	102	99
1977		100	95	92	93	98	102	101	94	96	95	90	93	93	92	90	96
1978		93	95	93	98	104	79	95	95	94	95	92	93	93	97	101	94
1979		87	108	106	108	75	85	101	105	111	107	109	104	105	109	105	111
1980		108	102	97	93	98	117	110	104	102	99	98	94	99	99	94	86
1981		92	98	94	87	87	94	95	100	98	95	95	94	95	91	89	80
1982		86	88	89	90	78	92	89	89	89	87	87	90	89	86	89	94
1983		84	84	89	89	96	76	79	80	84	88	88	91	88	88	90	89

Production: passenger cars — Production : voitures de tourisme

thousands, monthly averages — milliers, moyennes mensuelles

	Year	Q.1	Q.2	Q.3	Q.4	JAN	FEB	MAR	APR	MAY	JUN	JUL	AUG	SEP	OCT	NOV	DEC
1964	197.5	202.4	204.0	173.8	210.0	209.0	159.4	198.7	214.6	179.6	217.8	152.5	149.0	219.8	229.1	208.6	192.2
1965	203.4	210.7	211.1	171.9	219.3	198.7	203.2	230.1	208.9	210.9	213.4	132.9	157.7	225.2	229.9	219.1	210.5
1966	209.6	222.7	224.7	186.3	204.7	212.7	205.7	249.7	211.8	231.4	230.8	129.5	188.3	241.1	226.7	208.0	179.5
1967	170.2	157.4	174.8	155.9	192.9	175.8	144.2	152.3	167.4	172.2	184.8	121.6	138.0	208.0	211.8	202.3	164.5
1968	211.3	215.1	213.6	189.3	227.1	219.3	214.0	212.1	212.3	233.5	194.8	164.0	165.8	238.2	263.8	232.7	184.8
1969	244.7	247.8	252.5	216.6	261.8	248.0	237.5	258.1	249.9	249.2	258.3	207.5	160.9	281.4	303.2	257.7	224.6
1970	260.6	261.8	285.7	209.7	285.3	255.3	254.8	275.4	308.3	248.5	300.4	184.5	163.8	280.9	306.8	287.2	261.8
1971	274.1	293.5	295.5	249.5	258.1	274.8	285.9	319.8	288.8	284.3	313.2	278.7	145.7	323.9	313.3	290.0	170.9
1972	263.9	284.3	278.5	217.3	275.4	252.4	293.7	306.8	266.8	279.2	289.6	182.3	195.5	274.0	296.0	303.2	226.9
1973	280.0	313.0	299.0	231.4	276.5	303.0	301.6	334.3	286.5	330.7	279.8	186.2	210.4	297.6	325.5	299.0	205.2
1974	214.7	257.4	225.5	175.2	200.5	268.0	239.9	264.4	229.7	255.9	191.0	167.1	142.5	215.8	250.0	203.2	148.2
1975	224.2	186.4	247.9	202.0	260.5	172.9	176.9	209.3	266.3	226.1	251.3	147.3	183.4	275.2	301.1	268.4	212.2
1976	275.7	286.7	286.8	238.7	290.7	260.1	281.6	318.5	287.7	292.5	280.2	170.3	226.5	319.2	313.1	302.6	256.3
1977	297.7	325.9	307.0	247.9	310.1	309.7	306.4	361.4	298.6	308.7	313.8	195.3	213.6	334.7	326.0	330.1	274.1
1978	303.2	327.4	316.8	261.5	307.0	343.9	314.8	323.5	293.3	303.5	353.6	246.0	196.9	341.5	338.5	322.1	260.4
1979	305.7	344.7	327.6	254.2	296.3	354.1	314.3	365.6	318.0	345.7	318.9	223.4	224.2	315.1	342.0	331.9	214.9
1980	271.0	312.7	293.1	225.4	252.9	324.1	303.4	310.7	314.8	278.0	236.5	212.3	177.4	286.7	293.2	266.8	198.7
1981	274.6	283.8	277.6	234.4	302.7	256.4	284.9	310.0	285.3	272.7	274.7	194.1	196.0	313.2	333.2	319.6	255.4
1982	292.0	331.8	322.0	246.3	268.0	306.5	317.5	371.3	331.1	308.8	326.1	219.3	203.0	316.5	279.8	287.1	237.2
1983	297.3	305.3	323.3	253.9	306.7	280.1	288.5	347.4	308.6	322.8	333.5	198.5	222.4	340.8	320.0	322.7	277.6

GERMANY

Production: crude steel
thousand tons, monthly averages

Production : acier brut
milliers de tonnes, moyennes mensuelles

	Year	Q.1	Q.2	Q.3	Q.4	JAN	FEB	MAR	APR	MAY	JUN	JUL	AUG	SEP	OCT	NOV	DEC
1964																	
1965																	
1966																	
1967																	
1968																	
1969	3776	3689	3679	3852	3885	3688	3444	3936	3573	3640	3823	3907	3857	3791	4084	3959	3613
1970	3753	3862	3894	3867	3390	3950	3750	3885	4037	3738	3908	4055	3927	3620	3655	3458	3058
1971	3360	3600	3455	3465	2918	3470	3448	3883	3369	3348	3647	3621	3438	3337	3197	3030	2526
1972	3642	3408	3603	3801	3756	3071	3415	3738	3408	3548	3854	3804	3876	3723	3955	3816	3497
1973	4127	4003	3987	4273	4244	3894	3761	4354	3901	4225	3834	4333	4315	4171	4381	4353	3997
1974	4436	4457	4301	4568	4418	4415	4213	4742	4174	4559	4169	4667	4564	4474	4744	4506	4005
1975	3368	3802	3408	3190	3071	4270	3609	3527	3726	3169	3330	3267	3116	3186	3288	3262	2662
1976	3534	3491	3633	3828	3185	3241	3473	3760	3462	3814	3623	3979	3863	3642	3425	3298	2833
1977	3249	3234	3371	3247	3143	3109	2987	3606	3085	3403	3625	3448	3107	3136	3234	3218	2976
1978	3437	3388	3727	3596	3036	3324	3186	3653	3883	3585	3714	3525	3558	3704	3707	3446	1956
1979	3837	3605	3922	4075	3745	2986	3694	4136	3826	4128	3811	4066	4091	4067	4067	3883	3285
1980	3653	3869	3824	3625	3296	3649	3813	4144	3798	3849	3325	3624	3675	3575	3633	3496	2759
1981	3468	3479	3441	3511	3440	3185	3417	3834	3264	3615	3443	3586	3404	3542	3614	3614	3092
1982	2990	3589	3327	2665	2379	3387	3490	3890	3400	3340	3240	2886	2433	2676	2514	2522	2100
1983	2977	2955	3078	2804	3072	2573	2948	3344	3018	3100	3117	2751	2541	3120	3312	3280	2623

Ships completed
thousand gross register tons, quarterly averages

Navires achevés
milliers de tonneaux de jauge brut, moyennes trimestrielles

	Year	Q.1	Q.2	Q.3	Q.4	JAN	FEB	MAR	APR	MAY	JUN	JUL	AUG	SEP	OCT	NOV	DEC
1964	207	205	153	194	276												
1965	259	220	236	303	277												
1966	290	173	337	331	317												
1967	260	285	242	182	333												
1968	303	289	190	256	476												
1969	447	321	413	376	666												
1970	329	431	233	417	230												
1971	492	507	417	441	613												
1972	347	172	403	343	437												
1973	482	269	678	347	628												
1974	536	330	608	614	592												
1975	625	583	591	405	922												
1976	468	539	281	538	514												
1977	399	550	439	152	375												
1978	211	288	214	185	152												
1979	109	39	151	46	146												
1980	94	86	111	29	151												
1981	176	98	244	41	320												
1982	154	70	183	140	195												
1983	207	193	301	139	194												

Business climate (4)
manufacturing

Adjusted - Corrigé

Climat des affaires (4)
industries manufacturières

	Year	Q.1	Q.2	Q.3	Q.4	JAN	FEB	MAR	APR	MAY	JUN	JUL	AUG	SEP	OCT	NOV	DEC
1964																	
1965																	
1966																	
1967																	
1968																	
1969																	
1970						123.0	119.0	116.0	115.0	112.0	111.0	109.0	106.0	104.0	101.0	100.0	98.0
1971						97.0	95.0	95.0	93.0	91.0	89.0	87.0	84.0	81.0	78.0	79.0	81.0
1972						85.0	90.0	94.0	97.0	98.0	98.0	99.0	100.0	102.0	105.0	108.0	112.0
1973						116.0	116.0	115.0	114.0	109.0	104.0	98.0	94.0	89.0	80.0	74.0	73.0
1974						80.5	77.3	82.9	81.9	87.4	81.8	79.6	77.5	69.7	69.9	67.7	66.1
1975						62.8	64.1	62.5	63.2	60.1	61.8	67.6	70.5	78.7	86.9	92.7	93.1
1976						94.8	95.1	97.5	98.2	99.1	99.8	98.6	94.5	95.7	93.9	94.7	93.1
1977						89.8	85.1	84.5	80.2	82.1	80.4	80.6	78.5	83.7	82.9	85.7	84.1
1978						83.8	82.1	77.7	78.3	81.6	85.4	89.8	92.9	96.9	99.8	101.4	101.9
1979						99.6	100.0	101.9	104.7	104.3	104.0	106.0	103.8	103.5	104.9	100.8	97.2
1980						97.1	98.0	94.4	90.2	85.5	77.8	76.9	74.2	75.7	70.9	73.5	71.2
1981						67.3	68.1	68.6	68.2	68.6	70.7	74.8	74.0	78.3	78.6	75.9	77.6
1982						73.1	72.0	70.4	71.3	67.8	65.9	62.3	60.5	60.9	60.1	65.4	70.9
1983						73.2	79.6	84.5	83.3	84.2	88.4	90.4	93.4	97.6	99.3	104.4	106.8

Production: future tendency
manufacturing
per cent balance

Perspectives de production
industries manufacturières
solde en pourcentage

	Year	Q.1	Q.2	Q.3	Q.4	JAN	FEB	MAR	APR	MAY	JUN	JUL	AUG	SEP	OCT	NOV	DEC
1964						16	18	16	14	14	9	11	16	13	7	4	13
1965						22	21	19	16	12	10	12	17	11	5	-1	4
1966						11	11	8	7	1	1	-	1	-8	-23	-30	-36
1967						-23	-13	-11	-11	-12	-8	-2	7	3	1	3	9
1968						17	16	15	18	17	19	26	25	24	17	18	25
1969						30	28	28	25	21	18	21	21	20	11	12	17
1970						27	21	19	12	7	-2	4	8	-1	-7	-13	-5
1971						6	5	10	-	-8	-5	3	-5	-17	-31	-30	-9
1972						3	7	7	8	5	4	13	10	9	1	4	14
1973						24	25	22	18	9	8	9	8	-	-12	-29	-21
1974						-8	-1	-5	-5	-13	-15	-15	-14	-26	-38	-35	-30
1975						-24	-16	-15	-14	-16	-18	-10	-	-3	-4	-	13
1976						19	19	15	12	6	2	10	7	-	-10	-8	-4
1977						2	-	-7	-4	-7	-9	-8	-7	-10	-13	-13	-6
1978						-	3	-3	-4	-5	-3	5	3	4	-3	3	12
1979						9	13	8	6	3	6	6	9	-4	-4	-7	-3
1980						1	2	1	-4	-11	-20	-14	-15	-13	-24	-25	-16
1981						-18	-12	-15	-14	-18	-18	-13	-10	-15	-18	-19	-12
1982						-9	-10	-9	-14	-20	-20	-22	-28	-34	-32	-31	-17
1983						-5	5	8	3	-3	2	1	3	-	-	-1	10

Orders inflow or demand: tendency (2)
manufacturing
per cent balance

Commandes ou demande globale : tendance (2)
industries manufacturières
solde en pourcentage

	Year	Q.1	Q.2	Q.3	Q.4	JAN	FEB	MAR	APR	MAY	JUN	JUL	AUG	SEP	OCT	NOV	DEC
1964						6	18	24	20	9	16	10	-8	18	13	2	-8
1965						1	14	19	6	10	-7	-10	-6	19	7	-10	-22
1966						-17	2	12	-8	-4	-20	-27	-26	-6	-25	-38	-48
1967						-40	-22	-11	-13	-20	-13	-24	-8	19	21	6	-11
1968						-8	9	23	15	19	-1	15	9	30	27	7	-1
1969						24	25	34	25	15	18	9	-2	22	15	-2	-13
1970						-2	3	15	5	-5	-7	-21	-22	2	-8	-30	-20
1971						-11	-8	15	-17	-19	-18	-22	-32	-12	-21	-33	-25
1972						-5	-7	18	-7	-4	-	-17	-11	7	11	4	-7
1973						23	25	21	7	22	-9	-19	-13	-10	-5	-19	-41
1974						2	-6	6	-14	-7	-38	-21	-36	-28	-27	-47	-54
1975						-17	-19	-14	-19	-32	-7	-23	-29	3	12	-11	-8
1976						13	16	26	-6	-5	-5	-23	-18	4	-7	-13	-20
1977						-16	2	19	-27	-14	-20	-32	-23	-1	-10	-15	-13
1978						-7	-9	3	-16	-14	1	-22	-5	8	4	-3	-22
1979						10	10	31	-7	7	-1	-8	-8	-2	13	-11	-23
1980						13	4	7	-11	-27	-30	-29	-42	-14	-21	-32	-22
1981						-14	-8	-9	-21	-22	-21	-15	-27	-4	-9	-17	-20
1982						-15	-3	3	-27	-28	-24	-37	-34	-28	-27	-17	-8
1983						2	6	26	-6	4	3	-13	-4	12	2	9	5

Order books: level
manufacturing
per cent balance

Carnet de commandes : niveau
industries manufacturières
solde en pourcentage

	Year	Q.1	Q.2	Q.3	Q.4	JAN	FEB	MAR	APR	MAY	JUN	JUL	AUG	SEP	OCT	NOV	DEC
1964						-8	-4	-	1	3	5	6	4	7	6	5	1
1965						1	3	-	1	-	-3	-6	-5	-3	-5	-10	-12
1966						-15	-16	-15	-19	-19	-24	-27	-31	-31	-41	-46	-55
1967						-57	-55	-60	-62	-57	-56	-59	-50	-44	-40	-35	-33
1968						-34	-32	-25	-19	-14	-10	-7	2	8	9	8	8
1969						17	21	20	27	32	29	29	29	32	32	27	21
1970						19	18	20	15	9	8	6	4	6	-3	-12	-19
1971						-14	-17	-14	-19	-22	-23	-25	-28	-32	-35	-40	-44
1972						-36	-34	-27	-26	-29	-29	-26	-26	-26	-22	-20	-16
1973						-12	1	2	-1	2	4	-2	-4	-9	-11	-14	-23
1974						-18	-18	-19	-21	-24	-30	-31	-32	-42	-44	-54	-57
1975						-62	-61	-62	-63	-66	-62	-62	-61	-57	-53	-52	-50
1976						-41	-38	-28	-27	-27	-28	-29	-29	-32	-31	-33	-35
1977						-33	-35	-33	-35	-37	-41	-42	-43	-42	-43	-43	-43
1978						-42	-39	-38	-37	-37	-37	-34	-35	-35	-33	-30	-31
1979						-26	-19	-16	-14	-8	-4	-7	-8	-13	-11	-13	-12
1980						-10	-8	-11	-10	-16	-25	-28	-36	-38	-39	-47	-45
1981						-45	-43	-41	-42	-45	-44	-44	-43	-43	-46	-48	-47
1982						-48	-46	-45	-47	-50	-53	-54	-59	-60	-62	-60	-60
1983						-50	-48	-41	-38	-38	-37	-39	-37	-35	-33	-31	-30

GERMANY

Finished goods stocks: level
manufacturing
per cent balance

Stocks de produits finis : niveau
industries manufacturières
solde en pourcentage

	Year	Q.1	Q.2	Q.3	Q.4	JAN	FEB	MAR	APR	MAY	JUN	JUL	AUG	SEP	OCT	NOV	DEC
1964						5	-	-	-3	-6	-10	-9	-11	-16	-19	-15	-12
1965						-9	-8	-7	-6	-4	-1	2	3	-	-1	4	8
1966						14	11	12	14	16	20	20	23	21	26	30	38
1967						40	39	39	37	35	34	31	26	21	19	15	8
1968						11	10	9	6	3	1	-5	-10	-15	-19	-16	-13
1969						-10	-10	-14	-17	-18	-17	-18	-18	-19	-22	-18	-16
1970						-13	-10	-8	-5	-4	1	1	-3	3	5	10	12
1971						9	14	8	8	10	15	13	14	20	24	24	24
1972						23	17	18	15	16	17	16	11	12	9	9	8
1973						2	-	-4	-4	-9	-6	-4	-3	-	3	10	12
1974						10	12	10	10	13	16	19	21	25	33	38	40
1975						38	38	41	40	39	36	35	32	30	25	25	22
1976						16	14	14	14	11	7	8	10	9	8	13	12
1977						12	14	15	15	16	17	18	18	20	19	18	22
1978						17	16	17	16	17	15	14	13	9	11	9	9
1979						9	6	3	1	-2	-3	-2	-	2	2	4	8
1980						5	4	3	6	8	13	15	21	20	19	22	23
1981						24	23	24	24	24	25	26	25	26	25	25	22
1982						24	22	22	23	25	26	26	30	30	32	28	27
1983						23	24	20	13	15	13	13	12	9	11	10	11

Manufacturing sales: total (2)(5)
(volume)
1980 = 100

Ventes des industries manufacturières : total (2)(5)
(volume)
1980 = 100

	Year	Q.1	Q.2	Q.3	Q.4	JAN	FEB	MAR	APR	MAY	JUN	JUL	AUG	SEP	OCT	NOV	DEC
1964	56	52	55	56	60	50	51	54	57	51	57	57	51	61	62	60	60
1965	59	56	58	59	63	53	54	62	58	59	58	57	55	64	63	63	64
1966	60	59	60	60	62	55	55	66	59	60	62	57	57	65	62	61	61
1967	59	55	57	58	66	54	52	58	57	55	60	56	54	63	66	64	69
1968	66	59	64	67	75	55	57	64	63	67	62	65	64	72	78	75	73
1969	76	69	75	77	84	66	66	76	74	74	76	77	69	84	88	82	83
1970	81	75	81	81	88	72	74	81	85	75	84	83	72	89	89	85	88
1971	82	80	82	82	86	74	76	89	82	80	85	82	73	90	87	86	85
1972	85	82	84	82	92	75	80	90	81	84	88	79	79	89	93	92	91
1973	91	90	91	88	95	87	86	96	87	95	90	84	86	94	99	95	92
1974	89	89	90	87	91	87	86	95	90	94	86	89	80	92	97	89	87
1975	84	80	83	81	92	79	78	82	87	79	84	80	73	91	94	89	93
1976	91	87	90	87	98	82	84	96	89	89	93	82	81	99	95	95	105
1977	93	92	92	90	99	85	87	103	88	91	96	82	86	103	98	98	102
1978	95	92	95	93	101	91	87	98	91	89	103	85	87	107	104	101	98
1979	100	95	100	98	106	90	89	107	96	102	102	96	92	105	111	107	100
1980	100	102	100	96	102	97	101	108	101	99	99	96	84	108	109	98	100
1981	98	96	96	97	104	88	95	105	98	94	97	96	85	110	106	102	103
1982	96	96	96	93	98	85	92	109	98	93	98	91	84	103	95	98	100
1983	97	93	97	93	104	85	89	106	93	95	103	96	87	107	101	104	107

Manufacturing sales: (2)(5)
investment goods (volume)
1980 = 100

Ventes des industries manufacturières (2)(5)
biens d'équipement (volume)
1980 = 100

	Year	Q.1	Q.2	Q.3	Q.4	JAN	FEB	MAR	APR	MAY	JUN	JUL	AUG	SEP	OCT	NOV	DEC
1964	53	50	53	52	59	48	49	52	54	48	56	53	46	58	57	56	63
1965	57	53	56	55	62	49	51	59	55	57	57	54	50	61	59	60	68
1966	58	56	59	56	61	52	53	64	56	58	62	54	52	62	58	59	66
1967	56	50	54	52	66	49	48	54	52	51	58	51	48	58	61	61	76
1968	62	53	60	62	74	48	51	59	57	62	60	60	56	68	72	72	77
1969	73	64	72	72	83	59	61	71	70	71	76	73	63	81	84	79	87
1970	79	72	79	78	88	67	70	79	82	73	84	80	66	87	85	84	95
1971	80	77	81	79	85	71	74	87	79	79	85	81	67	89	83	83	89
1972	82	78	82	78	91	71	76	86	77	81	88	75	73	86	88	90	96
1973	87	85	88	83	94	81	81	93	83	93	88	79	79	91	93	92	98
1974	85	83	86	82	91	80	80	89	84	90	83	84	72	89	90	87	96
1975	83	75	83	79	95	72	72	80	84	77	86	79	69	91	91	89	103
1976	89	83	88	84	102	76	79	93	85	86	93	77	76	99	92	94	120
1977	92	88	91	88	103	80	85	100	85	89	98	79	81	104	96	100	114
1978	94	90	93	91	103	89	85	97	87	86	105	82	82	110	100	100	109
1979	98	92	98	94	108	87	85	105	94	99	102	92	83	105	107	106	112
1980	100	98	100	95	107	92	98	105	99	100	100	95	79	109	108	99	114
1981	99	93	96	97	111	83	93	104	96	94	98	95	83	113	106	106	120
1982	99	96	99	95	105	83	93	111	99	96	103	96	83	107	96	103	116
1983	99	94	99	93	111	83	90	108	93	97	108	86	83	109	101	108	123

Rate of capacity utilization
manufacturing
per cent

Taux d'utilisation de capacité
industries manufacturières
pourcentage

Year	Q.1	Q.2	Q.3	Q.4	JAN	FEB	MAR	APR	MAY	JUN	JUL	AUG	SEP	OCT	NOV	DEC
1964	86.0	88.0	88.0	89.0	86.0			88.0			88.0			89.0		
1965	87.0	88.0	88.0	89.0	87.0			88.0			88.0			89.0		
1966	85.0	87.0	86.0	84.0	85.0			87.0			86.0			84.0		
1967	77.0	77.0	79.0	82.0	77.0			77.0			79.0			82.0		
1968	81.0	84.0	86.0	88.0	81.0			84.0			86.0			88.0		
1969	87.0	90.0	90.0	91.0	87.0			90.0			90.0			91.0		
1970	90.9	92.3	90.6	90.1	90.9			92.3			90.6			90.1		
1971	87.0	88.2	86.0	85.7	87.0			88.2			86.0			85.7		
1972	83.4	85.4	84.8	86.6	83.4			85.4			84.8			86.6		
1973	86.2	88.1	86.7	87.5	86.2			88.1			86.7			87.5		
1974	83.7	84.0	81.6	80.6	83.7			84.0			82.6			80.6		
1975	75.6	75.9	74.8	77.7	75.6			75.9			74.8			77.7		
1976	77.6	81.0	80.3	81.9	77.6			81.0			80.3			81.9		
1977	80.8	81.2	79.1	79.8	80.8			82.2			79.8			81.6		
1978	80.3	81.4	82.2	80.9	80.3			81.4			82.2			80.9		
1979	83.5	85.6	85.3	84.5	83.5			85.6			85.3			84.5		
1980	85.9	83.8	81.2	78.6	85.9			83.8			82.2			78.6		
1981	79.8	79.4	78.8	77.9	79.8			79.4								
1982	78.6	77.7	74.7	74.3	78.6			77.7			74.7			74.3		
1983	76.7	78.4	78.8	79.5	76.7			78.4			78.8			79.5		

Manufacturing sales: total (2)(5)
(volume)
1980 = 100

Adjusted - Corrigé *

Ventes des industries manufacturières : total (2)(5)
(volume)
1980 = 100

Year	Q.1	Q.2	Q.3	Q.4	JAN	FEB	MAR	APR	MAY	JUN	JUL	AUG	SEP	OCT	NOV	DEC
1964	54	55	56	57	54	55	55	54	54	55	57	56	56	56	58	57
1965	59	59	59	60	59	59	58	58	60	58	59	59	59	59	60	60
1966	61	61	60	58	61	61	62	61	61	61	60	60	60	59	58	59
1967	58	57	59	63	59	57	57	57	57	58	59	58	59	60	60	68
1968	61	65	68	71	59	60	63	64	65	65	66	70	68	70	73	71
1969	72	75	78	79	71	72	74	75	75	76	77	78	78	79	81	79
1970	80	81	82	83	78	80	81	81	80	81	83	82	83	82	83	83
1971	82	83	83	82	82	83	83	82	83	83	84	81	83	83	82	81
1972	83	84	85	88	84	82	84	84	85	84	83	86	85	87	87	90
1973	91	91	91	91	92	92	90	90	92	92	88	93	91	91	91	91
1974	92	90	89	86	92	92	91	91	92	88	91	89	88	88	87	84
1975	83	82	83	87	83	83	83	84	81	82	82	83	85	86	89	87
1976	88	91	89	93	88	88	88	90	91	91	86	91	91	91	91	98
1977	94	93	92	95	94	94	94	92	94	92	89	94	94	93	94	98
1978	95	94	96	97	99	94	93	93	92	96	92	96	100	97	96	97
1979	97	101	101	101	96	95	99	100	100	102	102	101	100	102	102	99
1980	103	100	98	97	104	104	102	102	102	98	99	98	98	99	98	95
1981	98	97	99	99	97	101	97	98	96	97	98	99	100	98	100	98
1982	97	97	95	93	96	98	98	97	97	96	96	96	93	90	94	95
1983	95	98	96	100	96	95	94	94	99	100	93	98	97	97	100	103

Manufacturing sales: (2)(5)
investment goods (volume)
1980 = 100

Adjusted - Corrigé *

Ventes des industries manufacturières (2)(5)
biens d'équipement (volume)
1980 = 100

Year	Q.1	Q.2	Q.3	Q.4	JAN	FEB	MAR	APR	MAY	JUN	JUL	AUG	SEP	OCT	NOV	DEC
1964	52	53	54	54	52	53	52	52	53	53	54	53	53	54	55	54
1965	56	57	56	57	56	56	56	56	58	56	56	57	56	57	57	58
1966	59	59	57	57	60	59	59	59	59	59	58	58	57	56	56	57
1967	54	54	54	61	55	54	53	54	53	54	55	53	55	58	57	67
1968	55	60	64	68	53	55	58	58	61	61	62	65	64	66	70	67
1969	68	73	75	76	65	68	70	72	73	74	74	75	74	76	78	75
1970	77	78	80	81	75	78	79	80	78	78	81	79	80	80	82	81
1971	81	81	82	79	82	81	81	80	81	82	84	79	82	81	79	76
1972	81	81	82	85	82	80	81	81	82	81	81	85	81	84	84	86
1973	88	88	87	87	89	89	87	87	88	88	83	91	83	87	87	86
1974	87	86	85	83	87	88	87	87	88	83	87	85	84	83	84	82
1975	80	82	83	86	79	79	81	84	81	81	82	83	83	85	88	86
1976	86	89	87	93	85	86	86	88	89	90	83	90	89	89	89	99
1977	92	91	92	95	92	94	92	90	92	91	88	94	93	93	94	96
1978	95	92	96	95	100	93	93	90	91	95	91	95	101	95	94	96
1979	96	100	98	99	97	94	98	100	98	101	99	97	99	99	100	98
1980	102	101	98	98	102	103	101	102	104	97	99	97	98	100	98	96
1981	98	97	100	101	95	101	97	98	97	97	98	101	101	101	102	101
1982	100	100	99	96	98	101	101	101	101	99	101	99	96	94	97	98
1983	98	101	96	102	98	98	97	97	101	104	94	97	97	99	101	106

* Adjusted by the O.E.C.D.

* Corrigé par l'O.C.D.E.

GERMANY

Manufacturing sales: (2)(5)
consumer goods (volume)
1980 = 100

Ventes des industries manufacturières (2)(5)
biens de consommation (volume)
1980 = 100

	Year	Q.1	Q.2	Q.3	Q.4	JAN	FEB	MAR	APR	MAY	JUN	JUL	AUG	SEP	OCT	NOV	DEC
1964	64	61	60	65	72	60	60	63	66	55	59	63	59	72	78	73	63
1965	69	67	65	69	76	63	65	73	69	66	61	63	64	79	80	78	69
1966	70	72	67	71	71	68	67	80	70	67	64	65	67	80	79	73	62
1967	67	67	62	67	73	67	64	70	65	59	63	62	64	75	80	75	65
1968	76	72	71	76	85	71	71	76	74	75	64	70	74	85	95	86	73
1969	84	82	78	84	93	80	79	87	83	77	75	80	77	95	104	93	83
1970	88	85	84	87	95	81	84	89	93	77	82	85	79	97	103	96	85
1971	92	91	88	90	99	84	87	102	93	85	86	86	83	101	105	102	89
1972	95	96	92	92	100	90	94	104	93	91	91	85	89	102	110	103	88
1973	96	101	95	92	97	98	100	106	96	98	90	85	92	99	110	100	82
1974	91	96	90	87	90	93	94	101	96	94	80	87	80	95	104	91	75
1975	86	86	82	84	92	85	86	88	91	76	79	80	76	96	104	91	81
1976	93	95	90	90	97	88	93	103	94	89	86	82	84	104	104	99	88
1977	96	99	91	95	100	93	94	110	92	90	91	84	93	108	107	102	92
1978	98	99	94	96	103	99	94	103	97	88	98	86	94	108	113	105	90
1979	101	102	97	99	105	99	96	112	96	99	96	96	95	107	119	108	88
1980	100	108	95	98	99	104	106	112	102	92	92	96	86	111	115	98	86
1981	95	100	90	95	96	94	98	107	97	87	86	95	82	109	107	97	85
1982	92	96	88	90	91	88	92	109	93	85	86	84	84	102	96	93	85
1983	93	95	89	91	95	88	90	106	89	87	92	84	85	105	100	98	88

Manufacturing sales: (2)(5)
intermediate goods (volume)
1980 = 100

Ventes des industries manufacturières (2)(5)
biens intermédiaires (volume)
1980 = 100

	Year	Q.1	Q.2	Q.3	Q.4	JAN	FEB	MAR	APR	MAY	JUN	JUL	AUG	SEP	OCT	NOV	DEC
1964	55	50	55	58	57	49	50	51	57	52	56	60	54	59	60	58	53
1965	57	55	57	59	57	53	53	59	57	57	57	60	57	61	60	57	54
1966	58	56	59	60	56	52	53	63	58	59	61	60	60	62	60	57	52
1967	60	54	61	62	62	53	52	58	60	59	63	61	60	63	65	63	59
1968	68	61	68	72	73	57	60	66	67	71	65	72	71	72	78	74	66
1969	77	71	76	80	80	70	67	77	76	75	76	82	75	83	87	80	74
1970	81	75	83	85	82	74	74	79	87	77	85	87	80	87	88	81	77
1971	80	78	81	82	80	72	74	86	81	79	84	83	79	86	84	81	75
1972	84	79	84	84	87	74	77	87	81	85	87	81	83	88	92	89	82
1973	94	91	93	94	96	90	87	97	89	98	93	92	95	96	103	99	88
1974	95	96	97	96	91	97	92	100	97	102	93	99	94	96	103	91	77
1975	85	85	85	83	87	88	84	84	89	82	84	83	77	89	94	86	80
1976	92	90	93	92	92	87	87	98	93	93	95	90	87	98	96	94	86
1977	93	93	95	91	92	88	87	103	92	95	97	86	89	97	95	93	88
1978	95	92	98	95	96	91	88	96	96	95	103	90	93	102	104	102	83
1979	102	97	105	103	103	90	91	108	100	109	106	102	103	104	114	105	90
1980	100	106	102	97	96	103	104	110	104	101	100	98	89	103	108	94	87
1981	98	99	100	98	97	93	96	107	101	99	101	98	90	105	105	98	88
1982	93	95	97	90	89	87	91	108	98	93	99	88	84	96	92	91	84
1983	96	93	97	96	99	86	87	104	93	97	102	88	93	106	103	102	93

Manufacturing new orders: total (2)(5)
(volume)
1980 = 100

Commandes nouvelles (industries manufacturières) **: total** (2)(5)
(volume)
1980 = 100

	Year	Q.1	Q.2	Q.3	Q.4	JAN	FEB	MAR	APR	MAY	JUN	JUL	AUG	SEP	OCT	NOV	DEC
1964	56	54	57	55	60	53	54	56	60	54	58	58	50	57	62	59	58
1965	59	57	59	57	61	54	55	63	60	59	57	57	52	62	62	61	60
1966	57	59	59	55	56	54	56	67	60	60	59	54	52	58	59	57	53
1967	58	53	57	57	65	50	51	58	55	56	60	55	55	60	68	66	62
1968	71	64	69	71	79	60	63	67	69	73	64	71	67	74	84	78	75
1969	84	81	84	85	88	77	78	88	86	84	82	87	78	90	95	86	82
1970	83	83	83	80	84	78	83	88	87	78	84	82	73	85	86	84	83
1971	80	81	82	78	80	75	77	92	84	80	82	79	71	83	83	81	78
1972	84	81	84	79	92	74	80	90	82	83	86	77	76	85	94	92	90
1973	95	100	97	89	92	101	95	104	93	107	92	90	85	91	98	94	85
1974	90	98	93	85	84	94	95	104	95	96	87	87	83	86	95	83	74
1975	85	83	90	81	88	83	83	83	89	77	102	84	70	88	94	86	83
1976	94	93	91	95	95	87	89	103	92	90	91	103	86	96	96	94	97
1977	93	94	91	87	100	87	88	107	91	91	90	81	84	96	99	101	99
1978	96	95	96	92	101	94	89	102	96	92	99	85	90	101	105	103	96
1979	102	102	104	98	105	97	98	112	103	106	102	97	93	102	114	106	95
1980	100	109	100	92	99	105	107	116	103	99	98	95	82	100	108	94	94
1981	100	103	99	95	102	96	101	111	108	94	96	97	85	102	105	100	100
1982	94	100	93	86	96	92	96	113	97	88	93	87	80	92	92	96	102
1983	96	100	93	91	102	99	91	109	92	91	96	86	86	101	101	104	102

Manufacturing sales: (2)(5) — Ventes des industries manufacturières (2)(5)

consumer goods (volume) — biens de consommation (volume)

1980 = 100

Adjusted - Corrigé *

Year	Q.1	Q.2	Q.3	Q.4	JAN	FEB	MAR	APR	MAY	JUN	JUL	AUG	SEP	OCT	NOV	DEC
1964	62	63	65	67	61	62	63	63	62	63	66	64	65	66	67	67
1965	68	69	69	71	67	69	68	69	70	69	68	69	70	69	71	72
1966	72	71	71	68	72	71	73	72	72	70	72	70	71	69	67	67
1967	68	65	68	69	70	67	66	65	63	67	69	68	68	68	68	72
1968	71	75	77	80	72	70	72	75	75	76	73	80	78	79	81	79
1969	82	83	86	88	80	82	83	82	82	83	84	86	86	87	90	87
1970	86	87	88	90	84	87	87	87	86	87	89	88	88	89	90	90
1971	90	92	92	94	88	90	92	91	93	92	93	92	92	93	94	94
1972	94	95	95	97	96	92	94	94	94	96	95	95	96	96	95	99
1973	99	98	95	93	99	100	97	96	98	100	93	98	95	94	92	93
1974	94	93	90	86	93	94	94	95	93	92	94	88	89	89	87	83
1975	85	84	87	88	84	86	85	85	83	83	86	86	87	88	90	88
1976	91	93	92	94	90	91	91	92	94	93	91	93	93	93	94	95
1977	96	95	97	98	97	95	96	94	97	94	94	100	96	96	96	102
1978	97	97	98	100	100	95	94	97	95	99	96	101	98	100	99	103
1979	98	102	102	102	98	98	99	99	101	107	104	101	100	102	102	101
1980	103	100	99	97	103	103	103	102	100	99	100	98	100	97	98	95
1981	97	95	96	94	96	99	95	96	94	94	97	94	96	94	94	93
1982	93	93	91	90	92	93	94	93	94	91	89	94	90	87	90	93
1983	91	94	92	95	93	91	91	90	95	97	90	93	92	91	94	100

Manufacturing sales: (2)(5) — Ventes des industries manufacturières (2)(5)

intermediate goods (volume) — biens intermédiaires (volume)

1980 = 100

Adjusted - Corrigé *

Year	Q.1	Q.2	Q.3	Q.4	JAN	FEB	MAR	APR	MAY	JUN	JUL	AUG	SEP	OCT	NOV	DEC
1964	53	54	55	57	52	54	54	53	53	54	55	55	55	56	58	57
1965	58	57	57	57	59	58	57	56	57	57	56	57	57	57	56	58
1966	59	59	58	57	58	58	60	58	59	59	58	58	58	57	56	57
1967	58	59	60	63	58	58	58	59	58	60	60	59	61	61	61	66
1968	63	67	70	73	61	64	65	66	67	67	68	71	70	71	75	73
1969	74	75	78	80	74	74	75	75	75	76	77	78	79	79	83	79
1970	80	81	83	82	79	80	80	81	81	81	82	83	83	82	82	82
1971	80	81	81	80	79	81	80	80	81	81	81	81	81	81	80	80
1972	81	83	83	89	80	79	83	82	83	84	82	83	85	87	87	91
1973	92	93	94	97	92	93	91	91	94	93	92	95	96	95	97	99
1974	97	96	96	91	98	98	97	97	96	96	98	97	94	95	92	86
1975	88	83	83	87	88	89	86	84	82	82	83	82	85	86	89	87
1976	90	92	92	93	89	90	90	91	93	92	92	92	92	92	93	93
1977	93	93	91	94	93	92	94	92	95	92	91	92	91	92	92	98
1978	93	94	96	98	95	93	91	94	93	96	95	96	99	98	100	96
1979	96	102	105	104	92	96	99	100	103	104	106	106	103	104	104	105
1980	104	100	98	98	105	105	103	102	100	97	98	97	97	98	98	97
1981	99	98	99	98	98	102	97	98	98	98	98	98	99	98	99	97
1982	95	94	91	90	94	96	96	95	95	93	90	91	91	88	91	92
1983	92	95	97	102	94	92	92	92	97	96	93	98	100	99	101	105

Manufacturing new orders: total (2)(5) (volume) — Commandes nouvelles (industries manufacturières) : total (2)(5) (volume)

1980 = 100

Adjusted - Corrigé

Year	Q.1	Q.2	Q.3	Q.4	JAN	FEB	MAR	APR	MAY	JUN	JUL	AUG	SEP	OCT	NOV	DEC
1964	56	56	57	57	55	58	56	55	57	57	58	57	57	57	57	58
1965	59	58	59	59	60	59	58	59	58	57	59	58	61	59	59	59
1966	60	59	57	55	58	60	61	60	59	59	57	56	57	57	54	53
1967	54	56	59	64	52	54	56	54	56	58	58	59	61	63	64	65
1968	64	69	73	78	63	65	64	68	70	70	71	74	74	76	78	79
1969	82	84	89	86	81	82	83	84	84	84	88	90	88	86	87	84
1970	85	82	83	82	83	87	86	82	83	82	83	83	83	81	83	83
1971	81	82	81	78	82	80	81	83	81	82	83	79	81	80	79	75
1972	80	83	84	91	79	80	82	83	82	84	83	82	86	89	90	95
1973	98	97	93	91	103	97	95	94	103	94	94	92	94	90	92	92
1974	96	93	89	83	95	97	96	93	93	93	88	92	86	87	84	78
1975	83	89	84	86	85	84	81	83	81	103	86	81	86	86	87	85
1976	90	90	100	93	91	89	91	90	90	91	109	96	94	93	92	93
1977	91	91	91	98	90	89	93	92	91	90	88	92	93	96	99	98
1978	92	94	98	100	94	90	93	94	94	94	93	99	101	99	100	101
1979	98	105	104	103	96	99	99	104	105	105	104	103	105	105	103	102
1980	105	101	97	97	104	105	105	101	103	100	98	96	97	99	95	96
1981	100	101	100	99	99	101	99	106	98	98	101	99	99	99	98	99
1982	97	93	91	93	98	97	97	95	92	93	92	91	90	89	93	98
1983	95	94	96	100	101	92	93	93	93	95	94	96	98	98	101	101

* Adjusted by the O.E.C.D. — * Corrigé par l'O.C.D.E.

GERMANY

Manufacturing new orders: (2)(5) / Commandes nouvelles (industries manufacturières) : (2)(5)
domestic (volume) / marché intérieur (volume)
1980 = 100

	Year	Q.1	Q.2	Q.3	Q.4	JAN	FEB	MAR	APR	MAY	JUN	JUL	AUG	SEP	OCT	NOV	DEC
1964	66	62	67	65	70	60	62	65	70	63	67	68	59	69	73	69	67
1965	68	66	69	67	71	63	64	73	71	69	66	66	62	74	73	71	68
1966	65	67	67	63	62	61	63	77	68	68	66	62	59	66	67	63	56
1967	64	57	62	63	72	54	54	63	60	62	64	60	60	68	78	73	66
1968	78	70	76	79	87	66	69	75	77	82	70	78	74	83	94	86	81
1969	94	89	93	95	100	85	85	96	96	92	90	97	88	100	108	99	91
1970	93	93	93	90	95	86	93	99	99	88	93	92	83	95	98	94	92
1971	89	88	91	87	90	80	84	101	93	89	91	87	81	93	94	91	85
1972	92	89	93	88	99	82	88	99	92	91	95	86	84	94	103	98	94
1973	99	106	104	91	94	107	102	110	100	115	96	91	89	93	103	96	83
1974	90	98	93	84	85	94	96	104	96	98	85	87	80	86	95	84	75
1975	90	86	98	84	91	86	85	88	96	81	116	89	73	89	97	89	86
1976	94	96	93	90	97	88	92	109	96	93	90	36	86	98	99	96	97
1977	95	96	92	90	102	89	91	108	93	92	91	83	86	100	101	104	100
1978	98	98	98	95	103	97	92	103	99	93	100	88	92	105	109	105	96
1979	103	104	103	99	106	98	100	115	103	106	101	99	95	103	116	108	94
1980	100	110	98	94	98	105	108	117	103	96	97	96	86	101	111	94	90
1981	94	99	95	90	94	92	98	106	103	90	91	91	80	98	100	92	90
1982	89	93	88	83	94	85	88	105	92	85	87	83	77	88	89	92	100
1983	92	96	90	87	96	98	86	105	89	88	92	81	83	96	96	98	94

Manufacturing new orders: (2)(5) / Commandes nouvelles (industries manufacturières) : (2)(5)
export (volume) / étranger (volume)
1980 = 100

	Year	Q.1	Q.2	Q.3	Q.4	JAN	FEB	MAR	APR	MAY	JUN	JUL	AUG	SEP	OCT	NOV	DEC
1964	37	38	37	34	39	38	38	37	39	34	38	35	31	36	39	38	39
1965	39	38	38	37	42	35	37	43	38	39	38	38	33	39	40	40	45
1966	43	42	43	40	45	40	40	46	42	43	44	38	39	42	45	45	47
1967	47	46	47	45	51	43	45	49	45	44	53	43	45	46	48	52	53
1968	56	51	54	55	64	49	52	52	54	56	52	58	51	55	62	64	64
1969	65	65	66	65	63	61	63	69	67	66	67	67	59	70	67	60	63
1970	62	63	62	61	64	60	63	67	64	57	65	63	53	66	62	63	66
1971	62	66	64	58	60	63	61	73	66	61	65	63	52	61	60	60	61
1972	68	65	65	62	79	59	64	71	62	66	67	59	59	67	75	80	82
1973	86	87	85	84	88	90	79	92	80	91	83	88	77	83	88	88	89
1974	90	96	92	88	83	94	92	102	94	92	90	86	90	87	95	83	72
1975	76	76	73	74	81	77	77	73	76	69	74	73	64	36	88	78	77
1976	92	85	86	107	91	85	81	89	83	82	93	140	87	94	89	89	96
1977	89	90	88	81	95	83	83	105	87	89	89	76	81	86	93	96	97
1978	91	90	91	86	97	87	83	101	88	88	97	79	88	93	95	99	97
1979	100	98	105	94	103	94	93	107	102	107	104	94	89	100	110	103	97
1980	100	108	103	89	100	105	107	112	103	106	100	93	75	99	103	94	104
1981	111	111	109	106	118	103	109	122	117	102	106	110	97	110	115	117	122
1982	104	117	103	93	102	107	114	130	106	96	108	94	85	102	98	104	105
1983	106	107	100	100	116	101	102	118	97	99	105	96	93	111	113	115	120

Manufacturing new orders: (2)(5) / Commandes nouvelles (industries manufacturières) : (2)(5)
investments goods (volume) / biens d'équipement (volume)
1980 = 100

	Year	Q.1	Q.2	Q.3	Q.4	JAN	FEB	MAR	APR	MAY	JUN	JUL	AUG	SEP	OCT	NOV	DEC
1964	53	52	53	52	57	51	52	53	54	49	55	55	48	53	56	56	59
1965	56	56	55	55	59	54	55	60	56	55	55	55	50	59	56	58	61
1966	54	56	55	51	52	52	54	63	55	55	56	51	48	54	54	52	51
1967	54	48	52	53	63	45	47	52	49	50	56	51	52	55	64	63	62
1968	67	60	63	68	77	57	60	63	62	68	60	70	63	71	79	75	78
1969	85	81	84	88	88	77	78	87	84	83	84	91	82	92	95	85	83
1970	82	85	81	80	81	80	86	90	85	76	83	82	73	85	80	81	83
1971	76	80	77	74	73	74	74	91	78	75	80	77	66	78	72	75	73
1972	79	76	77	74	88	69	75	83	73	75	83	74	69	80	85	88	90
1973	92	99	96	86	87	105	92	100	89	109	90	90	81	88	91	88	83
1974	88	96	89	84	83	90	95	104	89	93	84	84	83	84	91	82	77
1975	85	84	93	81	83	85	85	82	86	74	119	88	68	87	85	80	83
1976	93	89	86	102	96	83	86	97	86	82	89	121	90	97	92	93	103
1977	92	94	87	85	102	86	89	106	85	87	88	80	84	92	96	104	108
1978	95	95	92	90	101	93	89	103	91	88	98	83	90	99	99	101	103
1979	102	103	102	96	106	97	101	110	101	104	101	95	91	102	112	106	100
1980	100	109	93	92	101	104	107	114	98	100	97	96	82	93	105	95	103
1981	102	103	99	96	107	96	103	112	110	92	96	99	86	103	103	105	114
1982	96	103	93	87	101	97	97	115	95	88	96	90	79	90	88	99	117
1983	96	103	90	88	103	108	92	109	89	88	95	84	82	97	96	104	108

Manufacturing new orders: (2)(5)
domestic (volume)
1980 = 100

Commandes nouvelles (industries manufacturières) : (2)(5)
marché intérieur (volume)
1980 = 100

Adjusted - Corrigé

	Year	Q.1	Q.2	Q.3	Q.4	JAN	FEB	MAR	APR	MAY	JUN	JUL	AUG	SEP	OCT	NOV	DEC
1964		65	65	66	67	63	66	65	64	66	66	67	66	65	66	66	69
1965		68	68	68	68	70	67	68	69	67	67	67	67	71	68	68	68
1966		68	67	64	60	67	67	71	68	66	66	65	63	64	62	60	57
1967		58	60	65	71	57	57	60	58	61	61	63	64	67	71	70	72
1968		70	76	81	85	69	70	71	74	77	77	78	82	82	84	84	88
1969		90	92	98	97	90	89	91	92	92	92	97	100	96	97	99	96
1970		95	91	92	92	93	97	96	90	93	91	92	93	92	90	92	94
1971		88	90	90	88	89	87	89	90	89	91	91	88	90	90	89	85
1972		89	91	92	98	88	88	90	91	90	93	92	90	94	96	95	102
1973		104	102	95	93	110	104	99	99	110	98	95	96	95	94	94	92
1974		97	93	88	84	96	98	96	92	95	92	89	88	86	86	84	81
1975		87	97	87	89	89	86	85	88	85	117	92	84	86	88	90	90
1976		93	92	93	95	93	92	95	93	93	91	91	95	94	95	94	96
1977		93	92	93	100	93	92	93	92	92	91	91	93	96	97	101	102
1978		95	97	100	102	99	93	93	97	96	97	96	100	103	102	102	103
1979		101	104	105	104	99	102	101	103	105	105	105	104	105	105	105	103
1980		105	100	98	97	105	106	105	100	100	100	99	99	96	101	95	94
1981		96	96	93	92	96	98	94	100	94	94	94	92	94	93	91	92
1982		90	89	86	91	91	88	90	90	89	88	88	87	84	85	90	99
1983		93	91	90	95	102	87	89	89	90	93	88	91	92	92	96	96

Manufacturing new orders: (2)(5)
export (volume)
1980 = 100

Commandes nouvelles (industries manufacturières) : (2)(5)
étranger (volume)
1980 = 100

Adjusted - Corrigé

	Year	Q.1	Q.2	Q.3	Q.4	JAN	FEB	MAR	APR	MAY	JUN	JUL	AUG	SEP	OCT	NOV	DEC
1964		38	36	36	37	38	39	36	36	36	36	36	36	37	38	37	37
1965		38	38	39	40	38	38	38	38	38	37	40	37	39	40	39	41
1966		41	43	42	44	41	40	41	43	42	43	41	42	43	45	43	44
1967		45	46	47	50	43	46	46	44	45	49	46	49	47	48	50	53
1968		49	54	58	63	49	51	48	54	54	55	58	58	57	60	65	64
1969		63	67	68	62	62	64	64	66	67	67	67	68	69	64	61	61
1970		63	61	64	62	62	63	64	61	61	62	63	63	65	61	63	62
1971		64	64	61	59	67	61	64	65	62	64	64	59	60	61	58	57
1972		62	64	65	79	61	63	63	64	65	64	63	66	67	75	78	84
1973		83	85	89	88	88	80	82	82	88	84	91	86	91	84	86	93
1974		93	93	93	83	93	93	93	94	89	96	88	102	88	91	83	74
1975		75	72	78	80	77	79	70	72	72	72	75	74	84	84	79	76
1976		82	85	113	89	87	82	78	83	81	91	150	97	92	90	87	89
1977		86	88	85	93	85	84	90	90	89	86	84	88	84	93	94	93
1978		88	89	92	95	87	84	92	88	90	89	87	95	94	92	96	98
1979		93	104	101	102	93	93	94	105	104	104	101	97	104	105	100	101
1980		103	104	95	98	104	105	101	103	110	100	98	88	98	97	95	101
1981		107	110	113	114	105	108	107	117	106	106	115	114	109	112	115	116
1982		112	104	99	99	112	114	110	106	100	105	101	97	100	98	101	98
1983		101	101	106	113	102	102	100	100	101	102	105	105	109	113	113	114

Manufacturing new orders: (2)(5)
investments goods (volume)
1980 = 100

Commandes nouvelles (industries manufacturières) : (2)(5)
biens d'équipement (volume)
1980 = 100

Adjusted - Corrigé

	Year	Q.1	Q.2	Q.3	Q.4	JAN	FEB	MAR	APR	MAY	JUN	JUL	AUG	SEP	OCT	NOV	DEC
1964		53	53	54	54	52	55	52	51	53	54	54	54	53	53	54	56
1965		57	55	56	56	58	57	55	56	55	55	56	54	57	55	56	57
1966		56	56	53	51	54	56	57	56	55	56	53	52	53	53	50	49
1967		49	51	55	62	47	49	50	49	52	53	53	56	55	61	61	63
1968		59	64	70	76	58	60	59	63	66	64	68	70	71	73	75	79
1969		80	85	91	86	79	80	82	85	85	85	89	94	89	89	86	82
1970		86	81	82	79	84	88	86	82	82	80	81	83	82	77	80	80
1971		78	73	75	72	80	75	80	79	77	79	78	73	75	72	74	69
1972		74	77	78	87	72	74	75	76	76	79	78	75	80	83	87	91
1973		96	97	90	87	106	91	91	93	107	91	92	87	90	87	87	86
1974		94	91	87	82	91	95	95	91	92	90	84	93	84	87	83	77
1975		84	93	84	81	86	85	80	83	78	118	88	78	85	82	82	80
1976		85	86	107	93	87	84	85	87	83	88	125	100	95	93	92	94
1977		90	88	89	100	89	88	92	89	88	88	86	91	90	97	102	100
1978		92	92	96	99	94	88	94	92	92	93	89	98	100	97	99	100
1979		98	104	102	103	96	101	97	105	104	104	100	100	106	108	103	99
1980		104	101	97	97	103	105	104	100	105	99	99	96	97	101	95	96
1981		100	102	101	103	98	102	100	112	97	98	102	101	101	102	102	104
1982		99	95	92	96	102	97	98	97	94	95	95	91	89	90	95	104
1983		98	93	93	99	110	92	93	93	91	94	91	93	95	98	100	98

GERMANY

Manufacturing new orders: (2)(5) — Commandes nouvelles (industries manufacturières) : (2)(5)
consumer goods (volume) — biens de consommation (volume)
1980 = 100

	Year	Q.1	Q.2	Q.3	Q.4	JAN	FEB	MAR	APR	MAY	JUN	JUL	AUG	SEP	OCT	NOV	DEC
1964	66	60	69	61	74	57	58	65	75	67	64	59	53	71	85	76	61
1965	70	64	73	65	78	56	61	76	77	77	64	59	56	80	90	80	65
1966	68	70	72	62	68	61	62	86	79	74	63	56	57	74	79	71	55
1967	68	61	69	63	79	58	58	69	72	68	66	56	58	75	89	81	65
1968	80	72	83	75	91	67	69	79	37	90	71	70	68	88	109	92	73
1969	88	84	89	81	97	79	80	93	98	89	78	77	70	97	114	97	79
1970	88	82	89	82	99	74	80	90	102	84	82	77	71	97	114	99	83
1971	94	90	97	86	103	79	84	106	109	95	87	80	77	101	117	103	88
1972	98	95	99	89	108	85	91	111	108	98	90	78	84	106	125	109	89
1973	97	105	101	85	98	93	102	119	108	106	89	80	82	93	112	102	81
1974	89	95	93	77	90	91	87	106	105	97	76	75	69	89	109	91	69
1975	86	81	88	77	99	76	77	90	105	83	77	69	68	95	118	98	82
1976	96	98	98	85	101	85	92	116	108	100	86	75	76	105	115	103	85
1977	96	96	97	90	103	86	89	113	105	98	89	77	85	107	116	104	88
1978	100	98	101	93	107	94	91	108	111	96	96	80	88	111	125	111	85
1979	103	103	105	95	108	93	95	121	112	108	96	90	89	107	127	111	86
1980	100	111	99	92	99	103	106	124	112	96	89	87	79	110	118	97	82
1981	96	101	94	90	97	92	98	115	106	90	86	86	79	106	113	98	81
1982	92	98	91	85	94	85	92	118	102	88	84	77	79	100	103	95	83
1983	95	97	93	90	99	86	91	115	97	92	90	79	84	108	108	100	88

Manufacturing new orders: (2)(5) — Commandes nouvelles (industries manufacturières) : (2)(5)
intermediate goods (volume) — biens intermédiaires (volume)
1980 = 100

	Year	Q.1	Q.2	Q.3	Q.4	JAN	FEB	MAR	APR	MAY	JUN	JUL	AUG	SEP	OCT	NOV	DEC
1964	56	54	58	57	56	53	55	56	61	54	59	61	53	56	59	55	54
1965	56	55	57	57	56	52	53	59	58	57	57	59	55	57	57	55	56
1966	58	58	60	58	56	54	55	64	58	61	61	59	57	57	57	56	55
1967	60	57	60	60	62	53	54	62	55	59	65	60	59	62	64	63	59
1968	71	66	71	73	75	63	66	68	71	74	67	75	73	71	78	76	72
1969	81	79	82	82	81	77	76	84	82	81	81	87	77	81	83	80	81
1970	81	79	82	80	82	75	79	84	83	78	86	85	76	80	81	81	84
1971	80	77	82	80	81	72	76	84	81	80	84	83	77	80	82	80	79
1972	86	83	87	83	91	78	82	90	84	88	90	81	83	84	91	92	91
1973	97	98	97	95	98	98	96	101	92	104	96	95	95	95	102	101	91
1974	94	101	100	93	83	103	99	102	100	103	97	99	92	89	94	82	72
1975	85	82	84	82	90	85	80	81	86	81	85	85	75	87	97	88	85
1976	93	98	97	89	91	95	92	107	94	98	98	90	86	91	91	91	91
1977	92	93	94	88	92	88	87	103	92	94	94	85	85	95	93	94	91
1978	96	94	98	95	97	95	89	97	95	96	103	92	93	98	102	100	89
1979	103	101	106	102	102	99	94	111	101	109	109	106	100	100	111	103	92
1980	100	109	103	93	95	107	103	113	105	100	104	97	85	97	107	91	88
1981	99	102	102	96	95	98	100	107	104	99	102	101	88	98	102	94	88
1982	92	98	93	86	89	89	96	107	96	88	95	87	82	91	91	90	87
1983	98	95	97	97	103	91	90	105	93	97	102	92	94	104	105	104	101

Construction permits issued: total (6)(7) — Permis de construire délivrés : total (6)(7)
billion DM, monthly averages — milliards de DM, moyennes mensuelles

	Year	Q.1	Q.2	Q.3	Q.4	JAN	FEB	MAR	APR	MAY	JUN	JUL	AUG	SEP	OCT	NOV	DEC
1964	3.40	2.65	3.43	3.81	3.67	2.49	2.58	2.89	3.34	3.32	3.62	3.82	3.87	3.72	4.01	3.55	3.46
1965	3.74	2.85	3.83	4.37	3.92	2.68	2.61	3.25	3.61	4.04	3.85	4.45	4.39	4.27	4.17	3.81	3.77
1966	3.72	3.31	3.88	4.07	3.64	2.95	2.97	4.00	3.75	3.85	4.04	4.15	4.03	4.04	4.13	3.33	3.47
1967	3.46	2.85	3.50	3.69	3.79	2.76	2.68	3.11	3.50	3.33	3.69	3.78	3.60	3.70	4.35	3.88	3.13
1968	3.60	2.99	3.74	4.01	3.66	2.35	2.99	3.63	3.88	3.72	3.63	4.16	3.90	3.97	3.98	3.64	3.35
1969	4.13	3.19	4.29	4.68	4.34	2.73	3.14	3.71	4.13	4.07	4.68	4.89	4.48	4.66	4.94	4.36	3.72
1970	4.92	3.64	5.04	5.86	5.14	3.21	3.49	4.22	5.29	4.58	5.26	6.03	5.75	5.79	5.68	5.23	4.51
1971	6.13	4.76	6.44	6.98	6.34	3.85	4.40	6.02	6.08	6.43	6.80	7.04	6.95	6.95	6.96	6.07	5.99
1972	7.27	6.11	7.43	8.14	7.39	5.58	5.85	6.91	7.08	6.93	8.28	8.20	7.98	8.25	7.93	7.21	7.04
1973	7.16	6.48	7.90	7.98	6.26	5.86	5.87	7.73	7.16	8.54	7.99	8.74	8.11	7.11	7.08	6.30	5.40
1974	6.02	4.96	6.50	6.89	5.71	4.65	4.52	5.70	5.96	6.84	6.69	7.36	6.92	6.39	6.63	5.19	5.29
1975	6.19	4.86	6.00	6.85	6.88	4.49	4.49	5.60	5.67	5.50	6.82	6.89	6.48	7.20	7.32	6.98	6.35
1976	6.07	6.00	6.54	6.32	5.39	5.10	6.13	6.77	6.27	6.76	6.58	7.36	5.87	5.72	5.77	5.16	5.23
1977	5.94	4.83	6.06	6.49	6.35	4.25	4.30	5.93	5.69	6.44	6.05	7.04	6.07	6.37	7.24	5.70	6.10
1978	7.38	5.64	7.69	8.14	7.95	5.25	5.43	6.23	6.75	7.36	8.95	8.30	7.84	8.27	8.13	7.40	8.30
1979	7.47	6.53	7.69	8.07	7.61	5.88	6.32	7.38	7.26	7.76	8.07	8.63	7.66	7.90	8.05	7.35	7.41
1980	8.05	7.12	8.51	8.69	7.91	6.03	7.22	8.10	8.21	8.64	8.67	9.01	8.22	8.84	9.33	7.23	7.17
1981	7.78	6.96	8.54	3.41	7.20	6.13	8.24	8.51	3.13	3.92	8.56	8.76	8.44	8.05	8.01	6.63	6.96
1982	7.42	6.82	7.59	7.78	7.54	6.24	6.58	7.66	7.10	7.26	8.40	8.17	7.65	7.53	8.31	7.25	7.06
1983	9.00	7.64	10.27	9.69	8.41	7.00	6.93	9.00	10.35	10.10	10.38	10.33	9.73	9.01	8.90	8.14	8.19

Manufacturing new orders: (2)(5)
consumer goods (volume)
1980 = 100

Adjusted - Corrigé

Commandes nouvelles (industries manufacturières) : (2)(5)
biens de consommation (volume)
1980 = 100

	Year	Q.1	Q.2	Q.3	Q.4	JAN	FEB	MAR	APR	MAY	JUN	JUL	AUG	SEP	OCT	NOV	DEC
1964		65	67	67	68	64	66	64	65	68	69	68	67	67	68	68	68
1965		68	70	71	72	67	68	70	70	72	69	70	69	75	74	71	71
1966		73	70	69	63	71	70	77	74	69	68	68	69	69	65	63	62
1967		65	66	70	74	65	65	65	65	65	68	68	70	72	71	73	77
1968		75	82	83	85	75	75	74	78	83	84	81	84	84	85	85	86
1969		88	87	89	90	88	89	87	87	87	87	90	88	90	89	91	90
1970		86	87	90	91	85	88	85	86	87	87	90	89	90	91	91	92
1971		92	95	95	95	92	92	92	97	94	94	96	94	95	97	94	95
1972		96	96	99	102	96	96	97	99	95	95	96	100	101	100	100	105
1973		105	99	95	93	101	109	104	98	99	100	96	98	91	87	94	98
1974		95	91	86	84	98	93	94	93	91	90	88	84	86	86	86	81
1975		83	86	85	94	82	83	84	88	85	84	82	86	87	93	94	94
1976		96	96	93	95	94	97	97	96	98	94	91	92	96	96	96	93
1977		94	96	98	98	94	94	93	96	97	96	95	101	98	97	97	99
1978		96	99	102	103	99	96	93	100	97	99	99	103	104	103	103	102
1979		99	105	105	104	96	99	101	103	105	107	107	104	103	102	104	105
1980		107	100	99	95	107	107	106	101	99	99	101	97	99	95	95	96
1981		98	95	97	93	98	100	96	96	94	95	99	96	96	95	93	92
1982		94	92	91	90	93	95	95	92	92	91	90	93	90	88	91	92
1983		92	94	97	96	92	93	92	92	94	97	96	97	97	93	96	100

Manufacturing new orders: (2)(5)
intermediate goods (volume)
1980 = 100

Adjusted - Corrigé

Commandes nouvelles (industries manufacturières) : (2)(5)
biens intermédiaires (volume)
1980 = 100

	Year	Q.1	Q.2	Q.3	Q.4	JAN	FEB	MAR	APR	MAY	JUN	JUL	AUG	SEP	OCT	NOV	DEC
1964		57	57	57	56	56	58	56	57	57	56	58	56	56	57	55	57
1965		56	56	57	56	58	55	56	57	56	55	57	57	58	57	55	57
1966		59	59	58	57	59	58	60	58	60	60	59	58	57	57	56	57
1967		58	58	62	63	56	57	61	54	58	61	60	61	64	63	63	64
1968		66	70	74	77	65	68	66	70	70	71	71	77	74	75	78	78
1969		80	81	83	83	80	79	82	80	81	81	83	84	82	80	83	85
1970		82	80	82	82	80	82	83	78	81	82	82	82	81	80	81	86
1971		78	80	81	81	78	79	77	80	80	81	82	82	80	83	80	80
1972		83	85	86	94	82	82	85	85	85	85	84	86	87	90	92	99
1973		97	95	98	99	98	98	96	94	98	94	95	99	101	97	100	101
1974		100	98	95	84	102	102	96	98	96	100	96	97	91	89	84	79
1975		83	82	85	92	85	82	81	81	82	82	84	83	87	92	92	91
1976		96	94	91	92	97	93	97	93	94	94	91	92	91	91	91	93
1977		90	91	91	94	89	89	92	93	91	90	89	89	95	92	95	96
1978		92	94	99	100	94	91	91	93	95	94	97	99	100	99	101	100
1979		98	103	106	105	97	95	101	101	103	106	108	107	104	105	104	105
1980		106	101	96	97	105	107	105	102	100	102	97	95	96	101	95	95
1981		99	100	99	96	100	100	98	101	99	100	101	98	97	99	96	94
1982		95	90	90	91	93	97	95	93	88	90	90	89	90	90	92	90
1983		92	95	100	105	92	90	93	93	94	97	98	100	103	104	105	107

Construction permits issued: (6)(7)
residential
billion DM, monthly averages

Permis de construire délivrés : (6)(7)
bâtiments résidentiels
milliards de DM, moyennes mensuelles

	Year	Q.1	Q.2	Q.3	Q.4	JAN	FEB	MAR	APR	MAY	JUN	JUL	AUG	SEP	OCT	NOV	DEC
1964	2.12	1.65	2.17	2.40	2.25	1.47	1.66	1.81	2.13	2.15	2.23	2.44	2.35	2.40	2.51	2.19	2.06
1965	2.38	1.80	2.49	2.73	2.49	1.61	1.67	2.13	2.38	2.58	2.50	2.82	2.68	2.70	2.79	2.39	2.30
1966	2.38	2.10	2.53	2.61	2.29	1.78	1.87	2.64	2.44	2.53	2.61	2.65	2.57	2.59	2.70	2.13	2.05
1967	2.17	1.79	2.32	2.36	2.22	1.66	1.71	1.99	2.35	2.16	2.46	2.42	2.40	2.26	2.52	2.31	1.82
1968	2.25	1.94	2.39	2.49	2.19	1.47	1.88	2.46	2.51	2.39	2.28	2.50	2.52	2.45	2.53	2.11	1.93
1969	2.46	1.93	2.63	2.77	2.52	1.55	1.89	2.34	2.55	2.58	2.75	2.89	2.66	2.76	3.01	2.50	2.06
1970	2.96	2.23	3.13	3.53	2.94	1.89	2.22	2.60	3.27	2.92	3.21	3.65	3.48	3.47	3.39	2.95	2.49
1971	3.92	2.91	4.15	4.61	4.01	2.21	2.81	3.70	3.92	4.12	4.40	4.59	4.64	4.59	4.46	4.00	3.58
1972	4.77	3.80	5.12	5.35	4.81	3.23	3.59	4.57	4.94	4.88	5.55	5.49	5.38	5.18	5.32	4.81	4.29
1973	4.64	4.36	5.38	5.33	3.50	3.77	4.00	5.32	4.99	5.87	5.28	5.89	5.49	4.60	4.25	3.59	2.65
1974	3.50	2.80	3.97	4.06	3.15	2.43	2.52	3.44	3.75	4.34	3.82	4.31	4.11	3.77	3.82	2.78	2.85
1975	3.37	2.75	3.48	3.73	3.54	2.37	2.60	3.27	3.41	3.26	3.76	3.76	3.61	3.82	3.84	3.64	3.14
1976	3.86	3.65	4.40	4.03	3.35	3.13	3.55	4.28	4.29	4.55	4.36	4.50	3.85	3.74	3.57	3.29	3.18
1977	3.90	3.13	4.10	4.33	4.00	2.62	2.95	3.82	3.84	4.31	4.14	4.47	4.33	4.20	4.49	3.71	3.81
1978	4.93	3.75	5.34	5.41	5.17	3.32	3.46	4.46	4.73	5.28	6.00	5.62	5.34	5.28	5.37	4.99	5.15
1979	5.00	4.48	5.38	5.34	4.81	4.00	4.33	5.11	5.17	5.45	5.52	5.61	5.24	5.16	5.17	4.68	4.56
1980	5.14	4.69	5.57	5.52	4.80	3.90	4.73	5.44	5.55	5.62	5.54	5.99	5.20	5.36	5.76	4.28	4.37
1981	4.99	4.57	5.76	5.39	4.23	3.98	4.03	5.70	5.44	6.11	5.73	5.87	5.36	4.95	4.86	3.88	3.96
1982	4.67	4.23	5.07	5.04	4.33	3.75	3.90	5.04	4.99	4.95	5.26	5.35	4.98	4.80	4.86	4.19	3.95
1983	5.86	4.76	6.87	6.31	5.52	4.13	4.27	5.88	6.64	6.82	7.15	6.60	6.58	5.74	5.96	5.47	5.13

GERMANY

Construction, work put in place: (8) — Construction, travaux effectués : (8)
residential — bâtiments résidentiels
billion DM, monthly averages — milliards de DM, moyennes mensuelles

	Year	Q.1	Q.2	Q.3	Q.4	JAN	FEB	MAR	APR	MAY	JUN	JUL	AUG	SEP	OCT	NOV	DEC
1964	1.26	0.82	1.27	1.43	1.52	0.76	0.79	0.91	1.19	1.20	1.42	1.52	1.34	1.42	1.50	1.40	1.65
1965	1.32	0.92	1.33	1.51	1.54	0.91	0.91	0.93	1.20	1.35	1.44	1.59	1.42	1.51	1.55	1.47	1.61
1966	1.41	1.04	1.45	1.55	1.60	0.92	0.91	1.28	1.29	1.49	1.56	1.58	1.51	1.55	1.58	1.50	1.73
1967	1.51	1.15	1.49	1.60	1.79	1.09	1.08	1.27	1.35	1.47	1.65	1.65	1.59	1.56	1.70	1.68	2.00
1968	0.95	0.26	0.95	1.12	1.48	0.11	0.25	0.41	0.58	0.78	1.50	1.10	1.06	1.20	1.23	1.30	1.91
1969	1.38	0.86	1.22	1.48	1.98	0.85	0.77	0.96	1.06	1.22	1.37	1.46	1.38	1.61	1.73	1.77	2.43
1970	1.67	1.01	1.47	1.84	2.33	1.04	0.91	1.08	1.34	1.38	1.69	1.78	1.72	2.03	2.02	2.11	3.00
1971	2.13	1.43	1.90	2.26	2.93	1.47	1.25	1.57	1.74	1.86	2.11	2.22	2.18	2.38	2.38	2.64	3.75
1972	2.58	1.87	2.34	2.66	3.45	1.77	1.72	2.12	2.02	2.29	2.70	2.63	2.62	2.73	2.99	3.08	4.28
1973	2.75	2.22	2.62	2.87	3.28	2.22	2.00	2.44	2.39	2.67	2.81	2.91	2.75	2.94	3.14	3.04	3.66
1974	2.50	2.03	2.35	2.56	3.05	2.04	1.89	2.17	2.21	2.49	2.35	2.53	2.50	2.64	2.82	2.64	3.70
1975	2.22	1.76	2.02	2.13	2.99	1.87	1.60	1.80	2.04	1.89	2.13	2.10	2.07	2.22	2.57	2.75	3.64
1976	2.36	1.68	2.15	2.31	3.31	1.79	1.46	1.79	1.96	2.19	2.29	2.17	2.25	2.49	2.79	2.95	4.19
1977	2.73	1.80	2.32	2.61	4.18	1.72	1.57	2.10	2.14	2.24	2.59	2.41	2.46	2.95	2.87	3.13	6.53
1978	2.46	1.57	2.18	2.50	3.59	1.83	1.16	1.71	1.92	2.06	2.57	2.38	2.27	2.84	3.08	3.30	4.38
1979	2.89	1.61	3.39	2.93	3.64	1.53	1.35	1.95	2.21	2.80	5.17	3.37	2.60	2.82	3.32	3.27	4.32
1980	3.55	2.42	3.45	3.78	4.55	2.23	2.11	2.92	3.18	3.46	3.72	3.81	3.37	4.16	4.41	4.07	5.18
1981	3.48	2.36	3.60	3.76	4.18	2.09	2.14	2.85	3.34	3.72	3.75	3.77	3.48	4.03	4.19	3.97	4.38
1982	3.22	2.12	3.26	3.41	4.10	1.86	1.73	2.76	3.00	3.16	3.60	3.47	3.13	3.63	3.79	3.93	4.57
1983	3.41	2.17	3.77	3.51	4.27	2.19	1.89	2.44	2.80	3.39	5.11	3.41	3.30	3.82	3.93	4.16	4.42

Construction, work put in place: (8)(9) — Construction, travaux effectués : (8)(9)
private non-residential — bâtiments non résidentiels, secteur privé
billion DM, monthly averages — milliards de DM, moyennes mensuelles

	Year	Q.1	Q.2	Q.3	Q.4	JAN	FEB	MAR	APR	MAY	JUN	JUL	AUG	SEP	OCT	NOV	DEC
1964	0.74	0.55	0.72	0.82	0.88	0.58	0.50	0.56	0.69	0.67	0.79	0.85	0.80	0.82	0.85	0.81	0.97
1965	0.81	0.62	0.76	0.90	0.97	0.62	0.61	0.62	0.69	0.76	0.82	0.89	0.87	0.94	0.95	0.91	1.05
1966	0.86	0.67	0.85	0.94	0.97	0.67	0.58	0.76	0.78	0.85	0.93	0.91	0.96	0.96	0.96	0.91	1.05
1967	0.76	0.65	0.73	0.78	0.89	0.69	0.58	0.68	0.70	0.71	0.79	0.76	0.80	0.79	0.83	0.80	1.03
1968	0.54	0.19	0.50	0.62	0.86	0.09	0.18	0.29	0.38	0.45	0.66	0.56	0.61	0.70	0.72	0.75	1.09
1969	0.84	0.54	0.71	0.92	1.19	0.55	0.47	0.59	0.65	0.70	0.80	0.86	0.85	1.04	1.09	1.06	1.42
1970	1.15	0.74	1.00	1.29	1.57	0.74	0.65	0.83	0.91	0.94	1.15	1.28	1.21	1.39	1.38	1.41	1.90
1971	1.49	1.12	1.37	1.61	1.86	1.19	0.98	1.19	1.24	1.39	1.48	1.52	1.59	1.71	1.61	1.72	2.26
1972	1.55	1.20	1.50	1.63	1.89	1.20	1.08	1.33	1.33	1.52	1.64	1.59	1.66	1.64	1.62	1.73	2.31
1973	1.66	1.32	1.62	1.75	1.95	1.35	1.17	1.44	1.58	1.58	1.71	1.70	1.66	1.89	1.77	1.83	2.25
1974	1.54	1.30	1.42	1.67	1.77	1.38	1.17	1.35	1.41	1.40	1.46	1.72	1.63	1.65	1.66	1.60	2.04
1975	1.46	1.21	1.30	1.46	1.89	1.23	1.17	1.24	1.27	1.24	1.38	1.52	1.29	1.56	1.71	1.73	2.22
1976	1.61	1.23	1.50	1.66	2.07	1.26	1.05	1.36	1.33	1.52	1.64	1.57	1.63	1.78	1.77	1.87	2.56
1977	1.69	1.20	1.57	1.69	2.31	1.16	1.08	1.35	1.33	1.43	1.96	1.72	1.63	1.73	1.78	1.85	3.29
1978	1.61	1.09	1.44	1.66	2.24	1.24	0.94	1.10	1.24	1.32	1.77	1.59	1.66	1.73	1.95	1.99	2.77
1979	1.90	1.19	1.90	1.99	2.50	1.25	0.95	1.37	1.44	1.70	2.57	2.04	1.87	2.07	2.19	2.34	2.98
1980	2.39	1.72	2.27	2.57	3.01	1.56	1.44	2.16	2.20	2.19	2.42	2.60	2.34	2.77	2.88	2.82	3.34
1981	2.41	1.73	2.33	2.59	2.94	1.67	1.54	1.99	2.26	2.37	2.51	2.69	2.38	2.69	2.79	2.96	3.08
1982	2.34	1.66	2.24	2.59	2.85	1.47	1.46	2.05	2.09	2.13	2.50	2.47	2.49	2.81	2.64	2.71	3.21
1983	2.43	1.73	2.42	2.55	3.01	1.76	1.51	1.92	2.00	2.21	3.05	2.40	2.48	2.76	2.73	2.90	3.41

Cost of construction: residential (6) — Coût de la construction : bâtiments résidentiels (6)
1980 = 100 — 1980 = 100

	Year	Q.1	Q.2	Q.3	Q.4	JAN	FEB	MAR	APR	MAY	JUN	JUL	AUG	SEP	OCT	NOV	DEC
1964	40	39	40	40	40		39			40			40			40	
1965	41	40	41	41	41		40			41			41			41	
1966	42	42	43	43	42		42			43			43			42	
1967	42	42	42	41	41		42			42			41			41	
1968	43	43	43	43	44		43			43			43			44	
1969	46	44	45	46	46		44			45			46			48	
1970	53	50	53	53	54		50			53			53			54	
1971	58	56	58	59	59		56			58			59			59	
1972	62	60	62	62	63		60			62			62			63	
1973	66	64	66	67	67		64			66			67			67	
1974	71	68	71	72	72		68			71			72			72	
1975	72	72	73	73	73		72			73			73			73	
1976	75	73	75	75	76		73			75			75			76	
1977	79	77	79	79	80		77			79			79			80	
1978	83	81	83	84	85		81			83			84			85	
1979	90	86	90	92	93		86			90			92			93	
1980	100	96	100	102	102		96			100			102			102	
1981	106	103	106	107	107		103			106			107			107	
1982	109	108	109	110	109		108			109			110			109	
1983	111	110	111	112	113		110			111			112			113	

Construction, work put in place: (8)
residential
billion DM, monthly averages

Construction, travaux effectués : (8)
bâtiments résidentiels
milliards de DM, moyennes mensuelles

Adjusted - Corrigé

	Year	Q.1	Q.2	Q.3	Q.4	JAN	FEB	MAR	APR	MAY	JUN	JUL	AUG	SEP	OCT	NOV	DEC
1964		1.17	1.28	1.26	1.28	1.10	1.18	1.24	1.29	1.25	1.29	1.27	1.25	1.25	1.26	1.25	1.32
1965		1.31	1.35	1.34	1.29	1.37	1.35	1.20	1.37	1.34	1.34	1.37	1.31	1.33	1.34	1.30	1.22
1966		1.45	1.49	1.39	1.32	1.35	1.36	1.63	1.51	1.49	1.46	1.41	1.39	1.37	1.37	1.32	1.26
1967		1.63	1.53	1.46	1.46	1.56	1.66	1.67	1.56	1.52	1.50	1.50	1.48	1.41	1.46	1.48	1.44
1968		0.36	1.00	1.03	1.17	0.16	0.39	0.54	0.68	0.79	1.52	0.98	1.02	1.09	1.04	1.17	1.31
1969		1.22	1.30	1.38	1.55	1.20	1.20	1.25	1.25	1.30	1.34	1.32	1.37	1.44	1.47	1.60	1.57
1970		1.43	1.56	1.72	1.83	1.46	1.41	1.43	1.52	1.56	1.60	1.63	1.72	1.82	1.77	1.86	1.87
1971		1.98	2.05	2.14	2.24	2.07	1.91	1.96	2.07	2.04	2.05	2.12	2.15	2.15	2.14	2.29	2.28
1972		2.54	2.50	2.56	2.68	2.40	2.53	2.68	2.44	2.47	2.58	2.61	2.56	2.52	2.63	2.65	2.76
1973		2.97	2.83	2.79	2.57	2.88	2.93	3.11	2.88	2.83	2.79	2.86	2.73	2.78	2.71	2.60	2.40
1974		2.74	2.56	2.49	2.36	2.63	2.79	2.80	2.60	2.64	2.44	2.47	2.55	2.44	2.41	2.29	2.37
1975		2.41	2.17	2.08	2.28	2.43	2.40	2.41	2.31	2.12	2.08	2.06	2.18	2.01	2.19	2.40	2.26
1976		2.29	2.29	2.25	2.48	2.41	2.24	2.22	2.29	2.34	2.23	2.17	2.32	2.25	2.44	2.49	2.51
1977		2.48	2.47	2.53	3.05	2.36	2.51	2.58	2.53	2.38	2.50	2.45	2.50	2.65	2.50	2.62	4.04
1978		2.21	2.26	2.43	2.73	2.54	1.91	2.19	2.20	2.19	2.38	2.41	2.31	2.58	2.60	2.74	2.85
1979		2.30	3.46	2.85	2.79	2.18	2.26	2.46	2.56	2.82	5.00	3.31	2.64	2.60	2.72	2.70	2.96
1980		3.51	3.58	3.61	3.51	3.27	3.51	3.76	3.58	3.58	3.57	3.62	3.57	3.65	3.59	3.41	3.53
1981		3.48	3.70	3.58	3.25	3.18	3.63	3.63	3.75	3.80	3.56	3.55	3.67	3.52	3.46	3.27	3.01
1982		3.10	3.29	3.23	3.19	2.92	2.95	3.42	3.34	3.20	3.34	3.31	3.22	3.16	3.18	3.21	3.17
1983		3.20	3.75	3.32	3.28	3.38	3.22	3.01	3.17	3.33	4.74	3.31	3.33	3.33	3.29	3.40	3.16

Construction, work put in place: (8)(9)
private non-residential
billion DM, monthly averages

Construction, travaux effectués : (8)(9)
bâtiments non résidentiels, secteur privé
milliards de DM, moyennes mensuelles

Adjusted - Corrigé

	Year	Q.1	Q.2	Q.3	Q.4	JAN	FEB	MAR	APR	MAY	JUN	JUL	AUG	SEP	OCT	NOV	DEC
1964		0.71	0.75	0.74	0.74	0.71	0.72	0.71	0.77	0.74	0.75	0.77	0.74	0.72	0.73	0.73	0.76
1965		0.80	0.80	0.82	0.81	0.78	0.88	0.75	0.80	0.80	0.80	0.82	0.80	0.83	0.83	0.80	0.80
1966		0.87	0.90	0.86	0.81	0.84	0.85	0.92	0.91	0.90	0.90	0.86	0.87	0.84	0.84	0.81	0.79
1967		0.86	0.78	0.72	0.74	0.86	0.86	0.85	0.81	0.77	0.75	0.72	0.73	0.70	0.72	0.71	0.78
1968		0.25	0.53	0.57	0.70	0.11	0.27	0.36	0.44	0.48	0.68	0.52	0.57	0.62	0.62	0.67	0.80
1969		0.70	0.77	0.85	0.97	0.69	0.69	0.72	0.76	0.76	0.80	0.82	0.82	0.91	0.95	0.96	1.00
1970		0.97	1.07	1.20	1.26	0.95	0.95	1.02	1.03	1.07	1.12	1.21	1.17	1.22	1.23	1.25	1.29
1971		1.46	1.48	1.50	1.50	1.54	1.44	1.39	1.44	1.54	1.46	1.46	1.53	1.52	1.47	1.52	1.51
1972		1.54	1.61	1.54	1.53	1.50	1.54	1.58	1.58	1.66	1.60	1.55	1.59	1.48	1.46	1.52	1.62
1973		1.67	1.76	1.66	1.59	1.64	1.67	1.70	1.87	1.69	1.72	1.64	1.60	1.74	1.57	1.60	1.60
1974		1.66	1.56	1.58	1.44	1.68	1.69	1.62	1.65	1.50	1.52	1.62	1.60	1.51	1.47	1.42	1.42
1975		1.53	1.40	1.38	1.52	1.50	1.71	1.54	1.44	1.39	1.38	1.43	1.30	1.41	1.51	1.54	1.51
1976		1.58	1.61	1.57	1.63	1.59	1.55	1.60	1.54	1.66	1.63	1.50	1.61	1.60	1.60	1.62	1.67
1977		1.57	1.69	1.60	1.82	1.50	1.64	1.57	1.56	1.56	1.94	1.66	1.59	1.55	1.62	1.62	2.23
1978		1.46	1.52	1.58	1.77	1.61	1.44	1.32	1.42	1.45	1.69	1.52	1.63	1.58	1.70	1.70	1.90
1979		1.59	2.02	1.88	1.99	1.66	1.49	1.63	1.69	1.81	2.55	1.92	1.82	1.90	1.87	1.98	2.12
1980		2.32	2.42	2.40	2.41	2.11	2.23	2.61	2.51	2.38	2.38	2.40	2.35	2.45	2.45	2.43	2.35
1981		2.37	2.53	2.40	2.36	2.30	2.41	2.40	2.56	2.57	2.46	2.48	2.37	2.36	2.41	2.51	2.17
1982		2.26	2.36	2.40	2.29	2.06	2.29	2.42	2.36	2.30	2.41	2.32	2.44	2.45	2.32	2.29	2.26
1983		2.36	2.52	2.36	2.43	2.45	2.37	2.26	2.28	2.34	2.94	2.30	2.40	2.39	2.39	2.45	2.46

GERMANY

Wholesale sales: value (6)(10) — Ventes du commerce de gros : valeur (6)(10)

1980 = 100

	Year	Q.1	Q.2	Q.3	Q.4	JAN	FEB	MAR	APR	MAY	JUN	JUL	AUG	SEP	OCT	NOV	DEC
1964	35	31	35	36	38	30	30	33	36	32	35	37	35	38	39	37	39
1965	38	34	38	40	41	31	32	38	38	37	39	39	39	42	40	41	42
1966	39	37	39	40	40	33	34	42	38	39	40	38	40	41	39	40	40
1967	39	35	38	39	43	33	33	38	37	38	40	38	40	40	42	41	46
1968	40	35	40	41	44	32	34	38	39	42	39	40	41	41	45	43	44
1969	45	39	45	47	50	37	36	43	45	45	44	47	45	50	52	48	52
1970	=50=	45	51	50	53	42	44	49	53	47	52	50	48	53	53	51	54
1971	53	49	53	54	57	43	47	56	54	51	55	53	52	57	56	56	58
1972	56	51	55	55	62	45	50	57	52	56	56	52	56	58	62	62	63
1973	65	60	64	64	71	56	57	65	61	67	63	62	65	64	73	73	69
1974	73	69	73	73	76	67	66	74	74	77	67	75	71	74	82	75	73
1975	71	67	70	71	76	68	66	68	74	68	69	70	67	75	79	72	76
1976	79	73	78	80	85	67	70	83	78	77	79	77	79	85	82	87	86
1977	82	78	81	81	87	71	73	89	79	81	84	76	80	86	83	86	90
1978	85	78	85	84	92	74	75	86	84	84	88	81	84	88	92	93	90
1979	95	85	97	95	102	79	80	96	91	100	100	94	95	97	108	103	94
1980	=100=	98	99	99	104	96	95	104	103	98	98	100	91	105	109	99	104
1981	106	101	102	108	113	93	101	110	103	99	104	107	102	115	118	109	110
1982	108	105	107	106	113	94	101	121	109	104	107	102	104	114	110	113	116
1983	109	104	110	108	117	95	96	120	106	109	114	98	109	117	116	117	117

Wholesale sales: volume (6)(10) — Ventes du commerce de gros : volume (6)(10)

1980 = 100

	Year	Q.1	Q.2	Q.3	Q.4	JAN	FEB	MAR	APR	MAY	JUN	JUL	AUG	SEP	OCT	NOV	DEC
1964	60	53	60	62	65	51	52	57	62	56	61	63	60	65	67	63	66
1965	64	57	63	67	68	52	54	64	63	62	64	65	65	70	67	68	70
1966	65	60	65	66	66	55	57	70	63	65	66	63	67	69	65	67	66
1967	64	57	63	65	72	55	54	63	61	63	66	63	67	66	70	69	77
1968	70	61	71	73	78	55	60	67	69	74	68	72	74	74	80	76	77
1969	78	68	77	81	86	66	64	75	78	77	76	81	78	85	89	82	88
1970	=84=	76	85	85	88	71	75	82	90	79	87	84	81	89	90	85	90
1971	87	80	86	89	93	72	77	92	87	83	88	87	86	93	92	93	95
1972	88	82	87	87	96	73	80	92	84	89	90	83	89	90	96	96	97
1973	93	89	92	91	100	84	85	96	89	97	90	88	94	91	104	102	94
1974	93	90	92	93	96	89	86	94	94	97	85	95	90	94	103	94	92
1975	88	84	87	87	93	85	82	85	92	84	85	87	83	91	96	88	93
1976	92	87	90	93	98	80	83	98	90	89	91	89	91	98	94	100	100
1977	93	89	92	93	100	81	83	101	89	91	95	87	93	99	97	100	104
1978	98	90	98	98	106	86	86	99	97	97	101	93	97	102	107	107	103
1979	102	95	105	101	107	90	90	105	99	108	108	100	101	102	115	109	98
1980	=100=	99	99	98	103	98	96	104	103	98	97	99	91	105	109	98	102
1981	98	97	95	99	101	90	96	104	96	92	97	99	93	104	107	98	99
1982	94	93	93	93	98	83	89	107	96	90	93	88	91	100	95	98	101
1983	96	92	97	94	101	84	85	107	94	96	100	86	95	102	101	101	101

Retail sales: value (6)(11) — Ventes au détail : valeur (6)(11)

1980 = 100

	Year	Q.1	Q.2	Q.3	Q.4	JAN	FEB	MAR	APR	MAY	JUN	JUL	AUG	SEP	OCT	NOV	DEC
1964	33	29	31	31	41	28	27	32	32	31	30	33	29	30	37	37	49
1965	36	31	35	35	44	29	29	34	37	35	34	37	33	35	39	41	52
1966	38	34	37	37	45	32	32	39	39	38	36	38	35	36	39	42	52
1967	39	35	37	37	46	33	32	39	37	38	37	38	36	37	39	42	56
1968	40	35	39	38	49	33	33	39	41	40	37	40	38	38	43	47	57
1969	44	38	43	43	54	37	35	42	43	44	40	44	41	43	49	50	64
1970	=49=	42	48	47	61	40	39	47	49	47	48	51	44	48	55	56	71
1971	55	48	54	52	65	45	44	54	56	53	52	55	48	53	59	63	73
1972	60	54	57	58	71	49	50	62	55	59	57	58	57	58	63	67	82
1973	64	58	64	60	75	56	55	65	64	64	63	61	58	60	69	72	84
1974	68	60	66	65	80	59	55	66	69	69	62	68	63	64	75	76	89
1975	74	65	72	70	88	64	61	71	74	73	69	73	66	72	82	81	100
1976	79	71	77	75	93	69	67	78	80	76	75	77	70	77	82	89	108
1977	85	76	82	81	100	71	70	86	82	83	82	83	77	83	86	95	118
1978	89	81	87	85	103	77	75	92	87	87	88	85	82	88	93	98	119
1979	95	86	95	88	110	82	78	98	93	96	94	89	83	88	102	106	123
1980	=100=	94	96	95	116	92	88	100	99	98	92	99	89	96	109	108	131
1981	104	96	100	98	121	92	91	104	104	99	97	104	93	99	113	112	138
1982	105	98	102	98	121	92	91	112	107	100	100	101	93	98	108	114	140
1983	108	101	105	101	124	93	92	119	104	105	109	99	97	106	112	118	142

Wholesale sales: value (6)(10) — Adjusted - Corrigé * — Ventes du commerce de gros : valeur (6)(10)

1980 = 100

	Year	Q.1	Q.2	Q.3	Q.4	JAN	FEB	MAR	APR	MAY	JUN	JUL	AUG	SEP	OCT	NOV	DEC
1964		34	34	35	36	34	34	34	34	34	34	35	35	36	36	36	36
1965		37	38	39	39	37	37	36	37	38	38	38	38	39	38	39	39
1966		40	39	39	38	39	39	40	39	39	39	39	39	39	38	38	38
1967		38	38	39	41	38	38	38	37	38	38	39	38	39	39	39	45
1968		37	40	40	42	36	37	38	39	40	40	40	41	40	41	42	42
1969		42	44	47	48	42	41	43	44	45	44	46	47	47	47	48	48
1970		49	50	50	50	48	50	49	50	49	50	50	50	50	50	50	50
1971		52	53	54	54	51	52	53	53	53	53	54	53	54	54	54	54
1972		54	54	56	60	52	53	56	52	54	55	55	56	57	58	59	63
1973		62	63	65	68	62	63	62	62	64	65	64	65	65	67	69	69
1974		72	73	74	73	73	72	73	74	73	71	75	73	73	74	73	72
1975		72	69	71	72	73	72	70	70	68	69	70	71	72	72	72	73
1976		76	78	80	81	74	76	77	77	78	79	79	82	81	79	82	81
1977		81	81	81	83	82	81	81	81	81	82	81	82	81	81	82	87
1978		83	84	86	88	83	83	82	84	84	85	86	84	86	87	87	90
1979		88	97	97	97	86	88	90	92	96	103	97	96	97	99	98	94
1980		101	100	99	99	103	100	100	102	99	99	100	98	99	99	100	99
1981		105	102	108	107	103	110	103	101	102	104	107	109	109	110	108	104
1982		109	107	107	108	107	110	109	108	108	106	105	108	107	106	108	110
1983		107	110	108	113	109	105	107	108	110	113	106	110	110	112	112	114

Wholesale sales: volume (6)(10) — Adjusted - Corrigé * — Ventes du commerce de gros : volume (6)(10)

1980 = 100

	Year	Q.1	Q.2	Q.3	Q.4	JAN	FEB	MAR	APR	MAY	JUN	JUL	AUG	SEP	OCT	NOV	DEC
1964		58	59	60	62	58	59	59	59	59	59	60	60	61	62	61	61
1965		62	63	64	65	62	62	61	63	64	64	64	64	65	65	65	65
1966		66	65	64	63	66	65	66	65	65	64	65	64	64	63	63	63
1967		63	63	64	69	64	63	63	62	62	64	64	64	64	66	65	76
1968		65	71	71	73	62	65	67	69	71	72	70	72	72	72	74	74
1969		74	77	80	82	74	73	76	77	77	76	79	80	81	81	82	82
1970		83	84	84	83	82	84	83	84	83	84	83	83	84	84	83	84
1971		86	86	88	88	85	86	86	86	86	86	88	87	88	89	88	89
1972		87	86	88	92	86	86	90	84	87	87	87	88	89	90	90	96
1973		93	93	92	94	93	94	92	91	93	93	91	93	92	94	95	94
1974		95	93	93	91	96	95	93	94	94	91	96	92	93	92	90	89
1975		90	86	87	87	91	91	88	88	86	85	87	88	87	86	88	88
1976		90	91	93	93	89	91	91	90	92	92	92	94	92	90	94	94
1977		93	92	93	96	93	92	93	91	93	93	93	94	93	92	94	101
1978		96	98	99	101	96	96	96	98	97	98	99	98	100	99	100	103
1979		99	106	103	101	98	99	99	102	105	111	104	102	102	103	102	98
1980		103	100	99	98	105	102	101	103	99	99	99	98	99	98	99	97
1981		101	96	99	96	99	106	97	95	96	97	99	100	98	98	96	93
1982		96	94	93	93	94	98	97	95	95	92	91	95	93	91	93	96
1983		95	98	95	97	96	94	96	97	98	99	93	96	94	96	96	98

Retail sales: value (6)(11) — Adjusted - Corrigé — Ventes au détail : valeur (6)(11)

1980 = 100

	Year	Q.1	Q.2	Q.3	Q.4	JAN	FEB	MAR	APR	MAY	JUN	JUL	AUG	SEP	OCT	NOV	DEC
1964		32	32	33	35	32	32	33	32	32	32	33	33	33	34	35	35
1965		35	36	37	37	35	35	34	37	36	36	37	37	37	37	37	37
1966		38	38	39	38	38	39	38	38	39	38	39	39	39	38	38	37
1967		39	38	39	39	40	39	39	37	38	39	39	39	39	38	38	41
1968		38	40	41	42	38	39	39	40	40	40	40	42	41	41	42	42
1969		42	44	45	47	42	42	43	43	44	44	45	46	46	46	47	47
1970		47	49	50	52	46	46	48	47	49	50	50	49	50	51	53	52
1971		53	54	55	56	53	53	53	54	55	54	55	54	56	56	57	54
1972		58	58	61	62	57	58	60	56	59	59	60	63	61	62	61	62
1973		64	64	64	65	63	65	63	65	64	64	63	64	65	65	65	65
1974		66	67	69	70	66	65	66	67	68	66	69	68	69	71	69	69
1975		72	73	74	77	71	72	72	72	72	74	74	74	75	77	77	76
1976		77	78	79	80	77	79	76	78	78	77	78	79	80	79	81	81
1977		82	84	86	86	82	82	83	80	86	85	86	85	86	84	87	88
1978		88	88	90	91	88	87	88	88	87	90	89	90	91	90	90	92
1979		92	96	95	96	91	91	93	95	96	97	94	96	95	96	96	96
1980		100	98	101	101	103	99	99	97	98	98	101	100	101	102	102	100
1981		104	102	105	106	102	107	103	103	103	100	105	105	104	106	106	105
1982		106	104	104	105	106	106	107	105	104	103	103	105	103	104	105	105
1983		109	109	107	108	106	107	114	102	110	114	103	106	111	109	108	106

* Adjusted by the O.E.C.D. — * Corrigé par l'O.C.D.E.

GERMANY

Retail sales: volume (6)(11) — Ventes au détail : volume (6)(11)

1980 = 100

	Year	Q.1	Q.2	Q.3	Q.4	JAN	FEB	MAR	APR	MAY	JUN	JUL	AUG	SEP	OCT	NOV	DEC
1964	57	50	54	53	71	48	47	55	56	54	53	57	50	53	64	64	85
1965	62	53	60	59	74	50	50	59	64	59	58	63	55	59	65	69	87
1966	64	57	62	61	74	53	53	64	64	63	59	64	59	61	66	70	87
1967	64	58	62	61	76	55	53	64	61	62	61	62	59	61	65	70	93
1968	67	58	65	64	81	54	54	64	68	66	61	66	64	63	72	77	93
1969	73	62	70	70	83	61	57	69	70	72	66	73	67	70	80	82	103
1970	78	67	76	75	95	65	62	75	77	75	75	80	69	75	87	88	110
1971	82	73	81	79	97	69	67	83	84	81	78	83	73	80	88	93	109
1972	86	78	83	83	100	72	73	90	81	86	83	83	83	84	90	95	116
1973	87	81	86	81	99	78	76	89	87	88	85	82	79	82	92	95	110
1974	85	77	84	81	99	76	71	85	87	87	78	85	79	80	93	94	109
1975	88	79	86	84	104	78	74	86	89	87	82	86	79	86	98	96	118
1976	92	84	89	86	107	81	78	91	93	88	86	90	81	89	95	103	124
1977	95	85	92	90	111	80	79	97	92	93	91	92	86	92	96	105	131
1978	97	89	95	92	112	84	82	100	95	94	96	92	89	96	101	107	129
1979	100	92	100	93	114	88	83	104	99	101	99	93	92	92	106	110	127
1980	100	95	96	94	114	94	90	101	99	98	91	99	88	96	108	106	129
1981	99	93	95	93	113	90	89	100	99	94	92	98	88	93	106	104	129
1982	95	90	92	88	108	85	83	103	98	90	89	91	84	88	97	102	126
1983	95	90	94	89	109	83	82	106	92	93	96	87	85	93	98	104	124

Employment: manufacturing (12)(13) (all employees) — Emploi : industries manufacturières (12)(13) (salariés)

thousands — milliers

	Year	Q.1	Q.2	Q.3	Q.4	JAN	FEB	MAR	APR	MAY	JUN	JUL	AUG	SEP	OCT	NOV	DEC
1964	7805	7695	7791	7841	7890	7678	7695	7714	7790	7792	7791	7815	7843	7866	7891	7918	7862
1965	7986	7896	8002	8024	8023	7862	7892	7934	8005	8005	7995	8008	8029	8036	8039	8051	7978
1966	7949	7966	8017	7985	7830	7957	7964	7977	8026	8019	8005	7997	7996	7961	7907	7846	7736
1967	7465	7573	7443	7429	7414	7640	7568	7510	7469	7445	7416	7411	7431	7445	7441	7433	7369
1968	7562	7397	7471	7625	7756	7369	7402	7420	7449	7473	7489	7556	7627	7691	7746	7778	7743
1969	7991	7824	7913	8053	8172	7771	7826	7874	7899	7908	7932	7998	8048	8114	8161	8188	8167
1970	8578	8498	8543	8633	8638	8456	8503	8533	8546	8539	8545	8594	8644	8660	8661	8659	8593
1971	8519	8560	8515	8532	8469	8562	8556	8562	8535	8506	8504	8513	8534	8549	8512	8485	8410
1972	8345	8356	8323	8348	8352	8357	8357	8353	8325	8321	8323	8328	8354	8364	8365	8372	8319
1973	8402	8352	8380	8447	8428	8323	8362	8371	8374	8381	8386	8417	8456	8467	8472	8450	8364
1974	8182	8292	8229	8183	8024	8310	8294	8273	8252	8232	8203	8201	8186	8162	8110	8026	7935
1975	7633	7790	7658	7586	7499	7842	7788	7739	7698	7657	7619	7598	7586	7576	7536	7505	7454
1976	7452	7402	7422	7489	7494	7393	7397	7414	7412	7419	7434	7449	7490	7528	7514	7505	7463
1977	7392	7363	7368	7427	7410	7352	7362	7375	7368	7363	7373	7395	7431	7455	7435	7419	7376
1978	7350	7336	7314	7372	7378	7341	7334	7335	7314	7307	7321	7334	7380	7404	7397	7390	7347
1979	7378	7321	7329	7416	7447	7311	7319	7332	7320	7328	7341	7373	7421	7455	7461	7461	7419
1980	7429	7419	7418	7462	7415	7403	7421	7433	7420	7414	7421	7449	7457	7482	7451	7423	7370
1981	7251	7307	7252	7264	7180	7323	7302	7296	7268	7247	7242	7255	7263	7275	7195	7203	7143
1982	6994	7068	7011	7002	6893	7083	7062	7058	7028	7006	7000	6999	7007	7000	6940	6900	6841
1983	6701	6738	6680	6704	6684	6758	6731	6725	6690	6677	6675	6675	6707	6730	6706	6693	6652

Unemployment (registered unemployed) (14) — Chômage (chômeurs inscrits) (14)

thousands — milliers

	Year	Q.1	Q.2	Q.3	Q.4	JAN	FEB	MAR	APR	MAY	JUN	JUL	AUG	SEP	OCT	NOV	DEC
1964	169	290	129	103	147	338	305	227	147	127	112	105	103	100	112	127	202
1965	147	260	110	87	130	286	291	201	127	107	95	89	86	85	92	119	178
1966	161	215	110	107	245	269	236	141	121	108	101	102	106	113	146	216	372
1967	460	624	454	359	427	621	674	576	501	459	401	377	360	341	361	395	526
1968	324	574	274	188	214	673	590	460	331	265	227	203	188	175	180	196	266
1969	179	329	130	104	140	369	374	243	155	123	111	108	104	101	108	119	192
1970	149	249	106	99	139	286	264	198	121	103	95	99	100	97	111	130	175
1971	185	249	146	145	216	286	255	207	160	143	135	142	146	147	170	208	270
1972	246	338	210	197	243	376	369	269	231	208	190	197	198	195	215	235	279
1973	274	330	218	219	362	356	347	287	241	211	201	217	222	219	267	332	486
1974	583	601	475	525	806	621	620	562	517	457	451	491	527	557	672	799	946
1975	1074	1151	1036	1024	1133	1154	1184	1114	1087	1018	1002	1035	1031	1006	1061	1114	1223
1976	1060	1296	989	928	1006	1351	1347	1190	1094	954	921	945	940	899	944	985	1090
1977	1030	1182	972	949	1017	1249	1214	1084	1039	947	931	973	964	911	954	1004	1091
1978	993	1179	930	904	945	1214	1224	1099	1000	913	877	922	924	864	902	927	1007
1979	876	1088	805	780	309	1171	1134	958	876	775	763	804	799	737	762	799	867
1980	889	968	791	847	991	1037	993	876	825	767	781	853	865	823	888	968	1118
1981	1272	1273	1127	1264	1520	1309	1300	1210	1147	1110	1126	1246	1289	1256	1366	1490	1704
1982	1833	1899	1669	1788	2061	1950	1935	1811	1710	1646	1650	1757	1787	1820	1920	2038	2223
1983	2258	2470	2177	2178	2230	2487	2536	2387	2254	2149	2127	2202	2196	2134	2148	2193	2349

Retail sales: volume (6)(11)
1980 = 100

Adjusted - Corrigé

Ventes au détail : volume (6)(11)
1980 = 100

	Year	Q.1	Q.2	Q.3	Q.4	JAN	FEB	MAR	APR	MAY	JUN	JUL	AUG	SEP	OCT	NOV	DEC
1964		56	56	57	60	55	55	57	55	56	56	57	56	57	59	59	61
1965		60	61	63	62	60	60	59	62	61	61	63	62	63	63	62	61
1966		64	64	64	63	63	64	64	63	65	64	65	64	64	64	63	61
1967		65	63	64	65	66	64	64	62	62	65	64	64	65	63	63	68
1968		64	66	68	69	63	64	65	67	66	66	66	69	68	68	69	70
1969		70	71	74	75	69	69	71	70	72	72	73	74	74	74	76	76
1970		75	77	79	81	73	74	77	76	77	79	80	78	79	80	82	81
1971		81	83	83	83	81	81	81	83	83	82	83	82	84	84	84	80
1972		86	84	88	87	85	85	88	81	86	86	86	90	87	87	86	88
1973		89	88	86	85	89	90	87	89	88	87	85	86	88	87	85	84
1974		85	85	86	86	86	85	85	86	86	84	86	86	86	88	85	84
1975		87	87	88	90	86	88	88	87	87	88	88	88	89	91	91	89
1976		90	91	92	92	90	92	89	91	91	90	91	91	93	90	94	92
1977		93	94	95	95	93	93	94	90	96	95	96	95	95	93	96	97
1978		97	96	98	98	97	96	97	96	95	98	97	98	99	98	97	99
1979		98	102	99	99	98	98	99	101	102	102	98	100	99	100	99	99
1980		102	98	100	100	105	101	100	98	98	98	101	99	100	101	100	98
1981		101	97	99	98	100	103	99	99	98	95	100	99	98	99	98	97
1982		98	94	93	93	98	97	98	96	94	93	92	94	93	93	93	94
1983		97	97	94	94	95	95	101	91	98	102	91	93	97	95	95	93

Employment: manufacturing (12)(13)
(all employees)
thousands

Adjusted - Corrigé *

Emploi : industries manufacturières (13)/(12)
(salariés)
milliers

	Year	Q.1	Q.2	Q.3	Q.4	JAN	FEB	MAR	APR	MAY	JUN	JUL	AUG	SEP	OCT	NOV	DEC
1964		7739	7783	7818	7875	7732	7741	7745	7782	7776	7791	7800	7819	7835	7852	7879	7893
1965		7944	7999	7998	8004	7918	7940	7974	7997	7997	8003	8000	7997	7996	7999	8003	8010
1966		8009	8020	7956	7806	8005	8012	8009	8026	8019	8013	7989	7964	7914	7859	7800	7760
1967		7605	7451	7408	7399	7682	7600	7533	7467	7452	7432	7409	7407	7408	7404	7396	7396
1968		7421	7484	7605	7739	7404	7425	7435	7450	7488	7512	7558	7605	7653	7708	7742	7767
1969		7843	7931	8034	8155	7804	7842	7882	7903	7929	7961	8003	8026	8073	8122	8151	8190
1970		8514	8566	8612	8618	8490	8517	8537	8555	8565	8577	8601	8620	8615	8620	8620	8615
1971		8578	8539	8509	8447	8596	8570	8567	8549	8533	8535	8517	8507	8503	8469	8444	8428
1972		8378	8348	8322	8327	8394	8377	8364	8344	8348	8351	8329	8323	8313	8317	8330	8334
1973		8381	8407	8416	8400	8363	8389	8391	8400	8409	8411	8416	8421	8410	8418	8405	8376
1974		8327	8256	8150	7994	8354	8327	8300	8283	8260	8226	8198	8150	8102	8055	7982	7944
1975		7826	7685	7554	7469	7885	7824	7769	7730	7685	7639	7595	7550	7516	7483	7463	7460
1976		7437	7450	7456	7463	7433	7433	7444	7446	7450	7454	7448	7454	7465	7460	7463	7466
1977		7398	7398	7393	7379	7391	7399	7403	7404	7396	7395	7394	7395	7390	7382	7377	7377
1978		7370	7346	7339	7347	7378	7370	7362	7350	7342	7344	7334	7345	7338	7345	7349	7348
1979		7353	7364	7381	7415	7348	7355	7358	7357	7367	7368	7375	7383	7386	7408	7419	7418
1980		7450	7449	7429	7386	7440	7456	7455	7455	7450	7443	7443	7427	7418	7403	7385	7371
1981		7338	7282	7232	7153	7359	7337	7316	7301	7282	7264	7249	7234	7213	7148	7167	7144
1982		7098	7042	6972	6867	7118	7097	7079	7061	7041	7024	6996	6980	6940	6895	6865	6842
1983		6767	6711	6679	6662	6792	6764	6745	6722	6712	6699	6673	6687	6676	6666	6660	6658

Unemployment (registered unemployed) (14)
thousands

Adjusted - Corrigé

Chômage (chômeurs inscrits) (14)
milliers

	Year	Q.1	Q.2	Q.3	Q.4	JAN	FEB	MAR	APR	MAY	JUN	JUL	AUG	SEP	OCT	NOV	DEC
1964		167	172	172	161	168	153	179	171	173	172	172	172	171	172	162	150
1965		143	143	152	145	133	143	153	141	142	147	149	151	155	151	153	131
1966		104	140	179	264	116	102	95	127	139	153	165	178	195	221	262	309
1967		434	522	498	460	382	439	482	516	533	517	509	499	486	477	456	447
1968		391	327	276	232	423	376	374	348	324	309	289	275	263	248	234	214
1969		197	171	164	148	196	212	183	174	168	170	168	163	160	152	143	149
1970		144	144	150	145	142	139	150	139	145	147	150	151	150	149	148	139
1971		152	184	203	222	152	142	163	175	184	192	198	203	209	215	227	225
1972		229	250	265	249	228	239	221	240	253	256	260	265	270	265	252	231
1973		223	253	293	364	214	221	234	239	254	267	281	293	304	325	351	415
1974		458	527	632	807	436	451	487	509	523	550	583	629	685	753	821	848
1975		957	1114	1162	1137	905	954	1011	1071	1122	1149	1159	1160	1167	1154	1137	1120
1976		1101	1061	1037	1011	1097	1111	1095	1080	1053	1050	1042	1038	1032	1020	1006	1008
1977		1008	1044	1044	1025	1018	1000	1006	1034	1045	1052	1053	1044	1036	1029	1029	1018
1978		1010	1003	987	956	990	1013	1027	1006	1012	992	990	990	982	974	953	941
1979		925	875	856	820	945	934	897	887	868	869	861	857	849	833	825	802
1980		812	863	928	1002	815	805	815	841	859	889	911	928	944	970	999	1038
1981		1089	1214	1365	1533	1054	1083	1131	1166	1219	1258	1319	1372	1405	1470	1530	1599
1982		1668	1776	1917	2077	1641	1661	1703	1735	1777	1815	1854	1905	1993	2042	2085	2103
1983		2201	2299	2319	2248	2145	2207	2252	2280	2298	2318	2319	2323	2314	2275	2242	2228

* Adjusted by the O.E.C.D.

* Corrigé par l'O.C.D.E.

GERMANY

Unemployment (registered unemployed) (14)(15)

as per cent of civilian labour force

Chômage (chômeurs inscrits) (14)(15)

en pourcentage de la main-d'œuvre civile

	Year	Q.1	Q.2	Q.3	Q.4	JAN	FEB	MAR	APR	MAY	JUN	JUL	AUG	SEP	OCT	NOV	DEC
1964	0.8	1.3	0.6	0.5	0.7	1.5	1.3	1.0	0.6	0.6	0.5	0.5	0.5	0.4	0.5	0.6	0.9
1965	0.7	1.2	0.5	0.4	0.6	1.3	1.3	0.9	0.6	0.5	0.4	0.4	0.4	0.4	0.4	0.5	0.8
1966	0.7	0.9	0.5	0.5	1.1	1.2	1.0	0.6	0.5	0.5	0.4	0.4	0.5	0.5	0.6	1.0	1.6
1967	2.1	2.9	2.1	1.7	2.0	2.9	3.1	2.7	2.3	2.1	1.9	1.8	1.7	1.6	1.7	1.8	2.4
1968	1.5	2.7	1.3	0.9	1.0	3.2	2.8	2.2	1.6	1.3	1.1	1.0	0.9	0.8	0.9	0.9	1.3
1969	0.9	1.6	0.6	0.5	0.7	1.8	1.8	1.2	0.7	0.6	0.5	0.5	0.5	0.5	0.5	0.6	0.9
1970	0.7	1.1	0.5	0.5	0.6	1.3	1.2	0.9	0.6	0.5	0.4	0.5	0.5	0.5	0.5	0.6	0.8
1971	0.9	1.2	0.7	0.7	1.0	1.3	1.2	1.0	0.7	0.7	0.6	0.7	0.7	0.7	0.8	1.0	1.2
1972	1.1	1.5	1.0	0.9	1.1	1.7	1.7	1.2	1.1	1.0	0.9	0.9	0.9	0.9	1.0	1.1	1.3
1973	1.3	1.5	1.0	1.0	1.6	1.6	1.5	1.3	1.1	0.9	0.9	1.0	1.0	1.0	1.2	1.5	2.2
1974	2.6	2.6	2.1	2.3	3.6	2.7	2.7	2.5	2.3	2.0	2.0	2.2	2.3	2.4	3.0	3.5	4.2
1975	4.7	5.0	4.5	4.5	4.9	5.0	5.2	4.9	4.7	4.4	4.4	4.5	4.5	4.4	4.6	4.9	5.3
1976	4.6	5.7	4.3	4.0	4.4	5.9	5.9	5.2	4.8	4.2	4.0	4.1	4.1	3.9	4.1	4.3	4.8
1977	4.5	5.2	4.3	4.2	4.5	5.5	5.3	4.8	4.6	4.2	4.1	4.3	4.3	4.0	4.2	4.4	4.8
1978	4.3	5.2	4.1	3.9	4.1	5.4	5.4	4.9	4.4	4.0	3.9	4.0	4.0	3.8	3.9	4.1	4.4
1979	3.8	4.8	3.5	3.4	3.5	5.1	5.0	4.2	3.8	3.4	3.3	3.5	3.5	3.2	3.3	3.5	3.8
1980	3.8	4.2	3.4	3.6	4.3	4.5	4.3	3.8	3.6	3.3	3.4	3.7	3.7	3.5	3.8	4.2	4.8
1981	5.5	5.5	4.8	5.4	6.5	5.6	5.6	5.2	4.9	4.8	4.8	5.3	5.5	5.4	5.9	6.4	7.3
1982	7.5	8.0	7.0	7.4	8.5	8.2	8.1	7.6	7.2	6.9	6.8	7.2	7.4	7.5	7.9	8.4	9.1
1983	9.1	10.1	8.9	8.8	9.0	10.2	10.4	9.8	9.2	8.8	8.7	8.9	8.9	8.6	8.7	8.8	9.5

Jobs vacant, unfilled vacancies (14)

thousands

Offres d'emploi non satisfaites (14)

milliers

	Year	Q.1	Q.2	Q.3	Q.4	JAN	FEB	MAR	APR	MAY	JUN	JUL	AUG	SEP	OCT	NOV	DEC
1964	609.2	569.8	634.4	676.0	566.7	500.7	585.9	622.9	614.3	627.1	661.9	676.5	680.9	670.6	627.3	571.1	501.7
1965	649.0	612.5	682.4	716.4	588.2	563.4	608.5	665.5	661.0	683.5	702.6	729.2	720.3	699.7	659.5	582.6	522.5
1966	539.8	587.1	608.2	583.0	335.6	548.0	591.5	621.8	595.7	607.5	621.3	618.7	594.2	536.1	436.2	318.9	251.8
1967	302.0	277.7	310.0	339.9	280.0	255.1	275.5	302.5	295.7	308.6	325.7	337.1	347.0	335.7	310.0	280.4	249.6
1968	488.3	359.8	497.0	600.3	535.8	303.2	364.8	411.5	443.3	499.4	548.2	586.9	604.4	609.5	582.1	538.2	487.1
1969	747.0	631.6	806.2	849.5	731.5	550.2	624.7	719.9	763.3	807.2	848.0	861.1	854.7	832.6	787.1	735.8	671.5
1970	794.8	781.9	865.9	845.4	674.6	722.8	788.4	834.6	846.4	859.7	891.7	872.2	852.5	811.5	748.1	672.8	602.8
1971	648.1	663.5	718.2	683.0	500.2	621.2	668.5	700.8	704.7	721.6	728.3	710.4	693.1	645.4	570.1	492.5	438.0
1972	545.8	499.6	577.4	596.9	516.0	460.7	501.6	536.6	554.9	576.6	600.8	600.8	596.2	593.6	558.4	512.1	477.6
1973	572.0	564.9	649.6	642.0	400.7	522.1	570.0	602.6	622.2	653.0	673.6	665.8	647.6	612.7	508.2	401.9	291.9
1974	315.4	329.1	367.5	330.3	218.2	307.6	330.7	349.1	361.5	367.4	373.7	353.3	339.1	298.4	247.9	213.1	193.7
1975	236.2	242.6	263.1	247.7	187.1	221.1	246.2	260.6	261.8	264.3	263.3	255.4	252.6	235.0	209.6	183.2	168.4
1976	235.0	213.0	269.1	257.7	203.0	190.6	208.5	239.9	252.1	274.5	280.8	276.2	263.8	233.1	221.1	202.1	185.9
1977	231.2	223.5	250.4	249.3	201.7	201.9	224.5	244.1	246.4	242.8	261.9	256.7	254.5	236.6	220.2	199.1	185.9
1978	245.6	225.3	263.9	264.3	234.8	204.7	223.8	247.5	257.1	254.9	279.7	272.1	269.3	251.5	248.1	233.9	222.3
1979	304.0	269.1	333.1	334.8	286.7	237.8	266.9	302.5	313.2	331.3	354.9	345.6	338.7	320.2	306.8	285.1	268.2
1980	308.4	310.6	347.4	319.3	249.1	282.2	312.6	337.0	345.8	343.7	352.8	334.9	323.8	299.1	274.9	246.3	226.1
1981	207.9	238.2	240.1	202.2	135.2	228.1	239.3	247.2	242.2	242.4	235.6	218.6	212.0	176.1	154.8	132.4	118.4
1982	104.9	129.5	121.8	95.0	63.0	122.2	132.0	134.3	127.5	120.2	117.7	106.4	97.6	81.0	69.8	61.5	57.8
1983	75.8	70.9	84.6	81.0	67.7	61.8	68.8	82.0	82.4	85.8	85.6	82.5	82.4	78.2	72.3	67.1	63.8

Weekly hours of work: (16)

manufacturing

1980 = 100

Durée hebdomadaire du travail : (16)

industries manufacturières

1980 = 100

	Year	Q.1	Q.2	Q.3	Q.4	JAN	FEB	MAR	APR	MAY	JUN	JUL	AUG	SEP	OCT	NOV	DEC
1964	104.8	103.0	104.8	104.9	106.3	103.0			104.8			104.9			106.3		
1965	105.8	105.6	105.0	106.1	106.7	105.6			105.0			106.1			106.7		
1966	104.9	104.7	104.8	105.6	104.3	104.7			104.8			105.6			104.3		
1967	101.0	98.9	100.7	101.8	102.3	98.9			100.7			101.8			102.3		
1968	103.4	101.5	103.0	104.0	105.0	101.5			103.0			104.0			105.0		
1969	105.3	104.0	105.4	105.5	106.0	104.0			105.4			105.5			106.0		
1970	105.3	105.1	105.6	104.8	105.5	105.1			105.6			104.8			105.5		
1971	103.4	103.2	102.9	103.5	103.8	103.2			102.9			103.5			103.8		
1972	102.4	100.9	103.0	103.0	103.1	100.9			103.0			103.0			103.1		
1973	102.9	102.4	103.3	102.9	102.8	102.4			103.3			102.9			102.8		
1974	100.7	100.7	100.9	101.3	99.9	100.7			100.9			101.3			99.9		
1975	97.1	95.8	97.1	98.0	97.4	95.8			97.1			98.0			97.4		
1976	99.6	97.6	99.2	100.4	101.2	97.6			99.2			100.4			101.2		
1977	100.1	99.6	100.0	100.1	100.5	99.6			100.0			100.1			100.5		
1978	99.9	99.1	100.1	100.0	100.4	99.1			100.1			100.0			100.4		
1979	100.3	99.4	100.3	100.7	100.8	99.4			100.3			100.7			100.8		
1980	100.0	100.0	100.3	100.2	99.5	100.0			100.3			100.2			99.5		
1981	98.7	98.2	98.6	99.2	98.9	98.2			98.6			99.2			98.9		
1982	97.6	98.2	97.9	98.3	95.8	98.2			97.9			98.3			95.8		
1983	97.0	94.7	97.1	98.3	98.0	94.7			97.1			98.3			98.0		

Unemployment (registered unemployed) (14)(15) — Chômage (chômeurs inscrits) (14)(15)

as per cent of civilian labour force — en pourcentage de la main-d'œuvre civile

Adjusted - Corrigé

	Year	Q.1	Q.2	Q.3	Q.4	JAN	FEB	MAR	APR	MAY	JUN	JUL	AUG	SEP	OCT	NOV	DEC
1964		0.7	0.8	0.8	0.7	0.7	0.7	0.8	0.8	0.8	0.8	0.8	0.8	0.8	0.8	0.7	0.7
1965		0.6	0.6	0.7	0.7	0.6	0.6	0.7	0.6	0.6	0.6	0.7	0.7	0.7	0.7	0.7	0.6
1966		0.5	0.6	0.8	1.2	0.5	0.5	0.4	0.6	0.6	0.7	0.8	0.8	0.9	1.0	1.2	1.4
1967		2.0	2.4	2.3	2.1	1.8	2.0	2.2	2.4	2.5	2.4	2.4	2.3	2.3	2.2	2.1	2.1
1968		1.9	1.6	1.3	1.1	2.0	1.8	1.6	1.7	1.6	1.5	1.4	1.3	1.3	1.2	1.1	1.0
1969		0.9	0.8	0.8	0.7	0.9	1.0	0.9	0.8	0.8	0.8	0.8	0.8	0.8	0.7	0.7	0.7
1970		0.7	0.7	0.7	0.7	0.7	0.7	0.7	0.7	0.7	0.7	0.7	0.7	0.7	0.7	0.7	0.7
1971		0.7	0.8	0.9	1.0	0.7	0.7	0.8	0.8	0.8	0.9	0.9	0.9	1.0	1.0	1.0	1.0
1972		1.0	1.2	1.2	1.1	1.0	1.1	1.0	1.1	1.2	1.2	1.2	1.2	1.2	1.2	1.1	1.1
1973		1.0	1.1	1.3	1.6	1.0	1.0	1.0	1.1	1.1	1.2	1.2	1.3	1.3	1.4	1.6	1.8
1974		2.0	2.3	2.8	3.5	1.9	2.0	2.1	2.2	2.3	2.4	2.6	2.8	3.0	3.3	3.6	3.7
1975		4.2	4.9	5.1	5.0	3.9	4.2	4.4	4.7	4.9	5.0	5.0	5.1	5.1	5.0	5.0	4.9
1976		4.8	4.6	4.5	4.4	4.8	4.9	4.8	4.7	4.6	4.6	4.6	4.5	4.5	4.5	4.4	4.4
1977		4.4	4.6	4.6	4.5	4.5	4.4	4.4	4.5	4.6	4.6	4.6	4.6	4.6	4.5	4.5	4.5
1978		4.5	4.4	4.3	4.2	4.4	4.5	4.5	4.4	4.5	4.4	4.3	4.3	4.3	4.3	4.2	4.1
1979		4.0	3.8	3.7	3.6	4.1	4.1	3.9	3.8	3.8	3.8	3.7	3.7	3.7	3.6	3.6	3.5
1980		3.5	3.7	4.0	4.3	3.5	3.5	3.5	3.6	3.7	3.8	3.9	4.0	4.1	4.2	4.3	4.5
1981		4.7	5.2	5.9	6.6	4.5	4.6	4.9	5.0	5.2	5.4	5.7	5.9	6.0	6.3	6.6	6.9
1982		7.0	7.4	7.9	8.5	6.9	7.0	7.1	7.3	7.4	7.4	7.6	7.8	8.2	8.4	8.5	8.6
1983		9.0	9.4	9.3	9.1	8.8	9.0	9.2	9.3	9.4	9.5	9.3	9.4	9.3	9.2	9.0	9.0

Jobs vacant, unfilled vacancies (14) — Offres d'emploi non satisfaites (14)

thousands — milliers

Adjusted - Corrigé

	Year	Q.1	Q.2	Q.3	Q.4	JAN	FEB	MAR	APR	MAY	JUN	JUL	AUG	SEP	OCT	NOV	DEC
1964		603.0	603.0	605.7	638.0	588.0	613.0	603.0	604.0	599.0	606.0	602.0	605.0	610.0	619.0	643.0	652.0
1965		655.7	646.7	635.3	667.7	667.0	650.0	650.0	652.0	650.0	638.0	641.0	632.0	633.0	651.0	666.0	686.0
1966		635.7	573.3	511.7	379.3	657.0	637.0	613.0	589.0	573.0	558.0	538.0	515.0	482.0	432.0	370.0	336.0
1967		302.3	289.7	299.0	322.7	309.0	299.0	299.0	291.0	288.0	290.0	292.0	301.0	304.0	310.0	325.0	333.0
1968		389.7	459.3	534.7	614.3	367.0	395.0	407.0	431.0	462.0	485.0	512.0	532.0	560.0	588.0	617.0	638.0
1969		681.3	744.0	766.3	831.0	659.0	674.0	711.0	735.0	745.0	752.0	759.0	763.0	777.0	801.0	835.0	857.0
1970		842.0	799.7	767.3	761.0	855.0	845.0	826.0	814.0	794.0	791.0	775.0	767.0	760.0	763.0	763.0	757.0
1971		715.3	663.3	617.7	566.0	732.0	717.0	697.0	678.0	666.0	646.0	631.0	622.0	600.0	581.0	563.0	554.0
1972		541.0	530.0	536.3	594.7	546.0	540.0	537.0	533.0	529.0	528.0	530.0	531.0	548.0	573.0	596.0	615.0
1973		615.0	590.7	573.0	463.3	625.0	617.0	603.0	594.0	592.0	586.0	583.0	571.0	565.0	528.0	478.0	384.0
1974		358.7	330.7	295.7	258.7	371.0	359.0	346.0	341.0	329.0	322.0	308.0	299.0	280.0	262.0	257.0	257.0
1975		261.0	235.3	224.7	222.0	264.0	265.0	254.0	244.0	235.0	227.0	224.0	224.0	226.0	224.0	221.0	221.0
1976		225.7	240.7	236.7	238.3	225.0	222.0	230.0	234.0	246.0	242.0	243.0	237.0	230.0	236.0	240.0	239.0
1977		235.0	225.0	232.0	233.7	236.0	237.0	232.0	228.0	221.0	226.0	228.0	232.0	236.0	234.0	233.0	234.0
1978		235.7	238.0	248.0	269.0	237.0	235.0	235.0	238.0	234.0	242.0	244.0	248.0	252.0	262.0	270.0	275.0
1979		280.7	301.0	315.7	328.7	275.0	279.0	288.0	291.0	304.0	308.0	312.0	314.0	321.0	326.0	330.0	330.0
1980		323.7	313.0	301.3	288.3	326.0	325.0	320.0	320.0	312.0	307.0	303.0	300.0	301.0	296.0	289.0	280.0
1981		248.0	215.0	188.7	158.3	264.0	248.0	232.0	223.0	217.0	205.0	198.0	190.0	178.0	169.0	158.0	148.0
1982		134.0	108.3	89.3	74.7	142.0	136.0	124.0	116.0	107.0	102.0	96.0	90.0	82.0	77.0	74.0	73.0
1983		72.7	75.0	77.0	80.7	72.0	71.0	75.0	75.0	76.0	74.0	75.0	76.0	80.0	80.0	81.0	81.0

Monthly hours worked: (13) — Heures effectuées par mois : (13)

mining and manufacturing — industries extractives et manufacturières

million man-hours — millions d'heures-homme

	Year	Q.1	Q.2	Q.3	Q.4	JAN	FEB	MAR	APR	MAY	JUN	JUL	AUG	SEP	OCT	NOV	DEC
1964	1051	1035	1042	1036	1090	1063	1010	1033	1097	988	1041	1064	973	1071	1120	1080	1069
1965	1055	1046	1055	1037	1079	1025	1011	1102	1073	1054	1039	1033	997	1082	1080	1084	1074
1966	1018	1036	1025	1000	1012	1023	988	1098	1021	1028	1025	980	977	1044	1031	1026	980
1967	916	929	905	893	935	964	890	934	903	882	930	881	876	921	968	955	883
1968	944	924	919	936	995	935	902	936	931	966	860	923	923	962	1054	1003	927
1969	996	977	977	984	1044	990	947	993	995	979	958	990	930	1031	1110	1036	987
1970	1044	1028	1051	1026	1072	1012	1017	1055	1107	998	1048	1048	962	1068	1111	1073	1031
1971	1001	1022	1004	974	1002	994	986	1087	1033	984	994	979	917	1026	1028	1016	960
1972	957	972	961	920	975	948	955	1014	944	964	976	900	904	956	1013	1005	906
1973	952	973	953	918	965	970	949	999	939	994	927	887	925	941	1034	1001	861
1974	893	927	902	862	879	942	904	933	926	947	832	871	827	888	964	892	782
1975	798	806	804	772	810	828	799	790	855	772	784	759	735	822	872	808	749
1976	804	804	802	780	832	772	784	855	811	801	792	747	751	844	844	845	806
1977	791	810	787	763	805	791	776	863	786	789	786	707	757	825	822	823	770
1978	772	781	777	745	786	800	756	786	778	750	803	711	736	789	834	815	710
1979	771	784	758	741	791	785	750	817	754	799	752	739	718	767	860	818	694
1980	762	793	756	735	765	791	783	806	738	747	732	748	668	790	840	762	694
1981	725	743	719	703	737	721	733	774	746	715	696	706	643	760	782	749	679
1982	690	717	696	664	681	683	692	777	724	683	679	639	638	716	702	697	645
1983	660	671	660	638	671	649	641	723	662	660	659	601	618	695	689	689	635

GERMANY

Labour disputes: time lost (17)
thousand man-days

Conflits du travail : journées perdues (17)
milliers de journées-homme

	Year	Q.1	Q.2	Q.3	Q.4	JAN	FEB	MAR	APR	MAY	JUN	JUL	AUG	SEP	OCT	NOV	DEC
1964	16.7	6.1	8.7	0.5	1.3												
1965	49.5	17.7	28.0	3.8	-												
1966	27.3	13.3	13.9	0.3	0.3												
1967	389.6	1.6	14.6	302.3	71.1												
1968	25.4	1.1	6.3	3.0	15.0												
1969	249.2	2.9	1.5	228.6	16.3												
1970	93.2	1.7	11.3	50.1	30.1							1.3	1.2	47.6	17.5	8.3	4.4
1971	4483.7	48.3	171.9	80.6	4182.9	15.2	32.8	0.3	0.5	6.2	165.3	80.6	-	-	3.9	808.8	3370.2
1972	66.0	5.7	2.1	6.6	51.6	5.3	0.0	0.4	-	0.2	1.9	1.2	1.9	3.6	25.3	25.7	0.6
1973	563.1	42.4	71.2	93.4	356.0	1.9	36.9	3.6	13.2	16.6	41.5	9.5	75.4	8.5	355.5	0.3	0.2
1974	1051.3	1024.1	6.7	0.5	9.9	18.2	482.1	533.8	1.0	5.3	0.4	0.5	-	-	0.6	7.8	1.5
1975	68.7	4.2	38.6	14.2	11.7	0.1	-	4.1	16.5	6.8	15.4	13.8	-	0.4	0.9	9.1	1.7
1976	533.7	8.8	524.4	0.0	0.4	0.2	2.3	6.3	99.7	421.4	3.3	0.0	-	-	-	0.3	0.1
1977	23.7	3.5	9.1	10.3	0.8	2.0	0.9	0.7	0.5	2.0	6.6	9.5	-	0.7	0.5	0.3	-
1978	4281.3	2983.5	2.5	78.8	1216.5	84.2	19.7	2879.7	1.9	0.4	0.2	-	78.6	0.2	0.1	124.0	1092.4
1979	483.1	480.1	0.6	2.4	-	480.1	0.0	-	0.1	0.4	0.2	0.9	1.5	-	-	-	-
1980	128.4	3.8	2.9	1.4	120.2	..	..	..	..	..	..	..	..	0.4	1.4	102.8	16.0
1981	58.4	38.0	17.5	-	3.1	0.2	0.2	37.7	16.2	0.4	1.0	-	-	-	-	1.8	1.3
1982	15.1	8.6	4.6	-	-	6.4	-	2.2	1.5	1.3	1.8	-	-	-	-	-	-
1983																	

Hourly rates: manufacturing (16)
1980 = 100

Taux horaires : industries manufacturières (16)
1980 = 100

	Year	Q.1	Q.2	Q.3	Q.4	JAN	FEB	MAR	APR	MAY	JUN	JUL	AUG	SEP	OCT	NOV	DEC
1964	30.3	29.5	30.0	30.3	31.3	29.5			30.0			30.3			31.3		
1965	32.4	31.6	31.9	32.8	33.4	31.6			31.9			32.8			33.4		
1966	34.9	34.2	34.7	35.1	35.4	34.2			34.7			35.1			35.4		
1967	36.7	36.4	36.6	36.7	36.9	36.4			36.6			36.7			36.9		
1968	38.3	37.1	38.3	38.8	38.9	37.1			38.3			38.8			38.9		
1969	40.8	39.5	40.1	40.7	42.7	39.5			40.1			40.7			42.7		
1970	45.8	43.3	44.5	46.0	49.2	43.3			44.5			46.0			49.2		
1971	51.9	50.9	51.4	52.5	53.0	50.9			51.4			52.5			53.0		
1972	56.3	55.0	56.1	56.8	57.3	55.0			56.1			56.8			57.3		
1973	61.8	60.0	61.5	62.8	63.2	60.0			61.5			62.8			63.2		
1974	69.3	66.8	68.9	70.3	71.0	66.8			68.9			70.3			71.0		
1975	75.5	74.1	75.3	76.2	76.4	74.1			75.3			76.2			76.4		
1976	79.7	78.1	79.6	80.6	80.8	78.1			79.6			80.6			80.8		
1977	85.7	84.1	85.5	86.6	86.8	84.1			85.5			86.6			86.8		
1978	89.6	87.6	89.1	90.8	91.1	87.6			89.1			90.8			91.1		
1979	94.3	93.1	94.2	95.0	95.2	93.1			94.2			95.0			95.2		
1980	100.0	95.9	100.2	101.8	102.1	95.9			100.2			101.8			102.1		
1981	105.5	102.5	105.2	107.0	107.3	102.5			105.2			107.0			107.3		
1982	110.2	107.5	110.4	111.4	111.6	107.5			110.4			111.4			111.6		
1983	114.0	111.8	114.2	115.0	115.2	111.8			114.2			115.0			115.2		

Hourly earnings: manufacturing (16)
1980 = 100

Gains horaires : industries manufacturières (16)
1980 = 100

	Year	Q.1	Q.2	Q.3	Q.4	JAN	FEB	MAR	APR	MAY	JUN	JUL	AUG	SEP	OCT	NOV	DEC
1964	29	28	29	30	31	28			29			30			31		
1965	32	31	32	33	33	31			32			33			33		
1966	35	33	35	35	35	33			35			35			35		
1967	36	36	36	36	36	36			36			36			36		
1968	38	36	37	38	39	36			37			38			39		
1969	41	39	40	41	43	39			40			41			43		
1970	46	45	46	47	49	45			46			47			49		
1971	52	50	51	52	53	50			51			52			53		
1972	56	55	56	57	57	55			56			57			57		
1973	62	60	62	63	64	60			62			63			64		
1974	69	64	69	71	71	64			69			71			71		
1975	74	72	74	75	75	72			74			75			75		
1976	79	76	79	80	81	76			79			80			81		
1977	85	82	85	86	86	82			85			86			86		
1978	89	86	89	91	91	86			89			91			91		
1979	94	92	94	95	95	92			94			95			95		
1980	100	96	101	102	102	96			101			102			102		
1981	105	103	104	107	107	103			104			107			107		
1982	110	108	111	112	112	108			111			112			112		
1983	114	112	114	115	115	112			114			115			115		

Unit labour cost: (18)
mining and manufacturing
1980 = 100

Adjusted - Corrigé

Coût unitaire de la main-d'œuvre : (18)
industries extractives et manufacturières
1980 = 100

	Year	Q.1	Q.2	Q.3	Q.4	JAN	FEB	MAR	APR	MAY	JUN	JUL	AUG	SEP	OCT	NOV	DEC
1964	46	46	46	46	47	46	45	46	46	47	46	45	46	46	47	47	47
1965	49	48	49	50	50	47	48	48	49	49	49	50	50	50	50	51	50
1966	52	50	52	53	53	50	50	51	52	52	51	52	53	53	52	53	53
1967	52	53	53	51	49	52	53	53	52	54	52	51	52	51	50	50	48
1968	51	51	51	51	50	52	51	51	51	51	52	52	50	51	51	50	50
1969	52	51	52	52	54	51	51	51	51	52	52	52	52	53	54	54	54
1970	59	57	58	60	63	56	57	58	57	57	59	59	60	60	62	64	63
1971	65	64	64	66	66	63	64	64	64	64	64	65	67	66	66	65	67
1972	67	67	67	67	67	67	67	66	66	67	67	66	67	69	68	67	67
1973	71	69	71	72	73	69	70	69	70	70	72	73	71	73	73	73	73
1974	80	76	78	81	84	74	74	79	78	78	79	79	83	81	82	84	86
1975	86	87	87	86	85	86	86	88	86	87	87	87	86	86	85	86	84
1976	85	83	84	85	86	84	82	84	85	84	83	86	85	85	86	86	87
1977	88	87	88	88	90	86	88	86	87	88	89	89	88	88	89	90	90
1978	92	91	93	91	91	89	91	92	94	93	93	92	91	91	92	92	89
1979	93	94	92	93	93	93	95	94	92	92	91	92	93	94	94	94	92
1980	100	95	99	102	103	93	95	98	97	99	101	100	101	104	103	104	103
1981	105	102	106	105	107	104	101	102	103	108	108	105	106	105	105	108	107
1982	109	107	108	111	112	108	106	107	106	107	110	112	111	111	111	112	112
1983	108	109	108	108	108	110	110	107	110	108	106	108	109	108	109	108	106

Producer prices : total (8)(19)
(manufacturing output)
1980 = 100

Prix à la production : total (8)(19)
(produits manufacturés)
1980 = 100

	Year	Q.1	Q.2	Q.3	Q.4	JAN	FEB	MAR	APR	MAY	JUN	JUL	AUG	SEP	OCT	NOV	DEC
1964	56.7	56.4	56.5	56.7	57.3	56.3	56.4	56.4	56.5	56.5	56.5	56.5	56.6	56.9	57.2	57.4	57.4
1965	58.1	57.6	58.0	58.2	58.4	57.4	57.6	57.7	57.9	58.0	58.1	58.1	58.2	58.2	58.4	58.4	58.5
1966	59.1	59.0	59.3	59.1	59.0	58.7	59.0	59.1	59.3	59.3	59.3	59.3	59.1	59.0	59.0	59.0	58.9
1967	58.5	58.9	58.4	58.3	58.3	59.0	58.9	58.8	58.4	58.4	58.4	58.4	58.4	58.2	58.2	58.4	58.4
1968	57.9	58.4	57.7	57.7	58.0	58.4	58.5	58.3	57.9	57.7	57.7	57.6	57.7	57.9	57.9	58.0	58.0
1969	59.2	58.3	58.7	59.2	60.4	58.3	58.4	58.4	58.5	58.7	58.8	59.0	59.2	59.5	60.0	60.5	60.7
1970	62.2	61.6	61.9	62.2	62.9	61.4	61.6	61.8	61.9	61.9	62.0	62.0	62.2	62.3	62.6	62.9	63.2
1971	64.8	64.4	64.8	65.0	64.8	64.1	64.4	64.6	64.8	64.8	64.9	65.0	64.9	65.0	64.9	64.8	64.9
1972	66.3	65.5	66.0	66.4	67.1	65.3	65.4	65.8	65.9	66.0	66.0	66.1	66.2	66.8	66.9	67.1	67.4
1973	70.8	68.8	70.2	71.4	72.7	68.1	68.9	69.4	69.8	70.2	70.6	71.3	71.4	71.5	72.0	72.8	73.5
1974	80.2	77.5	80.1	81.3	82.0	75.7	77.9	79.0	79.7	80.3	80.4	81.0	81.4	81.6	82.0	82.0	82.0
1975	82.8	82.7	82.8	82.8	83.0	82.7	82.7	82.6	82.8	82.8	82.8	82.7	82.8	83.0	83.0	82.8	83.0
1976	85.8	84.3	85.6	86.6	86.6	83.9	84.3	84.7	85.3	85.5	85.9	86.4	86.6	86.8	86.7	86.5	86.5
1977	88.2	87.7	88.5	88.4	88.2	87.3	87.7	88.1	88.4	88.5	88.5	88.5	88.3	88.3	88.3	88.2	88.1
1978	88.9	88.4	88.9	88.9	89.2	88.3	88.3	88.5	88.7	88.9	88.9	88.9	88.9	88.9	88.9	89.2	89.5
1979	93.4	90.8	92.8	94.5	95.7	90.1	90.7	91.5	92.3	92.8	93.3	94.1	94.4	94.9	95.3	95.6	96.1
1980	100.0	98.4	100.0	100.4	101.1	97.6	98.6	99.1	99.8	100.1	100.2	100.4	100.4	100.3	100.6	101.2	101.6
1981	106.0	103.2	105.5	107.3	108.1	102.4	103.2	104.1	104.9	105.5	106.0	106.7	107.5	107.8	107.8	108.1	108.3
1982	111.1	109.7	110.8	111.8	112.2	109.5	109.7	109.8	110.4	110.7	111.3	111.7	111.8	112.0	112.3	112.3	112.1
1983	112.8	111.8	112.2	113.1	114.0	112.0	111.8	111.5	112.0	112.1	112.4	112.5	113.3	113.6	113.8	114.0	114.3

Producer prices (manufacturing output): (8)(19)
food, beverages and tobacco
1980 = 100

Prix à la production (produits manufacturés) : (8)(19)
alimentation, boissons et tabac
1980 = 100

	Year	Q.1	Q.2	Q.3	Q.4	JAN	FEB	MAR	APR	MAY	JUN	JUL	AUG	SEP	OCT	NOV	DEC
1964	65.0	65.0	64.3	64.8	65.2	65.1	65.0	64.9	64.8	64.8	64.8	64.7	64.8	65.0	65.0	65.2	65.2
1965	65.9	65.4	65.6	66.1	66.5	65.3	65.5	65.5	65.5	65.5	65.7	65.8	66.1	66.4	66.5	66.5	66.6
1966	67.3	67.1	67.3	67.5	67.3	66.9	67.1	67.3	67.3	67.3	67.3	67.5	67.5	67.5	67.3	67.3	67.3
1967	67.9	67.6	68.3	67.9	67.7	67.3	67.3	68.3	68.3	68.3	68.4	68.0	67.9	67.7	67.7	67.7	67.7
1968	67.0	67.5	67.1	66.7	66.7	67.7	67.5	67.3	67.2	67.0	67.0	66.8	66.7	66.7	66.7	66.8	66.8
1969	67.7	67.2	67.3	67.6	68.5	67.0	67.2	67.3	67.2	67.3	67.4	67.5	67.5	67.8	68.1	68.7	68.8
1970	69.2	68.3	69.0	69.3	69.7	68.8	68.8	68.8	69.0	69.0	69.0	69.2	69.3	69.4	69.6	69.8	69.7
1971	71.7	70.7	71.5	72.2	72.4	70.1	70.9	71.1	71.4	71.5	71.7	72.1	72.2	72.2	72.4	72.4	72.4
1972	74.5	72.8	73.1	74.5	77.6	72.8	72.8	72.9	73.0	73.1	73.3	73.3	73.6	76.7	77.1	77.6	78.1
1973	80.7	79.2	80.5	81.4	81.7	78.7	79.6	79.4	79.7	80.5	81.2	81.6	81.5	81.1	81.2	81.4	82.5
1974	85.4	83.8	84.5	85.5	87.6	83.6	83.8	84.1	84.2	84.5	84.7	85.0	85.5	86.1	87.3	87.6	87.9
1975	88.6	87.6	88.0	89.1	89.7	87.7	87.5	87.5	87.9	88.1	88.2	88.5	89.1	89.7	89.7	89.7	89.8
1976	91.7	90.2	90.8	92.7	93.4	89.7	90.1	90.6	90.6	90.6	91.1	92.0	92.8	93.2	93.4	93.3	93.4
1977	98.1	96.7	98.6	98.7	98.2	96.1	96.7	97.4	98.4	98.5	98.9	98.6	98.5	98.8	98.2	98.1	98.4
1978	97.3	97.8	97.4	97.1	96.8	98.0	97.6	97.7	97.3	97.4	97.4	97.3	97.0	97.0	96.8	96.8	96.8
1979	97.6	96.8	97.2	97.9	98.4	96.8	96.8	96.8	96.9	97.3	97.5	97.9	97.8	98.1	98.3	98.5	98.5
1980	100.0	99.1	99.7	100.2	101.0	98.9	99.2	99.3	99.5	99.8	99.7	100.0	100.3	100.4	100.6	101.2	101.3
1981	104.6	102.2	104.1	105.6	106.4	101.9	102.3	102.4	103.5	104.1	104.7	105.2	105.4	106.1	106.3	106.3	106.7
1982	110.8	107.8	110.2	112.6	112.7	107.5	107.7	108.1	108.9	109.4	112.2	112.6	112.6	112.6	112.5	112.7	112.8
1983	113.2	112.6	112.4	113.3	114.5	112.7	112.7	112.4	112.5	112.3	112.5	112.5	113.3	114.2	114.3	114.4	114.7

GERMANY

Producer prices (manufacturing output): (8)(19)
investment goods
1980 = 100

Prix à la production (produits manufacturés) : (8)(19)
biens d'équipement
1980 = 100

	Year	Q.1	Q.2	Q.3	Q.4	JAN	FEB	MAR	APR	MAY	JUN	JUL	AUG	SEP	OCT	NOV	DEC
1964	54.8	54.2	54.5	54.8	55.6	54.2	54.2	54.3	54.4	54.5	54.5	54.6	54.7	55.0	55.2	55.7	55.7
1965	56.4	56.1	56.4	56.5	56.6	56.0	56.1	56.1	56.3	56.4	56.4	56.4	56.4	56.5	56.6	56.6	56.6
1966	57.5	57.0	57.7	57.8	57.4	56.8	56.9	57.1	57.6	57.8	57.8	57.8	57.8	57.6	57.5	57.4	57.4
1967	56.9	57.2	57.0	56.8	56.6	57.3	57.2	57.2	57.1	56.9	56.9	56.8	56.8	56.7	56.6	56.6	56.6
1968	56.9	56.9	56.7	56.8	57.0	56.6	57.1	57.1	56.8	56.6	56.7	56.7	56.8	56.9	56.9	57.0	57.1
1969	58.7	57.6	58.0	58.7	60.5	57.5	57.6	57.8	57.9	58.0	58.2	58.3	58.5	59.2	60.2	60.6	60.6
1970	63.3	62.4	62.9	63.4	64.7	62.1	62.4	62.6	62.8	63.0	63.0	63.2	63.4	63.5	64.2	64.7	65.3
1971	67.3	66.8	67.2	67.4	67.7	66.6	66.8	67.0	67.1	67.1	67.3	67.4	67.4	67.5	67.7	67.7	67.7
1972	69.1	68.8	69.1	69.2	69.2	68.5	68.9	69.0	69.0	69.2	69.2	69.2	69.2	69.2	69.2	69.2	69.2
1973	72.0	70.8	71.9	72.5	73.0	70.1	70.9	71.3	71.6	72.0	72.1	72.3	72.5	72.7	72.8	73.0	73.1
1974	78.7	76.0	78.6	79.9	80.6	74.7	75.8	77.3	78.2	78.6	78.9	79.6	79.9	80.1	80.4	80.7	80.7
1975	84.5	83.2	84.7	85.0	85.0	82.4	83.2	84.1	84.6	84.8	84.8	84.9	84.9	85.0	85.0	84.9	85.0
1976	87.4	86.0	87.4	88.0	88.2	85.7	85.9	86.4	87.2	87.5	87.6	87.9	88.0	88.1	88.2	88.2	88.3
1977	90.7	89.6	90.3	91.0	91.0	89.1	89.6	90.1	90.7	90.8	90.9	91.0	91.0	91.0	91.0	91.0	91.0
1978	92.7	91.8	92.7	93.1	93.2	91.5	91.8	92.0	92.3	92.8	93.0	93.0	93.1	93.2	93.2	93.2	93.3
1979	95.4	94.2	95.3	95.8	96.3	93.7	94.1	94.8	95.2	95.4	95.4	95.6	95.8	95.9	96.2	96.3	96.4
1980	100.0	98.3	100.1	100.6	101.0	97.6	98.3	99.1	99.9	100.1	100.2	100.4	100.7	100.7	100.9	101.0	101.0
1981	104.1	102.3	103.3	104.7	105.5	101.9	102.3	102.8	103.2	103.9	104.2	104.5	104.7	104.9	105.3	105.5	105.7
1982	110.0	108.1	110.1	110.7	111.1	107.4	108.2	108.8	109.8	110.1	110.3	110.5	110.7	110.8	111.1	111.0	111.1
1983	113.0	111.9	112.9	113.4	113.6	111.6	112.0	112.2	112.6	113.0	113.2	113.2	113.5	113.5	113.6	113.6	113.7

Producer prices (manufacturing output): (2)(8)(19)
consumer goods
1980 = 100

Prix à la production (produits manufacturés) : (2)(8)(19)
biens de consommation
1980 = 100

	Year	Q.1	Q.2	Q.3	Q.4	JAN	FEB	MAR	APR	MAY	JUN	JUL	AUG	SEP	OCT	NOV	DEC
1964	56.5	56.2	56.3	56.5	56.9	56.1	56.2	56.2	56.3	56.3	56.3	56.3	56.5	56.8	56.8	56.9	56.9
1965	57.8	57.3	57.6	57.9	58.3	57.1	57.3	57.4	57.5	57.6	57.6	57.8	58.0	58.1	58.3	58.3	58.5
1966	59.3	58.9	59.3	59.4	59.4	58.7	58.9	59.0	59.2	59.3	59.3	59.4	59.4	59.4	59.4	59.4	59.4
1967	58.9	59.3	59.0	58.7	58.6	59.4	59.3	59.2	59.1	58.9	58.9	58.8	58.6	58.6	58.6	58.6	58.7
1968	58.7	58.6	58.5	58.7	58.9	58.7	58.6	58.6	58.5	58.5	58.5	58.6	58.7	58.3	58.9	58.9	58.9
1969	59.8	59.2	59.5	60.0	60.5	59.1	59.1	59.3	59.4	59.6	59.7	59.9	60.0	60.2	60.3	60.5	60.6
1970	62.1	61.6	61.9	62.2	62.5	61.3	61.7	61.8	61.9	61.9	62.0	62.1	62.2	62.3	62.4	62.5	62.5
1971	64.5	63.7	64.3	64.9	65.0	63.4	63.7	64.0	64.2	64.3	64.4	64.7	64.8	65.3	65.0	65.0	65.0
1972	66.7	65.8	66.4	66.9	67.7	65.5	65.8	66.0	66.2	66.4	66.6	66.8	66.9	67.1	67.4	67.7	67.9
1973	71.7	69.7	71.2	72.4	73.4	69.2	69.7	70.2	70.7	71.2	71.7	72.0	72.4	72.8	73.0	73.3	73.8
1974	80.0	77.1	79.4	81.6	82.2	76.1	77.3	77.9	78.7	79.4	80.1	81.2	81.6	81.9	82.2	82.3	82.2
1975	82.2	82.4	82.2	82.1	82.3	82.5	82.5	82.3	82.3	82.3	82.1	82.0	82.1	82.1	82.2	82.2	82.4
1976	84.8	83.4	84.4	85.6	86.0	83.1	83.3	83.6	84.0	84.3	84.9	85.3	85.6	85.8	85.9	86.0	86.0
1977	87.3	86.9	87.3	87.5	87.4	86.8	86.9	86.9	87.2	87.3	87.4	87.5	87.6	87.5	87.5	87.4	87.4
1978	88.7	88.0	88.6	89.0	89.2	87.9	88.0	88.1	88.4	88.6	88.7	88.8	89.0	89.1	89.1	89.2	89.3
1979	93.0	90.3	92.3	94.1	95.6	89.8	90.3	90.8	91.7	92.4	92.8	93.6	94.2	94.6	95.4	95.6	95.8
1980	100.0	98.1	99.8	100.8	101.3	97.4	98.0	98.8	99.5	99.9	100.1	100.5	100.8	101.0	101.2	101.3	101.4
1981	104.9	102.9	104.4	105.6	106.8	102.4	102.9	103.3	103.8	104.5	104.9	105.3	105.6	106.0	106.6	106.8	106.9
1982	109.0	108.1	108.9	109.4	109.6	107.7	108.1	108.4	108.7	108.9	109.1	109.3	109.4	109.5	109.6	109.6	109.6
1983	111.0	110.1	110.6	111.3	112.0	109.9	110.2	110.2	110.4	110.6	110.7	111.0	111.3	111.5	111.9	112.0	112.1

Producer prices (manufacturing output): (8)(19)
intermediate goods
1980 = 100

Prix à la production (produits manufacturés) : (8)(19)
biens intermédiaires
1980 = 100

	Year	Q.1	Q.2	Q.3	Q.4	JAN	FEB	MAR	APR	MAY	JUN	JUL	AUG	SEP	OCT	NOV	DEC
1964	54.8	54.3	54.6	54.8	55.5	54.2	54.4	54.4	54.7	54.6	54.5	54.5	54.7	55.0	55.5	55.7	55.5
1965	55.9	55.6	56.1	56.0	56.2	55.2	55.7	55.8	56.1	56.2	56.1	55.9	56.0	56.1	56.2	56.1	56.3
1966	56.6	57.0	57.0	56.2	56.1	56.7	57.2	57.2	57.1	57.0	56.9	56.7	55.9	55.8	56.1	56.2	56.0
1967	55.1	55.9	54.5	55.0	55.2	56.2	55.9	55.5	54.4	54.3	54.7	55.0	55.1	54.9	55.0	55.3	55.4
1968	54.5	55.4	54.1	54.0	54.4	55.4	55.7	55.2	54.3	53.9	54.0	53.8	53.9	54.3	54.4	54.3	54.4
1969	55.3	54.5	54.8	55.4	56.3	54.6	54.6	54.3	54.7	54.8	54.9	55.1	55.4	55.7	55.7	56.4	56.6
1970	57.7	57.5	57.6	57.6	58.0	57.3	57.4	57.7	57.8	57.4	57.5	57.5	57.7	57.7	57.8	58.0	58.3
1971	59.1	59.4	59.7	59.1	58.3	59.1	59.3	59.7	59.9	59.7	59.5	59.4	59.1	58.8	58.5	58.1	58.4
1972	59.1	58.4	59.2	59.2	59.8	58.1	58.1	58.9	59.3	59.3	59.0	59.1	59.1	59.3	59.5	59.8	60.1
1973	64.3	61.4	63.0	65.0	67.9	60.7	61.4	62.1	62.6	62.9	63.6	64.8	65.0	65.1	66.1	68.2	69.5
1974	79.4	76.4	80.0	80.6	80.6	72.8	77.5	79.0	79.5	80.5	80.0	80.4	80.6	80.7	80.8	80.6	80.5
1975	78.7	79.8	78.6	78.2	78.0	80.8	79.8	78.7	78.8	78.6	78.5	78.1	77.9	78.5	78.1	77.7	78.1
1976	81.8	80.3	81.9	82.9	82.1	79.7	80.5	80.8	81.7	81.8	82.3	82.8	83.0	83.0	82.5	82.0	81.9
1977	81.7	82.1	82.1	81.5	81.1	81.8	82.2	82.2	82.2	82.2	81.9	81.7	81.4	81.3	81.3	81.2	80.9
1978	81.1	80.7	81.0	80.9	81.6	80.8	80.6	80.9	81.0	81.2	80.9	80.9	80.9	80.9	80.9	81.6	82.2
1979	89.7	84.7	88.5	91.7	93.7	83.2	84.7	86.2	87.5	88.5	89.7	91.0	91.7	92.4	93.0	93.5	94.7
1980	100.0	98.5	100.2	100.0	101.3	97.3	98.9	99.2	99.9	100.3	100.4	100.5	99.9	99.5	100.0	101.4	102.6
1981	109.7	105.0	108.7	112.4	112.7	103.3	104.9	106.9	108.2	108.6	109.4	111.0	112.9	113.2	112.3	112.7	113.0
1982	113.9	113.3	113.0	114.3	114.9	114.1	113.3	112.5	112.7	113.0	113.3	114.1	114.2	114.6	115.4	115.1	114.3
1983	113.4	112.1	112.1	113.9	115.5	113.2	112.2	111.0	111.8	111.9	112.5	112.6	114.3	114.7	114.9	115.5	116.1

Producer prices: agricultural goods (8)(20)
(input to manufacturing and construction)
1980 = 100

Prix à la production : produits agricoles (8)(20)
(produits de base pour les industries manufacturières et la construction)
1980 = 100

	Year	Q.1	Q.2	Q.3	Q.4	JAN	FEB	MAR	APR	MAY	JUN	JUL	AUG	SEP	OCT	NOV	DEC
1964	70.4																
1965	72.4																
1966	73.1																
1967	69.0	71.2	69.6	67.7	67.8	71.5	71.5	70.7	69.7	69.2	69.8	67.5	67.9	67.8	67.4	67.9	68.0
1968	68.4	68.0	67.1	68.1	70.1	68.0	67.9	68.0	66.8	67.2	67.3	67.5	68.1	68.6	69.3	70.6	70.6
1969	70.8	71.0	69.9	70.6	71.6	71.0	71.0	71.0	70.1	69.5	70.1	70.6	70.4	70.7	70.8	71.7	72.3
1970	68.8	70.5	68.9	68.5	67.1	70.4	70.4	70.6	69.5	68.8	68.5	69.1	68.4	68.1	67.5	66.8	67.1
1971	68.2	67.1	67.4	68.2	69.7	67.1	66.9	67.5	67.5	67.0	67.8	68.1	68.0	68.6	69.1	69.7	70.3
1972	74.9	71.6	73.4	75.8	78.7	70.8	71.7	72.3	72.3	73.6	74.3	74.3	75.7	77.2	78.0	78.3	79.8
1973	82.5	81.2	82.0	82.3	84.2	80.9	81.4	81.3	81.5	82.5	82.0	81.9	82.5	82.5	82.5	83.8	86.2
1974	83.4	86.7	81.8	81.5	83.3	87.1	87.0	86.0	82.8	81.6	81.1	80.3	81.4	82.8	83.5	83.4	83.0
1975	85.0	81.2	82.4	86.4	90.1	80.7	80.8	82.0	82.0	82.2	83.0	84.2	86.5	88.4	88.9	90.1	91.4
1976	=95.0=	92.2	93.3	95.8	98.6	91.5	92.1	92.9	92.8	93.0	94.2	94.4	96.1	96.8	97.8	98.2	99.9
1977	102.5	103.7	106.3	100.8	99.0	101.6	103.3	106.2	107.7	106.4	104.9	102.1	100.1	100.1	98.7	99.0	99.3
1978	95.5	98.0	95.8	94.1	94.3	98.4	98.2	97.4	96.0	96.2	95.2	94.5	93.2	94.5	93.6	94.6	94.6
1979	98.0	95.7	97.9	98.9	99.6	94.6	96.0	96.5	97.1	97.8	98.9	99.4	98.4	99.0	99.2	99.4	100.3
1980	100.0	100.7	99.2	98.2	101.8	100.1	100.9	101.1	100.1	99.1	98.6	98.6	97.7	98.4	100.4	102.2	102.9
1981	106.4	104.6	105.2	107.1	108.4	104.0	104.9	104.8	104.7	105.7	105.3	106.7	107.1	107.5	107.6	108.4	109.2
1982	108.8	109.5	108.5	108.3	108.9	109.9	109.5	109.0	108.7	108.3	108.6	108.4	108.3	108.3	108.8	109.3	108.5
1983	109.8	106.2	106.8	109.6	111.5	106.3	106.3	106.1	105.7	106.7	108.2	108.2	109.4	111.3	111.3	111.1	112.1

Producer prices: industrial goods (domestic) (8)(20)
(input to manufacturing and construction)
1980 = 100

Prix à la production : produits industriels d'origine nationale (8)(20)
(produits de base pour les industries manufacturières et la construction)
1980 = 100

	Year	Q.1	Q.2	Q.3	Q.4	JAN	FEB	MAR	APR	MAY	JUN	JUL	AUG	SEP	OCT	NOV	DEC
1964	55.2																
1965	56.4																
1966	57.0																
1967	55.1	56.0	54.7	54.7	55.1	56.2	56.1	55.6	54.7	54.7	54.7	54.7	54.8	54.7	54.8	55.2	55.2
1968	54.8	55.5	54.4	54.5	54.9	55.2	55.8	55.5	54.4	54.2	54.4	54.2	54.5	54.7	54.8	54.9	55.1
1969	56.5	55.4	55.9	56.8	58.0	55.4	55.4	55.4	55.6	55.8	56.1	56.4	56.8	57.0	57.6	58.0	58.3
1970	59.2	59.1	59.2	59.3	59.1	58.9	59.1	59.3	59.3	58.9	59.4	59.3	59.2	59.2	59.0	59.1	59.2
1971	60.6	59.9	60.7	60.9	60.7	59.6	59.8	60.3	60.7	60.5	60.9	61.0	61.0	60.8	60.7	60.6	60.7
1972	62.1	61.2	61.8	62.4	62.9	60.8	61.1	61.6	61.6	61.9	61.9	62.2	62.4	62.6	62.6	62.9	63.1
1973	68.0	65.0	66.7	68.7	71.5	64.2	65.1	65.9	66.4	66.5	67.2	68.1	69.0	69.0	70.0	71.8	72.9
1974	80.6	77.5	81.3	81.8	82.0	75.2	77.7	79.7	80.7	81.9	81.2	81.7	82.0	81.6	82.5	81.9	81.6
1975	81.5	82.2	81.5	81.2	81.1	82.8	82.3	81.6	81.7	81.6	81.2	81.2	81.1	81.2	81.1	81.0	81.4
1976	=85.8=	83.8	85.9	87.0	86.4	83.0	84.0	84.4	85.6	85.9	86.2	86.9	87.1	87.1	86.7	86.3	86.2
1977	85.6	86.1	86.1	85.5	84.8	85.9	86.1	86.2	86.2	86.1	85.9	85.7	85.5	85.4	85.3	84.7	84.5
1978	85.6	84.9	85.6	85.7	86.2	84.9	84.8	84.9	85.4	85.7	85.7	85.7	85.7	85.8	86.1	86.2	86.4
1979	91.7	88.5	90.9	92.9	94.5	87.2	88.5	89.7	90.5	90.9	91.3	92.4	92.8	93.6	94.0	94.3	95.0
1980	100.0	97.9	100.1	100.4	101.7	97.0	98.0	98.8	99.8	100.3	100.2	100.5	100.3	100.3	101.0	101.8	102.2
1981	108.4	104.4	107.4	110.4	111.7	103.3	104.3	105.7	106.8	107.4	107.9	109.4	110.6	111.4	111.2	111.6	112.3
1982	114.5	114.0	114.8	114.7	114.6	113.8	114.1	114.2	115.1	114.8	114.4	114.8	114.7	114.6	114.7	114.7	114.3
1983	115.4	114.1	114.7	115.8	116.9	114.2	114.1	114.0	114.5	114.6	114.9	115.2	116.0	116.2	116.6	116.7	117.3

Producer prices: industrial goods (imported) (8)(20)
(input to manufacturing and construction)
1980 = 100

Prix à la production : produits industriels importés (8)(20)
(produits de base pour les industries manufacturières et la construction)
1980 = 100

	Year	Q.1	Q.2	Q.3	Q.4	JAN	FEB	MAR	APR	MAY	JUN	JUL	AUG	SEP	OCT	NOV	DEC
1964	42.0																
1965	43.1																
1966	43.9																
1967	43.4	43.1	42.4	43.5	44.4	43.3	43.2	42.7	42.2	42.3	42.5	43.3	43.6	43.8	44.1	44.8	44.5
1968	44.0	44.8	43.8	43.9	43.5	44.5	44.9	45.0	44.0	43.6	43.9	43.7	43.8	44.1	44.0	43.8	42.9
1969	44.0	43.3	43.6	44.2	45.0	43.4	43.3	43.4	43.6	43.5	43.6	43.8	44.5	44.4	44.3	45.1	45.5
1970	45.2	45.8	45.6	44.8	44.5	45.4	45.7	46.1	46.1	45.7	45.1	44.9	44.6	44.7	44.5	44.4	44.4
1971	44.4	44.9	45.3	44.2	43.3	44.7	44.5	45.5	46.0	45.2	44.8	44.6	44.3	43.8	43.4	43.3	43.1
1972	43.3	42.8	42.3	43.2	44.2	42.6	42.8	42.9	42.8	42.9	42.9	42.8	43.2	43.5	43.8	44.2	44.6
1973	49.8	46.1	48.1	49.1	55.8	45.8	46.1	46.5	47.5	48.2	48.5	48.5	49.3	49.5	51.2	56.7	59.4
1974	73.2	71.4	74.3	73.9	73.3	68.6	72.1	73.5	75.4	74.3	73.3	73.3	74.0	74.5	74.1	73.3	72.4
1975	70.3	70.5	68.8	69.8	72.1	71.3	70.3	69.9	69.4	68.8	68.1	68.4	70.0	70.9	72.0	71.7	72.6
1976	=74.2=	73.3	74.5	75.4	73.5	73.1	73.4	73.5	73.9	74.5	75.2	75.9	75.2	75.0	73.7	73.5	73.2
1977	73.9	75.2	74.9	73.3	72.2	74.6	75.4	75.5	75.5	75.0	74.3	73.4	73.3	73.4	72.9	72.3	71.4
1978	69.9	70.1	70.0	69.9	69.6	70.7	70.0	69.5	69.5	70.2	70.4	70.2	69.7	69.7	69.4	69.6	69.9
1979	81.1	73.0	79.4	84.6	87.2	71.3	73.3	74.4	77.2	79.3	81.7	83.8	84.8	85.2	85.7	87.1	89.0
1980	100.0	97.4	99.6	99.5	103.7	95.4	97.6	99.1	100.3	99.0	99.4	99.2	99.3	99.9	101.8	104.2	105.1
1981	117.0	112.0	117.1	122.4	116.4	109.6	113.2	113.1	114.3	117.0	119.9	122.1	123.7	121.4	118.1	115.8	115.3
1982	116.8	116.7	115.1	117.3	118.3	116.0	117.5	116.8	116.2	114.0	115.1	116.8	116.8	118.3	119.1	119.2	116.4
1983	115.0	113.5	112.1	116.7	117.5	114.9	114.2	111.3	111.2	112.0	113.1	114.8	117.5	117.8	116.3	117.4	118.8

GERMANY

Producer prices: crude petroleum (8)(20) — Prix à la production : pétrole brut (8)(20)

(input to manufacturing and construction) — (produits de base pour les industries manufacturières et la construction)

1980 = 100

	Year	Q.1	Q.2	Q.3	Q.4	JAN	FEB	MAR	APR	MAY	JUN	JUL	AUG	SEP	OCT	NOV	DEC
1964	15.3																
1965	14.8																
1966	14.6																
1967	15.4	14.4	14.4	16.1	16.6	14.5	14.4	14.4	14.3	14.4	14.5	15.7	16.2	16.5	17.0	16.5	16.3
1968	16.0	16.2	15.9	16.0	15.8	16.3	16.2	16.1	16.0	15.9	15.9	16.1	16.0	15.9	16.0	15.8	15.4
1969	14.7	15.5	14.7	14.4	14.1	15.5	15.5	15.5	15.1	14.7	14.4	14.3	14.5	14.5	14.1	14.1	14.1
1970	14.5	14.1	14.2	14.3	15.3	14.0	14.1	14.3	14.1	14.2	14.3	14.1	14.3	14.6	15.1	15.1	15.5
1971	17.3	16.2	17.6	17.8	17.4	15.8	15.9	17.0	17.5	17.6	17.8	17.8	18.0	17.7	17.5	17.4	17.3
1972	16.6	16.9	16.7	16.3	16.4	16.8	17.0	17.0	16.9	16.7	16.6	16.4	16.3	16.2	16.3	16.5	16.5
1973	18.6	17.0	17.1	17.2	23.1	17.2	17.0	16.8	17.0	17.2	17.1	16.9	17.1	17.7	18.8	24.3	26.1
1974	48.3	44.3	46.7	50.7	51.3	41.8	45.5	45.6	48.1	46.2	45.9	50.0	50.2	52.0	51.8	51.2	50.9
1975	50.6	48.9	48.2	49.9	55.2	49.6	48.8	48.5	48.2	48.3	48.0	48.4	49.5	51.8	55.2	54.6	55.7
1976	55.0	55.9	55.5	55.4	53.3	56.0	56.1	55.5	55.1	55.4	56.1	55.9	55.3	55.0	53.7	53.2	52.9
1977	55.3	55.8	56.0	55.3	54.0	55.2	56.2	56.1	56.2	56.1	55.7	55.0	55.3	55.6	55.0	54.0	53.1
1978	48.5	50.2	49.5	48.2	45.9	51.4	50.4	49.0	49.0	49.8	49.8	49.2	48.1	47.3	46.3	45.4	46.0
1979	61.6	48.1	57.1	68.2	73.1	47.3	48.0	49.1	53.9	56.4	61.1	66.7	68.8	69.0	69.3	73.2	76.7
1980	100.0	90.7	100.1	100.9	108.2	85.3	91.1	95.7	100.5	99.3	100.6	100.1	101.1	101.7	104.8	109.0	110.6
1981	136.5	127.3	137.6	146.8	134.1	122.1	130.2	129.7	131.3	137.6	144.0	147.3	149.2	144.0	138.8	132.6	130.9
1982	134.2	134.2	129.3	135.1	138.2	132.2	135.2	135.0	131.7	126.5	129.7	135.0	134.1	136.3	138.9	140.5	135.1
1983	126.0	127.6	120.4	127.1	129.1	131.1	128.7	122.9	120.0	119.4	121.7	124.1	128.1	129.2	127.2	129.2	130.9

Wholesale prices: total (21) — Prix de gros : total (21)

1980 = 100

	Year	Q.1	Q.2	Q.3	Q.4	JAN	FEB	MAR	APR	MAY	JUN	JUL	AUG	SEP	OCT	NOV	DEC
1964	58.5	58.8	58.4	58.2	58.5	58.8	58.8	58.8	58.4	58.3	58.5	58.3	58.2	58.0	58.2	58.6	58.8
1965	59.7	59.3	59.8	59.6	59.9	59.2	59.3	59.5	59.5	59.7	60.3	59.7	59.4	59.6	59.6	59.9	60.1
1966	60.3	60.5	60.8	60.0	60.0	60.3	60.6	60.7	60.8	60.6	60.9	60.3	59.9	59.8	59.8	60.1	60.0
1967	60.0	60.3	60.3	59.8	59.7	60.0	60.5	60.4	60.4	60.2	60.4	59.9	59.7	59.8	59.6	59.8	59.7
1968	56.6	57.2	56.6	55.9	56.6	57.2	57.2	57.3	56.9	56.5	56.4	55.9	56.0	55.9	56.7	56.5	56.7
1969	57.8	57.1	57.8	58.0	58.3	56.8	57.1	57.3	57.5	57.8	58.0	58.0	57.9	58.1	58.1	58.3	58.6
1970	59.4	59.2	59.6	59.4	59.6	59.1	59.2	59.4	59.5	59.7	59.6	59.5	59.3	59.3	59.4	59.6	59.9
1971	61.1	61.0	61.7	61.1	60.8	60.6	60.9	61.4	61.7	61.5	61.8	61.5	60.9	61.0	60.8	60.8	60.7
1972	63.2	61.8	62.8	63.5	64.8	61.4	61.8	62.2	62.4	62.8	63.0	63.1	63.3	64.0	64.6	64.6	65.3
1973	69.4	67.2	69.1	69.9	71.6	66.4	67.2	68.0	68.5	69.0	69.7	70.0	69.9	69.7	70.2	71.5	73.1
1974	78.5	76.8	79.0	78.6	79.5	75.1	76.6	78.7	79.0	79.0	78.9	78.4	78.9	78.6	79.3	79.7	79.6
1975	81.1	80.2	81.0	81.2	82.1	80.4	80.0	80.1	80.8	80.7	81.5	80.8	80.9	82.0	82.1	81.9	82.2
1976	85.8	84.1	86.2	86.6	86.4	83.4	84.2	84.8	86.2	86.1	86.2	86.2	86.8	87.0	86.7	86.3	86.3
1977	87.4	87.6	88.7	87.0	86.1	87.1	87.7	88.0	88.8	88.8	88.4	87.4	86.8	86.7	86.2	85.8	86.4
1978	86.7	86.7	87.0	86.5	86.5	86.7	86.7	86.8	86.9	87.0	87.0	87.0	86.4	86.1	86.0	86.4	87.0
1979	92.7	89.4	92.4	94.0	95.0	88.1	89.2	90.9	91.8	92.2	93.1	93.8	93.8	94.3	94.3	94.8	95.9
1980	100.0	98.7	100.3	100.1	100.9	97.7	98.9	99.4	99.7	100.5	100.7	101.1	100.1	99.2	99.5	100.9	102.3
1981	108.2	104.8	107.2	109.5	111.4	103.3	104.6	106.4	107.1	107.2	107.4	108.2	109.6	110.6	111.0	111.6	111.6
1982	114.5	113.4	114.8	114.9	114.9	113.6	113.4	113.1	113.7	115.0	115.7	116.0	114.4	114.3	114.9	115.2	114.5
1983	114.2	112.6	113.5	114.5	115.9	113.4	112.5	111.9	112.8	113.5	114.3	113.7	114.6	115.3	115.1	116.1	116.5

Money supply (M1) (22)(23) — Disponibilités monétaires (M1) (22)(23)

billion DM, end of period — milliards de DM, fin de période

	Year	Q.1	Q.2	Q.3	Q.4	JAN	FEB	MAR	APR	MAY	JUN	JUL	AUG	SEP	OCT	NOV	DEC
1964	73.0	64.4	67.9	68.5	73.0	63.6	64.4	64.4	65.5	66.8	67.9	68.0	68.8	68.5	69.1	71.6	73.0
1965	78.5	70.3	74.2	74.4	78.5	69.5	70.5	70.3	71.5	73.4	74.2	74.3	74.3	74.4	75.2	77.6	78.5
1966	79.6	74.3	77.9	76.9	79.6	74.1	74.7	74.3	76.1	77.1	77.9	77.9	77.5	76.9	76.7	79.5	79.6
1967	87.9	75.8	79.0	80.4	87.9	74.6	76.5	75.8	77.2	77.9	79.0	79.5	79.9	80.4	80.6	84.4	87.9
1968	93.5	81.1	85.5	87.0	93.5	81.6	81.4	81.1	82.0	84.0	85.5	85.1	85.9	87.0	87.0	91.4	93.5
1969	99.4	87.6	92.8	94.3	99.4	86.6	87.2	87.6	88.3	91.5	92.8	93.2	94.3	94.3	94.4	99.7	99.4
1970	108.2	93.5	98.6	99.1	108.2	92.8	93.2	93.5	94.0	97.0	98.6	99.7	99.5	99.1	99.2	105.4	108.2
1971	121.5	101.9	110.2	112.4	121.5	100.6	101.8	101.9	104.8	109.7	110.2	112.9	113.0	112.4	113.3	119.4	121.5
1972	139.3	117.2	126.0	128.3	139.3	113.7	114.6	117.2	119.8	120.5	126.0	126.8	127.7	128.3	128.5	137.4	139.3
1973	142.9	133.4	133.4	129.1	142.9	127.9	128.6	133.4	133.9	130.8	133.4	132.9	128.8	129.1	128.3	137.6	142.9
1974	158.4	132.9	140.8	141.5	158.4	129.5	131.0	132.9	134.8	136.8	140.8	142.5	141.2	141.5	140.2	153.8	158.4
1975	179.9	149.3	160.6	164.4	179.9	144.6	144.9	149.3	151.8	156.0	160.6	160.7	161.6	164.4	163.9	178.1	179.9
1976	186.9	166.8	180.2	176.9	186.9	165.7	165.4	166.8	169.7	175.5	180.2	179.3	178.6	176.9	178.2	191.1	186.9
1977	208.1	179.7	190.5	193.1	208.1	178.1	179.4	179.7	182.6	187.0	190.5	193.9	192.0	193.1	195.0	210.8	208.1
1978	237.9	204.2	215.4	217.5	237.9	201.9	203.1	204.2	207.9	212.2	215.4	218.7	217.7	217.5	221.1	237.5	237.9
1979	247.9	225.5	233.1	230.2	247.9	223.9	225.5	225.5	228.2	230.6	233.1	233.7	231.3	230.2	230.7	248.2	247.9
1980	257.3	228.7	237.1	237.8	257.3	226.9	229.5	228.7	229.7	234.9	237.1	236.2	236.0	237.8	238.7	263.6	257.3
1981	255.3	232.4	242.5	234.3	255.3	241.0	240.6	232.4	233.3	237.7	242.5	239.8	239.6	234.3	234.5	258.2	255.3
1982	273.1	237.6	250.7	248.5	273.1	238.7	239.4	237.6	239.5	247.1	250.7	249.0	247.0	248.5	250.0	271.5	273.1
1983	295.8	263.4	277.9	274.0	295.8	261.8	263.7	263.4	266.6	271.9	277.9	277.9	275.9	274.0	277.0	295.3	295.8

Consumer prices: all items (24) / Prix à la consommation : total (24)

1980 = 100

	Year	Q.1	Q.2	Q.3	Q.4	JAN	FEB	MAR	APR	MAY	JUN	JUL	AUG	SEP	OCT	NOV	DEC
1964	51.6	51.3	51.5	51.7	51.9	51.2	51.3	51.4	51.5	51.5	51.6	51.7	51.7	51.7	51.7	52.0	52.1
1965	53.4	52.5	53.2	53.7	54.0	52.4	52.4	52.6	52.8	53.1	53.6	53.9	53.7	53.6	53.7	54.0	54.3
1966	55.2	54.7	55.4	55.3	55.5	54.6	54.7	54.9	55.2	55.5	55.5	55.5	55.2	55.1	55.2	55.6	55.7
1967	56.0	55.9	56.2	56.1	55.9	55.9	55.9	56.0	56.1	56.2	56.3	56.4	56.0	55.9	55.8	55.9	55.9
1968	57.6	57.5	57.6	57.5	57.8	57.5	57.6	57.6	57.6	57.6	57.7	57.6	57.5	57.4	57.6	57.9	58.0
1969	58.7	58.5	58.7	58.6	59.0	58.3	58.5	58.6	58.6	58.8	58.8	58.8	58.6	58.6	58.7	58.9	59.3
1970	60.7	60.1	60.6	60.8	61.3	59.9	60.1	60.3	60.5	60.6	60.8	60.8	60.8	60.8	61.0	61.3	61.6
1971	63.9	62.8	63.7	64.2	64.8	62.4	62.8	63.3	63.6	63.7	63.9	64.1	64.1	64.4	64.6	64.8	65.1
1972	67.4	66.2	66.9	67.8	68.9	65.8	66.2	66.5	66.7	66.8	67.1	67.5	67.6	68.2	68.5	68.8	69.2
1973	72.1	70.4	71.8	72.4	73.9	69.9	70.4	70.9	71.3	71.8	72.2	72.4	72.4	72.5	73.0	73.9	74.6
1974	77.2	75.6	76.9	77.6	78.6	75.1	75.8	76.0	76.4	76.9	77.2	77.4	77.5	77.8	78.2	78.7	79.0
1975	81.8	80.1	81.6	82.3	83.0	79.7	80.1	80.5	81.1	81.6	82.2	82.2	82.1	82.5	82.7	83.0	83.2
1976	85.5	84.5	85.5	85.7	86.2	84.1	84.6	84.8	85.3	85.5	85.6	85.5	85.7	85.8	86.0	86.2	86.5
1977	88.6	87.7	88.6	88.9	89.3	87.4	87.7	88.0	88.3	88.6	89.0	88.8	88.9	89.0	89.1	89.2	89.5
1978	91.0	90.4	91.1	91.1	91.4	90.0	90.4	90.7	90.9	91.1	91.4	91.2	91.1	91.0	91.1	91.4	91.7
1979	94.8	93.0	94.3	95.4	96.3	92.6	93.0	93.4	93.9	94.2	94.7	95.3	95.4	95.6	95.9	96.2	96.7
1980	100.0	98.1	99.9	100.6	101.4	97.2	98.2	98.8	99.4	99.8	100.3	100.5	100.6	100.6	100.8	101.4	102.0
1981	105.9	103.6	105.4	106.7	108.0	102.8	103.6	104.3	105.0	105.4	105.9	106.3	106.7	107.2	107.5	108.0	108.4
1982	111.5	109.5	111.1	112.3	113.1	109.3	109.6	109.7	110.3	110.9	112.1	112.3	112.1	112.5	112.8	113.1	113.3
1983	114.9	113.6	114.3	115.4	116.0	113.6	113.7	113.6	113.9	114.3	114.7	115.1	115.5	115.7	115.7	116.0	116.2

Central Bank money stock (25)(26) / Stock de monnaie Banque Centrale (26)/(25)

billion DM, end of period / milliards de DM, fin de période

Adjusted - Corrigé

	Year	Q.1	Q.2	Q.3	Q.4	JAN	FEB	MAR	APR	MAY	JUN	JUL	AUG	SEP	OCT	NOV	DEC
1964	44.2	41.6	42.3	43.3	44.2	41.1	41.2	41.6	41.7	42.0	42.3	42.7	43.0	43.3	43.6	43.9	44.2
1965	48.3	45.6	46.8	47.4	48.3	44.6	45.2	45.6	46.0	46.4	46.8	47.2	47.2	47.4	47.8	48.1	48.3
1966	50.9	49.0	49.9	50.6	50.9	48.3	48.8	49.0	49.4	49.8	49.9	50.3	50.4	50.6	50.8	50.9	50.9
1967	54.2	51.8	52.4	53.1	54.2	50.8	51.5	51.8	52.1	52.2	52.4	52.4	52.7	53.1	53.4	53.8	54.2
1968	59.4	55.4	56.5	57.3	59.4	54.6	55.0	55.4	55.7	55.8	56.5	56.5	56.8	57.3	57.8	58.4	59.4
1969	65.1	60.7	62.5	63.6	65.1	60.0	60.3	60.7	61.1	61.8	62.5	62.9	63.3	63.6	64.8	65.0	65.1
1970	69.4	66.1	66.5	68.5	69.4	65.7	65.8	66.1	65.7	66.0	66.5	67.4	67.6	68.5	68.6	68.8	69.4
1971	77.8	71.4	74.1	76.0	77.8	70.2	71.0	71.4	72.4	73.5	74.1	74.7	75.4	76.0	76.5	77.0	77.8
1972	88.1	80.0	82.6	86.2	88.1	78.5	79.3	80.0	80.9	81.8	82.6	84.1	85.7	86.2	86.7	87.5	88.1
1973	94.8	90.8	92.7	93.2	94.8	88.7	89.5	90.8	92.0	92.2	92.7	92.6	93.1	93.2	93.9	94.4	94.8
1974	100.8	95.9	97.9	99.4	100.8	94.9	95.1	95.9	96.8	97.7	97.9	98.6	99.5	99.4	99.5	99.8	100.8
1975	110.8	102.9	104.8	107.4	110.8	101.8	102.1	102.9	103.9	104.4	104.8	105.4	106.3	107.4	108.5	109.5	110.8
1976	120.1	112.0	114.7	117.6	120.1	111.6	111.7	112.0	113.0	113.6	114.7	116.0	116.5	117.6	118.6	119.8	120.1
1977	131.9	122.0	124.6	128.5	131.9	120.5	121.4	122.0	122.4	123.6	124.6	126.3	127.6	128.5	129.5	131.1	131.9
1978	143.1	131.4	134.7	138.6	143.1	133.8	135.0	131.4	132.2	133.5	134.7	135.6	137.3	138.6	140.2	142.0	143.1
1979	151.1	145.8	148.1	149.5	151.1	144.1	144.5	145.8	146.5	147.4	148.1	148.4	149.3	149.5	150.5	150.8	151.1
1980	159.3	153.7	154.5	156.3	159.3	151.9	152.4	153.7	154.1	154.0	154.5	155.1	155.5	156.3	157.1	157.8	159.3
1981	164.4	160.5	161.9	163.5	164.4	159.9	160.1	160.5	160.4	161.2	161.9	162.7	162.8	163.5	163.5	163.4	164.4
1982	174.1	167.1	169.7	172.1	174.1	165.1	166.4	167.1	168.0	168.9	169.7	170.6	171.0	172.1	173.2	174.0	174.1
1983	185.9	179.9	182.3	185.1	185.9	176.0	178.0	179.9	180.5	181.7	182.3	183.5	184.4	185.1	185.5	186.3	185.9

Money supply (M1) (22) / Disponibilités monétaires (M1) (22)

billion DM, end of period / milliards de DM, fin de période

Adjusted - Corrigé

	Year	Q.1	Q.2	Q.3	Q.4	JAN	FEB	MAR	APR	MAY	JUN	JUL	AUG	SEP	OCT	NOV	DEC
1964		66.1	67.6	68.6	69.8	65.2	65.4	66.1	66.4	66.9	67.6	67.8	68.5	68.6	69.2	69.6	69.8
1965		72.2	73.8	74.4	75.0	71.2	71.8	72.2	72.6	73.5	73.8	74.1	74.1	74.4	75.4	75.4	75.0
1966		76.4	77.4	77.0	76.1	75.9	76.1	76.4	77.2	77.2	77.4	77.7	77.3	77.0	76.9	77.1	76.1
1967		77.9	78.5	80.4	83.8	76.3	78.0	77.9	78.3	78.0	78.5	79.3	79.8	80.4	80.9	81.7	83.8
1968		83.4	85.0	87.0	89.0	83.6	83.2	83.4	83.3	84.2	85.0	84.9	85.7	87.0	87.4	88.4	89.0
1969		89.7	91.7	94.3	94.8	89.3	89.8	89.7	90.4	91.7	91.7	92.0	93.6	94.3	95.2	95.6	94.8
1970		95.8	97.5	99.6	103.2	95.6	95.9	95.8	96.2	97.3	97.5	98.2	98.6	99.6	100.0	100.8	103.2
1971		104.6	109.3	113.2	115.3	103.7	104.7	104.6	106.8	110.3	109.3	111.0	112.4	113.2	114.5	114.1	115.3
1972		120.0	124.8	129.0	131.8	116.9	117.8	120.0	121.8	121.5	124.8	126.4	128.0	129.0	130.1	131.7	131.8
1973		136.2	131.8	130.0	134.6	132.1	132.8	136.2	135.6	132.0	131.8	130.8	129.0	130.0	130.7	131.3	134.6
1974		135.7	139.2	142.2	149.4	133.7	135.3	135.7	136.7	137.8	139.2	141.0	141.5	142.2	143.0	146.0	149.4
1975		152.9	158.5	165.8	170.2	148.9	149.2	152.9	154.6	156.7	158.5	159.5	162.2	165.8	166.9	168.6	170.2
1976		171.1	179.1	179.4	176.8	170.0	169.9	171.1	172.9	175.6	179.1	177.6	179.2	179.4	180.9	180.4	176.8
1977		184.7	190.0	195.7	196.6	181.8	183.2	184.7	185.9	187.4	190.0	192.6	193.5	195.7	197.1	199.4	196.6
1978		209.5	214.7	220.4	224.8	206.1	207.1	209.5	211.8	213.5	214.7	217.1	219.8	220.4	223.8	224.5	224.8
1979		230.9	232.1	233.7	233.4	228.8	230.1	230.9	232.0	232.2	232.1	232.9	233.4	233.7	234.5	234.0	233.4
1980		233.5	235.1	241.4	243.7	231.5	233.2	233.5	235.0	235.8	235.1	237.0	238.1	241.4	242.7	248.0	243.7
1981		237.8	240.6	238.7	241.7	244.4	243.6	237.8	238.9	238.6	240.6	240.4	241.3	238.7	238.2	242.3	241.7
1982		244.2	249.3	253.6	258.0	241.8	242.4	244.2	245.1	248.6	249.3	249.4	249.3	253.6	254.2	255.3	258.0
1983		270.4	276.3	279.2	279.1	264.1	266.0	270.4	272.6	272.9	276.3	278.4	279.6	279.2	281.1	278.9	279.1

M1 plus quasi-money (22)(23)

billion DM, end of period

M1 plus quasi-monnaie (23)/(22)

milliards de DM, fin de période

	Year	Q.1	Q.2	Q.3	Q.4	JAN	FEB	MAR	APR	MAY	JUN	JUL	AUG	SEP	OCT	NOV	DEC
1964	100.8	91.0	94.7	95.1	100.8	91.1	92.0	91.0	92.4	94.4	94.7	95.3	96.2	95.1	95.7	98.5	100.8
1965	106.9	97.8	101.4	101.0	106.9	98.2	99.3	97.8	99.2	101.9	101.4	101.4	101.8	101.0	102.2	105.0	106.9
1966	113.4	103.3	107.6	108.5	113.4	103.6	104.3	103.3	105.6	107.2	107.6	108.2	109.0	108.5	108.8	111.9	113.4
1967	127.6	110.6	114.2	116.3	127.6	109.8	112.2	110.6	112.5	114.1	114.2	114.5	116.4	116.3	117.8	122.2	127.6
1968	142.3	123.0	129.4	133.0	142.3	122.9	124.1	123.0	125.2	129.1	129.4	129.3	131.3	133.0	135.7	141.0	142.3
1969	156.9	137.3	145.5	150.5	156.9	137.0	138.0	137.3	139.2	147.1	145.5	145.6	147.4	150.5	151.6	154.0	156.9
1970	173.4	148.8	159.0	160.3	173.4	149.8	150.9	148.8	151.7	156.7	159.0	162.9	163.5	160.3	161.4	168.2	173.4
1971	198.6	169.3	179.5	181.8	198.6	167.5	169.5	169.3	174.9	182.7	179.5	181.5	182.1	181.8	185.2	191.9	198.6
1972	232.3	192.1	204.7	210.4	232.3	191.5	193.3	192.1	195.5	199.4	204.7	210.0	211.0	210.4	212.9	222.2	232.3
1973	265.9	231.3	241.7	246.9	265.9	223.8	228.7	231.3	235.3	241.6	241.7	244.5	247.2	246.9	250.9	258.8	265.9
1974	279.6	255.8	262.2	258.0	279.6	256.3	258.5	255.8	262.4	264.6	262.2	262.2	261.0	258.0	258.6	269.9	279.6
1975	279.3	260.2	254.9	254.2	279.3	265.3	264.8	260.2	256.6	256.2	254.9	254.1	256.9	254.2	259.0	271.4	279.3
1976	298.2	260.6	274.6	276.0	298.2	261.6	263.1	260.6	265.7	270.7	274.6	273.3	278.0	276.0	284.4	295.7	298.2
1977	331.8	283.1	292.8	298.4	331.8	283.3	285.4	283.1	287.2	294.3	292.8	297.8	298.3	298.4	306.7	323.8	331.8
1978	375.4	311.0	324.5	335.7	375.4	315.6	315.8	311.0	316.6	323.5	324.5	331.1	335.3	335.7	349.0	369.8	375.4
1979	406.5	350.3	367.1	369.2	406.5	351.3	355.5	350.3	356.2	364.5	367.1	369.6	371.4	369.2	374.3	394.5	406.5
1980	440.6	389.6	399.5	401.3	440.6	384.1	390.8	389.6	391.4	400.4	399.5	402.1	405.7	401.3	407.1	434.4	440.6
1981	478.1	421.5	443.8	451.7	478.1	422.3	426.7	421.5	432.4	442.6	443.8	449.4	456.2	451.7	454.1	473.4	478.1
1982	502.2	460.0	473.4	477.3	502.2	463.0	465.3	460.0	464.7	473.9	473.4	477.0	479.1	477.3	481.3	494.6	502.2
1983	515.4	478.0	485.0	487.4	515.4	484.1	485.5	478.0	478.7	484.7	485.0	489.1	490.7	487.4	493.6	507.5	515.4

Personal savings deposits (22)(23)

billion DM, end of period

Dépôts d'épargne des particuliers (23)/(22)

milliards de DM, fin de période

	Year	Q.1	Q.2	Q.3	Q.4	JAN	FEB	MAR	APR	MAY	JUN	JUL	AUG	SEP	OCT	NOV	DEC
1964	84.3	75.8	77.6	79.7	84.3	74.1	75.1	75.8	76.5	76.9	77.6	78.4	79.0	79.7	80.7	81.3	84.3
1965	99.9	88.7	91.6	94.1	99.9	86.0	87.5	88.7	89.6	90.6	91.6	92.7	93.2	94.1	95.3	95.9	99.9
1966	115.6	103.4	106.1	108.9	115.6	101.6	102.8	103.4	104.4	105.1	106.1	107.3	108.2	108.9	110.3	110.6	115.6
1967	131.8	119.7	122.4	124.9	131.8	117.6	118.9	119.7	120.8	121.6	122.4	123.2	124.1	124.9	126.7	127.2	131.8
1968	151.4	137.0	139.3	142.6	151.4	134.2	136.0	137.0	137.7	138.6	139.3	140.6	141.7	142.6	144.3	145.1	151.4
1969	170.1	156.0	159.3	162.4	170.1	153.5	155.0	156.0	157.1	158.1	159.3	160.3	161.6	162.4	163.7	164.2	170.1
1970	189.9	173.7	175.9	178.2	189.9	171.8	173.2	173.7	174.6	175.0	175.9	176.1	177.3	178.2	179.5	180.6	189.9
1971	216.3	195.6	199.2	202.4	216.3	192.0	194.2	195.6	196.8	197.8	199.2	200.0	201.6	202.4	204.0	205.4	216.3
1972	245.7	221.5	227.8	232.3	245.7	218.4	220.5	221.5	224.1	225.7	227.8	229.7	231.1	232.3	234.4	235.6	245.7
1973	264.4	247.8	246.4	244.1	264.4	247.1	247.9	247.8	248.0	247.5	246.4	245.1	244.4	244.1	245.3	246.2	264.4
1974	294.9	265.9	269.1	272.1	294.9	264.8	265.8	265.9	266.8	268.0	269.1	269.6	270.9	272.1	274.4	276.7	294.9
1975	356.3	305.2	321.0	330.6	356.3	297.2	300.7	305.2	313.1	318.0	321.0	323.6	327.8	330.6	334.6	337.8	356.3
1976	388.7	362.2	365.8	368.5	388.7	359.4	362.4	362.2	362.7	364.3	365.8	366.6	368.1	368.5	370.9	372.5	388.7
1977	413.5	390.1	391.4	392.2	413.5	388.8	390.7	390.1	389.9	390.6	391.4	389.4	391.1	392.2	395.4	397.8	413.5
1978	441.5	412.4	415.9	420.1	441.5	411.6	413.1	412.4	413.6	414.6	415.9	416.9	419.2	420.1	423.2	425.5	441.5
1979	454.8	447.6	446.1	441.9	454.8	444.4	447.3	447.6	447.3	447.0	446.1	444.1	443.1	441.9	441.4	439.9	454.8
1980	464.0	446.0	439.3	438.3	464.0	450.7	449.5	446.0	441.4	439.7	439.3	437.2	438.1	438.3	439.8	441.5	464.0
1981	463.1	451.8	441.5	432.5	463.1	460.9	459.6	451.8	447.0	444.0	441.5	436.2	434.6	432.5	433.0	435.5	463.1
1982	498.0	462.3	464.2	462.5	498.0	461.5	462.9	462.3	463.1	463.9	464.2	461.7	462.1	462.5	464.8	468.0	498.0
1983	526.5	503.0	504.9	500.3	526.5	498.6	502.2	503.0	505.0	505.5	504.9	500.6	500.9	500.3	501.6	503.3	526.5

Bank credit to economy: (22)(23)(27) short-term

billion DM, end of period

Crédits bancaires à l'économie : (23)(27)/(22) court terme

milliards de DM, fin de période

	Year	Q.1	Q.2	Q.3	Q.4	JAN	FEB	MAR	APR	MAY	JUN	JUL	AUG	SEP	OCT	NOV	DEC
1964	60.7	56.1	58.3	58.8	60.7	54.7	55.1	56.1	56.2	56.9	58.3	57.5	57.4	58.8	58.5	59.0	60.7
1965	67.3	62.1	65.2	65.7	67.3	60.5	61.1	62.1	61.9	62.6	65.2	64.3	64.0	65.7	65.5	65.0	67.3
1966	72.3	69.3	72.7	72.7	72.3	66.5	67.8	69.3	70.1	70.2	72.7	71.9	71.0	72.7	71.5	71.1	72.3
1967	74.3	70.7	72.4	72.6	74.3	70.6	71.0	70.7	71.2	70.6	72.4	71.3	71.1	72.6	70.8	71.4	74.3
1968	81.0	73.5	76.7	78.1	81.0	71.7	72.0	73.5	72.9	74.0	76.7	75.2	76.2	78.1	78.2	78.9	81.0
1969	101.6	84.7	88.3	90.5	101.6	79.8	82.1	84.7	85.2	84.5	88.3	87.4	88.9	90.5	91.0	96.2	101.6
1970	113.6	103.9	109.9	109.9	113.6	101.1	103.1	103.9	104.5	106.4	109.9	109.1	108.8	109.9	108.5	109.4	113.6
1971	131.7	114.7	120.4	123.8	131.7	112.4	113.8	114.7	114.6	115.4	120.4	120.2	120.6	123.8	125.1	127.3	131.7
1972	155.9	135.0	145.2	146.3	155.9	129.5	130.7	135.0	137.8	139.8	145.2	143.0	141.4	146.3	146.4	150.0	155.9
1973	167.0	155.0	159.6	163.1	167.0	152.5	154.1	155.0	154.2	154.9	159.6	157.2	157.7	163.1	160.5	161.3	167.0
1974	179.7	169.1	176.7	177.9	179.7	165.0	167.1	169.1	168.8	168.5	176.7	174.4	174.7	177.9	174.6	176.3	179.7
1975	171.2	175.0	173.4	166.6	171.2	174.0	172.7	175.0	169.1	169.5	173.4	166.6	164.9	166.6	166.4	169.4	171.2
1976	182.8	165.6	174.2	176.6	182.8	167.2	166.7	165.6	166.4	165.6	174.2	172.4	173.1	176.6	177.9	178.4	182.8
1977	193.0	180.4	187.1	185.3	193.0	177.6	178.5	180.4	181.8	180.5	187.1	182.8	180.3	185.3	185.5	187.2	193.0
1978	205.6	187.4	196.2	197.1	205.6	182.7	184.8	187.4	187.6	189.7	196.2	193.5	190.2	197.1	195.0	199.0	205.6
1979	236.5	205.5	219.5	222.9	236.5	196.1	200.9	205.5	206.2	208.0	219.5	214.4	214.2	222.9	220.3	225.8	236.5
1980	268.2	233.5	247.5	248.6	268.2	225.8	228.7	233.5	234.5	237.5	247.5	243.1	242.9	248.6	249.5	255.9	268.2
1981	291.3	271.8	279.4	281.8	291.3	262.9	268.9	271.8	269.3	268.4	279.4	275.9	276.6	281.8	282.5	281.1	291.3
1982	303.7	288.1	296.8	298.7	303.7	287.5	287.5	288.1	285.6	285.2	296.8	295.7	293.7	298.7	299.4	295.8	303.7
1983	318.0	296.1	305.5	309.6	318.0	294.0	293.0	296.1	296.0	295.5	305.5	301.5	301.0	309.6	309.7	309.4	318.0

M1 plus quasi-money (22)
billion DM, end of period

Adjusted - Corrigé

M1 plus quasi-monnaie (22)
milliards de DM, fin de période

Year	Q.1	Q.2	Q.3	Q.4	JAN	FEB	MAR	APR	MAY	JUN	JUL	AUG	SEP	OCT	NOV	DEC
1964	92.6	94.8	95.9	97.9	92.0	92.3	92.6	93.1	93.7	94.8	95.4	95.9	95.9	96.4	97.0	97.9
1965	99.7	101.4	101.9	103.5	99.1	99.7	99.7	100.0	101.3	101.4	101.6	101.6	101.9	102.8	103.1	103.5
1966	105.3	107.6	109.3	109.7	104.6	104.9	105.3	106.5	106.5	107.6	108.6	108.8	109.3	109.4	109.7	109.7
1967	112.9	114.2	117.3	123.1	110.7	112.8	112.9	113.6	113.4	114.2	115.0	116.3	117.3	118.2	119.4	123.1
1968	125.9	129.4	134.2	140.9	124.0	124.9	125.9	126.6	128.3	129.4	129.8	131.0	134.2	136.3	137.9	140.9
1969	140.6	144.7	151.8	151.0	138.7	139.7	140.6	141.7	146.0	144.7	145.1	146.6	151.8	152.6	150.9	151.0
1970	152.5	158.3	162.2	166.8	151.3	152.3	152.5	154.2	155.6	158.3	162.3	162.6	162.2	162.5	164.6	166.8
1971	173.5	179.3	184.4	190.2	169.0	170.7	173.5	177.4	181.4	179.3	180.7	181.7	184.4	186.7	187.9	190.2
1972	196.4	204.7	213.3	221.6	192.7	194.4	196.4	197.9	199.0	204.7	209.2	211.6	213.3	214.8	217.8	221.6
1973	235.8	242.8	251.0	252.5	225.3	229.6	235.8	237.5	241.3	242.8	245.2	248.1	251.0	253.3	254.1	252.5
1974	260.2	264.5	262.1	264.5	256.9	258.6	260.2	265.3	264.2	264.5	264.3	262.3	262.1	260.8	263.0	264.5
1975	264.6	256.3	258.2	263.9	266.2	265.3	264.6	260.3	256.2	256.3	255.9	258.4	258.2	260.9	262.0	263.9
1976	266.4	277.3	281.4	281.2	263.5	264.8	266.4	269.9	270.2	277.3	274.9	279.4	281.4	285.5	284.5	281.2
1977	290.0	296.3	304.0	312.6	284.7	286.8	290.0	291.8	294.2	296.3	299.6	300.5	304.0	307.1	311.6	312.6
1978	318.5	327.6	341.6	353.9	317.7	317.8	318.5	322.1	324.3	327.6	332.4	337.9	341.6	350.0	355.9	353.9
1979	358.4	370.2	376.0	383.2	354.4	358.3	358.4	362.0	365.8	370.2	371.5	373.9	376.0	376.6	379.8	383.2
1980	397.0	402.4	406.5	420.2	386.9	392.9	397.0	399.5	401.0	402.4	404.6	406.5	406.5	408.5	420.8	420.2
1981	429.6	447.2	457.0	458.2	424.0	428.0	429.6	440.8	443.0	447.2	451.1	455.3	457.0	454.7	460.2	458.2
1982	469.7	477.4	482.5	482.1	465.0	466.6	469.7	473.0	474.7	477.4	477.9	478.2	482.5	482.5	481.7	482.1
1983	487.9	488.3	492.3	494.7	485.6	486.3	487.9	486.9	485.0	488.3	490.1	491.3	492.3	495.1	494.5	494.7

Bank credit to economy: (22)(27)
short-term
billion DM, end of period

Adjusted - Corrigé *

Crédits bancaires à l'économie : (27) (22)
court terme
milliards de DM, fin de période

Year	Q.1	Q.2	Q.3	Q.4	JAN	FEB	MAR	APR	MAY	JUN	JUL	AUG	SEP	OCT	NOV	DEC
1964	55.8	56.8	58.2	60.1	55.6	55.6	55.8	56.3	57.1	56.8	57.2	57.8	58.2	58.9	59.8	60.1
1965	61.9	63.6	65.1	66.6	61.3	61.6	61.9	62.0	62.9	63.6	64.0	64.4	65.1	66.0	65.9	66.6
1966	69.1	70.9	72.1	71.4	67.4	68.2	69.1	70.1	70.5	70.9	71.7	71.6	72.1	72.1	72.1	71.4
1967	70.6	70.8	72.3	73.2	71.3	71.4	70.6	71.2	70.9	70.8	71.2	71.7	72.3	71.5	72.2	73.2
1968	73.4	75.1	78.0	79.6	72.3	72.2	73.4	73.0	74.3	75.1	75.2	76.8	78.0	79.0	79.6	79.6
1969	84.5	86.5	90.5	99.7	80.3	82.1	84.5	85.4	84.8	86.5	87.5	89.7	90.5	92.1	96.8	99.7
1970	103.6	107.9	110.0	111.3	101.6	103.0	103.6	104.7	106.9	107.9	109.4	109.9	110.0	109.7	110.0	111.3
1971	114.5	118.2	123.9	128.9	112.9	113.7	114.5	115.1	116.0	118.2	120.6	121.9	123.9	126.5	127.8	128.9
1972	134.8	142.5	146.3	152.4	130.1	130.6	134.8	138.5	140.7	142.5	143.4	142.9	146.3	147.7	150.5	152.4
1973	155.0	156.6	162.8	163.0	153.0	154.2	155.0	155.1	156.2	156.6	157.8	159.5	162.8	161.8	161.4	163.0
1974	169.2	173.3	177.3	175.3	165.7	167.6	169.2	170.0	170.2	173.3	175.3	176.6	177.3	175.6	176.1	175.3
1975	175.5	170.0	165.8	166.9	174.7	173.6	175.5	170.3	171.2	170.0	167.3	166.9	165.8	167.2	168.9	166.9
1976	166.3	170.6	175.5	177.9	168.1	167.8	166.3	167.5	167.5	170.6	173.1	175.5	175.5	178.6	177.7	177.9
1977	181.1	183.1	184.2	187.4	178.9	180.1	181.1	183.1	182.3	183.1	183.3	183.0	184.2	186.4	186.3	187.4
1978	187.9	192.0	196.1	199.4	184.4	186.6	187.9	188.9	191.6	192.0	193.9	193.3	196.1	196.2	198.2	199.4
1979	205.7	214.6	221.8	229.2	198.0	202.9	205.7	207.7	209.9	214.6	214.9	217.7	221.8	221.6	225.1	229.2
1980	233.5	242.2	247.6	259.6	227.8	231.3	233.5	236.2	239.9	242.2	243.9	246.9	247.6	251.3	255.4	259.6
1981	271.5	273.4	281.0	282.2	265.3	271.9	271.5	271.5	271.1	273.4	276.8	280.9	281.0	284.7	280.5	282.2
1982	287.6	290.4	297.8	294.2	290.1	290.4	287.6	287.9	288.1	290.4	296.6	298.1	297.8	301.8	295.5	294.2
1983	295.5	299.0	308.7	308.1	296.6	296.0	295.5	298.4	298.5	299.0	302.4	305.6	308.7	312.1	309.1	308.1

* Adjusted by the O.E.C.D.

* Corrigé par l'O.C.D.E.

Bank credit to economy: (22)(23)(27) medium- and long-term

billion DM, end of period

Crédits bancaires à l'économie : (22)(23)(27) moyen et long terme

milliards de DM, fin de période

	Year	Q.1	Q.2	Q.3	Q.4	JAN	FEB	MAR	APR	MAY	JUN	JUL	AUG	SEP	OCT	NOV	DEC
1964	163.7	147.8	152.7	158.1	163.7	145.6	146.5	147.8	149.2	151.0	152.7	154.6	156.2	158.1	160.0	161.9	163.7
1965	183.9	167.4	172.2	178.2	183.9	164.6	165.8	167.4	169.0	171.0	172.2	174.5	176.7	178.2	180.0	181.9	183.9
1966	200.3	187.9	192.2	196.7	200.3	184.9	186.2	187.9	189.4	191.0	192.2	193.7	195.5	196.7	197.9	199.1	200.3
1967	216.2	202.7	206.0	209.9	216.2	200.6	201.7	202.7	203.5	205.0	206.0	206.9	208.8	209.9	211.8	213.7	216.2
1968	242.8	219.8	225.0	230.1	242.8	216.7	218.2	219.8	221.2	223.1	225.0	226.6	228.9	230.1	232.7	235.0	242.8
1969	272.4	247.4	254.1	261.4	272.4	244.1	245.8	247.4	249.9	251.8	254.1	256.9	259.7	261.4	264.4	268.0	272.4
1970	304.1	277.3	284.3	292.9	304.1	274.1	275.8	277.3	279.4	281.6	284.3	287.5	290.2	292.9	295.5	298.7	304.1
1971	345.4	310.1	318.4	331.3	345.4	305.2	307.1	310.1	312.8	315.1	318.4	322.2	327.1	331.3	335.1	338.2	345.4
1972	399.7	354.5	365.7	379.8	399.7	347.3	350.7	354.5	358.0	362.3	365.7	369.9	375.2	379.8	384.4	389.9	399.7
1973	449.7	416.1	428.4	437.5	449.7	403.6	410.6	416.1	421.0	424.6	428.4	431.7	435.4	437.5	440.9	444.6	449.7
1974	477.8	453.9	459.4	467.8	477.8	449.8	451.1	453.9	455.1	458.0	459.4	462.8	465.5	467.8	470.7	473.3	477.8
1975	519.0	481.2	488.9	500.7	519.0	478.1	478.5	481.2	483.9	486.8	488.9	493.4	496.4	500.7	506.1	511.1	519.0
1976	570.0	526.6	538.4	551.0	570.0	519.8	523.2	526.6	531.1	535.5	538.4	542.6	546.7	551.0	556.6	562.3	570.0
1977	627.4	576.8	590.7	606.3	627.4	569.7	572.6	576.8	580.9	586.0	590.7	596.7	602.3	606.3	613.1	619.2	627.4
1978	703.1	636.2	653.0	675.1	703.1	628.3	631.3	636.2	641.5	647.0	653.0	660.6	667.8	675.1	682.5	690.5	703.1
1979	785.7	717.6	739.6	760.3	785.7	705.4	710.9	717.6	724.9	733.6	739.6	748.0	755.0	760.3	768.6	775.0	785.7
1980	854.2	797.2	812.7	827.9	854.2	785.7	791.3	797.2	804.4	809.0	812.7	819.3	823.0	827.9	835.1	842.1	854.2
1981	914.6	867.0	882.7	897.0	914.6	855.9	862.4	867.0	872.9	878.2	882.7	887.1	892.1	897.0	900.6	905.4	914.6
1982	967.0	916.6	926.6	942.3	967.0	911.7	913.2	916.6	920.4	924.6	926.6	932.3	938.1	942.3	947.9	952.3	967.0
1983	1042.7	969.8	990.5	1011.1	1042.7	964.3	967.9	969.8	974.4	982.0	990.5	997.7	1005.3	1011.1	1017.4	1025.2	1042.7

Bank credit to manufacturing (23)(26)(28)

billion DM, end of period

Crédits bancaires aux industries manufacturières (23)(26)(28)

milliards de DM, fin de période

	Year	Q.1	Q.2	Q.3	Q.4	JAN	FEB	MAR	APR	MAY	JUN	JUL	AUG	SEP	OCT	NOV	DEC
1964																	
1965																	
1966																	
1967																	
1968	55.8				55.8												55.8
1969	71.6	57.9	60.3	62.7	71.6			57.9			60.3			62.7			71.6
1970	83.5	74.0	79.3	81.7	83.5			74.0			79.3			81.7			83.5
1971	95.1	84.2	87.4	90.4	95.1			84.2			87.4			90.4			95.1
1972	107.6	96.5	101.6	102.0	107.6			96.5			101.7			102.0			107.6
1973	113.3	107.0	108.6	111.1	113.3			107.0			108.6			111.1			112.9
1974	120.6	114.1	117.7	119.0	120.6			114.1			117.7			119.0			120.6
1975	114.7	117.1	115.3	112.7	114.7			117.1			115.3			112.7			114.7
1976	119.2	110.0	112.9	114.1	119.2			110.0			112.9			114.1			119.2
1977	125.2	116.6	119.2	119.2	125.2			116.6			119.2			119.2			125.2
1978	128.6	118.8	122.4	123.0	128.6			118.8			122.4			123.0			128.6
1979	144.0	127.4	133.1	134.9	144.0			127.4			133.1			134.9			144.0
1980	174.0	138.5	144.0	142.2	174.0			138.5			144.0			142.2			151.3
1981	181.4	175.6	178.9	178.1	181.4			175.6			178.9			178.1			181.4
1982	180.8	175.8	177.6	179.1	180.8			175.8			177.6			179.1			180.8
1983	181.9	173.1	176.1	177.1	181.9			173.1			176.1			177.1			181.9

Official discount rate

per cent per annum, end of period

Taux d'escompte officiel

pourcentage par an, fin de période

	Year	Q.1	Q.2	Q.3	Q.4	JAN	FEB	MAR	APR	MAY	JUN	JUL	AUG	SEP	OCT	NOV	DEC
1964	3.00	3.00	3.00	3.00	3.00	3.00	3.00	3.00	3.00	3.00	3.00	3.00	3.00	3.00	3.00	3.00	3.00
1965	4.00	3.50	3.50	4.00	4.00	3.50	3.50	3.50	3.50	3.50	3.50	3.50	4.00	4.00	4.00	4.00	4.00
1966	5.00	4.00	5.00	5.00	5.00	4.00	4.00	4.00	4.00	5.00	5.00	5.00	5.00	5.00	5.00	5.00	5.00
1967	3.00	4.00	3.00	3.00	3.00	4.50	4.00	4.00	3.50	3.00	3.00	3.00	3.00	3.00	3.00	3.00	3.00
1968	3.00	3.00	3.00	3.00	3.00	3.00	3.00	3.00	3.00	3.00	3.00	3.00	3.00	3.00	3.00	3.00	3.00
1969	6.00	3.00	5.00	6.00	6.00	3.00	3.00	3.00	4.00	4.00	5.00	5.00	5.00	6.00	6.00	6.00	6.00
1970	6.00	7.50	7.50	7.00	6.00	6.00	6.00	7.50	7.50	7.50	7.50	7.00	7.00	7.00	7.00	6.50	6.00
1971	4.00	6.00	5.00	5.00	4.00	6.00	6.00	6.00	5.00	5.00	5.00	5.00	5.00	5.00	4.50	4.50	4.00
1972	4.50	3.00	3.00	3.00	4.50	4.00	3.00	3.00	3.00	3.00	3.00	3.00	3.00	3.00	3.50	4.00	4.50
1973	7.00	5.00	7.00	7.00	7.00	5.00	5.00	5.00	5.00	6.00	7.00	7.00	7.00	7.00	7.00	7.00	7.00
1974	6.00	7.00	7.00	7.00	6.00	7.00	7.00	7.00	7.00	7.00	7.00	7.00	7.00	7.00	6.50	6.50	6.00
1975	3.50	5.00	4.50	3.50	3.50	6.00	5.50	5.00	5.00	4.50	4.50	4.50	4.00	3.50	3.50	3.50	3.50
1976	3.50	3.50	3.50	3.50	3.50	3.50	3.50	3.50	3.50	3.50	3.50	3.50	3.50	3.50	3.50	3.50	3.50
1977	3.00	3.50	3.50	3.50	3.00	3.50	3.50	3.50	3.50	3.50	3.50	3.50	3.50	3.50	3.50	3.50	3.00
1978	3.00	3.00	3.00	3.00	3.00	3.00	3.00	3.00	3.00	3.00	3.00	3.00	3.00	3.00	3.00	3.00	3.00
1979	6.00	4.00	4.00	5.00	6.00	3.00	3.00	4.00	4.00	4.00	4.00	5.00	5.00	5.00	5.00	6.00	6.00
1980	7.50	7.00	7.50	7.50	7.50	6.00	7.00	7.00	7.00	7.50	7.50	7.50	7.50	7.50	7.50	7.50	7.50
1981	7.50	7.50	7.50	7.50	7.50	7.50	7.50	7.50	7.50	7.50	7.50	7.50	7.50	7.50	7.50	7.50	7.50
1982	5.00	7.50	7.50	7.00	5.00	7.50	7.50	7.50	7.50	7.50	7.50	7.50	7.00	7.00	6.00	6.00	5.00
1983	4.00	4.00	4.00	4.00	4.00	5.00	5.00	4.00	4.00	4.00	4.00	4.00	4.00	4.00	4.00	4.00	4.00

Bank credit to economy: (22)(27) medium- and long-term

Crédits bancaires à l'économie : (22)(27) moyen et long terme

billion DM, end of period — milliards de DM, fin de période

Adjusted - Corrigé *

	Year	Q.1	Q.2	Q.3	Q.4	JAN	FEB	MAR	APR	MAY	JUN	JUL	AUG	SEP	OCT	NOV	DEC
1964		148.1	153.0	158.2	162.9	145.4	146.7	148.1	149.6	151.2	153.0	154.7	156.2	158.2	160.3	161.5	162.9
1965		167.4	172.3	179.0	183.2	164.3	165.6	167.4	169.0	170.8	172.3	174.7	176.9	179.0	180.9	182.2	183.2
1966		187.4	192.4	197.9	199.8	184.3	185.5	187.4	189.0	190.6	192.4	194.1	195.9	197.9	199.7	199.9	199.8
1967		201.5	206.0	211.4	215.5	199.8	200.3	201.5	202.7	204.3	206.0	207.6	209.4	211.4	213.9	215.0	215.5
1968		218.2	225.2	232.0	241.8	215.6	216.3	218.2	220.1	222.7	225.2	227.2	229.8	232.0	235.1	236.6	241.8
1969		245.7	254.6	263.3	270.7	242.6	243.6	245.7	248.6	251.6	254.6	258.0	260.8	263.3	266.8	269.6	270.7
1970		275.7	285.2	294.4	302.0	272.7	273.6	275.7	278.6	281.6	285.2	288.7	291.1	294.4	297.3	299.9	302.0
1971		308.8	319.4	332.3	343.0	303.7	305.3	308.8	312.2	315.4	319.4	323.2	328.1	332.3	336.1	338.9	343.0
1972		353.8	366.8	380.5	396.9	346.3	349.3	353.8	358.0	362.6	366.8	371.1	376.0	380.5	385.1	390.3	396.9
1973		415.7	429.7	438.4	446.6	402.4	409.8	415.7	421.0	425.0	429.7	433.0	436.3	438.4	441.3	444.6	446.6
1974		453.5	460.8	468.7	474.5	448.9	450.6	453.5	455.6	458.4	460.8	463.7	466.4	468.7	470.7	472.8	474.5
1975		481.2	490.4	501.7	514.9	477.1	478.5	481.2	484.4	487.3	490.4	494.4	497.4	501.7	506.1	510.6	514.9
1976		527.1	540.1	552.1	565.5	518.7	523.2	527.1	531.6	536.0	540.1	543.6	547.3	552.1	556.0	561.1	565.5
1977		577.4	592.5	607.5	622.4	568.6	573.1	577.4	582.0	586.6	592.5	597.3	602.9	607.5	612.5	618.0	622.4
1978		636.8	654.3	676.4	698.2	627.1	631.9	636.8	642.7	647.7	654.3	661.2	668.5	676.4	682.5	689.8	698.2
1979		718.4	741.1	761.8	779.5	704.7	711.6	718.4	725.6	734.3	741.1	748.7	755.7	761.8	768.6	774.2	779.5
1980		798.8	814.3	829.6	847.4	784.2	792.9	798.8	806.0	809.8	814.3	820.1	823.8	829.6	835.1	841.3	847.4
1981		867.9	884.4	898.8	908.3	854.1	864.2	867.9	874.7	879.1	884.4	888.0	893.0	898.8	901.5	905.4	908.3
1982		917.5	928.5	944.2	960.3	909.9	915.0	917.5	921.4	924.6	928.5	933.2	939.1	944.2	948.8	952.3	960.3
1983		970.7	992.5	1013.2	1035.5	962.3	969.3	970.7	975.4	982.0	992.5	998.7	1006.3	1013.2	1018.4	1025.2	1035.5

Call money rate (Frankfurt) (25)

Taux de l'argent au jour le jour (Francfort) (25)

per cent per annum, end of period — pourcentage par an, fin de période

	Year	Q.1	Q.2	Q.3	Q.4	JAN	FEB	MAR	APR	MAY	JUN	JUL	AUG	SEP	OCT	NOV	DEC
1964	3.33	3.26	3.33	3.63	3.33	2.64	2.87	3.26	3.36	3.33	3.33	3.26	3.63	3.63	3.72	3.10	3.33
1965	4.67	4.09	4.41	4.77	4.67	2.54	3.42	4.09	4.23	3.78	4.41	4.34	3.81	4.77	4.85	4.24	4.67
1966	5.85	5.07	6.11	5.61	5.85	4.12	4.47	5.07	5.33	5.07	6.11	6.20	5.33	5.61	5.72	5.19	5.85
1967	2.77	4.26	3.80	3.12	2.77	4.92	5.10	4.26	4.24	2.89	3.80	2.41	2.45	3.12	2.06	2.16	2.77
1968	1.84	2.69	2.58	2.66	1.84	2.26	2.85	2.69	2.72	2.99	2.68	2.43	3.07	2.66	3.18	1.55	1.84
1969	8.35	3.63	5.02	4.03	8.35	3.30	3.27	3.63	2.46	1.63	5.02	5.80	5.87	4.03	6.68	7.64	8.35
1970	7.47	9.53	8.72	9.14	7.47	9.09	8.48	9.53	9.65	9.18	8.72	8.80	7.83	9.14	7.44	8.43	7.47
1971	5.77	7.36	6.94	6.99	5.77	7.60	7.27	7.36	4.23	2.11	6.94	6.22	6.21	6.99	7.49	4.54	5.77
1972	6.69	3.88	2.65	4.83	6.69	4.20	4.15	3.88	3.77	2.95	2.65	2.24	4.48	4.83	6.07	5.71	6.69
1973	11.89	11.37	10.90	9.76	11.89	5.58	2.18	11.37	14.84	7.40	10.90	15.78	10.63	9.76	10.57	11.30	11.89
1974	8.35	11.63	8.79	9.22	8.35	10.40	9.13	11.63	5.33	8.36	8.79	9.40	9.30	9.22	9.10	7.38	8.35
1975	3.92	4.85	4.98	4.33	3.92	7.71	4.25	4.85	4.69	5.41	4.98	4.12	1.87	4.33	3.33	3.39	3.92
1976	5.03	3.64	4.31	4.33	5.03	3.58	3.28	3.64	2.81	3.71	4.31	4.48	4.21	4.33	3.26	3.98	5.03
1977	3.24	4.53	4.13	4.01	3.24	4.57	4.36	4.53	4.52	4.10	4.13	4.26	4.03	4.01	3.98	3.94	3.24
1978	3.56	3.55	3.55	3.51	3.56	3.37	3.34	3.55	3.53	3.54	3.55	3.40	3.23	3.51	3.07	2.67	3.56
1979	9.02	4.32	5.60	6.50	9.02	2.99	3.81	4.32	5.24	5.16	5.60	5.73	6.36	6.50	7.87	7.86	9.02
1980	9.16	8.61	10.04	9.27	9.16	8.25	8.06	8.61	9.05	9.80	10.04	9.80	8.92	9.27	9.01	8.76	9.16
1981	10.58	11.97	11.93	12.00	10.58	9.09	10.38	11.97	11.31	11.83	11.93	11.98	11.97	12.00	11.30	10.81	10.58
1982	6.15	9.83	9.02	7.97	6.15	10.10	10.06	9.83	9.47	9.11	9.02	9.02	8.78	7.97	7.46	7.02	6.15
1983	5.61	5.51	5.05	5.42	5.61	5.85	5.74	5.51	4.93	5.04	5.05	5.05	5.06	5.42	5.53	5.57	5.61

Rate on 3-month loans (Frankfurt) (25)

Taux de prêts à 3 mois (Francfort) (25)

per cent per annum, end of period — pourcentage par an, fin de période

	Year	Q.1	Q.2	Q.3	Q.4	JAN	FEB	MAR	APR	MAY	JUN	JUL	AUG	SEP	OCT	NOV	DEC
1964	5.36	3.46	3.75	4.08	5.36	3.33	3.33	3.46	3.55	3.69	3.75	3.69	3.91	4.08	5.42	5.50	5.36
1965	6.55	4.28	4.80	5.36	6.55	3.88	3.95	4.28	4.52	4.69	4.80	5.08	5.27	5.36	6.66	6.58	6.55
1966	7.57	5.69	6.81	6.80	7.57	5.23	5.36	5.69	6.21	6.35	6.81	6.89	7.00	6.80	7.88	7.73	7.57
1967	4.07	5.04	3.98	3.43	4.07	5.69	5.56	5.04	4.48	3.69	3.98	3.51	3.56	3.43	4.20	4.00	4.07
1968	4.25	3.52	3.72	3.54	4.25	3.32	3.45	3.52	3.64	3.68	3.72	3.59	3.55	3.54	4.75	4.50	4.25
1969	8.83	4.21	5.50	6.94	8.83	3.87	3.91	4.21	4.40	4.38	5.50	5.78	6.50	6.94	7.42	7.75	8.83
1970	8.12	9.81	9.88	9.40	8.12	9.38	9.51	9.81	9.86	9.93	9.88	9.59	9.16	9.40	9.53	8.84	8.12
1971	6.63	7.46	6.80	7.59	6.63	7.50	7.47	7.46	6.36	6.16	6.80	7.66	7.56	7.59	7.80	6.79	6.63
1972	8.60	4.80	4.65	5.32	8.60	5.19	4.88	4.80	4.78	4.71	4.65	4.65	4.60	5.32	6.88	8.07	8.60
1973	13.20	8.77	13.62	14.25	13.20	7.89	7.96	8.77	10.62	12.42	13.62	14.30	14.57	14.25	14.49	13.62	13.20
1974	8.60	11.20	9.46	9.69	8.60	12.09	10.67	11.20	10.07	9.10	9.46	9.48	9.65	9.69	9.78	9.04	8.60
1975	4.21	5.71	4.88	3.93	4.21	7.74	6.43	5.71	4.89	4.99	4.88	4.66	3.88	3.93	4.07	4.12	4.21
1976	4.93	3.74	4.14	4.56	4.93	3.93	3.72	3.74	3.62	3.77	4.14	4.47	4.56	4.56	4.85	4.69	4.93
1977	3.98	4.73	4.28	4.15	3.98	4.78	4.71	4.73	4.62	4.44	4.28	4.29	4.12	4.15	4.13	4.15	3.98
1978	4.06	3.51	3.68	3.70	4.06	3.58	3.46	3.51	3.56	3.60	3.68	3.75	3.70	3.70	3.95	3.85	4.06
1979	9.58	4.47	6.46	7.89	9.58	3.89	4.15	4.47	5.54	5.92	6.46	6.84	7.09	7.89	8.76	9.65	9.58
1980	10.20	9.64	10.11	8.97	10.20	8.86	8.97	9.64	10.22	10.26	10.11	9.70	8.98	8.97	9.08	9.45	10.20
1981	10.82	13.60	13.09	12.50	10.82	9.47	10.67	13.60	13.19	13.20	13.09	12.96	12.90	12.50	11.78	11.08	10.82
1982	6.62	9.87	9.28	8.18	6.62	10.46	10.27	9.87	9.33	9.18	9.28	9.46	9.00	8.18	7.58	7.31	6.62
1983	6.48	5.45	5.57	5.88	6.48	5.82	5.83	5.45	5.20	5.33	5.57	5.57	5.71	5.88	6.18	6.30	6.48

* Adjusted by the O.E.C.D. — * Corrigé par l'O.C.D.E.

GERMANY

Yield of long-term Government bonds (29)
per cent per annum, end of period

Rendement des bons d'État à long terme (29)
pourcentage par an, fin de période

	Year	Q.1	Q.2	Q.3	Q.4	JAN	FEB	MAR	APR	MAY	JUN	JUL	AUG	SEP	OCT	NOV	DEC
1964	6.4	6.0	6.3	6.4	6.4	5.9	5.9	6.0	6.2	6.3	6.3	6.3	6.3	6.4	6.4	6.4	6.4
1965	7.7	6.5	7.1	7.4	7.7	6.4	6.5	6.5	6.6	6.9	7.1	7.2	7.3	7.4	7.5	7.5	7.7
1966	7.7	7.7	8.4	8.5	7.7	7.6	7.6	7.7	8.0	8.2	8.4	8.6	8.6	8.5	8.4	8.2	7.7
1967	6.8	7.2	6.9	6.7	6.8	7.5	7.4	7.2	6.9	6.9	6.9	6.9	6.8	6.7	6.7	6.8	6.8
1968	6.3	6.7	6.4	6.3	6.3	6.7	6.7	6.7	6.6	6.4	6.4	6.4	6.3	6.3	6.3	6.3	6.3
1969	7.6	6.4	6.7	7.2	7.6	6.3	6.3	6.4	6.5	6.5	6.7	6.9	6.9	7.2	7.4	7.4	7.6
1970	8.2	8.1	8.7	8.5	8.2	7.6	7.8	8.1	8.1	8.4	8.7	8.7	8.4	8.5	8.7	8.6	8.2
1971	7.9	7.9	8.2	8.1	7.9	7.7	7.7	7.9	7.9	8.0	8.2	8.3	8.3	8.1	8.0	7.9	7.9
1972	8.6	7.4	7.9	7.9	8.6	7.6	7.3	7.4	7.7	7.8	7.9	8.0	7.9	7.9	8.0	8.4	8.6
1973	9.6	8.5	9.9	9.6	9.6	8.6	8.5	8.5	8.8	9.3	9.9	10.0	9.9	9.6	9.7	9.5	9.6
1974	9.8	10.4	10.7	10.7	9.8	9.6	9.9	10.4	10.4	10.6	10.7	10.7	10.7	10.7	10.7	10.4	9.8
1975	8.3	8.7	8.2	8.3	8.3	9.3	8.8	8.7	8.6	8.3	8.2	8.2	8.3	8.3	8.4	8.4	8.3
1976	7.3	7.6	8.0	7.9	7.3	8.1	7.9	7.6	7.6	7.8	8.0	8.1	8.1	7.9	7.8	7.4	7.3
1977	5.7	6.8	6.1	5.7	5.7	7.0	7.0	6.8	6.3	6.2	6.1	6.0	5.7	5.7	5.7	5.7	5.7
1978	6.3	5.2	5.6	6.0	6.3	5.5	5.4	5.2	5.2	5.4	5.6	5.9	6.1	6.0	6.0	6.2	6.3
1979	7.9	6.9	7.8	7.5	7.9	6.4	6.8	6.9	7.0	7.6	7.8	7.8	7.5	7.5	7.8	8.1	7.9
1980	8.9	9.4	8.2	8.1	8.9	8.1	8.5	9.4	9.4	8.7	8.2	7.9	7.8	8.1	8.3	8.7	8.9
1981	9.7	10.3	10.9	11.1	9.7	9.1	9.9	10.3	10.2	10.8	10.9	11.0	11.2	11.1	10.4	10.0	9.7
1982	7.9	9.5	9.1	8.7	7.9	9.9	9.8	9.5	9.0	8.8	9.1	9.3	9.0	8.7	8.3	8.1	7.9
1983	8.2	7.4	8.0	8.3	8.2	7.6	7.6	7.4	7.4	7.6	8.0	8.1	8.3	8.3	8.1	8.1	8.2

Share prices: industrials (25)(30)
(Federal Statistical Office)
1980 = 100

Cours des actions industrielles (30) (25)
(Office fédéral de statistique)
1980 = 100

	Year	Q.1	Q.2	Q.3	Q.4	JAN	FEB	MAR	APR	MAY	JUN	JUL	AUG	SEP	OCT	NOV	DEC
1964	99	99	98	100	95	97	99	102	100	98	97	99	101	100	95	94	95
1965	89	93	89	87	82	96	94	90	90	90	86	87	88	87	84	82	81
1966	73	84	75	69	66	84	85	82	79	76	70	66	69	71	66	67	66
1967	76	71	69	78	87	69	71	73	69	70	68	72	79	82	84	87	90
1968	99	94	100	102	101	93	94	96	100	98	103	102	103	101	103	99	100
1969	109	103	107	108	115	104	103	104	104	111	107	105	111	109	113	119	114
1970	96	107	96	93	88	108	106	107	102	95	90	94	94	92	90	87	86
1971	93	98	95	92	86	96	100	100	94	97	93	96	92	89	83	85	90
1972	101	99	103	103	99	94	100	104	103	104	101	105	104	101	98	99	99
1973	95	106	100	89	87	105	104	110	106	97	96	89	89	87	93	84	83
1974	81	85	85	78	78	88	83	84	87	85	82	79	79	75	76	78	79
1975	93	90	91	91	100	83	94	94	95	88	88	94	91	89	96	101	102
1976	101	107	103	99	94	105	106	109	103	102	103	100	98	98	91	96	96
1977	102	97	102	103	105	98	97	97	101	104	101	101	103	103	104	107	105
1978	100	107	106	112	114	107	108	106	106	105	107	110	112	115	116	113	113
1979	105	111	105	104	101	114	110	109	108	105	101	103	104	106	103	99	99
1980	100	100	99	102	100	99	103	98	97	99	101	102	102	101	102	99	98
1981	101	97	103	105	99	98	96	98	102	102	106	106	106	101	99	99	99
1982	100	100	100	97	104	98	100	102	102	100	97	97	96	99	102	102	107
1983	132	114	133	137	143	108	113	123	132	133	133	139	136	134	141	144	146

U.S. dollar exchange rate: spot
cents per DM, end of period

Taux de change du dollar É.-U. : au comptant
cents par DM, fin de période

	Year	Q.1	Q.2	Q.3	Q.4	JAN	FEB	MAR	APR	MAY	JUN	JUL	AUG	SEP	OCT	NOV	DEC
1964	25.15	25.16	25.16	25.16	25.15	25.17	25.17	25.16	25.16	25.17	25.16	25.15	25.15	25.16	25.15	25.15	25.15
1965	24.97	25.14	24.98	24.93	24.97	25.14	25.16	25.14	25.14	25.03	24.98	24.93	24.92	24.93	24.99	25.00	24.97
1966	25.14	24.90	25.00	25.07	25.14	24.90	24.91	24.90	24.88	24.93	25.00	25.06	25.07	25.07	25.14	25.17	25.14
1967	25.01	25.16	25.09	24.98	25.01	25.16	25.16	25.16	25.17	25.13	25.09	24.98	25.00	24.98	24.97	25.10	25.01
1968	25.00	25.12	25.03	25.15	25.00	24.98	24.98	25.12	25.08	25.11	25.03	24.88	25.17	25.15	25.15	25.07	25.00
1969	27.10	24.85	24.98	26.04	27.10	24.94	24.86	24.85	25.17	24.99	24.98	24.98	25.14	26.04	27.10	27.10	27.10
1970	27.41	27.30	27.54	27.53	27.41	27.11	27.10	27.30	27.51	27.53	27.54	27.54	27.54	27.53	27.54	27.54	27.41
1971	30.60	27.55	28.60	30.14	30.60	27.54	27.52	27.55	27.53	28.17	28.60	28.90	29.45	30.14	29.98	30.22	30.60
1972	31.24	31.56	31.69	31.23	31.24	31.16	31.37	31.56	31.46	31.48	31.69	31.50	31.35	31.23	31.21	31.29	31.24
1973	37.00	35.23	41.24	41.40	37.00	31.67	35.17	35.23	35.25	36.63	41.24	42.52	40.60	41.40	40.91	38.19	37.00
1974	41.50	39.64	39.14	37.70	41.50	35.94	37.49	39.64	40.87	39.54	39.14	38.66	37.54	37.70	38.76	40.37	41.50
1975	38.13	42.64	42.47	37.57	38.13	42.72	43.77	42.64	42.05	42.62	42.47	38.81	38.69	37.57	39.14	38.06	38.13
1976	42.33	39.40	38.85	41.04	42.33	38.55	38.99	39.40	39.43	38.54	38.85	39.32	39.57	41.04	41.58	41.58	42.33
1977	47.51	41.86	42.77	43.34	47.51	41.30	41.76	41.86	42.39	42.44	42.77	43.71	43.07	43.34	44.39	44.89	47.51
1978	54.71	49.43	48.19	51.58	54.71	47.35	49.12	49.43	48.36	47.60	48.19	48.99	50.34	51.58	57.58	53.99	54.71
1979	57.75	53.55	54.11	57.39	57.75	53.72	54.01	53.55	52.58	52.38	54.11	54.42	54.71	57.39	55.35	57.80	57.75
1980	51.05	51.50	56.88	55.21	51.05	57.49	56.42	51.50	55.51	55.99	56.88	56.02	55.79	55.21	52.38	51.93	51.05
1981	44.35	47.58	41.83	43.06	44.35	47.24	46.96	47.58	45.16	42.97	41.83	40.58	41.17	43.06	44.36	45.38	44.35
1982	42.08	41.42	40.65	39.56	42.08	43.32	41.91	41.42	42.87	42.64	40.65	40.74	40.05	39.56	38.96	40.21	42.08
1983	36.71	41.21	39.34	37.89	36.71	40.86	41.30	41.21	40.68	39.70	39.34	37.83	36.94	37.89	38.08	37.08	36.71

U.S. dollar exchange rate: forward (90 days) / Taux de change du dollar É.-U. : à terme (90 jours)

cents per DM, end of period / cents par DM, fin de période

	Year	Q.1	Q.2	Q.3	Q.4	JAN	FEB	MAR	APR	MAY	JUN	JUL	AUG	SEP	OCT	NOV	DEC
1964	25.19	25.21	25.23	25.16	25.19	25.21	25.23	25.21	25.19	25.19	25.23	25.20	25.18	25.16	25.15	25.17	25.19
1965	24.98	25.20	25.01	24.92	24.98	25.19	25.18	25.20	25.16	25.08	25.01	24.95	24.93	24.92	24.95	24.98	24.98
1966	25.14	24.91	24.96	25.07	25.14	24.91	24.91	24.91	24.89	24.91	24.96	25.05	25.08	25.07	25.11	25.14	25.14
1967	25.23	25.16	25.15	25.06	25.23	25.14	25.16	25.16	25.17	25.18	25.15	25.06	25.09	25.06	25.08	25.23	25.23
1968	25.27	25.30	25.25	25.28	25.27	25.13	25.11	25.30	25.28	25.33	25.25	25.08	25.33	25.28	25.29	25.25	25.27
1969	27.20	25.10	25.34	26.32	27.20	25.20	25.13	25.10	25.50	25.41	25.34	25.24	25.49	26.32	27.25	27.16	27.20
1970	27.47	27.23	27.53	27.54	27.47	27.14	27.13	27.23	27.44	27.48	27.53	27.54	27.53	27.54	27.52	27.52	27.47
1971	30.77	27.49	28.57	30.19	30.77	27.47	27.42	27.49	27.59	28.37	28.57	28.99	29.81	30.19	30.03	30.35	30.77
1972	31.37	31.73	32.00	31.47	31.37	31.23	31.52	31.73	31.59	31.57	32.00	31.87	31.65	31.47	31.39	31.37	31.37
1973	36.90	35.97	41.53	41.49	36.90	31.85	35.84	35.97	35.66	37.18	41.53	42.74	40.68	41.49	40.97	37.99	36.90
1974	41.70	39.59	39.40	37.91	41.70	35.77	37.29	39.59	41.09	39.75	39.40	39.00	37.98	37.91	38.84	40.52	41.70
1975	38.33	42.81	42.64	37.94	38.33	42.72	43.90	42.81	42.28	42.72	42.64	39.11	39.06	37.94	39.40	38.34	38.33
1976	42.34	39.60	39.00	41.14	42.34	38.69	39.17	39.60	39.62	38.82	39.00	39.43	39.67	41.14	41.67	41.62	42.34
1977	48.08	41.91	42.97	43.67	48.08	41.34	41.79	41.91	42.48	42.66	42.97	43.96	43.33	43.67	44.74	45.21	48.08
1978	55.80	49.93	48.80	52.33	55.80	47.87	49.63	49.93	48.88	48.15	48.80	49.58	51.02	52.33	58.69	52.99	55.80
1979	58.58	54.26	54.68	58.14	58.58	54.53	54.92	54.26	53.28	52.99	54.68	55.07	55.37	58.14	56.24	58.51	58.58
1980	52.11	52.74	56.88	55.90	52.11	58.34	57.47	52.74	56.21	56.05	56.88	56.21	56.31	55.90	53.19	52.97	52.11
1981	44.70	47.85	42.39	43.65	44.70	48.19	47.19	47.85	45.64	43.48	42.39	41.19	41.77	43.65	44.84	45.58	44.70
1982	42.43	42.05	41.36	39.94	42.43	43.78	42.43	42.05	43.52	43.25	41.36	41.19	40.37	39.94	39.23	40.49	42.43
1983	37.08	41.67	39.78	38.24	37.08	41.22	41.67	41.67	41.09	40.15	39.78	38.31	37.37	38.24	38.43	37.41	37.08

Official reserves excluding gold / Réserves officielles, or exclu

million SDR's, end of period / millions de DTS. fin de période

	Year	Q.1	Q.2	Q.3	Q.4	JAN	FEB	MAR	APR	MAY	JUN	JUL	AUG	SEP	OCT	NOV	DEC
1964	3634	3806	3777	3608	3634	3720	3929	3806	3547	3481	3777	3623	3576	3608	3537	3422	3634
1965	3020	3498	3075	2976	3020	3228	3322	3498	3459	3168	3075	2978	2894	2976	2998	3025	3020
1966	3737	2770	3103	3378	3737	2871	2824	2770	2781	2877	3103	3358	3355	3378	3551	3590	3737
1967	3925	3727	3502	3731	3925	3473	3658	3727	3685	3543	3502	3563	3614	3731	3788	3924	3925
1968	5409	4568	4572	4734	5409	3772	4110	4568	4556	4442	4572	4506	4507	4734	4592	6343	5409
1969	3050	3664	5595	7581	3050	4118	3944	3664	4316	7099	5595	5615	6182	7581	6201	4278	3050
1970	9630	3286	4736	7219	9630	2970	3137	3286	3414	3741	4736	5900	6164	7219	7803	9481	9630
1971	13108	11826	12649	12872	13108	10033	10875	11826	12705	14960	12649	12918	12634	12872	13100	13285	13108
1972	17800	14370	17043	18515	17800	13662	14357	14370	14428	14475	17043	19098	18903	18515	18275	17963	17800
1973	23381	22680	22626	25105	23381	17688	20471	22680	22401	21892	22626	24181	23545	25105	24928	24177	23381
1974	22346	23134	24254	23296	22346	22541	22419	23134	23917	24424	24254	24074	23851	23296	22670	22927	22346
1975	22394	23454	22289	22623	22394	22580	22920	23454	22958	22538	22289	22541	22400	22623	22625	22627	22394
1976	25838	25974	24960	26161	25838	22428	23075	25974	25823	25315	24960	24648	25687	26161	26908	26002	25838
1977	28573	25778	25262	25551	28573	25749	25747	25778	25613	25831	25262	25838	25933	25551	26112	27000	28573
1978	37208	30011	28704	30706	37208	29367	29985	30011	29556	28672	28704	28468	29730	30706	32586	36963	37208
1979	39891	37975	36529	39738	39891	36359	34682	37975	37677	35672	36529	37537	36494	39738	40813	37671	39891
1980	38099	37006	37562	37682	38099	39273	37675	37006	37430	36886	37562	38998	38915	37682	37008	38075	38099
1981	37560	40782	42280	41198	37560	39501	38745	40782	41390	42857	42280	42051	40556	41198	38435	37805	37560
1982	40578	36993	38273	37782	40578	36247	36471	36993	37125	37809	38273	37537	37454	37782	39464	40248	40578
1983	40760	46221	41093	40928	40760	42489	43941	46221	42100	41714	41093	41954	41006	40928	42009	42089	40760

Net foreign position: commercial banks / Position extérieure nette : banques commerciales

million DM, end of period / millions de DM, fin de période

	Year	Q.1	Q.2	Q.3	Q.4	JAN	FEB	MAR	APR	MAY	JUN	JUL	AUG	SEP	OCT	NOV	DEC
1964	-2468	-188	-576	-857	-2468	-752	-928	-188	142	423	-576	-333	-459	-857	-831	-554	-2468
1965	-2027	-378	-278	-1345	-2027	69	503	-378	-415	-295	-278	-757	-941	-1345	-1185	-950	-2027
1966	-1453	-604	-511	-110	-1453	-189	-149	-604	-518	-172	-511	-579	-460	-110	-22	682	-1453
1967	3370	1907	3280	3761	3370	1302	1859	1907	2458	3593	3280	4375	4127	3761	4238	4814	3370
1968	942	4936	3613	2636	942	6110	5694	4936	5244	5922	3613	3229	2545	2636	3144	-156	942
1969	-3946	5659	5465	1035	-3946	6727	5869	5659	3381	1587	5465	4125	1342	1035	2724	3800	-3946
1970	-12605	-5956	-7127	-8653	-12605	-3910	-4795	-5956	-5241	-5667	-7127	-7683	-7617	-8653	-7607	-8966	-12605
1971	-13970	-8121	-3994	-5716	-13970	-8118	-7690	-8121	-7107	-8606	-3994	-4021	-5665	-5716	-5838	-6202	-13970
1972	-14880	-6959	-9201	-10321	-14880	-8026	-7407	-6959	-6804	-6459	-9201	-11745	-10245	-10321	-11133	-9286	-14880
1973	-7744	-18049	-8960	-9792	-7744	-9042	-16131	-18049	-15383	-10489	-8960	-12013	-9240	-9792	-6438	1061	-7744
1974	2013	-7173	-5858	-2323	2013	-5548	-4857	-7173	-5380	-5873	-5858	-6675	-5744	-2323	-1296	911	2013
1975	3462	2766	6100	6701	3462	2152	4217	2766	7553	5775	6100	6785	7589	6701	5010	6423	3462
1976	-3154	-2262	472	-2980	-3154	2994	2813	-2262	-628	-429	472	-14	-2623	-2980	-3113	-457	-3154
1977	-11793	-960	-3341	-7053	-11793	-2694	-890	-960	-2966	-3672	-3341	-6752	-7637	-7053	-7768	-9718	-11793
1978	-22409	-8678	-8972	-14606	-22409	-9764	-8320	-8678	-10873	-9209	-8972	-10288	-11060	-14606	-16084	-12877	-22409
1979	-28382	-15050	-12710	-17812	-28382	-19280	-15794	-15050	-15539	-12210	-12710	-13893	-11287	-17812	-22056	-15709	-28382
1980	-20040	-19957	-21428	-26024	-20040	-24109	-23168	-19957	-19497	-19266	-21428	-21243	-22990	-26024	-22828	-19200	-20040
1981	-7619	-24334	-21663	-16734	-7619	-19559	-20600	-24334	-23350	-22792	-21663	-20505	-16967	-16734	-11806	-9805	-7619
1982	-14736	-12245	-14034	-16007	-14736	-10089	-9617	-12245	-11170	-12717	-14034	-15430	-17153	-16007	-15330	-12619	-14736
1983	-18672	-24259	-23144	-24995	-18672	-15290	-19786	-24259	-22213	-22825	-23144	-27379	-26471	-24995	-22056	-19347	-18672

GERMANY

Imports c.i.f. (31) — Importations c.a.f. (31)

billion DM, monthly averages — milliards de DM, moyennes mensuelles

	Year	Q.1	Q.2	Q.3	Q.4	JAN	FEB	MAR	APR	MAY	JUN	JUL	AUG	SEP	OCT	NOV	DEC
1964	4.90	4.39	4.75	4.93	5.54	4.31	4.23	4.63	4.92	4.39	4.93	5.25	4.56	4.98	5.48	5.47	5.68
1965	5.87	5.43	5.81	5.90	6.34	5.33	4.99	5.97	5.58	5.92	5.94	6.04	5.50	6.17	6.27	6.34	6.42
1966	5.97	5.70	6.08	5.88	6.23	5.79	5.59	5.74	5.91	6.17	6.18	5.91	5.79	5.93	6.43	6.12	6.13
1967	5.85	5.48	5.82	5.63	6.46	5.57	5.11	5.77	5.62	5.61	6.23	5.61	5.63	5.66	6.32	6.45	6.61
1968	6.77	6.33	6.47	6.84	7.42	6.21	6.15	6.63	6.60	6.76	6.05	7.34	6.47	6.71	7.84	7.20	7.22
1969	8.16	7.61	8.19	8.19	8.66	7.77	6.85	8.22	8.31	8.10	8.18	8.59	7.47	8.51	9.52	8.15	8.32
1970	9.13	8.59	9.27	8.86	9.82	8.60	8.10	9.06	9.65	8.61	9.57	9.29	8.07	9.21	9.84	9.74	9.88
1971	10.01	9.83	10.17	9.73	10.32	8.70	9.78	11.00	10.26	9.70	10.55	10.41	8.99	9.78	10.29	10.11	10.55
1972	10.73	10.23	10.90	10.18	11.60	9.32	10.13	11.24	10.34	11.17	11.20	10.02	10.04	10.49	11.79	11.67	11.33
1973	12.12	11.95	12.22	11.17	13.13	11.71	11.80	12.35	11.61	13.05	12.02	11.58	10.80	11.13	13.96	13.40	12.03
1974	14.98	13.80	15.06	15.25	15.79	13.96	12.37	15.09	14.77	16.08	14.34	15.95	15.05	14.74	16.77	15.74	14.87
1975	15.36	14.04	15.51	14.92	16.97	13.79	14.25	14.09	16.88	14.24	15.40	15.34	13.73	15.68	17.64	15.93	17.35
1976	18.51	17.32	18.44	18.43	19.87	16.00	16.98	18.99	18.63	18.08	18.61	18.79	18.08	18.42	19.33	19.24	21.04
1977	19.60	19.24	19.52	19.12	20.51	17.81	18.27	21.64	18.98	19.12	20.44	19.43	18.40	19.54	19.93	20.40	21.21
1978	20.31	19.49	20.59	19.53	21.64	19.38	18.72	20.36	20.67	19.45	21.66	19.66	18.83	20.10	21.87	21.84	21.19
1979	24.34	22.15	23.88	24.30	27.03	21.04	20.83	24.59	22.60	24.99	24.03	25.90	23.72	23.27	28.15	27.20	25.73
1980	28.45	28.69	28.62	27.14	29.35	27.63	29.14	29.29	29.04	28.61	28.21	29.18	24.37	27.87	30.34	28.43	29.26
1981	30.77	30.47	30.19	30.57	31.83	28.19	29.29	33.92	30.27	29.69	30.62	32.59	28.20	30.92	32.46	32.24	30.81
1982	31.37	32.15	31.68	29.90	31.76	30.29	30.82	35.35	33.05	30.57	31.42	30.74	27.99	30.96	31.88	31.78	31.62
1983	32.53	31.24	31.98	31.71	35.19	29.65	29.43	34.64	31.13	31.87	32.92	31.03	29.90	34.22	33.40	35.45	36.73

Exports f.o.b. (31) — Exportations f.o.b. (31)

billion DM, monthly averages — milliards de DM, moyennes mensuelles

	Year	Q.1	Q.2	Q.3	Q.4	JAN	FEB	MAR	APR	MAY	JUN	JUL	AUG	SEP	OCT	NOV	DEC
1964	5.41	5.19	5.41	5.16	5.89	4.96	5.16	5.45	5.69	5.13	5.40	5.47	4.69	5.32	5.95	5.56	6.15
1965	5.97	5.79	5.80	5.75	6.54	5.46	5.41	6.51	5.59	6.18	5.63	6.14	5.19	5.92	6.33	6.23	7.07
1966	6.72	6.32	6.54	6.63	7.39	5.97	5.96	7.03	6.24	6.81	6.58	6.83	6.15	6.91	7.24	6.88	8.05
1967	7.25	6.93	7.30	6.90	7.89	7.00	6.52	7.26	7.47	6.90	7.54	6.91	6.62	7.17	7.96	7.62	8.10
1968	8.30	7.78	7.62	8.22	9.57	7.48	7.45	8.41	7.71	8.06	7.08	8.74	7.71	8.23	9.56	9.24	9.91
1969	9.46	8.54	9.50	9.52	10.30	7.88	7.91	9.81	9.63	9.53	9.35	10.24	8.48	9.83	10.97	9.60	10.33
1970	10.44	9.57	10.39	10.28	11.52	8.74	9.41	10.56	10.77	9.72	10.70	11.26	9.02	10.56	11.55	10.41	12.58
1971	11.33	11.05	11.25	11.28	11.76	9.53	10.72	12.90	11.33	10.93	11.49	11.81	10.32	11.71	11.82	11.05	12.42
1972	12.42	11.74	12.21	11.71	14.01	10.39	11.89	12.93	11.70	12.50	12.44	11.64	11.38	12.11	14.43	13.37	14.24
1973	14.87	13.91	14.54	14.48	16.53	13.31	13.74	14.69	14.18	15.81	13.64	14.51	14.02	14.91	17.92	16.61	15.06
1974	19.22	18.23	19.06	19.16	20.41	17.52	17.44	19.73	19.36	20.97	16.86	20.41	18.22	18.84	21.41	19.67	20.16
1975	18.47	17.56	18.58	17.67	20.05	17.40	17.75	17.54	19.69	17.50	18.55	19.06	15.47	18.50	20.50	19.08	20.58
1976	21.39	20.20	20.97	21.25	23.13	18.48	19.16	22.95	20.94	21.35	20.63	21.37	19.27	23.10	22.89	22.21	24.30
1977	22.80	22.21	22.67	21.78	24.55	19.79	20.99	25.83	21.92	22.76	23.34	21.17	20.94	23.22	24.74	23.48	25.44
1978	23.74	22.55	24.01	22.72	25.69	21.50	21.54	24.60	23.92	22.48	25.62	21.40	21.94	24.82	26.67	25.39	25.02
1979	26.20	24.74	26.22	25.45	28.39	22.97	23.22	28.03	25.87	26.99	25.79	26.51	24.70	25.15	29.95	28.71	26.52
1980	29.19	29.60	29.17	27.64	30.37	27.95	29.56	31.28	30.13	28.90	28.49	29.28	24.20	29.43	32.02	28.81	30.27
1981	33.08	30.39	32.38	32.93	36.60	27.26	30.16	33.75	33.55	31.23	32.36	36.25	28.14	34.40	37.74	36.12	35.95
1982	35.65	35.87	36.09	33.78	36.84	31.43	34.45	41.75	36.50	35.57	36.20	34.50	30.70	36.15	35.87	36.63	38.01
1983	36.03	35.20	35.38	34.48	39.05	32.35	33.16	40.09	33.81	35.50	36.84	33.18	32.43	37.82	37.57	38.76	40.83

Trade balance (f.o.b. — c.i.f.) (31) — Balance commerciale (f.o.b. — c.a.f.) (31)

billion DM, monthly averages — milliards de DM, moyennes mensuelles

	Year	Q.1	Q.2	Q.3	Q.4	JAN	FEB	MAR	APR	MAY	JUN	JUL	AUG	SEP	OCT	NOV	DEC
1964	0.51	0.80	0.66	0.23	0.35	0.65	0.92	0.82	0.77	0.74	0.47	0.23	0.13	0.33	0.47	0.09	0.47
1965	0.10	0.37	-0.02	-0.15	0.20	0.13	0.43	0.54	0.00	0.26	-0.31	0.10	-0.31	-0.25	0.07	-0.11	0.65
1966	0.75	0.62	0.46	0.75	1.16	0.19	0.37	1.29	0.33	0.64	0.41	0.92	0.36	0.98	0.81	0.76	1.92
1967	1.41	1.44	1.48	1.27	1.43	1.43	1.41	1.49	1.85	1.29	1.31	1.30	0.99	1.51	1.64	1.17	1.49
1968	1.53	1.45	1.14	1.38	2.15	1.27	1.30	1.78	1.10	1.30	1.03	1.40	1.24	1.52	1.72	2.04	2.69
1969	1.30	0.92	1.31	1.33	1.64	0.12	1.06	1.60	1.31	1.43	1.17	1.66	1.01	1.32	1.45	1.45	2.01
1970	1.31	0.98	1.12	1.42	1.70	0.14	1.31	1.51	1.12	1.11	1.13	1.97	0.95	1.35	1.71	0.67	2.70
1971	1.32	1.22	1.08	1.55	1.45	0.83	0.94	1.90	1.07	1.23	0.93	1.40	1.33	1.93	1.53	0.94	1.87
1972	1.69	1.50	1.31	1.53	2.42	1.07	1.76	1.68	1.36	1.32	1.24	1.63	1.34	1.62	2.63	1.71	2.91
1973	2.75	1.96	2.32	3.31	3.40	1.61	1.94	2.34	2.57	2.77	1.62	2.93	3.22	3.78	3.96	3.22	3.03
1974	4.24	4.42	4.00	3.91	4.62	3.56	5.07	4.64	4.59	4.89	2.52	4.46	3.16	4.10	4.64	3.93	5.29
1975	3.11	3.52	3.07	2.76	3.08	3.61	3.50	3.45	2.81	3.26	3.14	3.72	1.74	2.82	2.86	3.15	3.23
1976	2.87	2.88	2.53	2.82	3.26	2.48	2.18	3.97	2.31	3.27	2.02	2.58	1.20	4.68	3.57	2.97	3.25
1977	3.20	2.97	3.16	2.65	4.04	1.98	2.73	4.20	2.93	3.64	2.90	1.75	2.53	3.68	4.81	3.08	4.22
1978	3.43	3.06	3.41	3.19	4.06	2.12	2.83	4.24	3.25	3.03	3.97	1.74	3.12	4.72	4.80	3.55	3.83
1979	1.86	2.59	2.34	1.16	1.37	1.93	2.40	3.44	3.27	2.00	1.76	0.61	0.98	1.88	1.80	1.51	0.79
1980	0.75	0.91	0.56	0.50	1.02	0.32	0.42	1.99	1.10	0.29	0.27	0.10	-0.17	1.56	1.67	0.38	1.01
1981	2.31	-0.08	2.19	2.36	4.77	-0.93	0.87	-0.17	3.28	1.54	1.74	3.67	-0.06	3.48	5.28	3.88	5.14
1982	4.27	3.72	4.41	3.89	5.08	1.14	3.63	6.40	3.45	5.00	4.78	3.76	2.71	5.19	4.00	4.85	6.39
1983	3.50	3.96	3.41	2.76	3.86	2.70	3.73	5.46	2.68	3.63	3.92	2.16	2.54	3.60	4.18	3.31	4.10

Imports c.i.f. (31)
billion DM, monthly averages

Adjusted - Corrigé

Importations c.a.f. (31)
milliards de DM, moyennes mensuelles

Year	Q.1	Q.2	Q.3	Q.4	JAN	FEB	MAR	APR	MAY	JUN	JUL	AUG	SEP	OCT	NOV	DEC
1964	4.57	4.66	4.99	5.32	4.45	4.63	4.63	4.66	4.62	4.69	4.97	5.00	5.00	5.23	5.33	5.41
1965	5.59	5.72	5.99	6.07	5.83	5.46	5.48	5.56	5.80	5.81	5.90	5.88	6.20	6.13	6.11	5.96
1966	6.14	6.02	5.98	6.07	6.15	6.10	6.17	6.04	6.06	5.96	5.95	6.04	5.96	6.28	5.91	6.02
1967	5.63	5.64	5.80	6.37	5.78	5.55	5.57	5.57	5.60	5.76	5.65	5.90	5.86	5.98	6.25	6.89
1968	6.43	6.45	6.98	7.24	6.45	6.47	6.38	6.51	6.48	6.35	6.99	7.00	6.95	7.20	7.20	7.32
1969	7.78	8.16	8.37	8.40	8.08	7.38	7.89	8.18	8.21	8.09	8.18	8.34	8.58	8.73	8.28	8.20
1970	8.81	9.03	9.24	9.48	9.15	8.34	8.93	8.90	9.19	9.00	9.11	9.23	9.38	9.29	9.53	9.62
1971	9.84	10.00	10.14	9.92	9.56	10.07	9.89	10.06	9.77	10.17	10.51	9.95	9.97	10.01	9.80	9.96
1972	10.16	10.62	10.76	11.38	9.93	10.12	10.43	10.45	10.93	10.48	10.43	10.82	11.02	11.14	11.33	11.67
1973	11.87	12.04	11.78	12.85	11.99	12.03	11.60	11.72	12.43	11.96	11.65	11.63	12.06	12.82	13.01	12.73
1974	13.85	15.02	15.90	15.44	14.30	12.79	14.45	14.46	15.37	15.24	15.54	16.70	15.47	15.42	15.78	15.12
1975	14.48	15.14	15.54	16.45	14.26	14.77	14.42	15.58	14.85	14.99	14.94	15.72	15.97	16.26	16.14	16.96
1976	17.27	18.09	19.17	19.00	17.03	17.42	17.35	18.28	17.85	18.15	18.82	19.91	18.77	18.99	18.72	19.28
1977	19.16	19.33	19.90	19.83	18.91	19.02	19.54	19.22	18.90	19.87	20.05	19.75	19.89	19.64	19.85	20.01
1978	19.65	20.00	20.49	21.20	19.91	19.50	19.53	20.27	19.73	19.99	20.24	20.19	21.03	20.94	21.28	21.37
1979	21.96	23.67	25.42	26.57	21.33	21.72	22.83	22.81	24.05	24.16	25.79	25.44	25.04	26.20	26.50	27.02
1980	28.47	28.67	28.04	28.71	27.92	29.50	27.99	28.38	29.26	28.36	28.17	27.85	28.09	28.31	28.81	29.00
1981	30.50	30.23	31.55	30.90	29.53	30.20	31.77	29.57	30.33	30.80	31.47	32.07	31.11	31.26	31.73	29.72
1982	32.19	31.38	30.87	30.79	32.67	32.17	31.72	32.29	31.18	30.67	30.63	30.88	31.11	31.71	30.98	29.68
1983	30.89	31.57	32.83	34.45	30.92	30.67	31.08	31.36	31.51	32.15	31.95	32.21	34.34	33.25	34.55	35.56

Exports f.o.b. (31)
billion DM, monthly averages

Adjusted - Corrigé

Exportations f.o.b. (31)
milliards de DM, moyennes mensuelles

Year	Q.1	Q.2	Q.3	Q.4	JAN	FEB	MAR	APR	MAY	JUN	JUL	AUG	SEP	OCT	NOV	DEC
1964	5.35	5.36	5.33	5.55	5.25	5.55	5.25	5.37	5.30	5.41	5.28	5.36	5.34	5.60	5.54	5.52
1965	5.91	5.78	5.92	6.14	6.08	5.81	5.83	5.54	6.01	5.78	6.04	5.79	5.94	6.09	6.15	6.19
1966	6.40	6.55	6.83	7.05	6.50	6.40	6.29	6.34	6.65	6.66	6.85	6.71	6.94	6.94	6.82	7.39
1967	7.09	7.21	7.17	7.61	7.47	6.98	6.83	7.42	6.86	7.34	6.89	7.24	7.38	7.42	7.61	7.81
1968	7.88	7.70	8.47	9.16	7.99	7.75	7.90	7.65	7.75	7.70	8.28	8.65	8.48	8.68	9.50	9.29
1969	8.69	9.62	9.77	9.80	8.45	8.40	9.22	9.58	9.65	9.64	9.68	9.75	9.88	9.94	10.03	9.42
1970	9.93	10.28	10.61	10.92	9.64	9.70	10.44	9.90	10.46	10.49	10.79	10.52	10.52	10.71	10.58	11.46
1971	11.13	11.24	11.66	11.12	10.92	11.07	11.40	11.18	10.95	11.59	11.75	11.58	11.66	11.40	11.05	10.92
1972	11.72	12.05	12.32	13.58	11.46	11.87	11.82	11.99	12.09	12.08	12.06	12.41	12.50	13.42	13.32	14.00
1973	13.89	14.51	15.26	16.00	13.99	14.06	13.62	14.51	14.79	14.23	14.51	15.30	15.96	16.06	16.51	15.42
1974	18.43	19.24	19.91	19.75	18.44	18.18	18.66	19.02	19.70	19.00	19.75	20.63	19.36	19.18	20.20	19.88
1975	18.35	18.31	18.33	19.24	18.53	18.56	17.95	17.95	18.29	18.69	18.51	18.21	18.28	18.40	19.73	19.59
1976	20.20	20.69	22.03	21.84	20.41	19.77	20.43	20.44	20.90	20.73	21.60	21.70	22.80	22.17	21.74	21.60
1977	22.16	22.57	22.71	23.45	21.85	22.01	22.63	22.22	22.30	23.20	22.27	22.96	22.90	23.99	22.86	23.50
1978	22.37	23.30	24.01	24.83	22.86	22.61	23.15	23.37	22.76	23.76	22.55	24.14	25.35	24.95	24.65	25.03
1979	24.62	26.09	26.95	27.50	24.10	24.39	25.38	26.26	25.65	26.37	26.96	27.26	26.64	27.00	27.82	27.69
1980	29.51	29.36	28.83	29.16	29.30	29.93	29.29	29.44	29.61	29.02	28.80	28.86	28.84	28.88	29.31	29.30
1981	30.67	32.56	34.25	34.80	29.96	31.17	30.87	32.76	32.02	32.90	35.71	33.35	33.68	35.34	35.45	33.62
1982	36.09	35.83	35.25	34.95	35.88	36.10	36.29	35.65	36.44	35.39	35.27	35.08	35.40	34.98	35.47	34.40
1983	35.00	35.11	36.10	37.50	35.46	34.67	34.87	34.36	34.98	35.98	35.27	36.04	37.00	36.68	37.48	38.33

Trade balance (f.o.b. — c.i.f.) (31)
billion DM, monthly averages

Adjusted - Corrigé

Balance commerciale (f.o.b. — c.a.f.) (31)
milliards de DM, moyennes mensuelles

Year	Q.1	Q.2	Q.3	Q.4	JAN	FEB	MAR	APR	MAY	JUN	JUL	AUG	SEP	OCT	NOV	DEC
1964	0.78	0.70	0.34	0.23	0.80	0.92	0.62	0.71	0.68	0.72	0.31	0.36	0.34	0.37	0.21	0.11
1965	0.32	0.05	-0.07	0.08	0.25	0.35	0.35	-0.02	0.21	-0.03	0.14	-0.09	-0.26	-0.04	0.04	0.23
1966	0.26	0.53	0.85	0.98	0.35	0.30	0.12	0.30	0.59	0.70	0.90	0.67	0.98	0.66	0.91	1.37
1967	1.46	1.56	1.37	1.24	1.69	1.43	1.26	1.85	1.26	1.58	1.24	1.34	1.52	1.44	1.36	0.92
1968	1.45	1.25	1.49	1.92	1.54	1.28	1.52	1.14	1.27	1.35	1.29	1.65	1.53	1.48	2.30	1.97
1969	0.91	1.46	1.40	1.39	0.37	1.02	1.33	1.40	1.44	1.55	1.50	1.41	1.30	1.21	1.75	1.22
1970	1.12	1.25	1.37	1.44	0.49	1.36	1.51	1.00	1.27	1.49	1.68	1.29	1.14	1.42	1.05	1.84
1971	1.29	1.24	1.52	1.20	1.36	1.00	1.51	1.12	1.18	1.42	1.24	1.63	1.69	1.39	1.25	0.96
1972	1.56	1.43	1.57	2.20	1.53	1.75	1.39	1.54	1.16	1.60	1.63	1.59	1.48	2.28	1.99	2.33
1973	2.02	2.47	3.48	3.14	2.00	2.03	2.02	2.79	2.36	2.27	2.86	3.67	3.90	3.24	3.50	2.69
1974	4.58	4.22	4.01	4.31	4.14	5.39	4.21	4.56	4.33	3.76	4.21	3.93	3.89	3.76	4.42	4.76
1975	3.86	3.17	2.79	2.79	4.27	3.79	3.53	2.37	3.44	3.70	3.57	2.49	2.31	2.14	3.59	2.63
1976	2.94	2.60	2.87	2.84	3.38	2.35	3.08	2.16	3.05	2.58	2.78	1.79	4.03	3.18	3.02	2.32
1977	3.01	3.24	2.81	3.62	2.94	2.99	3.09	3.00	3.40	3.33	2.22	3.21	3.01	4.35	3.01	3.49
1978	3.23	3.30	3.53	3.68	2.95	3.11	3.62	3.10	3.03	3.77	2.31	3.95	4.32	4.01	3.37	3.66
1979	2.66	2.42	1.53	0.93	2.77	2.67	2.55	3.45	1.60	2.21	1.17	1.82	1.60	0.80	1.32	0.67
1980	1.04	0.69	0.80	0.46	1.38	0.43	1.30	1.06	0.35	0.66	0.63	1.01	0.75	0.57	0.50	0.30
1981	0.17	2.33	2.70	3.90	0.43	0.97	-0.90	3.19	1.69	2.10	4.24	1.28	2.57	4.08	3.72	3.90
1982	3.90	4.45	4.38	4.16	3.21	3.93	4.57	3.36	5.26	4.72	4.64	4.20	4.29	3.27	4.49	4.72
1983	4.11	3.43	3.27	3.04	4.54	4.00	3.79	3.00	3.47	3.83	3.32	3.83	2.66	3.43	2.93	2.77

GERMANY

Balance of payments: net services
million DM

Balance des paiements : services, nets
millions de DM

	Year	Q.1	Q.2	Q.3	Q.4	JAN	FEB	MAR	APR	MAY	JUN	JUL	AUG	SEP	OCT	NOV	DEC
1964	654	305	283	-151	217	29	183	93	92	237	-46	-169	-76	94	3	295	-81
1965	-607	252	-592	-590	323	43	160	49	50	-537	-105	-211	-175	-204	199	90	34
1966	-474	104	-100	-744	266	92	34	-22	53	-69	-84	-360	-160	-224	143	45	78
1967	18	197	-34	-856	711	-43	210	30	26	-114	54	-211	-441	-204	184	183	344
1968	1498	605	480	-599	1012	86	308	211	100	82	298	-434	-184	19	346	456	210
1969	1086	161	691	-309	543	95	35	31	112	534	45	-421	-57	169	159	183	201
1970	-1127	-437	181	-1299	428	24	-370	-91	-98	165	114	-300	-544	-455	161	108	159
1971	-1763	809	-22	-2146	-405	233	67	510	265	-214	-73	-1042	-722	-381	-173	10	-242
1972	-3110	-486	-280	-2123	-221	126	-331	-281	-118	-72	-89	-506	-888	-730	-67	-367	213
1973	-5016	-608	-980	-3227	-201	-330	124	-402	-222	-226	-533	-1390	-1306	-530	-559	107	250
1974	-6951	-1582	-1246	-4390	267	-660	-435	-487	-770	-289	-187	-1420	-2269	-701	-677	-146	1091
1975	-8278	-1277	-2272	-4463	-267	-402	-112	-763	-452	-622	-1197	-1644	-2240	-579	-1094	-13	840
1976	-6564	-1235	-1197	-3650	-483	-763	-616	145	-621	-181	-395	-1075	-1509	-1066	-765	509	-227
1977	-10750	-1796	-2114	-7023	183	-617	-480	-698	-638	-388	-1088	-2222	-1866	-2935	-235	123	295
1978	-7358	-831	-1157	-5124	-246	109	-353	-588	-74	-233	-851	-1651	-1624	-1849	83	-301	-28
1979	-12588	-1439	-4185	-6652	-312	-479	234	-1195	-1075	-851	-2259	-1868	-2736	-2048	-508	-191	386
1980	-13020	-3074	-1791	-7466	-690	-682	-794	-1598	-1168	-1	-622	-2962	-2405	-2099	-997	-331	638
1981	-15067	-3455	-3967	-9000	1356	-1188	-451	-1816	-798	-666	-2503	-3624	-2391	-2985	-1283	572	2067
1982	-16461	-5255	-4416	-8436	1646	-1992	-1344	-1919	-721	-1117	-2578	-3390	-2508	-2539	-1056	1108	1595
1983	-10299	-3492	-2520	-7259	2971	-1342	-896	-1254	-865	-332	-1323	-2801	-2100	-2358	-129	271	2829

Balance of payments: current balance
million DM

Balance des paiements : opérations courantes, nettes
millions de DM

	Year	Q.1	Q.2	Q.3	Q.4	JAN	FEB	MAR	APR	MAY	JUN	JUL	AUG	SEP	OCT	NOV	DEC
1964	524	1152	556	-1020	-164	133	659	360	109	552	-105	-603	-441	24	55	-52	-167
1965	-6223	-343	-2743	-2716	-421	-479	88	48	-903	-837	-1003	-712	-1137	-867	-175	-465	219
1966	488	-1189	-639	49	2267	-438	-318	-433	-315	50	-374	75	-312	286	554	232	1481
1967	10006	2675	2540	1469	3322	834	951	890	1341	540	659	652	36	781	1367	942	1013
1968	11856	3156	2079	1711	4910	641	1089	1426	737	758	584	322	409	980	1541	1774	1595
1969	7498	1287	2252	1546	2413	-568	672	1183	687	1301	264	331	209	1006	944	949	520
1970	3183	-174	699	-80	2738	-793	-30	649	38	503	158	524	-664	60	1080	-81	1739
1971	2770	1722	558	-230	720	231	65	1426	543	66	-51	-489	-242	501	554	-299	465
1972	2731	301	83	-1141	3488	125	278	-102	39	-66	110	-289	-629	-224	1504	82	1901
1973	12354	1836	3149	2326	5043	237	940	660	1628	1602	-82	-382	933	1775	2050	1635	1359
1974	26581	7707	6060	2732	10083	1576	3198	2932	2495	2910	655	1221	-646	2156	2950	2398	4735
1975	9932	5123	1929	-928	3808	1739	1922	1463	1090	731	108	-11	-1746	829	-2	1585	2225
1976	9915	3721	2006	-608	4796	189	677	2855	131	1714	161	-585	-2105	2082	1476	2070	1250
1977	9498	3275	2462	-4161	7922	-152	753	2674	899	1211	352	-2219	-1116	-826	3860	1377	2686
1978	18111	5075	3725	849	8461	1074	1410	2592	1225	1060	1441	-1036	748	1138	3698	2496	2268
1979	-11189	3204	-2506	-9280	-2606	513	1570	1121	756	-671	-2591	-2917	-3874	-2489	-642	-669	-1295
1980	-28617	-4993	-6696	-12374	-4555	-2063	-2193	-737	-2535	-1083	-3078	-4696	-4952	-2725	-2029	-1701	-825
1981	-13135	-8743	-5338	-10207	11152	-5092	-764	-2887	65	-1900	-3503	-3595	-5532	-1080	3317	1808	6027
1982	8663	-511	1225	-4344	12293	-2512	-382	2383	788	1036	-599	-1478	-3325	459	1553	5234	5506
1983	10060	5226	1863	-6073	9045	-244	2091	3378	2	1719	141	-3277	-2247	-548	3563	714	4768

Balance of payments: net capital movements
million DM

Balance des paiements : mouvements de capitaux, nets
millions de DM

	Year	Q.1	Q.2	Q.3	Q.4	JAN	FEB	MAR	APR	MAY	JUN	JUL	AUG	SEP	OCT	NOV	DEC
1964	-1325	-1902	-514	188	903	-1383	115	-634	-681	-708	875	-158	180	166	-331	-541	1775
1965	2142	-1558	509	1896	1295	-1853	-115	410	459	35	15	556	538	802	149	425	721
1966	-599	-1382	367	739	-323	-1307	-275	200	-210	-432	1009	472	455	-188	-36	-539	252
1967	-11848	-3877	-3270	-1843	-2858	-2876	-645	-356	-1257	-1600	-413	-1302	-239	-302	-1206	-1514	-138
1968	-6125	-2742	-1122	-1731	-530	-2603	-103	-36	-584	-1572	1034	-532	-385	-814	-1626	4292	-3196
1969	-18679	-9368	-1204	3484	-11591	-6395	-1047	-1926	1211	2919	-5334	-292	967	2809	-4639	-6754	-198
1970	15113	-701	3126	5683	7005	-2097	872	524	-709	1264	2571	1793	1675	2215	1585	3248	2172
1971	10884	270	2746	1618	6251	-2906	1187	1989	2851	4700	-4805	2037	550	-969	24	792	5435
1972	11932	-1522	9348	6697	-2592	-2901	2041	-661	411	849	8087	6554	743	-601	-1217	-1351	-24
1973	13143	14078	580	4200	-5714	-2823	11785	5116	-1482	-1980	4043	3262	-1743	2681	-3295	-3445	1025
1974	-25298	-10055	-2262	-7496	-5486	-6418	-2905	-731	-984	-1187	-91	-1030	-2426	-4040	-2358	-1249	-1878
1975	-13282	-1775	-7911	969	-4565	-607	-288	-879	-4585	-1850	-1476	-557	1083	442	1198	-3150	-2613
1976	-1033	6303	-6277	4383	-5442	-14	1585	4732	-2959	-3252	-66	-102	5111	-627	-95	-4278	-1068
1977	-287	-4374	-5640	4809	4918	-1737	-802	-1835	-1608	-1910	-2122	5623	1004	-1818	286	1537	3095
1978	5436	-143	-6242	7051	4771	-332	1401	-1213	-215	-3120	-2908	2192	2238	2621	5024	-790	537
1979	10504	-9815	1837	18809	-327	-3096	-1074	-5646	-228	-5823	7887	5810	487	12512	265	-9242	8651
1980	4089	-3999	1365	9923	-3201	-2116	-615	-1268	-1283	-312	2961	4920	6154	-1150	-970	-2086	-145
1981	9244	14795	4827	6349	-16728	5326	-2190	11659	-1104	4717	1214	5385	2994	-2029	-9260	-1722	-5746
1982	-4433	-1592	-1067	4983	-6757	1951	-569	-2974	-1954	-684	1572	2345	4062	-1424	1827	-2905	-5680
1983	-15903	4779	-12564	761	-8879	4378	1845	-1444	-8436	-1995	-2133	3657	-241	-2655	1463	-3055	-7287

NOTES

1. The original base of the index is 1970 to 1969, 1976 from 1970 to 1979 and 1980 from 1980.
2. Excluding food, beverages and tobacco.
3. Not included in total index.
4. Geometric mean of present and future business situation. 100 = normal.
5. The original base of the index is 1976 to 1975 and 1980 from 1976. From 1977, enterprises with 20 or more employees (10 previously) including handicraft (previously excluded), and a revised industrial classification is used.
6. The discontinuity between 1967 and 1968 is due to the replacement of turnover tax by value added tax.
7. From 1979, new survey procedures.
8. From 1968, excluding indirect taxes.
9. Agricultural, industrial and commercial buildings.
10. The original base of the index is 1962 to 1970, 1970 from 1971 to 1980, and 1980 from 1981.
11. The original base of the index is 1962 to 1970, 1970 from 1971 to 1979 and 1980 from 1980. Prior to 1965, excluding West Berlin.
12. Monthly data refer to last pay period of month.
13. From 1970, enterprises with 20 or more employees. Previously, enterprises with 10 or more employees were covered, but handicraft was excluded.
14. Monthly data refer to last day of month; annual data are centred averages from December of previous year to December of current year.
15. The self-employed are excluded from the civilian labour force.
16. Weighting pattern based on 1970 to 1976, and on 1976 from 1977.
17. Monthly and quarterly data are provisional.
18. Wages and salaries per unit of output.
19. Home market. Weighting pattern based on 1962 to 1967, on 1970 from 1968 to 1979, and on 1980 from 1980.
20. Including semi-manufactured goods for further processing. Weighting pattern based on 1958 to 1966, on 1962 from 1967 to 1974, and on 1976 from 1975.
21. The original base of the index is 1962 to 1967, 1970 from 1968 to 1975, and 1976 from 1976.

NOTES

1. La base originale de l'indice est 1970 jusqu'en 1969, 1976 de 1970 à 1979 et 1980 à partir de 1980.
2. Non compris l'alimentation, les boissons et le tabac.
3. Non compris dans l'indice total.
4. Moyenne géométrique du climat des affaires actuel et à venir. 100 = normal.
5. La base originale de l'indice est 1976 jusqu'en 1975 et 1980 à partir de 1976. A partir de 1977, entreprises ayant 20 salariés ou plus (10 auparavant), y compris l'artisanat (non compris auparavant); en outre, une classification industrielle révisée est utilisée.
6. La discontinuité entre 1967 et 1968 est due au remplacement de la taxe sur le chiffre d'affaires par la taxe sur la valeur ajoutée.
7. A partir de 1979, nouvelle procédure d'enquête.
8. A partir de 1968, non compris les impôts indirects.
9. Bâtiments agricoles, industriels et commerciaux.
10. La base originale de l'indice est 1962 jusqu'en 1970, 1970 de 1971 à 1980, et 1980 à partir de 1981.
11. La base originale de l'indice est 1962 jusqu'en 1970, 1970 de 1971 à 1979 et 1980 à partir de 1980. Avant 1965, non compris Berlin-Ouest.
12. Les données mensuelles se réfèrent à la dernière période de paie du mois.
13. A partir de 1970, entreprises ayant 20 salariés ou plus. Avant 1970, la série se référait aux entreprises ayant 10 salariés ou plus, et l'artisanat était exclu.
14. Les données mensuelles se réfèrent au dernier jour du mois. Les données annuelles sont des moyennes centrées de décembre de l'année précédente à décembre de l'année en cours.
15. Les travailleurs indépendants ne sont pas compris dans la main-d'œuvre civile.
16. La pondération se réfère à 1970 jusqu'en 1976, et à 1976 à partir de 1977.
17. Les données mensuelles et trimestrielles sont provisoires.
18. Salaires par unité produite.
19. Marché intérieur. La pondération se réfère à 1962 jusqu'en 1967, à 1970 de 1968 à 1979, et à 1980 à partir de 1980.
20. Y compris les produits semi-ouvrés destinés à être ultérieurement transformés. La pondération se réfère à 1958 jusqu'en 1966, à 1962 de 1967 à 1974, et à 1976 à partir de 1975.
21. La base originale de l'indice est 1962 jusqu'en 1967, 1970 de 1968 à 1975, et 1976 à partir de 1976.

NOTES

22. A change in bank reporting was partially introduced in 1968 and fully implemented from 1969.

23. A change in the reporting requirement for credit cooperatives was introduced in December 1973. On the new basis, the December 1973 data are as follows:

	Billion DM
Money supply (M1)	132.9
M1 plus quasi-money	233.3
Personal savings deposits	264.4
Bank credit to economy:	
Short-term	167.0
Medium and long-term	449.7
Bank credit to manufacturing	113.3
Consumer credit outstanding	36.0

24. Weighting pattern based on 1962 to 1967, on 1970 from 1968 to 1975, and on 1976 from 1976.

25. Monthly data are daily averages.

26. From March 1978, excluding domestic currency held by banks.

27. Excluding Central Bank.

28. Excluding mortgage loans secured by real estate used for industrial purposes. From March 1981, change in classification.

29. From 1971, only bonds with a maximum maturity of four years are included.

30. The original base of the index is 31st December 1965 to 1965, and 29th December 1972 from 1966. Monthly data refer to last working day of month.

31. Excluding trade with Democratic Republic of Germany; including non-monetary gold.

NOTES

22. Un changement de procédure de notification par les banques a été introduit partiellement en 1968 et entièrement à partir de 1969.

23. Un changement dans les notifications obligatoires pour les coopératives de crédit a été introduit en décembre 1973. Sur la nouvelle base, les chiffres de décembre 1973 sont les suivants:

	Milliards de DM
Disponibilités monétaires (M1)	132,9
M1 plus quasi-monnaie	233,3
Dépôts d'épargne des particuliers	264,4
Crédits bancaires à l'économie:	
Court terme	167,0
Moyen et long terme	449,7
Crédits bancaires aux industries manufacturières	113,3
Crédits à la consommation en cours	36,0

24. La pondération se réfère à 1962 jusqu'en 1967, à 1970 de 1968 à 1975, et à 1976 à partir de 1976.

25. Les données mensuelles sont des moyennes journalières.

26. A partir de mars 1978, non compris la monnaie nationale détenue par les banques.

27. Non compris la Banque Centrale.

28. Non compris les prêts hypothécaires garantis par des biens immobiliers à usage industriel. A partir de mars 1981, changement de classification.

29. A partir de 1971, seuls sont inclus les bons ayant une échéance égale ou inférieure à 4 ans.

30. La base originale de l'indice est le 31 décembre 1965 jusqu'en 1965, et le 29 décembre 1972 à partir de 1966.

31. Non compris le commerce avec la République Démocratique de l'Allemagne; y compris l'or non monétaire.

MAIN SOURCES

PRINCIPALES SOURCES

Series	Séries	Sources
National product	Produit national	
Industrial production, adj.	Production industrielle, corr.	
Orders, adj.	Commandes, corr.	
Construction, work put in place, adj.	Construction, travaux effectués, corr	Deutsche Bundesbank
Retail sales, adj.	Ventes au détail, corr.	*Statistische Beihefte zu den*
Unemployment, adj.	Chômage, corr.	*Monatsberichten der Deutschen*
Job vacancies, adj.	Offres d'emploi, corr.	*Bundesbank, Reihe 4*
Unit labour cost	Coût unitaire de la main-d'œuvre	
Money supply, adj.	Disponibilités monétaires, corr.	
Foreign trade, adj.	Commerce extérieur, corr.	
Industrial production	Production industrielle	
Internal trade	Commerce intérieur	
Unemployment	Chômage	
Job vacancies	Offres d'emploi	Statistisches Bundesamt
Monthly hours worked	Heures effectuées par mois	*Wirtschaft und Statistik*
Hourly rates	Taux horaires	
Prices	Prix	
Share prices	Cours des actions	
Business surveys	Enquêtes de conjoncture	Institut für Wirtschaftsforschung *Konjunkturtest*
Sales and orders	Ventes et commandes	Statistisches Bundesamt *Indikatoren zur Wirtschaftsentwicklung*
Construction	Construction	Statistiches Bundesamt *Ausgewählte Zahlen für die Bauwirtschaft*
Employment	Emploi	Bundesministerium für Wirtschaft *Die Wirtschaftliche Lage in der Bundesrepublik Deutschlands*
Unemployment rate	Taux de chômage	
Home finance	Finances internes	
Interest rates	Taux d'intérêts	Deutsche Bundesbank
Net foreign position of commercial banks	Position extérieure nette des banques commerciales	*Monatsberichte*
Balance of payments	Balance des paiements	
Weekly hours of work	Durée hebdomadaire du travail	Statistisches Bundesamt
Hourly earnings	Gains horaires	*Löhne und Gehälter*
Foreign trade	Commerce extérieur	Statistisches Bundesamt *Aussenhandel, Reihe 1*

Greece — Grèce

GREECE

Industrial production: total (1) — Production industrielle : total (1)

1980 = 100

	Year	Q.1	Q.2	Q.3	Q.4	JAN	FEB	MAR	APR	MAY	JUN	JUL	AUG	SEP	OCT	NOV	DEC
1964	29.2	25.4	28.5	33.0	29.8	24.6	25.3	26.3	27.7	26.7	31.1	34.1	33.0	31.8	30.5	29.7	29.2
1965	31.8	28.3	32.2	34.7	31.7	27.2	28.0	29.6	29.4	30.9	36.4	36.4	33.5	34.2	32.5	31.8	30.9
1966	36.7	31.7	38.7	39.9	36.6	29.7	31.7	33.7	34.1	39.3	42.6	42.3	39.0	38.6	37.6	36.4	35.7
1967	38.4	35.6	39.7	40.2	38.2	34.1	35.5	37.3	36.9	39.6	42.5	41.9	40.2	38.6	39.2	38.6	37.0
1968	41.4	36.7	42.2	44.6	42.2	34.1	37.4	38.8	38.5	41.6	46.4	46.1	44.2	43.5	43.0	42.1	41.4
1969	46.3	41.2	47.1	49.9	47.1	38.7	41.9	42.9	43.7	46.4	51.1	51.8	49.2	48.7	48.2	48.0	45.0
1970	51.1	46.6	51.1	53.9	52.7	44.3	47.1	48.4	49.3	50.5	53.7	55.0	52.7	54.0	52.3	53.6	52.0
1971	56.9	52.0	56.0	60.9	58.6	49.3	53.0	53.5	52.6	55.8	59.6	61.9	60.7	60.1	57.9	59.2	58.6
1972	65.0	59.6	64.7	66.2	69.3	55.7	61.0	62.2	62.3	65.1	66.6	66.2	63.3	68.9	68.3	68.6	70.9
1973	74.9	69.2	75.3	78.1	77.1	64.8	70.1	72.8	74.2	75.2	76.4	77.0	75.4	81.8	79.3	76.4	75.5
1974	73.7	75.1	74.4	71.6	74.2	71.5	77.6	76.1	73.7	75.6	74.0	67.3	70.3	77.2	74.7	73.4	74.6
1975	77.0	73.9	76.6	77.5	80.0	69.9	74.1	77.6	77.9	74.6	77.3	76.2	74.6	81.7	78.3	81.1	80.6
1976	85.1	80.3	84.6	85.1	90.2	76.3	79.9	84.8	83.9	82.2	87.7	83.3	80.2	91.7	89.4	91.0	90.3
1977	86.8	83.8	84.6	87.5	91.3	81.7	84.2	85.4	82.4	82.8	88.6	86.2	81.1	95.2	92.1	90.7	91.2
1978	93.4	89.6	92.4	92.1	99.5	81.8	91.0	95.9	93.5	90.6	93.0	90.3	86.3	99.8	98.3	100.8	99.5
1979	99.0	96.5	100.6	98.2	101.1	93.3	95.3	101.0	100.2	101.6	100.0	95.0	92.7	106.8	104.4	98.4	100.5
1980	100.0	98.6	101.4	99.1	101.2	94.5	100.1	101.1	101.2	101.1	101.9	97.2	90.4	109.5	100.1	100.6	102.8
1981	99.3	94.6	100.2	99.6	102.7	88.0	96.5	99.4	96.5	101.4	102.7	97.6	92.1	109.0	101.2	105.4	101.6
1982	94.9	97.2	95.3	90.3	96.9	93.3	98.8	99.5	95.8	96.1	93.9	87.5	79.5	104.0	97.0	98.7	94.8
1983		94.5	95.3	93.5		91.2	94.9	97.5	95.8	92.6	97.6	89.2	87.4	103.8	98.1		

Industrial production: investment goods (1) — Production industrielle : biens d'équipement (1)

1980 = 100

	Year	Q.1	Q.2	Q.3	Q.4	JAN	FEB	MAR	APR	MAY	JUN	JUL	AUG	SEP	OCT	NOV	DEC
1964	26.4	24.2	27.4	25.6	28.3	22.6	24.4	25.7	28.2	27.5	26.4	25.8	24.6	26.5	28.4	28.3	28.2
1965	29.6	27.6	30.0	29.8	31.2	26.5	27.0	29.2	29.4	29.5	31.0	29.7	28.5	31.3	31.4	31.5	30.6
1966	34.1	30.6	33.9	35.2	36.4	28.6	30.5	32.7	32.7	34.0	35.1	35.7	33.4	36.6	36.5	36.1	36.7
1967	35.2	34.1	36.4	33.7	36.5	32.2	33.9	36.0	36.7	37.4	35.0	32.9	33.1	35.0	36.5	37.8	35.3
1968	39.0	35.3	38.5	40.0	42.1	32.5	35.4	38.0	37.8	39.3	38.4	38.4	38.7	42.9	44.0	40.9	41.4
1969	46.9	40.7	48.6	49.2	48.9	37.2	41.1	43.9	45.3	50.5	49.9	49.7	48.1	49.8	50.5	49.9	46.3
1970	53.2	49.7	54.8	53.9	54.5	46.2	50.8	52.2	53.9	55.5	54.8	53.3	52.5	56.0	54.6	56.8	52.1
1971	58.2	53.4	57.6	60.2	61.6	49.1	55.1	56.0	54.7	59.6	58.6	60.6	60.0	60.1	60.3	63.5	60.9
1972	69.9	63.2	71.1	69.4	75.9	59.2	65.2	65.1	70.0	72.1	71.3	71.2	64.6	72.5	78.3	74.2	75.2
1973	80.1	74.1	80.3	82.0	84.1	68.8	75.6	77.9	79.2	81.5	80.2	80.7	78.6	86.6	85.3	84.0	83.0
1974	79.2	81.8	81.7	75.0	78.9	74.6	86.5	84.3	81.8	83.3	80.0	70.3	75.3	79.4	78.0	78.7	79.9
1975	80.4	77.4	81.2	80.3	82.8	71.5	75.6	85.0	82.9	81.5	79.1	78.8	75.3	86.8	78.8	83.4	86.3
1976	85.9	80.9	88.0	85.8	89.0	77.0	79.7	86.0	90.1	85.1	88.8	83.1	84.5	89.7	88.5	90.3	88.3
1977	84.3	78.6	81.8	86.5	90.4	79.2	77.0	79.7	78.6	80.5	86.4	86.1	77.5	95.8	90.2	88.7	92.4
1978	91.2	89.9	92.4	86.3	96.5	79.3	91.1	99.2	95.6	91.5	90.1	86.5	80.4	91.9	94.5	98.3	96.7
1979	96.9	93.5	102.6	93.5	98.0	88.0	91.5	101.0	104.2	104.2	99.3	93.0	85.5	102.0	103.7	91.0	99.4
1980	100.0	97.9	104.9	97.3	99.8	88.5	101.5	103.7	103.3	107.5	104.0	97.7	89.8	104.3	99.6	97.1	102.8
1981	96.0	88.2	99.3	94.6	101.7	78.1	89.5	96.9	95.2	101.6	101.0	95.2	86.3	102.1	98.4	103.3	103.5
1982	86.7	94.6	90.6	75.0	86.5	91.2	96.9	95.8	92.0	92.0	87.8	75.6	66.6	82.8	84.0	86.3	89.1
1983		86.3	92.3	83.7		81.4	87.3	90.4	92.9	90.1	93.9	80.2	74.8	96.0	93.2		

Industrial production: consumer goods (1) — Production industrielle : biens de consommation (1)

1980 = 100

	Year	Q.1	Q.2	Q.3	Q.4	JAN	FEB	MAR	APR	MAY	JUN	JUL	AUG	SEP	OCT	NOV	DEC
1964	31.8	25.9	30.4	39.3	31.7	25.1	25.5	26.9	28.1	27.0	36.0	41.2	40.2	36.5	33.9	31.2	29.9
1965	34.0	28.5	35.3	39.5	32.4	27.3	23.1	30.1	30.2	33.2	42.5	43.0	38.2	37.3	33.8	32.3	31.2
1966	39.1	32.3	43.4	43.9	36.6	29.9	32.4	34.5	35.4	44.9	49.7	48.5	43.0	40.3	38.4	36.7	34.6
1967	40.1	35.3	42.3	44.0	38.9	33.8	34.9	37.2	36.1	41.9	48.8	48.3	44.3	39.3	39.8	39.3	37.6
1968	42.6	36.8	45.0	47.4	41.4	33.8	37.8	38.9	38.5	43.1	53.3	52.3	47.2	42.6	42.0	41.7	40.4
1969	46.1	40.4	47.1	51.2	45.8	37.7	41.2	42.2	41.9	45.2	54.1	54.7	50.4	48.5	46.7	46.3	44.2
1970	50.8	45.0	50.5	55.9	51.8	42.7	45.3	47.0	47.3	49.3	55.1	58.4	54.3	54.9	52.1	52.2	51.2
1971	56.1	50.4	55.2	62.2	56.2	47.9	50.9	52.4	51.3	53.1	61.2	65.0	61.7	59.8	56.2	56.5	56.0
1972	63.5	58.2	62.8	65.7	67.1	53.7	59.3	61.6	60.0	63.0	65.3	65.1	63.5	68.7	65.1	66.7	69.5
1973	73.9	67.5	74.7	78.7	75.0	63.1	68.2	71.3	73.7	74.2	76.1	77.6	75.7	82.7	78.3	73.8	72.9
1974	72.1	72.8	71.7	71.5	72.8	70.3	74.8	73.2	70.5	72.9	71.9	67.0	69.4	78.1	74.3	71.5	72.6
1975	76.5	72.8	75.2	77.7	80.2	68.8	74.2	75.5	76.3	72.0	77.4	76.0	75.4	81.5	79.7	81.8	79.2
1976	85.7	79.9	84.5	86.1	92.3	75.2	79.7	84.7	82.4	81.5	89.5	84.6	78.9	95.0	91.3	93.3	92.3
1977	88.0	85.8	85.7	87.9	91.9	81.1	88.1	88.2	84.4	83.3	89.4	84.6	81.8	97.3	93.9	91.7	90.0
1978	94.5	88.5	92.8	95.4	101.3	80.4	90.1	95.0	93.5	90.3	94.6	91.5	88.9	105.9	101.6	101.8	100.5
1979	100.2	96.8	100.2	101.2	102.9	94.1	95.7	100.7	98.9	101.1	100.6	95.8	95.9	111.9	106.5	101.9	100.4
1980	100.0	97.6	100.3	99.7	102.6	95.5	98.2	99.1	100.6	98.5	101.7	95.9	88.9	114.2	101.3	103.2	103.5
1981	100.4	96.0	100.9	101.7	102.3	89.3	98.1	100.7	97.0	101.9	103.9	97.8	93.7	113.6	103.0	105.8	99.5
1982	97.4	95.0	96.5	96.8	101.2	90.0	95.5	99.4	96.4	97.3	95.7	91.3	82.7	116.4	103.5	104.2	95.9
1983		96.2	96.8	97.9		92.6	96.0	100.2	96.7	93.5	100.2	92.3	92.3	109.1	100.4		

Industrial production: total (1) — Adjusted - Corrigé * — Production industrielle : total (1)

1980 = 100

	Year	Q.1	Q.2	Q.3	Q.4	JAN	FEB	MAR	APR	MAY	JUN	JUL	AUG	SEP	OCT	NOV	DEC
1964		27.8	28.1	30.2	30.4	27.9	27.7	27.8	29.1	27.1	28.3	29.9	30.8	29.9	29.8	30.5	31.0
1965		30.9	31.6	32.0	32.5	30.9	30.6	31.1	30.7	31.1	33.1	31.9	31.5	32.5	32.0	32.6	32.8
1966		34.4	37.8	37.0	37.5	33.6	34.4	35.2	35.7	39.2	38.6	37.2	36.9	36.9	37.2	37.4	37.8
1967		38.4	38.7	37.6	39.2	38.4	38.2	38.7	38.4	39.3	38.6	37.2	38.4	37.2	39.0	39.4	39.1
1968		39.3	41.1	42.0	43.1	38.2	39.8	40.0	39.8	41.1	42.3	41.5	42.5	42.2	43.0	42.8	43.6
1969		43.8	45.9	47.5	47.9	43.1	44.1	44.1	44.9	45.8	47.1	47.3	47.7	47.3	48.3	48.5	46.9
1970		49.2	50.1	51.7	53.4	49.1	48.9	49.5	50.2	49.8	50.1	51.2	51.6	52.4	52.4	54.1	53.9
1971		54.3	54.9	59.0	59.2	54.2	54.6	54.2	53.2	55.1	56.5	58.7	60.2	58.0	57.8	59.5	60.2
1972		61.8	63.7	64.6	69.6	60.7	62.3	62.4	62.5	64.6	64.1	64.0	63.6	66.2	67.8	68.8	72.3
1973		71.2	74.4	76.9	76.9	70.0	71.3	72.2	74.0	75.0	74.3	75.7	76.8	78.2	78.2	76.3	76.2
1974		76.8	73.9	71.0	73.6	76.8	78.8	75.0	73.2	75.9	72.5	67.1	72.7	73.4	73.2	73.0	74.7
1975		75.3	76.2	77.4	78.9	74.4	75.2	76.2	77.1	75.5	75.9	76.8	78.2	77.3	76.3	80.2	80.2
1976		81.7	84.3	85.4	88.6	81.0	80.9	83.2	82.9	83.6	86.3	84.6	85.1	86.5	86.9	89.4	89.5
1977		85.2	84.3	88.2	89.4	86.4	85.2	84.0	81.5	84.2	87.3	88.2	87.0	89.4	89.4	88.5	90.1
1978		91.0	92.0	93.2	97.3	86.5	91.8	94.5	92.5	91.7	91.7	92.9	93.3	93.3	95.5	97.9	98.4
1979		98.1	100.1	99.5	98.8	98.7	95.9	99.7	99.5	102.1	98.7	98.3	100.9	99.2	101.7	95.3	99.4
1980		100.2	100.8	100.4	98.9	100.0	100.7	99.8	100.7	100.8	100.9	101.1	98.7	101.3	97.8	97.1	101.9
1981		96.0	99.5	101.1	100.5	93.1	97.0	98.0	96.3	100.5	101.6	101.9	100.9	100.4	99.0	101.5	100.8
1982		98.7	94.5	91.5	94.8	98.6	99.3	98.1	95.7	95.0	92.7	91.6	87.3	95.5	95.1	95.0	94.2
1983		96.0	94.6	94.9		96.4	95.4	96.0	95.9	91.6	96.4	93.5	96.1	95.2	96.2		

Industrial production: investment goods (1) — Adjusted - Corrigé * — Production industrielle : biens d'équipement (1)

1980 = 100

	Year	Q.1	Q.2	Q.3	Q.4	JAN	FEB	MAR	APR	MAY	JUN	JUL	AUG	SEP	OCT	NOV	DEC
1964		25.6	26.7	25.4	27.9	25.4	25.9	25.6	28.1	26.4	25.5	25.5	25.3	25.3	27.5	27.9	28.3
1965		29.0	29.2	29.7	30.7	29.7	28.4	29.0	29.1	28.4	30.1	29.5	29.4	30.1	30.3	31.1	30.7
1966		32.1	33.0	35.1	35.9	31.9	32.0	32.4	32.3	32.6	34.2	35.4	34.5	35.4	35.2	35.6	36.9
1967		35.7	35.4	33.6	36.1	35.9	35.4	35.6	36.3	35.7	34.1	32.7	34.1	34.0	35.4	37.3	35.7
1968		36.9	37.3	39.9	41.8	36.3	36.8	37.6	37.2	37.3	37.4	38.0	39.7	41.9	42.9	40.4	42.1
1969		42.5	47.0	49.0	48.8	41.5	42.4	43.6	44.5	47.8	48.6	49.0	49.2	48.8	49.6	49.3	47.4
1970		51.8	53.0	53.7	54.4	51.5	52.1	52.0	53.0	52.5	53.5	52.5	53.7	55.0	54.0	56.0	53.3
1971		55.4	55.8	60.1	61.4	54.5	56.1	55.6	53.6	56.7	57.3	59.9	61.5	59.0	59.8	62.5	62.0
1972		65.3	69.2	69.4	75.5	65.4	66.2	64.3	68.4	69.0	70.1	70.6	66.7	70.8	77.6	73.1	75.8
1973		76.4	78.3	82.3	83.1	75.6	77.1	76.5	77.2	78.6	79.2	80.8	81.8	84.2	84.3	82.6	82.4
1974		84.4	79.9	75.6	77.4	81.8	88.9	82.6	79.3	81.1	79.2	70.7	79.4	76.6	76.7	77.3	78.2
1975		80.0	79.3	81.2	80.7	78.3	78.4	83.3	79.8	80.0	78.1	79.8	80.4	83.4	77.1	81.5	83.7
1976		84.0	85.7	87.4	86.5	84.3	83.4	84.3	86.1	83.7	87.4	84.4	91.7	86.0	86.2	87.8	85.5
1977		81.9	79.5	88.3	87.7	87.0	80.7	78.1	74.8	79.0	84.7	87.8	85.1	92.0	87.7	85.9	89.5
1978		93.3	89.3	88.8	93.7	87.3	95.5	97.2	91.1	88.9	88.0	88.6	89.5	88.3	91.9	95.3	93.8
1979		96.9	98.9	96.6	95.3	97.0	95.1	98.5	99.8	100.2	96.8	95.5	95.8	98.4	101.2	88.3	96.5
1980		100.9	101.1	100.9	97.3	97.2	104.7	100.9	99.7	102.4	101.1	100.7	101.3	100.9	97.7	94.3	99.8
1981		90.3	95.6	98.4	99.2	85.4	91.3	94.1	92.4	96.5	97.9	98.5	97.7	99.1	96.9	100.4	100.2
1982		96.9	87.4	78.0	84.4	99.1	98.4	93.1	89.8	87.5	84.8	78.3	75.5	80.3	83.0	84.1	86.1
1983		88.2	89.2	87.0		88.3	88.3	87.9	90.9	85.9	90.6	83.0	84.8	93.1	92.2		

Industrial production: consumer goods (1) — Adjusted - Corrigé * — Production industrielle : biens de consommation (1)

1980 = 100

	Year	Q.1	Q.2	Q.3	Q.4	JAN	FEB	MAR	APR	MAY	JUN	JUL	AUG	SEP	OCT	NOV	DEC
1964		29.8	29.8	34.1	33.1	30.1	29.5	29.9	30.9	27.8	30.7	33.4	35.4	33.5	33.0	33.0	33.3
1965		32.8	34.3	34.4	34.2	32.7	32.4	33.1	33.1	33.7	36.1	34.7	33.9	34.5	33.5	34.3	34.8
1966		36.7	41.9	38.5	38.7	35.7	37.0	37.6	38.7	45.0	42.0	39.2	38.6	37.8	38.7	38.8	38.5
1967		39.7	40.7	39.1	41.2	39.9	39.2	40.1	39.1	41.8	41.2	39.5	40.3	37.3	40.6	41.4	41.5
1968		40.9	43.2	42.6	43.7	39.5	41.7	41.3	41.5	42.9	45.3	43.6	43.5	40.8	43.1	43.7	44.2
1969		44.1	45.5	46.8	47.9	43.5	44.6	44.3	44.7	44.9	46.8	46.7	47.3	46.6	47.9	48.1	47.7
1970		48.5	49.2	51.8	53.8	48.6	48.2	48.7	49.9	49.0	48.8	51.2	51.8	52.5	53.2	53.9	54.5
1971		53.5	54.0	58.5	57.9	53.8	53.2	53.5	53.5	52.7	55.8	58.6	60.1	56.7	56.9	58.0	58.9
1972		60.9	61.9	62.7	68.6	59.4	61.1	62.2	62.0	62.5	61.2	60.5	62.9	64.7	65.3	68.1	72.3
1973		69.8	74.1	75.9	75.8	68.9	69.4	71.2	75.4	73.9	73.1	74.2	76.3	77.3	77.8	74.6	75.0
1974		74.8	71.6	69.7	72.8	76.2	75.5	72.6	71.7	73.1	70.0	65.7	71.0	72.5	73.0	71.5	74.1
1975		74.4	75.4	76.5	79.4	74.1	74.6	74.5	77.3	73.0	76.0	76.0	78.2	75.2	77.5	80.9	79.9
1976		81.4	84.9	85.3	90.7	80.7	80.2	83.3	83.2	83.3	88.1	85.9	82.7	87.1	88.1	91.5	92.6
1977		87.6	86.2	87.4	89.7	86.9	89.1	86.7	85.1	85.4	88.0	86.9	86.8	88.6	90.1	89.2	89.8
1978		90.5	93.3	95.1	98.6	86.4	91.5	93.7	94.4	92.3	93.2	94.6	95.3	95.5	97.3	98.6	100.0
1979		99.4	100.6	101.1	100.0	101.4	97.4	99.5	99.8	102.7	99.3	99.5	103.6	100.1	102.0	98.2	99.7
1980		100.6	100.5	99.3	99.6	103.2	100.4	98.2	101.8	99.2	100.6	99.9	96.5	101.5	97.1	99.0	102.8
1981		99.1	100.9	101.6	99.7	96.8	100.5	99.9	98.1	102.0	102.7	102.1	102.1	100.6	99.0	101.3	98.8
1982		98.1	96.5	96.2	93.2	97.8	97.9	98.6	97.9	97.0	94.5	95.4	90.3	102.8	99.6	99.5	95.3
1983		99.5	96.9	97.8		100.9	98.3	99.3	98.4	93.2	99.0	96.4	100.9	96.2	96.7		

* Adjusted by the O.E.C.D.

* Corrigé par l'O.C.D.E.

GREECE

Industrial production: manufacturing (1) — Production industrielle : industries manufacturières (1)

1980 = 100

	Year	Q.1	Q.2	Q.3	Q.4	JAN	FEB	MAR	APR	MAY	JUN	JUL	AUG	SEP	OCT	NOV	DEC
1964	30.5	25.9	29.9	35.2	31.0	25.0	25.7	27.1	28.7	27.7	33.2	36.6	35.5	33.6	32.1	30.8	30.0
1965	33.0	28.7	33.9	36.7	32.6	27.5	28.2	30.3	30.4	32.4	38.9	38.8	35.4	35.8	33.6	32.6	31.6
1966	37.8	32.4	40.5	41.4	37.0	30.1	32.4	34.5	35.1	41.4	45.1	44.3	40.2	39.5	38.2	36.9	35.7
1967	38.8	35.2	40.5	40.9	38.6	33.7	34.9	37.2	36.7	40.5	44.2	43.4	41.0	38.4	39.2	39.1	37.4
1968	41.6	36.7	43.0	45.1	41.8	33.8	37.3	38.9	38.6	42.2	48.3	47.7	44.6	42.9	42.8	41.7	40.8
1969	46.3	40.6	47.3	50.4	46.8	37.7	41.2	42.8	43.0	46.7	52.2	52.5	49.7	49.1	48.0	47.4	45.0
1970	51.4	46.4	51.5	55.1	52.5	43.7	46.9	48.5	49.2	50.9	54.4	56.3	53.7	55.2	52.8	53.4	51.4
1971	56.4	51.2	55.6	61.0	57.6	48.2	52.0	53.3	52.2	54.9	59.7	62.8	60.8	59.6	57.2	58.3	57.3
1972	65.2	59.6	65.2	66.5	69.7	55.2	61.0	62.5	63.0	65.7	67.0	66.6	63.3	69.5	69.0	69.0	71.1
1973	75.5	69.4	76.1	79.1	77.7	64.7	70.4	73.1	75.2	76.1	77.0	78.0	75.9	83.4	80.2	76.9	75.9
1974	74.0	75.6	74.8	71.8	74.2	71.4	78.5	76.8	74.1	76.1	74.2	67.4	70.4	77.8	74.9	73.2	74.5
1975	77.3	73.8	76.9	77.9	80.8	69.2	74.2	78.2	78.2	74.8	77.7	76.3	74.7	82.7	79.1	82.0	81.3
1976	85.5	80.1	85.5	85.5	90.9	75.6	79.7	85.0	84.8	82.7	89.0	83.6	80.0	92.8	90.0	92.0	90.8
1977	86.8	83.6	85.0	87.1	91.3	80.7	84.3	85.8	83.0	83.2	88.6	85.7	79.8	95.8	92.2	90.9	90.9
1978	93.4	89.1	92.8	92.0	99.6	80.2	90.6	96.5	94.4	90.9	93.3	89.7	85.4	100.9	99.0	100.6	99.3
1979	99.1	96.0	101.0	98.2	101.3	92.3	94.6	101.2	100.7	102.2	100.1	94.7	91.7	108.1	105.4	98.6	100.0
1980	100.0	97.9	102.0	98.5	101.6	93.4	99.6	100.8	101.8	101.7	102.6	96.5	88.6	110.5	100.6	101.0	103.1
1981	98.8	93.6	100.5	99.0	102.3	85.6	95.5	99.5	96.7	102.0	102.8	96.7	90.7	109.6	101.3	104.9	100.6
1982	93.8	94.9	94.8	89.2	96.4	90.5	96.0	98.3	95.2	95.9	93.3	85.9	76.9	104.8	97.2	98.4	93.6
1983		92.8	95.2	92.6		88.8	92.8	96.8	95.5	92.3	97.9	87.8	85.5	104.3	97.8		

Production: cement — Production : ciment

thousand tons, monthly averages — milliers de tonnes, moyennes mensuelles

	Year	Q.1	Q.2	Q.3	Q.4	JAN	FEB	MAR	APR	MAY	JUN	JUL	AUG	SEP	OCT	NOV	DEC
1964	222	158	240	253	235	132	157	185	254	235	231	243	259	257	271	234	200
1965	268	176	275	329	290	155	136	237	256	285	284	318	309	361	338	296	235
1966	299	229	321	353	293	140	250	296	291	331	341	357	339	362	366	292	222
1967	308	261	332	351	288	191	229	363	361	302	332	322	353	378	364	293	208
1968	338	227	367	423	335	138	220	322	345	382	374	398	417	453	426	338	241
1969	400	282	449	476	393	193	279	375	379	507	461	468	493	468	502	413	263
1970	404	293	428	484	411	219	318	341	402	443	440	459	491	503	481	443	309
1971	461	312	495	549	489	263	304	370	433	526	525	546	570	532	563	487	418
1972	528	419	586	578	530	330	429	498	501	668	589	594	568	572	541	537	511
1973	537	439	578	614	518	361	442	514	570	591	572	573	639	629	578	529	447
1974	585	550	621	617	554	499	569	581	571	642	649	553	615	684	648	562	451
1975	662	520	752	760	614	459	469	632	766	707	784	791	770	720	707	599	536
1976	726	608	787	788	722	552	563	708	748	811	801	787	800	777	777	730	660
1977	880	786	935	943	856	657	795	905	863	999	942	965	962	901	955	877	737
1978	953	821	1024	1031	936	611	790	1063	1086	1001	986	1083	994	1016	985	1009	815
1979	1005	876	1094	1085	966	748	820	1061	1121	1100	1061	1129	1060	1066	1048	901	949
1980	1056	972	1154	1162	937	830	1024	1063	1069	1231	1162	1202	1152	1131	910	994	908
1981	1105	821	1204	1232	1162	636	842	986	1189	1207	1217	1150	1260	1286	1251	1119	1116
1982	1101	1025	1178	1130	1073	1055	953	1067	1145	1201	1187	1115	1046	1228	1176	1020	1023
1983	1190	979	1275	1306	1200	1105	771	1060	1393	1264	1169	1226	1346	1346	1294	1183	1124

Production: future tendency manufacturing — Perspectives de production industries manufacturières

per cent balance — solde en pourcentage

	Year	Q.1	Q.2	Q.3	Q.4	JAN	FEB	MAR	APR	MAY	JUN	JUL	AUG	SEP	OCT	NOV	DEC
1964																	
1965																	
1966																	
1967																	
1968																	
1969																	
1970																	
1971																	
1972																	
1973																	
1974																	
1975																	
1976																	
1977																	
1978																	
1979																	
1980																	
1981						20	29	32	23	24	9	9	12	12	17	10	7
1982						7	11	26	17	18	-9	-7	2	10	3	2	-7
1983						7	3	13	22	14	15	8	13	18	17	10	28

Industrial production: manufacturing (1) | Adjusted - Corrigé * | Production industrielle : industries manufacturières (1)

1980 = 100 | 1980 = 100

	Year	Q.1	Q.2	Q.3	Q.4	JAN	FEB	MAR	APR	MAY	JUN	JUL	AUG	SEP	OCT	NOV	DEC
1964		28.9	29.3	32.0	31.6	28.8	28.8	29.0	30.3	28.0	29.7	31.4	33.1	31.5	31.2	31.8	31.9
1965		31.9	33.1	33.4	33.5	31.9	31.5	32.3	32.1	32.5	34.6	33.3	33.1	33.7	33.0	33.6	33.8
1966		35.7	39.3	37.9	38.1	34.9	35.9	36.4	36.9	41.2	39.9	38.2	37.8	37.5	37.9	38.0	38.3
1967		38.7	39.3	37.8	39.8	38.8	38.3	38.9	38.5	40.0	39.2	37.8	38.7	36.7	39.2	40.2	40.0
1968		39.8	41.6	42.0	43.1	38.7	40.4	40.3	40.3	41.5	43.1	42.2	42.5	41.3	43.0	42.7	43.5
1969		43.6	45.9	47.5	48.0	42.9	43.9	44.1	44.5	45.9	47.2	47.3	47.8	47.3	48.2	48.3	47.5
1970		49.4	50.1	52.4	53.7	49.3	49.2	49.6	50.3	50.0	50.0	51.8	52.3	53.1	52.9	54.2	53.9
1971		53.9	54.3	58.7	58.6	53.7	53.9	53.9	52.9	53.9	56.1	59.0	60.0	57.1	57.2	59.0	59.5
1972		62.1	63.9	64.6	70.4	60.9	62.6	62.6	63.1	64.7	64.0	64.0	63.5	66.3	68.6	69.5	73.1
1973		71.6	75.0	77.6	77.8	70.6	71.8	72.4	74.8	75.3	74.8	76.4	77.4	79.1	79.2	77.0	77.1
1974		77.6	73.9	71.1	73.8	77.5	79.9	75.5	73.2	75.9	72.7	67.1	73.0	73.4	73.6	72.9	74.9
1975		75.5	76.2	77.8	79.8	74.5	75.4	76.6	77.0	75.2	76.5	76.8	78.8	77.7	77.3	81.0	81.0
1976		81.7	84.9	85.7	89.3	81.2	80.9	83.2	83.3	83.6	87.8	85.0	85.4	86.7	87.6	90.3	90.1
1977		85.3	84.4	87.8	89.3	86.4	85.5	84.1	81.6	84.1	87.4	87.9	86.4	89.2	89.3	88.6	90.1
1978		90.8	92.1	93.1	97.2	85.8	91.7	94.9	92.8	91.4	92.0	92.7	93.3	93.3	95.7	97.6	98.4
1979		98.1	100.0	99.6	98.8	98.8	95.7	99.8	99.4	101.9	98.6	98.4	101.1	99.4	101.9	95.2	99.1
1980		100.1	100.9	100.1	99.0	100.2	100.8	99.4	100.8	100.6	101.1	101.0	98.0	101.2	97.4	97.1	102.4
1981		95.6	99.2	100.8	99.6	91.9	96.9	98.0	96.1	100.2	101.2	101.6	100.6	100.2	98.3	100.5	100.0
1982		97.1	93.5	90.5	93.9	97.1	97.5	96.8	94.8	94.0	91.6	90.5	85.6	95.5	94.4	94.2	93.1
1983		95.0	93.9	94.3		95.3	94.3	95.2	95.3	90.4	96.1	92.6	95.2	95.0	95.1		

Sales: prospects | Perspectives de vente

manufacturing | industries manufacturières

per cent balance | solde en pourcentage

	Year	Q.1	Q.2	Q.3	Q.4	JAN	FEB	MAR	APR	MAY	JUN	JUL	AUG	SEP	OCT	NOV	DEC
1964																	
1965																	
1966																	
1967																	
1968																	
1969																	
1970																	
1971																	
1972																	
1973																	
1974																	
1975																	
1976																	
1977																	
1978																	
1979																	
1980																	
1981						25	33	33	29	31	10	10	13	13	27	12	4
1982						7	13	15	17	9	-10	-	7	13	8	1	-6
1983						17	3	15	18	9	12	10	24	39	37	14	10

Order books: level | Carnet de commandes : niveau

manufacturing | industries manufacturières

per cent balance | solde en pourcentage

	Year	Q.1	Q.2	Q.3	Q.4	JAN	FEB	MAR	APR	MAY	JUN	JUL	AUG	SEP	OCT	NOV	DEC
1964																	
1965																	
1966																	
1967																	
1968																	
1969																	
1970																	
1971																	
1972																	
1973																	
1974																	
1975																	
1976																	
1977																	
1978																	
1979																	
1980																	
1981						-10	-25	-24	-30	-30	-35	-48	-39	-39	-31	-31	-28
1982						-27	-30	-15	-21	-27	-42	-38	-37	-38	-35	-37	-38
1983						-32	-33	-32	-23	-34	-37	-33	-25	-19	-15	-24	-22

* Adjusted by the O.E.C.D. | * Corrigé par l'O.C.D.E.

GREECE

Finished goods stocks
manufacturing
per cent balance

Stocks de produits finis : niveau
industries manufacturières
solde en pourcentage

	Year	Q.1	Q.2	Q.3	Q.4	JAN	FEB	MAR	APR	MAY	JUN	JUL	AUG	SEP	OCT	NOV	DEC
1964																	
1965																	
1966																	
1967																	
1968																	
1969																	
1970																	
1971																	
1972																	
1973																	
1974																	
1975																	
1976																	
1977																	
1978																	
1979																	
1980																	
1981						22	34	28	25	30	33	32	19	19	16	20	29
1982						27	22	20	19	26	23	16	15	12	9	6	8
1983						10	19	13	5	6	17	18	20	20	22	6	4

Rate of capacity utilization
manufacturing
per cent

Taux d'utilisation des capacités
industries manufacturières
pourcentage

	Year	Q.1	Q.2	Q.3	Q.4	JAN	FEB	MAR	APR	MAY	JUN	JUL	AUG	SEP	OCT	NOV	DEC
1964																	
1965																	
1966																	
1967																	
1968																	
1969																	
1970																	
1971																	
1972																	
1973																	
1974																	
1975																	
1976																	
1977																	
1978																	
1979																	
1980																	
1981						83.8	82.1	82.0	79.8	79.4	79.3	79.7	76.9	76.9	78.3	78.7	76.3
1982						76.5	75.8	76.7	75.3	75.4	74.3	76.1	76.0	75.9	72.5	74.3	73.2
1983						73.2	72.7	74.9	75.7	74.6	74.2	73.9	76.0	78.0	77.2	76.5	73.7

Construction permits issued: total
million cubic metres, monthly averages

Permis de construire délivrés : total
millions de mètres cubes, moyennes mensuelles

	Year	Q.1	Q.2	Q.3	Q.4	JAN	FEB	MAR	APR	MAY	JUN	JUL	AUG	SEP	OCT	NOV	DEC
1964	2.30	1.79	2.56	2.59	2.28	1.68	1.86	1.83	2.67	2.34	2.66	4.27	1.47	2.02	2.59	2.12	2.12
1965	2.61	2.21	2.86	2.79	2.58	2.08	1.92	2.62	2.54	2.90	3.13	4.25	1.78	2.34	2.51	2.84	2.38
1966	2.86	2.59	3.29	3.14	2.40	1.71	2.40	3.66	2.87	3.46	3.55	4.86	1.36	3.21	2.45	2.58	2.19
1967	2.78	2.14	2.96	3.00	3.04	1.83	1.95	2.64	2.51	3.24	3.14	4.22	1.94	2.84	3.21	3.21	2.69
1968	3.76	2.86	4.37	4.22	3.62	2.22	2.65	3.70	4.00	4.66	4.45	4.32	4.38	3.95	4.19	3.71	2.95
1969	4.45	3.66	5.36	5.12	3.65	2.79	3.66	4.52	5.03	5.74	5.32	5.94	4.85	4.57	4.21	3.80	2.95
1970	4.25	3.69	4.68	4.66	3.96	2.99	3.52	4.55	4.35	4.83	4.86	5.16	4.41	4.42	4.38	3.97	3.51
1971	4.63	3.61	4.94	5.17	4.77	3.41	3.28	4.15	4.22	5.52	5.10	5.35	5.10	5.05	4.61	5.11	4.59
1972	6.41	5.05	6.68	6.15	7.76	4.24	4.31	6.60	5.21	7.26	7.57	6.64	5.60	6.20	6.47	7.19	9.63
1973	7.24	7.70	9.58	6.41	5.25	6.61	7.49	9.00	10.57	10.11	8.07	7.25	6.41	5.56	5.70	5.36	4.70
1974	3.94	3.88	3.60	3.86	4.40	3.55	4.35	3.75	3.12	3.69	3.98	3.56	2.60	5.41	5.02	4.81	3.36
1975	4.87	4.36	4.96	5.20	4.96	3.31	4.93	4.83	5.30	4.02	5.55	5.30	5.14	5.17	5.95	4.85	4.07
1976	5.29	5.88	5.26	4.63	5.40	5.65	5.54	6.44	6.02	6.16	3.60	4.12	4.48	5.28	5.41	5.40	5.39
1977	6.44	5.96	6.92	6.40	6.46	4.98	5.79	7.11	6.57	6.99	7.20	8.94	4.15	6.10	6.06	6.97	6.36
1978	7.50	5.95	8.05	7.72	8.27	5.27	5.59	7.00	8.10	7.72	8.33	11.41	4.79	6.95	7.67	9.05	8.09
1979	7.89	9.03	8.76	7.19	6.57	8.35	9.78	8.97	7.98	8.95	9.35	10.15	5.21	6.22	7.38	6.55	5.79
1980	5.95	6.21	6.84	5.77	4.98	6.00	4.60	8.01	6.79	7.16	6.56	8.42	4.19	4.71	5.66	4.62	4.66
1981	4.91	4.11	5.01	5.59	4.92	3.76	4.55	4.03	4.67	4.75	5.62	7.31	3.99	5.48	5.54	4.68	4.54
1982	4.39	4.47	4.35	4.59	4.13	3.96	4.46	5.01	4.51	4.87	3.68	6.32	3.10	4.36	3.77	4.54	4.07
1983		4.21	5.47	5.92		3.39	4.11	5.12	6.04	4.52	5.86	6.16	5.52	6.09	5.20		

Construction permits issued: dwellings
thousands, monthly averages

Permis de construire délivrés : logements
milliers, moyennes mensuelles

	Year	Q.1	Q.2	Q.3	Q.4	JAN	FEB	MAR	APR	MAY	JUN	JUL	AUG	SEP	OCT	NOV	DEC
1964	5.52	4.37	5.72	6.12	5.87	4.30	4.63	4.19	6.25	5.26	5.65	9.93	3.60	4.82	6.29	5.73	5.60
1965	6.62	5.36	7.19	7.18	6.74	5.32	4.81	5.96	6.29	7.25	8.04	11.27	4.42	5.85	6.60	7.72	5.91
1966	7.00	6.51	8.37	7.11	6.01	4.28	5.78	9.46	7.56	8.59	8.95	12.00	2.79	6.53	6.51	6.44	5.06
1967	6.83	4.84	6.99	7.60	7.88	4.15	4.83	5.54	5.73	7.67	7.58	10.12	5.08	7.58	8.45	8.12	7.08
1968	9.34	7.03	10.61	10.84	8.87	6.13	6.51	8.45	9.80	11.27	10.74	11.16	11.08	10.28	10.64	9.08	6.89
1969	10.69	9.02	12.85	11.97	8.91	6.76	9.19	11.10	12.18	13.87	12.50	13.07	11.76	11.08	10.71	9.16	6.87
1970	9.55	8.69	10.84	10.08	8.60	7.04	8.36	10.68	10.09	10.86	11.56	11.17	9.48	9.60	9.46	9.13	7.20
1971	10.41	8.49	11.07	11.52	10.56	8.29	7.74	9.45	9.56	11.54	12.11	11.62	11.68	11.26	10.10	11.14	10.45
1972	14.88	11.53	14.80	13.90	19.29	10.46	9.80	14.32	11.89	15.93	16.58	14.76	13.09	13.84	14.81	19.11	23.96
1973	15.68	20.65	20.70	12.42	8.93	19.01	20.57	22.37	23.99	21.66	16.45	14.28	12.35	10.63	10.73	8.99	7.08
1974	6.80	6.03	5.68	6.49	9.01	6.34	6.81	4.93	4.86	5.16	7.00	6.19	3.97	9.32	10.24	10.06	6.73
1975	10.07	8.96	10.02	10.63	10.68	6.95	10.37	9.56	10.59	8.66	10.81	10.60	10.67	10.62	11.92	10.69	9.42
1976	10.72	12.52	10.40	8.94	11.01	12.53	11.15	13.89	11.62	12.42	7.15	7.49	9.12	10.21	11.23	10.57	11.24
1977	13.19	12.34	13.85	13.25	13.32	10.46	11.83	14.72	12.77	13.44	15.35	19.28	8.38	12.11	12.65	13.99	13.30
1978	15.58	12.71	16.37	16.20	17.05	11.34	12.26	14.53	15.96	15.88	17.26	23.93	9.79	14.88	16.22	18.30	16.64
1979	15.75	18.63	17.13	14.30	12.91	16.51	20.33	19.05	15.73	17.43	18.23	20.12	10.17	12.63	14.57	12.52	11.64
1980	11.34	12.00	13.29	10.62	9.44	12.11	8.66	15.23	13.22	13.67	12.98	15.07	7.72	9.07	10.88	9.10	8.33
1981	9.02	7.48	8.95	10.19	9.44	7.30	7.99	7.14	8.03	8.52	10.30	13.35	7.08	10.15	10.88	9.08	8.36
1982	8.51	8.98	8.27	8.79	8.00	8.05	8.97	9.92	8.31	9.14	7.36	12.06	5.81	8.51	7.76	8.67	7.56
1983		8.04	10.22	11.24		6.61	7.78	9.74	10.91	8.26	11.50	11.89	9.98	11.85	9.95		

Cost of construction: residential (2)
1980 = 100

Coût de la construction : bâtiments résidentiels (2)
1980 = 100

	Year	Q.1	Q.2	Q.3	Q.4	JAN	FEB	MAR	APR	MAY	JUN	JUL	AUG	SEP	OCT	NOV	DEC
1964																	
1965																	
1966																	
1967																	
1968																	
1969																	
1970																	
1971																	
1972	23.9																
1973	30.9																
1974	40.2	38.7	40.7	40.7	40.7	38.1	38.6	39.4	40.2	40.9	40.9	40.8	40.8	40.7	40.6	40.7	40.8
1975	41.2	40.9	40.9	41.3	41.6	40.8	40.7	41.0	41.0	41.0	40.9	41.2	41.3	41.3	41.5	41.6	41.8
1976	47.1	43.7	46.0	48.5	50.4	43.3	43.5	44.2	44.9	45.8	47.3	47.9	48.5	49.0	49.9	50.3	51.0
1977	55.0	52.9	54.2	56.0	56.7	52.0	53.2	53.4	53.4	54.3	55.0	55.8	55.8	56.3	56.6	56.7	56.8
1978	61.3	58.4	60.8	62.2	63.8	57.9	58.1	59.3	60.1	61.0	61.4	62.0	62.1	62.4	63.0	64.0	64.4
1979	76.7	69.4	72.9	79.6	85.0	68.3	69.6	70.2	71.1	72.6	75.1	77.3	78.4	82.9	83.6	84.9	86.6
1980	100.0	92.1	97.2	104.0	106.8	89.2	92.8	94.2	95.4	96.4	99.6	102.3	104.0	105.8	106.1	106.6	107.7
1981	119.7	111.6	117.8	122.5	127.2	108.7	112.4	113.7	115.6	118.3	119.6	120.3	122.9	124.2	126.6	127.1	127.8
1982	139.8	131.0	136.4	143.1	148.7	128.7	130.8	133.6	135.0	136.1	138.0	140.6	142.9	145.8	147.6	148.9	149.7
1983	169.8	157.3	165.8	173.7	181.9	154.0	158.1	161.5	163.5	165.8	168.2	171.2	173.8	176.1	179.2	181.9	184.7

Retail sales: value (3) / Ventes au détail : valeur (3)

1980 = 100

	Year	Q.1	Q.2	Q.3	Q.4	JAN	FEB	MAR	APR	MAY	JUN	JUL	AUG	SEP	OCT	NOV	DEC
1964																	
1965																	
1966																	
1967																	
1968																	
1969																	
1970																	
1971																	
1972																	
1973																	
1974				33.1	42.9						35.9	33.6	32.5	33.3	37.6	39.2	52.0
1975	43.0	39.7	42.4	39.0	50.8	38.0	42.4	38.7	41.5	44.5	41.1	36.7	41.4	38.9	45.4	47.8	59.1
1976	50.4	45.8	48.8	47.3	59.6	45.0	48.6	43.8	54.8	45.0	46.5	45.3	48.1	48.6	54.9	55.5	68.5
1977	59.8	55.5	56.2	56.8	70.6	54.3	59.6	52.5	59.7	54.2	54.8	54.1	57.5	58.8	67.3	64.6	79.9
1978	70.1	65.2	68.2	64.4	82.6	62.9	70.4	62.3	76.0	64.2	64.3	61.6	64.2	67.5	75.1	75.2	97.6
1979	82.0	74.8	80.2	76.7	96.4	74.5	80.0	69.8	88.1	75.8	76.8	73.0	77.9	79.0	83.1	88.8	117.2
1980	100.0	92.0	96.9	94.0	117.4	89.6	93.5	92.8	103.1	91.8	96.0	88.8	96.6	96.7	104.3	110.4	137.4
1981	120.3	112.7	118.3	111.3	138.9	117.4	110.7	109.9	129.8	114.7	110.5	107.2	112.0	114.6	123.0	134.3	159.4
1982	139.5	130.8	134.3	128.9	164.0	137.9	128.9	125.6	143.9	130.4	128.5	122.9	127.0	136.7	149.9	161.8	180.3
1983	167.0	155.9	162.5	156.5	193.2	169.0	152.6	146.2	160.8	172.4	154.2	148.9	153.5	167.1	181.6	177.8	220.1

New passenger car registrations (4) / Immatriculations de voitures de tourisme neuves (4)

thousands, monthly averages / milliers, moyennes mensuelles

	Year	Q.1	Q.2	Q.3	Q.4	JAN	FEB	MAR	APR	MAY	JUN	JUL	AUG	SEP	OCT	NOV	DEC
1964	1.17	0.96	1.32	1.62	1.05	1.27	0.98	0.63	1.65	1.47	0.86	2.32	1.54	0.99	1.38	0.97	0.80
1965	1.89	0.90	1.89	1.25	3.35	1.39	0.61	0.71	3.15	1.37	1.16	1.21	1.55	1.00	2.11	2.43	5.49
1966	1.52	1.01	..	2.04	1.64	0.74	1.08	1.19	..	1.64	1.53	2.90	1.98	1.23	2.23	1.55	1.14
1967	1.83	1.86	2.20	1.89	1.74	2.25	1.98	1.35	2.90	1.97	1.73	2.75	1.89	1.03	2.26	1.65	1.30
1968	2.13	2.13	2.27	2.36	1.68	2.59	2.26	1.53	3.01	2.39	1.43	3.52	2.34	1.22	2.46	1.81	0.78
1969	2.11	1.70	2.39	2.43	2.04	2.33	1.55	1.21	3.27	2.38	1.52	3.80	2.27	1.22	2.94	2.03	1.15
1970	2.64	2.10	2.85	3.12	2.68	2.82	2.18	1.30	4.03	2.78	1.75	4.64	2.89	1.83	3.69	2.69	1.67
1971	3.10	2.58	4.02	3.03	2.83	3.79	2.18	1.78	4.95	3.84	3.25	4.01	3.27	1.80	3.63	2.91	1.96
1972	3.30	2.95	3.47	3.29	3.48	4.05	2.44	2.37	4.52	3.52	2.38	4.72	3.21	1.94	4.05	3.47	2.92
1973	3.70	3.33	4.04	3.89	3.55	4.32	2.76	2.90	5.43	3.34	3.37	4.98	3.88	2.82	4.57	3.39	2.70
1974	2.82	3.09	2.64	2.85	2.70	4.54	2.70	2.02	3.23	2.46	2.23	3.68	2.99	1.88	3.01	2.60	2.50
1975	5.01	4.66	4.02	5.15	5.93	6.44	4.78	2.76	5.43	3.69	2.94	6.11	5.53	3.81	6.10	4.56	7.13
1976	5.83	4.37	5.61	6.32	7.53	4.26	3.59	5.26	5.61	5.21	6.02	7.84	6.37	4.76	8.07	8.44	6.07
1977	9.20	7.92	9.50	9.45	9.70	8.56	7.76	7.43	10.02	9.12	9.35	12.22	8.95	7.19	10.86	9.40	8.85
1978	10.62	10.95	11.42	9.88	10.24	11.18	9.87	11.80	14.78	9.75	9.75	12.20	9.91	7.53	10.06	10.95	9.71
1979	8.01	9.44	10.82	7.04	4.72	12.76	7.53	8.04	13.02	11.24	8.20	7.77	8.38	4.96	5.83	4.27	4.07
1980	3.49	3.87	3.66	3.18	3.23	4.57	3.34	3.70	4.36	3.55	3.08	4.01	3.02	2.51	4.11	2.88	2.71
1981	4.57	3.21	5.23	4.73	5.12	3.26	3.06	3.32	6.32	4.50	4.86	6.15	4.19	3.87	5.13	4.86	5.39
1982	7.66	6.63	7.21	7.61	9.19	6.57	6.74	6.57	8.62	7.05	5.97	8.69	7.28	6.87	8.66	9.68	9.23
1983	6.27	4.88	6.27	8.11	5.82	7.45	3.85	3.34	8.89	5.47	4.44	9.73	7.43	7.17	6.06	6.75	4.64

Retail sales: volume / Ventes au détail : volume

Adjusted - Corrigé *

1980 = 100

	Year	Q.1	Q.2	Q.3	Q.4	JAN	FEB	MAR	APR	MAY	JUN	JUL	AUG	SEP	OCT	NOV	DEC
1964																	
1965																	
1966																	
1967																	
1968																	
1969																	
1970																	
1971																	
1972																	
1973																	
1974				87	89						90	91	86	85	87	88	94
1975	91	89	93	92	91	89	90	88	83	103	92	91	96	90	90	91	92
1976	95	90	93	98	97	92	86	90	96	88	93	97	98	98	97	98	96
1977	100	99	96	104	102	97	101	99	93	97	97	101	105	106	104	101	100
1978	104	102	102	105	106	100	106	101	103	101	102	102	106	107	107	105	107
1979	102	102	103	103	101	102	105	98	102	103	103	103	106	102	98	102	102
1980	100	100	99	103	98	100	98	102	98	99	99	102	104	103	100	98	97
1981	97	98	97	97	95	102	96	98	98	97	96	98	97	97	95	96	93
1982	93	94	90	93	94	96	94	93	90	90	90	92	92	95	95	99	88
1983	92	93	91	94	92	98	92	89	82	99	90	92	93	97	94	90	90

* Adjusted by the O.E.C.D.

* Corrigé par l'O.C.D.E.

Retail sales: value

Adjusted - Corrigé *

1980 = 100

Ventes au détail : valeur

1980 = 100

	Year	Q.1	Q.2	Q.3	Q.4	JAN	FEB	MAR	APR	MAY	JUN	JUL	AUG	SEP	OCT	NOV	DEC
1964																	
1965																	
1966																	
1967																	
1968																	
1969																	
1970																	
1971																	
1972																	
1973																	
1974				36.3	38.6						37.7	37.9	35.1	35.8	37.2	37.8	40.9
1975		40.1	43.2	42.9	45.5	39.4	40.1	40.7	38.5	47.9	43.0	42.0	43.9	42.9	44.3	45.5	46.7
1976		46.0	49.3	51.9	53.8	46.9	43.9	47.1	50.8	47.1	50.0	51.6	51.4	52.9	52.8	54.4	54.1
1977		56.2	56.9	62.2	63.9	54.9	56.7	57.1	54.8	57.5	58.4	60.6	62.0	64.1	64.6	63.5	63.4
1978		66.1	68.7	70.5	74.4	64.2	67.5	66.6	68.6	68.2	69.3	68.5	70.3	72.6	73.8	73.5	76.0
1979		76.0	80.7	83.5	87.1	75.7	77.7	74.7	79.0	81.3	81.7	82.6	84.5	83.3	82.8	87.8	90.6
1980		92.1	97.5	103.5	106.5	90.8	89.2	96.2	94.8	97.3	100.3	102.2	103.4	104.7	104.7	106.2	108.8
1981		114.1	118.6	121.7	127.0	116.5	110.5	115.4	118.2	118.9	118.8	121.7	119.4	124.0	124.7	128.4	127.9
1982		131.6	134.8	141.6	150.4	132.8	129.6	132.5	132.4	134.1	138.0	140.2	137.9	146.7	149.3	159.1	143.0
1983		157.0	163.8	171.6	176.6	160.6	154.3	156.1	146.4	180.5	164.4	166.0	167.7	181.0	179.8	174.3	175.7

Employment: manufacturing (5)(6)

(employees on payrolls)

1980 = 100

Emploi : industries manufacturières (5)(6)

(salariés sur bordereaux)

1980 = 100

	Year	Q.1	Q.2	Q.3	Q.4	JAN	FEB	MAR	APR	MAY	JUN	JUL	AUG	SEP	OCT	NOV	DEC
1964	62	59	61	64	63	59	58	59	59	60	63	64	64	64	64	63	61
1965	64	61	64	67	64	61	61	61	62	64	66	67	66	67	66	65	63
1966	66	63	66	69	67	62	63	63	64	66	68	69	68	68	68	67	65
1967	65	64	66	67	65	64	64	64	65	66	69	67	66	67	66	65	63
1968	65	62	65	67	65	62	62	63	63	65	67	68	67	67	67	66	64
1969	67	64	67	70	69	63	64	64	65	67	69	70	70	70	70	69	68
1970	71	67	70	73	72	66	67	67	68	70	71	73	73	73	73	73	72
1971	75	72	75	76	76	71	72	73	73	75	77	76	77	77	77	76	75
1972	78	75	78	79	79	74	75	75	76	78	79	79	79	79	79	80	78
1973	82	79	82	85	84	77	79	80	80	83	83	85	86	85	84	85	83
1974	83	82	83	85	84	82	83	82	80	83	84	85	85	86	84	84	83
1975	84	81	82	87	86	82	80	82	81	82	85	87	87	86	85	86	86
1976	89	85	88	92	92	86	86	85	86	87	89	92	93	92	91	92	92
1977	93	90	92	96	96	90	89	91	91	92	93	95	96	96	97	96	94
1978	96	94	95	99	98	93	94	94	93	94	97	98	100	99	98	97	98
1979	99	96	99	102	98	95	96	97	97	98	103	101	104	101	99	98	98
1980	100	98	99	103	100	97	98	99	98	99	101	104	103	103	100	100	99
1981	101	99	100	105	100	98	100	99	99	100	103	106	106	104	101	100	100
1982	101	99	100	105	101	99	99	99	98	100	101	104	106	106	102	101	101
1983	100	98	100	103	100	98	98	98	98	99	101	101	104	103	101	100	99

Weekly hours of work: (5)

manufacturing (wage earners)

hours

Durée hebdomadaire du travail : (5)

industries manufacturières (ouvriers)

heures

	Year	Q.1	Q.2	Q.3	Q.4	JAN	FEB	MAR	APR	MAY	JUN	JUL	AUG	SEP	OCT	NOV	DEC
1964	44.0	43.6	43.5	43.9	44.3		43.6			43.5			43.9			44.8	
1965	43.8	44.0	43.7	43.3	44.1		44.0			43.7			43.3			44.1	
1966	43.3	43.9	43.5	42.1	43.7		43.9			43.5			42.1			43.7	
1967	43.6	43.7	42.9	43.1	44.5		43.7			42.9			43.1			44.5	
1968	43.7	44.3	43.8	42.7	44.0		44.3			43.8			42.7			44.0	
1969	43.8	43.6	43.5	43.7	44.4		43.6			43.5			43.7			44.4	
1970	44.6	44.9	45.7	43.3	44.6		44.9			45.7			43.3			44.6	
1971	44.1	44.7	45.2	42.3	44.3		44.7			45.2			42.3			44.3	
1972	44.6	44.9	46.5	43.3	43.6		44.9			46.5			43.3			43.6	
1973	43.7	45.4	44.6	40.0	44.9		45.4			44.6			40.0			44.9	
1974	43.8	44.6	44.3	42.5	43.8		44.6			44.3			42.5			43.8	
1975	42.7	44.9	41.2	41.7	43.0		44.9			41.2			41.7			43.0	
1976	41.8	43.3	41.9	40.2	41.9		43.3			41.9			40.2			41.9	
1977	41.1	41.4	41.2	40.4	41.2												
1978	41.3	41.4	41.8	39.6	42.2												
1979	41.2	41.3	41.7	41.2	40.5												
1980	40.7	40.4	42.0	40.1	40.3												
1981	39.5	39.8	39.0	39.0	40.3												
1982	38.6	38.9	39.1	37.8	38.6												
1983		38.4	38.7	38.0													

* Adjusted by the O.E.C.D.

* Corrigé par l'O.C.D.E.

Unemployment (registered unemployed) (7)

thousands

Chômage (chômeurs inscrits) (7)

milliers

	Year	Q.1	Q.2	Q.3	Q.4	JAN	FEB	MAR	APR	MAY	JUN	JUL	AUG	SEP	OCT	NOV	DEC
1964	65	75	68	55	61	75	76	73	73	69	63	60	56	50	53	60	69
1965	64	80	67	51	60	79	83	79	74	68	58	54	50	48	53	59	68
1966	65	77	63	54	66	78	79	75	70	62	56	53	54	54	57	65	75
1967	84	91	84	76	83	90	93	91	90	83	78	77	77	75	75	82	91
1968	74	98	76	57	64	103	98	93	86	76	65	61	57	54	55	59	78
1969	67	89	71	51	56	91	88	87	82	71	59	53	49	50	50	52	67
1970	49	73	51	33	38	78	74	68	61	51	39	35	32	32	32	36	47
1971	30	51	30	16	24	54	52	47	40	30	20	18	16	15	16	23	33
1972	24	40	21	13	21	44	39	38	29	20	14	13	13	13	15	19	28
1973	21	34	18	13	21	37	35	30	24	17	13	13	13	13	14	19	30
1974	27	35	23	19	31	37	35	32	28	22	18	18	20	20	24	29	41
1975	35	48	34	24	33	50	50	46	41	34	26	25	24	25	26	32	42
1976	29	46	22	17	29	49	48	42	29	19	17	17	17	18	19	29	38
1977	28	38	19	19	34	43	39	33	23	17	17	18	19	20	23	34	46
1978	31	44	23	20	36	51	45	36	30	20	19	20	20	21	24	38	47
1979	32	48	22	18	38	55	50	40	28	19	18	18	18	19	23	40	49
1980	37	57	26	22	44	61	57	53	34	22	22	22	22	22	27	47	60
1981	43	66	35	23	46	71	68	61	47	30	26	25	22	22	28	48	61
1982	51	69	40	32	61	71	70	65	52	36	32	32	32	33	39	62	83
1983	62	84	53	40	70	91	85	75	65	50	44	40	39	42	49	71	90

Hourly earnings: (5)

manufacturing (wage earners)

1980 = 100

Gains horaires : (5)

industries manufacturières (ouvriers)

1980 = 100

	Year	Q.1	Q.2	Q.3	Q.4	JAN	FEB	MAR	APR	MAY	JUN	JUL	AUG	SEP	OCT	NOV	DEC
1964	9	9	9	9	10		9			9			9			10	
1965	10	10	10	10	10		10			10			10			10	
1966	11	11	11	11	12		11			11			11			12	
1967	12	12	12	13	13		12			12			13			13	
1968	13	13	13	13	14		13			13			13			14	
1969	15	14	15	15	15		14			15			15			15	
1970	16	15	15	16	16		15			15			16			16	
1971	17	16	17	17	17		16			17			17			17	
1972	19	18	18	19	19		18			18			19			19	
1973	22	20	21	22	23		20			21			22			23	
1974	27	26	27	28	29		26			27			28			29	
1975	34	30	33	35	38		30			33			35			38	
1976	44	40	43	45	47		40			43			45			47	
1977	53	49	52	54	55												
1978	65	60	64	68	69												
1979	79	73	78	79	85												
1980	100	94	99	101	106												
1981	127	119	124	131	135												
1982	170	148	170	177	185												
1983		182	197	206													

Wholesale prices (home market): (8)

imported goods

1980 = 100

Prix de gros (marché intérieur) : (8)

produits importés

1980 = 100

	Year	Q.1	Q.2	Q.3	Q.4	JAN	FEB	MAR	APR	MAY	JUN	JUL	AUG	SEP	OCT	NOV	DEC
1964	17.7	18.1	17.9	17.4	17.4	18.3	18.0	18.1	18.0	17.9	17.8	17.3	17.5	17.4	17.4	17.5	17.4
1965	17.4	17.4	17.4	17.4	17.2	17.4	17.4	17.4	17.4	17.4	17.4	17.4	17.4	17.3	17.3	17.2	17.2
1966	17.4	17.4	17.4	17.4	17.2	17.4	17.4	17.4	17.4	17.4	17.4	17.4	17.4	17.4	17.3	17.2	17.2
1967	17.2	17.2	17.2	17.2	17.1	17.2	17.2	17.3	17.2	17.2	17.2	17.2	17.2	17.2	17.2	17.2	17.1
1968	17.0	17.1	17.0	17.0	17.1	17.1	17.1	17.0	17.0	17.0	17.0	17.0	17.0	17.0	17.0	17.1	17.1
1969	17.7	17.2	17.5	17.8	18.2	17.1	17.2	17.2	17.5	17.5	17.6	17.7	17.9	18.0	18.1	18.3	18.3
1970	19.2	18.7	19.1	19.4	19.6	18.5	18.7	18.8	19.0	19.1	19.2	19.3	19.4	19.4	19.5	19.6	19.8
1971	21.2	20.7	21.0	21.4	21.8	20.5	20.7	20.8	20.9	21.0	21.1	21.3	21.4	21.5	21.6	21.8	21.9
1972	23.6	22.8	23.5	23.9	24.2	22.3	22.8	23.3	23.2	23.7	23.7	23.8	23.9	24.0	24.1	24.2	24.3
1973	29.0	25.6	27.4	29.7	33.2	24.9	25.3	26.4	26.8	27.4	28.0	29.0	29.5	30.6	30.8	33.5	35.4
1974	40.0	38.3	40.0	40.6	41.1	36.9	38.5	39.6	39.4	40.1	40.5	40.5	40.6	40.7	40.8	41.1	41.4
1975	44.6	44.3	43.5	44.2	46.2	45.4	45.0	44.0	44.2	43.0	43.1	43.7	44.0	44.8	45.7	46.2	46.6
1976	51.3	49.1	50.8	52.1	53.3	48.3	49.0	49.9	50.3	50.8	51.4	51.7	52.1	52.5	53.2	53.3	53.4
1977	57.5	54.8	56.6	58.9	59.9	54.1	54.7	55.6	56.0	56.3	57.4	58.6	58.8	59.1	59.4	60.1	60.1
1978	65.0	62.5	64.5	65.6	67.2	61.3	62.5	63.8	64.0	64.6	65.0	65.1	65.5	66.2	66.6	67.0	67.9
1979	77.9	71.8	76.1	79.3	83.4	69.5	71.4	74.6	75.2	75.5	77.5	77.8	79.2	80.8	82.2	83.5	84.5
1980	100.0	87.3	97.1	106.0	109.6	85.5	87.5	88.9	91.5	96.8	102.9	105.4	106.2	106.5	107.5	109.1	112.3
1981	131.0	121.4	131.4	136.5	134.7	117.2	122.2	124.7	127.2	132.0	135.0	136.0	138.2	135.2	134.3	135.0	134.9
1982	151.2	140.2	148.3	156.8	159.5	138.1	140.6	142.0	145.5	147.7	151.6	156.8	156.4	157.3	158.8	159.8	159.8
1983	183.2	178.7	178.0	181.4	194.7	174.9	180.8	180.3	178.8	177.6	177.6	176.7	181.4	186.1	188.6	192.4	203.1

Unemployment (registered unemployed) (7)
thousands

Adjusted - Corrigé *

Chômage (chômeurs inscrits) (7)
milliers

	Year	Q.1	Q.2	Q.3	Q.4	JAN	FEB	MAR	APR	MAY	JUN	JUL	AUG	SEP	OCT	NOV	DEC
1964		61	68	68	64	60	61	61	65	68	71	70	68	65	64	64	63
1965		66	66	63	64	64	67	66	66	66	65	63	62	63	64	63	63
1966		63	52	66	69	63	62	62	61	61	63	63	66	68	69	70	69
1967		76	83	89	87	73	76	78	81	82	85	88	90	89	88	87	86
1968		82	76	70	67	86	81	79	78	76	73	72	69	68	68	64	71
1969		73	71	63	59	73	71	73	74	71	68	64	61	63	61	56	60
1970		57	52	45	41	60	57	55	54	52	49	47	44	45	43	40	39
1971		35	32	28	26	36	35	35	33	31	30	29	28	27	26	26	25
1972		25	23	24	22	27	23	26	24	22	24	24	25	24	24	22	20
1973		20	21	23	22	20	20	19	19	21	22	24	24	23	22	21	21
1974		21	26	30	31	20	20	22	24	27	28	29	30	30	31	30	32
1975		34	38	35	33	33	35	35	39	40	36	35	35	35	34	32	32
1976		31	27	28	27	31	32	31	27	26	27	28	28	29	28	28	27
1977		23	25	31	32	24	23	22	22	26	28	29	31	32	32	31	33
1978		27	30	33	34	30	27	25	29	30	31	33	33	34	34	34	33
1979		31	29	32	35	33	31	28	27	30	31	32	33	33	34	35	35
1980		37	34	37	41	36	36	40	32	34	35	36	37	37	39	41	44
1981		46	43	39	43	45	47	47	45	42	40	40	39	37	40	43	46
1982		48	48	48	58	45	48	50	49	49	47	48	48	48	51	57	67
1983		63	61	56	67	65	63	60	63	62	58	55	56	58	61	66	74

Wholesale prices (home market): (8) (9)
industrial goods
1980 = 100

Prix de gros (marché intérieur) : (8) (9)
produits industriels
1980 = 100

	Year	Q.1	Q.2	Q.3	Q.4	JAN	FEB	MAR	APR	MAY	JUN	JUL	AUG	SEP	OCT	NOV	DEC
1964	21.7	21.5	21.6	21.8	22.0	21.5	21.5	21.5	21.5	21.6	21.6	21.7	21.8	22.0	22.0	22.0	22.0
1965	22.1	22.0	22.1	22.1	22.2	22.0	22.1	22.0	22.1	22.1	22.1	22.0	22.1	22.2	22.2	22.2	22.2
1966	22.7	22.4	22.6	22.9	22.9	22.3	22.4	22.5	22.6	22.6	22.8	22.8	22.9	22.9	22.9	22.9	22.9
1967	22.9	23.0	23.0	22.8	22.7	23.0	23.0	23.0	23.1	23.0	23.0	23.0	22.7	22.7	22.7	22.8	22.8
1968	22.9	22.8	22.8	22.9	23.0	22.8	22.8	22.8	22.8	22.8	22.8	22.9	22.9	22.9	22.9	23.0	23.1
1969	23.5	23.2	23.4	23.6	23.8	23.2	23.2	23.2	23.3	23.4	23.4	23.5	23.6	23.7	23.8	23.8	23.9
1970	24.2	24.0	24.1	24.3	24.4	23.9	24.0	24.1	24.1	24.1	24.2	24.2	24.3	24.4	24.4	24.4	24.5
1971	24.8	24.5	24.6	24.9	25.0	24.5	24.5	24.5	24.5	24.5	24.8	24.9	24.9	24.9	25.0	25.0	25.0
1972	25.5	25.2	25.5	25.6	25.8	25.1	25.3	25.3	25.4	25.5	25.6	25.6	25.6	25.7	25.8	25.8	25.9
1973	29.8	26.0	27.6	30.4	35.3	25.9	26.0	26.2	26.5	27.6	28.6	29.3	29.9	32.0	33.4	35.9	36.5
1974	43.1	41.8	43.3	43.6	43.8	41.1	41.8	42.4	43.0	43.4	43.6	43.4	43.6	43.8	43.7	43.7	43.9
1975	46.6	45.4	46.3	46.9	47.9	44.5	45.7	45.9	46.1	46.3	46.6	46.7	46.9	47.1	47.7	48.0	48.1
1976	51.7	49.7	50.9	52.3	53.7	49.3	49.7	50.1	50.4	50.8	51.5	51.9	52.3	52.8	53.4	53.7	54.1
1977	58.1	55.4	57.7	59.3	60.1	54.9	55.3	55.9	57.1	57.9	58.2	58.8	59.3	59.7	59.9	60.0	60.3
1978	63.8	61.6	63.0	64.6	65.9	61.1	61.6	62.2	62.5	62.9	63.6	63.9	64.5	65.2	65.5	66.0	66.3
1979	76.7	69.9	73.7	80.0	83.0	69.1	70.1	70.7	72.5	73.5	75.0	78.8	79.5	81.7	82.3	82.9	83.8
1980	100.0	90.5	96.4	105.0	108.0	87.1	91.5	93.0	93.5	94.9	100.9	102.9	105.3	106.7	107.4	107.8	108.8
1981	124.2	117.6	121.4	126.2	131.5	115.9	117.7	119.2	120.2	121.3	122.6	124.2	125.9	128.3	130.1	131.3	133.1
1982	145.1	136.6	143.0	147.9	152.7	134.3	136.4	139.2	141.5	142.9	144.7	145.5	147.2	151.0	152.1	152.8	153.2
1983	175.3	165.3	172.6	178.5	184.5	161.2	165.3	169.5	171.2	172.8	173.8	176.2	178.5	180.9	183.5	184.8	185.3

Wholesale prices (home market): (8)
petroleum products
1980 = 100

Prix de gros (marché intérieur) : (8)
dérivés du pétrole
1980 = 100

	Year	Q.1	Q.2	Q.3	Q.4	JAN	FEB	MAR	APR	MAY	JUN	JUL	AUG	SEP	OCT	NOV	DEC
1964	6.5	6.6	6.7	6.4	6.3	6.6	6.6	6.6	6.7	6.6	6.7	6.5	6.4	6.4	6.3	6.3	6.3
1965	6.1	6.1	6.2	6.1	6.1	6.1	6.1	6.1	6.2	6.2	6.2	6.1	6.0	6.1	6.1	6.1	6.1
1966	6.0	6.0	6.1	6.1	5.9	6.0	6.0	6.0	6.1	6.1	6.1	6.1	6.1	6.1	5.9	5.9	5.9
1967	6.0	6.0	6.0	6.0	6.1	6.0	6.0	6.0	6.0	6.0	6.0	6.0	6.0	6.0	6.0	6.1	6.1
1968	5.9	5.9	5.9	6.0	6.0	5.9	5.9	5.9	5.9	5.9	5.9	6.0	6.0	6.0	6.0	6.0	6.0
1969	6.0	6.0	6.0	6.0	6.0	6.0	6.0	6.0	6.0	6.0	6.0	6.0	6.0	6.0	6.0	6.0	6.0
1970	6.1	6.0	6.1	6.1	6.1	6.0	6.1	6.1	6.1	6.1	6.1	6.1	6.1	6.1	6.1	6.1	6.1
1971	6.9	6.1	6.6	7.6	7.5	6.1	6.1	6.1	6.1	6.1	7.6	7.6	7.5	7.6	7.5	7.5	7.5
1972	7.6	7.5	7.5	7.6	7.6	7.5	7.5	7.5	7.5	7.5	7.6	7.5	7.6	7.6	7.6	7.6	7.6
1973	9.6	7.5	8.5	9.0	13.4	7.5	7.5	7.5	7.5	9.0	9.0	9.0	9.0	9.0	9.1	15.5	15.5
1974	30.5	30.5	30.5	30.5	30.5	30.4	30.6	30.6	30.6	30.5	30.5	30.5	30.5	30.5	30.5	30.5	30.6
1975	35.4	33.7	35.3	35.3	37.2	30.5	35.2	35.3	35.3	35.3	35.3	35.3	35.3	35.3	37.2	37.2	37.2
1976	37.2	37.2	37.2	37.2	37.2	37.2	37.2	37.2	37.2	37.2	37.2	37.2	37.2	37.2	37.2	37.2	37.2
1977	40.7	37.2	41.9	42.0	41.9	37.2	37.2	37.2	41.8	42.0	42.0	42.0	42.0	42.0	41.9	41.9	41.9
1978	42.4	41.9	42.0	42.7	43.0	41.9	41.9	41.9	41.9	41.9	42.0	42.0	43.0	43.0	43.0	42.9	42.9
1979	58.1	42.9	50.8	69.3	69.3	42.9	42.9	42.9	50.8	50.8	50.8	69.3	69.3	69.3	69.3	69.3	69.4
1980	100.0	79.1	93.2	113.8	113.9	69.4	83.9	83.9	84.0	84.0	111.7	113.8	113.8	113.8	113.9	113.9	113.9
1981	129.3	128.2	128.3	128.6	131.9	128.2	128.2	128.2	128.2	128.4	128.5	128.5	128.5	128.9	128.9	128.9	138.0
1982	139.2	138.5	139.2	139.4	139.7	138.0	138.2	139.2	139.2	139.2	139.2	139.3	139.3	139.7	139.7	139.7	139.7
1983	170.1	169.0	170.4	170.4	170.4	167.3	169.8	169.8	170.4	170.4	170.4	170.4	170.4	170.4	170.4	170.4	170.4

* Adjusted by the O.E.C.D.

* Corrigé par l'O.C.D.E.

Consumer prices: all items (10)
1980 = 100

Prix à la consommation : total (10)
1980 = 100

	Year	Q.1	Q.2	Q.3	Q.4	JAN	FEB	MAR	APR	MAY	JUN	JUL	AUG	SEP	OCT	NOV	DEC
1964	22.6	22.5	22.6	22.5	22.7	22.5	22.5	22.6	22.6	22.7	22.6	22.5	22.4	22.6	22.7	22.6	22.8
1965	23.3	22.8	23.2	23.3	23.7	22.8	22.7	22.9	23.1	23.2	23.2	23.3	23.3	23.4	23.7	23.7	23.9
1966	24.4	24.0	24.4	24.4	24.9	24.0	23.8	24.2	24.5	24.5	24.4	24.3	24.2	24.6	24.8	24.8	25.0
1967	24.8	25.1	25.1	24.6	24.6	25.1	24.9	25.2	25.3	25.1	24.8	24.7	24.5	24.7	24.7	24.5	24.7
1968	24.9	24.7	25.0	24.9	25.1	24.7	24.6	24.9	25.0	25.0	24.9	24.9	24.8	25.0	25.1	25.0	25.3
1969	25.5	25.3	25.7	25.5	25.8	25.3	25.1	25.4	25.7	25.6	25.6	25.6	25.2	25.6	25.7	25.7	25.9
1970	26.4	25.9	26.6	26.2	26.7	26.0	25.6	26.1	26.5	26.6	26.6	26.3	25.9	26.4	26.6	26.6	26.9
1971	27.1	26.7	27.5	26.9	27.4	26.9	26.4	26.9	27.3	27.7	27.5	27.1	26.6	27.2	27.3	27.3	27.7
1972	28.3	27.7	28.5	28.0	29.1	27.7	27.3	28.1	28.4	28.6	28.4	28.1	27.7	28.3	28.7	29.0	29.5
1973	32.7	29.7	31.5	32.5	37.1	29.6	29.3	30.3	30.8	31.4	32.2	31.8	31.9	33.8	35.4	37.5	38.6
1974	41.5	39.7	41.4	41.7	43.2	39.6	39.1	40.4	40.8	41.4	41.9	41.9	41.0	42.2	42.7	43.2	43.7
1975	47.1	44.9	46.7	46.7	49.9	44.3	44.4	46.1	46.6	46.7	46.8	46.4	45.9	47.8	49.1	49.8	50.6
1976	53.3	51.3	53.3	53.1	55.6	50.9	50.8	52.2	52.8	53.3	53.7	53.0	52.3	53.9	54.8	55.5	56.5
1977	59.8	57.0	59.5	59.8	62.9	56.7	56.4	57.9	59.1	59.6	60.0	59.8	59.0	60.6	62.0	62.8	63.7
1978	67.3	64.6	67.5	67.0	70.1	64.3	63.8	65.6	66.9	67.4	68.1	67.1	66.1	67.9	69.2	70.0	71.1
1979	80.1	74.6	78.6	80.8	86.3	73.9	73.9	76.2	77.8	78.7	79.5	80.5	79.8	82.1	84.4	85.9	88.7
1980	100.0	92.3	98.3	100.6	103.4	91.2	91.5	94.3	97.2	98.3	100.9	100.3	99.3	102.1	104.8	108.4	111.9
1981	124.5	116.3	122.5	124.9	134.3	114.7	115.7	118.5	120.8	122.3	124.4	123.8	122.8	128.1	131.4	134.2	137.1
1982	150.6	139.9	149.7	152.1	160.6	138.6	138.3	142.9	147.1	149.1	152.9	152.1	150.0	154.0	157.7	160.9	163.3
1983	181.5	169.4	181.0	182.4	193.1	164.6	167.7	175.8	178.8	182.0	182.1	180.5	180.0	186.8	190.5	192.9	195.9

Money supply (M1)
billion drachmae, end of period

Disponibilités monétaires (M1)
milliards de drachmes, fin de période

	Year	Q.1	Q.2	Q.3	Q.4	JAN	FEB	MAR	APR	MAY	JUN	JUL	AUG	SEP	OCT	NOV	DEC
1964	28.2	22.7	24.9	27.3	28.2	22.9	22.9	22.7	24.3	24.2	24.9	25.1	26.4	27.3	27.1	26.6	28.2
1965	32.3	25.9	27.6	30.1	32.3	26.8	26.1	25.9	27.7	27.2	27.6	28.1	29.6	30.1	30.8	30.6	32.3
1966	35.9	31.1	32.1	33.9	35.9	30.8	30.6	31.1	32.4	32.3	32.1	32.4	33.2	33.9	33.4	33.0	35.9
1967	43.4	33.1	37.6	38.5	43.4	33.9	32.8	33.1	38.3	37.6	37.6	37.5	38.2	38.5	38.1	40.1	43.4
1968	45.2	39.5	41.4	42.8	45.2	40.8	39.7	39.5	41.5	41.0	41.4	41.0	42.0	42.8	41.7	41.3	45.2
1969	49.0	41.9	44.2	45.7	49.0	42.5	41.5	41.9	42.8	42.4	44.2	44.8	45.1	45.7	45.2	45.1	49.0
1970	54.3	44.7	47.2	50.1	54.3	45.9	45.2	44.7	47.6	47.2	47.2	47.9	49.0	50.1	49.6	49.6	54.3
1971	61.8	50.6	54.0	56.0	61.8	50.4	49.8	50.6	52.5	52.6	54.0	55.2	55.3	56.0	56.6	54.8	61.8
1972	76.1	57.6	61.3	65.6	76.1	56.9	56.0	57.6	59.0	59.4	61.3	62.5	63.3	65.6	65.1	65.6	76.1
1973	93.1	71.8	80.7	85.6	93.1	69.4	70.5	71.8	77.3	74.8	80.7	86.6	84.8	85.6	84.4	83.9	93.1
1974	111.5	86.0	87.1	105.9	111.5	87.6	85.3	86.0	87.7	93.7	87.1	91.1	108.1	105.9	103.9	104.2	111.5
1975	128.9	106.9	111.6	118.2	128.9	109.6	109.2	106.9	115.3	111.9	111.6	115.8	117.2	118.2	118.7	119.3	128.9
1976	160.0	118.0	127.7	146.1	160.0	121.0	119.6	118.0	127.5	125.5	127.7	138.7	145.8	146.1	144.3	144.7	160.0
1977	187.0	151.3	157.7	171.5	187.0	148.6	147.6	151.3	156.5	153.1	157.7	164.7	166.1	171.5	171.2	173.6	187.0
1978	228.6	180.1	195.0	205.1	228.6	175.1	173.2	180.1	193.8	187.7	195.0	200.5	201.9	205.1	201.8	205.9	228.6
1979	264.5	214.3	233.6	248.1	264.5	204.4	207.9	214.3	223.7	224.8	233.6	248.1	249.1	248.1	245.9	239.4	264.5
1980	313.1	278.4	262.5	286.3	313.1	265.0	294.1	278.4	259.8	258.6	262.5	279.3	283.1	286.3	279.8	282.8	313.1
1981	385.9	300.6	326.6	348.8	385.9	293.2	289.8	300.6	316.5	312.6	326.6	331.1	334.7	348.8	360.3	345.6	385.9
1982	471.2	357.8	462.8	432.3	471.2	346.3	353.2	357.8	366.4	367.9	462.8	446.8	425.8	432.3	420.2	422.5	471.2
1983		416.5	457.1	476.4		444.6	431.7	416.5	440.1	443.9	457.1	456.2	459.9	476.4	484.1	473.1	

M1 plus quasi-money
billion drachmae, end of period

M1 plus quasi-monnaie
milliards de drachmes, fin de période

	Year	Q.1	Q.2	Q.3	Q.4	JAN	FEB	MAR	APR	MAY	JUN	JUL	AUG	SEP	OCT	NOV	DEC
1964	55.9	47.7	51.2	52.9	55.9	47.2	47.6	47.7	49.7	50.1	51.2	51.7	52.7	52.9	53.1	53.0	55.9
1965	62.8	55.0	57.7	59.7	62.8	55.3	54.9	55.0	57.1	56.8	57.7	58.0	59.4	59.7	60.8	60.6	62.8
1966	75.1	62.8	66.0	69.8	75.1	62.3	62.4	62.8	64.9	65.5	66.0	66.9	68.5	69.8	69.8	70.2	75.1
1967	86.4	74.5	78.1	81.2	86.4	74.5	73.9	74.5	77.3	77.2	78.1	78.9	80.4	81.2	81.2	81.0	86.4
1968	101.8	86.2	91.2	95.0	101.8	85.6	85.4	86.2	89.1	89.1	91.2	91.8	93.5	95.0	94.9	95.0	101.8
1969	118.1	101.7	107.0	110.9	118.1	100.7	100.5	101.7	103.9	104.1	107.0	108.5	109.7	110.9	110.9	111.1	118.1
1970	140.8	117.1	123.9	130.4	140.8	116.9	116.9	117.1	121.2	121.6	123.9	126.0	128.4	130.4	130.6	131.5	140.8
1971	172.2	141.6	150.5	157.9	172.2	139.6	139.9	141.6	145.5	146.3	150.5	153.7	155.9	157.9	160.0	159.3	172.2
1972	212.8	173.8	184.7	195.1	212.8	170.6	171.1	173.8	177.6	179.3	184.7	188.3	191.5	195.1	195.4	196.6	212.8
1973	244.0	210.7	217.0	226.9	244.0	208.5	209.9	210.7	215.3	212.0	217.0	222.6	224.6	226.9	227.9	227.8	244.0
1974	296.3	241.4	253.5	266.4	296.3	239.7	238.9	241.4	246.2	243.7	253.5	257.3	263.6	266.4	269.8	275.5	296.3
1975	376.8	296.9	318.8	343.4	376.8	293.3	294.8	296.9	307.7	309.4	318.8	328.7	337.0	343.4	347.6	351.6	376.8
1976	472.1	376.2	400.3	428.8	472.1	376.4	377.2	376.2	388.2	389.2	400.3	412.0	420.5	428.8	432.9	437.7	472.1
1977	578.7	477.3	502.5	535.6	578.7	467.9	471.0	477.3	488.7	487.2	502.5	516.5	525.4	535.6	539.4	545.0	578.7
1978	728.9	583.4	621.5	662.9	728.9	574.8	574.7	583.4	602.7	601.8	621.5	637.2	650.9	662.9	666.6	674.5	728.9
1979	862.7	729.4	776.6	800.8	862.7	715.3	721.1	729.4	745.8	749.2	776.6	787.0	794.8	800.8	804.6	800.2	862.7
1980	1073.7	875.5	905.9	972.1	1073.7	863.9	885.7	875.5	871.8	874.9	905.9	938.2	959.1	972.1	975.2	982.0	1073.7
1981	1443.2	1093.8	1194.0	1284.2	1443.2	1068.9	1072.9	1093.8	1130.0	1136.9	1194.0	1225.2	1252.9	1284.2	1307.0	1313.3	1443.2
1982	1860.4	1455.0	1614.2	1690.7	1860.4	1426.1	1442.4	1455.0	1488.5	1496.9	1614.2	1648.1	1658.6	1690.7	1696.9	1710.7	1860.4
1983		1806.1	1927.7	2014.7		1832.4	1816.3	1806.1	1835.4	1854.0	1927.7	1951.1	1979.1	2014.7	2043.7	2046.8	

Share prices: industrials (11) / Cours des actions industrielles (11)

Athens Stock Exchange / Bourse d'Athènes

1980 = 100

	Year	Q.1	Q.2	Q.3	Q.4	JAN	FEB	MAR	APR	MAY	JUN	JUL	AUG	SEP	OCT	NOV	DEC
1964	24	25	24	24	24	24	25	25	24	24	25	24	23	24	23	24	24
1965	23	25	24	22	22	25	25	25	25	24	24	22	22	22	22	22	22
1966	23	24	24	23	23	24	24	24	24	24	24	23	23	23	23	22	22
1967	23	22	21	23	25	22	22	22	22	22	21	22	24	24	25	25	26
1968	29	27	27	29	34	27	27	27	27	26	28	29	29	30	33	35	34
1969	55	36	51	64	67	35	36	37	42	49	61	61	62	69	67	69	66
1970	67	65	66	67	69	66	64	66	70	64	64	65	67	69	69	69	68
1971	64	67	66	62	60	67	66	67	68	67	64	61	62	62	61	59	59
1972	120	70	109	139	161	65	69	77	96	105	124	139	139	140	132	156	195
1973	211	193	218	228	206	178	194	208	214	218	222	230	226	229	217	212	189
1974	201	217	201	..	192	202	225	223	214	200	188	188	..	194	187	200	188
1975	181	183	180	183	178	179	178	190	185	182	175	174	184	193	181	177	175
1976	169	176	166	167	165	177	174	177	173	167	159	167	170	165	162	170	163
1977	166	164	172	164	164	163	164	163	178	174	165	162	165	166	165	165	162
1978	144	159	147	139	130	161	159	157	150	149	144	141	141	135	134	129	128
1979	116	130	121	112	100	133	132	126	124	122	118	116	114	108	103	102	96
1980	100	101	100	100	99	97	102	104	102	100	97	95	101	106	101	99	98
1981	91	97	98	85	84	96	96	98	99	99	96	91	85	79	80	84	87
1982	83	85	79	84	85	87	84	83	81	80	78	79	85	88	89	83	84
1983	72	86	78	66	58	86	87	85	83	79	71	67	67	65	59	58	56

Money supply (M1) / Disponibilités monétaires (M1)

Adjusted - Corrigé *

billion drachmae, end of period / milliards de drachmes, fin de période

	Year	Q.1	Q.2	Q.3	Q.4	JAN	FEB	MAR	APR	MAY	JUN	JUL	AUG	SEP	OCT	NOV	DEC
1964		23.7	25.1	26.7	26.7	23.2	23.7	23.7	24.1	24.5	25.1	25.4	26.1	26.7	26.6	26.6	26.7
1965		27.1	27.8	29.5	30.6	27.0	27.0	27.1	27.5	27.5	27.8	28.5	29.3	29.5	30.4	30.6	30.6
1966		32.4	32.3	33.3	33.8	31.1	31.7	32.4	32.2	32.5	32.3	32.7	32.9	33.3	33.0	33.2	33.8
1967		34.4	37.7	37.9	40.3	34.1	34.0	34.4	38.1	37.8	37.7	37.8	37.8	37.9	37.9	40.5	40.8
1968		41.0	41.5	42.1	42.3	41.0	41.1	41.0	41.3	41.2	41.5	41.2	41.7	42.1	41.6	41.8	42.3
1969		43.4	44.2	45.0	45.6	42.7	42.9	43.4	42.8	42.7	44.2	44.8	44.8	45.0	45.2	45.8	45.6
1970		46.3	47.3	49.3	50.5	46.2	46.7	46.3	47.6	47.7	47.3	47.8	48.7	49.3	49.6	50.4	50.5
1971		52.3	54.2	54.9	57.4	50.7	51.4	52.3	52.7	53.5	54.2	54.9	54.8	54.9	56.6	55.8	57.4
1972		59.4	61.9	64.2	70.6	57.3	57.7	59.4	59.2	60.8	61.9	62.0	62.6	64.2	65.0	66.7	70.6
1973		74.1	81.9	83.6	86.6	69.9	72.6	74.1	77.4	76.9	81.9	85.9	83.5	83.6	84.2	85.2	86.6
1974		88.7	88.8	103.2	103.8	88.1	87.8	88.7	87.9	86.4	88.8	90.2	106.2	103.2	103.6	105.4	103.8
1975		110.5	114.0	115.1	120.1	110.3	112.6	110.5	115.1	115.8	114.0	114.5	114.8	115.1	118.5	120.2	120.1
1976		121.7	130.3	142.7	149.3	122.3	123.4	121.7	127.1	130.0	130.3	136.8	142.8	142.7	144.3	145.9	149.3
1977		155.5	160.4	168.0	174.5	150.5	152.7	155.5	155.7	158.2	160.4	161.9	162.9	168.0	172.1	175.3	174.5
1978		184.2	197.6	201.7	213.4	177.9	179.1	184.2	192.7	193.8	197.6	196.8	198.3	201.7	203.6	208.6	213.4
1979		218.0	236.0	244.7	246.9	207.7	214.7	218.0	221.9	231.8	236.0	243.3	244.7	244.7	249.4	243.6	246.9
1980		282.1	264.9	292.6	292.3	269.3	303.2	282.1	257.4	266.4	264.9	273.8	278.3	282.6	284.4	288.3	292.3
1981		304.0	329.9	344.7	360.3	298.0	298.5	304.0	314.0	322.3	329.9	324.6	329.1	344.7	366.5	352.3	360.3
1982		361.4	468.0	427.2	440.0	351.9	363.3	361.4	363.5	379.3	468.0	438.0	418.7	427.2	427.5	430.7	440.0
1983		420.7	462.2	470.8		451.8	444.1	420.7	436.6	457.6	462.2	447.3	452.2	470.8	492.4	482.3	

M1 plus quasi-money / M1 plus quasi-monnaie

Adjusted - Corrigé *

billion drachmae, end of period / milliards de drachmes, fin de période

	Year	Q.1	Q.2	Q.3	Q.4	JAN	FEB	MAR	APR	MAY	JUN	JUL	AUG	SEP	OCT	NOV	DEC
1964		48.6	51.2	52.6	54.3	47.1	48.2	48.6	49.4	50.4	51.2	51.8	52.5	52.6	53.2	53.7	54.3
1965		56.0	57.6	59.4	61.0	55.1	55.4	56.0	56.7	57.0	57.6	58.1	59.1	59.4	61.0	61.6	61.0
1966		63.8	66.0	69.4	72.8	62.0	63.0	63.8	64.5	65.9	66.0	67.1	68.1	69.4	70.2	71.5	72.8
1967		75.5	78.0	80.8	83.7	74.1	74.5	75.5	76.8	77.6	78.0	79.1	80.0	80.8	81.8	82.6	83.7
1968		87.3	91.1	94.6	98.5	84.9	86.1	87.3	88.5	89.6	91.1	91.9	93.2	94.6	95.7	96.9	98.5
1969		102.8	106.9	110.5	114.2	99.9	101.2	102.8	103.5	104.8	106.9	108.5	109.3	110.5	112.0	113.3	114.2
1970		118.3	123.9	130.1	136.0	115.9	117.6	118.3	120.8	122.8	123.9	125.9	128.1	130.1	131.9	134.2	136.0
1971		142.9	150.6	157.8	165.9	138.3	140.5	142.9	145.2	147.7	150.6	153.4	155.4	157.8	161.7	162.4	165.9
1972		175.2	185.2	194.9	204.8	168.9	171.6	175.2	177.5	181.5	185.2	187.9	191.2	194.9	197.2	200.2	204.8
1973		212.6	217.9	226.7	234.3	206.2	210.3	212.6	215.3	215.0	217.9	222.4	224.2	226.7	230.0	231.7	234.3
1974		243.8	255.0	266.1	284.7	236.8	239.3	243.8	246.2	247.6	255.0	257.0	262.8	266.1	271.7	279.7	284.7
1975		300.5	321.0	341.4	362.6	289.8	295.3	300.5	308.3	315.1	321.0	328.4	335.3	341.4	349.0	356.3	362.6
1976		381.6	403.1	422.1	456.6	372.6	381.0	381.6	389.7	397.2	403.1	410.4	415.6	422.1	431.6	443.0	456.6
1977		486.0	506.6	515.5	564.0	466.5	484.5	486.0	489.7	499.2	506.6	511.9	512.6	515.5	527.7	548.3	564.0
1978		603.3	622.1	623.6	716.7	585.9	619.3	603.3	596.1	617.3	622.1	626.6	625.3	623.6	639.1	674.5	716.7
1979		767.0	769.7	738.1	854.2	749.0	820.4	767.0	724.8	767.6	769.7	767.0	754.1	738.1	757.6	793.8	854.2
1980		938.4	887.3	887.8	1067.3	930.9	1067.1	938.4	831.9	891.9	887.3	907.4	903.2	887.8	911.4	972.3	1067.3
1981		1180.0	1163.7	1167.4	1437.4	1164.4	1327.8	1180.0	1070.1	1156.6	1163.7	1180.4	1174.2	1167.4	1217.0	1299.0	1437.4
1982		1574.7	1568.8	1523.2	1856.7	1563.7	1809.8	1574.7	1404.2	1521.2	1563.8	1584.7	1550.1	1523.2	1577.0	1690.4	1856.7
1983		1954.6	1873.4	1815.1		2009.2	2278.9	1954.6	1731.5	1884.1	1873.4	1876.1	1849.6	1815.1	1904.0	2022.6	

* Adjusted by the O.E.C.D.

* Corrigé par l'O.C.D.E.

GREECE

Bank credit to private sector: total

billion drachmae, end of period

Crédits bancaires au secteur privé : total

milliards de drachmes, fin de période

	Year	Q.1	Q.2	Q.3	Q.4	JAN	FEB	MAR	APR	MAY	JUN	JUL	AUG	SEP	OCT	NOV	DEC
1964	45.4	40.4	44.0	44.6	45.4	39.6	39.8	40.4	41.6	42.4	44.0	44.2	44.0	44.6	44.7	44.7	45.4
1965	49.8	46.0	48.5	49.2	49.8	45.2	45.4	46.0	46.7	47.3	48.5	48.6	48.4	49.2	49.3	49.4	49.8
1966	56.6	50.2	53.3	54.7	56.6	49.3	49.2	50.2	51.2	52.1	53.3	53.7	54.0	54.7	55.0	55.3	56.6
1967	67.5	57.5	60.7	63.0	67.5	56.3	56.3	57.5	58.9	59.2	60.7	61.1	61.8	63.0	63.9	64.9	67.5
1968	76.0	68.2	73.6	76.2	76.0	66.8	67.2	68.2	69.6	71.6	73.6	74.0	75.3	76.2	76.0	75.5	76.0
1969	92.4	78.4	83.8	88.2	92.4	76.1	76.6	78.4	79.6	81.4	83.8	84.7	86.1	88.2	88.9	91.0	92.4
1970	113.3	95.6	101.9	107.4	113.3	92.7	94.0	95.6	97.4	99.2	101.9	103.6	105.0	107.4	109.6	110.6	113.3
1971	138.5	117.8	126.3	131.7	138.5	114.3	115.6	117.8	120.1	123.1	126.3	127.9	129.1	131.7	133.2	135.2	138.5
1972	171.7	143.6	151.8	159.2	171.7	139.5	140.8	143.6	145.7	148.1	151.8	153.7	155.7	159.2	161.8	164.3	171.7
1973	202.6	176.9	187.6	194.2	202.6	171.1	173.3	176.9	180.3	182.8	187.6	189.1	190.4	194.2	195.4	198.0	202.6
1974	243.2	207.2	218.1	229.0	243.2	203.6	205.5	207.2	209.0	212.0	213.1	220.7	222.9	229.0	232.0	236.1	243.2
1975	302.8	253.3	270.4	285.6	302.3	245.0	246.9	253.3	259.5	263.9	270.4	275.8	278.3	285.6	288.9	292.8	302.8
1976	379.3	313.6	337.7	357.4	379.3	304.6	307.4	313.6	320.5	326.3	337.7	343.2	349.6	357.4	364.4	366.6	379.3
1977	475.8	396.6	424.8	445.5	475.8	383.5	386.3	396.6	404.9	411.2	424.8	431.3	436.5	445.5	452.8	459.7	475.8
1978	585.1	502.0	532.7	546.9	585.1	480.6	488.2	502.0	515.5	518.5	532.7	537.5	534.1	546.9	552.0	561.9	585.1
1979	691.8	607.0	640.0	662.1	691.8	587.7	594.1	607.0	615.3	624.6	640.0	646.5	649.0	662.1	665.9	672.8	691.8
1980	828.1	722.1	745.0	771.0	828.1	699.5	705.0	722.1	725.9	732.3	745.0	752.5	756.3	771.0	774.4	790.1	828.1
1981	1040.1	867.2	922.3	970.2	1040.1	837.7	846.6	867.2	877.1	887.3	922.3	934.2	946.0	970.2	986.6	994.3	1040.1
1982	1277.9	1079.7	1131.2	1202.5	1277.9	1053.4	1053.8	1079.7	1095.7	1109.7	1131.2	1171.6	1174.0	1202.5	1213.5	1229.0	1277.9
1983		1333.9	1389.3	1410.2		1299.7	1305.3	1333.9	1347.2	1357.1	1389.3	1392.3	1390.8	1410.2	1421.8	1429.0	

Bank credit to private sector: agriculture

billion drachmae, end of period

Crédits bancaires au secteur privé : agriculture

milliards de drachmes, fin de période

	Year	Q.1	Q.2	Q.3	Q.4	JAN	FEB	MAR	APR	MAY	JUN	JUL	AUG	SEP	OCT	NOV	DEC
1964	11.4	10.9	10.9	10.4	11.4	10.4	10.7	10.9	11.0	10.9	10.9	10.6	10.4	10.4	10.7	11.1	11.4
1965	12.7	11.9	12.3	12.1	12.7	11.7	11.9	11.9	12.0	12.0	12.3	12.3	12.1	12.1	12.3	12.6	12.7
1966	13.8	13.0	13.2	13.2	13.8	12.9	12.9	13.0	12.8	13.0	13.2	13.2	13.2	13.2	13.2	13.5	13.8
1967	15.3	14.3	14.5	14.1	15.3	14.0	14.1	14.3	14.2	14.4	14.5	14.5	14.3	14.1	14.2	14.6	15.3
1968	13.5	15.4	16.8	16.0	13.5	15.3	15.4	15.4	16.0	16.4	16.8	16.6	16.9	16.0	15.0	14.2	13.5
1969	15.0	13.9	14.3	14.3	15.0	13.6	13.7	13.9	14.2	14.2	14.3	14.0	14.1	14.3	14.4	14.8	15.0
1970	17.7	16.1	17.0	17.0	17.7	15.6	15.8	16.1	16.7	17.1	17.0	16.7	16.7	17.0	17.1	17.2	17.7
1971	21.4	19.0	20.0	20.4	21.4	18.1	18.6	19.0	19.7	20.0	20.0	19.5	19.7	20.4	20.8	20.9	21.4
1972	26.4	22.9	24.4	25.1	26.4	21.8	22.3	22.9	23.6	24.2	24.4	23.9	24.2	25.1	25.6	25.9	26.4
1973	33.7	27.4	29.8	32.0	33.7	26.5	27.0	27.4	28.2	29.1	29.8	30.3	30.8	32.0	32.2	32.8	33.7
1974	44.5	36.0	40.0	41.5	44.5	34.1	34.9	36.0	37.9	39.3	40.0	40.3	40.7	41.5	42.7	43.5	44.5
1975	55.3	47.9	52.2	52.6	55.3	44.9	46.4	47.9	49.3	50.7	52.2	51.9	51.7	52.6	52.7	53.6	55.3
1976	66.5	58.5	63.5	63.9	66.5	56.5	57.7	58.5	61.0	62.6	63.5	63.3	62.9	63.9	64.9	64.3	66.5
1977	90.2	73.4	79.0	81.2	90.2	68.7	70.9	73.4	75.4	76.9	79.0	79.2	79.7	81.2	83.2	87.3	90.2
1978	110.2	99.4	106.3	102.0	110.2	92.5	95.8	99.4	103.4	105.8	106.3	105.2	99.0	102.0	104.0	106.4	110.2
1979	125.8	116.5	122.4	124.2	125.8	111.9	113.8	116.5	119.8	121.7	122.4	121.5	120.9	124.2	125.6	128.2	125.8
1980	141.9	136.5	135.6	136.9	141.9	131.5	133.2	136.5	139.1	139.0	135.6	134.7	134.6	136.9	137.5	139.6	141.9
1981	161.7	154.3	153.6	156.6	161.7	149.4	151.0	154.3	152.8	153.2	153.6	151.7	152.8	156.6	161.5	157.7	161.7
1982	199.6	166.8	178.5	183.9	199.6	171.1	163.5	166.8	170.8	175.4	173.5	180.7	179.2	183.9	190.6	194.6	199.6
1983		222.7	238.4	240.3		213.2	215.8	222.7	228.7	234.7	238.4	240.1	240.6	240.3	245.3	245.8	

Bank credit to private sector: manufacturing

billion drachmae, end of period

Crédits bancaires au secteur privé : industries manufacturières

milliards de drachmes, fin de période

	Year	Q.1	Q.2	Q.3	Q.4	JAN	FEB	MAR	APR	MAY	JUN	JUL	AUG	SEP	OCT	NOV	DEC
1964	19.1	17.0	18.0	18.5	19.1	16.7	16.6	17.0	17.2	17.3	18.0	18.3	18.2	18.5	18.5	18.6	19.1
1965	20.8	19.4	19.8	20.1	20.8	19.0	19.1	19.4	19.5	19.5	19.8	19.8	19.8	20.1	20.2	20.4	20.8
1966	24.2	21.1	21.8	22.6	24.2	20.6	20.8	21.1	21.0	21.2	21.8	22.0	22.1	22.6	23.0	23.2	24.2
1967	29.1	24.9	25.8	27.3	29.1	24.2	24.3	24.9	25.3	25.1	25.8	25.9	26.5	27.3	27.8	28.1	29.1
1968	33.8	29.2	30.2	32.4	33.8	28.6	28.7	29.2	29.4	29.3	30.2	30.9	31.3	32.4	32.8	33.0	33.8
1969	40.1	34.2	35.4	38.1	40.1	33.5	33.6	34.2	34.2	34.4	35.4	36.2	37.0	38.1	37.9	39.0	40.1
1970	48.8	40.7	42.7	45.7	48.8	40.0	40.3	40.7	41.1	41.2	42.7	44.0	44.7	45.7	46.9	47.3	48.8
1971	60.0	50.4	53.3	56.5	60.0	49.2	49.6	50.4	51.0	51.8	53.3	54.9	55.7	56.5	57.3	58.3	60.0
1972	72.8	61.7	63.9	67.1	72.8	60.2	60.5	61.7	61.9	61.8	63.9	65.3	66.1	67.1	67.4	68.4	72.8
1973	84.7	74.7	77.5	80.3	84.7	72.2	73.0	74.7	75.3	75.1	77.5	78.3	78.9	80.3	80.7	82.1	84.7
1974	104.5	86.5	90.7	97.5	104.5	85.2	85.9	86.5	87.0	88.0	90.7	92.7	94.2	97.5	98.2	100.1	104.5
1975	136.8	110.4	117.0	127.5	136.8	106.1	106.9	110.4	113.4	113.9	117.0	121.1	123.4	127.5	129.5	131.4	136.8
1976	170.8	140.9	149.7	159.8	170.8	136.8	137.5	140.9	143.2	144.4	149.7	153.1	156.4	159.8	162.1	163.2	170.8
1977	214.2	177.4	188.1	200.8	214.2	172.2	172.3	177.4	180.2	181.3	188.1	192.0	196.1	200.8	204.2	206.0	214.2
1978	269.3	224.1	236.1	249.6	269.3	215.3	218.0	224.1	228.4	227.1	236.1	241.3	243.4	249.6	251.4	256.2	269.3
1979	325.9	277.6	289.1	306.4	325.9	269.4	271.9	277.6	280.5	281.0	289.1	296.9	299.8	306.4	307.8	311.4	325.9
1980	410.3	340.6	350.0	372.2	410.3	327.2	330.8	340.6	340.3	340.7	350.0	359.1	363.4	372.2	375.8	385.9	410.3
1981	541.4	427.4	457.2	495.1	541.4	412.9	416.5	427.4	433.4	435.5	457.2	469.1	479.2	495.1	505.5	512.9	541.4
1982	665.1	557.8	576.3	622.8	665.1	545.4	546.3	557.8	564.6	566.0	576.3	598.4	601.7	622.8	628.2	633.9	665.1
1983		682.6	704.0	716.5		670.0	668.3	682.6	684.7	684.6	704.0	703.7	701.2	716.5	722.8	726.0	

U.S. dollar exchange rate

cents per drachme, end of period

Taux de change du dollar É.-U.

cents par drachme, fin de période

	Year	Q.1	Q.2	Q.3	Q.4	JAN	FEB	MAR	APR	MAY	JUN	JUL	AUG	SEP	OCT	NOV	DEC
1964	3.333	3.333	3.333	3.333	3.333	3.333	3.333	3.333	3.333	3.333	3.333	3.333	3.333	3.333	3.333	3.333	3.333
1965	3.333	3.333	3.333	3.333	3.333	3.333	3.333	3.333	3.333	3.333	3.333	3.333	3.333	3.333	3.333	3.333	3.333
1966	3.333	3.333	3.333	3.333	3.333	3.333	3.333	3.333	3.333	3.333	3.333	3.333	3.333	3.333	3.333	3.333	3.333
1967	3.333	3.333	3.333	3.333	3.333	3.333	3.333	3.333	3.333	3.333	3.333	3.333	3.333	3.333	3.333	3.333	3.333
1968	3.333	3.333	3.333	3.333	3.333	3.333	3.333	3.333	3.333	3.333	3.333	3.333	3.333	3.333	3.333	3.333	3.333
1969	3.333	3.333	3.333	3.333	3.333	3.333	3.333	3.333	3.333	3.333	3.333	3.333	3.333	3.333	3.333	3.333	3.333
1970	3.333	3.333	3.333	3.333	3.333	3.333	3.333	3.333	3.333	3.333	3.333	3.333	3.333	3.333	3.333	3.333	3.333
1971	3.333	3.333	3.333	3.333	3.333	3.333	3.333	3.333	3.333	3.333	3.333	3.333	3.333	3.333	3.333	3.333	3.333
1972	3.333	3.333	3.333	3.333	3.333	3.333	3.333	3.333	3.333	3.333	3.333	3.333	3.333	3.333	3.333	3.333	3.333
1973	3.367	3.333	3.333	3.333	3.367	3.333	3.333	3.333	3.333	3.333	3.333	3.333	3.333	3.333	3.704	3.509	3.367
1974	3.333	3.333	3.333	3.333	3.333	3.333	3.333	3.333	3.333	3.333	3.333	3.333	3.333	3.333	3.333	3.333	3.333
1975	2.805	3.333	3.305	2.888	2.805	3.333	3.333	3.333	3.303	3.324	3.305	3.029	2.995	2.888	2.898	2.807	2.805
1976	2.700	2.767	2.724	2.698	2.700	2.831	2.827	2.767	2.745	2.722	2.724	2.721	2.711	2.698	2.689	2.682	2.700
1977	2.816	2.678	2.702	2.722	2.816	2.673	2.676	2.678	2.694	2.695	2.702	2.740	2.724	2.722	2.752	2.767	2.816
1978	2.777	2.708	2.708	2.732	2.777	2.764	2.761	2.708	2.662	2.661	2.708	2.726	2.698	2.732	2.853	2.702	2.777
1979	2.612	2.717	2.720	2.717	2.612	2.744	2.738	2.717	2.694	2.671	2.720	2.727	2.715	2.717	2.652	2.648	2.612
1980	2.149	2.387	2.314	2.308	2.149	2.581	2.544	2.387	2.356	2.296	2.314	2.305	2.317	2.308	2.290	2.176	2.149
1981	1.735	1.949	1.712	1.743	1.735	2.024	1.950	1.949	1.861	1.762	1.712	1.661	1.678	1.743	1.755	1.794	1.735
1982	1.417	1.587	1.447	1.392	1.417	1.683	1.623	1.587	1.579	1.449	1.447	1.443	1.412	1.392	1.374	1.396	1.417
1983	1.014	1.190	1.183	1.079	1.014	1.191	1.197	1.190	1.192	1.185	1.183	1.177	1.077	1.079	1.063	1.030	1.014

Official reserves excluding gold

million SDR's

Réserves officielles, or exclu

millions de DTS

	Year	Q.1	Q.2	Q.3	Q.4	JAN	FEB	MAR	APR	MAY	JUN	JUL	AUG	SEP	OCT	NOV	DEC
1964	204	214	217	191	204	217	216	214	209	220	217	206	206	191	183	186	204
1965	173	183	180	180	173	201	190	183	185	187	180	178	181	180	178	175	173
1966	153	161	157	156	153	180	173	161	166	168	157	151	156	156	160	156	153
1967	156	143	111	140	156	161	158	143	138	133	111	109	115	140	137	145	156
1968	182	131	111	156	182	141	138	131	123	118	111	131	147	156	158	173	182
1969	187	153	138	183	187	182	168	153	150	144	138	167	178	183	178	164	187
1970	194	161	158	195	194	185	170	161	160	161	158	153	186	195	196	200	194
1971	380	199	231	353	380	197	187	199	234	236	231	239	275	353	363	373	380
1972	828	413	557	656	828	408	415	413	431	537	557	570	630	656	686	765	828
1973	745	786	792	812	745	848	780	786	802	807	792	809	823	812	824	799	745
1974	639	663	669	707	639	716	694	663	669	681	669	684	704	707	673	633	639
1975	668	601	594	707	668	627	619	601	574	586	594	645	675	707	694	678	668
1976	668	643	632	691	668	646	634	643	624	620	632	640	671	691	699	685	668
1977	709	671	650	751	709	672	672	671	633	641	650	666	722	751	744	741	709
1978	1002	827	898	1023	1002	833	815	827	892	912	898	930	964	1023	959	982	1002
1979	1019	1012	1002	1009	1019	945	947	1012	1056	1058	1002	1056	1016	1009	1063	1066	1019
1980	1055	1250	1206	1059	1055	1083	1232	1250	1199	1241	1206	1141	1056	1059	1017	929	1055
1981	878	1186	1200	1227	878	1124	1225	1186	1288	1273	1200	1277	1223	1227	1073	950	878
1982	781	850	712	840	781	877	872	850	779	737	712	698	854	840	882	861	781
1983	860	660	749	833	860	706	680	660	638	679	749	821	874	833	823	808	860

Net foreign position: (12)

commercial banks

billion drachmae, end of period

Position extérieure nette : (12)

banques commerciales

milliards de drachmes, fin de période

	Year	Q.1	Q.2	Q.3	Q.4	JAN	FEB	MAR	APR	MAY	JUN	JUL	AUG	SEP	OCT	NOV	DEC
1964	-0.1	0.2	-0.0	-0.1	-0.1	0.4	0.4	0.2	0.3	-0.0	-0.0	-0.0	-0.2	-0.1	0.2	0.2	-0.1
1965	0.2	0.1	0.2	0.1	0.2	-0.0	0.0	0.1	-0.0	0.0	0.2	0.1	0.2	0.1	0.1	0.2	0.2
1966	0.1	0.1	0.1	-0.0	0.1	0.1	0.1	0.1	0.1	0.1	0.1	0.0	-0.0	-0.0	0.2	0.1	0.1
1967	-0.3	0.2	-0.1	-0.2	-0.3	0.2	0.1	0.2	-0.1	0.0	-0.1	-0.1	-0.2	-0.2	-0.1	-0.2	-0.3
1968	-0.5	-0.1	-0.3	-0.5	-0.5	-0.3	0.1	-0.1	0.0	-0.3	-0.3	-0.4	-0.4	-0.5	-0.4	-0.5	-0.5
1969	-0.5	-0.6	-0.6	-0.5	-0.5	-0.3	-0.6	-0.6	-0.6	-0.5	-0.6	-0.6	-0.5	-0.5	-0.3	-0.1	-0.5
1970	-1.1	-0.5	-0.4	-0.2	-1.1	-0.5	-0.6	-0.5	-0.7	-0.4	-0.4	0.0	-0.1	-0.2	-0.3	-0.1	-1.1
1971	-4.4	-0.9	-1.6	-2.3	-4.4	0.4	0.2	-0.9	-1.0	-1.2	-1.6	-2.2	-2.2	-2.3	-2.5	-2.2	-4.4
1972	-7.3	-5.3	-7.2	-7.6	-7.3	-4.2	-4.6	-5.3	-6.1	-6.7	-7.2	-7.1	-7.2	-7.6	-7.2	-7.2	-7.3
1973	-9.2	-8.2	-9.7	-8.1	-9.2	-7.8	-7.9	-8.2	-8.8	-9.1	-9.7	-8.5	-9.2	-8.1	-8.8	-7.7	-9.2
1974	-15.4	-8.7	-11.9	-12.6	-15.4	-8.8	-8.3	-8.7	-10.6	-11.8	-11.9	-12.6	-13.0	-12.6	-12.4	-14.1	-15.4
1975	-25.0	-15.6	-18.9	-20.6	-25.0	-15.3	-15.6	-15.6	-16.8	-17.8	-18.9	-20.2	-20.4	-20.6	-20.9	-21.8	-25.0
1976	-45.1	-28.9	-30.0	-34.8	-45.1	-24.5	-25.1	-28.9	-29.9	-30.0	-30.0	-32.1	-33.6	-34.8	-35.4	-36.1	-45.1
1977	-64.7	-50.8	-55.3	-56.5	-64.7	-47.5	-49.3	-50.8	-52.9	-53.9	-55.3	-56.0	-55.6	-56.5	-56.8	-57.1	-64.7
1978	-90.9	-67.8	-74.4	-79.5	-90.9	-65.6	-65.5	-67.8	-70.7	-71.8	-74.4	-77.0	-78.1	-79.5	-80.0	-82.6	-90.9
1979	-107.9	-92.0	-96.0	-95.6	-107.9	-89.5	-91.0	-92.0	-92.3	-92.9	-96.0	-95.7	-97.6	-95.6	-95.8	-100.4	-107.9
1980	-130.9	-104.1	-105.6	-110.8	-130.9	-106.8	-104.7	-104.1	-103.0	-104.9	-105.6	-109.2	-109.2	-110.8	-110.1	-115.7	-130.9
1981	-173.4	-143.4	-158.6	-164.9	-173.4	-132.6	-142.9	-143.4	-151.2	-153.5	-158.6	-164.8	-172.3	-164.9	-83.7	-160.9	-173.4
1982	-247.6	-181.6	-189.4	-197.5	-247.6	-173.8	-174.1	-181.6	-186.1	-187.3	-189.4	-188.3	-199.3	-197.5	-205.4	-210.8	-247.6
1983		-256.4	-265.5	-283.1		-253.8	-256.6	-256.4	-254.8	-259.0	-265.5	-278.9	-282.8	-283.1	-285.9	-289.0	

GREECE

Imports c.i.f. / Importations c.a.f.

billion drachmae, monthly averages / milliards de drachmes, moyennes mensuelles

	Year	Q.1	Q.2	Q.3	Q.4	JAN	FEB	MAR	APR	MAY	JUN	JUL	AUG	SEP	OCT	NOV	DEC
1964	2.21	1.86	2.11	2.39	2.49	1.52	2.00	2.06	2.00	1.94	2.39	2.53	2.32	2.32	2.18	2.45	2.84
1965	2.83	2.45	2.98	2.65	3.26	2.13	2.21	3.02	2.67	3.19	3.08	2.51	2.44	2.99	3.43	3.14	3.22
1966	3.06	2.73	3.00	3.00	3.50	2.92	2.25	3.02	2.23	3.10	3.67	3.14	2.69	3.18	2.95	3.81	3.73
1967	2.97	2.67	2.99	2.76	3.45	2.23	2.67	3.11	2.81	3.36	2.79	2.42	2.97	2.88	2.61	3.30	4.44
1968	3.48	2.68	3.37	3.41	4.48	2.48	2.92	2.62	2.72	3.70	3.69	3.95	3.37	2.92	4.39	4.31	4.75
1969	3.99	4.16	3.79	3.64	4.35	3.91	4.27	4.31	3.12	3.97	4.28	3.74	3.08	4.10	4.12	3.99	4.95
1970	4.90	4.66	4.58	4.83	5.52	4.61	4.59	4.76	4.50	4.53	4.70	5.37	4.36	4.76	5.40	6.26	4.91
1971	5.25	3.48	6.57	4.69	6.24	3.71	3.28	3.45	3.78	7.14	8.80	5.29	4.10	4.67	4.67	7.39	6.67
1972	5.86	4.54	6.01	5.76	7.15	4.25	4.21	5.17	5.24	7.13	5.65	5.14	5.96	6.13	7.78	6.43	7.24
1973	8.57	7.07	8.24	8.99	9.98	6.54	6.46	8.21	6.72	8.82	9.17	9.45	8.47	9.05	10.32	8.68	10.96
1974	11.02	9.38	12.17	9.62	12.89	8.83	8.99	10.31	9.20	13.69	13.63	10.04	9.25	9.58	12.99	11.18	14.50
1975	14.33	12.90	14.10	13.21	17.13	12.07	12.35	14.27	14.53	13.67	14.10	12.58	11.27	15.79	16.70	15.44	19.25
1976	18.49	14.61	16.80	18.88	23.67	14.63	14.41	14.79	15.92	17.93	16.56	19.58	15.30	21.77	21.41	22.10	27.50
1977	21.01	17.37	22.01	21.65	23.03	18.77	16.17	17.16	16.70	22.24	27.10	24.80	20.33	19.81	21.78	24.75	22.54
1978	23.36	19.48	24.35	22.43	27.18	18.84	16.60	23.00	25.64	23.68	23.74	20.11	18.23	28.94	32.30	29.08	20.15
1979	29.74	22.13	26.80	33.36	36.66	20.62	21.34	24.42	20.97	30.89	28.53	31.10	34.23	34.75	30.31	35.11	44.56
1980	37.74	28.13	35.61	37.71	49.51	29.80	23.85	30.74	30.11	37.78	38.94	33.53	32.29	47.32	50.88	41.48	56.16
1981	40.18	18.18	47.34	43.21	52.02	8.28	15.18	31.07	56.21	45.53	40.27	46.95	35.39	47.29	47.43	47.37	61.26
1982	55.49	61.04	46.72	54.51	59.71	53.31	63.92	65.88	50.58	56.06	33.51	48.20	41.42	73.91	51.35	62.81	64.97
1983		55.09	71.97	52.49		52.89	50.35	62.02	82.20	60.71	73.01	48.73	44.05	64.68	74.81	66.10	

Exports f.o.b. / Exportations f.o.b.

billion drachmae, monthly averages / milliards de drachmes, moyennes mensuelles

	Year	Q.1	Q.2	Q.3	Q.4	JAN	FEB	MAR	APR	MAY	JUN	JUL	AUG	SEP	OCT	NOV	DEC
1964	0.77	0.89	0.52	0.41	1.27	1.08	0.79	0.79	0.64	0.55	0.36	0.38	0.42	0.44	0.66	1.65	1.51
1965	0.82	0.84	0.74	0.50	1.19	0.98	0.85	0.70	0.79	0.75	0.67	0.56	0.40	0.55	1.10	1.19	1.29
1966	1.02	1.09	0.87	0.67	1.43	1.13	1.13	1.00	0.89	0.98	0.75	0.67	0.54	0.81	1.31	1.42	1.55
1967	1.24	1.29	0.91	0.98	1.78	1.58	1.08	1.20	1.13	0.86	0.73	0.87	0.74	1.32	1.78	1.61	1.96
1968	1.17	1.08	0.98	0.99	1.63	0.94	1.27	1.03	1.16	0.94	0.84	0.85	0.98	1.13	1.39	1.37	2.14
1969	1.38	1.05	1.18	1.20	2.11	1.07	1.18	0.91	1.15	1.33	1.05	1.23	1.18	1.19	1.51	1.75	3.06
1970	1.61	1.39	1.39	1.51	2.14	1.50	1.26	1.40	1.33	1.44	1.39	1.97	1.23	1.34	1.96	2.06	2.40
1971	1.66	1.28	1.35	1.50	2.47	1.41	1.28	1.16	1.42	1.32	1.31	1.38	1.74	1.36	1.91	2.57	3.00
1972	2.18	1.95	1.95	1.84	2.97	1.75	2.05	2.05	1.95	1.91	1.98	1.78	1.72	2.03	2.35	2.97	3.59
1973	3.57	2.81	2.60	3.23	5.64	2.47	2.41	3.54	2.67	2.58	2.55	3.45	3.54	2.70	3.75	3.72	9.43
1974	5.08	4.08	5.53	4.46	6.24	3.31	3.53	5.41	4.94	5.72	5.92	4.30	4.90	4.20	5.16	6.38	7.17
1975	6.20	5.15	5.27	6.16	8.23	6.03	4.60	4.81	5.00	4.24	6.58	6.45	5.89	6.15	5.96	6.71	12.02
1976	7.82	5.93	7.27	7.14	10.94	5.84	6.17	5.79	7.19	7.21	7.40	6.96	6.61	7.83	9.05	9.39	14.38
1977	8.44	7.39	7.98	7.63	10.78	7.23	7.10	7.85	8.01	6.74	9.17	8.62	7.60	6.68	9.10	9.12	14.11
1978	10.31	8.49	9.43	9.76	13.57	6.79	9.23	9.44	8.50	9.88	9.92	9.30	8.99	10.98	11.02	11.38	18.30
1979	12.02	10.73	11.53	9.85	15.97	9.36	10.91	11.94	10.21	11.84	12.55	11.82	9.09	8.63	14.25	13.69	19.97
1980	16.43	15.20	16.78	16.23	25.49	16.66	13.92	15.02	15.10	15.11	20.14	17.04	16.52	15.14	25.92	17.92	32.63
1981	19.86	12.35	22.77	20.70	23.62	5.44	11.60	20.01	20.07	20.66	27.58	22.72	18.05	21.33	24.33	19.40	27.13
1982	23.86	23.86	20.56	27.62	23.39	23.52	22.13	25.91	19.63	22.74	19.30	37.04	22.23	23.61	28.26	21.39	20.53
1983		27.58	28.77	27.22		25.23	27.28	30.22	31.17	28.59	26.54	24.55	26.52	30.58	48.45	30.71	

Trade balance (f.o.b. — c.i.f.) / Balance commerciale (f.o.b. — c.a.f.)

billion drachmae, monthly averages / milliards de drachmes, moyennes mensuelles

	Year	Q.1	Q.2	Q.3	Q.4	JAN	FEB	MAR	APR	MAY	JUN	JUL	AUG	SEP	OCT	NOV	DEC
1964	-1.44	-0.98	-1.59	-1.98	-1.22	-0.44	-1.21	-1.27	-1.36	-1.39	-2.03	-2.15	-1.90	-1.88	-1.53	-0.80	-1.33
1965	-2.02	-1.61	-2.24	-2.14	-2.07	-1.15	-1.36	-2.32	-1.88	-2.44	-2.40	-1.95	-2.04	-2.44	-2.33	-1.95	-1.93
1966	-2.04	-1.64	-2.13	-2.33	-2.07	-1.79	-1.12	-2.01	-1.34	-2.12	-2.92	-2.46	-2.15	-2.38	-1.65	-2.39	-2.19
1967	-1.73	-1.39	-2.08	-1.78	-1.67	-0.66	-1.59	-1.90	-1.67	-2.51	-2.06	-1.55	-2.23	-1.56	-0.84	-1.69	-2.47
1968	-2.31	-1.60	-2.39	-2.42	-2.85	-1.55	-1.65	-1.60	-1.56	-2.76	-2.85	-3.10	-2.38	-1.79	-2.99	-2.93	-2.61
1969	-2.60	-3.11	-2.61	-2.44	-2.24	-2.84	-3.09	-3.40	-1.97	-2.64	-3.23	-2.51	-1.89	-2.92	-2.60	-2.24	-1.89
1970	-3.29	-3.27	-3.19	-3.31	-3.39	-3.11	-3.33	-3.36	-3.17	-3.09	-3.31	-3.39	-3.13	-3.42	-3.45	-4.20	-2.51
1971	-3.59	-2.20	-5.22	-3.19	-3.75	-2.30	-2.00	-2.29	-2.36	-5.82	-7.49	-3.91	-2.36	-3.30	-2.76	-4.82	-3.67
1972	-3.69	-2.59	-4.06	-3.91	-4.19	-2.49	-2.16	-3.12	-3.23	-5.22	-3.68	-3.36	-4.23	-4.15	-5.44	-3.47	-3.65
1973	-5.00	-4.27	-5.64	-5.76	-4.35	-4.07	-4.05	-4.67	-4.04	-6.25	-6.62	-6.00	-4.94	-6.35	-6.56	-4.95	-1.53
1974	-5.94	-5.29	-6.65	-5.16	-6.65	-5.52	-5.46	-4.90	-4.26	-7.98	-7.70	-5.74	-4.35	-5.38	-7.83	-4.80	-7.33
1975	-8.13	-7.75	-8.83	-7.05	-8.90	-6.04	-7.76	-9.45	-9.53	-9.43	-7.52	-6.13	-5.38	-9.65	-10.74	-8.73	-7.24
1976	-10.67	-8.68	-9.53	-11.75	-12.73	-8.30	-8.24	-9.00	-8.72	-10.72	-9.16	-12.62	-8.69	-13.94	-12.36	-12.71	-13.12
1977	-12.57	-9.97	-14.04	-14.02	-12.25	-11.54	-9.07	-9.31	-8.69	-15.50	-17.92	-16.18	-12.73	-13.13	-12.68	-15.63	-8.44
1978	-13.05	-10.99	-14.92	-12.67	-13.61	-12.05	-7.37	-13.56	-17.14	-13.80	-13.82	-10.81	-9.24	-17.96	-21.28	-17.70	-1.85
1979	-17.72	-11.39	-15.27	-23.51	-20.69	-11.26	-10.43	-12.48	-10.76	-19.06	-15.99	-19.28	-25.14	-26.11	-16.06	-21.43	-24.59
1980	-19.31	-12.93	-18.83	-21.48	-24.02	-13.14	-9.93	-15.72	-15.01	-22.67	-18.80	-16.49	-15.77	-32.19	-24.97	-23.56	-23.53
1981	-20.33	-5.83	-24.57	-22.51	-28.40	-2.84	-3.58	-11.06	-36.14	-24.87	-12.69	-24.23	-17.34	-25.96	-23.10	-27.97	-34.12
1982	-31.64	-37.18	-26.16	-26.89	-36.32	-29.79	-41.79	-39.97	-30.95	-33.32	-14.20	-11.16	-19.19	-50.30	-23.09	-41.42	-44.44
1983		-27.51	-43.21	-25.27		-27.66	-23.07	-31.80	-51.03	-32.12	-46.47	-24.18	-17.53	-34.10	-26.36	-35.39	

Imports c.i.f. / Importations c.a.f.

Adjusted - Corrigé *

billion drachmae, monthly averages / milliards de drachmes, moyennes mensuelles

	Year	Q.1	Q.2	Q.3	Q.4	JAN	FEB	MAR	APR	MAY	JUN	JUL	AUG	SEP	OCT	NOV	DEC
1964		2.02	2.10	2.38	2.27	1.75	2.20	2.10	2.06	1.88	2.35	2.46	2.43	2.24	2.11	2.28	2.44
1965		2.68	2.94	2.67	3.05	2.57	2.55	2.92	3.03	2.92	2.87	2.49	2.74	2.78	3.50	2.92	2.75
1966		2.95	2.[illegible]2	3.12	3.19	3.35	2.57	2.94	2.53	2.98	3.25	3.25	2.90	3.19	2.87	3.44	3.25
1967		2.89	2.97	2.84	3.18	2.65	2.98	3.04	3.20	3.05	2.67	2.37	3.30	2.84	2.67	2.89	3.97
1968		2.34	3.33	3.51	4.19	2.74	3.07	2.69	3.21	3.35	3.42	3.82	3.86	2.86	4.20	4.09	4.27
1969		4.42	3.74	3.78	3.97	4.32	4.67	4.25	3.60	3.62	4.02	3.61	3.60	4.14	3.86	3.84	4.20
1970		5.08	4.52	4.92	5.19	5.20	5.10	4.93	4.97	4.15	4.46	5.20	4.82	4.74	5.06	6.28	4.22
1971		3.78	6.21	4.87	5.94	4.28	3.72	3.34	4.46	6.11	8.05	5.27	4.76	4.56	4.39	7.69	5.75
1972		4.84	5.74	6.05	6.69	4.69	4.86	4.98	5.90	6.00	5.33	5.10	6.58	6.46	7.33	6.31	6.44
1973		7.60	7.83	9.62	9.12	7.22	7.47	8.12	7.45	7.49	8.55	10.12	9.46	9.28	9.07	9.17	9.13
1974		10.23	11.58	10.16	11.87	9.74	10.32	10.63	10.28	11.95	12.52	10.08	10.64	9.77	11.60	11.36	12.65
1975		13.90	13.77	14.03	15.19	13.16	14.20	14.34	15.57	12.56	13.16	12.64	13.55	15.90	15.00	14.86	15.71
1976		15.97	16.54	19.40	21.28	16.22	16.56	15.13	17.81	16.50	15.32	19.68	18.73	19.79	20.57	20.91	22.38
1977		19.35	21.51	22.58	20.24	20.49	19.48	18.08	18.39	21.83	24.30	25.54	23.53	18.67	19.98	22.16	18.57
1978		22.49	24.35	22.24	24.54	22.13	20.64	24.68	28.21	21.76	23.11	19.41	21.12	26.19	31.58	24.86	17.18
1979		25.51	26.39	34.01	32.37	22.96	27.18	26.40	23.32	28.29	27.54	32.09	39.95	29.98	27.86	32.60	36.65
1980		32.13	35.16	37.85	43.96	33.67	30.62	32.09	32.76	34.88	37.84	32.91	39.52	41.12	47.64	37.74	46.49
1981		20.90	46.93	42.52	46.88	9.47	19.39	33.85	57.12	43.12	40.55	46.81	41.49	39.27	45.26	43.86	51.52
1982		70.53	45.88	53.22	54.92	62.42	81.33	67.84	54.27	50.33	33.04	48.98	51.45	59.22	50.10	59.37	55.29
1983		62.26	70.74	52.83		58.57	64.06	64.13	85.27	57.55	69.40	50.81	51.58	56.10	69.40	60.92	

Exports f.o.b. / Exportations f.o.b.

Adjusted - Corrigé *

billion drachmae, monthly averages / milliards de drachmes, moyennes mensuelles

	Year	Q.1	Q.2	Q.3	Q.4	JAN	FEB	MAR	APR	MAY	JUN	JUL	AUG	SEP	OCT	NOV	DEC
1964		0.80	0.67	0.69	0.83	0.87	0.71	0.81	0.71	0.67	0.62	0.64	0.83	0.59	0.54	1.06	0.88
1965		0.76	0.96	0.79	0.81	0.79	0.78	0.72	0.86	0.91	1.10	0.90	0.74	0.72	0.87	0.81	0.76
1966		1.03	1.09	0.97	1.00	0.94	1.07	1.07	0.95	1.17	1.16	0.99	0.91	1.00	1.03	1.02	0.95
1967		1.23	1.10	1.30	1.27	1.37	1.05	1.28	1.24	1.00	1.05	1.22	1.14	1.55	1.39	1.22	1.19
1968		1.08	1.16	1.25	1.16	0.86	1.25	1.14	1.25	1.08	1.16	1.09	1.37	1.30	1.13	1.05	1.31
1969		1.10	1.37	1.47	1.50	1.03	1.23	1.04	1.25	1.51	1.35	1.53	1.51	1.35	1.26	1.38	1.86
1970		1.51	1.58	1.77	1.61	1.54	1.37	1.61	1.44	1.61	1.70	2.27	1.49	1.55	1.72	1.60	1.50
1971		1.41	1.50	1.73	1.88	1.50	1.43	1.29	1.54	1.46	1.51	1.56	2.02	1.62	1.74	2.01	1.88
1972		2.14	2.12	2.10	2.30	1.95	2.26	2.22	2.13	2.06	2.15	1.95	1.95	2.41	2.24	2.37	2.30
1973		3.12	2.76	3.61	4.26	2.79	2.78	3.78	2.86	2.79	2.64	3.73	3.88	3.23	3.65	3.06	6.07
1974		4.57	5.77	4.94	5.06	3.87	4.11	5.73	5.26	6.01	6.06	4.50	5.41	4.91	5.21	5.46	4.51
1975		5.87	5.41	6.83	6.47	7.10	5.38	5.13	5.33	4.44	6.45	6.84	6.54	7.10	5.89	6.11	7.42
1976		6.70	7.45	7.95	8.81	7.07	6.92	6.10	7.69	7.53	7.13	7.23	7.52	9.11	8.89	8.72	8.80
1977		8.46	8.11	8.44	8.76	8.94	8.05	8.38	8.60	6.96	8.77	8.89	8.74	7.68	8.67	8.67	8.94
1978		9.52	9.55	10.96	11.07	8.39	10.43	9.75	9.34	10.14	9.17	9.55	10.60	12.72	10.02	11.17	12.01
1979		11.99	11.58	10.88	13.37	11.41	12.37	12.18	11.17	12.33	11.23	12.01	10.50	10.12	12.39	13.69	14.04
1980		16.84	16.59	17.86	21.59	20.24	15.17	15.12	16.61	15.66	17.52	17.12	19.14	17.32	22.02	18.90	23.86
1981		13.22	22.34	22.41	20.79	6.39	13.38	19.89	22.23	21.37	23.43	22.27	21.03	23.91	20.62	20.81	20.95
1982		26.06	20.43	29.62	20.90	26.85	25.86	25.48	21.32	23.89	16.10	36.63	25.67	26.56	23.49	23.30	15.91
1983		30.32	28.57	29.44		28.83	32.09	30.04	33.63	29.97	22.12	24.07	30.31	33.94	40.51	33.71	

Trade balance (f.o.b. — c.i.f.) / Balance commerciale (f.o.b. — c.a.f.)

Adjusted - Corrigé *

billion drachmae, monthly averages / milliards de drachmes, moyennes mensuelles

	Year	Q.1	Q.2	Q.3	Q.4	JAN	FEB	MAR	APR	MAY	JUN	JUL	AUG	SEP	OCT	NOV	DEC
1964		-1.22	-1.43	-1.69	-1.45	-0.88	-1.49	-1.30	-1.35	-1.21	-1.73	-1.83	-1.59	-1.65	-1.57	-1.22	-1.55
1965		-1.92	-1.99	-1.88	-2.24	-1.78	-1.77	-2.20	-2.[illegible]8	-2.01	-1.77	-1.60	-2.00	-2.06	-2.63	-2.11	-1.99
1966		-1.93	-1.82	-2.15	-2.19	-2.41	-1.50	-1.87	-1.58	-1.81	-2.09	-2.26	-2.00	-2.19	-1.85	-2.42	-2.30
1967		-1.66	-1.88	-1.54	-1.91	-3.28	-1.93	-1.76	-1.96	-2.05	-1.62	-1.15	-2.17	-1.29	-1.28	-1.67	-2.78
1968		-1.75	-2.17	-2.26	-3.02	-1.89	-1.82	-1.56	-1.96	-2.28	-2.26	-2.73	-2.49	-1.55	-3.07	-3.04	-2.96
1969		-3.32	-2.37	-2.32	-2.47	-3.30	-3.44	-3.21	-2.35	-2.10	-2.66	-2.08	-2.09	-2.79	-2.61	-2.46	-2.34
1970		-3.57	-2.94	-3.15	-3.58	-3.66	-3.73	-3.32	-3.52	-2.54	-2.76	-2.93	-3.33	-3.19	-3.34	-4.67	-2.72
1971		-2.37	-4.71	-3.13	-4.07	-2.78	-2.29	-2.05	-2.93	-4.65	-6.54	-3.71	-2.75	-2.94	-2.65	-5.68	-3.86
1972		-2.70	-3.63	-3.95	-4.3[illegible]	-2.74	-2.60	-2.77	-3.77	-3.94	-3.17	-3.15	-4.63	-4.05	-5.09	-3.94	-4.14
1973		-4.49	-5.07	-6.00	-4.86	-4.43	-4.69	-4.34	-4.59	-4.70	-5.92	-6.38	-5.57	-6.05	-5.41	-6.12	-3.06
1974		-5.66	-5.81	-5.22	-6.81	-5.86	-6.21	-4.90	-5.02	-5.94	-6.47	-5.58	-5.23	-4.85	-6.39	-5.90	-8.14
1975		-8.04	-8.36	-7.21	-8.72	-6.07	-8.83	-9.21	-10.25	-8.12	-6.71	-5.80	-7.01	-8.31	-9.11	-8.75	-8.29
1976		-9.28	-9.09	-11.45	-12.48	-9.16	-9.64	-9.03	-10.[illegible]	-8.97	-8.19	-12.45	-11.21	-10.68	-11.68	-12.18	-13.57
1977		-10.90	-13.40	-14.14	-11.48	-11.55	-11.43	-9.70	-9.79	-14.87	-15.53	-16.65	-14.79	-10.99	-11.31	-13.49	-9.63
1978		-12.96	-14.81	-11.28	-13.47	-13.74	-10.21	-14.93	-18.87	-11.62	-13.94	-9.86	-10.52	-13.46	-21.56	-13.69	-5.17
1979		-13.53	-14.81	-23.13	-19.00	-11.55	-14.81	-14.22	-12.[illegible]6	-15.96	-16.31	-20.08	-29.45	-19.86	-15.46	-18.92	-22.61
1980		-15.28	-18.57	-19.99	-22.37	-13.43	-15.45	-16.97	-16.16	-19.22	-20.33	-15.78	-20.38	-23.80	-25.63	-18.84	-22.64
1981		-7.68	-24.59	-20.12	-26.09	-3.09	-6.01	-13.96	-34.90	-21.75	-17.12	-24.53	-20.46	-15.36	-24.64	-23.05	-30.57
1982		-44.47	-25.45	-23.60	-34.02	-35.57	-55.47	-42.37	-32.96	-26.44	-16.95	-12.35	-25.79	-32.67	-26.61	-36.07	-39.38
1983		-31.93	-42.17	-23.39		-29.74	-31.97	-34.09	-51.64	-27.58	-47.23	-26.75	-21.27	-22.16	-28.89	-27.21	

* Adjusted by the O.E.C.D. / * Corrigé par l'O.C.D.E.

GREECE

Balance of payments: net trade (13) / Balance des paiements : balance commerciale (13)

million dollars / millions de dollars

	Year	Q.1	Q.2	Q.3	Q.4	JAN	FEB	MAR	APR	MAY	JUN	JUL	AUG	SEP	OCT	NOV	DEC
1964																	
1965																	
1966																	
1967																	
1968	-784	-176	-234	-219	-155												
1969	-903	-228	-240	-244	-192												
1970	-1093	-212	-296	-285	-300												
1971	-1320	-323	-336	-332	-329												
1972	-1582	-336	-345	-443	-458												
1973	-2817	-492	-734	-764	-827												
1974	-2885	-839	-733	-525	-788												
1975	-2923	-745	-815	-608	-755												
1976	-3333	-797	-771	-915	-850												
1977	-3903	-832	-1129	-863	-1080												
1978	-4343	-1054	-1082	-1216	-991												
1979	-6177	-1369	-1523	-1644	-1642												
1980	-6810	-1523	-1787	-1576	-1925												
1981	-6697	-1518	-1776	-1650	-1752												
1982	-5911	-1410	-1123	-1844	-1534												
1983	-5409	-1460	-1086	-1324	-1539												

Balance of payments: current balance (13) / Balance des paiements : opérations courantes, nettes (13)

million dollars / millions de dollars

	Year	Q.1	Q.2	Q.3	Q.4	JAN	FEB	MAR	APR	MAY	JUN	JUL	AUG	SEP	OCT	NOV	DEC
1964																	
1965																	
1966																	
1967																	
1968	-54	-72	81	-44	-20												
1969	-349	-119	-100	-84	-46												
1970	-414	-99	-134	-68	-113												
1971	-362	-168	-114	-14	-65												
1972	159	-120	93	38	149												
1973	-1188	-208	-352	-189	-439												
1974	-1239	-515	-261	-14	-448												
1975	-999	-402	-372	70	-295												
1976	-1084	-407	-271	-122	-285												
1977	-1278	-366	-467	14	-458												
1978	-1249	-528	-346	-154	-221												
1979	-2111	-625	-560	-370	-556												
1980	-2216	-780	-701	22	-757												
1981	-2408	-733	-668	-182	-774												
1982	-1885	-637	-290	-390	-568												
1983	-1916	-921	-230	-173	-592												

Balance of payments: net capital movements (13) / Balance des paiements : mouvements de capitaux, nets (13)

million dollars / millions de dollars

	Year	Q.1	Q.2	Q.3	Q.4	JAN	FEB	MAR	APR	MAY	JUN	JUL	AUG	SEP	OCT	NOV	DEC
1964	178	25	37	51	65												
1965	228	51	69	67	41												
1966	264	97	68	53	47												
1967	186	32	62	47	45												
1968	276	48	82	82	64												
1969	328	82	86	107	55												
1970	381	35	125	128	92												
1971	496	136	159	96	106												
1972	874	136	286	130	322												
1973	1051	223	247	181	400												
1974	929	286	379	123	141												
1975	1021	339	215	256	211												
1976	927	278	205	142	301												
1977	1340	345	370	354	271												
1978	1352	303	287	559	203												
1979	1542	318	335	206	683												
1980	2271	589	682	237	762												
1981	1901	437	604	523	338												
1982	1809	487	365	325	632												
1983	2312	790	415	367	740												

NOTES

1. From 1972, index (original base 1970) linked on 1970 to previous index (original base 1959).
2. Construction material only. The original base of the index is 1971 to 1980 and 1981 from 1981.
3. Series adjusted for unequal number of working days in the month.
4. Including imported used cars. Annual data are based on more complete information than monthly and quarterly data.
5. Enterprises employing at least 10 persons.
6. Monthly data refer to the week including the 18th of the month.
7. Monthly data refer to end of period. Excluding sailors. Including part-time workers looking for a full-time job. An administrative change in April 1976 led to a significant decrease in the level of the series. However, the increase in the number of employment offices by about 60 per cent during the 1970's, may have introduced an upward bias in the series.
8. Weighting pattern based on 1952 to 1965, on 1961 from 1966 to 1973, and on 1970 from 1974.
9. Including petroleum products; excluding raw materials.
10. Weighting pattern based on 1959 to 1969, on 1969 from 1970 to 1972, on 1973 for 1973, and on 1974 from 1974.
11. The original base of the index is 1952 to 1977 and 1978 from 1978.
12. From May 1973, liabilities include foreign security deposits.
13. Settlements basis.

NOTES

1. A partir de 1972, indice (base originale 1970) raccordé sur 1970 à l'indice précédent (base originale 1959).
2. Matériaux de construction seulement. La base originale de l'indice est 1971 jusqu'en 1980 et 1981 à partir de 1981.
3. Série corrigée de l'inégalité du nombre de jours ouvrables dans le mois.
4. Y compris les voitures d'occasion importées. Les données annuelles sont établies à partir d'informations plus complètes que les données mensuelles et trimestrielles.
5. Entreprises employant 10 personnes ou plus.
6. Les données mensuelles se réfèrent à la semaine comprenant le 18 du mois.
7. Situation en fin de mois. Non compris les marins. Y compris les salariés travaillant à temps partiel mais qui cherchent un travail à temps complet. Un changement administratif en avril 1976 a baissé le niveau de la série de façon significative. Toutefois, l'augmentation d'environ 60% du nombre des bureaux de placement dans les années 1970 a sans doute entraîné une dérive ascendante de la série.
8. La pondération se réfère à 1952 jusqu'en 1965, à 1961 de 1966 à 1973, et à 1970 à partir de 1974.
9. Y compris les dérivés du pétrole; non compris les matières premières.
10. La pondération se réfère à 1959 jusqu'en 1969, à 1969 de 1970 à 1972, à 1973 en 1973, et à 1974 à partir de 1974.
11. La base originale de l'indice est 1952 jusqu'en 1977 et 1978 à partir de 1978.
12. A partir de mai 1973, les dettes comprennent les dépôts en valeurs étrangères.
13. Sur la base des règlements.

MAIN SOURCES

PRINCIPALES SOURCES

Series	Séries	Sources
Industrial production	Production industrielle	National Statistical Service of Greece *Monthly Statistical Bulletin*
Construction	Construction	
Internal trade	Commerce intérieur	
Labour and wages	Main-d'œuvre et salaires	
Prices	Prix	
Foreign trade	Commerce extérieur	
Business surveys	Enquêtes de conjoncture	Institute of Economic and Industrial Research *Business Survey in Industry*
Home finance	Finances internes	Bank of Greece *Monthly Statistical Bulletin*
Share prices	Cours des actions	
Net foreign position of commercial banks	Position extérieure nette des banques commerciales	
Balance of payments	Balance des paiements	

Iceland — Islande

ICELAND

Total fish catch — Pêche maritime

thousand tons, monthly averages — milliers de tonnes, moyennes mensuelles

	Year	Q.1	Q.2	Q.3	Q.4	JAN	FEB	MAR	APR	MAY	JUN	JUL	AUG	SEP	OCT	NOV	DEC
1964	81.0	66.9	93.0	116.0	48.0	50.7	69.2	80.8	144.6	37.5	96.9	156.9	85.3	105.7	76.6	28.1	39.3
1965	101.3	68.7	84.7	127.7	124.3	45.9	74.6	85.5	102.6	30.4	121.2	127.2	123.4	132.4	124.9	150.0	97.9
1966	99.3	79.9	90.4	123.1	103.8	28.8	85.8	125.1	92.9	72.2	106.1	94.6	148.9	126.8	148.8	102.6	59.9
1967	73.5	75.4	65.3	100.7	52.3	52.1	58.5	115.7	75.9	36.2	83.9	116.6	88.8	96.7	77.2	51.8	28.0
1968	45.5	52.1	52.0	44.5	33.6	12.2	39.0	105.0	87.8	38.4	29.8	49.2	40.9	43.3	30.3	47.2	23.3
1969	54.4	94.9	62.7	35.7	24.2	11.6	68.1	205.1	92.6	54.4	41.0	43.1	31.6	32.5	24.8	25.3	22.5
1970	58.1	89.7	85.2	34.5	23.1	22.5	53.7	192.8	171.1	43.7	40.7	48.1	28.6	26.8	27.5	23.8	18.1
1971	54.8	94.9	62.7	36.6	24.9	23.5	75.9	185.4	85.8	52.2	50.2	49.0	36.5	24.3	31.6	25.5	17.6
1972	59.1	132.6	49.1	33.7	21.1	48.1	232.7	116.9	76.4	32.1	38.9	46.9	33.7	20.5	25.5	22.7	15.0
1973	73.9	167.9	61.4	40.7	25.6	44.1	200.0	259.6	114.5	32.6	37.0	52.7	39.3	30.2	34.3	25.6	16.8
1974	78.0	186.1	52.4	41.2	32.1	124.9	258.0	175.4	79.8	42.6	34.8	49.1	42.7	31.8	38.8	33.7	23.9
1975	77.9	175.4	58.9	43.2	34.1	59.2	236.9	230.1	77.4	65.7	33.5	46.5	52.1	30.9	40.8	42.2	19.3
1976	81.2	149.0	51.9	79.3	44.5	85.2	126.7	235.2	75.2	42.9	37.6	78.2	77.2	82.5	25.9	64.4	43.3
1977	112.7	230.9	51.2	94.3	74.3	151.1	251.1	250.4	64.7	49.1	39.7	71.2	117.3	94.5	108.2	55.0	59.8
1978	128.8	195.6	65.1	131.7	122.9	97.4	231.0	258.3	91.9	58.5	44.9	93.7	162.2	139.2	178.6	118.8	71.4
1979	135.7	235.7	62.2	113.9	130.9	147.0	303.8	256.2	82.2	51.3	53.0	66.8	90.3	184.7	298.7	61.2	32.7
1980	123.6	205.5	65.3	69.2	154.3	179.5	207.2	229.7	87.4	56.6	52.0	43.5	41.7	122.5	207.8	186.0	69.0
1981	118.1	116.6	91.5	88.6	175.8	98.0	93.8	157.9	132.5	77.1	64.9	62.0	89.3	114.6	209.1	240.8	77.6
1982	63.6	70.6	71.1	56.5	56.2	30.9	68.6	112.4	96.3	59.1	58.0	60.3	60.9	48.4	61.0	71.0	36.7
1983	68.3	60.0	63.5	53.7	95.9	32.6	54.2	93.1	79.1	56.1	55.4	56.1	52.5	52.4	53.0	129.9	104.8

Money supply (M1) (1) — Disponibilités monétaires (M1) (1)

million kronur, end of period — millions de couronnes, fin de période

	Year	Q.1	Q.2	Q.3	Q.4	JAN	FEB	MAR	APR	MAY	JUN	JUL	AUG	SEP	OCT	NOV	DEC
1964	22	19	20	23	22	19	18	19	20	21	20	22	22	23	23	23	22
1965	27	21	25	26	27	22	21	21	24	24	25	26	25	26	27	28	27
1966	28	26	28	29	28	28	27	26	27	28	28	29	28	29	30	30	28
1967	26	27	28	27	26	27	26	27	28	29	28	28	27	27	27	27	26
1968	29	25	28	28	29	25	25	25	27	29	28	29	28	28	27	27	29
1969	38	31	35	37	38	28	29	31	33	36	35	36	36	37	38	39	38
1970	46	41	48	49	46	38	40	41	46	51	48	51	49	49	50	51	46
1971	57	51	60	63	57	48	49	51	55	58	60	62	65	63	62	63	57
1972	69	64	72	74	69	57	57	64	68	69	72	73	70	74	73	75	69
1973	96	81	95	99	96	68	73	81	93	94	95	95	98	99	99	105	96
1974	125	109	126	128	125	98	101	109	113	123	126	126	126	128	130	136	125
1975	167	134	151	161	167	126	128	134	140	147	151	159	163	161	169	170	167
1976	208	183	212	211	208	172	178	183	193	202	212	225	208	211	213	211	208
1977	305	246	276	279	305	208	224	246	261	281	276	284	268	279	295	309	305
1978	430	340	371	385	430	296	316	340	345	352	371	378	344	385	403	444	430
1979	629	502	550	542	629	422	445	502	526	545	550	564	546	542	573	628	629
1980	1010	692	770	792	1010	598	649	692	788	798	770	794	765	792	860	930	1010
1981	1628	1082	1351	1357	1628	1035	1092	1082	1302	1335	1351	1416	1395	1357	1423	1671	1628
1982	2076	1619	1781	1826	2076	1561	1582	1619	1721	1789	1781	1828	1856	1826	1913	1969	2076
1983		2514	2861	2999		2036	2179	2514	2434	2689	2861	2947	2876	2999	3086	3231	

Quasi-money (1) — Quasi-monnaie (1)

million kronur, end of period — millions de couronnes, fin de période

	Year	Q.1	Q.2	Q.3	Q.4	JAN	FEB	MAR	APR	MAY	JUN	JUL	AUG	SEP	OCT	NOV	DEC
1964	50	43	45	46	50												
1965	62	53	54	56	62												
1966	72	65	66	67	72	64	64	65	67	66	66	67	67	67	67	67	72
1967	78	73	73	74	78	73	73	73	74	73	73	74	74	74	74	72	78
1968	84	79	80	80	84	79	79	79	80	80	80	81	81	80	79	78	84
1969	101	87	90	93	101	85	86	87	88	89	90	92	93	93	94	94	101
1970	126	107	113	116	126	103	105	107	109	111	113	114	115	116	118	118	126
1971	152	132	137	142	152	128	130	132	134	136	137	139	140	142	144	144	152
1972	178	159	163	169	178	155	157	159	162	163	163	166	167	169	169	169	178
1973	231	188	202	213	231	181	184	188	191	197	202	207	210	213	216	217	231
1974	296	244	247	259	296	239	244	244	248	247	247	252	255	259	263	266	296
1975	375	308	315	334	375	304	305	308	312	312	315	322	329	334	337	337	375
1976	513	388	414	446	513	382	391	388	395	406	414	432	442	446	452	458	513
1977	732	553	582	604	732	432	442	553	568	583	582	593	590	604	616	631	732
1978	1110	782	847	871	1110	749	761	782	811	828	847	859	859	871	897	918	1110
1979	1792	1244	1348	1409	1792	1150	1187	1244	1279	1323	1348	1373	1384	1409	1440	1458	1792
1980	2993	1944	2070	2205	2993	1899	1950	1944	2016	2071	2070	2130	2159	2205	2266	2324	2993
1981	5240	3406	3854	4207	5240	3149	3277	3406	3516	3665	3854	4078	4145	4207	4342	4356	5240
1982	8780	5820	6314	6868	8780	5490	5620	5820	5978	6118	6314	6504	6638	6868	7103	7292	8780
1983	15750	9766	11742	13321	15750	9073	9318	9766	10223	10913	11742	12361	13159	13321	13851	13927	15750

Consumer prices: all items (2) — Prix à la consommation : total (2)

1980 = 100

	Year	Q.1	Q.2	Q.3	Q.4	JAN	FEB	MAR	APR	MAY	JUN	JUL	AUG	SEP	OCT	NOV	DEC
1964	3	3	3	3	3	3	3	3	3	3	3	3	3	3	3	3	3
1965	3	3	3	3	3	3	3	3	3	3	3	3	3	3	3	3	3
1966	4	3	4	4	4	3	3	3	3	4	4	4	4	4	4	4	4
1967	4	4	4	4	4	4	4	4	4	4	4	4	4	4	4	4	4
1968	4	4	4	4	4	=4=	4			4			4			4	
1969	5	5	5	5	5		5			5			5			5	
1970	6	6	6	6	6		6			6			6			6	
1971	6	6	6	6	6		6			6			6			6	
1972	7	6	7	7	7		6			7			7			7	
1973	8	7	8	9	9		7			8			9			9	
1974	12	10	12	12	14		10			12			12			14	
1975	18	15	17	19	20		15			17			19			20	
1976	23	20	23	24	26		20			23			24			26	
1977	30	28	30	31	34		28			30			31			34	
1978	44	38	42	47	50		38			42			47			50	
1979	64	52	59	66	77		52			59			66			77	
1980	100	84	95	105	116		84			95			105			116	
1981	152	133	144	157	171	=131=	133			144			157			171	
1982	226	188	209	234	274		188			209			234			274	
1983	422	316	389	474	506		316			389			474			506	

Money supply (M1) (1) — Disponibilités monétaires (M1) (1)

Adjusted - Corrigé *

million kronur, end of period — millions de couronnes, fin de période

	Year	Q.1	Q.2	Q.3	Q.4	JAN	FEB	MAR	APR	MAY	JUN	JUL	AUG	SEP	OCT	NOV	DEC
1964		20	21	22	22	19	19	20	20	20	21	21	22	22	22	22	22
1965		23	25	25	27	23	23	23	23	24	25	25	25	25	26	27	27
1966		28	27	29	29	30	29	28	27	27	27	28	27	29	30	30	29
1967		29	27	27	27	29	28	29	28	28	27	27	26	27	27	27	27
1968		26	27	28	30	27	27	26	27	27	27	28	27	28	27	27	30
1969		33	34	36	40	30	31	33	32	34	34	34	35	36	38	39	40
1970		43	46	48	49	41	43	43	45	48	46	48	48	48	50	50	49
1971		53	57	62	61	52	53	53	54	55	57	59	64	62	61	62	61
1972		66	69	72	75	62	62	66	66	66	69	69	69	72	72	74	75
1973		83	90	97	104	74	79	83	91	90	90	90	96	97	98	103	104
1974		112	120	126	134	106	108	112	111	117	120	120	125	126	129	134	134
1975		137	144	160	177	136	136	137	137	140	144	152	163	160	168	167	177
1976		185	202	213	218	185	188	185	189	192	202	215	210	213	212	208	218
1977		248	264	284	315	224	234	248	253	267	264	272	273	284	296	304	315
1978		341	357	396	438	319	328	341	333	332	357	365	354	396	413	434	438
1979		502	531	562	636	455	459	502	504	513	531	547	565	562	584	612	636
1980		691	746	825	1017	644	668	691	753	749	746	772	794	825	878	904	1017
1981		1031	1312	1417	1636	1115	1122	1081	1241	1252	1312	1380	1450	1417	1457	1621	1636
1982		1617	1731	1906	2086	1680	1624	1617	1639	1678	1731	1783	1931	1906	1960	1908	2086
1983		2512	2780	3131		2192	2237	2512	2318	2523	2780	2875	2993	3131	3162	3131	

M1 plus quasi-money (1) — M1 plus quasi-monnaie (1)

Adjusted - Corrigé *

million kronur, end of period — millions de couronnes, fin de période

	Year	Q.1	Q.2	Q.3	Q.4	JAN	FEB	MAR	APR	MAY	JUN	JUL	AUG	SEP	OCT	NOV	DEC
1964																	
1965																	
1966		92	93	97	100	93	92	92	92	92	93	94	95	97	99	100	100
1967		101	100	102	104	101	100	101	101	100	100	101	101	102	103	102	104
1968		104	107	109	114	105	102	104	105	107	107	109	109	109	108	108	114
1969		119	124	131	140	114	116	119	119	122	124	126	128	131	134	137	140
1970		149	159	166	175	143	147	149	154	158	159	162	164	166	170	173	175
1971		184	195	206	212	178	181	184	186	190	195	197	205	206	208	212	212
1972		223	231	243	250	215	209	223	227	228	231	236	238	243	245	250	250
1973		269	292	314	332	252	261	269	281	286	292	297	307	314	320	328	332
1974		352	369	391	424	341	350	352	356	362	369	373	381	391	401	411	424
1975		442	460	503	544	433	440	442	445	447	460	474	494	503	516	524	544
1976		568	616	675	715	557	557	568	573	593	616	645	659	675	682	695	715
1977		792	845	910	1022	645	673	792	803	836	845	860	877	910	949	981	1022
1978		1099	1191	1306	1510	1050	1086	1099	1117	1138	1191	1222	1239	1306	1367	1428	1510
1979		1705	1855	2052	2381	1582	1639	1705	1734	1798	1855	1916	1988	2052	2123	2175	2381
1980		2577	2787	3161	3921	2512	2497	2577	2688	2746	2787	2904	3014	3161	3291	3415	3921
1981		4370	5108	5875	6720	4192	4300	4370	4606	4789	5108	5445	5735	5875	6088	6318	6720
1982		7265	7913	9181	10622	7094	7231	7265	7396	7610	7913	8241	8748	9181	9541	9708	10622
1983		11992	14275	17233		11176	11543	11992	12159	13091	14275	15141	16514	17233	17923	17985	

* Adjusted by the O.E.C.D. — * Corrigé par l'O.C.D.E.

Credit to private sector: commercial and savings banks

million kronur, end of period

Crédits au secteur privé : banques commerciales et d'épargne

millions de couronnes, fin de période

	Year	Q.1	Q.2	Q.3	Q.4	JAN	FEB	MAR	APR	MAY	JUN	JUL	AUG	SEP	OCT	NOV	DEC
1964	66	60	63	67	66	59	60	60	61	63	63	65	66	67	68	68	66
1965	32	69	73	77	82	68	69	69	71	73	73	74	76	77	80	83	82
1966	96	84	89	95	96	83	83	84	86	89	89	91	93	95	96	97	96
1967	99	91	94	96	99	91	91	92	91	93	94	94	95	96	97	99	99
1968	113	100	106	109	113	100	100	100	102	105	106	107	109	109	110	114	113
1969	124	115	119	121	124	112	113	115	116	120	119	121	122	121	120	123	124
1970	143	124	132	138	143	122	122	124	128	133	132	136	136	138	141	142	143
1971	176	153	157	171	176	146	150	153	159	164	167	168	170	171	176	177	176
1972	215	188	203	207	215	178	182	188	193	197	203	203	203	207	211	216	215
1973	293	239	257	274	293	221	229	239	247	256	257	260	270	274	282	296	293
1974	465	337	388	425	465	303	322	337	351	381	388	397	412	425	446	462	465
1975	615	517	549	564	615	484	506	517	537	542	549	549	550	564	586	613	615
1976	785	664	721	765	785	634	647	664	683	709	721	724	737	765	794	797	785
1977	1103	890	935	1035	1103	821	847	890	879	913	935	960	976	1035	1070	1119	1103
1978	1646	1247	1410	1595	1646	1162	1203	1247	1266	1359	1410	1452	1474	1595	1583	1703	1646
1979	2599	1784	2037	2279	2599	1675	1737	1784	1844	1890	2037	2097	2107	2279	2390	2589	2599
1980	4294	2931	3383	3799	4294	2699	2825	2931	3105	3274	3383	3481	3587	3799	3911	4160	4294
1981	7313	4843	5796	6423	7313	4393	4558	4843	5140	5546	5796	5977	6204	6423	6801	7185	7313
1982	14261	8654	10060	11954	14261	7639	7871	8654	9114	9801	10060	10368	10670	11954	12598	13291	14261
1983	26034	15891	19677	22731	26034	14759	15017	15891	16484	18185	19677	20704	21754	22731	23691	25701	26034

U.S. dollar exchange rate: spot

cents per krona, end of period

Taux de change du dollar É.-U. : au comptant

cents par couronne, fin de période

	Year	Q.1	Q.2	Q.3	Q.4	JAN	FEB	MAR	APR	MAY	JUN	JUL	AUG	SEP	OCT	NOV	DEC
1964	232.2	232.2	232.2	232.2	232.2	232.2	232.2	232.2	232.2	232.2	232.2	232.2	232.2	232.2	232.2	232.2	232.2
1965	232.2	232.2	232.2	232.2	232.2	232.2	232.2	232.2	232.2	232.2	232.2	232.2	232.2	232.2	232.2	232.2	232.2
1966	232.2	232.2	232.2	232.2	232.2	232.2	232.2	232.2	232.2	232.2	232.2	232.2	232.2	232.2	232.2	232.2	232.2
1967	175.2	232.2	232.2	232.2	175.2	232.2	232.2	232.2	232.2	232.2	232.2	232.2	232.2	232.2	232.2	175.2	175.2
1968	113.5	175.2	175.2	175.2	113.5	175.2	175.2	175.2	175.2	175.2	175.2	175.2	175.2	175.2	175.2	113.5	113.5
1969	113.5	113.5	113.5	113.5	113.5	113.5	113.5	113.5	113.5	113.5	113.5	113.5	113.5	113.5	113.5	113.5	113.5
1970	113.5	113.5	113.5	113.5	113.5	113.5	113.5	113.5	113.5	113.5	113.5	113.5	113.5	113.5	113.5	113.5	113.5
1971	114.4	113.5	113.5	114.4	114.4	113.5	113.5	113.5	113.5	113.5	113.5	113.5	114.3	114.4	114.4	114.4	114.4
1972	102.2	114.4	114.4	114.4	102.2	114.4	114.4	114.4	114.4	114.4	114.4	114.4	114.4	114.4	114.4	114.4	102.2
1973	119.1	102.2	113.3	119.1	119.1	102.2	102.2	102.2	109.5	109.5	113.3	114.9	114.9	119.1	119.1	119.1	119.1
1974	84.4	115.3	105.5	84.4	84.4	114.7	116.8	115.3	113.0	106.4	105.5	103.7	101.6	84.4	84.8	85.3	84.4
1975	58.6	66.8	64.8	60.8	58.6	84.2	66.9	66.8	66.3	65.7	64.8	62.9	62.2	60.8	60.4	59.1	58.6
1976	52.7	56.6	54.3	53.3	52.7	58.5	58.5	56.6	55.6	54.6	54.3	54.2	53.9	53.3	52.8	52.7	52.7
1977	46.9	52.2	51.4	48.0	46.9	52.3	52.2	52.2	51.9	51.8	51.4	50.9	48.8	48.0	47.6	47.2	46.9
1978	31.4	39.3	38.5	32.5	31.4	45.8	39.5	39.3	39.0	38.5	38.5	38.5	38.5	32.5	32.1	31.5	31.4
1979	25.3	30.6	29.1	26.3	25.3	31.1	30.9	30.6	30.3	29.6	29.1	27.9	26.6	26.3	25.6	25.5	25.3
1980	16.0	23.3	21.0	19.0	16.0	25.0	24.6	23.3	22.5	22.1	21.0	20.3	20.0	19.0	18.0	17.2	16.0
1981	12.2	15.3	13.6	12.9	12.2	16.0	15.2	15.3	14.9	14.0	13.6	13.3	12.8	12.9	13.0	12.2	12.2
1982	6.0	9.8	8.7	6.9	6.0	10.6	10.2	9.8	9.6	9.3	8.7	8.2	7.0	6.9	6.3	6.2	6.0
1983	3.5	4.7	3.7	3.6	3.5	5.3	5.1	4.7	4.6	3.7	3.7	3.6	3.6	3.6	3.6	3.5	3.5

Official reserves excluding gold
million SDR's, end of period

Réserves officielles, or exclu
millions de DTS, fin de période

	Year	Q.1	Q.2	Q.3	Q.4	JAN	FEB	MAR	APR	MAY	JUN	JUL	AUG	SEP	OCT	NOV	DEC
1964	43	36	34	36	43	36	37	36	34	33	34	33	35	36	38	41	43
1965	53	43	46	49	53	42	44	43	41	42	46	44	47	49	49	48	53
1966	57	56	54	48	57	55	56	56	56	56	54	52	51	48	51	54	57
1967	34	58	43	38	34	59	61	58	55	52	43	43	41	38	35	34	34
1968	27	30	30	24	27	32	32	30	27	26	30	27	24	24	22	30	27
1969	38	34	31	35	38	26	30	34	35	34	31	31	33	35	37	40	38
1970	53	45	51	55	53	39	43	45	44	50	51	54	54	55	59	54	53
1971	63	60	66	71	63	61	61	60	62	62	66	67	70	71	69	64	63
1972	77	67	64	76	77	64	67	67	69	64	64	65	75	76	76	77	77
1973	82	63	76	82	82	72	64	63	68	72	76	87	86	82	93	88	82
1974	39	63	58	37	39	75	67	63	61	55	58	55	43	37	36	34	39
1975	39	28	33	34	39	31	30	28	28	31	33	41	38	34	34	33	39
1976	68	59	71	77	68	40	52	59	64	67	71	90	90	77	74	71	68
1977	81	77	92	79	81	67	73	77	102	104	92	88	80	79	82	77	81
1978	104	85	67	65	104	79	74	85	92	83	67	52	48	65	81	103	104
1979	123	103	107	107	123	99	93	103	108	116	107	108	112	107	110	104	123
1980	136	114	98	109	136	124	116	114	110	117	98	112	106	109	120	131	136
1981	197	168	170	194	197	167	163	168	272	160	170	188	202	194	195	215	197
1982	132	184	199	166	132	205	193	184	165	179	199	175	169	166	156	131	132
1983	143	119	136	130	143	133	134	119	116	117	136	130	129	130	141	140	143

Net foreign position: commercial banks
million kronur, end of period

Position extérieure nette : banques commerciales
millions de couronnes, fin de période

	Year	Q.1	Q.2	Q.3	Q.4	JAN	FEB	MAR	APR	MAY	JUN	JUL	AUG	SEP	OCT	NOV	DEC
1964	-2	-3	-3	-3	-2	-3	-3	-3	-2	-2	-3	-2	-2	-3	-2	-2	-2
1965	-1	-2	-2	-2	-1	-3	-3	-2	-2	-2	-2	-1	-1	-2	-2	-2	-1
1966	-3	-2	-3	-3	-3	-1	-2	-2	-2	-3	-3	-2	-3	-3	-3	-3	-3
1967	-6	-5	-4	-5	-6	-5	-4	-5	-4	-5	-4	-4	-4	-5	-4	-6	-6
1968	-10	-5	-5	-6	-10	-5	-5	-5	-4	-5	-5	-5	-6	-6	-8	-9	-10
1969	-1	-9	-5	-3	-1	-9	-10	-9	-8	-8	-5	-4	-4	-3	-4	-2	-1
1970	-3	1	1	-1	-3	-	1	1	3	2	1	1	-1	-1	-2	-3	-3
1971	-5	-4	-6	-6	-5	-5	-6	-4	-6	-6	-6	-6	-5	-6	-6	-6	-5
1972	-11	-8	-9	-10	-11	-6	-9	-8	-6	-7	-9	-6	-8	-10	-10	-10	-11
1973	-15	-14	-14	-18	-15	-12	-13	-14	-12	-13	-14	-14	-17	-18	-18	-20	-15
1974	-34	-20	-27	-29	-34	-19	-24	-20	-22	-25	-27	-27	-24	-29	-26	-27	-34
1975	-84	-56	-69	-69	-84	-41	-52	-56	-62	-70	-69	-70	-65	-69	-71	-82	-84
1976	-93	-96	-94	-90	-93	-93	-90	-96	-99	-98	-94	-85	-99	-90	-88	-82	-93
1977	-137	-104	-119	-120	-137	-110	-103	-104	-100	-113	-119	-114	-112	-120	-125	-126	-137
1978	-272	-171	-191	-234	-272	-159	-172	-171	-167	-194	-191	-188	-163	-234	-205	-264	-272
1979	-407	-242	-273	-317	-407	-243	-256	-242	-246	-263	-273	-281	-273	-317	-329	-369	-407
1980	-894	-371	-434	-620	-894	-428	-425	-371	-364	-486	-434	-516	-515	-620	-651	-725	-894
1981	-1422	-984	-1086	-1224	-1422	-939	-896	-984	-919	-983	-1086	-1091	-1224	-1224	-1273	-1383	-1422
1982	-3062	-1756	-1856	-2706	-3062	-1512	-1496	-1756	-1663	-2112	-1856	-1683	-1763	-2706	-2857	-2817	-3062
1983	-7119	-3490	-4626	-5422	-7119	-3284	-3445	-3490	-3281	-3756	-4626	-4927	-5138	-5422	-5581	-7103	-7119

Imports c.i.f.

million kronur, monthly averages

Importations c.a.f.

millions de couronnes, moyennes mensuelles

	Year	Q.1	Q.2	Q.3	Q.4	JAN	FEB	MAR	APR	MAY	JUN	JUL	AUG	SEP	OCT	NOV	DEC
1964	5	3	6	4	6	3	3	3	4	4	10	4	4	4	4	4	9
1965	5	3	6	5	6	3	3	4	4	5	10	5	4	5	5	5	7
1966	6	4	7	5	7	4	4	5	5	6	10	5	5	5	7	6	7
1967	6	4	8	5	7	4	4	5	5	6	12	6	5	5	5	9	6
1968	7	5	8	7	8	5	5	5	6	6	10	8	5	9	7	7	10
1969	9	7	9	10	11	7	7	7	10	8	9	11	8	9	9	13	10
1970	12	8	11	11	16	7	7	10	14	10	9	12	10	12	12	14	23
1971	16	12	17	15	21	10	11	14	13	17	22	14	16	15	13	19	30
1972	17	13	19	16	20	11	13	14	17	18	22	15	17	15	18	17	26
1973	27	19	30	23	35	17	19	20	18	25	49	24	22	22	32	25	47
1974	44	28	48	40	60	26	27	32	33	41	70	40	29	51	60	42	76
1975	63	48	70	58	75	36	31	76	56	54	99	73	45	56	67	68	90
1976	71	53	69	73	90	49	37	73	56	70	81	64	83	73	66	39	116
1977	101	72	109	96	126	63	64	90	82	89	157	93	98	98	83	122	172
1978	153	116	159	148	190	94	118	138	126	163	187	138	154	152	171	194	207
1979	243	176	209	274	315	168	167	193	159	232	236	212	289	321	272	350	324
1980	400	304	425	405	466	315	301	297	296	357	623	438	387	391	470	418	509
1981	624	454	630	592	819	356	435	572	483	569	837	596	494	685	696	764	998
1982	971	683	990	1008	1202	540	764	744	831	825	1314	938	939	1146	1088	1378	1139
1983	1716	1152	1605	1928	2180	1118	992	1346	1400	1436	1981	2086	1837	1860	2186	2058	2296

Exports f.o.b.

million kronur, monthly averages

Exportations f.o.b.

millions de couronnes, moyennes mensuelles

	Year	Q.1	Q.2	Q.3	Q.4	JAN	FEB	MAR	APR	MAY	JUN	JUL	AUG	SEP	OCT	NOV	DEC
1964	4	3	4	4	5	3	3	4	4	3	4	4	3	5	5	5	5
1965	5	3	5	4	6	3	3	5	5	5	5	4	5	4	5	5	8
1966	5	4	5	4	7	4	4	5	4	5	5	4	4	5	6	6	9
1967	4	3	4	3	4	3	4	4	5	4	3	3	3	3	4	4	5
1968	4	3	4	3	7	2	4	3	5	5	3	4	3	3	5	3	12
1969	8	5	7	9	11	4	5	7	6	6	9	8	9	9	9	12	11
1970	11	8	12	12	11	8	8	8	13	13	9	14	11	12	12	10	12
1971	11	8	13	13	10	8	8	8	11	13	15	16	12	10	12	11	8
1972	14	11	15	15	14	9	11	15	15	18	13	16	17	12	16	13	13
1973	22	17	28	20	22	9	14	29	22	28	33	23	23	14	28	17	21
1974	27	20	31	28	31	20	15	24	25	34	35	29	29	26	28	28	35
1975	40	23	48	40	47	23	13	33	59	41	46	58	33	29	53	38	50
1976	61	37	72	69	67	30	29	52	63	72	81	75	50	82	73	64	64
1977	85	72	87	88	92	46	71	100	80	102	79	87	106	71	82	71	123
1978	147	99	127	157	204	96	104	98	126	125	131	167	143	162	192	166	254
1979	232	169	201	248	311	143	170	192	242	146	214	249	300	195	297	268	368
1980	372	245	376	396	469	204	214	317	384	376	369	398	426	365	379	383	645
1981	545	370	563	563	683	316	348	446	524	555	609	641	407	642	433	735	881
1982	707	495	731	661	939	364	568	552	748	694	752	637	504	843	664	934	1220
1983	1553	1074	1506	1862	1769	734	1253	1237	1201	1282	2035	1417	2121	2049	1348	1942	2016

Trade balance (f.o.b. — c.i.f.)

million kronur, monthly averages

Balance commerciale (f.o.b. — c.a.f.)

millions de couronnes, moyennes mensuelles

	Year	Q.1	Q.2	Q.3	Q.4	JAN	FEB	MAR	APR	MAY	JUN	JUL	AUG	SEP	OCT	NOV	DEC
1964	-1	0	-2	-0	-1	0	0	1	-0	-1	-6	-1	-0	0	1	1	-4
1965	-0	0	-1	-0	0	-0	-0	1	1	0	-5	-1	1	-0	-0	0	1
1966	-1	0	-2	-1	0	0	-0	0	-1	-1	-5	-1	-2	-1	-1	0	2
1967	-2	-1	-4	-2	-2	-2	-1	-1	-1	-2	-9	-3	-2	-2	-2	-4	-0
1968	-3	-2	-4	-4	-1	-2	-1	-2	-2	-2	-7	-4	-2	-6	-2	-4	1
1969	-1	-2	-2	-1	-0	-3	-2	-0	-3	-2	0	-2	1	-1	-1	-1	1
1970	-1	0	1	1	-5	1	1	-2	-1	4	-1	2	2	0	0	-5	-11
1971	-5	-4	-5	-2	-10	-2	-4	-6	-2	-4	-7	3	-4	-5	-1	-8	-23
1972	-3	-1	-4	-0	-7	-2	-3	0	-3	0	-10	1	1	-3	-2	-5	-13
1973	-5	-1	-3	-3	-13	-8	-5	9	4	3	-16	-1	1	-8	-5	-6	-26
1974	-16	-9	-16	-12	-29	-5	-13	-7	-7	-7	-35	-11	0	-25	-32	-14	-42
1975	-23	-25	-21	-19	-28	-13	-18	-42	3	-14	-53	-15	-13	-29	-14	-30	-39
1976	-10	-16	3	-4	-23	-19	-8	-22	8	1	0	12	-33	9	7	-24	-52
1977	-16	1	-22	-8	-34	-17	8	11	-2	13	-78	-7	9	-27	-0	-51	-49
1978	-6	-17	-31	9	14	2	-14	-39	1	-38	-56	29	-10	10	21	-28	47
1979	-11	-7	-8	-26	-4	-25	4	-1	83	-86	-22	37	11	-126	26	-83	45
1980	-29	-59	-49	-9	3	-111	-87	20	88	19	-254	-40	39	-26	-91	-35	136
1981	-79	-84	-67	-29	-136	-39	-87	-126	41	-15	-228	45	-68	-43	-263	-29	-117
1982	-264	-188	-259	-346	-263	-177	-196	-192	-83	-132	-562	-302	-435	-302	-425	-445	81
1983	-164	-78	-100	-65	-412	-384	261	-110	-199	-154	54	-669	284	189	-838	-116	-280

Imports c.i.f.

million kronur, monthly averages

Adjusted - Corrigé *

Importations c.a.f.

millions de couronnes, moyennes mensuelles

	Year	Q.1	Q.2	Q.3	Q.4	JAN	FEB	MAR	APR	MAY	JUN	JUL	AUG	SEP	OCT	NOV	DEC
1964		4	5	4	5	4	4	4	4	4	6	4	4	4	4	4	6
1965		4	5	5	5	4	4	5	4	5	5	5	5	5	5	5	5
1966		6	6	6	6	6	6	6	6	6	6	5	6	6	7	6	6
1967		6	6	6	6	6	6	5	6	6	7	6	6	6	6	8	4
1968		6	6	8	7	6	6	6	6	6	7	7	6	10	7	8	7
1969		9	8	10	10	9	9	9	9	9	6	10	10	10	10	14	7
1970		10	10	12	14	10	9	11	14	10	6	12	11	12	13	14	15
1971		15	15	16	18	14	15	15	14	17	14	15	17	16	15	19	21
1972		15	17	17	18	15	16	16	19	17	16	17	18	18	18	18	19
1973		23	26	25	30	23	23	22	20	23	34	25	25	25	30	27	33
1974		34	41	44	52	33	34	36	36	40	47	40	35	57	56	46	53
1975		57	61	63	66	49	39	82	61	57	65	73	57	60	66	72	61
1976		62	63	80	81	69	46	72	65	74	51	70	94	75	73	85	85
1977		84	97	105	113	85	78	87	100	89	103	105	103	106	90	110	138
1978		133	147	158	176	119	142	140	153	155	132	149	157	168	180	174	176
1979		201	194	291	292	200	195	209	189	219	175	223	304	345	266	335	276
1980		346	382	423	428	371	345	322	329	372	446	435	441	394	470	404	410
1981		521	574	610	753	458	498	609	530	608	582	611	549	671	725	717	818
1982		785	896	1052	1129	709	883	764	949	856	882	1009	1013	1134	1153	1259	975
1983		1321	1465	2050	2048	1430	1147	1385	1618	1440	1337	2287	1900	1964	2233	1829	2080

Exports f.o.b.

million kronur, monthly averages

Adjusted - Corrigé *

Exportations f.o.b.

millions de couronnes, moyennes mensuelles

	Year	Q.1	Q.2	Q.3	Q.4	JAN	FEB	MAR	APR	MAY	JUN	JUL	AUG	SEP	OCT	NOV	DEC
1964		4	4	4	4	4	4	4	4	3	5	4	4	5	4	4	3
1965		4	5	5	5	4	3	5	5	5	5	5	6	4	4	4	6
1966		5	5	5	6	6	5	6	4	5	5	5	4	5	5	5	7
1967		4	4	3	4	4	4	4	4	3	3	3	3	3	3	4	4
1968		4	4	4	6	3	5	3	4	4	3	4	3	3	5	3	9
1969		6	7	9	9	5	6	8	6	6	9	8	10	10	8	11	9
1970		10	11	12	11	11	10	10	12	12	8	12	11	13	11	10	11
1971		10	11	12	10	12	10	9	11	11	12	14	11	11	12	12	7
1972		14	13	15	14	12	14	16	14	14	10	14	16	14	15	14	14
1973		21	23	20	22	12	19	31	21	22	26	20	22	18	24	21	21
1974		24	26	29	31	27	20	25	23	27	28	24	29	33	25	34	34
1975		28	41	40	45	32	17	33	52	34	37	50	35	34	48	45	43
1976		44	61	72	66	44	37	49	59	60	66	68	54	95	70	73	53
1977		85	77	90	85	67	88	99	73	89	69	80	106	84	78	78	100
1978		123	116	159	190	144	125	99	118	105	127	149	143	185	188	179	202
1979		203	186	247	286	201	204	204	220	129	210	230	295	218	287	295	276
1980		294	350	392	419	293	252	337	338	350	361	361	438	376	395	412	451
1981		459	522	545	625	469	425	483	463	532	570	595	404	636	483	755	637
1982		601	678	649	864	550	698	556	706	638	689	617	502	827	777	927	886
1983		1297	1391	1828	1651	1072	1533	1285	1127	1184	1863	1414	1971	2099	1544	1894	1514

Trade balance (f.o.b. — c.i.f.)

million kronur, monthly averages

Adjusted - Corrigé *

Balance commerciale (f.o.b. — c.a.f.)

millions de couronnes, moyennes mensuelles

	Year	Q.1	Q.2	Q.3	Q.4	JAN	FEB	MAR	APR	MAY	JUN	JUL	AUG	SEP	OCT	NOV	DEC
1964		-0	-1	0	-1	-1	-1	-0	-0	-1	-2	0	-0	0	-0	0	-2
1965		-1	0	0	-1	-1	-1	-0	1	-0	-0	-1	1	-0	-1	-1	1
1966		-0	-1	-1	-1	0	-1	-0	-2	-1	-1	-1	-2	-1	-2	-1	1
1967		-2	-3	-3	-3	-2	-1	-2	-1	-3	-4	-3	-3	-3	-2	-5	-0
1968		-2	-3	-4	-2	-3	-2	-3	-2	-2	-3	-3	-3	-6	-2	-5	2
1969		-2	-1	-1	-1	-4	-3	-1	-4	-3	3	-3	-1	-1	-2	-2	2
1970		0	1	0	-4	2	1	-2	-2	2	2	-0	-0	1	-2	-5	-4
1971		-4	-4	-4	-8	-3	-4	-6	-4	-7	-2	-0	-6	-5	-3	-7	-13
1972		-2	-4	-3	-4	-3	-2	0	-5	-3	-5	-3	-2	-3	-3	-4	-5
1973		-2	-3	-5	-8	-11	-4	8	1	-2	-8	-5	-3	-7	-6	-7	-12
1974		-10	-15	-15	-21	-6	-14	-11	-13	-14	-19	-15	-6	-24	-31	-13	-19
1975		-29	-20	-23	-21	-17	-22	-49	-9	-24	-28	-22	-21	-26	-18	-26	-18
1976		-19	-2	-8	-15	-25	-8	-23	-7	-14	15	-2	-41	20	-3	-12	-31
1977		1	-20	-15	-28	-17	10	12	-27	-0	-33	-25	3	-22	-12	-32	-38
1978		-11	-31	1	13	26	-18	-41	-36	-51	-5	-0	-14	18	8	5	26
1979		2	-8	-43	-7	1	9	-6	31	-90	35	7	-9	-128	20	-40	0
1980		-52	-33	-32	-9	-77	-93	15	9	-22	-86	-74	-3	-13	-75	8	40
1981		-63	-52	-65	-128	12	-73	-126	-67	-76	-12	-15	-145	-35	-242	38	-181
1982		-184	-218	-403	-265	-159	-185	-208	-243	-218	-193	-392	-511	-308	-376	-332	-89
1983		-24	-74	-222	-397	-358	386	-100	-491	-256	527	-873	71	135	-689	65	-567

* Adjusted by the O.E.C.D.

* Corrigé par l'O.C.D.E.

NOTES

1. Prior to 1967, including inter-bank deposits.
2. Cost of living in Reykjavik. Prior to 1968, including direct taxes. Prior to 1981, social and pension fund contributions are included with a positive weight, and family allowances with a negative weight. Weighting pattern based on March 1959 to 1968, on 1964-65 from 1969.

NOTES

1. Avant 1967, y compris les dépôts entre banques.
2. Coût de la vie à Reykjavik. Avant 1968, y compris les impôts directs. Avant 1981, les contributions aux assurances sociales et fonds de pension sont comprises avec une pondération positive, et les allocations familiales avec une pondération négative. La pondération se réfère à mars 1959 jusqu'en 1968, et à 1964-65 à partir de 1969.

MAIN SOURCES

PRINCIPALES SOURCES

Series	Séries	Sources
Sea fisheries	Pêche maritime	Statistical Bureau of Iceland and Central Bank of Iceland *Statistical Bulletin*
Consumer prices	Prix à la consommation	
Net foreign position of commercial banks	Position extérieure nette des banques commerciales	
Foreign trade	Commerce extérieur...............	
Home finance	Finances internes	International Monetary Fund *International Financial Statistics*

Ireland — Irlande

IRELAND

Industrial production: (1)
mining and manufacturing
1980 = 100

Production industrielle : (1)
industries extractives et manufacturières
1980 = 100

	Year	Q.1	Q.2	Q.3	Q.4	JAN	FEB	MAR	APR	MAY	JUN	JUL	AUG	SEP	OCT	NOV	DEC
1964	44	41	45	44	46												
1965	46	43	47	45	47												
1966	48	44	47	49	50												
1967	52	49	54	51	54												
1968	58	52	60	59	61												
1969	62	54	66	63	64												
1970	64	59	66	65	68												
1971	67	62	70	66	70												
1972	70	63	71	70	75												
1973	77	72	80	77	79												
1974	78	76	82	77	78												
1975	75	70	76	73	78							75	68	76	76	83	74
1976	82	75	84	83	85	73	73	77	79	87	87	83	78	89	90	88	78
1977	88	81	92	87	94	75	83	85	87	92	98	88	79	94	97	95	89
1978	95	89	100	93	99	85	88	94	96	97	107	99	79	102	101	102	93
1979	102	95	108	100	104	88	96	103	105	107	111	101	89	111	108	109	94
1980	100	99	109	95	97	94	101	103	106	110	110	97	87	100	100	101	90
1981	101	97	108	100	101	91	100	99	105	108	111	104	88	107	101	107	97
1982	102	99	109	98	103	88	103	106	107	109	111	102	85	105	107	107	94
1983	109	106	112	105	113	101	108	109	108	110	117	112	91	112	111	114	113

Industrial production: (1)
manufacturing
1980 = 100

Production industrielle : (1)
industries manufacturières
1980 = 100

	Year	Q.1	Q.2	Q.3	Q.4	JAN	FEB	MAR	APR	MAY	JUN	JUL	AUG	SEP	OCT	NOV	DEC
1964	45	43	46	44	47												
1965	47	45	47	45	49												
1966	48	46	47	48	52												
1967	52	49	53	50	55												
1968	57	53	58	57	61												
1969	61	54	64	61	65												
1970	63	59	64	64	68												
1971	66	61	67	65	70												
1972	69	63	70	68	75												
1973	77	73	80	76	80												
1974	78	77	81	76	78												
1975	75	71	74	71	79							72	65	76	78	85	75
1976	82	76	85	82	85	74	75	78	80	87	88	83	74	88	91	90	79
1977	89	82	93	86	94	76	84	86	88	93	96	86	77	94	97	97	89
1978	96	89	99	93	101	86	89	94	97	97	104	97	79	102	103	104	95
1979	102	96	108	99	105	90	96	103	106	108	111	98	88	111	109	109	95
1980	100	100	108	94	98	96	102	104	106	108	109	96	86	100	101	102	91
1981	102	98	109	99	104	92	101	100	106	109	112	104	86	107	103	109	99
1982	103	102	109	96	105	92	106	108	108	110	110	100	82	107	109	110	96
1983	110	108	114	104	115	103	110	111	110	113	119	110	89	114	113	117	116

Production: future tendency
manufacturing
per cent balance

Perspectives de production
industries manufacturières
solde en pourcentage

	Year	Q.1	Q.2	Q.3	Q.4	JAN	FEB	MAR	APR	MAY	JUN	JUL	AUG	SEP	OCT	NOV	DEC
1964																	
1965																	
1966																	
1967																	
1968																	
1969				61	46												
1970		50	44	45	45												
1971		41	48	57	37												
1972		35	27	67	61												
1973		77	83	82	87												
1974		60	78					48	40	25	22	22	10	3	-15	-17	-25
1975						-11	2	10	-4	-6	9	12	15	7	-4	-13	-6
1976						16	12	28	20	12	14	16	31	31	20	4	22
1977						31	35	36	33	21	19	32	37	27	19	9	24
1978						35	38	40	34	26	27	32	13	26	23	12	16
1979						26	..	..	..	..	..	26	33	13	21	-2	2
									S								
1980						7	-7	8	-5	-28	-27	-35	-11	-21	-23	-27	-25
1981						-10	13	-5	-	-5	-20	-6	-1	1	-10	-	-13
1982						8	4	11	3	-16	-4	-8	-17	-3	12	-12	10
1983						-2	-5	4	13	2	-1	4	25	12	-1	2	21

Industrial production: (1)(2)
mining and manufacturing
1980 = 100

Production industrielle : (1)(2)
industries extractives et manufacturières
1980 = 100

Adjusted - Corrigé

	Year	Q.1	Q.2	Q.3	Q.4	JAN	FEB	MAR	APR	MAY	JUN	JUL	AUG	SEP	OCT	NOV	DEC
1964		43	43	44	45												
1965		45	45	45	46												
1966		47	45	50	49												
1967		51	52	52	53												
1968		56	57	58	59												
1969		58	63	63	63												
1970		63	64	65	66												
1971		66	67	66	68												
1972		67	68	71	73												
1973		77	77	77	78												
1974		80	79	78	77												
1975		73	73	75	76							75	75	73	73	79	78
1976		78	80	85	84	80	78	78	79	82	78	83	87	85	86	85	83
1977		85	87	89	93	83	87	85	86	87	88	88	89	90	92	92	95
1978		93	94	95	98	94	92	94	94	92	96	99	89	98	97	98	100
1979		100	101	103	103	97	99	102	102	101	100	102	102	106	104	105	101
1980		104	102	97	97	105	104	103	102	103	100	97	100	95	97	98	97
1981		100	101	103	102	100	103	98	101	101	101	104	102	102	98	103	104
1982		101	102	101	103	97	102	104	103	102	102	103	100	102	104	103	103
1983		108	105	109	113	111	107	107	104	104	107	112	108	109	108	110	123

Industrial production: (1)(2)
manufacturing
1980 = 100

Production industrielle : (1)(2)
industries manufacturières
1980 = 100

Adjusted - Corrigé

	Year	Q.1	Q.2	Q.3	Q.4	JAN	FEB	MAR	APR	MAY	JUN	JUL	AUG	SEP	OCT	NOV	DEC
1964		44	45	45	45												
1965		46	46	46	47												
1966		47	46	49	50												
1967		51	52	52	53												
1968		55	57	58	59												
1969		57	63	62	62												
1970		62	62	66	65												
1971		65	66	66	67												
1972		66	68	69	72												
1973		76	77	78	77												
1974		81	79	78	76												
1975		73	71	74	77							74	75	73	74	79	79
1976		79	81	85	85	81	78	78	79	82	81	85	85	85	86	85	83
1977		85	88	89	93	83	87	85	87	88	88	88	89	90	92	92	94
1978		93	94	96	99	94	92	94	94	91	96	100	92	93	97	99	101
1979		100	102	103	103	98	99	102	102	101	102	101	103	106	104	104	101
1980		104	101	98	97	105	104	103	102	101	100	98	102	95	97	97	97
1981		101	102	104	103	100	103	99	101	102	103	106	103	103	99	104	106
1982		103	103	102	104	99	104	105	104	103	102	101	101	103	105	105	104
1983		109	107	111	115	112	109	108	106	107	109	112	110	111	109	111	125

Orders inflow: tendency
manufacturing
per cent balance

Commandes : tendance
industries manufacturières
solde en pourcentage

	Year	Q.1	Q.2	Q.3	Q.4	JAN	FEB	MAR	APR	MAY	JUN	JUL	AUG	SEP	OCT	NOV	DEC
1964																	
1965																	
1966																	
1967																	
1968																	
1969																	
1970																	
1971																	
1972																	
1973																	
1974																	
1975																	
1976																	
1977																	
1978									S	10	16	9	4	24	15	2	4
1979						4	..	..	..	..	..	2	5	-8	-	-2	-20
1980						-10	-20	-24	-24	-33	-45	-44	-45	-37	-27	-25	-27
1981						-11	-4	-16	-4	-22	-11	-16	-17	4	-24	-13	-20
1982						-18	-23	-13	-15	-23	-43	-34	-36	-35	-31	-42	-31
1983						-33	-37	-21	-50	-33	-14	-34	-23	-21	-15	-18	-13

IRELAND

Order books: level
manufacturing
per cent balance

Carnet de commandes : niveau
industries manufacturières
solde en pourcentage

	Year	Q.1	Q.2	Q.3	Q.4	JAN	FEB	MAR	APR	MAY	JUN	JUL	AUG	SEP	OCT	NOV	DEC
1964																	
1965																	
1966																	
1967																	
1968																	
1969																	
1970																	
1971																	
1972																	
1973																	
1974								25	16	2	-4	-13	-21	-25	-31	-32	-38
1975						-46	-46	-62	-58	-66	-50	-47	-39	-37	-33	-32	-24
1976						-38	-29	-26	-25	-28	-14	-19	-8	-13	-4	-1	-7
1977						-8	-17	-13	-18	-22	-5	-6	-4	3	-	-7	-6
1978						8	-6	3	-4	5	12	-2	3	9	4	-2	-11
1979						4	..	..	..	..	..	5	-	-11	-11	-2	-10
									S								
1980						-8	-23	-33	-37	-48	-55	-51	-54	-49	-51	-43	-42
1981						-22	-24	-46	-29	-33	-27	-25	-28	-15	-25	-29	-25
1982						-25	-20	-16	-20	-31	-37	-41	-46	-55	-37	-57	-51
1983						-34	-50	-44	-53	-47	-46	-50	-43	-39	-37	-22	-19

Finished goods stocks: level
manufacturing
per cent balance

Stocks de produits finis : niveau
industries manufacturières
solde en pourcentage

	Year	Q.1	Q.2	Q.3	Q.4	JAN	FEB	MAR	APR	MAY	JUN	JUL	AUG	SEP	OCT	NOV	DEC
1964																	
1965																	
1966																	
1967		1	8	4	2												
1968		-3	-15	-21	-14												
1969		-8	1	-5	-2												
1970		2	6	-6	-3												
1971		9	6	9	8												
1972		-5	-9	-17	-10												
1973		-11	-18	-25	-13												
1974								-21	-16	-11	1	-1	-1	13	8	24	17
1975						20	12	29	21	22	21	15	7	16	3	5	8
1976						-1	4	10	11	8	9	13	4	-2	2	-4	-2
1977						2	1	1	14	8	4	4	3	-2	-6	-2	-1
1978						-1	4	-6	3	6	1	-5	-	-1	-4	-12	-10
1979						-4	..	..	..	..	..	-3	-10	-6	-12	6	8
									S								
1980						12	9	17	19	20	25	34	32	21	26	22	17
1981						10	17	13	10	9	9	6	1	4	4	10	6
1982						4	5	10	6	8	13	14	16	14	13	13	6
1983						10	16	11	22	18	17	7	11	12	9	4	-6

Rate of capacity utilization
manufacturing
per cent

Taux d'utilisation des capacités
industries manufacturières
pourcentage

	Year	Q.1	Q.2	Q.3	Q.4	JAN	FEB	MAR	APR	MAY	JUN	JUL	AUG	SEP	OCT	NOV	DEC
1964																	
1965																	
1966																	
1967																	
1968																	
1969																	
1970																	
1971																	
1972																	
1973																	
1974																	
1975																	
1976																	
1977																	
1978									S	62.7	67.6	60.8	61.0	69.1	68.2	68.5	65.4
1979						66.0	..	..	..	..	..	71.5	67.3	64.1	62.5	65.3	63.2
1980						67.4	55.9	64.5	64.4	65.8	60.3	60.3	60.0	59.2	58.9	56.5	55.0
1981						63.4	60.8	53.7	61.5	61.8	61.4	59.0	56.7	61.1	60.9	59.9	59.6
1982						58.3	59.9	58.0	63.1	58.8	58.6	59.6	58.7	56.7	56.2	56.8	53.6
1983						58.0	57.9	60.3	59.4	57.9	57.9	59.2	56.9	57.6	56.7	57.7	57.1

Firms operating at full capacity — Entreprises travaillant à pleine capacité

manufacturing — industries manufacturières

per cent — pourcentage

	Year	Q.1	Q.2	Q.3	Q.4	JAN	FEB	MAR	APR	MAY	JUN	JUL	AUG	SEP	OCT	NOV	DEC
1964																	
1965																	
1966																	
1967		19	19	31	26												
1968		24	34	50	51												
1969		51	48	56	47												
1970		37	30	37	35												
1971		31	35	38	20												
1972		24	31	38	39												
1973		35	43	53	58												
1974		62						33	37	34	34	33	33	26	25	28	27
1975						25	25	30	35	37	30	27	34	35	30	35	30
1976						34	26	31	29	26	31	31	29	29	34	28	24
1977						20	26	30	27	28	28	22	25	17	21	19	21
1978						23	24	18	21	25	25	21	29	26	36	30	33
1979						31	..	..	..	..	..	24	28	32	20	32	24
									S								
1980						26	26	22	28	30	29	33	37	33	35	33	27
1981						30	34	35	29	28	36	32	33	30	20	29	35
1982						24	33	32	34	31	32	22	37	36	31	35	30
1983						25	28	30	33	35	33	32	31	27	29	29	27

Construction, dwellings completed (3) — Construction, logements achevés (3)

thousands, monthly averages — milliers, moyennes mensuelles

	Year	Q.1	Q.2	Q.3	Q.4	JAN	FEB	MAR	APR	MAY	JUN	JUL	AUG	SEP	OCT	NOV	DEC
1964	0.67	0.66	0.72	0.58	0.73	0.75	0.69	0.56	0.73	0.59	0.83	0.72	0.55	0.48	0.61	0.85	0.72
1965	0.98	1.00	1.05	0.91	0.98	0.79	1.00	1.20	1.13	0.92	1.09	1.17	0.69	0.87	0.89	0.89	1.16
1966	0.85	0.81	0.91	0.77	0.90	0.88	0.71	0.85	1.13	0.87	0.74	0.91	0.58	0.81	0.98	1.00	0.73
1967	1.03	1.07	1.00	0.95	1.08	0.99	0.95	1.29	1.04	0.95	1.02	0.87	0.96	1.03	1.15	1.22	0.88
1968	0.99	0.97	0.92	0.98	1.10	0.89	1.07	0.94	0.88	0.98	0.89	1.18	0.73	1.03	1.25	1.16	0.88
1969	1.17	1.35	0.94	1.04	1.33	1.07	1.04	1.95	0.83	0.99	1.00	1.18	0.89	1.04	1.28	1.42	1.31
1970	1.13	1.24	1.12	1.09	1.08	1.03	1.06	1.63	1.05	1.27	1.03	1.30	0.83	1.14	1.05	0.91	1.29
1971	1.25	1.27	1.11	1.21	1.41	0.82	1.33	1.67	0.70	1.60	1.04	1.39	1.02	1.21	1.05	1.37	1.80
1972	1.74	1.58	1.86	1.52	1.98	1.59	0.96	2.20	1.30	2.65	1.64	1.70	1.08	1.79	2.34	2.48	1.10
1973	2.06	1.93	1.59	2.62	2.09	1.59	2.07	2.12	1.10	2.00	1.68	3.59	1.97	2.30	2.08	2.64	1.54
1974	2.19	2.45	1.62	2.21	2.48	1.83	1.93	3.58	1.58	1.52	1.74	2.86	1.58	2.19	2.44	2.68	2.33
1975	2.24	2.79	1.74	2.12	2.31	2.44	2.48	3.45	1.54	1.92	1.76	2.05	2.20	2.11	2.48	2.26	2.19
1976	2.00	2.15	1.99	1.69	2.18	1.94	1.43	3.07	1.78	1.82	2.37	2.05	1.60	1.43	1.77	2.01	2.75
1977	2.05	1.89	1.58	2.63	2.08	2.04	2.47	1.17	1.82	2.10	0.82	3.08	2.44	2.37	2.05	2.52	1.67
1978	2.12	2.23	2.06	2.08	2.12	3.41	1.83	1.44	2.03	2.14	2.00	1.15	3.53	1.55	3.12	2.03	1.22
1979	2.21	2.67	1.96	1.89	2.33	4.37	1.98	1.67	1.85	2.03	2.00	2.00	1.33	2.34	2.01	4.11	0.87
1980	2.32	2.82	2.40	2.04	2.01	4.23	2.15	2.06	2.39	2.47	2.32	2.22	2.58	1.34	3.10	1.60	1.32
1981	2.41	2.44	1.99	2.39	2.82	2.91	3.64	0.78	1.73	1.92	2.31	2.21	2.53	2.42	2.46	4.00	2.01
1982	2.23	2.36	2.15	2.23	2.19	2.10	2.93	2.03	1.99	2.32	2.14	2.45	2.12	2.13	2.26	2.34	1.99
1983	2.18	2.05	2.34	2.10	2.22	2.66	1.69	1.81	1.70	2.89	2.42	1.86	2.12	2.32	1.98	2.30	2.39

Retail sales: value (4) — Ventes au détail : valeur (4)

Adjusted - Corrigé

1980 = 100

	Year	Q.1	Q.2	Q.3	Q.4	JAN	FEB	MAR	APR	MAY	JUN	JUL	AUG	SEP	OCT	NOV	DEC
1964																	
1965																	
1966																	
1967																	
1968	19	18	18	19	19	17	18	18	18	18	19	19	20	19	19	19	20
1969	21	19	21	21	21	19	19	19	20	22	21	21	21	21	21	21	21
1970	23	22	22	23	24	22	22	22	23	21	22	22	22	23	24	23	24
1971	25	24	25	25	26	24	24	24	25	24	25	25	25	25	25	26	27
1972	28	27	27	28	30	26	27	28	26	27	28	28	28	29	31	29	30
1973	33	31	33	34	34	31	31	32	31	33	34	32	36	33	34	35	35
1974	38	35	37	38	39	35	36	36	37	36	37	38	39	39	39	39	39
1975	44	41	42	45	48	40	40	41	41	43	43	44	44	46	47	47	49
1976	53	50	52	52	57	50	51	48	51	51	53	49	51	56	56	58	58
1977	63	58	61	65	68	57	59	59	60	62	62	63	65	66	66	68	69
1978	75	69	75	78	79	70	66	71	71	77	76	76	78	78	79	80	78
1979	87	82	86	89	92	80	83	84	85	87	87	88	89	90	92	91	92
1980	=100=	96	98	99	106	96	96	95	98	98	98	99	98	100	103	106	109
1981	118	111	115	123	122	110	109	113	114	115	117	121	135	112	120	121	126
1982	129	125	127	128	135	121	126	128	132	123	126	122	129	132	134	134	137
1983	137	137	132	135	144	135	152	124	126	134	135	130	134	141	143	143	146

IRELAND

Retail sales: volume (4) / Ventes au détail : volume (4)

at 1975 prices / *aux prix de 1975*

1980 = 100

Adjusted - Corrigé

	Year	Q.1	Q.2	Q.3	Q.4	JAN	FEB	MAR	APR	MAY	JUN	JUL	AUG	SEP	OCT	NOV	DEC
1964																	
1965																	
1966																	
1967																	
1968	77	74	76	79	77	73	74	74	75	76	78	78	84	76	76	78	79
1969	79	75	81	81	80	77	73	76	78	85	80	80	81	80	80	80	79
1970	81	81	80	80	82	81	81	82	85	77	77	79	79	82	83	81	83
1971	82	82	82	82	83	83	81	81	83	81	82	83	81	82	82	82	84
1972	86	84	85	86	88	82	84	87	83	85	86	85	85	87	92	84	86
1973	90	90	92	91	88	90	90	91	90	93	95	88	96	87	88	89	88
1974	86	88	87	87	84	87	89	87	90	86	86	87	88	86	86	84	82
1975	84	81	81	84	86	82	80	81	81	82	82	83	83	85	86	86	87
1976	86	86	85	83	88	88	88	82	86	84	86	80	82	88	87	88	88
1977	90	87	89	91	92	86	87	88	88	90	89	89	91	92	91	92	94
1978	98	93	99	100	99	94	90	96	95	103	100	99	101	99	99	100	97
1979	101	99	102	101	101	98	101	100	101	103	101	102	101	101	102	101	100
1980	=100=	102	100	97	101	103	103	100	101	99	98	98	96	97	99	101	101
1981	99	100	100	102	96	101	98	101	100	100	100	102	112	91	95	95	97
1982	94	96	94	92	94	94	97	96	99	91	92	88	92	94	95	94	94
1983	90	93	88	88	92	93	103	83	85	89	90	85	88	91	92	92	92

New passenger car registrations / Immatriculations de voitures de tourisme neuves

thousands, monthly averages / milliers, moyennes mensuelles

	Year	Q.1	Q.2	Q.3	Q.4	JAN	FEB	MAR	APR	MAY	JUN	JUL	AUG	SEP	OCT	NOV	DEC
1964	3.45	3.36	4.29	3.41	2.73	4.45	2.39	3.23	4.63	4.08	4.17	4.98	2.47	2.78	3.48	2.83	1.87
1965	3.61	4.26	4.65	3.54	1.97	5.78	3.30	3.72	5.38	4.34	4.22	5.39	2.50	2.73	2.78	1.98	1.15
1966	3.30	4.15	3.29	3.78	1.97	4.78	2.43	5.26	2.77	3.53	3.56	4.25	3.04	4.04	3.05	1.68	1.17
1967	3.36	3.58	4.25	3.14	2.46	4.30	2.82	3.62	4.56	4.26	3.93	4.01	2.89	2.53	3.28	2.61	1.50
1968	4.28	4.43	5.02	3.99	3.67	5.33	3.75	4.22	5.63	5.13	4.31	5.43	3.19	3.37	4.30	3.68	3.03
1969	4.21	4.40	5.49	3.74	3.21	6.85	2.98	3.38	5.26	5.61	5.60	4.93	3.07	3.22	4.16	3.41	2.05
1970	4.41	4.64	5.67	4.00	3.34	5.22	3.93	4.76	6.82	5.64	4.55	5.01	3.49	3.51	4.82	3.35	1.86
1971	4.32	4.67	5.12	4.25	3.23	5.49	3.98	4.55	5.64	5.20	4.52	5.23	3.78	3.73	3.95	3.53	2.21
1972	5.22	5.41	6.13	5.36	3.97	6.55	4.31	5.37	5.80	6.26	6.32	6.50	4.95	4.62	5.69	4.25	1.97
1973	6.23	6.64	7.45	7.31	3.37	7.47	5.97	6.47	6.85	9.83	5.67	8.06	7.55	6.32	4.92	3.37	1.81
1974	5.09	4.72	6.41	5.81	3.40	4.90	4.15	5.11	6.57	6.78	5.87	6.69	5.65	5.09	5.13	3.44	1.63
1975	4.42	4.81	5.43	4.24	3.22	6.35	4.05	4.03	5.03	5.20	6.05	4.90	3.65	4.16	4.49	3.43	1.74
1976	5.79	7.44	6.42	5.14	4.18	8.93	10.27	3.11	6.10	6.28	6.87	5.76	4.87	4.78	5.74	4.77	2.04
1977	6.86	7.78	7.60	7.12	4.94	9.04	7.27	7.04	7.74	8.32	6.74	6.26	7.34	7.75	6.80	5.72	2.30
1978	8.80	10.02	10.55	9.07	5.18	12.60	8.36	9.11	9.18	11.20	11.26	10.38	8.53	8.29	7.73	5.73	2.08
1979	7.99	10.52	9.45	7.89	4.12	12.17	10.02	9.36	8.37	11.16	8.82	9.13	8.13	6.41	5.79	4.83	1.73
1980	7.64	11.56	7.91	6.89	4.22	12.81	12.20	9.68	7.96	8.63	7.14	8.11	6.13	6.44	6.16	4.50	1.99
1981	8.67	11.89	9.77	10.78	2.39	13.34	13.01	9.33	10.35	10.11	8.85	10.20	16.29	5.87	3.19	2.75	1.22
1982	6.11	9.35	7.07	4.67	3.33	9.71	8.74	9.59	9.62	6.61	5.00	4.85	4.38	4.79	6.00	2.95	1.04
1983	5.08	9.85	4.05	3.98	2.29	8.76	12.28	8.50	2.99	4.60	4.57	4.83	3.76	3.33	3.19	2.58	1.09

Unemployment (registered unemployed) (5)(6) / Chômage (chômeurs inscrits) (5)(6)

thousands / milliers

	Year	Q.1	Q.2	Q.3	Q.4	JAN	FEB	MAR	APR	MAY	JUN	JUL	AUG	SEP	OCT	NOV	DEC
1964	48.3	59.9	46.9	38.0	48.2	61.6	60.8	57.3	53.7	47.2	39.9	37.1	37.5	39.5	42.3	51.5	50.7
1965	49.7	59.0	46.4	40.1	53.2	61.1	58.7	57.2	52.1	46.7	40.4	41.5	41.2	37.5	42.5	53.4	63.7
1966	48.1	56.7	47.6	37.0	51.2	59.2	56.6	54.4	52.3	49.0	41.4	38.0	36.7	36.3	41.6	50.8	61.3
1967	50.0	57.8	47.6	42.9	51.7	58.7	57.9	56.9	51.4	47.7	43.8	42.4	43.7	42.5	47.3	50.5	57.4
1968	53.1	62.4	51.9	46.2	51.7	61.3	60.6	65.3	56.7	51.1	48.0	46.3	46.6	45.6	48.5	51.9	54.8
1969	51.3	60.0	48.9	44.4	52.1	60.2	63.2	56.5	53.1	48.1	45.5	44.3	44.7	44.2	47.9	51.0	57.3
1970	58.8	62.3	62.2	53.5	57.1	59.6	62.4	65.0	64.0	61.6	60.9	55.2	53.6	51.7	53.4	55.8	62.2
1971	57.3	64.3	52.0	50.0	62.7	64.8	64.4	63.6	54.4	51.9	49.8	49.9	50.3	49.7	54.7	62.4	71.1
1972	66.6	72.4	66.0	62.1	65.7	73.3	72.4	71.5	69.3	65.5	63.3	62.0	63.2	61.1	62.6	65.0	69.6
1973	62.0	69.2	60.7	57.4	60.9	70.5	70.5	66.5	64.2	60.5	57.5	57.5	58.3	56.4	58.1	59.9	64.6
1974	67.2	67.3	62.9	64.4	74.1	68.2	68.1	65.5	64.3	63.0	61.3	62.5	64.5	66.1	67.8	73.5	81.1
1975	96.2	90.9	93.6	96.4	103.8	89.7	91.2	91.8	93.0	93.8	93.9	94.8	97.5	97.0	99.6	102.4	109.3
1976	107.8	110.9	107.0	105.9	107.5	110.5	111.5	110.7	109.6	107.0	104.5	106.5	107.1	104.0	104.3	106.5	111.6
1977	106.4	112.3	106.0	103.0	104.3	113.3	112.5	111.2	108.7	105.8	103.5	103.8	104.4	100.7	101.6	103.2	108.2
1978	99.2	108.7	99.2	93.7	95.3	109.4	108.8	107.9	103.2	99.3	95.1	95.2	95.9	90.1	92.2	95.4	98.4
1979	89.6	97.7	89.8	85.6	85.4	100.2	93.2	94.7	92.5	89.6	87.4	87.2	87.1	82.6	82.9	84.7	88.6
1980	101.5	92.0	94.0	103.9	116.0	92.1	92.4	92.6	92.0	93.5	96.5	100.8	105.2	105.6	110.9	115.0	122.2
1981	127.9	125.8	124.3	126.8	134.5	125.1	126.3	126.0	126.0	123.5	123.5	125.7	127.5	127.3	129.2	133.1	141.2
1982	156.6	146.8	149.0	159.0	171.6	146.6	145.7	143.0	148.4	147.7	150.9	156.1	160.8	160.2	165.0	169.9	179.9
1983	192.7	188.3	188.1	193.0	201.3	187.0	188.4	189.4	187.9	187.4	189.1	192.0	193.9	193.2	196.3	199.6	208.0

Employment: manufacturing (7)
(all employees)
thousands

Emploi : industries manufacturières (7)
(salariés)
milliers

	Year	Q.1	Q.2	Q.3	Q.4	JAN	FEB	MAR	APR	MAY	JUN	JUL	AUG	SEP	OCT	NOV	DEC
1964	171.9	169.4	170.9	173.4	173.9			169.4			170.9			173.4			173.9
1965	173.7	172.7	173.1	174.3	174.8			172.7			173.1			174.3			174.8
1966	175.3	173.4	172.4	177.1	178.1			173.4			172.4			177.1			178.1
1967	177.3	175.9	176.2	177.9	178.9			175.9			176.2			177.9			178.9
1968	183.9	179.2	182.3	185.6	188.6			179.2			182.3			185.6			188.6
1969	194.5	190.1	193.3	196.4	198.2			190.1			193.3			196.4			198.2
1970	197.2	194.6	196.3	199.3	198.8			194.6			196.3			199.3			198.8
1971	196.4	196.6	196.6	196.7	195.8			196.6			196.6			196.7			195.8
1972	197.3	194.1	196.9	198.7	199.7			194.1			196.9			198.7			199.7
1973	203.4	212.6	216.2	217.6	220.4			212.6			216.2			217.6			220.4
1974	205.2	220.8	221.8	220.2	218.6			220.8			221.8			220.2			218.6
1975	190.9	211.9	206.9	204.4	205.0			211.9			206.9			204.4			205.0
1976	190.6	202.3	205.0	207.2	210.0			202.3			205.0			207.2			210.0
1977	202.8	210.3	211.7	214.0	214.3			210.3			211.7			214.0			214.3
1978	206.8	213.8	215.8	217.6	220.2			213.8			215.8			217.6			220.2
1979	225.1	221.5	225.4	228.0	230.6			221.5			225.4			228.0			230.6
1980	224.5	227.4	225.7	223.4	221.4			227.4			225.7			223.4			221.4
1981	217.0	217.6	216.2	217.2	216.8			217.6			216.2			217.2			216.8
1982	209.5	213.1	210.5	209.0	205.2			213.1			210.5			209.0			205.2
1983		198.3	195.8	196.4				198.3			195.8			196.4			

Unemployment (insured unemployed) (6)(8)
thousands

Chômage (chômeurs assurés) (6)(8)
milliers

	Year	Q.1	Q.2	Q.3	Q.4	JAN	FEB	MAR	APR	MAY	JUN	JUL	AUG	SEP	OCT	NOV	DEC
1964	28.6	33.4	28.4	24.1	28.5	33.6	33.4	33.3	31.3	28.9	24.9	23.4	24.4	24.6	28.3	29.1	28.0
1965	28.6	33.3	28.1	24.3	28.6	33.8	33.9	32.1	32.0	27.8	24.4	24.1	25.5	23.2	25.8	29.1	31.0
1966	31.8	36.0	32.7	27.1	31.6	36.3	36.0	35.7	34.5	33.6	29.9	27.8	28.1	25.5	28.1	32.3	34.3
1967	36.2	41.3	35.4	32.5	35.7	41.7	41.0	41.1	38.2	35.7	32.3	32.0	34.3	31.2	32.9	36.8	37.5
1968	37.3	42.4	37.4	33.5	35.8	42.4	42.9	42.0	41.5	37.2	33.6	33.3	35.0	32.1	34.4	36.3	36.6
1969	36.1	42.1	34.8	31.9	35.7	40.4	43.8	42.0	37.7	34.7	32.0	31.9	33.4	30.5	33.9	36.0	37.2
1970	41.6	42.4	45.1	39.6	39.2	40.8	41.9	44.4	46.0	45.7	43.5	41.2	40.1	37.6	38.6	39.1	39.9
1971	42.4	45.0	40.6	38.8	45.1	44.8	45.0	45.2	43.4	40.4	37.9	38.0	39.9	38.6	42.0	45.3	48.1
1972	48.2	52.4	48.3	45.5	46.6	52.8	53.0	51.5	50.7	48.3	46.0	45.8	46.5	44.2	45.3	46.9	47.6
1973	44.0	49.7	43.6	41.0	41.6	50.6	50.2	48.4	46.2	43.4	41.2	40.8	42.2	40.1	40.2	42.0	42.7
1974	48.1	47.9	44.8	45.3	54.5	48.5	48.4	46.7	46.4	44.4	43.6	43.1	46.0	46.8	49.7	54.8	59.1
1975	75.4	73.5	74.4	74.9	78.8	70.7	74.9	74.8	74.5	74.3	74.4	74.0	75.4	75.3	76.8	79.1	80.6
1976	83.6	87.0	84.1	81.5	81.5	87.0	88.1	86.0	86.5	84.8	81.0	81.6	83.1	79.9	80.1	81.5	83.0
1977	81.9	86.8	83.1	79.6	77.9	86.9	87.1	86.5	84.9	83.6	80.9	80.1	80.9	77.7	76.7	78.9	78.2
1978	74.7	82.3	76.2	71.1	69.3	83.1	82.7	81.2	79.5	76.8	72.2	71.3	72.9	69.0	68.3	70.0	69.7
1979	66.4	72.7	66.0	64.1	62.7	74.7	72.6	70.8	68.6	65.9	63.4	64.8	65.2	62.4	61.0	62.6	64.4
1980	73.7	66.0	68.3	75.4	85.0	66.3	65.7	66.1	67.5	67.6	69.7	72.3	76.3	77.7	80.8	86.2	88.0
1981	96.1	95.1	94.5	95.7	99.2	93.6	95.7	96.0	95.8	94.6	93.0	95.8	96.0	95.2	96.2	99.2	102.1
1982	117.8	111.0	113.0	119.4	127.8	109.0	112.0	111.9	114.8	112.3	112.0	116.7	120.2	121.4	122.0	127.8	133.5
1983	148.7	146.3	147.9	147.5	152.9	144.4	146.3	148.2	149.5	147.7	146.6	147.2	147.3	148.0	149.6	153.0	156.1

Unemployment (registered unemployed) (5)(6)
thousands

Adjusted - Corrigé

Chômage (chômeurs inscrits) (5)(6)
milliers

	Year	Q.1	Q.2	Q.3	Q.4	JAN	FEB	MAR	APR	MAY	JUN	JUL	AUG	SEP	OCT	NOV	DEC
1964																	
1965																	
1966																	
1967		50.3	48.4	49.3	52.0	50.5	50.5	49.9	48.2	48.9	48.2	48.5	49.7	49.7	51.4	51.8	52.9
1968		55.0	52.7	52.5	51.9	53.3	53.2	58.4	53.5	52.3	52.3	52.3	52.5	52.8	52.5	53.1	50.2
1969		52.8	49.6	50.5	52.3	52.4	56.2	49.9	50.0	49.2	49.6	50.0	50.3	51.2	51.9	52.2	52.7
1970		55.5	62.9	59.2	57.3	52.1	55.5	58.9	61.1	62.7	64.8	60.5	58.9	58.3	57.3	57.0	57.6
1971		57.8	52.8	55.3	62.9	57.5	57.8	58.2	51.8	53.0	53.6	54.8	55.0	56.1	58.5	63.5	66.6
1972		66.3	66.9	67.0	65.9	66.4	65.9	66.7	67.0	66.6	67.1	66.5	67.4	67.1	66.3	66.2	65.1
1973		63.4	61.6	61.8	61.1	63.7	64.2	62.3	62.2	61.5	61.2	61.6	61.9	62.0	61.8	61.2	60.2
1974		61.8	63.9	68.4	74.4	61.7	61.9	61.7	62.5	64.1	65.1	66.3	67.7	71.3	71.4	74.9	76.9
1975		85.6	94.6	100.2	104.2	83.4	85.3	88.2	91.3	94.8	97.6	98.3	100.2	102.1	103.4	103.9	105.3
1976		105.8	108.0	109.5	108.0	104.4	105.8	107.1	108.0	108.0	108.1	109.7	109.5	109.2	108.2	108.1	107.7
1977		107.4	107.0	106.3	105.0	107.4	107.0	107.7	107.1	106.8	107.0	106.6	106.5	105.8	105.6	104.9	104.6
1978		104.2	100.3	96.7	95.7	103.7	103.9	105.0	101.9	100.6	98.3	97.6	97.5	94.9	95.8	96.5	94.7
1979		93.3	91.1	88.5	85.6	94.5	93.4	91.9	91.5	91.2	90.5	89.6	88.6	87.2	86.3	85.7	84.9
1980		87.5	95.5	106.5	116.3	86.0	87.6	89.0	91.4	95.5	99.7	103.0	106.5	110.1	114.3	116.1	118.4
1981		121.0	126.0	129.6	134.9	118.5	121.4	123.1	125.5	125.8	126.6	127.9	129.0	132.0	132.8	134.7	137.2
1982		141.9	150.7	161.8	172.0	139.7	140.9	145.0	147.9	150.2	154.0	158.3	162.3	164.8	168.6	171.7	175.8
1983		183.3	189.9	195.9	201.7	179.9	183.6	186.3	187.4	190.0	192.3	194.3	195.5	197.8	199.9	201.4	203.9

IRELAND

Unemployment (insured unemployed) (8)
as per cent of insured labour force

Chômage (chômeurs assurés) (8)
en pourcentage de la main-d'œuvre assurée

	Year	Q.1	Q.2	Q.3	Q.4	JAN	FEB	MAR	APR	MAY	JUN	JUL	AUG	SEP	OCT	NOV	DEC
1964	5.7	6.7	5.7	4.8	5.7	6.8	6.7	6.7	6.3	5.8	5.0	4.7	4.9	4.9	5.6	5.8	5.6
1965	5.6	6.6	5.5	4.7	5.6	6.7	6.7	6.3	6.3	5.5	4.8	4.7	5.0	4.5	5.0	5.7	6.0
1966	6.1	6.9	6.3	5.2	6.0	7.0	6.9	6.9	6.6	6.5	5.7	5.3	5.4	4.9	5.4	6.2	6.5
1967	6.7	7.7	6.5	6.0	6.6	7.8	7.6	7.6	7.1	6.6	5.9	5.9	6.3	5.7	6.0	6.8	6.9
1968	6.7	7.7	6.8	6.0	6.4	7.7	7.8	7.6	7.6	6.8	6.0	6.0	6.3	5.8	6.2	6.5	6.6
1969	6.4	7.5	6.2	5.6	6.2	7.2	7.8	7.5	6.7	6.2	5.6	5.6	5.9	5.4	6.0	6.3	6.4
1970	7.2	7.5	7.9	6.8	6.8	7.2	7.4	7.8	8.1	8.0	7.5	7.1	6.9	6.5	6.7	6.7	6.9
1971	7.2	7.6	6.9	6.5	7.6	7.6	7.6	7.7	7.4	6.9	6.4	6.4	6.7	6.5	7.1	7.6	8.1
1972	8.1	8.8	8.1	7.6	7.8	8.9	8.9	8.7	8.5	8.1	7.7	7.7	7.8	7.4	7.6	7.9	8.0
1973	7.2	8.1	7.1	6.6	6.7	8.3	8.2	7.9	7.5	7.1	6.7	6.6	6.8	6.5	6.5	6.8	6.9
1974	7.9	7.8	7.3	7.4	8.9	7.9	7.9	7.6	7.6	7.3	7.1	7.1	7.5	7.7	8.1	9.0	9.7
1975	12.2	12.0	12.1	12.1	12.8	11.5	12.2	12.2	12.1	12.1	12.1	12.0	12.2	12.2	12.4	12.8	13.1
1976	12.3	12.9	12.4	12.0	12.0	12.9	13.0	12.7	12.8	12.5	11.9	12.0	12.2	11.7	11.8	12.0	12.2
1977	11.9	12.8	12.0	11.5	11.2	12.8	12.8	12.7	12.3	12.1	11.7	11.6	11.7	11.2	11.0	11.3	11.2
1978	10.7	11.8	10.9	10.1	9.9	11.9	11.8	11.6	11.4	11.0	10.3	10.1	10.4	9.8	9.7	10.0	9.9
1979	9.3	10.2	9.3	9.0	8.8	10.5	10.2	9.9	9.6	9.3	8.9	9.1	9.2	8.8	8.6	8.8	9.0
1980	10.3	9.3	9.6	10.6	11.9	9.3	9.2	9.3	9.5	9.5	9.8	10.1	10.7	10.9	11.3	12.1	12.4
1981	13.5	13.3	13.2	13.4	13.9	13.1	13.4	13.5	13.4	13.3	13.0	13.4	13.5	13.4	13.5	13.9	14.3
1982	16.5	15.6	15.9	16.8	17.9	15.3	15.7	15.7	16.1	15.8	15.7	16.4	16.9	17.0	17.1	17.9	18.7
1983	20.9	20.5	20.8	20.7	21.5	20.3	20.5	20.8	21.0	20.7	20.6	20.6	20.7	20.8	21.0	21.5	21.9

Weekly hours of work: (7)
manufacturing
hours

Durée hebdomadaire du travail : (7)
industries manufacturières
heures

	Year	Q.1	Q.2	Q.3	Q.4	JAN	FEB	MAR	APR	MAY	JUN	JUL	AUG	SEP	OCT	NOV	DEC
1964	44.1	44.0	44.4	44.1	44.2			44.0			44.4			44.1			44.2
1965	43.7	43.0	43.9	43.9	44.1			43.0			43.9			43.9			44.1
1966	43.7	43.2	43.6	44.0	44.0			43.2			43.6			44.0			44.0
1967	43.5	43.2	43.3	43.6	43.8			43.2			43.3			43.6			43.8
1968	43.5	43.0	43.4	43.7	43.9			43.0			43.4			43.7			43.9
1969	43.1	43.3	43.5	43.5	42.8			43.3			43.5			42.9			42.8
1970	42.5	42.2	42.3	42.7	42.6			42.2			42.3			42.7			42.6
1971	42.1	41.7	42.0	42.3	42.3			41.7			42.0			42.3			42.3
1972	42.3	41.9	42.3	42.3	42.5			41.9			42.3			42.3			42.5
1973	42.4	42.2	42.5	42.2	42.6			42.2			42.5			42.2			42.6
1974	41.5	41.6	41.8	41.5	41.0			41.6			41.8			41.5			41.0
1975	41.2	40.4	41.2	41.3	41.8			40.4			41.2			41.3			41.8
1976	41.8	40.8	41.7	42.1	42.6			40.8			41.7			42.1			42.6
1977	42.4	42.0	42.4	42.6	42.0			42.0			42.4			42.6			42.0
1978	42.5	42.3	42.6	42.3	42.7			42.3			42.6			42.3			42.7
1979	42.3	42.3	42.6	42.4	42.0			42.3			42.6			42.4			42.0
1980	41.3	41.2	41.6	41.1	41.3			41.2			41.6			41.1			41.3
1981	41.3	40.6	41.5	41.6	41.5			40.6			41.5			41.6			41.5
1982	40.6	40.6	40.8	40.5	40.5			40.6			40.8			40.5			40.5
1983		40.1	40.7					40.1			40.7						

Hourly earnings: manufacturing (7)
1980 = 100

Gains horaires : industries manufacturières (7)
1980 = 100

	Year	Q.1	Q.2	Q.3	Q.4	JAN	FEB	MAR	APR	MAY	JUN	JUL	AUG	SEP	OCT	NOV	DEC
1964	11	10	11	11	11			10			11			11			11
1965	11	11	11	11	11			11			11			11			11
1966	12	11	12	12	13			11			12			12			13
1967	13	13	13	13	13			13			13			13			13
1968	14	13	14	14	15			13			14			14			15
1969	16	15	16	16	17			15			16			16			17
1970	18	17	18	19	20			17			18			19			20
1971	21	20	21	22	22			20			21			22			22
1972	25	23	24	25	26			23			24			25			26
1973	29	27	29	30	31			27			29			30			31
1974	35	32	35	36	38			32			35			36			38
1975	45	41	44	47	49			41			44			47			49
1976	53	50	51	53	57			50			51			53			57
1977	63	59	62	63	66			59			62			63			66
1978	72	67	71	73	75			67			71			73			75
1979	83	77	79	86	89			77			79			86			89
1980	100	94	98	100	108			94			98			100			108
1981	116	110	116	119	122			110			116			119			122
1982	133	125	132	135	141			125			132			135			141
1983		142	145	150				142			145			150			

Wholesale prices: total (9) / Prix de gros : total (9)

1980 = 100

	Year	Q.1	Q.2	Q.3	Q.4	JAN	FEB	MAR	APR	MAY	JUN	JUL	AUG	SEP	OCT	NOV	DEC
1964																	
1965																	
1966																	
1967																	
1968	24.2	23.8	24.2	24.2	24.6	23.7	23.8	24.0	24.3	24.2	24.2	24.3	24.1	24.3	24.3	24.6	24.8
1969	26.0	25.4	26.0	26.1	26.3	25.2	25.4	25.7	25.9	26.1	26.1	26.0	26.0	26.2	26.2	26.2	26.4
1970	27.3	26.9	27.5	27.4	27.4	26.7	26.9	27.2	27.4	27.6	27.5	27.5	27.4	27.4	27.4	27.4	27.6
1971	28.8	28.3	28.9	28.9	29.2	27.9	28.3	28.7	28.9	28.9	28.9	28.8	28.8	29.0	29.0	29.1	29.4
1972	31.8	30.6	31.2	32.0	33.4	30.2	30.6	30.9	31.0	31.2	31.5	31.8	32.1	32.1	32.2	33.7	34.2
1973	37.4	35.8	37.5	38.0	38.2	35.7	35.6	36.0	36.9	37.7	38.0	38.1	38.1	38.0	38.0	38.2	38.5
1974	42.5	40.4	42.3	42.7	44.4	39.9	40.2	41.2	42.2	42.5	42.1	42.5	42.9	42.8	43.1	44.4	45.6
1975	52.9	50.0	52.7	53.4	55.4	48.3	49.8	51.9	52.7	52.8	52.5	53.2	53.1	53.8	54.6	55.4	56.2
1976	63.2	58.7	61.9	64.3	67.3	57.5	58.8	60.0	60.9	62.0	62.8	63.4	64.3	65.3	67.2	67.7	68.5
1977	74.1	71.6	74.1	75.0	75.4	70.4	71.6	72.9	73.6	74.2	74.6	75.0	74.9	75.1	75.3	75.3	75.7
1978	80.7	77.8	80.1	81.8	83.0	77.0	77.6	78.7	79.6	80.2	80.6	81.4	81.7	82.2	82.4	83.0	83.6
1979	90.5	87.6	90.4	91.8	92.1	85.8	88.0	89.1	89.4	90.6	91.2	91.5	91.8	92.1	92.1	91.9	92.3
1980	100.0	96.4	99.8	100.5	103.2	94.3	95.6	99.4	100.1	99.8	99.4	99.9	100.4	101.2	101.8	103.2	104.7
1981	117.3	111.2	115.9	119.8	122.4	107.9	111.7	113.9	115.4	116.0	116.4	118.3	120.2	120.8	121.3	122.2	123.6
1982	130.4	127.4	130.3	131.5	132.7	126.3	127.3	128.7	130.1	129.8	130.8	130.8	131.5	132.4	132.6	132.7	132.7
1983	138.7	134.2	136.2	140.9	143.4	134.4	134.1	134.1	135.2	135.7	137.6	139.4	141.2	142.2	142.6	143.6	143.9

Wholesale prices: manufactured goods / Prix de gros : produits manufacturés

1980 = 100

	Year	Q.1	Q.2	Q.3	Q.4	JAN	FEB	MAR	APR	MAY	JUN	JUL	AUG	SEP	OCT	NOV	DEC
1964																	
1965																	
1966																	
1967																	
1968	24.2	23.8	24.2	24.2	24.6	23.7	23.8	24.0	24.3	24.2	24.2	24.3	24.1	24.3	24.3	24.6	24.8
1969	26.0	25.4	26.0	26.1	26.3	25.2	25.4	25.7	25.9	26.1	26.1	26.0	26.0	26.2	26.2	26.2	26.4
1970	27.3	26.9	27.5	27.4	27.4	26.7	26.9	27.2	27.4	27.6	27.5	27.5	27.4	27.4	27.4	27.4	27.6
1971	28.8	28.3	28.9	28.9	29.2	27.9	28.3	28.7	28.9	28.9	28.9	28.8	28.8	29.0	29.0	29.1	29.4
1972	31.8	30.6	31.2	32.0	33.4	30.2	30.6	30.9	31.0	31.2	31.5	31.8	32.1	32.1	32.2	33.7	34.2
1973	37.4	35.8	37.5	38.0	38.2	35.7	35.6	36.0	36.9	37.7	38.0	38.1	38.1	38.0	38.0	38.2	38.5
1974	42.5	40.4	42.3	42.7	44.4	39.9	40.2	41.2	42.2	42.5	42.1	42.5	42.9	42.8	43.1	44.4	45.6
1975	53.1	50.1	53.1	53.7	55.4	48.4	49.8	52.0	52.9	53.3	53.1	53.6	53.3	54.1	54.8	55.4	56.0
1976	62.8	58.4	61.5	64.1	67.2	57.4	58.5	59.4	60.2	61.6	62.6	63.4	63.9	65.0	66.6	67.2	67.9
1977	74.0	71.0	73.7	75.3	75.8	70.1	71.0	71.9	72.6	74.0	74.6	75.0	75.3	75.5	75.6	75.8	76.1
1978	80.6	77.8	80.0	81.8	82.9	77.4	77.7	78.3	79.3	80.1	80.7	81.4	81.8	82.3	82.3	82.9	83.3
1979	90.2	86.9	89.9	91.4	92.7	85.0	87.3	88.4	88.8	90.0	90.8	91.0	91.3	91.8	92.5	92.5	93.1
1980	100.0	96.6	99.6	100.9	102.9	95.0	95.8	98.9	99.7	99.5	99.7	100.5	101.1	101.2	102.1	102.9	103.8
1981	116.7	109.7	115.4	119.3	122.3	106.5	110.2	112.5	114.5	115.4	116.3	117.9	119.8	120.3	121.2	122.3	123.2
1982	130.5	126.4	130.1	132.0	133.5	125.4	126.2	127.6	129.7	129.9	130.7	130.9	132.4	132.7	133.1	133.4	134.0
1983	139.1	135.6	137.3	140.3	142.9	136.1	135.5	135.2	136.6	137.0	138.4	139.3	140.6	141.1	141.8	143.1	143.8

Wholesale prices: food / Prix de gros : produits alimentaires

1980 = 100

	Year	Q.1	Q.2	Q.3	Q.4	JAN	FEB	MAR	APR	MAY	JUN	JUL	AUG	SEP	OCT	NOV	DEC
1964																	
1965																	
1966																	
1967																	
1968																	
1969																	
1970																	
1971																	
1972																	
1973																	
1974																	
1975	53.8	50.1	55.3	53.6	56.1	47.5	48.7	54.1	55.6	55.7	54.6	53.9	53.0	54.0	55.2	56.1	56.9
1976	64.4	58.8	62.6	65.5	70.7	58.3	58.6	59.5	60.7	63.2	64.0	64.7	65.1	66.7	69.9	70.7	71.6
1977	79.3	75.1	79.4	81.4	81.0	74.0	75.1	76.2	77.6	79.6	81.1	81.2	81.5	81.5	80.8	80.8	81.5
1978	88.2	83.8	87.1	90.3	91.4	83.3	83.4	84.7	85.7	87.2	88.5	90.0	90.2	90.9	90.5	91.5	92.0
1979	97.4	96.2	98.8	97.9	96.8	94.8	96.1	97.6	97.5	99.0	99.9	98.7	97.7	97.3	97.0	96.1	97.3
1980	100.0	98.8	99.5	100.0	101.7	98.4	98.8	99.3	100.2	99.4	99.0	99.7	100.4	100.0	100.5	101.5	103.1
1981	116.2	108.9	116.1	118.8	121.3	107.0	108.3	111.3	114.8	116.2	117.1	118.0	119.3	119.2	119.4	121.1	123.4
1982	130.1	126.9	128.8	131.8	132.6	126.9	127.3	126.5	128.7	127.6	130.1	130.7	132.1	132.7	132.4	132.2	133.3
1983	136.1	131.9	134.9	137.6	140.0	133.7	131.0	131.0	133.6	134.0	137.0	137.7	137.3	137.9	138.7	140.3	141.1

IRELAND

Wholesale prices: investment goods / Prix de gros : biens d'investissement

1980 = 100

	Year	Q.1	Q.2	Q.3	Q.4	JAN	FEB	MAR	APR	MAY	JUN	JUL	AUG	SEP	OCT	NOV	DEC
1964																	
1965																	
1966																	
1967																	
1968																	
1969																	
1970																	
1971																	
1972																	
1973																	
1974																	
1975	49.7	46.8	48.4	50.6	52.8	46.2	47.0	47.4	48.2	48.4	48.6	50.0	50.2	51.7	52.3	52.8	53.3
1976	59.0	54.0	57.8	61.1	63.2	53.5	53.7	54.9	56.6	57.1	59.8	60.5	61.2	61.6	62.7	63.0	64.0
1977	69.5	66.1	69.2	70.8	71.7	65.0	66.0	67.1	68.6	69.4	69.7	70.4	70.6	71.3	71.5	71.8	72.0
1978	77.2	74.5	76.3	78.0	79.9	73.7	74.4	75.3	75.7	76.1	77.0	77.4	78.1	78.6	79.3	79.8	80.5
1979	87.7	83.3	85.1	88.2	93.9	82.5	83.6	83.8	84.5	84.7	86.1	86.8	87.9	89.9	93.4	94.0	94.4
1980	100.0	96.9	98.8	100.8	103.5	95.9	96.8	97.8	98.7	98.7	98.9	100.4	100.7	101.3	102.7	103.7	104.2
1981	112.6	109.7	112.2	113.2	115.1	108.3	109.9	110.7	111.6	112.3	112.9	112.6	113.4	113.7	114.4	115.3	115.7
1982	121.5	119.2	120.9	122.2	123.6	117.7	119.6	120.3	120.6	120.8	121.3	122.0	122.2	122.4	123.2	123.4	124.1
1983	129.8	126.0	128.9	131.5	132.7	125.1	125.7	127.1	127.8	129.1	129.9	131.0	131.2	132.4	132.4	132.7	133.1

Money supply (M1) (10) / Disponibilités monétaires (M1) (10)

£ million, end of period / millions de £, fin de période

	Year	Q.1	Q.2	Q.3	Q.4	JAN	FEB	MAR	APR	MAY	JUN	JUL	AUG	SEP	OCT	NOV	DEC
1964	302	280	278	286	302	263	263	280	270	263	278	275	279	286	291	290	302
1965	308	286	293	299	308	290	279	286	288	284	298	290	S 292	299	301	300	308
1966	336	301	..	..	336	304	298	301	309	..	..	..	..	..	333	322	336
1967	357	335	334	356	357	315	305	335	312	309	334	320	325	356	344	343	357
1968	384	365	353	383	384	341	332	365	336	337	353	343	357	383	372	373	384
1969	395	398	382	391	395	362	357	398	366	362	382	369	S 373	391	381	383	395
1970	..	..	..	..	..	382	373	..	..	..	..	..	..	..	..	..	..
1971	430	..	399	409	430	..	..	..	391	383	399	389	398	409	409	411	430
1972	499	450	448	477	499	418	S 412	450	430	428	448	446	452	477	470	486	499
1973	535	513	504	532	535	493	474	513	422	482	504	500	507	532	520	526	535
1974	563	533	512	527	563	521	500	533	511	503	512	508	515	527	522	537	563
1975	677	562	593	637	677	549	534	562	560	562	593	581	601	637	635	642	677
1976	789	664	..	..	789	660	657	664	668	664	..	..	S ..	..	740	742	789
1977	981	765	822	901	981	748	733	765	765	787	822	814	827	901	883	926	981
1978	1224	995	1025	1114	1224	947	928	995	949	983	1025	1006	1033	1114	1109	1118	1224
1979	1352	1259	1321	1296	1352	1178	1151	1259	1229	1259	1321	1318	1318	1296	1264	1242	1352
1980	1492	1278	1310	1383	1492	1261	1235	1278	1265	1255	1310	1290	1315	1383	1386	1402	1492
1981	1614	1464	1508	1543	1614	1433	1401	1464	1458	1465	1508	1482	1533	1543	1507	1536	1614
1982	1729	1549	1558	1693	1729	1577	1511	1549	1511	1502	1558	1556	1598	1693	1661	1671	1729
1983	1851	1659	1676	1734	1851	1640	1609	1659	1643	1665	1676	1700	1699	1734	1729	1751	1851

M1 plus quasi-money (10)(11)(12) / M1 plus quasi-monnaie (10) (11)(12)

£ million, end of period / million de £, fin de période

	Year	Q.1	Q.2	Q.3	Q.4	JAN	FEB	MAR	APR	MAY	JUN	JUL	AUG	SEP	OCT	NOV	DEC
1964	559	526	528	540	559	506	508	526	515	509	528	523	529	540	547	547	559
1965	582	547	565	571	582	549	540	547	548	545	565	556	S 560	571	576	568	582
1966	686	579	..	..	686	579	575	579	592	..	..	..	..	..	631	625	686
1967	767	697	712	753	767	..	..	697	..	..	712	..	..	753	..	..	767
1968	887	796	810	869	887	..	..	796	..	..	S 810	..	..	869	..	..	887
1969	983	919	920	949	983	..	870	919	888	889	920	904	S 923	949	947	958	983
1970	..	..	..	..	..	963	963	..	..	..	..	..	..	..	..	..	..
1971	1191	..	1116	1164	1191	..	..	..	1106	1102	1116	1109	1129	1164	1167	1164	1191
1972	1360	1191	1228	1307	1360	1175	S 1178	1191	1184	1189	1228	1237	1255	1307	1299	1333	1360
1973	1714	1473	1503	1536	1714	1378	1384	1473	1455	1456	1503	1513	1553	1536	1645	1689	1714
1974	2067	1812	1842	1942	2067	1719	1726	1812	1795	1805	1842	1840	1876	1942	1963	1999	2067
1975	2459	2128	2183	2314	2459	2067	2059	2128	2110	2134	2183	2169	2220	2314	2349	2417	2459
1976	2814	2489	..	..	2814	2438	2461	2489	2511	2529	..	..	..	..	2697	2763	2814
1977	3294	2877	2987	3102	3294	2789	2774	2877	2886	2932	2987	3017	3018	3102	3132	3263	3294
1978	4249	3381	3488	3750	4249	3313	3261	3381	3384	3453	3488	3501	3573	3750	3819	3942	4249
1979	5044	4431	4730	4761	5044	4265	4236	4431	4472	4586	4730	4777	4730	4761	4853	4900	5044
1980	5939	5094	5181	5500	5939	4963	4902	5094	5084	5061	5181	5209	5328	5500	5548	5890	5939
1981	6973	6148	6370	6680	6973	5991	6129	6148	6238	6277	6370	6475	6626	6680	6661	6782	6973
1982	7876	7098	7142	7499	7876	7050	7056	7098	7147	7107	7142	7227	7292	7499	7499	7903	7876
1983	7697	7229	7346	7440	7697	7269	7314	7229	7230	7379	7346	7393	7366	7440	7429	7621	7697

Consumer prices: all items (13)
1980 = 100

Prix à la consommation : total (13)
1980 = 100

	Year	Q.1	Q.2	Q.3	Q.4	JAN	FEB	MAR	APR	MAY	JUN	JUL	AUG	SEP	OCT	NOV	DEC
1964	20.4	19.7	20.5	20.7	20.9		19.7			20.5			20.7			20.9	
1965	21.5	21.2	21.5	21.6	21.6		21.2			21.5			21.6			21.6	
1966	22.1	21.6	22.0	22.4	22.4		21.6			22.0			22.4			22.4	
1967	22.8	22.5	22.9	22.9	23.0		22.5			22.9			22.9			23.0	
1968	23.9	23.5	23.9	23.9	24.3		23.5			23.9			23.9			=24.3=	
1969	25.7	25.1	25.5	25.9	26.1		25.1			25.5			25.9			26.1	
1970	27.8	26.6	27.7	28.1	28.8		26.6			27.7			28.1			28.8	
1971	30.3	29.2	30.0	30.6	31.2		29.2			30.0			30.6			31.2	
1972	32.9	31.9	32.4	33.3	33.8		31.9			32.4			33.3			33.8	
1973	36.6	35.1	36.2	37.1	38.1		35.1			36.2			37.1			38.1	
1974	42.8	39.9	42.1	43.7	45.7		39.9			42.1			43.7			45.7	
1975	51.8	49.4	52.4	52.0	53.4		49.4			52.4			52.0			=53.4=	
1976	61.1	57.3	60.9	61.8	64.4		57.3			60.9			61.8			64.4	
1977	69.4	66.8	69.4	70.1	71.3		66.8			69.4			70.1			71.3	
1978	74.7	72.3	73.6	75.9	77.0		72.3			73.6			75.9			77.0	
1979	84.6	80.2	82.8	86.2	89.3		80.2			82.8			86.2			89.3	
1980	100.0	92.6	99.5	102.4	105.6		92.6			99.5			102.4			105.6	
1981	120.5	112.1	116.4	123.0	130.2		112.1			116.4			123.0			130.2	
1982	141.1	133.2	140.9	143.9	146.2		133.2			140.9			143.9			=146.2=	
1983	155.8	149.8	153.9	158.3	161.2		149.8			153.9			158.3			161.2	

Money supply (M1) (10)
£ million, end of period

Adjusted - Corrigé *

Disponibilités monétaires (M1) (10)
millions de £, fin de période

	Year	Q.1	Q.2	Q.3	Q.4	JAN	FEB	MAR	APR	MAY	JUN	JUL	AUG	SEP	OCT	NOV	DEC
1964																	
1965																	
1966																	
1967																	
1968																	
1969																	
1970																	
1971			393	399	414				398	396	398	396	401	399	407	405	414
1972		444	446	465	480	415	425	444	438	443	446	455	456	465	467	479	480
1973		507	502	519	512	489	489	507	491	498	502	511	512	519	517	518	512
1974		527	511	513	537	517	516	527	520	519	511	520	521	513	519	530	537
1975		558	570	619	644	545	551	558	570	578	590	594	609	619	631	635	644
1976		661	691	720	747	656	679	661	681	681	..	..	..	..	736	738	747
1977		763	814	873	927	746	759	763	780	805	814	831	839	873	879	926	927
1978		995	1014	1078	1155	946	962	995	966	1003	1014	1023	1047	1078	1107	1121	1155
1979		1259	1303	1257	1277	1181	1194	1259	1250	1281	1303	1334	1338	1257	1264	1249	1277
1980		1279	1291	1342	1409	1265	1281	1279	1286	1276	1291	1301	1334	1342	1388	1414	1409
1981		1465	1486	1498	1526	1437	1455	1465	1482	1490	1486	1493	1555	1498	1508	1550	1526
1982		1551	1535	1644	1635	1582	1569	1551	1534	1528	1535	1567	1621	1644	1663	1688	1635
1983		1660	1651	1684	1750	1645	1671	1660	1668	1693	1651	1712	1723	1684	1731	1769	1750

* Adjusted by the O.E.C.D.

* Corrigé par l'O.C.D.E.

IRELAND

Bank credit to domestic sector (11)(14)

£ million, end of period

Crédits bancaires au secteur intérieur (14) (11)

millions de £, fin de période

	Year	Q.1	Q.2	Q.3	Q.4	JAN	FEB	MAR	APR	MAY	JUN	JUL	AUG	SEP	OCT	NOV	DEC
1964	307	276	288	288	307	266	270	276	271	274	288	292	282	289	288	291	307
1965	309	312	323	310	309	307	311	312	310	314	323	S 315	312	310	302	300	309
1966	384	302	..	..	384	304	304	302	297	..	..	..	..	..	319	312	384
1967	422	389	406	404	422	..	..	389	..	..	406	..	..	404	..	..	422
1968	509	443	462	478	509	..	..	443	..	..	462	..	..	478	..	..	509
1969	616	553	594	586	616	..	518	553	539	561	594	581	S 581	586	588	592	616
1970	..	..	..	..	..	605	516	..	..	..	..	..	..	..	..	..	..
1971	760	..	708	716	760	..	..	..	705	701	708	702	701	716	710	718	760
1972	1001	790	863	914	1001	729	S 741	790	802	821	863	852	863	914	908	931	1001
1973	1237	1078	1112	1169	1237	996	1028	1078	1065	1065	1112	1105	1116	1169	1155	1199	1237
1974	1446	1353	1391	1398	1446	1218	1254	1353	1346	1355	1391	1369	1360	1398	1407	1405	1446
1975	1698	1502	1533	1599	1698	1426	1435	1502	1490	1472	1533	1548	1546	1599	1608	1659	1698
1976	2088	1753	..	..	2088	1669	1670	1753	1762	1773	..	S ..	..	..	2018	2047	2088
1977	2640	2179	2313	2476	2640	2077	2082	2179	2202	2227	2313	2332	2354	2476	2490	2518	2640
1978	3475	2816	3007	3300	3475	2641	2671	2816	2856	2917	3007	3055	3111	3300	3330	3370	3475
1979	4351	3794	4058	4256	4351	3454	3571	3794	3834	3915	4058	4051	4065	4256	4256	4296	4351
1980	5051	4608	4586	4773	5051	4312	4398	4608	4581	4369	4586	4589	4563	4773	4743	4823	5051
1981	6054	5392	5512	5785	6054	5014	5299	5382	5441	5452	5512	5526	5495	5785	5786	5833	6054
1982	6677	6367	6348	6458	6677	6030	6111	6367	6302	6340	6348	6266	6203	6458	6443	6429	6677
1983	7290	6732	6834	7063	7290	6538	6762	6732	6681	6782	6334	6835	6876	7063	7032	7204	7290

Instalment credit outstanding

(all credit institutions)

£ million, end of period

Crédits remboursables par tranches, en cours

(ensemble des institutions de crédit)

millions de £, fin de période

	Year	Q.1	Q.2	Q.3	Q.4	JAN	FEB	MAR	APR	MAY	JUN	JUL	AUG	SEP	OCT	NOV	DEC
1964																	
1965																	
1966																	
1967	58.5	51.9	53.7	54.5	58.5			51.9			53.7			54.5			58.5
1968	67.0	61.4	63.2	64.5	67.0			61.4			63.2			64.5			67.0
1969	88.1	72.2	78.5	82.5	88.1			72.2			73.5	S		82.5			88.1
1970	..	..	..	..	..			..			..			..			..
1971	105.6	101.8	103.4	103.9	105.6			101.8			103.4			103.9			105.6
1972	129.2	109.5	118.3	125.3	129.2			109.5			118.3			125.3			129.2
1973	178.5	136.1	151.6	166.6	178.5			136.1			151.6			166.6			178.5
1974	215.2	183.4	198.6	209.2	215.2			183.4			198.6			209.2			215.2
1975	237.2	211.4	217.5	224.6	237.2			211.4			217.5			224.6			237.2
1976	286.6	242.7	258.6	273.9	286.6			242.7			258.6			273.9			286.6
1977	385.7	306.6	334.3	361.0	385.7			306.6			334.3			361.0			385.7
1978	535.9	411.3	462.2	503.0	535.9			411.3			462.2			503.0			535.9
1979	648.2	560.0	604.6	630.6	648.2			560.0			604.6			630.6			648.2
1980	686.3	671.9	673.7	694.5	686.3			671.9			673.7			694.5			686.3
1981	723.4	692.1	708.3	733.0	723.4			692.1			708.3			733.0			723.4
1982	717.3	734.6	750.9	730.6	717.3			734.6			750.9			730.6			717.3
1983		670.6	667.5	649.1				670.6			667.5			649.1			

New consumer credit

(finance houses)

£ million

Nouveaux crédits à la consommation

(établissements financiers)

millions de £

	Year	Q.1	Q.2	Q.3	Q.4	JAN	FEB	MAR	APR	MAY	JUN	JUL	AUG	SEP	OCT	NOV	DEC
1964																	
1965																	
1966																	
1967																	
1968																	
1969																	
1970																	
1971	16.4	4.1	4.2	4.0	4.2												
1972	19.6	4.9	5.6	4.9	4.3												
1973	20.9	4.7	5.3	5.7	4.7												
1974	17.3	4.2	4.9	4.3	4.0												
1975	18.3	3.9	4.3	4.8	5.3												
1976	30.2	6.7	7.5	8.3	7.7												
1977	38.6	7.9	10.0	10.3	10.4												
1978	55.6	10.6	16.7	13.6	14.7												
1979	66.3	14.6	17.8	18.0	15.9												
1980	59.7	20.1	14.3	13.5	11.8												
1981	62.8	16.9	19.4	15.5	11.0												
1982	56.8	17.9	14.2	12.7	12.0												
1983		13.9	10.8	9.9													

Official discount rate

per cent per annum, end of period

Taux d'escompte officiel

pourcentage par an, fin de période

	Year	Q.1	Q.2	Q.3	Q.4	JAN	FEB	MAR	APR	MAY	JUN	JUL	AUG	SEP	OCT	NOV	DEC
1964	6.81	4.55	4.59	4.89	6.81	3.94	3.94	4.55	4.50	4.62	4.69	4.87	4.87	4.39	4.94	6.87	6.81
1965	5.88	6.31	5.92	5.84	5.88	6.81	6.75	6.81	6.69	6.50	5.92	6.00	5.81	5.34	5.08	5.81	5.88
1966	6.87	5.91	5.94	7.00	6.87	5.75	5.75	5.91	5.94	5.87	5.94	6.87	6.87	7.00	6.81	6.87	6.87
1967	7.78	5.88	5.50	5.53	7.78	6.50	6.25	5.88	5.56	5.44	5.50	5.56	5.50	5.53	5.94	7.75	7.78
1968	7.17	7.39	7.44	6.86	7.17	7.69	7.62	7.39	7.38	7.31	7.44	7.44	7.25	6.86	6.81	7.00	7.17
1969	8.25	8.75	8.50	8.38	8.25	7.12	8.00	8.75	8.38	8.38	8.50	8.44	8.38	8.38	8.38	8.25	8.25
1970	7.31	7.81	7.38	7.31	7.31	8.62	8.19	7.81	7.19	7.31	7.38	7.38	7.31	7.31	7.31	7.31	7.31
1971	4.81	7.25	6.00	5.12	4.81	7.25	7.25	7.25	6.19	6.06	6.00	5.94	6.12	5.12	5.12	4.94	4.81
1972	8.00	4.81	6.06	7.19	8.00	4.81	4.81	4.81	4.81	4.81	6.06	5.19	6.19	7.19	7.44	7.44	8.00
1973	12.75	8.75	8.00	10.50	12.75	8.75	8.75	8.75	8.75	8.75	3.00	10.50	10.50	10.50	10.50	12.75	12.75
1974	12.00	12.75	12.00	12.00	12.00	12.75	12.75	12.75	12.00	12.00	12.00	12.00	12.00	12.00	12.00	12.00	12.00
1975	10.00	10.00	10.00	10.00	10.00	11.00	11.00	10.00	10.00	10.00	10.00	10.00	10.00	10.00	10.00	10.00	10.00
1976	14.75	10.00	11.25	11.25	14.75	10.00	10.00	10.00	10.00	10.00	11.25	11.25	11.25	11.25	11.25	14.75	14.75
1977	6.75	11.00	7.75	6.60	6.75	14.25	12.50	11.00	8.80	7.75	7.75	7.75	7.75	6.60	5.10	5.10	6.75
1978	11.85	6.75	9.05	9.60	11.85	6.75	6.75	6.75	6.75	8.50	9.05	9.60	9.60	9.60	9.60	11.75	11.85
1979	16.40	11.85	13.70	13.70	16.40	11.85	11.85	11.85	11.85	11.85	13.70	13.70	13.70	13.70	13.70	13.70	16.40
1980	12.75	16.85	16.85	13.50	12.75	16.40	16.40	16.85	16.85	16.85	16.85	16.10	15.00	13.50	12.75	12.75	12.75
1981	17.15	13.15	14.40	16.45	17.15	12.75	13.15	13.15	13.90	14.40	14.40	15.00	15.90	16.45	17.15	17.15	17.15
1982	14.35	18.30	18.30	14.55	14.35	17.15	17.70	18.30	18.30	18.30	18.30	17.30	15.95	14.55	12.85	12.85	14.35
1983	11.50	14.35	13.80	12.20	11.50	14.35	14.35	14.35	14.35	13.80	13.80	13.00	13.00	12.20	12.20	11.50	11.50

Call money rate (5)

per cent per annum, end of period

Taux de l'argent au jour le jour (5)

pourcentage par an, fin de période

	Year	Q.1	Q.2	Q.3	Q.4	JAN	FEB	MAR	APR	MAY	JUN	JUL	AUG	SEP	OCT	NOV	DEC
1964																	
1965																	
1966																	
1967																	
1968																	
1969																	
1970																	
1971	5.00	7.75	6.00	4.88	5.00	7.50	7.63	7.75	6.13	7.00	6.00	6.13	6.00	4.88	4.75	4.38	5.00
1972	7.62	6.25	8.50	7.12	7.62	4.75	5.38	6.25	4.50	4.75	8.50	7.00	6.38	7.12	6.12	7.75	7.62
1973	13.50	16.00	12.00	12.75	13.50	9.88	10.88	16.00	9.38	10.00	12.00	8.62	12.50	12.75	14.00	13.00	13.50
1974	11.25	18.50	25.00	12.00	11.25	14.00	12.25	18.50	12.50	12.25	25.00	13.25	10.75	12.00	11.38	14.00	11.25
1975	10.88	10.50	9.50	9.88	10.88	18.50	13.75	10.50	9.88	9.38	9.50	9.25	10.12	9.88	10.88	11.69	10.88
1976	14.81	8.50	11.50	13.25	14.81	10.62	5.75	8.50	9.50	8.00	11.50	11.00	10.12	13.25	13.62	15.19	14.81
1977	8.00	10.75	7.62	7.00	8.00	16.50	11.88	10.75	8.62	7.50	7.62	7.12	6.88	7.00	4.75	3.12	8.00
1978	12.12	6.88	12.50	10.38	12.12	7.00	5.75	6.88	7.50	8.62	12.50	10.88	9.12	10.38	10.25	11.88	12.12
1979	16.88	19.00	27.50	17.62	16.88	11.38	19.00	19.00	13.12	11.88	27.50	15.75	16.38	17.62	14.75	16.75	16.88
1980	13.31	24.00	17.75	13.62	13.31	24.00	16.88	24.00	17.62	17.56	17.75	17.62	14.38	13.62	13.25	13.38	13.31
1981	18.12	13.38	14.12	21.50	18.12	13.44	13.38	13.88	14.44	14.53	14.12	16.00	17.25	21.50	16.00	16.82	18.12
1982	18.50	21.00	19.50	15.62	18.50	16.31	21.00	21.00	19.31	19.88	19.50	18.25	16.50	15.62	15.50	12.25	18.50
1983	11.75	30.00	14.25	12.38	11.75	16.25	13.12	30.00	15.88	14.38	14.25	13.88	13.56	12.38	12.50	11.88	11.75

IRELAND

Treasury bill rate (3 months)

per cent per annum, end of period

Bons du Trésor (3 mois)

pourcentage par an, fin de période

	Year	Q.1	Q.2	Q.3	Q.4	JAN	FEB	MAR	APR	MAY	JUN	JUL	AUG	SEP	OCT	NOV	DEC
1964																	
1965																	
1966																	
1967																	
1968																	
1969	8.23				8.23												8.23
1970	7.27	7.80	7.36	7.27	7.27	..	..	7.80	..	..	7.36	..	..	7.27	..	..	7.27
1971	4.58	7.10	5.96	5.17	4.58	..	..	7.10	6.13	6.01	5.96	5.89	6.09	5.17	4.89	4.83	4.58
1972	7.98	4.61	5.15	6.50	7.93	4.62	4.63	4.61	4.56	4.51	5.15	5.76	6.14	6.50	7.13	7.32	7.98
1973	12.67	8.78	7.34	11.19	12.67	8.80	8.62	8.78	7.66	7.54	7.34	7.14	11.11	11.19	10.99	12.43	12.67
1974	11.19	12.15	11.39	11.43	11.19	12.27	12.15	12.15	11.67	11.63	11.39	11.39	11.39	11.43	11.15	11.19	11.19
1975	11.23	9.83	9.59	10.47	11.23	11.03	10.27	9.83	9.47	9.67	9.59	9.67	10.67	10.47	11.55	11.47	11.23
1976	14.28	8.74	11.23	11.19	14.28	10.50	9.02	8.74	8.73	10.19	11.23	11.15	11.07	11.19	14.64	14.56	14.28
1977	6.74	10.91	7.70	6.54	6.74	13.52	11.47	10.91	8.78	7.66	7.70	7.70	7.06	6.54	5.01	4.73	6.74
1978	11.83	6.22	9.02	9.31	11.83	6.14	6.18	6.22	6.26	3.46	9.02	9.55	9.23	9.31	9.59	11.03	11.83
1979	16.36	12.23	11.67	13.60	16.36	11.84	12.75	12.23	11.39	11.31	11.67	13.48	13.60	13.60	13.56	13.72	16.36
1980	12.84	16.76	16.57	13.43	12.84	16.08	16.45	16.76	16.88	16.69	16.57	15.82	14.98	13.43	12.72	12.78	12.84
1981	17.35	12.70	14.72	17.47	17.35	12.33	12.84	12.70	13.85	14.65	14.72	15.42	16.20	17.47	17.14	17.27	17.35
1982	14.70	18.38	18.25	14.48	14.70	17.46	17.85	18.38	18.28	18.25	18.25	16.76	15.94	14.48	12.74	12.83	14.70
1983	11.66	14.39	12.95	12.12	11.66	15.38	13.76	14.39	13.81	14.01	12.95	13.09	13.01	12.12	11.96	11.66	11.66

Yield of long-term Government bonds

per cent per annum, end of period

Rendement des bons d'État à long terme

pourcentage par an, fin de période

	Year	Q.1	Q.2	Q.3	Q.4	JAN	FEB	MAR	APR	MAY	JUN	JUL	AUG	SEP	OCT	NOV	DEC
1964																	
1965																	
1966																	
1967																	
1968																	
1969	9.71				9.71												9.71
1970	9.86				9.86												9.86
1971	8.48	9.51	9.30	9.11	8.48	9.82	9.85	9.51	9.40	9.29	9.30	9.36	9.35	9.11	8.78	8.61	8.48
1972	9.46	8.38	9.81	9.46	9.46	8.37	8.25	8.38	8.30	8.64	9.81	9.76	9.51	9.46	9.45	9.47	9.46
1973	12.33	10.01	10.18	11.42	12.33	9.56	9.61	10.01	10.00	10.04	10.18	10.76	11.34	11.42	11.44	11.92	12.33
1974	16.86	13.80	14.61	14.66	16.86	13.24	13.37	13.80	14.04	13.76	14.61	14.48	14.95	14.66	15.32	16.35	16.86
1975	14.64	13.18	13.76	13.81	14.64	15.20	14.06	13.18	13.88	13.64	13.76	13.16	13.36	13.81	14.47	14.45	14.64
1976	15.49	14.11	13.89	15.23	15.49	13.77	13.78	14.11	14.23	14.14	13.89	14.14	14.37	15.23	16.37	15.84	15.49
1977	11.30	12.70	13.58	11.87	11.30	14.09	14.28	12.70	13.14	13.45	13.58	13.86	13.17	11.37	11.24	11.96	11.30
1978	13.44	12.28	13.31	13.08	13.44	11.68	12.29	12.28	12.39	13.26	13.31	12.62	12.90	13.08	12.92	13.34	13.44
1979	16.29	13.33	15.37	15.72	16.29	14.35	13.48	13.33	13.46	13.81	15.37	15.99	15.92	15.72	16.64	16.42	16.29
1980	15.63	16.82	14.64	14.57	15.63	15.95	16.39	16.82	16.20	15.78	14.64	14.08	14.49	14.57	14.77	14.91	15.63
1981	18.34	16.18	17.31	18.22	18.34	16.13	15.99	16.18	16.60	16.99	17.31	17.44	17.61	18.22	18.24	18.16	18.34
1982	14.54	18.83	18.58	15.17	14.54	19.11	19.16	18.83	18.28	18.28	18.58	17.33	15.93	15.17	13.95	15.53	14.54
1983	14.24	13.96	13.61	13.72	14.24	14.98	14.26	13.96	13.62	13.51	13.61	13.81	13.60	13.72	13.82	13.72	14.24

Share prices: common stocks (15)

Irish Stock Exchange

1980 = 100

Cours des actions ordinaires (15)

Bourse d'Irlande

1980 = 100

	Year	Q.1	Q.2	Q.3	Q.4	JAN	FEB	MAR	APR	MAY	JUN	JUL	AUG	SEP	OCT	NOV	DEC
1964	36	34	36	37	36	33	34	34	35	36	37	37	36	37	37	36	36
1965	35	37	36	33	33	36	37	37	36	36	36	35	32	33	33	33	32
1966	32	34	33	32	30	33	33	34	33	34	34	34	33	30	30	30	30
1967	32	30	31	33	35	30	30	30	31	31	31	33	33	33	34	35	37
1968	46	39	45	49	51	38	39	41	42	46	47	48	49	50	51	51	50
1969	49	52	51	47	45	50	52	53	51	51	50	49	46	46	46	45	44
1970	43	45	42	43	41	46	46	44	43	42	41	42	42	44	44	41	39
1971	42	38	40	44	44	39	38	39	39	40	42	44	44	43	45	45	43
1972	61	47	57	69	71	45	48	48	50	58	63	64	68	76	69	71	74
1973	72	77	74	72	66	76	77	77	74	74	73	73	73	70	69	68	62
1974	49	59	55	46	34	60	57	59	57	57	52	47	46	43	36	36	31
1975	47	37	52	48	52	30	38	42	48	53	54	48	48	50	50	52	54
1976	50	54	53	50	43	53	54	55	54	54	52	50	50	48	46	42	42
1977	63	52	58	65	77	46	55	55	56	56	61	63	62	69	78	79	75
1978	95	85	90	101	106	86	86	82	88	90	93	93	100	110	106	107	104
1979	102	107	109	98	94	104	104	111	112	111	104	100	95	97	97	93	92
1980	100	97	97	100	105	93	98	101	99	99	94	94	103	103	105	106	105
1981	104	103	111	105	95	101	103	106	109	113	111	107	104	104	95	95	97
1982	85	91	82	83	84	95	91	86	82	82	83	79	82	87	83	87	81
1983	95	81	97	118	126	83	79	81	90	98	104	112	118	123	127	122	130

U.S. dollar exchange rate: spot / Taux de change du dollar É.-U. : au comptant

cents per £, end of period / cents par £, fin de période

	Year	Q.1	Q.2	Q.3	Q.4	JAN	FEB	MAR	APR	MAY	JUN	JUL	AUG	SEP	OCT	NOV	DEC
1964	279.01	279.84	279.17	273.33	279.01	279.78	279.82	279.84	279.99	279.79	279.17	278.82	278.39	278.33	278.50	279.12	279.01
1965	280.28	279.05	279.17	280.18	280.28	279.20	279.41	279.05	279.91	279.27	279.17	279.20	279.07	280.18	280.38	280.28	280.28
1966	279.02	279.31	278.96	279.14	279.02	280.36	280.00	279.31	279.37	279.11	278.96	279.02	278.91	279.14	279.09	279.05	279.02
1967	240.63	279.73	279.00	278.34	240.63	279.43	279.33	279.73	279.86	279.48	279.00	278.58	278.54	278.34	278.27	242.00	240.63
1968	238.44	240.11	238.26	238.96	238.44	241.23	240.30	240.11	239.71	238.34	238.26	239.49	238.36	238.96	239.11	238.46	238.44
1969	240.07	239.43	239.13	238.27	240.07	239.00	239.38	239.48	238.52	238.95	239.13	239.06	238.13	238.27	239.58	239.64	240.07
1970	239.37	240.67	239.52	238.79	239.37	240.25	240.71	240.67	240.59	240.15	239.52	239.09	238.34	238.79	239.03	238.87	239.37
1971	255.25	241.69	241.94	248.50	255.25	241.75	241.62	241.69	241.94	241.81	241.94	241.88	245.25	248.50	249.17	249.38	255.25
1972	234.81	261.58	244.40	242.03	234.81	259.38	260.60	261.58	261.11	261.29	244.40	245.01	244.85	242.03	234.20	235.27	234.81
1973	232.32	247.77	258.20	241.35	232.32	238.22	249.00	247.77	248.95	256.70	258.20	251.30	245.85	241.35	243.90	234.30	232.32
1974	234.85	239.40	239.05	233.23	234.85	227.70	230.55	239.40	243.28	239.30	239.05	237.61	231.78	233.23	233.38	232.37	234.85
1975	202.35	240.90	219.80	204.09	202.35	237.78	242.68	240.90	235.31	231.14	219.80	214.72	211.10	204.09	207.57	201.68	202.35
1976	170.24	191.57	178.13	167.75	170.24	202.91	202.71	191.57	184.40	176.40	178.13	178.43	177.46	167.75	160.60	164.84	170.24
1977	190.60	172.01	172.02	174.65	190.60	171.42	170.92	172.01	171.93	171.76	172.02	173.74	174.29	174.65	183.20	181.50	190.60
1978	203.45	185.63	186.02	197.21	203.45	195.04	193.43	185.63	183.13	182.22	186.02	193.17	194.25	197.21	209.00	194.93	203.45
1979	214.50	205.25	204.40	213.70	214.50	199.56	202.34	205.25	200.60	197.40	204.40	204.70	206.00	213.70	205.50	213.20	214.50
1980	189.75	193.80	212.85	207.40	189.75	212.50	208.20	193.80	205.35	208.10	212.85	210.95	209.30	207.40	196.20	193.45	189.75
1981	158.00	173.85	152.42	156.62	158.00	176.65	171.85	173.85	165.50	157.70	152.42	148.20	150.30	156.62	157.20	161.35	158.00
1982	139.65	143.75	140.00	134.75	139.65	152.27	148.00	143.75	148.10	147.55	140.00	140.00	137.55	134.75	132.85	135.55	139.65
1983	113.50	130.10	123.80	118.45	113.50	135.90	136.95	130.10	128.50	125.40	123.80	119.40	116.30	118.45	118.63	115.25	113.50

Official reserves excluding gold / Réserves officielles, or exclu

million SDR's, end of period / millions de DTS, fin de période

	Year	Q.1	Q.2	Q.3	Q.4	JAN	FEB	MAR	APR	MAY	JUN	JUL	AUG	SEP	OCT	NOV	DEC
1964	427	410	413	420	427	381	404	410	399	406	413	420	425	420	425	448	427
1965	388	431	380	388	388	425	423	431	408	384	380	381	375	388	372	387	388
1966	471	419	398	444	471	390	391	419	416	404	398	392	387	444	432	474	471
1967	414	464	445	493	414	491	484	464	432	433	445	433	435	493	457	431	414
1968	466	375	316	347	466	422	418	375	354	324	316	294	299	347	333	449	466
1969	652	511	463	564	652	468	468	511	479	461	463	453	546	564	599	635	652
1970	681	691	687	728	681	682	663	691	711	695	687	685	697	728	724	727	681
1971	901	785	787	882	901	688	774	785	785	779	787	781	848	882	894	950	901
1972	1022	963	941	892	1022	950	940	963	974	956	941	926	907	892	911	956	1022
1973	835	827	845	882	835	989	865	827	833	859	845	838	856	882	885	861	835
1974	1019	852	788	974	1019	798	775	852	816	825	788	926	1032	974	1001	1012	1019
1975	1292	968	1065	1130	1292	987	972	968	968	1016	1065	1112	1098	1130	1106	1132	1292
1976	1565	1456	1329	1436	1565	1406	1386	1456	1441	1404	1329	1259	1306	1436	1416	1510	1565
1977	1936	1612	1509	1810	1936	1613	1552	1612	1540	1545	1509	1590	1696	1810	1849	1746	1936
1978	2048	1854	1586	1831	2048	1734	1839	1854	1735	1727	1586	1661	1794	1831	1892	2027	2048
1979	1679	1901	1688	1599	1679	1951	2062	1901	1798	1561	1688	1666	1561	1599	1488	1599	1679
1980	2243	1626	1684	1968	2243	1690	1653	1626	1557	1595	1684	1895	2028	1968	1947	1976	2243
1981	2278	2049	1851	1717	2278	2160	2208	2049	1854	1969	1851	1959	1936	1717	1989	2288	2278
1982	2377	2151	2219	2277	2377	2190	2220	2151	2408	2442	2219	2444	2360	2277	2445	2138	2377
1983	2521	1879	1957	2547	2521	2145	2212	1879	1834	1749	1957	2219	2311	2547	2515	2521	2521

Net foreign position: commercial banks (11)(16) / Position extérieure nette : banques commerciales (11) (16)

£ million, end of period / millions de £, fin de période

	Year	Q.1	Q.2	Q.3	Q.4	JAN	FEB	MAR	APR	MAY	JUN	JUL	AUG	SEP	OCT	NOV	DEC
1964	93	98	87	94	93	100	97	98	94	94	87	94	90	94	94	94	93
1965	89	84	76	84	89	92	87	84	79	75	76	S 77	80	84	92	89	89
1966	75	94	..	..	75	93	92	94	98	..	..	..	..	..	86	82	75
1967	119	85	-94	-109	119	..	..	85	..	..	-94	..	..	-109	..	..	119
1968	114	120	123	129	114	..	..	120	..	..	123	..	..	129	..	..	114
1969	-28	72	58	-10	-28	..	99	72	80	67	58	S 54	-5	-10	-12	-18	-28
1970	..	..	..	..	..	-46	-45	..	..	..	..	..	..	..	..	..	..
1971	-89	..	-87	-86	-89	..	.. S	..	-80	-83	-87	-83	-84	-86	-81	-97	-89
1972	-172	-108	-119	-103	-172	-128	-106	-108	-120	-126	-119	-107	-112	-103	-123	-129	-172
1973	-146	-130	-150	-133	-146	-151	-147	-130	-142	-154	-150	-144	-119	-133	-129	-141	-146
1974	-148	-163	-163	-138	-148	-140	-146	-163	-168	-165	-163	-155	-170	-138	-133	-144	-148
1975	-184	-159	-154	-111	-184	-150	-158	-159	-185	-156	-154	-189	-192	-111	-92	-149	-184
1976	-278	-253	..	..	-278	-182	-215	-253	-222	-205	..	..	..	..	-218	-219	-278
1977	-542	-362	-385	-466	-542	-286	-331	-362	-345	-370	-385	-396	-431	-466	-482	-481	-542
1978	-538	-546	-534	-593	-538	-467	-474	-546	-549	-543	-534	-540	-558	-593	-554	-566	-538
1979	-563	-527	-439	-561	-563	-535	-579	-527	-468	-449	-489	-481	-497	-561	-520	-562	-563
1980	-879	-673	-723	-749	-879	-555	-621	-673	-687	-723	-723	-731	-749	-749	-792	-755	-879
1981	-961	-913	-906	-718	-961	-795	-940	-913	-858	-874	-906	-888	-846	-718	-820	-848	-961
1982	-981	-1203	-1215	-1026	-981	-967	-1012	-1203	-1209	-1150	-1215	-1135	-1004	-1026	-1043	-933	-981
1983	-2807	-2205	-2367	-2691	-2807	-1986	-2145	-2205	-2140	-2133	-2367	-2401	-2520	-2691	-2636	-2699	-2807

IRELAND

Imports c.i.f. (17) — Importations c.a.f. (17)

£ million, monthly averages — millions de £, moyennes mensuelles

	Year	Q.1	Q.2	Q.3	Q.4	JAN	FEB	MAR	APR	MAY	JUN	JUL	AUG	SEP	OCT	NOV	DEC
1964	29.0	29.2	30.2	27.3	29.3	29.7	28.8	29.2	30.2	27.4	32.9	31.3	23.1	27.3	30.5	29.2	29.1
1965	31.0	31.1	33.0	29.6	30.3	27.3	30.6	35.5	34.9	33.5	30.7	31.6	27.8	29.5	31.1	31.0	28.9
1966	31.1	30.1	28.6	32.3	33.3	25.2	23.3	36.9	31.8	29.3	24.6	33.3	31.4	32.3	32.7	36.2	31.0
1967	32.6	33.4	32.8	31.0	33.0	34.0	31.4	35.0	32.5	33.4	32.6	33.1	29.9	29.9	31.1	36.5	31.4
1968	41.3	38.8	41.3	39.3	45.2	36.8	41.1	38.4	42.3	45.7	37.4	43.3	37.1	37.4	45.8	45.8	44.0
1969	49.2	44.9	53.3	46.7	51.8	48.4	40.1	46.0	58.2	53.0	48.6	53.0	39.4	47.7	57.1	48.5	49.9
1970	56.3	52.7	57.6	53.3	61.6	52.3	54.1	51.8	61.0	58.6	53.2	56.2	49.1	54.6	65.1	60.4	59.3
1971	62.8	68.3	63.8	57.4	61.9	58.8	61.0	85.1	64.2	67.7	59.5	61.6	52.3	58.2	62.1	63.5	60.0
1972	70.3	64.9	69.0	63.9	83.6	60.9	63.2	70.7	63.7	74.6	68.6	63.5	56.5	71.6	84.2	82.5	84.0
1973	94.9	89.5	93.9	91.3	104.8	86.5	89.5	92.6	88.8	102.8	90.2	100.3	88.2	85.2	115.2	109.4	88.9
1974	135.6	124.7	149.3	136.9	131.5	109.0	119.9	145.3	152.1	162.1	133.8	150.0	131.7	128.9	147.2	124.4	122.9
1975	142.0	138.2	140.1	131.4	158.3	144.6	145.1	125.0	143.6	150.0	126.6	145.8	114.1	134.4	161.2	158.8	154.9
1976	194.7	176.3	193.2	187.0	222.5	155.6	170.3	203.0	190.6	197.8	191.3	190.4	170.5	200.0	215.9	246.8	203.8
1977	257.6	255.0	257.8	252.7	264.9	243.6	242.2	279.2	247.1	274.1	252.1	260.3	234.1	263.6	257.2	276.6	250.8
1978	309.2	281.0	327.6	306.7	321.6	291.0	266.7	285.3	288.0	372.5	322.3	302.7	306.3	311.1	339.7	372.3	252.8
1979	401.5	368.9	419.7	405.7	411.6	365.5	340.9	400.3	382.1	467.9	409.1	418.7	399.8	398.5	479.2	456.5	299.0
1980	451.7	476.6	440.0	432.1	458.1	493.4	480.1	456.2	438.5	488.2	393.2	457.8	382.9	455.5	431.0	513.1	430.2
1981	548.1	512.6	557.7	573.1	549.2	492.1	496.5	549.1	527.0	573.7	572.2	633.9	493.7	591.6	583.0	617.0	447.6
1982	567.6	597.5	589.7	532.5	550.8	566.5	567.3	658.6	624.7	579.4	565.0	552.9	518.6	525.9	525.3	607.2	519.9
1983	613.4	585.9	592.1	602.6	673.1	559.8	574.9	622.8	560.1	627.4	588.9	568.1	618.3	621.3	672.2	770.5	576.8

Exports f.o.b. (17) — Exportations f.o.b. (17)

£ million, monthly averages — millions de £, moyennes mensuelles

	Year	Q.1	Q.2	Q.3	Q.4	JAN	FEB	MAR	APR	MAY	JUN	JUL	AUG	SEP	OCT	NOV	DEC
1964	18.5	18.6	17.7	19.1	18.7	18.8	20.1	16.8	15.8	17.7	19.5	19.7	16.8	20.9	19.8	20.8	15.4
1965	18.3	16.5	15.8	20.8	20.1	17.0	15.3	17.1	14.4	15.4	17.7	22.3	18.6	21.4	21.2	21.2	18.0
1966	20.2	19.1	17.0	21.9	23.0	17.8	18.7	20.8	17.4	15.9	17.8	23.3	19.0	23.4	22.4	26.0	20.6
1967	23.6	21.5	22.4	25.5	25.1	21.2	20.3	22.9	21.7	23.0	22.5	24.0	25.0	27.4	25.8	28.6	21.0
1968	27.6	24.8	26.7	29.2	29.7	23.3	23.5	27.7	26.0	28.6	25.5	31.2	27.3	29.2	31.3	32.7	25.3
1969	30.8	26.7	30.6	32.2	33.7	29.0	22.0	29.3	30.6	32.2	29.1	33.5	27.1	36.0	36.1	34.8	30.1
1970	38.9	36.2	37.9	39.0	42.6	37.0	35.8	35.7	36.9	40.4	36.3	38.1	35.4	43.4	45.8	42.2	39.8
1971	44.7	41.8	45.1	44.6	47.4	43.1	38.3	43.9	39.6	47.6	48.0	45.2	40.4	48.3	45.1	46.3	50.8
1972	53.7	46.2	50.1	56.5	62.2	41.5	46.1	51.0	39.6	54.6	56.1	56.6	50.0	63.0	65.1	67.3	54.3
1973	72.4	62.5	68.9	73.2	84.9	56.0	61.2	70.3	59.5	76.4	70.9	72.2	68.6	78.7	90.7	86.1	78.0
1974	94.6	83.3	90.9	95.8	108.6	79.7	83.2	86.9	83.5	96.4	92.7	104.4	87.6	95.3	109.1	111.3	105.3
1975	120.6	103.9	111.4	125.7	141.4	112.8	106.7	92.3	108.4	124.6	101.3	133.4	108.3	135.6	171.1	139.7	113.4
1976	154.9	116.8	153.5	158.5	190.7	108.8	117.8	123.7	148.8	158.6	153.1	160.3	127.8	187.3	211.9	195.8	164.6
1977	209.9	174.5	199.7	229.4	235.8	153.6	178.8	191.0	186.0	206.5	206.7	244.5	202.0	241.8	229.4	253.9	224.0
1978	246.8	218.9	244.6	252.3	271.3	220.2	201.5	235.0	240.2	247.3	245.3	256.3	217.1	283.6	265.9	311.3	236.6
1979	290.2	246.5	275.3	307.5	331.6	216.0	257.6	266.0	259.9	314.0	252.0	357.9	258.4	306.3	357.1	360.9	276.7
1980	340.2	316.5	332.1	354.1	358.0	290.0	321.2	338.1	333.3	331.1	331.9	374.6	302.6	385.2	387.8	367.9	318.2
1981	398.1	334.1	400.7	413.3	444.2	313.4	326.3	362.6	343.0	425.6	433.4	431.4	370.2	438.2	479.6	456.4	396.7
1982	474.0	411.1	503.5	475.0	506.5	345.3	419.4	468.5	461.8	492.4	556.3	506.5	396.9	521.5	520.3	522.4	476.9
1983	578.2	471.6	575.8	606.3	658.9	423.7	494.4	496.6	539.4	555.2	632.8	619.2	549.1	650.7	659.5	704.1	613.2

Trade balance (f.o.b. — c.i.f.) (17) — Balance commerciale (f.o.b. — c.a.f.) (17)

£ million, monthly averages — millions de £, moyennes mensuelles

	Year	Q.1	Q.2	Q.3	Q.4	JAN	FEB	MAR	APR	MAY	JUN	JUL	AUG	SEP	OCT	NOV	DEC
1964	-10.5	-10.7	-12.5	-8.1	-10.6	-10.9	-8.7	-12.3	-14.3	-9.7	-13.4	-11.6	-6.4	-6.4	-10.7	-8.4	-12.7
1965	-12.7	-14.7	-17.2	-8.9	-10.2	-10.2	-15.3	-18.4	-20.5	-18.1	-13.0	-9.3	-9.2	-8.1	-10.0	-9.8	-10.9
1966	-10.8	-11.0	-11.5	-10.4	-10.3	-7.4	-9.6	-16.1	-14.4	-13.5	-6.8	-10.0	-12.4	-8.9	-10.3	-10.2	-10.4
1967	-8.9	-12.0	-10.4	-5.5	-7.8	-12.7	-11.1	-12.1	-10.8	-10.4	-10.0	-9.2	-4.9	-2.4	-5.3	-7.9	-10.3
1968	-13.6	-13.9	-15.1	-10.0	-15.5	-13.5	-17.6	-10.7	-16.3	-17.1	-11.9	-12.1	-9.8	-8.3	-14.6	-13.1	-18.7
1969	-18.3	-18.1	-22.6	-14.5	-18.1	-19.5	-18.2	-16.7	-27.6	-20.8	-19.5	-19.5	-12.3	-11.6	-21.0	-13.6	-19.7
1970	-17.4	-16.5	-19.7	-14.3	-19.1	-15.3	-18.2	-16.0	-24.1	-18.2	-16.8	-18.1	-13.8	-11.2	-19.4	-18.2	-19.5
1971	-18.1	-26.6	-18.8	-12.8	-14.5	-15.8	-22.7	-41.2	-24.6	-20.2	-11.5	-16.4	-11.9	-9.9	-17.0	-17.2	-9.2
1972	-16.6	-18.8	-18.9	-7.3	-21.4	-19.4	-17.1	-19.8	-24.1	-20.0	-12.5	-6.9	-6.5	-8.6	-19.1	-15.2	-29.8
1973	-22.5	-27.1	-25.0	-18.1	-19.9	-30.5	-28.3	-22.3	-29.3	-26.4	-19.3	-28.1	-19.6	-6.5	-25.5	-23.3	-10.8
1974	-41.0	-41.4	-58.4	-41.1	-22.9	-29.3	-36.7	-58.4	-68.6	-65.7	-41.0	-45.5	-44.2	-33.5	-38.1	-13.0	-17.6
1975	-21.4	-34.3	-28.7	-5.7	-16.9	-31.8	-38.3	-32.7	-35.2	-25.5	-25.3	-12.5	-5.8	1.2	9.9	-19.1	-41.4
1976	-39.9	-59.5	-39.7	-28.5	-31.8	-46.8	-52.5	-79.2	-41.8	-39.2	-38.1	-30.1	-42.7	-12.7	-5.1	-51.1	-39.2
1977	-47.7	-80.5	-58.1	-23.2	-29.1	-90.0	-63.5	-88.2	-61.1	-67.6	-45.5	-15.8	-32.0	-21.8	-37.8	-22.6	-26.9
1978	-62.5	-62.1	-83.0	-54.4	-50.3	-70.9	-65.2	-50.3	-47.8	-125.2	-76.0	-48.5	-89.2	-27.5	-73.8	-61.0	-16.2
1979	-111.2	-122.3	-144.4	-98.1	-80.1	-149.5	-83.3	-134.3	-122.2	-153.8	-157.1	-60.8	-141.5	-92.1	-122.2	-95.7	-22.3
1980	-111.5	-160.1	-107.9	-77.9	-100.1	-203.4	-158.9	-118.1	-105.2	-157.1	-61.3	-23.2	-80.3	-70.3	-43.2	-145.2	-111.9
1981	-150.1	-178.5	-157.0	-159.8	-105.0	-178.8	-170.2	-186.6	-184.1	-148.1	-138.8	-202.5	-123.5	-153.4	-103.5	-160.6	-50.8
1982	-93.6	-186.4	-86.2	-57.5	-44.3	-221.2	-147.9	-190.1	-162.9	-87.0	-3.7	-46.3	-121.7	-4.4	-5.0	-84.8	-43.0
1983	-35.3	-114.3	-16.4	3.8	-14.2	-136.2	-80.5	-126.2	-20.8	-72.2	43.9	51.2	-69.2	29.4	-12.7	-66.4	36.5

Imports c.i.f. (17)(18) — Importations c.a.f. (17)(18)

£ million, monthly averages — millions de £, moyennes mensuelles

Adjusted - Corrigé

Year	Q.1	Q.2	Q.3	Q.4	JAN	FEB	MAR	APR	MAY	JUN	JUL	AUG	SEP	OCT	NOV	DEC
1964	28.6	29.5	28.3	29.1	29.1	29.0	27.6	27.9	27.4	33.3	29.1	27.6	28.2	29.0	29.0	29.3
1965	30.7	32.3	30.9	30.1	28.5	31.3	32.5	32.0	33.7	31.0	30.1	31.9	30.8	30.9	29.5	29.9
1966	29.8	27.8	33.7	33.4	26.4	28.9	34.1	30.0	28.5	24.8	33.0	34.3	33.9	32.8	34.4	33.0
1967	32.8	31.9	32.8	33.2	34.5	31.8	32.2	32.3	30.9	32.7	33.2	32.7	32.5	30.3	34.8	34.6
1968	37.9	40.4	41.4	45.0	35.7	39.9	38.1	39.2	41.4	40.6	40.9	41.6	41.7	42.8	44.9	47.3
1969	44.3	51.3	49.4	51.3	46.7	40.5	45.8	54.1	43.7	51.2	51.0	46.2	51.0	52.4	50.2	51.4
1970	52.3	55.3	57.2	60.6	52.9	53.0	51.0	57.6	53.1	55.3	55.2	57.8	58.6	60.6	60.2	61.0
1971	67.4	61.3	61.6	61.1	59.8	60.3	82.1	61.1	61.1	61.8	60.9	61.5	62.4	57.9	63.1	62.2
1972	63.8	66.5	68.7	82.9	62.0	62.7	66.8	61.1	66.9	71.5	62.7	66.5	77.0	78.9	81.7	88.1
1973	87.8	90.5	98.1	103.9	88.6	89.2	85.6	85.2	91.9	94.3	99.0	103.4	92.0	109.7	107.5	94.4
1974	121.0	143.9	147.1	131.4	111.2	119.5	132.2	146.4	145.5	139.9	147.7	154.4	139.1	140.2	121.7	132.4
1975	134.6	135.1	140.7	159.6	146.2	144.8	112.7	137.6	135.6	132.1	144.1	133.4	144.6	155.4	154.3	169.0
1976	168.8	187.5	200.3	224.5	154.8	169.6	182.1	182.6	180.4	199.5	188.5	199.2	213.2	211.6	238.7	223.1
1977	245.7	249.0	269.4	265.4	240.8	243.7	252.5	240.2	251.4	255.4	262.5	267.5	278.2	263.0	260.4	272.7
1978	274.3	315.3	323.9	323.1	287.4	275.5	260.1	287.7	335.5	322.7	306.8	338.7	326.2	337.1	349.4	282.7
1979	361.1	403.7	425.0	415.0	349.4	354.4	379.4	384.8	412.4	413.9	426.0	438.3	410.7	485.9	427.6	331.5
1980	467.6	425.9	445.8	469.0	470.5	457.1	435.1	442.9	437.1	397.8	445.1	426.8	465.4	435.9	476.5	494.6
1981	501.2	541.9	586.5	562.9	478.3	510.8	514.5	520.0	527.7	578.1	610.2	545.3	603.9	602.5	576.5	509.8
1982	586.8	573.3	547.4	567.1	540.8	588.3	631.4	630.4	516.1	573.5	532.6	576.2	533.4	530.6	562.7	608.0
1983	570.6	577.3	620.7	690.2	543.5	589.1	579.3	549.7	583.1	599.1	540.5	691.6	630.1	699.5	718.7	652.4

Exports f.o.b. (17)(18) — Exportations f.o.b. (17)(18)

£ million, monthly averages — millions de £, moyennes mensuelles

Adjusted - Corrigé

Year	Q.1	Q.2	Q.3	Q.4	JAN	FEB	MAR	APR	MAY	JUN	JUL	AUG	SEP	OCT	NOV	DEC
1964	19.0	19.1	17.9	18.1	19.2	21.0	16.7	18.6	19.0	19.6	17.4	17.6	18.6	17.9	19.6	16.8
1965	17.0	17.0	19.4	19.5	17.8	16.7	16.6	16.5	16.6	17.9	19.5	19.6	19.2	19.7	18.8	20.1
1966	19.9	18.1	20.5	22.3	19.0	20.6	19.9	19.2	16.7	18.5	21.0	19.6	21.0	21.3	22.7	22.9
1967	22.4	23.6	24.2	24.7	22.5	22.3	22.2	24.1	23.1	23.5	22.4	25.7	24.5	24.3	25.6	24.1
1968	25.6	27.5	28.3	28.9	24.1	25.1	27.5	27.6	27.9	27.1	28.8	28.4	27.7	28.2	29.3	29.2
1969	27.9	31.1	31.2	33.1	29.8	24.3	29.7	31.7	30.3	31.2	31.1	29.4	32.9	32.9	32.6	33.7
1970	36.8	37.9	38.8	42.0	37.2	33.1	35.2	38.7	37.6	37.2	36.8	39.3	40.2	41.3	40.9	43.9
1971	42.6	45.0	44.6	46.8	43.8	40.6	43.3	42.1	44.5	48.4	43.9	44.9	45.1	40.6	44.5	55.3
1972	47.3	49.9	56.6	60.1	42.9	43.7	50.3	42.8	51.0	56.0	54.9	55.5	59.3	58.0	63.7	58.5
1973	64.6	68.9	73.3	81.3	59.3	64.7	69.9	64.7	71.5	70.6	69.4	76.1	74.3	80.0	80.2	83.7
1974	87.5	91.4	95.3	103.4	87.1	88.2	87.2	90.8	90.7	92.8	98.9	97.2	89.8	95.0	102.4	112.9
1975	111.4	112.1	124.0	132.0	125.7	114.1	94.3	116.8	117.7	101.8	124.5	120.3	127.1	147.3	127.4	121.3
1976	126.0	155.0	154.8	178.2	122.9	127.5	127.7	159.6	150.6	154.7	147.9	142.0	174.4	180.8	178.0	175.7
1977	186.3	198.9	222.1	226.6	173.6	193.2	198.2	194.7	196.6	205.3	225.0	224.1	217.2	215.1	223.2	241.4
1978	238.6	244.6	246.6	256.2	255.0	217.5	243.4	252.7	234.6	246.6	236.0	243.7	260.1	240.1	270.2	253.3
1979	262.6	275.4	301.1	316.3	248.9	268.9	270.1	268.5	303.4	254.3	330.5	292.6	280.3	327.9	319.1	303.4
1980	337.7	331.4	348.4	343.5	331.8	339.2	342.2	349.8	316.3	328.0	347.8	341.1	356.3	347.5	332.1	350.9
1981	358.6	393.3	407.3	429.9	362.7	348.5	364.5	357.5	403.4	418.9	397.9	422.1	402.0	430.4	423.0	436.2
1982	436.4	500.5	468.8	487.2	393.1	442.6	473.4	485.3	467.9	548.3	472.5	450.0	483.8	459.6	472.7	529.3
1983	507.7	565.9	600.9	641.3	497.2	529.4	496.6	562.5	525.7	609.6	569.1	630.5	603.0	592.0	661.1	670.9

Trade balance (f.o.b. — c.i.f.) (17)(18) — Balance commerciale (f.o.b. — c.a.f.) (17)(18)

£ million, monthly averages — millions de £, moyennes mensuelles

Adjusted - Corrigé

Year	Q.1	Q.2	Q.3	Q.4	JAN	FEB	MAR	APR	MAY	JUN	JUL	AUG	SEP	OCT	NOV	DEC
1964	-9.6	-10.5	-10.4	-11.0	-9.9	-8.1	-10.9	-9.2	-8.5	-13.6	-11.6	-10.0	-9.7	-11.2	-9.4	-12.5
1965	-13.7	-15.3	-11.5	-10.6	-10.8	-14.5	-15.9	-15.6	-17.1	-13.1	-10.6	-12.3	-11.5	-11.2	-10.7	-9.8
1966	-10.0	-9.6	-13.2	-11.1	-7.4	-8.3	-14.2	-10.8	-11.8	-6.3	-12.0	-14.7	-13.0	-11.6	-11.7	-10.2
1967	-10.5	-8.4	-8.6	-8.6	-12.0	-9.5	-10.0	-8.2	-7.8	-9.2	-10.8	-7.0	-8.1	-6.0	-9.1	-10.5
1968	-12.4	-12.9	-13.1	-16.1	-11.7	-14.9	-10.6	-11.6	-13.5	-13.5	-12.1	-13.2	-13.9	-14.6	-15.6	-18.2
1969	-16.4	-20.3	-18.2	-18.2	-16.9	-16.2	-16.1	-22.4	-18.5	-19.9	-19.9	-16.8	-18.0	-19.5	-17.6	-17.7
1970	-15.5	-17.4	-18.4	-18.6	-15.7	-14.9	-15.8	-18.9	-15.3	-18.1	-18.4	-18.5	-18.4	-19.3	-19.3	-17.1
1971	-24.8	-16.7	-17.0	-14.3	-16.0	-19.7	-38.8	-19.0	-16.6	-13.4	-17.0	-16.6	-17.3	-17.3	-18.6	-6.9
1972	-16.5	-16.6	-12.2	-22.8	-19.1	-14.0	-16.5	-18.3	-15.9	-15.5	-7.8	-11.0	-17.7	-20.9	-18.0	-29.6
1973	-23.2	-21.5	-24.9	-22.6	-29.3	-24.5	-15.7	-20.5	-20.4	-23.7	-29.6	-27.3	-17.7	-29.7	-27.3	-10.7
1974	-33.5	-52.5	-51.8	-28.0	-24.1	-31.3	-45.0	-55.6	-54.8	-47.1	-48.8	-57.2	-49.3	-45.2	-19.3	-19.5
1975	-23.2	-23.0	-16.7	-27.6	-20.5	-30.7	-13.4	-20.8	-17.9	-30.3	-19.6	-13.1	-17.5	-8.1	-26.9	-47.7
1976	-42.8	-32.5	-45.5	-45.3	-31.9	-42.1	-54.4	-23.0	-29.6	-44.8	-40.6	-57.2	-38.8	-30.8	-60.7	-47.4
1977	-57.3	-50.1	-47.3	-38.8	-67.2	-50.5	-54.3	-45.5	-54.8	-50.1	-37.5	-43.4	-61.0	-47.9	-37.2	-31.3
1978	-35.7	-70.7	-77.3	-66.9	-32.4	-58.0	-16.7	-35.0	-100.9	-76.1	-70.8	-95.0	-66.1	-97.0	-79.2	-24.4
1979	-98.4	-128.3	-123.9	-98.2	-100.5	-85.5	-109.3	-116.3	-109.0	-159.6	-95.5	-145.7	-130.4	-158.0	-108.5	-28.1
1980	-129.8	-94.6	-97.4	-125.5	-138.7	-157.9	-92.9	-93.1	-120.8	-69.8	-97.3	-85.7	-109.1	-88.4	-144.4	-143.7
1981	-142.6	-148.7	-179.1	-133.1	-215.6	-162.3	-150.0	-162.5	-124.3	-159.2	-212.3	-123.2	-201.9	-172.1	-153.5	-73.6
1982	-150.5	-72.8	-78.6	-79.9	-147.7	-145.7	-158.0	-145.1	-48.2	-25.2	-60.1	-126.2	-49.6	-71.0	-90.0	-78.7
1983	-62.9	-11.4	-19.9	-48.9	-46.3	-59.7	-82.7	12.8	-57.4	10.5	28.6	-61.1	-27.1	-107.5	-57.6	18.5

NOTES

1. Annual indices of Fisher chain type. Quarterly and monthly indices of Laspeyres chain type adjusted to bring their average into line with annual figures.
2. Prior to 1968, seasonally adjusted by the OECD Secretariat.
3. From April 1970, including demountable, prefabricated and mobile dwellings built by local authorities.
4. The original base of the index is 1975 to 1979, and 1980 from 1980.
5. Monthly data refer to end of period.
6. Due to numerous changes in coverage, the series is only broadly comparable over time.
7. Series based on the results of annual censuses of Industrial production. Quarterly data refer to a week near the middle of the 3rd month of the quarter. Extended coverage from 1973.
8. Monthly data refer to mid-month.
9. The original base of the index is 1953 to 1974, and 1975 from 1975.
10. From 1983, Government and non-resident deposits are excluded; foreign currency deposits and accrued interest are included.
11. Prior to December 1966, excluding non-associated banks. The amounts attributable to these banks in December 1966 are as follows:

	Million £
Net foreign position	—10.7
Domestic credit	54.8
Deposits included in *M1 plus quasi-money*	48.7

12. New accounting procedures were introduced in March 1972. This has had a downward effect of the order of £ 40 million on the data.
13. Weighting pattern based on 1951-52 to August 1968, on 1965-66 from November 1968 to August 1975, on 1973 from November 1975 to August 1982, and on November 1982 from November 1982.
14. Excluding central Government. From April 1972, including acceptances. From 1983, including credit in foreign currencies and accrued interest.
15. Monthly data refer to beginning of month. From 1967, excluding companies with a market capitalisation of less than £ 500,000.

NOTES

1. Indices annuels en chaîne de type Fisher. Indices trimestriels et mensuels en chaîne de type Laspeyre, ajustés pour être rendus compatibles avec l'indice annuel.
2. Avant 1968, corrigée des variations saisonnières par le Secrétariat de l'OCDE.
3. A partir d'avril 1970, les statistiques comprennent les logements démontables, préfabriqués et transportables construits par les collectivités locales.
4. La base originale de l'indice est 1975 jusqu'en 1979, et 1980 à partir de 1980.
5. Situation en fin de mois.
6. En raison de nombreux changements de couverture, les données ne peuvent être comparées qu'avec prudence.
7. Série établie d'après les recensements annuels de la Production industrielle. Les données trimestrielles se réfèrent à une semaine proche du milieu du 3e mois du trimestre. La couverture a été élargie à partir de 1973.
8. Les données mensuelles se réfèrent au milieu du mois.
9. La base originale de l'indice est 1953 jusqu'en 1974, et 1975 à partir de 1975.
10. A partir de 1983, non compris les dépôts de l'administration centrale et des non-résidents; y compris les dépôts en devises et les intérêts courus.
11. Avant décembre 1966, non compris les banques non associées. Les montants concernant ces banques en décembre 1966 sont les suivants:

	Millions de £
Position extérieure nette	—10.7
Crédits au secteur intérieur	54.8
Dépôts inclus dans *M1 plus quasi-monnaie*	48.7

12. En mars 1972, de nouvelles procédures de comptabilisation ont été introduites, entraînant une baisse du niveau de la série d'environ 40 millions de £.
13. La pondération se réfère à 1951-52 jusqu'en août 1968, à 1965-66 de novembre 1968 à août 1975, à 1973 de novembre 1975 à août 1982, et à novembre 1982 à partir de novembre 1982.
14. Non compris l'administration centrale. A partir d'avril 1972, y compris les traites acceptées. A partir de 1983, y compris les crédits en devises et les intérêts courus.
15. Les données mensuelles se réfèrent au début du mois. A partir de 1967, non compris les sociétés d'une capitalisation boursière inférieure à 500,000 £.

NOTES

16. From 1983, new definition of non-residents.

17. General imports; exports calculated as domestic exports plus re-exports.

18. Prior to 1970, seasonally adjusted by the OECD Secretariat.

NOTES

16. A partir de 1983, nouvelle définition des non-résidents.

17. Importations générales; les exportations sont la somme des exportations de marchandises d'origine nationale et des réexportations.

18. Avant 1970, corrigée des variations saisonnières par le Secrétariat de l'OCDE.

MAIN SOURCES

PRINCIPALES SOURCES

Series	Séries	Sources
Industrial production	Production industrielle	Central Statistics Office *Irish Statistical Bulletin*
Internal trade	Commerce intérieur	
Labour and wages	Main-d'œuvre et salaires	
Prices	Prix	
Share prices	Cours des actions	
Foreign trade	Commerce extérieur	
Business surveys	Enquêtes de conjoncture	Confederation of Irish Industries, Economic and Social Research Institute *Monthly Industrial Survey*
Construction	Construction	Department of the Environment *Quarterly Bulletin of Housing Statistics*
Home finance	Finances internes	Central Bank of Ireland *Quarterly Bulletin*
Interest rates	Taux d'intérêts	
Net foreign position of commercial banks	Position extérieure nette des banques commerciales	

Italy — Italie

ITALY

Gross domestic product / Produit intérieur brut

at current market prices / *aux prix courants du marché*

billion lire, annual rates / milliards de lires, taux annuels

Adjusted - Corrigé

	Year	Q.1	Q.2	Q.3	Q.4	JAN	FEB	MAR	APR	MAY	JUN	JUL	AUG	SEP	OCT	NOV	DEC
1964	36360	36004	36116	36436	36884												
1965	39124	37908	38684	39508	40396												
1966	42391	40996	41800	43216	43552												
1967	46695	45000	46396	47200	48184												
1968	50614	48684	49928	51236	52608												
1969	55876	54020	55792	57168	56524												
1970	62883	61372	62264	63080	64816												
1971	68510	66524	67632	68676	71208												
1972	75124	72736	73224	74900	79636												
1973	89746	81744	86943	93084	97203												
1974	110719	102320	107944	115208	117404												
1975	125376	119952	122056	126552	132952												
1976	156656	142584	151920	158900	173224												
1977	190084	185932	184892	190312	199196												
1978	222252	207588	215980	226288	239160												
1979	270200	250368	258332	275228	296864												
1980	338744	323236	332832	339080	359824												
1981	401300	384772	396620	396456	427352												
1982	469797	457224	467140	468448	486376												
1983		505880	518760	531040													

Industrial production: total (1) / Production industrielle : total (1)

1980 = 100

	Year	Q.1	Q.2	Q.3	Q.4	JAN	FEB	MAR	APR	MAY	JUN	JUL	AUG	SEP	OCT	NOV	DEC
1964	49.0	50.7	50.4	44.8	50.1	50.5	49.9	51.9	51.2	50.7	49.4	48.6	36.5	49.3	49.1	51.2	50.0
1965	51.3	50.0	52.5	48.0	54.7	48.8	50.6	50.6	51.5	53.0	53.1	52.0	39.0	52.9	53.1	56.2	54.7
1966	57.3	56.3	59.0	53.1	60.6	54.3	56.1	58.4	57.3	59.9	59.9	57.4	41.0	61.0	60.2	61.6	60.1
1967	61.8	61.9	64.8	56.0	64.5	59.8	62.8	63.0	64.3	65.3	64.9	61.7	42.4	63.8	64.4	66.1	62.9
1968	65.4	64.6	68.2	59.9	69.0	62.8	64.9	66.1	67.5	68.7	68.4	65.6	44.7	69.4	69.8	68.8	68.4
1969	67.8	70.2	73.4	62.5	64.9	69.0	69.1	72.4	73.1	72.5	74.5	70.6	48.6	68.3	64.9	65.2	64.5
1970	72.2	74.1	75.2	65.2	74.2	71.5	74.3	75.8	75.4	75.0	75.0	72.7	47.3	75.5	73.8	76.2	72.7
1971	71.8	72.5	74.2	64.4	76.0	70.4	73.1	74.0	72.8	74.7	75.0	70.7	44.2	78.4	75.5	77.5	75.0
1972	75.3	75.1	78.1	66.3	81.7	74.0	75.5	75.9	76.3	78.9	79.1	73.7	48.0	77.2	83.0	82.8	79.2
1973	82.6	76.6	86.4	77.6	89.7	75.0	77.0	77.9	84.0	86.6	88.7	86.7	55.8	90.4	91.6	91.5	86.2
1974	85.9	89.1	93.6	78.1	82.7	88.7	88.5	90.0	93.7	92.8	94.4	88.3	52.5	93.6	88.0	83.7	76.3
1975	78.3	80.3	81.2	68.9	82.7	78.4	82.7	79.7	82.0	78.7	83.0	79.9	42.7	84.1	84.5	85.6	78.1
1976	87.4	84.9	92.4	78.8	95.1	79.8	87.1	88.0	89.7	94.3	93.3	85.8	49.9	96.8	93.9	97.8	93.5
1977	87.4	94.5	91.9	76.2	86.5	93.5	96.0	93.9	92.8	93.5	89.5	85.5	49.6	93.4	89.3	89.5	80.8
1978	89.1	89.7	92.6	78.4	95.9	86.5	91.3	91.3	90.9	92.8	94.0	88.7	50.7	95.7	98.2	98.9	90.6
1979	95.1	96.4	96.9	83.6	103.4	92.1	99.8	97.4	99.0	97.8	93.9	92.5	54.5	103.8	105.5	106.4	98.2
1980	100.0	106.2	106.9	84.8	102.1	101.3	109.0	108.2	110.2	103.7	106.9	101.0	49.4	104.1	103.6	107.9	94.9
1981	97.8	101.9	103.0	84.4	102.0	95.2	105.6	105.0	105.6	101.1	102.4	100.4	46.8	106.1	101.8	108.6	95.5
1982	95.2	102.6	102.0	80.4	95.6	96.6	107.0	104.1	104.6	102.9	98.4	95.9	46.6	98.7	96.2	100.5	90.0
1983	90.5	95.2	91.0	78.3	94.9	90.8	98.5	96.4	93.1	91.1	89.0	90.2	46.7	98.1	95.3	102.2	87.2

Industrial production: investment goods (1)(2) / Production industrielle : biens d'équipement (1)(2)

1980 = 100

	Year	Q.1	Q.2	Q.3	Q.4	JAN	FEB	MAR	APR	MAY	JUN	JUL	AUG	SEP	OCT	NOV	DEC
1964	43.6	46.6	43.1	41.6	43.1	47.5	47.1	45.3	43.7	43.3	42.4	42.9	38.8	43.2	43.2	42.7	43.4
1965	46.5	43.8	46.5	47.5	48.3	43.0	44.8	43.5	45.7	46.6	47.2	47.1	47.2	48.2	48.1	48.8	48.0
1966	50.4	47.8	49.1	52.0	52.9	48.0	47.3	48.2	47.4	50.0	49.8	50.0	52.9	53.0	52.3	52.5	54.0
1967	57.1	55.1	57.1	57.4	58.8	54.5	55.3	55.7	56.3	57.4	57.5	57.5	56.9	57.7	55.4	59.2	57.7
1968	60.8	58.6	59.7	62.3	62.8	57.9	58.9	59.1	59.0	59.7	60.3	61.6	61.5	63.7	64.0	60.4	64.0
1969	61.9	63.6	65.9	64.0	54.1	63.6	62.6	64.8	65.9	64.6	67.1	66.4	65.8	59.7	54.1	52.0	56.1
1970	67.0	67.6	66.3	67.5	66.6	66.1	68.3	68.3	67.5	65.7	65.8	67.0	66.7	68.7	67.5	67.3	65.1
1971	66.9	68.4	66.7	65.8	66.4	67.9	67.4	69.9	66.8	67.3	66.1	64.4	65.9	67.1	64.0	66.8	68.6
1972	65.8	66.2	65.9	66.2	65.2	67.9	65.1	65.8	64.6	66.6	66.3	66.0	67.4	65.1	67.7	63.6	64.4
1973	70.5	55.7	71.2	76.4	78.6	57.7	54.1	55.1	66.5	71.5	75.6	77.1	76.3	75.9	79.0	77.0	79.8
1974	78.3	77.8	81.2	79.9	74.4	81.0	75.6	76.8	80.4	81.0	82.2	80.9	77.9	80.9	76.4	72.8	74.0
1975	71.4	74.8	70.3	71.1	69.4	75.0	76.4	72.9	72.0	67.1	71.8	72.9	69.5	70.9	70.3	70.1	67.8
1976	74.6	69.0	72.6	77.4	79.5	66.4	70.4	70.2	66.4	75.2	76.3	76.6	77.3	78.4	75.6	79.6	93.4
1977	78.6	82.8	78.1	77.9	76.0	83.9	81.2	83.2	74.7	83.0	76.5	75.2	78.9	79.5	75.7	77.4	74.9
1978	82.0	80.7	80.4	81.3	85.5	80.9	80.0	81.3	77.4	83.0	80.6	80.0	82.8	81.0	89.2	84.4	83.1
1979	87.6	84.8	81.9	86.9	96.9	83.7	86.2	84.4	85.2	82.3	73.2	85.3	87.7	87.3	95.2	97.1	98.5
1980	100.0	100.6	100.9	96.0	102.6	101.1	99.3	101.3	106.6	95.8	100.4	100.9	88.5	98.6	98.3	107.3	102.3
1981	106.6	108.5	101.4	105.1	111.4	100.4	112.5	112.7	106.4	95.8	102.0	110.1	90.4	114.9	104.9	117.4	111.8
1982	104.2	108.4	105.5	98.2	104.9	102.3	114.8	108.0	107.7	103.0	100.7	100.7	93.8	100.0	100.5	109.3	105.0
1983	96.3	98.4	92.0	93.6	101.3	92.4	103.6	99.1	94.0	95.9	86.1	96.2	86.2	98.3	97.1	108.4	98.5

Gross domestic product
implicit price level
1980 = 100

Adjusted - Corrigé

Produit intérieur brut
niveau implicite des prix
1980 = 100

	Year	Q.1	Q.2	Q.3	Q.4	JAN	FEB	MAR	APR	MAY	JUN	JUL	AUG	SEP	OCT	NOV	DEC
1964	20.4	20.0	20.3	20.5	20.3												
1965	21.3	21.1	21.1	21.3	21.5												
1966	21.7	21.6	21.7	21.8	21.9												
1967	22.3	22.1	22.4	22.4	22.4												
1968	22.7	22.6	22.7	22.7	22.8												
1969	23.6	23.1	23.4	23.9	24.1												
1970	25.3	24.8	25.1	25.3	25.8												
1971	27.1	26.5	27.0	27.2	27.7												
1972	28.8	28.2	28.4	28.9	29.6												
1973	32.1	30.7	31.5	32.6	33.4												
1974	38.0	34.8	36.6	39.4	41.4												
1975	44.7	42.7	44.0	45.3	46.7												
1976	52.8	49.0	51.4	53.4	57.0												
1977	62.8	60.7	61.4	63.2	66.1												
1978	71.5	67.7	70.2	73.0	75.1												
1979	82.9	78.0	80.7	84.3	88.3												
1980	100.0	94.3	97.8	101.5	106.5												
1981	118.3	112.9	117.0	117.9	125.4												
1982	139.0	132.3	137.1	140.6	146.3												
1983		151.2	157.7	160.0													

Industrial production: total (1)
1980 = 100

Adjusted - Corrigé

Production industrielle : total (1)
1980 = 100

	Year	Q.1	Q.2	Q.3	Q.4	JAN	FEB	MAR	APR	MAY	JUN	JUL	AUG	SEP	OCT	NOV	DEC
1964		50.2	49.1	48.1	48.9	50.9	49.3	50.4	49.7	49.2	48.3	49.2	46.2	48.8	48.6	49.0	49.1
1965		49.2	50.9	52.0	53.3	49.0	49.6	48.9	49.6	51.3	51.8	52.2	51.5	52.2	52.4	53.8	53.6
1966		55.1	56.2	58.6	59.2	54.8	54.6	56.0	54.8	56.9	57.1	57.6	59.1	59.2	58.6	58.9	60.1
1967		60.7	61.7	61.8	62.6	60.3	61.3	60.4	61.5	62.0	61.7	61.8	62.0	61.7	62.4	62.8	62.7
1968		63.3	64.9	66.1	67.2	63.2	63.3	63.3	64.4	65.2	65.1	65.6	65.4	67.3	67.8	65.4	68.3
1969		68.9	69.8	68.9	63.0	69.6	67.5	69.6	70.0	68.8	70.6	70.9	69.8	66.0	63.0	61.6	64.3
1970		72.6	71.3	72.4	72.3	72.1	72.9	72.7	72.0	70.9	71.0	72.9	71.1	73.2	71.6	72.5	72.7
1971		71.4	70.8	72.1	74.0	71.7	70.9	71.7	69.6	71.4	71.3	70.6	72.0	73.7	71.7	73.6	76.6
1972		73.5	74.1	74.0	79.3	74.8	72.8	73.1	72.3	75.0	74.8	73.1	75.7	73.1	79.2	78.4	80.3
1973		74.8	82.2	85.8	87.2	75.6	74.0	74.9	79.9	82.5	84.2	86.4	85.5	85.5	87.2	86.8	87.5
1974		87.5	89.4	87.7	80.2	89.8	85.6	87.1	89.5	88.7	89.9	88.2	86.4	88.5	83.6	78.9	78.2
1975		78.0	76.5	78.6	80.0	79.1	79.0	76.0	77.3	74.1	78.0	79.3	78.1	78.5	79.6	80.2	80.1
1976		82.5	87.5	89.5	92.5	80.6	83.0	84.0	84.7	89.5	88.2	89.3	88.0	91.3	89.2	92.3	96.1
1977		91.7	83.7	89.0	85.3	93.2	90.6	91.9	86.9	91.7	87.5	88.0	89.0	90.0	86.7	86.9	85.2
1978		88.4	89.1	90.9	94.3	88.5	88.2	83.5	87.2	89.5	90.6	90.4	91.9	90.5	94.6	94.4	93.9
1979		95.1	93.2	96.7	101.9	94.2	95.7	94.4	95.0	94.3	90.2	94.2	97.6	98.4	102.2	101.8	101.6
1980		105.6	103.8	98.6	100.2	104.4	106.4	106.0	106.9	100.7	104.0	103.6	93.7	98.6	99.4	102.9	98.3
1981		101.2	99.9	97.9	100.1	98.1	102.9	102.7	102.2	98.1	99.3	102.6	90.3	100.7	97.7	103.8	98.9
1982		102.3	99.2	94.6	94.0	99.9	104.8	102.2	101.6	100.4	95.6	98.5	90.3	95.0	92.4	95.9	93.7
1983		94.6	90.2	91.8	93.1	93.8	95.8	94.1	89.5	91.9	89.1	92.4	90.3	92.6	91.1	97.3	90.7

Industrial production: consumer goods (1)
1980 = 100

Adjusted - Corrigé

Production industrielle : biens de consommation (1)
1980 = 100

	Year	Q.1	Q.2	Q.3	Q.4	JAN	FEB	MAR	APR	MAY	JUN	JUL	AUG	SEP	OCT	NOV	DEC
1964	49.4	51.4	50.0	48.3	47.9	51.6	51.3	51.5	51.7	49.7	48.6	50.4	46.0	48.4	47.7	48.4	47.7
1965	49.6	46.7	49.8	51.2	50.8	46.4	46.7	47.0	48.3	49.9	51.3	51.6	50.7	51.2	49.5	51.8	51.2
1966	55.8	54.6	54.9	56.7	57.1	53.8	54.0	56.1	54.0	55.3	55.6	56.5	56.7	56.9	56.7	56.5	57.9
1967	58.1	57.9	58.0	57.9	58.4	57.8	58.9	57.0	58.3	58.1	57.5	57.9	58.3	57.5	57.5	58.1	59.7
1968	60.7	58.9	61.0	61.2	62.0	59.7	58.3	58.5	61.1	61.3	60.5	61.3	60.5	61.9	62.4	60.7	62.7
1969	63.7	64.1	64.6	64.2	61.7	65.8	61.9	64.5	64.6	63.5	65.7	65.5	64.1	63.1	62.0	61.5	61.7
1970	66.5	67.2	65.9	66.6	66.0	67.2	67.4	66.9	65.6	66.3	66.0	68.4	65.0	66.6	64.6	66.0	67.4
1971	66.8	66.3	65.0	67.2	68.3	68.0	65.1	65.6	63.4	66.1	65.5	64.9	66.1	70.6	66.6	67.9	71.8
1972	69.9	68.7	68.5	67.2	75.3	70.4	67.6	68.0	66.5	69.7	69.4	66.2	69.2	66.4	75.4	74.6	76.0
1973	76.7	70.3	76.9	79.4	79.9	71.7	70.4	70.4	74.4	77.4	78.8	80.1	78.6	79.5	79.7	79.9	80.2
1974	79.6	80.3	82.8	81.5	73.8	82.1	78.7	80.1	82.9	81.5	83.9	81.2	79.9	83.5	77.0	71.6	72.8
1975	73.3	72.0	70.7	74.5	75.9	72.8	72.6	70.6	71.4	69.2	71.6	74.0	75.5	74.0	74.8	76.7	76.3
1976	84.0	78.7	83.2	84.5	89.8	77.3	79.3	79.3	81.1	85.9	82.5	84.0	82.5	86.9	86.5	90.0	92.8
1977	84.7	87.5	84.0	85.6	81.6	89.0	86.2	87.2	82.3	86.5	83.1	84.7	85.4	86.8	82.8	82.5	79.5
1978	86.5	83.3	85.1	87.4	90.1	83.1	82.7	84.2	82.3	85.1	87.9	87.2	88.9	86.1	90.3	90.1	90.0
1979	94.4	92.1	91.4	94.3	100.0	90.8	94.0	91.5	92.6	92.9	88.7	92.1	94.6	96.2	100.0	99.7	100.3
1980	100.0	104.2	102.0	96.2	97.7	102.9	105.7	104.1	104.5	98.6	103.0	101.9	91.8	94.9	97.2	100.2	95.6
1981	96.0	97.3	97.9	93.1	95.9	94.0	98.9	99.1	99.7	97.6	96.2	99.5	86.0	93.9	93.2	99.3	95.1
1982	94.9	98.9	97.3	92.1	91.3	97.5	101.3	97.7	99.5	99.2	93.2	98.5	87.0	90.8	88.8	93.0	92.0
1983	90.7	95.7	89.3	88.9	88.9	96.9	95.0	95.2	89.2	91.4	87.3	89.9	88.3	88.4	86.4	94.2	86.3

ITALY

Industrial production: manufacturing (1) (20)

1980 = 100

Production industrielle : industries manufacturières (1) (20)

1980 = 100

	Year	Q.1	Q.2	Q.3	Q.4	JAN	FEB	MAR	APR	MAY	JUN	JUL	AUG	SEP	OCT	NOV	DEC
1964	47.4	48.6	47.8	44.5	48.4	49.1	47.5	49.4	49.6	47.2	46.6	49.9	34.9	48.8	50.2	47.9	47.2
1965	49.5	47.4	49.7	48.1	53.0	45.9	46.0	50.3	49.6	50.6	48.8	53.5	38.3	52.5	53.2	52.8	53.1
1966	55.5	52.9	56.4	54.2	58.6	49.4	50.8	58.5	54.3	59.6	55.3	59.1	42.6	60.8	60.1	57.6	58.0
1967	60.2	59.5	62.4	56.9	62.0	56.9	57.5	64.2	61.4	63.2	62.6	63.3	43.7	63.7	65.5	62.7	57.7
1968	63.9	62.5	65.2	60.6	67.5	59.7	62.4	65.3	64.3	68.0	63.3	68.5	45.8	67.4	72.8	65.1	64.6
1969	66.4	67.3	71.5	64.4	62.4	66.1	63.9	71.9	71.0	73.5	69.8	75.9	48.7	68.7	67.2	59.1	60.9
1970	70.8	70.6	72.9	67.0	72.9	69.3	69.3	73.1	75.5	71.1	72.2	77.4	47.6	75.9	77.3	72.3	69.0
1971	70.5	70.2	70.9	66.3	74.7	66.6	68.5	75.5	71.9	74.7	69.0	74.8	43.6	80.5	77.3	73.4	73.3
1972	73.4	74.4	73.7	67.2	78.5	69.8	73.3	80.0	69.8	78.3	72.8	75.5	47.3	78.8	85.1	78.4	72.0
1973	80.8	74.4	81.7	78.3	88.7	72.8	71.6	78.8	77.1	86.3	81.9	89.7	55.5	89.8	97.2	90.1	78.7
1974	84.6	87.4	90.1	79.8	81.1	90.2	83.0	89.1	89.8	92.9	87.6	94.3	51.8	93.1	93.0	78.8	71.4
1975	76.1	76.1	78.3	70.3	79.8	76.1	76.8	75.3	80.7	75.1	79.2	84.8	40.1	86.1	89.0	77.4	72.8
1976	85.8	81.8	87.4	80.6	93.2	76.5	80.5	83.5	87.4	89.7	85.0	94.5	48.2	99.3	96.1	92.2	91.4
1977	86.8	92.5	91.9	77.1	85.4	88.2	90.0	99.3	88.0	96.2	91.5	87.6	48.3	95.3	90.8	87.8	77.8
1978	88.2	87.8	92.6	79.4	93.0	86.4	84.4	92.6	85.8	95.4	96.6	91.1	49.4	97.7	101.0	96.5	81.6
1979	94.3	95.4	95.7	83.7	102.6	91.8	92.8	101.8	90.4	100.6	96.0	94.8	53.4	102.3	113.2	105.1	89.5
1980	100.0	106.5	106.4	87.0	100.2	102.5	106.7	110.4	105.4	106.9	106.7	107.9	46.0	106.9	109.8	102.1	88.8
1981	97.8	100.7	102.6	86.7	101.4	95.5	98.7	108.0	101.5	100.9	105.5	107.1	43.3	109.6	108.2	106.6	89.4
1982	95.3	101.0	102.3	83.1	94.6	93.6	99.7	109.8	103.6	102.5	100.8	102.1	44.8	102.4	98.5	98.2	87.0
1983	89.9	93.2	93.3	79.3	93.8	87.5	91.0	101.0	88.0	97.5	94.3	92.4	44.7	100.9	97.7	99.9	83.9

Industrial production: (1)

industrial materials

1980 = 100

Adjusted - Corrigé

Production industrielle : (1)

produits de base pour l'industrie

1980 = 100

	Year	Q.1	Q.2	Q.3	Q.4	JAN	FEB	MAR	APR	MAY	JUN	JUL	AUG	SEP	OCT	NOV	DEC
1964	47.7	45.5	47.5	48.0	49.5	46.8	42.3	47.5	46.9	48.0	47.6	47.7	48.0	48.4	48.8	49.8	50.1
1965	51.3	51.1	49.9	50.5	53.9	51.9	51.2	50.2	48.4	50.9	50.2	51.2	50.1	50.4	53.2	54.0	54.4
1966	58.6	57.0	57.4	59.1	60.6	57.1	56.5	57.4	56.8	57.6	57.9	57.7	60.0	59.8	58.7	60.8	62.2
1967	62.3	61.4	62.0	62.0	64.1	61.6	61.5	61.0	62.2	62.3	61.5	61.0	62.5	62.5	63.5	64.5	64.4
1968	66.9	65.2	66.0	67.1	69.3	64.4	65.0	66.1	65.4	66.5	66.0	66.0	66.4	69.1	69.9	68.6	69.4
1969	70.8	70.3	71.4	72.0	69.4	69.4	70.5	71.1	71.3	71.2	71.8	72.1	73.4	70.5	69.4	67.7	71.2
1970	75.5	74.3	75.5	75.9	76.2	74.0	74.0	74.9	76.7	74.9	74.9	76.6	74.9	76.2	76.1	76.5	76.1
1971	75.0	73.5	73.8	75.2	77.6	72.8	73.6	74.1	72.5	74.1	74.7	74.5	75.9	75.3	75.3	77.4	80.2
1972	79.6	76.9	78.2	79.0	84.2	77.6	76.6	76.6	76.5	79.1	79.0	78.1	80.6	73.2	82.9	83.5	86.1
1973	87.9	81.8	87.0	90.6	92.3	82.0	81.0	82.4	85.8	87.1	88.1	91.0	90.7	90.1	92.3	92.2	92.4
1974	90.6	93.0	93.8	91.7	84.0	95.2	91.0	92.7	94.3	93.5	93.7	92.7	91.0	91.5	87.7	83.5	80.8
1975	81.4	80.7	80.0	81.3	83.6	82.2	81.7	78.2	80.6	77.4	82.0	82.4	79.9	81.5	83.3	83.3	84.2
1976	92.2	86.9	92.5	94.1	95.5	84.8	86.9	89.0	90.6	93.7	93.2	94.4	92.5	95.6	92.5	94.8	99.3
1977	92.3	94.8	92.5	92.0	90.0	95.9	93.7	94.7	91.1	95.2	91.1	91.5	91.8	92.6	90.0	90.3	89.8
1978	93.2	91.3	91.5	93.4	96.7	91.7	91.6	90.6	90.7	91.4	92.5	92.9	93.7	93.5	96.0	97.4	96.8
1979	97.7	97.2	94.6	98.0	100.7	96.8	98.5	96.5	96.2	95.7	91.9	94.9	99.3	99.8	101.9	100.8	99.4
1980	100.0	104.0	101.8	97.3	97.0	102.3	105.0	104.6	104.2	99.8	101.6	101.4	93.2	97.2	97.3	98.9	94.7
1981	96.0	97.3	96.6	94.9	95.1	96.3	98.1	97.6	98.3	95.0	95.5	98.3	89.7	96.6	94.4	97.9	93.1
1982	93.0	98.5	94.2	91.3	88.1	96.7	99.4	99.4	96.8	94.2	91.6	93.4	87.9	92.5	88.2	89.3	86.9
1983	88.3	88.3	86.2	89.5	89.2	87.8	89.5	87.5	84.2	86.7	87.8	89.1	89.4	89.9	88.8	91.6	87.2

Production: crude steel

thousand tons, monthly averages

Production : acier brut

milliers de tonnes, moyennes mensuelles

	Year	Q.1	Q.2	Q.3	Q.4	JAN	FEB	MAR	APR	MAY	JUN	JUL	AUG	SEP	OCT	NOV	DEC
1964																	
1965																	
1966																	
1967																	
1968																	
1969	1366	1500	1524	1333	1107	1532	1378	1590	1494	1583	1496	1443	1263	1293	1020	1039	1263
1970	1440	1436	1525	1438	1360	1516	1318	1475	1524	1520	1530	1520	1280	1515	1460	1330	1289
1971	1454	1425	1419	1371	1603	1418	1359	1497	1353	1492	1412	1452	1158	1502	1615	1578	1617
1972	1651	1640	1675	1618	1672	1579	1592	1749	1610	1743	1673	1730	1368	1756	1817	1641	1557
1973	1750	1392	1829	1798	1982	1461	1255	1460	1697	1922	1867	1890	1600	1905	2013	1969	1965
1974	1984	1995	2005	1913	2022	2120	1823	2043	1968	2046	2001	2025	1647	2066	2104	1925	2036
1975	1822	2027	1877	1620	1764	2178	1929	1973	2055	1820	1756	1709	1302	1850	1861	1696	1736
1976	1949	1825	1956	2004	2009	1819	1748	1909	1729	2090	2050	2163	1681	2169	2230	1833	1915
1977	1944	2034	1938	1857	1947	2033	1958	2112	1867	2008	1920	1976	1519	2075	1994	1917	1930
1978	2021	2067	2125	1826	2067	2123	2009	2068	2125	2183	2067	2031	1357	2039	2168	2119	1914
1979	2021	2115	1940	1875	2152	2161	2025	2160	1953	2019	1944	1964	1465	2197	2275	2138	1994
1980	2210	2392	2334	2009	2106	2266	2388	2522	2336	2436	2231	2329	1453	2244	2348	2100	1869
1981	2047	2051	2146	1863	2127	2145	1884	2123	2098	2241	2100	1973	1479	2139	2200	2157	2013
1982	1998	2260	2177	1747	1810	2207	2182	2392	2271	2280	1979	1894	1372	1974	1918	1834	1678
1983	1806	1772	1802	1715	1935	1779	1728	1810	1622	1921	1864	1750	1403	1938	2087	1993	1724

Industrial production: manufacturing (1) — Production industrielle : industries manufacturières (1)

1980 = 100

Adjusted - Corrigé

	Year	Q.1	Q.2	Q.3	Q.4	JAN	FEB	MAR	APR	MAY	JUN	JUL	AUG	SEP	OCT	NOV	DEC
1964		48.6	47.4	46.4	47.1	49.4	47.6	48.7	48.1	47.5	46.6	47.5	44.4	47.1	46.8	47.1	47.3
1965		47.3	49.1	50.4	51.4	47.2	47.6	47.0	47.9	49.4	50.1	50.6	49.9	50.6	50.7	51.9	51.7
1966		54.3	55.5	58.0	58.4	53.9	53.8	55.2	53.9	56.2	56.3	57.0	58.5	58.6	57.9	58.0	59.2
1967		60.0	61.0	61.1	61.7	59.6	60.6	59.7	60.8	61.3	60.9	61.1	61.3	60.9	61.5	61.9	61.7
1968		62.2	63.9	65.0	66.1	62.2	62.2	62.1	63.4	64.2	64.2	64.7	64.1	66.2	66.6	64.3	67.3
1969		67.8	68.7	67.7	60.9	68.7	66.2	68.5	68.9	67.6	69.6	69.9	68.6	64.5	60.6	59.8	62.3
1970		71.6	69.9	71.0	70.8	71.1	72.0	71.7	70.5	69.6	69.6	71.5	69.6	71.9	70.0	71.0	71.5
1971		70.1	69.2	70.4	72.3	70.6	69.5	70.2	67.9	69.9	69.7	68.8	70.4	72.1	69.9	72.0	75.0
1972		71.8	72.2	72.1	77.6	73.3	71.0	71.2	70.5	73.1	73.1	71.3	73.9	71.0	77.3	76.6	78.7
1973		72.7	80.6	84.2	85.6	73.6	72.0	72.6	78.3	80.9	82.7	85.0	83.9	83.9	85.4	85.1	86.2
1974		86.0	88.1	86.2	78.1	88.3	84.0	85.6	88.2	87.3	88.7	86.7	84.8	87.0	81.4	76.8	76.1
1975		75.9	74.2	76.7	77.6	77.1	76.8	73.9	75.0	71.7	75.8	77.3	76.3	76.4	77.2	78.0	77.3
1976		80.1	85.1	87.3	90.6	78.2	80.7	81.4	82.1	87.4	85.8	87.0	85.8	89.1	87.1	90.4	94.2
1977		90.1	86.3	86.8	83.8	91.4	86.8	90.0	84.4	89.6	85.0	85.8	86.8	87.8	84.4	84.6	82.4
1978		85.9	86.5	88.6	91.9	86.1	85.6	86.1	84.4	87.0	88.2	88.2	89.5	88.0	92.5	91.6	91.5
1979		92.5	90.6	94.4	100.0	91.4	94.3	91.6	92.5	91.9	87.4	91.9	95.0	96.3	100.4	99.9	99.9
1980		103.8	101.9	96.4	98.1	102.5	104.9	103.9	105.0	98.4	102.1	101.7	91.1	96.3	97.2	100.9	96.1
1981		99.5	98.0	95.8	98.1	95.9	101.1	101.5	100.9	96.0	97.1	100.7	87.5	99.1	95.9	101.8	96.6
1982		100.2	96.8	92.1	91.8	97.7	102.6	100.3	99.7	98.1	92.8	96.3	87.5	92.6	90.3	93.8	91.3
1983		92.0	87.4	89.3	90.7	91.4	93.1	91.6	86.8	89.3	86.2	85.9	87.3	90.6	89.2	95.0	87.8

Production: commercial vehicles — Production : véhicules utilitaires

thousands, monthly averages — milliers, moyennes mensuelles

	Year	Q.1	Q.2	Q.3	Q.4	JAN	FEB	MAR	APR	MAY	JUN	JUL	AUG	SEP	OCT	NOV	DEC
1964	5.1	6.0	5.4	4.5	4.6	6.2	5.8	6.1	6.4	4.7	5.0	6.1	2.0	5.4	5.3	4.6	3.9
1965	6.0	6.3	6.2	5.3	6.1	5.5	6.8	6.5	6.5	6.8	5.3	7.2	2.2	6.4	5.9	6.7	5.8
1966	7.0	6.7	7.6	6.6	7.0	5.7	6.7	7.7	7.0	8.4	7.3	8.1	3.2	8.6	7.6	7.0	6.3
1967	8.6	8.5	9.6	7.8	8.6	7.7	7.9	9.8	9.4	9.8	9.6	9.5	4.0	10.0	10.0	9.2	6.6
1968	9.9	9.4	10.1	9.0	11.1	8.1	9.9	10.3	9.5	9.9	10.8	11.6	4.2	11.1	12.9	10.4	10.1
1969	9.9	11.8	11.7	8.9	7.1	11.6	11.0	12.8	11.6	12.3	11.3	12.9	4.1	9.6	7.8	6.5	7.1
1970	11.2	11.6	11.2	10.2	11.8	10.8	12.0	11.9	12.2	10.1	11.3	12.4	5.2	13.0	12.7	10.7	12.0
1971	9.7	10.3	9.9	8.7	9.6	9.5	10.1	11.4	10.6	9.9	9.3	11.4	3.8	10.8	9.8	9.5	9.6
1972	9.0	9.3	9.2	7.5	9.8	8.7	9.3	9.8	8.5	9.9	9.1	8.6	4.1	9.9	10.7	9.8	8.8
1973	11.2	8.4	11.9	10.8	13.7	8.5	8.0	8.8	11.2	12.8	11.8	14.1	5.9	12.3	14.8	14.8	11.6
1974	11.8	11.6	13.1	11.4	11.2	12.4	9.5	12.8	15.1	13.1	11.2	12.5	8.5	13.2	11.7	11.3	10.7
1975	9.2	8.4	10.4	9.1	9.2	7.9	10.0	7.2	12.0	9.2	10.0	12.7	2.4	12.3	11.9	9.0	6.8
1976	10.0	8.6	10.1	9.3	11.9	7.1	8.8	9.8	8.8	11.1	10.3	11.9	4.2	11.8	12.0	12.9	10.8
1977	12.0	14.0	11.7	10.1	12.0	13.8	13.2	14.9	10.3	13.9	11.0	12.3	4.6	13.4	12.8	12.5	10.8
1978	12.3	12.7	13.3	9.5	12.5	12.7	11.3	14.1	11.9	14.2	13.9	12.4	3.0	13.1	14.5	13.2	9.7
1979	12.6	13.3	12.4	10.0	14.6	13.5	12.7	13.8	11.8	13.3	12.2	10.8	4.3	14.9	17.1	15.1	11.5
1980	13.9	15.6	15.9	10.6	13.5	15.4	15.3	16.0	14.5	17.0	16.2	0.0	18.6	13.1	10.9	17.1	12.5
1981	15.2	16.9	16.0	12.4	15.0	17.4	16.3	16.9	14.9	17.1	16.0	18.2	0.6	18.4	17.5	16.3	11.1
1982	13.0	13.7	14.3	10.3	13.5	14.8	12.5	13.9	14.7	13.8	14.5	14.5	1.4	15.0	12.7	14.4	13.4
1983		14.2				10.9	14.4	17.4	14.7	16.8							

Production: passenger cars — Production : voitures de tourisme

thousands, monthly averages — milliers, moyennes mensuelles

	Year	Q.1	Q.2	Q.3	Q.4	JAN	FEB	MAR	APR	MAY	JUN	JUL	AUG	SEP	OCT	NOV	DEC
1964	85.7	100.4	90.2	72.2	80.1	101.0	102.6	97.6	98.1	86.0	86.5	99.3	25.9	91.5	52.6	88.9	58.8
1965	92.0	88.4	106.3	90.1	82.7	80.3	86.7	98.3	107.1	111.2	102.0	122.8	37.2	110.2	83.2	92.1	72.8
1966	106.9	94.4	117.2	106.2	107.7	83.6	96.6	103.1	105.8	127.7	118.1	138.8	51.1	134.7	121.6	112.5	88.9
1967	119.9	123.5	135.6	113.7	107.0	111.6	121.0	137.8	132.1	138.7	136.0	152.0	52.8	136.2	126.5	119.0	75.5
1968	128.7	128.8	138.4	115.0	132.7	116.7	136.6	133.1	126.5	148.7	140.1	153.9	46.2	144.9	150.5	126.2	121.4
1969	123.1	148.5	140.1	115.0	88.8	142.0	143.5	160.1	151.2	146.1	123.1	178.3	49.7	117.1	102.4	81.1	82.8
1970	143.3	146.5	136.8	130.5	159.4	148.0	144.9	146.6	155.8	121.8	132.8	157.9	55.7	178.0	167.9	157.7	152.6
1971	141.8	142.5	137.9	124.3	162.1	137.2	128.6	171.6	157.4	134.1	122.2	156.9	45.2	170.7	168.6	165.6	152.2
1972	144.4	159.2	156.4	124.1	137.8	147.0	157.3	173.4	148.4	171.9	148.9	155.2	61.1	155.9	155.5	137.4	120.4
1973	152.1	114.5	167.8	148.5	177.6	117.4	113.3	112.8	141.3	191.5	170.6	186.1	83.8	175.5	213.0	189.6	130.3
1974	135.9	150.7	158.0	130.3	104.8	179.3	126.3	146.5	154.6	166.8	152.5	163.1	69.7	158.0	120.8	95.7	98.0
1975	112.4	91.4	122.6	108.3	127.1	87.4	99.1	87.7	128.1	119.4	120.4	143.3	38.1	143.5	147.3	117.4	116.7
1976	122.6	115.6	124.2	117.3	133.3	110.3	111.2	125.3	109.1	135.4	128.2	152.2	48.9	150.8	133.4	140.0	126.5
1977	120.0	137.2	121.7	99.7	121.5	138.0	132.2	141.3	106.1	142.4	116.6	118.7	39.3	141.2	128.6	124.9	111.1
1978	125.7	134.1	134.5	99.2	135.0	139.7	123.9	138.7	121.1	140.5	142.0	129.4	31.1	137.1	145.6	139.8	119.7
1979	123.4	140.9	123.7	87.0	141.9	149.6	131.6	141.4	117.7	134.7	118.8	101.1	29.2	130.6	153.7	151.4	120.7
1980	132.9	150.2	143.1	122.3	116.1	145.9	149.9	154.7	144.6	149.8	134.8	145.7	149.7	67.6	98.0	134.1	116.1
1981	104.5	128.3	123.6	83.2	82.7	129.9	127.3	127.7	121.0	128.4	121.4	125.7	3.4	120.5	92.0	88.5	67.7
1982	108.0	116.1	123.0	92.3	100.8	103.3	117.6	127.5	120.3	114.9	133.9	130.9	17.4	128.7	108.8	102.8	90.7
1983		115.0	128.2			106.5	106.8	131.7	115.3	133.4	136.0						

ITALY

Ships completed

thousand gross register tons, quarterly averages

Navires achevés

milliers de tonneaux de jauge brute, moyennes trimestrielles

	Year	Q.1	Q.2	Q.3	Q.4	JAN	FEB	MAR	APR	MAY	JUN	JUL	AUG	SEP	OCT	NOV	DEC
1964	115	129	163	70	100												
1965	100	85	124	135	55												
1966	133	140	62	174	135												
1967	124	157	91	133	115												
1968	125	65	131	200	103												
1969	91	102	135	59	69												
1970	137	42	305	62	137												
1971	218	190	190	238	256												
1972	225	254	90	180	375												
1973	209	62	336	170	267												
1974	238	210	239	226	275												
1975	198	203	96	216	277												
1976	179	171	276	35	233												
1977	194	202	194	217	161												
1978	85	53	107	76	117												
1979	58	86	63	32	50												
1980	62	89	104	19	36												
1981	68	68	24	80	98												
1982	44	44	51	16	69												
1983	62	88	103	55	3												

Prospects for total economy (3)

mining and manufacturing

per cent balance

Perspectives économiques (3)

industries extractives et manufacturières

solde en pourcentage

	Year	Q.1	Q.2	Q.3	Q.4	JAN	FEB	MAR	APR	MAY	JUN	JUL	AUG	SEP	OCT	NOV	DEC
1964						-24	-39	-45	-42	-49	-50	-56	-50	-41	-43	-37	-40
1965						-39	-40	-22	-14	-13	-19	-21	-13	-14	-13	-8	[illegible]
1966						5	1	13	12	10	9	10	14	23	20	15	19
1967						25	22	31	24	24	26	33	31	32	29	24	22
1968						17	12	18	22	15	12	11	12	14	13	11	22
1969						22	22	31	32	36	23	22	19	14	-6	-13	-1
1970						1	-3	-1	-2	-14	-26	-22	-10	-11	-12	-26	-14
1971						-25	-26	-34	-48	-51	-49	-51	-52	-59	-53	-42	-35
1972						-42	-35	-26	-19	-22	-27	-27	-24	-17	-21	-11	-13
1973						-9	-10	-10	-4	2	1	5	14	11	10	-30	-34
1974						-35	-35	-19	-35	-45	-50	-56	-57	-66	-69	-68	-69
1975						-62	-57	-41	-31	-40	-49	-53	-52	-58	-45	-44	-44
1976						-47	-43	-54	-41	-39	-19	-17	-18	-29	-47	-37	-38
1977						-38	-41	-38	-37	-39	-46	-45	-41	-47	-49	-54	-47
1978						-46	-38	-36	-28	-25	-26	-25	-23	-17	-16	-25	-13
1979						-20	-16	-14	-19	-17	-16	-24	-23	-29	-28	-35	-41
1980						-30	-26	-32	-32	-51	-61	-59	-60	-62	-55	-56	-55
1981						-53	-50	-61	-53	-58	-56	-54	-54	-53	-62	-51	-47
1982						-42	-30	-30	-33	-33	-40	-43	-51	-52	-56	-57	-56
1983						-43	-33	-34	-44	-41	-44	-39	-38	-34	-32	-28	-17

Production: future tendency (3)

mining and manufacturing

per cent balance

Perspectives de production (3)

industries extractives et manufacturières

solde en pourcentage

	Year	Q.1	Q.2	Q.3	Q.4	JAN	FEB	MAR	APR	MAY	JUN	JUL	AUG	SEP	OCT	NOV	DEC
1964						14	-2	-16	-8	-21	-37	-32	-30	-32	-31	-25	-26
1965						-25	-23	-9	-1	-8	-18	-15	-9	-4	-12	-4	7
1966						11	17	18	23	16	6	2	7	3	7	10	17
1967						24	23	21	14	5	1	2	7	6	5	10	16
1968						17	15	14	9	4	1	4	9	12	12	14	24
1969						23	27	29	33	20	16	14	22	14	12	16	41
1970						34	24	26	18	9	1	8	14	2	-4	-9	2
1971						7	7	-3	-13	-15	-8	-10	-5	-12	-17	-6	-4
1972						7	7	9	8	3	-2	5	11	9	6	9	2
1973						17	26	38	37	34	25	24	24	24	16	-4	13
1974						14	20	19	16	4	-1	-14	-15	-16	-32	-39	-36
1975						-32	-19	-10	-8	-15	-21	-32	-22	-21	-19	-13	-3
1976						2	4	3	10	3	7	4	11	1	-8	-5	-5
1977						2	1	-4	-3	-13	-20	-22	-16	-19	-24	-26	-12
1978						-3	6	2	1	-	-2	-1	12	8	3	1	13
1979						13	19	8	17	3	14	19	18	13	7	2	3
1980						15	14	11	-2	-15	-24	-15	-8	-15	-12	-18	-10
1981						-7	2	-6	-15	-22	-22	-18	-10	-18	-19	-14	-1
1982						-	-2	-9	-2	-12	-26	-22	-17	-25	-26	-30	-17
1983						-8	-6	-11	-9	-16	-21	-13	3	-4	-17	-14	10

Order books or demand: futury tendency (3)
mining and manufacturing
per cent balance

Carnet de commandes ou demande globale : perspectives (3)
industries extractives et manufacturières
solde en pourcentage

Year	Q.1	Q.2	Q.3	Q.4	JAN	FEB	MAR	APR	MAY	JUN	JUL	AUG	SEP	OCT	NOV	DEC
1964					6	-16	-25	-23	-34	-45	-40	-38	-33	-34	-26	-27
1965					-23	-21	-14	-4	-14	-20	-17	-7	-7	-7	-2	3
1966					13	13	18	19	12	3	1	6	9	6	8	15
1967					20	21	17	10	1	-3	3	8	8	6	3	10
1968					17	16	13	10	5	-1	2	9	14	9	13	19
1969					25	24	30	27	19	9	12	23	14	4	8	16
1970					15	15	15	12	-4	-10	1	1	-3	-4	-13	-6
1971					-1	2	-10	-25	-23	-20	-17	-17	-21	-23	-11	-3
1972					-3	4	3	2	-2	-5	2	5	7	8	3	3
1973					21	23	25	28	29	21	23	24	22	16	-2	5
1974					7	7	6	3	-10	-21	-31	-32	-35	-47	-48	-50
1975					-36	-25	-11	-8	-14	-24	-32	-22	-19	-16	-12	-3
1976					2	6	-2	-5	-7	-8	-5	3	-11	-22	-17	-14
1977					-11	-8	-13	-12	-25	-29	-26	-22	-23	-32	-35	-20
1978					-8	-5	-	-1	-4	-11	-	6	3	-3	-8	7
1979					14	16	11	6	-3	-	2	-4	-6	-7	-9	-5
1980					6	6	3	-8	-25	-38	-30	-29	-30	-30	-24	-16
1981					-8	-5	-7	-5	-11	-18	-13	-11	-18	-24	-24	-6
1982					1	2	-2	-9	-9	-21	-16	-16	-17	-29	-32	-26
1983					-12	-8	-8	-8	-15	-14	-9	-	-3	-12	-10	8

Order books or demand: level (3)
mining and manufacturing
per cent balance

Carnet de commandes ou demande globale : niveau (3)
industries extractives et manufacturières
solde en pourcentage

Year	Q.1	Q.2	Q.3	Q.4	JAN	FEB	MAR	APR	MAY	JUN	JUL	AUG	SEP	OCT	NOV	DEC
1964					-17	-21	-37	-37	-47	-51	-46	-59	-56	-55	-54	-54
1965					-65	-57	-49	-42	-42	-41	-36	-40	-34	-31	-31	-25
1966					-22	-18	-8	-4	-3	-5	-2	-11	-1	-4	-4	-2
1967					-	-6	-3	-5	-6	-6	-8	-14	-15	-16	-20	-16
1968					-16	-14	-10	-9	-8	-9	-8	-12	-3	-2	6	6
1969					6	13	18	21	27	27	28	15	19	13	8	2
1970					7	10	12	6	-3	-7	-14	-21	-18	-21	-31	-30
1971					-35	-32	-30	-38	-40	-42	-44	-47	-53	-47	-39	-38
1972					-39	-37	-28	-29	-27	-26	-24	-30	-17	-10	-1	1
1973					-9	-9	1	3	13	22	23	5	16	23	20	16
1974					14	10	5	1	-4	-12	-21	-32	-35	-45	-57	-68
1975					-69	-68	-68	-70	-66	-65	-64	-74	-59	-54	-54	-56
1976					-45	-34	-21	-22	-20	-20	-18	-21	-15	-20	-26	-24
1977					-36	-35	-36	-35	-43	-45	-46	-49	-46	-50	-54	-51
1978					-46	-47	-40	-38	-29	-31	-30	-33	-24	-15	-14	-19
1979					-14	1	-3	-7	3	2	1	-11	-7	1	-3	1
1980					-4	4	-4	-11	-26	-37	-30	-44	-41	-41	-53	-43
1981					-47	-46	-42	-43	-51	-44	-42	-52	-39	-44	-53	-46
1982					-49	-48	-40	-43	-52	-50	-55	-58	-56	-60	-59	-61
1983					-58	-61	-53	-58	-51	-51	-47	-57	-49	-44	-43	-43

Finished goods stocks: level (3)
mining and manufacturing
per cent balance

Stocks de produits finis : niveau (3)
industries extractives et manufacturières
solde en pourcentage

Year	Q.1	Q.2	Q.3	Q.4	JAN	FEB	MAR	APR	MAY	JUN	JUL	AUG	SEP	OCT	NOV	DEC
1964					6	9	16	16	18	25	24	27	31	31	34	36
1965					37	35	30	26	25	28	19	18	21	19	18	19
1966					22	16	18	11	12	8	7	12	8	11	10	10
1967					11	14	11	15	12	10	12	8	18	18	19	17
1968					12	12	14	9	7	12	10	-	1	2	-1	5
1969					5	-2	-	-10	-6	-13	-14	-9	-17	-18	-19	-18
1970					-17	-14	-14	-7	-7	-1	2	1	6	11	16	13
1971					17	26	23	27	22	24	29	27	35	33	30	25
1972					19	22	16	14	16	15	11	10	11	5	-	-6
1973					-6	-13	-17	-14	-9	-13	-17	-15	-14	-12	-11	-11
1974					-15	-11	-10	-9	-9	-4	-3	2	13	26	28	35
1975					41	43	45	40	42	41	39	39	33	31	25	26
1976					22	19	9	9	8	7	15	11	11	9	6	10
1977					20	22	25	27	32	32	31	30	28	31	35	26
1978					31	33	29	25	22	21	22	23	23	18	16	9
1979					12	5	11	1	-2	-5	-7	-1	-5	-6	-1	-
1980					3	-3	-4	8	18	19	16	16	21	19	24	19
1981					21	25	26	27	29	27	25	27	28	24	21	20
1982					24	25	23	21	25	32	26	28	33	26	23	23
1983					23	24	25	23	30	27	24	23	22	18	13	15

ITALY

Rate of capacity utilization (3) / Taux d'utilisation de capacité (3)

mining and manufacturing — industries extractives et manufacturières

per cent — pourcentage

	Year	Q.1	Q.2	Q.3	Q.4	JAN	FEB	MAR	APR	MAY	JUN	JUL	AUG	SEP	OCT	NOV	DEC
1964																	
1965																	
1966																	
1967																	
1968					81.3										81.3		
1969		81.1	84.2	82.7	75.5	81.1			84.2			82.7			75.5		
1970		81.2	81.5	80.4	78.9	81.2			81.5			80.4			78.9		
1971		78.0	76.9	76.4	76.6	78.0			76.9			76.4			76.6		
1972		75.0	77.2	77.3	76.4	75.0			77.2			77.3			76.4		
1973		73.7	78.8	78.5	78.8	73.7			78.8			78.5			78.8		
1974		78.2	78.3	77.2	73.1	78.2			78.3			77.2			73.1		
1975		70.4	70.6	68.3	68.0	70.4			70.6			68.3			68.0		
1976		71.7	73.9	74.8	75.6	71.7			73.9			74.8			75.6		
1977		75.1	73.1	71.6	71.5	75.1			73.1			71.6			71.5		
1978		72.9	73.6	73.5	75.4	72.9			73.6			73.5			75.4		
1979		76.4	75.2	75.9	77.6	76.4			75.2			75.9			77.6		
1980		77.7	76.6	70.8	73.0	77.7			76.6			70.8			73.0		
1981		72.3	73.3	72.7	72.1	72.3			73.3			72.7			72.1		
1982		72.3	72.6	70.6	70.3	72.3			72.6			70.6			70.3		
1983		70.4	70.0	69.5	70.5	70.4			70.0			69.5			70.5		

Sales: total / Ventes : total

mining and manufacturing — industries extractives et manufacturières

1980 = 100

	Year	Q.1	Q.2	Q.3	Q.4	JAN	FEB	MAR	APR	MAY	JUN	JUL	AUG	SEP	OCT	NOV	DEC
1964																	
1965																	
1966																	
1967																	
1968																	
1969																	
1970																	
1971																	
1972																	
1973	24.7	19.5	23.9	24.4	30.9	16.6	19.4	22.6	21.6	25.7	24.4	27.7	17.8	27.7	31.4	29.5	31.8
1974	35.0	31.2	36.6	34.1	37.9	29.0	30.3	34.2	35.4	37.9	36.6	40.2	23.3	38.9	41.7	34.7	37.3
1975	36.6	34.3	36.6	33.9	41.6	32.1	34.9	36.0	36.9	35.1	37.9	40.5	20.9	40.3	42.0	36.9	45.1
1976	49.0	41.8	49.5	46.8	53.1	35.5	41.0	48.8	48.8	50.4	49.2	54.8	30.7	54.7	57.2	55.3	61.9
1977	57.8	57.9	59.6	52.5	61.2	51.3	57.8	64.7	57.2	61.7	59.9	59.7	34.6	63.3	61.9	59.0	62.6
1978	66.1	63.0	67.1	60.4	73.3	57.9	61.9	69.2	62.7	68.6	70.0	69.7	38.8	72.7	75.5	74.7	71.1
1979	81.9	75.9	80.5	75.4	95.9	68.7	74.0	84.9	75.5	85.1	81.1	86.0	50.2	89.9	101.4	95.4	90.8
1980	100.0	100.1	103.9	89.0	107.0	91.3	102.2	106.7	104.2	104.3	103.1	110.7	48.3	103.0	112.8	101.8	106.6
1981	116.3	113.8	113.9	105.5	127.1	102.3	111.2	127.9	119.4	113.1	124.2	131.3	55.9	129.1	130.4	125.4	125.5
1982	128.4	129.9	133.0	113.2	137.5	115.7	125.8	148.0	136.5	130.8	131.7	137.1	62.2	140.4	137.2	133.9	141.4
1983		135.4	140.6	127.4		120.0	131.9	154.2	132.8	141.0	149.1	147.9	74.0	160.2	152.9		

Sales: investment goods / Ventes : biens d'équipement

mining and manufacturing — industries extractives et manufacturières

1980 = 100

	Year	Q.1	Q.2	Q.3	Q.4	JAN	FEB	MAR	APR	MAY	JUN	JUL	AUG	SEP	OCT	NOV	DEC
1964																	
1965																	
1966																	
1967																	
1968																	
1969																	
1970																	
1971																	
1972																	
1973	24.3	16.7	24.1	24.1	32.5	13.3	16.6	20.3	20.8	26.2	25.3	28.1	16.4	27.6	31.1	28.9	37.5
1974	32.6	27.1	34.1	30.5	38.5	25.7	25.6	30.1	31.2	35.3	36.0	37.4	20.6	33.4	39.1	32.7	43.8
1975	39.0	35.3	39.2	34.7	46.6	32.1	36.3	37.4	38.9	38.0	40.7	44.7	18.6	40.7	42.6	39.4	57.8
1976	50.0	41.2	52.1	45.5	61.0	36.2	39.0	48.4	48.2	55.1	53.0	57.6	26.1	52.7	58.0	56.2	68.9
1977	59.4	56.3	63.5	51.1	66.7	49.1	57.0	62.9	59.2	67.7	63.7	61.5	30.0	61.6	62.8	63.1	74.3
1978	69.0	64.6	71.8	61.5	78.1	59.4	61.3	73.0	66.2	73.5	75.6	75.1	35.5	74.0	73.8	79.2	81.2
1979	80.4	73.3	78.3	70.9	99.3	68.5	70.3	81.1	72.3	84.7	78.0	83.3	44.5	84.8	96.0	96.3	105.7
1980	100.0	94.4	106.8	85.4	113.5	87.6	93.6	101.8	105.1	108.2	107.1	112.4	45.6	98.1	107.0	105.7	127.7
1981	115.9	113.5	120.8	102.2	127.1	97.5	108.6	134.5	122.6	113.4	126.4	139.2	44.3	123.3	122.5	123.5	135.2
1982	127.7	122.7	136.1	107.3	144.9	108.4	116.6	143.1	134.9	133.0	140.5	138.7	49.9	133.2	130.3	133.0	171.4
1983		129.9	144.1	117.9		114.0	124.3	151.4	135.5	142.1	154.7	150.5	53.6	149.5	145.8		

Sales: consumer goods
mining and manufacturing
1980 = 100

Ventes : biens de consommation
industries extractives et manufacturières
1980 = 100

	Year	Q.1	Q.2	Q.3	Q.4	JAN	FEB	MAR	APR	MAY	JUN	JUL	AUG	SEP	OCT	NOV	DEC
1964																	
1965																	
1966																	
1967																	
1968																	
1969																	
1970																	
1971																	
1972																	
1973	26.4	21.8	25.2	26.6	32.0	18.1	21.8	25.6	23.6	26.8	25.0	29.0	20.5	30.1	33.8	31.2	31.0
1974	35.2	31.2	34.0	35.9	39.5	28.2	30.9	34.5	34.9	34.9	32.4	38.9	26.1	42.8	45.5	36.3	36.6
1975	37.1	34.6	35.3	36.6	42.0	31.1	35.3	37.4	36.3	33.3	36.2	40.0	25.3	44.5	46.5	37.0	42.4
1976	49.2	42.6	46.7	48.9	58.6	35.2	43.2	49.4	48.2	46.0	45.8	53.1	35.0	58.7	60.8	55.3	59.7
1977	58.6	56.9	57.1	58.1	62.2	48.0	57.1	65.5	54.3	58.3	58.2	60.7	42.8	70.6	66.9	58.8	61.0
1978	67.4	61.7	65.9	65.9	76.1	54.4	60.9	69.8	60.5	67.8	69.6	71.0	47.7	78.9	83.4	75.5	69.3
1979	82.7	75.2	79.8	80.1	95.7	65.0	74.4	86.2	75.7	83.7	80.1	87.7	57.5	95.2	109.5	94.0	83.7
1980	100.0	97.7	97.4	97.5	107.4	85.3	101.3	106.5	98.3	96.5	97.4	111.2	59.6	121.5	125.2	99.7	97.4
1981	116.0	107.1	115.2	114.8	127.0	92.9	105.4	122.9	116.0	109.5	120.3	130.0	71.8	142.6	140.2	121.5	119.2
1982	130.8	125.0	130.1	127.4	140.5	106.1	122.0	147.0	134.8	126.0	129.7	143.6	80.1	158.4	151.5	137.0	133.0
1983		140.8	141.2	145.5		118.2	138.2	165.9	136.1	140.2	147.4	154.4	100.4	181.8	161.9		

Sales: intermediate goods
mining and manufacturing
1980 = 100

Ventes : biens intermédiaires
industries extractives et manufacturières
1980 = 100

	Year	Q.1	Q.2	Q.3	Q.4	JAN	FEB	MAR	APR	MAY	JUN	JUL	AUG	SEP	OCT	NOV	DEC
1964																	
1965																	
1966																	
1967																	
1968																	
1969																	
1970																	
1971																	
1972																	
1973	24.0	20.0	23.2	23.5	29.5	17.7	19.9	22.4	21.0	24.8	23.7	26.8	17.2	26.4	30.4	29.0	29.0
1974	36.2	33.4	39.2	35.3	36.8	31.3	32.7	36.3	37.9	40.7	39.1	42.3	23.5	40.1	41.4	35.1	34.1
1975	35.0	33.6	35.8	32.2	38.6	32.4	34.0	34.4	36.0	34.3	37.0	38.3	20.2	38.0	41.1	35.5	39.2
1976	48.4	41.7	49.3	46.5	56.3	35.2	41.1	43.8	49.5	49.8	48.6	54.0	31.4	53.9	55.0	54.7	59.1
1977	56.5	59.4	58.6	50.7	57.6	54.2	58.6	65.3	57.2	59.9	58.6	58.2	33.2	60.7	58.9	56.9	57.0
1978	63.8	62.8	65.1	57.1	70.2	58.9	62.8	66.8	61.8	66.3	67.1	65.9	36.4	69.0	72.5	71.9	65.3
1979	82.2	77.7	82.1	75.6	94.0	70.7	75.0	86.3	77.3	85.9	83.2	86.8	49.9	90.1	100.5	95.5	86.0
1980	100.0	104.5	105.3	86.9	103.3	96.3	107.5	109.6	106.5	105.9	103.5	109.4	44.5	107.0	110.0	100.6	99.2
1981	116.7	117.2	119.6	102.8	127.3	109.5	115.5	126.6	119.4	114.8	124.7	127.5	55.0	125.9	130.1	128.5	123.2
1982	128.0	136.3	133.7	109.8	132.0	124.7	133.1	151.3	138.3	132.0	130.9	133.1	60.6	135.6	134.3	133.0	128.9
1983		136.0	138.5	124.1		124.5	133.3	150.1	129.8	140.9	144.8	143.4	73.0	155.8	152.5		

New orders: total
manufacturing
1980 = 100

Commandes nouvelles : total
industries manufacturières
1980 = 100

	Year	Q.1	Q.2	Q.3	Q.4	JAN	FEB	MAR	APR	MAY	JUN	JUL	AUG	SEP	OCT	NOV	DEC
1964																	
1965																	
1966																	
1967																	
1968																	
1969																	
1970																	
1971																	
1972																	
1973	25.8	23.0	25.7	24.3	30.3	21.2	21.5	26.2	23.9	27.1	26.1	27.7	18.0	27.1	31.8	28.9	30.3
1974	33.3	35.4	35.7	28.3	33.8	34.5	34.8	36.8	36.8	36.0	34.2	32.4	19.1	33.2	35.1	31.6	34.7
1975	36.5	34.5	36.0	31.1	44.5	33.1	33.6	36.7	35.8	37.8	34.4	36.1	18.5	38.7	46.2	38.2	49.3
1976	51.3	45.8	51.1	44.8	63.5	41.1	43.5	52.8	53.1	51.2	48.9	50.4	27.7	56.2	62.4	67.4	60.7
1977	56.2	60.3	57.2	46.1	61.3	58.7	57.5	64.7	57.6	60.2	54.0	51.0	27.3	60.0	60.1	62.1	61.6
1978	67.5	68.7	66.2	60.5	74.6	71.5	63.6	71.1	66.9	67.8	63.8	62.4	34.6	84.5	75.2	76.2	72.4
1979	84.8	82.2	83.9	73.1	100.1	77.1	80.7	88.9	79.8	90.4	81.4	85.7	43.8	89.8	104.6	100.3	95.3
1980	100.0	109.8	101.4	83.8	104.9	104.4	103.6	116.5	105.5	98.4	100.2	103.5	43.8	104.3	109.8	103.1	101.9
1981	118.5	123.6	119.5	101.6	129.2	105.9	114.0	150.8	123.5	112.8	122.2	128.4	49.4	127.1	138.0	122.7	126.8
1982	127.6	133.2	137.8	104.0	135.4	118.2	128.7	152.7	142.2	135.1	136.1	121.8	55.1	134.9	143.4	127.8	134.9
1983		140.9	138.2	114.3		131.2	129.0	162.6	142.1	133.8	133.8	130.7	62.6	149.8	145.7		

ITALY

Construction permits issued: total

million cubic metres, monthly averages

Permis de construire délivrés : total

millions de mètres cubes, moyennes mensuelles

	Year	Q.1	Q.2	Q.3	Q.4	JAN	FEB	MAR	APR	MAY	JUN	JUL	AUG	SEP	OCT	NOV	DEC
1964																	
1965																	
1966	25.2	26.2	26.7	23.8	24.2	18.8	28.7	30.9	26.6	28.3	25.4	25.4	22.0	23.9	26.0	24.4	22.1
1967	29.4	26.6	33.0	27.4	30.6	21.9	27.2	30.8	33.6	33.6	31.9	28.5	27.2	26.4	26.2	31.3	34.4
1968	60.7	37.4	51.5	137.9	15.7	26.9	40.0	45.3	56.0	51.6	47.0	66.5	332.6	14.7	15.1	15.6	16.4
1969	24.5	21.6	26.3	25.5	24.7	18.0	22.2	24.7	23.6	29.6	25.6	29.4	22.9	24.3	28.6	23.1	22.3
1970	24.3	24.8	28.1	20.5	23.9	22.4	24.1	27.9	30.5	28.4	25.3	23.7	17.2	20.7	21.1	22.3	28.2
1971	26.5	20.9	26.3	27.4	30.7	15.5	22.5	24.7	27.4	26.2	26.9	28.5	26.6	27.0	25.2	24.3	42.7
1972	29.9	26.1	33.8	25.7	34.1	19.4	23.1	35.9	28.8	35.6	37.0	29.4	22.5	25.1	31.1	32.3	38.9
1973	36.1	31.7	37.3	34.6	40.7	24.8	33.0	37.4	33.7	42.3	35.9	40.0	27.7	36.1	35.8	32.9	53.5
1974	27.7	28.9	33.7	26.0	22.2	23.7	27.8	35.0	33.0	36.3	31.9	36.3	20.5	21.3	24.9	21.1	20.6
1975	22.6	20.6	29.0	18.1	22.4	16.6	18.2	27.0	25.7	33.0	28.3	20.2	15.1	19.1	25.9	19.5	21.8
1976	23.1	27.2	22.7	20.0	22.7	18.9	33.7	29.0	25.4	23.0	19.8	23.2	17.0	19.8	22.0	20.1	26.0
1977	23.7	22.0	27.2	24.5	21.1	26.5	18.5	21.1	21.9	31.3	28.4	28.8	21.7	22.9	22.4	18.8	22.0
1978	16.1	16.0	17.6	15.6	15.3	17.4	15.4	15.3	15.8	17.7	19.4	20.1	13.1	13.8	12.7	12.5	20.7
1979	15.9	16.1	16.4	13.9	17.2	13.3	16.8	18.0	16.5	18.9	13.7	15.0	12.9	13.8	15.0	15.9	20.7
1980	21.3	20.1	26.7	19.7	18.8	16.6	20.2	23.5	24.7	27.7	27.8	27.5	14.5	17.2	21.6	17.6	17.2
1981	17.9	18.9	19.2	16.8	16.8	19.5	16.5	20.6	18.3	19.5	19.7	19.6	13.9	17.0	17.7	16.8	15.8
1982	15.8	17.2	18.1	14.3	13.5	16.2	16.3	18.7	18.4	17.6	18.3	17.2	10.2	15.5	14.1	12.3	14.3
1983																	

Construction permits issued: residential

million cubic metres, monthly averages

Permis de construire délivrés : bâtiments résidentiels

millions de mètres cubes, moyennes mensuelles

	Year	Q.1	Q.2	Q.3	Q.4	JAN	FEB	MAR	APR	MAY	JUN	JUL	AUG	SEP	OCT	NOV	DEC
1964																	
1965																	
1966	17.1	18.0	18.8	16.0	15.5	13.6	18.4	22.0	19.0	19.5	17.8	17.7	14.7	15.6	17.1	14.8	14.6
1967	19.5	18.0	22.2	18.6	19.6	14.9	17.7	21.3	22.1	23.4	21.1	18.6	20.2	16.9	17.3	20.0	21.5
1968	41.8	25.1	33.7	99.3	9.2	17.1	27.6	30.5	36.4	32.3	32.3	47.6	240.5	9.8	8.7	9.7	9.3
1969	12.8	12.2	13.4	12.6	13.1	11.1	11.7	13.9	12.4	14.9	12.8	12.9	12.3	12.5	14.3	12.4	12.5
1970	13.6	13.1	15.5	11.3	14.6	11.9	13.0	14.4	16.6	15.9	14.0	12.1	9.7	12.0	11.9	13.5	18.6
1971	15.5	12.7	15.2	14.3	19.8	9.3	12.9	15.7	14.4	15.4	15.8	17.5	12.6	12.9	15.4	14.4	29.7
1972	16.4	13.9	18.5	14.0	19.1	11.0	13.0	17.9	15.9	17.0	22.6	15.0	12.4	14.6	16.8	17.7	22.8
1973	19.2	16.7	19.2	17.1	23.7	13.8	17.6	18.7	17.6	20.6	19.3	20.6	14.0	16.7	13.5	18.6	33.9
1974	14.2	14.5	16.9	13.5	12.0	11.6	13.5	18.4	16.8	17.2	16.8	18.1	10.4	11.8	13.4	11.5	11.3
1975	13.1	11.5	16.1	10.2	14.8	10.0	10.3	14.1	15.2	16.6	16.5	11.2	8.9	10.5	18.1	13.1	13.2
1976	13.4	16.9	12.8	11.2	13.0	10.8	23.9	15.9	14.5	12.9	11.0	12.2	10.0	11.3	12.9	11.7	14.3
1977	13.4	12.9	15.3	13.8	11.3	16.2	10.4	12.0	12.7	18.8	14.5	16.2	11.9	13.2	12.1	11.2	12.2
1978	9.0	8.8	10.3	8.6	8.2	9.7	8.1	8.5	9.5	9.6	11.6	11.8	7.5	7.1	6.7	7.1	10.9
1979	8.2	8.5	8.9	6.9	8.7	7.2	9.2	9.0	9.3	10.0	7.5	7.7	6.0	6.8	7.0	8.3	10.7
1980	10.1	9.9	12.2	9.3	9.0	9.5	9.7	10.7	11.2	12.7	12.8	13.5	7.0	7.3	10.1	8.5	8.5
1981	8.9	9.3	9.6	8.1	8.7	9.7	8.1	10.2	9.0	10.0	9.8	9.2	6.6	8.4	9.4	8.6	8.2
1982	8.3	8.8	9.6	7.6	7.4	8.2	8.3	9.9	10.1	9.2	9.4	9.7	5.7	7.4	7.6	7.1	7.5
1983																	

Retail sales: value (4)

major outlets

1980 = 100

Ventes au détail : valeur (4)

grande distribution

1980 = 100

	Year	Q.1	Q.2	Q.3	Q.4	JAN	FEB	MAR	APR	MAY	JUN	JUL	AUG	SEP	OCT	NOV	DEC
1964																	
1965																	
1966																	
1967																	
1968																	
1969																	
1970	19	17	18	18	24	17	15	19	18	18	19	19	15	19	23	20	29
1971	21	18	21	20	27	18	16	19	22	20	20	21	16	23	24	22	33
1972	24	21	22	23	30	20	19	24	21	23	22	22	20	26	27	25	39
1973	29	24	27	27	39	22	22	27	27	28	27	26	24	31	35	34	49
1974	36	31	34	35	45	29	29	34	35	34	33	35	31	38	43	38	55
1975	40	35	37	37	51	32	33	40	36	39	37	38	32	41	49	41	62
1976	48	40	46	45	61	39	38	44	47	45	46	43	41	50	56	52	77
1977	58	49	57	55	71	48	46	54	56	56	57	55	49	61	62	60	89
1978	67	58	65	63	83	55	53	65	61	65	67	63	55	71	73	71	105
1979	82	70	79	77	102	65	64	80	76	80	81	75	70	87	92	85	130
1980	100	86	96	95	123	82	83	93	93	98	96	98	87	102	115	105	149
1981	121	104	116	113	149	105	99	108	116	115	116	113	103	124	138	128	181
1982	145	126	142	135	178	124	116	139	143	140	142	143	122	140	158	152	224
1983		147	161	158		139	134	167	155	159	169	154	149	170	185	178	

Cost of construction: residential (5) — Coût de la construction : bâtiments résidentiels (5)

1980 = 100

	Year	Q.1	Q.2	Q.3	Q.4	JAN	FEB	MAR	APR	MAY	JUN	JUL	AUG	SEP	OCT	NOV	DEC
1964																	
1965																	
1966	15																
1967	16	16	16	16	16	16	16	16	16	16	16	16	16	16	16	16	16
1968	16	16	16	16	16	16	16	16	16	16	16	16	16	16	16	16	16
1969	18	17	17	18	18	17	17	17	17	17	18	18	18	18	18	18	18
1970	20	20	20	20	20	20	20	20	20	20	20	20	20	20	20	21	20
1971	21	21	21	21	22	21	21	21	21	21	21	21	21	21	21	22	22
1972	22	22	22	16	23	22	22	22	22	22	22	22	23	2	23	23	23
1973	27	26	27	28	29	25	26	26	26	27	27	28	28	29	29	29	30
1974	35	31	34	37	38	31	32	32	33	34	35	36	37	37	38	39	39
1975	41	40	41	42	42	39	41	41	41	41	41	41	42	42	42	42	42
1976	50	44	49	52	54	43	44	45	48	49	49	51	52	52	53	54	54
1977	59	56	59	60	62	54	56	57	58	59	59	59	61	61	61	62	62
1978	67	63	65	68	71	63	64	64	64	66	66	67	69	70	70	71	72
1979	80	73	77	82	83	72	74	74	75	77	78	79	83	84	85	88	89
1980	100	93	98	102	103	90	94	94	95	98	100	100	102	104	105	108	110
1981	123	115	121	125	131	113	115	116	118	122	123	123	126	127	128	133	133
1982	144	137	141	147	152	135	138	138	139	142	143	144	148	149	150	153	154
1983	164	157	161	167	171	155	158	159	159	161	162	166	168	169	169	171	172

New passenger car registrations — Immatriculations de voitures de tourisme neuves

thousands, monthly averages — milliers, moyennes mensuelles

	Year	Q.1	Q.2	Q.3	Q.4	JAN	FEB	MAR	APR	MAY	JUN	JUL	AUG	SEP	OCT	NOV	DEC
1964	69	93	71	60	54	97	89	93	78	64	70	76	58	44	62	54	44
1965	74	76	90	73	57	78	69	81	93	89	87	98	70	52	68	57	45
1966	85	86	74	109	69	90	74	95	92	100	30	162	95	70	80	70	57
1967	97	110	114	94	70	112	101	118	114	113	113	117	93	71	88	73	49
1968	97	102	116	89	83	106	92	106	120	124	103	115	94	58	88	86	76
1969	102	106	123	98	80	102	100	115	126	129	112	123	111	58	107	71	62
1970	114	105	125	114	111	89	112	114	131	121	124	138	115	83	123	112	97
1971	120	121	125	121	112	109	119	134	133	130	113	147	124	91	121	115	99
1972	123	126	125	121	119	116	121	140	112	141	122	136	122	105	121	115	120
1973	121	120	119	132	113	149	102	108	106	132	118	156	128	112	133	96	109
1974	107	121	118	113	76	141	113	108	100	128	126	128	113	98	89	73	65
1975	88	87	94	83	86	72	86	103	98	88	96	98	78	73	100	83	76
1976	99	111	102	90	93	96	114	123	117	104	85	90	87	94	95	90	93
1977	102	100	113	101	93	88	96	116	101	128	110	104	91	108	93	97	89
1978	101	89	105	99	113	89	72	105	102	111	101	100	87	109	134	115	92
1979	116	101	120	121	124	94	92	117	111	125	124	127	112	124	138	128	108
1980	128	113	122	126	144	109	123	122	113	124	129	129	94	155	156	141	135
1981	151	144	152	147	160	144	137	152	135	154	168	150	120	170	173	156	151
1982	158	158	161	154	161	138	149	188	159	157	168	158	128	176	175	155	153
1983	126	123	144	113	124	105	115	150	132	156	145	129	91	118	122	134	116

Retail sales: value (4) — Ventes au détail : valeur (4)

major outlets — grande distribution

Adjusted - Corrigé *

1980 = 100

	Year	Q.1	Q.2	Q.3	Q.4	JAN	FEB	MAR	APR	MAY	JUN	JUL	AUG	SEP	OCT	NOV	DEC
1964																	
1965																	
1966																	
1967																	
1968																	
1969																	
1970		18	19	20	20	18	18	19	20	18	20	20	19	19	20	20	20
1971		20	21	21	22	21	20	20	22	21	22	21	20	22	22	22	22
1972		23	23	24	25	22	22	24	22	24	23	24	25	25	24	25	26
1973		26	28	29	33	25	26	27	28	28	28	28	29	30	32	33	33
1974		34	35	38	38	34	35	34	35	35	36	38	37	37	39	37	38
1975		38	39	40	43	37	39	39	38	39	39	40	39	40	44	42	43
1976		44	47	48	52	43	44	45	46	46	48	44	50	50	51	52	52
1977		55	58	59	60	55	54	55	56	58	59	58	60	60	58	61	60
1978		63	66	68	71	63	62	63	65	66	67	68	66	69	68	72	73
1979		76	79	84	87	73	75	79	78	80	81	80	83	88	87	84	92
1980		92	97	103	106	91	92	94	96	96	100	104	104	102	107	106	105
1981		113	116	123	128	113	115	113	115	116	118	119	124	126	126	131	126
1982		137	144	146	152	136	135	141	141	143	148	147	147	142	150	152	156
1983		158	155	170		153	156	165	157	162	175	163	179	168	176	181	

* Adjusted by the O.E.C.D. — * Corrigé par l'O.C.D.E.

ITALY

Retail sales: volume (4) — Ventes au détail : volume (4)
major outlets — grande distribution
1980 = 100

Adjusted - Corrigé *

	Year	Q.1	Q.2	Q.3	Q.4	JAN	FEB	MAR	APR	MAY	JUN	JUL	AUG	SEP	OCT	NOV	DEC
1964																	
1965																	
1966																	
1967																	
1968																	
1969																	
1970	71	70	71	72	72	70	69	70	74	66	73	75	72	69	73	72	70
1971	75	73	76	75	76	74	72	71	77	74	77	75	71	78	75	76	77
1972	81	79	73	82	83	77	76	83	76	81	78	80	83	84	81	83	86
1973	89	85	86	88	94	83	84	87	87	87	85	85	88	91	93	96	93
1974	88	92	88	88	84	93	95	88	90	86	87	90	88	86	87	82	84
1975	85	84	84	85	89	81	84	86	83	84	85	86	84	84	92	87	88
1976	91	91	90	90	90	90	92	92	90	89	91	84	94	93	90	89	89
1977	93	92	93	94	92	93	91	90	92	93	94	92	95	94	90	94	92
1978	96	94	96	97	99	95	93	93	95	96	96	97	95	98	96	99	101
1979	103	102	104	104	101	99	101	106	103	104	104	103	104	106	102	97	104
1980	100	99	100	101	99	99	99	99	100	99	101	103	102	93	102	99	96
1981	103	102	101	104	103	103	103	100	102	100	101	102	105	106	104	105	100
1982	107	106	109	105	105	106	104	108	108	108	110	108	106	101	104	104	106
1983		104	106	106		102	102	107	101	104	111	103	112	104	108	109	

Unemployment (6) (7) — Chômage (6) (7)
thousands — milliers

	Year	Q.1	Q.2	Q.3	Q.4	JAN	FEB	MAR	APR	MAY	JUN	JUL	AUG	SEP	OCT	NOV	DEC
1964	904	1104	812	827	872	1104			812			827			872		
1965	1110	1186	1006	1128	1120	1186			1006			1128			1120		
1966	1193	1412	1031	1209	1151	1412			1001			1209			1151		
1967	1105	1306	1003	980	1131	1306			1003			980			1131		
1968	1172	1229	1041	1199	1220	1229			1041			1199			1220		
1969	1160	1270	1036	1171	1162	1270			1036			1171			1162		
1970	1111	1181	959	1167	1137	1181			959			1167			1137		
1971	1110	1149	985	1108	1196	1149			985			1108			1196		
1972	1297	1304	1138	1386	1359	1304			1138			1386			1359		
1973	1305	1352	1393	1265	1211	1352			1393			1265			1211		
1974	1113	1149	935	1151	1216	1149			935			1151			1216		
1975	1230	1141	1162	1253	1365	1141			1162			1253			1365		
1976	1426	1309	1323	1523	1549	1309			1323			1523			1549		
1977	1545	1459	1432	1692	1598	1459			1432			1692			1598		
1978	1571	1520	1455	1658	1651	1520			1455			1658			1651		
1979	1698	1632	1530	1880	1701	1632			1530			1880			1701		
1980	1698	1703	1554	1812	1722	1703			1554			1812			1722		
1981	1913	1717	1826	2013	2096	1717			1826			2013			2096		
1982	2068	2089	1954	2119	2110	2089			1954			2119			2110		
1983	2278	2217	2262	2258	2373	2217			2262			2258			2373		

Unemployment (6) (7) — Chômage (6) (7)
as per cent of total labour force — en pourcentage de la population active

	Year	Q.1	Q.2	Q.3	Q.4	JAN	FEB	MAR	APR	MAY	JUN	JUL	AUG	SEP	OCT	NOV	DEC
1964	4.3	5.3	3.9	3.9	4.2	5.3			3.9			3.9			4.2		
1965	5.4	5.8	4.9	5.4	5.4	5.8			4.9			5.4			5.4		
1966	5.9	7.0	5.0	5.9	5.6	7.0			5.0			5.9			5.6		
1967	5.4	6.4	4.9	4.8	5.5	6.4			4.9			4.8			5.5		
1968	5.7	6.0	5.1	5.8	5.9	6.0			5.1			5.8			5.9		
1969	5.7	6.3	5.1	5.7	5.7	6.3			5.1			5.7			5.7		
1970	5.4	5.9	4.7	5.6	5.5	5.9			4.7			5.6			5.5		
1971	5.4	5.7	4.8	5.4	5.9	5.7			4.8			5.4			5.9		
1972	6.4	6.5	5.7	6.7	6.6	6.5			5.7			6.7			6.6		
1973	6.4	6.7	6.9	6.1	5.8	6.7			6.9			6.1			5.8		
1974	5.4	5.6	4.6	5.5	5.8	5.6			4.6			5.5			5.8		
1975	5.9	5.5	5.6	5.9	6.4	5.5			5.6			5.9			6.4		
1976	6.7	6.3	6.3	7.0	7.2	6.3			6.3			7.0			7.2		
1977	7.2	6.8	6.6	7.7	7.4	6.8			6.6			7.7			7.4		
1978	7.2	7.1	6.8	7.5	7.5	7.1			6.8			7.5			7.5		
1979	7.7	7.6	7.3	8.3	7.6	7.6			7.3			8.3			7.6		
1980	7.6	7.8	7.0	8.0	7.6	7.8			7.0			8.0			7.6		
1981	8.4	7.7	8.1	8.8	9.1	7.7			8.1			8.8			9.1		
1982	9.1	9.3	8.6	9.2	9.2	9.3			8.6			9.2			9.2		
1983	9.9	9.8	9.9	9.8	10.2	9.8			9.9			9.8			10.2		

* Adjusted by the O.E.C.D. — * Corrigé par l'O.C.D.E.

Employment: industry (6)(8) — Emploi : industrie (6)(8)

thousands — milliers

	Year	Q.1	Q.2	Q.3	Q.4	JAN	FEB	MAR	APR	MAY	JUN	JUL	AUG	SEP	OCT	NOV	DEC
1964	6184	6192	6208	6201	6134	6192			6208			6201			6134		
1965	5920	5949	5983	5858	5890	5949			5983			5858			5890		
1966	5839	5643	5849	5927	5936	5643			5849			5927			5936		
1967	5998	5890	6056	6052	5994	5890			6056			6052			5994		
1968	6073	5918	6022	6152	6200	5918			6022			6152			6200		
1969	6283	6202	6277	6314	6339	6202			6277			6314			6339		
1970	6424	6330	6434	6436	6496	6330			6434			6436			6496		
1971	6516	6472	6561	6524	6506	6472			6561			6524			6506		
1972	6423	6453	6449	6416	6375	6453			6449			6416			6375		
1973	6443	6381	6300	6514	6578	6381			6300			6514			6578		
1974	6618	6567	6575	6661	6670	6567			6575			6661			6670		
1975	6627	6699	6551	6608	6650	6699			6551			6608			6650		
1976	6534	6395	6497	6635	6609	6395			6497			6635			6609		
1977	6602	6536	6605	6715	6551	6536			6605			6715			6551		
1978	6537	6519	6499	6629	6502	6519			6499			6629			6502		
1979	6557	6454	6496	6644	6634	6454			6496			6644			6634		
1980	6597	6512	6590	6727	6558	6512			6590			6727			6558		
1981	6535	6557	6548	6561	6472	6557			6548			6561			6472		
1982	6386	6411	6452	6392	6290	6411			6452			6392			6290		
1983	6196	6201	6200	6219	6162	6201			6200			6219			6162		

Unemployment (6)(7) — Chômage (6)(7)

Adjusted - Corrigé *

thousands — milliers

	Year	Q.1	Q.2	Q.3	Q.4	JAN	FEB	MAR	APR	MAY	JUN	JUL	AUG	SEP	OCT	NOV	DEC
1964		876	908	909	915	876			908			909			915		
1965		964	1130	1204	1159	964			1130			1204			1159		
1966		1134	1126	1261	1169	1134			1126			1261			1169		
1967		1132	1130	1002	1128	1132			1130			1002			1128		
1968		1098	1170	1209	1201	1098			1170			1209			1201		
1969		1161	1165	1165	1134	1161			1165			1165			1134		
1970		1103	1073	1151	1105	1103			1073			1151			1105		
1971		1087	1101	1082	1160	1087			1101			1082			1160		
1972		1253	1259	1351	1311	1253			1259			1351			1311		
1973		1318	1531	1229	1161	1318			1531			1229			1161		
1974		1140	1016	1115	1161	1140			1016			1115			1161		
1975		1148	1258	1206	1303	1148			1258			1206			1303		
1976		1334	1421	1459	1480	1334			1421			1459			1480		
1977		1493	1540	1601	1546	1493			1540			1601			1546		
1978		1557	1565	1557	1609	1557			1565			1557			1609		
1979		1665	1706	1755	1664	1665			1706			1755			1664		
1980		1732	1670	1694	1693	1731			1670			1694			1698		
1981		1742	1960	1885	2068	1741			1960			1885			2067		
1982		2116	2097	1986	2082	2117			2097			1986			2083		
1983		2244	2428	2117	2343	2244			2427			2116			2343		

Unemployment (6)(7) — Chômage (6)(7)

Adjusted - Corrigé *

as per cent of total labour force — en pourcentage de la population active

	Year	Q.1	Q.2	Q.3	Q.4	JAN	FEB	MAR	APR	MAY	JUN	JUL	AUG	SEP	OCT	NOV	DEC
1964		4.1	4.4	4.4	4.5	4.1			4.4			4.4			4.5		
1965		4.7	5.5	5.8	5.6	4.7			5.5			5.8			5.6		
1966		5.8	5.6	6.2	5.8	5.8			5.6			6.2			5.8		
1967		5.5	5.5	4.9	5.5	5.5			5.5			4.9			5.5		
1968		5.4	5.7	5.9	5.9	5.4			5.7			5.9			5.9		
1969		5.7	5.7	5.7	5.6	5.7			5.7			5.7			5.6		
1970		5.4	5.3	5.6	5.4	5.4			5.3			5.6			5.4		
1971		5.3	5.4	5.3	5.7	5.3			5.4			5.3			5.7		
1972		6.2	6.3	6.6	6.4	6.2			6.3			6.6			6.4		
1973		6.5	7.5	6.0	5.6	6.5			7.5			6.0			5.6		
1974		5.5	4.9	5.4	5.5	5.5			4.9			5.4			5.5		
1975		5.5	6.0	5.8	6.2	5.5			6.0			5.8			6.2		
1976		6.4	6.7	6.8	6.9	6.4			6.7			6.8			6.9		
1977		6.9	7.1	7.4	7.2	6.9			7.1			7.4			7.2		
1978		7.2	7.2	7.2	7.4	7.2			7.2			7.2			7.4		
1979		7.6	7.8	7.9	7.5	7.6			7.8			7.9			7.5		
1980		7.8	7.5	7.6	7.5	7.8			7.5			7.6			7.5		
1981		7.7	8.6	8.4	9.0	7.7			8.6			8.4			9.0		
1982		9.3	9.2	8.8	9.1	9.3			9.2			8.8			9.1		
1983		9.8	10.5	9.3	10.1	9.8			10.5			9.3			10.1		

* Adjusted by the O.E.C.D. — * Corrigé par l'O.C.D.E.

ITALY

Labour disputes: time lost
thousand man-hours

Conflits du travail : heures perdues
milliers d'heures-homme

	Year	Q.1	Q.2	Q.3	Q.4	JAN	FEB	MAR	APR	MAY	JUN	JUL	AUG	SEP	OCT	NOV	DEC
1964	104709	32573	38596	18771	14769	10137	16069	6367	7035	10773	20788	10446	2000	6325	7688	4405	2676
1965	55943	16226	16879	10987	11851	4204	8035	3987	5257	5468	6154	7815	1709	1463	3985	3543	4323
1966	115788	31953	42069	22172	19594	5353	13103	13497	14148	11869	16052	16535	2254	3333	7325	7426	4843
1967	68548	16938	22152	8859	20599	2641	5755	8542	5740	11211	5201	6481	972	1406	6734	6798	7067
1968	73918	15219	12558	10120	36021	3384	5170	6665	5271	3184	4103	5572	1211	3337	6777	19698	9546
1969	302597	60121	27626	54851	159999	19543	30395	10183	7957	10941	8728	10795	2326	41730	73323	48039	38637
1970	146212	37158	57674	12019	39361	6293	13493	17372	24021	23607	10046	5236	1301	5482	14719	14727	9915
1971	103590	25621	27549	25303	25117	6882	9535	9204	8632	11265	7652	17579	3516	4208	5258	8732	11127
1972	136480	25390	17005	21404	72681	5060	8281	12049	4499	4406	8100	9466	2549	9389	10981	33348	28352
1973	163935	93280	42454	8915	19286	23508	40216	29156	14924	16896	10634	5726	952	2237	6111	6577	6598
1974	136267	28841	26558	12973	67895	7487	10990	10364	6974	9349	10235	7266	856	4851	21813	18940	27142
1975	190324	72499	44048	25244	48533	25247	26012	21240	22121	13741	8186	16743	1415	7086	7247	13523	27763
1976	177643	68501	36964	24895	47283	17314	22151	29036	23390	7232	6342	18132	3612	3151	18267	26752	2264
1977	115963	29291	22222	19640	44810	1937	7567	19787	7245	3978	10999	14734	266	4640	6993	23733	14084
1978	71239	17793	21207	6737	25502	4218	4322	9253	5002	11066	5139	3683	382	2672	10092	9526	5884
1979	192713	33975	80265	33282	45191	9222	7700	17053	21431	26295	32539	20046	565	12671	10696	20945	13550
1980	115201	41601	13375	33695	26530	28192	8391	5018	6418	3494	3463	12991	3731	16973	22510	2579	1441
1981	73691	28859	14402	8281	22149	3500	13663	11696	10123	2263	1956	4875	419	2987	13549	3102	5498
1982	129934	26991	57882	11820	33241	8125	8359	10507	8885	14452	34545	3294	178	9343	11416	14193	7532
1983	93184	41088	39903	3830	8363	20878	7619	12591	10652	14508	14743	2014	118	1698	2503	3770	2090

Hourly rates: industry (9)
1980 = 100

Taux horaires : industrie (9)
1980 = 100

	Year	Q.1	Q.2	Q.3	Q.4	JAN	FEB	MAR	APR	MAY	JUN	JUL	AUG	SEP	OCT	NOV	DEC
1964	9.9	9.3	9.8	10.0	10.3	9.0	9.3	9.7	9.7	9.8	9.8	9.8	10.1	10.1	10.1	10.4	10.4
1965	10.7	10.5	10.6	10.8	10.9	10.4	10.6	10.6	10.6	10.6	10.6	10.6	10.8	10.8	10.8	10.9	10.9
1966	11.1	11.0	11.0	11.1	11.3	10.9	11.0	11.0	11.0	11.0	11.0	11.1	11.1	11.1	11.1	11.3	11.5
1967	11.7	11.5	11.6	11.8	11.8	11.4	11.6	11.6	11.6	11.6	11.6	11.7	11.8	11.8	11.8	11.8	11.8
1968	12.1	12.0	12.1	12.1	12.2	11.9	12.0	12.0	12.0	12.1	12.1	12.1	12.2	12.2	12.2	12.2	12.2
1969	13.0	12.4	12.9	13.3	13.5	12.3	12.4	12.5	12.7	13.1	13.1	13.1	13.3	13.4	13.4	13.4	13.6
1970	15.8	15.1	15.7	16.0	16.5	15.0	15.2	15.2	15.2	15.9	15.9	15.9	16.1	16.1	16.3	16.6	16.6
1971	18.0	17.5	17.8	18.2	18.5	17.3	17.5	17.6	17.6	17.9	17.9	17.9	18.3	18.3	18.3	18.5	18.6
1972	19.8	19.0	19.4	20.1	20.8	18.8	19.1	19.2	19.2	19.4	19.5	19.9	20.2	20.2	20.3	20.9	21.2
1973	24.6	21.9	24.0	25.8	26.8	21.3	22.1	22.4	23.6	24.2	24.3	25.2	25.9	26.2	26.2	27.1	27.1
1974	30.2	28.1	29.3	31.0	32.3	27.6	28.2	28.4	28.5	29.6	30.0	30.3	31.3	31.3	31.3	32.7	33.0
1975	38.2	36.0	38.1	39.1	39.8	33.1	37.4	37.4	37.5	38.3	38.3	38.5	39.4	39.4	39.4	40.0	40.0
1976	46.2	40.8	44.2	48.9	50.9	40.1	41.1	41.1	41.5	45.6	45.6	47.1	49.8	49.8	49.9	51.4	51.5
1977	59.1	54.4	57.9	60.9	63.0	51.7	55.8	55.8	56.0	58.9	58.9	59.5	61.7	61.7	61.8	63.6	63.6
1978	68.6	65.1	67.3	69.9	72.3	64.0	65.7	65.7	65.7	68.1	68.1	68.1	70.8	70.8	70.8	73.0	73.0
1979	81.7	75.4	78.8	84.1	88.3	73.6	76.3	76.3	76.4	80.0	80.0	80.9	85.5	85.8	85.8	89.6	89.6
1980	100.0	92.3	97.0	103.0	107.5	89.9	93.5	93.5	93.5	98.8	98.8	100.5	104.2	104.3	104.3	109.3	109.3
1981	123.7	113.6	121.1	127.8	132.1	109.6	114.4	116.9	116.9	123.2	123.4	124.8	129.3	129.4	129.4	133.4	133.4
1982	144.9	136.8	141.8	147.5	153.3	134.1	138.1	138.1	138.2	143.6	143.6	143.7	149.5	149.5	149.5	155.3	155.3
1983	156.3	158.6	162.9	169.7	174.0	155.5	160.2	160.2	160.4	164.1	164.3	167.4	170.2	171.6	171.6	175.2	175.2

Wholesale prices: total (10) (11)
1980 = 100

Prix de gros : total (10) (11)
1980 = 100

	Year	Q.1	Q.2	Q.3	Q.4	JAN	FEB	MAR	APR	MAY	JUN	JUL	AUG	SEP	OCT	NOV	DEC
1964	21.0	20.9	20.9	20.9	21.2	20.9	20.9	20.9	20.9	20.9	20.8	20.8	20.9	21.0	21.1	21.1	21.2
1965	21.3	21.2	21.2	21.3	21.5	21.2	21.2	21.1	21.1	21.3	21.3	21.2	21.2	21.4	21.5	21.5	21.6
1966	21.6	21.7	21.7	21.5	21.6	21.6	21.7	21.7	21.8	21.7	21.6	21.5	21.6	21.5	21.5	21.6	21.6
1967	21.6	21.6	21.5	21.5	21.8	21.6	21.6	21.6	21.5	21.5	21.5	21.4	21.5	21.7	21.7	21.8	21.8
1968	21.7	21.8	21.6	21.5	21.7	21.8	21.8	21.8	21.8	21.6	21.6	21.5	21.5	21.6	21.6	21.7	21.8
1969	22.5	21.9	22.2	22.7	23.2	21.8	21.9	22.0	22.1	22.2	22.4	22.5	22.7	22.9	23.0	23.2	23.4
1970	24.1	23.8	24.1	24.2	24.5	23.7	23.8	24.0	24.1	24.2	24.1	24.1	24.2	24.3	24.4	24.5	24.6
1971	25.0	24.8	24.9	25.1	25.2	24.7	24.8	24.8	24.9	24.8	24.9	25.0	25.1	25.1	25.2	25.2	25.2
1972	26.0	25.5	25.7	26.0	26.8	25.4	25.5	25.5	25.6	25.7	25.7	25.8	26.0	26.3	26.5	26.7	27.1
1973	30.4	27.9	29.5	32.2	33.1	27.3	27.9	28.4	28.8	29.4	30.2	30.9	31.3	31.5	32.1	32.7	34.3
1974	42.8	38.8	42.2	44.5	45.3	36.5	39.0	40.9	41.7	41.9	42.8	43.8	44.6	45.2	45.7	45.8	45.8
1975	46.5	45.9	46.0	46.4	47.5	45.8	45.9	46.0	46.1	45.9	45.9	46.0	46.3	46.8	47.1	47.4	48.1
1976	57.1	50.7	56.5	58.8	62.3	48.9	50.4	52.7	55.4	56.6	57.5	58.1	58.7	59.7	61.2	62.5	63.2
1977	66.6	64.6	66.1	67.1	68.4	63.7	64.7	65.2	65.8	66.2	66.4	66.6	67.0	67.8	68.2	68.4	68.7
1978	72.2	69.9	71.5	72.8	74.4	69.4	69.9	70.3	71.0	71.6	71.9	72.3	72.7	73.4	73.8	74.4	75.1
1979	83.3	77.7	81.3	84.7	89.5	76.4	77.7	78.9	80.2	81.5	82.2	83.0	84.8	86.4	88.2	89.3	91.0
1980	100.0	95.4	98.8	101.0	104.8	94.0	95.7	96.6	97.9	98.7	99.8	100.1	100.9	102.1	102.9	105.1	106.6
1981	116.6	109.2	114.3	118.9	123.6	107.5	109.2	111.0	112.9	115.2	116.4	117.4	118.8	120.4	121.8	123.9	125.0
1982	132.8	127.6	130.2	134.4	138.9	126.6	127.7	128.5	129.6	130.3	130.7	132.6	134.5	136.0	137.4	139.3	139.9
1983	145.7	141.1	143.4	146.7	151.6	140.6	141.2	141.6	142.7	143.4	144.1	145.1	146.2	148.9	150.4	151.7	152.8

Wholesale prices: finished investment goods (12) — Prix de gros : produits finis, biens d'équipement (12)

1980 = 100

	Year	Q.1	Q.2	Q.3	Q.4	JAN	FEB	MAR	APR	MAY	JUN	JUL	AUG	SEP	OCT	NOV	DEC
1964																	
1965																	
1966																	
1967																	
1968																	
1969																	
1970																	
1971																	
1972																	
1973																	
1974																	
1975	50.6																
1976	58.5	54.2	57.1	60.5	62.1	53.4	54.0	55.2	55.7	57.0	58.7	60.3	60.4	60.7	60.9	62.4	=63.0=
1977	68.0	65.3	67.5	68.8	70.5	64.5	65.3	66.1	66.6	67.7	68.0	68.4	68.5	69.3	70.1	70.6	70.8
1978	75.2	72.1	74.3	76.4	78.1	71.8	72.1	72.2	73.2	74.6	75.0	75.8	76.0	77.3	77.4	78.1	78.8
1979	84.5	80.7	83.2	85.5	88.7	80.2	80.5	81.5	82.4	83.4	83.9	84.7	85.3	86.4	87.3	88.1	90.5
1980	100.0	93.9	98.5	102.3	105.4	92.4	94.0	95.4	96.8	98.8	99.8	101.5	102.0	103.5	104.4	105.4	=106.2=
1981	119.4	111.4	117.6	122.5	126.1	109.7	110.8	113.6	116.0	117.9	119.0	121.0	122.4	124.2	125.0	126.5	126.9
1982	137.1	132.2	135.5	138.6	143.3	129.0	131.3	133.4	134.2	136.1	136.2	137.2	138.5	140.2	141.4	144.2	144.3
1983	155.0	148.6	153.3	156.8	161.2	147.4	148.5	149.9	151.7	153.9	154.3	155.9	156.6	158.0	160.0	161.6	162.1

Wholesale prices: finished consumer goods (12) — Prix de gros : produits finis, biens de consommation (12)

1980 = 100

	Year	Q.1	Q.2	Q.3	Q.4	JAN	FEB	MAR	APR	MAY	JUN	JUL	AUG	SEP	OCT	NOV	DEC
1964																	
1965																	
1966																	
1967																	
1968																	
1969																	
1970																	
1971																	
1972																	
1973																	
1974																	
1975	46.9																
1976	57.8	51.4	56.4	58.9	64.7	49.9	51.0	53.2	55.6	56.6	57.0	57.8	58.4	60.6	63.5	64.9	=65.7=
1977	69.3	66.6	68.4	70.1	72.1	65.5	65.9	67.3	67.9	68.4	68.9	69.2	70.0	71.1	71.8	72.2	72.5
1978	76.5	73.8	75.8	77.3	78.8	73.2	73.9	74.4	75.4	75.8	76.3	76.8	77.2	77.9	78.4	78.7	79.3
1979	85.4	81.3	83.4	86.2	90.7	80.5	81.4	82.0	82.8	83.4	83.9	84.6	86.4	87.7	89.7	90.3	92.1
1980	100.0	95.7	98.3	100.8	105.3	94.9	95.8	96.3	97.5	98.2	99.1	99.8	100.4	102.1	103.1	105.6	=107.1=
1981	114.9	108.4	113.1	116.0	122.0	107.0	108.2	109.9	111.4	113.5	114.3	114.6	115.8	117.6	120.1	122.2	123.6
1982	131.9	125.8	128.6	133.8	139.5	125.1	125.8	126.6	127.8	128.6	129.5	131.6	133.9	135.8	137.9	139.6	140.4
1983	146.8	142.4	144.7	147.8	152.3	142.0	142.4	142.8	144.1	144.7	145.4	146.3	147.3	149.9	151.3	152.3	153.2

Wholesale prices: intermediate goods (12) — Prix de gros : biens intermédiaires (12)

1980 = 100

	Year	Q.1	Q.2	Q.3	Q.4	JAN	FEB	MAR	APR	MAY	JUN	JUL	AUG	SEP	OCT	NOV	DEC
1964																	
1965																	
1966																	
1967																	
1968																	
1969																	
1970																	
1971																	
1972																	
1973																	
1974																	
1975																	
1976	56.2	49.4	56.3	58.3	60.3	47.2	49.2	51.7	55.2	56.4	57.3	57.7	58.3	58.8	59.8	61.0	=61.6=
1977	64.0	62.8	64.0	64.4	65.1	62.1	62.9	63.4	63.8	64.0	64.0	64.0	64.4	64.8	64.9	64.9	65.3
1978	68.2	66.3	67.6	68.5	70.2	66.0	66.4	66.6	67.2	67.6	67.9	68.0	68.5	69.0	69.4	70.2	71.1
1979	81.4	74.3	79.2	83.4	88.7	72.5	74.3	76.0	77.8	79.4	80.5	81.4	83.5	85.5	87.3	88.6	90.2
1980	100.0	95.5	99.2	100.9	104.3	93.5	95.8	97.1	98.4	99.1	100.2	99.9	101.0	101.9	102.3	104.6	=106.2=
1981	117.5	109.4	115.3	120.5	124.3	107.5	109.6	111.2	113.6	116.0	117.7	119.1	120.4	121.9	122.5	124.6	125.7
1982	132.6	128.4	130.5	134.0	137.7	127.4	128.5	129.2	130.2	130.6	130.7	132.5	134.2	135.3	136.3	138.1	138.7
1983	143.2	138.8	140.5	144.0	149.3	138.3	139.0	139.2	139.9	140.5	141.2	142.1	143.5	146.5	148.0	149.1	150.7

ITALY

Wholesale prices: petroleum products (10)(11)

Prix de gros : dérivés du pétrole (10)(11)

1980 = 100

	Year	Q.1	Q.2	Q.3	Q.4	JAN	FEB	MAR	APR	MAY	JUN	JUL	AUG	SEP	OCT	NOV	DEC
1964	12.9	12.7	13.0	13.0	13.1	12.4	12.6	13.2	13.1	12.9	13.0	13.0	12.9	13.0	13.1	13.1	13.1
1965	13.0	13.1	12.9	12.9	13.1	13.1	13.1	13.1	12.9	12.8	12.9	12.9	12.9	13.0	13.0	13.0	13.1
1966	13.2	13.2	13.0	13.1	13.4	13.1	13.2	13.2	13.1	13.0	13.0	13.0	13.1	13.1	13.2	13.5	13.7
1967	13.9	13.7	13.7	14.0	14.0	13.7	13.7	13.7	13.6	13.6	13.8	14.0	14.1	14.1	14.1	14.0	14.0
1968	13.8	14.0	13.7	13.7	13.7	14.0	14.0	14.0	13.8	13.7	13.7	13.7	13.7	13.7	13.7	13.7	13.7
1969	14.3	14.1	14.4	14.4	14.5	13.7	14.0	14.4	14.4	14.3	14.4	14.4	14.4	14.5	14.5	14.5	14.5
1970	15.2	14.5	14.5	15.2	16.4	14.5	14.5	14.5	14.5	14.5	14.5	14.6	14.9	16.2	16.4	16.4	16.5
1971	16.4	16.5	16.5	16.4	16.2	16.5	16.5	16.5	16.5	16.5	16.4	16.4	16.4	16.3	16.2	16.2	16.3
1972	16.3	16.3	16.4	16.3	16.2	16.3	16.3	16.4	16.4	16.4	16.3	16.3	16.3	16.3	16.2	16.2	16.2
1973	16.8	15.5	15.9	15.9	19.8	15.5	15.5	15.5	16.0	15.9	15.9	15.9	15.9	16.0	18.3	18.3	22.8
1974	32.2	26.8	31.9	34.3	35.9	22.9	25.6	32.0	32.0	31.9	31.9	33.5	34.2	35.2	35.9	35.9	35.9
1975	36.8	36.8	36.7	36.4	37.0	36.9	36.8	36.8	36.7	36.7	36.8	36.4	36.4	36.6	36.6	36.7	37.8
1976	47.2	39.1	47.1	47.6	55.0	37.7	38.2	41.3	45.1	47.2	48.9	47.9	47.5	47.4	52.0	56.8	56.3
1977	58.1	57.1	58.0	58.7	58.7	56.2	57.5	57.7	57.7	57.7	58.5	58.7	58.7	58.7	58.7	58.7	58.6
1978	59.2	59.7	58.9	59.3	59.0	59.7	59.7	59.7	58.9	58.9	58.9	59.6	59.3	58.9	59.0	59.0	59.0
1979	68.8	59.9	63.2	72.5	79.7	59.7	60.0	60.1	60.2	64.0	65.4	65.4	75.1	77.0	79.2	79.9	79.9
1980	100.0	93.1	97.8	101.7	107.4	93.1	93.3	93.2	96.3	96.5	100.7	101.7	101.7	101.7	101.3	108.2	112.7
1981	128.5	117.7	127.1	131.1	138.1	115.5	116.3	121.4	122.4	129.3	129.7	129.6	131.9	131.9	131.9	140.3	142.2
1982	149.8	138.7	139.0	154.0	167.5	142.0	137.0	137.1	137.1	137.1	142.8	146.7	156.4	159.0	163.2	169.9	169.5
1983	168.1	164.4	165.2	168.5	174.1	165.6	163.8	163.8	164.5	165.6	165.6	165.7	166.1	173.8	173.8	174.0	174.5

Money supply (M1)

Disponibilités monétaires (M1)

billion lire, end of period — milliards de lires, fin de période

	Year	Q.1	Q.2	Q.3	Q.4	JAN	FEB	MAR	APR	MAY	JUN	JUL	AUG	SEP	OCT	NOV	DEC
1964	12436	11069	11228	11410	12436	11139	11014	11069	10968	11140	11228	11301	11245	11410	11514	11726	12436
1965	14435	12130	12682	13158	14435	12078	11941	12130	12286	12562	12682	12971	12893	13158	13331	13512	14435
1966	16371	14118	14624	15128	16371	14112	14022	14118	14254	14397	14624	14948	14820	15128	15272	15410	16371
1967	18562	16096	16657	17163	18562	15992	15307	16096	16304	16545	16657	16850	16748	17163	17123	17204	18562
1968	21126	18134	18948	19512	21126	18028	17833	18134	18404	18724	18948	19093	19162	19512	19595	19942	21126
1969	24449	21020	21749	22426	24449	20738	20616	21020	21107	21726	21749	21834	21999	22426	22656	23161	24449
1970	31105	24767	26313	27468	31105	24236	24420	24767	25104	25820	26313	26752	26903	27468	28079	28606	31105
1971	36957	30652	32299	33429	36957	30678	30412	30652	31253	31790	32299	32811	32812	33429	33955	34264	36957
1972	43411	36527	38091	39099	43411	36039	36046	36527	37410	37801	38091	38558	38293	39099	39747	40504	43411
1973	53875	43083	46562	48227	53875	42703	42596	43083	44018	45352	46562	47199	47157	48227	48850	49734	53875
1974	59498	52973	55163	55152	59498	52024	52297	52973	53909	54308	55163	55294	54878	55152	55523	55728	59498
1975	66744	56724	57345	60139	66744	58686	57671	56724	55203	55767	57345	58133	58622	60139	60579	61072	66744
1976	79915	68568	70216	71894	79915	66372	67164	68568	69076	70030	70216	70819	70826	71894	73327	74567	79915
1977	97190	80908	83963	86800	97190	79441	79592	80908	82185	83240	83963	85955	85535	86800	88801	88556	97190
1978	122879	99210	104331	108515	122879	96009	96926	99210	100930	102570	104331	106420	105901	108515	109748	110911	122879
1979	151786	121836	127868	133047	151786	118489	120606	121836	124584	126585	127868	132113	131951	133047	137654	139940	151786
1980	172149	146838	150311	149997	172149	144282	144255	146838	148887	147399	150311	152525	150089	149997	153369	155172	172149
1981	189446	167023	168036	165780	189446	165742	165751	167023	166762	165805	168036	168113	163619	165780	166451	166726	189446
1982	221448	179098	183896	188837	221448	181091	179342	179098	180083	179115	183896	187195	184998	188837	191510	197494	221448
1983	250011	207181	212385	219759	250011	211241	207869	207181	207989	205896	212385	217523	216123	219759	221571	229335	250011

M1 plus quasi-money

M1 plus quasi-monnaie

billion lire, end of period — milliards de lires, fin de période

	Year	Q.1	Q.2	Q.3	Q.4	JAN	FEB	MAR	APR	MAY	JUN	JUL	AUG	SEP	OCT	NOV	DEC
1964	25028	22646	22841	23229	25028	22645	22567	22646	22564	22749	22841	22958	22989	23229	23410	23708	25028
1965	28887	24989	25723	26572	28887	24744	24693	24989	25221	25541	25723	26133	26187	26572	26903	27225	28887
1966	32875	28892	29636	30594	32875	28660	28685	28892	29094	29328	29636	30119	30159	30594	30846	31107	32875
1967	36979	32858	33675	34567	36979	32545	32450	32858	33153	33484	33675	33989	34055	34567	34644	34852	36979
1968	41557	36819	37886	38851	41557	36514	36427	36819	37176	37582	37886	38160	38383	38851	39037	39510	41557
1969	46308	41592	42387	43424	46308	41212	41139	41592	41696	42325	42387	42586	42929	43424	43706	44259	46308
1970	52612	46358	47433	48288	52612	45979	46097	46358	46544	47092	47433	47755	47872	48288	48771	49280	52612
1971	61598	52112	54309	56332	61598	52108	51782	52112	52857	53589	54309	55149	55474	56332	57090	57659	61598
1972	72842	61999	64438	66466	72842	60983	61267	61999	63162	63889	64438	65291	65356	66466	67443	68429	72842
1973	89619	73500	77753	80539	89619	72469	72682	73500	74662	76284	77753	78780	79193	80539	81462	82706	89619
1974	103371	90747	94100	95177	103371	88724	89542	90747	92258	92988	94100	94749	94696	95177	96153	96848	103371
1975	127672	105593	110075	115672	127672	103499	103991	105593	106256	107704	110075	111871	113514	115672	116779	117938	127672
1976	154254	132092	134854	138955	154254	128837	129996	132092	132963	134086	134854	136191	137250	138955	141347	143476	154254
1977	187860	157911	162598	167712	187860	154936	155893	157911	159796	161494	162598	165130	165841	167712	170670	171444	187860
1978	231071	192450	199554	206661	231071	187383	189256	192450	194887	197320	199554	202470	203261	206661	208819	210851	231071
1979	278112	232227	239791	247970	278112	227419	229786	232227	235343	237848	239791	244794	246096	247970	253678	256846	278112
1980	313313	272546	275777	277509	313313	270729	270149	272546	274673	272913	275777	278315	277161	277509	281509	284426	313313
1981	344453	306980	306470	305149	344453	306958	306063	306980	305952	304436	306470	306313	302848	305149	305567	307649	344453
1982	402917	333726	339061	348403	402917	335906	333575	333726	334981	333776	339061	343163	342916	348403	352467	360370	402917
1983	456227	388708	395337	407268	456227	392985	389372	388708	389891	387904	395337	401576	402443	407268	409781	407922	456227

Consumer prices: all items (11) — Prix à la consommation : total (11)

1980 = 100

	Year	Q.1	Q.2	Q.3	Q.4	JAN	FEB	MAR	APR	MAY	JUN	JUL	AUG	SEP	OCT	NOV	DEC
1964	22.7	22.2	22.5	22.8	23.1	22.1	22.2	22.3	22.4	22.4	22.7	22.8	22.8	22.9	23.1	23.1	23.2
1965	23.6	23.4	23.6	23.7	23.8	23.4	23.4	23.5	23.5	23.6	23.6	23.7	23.7	23.8	23.8	23.8	23.9
1966	24.1	24.0	24.1	24.1	24.3	24.0	24.0	24.0	24.1	24.1	24.1	24.1	24.1	24.1	24.2	24.3	24.3
1967	24.6	24.4	24.5	24.7	24.7	24.4	24.4	24.4	24.5	24.5	24.6	24.6	24.7	24.8	24.7	24.7	24.7
1968	24.9	24.8	24.9	24.9	25.0	24.8	24.8	24.8	24.9	24.9	24.9	24.9	24.9	24.9	25.0	25.0	25.1
1969	25.6	25.2	25.4	25.8	26.1	25.2	25.2	25.2	25.4	25.4	25.5	25.7	25.8	25.8	25.9	26.0	26.2
1970	26.9	26.5	26.8	27.0	27.4	26.3	26.5	26.6	26.7	26.8	26.8	26.9	27.0	27.2	27.3	27.4	27.6
1971	28.3	27.8	28.1	28.4	28.8	27.7	27.7	27.9	28.0	28.1	28.2	28.3	28.4	28.6	28.7	28.8	28.8
1972	29.8	29.1	29.5	30.0	30.8	29.0	29.1	29.2	29.3	29.5	29.7	29.8	30.0	30.2	30.7	30.9	30.9
1973	32.9	31.6	32.6	33.3	34.2	31.3	31.6	31.9	32.3	32.7	32.9	33.1	33.3	33.4	33.8	34.2	34.7
1974	39.3	35.9	37.9	40.5	43.0	35.2	35.8	36.8	37.3	37.8	38.6	39.5	40.3	41.6	42.5	43.1	43.5
1975	46.1	44.4	45.6	46.5	47.9	44.0	44.5	44.6	45.2	45.5	46.0	46.2	46.5	46.9	47.5	47.9	48.4
1976	53.7	49.7	52.9	54.3	58.0	48.8	49.6	50.7	52.2	53.1	53.3	53.7	54.1	55.1	56.9	58.2	58.9
1977	63.4	60.3	62.7	64.4	66.4	59.1	60.4	61.3	62.0	62.8	63.4	63.9	64.3	65.0	65.7	66.7	67.0
1978	71.3	68.3	70.5	72.2	74.4	67.6	68.3	69.0	69.8	70.5	71.1	71.6	72.0	72.9	73.7	74.4	74.9
1979	82.6	77.4	80.7	83.6	88.4	76.4	77.5	78.5	79.8	80.8	81.6	82.3	83.1	85.2	87.2	88.3	89.7
1980	100.0	94.1	97.6	101.5	107.0	92.7	94.3	95.2	96.7	97.5	98.4	100.1	101.1	103.3	105.1	107.3	108.7
1981	118.7	112.0	116.7	120.2	125.8	110.1	112.1	113.7	115.2	116.9	118.1	119.1	119.9	121.6	124.0	126.1	127.4
1982	138.1	130.6	134.6	140.3	146.9	129.1	130.8	132.0	133.2	134.7	136.0	138.0	140.5	142.5	145.3	147.2	148.2
1983	158.8	152.1	156.6	160.3	166.0	150.3	152.3	153.7	155.3	156.8	157.7	159.2	159.8	161.9	164.6	166.3	167.1

Money supply (M1) — Disponibilités monétaires (M1)

billion lire, end of period — milliards de lires, fin de période

Adjusted - Corrigé *

	Year	Q.1	Q.2	Q.3	Q.4	JAN	FEB	MAR	APR	MAY	JUN	JUL	AUG	SEP	OCT	NOV	DEC
1964		11125	11273	11467	11855	11029	11092	11125	11023	11174	11273	11278	11393	11467	11619	11797	11855
1965		12203	12720	13237	13774	11970	12037	12203	12360	12600	12720	12958	13063	13237	13452	13594	13774
1966		14203	14663	15219	15636	13972	14149	14203	14340	14411	14668	14933	15015	15219	15411	15503	15636
1967		16193	16674	17284	17729	15834	15951	16193	16402	16545	16674	16850	16969	17284	17296	17325	17729
1968		18225	18967	19669	20173	17832	17995	18225	18515	18705	18967	19093	19434	19669	19793	20103	20178
1969		21126	21749	22630	23329	20512	20782	21126	21213	21704	21749	21856	22311	22630	22908	23371	23329
1970		24892	26287	27746	29680	23972	24592	24892	25230	25769	26287	26779	27313	27746	28391	28866	29680
1971		30806	32235	33835	35231	30314	30596	30806	31410	31758	32235	32844	33346	33835	34367	34610	35231
1972		36711	38015	39574	41423	35541	36191	36711	37560	37801	38015	38597	38916	39574	40230	40996	41423
1973		43256	46516	48862	51407	42072	42681	43256	44151	45352	46516	47246	47973	48862	49493	50440	51407
1974		53079	55163	55878	56773	51205	52297	53079	54017	54362	55163	55405	55827	55878	56311	56634	56773
1975		56667	57402	61055	63626	57705	57556	56667	55338	55823	57402	58250	59636	61055	61502	62255	63626
1976		68363	70427	73063	76037	65327	66896	68363	69007	70030	70427	70961	72124	73063	74444	76244	76037
1977		80586	84300	88391	92123	78267	79275	80586	81939	83240	84300	86041	87192	88391	90153	90641	92123
1978		98815	104855	110730	116033	94777	96540	98815	100528	102570	104855	106420	108062	110730	111306	113522	116033
1979		121351	128382	136179	142925	117084	120245	121351	124088	126585	128382	131849	134644	136179	139750	143234	142925
1980		146253	150763	153528	161946	142712	143824	146253	148294	147694	150763	152069	153309	153528	155705	158825	161946
1981		166358	168542	169683	178051	164101	165255	166358	166098	166137	168542	167610	167129	169683	168986	170651	178051
1982		178562	184449	193283	208128	179298	178806	178562	179366	179654	184449	186635	188966	193283	194426	202133	208128
1983		206561	213024	224932	234973	209150	207247	206561	207160	206516	213024	216872	220759	224932	224945	224499	234973

M1 plus quasi-money — M1 plus quasi-monnaie

billion lire, end of period — milliards de lires, fin de période

Adjusted - Corrigé *

	Year	Q.1	Q.2	Q.3	Q.4	JAN	FEB	MAR	APR	MAY	JUN	JUL	AUG	SEP	OCT	NOV	DEC
1964		22578	22956	23416	24158	22332	22477	22578	22564	22795	22956	23050	23245	23416	23694	23972	24158
1965		24939	25852	26813	27910	24402	24619	24939	25236	25592	25852	26238	26478	26813	27230	27556	27910
1966		28834	29785	30872	31763	28264	28628	28834	29123	29357	29785	30240	30494	30872	31189	31485	31763
1967		32792	33810	34881	35729	32096	32385	32792	33191	33484	33810	34126	34434	34881	35029	35275	35729
1968		36746	38000	39204	40113	36010	36391	36746	37213	37545	38000	38313	38810	39204	39511	40030	40113
1969		41550	42515	43863	44699	40643	41098	41550	41738	42283	42515	42757	43407	43863	44237	44887	44699
1970		46312	47523	48825	50735	45344	46005	46312	46591	47045	47528	47899	48404	48825	49413	50031	50735
1971		52060	54363	57016	59343	51389	51679	52060	52857	53482	54363	55315	56148	57016	57901	58656	59343
1972		61937	64438	67341	70175	60141	61084	61937	63099	63762	64438	65422	66190	67341	68540	69754	70175
1973		73353	77753	81766	86255	71398	72320	73353	74439	76132	77753	79017	80236	81766	82871	84430	86255
1974		90386	94100	96725	99395	87241	88920	90386	91890	92802	94100	95130	96041	96725	98015	99128	99395
1975		104963	110185	117792	122644	101669	103063	104963	105727	107489	110185	112433	115243	117792	119162	120838	122644
1976		131044	135260	141646	147895	126435	128582	131044	132170	133952	135260	137013	139482	141646	144379	147155	147895
1977		156503	163251	171310	179770	151898	154045	156503	158843	161333	163251	166127	168709	171310	174331	175840	179770
1978		190733	200557	211094	220488	183529	187012	190733	193725	197320	200557	203897	206987	211094	213081	216257	220488
1979		229928	240996	253808	265121	222741	227061	229928	233939	237846	240996	246272	250607	253808	253855	263432	265121
1980		270115	277163	284042	298393	265161	266946	270115	273035	273186	277163	279995	282241	284042	287254	291719	298393
1981		304242	308010	312333	328051	300645	302454	304242	304127	304741	308010	308162	308714	312333	312824	315537	328051
1982		330749	341108	356605	383731	328997	329620	330749	332983	334447	341108	345234	349558	356605	359660	369610	383731
1983		385241	397723	416856	434502	384902	384755	385241	387566	388681	397723	404000	410238	416856	418144	418382	434502

* Adjusted by the O.E.C.D. — * Corrigé par l'O.C.D.E.

ITALY

Net new bond issues (13) — Nouvelles émissions d'obligations, nettes (13)

billion lire — milliards de lires

	Year	Q.1	Q.2	Q.3	Q.4	JAN	FEB	MAR	APR	MAY	JUN	JUL	AUG	SEP	OCT	NOV	DEC
1964																	
1965																	
1966																	
1967	1415	460	150	405	400	318	101	41	32	85	33	304	29	73	173	137	90
1968	1772	532	327	633	280	282	119	132	127	74	127	329	42	261	49	86	145
1969	1799	555	409	570	266	355	47	153	30	129	250	456	19	95	43	137	86
1970	1526	675	315	45	492	289	303	83	63	71	181	-73	24	94	3	242	246
1971	2774	916	518	457	883	193	611	112	261	141	117	254	72	131	56	439	388
1972	3309	1074	733	777	726	486	137	451	211	173	350	505	144	127	216	118	392
1973	7274	962	445	1859	4007	635	158	170	52	131	263	552	320	985	599	1007	2401
1974	2247	48	78	606	1514	-75	-98	221	-107	-12	198	26	113	467	450	272	792
1975	6806	2095	1635	1764	1313	-19	386	1728	231	128	1276	149	-46	1661	-25	494	843
1976	5155	2484	675	765	1231	917	317	1251	-79	7	746	-58	-146	968	-181	134	1278
1977	5699	2214	890	889	1706	-21	47	2188	-148	-49	1087	-95	-25	1010	-138	344	1500
1978	5918	2281	1457	807	1373	-110	279	2112	-156	484	1129	368	-217	656	-210	253	1331
1979	5299	632	2758	56	1842	55	228	349	-8	692	2084	-116	239	-58	-242	527	1558
1980	5398	659	2212	1822	705	-129	273	515	292	239	1680	-191	1271	742	-560	372	393
1981	3211	574	2179	2995	2463	118	345	111	157	230	1792	1046	340	1610	-22	762	1723
1982	8147	3850	2576	2808	-1036	-174	1042	2981	-16	623	1968	890	582	1336	-855	-130	-50
1983	8627	874	1748	1111	4894	-267	-11	1151	-231	993	986	232	74	805	-122	1572	3444

Domestic credit: (14) — Crédits au secteur intérieur : (14)

commercial and savings banks — banques commerciales et d'épargne

billion lire, end of period — milliards de lires, fin de période

	Year	Q.1	Q.2	Q.3	Q.4	JAN	FEB	MAR	APR	MAY	JUN	JUL	AUG	SEP	OCT	NOV	DEC
1964	13521	12930	12893	12800	13521	12864	12859	12930	12905	12851	12893	12794	12697	12800	12933	12873	13521
1965	14430	13144	13328	13487	14430	13103	13069	13144	13261	13165	13328	13415	13298	13487	13640	13618	14430
1966	16565	14394	14848	15249	16565	14112	14162	14394	14515	14485	14848	15026	15006	15249	15415	15555	16565
1967	19129	16576	17397	17650	19129	16266	16372	16576	16837	16884	17397	17472	17473	17650	17944	17961	19129
1968	21176	18801	19492	19767	21176	18722	18808	18801	18835	19034	19492	19809	19706	19767	19942	20071	21176
1969	24318	21080	22173	22481	24318	20844	20997	21080	21454	21650	22173	22356	22290	22481	22812	22873	24318
1970	27683	24000	25045	25389	27683	23868	23920	24000	24322	24461	25045	25564	25255	25389	25788	25850	27683
1971	31255	27067	27880	28399	31255	27047	27075	27067	27397	27206	27880	28323	28209	28399	29056	28894	31255
1972	37067	31136	32039	32987	37067	30756	30871	31136	31485	31448	32039	32834	32787	32987	33702	34170	37067
1973	44021	37134	39583	40552	44021	36179	36443	37134	37799	38513	39583	41001	40374	40552	40941	41222	44021
1974	53396	46733	48366	47957	53396	45813	46300	46733	47531	48138	48366	49183	48933	47957	50861	51093	53396
1975	60994	51789	54165	55882	60994	54132	53762	51789	53440	53645	54165	56356	55962	55882	56864	57316	60994
1976	74543	63805	65920	70026	74543	63856	63048	63805	64128	63794	65920	69223	69446	70026	72269	71038	74543
1977	81590	77146	78377	79306	81590	75027	75335	77146	78063	76920	78377	80657	80553	79306	81586	81285	81590
1978	90032	80146	81205	82986	90032	80990	80830	80146	80312	79986	81205	83428	83452	82986	85314	86030	90032
1979	109227	91931	95030	98621	109227	90111	91431	91931	93114	93797	95030	98075	99037	98621	102726	102592	109227
1980	131667	111259	119684	119785	131667	109037	113224	111259	116540	114815	119684	119465	119637	119785	123552	125080	131667
1981	148482	134352	137980	138937	148482	133650	133987	134352	135666	136740	137980	143211	141605	138937	143557	145082	148482
1982	163748	147185	148109	151796	163748	148326	147319	147185	147046	146280	148109	152624	152090	151796	155428	156772	163748
1983		167286	172021	175329		164351	164454	167286	170137	171310	172021	180005	176274	175329	182006	185595	

Credit to private sector: (14) — Crédits au secteur privé : (14)

commercial and savings banks — banques commerciales et d'épargne

billion lire, end of period — milliards de lires, fin de période

	Year	Q.1	Q.2	Q.3	Q.4	JAN	FEB	MAR	APR	MAY	JUN	JUL	AUG	SEP	OCT	NOV	DEC
1964	11647	11253	11172	10987	11647	11208	11214	11253	11210	11156	11172	11032	10898	10987	11078	10992	11647
1965	12385	11219	11417	11491	12385	11201	11155	11219	11336	11254	11417	11447	11337	11491	11615	11591	12385
1966	14288	12369	12784	13054	14288	12132	12187	12369	12520	12486	12784	12884	12863	13054	13252	13361	14288
1967	16318	14269	14883	15091	16318	13974	14045	14269	14501	14468	14883	14981	14965	15091	15318	15315	16318
1968	18083	16209	16738	16846	18083	15879	16128	16209	16281	16372	16738	16888	16804	16846	16988	17069	18083
1969	20768	17965	18965	19204	20768	17710	17879	17965	18254	18478	18965	19093	19043	19204	19461	19501	20768
1970	23399	20429	21242	21445	23399	20375	20356	20429	20674	20758	21242	21649	21299	21445	21774	21785	23399
1971	25959	22625	23145	23683	25959	22659	22632	22625	22845	22662	23145	23500	23282	23683	24178	23943	25959
1972	30267	25714	26282	27065	30267	25416	25540	25714	25936	25851	26282	26950	26898	27065	27579	27919	30267
1973	35513	30264	32177	32446	35513	29521	29771	30264	30710	31277	32177	33182	32447	32446	32536	32707	35513
1974	43471	38650	39915	38836	43471	37950	38297	38650	39199	39705	39915	40484	40101	38836	41402	41503	43471
1975	50217	42758	44642	45106	50217	43835	44056	42758	44108	44236	44642	46611	46051	46106	46923	47389	50217
1976	61477	52864	54868	58246	61477	52817	52129	52864	53291	52818	54868	57546	57717	58246	60355	58944	61477
1977	72304	64389	65785	66721	72304	61646	62370	64389	65405	64432	65785	67630	67537	66721	68788	68902	72304
1978	82842	72506	74262	76624	82842	71829	72221	72506	73340	73050	74262	76956	76989	76624	78685	79443	82842
1979	101162	85118	88454	91561	101162	82952	84556	85118	86100	86847	88454	91205	92016	91561	95098	95040	101162
1980	122297	103385	111416	110825	122297	100919	104926	103385	108246	106677	111416	111221	111003	110825	114606	116127	122297
1981	139861	124833	128369	128954	139861	124138	124457	124833	125671	126889	128369	132858	131520	128954	133441	135016	139861
1982	153223	138463	139186	142256	153223	139368	138361	138463	138134	137303	139186	143282	142904	142256	145320	146413	153223
1983		157662	162148	166229		154081	154510	157662	159415	159679	162148	170178	167240	166229	171641	175359	

Official discount rate / Taux d'escompte officiel

per cent per annum, end of period / pourcentage par an, fin de période

	Year	Q.1	Q.2	Q.3	Q.4	JAN	FEB	MAR	APR	MAY	JUN	JUL	AUG	SEP	OCT	NOV	DEC
1964	3.50	3.50	3.50	3.50	3.50	3.50	3.50	3.50	3.50	3.50	3.50	3.50	3.50	3.50	3.50	3.50	3.50
1965	3.50	3.50	3.50	3.50	3.50	3.50	3.50	3.50	3.50	3.50	3.50	3.50	3.50	3.50	3.50	3.50	3.50
1966	3.50	3.50	3.50	3.50	3.50	3.50	3.50	3.50	3.50	3.50	3.50	3.50	3.50	3.50	3.50	3.50	3.50
1967	3.50	3.50	3.50	3.50	3.50	3.50	3.50	3.50	3.50	3.50	3.50	3.50	3.50	3.50	3.50	3.50	3.50
1968	3.50	3.50	3.50	3.50	3.50	3.50	3.50	3.50	3.50	3.50	3.50	3.50	3.50	3.50	3.50	3.50	3.50
1969	4.00	3.50	3.50	4.00	4.00	3.50	3.50	3.50	3.50	3.50	3.50	3.50	4.00	4.00	4.00	4.00	4.00
1970	5.50	5.50	5.50	5.50	5.50	4.00	4.00	5.50	5.50	5.50	5.50	5.50	5.50	5.50	5.50	5.50	5.50
1971	4.50	5.50	5.00	5.00	4.50	5.50	5.50	5.50	5.00	5.00	5.00	5.00	5.00	5.00	4.50	4.50	4.50
1972	4.00	4.50	4.00	4.00	4.00	4.50	4.50	4.50	4.00	4.00	4.00	4.00	4.00	4.00	4.00	4.00	4.00
1973	6.50	4.00	4.00	6.50	6.50	4.00	4.00	4.00	4.00	4.00	4.00	4.00	4.00	6.50	6.50	6.50	6.50
1974	8.00	9.00	9.00	9.00	8.00	6.50	6.50	9.00	9.00	9.00	9.00	9.00	9.00	9.00	9.00	9.00	8.00
1975	6.00	8.00	7.00	6.00	6.00	8.00	8.00	8.00	8.00	7.00	7.00	7.00	7.00	6.00	6.00	6.00	6.00
1976	15.00	12.00	12.00	12.00	15.00	6.00	8.00	12.00	12.00	12.00	12.00	12.00	12.00	12.00	15.00	15.00	15.00
1977	11.50	15.00	13.00	11.50	11.50	15.00	15.00	15.00	15.00	15.00	13.00	13.00	11.50	11.50	11.50	11.50	11.50
1978	10.50	11.50	11.50	10.50	10.50	11.50	11.50	11.50	11.50	11.50	11.50	11.50	11.50	10.50	10.50	10.50	10.50
1979	15.00	10.50	10.50	10.50	15.00	10.50	10.50	10.50	10.50	10.50	10.50	10.50	10.50	10.50	12.00	12.00	15.00
1980	16.50	15.00	15.00	16.50	16.50	15.00	15.00	15.00	15.00	15.00	15.00	15.00	15.00	16.50	16.50	16.50	16.50
1981	19.00	19.00	19.00	19.00	19.00	16.50	16.50	19.00	19.00	19.00	19.00	19.00	19.00	19.00	19.00	19.00	19.00
1982	18.00	19.00	19.00	18.00	18.00	19.00	19.00	19.00	19.00	19.00	19.00	19.00	18.00	18.00	18.00	18.00	18.00
1983	17.00	18.00	17.00	17.00	17.00	18.00	18.00	18.00	17.00	17.00	17.00	17.00	17.00	17.00	17.00	17.00	17.00

Treasury bill rate (6 months) (15) / Bons du Trésor (6 mois) (15)

per cent per annum, end of period / pourcentage par an, fin de période

	Year	Q.1	Q.2	Q.3	Q.4	JAN	FEB	MAR	APR	MAY	JUN	JUL	AUG	SEP	OCT	NOV	DEC
1964	3.63	3.63	3.63	3.63	3.63	3.63	3.63	3.63	3.63	3.63	3.63	3.63	3.63	3.63	3.63	3.63	3.63
1965	3.63	3.63	3.63	3.63	3.63	3.63	3.63	3.63	3.63	3.63	3.63	3.63	3.63	3.63	3.63	3.63	3.63
1966	3.52	3.63	3.52	3.52	3.52	3.63	3.63	3.63	3.63	3.63	3.52	3.63	3.52	3.52	3.63	3.52	3.52
1967	3.63	3.52	3.63	3.52	3.63	3.63	3.52	3.52	3.63	3.63	3.63	3.63	3.52	3.52	3.63	3.52	3.63
1968	3.63	3.63	3.63	3.52	3.63	3.63	3.41	3.63	3.63	3.63	3.63	3.63	3.52	3.52	3.41	3.41	3.63
1969	..	3.63	4.44	..	..	3.41	3.63	3.63	3.41	4.44	4.44	4.99	..	..	..	..	..
1970	..	6.95	..	..	..	..	6.95	6.95	..	..	..	..	..	..	..	..	..
1971	..	5.76	..	6.04	..	..	..	5.76	..	5.54	..	6.38	..	6.04	..	..	..
1972	..	..	..	4.49	..	..	..	..	..	..	..	4.60	..	4.49	..	5.82	..
1973	8.85	..	..	9.64	8.85	..	..	..	5.82	6.38	..	7.53	..	9.64	8.96	8.62	8.85
1974	..	..	..	15.62	..	9.64	..	..	..	..	..	..	..	15.62	..	..	..
1975	..	..	..	9.65	..	..	..	..	..	..	..	..	..	9.65	7.16	8.50	..
1976	17.38	15.62	17.89	17.89	17.38	9.76	12.46	15.62	17.38	17.89	17.89	17.89	17.89	17.89	17.89	17.89	17.38
1977	12.81	17.64	15.62	13.29	12.81	17.64	16.87	17.64	17.51	16.62	15.62	15.62	15.12	13.29	13.17	12.93	12.81
1978	11.74	12.93	12.10	11.62	11.74	12.69	12.69	12.93	12.66	12.22	12.10	12.10	11.86	11.62	11.62	11.62	11.74
1979	15.62	11.86	11.51	11.62	15.62	11.74	11.62	11.86	11.51	10.92	11.51	11.62	11.62	11.62	12.93	13.05	15.62
1980	17.02	15.87	16.12	16.00	17.02	13.17	15.62	15.87	16.12	15.75	16.12	16.25	16.12	16.00	16.37	16.87	17.02
1981	21.36	19.01	20.30	20.95	21.36	17.02	17.02	19.01	18.99	19.66	20.30	20.31	20.57	20.95	21.36	21.49	21.36
1982	19.11	19.66	19.25	17.67	19.11	20.95	20.41	19.66	19.78	20.05	19.25	19.27	18.19	17.67	18.07	19.09	19.11
1983	16.95	18.88	17.58	17.18	16.95	19.09	19.09	18.88	18.22	17.74	17.58	17.35	17.24	17.18	17.08	17.05	16.95

Yield of long-term Government bonds (16) / Rendement des bons d'État à long terme (16)

per cent per annum, end of period / pourcentage par an, fin de période

	Year	Q.1	Q.2	Q.3	Q.4	JAN	FEB	MAR	APR	MAY	JUN	JUL	AUG	SEP	OCT	NOV	DEC
1964	5.62	5.86	6.05	5.72	5.62	5.57	5.57	5.86	5.87	5.94	6.05	5.97	5.83	5.72	5.75	5.71	5.62
1965	5.42	5.35	5.46	5.48	5.42	5.35	5.35	5.35	5.44	5.49	5.46	5.45	5.50	5.48	5.41	5.40	5.42
1966	5.61	5.31	5.54	5.62	5.61	5.25	5.16	5.31	5.49	5.49	5.54	5.50	5.55	5.62	5.63	5.64	5.61
1967	5.61	5.56	5.62	5.60	5.61	5.56	5.52	5.56	5.60	5.62	5.62	5.61	5.60	5.60	5.60	5.61	5.61
1968	5.62	5.59	5.66	5.64	5.62	5.62	5.60	5.59	5.60	5.65	5.66	5.65	5.65	5.64	5.64	5.65	5.62
1969	6.33	5.62	5.65	5.90	6.33	5.61	5.60	5.62	5.63	5.64	5.65	5.66	5.68	5.90	6.15	6.28	6.33
1970	7.94	7.46	7.95	8.10	7.94	6.50	6.96	7.46	7.53	7.76	7.95	8.08	8.15	8.10	8.11	8.11	7.94
1971	6.76	6.95	7.11	7.14	6.76	7.38	7.01	6.95	6.96	7.06	7.11	7.15	7.16	7.14	6.95	6.83	6.76
1972	6.74	6.67	6.42	6.52	6.74	6.78	6.79	6.67	6.58	6.48	6.42	6.41	6.45	6.52	6.50	6.59	6.74
1973	7.06	6.70	6.92	6.88	7.06	6.72	6.66	6.70	6.68	6.76	6.92	6.87	6.88	6.88	6.97	7.04	7.06
1974	10.78	7.57	9.33	10.26	10.78	6.98	7.05	7.57	7.83	8.61	9.33	9.85	9.94	10.26	10.44	10.73	10.78
1975	9.65	10.16	9.93	10.21	9.65	10.57	10.24	10.16	10.35	10.22	9.93	9.85	10.04	10.21	9.86	9.62	9.65
1976	14.39	11.15	13.47	13.31	14.39	9.93	10.28	11.15	11.86	12.49	13.47	13.04	13.03	13.31	14.25	14.23	14.39
1977	13.54	15.11	15.16	14.44	13.54	14.67	14.98	15.12	15.37	15.18	15.16	15.05	14.99	14.44	14.21	13.86	13.54
1978	13.04	13.37	13.04	12.91	13.04	13.53	13.38	13.37	13.25	13.16	13.04	13.16	13.19	12.91	13.08	13.06	13.04
1979	14.00	12.92	12.83	13.22	14.00	12.87	12.85	12.92	12.89	12.82	12.83	12.94	13.11	13.22	13.41	13.59	14.00
1980	16.23	14.82	15.17	15.73	16.23	14.03	14.17	14.82	14.99	15.04	15.17	15.45	15.61	15.73	16.12	16.19	16.23
1981	21.39	17.15	19.56	21.03	21.39	16.24	16.51	17.15	18.37	18.70	19.56	20.35	20.62	21.03	20.86	21.45	21.39
1982	19.70	20.07	20.78	19.18	19.70	20.97	20.70	20.07	20.22	20.77	20.78	20.77	20.11	19.18	19.38	19.90	19.70
1983	17.69	18.74	18.22	17.82	17.69	19.33	19.13	18.74	18.11	18.13	18.22	18.34	18.11	17.82	17.65	17.78	17.69

ITALY

Bond yield: credit institutions (16)(17)

per cent per annum, end of period

Rendement des obligations : crédit mobilier (16)(17)

pourcentage par an, fin de période

	Year	Q.1	Q.2	Q.3	Q.4	JAN	FEB	MAR	APR	MAY	JUN	JUL	AUG	SEP	OCT	NOV	DEC
1964	7.12	7.17	8.06	7.01	7.12	6.63	6.78	7.17	7.15	7.25	8.06	7.69	7.33	7.01	7.15	7.15	7.12
1965	6.63	6.87	6.89	6.83	6.63	6.92	6.94	6.87	6.86	6.88	6.89	6.89	6.82	6.83	6.71	6.56	6.63
1966	6.52	6.44	6.49	6.49	6.52	6.49	6.43	6.44	6.43	6.46	6.49	6.48	6.47	6.49	6.46	6.51	6.52
1967	6.77	6.50	6.60	6.59	6.77	6.46	6.47	6.50	6.55	6.56	6.60	6.60	6.58	6.59	6.67	6.72	6.77
1968	6.78	6.76	6.83	6.79	6.73	6.74	6.74	6.76	6.74	6.79	6.83	6.81	6.79	6.79	6.77	6.78	6.78
1969	7.90	6.72	6.83	7.26	7.90	6.70	6.68	6.72	6.76	6.83	6.83	6.93	7.08	7.26	7.46	7.52	7.90
1970	8.92	8.58	9.78	9.21	8.92	7.79	8.09	8.58	8.54	9.07	9.78	10.19	9.77	9.21	9.38	9.28	8.92
1971	7.87	8.13	8.37	8.21	7.87	8.54	8.16	8.13	8.10	8.27	8.37	8.25	8.19	8.21	7.96	7.92	7.87
1972	7.63	7.52	7.21	7.32	7.63	7.77	7.72	7.52	7.37	7.13	7.21	7.30	7.21	7.32	7.26	7.30	7.63
1973	7.67	7.38	7.66	7.45	7.67	7.44	7.39	7.38	7.31	7.42	7.66	7.41	7.33	7.45	7.67	7.62	7.67
1974	12.49	8.22	11.02	11.30	12.49	7.49	7.50	8.22	8.52	9.60	11.02	11.00	10.45	11.30	12.09	12.72	12.49
1975	10.66	10.48	10.78	10.80	10.66	11.44	10.64	10.48	10.98	10.84	10.78	10.74	10.85	10.80	10.90	10.70	10.66
1976	14.18	12.60	13.87	13.71	14.18	11.24	11.77	12.60	13.25	13.39	13.87	13.67	13.57	13.71	14.82	14.59	14.18
1977	13.98	14.88	14.60	14.44	13.98	14.35	14.72	14.88	14.92	14.75	14.60	14.67	14.70	14.44	14.38	14.27	13.98
1978	13.39	13.60	13.23	12.93	13.39	13.70	13.68	13.60	13.53	13.44	13.23	13.20	13.18	12.93	12.96	13.18	13.39
1979	14.27	13.44	13.42	13.41	14.27	13.37	13.40	13.44	13.47	13.51	13.42	13.45	13.53	13.41	13.70	14.03	14.27
1980	16.30	14.75	15.20	15.96	16.30	14.23	14.47	14.75	14.78	14.96	15.20	15.59	15.72	15.96	16.36	16.30	16.30
1981	21.00	17.67	20.95	21.33	21.00	16.44	16.84	17.67	18.90	19.66	20.95	20.64	20.85	21.33	20.88	21.01	21.00
1982	19.86	20.43	20.75	19.80	19.86	20.57	20.44	20.43	20.50	20.71	20.75	20.44	20.20	19.30	19.66	19.96	19.86
1983	17.33	18.28	17.90	17.47	17.33	19.55	19.21	18.28	17.77	17.92	17.90	17.64	17.50	17.47	17.20	17.43	17.33

Share prices (18)

Milan Stock Exchange

1980 = 100

Cours des actions (18)

Bourse de Milan

1980 = 100

	Year	Q.1	Q.2	Q.3	Q.4	JAN	FEB	MAR	APR	MAY	JUN	JUL	AUG	SEP	OCT	NOV	DEC
1964	126	142	123	118	122	150	142	134	122	130	118	115	114	126	126	122	116
1965	125	122	128	123	127	112	120	134	132	129	123	120	126	124	124	123	133
1966	148	153	144	147	148	148	154	157	145	144	144	147	148	146	150	148	146
1967	136	138	132	135	140	144	142	129	130	134	131	130	134	140	144	140	136
1968	134	133	135	137	131	135	131	134	137	136	133	136	138	137	131	127	134
1969	150	135	152	151	161	135	134	136	152	154	151	147	152	153	163	164	156
1970	146	157	153	142	132	157	157	157	163	152	144	140	145	140	137	130	128
1971	114	126	116	110	104	124	127	127	120	115	113	113	111	106	106	102	104
1972	108	103	107	108	114	106	103	100	107	108	106	109	109	107	109	116	116
1973	140	113	150	149	142	112	114	126	131	148	170	160	143	145	148	146	131
1974	128	148	145	116	102	145	148	152	159	144	131	123	120	104	100	108	98
1975	95	106	104	88	82	97	108	111	107	106	99	90	87	87	82	80	83
1976	78	82	74	85	72	82	85	79	72	73	77	88	87	81	70	69	76
1977	63	69	61	63	59	72	68	66	63	60	59	60	62	69	63	59	54
1978	64	58	59	68	73	55	59	58	56	59	60	61	65	78	79	70	70
1979	79	75	77	83	80	71	75	79	74	77	79	80	84	86	85	80	75
1980	100	83	85	101	131	81	83	83	83	84	88	90	101	113	128	135	131
1981	152	163	178	139	128	150	166	171	180	185	168	135	147	135	124	128	132
1982	123	135	123	114	121	129	135	142	132	124	113	107	117	117	118	121	124
1983	153	147	153	160	153	130	149	162	158	152	150	154	164	161	152	153	154

U.S. dollar exchange rate: spot — Taux de change du dollar É.-U. : au comptant

cents par lira, end of period — cents par lire, fin de période

	Year	Q.1	Q.2	Q.3	Q.4	JAN	FEB	MAR	APR	MAY	JUN	JUL	AUG	SEP	OCT	NOV	DEC
1964	0.1601	0.1600	0.1600	0.1600	0.1601	0.1607	0.1606	0.1600	0.1600	0.1600	0.1600	0.1600	0.1600	0.1600	0.1600	0.1600	0.1601
1965	0.1601	0.1601	0.1601	0.1600	0.1601	0.1600	0.1601	0.1601	0.1601	0.1600	0.1501	0.1601	0.1601	0.1600	0.1600	0.1601	0.1601
1966	0.1601	0.1601	0.1602	0.1602	0.1601	0.1600	0.1601	0.1601	0.1602	0.1602	0.1602	0.1604	0.1604	0.1602	0.1600	0.1600	0.1601
1967	0.1603	0.1601	0.1602	0.1605	0.1603	0.1599	0.1600	0.1601	0.1601	0.1600	0.1602	0.1603	0.1605	0.1605	0.1607	0.1603	0.1603
1968	0.1604	0.1602	0.1607	0.1608	0.1604	0.1601	0.1600	0.1602	0.1604	0.1608	0.1607	0.1609	0.1607	0.1608	0.1605	0.1603	0.1604
1969	0.1599	0.1592	0.1596	0.1589	0.1599	0.1602	0.1594	0.1592	0.1596	0.1591	0.1596	0.1590	0.1591	0.1589	0.1599	0.1595	0.1599
1970	0.1605	0.1590	0.1590	0.1605	0.1605	0.1589	0.1589	0.1590	0.1590	0.1590	0.1590	0.1590	0.1603	0.1605	0.1607	0.1606	0.1605
1971	0.1684	0.1608	0.1604	0.1634	0.1684	0.1604	0.1606	0.1608	0.1610	0.1602	0.1604	0.1605	0.1627	0.1634	0.1633	0.1637	0.1684
1972	0.1717	0.1717	0.1722	0.1719	0.1717	0.1697	0.1703	0.1717	0.1713	0.1720	0.1722	0.1721	0.1721	0.1719	0.1710	0.1711	0.1717
1973	0.1645	0.1717	0.1712	0.1773	0.1645	0.1719	0.1765	0.1717	0.1692	0.1708	0.1712	0.1710	0.1766	0.1773	0.1752	0.1655	0.1645
1974	0.1540	0.1607	0.1544	0.1514	0.1540	0.1514	0.1547	0.1607	0.1582	0.1552	0.1544	0.1549	0.1513	0.1514	0.1498	0.1505	0.1540
1975	0.1463	0.1582	0.1586	0.1455	0.1463	0.1553	0.1592	0.1582	0.1579	0.1599	0.1586	0.1503	0.1495	0.1455	0.1486	0.1461	0.1463
1976	0.1143	0.1190	0.1190	0.1163	0.1143	0.1331	0.1304	0.1190	0.1115	0.1185	0.1190	0.1197	0.1189	0.1163	0.1157	0.1155	0.1143
1977	0.1147	0.1127	0.1130	0.1133	0.1147	0.1134	0.1131	0.1127	0.1128	0.1129	0.1130	0.1134	0.1134	0.1133	0.1137	0.1139	0.1147
1978	0.1205	0.1173	0.1170	0.1214	0.1205	0.1153	0.1172	0.1173	0.1153	0.1154	0.1170	0.1188	0.1197	0.1214	0.1267	0.1178	0.1205
1979	0.1244	0.1191	0.1201	0.1247	0.1244	0.1189	0.1190	0.1191	0.1180	0.1170	0.1201	0.1215	0.1224	0.1247	0.1200	0.1227	0.1244
1980	0.1075	0.1113	0.1192	0.1160	0.1075	0.1238	0.1218	0.1113	0.1130	0.1192	0.1192	0.1188	0.1171	0.1160	0.1108	0.1093	0.1075
1981	0.0833	0.0954	0.0839	0.0849	0.0833	0.0997	0.0975	0.0954	0.0907	0.0864	0.0839	0.0817	0.0822	0.0849	0.0833	0.0846	0.0833
1982	0.0730	0.0756	0.0723	0.0703	0.0730	0.0808	0.0781	0.0756	0.0772	0.0769	0.0723	0.0727	0.0710	0.0703	0.0680	0.0696	0.0730
1983	0.0603	0.0692	0.0653	0.0625	0.0603	0.0710	0.0715	0.0692	0.0684	0.0668	0.0663	0.0638	0.0619	0.0625	0.0626	0.0612	0.0603

Official reserves excluding gold — Réserves officielles, or exclu

million SDR's, end of period — millions de DTS, fin de période

	Year	Q.1	Q.2	Q.3	Q.4	JAN	FEB	MAR	APR	MAY	JUN	JUL	AUG	SEP	OCT	NOV	DEC
1964	1717	964	831	1254	1717	1128	944	964	797	823	831	866	1025	1254	1419	1588	1717
1965	2396	1768	1736	1991	2396	1763	1836	1768	1561	1609	1736	1947	2071	1991	1926	2041	2396
1966	2497	2234	2430	2643	2497	2247	2202	2234	2310	2320	2430	2636	2865	2643	2548	2479	2497
1967	3063	2355	2556	3044	3063	2340	2307	2355	2461	2523	2556	2718	2953	3044	3166	3147	3063
1968	2418	2926	2709	2800	2418	3014	2984	2926	2888	2903	2709	2732	2830	2800	2790	2593	2418
1969	2089	2126	2212	2289	2089	2266	2167	2126	2246	2071	2212	2276	2229	2289	2271	2050	2089
1970	2465	2102	1696	1541	2465	1983	2081	2102	2152	1306	1696	1241	1341	1541	1904	2006	2465
1971	3398	3150	3208	3787	3398	2890	2970	3150	3326	3241	3208	3212	3636	3787	3740	3554	3398
1972	2721	3250	3028	3032	2721	3333	3333	3250	3172	3153	3028	3066	3276	3032	2919	2723	2721
1973	2448	2295	2116	2615	2448	2414	2425	2295	2363	2281	2116	1790	2482	2615	2229	2156	2448
1974	2782	2697	1517	3516	2782	2087	1586	2697	2257	1707	1517	1729	1640	3516	2905	2436	2782
1975	1191	2562	2528	2097	1191	2464	2414	2562	2671	2537	2528	1787	1472	2097	1938	1589	1191
1976	2840	1355	1680	1503	2840	1038	994	1355	1473	1403	1680	2511	2626	1503	1748	2743	2840
1977	6672	2655	5457	5758	6672	2947	2703	2655	2918	3867	5457	6033	6172	5758	6491	6991	6672
1978	8527	5666	7731	8113	8527	6500	6409	5666	6325	7139	7731	7850	8838	8113	7583	8185	8527
1979	13814	12600	14709	14195	13814	9381	9428	12600	13904	14357	14709	14203	15110	14195	14482	13997	13814
1980	18143	15330	15551	16547	18143	14949	14568	15330	17613	16984	15551	17877	16970	16547	17138	17937	18143
1981	17298	14629	15104	16583	17298	17754	16860	14629	14685	13672	15104	15916	16486	16583	16324	15718	17298
1982	12773	13265	13076	14550	12773	16802	15953	13265	11426	11556	13076	14020	14974	14550	13548	12264	12773
1983	19204	13178	17279	18250	19204	13981	13666	13178	14840	15419	17279	19000	18832	18250	18326	19111	19204

Net foreign position : (19) — Position extérieure nette : (19)

commercial and savings banks — banques commerciales et d'épargne

billion lire, end of period — milliards de lires, fin de période

	Year	Q.1	Q.2	Q.3	Q.4	JAN	FEB	MAR	APR	MAY	JUN	JUL	AUG	SEP	OCT	NOV	DEC
1964	-508	-661	-569	-504	-508	-732	-703	-661	-637	-621	-569	-518	-518	-504	-498	-539	-508
1965	-111	-475	-337	-25	-111	-543	-537	-475	-433	-381	-337	-301	-174	-25	94	77	-111
1966	144	33	43	153	144	0	13	33	32	59	43	61	74	153	180	171	144
1967	22	64	-26	26	22	136	78	64	5	13	-26	-11	23	26	11	20	22
1968	452	10	68	312	452	12	8	10	57	53	68	123	244	312	348	391	452
1969	22	468	118	158	22	508	497	468	301	325	118	108	170	158	152	87	22
1970	11	105	77	183	11	-16	65	105	-1	-36	77	143	182	183	81	24	11
1971	-95	-155	-77	89	-95	-74	-74	-155	-218	-103	-77	36	87	89	83	56	-95
1972	-351	-56	-147	-102	-351	-12	-56	-56	-37	-18	-147	-61	-102	-102	-218	-134	-351
1973	-381	-481	-724	-375	-381	-405	-379	-481	-697	-768	-724	-510	-490	-375	-358	-482	-381
1974	-857	-666	-1423	-903	-857	-308	-483	-666	-861	-1119	-1423	-1384	-1222	-903	-860	-815	-857
1975	-500	-901	-1130	-373	-500	-785	-770	-901	-1042	-1053	-1130	-809	-332	-373	-264	-281	-500
1976	-2635	-818	-1621	-1722	-2635	-359	-622	-818	-1163	-1258	-1621	-1891	-1764	-1722	-2125	-2718	-2635
1977	-5729	-3868	-6390	-5740	-5729	-2872	-3247	-3868	-4512	-5643	-6390	-6514	-5802	-5740	-5745	-6242	-5729
1978	-5884	-6511	-7551	-6866	-5884	-6574	-6412	-6511	-6900	-7197	-7551	-7511	-7218	-6866	-6157	-6267	-5884
1979	-6887	-6983	-8148	-7192	-6887	-6489	-6759	-6983	-7521	-8019	-8148	-7366	-7417	-7192	-6357	-6791	-6887
1980	-14910	-9883	-9868	-10834	-14910	-7271	-8012	-9388	-10430	-10735	-9868	-10663	-10064	-10834	-11943	-13523	-14910
1981	-16069	-14731	-15848	-14301	-16069	-15399	-16016	-14731	-15241	-16080	-15848	-15979	-15222	-14301	-15014	-15282	-16069
1982	-14564	-15895	-16305	-16822	-14564	-16159	-16897	-15895	-14366	-14488	-16305	-16597	-17124	-16822	-14259	-15143	-14564
1983	-21305	-16796	-20476	-19436	-21305	-15875	-15403	-16796	-17833	-20500	-20476	-21504	-20153	-19436	-19848	-20726	-21305

ITALY

Imports c.i.f. / Importations c.a.f.

billion lire, monthly averages / milliards de lires, moyennes mensuelles

	Year	Q.1	Q.2	Q.3	Q.4	JAN	FEB	MAR	APR	MAY	JUN	JUL	AUG	SEP	OCT	NOV	DEC
1964	378	433	400	321	357	447	435	418	406	396	398	344	281	338	371	321	380
1965	384	368	372	376	421	341	370	394	372	385	358	393	351	384	401	425	437
1966	447	440	436	433	480	448	415	457	418	448	442	442	350	509	500	471	470
1967	512	496	500	485	565	517	475	496	507	488	506	532	430	494	545	548	605
1968	536	483	536	529	595	472	460	516	528	549	532	539	478	570	514	658	613
1969	648	603	651	642	698	636	588	585	623	655	675	686	547	694	668	730	696
1970	778	717	798	779	818	774	663	716	783	784	827	821	678	837	801	870	785
1971	825	833	818	779	869	768	793	936	738	912	805	770	773	793	844	829	933
1972	939	877	919	897	1062	871	831	930	881	975	900	927	826	938	999	961	1226
1973	1352	1024	1353	1411	1620	1013	1146	912	1114	1436	1511	1379	1275	1578	1477	1403	1982
1974	2226	1994	2206	2355	2350	1634	2046	2303	2382	2088	2149	2744	1994	2326	2395	2061	2593
1975	2100	1916	1959	2035	2490	1895	1764	2088	1868	1848	2160	2094	1627	2385	2274	2201	2995
1976	3061	2508	3110	2892	3734	2088	2338	3098	3070	3246	3013	2882	2574	3220	3289	3605	4308
1977	3536	3345	3689	3104	4005	2956	3201	3879	3649	3888	3530	3184	2782	3346	3744	3265	5006
1978	3989	3232	3848	3589	5286	2862	3132	3703	3815	4293	3436	4150	2863	3754	4216	4372	7271
1979	5383	4500	5081	4859	7092	3695	4417	5388	4305	5716	5223	4776	4451	5350	5751	6676	8850
1980	7130	6350	6907	7153	8111	5644	6402	7005	6924	7089	6709	7128	6595	7737	7514	7453	9365
1981	8640	6986	9176	8881	9515	6400	7455	7104	9616	9061	8352	8636	7384	10624	9031	9219	10294
1982	9684	9939	9947	9083	9769	9266	10513	10039	10163	9908	9770	9513	8017	9719	8992	10601	9714
1983	10167	9583	9896	9850	11337	11350	8457	8942	11379	8290	10018	9720	8582	11248	10339	10519	13154

Exports f.o.b. / Exportations f.o.b.

billion lire, monthly averages / milliards de lires, moyennes mensuelles

	Year	Q.1	Q.2	Q.3	Q.4	JAN	FEB	MAR	APR	MAY	JUN	JUL	AUG	SEP	OCT	NOV	DEC
1964	310	276	305	323	338	261	282	284	307	288	319	363	273	333	356	317	342
1965	375	349	372	377	401	288	356	403	377	356	382	396	349	387	401	407	395
1966	419	394	424	416	442	357	375	448	383	451	437	452	372	424	473	422	430
1967	453	442	457	430	484	413	431	483	449	480	441	465	379	448	511	472	470
1968	531	494	520	519	589	462	484	536	513	527	519	550	492	515	564	628	576
1969	611	589	649	615	591	555	573	639	642	674	631	726	500	618	604	630	538
1970	688	621	707	697	727	625	576	663	700	697	724	743	636	710	776	710	695
1971	780	720	765	791	844	648	732	779	749	823	724	806	764	804	795	799	937
1972	904	847	905	861	1004	762	837	941	867	921	926	944	767	872	959	905	1149
1973	1081	805	1059	1158	1302	786	877	751	865	1124	1188	1331	996	1148	1225	1188	1492
1974	1652	1343	1545	1788	1933	1144	1331	1552	1567	1514	1552	2158	1472	1735	1882	1690	2228
1975	1906	1714	1806	1930	2172	1546	1720	1877	1749	1713	1957	2111	1711	1969	2080	2000	2434
1976	2597	2053	2541	2645	3150	1769	1880	2511	2362	2737	2526	2594	2229	2712	2969	2981	3500
1977	3331	2885	3389	3215	3833	2539	2702	3415	3142	3415	3612	3467	3040	3138	3280	3518	4700
1978	3959	3099	3924	3555	5257	2739	3052	3507	3827	3998	3947	3776	3207	3683	4452	4607	6712
1979	4994	4262	4870	4784	6059	3374	4762	4651	4369	5014	5228	4390	5032	4929	5764	5228	7185
1980	5560	5091	5571	5210	6370	4511	5142	5621	5411	5597	5706	5371	4950	5307	5170	6051	7889
1981	7170	5358	7174	7535	8613	4909	5921	5244	7257	6195	8072	7863	6342	8399	8576	8098	9175
1982	8271	8056	8540	7781	8706	7650	7583	8934	8843	8041	8735	8785	7022	7537	7867	9660	8590
1983	9217	8215	9020	8774	10858	8741	7288	8615	9596	7394	9571	9651	7191	9480	10136	11197	11242

Trade balance (f.o.b. — c.i.f.) / Balance commerciale (f.o.b. — c.a.f.)

billion lire, monthly averages / milliards de lires, moyennes mensuelles

	Year	Q.1	Q.2	Q.3	Q.4	JAN	FEB	MAR	APR	MAY	JUN	JUL	AUG	SEP	OCT	NOV	DEC
1964	-67	-158	-95	2	-18	-186	-153	-134	-99	-108	-80	18	-8	-5	-15	-3	-37
1965	-9	-19	1	1	-20	-53	-14	10	5	-27	24	3	-2	3	0	-18	-42
1966	-29	-47	-12	-18	-38	-90	-40	-9	-35	3	-5	10	22	-85	-27	-49	-39
1967	-58	-54	-43	-55	-82	-104	-44	-13	-57	-8	-65	-67	-51	-47	-34	-76	-136
1968	-5	11	-16	-10	-6	-10	24	20	-15	-21	-13	11	15	-55	50	-30	-38
1969	-38	-14	-2	-28	-107	-81	-15	54	19	19	-43	41	-47	-77	-64	-100	-158
1970	-90	-96	-91	-82	-91	-148	-87	-53	-83	-87	-103	-78	-42	-126	-24	-160	-90
1971	-45	-113	-53	13	-25	-120	-61	-157	12	-89	-81	36	-9	11	-49	-30	4
1972	-35	-30	-14	-36	-58	-109	6	11	-14	-54	25	17	-60	-66	-40	-56	-77
1973	-271	-219	-295	-253	-319	-226	-269	-162	-249	-312	-324	-47	-280	-430	-252	-215	-490
1974	-574	-652	-662	-566	-417	-490	-714	-751	-815	-574	-597	-586	-522	-591	-514	-371	-365
1975	-194	-202	-153	-105	-319	-350	-44	-211	-119	-135	-204	17	84	-416	-194	-201	-560
1976	-464	-455	-568	-247	-584	-319	-459	-587	-708	-510	-487	111	-346	-508	-320	-624	-808
1977	-205	-460	-299	111	-172	-418	-500	-464	-507	-473	82	283	259	-208	-464	253	-306
1978	-30	-133	76	-34	-30	-123	-80	-196	12	-296	511	-374	344	-72	235	236	-560
1979	-389	-238	-211	-76	-1033	-321	345	-737	65	-702	5	-386	581	-422	13	-1448	-1665
1980	-1570	-1259	-1336	-1944	-1741	-1133	-1260	-1385	-1513	-1492	-1003	-1757	-1645	-2430	-2344	-1402	-1476
1981	-1470	-1628	-2002	-1345	-902	-1492	-1533	-1360	-2359	-2866	-781	-773	-1041	-2225	-456	-1131	-1118
1982	-1414	-1883	-1407	-1302	-1063	-1616	-2930	-1104	-1320	-1368	-1034	-728	-995	-2182	-1125	-942	-1124
1983	-950	-1369	-875	-1076	-479	-2610	-1169	-328	-1783	-396	-446	-69	-1391	-1768	-203	678	-1912

Imports c.i.f. — Importations c.a.f.

Adjusted - Corrigé *

billion lire, monthly averages — milliards de lires, moyennes mensuelles

Year	Q.1	Q.2	Q.3	Q.4	JAN	FEB	MAR	APR	MAY	JUN	JUL	AUG	SEP	OCT	NOV	DEC
1964	419	398	341	346	443	420	393	403	383	409	348	324	351	358	313	368
1965	362	371	397	409	337	373	376	367	371	376	389	408	393	394	404	429
1966	431	436	456	464	430	423	441	417	438	452	447	409	511	482	457	453
1967	491	499	509	551	493	489	490	513	480	503	527	505	496	527	520	606
1968	477	531	552	575	452	455	524	518	540	534	531	554	571	501	621	604
1969	608	639	668	681	615	620	588	628	622	667	675	652	678	664	702	676
1970	722	778	816	794	746	703	717	786	752	796	821	787	840	787	854	740
1971	850	792	810	848	782	846	923	732	845	799	759	889	784	860	823	863
1972	885	888	934	1037	898	851	905	897	891	876	932	949	922	997	1007	1106
1973	1054	1303	1484	1549	1079	1235	847	1117	1299	1493	1394	1495	1564	1469	1475	1703
1974	2063	2125	2472	2239	1795	2226	2169	2326	1905	2143	2803	2329	2285	2362	2202	2154
1975	2010	1880	2159	2338	2174	1940	1916	1846	1650	2145	2159	2002	2317	2254	2342	2419
1976	2596	2960	3132	3445	2405	2542	2842	2940	2927	3013	2987	3163	3246	3283	3652	3400
1977	3542	3510	3427	3603	3520	3549	3559	3495	3509	3526	3450	3430	3400	3689	3332	3789
1978	3448	3666	3945	4719	3436	3445	3464	3693	3900	3406	4443	3496	3895	4187	4372	5597
1979	4741	4876	5378	6347	4430	4796	4998	4123	5235	5270	5081	5428	5626	5797	6545	6700
1980	6680	6659	7802	7430	6679	6669	6691	6670	6509	6797	7495	8072	7839	7746	7438	7106
1981	7391	8875	9636	8726	7391	7939	6844	9141	8712	8774	9100	8832	10975	9235	9092	7852
1982	10613	9644	9729	9099	10927	11148	9765	9489	9463	9979	9757	9544	9887	9515	10253	7530
1983	10255	9598	10576	10426	13091	8959	8716	10715	7941	10139	10253	10217	11259	10781	10488	10011

Exports f.o.b. — Exportations f.o.b.

Adjusted - Corrigé *

billion lire, monthly averages — milliards de lires, moyennes mensuelles

Year	Q.1	Q.2	Q.3	Q.4	JAN	FEB	MAR	APR	MAY	JUN	JUL	AUG	SEP	OCT	NOV	DEC
1964	279	302	329	330	297	279	262	311	282	313	345	308	333	327	321	343
1965	356	366	385	397	329	372	367	377	340	382	369	399	387	385	400	404
1966	397	413	430	434	392	393	407	380	427	431	441	423	427	446	427	429
1967	451	443	444	481	451	453	449	449	448	432	442	433	457	487	473	483
1968	497	503	537	578	495	485	512	490	498	519	518	560	533	536	628	569
1969	604	626	630	582	608	606	599	629	621	628	683	593	615	589	642	515
1970	638	682	722	705	675	610	629	685	670	691	708	735	723	744	726	646
1971	752	739	812	818	743	779	733	737	773	707	742	883	811	793	798	863
1972	877	877	877	971	870	853	908	881	856	893	876	875	879	932	933	1048
1973	852	1026	1189	1231	907	943	704	885	1044	1150	1227	1162	1180	1169	1226	1299
1974	1434	1506	1807	1814	1339	1447	1514	1563	1434	1522	1953	1677	1790	1801	1739	1901
1975	1853	1759	1983	2031	1873	1900	1786	1785	1580	1911	1919	2044	1985	2029	2064	2000
1976	2190	2463	2730	2906	2113	2075	2382	2383	2567	2438	2749	2607	2834	2952	2919	2847
1977	3124	3282	3406	3441	3104	3009	3259	3164	3224	3456	3389	3519	3310	3188	3493	3641
1978	3395	3809	3760	4735	3369	3368	3449	3901	3797	3731	3666	3703	3909	4373	4517	5314
1979	4601	4732	5192	5401	4080	5221	4503	4387	4863	4946	4325	5934	5317	5645	5061	5497
1980	5482	5436	5547	5715	5389	5470	5587	5320	5547	5440	5240	5936	5466	5196	5968	5981
1981	5816	6977	8038	7788	5741	6478	5228	6978	6514	7439	7816	7418	8878	8491	7875	6999
1982	8797	8324	8199	7980	9228	8351	8811	8351	8341	8280	8513	8193	7892	8195	9045	6700
1983	8937	8757	9296	9898	10235	8080	8496	9002	8249	9021	9739	8275	9875	10354	10766	8575

Trade balance (f.o.b. — c.i.f.) — Balance commerciale (f.o.b. — c.a.f.)

Adjusted - Corrigé *

billion lire, monthly averages — milliards de lires, moyennes mensuelles

Year	Q.1	Q.2	Q.3	Q.4	JAN	FEB	MAR	APR	MAY	JUN	JUL	AUG	SEP	OCT	NOV	DEC
1964	-140	-96	-12	-16	-146	-141	-131	-92	-100	-97	-3	-16	-17	-31	7	-25
1965	-6	-5	-11	-13	-8	-1	-9	10	-32	6	-19	-9	-6	-9	-4	-25
1966	-34	-23	-26	-30	-38	-30	-34	-37	-11	-21	-6	13	-84	-36	-30	-24
1967	-40	-56	-65	-70	-42	-36	-41	-64	-33	-71	-84	-72	-39	-41	-47	-123
1968	20	-29	-15	2	44	29	-13	-28	-42	-15	-12	6	-38	35	7	-34
1969	-4	-13	-38	-99	-7	-14	11	2	-0	-39	8	-59	-63	-75	-60	-161
1970	-84	-96	-94	-89	-71	-93	-88	-100	-82	-105	-113	-52	-117	-44	-128	-94
1971	-98	-53	2	-31	-39	-66	-190	5	-72	-92	-16	-5	27	-67	-25	0
1972	-8	-11	-57	-66	-28	2	3	-16	-35	17	-56	-74	-43	-65	-73	-59
1973	-202	-277	-295	-318	-172	-292	-143	-232	-255	-344	-167	-334	-384	-300	-249	-403
1974	-630	-619	-666	-426	-456	-779	-655	-764	-471	-621	-850	-652	-495	-562	-464	-253
1975	-157	-122	-177	-307	-300	-40	-130	-62	-70	-235	-240	43	-333	-225	-278	-419
1976	-406	-497	-402	-539	-292	-467	-460	-557	-360	-575	-238	-556	-412	-331	-733	-552
1977	-419	-229	-20	-163	-416	-540	-300	-331	-285	-70	-60	89	-90	-501	162	-149
1978	-53	143	-185	16	-66	-77	-16	208	-103	325	-777	207	15	186	145	-283
1979	-140	-144	-186	-946	-350	425	-495	264	-372	-324	-756	506	-309	-152	-1484	-1202
1980	-1197	-1224	-2255	-1715	-1290	-1198	-1104	-1350	-962	-1358	-2256	-2136	-2373	-2551	-1471	-1125
1981	-1575	-1899	-1598	-938	-1649	-1460	-1616	-2163	-2196	-1334	-1284	-1414	-2097	-744	-1217	-853
1982	-1817	-1320	-1530	-1119	-1699	-2797	-954	-1139	-1123	-1699	-1244	-1351	-1995	-1320	-1208	-830
1983	-1318	-841	-1280	-528	-2857	-879	-220	-1713	308	-1118	-515	-1942	-1384	-427	279	-1436

* Adjusted by the O.E.C.D. — * Corrigé par l'O.C.D.E.

ITALY

Balance of payments: net trade

billion lire

Balance des paiements : balance commerciale

milliards de lires

	Year	Q.1	Q.2	Q.3	Q.4	JAN	FEB	MAR	APR	MAY	JUN	JUL	AUG	SEP	OCT	NOV	DEC
1964	-403	-358	-176	94	37												
1965	404	56	123	120	105												
1966	209	9	99	72	29												
1967	-13	-11	22	-22	-1												
1968	655	153	173	151	177												
1969	339	151	187	123	-122												
1970	-238	-108	-72	5	-64												
1971	71	-181	-5	208	50												
1972	32	64	103	-2	-134												
1973	-2314	-449	-627	-480	-758												
1974	-5521	-1540	-1607	-1389	-985												
1975	-762	-232	-71	69	-527												
1976	-3527	-981	-1180	-237	-1129												
1977	-118	-804	-270	832	124												
1978	2460	158	694	999	608												
1979	-791	591	164	-508	-1038												
1980	-13991	-4469	-3098	-3125	-3299												
1981	-12032	-4223	-3849	-1620	-2340												
1982	-10720	-4874	-2503	-1981	-1362												
1983		-2604	-1015	-1624													

Balance of payments: current balance

billion lire

Balance des paiements : opérations courantes, nettes

milliards de lires

	Year	Q.1	Q.2	Q.3	Q.4	JAN	FEB	MAR	APR	MAY	JUN	JUL	AUG	SEP	OCT	NOV	DEC
1964	387	-291	1	421	255												
1965	1381	164	347	548	322												
1966	1323	139	356	583	246												
1967	999	105	264	444	187												
1968	1643	278	391	553	422												
1969	1462	320	454	610	78												
1970	476	-64	94	365	79												
1971	981	-66	92	672	283												
1972	1169	356	400	488	-75												
1973	-1473	-405	-435	-9	-624												
1974	-5212	-1602	-1582	-941	-1088												
1975	-377	-329	77	578	-703												
1976	-2343	-1078	-1147	724	-843												
1977	2168	-905	282	2043	743												
1978	5261	257	1235	2506	1263												
1979	4553	1122	1824	1891	-284												
1980	-8291	-3747	-1420	-916	-2208												
1981	-9225	-4713	-2725	23	-1810												
1982	-7393	-5772	-1235	603	-939												
1983		-2784	880	1547													

Balance of payments: net capital movements

billion lire

Balance des paiements : mouvements de capitaux, nets

milliards de lires

	Year	Q.1	Q.2	Q.3	Q.4	JAN	FEB	MAR	APR	MAY	JUN	JUL	AUG	SEP	OCT	NOV	DEC
1964	69	-98	93	21	53												
1965	-284	-129	-17	-40	-98												
1966	-798	-168	-176	-155	-299												
1967	-640	-214	-180	-50	-196												
1968	-1057	-325	-245	-167	-320												
1969	-2265	-507	-647	-650	-461												
1970	-148	-278	11	5	113												
1971	-374	281	71	-112	-615												
1972	-1571	-621	-308	-244	-399												
1973	1737	-41	-44	971	851												
1974	1559	562	351	933	-236												
1975	-527	368	-326	-441	-129												
1976	1484	-8	-107	439	1159												
1977	-338	-699	-555	263	654												
1978	1328	113	-62	528	750												
1979	-2404	-279	-731	-712	-683												
1980	2749	2009	-65	965	-160												
1981	11386	1811	3291	4522	1762												
1982	3687	909	2255	1237	-714												
1983		7950	14860	34340													

NOTES

1. The original base of the index is 1953 to 1965, 1966 from 1966 to 1970, and 1970 from 1971. The coverage of the series was considerably extended at each change of base. Caution should therefore be used when comparing the three series.
2. Prior to 1971, excluding passenger cars.
3. From 1980, new survey; from 1978 data have been recalculated with revised weights.
4. Department stores, chain stores and co-operatives.
5. The original base of the index is 1966 to 1970, 1970 from 1971 to 1976, 1976 from 1977 to 1979, and 1980 from 1980.
6. Sample survey of population aged 14 or over, taken in the first week without public holidays in each quarter.
7. Including first job seekers.
8. Including construction; excluding the self-employed.
9. Monthly data refer to end of period. The original base of the index is 1938 to 1966, 1966 from 1967 to 1975, 1975 from 1976 to 1982, and 1982 from 1983. Prior to 1983, manufacturing only.
10. From 1973, excluding indirect taxes.
11. Weighting pattern based on 1953 to 1966, on 1965 from 1967 to 1970, on 1969 from 1971 to 1976, on 1975 from 1977 to 1980, and on 1979 from 1981.
12. Weighting pattern based on 1969 to 1976, on 1975 from 1977 to 1980, and on 1979 from 1981.
13. Including corporations partly owned by the Government.
14. From 1974, new system of banking statistics.
15. Auction rate on new issues. Prior to September 1973, 12-month bills.
16. From 1976, change of coverage and estimation procedure.
17. Institutions granting credit to economy, excluding those specialized in real estate credit.
18. Monthly data are daily averages.
19. Prior to 1978, including bills in course of collection.
20. Series not adjusted for unequal number of working days in the month.

NOTES

1. La base originale de l'indice est 1953 jusqu'en 1965, 1966 de 1966 à 1970, et 1970 à partir de 1971. La couverture des séries a été considérablement étendue à chaque changement de base. Par conséquent, les trois séries ne doivent être comparées qu'avec prudence.
2. Avant 1971, non compris les voitures de tourisme.
3. A partir de 1980, nouvelle enquête; à partir de 1978, les données ont été recalculées avec une pondération révisée.
4. Grands magasins, magasins populaires, et coopératives.
5. La base originale de l'indice est 1966 jusqu'en 1970, 1970 de 1971 à 1976, 1976 de 1977 à 1979, et 1980 à partir de 1980.
6. Enquête par sondage auprès de la population de 14 ans ou plus, portant sur la première semaine sans jours fériés de chaque trimestre.
7. Y compris les personnes en quête d'un premier emploi.
8. Y compris la construction; non compris les travailleurs indépendants.
9. Situation en fin de mois. La base originale de l'indice est 1938 jusqu'en 1966, 1966 de 1967 à 1975, 1975 de 1976 à 1982, et 1982 à partir de 1983. Avant 1983, industries manufacturières seulement.
10. A partir de 1973, non compris les impôts indirects.
11. La pondération se réfère à 1953 jusqu'en 1966, à 1965 de 1967 à 1970, à 1969 de 1971 à 1976, à 1975 de 1977 à 1980, et à 1979 à partir de 1981.
12. La pondération se réfère à 1969 jusqu'en 1976, à 1975 de 1977 à 1980 et à 1979 à partir de 1981.
13. Y compris les sociétés d'économie mixte.
14. A partir de 1974, nouveau système de statistiques bancaires.
15. Taux d'adjudication sur les nouvelles émissions. Avant septembre 1973, bons à 12 mois.
16. A partir de 1976, changement de couverture et de la méthode d'estimation.
18. Les indices mensuels sont des moyennes de données journalières.
19. Avant 1978, y compris les effets en cours de recouvrement.
20. La série n'est pas corrigée de l'inégalité du nombre de jours ouvrables dans le mois.

MAIN SOURCES
PRINCIPALES SOURCES

Series	Séries	Sources
National product	Produit national	Istituto Nazionale per lo Studio della Congiuntura
Industrial production unadjusted Sales and orders Construction Internal trade Labour and wages Prices Foreign trade	Production industrielle, indice brut Ventes et commandes Construction Commerce intérieur Main-d'œuvre et salaires Prix Commerce extérieur	Istituto Centrale di Statistica *Bolletino Mensile di Statistica*
Industrial production, adj.	Production industrielle corr.	Istituto Nazionale per lo Studio della Congiuntura *Congiuntura Italiana*
Business surveys	Enquêtes de conjoncture	Istituto Nazionale per lo Studio della Congiuntura *Inchiesta Congiunturale Mensile*
Home finance Interest rates Share prices Net foreign position of commercial and savings banks Balance of payments	Finances internes Taux d'intérêts Cours des actions Position extérieure nette des banques commerciales et d'épargne Balance des paiements	Banca d'Italia *Bolletino*

Luxembourg

LUXEMBOURG

Industrial production: total (1) / Production industrielle : total (1)

1980 = 100

	Year	Q.1	Q.2	Q.3	Q.4	JAN	FEB	MAR	APR	MAY	JUN	JUL	AUG	SEP	OCT	NOV	DEC
1964	85.5	81.7	88.9	85.3	86.2	78.5	80.3	85.8	87.7	90.0	88.9	85.8	83.9	86.2	87.7	85.4	85.4
1965	86.1	85.8	89.3	83.7	85.7	85.8	88.5	83.1	88.9	90.0	88.9	85.1	80.1	85.8	85.8	87.4	83.9
1966	82.9	82.5	85.7	81.0	82.5	82.8	83.1	81.6	83.9	87.0	86.2	82.4	77.4	83.1	93.5	82.4	81.6
1967	=83.2	=83.2	86.3	80.2	82.9	82.6	83.0	84.0	86.1	87.9	85.0	83.1	75.0	82.4	82.7	85.2	80.8
1968	88.2	82.8	91.5	87.3	91.3	79.8	81.6	87.0	89.5	92.7	92.2	87.9	82.3	91.7	90.6	92.0	91.3
1969	99.4	96.3	102.3	97.7	101.2	94.9	95.9	98.3	101.4	101.4	104.2	99.7	92.0	101.5	100.9	102.9	99.9
1970	=99.9	=102.7	107.1	97.0	92.9	98.9	102.9	106.2	107.1	108.3	105.9	102.1	92.6	96.2	90.6	94.3	93.9
1971	98.6	94.7	105.5	97.8	96.5	89.2	97.2	97.7	104.7	107.3	104.5	98.8	93.5	101.0	98.3	98.1	92.9
1972	102.7	96.6	107.6	101.3	105.5	92.9	96.5	100.3	107.6	108.1	106.9	101.6	98.0	104.3	105.4	105.3	105.6
1973	115.0	112.6	118.6	111.7	117.1	102.7	115.8	119.3	118.0	121.0	116.8	114.0	106.7	114.4	115.0	123.6	112.6
1974	119.0	122.5	125.9	116.9	110.8	117.4	127.7	122.2	125.5	125.9	126.1	120.4	109.8	120.3	118.1	112.5	101.7
1975	=93.0	=102.3	96.5	81.2	92.0	96.2	107.1	103.6	94.2	95.7	99.4	88.2	62.2	93.1	89.5	95.8	90.6
1976	96.5	95.0	105.6	90.4	94.9	92.5	97.7	95.0	100.6	111.1	105.2	91.6	75.7	103.9	102.3	99.4	83.0
1977	97.0	96.7	105.8	88.0	97.3	95.5	96.5	98.1	102.6	108.4	106.5	94.6	72.7	96.8	97.4	100.5	94.1
1978	100.1	100.0	105.5	94.4	100.4	99.5	100.6	99.8	105.5	105.4	105.5	100.6	80.4	102.3	100.5	102.8	97.9
1979	103.4	103.8	110.8	94.9	104.2	95.0	107.5	108.8	110.5	109.1	112.8	98.2	78.6	107.7	100.2	106.8	105.6
1980	100.0	108.0	111.1	86.9	94.1	103.2	110.1	110.6	113.6	111.5	108.2	96.9	69.3	94.5	94.7	100.4	87.1
1981	93.2	92.5	100.8	85.4	94.0	85.0	95.9	96.6	95.2	105.0	102.3	90.2	70.9	95.3	98.1	100.4	83.6
1982	89.8	96.7	97.4	80.5	84.6	90.7	104.6	94.7	94.2	100.1	97.9	86.0	66.1	89.5	95.4	88.3	70.1
1983	90.8	87.2	95.9	81.6	98.4	81.0	93.4	87.2	97.9	98.1	91.7	89.4	62.7	92.3	99.5	99.4	96.3

Industrial production: manufacturing (1) / Production industrielle : industries manufacturières (1)

1980 = 100

	Year	Q.1	Q.2	Q.3	Q.4	JAN	FEB	MAR	APR	MAY	JUN	JUL	AUG	SEP	OCT	NOV	DEC
1964	79.7	76.0	83.2	79.2	80.3	72.8	75.0	80.2	82.4	83.9	83.5	79.8	78.0	79.8	81.7	79.8	79.4
1965	80.3	80.2	83.2	77.5	80.3	79.8	83.1	77.6	82.8	84.2	82.8	78.7	73.9	79.1	80.2	82.0	78.7
1966	76.9	77.0	79.1	74.8	76.7	77.6	77.6	75.8	77.2	80.5	79.4	75.8	71.4	77.2	73.0	76.9	75.4
1967	=77.6	=77.9	80.0	75.0	77.5	77.1	77.9	78.7	78.9	81.6	79.5	77.5	69.9	77.5	77.0	79.9	75.6
1968	83.3	78.6	85.9	82.0	86.5	75.4	77.6	82.8	84.7	86.5	86.6	82.8	76.3	86.4	86.8	86.8	85.9
1969	94.3	91.3	96.9	92.5	96.3	89.9	91.2	93.0	95.8	96.1	98.7	94.5	86.8	96.3	95.8	97.9	95.1
1970	=95.0	=97.9	102.2	91.9	88.2	94.1	98.4	101.1	101.9	103.8	101.0	97.4	87.3	90.9	85.6	89.6	89.4
1971	94.3	90.4	101.1	93.5	92.1	85.0	93.0	93.2	100.2	102.6	100.6	94.9	89.2	96.5	93.2	93.8	89.3
1972	98.6	93.3	103.2	97.1	101.0	89.9	93.4	96.6	103.0	103.4	103.1	97.7	93.9	99.7	100.6	101.0	101.3
1973	110.8	108.5	114.3	107.6	112.9	98.6	111.6	115.4	113.4	116.6	112.8	110.2	102.4	110.3	110.8	119.8	108.3
1974	115.4	119.0	122.7	113.2	106.8	113.7	124.3	118.8	122.4	122.4	123.2	116.8	106.3	116.6	114.4	108.3	97.6
1975	=90.0	=98.4	93.9	78.5	89.1	92.2	103.5	99.4	91.1	93.2	97.5	85.3	59.7	90.6	86.7	93.0	87.5
1976	93.7	92.8	103.3	87.3	91.6	89.6	95.4	93.5	98.3	108.8	102.8	88.5	72.4	100.9	98.7	96.3	79.7
1977	95.4	94.7	104.3	86.9	95.7	92.6	94.4	96.9	100.3	106.9	105.7	93.5	71.0	96.0	95.8	99.0	92.5
1978	99.1	98.8	104.8	93.3	99.3	98.0	99.6	98.8	104.4	105.0	105.0	95.9	78.9	101.2	100.1	101.4	96.5
1979	103.0	102.6	111.2	94.6	103.5	93.5	106.5	107.8	110.0	109.2	114.6	98.8	77.5	107.6	99.5	106.0	105.0
1980	100.0	107.4	111.9	87.3	93.5	102.1	109.9	110.3	113.7	112.5	109.4	96.5	69.7	95.5	94.2	100.2	86.1
1981	92.8	92.2	100.5	84.9	93.4	84.3	95.4	96.8	95.8	104.7	101.2	89.9	70.2	94.6	97.2	100.3	82.8
1982	90.4	97.0	99.1	81.4	83.9	90.1	105.9	95.1	95.4	101.9	100.1	87.5	65.9	90.9	95.2	87.7	68.7
1983	91.6	87.4	97.2	82.5	99.5	80.9	93.8	87.6	98.4	99.3	93.8	90.4	62.2	94.3	101.4	100.5	96.7

Industrial production: construction (1)(2) / Production industrielle : construction (1)(2)

1980 = 100

	Year	Q.1	Q.2	Q.3	Q.4	JAN	FEB	MAR	APR	MAY	JUN	JUL	AUG	SEP	OCT	NOV	DEC
1964	144.7	104.7	176.6	169.1	128.5	80.4	95.2	138.4	171.1	177.1	181.5	183.0	160.7	163.7	157.7	122.0	105.7
1965	143.0	103.2	175.1	167.6	126.0	80.4	92.3	136.9	172.6	183.0	169.6	175.6	166.7	160.7	154.8	126.5	96.7
1966	137.5	105.2	167.2	158.7	119.0	75.9	87.8	151.8	165.2	163.1	168.1	160.7	159.2	156.2	144.3	122.0	90.8
1967	=110.2	=86.3	128.1	120.4	106.1	66.1	78.2	114.5	121.1	134.3	128.8	128.8	115.6	116.7	116.7	109.0	92.5
1968	107.1	85.2	119.4	119.4	104.3	66.3	80.5	103.9	123.7	124.1	110.6	127.0	116.6	114.7	122.3	101.0	89.6
1969	111.6	82.5	126.4	126.0	111.5	69.6	70.1	107.8	127.0	128.1	124.2	133.0	119.1	125.9	132.8	106.3	95.6
1970	=124.6	=92.7	148.3	139.9	117.5	72.8	84.1	121.2	141.1	154.1	149.8	143.1	137.7	138.9	129.6	122.8	100.1
1971	127.3	93.8	153.7	142.3	119.5	65.9	91.5	124.0	148.0	151.4	151.7	149.0	137.2	140.7	136.4	125.9	96.1
1972	130.9	106.5	159.9	138.5	118.9	75.7	93.1	145.6	153.7	169.0	156.9	142.5	137.5	135.5	137.7	119.7	99.3
1973	130.4	96.4	155.0	145.2	124.9	67.4	92.1	129.6	145.7	161.9	157.4	147.3	148.3	140.0	142.2	131.4	101.1
1974	137.6	109.4	166.2	147.3	127.6	79.7	102.8	145.6	156.3	131.9	160.4	157.3	139.6	144.3	149.1	133.9	99.8
1975	=108.8	=98.8	126.6	108.9	101.0	75.0	105.1	116.3	119.0	136.5	124.2	114.1	103.6	109.1	107.7	104.3	91.0
1976	91.8	81.2	104.6	90.6	90.7	70.9	82.0	90.7	100.7	106.8	106.2	93.5	84.6	93.7	93.4	95.1	83.5
1977	90.7	78.3	99.8	91.3	93.2	67.1	78.5	89.2	91.0	108.3	100.0	94.2	85.6	94.1	94.5	92.2	93.0
1978	92.4	80.8	100.0	92.5	96.4	74.2	75.6	91.6	93.7	106.4	99.9	96.1	86.4	94.9	96.2	99.5	93.1
1979	99.3	84.4	106.7	102.1	104.0	71.4	86.7	95.0	101.4	110.5	108.3	104.0	96.0	106.4	102.5	102.0	107.6
1980	100.0	91.5	109.1	99.3	100.1	83.5	92.0	99.0	104.0	115.2	103.2	101.5	98.3	98.0	100.8	99.8	99.8
1981	97.7	88.2	105.4	98.9	98.1	83.6	87.7	93.4	101.5	104.0	110.6	101.5	95.3	99.9	97.7	101.7	94.9
1982	94.5	88.0	100.9	94.1	95.0	81.8	90.8	91.4	96.5	105.8	100.5	97.8	91.3	93.3	93.9	97.8	93.4
1983	89.0	81.5	95.7	90.1	88.9	84.9	71.8	87.9	92.5	99.8	94.7	93.3	88.4	85.7	88.0	89.5	89.1

Industrial production: total (1)

1980 = 100

Adjusted - Corrigé *

Production industrielle : total (1)

1980 = 100

	Year	Q.1	Q.2	Q.3	Q.4	JAN	FEB	MAR	APR	MAY	JUN	JUL	AUG	SEP	OCT	NOV	DEC
1964		83.1	85.7	86.7	86.7	80.7	82.3	86.3	85.4	85.8	85.8	85.6	88.6	86.0	87.0	86.2	86.9
1965		87.2	85.8	85.3	86.4	88.2	89.9	83.5	86.4	85.5	85.6	85.0	85.2	85.6	85.3	88.3	85.5
1966		83.6	82.2	82.7	83.4	85.0	84.1	81.6	81.4	82.4	82.9	82.4	82.9	82.9	83.4	83.3	83.5
1967		84.1	82.6	82.1	84.0	85.1	83.6	83.5	83.4	83.0	81.5	83.3	80.8	82.2	82.9	86.1	83.0
1968		83.6	87.2	89.5	92.8	82.8	82.0	86.0	86.2	87.2	88.2	88.1	88.8	91.5	91.3	92.9	94.2
1969		97.4	97.1	100.3	103.2	99.3	96.0	96.9	97.0	95.0	99.4	100.1	99.3	101.5	101.9	104.2	103.4
1970		103.7	101.4	99.7	94.9	104.3	102.4	104.3	101.9	101.2	101.1	102.7	100.1	96.4	91.9	95.2	97.7
1971		95.4	99.9	100.8	98.5	94.5	95.9	95.8	99.3	100.4	99.9	99.6	101.5	101.4	99.6	98.8	97.2
1972		97.0	101.9	105.0	107.6	98.6	94.2	98.1	102.0	101.5	102.3	102.7	107.9	104.5	106.6	105.2	110.9
1973		112.4	112.5	116.6	118.9	108.7	112.0	116.5	111.9	114.1	111.3	115.7	120.3	113.9	115.8	122.7	118.3
1974		121.9	119.1	123.3	112.1	123.5	123.1	119.2	119.2	113.7	119.3	122.9	128.0	119.0	118.7	110.6	106.9
1975		101.5	91.0	85.6	92.9	99.9	103.3	101.3	89.6	90.1	93.3	90.2	75.0	91.7	89.7	93.9	95.1
1976		94.2	99.1	96.7	95.7	95.2	94.6	92.8	95.3	104.2	97.9	94.1	94.1	101.9	102.8	97.2	87.1
1977		95.6	98.8	95.0	98.4	97.3	93.7	95.9	96.7	101.2	98.6	97.3	92.6	95.0	98.1	98.1	98.9
1978		98.6	98.1	102.9	101.6	101.2	97.8	96.9	99.1	97.7	97.4	103.6	104.3	100.8	101.3	99.9	103.6
1979		101.9	102.9	103.6	105.5	96.5	104.1	105.2	103.9	100.6	104.3	101.1	103.0	106.6	100.6	103.3	112.7
1980		105.9	103.1	95.0	95.0	105.5	105.7	106.5	107.3	102.1	99.8	100.0	91.4	93.6	94.8	96.5	93.8
1981		90.5	93.4	93.9	94.8	87.5	91.2	93.0	90.2	95.5	94.4	93.4	94.0	94.3	97.9	96.1	90.5
1982		94.7	90.1	88.6	85.1	93.9	98.8	91.4	89.8	90.3	90.2	89.2	88.0	88.7	94.8	84.3	76.1
1983		85.5	88.7	89.5	99.4	84.0	88.1	84.4	93.7	88.0	84.5	92.9	83.7	92.0	98.8	94.6	104.7

Industrial production: manufacturing (1)

1980 = 100

Adjusted - Corrigé *

Production industrielle : industries manufacturières (1)

1980 = 100

	Year	Q.1	Q.2	Q.3	Q.4	JAN	FEB	MAR	APR	MAY	JUN	JUL	AUG	SEP	OCT	NOV	DEC
1964		77.1	80.1	80.9	80.8	74.8	76.3	80.2	80.1	79.8	80.3	79.9	83.0	79.8	80.9	80.4	81.1
1965		82.2	80.0	79.3	80.9	81.9	84.2	77.4	80.4	80.0	79.5	79.0	79.3	79.7	79.6	82.8	80.4
1966		77.7	75.9	76.8	77.5	79.6	78.3	75.2	75.0	76.4	76.3	76.1	77.2	77.0	77.7	77.6	77.2
1967		78.4	76.7	77.0	78.4	79.3	78.3	77.7	76.4	77.3	76.3	77.8	76.0	77.3	76.9	80.7	77.7
1968		79.0	82.0	84.3	87.9	78.0	77.7	81.5	81.8	81.6	82.8	82.9	83.8	86.2	87.2	87.7	88.7
1969		92.0	92.0	95.3	98.1	93.8	91.1	91.2	91.7	90.3	94.0	94.6	94.8	96.4	96.8	99.0	98.5
1970		98.6	96.7	94.8	90.1	99.0	97.9	99.0	96.9	97.1	96.1	97.5	95.8	91.2	86.8	90.4	93.0
1971		90.9	95.4	96.9	94.1	89.7	91.9	91.0	94.9	95.9	95.6	95.0	98.8	96.9	94.5	94.4	93.3
1972		93.5	97.4	101.3	103.0	95.2	91.2	94.1	97.4	96.9	97.9	98.1	105.9	99.9	101.9	100.8	106.4
1973		108.1	107.9	113.2	114.8	104.0	108.0	112.2	107.3	109.7	106.6	111.3	118.5	109.8	111.5	118.8	114.0
1974		118.2	115.6	120.4	108.0	119.5	119.7	115.4	116.0	115.2	115.5	118.9	127.1	115.4	114.7	106.5	102.9
1975		97.4	88.2	83.4	90.0	95.8	99.7	96.7	86.4	87.5	90.7	87.2	73.7	89.3	86.4	91.2	92.2
1976		91.9	96.5	93.9	92.3	92.5	92.1	91.0	93.0	101.8	94.8	90.9	91.8	99.1	98.5	94.4	84.0
1977		93.6	96.9	94.3	96.7	94.9	91.5	94.4	94.4	99.5	96.9	96.2	92.3	94.3	95.4	97.1	97.7
1978		97.6	97.0	102.3	100.5	100.3	96.7	95.7	98.0	96.8	96.1	102.9	104.3	99.6	99.8	99.1	102.6
1979		101.0	102.7	103.8	105.0	95.7	103.2	104.0	103.2	100.0	104.9	101.6	103.7	106.2	99.0	103.2	112.7
1980		105.6	103.1	95.8	94.6	105.1	105.6	106.1	107.0	102.3	100.1	99.3	93.8	94.3	93.6	97.0	93.2
1981		90.4	92.5	93.7	94.5	87.3	90.8	93.1	90.4	94.5	92.5	92.8	95.0	93.3	96.5	96.8	90.2
1982		95.2	91.0	89.9	84.6	93.9	100.1	91.7	90.5	91.2	91.4	90.5	89.5	89.7	94.4	84.3	75.1
1983		85.9	89.3	90.6	100.9	84.5	88.6	84.7	93.6	88.5	85.7	93.5	84.7	93.5	100.5	96.5	105.8

Industrial production: construction (1)(2)

1980 = 100

Adjusted - Corrigé *

Production industrielle : construction (1)(2)

1980 = 100

	Year	Q.1	Q.2	Q.3	Q.4	JAN	FEB	MAR	APR	MAY	JUN	JUL	AUG	SEP	OCT	NOV	DEC
1964		151.6	146.0	143.7	140.6	149.8	154.7	150.2	147.3	141.1	149.5	147.3	137.6	146.2	142.2	134.2	145.5
1965		145.7	145.3	144.2	136.4	147.3	144.9	144.8	147.6	147.7	140.6	142.6	145.7	144.3	140.8	137.9	130.5
1966		142.6	139.8	138.2	127.7	136.9	133.9	157.0	141.0	137.4	140.9	131.9	141.8	141.0	132.2	131.6	119.4
1967		116.5	107.9	105.9	114.0	117.0	116.0	116.6	103.8	111.0	108.8	107.2	104.5	105.3	107.2	116.2	118.6
1968		114.4	101.0	106.1	110.8	116.0	117.1	110.0	106.4	102.6	94.1	106.8	106.8	104.7	112.9	106.8	112.7
1969		109.7	107.0	113.0	118.0	120.7	100.1	108.4	109.8	105.5	105.7	113.4	110.2	115.5	123.1	112.0	119.0
1970		121.7	125.0	126.8	124.7	125.4	118.3	121.4	122.2	125.6	127.3	123.5	128.6	128.2	120.8	129.2	124.1
1971		121.0	129.0	130.4	126.1	112.5	127.1	123.5	128.5	129.8	128.6	130.7	129.5	131.0	127.9	131.6	118.9
1972		135.0	134.0	128.6	125.0	127.2	134.1	143.8	134.4	134.4	133.2	126.9	132.0	127.5	130.1	123.6	121.4
1973		120.1	130.5	137.4	129.8	130.3	122.8	127.1	129.1	128.4	134.0	133.5	145.4	133.3	134.9	133.7	120.8
1974		133.4	141.3	141.4	130.6	125.1	132.7	142.5	140.8	145.2	137.7	144.7	140.2	139.1	141.8	134.4	115.7
1975		119.1	109.2	106.1	102.7	112.3	131.0	113.9	109.4	110.4	107.8	106.5	106.4	105.4	103.0	103.1	101.9
1976		96.5	91.9	89.1	91.2	101.2	98.6	89.6	94.3	87.9	93.5	88.3	88.4	90.7	90.1	93.1	90.5
1977		90.6	88.8	90.5	93.2	91.6	91.4	88.8	86.4	90.8	89.1	90.0	90.1	91.4	91.7	89.9	97.9
1978		92.3	90.3	91.9	95.8	97.6	87.1	92.2	89.9	90.9	90.1	92.5	90.8	92.4	94.0	97.3	96.0
1979		94.6	97.4	101.6	103.0	90.8	97.3	96.4	97.8	95.6	98.8	100.4	100.2	104.2	100.6	99.2	109.3
1980		102.5	100.4	98.7	98.7	103.5	102.4	101.4	100.7	100.9	99.7	98.0	101.7	96.5	99.3	96.9	100.4
1981		98.4	97.5	98.2	96.8	101.6	97.4	96.2	92.4	91.8	102.4	97.9	97.8	98.9	96.7	98.6	95.1
1982		97.9	93.6	93.4	93.7	98.4	100.8	94.6	93.7	93.7	93.5	94.2	93.1	92.7	93.0	94.7	93.4
1983		90.8	88.9	89.4	87.6	101.4	79.8	91.2	89.9	88.5	88.2	89.8	90.0	88.5	87.2	86.6	89.1

* Adjusted by the O.E.C.D.

* Corrigé par l'O.C.D.E.

LUXEMBOURG

Production: crude steel / Production : acier brut

thousand tons, monthly averages / milliers de tonnes, moyennes mensuelles

	Year	Q.1	Q.2	Q.3	Q.4	JAN	FEB	MAR	APR	MAY	JUN	JUL	AUG	SEP	OCT	NOV	DEC
1964																	
1965																	
1966																	
1967																	
1968																	
1969	460	447	450	468	476	456	423	462	455	450	445	486	435	483	503	455	469
1970	455	475	480	451	415	482	453	489	509	442	489	482	427	443	427	413	406
1971	437	431	439	465	414	413	413	466	446	413	457	485	456	453	428	422	391
1972	455	442	453	471	453	432	420	475	440	453	465	460	474	479	476	449	435
1973	494	491	482	500	502	475	463	534	472	498	477	505	512	482	520	511	476
1974	537	529	536	554	530	536	497	554	550	560	497	580	541	541	581	529	481
1975	385	432	417	323	370	447	417	433	470	376	404	364	191	413	393	354	362
1976	380	391	406	369	355	383	376	414	421	407	401	380	306	422	400	352	313
1977	361	358	380	342	363	326	342	407	369	365	405	346	297	334	362	366	360
1978	399	389	436	381	390	388	368	410	424	431	454	405	363	376	389	413	369
1979	412	408	434	389	419	379	382	462	420	455	427	388	377	402	459	430	368
1980	385	436	429	345	330	450	400	457	444	420	422	421	257	357	365	321	304
1981	316	324	329	289	321	295	313	365	305	340	343	297	238	331	364	327	273
1982	292	338	313	284	235	272	348	394	323	291	325	299	242	311	265	262	177
1983	275	251	292	247	308	222	253	277	296	287	293	257	183	302	323	308	294

Construction permits issued / Permis de construire délivrés

number, monthly averages / nombre, moyennes mensuelles

	Year	Q.1	Q.2	Q.3	Q.4	JAN	FEB	MAR	APR	MAY	JUN	JUL	AUG	SEP	OCT	NOV	DEC
1964																	
1965																	
1966	104	118	151	91	56												
1967	81	96	85	76	65												
1968	100	92	157	81	69												
1969	115	104	135	126	95	70	115	126	138	119	149	227	67	84	108	30	96
1970	106	105	133	108	76	55	87	174	137	147	115	128	110	37	96	65	68
1971	150	136	157	172	123	105	108	196	182	168	151	167	189	160	97	118	155
1972	219	194	274	236	173	120	180	283	250	209	362	269	272	166	179	202	139
1973	232	252	286	216	172	205	220	332	292	318	247	261	210	178	208	146	162
1974	229	278	269	212	157	220	218	397	258	236	313	265	175	196	151	95	224
1975	194	182	229	167	199	141	147	258	282	221	183	179	168	154	180	235	181
1976	170	159	179	187	155	78	191	208	157	165	215	209	184	168	223	103	140
1977	172	169	226	160	131	114	155	238	265	211	202	207	153	121	146	134	114
1978	168	158	203	169	143	149	154	171	184	203	222	163	119	225	152	140	136
1979	159	143	208	173	110	70	161	199	220	194	209	200	142	178	130	112	89
1980	166	181	217	158	110	151	175	216	211	201	240	221	148	105	162	97	70
1981	152	162	182	150	113	108	164	215	220	155	171	167	76	206	133	105	102
1982	116	109	132	134	89	47	90	189	139	134	124	176	106	120	91	88	87
1983	121	113	137	138	96	91	91	156	169	112	129	190	121	103	111	89	88

New passenger car registrations / Immatriculations de voitures de tourisme neuves

number, monthly averages / nombre, moyennes mensuelles

	Year	Q.1	Q.2	Q.3	Q.4	JAN	FEB	MAR	APR	MAY	JUN	JUL	AUG	SEP	OCT	NOV	DEC
1964	677	694	913	539	563	404	718	960	925	746	1069	498	556	563	653	451	585
1965	654	673	799	627	518	508	680	830	997	739	661	739	527	566	593	471	489
1966	661	793	801	601	451	529	778	1071	765	938	701	596	644	562	578	402	373
1967	601	672	718	504	512	521	619	875	840	676	637	597	458	458	633	495	408
1968	717	715	881	672	599	474	798	874	1189	866	589	992	521	503	755	495	546
1969	815	786	994	767	714	476	684	1197	1165	909	907	1037	515	748	831	711	600
1970	907	790	1162	858	817	472	835	1064	1247	1056	1181	1050	711	812	806	706	940
1971	1051	1090	1389	954	772	474	1123	1673	1433	1429	1304	1159	760	943	885	711	720
1972	1146	1300	1370	1025	888	626	1457	1317	1276	1459	1374	1202	984	910	1052	742	370
1973	1230	1359	1576	1118	865	800	1432	1846	1681	1718	1330	1358	1003	994	1185	821	590
1974	1285	1469	1422	1208	1051	934	1097	2348	1383	1596	1288	1485	1043	1096	1277	971	905
1975	1348	1616	1545	1159	1074	1043	1363	1941	1522	1672	1440	1492	936	1043	1248	935	1039
1976	1456	1680	1769	1254	1281	1181	1753	2107	1929	1713	1664	1425	993	1344	1324	1329	1191
1977	1591	1990	1934	1279	1161	1221	2107	2643	2141	1873	1787	1498	1088	1250	1269	1181	1032
1978	1696	2006	2029	1443	1308	1408	2049	2560	2226	1939	1922	1727	1203	1399	1572	1331	971
1979	1715	2078	2038	1391	1304	1167	2171	2895	2291	2153	1820	1613	1199	1361	1748	1258	906
1980	1723	2213	2084	1395	1201	1501	2712	2426	2378	1957	1917	1824	1060	1301	1517	1129	957
1981	1765	2177	2036	1472	1376	1310	2515	2706	2500	1926	1681	1758	1100	1557	1667	1328	1134
1982	1994	2592	2372	1562	1450	1329	2826	3620	2887	2253	1975	2011	1219	1455	1668	1457	1225
1983	2052	2502	2615	1647	1443	1363	3010	3134	2777	2527	2541	1920	1361	1659	1654	1508	1168

Employment in industry: total (3) / Emploi dans l'industrie : total (3)

(all employees) / (salariés)

1980 = 100 / 1980 = 100

	Year	Q.1	Q.2	Q.3	Q.4	JAN	FEB	MAR	APR	MAY	JUN	JUL	AUG	SEP	OCT	NOV	DEC
1964																	
1965																	
1966																	
1967																	
1968																	
1969																	
1970	114.7	112.9	114.2	115.6	116.0	112.0	113.1	113.5	113.9	114.0	114.7	115.4	115.6	115.9	115.9	116.0	116.0
1971	116.3	115.8	116.3	116.4	116.7	115.7	115.6	116.2	116.5	116.6	115.8	116.0	116.2	117.0	116.7	116.8	116.6
1972	116.4	116.3	116.2	116.3	116.7	116.2	116.3	116.5	116.3	116.2	116.0	116.5	116.0	116.4	116.8	116.8	116.4
1973	118.2	116.5	117.1	119.0	120.3	116.3	116.3	116.8	117.0	117.1	117.3	118.2	119.0	119.8	120.2	120.5	120.2
1974	122.0	121.0	121.2	122.9	123.1	120.9	121.0	121.1	121.2	121.0	121.3	122.6	122.7	123.5	123.5	123.1	122.7
1975	120.1	121.9	120.6	119.5	118.2	122.2	122.0	121.5	121.1	120.7	119.9	119.7	119.3	119.5	118.7	118.2	117.6
1976	116.4	117.1	116.5	116.3	115.5	117.3	117.1	117.0	116.6	116.5	116.3	116.5	116.0	116.3	115.9	115.6	115.1
1977	113.4	114.7	114.1	113.5	111.2	114.8	114.8	114.4	114.8	113.9	113.6	114.0	113.7	112.8	112.0	111.1	110.5
1978	105.8	106.6	106.1	105.8	104.6	107.0	106.8	106.2	106.2	105.7	106.3	106.4	105.7	105.4	105.4	104.6	103.8
1979	102.8	104.4	103.4	101.6	101.4	104.7	104.3	104.2	103.7	103.5	103.1	102.9	101.0	101.1	101.7	101.4	101.1
1980	100.0	100.0	100.3	100.0	99.6	100.0	100.0	100.1	100.6	100.2	100.0	100.0	99.8	100.1	100.2	99.5	99.2
1981	97.0	97.9	97.0	97.2	96.0	98.0	98.0	97.7	97.4	97.0	96.8	97.6	97.2	96.8	96.6	95.9	95.4
1982	93.9	94.5	93.9	93.8	93.1	94.7	94.4	94.4	94.0	93.9	93.8	94.1	93.6	93.8	93.4	93.3	92.6
1983		91.0	89.0	88.9	83.0	91.6	91.0	90.3	89.9	83.5	88.7	89.0	88.8	88.8	88.4	88.5	87.0

Employment in industry: iron and steel (3) / Emploi dans l'industrie : sidérurgie (3)

(wage earners) / (ouvriers)

thousands / milliers

	Year	Q.1	Q.2	Q.3	Q.4	JAN	FEB	MAR	APR	MAY	JUN	JUL	AUG	SEP	OCT	NOV	DEC
1964	22.2	21.8	22.2	22.4	22.5	21.7	21.8	21.9	22.1	22.2	22.2	22.4	22.4	22.5	22.5	22.5	22.5
1965	22.4	22.4	22.3	22.4	22.5	22.5	22.4	22.3	22.3	22.3	22.3	22.4	22.4	22.5	22.5	22.4	22.5
1966	22.3	22.3	22.3	22.3	22.2	22.4	22.4	22.2	22.3	22.3	22.3	22.3	22.2	22.3	22.3	22.2	22.1
1967	21.8	22.0	21.9	21.7	21.6	22.0	22.0	22.0	21.9	21.9	21.8	21.8	21.6	21.7	21.6	21.6	21.5
1968	21.3	21.4	21.2	21.2	21.3	21.5	21.4	21.3	21.3	21.2	21.2	21.2	21.2	21.2	21.2	21.3	21.3
1969	21.3	21.2	21.2	21.3	21.4	21.2	21.2	21.2	21.3	21.2	21.2	21.2	21.2	21.4	21.4	21.4	21.4
1970	21.8	21.5	21.8	21.9	21.8	21.4	21.5	21.7	21.8	21.8	21.9	21.9	21.9	21.9	21.8	21.8	21.7
1971	21.4	21.6	21.5	21.3	21.3	21.6	21.6	21.5	21.5	21.5	21.4	21.3	21.3	21.4	21.3	21.3	21.2
1972	21.1	21.1	21.1	21.1	21.1	21.1	21.1	21.1	21.1	21.1	21.0	21.1	21.0	21.1	21.1	21.2	21.1
1973	21.5	21.2	21.4	21.5	21.8	21.2	21.2	21.3	21.4	21.4	21.4	21.5	21.5	21.6	21.7	21.8	21.8
1974	22.0	21.9	21.9	22.0	22.1	21.8	21.9	21.9	21.9	21.9	21.8	22.0	22.0	22.1	22.1	22.1	22.0
1975	20.7	21.1	20.8	20.6	20.3	21.2	21.1	21.0	20.9	20.8	20.7	20.6	20.5	20.6	20.5	20.3	20.2
1976	19.5	20.0	19.6	19.4	19.2	20.1	20.0	19.8	19.7	19.6	19.5	19.4	19.3	19.4	19.3	19.2	19.2
1977	18.7	19.1	18.8	18.6	18.2	19.1	19.1	19.0	18.9	18.8	18.7	18.6	18.5	18.6	18.5	18.3	17.8
1978	17.3	17.6	17.3	17.3	17.0	17.6	17.6	17.5	17.4	17.3	17.3	17.3	17.2	17.3	17.1	17.0	16.9
1979	16.4	16.7	16.4	16.2	16.1	16.8	16.7	16.6	16.5	16.4	16.4	16.3	16.2	16.2	16.1	16.1	16.0
1980	15.5	15.8	15.5	15.3	15.3	15.9	15.8	15.6	15.6	15.5	15.4	15.3	15.3	15.4	15.4	15.3	15.2
1981	14.9	15.2	15.0	14.8	14.6	15.2	15.2	15.1	15.0	15.0	14.9	14.8	14.8	14.3	14.7	14.6	14.5
1982	14.1	14.4	14.2	14.0	13.7	14.5	14.4	14.3	14.2	14.2	14.1	14.0	13.9	14.0	13.9	13.8	13.5
1983	12.5	13.1	12.5	12.4	12.2	13.2	13.1	13.0	12.5	12.5	12.4	12.4	12.3	12.4	12.3	12.3	11.9

Unemployment (registered unemployed) (3) / Chômage (chômeurs inscrits) (3)

number / nombre

	Year	Q.1	Q.2	Q.3	Q.4	JAN	FEB	MAR	APR	MAY	JUN	JUL	AUG	SEP	OCT	NOV	DEC
1964	45	39	14	9	69	197	55	15	20	11	11	3	14	9	5	13	189
1965	46	114	2	18	50	72	265	6	-	2	3	10	18	26	25	62	62
1966	22	23	6	13	45	34	23	12	6	2	9	4	9	27	35	33	67
1967	34	27	22	22	66	29	18	33	20	22	24	21	25	21	70	80	47
1968	88	167	52	68	63	218	167	116	77	50	29	48	69	86	73	60	57
1969	39	43	25	51	38	45	49	35	23	20	31	77	31	44	50	36	28
1970	40	49	24	50	38	63	50	35	25	20	27	36	42	71	45	37	33
1971	21	17	15	30	20	20	13	19	14	16	15	26	37	28	16	23	22
1972	42	27	14	50	78	28	33	21	18	13	11	24	48	77	116	70	48
1973	46	30	31	58	66	25	24	41	33	32	29	35	69	71	73	56	69
1974	58	37	17	56	120	43	35	34	16	15	20	43	46	79	75	144	140
1975	265	160	109	189	600	116	230	134	103	124	101	131	145	292	567	609	623
1976	457	467	364	376	620	521	429	452	363	399	331	346	427	356	541	622	696
1977	821	696	625	803	1158	737	677	674	674	609	593	703	825	881	1001	1182	1291
1978	1166	1332	1063	1144	1125	1397	1328	1271	1140	1046	1002	1099	1165	1167	1055	1132	1187
1979	1055	1201	872	962	1185	1261	1236	1106	938	882	795	929	938	1020	1161	1177	1217
1980	1094	1166	867	1002	1341	1260	1187	1051	942	821	837	946	983	1077	1227	1345	1451
1981	1559	1563	1252	1488	1925	1610	1544	1535	1317	1269	1199	1345	1438	1680	1806	1942	2028
1982	2039	2061	1781	1855	2460	2139	2078	1967	1923	1703	1716	1739	1749	2078	2419	2404	2558
1983	2476	2484	2195	2391	2833	2608	2533	2312	2257	2185	2142	2348	2398	2426	2703	2845	2952

LUXEMBOURG

Jobs vacant, unfilled vacancies (3)

Offres d'emploi non satisfaites (3)

number / nombre

	Year	Q.1	Q.2	Q.3	Q.4	JAN	FEB	MAR	APR	MAY	JUN	JUL	AUG	SEP	OCT	NOV	DEC
1964	800	955	939	796	511	961	1011	892	895	886	1037	829	823	730	579	542	411
1965	686	620	831	744	550	445	586	830	753	690	1050	915	719	597	711	470	468
1966	505	642	552	525	301	517	722	688	530	557	568	601	576	399	347	279	276
1967	351	385	381	379	260	384	350	420	440	376	327	321	440	377	336	243	200
1968	611	505	828	704	406	345	496	674	871	839	775	744	728	641	546	424	249
1969	822	836	937	853	664	723	740	1044	1018	992	300	980	837	742	671	643	679
1970	801	841	924	878	563	804	373	345	943	962	868	968	914	752	673	519	496
1971	516	570	567	527	401	519	648	544	501	550	651	552	556	473	443	350	409
1972	520	600	494	515	469	541	678	581	493	502	487	518	555	471	472	548	388
1973	664	796	760	628	472	733	786	368	776	744	761	690	592	603	541	471	405
1974	584	734	741	601	258	666	750	786	797	685	741	746	597	461	331	235	207
1975	236	240	345	251	106	233	221	266	332	321	381	273	292	139	112	101	106
1976	265	214	331	351	165	156	190	296	305	367	322	339	426	288	241	126	129
1977	192	212	228	185	142	177	248	210	241	224	219	198	201	155	124	171	130
1978	263	177	295	351	228	166	159	206	275	297	312	280	398	376	246	237	201
1979	252	222	277	328	182	206	193	268	229	274	328	371	347	265	252	158	135
1980	207	228	265	213	121	176	256	251	258	293	244	218	197	225	144	127	93
1981	150	140	172	184	103	133	140	148	168	196	153	152	228	172	113	112	33
1982	152	173	172	138	123	168	161	189	182	186	149	128	153	134	140	112	117
1983	170	189	189	178	124	163	193	211	189	207	172	194	190	149	131	130	112

Consumer prices: all items (4)

Prix à la consommation : total (4)

1980 = 100

	Year	Q.1	Q.2	Q.3	Q.4	JAN	FEB	MAR	APR	MAY	JUN	JUL	AUG	SEP	OCT	NOV	DEC
1964	43.9	43.4	43.6	44.2	44.3	43.2	43.6	43.4	43.5	43.5	43.8	43.8	44.2	44.6	44.2	44.2	44.5
1965	45.3	44.6	45.1	45.7	46.0	44.6	44.7	44.6	44.6	45.2	45.4	45.5	45.7	45.8	45.7	45.8	46.4
1966	46.9	46.7	46.9	46.8	47.0	46.8	46.7	46.6	46.9	47.1	46.7	46.8	46.7	46.9	47.0	47.0	47.1
1967	47.9	47.3	47.5	48.1	48.5	47.3	47.3	47.3	47.5	47.6	47.5	48.0	48.0	48.4	48.4	48.5	48.6
1968	49.1	48.8	49.0	49.1	49.5	48.6	48.9	48.9	49.0	49.0	49.0	49.1	49.1	49.2	49.4	49.5	49.7
1969	50.3	49.8	50.2	50.3	50.7	49.8	49.8	49.9	50.0	50.3	50.2	50.3	50.3	50.4	50.4	50.6	51.1
1970	52.6	51.8	52.5	52.8	53.2	51.6	51.9	52.0	52.2	52.5	52.7	52.9	52.7	52.9	53.1	53.2	53.3
1971	55.0	54.1	54.9	55.2	56.0	53.7	54.0	54.5	54.5	54.9	55.1	55.1	55.2	55.4	55.8	56.0	56.2
1972	57.9	56.7	57.3	58.5	59.3	56.5	56.7	56.8	56.9	57.1	57.8	58.2	58.4	58.7	59.0	59.3	59.5
1973	61.4	60.0	61.3	61.7	62.7	59.8	60.0	60.3	60.8	61.6	61.6	61.6	61.7	61.8	62.2	62.6	63.2
1974	67.3	64.7	66.7	68.0	69.7	63.8	65.0	65.4	66.3	66.9	67.0	67.8	67.9	68.3	69.0	69.8	70.3
1975	74.5	71.6	73.7	75.2	77.5	70.8	71.8	72.3	73.2	73.7	74.2	74.8	75.1	75.7	76.9	77.5	78.0
1976	81.8	79.5	81.2	82.5	84.0	79.2	79.5	79.7	80.9	81.3	81.4	82.1	82.7	82.8	83.4	84.0	84.6
1977	87.3	85.9	87.2	87.8	88.2	85.4	86.0	86.3	86.9	87.2	87.6	88.0	87.8	87.6	88.0	88.4	88.2
1978	90.0	88.8	89.8	90.3	91.1	88.6	88.8	89.1	89.6	89.7	90.0	90.1	90.2	90.4	90.9	91.2	91.2
1979	94.1	92.3	93.3	94.6	96.2	91.9	92.4	92.6	92.8	93.3	93.7	94.2	94.5	95.0	95.6	96.3	96.7
1980	100.0	97.8	99.4	100.4	102.4	97.1	97.9	98.4	98.9	99.5	99.8	100.2	100.5	100.6	101.4	102.3	103.4
1981	108.1	104.9	107.2	109.3	111.0	104.2	104.8	105.6	106.3	107.1	108.2	108.7	109.1	110.0	110.3	111.0	111.7
1982	118.2	114.0	116.3	119.7	122.7	113.2	114.3	114.5	114.8	116.4	117.8	119.0	119.6	120.5	121.8	123.0	123.4
1983	128.4	125.1	126.3	129.7	132.7	124.8	125.2	125.4	125.8	126.4	126.7	128.7	129.6	130.3	132.0	132.7	133.3

Sight deposits
billion francs, end of period

Dépôts à vue
milliards de francs, fin de période

	Year	Q.1	Q.2	Q.3	Q.4	JAN	FEB	MAR	APR	MAY	JUN	JUL	AUG	SEP	OCT	NOV	DEC
1964	10.2	8.2	8.7	9.4	10.2	7.7	7.7	8.2	8.7	8.7	8.7	8.7	8.6	9.4	9.0	9.5	10.2
1965	11.9	8.9	10.2	10.2	11.9	9.5	9.6	8.9	9.2	9.8	10.2	9.9	11.3	10.2	10.5	11.1	11.9
1966	12.2	12.4	13.0	12.4	12.2	11.5	12.5	12.4	11.8	12.0	13.0	12.3	11.9	12.4	13.0	12.1	12.2
1967	15.0	11.5	12.7	10.5	15.0	12.3	12.1	11.5	12.2	13.5	12.7	12.5	12.4	10.5	10.3	13.1	15.0
1968	17.2	14.6	14.5	15.5	17.2	14.3	14.6	14.6	15.7	14.6	14.5	15.2	15.6	15.5	16.3	17.2	17.2
1969	27.3	21.0	21.7	21.9	27.3	19.2	18.3	21.0	23.7	20.2	21.7	20.3	21.3	21.9	20.7	22.7	27.3
1970	28.9	27.6	29.8	27.7	28.9	24.9	26.2	27.6	..	..	29.8	..	..	27.7	..	..	28.9
1971	35.8	30.5	33.8	32.5	35.8	27.0	28.4	30.5	30.3	31.9	33.8	31.7	29.7	32.5	30.9	31.1	35.8
1972	53.9	32.6	35.5	39.4	53.9	30.9	32.5	32.6	34.4	35.2	35.5	39.6	35.9	39.4	43.1	44.0	53.9
1973	47.4	42.1	38.4	41.2	47.4	40.5	43.2	42.1	41.3	41.0	38.4	37.4	39.2	41.2	40.7	43.0	47.4
1974	86.6	54.2	53.2	59.7	86.6	46.6	48.8	54.2	52.1	53.2	53.2	56.1	57.7	59.7	62.1	76.3	86.6
1975	89.8	84.8	84.7	94.7	89.8	79.5	85.6	84.8	86.4	80.8	84.7	86.7	87.2	94.7	90.3	88.7	89.8
1976	104.2	93.3	91.7	95.3	104.2	91.9	87.6	93.3	91.6	89.6	91.7	92.6	90.4	95.3	89.4	98.1	104.2
1977	110.0	113.0	118.0	123.0	110.0	104.0	110.0	113.0	113.0	114.0	118.0	105.0	116.0	123.0	119.0	120.0	110.0
1978	178.0	172.3	178.1	185.5	178.0	156.1	168.2	172.3	176.8	181.5	173.1	178.7	186.5	185.5	181.4	176.2	173.0
1979	237.3	198.5	216.6	223.6	237.3	168.3	184.8	198.5	208.6	233.0	216.6	203.4	212.4	223.6	215.2	225.9	237.3
1980	360.0	299.7	308.4	345.8	360.0	254.6	263.0	299.7	302.6	320.6	308.4	307.3	326.3	345.8	358.2	359.6	360.0
1981	546.6	440.1	473.2	492.9	546.6	373.0	411.8	440.1	419.4	480.4	473.2	499.7	517.0	492.9	519.4	544.4	546.6
1982	685.3	667.1	697.4	691.7	685.3	561.6	606.1	667.1	623.1	666.4	697.4	650.2	701.9	691.7	722.4	720.4	685.3
1983	821.2	728.1	751.4	791.4	821.2	694.0	740.6	728.1	723.6	760.1	751.4	746.0	810.0	791.4	806.6	808.1	821.2

Savings and time deposits
billion francs, end of period

Dépôts à terme et d'épargne
milliards de francs, fin de période

	Year	Q.1	Q.2	Q.3	Q.4	JAN	FEB	MAR	APR	MAY	JUN	JUL	AUG	SEP	OCT	NOV	DEC
1964	18.4	17.0	17.4	18.2	18.4	16.7	17.0	17.0	17.0	17.2	17.4	17.8	18.2	18.2	18.4	18.2	18.4
1965	20.7	20.0	19.9	20.4	20.7	19.2	19.7	20.0	20.1	19.9	19.9	19.9	19.2	20.4	20.7	20.4	20.7
1966	24.2	21.4	21.4	23.5	24.2	21.5	21.1	21.4	21.4	21.3	21.4	22.2	22.9	23.5	23.5	24.2	24.2
1967	27.6	25.2	25.4	27.9	27.6	24.9	25.3	25.2	24.6	24.7	25.4	25.2	25.7	27.9	29.0	27.6	27.6
1968	31.8	27.8	28.4	28.8	31.8	28.9	28.6	27.8	27.9	28.2	28.4	28.1	28.5	28.8	30.2	31.8	31.8
1969	45.5	33.8	38.0	42.4	45.5	31.6	33.7	33.8	34.5	36.5	33.0	40.0	38.8	42.4	44.2	44.9	45.5
1970	58.3	46.4	49.1	53.6	58.3	47.0	47.8	46.4	..	..	49.1	..	..	53.6	..	..	58.3
1971	70.7	59.7	64.1	69.2	70.7	62.0	60.4	59.7	61.4	62.5	64.1	68.1	70.0	69.2	71.6	69.8	70.7
1972	87.1	70.5	71.5	106.0	87.1	69.6	69.4	70.5	68.7	71.4	71.5	72.0	75.0	106.0	78.9	81.1	87.1
1973	137.1	91.4	101.2	118.2	137.1	90.2	87.7	91.4	94.2	95.0	101.2	108.8	114.5	118.2	123.4	129.2	137.1
1974	198.7	169.0	190.5	215.0	198.7	150.3	152.3	169.0	175.1	179.9	190.5	202.3	208.9	215.0	223.3	214.1	198.7
1975	205.1	204.0	202.3	210.7	205.1	208.0	200.9	204.0	196.9	200.7	202.3	206.6	205.3	210.7	210.9	207.5	205.1
1976	218.7	205.0	227.1	227.8	218.7	200.2	199.3	205.0	199.5	213.7	227.1	232.7	229.6	227.8	226.5	224.7	218.7
1977	254.9	235.0	243.0	250.2	254.9	231.0	229.0	235.0	235.0	241.0	243.0	246.1	249.7	250.2	240.7	240.2	254.9
1978	248.3	212.8	232.2	236.4	248.3	218.7	214.8	212.8	215.8	217.6	232.2	232.9	226.7	236.4	239.8	241.8	248.3
1979	316.5	280.2	286.2	294.4	316.5	269.6	269.4	280.2	275.8	275.2	286.2	289.4	296.5	294.4	295.1	292.5	316.5
1980	398.1	377.0	360.1	353.6	398.1	335.8	348.9	377.0	377.7	360.9	360.1	368.2	358.4	353.6	370.3	376.2	398.1
1981	503.3	472.6	501.6	519.2	503.3	431.7	459.8	472.6	480.8	476.6	501.6	530.7	507.8	519.2	536.0	501.1	503.3
1982	543.4	611.9	579.2	606.2	543.4	546.6	566.9	611.9	585.8	564.9	579.2	605.6	580.3	606.2	592.5	568.5	543.4
1983	597.7	578.6	580.2	591.0	597.7	563.5	556.3	578.6	580.5	560.7	580.2	595.9	576.6	591.0	600.6	582.6	597.7

NOTES

1. The original base of the index is 1947 to 1966, 1967 from 1967 to 1970, 1970 from 1971 to 1977, and 1975 from 1978.
2. Not included in total index.
3. Monthly data refer to end of period.
4. Excluding rent. Weighting pattern based on 1948 to 1965, and on 1963-64 from 1966.

NOTES

1. La base originale de l'indice est 1947 jusqu'en 1966, 1967 de 1967 à 1970, 1970 de 1971 à 1977, et 1975 à partir de 1978.
2. Non compris dans l'indice total.
3. Situation en fin de mois.
4. Non compris les loyers. La pondération se réfère à 1948 jusqu'en 1965, et à 1963-64 à partir de 1966.

MAIN SOURCES

PRINCIPALES SOURCES

Series	Séries	Sources
All series	Toutes les séries	Service central de la Statistique et des Études économiques *Bulletin du Statec*

Netherlands — Pays-Bas

NETHERLANDS

Consumers' expenditure / Dépenses des consommateurs

at current market prices / *aux prix courants du marché*

1980 = 100

	Year	Q.1	Q.2	Q.3	Q.4	JAN	FEB	MAR	APR	MAY	JUN	JUL	AUG	SEP	OCT	NOV	DEC
1964	18	17	18	18	20	17	16	18	18	19	18	20	18	18	20	19	21
1965	21	18	20	21	23	19	17	19	20	21	20	23	19	21	21	22	25
1966	22	20	23	23	25	21	18	21	23	23	22	25	21	22	23	24	26
1967	25	23	25	25	26	23	21	24	24	25	25	25	24	25	25	26	28
1968	26	25	26	26	30	25	23	26	26	27	26	28	26	26	28	30	31
1969	30	28	31	30	33	27	26	30	30	32	30	31	30	30	32	32	35
1970	34	31	33	34	38	33	29	33	33	35	33	36	33	34	37	36	40
1971	38	35	38	38	42	35	33	36	38	38	38	40	37	38	42	41	44
1972	43	40	43	43	47	39	37	43	41	43	44	42	42	43	45	46	49
1973	48	45	48	48	54	45	42	47	45	50	50	48	48	48	52	53	56
1974	55	50	55	55	60	50	47	52	53	57	54	56	56	55	60	60	61
1975	63	58	62	63	69	58	55	60	60	64	61	63	62	64	69	67	73
1976	72	67	72	72	78	67	64	69	71	72	73	72	70	76	75	76	83
1977	80	74	80	81	85	75	70	77	79	80	82	80	80	82	82	83	89
1978	87	82	87	88	92	82	78	87	85	87	88	88	88	88	83	91	96
1979	94	89	92	93	100	89	83	94	89	95	93	92	95	92	97	98	104
1980	100	97	99	99	105	98	94	98	98	102	98	101	98	99	104	102	109
1981	104	101	102	102	110	105	97	101	102	103	101	104	102	101	110	104	116
1982	108	105	106	107	114	108	101	107	107	106	105	109	106	106	112	109	120
1983	111	109	110	109	115	109	105	112	110	110	109	109	109	110	112	111	123

Gross fixed investment / Formation brute de capital fixe

at current market prices / *aux prix courants du marché*

1980 = 100

	Year	Q.1	Q.2	Q.3	Q.4	JAN	FEB	MAR	APR	MAY	JUN	JUL	AUG	SEP	OCT	NOV	DEC
1964	22	19	23	22	23												
1965	24	21	24	24	26												
1966	27	24	28	28	29												
1967	30	27	31	30	32												
1968	34	30	34	34	37												
1969	35	30	36	36	38												
1970	42	35	43	43	47												
1971	47	45	48	47	49												
1972	49	45	49	48	53												
1973	54	51	53	54	58												
1974	58	54	58	59	62												
1975	62	56	61	60	70												
1976	65	58	65	64	76												
1977	82	75	81	81	91												
1978	89	82	90	89	97												
1979	94	70	106	95	105												
1980	100	97	104	96	104												
1981	96	94	98	92	102												
1982	95	90	98	90	102												
1983		89	100	94													

Industrial production: total (1) / Production industrielle : total (1)

1980 = 100

	Year	Q.1	Q.2	Q.3	Q.4	JAN	FEB	MAR	APR	MAY	JUN	JUL	AUG	SEP	OCT	NOV	DEC
1964	47	46	48	44	51	45	46	47	47	48	47	42	43	48	52	52	50
1965	50	49	50	47	54	48	49	49	49	51	50	44	45	51	55	55	53
1966	53	51	53	49	57	50	51	52	54	53	53	45	49	53	57	58	56
1967	55	53	55	51	60	52	53	54	55	54	55	46	52	56	59	61	61
1968	61	59	61	58	68	57	59	60	61	61	62	51	61	62	67	69	70
1969	69	67	68	64	76	64	67	68	68	68	68	59	64	68	73	78	77
1970	75	74	76	69	82	71	74	77	77	76	74	65	69	74	81	83	81
1971	80	80	80	73	85	79	80	80	80	80	79	66	74	80	86	86	83
1972	83	83	84	76	91	81	83	84	87	83	82	68	77	83	89	92	92
1973	89	90	90	82	98	88	92	89	92	89	89	74	82	91	96	99	98
1974	94	96	95	86	99	93	98	98	95	95	95	77	87	94	99	101	95
1975	89	92	89	78	98	88	93	95	93	88	88	70	77	87	93	100	102
1976	96	97	97	86	105	95	98	98	99	95	96	76	85	98	100	103	111
1977	96	99	98	85	104	98	100	100	102	96	96	78	83	95	99	102	110
1978	97	100	96	85	108	98	102	101	100	94	95	78	83	95	101	106	116
1979	100	104	101	88	108	102	105	104	107	98	98	80	86	100	104	111	111
1980	100	107	102	85	108	107	105	109	106	100	98	78	84	93	102	109	113
1981	98	104	99	85	107	101	109	103	104	96	96	81	81	93	102	105	113
1982	96	101	97	83	100	101	102	101	102	95	94	79	79	92	96	98	105
1983	96	99	97	85	105	95	103	101	101	97	93	80	81	93	99	105	111

Consumers' expenditure / Dépenses des consommateurs

at 1975 market prices / *aux prix du marché de 1975*

1980 = 100

	Year	Q.1	Q.2	Q.3	Q.4	JAN	FEB	MAR	APR	MAY	JUN	JUL	AUG	SEP	OCT	NOV	DEC
1964	49	47	48	50	53	48	44	48	47	55	47	53	47	48	53	51	56
1965	53	49	52	53	59	52	46	50	52	53	51	58	49	52	56	56	64
1966	55	51	55	55	59	53	47	53	56	55	53	59	52	54	56	58	62
1967	58	55	57	58	61	57	50	57	56	58	58	59	56	59	58	61	65
1968	61	57	60	61	66	59	54	60	60	63	59	64	60	59	64	67	70
1969	66	60	66	67	70	61	57	64	64	70	64	70	66	65	69	70	75
1970	71	67	70	70	77	70	62	70	70	73	70	74	68	70	76	73	82
1971	74	69	74	74	79	70	64	70	74	74	73	77	70	73	78	76	82
1972	77	74	77	76	82	74	70	79	75	77	79	76	75	77	79	81	86
1973	80	76	80	78	86	76	72	80	75	81	82	78	79	77	83	84	90
1974	82	77	82	82	86	78	73	81	80	86	81	84	83	80	86	86	87
1975	85	81	84	84	91	82	76	84	82	86	82	85	82	84	90	87	96
1976	90	86	90	90	91	87	81	88	89	90	91	90	86	92	90	91	92
1977	93	89	94	93	97	90	84	93	92	93	96	93	92	94	93	95	102
1978	97	94	97	97	100	94	89	99	95	97	98	97	97	97	97	99	105
1979	100	97	100	98	104	99	91	102	96	103	100	98	100	97	102	103	108
1980	100	99	100	98	103	101	96	99	98	103	98	100	97	98	102	100	107
1981	98	97	97	96	100	102	93	96	97	98	96	98	96	94	101	95	105
1982	96	95	95	95	99	97	91	96	96	95	94	97	94	93	98	95	105
1983	96	95	96	95	99	95	91	97	96	96	96	95	94	95	96	95	105

Gross fixed investment / Formation brute de capital fixe

at 1975 market prices / *aux prix du marché de 1975*

1980 = 100

	Year	Q.1	Q.2	Q.3	Q.4	JAN	FEB	MAR	APR	MAY	JUN	JUL	AUG	SEP	OCT	NOV	DEC
1964																	
1965																	
1966																	
1967																	
1968																	
1969																	
1970	94	81	96	95	103												
1971	97	96	100	94	98												
1972	93	88	95	89	100												
1973	98	95	97	96	101												
1974	95	91	96	94	97												
1975	91	84	91	88	101												
1976	89	80	88	85	100												
1977	102	95	101	99	110												
1978	105	98	106	102	111												
1979	103	79	116	103	112												
1980	100	100	104	94	101												
1981	90	89	92	85	94												
1982	86	82	88	81	91												
1983		80	89	83													

Industrial production: total (1) / Production industrielle : total (1)

Adjusted - Corrigé

1980 = 100

	Year	Q.1	Q.2	Q.3	Q.4	JAN	FEB	MAR	APR	MAY	JUN	JUL	AUG	SEP	OCT	NOV	DEC
1964		46	47	47	48	46	46	47	46	48	46	47	47	47	48	48	48
1965		49	49	50	51	49	49	48	48	50	49	50	49	51	51	51	51
1966		51	52	53	54	51	51	52	53	52	52	52	53	53	54	54	54
1967		53	54	56	57	53	54	54	55	53	55	55	55	57	56	57	58
1968		59	61	62	64	58	58	59	60	60	62	61	62	63	64	64	65
1969		65	68	70	72	65	65	66	67	68	69	70	70	70	71	73	72
1970		74	74	76	77	73	74	75	74	74	74	77	75	75	77	77	77
1971		79	79	80	80	80	79	78	78	79	80	80	80	80	81	80	79
1972		81	83	84	86	80	80	82	84	83	83	83	84	84	84	85	88
1973		88	89	90	92	88	89	86	89	88	89	89	89	92	92	92	92
1974		94	94	96	92	93	95	94	93	94	95	95	96	95	94	94	89
1975		90	89	88	91	89	89	90	88	89	89	88	88	88	89	93	90
1976		94	96	98	97	95	95	94	95	96	97	96	96	100	96	96	97
1977		96	97	96	96	97	96	96	97	96	97	97	96	96	96	95	97
1978		97	96	97	100	97	97	96	96	95	96	98	96	96	97	99	103
1979		99	101	100	101	99	100	99	103	100	99	100	99	102	100	104	99
1980		104	101	96	101	106	102	105	101	101	100	99	96	94	99	102	101
1981		101	98	96	99	100	105	99	99	97	97	100	96	94	99	98	101
1982		99	96	93	94	10[illegible]	98	97	98	96	94	96	91	93	93	93	96
1983		97	96	95	98	96	98	96	96	98	94	97	94	94	96	98	101

NETHERLANDS

Industrial production: manufacturing (1) / Production industrielle : industries manufacturières (1)

1980 = 100

	Year	Q.1	Q.2	Q.3	Q.4	JAN	FEB	MAR	APR	MAY	JUN	JUL	AUG	SEP	OCT	NOV	DEC
1964	52	50	52	48	56	48	50	51	51	54	52	46	48	52	57	57	55
1965	54	52	55	51	59	52	52	53	54	56	56	48	50	56	60	59	57
1966	57	54	59	54	61	53	54	57	59	59	58	49	54	58	62	62	59
1967	59	56	60	56	64	55	57	57	60	58	61	50	57	61	64	64	64
1968	65	61	66	62	71	58	61	63	65	65	68	55	64	67	71	71	71
1969	71	67	73	68	73	64	66	69	71	73	74	64	69	73	79	80	76
1970	=77=	74	79	72	83	71	74	78	78	80	79	67	72	78	83	84	81
1971	80	78	82	76	84	77	79	79	82	84	82	69	76	82	87	85	81
1972	82	79	85	77	89	76	79	82	87	84	84	69	78	83	88	89	89
1973	88	83	88	83	93	81	84	84	88	87	89	74	82	92	94	94	92
1974	92	91	95	86	93	88	93	93	94	95	96	77	88	93	95	96	89
1975	=86=	84	88	78	92	80	84	87	88	87	88	68	78	87	89	93	95
1976	92	88	96	87	99	86	89	90	96	95	98	76	86	98	98	97	102
1977	93	91	97	86	99	87	91	94	97	95	97	79	85	95	98	96	104
1978	96	91	93	89	105	86	91	96	99	96	100	80	87	98	102	102	110
1979	98	91	104	93	105	85	92	97	108	101	104	84	91	105	103	106	106
1980	100	99	106	90	104	95	99	103	107	105	105	80	91	93	103	103	106
1981	99	96	104	92	105	89	97	101	105	102	104	88	88	100	104	104	108
1982	98	96	104	91	102	92	96	99	106	103	103	86	86	100	103	100	103
1983	98	94	101	92	106	91	94	97	102	101	101	88	88	93	104	105	109

Production: crude steel / Production : acier brut

thousand tons, monthly averages / milliers de tonnes, moyennes mensuelles

	Year	Q.1	Q.2	Q.3	Q.4	JAN	FEB	MAR	APR	MAY	JUN	JUL	AUG	SEP	OCT	NOV	DEC
1964																	
1965																	
1966																	
1967																	
1968																	
1969	392	376	380	388	424	380	347	402	381	375	385	317	417	431	404	439	429
1970	420	425	429	409	418	423	399	452	425	447	414	373	435	419	426	422	407
1971	422	391	410	434	454	390	364	418	382	413	435	456	407	437	497	438	426
1972	464	448	478	463	468	419	440	484	507	495	432	461	451	476	466	443	494
1973	468	434	485	489	463	490	358	454	474	503	478	481	494	492	458	469	463
1974	486	504	464	468	509	476	483	552	527	451	415	442	488	475	512	492	524
1975	401	478	387	359	382	523	433	477	375	370	416	382	378	317	370	398	388
1976	432	419	406	429	473	411	400	445	473	404	340	376	453	457	462	482	476
1977	410	408	394	448	390	451	387	386	374	415	393	408	474	463	431	337	353
1978	465	393	474	496	497	372	374	434	481	481	460	494	510	484	512	508	472
1979	483	428	524	513	468	444	366	473	529	565	478	517	514	507	448	473	484
1980	439	459	499	434	363	466	445	466	512	505	480	422	435	445	446	338	304
1981	455	431	509	488	393	386	421	486	492	509	527	522	493	450	452	386	340
1982	362	406	400	333	309	405	378	435	391	435	374	364	314	322	346	339	243
1983	373	269	433	392	399	244	261	301	441	480	378	434	432	310	388	384	425

Production: crude petroleum / Production : pétrole brut

thousand tons, monthly averages / milliers de tonnes, moyennes mensuelles

	Year	Q.1	Q.2	Q.3	Q.4	JAN	FEB	MAR	APR	MAY	JUN	JUL	AUG	SEP	OCT	NOV	DEC
1964	189	184	188	192	193	187	179	186	178	195	190	193	194	188	198	186	194
1965	200	183	192	209	214	188	168	192	190	196	191	206	213	209	215	212	215
1966	197	201	196	201	192	211	187	204	192	199	196	204	203	197	200	183	192
1967	189	187	189	191	189	192	176	192	186	196	184	195	190	188	194	184	188
1968	179	183	181	177	174	185	178	187	177	184	181	181	179	172	178	169	174
1969	168	171	168	168	166	179	160	174	168	170	167	165	174	166	172	159	168
1970	160	159	162	161	158	164	149	163	160	165	160	165	162	156	162	154	158
1971	143	148	143	143	138	154	138	152	142	143	143	148	144	138	143	134	136
1972	133	139	132	131	130	142	135	141	133	134	130	133	134	126	132	126	131
1973	124	128	124	122	123	134	118	131	124	126	123	125	122	120	123	120	125
1974	122	120	121	124	121	122	113	125	119	123	121	125	126	122	124	119	121
1975	118	115	118	121	120	119	107	118	113	121	120	123	122	119	122	117	120
1976	114	112	113	116	116	118	107	110	113	114	113	117	118	113	118	115	116
1977	115	114	115	116	116	115	109	118	114	118	112	114	118	115	118	114	117
1978	117	115	121	120	112	117	106	121	119	122	122	123	121	115	113	109	115
1979	110	106	108	113	112	113	99	105	104	111	109	114	114	110	114	109	112
1980	107	109	103	108	108	111	106	109	100	104	104	110	111	103	107	109	107
1981	110	104	109	113	114	108	95	109	107	109	110	112	116	110	113	110	118
1982	136	122	124	122	178	121	113	133	124	128	119	121	125	120	176	175	183
1983	216	181	190	237	255	186	167	189	175	192	184	187	261	264	268	244	253

Industrial production: manufacturing (1) / Production industrielle : industries manufacturières (1)

1980 = 100

Adjusted - Corrigé

	Year	Q.1	Q.2	Q.3	Q.4	JAN	FEB	MAR	APR	MAY	JUN	JUL	AUG	SEP	OCT	NOV	DEC
1964		51	51	51	53	51	51	52	51	51	51	51	51	52	53	53	54
1965		54	54	54	55	54	54	54	53	54	54	54	53	55	55	56	56
1966		56	57	57	58	55	56	57	57	57	57	55	58	58	58	58	58
1967		58	58	60	60	58	58	58	58	57	59	58	61	60	60	60	61
1968		62	64	66	68	62	62	62	64	63	65	64	67	66	66	67	69
1969		68	70	73	74	68	68	69	69	70	72	75	72	72	73	74	74
1970		76	76	78	79	75	76	77	76	77	76	79	77	77	79	79	79
1971		80	80	81	80	82	80	79	79	81	79	80	81	81	81	79	79
1972		81	82	82	84	80	80	82	84	81	82	81	82	82	82	84	87
1973		86	87	89	90	86	87	86	88	86	88	89	88	91	89	89	90
1974		93	92	92	89	92	94	93	92	92	93	92	92	91	89	91	86
1975		87	85	84	87	87	86	87	84	86	85	82	85	85	85	90	87
1976		91	93	93	93	92	91	90	92	93	94	92	92	96	93	93	92
1977		94	93	92	93	94	93	94	92	92	93	94	92	92	94	92	95
1978		94	94	96	98	93	93	95	94	93	96	97	96	95	97	97	100
1979		94	100	101	99	92	95	96	103	98	100	101	100	102	98	101	97
1980		102	101	97	98	103	102	103	102	103	100	97	99	95	97	99	97
1981		99	99	99	99	97	101	100	100	99	99	103	98	97	99	99	98
1982		99	99	98	96	100	98	97	101	99	98	102	96	97	97	96	94
1983		97	97	99	100	99	97	97	97	98	97	103	98	95	99	101	101

Production: natural gas (2) / Production : gaz naturel (2)

thousand tons, monthly averages / milliers de tonnes, moyennes mensuelles

	Year	Q.1	Q.2	Q.3	Q.4	JAN	FEB	MAR	APR	MAY	JUN	JUL	AUG	SEP	OCT	NOV	DEC
1964	66																
1965	138																
1966	276																
1967	583	550	410	418	953	605	516	530	482	383	364	349	424	480	680	987	1191
1968	1171	1253	900	832	1701	1323	1253	1183	943	972	784	765	799	932	1282	1699	2121
1969	1825	2075	1442	1300	2481	2009	2043	2174	1672	1415	1238	1172	1205	1523	1788	2399	3256
1970	2641	3108	2152	1914	3382	3234	2942	3149	2711	1986	1758	1829	1767	2145	2868	3250	4028
1971	3650	4108	3017	2849	4626	4266	3752	4307	3394	2770	2886	2700	2782	3065	3925	4855	5097
1972	4868	5453	4274	3770	5975	5877	5242	5241	4793	4241	3788	3405	3637	4269	5352	5971	6603
1973	5903	6868	5167	4138	7439	7290	6709	6604	6208	5137	4157	3962	3999	4453	6450	7538	8328
1974	6977	7892	6096	5497	8423	8209	7498	7969	6517	6419	5353	5262	5140	6089	8195	8476	8597
1975	7571	9133	6875	5208	9067	9179	8801	9419	8194	6570	5860	5061	4816	5748	8003	9169	10029
1976	8109	10111	7025	5847	9451	10299	9836	10199	8289	6845	5941	5344	5487	6709	7727	9106	11521
1977	8075	10030	7611	5785	8874	11212	9620	9258	9155	7243	6404	5244	5485	6626	7346	9141	10134
1978	7394	9999	6167	4631	8779	11009	9901	9088	7329	6219	4953	4419	4240	5235	7008	8916	10414
1979	8041	11474	6631	4821	9237	13025	11073	10323	8069	6686	5137	4577	4352	5533	7808	9805	10099
1980	7679	10649	6508	4273	9237	12163	9527	10258	7706	6943	4874	4881	3577	4362	7190	9753	10919
1981	7052	10326	5528	3884	8472	11529	10769	8679	6955	5356	4273	3582	3661	4408	6952	8131	10332
1982	6003	8863	4321	3279	7048	10153	8443	7994	6249	4620	3594	2971	2892	3975	5235	6810	9100
1983	6378	8791	5674	3593	7453	8347	9496	8531	6916	5964	4141	3239	3095	4446	5424	7460	9475

Ships completed / Navires achevés

thousand gross register tons, quarterly averages / milliers de tonneaux de jauge brute, moyennes trimestrielles

	Year	Q.1	Q.2	Q.3	Q.4	JAN	FEB	MAR	APR	MAY	JUN	JUL	AUG	SEP	OCT	NOV	DEC
1964	69	41	114	73	49												
1965	37	16	63	46	24												
1966	81	73	104	52	96												
1967	73	73	87	79	52												
1968	66	97	84	32	51												
1969	122	137	34	140	160												
1970	158	133	84	244	174												
1971	143	33	193	269	75												
1972	187	149	235	274	94												
1973	213	184	349	38	280												
1974	236	282	185	162	307												
1975	257	48	331	280	367												
1976	159	81	76	269	206												
1977	60	42	77	31	87												
1978	79	155	50	41	69												
1979	69	103	67	21	79												
1980	31	25	29	37	29												
1981	43	19	48	71	33												
1982	53	62	26	47	79												
1983	56	58	51	52	64												

NETHERLANDS

Production: future tendency (3)
manufacturing
per cent balance

Perspectives de production (3)
industries manufacturières
solde en pourcentage

	Year	Q.1	Q.2	Q.3	Q.4	JAN	FEB	MAR	APR	MAY	JUN	JUL	AUG	SEP	OCT	NOV	DEC
1964						23	25	25	23	22	22	23	25	23	20	20	23
1965						27	27	23	22	17	15	17	18	17	15	20	27
1966						30	27	25	22	20	22	18	18	17	13	2	-8
1967						-7	5	17	13	8	2	8	15	22	18	20	17
1968						22	20	25	23	23	23	23	25	22	15	17	10
1969						18	18	25	25	23	25	22	22	20	23	25	23
1970						23	25	27	15	13	10	22	22	28	28	25	22
1971						18	25	22	23	20	18	12	3	8	8	10	6
1972						8	24	18	15	-2	1	18	6	12	18	9	11
1973						34	20	18	20	29	26	32	18	23	17	5	8
1974						19	14	11	24	8	2	14	5	-2	-8	-2	-22
1975						-18	-1	-19	-17	-2	-3	-13	-15	-15	7	-	-
1976						11	7	14	4	-4	8	5	1	1	-10	-3	-16
1977						-1	10	9	2	-1	-4	4	-1	-8	-8	-2	6
1978						-1	-1	4	-4	2	-2	8	5	2	2	-	15
1979						18	13	10	-1	4	2	5	8	3	5	-5	2
1980						5	6	1	-2	-3	-9	-6	-5	-9	-9	-11	-3
1981						-4	3	-4	-4	-10	-4	-2	1	-4	-13	-15	-5
1982						5	3	3	-5	-3	-7	-5	-6	-9	-19	-15	-1
1983						2	2	3	3	-6	-5	1	8	5	-6	-2	10

Orders inflow: tendency (3)
manufacturing
per cent balance

Commandes : tendance (3)
industries manufacturières
solde en pourcentage

	Year	Q.1	Q.2	Q.3	Q.4	JAN	FEB	MAR	APR	MAY	JUN	JUL	AUG	SEP	OCT	NOV	DEC
1964						22	25	28	22	18	17	17	22	27	30	23	10
1965						7	12	22	28	27	15	7	8	22	35	33	28
1966						17	18	15	13	12	13	8	10	13	13	3	-8
1967						-8	-12	-8	-3	3	5	3	5	10	12	17	10
1968						3	-	10	13	10	-2	-5	-2	15	22	13	-7
1969						-12	-	18	23	12	10	-2	15	12	32.	18	17
1970						2	15	18	30	17	8	-3	2	3	18	8	-
1971						-10	-3	2	3	5	-	-8	-5	-5	-	-5	4
1972						-4	-9	9	10	-14	8	-	-13	15	24	16	6
1973						3	5	12	21	25	14	-12	-17	29	19	4	10
1974						-7	27	12	22	-9	12	-18	-23	-11	-6	-28	-22
1975						-30	-6	-17	-33	-1	-3	-14	-32	3	16	10	-4
1976						-2	-8	22	-3	-15	16	-12	-21	22	12	-14	-3
1977						-3	-11	7	5	-19	-16	-10	-19	2	5	-15	8
1978						-14	-18	22	8	-13	1	4	-17	28	6	10	-1
1979						-6	-13	16	10	3	1	-7	-22	16	8	-	-15
1980						-4	1	13	-8	-20	-17	-25	-34	-	11	-9	-7
1981						-13	-8	1	7	-10	-14	8	-32	14	1	-10	-16
1982						-13	-8	8	-4	-27	-	-12	-24	10	-10	-10	-10
1983						-8	3	9	-8	-8	8	-14	-4	10	-1	-1	10

Order books: level (3)
manufacturing
per cent balance

Carnet de commandes : niveau (3)
industries manufacturières
solde en pourcentage

	Year	Q.1	Q.2	Q.3	Q.4	JAN	FEB	MAR	APR	MAY	JUN	JUL	AUG	SEP	OCT	NOV	DEC
1964						10	8	6	7	7	5	2	2	-	2	-	-
1965						-2	-3	-7	-8	-10	-10	-10	-8	-7	-3	-2	-2
1966						-3	-7	-5	-3	-2	-3	-7	-8	-13	-17	-20	-20
1967						-23	-25	-27	-27	-25	-23	-20	-20	-18	-17	-17	-17
1968						-15	-12	-10	-10	-8	-8	-7	-7	-3	-2	-2	-3
1969						-3	-2	-2	-3	-5	-5	-3	-2	-	-	-	2
1970						3	3	3	2	2	-	-	2	2	5	5	8
1971						7	5	2	-2	-3	-3	-3	-5	-10	-14	-17	-20
1972						-23	-23	-21	-22	-23	-20	-23	-20	-18	-16	-9	-13
1973						-2	-4	-2	1	-2	2	-2	-1	1	6	-1	3
1974						-3	-1	-	1	-1	-2	-7	-10	-18	-23	-26	-28
1975						-37	-37	-47	-47	-50	-49	-50	-51	-50	-45	-48	-47
1976						-35	-37	-34	-28	-31	-27	-28	-31	-33	-34	-32	-34
1977						-36	-31	-20	-26	-26	-23	-30	-31	-35	-35	-38	-35
1978						-28	-26	-27	-24	-27	-22	-25	-24	-25	-24	-23	-19
1979						-19	-20	-14	-15	-9	-6	-6	-12	-14	-13	-10	-8
1980						-11	-9	-9	-12	-16	-21	-25	-30	-35	-35	-39	-39
1981						-39	-37	-36	-36	-35	-35	-30	-31	-33	-35	-36	-38
1982						-41	-41	-37	-39	-40	-39	-40	-42	-35	-40	-41	-44
1983						-39	-37	-32	-30	-32	-27	-27	-27	-27	-27	-27	-27

Finished goods stocks: level (3) / Stocks de produits finis : niveau (3)

manufacturing / industries manufacturières

per cent balance / solde en pourcentage

	Year	Q.1	Q.2	Q.3	Q.4	JAN	FEB	MAR	APR	MAY	JUN	JUL	AUG	SEP	OCT	NOV	DEC
1964						-2	-	2	-	-2	-	2	3	3	3	2	-
1965						-	2	3	10	12	12	12	12	12	8	10	7
1966						8	12	12	12	10	12	15	17	17	22	28	35
1967						33	32	32	32	32	30	30	33	33	37	28	20
1968						12	12	13	12	10	10	8	8	7	7	5	5
1969						5	3	2	2	3	7	8	7	7	3	3	5
1970						5	5	5	8	10	8	12	17	23	27	28	30
1971						30	30	30	30	32	35	35	35	35	34	29	25
1972						20	23	18	21	17	19	19	15	13	12	7	7
1973						6	4	3	1	-	-	-1	-4	4	1	-	2
1974						-	-4	-1	3	6	4	2	11	18	23	38	43
1975						42	43	48	50	53	51	45	51	48	44	38	36
1976						33	34	31	33	33	29	32	36	32	24	23	24
1977						20	19	17	18	18	16	21	29	27	28	25	26
1978						27	19	19	16	16	15	14	16	15	12	11	10
1979						12	12	12	10	3	2	3	7	6	3	8	4
1980						8	10	6	9	14	14	15	21	25	25	29	29
1981						31	32	31	28	30	32	32	31	29	33	34	38
1982						41	40	35	34	34	30	31	29	23	24	23	20
1983						19	19	15	15	18	16	15	13	15	15	13	14

Rate of capacity utilization (3) / Taux d'utilisation de capacité (3)

manufacturing / industries manufacturières

per cent / pourcentage

	Year	Q.1	Q.2	Q.3	Q.4	JAN	FEB	MAR	APR	MAY	JUN	JUL	AUG	SEP	OCT	NOV	DEC
1964																	
1965																	
1966																	
1967																	
1968																	
1969																	
1970																	
1971															81		
1972						83				84					84		
1973						85				84					86		
1974						84				85					84		
1975						80				76					76		
1976						79				77					80		
1977						79				80					78		
1978						78				80					81		
1979		80	82	83	83	80			82			83			83		
1980		82	81	79	78	82			81			79			78		
1981		79	79	78	77	79			79			78			77		
1982		76	76	78	78	76			76			78			78		
1983		79	80	81	80	79			80			81			80		

Manufacturing sales: total (4) / Ventes des industries manufacturières : total (4)

1980 = 100

	Year	Q.1	Q.2	Q.3	Q.4	JAN	FEB	MAR	APR	MAY	JUN	JUL	AUG	SEP	OCT	NOV	DEC
1964																	
1965																	
1966																	
1967																	
1968																	
1969																	
1970																	
1971																	
1972																	
1973	55	51	54	53	62												
1974	69	64	70	69	73												
1975	68	64	67	65	75												
1976	76	71	76	75	82												
1977	80	78	81	76	84												
1978	81	77	82	79	87												
1979	93	82	93	91	103												
1980	100	99	100	94	106												
1981	110	101	109	110	117												
1982	111	107	112	107	115												
1983		106	112	110													

NETHERLANDS

Sales: investment goods
1980 = 100

Ventes : biens d'équipement
1980 = 100

	Year	Q.1	Q.2	Q.3	Q.4	JAN	FEB	MAR	APR	MAY	JUN	JUL	AUG	SEP	OCT	NOV	DEC
1964																	
1965																	
1966																	
1967																	
1968																	
1969																	
1970																	
1971																	
1972																	
1973	66	58	64	62	78	56	58	62	59	67	64	59	62	65	76	74	83
1974	75	65	73	72	90	59	62	73	70	77	72	66	68	81	87	85	99
1975	80	70	80	75	96	67	67	75	82	76	80	64	70	90	86	87	114
1976	88	76	85	83	108	66	73	87	81	80	94	78	77	94	99	98	128
1977	90	84	92	86	102	72	86	94	97	85	95	74	82	100	86	98	120
1978	92	81	92	87	104	70	82	90	88	83	105	74	85	102	97	102	114
1979	97	87	98	92	111	75	91	95	95	100	99	82	91	102	106	106	119
1980	100	90	98	96	117	79	91	99	100	93	102	82	98	105	106	107	138
1981	104	89	102	102	123	74	90	102	102	94	109	95	89	122	111	110	147
1982	107	98	103	100	121	84	97	114	107	104	111	85	98	116	106	116	142
1983	105	98	100	98	124	90	89	116	98	96	107	94	88	113	106	116	150

Net new orders: total
investment goods
1980 = 100

Commandes nouvelles nettes : total
biens d'équipement
1980 = 100

	Year	Q.1	Q.2	Q.3	Q.4	JAN	FEB	MAR	APR	MAY	JUN	JUL	AUG	SEP	OCT	NOV	DEC
1964																	
1965																	
1966																	
1967																	
1968																	
1969																	
1970																	
1971																	
1972																	
1973	74	72	75	68	79	71	73	72	71	80	75	67	63	74	84	77	75
1974	91	93	89	83	100	88	81	109	84	103	80	75	93	80	91	109	101
1975	82	83	77	75	93	93	81	75	90	74	67	57	77	92	88	79	112
1976	90	79	86	88	106	65	75	96	75	88	96	81	89	94	89	93	137
1977	91	92	94	81	96	89	88	98	98	87	98	71	83	89	91	94	103
1978	99	99	95	93	105	110	78	109	90	85	109	84	86	108	98	109	107
1979	96	88	97	95	103	80	86	98	93	107	90	97	92	97	98	101	111
1980	100	96	99	96	108	88	103	99	102	94	102	91	93	105	104	95	125
1981	113	104	104	109	130	99	96	116	103	97	112	113	96	119	104	99	186
1982	104	112	104	92	111	93	119	123	111	89	111	73	104	99	93	108	131
1983	109	99	103	106	123	98	95	103	101	96	113	96	98	123	115	124	146

Net new orders: domestic
investment goods
1980 = 100

Commandes nouvelles nettes : marché intérieur
biens d'équipement
1980 = 100

	Year	Q.1	Q.2	Q.3	Q.4	JAN	FEB	MAR	APR	MAY	JUN	JUL	AUG	SEP	OCT	NOV	DEC
1964																	
1965																	
1966																	
1967																	
1968																	
1969																	
1970																	
1971																	
1972																	
1973	83	88	82	76	84	89	94	82	81	94	70	68	71	89	84	88	81
1974	104	97	89	97	130	105	84	103	76	101	90	78	130	84	97	161	130
1975	87	83	82	84	99	90	84	76	99	67	79	64	85	104	83	81	134
1976	100	86	92	92	130	77	81	100	72	101	102	73	104	99	92	113	184
1977	105	101	104	95	122	97	102	104	117	84	110	84	95	106	108	117	143
1978	105	107	109	101	101	105	83	134	117	90	120	101	82	119	84	99	120
1979	93	86	93	88	106	77	87	92	84	108	87	84	84	97	98	106	115
1980	100	96	100	93	110	94	105	89	108	76	117	95	94	89	101	103	127
1981	109	97	92	120	125	97	93	101	92	95	89	148	95	117	97	99	179
1982	101	110	98	92	106	101	120	108	97	90	105	74	97	104	82	90	146
1983	109	101	105	104	126	119	92	91	103	101	110	104	109	100	104	117	157

Net new orders: export — investment goods — 1980 = 100

Commandes nouvelles nettes : étranger — biens d'équipement — 1980 = 100

	Year	Q.1	Q.2	Q.3	Q.4	JAN	FEB	MAR	APR	MAY	JUN	JUL	AUG	SEP	OCT	NOV	DEC
1964																	
1965																	
1966																	
1967																	
1968																	
1969																	
1970																	
1971																	
1972																	
1973	67	60	70	62	75	57	57	65	63	71	77	66	57	63	84	70	72
1974	82	89	88	72	79	75	80	113	90	102	73	72	66	77	86	71	79
1975	78	82	73	69	88	94	79	74	83	79	59	52	71	84	91	77	96
1976	82	74	82	85	89	56	72	94	76	78	92	87	77	90	86	77	103
1977	80	85	87	71	77	82	78	94	83	88	90	62	73	77	79	78	74
1978	93	92	84	87	106	112	75	91	70	81	101	72	88	100	107	116	96
1979	97	90	99	100	101	81	86	102	99	105	92	106	97	97	98	97	108
1980	100	97	98	99	106	84	100	106	97	107	91	88	94	116	106	89	124
1981	116	108	112	108	134	101	97	126	111	98	127	109	95	119	109	102	191
1982	106	113	107	92	113	87	119	133	119	88	114	72	109	95	101	120	120
1983	109	97	101	106	130	84	98	111	98	91	114	90	90	138	123	129	138

Construction permits issued: total (5) — million guilders, monthly averages

Permis de construire délivrés : total (5) — millions de florins, moyennes mensuelles

	Year	Q.1	Q.2	Q.3	Q.4	JAN	FEB	MAR	APR	MAY	JUN	JUL	AUG	SEP	OCT	NOV	DEC
1964	430	387	418	415	500												
1965	484	397	444	529	564												
1966	568	525	626	573	550												
1967	705	660	717	665	777												
1968	708	645	746	701	742												
1969	796	697	759	843	886												
1970	858	700	762	1020	950												
1971	942	832	983	915	1035												
1972	1130	1032	1027	1192	1270												
1973	1163	1056	1130	1196	1219												
1974	1040	1012	989	997	1162												
1975	1113	964	1161	1198	1130												
1976	1382	1217	1338	1384	1587												
1977	1588	1337	1652	1579	1784												
1978	1767	1661	1644	1820	1943												
1979	1891	1710	1997	1976	1879												
1980	1914	1977	1755	1634	2291												
1981	1902	1977	1899	1779	1952	2151	1756	2023	1652	1991	2053	2110	1617	1610	1811	1896	2149
1982	1629	1558	1454	1603	1899	1235	1613	1826	1190	1395	1778	1431	1749	1628	1719	1979	1999
1983		1531	1662	1469		1526	1454	1612	1203	1955	1828	1288	1505	1613	1740	1534	

Construction permits issued: residential (5) — million guilders, monthly averages

Permis de construire délivrés : bâtiments résidentiels (5) — millions de florins, moyennes mensuelles

	Year	Q.1	Q.2	Q.3	Q.4	JAN	FEB	MAR	APR	MAY	JUN	JUL	AUG	SEP	OCT	NOV	DEC
1964	214	196	194	211	253												
1965	267	216	257	282	311												
1966	288	280	291	280	301												
1967	361	365	337	331	410												
1968	368	344	391	355	384												
1969	403	356	386	413	457												
1970	426	374	338	517	477												
1971	518	425	499	519	627												
1972	676	612	657	697	736												
1973	672	641	698	684	663												
1974	542	546	517	516	590												
1975	574	512	625	571	588												
1976	731	584	702	761	878												
1977	790	675	828	763	893												
1978	879	826	802	869	1021												
1979	902	836	957	892	924												
1980	913	942	776	752	1184												
1981	1007	1076	988	920	1043	1210	937	1082	923	956	1084	1030	849	881	1030	1099	999
1982	861	754	680	865	1145	653	741	868	542	671	826	722	906	968	987	1134	1314
1983		767	935	824		697	746	859	637	1184	983	643	894	935	1090	984	

NETHERLANDS

Construction: housing starts
thousands, monthly averages

Construction : logements mis en chantier
milliers, moyennes mensuelles

	Year	Q.1	Q.2	Q.3	Q.4	JAN	FEB	MAR	APR	MAY	JUN	JUL	AUG	SEP	OCT	NOV	DEC
1964	9.1	7.6	10.1	8.5	10.1	7.1	7.3	8.4	9.2	9.4	11.7	7.1	7.6	10.7	10.6	8.8	10.8
1965	10.1	8.8	11.6	9.9	10.0	7.8	8.3	10.4	12.8	8.8	13.2	8.2	11.2	10.3	10.8	9.3	9.9
1966	9.5	8.1	11.3	9.6	9.2	6.2	7.2	10.9	11.5	12.2	10.3	7.5	10.8	10.4	9.9	8.4	9.2
1967	11.2	10.0	11.1	11.8	11.9	8.3	11.2	10.6	10.3	11.0	12.1	8.9	12.6	14.0	12.1	13.0	10.6
1968	10.6	9.6	11.1	10.9	11.0	8.3	9.7	10.8	11.1	12.6	9.5	7.5	13.1	12.1	12.1	11.1	9.8
1969	10.1	9.2	10.7	10.4	10.1	11.2	6.5	10.0	11.3	10.3	10.4	7.9	9.8	13.5	11.2	10.7	8.4
1970	10.6	9.4	11.5	11.3	10.3	7.7	3.4	12.0	11.5	11.3	11.8	8.7	12.1	13.0	10.9	11.3	8.8
1971	11.6	10.3	11.9	12.4	11.9	10.4	9.4	11.1	11.6	12.7	11.5	9.4	13.3	14.4	11.5	11.5	12.7
1972	13.0	12.8	13.7	11.9	13.7	9.8	14.5	14.2	14.4	13.8	12.8	9.5	13.7	12.5	16.1	13.5	11.5
1973	11.8	13.2	11.8	11.8	10.2	12.7	12.3	14.6	11.7	13.3	10.4	10.1	12.7	12.7	11.9	9.9	8.8
1974	9.5	9.6	10.4	9.8	8.3	9.3	8.4	11.0	11.3	9.5	10.3	10.5	9.9	9.0	9.0	8.6	7.3
1975	9.3	8.9	9.9	8.4	9.8	9.3	3.7	8.7	10.5	9.3	10.0	5.7	9.3	10.2	10.7	11.0	7.8
1976	9.9	9.4	9.1	10.1	11.0	8.0	8.1	12.2	9.9	8.7	8.7	5.9	12.7	11.3	11.2	12.3	9.4
1977	9.1	10.0	9.4	8.4	8.6	10.3	8.8	10.9	9.1	9.1	9.9	5.4	9.9	9.9	9.4	8.5	7.8
1978	8.6	8.5	8.6	8.4	8.3	7.8	6.0	11.6	8.5	8.7	8.7	4.7	10.2	10.3	10.8	9.8	5.9
1979	8.3	4.8	10.8	8.4	9.1	1.8	2.0	10.7	12.3	9.9	10.2	5.4	9.9	9.9	11.2	9.3	6.8
1980	8.8	8.5	9.1	8.2	9.4	6.7	9.5	9.3	8.3	9.4	9.7	4.8	9.0	10.7	12.0	8.0	8.1
1981	10.0	8.7	11.5	9.9	10.0	7.4	8.5	10.2	12.0	11.4	11.2	6.1	10.5	13.1	9.6	11.9	8.5
1982	9.3	8.3	10.0	8.0	10.7	5.8	8.8	10.4	11.8	9.2	9.1	5.0	8.3	10.3	11.5	9.8	10.7
1983		9.1	8.2	9.5													

Construction, work in progress: dwellings
thousands, end of period

Construction, travaux en cours : logements
milliers, fin de période

	Year	Q.1	Q.2	Q.3	Q.4	JAN	FEB	MAR	APR	MAY	JUN	JUL	AUG	SEP	OCT	NOV	DEC
1964	144	141	147	149	144	138	139	141	142	144	147	147	147	149	149	147	144
1965	149	147	153	155	149	145	145	147	150	149	153	153	156	155	155	153	149
1966	141	151	153	153	141	149	150	151	152	153	153	152	154	153	151	147	141
1967	145	140	139	146	145	139	140	140	139	140	139	141	143	146	147	147	145
1968	149	148	151	155	149	146	147	148	150	151	151	150	153	155	155	153	149
1969	146	152	152	153	146	152	151	152	153	153	152	149	150	153	152	150	146
1970	154	152	157	160	154	147	149	152	154	155	157	154	157	160	160	159	154
1971	154	158	159	162	154	156	156	158	158	160	159	160	162	162	160	157	154
1972	157	162	162	162	157	155	160	162	164	165	162	163	163	162	163	161	157
1973	142	161	154	155	142	158	159	161	160	158	154	156	156	155	151	148	142
1974	107	136	127	120	107	140	138	136	135	130	127	124	123	120	116	112	107
1975	97	105	102	101	97	107	106	105	104	103	102	101	100	101	100	100	97
1976	109	103	102	110	109	98	100	103	104	103	102	103	107	110	111	111	109
1977	107	115	112	113	107	111	112	115	114	114	112	112	113	113	112	110	107
1978	104	109	107	108	104	107	105	109	109	108	107	104	106	108	109	108	104
1979	115	107	117	120	115	102	101	107	113	115	117	116	119	120	121	119	115
1980	106	118	116	114	106	115	118	118	118	117	116	114	114	114	114	111	106
1981	107	112	118	118	107	107	109	112	114	116	118	116	118	118	115	113	107
1982	94	111	107	101	94	108	110	111	112	110	107	104	103	101	100	97	94
1983		99	95	109		101		99			95			109			

Retail sales: value (6)
1980 = 100

Ventes au détail : valeur (6)
1980 = 100

	Year	Q.1	Q.2	Q.3	Q.4	JAN	FEB	MAR	APR	MAY	JUN	JUL	AUG	SEP	OCT	NOV	DEC
1964	25	23	25	25	29	24	22	24	24	27	24	27	23	25	29	27	31
1965	28	25	28	28	33	26	22	26	28	29	26	31	24	28	31	31	37
1966	30	26	30	29	33	28	23	28	31	30	29	31	27	29	31	33	36
1967	32	29	32	31	35	30	25	31	31	32	32	31	30	32	32	36	38
1968	34	31	34	33	39	32	28	33	33	35	32	34	32	32	36	40	42
1969	38	33	38	37	43	33	30	37	38	41	36	38	36	37	42	42	46
1970	43	38	42	41	49	40	34	40	40	44	41	43	38	42	48	46	54
1971	47	41	47	45	54	42	37	44	47	48	46	47	42	47	52	52	57
1972	52	47	51	50	58	46	42	53	50	52	53	49	48	53	55	58	63
1973	58	52	58	55	66	52	48	57	55	60	60	54	56	56	63	66	71
1974	65	57	65	64	73	58	53	62	63	69	64	64	64	64	72	74	75
1975	73	65	73	71	84	66	61	69	70	77	70	69	69	74	83	79	91
1976	81	72	82	80	90	74	66	77	82	83	81	79	75	87	85	86	98
1977	89	81	91	88	96	83	72	88	89	88	96	88	85	91	93	95	99
1978	95	91	97	93	99	93	80	100	95	98	99	88	91	99	99	100	99
1979	98	94	101	92	104	93	82	106	98	103	101	89	95	93	103	106	102
1980	100	99	102	95	104	106	90	100	101	108	98	95	95	96	107	101	103
1981	100	97	103	96	104	105	88	99	104	105	100	101	90	96	109	96	106
1982	103	97	104	98	111	100	89	102	106	104	103	101	92	100	109	105	120
1983	102	95	103	100	109	95	87	102	102	102	104	100	96	104	104	104	120

Cost of construction: residential / Coût de la construction : bâtiments résidentiels

1980 = 100

	Year	Q.1	Q.2	Q.3	Q.4	JAN	FEB	MAR	APR	MAY	JUN	JUL	AUG	SEP	OCT		DEC
1964	27	26	26	26	27			26			26			26			27
1965	28	27	27	28	28			27			27			28			28
1966	29	29	29	30	29			29			29			30			29
1967	29	29	29	30	30			29			29			30			30
1968	31	31	31	31	32			31			31			31			32
1969	35	34	35	35	36			34			35			35			36
1970	39	37	38	39	40			37			38			39			40
1971	44	42	43	45	45			42			43			45			45
1972	48	47	47	48	48			47			47			48			48
1973	53	51	52	54	55			51			52			54			55
1974	60	58	60	61	62			58			60			61			62
1975	65	64	65	66	67			64			65			66			67
1976	71	69	70	71	73			69			70			71			73
1977	77	75	76	78	80			75			76			78			80
1978	85	82	84	85	87			82			84			85			87
1979	93	90	92	94	96			90			92			94			96
1980	100	98	100	101	102			98			100			101			102
1981	103	103	103	103	104			103			103			103			104
1982	101	102	101	99	102			102			101			99			102
1983		101	100	100				101			100			100			

Retail sales: durable goods / Ventes au détail : biens durables

1980 = 100

	Year	Q.1	Q.2	Q.3	Q.4	JAN	FEB	MAR	APR	MAY	JUN	JUL	AUG	SEP	OCT	NOV	DEC
1964																	
1965																	
1966																	
1967																	
1968																	
1969																	
1970																	
1971																	
1972																	
1973																	
1974																	
1975																	
1976																	
1977																	
1978																	
1979																	
1980	100																
1981	100	91	101	97	109	99	82	93	102	104	98	101	90	101	114	102	112
1982	98	91	98	96	108	97	81	94	98	100	97	98	90	101	109	103	111
1983	97	90	98	95	105	93	80	96	97	97	99	94	88	102	104	100	112

Retail sales: value (6) / Ventes au détail : valeur (6)

Adjusted - Corrigé *

1980 = 100

	Year	Q.1	Q.2	Q.3	Q.4	JAN	FEB	MAR	APR	MAY	JUN	JUL	AUG	SEP	OCT	NOV	DEC
1964		25	25	26	26	24	25	25	24	25	25	25	26	26	27	26	26
1965		27	28	28	30	27	27	27	27	28	28	28	28	29	29	30	31
1966		29	30	30	30	29	28	28	30	30	30	30	31	30	30	31	29
1967		31	32	32	32	32	31	31	32	31	32	31	33	32	32	33	32
1968		33	33	34	36	33	33	33	33	33	33	34	34	34	35	35	37
1969		36	38	38	39	34	37	37	38	38	38	37	39	38	39	39	40
1970		41	41	43	45	40	41	41	41	42	42	42	43	43	44	44	46
1971		44	46	47	49	44	44	45	46	47	46	46	47	43	49	49	48
1972		50	51	52	54	49	49	52	50	50	52	51	52	53	53	54	54
1973		56	57	58	61	56	57	56	56	57	58	58	59	58	60	61	63
1974		62	64	67	68	61	62	62	63	65	64	68	66	67	67	68	68
1975		70	72	73	78	68	71	70	72	71	72	72	72	76	77	76	82
1976		77	80	83	83	74	78	79	79	80	80	79	83	88	79	84	87
1977		86	89	91	89	86	85	87	85	88	94	92	91	90	89	92	87
1978		96	96	96	95	99	94	95	96	95	96	94	96	97	97	97	91
1979		97	98	97	99	95	96	101	99	98	96	97	99	96	99	101	97
1980		101	100	100	99	106	99	99	100	99	100	99	100	100	100	99	98
1981		101	100	100	99	101	102	101	100	99	99	104	97	99	100	98	100
1982		100	101	102	106	99	102	100	102	101	101	102	102	103	103	104	112
1983		98	100	104	104	96	100	97	97	102	102	104	104	105	101	103	109

* Adjusted by the O.E.C.D. — * Corrigé par l'O.C.D.E.

NETHERLANDS

Retail sales: volume
1980 = 100

Adjusted - Corrigé *

Ventes au détail : volume
1980 = 100

	Year	Q.1	Q.2	Q.3	Q.4	JAN	FEB	MAR	APR	MAY	JUN	JUL	AUG	SEP	OCT	NOV	DEC
1964	66	65	64	66	68	64	66	65	62	66	65	67	66	67	68	67	67
1965	72	70	70	72	75	70	70	70	69	70	70	73	71	73	74	74	79
1966	73	71	73	74	73	74	70	70	73	73	73	74	75	72	73	74	71
1967	75	75	75	75	75	79	74	73	74	74	76	74	77	76	74	76	76
1968	79	78	76	79	81	79	77	77	76	76	77	79	79	79	79	80	85
1969	81	73	81	82	83	76	80	79	79	81	82	82	83	82	82	82	84
1970	89	87	87	89	91	87	87	86	85	87	87	90	89	89	90	92	93
1971	91	88	90	91	92	89	88	87	89	91	89	90	91	92	92	92	91
1972	95	93	93	95	95	94	91	95	92	92	94	95	95	95	95	96	96
1973	99	99	97	99	101	99	100	97	95	97	98	100	101	97	99	100	103
1974	100	100	99	102	98	100	100	98	98	100	99	105	102	100	98	98	98
1975	100	99	98	100	104	98	102	97	98	97	99	100	100	102	102	101	108
1976	103	101	101	107	103	98	102	102	100	102	102	103	106	111	98	103	108
1977	107	106	107	109	104	108	105	105	102	105	113	112	109	107	104	107	102
1978	108	112	108	109	105	117	109	109	108	107	108	109	109	109	107	107	101
1979	107	109	106	106	105	108	108	111	108	107	104	107	109	103	105	106	102
1980	100	105	100	99	96	113	104	100	99	99	100	100	99	93	97	96	96
1981	93	97	92	94	90	98	97	95	93	92	92	99	92	91	91	89	90
1982	91	90	89	91	92	89	91	89	89	88	89	91	91	90	89	90	97
1983	88	85	86	90	89	84	87	84	83	87	87	90	89	90	86	87	93

Employment: manufacturing (7)
(all employees)
1980 = 100

Emploi : industries manufacturières (7)
(salariés)
1980 = 100

	Year	Q.1	Q.2	Q.3	Q.4	JAN	FEB	MAR	APR	MAY	JUN	JUL	AUG	SEP	OCT	NOV	DEC
1964	134	134	133	134	135			134			133			134			135
1965	135	134	134	135	135			134			134			135			135
1966	134	134	134	134	133			134			134			134			133
1967	129	130	127	129	127			130			127			129			127
1968	126	126	126	127	127			126			126			127			127
1969	129	127	127	129	129			127			127			129			129
1970	129	129	129	129	129			129			129			129			129
1971	127	128	127	127	126			128			127			127			126
1972	122	123	122	122	121			123			122			122			121
1973	120	120	120	120	120			120			120			120			120
1974	118	118	118	120	118			118			118			120			118
1975	114	116	115	114	112			116			115			114			112
1976	110	110	110	110	109			110			110			110			109
1977	108	108	108	108	107			108			108			108			107
1978	103	103	103	103	102			103			103			103			102
1979	102	102	101	102	101			102			101			102			101
1980	100	100	100	101	100			100			100			101			100
1981	97	98	98	97	96			98			98			97			96
1982	92	94	93	92	91			94			93			92			91
1983		89	88	86				89			88			86			

Unemployment (registered unemployed) (8)(9)
thousands

Chômage (chômeurs inscrits) (8)(9)
milliers

	Year	Q.1	Q.2	Q.3	Q.4	JAN	FEB	MAR	APR	MAY	JUN	JUL	AUG	SEP	OCT	NOV	DEC
1964	22	29	14	18	27	35	29	22	17	13	12	19	18	18	20	23	39
1965	27	36	18	21	31	42	38	28	22	18	16	22	20	21	22	29	43
1966	37	43	22	28	57	50	50	29	25	20	20	26	27	30	36	53	82
1967	79	93	65	68	88	100	97	83	73	62	60	69	66	67	73	84	106
1968	72	103	62	58	64	116	106	88	72	59	56	62	57	55	58	61	73
1969	53	71	43	43	54	77	75	62	48	41	38	44	43	42	45	51	68
1970	46	63	37	37	49	71	66	52	42	36	34	37	35	37	42	47	59
1971	62	64	45	53	86	71	65	56	47	44	45	51	52	56	66	84	108
1972	108	123	94	99	116	128	130	112	100	91	91	99	98	100	105	115	127
1973	110	131	98	97	114	136	135	121	107	95	93	98	96	96	101	110	131
1974	135	143	113	126	158	150	145	133	118	110	111	123	126	129	140	154	181
1975	260	259	242	259	280	260	263	254	247	237	241	256	259	261	267	277	295
1976	278	297	261	276	276	304	305	283	267	256	261	274	280	274	272	273	284
1977	271	282	251	273	277	293	286	268	255	247	253	268	276	273	271	275	284
1978	273	282	251	276	282	290	285	270	256	245	252	269	282	278	277	278	289
1979	281	292	263	285	283	299	297	280	263	257	268	282	289	283	278	281	289
1980	325	298	285	338	381	307	302	285	277	280	298	326	340	349	359	378	405
1981	480	432	434	503	551	428	434	432	423	426	453	493	504	512	529	545	578
1982	655	596	607	681	735	593	600	595	592	596	633	665	680	697	710	730	765
1983	801	774	768	822	839	776	779	768	757	753	793	810	828	827	825	837	856

* Adjusted by the O.E.C.D.

* Corrigé par l'O.C.D.E.

Unemployment (registered unemployed) (8)(9)(10) — Chômage (chômeurs inscrits) (8)(9)(10)

as per cent of total labour force — en pourcentage de la population active

	Year	Q.1	Q.2	Q.3	Q.4	JAN	FEB	MAR	APR	MAY	JUN	JUL	AUG	SEP	OCT	NOV	DEC
1964																	
1965																	
1966																	
1967																	
1968																	
1969																	
1970																	
1971	1.6	1.7	1.2	1.4	2.2	1.8	1.7	1.5	1.2	1.1	1.2	1.3	1.3	1.5	1.7	2.2	2.8
1972	2.8	3.2	2.4	2.5	3.0	3.3	3.3	2.9	2.6	2.4	2.3	2.5	2.5	2.6	2.7	3.0	3.3
1973	2.8	3.4	2.5	2.5	2.9	3.5	3.5	3.1	2.8	2.4	2.4	2.5	2.5	2.5	2.6	2.8	3.4
1974	3.5	3.7	2.9	3.2	4.1	3.9	3.7	3.4	3.0	2.8	2.8	3.2	3.2	3.3	3.6	4.0	4.6
1975	5.0	5.0	4.5	5.0	5.4	5.1	5.1	4.9	4.7	4.4	4.5	4.9	5.0	5.0	5.1	5.4	5.8
1976	5.3	5.8	4.9	5.3	5.3	6.0	6.0	5.5	5.0	4.8	4.9	5.2	5.4	5.2	5.2	5.2	5.5
1977	5.1	5.3	4.6	5.1	5.2	5.6	5.4	5.0	4.7	4.5	4.6	5.0	5.2	5.1	5.1	5.2	5.4
1978	5.1	5.3	4.6	5.2	5.2	5.5	5.4	5.0	4.7	4.4	4.6	5.0	5.3	5.2	5.1	5.2	5.4
1979	5.1	5.4	4.7	5.2	5.2	5.6	5.5	5.1	4.7	4.6	4.8	5.2	5.3	5.2	5.1	5.1	5.3
1980	5.9	5.3	5.0	6.2	7.2	5.6	5.4	5.0	4.8	4.9	5.3	6.0	6.3	6.4	6.7	7.1	7.7
1981	9.1	8.1	8.1	9.5	10.6	8.1	8.2	8.1	7.9	7.9	8.5	9.3	9.6	9.7	10.1	10.4	11.2
1982	12.6	11.3	11.5	13.1	14.3	11.3	11.4	11.3	11.2	11.3	12.1	12.8	13.1	13.5	13.7	14.2	15.0
1983	16.9	16.6	16.4	17.6	17.0	16.6	16.7	16.4	16.2	16.1	17.0	17.3	17.7	17.7	14.8	17.9	18.3

Labour disputes: time lost — Conflits du travail : journées perdues

thousand man-days — milliers de journées-homme

	Year	Q.1	Q.2	Q.3	Q.4	JAN	FEB	MAR	APR	MAY	JUN	JUL	AUG	SEP	OCT	NOV	DEC
1964	43.8	15.0	12.7	4.8	11.3	7.6	6.3	1.1	5.3	2.1	5.3	-	1.0	3.8	7.2	4.1	-
1965	54.7	18.4	34.6	1.2	0.5	0.6	15.9	1.9	33.6	0.7	0.3	-	-	1.2	-	-	0.5
1966	12.7	1.8	7.1	3.3	0.5	0.2	0.7	0.9	-	1.3	5.8	2.8	0.2	0.3	0.5	-	-
1967	6.2	0.2	1.0	0.2	4.8	-	-	0.2	1.0	-	-	-	-	0.2	4.8	-	-
1968	13.7	4.9	2.3	6.0	0.5	-	2.3	2.6	2.3	-	-	-	-	6.0	-	0.5	-
1969	21.6	5.2	1.6	1.8	13.0	3.9	0.5	0.8	0.5	0.8	0.3	-	-	1.8	4.4	5.0	3.6
1970	262.6	0.4	3.6	258.1	0.5	0.4	-	-	0.1	2.4	1.1	0.8	66.1	191.2	-	-	0.5
1971	96.7	2.6	91.8	0.8	1.5	0.1	2.5	-	35.4	56.2	0.2	-	0.6	0.2	1.3	0.2	-
1972	134.2	114.3	3.1	16.5	0.3	-	113.6	0.7	0.8	0.9	1.4	0.9	10.3	5.3	0.3	-	-
1973	589.8	293.0	295.6	0.3	0.9	-	15.7	277.3	292.4	3.2	-	0.2	-	0.1	0.9	-	-
1974	7.0	0.1	3.6	0.6	2.7	-	-	0.1	2.0	1.1	0.5	-	0.3	0.3	2.0	0.3	0.4
1975	0.5	0.1	0.1	-	0.3	0.1	-	-	-	-	0.1	-	-	-	0.2	-	0.1
1976	13.8	-	-	13.8	-	-	-	-	-	-	-	5.9	0.2	7.7	-	-	-
1977	236.0	228.0	6.7	-	1.3	0.3	227.7	-	0.8	5.8	0.1	-	-	-	-	-	1.3
1978	2.8	0.4	0.7	-	1.7	0.1	-	0.3	-	0.7	-	-	-	-	0.2	-	1.5
1979	306.7	0.3	3.2	294.7	8.5	0.3	-	-	2.8	0.1	0.3	-	74.9	219.8	8.1	0.4	-
1980	55.2	24.4	8.6	20.2	2.0	0.2	-	24.2	4.0	4.6	-	-	-	20.2	2.0	-	-
1981	23.6	1.5	21.5	-	0.6	-	-	1.5	0.8	19.5	1.2	-	-	-	0.4	0.1	0.1
1982	215.4	65.7	39.8	2.5	106.4	-	1.3	65.4	0.4	32.0	7.4	-	-	2.5	-	104.5	1.9
1983		-	7.6			-	-	-	-	7.6	-	-					

Unemployment (registered unemployed) (8)(9) — Chômage (chômeurs inscrits) (8)(9)

Adjusted - Corrigé

thousands — milliers

	Year	Q.1	Q.2	Q.3	Q.4	JAN	FEB	MAR	APR	MAY	JUN	JUL	AUG	SEP	OCT	NOV	DEC
1964		27	27	29	30	27	27	27	27	27	27	29	29	30	30	29	31
1965		31	32	33	34	31	32	31	32	33	32	33	33	33	33	35	34
1966		36	35	41	57	36	40	32	34	34	37	38	41	45	50	58	64
1967		74	88	89	89	70	74	79	86	88	89	88	88	91	93	89	85
1968		83	85	78	58	83	82	84	86	86	85	81	78	77	63	57	54
1969		52	48	47	48	52	53	52	50	48	47	48	48	46	46	47	50
1970		44	42	45	47	45	45	43	42	43	42	44	44	46	47	47	46
1971		48	55	64	81	49	47	49	51	55	59	60	63	68	74	82	88
1972		100	108	112	112	95	103	103	107	108	110	110	111	113	114	114	108
1973		109	111	109	110	106	110	112	111	110	111	110	109	109	109	109	113
1974		120	126	139	155	120	119	122	123	126	129	134	139	143	149	154	161
1975		238	261	267	274	230	237	246	258	261	264	266	266	269	272	275	275
1976		277	282	281	270	274	280	278	280	282	283	282	283	278	275	270	267
1977		266	272	274	271	267	265	267	269	272	274	274	275	274	272	272	270
1978		268	271	275	276	268	268	270	272	271	270	273	277	277	277	275	276
1979		281	282	282	278	278	282	282	281	283	284	282	282	280	277	278	277
1980		288	305	335	374	287	289	288	295	306	313	325	334	346	359	374	388
1981		419	459	500	542	403	417	436	446	460	471	491	499	510	529	540	556
1982		582	634	678	724	566	581	599	618	634	651	664	675	695	710	723	739
1983		760	796	819	828	747	760	773	784	794	811	809	823	824	825	830	829

NETHERLANDS

Jobs vacant, unfilled vacancies (8) — Offres d'emploi non satisfaites (8)

thousands — milliers

	Year	Q.1	Q.2	Q.3	Q.4	JAN	FEB	MAR	APR	MAY	JUN	JUL	AUG	SEP	OCT	NOV	DEC
1964	131.0	114.4	136.7	147.8	125.0	111.1	113.8	118.2	124.8	134.2	151.0	156.3	148.1	139.1	132.4	124.9	117.7
1965	129.2	118.0	134.8	141.9	122.0	116.3	117.1	120.6	124.5	132.1	147.7	148.5	142.1	135.2	128.4	121.8	115.7
1966	124.9	114.9	130.8	127.1	86.7	112.3	114.6	117.7	119.7	130.3	142.5	138.9	126.8	115.6	103.2	85.3	71.6
1967	68.2	64.5	74.5	75.3	58.5	63.8	63.9	65.7	67.9	73.7	82.0	80.9	76.2	68.9	61.8	58.3	55.4
1968	77.3	60.1	79.8	87.1	82.0	56.4	59.6	64.3	69.1	78.4	91.8	89.7	86.8	84.8	82.3	83.2	80.6
1969	106.3	84.2	108.9	122.5	109.7	80.9	83.0	83.7	94.2	106.9	125.6	126.1	122.9	118.6	114.0	109.9	105.2
1970	127.1	108.0	132.5	144.2	123.6	104.7	106.8	112.4	118.8	130.1	148.6	151.0	144.1	137.6	127.8	124.1	116.8
1971	106.6	112.2	121.1	115.4	77.7	112.6	112.2	111.9	114.0	120.7	128.7	124.9	117.3	104.0	90.7	77.1	65.4
1972	63.4	61.5	69.0	69.4	53.4	60.7	61.1	62.8	63.5	67.9	75.7	74.6	70.6	63.1	57.0	52.8	50.4
1973	67.1	52.0	67.2	80.3	68.7	51.3	51.6	53.2	56.4	66.9	78.3	82.4	80.7	77.3	74.8	70.1	61.3
1974	69.3	58.4	76.7	84.3	57.7	56.6	58.1	60.6	63.9	76.4	89.9	90.6	86.2	76.0	66.0	57.1	50.0
1975	47.2	45.0	54.8	48.0	41.1	45.6	44.7	44.7	54.5	56.2	53.6	49.5	48.6	45.8	46.0	41.5	35.7
1976	47.1	35.6	53.3	50.3	49.1	33.5	34.6	38.6	50.3	56.2	53.5	51.2	49.3	50.3	54.9	49.5	42.8
1977	55.4	43.1	57.6	64.3	56.6	41.8	42.2	45.4	46.5	60.9	65.4	67.4	65.0	60.4	52.9	56.3	50.6
1978	63.3	50.8	72.0	65.7	64.7	49.1	50.3	53.1	66.9	74.5	74.7	69.1	65.5	62.6	68.1	65.5	60.4
1979	68.1	57.9	73.7	70.7	70.0	56.6	57.3	59.8	64.5	79.3	77.3	73.8	70.3	68.0	70.0	71.8	68.3
1980	53.9	64.4	66.9	50.5	33.9	65.3	64.8	63.2	66.6	70.5	63.6	56.3	51.6	43.5	37.4	33.4	30.8
1981	20.9	25.2	24.5	19.0	15.0	27.4	25.4	22.9	24.6	25.4	23.5	20.9	18.5	17.7	16.6	14.8	13.6
1982	11.3	12.6	12.7	11.1	8.8	12.6	12.9	12.2	12.4	13.1	12.6	11.6	11.6	10.2	9.0	9.1	8.2
1983	9.5	8.5	9.4	10.1	10.0	8.5	8.3	8.6	9.0	9.1	10.1	8.9	10.3	11.1	10.7	9.9	9.4

Hourly rates: manufacturing (8)(11) — Taux horaires : industries manufacturières (8)(11)

1980 = 100

	Year	Q.1	Q.2	Q.3	Q.4	JAN	FEB	MAR	APR	MAY	JUN	JUL	AUG	SEP	OCT	NOV	DEC
1964																	
1965																	
1966																	
1967																	
1968																	
1969																	
1970	39	37	38	40	40	37	37	38	38	38	38	40	40	40	40	40	40
1971	44	42	43	44	45	42	42	42	43	43	43	44	44	45	45	45	45
1972	49	48	49	50	51	47	48	48	49	49	49	50	50	50	51	51	51
1973	56	54	55	57	58	53	54	54	55	55	55	57	57	57	58	58	58
1974	66	62	65	67	68	62	62	62	65	65	65	67	68	68	68	68	68
1975	74	72	73	76	76	71	71	72	73	73	73	76	76	76	76	76	76
1976	81	80	80	81	82	80	80	80	80	80	80	81	81	81	81	83	83
1977	87	84	85	88	88	84	84	85	85	85	85	88	88	88	88	88	88
1978	92	91	91	92	93	91	91	91	91	91	91	92	92	92	93	93	93
1979	96	95	95	97	97	95	95	95	95	95	95	97	97	97	97	97	97
1980	100	99	99	101	101	99	99	99	99	99	99	101	101	101	101	101	101
1981	103	101	102	105	105	101	101	102	102	102	102	104	105	105	105	105	105
1982	110	109	109	112	112	109	109	109	109	109	109	112	112	112	112	112	112
1983	113	113	113	113	113	113	113	113	113	113	113	113	113	113	113	113	113

Producer prices: total (12) (output of industry) — Prix à la production : total (12) (produits industriels)

1980 = 100

	Year	Q.1	Q.2	Q.3	Q.4	JAN	FEB	MAR	APR	MAY	JUN	JUL	AUG	SEP	OCT	NOV	DEC
1964																	
1965																	
1966																	
1967																	
1968																	
1969																	
1970																	
1971																	
1972																	
1973																	
1974																	
1975																	
1976	80	78	79	81	81	78	78	78	79	79	80	80	81	81	81	81	81
1977	83	82	84	84	83	82	83	83	83	84	84	84	84	84	83	83	84
1978	83	83	83	83	83	83	83	83	83	83	83	83	83	83	83	83	83
1979	89	86	88	91	93	85	86	86	87	88	88	90	91	91	92	93	93
1980	100	97	100	101	102	97	97	98	100	100	100	101	101	101	101	102	103
1981	114	108	112	117	113	107	108	109	111	112	113	116	117	117	118	118	118
1982	122	121	121	122	122	121	121	121	121	122	122	122	122	122	122	122	121
1983	122	121	121	122	124	121	121	121	121	121	121	122	122	123	124	124	125

Jobs vacant, unfilled vacancies (8)
thousands

Adjusted - Corrigé

Offres d'emploi non satisfaites (8)
milliers

	Year	Q.1	Q.2	Q.3	Q.4	JAN	FEB	MAR	APR	MAY	JUN	JUL	AUG	SEP	OCT	NOV	DEC
1964		128.8	129.3	131.9	133.8	128.6	129.0	128.7	129.5	128.8	129.6	131.7	132.1	132.0	133.3	134.2	133.9
1965		133.1	127.5	126.3	131.0	134.6	133.0	131.8	125.9	126.7	125.9	125.0	126.2	127.8	129.5	131.3	132.1
1966		130.0	123.3	112.9	92.9	130.6	130.5	128.8	125.4	124.1	120.5	116.8	112.5	109.4	104.6	92.3	81.9
1967		73.1	70.0	67.1	63.1	74.2	73.0	72.0	71.1	69.9	68.9	68.2	67.6	65.4	62.9	63.0	63.3
1968		68.0	74.6	77.8	88.3	65.5	68.1	70.4	72.5	74.3	77.2	75.8	77.3	80.3	83.7	89.3	91.8
1969		95.4	102.2	109.3	117.3	93.8	95.0	97.5	99.1	102.0	105.7	106.8	109.1	111.9	114.9	117.5	119.6
1970		123.2	124.6	127.7	132.8	122.8	123.1	123.9	125.2	123.9	124.7	127.4	126.9	129.0	130.8	133.1	134.4
1971		128.2	113.6	101.5	83.1	132.1	129.0	123.6	119.7	114.1	107.1	104.4	102.7	97.4	91.2	82.6	75.6
1972		70.1	64.3	61.3	57.3	70.7	70.0	69.6	66.5	64.2	63.8	62.7	62.0	59.0	57.0	56.5	58.4
1973		61.1	63.0	70.1	74.0	61.7	60.8	60.8	60.1	62.9	66.2	68.9	69.0	72.5	73.7	75.3	72.9
1974		69.6	71.8	74.0	61.7	69.6	69.4	69.7	67.6	70.9	76.8	76.7	74.7	70.6	64.3	61.1	59.8
1975		54.3	48.7	42.0	43.8	57.1	54.3	51.5	53.4	48.8	43.8	40.6	42.7	42.8	43.6	44.0	43.9
1976		44.1	46.6	45.9	51.6	43.7	43.7	44.9	47.7	47.5	44.5	44.1	45.2	48.5	52.0	51.7	51.3
1977		51.7	49.9	60.9	59.1	51.8	51.5	51.7	43.7	50.7	55.3	60.9	61.7	60.0	60.1	58.5	58.7
1978		59.4	63.6	62.8	67.5	59.1	59.7	59.4	64.7	62.5	63.7	62.7	62.5	63.2	66.9	67.9	67.5
1979		65.2	65.6	68.6	72.9	65.2	64.9	65.4	62.2	67.6	67.0	68.1	68.0	69.7	70.5	74.0	74.1
1980		70.8	60.2	48.9	35.9	73.1	71.0	63.1	64.5	60.7	55.5	52.4	49.7	44.5	38.8	35.1	33.6
1981		27.5	22.1	18.2	16.0	30.4	27.5	24.6	23.9	22.0	20.4	19.5	17.6	17.6	17.3	15.6	14.9
1982		13.6	11.6	10.7	9.3	13.9	13.9	13.0	12.0	11.6	11.1	11.1	10.9	10.0	9.4	9.5	9.1
1983		9.1	8.6	9.7	10.6	9.3	8.9	9.0	8.7	8.1	9.0	8.6	9.6	10.3	11.0	10.4	10.5

Producer prices: investment goods (12)(13)
(output of industry)
1980 = 100

Prix à la production : biens d'équipement (12) (13)
(produits industriels)
1980 = 100

	Year	Q.1	Q.2	Q.3	Q.4	JAN	FEB	MAR	APR	MAY	JUN	JUL	AUG	SEP	OCT	NOV	DEC
1964																	
1965																	
1966																	
1967																	
1968																	
1969																	
1970																	
1971	61	60	61	61	62	60	60	60	61	61	61	61	62	62	62	62	62
1972	64	64	64	64	64	64	64	64	64	64	64	64	64	64	64	64	64
1973	68	66	67	68	69	66	66	67	67	67	67	68	68	68	68	69	69
1974	75	72	74	76	77	72	72	73	74	74	74	76	76	76	76	77	77
1975	=81=	80	81	82	82	79	80	81	81	81	81	82	82	82	82	82	83
1976	86	85	86	87	88	84	84	85	86	86	86	87	87	87	87	87	88
1977	90	89	90	90	90	89	89	89	90	90	90	90	90	90	90	90	90
1978	92	92	92	93	93	92	92	92	92	92	92	92	93	93	93	93	93
1979	96	94	95	96	97	94	94	95	95	95	96	96	96	96	96	97	97
1980	100	99	100	100	101	99	100	100	100	100	100	100	100	101	101	101	101
1981	105	104	105	106	106	104	104	104	104	105	105	105	106	106	106	106	106
1982	110	110	110	111	111	109	110	110	110	110	110	111	111	111	111	111	111
1983	112	113	112	112	113	112	113	113	112	112	112	112	112	113	113	113	113

Producer prices: consumer goods (12)(13)
(output of industry)
1980 = 100

Prix à la production : biens de consommation (12) (13)
(produits industriels)
1980 = 100

	Year	Q.1	Q.2	Q.3	Q.4	JAN	FEB	MAR	APR	MAY	JUN	JUL	AUG	SEP	OCT	NOV	DEC
1964																	
1965																	
1966																	
1967																	
1968																	
1969																	
1970																	
1971	59	58	59	59	60	58	58	59	59	59	59	59	59	59	59	60	60
1972	62	62	62	62	63	61	62	62	62	62	62	62	62	62	63	63	63
1973	66	65	66	67	68	65	65	65	66	66	66	67	67	67	67	68	69
1974	73	71	72	73	75	70	71	71	72	72	72	72	74	74	75	75	75
1975	=78=	76	77	78	79	76	76	76	76	76	77	77	78	78	79	80	80
1976	84	82	83	84	85	82	82	83	83	83	84	84	85	85	85	85	85
1977	89	86	89	90	90	86	86	87	88	89	90	91	90	90	90	90	90
1978	90	90	90	90	90	90	90	90	90	90	90	90	90	90	90	90	90
1979	92	90	91	93	94	90	91	91	91	91	92	92	93	94	94	94	94
1980	100	98	100	101	102	98	98	99	99	100	100	101	101	101	101	102	102
1981	110	106	109	111	113	105	106	107	108	109	109	110	112	113	113	113	113
1982	117	116	117	118	118	116	116	116	116	117	118	118	118	118	118	118	118
1983	119	118	118	120	120	118	118	118	118	118	119	120	121	121	120	120	121

NETHERLANDS

Producer prices: intermediate goods (12)
(output of industry)
1980 = 100

Prix à la production : biens intermédiaires (12)
(produits industriels)
1980 = 100

	Year	Q.1	Q.2	Q.3	Q.4	JAN	FEB	MAR	APR	MAY	JUN	JUL	AUG	SEP	OCT	NOV	DEC
1964																	
1965																	
1966																	
1967																	
1968																	
1969																	
1970																	
1971																	
1972																	
1973																	
1974																	
1975																	
1976	77	76	77	78	78	75	76	76	77	77	77	78	78	79	78	78	78
1977	80	80	81	80	80	80	80	81	81	81	81	81	80	80	80	80	80
1978	80	79	80	80	80	80	80	79	80	80	80	80	80	80	80	80	80
1979	87	83	86	89	92	82	83	83	85	86	86	89	89	90	91	92	92
1980	100	97	100	101	102	96	97	97	100	100	100	101	101	101	101	102	103
1981	116	109	114	120	121	109	109	110	114	114	115	119	120	120	121	121	121
1982	125	125	125	125	124	125	125	125	124	125	125	125	124	125	125	124	124
1983	124	123	123	124	127	124	123	123	123	123	123	123	124	125	127	127	127

Producer prices: crude petroleum (12)(13)
(output of industry)
1980 = 100

Prix à la production : pétrole brut (12)(13)
(produits industriels)
1980 = 100

	Year	Q.1	Q.2	Q.3	Q.4	JAN	FEB	MAR	APR	MAY	JUN	JUL	AUG	SEP	OCT	NOV	DEC
1964																	
1965																	
1966																	
1967																	
1968	15	16	15	16	15	16	16	15	15	15	15	15	16	15	15	15	15
1969	14	14	14	13	14	14	14	14	14	14	14	14	13	13	13	14	14
1970	15	14	14	14	16	14	14	14	14	14	14	14	14	15	15	16	17
1971	18	17	18	18	17	17	17	18	18	18	19	19	18	18	17	17	17
1972	16	16	16	16	16	16	17	16	16	16	16	15	16	16	16	16	16
1973	19	17	18	18	24	17	17	16	18	18	18	16	18	20	20	22	31
1974	61	58	61	62	64	59	59	57	62	60	61	61	61	64	65	63	65
1975	65	61	61	65	72	63	60	59	60	61	61	62	67	67	69	72	73
1976	70	71	71	71	70	72	70	71	69	70	72	70	70	72	71	69	71
1977	76	76	74	76	75	75	77	77	75	74	74	77	76	75	76	74	75
1978	67	70	69	66	61	71	71	68	67	70	70	68	67	62	59	58	67
1979	65	60	58	64	76	60	63	56	53	54	67	65	64	64	61	85	81
1980	100	89	100	100	112	87	89	90	106	97	96	95	102	102	103	116	117
1981	141	127	137	152	147	119	128	133	130	137	144	149	155	152	153	145	143
1982	157	151	155	160	163	145	152	155	158	152	156	161	159	161	163	165	160
1983	125	122	121	128	130	128	121	117	118	120	124	123	129	130	128	130	132

Money supply (M1) (14)(15)
billion guilders, end of period

Disponibilités monétaires (M1) (14)(15)
milliards de florins, fin de période

	Year	Q.1	Q.2	Q.3	Q.4	JAN	FEB	MAR	APR	MAY	JUN	JUL	AUG	SEP	OCT	NOV	DEC
1964	15.44	14.28	15.07	15.12	15.44	14.29	14.30	14.28	14.50	14.97	15.07	15.09	15.09	15.12	15.00	15.25	15.44
1965	16.99	15.65	16.79	16.87	16.99	15.50	15.54	15.65	16.02	16.61	16.79	16.99	17.02	16.87	16.87	16.94	16.99
1966	18.16	16.87	18.41	17.82	18.16	16.91	16.90	16.87	17.35	17.92	18.41	18.27	17.89	17.82	17.58	17.87	18.16
1967	19.29	18.13	19.79	19.37	19.29	17.72	17.82	18.13	18.58	19.14	19.79	19.45	19.15	19.37	18.97	19.26	19.29
1968	21.49	19.54	21.46	20.96	21.49	19.39	19.10	19.54	19.96	20.74	21.46	21.10	21.00	20.96	20.74	21.14	21.49
1969	23.22	21.37	23.34	22.56	23.22	21.56	21.35	21.37	21.97	22.86	23.34	23.05	22.70	22.56	23.01	22.99	23.22
1970	25.95	23.41	25.67	25.54	25.95	23.15	22.86	23.41	24.24	25.33	25.67	25.77	25.40	25.54	25.44	25.81	25.95
1971	29.85	27.13	30.10	29.94	29.85	26.63	26.65	27.13	28.58	30.39	30.10	30.12	29.43	29.94	29.79	29.85	29.85
1972	35.12	32.27	35.69	36.11	35.12	30.16	30.03	32.27	33.62	34.97	35.69	35.94	36.07	36.11	34.72	35.44	35.12
1973	35.14	37.47	39.05	36.10	35.14	35.48	35.38	37.47	38.79	39.42	39.05	37.12	35.87	36.10	35.13	35.68	35.14
1974	39.43	36.05	39.74	38.49	39.43	35.02	35.27	36.05	37.08	39.59	39.74	38.61	38.17	38.49	38.12	38.64	39.43
1975	47.19	40.50	47.39	46.91	47.19	39.33	39.07	40.50	42.48	47.67	47.39	48.08	47.47	46.91	46.21	46.63	47.19
1976	50.26	49.04	52.84	48.73	50.26	47.89	48.34	49.04	51.37	54.16	52.84	51.60	47.92	48.73	50.02	49.83	50.26
1977	57.53	52.47	61.69	58.59	57.53	51.67	51.33	52.47	54.95	61.52	61.69	61.52	58.81	58.59	57.44	56.74	57.53
1978	60.24	57.83	64.36	60.97	60.24	57.29	56.74	57.83	60.17	63.73	64.36	62.95	60.89	60.97	57.63	59.67	60.24
1979	61.60	59.31	66.04	62.31	61.60	59.10	59.09	59.31	60.51	65.84	66.04	63.00	61.53	62.31	61.73	61.82	61.60
1980	65.59	62.19	68.36	65.03	65.59	61.47	61.88	62.19	63.08	68.78	68.36	66.10	64.68	65.03	65.28	64.85	65.59
1981	64.04	64.84	69.49	65.20	64.04	65.96	65.35	64.84	66.98	71.33	69.49	67.07	65.31	65.20	65.95	65.84	64.04
1982	70.49	67.65	73.78	70.05	70.49	66.37	65.70	67.65	68.93	73.42	73.78	71.28	69.56	70.05	69.91	70.08	70.49
1983	77.47	76.40	81.08	76.24	77.47	73.08	73.56	76.40	76.44	80.37	81.08	78.48	75.81	76.24	76.91	80.02	77.47

Producer prices: total (13)
(input to industry)
1980 = 100

Prix à la production : total (13)
(produits de base pour l'industrie)
1980 = 100

	Year	Q.1	Q.2	Q.3	Q.4	JAN	FEB	MAR	APR	MAY	JUN	JUL	AUG	SEP	OCT	NOV	DEC
1964																	
1965																	
1966																	
1967																	
1968																	
1969																	
1970																	
1971	45	45	45	45	45	44	44	45	45	45	45	45	45	45	45	45	45
1972	45	45	45	45	47	45	44	44	44	44	45	44	44	45	46	47	47
1973	52	48	50	52	56	48	48	48	49	50	51	51	52	53	54	57	58
1974	69	67	69	69	71	66	67	69	70	69	69	69	69	70	71	71	70
1975	70	69	69	70	73	70	69	69	69	69	68	69	71	71	73	73	74
1976	76	75	76	77	77	74	75	75	76	76	76	76	77	77	77	77	76
1977	78	78	79	78	78	78	78	79	79	79	79	78	78	78	78	78	78
1978	76	75	75	75	77	76	75	75	75	75	75	75	75	75	78	78	75
1979	84	77	82	86	90	76	77	78	80	82	83	85	87	87	89	90	91
1980	100	97	100	100	104	95	97	99	101	99	99	99	100	101	102	104	106
1981	120	112	119	125	124	109	112	114	117	120	121	125	126	125	124	124	124
1982	126	127	125	126	126	126	127	127	125	124	126	126	126	125	126	126	125
1983	124	122	121	124	128	124	122	120	120	121	122	122	125	126	127	128	129

Consumer prices: all items (16)
1980 = 100

Prix à la consommation : total (16)
1980 = 100

	Year	Q.1	Q.2	Q.3	Q.4	JAN	FEB	MAR	APR	MAY	JUN	JUL	AUG	SEP	OCT	NOV	DEC
1964	37.6	36.7	37.9	37.9	37.9	36.6	36.6	37.0	38.6	37.6	37.6	37.6	37.9	38.3	37.9	37.9	37.9
1965	39.1	38.3	39.0	39.4	39.8	38.1	38.3	38.5	38.8	39.0	39.1	39.1	39.4	39.6	39.6	39.8	40.0
1966	41.4	40.9	41.5	41.5	41.6	40.5	41.0	41.2	41.5	41.5	41.6	41.3	41.5	41.6	41.6	41.6	41.6
1967	42.8	42.1	42.6	43.1	43.3	41.9	42.2	42.4	42.6	42.6	42.7	42.8	43.1	43.3	43.4	43.3	43.3
1968	44.4	43.8	44.3	44.5	45.0	43.6	43.8	44.0	44.2	44.2	44.3	44.2	44.6	44.7	45.0	45.0	45.1
1969	47.7	47.1	47.8	47.7	48.1	46.7	47.1	47.5	47.9	47.8	47.8	47.4	47.7	48.0	48.2	48.1	48.1
1970	49.4	48.4	49.2	49.7	50.4	48.1	48.4	48.8	49.1	49.1	49.3	49.4	49.7	50.1	50.3	50.4	50.5
1971	53.1	51.6	52.9	53.5	54.5	51.0	51.7	52.0	52.7	52.9	53.0	53.1	53.5	53.9	54.3	54.5	54.8
1972	57.3	55.7	57.0	57.5	58.9	55.2	55.7	56.1	56.9	57.0	57.2	57.0	57.4	58.0	58.7	59.0	59.1
1973	61.9	59.9	61.7	62.2	63.6	59.6	59.8	60.4	61.4	61.8	61.9	61.8	62.1	62.7	63.3	63.6	64.0
1974	67.8	65.2	67.2	68.3	70.6	64.4	65.1	66.0	66.9	67.2	67.4	67.6	68.2	69.2	70.1	70.6	70.9
1975	74.7	72.1	74.1	75.5	77.3	71.6	71.8	72.8	73.7	74.2	74.3	74.7	75.5	76.4	77.1	77.3	77.4
1976	81.3	78.6	81.2	81.8	83.8	77.8	78.6	79.3	81.0	81.3	81.3	80.9	81.8	82.6	83.8	83.9	83.9
1977	86.6	84.5	86.6	87.1	88.1	83.9	84.5	84.9	86.4	86.6	86.7	86.7	87.1	87.6	88.0	88.1	88.1
1978	90.1	88.3	89.6	90.8	91.6	87.8	88.2	88.9	89.5	89.7	89.6	90.3	90.7	91.4	91.6	91.6	91.6
1979	93.9	92.1	93.4	94.3	95.8	91.4	91.9	92.8	93.4	93.4	93.4	93.7	94.2	95.0	95.7	95.8	96.0
1980	100.0	97.4	99.5	101.0	102.2	96.5	97.4	98.3	99.3	99.6	99.5	100.4	100.8	101.6	102.1	102.2	102.4
1981	106.7	103.9	105.9	107.6	109.6	103.1	103.7	104.8	105.6	106.1	106.1	107.0	107.3	108.5	109.3	109.7	109.7
1982	113.1	111.1	112.8	113.9	114.6	110.3	110.9	112.0	112.6	112.9	113.0	113.5	113.7	114.4	114.7	114.7	114.4
1983	116.2	114.7	115.5	116.6	117.8	114.5	114.7	114.9	115.3	115.5	115.6	116.2	116.6	117.1	117.6	117.9	117.9

Money supply (M1) (15)
billion guilders, end of period

Adjusted - Corrigé *

Disponibilités monétaires (M1) (15)
milliards de florins, fin de période

	Year	Q.1	Q.2	Q.3	Q.4	JAN	FEB	MAR	APR	MAY	JUN	JUL	AUG	SEP	OCT	NOV	DEC
1964		14.61	14.64	15.09	15.50	14.46	14.55	14.61	14.62	14.72	14.64	14.75	14.89	15.09	15.23	15.34	15.50
1965		16.02	16.24	16.83	17.10	15.71	15.85	16.02	16.15	16.30	16.24	16.59	16.82	16.83	17.12	17.06	17.10
1966		17.27	17.72	17.77	18.30	17.13	17.32	17.27	17.47	17.55	17.72	17.82	17.71	17.77	17.86	18.01	18.30
1967		18.56	18.97	19.31	19.50	17.97	18.31	18.56	18.70	18.71	18.97	18.96	18.98	19.31	19.28	19.44	19.50
1968		20.03	20.53	20.90	21.79	19.68	19.69	20.03	20.02	20.20	20.53	20.53	20.84	20.90	21.07	21.38	21.79
1969		21.90	22.32	22.47	23.67	21.91	22.08	21.90	21.97	22.18	22.32	22.38	22.52	22.47	23.38	23.29	23.67
1970		23.96	24.52	25.41	26.59	23.60	23.72	23.96	24.14	24.43	24.52	24.99	25.22	25.41	25.85	26.20	26.59
1971		27.71	28.70	29.79	30.71	27.29	27.73	27.71	28.35	29.11	28.70	29.21	29.23	29.79	30.31	30.39	30.71
1972		32.92	33.92	35.97	36.21	31.06	31.31	32.92	33.25	33.24	33.92	34.83	35.85	35.97	35.42	36.16	36.21
1973		38.24	36.93	36.06	36.26	36.65	36.93	38.24	38.33	37.22	36.98	35.94	35.65	36.06	35.95	36.49	36.26
1974		36.82	37.49	38.57	40.65	36.21	36.85	36.82	36.71	37.11	37.49	37.31	37.98	38.57	39.09	39.63	40.65
1975		41.50	44.58	47.15	48.55	40.67	40.78	41.50	42.14	44.46	44.58	46.37	47.33	47.15	47.44	47.92	48.55
1976		50.40	49.57	49.07	51.61	49.43	50.41	50.40	51.16	50.38	49.57	49.67	47.83	49.07	51.36	51.26	51.61
1977		53.98	57.82	59.00	58.95	53.27	53.41	53.98	54.90	57.23	57.82	59.27	58.81	59.00	58.85	58.32	58.95
1978		59.61	60.32	61.27	61.59	59.00	58.86	59.61	60.29	59.34	60.32	60.88	61.01	61.27	58.87	61.27	61.59
1979		61.15	61.89	62.63	62.85	60.37	61.11	61.15	60.75	61.36	61.89	61.17	61.72	62.63	62.99	63.41	62.85
1980		64.11	64.07	65.29	66.86	63.31	63.86	64.11	63.46	64.16	64.07	64.43	64.88	65.29	66.54	66.38	66.86
1981		66.85	65.19	65.39	65.21	68.00	67.37	66.85	67.45	66.60	65.19	65.50	65.50	65.39	67.16	67.39	65.21
1982		69.67	69.21	70.19	71.79	68.42	67.66	69.67	69.41	68.62	69.21	69.67	69.84	70.19	71.12	71.73	71.79
1983		78.69	76.06	76.39	78.89	75.34	75.76	78.69	76.97	75.11	76.06	76.72	76.11	76.39	78.24	81.90	78.89

* Adjusted by the O.E.C.D.

* Corrigé par l'O.C.D.E.

NETHERLANDS

M1 plus quasi-money (14)(15)

billion guilders, end of period

(15)
M1 plus quasi-monnaie (14)

milliards de florins, fin de période

	Year	Q.1	Q.2	Q.3	Q.4	JAN	FEB	MAR	APR	MAY	JUN	JUL	AUG	SEP	OCT	NOV	DEC
1964	21.97	20.30	20.62	21.31	21.97	20.28	20.31	20.30	20.53	20.56	20.62	21.12	21.29	21.31	21.02	21.20	21.97
1965	23.32	22.78	23.45	23.82	23.32	22.40	22.51	22.78	23.15	23.23	23.45	23.38	23.84	23.82	23.17	23.45	23.32
1966	24.70	23.24	24.69	24.52	24.70	23.39	23.38	23.24	23.89	24.19	24.69	24.92	24.94	24.52	23.67	24.18	24.70
1967	27.39	25.23	26.66	27.23	27.39	24.59	24.86	25.23	25.79	26.23	26.66	26.66	26.74	27.23	26.55	27.19	27.39
1968	31.45	28.62	30.77	31.09	31.45	28.01	28.08	28.62	29.24	30.02	30.77	31.08	31.21	31.09	30.50	31.03	31.45
1969	34.64	32.19	34.47	34.66	34.64	31.60	31.83	32.19	32.90	33.93	34.47	34.96	34.79	34.66	34.21	33.97	34.64
1970	38.46	36.07	38.45	38.53	38.46	35.04	34.86	36.07	36.90	38.12	38.45	39.17	38.82	38.53	37.81	37.79	38.46
1971	41.91	39.19	41.16	41.58	41.91	38.61	38.70	39.19	39.84	41.39	41.16	41.42	41.26	41.58	41.45	41.44	41.91
1972	46.90	43.22	46.36	46.64	46.90	42.97	41.55	43.22	43.94	45.39	46.36	46.49	46.83	46.64	45.82	46.94	46.90
1973	57.19	50.27	53.29	55.58	57.19	47.92	48.03	50.27	51.37	53.13	53.29	53.23	54.54	55.58	55.14	56.25	57.19
1974	68.66	61.01	67.11	68.44	68.66	58.36	59.34	61.01	62.27	66.67	67.11	67.81	68.49	68.44	67.51	68.14	68.66
1975	72.58	70.45	74.36	71.99	72.58	67.92	69.07	70.45	72.07	75.54	74.36	73.49	72.95	71.99	71.40	72.56	72.58
1976	90.74	76.69	83.43	87.66	90.74	74.98	75.48	76.69	80.05	82.47	83.43	84.98	86.87	87.66	88.48	88.53	90.74
1977	92.20	96.61	96.39	92.45	92.20	91.35	92.32	96.61	98.93	99.06	96.39	94.44	92.38	92.45	90.45	91.62	92.20
1978	96.17	96.02	100.09	97.53	96.17	93.50	93.71	96.02	97.63	99.57	100.09	99.12	97.84	97.53	95.48	96.39	96.17
1979	102.60	98.84	104.81	100.87	102.60	95.43	96.34	98.84	100.69	103.04	104.81	101.38	100.70	100.87	99.16	101.10	102.60
1980	106.83	104.94	110.48	107.11	106.83	102.09	103.37	104.94	107.02	112.50	110.48	107.31	107.31	107.11	106.42	106.81	106.83
1981	112.40	113.97	117.74	114.42	112.40	108.21	111.23	113.97	115.90	120.35	117.74	116.48	114.60	114.42	113.91	114.19	112.40
1982	121.05	122.03	127.33	123.73	121.05	116.07	118.47	122.03	125.55	128.22	127.33	125.38	123.01	123.73	123.40	123.13	121.05
1983	133.93	133.75	139.82	135.59	133.93	124.68	125.66	133.75	135.79	139.87	139.82	136.57	134.05	135.59	133.72	136.25	133.93

Savings deposits (14)

billion guilders, end of period

Dépôts d'épargne (14)

milliards de florins, fin de période

	Year	Q.1	Q.2	Q.3	Q.4	JAN	FEB	MAR	APR	MAY	JUN	JUL	AUG	SEP	OCT	NOV	DEC
1964	18.03	16.53	16.93	17.31	18.03	16.20	16.40	16.53	16.57	16.80	16.93	17.11	17.23	17.31	17.38	17.49	18.03
1965	20.04	18.44	18.81	19.31	20.04	18.16	18.35	18.44	18.45	18.67	18.81	19.02	19.21	19.31	19.41	19.50	20.04
1966	22.09	20.45	20.83	21.26	22.09	20.18	20.39	20.45	20.49	20.67	20.83	21.04	21.25	21.26	21.30	21.41	22.09
1967	25.19	22.59	23.31	24.06	25.19	22.25	22.46	22.59	22.70	23.02	23.31	23.61	23.87	24.06	24.22	24.33	25.19
1968	28.05	25.75	26.42	27.09	28.05	25.49	25.67	25.75	25.82	26.18	26.42	26.76	26.97	27.09	27.22	27.28	28.05
1969	31.33	28.92	29.54	30.16	31.33	28.42	28.74	28.92	29.04	29.29	29.54	29.79	30.02	30.16	30.28	30.34	31.33
1970	34.80	31.98	32.44	33.34	34.80	31.56	31.80	31.98	32.04	32.23	32.44	32.76	33.09	33.34	33.49	33.61	34.80
1971	40.17	35.87	37.28	38.26	40.17	35.16	35.52	35.87	36.21	36.78	37.28	37.65	38.01	38.26	38.46	38.69	40.17
1972	46.07	41.23	42.97	44.13	46.07	40.49	40.84	41.23	41.70	42.38	42.97	43.36	43.77	44.13	44.45	44.59	46.07
1973	49.64	47.10	48.52	48.64	49.64	46.40	46.76	47.10	47.31	47.99	48.52	48.70	48.67	48.64	48.59	48.49	49.64
1974	51.39	49.26	49.42	49.26	51.39	49.40	49.31	49.26	49.11	49.26	49.42	49.34	49.28	49.26	49.22	49.36	51.39
1975	61.20	52.05	55.99	58.30	51.20	51.54	51.78	52.05	52.63	54.22	55.99	56.96	57.64	58.30	58.76	59.00	61.20
1976	66.50	63.30	65.14	63.49	66.50	61.61	62.45	63.30	63.73	64.58	65.14	65.02	64.18	63.49	63.46	63.75	66.50
1977	78.64	68.00	73.10	75.88	78.64	67.12	67.56	68.00	68.55	71.16	73.10	74.09	75.17	75.88	76.42	76.44	78.64
1978	93.64	80.72	87.98	90.73	93.64	79.33	80.14	80.72	85.25	86.67	87.98	88.95	90.04	90.73	92.29	93.01	93.64
1979	104.94	96.47	99.34	101.99	104.94	94.83	95.73	96.47	96.90	98.13	99.34	100.41	101.33	101.99	103.03	104.11	104.94
1980	114.88	108.16	111.01	113.10	114.88	106.08	107.10	108.16	108.58	109.72	111.01	111.68	112.44	113.10	113.94	114.71	114.38
1981	127.07	118.24	121.58	125.02	127.07	116.12	117.07	118.24	118.63	120.14	121.58	122.50	123.97	125.02	125.97	126.95	127.07
1982	134.58	130.61	133.34	135.34	134.58	128.63	129.78	130.61	131.05	132.19	133.34	134.11	135.09	135.34	135.77	135.54	134.58
1983	135.11	133.92	135.49	135.83	135.11	134.21	134.28	133.92	134.04	134.85	135.49	135.28	135.77	135.83	135.82	135.97	135.11

Credit to private sector (commercial banks): (14)

short-term

billion guilders, end of period

Crédits au secteur privé (banques commerciales) : (14)

court terme

milliards de florins, fin de période

	Year	Q.1	Q.2	Q.3	Q.4	JAN	FEB	MAR	APR	MAY	JUN	JUL	AUG	SEP	OCT	NOV	DEC
1964	5.96	5.69	5.88	5.95	5.96	5.43	5.51	5.69	5.87	5.84	5.88	5.91	5.86	5.95	6.03	5.95	5.96
1965	6.56	6.24	6.23	6.32	6.56	6.13	6.20	6.24	6.35	6.30	6.23	6.29	6.26	6.32	6.48	6.54	6.56
1966	7.20	7.25	7.05	7.17	7.20	6.85	7.07	7.25	7.36	7.18	7.05	7.11	7.18	7.17	7.34	7.21	7.20
1967	8.91	7.66	8.03	8.34	8.91	7.32	7.49	7.66	7.78	7.84	8.08	8.21	8.30	8.34	8.73	8.68	8.91
1968	10.90	9.41	9.77	10.28	10.90	9.10	9.32	9.41	9.61	9.55	9.77	9.88	10.04	10.23	10.54	10.54	10.90
1969	11.95	10.96	11.50	11.84	11.95	10.58	10.71	10.96	11.11	11.32	11.50	11.60	11.70	11.84	11.82	11.82	11.95
1970	13.01	12.74	12.84	12.70	13.01	12.09	12.39	12.74	12.65	12.78	12.84	12.73	12.77	12.70	13.01	12.99	13.01
1971	14.55	13.08	13.43	13.80	14.55	12.92	13.26	13.08	13.08	13.45	13.43	13.39	13.64	13.80	14.47	14.34	14.55
1972	16.77	14.88	15.88	16.22	16.77	14.46	14.65	14.88	15.36	15.42	15.89	15.85	15.92	16.22	16.73	16.33	16.77
1973	22.55	17.88	19.61	21.43	22.55	16.93	17.40	17.88	18.31	18.58	19.61	19.89	20.50	21.43	22.04	21.83	22.55
1974	28.29	23.30	25.25	27.21	28.29	22.70	23.08	23.30	23.88	24.44	25.25	25.83	26.55	27.21	27.64	27.64	28.29
1975	29.99	29.32	29.54	29.47	29.99	28.52	28.99	29.32	29.64	29.60	29.54	28.92	29.17	29.47	29.67	29.77	29.99
1976	34.92	31.25	33.43	34.77	34.92	30.07	30.72	31.25	32.26	32.64	33.43	33.27	34.99	34.77	34.89	34.41	34.92
1977	44.12	38.58	40.22	41.65	44.12	35.43	36.65	38.58	39.68	40.20	40.22	39.34	40.79	41.65	42.50	42.97	44.12
1978	52.37	46.00	48.62	50.12	52.37	44.41	45.04	46.00	46.63	47.48	48.62	48.77	48.92	50.12	51.51	50.70	52.37
1979	60.28	54.14	55.31	57.13	60.28	52.88	53.62	54.14	55.46	55.03	55.31	55.84	56.46	57.13	59.02	58.93	60.28
1980	65.15	61.63	62.93	63.83	65.15	59.66	61.18	61.63	61.86	62.00	62.93	62.88	63.51	63.83	64.45	64.09	65.15
1981	68.56	65.09	66.82	65.96	68.56	64.38	64.97	65.09	66.47	66.46	66.82	67.15	67.00	66.96	67.75	67.65	68.56
1982	69.73	71.82	71.05	71.64	69.73	69.87	70.54	71.82	72.38	72.52	71.05	71.50	70.77	71.64	72.12	70.28	69.73
1983	70.09	71.32	71.08	71.32	70.09	71.47	71.98	71.32	72.32	70.42	71.08	70.53	69.10	71.32	72.25	70.31	70.09

M1 plus quasi-money / M1 plus quasi-monnaie

billion guilders, end of period — Adjusted - Corrigé * — milliards de florins, fin de période

	Year	Q.1	Q.2	Q.3	Q.4	JAN	FEB	MAR	APR	MAY	JUN	JUL	AUG	SEP	OCT	NOV	DEC
1964		20.46	20.45	21.22	22.13	20.35	20.34	20.46	20.40	20.44	20.45	20.70	20.95	21.22	21.46	21.59	22.13
1965		22.99	23.17	23.67	23.52	22.50	22.60	22.99	23.05	23.06	23.17	23.41	23.45	23.67	23.68	23.85	23.52
1966		23.48	24.29	24.33	24.93	23.55	23.55	23.48	23.82	23.97	24.29	24.40	24.54	24.33	24.20	24.58	24.93
1967		25.52	26.12	27.00	27.69	24.82	25.14	25.52	25.74	25.92	26.12	26.04	26.30	27.00	27.14	27.66	27.69
1968		28.96	30.06	30.83	31.83	28.37	28.50	28.96	29.21	29.56	30.06	30.30	30.71	30.83	31.12	31.61	31.83
1969		32.56	33.62	34.39	35.13	32.06	32.41	32.56	32.88	33.30	33.62	34.05	34.21	34.39	34.85	34.67	35.13
1970		36.43	37.49	38.25	39.08	35.60	35.58	36.43	36.87	37.27	37.49	38.18	38.20	38.25	38.46	38.59	39.08
1971		39.55	40.13	41.32	42.66	39.25	39.56	39.55	39.76	40.33	40.13	40.43	40.60	41.32	42.15	42.34	42.66
1972		43.58	45.20	46.40	47.83	43.71	42.48	43.58	43.78	44.06	45.20	45.50	46.15	46.40	46.61	47.93	47.83
1973		50.67	51.94	55.40	58.39	48.74	49.05	50.67	51.06	51.41	51.94	52.21	53.81	55.40	56.15	57.44	58.39
1974		61.40	65.42	68.38	70.15	59.36	60.51	61.40	61.69	64.33	65.42	66.69	67.74	68.38	68.85	69.59	70.15
1975		70.78	72.49	72.12	74.17	69.06	70.29	70.78	71.14	72.80	72.49	72.37	72.34	72.12	72.94	74.15	74.17
1976		76.84	81.29	88.03	92.79	76.30	76.63	76.84	78.77	79.37	81.29	83.79	86.46	88.03	90.55	90.44	92.79
1977		96.57	93.77	93.00	94.38	92.98	93.52	96.57	97.13	95.28	93.77	93.21	92.18	93.00	92.67	93.63	94.38
1978		95.71	97.20	98.21	98.68	95.34	94.79	95.71	95.70	95.63	97.20	97.92	97.87	98.21	97.92	98.51	98.68
1979		98.33	101.56	101.64	105.66	97.46	97.34	98.33	98.59	98.77	101.56	100.16	100.91	101.64	101.68	103.39	105.66
1980		104.24	106.78	108.02	110.59	104.53	104.41	104.24	104.65	107.49	106.78	105.99	107.73	108.02	109.17	109.30	110.59
1981		113.08	113.52	115.41	116.75	110.86	112.33	113.08	113.14	114.68	113.52	115.04	115.14	115.41	116.73	116.85	116.75
1982		121.01	122.63	124.86	126.15	119.13	119.80	121.01	122.41	121.91	122.63	123.32	123.71	124.86	126.43	126.01	126.15
1983		132.52	134.61	136.92	139.89	127.99	127.08	132.52	132.28	132.82	134.61	134.86	134.91	136.92	137.02	139.52	139.89

Credit to private sector (commercial banks): (14) medium- and long-term / Crédits au secteur privé (banques commerciales) : (14) moyen et long terme

billion guilders, end of period — milliards de florins, fin de période

	Year	Q.1	Q.2	Q.3	Q.4	JAN	FEB	MAR	APR	MAY	JUN	JUL	AUG	SEP	OCT	NOV	DEC
1964	0.99	0.74	0.84	0.94	0.99	0.70	0.69	0.74	0.75	0.81	0.84	0.87	0.92	0.94	0.96	0.98	0.99
1965	1.48	1.15	1.30	1.42	1.48	1.09	1.11	1.15	1.19	1.25	1.30	1.34	1.38	1.42	1.41	1.45	1.48
1966	2.12	1.66	1.89	1.98	2.12	1.56	1.59	1.66	1.69	1.79	1.89	1.90	1.93	1.98	1.98	2.02	2.12
1967	2.50	2.14	2.19	2.30	2.50	2.09	2.11	2.14	2.15	2.20	2.19	2.19	2.24	2.30	2.38	2.43	2.50
1968	2.78	2.49	2.59	2.66	2.78	2.47	2.47	2.49	2.50	2.56	2.59	2.60	2.63	2.66	2.69	2.72	2.78
1969	4.22	3.00	3.31	3.60	4.22	2.77	2.87	3.00	3.08	3.13	3.31	3.34	3.46	3.60	3.83	3.98	4.22
1970	5.51	4.44	4.99	5.23	5.51	4.25	4.26	4.44	4.61	4.76	4.99	5.10	5.17	5.23	5.35	5.44	5.51
1971	6.81	5.72	6.12	6.47	6.81	5.52	5.56	5.72	5.82	5.98	6.12	6.17	6.27	6.47	6.52	6.66	6.81
1972	8.13	6.99	7.26	7.64	8.13	6.84	7.00	6.99	7.06	7.11	7.26	7.33	7.46	7.64	7.79	7.13	8.13
1973	11.29	8.71	9.17	10.24	11.29	8.27	8.54	8.71	8.88	9.09	9.17	9.65	10.20	10.24	10.66	11.01	11.29
1974	14.44	12.02	12.84	13.71	14.44	11.39	11.74	12.02	12.35	12.61	12.84	13.19	13.56	13.71	14.00	14.30	14.44
1975	17.81	14.76	15.28	16.31	17.81	14.49	14.58	14.76	15.01	15.20	15.28	15.68	15.94	16.31	16.56	17.28	17.81
1976	23.67	18.62	19.81	21.95	23.67	18.12	18.38	18.62	18.73	19.36	19.81	20.39	21.35	21.95	22.56	23.10	23.67
1977	31.28	26.37	27.97	29.13	31.28	24.29	24.78	26.37	27.05	27.66	27.97	28.39	28.63	29.13	29.54	30.08	31.28
1978	40.01	32.97	34.82	36.62	40.01	32.06	32.59	32.97	33.41	34.09	34.82	35.58	36.07	36.62	37.37	38.24	40.01
1979	46.92	41.15	43.18	44.69	46.92	40.38	40.87	41.15	41.31	42.30	43.18	43.46	43.91	44.69	44.97	45.82	46.92
1980	53.49	49.11	50.32	51.76	53.49	47.89	48.27	49.11	49.55	50.09	50.32	50.35	50.96	51.76	52.06	52.77	53.49
1981	57.35	54.71	55.74	56.50	57.35	54.00	54.43	54.71	55.01	55.42	55.74	55.93	56.49	56.50	56.81	57.33	57.35
1982	60.71	57.89	58.64	59.69	60.71	57.41	57.70	57.89	58.03	58.24	58.64	58.81	59.33	59.69	60.06	60.31	60.71
1983	62.22	60.61	61.85	61.78	62.22	60.03	60.04	60.61	60.65	61.66	61.85	62.13	61.27	61.78	61.75	61.86	62.22

New consumer credit / Nouveaux crédits à la consommation

million guilders, monthly averages — millions de florins, moyennes mensuelles

	Year	Q.1	Q.2	Q.3	Q.4	JAN	FEB	MAR	APR	MAY	JUN	JUL	AUG	SEP	OCT	NOV	DEC
1964																	
1965																	
1966																	
1967																	
1968																	
1969																	
1970																	
1971																	
1972																	
1973																	
1974																	
1975																	
1976	379	348	395	365	408	319	323	402	391	392	403	354	341	400	383	425	414
1977	648	591	701	625	673	499	560	715	738	656	708	587	622	665	653	651	716
1978	737	684	777	724	760	662	638	753	810	767	754	700	706	767	776	784	721
1979	724	729	821	668	676	631	657	900	867	847	748	729	614	661	681	697	650
1980	675	705	684	665	646	650	701	765	750	622	679	707	612	677	680	614	643
1981	588	574	623	600	555	565	512	645	662	569	639	678	529	594	577	528	561
1982	572	546	608	585	550	447	542	649	650	545	628	633	551	570	565	545	539
1983	566	547	589	582	547	498	486	657	607	536	625	600	560	586	543	466	632

* Adjusted by the O.E.C.D. — * Corrigé par l'O.C.D.E.

NETHERLANDS

Official discount rate

per cent per annum, end of period

Taux d'escompte officiel

pourcentage par an, fin de période

	Year	Q.1	Q.2	Q.3	Q.4	JAN	FEB	MAR	APR	MAY	JUN	JUL	AUG	SEP	OCT	NOV	DEC
1964	4.50	4.00	4.50	4.50	4.50	4.00	4.00	4.00	4.00	4.00	4.50	4.50	4.50	4.50	4.50	4.50	4.50
1965	4.50	4.50	4.50	4.50	4.50	4.50	4.50	4.50	4.50	4.50	4.50	4.50	4.50	4.50	4.50	4.50	4.50
1966	5.00	4.50	5.00	5.00	5.00	4.50	4.50	4.50	4.50	5.00	5.00	5.00	5.00	5.00	5.00	5.00	5.00
1967	4.50	4.50	4.50	4.50	4.50	5.00	5.00	4.50	4.50	4.50	4.50	4.50	4.50	4.50	4.50	4.50	4.50
1968	5.00	4.50	4.50	4.50	5.00	4.50	4.50	4.50	4.50	4.50	4.50	4.50	4.50	4.50	4.50	4.50	5.00
1969	6.00	5.00	5.50	6.00	6.00	5.00	5.00	5.00	5.50	5.50	5.50	5.50	6.00	6.00	6.00	6.00	6.00
1970	6.00	6.00	6.00	6.00	6.00	6.00	6.00	6.00	6.00	6.00	6.00	6.00	6.00	6.00	6.00	6.00	6.00
1971	5.00	6.00	5.50	5.00	5.00	6.00	6.00	6.00	5.50	5.50	5.50	5.50	5.50	5.00	5.00	5.00	5.00
1972	4.00	4.00	4.00	3.00	4.00	4.50	4.50	4.00	4.00	4.00	4.00	4.00	4.00	3.00	3.00	4.00	4.00
1973	8.00	4.00	5.00	6.50	8.00	4.00	4.00	4.00	4.00	4.00	5.00	6.00	6.50	6.50	7.00	7.00	8.00
1974	7.00	8.00	8.00	8.00	7.00	8.00	8.00	8.00	8.00	8.00	8.00	8.00	8.00	8.00	7.00	7.00	7.00
1975	4.50	6.00	6.00	4.50	4.50	7.00	7.00	6.00	6.00	6.00	6.00	6.00	5.50	4.50	4.50	4.50	4.50
1976	6.00	4.00	5.00	7.00	6.00	4.50	4.00	4.00	4.00	4.00	5.00	5.00	7.00	7.00	7.00	6.00	6.00
1977	4.50	5.00	3.50	3.50	4.50	5.00	5.00	5.00	4.50	3.50	3.50	3.50	3.50	3.50	3.50	4.50	4.50
1978	6.50	4.50	4.00	5.50	6.50	4.50	4.50	4.50	4.00	4.00	4.00	4.50	4.50	5.50	6.50	6.50	6.50
1979	9.50	6.50	7.00	8.00	9.50	6.50	6.50	6.50	6.50	7.00	7.00	8.00	8.00	8.00	8.00	9.50	9.50
1980	8.00	9.50	9.50	8.50	8.00	9.50	9.50	9.50	9.50	10.00	9.50	9.00	9.00	8.50	8.00	8.00	8.00
1981	9.00	9.00	9.00	9.00	9.00	8.00	8.00	9.00	9.00	9.00	9.00	9.00	9.00	9.00	9.00	9.00	9.00
1982	5.00	8.00	8.00	7.00	5.00	8.50	8.50	8.00	8.00	8.00	8.00	8.00	7.00	7.00	6.00	5.50	5.00
1983	5.00	3.50	4.50	5.00	5.00	4.50	4.50	3.50	3.50	4.50	4.50	4.50	4.50	5.00	5.00	5.00	5.00

Call money rate (Amsterdam) (17)(18)

per cent per annum, end of period

Taux de l'argent au jour le jour (Amsterdam) (17) (18)

pourcentage par an, fin de période

	Year	Q.1	Q.2	Q.3	Q.4	JAN	FEB	MAR	APR	MAY	JUN	JUL	AUG	SEP	OCT	NOV	DEC
1964	2.09	2.55	2.06	2.09	2.09	1.67	1.92	2.55	2.48	2.98	2.06	3.72	2.06	2.09	3.24	2.88	2.09
1965	3.47	3.05	2.69	2.66	3.47	2.43	3.69	3.05	3.39	3.67	2.69	3.53	2.68	2.66	3.13	3.91	3.47
1966	3.68	4.05	4.87	3.89	3.68	3.72	4.25	4.05	4.33	4.90	4.87	5.11	4.65	3.39	4.70	5.22	3.68
1967	4.05	4.57	4.38	3.69	4.05	4.31	5.04	4.57	4.25	4.36	4.38	4.38	3.83	3.69	4.60	3.23	4.05
1968	4.96	3.10	4.69	3.74	4.96	3.12	3.65	3.10	3.49	4.53	4.69	4.40	3.81	3.74	4.19	4.86	4.96
1969	7.11	5.38	5.92	7.66	7.11	4.44	5.38	5.38	5.77	5.88	5.92	7.17	7.71	7.66	3.80	5.55	7.11
1970	6.73	7.04	6.92	6.31	6.73	6.76	7.05	7.04	5.57	7.07	6.92	6.96	6.03	6.31	6.89	4.33	6.73
1971	4.85	3.27	2.92	3.80	4.35	4.46	5.41	3.27	1.13	1.84	2.92	2.69	5.53	3.80	5.35	3.79	4.85
1972	3.11	0.82	1.18	0.29	3.11	4.34	3.37	0.82	0.46	2.87	1.18	0.36	0.14	0.29	2.80	3.38	3.11
1973	16.13	0.32	4.46	9.63	16.13	2.76	1.36	0.32	0.59	3.74	4.46	8.47	9.03	9.63	11.36	9.39	16.13
1974	8.20	9.07	9.70	6.04	8.20	11.82	10.86	9.07	9.86	9.87	9.70	10.06	8.30	6.04	8.93	7.74	8.20
1975	4.82	6.28	2.21	1.37	4.82	6.97	8.25	6.28	4.05	2.19	2.21	1.90	2.30	1.37	5.15	4.52	4.82
1976	6.89	2.03	5.62	13.89	6.89	3.92	3.30	2.03	2.98	4.39	5.62	7.45	17.16	13.89	11.08	8.66	6.89
1977	5.34	6.18	0.75	3.02	5.34	6.23	6.09	6.18	4.01	1.23	0.75	0.88	2.69	3.02	4.29	4.82	5.34
1978	10.29	5.33	3.99	5.59	10.29	5.11	5.45	5.33	4.56	4.65	3.99	4.10	3.47	5.59	13.56	8.76	10.29
1979	15.90	7.14	7.57	9.39	15.90	8.64	7.73	7.14	7.09	7.10	7.57	8.63	8.73	9.39	9.28	11.18	15.90
1980	8.60	9.50	10.97	9.89	8.60	11.18	10.99	9.50	10.47	11.14	10.97	10.31	10.09	9.89	9.34	9.05	8.60
1981	10.77	9.90	11.57	11.91	10.77	8.97	9.08	9.90	9.61	10.68	11.57	12.33	12.67	11.91	12.76	11.89	10.77
1982	5.19	7.76	8.14	7.37	5.19	10.18	9.98	7.76	8.43	8.87	8.14	8.78	8.51	7.37	7.24	6.29	5.19
1983	5.75	4.44	4.94	5.67	5.75	5.14	4.89	4.44	5.18	5.21	4.94	5.28	5.56	5.67	5.75	5.60	5.75

Rate on 3-month loans to local authorities (17)

per cent per annum, end of period

Taux de prêts à 3 mois aux autorités locales (17)

pourcentage par an, fin de période

	Year	Q.1	Q.2	Q.3	Q.4	JAN	FEB	MAR	APR	MAY	JUN	JUL	AUG	SEP	OCT	NOV	DEC
1964	4.99	3.52	4.56	4.61	4.99	3.31	3.10	3.52	3.63	4.34	4.56	5.01	4.67	4.61	5.21	5.30	4.99
1965	5.34	4.09	5.04	4.52	5.34	4.08	4.22	4.09	4.28	5.27	5.04	5.10	4.62	4.52	4.99	5.24	5.34
1966	6.75	5.46	7.14	6.58	6.75	5.06	5.03	5.46	5.82	6.76	7.14	7.46	6.97	6.58	6.87	7.20	6.75
1967	5.48	5.48	5.94	5.30	5.48	6.16	5.75	5.48	5.50	5.74	5.94	6.07	5.59	5.30	5.64	5.41	5.48
1968	6.26	4.65	5.64	4.89	6.26	5.11	4.76	4.65	4.59	4.96	5.64	5.64	5.07	4.89	5.15	5.57	6.26
1969	9.03	6.83	7.61	9.41	9.03	5.91	6.24	6.83	7.14	7.23	7.61	8.51	9.00	9.41	7.96	8.19	9.03
1970	7.13	8.69	8.38	7.69	7.13	8.39	8.44	8.69	8.01	8.34	8.38	8.07	7.34	7.69	8.00	6.98	7.13
1971	5.58	5.01	5.14	5.24	5.53	6.72	5.78	5.01	4.23	4.43	5.14	4.89	4.94	5.24	5.63	5.52	5.58
1972	4.63	2.83	2.56	1.63	4.63	4.94	4.33	2.83	2.26	2.52	2.56	1.52	0.89	1.63	2.89	4.56	4.63
1973	13.43	2.47	4.35	10.52	13.43	4.53	3.63	2.47	2.11	4.32	4.85	7.62	9.14	10.52	10.60	9.41	13.43
1974	8.23	9.30	10.44	10.94	8.23	12.43	10.66	9.30	9.97	10.57	10.44	11.76	11.54	10.94	9.97	8.33	8.23
1975	5.50	7.27	3.36	3.48	5.50	8.03	7.87	7.27	5.93	4.22	3.36	3.69	3.63	3.48	4.93	5.28	5.50
1976	6.32	2.99	6.20	12.22	6.32	5.15	3.43	2.99	3.27	3.87	6.20	8.44	12.11	12.22	10.40	8.21	6.32
1977	6.50	5.58	2.54	4.04	6.50	5.90	5.98	5.58	4.92	2.99	2.54	3.04	3.40	4.04	4.30	5.59	6.50
1978	10.38	5.40	4.61	6.91	10.38	4.89	5.17	5.40	4.68	4.49	4.61	5.51	6.36	6.91	11.18	8.93	10.38
1979	14.80	7.46	8.73	9.95	14.80	8.78	7.47	7.46	7.27	7.82	8.73	9.62	9.63	9.95	10.20	11.86	14.80
1980	9.77	11.63	10.82	10.45	9.77	11.94	12.07	11.63	10.28	11.23	10.82	10.19	10.04	10.45	9.76	9.65	9.77
1981	11.10	10.81	11.99	13.06	11.10	9.43	9.87	10.81	10.49	11.88	11.99	12.47	13.66	13.06	12.67	11.79	11.10
1982	5.73	8.97	8.84	7.87	5.73	10.56	10.10	8.97	8.27	8.74	8.84	8.99	8.68	7.87	7.20	6.38	5.73
1983	6.18	4.34	5.93	6.16	6.18	5.08	4.91	4.34	5.20	5.72	5.93	5.67	6.10	6.16	6.03	6.10	6.18

Yield of long-term Government bonds (19) / Rendement des bons d'État à long terme (19)

per cent per annum, end of period / pourcentage par an, fin de période

	Year	Q.1	Q.2	Q.3	Q.4	JAN	FEB	MAR	APR	MAY	JUN	JUL	AUG	SEP	OCT	NOV	DEC
1964	5.35	4.88	5.01	5.13	5.35	4.83	4.82	4.88	4.90	4.93	5.01	5.32	5.38	5.13	5.20	5.32	5.35
1965	6.09	5.12	5.48	5.54	6.09	5.16	5.07	5.12	5.21	5.39	5.48	5.64	5.56	5.54	5.76	5.99	6.09
1966	6.67	6.44	6.73	6.65	6.57	6.17	6.31	6.44	6.50	6.77	6.73	6.59	6.79	6.65	6.65	6.73	6.67
1967	6.39	6.42	6.49	6.38	6.39	6.45	6.53	6.42	6.33	6.38	6.49	6.44	6.41	6.38	6.38	6.49	6.39
1968	6.60	6.51	6.53	6.51	6.60	6.44	6.48	6.51	6.45	6.47	6.53	6.59	6.58	6.51	6.52	6.55	6.60
1969	7.90	7.09	7.53	7.92	7.90	6.72	6.93	7.09	7.27	7.28	7.53	7.64	7.70	7.92	7.94	7.76	7.90
1970	7.77	8.03	8.17	8.02	7.77	7.93	8.01	8.03	8.06	8.15	8.17	8.02	8.01	8.02	8.01	7.95	7.77
1971	7.79	7.56	7.55	7.85	7.79	7.55	7.57	7.56	7.38	7.55	7.56	7.61	7.59	7.85	7.74	7.76	7.79
1972	7.50	7.26	7.56	7.05	7.50	7.52	7.32	7.26	7.36	7.51	7.56	7.47	7.23	7.05	7.15	7.32	7.50
1973	9.01	7.28	7.80	8.42	9.01	7.46	7.40	7.28	7.41	7.45	7.80	8.00	8.44	8.42	8.24	8.09	9.01
1974	9.09	9.34	10.15	10.43	9.09	9.26	9.35	9.34	9.77	10.22	10.15	10.44	10.45	10.43	10.25	9.14	9.09
1975	8.61	8.82	8.33	8.97	8.61	8.95	8.80	8.82	8.89	8.54	8.33	8.75	8.94	8.97	8.97	8.87	8.61
1976	8.40	8.32	9.34	9.80	8.40	8.47	8.25	8.32	8.40	8.69	9.34	9.63	10.03	9.80	9.32	8.78	8.40
1977	8.11	8.29	8.17	7.83	8.11	8.40	8.38	8.29	8.11	8.12	8.17	7.93	7.70	7.83	8.03	8.14	8.11
1978	8.48	7.46	7.35	7.78	8.48	7.73	7.54	7.46	7.27	7.40	7.35	7.70	7.78	7.78	8.28	8.06	8.48
1979	9.29	8.52	9.01	8.77	9.29	8.27	8.37	8.52	8.58	8.77	9.01	8.98	8.73	8.77	8.83	9.18	9.29
1980	10.48	11.45	9.99	10.25	10.48	9.41	10.37	11.45	10.59	9.97	9.99	9.66	9.67	10.25	10.20	10.46	10.48
1981	11.28	11.38	11.43	12.30	11.28	10.43	10.96	11.38	11.29	11.90	11.43	11.57	12.12	12.30	12.10	11.87	11.28
1982	8.40	10.37	10.53	9.98	8.40	11.23	10.98	10.37	10.17	10.15	10.53	10.50	10.24	9.98	9.73	8.89	8.40
1983	8.58	8.03	9.22	8.80	8.58	7.98	8.20	8.03	8.46	8.85	9.22	9.08	9.03	8.80	8.53	8.57	8.58

Share prices: industrials (8)(20) / Cours des actions industrielles (8)(20)

Amsterdam Stock Exchange / Bourse d'Amsterdam

1980 = 100

	Year	Q.1	Q.2	Q.3	Q.4	JAN	FEB	MAR	APR	MAY	JUN	JUL	AUG	SEP	OCT	NOV	DEC
1964	128	130	130	126	126	130	129	130	132	132	127	124	127	128	125	124	129
1965	122	132	125	120	116	132	134	129	129	127	120	121	121	119	118	115	116
1966	102	116	107	93	93	120	117	111	113	106	101	98	87	96	95	91	94
1967	109	103	107	113	114	101	103	106	108	105	107	110	113	116	113	113	117
1968	124	114	119	129	135	114	114	115	117	119	123	122	129	137	134	136	136
1969	135	140	138	127	134	141	139	140	140	142	132	125	127	128	136	135	131
1970	136	134	133	144	132	128	132	143	140	129	130	142	147	141	139	127	130
1971	139	142	147	138	127	137	142	146	149	145	149	143	139	133	122	125	134
1972	183	153	181	197	201	145	154	160	166	188	188	201	201	189	197	199	206
1973	199	217	208	198	175	214	214	221	217	203	202	205	196	193	192	166	169
1974	147	162	162	138	126	165	159	161	169	161	154	152	138	125	122	127	130
1975	147	152	152	140	144	152	151	153	160	150	146	150	142	129	135	149	149
1976	141	154	147	134	130	154	155	153	155	145	142	144	134	126	128	133	129
1977	132	131	136	129	134	126	129	137	142	135	132	132	129	126	133	134	134
1978	137	133	136	146	133	136	132	130	130	139	138	143	151	144	132	132	135
1979	125	135	125	120	114	140	132	133	130	121	124	110	126	123	119	112	112
1980	100	104	104	101	92	111	102	98	107	106	99	108	102	93	94	91	90
1981	93	98	99	93	85	94	105	96	101	97	100	95	95	88	84	86	85
1982	99	93	97	95	111	92	92	95	100	98	93	94	95	95	104	111	119
1983	166	143	156	179	187	131	139	158	151	152	164	175	177	185	177	184	201

U.S. dollar exchange rate: spot / Taux de change du dollar É.-U. : au comptant

cents per guilder, end of period / cents par florin, fin de période

	Year	Q.1	Q.2	Q.3	Q.4	JAN	FEB	MAR	APR	MAY	JUN	JUL	AUG	SEP	OCT	NOV	DEC
1964	27.84	27.73	27.59	27.72	27.84	27.74	27.72	27.73	27.69	27.67	27.59	27.68	27.67	27.72	27.79	27.84	27.84
1965	27.69	27.78	27.76	27.79	27.69	27.83	27.82	27.78	27.76	27.73	27.76	27.76	27.77	27.79	27.76	27.75	27.69
1966	27.67	27.57	27.68	27.63	27.67	27.59	27.61	27.57	27.51	27.56	27.68	27.71	27.66	27.63	27.63	27.64	27.67
1967	27.81	27.68	27.75	27.80	27.81	27.69	27.69	27.68	27.72	27.76	27.76	27.77	27.80	27.80	27.79	27.81	27.81
1968	27.73	27.67	27.63	27.50	27.73	27.72	27.71	27.67	27.63	27.66	27.63	27.61	27.56	27.50	27.52	27.64	27.73
1969	27.59	27.53	27.42	27.72	27.59	27.61	27.56	27.53	27.49	27.41	27.42	27.54	27.64	27.72	27.74	27.72	27.59
1970	27.80	27.54	27.59	27.79	27.80	27.50	27.47	27.54	27.50	27.53	27.59	27.77	27.76	27.79	27.79	27.77	27.80
1971	30.69	27.82	28.05	29.65	30.69	27.80	27.82	27.82	27.82	28.08	28.05	28.15	29.04	29.65	29.87	30.18	30.69
1972	30.99	31.30	31.52	30.90	30.99	31.37	31.49	31.30	31.07	31.17	31.52	31.29	30.96	30.90	30.96	30.99	30.99
1973	35.41	33.96	38.17	39.46	35.41	31.45	35.03	33.96	33.72	35.31	38.17	38.48	37.26	39.46	39.34	36.22	35.41
1974	39.90	37.24	37.72	36.99	39.90	34.38	35.79	37.24	38.52	39.13	37.72	37.91	36.85	36.99	37.89	39.02	39.90
1975	37.20	41.76	40.98	36.55	37.20	41.07	42.61	41.76	41.14	41.56	40.98	37.67	37.79	36.55	38.13	37.11	37.20
1976	40.70	37.22	36.56	38.93	40.70	37.52	37.36	37.22	37.24	36.30	36.56	36.94	37.80	38.93	39.68	39.86	40.70
1977	43.86	40.13	40.45	40.71	43.86	39.46	40.01	40.13	40.79	40.56	40.45	40.98	40.79	40.71	41.26	41.55	43.86
1978	50.79	46.22	44.79	47.47	50.79	44.23	45.96	46.22	45.25	44.43	44.79	45.33	46.40	47.47	53.38	47.95	50.79
1979	52.48	49.65	49.26	51.77	52.48	49.76	50.00	49.65	48.72	47.82	49.26	49.58	49.90	51.77	49.88	51.84	52.48
1980	46.96	47.02	51.88	50.88	46.96	52.06	51.30	47.02	50.26	50.96	51.88	51.35	51.20	50.88	48.49	47.87	46.96
1981	40.51	42.96	37.57	38.73	40.51	43.54	42.44	42.96	40.76	38.67	37.57	36.54	36.98	38.73	40.23	41.54	40.51
1982	38.10	37.35	36.77	36.18	38.10	39.46	38.20	37.35	38.27	38.51	36.77	36.88	36.54	36.18	35.90	36.52	38.10
1983	32.63	36.58	35.11	33.90	32.63	37.17	37.36	36.58	36.12	35.34	35.11	33.33	33.04	33.90	33.92	33.10	32.63

NETHERLANDS

U.S. dollar exchange rate: forward (90 days) — Taux de change du dollar É.-U. : à terme (90 jours)

cents per guilder, end of period — cents par florin, fin de période

	Year	Q.1	Q.2	Q.3	Q.4	JAN	FEB	MAR	APR	MAY	JUN	JUL	AUG	SEP	OCT	NOV	DEC
1964	27.86	27.76	27.59	27.72	27.86	27.79	27.78	27.76	27.72	27.66	27.59	27.63	27.69	27.72	27.77	27.84	27.86
1965	27.72	27.85	27.78	27.86	27.72	27.87	27.85	27.85	27.79	27.75	27.78	27.78	27.80	27.86	27.77	27.75	27.72
1966	27.69	27.60	27.62	27.66	27.69	27.64	27.62	27.60	27.53	27.56	27.62	27.71	27.69	27.56	27.64	27.64	27.69
1967	27.90	27.68	27.75	27.81	27.90	27.69	27.69	27.68	27.69	27.75	27.75	27.77	27.80	27.81	27.83	27.94	27.90
1968	27.79	27.79	27.71	27.56	27.79	27.82	27.79	27.79	27.76	27.80	27.71	27.71	27.65	27.56	27.59	27.69	27.79
1969	27.72	27.63	27.56	27.76	27.72	27.71	27.67	27.63	27.37	27.65	27.56	27.55	27.69	27.76	27.93	27.86	27.72
1970	27.79	27.57	27.67	27.83	27.79	27.59	27.51	27.57	27.55	27.61	27.67	27.85	27.83	27.83	27.84	27.83	27.79
1971	30.77	27.89	28.16	..	30.77	27.83	27.83	27.89	27.92	28.28	28.16	28.41	..	..	29.90	30.25	30.77
1972	31.10	31.57	31.74	31.21	31.10	31.38	31.59	31.57	31.29	31.34	31.74	31.69	31.33	31.21	31.10	31.10	31.10
1973	35.11	34.67	38.27	39.46	35.11	31.61	35.58	34.67	34.13	35.66	38.27	38.69	37.34	39.46	39.31	36.16	35.11
1974	40.06	37.24	37.88	37.20	40.06	34.11	35.68	37.24	38.61	37.76	37.88	38.05	37.31	37.20	37.98	39.23	40.06
1975	37.23	41.77	41.29	36.87	37.23	41.05	42.55	41.77	41.29	41.81	41.29	37.99	38.14	36.87	38.29	37.24	37.23
1976	40.57	37.44	36.31	38.10	40.57	37.58	37.58	37.44	37.41	36.39	36.31	36.62	36.94	38.10	39.32	39.64	40.57
1977	44.01	40.05	40.70	40.92	44.01	39.34	39.97	40.05	40.90	40.87	40.70	41.32	41.02	40.92	41.51	41.63	44.01
1978	51.07	46.51	45.23	47.46	51.07	44.52	46.19	46.51	45.60	44.78	45.23	45.62	46.77	47.46	53.62	48.17	51.07
1979	52.80	50.10	49.55	52.19	52.80	50.13	50.43	50.10	49.12	48.01	49.55	49.85	50.25	52.19	50.56	51.10	52.80
1980	47.94	48.01	51.76	51.36	47.94	52.47	51.84	48.01	50.81	50.84	51.76	51.41	51.02	51.36	49.19	48.80	47.94
1981	40.80	43.44	38.14	39.20	40.80	41.29	42.97	43.44	41.29	39.22	38.14	37.06	37.38	39.20	40.52	41.62	40.30
1982	38.49	38.01	37.41	36.51	38.49	39.89	38.73	38.01	38.88	39.09	37.41	37.26	36.86	36.51	36.19	36.31	38.49
1983	32.95	37.08	35.49	34.18	32.95	37.55	37.76	37.08	36.40	35.64	35.49	34.24	33.37	34.18	34.21	33.40	32.95

Official reserves excluding gold — Réserves officielles, or exclu

million SDR's, end of period — millions de DTS, fin de période

	Year	Q.1	Q.2	Q.3	Q.4	JAN	FEB	MAR	APR	MAY	JUN	JUL	AUG	SEP	OCT	NOV	DEC
1964	658	453	404	604	658	459	439	453	421	435	404	438	498	604	589	676	658
1965	657	612	580	664	657	653	637	612	626	605	580	641	651	664	687	719	657
1966	718	613	602	679	718	576	581	613	574	637	602	696	693	679	685	718	718
1967	908	689	740	744	908	662	687	689	626	716	740	748	706	744	869	892	908
1968	766	839	780	774	766	802	812	839	798	755	780	793	815	774	746	705	766
1969	809	710	663	654	809	679	703	710	[illegible]	740	663	725	684	654	1156	925	809
1970	1454	939	953	1188	1454	955	942	939	883	926	953	1050	1194	1188	1444	1410	1454
1971	1588	1738	1629	1718	1588	1531	1723	1738	1538	1681	1629	1591	1616	1718	1701	1664	1588
1972	2511	2108	2127	2605	2511	1632	1721	2108	2079	2053	2127	2618	2608	2605	2579	2534	2511
1973	3525	3149	2970	2626	3525	2483	2709	3149	3088	2989	2970	2699	2584	2626	3319	3245	3525
1974	3782	3075	2678	3658	3782	2986	3138	3075	2861	2854	2678	2786	3052	3658	3926	4023	3782
1975	4172	3868	3567	3955	4172	3978	3991	3868	3836	3706	3567	3665	3933	3955	4168	4118	4172
1976	4457	4395	3419	3686	4457	4159	4634	4395	4253	4048	3419	3413	3553	3686	3996	4369	4457
1977	4727	4241	4694	4927	4727	4207	4148	4241	4245	4340	4694	4760	4907	4927	4823	5206	4727
1978	3905	4667	4572	4322	3905	4546	4508	4667	4550	4496	4572	4416	4342	4322	3654	3534	3905
1979	5762	6028	5739	5951	5762	4124	4156	6028	6077	5976	5739	5809	5840	5951	5891	5738	5762
1980	9131	6781	7972	8732	9131	6449	7134	6781	7915	7782	7972	8556	8632	8732	8750	8915	9131
1981	8024	8926	7715	7376	8024	9010	8883	8926	8477	7961	7715	8022	7201	7376	7675	7842	8024
1982	9185	8343	7736	7794	9185	7757	7713	8343	7837	7825	7736	7588	7735	7794	8458	8518	9185
1983	9715	10045	9903	9579	9715	10126	10589	10045	9992	10005	9903	10060	9980	9579	9816	9894	9715

Net foreign position (21) — Position extérieure nette (21)

million guilders, end of period — millions de florins, fin de période

	Year	Q.1	Q.2	Q.3	Q.4	JAN	FEB	MAR	APR	MAY	JUN	JUL	AUG	SEP	OCT	NOV	DEC
1964	1142	1785	1186	984	1142	1929	1761	1785	1722	1231	1186	1019	1206	984	975	828	1142
1965	962	1400	1133	1085	962	1339	1402	1400	1258	972	1133	844	988	1085	937	872	962
1966	548	556	581	501	548	1133	938	556	608	365	581	268	275	501	371	359	548
1967	244	494	10	338	244	713	745	494	413	162	10	69	202	338	86	308	244
1968	622	351	377	620	622	527	383	351	518	555	377	344	549	620	351	760	622
1969	1172	1105	1308	1217	1172	1031	981	1105	1042	785	1308	1262	1309	1217	-97	623	1172
1970	630	1024	1414	1445	630	1159	1172	1024	1372	1381	1414	1740	1475	1445	593	514	630
1971	2589	687	1677	1796	2589	1250	707	687	1547	1222	1677	1924	1886	1796	2230	2551	2589
1972	3170	1956	2690	2439	3170	3108	2930	1956	2142	2835	2690	1872	1931	2439	3052	3682	3170
1973	3290	1990	4781	4691	3290	3814	2044	1990	3222	3032	4781	5189	5159	4691	2313	2919	3290
1974	3642	3757	5617	3449	3642	3787	3204	3757	4417	5367	5617	5727	5036	3449	3125	3160	3642
1975	6871	4315	7398	7269	6871	3328	3827	4315	5136	6346	7398	7725	6982	7269	6437	7155	6871
1976	6781	7430	10651	8979	6781	7897	6446	7430	7926	8876	10651	10261	10089	8979	7552	6575	6781
1977	4217	8091	6549	6108	4217	7802	8275	8091	7633	7054	6549	7144	6566	6108	6068	4034	4217
1978	2155	5245	4011	4098	2155	5748	5818	5245	5531	5189	4011	3858	3138	4098	4180	3846	2155
1979	-341	1917	2225	413	-341	838	1331	1917	2295	2729	2225	1701	754	413	545	1093	-341
1980	-6757	-3603	-3273	-5746	-6757	-1527	-3443	-3603	-2861	-2878	-3273	-4062	-5050	-5746	-5593	-6001	-6757
1981	-830	-3566	-337	337	-830	-5724	-4854	-3566	[illegible]	-595	-337	-1579	-939	337	-1073	18	-830
1982	-1301	-1730	1176	1283	-1301	-38	100	-1730	-418	1211	1176	1656	1717	1283	1120	2734	-1301
1983		-1398	2103	2414		-2728	-4549	-1398	843	2388	2103	2543	3351	2414	3521	3778	

Balance of payments: net trade / Balance des paiements : balance commerciale

million guilders / millions de florins

	Year	Q.1	Q.2	Q.3	Q.4	JAN	FEB	MAR	APR	MAY	JUN	JUL	AUG	SEP	OCT	NOV	DEC
1964	-2775	-1010	-1126	-281	-358												
1965	-1926	-525	-635	-137	-629												
1966	-2272	-1002	-689	-198	-383												
1967	-1855	-658	-596	-59	-542												
1968	-1125	-420	-387	-214	-104												
1969	-1174	-304	-259	-99	-512												
1970	-3072	-527	-1054	-543	-948												
1971	-1787	-846	-512	-404	-25												
1972	3948	1370	915	703	960												
1973	3380	513	1175	-444	2136												
1974	1576	109	750	378	339												
1975	2272	-2	945	614	715												
1976	3553	1458	720	591	784												
1977	-600	326	-406	-900	380												
1978	-3183	-400	-698	-973	-1112												
1979	-2746	232	83	-1788	-1273												
1980	-2672	135	-1231	-1271	-305												
1981	9734	2537	1418	985	4794												
1982	10054	5938	2648	10	1458												
1983		4592	4672	739													

Balance of payments: current balance / Balance des paiements : opérations courantes, nettes

million guilders / millions de florins

	Year	Q.1	Q.2	Q.3	Q.4	JAN	FEB	MAR	APR	MAY	JUN	JUL	AUG	SEP	OCT	NOV	DEC
1964	-558	-523	-836	366	435												
1965	175	32	-349	557	-65												
1966	-776	-821	-389	298	136												
1967	-291	-412	-242	242	121												
1968	229	-184	-2	-88	503												
1969	230	-39	-59	-88	416												
1970	-1761	-309	-565	-353	-534												
1971	-414	-469	-430	232	253												
1972	4347	269	1126	1390	1562												
1973	6767	1490	2049	208	3020												
1974	5956	1348	1799	1613	1196												
1975	5027	327	2221	719	1760												
1976	7162	2311	1071	1308	2472												
1977	1504	784	-403	-166	1289												
1978	-3191	-394	-947	-2416	566												
1979	1361	-646	244	2592	-829												
1980	-5563	-1008	-1770	-2569	-216												
1981	7176	2052	1062	-535	4597												
1982	8412	4589	3513	-1047	1357												
1983		5331	4086	-8													

Balance of payments: net capital movements / Balance des paiements : mouvements de capitaux, nets

million guilders / millions de florins

	Year	Q.1	Q.2	Q.3	Q.4	JAN	FEB	MAR	APR	MAY	JUN	JUL	AUG	SEP	OCT	NOV	DEC
1964	1183	17	457	536	173												
1965	220	-8	135	151	-58												
1966	451	317	133	94	-93												
1967	341	114	149	-128	206												
1968	-867	-237	-110	89	-539												
1969	-510	-413	-823	182	544												
1970	2816	134	367	1176	1139												
1971	622	1267	-558	239	-326												
1972	-2327	571	-817	-531	-1550												
1973	-4435	451	-4191	-892	197												
1974	-2547	-960	-2595	1945	-937												
1975	-4479	-705	-3773	-271	270												
1976	-5162	-2091	-4078	58	949												
1977	-59	-1738	1202	1907	-1430												
1978	1314	-375	-388	564	1513												
1979	-1719	1446	-199	-2727	-239												
1980	10571	3747	638	2357	3329												
1981	-6849	-2334	-4590	191	-116												
1982	-3658	-1861	-4984	583	2604												
1983		-3469	-5698	1157													

NETHERLANDS

Imports c.i.f. (22) — Importations c.a.f. (22)

million guilders, monthly averages — millions de florins, moyennes mensuelles

	Year	Q.1	Q.2	Q.3	Q.4	JAN	FEB	MAR	APR	MAY	JUN	JUL	AUG	SEP	OCT	NOV	DEC
1964	2128	2061	2207	2044	2203	2134	2060	1989	2316	2033	2272	2302	1806	2023	2274	2051	2282
1965	2254	2111	2132	2197	2527	2006	2042	2284	2221	2090	2234	2406	1938	2246	2449	2262	2869
1966	2419	2426	2431	2374	2445	2263	2267	2749	2538	2230	2475	2362	2243	2518	2424	2419	2492
1967	2516	2460	2559	2395	2650	2462	2314	2603	2497	2511	2668	2353	2359	2473	2652	2699	2598
1968	2805	2779	2674	2766	3000	2978	2509	2852	2550	2949	2524	2804	2686	2807	3110	2955	2935
1969	3318	3034	3313	3246	3679	2955	2926	3221	3195	3315	3430	3234	2972	3530	3810	3495	3732
1970	4040	3677	4106	3925	4453	3631	3582	3818	3911	4040	4369	4015	3713	4048	4238	4573	4547
1971	4418	4351	4424	4343	4553	3997	4223	4833	4352	4242	4678	4151	4134	4744	4628	4480	4551
1972	4531	4386	4528	4278	4931	4084	4294	4781	4467	4331	4785	3948	4390	4495	5131	4949	4712
1973	5502	5355	5328	5442	5881	5315	5080	5670	5109	5656	5220	5338	5276	5712	6281	5950	5413
1974	7286	6686	7442	7479	7535	6326	6276	7456	7298	7656	7361	7709	6968	7761	8139	7302	7165
1975	7276	7216	7122	6770	7994	7504	6848	7296	7025	7033	7308	6566	5961	7784	7930	7967	8086
1976	8688	7932	8494	8322	10002	7522	7371	8904	8715	8049	8717	7991	8319	8656	9676	8840	11490
1977	9331	9533	9439	8860	9493	9398	9089	10111	9323	9059	9934	8334	8946	9301	9511	9547	9421
1978	9531	9278	9562	9182	10102	9374	8906	9553	9623	9547	9516	8807	9094	9645	10376	10343	9587
1979	11236	10098	11041	11079	12725	9479	9510	11304	10287	11646	11189	10459	11280	11498	13051	12755	12370
1980	12690	13051	12752	11771	13186	12345	12765	14042	12481	12542	13234	11715	11327	12272	13167	12604	13788
1981	13667	12904	14019	13415	14329	13780	12841	14090	13600	13196	15261	13659	12730	13855	14666	13796	14525
1982	13926	13395	14173	13390	14748	12319	12655	15210	14150	13098	15272	13095	12716	14358	13689	15425	15129
1983	14611	13883	14418	14358	15783	13179	13272	15197	13792	14182	15280	13442	14775	14858	15971	15699	15680

Exports f.o.b. (22) — Exportations f.o.b. (22)

million guilders, monthly averages — millions de florins, moyennes mensuelles

	Year	Q.1	Q.2	Q.3	Q.4	JAN	FEB	MAR	APR	MAY	JUN	JUL	AUG	SEP	OCT	NOV	DEC
1964	1752	1614	1719	1750	1925	1636	1614	1592	1733	1647	1777	1751	1467	2031	1999	1829	1948
1965	1930	1807	1884	1904	2126	1728	1770	1924	1833	1814	2005	1967	1586	2158	2149	2016	2213
1966	2037	1861	2083	2026	2179	1810	1702	2070	2064	1968	2216	1989	1802	2287	2163	2226	2148
1967	2199	2098	2191	2150	2355	2174	1927	2194	2108	2142	2324	1939	2191	2319	2483	2406	2175
1968	2517	2373	2396	2512	2786	2464	2228	2426	2399	2626	2164	2485	2364	2688	2974	2718	2666
1969	3008	2705	2977	3006	3345	2700	2525	2890	2828	2957	3148	2857	2762	3399	3661	3204	3170
1970	3551	3271	3525	3537	3870	3262	3121	3429	3602	3365	3609	3404	3303	3903	3786	3964	3858
1971	4061	3892	4008	4021	4326	3784	3569	4222	4015	3775	4232	3823	3977	4263	4357	4369	4251
1972	4491	4337	4541	4281	4806	4262	3980	4769	4227	4693	4702	3739	4433	4671	4992	4939	4586
1973	5573	5607	5584	5220	5882	5808	5494	5520	4977	6184	5590	4968	5061	5632	6322	6169	5156
1974	7327	6800	7597	7356	7555	6582	6438	7381	7455	7895	7442	7645	6672	7751	8079	7371	7214
1975	7377	7164	7485	6670	8189	7752	6787	6953	7870	7062	7523	6541	5979	7491	8578	8043	7947
1976	8835	8452	8645	8463	9781	8117	7759	9480	8690	8530	8714	8146	8105	9137	9246	10049	10047
1977	8933	9043	8929	8401	9359	8865	8655	9609	9131	8606	9051	7841	8387	8976	9160	9607	9310
1978	9017	9133	9028	8534	9374	9317	8658	9423	8960	8935	9189	7982	8227	9394	9593	9585	8943
1979	10636	9969	10573	10320	11682	9587	9255	11064	10044	10785	10889	9986	10163	10311	12149	12123	10774
1980	12238	12803	12207	11265	12673	12572	12563	13275	12557	12181	11882	11128	10538	12130	12871	12240	12923
1981	14231	13525	14054	13853	15492	12934	13108	14533	13858	13450	14853	13980	12678	14902	15657	15939	14881
1982	14738	15495	14867	13467	15122	14600	14720	17164	15454	14021	15125	12636	12710	15056	14401	15532	15432
1983	15554	15598	15359	14592	16668	14696	14662	17435	14947	15291	15839	13543	14218	16015	15901	17585	16518

Trade balance (f.o.b. — c.i.f.) (22) — Balance commerciale (f.o.b. — c.a.f.) (22)

million guilders, monthly averages — millions de florins, moyennes mensuelles

	Year	Q.1	Q.2	Q.3	Q.4	JAN	FEB	MAR	APR	MAY	JUN	JUL	AUG	SEP	OCT	NOV	DEC
1964	-376	-446	-438	-294	-277	-498	-445	-396	-583	-386	-495	-551	-339	8	-275	-222	-335
1965	-324	-303	-298	-293	-401	-278	-272	-360	-389	-276	-229	-440	-352	-88	-300	-246	-656
1966	-382	-566	-348	-349	-266	-452	-565	-679	-474	-313	-259	-373	-441	-234	-261	-193	-344
1967	-317	-361	-367	-245	-295	-288	-388	-409	-390	-368	-344	-414	-168	-154	-169	-293	-423
1968	-288	-407	-278	-253	-214	-514	-281	-426	-151	-323	-361	-320	-321	-119	-137	-237	-269
1969	-310	-329	-336	-240	-334	-255	-401	-332	-368	-358	-282	-378	-210	-131	-149	-291	-562
1970	-490	-406	-581	-388	-583	-369	-461	-389	-308	-675	-760	-611	-410	-144	-452	-609	-688
1971	-356	-459	-417	-322	-228	-213	-554	-611	-337	-467	-446	-328	-157	-432	-271	-111	-300
1972	-40	-49	13	3	-125	178	-314	-12	-240	362	-83	-209	43	176	-239	-10	-126
1973	72	252	255	-222	1	493	414	-150	-132	528	370	-370	-215	-30	41	219	-257
1974	42	114	156	-123	19	256	162	-75	157	229	81	-64	-296	-10	-60	69	49
1975	102	-52	363	-100	195	248	-61	-343	845	29	215	-25	18	-293	648	76	-139
1976	148	520	151	141	-221	595	388	576	-25	481	-3	155	-214	481	-430	1209	-1443
1977	-398	-490	-509	-459	-134	-533	-434	-502	-192	-453	-383	-493	-559	-325	-351	60	-111
1978	-514	-145	-534	-648	-728	-57	-248	-130	-663	-612	-327	-825	-867	-251	-782	-758	-644
1979	-600	-129	-468	-759	-1043	108	-255	-240	-243	-861	-300	-473	-1117	-687	-902	-632	-1596
1980	-452	-247	-546	-506	-508	227	-202	-767	76	-361	-1352	-587	-789	-142	-296	-364	-865
1981	565	621	35	439	1163	1154	267	443	258	254	-408	321	-52	1047	991	2143	356
1982	811	2100	693	78	374	2281	2065	1954	1304	923	-147	-459	-6	693	712	107	303
1983	944	1715	941	234	385	1517	1390	2238	1155	1109	559	101	-558	1157	-69	1886	339

Imports c.i.f. (22) — million guilders, monthly averages — Adjusted - Corrigé * — **Importations c.a.f.** (22) — millions de florins, moyennes mensuelles

Year	Q.1	Q.2	Q.3	Q.4	JAN	FEB	MAR	APR	MAY	JUN	JUL	AUG	SEP	OCT	NOV	DEC
1964	2055	2167	2106	2144	2048	2143	1973	2175	2118	2208	2184	2038	2096	2147	2074	2209
1965	2109	2174	2251	2465	2074	2142	2109	2144	2193	2184	2339	2137	2278	2408	2235	2754
1966	2414	2417	2450	2411	2362	2378	2501	2548	2331	2373	2420	2430	2498	2388	2409	2436
1967	2473	2500	2505	2609	2518	2433	2467	2485	2506	2510	2454	2521	2539	2552	2633	2643
1968	2739	2651	2868	2926	2996	2494	2727	2537	2874	2542	2841	2897	2864	2907	2958	2914
1969	3030	3280	3370	3599	2937	3067	3086	3244	3282	3314	3297	3317	3495	3535	3622	3641
1970	3728	3997	4091	4338	3694	3739	3750	3746	4148	4098	4105	4144	4024	3991	4610	4414
1971	4347	4378	4483	4459	4234	4398	4409	4326	4360	4447	4342	4489	4620	4520	4431	4427
1972	4328	4453	4476	4887	4313	4294	4378	4673	4246	4455	4324	4636	4468	4877	4890	4893
1973	5264	5294	5699	5764	5336	5314	5141	5278	5507	5098	5703	5536	5859	5843	5805	5644
1974	6626	7407	7753	7374	6251	6586	7041	7305	7443	7473	8106	7452	7699	7488	7391	7245
1975	7295	6965	7019	7324	7364	7224	7296	6710	6998	7186	6854	6631	7572	7249	8265	7959
1976	7788	8431	8639	9669	7545	7694	8124	8502	8393	8398	8510	8994	8412	9403	8566	11038
1977	9572	9351	9243	9243	9914	9628	9175	9446	9235	9372	9281	9437	9013	9261	9287	9182
1978	9405	9321	9691	9812	9704	9395	9116	9613	9547	8803	9818	9453	9802	9854	9898	9684
1979	10077	10894	11700	12237	9732	10021	10476	10465	11519	10697	11295	11677	12129	12186	12056	12470
1980	13019	12556	12302	12747	12688	12816	13554	12531	12592	12544	12241	12488	12175	12158	12888	13194
1981	13042	13730	14064	13759	12387	13545	13193	13452	13789	13950	14199	14098	13897	13888	13673	13716
1982	13618	13858	13940	14198	13537	13363	13954	13832	13730	14011	13901	13703	14216	13540	14889	14166
1983	14124	14103	15003	15369	14530	14015	13828	14045	14486	13778	14870	15586	14552	15844	15301	14961

Exports f.o.b. (22) — million guilders, monthly averages — Adjusted - Corrigé * — **Exportations f.o.b.** (22) — millions de florins, moyennes mensuelles

Year	Q.1	Q.2	Q.3	Q.4	JAN	FEB	MAR	APR	MAY	JUN	JUL	AUG	SEP	OCT	NOV	DEC
1964	1672	1703	1766	1839	1651	1736	1630	1696	1712	1701	1723	1738	1838	1803	1813	1900
1965	1859	1886	1938	2023	1836	1930	1812	1866	1893	1399	2005	1843	1965	1997	1946	2126
1966	1920	2080	2059	2106	1914	1862	1984	2136	2014	2091	2087	1995	2094	2023	2136	2159
1967	2172	2149	2228	2281	2232	2113	2170	2157	2109	2180	2070	2429	2186	2284	2298	2261
1968	2392	2389	2575	2690	2420	2360	2395	2423	2570	2174	2525	2618	2582	2681	2637	2751
1969	2743	2961	3095	3233	2626	2766	2836	2845	2984	3056	2988	3083	3213	3278	3259	3161
1970	3372	3434	3640	3790	3268	3396	3453	3421	3458	3424	3532	3674	3714	3542	3898	3929
1971	3890	3956	4184	4233	3865	3962	3842	3980	3864	4023	4129	4347	4075	4230	4217	4251
1972	4295	4425	4508	4784	4336	4120	4428	4318	4500	4457	4168	4777	4579	4686	4781	4884
1973	5509	5474	5557	5750	5516	5863	5149	4992	5992	5438	5424	5424	5824	5827	5937	5485
1974	6738	7455	7768	7391	6329	6827	7056	7238	7519	7609	8056	7488	7759	7529	7191	7453
1975	7179	7232	7081	7942	7334	7167	7037	7227	7006	7463	7003	6904	7337	7855	8149	7822
1976	8207	8542	9022	9428	7989	8091	8541	8388	8785	8452	8903	9179	8984	9012	9498	9773
1977	8937	8855	8901	9142	9018	9072	8720	9041	8702	8822	8800	9087	8817	9007	9063	9357
1978	9046	8822	9157	9192	9280	9028	8831	8837	8700	8930	8999	9021	9451	9287	9068	9220
1979	9623	10515	11110	11344	9183	9591	10095	10074	10657	10813	10986	10975	11368	11386	11480	11165
1980	12294	12129	12007	12382	12242	12257	12383	12275	12267	11847	11914	12155	11951	12074	12439	12633
1981	13143	13949	14718	15216	12831	13444	13152	13546	13895	14406	14731	14742	14682	15305	15565	14778
1982	14931	14750	14383	14760	14853	15067	14874	15062	14560	14628	13810	14476	14863	14473	14750	15056
1983	15103	15259	15506	16494	15011	14977	15321	14888	15572	15318	15183	15556	15778	16078	16684	16719

Trade balance (f.o.b. — c.i.f.) (22) — million guilders, monthly averages — Adjusted - Corrigé * — **Balance commerciale (f.o.b. — c.a.f.)** (22) — millions de florins, moyennes mensuelles

Year	Q.1	Q.2	Q.3	Q.4	JAN	FEB	MAR	APR	MAY	JUN	JUL	AUG	SEP	OCT	NOV	DEC
1964	-382	-464	-340	-305	-397	-407	-343	-479	-406	-507	-461	-300	-259	-345	-261	-309
1965	-249	-288	-314	-443	-238	-212	-297	-278	-299	-285	-334	-294	-313	-411	-289	-627
1966	-494	-337	-391	-305	-448	-517	-517	-412	-318	-282	-333	-435	-404	-365	-273	-277
1967	-301	-352	-276	-329	-285	-321	-297	-328	-397	-330	-384	-91	-354	-268	-335	-382
1968	-347	-262	-293	-237	-575	-134	-331	-114	-305	-368	-316	-279	-282	-226	-321	-163
1969	-287	-318	-275	-366	-311	-301	-250	-399	-298	-257	-309	-235	-283	-257	-362	-480
1970	-355	-563	-451	-549	-426	-343	-297	-325	-690	-674	-574	-470	-310	-449	-712	-485
1971	-458	-422	-300	-227	-369	-437	-568	-347	-496	-424	-213	-142	-545	-290	-214	-176
1972	-34	-33	32	-103	23	-174	50	-355	253	2	-156	141	111	-192	-109	-9
1973	246	180	-142	-14	179	550	9	-286	485	340	-279	-112	-34	-16	133	-159
1974	112	48	15	17	78	242	16	-67	76	136	-50	36	59	42	-200	208
1975	-115	268	63	118	-30	-57	-259	517	8	278	149	274	-235	607	-116	-137
1976	419	110	383	-241	445	397	417	-114	392	54	393	185	572	-392	932	-1264
1977	-636	-496	-342	-101	-895	-556	-456	-405	-533	-550	-480	-350	-195	-254	-224	175
1978	-358	-499	-534	-620	-424	-366	-284	-777	-847	127	-819	-432	-351	-567	-830	-464
1979	-454	-379	-591	-893	-549	-430	-382	-391	-862	116	-309	-702	-761	-800	-576	-1305
1980	-726	-427	-295	-365	-446	-560	-1171	-256	-326	-698	-327	-334	-224	-84	-449	-562
1981	101	219	654	1457	444	-101	-41	94	106	457	533	644	785	1417	1893	1062
1982	1313	892	443	562	1315	1703	919	1231	830	617	-91	774	647	933	-139	890
1983	979	1156	503	1125	481	962	1493	843	1085	1540	313	-30	1226	234	1383	1758

* Adjusted by the O.E.C.D. — * Corrigé par l'O.C.D.E.

NOTES

1. The original base of the index is 1963 to 1969, 1970 from 1970 to 1974 and 1975 from 1975.
2. At 0°C and 1013 millibars.
3. Excluding food, beverages and tobacco. From September 1982, new industry grouping.
4. Excluding sales tax. The original base of the index is 1973 to 1974 and 1975 from 1975.
5. Excluding value added tax. From 1967, excluding projects valued at under 10,000 guilders; previously those under 2,000 guilders were excluded.
6. The original base of the index is 1963 to 1969, 1970 from 1970 to 1971, 1975 from 1972 to 1978, and 1980 from 1979.
7. Industrial enterprises employing at least 10 persons.
8. Monthly data refer to end of period.
9. Minor administrative changes in 1970, 1978 and 1983. From 1975, including certain categories of workers which were not included previously. The total number concerned was 84,000 persons in May 1982.
10. The self-employed are excluded from the labour force.
11. Weighting pattern based on 1954 to 1971, and on 1972 from 1972.
12. Home market.
13. The original base of the index is 1970 to 1975 and 1975 from 1976.
14. The breaks indicated are due to changes in the reporting system.
15. From December 1965, excluding government deposits.
16. Weighting pattern based on 1959-60 to 1964, on 1963-65 from 1965 to 1969, on 1969 from 1970 to 1976, on 1974-75 from 1977 to 1982, and on 1980 from 1983.
17. Monthly data are daily averages.
18. Prior to December 1971, average on rates of covered and uncovered loans.
19. From 1981, monthly data are averages of daily rates; previously, averages of Friday quotations.
20. Industrial and commercial shares.

NOTES

1. La base originale de l'indice est 1963 jusqu'en 1969, 1970 de 1970 à 1974, et 1975 à partir de 1975.
2. A 0°C et 1013 millibars.
3. Non compris l'alimentation, les boissons et le tabac. A partir de septembre 1982, nouvelle classification industrielle.
4. Non compris la taxe sur le chiffre d'affaires. La base originale de l'indice est 1973 jusqu'en 1974 et 1975 à partir de 1975.
5. Non compris la taxe sur la valeur ajoutée. A partir de 1967, non compris les projets d'une valeur inférieure à 10 000 florins; auparavant, non compris ceux d'une valeur inférieure à 2 000 florins.
6. La base originale de l'indice est 1963 jusqu'en 1969, 1970 de 1970 à 1971, 1975 de 1972 à 1978, et 1980 à partir de 1979.
7. Entreprises industrielles employant au moins 10 personnes.
8. Situation en fin de mois.
9. Changements administratifs mineurs en 1970, 1978 et 1983. A partir de 1975, y compris certaines catégories de travailleurs qui n'étaient pas comprises auparavant. Le nombre de personnes concernées s'élevait à 84 000 en mai 1982.
10. Les travailleurs indépendants ne sont pas compris dans la population active.
11. La pondération se réfère à 1954 jusqu'en 1971, et à 1972 à partir de 1972.
12. Marché intérieur.
13. La base originale de l'indice est 1970 jusqu'en 1975 et 1975 à partir de 1976.
14. Les ruptures indiquées sont dues à des modifications dans le système de notification.
15. A partir de décembre 1965, non compris les dépôts du secteur public.
16. La pondération se réfère à 1959-60 jusqu'en 1964, à 1963-65 de 1965 à 1969, à 1969 de 1970 à 1976, à 1974-75 de 1977 à 1982, et à 1980 à partir de 1983.
17. Les données mensuelles sont la moyenne des taux quotidiens.
18. Avant décembre 1971, moyenne des taux contre effets et à découvert.
19. A partir de 1981, les données mensuelles sont la moyenne des taux quotidiens; avant cette date, il s'agissait de la moyenne des cotations du vendredi.
20. Actions industrielles et commerciales.

NOTES

21. The breaks in the series in December 1965, September 1971 and May 1972 are due to the increase in the number of banks taken into account, and to the merger of banks. From 1977, changes in the reporting system.

22. Data for December 1976 affected by change in recording date. Imports for January 1977 affected by change in recording procedure for crude oil.

NOTES

21. Les discontinuités en décembre 1965, septembre 1971 et mai 1972 sont dues à l'augmentation du nombre des banques prises en compte et à des fusions entre banques. A partir de 1977, modifications dans le système de notifications.

22. Les données de décembre 1976 sont affectées par le changement de la date d'enregistrement. En janvier 1977, les importations sont affectées par la modification de la procédure d'enregistrement quant au pétrole brut.

MAIN SOURCES

PRINCIPALES SOURCES

Series	Séries	Sources
Indicators of national product Employment	Indicateurs du produit national Emploi	Centraal Bureau voor de Statistiek *Maandschrift*
Industrial production Sales and orders Construction	Production industrielle Ventes et commandes Construction	Centraal Bureau voor de Statistiek *Maandstatistiek van de Industrie*
Business surveys	Enquêtes de conjoncture	Centraal Bureau voor de Statistiek *Conjunctuurtest*
Retail sales Producer prices	Ventes au détail Prix à la production	Centraal Bureau voor de Statistiek *Maandstatistiek van de Binnenlandse Handel*
Labour excl. employment Wages Consumer prices	Main-d'œuvre autre que l'emploi Salaires Prix à la consommation	Centraal Bureau voor de Statistiek *Sociale Maandstatistiek*
Home finance Interest rates Share prices Net foreign position of commercial banks Balance of payments	Finances internes Taux d'intérêts Cours des actions Position extérieure nette des banques commerciales Balance des paiements	Centraal Bureau voor de Statistiek *Maandstatistiek van het Financiewezen*
Foreign trade	Commerce extérieur	Centraal Bureau voor de Statistiek *Maandstatistiek van de Buitenlandse Handel per Land*

Norway — Norvège

NORWAY

Acquisition of fixed assets: all industries *(current prices)*
million kroner

Acquisition de biens de capital fixe : ensemble des industries *(prix courants)*
millions de couronnes

	Year	Q.1	Q.2	Q.3	Q.4	JAN	FEB	MAR	APR	MAY	JUN	JUL	AUG	SEP	OCT	NOV	DEC
1964																	
1965	2867	551	621	721	974												
1966	3217	593	705	857	1062												
1967	3628	761	929	890	1043												
1968	3149	778	730	731	910												
1969	3141	561	683	767	1130												
1970	4038	728	936	996	1378												
1971	5355	947	1097	1420	1891												
1972	5506	1056	1223	1249	1978												
1973	6711	1173	1347	1778	2413												
1974	10960	1979	2643	2880	3457												
1975	12586	2156	3121	3473	3836												
1976	15625	2632	4377	4328	4288												
1977	23518	3131	7655	5508	7223												
1978	19907	4677	5036	4531	5663												
1979	17415	3293	4526	4444	5153												
1980	19719	3520	4430	4943	6826												
1981	32481	5852	4359	12869	9402												
1982	27366	5467	5943	3594	7362												
1983		4534	5890	7027													

Industrial production: total (1)
1980 = 100

Production industrielle : total (1)
1980 = 100

	Year	Q.1	Q.2	Q.3	Q.4	JAN	FEB	MAR	APR	MAY	JUN	JUL	AUG	SEP	OCT	NOV	DEC
1964	45	44	46	42	49	43	45	43	47	43	48	30	45	49	50	51	45
1965	48	49	47	44	51	46	50	51	45	47	50	31	49	53	53	54	47
1966	50	52	49	46	54	48	52	54	45	47	54	32	50	56	56	57	50
1967	=52=	52	53	47	57	53	56	48	56	48	56	31	53	56	53	60	52
1968	54	57	53	49	53	53	58	59	50	53	56	35	54	58	61	60	53
1969	=56=	58	55	51	61	55	59	60	52	53	60	36	57	61	64	63	55
1970	59	58	61	53	63	56	62	54	65	55	62	37	59	63	65	66	57
1971	61	64	60	55	65	60	65	67	56	58	66	38	61	65	67	68	60
1972	65	67	67	58	70	66	70	65	68	62	71	39	64	70	72	73	64
1973	69	72	67	63	74	67	73	75	62	66	72	43	70	77	78	78	65
1974	72	76	71	66	77	71	78	79	65	71	76	45	74	78	81	83	68
1975	76	75	78	70	81	73	81	70	[illegible]	72	81	50	77	84	84	86	72
1976	81	85	76	74	86	79	87	87	71	74	83	51	83	89	90	88	[illegible]
1977	80	88	73	69	90	86	89	88	70	68	81	44	78	85	90	93	87
1978	88	89	87	80	96	92	95	82	94	78	88	56	89	98	97	101	90
1979	95	97	89	88	104	95	99	97	86	89	93	64	97	105	101	112	99
1980	100	111	100	87	104	108	114	110	96	96	107	59	99	103	107	112	96
1981	100	108	99	89	105	103	111	110	95	99	104	71	90	106	104	112	99
1982	99	110	97	87	103	107	112	111	97	92	102	66	94	100	100	109	99
1983	105	108	103	94	113	105	113	106	104	97	108	74	100	108	114	118	107

Industrial production: export goods (1)
1980 = 100

Production industrielle : biens d'exportation (1)
1980 = 100

	Year	Q.1	Q.2	Q.3	Q.4	JAN	FEB	MAR	APR	MAY	JUN	JUL	AUG	SEP	OCT	NOV	DEC
1964	33	32	34	32	34	30	32	33	33	32	36	28	33	35	35	36	32
1965	35	35	35	35	36	32	36	36	33	35	38	29	36	38	38	37	34
1966	38	39	38	36	39	34	41	41	35	36	42	30	38	41	41	40	36
1967	=41=	41	43	39	43	40	44	39	43	39	45	29	43	44	44	46	39
1968	43	43	44	41	46	40	43	45	41	44	47	33	44	46	49	48	42
1969	=46=	47	46	44	47	44	47	49	43	46	50	35	47	50	51	48	43
1970	49	47	51	47	50	44	50	47	54	48	52	37	51	54	53	52	46
1971	50	52	51	46	50	48	53	56	48	49	56	37	50	51	53	52	47
1972	58	59	59	52	60	57	62	56	60	55	63	39	56	61	62	62	55
1973	63	65	62	60	65	59	65	70	57	62	68	44	65	70	70	68	58
1974	63	65	63	60	65	61	67	68	58	63	68	44	67	69	69	69	58
1975	66	64	69	63	69	62	70	61	70	65	73	47	69	74	74	71	61
1976	77	78	73	74	81	72	80	82	68	72	80	55	82	85	85	82	77
1977	76	83	71	67	84	81	84	85	68	66	79	47	74	81	86	84	81
1978	86	86	86	80	92	86	90	82	91	80	87	61	86	94	93	96	87
1979	92	93	83	87	98	89	94	95	86	89	90	65	92	101	95	104	97
1980	100	110	102	88	100	107	113	109	97	99	109	64	98	101	103	104	93
1981	99	106	100	90	100	100	109	108	95	101	105	78	88	105	98	105	95
1982	97	107	99	86	97	102	109	109	98	94	104	71	90	96	94	102	95
1983	102	104	102	95	109	99	108	104	102	94	109	79	98	108	110	113	105

Acquisition of fixed assets: manufacturing industries *(current prices)*
million kroner

Acquisition de biens de capital fixe : industries manufacturières *(prix courants)*
millions de couronnes

	Year	Q.1	Q.2	Q.3	Q.4	JAN	FEB	MAR	APR	MAY	JUN	JUL	AUG	SEP	OCT	NOV	DEC
1964	1624	333	351	387	553												
1965	1955	357	411	519	668												
1966	2307	500	605	551	651												
1967	1774	506	428	376	464												
1968	1640	304	354	400	582												
1969	2388	467	552	571	793												
1970	2745	592	684	644	825												
1971	2602	574	634	577	817												
1972	2772	544	665	625	938												
1973	4438	775	1009	1170	1433												
1974	5463	1128	1375	1226	1735												
1975	5557	1099	1414	1375	1769												
1976	7373	1495	1893	1809	2176												
1977	6721	1692	1670	1442	1917												
1978	5478	1095	1258	1258	1868												
1979	6986	1289	1669	1788	2240												
1980	8405	1658	2070	1992	2686												
1981	7491	1728	1923	1761	2078												
1982	6225	1294	1490	1465	1976												
1983																	

Industrial production: total (1)(2)
1980 = 100

Adjusted - Corrigé

Production industrielle : total (1)(2)
1980 = 100

	Year	Q.1	Q.2	Q.3	Q.4	JAN	FEB	MAR	APR	MAY	JUN	JUL	AUG	SEP	OCT	NOV	DEC
1964		47	49	50	50	47	47	48	49	49	50	50	49	50	49	51	51
1965		51	53	53	53	50	52	50	55	53	49	52	53	54	52	53	52
1966		53	54	55	55	53	53	53	53	54	55	54	54	56	55	56	56
1967		56	56	56	58	57	57	56	57	55	57	54	57	57	58	59	58
1968		58	58	59	59	58	58	58	58	61	56	60	59	58	60	58	59
1969		61	60	62	63	61	60	61	59	60	61	61	62	62	62	63	63
1970		63	62	64	65	61	62	66	62	62	63	65	64	64	65	65	66
1971		64	65	67	67	64	65	65	66	66	67	69	66	66	66	66	68
1972		62	67	65	66	65	64	59	71	64	66	66	64	65	65	65	68
1973		66	68	70	70	66	66	67	67	69	68	70	70	72	70	70	69
1974		70	72	73	73	70	70	71	71	74	72	72	74	72	74	74	71
1975		72	75	77	76	71	73	73	76	76	78	78	76	78	77	77	75
1976		78	78	82	81	76	79	79	78	78	80	81	83	83	82	78	84
1977		81	76	77	84	82	80	80	77	73	79	74	78	79	82	82	88
1978		87	86	89	90	88	86	86	88	83	87	87	90	90	89	91	91
1979		89	92	97	98	89	89	89	92	93	92	95	97	99	94	99	100
1980		103	102	95	100	103	104	101	101	102	104	90	100	97	102	99	98
1981		99	101	98	100	97	100	101	100	104	100	101	91	101	100	100	101
1982		102	99	96	98	102	101	102	102	97	99	97	95	96	96	97	102
1983		102	103	103	108	100	102	104	102	102	105	104	101	104	109	107	109

Industrial production: export goods (1)(3)
1980 = 100

Adjusted - Corrigé

Production industrielle : biens d'exportation (1)(3)
1980 = 100

	Year	Q.1	Q.2	Q.3	Q.4	JAN	FEB	MAR	APR	MAY	JUN	JUL	AUG	SEP	OCT	NOV	DEC
1964		31	33	33	34	31	31	32	33	33	33	34	33	33	33	34	34
1965		34	35	36	36	34	34	34	36	36	35	36	36	36	36	36	37
1966		37	38	39	40	37	37	38	38	38	39	38	38	40	39	40	41
1967		40	40	40	42	41	40	40	40	39	40	38	41	40	41	42	42
1968		42	43	43	44	41	42	42	42	44	42	44	44	43	44	44	44
1969		49	49	51	51	50	48	48	48	50	50	51	51	51	50	50	51
1970		51	53	56	56	49	50	54	52	53	53	56	55	56	55	55	57
1971		53	55	57	55	54	53	53	54	54	55	61	55	55	54	53	57
1972		59	62	62	63	61	59	56	65	59	62	63	61	62	62	63	65
1973		66	68	70	71	65	66	67	67	69	67	69	69	71	71	72	71
1974		70	70	71	71	70	70	71	70	71	70	71	72	71	72	71	69
1975		69	67	65	64	69	70	67	68	67	67	66	66	64	65	64	63
1976		67	68	70	71	65	67	68	67	70	66	68	72	70	69	70	73
1977		69	66	66	66	70	67	68	66	66	67	65	66	67	65	65	67
1978		68	68	69	72	67	67	70	69	66	70	68	69	70	71	72	74
1979		68	68	70	70	67	69	67	68	70	67	71	69	69	70	69	70
1980		72	72	71	70	74	72	71	72	72	73	73	71	70	70	70	69
1981		70	71	72	70	70	70	71	70	74	70	70	73	72	70	71	70
1982		69	70	65	65	69	70	70	69	68	72	66	65	65	65	64	66
1983		65	69	68	71	66	64	67	67	67	71	68	67	70	70	71	72

NORWAY

Industrial production: investment goods (1) / Production industrielle : biens d'équipement (1)

1980 = 100

	Year	Q.1	Q.2	Q.3	Q.4	JAN	FEB	MAR	APR	MAY	JUN	JUL	AUG	SEP	OCT	NOV	DEC
1964	64	62	65	57	71	63	66	58	65	59	69	34	64	71	73	75	66
1965	69	72	67	61	75	68	74	73	64	66	71	32	72	78	79	80	68
1966	76	81	72	67	85	78	81	84	65	70	82	35	75	88	88	90	76
1967	74	76	75	62	80	80	83	65	81	65	80	28	77	82	83	85	72
1968	72	79	70	62	77	75	82	81	62	71	78	35	71	81	83	83	67
1969	75	78	72	67	84	75	80	79	66	70	82	36	77	86	89	90	73
1970	75	73	78	66	83	72	81	66	82	71	81	35	78	85	87	89	73
1971	81	86	73	69	88	82	88	90	70	75	89	37	79	91	93	93	79
1972	87	89	88	75	94	91	93	83	89	79	97	40	87	98	97	101	84
1973	104	110	99	93	116	105	113	114	90	98	110	47	109	123	123	127	98
1974	112	121	89	99	122	115	124	124	89	107	122	50	120	129	129	136	101
1975	114	118	120	98	121	120	131	102	126	109	126	50	120	126	127	133	104
1976	123	136	117	106	132	130	140	137	103	119	129	51	131	137	136	142	117
1977	131	151	125	110	138	147	151	154	115	119	142	56	131	142	146	145	122
1978	127	131	132	108	135	140	142	112	143	112	140	55	130	140	143	144	117
1979	128	137	123	115	136	133	140	140	110	120	139	64	135	145	144	148	115
1980	100	108	93	87	106	103	111	109	89	93	113	47	105	110	113	117	89
1981	100	108	97	88	103	101	111	111	85	98	107	46	107	111	115	117	91
1982	98	109	94	85	103	105	113	111	84	89	109	44	102	108	109	110	89
1983	92	99	94	78	93	103	105	90	92	88	101	40	92	101	103	103	88

Industrial production: consumer goods (1) / Production industrielle : biens de consommation (1)

1980 = 100

	Year	Q.1	Q.2	Q.3	Q.4	JAN	FEB	MAR	APR	MAY	JUN	JUL	AUG	SEP	OCT	NOV	DEC
1964	72	69	74	67	77	67	72	68	77	66	76	49	72	79	80	81	72
1965	72	73	72	66	79	67	75	77	70	71	75	46	74	79	82	82	72
1966	75	77	75	68	83	71	77	83	69	73	83	47	75	83	86	87	75
1967	77	77	80	69	85	75	82	72	83	72	84	49	77	82	88	89	77
1968	79	82	73	72	85	77	82	86	75	76	81	54	77	84	90	88	78
1969	82	83	81	74	88	76	84	89	78	77	87	57	76	86	92	92	81
1970	82	79	86	74	89	75	85	77	92	79	86	56	80	87	93	92	82
1971	85	86	84	76	92	79	88	91	81	81	90	58	81	90	94	96	87
1972	87	87	89	78	94	83	90	87	92	82	92	59	82	93	97	98	88
1973	89	90	86	82	97	84	93	95	83	83	92	61	87	99	102	103	87
1974	92	95	90	81	104	89	96	100	86	88	96	62	90	92	109	111	92
1975	93	92	94	85	101	91	98	87	100	87	95	65	89	100	106	107	89
1976	96	97	93	88	105	88	100	102	89	92	98	65	92	106	109	109	96
1977	100	104	96	89	110	99	106	108	90	92	105	64	94	110	116	116	99
1978	101	101	102	91	110	98	108	97	107	93	106	63	98	121	116	117	98
1979	102	105	98	95	111	98	108	108	93	96	104	68	101	115	120	118	96
1980	100	105	97	89	107	98	107	111	93	94	106	65	95	107	115	115	93
1981	101	105	97	91	110	95	107	112	94	97	101	66	96	112	116	118	96
1982	100	106	96	91	107	98	109	109	91	92	106	66	96	111	113	113	94
1983	102	104	99	93	110	102	107	102	101	92	105	65	100	114	115	117	97

Industrial production: intermediate goods (1) / Production industrielle : biens intermédiaires (1)

1980 = 100

	Year	Q.1	Q.2	Q.3	Q.4	JAN	FEB	MAR	APR	MAY	JUN	JUL	AUG	SEP	OCT	NOV	DEC
1964	50	49	52	48	54	47	51	48	53	49	54	37	51	55	55	57	51
1965	56	58	55	52	60	54	60	60	53	55	57	39	57	61	62	63	55
1966	59	60	58	55	64	57	61	63	54	57	63	40	59	65	66	66	59
1967	62	62	64	57	68	62	66	58	68	59	67	39	64	67	70	72	61
1968	64	66	64	59	70	63	67	69	60	64	67	43	64	69	74	73	63
1969	67	69	65	62	73	65	70	72	62	64	71	46	67	73	76	76	67
1970	71	69	73	65	76	66	74	66	78	67	74	48	70	76	79	79	70
1971	73	76	73	66	79	71	78	79	69	71	78	48	72	77	82	81	73
1972	73	75	75	66	79	73	78	72	77	69	79	46	71	79	81	82	73
1973	77	80	75	71	84	75	82	83	70	75	80	49	77	86	87	89	75
1974	86	90	84	77	92	85	92	94	79	84	91	54	87	91	96	99	80
1975	89	90	92	80	94	90	97	83	98	86	93	56	88	96	99	101	82
1976	86	91	84	77	92	83	94	95	82	83	87	51	86	94	95	96	84
1977	91	101	88	80	97	97	102	103	85	83	96	53	89	98	101	101	88
1978	87	89	89	77	94	89	94	83	96	79	92	51	86	94	97	99	85
1979	93	95	89	86	100	91	98	98	85	88	96	60	95	103	105	105	89
1980	100	108	99	90	105	103	111	110	95	94	109	64	99	106	111	112	93
1981	102	108	98	93	109	101	111	113	94	98	104	65	102	112	112	115	99
1982	100	109	98	90	105	105	114	110	92	93	109	64	97	108	108	110	95
1983	102	106	101	93	110	104	112	102	100	94	109	64	101	113	113	116	101

Industrial production: investment goods (1) / Production industrielle : biens d'équipement (1)

1980 = 100 — Adjusted - Corrigé

Year	Q.1	Q.2	Q.3	Q.4	JAN	FEB	MAR	APR	MAY	JUN	JUL	AUG	SEP	OCT	NOV	DEC
1964	60	63	65	66	61	59	60	64	63	64	67	63	65	65	66	68
1965	66	69	70	70	65	67	66	70	70	67	67	71	71	70	70	70
1966	75	74	77	79	74	74	76	72	74	77	77	74	80	78	80	79
1967	75	73	72	74	77	76	73	74	70	74	67	76	72	73	74	75
1968	73	73	72	71	72	73	73	71	76	71	75	71	71	72	71	70
1969	74	72	75	79	76	73	74	69	73	74	70	78	77	79	79	79
1970	70	72	78	80	65	68	75	71	73	73	78	79	76	79	79	81
1971	75	79	84	82	74	75	77	79	79	80	96	78	80	81	80	85
1972	79	89	90	88	84	80	72	95	83	88	99	85	86	85	87	91
1973	98	101	108	110	97	98	100	100	102	109	108	106	111	111	112	107
1974	108	111	115	116	107	108	109	108	112	113	113	116	116	117	121	110
1975	112	116	115	114	111	114	111	116	115	116	116	115	113	114	117	111
1976	122	121	123	124	121	123	123	118	126	119	120	126	124	121	125	126
1977	137	129	126	128	138	134	139	130	126	131	126	126	128	129	127	129
1978	127	124	123	125	131	124	127	126	118	126	122	123	124	125	124	125
1979	120	122	125	122	120	119	120	121	124	122	127	124	125	123	123	120
1980	96	101	101	96	97	97	96	103	100	100	110	97	96	94	98	94
1981	97	99	101	98	96	98	99	100	105	93	106	100	98	98	98	98
1982	99	96	98	92	99	99	98	99	94	96	105	94	94	92	91	94
1983	93	90	90	88	98	91	91	93	89	88	100	84	87	86	84	93

Industrial production: consumer goods (1) / Production industrielle : biens de consommation (1)

1980 = 100 — Adjusted - Corrigé

Year	Q.1	Q.2	Q.3	Q.4	JAN	FEB	MAR	APR	MAY	JUN	JUL	AUG	SEP	OCT	NOV	DEC
1964	71	70	72	72	71	69	72	70	70	71	72	70	72	71	71	73
1965	71	72	72	73	71	72	71	73	72	70	70	73	73	72	73	74
1966	74	75	75	76	74	73	75	73	75	78	72	75	77	75	78	76
1967	78	77	78	80	79	79	76	77	76	79	76	79	78	80	80	79
1968	79	79	80	79	80	79	79	80	82	76	82	80	79	80	78	79
1969	82	81	81	82	82	81	82	80	79	83	81	81	83	83	82	81
1970	82	80	82	83	79	81	86	77	82	82	80	83	83	83	82	82
1971	83	85	85	85	82	83	83	85	85	85	86	84	85	84	84	87
1972	85	89	87	87	87	85	82	94	86	88	87	87	87	87	87	88
1973	87	88	91	90	87	88	87	88	88	88	89	90	92	91	92	87
1974	92	92	90	96	92	91	93	92	93	92	92	94	84	97	98	94
1975	93	93	93	92	94	93	93	93	93	93	95	93	91	93	93	91
1976	93	95	96	96	92	94	93	95	97	94	96	96	97	95	94	98
1977	99	98	98	100	100	98	100	97	97	101	96	98	99	100	100	101
1978	100	100	99	101	100	100	95	102	98	101	95	101	100	101	101	100
1979	100	101	103	102	101	99	99	99	103	101	101	104	104	104	102	99
1980	101	101	99	99	101	99	102	101	100	101	100	99	97	99	99	98
1981	100	101	100	101	98	100	102	101	104	97	100	99	101	101	101	102
1982	102	99	100	93	102	103	100	100	97	100	100	100	101	96	96	100
1983	103	101	102	101	106	102	101	101	100	101	100	103	102	99	101	103

Industrial production: intermediate goods (1) / Production industrielle : biens intermédiaires (1)

1980 = 100 — Adjusted - Corrigé

Year	Q.1	Q.2	Q.3	Q.4	JAN	FEB	MAR	APR	MAY	JUN	JUL	AUG	SEP	OCT	NOV	DEC
1964	49	51	52	51	48	48	50	51	50	52	53	51	52	50	51	53
1965	55	56	57	57	55	56	55	58	57	54	56	57	57	56	57	58
1966	56	58	59	60	57	55	57	57	57	59	58	58	60	58	60	61
1967	62	62	62	64	63	63	62	62	61	63	60	63	63	63	65	64
1968	64	64	65	65	64	64	64	64	67	62	65	65	64	66	65	65
1969	69	67	69	70	70	68	69	67	67	68	68	70	70	70	71	71
1970	71	70	72	73	69	70	74	70	70	71	72	72	72	73	73	74
1971	72	75	75	75	72	73	72	74	75	75	77	75	75	76	75	76
1972	72	77	76	76	75	73	68	81	73	76	77	76	76	76	76	78
1973	76	73	81	81	75	76	77	77	80	77	81	80	82	81	82	79
1974	86	86	86	88	85	86	86	84	87	88	86	88	85	89	90	85
1975	90	90	88	88	90	91	90	90	91	89	88	89	87	89	90	86
1976	86	87	87	87	84	87	87	88	89	85	86	88	88	87	86	88
1977	95	93	90	92	97	93	96	93	91	94	88	91	92	92	92	93
1978	88	87	87	89	88	85	91	88	84	89	86	89	87	88	88	91
1979	89	92	95	95	89	89	89	91	93	93	94	95	96	96	94	94
1980	103	103	102	102	104	103	102	103	102	104	103	101	101	103	103	100
1981	103	103	105	106	101	103	105	102	108	100	103	105	106	105	106	106
1982	104	102	102	101	106	104	103	103	101	104	102	101	102	100	98	104
1983	104	103	104	106	106	103	103	102	102	105	103	103	106	105	106	109

Industrial production: manufacturing (1) — Production industrielle : industries manufacturières (1)

1980 = 100

	Year	Q.1	Q.2	Q.3	Q.4	JAN	FEB	MAR	APR	MAY	JUN	JUL	AUG	SEP	OCT	NOV	DEC
1964	66	63	68	61	71	62	66	61	69	63	72	44	67	73	73	75	65
1965	70	71	70	65	75	56	73	74	66	69	74	44	73	78	78	78	68
1966	74	75	72	68	80	69	76	79	65	70	82	47	74	83	83	83	73
1967	76	76	79	68	82	76	82	70	82	70	85	42	80	83	85	88	73
1968	78	80	78	71	83	76	82	84	71	78	83	47	80	85	88	87	74
1969	82	83	81	76	90	77	84	87	74	77	90	51	86	92	96	94	79
1970	86	83	91	79	92	80	90	78	96	82	95	52	88	95	97	97	83
1971	89	93	89	81	95	87	95	97	81	86	100	54	90	98	100	99	86
1972	94	94	96	84	100	92	99	90	97	88	105	55	94	103	104	106	91
1973	98	101	95	90	107	95	104	105	87	94	104	57	102	112	113	116	92
1974	103	108	102	94	109	102	110	113	93	102	112	61	109	112	116	118	93
1975	100	102	106	90	104	103	112	93	110	97	110	57	103	109	111	113	88
1976	100	105	98	90	107	97	109	110	90	98	106	54	105	113	112	114	96
1977	99	108	96	87	105	105	109	111	88	91	110	50	101	110	111	111	94
1978	98	97	101	87	105	100	104	87	107	88	109	50	102	109	111	112	92
1979	99	104	97	91	106	98	106	107	87	95	108	57	105	113	113	114	91
1980	100	107	100	90	104	102	110	109	92	94	113	57	104	110	111	113	88
1981	99	105	97	91	104	98	109	109	88	98	106	55	105	112	110	112	89
1982	97	106	95	87	100	99	110	108	86	89	111	53	99	109	106	106	87
1983	96	99	96	86	102	98	103	94	94	88	107	52	98	109	107	110	88

Industrial production: construction (1)(4) — Production industrielle : construction (1)(4)

1980 = 100

Adjusted - Corrigé

	Year	Q.1	Q.2	Q.3	Q.4	JAN	FEB	MAR	APR	MAY	JUN	JUL	AUG	SEP	OCT	NOV	DEC
1964																	
1965	59	59	59	58	58	58	62	58	61	61	56	57	60	59	58	59	57
1966	61	58	60	62	62	59	58	58	59	60	62	61	62	64	61	63	63
1967	64	65	63	64	65	65	65	64	63	61	64	62	66	63	63	66	65
1968	65	64	66	66	66	64	65	65	65	69	62	67	65	65	67	64	66
1969	72	69	69	74	76	71	68	67	66	70	70	71	76	75	75	77	77
1970	72	69	70	74	76	65	67	76	67	71	72	75	74	73	75	75	77
1971	80	77	81	81	82	77	78	77	82	81	81	84	79	80	82	80	84
1972	86	81	89	87	89	85	82	77	95	83	90	87	84	88	87	88	91
1973	89	85	89	92	92	82	86	86	85	92	89	92	93	93	91	93	91
1974	95	94	94	97	96	93	94	94	91	97	96	95	98	97	98	98	91
1975	98	100	99	98	98	98	101	99	101	99	97	98	98	96	97	101	95
1976	99	98	99	98	100	97	99	100	99	104	95	99	96	95	99	99	100
1977	103	105	103	103	103	109	103	102	103	101	104	101	105	102	101	102	105
1978	108	112	107	107	108	115	106	116	104	102	114	102	109	109	108	108	107
1979	104	101	104	106	106	103	100	99	103	105	105	104	107	108	107	105	105
1980	100	99	104	99	97	101	99	98	107	101	104	104	99	94	96	98	96
1981	98	99	99	98	97	99	99	99	98	103	96	101	97	97	98	97	97
1982	97	100	98	96	95	100	101	100	99	96	99	97	94	97	95	91	98
1983	96	98	96	94	96	104	96	94	99	94	95	94	91	99	94	93	99

Production: crude steel — Production : acier brut

thousand tons, monthly averages — milliers de tonnes, moyennes mensuelles

	Year	Q.1	Q.2	Q.3	Q.4	JAN	FEB	MAR	APR	MAY	JUN	JUL	AUG	SEP	OCT	NOV	DEC
1964																	
1965																	
1966																	
1967																	
1968																	
1969	71	76	70	62	75	75	72	81	67	69	74	32	73	80	75	75	75
1970	73	72	75	61	81	76	73	68	77	64	84	34	71	79	78	77	89
1971	71	76	68	60	79	75	77	77	65	64	76	34	70	76	80	81	77
1972	74	77	73	63	82	78	77	76	76	69	74	57	70	63	84	82	80
1973	78	81	75	71	84	83	79	80	72	79	74	58	80	75	88	86	78
1974	76	85	75	68	77	82	83	89	75	78	71	57	73	73	76	84	72
1975	74	77	73	65	82	81	79	71	76	65	78	39	71	84	88	79	80
1976	74	83	71	64	78	81	84	84	67	73	73	49	67	75	78	77	78
1977	59	76	56	37	66	74	74	79	56	51	60	18	34	59	66	66	67
1978	66	63	68	57	78	66	61	61	74	60	71	23	65	83	80	79	74
1979	74	82	72	67	75	80	78	89	71	73	73	43	83	76	63	85	77
1980	72	85	63	67	74	79	97	78	55	61	73	57	71	73	70	78	75
1981	71	74	71	56	81	66	73	83	69	74	70	28	62	79	79	83	82
1982	65	83	72	40	67	78	81	89	68	70	78	30	26	63	67	66	67
1983	75	73	77	65	84	74	67	78	70	73	88	34	77	83	85	94	73

Industrial production: manufacturing (1) — Production industrielle : industries manufacturières (1)

1980 = 100 — Adjusted - Corrigé

	Year	Q.1	Q.2	Q.3	Q.4	JAN	FEB	MAR	APR	MAY	JUN	JUL	AUG	SEP	OCT	NOV	DEC
1964		63	65	67	67	63	62	65	65	65	66	67	66	67	66	67	68
1965		68	70	70	70	67	69	68	71	71	67	68	71	71	70	70	71
1966		71	72	73	75	71	70	72	70	72	75	72	72	75	73	75	76
1967		77	76	76	78	78	77	75	77	74	77	73	78	76	77	79	78
1968		78	78	78	78	77	78	77	78	82	75	80	78	77	79	77	78
1969		81	80	84	85	82	79	81	80	81	81	84	85	84	85	85	86
1970		85	84	87	88	82	83	91	83	84	86	88	87	87	88	87	90
1971		88	90	91	90	87	88	88	89	89	91	92	90	91	90	89	92
1972		89	97	94	95	93	91	84	102	92	96	94	94	95	94	95	96
1973		96	97	101	100	95	96	96	96	98	96	99	100	104	101	103	97
1974		103	103	103	103	103	103	104	102	105	103	103	105	103	105	105	99
1975		103	102	100	97	103	104	101	104	101	101	101	100	99	99	99	94
1976		99	99	101	101	97	100	100	100	102	96	99	101	102	100	100	102
1977		102	98	98	98	104	101	101	99	95	99	97	98	100	98	98	99
1978		98	96	97	99	100	96	98	97	92	99	96	98	98	99	99	100
1979		98	99	101	100	97	99	97	98	100	98	102	101	102	101	101	99
1980		101	102	101	100	102	101	101	103	101	103	103	100	99	100	101	98
1981		100	100	100	100	98	100	101	99	105	96	99	101	101	100	100	99
1982		99	98	97	95	99	100	99	98	96	100	97	96	97	95	94	97
1983		96	96	95	97	98	94	96	96	95	97	96	94	96	96	98	99

Production: wood pulp — Production : pâte à papier

thousand tons, monthly averages — milliers de tonnes, moyennes mensuelles

	Year	Q.1	Q.2	Q.3	Q.4	JAN	FEB	MAR	APR	MAY	JUN	JUL	AUG	SEP	OCT	NOV	DEC
1964	151	145	143	147	160	154	146	135	150	139	154	133	137	169	159	165	155
1965	152	159	151	148	155	152	153	172	142	147	165	127	146	171	161	156	148
1966	149	154	142	141	161	146	149	168	129	134	162	102	148	172	163	162	159
1967	150	147	154	139	161	144	153	145	159	137	165	109	144	165	153	174	156
1968	167	169	157	156	179	162	166	177	137	172	162	131	169	169	192	182	162
1969	174	179	162	169	187	183	168	185	154	157	174	146	170	190	192	198	171
1970	182	173	137	186	191	181	176	162	201	172	188	180	177	199	204	190	178
1971	165	165	149	159	173	171	165	170	142	151	155	128	158	191	176	181	176
1972	160	164	156	152	164	161	168	162	151	143	175	119	163	173	170	170	151
1973	166	181	172	178	194	170	176	197	158	191	168	152	189	193	200	206	176
1974	172	180	160	167	182	183	174	183	144	180	156	149	171	182	191	196	159
1975	131	153	133	127	133	178	154	127	139	134	126	106	148	126	129	153	118
1976	133	137	128	127	140	126	139	146	121	132	131	90	130	162	145	140	134
1977	119	133	120	106	117	123	126	149	110	112	139	61	113	145	112	127	113
1978	116	115	115	108	126	118	112	117	119	99	128	65	117	136	123	144	112
1979	127	128	124	118	138	117	122	145	105	137	130	102	114	139	138	155	120
1980	124	132	122	111	129	134	131	132	113	126	128	102	101	130	132	136	120
1981	135	131	125	130	153	131	127	135	125	134	117	91	139	160	171	154	134
1982	126	146	129	109	122	147	146	146	122	128	138	85	103	138	119	125	121
1983	137	128	135	138	147	113	132	139	118	122	164	100	138	176	133	175	132

Production: crude petroleum — Production : pétrole brut

thousand tons, monthly averages — milliers de tonnes, moyennes mensuelles

	Year	Q.1	Q.2	Q.3	Q.4	JAN	FEB	MAR	APR	MAY	JUN	JUL	AUG	SEP	OCT	NOV	DEC
1964																	
1965																	
1966																	
1967																	
1968																	
1969																	
1970																	
1971				45	59							29	44	62	74	48	54
1972	136	103	164	163	112	40	123	146	165	168	159	171	173	146	146	85	105
1973	131	144	145	153	84	156	101	174	114	160	161	144	152	163	159	78	15
1974	142	57	107	201	204	8	95	70	59	107	154	208	195	201	184	236	191
1975	771	299	727	1044	1022	99	289	510	605	694	881	1055	906	1167	1089	925	1051
1976	1141	1098	873	1306	1287	1095	1084	1114	789	701	1128	1323	1350	1246	1451	964	1446
1977	1141	1340	800	1032	1390	1434	1261	1325	951	625	824	907	1131	1058	1257	1290	1624
1978	1432	1512	1316	1490	1411	1626	1428	1482	1469	1397	1083	1482	1561	1427	1413	1388	1432
1979	1569	1398	1450	1619	1807	1440	1319	1435	1524	1484	1342	1467	1607	1784	1380	1900	2139
1980	2034	2252	2117	1676	2092	2289	2259	2207	2055	2195	2100	1048	2086	1893	2074	2029	2172
1981	1965	2005	2096	1828	1930	2087	1900	2027	1935	2182	2172	2178	1356	1950	1703	2014	2074
1982	2049	2086	1994	1981	2134	2187	1928	2143	2191	1979	1811	2069	2075	1799	1677	2279	2447
1983	2554	2411	2560	2522	2719	2223	2407	2602	2546	2555	2580	2782	2379	2404	2685	2668	2803

NORWAY

Ships completed
thousand gross register tons, quarterly averages

Navires achevés
milliers de tonneaux de jauge brute, moyennes trimestrielles

	Year	Q.1	Q.2	Q.3	Q.4	JAN	FEB	MAR	APR	MAY	JUN	JUL	AUG	SEP	OCT	NOV	DEC
1964	92	95	81	93	100												
1965	115	136	117	21	185												
1966	110	122	39	73	207												
1967	132	164	90	77	199												
1968	153	150	115	175	170												
1969	154	48	192	171	206												
1970	176	144	81	185	273												
1971	221	111	242	216	317												
1972	214	82	377	108	260												
1973	246	196	166	217	401												
1974	241	280	190	159	319												
1975	263	313	221	140	380												
1976	190	253	234	31	233												
1977	142	160	114	190	102												
1978	81	92	83	32	119												
1979	91	102	121	108	50												
1980	52	61	23	15	107												
1981	78	93	49	121	52												
1982	87	77	147	27	98												
1983	46	43	94	32	17												

Business situation: prospects
mining and manufacturing
per cent balance

État des affaires : perspectives
industries extractives et manufacturières
solde en pourcentage

	Year	Q.1	Q.2	Q.3	Q.4	JAN	FEB	MAR	APR	MAY	JUN	JUL	AUG	SEP	OCT	NOV	DEC
1964																	
1965																	
1966																	
1967																	
1968																	
1969																	
1970																	
1971																	
1972																	
1973					-9										-9		
1974		19	7	4	-35	19			7			4			-35		
1975		-24	-33	-11	-25	-24			-33			-21			-25		
1976		16	23	12	-24	16			23			12			-24		
1977		5	-1	-10	-32	5			-1			-10			-32		
1978		-10	-2	1	-9	-10			-2			1			-9		
1979		19	15	21	-2	19			15			21			-2		
1980		15	-3	-4	-15	15			-3			-4			-15		
1981		6	1	12	-15	6			1			12			-15		
1982		-6	-9	-6	-20	-6			-9			-6			-20		
1983		18	14	22	-4	18			14			22			-4		

Production: future tendency
mining and manufacturing
per cent balance

Perspectives de production
industries extractives et manufacturières
solde en pourcentage

	Year	Q.1	Q.2	Q.3	Q.4	JAN	FEB	MAR	APR	MAY	JUN	JUL	AUG	SEP	OCT	NOV	DEC
1964																	
1965																	
1966																	
1967																	
1968																	
1969																	
1970																	
1971																	
1972																	
1973					15										15		
1974		27	7	25	-12	27			7			25			-12		
1975		-1	-22	1	-6	-1			-22			1			-6		
1976		22	13	30	-9	22			13			30			-9		
1977		8	-11	13	-15	8			-11			13			-15		
1978		2	-17	18	-7	2			-17			18			-7		
1979		11	-4	29	-4	11			-4			29			-4		
1980		13	-5	12	-13	13			-5			12			-13		
1981		10	-10	18	-13	10			-10			10			-13		
1982		9	-17	-2	-19	9			-17			-2			-19		
1983		20	-3	22	-11	20			-3			22			-11		

Domestic orders inflow: tendency
mining and manufacturing
per cent balance

Commandes intérieures : tendance
industries extractives et manufacturières
solde en pourcentage

	Year	Q.1	Q.2	Q.3	Q.4	JAN	FEB	MAR	APR	MAY	JUN	JUL	AUG	SEP	OCT	NOV	DEC
1964																	
1965																	
1966																	
1967																	
1968																	
1969																	
1970																	
1971																	
1972																	
1973					40										40		
1974		8	9	-5	-	8			9			-5			-		
1975		-27	-17	-16	6	-27			-17			-16			6		
1976		-4	21	1	8	-4			21			1			8		
1977		-7	2	3	3	-7			2			3			3		
1978		-13	-3	-2	-	-13			-3			-2			-		
1979		-12	16	14	23	-12			16			14			23		
1980		10	6	-4	-	10			6			-4			-		
1981		-26	-4	-	1	-26			-4			-			1		
1982		-12	-8	-22	1	-12			-8			-22			1		
1983		-25	5	-1	11	-25			5			-1			11		

Order books: level
mining and manufacturing
per cent balance

Carnet de commandes : niveau
industries extractives et manufacturières
solde en pourcentage

	Year	Q.1	Q.2	Q.3	Q.4	JAN	FEB	MAR	APR	MAY	JUN	JUL	AUG	SEP	OCT	NOV	DEC
1964																	
1965																	
1966																	
1967																	
1968																	
1969																	
1970																	
1971																	
1972																	
1973					27										27		
1974		26	25	14	-12	26			25			14			-12		
1975		-34	-44	-47	-47	-34			-44			-47			-47		
1976		-38	-33	-35	-42	-38			-33			-35			-42		
1977		-41	-38	-39	-47	-41			-38			-39			-47		
1978		-44	-41	-39	-34	-44			-41			-39			-34		
1979		-26	-18	-15	-15	-26			-18			-15			-15		
1980		-13	-16	-28	-35	-13			-16			-28			-35		
1981		-37	-34	-33	-33	-37			-34			-33			-33		
1982		-38	-39	-43	-46	-38			-39			-43			-46		
1983		-36	-34	-26	-29	-36			-34			-26			-29		

Finished goods stocks: level
mining and manufacturing
per cent balance

Stocks de produits finis: niveau
industries extractives et manufacturières
solde en pourcentage

	Year	Q.1	Q.2	Q.3	Q.4	JAN	FEB	MAR	APR	MAY	JUN	JUL	AUG	SEP	OCT	NOV	DEC
1964																	
1965																	
1966																	
1967																	
1968																	
1969																	
1970																	
1971																	
1972																	
1973					-14										-14		
1974		-13	-5	-5	14	-13			-5			-5			-4		
1975		29	40	39	37	29			40			39			37		
1976		36	20	20	20	36			20			20			20		
1977		24	25	24	25	24			25			24			25		
1978		26	23	19	14	26			23			19			14		
1979		15	7	-	-3	15			7						-3		
1980		-	6	17	24				6			17			24		
1981		35	28	33	26	35			28			33			26		
1982		37	38	35	31	37			38			35			31		
1983		26	21	13	15	26			21			13			15		

NORWAY

Firms operating at full capacity (5)
mining and manufacturing
per cent

Entreprises travaillant à pleine capacité (5)
industries extractives et manufacturières
pourcentage

	Year	Q.1	Q.2	Q.3	Q.4	JAN	FEB	MAR	APR	MAY	JUN	JUL	AUG	SEP	OCT	NOV	DEC
1964																	
1965																	
1966																	
1967																	
1968																	
1969																	
1970																	
1971																	
1972																	
1973					52										52		
1974		50	50	48	45	50			50			48			45		
1975		38	33	28	28	38			33			28			28		
1976		26	34	32	33	26			34			32			33		
1977		32	32	30	27	32			32			30			27		
1978		30	28	22	25	30			28			22			25		
1979		25	31	31	36	25			31			31			36		
1980		35	38	30	34	35			38			30			34		
1981		25	23	30	27	25			28			30			27		
1982		24	20	17	17	24			20			17			17		
1983		16	16	19	21	16			16			19			21		

Stocks: domestic goods (6)
volume (for domestic market)
1980 = 100

Stocks : produits d'origine nationale (6)
volume (pour le marché intérieur)
1980 = 100

	Year	Q.1	Q.2	Q.3	Q.4	JAN	FEB	MAR	APR	MAY	JUN	JUL	AUG	SEP	OCT	NOV	DEC
1964																	
1965																	
1966																	
1967																	
1968																	
1969																	
1970	84	82	82	87	87												
1971	92	89	93	92	93												
1972	92	92	93	92	92												
1973	88	91	89	86	87												
1974	86	84	82	85	92												
1975	98	98	96	99	101												
1976	108	106	105	109	112												
1977	108	107	107	108	108												
1978	103	108	100	102	99												
1979	98	101	97	96	96												
1980	100	95	94	105	106												
1981	111	113	107	113	109												
1982	115	113	113	119	115												
1983	116	122	111	119	112												

Stocks: domestic goods (6)
volume (for export)
1980 = 100

Stocks : produits d'origine nationale (6)
volume (pour l'étranger)
1980 = 100

	Year	Q.1	Q.2	Q.3	Q.4	JAN	FEB	MAR	APR	MAY	JUN	JUL	AUG	SEP	OCT	NOV	DEC
1964																	
1965																	
1966																	
1967																	
1968																	
1969																	
1970	74	62	69	84	82												
1971	116	97	113	129	126												
1972	120	130	130	117	102												
1973	94	96	93	100	85												
1974	90	79	87	94	99												
1975	147	119	148	167	151												
1976	137	139	136	139	135												
1977	149	142	143	156	153												
1978	130	156	141	119	104												
1979	89	96	89	87	82												
1980	100	89	93	113	106												
1981	115	115	111	118	115												
1982	124	115	124	144	115												
1983	92	102	91	93	82												

New orders: metal products (7)
domestic
1980 = 100

Commandes nouvelles : ouvrages en métaux (7)
marché intérieur
1980 = 100

	Year	Q.1	Q.2	Q.3	Q.4	JAN	FEB	MAR	APR	MAY	JUN	JUL	AUG	SEP	OCT	NOV	DEC
1964																	
1965																	
1966																	
1967																	
1968																	
1969																	
1970																	
1971																	
1972																	
1973	63	56	48	65	80												
1974	70	63	65	63	87												
1975	68	64	77	53	78												
1976	83	74	76	78	104												
1977	92	86	90	83	106												
1978	91	91	93	79	99												
1979	91	83	83	83	116												
1980	100	100	92	98	111												
1981	117	122	124	102	118												
1982	117	113	111	106	133												
1983	118	104	116	113	137												

New orders: metal products (7)
export
1980 = 100

Nouvelles commandes : ouvrages en métaux (7)
étranger
1980 = 100

	Year	Q.1	Q.2	Q.3	Q.4	JAN	FEB	MAR	APR	MAY	JUN	JUL	AUG	SEP	OCT	NOV	DEC
1964																	
1965																	
1966																	
1967																	
1968																	
1969																	
1970																	
1971																	
1972																	
1973	62	54	65	51	73												
1974	67	65	67	53	84												
1975	56	56	50	51	67												
1976	71	67	77	65	75												
1977	72	62	70	71	82												
1978	79	87	75	67	87												
1979	97	86	86	100	116												
1980	100	111	111	76	102												
1981	120	106	86	120	143												
1982	112	98	123	79	148												
1983	116	121	106	101	138												

Unfilled orders: transport equipment
1980 = 100, end of period

Commandes en carnet : matériel de transport
1980 = 100, fin de période

	Year	Q.1	Q.2	Q.3	Q.4	JAN	FEB	MAR	APR	MAY	JUN	JUL	AUG	SEP	OCT	NOV	DEC
1964																	
1965																	
1966																	
1967																	
1968																	
1969																	
1970																	
1971																	
1972																	
1973	212	130	151	167	212												
1974	176	224	222	226	176												
1975	120	138	118	123	120												
1976	87	117	114	103	87												
1977	86	90	90	96	86												
1978	65	79	74	73	65												
1979	85	65	67	74	85												
1980	100	95	96	103	100												
1981	116	111	122	117	116												
1982	70	101	87	78	70												
1983	52	55	52	53	52												

NORWAY

Construction, buildings started: total (8)(9)
thousand square metres, monthly averages

Construction, bâtiments mis en chantier : total (8)(9)
milliers de mètres carrés, moyennes mensuelles

	Year	Q.1	Q.2	Q.3	Q.4	JAN	FEB	MAR	APR	MAY	JUN	JUL	AUG	SEP	OCT	NOV	DEC
1964	366	241	415	424	423	246	280	196	378	407	460	377	433	462	476	465	342
1965	373	302	389	443	395	242	287	376	290	452	424	388	510	431	442	392	351
1966	394	241	399	465	455	263	187	274	259	431	506	347	518	532	517	494	355
1967	441	277	461	473	587	227	286	317	446	458	480	376	533	511	552	482	727
1968	379	257	388	422	445	227	243	301	283	440	441	310	401	555	493	487	355
1969	473	350	435	553	571	318	344	389	329	514	461	415	515	728	591	529	593
1970	474	334	448	523	620	346	396	260	385	456	504	401	504	664	657	584	619
1971	499	406	475	560	579	415	469	333	385	471	569	400	595	685	638	595	505
1972	500	331	506	615	584	323	338	333	349	555	614	439	611	796	613	591	548
1973	495	385	476	544	609	338	411	405	402	533	494	397	530	704	706	707	415
1974	530	436	574	574	556	354	422	531	563	524	636	403	735	583	637	556	474
1975	534	378	569	572	657	364	423	348	562	544	600	511	602	602	696	647	628
1976	511	384	504	560	628	372	331	449	406	502	605	406	657	618	703	585	596
1977	514	379	521	575	596	373	342	423	456	511	595	443	630	653	695	572	520
1978	480	354	493	547	544	384	362	315	409	506	564	414	633	595	566	614	451
1979	489	304	543	564	568	296	278	339	366	601	641	398	701	573	682	573	449
1980	477	332	444	561	585	353	315	328	373	490	469	464	663	557	597	564	594
1981	481	342	505	560	540	330	336	361	356	551	608	442	626	612	602	529	490
1982	513	420	502	521	632	305	398	557	486	482	537	407	567	588	554	468	374
1983		439	757	815		448	452	417	674	745	851	707	934	803	746	695	

Construction: housing starts (9)
thousands, monthly averages

Construction : logements mis en chantier (9)
milliers, moyennes mensuelles

	Year	Q.1	Q.2	Q.3	Q.4	JAN	FEB	MAR	APR	MAY	JUN	JUL	AUG	SEP	OCT	NOV	DEC
1964	2.5	1.6	2.8	2.9	2.4	1.8	1.5	1.4	2.3	2.6	3.3	2.4	2.9	3.3	2.6	3.0	1.8
1965	2.5	1.6	2.9	3.1	2.5	1.6	1.4	1.8	2.1	3.3	3.2	3.3	3.3	2.6	2.9	2.9	1.8
1966	2.6	1.5	3.1	3.2	2.5	1.6	1.3	1.7	1.8	3.3	4.0	2.5	3.8	3.2	3.0	2.7	2.0
1967	2.9	1.9	2.9	3.4	3.6	1.6	2.1	2.0	2.3	3.0	3.3	2.5	3.8	4.0	3.4	2.8	4.5
1968	2.6	1.5	2.7	3.1	3.0	1.1	1.5	1.8	1.6	3.0	3.5	2.6	3.1	3.7	3.7	3.0	2.2
1969	3.1	2.1	2.9	3.8	3.6	1.8	2.2	2.4	2.1	3.5	3.2	3.0	3.8	4.5	4.1	3.3	3.5
1970	3.3	2.0	3.2	4.0	4.2	2.1	2.0	2.0	2.8	3.1	3.8	3.6	3.8	4.7	5.1	3.8	3.6
1971	3.7	2.6	3.7	4.4	4.2	2.6	2.8	2.4	3.0	3.9	4.2	3.3	4.6	5.3	4.6	4.3	3.8
1972	3.6	2.3	3.8	4.2	4.2	2.3	2.1	2.5	2.9	4.0	4.5	3.4	4.7	4.5	4.3	4.4	3.8
1973	3.6	2.7	3.6	3.8	4.4	2.3	3.1	2.7	3.2	4.0	3.7	2.9	4.5	3.9	5.1	5.1	3.0
1974	3.6	2.9	3.9	4.1	3.7	2.1	2.8	3.7	3.2	3.8	4.8	3.3	4.8	4.1	4.3	3.7	3.1
1975	3.6	2.6	4.2	4.1	3.6	2.5	2.9	2.4	4.1	4.1	4.5	3.9	4.1	4.1	4.2	3.6	3.0
1976	3.3	2.5	3.5	4.0	3.6	2.2	2.1	3.1	2.8	3.6	4.1	3.2	4.6	4.2	4.1	3.8	2.8
1977	3.3	2.0	3.6	4.1	3.6	1.9	1.7	2.4	2.4	4.1	4.2	3.2	4.7	4.5	4.3	3.7	2.9
1978	3.2	2.0	3.6	3.9	3.2	2.1	2.0	1.9	2.8	4.0	4.0	3.1	4.4	4.1	4.0	3.3	2.4
1979	3.3	1.9	4.1	4.0	3.4	1.8	1.7	2.1	2.6	4.6	5.1	3.0	5.3	3.9	4.1	3.7	2.3
1980	3.0	1.8	2.8	3.8	3.6	2.2	1.6	1.6	2.4	3.0	3.0	3.1	4.9	3.6	3.7	3.5	3.6
1981	3.0	2.1	3.3	3.6	3.1	1.9	2.0	2.4	2.3	3.9	3.7	3.0	4.0	3.6	3.4	3.3	2.6
1982	3.1	2.3	3.2	3.1	3.8	1.5	2.2	3.1	2.9	3.2	3.5	2.6	3.4	3.4	3.6	2.8	5.0
1983	2.6	1.8	3.2	3.3	2.3	1.8	1.7	1.8	2.7	3.2	3.5	2.9	3.8	3.0	2.5	2.9	1.7

Construction, work in progress: total (8)(9)
thousand square metres, end of period

Construction, travaux en cours : total (8)(9)
milliers de mètres carrés, fin de période

	Year	Q.1	Q.2	Q.3	Q.4	JAN	FEB	MAR	APR	MAY	JUN	JUL	AUG	SEP	OCT	NOV	DEC
1964	4375	4379	4568	4732	4503	4478	4480	4379	4418	4494	4568	4656	4644	4732	4819	4848	4503
1965	4781	4670	4853	5122	4898	4500	4572	4670	4637	4783	4353	4947	5058	5122	5182	5181	4898
1966	5003	4749	4938	5418	5108	4862	4782	4749	4705	4831	4988	5271	5287	5418	5432	5443	5108
1967	5619	5143	5418	5497	5687	5057	5086	5143	5217	5351	5418	5473	5467	5497	5640	5646	5687
1968	4924	5438	5467	5273	4914	5581	5571	5438	5362	5392	5467	5455	5249	5273	5175	5145	4914
1969	5529	4999	5077	5318	5551	4950	4997	4999	4972	5067	5077	5140	5032	5318	5442	5571	5551
1970	5749	5574	5512	5689	5795	5556	5681	5574	5575	5487	5512	5557	5460	5689	5784	5806	5795
1971	5784	5754	5743	5971	5822	5830	5905	5754	5663	5665	5743	5780	5780	5971	6046	6041	5822
1972	5774	5487	5505	5914	5834	5701	5585	5487	5378	5374	5505	5591	5640	5914	5998	5985	5834
1973	5797	5646	5601	5830	5852	5730	5737	5646	5587	5550	5601	5580	5557	5830	5924	6032	5852
1974	6316	5938	6376	6596	6342	5835	5913	5938	6088	6137	6376	6349	6504	6596	6647	6597	6342
1975	6302	6189	6284	6415	6377	6248	6261	6189	6285	6295	6284	6394	6403	6415	6607	6655	6377
1976	6451	6169	6222	6499	6507	6231	6142	6169	6093	6083	6222	6292	6357	6499	6611	6588	6507
1977	6635	6328	6605	6766	6683	6392	6359	6328	6356	6468	6605	6618	6675	6766	6901	6961	6683
1978	6073	6472	6485	6471	6116	6621	6598	6472	6411	6392	6485	6409	6476	6471	6406	6370	6116
1979	6201	5803	6107	6507	6277	5995	5934	5803	5766	5911	6107	6147	6342	6507	6645	6628	6277
1980	5982	6097	5987	6286	6045	6235	6145	6097	6027	6013	5987	6119	6173	6286	6252	6173	6045
1981	6289	5919	6162	6515	6407	6045	5997	5919	5875	5979	6162	6255	6420	6515	6687	6654	6407
1982	6015	6351	6520	6484	5985	6262	6288	6351	6386	6334	6520	6500	6426	6484	6390	6235	5985
1983																	

Construction, work in progress: residential (9)
thousand square metres, end of period

Construction, travaux en cours : bâtiments résidentiels (9)
milliers de mètres carrés, fin de période

	Year	Q.1	Q.2	Q.3	Q.4	JAN	FEB	MAR	APR	MAY	JUN	JUL	AUG	SEP	OCT	NOV	DEC
1964	2086	1994	2100	2280	2113	2067	2047	1994	1999	2015	2100	2144	2194	2280	2293	2297	2113
1965	2269	2050	2215	2430	2296	2099	2086	2050	2039	2131	2215	2308	2390	2430	2483	2437	2296
1966	2388	2147	2347	2618	2413	2235	2221	2147	2108	2203	2347	2415	2546	2618	2637	2635	2413
1967	2831	2430	2556	2810	2847	2399	2434	2430	2439	2501	2556	2622	2709	2810	2883	2847	2847
1968	2526	2656	2631	2753	2528	2779	2723	2656	2570	2587	2631	2659	2671	2753	2805	2753	2528
1969	2886	2517	2504	2864	2892	2529	2544	2517	2464	2522	2504	2567	2670	2864	2945	2971	2892
1970	2966	2773	2716	3007	2981	2872	2853	2773	2758	2685	2716	2793	2852	3007	3093	3080	2981
1971	3235	2918	2965	3283	3245	2992	2986	2918	2896	2904	2965	3017	3117	3283	3355	3366	3245
1972	3217	3040	2993	3255	3232	3198	3110	3040	3003	2952	2993	3061	3156	3255	3345	3360	3232
1973	3077	3082	2926	3105	3097	3150	3163	3082	2989	2906	2926	2941	3031	3105	3212	3247	3097
1974	3204	3052	3148	3373	3222	3061	3063	3052	3023	3009	3148	3148	3264	3373	3432	3413	3222
1975	3241	3059	3207	3408	3273	3188	3149	3059	3135	3143	3207	3278	3341	3408	3478	3444	3273
1976	3149	3108	3048	3286	3165	3212	3138	3108	3028	2986	3048	3104	3187	3286	3352	3338	3165
1977	3287	2943	3040	3356	3304	3064	2998	2943	2892	2967	3040	3111	3235	3356	3451	3474	3304
1978	3169	3083	3108	3357	3188	3229	3170	3083	3045	3043	3108	3153	3269	3357	3433	3400	3188
1979	3434	2971	3187	3623	3456	3130	3058	2971	2918	3029	3187	3268	3486	3623	3707	3696	3456
1980	3306	3202	3059	3391	3328	3408	3312	3202	3122	3076	3059	3140	3298	3391	3421	3422	3328
1981	3406	3221	3326	3611	3478	3322	3269	3221	3173	3246	3326	3375	3499	3611	3678	3670	3478
1982	3398	3328	3381	3513	3352	3376	3360	3328	3298	3295	3381	3411	3463	3513	3540	3453	3352
1983																	

Cost of construction: (10)
multiple dwellings
1980 = 100

Coût de la construction : (10)
immeubles résidentiels
1980 = 100

	Year	Q.1	Q.2	Q.3	Q.4	JAN	FEB	MAR	APR	MAY	JUN	JUL	AUG	SEP	OCT	NOV	DEC
1964																	
1965																	
1966																	
1967																	
1968																	
1969																	
1970	47																
1971	50																
1972	53	52	53	53	53	52	52	52	53	53	53	53	53	53	53	53	53
1973	57	55	57	58	59	54	55	55	56	57	57	57	57	58	58	59	59
1974	64	61	64	65	67	60	61	61	63	64	64	65	65	66	66	67	68
1975	70	68	70	71	72	68	68	69	70	70	70	70	70	71	72	72	72
1976	78	74	78	79	80	73	73	75	77	78	79	79	79	80	80	80	80
1977	85	83	85	86	86	83	84	84	85	85	85	86	85	86	86	86	86
1978	90	89	90	90	91	89	89	89	90	90	90	90	90	91	91	91	91
1979	93	91	92	93	94	91	91	92	92	92	92	92	93	93	94	94	94
1980	100	96	99	102	104	95	95	97	98	99	100	101	102	102	103	104	104
1981	110	105	109	111	113	105	105	106	109	109	110	111	112	112	112	113	113
1982	120	116	120	121	123	114	116	116	119	120	120	121	121	122	122	123	123
1983	127	125	126	128	129	124	125	125	126	126	127	127	128	128	129	129	129

New passenger car registrations
thousands, monthly averages

Immatriculations de voitures de tourisme neuves
milliers, moyennes mensuelles

	Year	Q.1	Q.2	Q.3	Q.4	JAN	FEB	MAR	APR	MAY	JUN	JUL	AUG	SEP	OCT	NOV	DEC
1964	4.61	3.53	6.88	4.34	3.70	2.59	2.96	5.04	7.22	6.91	6.50	5.80	3.17	4.04	4.07	5.08	1.96
1965	4.69	3.53	7.17	4.57	3.51	2.32	3.07	5.20	6.84	7.00	7.66	5.71	3.77	4.21	4.30	3.44	2.80
1966	5.04	4.10	7.18	5.05	3.84	2.99	3.09	6.21	6.16	7.57	7.81	5.80	4.21	5.13	4.78	3.86	2.87
1967	5.43	4.08	8.04	5.15	4.46	3.27	3.59	5.37	7.99	8.02	8.10	6.13	4.36	4.97	4.78	4.76	3.85
1968	5.80	4.21	8.39	5.70	4.92	3.58	3.46	5.60	7.36	9.54	8.25	6.98	4.85	5.27	6.17	4.66	3.92
1969	8.49	6.24	10.32	7.97	9.43	5.20	5.03	8.51	8.99	10.89	11.05	9.77	5.91	8.22	11.10	8.15	9.04
1970	6.04	3.09	7.82	5.99	6.27	3.40	2.31	3.55	6.11	8.20	9.14	8.35	5.57	7.05	7.63	6.33	4.84
1971	6.99	5.42	9.46	7.87	5.22	4.36	4.89	7.00	8.75	9.43	10.18	9.91	6.95	6.74	6.09	5.15	4.41
1972	6.40	5.44	7.53	6.85	5.76	5.00	4.88	6.42	6.98	6.01	9.60	6.79	6.44	7.35	6.70	5.73	4.85
1973	7.58	7.06	9.15	8.03	6.08	6.22	6.31	8.66	8.08	9.29	10.07	8.53	8.23	7.33	8.02	6.28	3.95
1974	7.68	6.91	9.18	8.04	6.61	5.13	6.64	8.95	9.33	9.59	8.62	8.46	7.26	8.40	7.74	6.81	5.28
1975	8.74	7.26	10.16	8.75	8.77	7.17	7.04	7.58	9.97	10.03	10.48	8.64	7.65	9.99	11.63	7.97	6.73
1976	10.30	9.65	12.41	11.26	9.88	8.24	9.06	11.65	10.87	12.19	14.18	12.16	9.75	11.38	11.36	10.31	7.99
1977	12.39	11.97	15.00	11.60	11.01	10.74	10.12	15.05	13.35	15.17	16.46	12.17	10.27	12.36	11.57	10.76	10.71
1978	6.67	7.60	7.65	5.75	5.69	8.48	6.92	7.40	8.23	7.62	7.10	5.56	5.52	6.17	6.67	6.14	4.27
1979	7.56	6.62	8.86	7.22	7.56	5.97	6.07	7.82	7.22	9.69	9.66	7.17	6.84	7.64	9.61	7.69	5.39
1980	8.07	7.67	8.69	8.07	7.84	7.76	7.11	8.14	7.63	9.39	9.07	8.74	7.30	8.17	9.93	7.38	6.21
1981	8.90	8.66	9.67	8.70	8.56	8.14	8.60	9.23	8.80	10.25	9.95	10.51	7.07	8.52	9.77	8.91	7.00
1982	9.84	9.79	10.35	10.18	9.04	10.01	8.84	10.53	9.54	9.59	11.92	10.99	8.06	11.48	11.22	9.73	6.16
1983	9.36	10.15	9.92	9.02	8.34	10.03	9.28	11.16	9.23	9.99	10.55	8.73	8.35	9.98	10.64	8.73	5.65

NORWAY

Retail sales: value (11) — Ventes au détail : valeur (11)

1980 = 100

	Year	Q.1	Q.2	Q.3	Q.4	JAN	FEB	MAR	APR	MAY	JUN	JUL	AUG	SEP	OCT	NOV	DEC
1964	22	18	22	22	26	18	18	19	21	21	22	23	22	22	24	27	28
1965	23	19	24	24	28	18	19	21	23	23	25	25	23	23	24	24	34
1966	25	21	25	26	30	20	19	23	23	25	26	26	26	26	26	26	37
1967	27	22	27	28	32	22	21	24	26	27	29	28	28	28	28	28	39
1968	29	24	29	29	34	23	23	26	27	30	29	30	29	28	30	30	40
1969	33	27	31	32	40	25	25	29	28	32	33	34	31	32	34	34	53
1970	36	28	36	36	43	27	27	29	34	36	38	36	35	37	40	39	51
1971	40	33	40	40	47	32	31	37	38	40	43	42	39	41	43	43	56
1972	43	37	42	43	50	35	36	41	38	42	46	41	44	44	45	45	58
1973	46	40	45	46	54	40	38	43	41	45	49	44	48	46	50	50	62
1974	52	44	50	53	62	43	42	48	48	52	51	50	54	53	57	57	72
1975	61	50	59	61	72	50	49	52	58	60	59	59	61	62	67	64	85
1976	71	59	68	71	84	59	56	62	66	66	72	73	69	72	77	76	100
1977	81	67	79	81	96	66	63	74	72	30	85	91	81	82	86	86	117
1978	81	71	30	80	94	73	69	73	77	80	82	77	81	82	85	83	112
1979	89	76	85	87	107	75	72	80	77	88	90	84	89	88	99	97	123
1980	100	86	94	99	120	86	84	89	88	97	97	98	98	100	114	107	140
1981	115	98	109	113	138	97	96	101	107	108	113	115	112	113	129	122	163
1982	126	112	122	125	145	111	108	116	120	118	127	124	125	127	138	131	167
1983	134	120	128	132	156	119	114	128	120	127	137	126	133	136	146	143	180

Retail sales: volume — Ventes au détail : volume

Adjusted - Corrigé

1980 = 100

	Year	Q.1	Q.2	Q.3	Q.4	JAN	FEB	MAR	APR	MAY	JUN	JUL	AUG	SEP	OCT	NOV	DEC
1964																	
1965																	
1966																	
1967																	
1968	73	72	73	74	75	72	71	72	73	74	72	74	74	74	74	74	75
1969	82	78	78	81	87	75	80	79	77	77	80	81	80	81	81	84	97
1970	83	75	83	83	85	72	79	74	82	83	83	80	84	85	85	87	83
1971	86	84	87	89	85	83	83	86	88	86	86	95	84	87	86	86	82
1972	86	86	87	88	83	84	89	85	86	86	89	87	89	88	84	85	80
1973	87	89	87	88	84	90	87	88	86	86	89	87	90	87	87	87	77
1974	89	87	88	89	87	86	87	87	90	90	85	88	91	89	88	90	84
1975	93	91	91	94	93	90	91	94	89	94	88	95	93	94	95	92	93
1976	100	95	98	101	101	97	95	94	103	94	98	106	98	99	100	100	104
1977	105	100	106	106	108	98	99	102	103	104	109	108	106	106	104	106	113
1978	97	99	97	96	95	99	99	100	96	97	98	93	97	97	93	94	98
1979	100	97	100	99	103	97	96	98	97	100	101	97	102	99	103	103	102
1980	100	99	97	99	103	101	100	97	98	98	97	99	98	100	104	100	105
1981	102	99	101	102	107	99	100	97	104	99	100	102	101	101	104	103	113
1982	103	101	104	103	102	101	101	102	106	101	104	103	104	103	102	101	104
1983	101	101	100	101	104	100	98	104	98	100	103	98	103	103	101	103	107

Unemployment (registered unemployed) (13)(14) — Chômage (chômeurs inscrits) (13) (14)

thousands — milliers

	Year	Q.1	Q.2	Q.3	Q.4	JAN	FEB	MAR	APR	MAY	JUN	JUL	AUG	SEP	OCT	NOV	DEC
1964	15.5	26.6	10.1	7.2	18.2	31.8	25.7	22.4	16.4	8.0	5.9	5.3	7.6	8.7	11.3	16.3	27.1
1965	13.4	23.1	8.7	5.3	16.3	28.1	22.0	19.1	15.7	6.2	4.2	3.8	5.8	6.4	8.7	14.2	26.0
1966	11.9	24.3	7.9	4.0	11.6	28.4	26.3	18.2	14.2	6.1	3.3	2.7	4.3	5.0	6.1	9.7	18.9
1967	11.4	17.6	7.5	5.4	15.2	21.1	17.2	14.4	11.6	6.5	4.3	3.8	5.9	6.6	9.2	13.0	23.4
1968	16.5	24.2	12.2	9.1	20.4	26.4	24.4	21.8	18.2	10.9	7.4	6.8	9.6	10.8	14.0	19.6	27.5
1969	15.6	26.2	11.5	8.7	16.0	28.8	26.3	23.5	17.7	9.8	7.1	7.2	8.9	9.9	12.0	14.6	21.5
1970	12.5	19.3	9.0	7.4	14.1	21.8	19.5	16.7	12.9	7.7	6.5	6.2	7.6	8.3	10.0	12.8	19.5
1971	12.2	16.1	9.1	8.0	15.6	18.7	15.5	14.1	12.3	8.5	6.5	6.5	8.2	9.3	11.4	14.6	20.8
1972	14.8	18.9	11.1	10.1	19.2	20.2	18.4	18.1	14.7	10.2	8.5	8.2	10.7	11.5	14.4	17.9	25.3
1973	12.8	18.8	10.5	8.5	13.5	20.8	18.9	16.7	15.2	9.3	6.9	6.8	9.3	9.4	11.2	13.0	16.3
1974	10.7	14.4	7.3	8.2	12.8	17.1	14.4	11.7	9.8	6.4	5.6	6.3	8.7	9.6	10.9	12.3	15.1
1975	19.6	18.9	14.5	17.5	27.4	18.3	19.4	18.9	18.0	13.6	11.9	14.6	17.4	20.4	22.1	24.1	35.9
1976	19.9	26.2	17.6	16.3	19.3	29.6	26.6	22.5	21.4	16.5	14.9	14.1	18.1	16.7	17.2	18.1	22.6
1977	16.1	20.6	14.3	13.5	16.2	23.2	20.7	17.8	15.7	14.3	12.8	11.1	15.1	14.3	14.1	15.3	19.2
1978	20.0	21.1	15.3	18.0	25.6	22.2	21.3	19.8	17.8	13.9	14.3	14.4	20.0	19.6	21.9	24.5	30.4
1979	24.1	32.0	22.2	20.2	22.0	33.6	32.9	29.5	26.8	21.2	18.5	18.5	22.2	20.0	19.9	21.2	24.9
1980	22.3	25.2	17.6	20.5	25.7	27.0	25.5	23.2	20.5	16.5	15.9	17.4	23.7	20.4	22.6	24.4	30.1
1981	28.4	31.9	24.7	27.1	30.1	34.2	31.3	30.1	28.4	23.1	22.6	24.9	30.8	25.6	26.2	28.4	35.6
1982	41.4	39.0	33.5	40.3	52.3	42.1	38.5	36.5	37.8	31.2	31.5	34.0	45.1	41.8	45.2	50.2	62.9
1983	63.6	67.4	58.3	63.5	64.9	67.4	67.5	67.4	61.4	56.0	57.5	60.8	68.7	61.4	60.2	62.6	71.9

Retail sales: value (11)(12) — Ventes au détail : valeur (12) (11)

1980 = 100

Adjusted - Corrigé

	Year	Q.1	Q.2	Q.3	Q.4	JAN	FEB	MAR	APR	MAY	JUN	JUL	AUG	SEP	OCT	NOV	DEC
1964		21	22	22	23	21	21	21	22	21	21	22	22	22	23	28	20
1965		22	24	24	24	22	23	23	24	23	24	24	24	24	23	24	24
1966		24	25	26	26	24	24	25	24	25	25	25	26	26	26	26	26
1967		27	27	28	28	27	27	26	28	27	27	28	28	28	28	28	28
1968		28	29	29	29	28	28	28	28	29	28	29	29	29	29	29	30
1969		31	31	32	35	30	32	31	30	31	32	32	32	32	32	34	39
1970		32	36	36	38	31	34	32	36	36	36	35	37	38	38	39	38
1971		39	40	41	40	38	38	40	41	40	40	44	39	41	41	41	39
1972		42	43	44	42	41	43	42	43	43	44	43	44	44	43	43	41
1973		46	46	47	46	46	45	46	45	45	47	48	48	47	48	48	43
1974		50	51	53	53	49	50	50	52	52	50	52	54	53	53	55	51
1975		58	59	62	63	57	58	60	58	61	58	62	61	63	64	62	63
1976		66	69	72	74	56	66	66	72	66	69	75	70	72	73	74	76
1977		75	81	82	85	74	74	78	79	80	84	83	81	82	81	83	89
1978		81	81	81	81	81	81	82	80	81	81	79	82	83	80	81	84
1979		84	88	89	94	83	83	85	85	89	89	86	90	89	94	94	94
1980		95	97	100	107	95	97	95	96	97	97	100	99	102	108	104	110
1981		108	113	115	123	106	109	108	116	112	112	116	114	116	120	119	130
1982		121	126	127	129	120	120	123	128	122	127	126	127	128	128	127	132
1983		131	132	133	140	129	127	135	128	131	135	127	135	138	135	139	144

Employment: manufacturing (15) (all employees) — Emploi : industries manufacturières (15) (salariés)

thousands — milliers

	Year	Q.1	Q.2	Q.3	Q.4	JAN	FEB	MAR	APR	MAY	JUN	JUL	AUG	SEP	OCT	NOV	DEC
1964	347	342	349	351	349	338	343	345	345	348	353	352	349	351	350	350	345
1965	353	348	354	357	355	344	349	350	349	353	359	360	356	356	357	357	351
1966	360	355	360	363	362	351	356	358	356	358	365	366	360	361	363	364	358
1967	363	360	364	365	363	356	361	361	363	361	367	370	364	364	365	365	359
1968	362	351	363	364	361	350	362	362	361	361	366	368	361	362	363	363	358
1969	366	360	366	370	370	357	360	362	362	364	371	373	368	369	371	372	368
1970	378	370	378	382	381	366	371	374	375	376	382	385	380	381	381	383	378
1971	..	..	..	..	..	379											
1972	392	386	399	394	386												
1973	389	378	390	398	392												
1974	392	378	400	399	391												
1975	411	408	416	420	401												
1976	416	400	416	427	419												
1977	409	412	413	413	399												
1978	396	404	392	387	399												
1979	384	386	373	381	390												
1980	388	387	391	384	391												
1981	390	405	389	383	383												
1982	384	394	388	381	372												
1983	356	371	362	340	350												

Unemployment (registered unemployed) (13) (14) — Chômage (chômeurs inscrits) (14) (13)

thousands — milliers

Adjusted - Corrigé *

	Year	Q.1	Q.2	Q.3	Q.4	JAN	FEB	MAR	APR	MAY	JUN	JUL	AUG	SEP	OCT	NOV	DEC
1964		16.0	15.8	17.1	14.9	16.2	16.0	16.0	14.1	16.2	17.3	17.4	17.4	16.6	15.7	14.8	14.0
1965		13.9	12.8	12.6	12.8	14.3	13.7	13.6	13.5	12.6	12.4	12.5	13.2	12.1	12.1	12.9	13.5
1966		16.1	11.7	10.6	9.2	16.8	17.9	13.7	12.6	11.3	11.3	10.9	10.6	10.4	9.3	8.6	9.6
1967		9.5	11.4	11.9	12.7	9.7	8.9	10.0	10.2	11.7	12.2	11.8	12.1	11.8	12.2	11.8	14.1
1968		16.4	16.1	15.3	17.7	15.4	16.3	17.5	17.0	16.1	15.1	14.6	15.5	15.7	16.6	18.2	18.4
1969		18.9	15.4	14.5	13.2	18.6	18.7	19.5	16.7	14.9	14.5	14.6	14.4	14.4	14.1	13.0	12.6
1970		12.7	12.8	12.7	11.2	12.5	12.6	13.1	12.2	12.7	13.6	13.2	12.6	12.3	11.7	11.1	10.9
1971		10.2	12.7	12.8	12.7	10.4	9.3	11.0	11.8	13.3	13.1	13.1	12.6	12.8	12.7	12.9	12.5
1972		13.7	14.6	14.5	15.4	12.7	13.0	15.4	14.3	14.8	14.8	14.3	14.6	14.5	15.4	16.3	17.4
1973		14.1	13.8	12.3	10.9	14.0	14.0	14.2	14.9	13.7	12.8	12.5	12.6	11.9	12.0	11.6	9.2
1974		10.0	10.5	11.7	10.4	10.7	9.8	9.4	9.5	10.7	11.3	11.6	11.5	11.8	11.6	11.2	8.3
1975		14.6	17.7	20.7	25.2	12.1	15.0	16.8	17.9	17.9	17.3	20.0	19.7	22.3	22.8	23.3	29.5
1976		21.8	20.8	19.3	17.7	23.2	21.9	20.3	21.3	20.8	20.2	19.4	20.0	18.6	18.2	17.7	17.1
1977		16.0	17.3	16.5	14.9	16.8	15.8	15.5	15.6	18.5	17.9	16.5	16.6	16.4	15.4	15.1	14.1
1978		16.4	18.5	20.3	24.5	15.5	16.4	17.3	17.6	18.2	19.6	19.7	20.9	22.0	23.4	24.5	25.5
1979		27.1	25.4	23.0	21.1	26.7	27.8	26.9	26.5	25.6	23.9	23.6	22.6	22.7	21.6	21.4	20.3
1980		20.2	20.9	23.2	24.9	19.8	20.4	20.5	20.1	21.0	21.6	22.4	23.8	23.4	24.4	24.7	25.6
1981		26.8	28.0	29.7	29.3	26.9	26.1	27.3	27.9	27.7	28.4	29.7	30.7	28.7	28.0	28.7	31.2
1982		33.9	36.8	42.9	52.0	34.7	33.3	33.7	37.2	35.8	37.4	38.8	44.8	45.0	47.0	50.5	58.5
1983		62.3	61.6	66.1	64.1	60.0	62.3	64.6	60.8	60.6	63.4	65.4	68.4	64.7	62.0	62.8	67.5

* Adjusted by the O.E.C.D. — * Corrigé par l'O.C.D.E.

NORWAY

Unemployment (registered unemployed) (14)(16)
as per cent of civilian labour force

Chômage (chômeurs inscrits) (14)(16)
en pourcentage de la main-d'œuvre civile

	Year	Q.1	Q.2	Q.3	Q.4	JAN	FEB	MAR	APR	MAY	JUN	JUL	AUG	SEP	OCT	NOV	DEC
1964	1.4	2.4	0.9	0.7	1.6	2.9	2.3	2.0	1.5	0.7	0.5	0.5	0.7	0.8	1.0	1.5	2.5
1965	1.2	2.1	0.8	0.5	1.5	2.5	2.0	1.7	1.4	0.6	0.4	0.3	0.5	0.6	0.8	1.3	2.3
1966	1.1	2.2	0.7	0.4	1.0	2.5	2.3	1.6	1.3	0.6	0.3	0.2	0.4	0.4	0.5	0.9	1.7
1967	1.0	1.6	0.7	0.5	1.3	1.9	1.5	1.3	1.0	0.6	0.4	0.3	0.5	0.6	0.8	1.1	2.0
1968	1.4	2.1	1.1	0.8	1.7	2.3	2.1	1.9	1.6	0.9	0.6	0.6	0.8	0.9	1.2	1.7	2.4
1969	1.3	2.2	1.0	0.7	1.3	2.5	2.2	2.0	1.5	0.8	0.6	0.6	0.8	0.8	1.0	1.2	1.3
1970	1.0	1.6	0.8	0.6	1.1	1.8	1.6	1.4	1.1	0.6	0.5	0.5	0.6	0.7	0.8	1.0	1.6
1971	..	..	..	..	..												
1972	0.9	1.1	0.7	0.6	1.2												
1973	0.8	1.1	0.6	0.5	0.8												
1974	0.6	0.9	0.4	0.5	0.8												
1975	1.1	1.1	0.8	1.0	1.6												
1976	1.1	1.5	1.0	0.9	1.1												
1977	0.9	1.1	0.8	0.7	0.9												
1978	1.1	1.1	0.8	1.0	1.4												
1979	1.3	1.7	1.2	1.1	1.2												
1980	1.2	1.3	0.9	1.1	1.3												
1981	1.5	1.6	1.3	1.4	1.5												
1982	2.1	2.0	1.7	2.0	2.7												
1983	3.2	3.4	2.9	3.1	3.2												

Jobs vacant, unfilled vacancies (14)
thousands

Offres d'emploi non satisfaites (14)
milliers

	Year	Q.1	Q.2	Q.3	Q.4	JAN	FEB	MAR	APR	MAY	JUN	JUL	AUG	SEP	OCT	NOV	DEC
1964	4.6	3.5	6.3	4.8	3.8	3.1	3.3	4.1	5.5	7.0	6.4	5.3	4.9	4.1	3.8	3.9	3.6
1965	5.9	4.6	7.6	5.9	5.2	3.8	4.5	5.6	7.0	8.4	7.4	6.8	6.0	5.0	5.4	5.5	4.8
1966	7.6	6.0	10.1	8.0	6.2	5.3	5.2	7.6	9.1	10.7	10.6	8.8	8.3	6.9	6.6	6.5	5.6
1967	7.2	6.1	10.1	7.6	4.9	6.0	5.8	6.6	8.8	11.3	10.1	9.1	7.5	6.2	5.3	5.0	4.3
1968	5.1	4.6	7.5	4.9	3.4	4.2	4.5	5.2	6.4	8.9	7.2	6.1	4.6	3.9	3.4	3.5	3.3
1969	5.9	3.9	8.2	6.3	5.3	3.5	3.4	4.9	7.4	9.1	8.0	7.0	6.5	5.4	5.1	5.8	5.0
1970	9.6	7.2	12.7	10.2	8.4	5.7	7.1	8.9	11.8	13.8	12.6	11.4	9.8	9.3	8.6	8.8	7.9
1971	10.7	9.8	14.7	11.2	7.3	7.9	9.4	12.0	14.3	15.9	13.8	13.7	10.7	9.2	7.6	7.2	7.1
1972	8.5	7.8	11.2	8.9	6.0	7.3	7.6	8.6	10.7	12.1	10.9	10.5	9.1	7.0	6.2	6.0	5.8
1973	8.2	6.7	10.2	8.5	7.2	6.1	6.4	7.7	9.3	11.2	10.2	9.9	8.8	6.9	7.4	7.4	6.9
1974	9.9	8.8	13.4	10.3	7.2	7.7	8.1	10.7	12.7	14.3	13.3	11.7	10.3	8.9	7.8	7.0	6.8
1975	6.0	6.1	8.0	5.6	4.5	6.3	5.8	6.1	7.9	8.6	7.4	6.7	5.7	4.5	4.4	4.5	4.5
1976	6.8	5.4	8.6	7.1	6.1	5.1	5.3	5.8	7.6	9.0	9.1	8.2	6.8	6.4	6.3	6.4	5.6
1977	8.8	6.6	11.4	9.8	7.2	5.8	6.3	7.8	10.6	11.9	11.8	10.8	9.9	8.6	8.0	7.2	6.4
1978	7.2	7.2	9.7	6.6	5.2	6.9	7.1	7.6	9.2	9.6	10.3	7.3	6.7	5.9	5.3	4.8	5.4
1979	6.1	5.4	7.6	6.3	5.2	5.0	5.2	5.9	6.7	8.4	7.6	6.5	6.5	5.8	5.1	5.2	5.2
1980	7.2	6.6	9.0	7.1	6.1	6.0	6.6	7.3	9.3	9.5	8.1	7.7	7.4	6.2	6.8	6.1	5.3
1981	6.5	6.4	8.3	6.4	5.0	5.9	5.8	7.4	7.9	9.7	7.4	6.4	6.4	6.3	5.7	5.1	4.3
1982	5.0	5.8	6.5	4.7	3.2	5.2	5.6	6.5	7.1	6.7	5.7	4.7	4.9	4.5	3.6	3.3	2.7
1983	3.3	3.9	3.9	2.7	2.6	3.7	3.6	4.4	3.7	3.8	4.2	2.0	3.8	2.3	2.8	3.6	1.4

Weekly hours of work: manufacturing (17)
(males)
hours

Durée hebdomadaire du travail : (17)
industries manufacturières (hommes)
heures

	Year	Q.1	Q.2	Q.3	Q.4	JAN	FEB	MAR	APR	MAY	JUN	JUL	AUG	SEP	OCT	NOV	DEC
1964	38.8	40.2	38.8	35.8	40.5												
1965	38.4	40.8	36.9	35.3	40.5												
1966	38.1	40.7	35.8	34.7	41.2												
1967	37.8	38.4	38.4	34.6	39.7												
1968	36.7	39.9	36.2	33.0	37.7												
1969	35.6	37.4	35.0	32.8	37.2												
1970	35.7	35.2	35.5	34.5	37.5												
1971	34.9	36.5	33.7	31.8	37.5												
1972	34.4	35.8	33.6	31.3	36.8												
1973	34.0	35.8	32.7	31.2	36.2												
1974	33.6	35.5	32.2	30.9	35.7												
1975	33.6	34.4	33.5	31.0	35.5												
1976	32.7	35.6	30.7	29.5	34.8												
1977	31.7	33.9	30.4	28.6	34.0												
1978	31.3	32.0	31.5	28.3	33.4												
1979	31.1	33.0	29.5	28.7	33.0												
1980	31.0	32.8	29.8	28.6	32.8												
1981	30.8	32.5	29.3	28.5	33.0												
1982	30.8	32.6	28.9	28.2	33.3												
1983		31.8	29.0	28.2													

Jobs vacant, unfilled vacancies (14) | Adjusted - Corrigé * | Offres d'emploi non satisfaites (14)

thousands | milliers

	Year	Q.1	Q.2	Q.3	Q.4	JAN	FEB	MAR	APR	MAY	JUN	JUL	AUG	SEP	OCT	NOV	DEC
1964		4.2	4.6	4.6	5.0	4.1	4.2	4.3	4.4	4.6	4.7	4.5	4.7	4.7	4.9	5.0	5.2
1965		5.5	5.5	5.8	6.9	5.0	5.7	5.8	5.6	5.5	5.4	5.7	5.7	5.8	6.9	7.0	6.9
1966		7.2	7.4	7.8	8.2	7.1	6.6	8.0	7.4	7.0	7.7	7.4	8.0	8.1	8.4	8.2	8.0
1967		7.4	7.3	7.4	6.4	8.1	7.3	6.9	7.1	7.4	7.3	7.6	7.3	7.2	6.8	6.3	6.1
1968		5.6	5.4	4.7	4.5	5.7	5.6	5.5	5.2	5.8	5.2	5.1	4.5	4.5	4.4	4.5	4.7
1969		4.7	5.9	6.1	7.0	4.8	4.2	5.1	5.9	6.0	5.9	5.8	6.4	6.2	6.6	7.4	7.0
1970		8.5	9.3	9.9	11.2	7.7	8.6	9.1	9.4	9.2	9.4	9.3	9.6	10.8	11.2	11.3	11.0
1971		11.3	10.9	10.8	9.6	10.6	11.3	12.2	11.4	10.8	10.5	11.3	10.5	10.6	9.7	9.2	9.7
1972		9.1	8.5	8.5	7.8	9.5	9.1	8.7	8.6	8.4	8.4	8.7	8.8	8.0	7.8	7.7	7.8
1973		7.8	7.8	8.2	9.3	7.8	7.7	7.9	7.5	7.9	7.9	8.2	8.5	7.9	9.2	9.4	9.2
1974		10.2	10.3	9.9	9.1	9.7	9.8	11.1	10.3	10.2	10.3	9.7	9.9	10.2	9.5	8.9	9.1
1975		7.0	6.1	5.4	5.6	7.8	7.0	6.4	6.5	6.2	5.7	5.7	5.5	5.1	5.3	5.7	6.0
1976		6.2	6.6	6.9	7.7	6.3	6.3	6.0	6.2	6.5	7.0	7.1	6.5	7.2	7.5	8.1	7.4
1977		7.5	8.8	9.5	9.0	7.1	7.4	8.1	8.7	8.7	9.1	9.5	9.5	9.6	9.5	9.1	8.5
1978		8.1	7.5	6.5	6.5	8.3	8.2	7.8	7.6	7.1	8.0	6.6	6.5	6.5	6.2	6.0	7.2
1979		5.9	5.9	6.2	6.5	6.0	5.9	5.9	5.5	6.2	5.9	6.0	6.3	6.4	5.9	6.5	7.0
1980		7.2	7.0	7.1	7.5	7.1	7.5	7.1	7.7	7.1	6.3	7.3	7.2	6.9	7.8	7.5	7.2
1981		6.9	6.5	6.5	6.2	7.0	6.5	7.1	6.6	7.3	5.8	6.1	6.3	7.0	6.6	6.3	5.8
1982		6.2	5.1	4.8	3.9	6.1	6.3	6.2	5.9	5.0	4.5	4.5	4.8	5.0	4.1	4.1	3.7
1983		4.2	3.1	2.7	3.2	4.4	4.0	4.2	3.1	2.9	3.3	1.9	3.7	2.6	3.2	4.4	1.9

Weekly hours of work: manufacturing (females) | Durée hebdomadaire du travail : industries manufacturières (femmes)

hours | heures

	Year	Q.1	Q.2	Q.3	Q.4	JAN	FEB	MAR	APR	MAY	JUN	JUL	AUG	SEP	OCT	NOV	DEC
1964	34.5	35.4	35.1	30.8	36.8												
1965	33.9	36.2	32.8	30.5	36.2												
1966	33.9	36.2	32.7	30.2	36.5												
1967	33.2	33.7	34.4	29.5	35.0												
1968	32.4	35.5	31.3	28.3	34.1												
1969	31.6	33.2	31.3	28.2	33.7												
1970	30.9	30.7	31.9	28.0	32.8												
1971	30.1	31.8	29.1	26.8	32.5												
1972	29.9	31.4	29.5	26.7	32.1												
1973	29.6	32.0	28.5	26.3	31.6												
1974	28.8	30.8	27.6	25.8	30.8												
1975	28.2	28.6	28.3	25.5	30.2												
1976	27.9	30.5	26.5	24.8	29.7												
1977	27.0	29.3	25.8	24.0	28.9												
1978	26.4	26.6	27.0	23.5	28.5												
1979	26.1	28.1	24.3	23.5	28.1												
1980	25.8	27.4	24.9	23.5	27.3												
1981	25.3	26.5	24.3	22.9	27.3												
1982	25.0	26.8	23.3	22.7	27.2												
1983		26.0	24.1	22.8													

* Adjusted by the O.E.C.D. | * Corrigé par l'O.C.D.E.

NORWAY

Hourly earnings: manufacturing (males) — Gains horaires : industries manufacturières (hommes)

1980 = 100

	Year	Q.1	Q.2	Q.3	Q.4	JAN	FEB	MAR	APR	MAY	JUN	JUL	AUG	SEP	OCT	NOV	DEC
1964	20	19	20	20	21												
1965	22	21	22	22	23												
1966	24	22	23	24	24												
1967	25	24	25	26	26												
1968	27	26	27	28	29												
1969	30	29	30	30	31												
1970	34	31	33	35	36												
1971	38	36	38	38	39												
1972	41	39	41	42	43												
1973	45	43	45	45	47												
1974	53	48	52	55	57												
1975	64	60	64	64	67												
1976	74	68	75	76	78												
1977	82	79	83	83	85												
1978	89	86	89	90	91												
1979	91	91	92	91	91												
1980	100	93	96	106	105												
1981	110	106	108	114	113												
1982	121	114	120	126	127												
1983	132	127	131	133	136												

Hourly earnings: manufacturing (females) — Gains horaires : industries manufacturières (femmes)

1980 = 100

	Year	Q.1	Q.2	Q.3	Q.4	JAN	FEB	MAR	APR	MAY	JUN	JUL	AUG	SEP	OCT	NOV	DEC
1964	17	17	17	18	18												
1965	19	18	19	19	20												
1966	21	20	21	22	22												
1967	23	22	23	23	24												
1968	25	24	24	26	26												
1969	27	27	27	28	28												
1970	31	28	30	32	33												
1971	35	33	35	35	36												
1972	38	36	38	39	40												
1973	42	40	42	43	44												
1974	50	44	49	53	54												
1975	61	57	61	61	64												
1976	72	65	73	75	76												
1977	80	77	80	82	83												
1978	87	84	86	89	89												
1979	90	89	90	90	90												
1980	100	92	95	108	106												
1981	111	107	103	115	115												
1982	123	116	120	129	130												
1983		131	134	135													

Wholesale prices: investment goods (18) — Prix de gros : biens d'équipement (18)

1980 = 100

	Year	Q.1	Q.2	Q.3	Q.4	JAN	FEB	MAR	APR	MAY	JUN	JUL	AUG	SEP	OCT	NOV	DEC
1964	43	43	43	44	44	43	43	43	43	43	43	43	43	44	44	44	44
1965	44	44	44	44	44	44	44	44	44	44	44	44	44	44	44	44	44
1966	45	45	45	45	45	45	45	45	45	45	45	45	45	45	45	45	45
1967	46	45	46	46	46	45	45	45	46	46	46	45	46	46	46	46	46
1968	46	46	46	46	46	46	46	46	46	46	46	46	46	46	46	46	46
1969	47	46	46	47	47	46	46	46	46	46	46	47	47	47	47	47	47
1970	49	48	49	50	50	48	48	48	49	49	50	50	50	50	50	50	51
1971	52	51	52	52	52	51	51	51	51	51	52	52	52	52	52	52	52
1972	54	53	54	54	55	53	53	53	54	54	54	54	54	55	55	55	55
1973	57	56	55	57	58	56	56	56	56	56	56	56	57	57	58	58	58
1974	62	60	61	63	64	60	60	61	61	61	62	62	63	63	64	64	64
1975	70	69	70	71	72	69	69	69	69	70	70	70	70	71	72	72	72
1976	78	75	78	79	80	75	76	76	78	78	78	78	79	80	80	80	81
1977	82	81	82	83	84	81	81	81	82	82	82	83	83	83	84	84	84
1978	88	86	88	89	90	86	86	86	87	88	88	89	89	90	90	90	91
1979	93	91	92	94	95	91	91	92	92	92	92	93	93	94	95	95	96
1980	100	98	99	101	102	97	97	99	99	99	100	100	101	102	102	102	102
1981	106	105	105	107	107	104	105	105	105	105	106	106	107	107	107	108	107
1982	111	109	110	111	113	108	109	109	110	110	110	110	111	112	113	113	113
1983	117	115	116	117	118	114	114	116	116	116	116	117	117	117	118	118	118

Wholesale prices: consumer goods (18) — Prix de gros : biens de consommation (18)

1980 = 100

	Year	Q.1	Q.2	Q.3	Q.4	JAN	FEB	MAR	APR	MAY	JUN	JUL	AUG	SEP	OCT	NOV	DEC
1964	40	40	40	41	40	39	40	40	40	40	40	40	40	41	40	40	40
1965	40	40	40	40	40	40	40	40	40	40	40	40	40	40	40	40	40
1966	41	40	41	41	41	40	40	40	40	40	41	41	42	41	41	41	41
1967	42	42	42	43	43	42	42	42	42	42	42	43	43	43	43	43	43
1968	43	43	43	43	43	43	43	43	43	43	43	43	43	43	43	43	43
1969	44	44	44	44	45	44	44	44	44	44	44	44	44	44	44	45	45
1970	47	45	46	47	48	45	46	46	46	46	46	47	47	47	47	48	48
1971	49	49	49	49	50	48	48	49	49	49	49	49	49	49	50	50	50
1972	52	51	51	52	53	51	51	51	51	51	52	52	52	52	53	53	53
1973	56	54	55	56	57	53	54	55	55	55	55	56	56	56	57	57	58
1974	62	60	61	62	64	59	60	61	61	61	61	61	62	63	64	64	65
1975	69	67	68	69	70	66	67	67	68	68	68	69	69	70	70	70	70
1976	73	72	73	75	74	72	72	73	73	73	73	75	75	74	74	74	74
1977	79	77	78	80	80	77	77	78	78	78	78	80	79	80	80	80	80
1978	84	82	83	85	86	81	82	82	82	83	83	84	85	86	86	86	87
1979	90	87	89	90	92	87	87	88	88	89	89	90	90	91	91	92	92
1980	100	96	99	102	104	94	96	97	98	99	99	100	102	102	103	104	105
1981	113	110	112	115	116	109	109	110	112	112	112	114	115	115	115	116	116
1982	123	120	120	124	127	119	119	121	119	119	121	123	124	124	125	127	127
1983	131	129	130	132	133	128	130	130	130	130	130	132	132	133	133	133	134

Wholesale prices: petroleum products (18) — Prix de gros : dérivés du pétrole (18)

1980 = 100

	Year	Q.1	Q.2	Q.3	Q.4	JAN	FEB	MAR	APR	MAY	JUN	JUL	AUG	SEP	OCT	NOV	DEC
1964	15	15	15	15	15	15	15	16	15	15	15	15	15	15	15	15	15
1965	15	15	15	15	14	15	15	15	15	15	15	15	15	14	14	14	14
1966	14	14	14	14	14	14	14	14	14	14	14	15	14	14	14	14	14
1967	15	14	14	16	16	14	14	14	14	14	14	15	16	17	16	17	16
1968	15	15	15	15	16	16	15	15	15	15	15	15	15	15	16	16	16
1969	15	15	15	15	15	16	15	15	15	15	15	15	15	15	15	14	14
1970	15	14	14	15	16	14	14	14	14	14	14	14	14	15	16	16	18
1971	19	18	19	19	18	18	18	19	19	19	19	19	19	19	19	19	18
1972	18	18	18	18	17	17	18	18	18	18	18	18	18	18	17	17	18
1973	20	18	19	20	23	18	18	19	19	19	19	20	20	20	22	22	26
1974	38	35	42	39	37	29	34	43	43	41	41	39	40	39	37	37	38
1975	39	39	37	38	42	40	38	38	38	37	37	37	37	39	40	42	44
1976	45	45	44	45	45	44	44	45	45	44	44	45	45	45	45	45	44
1977	47	46	47	47	48	45	46	47	47	47	47	47	47	48	48	48	48
1978	48	47	48	48	48	47	48	47	47	48	49	49	48	48	47	47	49
1979	64	52	60	68	76	49	51	57	58	60	62	64	68	72	74	76	78
1980	100	91	99	104	107	86	92	94	96	100	102	104	103	104	104	106	110
1981	123	118	124	125	125	114	117	122	123	124	125	127	124	124	123	127	125
1982	128	125	118	128	140	127	125	124	119	114	119	124	129	132	137	143	140
1983	132	134	129	131	134	137	137	129	132	127	128	129	130	133	133	133	135

Consumer prices: all items (19) — Prix à la consommation : total (19)

1980 = 100

	Year	Q.1	Q.2	Q.3	Q.4	JAN	FEB	MAR	APR	MAY	JUN	JUL	AUG	SEP	OCT	NOV	DEC
1964	34	33	33	34	34	33	33	33	33	33	33	34	34	34	34	34	34
1965	35	35	35	35	35	35	35	35	35	35	35	36	35	35	35	35	35
1966	36	36	36	37	37	36	36	36	36	36	36	37	37	37	37	37	37
1967	38	37	33	38	38	37	37	37	37	38	38	38	38	38	38	38	39
1968	39	39	39	39	40	39	39	39	39	39	39	39	39	39	40	40	40
1969	40	40	40	41	41	40	40	40	40	40	40	41	41	41	41	41	41
1970	45	44	44	45	46	43	44	44	44	44	44	45	45	45	46	46	46
1971	48	47	47	48	49	47	47	47	47	47	47	48	48	48	48	49	49
1972	51	50	50	52	52	49	49	50	50	50	51	51	51	52	52	52	52
1973	55	53	54	55	56	53	53	54	54	54	55	55	55	55	56	56	56
1974	60	58	59	60	62	57	58	59	59	59	59	60	60	61	61	62	62
1975	67	65	66	68	69	64	64	65	66	66	67	68	68	69	69	69	69
1976	73	71	73	74	75	70	70	71	72	73	73	74	74	74	74	75	75
1977	80	77	79	81	82	76	77	78	78	79	80	81	81	81	81	81	82
1978	86	84	85	87	88	83	84	85	85	85	86	87	87	88	88	88	88
1979	90	88	90	91	92	88	88	89	89	90	90	90	91	91	92	92	92
1980	100	95	99	102	104	94	95	97	98	99	100	101	102	103	104	104	105
1981	114	109	113	116	117	108	109	111	112	112	114	115	115	116	117	117	118
1982	127	122	125	128	131	121	122	124	124	125	126	128	128	129	130	131	131
1983	137	134	136	138	140	133	134	135	136	136	137	138	138	139	140	140	141

NORWAY

Money supply (M1)

billion kroner, end of period

Disponibilités monétaires (M1)

milliards de couronnes, fin de période

	Year	Q.1	Q.2	Q.3	Q.4	JAN	FEB	MAR	APR	MAY	JUN	JUL	AUG	SEP	OCT	NOV	DEC
1964																	
1965																	
1966																	
1967																	
1968																	
1969																	
1970	21.85	18.59	20.24	20.42	21.85	18.88	18.82	18.59	18.97	19.04	20.24	20.33	20.14	20.42	20.95	21.35	21.85
1971	24.57	21.29	22.86	22.84	24.57	22.12	21.78	21.29	21.79	21.67	22.86	23.17	23.33	22.84	23.69	24.24	24.57
1972	27.93	23.91	25.44	26.04	27.93	24.86	24.57	23.91	24.70	24.37	25.44	26.14	25.88	26.04	26.41	26.69	27.93
1973	30.64	26.37	28.23	28.78	30.64	27.45	27.20	26.37	27.25	26.96	28.23	28.50	28.34	28.78	29.19	29.15	30.64
1974	34.42	29.54	31.11	31.55	34.42	30.72	30.61	29.54	29.91	29.59	31.11	31.05	31.16	31.55	33.59	32.75	34.42
1975	41.01	33.81	36.91	38.37	41.01	34.58	34.78	33.81	34.47	34.18	36.91	37.44	37.88	38.37	39.76	39.51	41.01
1976	47.69	40.82	44.45	44.62	47.69	42.76	42.05	40.82	41.69	41.35	44.45	44.54	44.06	44.62	47.20	46.07	47.69
1977	53.76	49.02	50.21	50.83	53.76	49.21	47.59	49.02	47.66	47.12	50.21	50.56	50.42	50.83	53.54	52.15	53.76
1978	57.79	52.55	54.30	55.00	57.79	54.55	52.18	52.55	51.20	51.51	54.30	55.06	53.87	55.00	57.31	56.52	57.79
1979	64.37	56.91	60.42	62.79	64.37	58.33	56.33	56.91	57.03	56.10	60.42	61.76	60.90	62.79	63.51	63.06	64.37
1980	71.36	63.64	66.54	67.63	71.36	65.20	62.64	63.64	62.47	63.13	66.54	66.15	65.99	67.63	70.55	67.82	71.36
1981	78.26	68.57	74.96	76.97	78.26	72.15	70.81	68.57	69.99	68.88	74.96	75.21	75.15	76.97	79.31	76.63	78.26
1982	87.76	78.97	83.48	85.08	87.76	81.41	78.02	78.97	78.58	79.08	83.48	83.81	81.90	85.08	86.30	86.20	87.76
1983	97.29	86.05	90.99	93.66	97.29	88.22	88.14	86.05	86.14	86.29	90.99	93.41	90.02	93.66	95.44	95.81	97.29

M1 plus quasi-money

billion kroner, end of period

M1 plus quasi-monnaie

milliards de couronnes, fin de période

	Year	Q.1	Q.2	Q.3	Q.4	JAN	FEB	MAR	APR	MAY	JUN	JUL	AUG	SEP	OCT	NOV	DEC
1964																	
1965																	
1966																	
1967																	
1968																	
1969																	
1970	50.02	44.07	46.33	47.31	50.02	43.65	43.88	44.07	44.65	44.98	46.33	46.79	46.81	47.31	48.12	48.25	50.02
1971	56.13	50.46	52.43	52.87	56.13	51.66	50.84	50.46	51.28	51.13	52.48	53.05	53.51	52.87	54.46	54.74	56.13
1972	62.74	56.67	58.60	59.52	62.74	57.12	57.26	56.67	57.77	57.38	58.60	59.65	59.74	59.52	60.29	60.13	62.74
1973	69.75	62.67	65.93	66.50	69.75	63.09	63.54	62.67	64.27	63.91	65.93	66.44	66.55	66.50	67.31	66.86	69.75
1974	77.42	70.05	72.17	73.36	77.42	70.84	71.54	70.05	71.15	70.29	72.17	72.43	73.09	73.36	75.93	74.23	77.42
1975	89.22	77.92	81.93	84.96	89.22	77.94	78.80	77.92	78.55	78.31	81.93	83.85	84.43	84.96	87.00	85.93	89.22
1976	104.47	90.74	95.97	97.31	104.47	91.89	91.86	90.74	92.66	92.31	95.97	97.14	97.49	97.31	101.11	99.40	104.47
1977	121.13	107.93	111.41	114.48	121.13	106.93	106.63	107.93	107.92	106.98	111.41	113.08	114.33	114.48	119.00	115.80	121.13
1978	134.56	121.92	124.91	127.12	134.56	123.08	121.70	121.92	121.71	122.11	124.91	126.50	126.52	127.12	130.66	129.13	134.56
1979	153.18	136.66	141.50	145.56	153.18	137.12	136.53	136.66	138.22	136.33	141.50	143.82	143.79	145.56	148.52	147.20	153.18
1980	172.08	154.19	157.90	162.00	172.08	155.79	154.18	154.19	154.10	154.41	157.90	159.30	160.95	162.00	165.46	163.20	172.08
1981	192.02	172.30	178.58	184.20	192.02	176.01	174.69	172.30	174.68	172.65	178.58	180.50	181.69	184.20	186.86	182.85	192.02
1982	212.15	195.79	198.39	201.75	212.15	196.95	193.73	195.79	194.43	194.52	198.39	200.68	198.86	201.75	203.18	200.00	212.15
1983	232.14	212.14	215.60	219.24	232.14	213.94	214.54	212.14	210.30	208.81	215.60	220.95	217.51	219.24	223.02	219.78	232.14

Unused credit:

commercial and savings banks

billion kroner, end of period

Ouvertures de crédit :

banques commerciales et d'épargne

milliards de couronnes, fin de période

	Year	Q.1	Q.2	Q.3	Q.4	JAN	FEB	MAR	APR	MAY	JUN	JUL	AUG	SEP	OCT	NOV	DEC
1964																	
1965																	
1966																	
1967																	
1968																	
1969	5.77				5.77												5.77
1970	6.42	5.45	5.69	5.89	6.42	5.67	5.65	5.45	5.49	5.59	5.69	6.07	5.93	5.89	6.24	6.36	6.42
1971	7.53	6.21	6.30	6.77	7.53	6.66	6.46	6.21	6.15	6.31	6.30	7.01	6.97	6.77	7.06	7.35	7.53
1972	8.36	7.08	7.33	7.88	8.36	7.73	7.44	7.08	7.21	7.32	7.33	8.01	7.94	7.88	8.03	8.24	8.36
1973	8.90	7.81	8.07	8.63	8.90	8.54	8.11	7.81	7.78	7.98	8.07	8.54	8.69	8.63	9.09	9.08	8.90
1974	9.32	8.89	8.63	9.03	9.82	9.53	9.35	8.89	8.87	8.70	8.63	8.96	9.12	9.03	9.91	9.56	9.82
1975	11.82	9.36	9.69	10.98	11.82	9.94	9.63	9.36	9.64	9.53	9.69	10.80	11.03	10.98	11.51	11.71	11.82
1976	13.66	11.40	11.93	12.69	13.66	12.57	11.97	11.40	11.45	11.44	11.93	12.52	12.61	12.69	13.47	13.50	13.66
1977	14.74	12.94	12.93	13.95	14.74	13.86	13.51	12.94	12.82	13.07	12.93	14.01	14.07	13.95	14.98	15.02	14.74
1978	15.80	14.23	14.52	15.28	15.80	15.02	14.80	14.23	14.31	13.89	14.52	15.43	15.02	15.28	15.82	15.92	15.80
1979	18.80	16.11	16.61	17.51	18.80	16.35	16.02	16.11	15.64	16.00	16.61	17.87	17.84	17.51	18.38	18.61	18.80
1980	19.77	18.01	17.98	18.64	19.77	18.88	18.67	18.01	18.09	17.34	17.98	18.55	18.71	18.64	19.67	19.40	19.77
1981	22.80	19.33	20.46	21.31	22.80	20.05	19.46	19.33	19.09	19.22	20.46	21.43	21.79	21.31	23.09	22.28	22.80
1982	25.41	22.22	22.86	23.56	25.41	23.72	22.79	22.22	22.24	22.40	22.86	24.28	23.67	23.56	24.51	24.89	25.41
1983	27.22	23.29	24.29	25.42	27.22	25.13	24.14	23.29	23.51	23.70	24.29	26.18	25.24	25.42	26.74	26.98	27.22

Money supply (M1) — Disponibilités monétaires (M1)

billion kroner, end of period — milliards de couronnes, fin de période

Adjusted - Corrigé *

	Year	Q.1	Q.2	Q.3	Q.4	JAN	FEB	MAR	APR	MAY	JUN	JUL	AUG	SEP	OCT	NOV	DEC
1964																	
1965																	
1966																	
1967																	
1968																	
1969																	
1970		19.16	20.14	20.52	21.24	18.41	18.79	19.16	19.26	19.67	20.14	20.07	20.26	20.52	20.85	21.22	21.24
1971		21.95	22.72	22.96	23.86	21.53	21.71	21.95	22.12	22.39	22.72	22.90	23.47	22.96	23.55	24.12	23.86
1972		24.64	25.29	26.17	27.12	24.20	24.47	24.64	25.08	25.20	25.29	25.88	26.01	26.17	26.17	26.58	27.12
1973		27.16	28.04	28.95	29.71	26.73	27.07	27.16	27.70	27.93	28.04	28.28	28.51	28.95	28.85	29.09	29.71
1974		30.36	30.86	31.74	33.42	29.35	30.45	30.36	30.43	30.76	30.86	30.87	31.38	31.74	33.03	32.75	33.42
1975		34.65	36.61	38.60	39.85	33.54	34.67	34.65	35.21	35.64	36.61	37.26	38.18	38.60	38.87	39.48	39.85
1976		41.70	44.05	44.84	46.44	41.39	42.10	41.70	42.71	43.21	44.05	44.28	44.46	44.84	45.92	45.97	46.44
1977		49.92	49.76	50.98	52.40	47.59	47.88	49.92	48.98	49.34	49.76	50.16	50.93	50.98	51.88	51.94	52.40
1978		53.40	53.82	55.00	56.38	52.81	52.71	53.40	52.73	54.05	53.82	54.62	54.41	55.00	55.37	56.24	56.38
1979		57.71	59.83	62.60	62.74	56.47	57.13	57.71	58.86	59.00	59.83	61.21	61.51	62.60	61.24	62.68	62.74
1980		64.54	65.88	67.23	69.55	63.31	63.72	64.54	64.54	66.45	65.88	65.56	66.59	67.23	68.03	67.35	69.55
1981		69.61	74.14	76.43	76.35	70.12	72.10	69.61	72.38	72.58	74.14	74.62	75.83	76.43	76.48	76.17	76.35
1982		80.18	82.58	84.41	85.62	79.19	79.45	80.18	81.26	83.42	82.58	83.15	82.64	84.41	83.22	85.69	85.62
1983		87.36	90.00	92.91	94.91	85.81	89.76	87.36	89.08	91.02	90.00	92.66	90.84	92.91	92.03	95.24	94.91

M1 plus quasi-money — M1 plus quasi-monnaie

billion kroner, end of period — milliards de couronnes, fin de période

Adjusted - Corrigé

	Year	Q.1	Q.2	Q.3	Q.4	JAN	FEB	MAR	APR	MAY	JUN	JUL	AUG	SEP	OCT	NOV	DEC
1964																	
1965																	
1966																	
1967																	
1968																	
1969																	
1970		44.46	46.19	47.78	49.42	42.85	43.40	44.46	44.67	45.58	46.19	46.57	46.78	47.78	48.29	49.04	49.42
1971		50.90	52.32	53.39	55.44	50.70	50.23	50.90	51.30	51.82	52.32	52.83	53.49	53.39	54.63	55.65	55.44
1972		57.16	58.41	60.06	61.88	56.06	56.52	57.16	57.80	58.24	58.41	59.42	59.71	60.06	60.38	61.12	61.88
1973		63.24	65.73	67.12	68.77	61.94	62.70	63.24	64.36	65.01	65.73	66.19	66.55	67.12	67.31	68.03	68.77
1974		70.61	71.94	74.05	76.28	69.46	70.54	70.61	71.33	71.67	71.94	72.19	73.11	74.05	75.76	75.59	76.28
1975		78.44	81.70	85.79	87.84	76.32	77.75	78.44	78.86	80.00	81.70	83.00	84.50	85.79	86.60	87.51	87.84
1976		91.19	95.76	98.25	102.82	89.85	90.75	91.19	93.17	94.46	95.76	96.86	97.64	98.25	100.49	101.20	102.82
1977		108.28	111.29	115.56	119.12	104.39	105.51	108.28	108.61	109.54	111.29	112.77	114.62	115.58	118.20	117.84	119.12
1978		122.16	124.90	128.25	132.27	120.01	120.54	122.16	122.52	125.08	124.90	126.23	126.99	128.25	129.85	131.47	132.27
1979		136.80	141.62	146.63	150.30	133.49	135.23	136.80	139.12	139.59	141.62	143.64	144.42	146.63	147.60	149.77	150.30
1980		154.41	158.13	162.97	168.72	151.71	152.79	154.41	155.14	158.16	158.13	159.23	161.78	162.97	164.54	166.10	168.72
1981		172.54	178.89	185.25	188.31	171.35	173.08	172.54	175.85	176.83	178.89	180.45	182.73	185.25	185.93	186.19	188.31
1982		195.99	198.99	202.97	207.99	191.77	192.00	195.99	195.80	199.31	198.99	200.68	200.06	202.97	202.17	203.67	207.99
1983		212.14	215.99	219.24	227.59	207.37	212.41	212.14	212.25	210.81	215.99	221.07	217.61	219.24	222.53	224.98	227.59

Credit to economy: commercial and savings banks — Crédits à l'économie : banques commerciales et d'épargne

billion kroner, end of period — milliards de couronnes, fin de période

	Year	Q.1	Q.2	Q.3	Q.4	JAN	FEB	MAR	APR	MAY	JUN	JUL	AUG	SEP	OCT	NOV	DEC
1964	16.08	15.36	15.96	16.02	16.08	14.99	15.20	15.36	15.52	15.84	15.96	15.93	15.85	16.02	16.01	16.21	16.08
1965	17.09	16.66	16.94	17.11	17.09	16.15	16.45	16.66	16.77	16.96	16.94	16.94	16.89	17.11	17.06	17.30	17.09
1966	18.85	17.77	18.45	18.67	18.85	17.22	17.51	17.77	18.01	18.32	18.45	18.47	18.62	18.67	18.62	18.83	18.85
1967	20.43	19.54	20.12	20.44	20.43	18.93	19.21	19.54	19.74	20.06	20.12	20.11	20.21	20.44	20.23	20.62	20.43
1968	22.21	21.00	21.75	22.06	22.21	20.44	20.64	21.00	21.07	21.50	21.75	21.59	21.72	22.06	22.01	22.34	22.21
1969	25.19	23.30	24.26	25.09	25.19	22.38	22.67	23.30	23.63	24.11	24.26	24.30	24.46	25.09	25.04	25.43	25.19
1970	27.73	26.07	27.12	27.69	27.73	25.37	25.64	26.07	26.43	26.80	27.12	26.92	27.31	27.69	27.61	27.92	27.73
1971	31.04	28.78	30.15	30.80	31.04	27.60	28.15	28.78	29.11	29.61	30.15	29.85	30.23	30.80	30.80	31.00	31.04
1972	34.89	32.11	33.46	34.17	34.89	30.96	31.46	32.11	32.45	32.80	33.46	33.20	33.54	34.17	34.23	34.67	34.89
1973	39.25	36.26	37.30	38.10	39.25	34.70	35.53	36.26	36.67	36.82	37.30	37.00	37.36	38.10	38.17	38.59	39.25
1974	44.23	40.66	42.79	43.43	44.23	38.99	39.80	40.66	41.42	42.07	42.79	42.64	42.97	43.43	43.04	43.99	44.23
1975	51.42	46.47	48.34	49.42	51.42	44.46	45.47	46.47	46.91	47.50	48.34	47.85	48.31	49.42	49.87	50.84	51.42
1976	59.37	53.69	56.36	57.99	59.37	51.04	52.29	53.69	54.47	55.29	56.36	56.35	56.95	57.99	57.59	58.88	59.37
1977	69.16	62.52	65.81	66.98	69.16	59.37	60.72	62.52	63.43	64.30	65.81	65.47	65.74	66.98	66.57	67.60	69.16
1978	75.04	71.39	72.66	73.50	75.04	69.04	70.20	71.39	71.82	72.58	72.66	72.26	72.57	73.50	73.09	73.70	75.04
1979	83.39	76.74	80.48	82.27	83.39	74.68	75.46	76.74	77.73	78.85	80.48	80.16	80.48	82.27	81.63	82.49	83.39
1980	91.88	85.32	88.50	90.57	91.88	83.29	83.64	85.32	85.69	87.04	88.50	88.66	88.96	90.57	89.47	91.00	91.88
1981	104.38	94.50	98.80	100.42	104.38	91.58	92.82	94.50	95.74	97.20	98.80	98.93	98.69	100.42	99.58	101.65	104.38
1982	116.49	107.99	111.84	113.88	116.49	103.51	105.06	107.99	108.36	109.49	111.84	111.30	111.61	113.88	113.00	113.15	116.49
1983	130.21	122.30	129.30	128.59	130.21	117.07	118.42	122.30	122.77	124.94	129.30	128.40	129.23	128.59	127.25	127.38	130.21

* Adjusted by the O.E.C.D. — * Corrigé par l'O.C.D.E.

NORWAY

Instalment credit outstanding
billion kroner, end of period

Crédits remboursables par tranches, en cours
milliards de couronnes, fin de période

	Year	Q.1	Q.2	Q.3	Q.4	JAN	FEB	MAR	APR	MAY	JUN	JUL	AUG	SEP	OCT	NOV	DEC
1964	0.79	0.70	0.75	0.77	0.79												
1965	0.87	0.77	0.81	0.84	0.87												
1966	1.02	0.87	0.94	0.98	1.02												
1967	1.07	1.00	1.05	1.05	1.07												
1968	1.05	1.02	1.05	1.05	1.05												
1969	1.28	1.05	1.11	1.17	1.28												
1970	1.45	1.22	1.34	1.39	1.45												
1971	1.60	1.42	1.51	1.56	1.60												
1972	1.69	1.58	1.62	1.67	1.69												
1973	1.73	1.66	1.71	1.69	1.73												
1974	1.90	1.70	1.77	1.85	1.90												
1975	2.43	2.12	2.26	2.33	2.43												
1976	2.84	2.37	2.49	2.66	2.84												
1977	3.40	2.88	3.08	3.25	3.40												
1978	2.91	3.37	3.10	2.98	2.91												
1979	2.62	2.77	2.69	2.63	2.62												
1980	2.66	2.58	2.56	2.60	2.66												
1981	2.65	2.59	2.58	2.63	2.65												
1982	2.63	2.55	2.50	2.47	2.63												
1983		2.63															

Yield of Government bonds: 5 %, 1961-96 (20)
per cent per annum, end of period

Rendement des bons d'État : 5 %, 1961-96 (20)
pourcentage par an, fin de période

	Year	Q.1	Q.2	Q.3	Q.4	JAN	FEB	MAR	APR	MAY	JUN	JUL	AUG	SEP	OCT	NOV	DEC
1964	4.95	4.55	4.55	4.93	4.95	4.55	4.55	4.55	4.55	4.55	4.55	4.93	4.93	4.93	4.93	4.93	4.95
1965	4.99	5.97	5.03	5.01	4.99	4.95	4.95	5.97	5.97	5.97	5.03	5.03	5.03	5.01	5.00	5.00	4.99
1966	5.03	5.00	5.00	5.00	5.03	5.00	5.00	5.00	5.00	5.00	5.00	5.00	5.00	5.00	5.00	5.03	5.03
1967	4.95	5.03	5.00	4.97	4.95	5.03	5.03	5.03	5.00	5.00	5.00	5.00	4.97	4.97	4.95	4.95	4.95
1968	4.89	4.95	4.95	4.95	4.89	4.95	4.95	4.95	4.95	4.95	4.95	4.95	4.95	4.95	4.89	4.89	4.89
1969	6.30	4.89	4.83	..	6.30	4.92	4.89	4.89	4.89	4.95	4.83	4.86	4.97	..	6.08	6.20	6.30
1970	6.41	6.30	6.25	6.25	6.41	6.35	6.35	6.30	6.27	6.24	6.25	6.26	6.26	6.25	6.29	6.29	6.41
1971	6.37	6.37	6.39	6.42	6.37	6.38	6.36	6.37	6.37	6.38	6.39	6.40	6.41	6.42	6.43	6.43	6.37
1972	6.13	6.40	6.29	5.24	6.13	6.39	6.39	6.40	6.34	6.31	6.29	6.23	6.23	6.24	6.14	6.15	6.13
1973	6.20	6.19	6.18	6.21	6.20	6.10	6.18	6.19	6.19	6.20	6.18	6.19	6.20	6.21	6.21	6.22	6.20
1974	7.26	6.22	7.43	7.40	7.26	6.24	6.22	6.22	7.42	7.44	7.43	7.45	7.42	7.40	7.29	7.30	7.26
1975	7.29	7.31	7.25	7.28	7.29	7.32	7.33	7.31	7.26	7.30	7.25	7.27	7.28	7.28	7.28	7.29	7.29
1976	7.24	7.30	7.20	7.20	7.24	7.31	7.32	7.30	7.31	7.33	7.20	7.17	7.19	7.20	7.22	7.24	7.24
1977	8.37	7.29	7.28	7.29	8.37	7.25	7.27	7.29	7.31	7.33	7.28	7.30	7.31	7.29	7.31	7.33	8.37
1978	8.19	8.46	8.54	8.37	8.19	8.40	8.43	8.46	8.59	8.63	8.54	8.57	8.39	8.37	8.40	8.38	8.19
1979	10.04	8.28	8.26	8.25	10.04	8.22	8.25	8.28	8.31	8.38	8.26	8.29	8.32	8.25	8.28	10.19	10.04
1980	10.28	10.20	10.16	10.40	10.28	10.10	10.15	10.20	10.26	10.31	10.16	10.21	10.73	10.40	10.44	10.44	10.28
1981	12.91	11.57	12.71	12.51	12.91	11.71	11.50	11.57	11.65	12.99	12.71	12.81	12.58	12.51	12.44	12.37	12.91
1982	12.92	13.21	12.95	13.27	12.92	13.34	13.45	13.21	13.21	13.26	12.95	13.06	13.16	13.27	13.29	13.32	12.92
1983	12.38	13.16	12.56	12.80	12.38	13.03	13.13	13.16	13.10	13.12	12.56	12.67	12.77	12.80	12.82	12.76	12.38

Share prices: industrials (21)
Oslo Stock Exchange
1980 = 100

Cours des actions industrielles (21)
Bourse d'Oslo
1980 = 100

	Year	Q.1	Q.2	Q.3	Q.4	JAN	FEB	MAR	APR	MAY	JUN	JUL	AUG	SEP	OCT	NOV	DEC
1964	66	66	64	66	67	66	66	65	65	64	63	65	65	69	68	67	66
1965	65	68	64	64	62	66	69	68	67	63	63	62	64	65	63	62	62
1966	60	62	61	60	56	62	63	62	62	61	59	61	61	58	57	56	56
1967	52	55	52	52	50	56	55	54	54	52	51	52	52	52	51	51	49
1968	53	50	50	56	56	51	49	50	50	48	51	53	58	59	56	57	56
1969	66	62	65	68	71	59	64	62	64	66	64	66	63	70	69	71	74
1970	81	76	77	83	89	75	76	76	78	75	76	77	84	88	92	88	87
1971	90	93	91	99	77	95	93	92	87	90	97	103	99	96	85	74	73
1972	84	79	82	91	83	=81=	77	77	81	78	88	89	95	89	84	81	82
1973	130	95	133	148	144	89	96	98	118	132	148	151	148	145	145	149	138
1974	121	152	130	107	95	160	151	145	138	127	124	113	113	93	102	97	88
1975	86	88	87	91	80	86	92	86	84	92	86	91	93	89	81	81	77
1976	90	91	89	94	84	92	95	87	87	87	92	95	97	90	85	85	83
1977	70	78	72	69	59	80	78	77	76	70	70	70	68	67	65	56	55
1978	59	54	57	65	60	53	55	53	55	58	57	56	66	73	61	60	59
1979	83	64	78	86	103	59	65	69	70	81	84	86	84	88	95	103	110
1980	100	106	99	98	96	108	112	97	96	100	101	97	101	96	98	97	93
1981	98	92	93	105	102	92	91	94	93	95	91	96	112	108	98	106	100
1982	91	94	93	91	89	98	95	88	88	97	93	91	90	91	93	89	85
1983	159	120	157	177	181	=101=	130	128	142	168	161	168	179	184	186	171	135

U.S. dollar exchange rate: spot
cents per krone, end of period

Taux de change du dollar É.-U. : au comptant
cents par couronne, fin de période

	Year	Q.1	Q.2	Q.3	Q.4	JAN	FEB	MAR	APR	MAY	JUN	JUL	AUG	SEP	OCT	NOV	DEC
1964	13.97	13.97	13.97	13.95	13.97	13.95	13.96	13.97	13.98	13.98	13.97	13.96	13.94	13.95	13.94	13.97	13.97
1965	13.99	13.97	13.96	13.99	13.99	13.96	13.97	13.97	13.98	13.96	13.96	13.97	13.97	13.99	13.59	13.99	13.99
1966	13.98	13.97	13.96	13.98	13.98	13.98	13.97	13.97	13.96	13.96	13.96	13.97	13.98	13.98	13.99	13.98	13.98
1967	13.99	13.98	13.98	13.97	13.99	13.97	13.97	13.98	13.98	13.98	13.98	13.97	13.97	13.97	13.97	13.99	13.99
1968	13.99	13.99	13.99	13.99	13.99	13.99	13.99	13.99	13.99	13.99	13.99	13.99	13.99	13.99	13.99	13.99	13.99
1969	13.99	14.00	14.01	13.98	13.99	13.97	13.99	14.00	14.01	13.99	14.01	14.00	13.99	13.98	13.97	13.98	13.99
1970	14.01	13.99	13.98	13.98	14.01	13.97	13.99	13.99	13.98	13.98	13.98	13.99	13.99	13.98	13.98	13.99	14.01
1971	14.90	14.01	14.06	14.56	14.90	13.98	13.99	14.01	14.01	14.05	14.06	14.06	14.47	14.56	14.58	14.63	14.90
1972	15.06	15.16	15.35	15.11	15.06	14.95	15.09	15.16	15.15	15.32	15.35	15.32	15.31	15.11	15.07	15.22	15.06
1973	17.46	16.94	18.59	18.08	17.46	15.31	16.74	16.94	16.84	17.56	18.59	18.67	17.89	18.08	18.03	17.87	17.46
1974	19.21	18.27	18.42	18.07	19.21	16.75	17.60	18.27	18.77	18.45	18.42	18.48	17.97	18.07	18.16	18.58	19.21
1975	17.91	20.35	20.22	17.54	17.91	19.78	20.39	20.35	19.92	20.23	20.22	18.37	18.12	17.54	18.31	17.92	17.91
1976	19.29	18.14	17.98	18.78	19.29	18.00	18.03	18.14	18.23	18.04	17.98	18.08	18.17	18.78	18.92	19.09	19.29
1977	19.46	19.10	18.82	19.17	19.46	18.77	18.95	19.10	18.97	19.00	18.82	18.96	18.30	18.17	18.33	18.51	19.46
1978	19.91	18.84	18.51	19.47	19.91	19.49	18.81	18.84	18.51	18.41	18.51	18.65	19.10	19.47	21.44	19.56	19.91
1979	20.30	19.58	19.62	20.47	20.30	19.57	19.68	19.58	19.31	19.27	19.62	19.82	19.89	20.47	19.95	20.16	20.30
1980	19.31	19.34	20.66	20.54	19.31	20.46	20.35	19.34	20.23	20.47	20.66	20.37	20.66	20.54	20.14	19.83	19.31
1981	17.22	18.61	16.65	16.79	17.22	18.39	18.33	18.61	18.01	17.45	16.65	16.29	16.53	16.79	16.81	17.58	17.22
1982	14.18	16.34	16.00	14.37	14.18	16.98	16.64	16.34	16.70	16.56	16.00	15.53	14.84	14.37	13.80	14.09	14.18
1983	12.92	13.39	13.71	13.59	12.92	13.99	14.02	13.89	14.07	14.00	13.71	13.54	13.30	13.59	13.55	13.34	12.92

Official reserves excluding gold
million SDR's, end of period

Réserves officielles, or exclu
million de DTS, fin de période

	Year	Q.1	Q.2	Q.3	Q.4	JAN	FEB	MAR	APR	MAY	JUN	JUL	AUG	SEP	OCT	NOV	DEC
1964	356	300	337	350	356	292	289	300	303	341	337	347	344	350	347	341	356
1965	445	360	391	369	445	304	313	360	354	374	391	391	374	369	379	394	445
1966	509	425	474	469	509	369	389	425	452	468	474	485	469	469	465	473	509
1967	659	502	583	606	659	442	460	502	533	557	583	594	611	606	589	579	659
1968	679	633	670	669	679	580	583	633	662	655	670	686	707	669	635	623	679
1969	685	611	633	574	685	561	579	611	615	611	633	619	627	574	577	608	685
1970	788	655	636	672	788	590	654	655	655	643	636	641	702	672	697	678	788
1971	1030	849	928	1088	1030	740	719	849	857	898	928	983	1091	1088	1081	1073	1030
1972	1186	1081	1154	1212	1186	1069	1054	1081	1084	1093	1154	1248	1250	1212	1184	1186	1186
1973	1271	1100	1275	1274	1271	1187	1102	1100	1182	1263	1275	1309	1293	1274	1220	1268	1271
1974	1541	1448	1314	1539	1541	1422	1473	1448	1368	1337	1314	1332	1403	1539	1733	1683	1541
1975	1876	1341	1644	1797	1876	1440	1327	1341	1447	1488	1644	1866	1860	1797	1727	1805	1876
1976	1885	1792	1950	1865	1885	1754	1894	1792	1869	1897	1950	2020	1857	1865	1775	1821	1885
1977	1808	1833	2405	2448	1808	1685	1826	1833	2002	2148	2405	2354	2423	2448	2302	1825	1808
1978	2196	1890	2517	2282	2196	1818	1616	1890	2161	2452	2517	2555	2463	2282	2106	1994	2196
1979	3200	2853	3040	3218	3200	2422	2578	2853	2917	3119	3040	3007	3080	3218	3381	3338	3200
1980	4742	3566	3717	3853	4742	3221	3251	3566	3647	3749	3717	3603	3616	3853	4345	4824	4742
1981	5372	4277	5398	4773	5372	4277	4022	4277	4959	5457	5398	4863	5015	4773	5540	5474	5372
1982	6231	5449	6128	6407	6231	5248	5152	5449	5767	6460	6128	6091	6172	6407	6763	6766	6231
1983	6332	5456	6103	5775	6332	6093	5841	5456	5933	6750	6103	5450	5691	5775	6236	6283	6332

Net foreign position:
commercial and savings banks
million kroner, end of period

Position extérieure nette :
banques commerciales et d'épargne
millions de couronnes, fin de période

	Year	Q.1	Q.2	Q.3	Q.4	JAN	FEB	MAR	APR	MAY	JUN	JUL	AUG	SEP	OCT	NOV	DEC
1964	-440	-204	-530	-290	-440	-244	-214	-204	-263	-459	-530	-448	-399	-290	-246	-260	-440
1965	66	-301	-429	31	66	-118	-172	-301	-427	-498	-429	-265	19	31	117	87	66
1966	-263	66	-167	-65	-263	454	390	66	-9	-152	-167	-207	-122	-65	-39	-105	-263
1967	-69	-158	-549	-124	-69	168	150	-158	-366	-346	-549	-350	-312	-124	57	121	-69
1968	756	416	341	608	756	474	450	416	421	523	341	479	324	608	899	1084	756
1969	321	1345	840	1169	321	1719	1601	1345	1168	1141	840	1076	801	1159	932	760	321
1970	708	640	1058	807	708	515	338	640	697	978	1058	1202	647	807	544	741	708
1971	-440	664	355	-524	-440	1256	1123	664	618	462	355	370	-303	-524	-371	-322	-440
1972	-499	-477	-343	-477	-499	-469	-544	-477	-250	-78	-343	-615	-469	-477	-625	-735	-499
1973	-148	-391	-250	157	-148	-528	-567	-391	-606	-730	-250	-38	-55	157	-3	-287	-148
1974	-511	-470	138	-406	-511	-694	-737	-470	96	-107	138	67	152	-406	-1253	-1005	-511
1975	-732	-589	-928	-393	-732	-1070	-530	-589	-943	-1044	-928	-622	-605	-393	-392	-262	-732
1976	-893	-304	-402	-440	-893	-967	-1129	-304	196	-316	-402	-288	102	-440	-366	-1030	-893
1977	1188	-2117	-1898	-2597	1188	-821	-1175	-2117	-1729	-1681	-1898	-978	-1394	-2597	-1947	-59	1188
1978	-483	-840	-1138	318	-483	852	78	-840	-545	-875	-1138	-1117	-197	318	2141	1720	-483
1979	-3216	-1301	-2866	-3112	-3216	-1027	-526	-1301	-1218	-2026	-2866	-2628	-3068	-3112	-4150	-3671	-3216
1980	-10983	-3528	-6118	-7725	-10983	-2444	-2410	-3528	-3232	-4395	-6118	-6421	-6946	-7725	-6693	-9527	-10983
1981	-9105	-11699	-14143	-11391	-9105	-8608	-5509	-11699	-8565	-11785	-14143	-10630	-12364	-11391	-6261	-7415	-9105
1982	-11585	-11147	-10517	-15040	-11585	-10484	-9875	-11147	-5232	-11256	-10517	-13725	-14631	-15040	-11012	-12199	-11585
1983	-14029	-13125	-15063	-12417	-14029	-11715	-12038	-13125	-11238	-13738	-15063	-11008	-13028	-12417	-9259	-13091	-14029

NORWAY

Imports c.i.f. (22)
billion kroner, monthly averages

Importations c.a.f. (22)
milliards de couronnes, moyennes mensuelles

	Year	Q.1	Q.2	Q.3	Q.4	JAN	FEB	MAR	APR	MAY	JUN	JUL	AUG	SEP	OCT	NOV	DEC
1964	1.18	1.08	1.18	1.11	1.35	1.21	1.02	1.03	1.28	1.03	1.32	1.07	1.09	1.18	1.32	1.30	1.43
1965	1.32	1.27	1.35	1.26	1.39	1.19	1.16	1.45	1.40	1.22	1.42	1.14	1.15	1.49	1.33	1.43	1.42
1966	1.43	1.36	1.35	1.30	1.71	1.35	1.17	1.57	1.22	1.38	1.44	1.19	1.28	1.45	1.73	1.48	1.93
1967	1.64	1.62	1.68	1.53	1.71	1.50	1.65	1.71	1.72	1.62	1.70	1.40	1.53	1.65	1.86	1.82	1.47
1968	1.61	1.62	1.66	1.49	1.68	1.64	1.42	1.79	1.66	1.78	1.55	1.24	1.63	1.60	1.78	1.72	1.54
1969	1.75	1.62	1.67	1.65	2.07	1.69	1.47	1.69	1.56	1.81	1.64	1.58	1.53	1.84	1.85	2.03	2.33
1970	2.20	1.91	2.23	1.96	2.70	1.86	1.96	1.93	2.23	2.19	2.29	1.81	1.96	2.13	2.93	2.78	2.40
1971	2.39	2.19	2.54	2.28	2.56	2.17	1.98	2.43	2.40	2.52	2.69	2.25	1.84	2.76	2.36	2.65	2.67
1972	2.40	2.21	2.50	2.17	2.73	2.12	2.13	2.37	2.48	2.29	2.73	1.79	2.37	2.34	2.82	3.03	2.35
1973	3.00	2.79	2.79	2.97	3.47	2.76	2.85	2.75	2.31	3.28	2.78	3.05	2.62	3.24	3.03	4.85	2.53
1974	3.88	3.74	3.92	3.49	4.37	3.64	3.51	4.07	3.77	4.34	3.66	3.28	3.52	3.66	4.82	4.23	4.06
1975	4.21	3.91	4.83	3.65	4.46	3.80	3.87	4.05	5.48	4.54	4.46	3.34	3.32	4.30	4.68	4.38	4.34
1976	5.04	4.93	4.77	4.70	5.78	5.03	4.69	5.06	4.67	4.47	5.18	4.14	5.11	4.86	5.54	5.24	6.55
1977	5.72	5.64	5.56	5.66	6.00	4.68	5.25	7.00	4.90	5.43	6.35	6.57	4.76	5.64	6.46	5.84	5.71
1978	5.01	5.03	5.54	4.17	5.32	5.23	4.95	4.92	6.02	5.62	4.97	3.48	4.42	4.62	5.50	5.69	4.77
1979	5.78	5.12	5.56	5.58	6.85	4.85	4.57	5.96	4.58	6.03	6.08	5.33	5.60	5.82	7.28	7.07	6.19
1980	6.97	7.01	6.95	5.47	7.44	6.94	6.75	7.33	6.36	5.84	7.66	6.51	6.36	6.53	7.70	7.09	7.54
1981	7.47	7.30	6.70	7.29	8.61	6.41	6.93	8.56	6.39	7.25	6.45	6.69	6.99	8.19	8.40	8.99	8.42
1982	8.30	7.95	8.19	8.01	9.03	7.31	7.73	8.82	8.40	6.82	9.35	7.73	7.24	9.07	8.15	9.83	9.11
1983	8.19	8.43	8.23	7.29	8.81	8.64	7.58	9.07	6.85	9.23	8.61	6.33	7.11	8.43	8.90	9.26	8.26

Exports f.o.b. (22)
billion kroner, monthly averages

Exportations f.o.b. (22)
milliards de couronnes, moyennes mensuelles

	Year	Q.1	Q.2	Q.3	Q.4	JAN	FEB	MAR	APR	MAY	JUN	JUL	AUG	SEP	OCT	NOV	DEC
1964	0.77	0.71	0.79	0.74	0.83	0.71	0.73	0.70	0.78	0.77	0.82	0.72	0.66	0.85	0.80	0.86	0.83
1965	0.86	0.83	0.85	0.81	0.95	0.80	0.73	0.96	0.79	0.81	0.96	0.82	0.76	0.84	0.95	0.90	1.00
1966	0.93	0.92	0.91	0.89	1.00	0.91	0.81	1.05	0.86	0.90	0.97	0.85	0.84	0.99	0.93	1.05	1.00
1967	1.03	0.96	1.07	0.96	1.15	1.01	0.91	0.98	1.08	1.06	1.06	0.87	1.01	0.99	1.10	1.17	1.17
1968	1.15	1.11	1.13	1.05	1.33	1.04	1.10	1.18	1.09	1.14	1.18	0.93	1.10	1.12	1.37	1.32	1.29
1969	1.31	1.37	1.30	1.21	1.37	1.36	1.30	1.45	1.32	1.28	1.30	1.16	1.13	1.34	1.36	1.34	1.41
1970	1.46	1.38	1.51	1.39	1.57	1.42	1.36	1.35	1.65	1.38	1.49	1.18	1.29	1.72	1.62	1.46	1.62
1971	1.50	1.48	1.48	1.39	1.65	1.37	1.27	1.81	1.42	1.42	1.61	1.31	1.29	1.56	1.46	1.64	1.85
1972	1.80	1.64	1.80	1.74	2.03	1.50	1.56	1.86	1.73	1.88	1.79	1.67	1.55	2.00	2.10	1.90	2.08
1973	2.26	2.11	2.22	2.00	2.70	2.07	2.01	2.24	1.80	2.36	2.49	1.91	2.09	2.01	2.79	2.98	2.44
1974	2.89	2.78	2.88	2.71	3.22	2.67	2.72	2.95	2.85	3.17	2.61	2.73	2.62	2.76	3.58	3.05	3.02
1975	3.16	2.74	2.83	3.29	3.79	2.92	3.16	2.24	3.15	2.39	2.95	3.49	3.41	2.96	3.78	3.75	3.83
1976	3.61	3.42	3.49	3.67	3.86	2.87	3.61	3.79	3.11	3.51	3.85	4.36	3.12	3.54	3.63	3.61	4.34
1977	3.94	3.60	3.88	3.77	4.51	3.31	3.63	3.86	3.07	2.99	5.58	3.75	3.73	3.83	4.26	3.94	5.32
1978	4.76	4.03	5.84	4.29	4.88	3.94	3.86	4.29	4.13	6.50	6.90	3.75	4.47	4.64	4.57	4.97	5.09
1979	5.71	5.18	5.44	5.69	6.53	5.03	4.84	5.68	5.25	5.93	5.13	5.02	5.82	6.24	6.34	6.81	6.45
1980	7.64	7.93	7.60	5.67	8.35	8.12	7.67	8.00	7.58	7.42	7.80	5.84	6.82	7.35	8.34	7.56	9.17
1981	8.69	8.32	9.06	7.94	9.44	8.30	7.59	9.08	8.84	8.45	9.87	8.38	6.37	9.07	9.28	9.49	9.55
1982	9.43	9.33	9.12	8.92	10.34	8.36	8.68	10.45	10.05	8.24	9.06	9.32	7.81	9.62	9.21	10.68	11.13
1983	10.91	10.38	10.77	10.21	12.28	10.13	9.83	11.19	11.03	10.87	10.41	10.59	9.67	10.36	11.91	12.11	12.82

Trade balance (f.o.b. — c.i.f.) (22)
billion kroner, monthly averages

Balance commerciale (f.o.b. — c.a.f.) (22)
milliards de couronnes, moyennes mensuelles

	Year	Q.1	Q.2	Q.3	Q.4	JAN	FEB	MAR	APR	MAY	JUN	JUL	AUG	SEP	OCT	NOV	DEC
1964	-0.41	-0.37	-0.39	-0.37	-0.52	-0.50	-0.29	-0.32	-0.40	-0.26	-0.51	-0.35	-0.44	-0.33	-0.52	-0.44	-0.60
1965	-0.46	-0.44	-0.49	-0.45	-0.44	-0.39	-0.43	-0.49	-0.61	-0.41	-0.46	-0.31	-0.39	-0.66	-0.38	-0.52	-0.42
1966	-0.50	-0.44	-0.43	-0.41	-0.72	-0.44	-0.36	-0.52	-0.35	-0.48	-0.47	-0.34	-0.44	-0.46	-0.79	-0.43	-0.93
1967	-0.60	-0.66	-0.61	-0.57	-0.56	-0.49	-0.75	-0.73	-0.64	-0.56	-0.63	-0.53	-0.52	-0.66	-0.75	-0.64	-0.29
1968	-0.46	-0.51	-0.53	-0.44	-0.35	-0.60	-0.33	-0.60	-0.57	-0.64	-0.37	-0.32	-0.54	-0.48	-0.41	-0.39	-0.25
1969	-0.44	-0.25	-0.37	-0.44	-0.70	-0.33	-0.18	-0.24	-0.25	-0.54	-0.34	-0.42	-0.40	-0.50	-0.48	-0.69	-0.93
1970	-0.74	-0.54	-0.73	-0.57	-1.13	-0.44	-0.60	-0.57	-0.57	-0.80	-0.80	-0.63	-0.67	-0.40	-1.31	-1.32	-0.77
1971	-0.89	-0.71	-1.06	-0.90	-0.91	-0.80	-0.72	-0.62	-0.98	-1.10	-1.08	-0.94	-0.55	-1.20	-0.90	-1.01	-0.82
1972	-0.60	-0.57	-0.70	-0.42	-0.71	-0.62	-0.58	-0.51	-0.75	-0.41	-0.93	-0.12	-0.82	-0.34	-0.72	-1.13	-0.27
1973	-0.75	-0.68	-0.57	-0.97	-0.77	-0.69	-0.84	-0.51	-0.51	-0.91	-0.29	-1.14	-0.53	-1.23	-0.24	-1.97	-0.10
1974	-0.99	-0.96	-1.05	-0.78	-1.15	-0.97	-0.79	-1.12	-0.91	-1.18	-1.05	-0.56	-0.89	-0.89	-1.24	-1.19	-1.04
1975	-1.05	-1.17	-2.00	-0.37	-0.68	-0.98	-0.71	-1.81	-2.33	-2.16	-1.51	0.14	0.10	-1.34	-0.90	-0.63	-0.51
1976	-1.43	-1.51	-1.28	-1.03	-1.92	-2.17	-1.08	-1.28	-1.55	-0.96	-1.32	0.21	-1.98	-1.32	-1.91	-1.63	-2.22
1977	-1.78	-2.04	-1.68	-1.89	-1.50	-1.37	-1.62	-3.14	-1.83	-2.44	-0.77	-2.83	-1.02	-1.81	-2.20	-1.90	-0.39
1978	-0.26	-1.01	0.31	0.12	-0.44	-1.29	-1.09	-0.63	-1.89	0.88	1.92	0.27	0.06	0.02	-0.94	-0.71	0.32
1979	-0.07	0.06	-0.13	0.11	-0.31	0.18	0.27	-0.28	0.67	-0.10	-0.94	-0.31	0.22	0.43	-0.94	-0.26	0.26
1980	0.67	0.93	0.65	0.20	0.91	1.19	0.92	0.67	1.21	0.58	0.14	-0.67	0.45	0.83	0.64	0.47	1.63
1981	1.22	1.02	2.36	0.65	0.84	1.88	0.66	0.52	2.45	1.20	3.42	1.69	-0.62	0.88	0.88	0.50	1.13
1982	1.13	1.38	0.93	0.91	1.31	1.35	0.95	1.63	1.65	1.42	-0.29	1.59	0.58	0.55	1.06	0.85	2.02
1983	2.72	1.95	2.54	2.92	3.48	1.49	2.25	2.12	4.18	1.64	1.80	4.26	2.56	1.93	3.01	2.85	4.56

Imports c.i.f. (22) — Importations c.a.f. (22)

billion kroner, monthly averages — milliards de couronnes, moyennes mensuelles

Adjusted - Corrigé *

Year	Q.1	Q.2	Q.3	Q.4	JAN	FEB	MAR	APR	MAY	JUN	JUL	AUG	SEP	OCT	NOV	DEC
1964	1.11	1.11	1.22	1.26	1.14	1.09	1.09	1.02	1.08	1.21	1.19	1.27	1.20	1.21	1.27	1.30
1965	1.27	1.34	1.34	1.32	1.22	1.28	1.30	1.40	1.26	1.36	1.28	1.29	1.45	1.30	1.33	1.34
1966	1.33	1.34	1.43	1.62	1.37	1.28	1.33	1.31	1.38	1.34	1.46	1.42	1.41	1.64	1.39	1.84
1967	1.67	1.61	1.67	1.62	1.50	1.79	1.73	1.64	1.59	1.62	1.68	1.61	1.72	1.72	1.59	1.54
1968	1.58	1.66	1.61	1.57	1.65	1.41	1.70	1.70	1.68	1.59	1.45	1.76	1.62	1.57	1.60	1.55
1969	1.62	1.65	1.78	1.97	1.69	1.60	1.58	1.64	1.68	1.63	1.77	1.78	1.79	1.70	1.86	2.34
1970	2.02	2.10	2.15	2.50	1.85	2.14	2.07	1.95	2.19	2.16	2.11	2.24	2.09	2.70	2.50	2.29
1971	2.26	2.47	2.44	2.43	2.36	2.15	2.26	2.39	2.44	2.57	2.64	2.07	2.62	2.35	2.29	2.64
1972	2.26	2.37	2.39	2.58	2.24	2.18	2.34	2.46	2.14	2.51	2.22	2.57	2.40	2.64	2.61	2.50
1973	2.78	2.68	3.35	3.23	2.83	3.02	2.48	2.38	2.93	2.73	3.74	2.95	3.37	2.76	4.28	2.63
1974	3.71	3.80	3.91	4.11	3.56	3.66	3.92	3.73	4.06	3.62	4.00	3.97	3.77	4.13	4.09	4.10
1975	4.04	4.51	4.08	4.22	3.85	3.97	4.30	4.90	4.27	4.34	3.86	4.06	4.32	4.08	4.26	4.32
1976	4.78	4.70	5.18	5.47	5.10	4.79	4.44	4.68	4.48	4.93	4.85	5.90	4.80	5.17	4.83	6.39
1977	5.43	5.50	6.40	5.61	5.00	5.44	5.85	5.36	5.40	5.74	8.20	5.36	5.65	5.81	5.51	5.51
1978	5.20	5.33	4.58	4.98	5.47	5.17	4.95	5.93	5.59	4.48	4.14	4.67	4.93	4.86	5.10	4.99
1979	5.01	5.57	6.11	6.34	5.04	4.79	5.21	5.17	5.70	5.85	6.10	6.05	6.17	6.48	6.29	6.24
1980	6.93	7.00	6.95	6.98	6.93	7.05	6.80	7.17	6.62	7.22	7.00	7.38	6.47	6.91	6.69	7.34
1981	7.25	6.78	7.85	7.90	6.61	7.31	7.82	6.93	7.60	5.81	7.45	7.83	8.26	7.65	8.29	7.76
1982	8.12	8.24	8.40	8.50	8.22	8.13	8.00	9.22	6.91	8.58	8.58	7.86	8.76	8.13	8.70	8.66
1983	8.42	8.25	7.83	8.27	9.47	7.94	7.83	8.07	9.10	7.59	7.66	7.64	8.19	8.66	8.36	7.79

Exports f.o.b. (22) — Exportations f.o.b. (22)

billion kroner, monthly averages — milliards de couronnes, moyennes mensuelles

Adjusted - Corrigé *

Year	Q.1	Q.2	Q.3	Q.4	JAN	FEB	MAR	APR	MAY	JUN	JUL	AUG	SEP	OCT	NOV	DEC
1964	0.73	0.77	0.77	0.80	0.67	0.78	0.74	0.71	0.81	0.79	0.76	0.77	0.79	0.74	0.88	0.77
1965	0.81	0.86	0.86	0.91	0.80	0.79	0.85	0.81	0.85	0.90	0.90	0.86	0.80	0.92	0.88	0.93
1966	0.91	0.92	0.95	0.96	0.93	0.88	0.91	0.91	0.92	0.92	0.97	0.92	0.96	0.93	0.99	0.97
1967	0.98	1.03	1.03	1.11	1.00	0.97	0.98	1.04	1.04	1.01	1.02	1.09	0.98	1.07	1.11	1.16
1968	1.07	1.14	1.13	1.26	0.99	1.13	1.09	1.11	1.12	1.19	1.03	1.22	1.14	1.26	1.27	1.26
1969	1.35	1.30	1.30	1.30	1.31	1.38	1.35	1.31	1.29	1.30	1.29	1.30	1.30	1.26	1.35	1.30
1970	1.42	1.45	1.49	1.49	1.42	1.45	1.40	1.48	1.42	1.44	1.30	1.52	1.64	1.52	1.46	1.49
1971	1.45	1.48	1.50	1.55	1.42	1.35	1.57	1.45	1.47	1.53	1.46	1.49	1.52	1.38	1.58	1.69
1972	1.63	1.77	1.89	1.91	1.60	1.56	1.74	1.78	1.78	1.75	1.93	1.71	2.02	1.94	1.79	2.01
1973	2.08	2.22	2.18	2.52	2.09	2.08	2.07	1.97	2.20	2.49	2.09	2.29	2.16	2.45	2.71	2.39
1974	2.79	2.90	2.91	2.96	2.73	2.74	2.89	3.07	2.93	2.71	2.80	2.93	3.00	3.12	2.91	2.84
1975	2.90	2.74	3.49	3.51	2.93	3.15	2.61	2.96	2.27	3.00	3.49	3.87	3.10	3.34	3.78	3.42
1976	3.42	3.50	3.87	3.60	3.09	3.59	3.59	3.37	3.49	3.63	4.47	3.46	3.67	3.50	3.50	3.79
1977	3.66	3.82	3.96	4.30	3.72	3.69	3.59	3.34	2.90	5.23	3.98	3.97	3.94	4.31	3.83	4.76
1978	4.24	5.51	4.56	4.74	4.20	3.99	4.52	4.04	6.09	6.39	4.13	4.73	4.82	4.58	4.93	4.71
1979	5.12	5.35	6.13	6.36	5.03	5.09	5.26	5.59	5.60	4.84	5.46	6.22	6.71	6.19	6.73	6.16
1980	7.77	7.46	7.11	8.03	7.87	7.73	7.70	7.36	7.34	7.68	6.11	7.75	7.48	8.17	7.80	8.29
1981	8.21	8.90	8.41	9.20	8.18	8.02	8.43	8.49	8.71	9.49	8.74	7.44	9.04	9.40	9.53	8.65
1982	9.13	8.98	9.52	9.97	8.91	9.15	9.34	9.58	8.70	8.67	9.95	8.88	9.73	9.55	10.26	10.11
1983	10.23	10.67	10.88	11.97	10.36	10.37	9.95	10.67	11.19	10.14	11.54	10.57	10.53	12.54	11.37	12.01

Trade balance (f.o.b. — c.i.f.) (22) — Balance commerciale (f.o.b. — c.a.f.) (22)

billion kroner, monthly averages — milliards de couronnes, moyennes mensuelles

Adjusted - Corrigé *

Year	Q.1	Q.2	Q.3	Q.4	JAN	FEB	MAR	APR	MAY	JUN	JUL	AUG	SEP	OCT	NOV	DEC
1964	-0.38	-0.34	-0.45	-0.47	-0.47	-0.31	-0.35	-0.31	-0.28	-0.42	-0.43	-0.50	-0.41	-0.47	-0.39	-0.53
1965	-0.45	-0.48	-0.48	-0.42	-0.42	-0.49	-0.45	-0.59	-0.40	-0.46	-0.37	-0.43	-0.65	-0.38	-0.45	-0.41
1966	-0.42	-0.43	-0.48	-0.66	-0.44	-0.40	-0.41	-0.40	-0.47	-0.42	-0.49	-0.50	-0.45	-0.71	-0.40	-0.88
1967	-0.69	-0.59	-0.64	-0.51	-0.50	-0.82	-0.74	-0.60	-0.55	-0.61	-0.66	-0.51	-0.74	-0.65	-0.49	-0.38
1968	-0.51	-0.52	-0.48	-0.31	-0.65	-0.28	-0.61	-0.59	-0.57	-0.40	-0.42	-0.55	-0.48	-0.30	-0.33	-0.29
1969	-0.28	-0.35	-0.48	-0.66	-0.38	-0.22	-0.23	-0.33	-0.39	-0.33	-0.48	-0.48	-0.49	-0.44	-0.51	-1.04
1970	-0.60	-0.65	-0.66	-1.01	-0.43	-0.69	-0.67	-0.47	-0.77	-0.72	-0.81	-0.72	-0.45	-1.18	-1.05	-0.81
1971	-0.81	-0.98	-0.95	-0.88	-0.94	-0.80	-0.70	-0.94	-0.98	-1.04	-1.16	-0.58	-1.11	-0.97	-0.71	-0.95
1972	-0.62	-0.60	-0.51	-0.67	-0.65	-0.62	-0.60	-0.68	-0.36	-0.75	-0.29	-0.85	-0.37	-0.70	-0.82	-0.49
1973	-0.70	-0.46	-1.17	-0.71	-0.74	-0.94	-0.41	-0.41	-0.73	-0.25	-1.64	-0.66	-1.22	-0.31	-1.57	-0.25
1974	-0.93	-0.90	-1.01	-1.15	-0.83	-0.92	-1.04	-0.66	-1.13	-0.91	-1.20	-1.04	-0.77	-1.01	-1.17	-1.26
1975	-1.14	-1.77	-0.59	-0.71	-0.92	-0.82	-1.69	-1.55	-2.00	-1.35	-0.36	-0.19	-1.22	-0.74	-0.48	-0.90
1976	-1.36	-1.20	-1.32	-1.87	-2.01	-1.21	-0.85	-1.31	-0.99	-1.30	-0.38	-2.45	-1.13	-1.68	-1.33	-2.60
1977	-1.77	-1.68	-2.44	-1.31	-1.28	-1.75	-2.26	-2.02	-2.50	-0.50	-4.22	-1.39	-1.71	-1.51	-1.69	-0.75
1978	-0.96	0.18	-0.02	-0.24	-1.28	-1.18	-0.42	-1.88	0.51	1.91	-0.01	0.07	-0.11	-0.28	-0.17	-0.28
1979	0.11	-0.23	0.02	0.02	-0.02	0.31	0.05	0.43	-0.11	-1.00	-0.64	0.16	0.53	-0.29	0.44	-0.09
1980	0.34	0.45	0.17	1.10	0.94	0.68	0.90	0.19	0.71	0.46	-0.85	0.37	1.01	1.26	1.10	0.95
1981	0.96	2.12	0.56	1.30	1.57	0.71	0.61	1.56	1.11	3.69	1.29	-0.39	0.79	1.76	1.24	0.90
1982	1.01	0.75	1.12	1.43	0.59	1.01	1.34	0.36	1.79	0.09	1.37	1.02	0.98	1.42	1.56	1.45
1983	1.31	2.41	3.05	3.70	0.88	2.42	2.12	2.60	2.06	2.56	3.88	2.93	2.35	3.88	3.01	4.21

* Adjusted by the O.E.C.D. — * Corrigé par l'O.C.D.E.

NORWAY

Balance of payments: net trade
million kroner

Balance des paiements : balance commerciale
millions de couronnes

	Year	Q.1	Q.2	Q.3	Q.4	JAN	FEB	MAR	APR	MAY	JUN	JUL	AUG	SEP	OCT	NOV	DEC
1964	-3673	-839	-902	-859	-1073												
1965	-3898	-912	-1096	-911	-979												
1966	-4534	-1034	-1053	-1021	-1426												
1967	-5190	-1203	-1427	-1338	-1222	-346	-397	-460	-481	-502	-444	-472	-400	-466	-485	-425	-312
1968	-4955	-1238	-1230	-1154	-1333	-596	-352	-290	-445	-490	-295	-371	-379	-404	-529	-453	-351
1969	-6078	-1098	-1625	-1431	-1924	-419	-311	-368	-534	-541	-550	-466	-432	-533	-563	-552	-809
1970	-8137	-1653	-2162	-1883	-2439	-482	-620	-551	-726	-708	-728	-411	-726	-746	-773	-888	-778
1971	-9028	-1985	-2246	-2288	-2509	-714	-631	-640	-626	-771	-349	-773	-596	-919	-814	-819	-876
1972	-7526	-1736	-1909	-1577	-2304	-654	-550	-532	-598	-730	-581	-449	-748	-380	-798	-898	-608
1973	-8603	-1944	-1813	-2195	-2651	-651	-670	-623	-627	-649	-537	-698	-521	-976	-872	-1146	-633
1974	-14646	-3503	-3654	-3753	-3736	-972	-1194	-1337	-1056	-1552	-1046	-971	-1475	-1307	-1506	-1116	-1114
1975	-17525	-4257	-5395	-3969	-3904	-1444	-1494	-1319	-2064	-1816	-1515	-1197	-1477	-1295	-1408	-1198	-1308
1976	-18139	-3952	-4739	-4367	-5081	-1378	-1151	-1423	-1302	-1710	-1727	-1187	-1876	-1304	-1549	-1964	-1568
1977	-23883	-5339	-5792	-7053	-5699	-1695	-1686	-1958	-1906	-1847	-2039	-3417	-1803	-1833	-1835	-2328	-1536
1978	-10326	-4008	-3707	-990	-1621	-1695	-1297	-1016	-1612	-1003	-1092	-364	-431	-195	-996	-518	-107
1979	-1029	-1038	335	449	-725	-279	-221	-586	328	735	-728	35	210	204	-681	-8	-36
1980	5924	2121	1444	372	1987	557	1038	526	763	612	69	-456	239	589	506	520	961
1981	16487	3200	5694	4093	3500	1991	696	513	1990	1032	2672	2129	656	1308	1015	800	1685
1982	14683	4190	3857	2191	4445	2026	1025	1139	2339	1592	-74	1266	605	317	895	1413	2137
1983	29942	6391	7954	7241	8356	2233	2514	1644	3812	2438	1704	3332	1844	2065	1906	3462	2988

Balance of payments: current balance
million kroner

Balance des paiements : opérations courantes, nettes
millions de couronnes

	Year	Q.1	Q.2	Q.3	Q.4	JAN	FEB	MAR	APR	MAY	JUN	JUL	AUG	SEP	OCT	NOV	DEC
1964	-516	-55	-164	46	-345												
1965	-949	-256	-382	-142	-169												
1966	-1395	-145	-154	45	-1141												
1967	-1737	-936	-673	-187	64	-128	-430	-378	-259	-199	-220	-134	1	-54	-211	-98	373
1968	664	67	-78	402	273	-21	176	-88	-62	-155	139	357	68	-23	15	-5	263
1969	911	665	321	457	-532	177	239	249	179	-47	189	209	155	93	-17	-211	-304
1970	-1728	-161	-429	268	-1406	19	-191	11	-50	-227	-152	65	-34	233	-685	-681	-40
1971	-3683	-444	-1324	-797	-1118	-331	-182	69	-410	-496	-418	-224	64	-637	-421	-463	-234
1972	-387	-156	-466	621	-386	-186	-8	38	-291	201	-376	558	-133	196	-146	-607	367
1973	-2002	-485	-12	-1317	-183	-155	-444	114	35	-328	281	-598	210	-929	323	-1276	765
1974	-6164	-795	-1639	-1349	-2381	-87	-263	-445	-325	-810	-514	-280	-293	-776	-538	-779	-1064
1975	-12692	-2941	-5848	-1162	-2741	-598	-698	-1645	-2219	-1972	-1657	283	5	-1450	-1049	-914	-778
1976	-20370	-4332	-5523	-4104	-6406	-2176	-1100	-1056	-2419	-1355	-1754	300	-2529	-1875	-1814	-2075	-2517
1977	-26802	-6575	-5904	-7884	-6439	-1695	-1674	-3206	-2184	-2454	-1266	-3552	-1591	-2741	-2561	-2259	-1619
1978	-11275	-4459	-2431	-1639	-2746	-1849	-1598	-1012	-2573	-531	673	-632	-133	-874	-1195	-1051	-500
1979	-5278	-1184	-1245	-1303	-1546	-186	103	-1101	416	-236	-1425	-639	-152	-512	-1226	-523	203
1980	5448	2540	1500	131	1277	995	1330	215	1425	132	-57	-1545	776	900	385	256	636
1981	12463	2708	5732	2735	1268	1545	764	399	1908	781	3063	1517	562	656	1001	-2	269
1982	4205	2744	203	373	385	545	1032	1167	176	1531	-1504	-311	302	382	1003	454	-572
1983	16281	1690	1926	5372	7293	-901	1960	731	2545	56	-677	3058	1325	989	2618	2339	2336

Balance of payments: (23)
change in gold and foreign exchange
million kroner

Balance des paiements : (23)
variations des avoirs en or et en devises
millions de couronnes

	Year	Q.1	Q.2	Q.3	Q.4	JAN	FEB	MAR	APR	MAY	JUN	JUL	AUG	SEP	OCT	NOV	DEC
1964	526	68	70	361	27												
1965	916	272	40	228	376												
1966	-92	-9	-94	132	-121												
1967	1444	222	107	635	480												
1968	1598	490	421	511	176												
1969	108	281	-213	237	-192												
1970	625	206	315	133	-29												
1971	-749	53	-268	-32	-502												
1972	1178	168	759	437	-186												
1973	2190	-134	1732	547	45	151	-859	574	633	436	663	388	172	-13	-36	614	-533
1974	-	805	-54	766	-1517	695	266	-156	436	-417	-73	240	511	15	209	-590	-1136
1975	1253	-831	337	790	957	-1036	374	-169	-287	-154	788	1440	-358	-292	-104	979	82
1976	-2020	-297	312	-498	-1537	-795	631	-133	1211	-624	-275	449	-983	36	-839	-585	-123
1977	-527	-2053	4086	-1300	-1260	-1904	621	-770	1381	1157	1548	146	-438	-1008	-357	126	-1029
1978	4091	1436	2901	464	-710	481	-67	1022	2061	944	-104	1218	44	-798	-2153	1433	10
1979	4608	2414	206	1528	460	5	1520	889	406	546	-746	-52	285	1295	314	-392	538
1980	5346	4339	568	1000	-561	877	2597	765	1252	63	-747	-1124	588	1536	823	-2225	841
1981	6549	532	-1771	3615	4173	557	-1661	1626	988	198	-2957	2363	1656	-404	1827	-47	2393
1982	7870	1106	2228	-271	4307	-921	-476	2503	1900	1840	-1512	-3339	196	2872	-198	-2008	7013
1983	-346	-4330	-555	3442	1097	-3707	979	-1602	-805	387	-137	1191	1237	1014	1358	-1620	1359

NOTES

1. The original base of the index is 1961 to 1966, 1970 from 1967 to 1968, and 1975 from 1969.
2. Prior to 1972, excluding extraction of petroleum and natural gas.
3. Excluding petroleum and natural gas.
4. Not included in total index.
5. From 1983, firms working at more than 95 per cent of capacity.
6. Stocks held by manufacturers and wholesalers, including raw materials. The original base of the index is 1970 to 1981 and 1982 from 1982.
7. Excluding transport equipment.
8. Excluding agricultural buildings.
9. Annual data are based on more complete information than monthly and quarterly data.
10. Prior to 1978, Oslo only.
11. The original base of the index is 1961 to 1966, 1966 from 1967 to 1969, and 1979 from 1970.
12. Prior to 1971, seasonally adjusted by the OECD Secretariat.
13. In January 1973, the retirement age was lowered from 70 to 67, which lowered the level of the series by about 2,000 persons.
14. Monthly data refer to end of period.
15. From 1972, based on quarterly labour force sample survey. Previously the series referred to employees registered with the health insurance scheme.
16. For definition of labour force, see note 15.
17. Prior to 1975, including mining.
18. Weighting pattern based on 1961 to 1976, on 1974 from 1977 to 1980, and on 1981 from 1981.
19. Weighting pattern based on 1958 to 1967, on 1967 from 1968 to 1973, and on 1973 from 1974 to 1978; from 1979, the weighting pattern is revised each year.
20. Monthly data refer to beginning of following period in source.
21. Monthly data refer to the 15th of the month. Prior to 1972, ratio to nominal value. The original base of the index is 1st January 1972 from 1972 to 1982, and 3rd January 1983 from 1983.
22. General trade.
23. Increase in assets (+).

NOTES

1. La base originale de l'indice est 1961 jusqu'en 1966, 1970 de 1967 à 1968, et 1975 à partir de 1969.
2. Avant 1972, non compris l'extraction du pétrole et du gaz naturel.
3. Non compris le pétrole et le gaz naturel.
4. Non compris dans l'indice total.
5. A partir de 1983, entreprises travaillant à plus de 95 % de leur capacité.
6. Stocks des producteurs et des grossistes; y compris les matières premières. La base originale de l'indice est 1970 jusqu'en 1981 et 1982 à partir de 1982.
7. Non compris le matériel de transport.
8. Non compris les bâtiments agricoles.
9. Les données annuelles sont établies à partir d'informations plus complètes que les données mensuelles et trimestrielles.
10. Avant 1978, Oslo seulement.
11. La base originale de l'indice est 1961 jusqu'en 1966, 1966 de 1967 à 1969 et 1979 à partir de 1970.
12. Avant 1971, série corrigée des variations saisonnières par le Secrétariat de l'OCDE.
13. En janvier 1973, l'abaissement de l'âge de la retraite de 70 à 67 ans a entraîné une diminution du niveau de la série de l'ordre de 2000 personnes.
14. Situation en fin de mois.
15. A partir de 1972, données établies d'après l'enquête trimestrielle par sondage de la maind'œuvre. Précédemment, la série concernait les travailleurs immatriculés à la Sécurité Sociale.
16. Voir la définition de la main-d'œuvre, note 15.
17. Avant 1975, y compris les industries extractives.
18. La pondération se réfère à 1961 jusqu'en 1976, à 1974 de 1977 à 1980, et à 1981 à partir de 1981.
19. La pondération se réfère à 1958 jusqu'en 1967, à 1967 de 1968 à 1973, et à 1973 de 1974 à 1978; à partir de 1979, la pondération est révisée chaque année.
20. Les données mensuelles sont désignées dans la source nationale comme se référant au début du mois suivant.
21. Les données mensuelles se réfèrent au 15 du mois. Avant 1972, rapport à la valeur nominale. La base originale de l'indice est le 1er janvier 1972 de 1972 à 1982, et le 3 janvier 1983 à partir de 1983.
22. Commerce général.
23. Augmentation des avoirs (+).

MAIN SOURCES
PRINCIPALES SOURCES

Series	Séries	Sources
Indicators of national product	Indicateurs de produit national	
Industrial production	Production industrielle	
Stocks and orders	Stocks et commandes	
Construction	Construction	
Internal trade	Commerce intérieur	
Labour, excl. job vacancies	Emploi sauf offres d'emploi	Statistisk Sentralbyrå
Wages	Salaires	*Statistisk månedshefte*
Prices	Prix	
Credit	Crédits	
Interest rates	Taux d'intérêts	
Share prices	Cours des actions	
Foreign trade	Commerce extérieur	
Balance of payments	Balance des paiements	
Business surveys	Enquêtes de conjoncture	Statistisk Sentralbyrå *Statistisk ukehefte*
Job vacancies	Offres d'emploi	Statistisk Sentralbyrå
Money	Monnaie	Norges Bank *Penger og kredit*
Net foreign position of commercial and savings banks	Position extérieure nette des banques commerciales et d'épargne	Norges Bank

Portugal

PORTUGAL

Industrial production: total (1)
1980 = 100

Production industrielle : total (1)
1980 = 100

	Year	Q.1	Q.2	Q.3	Q.4	JAN	FEB	MAR	APR	MAY	JUN	JUL	AUG	SEP	OCT	NOV	DEC
1964																	
1965																	
1966																	
1967																	
1968	46	43	45	48	49	42	43	45	45	46	46	45	45	52	50	49	49
1969	50	48	50	50	53	47	48	49	49	47	52	44	52	54	52	52	55
1970	53	51	55	52	54	50	50	53	55	53	57	51	49	57	56	53	55
1971	57	51	59	57	63	50	51	53	61	57	58	57	55	58	63	68	59
1972	65	61	64	68	67	57	60	64	65	63	64	64	66	74	68	67	66
1973	73	69	71	72	78	67	70	70	70	71	72	69	68	78	78	77	77
1974	75	79	76	69	74	78	77	82	80	74	74	71	65	71	77	72	74
1975	71	74	72	65	73	72	75	73	71	72	73	70	55	71	75	73	69
1976	73	73	75	66	79	70	74	75	75	76	74	70	53	76	77	81	79
1977	83	82	85	77	88	80	83	83	85	84	85	79	63	88	88	90	87
1978	89	90	91	79	93	90	90	91	93	91	90	85	64	89	90	96	94
1979	95	95	98	85	102	92	91	101	101	98	96	86	71	97	102	104	101
1980	100	105	104	89	102	104	106	103	105	102	104	98	74	96	104	103	100
1981	101	104	102	90	106	101	108	102	107	102	98	95	70	105	106	108	105
1982	105	111	106	95	109	109	107	116	111	101	105	103	77	104	108	110	109
1983		112	111	96		110	113	114	110	110	112	105	77	105	110	108	

Industrial production: (1)
manufacturing
1980 = 100

Production industrielle : (1)
industries manufacturières
1980 = 100

	Year	Q.1	Q.2	Q.3	Q.4	JAN	FEB	MAR	APR	MAY	JUN	JUL	AUG	SEP	OCT	NOV	DEC
1964																	
1965																	
1966																	
1967																	
1968	46	42	45	47	49	41	42	44	43	45	45	44	46	52	50	48	48
1969	50	47	49	50	52	45	47	48	49	47	52	43	52	55	51	51	54
1970	53	50	55	52	54	48	49	52	55	53	57	51	49	57	55	52	54
1971	57	50	58	57	63	48	49	52	61	57	58	57	55	58	63	68	58
1972	65	59	64	69	66	56	59	63	65	62	64	64	66	75	68	66	64
1973	72	68	71	72	78	67	69	70	70	71	73	69	68	79	79	77	76
1974	74	78	76	69	73	76	76	81	80	74	74	71	65	71	77	71	73
1975	70	72	71	66	72	70	74	72	70	71	72	70	55	73	76	73	68
1976	74	72	76	68	79	69	73	75	76	77	76	71	54	77	79	80	77
1977	82	80	85	77	87	78	81	81	85	84	85	80	63	88	88	89	84
1978	88	88	91	81	93	87	88	90	92	90	91	86	64	91	90	97	91
1979	94	92	97	85	101	89	89	99	99	97	96	87	70	98	101	102	99
1980	100	103	104	90	103	102	104	103	105	102	106	95	75	97	105	105	99
1981	102	104	105	92	106	100	109	104	108	104	101	98	70	107	107	108	104
1982	106	109	108	97	109	106	105	116	113	103	108	106	79	106	110	110	107
1983		112	111	95		109	112	114	111	109	113	105	75	105	110	106	

Production: crude steel
thousand tons, monthly averages

Production : acier brut
milliers de tonnes, moyennes mensuelles

	Year	Q.1	Q.2	Q.3	Q.4	JAN	FEB	MAR	APR	MAY	JUN	JUL	AUG	SEP	OCT	NOV	DEC
1964																	
1965																	
1966																	
1967																	
1968																	
1969																	
1970																	
1971																	
1972																	
1973																	
1974	33	39	43	17	34	43	32	41	43	42	44	34	10	11	24	38	40
1975	37	31	36	40	41	39	26	27	30	38	40	43	39	39	38	29	55
1976	38	37	34	41	42	34	34	42	36	30	36	42	37	43	46	43	38
1977	44	43	45	46	43	45	41	44	36	50	49	46	44	48	44	38	47
1978	51	52	50	53	48	54	49	54	54	49	46	55	56	49	50	49	46
1979	55	56	54	53	57	57	52	59	52	58	51	54	51	55	57	58	57
1980	55	59	48	54	59	61	56	59	57	41	47	55	54	53	58	59	59
1981	46	57	34	50	43	59	57	56	31	38	32	44	49	56	38	37	54
1982	42	55	53	24	36	55	49	60	57	51	51	26	24	22	27	29	53
1983	56	55	53	53	56	59	51	55	59	61	54	56	49	54	56	56	56

Industrial production: total (1)

1980 = 100

Adjusted - Corrigé *

Production industrielle : total (1)

1980 = 100

	Year	Q.1	Q.2	Q.3	Q.4	JAN	FEB	MAR	APR	MAY	JUN	JUL	AUG	SEP	OCT	NOV	DEC
1964																	
1965																	
1966																	
1967																	
1968		45	45	48	48	44	44	45	44	46	43	47	49	49	49	49	48
1969		49	49	51	52	50	50	49	49	48	50	46	56	51	50	52	54
1970		52	54	53	54	52	52	53	54	53	55	53	53	53	54	53	54
1971		52	58	58	63	52	52	52	59	58	56	59	60	55	61	68	59
1972		61	63	70	66	60	61	63	63	63	63	66	72	71	66	67	66
1973		69	70	75	77	69	70	68	68	71	72	71	77	76	75	77	78
1974		78	74	73	73	79	76	79	77	73	73	74	75	69	74	71	75
1975		72	70	69	71	73	74	71	68	71	72	73	65	70	73	72	70
1976		71	73	71	77	70	72	72	72	74	73	73	66	75	75	78	79
1977		80	82	84	86	80	80	80	81	82	83	82	81	88	86	86	87
1978		88	83	87	91	89	87	88	88	88	89	89	84	89	88	91	94
1979		91	95	94	99	90	87	98	95	95	94	90	95	98	99	99	100
1980		101	101	99	99	102	101	99	99	100	103	101	101	96	101	99	99
1981		100	99	100	103	98	103	98	101	100	97	98	96	106	103	103	103
1982		106	103	105	106	105	102	111	105	100	105	106	105	105	105	105	107
1983		108	108	106		106	108	109	104	108	112	108	105	106	106	103	

Industrial production: (1) manufacturing

1980 = 100

Adjusted - Corrigé *

Production industrielle : (1) industries manufacturières

1980 = 100

	Year	Q.1	Q.2	Q.3	Q.4	JAN	FEB	MAR	APR	MAY	JUN	JUL	AUG	SEP	OCT	NOV	DEC
1964																	
1965																	
1966																	
1967																	
1968		44	44	47	48	44	44	45	43	45	43	46	48	48	48	48	47
1969		49	43	50	51	49	50	48	48	47	49	45	55	50	49	51	54
1970		52	54	52	53	52	51	52	54	53	55	52	52	53	53	53	54
1971		52	57	57	62	51	51	52	59	57	55	58	59	54	60	69	58
1972		61	62	70	66	59	61	63	63	62	62	66	72	71	65	66	66
1973		70	70	74	77	70	70	69	68	71	71	71	76	75	75	77	78
1974		78	74	72	73	79	76	79	77	74	73	73	75	68	73	70	74
1975		72	70	69	71	72	74	70	67	70	71	72	65	70	73	71	69
1976		72	74	71	77	70	72	73	72	75	74	73	66	75	76	78	79
1977		79	82	83	86	79	80	79	81	82	83	82	80	86	85	86	85
1978		87	88	87	91	88	86	87	87	88	88	89	84	89	87	93	93
1979		90	94	93	99	89	86	95	93	94	93	85	93	95	98	98	100
1980		100	101	99	101	101	101	99	98	100	103	101	100	95	101	101	100
1981		101	101	100	104	99	105	99	102	103	99	95	95	105	103	104	104
1982		106	105	106	106	105	102	111	106	102	106	107	106	104	106	106	107
1983		108	108	104		107	108	109	104	108	110	106	102	103	106	103	

Production: future tendency manufacturing

per cent balance

Perspectives de production industries manufacturières

solde en pourcentage

	Year	Q.1	Q.2	Q.3	Q.4	JAN	FEB	MAR	APR	MAY	JUN	JUL	AUG	SEP	OCT	NOV	DEC
1964																	
1965																	
1966																	
1967																	
1968																	
1969																	
1970																	
1971																	
1972																	
1973																	
1974																	
1975																	
1976																	
1977		20	-3	17	7	20			-3			17			7		
1978		16	-9	15	7	16			-9			15			7		
1979		22	-3	24	19	22			-3			24			19		
1980		26	1	27	17	26			1			27			17		
1981		30	-1	25	13	30			-1			25			13		
1982		26	-7	17	13	26			-7			17			13		
1983		13	-13	12	-2	13			-13			12			-2		

* Adjusted by the O.E.C.D.

* Corrigé par l'O.C.D.E.

PORTUGAL

Order books or demand: level
manufacturing
per cent balance

Carnet de commandes ou demande globale : niveau
industries manufacturières
solde en pourcentage

	Year	Q.1	Q.2	Q.3	Q.4	JAN	FEB	MAR	APR	MAY	JUN	JUL	AUG	SEP	OCT	NOV	DEC
1964																	
1965																	
1966																	
1967																	
1968																	
1969																	
1970																	
1971																	
1972																	
1973																	
1974																	
1975																	
1976																	
1977		2	-10	-5	-10	2			-10			-5			-10		
1978		-11	-20	-15	-13	-11			-20			-15			-13		
1979		-5	-4	-3	-3	-5			-4			-3			-3		
1980		3	-11	-13	-18	3			-11			-13			-18		
1981		-13	-18	-18	-19	-13			-18			-18			-19		
1982		-20	-30	-30	-34	-20			-30			-30			-34		
1983		-29	-33	-34	-35	-29			-33			-34			-35		

Finished goods stocks: level
manufacturing
per cent balance

Stocks de produits finis : niveau
industries manufacturières
solde en pourcentage

	Year	Q.1	Q.2	Q.3	Q.4	JAN	FEB	MAR	APR	MAY	JUN	JUL	AUG	SEP	OCT	NOV	DEC
1964																	
1965																	
1966																	
1967																	
1968																	
1969																	
1970																	
1971																	
1972																	
1973																	
1974																	
1975																	
1976																	
1977		-8	2	-1	5	-8			2			-1			5		
1978		9	16	13	9	9			16			13			9		
1979		10	9	4	1	10			9			4			1		
1980		3	11	13	14	3			11			13			14		
1981		15	21	15	17	15			21			15			17		
1982		21	26	21	19	21			26			21			19		
1983		23	21	21	22	23			21			21			22		

Rate of capacity utilization
manufacturing
per cent

Taux d'utilisation des capacités
industries manufacturières
pourcentage

	Year	Q.1	Q.2	Q.3	Q.4	JAN	FEB	MAR	APR	MAY	JUN	JUL	AUG	SEP	OCT	NOV	DEC
1964																	
1965																	
1966																	
1967																	
1968																	
1969																	
1970																	
1971																	
1972																	
1973																	
1974																	
1975																	
1976																	
1977		76	76	78	78	76			76			78			78		
1978		78	78	79	77	78			78			79			77		
1979		78	79	79	78	78			79			79			78		
1980		79	80	79	79	79			80			79			79		
1981		78	77	78	77	78			77			78			77		
1982		79	77	77	76	79			77			77			76		
1983		77	76	76	75	77			76			76			75		

Construction permits issued: total (2)(3)
thousands, quarterly averages

Permis de construire délivrés : total (2)(3)
milliers, moyennes trimestrielles

	Year	Q.1	Q.2	Q.3	Q.4	JAN	FEB	MAR	APR	MAY	JUN	JUL	AUG	SEP	OCT	NOV	DEC
1964																	
1965																	
1966																	
1967																	
1968																	
1969																	
1970	10.20	8.72	10.91	11.38	9.81												
1971	10.77	9.55	12.59	10.99	9.95												
1972	10.85	8.60	11.95	12.20	10.65												
1973	12.28	11.37	12.76	13.15	11.83												
1974	11.76	10.94	12.03	12.91	11.16												
1975	11.94	10.69	12.63	13.22	11.23												
1976	13.54	12.18	13.96	15.53	12.51												
1977	16.01	12.80	17.79	18.55	14.83												
1978	16.92	15.22	18.55	19.11	14.79												
1979	16.09	14.04	17.68	18.69	13.95												
1980	15.83	15.05	16.24	17.51	14.53												
1981	15.40	15.32	15.57	16.23	14.49												
1982	15.31	14.91	16.06	16.85	13.42												
1983	15.88	15.33	15.88	17.87	14.42												

Construction permits issued: residential (2)(3)
thousands, quarterly averages

Permis de construire délivrés : bâtiments résidentiels (2)(3)
milliers, moyennes trimestrielles

	Year	Q.1	Q.2	Q.3	Q.4	JAN	FEB	MAR	APR	MAY	JUN	JUL	AUG	SEP	OCT	NOV	DEC
1964																	
1965																	
1966																	
1967																	
1968																	
1969																	
1970	7.81	6.39	8.43	8.88	7.53												
1971	8.35	7.22	10.34	8.45	7.39												
1972	8.42	6.54	9.33	9.61	8.20												
1973	9.48	8.71	9.90	10.33	8.97												
1974	9.05	8.29	9.33	10.01	8.56												
1975	9.73	8.27	10.28	11.05	9.31												
1976	11.35	9.95	11.85	13.30	10.30												
1977	13.17	10.38	14.58	15.52	12.22												
1978	14.12	12.61	15.47	16.20	12.20												
1979	13.24	11.43	14.58	15.61	11.34												
1980	12.93	12.06	13.29	14.59	11.77												
1981	12.76	12.40	12.89	13.82	11.92												
1982	12.58	12.09	13.25	14.06	10.90												
1983	13.03	12.40	13.14	14.85	11.71												

Construction, buildings completed: total (2)(4)
number, quarterly averages

Construction, bâtiments achevés : total (2)(4)
nombre, moyennes trimestrielles

	Year	Q.1	Q.2	Q.3	Q.4	JAN	FEB	MAR	APR	MAY	JUN	JUL	AUG	SEP	OCT	NOV	DEC
1964																	
1965																	
1966																	
1967																	
1968																	
1969																	
1970	6248																
1971	6482			6291	7309												
1972	7011	5999	6630	7049	8364												
1973	7335	6863	6423	6705	9346												
1974	7134	6465	6552	7360	8150												
1975	..	6705	6174	5015	..												
1976	5706	6179	5274	5102	6269												
1977	5716	4992	5150	6572	6146												
1978	4953	4968	4407	5330	5104												
1979	5491	5468	5196	5728	5570												
1980	6302	6537	6888	8200	5581												
1981	5503	5023	4819	5942	6225												
1982	6173	5315	5135	7613	6631												
1983		4971	5095														

PORTUGAL

Construction, buildings completed: residential (2)(4)
number, quarterly averages

Construction, bâtiments achevés : résidentiels (2)(4)
nombre, moyennes trimestrielles

	Year	Q.1	Q.2	Q.3	Q.4	JAN	FEB	MAR	APR	MAY	JUN	JUL	AUG	SEP	OCT	NOV	DEC
1964																	
1965																	
1966																	
1967																	
1968																	
1969																	
1970	5204																
1971	5095			5041	5625												
1972	5368	4612	5159	5404	6297												
1973	5778	5405	5120	5316	7270												
1974	5726	5144	5079	6017	6565												
1975	..	5011	4822	4868	..												
1976	4643	4943	4052	4497	5081												
1977	4683	4100	4100	5299	5232												
1978	4234	4111	3863	4645	4313												
1979	4725	4785	4413	4991	4708												
1980	5478	5199	5422	6667	4618												
1981	4386	3944	3764	4785	5051												
1982	5015	4171	4125	6467	5303												
1983		3769	3788														

Cost of construction: multiple dwellings (5)
1980 = 100

Coût de la construction : immeubles résidentiels (5)
1980 = 100

	Year	Q.1	Q.2	Q.3	Q.4	JAN	FEB	MAR	APR	MAY	JUN	JUL	AUG	SEP	OCT	NOV	DEC
1964	14.0	13.8	13.8	14.0	14.3			13.8			13.8			14.0			14.3
1965	16.5	16.3	16.4	16.6	16.9			16.3			16.4			16.6			16.9
1966	18.1	17.2	17.5	18.7	19.0			17.2			17.5			18.7			19.0
1967	19.7	19.2	19.5	19.9	20.1			19.2			19.5			19.9			20.1
1968	20.5	20.2	20.4	20.5	20.7			20.2			20.4			20.5			20.7
1969	21.5	20.8	21.3	21.8	22.2			20.8			21.3			21.8			22.2
1970	23.9	23.1	23.6	24.3	24.6			23.1			23.6			24.3			24.6
1971	25.9	25.8	25.7	26.4	25.9			25.8			25.7			26.4			25.9
1972	28.4	27.6	28.1	28.9	29.1			27.6			28.1			28.9			29.1
1973	31.0	29.9	30.5	30.6	32.9			29.9			30.5			30.6			32.9
1974	38.9	35.6	37.8	40.9	41.2			35.6			37.8			40.9			41.2
1975	43.6	42.7	44.1	43.1	44.5			42.7			44.1			43.1			44.5
1976	50.6	46.7	49.7	52.2	53.7			46.7			49.7			52.2			53.7
1977	62.0	56.3	61.4	64.1	66.4			56.3			61.4			64.1			66.4
1978	71.1	67.8	69.5	70.7	76.2			67.8			69.5			70.7			76.2
1979	81.3	78.4	79.9	81.6	85.0			78.4			79.9			81.6			85.0
1980	100.0	94.7	99.3	101.9	104.0			94.7			99.3			101.9			104.0
1981	122.1	119.2	119.1	120.5	129.4			119.2			119.1			120.5			129.4
1982	149.1	143.8	145.5	152.9	154.2			143.8			145.5			152.9			154.2
1983	178.5	169.7	177.4	181.9	184.8			169.7			177.4			181.9			184.8

Employment: manufacturing (6)
(all employees)
1980 = 100

Emploi : industries manufacturières (6)
(salariés)
1980 = 100

	Year	Q.1	Q.2	Q.3	Q.4	JAN	FEB	MAR	APR	MAY	JUN	JUL	AUG	SEP	OCT	NOV	DEC
1964																	
1965																	
1966					95.6												
1967			95.7		95.7												
1968			96.3		95.8												
1969			96.2	96.9	95.5												
1970	96.4	95.7	96.7	96.8	96.4												
1971	96.2	96.4	96.2	96.5	95.8												
1972	96.8	96.0	96.6	97.4	97.1												
1973	97.7	97.4	97.6	98.3	97.7												
1974	97.8	98.3	97.9	98.0	97.1												
1975	97.0	96.9	96.3	97.3	95.9												
1976	97.6	97.2	97.6	98.0	97.9												
1977	98.0	97.8	97.9	98.4	97.7												
1978	98.2	98.1	98.4	98.5	97.9												
1979	98.8	98.3	98.9	99.0	98.9												
1980	100.0	99.4	100.0	100.5	100.0												
1981	99.6	100.1	99.8	99.6	98.7												
1982	98.0	98.7	98.5	97.9	97.0												
1983		96.5	95.7	95.3													

Unemployment (registered unemployed) (7) (8) / Chômage (chômeurs inscrits) (7) (8)

thousands / milliers

	Year	Q.1	Q.2	Q.3	Q.4	JAN	FEB	MAR	APR	MAY	JUN	JUL	AUG	SEP	OCT	NOV	DEC
1964																	
1965																	
1966																	
1967																	
1968																	
1969																	
1970																	
1971																	
1972																	
1973																	
1974	37.0	27.4	29.4	37.2	54.0	27.3	27.5	27.4	27.4	28.2	32.6	32.9	36.9	41.8	48.9	54.7	58.5
1975	105.6	68.1	93.6	122.2	142.5	62.8	68.4	73.2	81.9	94.2	104.7	114.0	122.0	130.6	137.8	143.0	146.8
1976	182.7	160.5	176.4	189.7	204.2	153.8	161.7	165.9	171.6	176.8	180.9	184.6	189.5	195.0	200.6	204.5	207.5
1977	227.6	219.5	218.4	221.3	251.1	214.0	220.6	224.0	221.2	217.2	216.7	218.3	219.4	226.1	243.6	253.2	256.6
1978	282.6	269.4	278.1	284.3	298.7	263.4	270.7	274.1	276.5	277.9	279.9	282.1	283.4	287.4	294.0	299.7	302.5
1979	304.1	309.3	305.0	296.7	305.4	306.6	309.9	311.3	309.4	305.4	300.3	296.8	296.3	297.1	303.4	307.2	305.7
1980	285.4	309.2	287.7	277.2	267.3	308.2	310.5	308.9	293.7	286.9	282.6	281.2	280.5	269.8	267.4	267.4	267.2
1981	249.6	264.3	255.0	238.8	240.4	265.0	264.8	263.1	260.1	255.6	249.4	239.4	240.2	236.9	236.7	240.9	243.5
1982	244.9	252.9	253.0	239.6	233.9	249.1	253.6	256.1	255.1	253.0	250.9	246.4	245.3	227.0	231.8	234.0	236.0
1983	252.9	245.4	249.3	253.3	263.5	241.3	246.4	248.5	249.6	249.7	248.7	252.2	254.6	253.0	255.7	264.1	270.7

Jobs vacant, unfilled vacancies (8) / Offres d'emploi non satisfaites (8)

thousands / milliers

	Year	Q.1	Q.2	Q.3	Q.4	JAN	FEB	MAR	APR	MAY	JUN	JUL	AUG	SEP	OCT	NOV	DEC
1964																	
1965																	
1966																	
1967																	
1968																	
1969																	
1970																	
1971																	
1972																	
1973																	
1974	14.9	22.9	21.0	9.3	6.3	21.6	22.7	24.3	25.7	22.5	14.7	10.9	8.8	8.3	7.4	6.3	5.1
1975	3.7	4.4	3.5	3.7	3.2	4.5	4.4	4.4	3.4	3.6	3.5	3.6	4.0	3.5	3.4	3.2	3.0
1976	3.6	3.0	3.7	4.3	3.5	2.7	2.9	3.3	3.6	3.7	3.8	4.2	4.5	4.2	3.7	3.5	3.4
1977	4.4	2.8	3.7	5.8	5.4	2.9	2.6	2.9	3.1	3.8	4.1	5.3	6.0	6.2	5.6	5.5	5.2
1978	5.9	5.4	5.9	6.6	5.5	5.6	5.2	5.5	5.8	6.0	6.0	6.7	6.6	6.5	5.8	5.7	5.1
1979	6.7	5.3	5.9	7.6	7.3	5.3	5.3	5.3	5.4	5.7	6.7	7.1	7.7	8.1	8.2	7.8	7.5
1980	11.2	8.2	10.8	13.1	12.6	7.8	7.8	9.0	10.4	10.5	11.4	12.5	13.5	13.4	13.0	12.7	12.1
1981	11.3	12.2	11.5	11.3	10.3	12.6	12.6	11.3	11.2	11.6	11.8	10.6	11.3	11.8	11.0	10.7	9.3
1982	9.8	9.2	10.3	10.2	9.5	9.0	9.0	9.6	9.9	10.5	10.6	10.2	10.1	10.3	10.2	10.1	8.3
1983	8.2	9.5	10.3	7.7	5.3	8.0	10.0	10.4	11.8	9.2	10.0	9.4	7.1	6.7	5.9	5.3	4.7

Daily earnings: manufacturing (6) (all employees) / Gains journaliers : industries manufacturières (6) (salariés)

1980 = 100

	Year	Q.1	Q.2	Q.3	Q.4	JAN	FEB	MAR	APR	MAY	JUN	JUL	AUG	SEP	OCT	NOV	DEC
1964																	
1965																	
1966																	
1967																	
1968																	
1969																	
1970																	
1971																	
1972																	
1973	22.5	19.6	21.5	24.3	24.5												
1974	32.6	23.6	30.0	38.6	38.4												
1975	43.4	34.5	38.9	49.9	50.3												
1976	51.5	42.6	45.6	59.5	53.4												
1977	60.0	48.7	51.6	69.9	69.5												
1978	69.9	56.3	61.6	80.8	80.9												
1979	81.0	64.4	70.4	95.9	93.3												
1980	100.0	77.5	86.4	121.6	114.5												
1981	120.8	94.1	104.0	147.3	137.7												
1982	144.7	116.6	124.7	171.2	166.4												
1983		139.5	150.3	206.0													

PORTUGAL

Wholesale prices: total (5)(9)
(Lisbon area)
1980 = 100

Prix de gros : total (5)(9)
(région de Lisbonne)
1980 = 100

	Year	Q.1	Q.2	Q.3	Q.4	JAN	FEB	MAR	APR	MAY	JUN	JUL	AUG	SEP	OCT	NOV	DEC
1964	17	17	17	17	17	17	17	17	17	17	17	17	17	17	17	17	17
1965	17	17	17	17	17	17	17	17	17	17	17	17	17	17	17	17	17
1966	18	18	18	18	18	18	18	18	18	18	18	18	18	18	18	18	18
1967	19	19	18	18	19	19	19	19	19	18	18	18	18	19	19	19	19
1968	19	19	19	19	19	19	19	19	19	19	19	19	19	19	19	19	19
1969	20	20	20	20	20	19	20	20	20	20	20	20	19	20	20	20	21
1970	21	21	21	20	20	21	21	21	21	21	21	20	20	21	20	20	20
1971	21	21	21	21	21	21	20	21	21	21	21	21	21	21	22	22	21
1972	22	22	22	22	22	22	22	22	22	23	22	22	22	22	22	22	23
1973	25	24	24	25	26	23	24	24	24	24	24	24	25	25	26	26	27
1974	32	30	31	32	34	28	30	30	31	31	31	31	31	34	34	35	34
1975	36	35	36	36	37	34	34	36	36	36	36	36	35	36	37	37	38
1976	43	41	41	43	46	41	40	41	41	41	41	42	42	44	46	46	48
1977	55	51	56	55	59	49	51	53	55	56	56	54	54	56	58	59	62
1978	72	64	68	74	84	64	63	64	67	68	70	72	73	76	80	86	86
1979	94	89	94	96	97	88	89	91	92	96	92	94	95	98	97	99	95
1980	100	96	98	101	105	93	97	98	99	99	97	99	101	102	103	104	109
1981	121	113	116	126	131	111	113	115	115	117	117	120	128	129	130	130	132
1982	145	137	143	146	152	135	137	139	144	143	143	143	145	150	151	152	154
1983	182	163	171	189	200	159	162	168	168	169	176	183	191	192	194	200	206

Wholesale prices: manufactured goods (5)(9)(10)
(Lisbon area)
1980 = 100

Prix de gros : produits manufacturés (5)(9)(10)
(région de Lisbonne)
1980 = 100

	Year	Q.1	Q.2	Q.3	Q.4	JAN	FEB	MAR	APR	MAY	JUN	JUL	AUG	SEP	OCT	NOV	DEC
1964	22	22	22	22	23	22	22	22	22	22	22	22	22	23	23	23	23
1965	23	22	23	23	23	22	22	22	23	23	23	23	23	23	23	23	23
1966	25	25	24	25	25	25	25	25	24	24	25	24	25	25	25	25	25
1967	25	26	26	26	26	26	26	26	26	26	26	26	26	26	26	26	27
1968	26	27	26	26	26	27	27	27	26	26	26	26	26	26	26	26	26
1969	26	26	26	26	26	26	26	26	26	26	26	26	26	26	26	26	26
1970	26	27	26	26	26	27	27	27	27	26	26	26	26	26	26	26	26
1971	29	26	27	27	27	26	26	27	27	27	27	27	27	27	27	27	27
1972	29	28	28	29	30	28	28	28	28	28	28	29	29	29	29	30	31
1973	32	31	31	32	34	31	31	31	32	31	31	31	32	32	33	34	34
1974	37	36	37	37	37	35	36	36	37	37	37	37	37	37	37	37	37
1975	38	37	38	38	38	37	37	38	38	38	38	38	38	38	38	38	38
1976	42	39	41	44	45	38	39	39	40	42	42	44	45	45	45	45	45
1977	51	46	50	53	55	45	45	47	49	51	51	54	53	53	55	55	55
1978	62	57	61	64	65	55	58	59	60	62	62	64	64	65	65	65	65
1979	76	69	74	78	83	66	71	71	72	75	75	76	77	79	82	83	85
1980	100	91	98	105	107	87	92	93	97	97	99	105	104	105	107	107	107
1981	119	114	117	121	125	112	114	115	116	117	119	119	122	123	124	126	125
1982	136	127	132	140	145	125	125	132	131	131	133	135	143	144	144	145	145
1983	181	157	174	193	201	145	156	169	170	172	179	182	193	199	200	202	202

Wholesale prices: food (5)(9)
(Lisbon area)
1980 = 100

Prix de gros : alimentation (5)(9)
(région de Lisbonne)
1980 = 100

	Year	Q.1	Q.2	Q.3	Q.4	JAN	FEB	MAR	APR	MAY	JUN	JUL	AUG	SEP	OCT	NOV	DEC
1964	16	16	16	16	16	16	16	16	16	16	16	16	16	16	16	16	16
1965	17	16	16	16	17	16	16	16	16	16	16	16	16	17	17	17	17
1966	17	17	17	17	18	17	17	17	17	18	17	17	17	17	17	18	18
1967	17	18	17	17	18	17	18	18	17	17	17	17	17	17	17	18	18
1968	18	18	18	17	18	18	18	18	18	18	17	17	17	17	18	18	18
1969	19	19	19	18	19	18	19	19	19	19	19	18	18	19	19	19	19
1970	19	19	19	19	19	19	19	19	19	19	19	19	19	19	19	19	19
1971	20	20	20	20	21	19	19	20	20	20	20	20	20	21	21	21	21
1972	21	21	22	21	21	21	21	22	21	23	22	21	21	21	21	21	21
1973	23	22	22	22	24	22	22	22	22	22	22	22	22	23	23	24	25
1974	29	26	28	29	33	25	27	27	28	28	27	28	29	32	32	34	33
1975	39	35	38	39	42	34	34	38	38	38	38	38	38	40	41	41	44
1976	47	45	44	46	51	47	45	45	45	44	44	45	45	47	51	51	52
1977	60	56	64	58	62	54	56	60	63	65	63	59	56	58	60	62	63
1978	64	63	69	70	77	64	62	63	67	70	70	68	71	71	75	78	78
1979	91	81	90	95	98	79	80	83	86	94	90	93	94	96	98	98	99
1980	100	98	98	100	103	97	97	99	100	101	95	95	102	100	103	101	106
1981	122	112	115	127	132	109	113	113	115	116	115	118	131	131	132	133	133
1982	147	139	147	145	155	135	139	144	151	147	144	142	143	150	153	155	153
1983	189	168	175	196	216	162	168	173	172	173	180	188	201	200	204	216	229

Wholesale prices: raw materials (5)(9)(11)
(Lisbon area)
1980 = 100

Prix de gros : matières premières (5)(9)(11)
(région de Lisbonne)
1980 = 100

	Year	Q.1	Q.2	Q.3	Q.4	JAN	FEB	MAR	APR	MAY	JUN	JUL	AUG	SEP	OCT	NOV	DEC
1964	20	20	20	20	20	20	20	20	20	20	20	20	20	20	20	20	20
1965	20	20	20	20	21	20	20	20	20	20	20	20	20	20	20	21	21
1966	21	21	21	21	21	21	21	21	21	21	21	21	21	21	21	21	21
1967	20	21	20	20	20	21	20	20	20	20	20	20	20	20	20	20	20
1968	20	20	20	20	20	20	20	20	20	20	20	20	20	20	20	20	19
1969	20	19	19	20	19	19	19	19	19	19	19	19	20	19	19	19	19
1970	19	20	19	19	19	20	20	19	19	19	19	19	19	19	19	19	19
1971	19	19	19	19	19	19	19	19	19	19	19	19	19	19	19	19	19
1972	20	20	20	21	21	19	20	20	20	20	20	20	21	21	21	22	21
1973	26	23	24	26	30	22	23	23	23	23	24	25	26	26	27	28	36
1974	35	35	36	34	34	37	33	36	35	36	36	36	33	33	34	35	33
1975	33	34	32	32	33	35	34	33	33	30	32	31	32	33	32	33	34
1976	37	33	36	38	41	31	33	35	36	35	37	38	38	38	38	42	43
1977	55	48	55	58	61	43	50	51	54	55	57	57	58	59	60	61	61
1978	65	63	64	66	68	62	62	64	64	64	65	66	66	66	67	68	69
1979	77	69	76	81	84	59	69	69	71	75	81	81	81	81	82	85	85
1980	100	93	99	101	107	89	95	95	99	99	99	100	100	104	104	106	110
1981	114	110	113	116	118	110	110	111	112	112	114	115	116	118	118	118	118
1982	124	118	120	129	131	118	118	118	118	120	122	129	129	129	129	132	132
1983	142	133	138	143	155	132	133	135	138	138	138	139	142	147	153	154	158

Wholesale prices: liquid fuel (5)(9)
(Lisbon area)
1980 = 100

Prix de gros : combustibles liquides (5)(9)
(région de Lisbonne)
1980 = 100

	Year	Q.1	Q.2	Q.3	Q.4	JAN	FEB	MAR	APR	MAY	JUN	JUL	AUG	SEP	OCT	NOV	DEC
1964	12	12	12	12	12	12	12	12	12	12	12	12	12	12	12	12	12
1965	12	12	12	12	12	12	12	12	12	12	12	12	12	12	12	12	12
1966	12	12	12	12	12	12	12	12	12	12	12	12	12	12	12	12	12
1967	13	12	12	13	13	12	12	12	12	12	12	12	13	13	13	13	13
1968	13	13	13	13	13	13	13	13	13	13	13	13	13	13	13	13	13
1969	13	13	13	13	13	13	13	13	13	13	13	13	13	13	13	13	13
1970	13	13	13	12	12	13	13	13	13	12	12	12	12	12	12	12	12
1971	13	12	13	13	13	12	12	13	13	13	13	13	13	13	13	13	13
1972	13	13	13	13	13	13	13	13	13	13	13	13	13	13	13	13	13
1973	13	13	13	13	13	13	13	13	13	13	13	13	13	13	13	14	14
1974	20	18	20	20	23	14	20	20	20	20	20	20	17	23	23	23	23
1975	23	23	23	23	23	23	23	23	23	23	23	23	23	23	23	23	23
1976	31	29	29	32	32	29	29	29	29	29	29	32	32	32	32	32	32
1977	40	36	37	41	48	32	37	37	37	37	37	37	37	48	48	48	48
1978	51	48	48	48	61	48	48	48	48	48	48	48	48	48	61	61	61
1979	67	61	61	67	79	61	61	61	61	61	61	61	61	79	79	79	79
1980	100	93	100	100	106	79	100	100	100	100	100	100	100	100	100	100	118
1981	125	118	118	131	135	118	118	118	118	118	118	131	131	131	131	131	144
1982	152	144	150	158	158	144	144	144	146	146	158	158	158	158	158	158	158
1983	206	187	192	222	222	184	184	192	192	192	192	222	222	222	222	222	222

Consumer prices: all items, *less rent* (12)
1980 = 100

Prix à la consommation : total, *sauf loyers* (12)
1980 = 100

	Year	Q.1	Q.2	Q.3	Q.4	JAN	FEB	MAR	APR	MAY	JUN	JUL	AUG	SEP	OCT	NOV	DEC
1964	13.5	13.4	13.4	13.5	13.7	13.3	13.4	13.5	13.5	13.3	13.4	13.4	13.6	13.6	13.7	13.7	13.8
1965	14.0	13.8	13.9	13.9	14.3	13.8	13.7	14.0	13.9	13.8	13.9	13.8	13.9	14.1	14.1	14.4	14.3
1966	14.8	14.7	14.6	14.6	15.1	14.5	14.8	14.9	14.8	14.6	14.4	14.5	14.6	14.9	15.2	15.1	14.9
1967	15.3	15.2	15.0	15.3	15.8	15.0	15.1	15.4	15.2	14.9	14.9	15.0	15.3	15.7	15.7	15.8	15.9
1968	16.0	16.0	15.8	15.9	16.4	15.9	16.0	16.1	16.0	15.9	15.7	15.7	15.9	16.1	16.2	16.6	16.5
1969	17.2	17.0	16.9	17.0	17.8	16.6	17.1	17.2	16.9	17.1	16.7	16.8	16.8	17.2	17.6	18.0	17.9
1970	18.2	18.0	17.9	18.3	18.7	18.0	17.3	18.2	18.0	17.9	17.9	18.1	18.3	18.4	18.5	18.6	18.8
1971	19.7	19.1	19.4	19.8	20.8	19.0	18.9	19.3	19.5	19.4	19.3	19.4	19.6	20.2	20.5	20.9	20.8
1972	21.5	21.1	21.5	21.5	21.9	20.9	21.1	21.4	21.2	21.9	21.3	21.4	21.4	21.7	21.9	21.6	22.2
1973	24.0	22.8	23.3	24.1	25.6	22.6	22.9	23.0	23.1	23.4	23.4	23.8	24.0	24.6	25.0	25.6	26.3
1974	31.0	27.9	29.9	32.2	33.9	26.6	28.1	29.0	29.7	29.9	30.0	31.1	31.6	33.9	33.9	34.0	34.0
1975	37.3	35.8	36.8	37.6	38.9	35.5	35.5	36.4	36.9	36.4	37.0	37.0	37.5	38.3	38.2	38.5	39.9
1976	44.4	42.4	42.2	44.4	48.7	42.8	41.9	42.5	42.7	41.8	42.2	43.2	44.2	45.7	47.6	48.4	50.7
1977	56.5	51.2	57.0	57.7	60.1	48.7	50.3	54.7	56.8	57.2	57.2	57.2	58.1	57.9	59.2	60.0	61.3
1978	69.2	62.9	68.2	70.8	75.4	62.6	62.8	63.4	67.7	68.5	68.5	65.6	70.3	71.9	74.3	75.2	76.7
1979	85.8	78.4	84.1	87.6	92.7	77.0	78.4	79.8	82.3	84.9	85.1	85.4	87.4	90.1	91.5	92.6	93.9
1980	100.0	96.2	98.6	101.1	104.0	94.5	96.4	97.6	98.4	98.2	99.3	100.4	101.4	101.5	102.5	103.2	106.2
1981	120.0	110.8	116.1	123.1	130.0	109.2	110.8	112.3	115.4	116.0	116.8	120.2	123.5	125.5	127.8	129.4	132.8
1982	146.8	139.0	146.0	149.3	154.7	135.1	139.1	142.7	145.4	145.6	147.0	146.9	149.5	151.6	152.5	153.8	157.8
1983	184.3	167.8	176.4	188.4	204.2	164.1	167.6	171.7	175.6	175.2	178.4	182.3	188.2	194.7	198.4	203.1	211.2

Money supply (M1) (13) / Disponibilités monétaires (M1) (13)

billion escudos, end of period / milliards d'escudos, fin de période

	Year	Q.1	Q.2	Q.3	Q.4	JAN	FEB	MAR	APR	MAY	JUN	JUL	AUG	SEP	OCT	NOV	DEC
1964																	
1965	62.3				62.3												62.3
1966	70.3				70.3												70.3
1967	75.4	69.2	71.5	74.1	75.4			69.2			71.5			74.1			75.4
1968	80.9	71.1	72.2	74.5	80.9			71.1			72.2			74.5			80.9
1969	91.4	77.3	83.1	83.7	91.4			77.3			83.1			83.7			91.4
1970	92.6	89.1	86.9	83.9	92.6			89.1			86.9			83.9			92.6
1971	104.9	87.0	89.5	92.6	104.9			87.0			89.5			92.6			104.9
1972	122.3	97.6	103.3	109.8	122.3			97.6			103.3			109.8			122.3
1973	165.6	126.3	130.7	141.1	165.6			126.3			130.7			141.1			165.6
1974	182.5	155.6	158.4	161.6	182.5			155.6			158.4			161.6			182.5
1975	227.2	176.7	185.9	204.7	227.2			176.7			185.9			204.7			227.2
1976	251.5	216.8	222.5	228.6	251.5			216.8			222.5			228.6			251.5
1977	274.8	238.7	249.9	253.1	274.3	240.3	238.9	238.7	237.9	241.0	249.9	255.1	255.4	253.1	247.9	252.3	274.8
1978	314.9	265.6	264.5	280.3	314.9	263.8	257.0	265.6	259.6	257.1	264.5	274.6	280.0	280.3	279.1	285.8	314.9
1979	390.9	285.2	308.5	335.1	390.9	291.7	286.3	285.2	289.7	295.5	308.5	322.9	329.7	335.1	337.2	349.3	390.9
1980	477.4	367.2	385.7	415.1	477.4	366.3	358.9	367.2	366.3	371.8	385.7	404.4	413.3	415.1	415.9	429.9	477.4
1981	517.3	444.7	471.7	491.4	517.3	450.3	438.6	444.7	442.1	451.1	471.7	490.8	499.8	491.4	478.8	491.1	517.3
1982	599.9	504.0	526.9	556.1	599.9	509.0	501.9	504.0	498.8	503.9	526.9	552.3	561.3	556.1	550.8	563.3	599.9
1983	653.0	587.6	600.9	616.1	653.0	579.8	576.3	587.6	590.7	586.6	600.9	613.6	621.7	616.1	602.9	618.9	653.0

M1 plus quasi-money (13) / M1 plus quasi-monnaie (13)

billion escudos, end of period / milliards d'escudos, fin de période

	Year	Q.1	Q.2	Q.3	Q.4	JAN	FEB	MAR	APR	MAY	JUN	JUL	AUG	SEP	OCT	NOV	DEC
1964																	
1965	81.1				81.1												81.1
1966	91.0				91.0												91.0
1967	102.1	90.5	93.2	96.6	102.1			90.5			93.2			96.6			102.1
1968	116.6	101.9	103.9	108.2	116.6			101.9			103.9			108.2			116.6
1969	137.6	116.5	122.6	126.7	137.6			116.5			122.6			126.7			137.6
1970	155.7	136.0	141.0	144.3	155.7			136.0			141.0			144.3			155.7
1971	189.0	156.4	163.5	172.1	189.0			156.4			163.5			172.1			189.0
1972	234.7	189.4	200.7	213.6	234.7			189.4			200.7			213.6			234.7
1973	301.3	243.5	255.7	272.2	301.3			243.5			255.7			272.2			301.3
1974	342.3	300.9	307.5	319.6	342.3			300.9			307.5			319.6			342.3
1975	385.4	341.6	351.0	364.5	385.4			341.6			351.0			364.5			385.4
1976	453.1	390.1	400.1	420.9	453.1			390.1			400.1			420.9			453.1
1977	567.5	474.5	502.0	526.8	567.5	462.9	470.0	474.5	479.6	488.7	502.0	512.2	520.0	526.8	528.6	537.6	567.5
1978	726.6	595.3	620.9	666.0	726.6	569.4	577.4	595.3	598.2	606.7	620.9	641.5	654.3	666.0	675.9	691.6	726.6
1979	994.2	755.2	822.1	892.2	994.2	731.1	740.4	755.2	768.9	791.1	822.1	849.7	873.4	892.2	908.3	936.4	994.2
1980	1340.4	1031.6	1105.3	1206.1	1340.4	991.0	1005.5	1031.6	1049.9	1068.9	1105.3	1143.4	1176.0	1206.1	1234.8	1266.6	1340.4
1981	1723.7	1408.7	1520.1	1628.5	1723.7	1350.0	1371.0	1408.7	1436.4	1476.4	1520.1	1565.5	1604.9	1628.5	1634.8	1667.8	1723.7
1982	2177.7	1814.7	1924.1	2053.7	2177.7	1752.1	1777.2	1814.7	1839.6	1874.4	1924.1	1977.7	2023.2	2053.7	2079.0	2119.3	2177.7
1983	2611.6	2272.0	2372.7	2477.8	2611.6	2200.8	2230.6	2272.0	2304.9	2328.2	2372.7	2407.2	2450.5	2477.8	2489.9	2538.4	2611.6

Bank credit to economy (13) / Crédits bancaires à l'économie (13)

billion escudos, end of period / milliards d'escudos, fin de période

	Year	Q.1	Q.2	Q.3	Q.4	JAN	FEB	MAR	APR	MAY	JUN	JUL	AUG	SEP	OCT	NOV	DEC
1964																	
1965	60.8				60.8												60.8
1966	70.0				70.0												70.0
1967	74.3	70.1	72.0	74.0	74.3			70.1			72.0			74.0			74.3
1968	86.8	74.9	78.0	80.8	86.8			74.9			78.0			80.8			86.8
1969	105.1	87.6	93.6	96.6	105.1			87.6			93.6			96.6			105.1
1970	125.5	106.3	111.9	117.0	125.5			106.3			111.9			117.0			125.5
1971	153.3	125.6	132.1	138.1	153.3			125.6			132.1			138.1			153.3
1972	187.7	155.2	164.7	174.4	187.7			155.2			164.7			174.4			187.7
1973	249.5	201.9	209.0	222.9	249.5			201.9			209.0			222.9			249.5
1974	293.8	256.6	260.9	271.2	293.8			256.6			260.9			271.2			293.8
1975	326.3	299.9	309.5	314.7	326.3			299.9			309.5			314.7			326.3
1976	389.9	329.9	347.2	359.2	389.9			329.9			347.2			359.2			389.9
1977	579.3	459.9	491.5	527.7	579.3	440.9	451.5	459.9	465.8	478.5	491.5	504.6	520.9	527.7	535.1	547.1	579.3
1978	703.2	601.5	640.8	664.9	703.2	582.3	592.5	601.5	617.5	631.0	640.8	653.0	661.7	664.9	670.3	681.9	703.2
1979	852.5	722.2	763.3	789.3	852.5	704.3	712.3	722.2	734.2	750.6	763.3	776.3	784.1	789.3	800.1	821.4	852.5
1980	1075.1	907.2	944.2	985.5	1075.1	863.5	882.3	907.2	918.1	931.9	944.2	963.3	969.0	985.5	1003.4	1032.5	1075.1
1981	1345.8	1148.2	1223.3	1273.6	1345.8	1092.9	1124.1	1148.2	1170.7	1192.9	1223.3	1253.6	1261.8	1273.6	1291.8	1312.9	1345.8
1982	1686.7	1412.4	1486.5	1571.8	1686.7	1367.0	1387.7	1412.4	1431.7	1448.7	1486.5	1526.9	1548.7	1571.8	1597.6	1632.6	1686.7
1983	2109.9	1751.0	1839.0	1936.3	2109.9	1697.1	1716.4	1751.0	1771.3	1793.3	1839.0	1870.4	1906.3	1936.3	1983.9	2033.7	2109.9

Money supply (M1) (13)

billion escudos, end of period

Adjusted - Corrigé *

Disponibilités monétaires (M1) (13)

milliards d'escudos, fin de période

Year	Q.1	Q.2	Q.3	Q.4	JAN	FEB	MAR	APR	MAY	JUN	JUL	AUG	SEP	OCT	NOV	DEC
1964																
1965																
1966				67.7												
1967	70.1	72.2	75.3	72.5												
1968	72.0	72.9	76.0	77.4												
1969	78.4	84.1	85.5	86.9												
1970	90.5	88.3	85.9	87.5												
1971	88.6	91.1	94.8	98.7												
1972	59.6	105.7	112.4	114.6												
1973	129.0	134.1	143.9	155.2												
1974	159.3	162.7	164.4	171.4												
1975	180.9	190.8	207.8	213.6												
1976	222.4	228.2	231.6	236.2												
1977	243.3	254.0	251.9	251.0	236.5	243.5	243.3	246.5	250.8	254.0	253.1	252.4	251.9	251.1	252.0	251.0
1978	270.8	268.8	278.9	287.0	259.4	261.9	270.8	268.7	267.6	268.8	272.6	276.4	278.9	282.8	285.2	287.0
1979	291.1	313.5	333.8	356.4	286.6	292.1	291.1	300.2	307.8	313.5	320.0	325.1	333.8	341.7	348.6	356.4
1980	374.7	392.4	413.4	435.2	359.8	366.2	374.7	379.6	387.3	392.4	400.8	407.6	413.4	420.9	428.6	435.2
1981	453.8	480.4	489.5	471.6	442.3	447.5	453.8	458.1	469.9	480.4	486.4	492.9	489.5	485.1	489.7	471.6
1982	514.3	536.6	554.4	546.9	500.0	512.1	514.3	517.5	524.9	536.6	548.0	553.5	554.4	558.1	561.6	546.9
1983	599.6	611.9	614.3	595.3	569.5	588.0	599.6	612.8	611.1	611.9	608.7	613.1	614.3	610.9	617.1	595.3

M1 plus quasi-money (13)

billion escudos, end of period

Adjusted - Corrigé *

M1 plus quasi-monnaie (13)

milliards d'escudos, fin de période

Year	Q.1	Q.2	Q.3	Q.4	JAN	FEB	MAR	APR	MAY	JUN	JUL	AUG	SEP	OCT	NOV	DEC
1964																
1965																
1966				88.6												
1967	91.3	94.0	97.4	99.3												
1968	102.8	105.0	109.2	113.3												
1969	117.7	123.8	128.0	133.6												
1970	137.4	142.4	145.9	151.1												
1971	158.0	165.1	174.0	183.5												
1972	191.2	202.9	215.7	228.1												
1973	245.2	258.8	274.7	293.4												
1974	302.8	311.2	322.1	334.3												
1975	343.0	355.3	367.1	377.1												
1976	351.6	404.5	423.4	444.2												
1977	475.9	504.6	526.3	553.1	459.6	471.0	475.9	484.5	494.6	504.6	510.7	518.0	526.3	532.9	540.3	553.1
1978	596.5	624.1	665.4	707.5	564.9	578.0	596.5	603.7	614.1	624.1	639.6	651.7	665.4	680.6	694.4	707.5
1979	757.4	827.0	390.4	968.0	726.0	741.9	757.4	776.7	800.7	827.0	847.2	870.0	890.4	915.6	940.1	968.0
1980	1034.7	1112.0	1203.7	1306.5	983.2	1007.5	1034.7	1060.5	1081.8	1112.0	1140.0	1170.1	1203.7	1243.5	1271.7	1306.5
1981	1413.0	1529.3	1626.9	1680.0	1339.3	1373.7	1413.0	1450.9	1494.4	1529.3	1566.3	1598.5	1626.9	1646.3	1674.5	1680.0
1982	1820.1	1935.7	2051.7	2122.5	1738.2	1780.8	1820.1	1858.1	1897.1	1935.7	1973.7	2015.2	2051.7	2095.8	2127.8	2122.5
1983	2278.8	2387.0	2475.3	2545.4	2183.3	2235.1	2278.8	2328.2	2356.5	2387.0	2402.4	2440.7	2475.3	2510.0	2548.6	2545.4

* Adjusted by the O.E.C.D.

* Corrigé par l'O.C.D.E.

PORTUGAL

U.S. dollar exchange rate: spot
cents per escudo, end of period

Taux de change du dollar É.-U. : au comptant
cents par escudo, fin de période

	Year	Q.1	Q.2	Q.3	Q.4	JAN	FEB	MAR	APR	MAY	JUN	JUL	AUG	SEP	OCT	NOV	DEC
1964	3.454	3.463	3.454	3.445	3.454	3.463	3.463	3.463	3.464	3.461	3.454	3.451	3.446	3.445	3.447	3.453	3.454
1965	3.469	3.455	3.455	3.467	3.469	3.455	3.458	3.455	3.465	3.457	3.455	3.455	3.454	3.467	3.470	3.470	3.469
1966	3.451	3.457	3.451	3.452	3.451	3.470	3.466	3.457	3.455	3.452	3.451	3.451	3.448	3.452	3.452	3.451	3.451
1967	3.465	3.459	3.451	3.445	3.465	3.455	3.453	3.459	3.461	3.457	3.451	3.446	3.446	3.445	3.445	3.464	3.465
1968	3.476	3.467	3.466	3.465	3.476	3.465	3.464	3.467	3.465	3.467	3.466	3.469	3.465	3.466	3.466	3.472	3.476
1969	3.490	3.489	3.484	3.490	3.490	3.484	3.487	3.489	3.487	3.483	3.484	3.488	3.489	3.490	3.490	3.490	3.490
1970	3.478	3.488	3.476	3.471	3.478	3.490	3.490	3.488	3.486	3.481	3.476	3.471	3.469	3.471	3.473	3.475	3.478
1971	3.628	3.490	3.490	3.615	3.628	3.490	3.488	3.490	3.489	3.490	3.490	3.490	3.560	3.615	3.628	3.630	3.628
1972	3.704	3.683	3.682	3.687	3.704	3.650	3.662	3.683	3.677	3.682	3.682	3.700	3.701	3.687	3.686	3.697	3.704
1973	3.869	3.949	4.357	4.267	3.869	3.738	3.985	3.949	3.921	4.091	4.357	4.436	4.245	4.267	4.293	4.003	3.869
1974	4.066	4.058	3.989	3.866	4.066	3.740	3.922	4.058	4.050	4.026	3.989	3.966	3.863	3.866	3.936	4.026	4.066
1975	3.640	4.092	4.074	3.641	3.640	4.082	4.163	4.092	4.050	4.097	4.074	3.768	3.749	3.641	3.755	3.687	3.640
1976	3.170	3.408	3.177	3.208	3.170	3.648	3.585	3.408	3.359	3.256	3.177	3.195	3.205	3.208	3.187	3.169	3.170
1977	2.509	2.581	2.589	2.451	2.509	3.091	2.573	2.581	2.583	2.582	2.589	2.597	2.509	2.451	2.470	2.451	2.509
1978	2.173	2.439	2.190	2.204	2.173	2.493	2.403	2.439	2.383	2.187	2.190	2.205	2.204	2.204	2.301	2.136	2.173
1979	2.009	2.073	2.039	2.048	2.009	2.118	2.100	2.073	2.034	2.007	2.039	2.045	2.029	2.048	1.977	2.010	2.009
1980	1.885	1.956	2.045	1.991	1.885	1.991	2.074	1.956	2.028	2.034	2.045	2.016	2.009	1.991	1.941	1.908	1.885
1981	1.533	1.762	1.578	1.538	1.533	1.808	1.758	1.762	1.689	1.626	1.578	1.526	1.527	1.538	1.545	1.574	1.533
1982	1.123	1.403	1.195	1.133	1.123	1.495	1.441	1.403	1.415	1.396	1.195	1.185	1.157	1.133	1.099	1.104	1.123
1983	0.761	1.024	0.855	0.806	0.761	1.037	1.081	1.024	1.019	0.998	0.855	0.827	0.802	0.806	0.799	0.776	0.761

Official reserves excluding gold
million SDR's, end of period

Réserves officielles, or exclu
millions de DTS, fin de période

	Year	Q.1	Q.2	Q.3	Q.4	JAN	FEB	MAR	APR	MAY	JUN	JUL	AUG	SEP	OCT	NOV	DEC
1964	431	358	355	387	431	352	358	358	357	360	355	384	377	387	402	406	431
1965	433	406	386	403	433	415	415	406	389	386	386	387	393	403	407	414	433
1966	434	337	323	364	434	354	348	337	328	322	323	332	352	364	360	376	434
1967	535	408	422	471	535	412	412	408	406	405	422	428	446	471	501	492	535
1968	507	509	527	462	507	535	519	509	505	509	527	511	464	462	477	506	507
1969	570	493	503	517	570	509	495	493	485	486	503	506	531	517	513	532	570
1970	602	502	487	559	602	544	521	502	502	486	487	490	534	559	556	566	602
1971	870	607	646	820	870	610	598	607	613	641	646	695	749	820	838	865	870
1972	1189	890	915	1112	1189	880	887	890	893	895	915	981	1058	1112	1142	1179	1189
1973	1390	1226	1242	1340	1390	1203	1178	1226	1225	1234	1242	1296	1299	1340	1337	1355	1390
1974	948	1243	1146	1127	948	1361	1319	1243	1171	1187	1146	1139	1139	1127	1055	964	948
1975	340	760	737	558	340	871	881	760	790	757	737	752	641	558	404	303	340
1976	151	238	136	191	151	434	357	238	237	166	136	207	214	191	111	109	151
1977	301	116	65	136	301	77	113	116	108	139	65	138	104	136	151	218	301
1978	669	214	232	624	669	278	232	214	140	269	232	441	614	624	675	784	669
1979	707	512	483	813	707	690	592	512	460	434	483	538	695	813	876	807	707
1980	624	485	338	839	624	692	528	485	440	353	338	359	670	839	846	755	624
1981	459	463	501	711	459	559	451	463	397	345	501	726	767	711	535	279	459
1982	405	279	444	546	405	411	339	279	308	354	444	522	644	546	470	368	405
1983	368	619	356	607	368	279	452	619	464	447	356	198	534	607	498	321	368

Net foreign position:
commercial and savings banks
million escudos, end of period

Position extérieure nette :
banques commerciales et d'épargne
millions d'escudos, fin de période

	Year	Q.1	Q.2	Q.3	Q.4	JAN	FEB	MAR	APR	MAY	JUN	JUL	AUG	SEP	OCT	NOV	DEC
1964																	
1965																	
1966																	
1967																	
1968																	
1969																	
1970																	
1971																	
1972																	
1973																	
1974																	
1975																	
1976	1949				1949												1949
1977	-20107	-2795	-7636	-15071	-20107	622	-1303	-2795	-5476	-10939	-7636	-7946	-10797	-15071	-17845	-17921	-20107
1978	-13953	-28315	-28696	-26769	-13953	-24397	-26735	-28315	-30287	-31677	-28696	-28573	-28056	-26769	-23991	-21294	-13953
1979	34455	-4600	1870	19324	34455	-11570	-8891	-4600	-514	-2733	1870	8143	18469	19324	22461	25916	34455
1980	63130	21033	30919	54135	63130	24590	17395	21033	20574	22817	30919	45465	54236	54135	54669	51944	63130
1981	74932	53959	61273	69343	74932	58434	54161	53959	57229	58364	61273	65745	69012	69343	63412	65253	74932
1982	103584	72457	92937	95146	103584	65680	66466	72457	77668	77647	92937	99597	101114	95146	100755	95808	103584
1983	184622	102292	140740	152830	184622	99922	98047	102292	108301	117917	140740	157296	170655	152830	156323	157809	184622

Balance of payments: net trade
billion escudos

Balance des paiements : balance commerciale
milliards d'escudos

	Year	Q.1	Q.2	Q.3	Q.4	JAN	FEB	MAR	APR	MAY	JUN	JUL	AUG	SEP	OCT	NOV	DEC
1964																	
1965																	
1966																	
1967																	
1968																	
1969																	
1970																	
1971																	
1972																	
1973																	
1974																	
1975	-41.0	-9.9	-11.2	-9.2	-10.7												
1976	-66.0	-13.7	-14.3	-17.0	-21.0												
1977	-97.3	-18.5	-25.5	-28.9	-24.5												
1978	-105.7	-25.8	-29.9	-26.8	-23.2												
1979	-122.1	-27.1	-23.2	-36.3	-35.6												
1980	-210.8	-47.5	-47.2	-60.2	-55.9												
1981	-317.2	-79.8	-85.0	-74.1	-78.3												
1982	-377.6	-96.9	-101.1	-107.7	-71.9												
1983	-329.1	-98.0	-85.3	-71.7	-74.1												

Balance of payments: current balance
billion escudos

Balance des paiements : opérations courantes, nettes
milliards d'escudos

	Year	Q.1	Q.2	Q.3	Q.4	JAN	FEB	MAR	APR	MAY	JUN	JUL	AUG	SEP	OCT	NOV	DEC
1964																	
1965																	
1966																	
1967																	
1968																	
1969																	
1970																	
1971																	
1972																	
1973																	
1974																	
1975	-19.1	-4.1	-5.7	-1.8	-7.5												
1976	-38.8	-10.4	-9.2	-5.4	-13.8												
1977	-57.4	-11.7	-17.0	-13.2	-15.5												
1978	-34.8	-17.6	-18.1	0.5	0.4												
1979	-2.4	-6.8	-4.4	13.1	-4.3												
1980	-62.8	-20.0	-19.0	-6.0	-17.8												
1981	-171.9	-52.5	-51.3	-19.5	-48.7												
1982	-249.3	-71.4	-85.5	-44.4	-48.0												
1983	-170.2	-70.2	-65.8	2.3	-36.5												

Balance of payments: net capital movements (14)
billion escudos

Balance des paiements : mouvements de capitaux, nets (14)
milliards d'escudos

	Year	Q.1	Q.2	Q.3	Q.4	JAN	FEB	MAR	APR	MAY	JUN	JUL	AUG	SEP	OCT	NOV	DEC
1964																	
1965																	
1966																	
1967																	
1968																	
1969																	
1970																	
1971																	
1972																	
1973																	
1974																	
1975	-6.8	-3.5	-2.5	-1.4	0.6												
1976	4.3	-0.2	-4.0	4.6	4.0												
1977	2.9	-1.9	1.5	-1.9	5.3												
1978	44.4	1.4	10.1	17.5	15.4												
1979	67.5	9.1	10.3	30.2	17.3												
1980	105.2	-5.3	27.6	67.5	15.4												
1981	167.6	22.9	70.7	46.1	27.9												
1982	262.9	52.7	101.7	55.7	52.8												
1983	83.8	42.9	10.2	-17.9	43.5												

PORTUGAL

Imports c.i.f. — Importations c.a.f.

billion escudos, monthly averages — milliards d'escudos, moyennes mensuelles

	Year	Q.1	Q.2	Q.3	Q.4	JAN	FEB	MAR	APR	MAY	JUN	JUL	AUG	SEP	OCT	NOV	DEC
1964	1.85	1.44	1.79	1.91	2.25	0.87	1.57	1.88	1.71	1.78	1.87	2.11	1.51	2.10	1.68	2.14	2.94
1965	2.14	1.78	2.11	2.09	2.60	1.14	1.93	2.28	2.12	2.28	1.93	1.94	1.83	2.50	1.89	2.58	3.33
1966	2.43	1.76	2.43	2.27	3.25	0.85	1.88	2.55	2.30	2.71	2.27	2.59	2.00	2.22	2.70	2.58	4.48
1967	2.41	1.75	2.61	2.28	2.99	0.87	2.02	2.35	2.88	2.84	2.11	2.42	2.48	1.94	2.34	2.82	3.82
1968	2.50	1.91	2.63	2.40	3.06	0.72	2.19	2.81	2.63	2.44	2.81	2.46	2.16	2.57	3.16	3.21	2.81
1969	2.95	1.66	2.68	2.47	5.01	0.66	2.00	2.32	2.65	2.79	2.58	2.51	2.41	2.48	3.51	4.49	7.02
1970	3.73	2.52	3.36	4.03	5.01	1.37	2.55	3.63	3.85	2.68	3.55	3.67	3.98	4.43	3.50	4.08	7.44
1971	4.25	2.62	3.82	3.92	6.66	1.18	2.75	3.92	3.99	3.31	4.16	4.23	3.75	3.79	4.79	4.92	10.27
1972	4.96	3.64	5.12	4.40	6.68	0.81	4.09	6.01	4.44	4.72	6.18	4.41	3.96	4.82	5.02	4.83	10.18
1973	6.12	2.68	5.51	6.45	9.85	1.13	2.46	4.47	5.71	5.38	5.44	7.35	5.90	6.06	6.70	7.16	15.69
1974	9.56	5.09	8.40	8.56	16.20	1.37	5.58	8.32	7.56	9.28	8.35	8.51	8.70	8.47	12.47	10.83	25.30
1975	8.29	5.47	8.21	7.46	8.01	9.80	9.58	9.04	9.42	8.44	6.77	6.86	7.33	8.20	10.18	7.52	6.33
1976	10.91	5.58	9.93	11.09	13.02	8.74	9.20	10.79	8.68	11.07	10.04	11.75	10.93	10.59	11.23	14.60	13.24
1977	15.90	13.01	16.34	17.09	17.15	12.83	10.23	15.98	14.76	16.65	17.61	16.50	16.92	17.86	15.64	17.69	18.14
1978	19.14	17.82	20.44	18.74	19.54	18.95	15.93	18.58	18.56	22.28	20.50	18.78	18.36	19.08	20.27	22.99	15.36
1979	27.66	23.88	26.54	28.32	31.90	25.73	18.51	27.39	21.96	30.27	27.39	27.89	28.20	28.89	32.85	34.48	28.38
1980	38.82	38.28	38.23	39.80	38.98	43.56	31.47	39.82	42.54	36.65	35.48	42.99	31.81	44.59	44.11	35.14	37.69
1981	49.81	47.83	53.19	47.05	51.17	46.71	50.47	46.30	57.08	53.11	49.38	55.13	32.72	53.29	55.82	50.27	43.42
1982	61.59	60.71	61.22	64.41	60.02	54.99	55.59	71.56	59.50	53.64	70.53	62.09	63.68	67.46	58.97	63.92	57.19
1983	73.79	72.05	73.71	72.22	77.18	76.15	62.80	77.20	65.09	81.34	74.70	80.62	65.46	70.58	89.94	79.28	62.32

Exports f.o.b. — Exportations f.o.b.

billion escudos, monthly averages — milliards d'escudos, moyennes mensuelles

	Year	Q.1	Q.2	Q.3	Q.4	JAN	FEB	MAR	APR	MAY	JUN	JUL	AUG	SEP	OCT	NOV	DEC
1964	1.24	0.95	1.18	1.18	1.65	0.68	0.96	1.21	1.22	1.12	1.22	1.25	1.00	1.29	1.38	1.38	2.19
1965	1.42	1.09	1.28	1.44	1.87	0.76	1.12	1.40	1.35	1.41	1.09	1.21	1.33	1.78	1.66	1.58	2.37
1966	1.50	1.20	1.38	1.38	2.06	0.74	1.18	1.68	1.31	1.63	1.20	1.43	1.41	1.29	1.68	1.61	2.87
1967	1.63	1.16	1.43	1.51	2.42	0.69	1.25	1.53	1.69	1.63	0.99	1.52	1.61	1.40	2.03	2.36	2.87
1968	1.76	1.32	1.63	1.76	2.33	0.64	1.62	1.68	1.62	1.63	1.63	1.68	1.74	1.88	2.10	2.21	2.68
1969	1.97	1.39	2.03	1.85	2.62	0.52	1.83	1.82	2.28	1.96	1.84	1.89	1.93	1.72	2.05	2.64	3.18
1970	2.27	1.56	2.20	1.97	3.33	1.11	1.77	1.81	2.34	2.03	2.22	1.81	1.98	2.13	2.13	3.49	4.38
1971	2.48	1.69	2.40	2.42	3.39	0.84	2.01	2.24	2.62	2.33	2.26	2.67	2.39	2.20	2.33	2.66	5.19
1972	2.92	1.76	2.77	2.71	4.45	0.52	2.23	2.43	3.09	2.49	2.73	2.83	2.53	2.77	3.39	3.25	6.72
1973	3.73	2.06	3.91	3.86	5.10	1.04	2.15	3.00	3.52	3.70	4.50	3.96	2.88	4.75	3.39	4.18	7.74
1974	4.83	3.46	4.45	4.07	7.35	1.49	3.61	5.28	4.28	5.14	3.94	4.46	3.84	3.91	6.29	5.84	9.92
1975	4.11	4.42	4.13	3.75	4.15	4.50	4.41	4.35	4.31	3.90	4.18	4.55	3.05	3.64	4.65	3.93	3.87
1976	4.59	4.37	4.43	4.45	5.12	4.65	4.05	4.40	4.68	4.20	4.42	5.30	3.80	4.24	4.75	5.12	5.49
1977	6.47	5.69	6.47	6.09	7.65	5.09	4.99	7.00	6.03	6.45	6.93	7.27	4.61	6.37	7.18	8.36	7.41
1978	8.93	7.50	8.69	8.35	11.20	7.17	7.15	8.17	7.48	9.11	9.48	9.95	6.57	8.53	10.94	12.27	10.39
1979	14.68	12.56	14.59	14.09	17.46	12.09	10.69	14.88	13.50	14.64	15.64	16.70	12.47	13.11	18.43	18.01	15.95
1980	19.35	19.43	19.83	17.64	20.50	18.27	19.59	20.43	20.80	18.28	20.42	22.55	13.49	16.88	21.34	18.47	21.69
1981	21.24	18.92	22.19	20.33	23.53	17.86	18.15	20.75	21.75	21.68	23.12	24.66	15.92	20.41	26.29	23.60	20.70
1982	27.60	23.47	25.67	27.22	34.04	18.79	23.18	28.43	24.64	24.30	28.07	33.06	21.75	26.86	32.39	33.56	36.16
1983	42.04	35.37	39.59	43.30	49.90	31.55	32.48	42.09	35.69	44.98	38.10	50.47	32.81	46.61	50.15	49.16	50.37

Trade balance (f.o.b. — c.i.f.) — Balance commerciale (f.o.b. — c.a.f.)

billion escudos, monthly averages — milliards d'escudos, moyennes mensuelles

	Year	Q.1	Q.2	Q.3	Q.4	JAN	FEB	MAR	APR	MAY	JUN	JUL	AUG	SEP	OCT	NOV	DEC
1964	-0.61	-0.49	-0.60	-0.73	-0.60	-0.19	-0.61	-0.68	-0.49	-0.67	-0.65	-0.87	-0.52	-0.80	-0.29	-0.76	-0.76
1965	-0.72	-0.69	-0.83	-0.65	-0.73	-0.38	-0.81	-0.88	-0.77	-0.87	-0.84	-0.72	-0.50	-0.72	-0.23	-1.00	-0.96
1966	-0.93	-0.56	-1.05	-0.90	-1.20	-0.11	-0.69	-0.87	-0.99	-1.08	-1.07	-1.16	-0.59	-0.94	-1.02	-0.97	-1.61
1967	-0.78	-0.59	-1.17	-0.77	-0.57	-0.18	-0.77	-0.83	-1.19	-1.21	-1.12	-0.90	-0.87	-0.53	-0.31	-0.46	-0.55
1968	-0.74	-0.59	-1.00	-0.64	-0.73	-0.08	-0.57	-1.13	-1.01	-0.81	-1.19	-0.80	-0.42	-0.70	-1.06	-1.00	-0.13
1969	-0.98	-0.27	-0.65	-0.62	-2.38	-0.15	-0.17	-0.50	-0.37	-0.94	-0.74	-0.62	-0.48	-0.76	-1.46	-1.35	-3.84
1970	-1.46	-0.96	-1.16	-2.06	-1.67	-0.26	-0.79	-1.82	-1.50	-0.64	-1.33	-1.86	-2.00	-2.31	-1.37	-0.60	-3.05
1971	-1.78	-0.92	-1.42	-1.50	-3.27	-0.35	-0.74	-1.68	-1.36	-0.98	-1.90	-1.56	-1.36	-1.60	-2.46	-2.26	-5.08
1972	-2.03	-1.88	-2.35	-1.69	-2.23	-0.20	-1.85	-3.58	-1.35	-2.23	-3.46	-1.59	-1.43	-2.05	-1.63	-1.58	-3.46
1973	-2.39	-0.62	-1.60	-2.59	-4.75	-0.09	-0.31	-1.47	-2.19	-1.68	-0.94	-3.43	-3.02	-1.31	-3.30	-2.98	-7.96
1974	-4.73	-1.63	-3.95	-4.49	-8.85	0.12	-1.97	-3.04	-3.28	-4.14	-4.42	-4.05	-4.87	-4.55	-6.18	-4.99	-15.38
1975	-4.18	-5.06	-4.03	-3.72	-3.86	-5.31	-5.17	-4.69	-5.11	-4.55	-2.59	-2.30	-4.29	-4.56	-5.53	-3.59	-2.47
1976	-6.31	-5.21	-5.50	-6.64	-7.90	-4.09	-5.15	-6.39	-4.01	-6.87	-5.62	-6.45	-7.13	-6.35	-6.48	-9.48	-7.75
1977	-9.43	-7.32	-9.87	-11.01	-9.50	-7.74	-5.24	-8.97	-8.74	-10.20	-10.69	-9.22	-12.31	-11.49	-8.45	-9.33	-10.73
1978	-10.20	-10.33	-11.76	-10.39	-8.34	-11.78	-8.78	-10.41	-11.07	-13.17	-11.02	-8.83	-11.79	-10.55	-9.33	-10.72	-4.97
1979	-12.99	-11.32	-11.95	-14.23	-14.44	-13.64	-7.82	-12.51	-8.46	-15.63	-11.76	-11.19	-15.72	-15.78	-14.42	-16.47	-12.43
1980	-19.47	-18.85	-18.40	-22.15	-18.48	-25.29	-11.88	-19.38	-21.75	-18.38	-15.07	-20.44	-18.32	-27.71	-22.77	-16.66	-16.00
1981	-28.57	-28.91	-31.00	-25.72	-27.64	-28.85	-32.32	-25.55	-35.32	-31.43	-26.26	-30.48	-16.80	-32.89	-33.53	-26.67	-22.71
1982	-33.99	-37.25	-35.55	-37.19	-25.99	-36.20	-32.42	-43.13	-34.86	-29.34	-42.46	-29.03	-41.94	-40.60	-26.57	-30.36	-21.02
1983	-31.75	-36.68	-34.12	-23.92	-27.28	-44.59	-30.31	-35.12	-29.40	-36.36	-36.60	-30.15	-32.65	-23.97	-39.79	-30.12	-11.95

Imports c.i.f. — Importations c.a.f.

billion escudos, monthly averages — milliards d'escudos, moyennes mensuelles

Adjusted - Corrigé *

Year	Q.1	Q.2	Q.3	Q.4	JAN	FEB	MAR	APR	MAY	JUN	JUL	AUG	SEP	OCT	NOV	DEC
1964	1.74	1.74	2.01	1.84	1.72	1.73	1.78	1.67	1.64	1.92	2.07	1.81	2.15	1.71	1.96	1.84
1965	2.26	2.05	2.24	2.08	2.43	2.18	2.17	2.05	2.13	1.97	1.93	2.15	2.63	1.86	2.31	2.07
1966	2.20	2.36	2.46	2.52	2.07	2.14	2.39	2.23	2.45	2.38	2.56	2.42	2.40	2.65	2.17	2.75
1967	2.32	2.53	2.52	2.24	2.34	2.37	2.25	2.70	2.66	2.22	2.48	2.93	2.16	2.19	2.37	2.17
1968	2.50	2.58	2.67	2.39	2.21	2.58	2.70	2.49	2.33	2.91	2.57	2.59	2.86	2.95	2.72	1.50
1969	2.33	2.65	2.70	3.58	2.20	2.51	2.27	2.50	2.83	2.64	2.57	2.78	2.76	3.32	3.76	3.66
1970	3.89	3.37	4.40	3.52	4.88	3.30	3.47	3.73	2.72	3.65	3.81	4.60	4.79	3.40	3.52	3.65
1971	3.91	3.88	4.22	4.65	4.27	3.65	3.82	3.98	3.48	4.18	4.44	4.15	4.11	4.55	4.48	4.93
1972	4.74	5.25	4.73	4.65	3.08	5.27	5.86	4.40	4.96	6.40	4.47	4.38	5.34	4.70	4.54	4.72
1973	4.05	5.67	5.80	6.86	4.38	3.36	4.41	5.77	5.54	5.72	7.25	6.63	6.51	6.34	6.94	7.31
1974	6.96	8.66	9.23	11.22	5.33	7.62	7.95	7.80	9.65	8.54	8.55	10.00	9.15	11.54	10.72	11.39
1975	9.57	7.90	7.45	8.30	9.49	10.18	9.03	8.87	7.68	7.15	6.23	8.07	8.05	10.04	7.94	6.91
1976	9.44	9.57	11.12	13.62	8.70	10.14	9.47	8.43	10.61	9.66	11.37	11.41	10.58	12.30	13.59	14.96
1977	12.82	15.70	17.22	18.33	13.20	11.29	13.97	14.76	15.22	17.11	16.94	16.82	17.91	16.94	16.54	21.51
1978	17.50	19.57	19.15	20.96	18.13	18.08	16.29	19.66	19.10	19.96	19.12	18.83	19.49	20.83	22.30	19.74
1979	22.76	25.24	29.48	34.17	22.53	21.23	24.52	21.98	26.46	27.28	26.97	30.19	31.27	31.37	34.35	36.80
1980	36.49	36.39	39.90	42.15	38.01	34.31	37.14	38.85	34.10	36.21	39.37	38.23	42.11	43.33	39.35	43.77
1981	46.63	50.74	47.01	55.61	42.85	56.39	40.65	53.10	52.79	46.32	51.62	39.28	50.13	61.04	54.82	50.96
1982	57.82	58.26	65.94	65.78	53.70	61.16	58.60	56.02	52.59	66.16	60.39	72.86	64.55	64.10	64.83	68.40
1983	68.69	70.14	73.87	85.08	73.93	68.18	63.96	63.07	75.73	71.62	83.54	70.01	68.06	96.92	80.81	77.51

Exports f.o.b. — Exportations f.o.b.

billion escudos, monthly averages — milliards d'escudos, moyennes mensuelles

Adjusted - Corrigé *

Year	Q.1	Q.2	Q.3	Q.4	JAN	FEB	MAR	APR	MAY	JUN	JUL	AUG	SEP	OCT	NOV	DEC
1964	1.13	1.26	1.23	1.27	1.16	1.09	1.15	1.22	1.09	1.47	1.30	1.09	1.31	1.22	1.26	1.34
1965	1.36	1.34	1.50	1.45	1.38	1.32	1.38	1.34	1.39	1.29	1.28	1.40	1.82	1.45	1.44	1.45
1966	1.49	1.44	1.46	1.55	1.47	1.40	1.59	1.34	1.57	1.40	1.52	1.51	1.36	1.49	1.39	1.76
1967	1.48	1.46	1.61	1.83	1.48	1.47	1.50	1.63	1.63	1.13	1.63	1.64	1.55	1.79	1.96	1.74
1968	1.68	1.66	1.89	1.78	1.54	1.79	1.71	1.57	1.61	1.80	1.81	1.82	2.04	1.88	1.88	1.57
1969	1.78	2.03	1.96	1.99	1.30	2.12	1.93	2.12	1.99	2.00	1.94	2.03	1.90	1.93	2.19	1.84
1970	2.33	2.20	2.10	2.47	3.00	2.08	1.92	2.11	2.06	2.40	1.85	2.16	2.30	2.08	2.99	2.33
1971	2.39	2.38	2.56	2.47	2.33	2.40	2.45	2.37	2.38	2.38	2.71	2.63	2.35	2.32	2.39	2.70
1972	2.32	2.74	2.93	3.21	1.78	2.60	2.57	2.83	2.52	2.88	2.83	2.83	3.15	3.35	2.88	3.41
1973	2.96	3.93	4.14	3.70	3.07	2.63	3.18	3.31	3.52	4.97	3.93	3.36	5.23	3.41	3.78	3.92
1974	4.76	4.43	4.46	5.46	4.26	4.46	5.55	4.10	4.96	4.21	4.41	4.58	4.38	5.98	5.50	4.90
1975	4.40	3.98	4.12	3.98	4.33	4.61	4.26	4.13	3.78	4.04	3.85	4.42	4.08	4.14	3.91	3.88
1976	4.31	4.27	4.88	4.91	4.73	4.22	3.99	4.35	4.26	4.18	4.57	5.42	4.64	4.62	4.77	5.35
1977	5.68	6.21	6.57	7.49	5.42	5.30	6.33	5.92	6.34	6.37	6.51	6.29	6.93	7.06	7.77	7.63
1978	7.40	8.31	9.25	10.91	7.46	7.69	7.06	7.78	8.56	8.59	9.06	8.93	9.76	10.40	11.17	11.17
1979	12.39	13.98	15.62	16.82	12.16	11.51	13.51	13.31	13.80	14.85	14.78	16.20	15.87	16.66	16.37	17.41
1980	19.23	19.06	19.04	19.83	18.62	19.78	19.30	20.31	17.62	19.24	19.23	18.87	19.03	18.49	18.87	22.13
1981	19.02	21.40	21.80	22.71	18.76	19.37	18.94	20.88	21.84	21.48	20.23	22.26	22.90	24.01	23.00	21.13
1982	23.35	24.78	29.15	32.83	20.61	24.71	24.74	23.58	24.80	25.97	28.65	29.39	29.42	30.65	32.36	35.49
1983	35.51	38.37	46.10	49.16	35.21	34.52	36.79	36.05	44.58	34.48	45.35	42.33	50.61	47.99	47.27	52.20

Trade balance (f.o.b. — c.i.f.) — Balance commerciale (f.o.b. — c.a.f.)

billion escudos, monthly averages — milliards d'escudos, moyennes mensuelles

Adjusted - Corrigé *

Year	Q.1	Q.2	Q.3	Q.4	JAN	FEB	MAR	APR	MAY	JUN	JUL	AUG	SEP	OCT	NOV	DEC
1964	-0.61	-0.49	-0.78	-0.56	-0.56	-0.64	-0.63	-0.46	-0.55	-0.46	-0.76	-0.73	-0.84	-0.49	-0.70	-0.50
1965	-0.90	-0.71	-0.73	-0.64	-1.05	-0.86	-0.79	-0.71	-0.75	-0.68	-0.64	-0.75	-0.81	-0.41	-0.88	-0.62
1966	-0.71	-0.92	-1.00	-0.98	-0.60	-0.74	-0.80	-0.89	-0.89	-0.98	-1.04	-0.91	-1.05	-1.17	-0.78	-0.98
1967	-0.84	-1.06	-0.92	-0.41	-0.86	-0.90	-0.75	-1.06	-1.03	-1.09	-0.85	-1.30	-0.61	-0.40	-0.41	-0.42
1968	-0.82	-0.92	-0.78	-0.61	-0.67	-0.79	-1.00	-0.92	-0.72	-1.11	-0.76	-0.77	-0.81	-1.07	-0.83	0.07
1969	-0.54	-0.62	-0.75	-1.59	-0.90	-0.39	-0.34	-0.38	-0.84	-0.64	-0.63	-0.75	-0.86	-1.39	-1.57	-1.31
1970	-1.55	-1.17	-2.29	-1.05	-1.88	-1.22	-1.56	-1.62	-0.64	-1.25	-1.95	-2.44	-2.49	-1.32	-0.52	-1.32
1971	-1.52	-1.50	-1.66	-2.19	-1.94	-1.25	-1.37	-1.60	-1.10	-1.81	-1.71	-1.51	-1.76	-2.23	-2.09	-2.23
1972	-2.42	-2.51	-1.80	-1.44	-1.30	-2.67	-3.29	-1.57	-2.44	-3.52	-1.64	-1.55	-2.20	-1.35	-1.66	-1.30
1973	-1.09	-1.74	-2.65	-3.16	-1.31	-0.72	-1.23	-2.46	-2.02	-0.75	-3.42	-3.26	-1.28	-2.93	-3.16	-3.39
1974	-2.21	-4.24	-4.78	-5.75	-1.07	-3.15	-2.39	-3.70	-4.68	-4.33	-4.14	-5.42	-4.77	-5.56	-5.21	-6.48
1975	-5.17	-3.92	-3.33	-4.32	-5.16	-5.57	-4.78	-4.74	-3.90	-3.12	-2.38	-3.64	-3.97	-5.90	-4.02	-3.03
1976	-5.13	-5.30	-6.24	-8.70	-3.98	-5.91	-5.49	-4.08	-6.35	-5.48	-6.80	-5.58	-5.95	-7.68	-8.82	-9.61
1977	-7.13	-9.49	-10.65	-10.84	-7.77	-5.99	-7.64	-8.85	-8.87	-10.74	-10.43	-10.53	-10.99	-9.88	-8.76	-13.88
1978	-10.10	-11.26	-9.90	-10.04	-10.67	-10.39	-9.23	-11.88	-10.55	-11.37	-10.07	-9.91	-9.73	-10.44	-11.13	-8.57
1979	-10.37	-11.26	-13.86	-17.36	-10.37	-9.72	-11.01	-3.67	-12.66	-12.44	-12.19	-13.99	-15.39	-14.71	-17.97	-19.39
1980	-17.25	-17.33	-20.86	-22.32	-19.39	-14.53	-17.85	-18.54	-16.47	-16.96	-20.14	-19.35	-23.07	-24.84	-20.48	-21.64
1981	-27.61	-29.34	-25.21	-32.89	-24.09	-37.02	-21.72	-32.22	-30.96	-24.84	-31.40	-17.01	-27.23	-37.03	-31.82	-29.83
1982	-34.47	-33.48	-36.79	-32.94	-33.09	-36.45	-33.86	-32.45	-27.79	-40.19	-31.75	-43.48	-35.14	-33.45	-32.46	-32.92
1983	-33.18	-31.77	-27.77	-35.93	-38.71	-33.66	-27.18	-27.02	-31.16	-37.14	-38.20	-27.67	-17.45	-48.93	-33.54	-25.31

* Adjusted by the O.E.C.D. — * Corrigé par l'O.C.D.E.

NOTES

1. Excluding the clothing, furniture and printing industries.
2. Including alterations and additions.
3. From 1976, continental Portugal only.
4. From 1978, continental Portugal only.
5. Lisbon area.
6. Establishment data.
7. Unemployment benefits were introduced in 1975. In 1977, they were extended to the unemployed who had worked in the Portuguese colonies.
8. Monthly data refer to end of period.
9. Weighting pattern based on 1948 to 1973, and on 1963 from 1974. The two indices have been linked on 1963.
10. Excluding food and chemicals.
11. Excluding food and fuel.
12. Prior to 1977, Lisbon area only. Weighting pattern based on 1948-49 to 1976, and on 1973-74 from 1977.
13. From 1979, new reporting system.
14. Including errors and omissions.

NOTES

1. Non compris l'habillement, l'industrie du meuble et l'imprimerie.
2. Y compris les transformations et les agrandissements.
3. A partir de 1976, Portugal continental seulement.
4. A partir de 1978, Portugal continental seulement.
5. Région de Lisbonne.
6. Statistiques d'établissement.
7. L'allocation de chômage a été introduite en 1975. En 1977 elle a été étendue aux chômeurs qui avaient travaillé dans les colonies portugaises.
8. Situation en fin de mois.
9. La pondération se réfère à 1948 jusqu'en 1973, et à 1963 à partir de 1974. Les deux indices ont été raccordés sur 1963.
10. Non compris l'alimentation et les produits chimiques.
11. Non compris l'alimentation et les combustibles.
12. Avant 1977, région de Lisbonne seulement. La pondération se réfère à 1948-49 jusqu'en 1976, et à 1973-74 à partir de 1977.
13. A partir de 1979, nouveau système de notification.
14. Y compris erreurs et omissions.

MAIN SOURCES

PRINCIPALES SOURCES

Series	Séries	Sources
Industrial production Construction permits issued Prices	Production industrielle Construction, permis de construire délivrés Prix	Instituto Nacional de Estatística *Boletim Mensal de Estatística*
Business surveys	Enquêtes de conjoncture	Instituto Nacional de Estatística *Inquierito Trimestral de Conjuntura a Industria Transformadora*
Construction, buildings completed Cost of construction	Construction, bâtiments achevés Coût de la construction	Instituto Nacional de Estatística
Labour and wages Share prices	Main-d'œuvre et salaires Cours des actions	Banco de Portugal *Boletim Trimestral*
Home finance Net foreign position of commercial and savings banks Balance of payments	Finances internes Position extérieure nette des banques commerciales et d'épargne Balance des paiements	Instituto Nacional de Estatística *Boletim Trimestral das Estatísticas Monetarias e Financiarias*
Foreign trade	Commerce extérieur	Instituto Nacional de Estatística *Boletim Mensal das Estatísticas do Comercio Externo*

Spain — Espagne

Industrial production: total (1)

Production industrielle : total (1)

1980 = 100

	Year	Q.1	Q.2	Q.3	Q.4	JAN	FEB	MAR	APR	MAY	JUN	JUL	AUG	SEP	OCT	NOV	DEC
1964	32.6	32.5	32.4	30.6	34.9	33.3	33.1	31.0	32.5	32.4	32.3	31.6	28.2	32.0	33.4	35.0	36.3
1965	37.8	36.2	37.9	36.7	40.4	34.5	36.2	38.0	37.4	38.8	37.5	39.0	32.9	38.3	39.4	40.4	41.5
1966	43.7	42.3	43.9	41.4	46.9	41.1	41.3	44.5	43.1	44.4	44.2	42.0	37.3	45.0	46.5	46.1	48.2
1967	46.2	45.5	48.1	43.6	47.5	46.4	43.8	46.3	48.0	47.5	48.7	45.9	38.8	46.1	46.8	47.9	47.8
1968	49.5	48.6	49.8	45.6	53.9	47.9	48.6	49.4	48.9	51.1	49.5	47.6	40.0	49.1	52.9	53.2	55.6
1969	57.2	55.6	58.1	54.2	60.9	55.4	53.2	58.1	57.0	59.2	58.2	57.8	46.6	58.3	62.5	60.0	60.2
1970	63.2	62.6	65.5	59.2	65.4	62.3	63.2	62.3	66.9	63.9	65.5	64.7	48.8	64.1	66.3	66.4	63.6
1971	65.1	64.0	65.8	61.9	68.6	62.1	63.2	66.9	65.2	65.9	66.3	68.6	51.9	65.2	67.2	69.8	68.9
1972	75.5	73.6	76.9	70.4	81.0	70.8	72.9	77.3	74.5	76.8	79.2	74.6	59.0	77.7	79.6	82.8	80.4
1973	86.8	85.8	88.1	81.2	92.2	84.3	83.8	89.2	84.4	89.8	90.1	86.1	68.2	89.4	92.7	94.9	89.1
1974	94.9	98.5	100.4	87.4	93.3	98.6	95.6	101.2	98.8	101.0	101.5	94.1	74.9	93.2	99.7	92.5	87.7
1975	86.6	87.0	88.7	77.7	93.1	84.4	86.1	90.4	89.4	88.6	88.1	83.9	58.5	90.6	97.7	91.8	89.7
1976	91.0	88.5	93.2	83.9	98.4	84.7	87.1	93.7	92.6	94.6	92.5	93.7	61.4	96.7	98.6	100.3	96.4
1977	95.8	98.7	98.9	84.5	101.1	92.8	97.1	106.3	97.0	102.3	97.3	90.2	62.3	101.1	101.1	100.5	101.7
1978	98.0	99.1	101.3	86.8	104.8	98.1	98.4	100.9	99.4	100.4	104.0	93.4	63.9	103.2	106.9	107.8	99.6
1979	98.8	100.2	102.2	88.3	104.4	101.7	95.0	103.9	95.6	107.6	103.3	98.9	65.1	100.9	107.2	109.3	96.8
1980	100.0	104.2	102.0	87.7	106.1	103.9	103.6	105.0	100.0	105.2	100.8	100.4	60.3	102.5	111.3	106.3	100.7
1981	98.9	101.4	102.1	88.1	104.3	98.4	100.2	105.7	99.9	103.3	103.3	105.3	58.0	101.0	107.4	105.2	100.3
1982	97.9	100.1	100.9	87.9	102.5	95.3	97.6	107.6	98.6	103.6	100.6	101.5	57.2	105.0	102.4	105.7	99.3
1983	100.5	103.1	104.1	88.4	106.1	100.4	100.1	108.8	101.2	107.0	103.9	99.8	59.7	105.8	105.8	108.2	104.4

Industrial production: manufacturing (1)

Production industrielle : industries manufacturières (1)

1980 = 100

	Year	Q.1	Q.2	Q.3	Q.4	JAN	FEB	MAR	APR	MAY	JUN	JUL	AUG	SEP	OCT	NOV	DEC
1964	32.4	31.9	32.3	30.4	34.9	32.8	32.6	30.5	32.1	32.7	32.2	31.6	27.8	31.9	33.3	35.1	36.3
1965	38.0	36.1	38.1	36.9	40.8	34.3	36.2	37.9	37.6	39.0	37.7	39.3	32.8	38.7	39.7	40.8	42.0
1966	44.0	42.4	44.4	41.9	47.3	41.0	41.6	44.7	43.5	45.0	44.6	42.7	37.4	45.7	47.3	46.3	48.4
1967	46.6	45.8	48.8	44.1	47.9	46.6	44.1	46.6	48.7	48.3	49.5	46.6	38.7	46.8	47.4	48.4	47.9
1968	49.9	48.7	50.5	45.8	54.5	47.7	48.8	49.5	49.3	51.8	50.3	48.1	39.7	49.6	53.4	53.7	56.3
1969	58.0	56.0	59.2	55.1	61.9	55.7	53.6	58.6	57.8	60.4	59.4	59.0	46.7	59.6	63.9	61.0	60.8
1970	64.4	63.6	67.1	60.3	66.6	63.2	64.4	63.2	68.4	65.6	67.3	66.5	48.9	65.6	67.8	67.9	64.2
1971	66.1	64.7	66.9	62.9	69.8	62.5	64.0	67.6	66.2	67.1	67.4	70.2	51.8	66.6	68.9	71.1	69.5
1972	77.2	74.7	79.0	72.1	83.0	71.5	73.9	78.7	76.3	78.8	81.8	76.8	59.5	80.0	81.9	85.0	81.9
1973	89.5	87.8	91.2	83.8	95.1	85.9	86.0	91.5	87.1	92.8	93.6	89.3	69.4	92.7	95.8	98.1	91.5
1974	98.0	101.5	104.6	90.1	95.8	101.4	98.5	104.7	102.8	105.0	106.0	97.7	76.4	96.2	102.9	94.9	89.4
1975	88.5	89.0	91.1	78.8	95.0	85.6	88.7	92.7	91.6	91.2	90.6	85.6	57.6	93.3	100.7	93.8	90.6
1976	92.6	89.9	95.7	85.1	99.7	85.1	88.8	95.8	94.9	97.3	94.9	95.9	60.3	99.1	100.5	101.7	97.0
1977	97.8	100.4	101.6	86.0	103.0	92.8	99.2	109.2	99.6	105.2	100.0	92.2	61.4	104.3	103.7	102.3	103.1
1978	99.6	100.5	104.0	87.7	105.3	98.7	100.1	102.8	102.0	103.0	107.1	95.2	62.1	105.8	109.3	109.4	100.2
1979	99.7	100.8	104.1	88.8	105.2	102.1	95.6	104.7	96.8	110.2	105.4	100.6	63.1	102.7	109.0	110.4	96.2
1980	100.0	104.6	102.7	86.9	105.9	103.4	104.6	105.7	100.5	106.1	101.5	100.6	56.3	103.0	112.1	106.5	99.3
1981	98.2	100.6	102.5	86.3	103.6	96.7	99.2	105.9	100.1	103.9	103.5	105.2	53.2	100.5	107.4	104.8	98.5
1982	96.5	99.0	100.1	85.6	101.4	93.4	96.8	106.9	97.8	102.7	99.9	100.4	51.7	104.6	102.4	105.1	96.8
1983	98.3	100.3	102.6	85.9	104.5	96.4	97.2	107.2	99.4	105.3	103.0	98.1	54.8	104.8	104.6	107.5	101.4

Production: crude steel

Production : acier brut

thousand tons, monthly averages

milliers de tonnes, moyennes mensuelles

	Year	Q.1	Q.2	Q.3	Q.4	JAN	FEB	MAR	APR	MAY	JUN	JUL	AUG	SEP	OCT	NOV	DEC
1964																	
1965																	
1966																	
1967																	
1968																	
1969	479	428	487	484	515	453	361	460	509	475	478	496	470	487	509	490	547
1970	616	573	636	571	685	572	556	591	634	643	631	599	515	598	611	636	808
1971	669	613	680	663	719	658	577	605	615	706	720	704	620	664	723	716	717
1972	794	743	789	760	878	746	723	774	776	789	802	762	715	804	871	885	879
1973	931	935	929	829	1031	920	893	991	928	945	915	881	765	840	903	1150	1039
1974	959	917	975	929	1013	871	878	1002	952	1006	968	966	835	985	1064	976	1000
1975	925	906	999	870	925	774	944	1001	1023	995	980	951	747	911	939	875	962
1976	915	851	1004	867	938	842	890	820	967	1050	994	993	720	888	961	926	926
1977	925	938	963	845	954	935	918	961	933	964	991	923	709	904	986	969	907
1978	940	936	954	847	1023	971	879	958	943	953	966	887	668	987	1035	1008	1027
1979	1014	1010	1045	939	1061	1059	924	1046	1006	1109	1020	1005	726	1095	1061	1053	1059
1980	1056	1029	1138	941	1116	1080	900	1107	1132	1162	1121	1065	653	1105	1184	1117	1046
1981	1077	1078	1149	970	1110	1108	1049	1078	1178	1130	1139	1105	709	1096	1099	1127	1104
1982	1097	1124	1159	950	1154	1104	1099	1168	1101	1217	1160	1117	601	1132	1183	1120	1158
1983	1061	1156	1112	909	1068	1175	1095	1197	1131	1086	1119	1089	612	1026	1085	1067	1053

Industrial production: total (1) — Production industrielle : total (1)

1980 = 100 | Adjusted - Corrigé *

	Year	Q.1	Q.2	Q.3	Q.4	JAN	FEB	MAR	APR	MAY	JUN	JUL	AUG	SEP	OCT	NOV	DEC
1964		31.4	31.8	33.0	33.8	31.2	31.9	31.0	31.2	31.8	32.3	32.7	33.2	33.1	32.9	34.8	33.9
1965		35.4	37.4	39.2	39.5	33.6	36.0	36.5	36.6	38.2	37.5	40.1	38.9	38.8	39.8	39.6	39.0
1966		41.3	43.1	44.5	46.0	40.5	41.4	41.9	42.9	43.2	43.1	44.1	44.3	45.0	46.7	45.4	45.8
1967		44.9	46.5	47.0	46.7	45.7	44.2	44.7	46.7	45.9	46.9	48.0	46.1	46.9	46.4	46.4	47.3
1968		47.1	48.5	49.0	52.9	47.1	46.7	47.6	47.9	48.5	49.2	48.6	48.4	50.1	51.0	52.4	55.2
1969		54.5	56.4	58.4	60.0	53.6	53.9	56.0	56.0	56.2	57.1	57.6	59.1	58.5	60.2	59.8	59.9
1970		61.9	62.8	63.8	64.1	60.5	63.9	61.3	62.8	62.4	63.1	64.1	63.0	64.2	63.9	65.7	62.7
1971		62.9	63.7	66.6	67.6	61.9	63.6	63.2	62.8	64.5	63.9	68.0	67.6	64.2	66.5	68.1	68.3
1972		71.6	73.6	76.8	80.1	70.5	70.3	73.9	72.4	74.0	74.5	76.4	76.6	77.3	77.9	79.9	82.4
1973		83.0	85.2	89.5	90.4	82.5	83.8	82.7	84.0	85.0	86.6	87.9	90.8	89.9	89.2	90.5	91.4
1974		95.6	97.2	97.1	90.6	95.2	95.5	96.1	97.0	95.3	99.2	95.9	102.8	92.5	93.5	89.7	88.7
1975		85.5	84.9	86.1	89.3	81.7	86.1	88.7	85.3	83.5	85.8	84.6	85.3	88.3	90.5	89.6	89.4
1976		85.1	90.1	93.1	94.1	82.5	85.1	87.7	89.6	91.5	89.4	95.1	91.6	92.5	93.3	95.1	93.9
1977		96.2	95.7	94.9	96.5	93.4	97.2	98.0	96.4	97.7	92.9	94.0	94.6	95.9	95.5	94.8	99.1
1978		97.6	97.1	98.3	99.7	98.0	98.4	96.3	97.7	94.8	98.9	97.1	97.6	100.1	99.9	99.5	99.8
1979		97.4	99.1	100.5	98.8	100.8	95.0	96.3	96.8	100.0	100.5	101.1	100.9	99.4	99.1	99.7	97.5
1980		100.4	99.1	98.6	100.6	101.6	99.7	100.1	100.8	98.0	98.6	99.3	97.6	99.0	101.1	100.4	100.1
1981		98.7	99.3	98.8	98.3	96.6	100.1	99.5	99.2	99.1	99.8	103.4	95.0	98.0	98.0	98.5	98.2
1982		98.0	98.2	97.7	97.0	96.5	97.4	100.0	97.4	99.6	97.6	99.7	93.0	100.5	96.1	97.5	97.4
1983		100.4	101.3	99.3	100.7	102.3	99.8	99.2	102.4	102.0	99.4	100.7	96.6	100.7	99.5	100.1	102.6

Industrial production: manufacturing (1) — Production industrielle : industries manufacturières (1)

1980 = 100 | Adjusted - Corrigé *

	Year	Q.1	Q.2	Q.3	Q.4	JAN	FEB	MAR	APR	MAY	JUN	JUL	AUG	SEP	OCT	NOV	DEC
1964		31.0	31.6	32.8	33.8	31.1	31.3	30.7	30.9	32.0	32.0	32.5	33.0	32.9	32.7	34.7	33.9
1965		35.5	37.5	39.4	39.9	33.7	36.0	36.7	36.9	38.0	37.5	39.9	39.1	39.1	40.0	39.9	39.8
1966		41.6	43.4	44.9	46.4	40.7	41.7	42.5	43.3	43.4	43.4	44.2	45.0	45.5	47.3	45.6	46.4
1967		45.5	47.0	47.4	47.1	46.2	44.6	45.6	47.2	46.3	47.5	48.1	46.8	47.4	46.7	47.0	47.7
1968		47.5	48.9	49.2	53.5	47.4	47.0	48.0	48.1	49.0	49.6	48.5	48.9	50.4	51.4	52.9	56.1
1969		55.2	57.2	59.2	61.0	54.6	54.4	56.6	56.6	57.1	57.8	58.3	60.0	59.4	61.4	60.8	60.8
1970		63.1	64.1	65.0	65.4	62.0	65.2	62.0	64.3	63.7	64.3	65.6	63.8	65.6	65.1	67.2	63.9
1971		63.7	64.6	67.6	68.9	63.0	64.6	63.4	64.0	65.2	64.6	69.1	68.2	65.4	67.8	69.3	69.6
1972		72.7	75.4	78.5	82.1	72.2	71.3	74.6	74.3	75.5	76.4	77.9	78.2	79.4	79.6	82.2	84.5
1973		85.1	88.0	92.3	93.2	85.9	86.0	83.3	87.3	87.5	89.1	90.2	94.2	92.6	91.9	93.6	94.2
1974		99.8	99.9	100.3	93.0	100.5	98.3	100.6	98.5	98.8	102.3	98.9	107.1	94.7	96.3	92.0	90.9
1975		86.7	88.0	87.2	91.9	85.4	88.4	86.2	91.4	85.4	87.2	85.8	86.1	89.8	93.3	91.4	91.0
1976		87.5	91.3	94.4	95.5	85.2	86.4	91.1	89.9	93.2	90.9	96.5	92.5	94.2	94.8	96.1	95.5
1977		98.1	98.0	96.7	98.2	95.4	99.1	99.6	99.5	99.6	94.9	95.3	96.6	98.1	97.2	96.5	101.0
1978		99.4	99.2	99.4	101.0	100.4	100.2	97.7	100.0	96.7	101.0	98.1	98.6	101.6	101.1	101.1	100.9
1979		98.4	100.3	101.4	99.3	103.0	95.8	96.5	97.5	101.9	101.6	101.9	102.1	100.2	100.0	100.8	97.3
1980		101.3	99.0	97.9	100.3	102.7	101.1	100.2	100.6	98.1	98.4	99.3	95.5	98.6	101.4	100.1	99.5
1981		98.3	98.8	96.9	97.4	96.2	99.6	99.2	98.8	98.7	98.9	103.2	90.2	97.4	97.1	97.7	97.5
1982		97.3	96.6	95.1	96.0	95.5	97.2	99.3	95.8	97.7	96.3	98.1	87.1	100.2	95.1	96.5	96.2
1983		98.1	98.9	96.8	99.1	98.8	97.5	97.9	99.4	99.3	98.1	98.3	92.1	99.8	97.2	99.3	100.8

Production: passenger cars — Production : voitures de tourisme

thousands, monthly averages — milliers, moyennes mensuelles

	Year	Q.1	Q.2	Q.3	Q.4	JAN	FEB	MAR	APR	MAY	JUN	JUL	AUG	SEP	OCT	NOV	DEC
1964	10.4	8.0	10.5	11.2	11.9	7.3	8.9	7.9	10.5	10.0	11.0	11.1	11.1	11.4	12.6	12.0	11.2
1965	12.8	12.3	13.0	11.4	14.6	10.6	12.9	13.4	12.3	13.7	13.0	13.2	7.0	13.9	13.8	15.0	15.0
1966	21.0	17.7	21.0	21.1	24.1	13.9	18.1	21.2	18.9	22.1	21.9	22.4	16.0	24.9	26.6	24.1	21.5
1967	22.9	22.9	24.9	19.7	24.1	23.8	22.3	22.5	25.4	23.3	26.2	22.5	11.3	25.4	25.2	25.7	21.5
1968	26.0	25.4	24.2	22.2	32.1	24.8	26.4	25.1	24.6	25.3	22.9	25.3	13.1	28.1	31.3	32.7	32.4
1969	30.8	30.9	32.3	25.9	34.1	32.8	28.8	31.0	29.5	34.7	32.7	32.3	13.0	32.5	39.8	35.4	27.2
1970	37.5	35.2	39.4	34.3	41.2	33.7	39.6	32.3	41.3	35.6	41.4	43.1	15.0	44.8	47.1	45.8	30.7
1971	37.4	38.1	40.0	33.6	38.0	35.8	37.0	41.6	38.8	42.6	38.5	48.7	14.1	37.9	34.5	43.0	36.5
1972	50.2	50.5	53.8	41.3	55.1	46.7	52.2	52.6	53.5	55.0	52.9	47.3	20.5	56.0	56.8	61.1	47.4
1973	58.9	63.7	55.2	49.3	67.4	60.6	64.0	66.4	51.8	57.6	56.3	56.9	24.2	66.8	71.6	72.4	53.2
1974	59.1	74.0	65.8	47.8	48.8	72.0	72.0	78.0	71.0	67.6	58.9	60.3	20.5	62.7	61.7	44.6	40.1
1975	58.1	57.3	59.2	49.8	65.9	53.1	68.5	50.4	53.0	62.0	62.6	69.8	13.9	65.9	74.5	68.0	55.2
1976	62.8	58.8	65.0	52.5	74.7	51.0	49.2	76.2	64.8	65.6	64.7	70.2	16.9	70.3	73.2	80.8	70.1
1977	82.6	84.7	88.4	66.6	90.7	70.9	83.3	95.0	83.6	86.8	94.7	85.6	20.4	93.9	90.9	96.5	84.6
1978	82.2	85.4	88.6	66.4	88.3	91.4	86.9	77.9	79.6	88.1	98.1	84.0	30.3	84.8	98.6	93.1	73.3
1979	80.7	77.1	89.0	65.4	91.4	74.2	68.7	88.5	80.8	97.2	89.1	85.3	35.5	79.4	96.6	97.6	80.1
1980	85.1	95.4	90.5	63.6	91.0	87.8	100.3	97.6	91.1	97.7	92.8	86.7	19.2	84.8	99.7	100.0	73.3
1981	71.5	76.3	76.3	55.9	77.7	78.1	76.6	74.1	69.8	75.8	83.4	83.5	14.1	70.0	89.8	76.9	66.3
1982	77.1	78.1	84.2	54.1	82.0	73.1	74.5	86.8	77.0	86.8	88.8	86.8	18.7	86.8	75.9	95.7	74.5
1983		97.2	106.3	30.4		88.6	96.1	106.9	98.1	111.0	109.7	104.3	27.0	105.9	107.8	103.4	

* Adjusted by the O.E.C.D. — * Corrigé par l'O.C.D.E.

SPAIN

Production: cement
thousand tons, monthly averages

Production : ciment
milliers de tonnes, moyennes mensuelles

	Year	Q.1	Q.2	Q.3	Q.4	JAN	FEB	MAR	APR	MAY	JUN	JUL	AUG	SEP	OCT	NOV	DEC
1964	675	602	672	717	707	580	589	637	649	706	662	710	729	711	732	706	684
1965	800	685	799	864	852	657	648	751	751	791	815	867	881	843	856	859	840
1966	985	857	1015	1046	1020	771	316	984	991	1040	1015	1040	1055	1042	1083	1009	969
1967	1092	977	1157	1141	1091	899	942	1091	1165	1136	1170	1108	1116	1200	1164	1078	1030
1968	1242	1119	1240	1309	1300	1027	1113	1217	1218	1303	1199	1298	1315	1315	1391	1294	1245
1969	1334	1213	1374	1415	1334	1144	1179	1316	1330	1418	1373	1429	1431	1399	1418	1342	1243
1970	1378	1248	1449	1431	1384	1076	1253	1414	1470	1472	1405	1426	1440	1428	1473	1428	1251
1971	1416	1249	1430	1498	1487	1066	1273	1406	1366	1467	1456	1513	1514	1467	1520	1496	1445
1972	1620	1417	1666	1740	1658	1269	1390	1591	1618	1704	1677	1678	1810	1731	1711	1680	1583
1973	1853	1729	1909	1886	1888	1553	1690	1943	1855	1955	1918	1889	1886	1894	1914	1903	1848
1974	1972	1863	2046	1965	2012	1864	1723	2001	2008	2116	2015	1962	1956	1978	2098	1995	1944
1975	1998	1768	2145	2119	1959	1689	1762	1852	1987	2177	2270	2167	2101	2038	2194	1943	1740
1976	2100	1885	2161	2172	2182	1715	1767	2174	2186	2214	2084	2194	2201	2120	2285	2174	2088
1977	2333	2231	2374	2394	2334	1955	2205	2532	2324	2427	2370	2415	2333	2435	2474	2390	2137
1978	2519	2316	2678	2646	2437	2158	2245	2535	2602	2625	2307	2755	2573	2611	2690	2572	2050
1979	2338	2199	2398	2451	2302	2008	2113	2476	2235	2567	2393	2556	2378	2418	2433	2367	2107
1980	2334	2314	2399	2370	2253	2179	2290	2474	2357	2519	2321	2549	2234	2327	2471	2327	1961
1981	2396	2256	2499	2360	2468	1873	2213	2683	2552	2594	2351	2308	2494	2277	2519	2492	2394
1982	2467	2422	2578	2410	2458	2317	2351	2599	2468	2668	2598	2325	2487	2419	2494	2388	2491
1983		2718	2707	2499		2382	2949	2824	2718	2868	2534	2520	2565	2411	2610	2326	

Ships completed
thousand gross register tons, quarterly averages

Navires achevés
milliers de tonneaux de jauge brute, moyennes trimestrielles

	Year	Q.1	Q.2	Q.3	Q.4	JAN	FEB	MAR	APR	MAY	JUN	JUL	AUG	SEP	OCT	NOV	DEC
1964	59	44	61	82	49												
1965	56	33	69	41	82												
1966	94	50	67	131	421												
1967	94	64	100	67	143												
1968	114	57	231	51	116												
1969	159	146	98	175	211												
1970	175	122	190	175	162												
1971	208	312	204	183	139												
1972	271	215	244	273	349												
1973	330	232	296	330	528												
1974	390	251	275	541	496												
1975	398	228	539	220	609												
1976	330	253	424	83	560												
1977	453	321	723	215	551												
1978	205	302	205	71	246												
1979	158	216	205	98	200												
1980	99	68	48	149	130												
1981	195	331	108	217	125												
1982	139	156	133	120	153												
1983	127	42	131	153	182												

Production: future tendency
mining and manufacturing
per cent balance

Perspectives de production
industries extractives et manufacturières
solde en pourcentage

	Year	Q.1	Q.2	Q.3	Q.4	JAN	FEB	MAR	APR	MAY	JUN	JUL	AUG	SEP	OCT	NOV	DEC
1964						16	23	28	27	31	30	25	23	27	23	20	17
1965						26	30	26	23	20	20	22	14	22	23	23	25
1966						26	32	33	28	23	20	17	15	19	18	13	13
1967						10	7	10	8	4	-1	-7	-2	2	1	-1	-
1968						-1	2	4	6	5	4	6	12	16	14	16	16
1969						19	26	25	23	22	19	21	23	28	25	23	23
1970						26	31	22	21	13	10	7	7	7	1	-1	-2
1971						2	8	8	11	6	5	10	15	15	16	6	10
1972						20	23	27	24	24	25	22	28	29	26	24	26
1973						30	32	29	29	26	24	26	29	24	24	19	18
1974						23	23	17	13	9	1	-1	-1	-8	-14	-20	-18
1975						-13	-10	-3	-2	-4	-6	-8	-5	-5	-4	-2	-2
1976						3	4	13	19	15	11	9	11	7	5	7	6
1977						8	22	17	9	-3	-12	-10	9	-2	-18	-25	-14
1978						-8	-1	-3	1	-3	-12	-7	-17	2	-4	-10	-
1979						8	7	10	9	-4	-17	-11	14	-3	-12	-16	2
1980						-1	-2	-3	-5	-13	-21	-9	15	-3	-13	-16	-1
1981						-1	-1	-4	-2	-13	-20	-7	18	5	-9	-9	8
1982						10	9	5	6	-8	-20	-14	24	-1	-10	-14	-5
1983						8	9	5	1	-8	-11	-4	22	8	-1	-4	3

Order books or demand: future tendency / Carnet de commandes ou demande globale : perspectives

mining and manufacturing / industries extractives et manufacturières

per cent balance / solde en pourcentage

Year	Q.1	Q.2	Q.3	Q.4	JAN	FEB	MAR	APR	MAY	JUN	JUL	AUG	SEP	OCT	NOV	DEC
1964					13	16	23	23	18	15	13	11	18	17	9	-1
1965					15	18	14	11	-11	5	2	6	9	10	12	4
1966					12	15	18	14	5	3	1	3	2	3	-	-8
1967					-5	-2	-1	-1	-4	-9	-15	-8	-2	1	-5	-7
1968					-2	2	3	8	6	2	2	3	10	13	10	8
1969					12	20	18	19	14	11	13	12	17	14	11	4
1970					11	16	15	3	-1	-10	-8	-3	-	-3	-5	-11
1971					-5	9	12	-9	8	6	2	7	10	9	-	-
1972					7	15	17	15	17	16	9	10	14	10	5	6
1973					14	16	18	20	11	9	8	7	8	9	-2	-9
1974					2	4	-	-5	-9	-14	-21	-19	-21	-21	-28	-31
1975					-19	-10	-4	-2	-3	-8	-10	-9	-8	-8	-4	-2
1976					2	6	9	12	15	6	-1	-	-4	-5	-8	-5
1977					2	14	11	-	-15	-20	-15	-6	-17	-30	-30	-20
1978					-10	-9	-7	-8	-13	-14	-6	-1	-5	-11	-10	-4
1979					1	3	-2	-6	-15	-23	-19	-7	-12	-16	-17	-9
1980					-4	-3	-4	-7	-20	-20	-13	-1	-5	-11	-15	-5
1981					1	2	-7	-6	-12	-16	-4	2	-2	-6	-9	-
1982					7	8	2	-	-7	-10	-5	2	-10	-9	-15	-9
1983					5	-3	1	5	-13	-13	-14	-	-3	-7	-13	-8

Order books or demand: level / Carnet de commandes ou demande globale : niveau

mining and manufacturing / industries extractives et manufacturières

per cent balance / solde en pourcentage

Year	Q.1	Q.2	Q.3	Q.4	JAN	FEB	MAR	APR	MAY	JUN	JUL	AUG	SEP	OCT	NOV	DEC
1964					-1	-5	-3	-2	1	1	2	1	1	1	1	1
1965					-2	-3	1	-3	-2	-2	-1	-2	-3	1	-3	-3
1966					-6	-2	-4	-5	-6	-8	-8	-12	-12	-14	-14	-17
1967					-24	-24	-22	-24	-26	-27	-28	-31	-32	-31	-33	-37
1968					-35	-35	-34	-34	-29	-27	-26	-23	-19	-14	-9	-11
1969					-12	-8	-4	1	2	5	7	4	4	7	8	6
1970					3	5	4	3	-2	-4	-7	-16	-17	-13	-17	-24
1971					-29	-29	-27	-25	-25	-23	-17	-17	-17	-14	-14	-15
1972					-16	-12	-6	-3	-	5	3	4	7	11	11	11
1973					10	11	16	16	20	20	18	16	22	26	24	16
1974					11	9	10	8	5	2	-4	-11	-18	-20	-26	-32
1975					-37	-40	-40	-39	-40	-45	-42	-42	-43	-40	-39	-41
1976					-38	-33	-26	-20	-20	-23	-23	-22	-24	-27	-25	-28
1977					-25	-23	-22	-27	-33	-36	-40	-37	-43	-45	-48	-49
1978					-53	-52	-53	-51	-46	-41	-42	-43	-38	-34	-37	-39
1979					-37	-33	-33	-35	-32	-39	-47	-46	-42	-42	-47	-46
1980					-43	-43	-49	-48	-52	-54	-48	-48	-53	-52	-50	-54
1981					-49	-50	-55	-53	-54	-51	-47	-47	-45	-46	-47	-41
1982					-39	-34	-34	-31	-38	-41	-41	-43	-46	-44	-40	-40
1983					-38	-38	-40	-44	-50	-49	-45	-48	-41	-43	-39	-40

Finished goods stocks: level / Stocks de produits finis : niveau

mining and manufacturing / industries extractives et manufacturières

per cent balance / solde en pourcentage

Year	Q.1	Q.2	Q.3	Q.4	JAN	FEB	MAR	APR	MAY	JUN	JUL	AUG	SEP	OCT	NOV	DEC
1964					8	3	6	5	6	6	6	7	8	5	6	7
1965					5	4	6	7	8	6	7	9	7	4	1	4
1966					6	10	10	11	13	14	13	14	14	14	11	13
1967					16	15	18	20	20	23	21	21	23	20	25	25
1968					25	25	24	24	26	23	21	20	16	14	9	7
1969					7	6	3	4	4	4	3	-2	-3	-2	-4	-4
1970					-2	-	-1	2	7	7	6	12	11	9	12	15
1971					20	19	22	17	21	19	14	11	14	10	9	7
1972					7	6	6	4	2	1	-	3	4	5	8	3
1973					4	4	5	7	6	6	10	11	11	15	16	17
1974					12	11	10	10	9	2	1	2	11	8	12	14
1975					16	19	21	24	23	20	19	18	20	22	16	17
1976					16	15	10	8	7	8	4	5	7	8	9	9
1977					8	11	8	12	14	21	20	21	17	22	25	27
1978					33	35	38	20	29	26	23	17	19	17	14	19
1979					18	18	20	19	15	22	21	21	19	25	24	25
1980					25	24	26	28	33	38	33	25	29	28	27	30
1981					29	28	35	28	34	32	27	24	23	24	25	23
1982					28	24	23	25	23	29	20	20	24	24	18	20
1983					14	15	21	22	28	24	23	21	17	21	19	19

SPAIN

Rate of capacity utilization
mining and manufacturing
per cent

Taux d'utilisation des capacités
industries extractives et manufacturières
pourcentage

	Year	Q.1	Q.2	Q.3	Q.4	JAN	FEB	MAR	APR	MAY	JUN	JUL	AUG	SEP	OCT	NOV	DEC
1964																	
1965		83	83	83	84			83			83			83			84
1966		83	83	83	83			83			83			83			83
1967		81	80	81	78			81			80			81			78
1968		79	80	81	82			79			80			81			82
1969		81	85	84	85			81			85			84			85
1970		84	83	84	84			84			83			84			84
1971		81	82	82	84			81			82			82			84
1972		83	86	89	89			83			86			89			89
1973		90	89	88	88			90			89			88			88
1974		86	86	83	81			86			86			83			81
1975		79	78	80	81			79			78			80			81
1976		80	81	82	83			80			81			82			83
1977		83	84	82	82			83			84			82			82
1978		79	80	80	81			79			80			80			81
1979		79	81	79	80			79			81			79			80
1980		79	79	77	80			79			79			78			80
1981		79	78	78	80			79			78			78			80
1982		80	82	78	80			80			82			78			80
1983		81	78	77	79			81			78			77			79

Retail sales: value
department stores
1980 = 100

Ventes au détail : valeur
grands magasins
1980 = 100

	Year	Q.1	Q.2	Q.3	Q.4	JAN	FEB	MAR	APR	MAY	JUN	JUL	AUG	SEP	OCT	NOV	DEC
1964																	
1965	6.0	5.6	5.4	6.3	6.6	8.1	4.0	4.6	5.2	5.4	5.6	8.4	5.0	5.4	6.2	6.1	7.4
1966	6.6	6.5	5.6	6.6	7.6	9.4	4.8	5.4	5.6	5.7	5.6	8.1	6.2	5.6	7.4	6.5	8.8
1967	7.5	8.0	6.4	7.3	8.3	12.0	6.1	5.8	5.8	6.6	6.7	9.7	6.5	5.9	7.7	7.6	9.7
1968	8.0	8.2	6.8	7.8	9.2	12.9	5.9	5.9	6.1	7.0	7.2	10.5	6.0	6.8	8.6	8.3	10.7
1969	10.6	10.0	8.8	11.4	12.2	13.5	7.3	9.0	8.1	9.7	8.6	13.7	9.7	10.8	12.1	11.8	12.7
1970	14.2	12.0	12.5	15.5	16.6	16.1	9.3	10.4	11.5	12.0	14.1	18.6	13.8	13.8	16.6	14.7	18.4
1971	17.8	16.2	14.6	18.7	21.8	22.7	13.2	12.7	14.2	13.8	15.8	22.9	16.6	16.5	21.2	19.0	25.1
1972	24.8	23.1	21.1	25.6	29.4	27.1	20.0	22.3	19.9	21.6	21.8	28.1	21.2	27.6	28.6	26.3	33.2
1973	29.2	25.1	24.4	30.2	37.0	36.5	18.5	20.1	23.2	25.0	24.9	35.1	27.2	28.3	37.2	32.6	41.0
1974	37.8	32.2	32.8	39.7	46.5	44.2	25.8	26.7	30.7	35.3	32.5	47.6	37.0	34.5	46.2	41.3	51.9
1975	43.6	41.9	37.7	43.7	51.1	56.8	34.2	34.8	35.9	38.0	39.3	51.8	35.4	43.9	49.1	42.5	61.8
1976	52.4	49.1	46.0	53.3	61.5	62.7	42.4	42.2	44.0	45.8	48.1	62.6	46.0	51.2	59.2	53.9	71.3
1977	62.8	59.3	53.4	64.9	73.3	80.2	48.9	48.9	52.1	53.1	55.1	77.6	58.3	58.8	70.2	64.0	85.8
1978	72.5	69.3	63.8	73.8	83.2	94.0	55.8	57.9	57.3	66.2	68.0	88.0	62.2	71.0	79.8	72.4	97.6
1979	80.4	76.8	71.1	75.7	93.3	103.5	64.7	62.2	65.6	72.5	75.3	88.0	67.3	71.6	89.8	88.5	116.6
1980	100.0	98.7	84.5	96.4	120.5	132.9	80.9	82.2	76.5	86.6	90.4	117.6	83.1	88.5	116.6	105.1	139.9
1981	115.4	109.6	100.5	114.5	136.9	148.0	92.0	88.9	95.8	97.4	108.2	132.9	99.3	111.4	141.5	108.1	161.1
1982	129.4	123.7	113.3	134.0	146.7	163.8	103.5	103.9	110.2	113.2	116.4	163.9	113.3	124.8	149.7	115.7	174.6
1983	147.7	145.0	127.7	147.5	170.7	187.2	123.8	124.0	118.9	128.3	135.8	174.7	134.6	133.1	159.2	144.6	208.4

Retail sales: volume
department stores
1980 = 100

Ventes au détail : volume
grands magasins
1980 = 100

	Year	Q.1	Q.2	Q.3	Q.4	JAN	FEB	MAR	APR	MAY	JUN	JUL	AUG	SEP	OCT	NOV	DEC
1964																	
1965	39	38	36	41	42	56	27	31	35	36	37	55	33	35	40	39	47
1966	40	41	34	40	45	59	30	34	35	35	34	50	38	34	45	38	52
1967	42	46	36	41	45	70	35	34	33	37	38	54	36	32	42	41	52
1968	42	44	36	42	43	59	32	31	32	37	38	56	32	36	45	43	56
1969	55	52	46	59	61	71	39	47	42	51	44	71	51	56	62	59	63
1970	67	59	61	74	76	80	46	51	56	58	68	90	65	65	76	67	83
1971	78	73	64	81	92	103	59	57	63	61	69	100	72	71	90	81	105
1972	100	96	86	104	115	114	83	92	82	88	89	114	86	111	113	103	129
1973	107	97	91	110	129	141	71	77	88	94	92	129	99	102	132	113	142
1974	118	109	104	122	136	151	87	87	98	112	102	148	114	104	137	121	149
1975	116	118	102	115	129	161	96	96	98	103	105	136	94	114	126	107	154
1976	119	119	108	120	127	154	103	101	104	107	112	143	104	114	125	111	145
1977	110	114	96	112	118	158	94	92	96	96	98	135	100	99	115	102	135
1978	104	107	94	102	112	146	86	88	85	97	99	127	87	91	110	98	129
1979	96	99	86	89	109	135	83	79	81	88	90	104	79	83	101	98	128
1980	100	105	85	95	115	143	85	86	78	88	91	117	82	86	112	100	132
1981	101	102	89	99	115	139	85	81	86	86	95	118	86	96	120	91	134
1982	99	101	88	101	107	135	84	83	87	87	89	125	86	93	111	85	126
1983	99	103	87	98	110	134	87	87	92	87	92	117	90	88	104	93	133

Construction: dwellings authorized (2)
thousands, monthly averages

Construction : logements autorisés (2)
milliers, moyennes mensuelles

	Year	Q.1	Q.2	Q.3	Q.4	JAN	FEB	MAR	APR	MAY	JUN	JUL	AUG	SEP	OCT	NOV	DEC
1964																	
1965					5.5										2.9	6.8	6.7
1966	8.5	5.9	9.3	8.9	9.9	6.0	6.0	5.7	9.7	8.9	9.2	9.5	8.3	8.8	8.6	11.9	9.2
1967	12.5	6.2	6.4	13.7	23.9	10.0	6.5	2.2	5.9	7.3	6.1	7.2	10.8	23.0	20.7	16.1	34.3
1968	24.0	20.5	14.3	13.1	48.2	18.8	29.5	13.3	15.6	15.3	12.1	9.0	9.0	21.4	39.2	46.5	58.8
1969	13.8	17.6	16.7	7.9	13.1	12.6	18.3	21.8	21.8	13.5	14.7	10.4	8.9	4.4	17.8	7.1	14.3
1970	22.8	23.5	31.1	11.6	24.9	20.5	22.7	27.3	32.4	33.2	27.6	17.5	4.1	13.1	16.7	16.2	41.9
1971	17.6	15.3	16.7	14.3	24.1	17.4	10.6	18.0	14.7	15.9	19.5	18.6	4.6	19.8	17.0	22.6	32.8
1972	16.9	17.7	9.9	7.2	32.8	17.2	22.0	13.8	9.2	9.7	10.7	10.4	1.6	9.6	16.8	21.8	59.8
1973	21.6	25.8	23.9	17.8	18.7	21.6	28.6	27.2	22.6	29.0	20.2	15.4	17.4	20.7	19.6	16.7	19.9
1974	19.1	23.4	21.0	15.5	16.4	17.6	22.4	30.1	23.7	20.1	19.3	18.4	6.9	21.0	22.8	13.3	13.0
1975	18.2	15.7	27.6	14.2	15.3	11.7	19.2	16.3	41.4	24.4	17.0	19.0	4.4	19.3	17.1	14.2	14.6
1976	16.8	18.7	14.0	11.8	22.4	15.8	22.6	17.8	11.6	15.0	15.5	19.3	2.2	14.1	20.8	21.7	24.9
1977	13.8	12.6	16.1	12.0	14.3	11.6	10.0	16.1	16.6	15.4	16.3	11.0	1.7	23.4	14.6	14.9	13.5
1978	11.0	9.9	12.1	6.1	15.9	10.7	9.8	9.2	14.8	9.4	12.0	5.7	3.8	8.8	10.3	22.1	15.4
1979	14.6	11.5	12.1	14.7	20.3	9.4	11.7	13.4	7.1	14.7	14.4	19.0	2.6	22.5	21.6	18.3	20.9
1980	11.3	11.5	17.0	8.6	9.3	12.7	10.2	11.7	11.7	27.1	12.1	15.3	3.7	6.9	8.4	8.7	7.7
1981	11.3	8.5	12.2	11.7	12.7	7.3	8.5	9.8	10.1	11.7	14.9	17.4	4.2	13.4	13.0	12.1	12.8
1982	11.8	10.7	11.9	12.0	12.3	10.7	11.3	10.0	12.0	12.1	11.7	15.4	4.9	11.7	13.2	11.3	14.0
1983	10.3	9.6	11.9	8.5	11.3	8.2	10.4	10.3	10.8	12.9	12.0	12.5	6.0	7.2	10.9	10.0	13.0

Retail sales: value
department stores
1980 = 100

Adjusted - Corrigé

Ventes au détail : valeur
grands magasins
1980 = 100

	Year	Q.1	Q.2	Q.3	Q.4	JAN	FEB	MAR	APR	MAY	JUN	JUL	AUG	SEP	OCT	NOV	DEC
1964																	
1965		5.4	6.2	6.2	6.1	5.2	5.2	5.7	6.2	6.1	6.3	6.5	5.6	6.5	6.0	6.3	6.0
1966		6.3	6.4	6.6	7.0	6.0	6.2	6.7	6.7	6.4	6.2	6.3	6.9	6.7	7.1	6.6	7.2
1967		7.6	7.3	7.2	7.7	7.8	7.9	7.2	7.0	7.3	7.5	7.5	7.2	7.0	7.4	7.8	7.9
1968		7.8	7.7	7.6	8.5	8.5	7.6	7.3	7.4	7.9	7.9	8.2	6.7	8.0	8.1	8.4	8.8
1969		9.9	10.0	11.3	11.3	9.1	9.3	11.2	9.8	10.9	9.2	10.7	10.9	12.5	11.4	12.0	10.5
1970		12.9	14.2	15.4	15.2	11.1	11.7	13.1	13.8	13.5	15.3	14.8	15.5	15.7	15.3	15.0	15.2
1971		16.1	16.5	18.5	19.7	15.9	16.4	15.9	16.7	15.6	17.3	18.4	18.6	18.5	19.2	19.3	20.6
1972		24.0	23.8	25.3	25.4	19.3	24.8	28.0	23.2	24.2	24.1	22.6	23.9	30.9	25.6	26.6	26.9
1973		24.9	27.5	30.4	33.0	26.3	22.8	25.5	27.1	27.9	27.6	28.6	30.9	31.4	33.3	33.1	32.7
1974		32.3	37.1	40.0	41.4	32.1	31.6	33.3	35.7	39.3	36.2	39.3	42.5	38.2	41.3	42.1	40.9
1975		42.1	42.6	44.1	45.5	41.6	41.8	42.9	41.9	42.1	43.7	43.0	41.0	48.3	44.4	43.5	48.5
1976		49.6	51.7	54.0	55.2	45.8	51.4	51.4	51.4	50.8	53.0	52.0	53.9	56.2	54.4	55.6	55.6
1977		58.7	60.0	66.2	66.0	58.4	58.7	58.9	61.3	58.8	60.0	64.9	69.1	64.6	65.2	66.2	66.8
1978		68.0	71.5	75.6	74.8	68.0	65.3	69.6	67.4	73.6	73.5	74.3	74.3	78.2	74.2	74.9	75.4
1979		75.3	79.7	78.2	88.2	74.5	76.6	74.7	77.2	80.9	81.1	74.7	80.8	79.2	83.2	91.7	89.6
1980		96.7	94.7	99.5	107.7	95.7	95.5	99.0	89.8	97.2	97.0	100.3	100.1	98.1	107.1	109.4	106.7
1981		107.5	112.8	119.0	121.6	106.8	109.4	107.1	112.3	110.1	116.1	113.6	119.8	123.5	129.2	113.1	122.4
1982		121.8	127.5	138.5	129.9	118.3	121.9	125.2	128.7	128.7	125.0	140.2	136.3	138.6	136.1	121.3	132.5
1983		143.4	143.6	153.3		135.2	145.6	149.4	138.6	146.3	145.9	149.4	162.5	148.1			

Retail sales: volume
department stores
1980 = 100

Adjusted - Corrigé *

Ventes au détail : volume
grands magasins
1980 = 100

	Year	Q.1	Q.2	Q.3	Q.4	JAN	FEB	MAR	APR	MAY	JUN	JUL	AUG	SEP	OCT	NOV	DEC
1964																	
1965	40	37	42	40	39	36	36	39	42	42	42	42	38	41	39	40	38
1966	40	40	40	40	41	38	40	42	42	40	38	39	43	39	43	39	42
1967	42	44	41	40	42	45	46	42	42	41	42	42	41	37	40	42	43
1968	42	41	41	40	45	44	39	40	39	42	43	43	36	41	43	45	46
1969	55	52	52	58	57	47	49	59	52	57	49	55	57	62	58	62	52
1970	67	59	70	72	69	54	58	65	68	67	74	71	73	72	70	70	68
1971	77	73	73	79	84	73	74	71	74	70	77	79	81	78	84	81	86
1972	101	99	98	103	104	81	100	116	98	99	98	93	95	121	102	105	106
1973	106	95	104	110	115	101	88	97	104	105	102	106	111	114	116	115	114
1974	118	109	118	121	121	109	107	112	114	125	115	121	128	116	122	124	119
1975	116	118	116	115	115	117	118	121	115	115	118	113	108	124	113	112	119
1976	119	120	122	121	114	111	124	124	122	121	123	117	120	126	116	114	113
1977	110	113	109	113	105	115	114	111	113	108	106	114	115	110	107	106	104
1978	104	105	106	104	101	106	103	106	103	108	106	107	103	101	102	101	102
1979	96	97	97	92	97	96	99	95	97	99	97	88	92	94	92	101	99
1980	100	102	97	97	102	103	98	104	93	98	98	99	99	95	101	106	100
1981	101	100	101	103	101	99	101	99	103	100	101	99	103	106	107	95	102
1982	99	99	100	103	95	100	99	99	103	101	96	106	102	103	100	87	97
1983	100	102	99	101	97	98	103	104	98	101	98	102	105	96	93	98	101

* Adjusted by the O.E.C.D.

* Corrigé par l'O.C.D.E.

SPAIN

New passenger car registrations — Immatriculations de voitures de tourisme neuves

thousands, monthly averages — milliers, moyennes mensuelles

	Year	Q.1	Q.2	Q.3	Q.4	JAN	FEB	MAR	APR	MAY	JUN	JUL	AUG	SEP	OCT	NOV	DEC
1964	10.6																
1965	13.3	12.1	13.6	12.2	15.2	10.2	12.1	14.0	13.1	13.4	14.4	16.1	8.8	11.6	14.4	15.0	16.1
1966	20.9	16.4	21.4	20.5	25.2	13.5	15.8	19.9	18.3	22.6	23.4	24.0	18.6	18.9	24.1	25.7	25.9
1967	23.9	24.8	26.6	21.0	24.3	22.3	24.5	27.5	27.1	25.6	27.2	25.4	15.5	22.3	23.8	24.3	24.8
1968	25.8	23.5	28.0	24.3	27.0	20.1	22.7	27.6	27.5	28.8	27.8	32.0	20.1	22.4	28.9	26.4	25.8
1969	31.2	30.1	35.8	29.4	30.6	27.1	27.5	35.8	32.3	37.0	38.0	38.1	25.9	24.3	35.1	28.5	28.2
1970	33.3	35.7	38.9	32.1	26.5	30.0	37.2	39.8	41.6	36.7	38.4	40.5	28.8	26.9	29.5	25.1	24.8
1971	36.1	35.4	42.3	35.2	31.6	28.8	33.9	43.3	40.7	41.1	45.0	45.7	30.2	29.7	32.6	32.2	29.9
1972	42.2	40.3	45.1	40.5	43.0	32.0	38.4	50.4	41.2	44.5	49.6	49.7	34.3	37.5	42.4	42.0	44.6
1973	49.6	51.2	51.3	42.9	53.0	50.9	44.9	57.7	50.6	50.0	53.4	52.0	33.6	42.9	54.8	54.6	49.7
1974	48.0	51.7	51.4	46.3	42.4	47.8	47.7	59.8	50.3	49.3	54.7	61.0	37.7	40.4	44.3	43.0	39.9
1975	47.7	45.9	49.1	46.2	49.6	44.0	47.2	46.4	51.5	43.7	52.1	62.0	40.6	36.0	50.7	48.5	49.6
1976	51.6	50.7	55.8	45.6	54.4	49.8	42.8	59.7	58.4	56.9	52.2	63.5	30.3	43.1	53.5	53.3	56.4
1977	55.2	59.4	62.7	49.9	49.0	50.0	59.2	69.1	59.6	64.9	63.6	65.4	37.5	46.7	49.9	50.1	47.0
1978	54.5	57.0	63.9	47.7	49.4	50.6	51.0	69.5	72.8	60.2	58.8	53.7	41.4	48.0	51.8	52.2	44.0
1979	51.7	53.0	58.2	48.5	47.2	59.4	43.4	56.1	51.7	67.1	56.0	54.7	43.8	47.0	45.0	60.0	36.6
1980	47.9	44.6	50.0	44.3	52.4	37.9	45.2	50.8	47.5	58.3	44.4	51.8	35.5	45.7	59.9	50.4	46.8
1981	42.2	39.8	47.3	37.9	43.5	39.5	39.1	40.9	47.6	49.4	45.0	48.7	30.5	34.7	42.9	39.9	47.7
1982	44.6	46.2	45.8	39.2	47.3	41.9	43.1	53.7	44.9	45.7	46.9	53.2	30.7	33.8	45.8	48.9	47.1
1983	46.0	48.7	48.2	41.3	45.9	48.6	42.3	55.1	45.0	53.6	46.0	49.8	37.0	37.3	46.0	44.2	47.5

Unemployment (registered unemployed) (3) — Chômage (chômeurs inscrits) (3)

thousands — milliers

	Year	Q.1	Q.2	Q.3	Q.4	JAN	FEB	MAR	APR	MAY	JUN	JUL	AUG	SEP	OCT	NOV	DEC
1964	130	118	116	129	156	109	120	124	119	116	112	117	132	138	144	154	170
1965	147	171	136	132	149	130	172	162	149	136	123	129	134	134	143	158	146
1966	123	150	114	105	123	135	159	135	127	111	103	105	107	108	117	126	127
1967	146	140	133	139	173	136	143	142	137	134	128	131	138	147	163	179	179
1968	182	212	177	167	173	204	226	206	192	177	162	162	170	168	166	175	177
1969	159	183	161	147	146	177	183	187	175	158	149	145	147	148	148	147	143
1970	146	154	138	135	154	163	152	149	143	140	132	134	136	137	142	156	166
1971	190	181	192	186	202	181	179	183	194	194	188	185	186	188	192	201	212
1972	191	221	199	178	166	220	221	221	212	199	186	182	178	173	169	167	163
1973	150	169	157	141	132	169	170	169	168	158	143	141	144	139	134	132	129
1974	150	135	139	148	179	133	134	139	142	140	135	140	149	154	161	181	196
1975	257	232	244	258	292	224	232	240	243	244	244	251	258	266	275	301	302
1976	376	331	362	375	437	317	330	346	362	363	361	366	376	382	414	448	447
1977	540	481	497	551	630	471	484	488	488	495	507	535	549	568	600	630	662
1978	817	741	786	837	903	702	745	776	778	780	799	820	833	857	891	914	905
1979	1037	947	1015	1070	1117	926	942	972	1006	1009	1030	1053	1066	1093	1107	1112	1130
1980	1277	1195	1244	1278	1393	1164	1198	1222	1245	1242	1244	1254	1268	1313	1360	1402	1416
1981	1566	1499	1515	1555	1696	1478	1500	1518	1527	1515	1504	1524	1547	1594	1649	1695	1744
1982	1873	1802	1793	1835	2061	1787	1817	1802	1801	1793	1786	1807	1827	1870	1967	2055	2151
1983	2207	2192	2147	2188	2302	2196	2208	2172	2175	2128	2138	2156	2187	2222	2266	2298	2342

Hourly earnings: all activities (4) (all employees) — Gains horaires : ensemble des activités (4) (salariés)

1980 = 100

	Year	Q.1	Q.2	Q.3	Q.4	JAN	FEB	MAR	APR	MAY	JUN	JUL	AUG	SEP	OCT	NOV	DEC
1964	5.6	5.0	5.3	6.1	6.1												
1965	6.5	5.8	6.1	7.0	7.1												
1966	7.6	6.8	7.0	8.2	8.5												
1967	8.8	7.9	8.1	9.6	9.7												
1968	9.6	8.7	8.9	10.4	10.5												
1969	10.8	9.5	9.9	11.9	11.8												
1970	12.3	10.7	11.1	13.7	13.6												
1971	14.0	12.4	12.9	15.5	15.3												
1972	16.4	14.2	14.9	18.5	18.1												
1973	19.6	16.9	17.8	22.0	22.0												
1974	24.9	20.8	22.4	28.3	28.1												
1975	32.6	28.0	28.3	37.7	36.4												
1976	42.4	34.4	37.9	49.2	43.1												
1977	55.0	46.6	48.1	59.8	65.5												
1978	70.1	59.7	61.4	77.3	82.1												
1979	86.7	74.8	79.7	95.4	96.7												
1980	100.0	78.5	97.1	107.4	117.1												
1981	124.7	109.0	119.4	134.7	135.7												
1982	144.5	127.7	136.6	151.6	162.0												
1983		144.5	153.4	177.6													

Unemployment (5) — Chômage (5)

as per cent of total labour force — en pourcentage de la population active

	Year	Q.1	Q.2	Q.3	Q.4	JAN	FEB	MAR	APR	MAY	JUN	JUL	AUG	SEP	OCT	NOV	DEC
1964	1.8		1.5	2.9	2.0												
1965	1.6	2.3	1.4	1.4	1.3												
1966	0.9	..	0.9	..	0.9												
1967	1.1	..	1.0	..	1.1												
1968	1.1	..	1.0	..	1.1												
1969	1.0	..	1.0	..	1.0												
1970	1.1	..	1.0	..	1.2												
1971	1.5	..	..	..	1.5												
1972	2.1	..	..	..	2.1												
1973	2.3	..	2.1	..	2.4												
1974	2.6	..	2.3	..	2.9												
1975	4.0	..	3.3	3.4	4.7												
1976	4.8	4.7	4.8	4.6	4.9												
1977	5.3	5.0	4.9	5.5	5.8												
1978	7.1	6.5	6.7	7.3	7.7												
1979	8.7	8.2	8.3	8.8	9.6												
1980	11.5	10.6	11.2	11.6	12.6												
1981	14.4	13.6	13.9	14.6	15.4												
1982	16.3	15.9	15.8	16.4	17.1												
1983	17.8	17.8	17.3	17.8	18.4												

Unemployment (registered unemployed) (3) — Chômage (chômeurs inscrits) (3)

thousands — milliers

Adjusted - Corrigé

	Year	Q.1	Q.2	Q.3	Q.4	JAN	FEB	MAR	APR	MAY	JUN	JUL	AUG	SEP	OCT	NOV	DEC
1964		105	124	143	150	98	106	111	116	125	132	136	146	147	145	145	158
1965		153	145	146	143	162	152	147	146	146	144	147	146	143	144	150	136
1966		134	119	117	119	139	141	123	124	119	113	119	116	115	118	120	120
1967		127	140	151	170	122	128	131	134	141	145	147	149	157	166	172	170
1968		193	184	180	171	184	204	191	187	184	180	180	182	178	171	171	170
1969		168	165	157	146	151	167	174	169	162	163	158	157	157	153	146	133
1970		143	141	144	155	150	140	138	137	142	142	144	144	144	148	156	162
1971		171	190	196	206	174	169	170	181	191	197	195	194	198	205	202	212
1972		209	196	186	169	212	210	206	199	195	195	192	186	181	177	167	164
1973		161	155	147	134	163	162	159	159	156	149	147	149	144	140	132	129
1974		130	138	156	183	129	128	131	133	137	142	148	156	165	171	181	196
1975		220	240	268	295	216	221	224	228	240	254	263	267	276	283	301	302
1976		319	359	388	442	310	319	330	346	358	373	380	389	398	429	448	448
1977		465	496	564	636	456	468	473	477	494	516	544	563	584	608	632	667
1978		723	787	854	907	639	727	754	770	779	813	833	854	875	898	913	909
1979		928	1018	1090	1114	909	923	951	992	1014	1047	1069	1092	1109	1108	1105	1128
1980		1172	1248	1305	1336	1142	1176	1198	1228	1249	1267	1277	1302	1335	1361	1391	1405
1981		1471	1521	1589	1684	1451	1473	1490	1506	1522	1535	1556	1591	1621	1649	1677	1726
1982		1769	1803	1876	2045	1753	1785	1770	1781	1804	1824	1846	1881	1899	1965	2040	2129
1983		2156	2158	2237	2280	2160	2172	2138	2152	2141	2181	2204	2254	2253	2258	2266	2316

Hourly earnings: all activities (4) — Gains horaires : ensemble des activites (4)

(all employees) — (salariés)

1980 = 100

Adjusted - Corrigé *

	Year	Q.1	Q.2	Q.3	Q.4	JAN	FEB	MAR	APR	MAY	JUN	JUL	AUG	SEP	OCT	NOV	DEC
1964		5.3	5.5	5.7	5.9												
1965		6.2	6.5	6.6	6.8												
1966		7.2	7.5	7.7	8.1												
1967		8.4	8.6	8.9	9.2												
1968		9.3	9.5	9.7	10.0												
1969		10.2	10.6	11.0	11.2												
1970		11.5	11.9	12.6	12.9												
1971		13.3	13.9	14.1	14.6												
1972		15.3	16.0	16.8	17.4												
1973		18.1	19.2	19.9	21.2												
1974		22.4	24.2	25.6	27.0												
1975		30.0	30.7	34.2	34.9												
1976		36.8	41.0	44.8	45.9												
1977		50.0	52.1	54.9	62.1												
1978		64.2	66.1	71.6	77.3												
1979		80.6	85.1	89.2	90.9												
1980		84.6	102.8	101.0	110.1												
1981		117.6	125.5	127.4	127.8												
1982		137.7	142.9	143.7	152.7												
1983		155.7	160.2	158.7													

* Adjusted by the O.E.C.D. — * Corrigé par l'O.C.D.E.

Agricultural prices: total (6)

1980 = 100

Prix agricoles : total (6)

1980 = 100

	Year	Q.1	Q.2	Q.3	Q.4	JAN	FEB	MAR	APR	MAY	JUN	JUL	AUG	SEP	OCT	NOV	DEC
1964	27.3	26.0	26.2	27.0	27.6	26.4	26.0	25.6	26.5	26.3	26.0	27.0	26.9	27.1	28.7	29.7	30.3
1965	32.0	31.0	33.0	30.9	32.8	30.2	31.2	31.8	32.7	34.1	32.2	31.9	30.2	30.7	32.1	32.6	33.7
1966	33.1	32.4	34.4	32.6	33.0	33.0	32.0	32.3	32.6	34.4	36.2	34.9	31.6	31.4	32.0	33.4	33.5
1967	32.3	32.6	34.1	31.3	31.8	32.7	32.7	32.6	33.5	35.8	33.0	32.1	31.1	30.7	31.1	31.7	32.4
1968	34.3	34.0	36.1	32.9	34.2	33.4	33.9	34.8	35.4	36.7	36.1	34.1	32.3	32.4	33.3	34.4	35.0
1969	35.9	35.6	37.7	35.1	35.3	35.1	35.9	35.7	36.5	38.4	38.2	37.0	33.9	34.2	34.9	34.9	36.0
1970	35.0	35.1	36.6	35.2	34.0	35.3	35.3	34.7	35.7	36.9	37.1	36.3	34.9	34.3	34.5	34.1	33.4
1971	37.1	35.4	39.0	35.5	38.2	35.0	35.0	36.2	37.8	39.6	39.7	36.6	34.5	35.5	36.9	37.6	40.2
1972	41.1	40.6	43.8	39.7	40.3	40.1	40.2	41.4	42.0	45.6	43.9	40.7	39.2	39.4	39.8	40.3	40.7
1973	45.8	42.2	48.9	45.5	46.5	41.1	41.9	43.6	46.9	49.9	49.9	46.3	44.7	45.6	46.8	45.9	46.7
1974	49.9	47.2	52.4	48.0	52.1	45.5	47.0	49.2	51.3	53.3	52.7	49.5	46.6	47.8	49.6	53.0	53.6
1975	57.7	53.8	59.5	57.6	59.9	53.4	53.1	54.9	58.4	60.6	59.6	59.2	56.1	57.5	58.7	59.6	61.2
1976	63.8	65.0	65.6	60.8	64.9	62.2	66.1	66.8	67.3	66.9	62.7	61.6	59.5	61.1	61.8	65.2	67.8
1977	77.8	69.7	75.5	87.0	78.9	68.5	69.4	71.2	74.4	72.0	80.1	89.7	86.5	84.7	82.5	76.8	77.2
1978	86.6	81.8	86.0	91.7	86.9	79.6	83.1	82.8	84.6	85.4	88.1	93.6	93.4	88.0	86.4	87.1	87.1
1979	97.8	98.9	104.9	94.3	93.0	95.6	98.7	102.4	104.5	104.7	105.4	100.8	93.6	88.6	91.6	93.0	94.5
1980	100.0	101.5	98.0	99.3	101.2	99.5	101.3	103.5	100.4	93.0	100.6	100.7	98.3	98.9	97.8	100.5	105.2
1981	113.0	112.6	114.6	110.9	113.9	107.7	113.9	116.2	121.3	111.7	110.9	114.7	110.2	107.9	111.9	113.5	116.3
1982	130.8	124.6	136.0	131.7	130.6	120.2	125.1	128.6	130.8	137.2	140.1	139.8	130.3	125.0	129.4	128.7	133.7
1983	142.8	139.3	140.1	137.1	153.0	139.2	139.1	139.4	142.1	137.7	140.5	137.6	135.6	138.2	148.7	153.5	156.7

Producer prices: investment goods

1980 = 100

Prix à la production : biens d'équipement

1980 = 100

	Year	Q.1	Q.2	Q.3	Q.4	JAN	FEB	MAR	APR	MAY	JUN	JUL	AUG	SEP	OCT	NOV	DEC
1964																	
1965																	
1966																	
1967																	
1968																	
1969																	
1970																	
1971																	
1972																	
1973																	
1974																	
1975	46.2	44.7	45.7	46.5	47.9	44.1	44.9	45.3	45.4	45.8	45.9	46.3	46.5	46.8	47.9	47.8	48.1
1976	52.9	50.0	52.0	53.8	55.8	49.1	50.2	50.7	51.4	52.0	52.6	53.4	54.0	54.1	55.5	55.8	56.1
1977	64.0	59.3	62.5	65.8	68.4	57.9	59.3	60.5	61.6	62.7	63.0	64.8	65.9	66.7	67.2	68.6	69.3
1978	76.1	72.1	74.9	77.2	80.2	71.4	72.0	72.7	73.5	74.9	76.2	76.7	77.0	77.8	79.8	80.2	80.7
1979	88.1	84.4	86.7	89.3	91.8	83.4	84.5	85.3	85.9	86.4	87.9	88.8	89.3	90.0	90.9	91.9	92.7
1980	100.0	95.3	98.6	101.7	104.5	94.0	95.5	96.3	97.7	98.4	99.9	101.0	101.5	102.5	103.8	104.7	105.0
1981	114.3	109.3	112.9	115.9	118.3	108.1	109.4	110.5	112.0	112.6	114.3	115.2	115.7	116.8	117.8	118.4	118.6
1982	128.8	123.9	127.7	130.3	133.2	121.8	124.1	125.8	126.5	127.7	129.0	129.8	130.0	131.3	132.2	133.1	134.2
1983	145.6	140.5	144.5	147.3	150.2	138.2	141.0	142.2	143.0	144.5	146.0	146.6	147.1	148.2	149.1	150.4	151.1

Producer prices: consumer goods

1980 = 100

Prix à la production : biens de consommation

1980 = 100

	Year	Q.1	Q.2	Q.3	Q.4	JAN	FEB	MAR	APR	MAY	JUN	JUL	AUG	SEP	OCT	NOV	DEC
1964																	
1965																	
1966																	
1967																	
1968																	
1969																	
1970																	
1971																	
1972																	
1973																	
1974																	
1975	47.9	46.4	47.5	48.4	49.1	46.0	46.5	46.8	47.2	47.6	47.7	47.9	48.5	48.8	49.0	49.1	49.3
1976	53.4	50.4	52.6	54.3	56.3	49.9	50.4	51.0	51.9	52.4	53.5	54.0	54.3	54.7	55.9	56.3	56.6
1977	65.6	60.1	63.4	67.5	71.2	59.0	59.7	61.8	62.6	63.3	64.2	65.9	67.8	68.9	70.7	71.4	71.6
1978	76.7	73.2	75.8	77.8	80.1	72.5	73.2	73.9	74.9	75.8	76.6	77.3	77.7	78.4	79.6	80.1	80.5
1979	87.5	83.1	85.7	88.7	92.3	82.1	83.2	83.9	85.0	85.6	86.7	87.3	88.5	90.5	91.8	92.1	93.1
1980	100.0	97.3	98.6	100.5	103.6	95.9	97.8	98.3	98.3	98.4	99.2	99.7	100.3	101.4	102.8	103.3	104.8
1981	112.1	106.7	109.4	112.7	115.3	106.2	106.7	107.3	108.6	109.0	110.5	111.5	112.7	114.0	115.4	116.4	117.1
1982	126.3	121.4	124.1	127.1	131.4	120.0	121.6	122.4	123.3	124.2	124.8	126.0	127.0	128.1	129.8	131.7	132.6
1983	142.3	136.6	140.7	144.0	148.1	135.0	137.0	137.7	140.3	140.2	141.5	142.8	143.8	145.5	146.9	148.1	149.5

Producer prices: intermediate goods — Prix à la production : biens intermédiaires

1980 = 100

	Year	Q.1	Q.2	Q.3	Q.4	JAN	FEB	MAR	APR	MAY	JUN	JUL	AUG	SEP	OCT	NOV	DEC
1964																	
1965																	
1966																	
1967																	
1968																	
1969																	
1970																	
1971																	
1972																	
1973																	
1974																	
1975	46.3	45.6	46.2	46.4	47.0	44.5	46.0	46.2	46.1	46.3	46.2	46.4	46.4	46.4	46.3	46.6	48.2
1976	52.9	49.4	53.1	54.3	54.8	48.6	49.4	50.3	52.3	53.3	53.7	54.3	54.3	54.4	54.7	54.8	54.9
1977	62.4	56.7	61.4	64.2	67.4	55.5	56.3	58.3	61.1	61.5	61.8	62.2	64.4	65.9	67.0	67.4	67.8
1978	71.9	68.8	71.4	73.1	74.2	68.3	68.8	69.2	70.0	71.8	72.6	72.9	73.0	73.3	73.9	74.2	74.6
1979	82.4	77.2	79.8	85.1	87.6	76.0	77.4	78.2	78.8	79.5	81.1	83.5	85.6	86.3	87.2	87.6	88.1
1980	100.0	94.2	97.9	102.7	105.1	89.4	96.1	97.2	97.5	97.9	98.3	101.1	103.2	104.0	104.7	105.0	105.6
1981	118.7	110.6	119.6	122.9	125.6	109.1	111.0	111.8	118.7	119.8	120.4	121.0	123.6	124.2	124.6	125.8	126.4
1982	132.8	129.2	132.6	133.9	135.7	126.5	129.9	131.1	131.9	132.9	132.9	133.4	134.0	134.2	134.9	135.8	136.3
1983	153.2	146.4	150.9	154.3	161.4	144.1	146.8	148.3	149.7	150.9	152.0	153.2	154.4	155.2	159.0	160.5	164.8

Producer prices: energy — Prix à la production : énergie

1980 = 100

	Year	Q.1	Q.2	Q.3	Q.4	JAN	FEB	MAR	APR	MAY	JUN	JUL	AUG	SEP	OCT	NOV	DEC
1964																	
1965																	
1966																	
1967																	
1968																	
1969																	
1970																	
1971																	
1972																	
1973																	
1974																	
1975	42.1	40.1	42.0	42.1	44.1	36.8	41.6	41.8	41.8	42.1	42.1	42.1	42.1	42.1	42.1	42.1	48.0
1976	49.3	48.6	49.4	49.6	49.6	48.3	48.3	49.1	49.3	49.5	49.5	49.6	49.6	49.6	49.6	49.7	49.7
1977	57.9	51.1	56.5	60.8	63.2	49.9	50.0	53.3	56.4	56.6	56.6	56.8	62.5	63.2	63.2	63.2	63.2
1978	63.7	63.6	63.6	63.7	63.8	63.6	63.6	63.6	63.6	63.6	63.6	63.6	63.6	63.8	63.8	63.8	63.8
1979	71.5	64.2	65.8	77.3	78.5	64.0	64.1	64.4	64.4	64.4	68.7	75.4	78.3	78.3	78.4	78.5	78.5
1980	100.0	89.8	95.3	107.1	107.8	78.9	95.3	95.3	95.3	95.3	95.3	104.7	108.3	108.3	107.8	107.8	107.8
1981	139.0	118.8	141.5	146.7	149.0	116.6	119.9	119.9	141.3	141.5	141.6	142.3	149.0	149.0	149.0	149.0	149.1
1982	154.5	152.3	155.2	155.3	155.3	149.1	153.9	153.9	155.1	155.2	155.2	155.2	155.3	155.3	155.3	155.4	155.4
1983	185.9	181.6	183.7	183.7	194.7	179.4	181.6	183.7	183.7	183.7	183.7	183.8	183.7	183.7	191.1	191.1	202.0

Consumer prices: all items (7) — Prix à la consommation : total (7)

1980 = 100

	Year	Q.1	Q.2	Q.3	Q.4	JAN	FEB	MAR	APR	MAY	JUN	JUL	AUG	SEP	OCT	NOV	DEC
1964	16.6	15.9	16.1	16.9	17.7	15.9	15.9	16.0	16.0	16.1	16.3	16.6	16.9	17.1	17.3	17.7	17.9
1965	18.8	18.4	18.7	18.9	19.4	18.1	18.4	18.6	18.7	18.8	18.7	18.7	18.8	19.0	19.1	19.5	19.6
1966	20.0	19.6	20.0	20.1	20.5	19.6	19.6	19.6	19.8	20.1	20.1	20.1	20.1	20.1	20.2	20.5	20.7
1967	21.3	20.8	21.2	21.3	21.9	20.7	20.8	20.9	21.2	21.3	21.1	21.1	21.4	21.5	21.6	22.0	22.0
1968	=22.3=	22.1	22.5	22.3	22.5	22.1	22.1	22.3	22.5	22.4	22.5	22.3	22.3	22.3	22.3	22.5	22.6
1969	22.8	22.6	22.8	22.8	23.2	22.6	22.5	22.6	22.9	22.9	22.6	22.8	22.8	22.9	23.0	23.2	23.4
1970	24.1	23.5	23.7	24.4	24.9	23.5	23.4	23.6	23.8	23.6	23.7	24.1	24.5	24.6	24.9	24.9	25.0
1971	26.1	25.4	25.9	26.2	27.1	25.3	25.3	25.5	25.8	25.9	26.1	26.1	26.1	26.4	26.7	27.1	27.4
1972	28.3	27.5	27.8	28.6	29.3	27.4	27.4	27.7	27.7	27.8	27.9	28.3	28.6	29.0	29.2	29.2	29.4
1973	31.5	29.8	30.8	32.2	33.4	29.7	29.7	29.9	30.4	30.8	31.3	31.6	32.1	32.7	33.2	33.3	33.6
1974	36.5	34.1	35.8	37.0	38.9	33.8	33.9	34.7	35.4	35.9	36.0	36.4	37.1	37.6	38.0	39.1	39.6
1975	42.6	40.5	41.9	43.5	44.6	40.2	40.6	40.8	41.5	42.1	42.2	42.8	43.5	44.2	44.2	44.5	45.2
1976	50.2	46.5	49.7	51.1	53.5	45.8	46.3	47.3	48.3	50.5	50.2	50.5	50.9	51.9	52.6	53.6	=54.1=
1977	62.5	56.9	60.1	65.0	67.9	55.9	56.8	58.1	59.2	59.7	61.4	63.4	65.4	66.3	67.3	67.9	68.4
1978	74.8	70.3	73.3	76.7	78.8	69.5	70.2	71.1	72.6	73.3	74.1	75.7	77.0	77.5	78.2	78.5	79.7
1979	86.6	81.8	84.7	88.4	91.2	81.1	81.7	82.6	83.8	84.8	85.6	87.5	88.3	89.5	90.5	90.9	92.2
1980	100.0	95.5	97.9	101.7	104.3	94.7	95.6	96.1	97.0	97.6	99.2	100.5	101.8	102.9	103.7	104.6	106.2
1981	114.6	109.4	112.6	116.3	120.0	108.3	108.9	111.0	112.2	112.7	112.8	115.1	116.5	117.4	118.7	119.7	121.5
1982	131.1	124.9	129.5	133.3	136.4	123.7	124.7	126.3	127.9	129.7	131.0	132.7	133.6	133.8	135.1	135.6	138.6
1983	147.0	141.5	145.0	148.0	153.4	140.6	141.4	142.4	144.4	145.0	145.8	146.3	148.3	149.5	151.5	153.1	155.4

SPAIN

Money supply (M1) (8)(9)

billion pesetas, end of period

Disponibilités monétaires (M1) (8)(9)

milliards de pesetas, fin de période

	Year	Q.1	Q.2	Q.3	Q.4	JAN	FEB	MAR	APR	MAY	JUN	JUL	AUG	SEP	OCT	NOV	DEC
1964	372	306	322	338	372	299	298	306	310	315	322	325	332	338	342	338	372
1965	429	353	377	392	429	353	352	353	358	366	377	388	388	392	396	399	429
1966	480	409	424	442	480	408	405	409	411	414	424	436	435	442	442	447	480
1967	544	464	485	503	544	455	456	464	469	471	485	495	491	503	506	505	544
1968	611	515	539	556	611	511	509	515	517	523	539	546	547	556	561	566	611
1969	700	588	612	631	700	574	578	588	592	597	612	628	627	631	635	643	700
1970	741	654	661	676	741	657	655	654	646	645	661	678	665	676	676	677	741
1971	929	709	766	800	929	695	695	709	718	730	766	784	777	800	801	820	929
1972	1146	890	955	998	1146	859	858	890	907	916	955	977	966	998	1000	1016	1146
1973	1412	1126	1216	1257	1412	1086	1086	1126	1138	1157	1215	1252	1221	1257	1264	1276	1412
1974	1658	1368	1445	1455	1658	1328	1326	1368	1395	1393	1445	1471	1432	1455	1482	1436	1658
1975	1978	1559	1657	1718	1978	1552	1525	1559	1575	1594	1657	1730	1698	1718	1753	1774	1978
1976	2353	1849	1982	2043	2353	1861	1830	1849	1900	1911	1982	2044	1989	2043	2078	2109	2353
1977	2806	2237	2389	2480	2806	2207	2191	2237	2274	2304	2389	2512	2437	2480	2472	2542	2806
1978	3260	2681	2884	2929	3260	2611	2584	2681	2718	2748	2884	2975	2864	2929	2946	2960	3260
1979	3545	3115	3305	3268	3545	3059	3107	3115	3175	3162	3305	3384	3220	3268	3247	3252	3545
1980	4015	3380	3583	3639	4015	3306	3302	3380	3427	3408	3583	3700	3565	3639	3684	3705	4015
1981	4520	3730	3948	4033	4520	3733	3693	3730	3829	3812	3948	4093	3956	4033	4058	4092	4520
1982	4833	4256	4505	4568	4833	4204	4189	4256	4367	4370	4505	4615	4460	4568	4614	4606	4833
1983	5248	4753	4812	4835	5248	4575	4558	4753	4670	4683	4812	4878	4733	4835	4725	4775	5248

M1 plus quasi-money (8)(9)

billion pesetas, end of period

M1 plus quasi-monnaie (8)(9)

milliards de pesetas, fin de période

	Year	Q.1	Q.2	Q.3	Q.4	JAN	FEB	MAR	APR	MAY	JUN	JUL	AUG	SEP	OCT	NOV	DEC
1964	773	648	676	709	773	630	635	648	656	664	676	688	696	709	719	727	773
1965	913	773	811	851	913	754	768	773	782	795	811	830	840	851	860	870	913
1966	1042	911	936	976	1042	900	902	911	917	922	936	955	962	976	984	994	1042
1967	1203	1047	1081	1127	1203	1026	1033	1047	1056	1063	1081	1103	1108	1127	1139	1145	1203
1968	1429	1214	1267	1327	1429	1137	1197	1214	1228	1243	1267	1291	1306	1327	1346	1362	1429
1969	1697	1449	1510	1575	1697	1409	1427	1449	1464	1480	1510	1539	1557	1575	1596	1613	1697
1970	1953	1689	1740	1814	1953	1670	1676	1689	1696	1708	1740	1778	1787	1814	1834	1851	1953
1971	2432	1934	2100	2215	2432	1931	1949	1984	2013	2043	2100	2146	2168	2215	2241	2275	2432
1972	2984	2468	2603	2730	2984	2390	2411	2468	2509	2540	2603	2657	2671	2730	2763	2798	2984
1973	3699	3060	3254	3420	3699	2956	2987	3060	3103	3156	3254	3338	3349	3420	3470	3510	3699
1974	4398	3753	3922	4039	4398	3652	3680	3753	3811	3832	3922	3996	3986	4039	4110	4145	4398
1975	5231	4431	4622	4822	5231	4343	4357	4431	4475	4521	4622	4764	4773	4822	4889	4935	5231
1976	6202	5217	5463	5686	6202	5164	5165	5217	5309	5356	5463	5609	5603	5686	5775	5843	6202
1977	7371	6246	6542	6832	7371	6117	6148	6246	6337	6412	6542	6763	6740	6832	6867	6978	7371
1978	8832	7432	7859	8205	8832	7250	7278	7432	7546	7642	7859	8103	8068	8205	8278	8340	8832
1979	10422	8954	9406	9662	10422	8713	8833	8954	9097	9161	9406	9643	9543	9662	9800	9905	10422
1980	12156	10575	11000	11413	12156	10230	10381	10575	10712	10745	11000	11295	11259	11413	11528	11603	12156
1981	14071	12158	12641	13127	14071	11953	12013	12158	12340	12410	12641	12591	12947	13127	13240	13345	14071
1982	16016	14167	14826	15346	16016	13867	13959	14167	14425	14547	14826	15159	15122	15346	15433	15506	16016
1983	18734	16739	17068	17680	18734	16358	16437	16739	16749	16816	17068	17388	17418	17680	17702	17883	18734

Net new capital issues

billion pesetas, monthly averages

Nouvelles émissions sur le marché des capitaux, nettes

milliards de pesetas, moyennes mensuelles

	Year	Q.1	Q.2	Q.3	Q.4	JAN	FEB	MAR	APR	MAY	JUN	JUL	AUG	SEP	OCT	NOV	DEC
1964																	
1965																	
1966																	
1967																	
1968																	
1969																	
1970																	
1971																	
1972																	
1973																	
1974																	
1975																	
1976																	
1977																	
1978																	
1979																	
1980																	
1981					39.78								16.06	3.14	15.75	29.08	74.50
1982	33.26	15.57	19.62	40.83	57.00	12.48	22.74	11.49	10.28	26.53	22.07	55.71	39.91	26.38	12.27	44.44	114.30
1983	38.94	33.46	39.19	32.37	50.74	33.47	35.07	31.83	10.61	54.68	52.27	51.66	31.03	14.37	15.80	31.98	104.43

Money supply (M1) (8)(9)

billion pesetas, end of period

Adjusted - Corrigé *

Disponibilités monétaires (M1) (8)(9)

milliards de pesetas, fin de période

	Year	Q.1	Q.2	Q.3	Q.4	JAN	FEB	MAR	APR	MAY	JUN	JUL	AUG	SEP	OCT	NOV	DEC
1964		308	324	337	351	299	302	308	314	319	324	328	333	337	343	339	351
1965		357	379	391	404	354	358	357	363	372	379	385	390	391	397	401	404
1966		414	424	441	451	409	411	414	417	421	424	432	436	441	443	448	451
1967		470	486	502	511	456	463	470	477	480	486	490	492	502	508	507	511
1968		521	539	555	572	514	517	521	526	533	539	540	550	555	563	569	572
1969		595	611	631	654	577	588	595	602	609	611	620	631	631	639	648	654
1970		661	658	676	691	650	666	661	656	657	658	666	671	676	681	684	691
1971		716	761	800	864	698	707	716	730	744	761	771	786	800	809	831	864
1972		897	947	1000	1064	862	876	897	921	932	947	960	979	1000	1010	1032	1064
1973		1137	1205	1260	1308	1098	1110	1137	1154	1177	1205	1228	1240	1260	1277	1296	1308
1974		1383	1432	1461	1537	1331	1359	1383	1413	1417	1432	1439	1453	1461	1497	1509	1537
1975		1578	1643	1725	1833	1555	1564	1578	1596	1621	1643	1687	1722	1725	1770	1801	1833
1976		1877	1962	2051	2182	1866	1879	1877	1925	1946	1962	1986	2015	2051	2097	2141	2182
1977		2273	2361	2490	2610	2218	2252	2273	2301	2346	2361	2434	2469	2490	2495	2581	2610
1978		2727	2847	2937	3039	2632	2655	2727	2748	2801	2847	2881	2899	2937	2973	3005	3039
1979		3169	3256	3275	3316	3090	3193	3169	3207	3223	3256	3266	3256	3275	3274	3299	3316
1980		3442	3530	3647	3760	3349	3394	3442	3458	3474	3530	3568	3601	3647	3713	3757	3760
1981		3798	3886	4041	4236	3782	3795	3798	3864	3885	3886	3947	4000	4041	4095	4150	4236
1982		4339	4434	4577	4529	4263	4305	4339	4402	4455	4434	4450	4510	4577	4656	4672	4529
1983		4845	4737	4845	4918	4640	4685	4845	4708	4773	4737	4704	4786	4845	4768	4843	4918

M1 plus quasi-money (8)(9)

billion pesetas, end of period

Adjusted - Corrigé *

M1 plus quasi-monnaie (8)(9)

milliards de pesetas, fin de période

	Year	Q.1	Q.2	Q.3	Q.4	JAN	FEB	MAR	APR	MAY	JUN	JUL	AUG	SEP	OCT	NOV	DEC
1964		648	681	710	750	627	636	648	659	670	681	689	699	710	722	731	750
1965		773	816	852	886	759	768	773	785	802	816	831	844	852	863	874	886
1966		912	941	977	1011	896	904	912	921	931	941	954	965	977	987	999	1011
1967		1049	1087	1128	1166	1022	1035	1049	1063	1074	1087	1102	1111	1128	1143	1151	1166
1968		1216	1272	1328	1386	1182	1200	1216	1235	1256	1272	1288	1310	1328	1350	1370	1386
1969		1452	1515	1577	1646	1404	1430	1452	1472	1493	1515	1534	1561	1577	1601	1625	1646
1970		1692	1743	1816	1894	1665	1681	1692	1706	1724	1743	1772	1794	1816	1841	1865	1894
1971		1988	2102	2219	2357	1925	1957	1988	2024	2062	2102	2136	2176	2219	2253	2296	2357
1972		2473	2603	2736	2891	2383	2421	2473	2522	2563	2603	2641	2684	2736	2777	2827	2891
1973		3066	3254	3430	3581	2947	3002	3066	3116	3181	3254	3312	3366	3430	3491	3546	3581
1974		3760	3922	4055	4258	3641	3702	3760	3827	3863	3922	3960	4006	4055	4135	4187	4258
1975		4444	4622	4841	5064	4330	4384	4444	4493	4557	4622	4713	4792	4841	4919	4989	5064
1976		5238	5463	5709	6009	5149	5201	5238	5330	5405	5463	5537	5625	5709	5810	5908	6009
1977		6271	6542	6853	7150	6105	6191	6271	6363	6470	6542	6670	6760	6853	6908	7056	7150
1978		7461	7859	8230	8575	7243	7330	7461	7568	7711	7859	7983	8092	8230	8328	8432	8575
1979		8990	9406	9681	10138	8704	8895	8990	9125	9244	9406	9501	9570	9681	9849	10015	10138
1980		10618	10989	11436	11837	10291	10454	10618	10733	10843	10989	11137	11293	11436	11585	11720	11837
1981		12206	12628	13154	13701	11975	12098	12206	12365	12523	12628	12799	12986	13154	13320	13497	13701
1982		14223	14811	15377	15595	13881	14058	14223	14454	14679	14811	14935	15167	15377	15526	15679	15595
1983		16806	17050	17715	18241	16384	16553	16806	16783	16969	17050	17131	17471	17715	17809	18082	18241

Credit to private sector: (9)(10)(11)

commercial banks

billion pesetas, end of period

Crédits au secteur privé : (11)(10)

banques commerciales (9)

milliards de pesetas, fin de période

	Year	Q.1	Q.2	Q.3	Q.4	JAN	FEB	MAR	APR	MAY	JUN	JUL	AUG	SEP	OCT	NOV	DEC
1964	383	324	344	351	383	322	323	324	331	336	344	346	347	351	358	366	383
1965	485	390	421	445	485	379	384	390	402	411	421	438	440	445	459	468	485
1966	553	491	508	519	553	482	487	491	497	499	508	515	514	519	530	538	553
1967	631	559	584	597	631	549	555	559	571	572	584	589	589	597	604	617	631
1968	756	634	658	677	756	626	629	634	639	646	658	668	670	677	693	712	756
1969	915	766	813	853	915	753	762	766	780	798	813	833	839	853	874	891	915
1970	1043	926	962	973	1043	914	923	926	937	946	962	976	970	973	993	1012	1043
1971	1243	1051	1108	1143	1243	1033	1040	1051	1069	1081	1108	1133	1124	1143	1160	1185	1243
1972	1595	1272	1363	1445	1595	1230	1243	1272	1298	1322	1363	1407	1410	1445	1479	1522	1595
1973	2062	1657	1793	1905	2062	1576	1606	1657	1690	1726	1793	1858	1861	1905	1956	2006	2062
1974	2615	2140	2272	2403	2615	2054	2081	2140	2194	2211	2272	2388	2377	2403	2464	2520	2615
1975	3201	2704	2837	2937	3201	2616	2656	2704	2740	2774	2837	2925	2917	2937	3008	3075	3201
1976	3914	3269	3463	3571	3914	3184	3220	3269	3342	3401	3463	3580	3551	3571	3680	3758	3914
1977	4756	4045	4309	4457	4756	3928	3983	4045	4157	4232	4309	4484	4427	4457	4520	4604	4756
1978	5225	4753	4978	5001	5225	4684	4719	4753	4845	4867	4978	5090	4989	5001	5038	5056	5225
1979	6075	5268	5516	5682	6075	5145	5236	5268	5310	5367	5516	5671	5613	5682	5782	5873	6075
1980	7252	6250	6533	6774	7252	6020	6127	6250	6326	6393	6533	6748	6727	6774	6931	7078	7252
1981	8442	7264	7639	7843	8442	7206	7264	7264	7448	7513	7639	7898	7786	7843	7997	8144	8442
1982	9502	8494	8856	9052	9502	8383	8438	8494	8655	8703	8856	9110	9011	9052	9194	9374	9502
1983	10194	9539	9688	9808	10194	9391	9429	9539	9621	9613	9688	9900	9794	9808	9977	10053	10194

* Adjusted by the O.E.C.D.

* Corrigé par l'O.C.D.E.

SPAIN

Credit to private sector: (9) / Crédits au secteur privé : (9)

other credit institutions / autres institutions de crédit

billion pesetas, end of period / milliards de pesetas, fin de période

	Year	Q.1	Q.2	Q.3	Q.4	JAN	FEB	MAR	APR	MAY	JUN	JUL	AUG	SEP	OCT	NOV	DEC
1964	142	119	126	132	142	114	116	119	121	123	126	128	130	132	135	138	142
1965	183	149	160	168	183	143	145	149	153	156	160	163	165	168	172	177	183
1966	231	196	210	219	231	186	190	196	200	205	210	213	216	219	222	225	231
1967	281	239	253	265	281	231	235	239	244	248	253	256	260	265	267	273	281
1968	349	295	311	327	349	232	288	295	298	304	311	315	321	327	332	338	349
1969	424	365	385	402	424	352	357	365	370	377	385	389	395	402	407	413	424
1970	481	435	450	464	481	425	428	435	437	442	450	453	458	464	467	472	481
1971	541	495	508	521	541	432	487	495	497	503	508	510	514	521	522	528	541
1972	602	545	559	574	602	542	535	545	544	551	559	562	568	574	579	586	602
1973	721	621	644	678	721	603	612	621	624	637	644	653	664	678	685	699	721
1974	893	756	800	837	893	728	741	756	770	736	800	809	822	837	850	869	893
1975	1088	931	981	1031	1088	902	917	931	946	963	981	995	1013	1031	1043	1058	1088
1976	1351	1130	1187	1255	1351	1091	1109	1130	1142	1165	1187	1212	1234	1255	1274	1307	1351
1977	1671	1411	1485	1566	1671	1361	1382	1411	1420	1454	1485	1511	1533	1566	1593	1626	1671
1978	2139	1755	1853	1947	2139	1688	1722	1755	1779	1815	1853	1891	1914	1947	1975	2012	2139
1979	2459	2210	2276	2356	2459	2138	2164	2210	2229	2255	2276	2293	2320	2356	2379	2420	2459
1980	2898	2551	2681	2771	2898	2480	2508	2551	2568	2622	2681	2696	2724	2771	2792	2853	2898
1981	3427	3023	3156	3255	3427	2921	2961	3023	3043	3092	3156	3182	3211	3255	3300	3370	3427
1982	4197	3552	3760	3917	4197	3448	3488	3552	3591	3642	3760	3800	3841	3917	3966	4037	4197
1983	5086	4365	4613	4781	5086	4214	4269	4365	4407	4485	4613	4648	4693	4781	4834	4934	5086

Official discount rate / Taux d'escompte officiel

per cent per annum, end of period / pourcentage par an, fin de période

	Year	Q.1	Q.2	Q.3	Q.4	JAN	FEB	MAR	APR	MAY	JUN	JUL	AUG	SEP	OCT	NOV	DEC
1964	4.60	4.60	4.60	4.60	4.60	4.60	4.60	4.60	4.60	4.60	4.60	4.60	4.60	4.60	4.60	4.60	4.60
1965	4.60	4.60	4.60	4.60	4.60	4.60	4.60	4.60	4.60	4.60	4.60	4.60	4.60	4.60	4.60	4.60	4.60
1966	4.60	4.60	4.60	4.60	4.60	4.50	4.60	4.60	4.60	4.60	4.60	4.60	4.60	4.60	4.60	4.60	4.60
1967	5.10	4.60	4.60	4.60	5.10	4.60	4.60	4.60	4.60	4.60	4.60	4.60	4.60	4.60	4.60	5.10	5.10
1968	5.10	5.10	5.10	5.10	5.10	5.10	5.10	5.10	5.10	5.10	5.10	5.10	5.10	5.10	5.10	5.10	5.10
1969	5.50	5.10	5.10	5.50	5.50	5.10	5.10	5.10	5.10	5.10	5.10	5.50	5.50	5.50	5.50	5.50	5.50
1970	6.50	6.50	6.50	6.50	6.50	5.50	5.50	6.50	6.50	6.50	6.50	6.50	6.50	6.50	6.50	6.50	6.50
1971	5.00	6.25	6.00	6.00	5.00	6.25	6.25	6.25	6.00	6.00	6.00	6.00	6.00	6.00	5.00	5.00	5.00
1972	5.00	5.00	5.00	5.00	5.00	5.00	5.00	5.00	5.00	5.00	5.00	5.00	5.00	5.00	5.00	5.00	5.00
1973	6.00	5.00	5.00	6.00	6.00	5.00	5.00	5.00	5.00	5.00	5.00	6.00	6.00	6.00	6.00	6.00	6.00
1974	7.00	6.00	6.00	7.00	7.00	6.00	6.00	6.00	6.00	6.00	6.00	6.00	7.00	7.00	7.00	7.00	7.00
1975	7.00	7.00	7.00	7.00	7.00	7.00	7.00	7.00	7.00	7.00	7.00	7.00	7.00	7.00	7.00	7.00	7.00
1976	7.00	7.00	7.00	7.00	7.00	7.00	7.00	7.00	7.00	7.00	7.00	7.00	7.00	7.00	7.00	7.00	7.00
1977	8.00	7.00	7.00	8.00	8.00	7.00	7.00	7.00	7.00	7.00	7.00	8.00	8.00	8.00	8.00	8.00	8.00
1978	8.00	8.00	8.00	8.00	8.00	8.00	8.00	8.00	8.00	8.00	8.00	8.00	8.00	8.00	8.00	8.00	8.00
1979	8.00	8.00	8.00	8.00	8.00	8.00	8.00	8.00	8.00	8.00	8.00	8.00	8.00	8.00	8.00	8.00	8.00
1980	8.00	8.00	8.00	8.00	8.00	8.00	8.00	8.00	8.00	8.00	8.00	8.00	8.00	8.00	8.00	8.00	8.00
1981	8.00	8.00	8.00	8.00	8.00	8.00	8.00	8.00	8.00	8.00	8.00	8.00	8.00	8.00	8.00	8.00	8.00
1982	8.00	8.00	8.00	8.00	8.00	8.00	8.00	8.00	8.00	8.00	8.00	8.00	8.00	8.00	8.00	8.00	8.00
1983	8.00	8.00	8.00	8.00	8.00	8.00	8.00	8.00	8.00	8.00	8.00	8.00	8.00	8.00	8.00	8.00	8.00

Call money rate (12) / Taux de l'argent au jour le jour (12)

per cent per annum, end of period / pourcentage par an, fin de période

	Year	Q.1	Q.2	Q.3	Q.4	JAN	FEB	MAR	APR	MAY	JUN	JUL	AUG	SEP	OCT	NOV	DEC
1964																	
1965																	
1966																	
1967																	
1968																	
1969																	
1970																	
1971																	
1972																	
1973	11.75		6.48	9.17	11.75						6.48	8.64	8.98	9.17	10.27	14.78	11.75
1974	5.58	6.67	14.90	10.34	5.58	8.56	8.53	6.67	3.91	15.77	14.90	12.38	14.02	10.34	4.83	5.13	5.58
1975	8.28	6.39	5.44	6.68	8.28	5.56	8.55	6.39	6.10	6.60	5.44	5.98	6.19	6.68	6.70	7.94	8.28
1976	8.44	6.84	12.56	8.54	8.44	11.73	14.04	6.84	5.67	7.88	12.56	18.21	14.66	8.54	7.17	7.45	8.44
1977	7.78	12.40	8.29	15.43	7.78	12.34	18.39	12.40	9.63	9.49	8.29	12.77	18.51	16.43	20.21	10.73	7.78
1978	16.49	1.91	18.03	27.54	16.49	9.11	3.26	1.91	6.71	12.21	18.03	28.01	42.57	27.54	42.86	40.56	16.49
1979	10.75	12.78	10.07	11.87	10.75	11.52	9.72	12.78	19.27	21.41	10.07	15.23	15.74	11.87	8.85	10.39	10.75
1980	18.60	16.65	15.21	14.34	18.60	11.70	12.83	16.65	16.39	19.25	15.21	13.95	14.13	14.34	15.44	16.79	18.60
1981	18.73	12.91	18.53	17.36	18.73	17.10	13.51	12.91	13.89	16.80	18.53	16.66	17.42	17.36	17.27	18.52	18.73
1982	15.81	15.19	22.34	13.78	15.81	14.70	14.98	15.19	12.42	17.84	22.34	17.29	13.96	13.78	20.54	20.28	15.81
1983	16.77	14.14	20.05	20.31	16.77	14.30	15.22	14.14	18.93	20.37	20.05	21.04	23.31	20.31	19.78	17.97	16.77

Rate on 3-month loans (12)
per cent per annum, end of period

Taux de prêts à 3 mois (12)
pourcentage par an, fin de période

	Year	Q.1	Q.2	Q.3	Q.4	JAN	FEB	MAR	APR	MAY	JUN	JUL	AUG	SEP	OCT	NOV	DEC
1964																	
1965																	
1966																	
1967																	
1968																	
1969																	
1970																	
1971																	
1972																	
1973																	
1974																	
1975																	
1976																	
1977	16.37	13.34	13.34	17.61	16.37	14.25	13.38	13.34	13.25	13.88	13.34	15.48	16.61	17.61	20.88	17.95	16.37
1978	17.00	8.58	16.29	24.61	17.00	14.66	10.00	8.58	10.53	13.31	16.29	21.04	26.24	24.61	20.87	30.83	17.00
1979	15.64	13.83	18.63	16.94	15.64	14.10	14.59	13.83	10.60	19.44	18.63	17.84	15.69	16.94	14.54	14.30	15.64
1980	17.76	17.06	18.18	15.29	17.76	15.69	14.34	17.06	17.75	18.78	18.18	16.06	15.59	15.29	15.76	16.32	17.76
1981	16.12	14.94	17.22	16.29	16.12	17.73	16.06	14.94	14.67	16.59	17.22	16.79	16.38	16.29	15.58	16.00	16.12
1982	16.97	14.65	17.73	15.15	16.97	15.76	15.19	14.65	15.51	16.05	17.73	17.45	15.86	15.15	17.12	17.97	16.97
1983	18.99	16.61	20.87	22.40	18.99	16.75	16.96	16.61	18.31	21.20	20.87	22.40	23.41	22.40	21.82	20.59	18.99

Share prices
Madrid Stock Exchange
1980 = 100

Cours des actions
Bourse de Madrid
1980 = 100

	Year	Q.1	Q.2	Q.3	Q.4	JAN	FEB	MAR	APR	MAY	JUN	JUL	AUG	SEP	OCT	NOV	DEC
1964	88	88	87	89	91	89	87	88	87	86	86	88	89	89	90	92	90
1965	92	91	89	94	95	92	90	90	91	90	87	92	95	95	95	95	95
1966	96	97	93	96	97	98	97	96	93	93	94	95	97	96	95	99	98
1967	100	99	98	101	101	99	100	98	100	98	96	95	102	102	104	101	99
1968	117	106	116	122	126	104	106	107	113	118	116	119	125	124	123	125	129
1969	170	149	160	181	189	143	149	156	159	158	161	178	181	133	186	191	190
1970	181	199	176	175	172	195	204	199	182	171	176	178	177	170	174	174	170
1971	183	177	173	186	192	177	179	174	176	179	177	185	189	186	192	191	195
1972	240	213	237	250	260	206	214	220	230	241	240	244	255	249	263	259	257
1973	304	294	306	311	304	279	291	311	317	297	305	298	308	328	330	292	290
1974	308	324	335	304	267	319	331	324	344	326	335	326	312	275	262	279	260
1975	264	276	268	249	265	269	284	274	281	268	254	252	254	242	248	276	270
1976	228	244	245	223	202	257	245	228	254	250	232	230	221	219	202	210	193
1977	157	184	174	143	127	182	190	180	179	172	171	154	147	129	126	125	130
1978	127	121	132	133	120	124	119	121	131	134	132	137	133	128	125	118	116
1979	110	117	116	109	97	111	115	127	118	115	115	110	110	105	99	94	98
1980	100	100	96	105	105	99	102	98	94	96	100	102	104	108	107	104	104
1981	132	117	131	147	133	113	119	119	122	126	143	144	152	144	134	135	130
1982	121	135	127	112	108	135	137	132	131	128	123	121	113	104	108	110	106
1983	124	114	123	126	132	110	111	121	118	126	125	125	122	126	135	135	127

SPAIN

U.S. dollar exchange rate: spot / Taux de change du dollar É.-U. : au comptant

cents per peseta, end of period / cents par peseta, fin de période

	Year	Q.1	Q.2	Q.3	Q.4	JAN	FEB	MAR	APR	MAY	JUN	JUL	AUG	SEP	OCT	NOV	DEC
1964	1.668	1.668	1.668	1.667	1.668	1.668	1.668	1.668	1.668	1.668	1.668	1.667	1.667	1.667	1.668	1.668	1.668
1965	1.667	1.667	1.666	1.665	1.667	1.668	1.668	1.667	1.667	1.666	1.666	1.667	1.667	1.666	1.667	1.667	1.667
1966	1.667	1.666	1.665	1.667	1.667	1.666	1.666	1.666	1.666	1.666	1.665	1.666	1.667	1.667	1.667	1.667	1.667
1967	1.435	1.665	1.664	1.665	1.435	1.666	1.665	1.665	1.664	1.664	1.664	1.665	1.667	1.665	1.666	1.434	1.435
1968	1.432	1.433	1.432	1.433	1.432	1.434	1.432	1.433	1.434	1.433	1.432	1.433	1.434	1.433	1.433	1.433	1.432
1969	1.427	1.430	1.428	1.431	1.427	1.432	1.432	1.430	1.428	1.426	1.428	1.429	1.431	1.431	1.426	1.425	1.427
1970	1.434	1.430	1.434	1.435	1.434	1.428	1.430	1.430	1.431	1.434	1.434	1.434	1.434	1.435	1.434	1.434	1.434
1971	1.515	1.435	1.435	1.456	1.515	1.434	1.434	1.435	1.435	1.435	1.435	1.436	1.438	1.456	1.456	1.457	1.515
1972	1.573	1.546	1.571	1.573	1.573	1.515	1.515	1.546	1.547	1.547	1.571	1.573	1.573	1.573	1.573	1.573	1.573
1973	1.756	1.713	1.721	1.759	1.756	1.573	1.712	1.713	1.719	1.712	1.721	1.760	1.758	1.759	1.746	1.742	1.756
1974	1.782	1.688	1.748	1.738	1.782	1.690	1.686	1.688	1.724	1.745	1.748	1.754	1.733	1.738	1.742	1.762	1.782
1975	1.673	1.786	1.783	1.673	1.673	1.778	1.797	1.786	1.780	1.793	1.783	1.714	1.713	1.673	1.699	1.677	1.673
1976	1.464	1.494	1.473	1.476	1.464	1.672	1.502	1.494	1.483	1.474	1.473	1.467	1.472	1.476	1.466	1.464	1.464
1977	1.236	1.456	1.437	1.181	1.236	1.453	1.448	1.456	1.454	1.448	1.437	1.177	1.183	1.181	1.200	1.211	1.236
1978	1.426	1.250	1.269	1.384	1.426	1.241	1.246	1.250	1.237	1.245	1.269	1.302	1.357	1.384	1.481	1.398	1.426
1979	1.512	1.466	1.515	1.515	1.512	1.431	1.448	1.466	1.515	1.512	1.515	1.515	1.515	1.515	1.506	1.506	1.512
1980	1.262	1.383	1.427	1.353	1.262	1.509	1.492	1.383	1.421	1.425	1.427	1.391	1.374	1.353	1.330	1.290	1.262
1981	1.026	1.172	1.051	1.037	1.026	1.211	1.152	1.172	1.120	1.087	1.051	1.015	1.025	1.037	1.037	1.059	1.026
1982	0.796	0.936	0.901	0.877	0.796	1.016	0.968	0.936	0.966	0.954	0.901	0.894	0.885	0.877	0.851	0.845	0.796
1983	0.638	0.732	0.688	0.658	0.638	0.773	0.765	0.732	0.731	0.715	0.688	0.667	0.654	0.658	0.657	0.644	0.638

Official reserves excluding gold / Réserves officielles, or exclu

million SDR's, end of period / millions de DTS, fin de période

	Year	Q.1	Q.2	Q.3	Q.4	JAN	FEB	MAR	APR	MAY	JUN	JUL	AUG	SEP	OCT	NOV	DEC
1964	898	638	690	884	893	610	614	638	642	648	690	738	819	884	911	914	898
1965	599	803	672	713	599	910	862	803	734	664	672	655	693	713	667	635	599
1966	421	480	408	492	421	557	517	480	437	436	408	416	464	492	462	433	421
1967	264	253	205	323	264	377	319	253	204	198	205	281	333	323	285	247	264
1968	364	276	269	381	364	307	280	276	307	271	269	301	356	381	381	347	364
1969	497	311	333	321	497	343	352	311	312	315	333	402	377	321	324	326	497
1970	1319	530	606	1057	1319	566	584	580	560	573	606	811	969	1057	1133	1199	1319
1971	2512	1579	1860	2450	2512	1484	1511	1579	1635	1743	1860	2082	2327	2450	2556	2638	2512
1972	4120	2851	3282	3826	4120	2625	2718	2851	2903	3027	3282	3499	3718	3826	3924	4025	4120
1973	5114	3928	4284	5001	5114	4257	3910	3928	4048	4162	4284	4795	4914	5001	5067	5050	5114
1974	4798	4864	4558	4940	4798	4969	4978	4864	4697	4624	4558	4762	4848	4940	4809	4701	4798
1975	4703	4524	4555	4973	4703	4583	4463	4524	4325	4380	4555	4709	4957	4973	4814	4595	4703
1976	4049	4608	4124	4280	4049	4739	4794	4608	4477	4312	4124	4169	4411	4230	4152	4140	4049
1977	4920	3746	2857	4645	4920	3890	3779	3746	3664	3420	2857	3439	4260	4645	4769	5005	4920
1978	7762	5403	6275	7578	7762	5178	5374	5403	5672	5813	6275	6734	7356	7578	7360	7457	7762
1979	10039	8492	9346	10109	10039	7927	8108	8492	8703	9008	9346	9500	9907	10109	10244	10225	10039
1980	9302	9301	8898	9715	9302	10197	9716	9301	8969	9055	8898	9704	9963	9715	9544	9375	9302
1981	9283	8816	9062	9876	9283	9296	9170	8816	8777	8497	9062	9553	9727	9876	9868	9463	9283
1982	6939	8360	8001	8116	6939	9305	8998	8360	8235	7960	8001	8243	8356	8116	7163	6493	6939
1983	7070	5726	5430	6473	7070	6893	6574	5726	5584	5660	5430	5783	6352	6473	6740	6755	7070

Net foreign position: (9)(11)(13) commercial banks / Position extérieure nette : banques commerciales (13)(11)(9)

billion pesetas, end of period / milliards de pesetas, fin de période

	Year	Q.1	Q.2	Q.3	Q.4	JAN	FEB	MAR	APR	MAY	JUN	JUL	AUG	SEP	OCT	NOV	DEC
1964	-4	-4	-4	-3	-4	-4	-5	-4	-4	-4	-4	-3	-4	-3	-3	-3	-4
1965	-7	-5	-5	-6	-7	-4	-4	-5	-5	-5	-5	-5	-5	-6	-6	-7	-7
1966	-7	-8	-10	-8	-7	-6	-7	-8	-9	-9	-10	-10	-8	-8	-9	-8	-7
1967	-11	-8	-10	-9	-11	-8	-8	-8	-8	-8	-10	-9	-9	-9	-9	-8	-11
1968	-8	-8	-10	-8	-8	-10	-9	-8	-9	-9	-10	-9	-10	-8	-7	-7	-8
1969	-5	-8	-7	-6	-5	-7	-6	-8	-6	-5	-7	-8	-7	-6	-6	-6	-5
1970	-15	-8	-13	-10	-15	-6	-7	-8	-10	-10	-13	-11	-11	-10	-10	-12	-15
1971	-31	-18	-24	-27	-31	-18	-19	-18	-22	-19	-24	-22	-27	-27	-28	-30	-31
1972	-41	-35	-38	-36	-41	-31	-31	-35	-33	-38	-38	-41	-37	-36	-35	-38	-41
1973	-4	-8	-16	-13	-4	-14	-12	-8	-10	-14	-16	-15	-10	-13	-12	-10	-4
1974	58	-60	-58	-60	53	-52	-52	-60	-57	-58	-58	-52	-52	-60	-57	-58	58
1975	-103	-73	-74	-89	-103	-62	-68	-73	-73	-77	-74	-83	-87	-89	-87	-91	-103
1976	-170	-132	-144	-164	-170	-116	-131	-132	-130	-139	-144	-160	-165	-164	-171	-169	-170
1977	-261	-173	-162	-258	-261	-168	-162	-173	-170	-166	-162	-217	-251	-258	-273	-271	-261
1978	-181	-258	-233	-218	-181	-256	-269	-258	-246	-242	-238	-220	-239	-218	-225	-185	-181
1979	-180	-189	-207	-205	-180	-185	-190	-189	-190	-211	-207	-205	-194	-206	-218	-166	-180
1980	-225	-199	-226	-217	-225	-191	-198	-199	-189	-184	-226	-220	-219	-217	-233	-225	-225
1981	-267	-241	-265	-213	-267	-230	-261	-241	-265	-263	-265	-264	-211	-213	-213	-211	-267
1982	-236	-254	-186	-181	-236	-263	-298	-254	-224	-205	-186	-163	-193	-181	-94	-143	-236
1983	-259	-209	-276	-323	-259	-248	-207	-209	-257	-264	-276	-294	-239	-323	-357	-369	-259

Balance of payments: net trade (14) / Balance des paiements : balance commerciale (14)

billion pesetas / milliards de pesetas

	Year	Q.1	Q.2	Q.3	Q.4	JAN	FEB	MAR	APR	MAY	JUN	JUL	AUG	SEP	OCT	NOV	DEC
1964																	
1965																	
1966																	
1967																	
1968																	
1969	-148	-24	-40	-44	-40	-8	-6	-10	-12	-15	-13	-16	-14	-14	-17	-12	-10
1970	-132	-30	-35	-36	-31	-9	-10	-10	-12	-10	-13	-12	-12	-12	-12	-11	-9
1971	-126	-32	-41	-31	-22	-7	-13	-11	-15	-11	-15	-12	-9	-11	-8	-8	-6
1972	-164	-33	-44	-43	-44	-11	-11	-11	-16	-15	-13	-16	-15	-13	-19	-11	-15
1973	-212	-35	-49	-68	-61	-10	-9	-17	-17	-16	-16	-24	-25	-19	-22	-21	-18
1974	-429	-79	-126	-104	-119	-30	-22	-27	-44	-47	-35	-36	-32	-36	-41	-38	-41
1975	-412	-112	-106	-94	-99	-39	-39	-35	-40	-30	-37	-35	-27	-33	-37	-31	-32
1976	-489	-101	-117	-139	-132	-27	-21	-54	-34	-40	-43	-55	-40	-44	-43	-42	-46
1977	-515	-137	-153	-116	-110	-47	-45	-45	-44	-49	-60	-48	-29	-39	-28	-39	-42
1978	-303	-70	-82	-65	-86	-14	-25	-31	-22	-37	-24	-28	-19	-18	-34	-30	-22
1979	-491	-68	-107	-154	-161	-24	-22	-22	-28	-33	-46	-60	-51	-43	-56	-47	-58
1980	-915	-196	-240	-255	-224	-51	-79	-67	-73	-74	-93	-85	-76	-94	-85	-69	-70
1981	-1042	-264	-288	-246	-243	-58	-101	-105	-118	-87	-83	-85	-69	-92	-67	-77	-100
1982	-1157	-261	-298	-265	-334	-66	-88	-107	-83	-93	-122	-89	-82	-94	-127	-111	-96
1983	-1210	-331	-316	-278	-285	-87	-114	-131	-109	-106	-101	-83	-95	-101	-107	-95	-83

Balance of payments: current balance (14) / Balance des paiements : opérations courantes, nettes (14)

billion pesetas / milliards de pesetas

	Year	Q.1	Q.2	Q.3	Q.4	JAN	FEB	MAR	APR	MAY	JUN	JUL	AUG	SEP	OCT	NOV	DEC
1964																	
1965																	
1966																	
1967																	
1968																	
1969	-35	-7	-16	1	-14	-1	-1	-5	-5	-7	-4	0	1	-0	-7	-4	-3
1970	16	-6	-2	21	2	-1	-3	-2	-2	-1	1	10	7	4	2	0	0
1971	62	-2	3	40	21	3	-4	-1	-4	2	4	13	16	11	10	5	6
1972	39	6	6	31	-4	3	-0	3	-2	3	6	10	13	8	-2	1	-3
1973	33	4	13	25	-9	5	3	-4	1	2	10	14	8	3	-0	-6	-3
1974	-187	-38	-69	-14	-66	-16	-10	-12	-28	-26	-15	-6	1	-9	-20	-21	-25
1975	-171	-64	-45	-7	-55	-21	-24	-19	-23	-11	-12	-5	5	-8	-21	-19	-16
1976	-266	-54	-67	-66	-79	-15	-3	-35	-21	-23	-23	-33	-12	-22	-22	-25	-32
1977	-195	-107	-116	61	-34	-37	-38	-32	-29	-36	-51	14	43	3	0	-17	-19
1978	134	-7	17	118	7	11	-7	-11	7	-12	22	31	53	34	8	-4	3
1979	-44	9	-4	8	-56	4	-2	7	0	0	-5	-8	10	6	-10	-16	-30
1980	-414	-109	-135	-62	-107	-11	-58	-41	-39	-34	-62	-24	-3	-36	-32	-40	-35
1981	-529	-177	-193	-12	-143	-22	-73	-81	-86	-57	-51	-12	20	-20	-9	-53	-86
1982	-601	-162	-168	-18	-254	-26	-57	-79	-44	-49	-75	-1	17	-34	-88	-88	-78
1983	-473	-247	-162	29	-93	-35	-91	-121	-61	-51	-50	23	18	-12	-19	-14	-61

Balance of payments: net capital movements (14) / Balance des paiements : mouvements de capitaux, nets (14)

billion pesetas / milliards de pesetas

	Year	Q.1	Q.2	Q.3	Q.4	JAN	FEB	MAR	APR	MAY	JUN	JUL	AUG	SEP	OCT	NOV	DEC
1964																	
1965																	
1966																	
1967																	
1968																	
1969	30	7	8	7	8	2	3	1	1	3	4	4	3	1	3	2	4
1970	40	10	8	11	12	4	4	2	2	4	2	4	4	3	2	5	5
1971	39	21	16	9	-7	6	8	6	5	6	4	2	4	3	2	-7	-2
1972	51	7	12	9	23	1	2	4	7	2	3	3	4	2	11	5	7
1973	45	14	3	10	18	7	3	4	6	2	-5	0	5	5	4	7	6
1974	91	15	26	25	25	5	6	3	6	6	15	8	6	11	10	8	7
1975	140	37	41	28	35	3	10	23	8	12	21	7	17	4	13	5	16
1976	135	28	8	45	54	7	3	18	-3	4	7	10	27	8	11	25	19
1977	255	78	53	55	67	28	30	21	23	16	12	21	13	19	9	43	15
1978	134	64	76	-6	0	10	31	22	29	22	24	10	-3	-14	-13	-10	23
1979	162	33	53	37	38	11	-1	23	19	5	29	22	4	11	8	15	15
1980	303	39	99	100	64	11	12	16	26	33	41	40	31	29	14	26	24
1981	444	114	172	112	46	29	34	52	60	42	70	53	30	29	15	16	15
1982	280	59	119	7	96	34	4	21	33	13	74	17	-22	12	7	27	62
1983	438	79	44	101	214	13	64	3	15	48	-19	14	62	25	49	39	126

SPAIN

Imports c.i.f. / Importations c.a.f.

billion pesetas, monthly averages / milliards de pesetas, moyennes mensuelles

	Year	Q.1	Q.2	Q.3	Q.4	JAN	FEB	MAR	APR	MAY	JUN	JUL	AUG	SEP	OCT	NOV	DEC
1964	11.3	11.0	10.7	11.3	12.2	11.4	10.9	10.6	10.7	10.2	11.3	12.1	11.0	10.6	11.0	11.5	14.2
1965	15.1	13.0	15.3	15.4	16.7	13.0	12.6	13.5	15.7	15.2	14.9	15.3	15.3	15.6	15.7	16.1	18.3
1966	18.0	19.1	18.8	16.6	17.4	18.7	18.4	20.2	18.7	19.1	18.5	17.2	16.2	16.3	16.4	16.9	18.9
1967	17.7	17.7	18.7	16.9	17.4	17.6	17.8	17.7	17.9	19.1	19.0	17.4	17.0	16.2	14.7	17.8	19.7
1968	20.6	20.3	20.3	19.8	21.3	22.4	18.9	19.7	21.4	21.1	18.3	19.0	21.0	19.4	21.9	22.0	21.6
1969	24.7	21.7	24.6	24.4	28.0	23.3	19.4	22.5	24.8	25.9	23.2	23.2	25.1	24.9	29.3	28.0	25.9
1970	27.7	26.8	29.6	26.0	28.4	28.7	25.3	26.5	33.5	24.7	30.6	28.5	24.2	25.2	29.4	28.0	27.6
1971	29.0	27.3	29.6	28.6	30.5	28.2	25.6	28.2	28.0	29.3	31.6	30.6	24.7	30.3	31.5	31.6	28.4
1972	36.5	35.1	38.0	34.7	38.2	33.0	36.8	35.4	37.7	36.4	39.9	36.5	35.1	32.6	38.6	40.1	35.8
1973	46.8	42.4	46.9	46.3	51.7	39.9	44.4	42.8	42.7	48.2	49.8	43.9	47.1	47.9	51.5	51.4	52.1
1974	74.1	62.3	81.2	74.2	78.7	60.3	55.7	70.8	80.6	81.4	81.6	82.6	67.2	72.4	76.8	81.7	77.5
1975	77.7	77.6	84.7	70.2	78.3	74.6	79.1	79.1	90.9	83.3	79.8	72.8	70.9	66.8	84.7	78.6	71.7
1976	97.5	86.5	99.8	96.4	107.4	81.3	90.7	87.3	92.3	108.8	98.4	98.1	97.4	95.9	93.8	105.3	123.2
1977	112.5	96.5	116.0	116.0	121.7	77.8	108.6	102.9	107.1	126.4	114.5	103.2	121.8	123.0	118.2	122.5	124.5
1978	119.3	119.0	125.4	110.7	122.1	122.3	131.5	103.3	110.2	129.6	136.3	127.7	96.1	108.3	126.1	125.0	115.2
1979	142.0	123.9	130.1	142.8	171.3	118.1	137.3	116.3	125.7	141.2	123.4	159.3	130.3	138.9	163.4	171.8	178.7
1980	204.2	180.8	207.3	195.4	233.4	160.0	189.9	192.6	224.9	189.3	207.6	188.1	153.0	245.2	208.3	224.3	267.6
1981	247.5	215.8	262.3	231.1	280.9	174.3	225.4	247.7	245.0	272.9	269.0	258.7	227.7	206.9	323.6	231.9	287.3
1982	288.8	266.8	289.5	262.4	336.5	244.0	261.1	295.3	298.8	270.4	299.4	292.1	228.9	266.1	238.9	361.3	409.3
1983	348.0	334.9	357.0	305.6	394.6	312.1	336.8	356.0	341.2	382.7	347.1	329.3	300.7	286.8	336.3	395.0	452.6

Exports f.o.b. / Exportations f.o.b.

billion pesetas, monthly averages / milliards de pesetas, moyennes mensuelles

	Year	Q.1	Q.2	Q.3	Q.4	JAN	FEB	MAR	APR	MAY	JUN	JUL	AUG	SEP	OCT	NOV	DEC
1964	4.8	5.1	4.6	3.3	6.1	5.4	5.0	4.9	5.1	4.8	3.9	3.3	3.3	3.4	4.5	5.6	8.1
1965	4.8	4.4	4.3	3.8	6.9	4.0	4.5	4.7	4.5	4.4	4.1	4.3	3.4	3.6	4.7	5.9	10.1
1966	6.3	5.0	7.0	5.3	7.8	3.8	4.8	6.3	6.7	7.9	6.4	5.6	5.0	5.2	5.4	8.3	9.8
1967	7.1	7.0	6.3	6.0	8.9	6.6	7.3	7.0	6.1	6.5	6.4	5.9	5.9	6.1	6.3	9.3	11.3
1968	9.3	9.0	8.5	8.2	11.3	9.0	8.2	9.7	9.2	8.8	7.6	8.5	8.6	7.6	9.9	10.6	13.5
1969	11.1	11.0	10.5	9.4	13.4	10.7	9.9	12.5	11.6	10.2	9.7	10.4	9.7	8.1	10.4	12.7	17.2
1970	13.9	12.9	14.4	11.8	16.6	14.4	10.9	13.3	14.1	14.2	14.8	11.9	11.3	12.3	12.7	16.7	20.5
1971	17.1	16.4	17.4	14.7	20.1	19.3	14.1	15.9	18.9	18.0	15.4	16.9	13.4	13.7	16.7	19.2	24.2
1972	20.4	21.3	19.9	18.0	22.6	23.6	18.7	21.5	19.5	22.4	17.9	18.2	15.4	20.3	20.9	22.7	24.1
1973	25.2	25.2	24.2	24.1	27.4	26.3	24.7	24.5	21.5	26.4	24.7	26.0	22.0	24.5	27.8	25.8	28.5
1974	34.1	30.6	33.6	29.8	42.2	34.8	26.3	30.6	34.3	35.2	31.3	26.7	28.3	34.4	44.4	41.8	40.6
1975	35.8	37.3	36.6	30.1	43.2	41.2	39.2	31.4	36.0	38.6	35.2	35.7	21.5	33.1	44.2	41.1	44.2
1976	48.6	47.8	41.8	46.4	58.6	49.4	48.7	45.1	38.1	39.8	47.5	52.0	41.6	45.4	44.3	55.3	76.3
1977	64.6	58.9	59.8	60.8	78.9	51.3	62.1	63.4	56.2	68.7	54.5	60.2	60.3	61.9	73.6	71.5	91.7
1978	83.5	82.0	85.2	73.9	92.9	77.2	88.5	80.2	86.9	84.8	83.8	84.6	70.1	66.9	80.4	93.2	105.1
1979	101.8	98.1	99.9	92.1	117.0	92.0	103.4	98.9	94.3	101.2	104.4	103.1	95.7	77.3	92.3	120.0	138.7
1980	124.4	114.4	122.7	102.2	158.5	96.8	119.5	126.8	120.9	123.5	123.8	102.7	96.9	105.9	133.5	125.6	216.3
1981	157.4	122.9	156.9	163.5	186.2	97.6	129.6	141.6	132.5	161.8	176.4	212.7	150.9	126.8	151.8	175.5	231.2
1982	188.2	182.1	171.6	174.4	224.6	146.1	203.7	196.6	170.5	183.6	160.6	220.7	130.8	171.7	168.1	225.9	279.7
1983	236.6	206.8	236.5	219.6	283.4	162.5	188.4	269.5	173.6	283.8	252.0	234.2	196.3	228.2	251.1	292.6	306.4

Trade balance (f.o.b. — c.i.f.) / Balance commerciale (f.o.b. — c.a.f.)

billion pesetas, monthly averages / milliards de pesetas, moyennes mensuelles

	Year	Q.1	Q.2	Q.3	Q.4	JAN	FEB	MAR	APR	MAY	JUN	JUL	AUG	SEP	OCT	NOV	DEC
1964	-6.5	-5.9	-6.1	-7.9	-6.2	-6.0	-5.9	-5.7	-5.7	-5.4	-7.3	-8.9	-7.7	-7.2	-6.5	-5.9	-6.1
1965	-10.3	-8.7	-10.9	-11.6	-9.8	-9.1	-8.1	-8.8	-11.2	-10.8	-10.8	-11.1	-11.8	-12.0	-11.0	-10.2	-8.3
1966	-11.7	-14.2	-11.8	-11.3	-9.6	-14.9	-13.7	-13.9	-12.0	-11.2	-12.1	-11.5	-11.2	-11.0	-11.0	-8.6	-9.1
1967	-10.6	-10.7	-12.3	-10.9	-8.5	-11.0	-10.4	-10.8	-11.8	-12.6	-12.6	-11.5	-11.1	-10.0	-8.4	-8.6	-8.4
1968	-11.3	-11.3	-11.7	-11.5	-10.5	-13.3	-10.6	-10.0	-12.2	-12.3	-10.7	-10.5	-12.3	-11.8	-12.0	-11.4	-8.2
1969	-13.6	-10.7	-14.1	-15.0	-14.6	-12.5	-9.5	-10.1	-13.2	-15.7	-13.5	-12.9	-15.4	-16.8	-18.9	-15.2	-9.7
1970	-13.8	-14.0	-15.2	-14.1	-11.7	-14.4	-14.4	-13.2	-19.4	-10.5	-15.8	-16.6	-12.9	-12.9	-16.8	-11.3	-7.2
1971	-11.9	-10.9	-12.2	-13.9	-10.5	-8.9	-11.4	-12.3	-9.1	-11.3	-16.2	-13.7	-11.3	-16.6	-14.8	-12.3	-4.3
1972	-16.1	-13.8	-18.1	-16.7	-15.6	-9.5	-18.1	-13.8	-18.1	-14.1	-22.0	-18.3	-19.7	-12.3	-17.7	-17.4	-11.7
1973	-21.6	-17.2	-22.7	-22.2	-24.3	-13.6	-19.7	-18.3	-21.2	-21.8	-25.1	-18.0	-25.2	-23.4	-23.7	-25.5	-23.6
1974	-40.0	-31.7	-47.7	-44.3	-36.4	-25.5	-29.4	-40.2	-46.4	-46.3	-50.3	-56.1	-38.9	-38.0	-32.5	-39.9	-36.9
1975	-40.9	-40.3	-48.1	-40.1	-35.1	-33.4	-39.9	-47.7	-54.9	-44.7	-44.6	-37.1	-49.4	-33.8	-40.4	-37.4	-27.4
1976	-48.9	-38.7	-58.0	-50.1	-43.8	-31.9	-42.1	-42.2	-54.2	-69.0	-50.9	-44.0	-55.8	-50.5	-49.4	-50.0	-46.9
1977	-47.9	-37.6	-56.2	-55.1	-42.8	-26.6	-46.6	-39.6	-50.9	-57.7	-60.0	-43.0	-61.4	-61.0	-44.6	-51.0	-32.8
1978	-35.8	-37.1	-40.2	-36.8	-29.2	-45.2	-43.0	-23.1	-23.3	-44.8	-52.5	-43.0	-25.9	-41.4	-45.7	-31.8	-10.2
1979	-40.2	-25.8	-30.1	-50.7	-54.3	-26.0	-33.9	-17.3	-31.4	-40.0	-19.0	-56.1	-34.6	-61.5	-71.2	-51.8	-40.0
1980	-79.8	-66.4	-84.5	-93.3	-75.0	-63.2	-70.3	-65.8	-104.0	-65.8	-83.8	-84.4	-56.1	-139.3	-74.8	-98.7	-51.4
1981	-90.2	-92.9	-105.4	-67.6	-94.8	-76.8	-95.8	-106.1	-112.5	-111.1	-92.7	-46.0	-76.8	-80.0	-171.9	-56.4	-56.0
1982	-100.6	-64.7	-117.9	-87.9	-111.9	-97.9	-57.5	-98.7	-128.3	-86.7	-133.8	-71.4	-98.0	-94.4	-70.8	-135.4	-129.6
1983	-111.5	-128.1	-120.5	-86.0	-111.3	-149.6	-148.4	-86.5	-167.6	-98.9	-95.1	-95.0	-104.5	-58.6	-85.2	-102.4	-146.2

Imports c.i.f. / Importations c.a.f.

billion pesetas, monthly averages — Adjusted - Corrigé — milliards de pesetas, moyennes mensuelles

Year	Q.1	Q.2	Q.3	Q.4	JAN	FEB	MAR	APR	MAY	JUN	JUL	AUG	SEP	OCT	NOV	DEC
1964	10.9	10.5	11.7	12.2	11.5	10.9	10.4	10.3	9.9	11.2	12.5	11.2	11.3	11.6	11.8	13.1
1965	13.0	14.8	16.0	16.7	13.0	12.7	13.4	15.1	14.6	14.6	15.8	15.7	16.5	16.4	16.6	17.0
1966	19.1	18.0	17.4	17.4	18.4	18.8	20.2	17.9	18.2	18.0	17.8	16.8	17.5	16.9	17.4	17.9
1967	17.7	17.8	17.8	17.3	17.0	18.4	17.7	17.1	18.1	18.2	18.1	17.8	17.5	14.8	18.1	18.9
1968	20.0	19.3	20.9	21.7	20.9	19.4	19.8	20.5	19.9	17.5	19.7	22.0	21.0	21.5	22.1	21.4
1969	21.9	23.4	25.8	27.8	22.5	20.7	22.7	23.7	24.5	21.8	23.8	26.3	27.2	28.4	27.8	27.3
1970	27.2	28.0	27.3	28.4	28.0	27.1	26.6	32.2	23.4	28.4	28.9	25.4	27.6	28.4	27.9	28.9
1971	27.7	27.8	29.9	30.8	27.7	27.1	28.2	26.8	27.7	29.0	30.5	26.0	33.2	30.7	31.4	30.3
1972	35.5	35.6	36.5	39.0	33.0	38.3	35.0	36.1	34.2	36.5	37.0	36.9	35.7	38.3	40.2	38.7
1973	42.6	43.7	48.5	53.3	40.4	45.1	42.1	40.7	44.7	45.8	43.4	49.4	52.6	52.1	51.4	56.5
1974	63.6	77.5	77.3	78.2	62.7	56.9	71.3	79.2	74.7	78.7	79.8	73.5	78.5	78.5	79.9	76.1
1975	79.1	81.2	73.3	77.7	77.8	79.7	79.8	89.0	77.5	77.0	69.6	77.7	72.5	86.2	77.1	69.7
1976	88.0	95.6	100.3	105.8	85.3	90.8	87.9	91.2	100.9	94.6	92.8	105.8	102.2	95.4	103.2	118.9
1977	98.3	111.8	121.4	119.8	82.7	108.4	103.7	105.7	118.8	110.8	100.2	133.6	130.3	120.0	119.4	120.1
1978	121.3	121.0	116.1	119.5	128.8	131.5	103.8	107.6	122.8	132.6	124.9	108.8	114.5	128.1	121.1	109.2
1979	126.0	125.4	150.1	166.9	124.8	137.8	115.3	121.6	134.1	120.5	155.8	149.5	145.0	166.1	166.1	168.6
1980	183.2	201.5	203.4	226.4	169.5	191.3	188.8	219.5	180.9	204.0	183.8	173.5	252.9	212.3	216.9	249.9
1981	218.2	256.4	243.7	271.6	185.3	227.8	241.3	240.5	262.9	265.9	252.3	263.9	214.9	330.3	222.3	262.2
1982	269.4	281.4	275.6	323.4	258.7	264.6	284.9	291.5	256.7	295.9	285.5	264.5	276.7	248.8	347.7	373.5
1983	337.5	348.1	324.1	378.5	330.3	340.8	341.5	335.5	364.9	343.9	323.0	349.7	299.5	350.2	377.0	408.2

Exports f.o.b. / Exportations f.o.b.

billion pesetas, monthly averages — Adjusted - Corrigé — milliards de pesetas, moyennes mensuelles

Year	Q.1	Q.2	Q.3	Q.4	JAN	FEB	MAR	APR	MAY	JUN	JUL	AUG	SEP	OCT	NOV	DEC
1964	4.7	4.7	4.4	5.0	5.0	4.7	4.5	4.7	4.8	4.7	4.2	4.4	4.4	4.7	4.7	5.7
1965	4.1	4.4	4.9	5.7	3.7	4.3	4.4	4.3	4.4	4.6	5.4	4.6	4.6	5.1	4.9	7.1
1966	4.7	7.2	6.6	6.6	3.6	4.7	5.9	6.5	7.9	7.1	6.8	6.4	6.7	5.8	7.1	6.9
1967	6.7	6.5	7.3	7.7	6.2	7.4	6.4	5.9	6.6	7.0	6.9	7.3	7.8	7.0	8.0	8.0
1968	8.7	8.7	9.8	10.1	8.4	8.6	9.0	8.8	8.8	8.4	9.6	10.5	9.5	11.1	9.4	9.7
1969	10.6	10.6	11.1	12.0	9.7	10.5	11.6	11.1	10.0	10.8	11.5	11.7	10.0	11.6	11.6	12.8
1970	12.2	14.6	13.9	15.1	12.6	11.7	12.5	13.5	13.8	16.5	13.0	13.8	15.0	13.8	15.6	15.8
1971	15.6	17.4	17.0	18.4	16.4	15.2	15.1	18.3	17.1	17.0	18.0	16.7	16.4	17.5	18.2	19.6
1972	20.1	20.0	20.8	21.1	19.8	19.8	20.8	19.3	21.0	19.5	19.2	19.5	23.7	21.0	21.7	20.6
1973	23.8	24.4	27.6	25.7	22.1	25.4	23.9	21.9	24.7	26.6	27.0	27.8	28.0	26.8	24.9	25.6
1974	29.9	33.8	34.8	38.0	32.0	26.2	31.4	34.7	34.0	32.7	29.1	37.0	38.3	41.2	38.7	34.1
1975	36.1	37.1	34.5	39.2	38.3	38.0	32.0	37.0	37.6	36.6	37.8	28.3	37.3	42.2	38.6	36.7
1976	46.0	42.6	52.9	52.8	47.1	46.0	45.0	39.7	39.0	49.1	53.6	52.8	52.1	44.1	52.5	61.7
1977	57.1	60.4	69.5	72.2	51.1	58.3	62.0	58.4	66.5	56.3	61.8	74.4	72.5	74.8	68.5	73.4
1978	80.0	85.4	83.7	85.2	79.5	82.9	77.7	89.5	81.6	85.0	85.4	85.3	80.2	83.5	88.9	83.2
1979	96.8	99.4	103.9	106.0	98.5	97.6	94.5	97.5	96.6	103.9	102.4	115.3	93.8	97.0	113.8	107.1
1980	114.3	121.7	115.4	140.7	108.8	114.6	119.4	126.5	116.8	121.9	101.0	117.6	127.6	140.2	119.5	162.5
1981	124.4	155.5	178.4	166.9	114.6	126.5	132.2	142.0	151.4	173.1	199.2	184.2	151.7	161.2	165.1	174.4
1982	184.6	171.8	189.7	200.3	174.3	159.7	179.8	186.5	169.7	159.1	205.0	162.9	201.0	179.3	208.8	212.9
1983	208.6	233.0	242.9	257.0	195.8	188.2	241.7	194.4	257.0	247.6	220.1	244.7	264.0	265.8	268.1	237.1

Trade balance (f.o.b. — c.i.f.) / Balance commerciale (f.o.b. — c.a.f.)

billion pesetas, monthly averages — Adjusted - Corrigé — milliards de pesetas, moyennes mensuelles

Year	Q.1	Q.2	Q.3	Q.4	JAN	FEB	MAR	APR	MAY	JUN	JUL	AUG	SEP	OCT	NOV	DEC
1964	-6.2	-5.8	-7.3	-7.1	-6.5	-6.2	-5.9	-5.6	-5.1	-6.6	-8.3	-6.8	-6.9	-6.8	-7.2	-7.4
1965	-8.9	-10.3	-11.2	-11.0	-9.3	-8.4	-9.0	-10.8	-10.2	-10.0	-10.5	-11.1	-12.0	-11.3	-11.7	-9.9
1966	-14.4	-10.9	-10.8	-10.8	-14.8	-14.0	-14.3	-11.4	-10.3	-10.8	-11.0	-10.5	-10.8	-11.1	-10.3	-10.9
1967	-11.0	-11.3	-10.5	-9.6	-10.8	-10.9	-11.3	-11.2	-11.6	-11.2	-11.2	-10.5	-9.7	-7.8	-10.1	-10.9
1968	-11.4	-10.6	-11.0	-11.6	-12.5	-10.8	-10.8	-11.7	-11.1	-9.0	-10.1	-11.5	-11.5	-10.4	-12.6	-11.6
1969	-11.3	-12.7	-14.7	-15.8	-12.8	-10.2	-11.1	-12.7	-14.5	-11.0	-12.3	-14.6	-17.2	-16.8	-16.2	-14.5
1970	-15.0	-13.4	-13.3	-13.3	-15.4	-15.4	-14.1	-18.7	-9.6	-11.9	-15.9	-11.5	-12.6	-14.6	-12.3	-13.1
1971	-12.1	-10.4	-12.9	-12.4	-11.3	-11.9	-13.1	-8.5	-10.6	-12.0	-12.5	-9.3	-16.9	-13.2	-13.3	-10.7
1972	-15.3	-15.6	-15.8	-18.0	-13.2	-18.5	-14.3	-16.8	-13.2	-17.0	-17.6	-17.4	-12.1	-17.3	-18.5	-18.1
1973	-18.8	-19.4	-20.9	-27.6	-18.3	-19.7	-18.2	-18.8	-20.1	-19.2	-16.4	-21.6	-24.6	-25.3	-26.5	-30.9
1974	-33.8	-43.7	-42.4	-40.2	-30.7	-30.7	-39.9	-44.4	-40.6	-46.0	-50.6	-36.5	-40.2	-37.3	-41.2	-42.0
1975	-43.0	-44.1	-38.8	-38.5	-39.4	-41.7	-47.7	-52.0	-39.8	-40.5	-31.8	-49.5	-35.2	-44.0	-38.5	-33.1
1976	-42.0	-53.0	-47.4	-53.1	-38.2	-44.8	-43.0	-51.5	-61.9	-45.6	-39.1	-53.0	-50.2	-51.3	-50.7	-57.2
1977	-41.1	-51.4	-51.8	-47.6	-31.6	-50.1	-41.7	-47.3	-52.3	-54.5	-38.5	-59.3	-57.8	-45.2	-50.9	-46.7
1978	-41.3	-35.6	-32.4	-34.3	-49.4	-48.6	-26.1	-18.1	-41.1	-47.6	-39.5	-23.5	-34.2	-44.6	-32.3	-26.0
1979	-29.1	-26.1	-46.3	-61.0	-26.3	-40.3	-20.8	-24.1	-37.5	-16.6	-53.5	-34.2	-51.2	-69.1	-52.3	-61.5
1980	-68.9	-79.3	-88.0	-85.7	-60.7	-76.7	-69.4	-93.1	-64.1	-82.2	-82.8	-56.0	-125.3	-72.1	-97.4	-87.5
1981	-93.8	-100.9	-65.3	-104.7	-70.8	-101.4	-109.1	-98.5	-111.5	-92.8	-53.1	-79.7	-63.2	-169.1	-57.2	-87.8
1982	-84.8	-109.6	-85.9	-123.0	-84.3	-64.9	-105.1	-105.0	-87.0	-136.8	-80.5	-101.6	-75.7	-69.6	-138.9	-160.7
1983	-128.9	-115.1	-81.1	-121.4	-134.5	-152.6	-99.8	-141.1	-107.9	-96.3	-102.9	-105.0	-35.5	-84.4	-108.9	-171.1

NOTES

1. The original base of the index is 1962 to 1974, and 1972 from 1975. The seasonally unadjusted series is not adjusted for unequal number of working days in the month.
2. Dwellings for which state aid has been authorized.
3. Monthly data refer to end of period. From March 1980, minimum age raised from 14 to 16.
4. Excluding government and agriculture. Weighting pattern based on 1967 to 1970 and on January 1981 from 1971.
5. Quarterly labour force sample survey. Prior to 3rd quarter 1976, covers persons aged 14 or over. From 3rd quarter 1976, covers persons aged 16 or over, and excludes conscripts and Spaniards having legal residence in Spain but working abroad.
6. The original base of the index is 1964 to 1975, and 1976 from 1976.
7. Weighting pattern based on 1958 to 1968, on 1968 from 1969 to 1975, and on 1976 from 1976.
8. From 1975, new reporting system. Government deposits are excluded from savings bank deposits from December 1981 and from commercial bank deposits from December 1982. From 1983, including deposits in cooperative credit unions.
9. Prior to December 1982, transactions of foreign branches of Spanish banks are included.
10. From December 1968, improved accounting procedures.
11. From 1973, new reporting system.
12. Monthly data are averages of daily rates.
13. To June 1966, data partly estimated; to October 1967, excluding foreign banks' assets in pesetas. Data concerning certain items which are included in the series from December 1968 were not available before that date. The net amount involved was — 1 billion pesetas in December 1968. Prior to July 1974, including foreign exchange credits to and deposits from residents other than banks.
14. Settlements basis.

NOTES

1. La base originale de l'indice est 1962 jusqu'en 1974, et 1972 à partir de 1975. La série brute n'est pas corrigée de l'inégalité du nombre de jours ouvrables dans le mois.
2. Logements pour lesquels l'aide de l'État a été accordée.
3. Situation en fin de mois. A partir de mars 1980, l'âge minimum a été élevé de 14 à 16 ans.
4. Administration et agriculture exclues. La pondération se réfère à 1967 jusqu'en 1970 et à janvier 1981 à partir de 1971.
5. Enquête trimestrielle par sondage. Avant le 3e trimestre 1976, l'enquête couvre les personnes âgées de 14 ans ou plus; à partir du 3e trimestre 1976, elle couvre les personnes âgées de 16 ans ou plus, mais ne comprends pas les conscrits et les espagnols ayant résidence légale en Espagne mais travaillant à l'étranger.
6. La base originale de l'indice est 1964 jusqu'en 1975, et 1976 à partir de 1976.
7. La pondération se réfère à 1958 jusqu'en 1968, à 1968 de 1969 à 1975, et à 1976 à partir de 1976.
8. A partir de 1975, nouveau système de notification. Non compris les dépôts du gouvernement auprès des caisses d'épargne à partir de décembre 1981, et auprès des banques commerciales à partir de décembre 1982. A partir de 1983, y compris les dépôts dans les coopératives de crédit.
9. Avant décembre 1982, les transactions des filiales étrangères des banques espagnoles sont comprises.
10. A partir de décembre 1968, système de comptabilité amélioré.
11. A partir de 1973, nouveau système de notification.
12. Les données mensuelles sont la moyennes des taux journaliers.
13. Jusqu'en juin 1966, données partiellement estimées; jusqu'en octobre 1967, non compris les avoirs en pesetas des banques étrangères. Les données concernant certains postes qui sont inclus dans les séries à partir de décembre 1968 n'étaient pas disponibles avant cette date. Le montant net de ces avoirs représentaient — 1 milliard de pesetas en décembre 1968. Avant juillet 1974, y compris les crédits et dépôts en devises des résidents autres que les banques.
14. Sur la base des règlements.

MAIN SOURCES

PRINCIPALES SOURCES

Series	Séries	Sources
Industrial production	Production industrielle	Instituto Nacional de Estadística *Boletin Mensual de Estadística*
Internal trade, value	Commerce intérieur, valeur	
Construction	Construction	
Consumer prices	Prix à la consommation	
Foreign trade	Commerce extérieur	
Business surveys	Enquêtes de conjoncture	Ministerio de Economia y Energia *Coyuntura Industrial*
Internal trade, volume	Commerce intérieur, volume	Instituto Nacional de Estadística
Labour and wages	Main-d'œuvre et salaires	Banco de España *Boletin Estadístico*
Producer prices	Prix à la production	
Home finance	Finances internes	
Interest rates	Taux d'intérêts	
Share prices	Cours des actions	
Net foreign position of commercial banks	Position extérieure nette des banques commerciales	
Balance of payments	Balance des paiements	

Sweden — Suède

SWEDEN

Gross domestic product / Produit intérieur brut

at 1980 market prices / *aux prix du marché de 1980*

million kronor, annual rates / millions de couronnes, taux annuels

Adjusted - Corrigé

	Year	Q.1	Q.2	Q.3	Q.4	JAN	FEB	MAR	APR	MAY	JUN	JUL	AUG	SEP	OCT	NOV	DEC
1964																	
1965																	
1966																	
1967																	
1968																	
1969																	
1970	432.8	417.3	426.0	440.2	447.7												
1971	436.5	434.3	432.5	441.9	437.1												
1972	446.9	444.7	442.7	447.2	452.9												
1973	464.4	467.0	466.5	459.6	464.7												
1974	479.4	468.3	482.6	483.4	483.4												
1975	491.4	490.5	490.1	490.8	494.1												
1976	496.8	494.4	499.3	497.3	496.1												
1977	488.8	486.6	487.6	493.1	488.0												
1978	497.4	500.3	497.7	495.0	496.8												
1979	516.6	510.5	518.8	518.2	518.8												
1980	525.1	526.9	517.0	529.7	526.7												
1981	522.1	519.3	524.2	522.8	522.0												
1982	524.7	519.4	526.7	524.6	527.9												
1983	536.6	528.1	535.5	535.5	547.4												

Industrial production: mining and manufacturing / Production industrielle : industries extractives et manufacturières

1980 = 100

	Year	Q.1	Q.2	Q.3	Q.4	JAN	FEB	MAR	APR	MAY	JUN	JUL	AUG	SEP	OCT	NOV	DEC
1964	66	68	70	57	74	67	68	69	70	71	70	34	66	70	73	74	74
1965	72	74	76	60	73	74	74	74	76	76	76	34	70	77	78	79	76
1966	74	77	79	61	80	76	75	78	78	79	79	32	71	80	81	81	78
1967	76	78	82	64	82	77	78	80	82	83	82	35	74	82	82	83	81
1968	80	80	83	67	88	78	79	82	88	88	88	42	76	84	87	89	89
1969	86	86	94	73	96	86	85	88	94	94	93	46	81	89	95	98	95
1970	91	94	100	76	99	91	94	96	100	103	97	49	87	93	98	100	98
1971	92	96	101	74	93	96	96	96	101	101	100	45	85	93	99	98	96
1972	94	95	101	79	103	92	95	97	101	101	100	44	93	101	102	104	103
1973	100	101	109	85	110	98	101	103	108	109	109	48	99	109	110	111	109
1974	105	107	116	89	112	105	108	108	116	114	118	52	104	110	114	115	106
1975	102	110	111	86	110	109	109	112	112	110	110	49	102	106	110	113	106
1976	102	102	110	85	109	99	103	103	111	108	112	49	102	105	111	110	106
1977	96	100	104	79	101	98	101	100	106	103	104	41	95	102	103	102	97
1978	94	95	101	78	105	95	95	96	104	99	100	36	95	103	106	107	102
1979	100	97	109	86	111	95	98	99	109	107	111	44	104	111	110	113	111
1980	100	105	104	85	109	103	105	107	113	87	111	48	101	106	110	112	105
1981	98	101	107	81	107	99	102	102	109	105	106	42	99	103	108	109	104
1982	97	97	106	79	106	95	98	98	107	105	106	40	95	103	107	107	104
1983	103	99	111	84	115	98	100	100	113	109	110	42	100	109	117	117	112

Industrial production: manufacturing / Production industrielle : industries manufacturières

1980 = 100

	Year	Q.1	Q.2	Q.3	Q.4	JAN	FEB	MAR	APR	MAY	JUN	JUL	AUG	SEP	OCT	NOV	DEC
1964	66	68	70	57	73	67	68	69	70	71	70	34	65	70	72	74	74
1965	72	74	76	60	73	74	74	74	76	76	76	34	70	77	78	79	76
1966	74	77	79	61	80	76	76	78	78	79	79	32	71	80	81	82	78
1967	76	79	82	64	82	78	78	80	82	83	82	34	74	82	82	84	81
1968	80	79	88	67	83	77	79	81	88	87	88	42	76	84	87	89	89
1969	85	86	93	72	95	85	84	88	94	93	93	47	80	89	95	97	95
1970	91	94	99	76	98	91	94	96	99	102	97	49	85	92	98	99	93
1971	92	95	100	74	97	95	96	95	101	101	99	45	85	92	98	98	95
1972	94	95	100	79	102	92	95	97	101	100	100	44	92	100	102	103	102
1973	100	101	108	85	110	98	101	103	107	109	108	48	99	109	110	110	109
1974	104	107	115	88	111	105	107	108	115	113	118	51	104	109	113	115	106
1975	102	109	111	86	110	109	108	111	112	110	110	49	102	106	110	113	105
1976	102	101	110	85	109	99	102	103	[illegible]	108	112	49	102	105	111	110	106
1977	96	99	104	79	101	98	100	100	106	103	104	41	95	102	103	102	98
1978	95	95	101	79	105	95	95	96	104	99	100	37	96	103	106	107	102
1979	100	97	109	85	112	95	98	99	109	107	111	44	104	111	111	113	111
1980	100	105	104	85	109	103	105	107	114	86	111	47	102	106	110	112	105
1981	98	101	106	81	107	99	102	102	107	104	106	42	99	103	108	110	104
1982	97	98	106	80	107	95	99	99	108	105	106	40	96	104	108	108	105
1983	103	100	111	84	116	98	101	100	113	109	111	42	101	110	118	118	112

Production: passenger cars (1)

thousands, monthly averages

Production : voitures de tourisme (1)

milliers, moyennes mensuelles

	Year	Q.1	Q.2	Q.3	Q.4	JAN	FEB	MAR	APR	MAY	JUN	JUL	AUG	SEP	OCT	NOV	DEC
1964																	
1965																	
1966																	
1967																	
1968				15	22							6	17	22	24	23	18
1969	20	19	21	15	24	18	19	21	24	19	22	8	18	20	26	24	24
1970	22	22	23	18	25	22	23	22	24	22	24	8	21	25	27	24	26
1971	22	21	23	17	25	19	21	24	22	23	25	9	19	23	25	26	24
1972	27	30	27	20	32	27	29	33	28	27	25	11	25	25	31	35	30
1973	28	32	29	21	32	32	32	31	30	33	24	15	20	24	34	36	26
1974	27	29	27	21	32	24	26	36	47	21	14	20	20	24	33	31	32
1975	27	26	27	23	30												
1976	26	30	26	23	24												
1977	20	24	19	14	22												
1978	22	22	21	16	27												
1979	26	27	26	22	28												
1980	21	24	21	16	24												
1981	19	16	20	17	24												
1982	22	22	23	17	27												
1983	23	22	25	20	27												

Industrial production: mining and manufacturing

1980 = 100

Adjusted - Corrigé

Production industrielle : industries extractives et manufacturières

1980 = 100

	Year	Q.1	Q.2	Q.3	Q.4	JAN	FEB	MAR	APR	MAY	JUN	JUL	AUG	SEP	OCT	NOV	DEC
1964		65	65	66	69	65	65	65	64	65	65	65	68	67	68	69	69
1965		71	70	70	72	72	71	69	69	70	71	66	72	73	72	72	72
1966		73	73	72	74	73	72	74	72	72	74	68	72	76	75	74	72
1967		75	76	75	76	74	75	75	75	76	76	73	76	77	76	76	76
1968		75	78	83	82	75	74	76	78	77	80	87	81	81	80	81	84
1969		82	85	88	90	83	81	83	84	84	86	92	85	87	89	91	89
1970		89	91	92	92	87	90	91	90	93	89	95	91	90	91	92	93
1971		93	93	92	92	95	93	92	93	93	93	93	91	91	93	92	91
1972		92	93	96	97	91	92	93	93	93	93	94	97	97	96	97	98
1973		98	101	103	104	97	98	99	100	102	101	101	102	105	104	103	104
1974		105	108	106	105	105	105	105	107	107	110	106	106	106	107	107	101
1975		108	103	103	102	109	107	109	104	104	102	104	104	102	102	104	100
1976		100	103	102	102	99	101	100	102	102	104	104	102	100	103	101	101
1977		99	97	96	93	99	99	98	97	97	96	96	95	96	94	93	93
1978		94	93	95	97	95	94	94	94	93	92	92	95	97	97	97	97
1979		97	101	103	104	96	97	97	100	101	103	101	104	105	102	103	106
1980		105	95	102	101	105	104	105	103	80	103	105	102	100	101	102	99
1981		100	93	99	99	100	101	100	99	97	97	95	99	98	99	100	99
1982		97	97	97	98	97	97	97	96	97	97	97	96	98	98	97	98
1983		99	101	102	107	99	99	99	101	101	102	100	102	104	107	108	106

Industrial production: manufacturing

1980 = 100

Adjusted - Corrigé *

Production industrielle : industries manufacturières

1980 = 100

	Year	Q.1	Q.2	Q.3	Q.4	JAN	FEB	MAR	APR	MAY	JUN	JUL	AUG	SEP	OCT	NOV	DEC
1964		65	66	68	69	65	65	66	65	67	66	67	68	68	68	69	71
1965		72	71	71	73	72	72	70	71	71	72	67	73	74	73	74	73
1966		74	74	72	75	74	74	75	73	74	74	64	74	77	76	76	74
1967		76	77	75	78	76	76	77	76	77	76	65	78	79	77	78	77
1968		77	81	82	83	76	77	78	81	80	82	85	80	82	82	83	85
1969		84	86	89	90	84	82	84	86	85	87	95	84	87	89	90	90
1970		91	91	94	92	90	91	92	91	93	90	100	90	90	92	92	93
1971		93	93	90	91	94	93	91	93	93	92	92	89	90	92	91	90
1972		92	93	95	96	91	92	93	93	92	93	91	95	98	95	96	97
1973		98	100	103	103	97	98	99	98	101	101	100	102	106	102	102	103
1974		104	107	105	104	105	104	104	106	105	110	107	106	105	105	106	101
1975		103	103	103	102	109	106	108	103	103	102	105	103	102	102	104	101
1976		100	102	103	101	99	100	101	102	102	104	106	102	100	102	101	101
1977		93	97	94	94	99	99	98	97	97	96	90	95	97	95	93	93
1978		95	94	92	97	96	94	94	95	94	93	82	96	97	97	98	97
1979		97	101	103	103	96	97	97	99	101	103	95	104	105	102	103	105
1980		105	96	103	101	105	104	105	104	81	103	107	102	100	101	102	100
1981		101	93	98	99	101	101	100	99	98	98	96	99	98	99	100	98
1982		97	93	96	99	97	98	98	98	99	98	92	96	99	99	98	99
1983		99	103	101	107	100	100	99	102	102	103	97	101	105	108	107	106

* Adjusted by the O.E.C.D.

* Corrigé par l'O.C.D.E.

SWEDEN

Production: wood pulp (2)
thousand tons, monthly averages

Production : pâte à papier (2)
milliers de tonnes, moyennes mensuelles

	Year	Q.1	Q.2	Q.3	Q.4	JAN	FEB	MAR	APR	MAY	JUN	JUL	AUG	SEP	OCT	NOV	DEC
1964	241	237	235	234	253	244	238	228	253	232	219	197	241	264	280	258	235
1965	253	263	244	242	262	263	251	274	243	269	221	221	237	269	274	268	243
1966	254	261	236	236	283	257	242	283	[illegible]	246	253	187	242	279	297	294	258
1967	284	283	285	290	277	291	280	278	302	282	272	250	317	304	303	286	241
1968	298	303	285	276	328	287	296	327	284	325	246	222	289	318	339	335	309
1969	339	342	315	340	358	346	316	364	320	334	292	304	357	360	382	364	329
1970	371	353	358	386	337	366	348	346	375	358	342	362	400	397	406	395	360
1971	361	394	349	345	356	396	369	418	347	366	335	271	358	406	370	366	333
1972	391	395	355	377	437	390	393	403	[illegible]	384	363	320	400	412	455	435	422
1973	447	451	412	470	454	453	433	468	398	468	371	454	489	467	480	457	426
1974	458	468	432	476	457	457	452	495	427	474	396	474	483	470	480	468	424
1975	406	446	388	387	401	465	442	430	425	401	339	361	406	394	392	420	391
1976	421	430	402	447	404	421	425	445	362	436	409	404	484	452	420	427	365
1977	390	410	370	394	387	404	394	431	325	396	388	319	433	430	410	387	364
1978	435	411	424	419	436	436	413	384	450	424	398	258	500	498	491	520	446
1979	462	479	429	461	478	464	453	520	429	468	389	401	498	483	489	496	450
1980	448	487	375	477	451	467	474	521	412	304	408	434	499	497	481	453	420
1981	453	470	443	459	440	478	461	470	434	484	410	383	489	506	476	444	401
1982	413	445	404	366	438	439	417	478	406	434	373	333	372	392	398	465	452
1983	470	489	447	462	481	485	466	516	401	470	471	388	452	507	469	486	489

Production: crude steel
thousand tons, monthly averages

Production : acier brut
milliers de tonnes, moyennes mensuelles

	Year	Q.1	Q.2	Q.3	Q.4	JAN	FEB	MAR	APR	MAY	JUN	JUL	AUG	SEP	OCT	NOV	DEC
1964																	
1965																	
1966																	
1967																	
1968																	
1969	446	478	434	368	504	512	460	462	505	426	372	238	408	457	577	467	467
1970	458	490	451	406	436	450	468	552	451	421	480	209	436	572	451	469	538
1971	438	494	445	359	452	514	477	491	435	505	396	158	429	490	462	467	426
1972	436	434	435	345	481	462	483	506	450	466	390	102	439	494	494	472	476
1973	472	518	469	403	499	505	509	540	471	521	414	180	517	513	524	517	455
1974	499	547	478	438	534	546	526	569	496	540	397	246	525	542	554	535	512
1975	468	534	487	384	465	554	521	528	534	524	403	207	464	482	465	500	429
1976	428	480	471	316	447	450	464	527	486	512	415	94	417	436	432	481	427
1977	331	413	299	233	377	404	387	449	276	342	280	22	309	368	388	393	350
1978	360	387	358	279	417	400	381	381	410	385	280	30	386	421	451	424	376
1979	394	426	410	288	454	403	393	481	427	462	341	47	373	444	489	439	434
1980	353	471	342	237	362	473	435	506	418	300	309	39	320	351	357	372	357
1981	314	352	330	214	361	340	342	374	328	371	290	28	289	325	380	359	345
1982	325	380	358	235	327	349	363	427	348	383	343	43	299	363	363	317	301
1983	351	342	372	268	421	307	310	409	356	420	340	33	364	408	430	437	396

Ships completed
thousand gross register tons, quarterly averages

Navires achevés
milliers de tonneaux de jauge brute, moyennes trimestrielles

	Year	Q.1	Q.2	Q.3	Q.4	JAN	FEB	MAR	APR	MAY	JUN	JUL	AUG	SEP	OCT	NOV	DEC
1964	259	169	321	124	420												
1965	316	240	342	167	517												
1966	283	247	262	200	421												
1967	340	290	402	236	434												
1968	274	209	421	177	290												
1969	316	252	250	134	633												
1970	385	230	431	232	639												
1971	466	404	565	336	559												
1972	507	499	505	292	733												
1973	573	446	685	305	854												
1974	545	407	751	340	685												
1975	547	554	835	484	314												
1976	629	805	531	584	595												
1977	578	664	534	558	555												
1978	352	139	563	333	373												
1979	115	77	250	50	84												
1980	87	111	59	52	123												
1981	113	73	157	27	197												
1982	72	74	155	32	29												
1983	83	117	105	54	57												

Production: future tendency (3) / Perspectives de production (3)

manufacturing / industries manufacturières

per cent balance / solde en pourcentage

Year	Q.1	Q.2	Q.3	Q.4	JAN	FEB	MAR	APR	MAY	JUN	JUL	AUG	SEP	OCT	NOV	DEC
1964	21	20	26	20			21			20			26			20
1965	22	12	22	15			22			12			22			15
1966	11	4	9	3			11			4			9			3
1967	7	9	14	7			7			9			14			7
1968	15	16	25	25			15			16			25			25
1969	32	37	34	31			32			37			34			31
1970	27	20	16	4			27			20			16			4
1971	5	-5	3	-7			5			-5			3			-7
1972	7	10	14	9			7			10			14			9
1973	17	23	26	12			17			23			26			12
1974	26	22	20	1			26			22			20			1
1975	2	-4	-6	-16			2			-4			-6			-16
1976	3	9	8	-17			3			9			8			-17
1977	-2	-11	-10	-11			-2			-11			-10			-11
1978	5	8	16	17			5			8			16			17
1979	20	21	21	6			20			21			21			6
1980	11	6	-3	-17			11			6			-3			-17
1981	-1	-6	-1	-6			-1			-6			-1			-6
1982	8	-1	2	-11			8			-1			2			-11
1983	15	11	13	9			15			11			13			9

Orders inflow: tendency (3) / Commandes : tendance (3)

manufacturing / industries manufacturières

per cent balance / solde en pourcentage

Year	Q.1	Q.2	Q.3	Q.4	JAN	FEB	MAR	APR	MAY	JUN	JUL	AUG	SEP	OCT	NOV	DEC
1964	20	20	17	17			20			20			17			17
1965	12	4	1	1			12			4			1			1
1966	-12	-9	-1	8			-12			-9			-1			8
1967	-1	5	9	-7			-1			5			9			-7
1968	8	18	18	21			8			18			18			21
1969	29	28	22	22			29			28			22			22
1970	10	1	-6	-13			10			1			-6			-13
1971	-24	-23	-16	-6			-24			-23			-16			-6
1972	-5	10	11	15			-5			10			11			15
1973	24	23	24	16			24			23			24			16
1974	23	11	-1	-13			23			11			-1			-13
1975	-25	-25	-24	-14			-25			-25			-24			-14
1976	-2	13	11	-9			-2			13			11			-9
1977	-12	-7	-14	-11			-12			-7			-14			-11
1978	3	13	15	14			3			13			15			14
1979	18	26	18	5			18			26			18			5
1980	11	-12	-26	-39			11			-12			-26			-39
1981	-25	-14	-14	-7			-25			-14			-14			-7
1982	-6	-5	-9	-7			-6			-5			-9			-7
1983	11	11	17	15			11			11			17			15

Order books: level (3) / Carnet de commandes : niveau (3)

manufacturing / industries manufacturières

per cent balance / solde en pourcentage

Year	Q.1	Q.2	Q.3	Q.4	JAN	FEB	MAR	APR	MAY	JUN	JUL	AUG	SEP	OCT	NOV	DEC
1964	-4	2	5	8			-4			2			5			8
1965	2	-1	-2	-10			2			-1			-2			-10
1966	-19	-28	-31	-37			-19			-28			-31			-37
1967	-40	-29	-30	-41			-40			-29			-30			-41
1968	-38	-30	-24	-14			-38			-30			-24			-14
1969	-1	14	20	23			-1			14			20			23
1970	18	15	6	-11			18			15			6			-11
1971	-27	-34	-42	-43			-27			-34			-42			-43
1972	-43	-34	-37	-32			-43			-34			-37			-32
1973	-22	-5	7	16			-22			-5			7			16
1974	23	27	23	-6			23			27			23			-6
1975	-22	-37	-48	-53			-22			-37			-48			-53
1976	-54	-53	-50	-57			-54			-53			-50			-57
1977	-66	-66	-68	-71			-66			-66			-68			-71
1978	-69	-57	-49	-45			-69			-57			-49			-45
1979	-33	-9	-12	-13			-33			-9			-12			-13
1980	-11	-12	-25	-49			-11			-12			-25			-49
1981	-53	-55	-59	-62			-53			-55			-59			-62
1982	-64	-60	-56	-55			-64			-60			-56			-55
1983	-54	-36	-28	-24			-54			-36			-28			-24

SWEDEN

Finished goods stocks: level (3)
manufacturing
per cent balance

Stocks de produits finis : niveau (3)
industries manufacturières
solde en pourcentage

	Year	Q.1	Q.2	Q.3	Q.4	JAN	FEB	MAR	APR	MAY	JUN	JUL	AUG	SEP	OCT	NOV	DEC
1964		4	-	-6	-			4			-			-6			-
1965		-1	10	10	19			-1			10			10			19
1966		28	28	31	39			28			28			31			39
1967		38	34	30	30			38			34			30			30
1968		26	21	11	6			26			21			11			6
1969		7	-8	-16	-13			7			-8			-16			-13
1970		-6	1	6	18			-6			1			6			18
1971		25	35	38	37			25			35			38			37
1972		33	28	24	20			33			28			24			20
1973		17	10	-2	-6			17			10			-2			-6
1974		-9	-10	-5	5			-9			-10			-5			5
1975		16	29	34	38			16			29			34			38
1976		38	34	37	43			38			34			37			43
1977		49	50	48	49			49			50			48			49
1978		43	37	26	24			43			37			26			24
1979		16	8	2	-			16			8			2			-
1980		7	15	13	34			7			15			13			34
1981		32	36	36	41			32			36			36			41
1982		37	38	34	35			37			38			34			35
1983		38	30	22	25			38			30			22			25

Firms operating at full capacity (3)
manufacturing
per cent balance

Entreprises travaillant à pleine capacité (3)
industries manufacturières
solde en pourcentage

	Year	Q.1	Q.2	Q.3	Q.4	JAN	FEB	MAR	APR	MAY	JUN	JUL	AUG	SEP	OCT	NOV	DEC
1964		65	70	68	69			65			70			68			69
1965		72	75	72	69			72			75			72			69
1966		64	62	58	56			64			62			58			56
1967		53	55	57	50			53			55			57			50
1968		52	51	53	55			52			51			53			55
1969		59	68	70	73			59			68			70			73
1970		75	71	69	65			75			71			69			65
1971		56	52	47	41			56			52			47			41
1972		43	47	45	46			43			47			45			46
1973		49	57	60	63			49			57			60			63
1974		67	71	67	61			67			71			67			61
1975		52	42	35	32			52			42			35			32
1976		29	34	35	30			29			34			35			30
1977		25	26	26	25			25			26			26			25
1978		24	28	30	35			24			28			30			35
1979		34	42	46	47			34			42			46			47
1980		47	49	42	34			47			49			42			34
1981		29	29	27	23			29			29			27			34
1982		22	24	22	22			22			24			22			22
1983		24	28	34	37			24			28			34			37

Deliveries: manufacturing
1980 = 100

Livraisons : industries manufacturières
1980 = 100

	Year	Q.1	Q.2	Q.3	Q.4	JAN	FEB	MAR	APR	MAY	JUN	JUL	AUG	SEP	OCT	NOV	DEC
1964																	
1965																	
1966																	
1967																	
1968																	
1969																	
1970	35	32	37	32	40	30	31	34	39	34	39	25	35	38	40	38	42
1971	36	34	37	33	41	31	32	38	36	35	40	24	35	39	39	40	44
1972	38	35	39	35	44	30	34	40	36	38	41	24	38	42	44	44	46
1973	45	41	45	41	54	38	39	45	42	47	46	30	45	47	55	55	53
1974	58	52	53	53	66	48	51	58	56	60	59	37	60	63	67	66	66
1975	60	58	63	53	68	55	58	61	65	59	64	36	58	65	67	67	71
1976	67	62	69	60	77	55	62	70	67	67	72	36	68	73	72	76	81
1977	71	66	73	62	81	59	64	77	69	72	77	36	71	77	75	78	90
1978	77	70	78	68	90	65	68	77	79	73	83	40	83	83	87	89	94
1979	91	82	93	81	106	74	79	94	88	93	99	54	95	97	107	106	105
1980	100	101	96	90	113	93	98	111	99	80	110	62	101	108	116	107	117
1981	106	99	109	95	123	87	97	114	111	100	114	63	104	114	120	119	130
1982	119	109	123	105	133	93	107	126	123	114	132	73	115	126	131	137	146
1983	141	130	143	125	163	115	125	150	133	141	155	81	138	157	157	161	177

Deliveries: metal products (4) / Livraisons : ouvrages en métaux (4)

1980 = 100

	Year	Q.1	Q.2	Q.3	Q.4	JAN	FEB	MAR	APR	MAY	JUN	JUL	AUG	SEP	OCT	NOV	DEC
1964																	
1965																	
1966																	
1967																	
1968																	
1969																	
1970	31	28	32	27	38	24	28	32	33	29	34	18	30	33	36	35	41
1971	34	31	35	28	40	26	30	37	33	33	39	19	31	36	37	37	45
1972	36	33	36	30	43	28	32	38	35	33	40	19	34	38	42	40	47
1973	41	38	40	35	50	35	36	43	38	42	41	23	40	43	48	49	52
1974	51	46	52	45	63	40	44	53	48	51	56	26	52	56	59	60	70
1975	59	53	62	50	71	47	53	60	63	59	65	31	55	63	66	67	81
1976	66	60	68	55	80	50	59	71	65	65	74	29	67	70	72	74	93
1977	71	65	73	59	85	58	63	75	68	72	78	29	71	77	75	78	100
1978	77	69	78	65	97	63	67	77	78	69	86	32	79	83	89	93	109
1979	91	81	94	77	111	71	76	95	88	90	103	40	93	99	106	107	121
1980	100	97	96	85	122	86	96	110	97	76	115	48	100	108	118	115	132
1981	108	100	110	89	135	81	98	119	107	100	122	52	102	115	124	126	154
1982	124	113	130	101	153	94	112	132	127	117	145	58	114	131	136	152	169
1983	147	133	147	122	185	114	130	157	137	144	162	63	136	166	165	174	216

Change in stocks (manufacturing): finished goods *at 1968 prices* / Variations des stocks (industries manufacturières) : produits finis *aux prix de 1968*

million kronor / millions de couronnes

	Year	Q.1	Q.2	Q.3	Q.4	JAN	FEB	MAR	APR	MAY	JUN	JUL	AUG	SEP	OCT	NOV	DEC
1964																	
1965																	
1966																	
1967																	
1968																	
1969																	
1970																	
1971																	
1972	-140	425	-217	-418	70												
1973	-847	109	-298	-485	-173												
1974	660	90	195	-79	455												
1975	2669	973	675	577	444												
1976	1814	730	297	-106	394												
1977	-28	508	146	-277	-405												
1978	-1535	77	-609	-797	-206												
1979	-881	358	-739	-424	-77												
1980	859	716	-73	-362	617												
1981	396	538	-128	-175	160												
1982	-694	110	-329	-390	-85												
1983	-707	45	-287	-633	168												

Change in stocks (manufacturing): work in progress *at 1968 prices* / Variations des stocks (industries manufacturières) : produits en cours de fabrication *aux prix de 1968*

million kronor / millions de couronnes

	Year	Q.1	Q.2	Q.3	Q.4	JAN	FEB	MAR	APR	MAY	JUN	JUL	AUG	SEP	OCT	NOV	DEC
1964																	
1965																	
1966																	
1967																	
1968																	
1969																	
1970																	
1971																	
1972	137	539	-50	82	-435												
1973	-199	189	-40	77	-425												
1974	1070	430	94	531	16												
1975	1419	437	25	650	307												
1976	901	52	459	461	-72												
1977	-960	-266	-285	433	-841												
1978	-220	179	219	-214	-405												
1979	279	449	-236	314	-249												
1980	113	441	156	382	-365												
1981	-1018	105	-366	86	-343												
1982	-1051	1	-465	-4	-584												
1983	-482	-191	-246	377	-422												

SWEDEN

Change in stocks (manufacturing):
intermediate goods *at 1968 prices*
million kronor

Variations des stocks (industries manufacturières) :
biens intermédiaires *aux prix de 1968*
millions de couronnes

	Year	Q.1	Q.2	Q.3	Q.4	JAN	FEB	MAR	APR	MAY	JUN	JUL	AUG	SEP	OCT	NOV	DEC
1964																	
1965																	
1966																	
1967																	
1968																	
1969																	
1970																	
1971																	
1972	-197	-212	-61	43	32												
1973	-201	-336	-41	-33	209												
1974	382	-248	163	333	134												
1975	921	98	247	308	269												
1976	343	82	-22	115	168												
1977	-270	-314	-61	146	-42												
1978	-691	-510	-212	-19	50												
1979	163	-144	54	183	70												
1980	385	-152	120	96	321												
1981	58	-131	89	64	36												
1982	98	-338	91	-75	419												
1983	-369	-389	-179	-63	262												

Net new orders:
manufacturing
1980 = 100

Commandes nouvelles nettes :
industries manufacturières
1980 = 100

	Year	Q.1	Q.2	Q.3	Q.4	JAN	FEB	MAR	APR	MAY	JUN	JUL	AUG	SEP	OCT	NOV	DEC
1964																	
1965																	
1966																	
1967																	
1968																	
1969																	
1970	36	34	38	32	40	35	32	35	38	34	43	25	36	37	40	39	40
1971	35	35	35	32	40	34	33	38	33	33	38	27	33	37	37	39	43
1972	39	36	39	34	48	34	35	38	35	41	40	24	35	42	44	51	50
1973	52	50	50	50	60	47	50	54	43	50	55	44	52	55	59	59	61
1974	61	61	61	54	68	60	59	64	59	61	63	40	61	62	69	66	68
1975	58	59	58	50	66	63	58	56	58	52	63	35	56	60	66	62	72
1976	65	63	68	58	72	59	61	70	65	66	72	39	66	69	70	70	76
1977	69	67	69	61	73	63	64	74	68	70	71	42	72	71	73	75	85
1978	81	79	84	71	91	75	75	87	80	84	87	45	83	85	90	88	94
1979	96	92	98	87	107	93	84	100	92	94	107	63	102	98	113	106	101
1980	100	112	98	85	105	115	105	114	99	88	108	60	92	101	104	101	109
1981	110	109	111	97	123	104	103	121	121	103	118	68	102	121	129	118	122
1982	125	121	127	109	140	116	118	130	117	109	155	82	118	127	135	133	153
1983	145	143	141	130	164	133	135	161	135	136	153	85	148	159	157	161	176

Net new orders: (4)(5)
metal products
1980 = 100

Commandes nouvelles nettes : (4)(5)
ouvrages en métaux
1980 = 100

	Year	Q.1	Q.2	Q.3	Q.4	JAN	FEB	MAR	APR	MAY	JUN	JUL	AUG	SEP	OCT	NOV	DEC
1964	27	25	27	26	30												
1965	27	27	27	25	30												
1966	26	25	27	25	26												
1967	25	24	26	22	26												
1968	28	32	28	24	27	24	24	47	25	28	30	20	25	27	29	28	25
1969	31	28	31	29	34	28	25	32	28	28	37	25	29	32	35	32	35
1970	33	31	35	31	35	30	30	31	34	31	38	22	33	39	35	35	35
1971	33	34	33	29	37	30	34	38	32	29	38	21	32	33	33	40	39
1972	35	33	35	31	41	31	33	35	34	32	38	20	33	40	39	42	43
1973	46	42	44	47	51	42	41	45	43	44	44	38	53	50	48	53	52
1974	59	59	60	52	64	58	59	61	55	59	66	35	61	57	64	61	66
1975	62	65	61	50	70	65	68	62	58	54	72	31	58	59	66	63	81
1976	65	60	69	54	76	56	57	67	67	68	71	28	67	67	68	70	89
1977	68	65	72	57	79	62	62	71	70	73	74	31	76	65	71	72	95
1978	82	77	91	69	91	68	69	93	82	98	92	38	83	87	85	90	97
1979	99	93	103	89	110	91	82	105	97	90	123	62	106	99	115	108	107
1980	100	110	101	83	107	109	106	115	96	93	115	51	100	97	100	105	114
1981	115	114	119	93	136	106	110	125	110	119	127	54	105	121	147	126	134
1982	135	129	148	109	154	127	118	141	118	112	214	74	117	137	138	141	183
1983	149	151	139	129	177	136	145	173	137	133	148	65	154	165	162	166	204

Unfilled orders: shipbuilding — Commandes en carnet : construction navale

1980 = 100, end of period — 1980 = 100, fin de période

	Year	Q.1	Q.2	Q.3	Q.4	JAN	FEB	MAR	APR	MAY	JUN	JUL	AUG	SEP	OCT	NOV	DEC
1964																	
1965																	
1966																	
1967																	
1968																	
1969																	
1970	106	73	80	88	106	73	72	73	75	75	80	79	87	88	97	104	106
1971	96	104	95	100	96	107	105	104	102	98	95	99	99	100	99	96	96
1972	122	93	97	97	122	96	96	93	92	99	97	96	96	97	98	112	122
1973	209	161	169	198	209	127	145	161	161	159	169	185	185	198	202	198	209
1974	213	220	218	218	213	214	218	220	219	214	218	217	219	218	216	212	213
1975	175	202	186	180	175	212	209	202	199	192	186	185	185	180	178	173	175
1976	114	156	137	128	114	164	158	156	148	145	137	138	136	128	129	121	114
1977	76	103	91	90	76	111	109	103	96	91	91	93	91	90	88	85	76
1978	91	90	89	83	91	80	90	90	83	82	89	91	86	83	90	89	91
1979	107	94	101	100	107	96	99	94	91	102	101	101	106	100	107	108	107
1980	100	107	112	106	100	113	113	107	109	112	112	111	107	106	97	102	100
1981	103	105	104	110	103	107	100	105	100	98	104	101	99	110	107	105	103
1982	119	112	98	110	119	103	118	112	107	101	98	107	112	110	119	120	119
1983	111	104	103	115	111	101	99	104	104	96	103	101	108	115	111	111	111

Construction: housing starts (6) — Construction : logements mis en chantier (6)

thousands, monthly averages — milliers, moyennes mensuelles

	Year	Q.1	Q.2	Q.3	Q.4	JAN	FEB	MAR	APR	MAY	JUN	JUL	AUG	SEP	OCT	NOV	DEC
1964	8.1	3.9	10.2	10.6	7.6	4.6	2.7	4.5	8.7	9.6	12.3	6.1	12.5	13.2	9.8	8.5	4.4
1965	7.8	5.0	8.0	7.0	11.0	6.3	3.9	4.8	7.2	9.0	7.7	3.6	9.1	8.3	12.9	10.6	9.6
1966	7.8	4.2	6.7	7.3	13.1	4.1	3.3	5.2	4.3	7.5	8.3	3.4	7.3	11.3	11.3	15.2	12.9
1967	8.3	4.8	10.6	10.9	7.0	4.3	4.9	5.3	9.9	10.7	11.1	5.0	10.8	16.8	9.0	6.6	5.4
1968	9.0	6.6	10.0	10.7	8.5	6.8	5.8	7.2	8.7	11.4	9.9	5.4	11.0	15.8	10.5	7.7	7.2
1969	8.8	6.7	9.7	10.4	8.3	7.8	4.5	7.8	9.6	10.5	9.0	5.1	11.6	14.6	12.1	7.4	5.5
1970	8.9	6.7	10.7	8.6	9.4	6.7	4.4	9.1	10.7	10.8	10.7	3.5	10.5	11.4	10.4	9.8	8.0
1971	8.7	5.3	8.9	9.0	11.6	4.5	4.9	6.6	8.2	9.2	9.4	4.1	11.1	11.7	13.5	11.3	10.1
1972	8.2	5.4	8.6	8.0	10.9	6.1	4.6	5.5	8.7	8.6	8.6	3.3	9.6	11.1	11.6	11.3	9.7
1973	6.7	5.7	6.4	6.8	7.9	6.0	4.9	6.0	5.3	7.3	6.6	3.6	8.1	8.6	9.1	8.2	6.5
1974	6.8	4.6	6.2	5.3	11.0	4.7	4.2	4.8	6.0	6.6	5.9	3.5	6.3	6.0	8.2	9.4	15.4
1975	4.3	2.9	3.8	4.1	6.5	3.3	2.6	2.7	3.2	3.9	4.2	2.5	4.6	5.1	7.0	6.5	5.8
1976	4.8	3.6	5.4	4.5	5.6	3.5	3.8	3.4	4.7	5.7	5.7	3.5	5.0	5.2	6.2	6.6	4.0
1977	4.5	3.1	4.4	4.3	6.2	3.3	2.4	3.8	3.9	4.7	4.6	2.3	4.7	5.8	6.3	6.5	5.9
1978	4.8	3.8	5.0	4.8	5.6	4.5	2.9	3.9	4.9	5.2	4.8	2.1	5.2	7.0	6.1	6.8	3.9
1979	4.7	3.5	5.2	4.5	5.5	3.8	2.6	4.1	4.8	5.4	5.4	2.2	6.1	5.5	6.4	6.1	4.0
1980	4.2	3.4	4.3	4.1	5.0	3.6	2.6	3.8	4.3	3.9	4.6	1.7	5.1	5.5	5.8	5.2	4.0
1981	3.7	3.0	3.6	3.7	4.5	2.6	2.8	3.5	3.0	4.2	3.7	2.2	4.6	4.3	4.4	6.0	3.2
1982	3.5	3.0	3.4	3.4	4.1	2.8	2.8	3.4	2.9	3.4	4.0	1.3	4.3	4.7	3.9	5.2	3.2
1983	3.1	3.0	3.0	2.8	3.6	2.9	3.2	2.9	2.5	3.7	2.8	1.7	3.6	3.3	3.8	3.3	3.7

Construction: dwellings in progress (6) — Construction : travaux en cours (logements) (6)

thousands, end of period — milliers, fin de période

	Year	Q.1	Q.2	Q.3	Q.4	JAN	FEB	MAR	APR	MAY	JUN	JUL	AUG	SEP	OCT	NOV	DEC
1964	115.1	97.2	105.8	119.1	115.1	104.5	100.8	97.2	98.7	101.1	105.8	106.8	113.6	119.1	121.7	122.3	115.1
1965	120.4	108.5	106.3	108.4	120.4	116.1	113.0	108.5	107.9	109.3	106.3	105.6	109.1	108.4	112.3	114.1	120.4
1966	116.1	102.0	99.1	103.5	116.1	109.0	104.9	102.0	98.7	99.3	99.1	98.5	100.8	103.5	107.9	114.1	116.1
1967	115.6	105.3	112.3	124.0	115.6	113.7	110.6	105.3	107.0	110.1	112.3	111.4	116.9	124.0	123.3	121.1	115.6
1968	116.8	111.5	115.3	123.4	116.8	116.0	114.4	111.5	112.2	114.9	115.3	114.8	117.4	123.4	123.6	120.6	116.8
1969	113.3	112.2	111.1	120.1	113.3	117.2	113.9	112.2	112.0	112.9	111.1	111.3	115.1	120.1	121.8	118.9	113.3
1970	96.9	94.9	97.2	100.7	96.9	98.9	95.1	94.9	95.8	96.7	97.2	95.2	99.1	100.7	101.8	102.0	96.9
1971	94.3	88.8	86.6	89.7	94.3	94.5	91.4	88.8	86.6	86.2	86.6	85.5	87.3	89.7	94.0	95.0	94.3
1972	88.8	84.1	82.6	86.1	88.8	92.0	88.7	84.1	84.0	83.6	82.6	81.1	81.5	86.1	87.3	89.1	88.8
1973	71.4	81.4	71.8	72.2	71.4	87.7	85.0	81.4	77.6	75.2	71.8	70.4	72.8	72.2	73.1	73.0	71.4
1974	67.1	62.8	57.5	57.1	67.1	68.6	65.9	62.8	61.0	60.8	57.5	57.2	58.1	57.1	57.1	60.1	67.1
1975	44.0	59.5	49.2	46.9	44.0	64.9	62.2	59.5	56.7	54.1	49.2	48.7	48.7	46.9	47.5	47.5	44.0
1976	45.4	41.8	41.2	44.1	45.4	42.8	42.7	41.8	41.8	42.6	41.2	42.6	43.7	44.1	46.1	47.1	45.4
1977	44.5	40.5	36.9	39.9	44.5	44.0	42.4	40.5	40.2	39.8	36.9	36.9	38.3	39.9	42.0	43.6	44.5
1978	48.1	43.2	42.4	46.5	48.1	44.6	43.9	43.2	43.6	43.1	42.4	42.3	44.1	46.5	48.1	49.6	48.1
1979	48.6	45.3	45.3	47.8	48.6	47.1	45.7	45.3	44.9	45.2	45.3	45.1	47.3	47.8	49.2	50.0	48.6
1980	47.3	46.2	45.6	46.9	47.3	48.2	46.8	46.2	45.8	45.9	45.6	44.7	46.1	46.9	47.7	48.0	47.3
1981	40.2	43.2	40.4	39.7	40.2	45.1	44.0	43.2	41.4	41.0	40.4	40.1	40.6	39.7	39.7	41.5	40.2
1982	36.9	37.4	35.7	37.5	36.9	38.8	37.6	37.4	36.4	35.5	35.7	35.0	36.2	37.5	37.1	37.8	36.9
1983	30.3	33.6	31.2	31.5	30.3	35.6	35.3	33.6	32.3	32.2	31.2	31.2	31.5	31.5	31.2	31.0	30.3

SWEDEN

Construction: dwellings completed / Construction : logements achevés

thousands, monthly averages / milliers, moyennes mensuelles

	Year	Q.1	Q.2	Q.3	Q.4	JAN	FEB	MAR	APR	MAY	JUN	JUL	AUG	SEP	OCT	NOV	DEC
1964	7.3	6.6	7.4	6.1	8.9	5.5	6.4	8.0	7.2	7.1	7.8	6.1	4.6	7.7	7.3	7.9	11.6
1965	8.1	7.2	8.7	6.3	10.0	5.4	7.0	9.3	7.8	7.7	10.6	4.3	5.6	9.0	8.9	8.9	12.3
1966	7.4	7.3	7.7	5.8	8.9	6.6	7.4	8.0	7.6	6.9	8.6	3.6	5.3	8.6	6.9	9.0	10.9
1967	8.4	8.4	8.2	7.0	9.3	6.6	8.1	10.6	8.2	7.5	8.9	5.9	5.3	9.7	9.7	8.9	10.8
1968	8.9	8.0	8.8	8.0	10.7	6.5	7.5	10.0	8.1	8.7	9.5	5.8	8.4	9.8	10.4	10.7	10.9
1969	9.1	8.2	10.1	7.5	10.6	7.4	7.8	9.4	9.8	9.7	10.8	4.9	7.0	10.6	10.3	10.3	11.1
1970	9.2	8.5	9.9	7.5	10.7	7.9	8.1	9.4	9.7	10.0	10.1	6.0	6.6	9.9	9.3	9.6	13.1
1971	8.9	8.0	9.6	7.9	10.1	6.7	8.0	9.3	10.3	9.6	8.9	5.3	9.3	9.2	9.3	10.2	10.9
1972	8.7	8.8	9.1	6.8	10.0	8.3	8.0	10.0	8.8	9.0	9.6	4.8	7.1	8.6	10.4	9.5	10.1
1973	8.1	8.1	9.6	6.6	8.2	7.1	7.6	9.7	9.1	9.7	10.1	5.0	5.7	9.2	8.2	8.3	8.0
1974	7.1	7.4	8.0	5.4	7.7	7.5	5.9	8.8	7.8	6.8	9.3	3.7	5.4	7.0	8.1	6.5	8.4
1975	6.2	5.4	7.2	4.9	7.4	5.4	5.3	5.4	6.0	6.5	9.1	3.0	4.5	7.0	6.4	6.5	9.4
1976	4.7	4.3	5.6	3.6	5.2	4.8	3.8	4.3	4.7	4.9	7.1	2.1	3.8	4.8	4.3	5.5	5.7
1977	4.6	4.8	5.6	3.3	4.7	4.7	4.0	5.6	4.2	5.1	7.5	2.3	3.3	4.2	4.2	4.8	4.9
1978	4.5	4.2	5.2	3.4	5.1	4.4	3.7	4.5	4.5	5.7	5.5	2.2	3.4	4.5	4.6	5.2	5.5
1979	4.6	4.4	5.2	3.8	5.2	4.7	4.0	4.4	5.2	5.0	5.3	2.4	3.9	5.0	4.9	5.3	5.3
1980	4.3	4.2	4.5	3.7	4.9	4.0	4.0	4.4	4.7	3.9	4.8	2.6	3.7	4.7	5.0	4.9	4.7
1981	4.3	4.3	4.6	4.0	4.4	4.8	4.0	4.2	4.8	4.6	4.3	2.5	4.1	5.3	4.4	4.2	4.5
1982	3.8	3.9	4.0	2.9	4.3	4.1	4.0	3.6	3.9	4.3	3.7	2.1	3.1	3.5	4.4	4.4	4.2
1983	3.6	4.1	3.8	2.7	3.9	4.3	3.4	4.6	3.9	3.7	3.7	1.7	3.2	3.3	4.0	3.3	4.2

Retail sales: value (7) / Ventes au détail : valeur (7)

1980 = 100

	Year	Q.1	Q.2	Q.3	Q.4	JAN	FEB	MAR	APR	MAY	JUN	JUL	AUG	SEP	OCT	NOV	DEC
1964	28	24	27	27	33												
1965	30	25	31	27	35												
1966	32	27	31	31	33												
1967	33	29	33	32	39												
1968	34	30	34	33	40												
1969	36	31	35	34	43												
1970	38	33	37	37	46												
1971	40	33	39	39	48												
1972	43	39	42	41	50												
1973	47	41	45	44	56	41	38	44	45	45	46	44	44	44	55	55	57
1974	54	46	52	53	64	46	44	48	53	54	49	52	53	55	58	58	76
1975	61	51	59	60	75	52	49	54	58	60	59	61	59	60	71	65	90
1976	70	61	68	67	83	62	57	63	69	68	68	66	65	69	75	74	100
1977	76	67	75	73	91	56	64	71	74	79	72	70	73	75	81	82	111
1978	83	73	80	79	98	73	68	78	73	81	82	75	80	82	87	89	119
1979	90	80	88	85	108	80	76	86	86	89	88	83	87	84	98	97	129
1980	100	89	95	96	119	90	86	91	97	95	94	93	97	96	110	103	146
1981	110	97	108	105	130	100	92	100	109	107	108	105	104	107	117	114	158
1982	122	108	119	117	144	104	102	117	121	114	122	118	117	117	127	128	177
1983	134	118	129	131	158	111	110	132	122	132	134	128	132	132	138	145	191

New passenger car registrations / Immatriculations de voitures de tourisme neuves

thousands, monthly averages / milliers, moyennes mensuelles

	Year	Q.1	Q.2	Q.3	Q.4	JAN	FEB	MAR	APR	MAY	JUN	JUL	AUG	SEP	OCT	NOV	DEC
1964	20.3	16.2	23.2	23.0	18.8												
1965	23.8	23.5	25.9	24.6	21.2												
1966	17.3	17.6	16.7	16.7	13.0												
1967	15.6	17.4	15.3	15.1	14.8												
1968	16.8	13.6	18.6	17.4	17.5												
1969	19.3	18.6	21.4	18.6	13.6												
1970	17.7	22.0	13.4	17.0	18.3												
1971	15.4	13.2	15.0	15.2	18.2												
1972	19.4	19.2	18.6	21.2	13.4												
1973	19.6	21.2	19.0	17.2	21.1	20.2	23.9	19.6	17.9	20.2	19.0	16.2	15.5	19.9	23.8	21.7	17.7
1974	22.0	16.1	25.1	28.7	18.0	13.9	14.4	20.1	30.2	23.6	21.4	20.4	27.2	38.5	17.5	19.2	17.4
1975	24.5	23.5	23.5	24.6	26.3	22.0	22.4	26.0	23.9	20.6	25.9	20.7	21.2	31.8	28.5	23.7	26.7
1976	26.8	25.0	28.9	24.3	29.0	20.2	24.7	30.0	29.4	28.0	29.4	20.9	21.2	30.7	30.1	29.8	27.0
1977	20.6	22.7	26.3	16.2	17.2	21.0	23.5	23.5	27.7	29.7	21.5	11.6	14.2	22.7	19.2	17.5	14.8
1978	17.0	15.2	18.3	15.9	13.5	13.0	13.9	18.6	19.9	16.5	18.6	13.3	14.8	19.7	20.0	19.2	16.4
1979	18.2	17.5	20.6	16.3	18.3	15.3	16.4	20.7	19.2	22.7	20.0	16.1	14.6	18.2	20.6	19.6	14.6
1980	16.1	17.3	15.4	15.8	15.8	16.5	15.9	19.6	20.0	9.6	16.6	16.3	13.6	17.6	17.0	14.6	15.7
1981	16.0	15.8	16.6	13.6	17.8	12.7	17.2	17.5	18.2	15.4	16.2	12.1	12.4	16.4	18.5	18.0	17.0
1982	18.4	17.4	19.4	14.6	22.3	13.8	17.1	21.2	20.5	17.5	20.2	13.2	12.9	17.7	24.0	21.5	21.4
1983	18.4	17.3	18.7	15.4	22.2	15.7	14.6	21.6	18.7	18.5	18.9	11.1	14.5	20.5	20.8	22.9	22.8

Cost of construction: (8) multiple dwellings

Coût de la construction : (8) immeubles résidentiels

1980 = 100

	Year	Q.1	Q.2	Q.3	Q.4	JAN	FEB	MAR	APR	MAY	JUN	JUL	AUG	SEP	OCT	NOV	DEC
1964																	
1965																	
1966																	
1967																	
1968	29	29	29	29	29		29			29			29			29	
1969	31	30	30	31	32		30			30			31			32	
1970	33	33	34	34	34		33			34			34			34	
1971	35	34	35	35	36		34			35			35			36	
1972	38	37	38	38	38		37			38			38			38	
1973	42	40	42	43	44		40			42			43			44	
1974	50	47	50	51	52		47			50			51			52	
1975	56	54	56	58	58		54			56			58			58	
1976	65	61	65	67	69		61			65			67			69	
1977	75	73	74	76	77		73			74			76			77	
1978	81	80	81	81	82		80			81			81			82	
1979	88	85	86	89	92		85			86			89			92	
1980	100	96	99	102	104		96			99			102			104	
1981	111	108	111	113	114		108			111			113			114	
1982	120	117	118	120	123		117			118			120			123	
1983	131	126	130	133	135		126			130			133			135	

Retail sales: value (7)

Ventes au détail : valeur (7)

Adjusted - Corrigé *

1980 = 100

	Year	Q.1	Q.2	Q.3	Q.4	JAN	FEB	MAR	APR	MAY	JUN	JUL	AUG	SEP	OCT	NOV	DEC
1964		27	27	28	28												
1965		29	31	29	31												
1966		30	31	32	33												
1967		33	33	34	34												
1968		34	34	34	34												
1969		35	35	36	37												
1970		37	38	38	40												
1971		37	39	41	42												
1972		43	42	43	43												
1973		45	46	46	49												
1974		51	53	56	56												
1975		57	60	63	65												
1976		66	69	71	72												
1977		74	76	75	79												
1978		80	81	83	86												
1979		87	89	90	94												
1980		96	97	101	104												
1981		106	110	111	113												
1982		117	121	123	124												
1983		129	131	137	138												

Retail sales: volume

Ventes au détail : volume

Adjusted - Corrigé *

1980 = 100

	Year	Q.1	Q.2	Q.3	Q.4	JAN	FEB	MAR	APR	MAY	JUN	JUL	AUG	SEP	OCT	NOV	DEC
1964	87	86	86	87	88												
1965	91	89	96	86	92												
1966	91	88	90	93	92												
1967	92	92	91	92	92												
1968	93	93	93	92	93												
1969	96	94	94	95	98												
1970	97	96	96	96	93												
1971	93	88	92	96	95												
1972	96	98	94	96	94												
1973	96	96	97	96	93												
1974	99	97	98	103	97												
1975	103	100	103	104	106												
1976	107	104	106	107	107												
1977	106	108	107	104	105												
1978	103	102	102	103	104												
1979	104	104	104	103	103												
1980	100	100	99	101	98												
1981	99	98	100	99	99												
1982	101	100	101	102	100												
1983	101	100	101	103	101												

* Adjusted by the O.E.C.D.

* Corrigé par l'O.C.D.E.

SWEDEN

Employment: industry (9)

thousands

Emploi : industrie (9)

milliers

	Year	Q.1	Q.2	Q.3	Q.4	JAN	FEB	MAR	APR	MAY	JUN	JUL	AUG	SEP	OCT	NOV	DEC
1964	1205	1183	1190	1221	1226		1183			1190			1221			1226	
1965	1255	1255	1249	1260	1255		1255			1249			1260			1255	
1966	1221	1236	1227	1222	1193		1236			1227			1222			1198	
1967	1186	1172	1154	1195	1220		1172			1154			1196			1220	
1968	1198	1220	1177	1185	1209		1220			1177			1185			1209	
1969	1190	1196	1182	1192	1191		1196			1182			1192			1191	
1970	1109	1102	1105	1115	1113	1084	1123	1100	1103	1095	1116	1126	1117	1103	1107	1107	1126
1971	1099	1094	1107	1100	1095	1087	1083	1112	1109	1088	1123	1128	1081	1092	1111	1083	1092
1972	1091	1080	1092	1095	1098	1086	1062	1092	1094	1060	1122	1125	1064	1091	1106	1075	1113
1973	1112	1091	1104	1123	1129	1097	1064	1112	1121	1074	1126	1142	1097	1129	1134	1104	1149
1974	1172	1150	1172	1186	1179	1150	1119	1180	1156	1139	1221	1200	1177	1181	1192	1153	1192
1975	1191	1193	1199	1185	1185	1202	1168	1208	1199	1174	1224	1194	1165	1197	1199	1166	1190
1976	1155	1159	1164	1153	1144	1151	1146	1179	1149	1140	1204	1160	1140	1159	1141	1134	1156
1977	1110	1128	1119	1108	1086	1121	1127	1135	1108	1117	1132	1111	1122	1090	1083	1097	1078
1978	1070	1071	1073	1077	1060	1063	1088	1062	1060	1082	1077	1082	1099	1050	1058	1085	1036
1979	1076	1065	1076	1083	1079	1062	1088	1046	1066	1088	1075	1081	1107	1061	1076	1102	1060
1980	..	1075	..	1083	1061	1062	1097	1066	..	1098	1089	1039	1109	1051	1054	1075	1053
1981	1036	1052	1040	1041	1011	1046	1067	1042	1031	1045	1045	1048	1053	1022	1004	1017	1012
1982	1000	999	1008	1005	988	989	1005	1002	992	1000	1032	1004	1014	997	974	997	992
1983	995	985	999	1008	989	970	990	994	975	999	1023	1019	1011	994	988	990	990

Unemployment: total (9)

thousands

Chômage : total (9)

milliers

	Year	Q.1	Q.2	Q.3	Q.4	JAN	FEB	MAR	APR	MAY	JUN	JUL	AUG	SEP	OCT	NOV	DEC
1964	58	64	56	61	51		64			56			61			51	
1965	44	45	43	44	44		45			43			44			44	
1966	59	65	59	57	56		65			59			57			56	
1967	80	96	67	82	73		96			67			82			73	
1968	85	103	74	86	77		103			74			86			77	
1969	73	86	75	66	64		86			75			66			64	
1970	59	69	52	56	59	74	68	65	62	54	41	46	57	65	59	60	57
1971	101	99	88	102	114	105	94	99	87	84	93	85	107	113	116	120	106
1972	107	123	95	106	105	136	122	109	109	90	87	78	118	121	110	107	100
1973	98	119	87	94	92	128	126	103	103	83	74	82	104	97	95	95	87
1974	80	101	73	78	69	115	101	88	83	61	75	72	81	83	76	68	62
1975	67	71	63	65	69	77	77	60	65	62	63	53	67	76	72	71	64
1976	66	76	60	64	66	92	74	62	70	49	62	54	67	70	74	62	61
1977	75	78	61	80	81	95	74	65	66	53	62	69	89	83	88	78	77
1978	94	99	86	106	84	110	92	96	89	77	91	97	113	108	89	78	86
1979	88	100	85	92	76	117	94	88	86	72	96	86	102	89	78	76	74
1980	..	84	..	87	91	94	82	76	..	70	85	80	88	92	92	96	86
1981	108	101	85	116	129	108	106	90	87	81	86	104	116	127	133	128	125
1982	137	137	120	158	134	153	135	124	112	116	131	133	166	176	127	134	140
1983	151	150	139	170	146	147	155	149	122	135	158	154	179	177	149	142	147

Unemployment (insured unemployed) (10)

thousands

Chômage (chômeurs assurés) (10)

milliers

	Year	Q.1	Q.2	Q.3	Q.4	JAN	FEB	MAR	APR	MAY	JUN	JUL	AUG	SEP	OCT	NOV	DEC
1964	17.0	23.0	17.1	11.3	16.6	24.1	23.0	21.9	22.3	18.1	10.9	8.8	12.2	12.9	13.6	17.0	19.2
1965	15.6	25.4	14.8	8.7	17.6	28.3	24.1	23.8	19.9	15.4	9.2	6.8	9.2	10.2	10.9	16.5	25.4
1966	22.2	38.4	19.0	10.6	20.7	33.8	49.9	31.7	28.7	17.3	11.1	7.7	11.8	12.4	14.0	20.9	27.1
1967	28.8	39.5	26.2	18.7	30.8	40.5	41.8	36.1	32.2	26.6	19.9	15.6	20.0	20.5	25.2	30.5	36.8
1968	33.4	48.5	29.4	23.9	31.6	55.5	45.8	44.3	37.2	28.3	22.7	22.1	25.0	24.8	27.3	32.5	34.9
1969	29.9	44.6	28.1	20.5	25.2	47.6	43.4	42.8	36.3	28.3	19.7	21.5	20.5	19.6	20.4	25.6	32.6
1970	29.5	40.3	26.2	21.7	29.9	39.4	44.6	37.0	33.1	26.9	18.5	23.8	20.8	20.4	22.2	31.1	36.4
1971	45.3	50.0	43.7	38.2	49.6	47.7	48.7	53.5	52.5	42.2	36.2	36.5	38.6	39.4	43.2	50.3	55.4
1972	48.2	60.9	45.2	39.3	47.6	64.8	59.3	58.8	54.4	43.6	37.5	36.6	40.7	40.6	42.8	48.1	52.0
1973	46.0	59.2	44.8	37.7	42.3	60.5	60.2	56.8	51.4	43.6	39.4	36.7	38.7	37.8	38.1	42.0	46.9
1974	39.0	49.7	34.1	33.7	38.6	52.9	50.5	45.6	41.0	32.2	29.2	33.2	34.0	33.9	34.7	36.7	44.3
1975	36.7	41.0	32.7	32.7	40.2	43.6	41.0	38.6	36.2	32.0	29.7	30.9	33.2	34.0	35.8	38.4	46.5
1976	32.7	44.9	32.3	23.6	29.9	47.1	45.0	42.5	37.9	31.6	27.2	22.6	24.2	24.0	25.6	28.4	35.7
1977	34.2	35.4	28.7	31.2	41.6	36.8	35.8	33.6	31.8	27.4	26.9	29.1	31.9	32.6	35.9	40.9	48.1
1978	45.7	49.5	41.0	44.0	48.2	49.9	49.8	48.9	44.4	38.3	40.2	43.6	44.3	44.2	44.8	46.6	53.2
1979	45.1	53.7	41.5	42.3	42.9	55.7	54.4	50.9	45.5	39.0	40.1	43.5	42.6	41.0	40.2	41.5	46.9
1980	43.6	46.7	38.5	40.5	48.5	49.3	47.1	43.7	39.9	38.0	37.6	39.8	40.8	40.8	42.8	46.7	56.2
1981	58.9	55.4	49.0	58.5	72.5	57.8	54.5	54.0	50.1	45.7	51.2	55.0	58.5	62.2	65.1	70.3	82.1
1982	80.4	80.5	70.7	82.5	87.7	83.3	80.7	77.4	71.5	67.0	73.8	79.3	85.3	82.9	82.7	85.0	95.5
1983	91.7	93.0	83.2	94.1	96.4	96.2	92.5	90.3	84.5	78.4	86.7	94.4	96.5	91.4	90.1	94.3	104.8

Unemployment: total (9)
as per cent of total labour force

Chômage : total (9)
en pourcentage de la population active

	Year	Q.1	Q.2	Q.3	Q.4	JAN	FEB	MAR	APR	MAY	JUN	JUL	AUG	SEP	OCT	NOV	DEC
1964	1.6	1.7	1.5	1.7	1.4		1.7			1.5			1.7			1.4	
1965	1.2	1.2	1.2	1.2	1.2		1.2			1.2			1.2			1.2	
1966	1.6	1.7	1.5	1.5	1.3		1.7			1.5			1.5			1.5	
1967	2.1	2.6	1.8	2.2	1.9		2.6			1.8			2.2			1.9	
1968	2.2	2.7	1.9	2.2	2.0		2.7			1.9			2.2			2.0	
1969	1.9	2.3	1.9	1.7	1.7		2.3			1.9			1.7			1.7	
1970	1.5	1.8	1.3	1.4	1.5	1.9	1.8	1.7	1.6	1.4	1.0	1.2	1.4	1.7	1.5	1.5	1.4
1971	2.5	2.5	2.2	2.5	2.9	2.7	2.4	2.5	2.2	2.1	2.3	2.1	2.7	2.8	2.9	3.0	2.7
1972	2.7	3.1	2.4	2.6	2.7	3.5	3.1	2.8	2.8	2.3	2.2	1.9	3.0	3.0	2.8	2.7	2.5
1973	2.5	3.0	2.2	2.3	2.3	3.3	3.2	2.6	2.6	2.1	2.0	2.0	2.6	2.4	2.4	2.4	2.2
1974	2.0	2.6	1.8	1.9	1.7	2.9	2.6	2.2	2.1	1.5	1.7	1.7	2.0	2.0	1.9	1.7	1.5
1975	1.6	1.8	1.5	1.5	1.7	1.9	1.9	1.5	1.6	1.5	1.5	1.2	1.5	1.8	1.7	1.7	1.6
1976	1.6	1.8	1.5	1.5	1.6	2.2	1.8	1.5	1.7	1.2	1.5	1.3	1.6	1.7	1.8	1.5	1.5
1977	1.8	1.9	1.5	1.9	1.9	2.3	1.8	1.6	1.6	1.3	1.5	1.6	2.1	2.0	2.1	1.9	1.3
1978	2.2	2.4	2.0	2.5	2.0	2.6	2.2	2.3	2.1	1.9	2.1	2.2	2.7	2.6	2.1	1.9	2.1
1979	2.1	2.4	2.0	2.2	1.8	2.8	2.2	2.1	2.0	1.7	2.2	2.0	2.4	2.1	1.8	1.8	1.7
1980	..	2.0	..	2.0	2.1	2.2	1.9	1.8	..	1.6	1.9	1.8	2.0	2.1	2.1	2.3	2.0
1981	2.5	2.4	2.0	2.6	3.0	2.5	2.5	2.1	2.0	1.9	2.0	2.3	2.6	2.9	3.0	3.0	2.9
1982	3.2	3.2	2.8	3.6	3.1	3.6	3.1	2.9	2.6	2.7	3.0	3.0	3.7	4.0	3.0	3.1	3.2
1983	3.5	3.5	3.1	3.8	3.4	3.4	3.6	3.4	2.8	3.1	3.5	3.4	4.0	4.1	3.4	3.3	3.4

Unemployment: total (9)
thousands

Adjusted - Corrigé *

Chômage : total (9)
milliers

	Year	Q.1	Q.2	Q.3	Q.4	JAN	FEB	MAR	APR	MAY	JUN	JUL	AUG	SEP	OCT	NOV	DEC
1964		56	61	60	55												
1965		39	47	44	49												
1966		56	63	58	62												
1967		82	72	83	81												
1968		87	80	86	84												
1969		73	81	68	68												
1970		59	57	58	61												
1971		86	97	105	127												
1972		106	106	109	107												
1973		104	98	95	93												
1974		89	82	80	69												
1975		64	71	65	70												
1976		68	68	63	67												
1977		70	69	78	83												
1978		89	99	101	86												
1979		90	101	87	77												
1980		76	..	81	91												
1981		93	103	108	127												
1982		125	147	148	131												
1983		137	171	158	142												

Unemployment (insured unemployed) (10)
thousands

Adjusted - Corrigé *

Chômage (chômeurs assurés) (10)
milliers

	Year	Q.1	Q.2	Q.3	Q.4	JAN	FEB	MAR	APR	MAY	JUN	JUL	AUG	SEP	OCT	NOV	DEC
1964		14.8	18.1	20.0	18.2	14.2	14.5	15.7	17.0	18.5	13.8	19.8	20.1	20.2	19.5	18.5	16.6
1965		16.3	15.6	15.5	13.4	16.7	15.4	16.8	15.3	15.7	15.8	15.4	15.1	15.9	15.7	17.9	21.7
1966		24.8	19.6	18.7	22.0	20.0	32.1	22.4	22.1	17.5	19.2	17.5	19.4	19.3	20.3	22.7	23.1
1967		26.9	28.7	27.7	32.0	26.1	28.9	25.6	27.3	29.1	29.6	24.9	28.7	29.5	31.7	31.4	32.8
1968		36.0	31.8	32.9	32.7	41.2	33.0	33.9	32.3	30.6	32.4	31.5	33.6	33.7	33.8	33.3	30.8
1969		32.2	30.5	29.4	27.1	33.4	30.9	32.4	31.2	30.7	29.4	31.1	28.9	28.3	26.9	26.1	28.4
1970		28.2	28.5	30.4	30.6	25.5	32.6	26.7	28.1	29.4	28.1	33.4	28.9	28.8	28.5	31.4	31.9
1971		38.3	46.2	46.5	50.0	34.1	37.1	43.7	47.8	45.1	45.7	46.2	46.1	47.2	49.0	50.3	50.6
1972		50.0	47.9	47.1	47.4	51.8	48.2	50.0	50.2	46.8	46.7	46.0	47.7	47.5	47.8	47.9	46.6
1973		49.0	47.8	44.9	41.6	48.2	49.8	49.1	48.0	47.2	48.1	46.0	44.9	43.8	42.2	41.6	40.9
1974		40.5	37.3	40.3	37.4	41.6	40.9	38.9	38.4	36.1	37.3	41.9	39.7	39.3	38.2	36.4	37.7
1975		32.9	36.0	38.4	38.3	33.3	32.5	33.0	34.5	36.2	37.2	38.3	38.2	38.7	38.7	38.1	39.6
1976		37.5	35.7	28.7	28.4	37.8	37.2	37.6	36.9	35.9	34.1	29.2	28.6	28.3	28.3	28.2	28.7
1977		28.6	32.3	35.8	40.0	28.0	28.6	29.2	31.4	32.2	33.3	34.9	35.8	36.6	38.5	40.7	40.7
1978		43.1	44.8	48.2	46.5	41.4	43.0	44.9	44.7	43.4	46.2	48.8	47.9	47.9	47.3	46.3	45.7
1979		47.4	45.7	46.1	41.1	47.1	47.7	47.3	46.5	44.5	45.9	48.1	45.9	44.4	42.6	41.3	39.4
1980		40.5	42.9	44.0	46.7	40.5	40.6	40.5	41.5	43.9	43.4	44.0	43.9	44.0	45.2	46.4	48.6
1981		49.3	53.6	61.9	70.7	48.8	48.0	51.0	52.2	51.7	57.0	59.0	61.5	65.2	67.5	70.1	74.5
1982		74.4	75.4	35.8	85.9	74.2	74.3	74.6	73.7	73.0	79.5	83.[illegible]	88.4	85.8	85.1	84.8	87.8
1983		86.9	87.9	97.3	94.5	87.0	86.1	87.7	86.8	34.5	92.5	98.1	99.5	94.3	92.4	94.1	97.0

* Adjusted by the O.E.C.D.

* Corrigé par l'O.C.D.E.

SWEDEN

Jobs vacant, unfilled vacancies (10)
thousands

Offres d'emploi non satisfaites (10)
milliers

	Year	Q.1	Q.2	Q.3	Q.4	JAN	FEB	MAR	APR	MAY	JUN	JUL	AUG	SEP	OCT	NOV	DEC
1964	47.1	39.4	53.5	51.0	44.6	36.1	38.9	43.2	47.8	55.0	57.8	52.6	52.7	47.7	44.8	44.4	44.5
1965	53.8	45.1	62.3	59.5	48.2	41.2	44.9	49.1	55.4	64.1	67.4	61.4	60.5	56.8	51.0	48.3	45.4
1966	44.6	41.4	53.5	48.7	34.9	40.8	40.2	43.1	47.7	56.2	56.6	54.2	48.9	43.0	38.1	33.4	33.2
1967	32.6	28.7	38.8	36.0	26.9	28.1	27.8	30.1	33.5	40.3	42.6	40.5	36.7	30.9	26.1	26.3	28.3
1968	36.3	26.5	42.6	40.6	35.4	25.0	26.9	27.5	34.2	46.4	47.3	43.9	41.0	36.9	34.5	34.6	37.0
1969	56.9	39.6	65.5	54.1	58.5	36.4	39.0	43.3	54.9	68.1	73.7	65.7	66.2	60.4	58.5	56.7	60.3
1970	62.2	57.1	78.3	66.3	47.3	54.7	56.6	60.0	71.1	82.6	81.3	72.1	68.6	58.1	52.2	46.2	43.5
1971	36.0	34.8	46.9	35.9	26.4	36.5	33.3	34.5	43.0	49.9	47.7	41.5	36.3	29.9	25.5	25.6	28.0
1972	31.7	25.6	41.3	34.0	25.9	23.9	24.8	28.1	35.2	43.7	45.0	38.1	35.1	28.7	25.0	25.0	27.6
1973	35.3	26.2	42.1	38.2	34.8	24.9	26.1	27.5	37.5	44.0	44.7	40.5	39.1	35.1	32.7	35.6	36.2
1974	48.9	35.9	65.3	50.2	44.0	30.7	35.3	41.8	58.4	68.9	68.7	53.6	52.1	44.9	45.2	44.6	42.2
1975	50.3	48.7	73.0	45.2	34.2	42.7	47.7	55.7	78.3	79.3	61.5	49.7	48.8	37.3	33.9	35.9	32.9
1976	46.4	39.9	64.8	44.6	36.4	33.4	37.3	49.1	64.0	69.8	60.6	49.0	45.7	39.1	38.4	37.8	33.2
1977	38.0	38.7	57.6	30.9	25.0	31.1	35.9	49.3	63.4	60.0	49.3	37.1	32.0	23.7	23.1	27.5	24.3
1978	34.6	31.9	50.3	28.4	27.8	23.7	29.2	42.8	58.3	54.0	38.7	29.8	30.6	25.0	25.4	31.0	26.9
1979	49.5	45.1	68.3	41.9	42.4	30.1	45.0	60.3	76.5	71.3	57.2	44.5	42.6	38.7	40.2	46.2	40.9
1980	54.0	64.5	75.7	42.2	33.5	45.9	66.6	80.9	90.5	77.9	58.7	46.9	45.4	34.3	32.6	38.8	29.3
1981	30.0	45.7	38.3	19.0	17.1	32.4	50.1	54.6	46.9	43.0	25.1	20.3	19.5	17.2	16.8	21.3	13.1
1982	19.9	27.6	25.5	13.5	12.9	16.8	32.2	33.8	30.5	25.6	20.6	13.7	14.5	12.1	12.1	16.7	10.1
1983	20.8	26.9	25.4	14.8	16.0	15.9	34.9	30.0	28.8	25.5	22.0	15.2	15.8	13.5	15.0	19.4	13.6

Monthly hours worked: (11)(12)(13)
mining and manufacturing
1980 = 100

Heures effectuées par mois : (13) (12) (11)
industries extractives et manufacturières
1980 = 100

	Year	Q.1	Q.2	Q.3	Q.4	JAN	FEB	MAR	APR	MAY	JUN	JUL	AUG	SEP	OCT	NOV	DEC
1964																	
1965																	
1966																	
1967																	
1968	137.6	147.9	144.9	114.3	143.3	147.3	147.1	149.2	148.3	145.5	140.8	59.8	137.4	145.8	147.4	150.1	132.3
1969	137.7	142.8	143.9	117.3	146.7	142.7	141.5	144.2	144.8	141.8	145.1	72.0	135.9	144.0	145.5	149.6	144.9
1970	141.0	147.1	148.8	121.0	147.1	143.2	148.9	149.2	150.8	149.9	145.7	75.9	139.3	147.7	147.4	149.2	144.6
1971	133.1	144.3	141.0	110.3	136.7	145.5	144.8	142.6	143.2	140.4	139.6	63.8	128.9	138.3	139.6	138.4	132.1
1972	126.1	133.3	132.2	105.6	133.2	131.4	135.2	133.3	136.2	131.5	128.8	56.2	125.6	135.1	133.9	134.4	131.4
1973	126.0	131.6	132.2	105.8	134.3	130.3	131.8	132.8	130.5	134.1	132.0	55.8	125.7	136.0	135.6	136.4	131.0
1974	128.4	134.8	135.1	108.9	134.7	133.9	135.5	134.9	134.4	132.5	138.3	60.4	129.7	136.7	137.4	139.8	127.0
1975	125.7	134.8	132.0	106.0	129.8	134.3	134.7	135.5	135.2	128.8	132.1	58.8	126.8	132.5	130.9	133.3	125.0
1976	120.2	127.0	127.2	101.7	124.8	124.9	128.1	128.1	128.4	124.8	128.5	57.7	121.3	126.0	126.1	126.4	122.0
1977	112.6	122.6	119.5	93.4	114.9	120.2	124.4	123.2	122.4	116.1	120.1	47.3	113.9	119.1	118.6	118.5	107.5
1978	104.4	112.2	110.7	85.5	109.3	113.8	112.1	110.7	114.6	106.7	110.7	39.6	105.8	111.1	110.7	111.4	105.9
1979	101.2	109.1	107.7	85.9	102.0	108.3	110.0	109.0	107.2	105.9	109.9	42.7	104.2	110.7	109.8	111.2	84.9
1980	100.0	108.4	98.9	86.8	105.9	108.6	108.2	108.6	107.5	81.9	107.2	51.5	102.0	106.7	107.2	109.6	100.7
1981	95.9	102.4	101.9	79.1	100.0	99.2	104.3	103.6	103.6	100.5	101.6	38.4	97.5	101.3	101.5	102.1	96.4
1982	91.0	97.2	97.5	73.9	95.6	96.0	98.7	96.9	99.1	94.5	99.1	35.5	90.1	96.0	96.7	96.4	93.7
1983	88.2	92.6	94.9	71.4	94.0	92.2	93.7	91.7	96.9	92.8	95.1	33.1	86.8	94.2	95.1	95.1	91.8

Hourly earnings: (12)
mining and manufacturing
1980 = 100

Gains horaires : (12)
industries extractives et manufacturières
1980 = 100

	Year	Q.1	Q.2	Q.3	Q.4	JAN	FEB	MAR	APR	MAY	JUN	JUL	AUG	SEP	OCT	NOV	DEC
1964																	
1965																	
1966																	
1967																	
1968	30.0	29.2	30.2	30.1	30.6	28.6	29.3	29.7	30.3	30.1	30.3	30.1	29.9	30.2	30.3	30.5	31.0
1969	32.3	31.2	32.0	32.2	33.8	31.1	31.2	31.4	31.9	32.2	31.9	31.6	31.9	32.8	33.3	33.9	34.3
1970	36.6	35.2	36.8	36.7	37.5	34.2	35.4	36.2	36.3	37.4	36.8	36.6	36.5	36.9	37.3	37.5	37.9
1971	39.3	37.9	38.5	39.4	41.5	37.9	37.9	37.9	38.5	38.7	38.3	38.5	39.3	40.3	41.0	41.5	41.9
1972	45.2	43.9	45.5	45.3	46.1	42.8	44.2	44.6	45.5	45.8	45.2	45.8	44.7	45.3	45.7	45.9	46.6
1973	49.0	47.6	49.3	48.9	50.0	46.6	48.1	48.3	49.2	49.1	49.6	49.0	48.4	49.3	49.4	49.9	50.7
1974	54.4	50.7	55.0	55.0	56.7	50.2	50.6	51.4	54.3	55.1	55.6	54.8	54.7	55.6	55.9	56.5	57.7
1975	62.4	57.8	59.4	64.9	67.5	57.5	57.6	58.4	58.1	59.5	60.7	63.8	64.9	66.0	66.5	67.6	68.4
1976	73.6	70.4	74.3	74.4	75.4	68.5	71.0	71.8	73.7	74.5	74.5	75.3	73.6	74.3	75.0	75.3	76.0
1977	78.5	76.1	77.0	78.9	82.0	76.4	76.2	75.8	77.4	77.1	76.6	79.0	77.9	79.8	81.5	81.8	82.7
1978	85.3	83.3	85.0	86.0	86.8	83.0	83.3	83.7	84.0	85.7	85.2	87.1	84.8	86.1	86.2	86.5	87.8
1979	91.9	88.7	92.9	92.4	93.5	87.3	88.8	90.0	92.9	92.7	93.0	93.2	91.2	92.7	92.3	92.9	95.2
1980	100.0	96.4	98.5	100.3	104.7	96.2	96.2	95.9	99.0	98.9	97.5	99.0	99.8	102.3	102.9	104.8	105.5
1981	110.5	107.2	110.4	111.4	113.1	107.7	107.1	106.9	108.7	110.8	111.5	112.5	110.4	111.4	112.3	113.0	113.8
1982	119.2	115.8	120.3	120.0	120.7	115.3	115.4	116.7	119.9	121.7	119.4	121.5	119.0	119.6	120.3	120.1	121.6
1983	128.6	127.0	129.0	128.5	129.9	127.6	127.0	126.3	128.8	129.7	128.5	130.9	126.5	128.3	129.3	129.4	131.1

Jobs vacant, unfilled vacancies (10) — Offres d'emploi non satisfaites (10)

thousands — milliers

Adjusted - Corrigé *

	Year	Q.1	Q.2	Q.3	Q.4	JAN	FEB	MAR	APR	MAY	JUN	JUL	AUG	SEP	OCT	NOV	DEC
1964		46.4	46.5	46.3	49.5	45.1	46.2	47.8	46.8	46.5	46.3	45.7	46.9	46.3	48.2	49.7	50.7
1965		53.5	54.2	53.8	53.6	51.9	54.0	54.5	54.5	53.8	54.2	52.1	53.9	55.3	54.4	54.4	51.8
1966		49.9	46.1	43.6	39.2	51.8	49.5	48.3	47.3	46.6	44.5	44.9	43.5	42.2	40.9	38.7	37.9
1967		34.9	32.9	32.3	30.6	36.1	34.6	34.1	33.2	32.6	32.7	33.2	32.6	31.0	28.6	31.1	32.3
1968		32.2	35.4	37.0	40.5	32.1	33.2	31.4	33.4	37.1	35.6	36.8	36.6	37.6	38.3	41.0	42.3
1969		47.9	53.9	59.2	67.2	46.4	47.8	49.5	52.6	53.9	55.3	56.2	59.5	61.8	65.9	66.5	69.3
1970		69.7	63.6	61.1	54.9	69.1	70.5	69.6	66.0	63.9	61.0	61.5	61.6	60.3	60.6	54.8	49.4
1971		43.0	37.5	33.1	31.3	47.0	42.3	39.7	39.4	37.7	35.2	35.0	32.6	31.6	30.8	31.2	32.1
1972		31.6	32.1	31.6	31.5	31.0	31.5	32.4	31.1	32.2	33.0	31.9	31.9	31.0	30.8	31.2	32.5
1973		32.1	32.0	36.8	43.4	32.9	32.7	30.6	31.7	31.8	32.5	35.2	36.2	38.8	40.1	44.7	45.4
1974		43.3	47.6	50.2	56.8	42.0	43.2	44.7	45.2	47.7	50.0	48.6	50.3	51.7	58.2	56.2	56.1
1975		57.0	51.6	47.3	45.5	58.4	57.7	55.0	56.8	52.8	45.3	47.3	49.5	45.1	45.7	45.5	45.3
1976		45.1	45.0	48.8	49.7	45.9	44.7	44.8	43.3	45.8	45.9	47.7	48.4	50.3	54.3	48.1	46.7
1977		42.0	39.5	35.1	34.6	43.7	41.0	41.4	41.0	38.7	38.9	37.4	35.4	32.4	34.0	35.0	34.9
1978		32.6	34.5	34.2	38.8	33.5	30.8	33.6	36.2	35.3	31.8	31.6	35.3	35.8	37.8	39.4	39.2
1979		42.8	48.4	52.9	58.7	40.9	42.7	44.7	47.1	48.1	50.1	50.6	50.7	57.5	59.7	56.9	59.6
1980		57.4	55.5	54.8	45.3	59.0	57.6	55.7	57.4	55.6	53.4	57.2	56.4	50.9	47.9	45.6	42.4
1981		38.9	28.8	25.6	22.6	40.8	40.7	35.3	30.7	32.2	23.5	26.3	24.7	25.8	24.7	23.9	19.1
1982		22.5	19.7	18.4	16.9	21.2	25.4	21.0	20.5	19.5	19.2	18.5	18.7	18.0	17.7	18.3	14.7
1983		21.8	19.9	20.5	21.0	20.1	27.1	18.3	19.7	19.6	20.5	20.5	20.5	19.9	22.1	21.0	19.9

Monthly hours worked: (11)(12) — Heures effectuées par mois : (12)(11)

mining and manufacturing — industries extractives et manufacturières

1980 = 100

Adjusted - Corrigé *

	Year	Q.1	Q.2	Q.3	Q.4	JAN	FEB	MAR	APR	MAY	JUN	JUL	AUG	SEP	OCT	NOV	DEC
1964																	
1965																	
1966																	
1967																	
1968		140.8	138.0	135.2	135.9												
1969		136.0	137.0	138.7	139.0												
1970		140.1	141.7	143.2	139.3												
1971		137.5	134.3	130.7	129.5												
1972		127.0	125.9	125.2	126.2												
1973		125.4	125.9	125.4	127.2												
1974		128.3	128.6	129.1	127.6												
1975		128.4	125.8	125.5	123.1												
1976		121.0	121.2	120.3	118.4												
1977		116.1	114.0	110.8	109.2												
1978		106.0	105.9	101.3	103.9												
1979		102.9	103.4	101.7	96.7												
1980		102.2	95.1	102.7	100.3												
1981		96.5	98.3	93.5	94.3												
1982		91.5	94.2	87.2	90.6												
1983		87.1	91.8	84.2	82.1												

Hourly labour cost: — Coût horaire de la main-d'œuvre :

mining and manufacturing — industries extractives et manufacturières

1980 = 100

	Year	Q.1	Q.2	Q.3	Q.4	JAN	FEB	MAR	APR	MAY	JUN	JUL	AUG	SEP	OCT	NOV	DEC
1964																	
1965																	
1966																	
1967																	
1968	23	22	23	23	23		22			23			23			23	
1969	26	25	25	26	26		25			25			26			26	
1970	29	28	29	29	29		28			29			29			29	
1971	32	32	32	32	33		32			32			32			33	
1972	36	35	36	35	37		35			36			35			37	
1973	40	39	40	40	41		39			40			40			41	
1974	47	46	48	47	49		46			48			47			49	
1975	58	56	58	59	60		56			58			59			60	
1976	67	65	68	67	68		65			68			67			68	
1977	74	72	74	75	77		72			74			75			77	
1978	83	82	84	81	83		82			84			81			83	
1979	91	89	90	89	93		89			90			89			93	
1980	100	95	102	101	103		95			102			101			103	
1981	110	109	111	109	111		109			111			109			111	
1982	118	118	120	117	118		118			120			117			118	
1983	127	126	129	126	129		126			129			126			129	

* Adjusted by the O.E.C.D. — * Corrigé par l'O.C.D.E.

Producer prices (home market): (14)
manufactured goods
1980 = 100

Prix à la production (marché intérieur) : (14)
produits manufacturés
1980 = 100

	Year	Q.1	Q.2	Q.3	Q.4	JAN	FEB	MAR	APR	MAY	JUN	JUL	AUG	SEP	OCT	NOV	DEC
1964	33																
1965	34																
1966	35	35	35	35	35	35	35	35	35	35	35	35	35	35	35	35	35
1967	35	35	35	35	35	35	35	35	35	35	35	35	35	35	35	35	35
1968	35	36	35	35	36	35	36	36	35	35	35	35	35	35	35	36	36
1969	37	36	36	37	38	36	36	36	36	36	37	37	37	37	38	38	38
1970	40	39	40	40	40	39	39	39	40	40	40	40	40	40	40	40	40
1971	40	40	40	41	41	40	40	40	40	40	40	40	41	41	41	41	41
1972	42	42	42	42	43	41	42	42	42	42	42	42	42	43	43	43	43
1973	47	44	46	48	50	44	44	45	46	46	46	47	48	48	49	50	51
1974	58	55	57	59	60	53	55	57	57	57	58	59	59	59	60	60	60
1975	62	61	61	61	62	61	61	61	61	61	61	61	61	62	62	63	63
1976	67	65	66	68	69	64	65	65	66	66	67	68	68	68	69	69	69
1977	73	71	72	74	76	70	71	71	72	72	73	74	74	75	75	76	76
1978	79	78	79	80	81	77	78	78	78	78	79	79	80	80	81	81	82
1979	88	84	87	90	93	83	84	85	86	87	88	89	91	91	92	93	93
1980	100	97	99	101	103	95	97	98	99	99	100	100	101	101	102	103	103
1981	111	106	109	112	116	105	107	107	108	109	109	110	112	113	115	116	116
1982	125	120	122	124	132	120	120	121	122	122	123	124	124	125	130	132	133
1983	139	135	137	141	143	135	135	135	136	137	138	140	141	141	142	143	144

Producer prices (home market): (14)
food
1980 = 100

Prix à la production (marché intérieur) : (14)
alimentation
1980 = 100

	Year	Q.1	Q.2	Q.3	Q.4	JAN	FEB	MAR	APR	MAY	JUN	JUL	AUG	SEP	OCT	NOV	DEC
1964	39																
1965	41																
1966	41	41	41	41	42	41	41	42	42	41	41	41	41	42	42	42	42
1967	42	42	41	42	42	41	42	42	41	41	42	42	41	42	42	42	42
1968	42	42	42	42	43	42	42	42	42	42	42	42	42	43	43	43	43
1969	43	43	43	43	45	43	43	43	43	43	43	43	43	44	44	45	45
1970	47	45	46	48	48	45	45	46	46	46	46	48	48	48	48	48	48
1971	48	47	47	49	49	47	47	47	47	47	47	48	49	49	49	49	49
1972	52	51	52	53	54	51	51	51	52	52	52	52	52	54	54	54	54
1973	58	56	57	58	58	56	57	56	57	57	58	58	58	58	58	58	59
1974	61	61	61	62	62	60	61	62	61	61	61	61	62	61	61	62	62
1975	64	62	62	64	65	62	62	62	62	62	62	64	64	65	65	66	66
1976	72	69	70	73	74	69	69	69	70	70	71	73	73	73	74	74	75
1977	81	78	81	83	84	77	78	79	80	81	82	84	83	83	84	84	84
1978	87	87	86	87	88	87	87	87	86	86	86	87	87	87	88	88	88
1979	91	89	90	93	94	88	89	89	89	90	91	92	93	93	94	94	94
1980	100	98	99	101	103	97	98	99	99	99	99	101	102	101	102	103	103
1981	114	109	111	116	119	107	109	109	110	111	111	115	116	117	119	119	119
1982	131	127	129	133	136	126	127	128	128	129	129	132	133	134	135	136	137
1983	144	139	142	146	150	137	140	140	141	142	143	146	146	146	147	149	153

Producer prices (home market): (14)
textiles, clothing and leather
1980 = 100

Prix à la production (marché intérieur) : (14)
textiles, habillement et cuir
1980 = 100

	Year	Q.1	Q.2	Q.3	Q.4	JAN	FEB	MAR	APR	MAY	JUN	JUL	AUG	SEP	OCT	NOV	DEC
1964	40																
1965	40																
1966	41	41	41	41	41	41	41	41	41	41	41	41	41	41	41	41	41
1967	41	41	41	41	41	41	41	41	41	41	41	41	41	41	41	41	41
1968	42	42	42	42	41	42	41	42	42	42	42	42	42	42	42	41	42
1969	42	42	42	42	42	42	42	42	42	42	42	42	42	42	42	42	42
1970	43	43	43	44	44	43	43	43	43	43	43	44	44	44	44	44	44
1971	45	44	44	45	45	44	44	44	45	44	45	45	45	45	45	45	46
1972	47	47	47	47	48	46	47	47	47	47	47	47	47	48	48	48	48
1973	52	50	51	52	54	50	50	50	51	51	51	52	53	53	54	54	54
1974	60	57	59	61	61	56	58	58	58	59	59	61	61	61	61	61	61
1975	63	63	63	63	64	62	63	63	63	63	63	63	64	64	64	64	64
1976	68	66	67	69	70	66	65	66	66	67	67	68	69	69	69	70	70
1977	75	73	74	75	77	73	73	73	73	73	74	75	75	76	76	77	78
1978	82	81	82	83	83	80	82	82	82	82	82	82	83	83	83	83	83
1979	90	87	89	91	92	86	87	88	88	89	89	91	91	92	92	92	93
1980	100	97	98	102	103	95	98	98	98	98	99	100	102	103	103	103	104
1981	111	107	109	112	115	106	107	108	108	109	109	114	112	114	115	115	116
1982	124	120	122	124	130	118	119	121	121	122	122	123	124	125	129	130	130
1983	141	137	139	142	145	136	137	138	138	139	139	141	142	142	143	143	148

Producer prices (home market): (14)
wood and wood products
1980 = 100

Prix à la production (marché intérieur) : (14)
bois et ouvrages en bois
1980 = 100

	Year	Q.1	Q.2	Q.3	Q.4	JAN	FEB	MAR	APR	MAY	JUN	JUL	AUG	SEP	OCT	NOV	DEC
1964	31																
1965	33																
1966	33	33	33	33	33	33	33	33	33	33	33	33	33	33	33	32	32
1967	32	32	32	32	32	32	32	32	32	32	32	32	32	32	32	32	32
1968	32	32	32	32	33	32	32	32	32	32	32	32	32	32	32	33	33
1969	34	33	33	34	34	33	33	33	33	33	34	34	34	34	34	34	34
1970	36	35	35	36	36	35	35	35	35	36	36	36	36	36	36	36	36
1971	36	36	36	36	36	36	36	36	36	36	36	36	36	36	36	36	36
1972	38	37	37	38	39	36	37	37	37	37	38	38	38	38	39	39	39
1973	47	41	45	49	51	40	41	42	44	45	47	49	50	50	51	51	52
1974	56	55	56	57	58	54	55	56	56	56	56	57	57	57	58	58	57
1975	59	58	59	58	60	58	58	59	59	59	59	58	58	58	60	60	61
1976	66	63	65	68	69	62	63	64	65	65	66	67	68	68	69	70	70
1977	74	72	74	74	74	71	73	73	74	74	74	74	74	74	74	74	74
1978	77	76	77	78	79	75	75	77	77	77	77	78	78	78	78	79	79
1979	86	83	85	88	91	81	83	84	85	85	85	86	88	89	90	91	92
1980	100	95	99	102	104	94	95	96	98	99	99	100	102	103	104	104	105
1981	108	106	107	108	110	106	106	106	107	107	107	107	109	109	109	110	110
1982	115	112	113	115	119	111	112	112	113	113	113	115	115	116	117	119	120
1983	127	122	126	129	132	121	122	123	125	126	127	128	130	130	131	133	133

Producer prices (home market): (14)
pulp, paper and paper products
1980 = 100

Prix à la production (marché intérieur) : (14)
pâte à papier, papier et articles en papier
1980 = 100

	Year	Q.1	Q.2	Q.3	Q.4	JAN	FEB	MAR	APR	MAY	JUN	JUL	AUG	SEP	OCT	NOV	DEC
1964	28																
1965	29																
1966	31	30	30	31	31	30	30	30	30	30	30	31	31	31	31	31	31
1967	32	32	32	32	33	31	32	32	32	32	32	32	32	32	33	33	33
1968	33	33	33	33	33	33	33	33	33	33	33	33	33	33	33	33	33
1969	34	34	34	34	34	34	34	34	34	34	34	34	34	34	34	34	34
1970	36	35	36	37	37	35	35	36	36	36	36	37	36	37	37	37	37
1971	39	38	39	39	39	38	38	39	39	39	39	39	39	39	39	39	39
1972	40	39	40	40	41	39	39	40	40	40	40	40	40	40	40	41	41
1973	43	42	43	44	45	41	42	42	42	42	43	43	44	44	45	45	46
1974	55	49	53	58	61	47	49	50	51	53	54	57	58	59	60	61	62
1975	64	63	64	65	66	62	63	63	64	64	64	64	65	65	65	66	66
1976	69	67	69	69	70	67	67	68	69	69	69	69	69	69	70	70	71
1977	75	73	75	75	76	73	73	74	74	75	75	75	75	75	76	76	76
1978	80	77	79	80	83	77	77	77	78	78	79	79	80	82	83	83	83
1979	87	85	86	88	91	84	85	85	86	86	87	88	88	89	90	91	92
1980	100	96	99	102	104	94	96	96	98	99	100	100	102	103	103	104	105
1981	113	108	112	114	117	106	106	111	111	112	113	112	114	115	116	117	117
1982	126	123	126	125	129	123	124	124	126	126	125	125	126	126	127	129	129
1983	139	134	137	141	144	134	134	134	134	137	139	140	141	141	144	145	145

Producer prices (home market): (14)
chemicals
1980 = 100

Prix à la production (marché intérieur) : (14)
produits chimiques
1980 = 100

	Year	Q.1	Q.2	Q.3	Q.4	JAN	FEB	MAR	APR	MAY	JUN	JUL	AUG	SEP	OCT	NOV	DEC
1964	26																
1965	27																
1966	27	27	27	27	27	27	27	27	27	27	27	27	27	27	27	27	27
1967	27	27	27	27	27	27	27	27	27	27	27	27	27	27	27	27	27
1968	27	27	27	27	27	27	27	27	27	27	27	27	27	27	27	27	27
1969	27	27	27	27	27	27	27	27	27	27	27	27	27	27	27	27	27
1970	28	27	28	28	28	27	27	27	27	28	28	28	28	28	28	28	28
1971	29	29	29	29	29	29	29	29	29	29	29	29	29	29	29	29	29
1972	30	30	30	30	30	30	30	30	30	30	30	30	30	30	30	30	30
1973	33	31	32	33	37	30	30	31	31	32	32	33	33	34	35	37	39
1974	51	48	51	53	53	42	51	52	53	50	51	52	52	53	53	53	53
1975	54	54	53	52	54	54	54	54	54	53	53	52	52	52	53	54	54
1976	57	57	57	58	58	56	57	57	57	57	57	57	58	58	58	58	58
1977	62	60	61	62	64	59	60	60	61	61	61	61	61	64	64	65	65
1978	66	65	65	66	68	65	65	65	65	65	65	66	66	67	67	68	68
1979	82	71	78	88	91	69	71	73	74	77	83	86	89	90	91	91	92
1980	100	96	99	101	104	95	96	98	98	99	100	101	100	100	102	104	106
1981	117	110	113	118	125	108	111	112	112	114	114	116	118	121	124	125	126
1982	134	129	128	132	147	129	129	128	127	127	129	130	132	133	145	149	148
1983	150	146	146	151	155	149	146	143	145	146	148	149	152	153	154	155	156

SWEDEN

Producer prices (home market): (14)

basic metals

1980 = 100

Prix à la production (marché intérieur) : (14)

métaux de base

1980 = 100

	Year	Q.1	Q.2	Q.3	Q.4	JAN	FEB	MAR	APR	MAY	JUN	JUL	AUG	SEP	OCT	NOV	DEC
1964	34																
1965	36																
1966	37	38	38	36	36	37	38	38	39	38	38	37	36	35	36	36	36
1967	35	36	35	35	35	36	36	35	35	35	35	35	35	35	35	36	36
1968	=36=	37	35	35	35	36	38	38	36	35	35	35	35	35	35	35	36
1969	41	37	39	42	46	36	37	37	39	39	41	41	43	44	45	46	47
1970	46	47	48	45	43	47	47	48	49	48	47	46	45	45	44	43	43
1971	42	43	43	43	41	42	42	43	44	43	43	43	43	42	42	41	41
1972	42	41	42	42	43	41	41	42	41	41	42	42	42	42	42	42	43
1973	51	45	48	52	58	43	44	47	48	48	49	51	53	53	55	58	60
1974	69	66	71	69	69	62	65	70	72	71	69	69	70	68	69	69	69
1975	64	58	65	62	61	69	69	67	66	65	63	63	63	61	61	61	61
1976	67	62	68	70	69	61	63	63	67	68	69	70	70	70	70	69	69
1977	69	69	69	68	69	69	69	70	69	69	68	68	68	70	70	69	69
1978	72	70	72	74	75	70	70	70	71	72	72	73	74	74	75	75	76
1979	87	81	86	89	93	78	81	83	85	86	86	88	88	90	91	93	94
1980	100	99	100	101	100	97	101	101	99	100	100	101	101	101	101	101	99
1981	102	100	100	102	106	100	100	100	100	100	100	101	103	103	105	105	107
1982	116	113	116	116	118	110	113	115	116	117	117	116	116	115	117	119	119
1983	129	123	128	132	133	121	122	124	126	128	129	131	133	133	133	134	133

Producer prices (home market): (14)

metal products

1980 = 100

Prix à la production (marché intérieur) : (14)

ouvrages en métaux

1980 = 100

	Year	Q.1	Q.2	Q.3	Q.4	JAN	FEB	MAR	APR	MAY	JUN	JUL	AUG	SEP	OCT	NOV	DEC
1964	36																
1965	36																
1966	36	36	36	36	37	36	36	36	36	37	36	37	37	36	37	37	37
1967	36	36	36	36	36	36	36	36	36	36	36	36	36	36	36	36	36
1968	=37=	37	37	37	37	37	37	37	37	37	37	37	37	37	37	37	37
1969	40	37	39	41	43	37	37	38	38	39	39	39	41	42	43	43	44
1970	46	45	46	46	46	45	45	46	46	46	46	46	46	46	46	46	46
1971	46	45	46	46	45	45	45	46	46	46	46	46	46	46	46	46	46
1972	48	47	48	49	50	47	47	47	48	48	48	48	49	49	50	50	50
1973	50	47	49	50	52	47	48	48	49	49	49	50	51	51	52	52	52
1974	59	55	58	61	62	55	55	56	58	58	59	60	61	61	62	62	62
1975	65	64	64	65	66	63	64	64	64	64	65	65	65	66	66	66	66
1976	70	68	70	71	72	67	68	68	69	70	70	71	71	72	72	72	73
1977	76	74	75	77	80	73	74	74	75	75	76	76	77	78	79	80	80
1978	85	83	84	85	87	82	83	83	84	84	84	85	86	86	87	87	87
1979	91	89	90	92	94	89	89	90	90	91	91	91	92	93	94	94	95
1980	100	97	100	101	102	96	97	98	99	100	100	100	101	102	102	102	103
1981	107	105	106	108	111	104	105	105	106	106	107	107	107	109	111	111	112
1982	120	115	118	119	127	114	115	117	118	118	118	119	119	120	124	127	130
1983	135	132	134	136	138	130	132	133	134	135	135	136	136	137	137	138	138

M1 plus quasi-money

billion kronor, end of period

M1 plus quasi-monnaie

milliards de couronnes, fin de période

	Year	Q.1	Q.2	Q.3	Q.4	JAN	FEB	MAR	APR	MAY	JUN	JUL	AUG	SEP	OCT	NOV	DEC
1964	65.03	61.03	60.94	61.50	65.03	61.21	61.56	61.03	61.63	60.13	60.94	60.92	61.49	61.50	62.56	62.57	65.03
1965	68.91	65.90	66.63	65.78	68.91	66.10	66.54	65.90	66.69	64.74	66.63	65.68	66.08	65.78	66.74	66.60	68.91
1966	75.12	70.20	71.64	71.78	75.12	70.08	70.73	70.20	71.13	69.94	71.64	71.39	71.79	71.78	73.02	72.68	75.12
1967	84.58	77.24	78.72	80.23	84.58	77.08	77.81	77.24	78.14	77.31	78.72	79.02	79.77	80.23	81.87	81.48	84.58
1968	94.47	86.76	88.47	90.16	94.47	86.31	86.92	86.76	88.26	86.98	88.47	88.90	89.42	90.16	91.24	90.96	94.47
1969	98.43	96.81	96.16	95.80	98.43	96.31	96.76	96.81	97.35	95.10	96.16	96.98	96.36	96.80	96.78	96.35	98.43
1970	103.80	100.92	99.36	99.18	103.80	101.96	101.08	100.92	100.63	98.49	99.36	98.97	98.91	99.18	100.07	100.66	103.80
1971	114.30	107.49	107.38	109.85	114.30	108.26	106.94	107.49	107.65	107.11	107.38	108.79	108.29	109.85	110.38	112.34	114.30
1972	128.16	120.41	120.39	122.69	128.16	119.72	118.58	120.41	120.97	119.96	120.39	122.19	121.07	122.69	123.89	125.31	128.16
1973	145.84	133.86	135.43	139.48	145.84	133.60	132.45	133.86	134.75	134.85	135.43	138.19	136.73	139.48	139.28	142.31	145.84
1974	159.52	153.32	153.75	156.48	159.52	151.08	150.29	153.32	153.37	153.15	153.75	154.71	153.47	156.48	154.07	156.93	159.52
1975	178.66	167.79	167.10	172.04	178.66	165.78	163.23	167.79	167.37	166.16	167.10	169.84	168.71	172.04	171.83	175.05	178.66
1976	187.54	187.53	183.87	187.98	187.54	186.49	183.04	187.53	187.25	185.60	183.87	187.12	184.11	187.98	185.98	187.73	187.54
1977	205.08	198.59	190.30	193.26	205.08	197.77	193.18	198.59	197.10	194.08	190.30	196.14	191.22	198.26	198.36	203.81	205.08
1978	240.28	221.86	219.30	229.10	240.28	218.35	213.41	221.86	221.75	220.39	219.30	227.27	223.38	229.10	226.91	236.72	240.28
1979	279.89	258.56	249.45	260.99	279.89	255.35	250.34	258.56	254.91	253.67	249.45	256.21	252.39	260.99	258.12	265.66	279.89
1980	314.38	290.50	279.17	289.17	314.38	287.06	280.40	290.50	284.76	284.77	279.17	289.22	281.14	289.17	287.29	295.52	314.38
1981	357.87	322.31	309.13	316.27	357.87	318.96	309.39	322.31	319.45	316.56	309.13	310.09	309.09	316.27	319.56	321.49	357.87
1982	385.65	364.75	362.63	357.80	385.65	357.09	357.69	364.75	361.08	355.85	362.63	361.43	357.55	357.80	364.02	359.11	385.65
1983	417.03	401.29	393.17	394.26	417.03	394.83	395.99	401.29	393.70	390.18	393.17	397.07	393.11	394.26	396.32	396.22	417.03

Consumer prices: all items (15)

excluding indirect taxes
1980 = 100

Prix à la consommation : total (15)

non compris les impôts indirects
1980 = 100

	Year	Q.1	Q.2	Q.3	Q.4	JAN	FEB	MAR	APR	MAY	JUN	JUL	AUG	SEP	OCT	NOV	DEC
1964	33.5	33.0	33.2	33.7	34.1		33.0			33.2			33.7			34.1	
1965	35.0	34.4	35.0	35.0	35.3		34.4			35.0	35.1	35.0	35.0			35.3	
1966	36.7	36.2	36.5	36.7	37.0		36.2			36.5			36.7			37.0	
1967	37.9	37.9	37.9	38.2	38.2		37.9	37.7		37.9			38.2			38.2	
1968	38.2	37.9	38.2	38.2	38.2	38.0	37.9			38.2	38.1	38.4	38.2			38.2	38.6
1969	39.4	38.8	39.1	39.7	40.0	38.7	38.8			39.1			39.7			40.0	
1970	42.1	41.2	41.8	42.5	42.8		41.2			41.8			42.5			42.8	43.1
1971	43.3	42.8	42.6	43.6	44.1	42.7	42.8			42.6			43.6			44.1	
1972	46.1	45.2	45.7	46.5	46.9		45.2			45.7			46.5			46.9	47.7
1973	48.9	47.5	48.2	49.2	50.6	47.3	47.5			48.2			49.2			50.6	
1974	55.6	53.4	54.9	56.3	58.0		53.4			54.9			56.3			58.0	58.3
1975	60.7	58.8	59.9	61.4	62.9		58.8			59.9			61.4			62.9	
1976	66.9	64.5	66.2	67.5	69.4		64.5			66.2			67.5			69.4	
1977	74.0	71.5	73.2	74.7	76.5		71.5			73.2			74.7			76.6	
1978	82.3	81.0	81.4	82.6	84.1		81.0			81.4			82.6			84.1	
1979	89.1	86.0	87.6	89.9	92.3	85.4	86.1	86.6	87.1	87.6	88.1	88.8	90.2	90.6	91.5	92.3	93.2
1980	=100.0=	96.9	98.8	101.1	102.8	95.6	97.3	97.8	98.5	98.9	99.2	100.5	101.1	101.7	102.2	102.9	103.4
1981	111.0	107.6	110.0	112.2	114.2	105.9	108.2	108.8	109.4	110.1	110.6	111.2	112.2	113.1	113.7	114.1	114.7
1982	121.7	119.1	120.4	122.0	125.3	117.9	119.5	119.7	120.1	120.4	120.9	121.5	121.8	122.5	124.5	125.5	125.8
1983	132.6	126.6	128.6	130.6	132.9	126.7	125.3	126.7	127.8	128.6	129.3	129.6	130.5	131.5	132.7	132.9	133.0

New share issues

billion kronor

Nouvelles émissions d'actions

milliards de couronnes

	Year	Q.1	Q.2	Q.3	Q.4	JAN	FEB	MAR	APR	MAY	JUN	JUL	AUG	SEP	OCT	NOV	DEC
1964	1.00	0.15	0.24	0.35	0.26	0.03	0.07	0.05	0.03	0.05	0.17	0.14	0.08	0.12	0.09	0.06	0.12
1965	1.90	0.18	0.73	0.40	0.59	0.04	0.06	0.08	0.04	0.33	0.36	0.15	0.14	0.08	0.07	0.08	0.44
1966	1.32	0.28	0.30	0.39	0.35	0.13	0.07	0.08	0.12	0.08	0.11	0.14	0.15	0.11	0.08	0.14	0.13
1967	1.85	0.28	0.33	0.45	0.79	0.13	0.09	0.06	0.07	0.13	0.15	0.17	0.19	0.09	0.08	0.06	0.66
1968	1.06	0.17	0.33	0.22	0.35	0.07	0.07	0.04	0.08	0.08	0.18	0.08	0.06	0.07	0.08	0.14	0.13
1969	3.31	0.55	0.66	0.65	1.45	0.16	0.16	0.23	0.11	0.10	0.44	0.35	0.10	0.20	0.09	0.36	1.01
1970	2.86	0.49	0.72	1.16	0.49	0.40	0.04	0.05	0.20	0.18	0.34	0.84	0.09	0.23	0.08	0.28	0.13
1971	1.65	0.26	0.37	0.54	0.49	0.20	0.01	0.04	0.08	0.06	0.22	0.14	0.31	0.12	0.09	0.08	0.31
1972	1.59	0.32	0.32	0.41	0.54	0.09	0.12	0.11	0.11	0.10	0.11	0.10	0.13	0.18	0.19	0.26	0.09
1973	2.61	0.41	0.54	0.96	0.71	0.13	0.07	0.21	0.25	0.16	0.13	0.50	0.16	0.29	0.31	0.19	0.21
1974	3.71	0.58	0.66	1.41	1.06	0.15	0.37	0.06	0.18	0.24	0.24	0.69	0.39	0.33	0.45	0.13	0.48
1975	4.97	0.95	1.23	1.32	1.47	0.25	0.27	0.43	0.40	0.47	0.37	0.45	0.47	0.41	0.28	0.40	0.79
1976	6.89	0.70	1.19	1.76	3.24	0.11	0.18	0.41	0.21	0.47	0.51	0.64	0.71	0.42	1.77	0.75	0.71
1977	4.73	0.72	0.92	1.26	1.83	0.28	0.25	0.19	0.27	0.36	0.29	0.48	0.44	0.35	0.48	0.52	0.83
1978	5.32	0.52	3.12	0.71	0.97	0.26	0.11	0.15	0.08	2.13	0.91	0.10	0.36	0.26	0.33	0.31	0.33
1979	4.85	0.68	1.25	0.89	2.04	0.30	0.11	0.27	0.56	0.50	0.19	0.23	0.37	0.29	0.26	0.66	1.12
1980	7.55	1.47	2.06	2.30	1.73	0.65	0.41	0.41	0.47	0.08	1.51	1.23	0.46	0.61	0.72	0.35	0.65
1981	8.38	1.15	0.87	2.73	3.63	0.33	0.36	0.47	0.25	0.30	0.32	1.72	0.17	0.84	0.76	1.14	1.73
1982	11.75	2.12	2.47	2.62	4.55	0.67	0.62	0.83	0.40	0.71	1.35	0.35	1.36	0.92	0.98	1.82	1.74
1983	14.94	2.09	3.36	5.23	4.22	0.51	0.56	1.02	1.56	1.09	0.71	2.01	1.41	1.86	1.50	0.81	1.91

M1 plus quasi-money

billion kronor, end of period

Adjusted - Corrigé *

M1 plus quasi-monnaie

milliards de couronnes, fin de période

	Year	Q.1	Q.2	Q.3	Q.4	JAN	FEB	MAR	APR	MAY	JUN	JUL	AUG	SEP	OCT	NOV	DEC
1964		60.48	61.24	62.56	64.32	59.89	60.18	60.48	60.78	60.92	61.24	61.54	62.05	62.56	63.07	63.65	64.32
1965		65.32	66.90	66.92	68.23	64.68	65.05	65.32	65.77	65.52	66.90	66.34	66.68	66.92	67.27	67.82	68.23
1966		69.57	71.93	72.95	74.45	68.58	69.14	69.57	70.21	70.72	71.93	72.04	72.51	72.95	73.69	74.09	74.45
1967		76.55	78.96	81.45	83.91	75.35	76.14	76.55	77.14	78.09	78.96	79.66	80.66	81.45	82.69	83.06	83.91
1968		85.81	88.83	91.53	93.91	84.28	85.13	85.81	87.12	87.68	88.83	89.53	90.50	91.53	92.35	92.72	93.91
1969		95.57	96.55	98.28	98.03	94.06	94.86	95.57	96.10	95.78	96.55	97.56	97.73	98.28	98.05	98.21	98.03
1970		99.43	99.86	100.59	103.59	99.18	99.20	99.43	99.34	99.98	99.86	99.36	100.52	100.59	101.59	102.51	103.59
1971		105.79	108.03	111.41	114.18	105.11	105.15	105.79	106.27	107.54	108.03	109.12	110.27	111.41	112.29	114.17	114.18
1972		118.28	121.24	124.31	128.16	116.01	116.83	118.28	119.53	120.20	121.24	122.44	123.29	124.31	126.29	127.22	128.16
1973		131.24	136.53	141.17	145.99	129.45	130.75	131.24	133.03	134.99	136.53	138.47	139.38	141.17	142.27	144.33	145.99
1974		150.02	155.30	158.22	159.52	146.39	148.65	150.02	151.25	153.15	155.30	155.02	156.60	158.22	157.54	159.16	159.52
1975		163.85	169.13	173.95	178.49	160.48	161.77	163.85	164.90	166.16	169.13	170.01	172.50	173.96	176.05	177.53	178.49
1976		182.60	186.57	190.07	186.97	180.19	181.58	182.60	184.30	185.60	186.67	187.49	188.83	190.07	190.75	190.39	186.97
1977		192.62	193.79	200.67	203.86	190.53	191.65	192.62	193.80	194.08	193.79	196.53	196.73	200.67	204.08	206.92	203.86
1978		214.57	224.00	232.12	238.14	210.43	211.51	214.57	218.04	220.17	224.00	227.96	230.53	232.12	233.93	240.57	238.14
1979		249.34	255.32	264.96	276.30	245.05	247.86	249.34	250.65	253.16	255.32	256.98	261.00	264.96	266.38	269.70	276.30
1980		279.87	286.32	293.87	309.74	274.70	277.63	279.87	280.00	284.49	286.32	290.39	291.04	293.87	296.48	300.33	309.74
1981		310.51	317.06	321.74	352.23	304.94	306.33	310.51	314.42	315.93	317.06	311.33	319.97	321.74	330.13	326.72	352.23
1982		351.06	371.93	363.99	379.58	341.38	354.15	351.06	355.39	355.14	371.93	363.25	370.51	363.99	376.05	364.95	379.58
1983		386.22	403.25	401.07	410.46	377.47	392.07	386.22	387.50	389.40	403.25	399.07	407.37	401.07	409.42	402.67	410.46

* Adjusted by the O.E.C.D.

* Corrigé par l'O.C.D.E.

SWEDEN

Domestic credit: commercial and major savings banks

billion kronor, end of period

Crédits au secteur intérieur : banques commerciales et grandes caisses d'épargne

milliards de couronnes, fin de période

	Year	Q.1	Q.2	Q.3	Q.4	JAN	FEB	MAR	APR	MAY	JUN	JUL	AUG	SEP	OCT	NOV	DEC
1964	43.13	40.79	41.32	42.57	43.13	39.83	40.15	40.79	40.22	41.28	41.32	41.75	41.85	42.57	42.44	43.12	43.13
1965	48.00	44.72	46.36	46.82	48.00	43.61	43.89	44.72	45.00	45.90	46.36	46.54	46.33	46.82	46.99	47.66	48.00
1966	52.48	50.15	51.32	51.96	52.48	48.82	49.12	50.15	50.23	51.23	51.32	51.76	51.59	51.96	51.87	52.43	52.48
1967	58.35	53.42	54.94	56.75	58.35	52.60	52.53	53.42	53.68	54.57	54.94	55.78	55.49	56.75	56.62	57.64	58.35
1968	66.74	60.31	62.47	64.74	66.74	58.94	58.86	60.31	60.66	61.99	62.47	63.27	63.57	64.74	64.65	65.98	66.74
1969	69.86	67.86	70.99	70.75	69.86	67.57	68.21	67.86	68.59	69.94	70.99	70.51	70.15	70.75	70.05	69.78	69.86
1970	72.99	71.34	70.92	71.13	72.99	70.93	70.95	71.34	71.45	71.22	70.92	71.00	71.03	71.13	71.28	71.61	72.99
1971	79.06	73.02	74.89	75.96	79.06	72.41	72.51	73.02	72.90	74.13	74.89	74.93	75.11	75.96	76.60	77.75	79.06
1972	88.12	81.91	85.07	86.49	88.12	80.48	81.10	81.91	82.98	83.72	85.07	85.74	85.53	86.49	87.03	87.86	88.12
1973	98.92	91.29	93.86	97.11	98.92	89.14	90.45	91.29	92.42	92.76	93.86	94.45	95.50	97.11	97.51	98.45	98.92
1974	109.83	103.05	107.93	108.85	109.83	100.47	101.47	103.05	104.78	106.22	107.93	108.19	108.19	108.85	109.27	110.36	109.83
1975	123.13	113.07	116.36	118.38	123.13	111.22	112.49	113.07	114.70	114.87	116.36	116.45	117.15	118.38	119.47	121.76	123.13
1976	138.23	125.14	134.32	139.05	138.23	123.79	124.35	125.14	128.75	131.24	134.32	134.58	137.36	139.05	140.50	140.41	138.23
1977	157.23	141.63	149.77	152.66	157.23	140.89	141.87	141.63	144.41	146.75	149.77	149.32	152.01	152.66	154.78	155.85	157.23
1978	175.18	162.04	166.28	169.33	175.18	159.06	161.78	162.04	163.53	164.15	166.28	165.90	167.37	169.33	170.99	172.58	175.18
1979	200.41	183.12	190.68	195.91	200.41	177.10	179.50	183.12	185.34	187.62	190.68	189.92	192.12	195.91	196.54	197.24	200.41
1980	222.35	209.43	213.79	217.42	222.35	199.93	204.68	209.43	211.15	211.89	213.79	211.99	214.21	217.42	218.51	220.16	222.35
1981	246.62	222.82	233.67	244.84	246.62	220.78	224.07	222.82	226.13	228.50	233.67	231.67	233.58	244.84	241.91	241.70	246.62
1982	283.38	256.04	261.80	271.15	283.38	244.81	248.65	256.04	251.87	256.99	261.80	262.23	267.26	271.15	280.26	280.51	283.38
1983	309.26	292.04	297.40	298.01	309.26	287.16	289.73	292.04	290.24	292.49	297.40	295.04	295.59	298.01	299.00	301.55	309.26

Official discount rate

per cent per annum, end of period

Taux d'escompte officiel

pourcentage par an, fin de période

	Year	Q.1	Q.2	Q.3	Q.4	JAN	FEB	MAR	APR	MAY	JUN	JUL	AUG	SEP	OCT	NOV	DEC
1964	5.00	4.50	4.50	4.50	5.00	4.50	4.50	4.50	4.50	4.50	4.50	4.50	4.50	4.50	4.50	5.00	5.00
1965	5.50	5.00	5.50	5.50	5.50	5.00	5.00	5.00	5.50	5.50	5.50	5.50	5.50	5.50	5.50	5.50	5.50
1966	6.00	5.50	6.00	6.00	6.00	5.50	5.50	5.50	5.50	5.50	6.00	6.00	6.00	6.00	6.00	6.00	6.00
1967	6.00	5.00	5.00	5.00	6.00	6.00	5.50	5.00	5.00	5.00	5.00	5.00	5.00	5.00	5.00	5.00	6.00
1968	5.00	5.50	5.50	5.50	5.00	6.00	5.50	5.50	5.50	5.50	5.50	5.50	5.50	5.50	5.00	5.00	5.00
1969	7.00	6.00	6.00	7.00	7.00	5.00	6.00	6.00	6.00	6.00	6.00	7.00	7.00	7.00	7.00	7.00	7.00
1970	7.00	7.00	7.00	7.00	7.00	7.00	7.00	7.00	7.00	7.00	7.00	7.00	7.00	7.00	7.00	7.00	7.00
1971	5.00	6.50	6.00	5.50	5.00	7.00	7.00	6.50	6.00	6.00	6.00	6.00	6.00	5.50	5.00	5.00	5.00
1972	5.00	5.00	5.00	5.00	5.00	5.00	5.00	5.00	5.00	5.00	5.00	5.00	5.00	5.00	5.00	5.00	5.00
1973	5.00	5.00	5.00	5.00	5.00	5.00	5.00	5.00	5.00	5.00	5.00	5.00	5.00	5.00	5.00	5.00	5.00
1974	7.00	5.00	6.00	7.00	7.00	5.00	5.00	5.00	6.00	6.00	6.00	6.00	7.00	7.00	7.00	7.00	7.00
1975	6.00	7.00	7.00	6.00	6.00	7.00	7.00	7.00	7.00	7.00	7.00	7.00	6.00	6.00	6.00	6.00	6.00
1976	8.00	5.50	6.00	6.00	8.00	5.50	5.50	5.50	5.50	5.50	6.00	6.00	6.00	6.00	8.00	8.00	8.00
1977	8.00	8.00	8.00	8.00	8.00	8.00	8.00	8.00	8.00	8.00	8.00	8.00	8.00	8.00	8.00	8.00	8.00
1978	6.50	7.50	7.00	6.50	6.50	8.00	7.50	7.50	7.00	7.00	7.00	6.50	6.50	6.50	6.50	6.50	6.50
1979	9.00	6.50	6.50	8.00	9.00	6.50	6.50	6.50	6.50	6.50	6.50	7.00	7.00	8.00	8.00	9.00	9.00
1980	10.00	10.00	10.00	10.00	10.00	10.00	10.00	10.00	10.00	10.00	10.00	10.00	10.00	10.00	10.00	10.00	10.00
1981	11.00	12.00	12.00	12.00	11.00	12.00	12.00	12.00	12.00	12.00	12.00	12.00	12.00	12.00	11.00	11.00	11.00
1982	10.00	10.00	10.00	10.00	10.00	11.00	11.00	10.00	10.00	10.00	10.00	10.00	10.00	10.00	10.00	10.00	10.00
1983	8.50	9.00	8.50	8.50	8.50	9.00	9.00	9.00	8.50	8.50	8.50	8.50	8.50	8.50	8.50	8.50	8.50

Treasury bill rate (3 months) (16)

per cent per annum, end of period

Bons du Trésor (3 mois) (16)

pourcentage par an, fin de période

	Year	Q.1	Q.2	Q.3	Q.4	JAN	FEB	MAR	APR	MAY	JUN	JUL	AUG	SEP	OCT	NOV	DEC
1964	4.80	4.70	4.90	5.00	4.80	4.20	4.70	4.70	4.70	4.70	4.90	4.90	5.00	5.00	5.00	5.70	4.80
1965	5.70	5.50	6.20	6.20	5.70	5.50	5.50	5.50	..	..	6.20	6.20	6.20	6.20	6.20	6.20	5.70
1966	6.00	6.00	6.70	6.50	6.00	6.20	6.00	6.00	6.00	6.00	6.70	6.70	6.50	6.50	5.80	5.80	6.00
1967	6.80	4.50	4.25	4.00	6.80	6.70	5.00	4.50	..	..	4.25	..	4.00	4.00	4.00	..	6.80
1968	5.25	6.50	6.00	5.75	5.25	6.80	6.30	6.50	6.00	5.00	6.00	6.00	5.75	5.75	5.25	5.25	5.25
1969	8.50	6.50	6.50	7.75	8.50	5.50	5.25	6.50	6.50	6.50	6.50	8.00	8.00	7.75	7.75	7.75	8.50
1970	8.25	..	8.50	8.25	8.25	8.50	8.50	..	8.50	8.50	8.50	8.50	8.50	8.25	8.25	8.25	8.25
1971	4.00	6.75	6.25	5.50	4.00	7.50	6.75	6.75	6.25	6.25	6.25	6.00	6.00	5.50	4.75	3.75	4.00
1972	2.75	3.50	4.00	3.50	2.75	3.75	4.00	3.50	3.50	4.00	4.00	4.00	4.00	3.50	3.50	3.00	2.75
1973	2.75	2.25	3.00	2.75	2.75	2.75	2.75	2.25	2.50	3.00	3.00	2.75	2.75	2.75	3.00	2.75	2.75
1974	8.75	2.00	8.00	8.75	8.75	2.00	2.00	2.00	8.00	8.00	8.00	8.00	8.75	8.75	8.75	8.75	8.75
1975	4.75	8.75	8.25	6.25	4.75	8.75	8.75	8.75	8.75	8.25	8.25	8.25	6.25	6.25	6.00	4.75	4.75
1976	9.50	5.00	5.50	7.50	9.50	4.75	4.50	5.00	5.00	5.00	5.50	5.50	7.50	7.50	9.50	9.50	9.50
1977	9.00	9.50	9.50	9.50	9.00	9.50	9.50	9.50	9.50	9.50	9.50	9.50	9.50	9.50	9.50	9.00	9.00
1978	5.75	8.00	6.50	5.75	5.75	8.30	8.00	8.00	7.50	6.50	6.50	6.00	6.00	5.75	5.75	5.75	5.75
1979	9.50	5.75	5.75	8.50	9.50	5.75	5.75	5.75	5.75	5.75	5.75	6.50	6.50	8.50	8.50	9.50	9.50
1980	12.35	10.50	12.30	12.50	12.35	10.50	10.50	10.50	10.50	10.50	12.30	12.30	12.15	12.50	12.30	12.50	12.35
1981	9.00	15.10	13.50	10.50	9.00	16.10	16.10	15.10	..	15.10	13.50	11.50	10.50	10.50	9.00	9.00	9.00
1982	8.00	9.00	9.00	10.00	8.00	9.00	9.00	9.00	9.00	9.00	9.00	10.00	10.00	10.00	9.00	9.00	8.00
1983	7.00	7.00	7.00	7.00	7.00	7.00	7.00	7.00	7.00	7.00	7.00	7.00	7.00	7.00	7.00	7.00	7.00

Yield of long-term Government bonds (17)

Rendement des bons d'État à long terme (17)

per cent per annum, end of period

pourcentage par an, fin de période

	Year	Q.1	Q.2	Q.3	Q.4	JAN	FEB	MAR	APR	MAY	JUN	JUL	AUG	SEP	OCT	NOV	DEC
1964	5.87	5.58	5.64	5.64	5.87	5.22	5.60	5.58	5.64	5.64	5.64	5.64	5.67	5.64	5.66	5.87	5.87
1965	6.38	5.87	6.27	6.27	6.38	5.87	5.87	5.87	6.27	6.27	6.27	6.27	6.27	6.27	6.27	6.27	6.38
1966	6.35	6.55	6.80	6.52	6.35	6.51	6.55	6.55	6.55	6.55	6.80	6.80	6.65	6.52	6.52	6.48	6.35
1967	6.80	5.89	5.90	5.95	6.80	6.35	6.26	5.89	5.90	5.90	5.90	5.96	5.95	5.95	5.95	5.92	6.80
1968	6.19	6.29	6.29	6.33	6.19	6.59	6.29	6.29	6.34	6.33	6.29	6.31	6.31	6.33	6.18	6.19	6.19
1969	7.27	6.72	6.98	7.28	7.27	6.27	6.27	6.72	6.78	7.02	6.98	7.25	7.27	7.28	7.29	7.25	7.27
1970	7.32	7.29	7.43	7.52	7.32	7.28	7.28	7.29	7.29	7.31	7.43	7.48	7.51	7.52	7.52	7.47	7.32
1971	7.14	7.30	7.28	7.10	7.14	7.29	7.29	7.30	7.30	7.29	7.28	7.29	7.30	7.10	7.11	7.12	7.14
1972	7.34	7.25	7.27	7.34	7.34	7.21	7.24	7.25	7.26	7.27	7.27	7.29	7.33	7.34	7.34	7.36	7.34
1973	7.37	7.36	7.40	7.41	7.37	7.35	7.36	7.36	7.37	7.40	7.40	7.40	7.41	7.41	7.42	7.37	7.37
1974	8.17	7.15	7.86	8.10	8.17	7.30	7.27	7.15	7.73	7.83	7.86	7.87	7.87	8.10	8.12	8.15	8.17
1975	9.15	8.18	9.04	9.11	9.15	8.18	8.17	8.18	8.22	9.00	9.04	9.05	9.08	9.11	9.13	9.14	9.15
1976	9.61	9.11	9.19	9.22	9.61	9.19	9.12	9.11	9.13	9.14	9.19	9.20	9.22	9.22	10.06	9.63	9.61
1977	9.84	9.69	9.74	9.78	9.84	9.50	9.63	9.69	9.73	9.75	9.74	9.76	9.75	9.78	9.81	9.83	9.84
1978	10.09	10.08	10.33	10.03	10.09	9.86	9.87	10.08	10.17	10.19	10.33	10.35	10.08	10.03	10.06	10.07	10.09
1979	11.22	10.15	10.21	10.49	11.22	10.12	10.12	10.15	10.18	10.20	10.21	10.41	10.44	10.49	11.01	11.04	11.22
1980	12.61	11.26	11.38	12.63	12.61	10.92	11.24	11.26	11.33	11.31	11.38	11.36	11.46	12.61	12.68	12.71	12.61
1981	12.80	13.43	13.63	13.73	12.80	12.66	13.60	13.43	13.49	13.56	13.63	13.70	13.74	13.73	13.73	13.77	12.80
1982	13.01	12.78	13.00	13.27	13.01	12.84	12.76	12.78	12.82	12.79	13.00	13.18	13.23	13.27	13.73	13.09	13.01
1983	12.08	12.51	12.17	12.20	12.08	13.10	12.83	12.51	12.22	12.14	12.17	11.85	11.84	12.20	12.24	12.44	12.08

Share prices (16)

Cours des actions (16)

Stockholm Stock Exchange

Bourse de Stockholm

1980 = 100

	Year	Q.1	Q.2	Q.3	Q.4	JAN	FEB	MAR	APR	MAY	JUN	JUL	AUG	SEP	OCT	NOV	DEC
1964	57	55	56	58	59	55	55	56	57	55	55	57	58	58	58	59	61
1965	66	65	65	67	65	67	65	65	64	65	65	67	68	67	65	65	65
1966	58	64	61	57	52	64	63	64	60	61	62	60	55	56	55	52	50
1967	55	54	54	56	54	54	54	54	54	54	54	56	57	55	56	54	52
1968	62	54	60	65	68	53	54	55	58	61	62	65	65	64	65	68	70
1969	76	77	81	73	72	76	77	77	81	82	60	74	73	73	73	72	72
1970	60	66	58	61	55	68	64	65	59	56	60	64	60	58	52	56	56
1971	63	62	63	63	66	59	62	63	60	63	64	63	63	61	64	67	68
1972	74	71	73	75	75	70	69	73	75	73	72	75	75	75	74	77	74
1973	77	77	80	78	75	77	77	76	78	80	81	80	77	76	79	74	74
1974	81	84	85	79	76	79	85	86	88	93	83	84	78	75	80	75	73
1975	87	82	85	89	93	80	84	83	85	84	87	89	87	91	92	93	94
1976	100	99	109	102	92	97	98	101	[illegible]	108	108	108	[illegible]	96	89	91	95
1977	87	95	94	83	78	90	97	99	97	96	88	85	81	84	80	74	80
1978	92	87	93	98	92	87	84	90	95	91	93	99	100	96	91	92	93
1979	92	97	90	90	91	100	95	95	90	91	89	94	90	89	89	91	92
1980	100	97	98	97	103	98	97	96	93	98	99	100	97	96	101	109	113
1981	150	124	140	160	175	113	127	131	127	139	154	163	163	153	168	181	177
1982	186	174	167	180	223	177	175	171	163	169	169	177	176	187	202	226	239
1983	361	[illegible]	343	385	399	275	326	328	355	352	338	368	399	392	385	414	397

SWEDEN

U.S. dollar exchange rate: spot
cents per krona, end of period

Taux de change du dollar É.-U. : au comptant
cents par couronne, fin de période

	Year	Q.1	Q.2	Q.3	Q.4	JAN	FEB	MAR	APR	MAY	JUN	JUL	AUG	SEP	OCT	NOV	DEC
1964	19.425	19.410	19.436	19.399	19.423	19.249	19.305	19.410	19.448	19.448	19.436	19.416	19.448	19.399	19.350	19.399	19.425
1965	19.305	19.448	19.313	19.335	19.307	19.448	19.448	19.448	19.372	19.350	19.313	19.335	19.305	19.335	19.305	19.313	19.305
1966	19.305	19.350	19.342	19.313	19.305	19.305	19.335	19.350	19.342	19.361	19.342	19.342	19.313	19.313	19.305	19.313	19.305
1967	19.361	19.350	19.361	19.342	19.361	19.335	19.313	19.350	19.361	19.380	19.361	19.387	19.342	19.342	19.305	19.305	19.361
1968	19.305	19.324	19.335	19.342	19.305	19.350	19.313	19.324	19.324	19.350	19.335	19.335	19.342	19.342	19.305	19.305	19.305
1969	19.342	19.342	19.313	19.335	19.342	19.313	19.305	19.342	19.335	19.342	19.313	19.342	19.305	19.335	19.342	19.313	19.342
1970	19.342	19.223	19.260	19.194	19.342	19.324	19.201	19.223	19.212	19.223	19.260	19.275	19.268	19.194	19.275	19.313	19.342
1971	20.555	19.342	19.361	19.861	20.555	19.335	19.342	19.342	19.350	19.342	19.361	19.361	19.666	19.861	19.901	20.129	20.555
1972	21.084	20.937	21.221	21.078	21.084	20.810	20.871	20.937	20.937	21.131	21.221	21.154	21.172	21.078	21.063	21.108	21.084
1973	21.798	22.256	24.450	23.798	21.798	21.250	22.432	22.256	22.097	23.087	24.450	24.579	23.688	23.798	23.901	22.686	21.798
1974	24.507	22.766	22.831	22.422	24.507	20.912	21.582	22.766	23.529	23.148	22.831	22.847	22.307	22.422	22.821	23.337	24.507
1975	22.802	25.368	25.384	22.183	22.802	24.931	25.648	25.368	25.211	25.413	25.384	23.202	22.928	22.183	22.989	22.594	22.802
1976	24.234	22.725	22.466	23.348	24.234	22.810	22.830	22.725	22.797	22.507	22.466	22.520	22.740	23.348	23.691	23.869	24.234
1977	21.416	23.821	22.735	20.692	21.416	23.422	23.649	23.821	23.076	22.865	22.735	22.986	20.623	20.692	20.908	20.814	21.416
1978	23.280	21.792	21.856	22.707	23.280	21.524	21.671	21.792	21.654	21.494	21.856	22.176	22.535	22.707	24.489	22.612	23.280
1979	24.117	22.875	23.366	24.219	24.117	22.871	22.946	22.875	22.716	22.821	23.366	23.757	23.725	24.219	23.508	23.929	24.117
1980	22.869	22.437	24.095	24.020	22.869	23.993	23.732	22.437	23.691	23.821	24.095	23.952	23.972	24.020	23.471	23.111	22.869
1981	17.950	21.775	19.666	17.864	17.950	21.875	21.547	21.775	20.954	20.259	19.666	19.126	19.205	17.864	17.979	18.433	17.950
1982	13.709	16.804	16.415	15.897	13.709	17.696	17.268	16.804	17.206	17.066	16.415	16.416	16.211	15.897	13.452	13.403	13.709
1983	12.498	13.317	13.085	12.785	12.498	13.419	13.442	13.317	13.346	13.278	13.085	12.908	12.574	12.785	12.793	12.563	12.498

Official reserves excluding gold
million SDR's, end of period

Réserves officielles, or exclu
millions de DTS, fin de période

	Year	Q.1	Q.2	Q.3	Q.4	JAN	FEB	MAR	APR	MAY	JUN	JUL	AUG	SEP	OCT	NOV	DEC
1964	776	599	632	714	776	586	588	599	597	605	632	645	658	714	699	735	776
1965	770	870	839	838	770	796	824	870	871	857	839	842	837	838	820	796	770
1966	824	809	840	851	824	772	776	809	814	835	840	845	848	851	822	829	824
1967	638	786	805	825	638	779	783	786	790	802	805	806	812	826	793	661	638
1968	590	706	730	724	590	679	689	706	723	747	730	727	725	724	712	656	590
1969	470	525	362	320	470	594	544	525	517	430	362	325	362	320	405	462	470
1970	561	429	421	446	561	520	481	429	421	417	421	444	456	446	421	487	561
1971	822	667	765	798	822	637	650	667	717	732	765	795	798	798	798	807	822
1972	1251	1030	1084	1091	1251	881	940	1030	1032	1048	1084	1087	1090	1091	1104	1190	1251
1973	1894	1551	1770	1758	1894	1275	1374	1551	1630	1689	1770	1812	1753	1758	1677	1780	1894
1974	1215	1694	1279	1192	1215	1912	1399	1694	1462	1415	1279	1248	1190	1192	1192	1195	1215
1975	2425	1262	1723	2186	2425	1244	1234	1262	1503	1617	1723	2038	2136	2186	2211	2323	2425
1976	1941	2610	2673	2306	1941	2523	2558	2610	2617	2669	2673	2646	2477	2306	1714	1820	1941
1977	2811	2057	2563	2653	2811	1946	1947	2057	2311	2652	2563	2215	2124	2653	2913	3221	2811
1978	3165	2951	3375	3285	3165	2852	2894	2951	3219	3346	3375	3345	3345	3285	2982	3260	3165
1979	2667	2959	2957	2750	2667	3119	3027	2959	3054	3145	2957	2872	2956	2750	2855	2669	2667
1980	2680	2697	2773	2724	2580	2652	2793	2697	2696	2522	2773	2686	2703	2724	2717	2725	2680
1981	3094	3368	3315	3538	3094	2406	3063	3368	3413	3531	3315	3223	3156	3538	3265	3030	3094
1982	3184	3066	2959	3001	3184	2952	3086	3066	3015	3038	2959	2570	2993	3001	3740	3286	3184
1983	3853	3203	3237	3207	3853	3120	3339	3203	3164	3264	3237	3407	3097	3207	3482	3729	3853

Net foreign position:
commercial banks
million kronor, end of period

Position extérieure nette :
banques commerciales
millions de couronnes, fin de période

	Year	Q.1	Q.2	Q.3	Q.4	JAN	FEB	MAR	APR	MAY	JUN	JUL	AUG	SEP	OCT	NOV	DEC
1964	787	920	949	918	787	939	1003	920	779	828	949	1021	941	918	936	901	787
1965	963	449	647	777	963	853	735	449	462	540	647	686	755	777	667	945	963
1966	1241	913	770	992	1241	980	377	913	817	759	770	943	964	992	1053	1321	1241
1967	2097	1280	1532	1789	2097	1449	1420	1280	1544	1508	1532	1518	1886	1789	2105	2202	2097
1968	2106	1668	1636	1813	2106	1913	1661	1668	1633	1848	1636	1639	1894	1813	2031	1932	2106
1969	1059	1798	1879	1667	1059	1941	1768	1798	1873	1856	1879	1959	1706	1667	1200	949	1059
1970	1507	1181	1555	1372	1507	1205	1136	1181	1005	1123	1555	1655	1340	1372	1537	1497	1507
1971	1407	1424	1315	1598	1407	1318	1222	1424	1549	1475	1315	1554	1487	1598	1487	1615	1407
1972	2121	1366	1734	1669	2121	1430	1459	1366	1608	1661	1734	1805	1780	1669	1976	1997	2121
1973	3932	2219	2588	3331	3932	2493	2041	2219	2404	2288	2588	3159	2977	3331	4094	4118	3932
1974	5433	5678	5947	5652	5433	3954	4297	5678	5307	5796	5947	6039	6032	5652	5352	5317	5433
1975	3971	5615	5329	4851	3971	5101	5199	5615	5849	5698	5329	5337	5115	4851	3908	3649	3971
1976	2457	4463	3214	3926	2457	3617	4336	4463	4397	3674	3214	3104	3063	3926	4181	3140	2457
1977	-715	1466	821	-566	-715	2499	2170	1466	1072	457	821	1914	-141	-566	-2353	-2163	-715
1978	-6005	-3097	-4334	-5667	-6005	-1449	-2795	-3097	-3470	-4305	-4334	-4640	-5405	-5667	-5093	-5860	-6005
1979	-13279	-8862	-10424	-12205	-13279	-7008	-7755	-8862	-9583	-10032	-10424	-10044	-11319	-12205	-13359	-13292	-13279
1980	-18279	-16946	-16470	-15324	-18279	-13639	-15677	-16946	-16734	-15610	-16470	-15869	-15463	-16324	-18184	-18132	-18279
1981	-32746	-21114	-26465	-33692	-32746	-16446	-15233	-21114	-23469	-23559	-26465	-27135	-27027	-33692	-33244	-32566	-32746
1982	-48551	-33280	-32631	-34748	-48551	-32261	-31994	-33280	-33480	-32534	-32631	-32012	-35013	-34748	-46135	-48470	-48551
1983	-54466	-52397	-51197	-52075	-54466	-53733	-55349	-52397	-50797	-49398	-51197	-50513	-50592	-52075	-49934	-52554	-54466

Balance of payments: net trade (18) — Balance des paiements : balance commerciale (18)

million kronor — millions de couronnes

	Year	Q.1	Q.2	Q.3	Q.4	JAN	FEB	MAR	APR	MAY	JUN	JUL	AUG	SEP	OCT	NOV	DEC
1964																	
1965																	
1966	-1500	-1001	-146	-284	-69												
1967	-756	-682	498	-566	-6												
1968	-913	-626	80	-180	-137												
1969	-961	-378	-149	-372	-62												
1970	-965	-982	-375	75	317												
1971	2048	437	814	358	439												
1972	3082	39	845	832	1316												
1973	5653	2118	1427	1196	912	645	490	983	90	829	508	1125	-233	304	359	83	470
1974	-3419	-1528	-632	-121	-1138	-946	-444	-138	53	-339	-296	-125	-51	55	-262	-521	-355
1975	-378	151	629	-1701	543	-603	585	169	395	-105	339	-78	-813	-810	-425	164	804
1976	-5105	-824	-898	-670	-2713	-378	-295	-151	-470	-835	407	596	-1124	-142	-575	-1024	-1114
1977	-4544	-2170	-601	-2410	637	-947	-428	-795	-398	-362	159	-475	-1513	-422	-388	369	656
1978	5456	975	2961	98	1422	-67	542	400	1184	494	1303	-87	-771	956	-76	750	748
1979	-4753	499	303	-3135	-2420	-21	126	394	576	-449	176	-1038	-2493	396	-1109	-737	-574
1980	-10696	-2380	-3266	-4070	-980	-1866	-51	-463	-213	-2162	-891	-757	-2022	-1291	-977	-137	134
1981	-1165	-100	2139	-2365	-839	-731	-141	822	1131	216	792	-32	-1991	-342	-497	-189	-153
1982	-5800	545	2529	-3435	-5439	-1001	433	1113	1973	99	457	1500	-4214	-721	-1060	-3074	-1305
1983	10086	2837	6443	-908	1714	172	299	2366	1022	1942	3489	1029	-3404	1467	1490	662	-433

Balance of payments: current balance (18) — Balance des paiements : opérations courantes, nettes (18)

million kronor — millions de couronnes

	Year	Q.1	Q.2	Q.3	Q.4	JAN	FEB	MAR	APR	MAY	JUN	JUL	AUG	SEP	OCT	NOV	DEC
1964																	
1965																	
1966																	
1967																	
1968																	
1969	-1019	-488	-89	-488	45												
1970	-1367	-1027	-426	-137	223												
1971	1794	204	641	-39	283												
1972	1271	-430	439	239	1023												
1973	5312	998	1840	677	1797												
1974	-4214	-1146	416	-1793	-1691												
1975	72	-178	250	-	-												
1976	-7343	-1508	-1331	-1446	-3058												
1977	-9837	-3593	-1891	-3766	-587												
1978	-1524	-805	134	-1462	609												
1979	-10483	-809	-1549	-4869	-3256												
1980	-19207	-4200	-5469	-5903	-3635												
1981	-14177	-2645	-1384	-5416	-4732												
1982	-22755	-2842	-1628	-7372	-10913												
1983	-8241	-1732	1807	-4675	-3641												

Balance of payments: net capital movements (18) — Balance des paiements : mouvements de capitaux, nets (18)

million kronor — millions de couronnes

	Year	Q.1	Q.2	Q.3	Q.4	JAN	FEB	MAR	APR	MAY	JUN	JUL	AUG	SEP	OCT	NOV	DEC
1964																	
1965																	
1966																	
1967																	
1968																	
1969	829	292	-469	323	683												
1970	739	265	-75	511	38												
1971	657	294	-93	-115	571												
1972	812	1031	-272	93	-90												
1973	-1368	804	-603	-1450	-119												
1974	349	-1842	-665	582	2274												
1975	7953	948	2755	2765	1485												
1976	4437	582	1004	-350	3201												
1977	13066	2932	4879	4409	846												
1978	4955	3001	1070	1400	-516												
1979	7706	-1781	2653	5244	1590												
1980	21077	3906	8196	6472	2503												
1981	15044	7431	-926	5668	2871												
1982	20280	1335	1331	6248	11366												
1983	7453	2289	-2681	3469	4376												

SWEDEN

Imports c.i.f. (19)

billion kronor, monthly averages

Importations c.a.f. (19)

milliards de couronnes, moyennes mensuelles

	Year	Q.1	Q.2	Q.3	Q.4	JAN	FEB	MAR	APR	MAY	JUN	JUL	AUG	SEP	OCT	NOV	DEC
1964	1.66	1.61	1.65	1.55	1.84	1.75	1.66	1.43	1.79	1.59	1.60	1.50	1.45	1.69	1.74	1.90	1.86
1965	1.89	1.88	1.85	1.80	2.02	1.81	1.85	1.99	1.81	1.92	1.82	1.76	1.78	1.88	2.05	2.04	1.96
1966	1.97	2.04	1.94	1.82	2.09	1.94	1.82	2.35	1.87	1.95	2.01	1.63	1.80	2.03	2.03	2.23	2.02
1967	2.03	2.04	1.97	1.96	2.14	2.20	1.96	1.96	1.99	1.98	1.95	1.73	2.09	2.14	2.09	2.30	2.03
1968	2.21	2.23	2.07	2.12	2.42	2.34	2.21	2.13	2.07	2.22	1.92	1.91	2.08	2.36	2.53	2.43	2.31
1969	2.55	2.40	2.53	2.47	2.79	2.53	2.19	2.49	2.46	2.45	2.67	2.39	2.16	2.86	2.85	2.72	2.81
1970	3.02	2.93	3.11	2.80	3.25	3.02	2.82	2.94	3.30	3.06	2.98	2.74	2.62	3.07	3.26	3.27	3.23
1971	3.02	2.98	2.99	2.81	3.28	3.09	2.68	3.18	3.06	2.74	3.18	2.73	2.62	3.08	3.32	3.20	3.32
1972	3.22	3.16	3.15	2.96	3.59	3.10	3.04	3.35	3.03	3.24	3.19	2.72	3.03	3.13	3.85	3.79	3.15
1973	3.87	3.76	3.38	3.68	4.65	4.01	3.34	3.93	2.84	3.86	3.43	3.29	3.73	4.03	4.79	4.58	4.57
1974	5.84	4.78	5.74	6.16	6.67	4.42	4.68	5.26	6.07	6.23	4.92	5.83	6.38	6.27	7.21	6.97	5.84
1975	6.24	6.51	6.35	5.65	6.45	7.98	5.93	5.61	7.08	5.16	5.80	5.82	4.98	6.15	7.02	6.03	6.29
1976	7.01	6.38	6.79	6.86	7.99	5.96	6.00	7.19	6.79	6.30	6.77	6.06	6.85	7.68	7.27	8.27	8.44
1977	7.52	7.51	7.41	7.03	8.14	7.17	7.01	8.34	7.11	7.59	7.52	5.57	7.56	7.95	8.45	7.86	8.12
1978	7.73	7.35	7.57	7.11	8.89	7.28	6.93	7.84	7.61	7.55	7.55	5.68	7.90	7.75	9.47	8.83	8.36
1979	10.25	8.81	9.92	10.01	12.25	8.23	8.12	10.07	9.28	10.48	9.99	8.89	10.76	10.39	12.88	12.60	11.28
1980	11.81	12.28	11.08	11.62	12.27	12.62	11.57	12.66	11.13	9.22	12.88	10.70	11.01	13.16	13.37	11.62	11.82
1981	12.17	11.51	11.30	11.53	14.34	10.88	11.21	12.44	11.44	10.84	11.61	9.78	11.74	13.08	14.49	13.90	14.62
1982	14.49	13.34	13.26	13.41	17.94	12.58	12.62	14.72	12.83	12.94	14.02	10.70	14.64	14.89	16.57	19.15	18.09
1983	16.55	15.95	15.46	15.83	18.96	15.93	15.23	16.69	15.55	15.30	15.53	12.37	17.31	17.82	17.78	19.09	20.00

Exports f.o.b. (19)

billion kronor, monthly averages

Exportations f.o.b. (19)

milliards de couronnes, moyennes mensuelles

	Year	Q.1	Q.2	Q.3	Q.4	JAN	FEB	MAR	APR	MAY	JUN	JUL	AUG	SEP	OCT	NOV	DEC
1964	1.59	1.40	1.63	1.47	1.84	1.53	1.32	1.34	1.55	1.48	1.86	1.41	1.42	1.58	1.71	1.92	1.90
1965	1.71	1.62	1.68	1.62	1.93	1.62	1.56	1.69	1.56	1.65	1.82	1.62	1.52	1.71	1.88	2.01	1.90
1966	1.85	1.70	1.90	1.72	2.07	1.60	1.40	2.09	1.67	1.90	2.14	1.59	1.69	1.88	1.85	2.09	2.27
1967	1.95	1.80	2.13	1.75	2.13	1.79	1.78	1.82	2.07	1.98	2.32	1.66	1.67	1.93	2.00	2.09	2.31
1968	2.13	2.01	2.09	2.09	2.34	1.79	2.02	2.20	1.92	2.22	2.11	1.88	1.92	2.46	2.39	2.40	2.23
1969	2.46	2.27	2.47	2.33	2.75	2.33	2.07	2.41	2.21	2.55	2.65	2.29	2.17	2.52	2.60	2.80	2.86
1970	2.92	2.57	2.95	2.81	3.34	2.35	2.65	2.71	2.89	2.76	3.21	2.74	2.68	3.02	3.13	3.59	3.29
1971	3.19	3.10	3.27	2.93	3.44	3.12	2.71	3.48	2.96	3.09	3.77	2.72	2.75	3.30	3.46	3.53	3.33
1972	3.48	3.21	3.44	3.25	4.02	3.17	3.09	3.36	3.29	3.35	3.68	2.92	3.32	3.50	3.92	4.45	3.69
1973	4.42	4.22	4.35	4.01	5.11	4.12	3.89	4.66	3.63	4.94	4.48	4.08	3.80	4.16	5.29	5.22	4.83
1974	5.87	5.20	5.93	5.82	6.53	4.79	5.09	5.71	6.30	5.87	5.63	5.55	5.80	6.12	7.35	6.08	6.15
1975	6.00	6.09	6.17	5.22	6.52	6.20	6.25	5.80	6.71	5.90	5.90	5.33	4.28	6.06	6.54	6.14	6.83
1976	6.70	6.44	6.78	5.45	7.12	5.70	6.39	7.22	6.20	6.59	7.56	5.60	6.10	7.64	6.91	7.43	7.02
1977	7.14	6.78	7.21	6.22	8.35	6.22	6.58	7.54	6.71	7.23	7.68	5.09	6.05	7.53	8.06	8.22	8.77
1978	8.18	7.67	8.56	7.15	9.35	7.21	7.57	8.24	8.77	8.05	8.86	5.61	7.13	8.71	9.39	9.57	9.10
1979	9.85	8.97	10.02	9.97	11.45	8.21	8.25	10.46	9.86	10.03	10.16	7.35	8.26	10.79	11.77	11.36	10.71
1980	10.90	11.47	9.93	10.26	11.91	10.59	11.52	12.19	10.91	7.05	11.99	9.93	8.98	11.86	12.30	11.48	11.95
1981	12.07	11.48	12.01	10.75	14.06	10.10	11.07	13.26	12.57	11.06	12.40	9.75	9.75	12.74	14.00	13.71	14.47
1982	14.01	13.53	14.11	12.27	16.14	11.68	13.06	15.85	14.81	13.04	14.48	12.21	10.43	14.18	15.51	16.09	16.81
1983	17.53	16.93	17.86	15.73	19.61	16.22	15.54	19.04	16.68	17.80	19.10	13.41	14.30	19.47	19.41	19.86	19.56

Trade balance (f.o.b. — c.i.f.) (19)

billion kronor, monthly averages

Balance commerciale (f.o.b. — c.a.f.) (19)

milliards de couronnes, moyennes mensuelles

	Year	Q.1	Q.2	Q.3	Q.4	JAN	FEB	MAR	APR	MAY	JUN	JUL	AUG	SEP	OCT	NOV	DEC
1964	-0.08	-0.21	-0.03	-0.08	0.01	-0.22	-0.33	-0.09	-0.24	-0.11	0.27	-0.06	-0.03	-0.11	-0.03	0.02	0.03
1965	-0.18	-0.26	-0.17	-0.19	-0.08	-0.19	-0.29	-0.30	-0.25	-0.27	0.01	-0.15	-0.26	-0.16	-0.17	-0.03	-0.06
1966	-0.13	-0.34	-0.04	-0.10	-0.02	-0.34	-0.43	-0.26	-0.20	-0.05	0.13	-0.05	-0.11	-0.15	-0.18	-0.14	0.25
1967	-0.08	-0.24	0.16	-0.20	-0.01	-0.41	-0.18	-0.14	0.09	0.00	0.38	-0.06	-0.33	-0.20	-0.09	-0.22	0.28
1968	-0.08	-0.22	0.01	-0.03	-0.08	-0.55	-0.19	0.07	-0.15	-	0.20	-0.02	-0.16	0.10	-0.14	-0.03	-0.08
1969	-0.09	-0.13	-0.06	-0.14	-0.04	-0.20	-0.12	-0.08	-0.25	0.10	-0.02	-0.10	0.02	-0.34	-0.24	0.08	0.05
1970	-0.10	-0.36	-0.16	0.01	0.09	-0.67	-0.17	-0.22	-0.41	-0.30	0.23	0.03	0.06	-0.05	-0.13	0.33	0.06
1971	0.17	0.12	0.28	0.12	0.16	0.03	0.03	0.30	-0.10	0.34	0.60	-0.01	0.14	0.22	0.14	0.33	0.01
1972	0.26	0.04	0.29	0.29	0.43	0.07	0.05	0.01	0.26	0.12	0.49	0.20	0.29	0.37	0.07	0.67	0.54
1973	0.56	0.46	0.98	0.33	0.46	0.11	0.55	0.73	0.80	1.07	1.06	0.79	0.07	0.13	0.50	0.63	0.26
1974	0.03	0.41	0.20	-0.34	-0.15	0.37	0.41	0.46	0.23	-0.36	0.71	-0.28	-0.58	-0.15	0.14	-0.89	0.32
1975	-0.24	-0.42	-0.18	-0.43	0.07	-1.78	0.32	0.19	-0.37	-0.26	0.10	-0.49	-0.70	-0.09	-0.48	0.11	0.59
1976	-0.31	0.05	-0.01	-0.42	-0.37	-0.26	0.39	0.03	-0.59	-0.22	0.79	-0.46	-0.75	-0.04	-0.36	-0.84	-1.42
1977	-0.38	-0.73	-0.20	-0.80	0.21	-0.95	-0.43	-0.80	-0.40	-0.36	0.16	-0.48	-1.51	-0.42	-0.39	0.36	0.65
1978	0.46	0.32	0.99	0.04	0.47	-0.07	0.64	0.40	1.16	0.50	1.31	-0.07	-0.77	0.96	-0.08	0.74	0.74
1979	-0.40	0.17	0.10	-1.05	-0.81	-0.02	0.13	0.39	0.58	-0.45	0.17	-1.04	-2.50	0.40	-1.11	-0.74	-0.57
1980	-0.91	-0.32	-1.09	-1.37	-0.36	-1.93	-0.05	-0.47	-0.22	-2.17	-0.89	-0.77	-2.03	-1.30	-1.07	-0.14	0.13
1981	-0.10	-0.03	0.71	-0.79	-0.28	-0.78	-0.14	0.82	1.13	0.22	0.79	-0.03	-1.99	-0.34	-0.49	-0.19	-0.15
1982	-0.48	0.19	0.85	-1.14	-1.80	-1.00	0.44	1.13	1.98	0.10	0.46	1.51	-4.21	-0.71	-1.06	-3.06	-1.28
1983	0.98	0.98	2.40	-0.11	0.65	0.29	0.31	2.35	1.13	2.50	3.57	1.04	-3.01	1.65	1.63	0.77	-0.44

Imports c.i.f. (19)

billion kronor, monthly averages

Adjusted - Corrigé *

Importations c.a.f. (19)

milliards de couronnes, moyennes mensuelles

Year	Q.1	Q.2	Q.3	Q.4	JAN	FEB	MAR	APR	MAY	JUN	JUL	AUG	SEP	OCT	NOV	DEC
1964	1.61	1.64	1.67	1.72	1.62	1.71	1.50	1.66	1.65	1.60	1.66	1.64	1.70	1.63	1.76	1.75
1965	1.84	1.89	1.93	1.95	1.77	1.93	1.83	1.85	1.90	1.92	1.95	1.95	1.84	2.02	1.83	1.83
1966	1.97	1.99	1.94	2.01	1.98	1.89	2.14	1.99	1.97	2.01	1.93	1.92	1.96	2.01	2.03	2.00
1967	2.03	1.95	2.09	2.06	2.06	2.04	2.00	1.96	1.97	1.93	2.04	2.12	2.11	2.00	2.09	2.10
1968	2.13	2.11	2.24	2.31	2.14	2.18	2.08	2.10	2.11	2.13	2.13	2.28	2.32	2.32	2.31	2.30
1969	2.34	2.58	2.62	2.66	2.31	2.30	2.41	2.50	2.50	2.74	2.63	2.49	2.72	2.59	2.56	2.72
1970	2.96	3.07	3.00	3.06	2.84	3.00	3.05	3.00	3.26	2.94	3.00	3.03	2.97	2.98	3.13	3.06
1971	2.95	3.04	2.99	3.07	3.09	2.86	2.89	3.05	2.90	3.16	3.08	2.92	2.98	3.13	2.95	3.14
1972	3.15	3.15	3.19	3.38	3.15	3.11	3.20	3.08	3.24	3.14	3.19	3.21	3.17	3.47	3.50	3.16
1973	3.72	3.42	3.95	4.32	3.93	3.58	3.65	2.94	3.62	3.69	3.75	3.90	4.21	4.19	4.21	4.55
1974	4.83	5.80	6.52	6.17	4.35	5.01	5.13	6.05	5.87	5.48	6.52	6.69	6.34	6.20	6.70	5.62
1975	6.32	6.22	5.96	5.98	8.04	6.36	6.06	6.47	6.18	6.01	6.49	5.39	5.99	6.07	5.97	5.89
1976	6.38	6.89	7.19	7.40	6.15	6.41	6.58	6.76	6.80	7.12	7.01	7.12	7.45	6.66	7.69	7.86
1977	7.59	7.54	7.38	7.58	7.73	7.58	7.47	7.42	7.74	7.45	6.81	7.64	7.70	7.68	7.36	7.72
1978	7.63	7.49	7.55	8.27	7.60	7.48	7.82	7.48	7.58	7.41	6.95	7.87	7.79	8.32	8.18	8.32
1979	8.74	10.19	10.74	11.25	8.35	8.70	9.16	9.88	10.00	10.67	10.70	10.76	10.76	11.08	11.56	11.14
1980	12.15	11.42	12.33	11.20	12.56	11.84	12.05	11.55	9.55	13.16	12.53	11.69	12.78	11.49	11.37	10.99
1981	11.46	11.69	12.28	13.08	11.02	11.85	11.52	11.62	11.27	11.99	11.63	12.38	12.81	12.74	13.16	13.34
1982	13.33	13.77	14.14	15.44	13.33	13.27	13.38	13.23	14.10	13.99	13.07	14.95	14.41	15.31	17.44	16.57
1983	15.86	16.10	15.77	17.51	16.61	15.95	15.02	16.72	16.17	15.41	15.90	17.24	17.17	16.39	17.50	18.64

Exports f.o.b. (19)

billion kronor, monthly averages

Adjusted - Corrigé *

Exportations f.o.b. (19)

milliards de couronnes, moyennes mensuelles

Year	Q.1	Q.2	Q.3	Q.4	JAN	FEB	MAR	APR	MAY	JUN	JUL	AUG	SEP	OCT	NOV	DEC
1964	1.51	1.54	1.56	1.68	1.54	1.45	1.55	1.49	1.51	1.63	1.51	1.59	1.59	1.62	1.73	1.69
1965	1.71	1.64	1.73	1.78	1.73	1.74	1.68	1.65	1.63	1.65	1.78	1.70	1.71	1.86	1.77	1.69
1966	1.75	1.86	1.86	1.91	1.59	1.54	2.03	1.81	1.89	1.87	1.83	1.87	1.87	1.82	1.88	2.03
1967	1.91	2.02	1.91	1.99	1.87	1.95	1.92	2.10	1.91	2.05	1.89	1.86	1.97	1.95	1.88	2.15
1968	2.03	2.05	2.25	2.18	1.82	2.09	2.17	2.03	2.10	2.03	2.08	2.17	2.49	2.28	2.22	2.05
1969	2.30	2.43	2.52	2.58	2.35	2.25	2.30	2.36	2.51	2.44	2.55	2.54	2.48	2.49	2.63	2.62
1970	2.68	2.83	3.06	3.12	2.36	2.88	2.80	2.77	2.83	2.90	3.06	3.07	3.04	2.98	3.27	3.10
1971	3.10	3.24	3.16	3.23	3.23	2.92	3.15	3.10	3.14	3.49	3.06	3.11	3.31	3.36	3.11	3.23
1972	3.21	3.37	3.54	3.80	3.24	3.16	3.21	3.39	3.31	3.41	3.34	3.67	3.60	3.64	3.98	3.77
1973	4.15	4.32	4.40	4.78	4.11	4.08	4.27	3.79	4.78	4.39	4.64	4.22	4.35	4.74	4.72	4.87
1974	5.18	5.90	6.33	6.10	4.85	5.26	5.41	6.34	5.71	5.65	6.24	6.57	6.18	6.60	5.69	6.02
1975	6.27	5.93	5.69	6.10	6.43	6.39	5.98	6.21	5.98	5.59	6.14	5.04	5.38	5.91	5.91	6.49
1976	6.32	6.68	7.05	6.63	6.05	6.46	5.44	6.20	6.62	7.22	6.72	7.11	7.33	6.55	6.81	6.52
1977	6.76	7.08	6.85	7.78	6.81	6.78	6.70	6.80	7.40	7.03	6.45	6.97	7.13	7.55	7.61	8.17
1978	7.91	8.11	7.99	8.72	7.30	7.83	8.06	8.17	8.08	8.08	7.17	8.39	8.41	8.67	8.78	8.72
1979	8.86	9.79	10.18	10.52	8.72	8.64	9.23	9.71	9.88	9.78	9.94	9.89	10.72	10.57	10.88	10.11
1980	11.30	9.67	11.65	10.99	11.38	11.64	10.88	10.45	7.29	11.27	12.25	13.41	11.25	11.07	11.05	10.84
1981	11.34	11.71	12.23	12.95	10.92	11.51	11.60	11.89	11.58	11.67	12.05	12.31	12.33	12.74	12.90	13.20
1982	13.34	13.77	13.98	14.92	13.08	13.46	13.49	14.01	13.87	13.42	15.24	13.02	13.67	14.61	14.75	15.41
1983	16.69	17.47	17.87	18.20	17.90	15.94	16.22	16.10	18.72	17.60	17.33	17.46	18.83	18.01	18.47	18.13

Trade balance (f.o.b. — c.i.f.) (19)

billion kronor, monthly averages

Adjusted - Corrigé *

Balance commerciale (f.o.b. — c.a.f.) (19)

milliards de couronnes, moyennes mensuelles

Year	Q.1	Q.2	Q.3	Q.4	JAN	FEB	MAR	APR	MAY	JUN	JUL	AUG	SEP	OCT	NOV	DEC
1964	-0.10	-0.09	-0.10	-0.04	-0.08	-0.27	0.05	-0.18	-0.14	0.04	-0.15	-0.05	-0.11	-0.01	-0.03	-0.07
1965	-0.13	-0.25	-0.20	-0.14	-0.04	-0.19	-0.16	-0.20	-0.28	-0.27	-0.21	-0.24	-0.14	-0.16	-0.06	-0.19
1966	-0.22	-0.13	-0.08	-0.10	-0.20	-0.35	-0.11	-0.18	-0.09	-0.13	-0.10	-0.06	-0.08	-0.19	-0.15	0.04
1967	-0.12	0.07	-0.18	-0.07	-0.19	-0.09	-0.08	0.14	-0.06	0.12	-0.35	-0.26	-0.14	-0.05	-0.21	0.05
1968	-0.11	-0.06	0.01	-0.13	-0.33	-0.09	0.09	-0.08	-0.01	-0.10	-0.05	-0.11	0.17	-0.04	-0.09	-0.26
1969	-0.04	-0.15	-0.09	-0.08	0.04	-0.05	-0.11	-0.15	0.01	-0.30	-0.09	0.04	-0.24	-0.11	-0.03	-0.10
1970	-0.28	-0.23	0.06	0.06	-0.48	-0.12	-0.25	-0.23	-0.43	-0.04	0.06	0.04	0.07	-0.00	0.14	0.04
1971	0.16	0.21	0.17	0.16	0.15	0.06	0.26	0.04	0.24	0.34	-0.02	0.19	0.33	0.23	0.16	0.08
1972	0.05	0.22	0.35	0.42	0.10	0.06	0.01	0.31	0.07	0.28	0.16	0.47	0.44	0.16	0.49	0.61
1973	0.44	0.90	0.45	0.46	0.19	0.50	0.62	0.85	1.16	0.70	0.89	0.32	0.14	0.56	0.51	0.32
1974	0.35	0.10	-0.19	-0.07	0.51	0.25	0.29	0.29	-0.16	0.17	-0.28	-0.12	-0.18	0.39	-1.01	0.40
1975	-0.55	-0.29	-0.27	0.12	-1.61	0.03	-0.08	-0.26	-0.20	-0.42	-0.35	-0.35	-0.11	-0.16	-0.07	0.59
1976	-0.07	-0.21	-0.14	-0.78	-0.11	0.05	-0.14	-0.56	-0.18	0.10	-0.29	-0.00	-0.12	-0.12	-0.39	-1.33
1977	-0.83	-0.46	-0.52	0.20	-0.92	-0.80	-0.78	-0.62	-0.34	-0.42	-0.32	-0.67	-0.57	-0.12	0.25	0.46
1978	0.28	0.63	0.44	0.45	0.20	0.40	0.23	0.70	0.50	0.68	0.18	0.52	0.62	0.35	0.60	0.40
1979	0.13	-0.40	-0.56	-0.74	0.37	-0.06	0.08	-0.18	-0.12	-0.89	-0.76	-0.87	-0.04	-0.51	-0.68	-1.02
1980	-0.85	-1.75	-0.68	-0.29	-1.17	-0.21	-1.16	-1.10	-2.26	-1.89	-0.24	-0.28	-1.52	-0.42	-0.32	-0.14
1981	-0.12	0.02	-0.04	-0.14	-0.09	-0.34	0.08	0.07	0.31	-0.33	0.42	-0.07	-0.48	-0.01	-0.27	-0.14
1982	0.02	-0.00	-0.17	-1.52	-0.25	0.19	0.11	0.79	-0.22	-0.57	2.18	-1.93	-0.74	-0.71	-2.69	-1.16
1983	0.83	1.37	1.10	0.70	1.29	-0.01	1.21	-0.62	2.54	2.20	1.43	0.22	1.66	1.62	0.98	-0.51

* Adjusted by the O.E.C.D.

* Corrigé par l'O.C.D.E.

NOTES

1. Deliveries.
2. Excluding dissolving pulp.
3. From 3rd quarter 1982, new sample.
4. Excluding shipbuilding.
5. The original base of the index is September-November 1954 to 1967, 1968 from 1968 to 1970, and 1970 from 1971.
6. The break between 1969 and 1970 is due to a change in the definition of when work is started: from 1970, the laying of foundations replaced the start of excavations. Certain types of small houses (about 30 per cent) are excluded from the series.
7. Excluding sales of passenger cars, gasoline, pharmaceutical preparations and alcoholic beverages. From 1973, index (original base May 1970) linked on 1973 to previous index (original base 1968). From 1974, new sample.
8. Excluding indirect taxes; including wage-drift.
9. Labour force sample survey of population aged 16-74 from January 1970, 14 and over previously. The sample is revised every few years.
10. Monthly data refer to end of month from July 1974, and to mid-month previously.
11. Excluding hours paid for but not worked.
12. Weighting pattern based on January 1968 to 1971, on January 1972 from 1972 to 1973, and on January 1974 from 1974. New industrial classification in conformity with 1968 ISIC from 1972.
13. Series adjusted for unequal number of working days in the month.
14. Weighting pattern based on 1968 from 1973 and on 1963 previously. From 1973 excluding exports and including imports.
15. The original base of the index is 1949 to 1980, and 1980 from 1981. Weighting pattern revised each January.
16. Monthly data refer to end of period.
17. Monthly data refer to mid-month.
18. Annual data have a larger coverage than quarterly data.
19. General trade. From 1977, new recording procedure.

NOTES

1. Livraisons.
2. Non compris la pâte textile.
3. A partir du 3e trimestre 1982, nouvel échantillon.
4. Non compris la construction navale.
5. La base originale de l'indice est septembre-novembre 1954 jusqu'en 1967, 1968 de 1968 à 1970, et 1970 à partir de 1971.
6. La discontinuité entre 1969 et 1970 est due à un changement dans la définition des mises en chantier : à partir de 1970, la pose des fondations remplace le début des travaux d'excavation. Certains types de petites maisons (environ 30 %) sont exclus de la série.
7. Non compris les ventes de voitures de tourisme, d'essence, de préparations pharmaceutiques et de boissons alcoolisées. A partir de 1973, indice (base originale mai 1970) raccordé sur 1973 à l'indice précédent (base originale 1968). A partir de 1974, nouvel échantillon.
8. Non compris les impôts indirects; y compris la dérive des salaires.
9. Enquête par sondage auprès de la population âgée de 16 à 74 ans à partir de janvier 1970, de 14 ans ou plus auparavant. L'échantillon est révisé de temps à autre.
10. Situation en fin de mois à partir de juillet 1974, et en milieu de mois auparavant.
11. Non compris les heures payées mais non ouvrées.
12. La pondération se réfère à janvier 1968 jusqu'en 1971, à janvier 1972 de 1972 à 1973, et à janvier 1974 à partir de 1974. Nouvelle classification industrielle, conforme à la CITI de 1968, à partir de 1972.
13. Série corrigée de l'inégalité du nombre de jours ouvrables dans le mois.
14. La pondération se réfère à 1968 à partir de 1973, et à 1963 auparavant. A partir de 1973, non compris les exportations, y compris les importations.
15. La base originale de l'indice est 1949 jusqu'en 1980, et 1980 à partir de 1981. La pondération est révisée chaque année en janvier.
16. Situation en fin de mois.
17. Situation en milieu de mois.
18. Les données annuelles ont une couverture plus étendue que les données trimestrielles.
19. Commerce général. A partir de 1977, nouvelle procédure d'enregistrement.

MAIN SOURCES

PRINCIPALES SOURCES

Series	Séries	Sources
National product	Produit national	Statistiska Centralbyrån
Industrial production Internal trade Labour excl. hours worked Capital issues Credit Interest rates Share prices	Production industrielle Commerce intérieur Main-d'œuvre sauf heures effectuées Émissions de capital Crédits Taux d'intérêts Cours des actions	Statistiska Centralbyrån *Allmän Månadsstatistik*
Business surveys	Enquêtes de conjoncture	Konjunkturinstitutet *Konjunkturbarometern*
Deliveries, stocks and orders Construction Monthly hours worked Prices Foreign trade	Livraisons, stocks et commandes Construction Heures effectuées par mois Prix Commerce extérieur	Statistiska Centralbyrån *Statistiska Meddelanden*
Money supply	Disponibilités monétaires	Sveriges Riksbank
Net foreign position of commercial banks	Position extérieure nette des banques commerciales	Statistiska Centralbyrån
Balance of payments	Balance des paiements	Sveriges Riksbank *Ur Tidningarna*

Switzerland — Suisse

SWITZERLAND

Industrial production: total (1) / Production industrielle : total (1)

1980 = 100

	Year	Q.1	Q.2	Q.3	Q.4	JAN	FEB	MAR	APR	MAY	JUN	JUL	AUG	SEP	OCT	NOV	DEC
1964	65	62	67	65	67												
1965	68	65	69	67	70												
1966	70	65	72	69	74												
1967	73	70	74	71	76												
1968	76	71	76	76	82												
1969	83	75	83	84	89												
1970	90	84	93	89	95												
1971	92	87	93	89	96												
1972	94	91	94	91	99												
1973	99	96	99	96	105												
1974	100	99	104	95	100												
1975	87	81	86	84	99												
1976	88	82	88	86	95												
1977	93	87	94	91	99												
1978	93	87	96	89	100												
1979	95	89	94	92	104												
1980	100	97	101	96	105												
1981	99	93	100	99	106												
1982	96	93	98	93	98												
1983		91	97	93													

Industrial production: manufacturing / Production industrielle : industries manufacturières

1980 = 100

	Year	Q.1	Q.2	Q.3	Q.4	JAN	FEB	MAR	APR	MAY	JUN	JUL	AUG	SEP	OCT	NOV	DEC
1964	67	63	69	66	70												
1965	69	67	70	68	72												
1966	71	67	73	69	76												
1967	74	72	74	70	77												
1968	77	72	76	76	84												
1969	85	78	85	85	92												
1970	92	87	94	89	97												
1971	94	90	95	91	100												
1972	96	94	96	93	102												
1973	101	98	101	97	108												
1974	102	101	106	99	103												
1975	87	81	86	82	101												
1976	89	82	90	87	97												
1977	93	87	94	89	100												
1978	94	87	97	88	102												
1979	95	90	94	91	104												
1980	100	97	102	95	106												
1981	99	93	99	97	106												
1982	94	92	93	89	98												
1983		90	96	89													

Business climate (2)(3) manufacturing / Climat des affaires (2)(3) industries manufacturières

per cent balance / solde en pourcentage

	Year	Q.1	Q.2	Q.3	Q.4	JAN	FEB	MAR	APR	MAY	JUN	JUL	AUG	SEP	OCT	NOV	DEC
1964																	
1965																	
1966																	
1967																-13	-14
1968						-11	-5	-1	2	5	1	7	13	18	20	17	23
1969						22	32	40	37	35	36	44	40	35	21	38	31
1970						30	27	25	29	27	24	22	19	17	9	7	4
1971						8	6	2	-5	-1	-2	-10	-8	-11	-12	-14	-14
1972						-15	-9	-10	-13	-11	-7	-1	-3	1	7	9	10
1973						7	6	15	14	18	14	10	12	8	14	14	10
1974						15	9	6	9	8	4	7	-4	-8	-15	-26	-30
1975						-36	-42	-45	-52	-56	-50	-50	-54	-50	-49	-50	-45
1976						-35	-33	-13	-18	-13	-9	-12	-11	-4	-8	-4	-6
1977						-11	-8	-5	-6	-5	2	-9	-10	-9	-8	-10	-11
1978						-7	-16	-19	-16	-13	-10	-4	-15	-19	-21	-21	-23
1979						-18	-15	-9	-10	1	-3	2	5	7	12	10	2
1980						9	14	16	15	5	9	5	-3	4	-1	-7	-2
1981						-5	-8	-4	-4	-9	-4	-9	-9	-9	-13	-11	-16
1982						-21	-22	-20	-27	-34	-32	-36	-35	-34	-39	-40	-33
1983						-32	-31	-26	-19	-16	-12	-18	-13	-11	-9	-4	-9

Industrial production: total (1)

1980 = 100

Adjusted - Corrigé *

Production industrielle : total (1)

1980 = 100

	Year	Q.1	Q.2	Q.3	Q.4	JAN	FEB	MAR	APR	MAY	JUN	JUL	AUG	SEP	OCT	NOV	DEC
1964		64	65	66	65												
1965		67	67	66	68												
1966		68	71	70	71												
1967		73	73	72	73												
1968		73	74	77	79												
1969		79	82	85	85												
1970		87	91	91	91												
1971		91	92	92	92												
1972		94	93	93	95												
1973		99	98	99	100												
1974		103	103	100	95												
1975		84	85	86	93												
1976		86	87	88	90												
1977		91	93	94	93												
1978		92	95	91	94												
1979		94	93	94	93												
1980		102	100	99	98												
1981		98	99	101	100												
1982		98	97	95	92												
1983		96	95	95													

Industrial production: manufacturing

1980 = 100

Adjusted - Corrigé *

Production industrielle : industries manufacturières

1980 = 100

	Year	Q.1	Q.2	Q.3	Q.4	JAN	FEB	MAR	APR	MAY	JUN	JUL	AUG	SEP	OCT	NOV	DEC
1964		66	68	68	67												
1965		69	69	67	69												
1966		69	72	71	72												
1967		74	73	72	74												
1968		75	75	78	80												
1969		81	84	88	87												
1970		89	93	92	93												
1971		93	94	94	95												
1972		97	95	96	97												
1973		101	100	100	102												
1974		105	105	103	95												
1975		84	85	85	94												
1976		86	89	90	90												
1977		91	93	93	93												
1978		92	96	92	95												
1979		94	93	95	97												
1980		102	101	99	99												
1981		98	98	100	99												
1982		97	96	92	91												
1983		94	94	92													

Production: future tendency (2)

manufacturing

per cent balance

Perspectives de production (2)

industries manufacturières

solde en pourcentage

	Year	Q.1	Q.2	Q.3	Q.4	JAN	FEB	MAR	APR	MAY	JUN	JUL	AUG	SEP	OCT	NOV	DEC
1964																	
1965															13	-10	21
1966						50	39	28	55	-10	-21	84	69	52	16	18	37
1967						24	43	37	33	10	-	32	42	44	23	9	30
1968						26	19	22	18	19	16	20	20	24	20	16	35
1969						41	39	46	31	14	18	23	30	27	18	19	14
1970						18	38	33	34	21	5	18	28	19	16	7	14
1971						31	29	15	12	9	-3	7	18	18	2	-6	-2
1972						6	21	20	12	-7	-7	17	38	23	17	1	21
1973						34	33	18	2	2	-6	18	25	13	5	-1	14
1974						15	11	4	4	-10	-16	12	21	5	-15	-24	-19
1975						-29	-21	-28	-30	-34	-31	-2	-12	-16	-14	-14	-3
1976						7	9	17	9	-4	-12	2	15	19	-	-23	-5
1977						1	9	6	5	-8	-15	4	25	13	-3	-12	-
1978						5	5	8	1	-11	-22	8	15	3	-21	-17	-3
1979						9	16	19	15	-4	-12	18	23	27	11	9	7
1980						26	29	24	8	-14	-17	5	22	13	-2	-13	-2
1981						14	19	12	5	-14	-20	1	21	10	-14	-13	-13
1982						5	3	-2	-11	-25	-35	-16	7	-7	-27	-26	-27
1983						-5	4	7	6	-15	-13	6	14	13	2	-3	3

* Adjusted by the O.E.C.D.

* Corrigé par l'O.C.D.E.

SWITZERLAND

Orders inflow: tendency (2)
manufacturing
per cent balance

Commandes : tendance (2)
industries manufacturières
solde en pourcentage

	Year	Q.1	Q.2	Q.3	Q.4	JAN	FEB	MAR	APR	MAY	JUN	JUL	AUG	SEP	OCT	NOV	DEC
1964																	
1965																	
1966															8	8	-
1967						-5	-2	5	11	-1	18	-7	-14	11	11	-1	-6
1968						2	3	21	14	27	-2	20	19	39	35	16	20
1969						20	46	39	38	25	37	42	10	36	24	35	21
1970						22	18	12	28	1	3	2	-1	15	6	5	-5
1971						-	11	11	8	9	4	-12	-16	-4	-12	-9	-11
1972						-2	9	23	-6	9	16	11	6	41	39	25	26
1973						19	14	28	8	25	18	10	6	11	25	21	-11
1974						16	1	16	3	-4	1	2	-13	1	-6	-30	-45
1975						-31	-38	-38	-31	-41	-26	-36	-42	-13	-12	-26	-22
1976						-5	-8	29	-5	7	16	-4	-14	24	4	30	-3
1977						-16	14	13	9	12	13	-21	3	-1	4	1	-17
1978						12	-9	-6	-5	-6	3	-6	-6	-1	-12	1	-18
1979						-7	13	18	-4	18	-3	3	8	17	29	19	-11
1980						12	24	24	15	-8	4	-6	-11	9	4	-13	-1
1981						3	3	19	-	-2	12	-5	-3	9	-3	-3	-6
1982						-8	-6	5	-21	-31	-13	-28	-24	-4	-19	-24	-8
1983						-14	-12	6	-9	8	13	-23	15	15	10	20	1

Orders books: level (2)
manufacturing
per cent balance

Carnet de commandes : niveau (2)
industries manufacturières
solde en pourcentage

	Year	Q.1	Q.2	Q.3	Q.4	JAN	FEB	MAR	APR	MAY	JUN	JUL	AUG	SEP	OCT	NOV	DEC
1964																	
1965																	
1966															-16	-15	-16
1967						-24	-30	-32	-34	-34	-33	-28	-31	-28	-40	-31	-43
1968						-27	-29	-24	-17	-15	-15	-15	-9	-2	4	2	-7
1969						-	12	18	14	21	22	24	29	30	19	25	26
1970						23	18	25	28	24	26	25	23	13	10	8	5
1971						4	7	-4	-5	1	-1	-7	-8	-7	-17	-22	-23
1972						-24	-22	-23	-25	-24	-22	-18	-17	-18	-12	-14	-9
1973						-7	-12	-8	-5	-3	-3	-5	-1	-2	-2	-7	-7
1974						-3	-9	-4	-5	-8	-10	-13	-13	-22	-31	-34	-32
1975						-46	-54	-52	-59	-62	-64	-55	-63	-61	-58	-62	-63
1976						-50	-49	-42	-37	-43	-38	-41	-42	-41	-40	-54	-43
1977						-48	-46	-42	-38	-39	-34	-36	-37	-35	-36	-31	-36
1978						-30	-37	-36	-27	-33	-27	-28	-31	-40	-40	-42	-43
1979						-40	-38	-31	-27	-21	-15	-18	-16	-14	-9	-10	-12
1980						-12	-3	-7	-9	-10	-5	-10	-17	-10	-7	-15	-23
1981						-21	-19	-19	-15	-19	-17	-15	-24	-24	-24	-28	-31
1982						-32	-38	-36	-35	-38	-42	-50	-53	-51	-47	-54	-53
1983						-30	-44	-43	-39	-37	-32	-38	-41	-42	-41	-37	-36

Finished goods stocks: level (2)
manufacturing
per cent balance

Stocks de produits finis : niveau (2)
industries manufacturières
solde en pourcentage

	Year	Q.1	Q.2	Q.3	Q.4	JAN	FEB	MAR	APR	MAY	JUN	JUL	AUG	SEP	OCT	NOV	DEC
1964																	
1965																	
1966																	
1967						10	14	8	14	14	15	17	19	14	16	12	16
1968						12	7	12	11	10	9	-	9	5	1	-3	1
1969						4	-13	-25	-9	-10	-14	-19	-19	-21	-13	-13	-13
1970						-22	-8	-7	-11	-17	-9	-15	-7	-7	-	-	-4
1971						3	2	-1	3	-6	7	15	6	10	16	20	23
1972						35	32	21	32	24	29	16	23	16	5	5	-1
1973						1	-	-3	-2	1	-2	-8	-7	-10	-7	-4	-14
1974						-7	-8	-7	-5	-3	7	12	12	25	32	34	38
1975						43	49	52	55	56	54	56	61	56	53	55	45
1976						43	38	28	23	27	19	15	20	19	15	22	24
1977						15	19	20	19	24	13	14	24	20	22	20	16
1978						16	18	18	25	15	16	16	14	18	22	26	29
1979						23	24	14	13	9	7	5	-1	-1	2	2	3
1980						-3	-1	2	3	6	2	7	11	8	16	14	13
1981						15	19	16	17	21	19	25	24	27	22	27	26
1982						27	28	27	31	35	34	34	32	36	37	37	34
1983						26	28	29	26	23	21	17	16	15	17	17	14

Rate of capacity utilization (2) — **Taux d'utilisation des capacités (2)**
manufacturing — industries manufacturières
per cent — pourcentage

	Year	Q.1	Q.2	Q.3	Q.4	JAN	FEB	MAR	APR	MAY	JUN	JUL	AUG	SEP	OCT	NOV	DEC
1964																	
1965																	
1966																	
1967																	
1968																	
1969																	
1970					90										90		
1971		84	90	82	88	84			90			82			88		
1972		85	87	86	87	85			87			86			87		
1973		82	79	86	86	82			79			86			86		
1974		90	88	85	82	90			88			85			82		
1975		81	76	75	75	81			76			75			75		
1976		76	80	78	78	76			80			78			78		
1977		78	80	80	81	78			80			80			81		
1978		80	80	78	80	80			80			78			80		
1979		81	82	83	84	81			82			83			84		
1980		86	87	85	87	86			87			86			87		
1981		85	85	85	84	85			85			85			84		
1982		81	80	78	80	81			80			78			80		
1983		79	80	80	81	79			80			80			81		

Manufacturing sales — **Ventes des industries manufacturières**
1980 = 100 — 1980 = 100

	Year	Q.1	Q.2	Q.3	Q.4	JAN	FEB	MAR	APR	MAY	JUN	JUL	AUG	SEP	OCT	NOV	DEC
1964																	
1965																	
1966																	
1967																	
1968																	
1969																	
1970																	
1971																	
1972																	
1973																	
1974																	
1975	84.7	79.3	82.3	80.0	97.3												
1976	84.4	78.0	85.3	82.3	91.9												
1977	88.9	84.0	89.2	85.8	96.7												
1978	90.0	83.4	91.2	86.5	98.9												
1979	91.7	84.5	91.0	88.6	102.6												
1980	100.0	93.8	99.7	96.8	109.7												
1981	104.4	95.7	104.2	102.5	115.2												
1982	104.4	100.0	105.0	101.7	111.0												
1983	106.3	98.3	105.0	103.4	118.6												

Net new orders, manufacturing — **Commandes nouvelles nettes (industries manufacturières)**
1980 = 100 — 1980 = 100

	Year	Q.1	Q.2	Q.3	Q.4	JAN	FEB	MAR	APR	MAY	JUN	JUL	AUG	SEP	OCT	NOV	DEC
1964																	
1965																	
1966																	
1967																	
1968																	
1969																	
1970																	
1971																	
1972																	
1973																	
1974																	
1975	74.9	73.1	76.0	70.8	79.5												
1976	80.9	81.1	80.1	77.5	85.0												
1977	87.5	84.0	87.1	87.9	91.0												
1978	85.1	84.5	90.3	77.0	88.6												
1979	88.9	85.7	87.9	84.7	97.4												
1980	100.0	103.4	100.8	93.0	102.8												
1981	101.8	98.8	105.6	97.3	105.6												
1982	98.6	106.3	97.3	90.6	100.3												
1983	100.3	98.8	101.8	95.8	104.8												

SWITZERLAND

Construction permits issued: dwellings (4)

thousands, monthly averages

Permis de construire délivrés : logements (4)

milliers, moyennes mensuelles

	Year	Q.1	Q.2	Q.3	Q.4	JAN	FEB	MAR	APR	MAY	JUN	JUL	AUG	SEP	OCT	NOV	DEC
1964	2.24	3.48	1.94	1.98	1.56	4.44	3.15	2.85	1.66	1.63	2.53	2.37	1.65	1.92	1.38	2.17	1.12
1965	1.72	1.52	1.97	1.59	1.31	1.41	1.55	1.59	2.38	1.64	1.90	1.52	1.70	1.54	1.48	1.24	2.71
1966	1.76	2.07	1.61	1.56	1.78	2.03	1.66	2.53	1.31	1.45	2.06	1.65	1.59	1.42	1.22	2.50	1.64
1967	1.80	1.65	1.98	1.60	1.97	1.46	2.06	1.42	1.73	1.98	2.21	1.50	1.15	2.15	2.09	2.05	1.77
1968	2.07	1.66	2.24	2.26	[illegible]	1.47	1.51	2.00	2.59	1.65	2.49	2.35	1.79	2.63	2.24	2.16	1.92
1969	2.45	1.93	2.20	2.48	3.20	1.40	2.15	2.25	1.92	1.86	2.82	2.89	2.06	2.50	3.29	2.67	3.63
1970	2.88	3.16	3.17	2.64	2.53	3.35	2.97	3.15	3.28	2.38	3.85	2.69	3.00	2.24	2.30	2.69	2.62
1971	2.74	2.49	2.37	2.54	3.03	2.54	2.84	2.09	2.39	2.17	4.05	2.79	2.41	2.42	2.86	2.93	3.45
1972	2.84	2.62	3.11	2.65	2.97	2.15	2.32	3.37	3.15	2.70	3.48	1.87	2.89	3.19	2.62	3.07	3.23
1973	2.44	2.45	2.87	2.58	1.88	2.18	2.34	2.83	2.82	2.19	3.60	2.27	3.18	2.29	2.42	1.83	1.38
1974	1.84	1.89	2.13	1.78	1.55	1.47	2.13	2.07	2.55	1.67	2.19	2.17	1.40	1.77	1.54	1.56	1.55
1975	1.26	1.28	1.56	1.11	1.10	1.38	1.55	0.92	1.33	1.66	1.68	0.82	1.65	0.85	1.15	1.03	1.14
1976	0.90	1.03	0.73	0.91	0.95	0.85	1.02	1.21	0.75	0.55	0.89	0.92	1.07	0.75	1.09	0.65	1.11
1977	0.82	0.84	0.99	0.85	0.60	0.58	0.87	1.07	0.96	0.91	1.11	1.01	0.81	0.71	0.58	0.73	0.48
1978	0.92	0.89	1.05	0.77	0.95	0.87	0.89	0.92	0.78	1.09	1.29	0.68	0.74	0.89	0.84	0.80	1.24
1979	1.29	1.14	1.46	1.39	1.19	0.91	1.15	1.36	1.60	1.50	1.28	1.70	1.43	1.04	1.21	1.17	1.19
1980	1.32	1.35	1.41	1.14	1.37	1.15	1.39	1.52	1.47	1.37	1.39	1.04	0.97	1.39	1.49	1.42	1.19
1981	1.28	1.24	1.27	1.26	1.37	0.85	1.56	1.32	1.24	1.11	1.44	1.47	1.08	1.24	1.58	1.07	1.45
1982	1.24	1.07	1.41	1.07	1.41	1.04	0.94	1.22	1.27	1.32	1.64	1.26	0.96	0.97	1.49	1.56	1.18
1983	1.36	1.25	1.49	1.31	1.38	1.09	1.06	1.59	1.32	1.83	1.33	1.35	1.51	1.07	1.61	1.29	1.23

Retail sales: value (5)

1980 = 100

Ventes au détail : valeur (5)

1980 = 100

	Year	Q.1	Q.2	Q.3	Q.4	JAN	FEB	MAR	APR	MAY	JUN	JUL	AUG	SEP	OCT	NOV	DEC
1964	47.7	44.5	45.8	43.0	58.1	45.3	39.7	48.5	44.7	49.4	43.2	44.6	40.6	43.8	50.4	51.9	71.9
1965	50.7	45.8	50.5	46.3	60.5	49.5	41.4	46.4	53.4	49.5	48.5	49.2	42.9	46.9	52.2	56.4	72.9
1966	53.3	48.9	52.6	48.6	63.5	52.5	44.1	50.1	55.3	53.0	49.5	51.7	45.7	48.2	53.5	60.5	76.4
1967	55.9	53.2	54.2	50.3	65.8	54.1	46.6	59.0	53.7	56.1	52.8	53.1	47.3	52.2	53.1	60.9	83.5
1968	57.9	53.6	57.0	52.5	69.0	56.1	47.1	57.7	59.3	55.6	56.2	54.1	51.0	52.5	55.9	66.6	84.6
1969	62.1	57.4	61.2	55.9	74.5	59.3	50.3	62.5	61.7	64.3	57.5	57.8	55.2	54.6	60.4	71.9	91.1
1970	65.7	62.6	64.2	59.9	80.8	63.8	54.8	69.3	61.8	68.5	62.2	62.1	58.4	59.2	69.3	73.8	98.8
1971	72.2	66.1	72.3	65.0	85.9	70.7	59.6	67.8	75.6	73.2	68.1	68.3	61.5	65.4	74.1	81.5	102.2
1972	79.7	73.9	77.6	73.2	94.9	73.3	66.1	82.3	77.8	78.4	76.7	75.3	69.7	74.5	79.8	88.4	116.5
1973	85.5	79.2	85.2	75.5	103.3	82.2	72.3	83.1	88.3	82.6	84.7	78.4	71.6	76.5	86.1	95.5	128.2
1974	90.1	84.8	90.4	82.0	104.3	88.1	77.6	88.8	92.5	88.5	90.2	82.5	80.3	83.3	92.7	97.4	122.7
1975	87.2	88.0	85.3	78.7	93.2	90.0	80.4	93.6	83.6	90.1	82.4	80.1	79.7	76.3	84.4	91.9	118.3
1976	86.3	82.6	87.2	79.0	97.4	87.6	76.8	83.2	91.0	84.9	85.7	79.3	78.0	79.8	83.6	91.0	117.7
1977	89.2	85.3	89.0	82.8	100.5	87.0	81.0	88.0	91.4	87.9	87.8	84.0	82.4	82.1	86.8	95.5	119.1
1978	90.4	89.2	89.4	81.6	102.6	89.3	82.0	96.3	88.1	90.7	89.3	83.8	80.0	81.0	86.2	95.1	126.5
1979	93.7	89.3	93.0	84.8	108.6	92.6	84.8	90.6	93.6	92.3	93.1	84.7	85.0	84.9	91.0	102.8	131.9
1980	100.0	96.0	97.8	89.8	117.6	99.4	90.4	98.0	97.1	100.8	95.5	93.1	90.2	86.2	101.8	110.9	140.0
1981	106.6	102.0	105.4	96.0	124.2	106.3	96.8	102.7	108.3	103.2	104.6	98.0	93.5	96.6	111.0	114.2	147.4
1982	109.5	106.7	109.4	98.1	126.4	109.3	100.0	110.7	112.3	110.7	105.1	100.6	96.5	97.2	113.8	118.2	147.3
1983	112.9	110.6	111.8	101.9	128.7	110.6	103.7	117.4	110.9	113.9	110.8	103.8	98.6	103.3	113.4	122.8	149.8

New passenger car registrations

thousands, monthly averages

Immatriculations de voitures de tourisme neuves

milliers, moyennes mensuelles

	Year	Q.1	Q.2	Q.3	Q.4	JAN	FEB	MAR	APR	MAY	JUN	JUL	AUG	SEP	OCT	NOV	DEC
1964	11.1	11.4	14.9	9.8	8.5	7.6	11.1	15.4	17.7	13.8	13.3	12.2	7.9	9.2	9.6	7.7	8.1
1965	11.6	11.1	15.6	10.4	9.4	6.7	10.0	16.6	18.4	14.4	14.0	12.3	8.8	10.0	10.7	9.2	8.3
1966	12.2	12.6	15.8	10.3	10.3	7.0	11.7	19.1	17.0	15.9	14.5	11.7	8.8	10.5	11.9	9.9	8.9
1967	12.8	13.1	17.1	10.3	10.5	8.1	11.9	19.4	18.4	17.2	15.6	11.2	9.5	10.2	11.8	10.7	9.1
1968	14.0	13.4	19.2	12.0	11.3	8.1	12.7	19.4	21.5	21.1	14.8	15.3	10.5	10.3	13.6	11.6	8.9
1969	16.6	17.8	16.6	14.9	17.1	16.8	17.2	19.2	18.4	16.2	15.3	16.4	11.1	17.1	19.8	17.9	13.6
1970	18.9	17.9	20.7	16.0	20.3	16.0	15.9	21.8	24.7	17.7	19.7	19.2	10.4	18.4	22.3	20.2	20.0
1971	19.6	18.9	25.6	17.3	16.6	12.0	16.4	28.4	29.4	23.8	23.7	20.1	15.4	16.5	18.5	16.7	14.6
1972	21.6	23.2	28.1	17.8	17.3	14.6	20.9	33.9	28.3	27.4	28.6	20.1	16.7	16.5	18.6	17.3	16.1
1973	19.9	22.0	26.5	16.3	14.8	17.0	18.5	30.5	28.7	28.4	22.5	19.3	14.7	14.8	17.8	13.7	12.7
1974	16.9	15.3	24.9	14.9	12.4	11.8	10.4	23.6	28.4	26.3	19.9	17.8	13.0	13.8	15.2	11.4	10.6
1975	15.8	14.5	19.0	16.9	12.9	10.7	14.3	18.5	19.7	15.3	22.1	17.5	17.5	15.7	13.1	12.0	13.7
1976	17.0	14.8	21.9	15.7	15.6	10.9	14.6	18.7	25.3	20.1	20.2	18.6	13.9	14.5	15.9	15.9	15.1
1977	19.5	16.5	26.4	18.6	16.7	11.4	14.3	23.6	31.1	27.9	20.0	21.5	19.5	14.7	18.1	19.0	13.1
1978	23.0	20.4	27.3	22.5	21.9	15.2	15.8	30.2	28.2	23.2	30.4	23.7	23.7	20.0	25.1	24.0	16.6
1979	23.3	24.4	30.8	19.6	18.6	18.2	20.1	34.8	33.3	32.4	26.8	20.9	19.5	18.3	21.3	20.4	14.1
1980	23.4	24.2	29.0	20.9	19.3	19.3	21.3	32.1	30.5	27.7	28.8	23.8	19.2	19.7	23.6	18.1	16.3
1981	24.3	23.2	33.4	21.4	19.0	18.1	21.5	30.2	28.0	29.3	42.9	25.4	17.9	20.8	22.7	18.5	15.8
1982	24.2	24.5	31.9	22.6	18.0	19.6	20.5	33.3	37.1	28.5	30.0	25.4	18.9	23.6	20.2	17.8	16.1
1983	22.8	28.7	25.9	18.7	18.0	20.3	19.2	46.8	19.7	27.1	30.8	19.8	17.3	19.0	19.5	19.8	14.7

Construction: dwellings completed (4) / Construction : logements achevés (4)

thousands, monthly averages / milliers, moyennes mensuelles

	Year	Q.1	Q.2	Q.3	Q.4	JAN	FEB	MAR	APR	MAY	JUN	JUL	AUG	SEP	OCT	NOV	DEC
1964	1.74	1.48	1.94	1.60	1.94	1.04	1.43	1.96	2.47	1.49	1.87	1.73	1.12	1.96	1.52	1.94	2.36
1965	1.84	1.54	2.11	1.71	2.07	0.92	1.45	2.23	2.42	1.75	2.17	1.12	2.07	1.93	2.26	1.78	1.96
1966	1.74	1.46	2.15	1.57	1.78	0.94	1.36	2.09	2.15	1.73	2.57	1.01	1.54	2.17	1.49	1.65	2.20
1967	1.56	1.30	1.62	1.58	1.75	1.04	1.34	1.51	2.17	1.19	1.50	1.33	1.42	1.98	1.90	1.82	1.54
1968	1.58	1.43	1.93	1.43	1.47	1.17	1.03	2.10	2.33	1.46	2.16	0.94	1.25	2.09	1.91	1.37	1.12
1969	1.71	1.37	1.79	1.78	1.88	1.02	0.83	2.26	1.70	1.99	1.69	1.54	1.85	1.95	2.45	1.77	1.41
1970	2.31	1.76	2.71	1.82	2.95	1.21	1.50	2.57	2.92	2.52	2.68	1.82	1.43	2.21	2.69	2.76	3.41
1971	2.26	1.68	2.56	1.81	2.93	1.32	1.20	2.53	2.75	2.08	2.83	2.00	1.49	1.95	3.41	2.58	2.94
1972	2.32	1.91	2.54	2.21	2.59	1.66	1.67	2.41	2.89	1.75	3.00	2.34	2.11	2.19	2.48	2.72	2.58
1973	2.57	2.37	2.53	2.33	3.06	2.22	2.11	2.78	2.28	2.42	2.90	1.83	1.77	3.40	3.07	2.40	3.71
1974	2.35	2.22	2.50	2.20	2.49	2.07	1.99	2.61	2.40	1.86	3.24	2.09	2.11	2.41	2.55	2.12	2.80
1975	1.92	2.08	2.16	1.69	1.75	1.95	1.95	2.33	1.50	1.58	3.01	1.37	1.52	2.18	1.99	1.83	1.44
1976	1.14	1.22	1.45	0.84	1.03	0.58	0.90	2.09	1.04	1.24	2.08	0.58	0.88	1.04	0.98	0.98	1.15
1977	0.94	0.67	1.04	0.97	1.07	0.44	0.41	1.16	1.05	1.23	0.85	0.82	0.73	1.36	1.43	0.37	0.91
1978	0.91	0.91	1.14	0.69	0.93	0.45	0.68	1.58	1.23	0.95	1.24	0.38	0.62	1.06	0.80	0.84	1.14
1979	1.00	0.98	0.95	0.96	1.13	0.58	0.67	1.69	0.79	0.92	1.12	0.63	0.67	1.57	1.22	1.25	0.92
1980	0.99	0.75	1.03	1.10	1.08	0.50	0.41	1.35	0.98	0.69	1.42	0.89	0.69	1.73	0.89	1.05	1.29
1981	1.10	0.90	1.22	1.10	1.17	0.65	0.67	1.37	1.01	0.99	1.65	1.00	0.81	1.51	1.22	1.29	0.98
1982	1.17	1.18	1.22	1.03	1.25	0.98	0.85	1.71	1.00	0.88	1.77	0.99	0.78	1.31	1.68	0.99	1.08
1983	1.11	1.03	1.01	1.20	1.21	0.70	0.91	1.49	0.90	0.73	1.41	0.61	1.06	1.91	1.34	0.95	1.34

Retail sales: value (5) / Ventes au détail : valeur (5)

1980 = 100

Adjusted - Corrigé *

	Year	Q.1	Q.2	Q.3	Q.4	JAN	FEB	MAR	APR	MAY	JUN	JUL	AUG	SEP	OCT	NOV	DEC
1964		46.2	47.0	47.9	49.7	46.1	45.3	47.2	46.6	47.8	46.8	47.0	48.3	48.4	50.5	48.6	50.0
1965		49.4	50.4	51.5	51.9	49.3	49.5	49.5	50.2	50.3	50.5	51.1	51.0	52.2	52.4	52.3	50.9
1966		52.2	53.1	53.9	54.3	52.9	52.6	51.0	53.2	53.5	52.7	53.9	54.6	53.3	54.7	55.8	52.5
1967		55.5	56.1	56.4	56.2	54.9	55.6	56.0	55.7	55.5	57.0	56.1	55.7	57.3	55.0	56.1	57.4
1968		56.6	57.2	58.8	59.1	57.4	54.4	57.8	57.2	56.4	57.9	58.3	58.7	59.4	58.1	59.7	59.6
1969		60.4	62.0	62.4	64.1	60.5	60.0	60.7	62.0	63.0	61.2	62.1	63.3	61.7	62.8	64.7	65.0
1970		64.7	65.8	67.2	69.6	63.8	65.3	65.2	64.9	65.8	66.9	66.9	67.3	67.0	70.6	67.9	70.4
1971		69.7	72.6	72.8	74.3	70.6	70.6	67.8	73.9	72.8	71.2	72.2	71.9	74.3	74.5	75.0	73.4
1972		75.6	79.1	81.5	82.1	73.9	74.5	78.6	78.7	78.1	80.6	80.6	81.4	82.5	81.5	82.3	82.5
1973		84.4	84.3	84.2	89.9	84.0	83.9	85.2	83.5	85.1	84.2	85.0	83.1	84.6	88.7	88.6	92.5
1974		88.6	90.4	91.7	91.5	88.9	88.8	88.0	90.4	90.0	90.9	90.6	90.3	94.1	95.2	89.8	89.6
1975		89.9	87.3	87.3	86.7	90.8	90.7	88.3	87.5	87.5	86.9	87.5	88.6	85.7	87.3	85.5	87.4
1976		85.4	86.7	87.7	86.0	86.4	82.7	87.2	86.7	86.6	86.7	85.4	87.6	90.3	85.1	86.4	86.5
1977		88.2	89.5	91.7	88.8	86.6	89.6	88.5	88.9	89.0	90.6	90.2	93.0	91.9	89.7	90.7	86.0
1978		90.1	92.1	90.2	90.6	89.3	90.2	90.8	92.4	90.0	93.7	91.0	89.9	89.7	89.7	90.8	91.3
1979		92.6	93.0	94.4	96.1	93.3	93.1	91.2	91.4	94.4	93.1	92.8	96.2	94.2	94.9	96.6	96.7
1980		96.8	99.2	100.0	104.0	99.5	95.2	95.6	98.5	99.3	99.8	102.2	100.5	97.3	104.7	103.0	104.4
1981		105.7	104.9	107.6	109.6	104.5	106.0	106.7	104.3	104.0	106.3	107.8	105.9	109.0	111.2	108.3	109.4
1982		109.5	110.1	109.8	111.4	107.8	109.2	111.5	110.8	111.3	108.3	108.7	110.6	110.1	113.4	111.6	109.3
1983		112.4	114.0	114.0	113.1	110.7	113.1	113.3	111.7	113.7	116.5	112.0	114.3	115.5	114.3	115.9	109.0

Retail sales: volume / Ventes au détail : volume

1980 = 100

Adjusted - Corrigé *

	Year	Q.1	Q.2	Q.3	Q.4	JAN	FEB	MAR	APR	MAY	JUN	JUL	AUG	SEP	OCT	NOV	DEC
1964	95	93	94	95	98	93	91	95	93	95	93	94	96	96	100	96	99
1965	98	97	98	98	98	97	97	97	98	97	97	98	98	100	100	99	96
1966	98	97	98	99	98	99	98	95	99	98	97	95	100	98	100	101	94
1967	99	100	100	99	98	98	100	100	100	98	101	99	97	101	97	98	100
1968	100	98	99	102	101	100	94	100	99	98	100	101	101	103	100	102	101
1969	105	102	105	105	107	102	102	103	105	106	103	104	107	104	105	108	108
1970	108	107	108	109	110	106	108	108	107	108	109	105	110	108	113	107	111
1971	110	109	112	111	111	110	110	105	114	112	109	110	109	112	112	111	103
1972	114	111	114	116	114	108	109	115	115	112	116	116	116	117	114	114	114
1973	112	114	112	111	113	115	114	115	112	114	112	112	110	111	114	111	114
1974	108	109	110	109	106	109	110	108	112	109	110	109	103	110	111	103	103
1975	98	102	98	98	96	104	103	100	99	98	97	98	99	95	97	95	97
1976	95	94	96	97	95	95	91	96	96	96	96	94	96	100	94	95	95
1977	97	97	98	100	96	95	98	97	97	97	99	98	101	100	97	98	93
1978	97	97	99	97	98	97	98	98	100	97	101	98	97	97	97	98	98
1979	98	98	97	97	99	100	99	96	96	99	96	98	99	97	98	99	99
1980	100	99	100	99	102	102	97	97	100	100	100	102	100	96	104	101	102
1981	100	102	99	100	101	101	102	102	100	99	100	101	98	100	103	100	101
1982	97	100	99	96	97	99	100	102	100	100	96	96	97	98	99	97	95
1983	97	98	99	98	97	97	99	99	97	99	100	97	99	99	98	99	93

* Adjusted by the O.E.C.D. / * Corrigé par l'O.C.D.E.

SWITZERLAND

Employment: manufacturing (6)
(wage earners)
1980 = 100

Emploi : industries manufacturières (6)
(ouvriers)
1980 = 100

	Year	Q.1	Q.2	Q.3	Q.4	JAN	FEB	MAR	APR	MAY	JUN	JUL	AUG	SEP	OCT	NOV	DEC
1964	131.7	131.6	132.4	132.4	130.7			131.6			132.4			132.4			130.7
1965	130.1	131.6	130.7	129.8	128.2			131.6			130.7			129.8			128.2
1966	127.3	127.3	128.2	127.3	126.4			127.3			128.2			127.3			126.4
1967	125.9	126.1	126.7	126.0	124.9			126.1			126.7			126.0			124.9
1968	125.1	124.7	125.4	125.5	124.6			124.7			125.4			125.5			124.6
1969	124.9	124.2	125.3	125.1	124.9			124.2			125.3			125.1			124.9
1970	124.2	124.9	124.9	124.1	123.0			124.9			124.9			124.1			123.0
1971	122.5	122.8	123.3	122.7	121.1			122.8			123.3			122.7			121.1
1972	119.4	120.7	120.2	119.0	117.6			120.7			120.2			119.0			117.6
1973	118.3	118.4	118.5	118.4	117.9			118.4			118.5			118.4			117.9
1974	118.0	117.9	119.0	118.6	116.3			117.9			119.0			118.6			116.3
1975	107.4	113.2	109.0	105.3	102.0			113.2			109.0			105.3			102.0
1976	99.8	100.1	99.9	99.9	99.3			100.1			99.9			99.9			99.3
1977	99.6	98.7	99.5	100.0	99.9			98.7			99.5			100.0			99.9
1978	99.5	99.5	100.2	99.8	98.5			99.5			100.2			99.8			98.5
1979	98.4	97.8	98.6	98.6	98.4			97.8			98.6			98.6			98.4
1980	100.0	99.0	100.1	100.6	100.2			99.0			100.1			100.6			100.2
1981	101.4	100.3	100.3	101.4	100.5			100.3			100.3			101.4			100.5
1982	97.7	99.4	98.5	97.6	95.8			99.4			98.5			97.6			95.8
1983	93.9	94.3	94.4	93.7	93.0			94.3			94.4			93.7			93.0

Jobs vacant, unfilled vacancies (7)(8)
thousands

Offres d'emploi non satisfaites (7)(8)
milliers

	Year	Q.1	Q.2	Q.3	Q.4	JAN	FEB	MAR	APR	MAY	JUN	JUL	AUG	SEP	OCT	NOV	DEC
1964	6.3	6.7	6.5	6.1	5.8	6.0	7.1	7.0	6.8	6.4	6.2	6.0	6.1	6.3	6.0	5.8	5.7
1965	5.3	5.9	5.5	5.2	4.4	6.5	5.4	5.9	5.7	5.4	5.5	5.3	5.2	5.0	4.8	4.4	3.9
1966	4.6	4.7	4.9	4.7	4.2	4.4	4.8	4.8	5.0	5.0	4.8	4.6	4.8	4.7	4.5	4.2	3.8
1967	4.1	4.4	4.3	4.2	3.6	4.3	4.4	4.4	4.3	4.3	4.2	4.0	4.3	4.3	3.8	3.8	3.2
1968	4.0	4.0	4.1	4.0	3.6	3.5	4.2	4.4	4.1	4.2	4.1	4.2	4.1	3.7	3.9	3.6	3.4
1969	4.3	3.7	4.4	4.7	4.2	3.5	3.8	3.9	4.1	4.5	4.7	4.7	4.7	4.8	4.6	4.3	3.8
1970	4.8	4.6	5.3	4.9	4.3	4.2	4.5	5.1	5.2	5.3	5.3	5.0	4.8	5.0	4.9	3.8	4.2
1971	4.0	4.2	4.0	3.8	3.8	4.1	4.3	4.1	4.1	4.1	3.9	3.7	3.8	3.9	3.8	3.8	3.9
1972	4.5	3.9	5.5	4.6	3.9	4.1	3.9	3.8	3.7	6.6	6.1	5.2	4.6	4.1	4.0	3.9	3.7
1973	3.8	4.0	3.9	3.8	3.5	3.9	4.1	4.1	4.0	4.0	3.8	3.8	3.8	3.7	3.6	3.6	3.3
1974	2.8	3.6	3.1	2.6	1.8	3.5	3.8	3.6	3.4	3.0	2.9	2.7	2.7	2.4	2.2	1.7	1.5
1975	2.8	2.4	2.8	3.3	2.3	2.1	2.4	2.6	2.6	2.8	3.1	3.1	3.5	3.4	2.9	2.8	2.7
1976	4.6	4.2	5.1	5.1	4.1	3.6	4.4	4.7	5.0	5.2	5.1	5.3	5.1	4.8	4.4	4.0	4.0
1977	6.5	5.4	6.4	7.0	7.1	4.6	5.5	6.1	6.0	6.4	6.9	6.7	6.9	7.3	7.5	7.1	6.7
1978	8.3	7.9	8.4	8.3	8.5	7.2	8.3	8.3	8.3	8.2	8.6	8.3	8.7	8.0	9.1	8.7	7.8
1979	8.9	8.2	8.4	9.0	10.1	8.0	8.1	8.4	8.2	8.8	8.3	8.4	8.8	9.7	10.7	9.9	9.7
1980	12.3	11.0	12.3	12.3	13.6	10.4	11.1	11.5	11.4	12.3	13.2	12.0	12.2	12.7	12.3	14.6	13.9
1981	11.9	13.6	12.9	11.1	9.9	14.1	13.4	13.3	13.1	13.0	12.6	11.1	11.2	11.1	10.6	10.1	8.9
1982	6.3	8.4	6.8	5.6	4.6	8.4	8.8	8.0	7.3	6.7	6.3	5.7	5.7	5.4	5.2	4.3	4.3
1983	5.1	5.5	5.0	5.2	4.7	5.2	5.7	5.6	5.1	4.9	5.0	5.0	5.1	5.4	5.2	4.6	4.3

Weekly hours of work: manufacturing (9)
(wage earners)
hours

Durée hebdomadaire du travail : (9)
industries manufacturières (ouvriers)
heures

	Year	Q.1	Q.2	Q.3	Q.4	JAN	FEB	MAR	APR	MAY	JUN	JUL	AUG	SEP	OCT	NOV	DEC
1964																	
1965																	
1966																	
1967																	
1968																	
1969																	
1970																	
1971																	
1972																	
1973	44.9	44.8	45.0	45.0	44.9												
1974	44.9	44.8	44.9	44.9	44.8												
1975	44.5	44.6	44.5	44.6	44.3												
1976	44.5	44.2	44.5	44.6	44.5												
1977	44.6	44.5	44.6	44.6	44.5												
1978	44.4	44.4	44.5	44.4	44.3												
1979	44.2	44.1	44.2	44.2	44.1												
1980	43.9	43.8	43.9	43.9	43.8												
1981	43.8	43.7	43.8	43.9	43.8												
1982	43.7	43.6	43.8	43.6	43.6												
1983	43.2	43.1	43.3	43.3	43.2												

Unemployment: registered unemployed (7) — Chômage : chômeurs inscrits (7)

thousands — milliers

	Year	Q.1	Q.2	Q.3	Q.4	JAN	FEB	MAR	APR	MAY	JUN	JUL	AUG	SEP	OCT	NOV	DEC
1964	0.3	0.5	0.2	0.1	0.4	1.1	0.3	0.2	0.2	0.1	0.1	0.1	0.1	0.1	0.2	0.2	0.6
1965	0.3	0.6	0.1	0.1	0.4	0.8	0.7	0.3	0.2	0.1	0.1	0.1	0.1	0.1	0.2	0.3	0.6
1966	0.3	0.7	0.1	0.1	0.3	1.5	0.3	0.2	0.2	0.1	0.1	0.1	0.1	0.1	0.2	0.2	0.4
1967	0.3	0.4	0.2	0.1	0.3	0.7	0.3	0.2	0.2	0.2	0.1	0.1	0.1	0.1	0.2	0.2	0.6
1968	0.3	0.7	0.2	0.1	0.2	1.3	0.5	0.3	0.2	0.2	0.1	0.1	0.1	0.1	0.2	0.2	0.4
1969	0.2	0.4	0.1	0.1	0.1	0.6	0.4	0.2	0.1	0.1	0.1	0.1	0.1	0.1	0.1	0.1	0.2
1970	0.1	0.2	0.1	0.0	0.1	0.3	0.3	0.1	0.1	0.1	0.0	0.0	0.0	0.1	0.1	0.1	0.1
1971	0.1	0.1	0.1	0.1	0.2	0.2	0.1	0.1	0.1	0.1	0.0	0.1	0.1	0.1	0.1	0.1	0.2
1972	0.1	0.2	0.1	0.1	0.1	0.3	0.2	0.1	0.1	0.1	0.1	0.1	0.1	0.1	0.1	0.1	0.1
1973	0.1	0.1	0.1	0.1	0.1	0.2	0.1	0.1	0.1	0.1	0.1	0.1	0.1	0.1	0.1	0.1	0.1
1974	0.2	0.1	0.1	0.1	0.6	0.1	0.1	0.1	0.1	0.1	0.1	0.1	0.1	0.1	0.3	0.6	1.0
1975	10.2	3.0	6.6	10.4	20.8	2.1	2.8	4.0	5.7	6.5	7.5	8.5	10.1	12.5	15.8	20.3	26.3
1976	20.7	30.6	22.8	14.2	15.2	31.6	32.2	28.0	25.9	22.9	19.7	15.4	14.1	13.0	13.0	15.3	17.4
1977	12.0	17.5	12.1	8.3	10.2	21.0	17.5	14.1	13.8	12.3	10.2	8.8	8.3	7.6	8.5	10.6	11.6
1978	10.5	13.6	9.3	7.9	11.2	15.1	14.4	11.2	10.1	9.4	8.4	7.6	7.3	8.1	9.3	11.3	13.0
1979	10.3	14.5	10.3	8.1	8.4	17.2	14.2	12.1	11.1	10.6	9.3	8.6	8.1	7.7	7.8	8.4	8.9
1980	6.3	9.1	5.7	4.7	5.5	11.4	8.6	7.2	6.4	5.7	5.0	4.7	4.7	4.6	4.8	5.5	6.3
1981	5.9	6.9	4.7	4.6	7.3	8.8	6.5	5.3	5.0	4.7	4.5	4.3	4.6	4.9	5.7	7.1	9.2
1982	13.2	10.3	10.3	12.3	20.0	11.7	9.7	9.4	9.3	10.5	10.6	10.8	12.3	13.6	16.2	20.4	23.6
1983	26.3	27.2	25.8	23.9	28.3	27.9	27.8	25.9	25.9	26.4	25.1	23.4	23.9	24.5	25.4	29.0	30.4

Jobs vacant, unfilled vacancies (7) (8) — Offres d'emploi non satisfaites (7) (8)

Adjusted - Corrigé *

thousands — milliers

	Year	Q.1	Q.2	Q.3	Q.4	JAN	FEB	MAR	APR	MAY	JUN	JUL	AUG	SEP	OCT	NOV	DEC
1964		6.6	6.2	6.0	5.3	6.3	5.9	6.6	6.4	6.2	6.1	6.0	5.9	6.1	6.1	6.2	6.5
1965		5.9	5.3	5.0	4.7	6.8	5.2	5.6	5.4	5.2	5.4	5.3	5.0	4.8	4.9	4.7	4.6
1966		4.6	4.7	4.5	4.5	4.7	4.7	4.5	4.8	4.8	4.6	4.5	4.6	4.5	4.5	4.5	4.5
1967		4.4	4.1	4.0	3.9	4.6	4.3	4.2	4.1	4.1	4.0	3.9	4.1	4.1	3.8	4.1	3.8
1968		4.1	3.9	3.8	3.9	3.8	4.2	4.2	3.9	3.9	3.9	4.1	3.9	3.5	3.9	3.9	4.0
1969		3.8	4.2	4.6	4.5	3.9	3.8	3.8	3.9	4.2	4.4	4.6	4.6	4.6	4.6	4.6	4.3
1970		4.7	5.0	4.8	4.6	4.6	4.6	5.0	5.0	5.0	5.0	4.8	4.7	4.9	5.0	4.1	4.7
1971		4.3	3.3	3.7	4.1	4.4	4.4	4.0	3.9	3.8	3.6	3.5	3.8	3.8	3.9	4.1	4.4
1972		4.0	5.2	4.5	4.2	4.4	3.9	3.7	3.5	6.3	5.8	5.0	4.5	4.0	4.2	4.3	4.2
1973		4.0	3.7	3.6	3.9	4.1	4.1	3.9	3.9	3.7	3.6	3.6	3.7	3.6	3.8	4.0	3.8
1974		3.6	2.9	2.4	2.3	3.7	3.7	3.4	3.2	2.7	2.6	2.5	2.5	2.3	2.4	2.2	2.2
1975		2.3	2.6	3.2	3.3	2.4	2.2	2.3	2.4	2.6	2.8	2.9	3.3	3.3	3.0	3.3	3.5
1976		4.2	4.9	4.9	4.6	3.9	4.2	4.4	4.8	5.0	4.8	5.2	4.9	4.7	4.4	4.4	4.8
1977		5.4	6.2	6.9	7.4	5.0	5.3	5.8	5.8	6.1	6.6	6.7	6.9	7.2	7.4	7.4	7.5
1978		7.9	8.1	8.4	8.8	7.6	8.1	8.0	8.2	7.9	8.3	8.5	8.7	7.9	8.9	8.9	8.5
1979		8.1	8.2	9.1	10.2	8.3	7.9	8.1	8.1	8.5	8.1	8.7	8.9	9.6	10.5	9.9	10.3
1980		10.9	12.1	12.5	13.7	10.7	10.9	11.2	11.4	12.0	13.0	12.4	12.4	12.6	12.0	14.5	14.4
1981		13.5	12.8	11.3	9.9	14.3	13.2	13.1	13.1	12.7	12.5	11.6	11.4	11.0	10.3	10.0	9.4
1982		8.3	6.6	5.8	4.6	8.6	8.6	7.8	7.3	6.4	6.2	6.2	6.0	5.3	4.9	4.1	4.8
1983		5.4	4.9	5.4	4.7	5.4	5.5	5.4	5.1	4.6	4.9	5.5	5.4	5.2	4.9	4.4	4.7

Monthly earnings: manufacturing (10) (wage earners) — Gains mensuels : industries manufacturières (10) (ouvriers)

1980 = 100

	Year	Q.1	Q.2	Q.3	Q.4	JAN	FEB	MAR	APR	MAY	JUN	JUL	AUG	SEP	OCT	NOV	DEC
1964	40.4	39.9	40.3	40.6	41.0			39.9			40.3			40.6			41.0
1965	42.4	41.9	42.2	42.6	43.0			41.9			42.2			42.6			43.0
1966	44.9	44.4	44.8	45.0	45.5			44.4			44.8			45.0			45.5
1967	47.3	46.9	47.2	47.4	47.8			46.9			47.2			47.4			47.8
1968	49.3	48.9	49.1	49.3	49.8			48.9			49.1			49.3			49.8
1969	51.4	51.0	51.2	51.5	51.8			51.0			51.2			51.5			51.8
1970	54.6	53.6	54.2	55.0	56.1			53.5			54.1			55.0			56.1
1971	59.9	58.8	59.4	60.3	61.1			58.8			59.4			60.3			61.1
1972	65.2	64.2	64.8	65.6	66.4			64.2			64.8			65.6			66.4
1973	71.2	70.2	70.4	71.7	72.6												
1974	81.1	80.1	80.3	81.6	82.5												
1975	87.1	87.1	86.6	87.6	87.1												
1976	88.5	88.8	88.5	88.3	88.6												
1977	90.0	90.6	89.6	89.7	90.1												
1978	93.1	93.4	92.3	93.5	93.2												
1979	95.1	95.4	94.5	95.2	95.3												
1980	100.0	100.1	99.1	99.9	100.9												
1981	105.1	105.4	104.2	105.0	105.7												
1982	111.6	111.8	111.0	111.5	112.3												
1983	119.2	119.7	118.5	119.5	119.1												

* Adjusted by the O.E.C.D. — * Corrigé par l'O.C.D.E.

SWITZERLAND

Wholesale prices: agricultural products — Prix de gros : produits agricoles

1980 = 100

	Year	Q.1	Q.2	Q.3	Q.4	JAN	FEB	MAR	APR	MAY	JUN	JUL	AUG	SEP	OCT	NOV	DEC
1964	68.1																
1965	68.9																
1966	69.7																
1967	70.8																
1968	71.0																
1969	72.5																
1970	74.0	73.7	74.2	73.5	74.7	73.5	73.6	73.8	73.4	75.2	73.9	74.0	73.3	73.4	74.4	74.7	75.0
1971	76.4	75.9	76.5	76.1	77.0	75.8	76.0	76.0	76.1	76.9	76.6	76.2	75.8	76.2	76.9	77.0	77.1
1972	80.0	77.7	79.9	80.5	82.2	77.4	77.5	78.3	78.8	80.6	80.2	79.8	80.5	81.1	81.5	81.7	83.4
1973	87.5	84.7	87.0	87.6	90.6	84.3	84.9	85.0	86.0	87.5	87.5	88.0	87.6	87.1	89.4	89.9	92.5
1974	94.0	93.8	93.7	93.3	95.3	93.8	93.6	94.0	93.7	94.6	92.7	93.0	93.1	93.8	96.2	95.7	94.0
1975	94.4	94.1	94.6	94.4	94.4	93.6	94.2	94.4	95.2	95.3	93.3	94.4	94.1	94.7	95.0	94.0	94.2
1976	97.1	95.5	96.8	97.5	98.9	94.4	96.1	95.9	96.6	96.5	97.3	97.6	96.9	98.1	97.5	98.7	100.4
1977	103.4	103.9	106.6	102.5	100.7	102.6	103.2	105.9	106.4	106.4	107.0	104.7	100.1	102.8	100.8	101.2	100.2
1978	97.9	99.0	100.0	95.9	96.5	99.5	98.4	99.2	99.9	100.0	100.0	97.6	94.9	95.1	95.2	97.1	97.1
1979	98.4	97.6	98.9	98.2	98.6	97.3	97.1	98.4	98.3	99.1	99.2	98.9	98.0	97.7	97.4	99.1	99.4
1980	100.0	99.8	100.1	99.6	100.5	99.9	99.2	100.4	101.0	100.1	99.1	101.0	99.3	98.6	99.0	100.3	102.2
1981	105.4	105.6	105.5	104.4	106.0	105.4	105.7	105.6	106.2	106.1	104.2	104.1	104.5	104.4	106.2	105.6	106.2
1982	106.6	106.5	107.8	105.8	106.1	106.6	106.6	106.4	108.1	108.2	107.2	107.1	105.2	105.0	105.4	106.3	106.7
1983	110.5	107.6	109.8	111.7	112.3	107.1	107.6	108.2	108.4	109.6	111.3	110.3	111.5	113.2	111.8	112.3	114.3

Wholesale prices: processed foods — Prix de gros : produits alimentaires manufacturés

1980 = 100

	Year	Q.1	Q.2	Q.3	Q.4	JAN	FEB	MAR	APR	MAY	JUN	JUL	AUG	SEP	OCT	NOV	DEC
1964	63.8																
1965	64.2																
1966	67.5																
1967	69.0																
1968	67.8																
1969	69.8																
1970	70.3	70.3	70.3	70.5	69.6	70.1	70.1	70.8	70.8	70.9	70.5	70.6	70.3	70.7	69.1	69.7	70.0
1971	71.6	70.6	71.5	72.0	72.5	70.3	70.5	70.8	71.4	71.5	71.5	71.9	72.0	72.0	72.2	72.2	73.1
1972	75.4	74.7	75.5	75.4	76.2	74.2	74.4	75.5	75.6	75.5	75.3	75.1	75.3	75.7	76.0	76.1	76.4
1973	82.3	80.2	81.7	82.6	84.8	79.5	79.9	81.3	81.6	81.7	81.7	82.4	82.7	82.9	83.8	84.5	86.0
1974	94.8	89.6	92.6	96.7	100.4	88.0	90.0	90.7	90.9	92.1	94.7	95.5	96.8	97.9	99.2	102.4	99.5
1975	97.2	99.3	97.6	96.8	95.3	99.1	100.1	98.8	95.0	97.5	96.2	96.7	97.3	96.5	95.5	95.2	95.0
1976	93.4	94.3	93.6	93.2	92.6	94.8	94.0	94.2	93.7	93.5	93.5	93.8	93.1	92.6	92.5	92.4	92.8
1977	93.8	93.2	93.6	93.6	94.9	93.1	93.0	93.5	93.7	93.7	93.4	93.0	93.1	94.7	94.8	94.9	94.8
1978	95.2	95.1	94.8	94.6	96.2	94.8	95.2	95.3	94.8	94.8	94.8	94.7	94.6	94.5	96.2	96.2	96.2
1979	96.7	96.2	96.4	97.0	97.1	96.2	96.0	96.3	96.3	96.4	96.6	96.9	97.0	97.1	97.0	97.2	97.2
1980	100.0	98.1	99.1	100.3	102.4	97.7	98.3	98.2	98.3	99.1	99.8	99.6	100.4	100.9	102.3	102.5	102.5
1981	105.7	104.2	104.5	105.8	108.0	103.8	104.0	104.7	104.5	104.5	104.5	105.8	105.8	105.8	108.1	108.0	108.1
1982	111.4	108.9	110.9	112.4	113.5	108.6	108.8	109.5	109.5	111.5	111.6	112.5	112.5	112.3	113.4	113.5	113.5
1983	114.2	113.4	113.6	115.0	114.9	113.5	113.6	113.2	113.4	113.7	113.9	114.6	115.1	115.2	114.9	114.8	114.9

Wholesale prices: textiles — Prix de gros : textiles

1980 = 100

	Year	Q.1	Q.2	Q.3	Q.4	JAN	FEB	MAR	APR	MAY	JUN	JUL	AUG	SEP	OCT	NOV	DEC
1964	90.0																
1965	86.7																
1966	84.9																
1967	81.6																
1968	82.2																
1969	83.0																
1970	85.8	85.5	86.0	86.2	85.4	85.2	85.6	85.6	85.7	86.3	86.1	86.2	86.3	86.0	85.0	85.6	85.7
1971	85.8	85.6	85.8	85.9	85.9	85.8	85.4	85.8	85.8	85.8	85.7	85.8	85.8	86.0	85.8	85.8	86.1
1972	89.5	86.6	87.2	88.9	95.2	86.0	86.9	87.0	86.7	87.3	87.6	88.3	88.7	89.7	94.3	94.8	96.4
1973	112.0	104.2	110.0	113.0	120.7	100.8	102.0	109.7	109.1	109.8	111.2	111.5	113.5	114.1	120.5	119.8	121.6
1974	119.7	125.0	123.3	119.7	110.5	126.2	124.7	124.3	124.3	122.9	122.7	121.6	120.3	117.1	112.6	110.6	108.2
1975	97.6	101.6	96.8	96.0	95.1	104.3	101.3	99.3	96.8	97.0	96.5	96.6	95.8	95.6	95.8	95.8	96.7
1976	101.9	98.4	99.7	103.8	105.3	97.4	98.5	99.5	98.8	98.9	101.5	102.7	104.3	104.3	105.1	105.2	105.5
1977	102.9	104.9	104.5	103.4	98.8	104.9	104.9	104.9	104.6	104.3	104.5	104.3	103.7	102.3	99.8	98.9	97.6
1978	91.2	94.0	92.1	90.7	87.9	95.2	93.5	93.3	92.1	92.1	92.0	92.2	90.4	89.5	87.7	88.1	88.0
1979	92.1	88.3	91.7	93.4	95.0	88.0	88.3	88.7	90.8	91.9	92.5	93.1	93.5	93.5	94.4	95.2	95.2
1980	100.0	97.6	99.4	100.8	102.0	96.5	97.7	98.8	99.2	99.1	100.0	100.2	100.9	101.2	101.5	101.9	102.7
1981	105.2	103.4	105.4	107.2	105.0	102.7	103.9	103.6	104.8	105.9	105.5	107.0	107.8	106.8	106.1	104.7	104.3
1982	104.3	103.5	103.7	105.2	104.6	103.5	103.5	103.3	103.1	103.6	104.3	105.2	105.1	105.2	105.0	104.8	104.1
1983	105.1	103.6	104.0	106.0	107.0	103.7	103.5	103.5	103.5	104.0	104.6	105.2	105.9	106.9	106.5	106.9	107.5

Wholesale prices: chemicals

Prix de gros : produits chimiques

1980 = 100

	Year	Q.1	Q.2	Q.3	Q.4	JAN	FEB	MAR	APR	MAY	JUN	JUL	AUG	SEP	OCT	NOV	DEC
1964	74.0																
1965	75.0																
1966	75.0																
1967	76.3																
1968	76.6																
1969	73.9																
1970	73.9	73.5	73.9	73.9	73.9	73.2	73.2	73.9	73.9	73.9	73.9	73.9	73.9	73.9	73.9	73.9	73.9
1971	75.7	74.6	75.9	76.0	76.3	73.9	73.9	75.9	75.9	75.9	75.9	75.9	75.9	76.1	76.3	76.3	76.3
1972	75.8	76.1	75.7	75.7	75.9	76.3	76.3	75.7	75.7	75.7	75.7	75.7	75.7	75.9	75.9	75.9	75.9
1973	80.1	76.7	78.4	80.4	84.5	75.9	75.9	78.4	78.4	78.4	78.4	78.4	78.4	84.5	84.5	84.5	84.5
1974	104.9	91.7	106.2	108.5	113.2	84.5	84.5	106.2	106.2	106.2	106.2	106.2	106.2	113.2	113.2	113.2	113.2
1975	103.1	109.8	103.0	101.4	98.1	113.2	113.2	103.0	103.0	103.0	103.0	103.0	103.0	98.1	98.1	98.1	98.1
1976	98.1	98.3	98.6	98.2	97.5	98.1	98.1	98.6	98.6	98.6	98.6	98.6	98.6	97.5	97.5	97.5	97.5
1977	96.8	97.4	97.1	96.8	96.2	97.5	97.5	97.1	97.1	97.1	97.1	97.1	97.1	96.2	96.2	96.2	96.2
1978	91.8	94.9	92.4	91.2	88.8	96.2	96.2	92.4	92.4	92.4	92.4	92.4	92.4	88.8	88.8	88.8	88.8
1979	93.5	89.9	92.0	94.1	93.2	88.8	88.8	92.0	92.0	92.0	92.0	92.0	92.0	98.2	98.2	98.2	98.2
1980	100.0	99.1	100.9	100.5	99.6	98.2	98.2	100.9	100.9	100.9	100.9	100.9	100.9	99.6	99.6	99.6	99.6
1981	104.9	101.1	104.2	105.5	108.6	99.6	99.6	104.2	104.2	104.2	104.2	104.2	104.2	108.6	108.6	108.6	108.6
1982	106.8	107.6	105.6	106.3	107.6	108.6	108.6	105.6	105.6	105.6	105.6	105.6	105.6	107.6	107.6	107.6	107.6
1983	106.4	107.1	105.9	106.1	105.6	107.6	107.6	105.9	105.9	105.9	105.9	105.9	105.9	106.6	106.6	106.6	106.6

Wholesale prices: metals and metal products

Prix de gros : métaux et ouvrages en métaux

1980 = 100

	Year	Q.1	Q.2	Q.3	Q.4	JAN	FEB	MAR	APR	MAY	JUN	JUL	AUG	SEP	OCT	NOV	DEC
1964	62.6																
1965	63.9																
1966	66.1																
1967	64.3																
1968	64.8																
1969	73.4																
1970	81.0	82.3	82.8	80.5	78.4	81.6	82.1	83.2	83.5	83.1	81.7	81.1	80.3	80.0	78.0	78.8	78.4
1971	78.1	78.5	79.4	77.8	76.7	78.0	78.0	79.6	79.9	79.4	79.1	78.2	77.9	77.2	76.6	76.5	76.9
1972	79.2	77.9	79.0	79.4	80.7	77.3	77.7	78.6	78.8	79.0	79.1	79.2	79.4	79.7	79.7	80.9	81.5
1973	91.3	85.1	89.2	92.5	98.6	83.6	84.8	86.9	88.0	89.1	90.4	91.6	92.7	93.0	95.8	100.4	99.6
1974	110.5	106.7	114.2	112.4	108.6	102.6	107.1	110.4	113.6	115.2	113.7	113.1	112.9	111.1	110.0	109.2	106.7
1975	98.5	101.8	99.1	97.5	95.3	103.5	101.4	100.5	99.5	99.2	98.5	97.7	97.9	96.9	95.2	95.5	95.2
1976	97.6	96.1	98.9	98.9	96.5	95.1	96.1	97.1	98.7	98.8	99.2	99.4	99.1	98.2	97.3	96.4	95.7
1977	93.6	95.3	94.5	93.2	91.4	95.5	95.2	95.2	94.6	94.6	94.4	93.5	93.1	92.9	92.2	91.3	90.6
1978	90.9	91.3	91.8	91.0	89.6	91.0	91.3	91.7	91.6	92.2	91.5	91.6	91.3	90.0	89.3	89.5	89.8
1979	94.2	91.4	93.6	95.0	96.3	90.9	90.7	92.5	92.9	93.8	94.1	94.2	95.2	95.7	95.6	96.5	96.8
1980	100.0	99.5	99.9	100.3	100.2	98.8	100.1	99.5	99.2	100.5	99.9	100.4	100.5	100.1	99.9	100.5	100.3
1981	104.2	101.1	103.5	105.8	106.3	100.7	101.0	101.6	102.0	104.3	104.3	105.1	106.5	105.7	105.7	106.5	106.5
1982	106.8	106.9	107.2	107.2	105.7	107.1	107.2	106.5	106.6	107.9	107.1	107.4	107.2	106.9	106.5	105.5	105.2
1983	106.2	105.1	106.4	106.8	106.4	105.1	104.9	105.1	105.8	106.7	106.8	106.6	106.3	106.7	106.0	106.3	106.9

Wholesale prices: liquid fuel

Prix de gros : combustibles liquides

1980 = 100

	Year	Q.1	Q.2	Q.3	Q.4	JAN	FEB	MAR	APR	MAY	JUN	JUL	AUG	SEP	OCT	NOV	DEC
1964	31.2																
1965	31.6																
1966	33.3																
1967	37.6																
1968	39.5																
1969	39.1																
1970	41.1	39.5	39.4	41.2	44.5	39.9	39.7	38.8	39.1	39.3	39.6	39.3	41.5	42.9	44.0	44.8	44.8
1971	44.1	45.8	45.4	42.3	42.8	45.1	45.8	46.4	46.2	45.5	44.4	43.0	42.1	41.9	41.9	41.6	44.8
1972	44.9	45.7	43.8	43.3	46.6	46.6	45.0	45.5	44.8	43.7	43.0	42.7	42.9	44.4	46.0	46.7	47.2
1973	53.6	47.5	49.0	51.6	66.4	47.3	48.1	47.0	47.1	49.2	50.6	51.0	50.3	52.9	58.6	66.5	74.0
1974	71.2	72.7	70.2	70.3	71.6	76.5	68.5	72.9	71.0	70.0	69.4	69.1	67.0	74.9	73.3	71.5	70.0
1975	69.3	67.3	68.5	70.0	71.5	68.3	67.2	66.2	67.8	68.9	68.8	68.0	70.2	71.9	72.0	71.5	71.1
1976	71.9	71.0	73.0	72.2	71.5	70.8	70.4	71.8	73.2	73.1	72.7	72.0	72.3	72.4	71.7	71.3	71.5
1977	71.5	72.5	72.8	71.3	69.4	72.4	72.6	72.4	72.9	73.1	72.4	71.6	71.3	70.7	70.5	69.6	68.1
1978	65.6	65.4	65.7	63.4	67.8	65.9	64.7	65.6	65.9	66.1	65.1	64.6	63.1	62.6	62.6	70.8	69.9
1979	95.3	83.7	97.6	97.3	102.5	75.5	92.5	83.1	88.7	100.5	103.7	100.2	96.6	95.2	97.9	105.3	104.2
1980	100.0	100.4	101.3	94.9	103.4	101.8	98.4	101.1	105.0	99.4	99.5	96.9	93.0	94.8	98.9	106.2	105.1
1981	111.1	109.1	109.5	115.7	110.1	107.6	110.1	109.5	108.3	109.1	111.2	116.6	118.2	112.1	112.0	108.5	109.7
1982	110.3	104.1	109.3	112.5	115.4	107.4	103.4	102.5	106.5	110.2	111.3	109.5	111.3	116.8	120.0	114.7	111.4
1983	103.8	101.5	103.0	104.7	105.8	105.5	98.8	100.3	103.7	101.2	104.1	103.1	105.7	105.3	104.8	107.1	105.5

SWITZERLAND

Consumer prices: all items (11) / Prix à la consommation : total (11)

1980 = 100

	Year	Q.1	Q.2	Q.3	Q.4	JAN	FEB	MAR	APR	MAY	JUN	JUL	AUG	SEP	OCT	NOV	DEC
1964	50.2	49.7	50.2	50.4	50.7	49.6	49.7	49.7	50.0	50.3	50.2	50.2	50.4	50.5	50.6	50.7	50.7
1965	51.9	50.9	51.6	52.3	53.0	50.8	50.9	51.0	51.1	51.7	51.9	52.0	52.3	52.5	52.6	53.1	53.2
1966	54.4	53.6	54.2	54.5	55.3	53.5	53.7	53.7	53.8	54.5	54.4	54.4	54.6	=54.6=	54.7	55.4	55.7
1967	56.6	55.7	56.3	57.0	57.3	55.8	55.7	55.7	55.8	56.4	56.8	57.0	57.2	57.0	56.9	57.5	57.6
1968	58.0	57.7	57.7	57.9	58.6	57.7	57.8	57.6	57.6	57.7	57.8	57.7	57.9	58.0	58.2	58.7	58.9
1969	59.4	59.1	59.2	59.4	59.9	59.0	59.2	59.0	58.9	59.2	59.5	59.5	59.4	59.4	59.5	60.0	60.2
1970	61.6	60.4	61.0	61.8	63.1	60.4	60.4	60.5	60.5	61.1	61.3	61.5	61.7	62.1	62.4	63.2	63.5
1971	65.6	64.2	65.1	65.9	67.2	63.9	64.2	64.6	64.6	65.3	65.4	65.7	65.8	66.3	66.5	67.4	67.7
1972	70.0	68.4	69.3	70.2	71.9	68.2	68.5	68.7	68.7	69.4	69.8	69.9	70.1	70.7	71.4	72.0	72.4
1973	76.1	73.7	75.0	76.0	79.7	73.2	73.7	74.3	74.4	75.0	75.5	75.6	75.9	76.6	78.2	79.8	81.0
1974	83.5	81.4	82.0	84.1	86.6	81.7	81.1	81.4	80.9	82.4	82.8	83.1	83.9	85.3	85.8	87.0	87.1
1975	89.1	87.9	89.0	89.5	90.1	87.6	87.9	88.2	88.4	89.1	89.4	89.2	89.5	89.8	90.0	90.2	90.1
1976	90.7	90.5	90.3	90.7	91.1	90.6	90.6	90.4	90.4	90.2	90.4	90.6	90.9	90.7	90.9	91.0	91.3
1977	91.8	91.4	91.6	92.0	92.3	91.4	91.5	91.3	91.4	91.4	92.0	92.0	92.0	=92.1=	92.3	92.2	92.4
1978	92.8	92.5	92.9	93.0	92.3	92.4	92.5	92.5	92.7	92.8	93.0	93.0	93.1	92.8	92.6	92.8	93.0
1979	96.1	94.2	95.8	97.1	97.5	93.4	94.4	94.8	95.1	95.5	96.8	97.1	96.9	97.3	97.2	97.6	97.8
1980	100.0	98.3	99.5	100.7	101.6	98.1	98.3	98.5	99.0	99.6	99.9	100.3	100.9	101.0	100.8	101.8	102.1
1981	106.5	104.0	105.5	108.0	108.6	103.1	104.1	104.8	104.6	105.5	106.3	106.8	108.5	108.6	108.2	108.8	108.8
1982	112.5	109.6	111.7	114.0	115.0	109.4	109.6	109.8	110.4	111.8	112.8	113.3	114.1	114.6	114.8	115.2	=114.8=
1983	115.9	114.9	115.6	116.0	117.0	114.7	114.8	115.1	115.4	115.5	116.0	115.7	116.1	116.2	116.4	117.2	117.2

Money supply (M1) / Disponibilités monétaires (M1)

billion francs, end of period / milliards de francs, fin de période

	Year	Q.1	Q.2	Q.3	Q.4	JAN	FEB	MAR	APR	MAY	JUN	JUL	AUG	SEP	OCT	NOV	DEC
1964	23.62	21.99	22.50	22.46	23.62	21.91	21.73	21.99	22.26	22.24	22.50	22.43	22.41	22.46	22.67	22.98	23.62
1965	24.53	23.08	23.44	23.53	24.53	23.43	22.93	23.08	23.02	23.24	23.44	23.26	23.22	23.53	23.74	23.88	24.53
1966	25.05	23.78	24.20	24.03	25.05	23.91	23.64	23.78	23.82	24.07	24.20	23.80	23.76	24.03	24.30	24.41	25.05
1967	26.25	24.37	24.42	25.16	26.25	24.21	24.05	24.37	24.09	24.26	24.42	24.53	24.75	25.16	25.54	25.81	26.25
1968	29.11	26.62	27.27	27.34	29.11	26.17	26.01	26.62	26.80	27.10	27.27	27.11	26.78	27.34	27.45	28.00	29.11
1969	30.80	27.86	28.12	28.70	30.80	28.07	27.89	27.86	27.97	28.18	28.12	28.10	28.21	28.70	29.60	29.83	30.80
1970	32.93	29.35	29.83	30.00	32.93	29.51	28.91	29.35	29.54	29.50	29.83	29.69	29.60	30.00	30.47	31.02	32.93
1971	39.91	32.27	34.84	36.56	39.91	31.93	31.78	32.27	33.10	33.05	34.84	34.70	35.50	36.56	37.27	38.90	39.91
1972	43.32	40.69	40.81	41.27	43.32	39.93	40.00	40.69	40.22	40.53	40.81	41.19	41.35	41.27	41.55	42.20	43.32
1973	44.21	41.59	42.31	41.80	44.21	41.95	41.38	41.59	41.50	41.74	42.31	41.42	41.15	41.80	42.29	42.85	44.21
1974	44.70	41.49	41.97	41.66	44.70	42.41	41.54	41.49	41.96	41.59	41.97	41.29	41.21	41.66	42.09	42.97	44.70
1975	47.35	43.49	43.89	43.30	47.35	43.38	42.91	43.49	43.53	43.62	43.89	43.01	42.47	43.30	43.96	45.42	47.35
1976	51.19	46.39	48.12	47.00	51.19	46.41	45.09	46.39	46.87	46.68	48.12	46.90	46.41	47.00	47.44	48.33	51.19
1977	53.27	49.68	49.88	49.09	53.27	49.70	49.41	49.68	49.85	48.89	49.88	48.34	48.05	49.09	50.27	50.97	53.27
1978	65.46	57.60	57.20	57.68	65.46	53.14	54.12	57.60	57.69	57.29	57.20	54.44	56.09	57.68	61.05	63.12	65.46
1979	60.90	66.43	62.38	61.21	60.90	65.40	65.30	66.43	63.88	61.55	62.38	62.10	60.73	61.21	62.10	62.12	60.90
1980	60.75	57.10	57.17	57.14	60.75	58.65	57.68	57.10	56.00	55.57	57.17	54.95	54.64	57.14	57.61	58.72	60.75
1981	56.54	56.38	55.77	54.31	56.54	57.58	55.93	56.38	56.02	56.58	55.77	53.67	52.63	54.31	53.42	54.68	56.54
1982	62.93	54.66	57.48	58.33	62.93	52.72	52.70	54.66	55.38	55.87	57.48	55.31	55.23	58.33	59.39	61.44	62.93
1983	63.67	62.46	61.29	60.68	63.67	61.26	60.74	62.46	61.13	61.06	61.29	58.61	58.47	60.68	60.84	62.71	63.67

M1 plus quasi-money / M1 plus quasi-monnaie

billion francs, end of period / milliards de francs, fin de période

	Year	Q.1	Q.2	Q.3	Q.4	JAN	FEB	MAR	APR	MAY	JUN	JUL	AUG	SEP	OCT	NOV	DEC
1964																	
1965																	
1966																	
1967																	
1968																	
1969																	
1970																	
1971																	
1972																	
1973																	
1974																	
1975	148.23		139.17	139.76	148.23						139.17	139.01	138.59	139.76	141.25	142.99	148.23
1976	159.28	149.52	151.06	152.37	159.28	148.45	148.20	149.62	150.93	151.09	151.06	151.10	151.30	152.37	153.30	154.67	159.28
1977	172.26	161.47	164.89	165.99	172.26	159.90	159.90	161.47	162.63	163.33	164.89	165.12	164.95	166.99	168.08	168.13	172.26
1978	189.98	177.09	179.52	180.44	189.98	172.49	173.54	177.09	178.62	179.13	179.52	178.00	179.28	180.44	183.21	185.88	189.98
1979	206.72	192.26	196.08	198.13	206.72	190.50	190.92	192.26	194.47	194.52	196.08	197.23	196.53	198.13	200.37	201.87	206.72
1980	215.53	211.70	207.65	208.22	215.53	208.79	210.04	211.70	211.24	208.51	207.65	206.22	205.26	208.22	209.43	210.66	215.53
1981	224.50	218.17	221.55	222.24	224.50	214.97	216.09	218.17	219.75	220.14	221.55	222.06	221.34	222.24	222.85	221.92	224.50
1982	236.48	225.48	226.51	229.83	236.48	223.07	224.85	225.48	227.02	225.09	226.51	225.37	226.28	229.83	233.31	234.85	236.48
1983	251.31	241.34	244.77	245.39	251.31	236.65	238.25	241.34	242.47	244.13	244.77	243.26	243.59	245.39	244.77	247.16	251.31

Savings deposits

billion francs, end of period

Dépôts d'épargne

milliards de francs, fin de période

	Year	Q.1	Q.2	Q.3	Q.4	JAN	FEB	MAR	APR	MAY	JUN	JUL	AUG	SEP	OCT	NOV	DEC
1964	25.26	23.96	24.20	24.62	25.26	23.78	23.89	23.96	24.09	24.18	24.20	24.33	24.51	24.62	24.72	24.80	25.26
1965	27.34	25.89	26.11	26.50	27.34	25.52	25.73	25.89	25.99	26.06	26.11	26.27	26.41	26.50	26.59	26.71	27.34
1966	29.48	27.99	28.27	28.59	29.48	27.85	27.88	27.99	28.12	28.20	28.27	28.37	28.49	28.59	28.73	28.81	29.48
1967	32.03	30.02	30.23	30.73	32.03	29.74	30.42	30.02	[illegible]	30.19	30.23	30.34	30.55	30.73	31.00	31.14	32.03
1968	34.94	32.92	33.34	33.86	34.94	32.45	32.69	32.92	33.10	33.25	33.34	33.55	33.69	33.86	34.04	34.17	34.94
1969	37.75	35.79	36.06	36.42	37.75	35.30	35.66	35.79	35.99	36.09	36.06	36.13	36.27	36.42	36.66	36.78	37.75
1970	40.69	38.49	38.70	39.36	40.69	38.11	38.31	38.49	38.58	38.68	38.70	39.41	39.45	39.36	39.53	39.68	40.69
1971	47.95	42.04	43.33	44.95	47.95	41.25	41.64	42.04	42.55	42.65	43.33	43.64	44.31	44.95	45.51	46.14	47.95
1972	57.22	50.76	52.63	54.32	57.22	49.12	49.93	50.76	51.57	52.26	52.63	53.16	53.73	54.32	54.78	55.19	57.22
1973	62.60	58.90	59.63	60.35	62.60	58.21	58.61	58.90	[illegible]	57.45	59.63	59.93	60.19	60.35	60.55	60.92	62.60
1974	65.18	62.97	62.34	62.94	65.13	63.18	63.09	62.97	63.08	62.63	62.34	62.28	62.69	62.94	63.15	63.59	65.13
1975	75.48	66.95	69.04	70.90	75.48	65.98	66.42	66.95	67.70	68.31	69.04	69.65	70.45	70.90	71.48	72.57	75.48
1976	85.33	78.31	79.36	81.38	85.33	76.94	77.97	78.31	78.79	79.40	79.36	80.21	80.95	81.38	82.09	82.80	85.33
1977	94.08	88.37	88.97	90.38	94.08	86.85	87.96	88.37	89.03	89.31	88.97	89.38	89.97	90.38	91.14	91.18	94.08
1978	103.84	97.05	98.43	100.08	103.84	95.42	96.69	97.05	97.87	98.37	98.43	99.09	99.68	100.08	100.87	101.83	103.84
1979	110.12	106.82	107.46	108.87	110.12	105.09	106.25	106.82	107.53	108.09	107.46	108.02	108.56	108.87	109.19	108.71	110.12
1980	105.65	106.91	103.30	103.41	105.65	109.29	108.81	106.91	105.59	104.43	103.30	103.09	103.35	103.41	103.24	103.87	105.65
1981	100.22	105.45	102.23	99.87	100.22	106.57	106.67	105.45	104.55	104.01	102.23	101.10	101.01	99.87	99.02	98.80	100.22
1982	116.06	100.15	103.77	107.83	116.06	100.18	100.72	100.15	101.04	103.57	103.77	104.63	105.92	107.83	109.78	111.80	116.06
1983	129.64	124.34	124.73	125.19	129.64	119.52	122.51	124.34	126.28	127.17	124.73	124.72	125.02	125.19	125.21	126.50	129.64

Money supply (M1)

billion francs, end of period

Adjusted - Corrigé *

Disponibilités monétaires (M1)

milliards de francs, fin de période

	Year	Q.1	Q.2	Q.3	Q.4	JAN	FEB	MAR	APR	MAY	JUN	JUL	AUG	SEP	OCT	NOV	DEC
1964		22.05	22.48	22.57	22.93	21.93	21.93	22.05	22.33	22.26	22.48	22.57	22.66	22.57	22.61	22.84	22.93
1965		23.17	23.42	23.65	23.74	23.41	23.14	23.17	23.11	23.29	23.42	23.42	23.53	23.65	23.67	23.72	23.74
1966		23.88	24.20	24.15	24.18	23.86	23.86	23.88	23.94	24.12	24.20	24.02	24.10	24.15	24.25	24.19	24.18
1967		24.47	24.44	25.29	25.27	24.14	24.26	24.47	24.21	24.31	24.44	24.78	25.16	25.29	25.52	25.55	25.27
1968		26.76	27.30	27.51	27.93	26.06	26.25	26.76	26.93	27.18	27.30	27.41	27.24	27.51	27.42	27.70	27.93
1969		28.00	28.15	28.90	29.50	27.93	28.15	28.00	28.08	28.29	28.15	28.44	28.73	28.90	29.63	29.48	29.50
1970		29.49	29.83	30.24	31.54	29.34	29.15	29.49	29.66	29.68	29.83	30.08	30.14	30.24	30.53	30.62	31.54
1971		32.43	34.80	36.89	38.19	31.71	32.04	32.43	33.20	33.28	34.80	35.16	36.19	36.89	37.38	38.40	38.19
1972		40.89	40.69	41.73	41.49	39.51	40.28	40.89	40.31	40.78	40.69	41.77	42.24	41.73	41.72	41.70	41.49
1973		41.71	42.10	42.35	42.34	41.58	41.67	41.71	41.50	41.99	42.10	42.05	42.12	42.35	42.55	42.38	42.34
1974		41.49	41.72	42.33	42.81	41.99	41.79	41.49	41.88	41.80	41.72	41.96	42.36	42.33	42.38	42.48	42.81
1975		43.36	43.59	44.18	45.40	42.91	43.08	43.36	43.31	43.75	43.59	43.80	43.83	44.18	44.27	45.06	45.40
1976		46.02	47.88	48.10	49.17	45.81	45.13	46.02	46.54	46.82	47.88	47.90	48.04	48.10	47.72	47.90	49.17
1977		49.04	49.73	50.30	51.27	48.97	49.26	49.04	49.55	49.08	49.73	49.47	49.90	50.30	50.42	50.36	51.27
1978		56.75	57.14	58.92	63.01	52.36	53.80	56.75	57.52	57.58	57.14	55.89	58.43	58.92	61.11	62.18	63.01
1979		65.39	62.45	62.27	58.50	64.50	64.78	65.39	63.94	61.86	62.45	63.89	63.33	62.27	61.98	60.91	58.50
1980		56.25	57.40	57.90	58.30	57.96	57.28	56.25	56.28	55.91	57.40	56.63	56.98	57.90	57.43	57.40	58.30
1981		55.54	56.05	54.97	54.26	56.90	55.59	55.54	56.48	56.98	56.05	55.33	54.88	54.97	53.26	53.40	54.26
1982		53.91	57.77	58.98	60.45	52.09	52.39	53.91	55.68	56.27	57.77	57.02	57.59	58.98	59.21	59.94	60.45
1983		61.60	61.60	61.35	61.16	60.53	60.33	61.60	61.68	61.49	61.60	60.42	60.97	61.35	60.66	61.18	61.16

M1 plus quasi-money

billion francs, end of period

Adjusted - Corrigé *

M1 plus quasi-monnaie

milliards de francs, fin de période

	Year	Q.1	Q.2	Q.3	Q.4	JAN	FEB	MAR	APR	MAY	JUN	JUL	AUG	SEP	OCT	NOV	DEC
1964																	
1965																	
1966																	
1967																	
1968																	
1969																	
1970																	
1971																	
1972																	
1973																	
1974																	
1975			140.44	139.34	147.64						140.44	137.50	137.49	139.34	140.13	141.72	147.64
1976		151.44	152.43	151.91	158.80	148.15	148.94	151.44	152.61	152.46	152.43	149.45	150.10	151.91	151.93	153.29	158.80
1977		163.60	166.39	166.16	171.57	159.58	160.71	163.60	164.44	164.81	166.39	163.32	163.64	166.16	166.41	166.47	171.57
1978		179.79	181.15	179.36	189.41	172.49	174.76	179.79	180.79	180.76	181.15	176.06	177.68	179.36	181.04	183.86	189.41
1979		195.19	197.66	196.95	206.10	190.50	192.27	195.19	196.64	196.09	197.66	194.89	194.97	196.95	197.99	199.67	206.10
1980		215.14	209.32	206.78	215.10	208.79	211.74	215.14	213.59	210.19	209.32	203.78	203.63	206.78	206.95	208.37	215.10
1981		221.94	223.34	220.70	224.05	215.19	217.83	221.94	222.42	222.14	223.34	219.66	219.59	220.70	220.21	219.50	224.05
1982		229.38	228.33	228.23	236.01	223.29	226.66	229.38	229.78	227.14	228.33	222.92	224.48	228.23	230.55	232.29	236.01
1983		245.51	246.74	243.69	250.81	236.88	240.17	245.51	245.42	246.35	246.74	240.62	241.65	243.69	241.86	244.47	250.81

* Adjusted by the O.E.C.D.

* Corrigé par l'O.C.D.E.

SWITZERLAND

Net new capital issues

billion francs

Nouvelles émissions sur le marché des capitaux, nettes

milliards de francs

	Year	Q.1	Q.2	Q.3	Q.4	JAN	FEB	MAR	APR	MAY	JUN	JUL	AUG	SEP	OCT	NOV	DEC
1964	3.03	1.11	0.85	0.66	0.41	0.24	0.34	0.54	0.21	0.35	0.29	0.17	0.17	0.32	0.23	0.12	0.06
1965	2.68	0.64	0.83	0.50	0.71	0.09	0.26	0.30	0.42	0.34	0.07	0.13	0.13	0.24	0.29	0.27	0.16
1966	2.71	0.88	0.58	0.56	0.69	0.19	0.28	0.40	0.05	0.37	0.16	0.15	0.18	0.23	0.31	0.21	0.17
1967	3.40	0.73	0.98	0.64	1.05	0.27	0.15	0.32	0.21	0.44	0.34	0.12	0.21	0.30	0.34	0.48	0.23
1968	3.92	0.82	1.23	0.89	0.98	0.24	0.26	0.32	0.36	0.56	0.31	0.14	0.39	0.35	0.67	0.22	0.10
1969	3.81	1.19	0.77	0.78	1.08	0.20	0.47	0.52	0.25	0.22	0.30	0.33	0.18	0.27	0.51	0.45	0.13
1970	3.57	0.99	0.61	0.76	1.21	0.33	0.31	0.35	0.36	0.13	0.12	0.27	0.18	0.31	0.48	0.43	0.30
1971	6.48	1.51	1.90	1.44	1.63	0.32	0.46	0.73	0.46	0.45	0.99	0.28	0.52	0.64	0.56	0.58	0.49
1972	7.38	1.59	2.45	1.70	1.64	0.43	0.41	0.75	0.93	0.79	0.73	0.35	0.50	0.85	0.68	0.47	0.49
1973	6.47	1.43	2.00	1.49	1.55	0.46	0.25	0.72	0.61	0.86	0.52	0.37	0.39	0.72	0.68	0.53	0.35
1974	4.91	1.50	1.25	0.62	1.53	0.52	0.53	0.45	0.35	0.64	0.26	0.10	0.10	0.42	0.27	0.86	0.41
1975	8.57	1.69	2.69	1.95	2.22	0.29	0.81	0.60	0.85	0.78	1.06	0.36	0.51	1.09	0.60	0.87	0.75
1976	10.49	2.96	2.72	2.24	2.56	1.11	0.85	0.99	1.07	0.66	0.99	0.52	0.77	0.96	0.44	0.82	1.31
1977	5.32	1.32	1.12	1.18	1.70	0.39	0.84	0.09	0.55	0.13	0.44	0.10	0.50	0.57	0.21	0.79	0.71
1978	3.07	1.30	0.95	0.55	-0.23	0.71	0.78	0.31	0.71	0.09	0.15	-0.32	0.44	0.43	0.08	-0.20	-0.10
1979	3.96	0.79	1.25	1.50	0.41	0.08	0.38	0.34	-0.05	0.73	0.58	0.20	0.75	0.55	0.95	-0.47	-0.07
1980	12.16	2.34	4.02	2.97	2.84	0.45	1.07	0.82	2.09	0.40	1.52	0.77	1.15	1.06	1.20	1.03	0.61
1981	14.23	3.07	3.63	3.21	4.33	0.85	1.12	1.10	1.25	1.17	1.22	1.08	1.17	0.96	1.94	1.25	1.14
1982	16.16	3.73	4.65	2.91	4.88	0.70	1.28	1.75	1.36	1.53	1.76	0.22	1.28	1.40	1.66	2.02	1.20
1983	12.57	4.95	2.44	2.49	2.69	1.38	1.59	1.98	0.29	1.11	1.04	0.85	0.72	0.88	1.18	0.80	0.71

Short-term bank credit to private sector (12)

billion francs, end of period

Crédits bancaires à court terme au secteur privé (12)

milliards de francs, fin de période

	Year	Q.1	Q.2	Q.3	Q.4	JAN	FEB	MAR	APR	MAY	JUN	JUL	AUG	SEP	OCT	NOV	DEC
1964	25.59	23.51	24.35	24.68	25.59	23.33	23.30	23.51	24.01	24.18	24.35	24.36	24.60	24.68	25.11	25.21	25.59
1965	28.01	25.99	26.59	27.06	28.01	25.78	25.94	25.99	26.19	26.42	26.59	26.71	26.81	27.06	27.49	27.49	28.01
1966	31.25	28.84	29.67	30.34	31.25	28.58	28.91	28.84	29.12	29.31	29.67	30.20	30.15	30.34	30.49	30.69	31.25
1967	34.94	31.89	32.64	33.16	34.94	31.20	31.25	31.89	31.92	32.30	32.64	32.73	32.82	33.16	33.69	34.04	34.94
1968	38.76	35.63	36.83	37.27	38.76	34.71	34.82	35.63	35.73	35.96	36.83	36.91	36.84	37.27	37.10	37.69	38.76
1969	45.81	39.86	42.81	45.43	45.81	39.09	39.48	39.86	40.81	41.72	42.81	43.83	45.56	45.43	45.64	45.29	45.81
1970	52.47	47.14	48.99	49.74	52.47	46.53	47.03	47.14	47.89	48.93	48.99	49.66	49.64	49.74	50.08	50.59	52.47
1971	56.22	53.22	54.63	54.42	56.22	52.15	52.98	53.22	53.78	53.65	54.63	54.42	54.84	54.42	54.28	54.85	56.22
1972	60.18	56.03	57.44	58.32	60.18	55.66	55.67	56.03	55.88	56.60	57.44	58.01	58.02	58.32	62.81	59.08	60.18
1973	65.76	59.30	60.43	62.23	65.76	59.30	59.57	59.80	59.66	59.96	60.43	59.90	60.85	62.23	62.65	63.92	65.76
1974	71.57	66.95	68.17	69.36	71.57	66.62	66.93	66.95	67.17	67.13	68.17	67.39	68.44	69.36	69.45	70.06	71.57
1975	76.68	72.89	73.66	74.40	76.68	71.98	72.98	72.89	72.83	74.24	73.66	73.39	73.41	74.40	75.14	75.25	76.68
1976	81.48	76.48	77.56	78.87	81.48	76.96	76.68	76.48	76.25	75.67	77.56	77.22	77.31	78.87	79.88	81.23	81.48
1977	87.00	81.56	86.21	86.85	87.00	81.92	83.05	81.56	83.35	84.53	86.21	88.60	86.45	86.85	87.18	88.68	87.00
1978	94.93	89.02	90.17	89.16	94.93	87.93	88.94	89.02	90.45	89.64	90.17	89.92	89.81	89.16	91.78	95.00	94.93
1979	107.57	96.72	100.82	102.18	107.57	94.51	95.43	96.72	97.89	99.98	100.82	101.83	100.90	102.18	103.18	104.51	107.57
1980	125.90	116.22	116.29	118.80	125.90	110.60	112.49	116.22	115.10	115.35	116.29	117.43	117.75	118.80	120.71	124.31	125.90
1981	140.19	132.48	139.02	140.88	140.19	128.48	129.01	132.48	134.59	136.95	139.02	138.67	139.48	140.88	138.76	138.50	140.19
1982	142.19	140.07	144.43	142.01	142.19	140.37	140.53	140.07	140.67	140.84	144.43	141.20	138.81	142.01	141.57	143.81	142.19
1983	152.03	144.25	148.34	144.93	152.03	141.19	142.97	144.25	143.52	145.66	148.34	146.85	146.19	144.93	146.27	148.16	152.03

Official discount rate

per cent per annum, end of period

Taux d'escompte officiel

pourcentage par an, fin de période

	Year	Q.1	Q.2	Q.3	Q.4	JAN	FEB	MAR	APR	MAY	JUN	JUL	AUG	SEP	OCT	NOV	DEC
1964	2.50	2.00	2.00	2.50	2.50	2.00	2.00	2.00	2.00	2.00	2.00	2.50	2.50	2.50	2.50	2.50	2.50
1965	2.50	2.50	2.50	2.50	2.50	2.50	2.50	2.50	2.50	2.50	2.50	2.50	2.50	2.50	2.50	2.50	2.50
1966	3.50	2.50	2.50	3.50	3.50	2.50	2.50	2.50	2.50	2.50	2.50	3.50	3.50	3.50	3.50	3.50	3.50
1967	3.00	3.50	3.50	3.00	3.00	3.50	3.50	3.50	3.50	3.50	3.50	3.00	3.00	3.00	3.00	3.00	3.00
1968	3.00	3.00	3.00	3.00	3.00	3.00	3.00	3.00	3.00	3.00	3.00	3.00	3.00	3.00	3.00	3.00	3.00
1969	3.75	3.00	3.00	3.75	3.75	3.00	3.00	3.00	3.00	3.00	3.00	3.00	3.00	3.75	3.75	3.75	3.75
1970	3.75	3.75	3.75	3.75	3.75	3.75	3.75	3.75	3.75	3.75	3.75	3.75	3.75	3.75	3.75	3.75	3.75
1971	3.75	3.75	3.75	3.75	3.75	3.75	3.75	3.75	3.75	3.75	3.75	3.75	3.75	3.75	3.75	3.75	3.75
1972	3.75	3.75	3.75	3.75	3.75	3.75	3.75	3.75	3.75	3.75	3.75	3.75	3.75	3.75	3.75	3.75	3.75
1973	4.50	4.50	4.50	4.50	4.50	4.50	4.50	4.50	4.50	4.50	4.50	4.50	4.50	4.50	4.50	4.50	4.50
1974	5.50	5.50	5.50	5.50	5.50	5.50	5.50	5.50	5.50	5.50	5.50	5.50	5.50	5.50	5.50	5.50	5.50
1975	3.00	5.00	4.50	3.50	3.00	5.50	5.50	5.00	5.00	4.50	4.50	4.50	4.00	3.50	3.00	3.00	3.00
1976	2.00	2.50	2.00	2.00	2.00	2.50	2.50	2.50	2.50	2.50	2.00	2.00	2.00	2.00	2.00	2.00	2.00
1977	1.50	2.00	2.00	1.50	1.50	2.00	2.00	2.00	2.00	2.00	2.00	1.50	1.50	1.50	1.50	1.50	1.50
1978	1.00	1.00	1.00	1.00	1.00	1.50	1.00	1.00	1.00	1.00	1.00	1.00	1.00	1.00	1.00	1.00	1.00
1979	2.00	1.00	1.00	1.00	2.00	1.00	1.00	1.00	1.00	1.00	1.00	1.00	1.00	1.00	1.00	2.00	2.00
1980	3.00	3.00	3.00	3.00	3.00	2.00	3.00	3.00	3.00	3.00	3.00	3.00	3.00	3.00	3.00	3.00	3.00
1981	6.00	4.00	5.00	6.00	6.00	3.00	4.00	4.00	4.00	5.00	5.00	5.00	5.00	6.00	6.00	6.00	6.00
1982	4.50	5.50	5.50	5.00	4.50	6.00	6.00	5.50	5.50	5.50	5.50	5.50	5.00	5.00	5.00	5.00	4.50
1983	4.00	4.00	4.00	4.00	4.00	4.50	4.50	4.00	4.00	4.00	4.00	4.00	4.00	4.00	4.00	4.00	4.00

Call money rate (Zürich) (7)(13) / Taux de l'argent au jour le jour (Zurich) (7)(13)

per cent per annum, end of period / pourcentage par an, fin de période

	Year	Q.1	Q.2	Q.3	Q.4	JAN	FEB	MAR	APR	MAY	JUN	JUL	AUG	SEP	OCT	NOV	DEC
1964	2.75	2.25	2.25	2.25	2.75	2.25	2.25	2.25	2.25	2.25	2.25	2.25	2.25	2.25	2.50	2.75	2.75
1965	3.00	2.25	2.88	2.75	3.00	2.38	2.38	2.25	2.50	2.63	2.88	2.88	2.75	2.75	2.75	2.88	3.00
1966	3.75	2.88	3.75	3.25	3.75	2.63	2.63	2.88	3.13	3.50	3.75	3.50	3.00	3.25	3.63	4.00	3.75
1967	2.50	3.75	3.38	2.50	2.50	4.12	3.75	3.75	4.00	3.75	3.38	1.50	1.25	2.50	1.75	2.25	2.50
1968	3.50	2.00	2.50	3.00	3.50	0.50	1.00	2.00	2.00	3.50	2.50	3.50	3.00	3.00	3.75	2.50	3.50
1969	6.00	4.75	5.00	5.00	6.00	3.00	3.75	4.75	2.50	2.50	5.00	3.75	4.50	5.00	2.00	3.50	6.00
1970	4.50	4.00	2.00	1.50	4.50	5.00	5.00	4.00	5.50	1.50	2.00	4.50	2.75	1.50	3.00	4.50	4.50
1971	-	2.25	3.25	-	-	6.00	3.50	2.25	1.50	1.50	3.25	5.00	-	-	-	-	-
1972	3.00	1.25	1.62	1.37	3.00	-	-	1.25	-	1.75	1.62	-	-	1.37	1.50	4.25	3.00
1973	2.50	0.50	1.55	0.50	2.50	2.25	3.25	0.50	1.00	-	1.55	2.00	1.00	0.50	4.00	8.50	2.50
1974	3.25	4.00	4.00	0.50	3.25	3.25	5.00	4.00	1.00	4.00	4.00	2.50	6.00	0.50	0.25	3.00	3.25
1975	2.00	1.00	0.25	2.50	2.00	0.50	1.00	1.00	7.00	0.75	0.25	9.00	0.37	2.50	0.75	2.00	2.00
1976	-	0.50	-	-	-	-	0.75	0.50	0.37	-	-	2.00	0.50	-	-	-	-
1977	-	-	1.00	-	-	-	1.25	-	3.50	1.50	1.00	1.00	0.50	-	-	-	-
1978	-0.38	-	0.25	-1.25	-0.38	-	-	-	-	-	0.25	0.25	-	-1.25	-	-0.50	-0.38
1979	0.69	-0.13	-	-	0.69	-0.06	-0.25	-0.13	0.25	1.25	-	0.25	-	-	0.31	-	0.69
1980	-	-	1.38	-	-	-	2.25	-	3.25	0.13	1.38	2.88	2.25	-	2.50	1.00	-
1981	4.75	1.00	1.88	3.50	4.75	0.63	6.75	1.00	3.38	0.31	1.88	0.63	0.50	3.50	3.19	2.06	4.75
1982	-	0.25	-	0.75	-	3.19	4.50	0.25	1.88	0.25	-	0.57	-	0.75	1.00	1.13	-
1983	0.94	3.06	2.13	0.38	0.94	0.50	0.69	3.06	0.13	2.68	2.18	2.63	1.38	0.38	0.25	0.50	0.94

3-month deposit rate: (7) major banks (Zürich) / Taux des dépôts à 3 mois : (7) grandes banques (Zurich)

per cent per annum, end of period / pourcentage par an, fin de période

	Year	Q.1	Q.2	Q.3	Q.4	JAN	FEB	MAR	APR	MAY	JUN	JUL	AUG	SEP	OCT	NOV	DEC
1964	3.63	3.19	3.25	3.38	3.63	2.94	3.13	3.19	3.38	3.44	3.25	3.13	3.25	3.38	3.50	3.69	3.63
1965	4.00	3.25	3.88	3.88	4.00	3.06	3.00	3.25	3.25	3.50	3.88	3.81	3.69	3.88	3.94	4.00	4.00
1966	4.50	4.00	4.19	4.25	4.50	3.81	3.88	4.00	4.06	4.13	4.19	4.25	4.19	4.25	4.25	4.50	4.50
1967	4.00	4.50	4.25	3.00	4.00	4.50	4.50	4.50	4.25	4.25	4.25	3.75	2.75	3.00	4.00	4.00	4.00
1968	4.25	2.75	3.75	3.75	4.25	2.75	2.75	2.75	2.75	3.25	3.75	3.75	3.75	3.75	4.00	4.25	4.25
1969	5.00	4.75	5.00	5.00	5.00	4.00	4.38	4.75	4.75	4.75	5.00	5.00	5.00	5.00	5.00	5.00	5.00
1970	5.25	5.50	5.50	5.50	5.25	5.00	5.00	5.50	5.50	5.50	5.50	5.50	5.50	5.50	5.50	5.25	5.25
1971	1.50	3.75	3.50	2.50	1.50	4.75	4.75	3.75	3.50	3.50	3.50	3.50	2.50	2.50	2.00	1.50	1.50
1972	4.00	0.50	2.00	1.50	4.00	1.50	0.50	0.50	1.50	1.50	2.00	2.00	1.50	1.50	2.50	4.00	4.00
1973	5.50	4.00	2.50	4.50	5.50	4.00	4.00	4.00	3.50	2.50	2.50	3.50	4.50	4.50	4.50	5.50	5.50
1974	6.00	6.00	6.00	6.00	6.00	6.00	6.00	6.00	6.00	6.00	6.00	6.00	6.00	6.00	6.00	6.00	6.00
1975	2.50	4.00	3.00	2.50	2.50	5.50	4.00	4.00	4.00	4.00	3.00	3.00	2.50	2.50	2.50	2.50	2.50
1976	1.50	1.25	1.00	1.00	1.50	1.50	1.50	1.25	1.00	1.00	1.00	1.00	1.00	1.00	1.00	1.50	1.50
1977	1.12	1.75	3.25	2.25	1.12	1.25	1.25	1.75	2.00	3.50	3.25	2.50	2.25	2.25	1.75	1.75	1.12
1978	0.13	0.50	1.00	0.50	0.13	1.00	0.50	0.50	0.50	1.00	1.00	1.25	0.50	0.50	0.50	0.13	0.13
1979	4.42	0.13	1.00	1.50	4.42	0.13	0.13	0.13	0.50	1.50	1.00	0.75	1.25	1.50	2.50	3.75	4.42
1980	5.75	5.75	4.75	5.00	5.75	5.00	5.00	5.75	5.50	5.08	4.75	4.75	4.75	5.00	4.75	4.75	5.75
1981	8.75	7.00	9.00	9.75	8.75	5.00	6.50	7.00	8.00	9.00	9.00	8.50	8.50	9.75	9.75	8.75	8.75
1982	3.00	5.00	4.75	3.25	3.00	7.50	8.00	5.00	3.75	3.25	4.75	3.50	3.50	3.25	3.00	3.00	3.00
1983	3.50	2.75	4.25	3.75	3.50	2.00	2.00	2.75	3.50	3.75	4.25	4.00	3.33	3.75	3.50	3.50	3.50

Yield of Confederation bonds (14)(15) / Rendement des obligations de la Confédération (14)(15)

per cent per annum, end of period / pourcentage par an, fin de période

	Year	Q.1	Q.2	Q.3	Q.4	JAN	FEB	MAR	APR	MAY	JUN	JUL	AUG	SEP	OCT	NOV	DEC
1964	4.07	3.39	4.05	4.05	4.07	3.64	3.80	3.89	3.88	4.02	4.05	4.04	4.05	4.05	4.08	4.08	4.07
1965	3.98	3.91	3.92	3.94	3.98	4.04	3.94	3.91	3.92	3.92	3.92	3.92	3.92	3.94	3.96	3.98	3.98
1966	4.53	3.98	4.04	4.27	4.53	3.98	3.98	3.98	4.01	4.02	4.04	4.16	4.24	4.27	4.36	4.40	4.53
1967	4.55	4.72	4.75	4.32	4.55	4.74	4.74	4.72	4.69	4.68	4.75	4.60	4.48	4.32	4.45	4.52	4.55
1968	4.33	4.35	4.34	4.34	4.33	4.59	4.39	4.35	4.37	4.35	4.34	4.35	4.35	4.34	4.38	4.33	4.33
1969	5.34	4.60	4.69	5.37	5.34	4.38	4.40	4.60	4.67	4.58	4.69	5.00	5.20	5.37	5.23	5.34	5.34
1970	5.70	5.66	5.87	5.74	5.70	5.33	5.55	5.66	5.88	5.86	5.87	5.81	5.76	5.74	5.75	5.68	5.70
1971	4.99	5.44	5.38	5.10	4.99	5.58	5.52	5.44	5.27	5.32	5.38	5.45	5.31	5.10	4.97	4.86	4.99
1972	5.27	4.77	5.06	4.98	5.27	4.76	4.60	4.77	4.94	4.93	5.06	4.95	4.93	4.98	5.08	5.29	5.27
1973	6.31	5.29	5.36	5.79	6.31	5.36	5.32	5.29	5.42	5.37	5.36	5.36	5.65	5.79	5.77	6.13	6.31
1974	7.17	7.09	7.28	7.41	7.17	6.38	6.59	7.09	7.23	7.30	7.28	7.23	7.36	7.41	7.32	7.19	7.17
1975	5.93	6.79	6.51	6.21	5.93	6.83	6.66	6.79	6.87	6.76	6.51	6.45	6.19	6.21	6.08	5.96	5.93
1976	4.46	5.14	5.12	4.89	4.46	5.40	5.29	5.14	5.19	5.21	5.12	5.09	4.99	4.89	4.60	4.41	4.46
1977	3.78	3.95	4.49	3.94	3.78	4.05	3.97	3.95	3.93	4.44	4.49	4.22	4.08	3.94	3.85	3.84	3.78
1978	3.03	3.49	3.39	3.25	3.03	3.65	3.45	3.49	3.40	3.48	3.39	3.37	3.31	3.25	3.07	3.03	3.03
1979	4.04	3.22	3.45	3.50	4.04	3.11	3.08	3.22	3.21	3.18	3.45	3.49	3.51	3.50	3.60	4.04	4.04
1980	4.63	5.10	4.72	4.87	4.63	4.48	4.72	5.10	4.97	4.82	4.72	4.60	4.87	4.87	4.69	4.68	4.63
1981	5.39	5.47	5.62	6.13	5.39	4.79	5.20	5.47	5.48	5.85	5.62	5.51	5.84	6.13	5.99	5.57	5.39
1982	4.23	5.15	5.22	4.43	4.23	5.44	5.56	5.15	5.01	4.98	5.22	4.95	4.65	4.43	4.30	4.27	4.23
1983	4.53	4.46	4.60	4.70	4.53	4.22	4.25	4.46	4.41	4.47	4.60	4.52	4.70	4.70	4.61	4.62	4.53

Share prices: all shares (14) — Cours des actions : ensemble des actions (14)

1980 = 100

	Year	Q.1	Q.2	Q.3	Q.4	JAN	FEB	MAR	APR	MAY	JUN	JUL	AUG	SEP	OCT	NOV	DEC
1964																	
1965																	
1966	60	67	61	57	54	69	67	64	63	61	60	58	57	56	55	53	54
1967	63	58	53	65	71	57	60	58	59	57	57	58	66	70	68	70	76
1968	87	78	86	87	95	76	76	82	83	88	88	85	88	89	91	97	98
1969	101	100	105	95	101	102	99	98	106	110	101	96	97	95	104	101	99
1970	89	96	86	90	85	97	96	95	87	85	86	88	92	89	87	83	86
1971	93	94	95	94	90	93	93	97	100	92	94	96	95	90	85	90	94
1972	110	105	109	114	112	101	105	107	107	114	104	111	115	116	114	109	115
1973	106	113	109	103	101	117	113	110	106	111	109	102	101	106	108	98	96
1974	80	96	84	75	66	98	96	93	90	80	82	84	74	68	69	66	63
1975	78	76	79	76	81	75	77	77	81	78	77	79	76	73	78	82	84
1976	86	87	85	88	86	87	87	88	85	83	86	87	88	87	84	85	90
1977	91	92	89	91	93	92	92	92	91	87	87	88	91	94	93	93	94
1978	93	97	91	92	91	97	99	93	90	92	93	93	94	90	89	91	93
1979	101	101	99	102	101	100	101	101	101	98	99	100	102	104	103	100	101
1980	100	100	97	101	102	104	102	93	96	97	99	101	101	102	102	101	102
1981	92	99	93	90	87	99	99	98	95	91	93	93	91	86	84	88	88
1982	89	87	87	86	95	86	86	87	88	89	85	85	87	86	93	95	99
1983	105	103	104	103	110	101	106	101	106	103	101	105	102	103	106	108	116

U.S. dollar exchange rate: spot — Taux de change du dollar É.-U. : au comptant

cents per franc, end of period — cents par franc, fin de période

	Year	Q.1	Q.2	Q.3	Q.4	JAN	FEB	MAR	APR	MAY	JUN	JUL	AUG	SEP	OCT	NOV	DEC
1964	23.18	23.10	23.17	23.15	23.18	23.16	23.10	23.10	23.18	23.18	23.17	23.17	23.14	23.15	23.18	23.18	23.18
1965	23.16	22.99	23.07	23.16	23.16	23.13	23.10	22.99	23.00	23.04	23.07	23.14	23.15	23.16	23.14	23.16	23.16
1966	23.11	23.02	23.17	23.10	23.11	23.07	23.05	23.02	23.16	23.17	23.17	23.15	23.11	23.10	23.08	23.16	23.11
1967	23.12	23.07	23.16	23.03	23.12	23.06	23.06	23.07	23.16	23.18	23.16	23.11	23.05	23.03	23.09	23.18	23.12
1968	23.25	23.15	23.23	23.23	23.25	22.99	22.99	23.15	23.03	23.28	23.28	23.23	23.26	23.23	23.27	23.24	23.25
1969	23.16	23.15	23.08	23.25	23.16	23.12	23.20	23.15	23.20	23.13	23.08	23.21	23.23	23.25	23.10	23.14	23.16
1970	23.17	23.21	23.16	23.11	23.17	23.23	23.23	23.21	23.25	23.13	23.16	23.23	23.25	23.11	23.07	23.19	23.17
1971	25.54	23.28	24.41	25.32	25.54	23.27	23.22	23.28	23.28	24.40	24.41	24.47	25.11	25.32	25.07	25.30	25.54
1972	26.50	26.04	26.50	25.31	26.50	25.83	25.84	26.04	25.89	26.02	26.50	26.50	26.46	26.31	26.34	26.48	26.50
1973	30.83	30.89	33.78	33.09	30.83	27.60	31.97	30.89	30.86	32.30	33.78	34.89	33.01	33.09	32.29	31.23	30.83
1974	39.37	33.33	33.36	33.94	39.37	30.40	32.03	33.33	34.31	33.60	33.36	33.61	33.25	33.94	34.85	36.82	39.37
1975	38.17	39.57	39.96	36.40	38.17	40.00	41.67	39.57	39.12	39.98	39.96	36.85	37.28	36.40	38.11	37.33	38.17
1976	40.81	39.46	40.44	40.75	40.81	38.46	39.03	39.46	39.80	40.97	40.44	40.33	40.37	40.75	41.05	40.93	40.81
1977	50.00	39.33	40.64	42.76	50.00	39.73	39.18	39.33	39.62	39.93	40.64	41.56	41.75	42.76	44.83	46.20	50.00
1978	61.73	53.52	53.81	64.81	61.73	50.48	53.39	53.52	51.73	52.45	53.81	57.41	60.75	64.31	67.87	58.14	61.73
1979	63.29	59.14	60.20	65.21	63.29	59.29	60.01	59.14	58.04	58.06	60.20	60.11	60.39	65.21	61.55	61.96	63.29
1980	56.71	54.59	61.79	60.55	56.71	61.52	59.26	54.59	59.92	60.10	61.79	60.39	60.57	60.55	58.15	57.49	56.71
1981	55.60	52.23	49.24	50.72	55.60	51.88	50.92	52.23	49.48	48.25	49.24	46.77	47.14	50.72	54.13	56.65	55.60
1982	50.14	51.70	47.54	46.13	50.14	54.22	52.84	51.70	51.14	50.09	47.54	47.81	47.19	46.13	45.14	46.78	50.14
1983	45.88	48.04	47.52	46.96	45.88	50.02	48.92	48.04	48.47	47.82	47.52	46.97	45.60	46.96	46.80	46.25	45.88

U.S. dollar exchange rate: forward (90 days) / Taux de change du dollar É.-U. : à terme (90 jours)

cents per franc, end of period / cents par franc, fin de période

	Year	Q.1	Q.2	Q.3	Q.4	JAN	FEB	MAR	APR	MAY	JUN	JUL	AUG	SEP	OCT	NOV	DEC
1964	23.22	23.13	23.21	23.16	23.22	23.21	23.15	23.13	23.17	23.18	23.21	23.15	23.19	23.16	23.18	23.19	23.22
1965	23.18	23.07	23.10	23.18	23.18	23.20	23.16	23.07	23.04	23.06	23.10	23.16	23.17	23.18	23.15	23.16	23.18
1966	23.13	23.05	23.19	23.14	23.13	23.13	23.10	23.05	23.15	23.17	23.19	23.21	23.17	23.14	23.11	23.16	23.13
1967	23.27	23.08	23.20	23.11	23.27	23.08	23.08	23.08	23.16	23.19	23.20	23.19	23.17	23.11	23.15	23.26	23.27
1968	23.36	23.31	23.45	23.31	23.36	23.15	23.11	23.31	23.21	23.40	23.45	23.34	23.37	23.31	23.33	23.33	23.36
1969	23.28	23.26	23.22	23.40	23.28	23.27	23.30	23.26	23.35	23.26	23.22	23.24	23.29	23.40	23.28	23.27	23.28
1970	23.23	23.25	23.30	23.26	23.23	23.25	23.28	23.25	23.27	23.25	23.30	23.34	23.35	23.26	23.21	23.23	23.23
1971	26.01	23.36	24.50	25.75	26.01	23.27	23.26	23.36	23.45	24.56	24.50	24.59	25.50	25.75	25.36	25.61	26.01
1972	26.59	26.32	26.62	26.55	26.59	26.11	26.15	26.32	26.10	26.16	26.62	26.82	26.74	26.56	26.49	26.53	26.59
1973	30.91	31.27	34.80	33.47	30.91	27.77	32.15	31.27	31.26	32.81	34.80	35.83	33.51	33.47	32.60	31.10	30.91
1974	39.48	33.25	33.59	34.10	39.48	30.72	31.91	33.25	34.38	33.83	33.59	33.78	33.47	34.10	34.97	36.96	39.48
1975	38.46	39.78	40.19	36.78	38.46	40.19	42.05	39.78	39.42	40.24	40.19	37.11	37.78	36.78	38.49	37.62	38.46
1976	41.05	39.86	40.95	41.10	41.05	38.87	39.42	39.86	40.23	41.53	40.95	40.75	40.82	41.10	41.43	41.25	41.05
1977	50.74	39.56	40.88	43.23	50.74	40.21	39.45	39.56	39.83	40.11	40.88	42.02	42.23	43.23	45.39	46.80	50.74
1978	63.61	54.47	54.77	66.23	63.61	51.28	54.38	54.47	52.63	53.36	54.77	58.41	62.00	66.23	65.83	59.77	63.61
1979	64.73	60.64	61.65	66.23	64.73	60.83	61.65	60.64	59.42	59.24	61.65	61.61	61.96	66.23	62.04	63.41	64.73
1980	58.17	56.37	62.31	61.92	58.17	62.89	60.94	56.37	61.24	60.90	62.31	61.28	61.58	61.92	59.56	59.28	58.17
1981	56.34	53.22	50.25	51.41	56.34	53.88	51.81	53.22	50.35	49.38	50.25	48.08	48.24	51.41	54.89	56.92	56.34
1982	50.92	52.83	48.90	46.95	50.92	55.13	53.97	52.83	52.58	51.44	48.90	48.88	47.78	46.95	46.06	47.42	50.92
1983	46.56	48.73	48.15	47.64	46.56	50.76	49.70	48.73	49.09	48.38	48.15	47.69	46.25	47.64	47.44	46.75	46.56

Official reserves excluding gold / Réserves officielles, or exclu

million SDR's, end of period / millions de DTS, fin de période

	Year	Q.1	Q.2	Q.3	Q.4	JAN	FEB	MAR	APR	MAY	JUN	JUL	AUG	SEP	OCT	NOV	DEC
1964	596	249	401	419	596	272	250	249	328	316	401	398	412	419	409	546	596
1965	402	395	358	424	402	453	437	395	319	314	358	420	443	424	418	391	402
1966	704	424	560	471	704	414	429	424	384	458	560	489	489	471	423	476	704
1967	607	650	549	456	607	478	469	650	402	538	549	489	480	456	462	527	607
1968	1669	790	1063	723	1669	511	468	790	655	660	1063	767	734	723	739	917	1669
1969	1783	856	978	1007	1783	815	644	856	827	749	978	730	698	1007	1100	1022	1783
1970	2401	1358	1629	1791	2401	966	951	1358	981	1213	1629	1267	1209	1791	1327	1307	2401
1971	3507	1817	2226	3640	3507	1414	1400	1817	1693	1832	2226	1547	3672	3640	3619	3622	3507
1972	4052	3303	3564	3935	4052	3438	3385	3303	3239	2851	3564	3856	3718	3935	3365	3032	4052
1973	4151	3826	4314	4257	4151	3588	3649	3826	3428	3614	4314	3580	3609	4257	3447	3312	4151
1974	4448	3737	4062	4071	4448	3034	3030	3737	3219	3164	4062	3438	3210	4071	3365	3355	4448
1975	5996	4283	4135	4201	5996	3707	3849	4283	3625	3824	4135	4004	4109	4201	4020	4079	5996
1976	8268	5720	6695	6556	8268	4914	4831	5720	5333	5496	6695	6154	5789	6556	5659	5929	8268
1977	8471	6549	6410	6160	8471	5747	5845	6549	5417	5331	6410	5552	5531	6160	5548	6061	8471
1978	13634	8081	8459	9259	13634	7702	8154	8081	7913	7665	8459	7244	8202	9259	10031	11531	13634
1979	12476	12928	11897	11383	12476	14005	13993	12928	11215	11257	11897	10586	10265	11383	10421	10674	12476
1980	12276	10777	10897	10824	12276	10154	10482	10777	9915	9148	10897	9576	9316	10824	9180	9975	12276
1981	12010	10488	10553	9495	12010	9966	9588	10488	9348	8919	10553	9073	8843	9495	8189	8833	12010
1982	14015	11450	12537	12474	14015	9573	9702	11450	11024	11584	12537	11282	11571	12474	12069	12533	14015
1983	14360	12921	12448	12502	14360	11736	12145	12921	11396	11758	12448	12805	11642	12502	11694	12250	14360

SWITZERLAND

Imports c.i.f. (16)

billion francs, monthly averages

Importations c.a.f. (16)

milliards de francs, moyennes mensuelles

	Year	Q.1	Q.2	Q.3	Q.4	JAN	FEB	MAR	APR	MAY	JUN	JUL	AUG	SEP	OCT	NOV	DEC
1964	1.30	1.25	1.32	1.27	1.34	1.25	1.25	1.26	1.39	1.21	1.37	1.37	1.19	1.26	1.37	1.31	1.33
1965	1.33	1.28	1.32	1.31	1.40	1.19	1.23	1.43	1.31	1.32	1.33	1.39	1.23	1.31	1.36	1.38	1.45
1966	1.42	1.36	1.41	1.41	1.49	1.20	1.36	1.53	1.33	1.42	1.47	1.42	1.35	1.47	1.48	1.50	1.48
1967	1.48	1.44	1.52	1.45	1.50	1.40	1.41	1.53	1.45	1.51	1.59	1.46	1.39	1.49	1.53	1.50	1.48
1968	1.62	1.54	1.56	1.62	1.76	1.48	1.53	1.60	1.52	1.61	1.54	1.79	1.47	1.60	1.89	1.66	1.73
1969	1.90	1.68	1.86	1.90	2.16	1.63	1.57	1.83	1.82	1.83	1.94	2.00	1.73	1.96	2.25	2.06	2.17
1970	2.32	2.16	2.39	2.25	2.49	1.99	2.17	2.33	2.54	2.15	2.48	2.48	1.97	2.30	2.54	2.41	2.53
1971	2.47	2.40	2.50	2.41	2.57	2.09	2.36	2.75	2.43	2.52	2.56	2.53	2.16	2.54	2.51	2.55	2.65
1972	2.70	2.59	2.71	2.62	2.88	2.38	2.60	2.80	2.58	2.72	2.81	2.43	2.61	2.81	2.89	2.91	2.84
1973	3.05	2.94	2.94	2.95	3.37	2.08	2.88	3.05	2.73	3.15	2.94	3.11	2.74	3.00	3.55	3.49	3.07
1974	3.58	3.60	3.71	3.52	3.48	3.53	3.42	3.86	3.71	3.85	3.56	3.88	3.19	3.51	3.91	3.36	3.16
1975	2.86	3.01	2.91	2.68	2.82	3.09	3.00	2.95	3.24	2.68	2.83	2.85	2.31	2.87	3.06	2.56	2.84
1976	3.07	2.88	2.96	3.04	3.40	2.58	2.77	3.30	2.94	2.87	3.08	3.00	2.84	3.29	3.32	3.35	3.53
1977	3.58	3.46	3.61	3.57	3.67	3.06	3.30	4.02	3.46	3.51	3.86	3.51	3.49	3.70	3.70	3.78	3.54
1978	3.53	3.51	3.73	3.30	3.58	3.36	3.29	3.86	3.57	3.62	3.98	3.30	3.19	3.41	3.59	3.75	3.39
1979	4.06	3.74	3.90	4.06	4.54	3.36	3.68	4.19	3.65	4.13	3.92	4.22	3.86	4.08	4.83	4.63	4.15
1980	5.07	5.20	5.03	4.90	5.17	4.59	5.32	5.68	5.39	4.67	5.02	5.30	4.21	5.19	5.50	4.74	5.27
1981	5.01	4.86	5.03	5.07	5.08	4.18	4.97	5.41	4.59	4.86	5.23	5.26	4.52	5.42	5.38	4.92	4.95
1982	4.84	4.72	4.90	4.65	5.11	4.03	4.62	5.51	5.09	4.56	5.05	4.66	4.14	5.15	4.90	5.27	5.15
1983	5.11	5.01	5.16	4.90	5.36	4.47	4.73	5.81	5.11	4.98	5.38	4.76	4.70	5.22	5.24	5.66	5.19

Exports f.o.b. (16)

billion francs, monthly averages

Exportations f.o.b. (16)

milliards de francs, moyennes mensuelles

	Year	Q.1	Q.2	Q.3	Q.4	JAN	FEB	MAR	APR	MAY	JUN	JUL	AUG	SEP	OCT	NOV	DEC
1964	0.96	0.87	0.94	0.93	1.09	0.79	0.90	0.91	0.98	0.87	0.98	0.98	0.79	1.01	1.13	1.05	1.08
1965	1.07	0.97	1.04	1.05	1.23	0.86	0.98	1.07	1.01	1.04	1.06	1.12	0.88	1.14	1.20	1.19	1.31
1966	1.18	1.10	1.17	1.15	1.32	0.99	1.08	1.24	1.12	1.15	1.23	1.21	0.98	1.25	1.33	1.30	1.34
1967	1.26	1.18	1.25	1.19	1.44	1.11	1.16	1.26	1.24	1.20	1.32	1.21	1.05	1.31	1.43	1.45	1.45
1968	1.45	1.32	1.39	1.42	1.66	1.21	1.29	1.46	1.35	1.40	1.41	1.53	1.22	1.51	1.71	1.70	1.57
1969	1.68	1.51	1.63	1.63	1.93	1.33	1.52	1.68	1.61	1.62	1.68	1.77	1.32	1.79	2.01	1.85	1.94
1970	1.85	1.67	1.89	1.77	2.06	1.49	1.70	1.82	1.94	1.71	2.01	1.94	1.45	1.92	2.06	2.01	2.09
1971	1.97	1.85	1.96	1.90	2.18	1.65	1.81	2.08	1.94	1.88	2.06	2.06	1.63	2.00	2.13	2.14	2.27
1972	2.18	2.04	2.15	2.07	2.48	1.83	2.01	2.29	2.03	2.12	2.31	2.14	1.81	2.25	2.43	2.50	2.51
1973	2.50	2.31	2.45	2.40	2.84	2.10	2.30	2.52	2.27	2.63	2.44	2.54	2.12	2.53	2.85	2.99	2.68
1974	2.95	2.83	3.03	2.83	3.11	2.56	2.87	3.07	2.97	3.22	2.89	3.16	2.42	2.91	3.30	3.17	2.86
1975	2.79	2.62	2.82	2.62	3.08	2.52	2.68	2.67	2.90	2.62	2.95	2.87	2.17	2.82	3.16	3.01	3.07
1976	3.10	2.86	3.08	2.91	3.53	2.47	2.80	3.30	3.12	3.06	3.08	3.08	2.52	3.13	3.62	3.59	3.40
1977	3.50	3.30	3.46	3.35	3.89	3.03	3.19	3.67	3.29	3.38	3.72	3.51	2.88	3.67	3.71	3.93	4.04
1978	3.48	3.34	3.62	3.30	3.68	3.15	3.34	3.54	3.45	3.52	3.87	3.34	3.03	3.53	3.60	3.76	3.67
1979	3.67	3.46	3.67	3.48	4.07	3.17	3.33	3.87	3.35	3.81	3.85	3.63	3.18	3.63	4.23	4.24	3.74
1980	4.14	4.11	4.13	3.86	4.44	3.67	4.22	4.45	4.13	4.00	4.28	4.31	3.18	4.09	4.69	4.24	4.39
1981	4.40	4.20	4.39	4.25	4.77	3.79	4.19	4.61	4.28	4.38	4.51	4.75	3.53	4.48	4.94	4.66	4.71
1982	4.39	4.35	4.49	3.97	4.76	3.79	4.25	5.01	4.41	4.35	4.70	4.26	3.36	4.27	4.52	4.83	4.92
1983	4.48	4.22	4.43	4.27	5.00	3.84	4.03	4.80	4.28	4.32	4.70	4.36	3.62	4.82	4.74	5.21	5.05

Trade balance (f.o.b. — c.i.f.) (16)

billion francs, monthly averages

Balance commerciale (f.o.b. — c.a.f.) (16)

milliards de francs, moyennes mensuelles

	Year	Q.1	Q.2	Q.3	Q.4	JAN	FEB	MAR	APR	MAY	JUN	JUL	AUG	SEP	OCT	NOV	DEC
1964	-0.34	-0.39	-0.38	-0.34	-0.25	-0.46	-0.35	-0.35	-0.41	-0.34	-0.39	-0.39	-0.40	-0.24	-0.23	-0.27	-0.25
1965	-0.26	-0.31	-0.28	-0.26	-0.16	-0.32	-0.25	-0.36	-0.30	-0.28	-0.27	-0.26	-0.35	-0.18	-0.16	-0.19	-0.14
1966	-0.23	-0.26	-0.24	-0.27	-0.17	-0.21	-0.28	-0.29	-0.22	-0.27	-0.24	-0.21	-0.37	-0.23	-0.14	-0.21	-0.15
1967	-0.21	-0.27	-0.27	-0.25	-0.06	-0.29	-0.25	-0.27	-0.21	-0.32	-0.27	-0.25	-0.34	-0.19	-0.10	-0.06	-0.03
1968	-0.17	-0.22	-0.17	-0.20	-0.10	-0.27	-0.24	-0.15	-0.17	-0.21	-0.14	-0.27	-0.25	-0.10	-0.18	0.04	-0.16
1969	-0.22	-0.17	-0.23	-0.27	-0.23	-0.30	-0.05	-0.15	-0.22	-0.22	-0.26	-0.23	-0.41	-0.17	-0.24	-0.20	-0.23
1970	-0.48	-0.49	-0.50	-0.48	-0.44	-0.50	-0.46	-0.51	-0.60	-0.43	-0.47	-0.54	-0.52	-0.38	-0.47	-0.40	-0.44
1971	-0.50	-0.56	-0.55	-0.51	-0.39	-0.44	-0.56	-0.67	-0.49	-0.65	-0.51	-0.47	-0.53	-0.54	-0.38	-0.42	-0.38
1972	-0.51	-0.55	-0.56	-0.55	-0.40	-0.55	-0.59	-0.51	-0.56	-0.60	-0.51	-0.29	-0.80	-0.56	-0.46	-0.41	-0.34
1973	-0.55	-0.63	-0.49	-0.55	-0.53	-0.78	-0.59	-0.53	-0.45	-0.52	-0.51	-0.57	-0.62	-0.47	-0.70	-0.50	-0.39
1974	-0.63	-0.77	-0.68	-0.69	-0.37	-0.97	-0.54	-0.80	-0.74	-0.62	-0.67	-0.72	-0.76	-0.60	-0.61	-0.20	-0.30
1975	-0.07	-0.39	-0.09	-0.06	0.26	-0.57	-0.32	-0.28	-0.34	-0.06	0.12	0.02	-0.14	-0.05	0.10	0.44	0.24
1976	0.02	-0.03	0.12	-0.13	0.13	-0.11	0.03	-	0.18	0.18	0.01	0.08	-0.33	-0.16	0.29	0.24	-0.13
1977	-0.08	-0.17	-0.15	-0.21	0.22	-0.03	-0.11	-0.35	-0.17	-0.13	-0.15	0.01	-0.61	-0.03	0.01	0.15	0.49
1978	-0.04	-0.16	-0.11	0.00	0.10	-0.21	0.05	-0.33	-0.12	-0.10	-0.11	0.04	-0.16	0.13	0.02	0.01	0.28
1979	-0.39	-0.29	-0.23	-0.58	-0.47	-0.19	-0.36	-0.32	-0.30	-0.32	-0.08	-0.55	-0.68	-0.46	-0.60	-0.39	-0.41
1980	-0.94	-1.09	-0.89	-1.04	-0.73	-0.92	-1.11	-1.23	-1.26	-0.68	-0.74	-0.99	-1.03	-1.09	-0.81	-0.51	-0.88
1981	-0.61	-0.66	-0.64	-0.82	-0.31	-0.39	-0.78	-0.80	-0.71	-0.48	-0.72	-0.51	-0.59	-0.94	-0.44	-0.26	-0.24
1982	-0.45	-0.37	-0.41	-0.68	-0.35	-0.24	-0.37	-0.50	-0.67	-0.21	-0.35	-0.38	-0.73	-0.88	-0.38	-0.44	-0.23
1983	-0.63	-0.79	-0.72	-0.63	-0.36	-0.63	-0.71	-1.02	-0.83	-0.56	-0.68	-0.42	-1.08	-0.40	-0.50	-0.44	-0.15

Imports c.i.f. (16) — Importations c.a.f. (16)

billion francs, monthly averages — milliards de francs, moyennes mensuelles

Adjusted - Corrigé *

	Year	Q.1	Q.2	Q.3	Q.4	JAN	FEB	MAR	APR	MAY	JUN	JUL	AUG	SEP	OCT	NOV	DEC
1964		1.28	1.23	1.29	1.31	1.27	1.29	1.27	1.28	1.27	1.29	1.27	1.33	1.27	1.32	1.33	1.29
1965		1.29	1.31	1.34	1.37	1.30	1.27	1.29	1.31	1.33	1.30	1.34	1.35	1.32	1.36	1.35	1.39
1966		1.37	1.40	1.44	1.47	1.32	1.41	1.38	1.38	1.40	1.41	1.42	1.42	1.49	1.46	1.47	1.43
1967		1.48	1.48	1.50	1.48	1.50	1.46	1.48	1.46	1.49	1.48	1.46	1.48	1.55	1.46	1.46	1.52
1968		1.53	1.55	1.66	1.71	1.53	1.53	1.54	1.52	1.53	1.61	1.67	1.64	1.66	1.74	1.68	1.73
1969		1.69	1.85	1.96	2.09	1.59	1.63	1.75	1.82	1.85	1.90	1.89	2.02	1.97	2.05	2.16	2.06
1970		2.24	2.31	2.32	2.42	2.15	2.24	2.32	2.35	2.27	2.31	2.34	2.32	2.30	2.42	2.42	2.43
1971		2.40	2.49	2.50	2.49	2.72	2.43	2.44	2.42	2.59	2.46	2.46	2.48	2.52	2.47	2.48	2.53
1972		2.59	2.66	2.74	2.83	2.62	2.56	2.58	2.67	2.65	2.67	2.47	2.91	2.85	2.74	2.82	2.94
1973		2.91	2.93	3.09	3.27	2.94	2.96	2.82	2.80	2.98	3.02	3.08	3.04	3.15	3.22	3.40	3.18
1974		3.61	3.71	3.62	3.38	3.63	3.51	3.68	3.69	3.71	3.73	3.70	3.64	3.53	3.57	3.39	3.19
1975		3.09	2.84	2.75	2.74	3.17	3.10	3.00	2.99	2.79	2.74	2.76	2.70	2.79	2.77	2.69	2.75
1976		2.83	2.96	3.14	3.31	2.77	2.84	2.87	2.91	2.99	2.99	3.02	3.20	3.20	3.25	3.25	3.44
1977		3.44	3.61	3.67	3.63	3.42	3.39	3.49	3.52	3.62	3.69	3.65	3.75	3.62	3.63	3.67	3.58
1978		3.54	3.65	3.44	3.53	3.68	3.36	3.57	3.54	3.72	3.69	3.43	3.45	3.43	3.42	3.64	3.53
1979		3.68	3.91	4.23	4.41	3.56	3.74	3.73	3.70	4.11	3.92	4.25	4.17	4.27	4.43	4.48	4.31
1980		5.12	5.03	5.02	5.02	4.99	5.14	5.23	5.26	4.89	4.93	5.18	4.90	4.99	5.03	4.94	5.08
1981		4.88	5.01	5.19	4.94	4.76	5.05	4.84	4.82	5.10	5.12	5.11	5.29	5.17	5.12	4.90	4.80
1982		4.75	4.87	4.77	4.94	4.78	4.72	4.74	4.92	4.83	4.85	4.73	4.69	4.89	4.80	5.08	4.95
1983		5.08	5.11	5.03	5.25	5.32	4.65	5.06	5.09	5.16	5.10	5.03	5.10	4.97	5.12	5.45	5.19

Exports f.o.b. (16) — Exportations f.o.b. (16)

billion francs, monthly averages — milliards de francs, moyennes mensuelles

Adjusted - Corrigé *

	Year	Q.1	Q.2	Q.3	Q.4	JAN	FEB	MAR	APR	MAY	JUN	JUL	AUG	SEP	OCT	NOV	DEC
1964		0.91	0.94	0.96	0.99	0.89	0.93	0.93	0.95	0.93	0.93	0.94	0.98	0.97	1.01	0.98	0.99
1965		1.01	1.05	1.09	1.12	1.00	1.04	0.99	1.04	1.06	1.05	1.09	1.09	1.10	1.08	1.10	1.19
1966		1.15	1.18	1.19	1.21	1.16	1.15	1.15	1.15	1.19	1.20	1.20	1.18	1.20	1.22	1.19	1.23
1967		1.25	1.24	1.25	1.33	1.29	1.23	1.23	1.24	1.25	1.23	1.21	1.26	1.27	1.30	1.33	1.36
1968		1.36	1.40	1.49	1.52	1.37	1.33	1.38	1.39	1.38	1.44	1.46	1.49	1.51	1.52	1.57	1.47
1969		1.57	1.65	1.70	1.77	1.49	1.63	1.60	1.63	1.66	1.65	1.71	1.64	1.76	1.77	1.78	1.76
1970		1.78	1.85	1.85	1.90	1.70	1.81	1.84	1.85	1.82	1.88	1.84	1.82	1.87	1.87	1.91	1.91
1971		1.91	1.96	2.00	2.01	1.92	1.91	1.91	1.96	1.93	1.98	1.95	2.04	1.97	1.98	1.97	2.06
1972		2.11	2.12	2.19	2.32	2.15	2.03	2.17	2.08	2.13	2.16	2.14	2.20	2.23	2.27	2.30	2.38
1973		2.37	2.43	2.56	2.64	2.35	2.40	2.35	2.38	2.49	2.43	2.52	2.56	2.61	2.58	2.73	2.60
1974		2.92	3.01	3.00	2.88	2.85	3.00	2.92	3.02	3.08	2.91	3.05	2.99	2.97	2.98	2.90	2.77
1975		2.77	2.74	2.78	2.85	2.76	2.80	2.74	2.75	2.66	2.82	2.75	2.73	2.81	2.81	2.85	2.91
1976		2.89	3.06	3.10	3.27	2.72	2.90	3.04	3.15	3.04	2.99	3.03	3.19	3.10	3.34	3.29	3.18
1977		3.39	3.43	3.57	3.63	3.46	3.34	3.38	3.36	3.40	3.52	3.54	3.54	3.62	3.47	3.59	3.84
1978		3.49	3.51	3.55	3.45	3.55	3.50	3.42	3.45	3.60	3.49	3.40	3.74	3.52	3.34	3.46	3.56
1979		3.49	3.63	3.77	3.79	3.47	3.47	3.54	3.52	3.68	3.68	3.65	3.90	3.76	3.81	3.91	3.66
1980		4.14	4.09	4.12	4.13	4.06	4.16	4.19	4.19	3.99	4.10	4.19	4.05	4.12	4.20	4.09	4.11
1981		4.28	4.34	4.55	4.45	4.24	4.34	4.27	4.34	4.32	4.37	4.56	4.59	4.50	4.48	4.46	4.42
1982		4.40	4.44	4.27	4.42	4.33	4.39	4.49	4.44	4.45	4.42	4.18	4.32	4.32	4.19	4.51	4.53
1983		4.30	4.33	4.58	4.68	4.45	4.16	4.30	4.33	4.44	4.37	4.35	4.52	4.87	4.44	4.83	4.77

Trade balance (f.o.b. — c.i.f.) (16) — Balance commerciale (f.o.b. — c.a.f.) (16)

billion francs, monthly averages — milliards de francs, moyennes mensuelles

Adjusted - Corrigé *

	Year	Q.1	Q.2	Q.3	Q.4	JAN	FEB	MAR	APR	MAY	JUN	JUL	AUG	SEP	OCT	NOV	DEC
1964		-0.36	-0.34	-0.33	-0.32	-0.39	-0.37	-0.34	-0.33	-0.34	-0.36	-0.33	-0.35	-0.30	-0.32	-0.35	-0.30
1965		-0.28	-0.26	-0.25	-0.24	-0.30	-0.24	-0.30	-0.27	-0.26	-0.25	-0.25	-0.26	-0.23	-0.27	-0.25	-0.20
1966		-0.22	-0.22	-0.25	-0.26	-0.16	-0.27	-0.23	-0.23	-0.22	-0.21	-0.23	-0.24	-0.29	-0.24	-0.28	-0.25
1967		-0.23	-0.24	-0.25	-0.15	-0.20	-0.23	-0.24	-0.22	-0.24	-0.25	-0.26	-0.22	-0.29	-0.16	-0.13	-0.16
1968		-0.17	-0.15	-0.17	-0.19	-0.16	-0.20	-0.16	-0.14	-0.15	-0.16	-0.21	-0.16	-0.16	-0.22	-0.11	-0.24
1969		-0.12	-0.21	-0.26	-0.32	-0.20	-0.01	-0.15	-0.19	-0.19	-0.25	-0.19	-0.37	-0.21	-0.28	-0.39	-0.30
1970		-0.45	-0.46	-0.47	-0.53	-0.46	-0.43	-0.48	-0.50	-0.45	-0.43	-0.49	-0.49	-0.43	-0.55	-0.51	-0.52
1971		-0.49	-0.53	-0.50	-0.49	-0.41	-0.52	-0.53	-0.46	-0.66	-0.49	-0.49	-0.44	-0.55	-0.49	-0.50	-0.47
1972		-0.48	-0.54	-0.56	-0.52	-0.48	-0.53	-0.42	-0.60	-0.53	-0.51	-0.33	-0.71	-0.63	-0.47	-0.52	-0.56
1973		-0.54	-0.50	-0.53	-0.63	-0.59	-0.56	-0.47	-0.42	-0.49	-0.59	-0.55	-0.48	-0.55	-0.64	-0.67	-0.58
1974		-0.69	-0.70	-0.62	-0.50	-0.79	-0.52	-0.76	-0.66	-0.63	-0.82	-0.65	-0.66	-0.56	-0.59	-0.49	-0.42
1975		-0.32	-0.10	0.03	0.12	-0.42	-0.30	-0.25	-0.24	-0.14	0.08	0.04	0.03	0.02	0.03	0.16	0.15
1976		0.06	0.10	-0.04	-0.04	-0.05	0.06	0.18	0.24	0.05	0.00	0.01	-0.01	-0.11	0.09	0.04	-0.26
1977		-0.04	-0.18	-0.11	0.01	0.03	-0.05	-0.11	-0.17	-0.21	-0.17	-0.12	-0.21	0.00	-0.17	-0.08	0.26
1978		-0.04	-0.14	0.11	-0.08	-0.13	0.15	-0.15	-0.09	-0.12	-0.21	-0.03	0.29	0.08	-0.08	-0.18	0.03
1979		-0.18	-0.28	-0.45	-0.61	-0.09	-0.27	-0.19	-0.18	-0.43	-0.24	-0.60	-0.27	-0.51	-0.62	-0.58	-0.65
1980		-0.98	-0.93	-0.90	-0.88	-0.93	-0.98	-1.04	-1.07	-0.90	-0.83	-0.98	-0.85	-0.87	-0.83	-0.85	-0.97
1981		-0.60	-0.67	-0.64	-0.49	-0.52	-0.71	-0.57	-0.48	-0.79	-0.75	-0.55	-0.70	-0.67	-0.64	-0.44	-0.38
1982		-0.34	-0.43	-0.50	-0.52	-0.45	-0.32	-0.26	-0.48	-0.39	-0.43	-0.55	-0.38	-0.58	-0.61	-0.57	-0.37
1983		-0.77	-0.73	-0.46	-0.58	-0.87	-0.69	-0.76	-0.76	-0.71	-0.72	-0.68	-0.58	-0.10	-0.68	-0.62	-0.42

* Adjusted by the O.E.C.D. — * Corrigé par l'O.C.D.E.

NOTES

1. Manufacturing, electricity and gas industries.
2. From August 1983, new survey questionnaire.
3. Synthesis of several business survey series.
4. Urban areas with 10,000 or more inhabitants.
5. Average sales per working day.
6. Weighting pattern based on industrial survey of 1955 to 2nd quarter 1966, of 1967 from 3rd quarter 1966 to 1972, of 1972 from 1973 to 2nd quarter 1975, and of 1975 from 3rd quarter 1975.
7. Monthly data refer to end of period.
8. Full time jobs only.
9. Based on accident reports to the Caisse nationale suisse d'Assurances en cas d'Accidents (CNA). It is compulsory for industrial firms to insure their personnel with the CNA and report all accidents. Reports include contractual weekly hours of work, excluding overtime, at the time of the accident.
10. Compensation payments to accident victims (see note 9). If actual earnings exceed maximum insured earnings, the latter are recorded.
11. Weighting pattern based on 1948 to September 1966, on 1966 from October 1966 to September 1977, on 1977 from October 1977 to 1982 and on June 1981-June 1982 from 1983. New calculation method from 1983.
12. From 1966, banks whose balance sheets exceed 100 million francs. From December 1981, including precious metals.
13. From 1971, rate on 2-day Euro-franc loans.
14. Monthly data refer to last Friday of month.
15. To 1969, weighting pattern based on amounts outstanding at beginning of year. From 1970, current weighted. From 1979, 5 to 12 year bonds.
16. Prior to 1978, including industrial gold. From 1981, excluding industrial silver.

NOTES

1. Industries manufacturières, électricité et gaz.
2. A partir d'août 1983, nouveau questionnaire d'enquête.
3. Synthèse des résultats de plusieurs séries de l'enquête conjoncturelle.
4. Zones urbaines de 10 000 habitants ou plus.
5. Ventes moyennes par jour ouvrable.
6. La pondération a été établie d'après l'enquête industrielle de 1955 jusqu'au 2e trimestre 1966, de 1967 du 3e trimestre 1966 jusqu'en 1972, de 1972 de 1973 jusqu'au 2e trimestre 1975, et de 1975 à partir du 3e trimestre 1975.
7. Situation en fin de mois.
8. Emplois à temps complet seulement.
9. Série basée sur les déclarations d'accidents à la Caisse nationale suisse d'Assurances en cas d'Accidents (CNA). Les entreprises industrielles ont l'obligation d'inscrire leur personnel à la CNA et de déclarer tout accident à cet organisme. Les déclarations font état de la durée hebdomadaire du travail contractuelle, non compris les heures supplémentaires, au moment de l'accident.
10. Paiements compensatoires aux victimes d'accidents (voir note 9). Si les gains effectifs dépassent le salaire maximum assuré, ce dernier est pris en compte.
11. La pondération se réfère à 1948 jusqu'en septembre 1966, à 1966 d'octobre 1966 à septembre 1977, à 1977 d'octobre 1977 à 1982, et à juin 1981-juin 1982 à partir de 1983. Nouvelle méthode de calcul à partir de 1983.
12. A partir de 1966, banques dont les bilans dépassent 100 millions de francs. A partir de décembre 1981, les comptes-métal sont inclus dans les statistiques.
13. A partir de 1971, taux de prêts à 2 jours en Eurofrancs.
14. Les données mensuelles se réfèrent au dernier vendredi du mois.
15. Jusqu'en 1969, pondération établie d'après le montant des obligations en circulation au début de l'année. A partir de 1970, pondération courante. A partir de 1979, obligations à terme de 5 à 12 ans.
16. Avant 1978, y compris l'or industriel. A partir de 1981, non compris l'argent industriel.

MAIN SOURCES

PRINCIPALES SOURCES

Series	Séries	Sources
Industrial production	Production industrielle	Département fédéral de l'Économie Publique *La Vie économique*
Sales and orders	Ventes et commandes	
Car registrations	Immatriculations de voitures	
Labour and wages	Main-d'œuvre et salaires	
Prices	Prix	
Share prices	Cours des actions	
Foreign trade	Commerce extérieur	
Business surveys	Enquêtes de conjoncture	Institut für Wirtschaftsforschung, Eidgnössische Technische Hochschule *Konjunkturtest*
Construction	Construction	Banque Nationale Suisse *Bulletin Mensuel*
Retail sales	Ventes au détail	
Home finance	Finances internes	
Interest rates	Taux d'intérêts	

Turkey — Turquie

TURKEY

Production: cement
thousand tons, monthly averages

Production : ciment
milliers de tonnes, moyennes mensuelles

	Year	Q.1	Q.2	Q.3	Q.4	JAN	FEB	MAR	APR	MAY	JUN	JUL	AUG	SEP	OCT	NOV	DEC
1964	245	155	284	284	256	126	123	216	277	290	284	291	276	286	297	275	155
1965	270	177	279	330	293	159	145	226	246	303	289	318	341	331	316	293	271
1966	321	240	362	364	318	172	228	320	356	380	351	381	359	352	357	298	299
1967	354	239	417	398	361	138	248	332	389	430	431	425	409	360	389	383	310
1968	394	229	467	490	392	135	224	328	426	478	496	493	507	469	467	426	284
1969	483	328	553	592	460	178	349	456	527	558	573	628	589	558	609	471	299
1970	531	334	623	672	494	269	271	462	573	664	632	650	674	693	668	514	301
1971	629	393	763	794	565	336	342	500	687	779	823	786	799	797	736	510	448
1972	702	450	862	835	560	305	362	683	839	865	883	883	838	784	760	625	594
1973	746	555	917	873	533	402	539	723	885	948	919	888	894	836	793	592	528
1974	745	510	907	871	691	361	464	706	782	963	976	899	855	859	810	799	464
1975	904	568	1074	1106	867	512	386	807	1033	1051	1139	1148	1110	1061	1077	937	586
1976	1028	716	1251	1201	945	516	650	982	1094	1319	1339	1316	1234	1052	1078	1040	718
1977	1153	958	1376	1216	1061	673	946	1255	1404	1461	1264	1414	1215	1019	1331	1098	753
1978	1279	1003	1475	1456	1181	704	927	1379	1392	1476	1556	1615	1491	1252	1440	1109	993
1979	1149	1016	1352	1301	926	885	1006	1158	1316	1388	1351	1344	1298	1261	1247	854	678
1980	1073	556	1334	1326	1075	255	521	893	1157	1381	1464	1367	1215	1396	1271	1175	780
1981	1253	721	1539	1491	1262	550	644	970	1408	1613	1596	1468	1441	1565	1472	1192	1122
1982	1315	1148	1434	1428	1200	1015	1000	1428	1507	1484	1460	1313	1488	1484	1442	1261	897
1983	1133	627	1465	1351	1038	415	514	952	1308	1611	1476	1217	1452	1384	1339	1057	867

Production: crude steel
thousand tons, monthly averages

Production : acier brut
milliers de tonnes, moyennes mensuelles

	Year	Q.1	Q.2	Q.3	Q.4	JAN	FEB	MAR	APR	MAY	JUN	JUL	AUG	SEP	OCT	NOV	DEC
1964																	
1965																	
1966																	
1967																	
1968																	
1969																	
1970																	
1971																	
1972																	
1973																	
1974	133	135	135	122	137	131	131	143	135	131	140	133	133	101	138	137	137
1975	142	136	133	150	149	140	129	139	112	148	138	146	152	153	155	148	143
1976	155	151	153	149	167	158	145	150	144	154	162	155	146	145	169	166	165
1977	155	155	161	153	152	155	144	167	158	170	156	151	160	148	185	134	137
1978	189	169	210	182	195	139	135	232	222	214	193	189	187	171	202	202	180
1979	203	218	199	194	201	200	215	240	196	208	193	198	200	184	200	197	207
1980	201	190	201	184	228	199	176	195	192	200	212	152	183	218	236	220	227
1981	201	212	204	176	209	189	200	247	194	205	213	176	160	197	202	200	226
1982	233	214	236	235	246	227	200	215	226	238	244	230	244	232	235	259	245
1983	295	287	288	282	322	293	272	297	305	288	272	300	279	268	316	306	345

Construction permits issued: total (1)
thousand square metres, monthly averages

Permis de construire délivrés : total (1)
milliers de mètres carrés, moyennes mensuelles

	Year	Q.1	Q.2	Q.3	Q.4	JAN	FEB	MAR	APR	MAY	JUN	JUL	AUG	SEP	OCT	NOV	DEC
1964	708	413	973	813	632	388	285	565	707	1059	1152	952	757	729	654	683	560
1965	909	539	1287	1120	690	371	434	812	938	1253	1669	1262	1047	1051	728	641	700
1966	1047	724	1359	1212	892	357	715	1091	1116	1370	1592	1259	1178	1129	974	927	774
1967	1061	577	1454	1339	873	411	579	740	1177	1645	1540	1213	1508	1297	1067	911	641
1968	1198	689	1301	1375	929	419	693	955	1720	2019	1673	1448	1440	1236	1063	953	772
1969	1430	839	1907	1739	1234	652	666	1200	1579	1910	2233	1897	1632	1688	1422	1137	1143
1970	1645	1332	2404	1508	1288	1192	1141	1813	2238	2172	2803	2131	1247	1145	994	958	1912
1971	1409	1019	1644	1557	1417	807	869	1380	1425	1633	1875	1472	1393	1806	1420	1378	1453
1972	1603	1218	2122	1888	1295	741	1007	1605	2101	2256	2010	1872	1825	1967	1435	1029	1421
1973	2041	1331	2494	2562	1777	1049	1194	1751	2379	2393	2709	2713	2717	2255	1872	1424	2036
1974	1696	1051	2160	1907	1434	875	1151	1126	2031	2237	2211	2082	1725	1914	1483	1378	1441
1975	1946	1380	2373	2392	1635	1175	1246	1718	2458	2054	2606	2538	2223	2414	1402	1820	1683
1976	2426	1618	2924	3003	2328	1253	1358	2242	2977	2736	3058	2521	3617	2871	2298	2899	1787
1977	2407	2003	3032	2314	2279	1272	1698	3038	3363	2934	2799	2174	2516	2252	1985	1985	2868
1978	2686	2199	3406	2835	2306	1629	1918	3049	2925	3666	3627	3094	2893	2517	2592	1745	2582
1979	2837	3169	3169	2702	2309	2450	3159	3887	3089	3352	3067	2747	2370	2988	2630	2036	2262
1980	2331	2186	2550	2271	2317	1849	2547	2163	2354	2504	2791	2526	1916	2371	2080	1593	2876
1981	1657	1339	2054	1621	1624	1357	1272	1388	1934	2149	2079	1782	1482	1600	1234	1703	1905
1982	1811	1218	2063	1791	2172	900	1033	1720	1926	2157	2115	1672	1946	1754	1720	1582	3213
1983	2112	1176	2311	2346	2616	975	1142	1411	1968	2387	2578	2135	2620	2282	2415	2321	3114

Construction permits issued: (1) residential

thousand square metres, monthly averages

Permis de construire délivrés : (1) bâtiments résidentiels

milliers de mètres carrés, moyennes mensuelles

	Year	Q.1	Q.2	Q.3	Q.4	JAN	FEB	MAR	APR	MAY	JUN	JUL	AUG	SEP	OCT	NOV	DEC
1964	507	277	729	600	421	245	169	418	555	732	899	702	560	537	462	473	328
1965	666	385	937	854	489	285	246	625	708	955	1148	578	772	811	556	457	454
1966	751	521	1016	850	591	255	494	813	818	1023	1208	868	843	838	689	638	445
1967	803	405	1157	1023	626	300	383	532	950	1299	1222	948	1134	987	820	631	428
1968	880	478	1380	1031	631	279	460	696	1303	1544	1292	1090	1083	921	756	648	490
1969	1078	642	1498	1254	917	507	499	919	1232	1483	1780	1412	1205	1145	1074	848	830
1970	1272	1022	1861	1192	1011	860	878	1328	1755	1694	2135	1669	1028	879	828	802	1403
1971	1175	854	1365	1322	1154	704	756	1102	1194	1350	1552	1290	1185	1492	1094	1170	1199
1972	1327	920	1809	1545	1045	594	838	1327	1790	1949	1687	1601	1441	1592	1206	807	1122
1973	1609	1077	2029	2044	1283	868	922	1441	2046	2015	2026	2123	2315	1694	1467	1079	1304
1974	1281	802	1730	1490	1101	675	891	839	1662	1734	1795	1697	1327	1445	1172	1089	1041
1975	1516	1077	1908	1871	1210	893	963	1375	1999	1676	2048	2000	1775	1838	1076	1342	1212
1976	1866	1284	2146	2243	1791	1010	1047	1796	1962	2088	2387	1968	2786	1976	1769	2250	1355
1977	1859	1538	2374	1806	1719	971	1364	2278	2653	2314	2156	1724	1956	1738	2301	895	1960
1978	2096	1773	2694	2159	1757	1302	1507	2511	2289	2908	2885	2422	2226	1829	1981	1324	1967
1979	2228	2602	2482	2032	1792	2056	2620	3129	2466	2626	2353	2204	1935	1956	1921	1669	1786
1980	1836	1725	2076	1790	1752	1498	2019	1657	1817	1987	2423	1953	1528	1889	1535	1478	2245
1981	1288	1029	1606	1264	1253	978	1016	1093	1467	1727	1623	1346	1152	1295	988	1412	1359
1982	1445	948	1667	1419	1744	691	801	1351	1480	1802	1720	1310	1570	1378	1408	1223	2600
1983	1566	884	1723	1714	1943	749	871	1032	1463	1809	1897	1439	1990	1712	1816	1665	2348

Construction, buildings completed: total

thousand square metres, monthly averages

Construction, bâtiments achevés : total

milliers de mètres carrés, moyennes mensuelles

	Year	Q.1	Q.2	Q.3	Q.4	JAN	FEB	MAR	APR	MAY	JUN	JUL	AUG	SEP	OCT	NOV	DEC
1964	155																
1965	343																
1966	447																
1967	522																
1968	672	570	612	700	805	663	595	452	598	629	610	724	619	758	885	804	727
1969	669	571	578	776	751	797	352	565	525	577	631	781	740	806	701	702	851
1970	674	624	673	642	759	787	388	696	577	663	779	709	596	620	700	529	1048
1971	672	542	635	737	774	506	497	624	544	666	696	798	552	861	639	716	968
1972	806	588	672	939	1027	581	590	594	616	603	796	879	887	1051	1127	956	989
1973	907	779	839	986	1021	746	791	801	739	818	961	921	1036	1001	824	1091	1149
1974	817	623	793	959	896	599	600	669	765	801	812	507	938	1031	883	891	913
1975	964	773	831	1179	1074	822	798	700	804	742	946	1204	1014	1318	995	1158	1070
1976	1023	875	912	1113	1191	860	886	880	822	883	1032	1071	1343	924	1259	1317	997
1977	1180	1082	1183	1212	1243	1073	1091	1081	1086	1131	1282	1139	1433	1063	1112	1061	1557
1978	1245	1151	1166	1245	1416	1097	1032	1323	1208	1119	1172	1326	1271	1138	1422	1102	1724
1979	1301	1302	1204	1351	1353	1311	1311	1283	1150	1268	1193	1461	1257	1336	1363	1145	1550
1980	1442	1379	1111	1295	1980	1236	1715	1187	1022	1036	1276	1494	1090	1303	1282	1734	2925
1981	1289	1393	1056	1224	1484	1676	1440	1061	986	1023	1159	1275	1169	1228	1192	1605	1655
1982	1329	1060	1066	1257	1799	1196	902	1081	1066	1040	1094	1156	1367	1249	1424	1603	2368
1983	1317	1014	1286	1287	1709	1082	927	1032	973	1322	1563	1187	1495	1179	1585	1780	1761

Construction, buildings completed: residential

thousand square metres, monthly averages

Construction, bâtiments achevés : bâtiments résidentiels

milliers de mètres carrés, moyennes mensuelles

	Year	Q.1	Q.2	Q.3	Q.4	JAN	FEB	MAR	APR	MAY	JUN	JUL	AUG	SEP	OCT	NOV	DEC
1964	121																
1965	266																
1966	341																
1967	414																
1968	495	376	476	547	580	435	373	320	432	495	500	597	443	601	504	618	518
1969	515	402	447	618	595	511	258	438	424	422	496	590	605	658	571	565	650
1970	542	477	540	519	631	598	296	538	455	532	633	561	482	513	554	430	908
1971	555	446	518	613	643	435	401	501	430	551	574	650	463	725	556	619	754
1972	678	473	564	819	855	465	469	484	502	520	670	757	795	905	986	734	845
1973	746	628	706	823	825	596	639	650	601	693	825	758	856	855	685	902	838
1974	667	507	619	799	725	492	478	552	608	602	646	761	786	850	754	711	711
1975	783	621	681	966	865	669	612	582	644	616	783	1000	842	1057	771	980	843
1976	816	678	742	897	947	689	680	665	687	713	827	853	1070	767	1025	1025	791
1977	956	847	966	996	1013	863	776	903	878	947	1072	948	1191	849	867	895	1277
1978	994	925	937	1000	1115	914	810	1051	929	914	968	1035	1044	920	1118	882	1346
1979	1038	1011	964	1119	1062	1038	1005	989	892	1019	980	1205	1049	1099	1059	963	1164
1980	1155	1205	875	1063	1576	1003	1334	976	822	802	1001	1214	925	1049	1032	1339	2356
1981	1012	1063	806	1002	1176	1255	1131	802	769	760	890	1021	980	1005	977	1281	1270
1982	1013	812	852	1012	1377	933	689	815	857	809	891	886	1128	1023	999	1236	1895
1983	1014	805	970	1031	1271	838	723	853	747	1014	1149	945	1190	958	1292	1267	1255

TURKEY

Employment: insured wage earners
thousands

Emploi : ouvriers assurés
milliers

	Year	Q.1	Q.2	Q.3	Q.4	JAN	FEB	MAR	APR	MAY	JUN	JUL	AUG	SEP	OCT	NOV	DEC
1964	670	600	692	774	614	583	587	629	649	714	713	838	718	765	681	717	445
1965	801	617	835	932	819	655	605	590	666	888	951	501	976	920	851	836	771
1966	872	816	811	965	890	771	868	809	758	825	850	517	986	992	972	932	789
1967	905	831	883	993	915	837	848	808	856	887	905	561	997	1020	1018	982	745
1968	1021	887	955	1182	1059	890	918	853	931	942	992	1148	1192	1206	1167	1104	906
1969	1139	969	1184	1279	1124	976	951	981	1117	1181	1253	1300	1275	1262	1239	1163	969
1970	1101	1012	1093	1213	1082	1021	1010	1005	1080	1093	1120	1170	1153	1316	1088	1093	1064
1971	1193	1046	1173	1298	1251	1035	1088	1014	1102	1189	1243	1245	1337	1312	1275	1266	1211
1972	1330	1222	1308	1394	1397	1233	1209	1223	1278	1333	1314	1378	1394	1409	1400	1388	1402
1973	1459	1355	1427	1543	1508	1359	1364	1343	1377	1452	1453	1492	1489	1649	1540	1461	1524
1974	1548	1460	1528	1631	1573	1404	1483	1492	1499	1566	1518	1589	1638	1667	1607	1573	1540
1975	1638	1520	1652	1702	1679	1525	1488	1548	1620	1654	1692	1678	1687	1741	1659	1669	1708
1976	1733	1624	1679	1826	1802	1619	1611	1643	1642	1681	1714	1769	1838	1871	1785	1826	1794
1977	1819	1732	1743	1890	1911	1752	1707	1738	1784	1719	1725	1503	1804	1962	1921	1958	1854
1978	1861	1816	1851	1844	1934	1939	1758	1752	1812	1828	1913	1797	1879	1856	1939	1946	1918
1979	1791	1752	1808	1799	1814	1832	1731	1692	1765	1787	1873	1734	1860	1776	1819	1842	1781
1980	1797	1708	1809	1840	1831	1622	1723	1780	1808	1737	1882	1803	1860	1858	1907	1858	1727
1981	1874	1775	1835	1950	1937	1620	1765	1939	1885	1921	1698	1878	1949	2024	2026	1910	1874
1982	1951	1896	1867	1955	2084	1997	1859	1833	1837	1843	1922	1927	1947	1992	2090	2058	2105
1983		1716	1907	2168		1439	1792	1918	1851	1918	1952	2126	2151	2226	2245	2149	

Unemployment (registered unemployed) (2)
thousands

Chômage (chômeurs inscrits) (2)
milliers

	Year	Q.1	Q.2	Q.3	Q.4	JAN	FEB	MAR	APR	MAY	JUN	JUL	AUG	SEP	OCT	NOV	DEC
1964	23.5	22.3	27.5	24.3	19.8	20.4	18.2	28.3	24.7	26.4	31.5	24.5	26.6	21.8	21.0	19.9	18.5
1965	22.5	23.2	23.5	21.7	21.7	18.0	19.8	31.7	22.6	25.5	22.5	22.1	21.1	22.0	19.7	22.4	22.9
1966	24.3	25.7	25.1	24.6	21.8	21.3	26.4	29.4	26.3	24.6	24.5	20.7	21.7	31.3	21.6	22.6	21.1
1967	26.8	26.4	31.7	26.0	23.1	22.1	26.5	30.5	36.1	31.5	27.6	27.3	24.7	26.1	25.5	24.0	19.7
1968	33.1	32.2	37.6	31.3	31.1	26.7	32.8	37.2	41.7	37.2	33.8	34.4	28.7	30.8	32.5	30.7	30.2
1969	39.0	47.2	42.9	32.5	33.6	43.2	40.0	58.3	45.9	41.4	37.3	33.6	29.7	34.2	33.8	33.0	34.0
1970	43.8	47.0	52.0	38.6	37.5	40.0	38.1	62.8	58.1	49.9	48.1	38.8	38.0	39.1	37.9	35.3	39.2
1971	45.0	51.0	50.2	40.0	38.6	45.9	45.1	62.1	53.6	50.9	46.1	42.6	37.9	39.5	36.5	37.8	41.5
1972	43.9	48.3	48.9	40.1	38.2	38.9	46.6	59.5	52.2	47.6	46.8	41.1	40.2	39.1	36.1	37.2	41.4
1973	44.8	50.1	48.0	40.3	40.7	40.9	49.7	59.7	53.1	48.4	42.5	40.3	39.6	40.9	35.5	42.3	44.3
1974	81.8	55.3	85.7	87.9	93.2	47.7	52.9	65.3	78.0	89.4	89.6	86.7	85.6	91.3	92.3	105.0	97.2
1975	116.8	115.8	127.7	110.8	112.8	106.1	110.9	130.3	133.1	130.4	119.5	109.7	113.7	109.1	106.7	114.7	116.9
1976	141.3	136.3	159.4	137.9	131.4	121.7	131.6	155.5	162.5	162.5	153.3	145.2	138.9	129.7	127.1	131.1	136.1
1977	142.6	152.6	158.2	133.5	126.2	141.8	149.1	166.8	172.4	160.1	142.2	134.4	133.4	132.8	126.3	121.0	131.4
1978	..	163.3	184.4	165.9	..	142.4	163.7	183.7	184.7	188.9	179.6	172.5	165.9	159.4	155.0	..	..
1979	170.7	163.2	180.4	158.1	181.1	150.8	158.1	180.6	185.3	186.2	169.7	163.9	151.6	158.8	169.0	184.7	189.5
1980	256.4	226.1	278.3	259.4	251.6	201.9	220.8	255.7	271.5	280.5	282.8	281.0	278.3	248.9	244.8	246.6	263.4
1981	267.0	248.2	240.0	262.4	317.6	250.6	248.9	245.0	241.6	233.3	245.0	248.0	260.7	278.4	294.5	317.0	341.3
1982	425.7	385.8	427.8	434.1	455.0	361.3	384.5	411.5	425.3	430.6	427.6	428.3	436.5	437.4	444.4	452.1	468.6
1983	549.1	504.2	530.7	553.7	607.6	486.3	502.2	524.2	529.0	527.4	535.8	538.4	553.6	569.1	587.7	608.9	626.2

Jobs vacant, new vacancies
thousands

Offres d'emploi nouvelles
milliers

	Year	Q.1	Q.2	Q.3	Q.4	JAN	FEB	MAR	APR	MAY	JUN	JUL	AUG	SEP	OCT	NOV	DEC
1964	28.8	15.7	39.3	39.6	20.9	13.6	13.3	20.2	31.0	45.5	41.3	26.7	35.6	56.4	27.1	20.3	15.1
1965	23.2	12.8	28.5	31.7	20.0	11.5	8.9	17.9	17.5	28.0	39.8	26.9	26.7	41.4	27.0	18.7	14.4
1966	23.8	12.2	28.3	34.1	20.2	9.3	12.0	15.3	21.8	30.9	33.6	22.1	30.8	49.5	27.2	20.7	12.7
1967	25.4	11.9	29.8	31.6	28.5	8.9	11.1	15.8	25.9	31.3	32.1	25.5	27.1	42.1	49.7	23.6	12.1
1968	30.5	13.5	36.7	42.1	29.6	10.1	12.5	18.0	28.9	46.6	34.5	33.6	42.3	50.6	44.5	29.5	14.8
1969	30.6	15.3	39.5	41.6	26.8	13.0	10.4	22.6	27.2	47.1	41.3	25.9	36.7	58.3	40.1	24.8	15.4
1970	28.9	17.7	37.0	38.0	22.9	14.7	13.2	25.2	33.9	42.2	34.8	29.0	43.5	41.5	32.5	21.0	15.2
1971	32.3	18.3	36.9	50.7	23.3	13.6	12.3	29.0	26.2	46.9	37.7	27.7	39.2	85.3	34.0	20.4	15.6
1972	35.3	15.5	41.1	53.2	31.6	10.5	13.9	22.1	31.8	51.1	40.2	25.6	40.0	93.7	45.7	29.0	20.1
1973	34.2	16.1	40.6	47.7	32.2	11.8	14.2	22.4	30.3	51.2	40.5	26.1	37.6	79.5	41.9	36.3	18.2
1974	35.3	17.4	45.1	48.6	30.3	13.8	15.2	23.2	34.7	54.8	45.7	27.2	39.2	79.3	43.1	33.1	14.8
1975	29.7	17.4	37.5	41.0	23.0	13.9	13.5	24.7	34.5	39.5	38.6	27.6	35.7	59.7	31.6	20.7	16.8
1976	34.3	19.4	45.0	44.6	28.2	15.8	16.8	25.7	36.3	48.8	49.9	34.4	37.8	61.4	38.6	25.5	20.5
1977	33.8	20.9	45.2	42.6	26.3	16.4	19.7	26.6	36.0	51.5	48.2	31.5	32.8	63.6	38.9	24.4	15.7
1978	26.5	14.1	32.8	36.5	22.5	11.7	11.6	19.0	22.1	36.4	40.1	25.5	27.3	56.8	31.9	22.4	13.3
1979	19.6	12.7	28.9	25.4	11.3	10.3	10.4	17.3	22.2	34.5	30.2	18.0	17.7	40.6	16.8	11.0	6.2
1980	15.0	6.1	19.3	21.5	12.9	4.5	5.2	8.5	12.5	22.9	22.4	15.2	11.4	38.0	22.5	10.7	5.6
1981	16.8	6.8	23.4	24.4	12.5	5.1	5.4	10.0	13.3	27.3	29.5	16.8	16.9	39.6	18.7	10.4	8.4
1982	15.8	9.8	22.6	19.7	10.9	6.9	9.6	12.8	17.8	28.8	21.2	13.1	14.5	31.5	13.1	11.4	8.2
1983	15.7	9.8	24.1	18.5	14.4	6.5	8.4	14.4	19.3	32.4	20.5	10.8	14.4	30.6	19.3	13.1	10.6

Workers abroad: new emigrations

thousands

Ouvriers à l'étranger : nouveaux émigrants

milliers

	Year	Q.1	Q.2	Q.3	Q.4	JAN	FEB	MAR	APR	MAY	JUN	JUL	AUG	SEP	OCT	NOV	DEC
1964																	
1965	51.7	14.2	11.4	14.3	11.9	4.2	3.7	6.3	3.9	3.6	3.9	5.1	4.3	4.9	5.9	4.3	1.7
1966	33.1	9.4	10.0	11.2	2.5	2.4	2.4	4.6	3.1	3.9	2.9	3.6	3.2	4.5	1.0	1.0	0.5
1967	10.7	1.2	3.5	2.8	3.2	0.5	0.2	0.5	0.5	2.4	0.6	0.5	1.2	1.2	1.4	1.3	0.5
1968	43.2	3.0	7.3	15.0	18.0	0.7	1.1	1.2	2.4	2.6	2.4	5.0	4.5	5.5	8.0	7.3	2.7
1969	104.4	18.3	23.1	36.2	26.8	5.1	6.6	6.7	6.5	8.2	8.4	10.7	11.6	13.9	12.1	10.8	3.8
1970	124.9	23.2	39.2	38.5	23.9	6.4	6.5	10.3	14.2	11.6	13.5	13.4	12.0	13.1	9.5	8.7	5.8
1971	88.4	21.0	25.0	28.2	14.3	7.3	4.7	9.0	8.7	6.9	9.3	10.0	8.3	9.9	6.5	4.9	3.0
1972	85.2	12.2	21.1	21.7	30.2	2.3	4.3	5.6	6.8	5.8	8.6	7.4	8.3	6.0	10.2	10.9	9.1
1973	135.8	22.6	42.6	45.0	25.7	5.1	8.4	9.1	15.9	12.7	14.1	15.5	15.0	14.6	13.0	8.2	4.6
1974	20.2	7.4	6.7	4.6	1.5	2.6	2.6	2.3	2.2	2.5	2.0	1.8	1.5	1.3	0.7	0.5	0.3
1975	4.4	1.0	1.0	0.9	1.6	0.3	0.4	0.3	0.3	0.3	0.3	0.3	0.3	0.3	0.3	0.6	0.7
1976	10.6	2.1	1.6	3.0	3.9	0.7	0.4	0.9	0.6	0.3	0.7	0.5	1.1	1.4	0.8	1.6	1.5
1977	19.1	4.1	3.8	3.9	7.3	1.2	1.4	1.5	1.6	1.3	1.0	1.6	1.6	0.7	2.3	3.0	2.0
1978	18.9	4.9	5.0	4.3	4.7	1.7	1.4	1.8	1.5	1.9	1.7	1.5	1.6	1.3	1.4	1.5	1.8
1979	23.6	4.5	6.1	6.6	6.5	1.5	1.4	1.7	1.8	2.4	1.8	1.9	2.0	2.7	2.4	2.0	2.1
1980	28.5	6.2	6.5	7.7	8.1	2.5	1.8	1.9	2.7	1.7	2.2	3.1	2.1	2.6	2.0	3.0	3.1
1981	58.8	9.4	13.1	17.0	19.2	3.2	2.9	3.3	4.2	4.0	5.0	5.1	5.4	6.5	7.2	5.6	6.5
1982	49.4	17.7	7.2	9.5	15.1	5.3	6.1	6.3	3.2	2.1	1.9	1.9	4.1	3.5	4.3	5.2	5.7
1983		14.9				5.2	4.7	5.0	5.0								

Unemployment (registered unemployed) (2)

thousands

Adjusted - Corrigé *

Chômage (chômeurs inscrits) (2)

milliers

	Year	Q.1	Q.2	Q.3	Q.4	JAN	FEB	MAR	APR	MAY	JUN	JUL	AUG	SEP	OCT	NOV	DEC
1964		22.6	24.3	25.1	22.0	23.6	20.5	23.7	20.4	23.9	28.6	24.3	27.5	23.2	23.0	21.7	21.4
1965		22.8	20.7	22.7	24.5	20.7	21.5	26.3	18.6	22.8	20.7	22.2	22.3	23.5	21.9	24.8	26.8
1966		25.3	22.0	26.1	24.9	24.3	27.4	24.1	21.2	21.7	23.1	21.0	23.6	33.6	24.3	25.6	24.9
1967		25.4	27.5	28.0	26.7	24.8	26.6	24.7	28.4	27.7	26.3	28.0	27.8	28.3	23.9	27.8	23.4
1968		30.4	32.5	34.2	36.3	29.4	32.2	29.5	32.3	32.7	32.5	35.5	33.3	33.9	37.1	36.3	35.7
1969		43.6	37.0	36.0	39.3	46.7	39.0	45.1	38.6	36.5	35.8	34.5	34.9	38.1	38.9	39.5	39.6
1970		42.4	45.3	42.9	43.7	42.8	37.1	47.5	45.5	44.2	46.3	40.6	44.4	43.7	44.3	42.1	44.6
1971		46.5	44.1	44.1	44.6	49.1	44.0	46.5	43.0	45.3	44.0	44.8	43.6	44.0	43.1	44.5	46.2
1972		44.1	43.3	43.9	43.7	41.7	45.8	44.9	42.9	42.4	44.6	43.3	45.1	43.2	42.7	42.9	45.5
1973		46.6	42.6	43.5	46.0	44.1	49.4	46.3	44.5	42.9	40.3	42.1	43.3	45.0	41.7	47.9	48.5
1974		52.2	76.6	93.8	110.3	51.4	53.0	52.4	66.0	78.8	85.1	89.8	91.9	99.8	107.5	116.9	106.6
1975		111.4	113.4	117.6	126.1	113.8	112.0	108.2	113.0	114.4	113.0	112.7	120.7	119.2	123.1	126.7	128.6
1976		131.6	141.9	145.8	146.3	129.3	132.7	132.7	138.0	142.4	145.5	146.5	146.1	142.8	144.3	144.7	149.9
1977		148.6	141.9	140.7	138.2	150.1	150.2	145.4	149.1	140.9	135.6	136.3	139.4	146.3	141.1	131.3	142.2
1978		159.1	167.2	173.9	..	150.0	164.4	162.8	161.6	167.6	172.3	174.2	172.6	174.9	171.1	..	..
1979		159.6	165.2	164.9	194.0	157.9	158.4	162.6	165.1	167.4	163.0	164.4	157.3	173.0	184.4	196.7	200.8
1980		221.3	257.4	279.8	267.3	209.7	220.6	233.7	245.6	254.6	272.0	281.7	288.3	269.4	264.6	260.5	276.9
1981		244.6	223.4	272.6	335.9	258.8	248.2	226.8	221.2	213.7	235.3	247.8	269.5	300.5	316.9	333.6	357.1
1982		379.4	399.6	449.8	480.4	371.7	382.8	383.7	391.5	396.4	410.8	427.3	450.7	471.4	477.2	474.9	489.2
1983		456.5	496.7	573.6	640.4	499.3	499.5	490.6	488.4	486.8	514.8	536.3	571.3	613.3	629.9	638.3	653.0

Jobs vacant, new vacancies

thousands

Adjusted - Corrigé *

Offres d'emploi nouvelles

milliers

	Year	Q.1	Q.2	Q.3	Q.4	JAN	FEB	MAR	APR	MAY	JUN	JUL	AUG	SEP	OCT	NOV	DEC
1964		30.0	31.8	28.1	25.6	31.7	31.7	26.7	34.9	34.8	25.8	25.0	29.8	29.4	25.2	25.9	25.8
1965		24.4	22.2	23.1	24.1	26.7	20.4	26.0	19.6	20.9	26.3	26.7	21.6	21.0	24.5	22.9	24.7
1966		23.8	23.6	24.8	22.7	22.5	26.9	22.0	23.6	24.6	22.7	21.3	26.3	27.0	19.5	24.6	24.1
1967		23.9	24.8	23.6	28.3	23.6	23.6	24.5	26.2	22.8	25.2	25.3	21.9	23.7	33.4	26.3	25.2
1968		27.9	29.6	32.5	31.7	26.4	30.5	26.8	29.5	32.0	27.3	32.8	35.2	29.7	29.2	34.1	31.8
1969		29.8	30.7	30.4	30.7	31.4	26.4	31.6	27.5	31.1	33.5	29.1	26.9	35.1	31.2	30.0	30.9
1970		32.3	31.1	28.0	29.0	32.7	33.7	30.5	36.4	28.7	28.1	30.6	33.0	20.5	27.7	29.0	30.1
1971		32.2	30.6	33.5	28.7	32.2	28.9	35.6	27.2	32.2	32.4	32.3	30.6	37.8	29.1	27.7	29.3
1972		29.8	34.8	35.1	37.6	27.7	32.9	28.8	35.6	34.3	34.5	33.1	35.1	37.2	38.9	35.3	38.7
1973		33.8	33.0	34.1	36.7	34.0	33.7	33.7	31.9	33.6	33.4	34.7	34.1	33.6	34.3	39.4	36.4
1974		36.0	36.1	34.4	34.9	36.8	37.3	33.8	34.9	37.5	35.9	32.8	34.3	36.2	37.2	37.5	30.2
1975		32.4	29.7	30.5	28.9	32.6	30.4	34.1	32.9	27.6	28.5	30.6	31.4	29.7	28.0	26.3	32.5
1976		34.3	34.8	34.1	34.9	34.8	34.4	33.6	33.9	34.7	36.0	36.0	34.3	31.9	33.7	34.1	36.8
1977		37.0	35.4	32.3	30.6	35.9	39.5	35.5	36.9	36.1	33.2	32.7	31.7	32.4	32.5	31.2	28.0
1978		26.3	25.4	26.8	27.3	27.6	25.1	26.4	23.8	24.9	27.6	27.2	27.2	26.0	27.0	27.9	26.9
1979		26.0	22.6	18.3	14.3	27.3	25.5	25.3	24.9	22.8	20.0	18.4	19.2	17.3	13.6	14.7	14.7
1980		13.6	14.1	14.5	16.3	13.2	14.2	13.4	14.2	14.2	14.0	15.3	12.5	16.0	19.1	16.3	13.6
1981		14.8	17.1	17.0	17.6	15.3	13.4	15.7	15.0	16.9	19.5	16.1	18.4	16.6	15.4	16.9	20.5
1982		20.7	17.8	13.7	16.6	20.0	22.2	19.9	20.1	18.2	15.1	12.2	15.7	13.3	10.7	19.3	19.8
1983		19.9	19.2	12.8	21.4	18.6	18.9	22.1	21.8	20.7	15.2	9.9	15.6	12.9	15.6	23.0	25.6

* Adjusted by the O.E.C.D.

* Corrigé par l'O.C.D.E.

TURKEY

Wholesale prices: food and feeds (3)

1980 = 100

Prix de gros : produits alimentaires et fourrages (3)

1980 = 100

	Year	Q.1	Q.2	Q.3	Q.4	JAN	FEB	MAR	APR	MAY	JUN	JUL	AUG	SEP	OCT	NOV	DEC
1964	4.5	4.6	4.6	4.3	4.5	4.6	4.7	4.6	4.5	4.6	4.5	4.4	4.3	4.3	4.4	4.5	4.6
1965	4.9	4.8	4.9	4.9	5.1	4.8	4.8	4.8	4.8	4.9	4.9	4.8	4.9	4.9	4.9	5.2	5.3
1966	5.2	5.5	5.3	5.0	5.1	5.5	5.6	5.4	5.4	5.4	5.1	5.0	4.9	4.9	5.1	5.1	5.2
1967	5.4	5.6	5.6	5.2	5.4	5.4	5.8	5.6	5.5	5.7	5.5	5.3	5.2	5.2	5.3	5.3	5.4
1968	5.9	5.9	5.9	5.8	6.1	5.8	5.9	5.9	6.0	6.0	5.9	5.7	5.8	5.8	6.0	6.0	6.2
1969	6.3	6.3	6.3	6.2	6.4	6.3	6.3	6.4	6.4	6.4	6.2	6.2	6.2	6.2	6.2	6.3	6.5
1970	6.5	6.8	6.6	6.3	6.6	6.7	6.8	6.8	6.8	6.6	6.4	6.2	6.3	6.3	6.4	6.5	6.8
1971	7.4	7.1	7.3	7.3	7.8	7.1	7.1	7.2	7.3	7.4	7.3	7.3	7.4	7.3	7.6	7.8	8.0
1972	8.6	8.4	8.5	8.5	8.9	8.2	8.5	8.5	8.5	8.6	8.5	8.4	8.5	8.6	8.6	8.9	9.1
1973	10.3	9.6	10.0	10.3	11.4	9.1	9.9	9.9	10.0	10.1	10.0	10.1	10.3	10.5	10.9	11.1	12.1
1974	14.0	12.9	14.0	14.0	15.0	12.4	13.1	13.3	13.9	14.4	13.7	13.7	13.8	14.6	14.7	14.9	15.3
1975	16.6	16.7	16.6	16.1	16.8	16.2	16.9	17.1	16.9	16.7	16.1	16.0	16.1	16.2	16.5	16.5	17.4
1976	19.1	18.1	19.3	18.7	20.2	17.9	18.3	18.1	18.9	19.5	19.6	18.4	18.7	19.2	19.7	20.2	20.5
1977	23.3	21.4	22.5	23.1	26.2	21.1	21.4	21.6	22.2	22.4	22.7	22.6	22.8	23.7	25.0	26.1	27.4
1978	33.3	29.8	32.4	34.3	36.5	28.9	30.0	30.5	31.7	32.6	33.0	33.5	34.3	35.3	35.8	36.3	37.4
1979	49.6	41.4	46.3	52.0	58.7	39.6	41.5	43.1	44.2	46.2	48.5	50.4	52.3	53.2	55.1	59.0	61.9
1980	100.0	81.9	95.1	101.8	121.2	68.6	85.4	91.8	91.4	95.5	98.4	97.8	100.8	106.8	115.9	120.6	127.0
1981	142.2	137.2	136.6	142.6	152.5	134.9	139.6	137.1	137.2	134.9	137.9	142.0	140.7	145.1	148.7	152.8	155.8
1982	172.5	165.9	174.9	175.0	178.8	162.4	165.4	169.8	174.1	175.9	174.8	174.6	174.5	175.7	173.0	178.5	185.0
1983	218.2	198.8	206.4	220.2	251.8	196.1	199.7	200.5	202.4	204.9	211.9	215.0	218.3	227.3	236.2	250.4	269.0

Wholesale prices: intermediate goods (3)

1980 = 100

Prix de gros : biens intermédiaires (3)

1980 = 100

	Year	Q.1	Q.2	Q.3	Q.4	JAN	FEB	MAR	APR	MAY	JUN	JUL	AUG	SEP	OCT	NOV	DEC
1964	3.2	3.2	3.2	3.2	3.3	3.2	3.2	3.2	3.2	3.2	3.2	3.2	3.2	3.2	3.3	3.3	3.4
1965	3.5	3.4	3.5	3.5	3.5	3.4	3.4	3.5	3.5	3.5	3.5	3.5	3.5	3.5	3.5	3.5	3.5
1966	3.6	3.5	3.6	3.6	3.6	3.5	3.5	3.5	3.5	3.6	3.6	3.6	3.6	3.6	3.6	3.6	3.6
1967	3.8	3.7	3.8	3.8	3.9	3.6	3.7	3.8	3.8	3.8	3.8	3.8	3.8	3.8	3.8	3.9	4.0
1968	4.0	4.0	3.9	4.0	4.2	4.0	4.0	4.0	4.0	3.9	3.9	4.0	4.0	4.1	4.1	4.2	4.2
1969	4.4	4.3	4.3	4.4	4.5	4.3	4.3	4.3	4.3	4.3	4.3	4.3	4.4	4.4	4.5	4.4	4.5
1970	4.9	4.5	4.6	4.8	5.0	4.5	4.5	4.5	4.5	4.6	4.6	4.7	4.8	4.9	5.0	5.0	5.0
1971	5.8	5.3	5.4	6.1	6.4	5.1	5.3	5.4	5.4	5.4	5.5	6.1	6.1	6.2	6.3	6.5	6.5
1972	7.1	6.7	6.8	7.4	7.5	6.6	6.8	6.7	6.7	6.8	7.0	7.4	7.4	7.4	7.4	7.5	7.5
1973	8.4	7.6	8.0	8.7	9.4	7.6	7.6	7.7	7.8	7.9	8.1	8.3	8.6	9.2	9.3	9.4	9.4
1974	10.2	9.8	10.5	10.5	10.1	9.5	9.5	10.4	10.5	10.5	10.6	10.6	10.6	10.4	10.2	10.1	10.1
1975	10.2	10.0	10.2	10.1	10.4	10.0	10.0	9.9	10.2	10.2	10.2	10.2	10.1	10.2	10.3	10.4	10.5
1976	11.9	11.0	11.8	12.3	12.6	10.7	10.9	11.4	11.7	11.8	12.0	12.2	12.4	12.4	12.5	12.7	12.8
1977	15.1	13.1	14.1	15.4	17.9	13.0	13.0	13.2	13.9	14.1	14.2	14.4	14.6	17.1	17.7	17.9	18.0
1978	24.6	19.6	22.6	26.3	29.7	18.3	19.4	21.2	21.8	22.7	23.2	25.4	25.9	27.6	28.8	29.6	30.7
1979	46.6	33.4	43.6	49.9	59.4	31.6	33.1	35.4	40.8	42.8	47.1	48.2	49.6	51.9	55.4	60.4	62.5
1980	100.0	83.0	100.5	103.9	112.6	67.1	90.5	91.5	99.0	100.2	102.4	103.6	103.6	104.3	110.0	113.8	114.0
1981	131.9	117.5	124.5	139.7	145.8	116.9	117.6	118.1	118.5	121.0	134.2	136.3	139.5	143.3	144.2	145.7	147.6
1982	171.8	156.4	167.6	176.9	187.5	152.0	154.4	162.7	167.0	168.1	167.7	172.5	177.2	180.9	183.2	183.9	195.3
1983	232.7	204.6	226.5	242.9	256.7	198.7	201.4	213.8	221.5	224.1	233.8	238.7	244.2	245.9	248.4	256.3	265.3

Wholesale prices: fuel (3)

1980 = 100

Prix de gros : combustibles (3)

1980 = 100

	Year	Q.1	Q.2	Q.3	Q.4	JAN	FEB	MAR	APR	MAY	JUN	JUL	AUG	SEP	OCT	NOV	DEC
1964	2.2	2.2	2.2	2.2	2.2	2.2	2.2	2.2	2.2	2.2	2.2	2.2	2.2	2.2	2.2	2.2	2.2
1965	2.2	2.2	2.2	2.2	2.2	2.2	2.2	2.2	2.2	2.2	2.2	2.2	2.2	2.2	2.2	2.2	2.2
1966	2.2	2.2	2.2	2.2	2.3	2.2	2.2	2.2	2.2	2.2	2.2	2.2	2.3	2.3	2.3	2.3	2.3
1967	2.7	2.4	2.6	2.6	3.1	2.3	2.3	2.6	2.6	2.6	2.6	2.6	2.6	2.6	2.7	3.3	3.3
1968	3.5	3.2	3.2	3.6	4.0	3.3	3.2	3.2	3.2	3.2	3.2	3.3	3.6	3.9	4.0	4.0	4.0
1969	3.9	3.7	3.3	3.9	4.0	3.7	3.8	3.8	3.8	3.8	3.8	3.8	3.9	4.0	4.0	4.1	4.1
1970	3.9	4.0	3.8	3.8	3.9	4.1	4.1	3.8	3.7	3.8	3.8	3.8	3.8	3.9	3.9	3.9	3.9
1971	4.7	3.9	4.0	5.3	5.7	3.9	3.9	4.0	4.0	4.0	4.1	5.1	5.3	5.3	5.3	5.9	5.9
1972	6.3	5.9	5.9	6.8	6.8	5.7	6.1	5.8	5.7	5.7	6.1	6.7	6.8	6.8	6.8	6.8	6.8
1973	7.1	6.8	6.8	7.1	7.5	6.8	6.8	6.8	6.8	6.8	6.8	6.9	7.1	7.3	7.5	7.5	7.5
1974	7.7	7.5	7.5	7.7	7.9	7.5	7.5	7.5	7.5	7.5	7.5	7.7	7.7	7.7	7.9	7.9	8.0
1975	8.1	8.0	8.1	8.1	8.2	8.0	8.0	8.0	8.1	8.1	8.1	8.1	8.1	8.1	8.1	8.1	8.5
1976	8.5	8.5	8.5	8.5	8.5	8.5	8.5	8.5	8.5	8.5	8.5	8.5	8.5	8.5	8.5	8.5	8.5
1977	9.9	8.4	8.4	9.7	12.9	8.5	8.4	8.4	8.4	8.4	8.4	8.4	8.4	12.4	12.8	13.0	13.0
1978	20.7	14.6	16.5	24.0	27.8	13.0	14.9	15.8	16.3	16.3	17.0	23.7	23.7	24.6	27.5	28.0	28.0
1979	37.1	28.5	32.1	35.8	52.0	28.2	28.7	28.7	30.5	32.1	33.6	34.4	35.3	37.6	42.8	56.1	57.2
1980	100.0	82.8	101.8	102.8	112.7	63.3	91.9	93.3	100.1	102.4	102.8	102.8	102.8	102.8	109.7	114.2	114.2
1981	129.2	114.1	114.4	144.2	144.1	114.2	114.1	114.1	114.1	114.1	115.1	144.2	144.2	144.2	143.3	143.3	145.6
1982	170.9	153.6	167.2	174.5	187.2	146.8	146.8	167.2	167.2	167.2	167.2	167.2	172.7	183.6	183.6	183.6	194.3
1983	235.2	201.2	233.3	253.1	253.1	194.3	194.3	214.9	225.2	225.3	249.3	253.1	253.1	253.1	253.1	253.1	253.1

Consumer prices: all items
(Ankara)
1980 = 100

Prix à la consommation : total
(Ankara)
1980 = 100

	Year	Q.1	Q.2	Q.3	Q.4	JAN	FEB	MAR	APR	MAY	JUN	JUL	AUG	SEP	OCT	NOV	DEC
1964																	
1965																	
1966																	
1967																	
1968																	
1969	5.7		5.7	5.7	5.8				5.6	5.7	5.7	5.7	5.6	5.6	5.7	5.7	5.8
1970	6.1	5.9	5.9	6.1	6.4	5.9	5.9	6.0	6.0	6.0	5.8	5.9	6.1	6.3	6.4	6.4	6.5
1971	7.1	6.6	6.8	7.3	7.7	6.5	6.6	6.7	6.8	6.8	6.9	7.0	7.4	7.5	7.7	7.7	7.6
1972	8.0	7.8	7.8	8.0	8.5	7.7	7.8	7.8	7.9	7.7	7.7	7.9	7.9	8.3	8.5	8.5	8.5
1973	9.4	8.7	9.1	9.7	10.0	8.7	8.7	8.6	8.9	9.1	9.4	9.5	9.5	9.9	10.0	9.9	9.9
1974	11.1	10.3	10.8	11.4	11.9	10.1	10.2	10.5	10.7	10.9	10.8	11.2	11.3	11.7	12.0	11.9	11.8
1975	13.3	12.6	13.4	13.4	13.9	12.1	12.6	13.1	13.4	13.5	13.3	13.2	13.3	13.7	13.9	14.0	13.9
1976	15.4	14.5	15.1	15.5	16.3	14.3	14.3	14.9	15.2	15.2	15.0	15.1	15.4	16.0	16.3	16.3	16.4
1977	19.7	17.1	18.3	20.2	23.4	16.9	16.8	17.5	17.8	18.3	18.8	19.3	19.6	21.6	22.8	23.5	23.7
1978	29.5	25.0	28.1	31.4	33.5	24.6	24.6	25.9	27.1	28.2	29.0	30.7	31.0	32.5	33.0	33.6	33.9
1979	46.2	35.7	41.8	49.0	58.1	34.9	35.0	37.3	40.4	41.7	43.3	46.2	48.1	52.7	55.0	58.7	60.7
1980	100.0	77.8	98.7	106.7	116.8	64.5	81.8	87.2	94.0	99.6	102.5	105.3	104.4	110.4	115.9	117.0	117.5
1981	136.0	124.5	130.9	140.4	148.0	122.5	124.1	127.0	128.3	130.1	134.4	138.2	138.0	144.9	146.8	147.9	149.3
1982	172.8	159.6	169.8	176.1	185.6	154.2	159.8	164.7	168.3	170.6	170.6	173.3	174.7	180.3	183.4	184.9	188.5
1983	221.2	198.2	208.2	224.2	254.2	194.4	197.4	202.6	203.5	207.6	213.6	217.3	222.1	233.1	242.8	252.3	267.6

Consumer prices: food
(Ankara)
1980 = 100

Prix à la consommation : alimentation
(Ankara)
1980 = 100

	Year	Q.1	Q.2	Q.3	Q.4	JAN	FEB	MAR	APR	MAY	JUN	JUL	AUG	SEP	OCT	NOV	DEC
1964																	
1965																	
1966																	
1967																	
1968																	
1969	5.7		5.8	5.7	5.7				5.8	5.8	5.9	5.7	5.6	5.6	5.7	5.7	5.8
1970	6.1	6.0	5.9	6.0	6.4	5.9	6.0	6.0	6.0	6.0	5.7	5.7	6.1	6.2	6.4	6.3	6.4
1971	7.0	6.6	6.3	7.1	7.4	6.5	6.6	6.6	6.8	6.7	6.8	7.0	7.1	7.3	7.4	7.4	7.3
1972	7.7	7.6	7.4	7.8	8.2	7.4	7.7	7.7	7.6	7.2	7.2	7.6	7.7	8.1	8.2	8.1	8.2
1973	9.3	8.4	9.0	9.9	9.8	8.4	8.4	8.4	8.5	9.0	9.4	9.8	9.8	10.0	10.0	9.7	9.7
1974	11.0	10.0	10.6	11.5	12.1	9.9	9.9	10.1	10.4	10.8	10.5	11.2	11.5	11.9	12.3	12.1	11.8
1975	14.4	13.5	14.4	14.4	15.1	12.4	13.9	14.1	14.5	14.6	14.2	14.0	14.5	14.8	15.2	15.1	14.9
1976	16.9	16.0	16.5	17.1	18.0	15.6	16.1	16.4	16.8	16.6	16.2	16.3	17.3	17.6	18.1	18.1	17.9
1977	22.1	18.8	20.6	23.3	25.7	18.4	18.8	19.3	19.6	20.6	21.5	22.3	23.3	24.2	25.5	26.0	25.7
1978	32.0	27.5	30.6	34.3	35.4	26.9	27.3	28.3	29.9	31.6	30.1	33.5	34.9	34.6	35.2	35.4	35.8
1979	48.4	38.5	44.2	52.3	58.5	37.0	38.5	40.0	42.5	44.5	45.8	49.5	53.0	54.3	58.0	57.7	59.8
1980	100.0	75.7	99.4	108.9	116.0	65.7	78.1	83.4	91.9	101.1	105.2	111.1	106.6	108.9	115.7	116.5	116.0
1981	140.7	127.4	134.3	148.1	153.1	123.9	127.9	130.4	130.4	132.3	140.0	146.0	147.0	151.5	151.7	152.9	154.6
1982	181.5	169.9	179.5	185.7	191.0	160.7	172.4	176.6	177.6	181.4	179.6	179.9	185.5	191.6	191.2	190.4	191.4
1983	235.2	209.6	221.6	239.5	270.1	202.0	211.5	215.4	216.6	221.4	226.7	229.5	238.7	250.2	255.0	266.8	288.6

TURKEY

Money supply (M1)

billion liras, end of period

Disponibilités monétaires (M1)

milliards de livres, fin de période

	Year	Q.1	Q.2	Q.3	Q.4	JAN	FEB	MAR	APR	MAY	JUN	JUL	AUG	SEP	OCT	NOV	DEC
1964																	
1965																	
1966																	
1967																	
1968																	
1969																	
1970																	
1971																	
1972																	
1973																	
1974																	
1975	117.6				117.6												117.6
1976	150.4				150.4												150.4
1977	209.1	152.0	169.9	187.3	209.1	145.6	147.2	152.0	156.9	159.6	169.9	179.5	181.4	187.3	192.6	195.7	209.1
1978	283.6	210.4	217.5	247.3	283.6	205.3	207.5	210.4	217.9	212.0	217.5	227.9	244.4	247.3	259.2	269.3	283.6
1979	444.5	305.1	350.7	376.6	444.5	282.4	290.5	305.1	317.1	337.2	350.7	348.6	361.3	376.6	428.9	413.3	444.5
1980	704.0	443.5	500.5	606.7	704.0	456.5	466.6	443.5	483.9	493.1	500.5	551.3	586.3	606.7	642.7	655.1	704.0
1981	972.0	623.2	722.1	791.7	972.0	653.0	663.5	623.2	692.8	717.4	722.1	815.8	779.9	791.7	822.5	777.8	972.0
1982	1341.9	821.4	889.2	1071.5	1341.9	837.3	860.7	821.4	891.1	879.9	889.2	985.7	1023.8	1071.5	1113.9	1099.7	1341.9
1983	1904.9	1233.4	1296.8	1382.2	1904.9	1177.1	1204.5	1233.4	1300.1	1288.3	1296.8	1395.1	1393.0	1382.2	1520.6	1573.2	1904.9

M1 plus quasi-money

billion liras, end of period

M1 plus quasi-monnaie

milliards de livres, fin de période

	Year	Q.1	Q.2	Q.3	Q.4	JAN	FEB	MAR	APR	MAY	JUN	JUL	AUG	SEP	OCT	NOV	DEC
1964																	
1965																	
1966																	
1967																	
1968																	
1969																	
1970																	
1971																	
1972																	
1973																	
1974																	
1975	166.1				166.1												166.
1976	206.6				206.6												206.6
1977	275.4	211.4	231.9	249.7	275.4	204.0	201.9	211.4	216.6	219.6	231.9	241.2	241.6	249.7	259.0	261.0	275.4
1978	383.4	282.3	295.1	334.7	383.4	274.4	273.2	282.3	292.7	288.1	295.1	307.3	319.3	334.7	347.2	360.1	383.4
1979	609.5	410.4	482.2	520.1	609.5	380.0	386.6	410.4	426.3	459.4	482.2	494.8	502.7	520.1	567.8	563.7	609.5
1980	1071.9	637.7	689.5	894.4	1071.9	625.3	633.1	637.7	665.0	680.3	689.5	813.5	845.1	894.4	959.5	977.9	1071.9
1981	2142.1	1120.3	1354.1	1567.5	2142.1	1047.6	1100.6	1120.3	1261.6	1325.8	1354.1	1525.8	1542.3	1567.5	1787.1	1839.3	2142.1
1982	3176.3	2146.9	2352.9	2647.1	3176.3	2057.3	2132.7	2146.9	2303.2	2309.7	2352.9	2458.1	2583.1	2647.1	2748.3	2804.2	3176.3
1983	3915.2	3113.4	3284.2	3357.8	3915.2	2948.4	2992.8	3113.4	3157.7	3239.3	3284.2	3334.2	3355.8	3357.8	3536.8	3611.7	3915.2

Bank credit to economy

billion liras, end of period

Crédits bancaires à l'économie

milliards de livres, fin de période

	Year	Q.1	Q.2	Q.3	Q.4	JAN	FEB	MAR	APR	MAY	JUN	JUL	AUG	SEP	OCT	NOV	DEC
1964																	
1965																	
1966																	
1967																	
1968																	
1969																	
1970																	
1971																	
1972																	
1973																	
1974																	
1975	148.7				148.7												148.7
1976	211.0				211.0												211.0
1977	277.3	219.4	240.8	256.3	277.3	206.6	212.0	219.4	226.5	232.2	240.8	243.4	248.8	256.3	262.6	266.0	277.3
1978	354.3	287.6	307.4	326.1	354.3	273.2	276.1	287.6	295.8	299.1	307.4	311.6	317.1	326.1	335.3	341.2	354.3
1979	558.0	378.6	423.8	454.5	558.0	351.4	359.3	378.6	386.9	395.1	423.8	435.2	438.3	454.5	483.6	496.6	558.0
1980	957.1	625.6	691.7	797.5	957.1	560.0	588.3	625.6	633.3	647.8	691.7	712.4	724.3	797.5	823.2	842.7	957.1
1981	1533.9	1012.3	1150.1	1332.7	1533.9	925.5	943.5	1012.3	1049.8	1105.7	1150.1	1212.0	1235.7	1332.7	1362.8	1386.4	1533.9
1982	2039.2	1581.0	1700.0	1831.3	2039.2	1502.3	1507.4	1581.0	1614.6	1608.8	1700.0	1701.2	1710.5	1831.3	1836.5	1803.0	2039.2
1983	2565.1	2048.3	2217.7	2301.5	2565.1	1968.1	1963.0	2048.3	2040.5	2061.3	2217.7	2198.3	2209.3	2301.5	2321.8	2338.1	2565.1

U.S. dollar exchange rate: spot — Taux de change du dollar É.-U : au comptant

cents par lira — cents par livre

	Year	Q.1	Q.2	Q.3	Q.4	JAN	FEB	MAR	APR	MAY	JUN	JUL	AUG	SEP	OCT	NOV	DEC
1964	11.062	11.062	11.062	11.062	11.062	11.062	11.062	11.062	11.062	11.062	11.062	11.062	11.062	11.062	11.062	11.062	11.062
1965	11.062	11.062	11.062	11.062	11.062	11.062	11.062	11.062	11.062	11.062	11.062	11.062	11.062	11.062	11.062	11.062	11.062
1966	11.062	11.062	11.062	11.062	11.062	11.062	11.062	11.062	11.062	11.062	11.062	11.062	11.062	11.062	11.062	11.062	11.062
1967	11.062	11.062	11.062	11.062	11.062	11.062	11.062	11.062	11.062	11.062	11.062	11.062	11.062	11.062	11.062	11.062	11.062
1968	11.062	11.062	11.062	11.062	11.062	11.062	11.062	11.062	11.062	11.062	11.062	11.062	11.062	11.062	11.062	11.062	11.062
1969	11.062	11.062	11.062	11.062	11.062	11.062	11.062	11.062	11.062	11.062	11.062	11.062	11.062	11.062	11.062	11.062	11.062
1970	6.700	11.062	11.062	6.700	6.700	11.062	11.062	11.062	11.062	11.062	11.062	11.062	6.700	6.700	6.700	6.700	6.700
1971	7.067	6.700	6.700	6.700	7.067	6.700	6.700	6.700	6.700	6.700	6.700	6.700	6.700	6.700	6.700	6.700	7.067
1972	7.067	7.067	7.067	7.067	7.067	7.067	7.067	7.067	7.067	7.067	7.067	7.067	7.067	7.067	7.067	7.067	7.067
1973	7.067	7.067	7.067	7.067	7.067	7.067	7.067	7.067	7.067	7.067	7.067	7.067	7.067	7.067	7.067	7.067	7.067
1974	7.148	7.067	7.334	7.148	7.148	7.067	7.067	7.067	7.067	7.334	7.334	7.334	7.334	7.148	7.148	7.148	7.148
1975	6.501	7.148	7.072	6.712	6.501	7.148	7.148	7.148	7.072	7.072	7.072	6.948	6.712	6.712	6.601	6.601	6.601
1976	6.001	6.338	6.188	6.188	6.001	6.601	6.601	6.388	6.188	6.188	6.183	6.188	6.185	6.188	6.001	6.001	6.001
1977	5.143	5.658	5.658	5.143	5.143	6.001	6.001	5.658	5.658	5.658	5.658	5.658	5.658	5.143	5.143	5.143	5.143
1978	3.960	3.960	3.960	3.960	3.960	5.143	5.143	3.960	3.960	3.960	3.960	3.960	3.960	3.960	3.960	3.960	3.960
1979	2.829	3.960	2.829	2.829	2.829	3.960	3.960	3.960	3.736	3.736	2.829	2.829	2.829	2.829	2.829	2.829	2.829
1980	1.109	1.414	1.269	1.238	1.109	1.414	1.414	1.414	1.343	1.338	1.269	1.269	1.238	1.238	1.168	1.126	1.109
1981	0.748	1.035	0.903	0.818	0.748	1.077	1.032	1.035	1.008	0.954	0.903	0.854	0.815	0.818	0.776	0.774	0.748
1982	0.535	0.676	0.604	0.566	0.535	0.708	0.691	0.676	0.670	0.655	0.604	0.590	0.579	0.566	0.556	0.541	0.535
1983	0.354	0.486	0.451	0.407	0.354	0.518	0.510	0.486	0.476	0.463	0.451	0.435	0.425	0.407	0.396	0.372	0.354

Official reserves excluding gold — Réserves officielles, or exclu

million SDR's, end of period — millions de DTS, fin de période

	Year	Q.1	Q.2	Q.3	Q.4	JAN	FEB	MAR	APR	MAY	JUN	JUL	AUG	SEP	OCT	NOV	DEC
1964	40	20	19	10	40	10	9	20	8	9	19	8	13	10	13	18	40
1965	25	16	20	16	25	19	15	16	12	16	20	11	14	16	25	14	25
1966	29	19	18	15	29	38	24	19	17	15	18	21	14	15	14	15	29
1967	22	16	20	15	22	17	14	16	15	24	20	12	11	15	14	13	22
1968	26	21	27	15	26	20	14	21	25	12	27	15	13	15	18	25	26
1969	128	12	53	80	128	29	17	12	14	26	53	45	62	80	107	121	128
1970	304	122	91	155	304	110	131	122	123	108	91	93	114	155	190	272	304
1971	582	308	316	435	582	307	333	308	256	313	316	350	387	435	484	530	582
1972	1165	751	679	932	1165	662	744	751	699	713	679	740	878	932	1002	1123	1165
1973	1632	1308	1389	1639	1632	1243	1237	1308	1299	1333	1389	1514	1635	1639	1659	1601	1632
1974	1395	1745	1673	1679	1395	1739	1717	1745	1727	1742	1673	1755	1728	1679	1620	1478	1395
1975	784	984	821	863	784	1248	1098	984	832	760	821	893	941	863	939	858	784
1976	842	654	672	790	842	756	645	654	651	716	672	668	824	790	611	614	842
1977	510	544	618	572	510	756	730	544	499	510	618	620	581	572	559	481	510
1978	640	601	634	901	640	569	574	601	751	667	634	645	772	901	818	776	640
1979	582	608	954	782	582	637	583	608	610	930	954	1016	930	782	696	612	582
1980	999	775	604	907	999	449	633	775	733	654	604	651	902	907	915	907	999
1981	1104	897	749	1290	1104	1049	991	897	920	772	749	914	1187	1290	1267	1145	1104
1982	837	1159	992	1147	837	1116	1046	1159	1117	1132	992	1072	1165	1147	1049	875	837
1983	1213	982	1079	1063	1213	984	929	982	1023	1075	1079	781	869	1063	1064	1213	1213

Imports c.i.f.

billion liras, monthly averages

Importations c.a.f.

milliards de livres, moyennes mensuelles

	Year	Q.1	Q.2	Q.3	Q.4	JAN	FEB	MAR	APR	MAY	JUN	JUL	AUG	SEP	OCT	NOV	DEC
1964	0.4	0.4	0.4	0.4	0.4	0.3	0.6	0.4	0.5	0.5	0.4	0.4	0.4	0.3	0.3	0.4	0.5
1965	0.4	0.4	0.4	0.5	0.4	0.4	0.4	0.4	0.4	0.5	0.5	0.5	0.4	0.4	0.4	0.4	0.5
1966	0.5	0.5	0.5	0.5	0.6	0.4	0.6	0.6	0.5	0.5	0.6	0.6	0.5	0.5	0.5	0.5	0.6
1967	0.5	0.5	0.5	0.6	0.5	0.4	0.5	0.5	0.6	0.5	0.5	0.4	0.6	0.6	0.5	0.5	0.6
1968	0.6	0.6	0.6	0.5	0.6	0.5	0.7	0.5	0.7	0.6	0.6	0.6	0.5	0.5	0.6	0.7	0.6
1969	0.6	0.6	0.6	0.5	0.5	0.6	0.6	0.7	0.6	0.6	0.7	0.6	0.5	0.5	0.5	0.5	0.5
1970	0.9	0.7	0.9	0.8	1.1	0.7	0.7	0.7	0.9	0.9	0.9	1.0	0.6	0.8	0.7	1.0	1.5
1971	1.5	1.4	1.6	1.5	1.4	1.5	1.4	1.5	1.6	1.5	1.8	1.8	1.2	1.4	1.3	1.2	1.6
1972	1.9	1.5	1.9	1.9	2.1	1.3	1.7	1.6	1.8	1.9	1.9	1.9	1.6	2.2	1.8	1.7	2.9
1973	2.5	2.1	2.3	2.3	3.0	1.8	1.8	2.8	2.2	2.1	2.6	2.5	1.9	2.6	2.7	3.2	3.2
1974	4.4	3.4	4.3	3.9	5.8	3.0	3.2	4.0	4.5	4.5	4.0	3.4	4.1	4.3	4.2	5.6	7.5
1975	5.8	5.5	5.9	5.6	6.0	4.9	5.2	6.5	5.6	4.5	7.7	6.1	5.2	5.5	4.9	7.3	5.7
1976	6.9	6.4	6.0	7.5	7.7	6.5	4.9	7.7	7.1	4.5	6.5	6.7	7.0	6.9	7.2	8.0	8.0
1977	8.7	8.0	9.3	9.2	8.5	9.1	6.8	8.2	10.8	6.7	10.4	7.6	11.3	8.6	7.3	6.9	11.3
1978	9.4	6.9	10.8	7.8	12.3	3.6	9.7	7.2	11.2	11.2	10.1	7.5	6.2	9.6	10.7	10.7	15.6
1979	14.9	10.2	11.2	17.5	20.7	7.1	9.9	13.4	10.0	9.1	14.6	12.0	14.6	25.8	19.0	15.8	27.2
1980	43.0	28.2	35.9	41.7	66.1	18.6	41.4	24.5	23.4	46.0	38.3	29.8	35.1	60.4	73.3	44.2	80.8
1981	83.9	72.6	73.7	84.4	104.8	70.3	82.1	65.3	63.6	78.4	79.1	88.6	80.5	83.9	83.0	104.1	127.5
1982	120.1	53.9	116.4	114.1	156.2	84.1	97.1	100.5	114.1	116.5	118.5	114.2	113.7	114.4	129.3	139.7	199.4
1983	177.6	154.0	152.0	164.6	239.8	141.1	147.5	173.3	139.4	156.3	160.3	143.1	182.3	168.4	198.1	216.4	304.8

Exports f.o.b.

billion liras, monthly averages

Exportations f.o.b.

milliards de livres, moyennes mensuelles

	Year	Q.1	Q.2	Q.3	Q.4	JAN	FEB	MAR	APR	MAY	JUN	JUL	AUG	SEP	OCT	NOV	DEC
1964	0.3	0.3	0.2	0.2	0.6	0.3	0.2	0.3	0.2	0.2	0.2	0.1	0.1	0.3	0.5	0.5	0.7
1965	0.3	0.3	0.3	0.3	0.5	0.3	0.3	0.4	0.4	0.3	0.2	0.2	0.2	0.4	0.3	0.5	0.7
1966	0.4	0.4	0.3	0.2	0.6	0.5	0.5	0.4	0.3	0.2	0.2	0.1	0.2	0.3	0.5	0.5	0.7
1967	0.4	0.4	0.3	0.3	0.6	0.5	0.4	0.4	0.4	0.3	0.2	0.2	0.2	0.3	0.5	0.7	0.7
1968	0.4	0.5	0.2	0.2	0.6	0.5	0.6	0.4	0.3	0.2	0.2	0.2	0.2	0.3	0.6	0.6	0.5
1969	0.4	0.4	0.4	0.3	0.6	0.5	0.4	0.3	0.4	0.4	0.3	0.2	0.3	0.4	0.5	0.6	0.6
1970	0.5	0.5	0.3	0.4	0.9	0.5	0.4	0.5	0.4	0.3	0.3	0.2	0.4	0.6	0.8	0.9	1.0
1971	0.8	0.8	0.5	0.5	1.3	0.8	0.8	0.8	0.5	0.4	0.4	0.4	0.5	0.7	0.8	1.2	1.8
1972	1.0	1.2	0.7	0.7	1.4	1.3	1.3	1.0	0.7	0.8	0.8	0.6	0.5	1.0	1.1	1.2	1.8
1973	1.5	1.4	1.4	1.3	2.0	1.4	1.3	1.5	1.5	1.3	1.3	1.1	1.2	1.5	2.1	1.6	2.3
1974	1.8	2.4	1.7	1.2	1.8	2.2	2.2	2.7	2.1	1.8	1.3	1.0	1.2	1.5	1.4	1.7	2.3
1975	1.7	1.6	1.2	1.7	2.0	1.6	1.7	1.6	1.1	1.1	1.5	1.4	1.7	2.0	1.6	2.0	2.5
1976	2.6	3.9	2.1	1.8	2.5	4.5	3.4	3.8	2.5	1.8	1.8	2.0	1.5	2.0	1.7	2.3	3.5
1977	2.6	2.8	2.3	1.8	3.6	3.0	2.6	2.7	2.6	2.0	2.2	1.8	1.9	1.7	2.6	3.1	5.1
1978	4.6	3.4	4.0	3.9	7.1	2.9	3.3	4.0	4.6	3.5	4.1	3.6	4.2	4.0	5.3	6.5	9.5
1979	6.3	5.5	4.8	6.7	8.3	5.4	6.2	4.9	4.8	4.3	5.3	6.3	6.8	7.0	7.1	8.7	9.0
1980	18.0	14.2	14.1	14.0	29.8	9.7	17.0	16.1	15.6	14.3	12.3	11.3	13.2	17.6	21.1	28.0	40.5
1981	44.2	31.7	31.9	41.4	71.9	36.8	29.2	29.2	30.6	30.0	35.0	35.8	40.4	48.1	60.6	70.2	84.9
1982	78.1	61.2	62.4	72.4	116.4	60.6	58.5	64.6	59.2	61.6	66.4	68.2	69.7	79.3	98.2	109.6	141.4
1983	108.3	87.2	92.3	96.1	157.4	89.5	77.8	94.2	99.3	89.3	88.3	78.4	98.9	111.1	139.1	148.6	184.6

Trade balance (f.o.b. — c.i.f.)

billion liras, monthly averages

Balance commerciale (f.o.b. — c.a.f.)

milliards de livres, moyennes mensuelles

	Year	Q.1	Q.2	Q.3	Q.4	JAN	FEB	MAR	APR	MAY	JUN	JUL	AUG	SEP	OCT	NOV	DEC
1964	-0.1	-0.2	-0.2	-0.2	0.2	-0.0	-0.3	-0.1	-0.2	-0.3	-0.2	-0.3	-0.2	-0.0	0.2	0.2	0.2
1965	-0.1	-0.1	-0.1	-0.2	0.1	-0.1	-0.1	-0.1	0.0	-0.2	-0.2	-0.2	-0.2	-0.1	-0.1	0.1	0.2
1966	-0.2	-0.1	-0.3	-0.3	0.0	0.1	-0.1	-0.2	-0.2	-0.3	-0.4	-0.5	-0.3	-0.2	-0.0	-0.1	0.1
1967	-0.1	-0.1	-0.2	-0.3	0.1	0.0	-0.1	-0.1	-0.2	-0.2	-0.3	-0.2	-0.4	-0.3	0.0	0.2	0.1
1968	-0.2	-0.1	-0.4	-0.3	-0.0	0.1	-0.1	-0.2	-0.4	-0.5	-0.4	-0.4	-0.3	-0.2	0.0	-0.0	-0.0
1969	-0.2	-0.2	-0.3	-0.2	0.0	-0.1	-0.2	-0.4	-0.1	-0.2	-0.4	-0.4	-0.2	-0.1	0.1	0.0	0.0
1970	-0.3	-0.3	-0.5	-0.4	-0.2	-0.2	-0.3	-0.2	-0.4	-0.6	-0.6	-0.7	-0.2	-0.2	0.1	-0.1	-0.5
1971	-0.7	-0.7	-1.2	-1.0	-0.1	-0.7	-0.6	-0.7	-1.1	-1.1	-1.4	-1.4	-0.7	-0.8	-0.5	0.1	0.2
1972	-0.9	-0.4	-1.1	-1.2	-0.8	-0.1	-0.4	-0.6	-1.1	-1.2	-1.2	-1.4	-1.1	-1.3	-0.7	-0.5	-1.1
1973	-0.9	-0.8	-0.9	-1.1	-1.1	-0.5	-0.4	-1.3	-0.7	-0.8	-1.3	-1.4	-0.7	-1.1	-0.6	-1.6	-1.0
1974	-2.6	-1.0	-2.6	-2.8	-4.0	-0.8	-1.0	-1.3	-2.4	-2.7	-2.7	-2.5	-3.0	-2.8	-2.8	-3.9	-5.3
1975	-4.1	-3.9	-4.7	-3.9	-3.9	-3.4	-3.5	-4.9	-4.5	-3.4	-6.2	-4.7	-3.4	-3.5	-3.4	-5.3	-3.2
1976	-4.4	-2.5	-4.0	-5.7	-5.2	-2.0	-1.5	-3.9	-4.7	-2.6	-4.7	-6.7	-5.6	-4.9	-5.5	-5.6	-4.5
1977	-6.1	-5.3	-7.0	-7.4	-4.9	-6.1	-4.3	-5.5	-8.1	-4.7	-8.2	-5.8	-9.4	-6.9	-4.7	-3.8	-6.2
1978	-4.8	-3.5	-6.8	-3.8	-5.2	-0.7	-6.5	-3.2	-6.6	-7.7	-6.1	-3.9	-2.1	-5.6	-5.3	-4.2	-6.0
1979	-8.6	-4.6	-6.4	-10.8	-12.4	-1.7	-3.7	-8.5	-5.2	-4.8	-9.3	-5.7	-7.8	-18.9	-12.0	-7.1	-18.2
1980	-24.9	-13.9	-21.8	-27.7	-36.2	-8.9	-24.5	-8.5	-7.9	-31.7	-26.0	-18.4	-21.9	-42.8	-52.2	-16.2	-40.3
1981	-39.6	-40.8	-41.8	-42.9	-32.9	-33.5	-52.9	-36.1	-33.0	-48.4	-44.1	-53.0	-40.0	-35.8	-22.4	-33.8	-42.6
1982	-42.0	-32.7	-54.0	-41.7	-39.8	-23.5	-38.7	-35.9	-54.9	-54.9	-52.1	-46.0	-44.1	-35.1	-31.2	-30.1	-58.0
1983	-69.3	-66.8	-59.7	-68.5	-82.4	-51.6	-69.7	-79.1	-40.1	-67.0	-72.0	-64.8	-83.4	-57.3	-59.0	-67.8	-120.3

Imports c.i.f. — Adjusted - Corrigé * — Importations c.a.f.

billion liras, monthly averages — milliards de livres, moyennes mensuelles

	Year	Q.1	Q.2	Q.3	Q.4	JAN	FEB	MAR	APR	MAY	JUN	JUL	AUG	SEP	OCT	NOV	DEC
1964		0.5	0.4	0.4	0.4	0.4	0.5	0.5	0.5	0.5	0.4	0.4	0.4	0.4	0.3	0.4	0.4
1965		0.4	0.4	0.4	0.4	0.5	0.4	0.5	0.4	0.4	0.5	0.4	0.5	0.4	0.4	0.5	0.5
1966		0.5	0.5	0.6	0.6	0.5	0.6	0.6	0.5	0.5	0.6	0.6	0.6	0.5	0.6	0.6	0.5
1967		0.5	0.5	0.6	0.5	0.5	0.5	0.5	0.6	0.5	0.5	0.4	0.7	0.6	0.6	0.5	0.6
1968		0.5	0.6	0.6	0.6	0.5	0.6	0.5	0.7	0.6	0.5	0.5	0.6	0.6	0.6	0.7	0.5
1969		0.6	0.6	0.5	0.5	0.6	0.6	0.6	0.5	0.5	0.6	0.5	0.6	0.5	0.6	0.6	0.5
1970		0.7	0.8	0.8	1.1	0.7	0.7	0.7	0.8	0.8	0.8	0.9	0.7	0.9	0.8	1.1	1.3
1971		1.4	1.5	1.6	1.4	1.5	1.4	1.4	1.5	1.4	1.7	1.6	1.5	1.5	1.5	1.3	1.5
1972		1.5	1.8	2.1	2.1	1.3	1.6	1.5	1.6	2.1	1.7	1.8	2.0	2.4	2.0	1.8	2.5
1973		2.1	2.2	2.5	3.0	2.0	1.9	2.4	2.1	2.2	2.4	2.5	2.3	2.6	3.1	3.1	2.6
1974		3.4	4.3	4.2	5.5	3.1	3.5	3.5	4.0	5.4	3.6	3.6	4.6	4.5	4.6	5.4	6.3
1975		5.5	5.9	6.0	5.7	5.3	5.7	5.6	5.2	5.2	7.2	6.2	6.0	5.6	5.6	6.7	4.9
1976		6.3	6.0	7.9	7.4	6.5	5.2	7.3	6.1	5.6	6.2	8.9	8.0	6.8	7.8	7.6	6.6
1977		8.1	9.2	10.1	7.6	9.6	7.0	7.7	9.7	8.3	9.4	8.7	13.6	8.0	7.1	7.3	8.5
1978		7.0	11.2	8.1	11.3	4.1	9.4	7.5	10.4	13.9	9.2	8.4	7.2	8.7	10.1	11.5	12.3
1979		10.3	11.4	18.1	13.4	8.5	8.8	13.4	10.5	10.0	13.8	14.2	18.1	21.9	17.7	17.6	20.0
1980		27.5	37.6	42.7	59.7	21.5	35.9	25.1	28.4	47.5	36.8	34.4	43.0	50.6	66.3	49.6	63.2
1981		71.8	80.5	92.2	94.2	79.4	68.7	67.3	82.6	84.0	74.9	107.9	94.9	73.8	68.0	119.9	94.9
1982		95.5	131.8	119.8	142.7	99.4	82.7	104.3	159.2	117.4	119.0	127.0	136.3	95.9	111.8	158.8	157.5
1983		151.2	172.6	178.4	215.4	157.0	126.2	170.4	204.1	159.8	153.8	169.4	225.6	140.4	163.3	259.8	223.2

Exports f.o.b. — Adjusted - Corrigé * — Exportations f.o.b.

billion liras, monthly averages — milliards de livres, moyennes mensuelles

	Year	Q.1	Q.2	Q.3	Q.4	JAN	FEB	MAR	APR	MAY	JUN	JUL	AUG	SEP	OCT	NOV	DEC
1964		0.3	0.3	0.3	0.4	0.3	0.2	0.4	0.3	0.3	0.3	0.2	0.2	0.3	0.3	0.4	0.4
1965		0.3	0.4	0.4	0.3	0.3	0.3	0.4	0.4	0.4	0.4	0.4	0.4	0.4	0.2	0.3	0.4
1966		0.4	0.3	0.3	0.4	0.4	0.4	0.4	0.4	0.3	0.3	0.3	0.4	0.3	0.4	0.3	0.4
1967		0.4	0.4	0.4	0.4	0.4	0.4	0.4	0.4	0.4	0.4	0.4	0.4	0.4	0.4	0.5	0.4
1968		0.4	0.3	0.3	0.4	0.4	0.5	0.4	0.3	0.3	0.3	0.3	0.3	0.4	0.4	0.4	0.3
1969		0.3	0.5	0.4	0.4	0.4	0.4	0.3	0.5	0.5	0.5	0.4	0.5	0.5	0.4	0.4	0.4
1970		0.4	0.5	0.6	0.7	0.4	0.4	0.5	0.5	0.4	0.4	0.4	0.6	0.7	0.6	0.7	0.7
1971		0.7	0.6	0.7	1.0	0.7	0.7	0.7	0.6	0.6	0.6	0.7	0.8	0.7	0.7	0.9	1.2
1972		1.0	0.9	0.9	1.1	1.1	1.1	0.9	0.8	1.0	1.0	1.0	0.7	1.0	1.0	1.0	1.2
1973		1.2	1.7	1.7	1.6	1.1	1.1	1.2	1.7	1.7	1.7	1.8	1.7	1.7	2.0	1.4	1.5
1974		2.0	2.0	1.5	1.5	1.9	1.8	2.4	2.2	2.2	1.7	1.4	1.6	1.6	1.4	1.6	1.5
1975		1.4	1.4	2.2	1.8	1.3	1.5	1.3	1.2	1.3	1.8	2.0	2.5	2.1	1.7	2.0	1.6
1976		3.3	2.4	2.3	2.1	3.9	2.9	3.1	2.5	2.3	2.2	2.6	2.0	2.2	2.0	2.2	2.2
1977		2.4	2.6	2.3	3.0	2.6	2.2	2.3	2.7	2.6	2.6	2.5	2.4	2.0	2.9	3.0	3.1
1978		3.0	4.6	4.9	6.0	2.6	2.9	3.5	4.8	4.2	4.8	4.5	5.4	4.7	5.8	5.9	6.2
1979		5.0	5.5	8.3	6.9	4.7	5.7	4.5	4.9	5.3	6.3	8.1	8.4	8.2	7.3	7.8	5.6
1980		13.2	16.0	16.6	24.6	8.6	15.7	15.3	16.5	16.8	14.7	14.2	16.7	18.8	22.2	25.7	25.8
1981		29.6	36.4	48.2	60.6	31.9	28.2	28.7	31.7	37.3	40.3	44.9	47.1	52.7	62.0	62.3	57.4
1982		58.0	71.3	83.1	99.3	54.7	57.7	61.7	61.6	71.2	81.0	83.5	82.8	82.9	106.7	93.1	98.1
1983		81.8	104.5	110.7	133.8	74.7	78.3	92.3	104.2	104.7	104.6	102.5	113.5	116.0	141.7	133.2	126.4

Trade balance (f.o.b. — c.i.f.) — Adjusted - Corrigé * — Balance commerciale (f.o.b. — c.a.f.)

billion liras, monthly averages — milliards de livres, moyennes mensuelles

	Year	Q.1	Q.2	Q.3	Q.4	JAN	FEB	MAR	APR	MAY	JUN	JUL	AUG	SEP	OCT	NOV	DEC
1964		-0.2	-0.1	-0.1	-0.0	-0.2	-0.3	-0.1	-0.2	-0.2	-0.1	-0.1	-0.2	-0.0	0.0	-0.0	-0.0
1965		-0.1	-0.0	-0.0	-0.1	-0.2	-0.1	-0.1	0.1	-0.0	-0.1	0.0	-0.1	-0.1	-0.2	-0.1	-0.1
1966		-0.1	-0.2	-0.2	-0.2	-0.1	-0.1	-0.2	-0.1	-0.2	-0.2	-0.3	-0.2	-0.2	-0.2	-0.2	-0.2
1967		-0.1	-0.1	-0.2	-0.1	-0.1	-0.1	-0.1	-0.2	-0.1	-0.1	0.0	-0.3	-0.3	-0.2	-0.1	-0.1
1968		-0.1	-0.3	-0.2	-0.2	-0.1	-0.1	-0.2	-0.4	-0.4	-0.2	-0.2	-0.3	-0.2	-0.2	-0.2	-0.2
1969		-0.3	-0.1	-0.1	-0.2	-0.2	-0.2	-0.3	-0.1	0.0	-0.2	-0.1	-0.2	-0.1	-0.1	-0.2	-0.2
1970		-0.3	-0.4	-0.3	-0.4	-0.3	-0.3	-0.2	-0.3	-0.4	-0.4	-0.5	-0.1	-0.2	-0.2	-0.4	-0.7
1971		-0.8	-0.9	-0.8	-0.5	-0.9	-0.7	-0.7	-0.9	-0.9	-1.0	-0.9	-0.8	-0.8	-0.8	-0.3	-0.3
1972		-0.5	-0.9	-1.1	-1.0	-0.3	-0.5	-0.6	-0.8	-1.0	-0.7	-0.9	-1.2	-1.3	-1.0	-0.7	-1.3
1973		-0.9	-0.6	-0.8	-1.3	-0.9	-0.7	-1.1	-0.4	-0.6	-0.7	-0.6	-0.6	-1.0	-1.1	-1.7	-1.2
1974		-1.3	-2.3	-2.7	-3.9	-1.2	-1.6	-1.2	-1.9	-3.2	-1.9	-2.2	-3.0	-2.9	-3.2	-3.8	-4.9
1975		-4.2	-4.4	-3.7	-4.0	-4.0	-4.2	-4.3	-4.0	-3.9	-5.4	-4.2	-3.5	-3.5	-3.9	-4.7	-3.3
1976		-3.1	-3.6	-5.6	-5.2	-2.6	-2.3	-4.2	-3.6	-3.3	-4.0	-6.2	-6.0	-4.6	-5.8	-5.4	-4.5
1977		-5.7	-6.5	-7.8	-4.6	-7.0	-4.8	-5.4	-7.0	-5.7	-6.8	-6.2	-11.2	-6.0	-4.2	-4.3	-5.4
1978		-3.9	-6.5	-3.2	-5.3	-1.4	-6.5	-3.9	-5.6	-9.7	-4.4	-3.5	-1.9	-4.0	-4.2	-5.7	-6.1
1979		-5.3	-5.9	-9.8	-11.5	-3.8	-3.1	-9.0	-5.6	-4.8	-7.5	-6.1	-9.7	-13.7	-10.4	-9.8	-14.4
1980		-14.3	-21.6	-26.1	-35.1	-12.9	-20.2	-9.8	-11.9	-30.7	-22.1	-20.2	-26.4	-31.8	-44.1	-23.9	-37.4
1981		-42.2	-44.1	-44.0	-33.7	-47.5	-40.6	-38.6	-50.9	-46.7	-34.7	-63.0	-47.8	-21.1	-6.0	-57.6	-37.5
1982		-37.5	-60.6	-36.7	-43.4	-44.7	-25.0	-42.7	-97.6	-46.2	-38.0	-43.5	-53.5	-13.0	-5.1	-65.7	-59.4
1983		-69.4	-68.1	-67.8	-81.7	-82.2	-47.8	-78.2	-99.9	-55.1	-49.3	-66.9	-112.1	-24.4	-21.7	-126.7	-96.8

* Adjusted by the O.E.C.D. — * Corrigé par l'O.C.D.E.

Balance of payments: invisible balance (4) / Balance des paiements : services et transferts, nets (4)

million dollars / millions de dollars

	Year	Q.1	Q.2	Q.3	Q.4	JAN	FEB	MAR	APR	MAY	JUN	JUL	AUG	SEP	OCT	NOV	DEC
1964																	
1965																	
1966																	
1967																	
1968	35	-5	3	26	7	1	-7	1	1	7	-0	12	8	6	2	7	-2
1969	43	6	-2	23	16	5	-1	2	2	-	-4	5	11	6	10	3	3
1970	72	12	7	-20	73	2	7	3	3	9	-5	-20	38	-38	22	25	26
1971	426	96	59	164	108	26	53	16	12	26	21	48	72	44	39	33	36
1972	654	102	92	309	152	28	37	37	21	41	30	101	127	81	50	56	46
1973	1234	177	234	513	310	69	54	54	74	80	80	220	183	110	85	84	141
1974	1499	285	343	610	261	119	82	84	80	138	124	222	232	156	86	74	101
1975	1448	317	272	556	303	161	96	60	96	82	94	187	219	150	113	82	108
1976	863	205	195	313	150	80	57	68	50	62	83	108	119	87	53	68	29
1977	613	172	164	191	86	56	57	49	37	58	70	63	77	51	10	58	19
1978	256	60	85	86	25	13	15	31	22	28	36	38	24	24	1	5	19
1979	349	61	78	65	144	32	16	13	26	36	16	22	37	7	23	49	72
1980	1795	324	310	852	309	71	159	94	87	75	148	302	299	251	111	85	112
1981	2212	408	577	1024	203	132	160	116	184	150	243	332	398	293	27	77	99
1982	1935	310	390	511	724	99	68	144	152	119	119	102	293	116	229	143	352
1983		232	1636	-826		-6	93	145	860	69	707	-1370	260	284	209	109	

Balance of payments: net capital movements (4) / Balance des paiements : mouvements de capitaux, nets (4)

million dollars / millions de dollars

	Year	Q.1	Q.2	Q.3	Q.4	JAN	FEB	MAR	APR	MAY	JUN	JUL	AUG	SEP	OCT	NOV	DEC
1964																	
1965																	
1966																	
1967																	
1968	217	43	37	58	79	27	10	7	14	22	2	19	21	18	45	30	4
1969	259	31	65	68	96	18	9	4	17	23	25	9	40	19	35	34	28
1970	385	60	43	134	148	22	17	21	28	6	9	26	71	37	58	65	25
1971	358	129	70	83	76	30	78	21	27	27	16	25	32	26	22	30	24
1972	177	34	-75	132	87	17	16	1	-67	8	-17	14	12	106	23	27	36
1973	396	92	67	103	135	24	23	44	21	40	6	39	24	39	37	14	84
1974	259	68	113	65	13	1	42	25	32	44	37	19	19	27	18	16	-20
1975	520	57	112	98	253	23	13	20	19	30	64	28	47	23	64	26	162
1976	520	85	159	123	253	26	11	48	12	7	140	5	44	73	7	26	220
1977	423	74	83	119	146	34	26	14	54	37	-7	-16	58	77	26	59	62
1978	1032	302	287	96	347	146	71	85	42	87	158	49	68	-21	-42	-6	394
1979	276	-8	-13	76	222	106	-166	52	-48	-19	54	21	9	45	6	100	116
1980	1926	918	234	456	319	231	291	396	36	155	43	105	158	193	81	113	125
1981	981	182	324	136	339	156	5	21	81	94	150	49	59	28	-15	178	175
1982	1176	535	-51	165	527	325	168	42	29	9	-88	117	119	-71	-69	30	566
1983		54	132	41		16	-2	39	-33	65	99	3	48	-10	10	177	

Balance of payments: change in official reserves (4)(5) / Balance des paiements : variation des réserves officielles (4)(5)

million dollars / millions de dollars

	Year	Q.1	Q.2	Q.3	Q.4	JAN	FEB	MAR	APR	MAY	JUN	JUL	AUG	SEP	OCT	NOV	DEC
1964																	
1965																	
1966																	
1967																	
1968	17	-24	38	8	-5	2	4	-30	24	16	-1	7	6	-6	7	-13	0
1969	-133	14	-53	-28	-66	14	-9	10	-1	-16	-36	7	-22	-13	-34	-27	-5
1970	-262	-39	39	-110	-152	-10	-14	-14	11	19	9	20	-74	-56	-48	-83	-21
1971	-380	-100	22	-72	-230	-24	-52	-25	15	0	7	19	-36	-56	-52	-43	-135
1972	-564	-121	56	-240	-259	-62	-52	-7	67	-20	9	-30	-111	-100	-72	-111	-76
1973	-726	-317	-110	-287	-13	-26	-123	-108	-6	-47	-57	-154	-126	-6	-1	19	-31
1974	431	-129	90	41	429	-46	-51	-33	22	-20	88	-65	7	99	98	109	222
1975	448	238	433	-239	-33	23	191	74	191	100	142	-54	-116	-70	-36	-56	59
1976	382	93	151	166	-28	53	35	6	37	30	84	26	39	101	158	73	-259
1977	544	377	-27	82	112	147	-24	254	46	-23	-50	10	52	20	62	51	-2
1978	-49	2	-73	-389	411	-61	54	9	-170	63	33	-40	-184	-165	58	20	333
1979	-112	71	-547	152	212	-68	149	-10	-19	-522	-6	-37	92	97	48	44	121
1980	-866	-457	105	-534	30	49	-284	-233	18	27	60	-176	-254	-104	-96	-69	195
1981	-430	-10	271	-828	133	-317	264	42	133	77	60	-266	-416	-146	-254	53	339
1982	-482	-475	211	-298	80	-355	74	-184	-12	53	170	-124	-82	-92	151	155	-225
1983		-28	234	-573		36	-229	165	-146	-77	458	-62	-154	-358	471	24	

NOTES

1. Excluding alterations and additions.
2. Monthly data refer to end of period. Including unemployed in Turkey seeking work abroad.
3. The original base of the index is 1958 to 1968, and 1963 from 1969. The two indices have been linked on 1963.
4. Settlements basis.
5. Increase in assets (—).

NOTES

1. Non compris les transformations et les agrandissements.
2. Situation en fin de mois. Y compris les chômeurs qui cherchent à travailler à l'étranger.
3. La base originale de l'indice est 1958 jusqu'en 1968, et 1963 à partir de 1969. Les deux indices ont été raccordés sur 1963.
4. Sur la base des règlements.
5. Augmentation des avoirs (—).

MAIN SOURCES

PRINCIPALES SOURCES

Series	Séries	Sources
Production	Production	State Institute of Statistics *Monthly Bulletin of Statistics*
Construction	Construction	
Employment	Emploi	
Unemployment	Chômage	
Job vacancies	Offres d'emploi	
Prices	Prix	
Foreign trade	Commerce extérieur	
Workers abroad	Ouvriers à l'étranger	State Institute of Statistics
Balance of payments	Balance des paiements	
Home finance	Finances internes	Central Bank of the Republic of Turkey *Quarterly Bulletin*

United Kingdom — Royaume-Uni

UNITED KINGDOM

Gross domestic product / Produit intérieur brut

at current market prices / *aux prix courants du marché*

£ million, annual rates / millions de £, taux annuels

Adjusted - Corrigé

	Year	Q.1	Q.2	Q.3	Q.4	JAN	FEB	MAR	APR	MAY	JUN	JUL	AUG	SEP	OCT	NOV	DEC
1964	33334	32108	33156	33496	34576												
1965	35826	35028	35324	35183	36764												
1966	38174	37180	37952	38408	39156												
1967	40389	39892	40344	40824	40496												
1968	43840	42672	42840	44428	45420												
1969	46835	45456	46340	47335	48208												
1970	51365	48676	50620	52264	53900												
1971	57638	54192	56576	59296	60488												
1972	63774	60784	62972	64072	67268												
1973	73493	72528	71784	74008	75652												
1974	83588	75956	81228	85792	90376												
1975	105422	97084	103596	107380	113628												
1976	125611	120116	121896	125876	133556												
1977	144793	136608	142304	146940	153320												
1978	166502	158636	164992	168468	173912												
1979	194428	176764	190860	201936	208152												
1980	227496	216124	224136	231088	238636												
1981	251612	245240	248296	252852	260060												
1982	275717	266464	273440	276724	286360												
1983	300617	296656	294996	301416	309980												

Industrial production: total (1)(2) / Production industrielle : total (1)(2)

1980 = 100

	Year	Q.1	Q.2	Q.3	Q.4	JAN	FEB	MAR	APR	MAY	JUN	JUL	AUG	SEP	OCT	NOV	DEC
1964	78.3	76.4	78.8	72.3	87.2	76.2	80.5	78.4	79.1	76.9	80.5	69.7	67.5	79.8	83.4	85.6	80.5
1965	80.8	83.0	80.8	74.5	84.9	80.5	84.2	84.2	78.4	84.2	79.8	72.6	68.9	82.0	85.6	87.1	82.0
1966	81.9	85.1	82.5	76.4	83.7	82.0	85.6	87.8	81.3	83.4	82.7	75.5	71.1	82.7	84.9	85.6	80.5
1967	82.1	82.2	83.4	75.7	87.1	80.5	84.2	82.0	84.9	82.0	83.4	74.7	68.9	83.4	86.3	89.2	85.6
1968	= 86.7	= 88.1	86.7	81.3	90.7	83.4	89.0	92.0	84.4	89.4	86.4	78.6	77.4	87.7	90.3	93.6	88.3
1969	89.7	92.0	90.5	83.5	92.7	88.3	92.5	95.1	88.6	90.8	92.1	81.7	79.0	89.7	91.5	96.0	90.6
1970	90.1	92.1	91.3	83.4	93.7	88.8	94.3	93.3	92.8	90.1	90.9	81.1	78.1	91.0	94.9	96.1	90.0
1971	89.6	93.2	90.0	82.7	92.7	91.2	93.5	94.9	88.3	91.6	90.0	80.2	77.6	90.2	93.2	95.8	89.2
1972	91.2	88.1	91.9	85.4	99.5	87.6	84.0	92.7	90.5	92.3	92.8	81.9	79.5	94.9	99.5	103.2	95.9
1973	99.4	103.1	99.0	92.5	103.1	98.3	103.6	107.5	96.4	98.9	101.6	85.9	86.3	101.2	106.1	108.0	95.3
1974	97.5	96.4	100.2	92.8	100.4	89.9	96.5	102.7	97.5	101.1	102.0	90.8	87.0	100.7	102.8	105.4	93.0
1975	92.2	98.7	91.5	82.9	95.5	95.4	102.1	98.5	93.3	90.3	90.8	81.2	75.7	91.8	97.3	99.9	89.5
1976	95.2	97.2	93.8	87.4	102.3	90.8	99.3	101.6	92.5	96.9	92.1	85.3	80.2	96.6	103.4	106.6	97.0
1977	100.1	105.4	99.3	92.1	103.7	99.6	107.1	109.4	98.4	104.2	95.2	90.0	85.3	101.0	105.2	107.2	98.8
1978	103.1	104.1	103.4	97.2	107.8	99.6	107.9	104.8	106.8	100.2	103.1	95.2	90.5	105.8	107.1	111.5	104.8
1979	107.0	109.7	108.3	100.0	109.9	97.6	114.1	117.5	105.2	106.9	112.9	101.5	92.2	106.4	109.9	115.8	104.1
1980	100.0	110.2	100.1	91.3	93.5	105.6	111.5	113.4	99.2	98.6	102.4	91.9	85.1	96.9	99.6	103.3	92.6
1981	96.3	99.7	94.1	90.6	100.9	92.7	102.2	104.1	94.0	91.5	96.8	89.3	84.7	97.9	103.4	105.4	94.0
1982	98.0	102.0	96.7	92.4	100.9	95.5	104.5	106.0	95.9	97.2	97.1	91.1	86.5	99.7	102.7	104.0	96.1
1983	100.8	104.4	97.8	95.5	105.5	97.8	107.8	107.7	97.3	98.6	97.5	94.3	89.3	102.9	106.5	109.7	100.7

Industrial production: (2) / Production industrielle : (2)

investment goods / biens d'équipement

1980 = 100

	Year	Q.1	Q.2	Q.3	Q.4	JAN	FEB	MAR	APR	MAY	JUN	JUL	AUG	SEP	OCT	NOV	DEC
1964																	
1965																	
1966																	
1967																	
1968	96.4	96.0	96.7	91.7	101.0	91.0	95.0	102.0	94.0	98.0	98.0	89.0	87.0	99.0	98.0	102.0	103.0
1969	101.9	101.7	103.0	96.7	106.0	95.0	101.0	109.0	98.0	103.0	108.0	94.0	92.0	104.0	102.0	108.0	108.0
1970	101.7	103.0	103.7	94.0	106.0	96.0	104.0	109.0	102.0	103.0	106.0	91.0	88.0	103.0	105.0	108.0	105.0
1971	98.3	102.0	101.7	90.7	99.0	97.0	101.0	108.0	98.0	103.0	104.0	88.0	85.0	99.0	98.0	101.0	98.0
1972	95.7	95.0	96.0	89.0	102.7	90.0	93.0	102.0	93.0	96.0	99.0	85.0	83.0	99.0	100.0	106.0	102.0
1973	105.3	109.7	103.7	97.7	110.3	101.0	109.0	119.0	99.0	103.0	109.0	94.0	92.0	107.0	110.0	114.0	107.0
1974	109.8	107.3	111.7	106.3	114.3	97.0	106.0	119.0	107.0	112.0	116.0	103.0	100.0	116.0	114.0	118.0	111.0
1975	106.5	112.3	108.0	97.3	103.3	106.0	113.0	118.0	108.0	107.0	109.0	96.0	89.0	107.0	109.0	111.0	105.0
1976	103.5	107.3	102.0	94.3	110.0	98.0	106.0	118.0	100.0	105.0	101.0	93.0	86.0	104.0	109.0	114.0	107.0
1977	105.8	111.3	104.7	98.0	109.3	101.0	110.0	123.0	102.0	109.0	103.0	95.0	90.0	109.0	110.0	112.0	106.0
1978	105.6	108.0	106.0	100.7	107.7	100.0	109.0	115.0	108.0	102.0	108.0	98.0	93.0	111.0	105.0	111.0	107.0
1979	104.3	108.3	106.7	95.0	107.0	89.0	112.0	124.0	101.0	103.0	116.0	100.0	84.0	101.0	104.0	112.0	105.0
1980	100.0	111.3	101.3	92.7	94.7	101.0	112.0	121.0	98.0	99.0	107.0	92.0	86.0	100.0	97.0	100.0	87.0
1981	90.5	93.0	89.3	87.7	92.7	82.0	94.0	103.0	87.0	85.0	96.0	86.0	81.0	96.0	95.0	97.0	86.0
1982	91.5	96.3	91.7	87.3	91.0	86.0	98.0	105.0	88.0	92.0	95.0	86.0	80.0	96.0	93.0	95.0	85.0
1983	91.3	95.7	89.0	87.7	92.7	87.0	97.0	103.0	86.0	89.0	92.0	87.0	81.0	95.0	93.0	96.0	89.0

Gross domestic product / Produit intérieur brut
implicit price level / niveau implicite des prix
1980 = 100

Adjusted - Corrigé

	Year	Q.1	Q.2	Q.3	Q.4	JAN	FEB	MAR	APR	MAY	JUN	JUL	AUG	SEP	OCT	NOV	DEC
1964	20.3	19.8	20.2	20.6	20.7												
1965	21.4	21.0	21.2	21.5	21.7												
1966	22.3	21.9	22.2	22.5	22.7												
1967	23.0	22.7	23.0	23.1	23.2												
1968	24.0	23.4	23.8	24.2	24.4												
1969	25.3	24.9	25.1	25.4	25.7												
1970	27.1	26.3	26.7	27.4	28.0												
1971	29.6	28.7	29.2	30.1	30.6												
1972	32.1	31.1	31.7	32.4	33.1												
1973	34.4	33.6	33.6	34.5	35.9												
1974	39.5	36.4	38.3	40.4	42.8												
1975	50.2	46.1	49.3	51.7	53.7												
1976	57.7	55.4	56.6	58.2	60.4												
1977	65.7	62.7	64.9	66.7	68.3												
1978	72.9	70.6	71.6	73.8	75.8												
1979	83.5	78.0	80.5	86.1	89.3												
1980	100.0	93.6	98.6	102.5	105.6												
1981	111.7	107.8	111.2	113.1	114.8												
1982	119.8	116.4	119.1	121.0	122.5												
1983	126.2	124.0	125.1	127.4	128.2												

Industrial production: total (1)(2) / Production industrielle : total (1)(2)
1980 = 100

Adjusted - Corrigé

	Year	Q.1	Q.2	Q.3	Q.4	JAN	FEB	MAR	APR	MAY	JUN	JUL	AUG	SEP	OCT	NOV	DEC
1964		76.7	78.1	78.1	80.1	76.2	76.9	75.9	77.6	77.6	79.1	77.6	77.6	79.1	79.8	79.8	80.5
1965		80.1	80.3	80.5	81.7	80.5	80.5	79.1	80.5	82.0	79.8	79.8	80.5	81.3	82.0	81.3	82.0
1966		82.2	82.2	82.2	80.5	82.0	82.0	82.7	82.7	82.7	81.3	82.7	82.0	82.0	81.3	79.8	80.5
1967		81.0	82.0	81.7	83.9	80.5	81.3	81.3	82.7	81.3	82.0	82.0	81.3	82.0	82.7	83.4	85.6
1968		85.4	86.5	87.3	87.5	84.5	85.6	86.2	85.9	86.8	86.9	87.0	87.6	87.4	86.8	87.5	88.3
1969		88.8	90.5	89.8	89.5	88.6	89.0	88.9	90.3	90.3	90.9	90.7	89.3	89.5	88.0	89.8	90.6
1970		89.8	90.0	90.2	90.6	88.4	90.0	90.9	90.5	89.6	89.9	90.3	90.3	89.9	91.2	89.8	90.7
1971		89.7	89.9	89.5	89.4	91.3	89.5	88.4	89.8	90.1	89.8	89.4	90.0	89.2	89.3	89.1	89.7
1972		85.1	91.6	92.5	95.7	87.1	80.2	88.1	90.2	92.0	92.5	91.4	92.4	93.7	94.9	95.7	96.4
1973		99.1	99.3	99.8	99.5	99.3	98.4	99.5	98.6	98.7	100.5	100.0	100.0	99.5	100.5	99.5	98.5
1974		92.5	100.4	100.3	96.5	91.4	91.4	94.6	99.5	100.7	101.1	100.7	101.0	99.2	97.3	97.0	95.5
1975		95.2	91.5	90.1	91.8	96.3	95.7	93.7	92.1	90.9	91.5	90.3	89.1	90.8	91.9	92.0	91.6
1976		93.0	94.7	94.7	98.4	92.2	93.2	93.5	94.3	95.8	93.9	94.3	94.1	95.6	97.7	98.5	99.1
1977		100.8	100.2	99.5	99.9	101.1	100.6	100.7	99.8	102.4	98.4	98.8	99.8	100.1	99.8	99.0	100.8
1978		100.3	103.3	104.2	104.6	100.9	100.6	99.5	105.4	102.3	102.3	103.2	104.8	104.5	103.1	103.8	106.8
1979		104.6	109.3	106.9	107.3	99.4	106.5	107.8	107.5	109.3	111.0	109.7	105.7	105.4	106.3	107.8	107.8
1980		105.1	101.3	97.8	95.7	106.9	104.3	104.1	101.7	101.1	101.2	99.5	97.6	96.3	96.1	95.9	95.2
1981		94.9	95.5	96.9	98.0	94.2	95.0	95.5	96.3	94.1	96.1	96.5	96.7	97.4	99.2	98.1	96.8
1982		97.0	98.3	98.5	98.2	96.6	97.0	97.4	98.4	98.9	97.7	98.0	98.6	99.2	98.5	97.0	99.0
1983		99.5	99.5	101.5	102.9	99.6	99.9	99.0	99.8	100.1	98.6	101.3	101.3	101.9	102.2	102.5	104.0

Industrial production: (2) / Production industrielle : (2)
investment goods / biens d'équipement
1980 = 100

Adjusted - Corrigé

	Year	Q.1	Q.2	Q.3	Q.4	JAN	FEB	MAR	APR	MAY	JUN	JUL	AUG	SEP	OCT	NOV	DEC
1964																	
1965																	
1966																	
1967																	
1968		94.0	96.0	97.3	93.3	95.0	94.0	93.0	97.0	96.0	95.0	97.0	97.0	98.0	98.0	98.0	99.0
1969		98.7	102.3	103.3	102.7	98.0	99.0	99.0	102.0	102.0	103.0	104.0	103.0	103.0	102.0	103.0	103.0
1970		101.3	101.3	101.0	103.0	100.0	101.0	103.0	101.0	102.0	101.0	101.0	101.0	101.0	104.0	103.0	102.0
1971		99.0	100.7	97.3	96.0	101.0	99.0	97.0	101.0	101.0	100.0	98.0	97.0	97.0	96.0	96.0	96.0
1972		92.7	95.0	95.3	99.7	93.0	91.0	94.0	94.0	96.0	95.0	94.0	95.0	97.0	98.0	100.0	101.0
1973		105.7	103.7	104.7	107.0	106.0	106.0	105.0	103.0	103.0	105.0	104.0	106.0	104.0	107.0	107.0	107.0
1974		103.3	111.3	113.7	111.0	102.0	103.0	105.0	110.0	112.0	112.0	113.0	115.0	113.0	111.0	111.0	111.0
1975		109.7	107.3	104.7	104.0	111.0	110.0	108.0	108.0	107.0	107.0	106.0	103.0	105.0	105.0	103.0	104.0
1976		103.3	103.0	101.3	106.0	103.0	103.0	104.0	104.0	103.0	102.0	102.0	101.0	101.0	105.0	106.0	107.0
1977		106.7	105.0	104.7	106.3	106.0	106.0	108.0	105.0	106.0	104.0	103.0	106.0	105.0	106.0	106.0	107.0
1978		105.0	105.7	106.3	105.7	106.0	105.0	104.0	108.0	105.0	104.0	105.0	108.0	106.0	103.0	105.0	109.0
1979		104.7	106.7	100.0	105.7	100.0	106.0	108.0	105.0	106.0	109.0	106.0	98.0	96.0	102.0	106.0	109.0
1980		107.3	102.0	97.3	93.3	109.0	107.0	106.0	103.0	102.0	101.0	98.0	98.0	96.0	95.0	94.0	91.0
1981		89.3	89.7	91.7	91.7	89.0	89.0	90.0	91.0	88.0	90.0	91.0	92.0	92.0	92.0	92.0	91.0
1982		92.7	92.7	91.0	90.0	92.0	93.0	93.0	92.0	94.0	92.0	91.0	90.0	92.0	90.0	90.0	90.0
1983		91.3	90.0	91.3	92.3	93.0	91.0	90.0	90.0	91.0	89.0	92.0	91.0	91.0	91.0	91.0	95.0

Industrial production: (2)
consumer goods
1980 = 100

Production industrielle : (2)
biens de consommation
1980 = 100

	Year	Q.1	Q.2	Q.3	Q.4	JAN	FEB	MAR	APR	MAY	JUN	JUL	AUG	SEP	OCT	NOV	DEC
1964																	
1965																	
1966																	
1967																	
1968	88.0	88.3	87.7	84.3	91.7	82.0	89.0	94.0	83.0	91.0	89.0	83.0	80.0	90.0	95.0	95.0	85.0
1969	90.6	89.7	90.7	87.3	94.3	87.0	90.0	92.0	88.0	91.0	93.0	86.0	84.0	92.0	97.0	98.0	88.0
1970	92.2	90.7	94.0	87.7	96.3	89.0	93.0	90.0	94.0	93.0	95.0	85.0	83.0	95.0	100.0	100.0	89.0
1971	94.4	93.7	94.3	90.3	99.3	92.0	93.0	96.0	91.0	97.0	95.0	87.0	85.0	99.0	103.0	103.0	92.0
1972	100.8	96.3	100.7	97.0	108.3	95.0	95.0	99.0	99.0	101.0	102.0	93.0	91.0	107.0	112.0	113.0	100.0
1973	109.4	108.7	109.3	105.3	114.3	105.0	109.0	112.0	105.0	110.0	113.0	102.0	99.0	115.0	120.0	121.0	102.0
1974	107.7	105.7	111.3	103.7	110.0	99.0	108.0	110.0	107.0	113.0	114.0	101.0	98.0	112.0	115.0	117.0	98.0
1975	100.9	104.7	99.7	95.0	104.3	103.0	110.0	101.0	101.0	98.0	100.0	92.0	88.0	105.0	109.0	110.0	94.0
1976	103.1	101.0	102.0	99.0	110.3	96.0	103.0	104.0	99.0	105.0	102.0	97.0	91.0	109.0	115.0	116.0	100.0
1977	106.3	108.3	105.0	100.7	111.0	104.0	110.0	111.0	103.0	111.0	101.0	97.0	94.0	111.0	115.0	116.0	102.0
1978	108.8	107.0	110.0	105.7	112.3	103.0	111.0	107.0	113.0	106.0	111.0	101.0	100.0	116.0	116.0	118.0	103.0
1979	108.3	107.0	109.7	104.3	112.3	96.0	110.0	115.0	106.0	108.0	115.0	102.0	96.0	115.0	116.0	120.0	101.0
1980	100.0	106.7	98.7	94.7	99.7	103.0	109.0	108.0	97.0	96.0	103.0	93.0	89.0	102.0	105.0	105.0	89.0
1981	95.9	96.7	93.3	93.0	100.7	91.0	100.0	99.0	92.0	90.0	98.0	90.0	88.0	101.0	107.0	107.0	88.0
1982	94.4	95.7	92.0	90.7	98.7	89.0	99.0	99.0	90.0	93.0	93.0	88.0	85.0	99.0	104.0	103.0	89.0
1983	96.6	96.3	93.7	93.3	103.0	92.0	98.0	99.0	92.0	93.0	96.0	90.0	88.0	102.0	108.0	109.0	92.0

Industrial production: (2)
intermediate goods
1980 = 100

Production industrielle : (2)
biens intermédiaires
1980 = 100

	Year	Q.1	Q.2	Q.3	Q.4	JAN	FEB	MAR	APR	MAY	JUN	JUL	AUG	SEP	OCT	NOV	DEC
1964																	
1965																	
1966																	
1967																	
1968	81.8	84.7	82.0	75.0	85.3	81.0	87.0	86.0	81.0	85.0	80.0	72.0	72.0	81.0	84.0	89.0	83.0
1969	83.6	89.3	84.7	75.3	85.3	87.0	91.0	90.0	85.0	85.0	84.0	74.0	70.0	82.0	83.0	89.0	84.0
1970	83.6	88.3	84.0	76.0	86.7	86.0	91.0	88.0	88.0	83.0	81.0	74.0	71.0	83.0	88.0	88.0	84.0
1971	82.9	89.3	81.7	74.7	86.0	89.0	91.0	88.0	82.0	83.0	80.0	73.0	70.0	81.0	86.0	89.0	83.0
1972	84.2	80.3	85.3	77.3	93.7	83.0	73.0	85.0	85.0	86.0	85.0	74.0	72.0	86.0	93.0	97.0	91.0
1973	91.4	97.3	91.0	83.0	93.7	94.0	98.0	100.0	90.0	91.0	92.0	81.0	77.0	91.0	97.0	98.0	86.0
1974	86.2	86.3	88.7	81.0	88.7	82.0	85.0	91.0	88.0	89.0	89.0	80.0	75.0	88.0	91.0	93.0	82.0
1975	80.9	89.3	79.3	69.7	85.7	87.0	93.0	88.0	82.0	79.0	77.0	69.0	63.0	77.0	86.0	90.0	81.0
1976	87.2	90.7	86.0	78.0	94.7	85.0	94.0	93.0	86.0	89.0	83.0	75.0	72.0	87.0	94.0	99.0	91.0
1977	94.3	101.3	93.3	84.7	97.3	97.0	104.0	103.0	94.0	98.0	88.0	84.0	78.0	92.0	98.0	100.0	94.0
1978	99.3	101.0	98.7	91.7	106.0	98.0	106.0	99.0	103.0	96.0	97.0	91.0	85.0	99.0	104.0	109.0	105.0
1979	107.8	111.7	108.7	100.7	110.3	102.0	117.0	116.0	107.0	108.0	111.0	102.0	94.0	106.0	110.0	116.0	105.0
1980	100.0	111.3	100.0	89.0	99.7	109.0	113.0	112.0	101.0	99.0	100.0	91.0	83.0	93.0	98.0	104.0	97.0
1981	99.2	104.3	96.7	90.7	105.0	99.0	107.0	107.0	98.0	95.0	97.0	90.0	85.0	97.0	106.0	109.0	100.0
1982	102.7	107.7	101.3	95.7	107.0	103.0	110.0	110.0	102.0	102.0	100.0	95.0	90.0	102.0	107.0	109.0	105.0
1983	107.3	112.3	103.3	100.3	113.0	106.0	117.0	114.0	105.0	105.0	100.0	100.0	94.0	107.0	112.0	117.0	110.0

Industrial production: construction (2)
1980 = 100

Adjusted - Corrigé

Production industrielle : construction (2)
1980 = 100

	Year	Q.1	Q.2	Q.3	Q.4	JAN	FEB	MAR	APR	MAY	JUN	JUL	AUG	SEP	OCT	NOV	DEC
1964	104.2	102.9	104.7	103.5	105.6												
1965	109.1	111.2	107.7	107.6	109.8												
1966	111.0	109.4	110.7	111.6	112.4												
1967	115.5	114.5	114.7	116.2	116.6												
1968	118.5	118.9	118.2	118.3	118.5												
1969	117.6	117.5	117.7	118.2	116.9												
1970	115.3	112.3	115.9	117.7	115.4												
1971	117.3	115.1	117.8	116.6	119.8												
1972	119.5	119.4	122.0	118.5	118.1												
1973	122.4	125.9	122.5	122.1	119.1												
1974	109.7	113.8	112.1	109.1	103.8												
1975	103.9	104.8	104.4	103.5	103.0												
1976	102.5	104.5	101.6	100.2	103.5												
1977	102.1	100.7	101.0	102.2	104.3												
1978	105.0	102.0	107.1	106.2	104.7												
1979	105.7	101.0	107.1	107.6	106.9												
1980	100.0	105.0	101.6	100.5	92.9												
1981	90.0	92.5	89.6	90.9	86.8												
1982	91.6	89.2	90.1	92.6	94.3												
1983	95.3	93.9	91.4	97.8	98.1												

Industrial production: (2) consumer goods — Production industrielle : (2) biens de consommation

1980 = 100 — Adjusted - Corrigé

	Year	Q.1	Q.2	Q.3	Q.4	JAN	FEB	MAR	APR	MAY	JUN	JUL	AUG	SEP	OCT	NOV	DEC
1964																	
1965																	
1966																	
1967																	
1968		88.0	87.3	88.0	88.7	85.0	88.0	91.0	85.0	88.0	89.0	89.0	87.0	88.0	88.0	89.0	89.0
1969		89.3	90.7	91.3	91.0	90.0	89.0	89.0	91.0	90.0	91.0	93.0	91.0	90.0	90.0	91.0	92.0
1970		90.7	92.7	91.7	93.3	90.0	91.0	91.0	92.0	92.0	94.0	92.0	92.0	91.0	93.0	93.0	94.0
1971		92.7	93.7	94.7	96.7	94.0	92.0	92.0	93.0	94.0	94.0	94.0	95.0	95.0	96.0	96.0	98.0
1972		96.0	100.7	101.7	105.0	97.0	93.0	98.0	100.0	101.0	101.0	101.0	102.0	102.0	104.0	105.0	106.0
1973		108.0	109.7	110.7	109.7	108.0	107.0	109.0	109.0	109.0	111.0	111.0	111.0	110.0	110.0	110.0	109.0
1974		105.3	111.3	109.0	105.3	104.0	105.0	107.0	110.0	112.0	112.0	110.0	110.0	107.0	105.0	106.0	105.0
1975		105.3	99.3	99.0	100.0	107.0	106.0	103.0	100.0	98.0	100.0	99.0	98.0	100.0	100.0	100.0	100.0
1976		100.3	102.7	103.7	105.7	100.0	100.0	101.0	102.0	103.0	103.0	105.0	102.0	104.0	106.0	105.0	106.0
1977		107.7	106.0	105.0	106.0	109.0	107.0	107.0	106.0	107.0	105.0	105.0	105.0	105.0	105.0	105.0	108.0
1978		107.3	110.0	109.3	107.7	107.0	107.0	108.0	111.0	110.0	109.0	108.0	111.0	109.0	107.0	107.0	109.0
1979		107.0	111.3	108.0	108.0	102.0	108.0	111.0	110.0	112.0	112.0	110.0	106.0	108.0	107.0	108.0	109.0
1980		106.0	100.3	98.3	95.3	108.0	106.0	104.0	101.0	99.0	101.0	100.0	98.0	97.0	96.0	95.0	95.0
1981		95.3	95.3	96.7	95.0	95.0	96.0	95.0	96.0	94.0	96.0	97.0	96.0	97.0	97.0	96.0	95.0
1982		95.0	94.0	94.3	94.3	94.0	96.0	95.0	94.0	95.0	93.0	94.0	94.0	95.0	95.0	93.0	95.0
1983		95.7	96.0	97.3	98.0	97.0	95.0	95.0	96.0	96.0	96.0	98.0	97.0	97.0	98.0	98.0	98.0

Industrial production: (2) intermediate goods — Production industrielle : (2) biens intermédiaires

1980 = 100 — Adjusted - Corrigé

	Year	Q.1	Q.2	Q.3	Q.4	JAN	FEB	MAR	APR	MAY	JUN	JUL	AUG	SEP	OCT	NOV	DEC
1964																	
1965																	
1966																	
1967																	
1968		80.0	82.0	82.7	82.3	79.0	80.0	81.0	81.0	83.0	82.0	82.0	84.0	82.0	81.0	82.0	84.0
1969		83.7	85.0	83.0	82.3	83.0	84.0	84.0	85.0	85.0	85.0	84.0	82.0	83.0	80.0	83.0	84.0
1970		83.7	83.3	84.0	83.7	82.0	84.0	85.0	85.0	83.0	82.0	84.0	84.0	84.0	85.0	82.0	84.0
1971		83.7	82.3	83.0	82.0	85.0	84.0	82.0	82.0	82.0	83.0	83.0	84.0	82.0	82.0	82.0	82.0
1972		75.3	85.7	86.7	89.0	79.0	67.0	80.0	84.0	86.0	87.0	85.0	87.0	88.0	89.0	89.0	89.0
1973		91.0	91.7	92.0	90.3	91.0	90.0	92.0	92.0	91.0	93.0	92.0	92.0	92.0	92.0	90.0	89.0
1974		80.3	89.7	89.7	85.0	80.0	78.0	83.0	89.0	90.0	90.0	90.0	90.0	89.0	87.0	85.0	83.0
1975		83.3	80.0	78.0	82.0	84.0	84.0	82.0	80.0	80.0	80.0	78.0	77.0	79.0	82.0	82.0	82.0
1976		84.3	86.7	87.0	91.0	83.0	85.0	85.0	86.0	89.0	85.0	85.0	87.0	89.0	90.0	91.0	92.0
1977		94.3	95.0	94.3	93.3	95.0	94.0	94.0	94.0	98.0	93.0	94.0	94.0	95.0	94.0	92.0	94.0
1978		94.3	99.0	100.7	102.3	95.0	95.0	93.0	101.0	98.0	98.0	100.0	101.0	101.0	101.0	102.0	104.0
1979		103.7	109.7	110.3	108.0	98.0	106.0	107.0	108.0	110.0	111.0	112.0	110.0	109.0	108.0	109.0	107.0
1980		104.3	101.3	97.7	96.7	106.0	103.0	104.0	102.0	101.0	101.0	100.0	97.0	96.0	96.0	97.0	97.0
1981		97.0	98.3	99.3	102.3	96.0	97.0	98.0	99.0	97.0	99.0	99.0	99.0	100.0	104.0	102.0	101.0
1982		100.0	103.0	104.3	103.7	100.0	99.0	101.0	103.0	103.0	103.0	103.0	105.0	105.0	104.0	102.0	105.0
1983		105.0	105.7	108.7	110.0	104.0	106.0	105.0	106.0	107.0	104.0	108.0	108.0	110.0	109.0	110.0	111.0

Production: crude steel — Production : acier brut

thousand tons, monthly averages — milliers de tonnes, moyennes mensuelles

	Year	Q.1	Q.2	Q.3	Q.4	JAN	FEB	MAR	APR	MAY	JUN	JUL	AUG	SEP	OCT	NOV	DEC
1964																	
1965																	
1966																	
1967																	
1968																	
1969	2237	2331	2382	1938	2247	2646	2261	2237	2737	2222	2186	2085	1762	1968	2614	2151	1977
1970	2319	2370	2593	2339	1976	2574	2269	2267	2848	2838	2094	2233	2031	2752	2321	2242	1364
1971	2024	2188	2065	1963	1880	2362	2111	2092	2124	2207	1863	1757	2006	2127	1975	1941	1724
1972	2119	1801	2267	2101	2306	1935	1389	2080	2320	2253	2227	1917	2003	2382	2423	2399	2097
1973	2227	2276	2231	2167	2235	2326	2190	2311	2156	2222	2274	2112	2068	2321	2430	2358	1917
1974	1867	1762	1985	1816	1905	1763	1669	1854	1960	1941	2054	1760	1792	1895	2019	1929	1768
1975	1653	2065	1580	1348	1620	2001	2012	2182	1807	1477	1457	1161	1372	1510	1777	1718	1364
1976	1888	1867	1990	1701	1996	1737	1866	1997	1979	2076	1916	1626	1650	1826	2088	2033	1866
1977	1708	1836	1679	1722	1593	1988	1698	1821	1631	1733	1673	1629	1644	1894	1782	1705	1292
1978	1689	1657	1812	1531	1755	1465	1584	1923	1889	1784	1764	1628	1183	1777	1849	1882	1534
1979	1795	1696	1963	1753	1770	1409	1701	1977	1992	1939	1958	1725	1541	1994	1986	1862	1461
1980	945	263	1432	1052	1034	287	131	371	1044	1589	1662	1250	1015	891	1008	1107	987
1981	1297	1224	1405	1193	1367	1039	1269	1363	1544	1272	1393	1263	1044	1272	1495	1439	1167
1982	1148	1357	1324	970	939	1255	1363	1454	1347	1421	1204	999	941	970	1023	1011	784
1983	1249	1268	1307	1178	1243	1159	1255	1389	1252	1400	1269	1046	1103	1385	1339	1329	1061

UNITED KINGDOM

Production: commercial vehicles (3)(4)

thousands, weekly averages

Production : véhicules utilitaires (3)(4)

milliers, moyennes hebdomadaires

	Year	Q.1	Q.2	Q.3	Q.4	JAN	FEB	MAR	APR	MAY	JUN	JUL	AUG	SEP	OCT	NOV	DEC
1964	8.8	8.8	9.3	7.5	9.4	9.3	8.9	8.3	9.2	9.1	9.7	5.4	7.8	9.0	9.7	9.8	8.8
1965	8.8	9.3	9.7	7.2	8.8	9.5	9.6	9.0	9.2	10.4	9.6	5.5	6.6	8.8	9.3	8.8	8.3
1966	8.4	9.3	9.5	7.5	7.5	8.3	9.3	10.0	9.0	10.0	9.5	6.0	7.3	8.7	8.1	7.5	7.1
1967	7.4	7.3	8.0	6.4	7.9	7.2	7.5	7.3	8.2	7.9	8.0	6.7	5.0	7.3	8.6	8.0	7.2
1968	7.9	8.0	8.0	6.8	8.6	7.0	7.9	8.9	7.9	8.4	7.8	6.3	5.3	8.4	8.5	8.9	8.5
1969	8.8	9.3	9.7	7.6	8.6	9.8	9.7	8.2	9.6	9.4	10.2	7.4	7.0	8.3	7.7	9.8	8.6
1970	8.8	8.9	10.2	5.8	10.4	10.2	8.8	7.9	9.8	10.4	10.3	5.6	6.3	5.5	11.3	11.3	8.9
1971	8.8	8.4	10.3	7.5	8.9	10.8	8.0	6.9	9.8	11.2	9.9	6.9	7.1	8.3	9.5	9.3	8.2
1972	7.9	7.3	8.6	6.2	9.3	7.7	6.3	7.8	7.9	9.6	8.2	5.5	5.5	7.3	9.2	10.3	8.7
1973	8.0	8.2	8.4	6.9	8.5	8.2	8.4	8.0	7.6	8.1	9.7	7.0	5.8	7.8	9.9	7.8	8.0
1974	7.7	6.9	8.4	6.9	8.8	5.9	6.9	7.7	8.0	9.0	8.3	7.0	6.3	7.4	8.8	9.6	8.0
1975	7.3	8.3	7.5	6.0	7.4	8.6	8.8	7.7	7.8	8.0	7.0	5.9	5.1	6.8	7.8	7.6	7.0
1976	7.0	7.2	7.5	5.8	7.5	6.5	7.6	7.5	6.8	8.6	7.2	6.5	4.5	6.4	7.9	8.4	6.3
1977	7.7	8.4	7.8	6.6	7.0	8.6	8.3	8.4	7.4	9.7	6.6	6.8	5.9	7.1	8.5	7.8	7.3
1978	7.4	8.0	8.6	6.3	6.6	7.8	7.7	8.4	8.7	9.5	7.9	6.8	5.3	6.8	6.6	6.1	7.2
1979	7.9	9.2	9.4	5.6	7.3	8.0	9.4	10.1	9.5	10.0	8.7	8.0	3.9	5.1	6.6	8.1	7.1
1980	7.5	9.4	8.6	6.1	5.8	9.3	10.7	8.6	8.1	8.9	8.8	8.3	4.6	5.5	6.9	6.5	4.3
1981	4.4	4.4	4.6	3.7	4.9	4.4	4.4	4.4	5.1	4.0	4.6	4.5	2.5	4.2	5.2	5.3	4.5
1982	5.2	5.4	5.3	4.5	5.5	4.4	5.7	5.9	5.1	5.8	5.1	5.2	3.0	5.2	5.8	6.2	4.6
1983	4.6	5.0	4.8	3.9	4.8	4.6	5.4	5.1	5.0	5.0	4.5	3.6	3.6	4.3	4.9	5.9	3.7

Production: passenger cars (3)(4)

thousands, weekly averages

Production : voitures de tourisme (3)(4)

milliers, moyennes hebdomadaires

	Year	Q.1	Q.2	Q.3	Q.4	JAN	FEB	MAR	APR	MAY	JUN	JUL	AUG	SEP	OCT	NOV	DEC
1964	35.2	37.0	39.8	29.0	35.0	37.1	38.6	35.7	41.0	38.3	40.1	22.2	30.7	33.1	35.6	37.1	32.9
1965	33.1	35.4	37.6	26.3	33.2	35.8	36.8	33.9	35.0	39.0	38.6	22.7	24.8	30.3	34.3	33.4	32.2
1966	30.8	35.6	37.2	25.7	24.8	32.2	36.3	37.7	35.9	39.5	36.5	22.2	26.9	27.6	27.0	22.8	24.8
1967	29.9	29.8	34.4	24.3	31.0	28.1	30.3	30.8	35.6	34.4	33.4	23.7	22.8	25.9	30.2	32.2	30.6
1968	35.2	36.0	37.6	30.0	36.1	30.5	35.8	40.5	36.3	40.5	36.4	27.8	25.2	35.6	36.5	37.6	34.7
1969	32.4	34.7	37.3	27.3	30.4	37.0	36.0	30.8	35.6	37.2	39.6	26.6	26.7	28.7	29.8	32.3	29.6
1970	31.6	33.6	36.2	21.3	35.2	36.6	33.9	30.9	34.2	34.4	39.1	20.2	24.0	20.1	35.0	38.8	32.4
1971	33.5	33.3	36.3	28.0	35.6	39.1	33.6	28.4	34.5	39.1	35.2	21.4	29.7	31.9	37.7	36.4	35.9
1972	37.0	36.9	39.5	30.5	40.8	35.1	32.9	41.6	36.3	43.1	39.3	25.5	29.7	35.2	42.1	43.7	37.5
1973	33.6	36.8	34.3	27.1	36.2	39.5	34.4	35.8	31.5	34.7	36.7	24.9	29.6	26.8	39.2	38.7	31.9
1974	29.5	29.8	33.8	23.6	30.8	27.4	31.1	32.8	28.8	39.5	33.2	23.4	28.3	20.0	30.7	35.1	27.4
1975	24.4	29.4	22.1	20.8	25.2	31.4	32.0	25.8	26.5	18.0	21.9	17.9	19.7	23.9	24.3	28.0	23.8
1976	25.2	27.6	26.9	19.5	26.5	24.1	30.0	28.5	23.2	31.8	25.9	22.7	16.2	19.6	28.3	30.1	22.0
1977	25.3	25.4	28.5	20.8	26.5	30.1	23.9	22.9	28.4	35.0	23.5	18.8	19.8	23.3	25.8	28.1	25.6
1978	23.5	27.6	27.9	20.1	18.5	27.9	27.0	27.8	29.8	30.4	24.4	16.2	22.2	21.5	19.8	14.4	20.7
1979	20.6	25.0	24.4	13.2	19.8	23.1	25.0	26.7	24.2	26.4	22.9	16.8	10.9	12.0	17.9	22.0	19.6
1980	17.8	23.0	19.3	14.0	14.9	24.6	25.4	19.8	20.1	18.9	19.1	17.3	12.8	12.2	16.7	15.7	12.6
1981	18.4	18.9	18.9	17.3	18.3	17.5	19.3	19.7	22.6	13.8	20.0	18.3	14.1	19.1	22.7	17.1	15.9
1982	17.1	19.8	17.6	13.5	17.4	17.6	22.1	19.7	16.4	20.2	16.4	14.8	12.9	13.0	19.5	18.4	15.0
1983	19.7	19.0	22.1	17.4	20.4	16.1	21.9	19.6	19.2	25.7	21.6	15.1	19.7	17.3	22.3	26.0	14.4

Ships completed

thousand gross register tons, quarterly averages

Navires achevés

milliers de tonneaux de jauge brute, moyennes trimestrielles

	Year	Q.1	Q.2	Q.3	Q.4	JAN	FEB	MAR	APR	MAY	JUN	JUL	AUG	SEP	OCT	NOV	DEC
1964	202	200	302	117	189												
1965	320	436	262	258	325												
1966	268	300	306	92	376												
1967	297	244	275	364	304												
1968	262	243	268	194	342												
1969	207	210	266	186	167												
1970	332	378	161	268	518												
1971	308	256	186	399	394												
1972	299	282	405	111	393												
1973	267	273	288	239	263												
1974	300	344	465	70	315												
1975	292	273	382	124	390												
1976	375	332	356	307	492												
1977	255	175	309	380	157												
1978	283	329	248	285	372												
1979	173	217	155	121	300												
1980	107	122	127	93	79												
1981	53	52	81	28	53												
1982	109	137	100	91	106												
1983	124	261	71	126	37												

Business climate — Climat des affaires
manufacturing — industries manufacturières
per cent balance — solde en pourcentage

Year	Q.1	Q.2	Q.3	Q.4	JAN	FEB	MAR	APR	MAY	JUN	JUL	AUG	SEP	OCT	NOV	DEC
1964																
1965																
1966																
1967																
1968																
1969																
1970																
1971																
1972	37	38	22	29	37			38			22			29		
1973	31	41	26	12	31			41			26			12		
1974	-75	-9	-43	-56	-75			-9			-43			-56		
1975	-63	-44	-35	-18	-63			-44			-35			-18		
1976	10	24	31	-9	10			24			31			-9		
1977	6	7	-7	-	6			7			-7			0		
1978	1	-3	-	6	1			-3			0			5		
1979	-5	6	-22	-40	-5			6			-22			-40		
1980	-45	-41	-70	-54	-45			-41			-70			-54		
1981	-27	-6	2	-9	-27			-6			2			-9		
1982	8	10	-22	-28	8			10			-22			-28		
1983	-5	31	24	7	-5			31			24			7		

Production: future tendency — Perspectives de production
manufacturing — industries manufacturières
per cent balance — solde en pourcentage

Year	Q.1	Q.2	Q.3	Q.4	JAN	FEB	MAR	APR	MAY	JUN	JUL	AUG	SEP	OCT	NOV	DEC
1964																
1965																
1966																
1967																
1968																
1969																
1970																
1971																
1972																
1973																
1974																
1975		-16	-11	-1		-11	-16	-16	-19	-13	-11	-11	-12	-1	10	2
1976	6	26	33	28	6	20	25	26	33	37	33	35	40	28	24	23
1977	22	23	17	23	22	22	25	23	19	18	17	16	21	23	19	24
1978	19	16	17	22	19	22	22	16	19	12	17	19	21	22	22	28
1979	10	24	4	4	10	19	25	24	27	20	4	1	2	4	3	-3
1980	-11	-14	-41	-31	-11	-11	-12	-14	-24	-36	-41	-43	-48	-31	-40	-36
1981	-16	-4	1	-	-16	-17	-13	-4	-1	-3	1	2	2	-	1	-1
1982	1	4	-3	-4	1	3	4	4	-2	-4	-3	-8	-7	-4	-9	-11
1983	-5	22	17	16	-5	8	16	22	18	19	17	19	20	16	24	27

Orders inflow: tendency — Commandes : tendance
manufacturing — industries manufacturières
per cent balance — solde en pourcentage

Year	Q.1	Q.2	Q.3	Q.4	JAN	FEB	MAR	APR	MAY	JUN	JUL	AUG	SEP	OCT	NOV	DEC
1964																
1965																
1966																
1967																
1968																
1969																
1970																
1971																
1972																
1973																
1974																
1975																
1976																
1977		22	10	6				22			10			6		
1978	3	-1	-1	2	3			-1			-1			2		
1979	6	11	6	-18	6			11			6			-18		
1980	-18	-26	-58	-61	-18			-26			-58			-61		
1981	-46	-30	-14	-10	-46			-30			-14			-10		
1982	-4	-4	-21	-30	-4			-4			-21			-30		
1983	-13	16	13	10	-13			16			13			10		

UNITED KINGDOM

Order books or demand: level
manufacturing
per cent balance

Carnet de commandes ou demande globale : niveau
industries manufacturières
solde en pourcentage

	Year	Q.1	Q.2	Q.3	Q.4	JAN	FEB	MAR	APR	MAY	JUN	JUL	AUG	SEP	OCT	NOV	DEC
1964																	
1965																	
1966																	
1967																	
1968																	
1969																	
1970																	
1971																	
1972																	
1973																	
1974																	
1975																	
1976																	
1977			-21	-31	-31	..	..	..	-21	-22	-20	-31	-28	-26	-31	-24	-23
1978		-34	-32	-29	-19	-34	-23	-23	-32	-28	-25	-29	-22	-15	-19	-15	-8
1979		-17	-10	-12	-28	-17	-17	-11	-10	-6	-4	-12	-18	-21	-28	-26	-30
1980		-40	-50	-71	-79	-40	-35	-39	-50	-57	-62	-71	-71	-72	-79	-74	-73
1981		-73	-73	-65	-62	-73	-71	-69	-73	-67	-65	-68	-62	-58	-62	-55	-53
1982		-60	-56	-58	-58	-60	-49	-42	-56	-48	-50	-58	-55	-52	-58	-57	-55
1983		-55	-41	-34	-33	-55	-46	-33	-41	-26	-24	-34	-24	-25	-33	-21	-14

Finished goods stocks: level
manufacturing
per cent balance

Stocks de produits finis : niveau
industries manufacturières
solde en pourcentage

	Year	Q.1	Q.2	Q.3	Q.4	JAN	FEB	MAR	APR	MAY	JUN	JUL	AUG	SEP	OCT	NOV	DEC
1964																	
1965																	
1966																	
1967																	
1968																	
1969																	
1970																	
1971																	
1972																	
1973																	
1974																	
1975																	
1976																	
1977		..	5	11	8	..	..	..	5	10	9	11	13	9	8	6	4
1978		8	10	10	8	8	9	9	10	13	7	10	9	7	8	5	7
1979		6	2	-	7	6	10	2	2	1	3	-	5	5	7	7	15
1980		15	26	36	33	15	16	18	26	26	30	38	38	35	33	35	32
1981		31	26	20	17	31	25	24	26	21	18	20	16	14	17	17	18
1982		18	18	18	19	18	24	18	18	19	18	18	23	23	19	23	16
1983		15	12	13	9	15	13	12	12	9	8	13	10	7	9	6	7

Firms operating at full capacity
manufacturing
per cent

Entreprises travaillant à pleine capacité
industries manufacturières
pourcentage

	Year	Q.1	Q.2	Q.3	Q.4	JAN	FEB	MAR	APR	MAY	JUN	JUL	AUG	SEP	OCT	NOV	DEC
1964		48	56		58		48				56				58		
1965		59	54		50		59				54				50		
1966		50	49		44		50				49				44		
1967		33	31		30		33				31				30		
1968		36	42		49		36				42				49		
1969		56	52		51		56				52				51		
1970		47	47		49		47				47				49		
1971			36								36			26			
1972		27	32	36	40	27			32			36			40		
1973		47	52	60	55	47			52			60			55		
1974		27	49	44	41	27			49			44			41		
1975		36	28	23	25	38			28			23			25		
1976		20	23	27	31	20			23			27			31		
1977		34	33	32	30	34			33			32			30		
1978		33	33	35	38	33			33			35			38		
1979		38	44	49	38	38			44			49			38		
1980		36	30	24	15	36			30			24			15		
1981		16	17	22	23	16			17			22					
1982		22	22	25	24	22			22			25			24		
1983		23	27	32	33	23			27			32			33		

Engineering sales (volume): (2)(5) total — Ventes, fabrications métalliques (volume) : (2)(5) total

1980 = 100

Adjusted - Corrigé

	Year	Q.1	Q.2	Q.3	Q.4	JAN	FEB	MAR	APR	MAY	JUN	JUL	AUG	SEP	OCT	NOV	DEC
1964	76	74	77	77	79	72	74	74	75	78	79	74	79	79	79	80	80
1965	80	80	78	80	81	82	81	76	78	78	77	78	81	80	82	81	81
1966	83	83	82	83	83	83	82	83	83	81	82	86	82	81	84	84	83
1967	84	82	85	85	84	81	83	83	86	86	83	85	85	84	81	83	88
1968	88	86	87	88	89	83	87	87	87	85	90	86	87	89	87	90	90
1969	91	88	90	92	93	90	88	88	88	90	92	92	91	92	93	95	93
1970	=95=	95	93	96	95	91	95	100	90	94	96	94	102	96	96	96	94
1971	97	97	101	97	94	100	100	93	100	105	96	97	101	94	97	93	93
1972	95	91	94	95	101	94	88	92	94	95	93	93	94	95	100	100	102
1973	105	103	105	106	107	100	103	105	104	105	107	107	104	108	106	108	108
1974	109	105	109	111	111	102	105	108	107	106	116	109	115	111	110	111	112
1975	107	112	107	106	104	111	112	115	107	108	106	107	106	104	105	107	99
1976	104	102	105	104	104	105	102	100	107	109	97	103	105	104	106	104	103
1977	104	105	103	104	103	109	105	100	105	101	104	106	103	104	106	101	103
1978	=106=	105	104	109	106	104	104	108	104	106	103	107	108	111	103	104	112
1979	106	102	109	103	108	92	107	107	106	108	114	105	99	100	103	108	114
1980	100	106	102	99	93	107	105	105	103	102	102	95	100	97	95	94	90
1981	88	88	89	89	89	87	88	89	91	97	90	88	90	88	91	89	87
1982	90	90	90	91	90	89	91	89	89	93	87	91	90	92	90	88	89
1983	91	91	90	93	94	93	91	88	91	92	87	96	92	91	94	92	95

Engineering sales (volume): (2)(5) domestic — Ventes, fabrications métalliques (volume) : (2)(5) marché intérieur

1980 = 100

Adjusted - Corrigé

	Year	Q.1	Q.2	Q.3	Q.4	JAN	FEB	MAR	APR	MAY	JUN	JUL	AUG	SEP	OCT	NOV	DEC
1964	85	82	85	86	88	80	82	83	84	86	87	82	89	88	87	89	90
1965	88	88	85	88	91	88	88	85	86	86	85	86	90	89	92	90	90
1966	92	92	92	92	91	93	91	92	92	90	91	94	90	91	92	91	91
1967	94	91	95	95	95	90	91	92	95	96	94	95	95	95	93	94	96
1968	97	95	97	96	93	93	97	97	96	95	100	96	96	96	97	98	99
1969	98	97	98	99	100	99	96	95	97	98	100	98	99	100	101	101	99
1970	=101=	101	100	102	101	96	101	106	95	102	101	98	107	101	101	102	100
1971	103	103	106	102	101	104	104	100	105	112	101	101	105	101	103	100	101
1972	104	98	103	105	108	102	96	97	104	103	103	104	105	105	107	107	112
1973	115	111	115	115	117	107	112	114	114	115	116	116	113	116	115	118	117
1974	114	112	115	116	115	108	111	115	112	112	120	115	118	116	113	116	115
1975	109	116	109	107	105	115	116	117	112	111	107	108	107	106	107	107	100
1976	104	103	105	104	104	105	102	100	107	109	97	103	106	105	106	103	102
1977	102	104	101	101	102	108	105	100	104	98	101	103	98	100	104	98	102
1978	=105=	104	104	109	106	103	103	107	104	105	103	107	107	113	104	104	110
1979	106	103	109	104	109	96	106	107	106	108	112	110	101	101	102	108	116
1980	100	106	102	99	93	108	107	104	103	101	103	100	100	97	94	93	90
1981	89	88	89	88	87	87	88	89	91	86	89	87	88	88	90	87	85
1982	89	89	89	91	90	88	90	89	88	93	86	91	90	92	91	89	89
1983	92	91	91	95	94	94	92	88	91	93	88	98	94	92	96	93	94

Engineering sales (volume): (2)(5) export — Ventes, fabrications métalliques (volume) : (2)(5) étranger

1980 = 100

Adjusted - Corrigé

	Year	Q.1	Q.2	Q.3	Q.4	JAN	FEB	MAR	APR	MAY	JUN	JUL	AUG	SEP	OCT	NOV	DEC
1964	58	56	59	58	61	55	56	57	58	59	59	57	58	60	61	61	59
1965	62	63	61	62	63	66	64	60	61	62	62	61	63	52	63	61	64
1966	66	63	63	66	69	64	63	63	64	62	64	65	67	63	70	71	66
1967	64	65	65	63	63	54	65	65	65	67	62	64	63	62	55	63	72
1968	69	66	67	70	70	63	67	67	68	65	69	67	69	74	68	73	71
1969	75	71	74	76	79	72	70	72	72	76	76	78	75	75	78	79	80
1970	=84=	84	83	85	85	81	85	87	80	77	89	74	91	89	88	85	83
1971	86	86	89	87	81	88	88	81	89	90	87	85	90	81	84	81	76
1972	77	75	75	74	83	79	69	79	75	77	74	70	71	82	82	84	82
1973	86	83	85	86	89	82	83	84	83	83	88	89	86	90	88	88	90
1974	99	92	99	102	104	88	94	94	97	95	105	97	107	102	104	101	106
1975	102	105	101	101	100	103	105	107	99	103	102	104	102	98	99	105	97
1976	103	102	103	102	104	104	102	101	106	107	97	102	101	102	105	105	103
1977	108	104	103	113	107	110	104	99	109	104	111	113	111	114	111	105	104
1978	=107=	107	105	108	107	105	106	111	106	106	105	107	112	106	100	104	115
1979	105	100	112	100	107	79	109	111	108	108	120	107	95	98	105	108	109
1980	100	105	103	99	94	106	101	107	103	104	100	98	100	98	96	95	91
1981	91	89	90	92	94	87	91	90	91	88	92	92	94	90	94	93	95
1982	91	92	92	92	89	93	93	90	91	94	91	93	89	93	89	87	89
1983	89	89	88	88	91	90	88	88	90	89	86	90	87	87	88	88	97

UNITED KINGDOM

Change in stocks (manufacturing):
finished goods *at 1980 prices*
£ million

Variations des stocks (industries manufacturières) :
produits finis *aux prix de 1980*
millions de £

Adjusted - Corrigé

	Year	Q.1	Q.2	Q.3	Q.4	JAN	FEB	MAR	APR	MAY	JUN	JUL	AUG	SEP	OCT	NOV	DEC
1964	370	64	210	39	57												
1965	518	124	197	124	73												
1966	584	162	70	286	66												
1967	-190	-54	34	-5	-165												
1968	205	-308	217	231	65												
1969	716	233	169	148	166												
1970	354	128	38	98	90												
1971	280	207	62	16	-5												
1972	-486	-284	-88	-42	-72												
1973	-112	-75	-9	-87	59												
1974	978	-449	443	605	379												
1975	70	249	-42	-108	-29												
1976	29	4	-136	-90	251												
1977	599	157	389	81	-28												
1978	126	34	155	76	-142												
1979	521	158	-121	151	333												
1980	-356	109	167	-56	-576												
1981	-491	-285	-270	-87	151												
1982	-223	86	-53	-122	-134												
1983	-163	-21	58	-232	32												

Change in stocks (manufacturing):
work in progress *at 1980 prices*
£ million

Variations des stocks (industries manufacturières) :
produits en cours de fabrication *aux prix de 1980*
millions de £

Adjusted - Corrigé

	Year	Q.1	Q.2	Q.3	Q.4	JAN	FEB	MAR	APR	MAY	JUN	JUL	AUG	SEP	OCT	NOV	DEC
1964	968	165	299	271	233												
1965	599	248	55	180	116												
1966	362	115	86	52	109												
1967	306	45	-6	44	223												
1968	329	-14	122	195	26												
1969	103	141	-27	1	-12												
1970	357	10	208	21	118												
1971	-313	-95	-188	-12	-18												
1972	85	-22	95	-3	15												
1973	722	265	73	204	180												
1974	455	-37	306	254	-18												
1975	-315	49	-41	-155	-168												
1976	408	-9	37	130	250												
1977	398	241	60	-64	161												
1978	176	-15	10	-103	284												
1979	-261	-68	1	-	-194												
1980	-714	-7	-234	-192	-281												
1981	-45	-135	-127	91	126												
1982	-293	-67	39	-101	-164												
1983	170	210	-76	4	33												

Change in stocks (manufacturing):
intermediate goods *at 1980 prices*
£ million

Variations des stocks (industries manufacturières) :
biens intermédiaires *aux prix de 1980*
millions de £

Adjusted - Corrigé

	Year	Q.1	Q.2	Q.3	Q.4	JAN	FEB	MAR	APR	MAY	JUN	JUL	AUG	SEP	OCT	NOV	DEC
1964	856	197	186	131	352												
1965	455	44	233	113	65												
1966	68	85	-23	209	-193												
1967	-45	128	-3	5	-175												
1968	365	49	4	131	181												
1969	367	83	196	-29	117												
1970	517	35	241	162	79												
1971	-655	-135	-174	-197	-149												
1972	-169	-101	-175	31	76												
1973	1408	361	434	244	369												
1974	691	132	168	268	123												
1975	-1580	-558	-237	-488	-247												
1976	-	-89	-78	58	109												
1977	357	207	118	32	-												
1978	174	121	-69	17	105												
1979	15	-45	135	32	-107												
1980	-1251	-270	-180	-387	-414												
1981	-922	-342	-356	-167	-57												
1982	-492	-55	18	-119	-336												
1983	-294	-167	-86	-153	113												

Net new orders: engineering (2)(5) (volume) total — Commandes nouvelles nettes : fabrications métalliques (2)(5) (volume) total

1980 = 100

Adjusted - Corrigé

	Year	Q.1	Q.2	Q.3	Q.4	JAN	FEB	MAR	APR	MAY	JUN	JUL	AUG	SEP	OCT	NOV	DEC
1964	94	88	96	95	97	88	81	96	98	96	95	94	98	93	96	99	95
1965	90	94	86	88	93	93	97	91	84	84	91	88	92	84	93	90	95
1966	90	95	85	90	91	102	91	92	77	90	90	91	91	88	95	88	89
1967	89	83	96	91	86	77	82	89	92	101	95	88	90	96	81	87	90
1968	98	93	95	102	100	86	94	99	106	86	96	104	98	102	95	98	106
1969	106	106	106	102	107	106	105	106	108	108	103	100	102	105	111	110	100
1970	=106=	112	106	104	105	113	111	111	102	107	110	96	112	103	105	109	103
1971	102	102	100	105	100	104	104	96	102	109	91	115	102	100	103	91	106
1972	107	103	105	107	117	104	104	99	100	110	105	106	105	110	119	117	116
1973	137	124	137	145	143	116	126	129	137	135	138	146	141	150	131	139	157
1974	122	130	130	117	109	129	126	133	132	122	136	117	118	116	116	110	103
1975	98	104	102	97	92	98	106	107	104	103	97	97	98	95	93	93	91
1976	109	100	104	115	115	103	102	97	103	105	104	115	113	111	122	120	102
1977	116	118	115	115	116	125	119	111	118	110	113	117	119	107	116	111	120
1978	=120=	119	115	117	129	126	119	113	115	117	113	115	110	125	111	131	145
1979	114	107	118	115	115	101	109	110	116	117	122	118	114	112	108	110	127
1980	100	109	109	94	88	105	108	113	103	112	110	99	88	95	87	84	95
1981	101	105	97	108	97	97	98	124	101	89	101	106	108	101	103	88	100
1982	95	93	98	90	100	119	96	86	109	104	83	93	87	93	107	89	101
1983	96	91	97	98	102	86	102	89	102	97	91	105	96	95	99	101	105

Net new orders: engineering (2)(5) (volume) domestic — Commandes nouvelles nettes : fabrications métalliques (2)(5) (volume) marché intérieur

1980 = 100

Adjusted - Corrigé

	Year	Q.1	Q.2	Q.3	Q.4	JAN	FEB	MAR	APR	MAY	JUN	JUL	AUG	SEP	OCT	NOV	DEC
1964	106	100	108	106	109	100	92	111	112	106	106	104	107	106	108	110	108
1965	100	102	95	99	103	102	102	101	93	94	100	98	106	93	105	100	103
1966	100	105	97	100	99	108	103	104	83	106	103	101	102	98	104	96	97
1967	97	92	103	100	94	86	91	99	105	105	100	98	96	107	87	97	97
1968	106	103	105	108	110	102	106	101	111	96	106	112	106	106	104	106	119
1969	112	115	112	110	112	120	118	106	114	113	111	109	112	109	117	118	110
1970	=113=	119	112	111	112	122	113	123	106	117	114	102	116	113	110	116	112
1971	111	108	108	115	111	111	111	102	108	121	97	129	111	107	112	101	121
1972	119	113	117	119	129	113	114	113	112	123	117	118	116	123	132	130	127
1973	147	138	147	153	150	128	140	145	149	149	145	160	147	155	136	142	169
1974	124	127	130	124	113	127	124	129	132	124	136	123	124	124	118	113	108
1975	101	110	104	99	94	104	110	114	107	108	96	97	97	100	97	93	91
1976	106	101	106	111	106	104	102	99	105	108	104	106	112	113	110	110	99
1977	114	118	108	113	114	124	122	108	112	107	107	118	117	104	116	112	114
1978	=122=	119	114	121	134	128	115	113	110	119	115	119	112	129	114	142	144
1979	117	107	121	121	117	104	111	105	120	119	124	125	120	117	105	113	134
1980	100	111	107	97	86	107	116	110	104	110	104	101	92	96	89	83	86
1981	102	109	99	102	97	99	97	130	99	89	109	110	87	100	100	87	102
1982	97	94	97	96	104	128	100	83	107	103	80	98	91	101	112	94	107
1983	98	88	97	102	105	86	94	87	97	100	94	108	102	96	103	105	108

Net new orders: engineering (2)(5) (volume) export — Commandes nouvelles nettes : fabrications métalliques (2)(5) (volume) étranger

1980 = 100

Adjusted - Corrigé

	Year	Q.1	Q.2	Q.3	Q.4	JAN	FEB	MAR	APR	MAY	JUN	JUL	AUG	SEP	OCT	NOV	DEC
1964	72	65	74	76	75	64	63	68	69	78	74	76	83	67	74	81	70
1965	73	80	69	67	74	77	90	74	67	64	78	69	67	67	71	72	81
1966	72	78	64	70	76	92	71	70	66	61	65	73	68	69	76	75	74
1967	75	67	84	75	73	59	67	73	69	96	89	68	81	76	71	68	80
1968	82	75	81	91	83	54	72	98	98	66	78	90	87	97	79	86	83
1969	92	87	95	89	99	72	81	107	96	99	90	84	87	97	101	97	100
1970	=94=	98	94	91	92	95	110	90	94	88	101	84	107	31	98	94	85
1971	84	38	85	85	78	89	89	85	90	85	81	87	83	88	84	73	75
1972	84	80	81	83	94	87	82	70	79	84	81	84	82	82	95	92	97
1973	118	97	117	131	128	93	100	97	115	108	127	122	130	143	120	134	131
1974	119	138	130	104	102	136	131	146	136	118	137	108	107	100	110	103	94
1975	94	95	98	95	90	89	102	95	99	95	99	95	101	85	85	94	90
1976	116	100	102	126	135	103	103	93	100	100	107	151	118	110	152	144	109
1977	121	120	127	119	121	127	116	118	133	117	131	115	127	117	120	109	134
1978	=118=	121	118	112	118	118	133	114	134	112	107	121	102	112	102	99	152
1979	107	107	113	98	108	94	101	126	106	116	116	99	97	99	114	101	111
1980	100	103	116	86	98	103	83	124	98	121	130	93	77	90	81	92	122
1981	104	99	94	127	100	92	101	103	111	91	79	102	173	107	115	91	95
1982	90	92	105	75	87	96	83	96	115	107	93	85	74	66	92	81	88
1983	96	104	98	88	92	88	128	99	122	87	84	98	78	91	83	91	100

UNITED KINGDOM

Construction (Great Britain): volume of new orders (6)
total, including civil engineering
1980 = 100

Construction (Grande-Bretagne) : commandes nouvelles (6)
(volume) total, y compris les travaux publics
1980 = 100

	Year	Q.1	Q.2	Q.3	Q.4	JAN	FEB	MAR	APR	MAY	JUN	JUL	AUG	SEP	OCT	NOV	DEC
1964	199	181	190	201	223												
1965	188	200	186	189	178												
1966	178	175	173	185	175												
1967	204	219	199	194	204												
1968	189	192	182	181	200												
1969	178	176	173	175	189												
1970	175	176	182	177	165												
1971	186	181	188	182	191												
1972	195	198	208	176	198												
1973	189	215	193	187	163												
1974	135	132	129	135	142												
1975	132	123	129	142	133												
1976	140	149	151	131	128												
1977	126	123	125	126	130												
1978	132	137	129	133	128												
1979	120	117	123	117	118	113	124	114	122	136	126	130	117	105	126	116	122
1980	100	108	101	95	96	108	109	107	109	94	101	96	87	100	85	94	110
1981	109	106	111	113	107	118	104	97	94	111	127	116	120	101	111	109	101
1982	113	112	106	111	124	110	108	118	103	106	109	112	98	124	110	122	140
1983	129	132	119	131	132	135	123	139	134	119	105	142	121	131	122	138	136

Construction (Great Britain): volume of new orders (6)
residential
1980 = 100

Adjusted - Corrigé

Construction (Grande-Bretagne) : commandes nouvelles (6)
(volume), bâtiments résidentiels
1980 = 100

	Year	Q.1	Q.2	Q.3	Q.4	JAN	FEB	MAR	APR	MAY	JUN	JUL	AUG	SEP	OCT	NOV	DEC
1964	307	279	285	316	350												
1965	298	321	278	302	293												
1966	273	260	279	286	268												
1967	329	366	336	299	315												
1968	284	310	281	275	270												
1969	230	241	213	235	233												
1970	233	228	240	245	219												
1971	239	210	226	245	274												
1972	267	273	279	258	259												
1973	253	305	246	244	219												
1974	166	166	153	165	172												
1975	198	132	187	207	216												
1976	203	243	211	188	170												
1977	167	155	163	165	176												
1978	175	133	177	175	162												
1979	148	137	154	161	140	129	144	137	146	160	157	180	153	150	146	134	140
1980	100	126	101	88	85	128	129	121	112	103	89	88	93	84	81	84	90
1981	95	92	88	95	104	84	102	90	81	94	89	94	93	98	114	101	96
1982	131	124	124	132	147	108	126	137	131	118	124	121	131	145	130	154	155
1983	157	176	149	154	148	181	168	178	169	133	144	154	146	162	148	159	137

Construction (Great Britain): housing starts
thousands, monthly averages

Construction (Grande-Bretagne) : logements mis en chantier
milliers, moyennes mensuelles

	Year	Q.1	Q.2	Q.3	Q.4	JAN	FEB	MAR	APR	MAY	JUN	JUL	AUG	SEP	OCT	NOV	DEC
1964	35.5	33.4	38.1	34.4	36.2	36.0	31.7	32.4	36.5	39.5	38.2	34.4	32.4	36.3	39.5	37.5	31.7
1965	32.7	32.4	37.0	30.4	31.2	29.1	33.5	34.4	40.1	36.5	34.4	29.8	30.1	31.1	37.2	29.2	27.2
1966	31.6	27.9	35.0	34.4	28.1	25.2	23.0	35.6	36.2	33.8	38.0	37.7	31.6	33.8	29.7	28.8	25.9
1967	37.3	35.7	45.3	36.7	31.5	25.9	33.2	48.2	51.0	40.5	44.1	38.0	35.8	36.4	33.1	34.0	27.5
1968	32.9	30.2	38.5	33.2	29.5	24.5	29.9	36.1	36.7	40.1	39.0	32.1	35.2	32.4	31.2	28.3	28.9
1969	28.6	23.6	35.7	30.7	24.5	24.8	20.5	25.5	35.8	32.8	38.5	32.8	29.0	30.4	29.8	22.9	20.6
1970	26.6	19.5	31.6	29.4	25.8	18.8	18.7	21.1	29.3	32.8	32.5	31.9	25.6	30.7	31.2	24.8	21.5
1971	28.7	23.6	30.3	30.9	30.0	20.5	23.0	27.3	31.0	29.8	30.2	32.1	27.9	32.6	31.8	27.6	30.5
1972	29.3	25.3	33.2	30.5	28.5	23.4	23.0	29.5	29.4	31.7	38.4	31.8	29.2	29.1	30.9	30.4	24.3
1973	27.4	27.3	31.5	28.0	22.7	25.4	27.3	29.3	31.5	30.8	32.3	28.2	27.0	28.9	26.2	24.0	17.8
1974	21.0	19.8	24.9	20.9	18.4	17.0	19.1	23.3	24.5	25.4	24.8	20.7	21.6	20.4	22.1	18.4	14.8
1975	25.9	21.4	28.9	29.4	27.9	20.2	22.9	21.2	27.1	29.0	30.5	31.0	26.9	30.4	33.0	27.6	23.2
1976	27.1	27.3	32.3	29.9	19.0	23.9	25.2	32.6	30.8	31.2	35.1	32.5	27.9	29.2	21.5	20.9	14.6
1977	22.2	17.8	25.1	25.4	20.6	15.7	14.7	22.9	22.9	26.7	25.9	26.0	22.0	28.3	24.7	21.1	16.1
1978	22.1	17.8	27.1	23.0	20.3	17.5	15.3	20.7	25.4	25.1	30.9	23.6	20.3	25.0	24.5	20.7	15.8
1979	18.8	12.9	21.5	21.0	19.6	10.1	12.7	15.9	18.6	20.1	25.9	22.5	18.2	22.4	21.7	20.2	16.9
1980	12.8	13.3	15.3	12.6	10.1	12.6	13.6	13.7	14.6	16.0	15.3	14.0	10.8	13.0	11.9	11.4	7.1
1981	12.7	11.1	14.1	14.2	11.3	10.4	11.3	11.4	12.4	13.8	16.0	14.5	12.6	15.5	13.2	13.9	7.8
1982	15.1	14.7	17.5	17.1	13.1	11.6	15.2	17.5	17.1	17.7	17.6	16.7	15.9	19.0	15.5	17.1	12.7
1983	17.9	18.1	19.9	17.3	15.9	15.6	18.2	26.1	17.3	19.4	22.8	27.3	16.8	18.3	18.6	18.2	11.0

Construction (Great Britain): volume of work put in place total, including civil engineering
1980 = 100

Adjusted - Corrigé

Construction (Grande-Bretagne) : travaux effectués (volume) total, y compris les travaux publics
1980 = 100

	Year	Q.1	Q.2	Q.3	Q.4	JAN	FEB	MAR	APR	MAY	JUN	JUL	AUG	SEP	OCT	NOV	DEC
1964	100	99	100	98	104												
1965	106	106	105	106	103												
1966	108	107	107	109	110												
1967	115	114	116	116	116												
1968	118	118	117	113	113												
1969	117	118	117	118	117												
1970	115	112	116	118	115												
1971	116	115	117	116	118												
1972	118	119	119	117	116												
1973	118	122	118	118	115												
1974	106	110	108	106	100												
1975	100	101	100	100	99												
1976	98	101	97	96	99												
1977	98	97	97	98	100												
1978	105	102	107	106	104												
1979	106	101	107	107	107												
1980	100	105	101	101	94												
1981	91	93	90	92	87												
1982	92	90	90	93	95												
1983	96	94	91	98	99												

Construction (Great Britain): volume of work put in place new dwellings, public sector
1980 = 100

Adjusted - Corrigé

Construction (Grande-Bretagne) : travaux effectués (volume) nouveaux logements, secteur public
1980 = 100

	Year	Q.1	Q.2	Q.3	Q.4	JAN	FEB	MAR	APR	MAY	JUN	JUL	AUG	SEP	OCT	NOV	DEC
1964	156	156	157	148	163												
1965	176	172	171	180	180												
1966	185	177	183	187	195												
1967	211	209	211	208	214												
1968	217	215	216	221	213												
1969	209	214	208	206	207												
1970	184	187	187	184	176												
1971	168	170	171	165	166												
1972	150	159	157	141	144												
1973	146	150	147	148	140												
1974	142	140	142	141	145												
1975	157	149	152	161	165												
1976	173	178	174	168	172												
1977	157	159	156	159	156												
1978	148	150	152	149	140												
1979	123	122	126	121	122												
1980	100	116	104	95	85												
1981	66	78	69	62	54												
1982	55	56	54	54	57												
1983	59	60	58	59	59												

Construction (Great Britain): volume of work put in place new dwellings, private sector
1980 = 100

Adjusted - Corrigé

Construction (Grande-Bretagne) : travaux effectués (volume) nouveaux logements, secteur privé
1980 = 100

	Year	Q.1	Q.2	Q.3	Q.4	JAN	FEB	MAR	APR	MAY	JUN	JUL	AUG	SEP	OCT	NOV	DEC
1964	151	145	150	150	160												
1965	155	164	152	152	151												
1966	147	150	148	145	147												
1967	160	154	158	166	164												
1968	169	169	170	166	170												
1969	155	164	161	154	141												
1970	142	139	140	142	147												
1971	163	153	161	166	172												
1972	178	180	175	177	180												
1973	186	189	189	188	176												
1974	134	155	134	127	119												
1975	121	117	122	121	122												
1976	128	135	127	122	131												
1977	122	118	119	123	126												
1978	138	134	141	140	136												
1979	127	121	129	128	130												
1980	100	118	99	97	86												
1981	91	93	93	91	87												
1982	104	92	101	104	121												
1983	125	124	121	124	131												

Retail sales (value): total (3)(7) — Ventes au détail (valeur) : total (3)(7)

(Great Britain) — (Grande-Bretagne)

1980 = 100

	Year	Q.1	Q.2	Q.3	Q.4	JAN	FEB	MAR	APR	MAY	JUN	JUL	AUG	SEP	OCT	NOV	DEC
1964	19	17	18	18	21	17	16	17	18	18	18	19	18	18	19	20	25
1965	20	18	19	19	23	18	18	18	19	19	19	20	19	19	20	21	26
1966	21	19	20	20	23	19	18	19	20	21	20	21	20	20	21	22	27
1967	21	20	21	21	25	20	19	20	20	21	21	21	20	21	22	23	29
1968	23	21	22	22	26	21	21	22	22	22	22	23	22	22	23	25	30
1969	24	22	24	24	28	23	21	23	24	24	24	24	24	24	25	27	32
1970	26	24	25	26	30	24	23	24	25	26	25	26	26	26	27	29	35
1971	29	25	28	29	34	26	24	26	28	29	28	29	29	28	30	32	39
1972	33	29	31	32	39	29	28	29	29	31	31	32	32	32	34	36	45
1973	37	33	34	36	44	33	32	35	33	35	35	36	36	36	39	41	51
1974	43	37	39	42	52	37	36	38	39	40	40	42	42	43	46	49	60
1975	51	45	49	50	60	45	44	45	52	47	48	50	49	50	53	57	69
1976	58	51	54	57	71	52	50	51	54	55	54	57	57	57	61	67	81
1977	67	59	61	66	80	60	58	59	61	62	62	66	65	65	68	74	95
1978	76	66	71	76	92	67	65	67	71	71	71	77	75	75	79	85	109
1979	89	76	85	87	108	76	73	77	82	83	88	87	87	86	93	101	127
1980	100	91	95	98	117	91	89	93	95	93	96	100	97	98	103	110	133
1981	108	100	103	105	125	102	97	100	103	100	104	105	106	105	111	118	143
1982	117	107	110	113	137	109	105	108	111	110	109	113	114	112	119	128	160
1983	128	116	120	124	151	117	113	118	120	120	120	124	124	124	130	141	177

New passenger car registrations (8) — Immatriculations de voitures de tourisme neuves (8)

thousands, monthly averages — milliers, moyennes mensuelles

	Year	Q.1	Q.2	Q.3	Q.4	JAN	FEB	MAR	APR	MAY	JUN	JUL	AUG	SEP	OCT	NOV	DEC
1964	99.2	106.5	121.5	92.9	76.0	98.2	100.0	121.3	130.0	116.6	117.8	113.4	78.2	87.3	86.2	82.8	59.0
1965	93.5	120.2	109.1	79.3	65.6	103.0	110.0	147.7	119.0	104.5	103.7	100.6	68.5	68.7	72.7	68.3	55.8
1966	88.8	116.1	119.9	71.0	48.2	107.7	103.5	137.1	137.0	120.1	102.5	99.5	59.3	54.3	52.8	52.6	39.1
1967	93.1	100.4	102.3	87.7	81.9	103.2	92.9	105.0	96.7	105.0	105.2	92.4	89.4	81.2	88.6	91.5	65.7
1968	93.1	129.7	88.1	80.3	74.2	122.0	131.4	135.8	86.5	102.3	75.5	73.6	94.1	73.1	85.0	79.1	58.5
1969	82.3	89.4	94.4	83.3	62.1	84.2	84.4	99.4	105.5	93.7	84.0	73.2	101.9	74.8	77.4	58.0	51.0
1970	91.4	95.9	102.8	91.0	76.0	84.8	92.2	110.7	107.8	100.5	100.1	87.0	102.3	83.7	82.2	77.7	68.1
1971	108.9	104.4	105.1	117.9	108.1	106.4	97.0	109.8	107.1	106.3	102.0	100.6	142.6	110.6	113.7	118.9	91.9
1972	138.6	133.7	156.3	142.0	122.4	137.5	120.4	143.2	147.6	164.6	156.6	116.4	183.3	125.8	134.8	135.3	97.0
1973	137.1	159.8	142.2	145.9	100.6	159.8	152.0	167.7	144.8	144.7	137.1	126.0	197.1	114.6	116.6	114.2	70.9
1974	102.8	109.1	110.1	110.5	81.7	100.9	107.5	118.9	101.4	115.1	113.7	91.2	134.2	106.2	94.5	90.2	60.2
1975	98.5	116.9	97.0	110.1	70.2	128.4	112.9	109.5	93.2	100.6	97.1	57.1	154.2	119.1	79.7	77.9	52.9
1976	106.5	117.4	111.5	108.4	83.9	129.0	105.6	116.6	117.9	119.8	96.8	55.1	182.3	87.8	97.3	107.0	62.3
1977	109.4	118.9	108.3	123.4	87.2	114.0	125.0	117.6	110.4	118.8	95.8	67.0	197.6	105.6	106.3	96.2	59.2
1978	131.6	148.6	132.2	150.1	95.5	151.3	133.4	161.2	136.6	125.6	134.3	63.7	246.0	140.8	119.1	102.7	64.7
1979	142.1	154.6	182.2	126.4	105.1	155.2	133.0	175.7	169.2	180.9	196.6	51.4	215.8	112.0	125.8	120.5	69.0
1980	126.6	164.4	123.1	137.0	82.0	156.8	143.4	192.9	118.3	130.2	120.9	42.4	236.1	132.4	95.5	95.6	54.8
1981	124.6	138.8	124.3	138.2	96.9	137.2	118.1	161.0	136.0	133.2	103.6	46.6	247.1	121.0	116.0	114.0	60.8
1982	132.0	139.2	122.8	158.3	107.9	116.7	125.4	175.5	136.0	123.4	108.9	46.7	311.1	117.2	136.0	119.4	68.2
1983	150.5	165.6	141.4	183.2	111.8	167.8	144.1	185.0	148.5	143.3	132.6	52.4	375.8	121.3	136.4	125.5	73.5

Retail sales (volume): total (3)(7) — Ventes au détail (volume) : total (3)(7)

(Great Britain) — (Grande-Bretagne)

1980 = 100

Adjusted - Corrigé

	Year	Q.1	Q.2	Q.3	Q.4	JAN	FEB	MAR	APR	MAY	JUN	JUL	AUG	SEP	OCT	NOV	DEC
1964	77	76	76	77	78	76	76	76	76	76	76	76	76	78	78	77	78
1965	79	78	78	79	80	78	78	78	78	78	78	79	79	79	79	80	79
1966	80	80	80	79	79	80	80	80	80	81	80	81	79	79	79	79	79
1967	82	80	80	82	83	80	81	80	80	80	81	82	82	83	83	83	84
1968	84	85	83	84	84	84	85	87	83	82	84	84	84	84	84	86	83
1969	85	84	85	85	85	85	83	84	85	86	85	84	85	85	84	85	84
1970	87	86	87	87	87	85	86	85	86	87	87	87	87	87	87	86	87
1971	88	86	89	88	88	87	84	87	89	90	88	88	89	89	89	88	88
1972	92	89	93	94	94	89	89	90	91	94	93	94	93	93	94	94	95
1973	97	97	96	96	97	95	97	100	94	96	97	97	96	96	97	97	97
1974	96	95	94	96	96	94	95	96	94	94	95	95	96	97	97	98	95
1975	94	96	95	91	91	96	96	95	105	93	91	91	91	92	92	91	92
1976	93	93	94	93	93	96	92	92	94	94	93	93	93	93	93	94	91
1977	92	91	90	92	93	92	91	90	89	90	90	92	92	92	91	92	94
1978	96	94	95	98	99	94	93	94	95	96	96	95	98	98	98	98	100
1979	101	98	104	99	102	97	97	99	102	102	109	98	99	100	101	103	101
1980	100	101	100	100	99	101	101	100	100	100	101	100	100	100	100	99	99
1981	100	102	100	101	99	104	101	101	100	100	101	100	101	101	101	100	98
1982	103	102	101	103	104	103	101	102	101	102	101	101	104	103	103	104	105
1983	108	106	107	108	110	105	105	106	107	107	107	107	108	110	109	111	111

Retail sales (value): total (3)(7) — Ventes au détail (valeur) : total (3)(7)

(Great Britain) — (Grande-Bretagne)

1980 = 100

Adjusted - Corrigé

	Year	Q.1	Q.2	Q.3	Q.4	JAN	FEB	MAR	APR	MAY	JUN	JUL	AUG	SEP	OCT	NOV	DEC
1964		18	18	19	19	18	18	18	18	18	18	19	19	19	19	19	19
1965		19	20	20	20	19	19	19	20	20	20	20	20	20	20	20	20
1966		20	21	21	21	20	20	21	21	21	21	21	21	21	21	21	21
1967		21	21	22	22	21	21	21	21	21	21	21	21	22	22	22	22
1968		23	23	23	24	22	23	23	23	22	23	23	23	23	23	24	23
1969		24	24	25	25	24	23	24	24	25	24	24	25	25	25	25	25
1970		26	26	27	27	25	26	26	26	26	26	27	27	27	27	27	27
1971		27	29	30	30	28	27	28	29	30	29	29	30	30	30	30	30
1972		31	32	33	34	30	30	31	31	32	32	33	33	33	34	34	35
1973		36	36	37	39	35	36	37	35	36	37	37	37	38	38	39	39
1974		40	41	44	46	39	39	41	41	41	42	43	44	45	46	47	46
1975		48	51	51	53	47	48	49	54	50	50	51	51	52	52	52	53
1976		55	57	59	62	56	55	55	57	58	57	58	59	60	61	62	62
1977		63	65	68	70	63	64	64	64	65	66	68	68	69	69	69	72
1978		72	74	78	80	71	71	72	73	75	75	78	78	79	79	80	82
1979		81	89	90	95	80	81	83	86	86	93	88	90	91	93	96	96
1980		97	100	102	102	95	97	98	99	99	101	101	101	102	103	102	102
1981		106	107	109	110	108	106	106	106	106	108	108	109	110	111	110	109
1982		115	115	118	121	115	114	115	115	116	115	116	119	118	119	120	122
1983		123	126	129	133	122	123	124	125	126	127	127	129	131	131	133	134

New passenger car registrations (8) — Immatriculations de voitures de tourisme neuves (8)

thousands, monthly averages — milliers, moyennes mensuelles

Adjusted - Corrigé

	Year	Q.1	Q.2	Q.3	Q.4	JAN	FEB	MAR	APR	MAY	JUN	JUL	AUG	SEP	OCT	NOV	DEC
1964		95.9	97.3	106.1	105.3	99.2	96.5	91.9	97.6	91.5	104.3	101.7	104.0	112.7	106.5	109.7	102.8
1965		104.8	91.4	92.2	94.4	99.0	105.8	109.6	92.8	88.0	93.4	93.1	91.9	91.7	93.1	91.5	98.6
1966		101.1	107.7	84.5	70.2	99.7	93.2	105.3	116.5	107.5	99.1	100.2	77.7	75.5	69.7	70.6	70.3
1967		82.1	91.5	99.1	103.3	87.2	81.0	78.2	82.8	90.4	101.2	95.4	98.3	103.6	104.8	112.9	107.1
1968		110.6	83.6	90.0	96.7	109.5	114.6	107.7	79.3	92.8	78.7	83.8	95.1	91.1	97.9	98.7	93.5
1969		79.7	90.1	88.7	78.2	79.0	78.6	81.6	95.6	87.1	87.7	85.1	93.5	87.6	85.7	71.4	77.5
1970		88.2	97.5	94.7	93.9	81.8	89.3	93.5	96.9	93.8	101.8	100.3	89.1	94.8	90.1	92.0	99.6
1971		97.2	100.2	114.4	132.3	96.1	97.4	98.1	103.8	99.8	97.0	112.8	112.9	117.4	123.3	128.3	145.2
1972		126.9	151.2	138.5	150.6	129.0	121.8	129.8	146.1	157.0	150.4	140.5	141.2	134.1	149.5	149.9	152.4
1973		150.5	140.3	142.4	123.1	145.1	151.6	154.9	144.6	139.6	136.7	141.7	154.7	130.9	130.8	130.5	122.9
1974		101.6	106.7	109.3	103.4	88.7	105.8	110.2	100.1	104.0	116.0	108.1	103.3	116.5	105.7	100.0	104.5
1975		100.1	94.7	108.1	95.2	104.2	100.7	95.4	88.8	93.2	102.1	108.1	89.4	126.7	90.0	95.5	100.1
1976		100.7	108.0	101.4	120.3	105.2	96.3	100.6	111.4	111.1	101.5	106.2	104.8	93.2	110.1	131.4	119.3
1977		102.7	104.7	119.7	117.9	94.3	115.1	98.7	103.1	110.7	100.4	136.0	111.1	112.0	120.4	118.0	115.4
1978		126.1	128.5	141.0	130.1	128.1	125.3	130.8	126.2	117.1	142.1	138.4	134.8	149.7	135.4	125.2	129.7
1979		132.5	179.1	118.4	143.3	133.4	127.6	136.6	155.7	171.1	210.5	121.0	115.0	119.2	142.3	145.9	141.7
1980		142.3	123.7	126.7	114.0	136.0	141.0	150.0	111.0	126.0	134.0	110.0	122.0	148.0	110.0	116.0	116.0
1981		119.7	123.3	126.0	129.3	119.0	113.0	122.0	127.0	129.0	114.0	124.0	119.0	135.0	128.0	134.0	126.0
1982		118.0	125.0	139.0	145.7	99.0	124.0	131.0	128.0	122.0	125.0	132.0	148.0	137.0	151.0	143.0	146.0
1983		144.0	149.0	156.7	152.0	145.0	146.0	141.0	144.0	147.0	156.0	152.0	174.0	144.0	149.0	150.0	157.0

Employment: manufacturing (2)(9) — Emploi : industries manufacturières (2)(9)

(all employees) — (salariés)

thousands — milliers

	Year	Q.1	Q.2	Q.3	Q.4	JAN	FEB	MAR	APR	MAY	JUN	JUL	AUG	SEP	OCT	NOV	DEC
1964	8454	8417	8452	8515	8596	8408	8419	8424	8449	8453	8454	8474	8512	8559	8581	8599	8507
1965	8564	8562	8562	8616	8667	8557	8567	8561	8548	8575	8564	8581	8619	8646	8657	8670	8674
1966	8587	8607	8592	8627	8573	8616	8612	8592	8599	8590	8587	8604	8640	8637	8615	8571	8533
1967	8323	8421	8352	8326	8326	8436	8418	8388	8380	8352	8323	8320	8329	8328	8323	8327	8329
1968	8242	8250	8240	8305	8366	8252	8254	8243	8233	8246	8242	8273	8317	8327	8348	8356	8384
1969	8356	8346	8364	8406	8459	8338	8349	8351	8371	8365	8356	8389	8410	8419	8448	8461	8468
1970	8342	8391	8364	8365	8358	8399	8392	8381	8385	8365	8342	8363	8370	8362	8367	8363	8346
1971	8058	..	8105	8049	7968	8277	..	8226	8153	8105	8058	8060	8058	8029	7999	7962	7942
1972	7779	7837	7789	7821	7840	7870	7842	7798	7759	7790	7779	7804	7829	7831	7834	7844	7842
1973	7830	7815	7825	7884	7940	7805	7818	7822	7821	7824	7830	7872	7890	7890	7908	7945	7966
1974	7873	7869	7863	7923	7883	7886	7868	7853	7858	7875	7873	7905	7932	7931	7908	7893	7850
1975	7490	7716	7547	7455	7388	7773	7714	7661	7605	7546	7490	7474	7459	7433	7406	7391	7365
1976	7246	7275	7238	7295	7329	7301	7272	7253	7238	7230	7246	7285	7295	7305	7327	7333	7327
1977	7292	7288	7288	7325	7320	7286	7290	7287	7286	7286	7292	7325	7324	7325	7324	7320	7317
1978	7257	7272	7255	7284	7276	7272	7268	7277	7261	7251	7257	7286	7283	7284	7279	7279	7270
1979	7193	7210	7188	7214	7145	7224	7209	7198	7186	7185	7193	7225	7219	7198	7165	7152	7123
1980	6840	7015	6879	6725	6498	7058	7015	6972	6919	6878	6840	6795	6726	6655	6574	6490	6430
1981	6087	6279	6131	6107	6111	6338	6277	6221	6171	6135	6087	6075	6064	6177	6149	6113	6071
1982	5764	5990	5920	5873	5781	6006	5988	5977	5935	5921	5903	5891	5874	5855	5816	5787	5741
1983	5598	5660	5614	5581	5537	5670	5663	5647	5627	5612	5603	5619	5572	5552	5537	5546	5528

UNITED KINGDOM

Unemployment (registered unemployed) (10) — **Chômage** (chômeurs inscrits) (10)

thousands — milliers

	Year	Q.1	Q.2	Q.3	Q.4	JAN	FEB	MAR	APR	MAY	JUN	JUL	AUG	SEP	OCT	NOV	DEC
1964	394	482	389	340	363	509	489	449	430	391	347	334	344	343	360	364	365
1965	339	386	324	305	339	395	389	374	345	328	298	293	308	315	330	340	343
1966	353	353	299	306	455	358	357	334	321	297	280	281	302	336	397	468	500
1967	547	565	530	515	578	551	573	562	557	532	501	499	519	528	558	584	593
1968	574	623	567	534	573	634	630	605	594	568	539	527	538	537	567	578	575
1969	566	612	545	526	583	621	613	602	578	541	515	511	529	537	568	583	593
1970	602	640	585	566	618	645	639	635	620	533	552	552	569	576	600	617	636
1971	744	693	709	730	845	682	691	705	713	719	695	702	725	763	806	852	875
1972	826	934	840	770	760	933	934	935	911	837	773	762	766	781	770	764	747
1973	591	729	603	531	502	773	723	691	655	600	555	535	535	521	510	502	495
1974	591	607	552	574	631	609	612	601	587	544	525	539	584	598	608	626	658
1975	902	762	813	943	1091	747	764	776	801	814	823	891	949	939	1046	1093	1135
1976	1229	1233	1194	1236	1255	1234	1240	1225	1220	1198	1163	1202	1250	1258	1241	1255	1268
1977	1313	1324	1254	1327	1347	1346	1329	1298	1286	1244	1233	1291	1330	1360	1342	1349	1349
1978	1299	1384	1271	1286	1255	1417	1387	1349	1323	1268	1221	1257	1302	1298	1267	1256	1246
1979	1227	1324	1184	1281	1220	1336	1340	1298	1242	1190	1120	1161	1187	1196	1211	1219	1230
1980	1561	1351	1372	1605	1914	1339	1360	1353	1379	1368	1370	1486	1619	1714	1795	1925	2022
1981	2420	2237	2321	2502	2520	2191	2244	2275	2319	2325	2318	2435	2501	2570	2592	2626	2642
1982	2793	2751	2699	2804	2919	2759	2759	2726	2732	2696	2671	2753	2796	2862	2875	2916	2966
1983	2970	3074	2941	2919	2945	3087	3076	3060	3035	2924	2865	2905	2898	2953	2926	2947	2961

Jobs vacant, unfilled vacancies (11) — **Offres d'emploi non satisfaites** (11)

thousands — milliers

	Year	Q.1	Q.2	Q.3	Q.4	JAN	FEB	MAR	APR	MAY	JUN	JUL	AUG	SEP	OCT	NOV	DEC
1964	222	183	231	244	230	167	179	204	214	228	252	251	240	240	235	232	223
1965	267	235	290	286	237	223	231	251	276	288	304	298	284	277	268	256	248
1966	257	262	297	274	194	247	262	276	291	297	302	298	275	249	219	197	175
1967	175	170	183	179	169	165	169	175	179	181	188	185	175	178	177	167	165
1968	190	168	196	199	195	151	166	178	187	195	204	206	194	197	193	195	197
1969	202	190	214	211	193	183	189	198	203	214	221	214	209	211	200	190	188
1970	188	184	200	196	173	182	184	187	195	199	207	203	192	194	185	171	161
1971	131	139	139	130	115	147	140	132	133	136	147	134	130	127	121	116	109
1972	147	113	144	157	176	105	114	120	132	142	158	155	155	160	168	176	182
1973	307	219	302	345	362	197	222	247	276	304	326	339	338	357	368	366	352
1974	303	276	323	318	..	289	270	270	302	326	340	334	307	311	303	275	.. S
1975	150	..	169	142	117	.. S	185	182	177	167	162	145	139	143	132	116	103
1976	121	99	124	134	..	99	100	109	120	124	127	129	130	142	140	.. S	.. S
1977	158	..	163	161	161	.. S	134	144	156	165	169	163	158	161	169	160	154
1978	210	172	216	222	231	159	172	186	204	216	228	219	214	233	241	232	221
1979	241	219	265	254	227	215	216	227	250	268	277	260	248	253	247	231	204
1980	143	130	173	124	95	136	179	177	175	177	165	133	119	119	109	93	84
1981	97	85	103	100	100	82	83	92	100	107	103	97	97	105	107	101	92
1982	111	99	121	114	111	92	99	106	115	123	124	115	112	115	120	111	103
1983	145	121	149	163	158	103	110	121	141	148	158	157	160	171	173	160	140

Unemployment (registered unemployed) (10)(12) — **Chômage** (chômeurs inscrits) (10)(12)

as per cent of civilian labour force — en pourcentage de la main-d'œuvre civile

Adjusted - Corrigé

	Year	Q.1	Q.2	Q.3	Q.4	JAN	FEB	MAR	APR	MAY	JUN	JUL	AUG	SEP	OCT	NOV	DEC
1964	1.7	1.8	1.7	1.7	1.5	1.9	1.8	1.7	1.7	1.7	1.7	1.7	1.7	1.6	1.6	1.5	1.4
1965	1.4	1.4	1.4	1.5	1.4	1.4	1.4	1.4	1.4	1.4	1.4	1.5	1.5	1.5	1.4	1.4	1.3
1966	1.5	1.3	1.3	1.5	1.9	1.3	1.2	1.3	1.3	1.3	1.4	1.4	1.4	1.6	1.7	1.9	2.0
1967	2.3	2.2	2.3	2.4	2.4	2.1	2.2	2.2	2.3	2.3	2.3	2.3	2.4	2.4	2.4	2.4	2.4
1968	2.4	2.4	2.5	2.4	2.4	2.4	2.4	2.4	2.4	2.5	2.5	2.4	2.4	2.4	2.4	2.4	2.4
1969	2.4	2.4	2.4	2.4	2.4	2.4	2.4	2.4	2.4	2.4	2.4	2.4	2.4	2.4	2.4	2.4	2.5
1970	2.6	2.5	2.5	2.6	2.6	2.5	2.5	2.5	2.5	2.5	2.6	2.6	2.6	2.6	2.6	2.6	2.7
1971	3.4	2.9	3.3	3.4	3.8	2.8	2.9	3.0	3.1	3.3	3.4	3.4	3.4	3.5	3.7	3.8	3.9
1972	3.7	4.0	3.8	3.6	3.4	3.9	4.0	4.0	4.0	3.8	3.7	3.6	3.6	3.6	3.5	3.4	3.3
1973	2.6	3.0	2.8	2.5	2.2	3.1	3.0	2.9	2.8	2.8	2.7	2.6	2.5	2.4	2.3	2.2	2.2
1974	2.6	2.5	2.5	2.6	2.8	2.4	2.5	2.5	2.5	2.5	2.6	2.6	2.6	2.7	2.7	2.8	2.9
1975	3.9	3.1	3.6	4.2	4.7	3.0	3.1	3.3	3.4	3.7	3.8	4.0	4.2	4.3	4.6	4.7	4.9
1976	5.3	5.1	5.3	5.4	5.4	5.0	5.1	5.1	5.2	5.3	5.3	5.3	5.4	5.4	5.3	5.4	5.4
1977	5.5	5.4	5.4	5.6	5.7	5.4	5.4	5.4	5.4	5.4	5.5	5.6	5.6	5.7	5.7	5.7	5.7
1978	5.5	5.6	5.5	5.5	5.3	5.6	5.6	5.6	5.5	5.5	5.5	5.5	5.5	5.4	5.4	5.3	5.2
1979	5.1	5.3	5.2	5.0	5.0	5.3	5.4	5.3	5.2	5.2	5.1	5.1	5.0	5.0	5.0	5.0	5.0
1980	6.4	5.3	5.8	6.7	7.9	5.1	5.3	5.4	5.6	5.8	6.0	6.3	6.7	7.0	7.4	7.9	8.3
1981	10.0	9.0	9.8	10.4	10.8	8.7	9.0	9.3	9.5	9.8	10.0	10.3	10.4	10.6	10.7	10.9	10.9
1982	11.7	11.2	11.5	11.9	12.2	11.2	11.2	11.3	11.4	11.5	11.6	11.8	11.9	12.0	12.1	12.2	12.4
1983	12.4	12.6	12.5	12.4	12.3	12.5	12.6	12.7	12.7	12.4	12.4	12.4	12.3	12.4	12.3	12.3	12.3

Unemployment (registered unemployed) (10)
thousands

Adjusted - Corrigé

Chômage (chômeurs inscrits) (10)
milliers

	Year	Q.1	Q.2	Q.3	Q.4	JAN	FEB	MAR	APR	MAY	JUN	JUL	AUG	SEP	OCT	NOV	DEC
1964		419	404	390	354	440	415	402	408	406	398	395	391	383	370	352	340
1965		332	338	353	328	329	328	338	325	343	347	352	353	353	338	325	321
1966		302	315	352	444	395	299	302	303	313	323	338	345	374	404	454	474
1967		516	545	560	567	499	519	529	540	547	547	554	561	565	565	572	571
1968		574	581	577	568	573	577	571	575	583	565	580	577	573	575	569	559
1969		562	557	567	580	550	561	565	557	555	560	562	567	571	577	578	536
1970		537	593	607	518	584	585	592	597	596	601	604	607	610	612	614	627
1971		661	743	788	864	636	661	684	710	753	766	776	785	803	836	869	883
1972		902	876	825	761	886	905	917	910	873	846	835	821	819	800	782	760
1973		699	642	580	524	726	695	676	657	639	629	602	582	557	540	522	510
1974		578	594	617	653	562	584	591	594	587	602	600	621	630	638	648	674
1975		736	860	981	1115	704	734	769	812	852	905	948	979	1016	1076	1116	1154
1976		1203	1246	1270	1273	1180	1208	1222	1234	1251	1252	1260	1275	1277	1271	1279	1283
1977		1292	1311	1359	1370	1290	1292	1295	1301	1301	1330	1349	1354	1374	1372	1371	1367
1978		1349	1331	1319	1273	1337	1346	1344	1337	1329	1326	1320	1325	1311	1297	1275	1262
1979		1285	1247	1218	1225	1271	1294	1289	1253	1254	1233	1227	1214	1212	1222	1216	1224
1980		1287	1417	1627	1913	1249	1290	1322	1368	1414	1469	1535	1631	1713	1807	1919	2014
1981		2166	2362	2515	2609	2094	2166	2238	2301	2368	2417	2477	2514	2555	2583	2616	2629
1982		2679	2743	2838	2923	2671	2680	2689	2715	2740	2773	2814	2832	2866	2885	2906	2949
1983		3003	2936	2950	2942	2983	3001	3026	3021	2970	2968	2957	2941	2951	2941	2939	2946

Jobs vacant, unfilled vacancies (11)
thousands

Adjusted - Corrigé

Offres d'emploi non satisfaites (11)
milliers

	Year	Q.1	Q.2	Q.3	Q.4	JAN	FEB	MAR	APR	MAY	JUN	JUL	AUG	SEP	OCT	NOV	DEC
1964		201	214	230	245	192	200	211	205	211	225	226	229	234	240	248	248
1965		251	272	273	272	248	250	256	268	271	278	272	275	272	272	272	273
1966		278	281	261	207	273	260	281	283	281	277	273	267	244	223	201	196
1967		135	168	167	181	190	165	179	171	167	165	163	168	172	180	179	182
1968		182	183	189	204	182	181	182	181	183	184	185	188	191	195	205	211
1969		203	203	202	200	202	203	204	204	204	202	198	203	205	201	199	200
1970		197	192	188	177	199	197	194	195	191	189	190	186	187	183	176	170
1971		152	129	122	121	165	152	139	131	128	128	121	125	121	119	121	121
1972		126	135	149	179	124	126	129	132	134	140	142	152	153	164	179	193
1973		234	297	336	361	207	235	259	279	299	312	328	334	346	358	364	360
1974		293	318	308	..	311	285	282	304	322	327	323	303	298	291	271	..
1975		..	163	134	116	..	199	192	177	161	150	136	135	131	119	114	113
1976		114	116	125	133	111	113	117	118	116	113	120	128	131	129	133	137
1977		147	153	155	164	142	148	151	151	155	153	155	157	152	160	163	170
1978		187	204	216	234	181	187	193	199	203	210	212	214	224	232	234	236
1979		233	252	250	231	235	230	233	244	253	259	255	249	245	239	234	220
1980		193	159	121	99	205	193	182	169	161	147	125	121	112	102	97	99
1981		97	90	97	104	100	96	95	93	92	86	93	98	100	101	104	106
1982		109	109	112	116	108	110	109	109	109	109	112	113	111	115	115	117
1983		122	137	161	162	118	121	125	134	134	143	154	161	167	168	163	153

Weekly hours of work: (2)(13)
manufacturing (Great Britain)
1980 = 100

Adjusted - Corrigé

Durée hebdomadaire du travail : (2)(13)
industries manufacturières (Grande-Bretagne)
1980 = 100

	Year	Q.1	Q.2	Q.3	Q.4	JAN	FEB	MAR	APR	MAY	JUN	JUL	AUG	SEP	OCT	NOV	DEC
1964	112	112	111	111	112	112	112	112	112	111	112	112	111	111	111	112	112
1965	110	111	110	109	110	111	111	111	111	110	110	110	109	110	110	109	110
1966	108	109	109	108	107	109	109	109	109	109	109	109	108	108	107	107	107
1967	108	107	108	108	108	107	107	108	107	107	108	108	108	108	108	108	108
1968	108	108	108	109	109	107	108	108	108	108	108	109	109	109	109	109	109
1969	109	109	109	109	108	109	108	108	109	109	109	108	109	108	109	108	108
1970	107	107	107	107	107	107	107	107	107	107	108	107	107	107	107	107	107
1971	105	106	105	105	105	107	106	106	105	106	106	105	105	105	105	105	105
1972	105	102	105	106	106	105	97	105	105	105	105	105	106	105	106	106	106
1973	107	107	107	107	107	107	108	107	107	107	107	107	107	107	107	107	107
1974	104	100	106	105	105	96	99	104	106	106	106	106	105	105	105	105	105
1975	103	104	102	102	102	105	104	103	103	102	102	102	102	102	102	102	103
1976	103	102	103	103	104	102	102	102	102	103	103	103	103	103	104	104	104
1977	104	104	104	104	104	104	104	104	104	104	104	104	104	104	104	104	104
1978	104	104	104	103	104	104	104	104	104	104	103	103	103	104	104	104	104
1979	103	104	104	103	104	103	104	104	104	104	104	104	102	102	103	104	104
1980	100	103	101	99	97	103	103	102	101	101	101	100	99	98	97	97	97
1981	99	97	98	100	100	97	97	97	98	98	99	99	100	100	100	100	100
1982	101	100	100	100	101	100	101	101	100	101	100	100	100	100	101	101	101
1983	101	101	101	101	102	101	101	101	101	101	101	101	101	102	102	102	102

UNITED KINGDOM

Labour disputes: time lost (14)
thousand man-days

Conflits du travail : journées perdues (14)
milliers de journées-hommes

	Year	Q.1	Q.2	Q.3	Q.4	JAN	FEB	MAR	APR	MAY	JUN	JUL	AUG	SEP	OCT	NOV	DEC
1964	2278	738	644	508	388	381	178	179	268	204	172	249	100	159	161	159	68
1965	2924	915	1094	501	414	123	371	421	263	503	328	183	169	149	195	145	74
1966	2400	486	1302	257	355	147	186	153	121	391	790	133	64	60	163	135	57
1967	2786	459	606	685	1036	133	171	155	184	227	195	164	142	379	600	321	115
1968	4689	714	2395	799	781	157	268	289	257	1861	277	179	217	403	377	289	115
1969	6846	1551	1117	1397	2781	354	433	754	310	402	405	434	563	400	1853	536	392
1970	10979	2201	2801	2408	3569	446	880	875	928	911	962	1105	530	773	1659	1600	310
1971	13552	9497	1469	1282	1304	2043	5119	2335	493	439	537	275	438	569	409	619	276
1972	23909	12522	2992	6833	1562	5486	6514	522	859	1003	1130	1184	3132	2517	956	374	232
1973	7198	2256	1903	1353	1686	400	695	1161	641	499	763	276	378	699	702	715	269
1974	14749	6494	2361	2018	3876	213	4085	2196	667	838	856	499	520	999	1656	1456	764
1975	6012	1438	2467	1400	707	339	388	711	668	864	935	631	469	300	352	220	135
1976	3283	867	722	925	769	324	240	303	298	200	224	219	321	385	254	327	188
1977	10142	2257	1811	2444	3630	434	781	1042	629	678	514	299	868	1277	998	1624	1008
1978	9404	1784	1574	1729	4317	836	571	377	595	527	452	379	472	878	1857	1918	542
1979	29474	6724	1965	16481	4304	2966	2425	1333	867	485	613	662	4103	11716	3508	606	190
1980	11964	9291	1744	496	433	2775	3254	3262	977	463	304	170	119	207	198	179	56
1981	4267	1368	1331	565	1002	249	473	646	565	408	358	289	108	169	336	506	160
1982	5315	1916	1205	1416	778	710	851	355	321	273	611	444	219	753	428	239	111
1983	3590	1600	639	683	668	327	746	527	385	136	118	183	202	298	264	297	107

Hourly rates: manufacturing (15)
(wage earners)
1980 = 100

Taux horaires: industries manufacturières (15)
(ouvriers)
1980 = 100

	Year	Q.1	Q.2	Q.3	Q.4	JAN	FEB	MAR	APR	MAY	JUN	JUL	AUG	SEP	OCT	NOV	DEC
1964	15.4	15.2	15.3	15.5	15.6	15.2	15.2	15.2	15.3	15.3	15.4	15.5	15.5	15.5	15.5	15.5	15.8
1965	16.3	15.9	16.1	16.6	15.7	15.9	15.9	16.0	16.1	16.1	16.2	16.6	16.6	16.6	16.7	16.7	16.8
1966	17.4	17.1	17.3	17.6	17.6	17.0	17.0	17.2	17.3	17.3	17.3	17.6	17.6	17.6	17.6	17.6	17.6
1967	18.1	17.8	17.8	18.4	18.5	17.8	17.8	17.8	17.8	17.8	17.9	18.4	18.4	18.4	18.5	18.5	18.6
1968	19.6	19.4	19.4	19.6	19.9	19.3	19.4	19.4	19.4	19.5	19.5	19.5	19.5	19.6	19.6	19.7	20.3
1969	20.7	20.4	20.5	20.7	21.1	20.4	20.4	20.4	20.4	20.5	20.5	20.7	20.7	20.7	20.8	20.8	21.6
1970	22.7	21.9	22.4	23.0	23.8	21.7	21.8	22.0	22.1	22.4	22.6	22.8	23.0	23.2	23.3	23.6	24.4
1971	25.6	24.8	25.3	25.8	26.4	24.7	24.8	24.8	25.0	25.4	25.5	25.7	25.8	26.0	26.0	26.2	27.1
1972	29.1	27.4	28.1	30.0	30.9	27.3	27.3	27.5	27.7	28.2	28.6	28.7	30.6	30.7	30.8	30.8	30.9
1973	32.9	31.0	32.0	33.7	34.6	30.9	31.0	31.1	31.7	32.1	32.3	32.4	34.3	34.5	34.5	34.6	34.7
1974	38.5	35.2	36.7	40.0	42.2	35.0	35.2	35.3	35.6	36.8	37.7	38.3	40.8	40.9	41.3	42.2	43.1
1975	50.0	44.5	49.3	51.8	54.5	43.6	43.7	46.3	46.7	50.0	51.3	51.5	51.8	52.0	52.2	55.6	55.8
1976	59.9	57.8	60.0	61.0	61.1	56.7	58.3	58.5	59.3	60.0	60.6	60.9	61.0	61.0	61.0	61.2	61.2
1977	62.8	61.9	62.5	63.2	63.6	61.8	61.9	62.0	62.2	62.5	62.8	62.9	63.3	63.4	63.4	63.7	63.7
1978	74.2	64.9	75.7	76.8	79.6	64.7	64.8	65.0	75.2	75.7	76.2	76.3	77.0	77.2	79.4	79.7	79.7
1979	85.3	81.6	83.5	85.0	91.2	81.4	81.7	81.8	82.8	83.5	84.4	84.5	85.1	85.4	85.6	93.9	94.2
1980	100.0	96.6	99.1	100.4	104.0	96.3	96.6	96.8	97.7	99.5	100.1	100.2	100.4	100.7	100.8	105.6	105.6
1981	109.8	107.0	109.0	110.1	113.3	106.9	107.1	107.1	108.2	108.9	109.8	109.9	110.1	110.4	111.0	114.5	114.5
1982	117.6	115.6	117.0	117.9	120.2	115.5	115.7	115.7	116.5	117.0	117.4	117.7	117.8	118.1	118.1	121.2	121.2
1983	124.2	122.6	123.5	124.3	126.5	122.5	122.6	122.7	123.1	123.6	124.0	124.2	124.4	124.4	124.4	127.5	127.5

Weekly earnings: manufacturing (2)(16)
(all employees) Great Britain
1980 = 100

Gains hebdomadaires: industries manufacturières (2)(16)
(salariés) Grande-Bretagne
1980 = 100

	Year	Q.1	Q.2	Q.3	Q.4	JAN	FEB	MAR	APR	MAY	JUN	JUL	AUG	SEP	OCT	NOV	DEC
1964	15.4	15.1	15.4	15.5	15.6	15.0	15.2	15.2	15.3	15.2	15.7	15.7	15.3	15.4	15.6	15.8	15.4
1965	16.5	16.2	16.4	16.5	16.3	16.0	16.1	16.4	16.0	16.6	16.7	16.6	16.3	16.5	16.8	16.9	16.6
1966	17.5	17.3	17.7	17.5	17.4	17.1	17.3	17.7	17.6	17.7	17.9	17.8	17.4	17.4	17.5	17.5	17.1
1967	18.1	17.5	18.0	18.2	18.5	17.5	17.7	17.4	17.8	17.9	18.2	18.4	17.9	18.2	18.5	18.7	18.4
1968	19.6	19.2	19.5	19.6	20.0	18.9	19.1	19.5	19.2	19.5	19.8	19.8	19.4	19.7	19.8	20.2	20.1
1969	21.2	20.6	21.0	21.2	21.8	20.5	20.4	20.9	20.9	20.8	21.4	21.3	21.0	21.3	21.6	21.9	21.9
1970	23.8	22.6	23.5	24.2	25.0	22.3	22.6	22.9	23.2	23.4	24.1	24.1	24.1	24.3	24.7	25.2	25.0
1971	26.5	25.7	26.4	26.8	27.3	25.5	25.7	25.8	26.0	26.4	26.7	26.8	26.6	26.9	27.2	27.4	27.3
1972	29.9	..	29.5	30.2	31.3	27.9	..	28.6	29.0	29.4	30.0	30.0	29.8	30.7	31.1	31.7	31.1
1973	33.7	32.0	33.2	34.2	35.5	31.6	32.0	32.4	32.1	33.3	34.2	34.2	33.8	34.5	35.1	35.8	35.6
1974	39.5	35.0	37.8	40.9	44.1	33.8	34.5	36.8	36.3	37.6	39.6	40.4	40.6	41.7	42.5	44.6	45.1
1975	49.9	46.2	48.2	51.3	53.7	45.4	46.2	47.0	47.3	47.9	49.3	51.1	50.9	51.8	52.8	54.0	54.5
1976	58.2	55.4	57.7	58.9	60.7	54.8	55.2	56.3	56.5	58.2	58.5	59.0	58.6	59.1	59.9	61.0	61.2
1977	64.2	62.1	63.5	64.0	67.2	61.6	61.8	62.8	62.7	64.1	63.7	64.3	63.3	64.3	65.5	67.8	68.1
1978	73.4	69.3	73.2	74.0	77.2	68.6	69.2	70.3	72.4	73.2	74.0	74.5	73.2	74.5	76.2	77.0	78.3
1979	84.9	79.5	84.5	84.3	91.2	76.9	79.2	82.3	82.0	84.6	86.9	86.7	83.0	83.2	88.7	91.6	93.3
1980	100.0	93.4	99.5	102.4	105.0	91.7	92.8	95.7	96.9	99.3	102.3	103.1	101.6	102.4	102.8	105.6	106.4
1981	113.3	107.5	111.2	115.4	119.2	106.1	107.5	109.0	108.5	110.9	114.1	114.9	115.5	115.7	117.9	119.9	119.9
1982	125.9	121.4	125.6	126.7	130.1	120.2	120.8	123.2	123.6	126.0	127.2	127.6	126.1	126.4	128.3	130.6	131.3
1983	137.2	131.9	136.3	138.1	142.6	131.0	131.7	133.0	134.5	136.8	137.7	138.6	137.4	138.3	140.5	143.5	143.9

Unit labour cost: (2)(17)
manufacturing
1980 = 100

Adjusted - Corrigé

Coût unitaire de la main-d'œuvre : (2)(17)
industries manufacturières
1980 = 100

	Year	Q.1	Q.2	Q.3	Q.4	JAN	FEB	MAR	APR	MAY	JUN	JUL	AUG	SEP	OCT	NOV	DEC
1964	20	20	20	20	20	20	20	20	20	20	20	20	20	20	20	20	20
1965	21	21	21	22	22	21	21	21	21	21	21	22	22	22	22	22	22
1966	22	22	22	22	23	22	22	22	22	22	22	22	22	22	23	23	23
1967	22	22	22	22	22	22	22	22	22	22	22	22	22	23	23	22	22
1968	22	23	23	23	23	23	23	22	23	23	23	23	23	23	23	23	24
1969	24	24	24	24	25	24	24	24	24	24	24	24	24	25	25	25	26
1970	28	27	28	29	29	27	27	27	27	28	28	28	29	29	29	29	30
1971	31	30	30	31	31	30	30	31	30	30	31	31	31	31	31	31	31
1972	33	33	32	33	33	32	34	32	32	32	32	33	33	33	33	33	33
1973	34	32	34	34	36	32	32	33	34	34	34	34	34	35	35	36	36
1974	40	37	38	41	46	37	37	38	36	38	39	40	41	42	44	46	47
1975	52	48	51	55	56	46	48	49	50	52	52	54	55	55	55	55	57
1976	58	56	57	59	59	56	56	57	56	56	59	59	60	59	59	59	59
1977	63	60	62	64	66	59	60	60	62	60	64	63	64	64	65	67	66
1978	71	69	70	72	74	67	69	70	69	70	71	72	71	72	75	74	74
1979	82	79	79	83	87	82	77	78	79	79	80	81	83	84	87	88	87
1980	100	91	98	104	107	88	91	94	96	98	100	103	104	105	106	107	109
1981	110	109	109	110	111	109	109	109	108	110	109	109	111	110	110	111	113
1982	116	113	115	116	113	114	112	114	115	114	116	116	116	116	113	118	117
1983	118	117	119	118	120	115	118	117	119	118	119	117	118	119	120	121	119

Producer prices (manufacturing output): total (2)(18)(19)
excluding food, beverages and tobacco
1980 = 100

Prix à la production (produits manufacturés) : total (19) (18)
alimentation, boissons et tabac exclus (2)
1980 = 100

	Year	Q.1	Q.2	Q.3	Q.4	JAN	FEB	MAR	APR	MAY	JUN	JUL	AUG	SEP	OCT	NOV	DEC
1964	21.2	21.0	21.1	21.2	21.3	21.0	21.0	21.1	21.1	21.1	21.1	21.2	21.2	21.2	21.2	21.3	21.3
1965	21.7	21.6	21.7	21.8	21.9	21.5	21.6	21.6	21.6	21.7	21.7	21.7	21.8	21.8	21.8	21.8	21.9
1966	22.3	22.1	22.3	22.4	22.3	22.0	22.1	22.1	22.3	22.3	22.3	22.4	22.4	22.4	22.3	22.3	22.3
1967	22.5	22.3	22.3	22.5	22.7	22.3	22.3	22.3	22.3	22.3	22.3	22.5	22.5	22.5	22.6	22.7	22.8
1968	23.3	23.1	23.4	23.4	23.5	23.0	23.1	23.3	23.4	23.3	23.4	23.4	23.4	23.4	23.5	23.5	23.5
1969	24.1	23.7	23.9	24.2	24.5	23.6	23.7	23.8	23.8	23.9	24.0	24.1	24.2	24.3	24.4	24.5	24.6
1970	25.9	24.9	25.6	26.1	26.8	24.7	24.9	25.1	25.5	25.6	25.7	25.9	26.1	26.3	26.6	26.9	27.0
1971	28.5	27.7	28.4	28.9	29.1	27.5	27.7	27.9	28.2	28.4	28.6	28.8	28.9	29.0	29.0	29.1	29.1
1972	30.2	29.4	29.9	30.4	31.1	29.3	29.4	29.6	29.7	29.9	30.1	30.2	30.5	30.7	30.9	31.2	31.3
1973	32.6	31.4	32.0	32.9	34.2	31.4	31.4	31.5	31.6	32.0	32.3	32.6	32.9	33.3	33.8	34.1	34.6
1974	42.4	38.7	41.2	43.5	45.9	37.9	38.7	39.5	40.5	41.2	42.0	42.6	43.5	44.3	45.3	45.9	46.5
1975	52.1	48.9	51.3	53.2	54.9	48.1	48.8	49.8	50.7	51.3	51.8	52.7	53.2	53.7	54.5	54.9	55.2
1976	59.9	56.6	58.6	60.9	63.4	56.0	56.7	57.2	57.9	58.7	59.2	60.1	61.0	61.6	62.7	63.5	64.1
1977	69.9	66.5	69.0	71.1	73.0	65.7	66.6	67.2	68.2	69.1	69.6	70.4	71.2	71.8	72.6	73.0	73.3
1978	77.3	75.0	76.6	78.2	79.7	74.5	75.0	75.5	76.1	76.6	77.0	77.6	78.2	78.7	79.3	79.7	80.0
1979	86.7	82.1	85.0	88.2	91.3	81.4	82.1	82.8	84.0	84.9	86.0	87.2	88.3	89.2	90.6	91.4	92.0
1980	100.0	95.8	99.1	101.7	103.3	94.4	95.8	97.2	98.1	99.2	100.1	101.2	101.7	102.3	103.0	103.3	103.6
1981	107.5	104.8	106.8	108.2	109.8	104.4	104.8	105.3	106.3	106.9	107.3	107.8	108.2	108.7	109.0	110.1	110.4
1982	114.9	112.8	114.5	115.6	116.7	112.0	112.9	113.4	114.2	114.6	114.6	115.1	115.5	116.2	116.5	116.7	116.9
1983	121.1	118.5	120.6	121.9	123.3	117.8	118.5	119.2	120.2	120.7	120.9	121.4	121.8	122.4	122.8	123.4	123.6

Producer prices: food (2)(18)(19)
(manufacturing output)
1980 = 100

Prix à la production : alimentation (19) (18)
(produits manufacturés) (2)
1980 = 100

	Year	Q.1	Q.2	Q.3	Q.4	JAN	FEB	MAR	APR	MAY	JUN	JUL	AUG	SEP	OCT	NOV	DEC
1964	20.8	20.5	20.7	20.9	21.0	20.6	20.5	20.5	20.7	20.7	20.7	20.9	20.9	20.8	20.9	21.0	21.1
1965	21.2	21.3	21.2	21.2	21.3	21.2	21.3	21.4	21.3	21.2	21.2	21.1	21.2	21.2	21.2	21.2	21.4
1966	21.6	21.5	21.6	21.6	21.6	21.5	21.5	21.5	21.6	21.6	21.6	21.6	21.6	21.6	21.6	21.6	21.7
1967	22.0	21.9	22.0	22.0	22.1	21.9	21.9	21.9	22.0	22.0	22.0	22.0	22.0	22.0	22.0	22.0	22.2
1968	22.9	22.6	22.9	23.0	23.1	22.4	22.7	22.8	22.8	22.9	23.0	23.0	23.0	23.0	23.1	23.1	23.2
1969	23.7	23.4	23.6	23.7	24.1	23.3	23.4	23.5	23.5	23.6	23.7	23.8	23.6	23.9	24.0	24.1	24.3
1970	25.6	24.7	25.2	26.0	26.7	24.6	24.6	24.8	24.9	25.1	25.5	25.8	25.9	26.2	26.4	26.7	27.0
1971	28.0	27.2	27.9	28.4	28.5	27.1	27.2	27.4	27.7	28.0	28.1	28.4	28.4	28.4	28.3	28.4	28.7
1972	29.2	28.7	28.7	29.4	30.2	28.8	28.7	28.7	28.6	28.7	28.8	29.0	29.6	29.7	30.1	30.1	30.4
1973	34.0	31.4	32.5	34.8	37.2	30.8	31.5	31.8	32.1	32.4	33.0	33.9	34.8	35.7	36.6	37.2	37.9
1974	43.2	41.8	42.3	43.0	45.7	40.8	41.8	42.7	42.6	42.4	42.0	42.6	42.9	43.6	44.3	45.8	46.9
1975	52.0	49.3	51.6	52.0	55.1	47.9	48.8	51.1	51.2	51.7	51.9	51.4	51.9	52.8	53.4	55.3	56.7
1976	61.9	57.4	59.8	62.6	67.6	57.0	57.3	58.0	59.2	59.8	60.4	60.8	62.1	64.8	66.7	67.5	68.5
1977	75.2	71.1	74.6	77.5	77.6	70.5	71.2	71.7	73.2	74.4	76.2	77.4	77.3	77.8	77.6	77.2	78.0
1978	82.3	79.4	82.0	83.6	84.3	78.7	79.5	80.0	81.1	82.2	82.8	83.4	83.5	83.8	83.8	84.1	85.1
1979	90.5	86.6	89.7	92.1	93.6	86.4	86.6	86.8	88.4	89.5	91.3	92.1	92.1	92.2	92.6	93.4	94.7
1980	100.0	96.9	100.2	100.8	102.0	95.9	96.7	98.2	99.5	100.5	100.7	100.9	100.7	100.9	101.1	101.6	103.4
1981	108.6	105.5	108.1	108.9	111.9	104.7	105.4	106.3	107.2	108.0	109.0	108.7	108.5	109.5	110.5	111.8	113.3
1982	115.4	115.2	115.7	116.7	118.1	114.6	115.2	115.7	115.8	115.8	115.4	116.5	116.6	116.9	117.3	117.9	119.2
1983	121.5	119.1	121.4	121.6	123.9	119.1	119.1	119.1	120.4	121.7	122.2	121.4	121.2	122.2	123.0	123.6	125.0

UNITED KINGDOM

Producer prices: chemicals (2)(18)(19)
(manufacturing output)
1980 = 100

Prix à la production : produits chimiques (19) (18)
(produits manufacturés) (2)
1980 = 100

	Year	Q.1	Q.2	Q.3	Q.4	JAN	FEB	MAR	APR	MAY	JUN	JUL	AUG	SEP	OCT	NOV	DEC
1964	24.9	24.8	24.8	24.9	24.9	24.8	24.8	24.8	24.8	24.8	24.8	24.8	24.9	24.9	24.9	24.9	25.0
1965	25.1	25.1	25.2	25.1	25.1	25.1	25.1	25.1	25.1	25.2	25.1	25.1	25.1	25.1	25.1	25.1	25.1
1966	25.3	25.3	25.3	25.3	25.2	25.2	25.3	25.3	25.3	25.3	25.3	25.3	25.3	25.3	25.3	25.2	25.2
1967	25.4	25.2	25.3	25.4	25.5	25.2	25.2	25.3	25.3	25.3	25.2	25.3	25.4	25.5	25.5	25.5	25.6
1968	26.2	26.1	26.3	26.3	26.2	25.9	26.0	26.2	26.3	26.3	26.2	26.3	26.3	26.3	26.2	26.2	26.2
1969	26.4	26.2	26.3	26.5	26.7	26.2	26.2	26.3	26.4	26.3	26.4	26.4	26.5	26.6	26.6	26.7	26.8
1970	27.8	27.1	27.6	28.1	28.5	27.0	27.1	27.2	27.5	27.6	27.7	28.0	28.1	28.2	28.4	28.5	28.6
1971	30.1	29.4	30.0	30.4	30.6	29.1	29.6	29.7	29.9	30.0	30.1	30.3	30.4	30.5	30.6	30.6	30.6
1972	31.6	31.0	31.4	31.8	32.4	30.8	31.0	31.1	31.3	31.4	31.3	31.6	31.8	32.0	32.3	32.4	32.5
1973	33.1	32.6	32.6	33.2	34.1	32.5	32.5	32.6	32.5	32.6	32.6	32.9	33.2	33.4	33.8	34.1	34.3
1974	44.0	39.4	43.1	45.5	48.1	37.4	39.5	41.3	42.7	43.2	43.5	44.7	45.5	46.2	47.5	48.2	48.7
1975	53.6	51.0	52.7	54.7	56.1	50.3	51.0	51.7	52.3	52.8	53.1	54.2	54.6	55.2	55.8	56.1	56.5
1976	60.9	57.8	59.6	61.9	64.3	57.1	58.0	58.2	58.9	59.5	60.5	61.4	61.9	62.4	63.5	64.3	65.0
1977	70.5	67.3	69.3	72.2	73.3	66.7	67.4	67.7	68.6	69.3	70.0	71.8	72.2	72.5	72.9	73.3	73.6
1978	76.3	75.1	76.0	76.5	77.6	74.7	75.3	75.4	75.9	76.0	76.0	76.3	76.4	76.7	77.1	77.7	78.1
1979	86.5	80.3	85.1	88.9	91.7	79.3	80.3	81.3	84.1	85.1	86.1	87.7	89.0	89.9	91.0	91.5	92.7
1980	100.0	96.9	99.8	101.4	102.0	95.4	97.0	98.4	99.2	99.7	100.5	101.1	101.5	101.5	101.6	102.0	102.3
1981	105.4	104.2	105.5	106.5	109.4	103.5	104.5	104.7	105.4	105.8	105.2	105.8	106.4	107.2	108.6	109.3	110.3
1982	113.5	111.9	113.0	113.8	115.2	111.5	111.8	112.5	113.0	113.2	112.8	113.2	113.8	114.4	114.9	115.2	115.5
1983	119.1	116.9	118.5	119.4	121.4	116.1	117.0	117.7	118.4	118.7	118.5	119.1	119.3	119.7	120.8	121.5	121.9

Producer prices: engineering (2)(18)(19)
(manufacturing output)
1980 = 100

Prix à la production : fabrications métalliques (19) (18)
(produits manufacturés) (2)
1980 = 100

	Year	Q.1	Q.2	Q.3	Q.4	JAN	FEB	MAR	APR	MAY	JUN	JUL	AUG	SEP	OCT	NOV	DEC
1964	21.7	21.6	21.6	21.7	21.8	21.5	21.5	21.6	21.6	21.6	21.6	21.6	21.7	21.7	21.8	21.8	21.9
1965	22.3	22.1	22.2	22.3	22.5	22.0	22.1	22.1	22.2	22.2	22.2	22.3	22.3	22.4	22.4	22.5	22.5
1966	23.0	22.7	23.0	23.2	23.1	22.6	22.6	22.8	22.9	23.0	23.1	23.2	23.2	23.2	23.1	23.1	23.1
1967	23.2	23.1	23.1	23.2	23.4	23.1	23.1	23.1	23.1	23.1	23.1	23.2	23.2	23.2	23.3	23.4	23.5
1968	24.0	23.8	24.1	24.1	24.2	23.7	23.8	24.0	24.1	24.1	24.1	24.1	24.1	24.1	24.2	24.2	24.2
1969	25.0	24.4	24.7	25.2	25.6	24.3	24.5	24.5	24.6	24.7	24.8	25.0	25.2	25.3	25.4	25.5	25.7
1970	27.2	26.0	27.0	27.5	28.3	25.8	26.0	26.3	26.8	27.0	27.1	27.4	27.5	27.7	28.1	28.4	28.6
1971	30.1	29.2	30.0	30.4	30.5	29.0	29.2	29.4	29.8	30.0	30.2	30.3	30.4	30.5	30.5	30.5	30.5
1972	31.6	30.9	31.3	31.8	32.5	30.8	30.9	31.0	31.1	31.3	31.5	31.6	31.9	32.0	32.3	32.6	32.7
1973	33.9	32.7	33.2	34.2	35.4	32.7	32.7	32.8	32.9	33.2	33.6	33.8	34.1	34.7	35.1	35.4	35.7
1974	41.9	38.0	40.7	43.3	45.6	37.2	37.9	38.8	39.7	40.6	41.9	42.6	43.2	44.1	45.0	45.6	46.2
1975	52.3	48.8	51.6	53.5	55.3	47.9	48.6	50.0	51.1	51.5	52.1	53.0	53.4	54.0	54.8	55.3	55.7
1976	60.7	57.1	59.4	61.8	64.5	56.4	57.2	57.8	58.6	59.5	60.1	61.0	61.8	62.5	63.6	64.7	65.2
1977	70.9	67.1	70.0	72.1	74.4	66.3	67.2	67.8	69.1	70.3	70.6	71.2	72.2	72.8	73.9	74.5	74.9
1978	78.8	76.4	78.0	79.7	81.2	75.9	76.5	76.9	77.6	78.0	78.4	79.2	79.7	80.2	80.7	81.2	81.8
1979	87.9	83.7	86.3	89.1	92.4	83.2	83.6	84.4	85.4	86.2	87.3	88.4	89.0	89.9	91.6	92.5	93.1
1980	100.0	96.2	99.0	101.5	103.3	94.8	96.3	97.4	98.2	98.9	100.0	101.2	101.5	101.9	102.7	103.3	103.8
1981	107.2	104.7	106.4	108.0	109.8	104.4	104.7	104.9	106.0	106.4	106.9	107.5	108.0	108.4	109.4	109.9	110.2
1982	113.2	111.9	113.5	114.5	115.4	111.2	112.2	112.4	113.1	113.6	113.7	114.2	114.4	114.9	115.3	115.4	115.6
1983	119.4	116.9	119.0	120.2	121.7	116.3	116.9	117.5	118.5	119.0	119.4	119.6	120.1	120.8	121.4	121.8	122.0

Producer prices (manufacturing input): total, (2)(19)
excluding food, beverages and tobacco
1980 = 100

Prix à la production (produits de base pour les ind. manufacturières) : (2)(19)
total, alimentation, boissons et tabac exclus
1980 = 100

	Year	Q.1	Q.2	Q.3	Q.4	JAN	FEB	MAR	APR	MAY	JUN	JUL	AUG	SEP	OCT	NOV	DEC
1964	14.2	14.1	14.1	14.2	14.5	14.0	14.1	14.2	14.2	14.1	14.1	14.2	14.2	14.3	14.5	14.6	14.4
1965	14.6	14.6	14.6	14.6	14.7	14.6	14.5	14.6	14.6	14.7	14.6	14.6	14.6	14.7	14.7	14.7	14.7
1966	15.1	15.0	15.4	15.1	14.9	14.9	15.1	15.0	15.3	15.5	15.5	15.4	15.0	14.8	14.9	14.9	14.8
1967	14.9	14.6	14.4	14.7	15.7	14.7	14.7	14.5	14.4	14.4	14.4	14.4	14.8	14.8	15.0	15.6	16.4
1968	16.5	16.8	16.4	16.3	16.5	16.5	16.9	17.1	16.5	16.2	16.4	16.3	16.3	16.4	16.4	16.5	16.6
1969	17.1	16.8	17.0	17.3	17.4	16.7	16.8	16.8	16.9	17.0	17.1	17.1	17.4	17.3	17.2	17.5	17.6
1970	17.6	17.6	17.7	17.6	17.5	17.5	17.6	17.8	17.7	17.7	17.6	17.6	17.4	17.6	17.6	17.5	17.5
1971	18.2	17.9	18.4	18.4	18.2	17.6	18.0	18.1	18.5	18.4	18.5	18.6	18.4	18.3	18.2	18.1	18.2
1972	19.0	18.3	18.5	19.1	20.0	18.2	18.3	18.4	18.5	18.4	18.5	18.8	19.1	19.4	19.8	20.0	20.2
1973	24.9	21.6	23.0	25.8	29.0	20.8	21.5	22.4	22.6	22.8	23.6	25.1	25.9	26.5	28.0	28.8	30.4
1974	48.4	45.2	48.7	49.1	50.3	43.5	45.4	46.7	48.9	48.8	48.3	49.0	49.3	49.0	49.9	50.8	51.7
1975	54.4	53.4	53.3	54.0	56.7	54.2	53.5	52.5	52.4	53.6	53.9	54.0	54.1	54.0	55.2	56.4	58.6
1976	67.2	60.2	65.8	68.8	73.9	59.3	60.0	61.4	64.5	65.8	67.1	67.8	68.6	70.0	72.7	74.4	74.7
1977	75.2	75.5	75.5	75.0	74.7	75.9	75.8	74.9	75.3	75.7	75.5	75.6	74.8	74.7	74.4	74.5	75.3
1978	76.8	74.1	76.1	76.5	80.3	74.1	74.1	74.1	75.4	76.2	76.6	76.2	76.4	76.9	78.8	80.4	81.8
1979	89.8	84.9	87.4	90.2	96.6	83.2	85.7	85.7	86.5	87.5	88.3	89.1	89.9	91.7	94.7	96.8	98.4
1980	100.0	102.2	99.4	98.5	99.3	102.4	103.3	100.8	100.0	99.1	99.2	98.8	98.6	98.1	98.1	100.1	101.3
1981	108.8	103.2	106.0	110.8	115.4	102.8	103.6	103.2	104.3	105.7	108.1	109.3	111.0	112.0	113.1	115.5	117.6
1982	116.3	117.2	113.6	114.5	119.8	117.8	118.1	115.8	114.0	113.3	113.4	114.2	114.5	115.1	116.2	119.5	123.8
1983	125.5	126.1	123.0	125.3	127.6	125.8	127.5	125.0	123.0	122.7	123.2	123.7	125.7	126.4	125.3	126.2	131.2

Producer prices: raw materials (2)(19) (manufacturing input) / Prix à la production : matières premières (2)(19) (produits de base pour les industries manufacturières)

1980 = 100

	Year	Q.1	Q.2	Q.3	Q.4	JAN	FEB	MAR	APR	MAY	JUN	JUL	AUG	SEP	OCT	NOV	DEC
1964	16.7	16.6	16.5	16.7	17.0	16.7	16.6	16.5	16.6	16.4	16.5	16.6	16.6	16.7	17.0	17.0	16.9
1965	16.7	16.8	16.8	16.6	16.8	16.9	16.8	16.8	16.8	16.8	16.7	16.6	16.5	16.7	16.8	16.7	16.8
1966	17.1	17.1	17.4	17.1	16.9	17.1	17.1	17.1	17.3	17.5	17.5	17.4	17.0	16.8	16.9	17.0	16.9
1967	17.0	16.8	16.6	16.7	17.7	16.8	16.8	16.6	16.6	16.7	16.6	16.6	16.8	16.6	17.0	17.7	18.6
1968	18.7	18.9	18.5	18.4	18.8	18.7	18.9	19.0	18.5	18.4	18.6	18.5	18.4	18.5	18.7	18.9	19.0
1969	19.4	19.1	19.2	19.4	19.9	19.1	19.1	19.1	19.2	19.2	19.3	19.3	19.5	19.5	19.7	19.9	20.1
1970	=20.1=	20.0	20.1	20.1	20.4	19.9	20.0	20.1	20.1	20.2	20.0	20.1	19.9	20.4	20.3	20.4	20.4
1971	21.0	20.7	21.0	21.2	21.0	20.5	20.8	20.8	21.1	21.0	21.1	21.4	21.1	21.0	20.9	21.0	21.0
1972	21.9	21.1	21.2	21.9	23.3	21.1	21.1	21.2	21.2	21.2	21.2	21.5	22.0	22.2	22.7	23.2	24.0
1973	29.7	25.6	27.3	31.2	34.9	24.8	25.6	26.3	26.6	27.1	28.2	29.9	31.5	32.0	33.6	34.5	36.5
1974	53.4	52.6	53.4	52.8	54.6	=51.5=	52.5	53.7	54.4	53.5	52.3	52.9	53.0	52.6	53.7	55.0	55.2
1975	58.3	55.8	56.8	58.2	62.1	56.4	54.8	56.2	56.6	57.0	56.9	56.9	58.4	59.4	60.5	62.5	63.4
1976	73.2	65.2	71.4	74.9	81.2	63.9	64.6	67.1	70.0	71.3	72.9	73.3	74.1	77.3	80.7	81.6	81.3
1977	83.1	83.5	85.6	82.5	80.7	82.6	83.0	84.9	86.1	85.6	85.1	83.7	81.8	81.9	81.1	80.4	80.5
1978	85.4	81.5	85.7	85.8	88.5	80.7	81.0	82.7	84.7	86.0	86.4	86.1	85.2	86.1	87.5	88.4	89.5
1979	96.1	92.9	96.1	95.8	99.7	91.1	93.1	94.4	95.4	96.4	96.6	95.4	95.4	96.5	98.7	99.9	100.4
1980	100.0	103.1	100.9	98.1	97.9	102.4	103.4	103.4	102.1	100.5	100.0	99.3	97.5	97.6	97.1	97.7	99.0
1981	105.1	100.8	105.4	107.7	110.6	99.4	100.5	102.5	103.8	105.4	107.1	106.9	107.5	108.8	109.6	110.5	111.6
1982	113.4	113.5	113.6	112.4	113.9	112.6	113.8	114.1	114.1	113.6	113.2	112.5	111.9	112.3	112.9	113.8	115.1
1983	121.3	118.3	120.3	121.3	125.2	116.7	118.4	119.7	119.9	120.4	120.7	119.7	121.1	123.0	123.5	125.0	127.1

Producer prices: fuel (2)(19) (manufacturing input) / Prix à la production : combustibles (2)(19) (produits de base pour les industries manufacturières)

1980 = 100

	Year	Q.1	Q.2	Q.3	Q.4	JAN	FEB	MAR	APR	MAY	JUN	JUL	AUG	SEP	OCT	NOV	DEC
1964	19.9	19.6	19.6	19.9	20.3	19.6	19.6	19.6	19.6	19.6	19.6	19.9	19.9	19.9	20.3	20.3	20.3
1965	21.2	21.1	21.1	21.2	21.4	21.0	21.1	21.1	21.1	21.1	21.1	21.2	21.2	21.2	21.4	21.4	21.4
1966	22.0	21.5	22.2	22.2	22.2	21.5	21.5	21.5	22.2	22.2	22.2	22.2	22.2	22.2	22.2	22.2	22.2
1967	22.5	22.3	22.3	22.2	23.4	22.3	22.3	22.3	22.3	22.3	22.3	22.2	22.2	22.2	23.4	23.4	23.4
1968	23.4	23.4	23.3	23.4	23.4	23.4	23.4	23.4	23.3	23.3	23.3	23.3	23.3	23.4	23.4	23.4	23.4
1969	23.4	23.4	23.4	23.4	23.6	23.4	23.4	23.4	23.4	23.4	23.4	23.4	23.4	23.4	23.6	23.6	23.6
1970	=24.5=	24.1	24.3	24.5	25.3	23.9	24.1	24.1	24.3	24.3	24.3	24.4	24.5	24.5	24.8	25.5	25.5
1971	26.5	25.7	26.6	26.7	26.8	25.6	25.7	25.7	26.5	26.7	26.7	26.7	26.7	26.7	26.8	26.8	26.8
1972	27.5	27.1	27.6	27.5	27.6	27.0	27.1	27.2	27.6	27.6	27.6	27.6	27.6	27.6	27.6	27.6	27.6
1973	27.8	27.6	27.6	28.0	28.2	27.6	27.6	27.6	27.6	27.6	27.6	28.0	28.0	28.0	28.2	28.2	28.2
1974	34.4	31.9	33.3	34.0	38.6	=30.0=	32.4	33.2	33.1	33.2	33.5	33.5	34.0	34.4	36.2	38.4	41.3
1975	43.5	42.4	41.8	42.4	47.4	42.7	43.1	41.5	40.5	42.5	42.4	42.4	42.4	42.4	44.3	46.5	51.3
1976	52.2	50.7	49.8	50.9	57.4	51.6	51.7	48.9	49.6	49.8	49.9	50.5	51.1	51.1	52.5	58.0	61.7
1977	64.4	62.4	62.9	64.3	68.1	63.7	63.3	60.1	61.6	63.2	64.0	64.4	64.3	64.3	65.3	68.0	71.1
1978	68.7	70.2	66.8	66.8	70.9	71.6	71.6	67.4	66.8	66.8	66.8	66.8	66.7	66.8	67.9	70.8	74.1
1979	78.8	73.3	72.8	80.2	88.8	74.1	74.8	71.0	70.7	72.6	75.2	75.0	79.9	81.7	84.5	88.7	93.2
1980	100.0	96.5	97.2	99.5	106.7	96.8	98.4	94.4	96.2	97.1	98.4	98.6	100.0	99.8	101.9	107.1	111.2
1981	119.8	116.0	115.7	118.3	129.4	116.7	117.8	113.5	114.7	115.2	117.3	117.6	118.1	119.2	122.4	129.8	135.9
1982	130.3	133.5	123.6	125.8	138.3	136.7	135.2	128.7	123.3	123.5	124.0	125.7	125.5	126.2	129.0	136.5	149.4
1983	139.3	146.1	135.0	136.7	139.3	149.5	149.6	139.3	134.3	135.3	135.3	135.1	136.8	138.2	135.0	135.7	147.2

Consumer prices: all items (20) / Prix à la consommation : total (20)

1980 = 100

	Year	Q.1	Q.2	Q.3	Q.4	JAN	FEB	MAR	APR	MAY	JUN	JUL	AUG	SEP	OCT	NOV	DEC
1964	21.4	21.0	21.3	21.6	21.8	20.9	21.0	21.0	21.2	21.4	21.4	21.5	21.6	21.6	21.6	21.8	21.9
1965	22.4	21.9	22.4	22.6	22.7	21.9	21.9	22.0	22.4	22.4	22.5	22.5	22.6	22.6	22.6	22.7	22.8
1966	23.2	22.9	23.1	23.4	23.5	22.8	22.9	22.9	23.1	23.3	23.2	23.2	23.4	23.4	23.5	23.5	23.5
1967	23.8	23.6	23.7	23.7	24.0	23.6	23.6	23.6	23.7	23.7	23.7	23.7	23.7	23.7	23.9	24.0	24.1
1968	24.9	24.3	24.9	25.1	25.4	24.2	24.3	24.4	24.8	24.9	25.0	25.0	25.1	25.2	25.3	25.3	25.6
1969	26.2	25.8	26.1	26.3	26.7	25.7	25.8	25.9	26.0	26.0	26.2	26.2	26.3	26.4	26.6	26.6	26.8
1970	27.9	27.1	27.6	28.1	28.8	27.0	27.1	27.2	27.5	27.6	27.7	28.0	28.1	28.3	28.6	28.8	29.0
1971	30.6	29.5	30.4	31.0	31.4	29.3	29.5	29.6	30.2	30.4	30.6	30.9	31.0	31.0	31.3	31.4	31.4
1972	32.7	31.8	32.3	32.9	33.7	31.7	31.8	31.9	32.2	32.3	32.5	32.6	32.9	33.1	33.6	33.7	33.8
1973	35.4	34.1	35.0	35.6	36.8	34.0	34.1	34.2	34.8	34.9	35.2	35.4	35.6	35.9	36.5	36.8	37.0
1974	41.0	38.3	40.5	41.7	43.6	37.7	38.4	38.8	40.1	40.6	40.9	41.5	41.6	42.0	42.9	43.6	44.3
1975	50.9	46.2	50.4	52.7	54.5	45.4	46.2	47.0	48.8	50.8	51.7	52.2	52.7	53.1	53.8	54.5	55.1
1976	59.0	56.1	58.0	59.7	62.1	55.6	56.2	56.4	57.4	58.1	58.6	59.1	59.7	60.3	61.4	62.1	62.9
1977	68.4	65.1	68.1	69.7	70.9	64.4	65.0	65.7	67.4	68.0	68.8	69.2	69.7	70.2	70.6	70.9	71.2
1978	74.6	72.1	73.9	75.5	76.8	71.7	72.1	72.5	73.5	73.9	74.3	74.9	75.5	75.9	76.3	76.8	77.3
1979	84.5	78.8	81.6	87.6	90.0	78.1	78.8	79.4	80.7	81.4	82.7	86.7	87.5	88.4	89.3	90.1	90.7
1980	100.0	94.1	99.7	102.0	104.0	92.8	94.2	95.4	98.8	99.8	100.7	101.5	102.0	102.6	103.3	104.2	104.6
1981	111.9	106.4	111.5	113.6	116.2	105.3	106.2	107.8	110.9	111.5	112.1	112.7	113.8	114.3	115.2	116.4	117.0
1982	121.4	117.8	121.5	122.7	123.8	117.4	117.5	118.4	120.7	121.4	122.3	122.4	122.8	122.8	123.5	124.1	123.8
1983	127.1	124.2	126.6	128.1	129.3	123.8	124.3	124.5	126.2	126.7	126.9	127.7	128.2	128.5	129.0	129.3	129.6

UNITED KINGDOM

Money supply (M1) (21)(22)(23)

£ million, end of period

Disponibilités monétaires (M1) (21)(22)(23)

millions de £, fin de période

	Year	Q.1	Q.2	Q.3	Q.4	JAN	FEB	MAR	APR	MAY	JUN	JUL	AUG	SEP	OCT	NOV	DEC
1964	7557	7146	7223	7376	7557												
1965	7848	7358	7461	7548	7848												
1966	7844	7764	7728	7806	7844												
1967	8442	7773	7899	8255	8442												
1968	8784	8210	8356	8461	8784												
1969	8812	8339	8188	8312	8812												
1970	9635	8507	8852	9032	9635												
1971	11088	9691	9831	10210	11088						9417	9592	9644	9742	10079	10230	10588
1972	12657	11225	11729	11930	12657	10382	10218	10596	10987	11051	11347	11425	11358	11403	11665	11671	12107
1973	13303	12333	13175	12882	13303	11850	11669	11798	12304	12240	12437	12789	12656	12392	12311	12469	12642
1974	14739	12772	13175	13513	14739	12435	12129	12123	12629	12468	12520	12768	12778	12798	13148	13318	13714
1975	17387	14735	15791	15664	17387	13736	13471	13763	14294	15041	15292	15659	15837	26032	16204	16140	16680
1976	19335	17687	18141	19081	19335	16059	16555	16906	17468	17397	17468	17905	18218	18560	18159	18452	18897
1977	23523	19416	20227	21887	23523	18116	18144	18392	19213	19381	19825	20001	20274	20796	21547	22030	22695
1978	27364	24107	24553	25850	27364	22432	22542	22886	23700	23908	23594	24354	24487	24621	25105	25149	26137
1979	29856	27299	27652	28727	29856	25585	25357	25659	27173	26999	26590	27350	27344	27376	28490	27709	28318
1980	31044	28979	29513	29567	31044	27536	26695	27188	27933	27612	27595	28709	28414	28388	28901	28855	30161
1981	36533	31441	32539	33090	36533	28699	29217	29398	31236	31259	31077	32319	31313	31727	31563	34298	34859
1982	40568	36341	37263	38205	40668	34353	34199	34244	34881	34945	35518	36010	36463	36645	37956	37858	38803
1983	45230	41727	42823	43292	45230	38450	38161	38733	40122	40334	40994	41293	41194	40954	42014	42147	43575

M1 plus quasi-money (21)(22)(23)

£ million, end of period

M1 plus quasi-monnaie (21)(22)(23)

millions de £, fin de période

	Year	Q.1	Q.2	Q.3	Q.4	JAN	FEB	MAR	APR	MAY	JUN	JUL	AUG	SEP	OCT	NOV	DEC
1964	12155	11271	11536	11765	12155												
1965	13083	11914	12337	12514	13083												
1966	13555	12992	13164	13312	13555												
1967	15003	13414	13825	14270	15003												
1968	16092	14748	15270	15444	16092												
1969	16596	15790	15737	15934	16596												
1970	18175	16161	16893	17281	18175												
1971	20541	18192	18662	19112	20541	17779	17737	18021	18063	18142	18287	18603	18662	18751	19146	19426	19771
1972	26245	21411	23105	24060	26245	20155	19822	20679	21440	21699	22579	23238	23262	23700	24116	24377	25227
1973	33478	27146	28674	31008	33478	25740	26160	26484	27034	27047	27800	29107	29698	30388	30943	31418	32347
1974	37698	33938	34880	35758	37698	32841	33086	33087	33226	33297	33533	34823	35091	35102	35347	35884	36270
1975	40477	37422	38072	39519	40477	36346	36238	36527	36700	37015	37220	37883	38303	38506	38936	38913	39242
1976	44997	40355	42129	44118	44997	38959	39283	39723	40496	40529	40868	42015	42559	43460	43875	44324	44551
1977	49429	44279	46308	47155	49429	43198	42728	42921	44345	44592	45033	45617	45564	46425	46859	47045	48278
1978	56792	50751	53146	54105	56792	47920	48387	49061	51379	52149	52433	53188	52281	52795	53451	54016	54973
1979	63806	56176	59130	60457	63806	55029	55167	54547	56129	56851	57686	58027	58255	58625	60130	60994	61159
1980	75748	63647	67988	70487	75748	60956	61030	61277	62779	64127	64713	67754	69181	68720	70098	71583	72625
1981	96373	76621	82702	87083	96373	73640	74420	74719	77280	79023	80284	82785	83829	84533	86729	93181	93453
1982	107215	96600	100436	102616	107215	93610	93537	93508	96387	96880	97573	99545	100125	99956	102477	103156	104672
1983	120721	110293	113759	115148	120721	104954	105494	106213	108781	108941	110810	112855	112864	112900	114696	115159	118286

Domestic bank deposits (21)(22)(23)

£ million, end of period

Dépôts bancaires (secteur intérieur) (21)(22)(23)

millions de £, fin de période

	Year	Q.1	Q.2	Q.3	Q.4	JAN	FEB	MAR	APR	MAY	JUN	JUL	AUG	SEP	OCT	NOV	DEC
1964	9704	8962	9210	9440	9704												
1965	10447	9504	9861	9981	10447												
1966	10860	10359	10465	10599	10860												
1967	12188	10663	11032	11510	12188												
1968	13233	11897	12360	12640	13233												
1969	13590	12876	12828	13077	13590												
1970	14855	13121	13812	14127	14855												
1971	16952	14868	15289	15658	16952						14965	15189	15308	15408	15794	16048	16301
1972	22166	17656	19245	20155	22166	16785	16395	17205	17927	18111	18943	19491	19544	19984	20377	20584	21221
1973	29101	22976	24325	26707	29101	21889	22261	22536	22941	23008	23711	24878	25516	26297	26834	27229	27978
1974	32613	29364	30113	30986	32613	28587	28814	28760	28783	28864	29034	30170	30373	30363	30574	30969	31202
1975	34669	31974	32812	34145	34669	31428	31247	31438	31548	31726	31915	32381	32771	33005	33420	33340	33512
1976	38415	34554	36090	37769	38415	33360	33569	33914	34531	34569	34796	35682	36236	37141	37570	37979	38020
1977	41866	37628	39412	40030	41866	36821	36300	36416	37749	37934	38241	38608	38578	39430	39868	39987	40697
1978	48059	42948	45062	45776	48059	40654	40970	41502	43789	44406	44571	44958	44108	44595	45222	45708	46242
1979	54295	47232	50065	51168	54295	46602	46535	45822	47232	47971	48840	48767	49075	49469	50821	51650	51445
1980	65509	54149	58420	60873	65509	51597	51623	51779	53175	54387	54974	57759	59217	58838	60234	61731	62370
1981	85606	66701	72694	76848	85606	63755	64467	64677	66781	68705	70011	72303	73361	74077	76351	82844	82758
1982	95983	86245	89957	91867	95983	83197	83154	83045	85932	86415	87020	88678	89375	89168	91775	92396	93476
1983	108813	98521	102353	103498	108813	94129	94529	95110	97587	97678	99482	101254	101357	101423	103223	103628	106167

Money supply (M1) (21)(22)

£ million, end of period

Adjusted - Corrigé

Disponibilités monétaires (M1) (21) (22)

millions de £, fin de période

	Year	Q.1	Q.2	Q.3	Q.4	JAN	FEB	MAR	APR	MAY	JUN	JUL	AUG	SEP	OCT	NOV	DEC
1964		7230	7330	7440	7450												
1965		7490	7570	7620	7610												
1966		7910	7830	7740	7600												
1967		7780	7880	8160	8180												
1968		8210	8340	8530	8640												
1969		8490	8310	8380	8560												
1970		8640	8920	9020	9420												
1971		9820	9900	10210	10710						9440	9490	9570	9780	10040	10140	10310
1972		11380	11720	12040	12360	10320	10420	10820	10720	11010	11460	11290	11330	11530	11580	11660	11820
1973		12460	13190	12950	13010	11790	12000	12080	12070	12250	12570	12580	12390	12210	12220	12400	12250
1974		12860	13220	13540	14450	12310	12440	12390	12390	12400	12470	12630	12880	12820	13060	13270	13380
1975		14850	15910	16630	17040	13710	13800	13920	13960	15000	15290	15550	16070	16150	16170	16120	16460
1976		17790	18350	18900	18970	16430	16990	17310	17310	17330	17540	17860	18220	18680	18020	18390	18580
1977		19350	20350	21860	23090	18270	18640	18820	18930	19320	19960	19940	20350	20990	21400	22000	22070
1978		24160	24860	25840	26360	22550	23010	23330	23270	23800	23830	24090	24500	24650	24820	25050	25350
1979		27330	27940	28820	29300	25660	26010	26180	26700	26900	26690	27000	27470	27410	28310	27760	27600
1980		29020	29760	29730	30490	27580	27190	27450	27580	27640	27660	28420	28400	28480	28810	28710	29490
1981		31510	32730	33390	35700	29220	29730	29820	30990	31190	31210	32040	31260	31890	31650	34260	34300
1982		36410	37420	38320	40130	34890	34750	34710	34620	34790	35650	35800	36460	36830	37800	37790	38190
1983		41640	42790	43600	44700	38510	38760	39210	39660	40210	41140	40960	41290	41200	41810	42040	42690

M1 plus quasi-money (21)(22)

£ million, end of period

Adjusted - Corrigé

M1 plus quasi-monnaie (21) (22)

millions de £, fin de période

	Year	Q.1	Q.2	Q.3	Q.4	JAN	FEB	MAR	APR	MAY	JUN	JUL	AUG	SEP	OCT	NOV	DEC
1964		11510	11610	11890	11970												
1965		12160	12420	12660	12750												
1966		13250	13250	13330	13210												
1967		13530	13810	14270	14640												
1968		14880	15270	15600	15830												
1969		16090	15910	16090	16280												
1970		16450	16980	17350	17810												
1971		18510	18780	19180	19960	18520	18710	18800	18880	19210	19460	18520	18710	18800	18880	19210	19460
1972		21960	23230	24110	25580	20000	20060	21010	21450	21910	22820	22590	23210	23700	23930	24350	25060
1973		27710	28830	31070	32820	25530	26450	26900	27150	27390	28170	28850	29420	30140	30820	31260	32190
1974		34610	34990	35850	37050	32630	33450	33540	33440	33620	33800	34610	35230	35090	35290	35860	35870
1975		38200	38060	39530	39950	36200	36650	36860	36790	37240	37520	37690	38540	38590	38880	38830	38880
1976		41030	42160	44030	44400	38980	40020	40450	40370	40910	41220	41800	42680	43330	43490	44060	43580
1977		44900	46160	47140	48800	43420	43620	43780	44430	44990	45370	45460	45720	46250	46510	46760	47500
1978		51310	53160	54150	56150	48150	49130	49810	51360	52350	52600	53140	52470	52740	53160	53790	54440
1979		56930	59190	60560	63140	55250	55870	55280	56220	57220	58080	58050	58550	58720	59880	60780	60870
1980		65090	68260	71330	75110	61050	61730	62670	63450	64820	65510	67770	69380	69410	70350	71950	72650
1981		78060	82720	87710	95550	73390	75090	76410	77910	79720	81000	82560	83700	85230	86750	93570	93600
1982		98300	100830	103340	106680	93740	94440	95350	96860	97850	98580	99250	100250	100790	102660	103360	104570
1983		111910	113880	115100	120190	105180	106440	107700	109010	109310	111070	112060	112180	111850	113820	114770	117640

Change in domestic bank deposits (21)(22)

£ million

Adjusted - Corrigé

Variations des dépôts bancaires (secteur intérieur) (21) (22)

millions de £

	Year	Q.1	Q.2	Q.3	Q.4	JAN	FEB	MAR	APR	MAY	JUN	JUL	AUG	SEP	OCT	NOV	DEC
1964	512	68	155	248	41												
1965	675	153	231	233	58												
1966	413	420	-18	90	-79												
1967	1220	238	287	457	238												
1968	1100	207	399	285	209												
1969	357	154	-92	214	81												
1970	1340	111	574	264	409												
1971	2018	511	270	409	810							-232	160	79	53	307	241
1972	4804	1481	1171	784	1377	365	-2	485	440	362	878	154	193	440	193	359	626
1973	6927	1932	999	2255	1552	417	888	411	242	210	753	652	587	765	654	383	882
1974	3512	1693	256	654	909	421	821	71	-135	161	136	768	495	-231	121	411	-18
1975	1590	968	-347	1091	130	233	370	149	-170	331	192	31	736	-42	206	-143	-10
1976	3235	906	527	1307	731	602	810	221	-213	331	304	558	788	604	-276	636	-414
1977	3967	408	985	835	1756	-196	112	258	464	489	475	-45	304	380	216	458	506
1978	6317	1695	1431	979	2195	304	830	551	321	761	349	511	-656	157	367	497	569
1979	6620	366	2231	1237	2556	802	534	-587	921	896	1016	125	284	-179	1000	1024	-64
1980	11617	1926	3242	3227	3378	249	671	690	834	1703	459	2356	1545	-39	997	1455	653
1981	11437	2743	3345	4008	839	996	1038	1218	1121	1464	846	1061	723	1498	1503	761	165
1982	9025	2163	1899	1883	3080	-68	404	741	1529	913	515	845	631	399	1806	-98	1339
1983	11063	2713	2751	708	4556	131	1012	866	1708	364	1419	1106	5	-627	1847	779	1983

UNITED KINGDOM

Domestic bank deposits: public sector (21)(22)(23)(24)

£ million, end of period

Dépôts bancaires : secteur public (secteur intérieur) (24) (23) (22) (21)

millions de £, fin de période

	Year	Q.1	Q.2	Q.3	Q.4	JAN	FEB	MAR	APR	MAY	JUN	JUL	AUG	SEP	OCT	NOV	DEC
1964																	
1965																	
1966																	
1967																	
1968	390	383	378	381	390												
1969	457	438	425	436	457												
1970	501	505	483	440	501												
1971	544	542	505	481	544						428	504	456	419	524	468	416
1972	625	558	525	490	625	563	500	460	493	519	507	531	477	540	467	508	472
1973	725	635	665	603	725	553	588	588	554	582	672	653	553	639	569	679	559
1974	656	733	621	623	656	664	765	719	696	670	677	695	777	647	630	752	569
1975	924	686	879	691	924	737	774	759	683	1022	753	782	1005	705	693	875	616
1976	921	933	1093	877	921	1129	898	817	1003	1094	912	1127	952	905	1059	881	737
1977	1278	1001	1150	1042	1270	1052	822	856	1188	1016	1086	1446	1024	1213	1253	1195	1167
1978	1312	1199	1270	1019	1312	1334	1164	1069	1280	1171	1456	1432	995	1190	1074	1104	1068
1979	1257	1155	1159	1007	1257	1153	1506	1182	1224	1073	1260	1050	947	911	978	1096	996
1980	1595	1060	1213	1098	1595	1162	1250	1010	963	1210	1100	1178	1426	1019	1062	1280	1054
1981	1729	1431	1568	1272	1729	1789	1218	1223	1303	1337	1259	1336	1239	1130	1490	1598	1418
1982	2185	1643	1804	1673	2185	1776	1593	1790	1682	1902	1733	1956	1680	1835	2168	2106	2202
1983	2282	1968	2561	2087	2282	2317	2251	2154	2103	1989	2463	2766	2324	2173	2165	2485	2376

Change in loans to domestic sector (21)(22)
(public sector)
£ million

Adjusted - Corrigé

Variations des prêts au secteur intérieur (22) (21)
(secteur public)
millions de £

	Year	Q.1	Q.2	Q.3	Q.4	JAN	FEB	MAR	APR	MAY	JUN	JUL	AUG	SEP	OCT	NOV	DEC
1964	-312	-19	98	15	-407												
1965	476	-26	191	85	232												
1966	233	195	-36	-5	72												
1967	574	452	340	-83	-135												
1968	-4	-126	121	210	-208												
1969	-373	-41	-25	-417	110												
1970	988	365	149	4	488												
1971	1735	458	214	352	700						-28	96	156	-81	2	76	369
1972	-1013	-116	-780	60	-181	32	-238	-102	-72	15	86	-662	-160	124	-108	20	18
1973	1838	550	507	617	132	-3	477	-43	1	228	184	-98	-49	170	455	41	270
1974	701	159	-535	-50	1127	-53	278	186	-275	-161	-303	55	557	-423	-128	549	281
1975	3379	855	707	1629	182	276	266	29	112	552	554	550	571	101	362	-141	212
1976	288	374	-578	835	-49	391	322	-141	-330	-53	-200	209	606	374	-859	275	-110
1977	2378	590	-38	938	903	-488	121	512	839	15	208	406	-235	655	501	294	-611
1978	-289	-109	-1593	302	1122	211	-286	-77	-210	-246	-783	519	-741	164	439	161	-187
1979	925	-956	360	485	808	219	68	-604	677	616	-485	287	101	-263	480	-174	-743
1980	1662	-402	554	-285	1902	-1103	436	141	95	506	-468	1627	-186	-147	310	228	221
1981	-510	1218	-1054	-107	-441	-343	172	968	75	-86	-812	1027	-218	614	-248	-440	-760
1982	-2102	881	-1238	-760	-1025	122	-35	1183	-1294	235	101	196	-395	645	-341	-841	-1997
1983	-1930	198	1823	-828	-115	-1752	-273	1397	508	-244	-652	-30	-1142	540	126	349	-413

Change in loans to domestic sector (21)(22)
(private sector)
£ million

Adjusted - Corrigé

Variations des prêts au secteur intérieur (22) (21)
(secteur privé)
millions de £

	Year	Q.1	Q.2	Q.3	Q.4	JAN	FEB	MAR	APR	MAY	JUN	JUL	AUG	SEP	OCT	NOV	DEC
1964	988	211	170	295	312												
1965	392	294	90	42	-40												
1966	39	325	-33	-127	-114												
1967	630	105	-43	359	209												
1968	858	178	252	161	266												
1969	597	228	-61	330	100												
1970	1315	276	475	255	309												
1971	1712	246	207	603	649	-77	200	237	275	301	285	-77	200	237	275	301	285
1972	6421	1747	1726	950	2011	503	402	539	545	706	549	706	346	355	400	559	585
1973	6985	1709	892	1954	2273	676	774	402	245	305	606	822	824	455	812	534	731
1974	4671	1727	1312	1200	432	865	329	274	594	290	555	494	271	482	461	120	-17
1975	124	290	25	-212	27	39	52	7	176	207	57	-206	-92	-81	67	-12	-59
1976	3387	314	504	708	1497	140	335	75	-37	439	230	331	156	426	647	579	98
1977	4707	1092	920	1207	1489	651	-44	261	273	281	333	276	402	380	560	456	806
1978	5730	1015	1798	1385	1532	455	558	326	531	785	700	234	351	310	163	527	985
1979	6475	2868	2534	2010	2063	674	742	951	581	435	1389	428	628	360	1026	985	549
1980	10902	3218	3422	3320	1040	2038	876	206	617	1574	1047	1563	1030	625	805	453	374
1981	11283	594	3374	3866	3531	444	128	131	872	624	1391	40	1253	1157	781	1808	1393
1982	14800	2632	4492	3310	4366	710	1410	-150	2286	1746	966	278	2282	738	1779	1294	2407
1983	14925	3326	4990	3205	3514	1859	2112	-328	-228	1640	2711	344	2009	-260	1135	1224	2294

Advances to industry (domestic sector) (21)(23)(25)(26)
£ million, end of period

Crédits à l'industrie (secteur intérieur) (21)(23)(25)(26)
millions de £, fin de période

	Year	Q.1	Q.2	Q.3	Q.4	JAN	FEB	MAR	APR	MAY	JUN	JUL	AUG	SEP	OCT	NOV	DEC
1964																	
1965																	
1966																	
1967																	
1968																	
1969																	
1970	4775			4772	4775								4772			4775	
1971	4999	5157	5033	5047	4999		5157			5033			5047			4999	
1972	6917	5188	6298	6745	6917		5188			6298			6745			6917	
1973	9168	7684	7735	8454	9168		7684			7735			8454			9168	
1974	13074	10655	11415	12638	13074		10655			11415			12638			13074	
1975	10600	13617	10757	10825	10600		13617			10730			10830			10605	
1976	12490	10454	10679	11495	12490		10454			10679			11495			12490	
1977	13857	12799	12849	13790	13857		12799			12849			13790			13857	
1978	15651	14365	14812	15408	15651		14365			14812			15408			15651	
1979	18783	16488	17301	18220	18783		16488			17301			18220			18783	
1980	22960	19872	20962	23297	22960		19872			20962			23297			22960	
1981	24594	22908	22813	24710	24594		22908			22813			24710			24594	
1982	29047	26418	26828	27984	29047		26361			26828			27984			29047	
1983	31355	29562	28915	30479	31355		29563			28915			30479			31355	

Advances to sectors other than industry (21)(23)(26)
(domestic sector)
£ million, end of period

Crédits aux secteurs autres que l'industrie (26)(23)
(secteur intérieur) (21)
millions de £, fin de période

	Year	Q.1	Q.2	Q.3	Q.4	JAN	FEB	MAR	APR	MAY	JUN	JUL	AUG	SEP	OCT	NOV	DEC
1964																	
1965																	
1966																	
1967																	
1968																	
1969																	
1970	3827			3870	3827								3870			3827	
1971	5254	4273	4565	4764	5254		4273			4565			4764			5254	
1972	9183	5968	7213	8395	9183		5968			7213			8395			9183	
1973	13874	10673	10891	12843	13874		10673			10891			12843			13874	
1974	18180	16721	17000	17804	18180		16721			17000			17744			18180	
1975	19509	18710	18433	19100	19509		18710			18492			19128			19538	
1976	22423	19612	20371	21182	22423		19612			20371			21182			22423	
1977	24247	22385	23108	23820	24247		22385			23108			23871			24247	
1978	26931	24612	26051	26047	26931		24612			26051			26047			26931	
1979	30758	27741	28619	29270	30758		27741			28619			29270			30758	
1980	35901	31714	33036	35177	35901		31714			33036			35177			35901	
1981	47211	37255	39314	43133	47211		37255			39364			43128			47239	
1982	65805	53936	58192	61844	65805		53976			58283			61961			65992	
1983	82307	71672	73419	77060	82307		71672			73419			77060			82307	

Consumer credit outstanding: total
(Great Britain)
£ million, end of period

Crédits à la consommation : crédits en cours
(Grande-Bretagne)
millions de £, fin de période

	Year	Q.1	Q.2	Q.3	Q.4	JAN	FEB	MAR	APR	MAY	JUN	JUL	AUG	SEP	OCT	NOV	DEC
1964																	
1965																	
1966																	
1967																	
1968																	
1969																	
1970																	
1971																	
1972																	
1973																	
1974																	
1975																	
1976	3775				3775												3775
1977	4810	..	4192	4470	4810	..	..	..	4039	4130	4192	4250	4388	4470	4571	4717	4810
1978	6357	5086	5541	5914	6357	4869	4963	5086	5231	5399	5541	5619	5789	5914	6062	6227	6357
1979	8123	6496	7047	7516	8123	6355	6414	6496	6626	6820	7047	7186	7375	7516	7707	7981	8123
1980	9326	8453	8846	9123	9326	8171	8274	8453	8607	8701	8846	8517	9035	9123	9232	9264	9326
1981	1002	9271	9449	9676	1002	9250	9247	9271	9321	9350	9449	9482	9591	9676	9795	9897	1002
1982	11531	1013	10453	11076	11631	9968	9981	1013	10228	10324	10453	10524	10820	11076	11317	11564	11631
1983		12116	12707	13408		11727	11861	12116	12227	12404	12707	12909	13119	13408	13713		

New consumer credit: retail shops
(Great Britain)
£ million, monthly averages

Crédits à la consommation : nouveaux crédits, commerces de détail (Grande-Bretagne)
millions de £, moyennes mensuelles

	Year	Q.1	Q.2	Q.3	Q.4	JAN	FEB	MAR	APR	MAY	JUN	JUL	AUG	SEP	OCT	NOV	DEC
1964																	
1965																	
1966																	
1967																	
1968																	
1969																	
1970																	
1971																	
1972																	
1973																	
1974																	
1975																	
1976																	
1977	191	178	176	180	231	186	169	180	179	182	168	171	180	189	215	244	234
1978	224	204	207	213	272	218	195	198	216	210	194	204	213	222	251	294	272
1979	251	223	243	231	305	231	213	225	245	241	244	224	230	238	287	327	301
1980	270	269	262	247	302	288	255	263	285	247	255	247	234	259	294	323	289
1981	262	266	253	229	301	281	252	265	255	244	260	224	217	247	292	313	297
1982	282	272	265	253	333	291	245	280	263	260	271	236	244	279	319	351	344
1983	307	299	297	266	366	331	269	296	304	292	295	248	247	303	339	376	382

New consumer credit: finance houses
(Great Britain)
£ million, monthly averages

Crédits à la consommation : nouveaux crédits, établissements financiers (Grande-Bretagne)
millions de £, moyennes mensuelles

	Year	Q.1	Q.2	Q.3	Q.4	JAN	FEB	MAR	APR	MAY	JUN	JUL	AUG	SEP	OCT	NOV	DEC
1964																	
1965																	
1966																	
1967																	
1968																	
1969																	
1970																	
1971																	
1972																	
1973																	
1974																	
1975																	
1976																	
1977	211	135	205	226	227	152	181	223	195	216	203	208	250	220	222	239	221
1978	289	260	308	302	286	239	240	300	294	319	311	267	348	291	303	322	232
1979	361	295	394	376	378	263	282	340	350	407	425	365	411	353	420	419	296
1980	330	391	412	386	331	361	385	428	429	390	416	385	395	377	377	305	312
1981	338	338	404	425	384	295	332	386	405	383	423	396	452	426	412	395	345
1982	470	402	462	523	493	317	381	508	474	436	476	413	607	549	503	534	441
1983	570	515	564	622	580	456	474	615	527	556	608	511	755	599	576	643	520

Call money rate (27)
per cent per annum, end of period

Taux de l'argent au jour le jour (27)
pourcentage par an, fin de période

	Year	Q.1	Q.2	Q.3	Q.4	JAN	FEB	MAR	APR	MAY	JUN	JUL	AUG	SEP	OCT	NOV	DEC
1964	5.88	3.82	3.88	3.94	5.88	3.07	3.82	3.82	3.82	3.82	3.88	3.76	3.88	3.94	4.01	5.94	5.88
1965	5.07	5.94	4.82	5.01	5.07	5.94	5.82	5.94	5.94	5.82	4.82	4.88	5.01	5.01	4.88	5.01	5.07
1966	6.07	4.94	5.07	6.07	6.07	5.01	4.94	4.94	4.94	5.01	5.07	5.82	6.07	6.07	6.01	6.01	6.07
1967	6.85	5.01	4.51	4.38	6.85	5.32	5.38	5.01	5.01	4.57	4.51	4.57	4.38	4.38	5.07	6.82	6.85
1968	6.04	6.51	6.54	5.01	6.04	6.38	6.85	6.51	6.44	6.54	6.54	6.51	6.44	6.01	5.94	6.01	6.04
1969	7.01	6.94	7.01	7.07	7.01	6.01	6.94	6.94	6.94	6.88	7.01	7.01	7.07	7.07	7.01	7.01	7.01
1970	6.01	6.57	6.13	6.13	6.01	7.07	7.13	6.57	6.07	6.13	6.13	6.13	6.13	6.13	6.07	6.01	6.01
1971	3.25	6.13	5.13	4.25	3.25	6.13	6.07	6.13	5.13	5.13	5.13	5.13	5.19	4.26	3.50	2.88	3.25
1972	6.00	3.00	3.94	5.75	6.00	4.00	4.13	3.00	4.50	4.63	3.94	5.38	4.94	5.75	4.50	6.13	6.00
1973	7.50	6.50	5.63	9.75	7.50	7.75	8.50	6.50	6.13	7.50	5.63	4.38	10.25	9.75	10.50	6.75	7.50
1974	5.75	9.75	6.33	9.50	5.75	6.38	7.25	9.75	7.25	9.88	6.38	10.38	8.75	9.50	9.75	9.75	5.75
1975	10.57	5.88	8.00	9.25	10.57	10.25	10.00	5.88	8.75	8.25	8.00	8.88	9.75	9.25	11.25	12.75	10.57
1976	10.50	7.88	10.82	12.13	10.50	10.63	9.25	7.88	9.00	8.75	10.82	10.75	9.82	12.13	14.00	13.38	10.50
1977	6.00	6.00	7.00	5.00	6.00	11.53	10.50	8.00	7.88	6.25	7.00	6.38	5.75	5.00	4.25	3.50	6.00
1978	11.00	3.50	8.75	7.00	11.00	6.38	5.75	3.50	6.25	6.00	8.75	9.00	8.25	7.00	9.25	11.50	11.00
1979	15.88	12.25	12.50	12.50	15.88	10.25	11.50	12.25	10.50	11.00	12.50	13.50	13.50	12.50	13.50	14.00	15.88
1980	13.50	15.50	15.50	15.00	13.50	16.50	16.38	15.50	16.50	14.50	15.50	15.50	13.00	15.00	14.38	13.00	13.50
1981	13.19	8.50	8.50	12.50	13.19	13.00	13.50	8.50	10.50	10.50	8.50	12.38	12.13	12.50	14.50	14.63	13.19
1982	10.00	11.75	12.44	10.50	10.00	13.00	13.50	11.75	13.00	12.88	12.44	12.25	11.00	10.50	9.50	8.75	10.00
1983	8.88	10.38	9.50	9.57	8.88	10.38	10.88	10.38	9.88	9.86	9.50	9.50	9.25	9.57	9.00	8.88	8.88

New consumer credit: retail shops (Great Britain)
£ million, monthly averages

Adjusted - Corrigé

Crédits à la consommation : nouveaux crédits, commerces de détail (Grande-Bretagne)
millions de £, moyennes mensuelles

	Year	Q.1	Q.2	Q.3	Q.4	JAN	FEB	MAR	APR	MAY	JUN	JUL	AUG	SEP	OCT	NOV	DEC
1964																	
1965																	
1966																	
1967																	
1968																	
1969																	
1970																	
1971																	
1972																	
1973																	
1974																	
1975																	
1976		153	158	157	178	151	155	154	153	161	159	150	157	165	173	181	180
1977		185	186	196	199	180	183	191	183	189	187	191	199	198	197	197	202
1978		210	217	233	235	212	210	209	220	219	213	228	238	233	231	239	235
1979		229	255	253	265	222	229	235	246	252	267	253	259	248	263	267	265
1980		272	274	271	263	274	273	270	286	259	276	277	267	269	269	265	254
1981		269	264	253	262	255	271	271	257	257	279	252	250	258	267	257	263
1982		274	278	280	295	274	263	285	265	276	292	266	284	290	292	290	304
1983		301	308	299	319	307	294	301	310	310	305	289	294	314	309	314	335

New consumer credit: finance houses (Great Britain)
£ million, monthly averages

Adjusted - Corrigé

Crédits à la consommation : nouveaux crédits, établissements financiers (Grande-Bretagne)
millions de £, moyennes mensuelles

	Year	Q.1	Q.2	Q.3	Q.4	JAN	FEB	MAR	APR	MAY	JUN	JUL	AUG	SEP	OCT	NOV	DEC
1964																	
1965																	
1966																	
1967																	
1968																	
1969																	
1970																	
1971																	
1972																	
1973																	
1974																	
1975																	
1976																	
1977		191	191	219	244	171	192	209	186	196	190	211	219	228	216	237	279
1978		275	286	289	305	277	266	283	280	291	288	275	300	293	299	327	290
1979		309	353	377	400	305	306	315	329	370	375	380	385	365	408	426	367
1980		416	385	369	351	429	423	395	402	370	383	392	346	368	368	312	372
1981		359	380	404	406	354	365	359	379	374	387	401	394	418	400	402	417
1982		419	434	494	528	386	412	460	440	427	434	412	546	525	490	553	541
1983		539	538	583	619	553	518	547	497	555	563	539	632	578	569	645	643

Treasury bill rate (91 days) (28)
per cent per annum, end of period

Bons du Trésor (91 jours) (28)
pourcentage par an, fin de période

	Year	Q.1	Q.2	Q.3	Q.4	JAN	FEB	MAR	APR	MAY	JUN	JUL	AUG	SEP	OCT	NOV	DEC
1964	6.63	4.30	4.46	4.65	6.63	3.76	4.31	4.30	4.30	4.38	4.46	4.65	4.66	4.65	4.70	6.63	6.63
1965	5.52	6.55	5.54	5.49	5.52	6.54	6.44	6.55	6.38	6.36	5.54	5.63	5.56	5.49	5.44	5.40	5.52
1966	6.53	5.60	5.73	6.75	6.53	5.48	5.62	5.60	5.64	5.66	5.73	6.68	6.73	6.75	6.51	6.74	6.53
1967	7.48	5.50	5.28	5.48	7.48	6.08	6.04	5.50	5.41	5.25	5.28	5.35	5.29	5.48	5.73	7.55	7.48
1968	6.78	7.11	7.24	6.58	6.78	7.52	7.37	7.11	7.08	7.24	7.24	7.06	6.95	6.58	6.49	6.79	6.78
1969	7.65	7.78	7.88	7.81	7.65	6.73	7.71	7.78	7.80	7.85	7.88	7.83	7.79	7.81	7.74	7.74	7.65
1970	6.82	7.18	6.85	6.81	6.82	7.51	7.59	7.18	6.77	6.86	6.85	6.83	6.82	6.81	6.81	6.92	6.82
1971	4.41	6.62	5.59	4.75	4.41	6.77	6.72	6.62	5.68	5.63	5.59	5.58	5.81	4.75	4.56	4.28	4.41
1972	8.31	4.31	5.64	6.63	8.31	4.35	4.36	4.31	4.27	4.30	5.64	5.76	5.83	6.63	6.89	6.93	8.31
1973	12.42	7.94	6.96	10.94	12.42	8.13	8.06	7.94	7.67	7.20	6.96	10.89	10.97	10.94	10.67	12.45	12.42
1974	10.99	11.98	11.24	10.98	10.99	12.03	11.82	11.98	11.48	11.21	11.24	11.19	11.25	10.98	10.89	10.98	10.99
1975	10.64	9.37	9.48	10.48	10.64	10.26	9.77	9.37	9.24	9.45	9.48	10.44	10.38	10.48	11.41	10.99	10.64
1976	13.51	8.42	10.99	12.35	13.51	9.30	8.62	8.42	9.94	11.00	10.99	10.87	10.94	12.35	14.43	14.03	13.51
1977	6.29	9.35	7.46	5.30	6.29	11.74	10.77	9.35	7.50	7.43	7.46	7.30	6.42	5.30	4.48	6.43	6.29
1978	11.56	5.99	9.27	9.17	11.56	5.77	5.98	5.99	6.99	8.48	9.27	9.11	8.83	9.17	10.28	11.56	11.56
1979	15.84	11.44	13.33	13.37	15.84	12.09	12.23	11.44	11.29	11.45	13.33	13.35	13.34	13.37	13.47	16.10	15.84
1980	13.02	16.28	15.68	14.33	13.02	15.74	16.12	16.28	16.06	16.06	15.68	14.44	14.95	14.33	14.36	12.95	13.02
1981	14.78	11.53	11.88	15.12	14.78	12.61	11.59	11.53	11.24	11.45	11.88	13.80	13.19	15.12	15.66	13.76	14.78
1982	9.72	12.51	12.27	9.97	9.72	13.52	13.29	12.51	12.98	12.67	12.27	11.08	9.92	9.97	8.83	10.00	9.72
1983	8.84	10.23	9.29	8.97	8.84	10.94	10.84	10.23	9.68	9.69	9.29	9.40	9.34	8.97	8.83	8.86	8.84

UNITED KINGDOM

Yield of Government bonds: 2 1/2 % consols (27)

per cent per annum, end of period

Rendement des bons d'État : 2,5 % consolidés (27)

pourcentage par an, fin de période

	Year	Q.1	Q.2	Q.3	Q.4	JAN	FEB	MAR	APR	MAY	JUN	JUL	AUG	SEP	OCT	NOV	DEC
1964	6.32	5.90	6.07	6.04	6.32	5.86	6.06	5.90	6.04	6.05	6.07	6.06	6.08	6.04	6.05	6.19	6.32
1965	6.46	6.40	6.68	6.25	6.46	6.27	6.30	6.40	6.48	6.69	6.68	6.66	6.45	6.25	6.26	6.30	6.46
1966	6.65	6.73	6.89	7.03	6.65	6.43	6.58	6.73	6.74	6.71	6.89	7.13	7.24	7.03	6.85	6.83	6.65
1967	7.06	6.41	6.83	6.87	7.06	6.55	6.41	6.41	6.37	6.60	6.83	6.86	6.80	6.87	6.91	7.09	7.06
1968	8.05	7.18	7.75	7.45	8.05	7.18	7.19	7.18	7.24	7.36	7.75	7.47	7.45	7.45	7.43	7.76	8.05
1969	8.88	8.69	9.25	9.12	8.88	8.39	8.45	8.69	8.94	9.45	9.25	8.94	9.40	9.12	8.68	9.10	8.88
1970	9.65	8.54	9.42	9.33	9.65	8.83	8.41	8.54	9.15	9.53	9.42	9.08	9.31	9.33	9.64	9.91	9.65
1971	8.47	9.00	9.33	8.64	8.47	9.64	9.18	9.00	9.16	9.40	9.33	9.33	9.14	8.64	8.71	8.48	8.47
1972	9.85	8.77	9.39	9.52	9.85	8.28	8.37	8.77	8.68	9.22	9.39	9.50	9.48	9.52	9.66	9.66	9.85
1973	12.25	10.25	10.47	11.48	12.25	9.77	9.90	10.25	10.28	10.36	10.47	11.20	11.38	11.48	11.32	12.25	12.25
1974	17.05	14.80	15.60	15.13	17.05	13.10	13.59	14.80	14.75	13.82	15.60	15.19	15.78	15.13	16.44	16.83	17.05
1975	14.78	14.07	14.58	14.26	14.78	15.23	14.73	14.07	15.19	14.84	14.58	13.92	14.00	14.26	14.89	14.72	14.78
1976	14.49	13.95	13.95	14.56	14.49	13.12	13.53	13.95	13.65	14.10	13.95	14.14	14.30	14.56	15.69	15.05	14.49
1977	10.47	12.63	12.95	10.41	10.47	13.20	13.61	12.63	12.54	12.58	12.95	13.03	12.67	10.41	10.78	11.43	10.47
1978	12.34	11.42	12.42	12.34	12.34	10.89	11.23	11.42	12.01	12.28	12.42	12.16	12.20	12.34	12.38	12.65	12.34
1979	11.75	10.75	11.42	10.74	11.75	12.53	12.26	10.75	10.72	11.30	11.42	10.84	10.60	10.74	11.39	11.85	11.75
1980	12.14	12.72	11.89	11.68	12.14	11.26	12.29	12.72	12.60	12.14	11.89	11.26	11.99	11.68	11.54	11.64	12.14
1981	13.89	12.03	13.13	14.05	13.89	12.02	12.06	12.03	12.14	12.59	13.13	13.48	13.44	14.05	14.14	13.17	13.89
1982	10.20	12.55	12.71	10.91	10.20	13.03	12.67	12.55	12.79	12.44	12.71	12.16	11.00	10.91	9.73	10.70	10.20
1983	9.90	10.24	9.83	10.00	9.90	10.96	10.93	10.24	10.13	9.96	9.83	10.56	10.42	10.00	10.13	9.95	9.90

Share prices: F.T. Actuaries (500 shares) (29)

1980 = 100

Cours des actions : «F.T. Actuaries» (500 actions) (29)

1980 = 100

	Year	Q.1	Q.2	Q.3	Q.4	JAN	FEB	MAR	APR	MAY	JUN	JUL	AUG	SEP	OCT	NOV	DEC
1964	40	39	40	41	39	40	39	40	40	40	39	41	41	41	40	38	37
1965	37	38	37	36	39	38	39	37	37	38	36	35	35	36	39	40	39
1966	38	40	41	36	34	39	41	40	40	41	41	39	35	35	34	33	34
1967	40	36	39	41	46	36	36	36	38	39	39	40	40	42	45	46	46
1968	57	47	56	62	62	46	48	49	54	56	57	60	62	63	61	62	64
1969	56	64	57	52	52	66	64	61	61	58	54	52	52	52	51	52	53
1970	50	54	48	47	50	56	54	53	52	47	45	46	48	49	52	48	49
1971	59	49	57	64	65	50	49	48	53	59	59	63	64	66	64	63	67
1972	75	73	76	76	75	71	72	75	77	78	74	75	79	74	72	75	77
1973	65	69	68	63	59	73	68	66	68	67	69	65	63	62	64	61	51
1974	38	49	44	34	26	51	50	47	45	45	42	38	33	30	29	26	23
1975	48	37	49	49	56	28	40	44	46	51	51	48	46	51	53	57	56
1976	57	61	61	56	50	61	61	61	62	63	59	59	56	53	47	49	53
1977	73	63	70	78	81	60	63	66	66	73	72	72	77	84	85	80	80
1978	82	77	80	87	86	80	76	75	77	82	81	82	89	90	88	84	86
1979	94	89	101	94	90	85	85	97	103	103	97	94	94	95	96	87	87
1980	100	93	94	104	109	91	97	93	92	93	97	103	103	106	108	112	108
1981	113	107	118	115	110	104	108	110	118	119	116	115	121	112	104	112	114
1982	131	119	125	131	147	117	121	120	122	127	127	126	129	138	145	150	147
1983	165	153	166	171	170	150	153	156	165	162	171	168	174	170	165	171	174

U.S. dollar exchange rate: spot — Taux de change du dollar É.-U. : au comptant

cents per £, end of period — cents par £, fin de période

	Year	Q.1	Q.2	Q.3	Q.4	JAN	FEB	MAR	APR	MAY	JUN	JUL	AUG	SEP	OCT	NOV	DEC
1964	279.01	275.84	279.17	278.33	279.01	279.78	279.82	279.84	279.59	279.79	279.17	278.82	278.39	278.33	278.50	279.12	279.01
1965	280.28	279.05	279.17	280.18	280.28	279.20	279.41	279.05	279.91	279.27	279.17	279.20	279.07	280.18	280.38	280.28	280.28
1966	279.02	279.31	278.96	279.14	279.02	280.36	280.00	279.31	279.37	279.11	278.96	279.02	278.91	279.14	279.09	279.05	279.02
1967	240.63	279.73	279.00	278.34	240.63	279.43	279.33	279.73	279.86	279.48	279.00	278.58	278.54	278.34	278.27	242.00	240.63
1968	238.44	240.11	238.26	238.96	238.44	241.23	240.30	240.11	239.71	238.34	238.26	239.49	238.36	238.96	239.11	238.46	238.44
1969	240.07	239.48	239.13	238.27	240.07	239.00	239.38	239.48	238.52	238.95	239.13	239.06	238.13	238.27	239.59	239.64	240.07
1970	239.37	240.67	239.52	238.79	239.37	240.25	240.71	240.67	240.59	240.15	239.52	239.05	238.34	238.79	239.03	238.87	239.37
1971	255.25	241.69	241.94	248.50	255.25	241.75	241.62	241.69	241.94	241.81	241.94	241.88	245.25	248.50	249.12	249.38	255.25
1972	234.81	261.58	244.40	242.03	234.81	259.38	260.60	261.58	261.11	261.29	244.40	245.01	244.85	242.03	234.20	235.27	234.81
1973	232.32	247.77	258.20	241.35	232.32	238.22	249.00	247.77	248.95	256.70	258.20	251.30	245.85	241.35	243.90	234.30	232.32
1974	234.85	239.40	239.05	233.23	234.85	227.70	230.55	239.40	243.28	239.30	239.05	237.61	231.78	233.23	233.38	232.37	234.85
1975	202.35	240.90	219.80	204.09	202.35	237.73	242.68	240.90	235.31	231.14	219.80	214.72	211.10	204.09	207.57	201.68	202.35
1976	170.24	191.57	178.13	167.75	170.24	202.91	202.71	191.57	184.40	176.40	178.13	178.43	177.46	167.75	160.60	164.84	170.24
1977	190.60	172.01	172.02	174.65	190.60	171.42	170.92	172.01	171.93	171.76	172.02	173.74	174.29	174.65	183.20	181.50	190.60
1978	203.45	185.63	186.02	197.21	203.45	195.04	193.43	185.63	183.13	182.22	186.02	193.17	194.25	197.21	209.00	194.93	203.45
1979	222.40	206.88	216.84	219.76	222.40	199.56	202.34	206.88	205.78	206.60	216.84	228.14	225.07	219.76	207.61	219.55	222.40
1980	238.50	216.68	236.20	238.83	238.50	226.83	227.87	216.68	226.60	233.00	236.20	233.30	237.26	238.83	243.83	235.95	238.50
1981	190.80	224.42	194.28	180.05	190.80	238.60	220.45	224.42	214.04	206.95	194.28	185.60	183.70	180.05	184.50	197.00	190.80
1982	161.45	178.17	173.83	169.27	161.45	188.35	181.57	178.17	178.85	179.10	173.83	174.00	172.05	169.27	167.34	161.20	161.45
1983	145.06	147.90	153.04	149.57	145.06	153.10	152.11	147.90	156.15	160.86	153.04	152.09	149.33	149.57	149.53	146.47	145.06

U.S. dollar exchange rate: forward (90 days) — Taux de change du dollar É.-U. : à terme (90 jours)

cents per £, end of period — cents par £, fin de période

	Year	Q.1	Q.2	Q.3	Q.4	JAN	FEB	MAR	APR	MAY	JUN	JUL	AUG	SEP	OCT	NOV	DEC
1964	277.11	279.32	278.78	278.87	277.11	279.52	279.35	279.32	279.44	279.25	278.78	278.35	277.96	278.87	277.91	277.11	277.11
1965	279.52	277.01	277.92	279.20	279.52	277.33	277.43	277.01	278.26	277.38	277.92	277.73	277.34	279.20	279.47	279.59	279.52
1966	278.50	278.62	278.54	278.48	278.50	279.79	279.26	278.62	278.76	278.74	278.54	277.92	278.11	278.48	278.72	278.62	278.50
1967	239.00	279.14	278.14	277.59	239.00	278.82	278.85	279.14	279.17	279.01	278.14	278.01	277.85	277.59	241.30	238.98	239.00
1968	236.08	235.86	235.11	237.97	236.08	239.52	238.67	235.86	237.06	234.14	235.11	238.2[illegible]	236.73	237.97	238.60	236.41	236.08
1969	239.75	237.75	237.26	236.07	239.75	237.48	237.81	237.75	235.02	235.37	237.26	237.46	233.08	236.07	238.86	239.35	239.75
1970	238.81	240.37	239.56	238.09	238.81	240.01	240.36	240.37	240.32	239.88	239.56	238.96	237.84	238.09	238.50	238.30	238.81
1971	255.57	240.12	241.39	249.75	255.57	240.12	239.69	240.12	240.67	241.26	241.39	241.48	247.53	249.75	248.79	250.32	255.57
1972	232.72	261.49	242.20	240.43	232.72	259.24	260.47	261.49	261.08	260.75	242.20	243.00	243.04	240.43	232.57	233.54	232.72
1973	228.52	246.05	256.97	238.63	228.52	235.90	246.81	246.05	247.45	255.71	256.97	249.35	243.15	238.63	241.25	231.08	228.52
1974	230.00	233.80	237.35	231.37	230.00	221.70	225.25	233.80	240.18	237.47	237.35	237.50	230.45	231.37	231.40	229.70	230.00
1975	199.78	237.19	216.25	202.68	199.78	234.97	239.10	237.19	231.73	228.72	216.25	212.91	209.24	202.68	205.30	199.56	199.78
1976	165.85	189.56	174.74	162.18	165.85	200.36	200.72	189.56	181.60	173.37	174.74	175.23	174.26	162.18	152.54	160.93	165.85
1977	192.14	170.29	170.67	175.06	192.14	168.05	167.96	170.29	170.45	169.17	170.67	172.83	173.77	175.06	184.87	181.47	192.14
1978	203.65	186.21	184.73	195.64	203.65	195.46	193.53	186.21	181.52	181.73	184.73	191.88	193.07	195.64	208.15	193.42	203.65
1979	221.29	207.36	215.26	219.50	221.29	197.73	201.36	207.36	207.51	206.57	215.26	224.07	224.38	219.50	208.26	218.53	221.29
1980	241.20	217.16	231.56	237.81	241.20	224.86	226.50	217.16	223.96	230.65	231.56	230.84	236.91	237.81	242.80	237.95	241.20
1981	190.38	225.54	196.47	181.51	190.38	239.34	222.57	225.54	216.86	209.88	196.47	186.74	186.82	181.51	184.39	194.62	190.38
1982	162.15	179.25	175.57	169.95	162.15	188.48	182.84	179.25	180.29	179.90	175.57	174.68	172.06	169.95	167.91	161.56	162.15
1983		148.47	153.42			153.34	152.51	148.47	156.68	160.92	153.42	151.90	149.13				

Official reserves excluding gold — Réserves officielles, or exclu

million SDR's, end of period — millions de DTS, fin de période

	Year	Q.1	Q.2	Q.3	Q.4	JAN	FEB	MAR	APR	MAY	JUN	JUL	AUG	SEP	OCT	NOV	DEC
1964	178	692	756	727	178	711	655	692	753	802	756	776	755	727	636	593	178
1965	739	218	567	615	739	117	216	218	241	652	567	503	344	615	733	707	739
1966	1158	1536	1236	1221	1158	850	1519	1536	1480	1447	1236	969	1021	1221	1260	1295	1158
1967	1405	1582	1125	901	1405	1197	1201	1582	1792	1242	1125	1095	910	901	1028	1869	1405
1968	949	1229	1209	1232	949	1417	1345	1229	1256	1235	1209	1249	1188	1232	1225	1039	949
1969	1055	994	971	973	1055	961	983	994	1023	942	971	998	967	973	1030	1063	1055
1970	1479	1242	1322	1211	1479	1107	1173	1242	1292	1299	1322	1327	1296	1211	1283	1450	1479
1971	7358	2693	4516	5536	7358	1756	1969	2693	3378	3569	4516	4858	5120	5536	6133	7045	7358
1972	4463	7792	7424	4871	4463	7725	7715	7792	7578	7595	7424	4852	4872	4871	4660	4693	4463
1973	4633	4256	5066	4555	4633	4465	4159	4256	4324	4839	5066	4747	4666	4555	4869	4774	4633
1974	4932	4606	4827	5319	4932	4386	4210	4606	5030	5000	4827	4871	5051	5319	5619	5824	4932
1975	3927	5135	4428	4295	3927	4931	5065	5135	5154	4637	4428	4569	4369	4295	4134	4072	3927
1976	2905	4381	3890	3773	2905	5105	5301	4381	3477	3995	3890	3548	3647	3773	3396	3804	2905
1977	16557	7609	9301	14149	16557	5543	6053	7609	8053	7868	9301	10863	12164	14149	16571	16731	16557
1978	12301	16224	13144	12961	12301	16829	16647	16224	13663	13389	13144	13170	12903	12961	12168	12402	12301
1979	14988	13851	13916	15072	14988	12838	13188	13851	13540	13621	13916	15562	15437	15072	14873	14810	14988
1980	16192	15959	16827	16428	16192	15584	15746	15959	16840	16851	16827	16955	16940	16428	16655	16812	16192
1981	13091	17016	14838	13359	13091	16796	16958	17016	16921	15550	14838	13599	13957	13359	13142	13183	13091
1982	11238	12958	11810	12366	11238	12991	13095	12958	12263	11956	11810	12032	12183	12366	12525	12104	11238
1983	10831	10590	10854	10974	10831	11483	10838	10590	10822	11030	10854	11002	11047	10974	11146	11113	10831

UNITED KINGDOM

External sterling liabilities, total (23)(30)
excluding international organisations
£ million, end of period

Dette extérieure en sterling, total (30) (23)
non compris les organisations internationales
millions de £, fin de période

	Year	Q.1	Q.2	Q.3	Q.4	JAN	FEB	MAR	APR	MAY	JUN	JUL	AUG	SEP	OCT	NOV	DEC
1964	4030	4166	4267	4364	4030												
1965	3970	3959	3848	3815	3970												
1966	3871	4120	4179	3800	3871												
1967	3589	4061	4062	3773	3589												
1968	3263	3631	3272	3272	3263												
1969	3553	3332	3454	3403	3553												3548
1970	4038	3847	4013	4027	4038	3635	3618	3847	3995	4015	4018	4054	4038	4027	4139	4126	4038
1971	5412	4330	4611	4934	5412	4176	4259	4330	4577	4588	4611	4705	4858	4934	5140	5231	5412
1972	5552	5616	5471	5382	5652	5403	5441	5616	5910	5880	5471	5371	5307	5382	5512	5523	5652
1973	5663	5810	5991	5495	5663	5676	5700	5810	6010	5954	5991	5930	5663	5495	5614	5556	5663
1974	7157	5890	6243	6867	7157	5763	5677	5890	6259	6128	6243	6537	6735	6867	7164	7162	7157
1975	6942	7031	7212	6843	6942	6537	6688	7031	6893	7186	7218	7055	7147	6928	6829	6808	6964
1976	5687	6854	5924	5806	5687	7000	6823	6793	6499	6292	5930	5885	5912	5766	5503	5468	5497
1977	7097	6083	6003	6406	7097	5626	5696	5798	5671	5734	5636	5873	6076	6303	6728	7114	6917
1978	7001	7182	6754	6914	7001	7130	6941	7145	7002	6927	6769	6733	6686	6842	6842	6770	6885
1979	10056	7596	8116	8872	10056	7054	7122	7351	7562	7729	7887	8176	8532	8684	8979	9102	9506
1980	13870	10724	12132	13293	13870	9949	10200	10564	10876	11361	11524	12326	12417	12722	13211	13534	13643
1981	17073	14251	15345	16396	17073	13860	14087	14173	14396	14557	14861	15378	16093	16203	15893	16159	16502
1982	21756	18384	19678	20881	21756												
1983	26039	23544	24024	24802	26039												

External sterling liabilities, (23)(30)
monetary authorities
£ million, end of period

Dette extérieure en sterling, (30) (23)
autorités monétaires
millions de £, fin de période

	Year	Q.1	Q.2	Q.3	Q.4	JAN	FEB	MAR	APR	MAY	JUN	JUL	AUG	SEP	OCT	NOV	DEC
1964	2326	2412	2449	2444	2326												
1965	2214	2249	2182	2157	2214												
1966	2187	2316	2301	2174	2187												
1967	2001	2234	2218	2104	2001												
1968	1803	2051	1762	1714	1803												
1969	2146	1976	2046	2095	2146												2146
1970	2365	2325	2414	2430	2365	2266	2224	2325	2445	2441	2414	2444	2452	2430	2503	2446	2365
1971	3030	2597	2881	2964	3030	2520	2542	2597	2802	2835	2881	2915	2894	2964	3108	3041	3030
1972	3361	3231	3253	3169	3361	3052	3134	3231	3481	3458	3253	3161	3103	3169	3352	3304	3361
1973	3379	3550	3654	3228	3379	3452	3473	3550	3715	3646	3654	3668	3425	3228	3374	3316	3379
1974	4725	3659	3857	4420	4725	3543	3483	3659	3939	3815	3857	4113	4320	4420	4703	4748	4725
1975	3714	4512	4228	3858	3714	4054	4190	4512	4368	4409	4308	4154	4172	3971	3819	3750	3732
1976	2203	3620	2701	2371	2203	3747	3596	3579	3231	3062	2761	2582	2544	2328	2178	2112	2165
1977	2132	2400	1970	2050	2132	2150	2180	2254	1976	2014	1913	1843	1921	1987	2077	2302	2135
1978	1735	2279	2003	2004	1735	2131	2234	2301	2225	2265	2064	1582	1944	2027	1846	1793	1841
1979	2218	1867	2028	2336	2218	1820	1874	1751	1873	1867	1899	1508	2087	2208	2304	2029	2228
1980	3561	2717	3142	3479	3561	2234	2384	2559	2605	2798	2812	2508	2938	3045	3401	3531	3585
1981	3612	3641	3833	3869	3612	3642	3618	3591	3590	3720	3654	3804	3884	3797	3567	3453	3698
1982	4126	3795	3589	3750	4126		3562			3640			3725			4127	
1983	4692	4425	4270	4645	4692		4390			4113			4275			4485	

Balance of payments: net trade / Balance des paiements : balance commerciale

£ million / millions de £

	Year	Q.1	Q.2	Q.3	Q.4	JAN	FEB	MAR	APR	MAY	JUN	JUL	AUG	SEP	OCT	NOV	DEC
1964	-510	-117	-98	-173	-122												
1965	-233	-78	-49	-87	-19												
1966	-77	-56	-81	-94	154												
1967	-567	-70	-86	-127	-284												
1968	-682	-207	-190	-189	-96												
1969	-172	-130	-17	-6	31												
1970	-34	25	-58	-107	106												
1971	190	-165	107	140	108												
1972	-748	-220	-49	-342	-137												
1973	-2586	-569	-438	-660	-919												
1974	-5351	-1334	-1406	-1300	-1311												
1975	-3333	-1050	-715	-995	-573												
1976	-3929	-658	-1040	-1183	-1043												
1977	-2284	-1088	-907	-137	-152												
1978	-1542	-722	-190	-476	-154												
1979	-3449	-1651	-557	-589	-652												
1980	1513	-623	-258	896	1503												
1981	3652	1541	1186	104	821												
1982	2384	76	30	645	1633												
1983	-500	-176	-690	-182	548												

Balance of payments: current balance / Balance des paiements : opérations courantes, nettes

£ million / millions de £

	Year	Q.1	Q.2	Q.3	Q.4	JAN	FEB	MAR	APR	MAY	JUN	JUL	AUG	SEP	OCT	NOV	DEC
1964	-357	-44	-65	-166	-82												
1965	-45	-20	1	-63	37												
1966	111	-10	-24	-70	215												
1967	-293	22	-37	-59	-219												
1968	-242	-139	-44	-54	-5												
1969	509	-8	178	165	174												
1970	823	253	190	115	265												
1971	1124	76	354	397	297												
1972	223	19	256	-104	52												
1973	-979	-386	-30	-227	-336												
1974	-3278	-870	-863	-707	-838												
1975	-1513	-642	-353	-467	-51												
1976	-836	-111	-342	-151	-232												
1977	54	-628	-454	701	435												
1978	1158	-408	335	604	627												
1979	-653	-904	-165	547	-131												
1980	3650	-208	-119	1557	2420												
1981	7272	2708	1793	842	1929												
1982	5551	1216	360	1214	2761												
1983	2049	1021	-687	663	1052												

Balance of payments: net capital movements / Balance des paiements : mouvements de capitaux, nets

£ million / millions de £

	Year	Q.1	Q.2	Q.3	Q.4	JAN	FEB	MAR	APR	MAY	JUN	JUL	AUG	SEP	OCT	NOV	DEC
1964	-311	-	83	63	-457												
1965	-317	-136	-201	-78	98												
1966	-580	55	-111	-452	-72												
1967	-504	355	-81	-363	-415												
1968	-759	-129	-375	66	-321												
1969	-175	53	-72	-94	-62												
1970	549	474	205	-156	28												
1971	1792	573	348	479	392												
1972	-673	-	-843	8	162												
1973	178	123	406	-587	236												
1974	1602	515	689	512	-114												
1975	154	103	101	264	-314												
1976	-2975	-543	-1734	-658	-40												
1977	4166	1620	14	1254	1278												
1978	-4263	-153	-2203	-454	-1453												
1979	2146	563	821	316	446												
1980	-1455	-501	371	192	-1517												
1981	-7352	-3911	-2002	-1164	-275												
1982	-3258	-132	131	-1032	-2225												
1983	-2044	-477	539	831	-2937												

UNITED KINGDOM

Imports c.i.f. (31) / Importations c.a.f. (31)

£ million, monthly averages / millions de £, moyennes mensuelles

	Year	Q.1	Q.2	Q.3	Q.4	JAN	FEB	MAR	APR	MAY	JUN	JUL	AUG	SEP	OCT	NOV	DEC
1964	461	461	466	443	470	505	432	445	481	450	468	452	444	448	492	457	461
1965	482	465	488	478	495	430	405	510	474	506	485	495	454	484	488	500	498
1966	499	515	499	502	478	524	472	549	496	508	494	518	494	495	479	454	500
1967	539	537	543	510	568	580	488	543	533	544	552	490	530	511	526	599	578
1968	661	665	649	653	677	691	639	666	647	718	583	700	653	607	718	686	627
1969	696	686	710	680	709	734	638	687	709	726	694	747	647	646	753	664	708
1970	759	720	792	728	798	747	684	729	811	749	814	641	739	803	823	782	739
1971	817	816	830	783	837	768	743	938	844	777	869	810	724	815	821	842	850
1972	923	901	908	842	1040	843	871	988	852	925	947	770	728	1028	1079	1103	939
1973	1310	1182	1235	1302	1522	1223	1016	1308	1087	1351	1266	1299	1339	1269	1572	1603	1390
1974	1928	1766	1994	1928	2025	1637	1689	1971	1956	2071	1957	2120	1812	1854	2147	2028	1899
1975	2004	1960	1958	1990	2107	2209	1902	1769	2037	1879	1959	2165	1858	1946	2276	1977	2070
1976	2590	2252	2606	2590	2913	2124	2102	2531	2534	2460	2823	2701	2359	2711	2801	3089	2850
1977	3018	3032	3173	2926	2942	3008	2728	3359	2880	3285	3354	3054	2726	3000	2980	2884	2963
1978	3297	3149	3466	3202	3369	3138	2893	3417	3070	3596	3731	3287	3057	3262	3444	3666	2998
1979	3910	3597	4048	3751	4245	3275	3303	4215	3876	4224	4044	3943	3717	3593	4646	4395	3695
1980	4157	4569	4371	3877	3812	4657	4617	4434	4517	4234	4361	4339	3530	3762	3997	3611	3828
1981	4264	3681	4024	4523	4829	3599	3579	3865	3665	3853	4553	4682	4324	4562	4985	4782	4719
1982	4747	4736	4939	4566	4749	4512	4340	5355	4822	4768	5225	4746	4185	4758	4691	4951	4604
1983	5497	5388	5567	5323	5710	5166	5116	5384	5178	5726	5797	5308	5174	5486	5856	5940	5334

Exports f.o.b. (31) / Exportations f.o.b. (31)

£ million, monthly averages / millions de £, moyennes mensuelles

	Year	Q.1	Q.2	Q.3	Q.4	JAN	FEB	MAR	APR	MAY	JUN	JUL	AUG	SEP	OCT	NOV	DEC
1964	367	373	377	337	383	342	370	407	357	412	361	339	358	314	375	380	394
1965	408	388	414	395	434	369	382	412	420	407	415	435	368	381	407	461	434
1966	436	439	416	416	475	393	428	497	400	458	389	408	419	420	461	513	451
1967	433	460	460	407	403	467	452	461	454	476	451	440	392	390	352	388	469
1968	532	519	519	522	569	500	528	530	510	523	524	550	510	506	537	626	544
1969	607	552	615	608	655	568	521	568	577	632	637	635	594	595	620	689	654
1970	675	652	689	613	744	641	620	695	694	673	701	705	460	675	719	764	750
1971	756	671	786	754	812	632	596	785	723	788	786	787	707	769	767	815	855
1972	800	762	831	668	940	754	761	770	740	864	889	760	478	766	982	989	850
1973	1007	919	1000	985	1126	945	872	939	945	1024	1029	1046	1005	903	1146	1198	1034
1974	1359	1296	1371	1388	1492	1085	1186	1317	1303	1463	1346	1506	1320	1338	1590	1420	1435
1975	1634	1513	1629	1575	1820	1576	1472	1490	1570	1745	1571	1766	1369	1589	1938	1652	1869
1976	2106	1895	2084	2055	2391	1748	1716	2221	1969	2022	2262	2071	1942	2151	2268	2465	2442
1977	2666	2511	2685	2743	2725	2295	2314	2934	2474	2850	2731	2788	2643	2799	2713	2806	2655
1978	2949	2762	3070	2857	3109	2532	2797	2956	2991	3025	3193	2933	2808	2829	3214	3233	2379
1979	3386	2838	3602	3375	3731	2846	2360	3307	3498	3707	3600	3633	3340	3154	3871	3817	3506
1980	3944	3993	3962	3808	4013	4007	4012	3960	3946	3957	3982	4298	3365	3761	4200	3797	4042
1981	4267	3898	4063	4308	4800	3804	3659	4230	4094	3856	4240	4487	3775	4662	4715	5084	4602
1982	4628	4456	4602	4476	4979	3905	4312	5152	4740	4370	4696	4650	4090	4688	4707	5173	5058
1983	5042	4883	4889	4865	5530	4190	4689	5770	4648	4764	5255	4652	4784	5161	5226	5640	5723

Trade balance (f.o.b. — c.i.f.) (31) / Balance commerciale (f.o.b. — c.a.f.) (31)

£ million, monthly averages / millions de £, moyennes mensuelles

	Year	Q.1	Q.2	Q.3	Q.4	JAN	FEB	MAR	APR	MAY	JUN	JUL	AUG	SEP	OCT	NOV	DEC
1964	-94	-88	-90	-111	-87	-164	-62	-38	-125	-37	-106	-112	-86	-134	-117	-77	-67
1965	-74	-77	-74	-83	-61	-111	-22	-99	-54	-98	-69	-60	-86	-103	-81	-39	-64
1966	-62	-76	-84	-86	-3	-132	-44	-52	-96	-50	-105	-109	-75	-75	-19	58	-50
1967	-107	-77	-83	-103	-164	-113	-36	-83	-79	-68	-101	-50	-138	-121	-174	-211	-109
1968	-129	-146	-130	-131	-108	-191	-110	-136	-137	-194	-60	-150	-143	-101	-181	-60	-83
1969	-89	-134	-94	-72	-54	-165	-118	-120	-132	-94	-57	-112	-53	-51	-133	25	-54
1970	-85	-68	-102	-115	-54	-106	-65	-34	-118	-76	-113	64	-279	-129	-104	-18	-40
1971	-61	-145	-45	-28	-25	-136	-147	-153	-61	11	-83	-22	-17	-45	-54	-27	5
1972	-123	-139	-77	-174	-100	-90	-110	-218	-112	-61	-58	-10	-249	-262	-97	-113	-89
1973	-303	-264	-235	-317	-396	-278	-144	-369	-142	-327	-237	-251	-334	-366	-426	-406	-356
1974	-569	-569	-624	-540	-543	-552	-503	-654	-653	-608	-611	-613	-492	-516	-557	-608	-464
1975	-370	-447	-330	-415	-288	-634	-430	-279	-466	-134	-389	-399	-489	-357	-338	-325	-201
1976	-484	-357	-522	-535	-522	-376	-386	-311	-565	-438	-562	-629	-417	-560	-534	-624	-408
1977	-352	-521	-488	-183	-218	-723	-414	-426	-406	-435	-622	-266	-82	-201	-267	-78	-308
1978	-348	-388	-396	-345	-260	-606	-96	-461	-79	-571	-539	-354	-249	-433	-230	-433	-119
1979	-524	-760	-446	-376	-514	-429	-942	-908	-378	-517	-444	-310	-378	-440	-775	-578	-190
1980	-213	-576	-409	-69	201	-649	-606	-474	-572	-276	-379	-41	-164	-1	203	186	213
1981	3	217	40	-215	-28	206	79	366	429	2	-313	-195	-549	100	-270	302	-117
1982	-119	-280	-337	-91	231	-608	-28	-204	-83	-399	-529	-96	-95	-81	17	222	454
1983	-455	-506	-678	-457	-180	-976	-427	-114	-530	-962	-542	-656	-390	-325	-630	-300	389

Imports c.i.f. (31) — Importations c.a.f. (31)

£ million, monthly averages — millions de £, moyennes mensuelles

Adjusted - Corrigé

Year	Q.1	Q.2	Q.3	Q.4	JAN	FEB	MAR	APR	MAY	JUN	JUL	AUG	SEP	OCT	NOV	DEC
1964	470	470	473	485	474	469	468	473	472	466	441	503	475	487	483	484
1965	456	482	488	491	462	437	469	472	489	485	481	486	495	485	492	496
1966	504	492	510	473	507	505	499	509	498	469	525	503	501	475	439	520
1967	525	524	526	570	535	520	522	538	509	525	495	543	536	503	583	622
1968	644	644	669	676	629	652	651	644	651	637	666	669	674	673	696	659
1969	674	699	695	703	667	681	675	700	704	692	705	690	687	701	701	707
1970	720	770	751	796	704	713	743	754	773	783	604	832	817	796	799	793
1971	791	830	809	836	760	778	835	855	803	833	808	787	833	834	821	852
1972	872	889	882	1049	838	873	904	900	868	899	800	761	1085	1043	1068	1036
1973	1132	1225	1367	1517	1121	1073	1202	1150	1273	1253	1287	1400	1413	1457	1552	1541
1974	1735	1968	1991	2019	1551	1771	1884	1957	1937	2009	2029	1968	1975	1991	2064	2003
1975	1980	1875	2062	2099	2072	1994	1873	1866	1841	1917	2071	2129	1987	2109	2093	2094
1976	2180	2576	2696	2909	2081	2218	2242	2554	2525	2649	2702	2615	2772	2825	2999	2904
1977	2959	3145	3017	2951	3057	2865	2956	3009	3036	3387	3135	2885	3032	2966	2743	3143
1978	3115	3333	3357	3373	3051	3016	3277	3064	3483	3453	3371	3257	3443	3268	3490	3360
1979	3474	4000	3945	4224	3090	3463	3868	4047	4054	3890	3861	3982	3991	4310	4254	4107
1980	4478	4350	3967	3796	4461	4653	4319	4583	4232	4236	4092	4038	3770	3744	3733	3911
1981	3648	3967	4704	4737	3597	3747	3601	3706	3997	4197	4565	4929	4615	4554	4976	4680
1982	4710	4896	4657	4716	4764	4590	4777	4857	4965	4336	4636	4589	4747	4762	4642	4745
1983	5393	5476	5429	5770	5483	5448	5248	5459	5632	5337	5416	5420	5451	5925	5581	5803

Exports f.o.b. (31) — Exportations f.o.b. (31)

£ million, monthly averages — millions de £, moyennes mensuelles

Adjusted - Corrigé

Year	Q.1	Q.2	Q.3	Q.4	JAN	FEB	MAR	APR	MAY	JUN	JUL	AUG	SEP	OCT	NOV	DEC
1964	376	384	375	388	363	379	387	379	392	380	345	391	388	374	380	410
1965	394	401	415	424	330	398	403	407	392	405	425	407	413	412	429	431
1966	428	417	442	465	403	444	438	435	440	375	417	453	451	466	473	455
1967	463	448	436	396	477	470	442	450	459	436	451	434	424	360	352	476
1968	519	510	552	563	513	530	514	510	510	511	540	555	562	552	580	557
1969	562	600	640	645	569	546	570	572	600	629	609	666	645	648	641	644
1970	668	660	639	732	658	661	684	672	645	664	687	515	715	729	717	749
1971	683	761	782	797	646	637	767	756	754	772	763	767	815	774	764	854
1972	767	795	709	930	772	776	754	750	798	837	774	512	840	954	940	895
1973	922	969	1039	1099	924	926	917	953	945	1010	1022	1052	1043	1060	1144	1093
1974	1205	1345	1437	1450	1087	1254	1274	1309	1350	1377	1405	1442	1463	1465	1424	1460
1975	1569	1551	1630	1786	1574	1553	1579	1429	1689	1535	1653	1575	1663	1787	1736	1834
1976	1873	2054	2139	2359	1831	1819	1970	1978	2056	2128	2033	2142	2243	2273	2388	2417
1977	2496	2656	2819	2693	2487	2422	2578	2563	2628	2777	2828	2756	2872	2680	2682	2717
1978	2791	2953	2976	3074	2637	2918	2817	2962	2924	2973	2982	2929	3016	3045	3092	3086
1979	2782	3570	3500	3693	2853	2477	3017	3600	3592	3518	3540	3474	3487	3570	3771	3739
1980	3991	3965	3901	3928	4077	4050	3847	3918	3994	3982	4065	3795	3842	3982	3896	4006
1981	3933	4042	4327	4598	4004	3839	3956	4039	4012	4074	4213	4363	4406	4603	4528	4662
1982	4499	4599	4556	4858	4308	4510	4680	4691	4567	4538	4556	4368	4745	4663	4905	5007
1983	4897	4862	4938	5407	4552	4369	5260	4760	4743	5082	4709	4905	5200	5160	5279	5782

Trade balance (f.o.b. — c.i.f.) (31) — Balance commerciale (f.o.b. — c.a.f.) (31)

£ million, monthly averages — millions de £, moyennes mensuelles

Adjusted - Corrigé

Year	Q.1	Q.2	Q.3	Q.4	JAN	FEB	MAR	APR	MAY	JUN	JUL	AUG	SEP	OCT	NOV	DEC
1964	-94	-87	-99	-97	-111	-91	-81	-94	-80	-86	-96	-113	-87	-114	-103	-75
1965	-62	-81	-73	-67	-83	-39	-66	-65	-97	-81	-57	-79	-82	-73	-63	-65
1966	-76	-75	-68	-13	-105	-61	-62	-74	-58	-94	-108	-44	-51	-8	35	-65
1967	-62	-76	-90	-174	-58	-50	-80	-89	-50	-89	-48	-109	-112	-145	-232	-146
1968	-125	-133	-117	-112	-116	-122	-137	-134	-141	-126	-127	-113	-112	-121	-116	-101
1969	-113	-99	-56	-58	-98	-136	-105	-128	-104	-63	-100	-24	-43	-53	-60	-63
1970	-52	-110	-112	-64	-46	-52	-59	-82	-128	-119	83	-317	-102	-67	-82	-44
1971	-108	-70	-28	-38	-114	-141	-68	-99	-49	-61	-45	-20	-18	-60	-57	2
1972	-104	-94	-173	-119	-66	-97	-150	-150	-70	-62	-26	-248	-245	-89	-128	-141
1973	-210	-256	-328	-418	-197	-147	-285	-197	-328	-243	-265	-348	-370	-397	-408	-443
1974	-530	-622	-554	-570	-464	-517	-610	-648	-587	-632	-624	-526	-512	-326	-640	-543
1975	-411	-324	-432	-313	-498	-441	-294	-437	-152	-382	-418	-554	-324	-322	-357	-260
1976	-307	-522	-557	-550	-250	-399	-272	-576	-469	-521	-669	-473	-529	-552	-611	-487
1977	-464	-489	-199	-258	-570	-443	-378	-446	-410	-610	-307	-129	-160	-286	-61	-426
1978	-324	-380	-381	-298	-414	-98	-460	-102	-559	-480	-389	-328	-427	-223	-398	-274
1979	-691	-430	-444	-530	-237	-986	-851	-447	-472	-372	-321	-508	-504	-740	-483	-368
1980	-486	-386	-66	132	-384	-603	-472	-665	-238	-254	-27	-242	72	138	163	95
1981	285	75	-377	-139	407	92	355	333	15	-123	-356	-566	-209	49	-448	-18
1982	-211	-297	-101	142	-456	-80	-97	-196	-398	-298	-80	-221	-2	-99	263	262
1983	-496	-614	-491	-363	-921	-579	12	-659	-889	-255	-707	-515	-251	-765	-302	-21

NOTES

1. The original base of the index is 1963 to 1967, and 1980 from 1968.
2. Data are based on the *UK Standard Industrial Classification* as from the following dates:

Industrial production	1968
Sales and orders	1974
Employment in manufacturing	September 1981
Weekly hours of work	1976
Weekly earnings	1980
Unit labour cost	1970
Producer prices	1974

For previous periods the 1968 or earlier versions of the SIC are used.

3. Averages of four or five weeks for months, thirteen for quarters.
4. From 1977, Land Rover Estate cars are included with commercial vehicles. Prior to this date, they are included with passenger cars.
5. Mechanical, instrument and electrical engineering, excluding transport equipment. The original base of the index is 1963 to 1969, 1975 from 1970 to 1977, and 1980 from 1978. The weighting pattern used is derived from gross output for the base year; the arithmetic base is the base year value of the sales series. The discontinuity in the series between June and July 1965 is due to the expansion of the number of product headings used in the inquiry; that between 1971 and 1972 is due to a major change in the inquiry method. Adjustments have been made to the data for 1969-71 to attempt to present them on the same basis as the post-1971 data but this was only possible to a limited extent.
6. Excluding work to be carried out by public authorities using their own labour (about 6 per cent of total work). From April 1976, new estimation procedure and minor changes in type of work classification.
7. Data are benchmarked on the 1961 Census of Distribution to 1965; on the 1966 Census from 1966 to 1970, and on the 1971 Census from 1971 to 1975; from 1976 to 1980 the data are benchmarked on an annual sample retail inquiry. From 1980 this inquiry is conducted only every second year.
8. Series based on taxation categories. From 1975, the series covers cars in all taxation classes; previously only private cars and vans were covered.

NOTES

1. La base originale de l'indice est 1963 jusqu'en 1967, et 1980 à partir de 1968.
2. Les données se réfèrent à la *Classification Type de l'Industrie du Royaume-Uni* de 1980 à partir des dates suivantes :

Production industrielle	1968
Ventes et commandes	1974
Emploi dans les industries manufacturières	Septembre 1981
Durée hebdomadaire du travail	1976
Gains hebdomadaires	1980
Coût unitaire de la main-d'œuvre	1970
Prix à la production	1974

Pour les périodes antérieures, la CTI de 1968, ou une version précédente, a été utilisée.

3. Moyenne de quatre ou cinq semaines pour les mois, treize pour les trimestres.
4. A partir de 1977, les voitures Land Rover Estate sont comprises dans les véhicules utilitaires. Avant cette date, elles font partie des voitures de tourisme.
5. Machines et matériel, à l'exclusion du matériel de transport. La base originale de l'indice est 1963 jusqu'en 1969, 1975 de 1970 à 1977, et 1980 à partir de 1978. La pondération se réfère à la production brute de l'année de base; la base arithmétique est la valeur de l'année de base des séries de ventes. La discontinuité dans les séries entre juin et juillet 1965 est due à l'extension du nombre de types de produits utilisés dans l'enquête; celle entre 1971 et 1972 est due à un changement important dans la méthode d'enquête. Les ajustements qui ont été faits sur les données pour la période 1969-71 pour essayer de les présenter sur la même base que les données postérieures à 1971 n'ont donné que des résultats partiels.
6. Non compris les travaux entrepris par le secteur public et effectués par ses propres salariés (environ 6 % des travaux totaux). A partir d'avril 1976, nouvelle méthode d'estimation et changements mineurs dans la classification par type de construction.
7. Les données sont établies à partir du Recensement de la distribution de 1961 jusqu'en 1965; à partir du Recensement de 1966 de 1966 à 1970, et à partir du Recensement de 1971 de 1971 à 1975; de 1976 à 1980, les données sont établies à partir d'enquêtes annuelles auprès des détaillants. A partir de 1980, cette enquête n'a lieu que tous les deux ans.
8. Série basée sur les catégories fiscales. A partir de 1975, la série couvre les voitures de tourisme de toutes les catégories fiscales; avant cette date, seulement les voitures de tourisme des particuliers et les camionettes étaient comprises.

NOTES

9. Annual data refer to mid-year employment.
10. Excluding school-leavers and adult students.
11. Vacancies intended mainly for adults.
12. The self-employed are excluded from the civilian labour force.
13. Revised methodology from 1976.
14. Excluding stoppages involving less than 10 workers or lasting less than one day, unless the total number of working days lost exceeds 100.
15. Including juveniles.
16. Prior to 1976, excluding some services and public administration.
17. Wages and salaries per unit of output.
18. Home market.
19. Weighting pattern based on 1963 to 1969, on 1968 from 1970 to 1973, and on 1980 from 1974.
20. Excluding items the prices of which show marked seasonal fluctuations. The weighting pattern is revised yearly and the indices linked on January.
21. Monthly data refer to third Wednesday of month (second in December).
22. Quarterly and annual data refer to last day of period.
23. Discontinuities in the series not mentioned elsewhere result from changes in the list of contributors to the banking statistics.
24. Excluding foreign currency deposits.
25. Including agriculture and construction.
26. From May 1975, excluding lending to some exporters and to the banking sector. From February 1983, including some market loans.
27. Last Friday of month.
28. Average rate of allotment on last issue of month.
29. Monthly data are daily averages.
30. Banking and money market liabilities and reserves in sterling held by foreign monetary authorities. From 1975, monthly data refer to third Wednesday of month (second in December). Quarterly and annual data refer to last day of period. A new reporting system was introduced in December 1974. On the new basis the data for December 1974 are £ 6,803 million for the total and £ 4,303 million for monetary authorities.
31. General trade. From 1981, including non-monetary gold.

NOTES

9. Les données annuelles se réfèrent à l'emploi en milieu d'année.
10. Non compris les jeunes arrivant en fin de scolarité et les étudiants.
11. Offres d'emploi destinées principalement aux adultes.
12. Les travailleurs indépendants ne sont pas compris dans la main-d'œuvre civile.
13. Méthodologie révisée à partir de 1976.
14. Non compris les arrêts de travail impliquant moins de 10 travailleurs, ou d'une durée inférieure à une journée, sauf si le nombre total de journées de travail perdues dépasse 100.
15. Y compris les personnes âgées de 18 ans ou moins.
16. Avant 1976, non compris certains services et l'administration publique.
17. Salaires et traitements par unité produite.
18. Marché intérieur.
19. La pondération se réfère à 1963 jusqu'en 1969, à 1968 de 1970 à 1973, et à 1980 à partir de 1974.
20. Non compris les articles dont les prix sont sujets à de fortes fluctuations saisonnières. La pondération est révisée chaque année et les indices raccordés sur janvier.
21. Les données mensuelles se réfèrent au troisième mercredi du mois (deuxième pour décembre).
22. Les données trimestrielles et annuelles se réfèrent au dernier jour de la période.
23. Les discontinuités dans les séries non citées ailleurs proviennent de changements dans la liste des banques figurant aux statistiques bancaires.
24. Non compris les dépôts en devises.
25. Y compris l'agriculture et la construction.
26. A partir de mai 1975, non compris les prêts à certains exportateurs et au secteur bancaire. A partir de février 1983, y compris certains emprunts sur le marché monétaire.
27. Dernier vendredi du mois.
28. Taux moyen d'adjudication de la dernière émission du mois.
29. Les données mensuelles sont des moyennes journalières.
30. Avoirs de l'étranger sur le système bancaire et le marché monétaire, et réserves en sterling des autorités monétaires étrangères. A partir de 1975, les données mensuelles se réfèrent au troisième mercredi du mois (deuxième pour décembre). Les données trimestrielles et annuelles se réfèrent au dernier jour de la période. Un nouveau système de notification a été introduit en décembre 1974. Les données de décembre 1974 sur la nouvelle base sont de 6803 millions de £ pour le total et de 4303 millions de £ pour les autorités monétaires.
31. Commerce général. A partir de 1981, y compris l'or non monétaire.

MAIN SOURCES

PRINCIPALES SOURCES

Series	Séries	Sources
Gross domestic product	Produit intérieur brut	
Industrial production	Production industrielle	
Engineering sales and orders	Industries mécaniques, ventes et commandes	Central Statistical Office *Monthly Digest of Statistics*
Retail sales	Ventes au détail	
Share prices	Cours des actions	
Business surveys	Enquêtes de conjoncture	Confederation of British Industry *Industrial Trends Survey*
Change in stocks	Variations des stocks	
Producer prices	Prix à la production	Department of Trade and Industry *British Business*
Instalment credit	Crédits remboursables par tranches	
Construction	Construction	Department of the Environment *Housing and Construction Statistics*
New passenger car registrations	Immatriculations de voiture de tourisme neuves	Department of Transport *Press Notice*
Labour and wages	Main-d'œuvre et salaires	Department of Employment *Employment Gazette*
Consumer prices	Prix à la consommation	
Money and credit	Monnaie et crédit	
Interest rates	Taux d'intérêts	Central Statistical Office *Financial Statistics*
External sterling liabilities	Dette extérieure en sterling	
Balance of payments	Balance des paiements	
Foreign trade	Commerce extérieur	Department of Trade *Overseas Trade Statistics*

Yugoslavia — Yougoslavie

YUGOSLAVIA

Gross fixed investment (1)
(socialized sector)
billion dinars

Formation brute de capital fixe (1)
(secteur socialisé)
milliards de dinars

	Year	Q.1	Q.2	Q.3	Q.4	JAN	FEB	MAR	APR	MAY	JUN	JUL	AUG	SEP	OCT	NOV	DEC
1964	18.8	2.5	4.8	4.8	6.8	0.5	0.8	1.1	1.5	1.4	1.9	1.6	1.5	1.7	1.8	1.5	3.5
1965	19.2	3.1	4.7	4.5	6.7	0.7	1.0	1.5	1.6	1.2	2.0	1.6	1.4	1.6	1.6	1.7	3.4
1966	21.2	3.1	5.6	5.6	6.9	0.5	1.0	1.6	1.7	1.4	2.4	1.6	2.0	1.9	1.9	1.7	3.3
1967	19.9	3.5	5.4	4.7	6.3	0.9	1.2	1.4	1.7	1.6	2.1	1.3	1.8	1.7	1.5	1.7	3.1
1968	25.2	3.7	6.7	6.3	8.6	1.0	1.1	1.5	1.9	2.4	2.4	2.0	2.1	2.1	2.4	2.1	4.1
1969	29.1	4.4	7.3	7.4	10.0	1.3	1.3	1.8	2.3	2.1	2.9	2.4	2.5	2.5	2.5	2.4	5.1
1970	38.5	6.8	9.6	9.6	12.4	1.8	2.3	2.7	3.0	2.9	3.7	3.2	3.2	3.3	3.4	3.1	5.8
1971	41.4	8.1	10.6	10.2	12.6	2.3	2.7	3.0	3.5	3.4	3.7	3.5	3.5	3.2	3.2	3.5	5.8
1972	48.8	8.6	12.6	11.4	16.2	2.7	2.9	3.0	4.8	3.5	4.3	3.6	4.0	3.9	4.0	4.1	8.1
1973	52.8	9.6	13.4	12.3	17.5	2.8	3.2	3.7	3.6	4.2	5.6	3.8	4.1	4.4	4.8	4.6	8.1
1974	79.1	12.6	18.8	20.3	27.4	3.6	4.0	5.0	6.0	6.2	6.6	6.9	6.4	6.9	7.4	7.1	12.9
1975	119.7	19.7	27.7	29.3	43.1	5.6	6.2	7.9	9.1	8.5	10.1	10.2	9.1	10.0	12.3	10.7	20.0
1976	157.4	28.2	37.4	40.2	51.7	8.9	8.1	11.2	11.7	11.6	14.1	13.5	12.6	14.1	13.2	12.9	25.6
1977	206.3	33.5	52.0	49.5	71.4	9.8	9.1	14.6	15.2	14.1	22.7	12.4	18.9	18.1	19.8	18.3	33.2
1978	278.1	49.5	67.2	70.7	90.7	14.4	14.7	20.4	19.2	20.4	27.6	24.5	22.1	24.1	28.1	22.4	40.3
1979	354.4	64.0	84.8	91.7	114.0	23.9	16.9	23.1	26.1	27.6	31.1	34.4	29.0	28.3	38.1	28.9	47.0
1980	445.6	83.9	106.9	110.9	143.8	33.0	22.1	28.8	33.5	30.0	43.4	43.6	31.2	36.2	45.0	36.4	62.4
1981	524.7	97.1	127.2	140.9	159.6	39.5	25.4	32.2	44.1	37.3	45.8	55.0	39.8	46.1	50.9	41.1	67.5
1982	661.0	123.5	162.6	159.7	205.2	46.8	30.2	46.5	54.8	46.4	61.4	67.6	46.7	55.4	63.1	49.6	92.6
1983	765.5	143.8	180.2	201.5	240.0	51.3	36.9	55.7	59.1	52.9	68.2	72.8	60.7	68.0	74.0	61.7	104.3

Industrial production: total (2)
(socialized sector)
1980 = 100

Production industrielle : total (2)
(secteur socialisé)
1980 = 100

	Year	Q.1	Q.2	Q.3	Q.4	JAN	FEB	MAR	APR	MAY	JUN	JUL	AUG	SEP	OCT	NOV	DEC
1964	35	30	34	34	38	28	30	33	34	33	35	32	33	36	38	36	40
1965	36	34	37	36	40	32	33	38	38	35	38	33	36	39	40	37	43
1966	38	36	39	38	41	33	35	40	39	37	40	34	38	41	40	39	44
1967	38	36	38	37	41	34	35	40	38	38	39	34	38	40	41	39	41
1968	40	37	41	40	45	34	36	40	40	41	41	38	40	42	46	43	46
1969	45	41	46	45	48	38	39	45	45	46	47	43	45	49	51	46	48
1970	49	45	50	48	54	42	45	50	49	49	51	45	48	52	54	52	55
1971	54	50	56	53	59	46	50	55	55	54	57	50	53	57	59	56	61
1972	59	56	60	57	63	51	55	61	58	60	62	51	58	61	63	61	64
1973	62	59	64	60	66	56	58	64	62	65	64	55	61	63	68	65	65
1974	69	65	70	66	75	62	63	70	70	70	70	62	65	71	75	71	78
1975	72	71	74	67	78	67	70	75	76	73	73	62	66	74	79	75	79
1976	75	72	73	71	81	69	71	78	72	72	76	63	71	78	81	78	86
1977	82	80	83	78	88	75	78	87	83	82	85	69	80	86	87	85	91
1978	89	86	91	85	96	80	84	95	89	91	92	74	87	94	97	93	97
1979	97	94	99	90	103	88	92	103	97	99	99	81	92	98	104	99	106
1980	100	99	101	92	108	92	100	105	102	101	101	82	92	102	110	105	108
1981	104	102	107	98	111	94	100	111	107	105	110	89	97	109	112	107	113
1982	104	104	107	97	109	97	102	114	110	104	107	87	97	109	110	103	114
1983	104	104	107	99	113	98	101	114	105	104	112	88	101	111	115	109	115

Industrial production: investment goods (2)
(socialized sector)
1980 = 100

Production industrielle : biens d'équipement (2)
(secteur socialisé)
1980 = 100

	Year	Q.1	Q.2	Q.3	Q.4	JAN	FEB	MAR	APR	MAY	JUN	JUL	AUG	SEP	OCT	NOV	DEC
1964	30	25	31	28	35	21	25	30	29	29	33	27	28	31	31	32	42
1965	32	28	33	30	40	23	27	34	34	30	35	27	28	35	34	36	48
1966	33	30	35	32	37	26	29	34	34	33	37	28	32	35	32	34	45
1967	34	30	34	32	39	26	29	36	32	34	36	32	30	34	36	34	45
1968	36	32	37	35	41	26	31	37	36	36	38	33	34	37	38	38	46
1969	40	35	41	39	46	29	35	40	39	42	43	38	38	41	45	42	50
1970	43	39	44	40	49	34	40	44	43	42	47	35	39	44	46	48	53
1971	48	43	49	44	53	38	43	48	48	47	52	42	43	47	51	48	60
1972	50	47	51	46	56	42	47	51	48	52	53	43	47	50	52	54	63
1973	53	50	56	48	59	45	50	55	53	56	58	46	43	53	56	57	62
1974	59	54	60	55	69	47	53	62	59	59	62	52	49	63	66	62	79
1975	67	61	70	61	78	53	63	69	69	68	73	59	57	67	74	74	85
1976	70	66	73	64	78	58	68	72	72	72	76	60	60	72	72	75	87
1977	77	71	79	71	86	61	70	83	77	78	84	64	69	80	81	77	100
1978	86	78	90	81	97	70	75	90	85	88	96	71	76	95	92	90	110
1979	96	92	101	87	105	79	91	106	94	100	103	82	81	98	100	100	116
1980	100	97	104	90	110	82	98	111	101	101	109	84	87	98	107	100	122
1981	105	98	112	96	114	86	96	111	107	108	122	90	92	107	107	106	128
1982	106	102	114	97	112	89	102	114	112	111	121	91	93	108	104	104	129
1983	106	101	111	95	110	88	100	116	105	105	123	83	93	108	102	102	124

Industrial production: consumer goods (2)
(socialized sector)
1980 = 100

Production industrielle : biens de consommation (2)
(secteur socialisé)
1980 = 100

	Year	Q.1	Q.2	Q.3	Q.4	JAN	FEB	MAR	APR	MAY	JUN	JUL	AUG	SEP	OCT	NOV	DEC
1964	33	30	33	32	39	28	31	31	33	32	33	29	31	37	40	38	39
1965	36	34	35	35	41	32	33	37	36	33	36	30	35	41	42	39	42
1966	38	35	37	38	44	33	34	39	38	35	39	31	38	44	45	41	46
1967	38	37	37	37	42	35	36	40	37	37	37	31	37	43	44	41	42
1968	41	37	40	39	47	36	37	39	40	39	40	35	39	43	49	45	47
1969	45	41	45	44	49	38	39	44	45	44	46	35	43	50	52	48	48
1970	49	46	49	48	55	43	45	49	48	47	51	42	48	53	56	53	56
1971	55	51	56	53	60	46	51	55	55	54	57	47	53	60	61	57	62
1972	60	57	61	58	64	52	56	62	58	61	63	50	60	64	66	62	64
1973	63	61	64	60	69	58	59	64	62	65	64	51	62	65	71	69	66
1974	69	66	71	65	76	63	64	69	72	70	72	59	66	72	77	72	80
1975	72	72	73	65	80	69	71	75	75	72	72	56	64	76	82	77	79
1976	75	72	73	71	86	69	71	77	71	71	76	59	72	82	85	84	89
1977	82	79	82	77	90	76	78	85	81	81	85	62	80	90	90	87	92
1978	88	36	89	82	97	80	84	93	86	90	91	67	85	93	98	95	99
1979	96	95	98	87	105	92	93	101	96	98	99	74	91	96	107	100	109
1980	100	99	98	89	114	98	100	100	99	97	99	72	89	105	118	112	111
1981	104	101	104	95	116	96	100	108	104	101	107	76	94	114	120	114	115
1982	104	103	105	95	114	98	101	111	107	101	106	75	96	113	116	112	112
1983	104	101	105	97	120	96	98	110	103	102	109	76	100	115	128	115	116

Industrial production: total (2)
(socialized sector)
1980 = 100

Adjusted - Corrigé *

Production industrielle : total (2)
(secteur socialisé)
1980 = 100

	Year	Q.1	Q.2	Q.3	Q.4	JAN	FEB	MAR	APR	MAY	JUN	JUL	AUG	SEP	OCT	NOV	DEC
1964		32	34	34	36	32	32	32	33	34	34	35	34	34	35	36	36
1965		36	36	37	38	37	36	36	37	36	36	36	37	37	37	37	39
1966		38	38	38	39	38	38	38	38	38	38	38	38	38	38	38	40
1967		39	38	38	39	39	39	38	38	38	38	38	38	38	39	39	38
1968		39	40	41	43	39	38	39	40	40	40	41	41	41	42	43	43
1969		43	45	47	46	42	43	44	44	45	46	47	47	47	47	47	44
1970		48	49	50	51	47	48	48	48	49	49	50	51	50	51	53	50
1971		52	54	55	56	52	53	52	54	54	54	56	55	55	56	55	56
1972		57	58	59	60	58	57	57	58	58	59	58	60	60	60	60	60
1973		61	62	63	63	61	61	61	61	63	61	63	63	63	64	65	61
1974		66	68	70	71	66	66	67	67	68	69	70	69	71	70	71	73
1975		72	72	71	74	71	73	72	73	72	72	71	71	72	74	76	73
1976		73	72	75	78	74	72	72	70	72	73	74	76	76	77	77	79
1977		81	81	83	84	82	81	81	31	82	82	83	84	84	84	84	85
1978		87	38	91	92	87	87	87	88	38	89	90	91	92	92	92	93
1979		94	96	97	99	93	94	96	96	96	96	97	96	97	97	98	102
1980		98	99	98	103	98	98	99	98	99	99	97	99	99	102	107	101
1981		102	105	105	106	101	103	103	104	104	106	105	106	105	105	108	105
1982		105	104	105	104	106	105	104	106	104	103	104	105	106	104	102	106
1983		105	104	106	108	108	104	104	103	103	107	104	107	108	110	106	108

Industrial production: intermediate goods (2)
(socialized sector)
1980 = 100

Production industrielle : biens intermédiaires (2)
(secteur socialisé)
1980 = 100

	Year	Q.1	Q.2	Q.3	Q.4	JAN	FEB	MAR	APR	MAY	JUN	JUL	AUG	SEP	OCT	NOV	DEC
1964	36	32	36	36	38	30	32	35	36	36	37	36	36	37	38	36	39
1965	38	36	39	38	39	34	34	40	40	38	40	36	39	39	39	36	42
1966	40	38	40	39	40	35	37	43	41	39	41	38	40	40	41	38	42
1967	39	38	41	39	40	35	37	43	40	41	41	37	41	40	41	39	39
1968	42	38	43	42	45	36	38	42	42	43	42	44	43	43	46	43	44
1969	47	43	48	48	48	41	41	47	43	48	49	47	43	50	53	47	45
1970	51	47	52	51	54	43	46	51	52	52	52	50	51	54	55	53	54
1971	56	52	57	56	59	48	51	57	57	56	59	55	55	58	59	56	61
1972	60	58	62	60	63	53	57	63	60	62	63	55	60	63	64	62	63
1973	64	62	66	64	66	59	60	66	65	66	66	61	65	65	70	65	63
1974	71	68	72	70	74	65	65	72	72	72	71	67	71	72	76	72	75
1975	74	73	75	72	76	71	71	78	78	75	72	68	72	75	78	72	77
1976	76	75	75	74	82	72	72	80	74	74	76	69	75	78	82	79	84
1977	83	81	85	81	86	76	79	89	86	85	84	74	82	86	86	84	87
1978	90	88	92	87	94	83	86	96	91	93	91	79	90	92	96	93	93
1979	96	94	98	92	100	87	91	103	97	99	97	85	95	97	102	98	101
1980	100	99	103	95	103	91	100	107	104	103	101	88	95	102	106	102	101
1981	105	104	108	101	106	96	101	113	111	107	107	96	101	107	108	104	107
1982	105	106	103	100	106	99	104	115	111	106	107	93	100	107	107	99	113
1983	105	107	109	102	109	102	104	116	109	107	111	92	105	109	110	106	112

* Adjusted by the O.E.C.D.

* Corrigé par l'O.C.D.E.

YUGOSLAVIA

Industrial production: construction (2)(3)(4)
(socialized sector) (hours worked)
1980 = 100

Production industrielle : construction (2)(3)(4)
(secteur socialisé) (heures ouvrées)
1980 = 100

	Year	Q.1	Q.2	Q.3	Q.4	JAN	FEB	MAR	APR	MAY	JUN	JUL	AUG	SEP	OCT	NOV	DEC
1964	89	63	94	98	87	52	61	77	91	93	98	96	99	97	94	87	73
1965	76	62	84	82	74	55	56	74	84	82	85	82	81	82	79	73	69
1966	68	53	71	73	67	43	51	64	70	69	73	70	75	75	72	67	63
1967	66	50	69	71	66	42	49	60	66	70	71	65	73	72	72	68	59
1968	68	49	72	75	69	39	48	60	69	72	74	74	75	75	77	69	62
1969	74	52	79	86	76	43	48	64	75	80	84	85	86	86	87	77	63
1970	75	54	81	86	79	45	52	66	78	79	86	95	85	87	86	79	73
1971	74	53	82	85	76	44	51	65	79	82	87	86	86	85	82	75	70
1972	79	52	86	88	80	49	59	78	81	88	91	86	88	88	86	80	74
1973	63	48	67	70	64	42	45	58	63	67	70	65	71	70	70	65	58
1974	65	53	68	71	67	52	49	59	65	68	70	70	71	72	71	66	63
1975	77	61	83	84	80	48	61	75	80	83	85	82	85	84	84	79	76
1976	74	59	77	83	77	45	61	71	75	77	80	83	81	84	82	77	74
1977	81	67	85	88	83	55	65	80	83	83	88	85	90	90	88	83	78
1978	89	74	93	98	91	69	68	86	90	94	96	94	100	100	98	93	83
1979	95	75	102	103	98	59	75	93	98	102	105	101	105	104	104	97	94
1980	100	81	107	110	101	62	83	99	107	106	109	109	108	112	111	100	93
1981	91	74	99	101	91	58	71	92	99	99	101	100	99	103	99	92	83
1982	89	73	97	97	89	57	71	91	95	95	100	95	97	98	93	89	86
1983	89	71	91	91	84	61	65	88	89	91	93	87	93	93	90	86	78

Production: cement
(socialized sector)
thousand tons, monthly averages

Production : ciment
(secteur socialisé)
milliers de tonnes, moyennes mensuelles

	Year	Q.1	Q.2	Q.3	Q.4	JAN	FEB	MAR	APR	MAY	JUN	JUL	AUG	SEP	OCT	NOV	DEC
1964	253	211	272	267	262	154	209	270	263	285	269	269	269	264	278	258	250
1965	259	193	286	293	262	160	172	247	275	286	297	290	293	296	277	268	241
1966	269	224	284	293	276	159	207	305	277	287	287	302	286	292	319	266	244
1967	276	228	305	303	271	161	203	319	303	304	307	306	304	298	297	300	215
1968	314	201	364	379	311	115	183	306	356	377	359	396	395	346	372	306	254
1969	330	239	332	374	327	173	182	363	380	379	387	374	358	339	380	355	245
1970	367	266	393	417	390	180	242	375	360	389	411	415	393	442	447	397	327
1971	413	305	469	474	403	240	278	397	474	462	471	493	476	453	461	405	344
1972	479	370	508	538	501	288	354	467	496	505	524	527	546	540	541	501	462
1973	516	427	593	564	484	306	389	587	595	604	581	559	588	544	559	512	382
1974	554	477	592	617	530	390	461	579	561	608	608	614	633	603	580	525	485
1975	589	436	662	659	548	401	446	611	661	671	655	667	649	661	649	562	432
1976	636	473	716	717	634	362	436	621	683	723	741	719	729	702	712	665	524
1977	667	520	751	728	669	390	503	668	745	746	762	747	737	701	730	684	592
1978	725	564	778	760	734	437	531	705	795	753	785	724	766	771	854	742	607
1979	757	606	816	825	780	457	564	798	821	837	790	796	836	842	819	754	767
1980	776	648	863	876	718	443	621	880	855	899	835	927	879	823	788	730	635
1981	815	643	917	927	773	409	666	854	832	922	998	1008	970	802	880	834	605
1982	810	671	926	882	760	533	703	778	937	960	880	923	901	822	928	675	677
1983	799	683	928	922	664	486	690	874	953	900	932	941	926	898	806	653	532

Ships completed
thousand gross register tons, quarterly averages

Navires achevés
milliers de tonneaux de jauge brute, moyennes trimestrielles

	Year	Q.1	Q.2	Q.3	Q.4	JAN	FEB	MAR	APR	MAY	JUN	JUL	AUG	SEP	OCT	NOV	DEC
1964	44	55	65	24	34												
1965	57	23	65	48	94												
1966	83	91	72	53	117												
1967	65	26	73	41	120												
1968	82	55	106	82	84												
1969	74	18	73	95	102												
1970	96	86	136	35	128												
1971	99	102	110	86	95												
1972	168	71	164	113	245												
1973	112	76	152	161	58												
1974	180	204	203	102	213												
1975	160	64	265	142	166												
1976	149	193	123	68	211												
1977	105	164	136	81	39												
1978	73	68	85	63	76												
1979	56	0	94	48	78												
1980	37	30	41	44	35												
1981	56	44	22	31	124												
1982	78	52	92	70	115												
1983	82	22	61	100	145												

Industrial production: construction (2)(3)(4) (socialized sector) (hours worked)

1980 = 100

Adjusted - Corrigé *

Production industrielle : construction (2)(3)(4) (secteur socialisé) (heures ouvrées)

1980 = 100

	Year	Q.1	Q.2	Q.3	Q.4	JAN	FEB	MAR	APR	MAY	JUN	JUL	AUG	SEP	OCT	NOV	DEC
1964		85	87	86	83	82	87	86	66	87	87	86	87	85	87	84	82
1965		84	77	72	71	90	81	80	79	77	75	74	72	71	71	69	72
1966		71	65	65	65	70	74	69	67	65	64	64	65	66	64	63	67
1967		68	64	63	64	68	70	65	64	64	62	63	63	63	64	64	63
1968		65	66	66	67	63	67	66	66	66	67	66	65	66	67	66	67
1969		70	73	76	73	68	70	71	71	73	74	76	76	75	75	75	68
1970		73	74	75	77	72	74	74	74	74	75	75	75	76	75	77	80
1971		71	76	75	74	70	72	71	75	76	76	76	76	74	74	73	76
1972		80	80	78	79	79	79	84	80	80	79	78	77	78	78	77	83
1973		63	62	63	64	65	61	62	62	62	62	63	62	63	63	64	64
1974		69	63	64	66	79	64	63	63	62	63	63	63	65	64	65	69
1975		76	77	76	79	71	77	79	77	77	77	74	77	75	76	80	81
1976		72	72	75	77	68	75	72	71	73	72	76	74	75	76	76	78
1977		82	79	80	83	84	81	81	79	79	79	79	80	81	82	82	84
1978		91	87	89	91	104	84	85	87	87	87	88	90	90	91	91	90
1979		91	95	95	97	88	93	93	94	95	96	95	94	95	95	96	101
1980		98	100	100	100	93	100	101	101	99	100	101	100	101	101	100	98
1981		90	93	92	90	87	89	93	93	94	92	92	92	92	91	92	87
1982		89	90	89	88	88	88	91	90	91	90	85	90	87	87	87	89
1983		88	85	83	83	94	81	88	86	86	83	83	84	83	85	84	82

Construction: work put in place, total (3)(4) (socialized sector)

million dinars, monthly averages

Construction: travaux effectués, total (3)(4) (secteur socialisé)

millions de dinars, moyennes mensuelles

	Year	Q.1	Q.2	Q.3	Q.4	JAN	FEB	MAR	APR	MAY	JUN	JUL	AUG	SEP	OCT	NOV	DEC
1964	804	312	672	777	710	194	277	465	572	663	780	705	759	868	725	650	755
1965	867	349	712	788	890	268	275	505	637	682	818	666	779	920	906	783	982
1966	1039	412	882	998	1001	267	358	612	715	847	1085	503	979	1113	987	922	1093
1967	1249	526	1040	1151	1150	315	452	810	906	1039	1174	1040	1125	1288	1245	1062	1144
1968	1413	558	1231	1332	1307	343	482	850	1057	1195	1441	1161	1360	1475	1296	1187	1438
1969	1645	630	1492	1625	1490	402	520	968	1226	1458	1792	1585	1532	1758	1690	1496	1284
1970	2075	818	1774	1971	2130	572	706	1176	1452	1671	2199	1731	1916	2266	2198	2050	2141
1971	2563	968	2292	2533	2450	712	833	1358	1955	2190	2732	2413	2399	2786	2509	2087	2753
1972	2920	1274	2601	2713	2746	872	1163	1786	2354	2369	3081	2574	2540	3024	2896	2383	2958
1973	3194	1454	2860	3144	3022	1007	1227	2128	2316	2785	3478	2933	3016	3484	3219	2813	3034
1974	4393	1922	3912	4371	4331	1191	1689	2885	3384	3861	4492	4065	4010	5038	4259	4083	4652
1975	6290	3075	5619	6170	6321	2013	2656	4555	4694	5386	6778	5920	5729	6860	5949	6195	6820
1976	7418	3516	6666	7443	8099	2700	2970	4878	5472	6560	7965	6874	6793	8662	7242	7817	9239
1977	9820	5325	9451	10158	11006	3299	4887	7789	7851	8906	11597	8732	9364	12378	10431	9551	13036
1978	13469	7173	13109	14896	14435	5038	5739	10743	11220	12327	15779	13110	14385	17193	14546	12309	16450
1979	18242	9246	17968	19162	18852	5820	7648	14270	14970	16973	21961	17390	17377	22719	17956	16607	21993
1980	22442	12916	21406	24038	23076	7954	10531	20262	18814	18710	26694	21213	22067	28834	21699	22684	24845
1981	29459	15088	29841	32286	29975	8961	11442	24861	23939	26397	39188	28806	29098	38954	26892	27623	35411
1982	34773	18680	34703	36401	36063	12420	14786	28833	26627	33028	44455	32127	32266	44810	32145	29953	46090
1983	35471	22391	38875	40001	41505	15915	17104	34155	31721	33815	51090	33448	38067	48439	39424	36326	49066

Construction, work in progress: dwellings (4) (socialized sector)

thousands, end of period

Construction, travaux en cours : logements (4) (secteur socialisé)

milliers, fin de période

	Year	Q.1	Q.2	Q.3	Q.4	JAN	FEB	MAR	APR	MAY	JUN	JUL	AUG	SEP	OCT	NOV	DEC
1964																	
1965																	
1966	55.51	66.12	67.66	66.44	52.78												
1967	50.51	52.82	55.14	55.86	48.83												
1968	56.24	56.72	59.00	61.60	57.55												
1969	65.98	62.12	70.66	73.98	67.56												
1970	67.82	70.86	71.47	74.64	68.03												
1971	75.21	73.54	74.47	77.84	71.94												
1972	75.86	76.91	79.70	79.63	72.41												
1973	88.14	77.66	82.59	91.68	85.75												
1974	91.21	89.55	97.51	98.59	87.94												
1975	87.27	96.96	99.75	95.98	85.26												
1976	78.53	93.37	94.76	95.29	77.98												
1977	90.86	88.65	91.11	95.88	86.[illegible]3												
1978	103.00	96.64	100.09	102.30	97.45												
1979	109.27	109.20	109.72	113.23	103.20												
1980	114.37	111.95	117.15	119.66	113.33												
1981	105.00	121.99	120.22	117.72	105.48												
1982	91.56	107.69	108.92	107.30	92.07												
1983	92.68	92.20	93.31	104.43	80.78												

* Adjusted by the O.E.C.D.

* Corrigé par l'O.C.D.E.

Construction: dwellings completed (4) / Construction : logements achevés (4)

(socialized sector) / (secteur socialisé)

thousands, quarterly averages / milliers, moyennes trimestrielles

	Year	Q.1	Q.2	Q.3	Q.4	JAN	FEB	MAR	APR	MAY	JUN	JUL	AUG	SEP	OCT	NOV	DEC
1964	12.88																
1965	11.15																
1966	12.58	5.66	8.86	10.10	20.90												
1967	11.29	6.13	7.59	11.21	16.40												
1968	10.95	3.72	8.45	12.49	17.45												
1969	9.98	4.39	6.22	9.78	16.11												
1970	11.10	4.68	9.05	9.56	17.39												
1971	9.78	3.77	8.35	7.54	16.28												
1972	10.94	5.19	6.54	10.22	18.73												
1973	11.17	5.58	8.66	9.02	17.50												
1974	13.78	7.83	8.23	13.96	22.70												
1975	13.96	7.05	9.79	14.86	22.12												
1976	15.23	6.17	10.27	12.87	30.96												
1977	13.15	5.62	8.97	13.05	23.14												
1978	12.60	6.34	10.12	11.92	20.99												
1979	13.88	6.88	9.50	11.57	26.08												
1980	12.15	5.26	10.02	12.48	18.14												
1981	14.46	5.04	12.31	12.45	27.18												
1982	13.33	5.87	9.21	10.44	25.76												
1983	12.56	7.98	10.41	10.82	21.01												

Retail sales: value (5) / Ventes au détail : valeur (5)

(socialized sector) / (secteur socialisé)

1980 = 100

	Year	Q.1	Q.2	Q.3	Q.4	JAN	FEB	MAR	APR	MAY	JUN	JUL	AUG	SEP	OCT	NOV	DEC
1964	3	3	3	3	4	2	2	3	3	3	3	3	3	4	4	4	5
1965	4	3	4	4	6	3	3	4	4	4	4	4	4	5	5	6	7
1966	5	4	5	5	6	4	4	5	5	5	5	5	6	6	6	6	7
1967	6	5	6	6	7	4	5	5	6	5	6	6	6	6	6	7	8
1968	7	5	7	7	8	5	5	6	7	6	7	7	7	7	8	8	9
1969	8	6	8	9	10	6	6	7	8	8	8	8	9	9	9	9	10
1970	10	7	10	11	12	7	7	8	9	9	10	10	10	11	12	12	13
1971	13	10	13	14	15	9	10	11	13	12	13	13	14	14	15	15	17
1972	17	13	16	18	20	12	13	15	16	16	17	17	18	19	19	19	22
1973	21	16	19	22	25	14	15	18	19	19	20	21	22	22	24	24	27
1974	28	21	27	30	34	19	20	24	27	26	27	28	30	30	32	32	38
1975	34	27	33	36	40	25	26	30	33	33	34	35	36	38	38	39	43
1976	39	31	38	42	46	29	30	35	37	36	39	41	42	43	44	44	51
1977	48	37	46	51	56	33	36	42	46	45	48	49	51	53	53	55	60
1978	58	45	57	63	70	40	42	52	55	56	59	59	63	65	66	68	75
1979	75	58	73	79	90	52	56	68	72	71	74	75	81	80	86	88	96
1980	100	76	94	108	121	67	75	85	94	90	98	101	108	115	120	117	126
1981	139	106	134	152	164	93	104	121	134	129	140	146	153	155	161	161	169
1982	183	144	179	197	214	129	138	165	177	175	184	192	198	200	204	208	229
1983	250	188	235	270	306	171	174	217	231	227	247	252	279	280	294	300	323

Retail sales: volume (5) / Ventes au détail : volume (5)

(socialized sector) / (secteur socialisé)

1980 = 100

	Year	Q.1	Q.2	Q.3	Q.4	JAN	FEB	MAR	APR	MAY	JUN	JUL	AUG	SEP	OCT	NOV	DEC
1964	38	31	37	39	46	27	29	35	39	35	37	37	38	41	44	44	50
1965	39	33	40	38	44	31	32	37	42	35	42	42	34	37	39	43	51
1966	39	32	38	41	46	27	31	37	40	35	39	39	42	42	42	45	52
1967	42	34	40	43	49	30	33	38	41	39	41	41	44	45	46	47	55
1968	46	36	44	48	55	32	36	40	46	42	45	46	50	50	51	52	61
1969	50	39	49	53	58	36	37	44	50	48	49	52	54	54	56	57	62
1970	57	44	55	60	68	40	42	50	55	52	57	57	60	63	66	64	73
1971	64	53	64	68	74	48	53	57	65	62	65	66	67	69	69	71	80
1972	70	59	68	74	80	53	58	66	68	67	70	70	74	78	77	76	86
1973	72	60	70	77	83	56	57	66	71	68	71	75	79	78	81	80	88
1974	78	65	78	80	85	59	63	72	80	76	76	80	80	79	82	80	92
1975	77	64	76	79	85	60	61	71	77	75	76	77	79	82	83	83	92
1976	81	66	78	87	92	62	63	73	78	75	80	85	86	89	89	88	100
1977	87	70	85	91	97	63	68	79	85	82	87	88	92	94	94	94	104
1978	94	75	92	100	105	68	72	87	90	91	95	96	101	103	102	103	111
1979	100	85	100	101	110	77	81	96	101	97	100	98	104	101	106	108	116
1980	100	86	99	105	105	79	84	94	102	96	100	100	106	108	107	102	107
1981	96	82	95	102	103	74	80	91	97	91	96	100	103	102	102	101	105
1982	96	86	100	99	102	79	83	96	102	97	99	98	100	99	100	98	107
1983	94	84	95	99	94	79	78	94	96	92	97	97	103	96	95	94	94

Employment: mining and manufacturing (6) (socialized sector) — Emploi : industries extractives et manufacturières (6) (secteur socialisé)

thousands — milliers

	Year	Q.1	Q.2	Q.3	Q.4	JAN	FEB	MAR	APR	MAY	JUN	JUL	AUG	SEP	OCT	NOV	DEC
1964	1322	1270	1303	1350	1366	1262	1273	1275	1292	1303	1313	1333	1353	1363	1367	1368	1363
1965	1375	1368	1386	1384	1362	1358	1372	1375	1387	1386	1385	1385	1386	1380	1372	1362	1352
1966	1359	1343	1358	1373	1361	1343	1342	1345	1353	1358	1364	1370	1377	1371	1368	1361	1353
1967	1348	1346	1350	1354	1340	1346	1346	1347	1349	1351	1350	1352	1353	1357	1350	1341	1330
1968	1348	1327	1337	1359	1369	1327	1326	1329	1335	1337	1340	1349	1358	1369	1375	1369	1362
1969	1400	1364	1394	1419	1421	1359	1363	1371	1384	1395	1404	1412	1418	1426	1428	1424	1412
1970	1457	1417	1444	1476	1492	1412	1418	1422	1437	1443	1453	1465	1473	1486	1494	1493	1488
1971	1532	1490	1520	1552	1566	1482	1490	1499	1510	1520	1529	1539	1555	1563	1568	1568	1563
1972	1613	1576	1604	1629	1641	1571	1574	1584	1595	1602	1614	1621	1628	1638	1645	1642	1636
1973	1667	1637	1656	1680	1695	1634	1636	1640	1649	1656	1663	1670	1682	1688	1695	1698	1693
1974	1758	1708	1733	1780	1804	1697	1708	1719	1729	1737	1748	1762	1783	1795	1803	1804	1806
1975	1808	1772	1794	1824	1843	1770	1770	1777	1785	1793	1803	1813	1820	1840	1842	1845	1842
1976	1869	1837	1854	1883	1902	1877	1836	1839	1847	1855	1861	1868	1885	1896	1904	1898	1903
1977	1959	1912	1928	1984	2011	1906	1911	1918	1908	1933	1944	1956	1992	2004	2011	2011	2010
1978	2031	2009	2011	2042	2064	2005	2008	2013	1999	2011	2022	2030	2041	2054	2062	2065	2065
1979	2103	2064	2090	2120	2138	2061	2062	2070	2079	2091	2099	2109	2117	2134	2136	2138	2139
1980	2163	2133	2151	2172	2194	2129	2133	2137	2144	2152	2158	2164	2170	2181	2191	2197	2194
1981	2239	2198	2221	2257	2280	2189	2193	2212	2213	2219	2230	2242	2256	2273	2280	2281	2280
1982	2310	2275	2300	2326	2340	2268	2273	2283	2290	2298	2311	2317	2323	2337	2338	2342	2339
1983	2369	2336	2354	2384	2402	2331	2335	2343	2344	2352	2366	2373	2382	2398	2401	2402	2403

Unemployment (registered unemployed) (7) — Chômage (chômeurs inscrits) (7)

thousands — milliers

	Year	Q.1	Q.2	Q.3	Q.4	JAN	FEB	MAR	APR	MAY	JUN	JUL	AUG	SEP	OCT	NOV	DEC
1964	212	273	196	174	206	273	288	259	223	193	172	172	171	180	188	202	228
1965	237	275	228	203	242	256	285	275	250	229	206	199	197	212	221	237	267
1966	258	304	256	220	251	292	310	309	283	256	230	220	214	225	236	251	265
1967	269	300	263	238	275	290	305	306	287	264	238	234	233	246	257	276	291
1968	311	334	304	292	315	319	338	344	329	303	280	288	292	295	303	314	327
1969	331	382	336	295	310	360	389	396	378	334	295	294	293	299	303	311	316
1970	320	368	327	292	291	350	374	379	358	330	294	289	291	297	294	289	290
1971	291	326	290	267	282	313	329	335	314	292	264	265	266	271	274	283	290
1972	315	327	306	303	326	313	334	335	323	306	289	296	301	311	316	327	334
1973	382	387	375	374	391	367	391	403	394	376	354	368	375	379	381	393	399
1974	449	445	435	444	471	429	449	456	450	436	418	434	443	456	462	473	479
1975	540	529	522	536	574	508	535	543	540	524	502	521	534	553	564	575	584
1976	635	622	622	633	664	605	624	636	636	627	604	622	630	647	660	667	665
1977	701	711	691	687	714	693	714	725	720	694	660	676	686	698	707	717	717
1978	735	744	725	727	743	734	748	751	738	729	708	720	724	737	747	744	738
1979	762	774	749	751	775	757	780	785	774	753	720	738	747	767	771	778	775
1980	785	799	771	777	795	788	804	805	792	770	751	768	771	792	794	801	789
1981	809	816	789	799	830	806	819	824	811	793	763	784	795	817	825	832	833
1982	863	859	848	855	888	844	859	874	867	848	828	843	852	871	882	894	888
1983		915	898	905		902	917	927	913	896	885	895	903	914	920	931	

Jobs vacant, new vacancies — Offres d'emploi nouvelles

thousands — milliers

	Year	Q.1	Q.2	Q.3	Q.4	JAN	FEB	MAR	APR	MAY	JUN	JUL	AUG	SEP	OCT	NOV	DEC
1964	83	85	105	90	52	58	73	125	120	103	91	92	81	97	71	49	36
1965	54	74	71	42	28	48	53	120	94	66	52	43	36	46	37	26	21
1966	44	43	57	47	29	23	35	70	66	56	48	47	47	47	42	27	18
1967	34	34	44	35	21	20	26	56	48	48	36	36	34	36	29	19	15
1968	36	31	44	39	28	17	29	48	51	44	37	39	36	42	36	25	22
1969	43	40	58	45	30	24	35	61	60	63	51	43	44	49	39	29	21
1970	46	44	63	47	32	27	39	65	68	62	58	51	42	49	40	30	25
1971	45	43	61	43	33	29	44	56	67	63	54	45	42	43	38	33	27
1972	45	46	54	47	34	30	42	65	54	54	55	45	45	52	40	33	29
1973	54	49	65	56	45	38	45	64	62	69	64	57	53	58	59	42	33
1974	58	56	69	62	46	42	59	66	78	66	64	63	57	67	57	43	39
1975	59	61	72	59	43	46	62	75	77	73	67	63	52	63	55	39	36
1976	54	46	64	58	47	38	43	57	64	64	63	57	53	63	56	46	39
1977	63	55	77	68	52	39	52	74	77	74	80	60	73	72	62	52	43
1978	72	63	86	76	65	52	56	80	89	83	86	68	77	83	77	62	55
1979	80	77	92	83	68	60	79	93	94	88	93	80	76	94	80	62	63
1980	79	81	89	76	68	59	91	94	95	80	93	76	71	82	84	71	48
1981	77	74	93	77	62	53	79	89	104	85	90	79	70	83	74	59	53
1982	72	69	90	68	59	45	75	87	93	87	90	65	62	74	72	50	54
1983		63	90	78		41	64	85	90	90	89	77	78	78	70	61	

YUGOSLAVIA

Monthly earnings: (6)(8)
mining and manufacturing
1980 = 100

Gains mensuels : (6)(8)
industries extractives et manufacturières
1980 = 100

	Year	Q.1	Q.2	Q.3	Q.4	JAN	FEB	MAR	APR	MAY	JUN	JUL	AUG	SEP	OCT	NOV	DEC
1964	5	4	5	5	6	4	4	5	5	5	5	6	5	5	6	6	7
1965	7	6	6	8	9	6	6	7	7	6	6	7	8	8	8	9	10
1966	10	9	10	10	11	8	9	9	10	10	10	11	10	10	11	11	11
1967	11	10	11	11	11	10	10	11	10	11	11	11	11	11	11	11	12
1968	12	11	12	12	13	11	11	11	11	12	11	13	12	12	13	13	13
1969	14	13	14	14	15	13	13	13	14	14	13	15	14	14	15	14	15
1970	16	15	16	16	18	14	15	15	16	15	16	17	16	16	18	17	19
1971	20	18	19	20	22	17	17	19	19	19	19	20	20	20	21	22	23
1972	23	22	22	23	25	21	21	23	22	23	23	23	24	23	24	25	25
1973	27	24	26	28	30	24	24	25	25	27	26	28	28	27	30	30	31
1974	35	31	34	36	39	30	30	32	33	34	33	37	36	35	39	39	40
1975	42	39	42	43	46	38	38	40	42	42	41	44	42	42	46	45	47
1976	48	45	46	49	53	44	45	47	46	46	47	49	49	49	51	52	54
1977	57	52	55	58	61	50	51	55	54	55	56	58	59	57	59	60	63
1978	68	64	67	69	73	61	62	67	65	69	68	69	70	68	72	73	73
1979	82	76	79	83	90	74	74	78	77	82	79	84	85	80	90	89	90
1980	100	88	95	102	115	88	87	90	95	97	94	103	99	103	113	112	119
1981	137	121	132	142	155	115	121	126	132	131	134	146	139	140	152	150	163
1982	175	162	171	178	189	153	162	170	171	170	173	182	177	174	180	187	200
1983	223	194	211	227	262	185	193	204	206	211	215	223	230	229	249	259	277

Producer prices: agricultural goods
(home market)
1980 = 100

Prix à la production : produits agricoles
(marché intérieur)
1980 = 100

	Year	Q.1	Q.2	Q.3	Q.4	JAN	FEB	MAR	APR	MAY	JUN	JUL	AUG	SEP	OCT	NOV	DEC
1964	8	7	8	9	9	7	7	7	8	8	8	9	9	9	9	9	9
1965	12	10	11	12	12	9	10	11	11	11	11	11	12	12	12	12	13
1966	14	15	15	14	14	14	14	15	15	15	14	15	14	14	14	14	14
1967	13	14	14	13	13	14	14	14	14	14	14	14	13	13	13	13	13
1968	13	13	13	13	13	13	13	13	13	13	13	13	13	13	13	13	13
1969	14	14	14	14	15	14	14	14	14	14	14	14	14	14	14	15	15
1970	16	16	16	17	17	15	16	16	16	16	16	16	17	17	17	17	17
1971	21	18	19	21	22	18	18	19	19	19	20	20	20	21	21	21	22
1972	25	23	25	26	27	22	23	23	24	25	26	26	26	27	27	27	27
1973	32	29	31	32	33	29	30	30	30	31	32	32	32	33	33	33	34
1974	36	34	35	36	37	34	34	34	34	34	35	36	36	36	36	36	37
1975	41	39	39	41	43	39	38	39	39	39	40	41	41	43	42	43	44
1976	47	46	47	48	49	45	46	46	47	47	47	48	48	49	49	49	50
1977	53	51	52	53	54	51	52	51	52	52	53	53	53	53	53	54	55
1978	58	56	58	58	60	55	56	57	58	58	58	58	59	59	59	60	62
1979	73	67	73	74	76	65	67	70	69	73	76	76	73	74	74	76	78
1980	100	86	92	100	112	85	86	88	89	91	95	95	98	103	110	111	115
1981	150	126	139	150	161	122	125	132	138	140	140	146	149	155	155	162	165
1982	197	178	192	199	216	175	177	183	181	195	200	200	199	199	212	212	222
1983	281	244	271	288	318	230	246	256	261	271	281	285	285	295	303	316	334

Producer prices: investment goods
(home market)
1980 = 100

Prix à la production : biens d'équipement
(marché intérieur)
1980 = 100

	Year	Q.1	Q.2	Q.3	Q.4	JAN	FEB	MAR	APR	MAY	JUN	JUL	AUG	SEP	OCT	NOV	DEC
1964	30	30	30	30	30	30	29	30	30	30	30	30	29	30	30	30	30
1965	32	32	33	32	32	32	32	32	32	32	33	32	32	32	32	32	32
1966	33	33	34	33	33	32	34	34	34	34	34	33	33	33	33	33	33
1967	34	34	34	34	34	34	34	34	34	34	34	34	34	34	34	34	34
1968	34	34	34	34	34	34	34	34	34	34	34	34	34	34	34	34	34
1969	34	34	34	34	35	34	34	34	34	34	34	34	34	34	34	35	35
1970	36	35	36	36	38	35	35	35	35	35	36	36	36	36	38	38	38
1971	40	38	40	42	42	38	38	38	39	39	41	41	42	42	42	42	42
1972	43	43	43	43	44	43	43	43	43	43	43	43	43	43	43	44	44
1973	47	46	46	48	49	45	45	46	45	46	46	47	47	48	48	49	49
1974	53	49	51	53	57	49	49	49	49	51	53	53	54	54	56	57	57
1975	64	58	64	67	67	58	58	58	60	64	67	67	67	67	67	67	68
1976	71	69	69	71	73	69	69	69	69	69	69	69	70	73	73	73	73
1977	77	75	77	78	80	73	74	77	77	77	77	77	78	79	80	80	80
1978	82	80	81	82	84	80	80	80	80	81	81	82	82	83	83	83	84
1979	87	85	86	88	88	84	84	86	86	86	86	88	88	88	88	88	88
1980	100	95	98	100	108	93	96	96	97	98	100	100	99	100	103	109	111
1981	125	119	123	128	131	116	119	121	121	123	125	126	128	130	130	131	131
1982	145	134	141	151	154	132	133	136	138	141	144	145	151	152	154	154	155
1983	177	159	167	183	199	157	160	161	164	167	171	174	183	193	197	197	202

Producer prices: consumer goods (home market)

1980 = 100

Prix à la production : biens de consommation (marché intérieur)

1980 = 100

	Year	Q.1	Q.2	Q.3	Q.4	JAN	FEB	MAR	APR	MAY	JUN	JUL	AUG	SEP	OCT	NOV	DEC
1964	19	18	19	19	20	18	18	18	18	19	19	19	19	20	20	20	20
1965	22	21	21	23	24	21	21	21	21	21	21	21	23	24	24	24	24
1966	25	24	24	25	25	24	24	24	24	24	24	25	25	25	25	25	25
1967	25	25	25	25	25	25	25	25	25	25	25	25	25	25	25	25	25
1968	25	24	25	25	25	24	24	24	25	25	25	25	25	25	25	25	25
1969	26	25	25	26	26	25	25	25	25	25	25	26	26	26	26	26	27
1970	28	27	27	28	28	27	27	27	27	27	28	28	28	28	28	28	28
1971	31	29	30	31	32	28	28	29	29	30	31	31	31	32	32	32	33
1972	35	33	34	35	37	33	33	33	34	34	34	35	35	35	36	37	37
1973	39	37	39	40	42	37	37	38	38	39	39	39	40	40	41	42	42
1974	48	43	46	50	53	42	43	43	45	46	47	47	51	52	52	52	54
1975	58	56	58	59	60	55	56	56	57	57	59	59	59	59	60	59	60
1976	61	60	60	61	63	60	60	60	60	60	61	61	62	62	62	63	64
1977	67	65	66	68	70	65	65	65	65	66	67	67	69	69	69	70	71
1978	74	72	73	74	76	71	72	72	72	72	73	73	75	75	76	76	76
1979	82	78	81	84	86	77	77	79	79	80	82	83	84	85	85	86	86
1980	100	91	95	101	113	89	90	93	94	95	97	98	101	104	109	114	116
1981	144	130	140	148	157	125	130	135	138	140	143	145	148	150	156	157	158
1982	180	163	173	188	196	160	162	166	169	173	176	184	187	193	194	196	198
1983	238	206	220	240	282	198	207	212	214	220	225	227	241	252	265	279	301

Producer prices: industrial goods (home market)

1980 = 100

Prix à la production : produits industriels (marché intérieur)

1980 = 100

	Year	Q.1	Q.2	Q.3	Q.4	JAN	FEB	MAR	APR	MAY	JUN	JUL	AUG	SEP	OCT	NOV	DEC
1964	16	16	16	16	17	16	16	16	16	16	16	16	16	17	17	17	17
1965	19	17	18	19	20	17	17	18	18	18	18	18	20	20	20	20	20
1966	21	21	21	21	21	21	21	21	21	21	21	21	21	21	21	21	21
1967	21	21	21	21	21	21	21	21	21	21	21	21	21	21	21	21	21
1968	21	21	21	21	21	21	21	21	21	21	21	21	21	21	21	22	22
1969	22	21	22	22	22	21	22	22	22	22	22	22	22	22	22	22	22
1970	24	23	24	24	25	23	23	23	23	24	24	24	24	24	25	25	25
1971	28	26	28	29	29	26	26	27	27	28	28	29	29	29	29	29	30
1972	31	30	30	33	32	29	30	30	30	30	30	31	31	35	32	32	32
1973	35	33	34	35	37	33	33	33	33	34	34	35	35	36	36	38	38
1974	45	39	43	48	50	39	39	40	41	43	44	46	48	50	50	50	51
1975	55	53	55	56	57	52	53	53	53	55	56	56	56	57	57	57	57
1976	58	57	57	59	60	57	57	57	57	57	58	58	59	60	60	60	61
1977	64	61	63	65	66	61	61	62	63	63	63	64	65	66	66	66	66
1978	69	67	68	70	72	67	67	68	68	68	69	69	70	71	71	72	72
1979	78	74	77	81	83	73	74	75	75	78	78	80	81	82	82	83	83
1980	100	89	94	103	114	86	90	91	92	94	96	100	102	107	111	115	116
1981	145	131	141	149	158	126	132	135	138	141	144	146	149	151	157	158	160
1982	181	163	175	189	197	161	163	165	170	176	179	185	190	192	194	198	199
1983	239	205	220	245	286	201	205	208	214	218	228	232	245	259	270	279	308

Producer prices: intermediate goods (home market)

1980 = 100

Prix à la production : biens intermédiaires (marché intérieur)

1980 = 100

	Year	Q.1	Q.2	Q.3	Q.4	JAN	FEB	MAR	APR	MAY	JUN	JUL	AUG	SEP	OCT	NOV	DEC
1964	14	14	14	14	14	14	14	14	14	14	14	14	14	14	14	14	14
1965	16	14	15	16	17	14	14	14	15	15	15	15	17	17	17	17	17
1966	18	18	18	18	18	18	18	18	18	18	18	18	18	18	18	18	18
1967	18	18	18	18	18	18	18	18	18	18	18	18	18	18	18	18	18
1968	18	18	18	18	18	18	18	18	18	18	18	18	18	18	18	18	18
1969	19	18	18	19	19	18	18	18	18	18	18	19	19	19	19	19	19
1970	21	20	20	21	22	19	20	20	20	20	21	21	21	21	22	22	22
1971	25	23	25	25	26	22	23	24	24	25	25	25	25	25	26	26	26
1972	27	26	26	27	28	26	26	26	26	26	26	27	27	28	28	28	28
1973	31	29	29	32	33	28	29	28	28	29	29	31	31	32	33	34	34
1974	42	36	40	46	48	36	36	36	38	40	41	44	46	47	48	47	48
1975	52	50	52	53	54	49	50	50	50	52	53	53	53	54	54	53	54
1976	55	54	54	56	57	54	55	55	54	54	54	55	56	56	56	57	57
1977	60	58	60	61	62	57	58	58	59	60	60	60	62	62	62	62	62
1978	66	63	64	66	68	63	64	64	64	64	65	66	66	67	68	68	69
1979	76	70	73	79	81	70	71	71	72	74	75	78	78	80	81	81	81
1980	100	86	93	105	115	82	88	89	91	94	95	101	104	109	113	116	117
1981	148	134	145	152	162	129	135	138	141	145	143	150	152	154	160	161	164
1982	188	169	182	196	204	155	169	173	177	184	186	190	197	199	201	205	207
1983	252	212	229	260	305	211	212	214	222	224	243	246	258	276	286	295	335

YUGOSLAVIA

Consumer prices: all items

1980 = 100

Prix à la consommation : total

1980 = 100

	Year	Q.1	Q.2	Q.3	Q.4	JAN	FEB	MAR	APR	MAY	JUN	JUL	AUG	SEP	OCT	NOV	DEC
1964	8	8	8	8	9	7	8	8	8	8	8	8	8	8	8	9	9
1965	11	9	10	11	13	9	9	9	9	10	10	10	12	12	12	13	13
1966	13	13	13	13	13	13	13	13	13	13	13	13	13	13	13	13	13
1967	14	14	14	14	14	14	14	14	14	14	15	14	14	14	14	14	14
1968	15	15	15	15	15	15	15	15	15	15	15	15	15	15	15	15	15
1969	16	15	16	16	16	15	16	16	16	16	16	16	16	16	16	16	17
1970	18	17	18	18	19	17	17	18	18	18	18	18	18	18	19	19	19
1971	20	19	21	21	22	19	19	20	20	20	21	21	20	21	21	22	22
1972	24	22	24	24	26	22	22	23	23	24	24	24	24	25	25	26	26
1973	29	27	29	29	31	27	28	28	29	29	30	29	29	29	30	31	32
1974	35	33	34	36	38	32	33	33	34	34	35	35	36	36	37	38	39
1975	43	40	43	45	46	40	40	41	41	43	44	45	45	45	45	46	46
1976	48	47	49	48	50	47	47	47	48	49	50	48	48	48	49	51	52
1977	56	54	56	56	58	54	54	55	55	56	57	56	56	56	57	59	59
1978	64	61	63	64	68	61	61	62	63	63	64	64	64	65	66	68	69
1979	77	71	76	79	82	70	71	74	74	76	78	78	78	80	80	82	84
1980	100	91	96	101	113	89	92	93	94	96	99	100	100	104	110	112	116
1981	141	128	139	144	155	124	128	133	134	140	142	142	142	147	152	155	158
1982	186	166	180	194	206	162	166	169	173	182	184	192	192	197	201	207	210
1983	216	183	204	220	259	176	184	190	198	205	208	210	218	233	244	257	277

Money supply (M1)

billion dinars, end of period

Disponibilités monétaires (M1)

milliards de dinars, fin de période

	Year	Q.1	Q.2	Q.3	Q.4	JAN	FEB	MAR	APR	MAY	JUN	JUL	AUG	SEP	OCT	NOV	DEC
1964	20.2				20.2										21.2	20.9	20.2
1965	20.7	21.8	20.7	20.2	20.7	20.2	20.9	21.8	21.5	21.1	20.7	20.2	20.1	20.2	20.1	20.2	20.7
1966	21.9	23.3	23.1	23.3	21.9	22.3	22.5	23.3	23.2	22.5	23.1	22.8	22.9	23.3	22.9	23.2	21.9
1967	22.1	22.3	22.6	23.0	22.1	22.6	22.5	22.3	22.8	22.7	22.6	22.8	22.8	23.0	22.8	22.6	22.1
1968	26.8	23.0	24.6	28.2	26.8	22.9	23.4	23.0	22.9	23.6	24.6	25.5	27.3	28.2	28.3	28.3	26.8
1969	30.3	29.4	29.9	30.3	30.3	28.3	29.3	29.4	29.8	29.9	29.9	30.3	30.9	30.3	30.6	30.7	30.3
1970	34.8	33.6	35.3	34.6	34.8	32.4	32.8	33.6	34.9	35.5	35.3	35.8	36.6	34.6	35.1	35.3	34.8
1971	40.7	35.7	37.5	39.2	40.7	35.8	36.3	35.7	37.1	37.9	37.5	38.8	39.4	39.2	40.0	41.2	40.7
1972	56.0	45.2	47.1	53.0	56.0	42.6	43.8	45.2	46.0	46.3	47.1	50.3	51.9	53.0	54.1	54.9	56.0
1973	78.2	61.5	68.0	76.0	78.2	58.5	61.0	61.5	64.7	65.3	68.0	71.0	74.0	76.0	76.0	76.3	78.2
1974	98.1	84.4	88.7	95.1	98.1	80.5	83.7	84.4	87.2	87.0	88.7	90.0	94.6	95.1	94.6	96.4	98.1
1975	130.7	103.0	105.9	118.4	130.7	100.8	103.0	103.0	104.3	105.4	105.9	113.5	117.0	118.4	122.1	125.6	130.7
1976	206.5	139.4	162.9	186.9	206.5	136.7	139.9	139.4	149.5	158.2	162.9	172.3	180.4	186.9	187.7	191.3	206.5
1977	251.1	208.7	220.0	230.6	251.1	209.6	207.4	208.7	210.5	211.9	220.0	222.6	226.1	230.6	233.2	238.6	251.1
1978	315.2	259.8	276.4	300.3	315.2	248.6	255.0	259.8	267.7	272.7	276.4	289.9	299.8	300.3	308.8	312.6	315.2
1979	375.1	323.1	321.0	346.5	375.1	321.4	324.1	323.1	330.5	325.9	321.0	330.8	344.5	346.5	355.0	361.9	375.1
1980	461.6	386.2	399.4	430.8	461.6	380.6	388.9	386.2	396.9	400.1	399.4	420.6	432.1	430.8	445.2	444.0	461.6
1981	584.3	477.1	506.0	545.6	584.3	471.5	481.8	477.1	497.5	508.1	506.0	538.3	550.7	545.6	557.0	573.2	584.3
1982	739.8	593.8	616.5	664.9	739.8	595.8	555.0	593.8	617.9	623.9	616.5	659.7	667.2	664.9	675.3	686.6	739.8
1983	888.7	747.3	764.4	833.5	888.7	740.9	743.6	747.3	757.8	760.4	764.4	829.6	830.3	833.5	852.8	868.0	888.7

Blocked deposits

billion dinars, end of period

Dépôts bloqués

milliards de dinars, fin de période

	Year	Q.1	Q.2	Q.3	Q.4	JAN	FEB	MAR	APR	MAY	JUN	JUL	AUG	SEP	OCT	NOV	DEC
1964																	
1965																	
1966																	
1967																	
1968																	
1969																	
1970	20.2			18.2	20.2									18.2	18.4	18.9	20.2
1971	24.9	22.4	23.3	22.5	24.9	20.6	21.8	22.4	21.8	22.1	23.3	23.0	22.1	22.5	22.5	22.6	24.9
1972	28.6	24.2	26.5	27.4	28.5	25.6	24.9	24.2	25.0	25.8	26.5	26.5	26.7	27.4	28.1	28.2	28.6
1973	33.6	30.2	31.3	32.0	33.6	27.9	27.5	30.2	29.6	30.7	31.3	31.1	31.8	32.0	31.6	32.5	33.6
1974	35.9	33.7	32.6	33.5	35.9	31.9	31.7	33.7	33.6	34.9	32.6	32.1	32.9	33.6	32.6	32.7	35.9
1975	40.9	40.6	39.7	38.6	40.9	37.1	38.3	40.6	40.8	41.0	39.7	37.3	38.3	38.6	39.2	39.4	40.9
1976	52.1	44.8	44.3	47.1	52.1	40.9	43.8	44.8	44.2	45.6	44.3	45.2	46.9	47.1	47.9	47.6	52.1
1977	52.1	49.3	46.1	49.7	52.1	46.5	47.0	49.3	47.8	48.4	46.1	47.5	49.2	49.7	50.1	50.8	52.1
1978	45.1	46.5	41.2	41.8	45.1	50.3	48.3	46.5	42.8	45.0	41.2	41.6	42.0	41.8	41.6	41.6	45.1
1979	60.9	47.8	51.1	54.8	60.9	47.9	46.7	47.8	45.3	45.6	51.1	52.5	53.5	54.8	56.1	57.3	60.9
1980	100.2	69.1	75.2	87.7	100.2	62.8	68.1	69.1	70.0	70.2	75.2	86.1	86.3	87.7	89.2	92.1	100.2
1981	139.2	107.2	118.5	124.7	139.2	98.5	105.4	107.2	110.4	119.4	118.5	119.7	127.9	124.7	125.0	131.1	139.2
1982	262.6	150.1	161.9	201.4	262.6	140.5	141.1	150.1	151.7	159.7	161.9	182.7	197.1	201.4	239.0	257.4	262.6
1983	365.2	288.5	341.5	316.3	365.2	255.6	256.6	288.5	277.8	297.2	341.5	323.5	323.8	316.3	315.2	328.5	365.2

Consumer credit outstanding (9)

billion dinars, end of period

Crédits à la consommation en cours (9)

milliards de dinars, fin de période

	Year	Q.1	Q.2	Q.3	Q.4	JAN	FEB	MAR	APR	MAY	JUN	JUL	AUG	SEP	OCT	NOV	DEC
1964	4.2	3.3	3.7	4.0	4.2	3.2	3.2	3.3	3.4	3.6	3.7	3.8	3.8	4.0	3.3	4.2	4.2
1965	3.9	4.0	4.0	3.8	3.9	4.1	4.0	4.0	4.0	4.0	4.0	3.9	3.9	3.8	3.8	3.8	3.9
1966	3.4	3.8	3.8	3.5	3.4	3.7	3.8	3.8	3.9	3.9	3.8	3.7	3.6	3.5	3.4	3.4	3.4
1967	2.6	3.0	2.9	2.7	2.6	3.2	3.1	3.0	2.9	2.9	2.9	2.8	2.7	2.7	2.6	2.6	2.6
1968	4.3	2.6	3.0	3.7	4.3	2.6	2.5	2.6	2.6	2.7	3.0	3.2	3.5	3.7	3.9	4.0	4.3
1969	4.9	4.4	4.6	4.6	4.9	4.3	4.4	4.4	4.4	4.5	4.6	4.5	4.5	4.6	4.6	4.7	4.9
1970	6.9	5.1	5.9	6.2	6.9	4.9	4.9	5.1	5.3	5.6	5.9	5.8	5.9	6.2	6.5	6.6	6.9
1971	7.0	7.0	7.3	7.2	7.0	6.9	7.0	7.0	7.0	7.1	7.3	7.4	7.3	7.2	7.0	7.0	7.0
1972	6.3	6.6	6.6	6.4	6.3	6.9	6.8	6.6	6.5	6.5	6.6	6.5	6.4	6.4	6.3	6.3	6.3
1973	8.0	6.2	6.8	7.4	8.0	6.2	6.2	6.2	6.4	6.6	6.8	7.0	7.1	7.4	7.5	7.7	8.0
1974	12.4	8.5	9.9	10.8	12.4	8.1	8.2	8.5	8.9	9.3	9.9	10.2	10.4	10.8	11.2	11.6	12.4
1975	18.7	13.4	15.1	16.1	18.7	12.5	12.7	13.4	14.3	14.7	15.1	15.3	15.3	16.1	16.9	17.2	18.7
1976	32.1	20.6	22.8	26.2	32.1	18.7	19.3	20.6	21.3	21.7	22.8	23.6	24.7	26.2	27.6	29.0	32.1
1977	40.0	34.5	37.8	37.7	40.0	32.0	32.8	34.5	35.2	36.1	37.8	36.7	36.9	37.7	38.1	38.5	40.0
1978	50.2	41.8	44.8	45.6	50.2	39.9	40.9	41.8	43.1	43.6	44.8	44.9	45.0	45.6	47.5	48.5	50.2
1979	54.8	54.1	55.0	54.4	54.8	49.4	51.8	54.1	54.3	54.0	55.0	54.9	54.2	54.4	54.8	54.6	54.8
1980	54.9	53.3	54.3	54.7	54.9	53.1	52.6	53.3	53.3	53.7	54.3	54.7	54.0	54.7	56.4	55.7	54.9
1981	51.4	53.5	51.8	50.1	51.4	54.2	53.6	53.5	52.9	52.0	51.8	51.4	50.4	50.1	50.3	51.1	51.4
1982	51.2	51.3	52.5	52.7	51.2	49.8	51.5	51.3	52.2	52.7	52.5	54.1	53.4	52.7	51.5	50.8	51.2
1983	47.7	49.0	47.9	47.1	47.7	51.0	49.9	49.0	46.6	48.0	47.9	47.4	47.2	47.1	47.1	46.7	47.7

U.S. dollar exchange rate (10)

cents per dinar, end of period

Taux de change du dollar É.-U. (10)

cents par dinar, fin de période

	Year	Q.1	Q.2	Q.3	Q.4	JAN	FEB	MAR	APR	MAY	JUN	JUL	AUG	SEP	OCT	NOV	DEC
1964	13.333	13.333	13.333	13.333	13.333	13.333	13.333	13.333	13.333	13.333	13.333	13.333	13.333	13.333	13.333	13.333	13.333
1965	8.000	13.333	13.333	8.000	8.000	13.333	13.333	13.333	13.333	13.333	13.333	8.000	8.000	8.000	8.000	8.000	8.000
1966	8.000	8.000	8.000	8.000	8.000	8.000	8.000	8.000	8.000	8.000	8.000	8.000	8.000	8.000	8.000	8.000	8.000
1967	8.000	8.000	8.000	8.000	8.000	8.000	8.000	8.000	8.000	8.000	8.000	8.000	8.000	8.000	8.000	8.000	8.000
1968	8.000	8.000	8.000	8.000	8.000	8.000	8.000	8.000	8.000	8.000	8.000	8.000	8.000	8.000	8.000	8.000	8.000
1969	8.000	8.000	8.000	8.000	8.000	8.000	8.000	8.000	8.000	8.000	8.000	8.000	8.000	8.000	8.000	8.000	8.000
1970	8.000	8.000	8.000	8.000	8.000	8.000	8.000	8.000	8.000	8.000	8.000	8.000	8.000	8.000	8.000	8.000	8.000
1971	5.882	6.667	6.667	6.667	5.882	6.667	6.667	6.667	6.667	6.667	6.667	6.667	6.667	6.667	6.667	6.667	5.882
1972	5.882	5.882	5.882	5.882	5.882	5.882	5.882	5.882	5.882	5.882	5.882	5.882	5.882	5.882	5.882	5.882	5.882
1973	6.410	5.882	5.882	6.579	6.410	5.882	5.882	5.882	5.882	5.882	5.882	6.452	6.579	6.579	6.579	6.452	6.410
1974	5.864	6.494	6.579	6.098	5.864	6.061	6.250	6.494	6.579	6.579	6.579	6.579	6.329	6.098	5.780	5.841	5.864
1975	5.556	5.882	5.882	5.583	5.556	5.882	5.865	5.882	5.879	5.882	5.882	5.764	5.673	5.583	5.617	5.598	5.556
1976	5.485	5.501	5.490	5.499	5.485	5.556	5.573	5.501	5.529	5.474	5.490	5.474	5.469	5.499	5.480	5.453	5.485
1977	5.422	5.486	5.483	5.462	5.422	5.437	5.437	5.486	5.486	5.476	5.483	5.500	5.456	5.462	5.461	5.478	5.422
1978	5.373	5.466	5.302	5.326	5.373	5.449	5.485	5.466	5.395	5.302	5.302	5.318	5.303	5.326	5.337	5.316	5.373
1979	5.218	5.348	5.242	5.247	5.218	5.375	5.348	5.348	5.247	5.221	5.242	5.242	5.227	5.247	5.227	5.234	5.218
1980	3.413	4.924	3.650	3.578	3.413	5.036	4.978	4.924	4.805	4.762	3.650	3.658	3.643	3.578	3.511	3.455	3.413
1981	2.391	3.138	2.947	2.609	2.391	3.392	3.285	3.138	3.037	2.994	2.947	2.709	2.556	2.609	2.583	2.556	2.391
1982	1.600	2.168	2.076	1.913	1.600	2.289	2.223	2.168	2.199	2.174	2.076	2.040	1.990	1.913	1.568	1.572	1.600
1983	0.796	1.292	1.105	0.917	0.796	1.476	1.365	1.292	1.232	1.178	1.105	1.016	0.976	0.917	0.850	0.803	0.796

Official reserves: total

million SDR's, end of period

Réserves officielles : total

millions de DTS, fin de période

	Year	Q.1	Q.2	Q.3	Q.4	JAN	FEB	MAR	APR	MAY	JUN	JUL	AUG	SEP	OCT	NOV	DEC
1964	74	64	64	73	74	89	77	64	57	68	64	84	76	73	69	71	74
1965	103	71	66	141	103	72	64	71	62	65	66	63	141	141	123	118	103
1966	115	92	77	107	115	73	71	92	82	84	77	85	104	107	139	125	115
1967	80	106	112	129	80	119	114	106	100	125	112	116	122	129	123	115	80
1968	132	149	131	116	132	143	153	149	144	132	131	107	123	116	124	141	132
1969	253	188	161	173	253	150	147	188	183	172	161	147	164	173	193	229	253
1970	140	264	217	217	140	302	295	264	230	217	217	221	213	217	191	190	140
1971	196	152	180	136	196	134	140	152	191	177	180	176	192	136	178	163	196
1972	674	351	431	519	674	218	271	351	408	431	431	446	513	519	587	631	674
1973	1109	718	864	1060	1109	663	645	718	787	855	864	926	1017	1060	1114	1118	1109
1974	937	938	799	996	937	1055	1035	938	830	841	799	854	903	996	932	910	937
1975	744	867	769	911	744	874	879	867	774	770	769	804	807	911	887	840	744
1976	1764	1038	1400	1712	1764	767	959	1038	1067	1313	1400	1512	1651	1712	1785	1873	1764
1977	1736	1745	1567	1706	1736	1737	1693	1745	1733	1691	1567	1610	1573	1706	1691	1751	1736
1978	1890	1831	1740	1918	1890	1921	1948	1831	1821	1829	1740	1741	1848	1918	1844	1909	1890
1979	1014	1594	1443	1369	1014	1916	1743	1594	1349	1406	1443	1379	1333	1369	1242	1058	1014
1980	1150	731	731	761	1150	797	763	731	690	646	731	745	798	761	1001	890	1150
1981	1437	1229	1313	1348	1437	1179	1269	1229	1105	1135	1313	1185	1300	1348	1437	1526	1437
1982	768	1034	845	859	768	1177	1058	1034	908	986	845	714	786	859	859	867	768
1983	998	777	648	753	998	709	634	777	646	727	648	560	695	753	1049	990	998

YUGOSLAVIA

Imports c.i.f.
billion dinars, monthly averages

Importations c.a.f.
milliards de dinars, moyennes mensuelles

	Year	Q.1	Q.2	Q.3	Q.4	JAN	FEB	MAR	APR	MAY	JUN	JUL	AUG	SEP	OCT	NOV	DEC
1964	1.38	1.29	1.46	1.51	1.25	1.36	1.13	1.39	1.40	1.46	1.51	1.55	1.48	1.46	1.19	1.15	1.42
1965	1.96	1.67	2.12	2.09	1.97	1.80	1.49	1.71	1.98	2.29	2.08	2.52	1.89	1.84	2.02	1.73	2.16
1966	2.40	2.23	2.42	2.36	2.57	2.21	2.29	2.19	2.29	2.48	2.49	2.47	2.50	2.12	2.35	2.31	3.06
1967	2.60	2.41	2.67	2.61	2.69	2.47	2.48	2.29	2.70	2.40	2.91	2.65	2.46	2.73	2.63	2.74	2.71
1968	2.73	2.27	2.83	2.82	3.02	2.30	2.24	2.27	2.84	2.90	2.74	2.76	3.11	2.58	2.75	2.95	3.36
1969	3.25	3.01	3.32	3.29	3.38	3.23	2.55	3.23	3.19	3.31	3.45	3.75	3.09	3.03	3.36	2.98	3.79
1970	4.37	3.21	4.32	4.95	5.01	3.18	3.00	3.45	4.16	3.95	4.85	5.62	4.76	4.47	5.27	4.51	5.24
1971	4.95	4.66	5.36	5.08	4.68	5.79	3.35	4.83	5.01	5.12	5.96	5.56	5.12	4.57	4.72	4.34	4.99
1972	4.92	4.27	4.52	5.05	5.82	3.88	4.05	4.88	4.12	4.34	5.11	4.98	5.01	5.16	5.78	5.57	6.12
1973	6.86	5.82	6.28	7.14	8.21	6.39	5.29	5.77	5.60	6.63	6.61	7.03	6.83	7.55	7.61	8.18	8.84
1974	11.54	10.00	11.26	12.19	12.72	10.16	9.69	10.16	11.07	10.62	12.08	13.27	12.05	11.25	12.92	12.52	12.73
1975	11.71	11.21	12.69	11.20	11.73	12.37	10.53	10.72	13.39	12.35	12.31	12.22	11.41	9.97	10.72	10.47	14.00
1976	11.20	10.22	11.06	10.78	12.76	12.29	8.62	9.74	10.49	9.67	13.02	9.93	11.14	11.27	11.70	10.77	15.80
1977	14.65	13.46	15.68	14.34	15.13	13.50	10.81	15.97	15.71	14.90	16.43	13.11	15.97	13.94	13.97	12.41	19.00
1978	15.19	14.11	14.74	14.67	17.25	15.20	12.64	14.49	13.89	15.39	14.94	12.15	16.39	15.47	16.60	15.23	19.92
1979	22.20	20.92	22.10	21.80	23.97	23.17	18.48	21.10	20.85	23.87	21.57	22.40	23.03	19.97	24.94	20.53	26.45
1980	29.18	25.05	21.55	34.06	36.07	27.03	25.05	23.07	22.26	19.50	22.90	35.71	35.35	31.12	38.93	30.53	38.74
1981	50.61	47.64	57.44	47.19	50.15	45.44	39.92	57.57	64.81	52.47	55.05	54.34	47.84	39.39	35.24	40.17	75.05
1982	67.36	63.15	70.69	63.00	72.59	62.52	58.15	68.79	75.65	59.73	76.69	67.90	68.52	52.57	55.48	50.95	111.34
1983	64.22	59.42	60.43	59.56	77.45	48.27	56.71	73.27	52.69	59.41	69.19	57.13	65.75	55.81	59.76	62.83	109.77

Exports f.o.b.
billion dinars, monthly averages

Exportations f.o.b.
milliards de dinars, moyennes mensuelles

	Year	Q.1	Q.2	Q.3	Q.4	JAN	FEB	MAR	APR	MAY	JUN	JUL	AUG	SEP	OCT	NOV	DEC
1964	0.93	0.86	0.88	0.88	1.10	0.93	0.80	0.84	0.90	0.88	0.88	0.92	0.92	0.82	0.98	1.01	1.31
1965	1.66	1.37	1.56	1.66	2.06	1.41	1.16	1.53	1.46	1.61	1.62	1.84	1.42	1.72	1.92	1.74	2.51
1966	1.86	1.62	1.81	1.81	2.19	1.56	1.47	1.83	1.87	1.57	1.97	1.84	1.76	1.84	1.97	1.74	2.85
1967	1.90	1.66	1.98	1.82	2.15	1.43	1.53	2.01	1.91	1.79	2.25	1.79	1.69	1.99	2.05	2.05	2.36
1968	1.92	1.56	1.86	2.00	2.27	1.70	1.32	1.66	1.90	1.84	1.83	2.25	1.93	1.84	2.15	1.96	2.69
1969	2.24	1.74	2.16	2.40	2.67	1.82	1.57	1.83	2.32	2.00	2.17	2.73	2.31	2.15	2.66	2.48	2.88
1970	2.55	2.32	2.53	2.52	2.84	2.38	2.35	2.24	2.65	2.23	2.70	2.72	2.05	2.80	2.52	2.51	3.49
1971	2.76	2.33	2.49	3.02	3.20	2.61	1.98	2.39	2.30	2.38	2.78	3.43	2.74	2.90	2.80	2.80	4.01
1972	3.40	2.99	3.56	3.26	3.80	2.93	2.84	3.20	3.17	3.60	3.92	3.56	2.85	3.38	3.63	3.38	4.38
1973	4.34	3.38	4.01	4.75	5.21	3.60	3.03	3.53	3.96	3.99	4.09	5.21	4.27	4.76	5.08	5.12	5.43
1974	5.79	5.55	5.76	5.75	6.08	5.80	5.38	5.48	5.86	5.51	5.92	7.17	4.72	5.36	5.49	5.54	7.21
1975	6.19	6.08	6.02	5.69	6.93	7.56	5.03	5.67	5.75	6.29	6.01	6.18	5.56	5.33	6.65	5.96	8.33
1976	7.42	6.57	8.37	6.73	8.00	8.19	4.86	6.67	8.01	7.48	9.63	7.32	5.90	6.96	7.33	7.81	8.86
1977	7.99	7.75	8.06	7.25	8.92	6.34	6.95	9.94	7.72	7.84	8.63	7.08	7.00	7.68	7.71	7.87	11.17
1978	8.63	7.71	7.93	8.73	10.13	7.45	7.11	8.56	7.55	7.97	8.27	9.77	7.55	8.88	9.71	8.26	12.42
1979	10.76	9.26	10.46	10.54	12.77	8.74	9.51	9.52	10.09	11.14	10.17	12.09	9.13	10.41	13.65	10.43	14.23
1980	17.59	13.16	12.84	20.06	24.29	13.93	12.83	12.72	13.25	12.59	12.67	25.15	17.19	17.84	22.97	21.91	28.00
1981	35.55	29.13	34.62	33.55	44.88	25.67	28.66	33.06	37.46	30.29	36.12	34.42	29.21	37.01	34.33	37.37	62.95
1982	52.43	45.12	54.82	46.07	63.70	38.78	41.21	55.36	57.97	45.74	60.77	49.12	41.13	47.95	51.62	48.25	91.23
1983	52.38	48.46	49.48	49.17	62.40	35.29	52.04	58.04	48.53	45.33	54.57	48.75	48.74	50.03	50.23	50.67	86.30

Trade balance (f.o.b. — c.i.f.)
billion dinars, monthly averages

Balance commerciale (f.o.b. — c.a.f.)
milliards de dinars, moyennes mensuelles

	Year	Q.1	Q.2	Q.3	Q.4	JAN	FEB	MAR	APR	MAY	JUN	JUL	AUG	SEP	OCT	NOV	DEC
1964	-0.45	-0.44	-0.57	-0.63	-0.15	-0.43	-0.33	-0.55	-0.50	-0.59	-0.63	-0.67	-0.57	-0.64	-0.21	-0.13	-0.12
1965	-0.30	-0.30	-0.55	-0.43	0.09	-0.39	-0.33	-0.18	-0.52	-0.68	-0.46	-0.68	-0.48	-0.13	-0.10	0.01	0.35
1966	-0.54	-0.61	-0.62	-0.55	-0.39	-0.35	-0.83	-0.36	-0.42	-0.91	-0.52	-0.63	-0.73	-0.28	-0.38	-0.57	-0.21
1967	-0.69	-0.75	-0.69	-0.79	-0.54	-1.04	-0.95	-0.27	-0.79	-0.61	-0.66	-0.86	-0.77	-0.74	-0.58	-0.65	-0.35
1968	-0.81	-0.71	-0.97	-0.81	-0.75	-0.60	-0.93	-0.61	-0.94	-1.05	-0.90	-0.51	-1.19	-0.74	-0.60	-0.99	-0.67
1969	-1.00	-1.27	-1.16	-0.89	-0.70	-1.42	-0.98	-1.41	-0.87	-1.32	-1.28	-1.01	-0.78	-0.88	-0.70	-0.50	-0.90
1970	-1.82	-0.89	-1.79	-2.43	-2.16	-0.80	-0.65	-1.21	-1.51	-1.72	-2.16	-2.90	-2.73	-1.67	-2.75	-1.99	-1.75
1971	-2.19	-2.33	-2.87	-2.06	-1.48	-3.18	-1.37	-2.44	-2.71	-2.73	-3.18	-2.14	-2.38	-1.67	-1.92	-1.55	-0.98
1972	-1.51	-1.28	-0.96	-1.79	-2.02	-0.96	-1.21	-1.68	-0.95	-0.74	-1.19	-1.42	-2.17	-1.79	-2.15	-2.19	-1.74
1973	-2.52	-2.43	-2.27	-2.39	-3.00	-2.79	-2.27	-2.25	-1.64	-2.64	-2.52	-1.81	-2.56	-2.79	-2.52	-3.06	-3.41
1974	-5.76	-4.45	-5.49	-6.44	-6.65	-4.35	-4.31	-4.69	-5.22	-5.11	-6.16	-6.11	-7.32	-5.89	-7.43	-6.98	-5.52
1975	-5.51	-5.13	-6.67	-5.51	-4.75	-4.82	-5.51	-5.05	-7.64	-6.06	-6.31	-6.03	-5.85	-4.64	-4.06	-4.51	-5.67
1976	-3.79	-3.64	-2.69	-4.05	-4.76	-4.10	-3.76	-3.08	-2.48	-2.19	-3.40	-2.61	-5.24	-4.30	-4.37	-2.96	-6.94
1977	-6.66	-5.71	-7.62	-7.09	-6.21	-7.26	-3.85	-6.03	-7.99	-7.06	-7.80	-6.04	-8.98	-6.27	-6.26	-4.54	-7.83
1978	-6.57	-6.40	-6.81	-5.94	-7.12	-7.75	-5.52	-5.92	-6.34	-7.42	-6.67	-2.38	-8.84	-6.59	-6.89	-6.97	-7.49
1979	-11.44	-11.66	-11.63	-11.26	-11.20	-14.44	-8.98	-11.58	-10.77	-12.73	-11.40	-10.31	-13.90	-9.56	-11.29	-10.10	-12.22
1980	-11.60	-11.90	-8.72	-14.00	-11.78	-13.11	-12.23	-10.35	-9.01	-6.91	-10.23	-10.56	-18.16	-13.29	-15.97	-8.61	-10.75
1981	-15.06	-18.52	-22.82	-13.64	-5.27	-19.78	-11.26	-24.51	-27.35	-22.18	-18.93	-19.91	-18.63	-2.37	-0.91	-2.80	-12.11
1982	-14.93	-18.04	-15.86	-16.93	-8.89	-23.74	-16.94	-13.43	-17.69	-13.99	-15.92	-18.77	-27.39	-4.62	-3.86	-2.70	-20.11
1983	-11.84	-10.96	-10.96	-10.39	-15.05	-12.98	-4.67	-15.23	-4.16	-14.08	-14.63	-8.38	-17.01	-5.78	-9.53	-12.16	-23.47

Imports c.i.f. — Importations c.a.f.

billion dinars, monthly averages — milliards de dinars, moyennes mensuelles

Adjusted - Corrigé *

Year	Q.1	Q.2	Q.3	Q.4	JAN	FEB	MAR	APR	MAY	JUN	JUL	AUG	SEP	OCT	NOV	DEC
1964	1.35	1.36	1.51	1.27	1.33	1.33	1.40	1.31	1.35	1.43	1.43	1.48	1.61	1.17	1.30	1.34
1965	1.30	2.02	2.05	1.95	1.81	1.69	1.88	1.87	2.24	1.94	2.25	1.97	1.93	2.08	1.84	1.94
1966	2.39	2.31	2.36	2.52	2.26	2.63	2.29	2.21	2.41	2.30	2.35	2.50	2.23	2.44	2.41	2.70
1967	2.61	2.55	2.60	2.68	2.53	2.87	2.43	2.68	2.29	2.67	2.56	2.33	2.91	2.70	2.81	2.54
1968	2.43	2.71	2.80	2.95	2.32	2.46	2.52	2.75	2.77	2.59	2.56	2.98	2.88	2.61	3.07	3.15
1969	3.28	3.19	3.22	3.30	3.24	3.01	3.58	3.08	3.18	3.31	3.34	3.13	3.19	3.26	3.18	3.46
1970	3.48	4.16	4.88	4.87	3.13	3.56	3.74	4.06	4.05	4.38	5.12	4.86	4.65	5.01	4.96	4.64
1971	4.99	5.21	4.97	4.61	5.96	3.96	5.04	4.98	5.33	5.34	4.97	5.21	4.73	4.74	4.51	4.57
1972	4.48	4.41	5.02	5.78	3.97	4.47	5.01	4.29	4.36	4.59	4.78	4.78	5.49	5.80	5.64	5.89
1973	6.05	6.14	7.25	8.10	6.16	6.13	5.86	5.92	6.40	6.11	6.76	6.74	8.24	7.48	8.33	8.48
1974	10.46	10.99	12.34	12.45	9.27	11.21	10.92	10.90	10.52	11.56	12.67	11.69	12.57	12.33	13.15	11.86
1975	11.73	12.36	11.25	11.55	11.48	12.21	11.49	12.83	12.02	12.22	11.48	11.69	10.59	10.58	11.57	12.49
1976	10.34	10.69	10.92	12.59	11.12	9.99	9.92	9.55	9.98	12.14	9.74	11.23	11.81	12.14	11.89	13.74
1977	13.61	15.28	14.63	14.94	12.99	12.47	15.38	15.28	15.05	15.50	13.76	15.40	14.72	14.45	13.99	16.39
1978	14.30	14.42	14.86	17.58	14.27	14.54	14.09	13.85	14.96	14.45	12.71	14.99	16.87	16.77	17.41	18.56
1979	20.77	21.61	22.27	24.62	21.26	21.22	19.82	21.19	22.25	21.40	22.61	21.46	22.74	24.38	23.87	25.60
1980	24.97	20.97	34.18	37.18	24.25	28.06	22.61	20.49	18.55	23.86	32.70	34.49	35.36	37.72	37.14	36.69
1981	47.59	55.11	47.35	51.29	42.35	46.05	54.36	58.02	53.65	53.66	50.26	46.67	45.12	34.12	50.33	69.43
1982	64.09	67.32	62.63	74.90	63.34	67.61	61.31	66.48	61.96	73.52	61.50	65.76	60.64	57.37	60.16	107.16
1983	59.32	57.80	60.32	80.18	50.07	66.17	61.73	46.51	61.12	65.77	54.77	61.05	65.13	62.45	73.14	104.94

Exports f.o.b. — Exportations f.o.b.

billion dinars, monthly averages — milliards de dinars, moyennes mensuelles

Adjusted - Corrigé *

Year	Q.1	Q.2	Q.3	Q.4	JAN	FEB	MAR	APR	MAY	JUN	JUL	AUG	SEP	OCT	NOV	DEC
1964	0.94	0.90	0.91	0.96	1.01	0.96	0.85	0.94	0.91	0.86	0.89	0.98	0.86	0.91	0.97	1.01
1965	1.53	1.61	1.67	1.78	1.56	1.49	1.53	1.44	1.87	1.53	1.72	1.59	1.69	1.77	1.74	1.83
1966	1.84	1.34	1.82	1.91	1.79	1.90	1.83	1.27	1.75	1.92	1.74	1.89	1.82	1.89	1.68	2.16
1967	1.87	2.02	1.85	1.91	1.60	1.99	2.03	1.97	1.92	2.16	1.75	1.77	2.02	1.91	2.01	1.81
1968	1.76	1.89	2.00	1.99	1.82	1.66	1.80	1.85	1.95	1.87	2.00	2.07	1.94	1.95	1.95	2.07
1969	2.01	2.18	2.37	2.40	1.90	2.05	2.08	2.20	2.16	2.18	2.38	2.52	2.19	2.46	2.58	2.15
1970	2.68	2.54	2.48	2.57	2.54	3.03	2.47	2.58	2.42	2.61	2.32	2.33	2.79	2.48	2.62	2.62
1971	2.60	2.49	3.00	2.91	2.77	2.49	2.55	2.24	2.65	2.59	3.01	3.03	2.95	2.84	2.86	3.03
1972	3.26	3.55	3.28	3.58	3.16	3.30	3.32	3.29	3.66	3.70	3.28	3.07	3.49	3.71	3.48	3.55
1973	3.64	3.97	4.84	4.96	3.57	3.61	3.75	4.08	3.94	3.91	4.67	4.68	5.16	5.03	5.27	4.60
1974	5.94	5.66	5.86	5.68	5.74	6.26	5.81	5.77	5.32	5.89	6.33	5.42	5.83	5.37	5.80	5.86
1975	6.48	5.88	5.90	6.49	7.56	5.72	6.15	5.48	6.25	5.91	5.49	6.59	5.61	6.45	6.51	6.50
1976	6.88	8.16	7.03	7.45	8.64	5.37	6.64	7.79	7.77	8.93	6.79	6.99	7.31	7.36	8.23	6.76
1977	8.18	7.94	7.58	8.27	7.13	7.66	9.75	7.69	7.86	8.26	6.66	8.05	8.03	7.87	8.13	8.80
1978	8.05	7.88	9.19	9.35	8.17	7.69	8.30	7.81	7.85	7.98	9.56	8.60	9.43	9.45	8.75	9.86
1979	9.66	10.46	11.11	11.83	9.41	10.16	9.42	10.21	11.19	9.97	11.40	10.38	11.54	13.00	10.84	11.64
1980	13.64	12.81	20.92	22.26	15.17	12.78	12.97	12.40	13.32	12.71	23.14	20.64	18.99	22.02	23.61	21.16
1981	30.38	34.25	35.79	40.33	29.30	29.92	31.72	35.48	32.92	34.34	32.32	36.29	38.76	34.89	38.80	47.29
1982	46.34	53.91	49.78	56.63	45.84	42.62	50.56	54.33	51.86	55.55	48.78	48.79	51.78	53.94	47.44	68.49
1983	45.81	48.76	53.11	56.67	43.45	53.87	52.10	46.05	49.48	50.76	49.60	55.70	54.03	54.72	47.98	67.31

Trade balance (f.o.b. — c.i.f.) — Balance commerciale (f.o.b. — c.a.f.)

billion dinars, monthly averages — milliards de dinars, moyennes mensuelles

Adjusted - Corrigé *

Year	Q.1	Q.2	Q.3	Q.4	JAN	FEB	MAR	APR	MAY	JUN	JUL	AUG	SEP	OCT	NOV	DEC
1964	-0.41	-0.46	-0.59	-0.30	-0.32	-0.36	-0.55	-0.37	-0.45	-0.57	-0.54	-0.50	-0.75	-0.26	-0.32	-0.33
1965	-0.27	-0.41	-0.38	-0.17	-0.25	-0.20	-0.35	-0.44	-0.37	-0.41	-0.52	-0.37	-0.24	-0.31	-0.10	-0.11
1966	-0.55	-0.46	-0.54	-0.61	-0.47	-0.72	-0.46	-0.34	-0.67	-0.39	-0.61	-0.61	-0.41	-0.55	-0.73	-0.55
1967	-0.74	-0.53	-0.75	-0.77	-0.94	-0.88	-0.40	-0.72	-0.37	-0.51	-0.81	-0.56	-0.89	-0.79	-0.80	-0.73
1968	-0.67	-0.81	-0.80	-0.96	-0.50	-0.80	-0.72	-0.90	-0.83	-0.72	-0.55	-0.90	-0.94	-0.66	-1.13	-1.09
1969	-1.27	-1.01	-0.85	-0.90	-1.34	-0.96	-1.50	-0.88	-1.01	-1.13	-0.95	-0.61	-1.00	-0.80	-0.60	-1.31
1970	-0.80	-1.63	-2.40	-2.30	-0.59	-0.53	-1.27	-1.48	-1.63	-1.77	-2.79	-2.54	-1.86	-2.53	-2.33	-2.02
1971	-2.39	-2.72	-1.97	-1.69	-3.19	-1.47	-2.50	-2.74	-2.68	-2.75	-1.96	-2.18	-1.78	-1.89	-1.65	-1.54
1972	-1.22	-0.86	-1.74	-2.20	-0.81	-1.17	-1.69	-1.00	-0.69	-0.89	-1.51	-1.72	-2.00	-2.10	-2.16	-2.34
1973	-2.41	-2.17	-2.41	-3.13	-2.58	-2.53	-2.10	-1.85	-2.46	-2.20	-2.09	-2.06	-3.07	-2.45	-3.06	-3.89
1974	-4.53	-5.33	-6.48	-6.77	-3.53	-4.95	-5.10	-5.13	-5.20	-5.66	-6.34	-6.27	-6.84	-6.96	-7.35	-6.00
1975	-5.25	-6.48	-5.35	-5.06	-3.92	-6.48	-5.34	-7.35	-5.77	-6.31	-5.99	-5.10	-4.98	-4.13	-5.06	-5.99
1976	-3.46	-2.52	-3.90	-5.14	-2.48	-4.62	-3.29	-2.15	-2.21	-3.21	-2.95	-4.24	-4.50	-4.78	-3.66	-6.99
1977	-5.43	-7.34	-7.05	-6.68	-5.86	-4.81	-5.64	-7.60	-7.19	-7.23	-7.10	-7.35	-6.69	-6.58	-5.86	-7.60
1978	-6.25	-6.54	-5.66	-8.23	-6.11	-6.85	-5.79	-6.03	-7.11	-6.47	-3.14	-6.40	-7.45	-7.32	-8.66	-8.70
1979	-11.10	-11.16	-11.16	-12.79	-11.85	-11.06	-10.40	-10.98	-11.05	-11.43	-11.21	-11.08	-11.20	-11.38	-13.03	-13.96
1980	-11.33	-8.16	-13.26	-14.92	-9.08	-15.28	-9.64	-8.09	-5.23	-11.15	-9.56	-13.85	-16.37	-15.71	-13.52	-15.53
1981	-17.21	-20.86	-11.56	-10.97	-12.85	-16.13	-22.64	-22.54	-20.72	-19.32	-17.94	-10.39	-6.36	0.77	-11.53	-22.14
1982	-17.75	-13.41	-12.85	-18.27	-17.51	-25.00	-10.75	-12.15	-10.10	-17.98	-12.72	-16.97	-8.86	-3.43	-12.71	-38.67
1983	-9.51	-9.04	-7.21	-23.51	-6.62	-12.30	-9.62	-0.46	-11.64	-15.01	-5.16	-5.35	-11.10	-7.73	-25.16	-37.63

* Adjusted by the O.E.C.D. — * Corrigé par l'O.C.D.E.

NOTES

1. Payments statistics.
2. Chain index with yearly links and a changing weighting pattern. Seasonally unadjusted series are not adjusted for unequal number of working days in the month.
3. Including civil engineering.
4. Annual data are based on more complete information than monthly and quarterly data.
5. Including some food sales in private sector. Chain index with yearly links and a changing weighting pattern.
6. From 1975, new definition of a reporting unit.
7. Monthly data refer to end of period.
8. Total cash earnings after payment of direct taxes and social insurance contributions.
9. Including credit to individuals for the purchase of capital goods, and for promoting tourism.
10. To June 1973, par values of official rates, thereafter spot market quotations.

NOTES

1. Sur la base des paiements.
2. Indice en chaîne raccordé chaque année et à pondération variable. Les séries brutes ne sont pas corrigées de l'inégalité du nombre de jours ouvrables dans le mois.
3. Y compris les travaux publics.
4. Les données annuelles sont établies à partir d'informations plus complètes que les données mensuelles et trimestrielles.
5. Y compris la vente par le secteur privé de certains produits alimentaires. Indice en chaîne raccordé chaque année et à pondération variable.
6. A partir de 1975, nouvelle définition de l'unité statistique.
7. Situation en fin de mois.
8. Total des gains en espèces après paiement des impôts directs et des contributions sociales.
9. Y compris les crédits accordés aux particuliers pour l'achat de moyens de production, et pour la promotion du tourisme.
10. Jusqu'en juin 1973, parités ou taux officiels; à partir de juillet 1973, taux du marché au comptant.

MAIN SOURCES

PRINCIPALES SOURCES

Series	Séries	Sources
All series	Toutes les séries	Savezni Zavod Za Statistiku *Indeks, Mesecni pregled privredne statistike S.F.R. Jugoslavije*

OECD SALES AGENTS
DÉPOSITAIRES DES PUBLICATIONS DE L'OCDE

ARGENTINA – ARGENTINE
Carlos Hirsch S.R.L., Florida 165, 4° Piso (Galería Guemes)
1333 BUENOS AIRES, Tel. 33.1787.2391 y 30.7122

AUSTRALIA – AUSTRALIE
Australia and New Zealand Book Company Pty, Ltd.,
10 Aquatic Drive, Frenchs Forest, N.S.W. 2086
P.O. Box 459, BROOKVALE, N.S.W. 2100. Tel. (02) 452.44.11

AUSTRIA – AUTRICHE
OECD Publications and Information Center
4 Simrockstrasse 5300 Bonn (Germany). Tel. (0228) 21.60.45
Local Agent/Agent local :
Gerold and Co., Graben 31, WIEN 1. Tel. 52.22.35

BELGIUM – BELGIQUE
Jean De Lannoy, Service Publications OCDE
avenue du Roi 202, B-1060 BRUXELLES. Tel. 02/538.51.69

BRAZIL – BRÉSIL
Mestre Jou S.A., Rua Guaipa 518,
Caixa Postal 24090, 05089 SAO PAULO 10. Tel. 261.1920
Rua Senador Dantas 19 s/205-6, RIO DE JANEIRO GB.
Tel. 232.07.32

CANADA
Renouf Publishing Company Limited,
2182 ouest, rue Ste-Catherine,
MONTRÉAL, Qué. H3H 1M7. Tel. (514)937.3519
OTTAWA, Ont. K1P 5A6, 61 Sparks Street

DENMARK – DANEMARK
Munksgaard Export and Subscription Service
35, Nørre Søgade
DK 1370 KØBENHAVN K. Tel. +45.1.12.85.70

FINLAND – FINLANDE
Akateeminen Kirjakauppa
Keskuskatu 1, 00100 HELSINKI 10. Tel. 65.11.22

FRANCE
Bureau des Publications de l'OCDE,
2 rue André-Pascal, 75775 PARIS CEDEX 16. Tel. (1) 524.81.67
Principal correspondant :
13602 AIX-EN-PROVENCE : Librairie de l'Université.
Tel. 26.18.08

GERMANY – ALLEMAGNE
OECD Publications and Information Center
4 Simrockstrasse 5300 BONN Tel. (0228) 21.60.45

GREECE – GRÈCE
Librairie Kauffmann, 28 rue du Stade,
ATHÈNES 132. Tel. 322.21.60

HONG-KONG
Government Information Services,
Publications/Sales Section, Baskerville House,
2nd Floor, 22 Ice House Street

ICELAND – ISLANDE
Snaebjörn Jönsson and Co., h.f.,
Hafnarstraeti 4 and 9, P.O.B. 1131, REYKJAVIK.
Tel. 13133/14281/11936

INDIA – INDE
Oxford Book and Stationery Co. :
NEW DELHI-1, Scindia House. Tel. 45896
CALCUTTA 700016, 17 Park Street. Tel. 240832

INDONESIA – INDONÉSIE
PDIN-LIPI, P.O. Box 3065/JKT., JAKARTA, Tel. 583467

IRELAND – IRLANDE
TDC Publishers – Library Suppliers
12 North Frederick Street, DUBLIN 1 Tel. 744835-749677

ITALY – ITALIE
Libreria Commissionaria Sansoni :
Via Lamarmora 45, 50121 FIRENZE. Tel. 579751/584468
Via Bartolini 29, 20155 MILANO. Tel. 365083
Sub-depositari :
Ugo Tassi
Via A. Farnese 28, 00192 ROMA. Tel. 310590
Editrice e Libreria Herder,
Piazza Montecitorio 120, 00186 ROMA. Tel. 6794628
Costantino Ercolano, Via Generale Orsini 46, 80132 NAPOLI. Tel. 405210
Libreria Hoepli, Via Hoepli 5, 20121 MILANO. Tel. 865446
Libreria Scientifica, Dott. Lucio de Biasio "Aeiou"
Via Meravigli 16, 20123 MILANO Tel. 807679
Libreria Zanichelli
Piazza Galvani 1/A, 40124 Bologna Tel. 237389
Libreria Lattes, Via Garibaldi 3, 10122 TORINO. Tel. 519274
La diffusione delle edizioni OCSE è inoltre assicurata dalle migliori librerie nelle città più importanti.

JAPAN – JAPON
OECD Publications and Information Center,
Landic Akasaka Bldg., 2-3-4 Akasaka,
Minato-ku, TOKYO 107 Tel. 586.2016

KOREA – CORÉE
Pan Korea Book Corporation,
P.O. Box n° 101 Kwangwhamun, SÉOUL. Tel. 72.7369

LEBANON – LIBAN
Documenta Scientifica/Redico,
Edison Building, Bliss Street, P.O. Box 5641, BEIRUT.
Tel. 354429 – 344425

MALAYSIA – MALAISIE
University of Malaya Co-operative Bookshop Ltd.
P.O. Box 1127, Jalan Pantai Baru
KUALA LUMPUR. Tel. 51425, 54058, 54361

THE NETHERLANDS – PAYS-BAS
Staatsuitgeverij, Verzendboekhandel,
Chr. Plantijnstraat 1 Postbus 20014
2500 EA S-GRAVENHAGE. Tel. nr. 070.789911
Voor bestellingen: Tel. 070.789208

NEW ZEALAND – NOUVELLE-ZÉLANDE
Publications Section,
Government Printing Office Bookshops:
AUCKLAND: Retail Bookshop: 25 Rutland Street,
Mail Orders: 85 Beach Road, Private Bag C.P.O.
HAMILTON: Retail: Ward Street,
Mail Orders, P.O. Box 857
WELLINGTON: Retail: Mulgrave Street (Head Office),
Cubacade World Trade Centre
Mail Orders: Private Bag
CHRISTCHURCH: Retail: 159 Hereford Street,
Mail Orders: Private Bag
DUNEDIN: Retail: Princes Street
Mail Order: P.O. Box 1104

NORWAY – NORVÈGE
J.G. TANUM A/S
P.O. Box 1177 Sentrum OSLO 1. Tel. (02) 80.12.60

PAKISTAN
Mirza Book Agency, 65 Shahrah Quaid-E-Azam, LAHORE 3.
Tel. 66839

PHILIPPINES
National Book Store, Inc.
Library Services Division, P.O. Box 1934, MANILA.
Tel. Nos. 49.43.06 to 09, 40.53.45, 49.45.12

PORTUGAL
Livraria Portugal, Rua do Carmo 70-74,
1117 LISBOA CODEX. Tel. 360582/3

SINGAPORE – SINGAPOUR
Information Publications Pte Ltd,
Pei-Fu Industrial Building,
24 New Industrial Road N° 02-06
SINGAPORE 1953, Tel. 2831786, 2831798

SPAIN – ESPAGNE
Mundi-Prensa Libros, S.A.
Castelló 37, Apartado 1223, MADRID-1. Tel. 275.46.55
Libreria Bosch, Ronda Universidad 11, BARCELONA 7.
Tel. 317.53.08, 317.53.58

SWEDEN – SUÈDE
AB CE Fritzes Kungl Hovbokhandel,
Box 16 356, S 103 27 STH, Regeringsgatan 12,
DS STOCKHOLM. Tel. 08/23.89.00
Subscription Agency/Abonnements:
Wennergren-Williams AB,
Box 13004, S104 25 STOCKHOLM.
Tel. 08/54.12.00

SWITZERLAND – SUISSE
OECD Publications and Information Center
4 Simrockstrasse 5300 BONN (Germany). Tel. (0228) 21.60.45
Local Agents/Agents locaux
Librairie Payot, 6 rue Grenus, 1211 GENÈVE 11. Tel. 022.31.89.50

TAIWAN – FORMOSE
Good Faith Worldwide Int'l Co., Ltd.
9th floor, No. 118, Sec. 2,
Chung Hsiao E. Road
TAIPEI. Tel. 391.7396/391.7397

THAILAND – THAILANDE
Suksit Siam Co., Ltd., 1715 Rama IV Rd,
Samyan, BANGKOK 5. Tel. 2511630

TURKEY – TURQUIE
Kültur Yayinlari Is-Türk Ltd. Sti.
Atatürk Bulvari No : 191/Kat. 21
Kavaklidere/ANKARA. Tel. 17 02 66
Dolmabahce Cad. No : 29
BESIKTAS/ISTANBUL. Tel. 60 71 88

UNITED KINGDOM – ROYAUME-UNI
H.M. Stationery Office,
P.O.B. 276, LONDON SW8 5DT.
(postal orders only)
Telephone orders: (01) 622.3316, or
49 High Holborn, LONDON WC1V 6 HB (personal callers)
Branches at: EDINBURGH, BIRMINGHAM, BRISTOL,
MANCHESTER, BELFAST.

UNITED STATES OF AMERICA – ÉTATS-UNIS
OECD Publications and Information Center, Suite 1207,
1750 Pennsylvania Ave., N.W. WASHINGTON, D.C.20006 – 4582
Tel. (202) 724.1857

VENEZUELA
Libreria del Este, Avda. F. Miranda 52, Edificio Galipan,
CARACAS 106. Tel. 32.23.01/33.26.04/31.58.38

YUGOSLAVIA – YOUGOSLAVIE
Jugoslovenska Knjiga, Knez Mihajlova 2, P.O.B. 36, BEOGRAD.
Tel. 621.992

Les commandes provenant de pays où l'OCDE n'a pas encore désigné de dépositaire peuvent être adressées à :
OCDE, Bureau des Publications, 2, rue André-Pascal, 75775 PARIS CEDEX 16.

Orders and inquiries from countries where sales agents have not yet been appointed may be sent to:
OECD, Publications Office, 2, rue André-Pascal, 75775 PARIS CEDEX 16.

67738-06-1984

PUBLICATIONS DE L'OCDE, 2, rue André-Pascal, 75775 PARIS CEDEX 16 - N° 43041 1984
IMPRIMÉ EN FRANCE
(31 84 21 3) ISBN 92-64-02616-9